The Researchers
Library *of* Ancient Texts
Volume 5

The Researchers Library of Ancient Texts
VOLUME 5

Preachers of the Great Awakenings

Select Works of Gilbert Tennent,
Jonathan Edwards, George Whitefield,
Charles H. Spurgeon, Charles Finney,
and Dwight L. Moody

DEFENSE
CRANE, MO 65633

The Researcher's Library of Ancient Texts
Volume V
Preachers of the Great Awakenings: Select Works of Gilbert Tennent, Jonathan Edwards, George Whitefield, Charles H. Spurgeon, Charles Finney, and Dwight L. Moody

Thomas Horn
Defense
Crane, MO

Defender
Crane, MO 65633
©2014 by Thomas Horn
All rights reserved. Published 2014.
Printed in the United States of America.

ISBN 13: 978-0-9856045-9-2

A CIP catalog record of this book is available from the Library of Congress.

Cover illustration and design by Daniel Wright.

Contents

Sermons and Essays

Gilbert Tennent	1
Samuel Blair	30
John Blair	58
William Tennent, Jr.	71
John Tennent	80
Robert Smith, D. D.	96
Samuel Finley, D. D.	110

Freedom of the Will
by Johathan Edwards

Author's Preface	118
Part One	121
Part Two	134
Part Three	180
Part Four	206

Sermons of George Whitefield 254

Sermons of Reverend Charles Haddon Spurgeon 601

Power From On High
  by Charles Finney 857

Weighed and Wanting
  Addresses on the Ten Commandments by D. L. Moody 891

SERMONS AND ESSAYS

By the Tennents and their Contemporaries, compiled for the Board, 1951

*Entered according to Act of Congress, in the year 1855,
by A. W. Mitchell, M. D., in the Clerk's Office of the District Court
for the Eastern District of Pennsylvania.*

GILBERT TENNENT.

Gilbert Tennent was the eldest son of the Rev. William Tennent, Sen., the founder of the Log College. From an original document, a small memorandum book, kept by his father, we learn that he was born in the County of Armagh, Ireland, on the 5th of Oct., 1703. lie was therefore thirteen or fourteen years old when his father immigrated to this country. He received his education under his father's roof, before the founding of the Log College, and when this school was opened, he assisted his father in teaching.

    His first religious impressions of any permanency, were experienced soon after his arrival in this country. And during the several years in which he was under serious concern, besides his other studies, he pursued a course of theological reading. But having doubts as to his spiritual condition, he was fearful of entering the holy ministry; and commenced the study of medicine, which he prosecuted for the space of a year. But about this time, it pleased God to reveal himself to him with so much clearness and comfort, that all his doubts, and sorrows, and fears were dispelled; and the Sun of Righteousness arose upon him with healing under his wings. And no sooner was he satisfied of his saving interest in Christ, than he felt himself called to seek the ministry, which he had before been deterred from thinking of. After due preparation and study, he was licensed to preach the gospel, by the Presbytery of Philadelphia, in May, 1726. After his licensure, he preached for several Sabbaths in New Castle on the Delaware.

    Declining a call to this church, he soon after accepted one from the Presbyterian Church of New Brunswick, and in the autumn of 1726 was ordained by the Presbytery of New Brunswick.

    From his first entrance on the public work of the ministry, the preaching of Gilbert Tennent was very popular and attractive, with all classes of hearers. He possessed uncommon advantages as a preacher. In person, he was taller than the common stature, and well proportioned in every respect. His aspect was grave and venerable, and his address prepossessing. His voice was clear and commanding, and his manner in the pulpit was exceedingly earnest and impressive. His reasoning powers, also, were strong, and his language often nervous, and indeed sublime. No one could hear him, without being convinced that he was deeply in earnest. His style was copious and sometimes elegant. Indeed, in the vigour of his age few preachers could equal him.

In the winter of 1740 and 1741, Mr. Tennent visited Boston with Mr. Whitefield, where he spent three months, preaching almost every day with extraordinary power and success.

In May, 1743, Mr. Tennent was called to a new church in Philadelphia, formed from those who were converted under the preaching of Mr. Whitefield. This call he accepted, and exercised his ministry with great fidelity and diligence for twenty years. The only interruption to his pastoral labours in Philadelphia was occasioned by a mission to Great Britain, in conjunction with the Rev. Samuel Davis of Virginia, for the College of New Jersey.

For about three years before his death, Mr. Tennent became very infirm, so that he was unable to go through the duties which devolved upon him as the pastor of a large city congregation. His death occurred in the year 1764.

SERMON I: THE JUSTICE OF GOD.

BY THE REV. GILBERT TENNENT.

"He is the rock; his work is perfect; for all his ways are judgment; a God of truth, and without iniquity, just and right is he."—Deut. xxxii. 4.

Moses introduces his song in this chapter with the most solemn and commanding magnificence, and yet with the softest charms of language. He summons the attention of the inanimate creation, partly to reprove the stupidity of Israel, and partly to bear witness to the truth of what he was about to deliver to them in the following song, either for their instruction or warning, as well as to witness to the justice and equity of the divine proceedings against that unhappy nation: "Give ear, heavens, and I will speak, and hear, earth, the words of my mouth."

In the second verse, the devout penman of this song wishes that the instructions contained in it, may be refreshing to and effectual upon his beloved nation, as the rain and dew upon the earth: "My doctrine shall drop as the rain, my speech shall distil as the dew." These words may be considered as a prayer of Moses, as if he had said, that it might do so! Thus Bishop Patrick understands the words. In the next verse, he signifies his intention to make known the glory of God, and therefore excites them to ascribe greatness to him; which intention he performs in the words of our text, wherein we have a representation of the divine glory and greatness apparent in the perfection of his works and equity of his government, in a variety of particulars, viz:

1. He is called a Rock, to signify the stability of his nature, the firmness of his counsels, the immutability of his promises, and the almightiness of his power; in all which respects he is a secure shelter and unshaken foundation for our resort and confidence.

2. His work is perfect. "His work of creation was so; all that he made in its original constitution was very good; his works of redemption and providence shall be so, when the mystery of God is finished." "God's works are true and cannot be blamed," saith Ainsworth upon the place: "God never recalls his counsels, but perfects them. God's work is called perfect, because he fulfilled what he promised to the fathers."

3. All his ways are judgment; i.e., saith Henry, "The ends of his ways are all righteous, and he is wise in the choice of the means in order to those ends." By God's ways, we are to understand all God's providential administrations towards intelligent creatures, and by judgment prudence, and justice. Hos. xiv. 9.

4. He is a God of truth; i.e., as Mr. Pool observes in his Synopsis, "Faithful in his promises; whose word we may depend upon, for he cannot lie."

5. Without iniquity—he is perfectly free from all moral blemish and defect. "He deceives none that confide in him, and wrongs none that apply for justice, and is hard upon none that cast themselves upon his mercy."

6. Just and right is he. God is holy and equal in his distributions; as he is just in himself, so he is just in all his dealings with mankind; none can with reason accuse him of insincerity, unrighteousness, or levity.

Now that attribute or perfection of God which is principally represented in our text, by a beautiful variety of expressions, is his justice; this, therefore, is the subject of our meditations. That God is just, the Scriptures prove many ways, particularly, 1. Metaphorically and figuratively, when he is therein called a consuming fire, an angry lion, a man of war. Deut. iv. 24. Isa. xxxviii. 13.

2. Affectively, by attributing to him zeal, anger, jealousy, fury. Num. xi. 10. Exo. xx. 5; xxxii. 10. The aforesaid affections suppose justice in creatures, and though they be passions in them, they are in God but an act of immutable justice.

3. Effectively, by showing that he renders to every one according to his works. 1 Sam. xxvi. 23.

4. Negatively, by removing from him all injustice and iniquity, all respect of persons; and in a word, all the causes and effects of injustice. "Doth God pervert judgment, or doth the almighty pervert justice?" Job viii. 3. Dan. ix. 13. Rom. iii. 4.

5. Positively, by affirming and extolling his justice, by calling him a revenger, holy, right. Jer. xii. 1. Ps. xi. 7.

For the Righteous Lord loveth righteousness, his countenance doth behold the upright. To these we may add the words of our text, than which nothing can be more full and express: "He is a rock, his work is perfect, for all his ways are judgment; a God of truth, and without iniquity, just and right is he;" and also that of the Psalmist, Ps. cxix. 137, "Righteous art thou, Lord, and upright are thy judgments." "And does not reason confirm the same truth? For, 1st, if God be not just, whence is there any justice? Either there would be no justice at all, or if there was any, it would not proceed from God; or if it did, it must proceed from one who had none; each of which particulars is absurd. Besides, 2d, inasmuch as the Lord is governor of the whole universe, he would degenerate into a tyrant if he was not just; and, 3d, seeing Jehovah is judge of all the earth, how could he judge aright without being just himself? Neither can it be otherwise but that God should be just, seeing that he is absolutely perfect. All confess justice to be an excellency, involving no imperfection in it, and therefore it cannot be wanting to that being, who is absolutely and infinitely perfect.

In discoursing upon this divine attribute of God's justice, I propose to consider its nature, kinds, properties, displays, and in the fifth place, to answer some objections, and then proceed to the improvement. And,

1. Justice in its general nature may be said to be an agreement with right and rule. It is opposed to crookedness and obliquity, by which any thing declines from its proper rule. Crookedness in morals is the same with sin; which the apostle John calls "a transgression of the law." 1 John iii. 4. Or, as the original word *anomia* may be rendered, a being without the law, or a wandering from the law. Justice, therefore, does coincide with rectitude or uprightness: "Lo, this only I have found, that God hath made man upright." Eccl. vii. 29. So that justice includes two things in it especially, viz: right, and an agreement with that right. 1st, I say, it includes right or that which belongs to every one: "Render therefore unto Caesar the things that are Caesar's, and unto God the things that are God's." Luke xx. 25. "Knowing the judgments of God, that they that do such things are worthy of death." Rom. i. 32. It is from this right that the very name of justice is derived. And, 2nd, it includes an agreement with this right, and in this the form of justice consists; and the contrary to this, viz: a disagreement from right, constitutes the form of injustice. From this general description it is evident that justice admits of no degrees, for the thing either agrees with the rule of right or not; if the former, it is just, if the latter, it is unjust. Undoubtedly the justice of God, as well as of creatures, consists in an agreement with right, but with this difference, that the creatures have their rule of right prescribed by another; whereas the divine nature is a rule of right to the Almighty. But let me pass to the second, and speak of the kinds of justice. And here it may be observed that justice may be considered under a threefold view, viz: as relating to God's will, word, and deeds. And, 1. Justice, as it relates to the will of God, is thus described by Wendeline, viz: "That it is that whereby God is just in himself and without himself gives to every one their own by a constant will." "Justice in man," saith Mr. Leigh, "is a settled will to do right in everything to every person." Thus God hath a settled will to do right,—"shall not the judge of all the earth do right?" This constant will of God to render to every one his own, coincides with the divine essence, and may be called his essential justice, and is no other but the essential rectitude of his nature. And that justice of God which respects his words and deeds, may be called his declarative or relative justice, because it is a manifestation of the former, and respects the transactions of God with creatures. But,

2. The justice of God, as it relates to his words, is called truth, faithfulness, and constancy; because it agrees with the rectitude of his nature to speak so and no otherwise. Faithfulness may be called justice, because it is a doing justice to his word.

3. The justice of God, as it respects his deeds, is twofold, viz: of dominion and jurisdiction. And, 1st, God's justice of dominion, or, as some divines term it, his disposing justice, is that whereby Jehovah, as the sole Monarch and supreme Lord of all, disposes and governs every thing in a just order; and in particular he disposes his own actions according to the rule of equity, requiring and prohibiting nothing but what is fit for intelligent creatures, in right reason, to do and forbear. In a word, this justice of dominion consists in governing reasonable creatures agreeable to the original rectitude of their natures. 2nd, God's justice of jurisdiction consists in prescribing to reasonable creatures their proper due, and in governing them accordingly: and this the Almighty doth by three things: 1. By prescribing laws, which are rules tending to direct mankind in their duty to God and man, agreeable to his own sanctity, attended with rewards and punishments. "There is one lawgiver who is able to save and to destroy." James iv. 12. 2. By establishing his laws by proper sanctions of rewards and punishments promised and threatened (Deut. xxx. 15); now the sanction consists in promises and threatenings. And, 3. By fulfilling the sanction, and that both as to the reward and punishment: the former is called remunerative, and the latter vindictive. And, 1st, "The remunerative justice of God is a most ready will to perform God's promises," as Wendeline observes; when God rewards the obedience of his creatures with a free reward, proceeding from his own pure and abounding goodness, not for any worth or condignity in his people's works, as the Papists vainly dream, but for the sake of his gracious promise, by which he makes himself a debtor to them. "Who will render to every man according to his deeds; to them who by patient continuing in well doing, seek for glory, and honour, and immortality, eternal life. But to them that are contentious, and do not obey the truth, indignation and wrath." Rom. ii. 6, 7, 8. "When we have done all that is

commanded, we must say that we are unprofitable servants; we have done that which was (but) our duty to do." Luke xvii. 10. "Or who hath first given to him, and it shall be recompensed to him again? For of him, and through him, and to him are all things." Rom. xi. 35, 36. Although there be no intrinsic worth in man's obedience to merit the glory or reward promised, yet God having promised it to the creature, and having a right and power to confer it, it is just and right in him to perform his own word. And certainly, he would wrong his truth if he did not. When happiness, in Scripture, is represented as a reward, it is only to encourage or excite to obedience, by showing the inseparable connection between grace wrought in us, and glory conferred upon us. It cannot intend any merit in our works; for if we ourselves be less than the least of God's mercies, then the best actions put forth by us must be so; for, as Dr. Ridgely observes, "The action cannot have more honour ascribed to it than the agent." Being God's creatures, we have derived all from him, and consequently can offer him no more than his own. And being corrupt criminals, our services are defective, and so cannot merit good at the hand of God; nay, on the contrary, for our transgressions we merit his wrath. And therefore in respect of us, the reward of happiness is wholly gracious; but indeed in respect of Christ, who has fully answered the demands of law for his people, by his obedience and suffering, and thereby, according to the covenant transaction between his Father and him, completely purchased for them everlasting life, it may be called an act of divine justice. Hence it is said, "That he might be just, and the justifier of him that believes in Jesus." Rom. ii. 26. But,

2. The vindictive justice of God is the Almighty's will to execute the threatenings of his law upon transgressors, by punishing or inflicting on them evils of suffering equal to their crimes. This is called wrath, hatred, revenge, and judgment. It is likewise termed God's "visiting iniquity." Jer. v. 9. His "setting his face against a person." Lev. xvii. 10. It is called the fire of God's jealousy, and those that are exposed to it, are said to fall into the hands of the living God. Some divines use the terms of rewarding and revenging justice, instead of remunerative and vindictive.

But here I would have it observed, that there is a less proper sense in which the word punishment is used in Scripture. Thus, when God corrects his people with his rod, this is often called punishment (Ps. lxxxix. 30, 33); and hence they are said to bear the indignation of the Lord, because they have sinned against him. Micah vii. 9. These afflictions are called punishments, because occasioned by sin and afflictive to sense; but they are not inflicted by God as a judge, with any demand of satisfaction, for that was made by Christ for those that believe in him; and surely, it is contrary to the nature of divine justice to require a double satisfaction for the same crimes! No! the afflictions of God's people spring from his fatherly love to them, and are sent either to prevent or correct sinful disorders. By these the Almighty humbles his people, by showing them the desert of their impieties; and by these he brings them nearer to himself, and deadens them more to a vain world, and all its varnished but empty entertainments. Afflictions are the medicines which the great Physician uses to cure his people's manifold disorders.

But that what has been said, concerning the nature of divine justice, may be further explained and illustrated, let these things following be considered: 1st. That justice among men is two-fold, viz: either commutative or distributive. Commutative respects trade and bargains among equals, and consists in observing the rules of equity and right therein. Distributive is that which is exercised by a superior towards his inferiors, and consists in the conformity of their administrations to rule and law, and, therefore, comprises these four things in it, viz: 1. A law to which the acts of government should be conformed. A law, says Maresius, "*est faciendorum et fugiendorum norma, sub ratione premii et poenae,*" i.e., "it is a rule of things to be done and avoided, on consideration of a reward or punishment." All justice, and especially distributive, has respect to a law; this is the foundation on which It is built, and the rule according to which It must be squared and accommodated.

Now the law that is the ground and foundation of justice among men, must have the following characters, viz: 1st, it must be bottomed upon natural equity, upon the nature, relation and reason of things, otherwise it will be a crooked rule, and so unworthy of observation. No human authority can alter the intrinsic goodness and badness of things; and therefore bad laws (in a moral sense) are but a recommending and enforcing iniquity by human authority. And, 2d, the law must be enacted by competent authority and power; because legislation as well as the execution thereof, are acts of government, which those that exercise should have a right so to do, either originally or by delegation, the contrary to which tends to open a scene of confusion and blood. And hence it is well observed by some, that however just any act of government be in itself, yet it is unjust for those to meddle with it, that have no right thereto: e.g. for a judge to condemn one guilty of a capital crime to death, is just; but for a private person divested of authority to do it, is murder. And, 3d, the law must be promulgated, that it may be known, "for where there is no law, there is no transgression." Rom. iv. 15. But the Second particular, that civil justice, or justice among men includes, is Conformity to the law in all administrations. When a judge does this, in all his inquiries and examinations respecting cases brought before him, he does his duty, and otherwise he perverts the ways of judgment. It is this kind of justice among men, that is an emblem or shadow of the justice of God, and therefore I have so long discoursed upon it. But to show the similitude, let me add a few words more, and inquire, what is God's declarative or relative justice, but his conformity to the law he has given his creatures in his transactions with them? Here observe, 1st, That the law which God gave to man to direct him in his service, is grounded on natural equity, or the nature and reason of things; which appears by the harmony of its precepts among themselves, and their direct tendency to promote the glory of God, and make the creature happy in his service; the contraries to which tend to dishonour God, debase our intelligent nature, and destroy our happiness. The moral law is but a transcript of his nature as it is imitable. And hence is the Apostle's just commendatory encomium concerning it: "Wherefore the law is holy, and the commandment holy, and just and good." Rom. vii. 12. And, 2d, That God had authority to enact laws, appears evidently from his creating all. As his infinite and eternal excellency makes him worthy of absolute sovereignty and dominion, so his producing all by his almightiness gives him an irrefragable right thereto. Human power is derived, delegated, and limited, but his is original and absolute. And, 3d, Almighty God having annexed the sanction of rewards and punishments to the law he has given his creatures, his truth stands engaged to execute the same upon suitable objects; which is likewise necessary to answer the designs of government. This execution, therefore, of the sanction of the law, or conformity thereto, in the dealings of God with his creatures, is his declarative justice, and with this even all his acts of sovereignty do really harmonize, which appears by considering, 3d. The properties of divine justice, which are these following, viz:

1. Divine justice is impartial; with him is no respect of persons in judgment: "For we must all appear before the judgment seat of Christ, that every one may receive the things done in his body, according to that he hath done, whether it be good or bad." 2 Cor. v. 10. Justice will not spare for the sake of the multitude, greatness, or nearness of the guilty. Did not Sodom and Gomorrah perish by fire, and was not the whole antediluvian world drowned with water? And what vast multitudes of people may we suppose did the aforesaid cities, together with Zeboim and Admah, contain? And how much more the whole world before the flood? And yet all were destroyed by a sudden and terrible stroke of divine justice. And when the angels, those spirits of excelling dignity, sinned, did not divine justice cast them into an abyss of woe? And does it not still confine them in chains of darkness to the judgment of the great day? When Adam, our federal head, had transgressed the covenant, was he not banished from that paradise of pleasure he before possessed, and kept out of it by a flaming sword? Divine justice scatters kings as snow in Salmon, and before its adverse edge, their pompous armies flee apace. Ps. lxviii. 12, 14. And were not Moses and David, though so near and dear to God, punished with awful severity? Hence is that solemn and soul-affecting saying of the prophet: "Hear this word that the Lord hath spoken against you, children of Israel. You only have I known of all the families of the earth, therefore I will punish you for all your iniquities." Amos iii. 1, 2. But divine justice is—

2. Universal, so that not one sin can escape severe punishment, either in the sinner or surety: "Cursed is every one that continueth not in all things that are written in the book of the law to do them." Gal. iii. 10.

3. Divine justice is inexorable, no importunities can alter its course. When once a sinner's season of mercy expires, Jehovah refuses to be entreated. "Though Noah, Daniel, and Job were in it, as I live, saith the Lord God, they shall deliver neither son nor daughter; they shall but deliver their own souls by their righteousness." Ez. xiv. 18, 20. This is twice repeated in that chapter, to show the infallible certainty and unspeakable importance of the truth delivered. The almighty cannot be corrupted or bribed. But that which further confirms this awful truth, is the 4th proposition, viz: The displays of divine justice. And here, to be as brief as I can, I shall only mention two instances thereof. The first of which was the sufferings our Lord endured when he stood in the sinner's room and place. How unspeakable were the tortures he endured in his sacred body, every part of which was put to exquisite pain! Deep furrows were made in his sacred back by cruel scourges, and his beauteous face exposed to contemptuous blows, yea, to shame and spitting, by the insulting herd; his venerable temples were pierced by thorns, his side and heart by a spear; the whole weight of

his body hung upon a few sinewy and sensible parts in his crucifixion, and his name was treated with the greatest ignominy and scorn. But, as Mr. Flavel justly observes, "The soul of our Lord's sufferings was his sufferings in his soul." When he who knew no sin was made sin for us, his soul was made an offering for sin, his soul became sorrowful even unto death. How inconceivable must be the anguish which our Lord endured in his soul, when in one instant of time, that whole weight of distress and pain, which was due to divine justice for all the sins of the elect world, were laid upon it, and in the meantime deserted by the Father in respect of his comfortable presence! This pressed a bloody shower from all the pores of our Lord's body in the garden of Gethsemane. This extorted that heart-rending outcry on the cross, "*Eloi, Eloi, lama sabachthani?* (My God, my God, why hast thou forsaken me?)" No wonder the earth's foundation trembled, and the dead awoke out of their long and silent slumbers, and the sun itself, that glorious orb of light and beauty, put on a funeral robe of darkness and obscurity, to testify their surprise and sorrow on so awful an occasion, and to complete the train of mourners. But secondly,

The vindictive justice of God has a dreadful display in the torments of the damned, who are punished with everlasting destruction, from the presence of the Lord, and from the glory of his power. As the damned are deprived of all the honours and comforts of the heavenly paradise, as they are burnt in a lake of fire, which is kindled by the breath of God, as by a river of brimstone; so their intolerable tortures, by God's inflamed jealousy, by their own guilty consciences, by wicked men and devils, will know no intermission and no end; "the smoke of their torment ascendeth up for ever and ever." But I hasten to the 5th proposition, which was to answer some objections offered against the justice of God. And

1st. It is objected by the Socinians, that, according to our doctrine, God punished the innocent in the room of the guilty, namely, our Saviour in the place of sinners.

Ans. Though our Saviour was personally innocent, yet he was, with his own consent, and by his Father's imputation, guilty. And, hence, he is said, to be "made sin for us;" he willingly became the sinner's surety, and so assumed their guilt, in order to satisfy for it, and save them from ruin; and to a willing person, who had a right to dispose of his own life, especially seeing so valuable an end was answered by it, as the salvation of sinners, no injury was done by his Father imputing him to death.

2d. It is objected that God sometimes punishes the sins of the parents in their children. Ex. xx. 5.

Ans. God never punishes the sins of the parents in innocent children. As to the sin of Adam, he being the federal head, or covenant representative of his whole offspring, they sinned in him. "But they, like Adam, (as the word should be rendered,) have transgressed the covenant." Hos. vi. 7. "Wherefore as by one man sin entered into the world, and death by sin, and so death passed upon all men, for that all have sinned" (i.e., in Adam). Rom. v. 12. And as to the sins of private parents, they are not punished in children unless they be propense to them or imitate them.

3d. It is objected that God is a respecter of persons in the affair of predestination, by dispensing unequal things to those that were in an equal state, choosing one and rejecting another, without any reason but his own pleasure.

Ans. To respect persons is when, in matters of judgment, equal things according to law and right are due to several persons, and yet we dispense unequal; but this is not the case with the Almighty. "Who hath given to him," saith the Apostle, "and it shall be repaid? for of him are all things." Rom. xi. 36. As to God's grace, he owes it to no creature as such. He is Lord of his own treasures, and may do with his own what he pleases. Rom. ix. 18, 21. And, therefore, such as favour the objection, do but reply against God, as the Apostle there observes.

Predestination is but an immanent act of God, which produces nothing without himself, and, consequently, dispenses neither good nor evil, though it be the pattern according to which his providence dispenses all things in time. But if we consider God's providence which dispenses salvation and damnation, that does not confer unequal things upon those that are equal; but it confers unequal things upon those that are unequal, viz: believers and unbelievers; for Christ's sake, salvation to the former, and for sin's sake, damnation to the latter. If a prince of a number of rebels, who all, according to law, deserve death, purposes and passes an act of pardon upon some to show his clemency, and lets the law take place upon others to show his justice, where is the wrong? And that is the case; for God in his purposes looked upon men as fallen, and meriting his displeasure; he might have left the whole race to perish for their sins with the devils, who after their fall had never an offer of mercy. And because Jehovah has chosen some, when he might have condemned all, shall our eye be evil because God is good?

4th. It is objected, that God suffers the wicked to prosper, and the pious to be afflicted and oppressed.

Ans. This world is a time of probation, and not of

recompense. The scales will turn at the conclusion of this short scene, this transient drama. Besides, the miseries of God's people are necessary physic to cure their maladies, to which end they are sanctified by the Spirit of God. Rom. viii., 29. They are also at times sweetened with the love of Christ, and shall soon expire, and then an everlasting salvation shall commence; whereas, on the contrary, the abused prosperity of the wicked tends but to secure and increase their destruction. But it is time to proceed to the improvement. And

1st. This subject speaks terror to all ungodly and Christless sinners of every kind. How deplorable is their case, "who must drink of the wine of the wrath of the Almighty, which is poured out without mixture into the cup of his indignation!" O! let the secure and impenitent transgressor think on the following particulars:

1. That God, upon the account of his justice and judgments, is called the "great and dreadful God." Dan. ix. 4. Likewise, "mighty and terrible." Deut. vii. 22. "With God," saith Job, "is terrible majesty." Job xxxvii. 22. 2. That the wages of every sin is death, and that you have been guilty of a prodigious multitude, attended with awful aggravations: sins against light and love, against law and gospel, mercy and judgments; your iniquities, for number, rival the stars, and for aggravation, are red as crimson. And, 8. That the justice of God will not, can not pass by one of them, except ye repent, but will surely proportion pains equal to all their number and heinousness. For, as has been observed, it is impartial universal, inexorable. And now, seeing every imagination of the thoughts of your hearts has been, since your birth until now, only evil continually, and all your words and actions evil; for a corrupt tree cannot bring forth good fruit, neither can he that is in the flesh please God, how dreadful must that wrath be which is proportioned to them all!

Surely it is, 1st, *Incomprehensible wrath*; the most fearful imagination cannot fully represent it by its most gloomy ideas. "Who knoweth the power of thine anger? even according to thy fear, so is thy wrath." Ps. xc. 11. 2d. It is unavoidable wrath. If we take the morning wings and flee to the uttermost ends of the earth, lo, there God's all-seeing eye will discern us, and his righteous arm arrest us. If we ascend to the top of Carmel, or descend into the deeps of the ocean, or seek to conceal ourselves with the curtain of obscurity, darkness and retirement, even there our persons and purposes will be open to the all-penetrating eye of God. "For the darkness is as the light to him, and the night shines as the day." Sinners, ye cannot escape by policy, for God is infinite in wisdom; nor by power, for he is infinite in strength, as Job observes, "lie is wise in heart, and mighty in strength, who hath hardened himself against God and prospered? Job ix. 4. Nor can ye escape by flight, for Jehovah is omnipresent. 3d. It is eternal wrath (Matt. xxv. 46.); it will continue as long as God endures; never, never, never shall it know a period. O! this gives it a dreadful and heart-rending accent! And, 4th, It is intolerable wrath. If the Redeemer, who was personally innocent and supported by the Godhead, cried so dolorously under this wrath, how can your hands be strong, or your hearts endure, when a jealous God deals with you, and pours out the vials of his unmixed wrath upon you, who are full of real and crimson guilt, and shall have none to succour you? And do you think that that just God, who spared not his own beloved Son, when he but stood in sinners' place, but smote him dead by the sword of his justice, and made all the waves of his almighty vengeance beat upon him, and roll over him, will spare you who are covered all over with real and scarlet guilt? No, friends, "be not deceived, God is not mocked; for whatsoever a man soweth that shall he also reap." He that sows to the flesh, shall of the flesh reap corruption. The intolerableness of the divine wrath, anger and hatred, as well as its terribleness, is represented in Scripture by a variety of bold and dreadful images of thought. I shall mention a few of them, and in the name of the great God charge the ungodly to think upon them: "For a fire is kindled in my anger, and shall burn to the lowest hell, and shall consume the earth with her increase, and set on fire the foundations of the mountains. I will drop mischiefs upon them. I will spend my arrows upon them." Deut. xxxii. 22, 23. "Which removeth the mountains and they know it not; which overturneth them in his anger; which shaketh the earth out of her place, and the pillars thereof tremble; which commandeth the sun and it riseth not, and sealeth up the stars." Job ix. 5, 6, 7. "Upon the wicked he shall rain snares, fire and brimstone, and a horrible tempest; this shall be the portion of their cup." Ps. xi. 6. Elsewhere Jehovah threatens to wound the hairy scalp of the wicked, and tear them in pieces when there shall be none to deliver them. Hos. v. 14. That he will be to them as a lion and as a leopard, and meet them as a bear bereaved of her whelps, devour them like a lion and rend the caul of their hearts. Hos. xiii. 8. And with what magnificence and grandeur of diction does the prophet Nahum speak upon this solemn subject: "God is jealous, and the Lord revengeth; the Lord revengeth, and is furious. The Lord will take vengeance on his adversaries, and he reserveth wrath for his enemies. The Lord is slow to anger, and great in power, and will not at all acquit the wicked: the Lord hath his way in the whirlwind and in the storm, and the clouds are the dust of his feet. He rebuketh the sea, and maketh it dry, and drieth up all the rivers: Bashan languisheth, and Carmel, and the flower of Lebanon languisheth. The mountains quake at him, and the hills melt, and the earth is burned at his presence, yea, the world, and all that dwell therein. Who can stand before his indignation? and who can abide in the fierceness of his anger? His fury is poured out like fire, and the rocks are thrown down by him." Nahum i. 2–7.

Now as the consideration of God's justice and wrath ministers terror to all the ungodly in general, so especially and particularly to these following, viz: 1. Epicures, who indulge a sensual security, and put the evil day far from them. Surely such treasure up to themselves wrath against the day of wrath, and the revelation of the righteous judgment of God. Surely the day of the Lord will be to them, as the prophet expresseth it, "cruel with wrath and fierce anger." Isa. xiii. 9. And, 2d. All unjust persons who are guilty of fraud in contracts, and dealings with men, or respecting of persons in judgment. "Woe to him that buildeth his house by unrighteousness, and his chambers by wrong." Jer. xxii. 13. Ps. lxxxii. 2, 5. 3d. All hypocrites, such as are unjust to God and their own souls, who cover their inward injustice with an outward show of piety. Such are an abomination to God, and may expect to be cut asunder by the sword of divine justice. Matt. xxiv. 50, 51. 4th. All murmurers, who call in question the justice of God in his judgments, and kick with the heel against the Most High, under frowns of providence. For this, the whole congregation of Israel fell in the wilderness, and never saw Canaan, two excepted. Num. xiv. 27–30. Now the use I would advise poor graceless sinners, of every age and order, to make of the justice of God, is to be excited by it to fly to Christ for security and defence. "He is a hiding place from the wind, and a covert from the storm." Isa. xxxii. 2. 1st. He was made sin for us, that we might be made the righteousness of God in him. In Him God the Father has declared his righteousness (Rom. iii. 25); and Him he is willing to make righteousness to such as accept of him. 1 Cor. i. 30. Well, seeing divine justice must be satisfied for the wrong done by our offences, either by us, or a surety in our place, or else we must perish eternally: then, seeing we ourselves cannot satisfy, because we are poor, imperfect and finite creatures, let us hasten to Christ and receive him by faith, as the gospel offers him, that so we may be justified by faith, and securely rest on and rejoice in that Jesus, who has fulfilled the righteousness of the law for his people. Rom. viii. 3. But, 2d. This subject speaks comfort to all believers in every one of their troubles; for from this they may see that they are afflicted less than their iniquities deserve, that a Father's love is the spring of them, who chastens them lest they should be condemned with the world. And particularly we may draw comfort from this subject, under calumnies and wrongs, when we think that we have a witness in heaven, a just Judge there, who will uphold us in a good cause, and reward us according to our righteousness, and make it sooner or later to "shine forth as the light, and our judgment as the noonday." Ps. xxxvii. 6. Yea, in troubles of conscience God's justice yields support, when we consider that it was once satisfied by our Lord, and that it is contrary to its nature to require a double satisfaction. Hence is the Apostle's query, "Who is he that condemneth? it is Christ that died." Rom. viii. 34.

But there are these following duties, which, from the consideration of divine justice, we should be exhorted to perform, viz: 1st. That we beware of depending upon our own righteousness, upon the one hand, with the Pharisee (Luke xviii. 11); and of the neglect of duty, on the other, with the sluggard whose hands refuse to labour: "for without holiness no man shall see the Lord." Heb. xii. 14. 2d. Let us walk with humble reverence and child-like fear before the righteous God, as with a consuming fire, avoiding every appearance of evil, and continually, in all our religious services, eyeing Jesus the Mediator and Intercessor, who alone is able to cover their defects, and render them acceptable to his Father by his abundant righteousness; in whom alone we are complete, and safe from every impending storm. For when in him, the flaming sword of divine justice, which before kept us out of paradise, guards and assists our entrance into it. And, 3d. Let us glorify God on account of his justice of every kind, whether essential, declarative, judicatory, legislative, remunerative, or vindictive; for transcendent beauty shines therein. Let us say with the Psalmist, "Justice and judgment are the habitation of thy throne." Ps. lxxxix. 24. And with Paul, "the depth of the riches of the wisdom and knowledge of God! his judgments are un-searchable, and his ways past finding out." Rom. xi. 33. Such is the strictness of divine justice in all his proceedings, that it is compared to mountains, and to the abyss. "Thy righteousness is as the great mountains, thy judgments are a great deep." Ps. xxxvi. 6. And let us join with the inhabitants of heaven in celebrating the justice of God. "And after these things I heard a great voice of much people, in heaven, saying, Hallelujah, salvation, and glory, and honour, and power, unto the Lord our God, for true and righteous are his judgments." Rev. xix. 1, 2.

In fine, let us labour to imitate the justice and righteousness of God, by seeking the righteousness of Christ to our justification, in the manner before expressed; also by seeking the inherent righteousness, which it pleased God at first to implant in our natures by creation (Ecc. vii. 29), which we have lost by sin. I say, let us fervently and frequently cry to God by humble supplications, in the name of Christ, that he would be pleased to implant or infuse into our souls, by regeneration, the habits or principles of that righteousness; and, having the same implanted, let us exercise them in our whole practice. 1. Towards God, by rendering him his due, viz: ourselves, and all that honour, love, trust, and service which he requires in his word. And 2. Towards our neighbor, in all matters of government, judgment, and commerce, ruling without oppression, judging without respect of persons, and dealing without fraud, falsehood, or imposition. And 3. Towards ourselves, in a right improvement of the seasons of mercy, thereby securing our salvation; and also in not suffering ourselves to be wronged in our temporal interest. A great part of the image of God, and beauty of religion, consists in justice: and as the blessing of God rests upon such here, so they shall receive from the just Judge of heaven and earth a crown of righteousness hereafter, which shall never fade away. That this may be the happy lot of us all, may God grant, for Christ's sake! Amen.

SERMON II: THE DIVINE MERCY.

BY THE REV. GILBERT TENNENT.

And the Lord passed by before him, and proclaimed, The Lord, the Lord God, merciful and gracious, longsuffering.—Exodus xxxiv. 6.

In discoursing upon this divine attribute of mercy, it will be necessary to speak upon its nature, kinds, and properties. And,

1st. Mercy, in respect of its nature, may be thus described, viz: That it is the goodness of God extended to the miserable. Here good and bad angels are excluded: the good, because they are not miserable, and the bad, because they are wholly given up to justice. "But God spared not the angels that sinned, but cast them down to hell, and delivered them into chains of darkness to be reserved unto judgment." 2 Pet. ii. 4. Or the mercy of God may be thus described, viz: That it is that property of the Supreme Being whereby he is inclined to succour his creatures in misery, together with its kind effects upon them. Here observe, 1st, that the special object of mercy is the creature in misery, and thus it is distinguished from Other attributes. Goodness considers its object as indigent and so communicates needed benefits, but mercy considers its object as miserable, because of sin; and therefore, though an innocent creature be the object of divine goodness and bounty, it is only a fallen and sinning creature that is the proper object of God's mercy. Grace is mercy or goodness freely dispensed, and therefore it considers its object, not only as miserable, but unworthy. Whereas, longsuffering consists in the suspension of merited vengeance, and the communication of unmerited benefits. Thus you may see that all these attributes of the Deity import the communication of some good to the creature, and are only distinguished in relation to the objects upon which they are exercised. Misery is the foil of mercy, it can have no other object; hence it is said, that "his soul was grieved for the misery of Israel." Judg. X. 16. Undoubtedly the virtue of mercy was in God from all eternity, but there was no room or occasion for its displays, till the creature's fatal fall from God, and misery consequent upon it, proved it an object to be exercised upon. Man by sin robbed himself of his beauty and happiness, and exposed himself to all the manifold miseries of this and the next life; all which are included in the sentence of death annexed to the breach of the first covenant. As man by sin had lost all right to happiness, and, on the contrary, rendered himself liable to all the threats of the divine law; so by this he likewise became "altogether unprofitable," (Rom. iii. 1, 2,) having lost all his original power to glorify God by active obedience, and thus he had no ground from himself to expect the divine favour.

2d. Seeing the misery of fallen mankind is twofold, viz: of sin, and punishment; consequently, the operations of mercy consist in affording suitable succours under these maladies. In respect of sin, the mercy of God succours in the following instances:

1. In reconciling sinners to himself, by the blood of his only begotten Son. 2 Cor. v. 18. For the purchase of which reconciliation, the eternal Father gave his beloved Son to shame, pain and death. John iii. 16. And for the application thereof, he confers faith upon the elect, whereby they are enabled to accept and rely upon the blessed Jesus as Mediator and Reconciler. And

2. By renewing sinners by his Spirit, whereby the tyranny and dominion of sin is broken, and the people of God enabled to overcome sin, and triumph over it. "Let not sin reign in your mortal bodies, that ye should obey it in the lusts thereof." Rom. vii. 12. "I thank God, through Jesus Christ our Lord." Rom. vii. 25.

In respect of punishment, divine mercy succours in the following manner:

1. By bearing with the sinner for a time before judgment is inflicted. "What if God, willing to show his wrath, and to make his power known, endured with much longsuffering; the vessels of wrath fitted to destruction?" Rom. ix. 22.

2. By threatening punishments against the impenitent, in order to reclaim them from their trespasses. God warns before he wounds, and sends his servants to slay sinners by his word, before he slays them by his sword.

3. By pointing to a remedy, whereby the impending stroke of divine justice may be averted. "At what instant I shall speak concerning a nation, and concerning a kingdom to pluck up, and to pull down, and to destroy it; if that nation against whom I have pronounced turn from their evil, I will repent of the evil I thought to do unto them." Jer. xviii. 7, 8. If sinners repent of the evil of sin, God will avert the evil of judgment.

4. By inviting, and expostulating with, sinners to accept of the remedy proposed. "Come now, and let us reason together; though your sins be as scarlet, they shall be as white as snow; though they be red like crimson, they shall be as wool." Isa. i. 18. "Thus saith the Lord, what iniquity have your fathers found in me, that they are gone far from me, and have walked after vanity and become vain?" Jer. ii. 5.

5. By receiving into favour those that comply with the remedy, how great soever their trespasses have been, by forgiving their sins, sanctifying and sweetening their sorrows, and supporting them under them by his Spirit, love and power. "Who forgiveth all thine iniquities, who healeth all thy diseases." Ps. ciii. 3. "And he said unto me, My grace is sufficient for thee." 2 Cor. xii. 9. "Blessed be God, even the Father of our Lord Jesus Christ, the Father of mercies, and the God of all comfort, who comforteth us in all our tribulation." 2 Cor. i. 3, 4. And,

6. When he begins to inflict deserved judgment, (in general,) he doth it by degrees, first he sends lighter calamities, and when those do not reclaim the sinner, he sends heavier. In the day of God's rough wind, he stays his east wind. First rods are tried, and if those do not avail, scorpions may be expected. Jehovah does not all at once stir up "all his wrath." Ps. lxxviii. 38. But the,

2d proposition was to speak of the *kinds* of mercy. Now the mercy of God may be said to be two-fold, viz: either common or special. Common mercy consists in conferring without distinction upon the children of men, the outward comforts and conveniences of life, and hence the Almighty is said to cause his sun to rise upon the evil and the good, and to send his rain upon the just and the unjust. Matt. v. 45. But the special mercy of God consists in conferring upon the elect, such things as do accompany salvation, and that through Christ, in the channel of the new covenant. "Blessed be the God and Father of our Lord Jesus Christ, who hath blessed us with all spiritual blessings, in heavenly places, in Christ." Eph. i. 3. But I proceed to the 3d proposition, which was to discourse upon the properties of divine mercy. And,

1. It is eternal. "The mercy of God is from everlasting to everlasting." Ps. ciii. 17. It is repeated twenty-six times in one psalm, "that his mercy endureth for ever." Ps. cxxxvi. And this may justly enhance our esteem of it, and desire after it. Though God may hide his face for a little moment, yet with everlasting kindness will he return to his people. And,

2. God's mercy is great, and hence God is said to be "plenteous in mercy." Ps. lxxxvi. 5. "Rich in mercy." Eph. ii. 4. And, in Psalm li. 1, we read of the multitude of his "tender mercies." And in 2 Sam. xxiv. 14, his mercies are expressly said to be "great." But methinks the greatness of God's mercy appears especially by considering these two things, viz: What is the sinner's due, according to strict

justice, and the mitigation thereof which he enjoys in this world? Surely "the wages of sin is death." Rom. vi. 23. Which includes all the miseries of this present life, as well as the pains of hell hereafter. Now, therefore, every mitigation of those miseries, every comfort the sinner enjoys, is mercy; it is what the sinner has forfeited a right to; it is what he deserves not.

3. The mercy of God is incomparable. "They say, if a man put away his wife, and she go from him and become another man's, shall he return unto her again? But thou hast played the harlot with many lovers, yet return unto me, saith the Lord." Jer. iii. 1. The merciful God exceeds his creatures both in giving and forgiving. And,

1st. In giving. Our donations are often extorted from us, but He gives of his own accord, without any incentive but what is in his own bosom. Isa. lxv. 1.

We give but small gifts, but He gives the greatest, viz: Himself, his Son, his Spirit, his kingdom. Job iii. 16.

We give to our friends, but Jehovah confers many donations on his enemies. Matt. v. 45.

We are soon weary of giving, but so is not God; he is unwearied in his mercy (to the penitent); "he giveth liberally and upbraideth not." James i. 5. And,

2d. The merciful God exceeds his creatures in forgiving.

Men are revengeful to those that wrong them, but God is "merciful and gracious, long suffering," as our text asserts. How remarkable, to this purpose, are these words of the prophet, "I will not execute the fierceness of mine anger, I will not return to destroy Ephraim, for I am God and not man!" Hos. xi. 9.

Men are difficultly drawn to forgive, and cannot forgive often; but God is ready to pardon (Neh. ix. 17); and does multiply pardons.

Sometimes men forgive when it is not in their power to revenge themselves, but sinners are always under God's control and within the reach of his arm.

4. The mercy of God is sure and infallible. "Incline your ear and come unto me, hear and your soul shall live; and I will make an everlasting covenant with you, even the sure mercies of David." Isa. lv. 3. And hence it is that the gifts and callings of God are said to be without repentance, and that the foundation of God stands sure. The Lord knoweth who are his. God's special mercy to his people is built upon the sure and invariable foundation of his purposes and promises, as well as the satisfaction and intercession of Christ. And

5. God's mercy is free. "In whom also we have obtained an inheritance, being predestinated, according to the purpose of him, who worketh all things after the counsel of his own will." Eph. i. 11. Albeit the virtue of mercy belongs to God, in respect of his being, yet the dispensation of it depends entirely upon God's good pleasure, and hence the apostle Paul informs us, that "it is not of him that willeth, nor of him that runneth, but of God that sheweth mercy," and that "he hath mercy upon whom he will have mercy, and whom he will, he hardeneth." Rom. ix. 16, 18. Now, because when such things as are really or seemingly contrary are put together, they illustrate each other; it may not be improper, before I proceed to the improvement of this subject, to discourse upon the severity of God in his judgments, which is seemingly opposed to his mercy. Of this, mention is made in Rom. xi. 22, and in many other places of scripture; and of this there are many examples upon sacred record, such as the instance of the fallen angels, our first parents, the old world, Pharaoh, the Egyptians, Korah, Dathan, Abiram, Achan, Ananias and Sapphira, and many others. From which we may gather that God's judgments, which he exercises by his severity, are no other than singular punishments, inflicted for singular offences. The meritorious cause of them is some aggravated iniquity, the nature of which is often pointed out by the punishment inflicted, which is not common but singular. Adonibezek, who had cut off the thumbs and great toes of threescore and ten kings, was served so himself. Judges i. 6, 7. And hence Samuel saith concerning Agag, that "as his sword made women childless, so his mother should be childless among women." 1 Sam. XV. 33. Hence the Lord elsewhere threatens that those who shed the blood of others, should themselves have blood to drink. Thus you see that the punishment does often resemble the sin that procured it. Now the judgments of God are of various kinds, viz: Spiritual or bodily, private or public. Spiritual judgments are such as these, viz: A famine of the word. Amos viii. 11, 12. Leanness and backsliding. Rev. ii. 5. Errors in judgment. "And for this cause God shall send them strong delusion, that they should believe a lie." 2 Thess. ii. 10, 11. Corporal judgments are war, pestilence, famine, drought and the like. Now the procuring causes of public and epidemical judgments are such as the following, viz: Ingratitude against God. Isa. i. 3. Contempt of his word. "Who gave Jacob for a spoil, and Israel to the robbers? did not the Lord, he against whom we have sinned? for they would not walk in his ways, neither were they obedient unto his law." Isa. xlii. 24. Another cause of judgments, is slighting of the ministers of God. "But they mocked the messengers of God, and despised his word, and misused his prophets, until the wrath of the

Lord arose against his people, till there was no remedy." 2 Chron. xxxvi. 16. Besides, pride and idolatry are procuring causes of divine judgments. "The lofty looks of man shall be humbled, and the haughtiness of men shall be brought down." Isa. ii. 11. Jer. ii. 13, 14. Likewise the following evils against our neighbour, are causes of divine judgments, viz: Oppression of the poor. "The Lord will enter into judgment with the ancients of his people, and the princes thereof; for ye have eaten up the vineyard, the spoil of the poor is in your houses." Isa. iii. 14. 2d. Wronging the widow and fatherless. "They judge not the fatherless, neither does the cause of the widow come before them." Isa. i. 23. 3d. Cheating the labourer of his hire. "Woe unto him that buildeth his house by unrighteousness, and his chambers by wrong, that useth his neighbour's service without wages, and giveth him not for his work." Jer. xxii. 13. The prophet Hosea mentions a number of causes together, in the fourth chapter of his book, verses 1, 2. "Hear the word of the Lord, ye children of Israel, for the Lord hath a controversy with the inhabitants of the land, because there is no truth, nor mercy, nor knowledge of God in the land. By swearing, and lying, and killing, and stealing, and committing adultery, they break out and blood toucheth blood, therefore shall the land mourn." To the aforesaid causes of divine judgments I may add covetousness and hypocrisy. "Woe unto them that join house to house—therefore my people are gone into captivity." Isa. V. 8, 13. "Assyrian, the rod of mine anger—I will send him against a hypocritical nation." Isa. x. 6. Here it may be observed, that judgments are not always sent, except the aforesaid evils become general, and are attended with impudence, after various warnings. Jer. v. 1. Isa. iii. 9. Ps. xcv. 10, 11. Now the judgments of God are always just, and sometimes unsearchable and wonderful; for sometimes he not only sends them on the ungodly, but upon his own people. Yea, as the apostle Peter observes, "Judgment begins at the house of God." The Lord threatened his people of old, that them only he had known of all the families of the earth, therefore he would punish them for their iniquities. Hence David tells us, that his flesh trembled for fear of God, and that he was afraid of God's judgments. I may add that the end of God's punishments is the glory of God's holiness, the conversion and humiliation of some, and the hardening of others. Witness the prodigal, Pharaoh, and others. But it is time to proceed to the improvement of this subject. And,

1st. We should be cautious of abusing God's mercy; let us beware that we suck not poison out of that sweet flower. To take encouragement to go on in sin, because of God's mercy, is the vilest instance of ingratitude, and justly exposes to an aggravated condemnation; abused mercy turns into enraged fury and vengeance. "If he bless himself, saying, I shall have peace, though I walk after the imagination of my heart, to add drunkenness to thirst; the Lord will not spare him, but the anger of the Lord and his jealousy shall smoke against that man, and all the curses that are written in this book shall lie upon him." Deut. xxix. 19.

2d. The mercy of God offers encouragement and support to the people of God, in all their distresses, whether outward or inward. Are they afflicted with outward straits? The merciful God, who is their Shepherd, will not suffer them to want, but make their bread and water sure. He that hears and feeds the ravens, will surely hear and help his children. Have they backslidden from God, and are they labouring to be sorrowfully sensible thereof? Then may they encourage themselves in this, that all God's ways are mercy and truth, and that the mercy of Jehovah endureth for ever. He will begin and end with mercy, and such as are under the first convictions of sin may take encouragement from the mercy of God, which is great above the heavens, and most freely dispensed upon the vilest creatures. Mercy considers not what one deserves, but what he needs. God is more inclined to mercy than wrath. Justice and judgment is his strange work, but mercy is his delight. Micah vii. 18. "It is delightful to the mother," saith Chrysostom, "to have her breasts drawn; so it is to God to have the breasts of his mercy drawn." The Almighty is slow to anger, but ready to forgive. Ps. lxxxvi. 5. Let us, therefore, entertain honourable thoughts of God's mercy, and trust in it for ever. Ps. lii. 8. What greater encouragement can there be to believe, than the mercy of God? Mercy is one of the most orient pearls of the crown of God; he reckons it his glory to be conferring pardons upon penitent transgressors; and, therefore, he invites poor sinners to come and lay hold on his mercy. "Whosoever will, let him come and take of the water of life freely." Rev. xxii. 17. Mercy woos sinners in the most importunate, moving and condescending strains. "Ho, every one that thirsteth, come ye to the waters, and he that hath no money; come ye, buy and eat: come, buy wine and milk without money and without price." Isa. lv. 1. And what joy does the Almighty express, when sinners accept of the proposals of his mercy! when the prodigal son returned from his wanderings, how much did it please the Indulgent father, who made a feast to express his joy on that occasion!

We should be induced to inquire into the state of our

souls, in order to know whether we have an interest in the special mercy of God or not. For it will be miserable and ruining to us in the issue, if we content ourselves with common mercies. Now we may be helped to determine this important point, by an impartial comparing of ourselves with the following particulars, viz:

1. Those who have an interest in the special mercy of God, have been (if of adult age when converted) made sensible of their misery without it, and their unworthiness of it, with the prodigal and publican.

2. They have been stirred up to solicitous inquiries, how they might obtain an interest therein. Acts ii. 37.

3. Such have, deliberately and without reserve, consented to embrace Christ Jesus (the fountain of mercy) in all his offices and relations, and resolved to bear his cross and obey his laws. Job i. 12.

4. And, in consequence hereof, they find the general bias of their affections going towards God, and an habitual carefulness to do the things that are pleasing to him. Now, those who, upon examination, find themselves destitute of the aforesaid characters, should, in order to obtain mercy, 1. Think seriously of all the kindnesses of heaven towards them, together with their innumerable sins against those mercies, and the dangers to which they are thereby exposed. 2. Attend with diligence upon the preached word; for it is by the foolishness of preaching that God saves those that believe. 3. Bewail your sins against the mercies of God; let the goodness of God lead you to repentance. 4. Try to reform your lives. "Let the wicked forsake his way, and the ungodly man his thoughts, and let him turn unto the Lord, for he will have mercy upon him, and to our God, for he will abundantly pardon." And, 5. Pray earnestly and frequently to God for mercy, in the name of Christ, with fear and hope.

And let me exhort those that have obtained the special mercy of God to walk worthy of it. 1. Praise God for his mercy in the Psalmist's language: "Bless the Lord, my soul, and all that is within me bless his holy name." Ps. ciii. 1. Such as have been monuments of mercy, should be trumpets of praise.

2. Love God. Mercy is a powerful excitant to this. "I will love thee, Lord, my strength." Ps. xviii. 1. Surely that heart is harder than marble and adamant, which mercy will not melt. "I would hate my own soul, (saith Austin,) if I did not find it loving God." We should love God for outward comforts, but much more for special and enduring mercies.

3. Let us imitate the mercy of God, in showing mercy to our fellow creatures. God is the Father of mercy, show yourselves to be his children by being like him. It was a just observation of Ambrose, "that the sum of religion is to be rich in works of mercy." let the lamp of our profession be filled with the oil of mercy! And to this our dear Lord exhorts us, "Be merciful, as your Father also is merciful." Matt. vi. 36. But let the despisers and abusers of mercy, who go on in a course of any of the evils before mentioned, which procure the judgments of God, be entreated to repent, and reform speedily, otherwise ye may expect the dreadful effects of divine severity in some or all of the instances thereof before expressed. By your ungrateful return for mercies received, "you treasure up wrath against the day of wrath, and the revelation of the righteous judgment of God." Though God be gracious and merciful, slow to wrath, yet will he by no means clear the guilty.

SERMON III: THE GRACE OF GOD.

BY THE REV. GILBERT TENNENT.

> "And the Lord passed by before him,
> and proclaimed, The Lord, the Lord God,
> merciful and gracious, longsuffering.
> —Exodus xxxiv. 6,

The next divine attribute that comes now, according to the order of our text, to be considered, is the grace of God. "The Lord is merciful and gracious."

There is nothing more frequently mentioned in Scripture, than the grace of God. I shall mention but a few passages, for if I should take notice of all, I must transcribe a great part of the Bible. "To the praise of the glory of his grace, wherein he has made us accepted in the beloved." Eph. i. 6. "He is gracious and full of compassion." Ps. cxii. 14. "The grace of our Lord Jesus Christ, and the love of God, be with you all." 2 Cor. xiii. 14. In speaking upon this subject, I purpose,

I. To explain its *nature*.

II. Show its *kinds*.

III. Mention some considerations, serving to manifest its *sovereignty* and *glory*.

IV. Consider what is really and seemingly *opposed* thereto, and then proceed to some improvement.

I. I return to consider the first proposed, which was to explain the nature of the grace of God. Now, the word grace signifies something that is free, as was observed in the preceding sermon, and it is taken two ways, either for an attribute of God, which is in God, or for the gift of God, which is from God. In the first sense, the grace of God signifies his free and sovereign benevolence, by which he peculiarly favours and doth good to his creatures, whence God is called gracious, as in our text, i.e., endued with grace; as from his goodness he is called good, and from his justice, just. The gifts of God, which are the effects of the grace that is in him, are metonymically called grace, especially such of them as are peculiar and special, i.e., such as are conferred upon some, rather than others. Hence, some divines observe, that the word grace intends either, 1. The grace freely giving (Mat. xi. 26), which they term (*gratiam gratis dantem*), or the free favour of God; or the grace freely given, which they call (*gratiam gratis datam*). And this imports any kind of benefits which the Almighty confers upon his creatures, whether good or bad, which makes them not in the least the more acceptable to God; or, 3. The grace which makes acceptable, which they term (*gratiam gratum faeientem*), viz: all the saving gifts of God, faith, hope, charity, by which we please him.

Now, the grace of God may be thus described, viz: that it is a property of the Deity, whereby he is inclined to dispense undeserved kindnesses upon his creatures freely, and in a sovereign way. The dispensations of grace have no dependence upon any dignity or merit of creatures, upon whom benefits are conferred (Rom. xi. 6.); but the whole reason thereof is the good pleasure of God's will, (Matt. xi. 26,) which respects all creatures, even to the noblest angels. Whatever any of these enjoy, they have it of grace; for who, among all created beings, has first given to God, "and it shall be recompensed to him again?" Rom. xi. 35. In the meantime, these things are more properly and peculiarly ascribed to grace, which are different from nature. Nature and grace should not be confounded: such things as by the kind constitution of God, belong to every creature, according to their different kinds, are not usually called grace, because, though they be undue, yet they belong to nature. But to make this more plain, let us consider

II. The kinds of grace: and here it may be observed, that grace is three-fold, viz: universal, common, and saving. And,

1. Universal grace Is that, whereby Jehovah dispenses natural things upon all his creatures. And hence he is called the "Saviour of men." 1 Tim. iv. 10. And is said to "preserve man and beast." Ps. xxxvi. 6. He causes his sun to rise upon the fields of the evil and the good, and sends his rain upon the just and unjust. He gives to man life, health, strength, and all the supports he enjoys therein, all which, being undeserved, may be called grace: but according to the usage of scripture and antiquity, they seldom and less properly bear that name.

2. Common grace consists in the communication of moral good things upon men promiscuously, whether they be good or bad, elect or not elect; such as natural wisdom and prudence and all the train of moral virtues, in which even some pagans have excelled. And to these we may add, all outward religious privileges and means of grace; together with those transient effects which are sometimes produced by them upon the unregenerate, such as some kind of illumination, and stirrings of religious affections. In a word, all those common operations of the Holy Spirit which are not followed by an habitual and saving change, must be ascribed hereto. Of these mention is made in Heb. vi. 4–6, and also in the parable of the sower: "But he that received the seed into stony

places, the same is he that heareth the word, and anon with joy receiveth it; yet hath he not root in himself, but dureth for a while, for when tribulation or persecution ariseth because of the word, by and by he is offended." Matt. xiii. 20, 21. But,

3. Saving grace is that undue or undeserved love of God, whereby he confers upon the elect only, saving benefits, of his own mere good pleasure. Here observe

First. That it is love, or the kind inclination or propension of God's will, to communicate good to his elect.

Secondly. It is undue, undeserved love. The objects of this love, considered as creatures, can merit no good at the hand of God. Seeing they have received their all from him, surely they cannot put the Almighty in their debt, by giving him what is his own; and considered as sinners, who, by their voluntary transgression, have fallen short of his glory, they deserve his high and dreadful displeasure.

Thirdly. It is distinguishing love, manifested to the elect in a sovereign way, according to the good pleasure of God's will. Eph. i. 9. That is given to one which is denied to another, and only because it is God's pleasure; hence is that query of one of Christ's disciples, "Lord, how is it that thou wilt manifest thyself to us, and not unto the world?" John xiv. 22. And does not our Lord himself thank his eternal Father for the displays of his sovereignty in this respect? "I thank thee, Father, Lord of heaven and earth, because thou hast hid these things from the wise and prudent, and hast revealed them unto babes; even so. Father, for so it seemed good in thy sight." Matt. xi. 25, 26. It is but a few, a remnant of the fallen race of mankind, upon whom God is pleased to vouchsafe, and in whom he is pleased to glorify, his special grace. Luke xiii. 24. Rom. ix. 2, 7. "Esaias crieth also concerning Israel, Though the number of the children of Israel be as the sand of the sea, a remnant shall be saved."

Fourthly. It is efficacious love, which confers saving benefits; hence it is called, "the grace of God, which bringeth salvation." Tit. ii. 11. And the blessings it vouchsafes, are termed "things that accompany salvation." Heb. vi. 9. And hence the Psalmist prays, "Remember me, Lord, with the favour that thou bearest unto thy people. visit me with thy salvation; that I may see the good of thy chosen, that I may rejoice in the gladness of thy nation, that I may glory with thine inheritance." Ps. cvi. 4. And here it may be necessary to observe particularly, that divine love confers freely upon the elect, or concerts for them, the following important benefits, viz:

1. Election; this is free and gracious, without faith or works foreseen. "Even so then, at this present time also, there is a remnant according to the election of grace." Rom. xi. 5. "Having predestinated us, unto the adoption of children, by Jesus Christ, to himself, according to the good pleasure of his will." Eph. i. 5. "If by grace, then is it no more of works, otherwise grace is no more grace, and work is no more work." Rom. xi. 6. To the same effect the apostle elsewhere observes, that "it is not of him that willeth nor of him that runneth, but of God that showeth mercy." Rom. ix. 16. It is inconsistent with the independency and immutability of God, to suppose that anything without him should alter or incline his will.

2. Redemption is likewise of free grace. The contrivance of this scheme of happiness, as well as the sending of the blessed Son of God to effect it, by his obedience and sufferings, were marvellous displays of the Father's pure affection to a miserable world. "Herein is love, not that we loved God, but that he loved us, and sent his Son to be the propitiation for our sins." 1 John vi. 10. And to what else than free grace can we ascribe God the Father's acceptance of the suretiship of Christ in the sinner's room and place? Strict justice certainly demands personal satisfaction; and does not the love of Christ pass knowledge, in that he who is over all, God blessed for ever, came into a state of the worst abasement, voluntarily to save worthless dust from perpetual ruin? How sweetly does the Apostle Paul speak to this effect: "For ye know the grace of our Lord Jesus Christ, that though he was rich, yet for your sakes he became poor, that ye through his poverty might be rich!" 2 Cor. viii. 9. Besides, it may be here observed, that redemption by the satisfaction of Christ is frequently, in Scripture, restrained to a certain number, who are called the people of God, the sheep of Christ, and such as were given him by his Father. Matt. i. 21. John X. 15; xvii. 9.

Albeit the blood of the Son of God be of infinite value, and, therefore, the satisfaction made by it may, in this respect, be said to be universal; yet, inasmuch as it was neither the design of the Father, nor the Son, that it should be spent for all, so as to be saved by it, it is, therefore, to be referred to singular grace. Moreover,

3. The application of redemption in all its branches, is of free grace, as may appear by the following induction of particulars, viz:

Effectual calling is said to be according to God's purpose. Rom. viii. 29.

Faith is called the gift of God. "For by grace are ye "saved through faith, and that not of yourselves, it is the gift of God." Eph. ii. 8.

Conversion is not of flesh nor blood, nor of the will of

man, but of God, None of these graces which I have mentioned, are the fruits of free will; "for we are not sufficient to think any thing as of ourselves, but our sufficiency is of God." 2 Cor. iii. 5. No, they are all the fruits of the Spirit (Gal, v. 22), who produces them not by moral suasion, like poor creatures, but by an almighty, creating power, taking away the stony heart, and giving a heart of flesh. 1 Cor. iii. 5, 6. Ps. li. 10. Ezek. xxxvi. 26, 27. And,

Justification, whereby an elect sinner is freed from the guilt of sin and hath a right to eternal happiness, is of free grace. "Being justified freely by his grace, through the redemption that is in Christ Jesus." Rom. iii. 24. It is entirely without works. "Knowing that a man is not justified by the works of the law, but by the faith of Jesus Christ—for by the works of the law shall no flesh be justified." Gal. ii. 16.

Our *adoption*, or right, to the important privileges of children, and joint heirship with Christ, is also of pure grace. "Having predestinated us unto the adoption of children, by Jesus Christ, to himself, according to the good pleasure of his will, to the praise of the glory of his grace, wherein he hath made us accepted in the beloved." Eph. i. 5, 6.

Our *salvation*, in regard to the right thereto, is of grace. And, hence, eternal life is said to be "the gift of God through Jesus Christ our Lord." Rom. vi. 23. And, elsewhere, we are said expressly to be "saved by grace," Eph. ii. 8. In the meantime it should be remembered, that good works are the way to the kingdom, though they be not the cause of our reigning, as Barnard of old observed, "Though our right to happiness is of grace, as was before observed, yet the Almighty hath, by his gracious constitution, so ordered the matter, that good works are necessary to the possession of it." Matt. xxv. 21, 34, 35. I proceed,

III. To mention some considerations serving to manifest the sovereignty and glory of God's grace. And 1. Methinks the glory of divine grace appears by considering the author of it, who is a being infinitely and invariably happy in himself, as well as essentially and eternally glorious; and so neither needs the services of creatures, nor can be benefitted by them. Our goodness extends not to him, neither is it any gain to the Almighty, that we are righteous. To acknowledge God's glory, adds no more to its lustre, than speaking well of the natural sun adds to its beauty.

It may be here also observed, that Jehovah would have had millions of angels to celebrate his praise and execute his pleasure, although he had made his justice triumph in the ruin of the whole human race, which, certainly, he might have done. Or, he could have formed innumerable creatures of a more noble order than any of the creation to celebrate the glory of his attributes, if it had so pleased his Majesty: for he is almighty in power, hath the residue of the Spirit, and can raise up children even out of the stones to Abraham. But,

2. Let us consider the object upon which this divine grace is conferred, and we shall find,

First. That it is man, not angels. Our Saviour took not on him the nature of angels, but the seed of Abraham; because he designed to save the one, and to reserve those that fell of the other, in chains under darkness, unto the judgment of the great day. What is man but dust and ashes? A worm that is crushed before the moth, altogether unworthy of the kind notice of the great and glorious God. How amazing is the distinguishing grace of God in passing by creatures of a higher order, and fixing his love upon man!

Secondly. It is sinners upon whom divine grace is conferred. Man, by creation, was but dust, but by sin he is become polluted dust, and so odious and loathsome, as well as wretched and miserable. And this doleful state he has wilfully brought himself into, and wilfully continues in, against all the remonstrances of conscience, against all the kind importunities of a condescending God and Saviour. Man by sin has brought this twofold misery upon himself: 1. That he deserves no good, and, 2. That he deserves all evil. How can these deserve good at the hand of God, whose persons and performances are covered with deformity and pollution? Indeed, we deserve not the least common mercy, how much less, then, can we merit special benefits? "I am not worthy of the least of all the mercies, and of all the truth, thou hast showed unto thy servant." Gen. xxxii. 10. Men in a state of nature are unprofitable creatures, they are neither prepared to receive benefits, nor able to prepare themselves, seeing they are dead in sins and trespasses. And by their multiplied impieties they deserve the divine displeasure, and provoke him to inflict it. As they are children of wrath by nature, so they weary the Almighty by continued iniquities in practice. Eph. ii. 3. Isa. xliii. 24. And

Thirdly. The persons to whom divine grace is given, are enemies to God, both in their minds and lives. "The carnal mind is enmity against God, for it is not subject to the law of God, neither indeed can be." Rom. viii. 7. Now, enmity imports a high degree of fixed and implacable spite. dreadful state! This inward enmity unregenerate sinners bewray by their rebellion against God in practice, and cruel confederacies with his declared enemies. "And you that were sometime alienated, and enemies in your mind by wicked works, yet now hath he reconciled." Col. i. 21.

Fourthly. It is generally the poorer and meaner sort of men, that are favoured with divine grace, while the rich, honourable, and great are passed by. Many who make a considerable figure in the world, by the keenness of their natural and acquired endowments, and by the splendour of their outward circumstances, are entirely destitute of special grace, while others, who are poor and despised, are favoured therewith. This subject the apostle Paul discourses largely upon. "Not many mighty, not many noble are called; but God hath chosen the foolish things of the world, to confound the wise, and the weak things of the world, to confound the things that are mighty; and base things of the world, and things which are despised, hath God chosen, and things that are not, to bring to nought things that are." 1 Cor. i. 26–28.

Fifthly. Many of those to whom divine grace is given were, before conversion, notorious sinners, some blasphemers, persecutors and injurious. These things the apostle Paul ascribes to himself; he shut up many of the saints in prison, consented to their death, punished them in every synagogue, compelled them to blaspheme, and being exceeding mad against them, he persecuted them to strange cities. Acts xxvi. 10, 11. 1 Tim. i. 13, 15. Some, before conversion, have been idolaters, as the Ephesians. Some, fornicators, adulterers, effeminate, abusers of themselves with mankind, thieves, covetous, drunkards, revilers, extortioners. Such were some of the Corinthians, and yet they were washed, sanctified, justified. 1 Cor. vi. 9, 11. rich and glorious grace! How admirable is the grace of God, in the instance of Manasseh's conversion! who, though a conjurer, a murderer, and one who despised God, and bid defiance to heaven in prosperity, yet when, in adversity, he humbled himself and made supplication to Jehovah, was graciously heard and accepted. 2 Chron. xxxiii. 9, 12, 13. I shall only add the famous instance of Mary Magdalene, who was a notorious sinner. This poor woman loved much, because much was forgiven her; her heart was so melted with a sense of divine goodness, that she could wash our Lord's feet with her tears. Luke vii.

3. The glory of divine grace appears, not only from its author and object, but also from the season in which it is vouchsafed. The Almighty bestows benefits upon his people, at such seasons when they are most suitable. In the mount of difficulty and distress the Lord is seen, yea, he is a very present help in trouble. When sinners have wearied themselves in the greatness of their "way, and through a series of disappointments are brought to the last extremity, the blessed God manifests his grace and mercy. And thus when gracious persons are encircled with manifold miseries outward and inward, and their sorrowful hearts are ready to sink into despondency, with a long continued, oppressive weight of woe, from which they can hardly see any way of deliverance; when they are desolate and afflicted, their hearts almost overwhelmed, then Jehovah sends deliverance; "and they are as those that dreamed." Ps. XXV. 16, 17. When the compassionate Jehovah returns to his people, after their sinful wanderings from him. Oh! it makes them admire the pure and glorious riches of divine grace. And truly the Lord teaches his people more and more of this doctrine, namely, the freeness of his grace, while they are in the world.

4. The freeness of divine grace appears likewise from the manner in which divine benefits are conferred; e.g., we contribute nothing to the change wrought upon us by conversion. The natural bias of our wills is against it, and this reluctance and opposition remains, until it be overcome by the almighty power of God, who is hence said to make his people "a willing people in the day of his power." Ps. ciii. That alteration of dispositions which is implied in conversion, is not desired by the sinner before it; though unregenerate sinners desire to be delivered from misery, yet they do not desire to be delivered from sin, the cause of it. For that is as their right eye, and right arm. Well then, seeing those benefits whereby the soul is sanctified are undeserved, undesired, yea, opposed by the unconverted, surely then they must be freely vouchsafed.

5. The riches of divine grace appear from the nature of the benefits conferred, which are attended with these two following properties, viz: freedom from the greatest evils, and a right to, and possession of, the greatest good. Sinners, while in a state of unregeneracy, are immersed in, and exposed to, the greatest evils, both moral and penal. They are under the dominion of sin, and all over tainted by it; and by reason thereof, they are exposed to the curse and wrath of God in this and the next world. They are in a dungeon of darkness and distress, in a pit in which there is no water; bound and shackled with the heavy curse of God, void of light and beauty, and covered with the basest deformity. Now the benefits of divine grace bring the sinner from this depth of woe, loose his shackles, and release him out of prison. Hereby he is freed from the guilt of sin, through the righteousness of Christ imputed to him, and hereby he is freed from the

dominion of it, through the sanctifying influences of the Holy Spirit; and as he is thus freed from the greatest evils by divine grace, so he is thereby entitled to, and made a possessor of, the greatest good, both physical and moral, being made a partaker of the divine love, and beautified with the divine image, viz: holiness. By the former, he is refreshed, and by the latter adorned. And as he is under the unerring conduct and almighty protection of God here, so he is entitled to the perfect enjoyment of God hereafter; which is the greatest good, that it is possible for a creature to receive. I proceed to the,

IV. Proposition, which was to consider what is really and seemingly opposed to the grace of God. Now, the things that are opposed really are these two, viz: nature and merit. And, 1. Nature. Hereby we are children of wrath, "being dead in trespasses and sins." Eph. ii. 1, 3. By nature we have blind minds and stony hearts, neither discern the things that be of God, nor are willing to be subject thereto. "The natural man understands not the things of the Spirit of God, neither can he know them, because they are spiritually discerned." 1 Cor. ii.

14. "The carnal mind is enmity against God; it is not subject to the law of God, neither indeed can be." Rom. viii. 7. Nature, in its present fallen and corrupt state, fights against the grace of God as long as it can; and, therefore, that citadel of man's heart must be taken by storm, if the King of glory takes possession of it. And, 2. The papal doctrine of the merit of works, in the business of justification, directly opposes the grace of God. For grace is undue and undeserved love, as was shown before. "We conclude that a man is justified by faith without the deeds of the law. If it be of works, it is no more of grace, otherwise work would be no more work, and grace would be no more grace." Rom. iii. 28. But to proceed, 3. The wrath of God is seemingly opposed to grace. Now, the wrath of God is no other than his vindictive justice, or disposition to punish the guilty, which includes three things:

First. A purpose of punishing the transgressor. "For the wrath of God is revealed from heaven, against all ungodliness and unrighteousness of men, who hold the truth in unrighteousness," Rom. i. 18.

Secondly. It includes the denunciation of the aforesaid purpose by threatenings. "God is angry with the wicked every day; if he turn not, he will whet his sword; he hath bent his bow, and made it ready. He hath also prepared for him the instruments of death; he ordaineth his arrows against the persecutors." Ps. vii. 11–13.

Thirdly. It includes the execution of the threatenings, by all kinds of revenge and judgments. "Let no man deceive you with vain words, for because" of these things cometh the wrath of God upon the children of disobedience" (Eph. v. 6.); that is, fruits and effects of wrath in divine judgments. Sin wrongs the Almighty by insulting his sovereignty and legislative authority, by contradicting his unspotted holiness, and by slighting the riches of his goodness. By sin God is wronged, and robbed of that tribute of honour and service which is due to him from all created beings, by the strongest claims of right, viz: creation, preservation, provision; and some are under the additional engagement of redeeming love. It is sin, therefore, that stirs up the divine wrath; and because there be various aggravations of sin, therefore, there are various degrees of wrath excited thereby and proportioned thereto. And hence, the Scriptures, speaking after the manner of men, make mention of God S hot displeasure, fury and rage. Ps. vi. 1. "Therefore, will I also deal in fury; mine eye shall not spare, neither will I have pity, and though they cry in mine ears with a loud voice, yet I will not hear them." Ezek. viii. 18. "Cast abroad the rage of thy wrath." Job xl. 11. These expressions do not signify any tumult of passion in God, for he is incapable of passion, being simple, immutable and perfect. They serve, therefore, only to represent the great contrariety of the nature of God to sin, as well as the more dreadful effects of his wrath upon heinous transgressors. But in the meantime, it may be observed, that the wrath of God, in every instance of it, is terrible and irresistible, because it proceeds from an infinite and almighty God. And hence, it is compared to a "burning fire," and to a whirlwind that sweeps all before it. Zeph. i. And except repentance intervene, it will be continual and eternal.

Although the doctrine of free grace has been abused into licentiousness by some sordid spirits, which the apostle Paul mentions with great abhorrence, "Shall we continue in sin that grace may abound? God forbid," (Rom.vi. 1, 2,) yet its design and tendency is to promote the contrary. And indeed nothing more powerfully incites an ingenuous mind to holiness than the consideration of God's free and distinguishing grace. And here it is to be noted, that though Almighty God gives his grace freely, that so no creature should have occasion of boasting or glorying in his presence, yet, ordinarily, he vouchsafes it in the use of appointed means; that so there may be no umbrage for negligence, but, on the contrary, all that excitement to duty, "which can consist with the divine sovereignty. These things are excellently represented in the thirty-sixth chapter of Ezekiel, from the twenty-sixth to the thirty-seventh verse. Though the Almighty promises to confer saving benefits, yet he tells them, that for all these things he will be enquired of by them. But it is time to offer a word of improvement. And

1. From what has been said we may learn, that all those doctrines which ascribe any part of our salvation to our endeavours, as meritorious causes thereof, are very derogatory to the glory of God, and the design of his gospel; which is to magnify the exceeding riches of God's grace. Eph. i. Such who seek after righteousness, as it were, by the works of the law, are not like to attain it. Justification is not to be attained by a dependence upon our endeavours, we must come to God as beggars, and ask an alms of free grace, otherwise we shall be rejected.

2. We should examine ourselves, whether we are partakers of God's special grace, in the instances before mentioned, of effectual calling, faith, justification, conversion, adoption; have we by these things been brought, to a high prizing of Christ above all others, to a child-like familiarity with God, to an habitual, holy, humble, heavenly, and loving temper of mind, and course of behaviour? If so, let us rejoice in Christ Jesus in all outward distresses, let us ever admire the sovereign and distinguishing grace of God, and give to God the glory of it in heart, speech and practice.

But such of you as have not found the aforesaid experiences, rejoice not for joy, as other people, for ye have gone a whoring from God. Let your laughter be turned into mourning, and your joy into heaviness. Cry frequently and earnestly to God for sovereign, saving grace, and rest in no duties or ordinances short of it.

Is the grace of God free? Then the greatest transgressors should not despair of God's mercy; though your iniquities rival the stars for multitude, and in their aggravations are red as crimson and scarlet, yet free grace can easily blot them out, as a thick cloud, and make them white as snow. Therefore let sensible sinners be encouraged to come to, and believe in, the God of grace, for "where sin has abounded, there grace has much more abounded. The greater your transgressions are, the greater glory God will get to his grace in forgiving them. The Psalmist was aware of this, and therefore pled with God to pardon his iniquities, because they were exceeding great.

And methinks the doctrine of free grace should powerfully induce us to humility, seeing that it is God only who has made us to differ from others, and that we have nothing but what we have received. We are his debtors for all we have in hand or hope. The nature of grace supposes the object upon whom it is vouchsafed unworthy of it. A continued, humbling sense of this would as much conduce to our benefit as ornament.

And, seeing the good God is pleased to heap many undeserved kindnesses freely upon us, why should we not imitate his grace by conferring benefits upon our fellow creatures, without any regard to dignity, or hopes of a reward from them? By this we should glorify God, and convince others that we are his children.

In fine, let me, in the name of the gracious God, my Lord and Master, earnestly beseech poor sinners of every order to hasten, as for their lives, to that fountain of grace that is in Christ. Think not to put the Almighty in your debt by your doings, for if grace be not free, it is not grace. Sinners, abuse not the grace of God by delays and other impieties, or expect his inflamed wrath to avenge the ingratitude. "Let the wicked man forsake his way, and the unrighteous man his thoughts, and turn unto God, and he will have mercy on him, and to our God, for he will abundantly pardon."

I add no more at present. May the almighty and gracious God bless his word that has been offered in his name to our special and enduring benefit! Amen.

SERMON IV: THE WISDOM OF GOD IN REDEMPTION.

BY THE REV. GILBERT TENNENT.

"But we preach Christ crucified, unto the Jews a stumbling block, and unto the Greeks foolishness; but unto them which are called, both Jews and Greeks, Christ the power of God, and the wisdom of God."—1 Cor. i. 23, 24.

The apostle observes in the preceding verses, with great beauty and propriety, that, "in the wisdom of God, the world by wisdom knew not God." The gentile sages, by the mere dint of reason and philosophy, could not form consistent notions of the Supreme Being, or how to obtain his favour. A deluge of the most absurd polytheism and gross profaneness overspread the greatest part of the infidel tribes, before the light of the gospel shone among them; no object was so despicable, as not to be thought worthy of divine honours; no vice so detestable, as not only to obtain in common conversation, but even to be admitted into their religious rites, and most solemn acts of worship; yea, to give sanction to the most brutish and crimson iniquities, they ascribed them to the gods they adored, as the learned Arnobius observes, with equal justice and elegance.

It is true, the corruption was not so universal, but that some noble souls raised themselves above the common level; they bewailed, and contemned the stupidity and credulity of the multitude, yet their number was small, and the efficacy of their singular sentiments even upon themselves but little; the effect of their discernment was but a state of perpetual scepticism, a floating in doubtful uncertainty between all opinions, discarding what was manifestly wrong, but not fixing their minds in what was good and right. Yea, in matters of moral good and evil, though some of the rules they have left us are truly excellent, yet in many important things they are very deficient; there is a deep silence in their writings of the nature and obliquity of several vices, such as pride, revenge, and self-murder; they are likewise silent about the right principle of action, love to God; the right end of action, the glory of God; the right mode of action, humility and dependence upon God, for light, strength and acceptance.

They were also at a loss respecting the gaining the friendship of the Almighty when offended, the certainty of a future state, and the strict account they must render of all their actions, to the sovereign Lord and Judge of the universe. Are not these things of inexpressible importance, the very governing principles of a Christian's conduct? This melancholy ignorance of the pagan masters was, doubtless, the source of that uncertainty they bewray in their discourses, and such inconsistency in their lives, concerning which, one of the greatest and best judges among them, viz: Tully, speaks thus, "Do you think," says he, "that these things [meaning the precepts of morality] had any influence upon those men, (except only a very few,) that thought, and wrote, and disputed about them? no; who is there of all the philosophers, whose mind and manners were conformable to right reason? who ever made his philosophy the law and rule of his life, and not a mere boast and show of his wit and parts? who observed his own instructions, and lived in obedience to his own precepts? On the contrary, many of them were slaves to filthy lusts."

Nay, even the things which they themselves knew, they had not authority enough to inculcate upon men's minds with such impression as to influence and govern their conduct; the truths they proved by a train of speculative reasonings were destitute of more sensible authority to enforce them with energy in practice; the precepts they proposed wanted weight, and evidently appeared to be no more than the precepts of men. This was, doubtless, the reason that none of the philosophers were ever able to work any remarkable change in the minds and lives of their hearers; nor does it appear in history that any of the followers of Socrates were ever so convinced by his instructions of the excellency of virtue, and the certainty and value of its final reward, as to be willing to lay down their lives for its sake, as innumerable disciples of the Lord Jesus Christ have done, with the greatest gladness and heroic fortitude. The truth is, the philosophers themselves were sensible of the defect of their own rules in this particular, and, therefore, confess that human nature was strangely corrupted, and that this corruption was a disease whose cause they knew not, and for which they could not find a sufficient remedy. So that the great duties of religion and virtue were proposed by them as matters of speculation, rather than rules of practice: not so much urged upon men's hearts and lives, as proposed to their admiration.

This was, apparently, the condition of mankind without a revelation; to recover them out of which degeneracy, into a state suitable to the original excellency of their nature, a supernatural discovery of their duty was plainly necessary; for if, as has been observed, the generality of the world were so ignorant and corrupt, so overrun with idolatry and licentiousness; if the best of the philosophers were not exempt from the general infection, and free from uncertainty respecting the doctrines they pretended to advance; if the points wherein they were certain, they were not able to prove clearly to vulgar understandings, and those they were able to prove, they had not sufficient authority to enforce; in a word, if there was so much inconsistency in themselves as to give scandal to others, and so much depravity in others as to make them despair of reforming them, there was, then, plainly a want of some revelation to supply these defects, and to discover in what manner, and with what kind of external service, the blessed God might be acceptably worshipped; a revelation to discover what expiation he would be pleased to accept of for sin, by which his honour is affronted and his authority opposed; a revelation to give intelligent beings an assurance of the great motives of religion, the rewards and punishments of a future state. In fine, some particular revelation was necessary to make the whole system of Christian doctrine clear and obvious to all capacities, to add weight and authority to the plainest precepts, and to furnish men with extraordinary assistance to enable them to overcome the corruptions of their nature; and, indeed, without the assistance of such a revelation, the wisest of men were always of opinion that the world could never be reformed. "Ye may even give over," says Socrates, "all hopes of amending men's manners for the future, unless God be pleased to send some other person to instruct you; for whatsoever is set right, says Plato, in the present ill state of the world, can only be done by the interposition of God."

This condescending and gracious interposure appears evidently in the Christian system, the plan of salvation by the Lord Jesus Christ, which, though it be despised by the ignorant, inconsiderate and prejudiced, is, by those that are awakened out of their security and divinely illuminated, experienced to be, indeed and in truth, a glorious display of the power of God, and the wisdom of God; the latter of which, let us for a little space fix our attention upon at present.

The blessed God, my brethren, foreseeing man's fall, and the misery consequent upon it, determined his recovery in a way worthy of himself, and suited to the circumstances of the apostate creature, in which his wisdom is eminently conspicuous. This will appear by considering the end that God proposed, and the means he concerted to compass it. All intelligent agents first propose an end, and then choose the means that tend to obtain it; now the more perfect the understanding is, the more noble is the end it designs, and the more apt the means it prescribes to acquire it. The end proposed by the gospel of the Lord Jesus Christ is most excellent, viz: the glory of God, and the happiness of mankind, or their restoration to his image and favour.

The glory of God, or the manifestation of his attributes, by their exercise, to the moral world, was his supreme scope; as God is the best of beings, of consequence his glory must be the best end, and therefore it is but reasonable he should aim at it in all his works; and hence he is said to have made all things for himself, and that of him, and through him, and to him are all things: seeing he is the Creator and Lord of all, it is but just and right that he should be the end of all; nothing can be more natural than that what was borrowed from him, should be directed to him or his honour; "the heavens" are, therefore, said to "declare the glory of God, and the firmament to show forth his handywork:" on this account, the revelation of the way to future happiness, by the dear, dear Lord Jesus Christ, is called "the glorious gospel of the blessed God;" because it is the clearest manifestation, the richest display of the transcendent excellency of his adorable attributes, which was ever given to the children of men: and hence Jehovah is said to "magnify his word (that is, the word of his grace) above all his name." The apostle Paul, in his epistle to the Corinthians, assures us, that the "ministration of righteousness exceeds in glory;" and that under this dispensation, "we all with open face beholding, as in a glass, the glory of the Lord, are changed into the same image from glory to glory, even as by the Spirit of the Lord." In the gospel we behold the Lord Jesus Christ, and the harmonious manifestation of the divine attributes in the scheme of salvation through him, not under the dark veil of types, shadows and prophecies, as the Jewish church, but with open face as in a glass, and are thereby gradually transformed into his image, through the Holy Spirit's concurring influence.

To the aforesaid manifestation of the divine attributes, which the Almighty proposed as his supreme end, we must add the praise and thanksgiving of reasonable creatures on account thereof. When intelligent beings acknowledge the displays of God's excellencies with adoring reverence and ardent affection, they glorify him; "he that offereth praise, glorifieth me," saith the Almighty by the Psalmist; and this, undoubtedly, the blessed God had likewise in view as his supreme end.

But the subordinate end in redemption is the restoration of man; and this, indeed, is inseparably connected with the former, as appears from the angels' anthem,

"Glory to God in the highest, on earth peace, good will towards men." Sin had broken the sacred alliance between God and man, and exposed man to the divine displeasure, an inexpressible and incomprehensible misery. Now, what is more becoming the Father of mercies, the God of love, than to compassionate and relieve the miserable—than to raise from the depths of ruin many monuments, in which his kindness and benignity might for ever triumph? To compass these truly valuable ends, divine wisdom projected the aptest means possible, which appears in the following easy light.

The misery of apostate man consists in the depravation of his whole nature by sin, and in his exposedness to the divine displeasure on account of it, which was a just and natural consequent of his crimson apostasy; and his happiness consisted in his restoring him to his original purity and fellowship with God, and to the full enjoyment of him. But the way to effect this, in consistency with the divine justice, law and government, was a depth which no human understanding could fathom. That God whose being is love, should show kindness to the angels, who never swerved from his statutes, is easy to imagine; for though they cannot merit his favour, yet they never incurred his displeasure by malconduct: and it must needs be natural to Jehovah to love the image of his purity wherever it appears.

Nor is it hard to conceive that the Almighty would be inclined to succour an innocent creature in misery; for in this case, there would be nothing to obstruct the free effluxes of his unexhausted goodness; but how to save a creature that is as guilty as miserable, by its own criminal choice, is a difficulty too hard to be solved by the wisdom of men or of angels. Heaven itself seemed to be divided on this occasion; mercy inclined to save, but justice interposed for satisfaction. Mercy regarded man with respect to his misery, and its pleas were such as these: Shall the most excellent creature in the lower world perish, the fault not being entirely his—perish for ever without any favour? Shall no compassion be shown to miserable mankind, who in their original state were the beauty and crown of all the numerous ranks of beings in this inferior system? Shall the malignant enemy forever triumph in the fatal success of his perfidy, and reduce the whole human race to the most deplorable and remediless ruin? On the other hand, justice, the nature of which is to give to every one his due, considered man as guilty of a most ungrateful, murderous and pregnant iniquity, the wages of which, agreeable to the dictates of reason and the law of God, is death: this divine attribute remonstrates against showing favour to the unhappy delinquents, and queries, "Shall not the Judge of all the earth do right?" All the other attributes seemed to be attendants on justice.

The wisdom of God enforced its plea; it being most indecent, that sin, which demerits the execution, should procure the abrogation, of the law, which would encourage the commission of it without fear. The majesty of God was likewise concerned; for it was not becoming excellent greatness and absolute sovereignty, to treat in this humble manner with inferiors and delinquents, and to offer pardon to presumptuous, ungrateful rebels, before they bow at his footstool, and make supplication to their judge.

The holiness of God confirms and corroborates incensed, lesed majesty, and urges justice to execute the threatening annexed to the violation of the law; for "Jehovah is of purer eyes than to behold iniquity." As purity is the essential object of his complacential will, which he loves immutably wherever it is, so, by the law of contraries, sin is the eternal object of his hatred, and consequently such as" are (with their full consent) under its habitual rule and government. Because of their connection with it, he will not, saith Job, take the wicked by the hand, or at all acquit them, as the prophet Nahum expresses it. Purity and pollution, by reason of their contrary natures, cannot mix or coalesce, but must maintain a perpetual jar and discord, till one or other is destroyed. Further,

The truth of God, being plighted in the covenant of works, stands engaged to see to the execution of the penalty denounced in case of trespass; and if it is not, the matter so requiring, divine truth fails; but that is impossible, and the attribute joins issue in the contest with divine justice, wisdom, majesty and purity, and requires the execution of the threatened punishment upon the offender himself; or, if extraordinarily dispensed with (in this respect), it must be on such terms as the honour of God's truth may be preserved inviolate.

This seeming conflict among the divine attributes, no created understanding could adjust, and find out a way to reconcile infinite mercy with inflexible justice; a way to satisfy the demands of the one, and grant the requests of the other. In this exigency divine wisdom interposed, and in its unsearchable depths cherished an expedient, to save man without any prejudice to the perfections of the Deity, without any injury to his government over the moral world, by constituting a mediator between the guilty creature and himself, that, by transferring the punishment on the surety, sin might be punished, and the sinner saved. Here mercy and justice salute each other, and shine with equal glory and lustre. The latter is fully satisfied, and the former exceedingly magnificent. These amiable attributes, in this mediatorial plan, joy in friendly harmony, to promote and secure the penitent and believing sinner's perpetual happiness. Nor is it unbecoming the majesty of God, to accept a returning sinner, when a mediator of infinite dignity intercedes for him.

The purity of God is not in the least degree disparaged by his clemency to transgressors, seeing the blessed Mediator is a principle and pattern of holiness to all that believe in him, and the truth of God, engaged to issue the threatenings of the broken law, is, by the sufferings of the sinner's surety, preserved inviolate. So that all the divine perfections concur herein, and express, to the eternal astonishment and delight of men and angels, inexpressible charms, beauty and magnificence. Here we may see the glory of the blessed God shining in the face of the venerable and dear Lord Jesus Christ. Who can fathom the un-searchable depths of this amazing wisdom? Who can unfold the boundless riches and treasures of this mysterious prodigy and miracle of mercy—this inexpressible, transcendent, incomprehensible and glorious grace and love?

Surely, no understanding, either human or angelical, is equal to this province; it is only the same infinite mind that concerted this illustrious scheme of salvation by a Redeemer, that can comprehend it.

The angels, those great ministers that attend the throne of God, stoop down with the deepest attention, the strongest desire, and noblest pleasure, to behold the rich and unsearchable variety of manifold wisdom and glorious grace that is herein contained. But though we cannot comprehend the depths of redeeming goodness, yet we may apprehend so much as to be thereby powerfully influenced to admiration, love and obedience; so much as to be thereby excited to cry out in the apostle's language, "the depths of the riches, both of the knowledge and wisdom of God! how unsearchable are his judgments, and his ways past finding out!" Surely, the "love of Christ passeth knowledge." But, more particularly.

The wisdom of God appears eminently in taking occasion from the sin of our progenitor, to bring a greater tribute of honour to God, and greater benefit to man, than if he had never transgressed. Sin naturally tends to God's dishonour and to the creature's ruin; but, contrary to its natural tendency, it is overruled by a wise providence to be the occasion of the greatest glory to God and good to man; so that "out of the eater comes forth meat, and out of the strong, sweetness;" as a medicine is extracted out of a poison by the alembic; or as the black ground in a picture, though in itself it contaminates, yet when fixed, with judgment, in its proper place as a shade, heightens the lustre of the brightest colours, and adds to the beauty of the whole piece.

Dear sirs, the glory of God is more illustriously apparent, in the recovery of fallen man, than if he had never sinned. Had Adam persevered inviolably in his duty and allegiance to his great Creator and Sovereign, he could only have been the subject of divine goodness, but not in its highest and most endearing acts, which are to pity and succour the guilty and miserable. Had he transgressed, and redemption not have taken place, justice, it is true, would have been honoured with a solemn sacrifice, a solemn triumph; but mercy, that amiable, benign, and indulgent attribute, would have been veiled with a total eclipse. But now the wisdom of Jehovah in the redemption of man appears, by according these attributes, and making them shine with rival charms. The honour of Jehovah appears as much in preserving the authority of his law, by punishing our surety in our room and place, as by the exercise of his mercy in pardoning the transgressor.

Nor is it less honourable, my brethren, to the divine wisdom, to restore fallen man with infinite advantage: though innocent man was holy, yet sad experience verifies, that he was mutably so; but holiness in the redeemed shall be perpetual, eternal. Adam's stock was in his own hand, and hence he became a bankrupt; but ours is in the hands of an almighty surety, who has undertaken for us, and will be faithful to his trust. Justice itself being satisfied becomes our friend, and ascertains our possession of paradise. I might add, that there are graces to be acted by us in our fallen state, for which there were no objects or occasions in innocence: such as compassion to the miserable, forgiveness of injuries, and patience; all which, being emblems of the divine perfections, must, of consequence, be ornamental to, and perfective of, our immortal souls, in conforming them to the great pattern and original of beauty and excellency.

Again, the wisdom of God appears in appointing such a mediator as is suitably qualified to reconcile God to man, and man to God; a mediator, that is God and man in one person, and therefore capable of the affections and sentiments of both the parties to be reconciled. The wisdom of the divine constitution in appointing a person to mediate, who is possessed of the divine and human natures, appears more particularly from the three offices he exercises in that character, viz: Prophetical, Priestly, and Kingly.

Considered as a Prophet, it was necessary that the mediator should be God, that he might deliver instructions with more authority and efficacy; it is God alone that can enlighten the mind, convince the conscience, teach, and change the heart. And it was likewise necessary, that he should be man, that he might converse with us, and convey his instructions to us, in such a familiar way, as we could receive. Such is the weakness of our present frame, that the majesty of God's appearance occasions a distressing panic, and, hence, when Israel had seen some glimpses of God's glory and majesty, at the giving of the law, they besought the Lord to speak no more to them, in such a manner, lest they died. And no doubt guilt increases our dread at the approach of God, and therefore renders us unfit to attend with due calmness to his immediate instructions. An instance of this we have in the prophet, who, when he heard the seraphs shout, "Holy, holy, holy, is the Lord of hosts, the heavens and earth are full of the majesty of his glory," lamented in this mournful language, "Woe is me, I am undone, for mine eyes have seen the King, the Lord of Hosts." Infinite purity, attended with awful majesty, so alarms our fears, as to render us unfit for instruction; but the Son of God appearing in our nature to make atonement for transgressors, the brightness of his divine majesty being veiled with the mantle of his humanity is thereby allayed, and so more accommodated to our present state of weakness. Hereby we are encouraged to draw near to him, and to hear with composure his gentle instructions, which drop as the rain, and distil as the dew upon the tender herb.

Nor was the union of the divine and human natures in the person of the Mediator less necessary, my brethren, in respect of his Priestly office. He must be man, that the sinning nature might suffer, and thereby acquire a right to the satisfaction made; for our title to the benefits of Christ's sufferings depends upon our union to him, which is not only spiritual by faith, but natural also; for, as the apostle observes, "He who sanctifies, and they who are sanctified, are all one;" i.e., they have communion in the same nature. Inasmuch as suffering, according to the divine declaration, was necessary to atone for sin, of which the Deity is incapable, it behoved our High Priest to be man, that he might have a capacity for it; and that those sufferings might be of sufficient dignity and value, and the human nature supported under them, it was as necessary he should be God.

Nor was it less needful that the Mediator should partake of both natures, in order to intercede for us as a Priest; that so he might have a sufficient interest in his Father's affection to prevail in his suit for us, and, at the same time, be possessed of tender affections towards us. Being the Son of God, him the Father always hears, and being the Son of man, he is touched with the feeling of our infirmities; we have, therefore, encouragement to come with boldness to the throne of his grace to obtain mercy, and find grace to help in time of need.

And is it not also requisite that the Mediator should be God and man, in regard to his Kingly office? For unless he be God, how can he apply the fruits of his death to us, dispossess the strong man armed, and subdue us to the obedience of faith? And if he had not been man, how could he have led us into the way of universal holiness, by the influence of his own example, which is, doubtless, an excellent method to reform mankind? It is not only necessary to enact rules of virtue by a kingly authority, but likewise, by example, to make precepts practicable and honourable. When brave generals, though of the noblest lineage, design to animate their armies to heroic achievements, they voluntarily submit their persons to all the humble offices and hardships of a state of war, courageously lead their troops into the high places of the field of battle, and expose their lives to the greatest perils. This our Lord has done for us; the Captain of our salvation, the King of the church, and Lord of the universe, has been made perfect through sufferings.

Another instance of divine wisdom in the redemption of man, by the Lord Jesus Christ, is in making the remedy to have some analogy and proportion to the cause of our ruin; i.e., as we fell in the first Adam, considered as our representative, so we are raised by the second, considered in the same character: "as by the disobedience of one, many were made sinners, so by the obedience of one, many are made righteous." As guilt and death came by the first, through imputation to all his natural offspring, that are united to him naturally by existence, so righteousness and life came by the second Adam, through imputation to all his spiritual offspring, that are united to him spiritually by faith.

Moreover, my brethren, divine wisdom is conspicuous in the manner whereby our redemption is accomplished, viz: by the humiliation of the Son of God; by this, Jehovah, as it were, counterworks the sin of angel and men. Pride is the malignity of every sin, for, by it, the sinner sets up his will against God. Now that our dear Redeemer might cure the disease we labour under, in its original source, by the nature of the remedy, he applied to our arrogance, humility. Man, who is but a worm and crushed before the moth, was vainly and wickedly guilty of high treason, in affecting to be like God; and thus he fell from the state of happiness in which he was at first created. And the eternal Son of God, who was in the form of God, and counted it not robbery to be equal with God, stooped to assume the humble form of a servant, that by his sufferings he might restore fallen man to his primitive purity and bliss; and by his example correct that arrogance, which was the fountain of his fatal apostasy, and all its unhappy consequences. "The word was made flesh," to banish the distance between God and it. stupendous abasement! the condescension of divine majesty herein is equal to the contrivance of divine wisdom. Both are indeed incomprehensible, both inexpressible. So dreadful was the malignity of our native arrogance, that such unparalleled, astonishing abasement, even of God himself, was necessary to its cure. By this, our Lord destroyed the first work of our grand enemy.

Further, the wisdom of God (in connection with almightiness) appears in appointing such contemptible, and, to appearance, contrary means, to accomplish such great and glorious effects. The way is as wonderful as the work: that Christ, by dying on the cross, a reputed malefactor, should be made our eternal righteousness; that by death, he should destroy him that had the power of death and purchase our life; that, by descending into the grave, he should purchase our resurrection from it, and immortal blessedness,—is truly amazing, and plainly shows that the thoughts and ways of God are far above ours, as the heavens are above the earth. Strange that immortal life should spring from death, honour from ignominy, healing from stripes, blessedness from a curse! This is so contrary to the usual course of things, that to render it credible, it was typified by many symbols, and foretold by many prophets before it came to pass, that, when it came, it might be esteemed an effect of God's eternal counsel, almighty power, and unsearchable wisdom. Though Christ crucified be to the Jews a stumbling-block, and to the Greeks foolishness, yet to those that are called, he is the power of God, and the wisdom of God. Surely great is the mystery of godliness, God manifest in the flesh; whatever our modern exalters of carnal reason, and monopolizers of wisdom, mutter to the contrary notwithstanding. These men say they are Christians, and yet with a show of wisdom, and pretext of friendship to Jesus Christ, they presume to confront the express testimony of his inspired apostles; they labour with art and address to rob his religion of its grand peculiars, and to substitute polished paganism in its place, and would have us to believe the jest, the juggle, that there is no material difference between them. But God forbid! we have not so learned Christ; while they profess themselves to be wise, they commence fools, they become vain in their imaginations, and their foolish hearts are darkened; "for in the wisdom of God, the world by wisdom knew not God; it pleased God by the foolishness of preaching to save those that believe;" i.e., the great Sovereign and Lord of all, who has a right to do with his own as he pleases, has, of his mere motion, so ordered the matter, that by the humble preaching of the cross of Christ, or, in other words, the mediatorial plan of salvation, by the sufferings and death of the Son of God (which some stumble at, and reckon inconsistent and foolish), those that believe shall obtain eternal happiness. Such who reckon the grand peculiars of the religion of Jesus foolish and absurd, would act a more candid and consistent part, if they renounced the name of Christianity altogether, (for what signifies the name without the thing?) and openly declared that they reject the Bible, as a sure and sufficient guide to heaven, and betake themselves to their Dagons, viz: their carnal reason, and graceless virtue,—to a dependence on the former as their supreme and sufficient guide in the matters of religion, and on the latter as their only Saviour. "My soul, come not into their secret; to their assembly, mine honour, be not thou united." Let Jewish, Grecian, and British infidels or pagans, (the most inexcusable of all the rest, who in the midst of light and day grope in Egyptian darkness,) in the pride and stoutness of their hearts deride and burlesque the mysterious and humble doctrines of Christ crucified, as a nonsensical scheme; yet they never will be able, by all their art, their eloquence, and sovereign contempt, to drive those that have experienced a gracious change (a divine birth) from the foundation of their hope. No, such have an inward witness, that "Christ crucified is the wisdom of God, and the power of God;" and in every successive period, till time concludes its drama, there will be such, who shall not be ashamed of the gospel of Christ, but glory in his cross, as a badge of honour; for "the foundation of God stands sure." Jehovah has graciously promised, that the gates of hell shall not prevail against his church, and that no weapon formed against her shall prosper. But to proceed:

The divine wisdom, my brethren, appears gloriously in forming the plan of the gospel, in such a manner, as at once to provide for the comfort of men's souls, and promote the purity of their manners. And this, indeed, is an inseparable character of divine doctrines, that they equally tend to promote God's glory and our benefit. Thus, as the way to blessedness by a mediator, effectually secures God's honour, so it powerfully incites the sinner's hope, love and joy, by representing the blessed God as amiable, benign, and gracious, by providing a complete satisfaction to injured justice, that thus a way might be opened for a liberal, consistent and honourable effusion of divine goodness, in all its innumerable instances, in all its various and valuable effects, adapted to every changing scene of life, adapted to every circumstance of the indigent and distressed; and sufficient to support, relieve, yea, refresh and content them, in the midst of miseries and woes; and under a train and complication of the greatest calamities, which this Bochim, this state of exile, affords. These primitive and faithful servants of Christ, the apostles, though they were by many reckoned deceivers, yet they were true; though they had nothing, yet they possessed all things; though they were sorrowful, yet they were always rejoicing. The mediatorial plan shows us how "God may be just, and yet the justifier of him that believeth in Jesus," because of his propitiation. This opens to our view the unspeakable gift of the Son of God, and assures us of the gift of all things with him, in case we believe; in particular, this fixes our final perseverance in goodness, a crowning mercy, upon the impregnable basis of the immutable purpose, the almighty power, and faithful promise of God; upon the sacred suretyship, the complete satisfaction, and perpetual intercession of the Lord Jesus Christ; and therefore this gospel scheme of grace and salvation opens an unfailing spring of joy, and lays a firm foundation for our hope and trust; this calms the guilty, restless mind, and makes it "rejoice in the hope of the glory of God, with joy unspeakable, and full of glory."

And as the gospel of Christ provides for our solace, so it incites to universal purity. Do not the sufferings of the Son of God for sin give us a dreadful representation of its malignity and danger, seeing nothing less could make a satisfaction for it, and, therefore, serve to deter us from it? We may judge of the danger of a disease by the difficulty of its cure; nothing less could heal our mortal malady than the blood of God; and seeing Christ has expressed such amazing love to us, does not this tend to beget love in us to him, and to constrain us to a voluntary, sincere and uniform obedience, from that truly noble principle?

Now, if the gospel of Christ be such as has been described, with what ardour should we celebrate the divine praises for this revelation, so worthy of God, so suited to the case of fallen man? The apostasy of our first parents was so fatal to us, that nothing less than infinite wisdom could find out a sufficient remedy. There is no discovery of this in the works of creation. The heavens and the earth do, indeed, prove the existence of a Supreme Being, by pointing to some of his adorable attributes; but cannot represent the design of redemption, which has no connection with the existence of creatures, but hangs altogether upon the sovereign pleasure of God. The doctrine of the Trinity, which is the foundation of the mediatorial plan of salvation, cannot be known by the frame of the universe.

Nor can natural reason, by its utmost force, attain to the knowledge of redeeming grace and love. It is true, there are some remains of the law of nature in the heart of man, some common notices (*rudera, vestigia*) of the differences between moral good and evil, otherwise the world would soon disband and turn into the wildest anarchy, the rudest chaos, and become an Aceldama. Though misery when felt, excites to look out for a remedy, yet, here reason is at a loss, at a plunge, and quite nonplussed. How could the Israelites imagine, that by looking to the brazen serpent, those that were stung should be healed? And how can a poor creature discover, by the mere dint of his own genius, or light within, the satisfaction of divine justice by Jesus Christ? No, they cannot, and hence it is called a "mystery, hid from ages and generations;" nay, though the human mind had never been corrupted, it could not, by the force of its reasonings, find it out; for this the very angels could not discover, till it was made known to them by the church. By the first coming of Christ, and the conversion of many to him, the depths of divine wisdom were unveiled.

The apostle informs us, that the case of the Gentiles was extremely dangerous: "their understandings were darkened, being alienated from the life of God, through the ignorance that is in them, because of the blindness of their hearts." The apostle Paul declares, that the Ephesians were formerly darkness, i.e., while pagans; and elsewhere assures us that "the natural man does not understand the things of the Spirit of God;" that they are foolishness to him, and he cannot know them, because they are spiritually discerned; and this was not only the case with the ruder sort, but of the more polite and learned; for, as has been before observed, "the world by wisdom knew not God." Natural reason cannot inform us whether God will pardon any transgressors at all, or not, or upon what terms. It is true, the modern Deists do now trump up a plausible scheme of natural religion, with design to overset revealed, but are not so candid as to inform us that they borrowed their lessons from the Bible; without the assistance of which, notwithstanding their pride and pretence to penetration (or superior acumen), they would speak as darkly, doubtingly, and confusedly, as their more ingenious and ingenuous forefathers, the pagan philosophers, long since.

What a horrid confusion of sentiments, what a rude, wild, and dark chaos, overwhelmed the pagan world before Christ's coming, in respect of the most important points of religion! Varro declares, that there were, among them, no less than three hundred different opinions about the chief good; nor did they inculcate internal purity, and the necessity of forgiving injuries; and the best of them offered but uncertain conjectures about the immortality of the soul. A view of their miseries may justly heighten our value for the mercies we enjoy. While many nations dwell in darkness, and in the shadow of death, the day-spring from on high has visited us, and the Sun of righteousness arisen with healing under his wings upon us. This distinguishing, important, and unmerited benefit should fire our souls with love and gratitude, and stir us up to the most affectionate thanksgiving. It is the prerogative of God to reveal the secrets of his kingdom to whom he pleases; how, then, can we reflect upon the divine goodness towards us, without the warmest emotion, the most admiring, grateful sentiments? Surely, by nature Ave are as blind, corrupt, and perverse as any other nation; what are we, then, that God should be so gracious to us? If the publication of the law to the people of Israel was justly reckoned their peculiar treasure, what, then, is the revelation of the gospel by the Son of God, which alone discovers our remedy, and of which there is no innate notice in human nature, nor any given otherwise universally.

Can this principle be easily justified, that there is something in mankind, which, if attended to, is sufficient to direct man to salvation without the Scriptures? It is no matter what this something be called, whether reason, conscience, or the light within, seeing the substance intended is the same. Do not the Scriptures positively declare that there is no name given under heaven, by which salvation can be obtained, but the name of Jesus; that faith comes by hearing, and hearing by the word of God; that we cannot hear without a preacher; that the heathen are darkness, without the covenants of promise, without God; that they perish for lack of vision, and that all the unregenerate before conviction are blind, dead, possessed with Satan; that the light in some is darkness, and that all men have not faith? Now, how can the aforesaid principles agree with those declarations?

And do not millions of facts (which are stubborn things) in the pagan world, in the present and past ages, and in various nations, confirm the aforesaid testimony of Scripture, that the pagans, whatever pains they take in their different ways of religion (unless they obtain some information from the sacred Scriptures), remain ignorant of the way of salvation by Christ? If the pagans had this knowledge, is it reasonable to think that they would be brought to the profession of what they believe with great difficulty, in places where this profession is not attended with any danger? And yet this has often been the case, and is so still; and why have so many opposed, with great vehemence, and without any sense of guilt, the profession of Christianity, (with Saul before his conversion,) if it be 60 universally known as is supposed? And why do none, among such vast multitudes, and during so many ages, give any account of this matter?

Further, is not one design of the sacred scriptures for "doctrine and instruction," "to make the man of God perfect and thoroughly furnished to every good work;" now what need is there of this, if there be sufficient light in every man to direct him without it? Is it not absurd to say, we need more than what is sufficient, or that we need more than we need? Is not the Bible, therefore, needless and superfluous, according to this principle? And is this principle safe, that, in its consequences, deprives us of our Bible? Pray is not the business of pastors after God's heart, to feed the people with knowledge and understanding? And is it not the design of their office to turn sinners from darkness to light? But what need is there of this institution at all, what need of any labours to instruct mankind, if men have sufficient light without it in themselves? Is not preaching at any time or place, on this plan, an absurdity, a mere farce? And why did the apostles take so much pains in travelling and preaching? Why did they run such risks and endure such hardships? Was it to do a superfluous business, to teach people what they knew already, or might know without their assistance? If so, was this prudent in them (seeing they carried on no business of merchandize, or traffic in their travels to enrich themselves), or a good argument that they had the full exercise of their reason? Pray did they suffer stripes, imprisonment, or death, like wise men or fools, for doing what was needless? Judge ye.

Upon this hypothesis, is it probable that we shall be duly sensible of the value of our religious privileges sincerely thankful for them, tenderly concerned for those that want them, and use diligence to proselyte them to Christianity, when we judge that they are unnecessary?

But to proceed, is not the incomprehensible mystery

of redeeming wisdom and grace, well worthy of our serious thoughts and study; seeing it excels all other sciences in the sublimity of its object, the certainty of its principle, the efficacy of its influence, and the value of its end? It is a doctrine that affects the soul with the highest admiration of the divine wisdom, love, and grace, and makes us speak in "the Psalmist's language, "How wonderful are thy thoughts to us-ward!" When the Almighty hereby turns our captivity, we are as those that dream. This opens before us the grandest theme, that was ever exposed to mortal eye or ear; a complication of wonders, the chief of all the ways of God; strange that He who fills heaven and earth, should be confined in a virgin's womb—that life should die and, being dead, revive—that mercy should triumph, without infringing on the rights of justice!

The principle of this mysterious doctrine is immutable, like God, the author and object of it; whereas, philosophical sciences are frequently shifting; almost every one, through pride and excessive self-love, is disposed to despise and pull down what another, with much labour, builds up.

And how precious and powerful is the influence of this doctrine upon those that believingly receive it! While they behold, as in a glass, the glory of the Lord, they are transformed into the same image from glory to glory—this is eternal life, to know God, and Jesus Christ whom he has sent.! let us cry earnestly to God, that Christ crucified may be more and more the wisdom of God, and the power of God to us! Amen, amen. Dear Lord Jesus Christ, say Amen.

SAMUEL BLAIR.

The Rev. Samuel Blair was a native of Ireland, but came early to this country, and received his education in the Log College, under Mr. William Tennent, Sen. He must have been among the first pupils of this institution. After finishing his classical and theological studies, Mr. Blair put himself under the care of the New Castle Presbytery, by which body he was in due time licensed to preach the gospel. Soon after his licensure, he was settled in the Presbyterian Congregation at Shrewsbury, in New Jersey, in 1734. He laboured in this field for five or six years, when he received an earnest call to settle in New Londonderry, otherwise called Faggs Manor, in the State of Pennsylvania. Here he instituted a classical school, similar in its purpose to that of Mr. Tennent, in Neshaminy, in which some of the ablest ministers of the Presbyterian Church received either the whole, or the more substantial parts of their education.

There are no records extant, from which we can learn any particulars respecting the fruits of Mr. Blair's labours, at Shrewsbury. Here he commenced his ministerial work; and, as he was a faithful, able and zealous preacher of the truth as it is in Jesus, we entertain no doubt that some of the good seed which he sowed, fell into good ground, and brought forth fruit.

Under his ministry at New Londonderry, there occurred a very remarkable revival of religion, of which he wrote a particular narrative.

The congregation at Faggs Manor consisted almost entirely of emigrants from the north of Ireland; and had been formed a number of years, but had never enjoyed the ministry of a stated pastor. His settlement among them took place in November, 1739; although he was not installed as their pastor until the month of April, 1740.

Mr. Blair was one of the most learned and profound, as well as pious, excellent, and venerable men of his day. His deep and clear views as a theologian, are sufficiently evident from his treatise on "Predestination," where this awful and mysterious doctrine is treated with the hand of a master. As a preacher, Mr. Blair was very eminent. There was a solemnity in his very appearance, which struck his hearers with awe, before he opened his mouth. And his manner of preaching, while it was truly evangelical and instructive, was exceedingly impressive—he spoke as in the view of eternity, as in the immediate presence of God,

He contracted the disease of which he died, by exposure in attending upon a meeting of the Trustees of the College of New Jersey. His last words, a minute or two before his departure, were, "The Bridegroom is come, and we shall now have all things." And thus, under a gleam of heaven, he breathed out his last. Though his life was protracted beyond the age attained by Davies and Brainerd, yet he may be said to have died young; for, from the inscription on his tomb, it appears that he was only thirty-nine years and twenty one days old, when he was taken away.

TREATISE ON THE DOCTRINE OF PREDESTINATION.

BY THE REV. SAMUEL BLAIR.

In order to speak clearly and to advantage upon any subject, and especially, if it be much controverted in the world, it is, in the first place, necessary that it be exactly defined and bounded by its proper limits; that it be represented properly, as it is maintained by those who contend for it, that so both parties may have the same fixed, determinate idea of what they reason about, and speak both still to the self same thing. Endless are the confusions and contentions that are introduced into the world, either for the want of this care in defining and rightly understanding the subject in debate, or for want of honesty in an opponent, when he will not keep close to the very thing, though he doth understand what it is. It is the readiest way to bring out controversy to a right issue, rightly to state and represent the case, and then to keep close to it, as so stated, and not suffer another thing, under the same name, to be shuffled in in its place, through the course of the argument. In this way, such objections, as suppose the case to be different from what it is, are easily answered by reducing the objector to the prefixed limits, and so showing his argument to be nothing to the purpose in hand. And I think there is nowhere more need of this care and attention, than about the doctrine of God's Decrees or Predestination, which is the subject of this small treatise. I know not any doctrine more furiously opposed, without being rightly understood, or by being disingenuously and uncandidly misrepresented. I shall, therefore, first of all, state the doctrine truly, and then defend and confirm it.

I. As to the true state of the doctrine, it may be taken up in these two or three propositions:

1. That as God, from everlasting, was pleased in his own free sovereignty to decree and to determine to create this world, and to make man in it, a reasonable creature, in his own image, holy and upright, every way fitted and impowered for that duty which was due from such a rational creature to the great God Creator, with full ability to preserve and continue in that happy state of integrity; and to enter into a covenant of life with him, wherein all the human race were to be concerned and engaged; and, Adam, their first father, constituted their public head and representative; so that, as he kept or broke the covenant, they were to enjoy or lose the promised blessings of it; and as God infallibly foreknew the fall and transgression of Adam, as what he had decreed to permit, and so the depravity and ruin of his posterity consequent thereupon, according to the covenant, with all the actual sins which every individual should ever be guilty of; so he was likewise pleased, of his own mere grace and free favour, to decree and determine to recover and save a number, only known to himself, of that fallen, wretched race, through the mediation of his own Son's redeeming them, by answering the precept and penalty of the broken law for them; and through the sanctification of his eternal Spirit making them fit for, and capable of, glorifying and enjoying him for ever.

2. That God's determining and appointing to save any of fallen mankind, or any in particular more than others, was not upon the foresight of any difference which he foresaw they would make among themselves, by the better improvement of any common helps and advantages, as the reason of it; but it was purely of his own sovereign, free, wise pleasure, and distinguishing grace.

3. The rest of fallen mankind, not thus chosen and ordained to eternal life, he was pleased of his sovereign, wise and righteous pleasure, as a just king and lawgiver, to determine to leave in their fallen state, and punish them according to all the sin and disobedience which they should be guilty of, and chargeable with.

This is, briefly, a just view of the case I am upon; which, I hope, with the divine direction and conduct, to maintain against all the arguments commonly opposed to the doctrine. I cannot, indeed, expect that this representation of it will render it generally acceptable and agreeable to those who have been long prejudiced against it; but that is not the question, whether we would incline or desire to have it so; but, whether it be truly and really so, whether we would desire to have it so, or not. Many of the laws and commands of God are very contrary to the will and inclination of depraved sinners; but they are not the less truly the commands of God for that. In the defence of this doctrine, I would first show, that it is a reasonable, and next, that it is a scriptural doctrine; and speak to the arguments which may be urged both for and against it, from both these topics, of reason and revelation.

II. Those who oppose the doctrine of absolute decrees, generally bring in a heavy indictment against it, as big with the most glaring absurdities, inconsistencies, and contradictions to the very light of reason; and these, such as involve in them the grossest impiety, and most horrid blasphemy against the Divine Majesty: as, that it is directly contrary to, and necessarily infers the exact reverse of most of, the glorious perfections and attributes which reason as well as scripture teaches us to ascribe to the great God; that it makes him unjust, and tyrannically cruel; some say, I dread to express it, worse than the very devil; that it makes him the author of sin, chargeable with most, if not all the guilt of it; that it makes him a most gross, hypocritical dissembler, &c. But, sure, it is not the proper Calvinistic doctrine upon that head, that these men bring in all these awful and shocking charges against; but some horrid composition of their own brain, which they will palm upon the Calvinists, whether they will or no: or else, they just resolve to bring a popular odium upon the doctrine, by such vile, bold, and daring methods; to impose upon such as are not well capable to reason clearly or closely upon such a sublime subject, that they may abhor the very thoughts of it. I readily own, that whatsoever notion infers any the least imperfection in God, is unreasonable, and worse than false. But let the account I have given of this doctrine, be but duly and unbiassedly considered; and then tell me, if there is any thing so dishonourable to God, or unreasonable in it; if there is, in which of the three propositions, or articles, is it? Is it in the first, when it is said, that God decreed to permit Adam's fall? But you must own that he did permit it: that is, that he did not prevent it, if you own that Adam did fall; and consequently, you must own that God decreed to permit or suffer him to fall; for it is highly absurd to say, that he did permit it without determining to permit it; that is the same thing as to say that he took no notice of it at all, till it was done; that it never once came under the view of his all-comprehending, all-discerning mind, how Adam would behave himself in such circumstances as he was in, when he did transgress, if left merely to his own use of his original powers; but this is to deny God's infinite and boundless perfection. Well then, if he had this view and knowledge of what Adam would do in such a case, if thus left to himself, that is, that he would sin; he determined either to hinder or suffer it, to prevent or permit it. It is manifest that he did not determine to prevent it, for if so, it would not have been; and his not determining or decreeing to prevent it, when he infallibly knew it would be if he did not, was decreeing to permit it. And then, upon this decree to permit the fall, proceeded God's certain foreknowledge of it, as future.

Moreover, this permissive decree and foreknowledge of man's transgression and apostasy, plainly appear from God's having foreordained a Redeemer before the foundation of the world, as according to 1 Pet. i. 18–20. And now, seeing these things are plainly so, viz: that God did thus determine to permit the fall of man, which, in his perfect and boundless knowledge, he saw would be, if he did not hinder it by his immediate, super-added influence; and consequently foresaw it, as a thing that would surely be; so plain, that he must have a strange art of managing his reason, who will carefully follow these few steps I have here taken, and not be constrained to yield his assent; then, surely, one would think there was more reverence and honour due to the great and glorious majesty of God, than for any poor worms of the dust to bring in their bold charges against him here, and say, that for these things he is the author of sin: either in that he created man at all, or in that he did not prevent his sin, when he could have done it. Who art thou, man, that repliest against God? Surely, it becomes us to entertain more honourable, exalting thoughts of God, than to give the least way to such a vile suggestion; even supposing our poor mole-eyes should not be able to discern, to our satisfaction, how it could be otherwise. We may, on the one hand, be clearly assured of God's permissive decree, and certain foreknowledge of man's sin; and, on the other hand, as well assured, that he is essentially and infinitely holy; and though we should not be able to reconcile these together, yet he can; and that ought to silence and satisfy us. It does not well befit us to put ourselves on a par with him; and think that he can know nothing but what we must know too. But yet, I see no need of leaving the case at this issue neither; for how unreasonable and ridiculous is this ground of the charge! God did not propose and determine to prevent Adam's sinning, when it was easy to his power to have prevented it; well, and what then? Did not the Lord give him sufficient power to have prevented it himself? And was not this enough to free the kind Creator from all blame in the case? Cannot God make a creature perfect, and complete in its order and rank, endowed with full ability and power to preserve its glory unstained, and put it in a state of probation and trial, without a criminal charge? Must he be called to answer at the creature's bar, for his own miscarriage, and voluntary rebellion, in such a case? Indeed, if we maintained that God did not give Adam sufficient power to preserve his fidelity, and withstand the temptation; or that God, by his immediate energy, overpowered him to a compliance; then, I confess, there would be no standing before the argument. But, as we assert no such thing, nor anything that will afford such a consequence, how unfair and inexcusable is it, to give out as if we did! which is the method of too many, either ignorantly or wilfully. And let me observe, that the Arminians, yea, men of all sorts of religions in the world, are no less obliged to answer this difficulty, than the Calvinists; for they must all acknowledge that there is sin in the world, and that God has permitted it, otherwise it could not be; yea, you must acknowledge yourselves to have been guilty of sins, and such as you might have avoided. But dare you lift up your face to God, and say to him, "I have done many evils, even such as I had power to refrain; but they are thy sins, and not mine, because thou didst not keep me from them?" Would not your own reason confound you with shame, at the thoughts of such a malapert, senseless speech to God? As little reason is there, whatever less, for charging the righteous God in the case of Adam's transgression.

Or, is it matter of just prejudice against this doctrine, that mankind are said to have been considered, in the divine decree, as universally fallen in Adam, in consequence of his breach and violation of the covenant of God, wherein he was appointed the covenant-head and representative of his posterity? But, sure, yourselves must acknowledge that all mankind did fall in Adam's transgression, if you profess to believe the holy Scriptures. So long as the fifth chapter of St. Paul's epistle to the Romans stands in the Bible, it will be impossible, with any face of modesty, to deny it; where we are told, that "by one man sin entered into the world, and death by sin; and so death passed upon all men, for that all have sinned;" and, that "by the offence of one judgment came upon all men to condemnation." When you say that all mankind are recovered again out of the condemnation and ruin which the sin of Adam brought upon them, by Jesus Christ, is it not an acknowledgment that they were at once fallen, and ruined by it? And inasmuch as yourselves acknowledge it was so, you must acknowledge it was reasonable and no way inconsistent with the perfections of God that it should be so; or else you say, point blank, that God was, at least once, unrighteous. And now, seeing mankind were fallen in Adam, which God's glorious perfections will not suffer us to think was any way unreasonable or unjust in him, it necessarily follows, that it would have been no way unreasonable or unjust in God, if he had so pleased, to have left them all in that fallen state, without restoring any. Seeing there was once a plain forfeiture of all rights and privileges, according to law and justice, it was at the free pleasure of the great Lawgiver to bestow them again upon any or not; unless you will say that our recovery by Christ was not of free and mere grace, but what God was bound to order and bring about, or else oppose his own nature, and be unjust; and so, that herein he did what we have no reason to thank him for: which to say, is not only a gross inconsistency in itself, but such an impiety against God, that few, I believe, would be so bold as to venture upon it. It is ridiculous to talk of our being redeemed by God out of a miserable state, which it was unjust for him either to suffer us to come into, or yet to leave us in. There is no need of a mediator and redeemer in such a case. Then, indeed, Christ is dead in vain! Thus far we have made our way clear. "Well then, I say again, if it would have been no way unbecoming God, if he had so pleased, to have determined to leave all mankind in that fallen state; no man will say, who duly considers what he says, that it would have been any way unbecoming him, had he so pleased, looking upon them in this fallen, guilty, apostate state, to have made this distinction among them, in his eternal purpose, which I am defending. And so the proper doctrine of predestination, in the right notion of it, must be owned to be entirely reasonable; and the very method, for what we know, that God (unless he has told us to the contrary) was pleased to take.

But, to make all this yet clearer, I would give this farther brief account of the reasonableness of mankind's partaking in the sad fruits of Adam's transgression. I would account for it, from his being set up as their public head and representative in the first covenant. If this constitution and appointment of God was reasonable, then all that was natively consequent upon it, according to the tenor of it, must be so too. To make it appear that this constitution was every way just and reasonable, let it be considered, that it was in its own nature adapted and directly calculated to the great good and advantage of mankind, securing to them a confirmed state of innocence and everlasting happiness, upon their first father's continuing obedient, so long as God saw fit to leave him in a state of probation and trial; so that none of them would have been any more in the danger of a probationary state for themselves. Adam was sufficiently impowered to manage this great trust, endowed with full ability to keep the covenant; yea, with as full as any of his offspring would have had, had they been to pass a time of trial for themselves; and his motives to care and watchfulness were as strong as theirs could have been, having his own eternal interest as much engaged in the case as theirs; so that their whole

Stock, all their everlasting concerns, were every whit as safe in his hands, as they would have been in their own. And, seeing their case was, this way, as safe as if it had been in their own management, and there was a rational prospect of a glorious, unspeakable advantage by it, though there was an awful evil on the other hand, in case of disobedience; yet, since the rational hope on the one hand, was far greater than the danger on the other, it was surely a reasonable, wise and good plan, and which, I am satisfied, we would all have admired and praised the glorious God for, had our representative fulfilled his part of the covenant, and we now been enjoying the happy consequences of it. If so, then, how unreasonable and wicked must it be now to quarrel with the scheme and its glorious Author on the account of it, because it has eventually proved, through our trustee's default, to our disadvantage? If it would have been just and altogether right had he obeyed, does his sin and disobedience make it wrong and unjust? One thing more may be observed here, to free the subject of all misapprehension, viz: that it is not imagined that the same degree of punishment is justly due to Adam's posterity, merely on account of his transgression, which was due to himself for it. Thus far only is certain in this matter, that beside our being exposed by it to the various miseries of this life, and death itself, we lost all right and title to the life and happiness which God promised in the covenant, and the glorious moral image of God in our souls, viz: our original righteousness; so that, instead of being now naturally holy and upright, we are naturally depraved and sinful; which is the awful foundation and spring of our numberless actual transgressions, whereby we deserve an awfully aggravated condemnation. I say, persons, for their actual sins, though they flow from their original corruption as the spring and fountain of them, deserve an awfully aggravated condemnation, or unspeakably greater than the law denounces only on the account of Adam's transgression; inasmuch as that man or woman cannot be found, of whom it could justly be said, that they had never been farther guilty of actual sin, than what was absolutely unavoidable from the original depravity of their nature. These things may suffice to evince the reasonableness of the doctrine of all mankind's being fallen in Adam; and of their being considered as such, in the decree and purpose of God concerning their eternal states; which, as has been already shown, proves the reasonableness of the doctrine of predestination; forasmuch as God might justly have determined, either to save none, or to save all, or to save only a part, as he pleased.

But farther, if any should yet be unwilling to yield the reasonableness of mankind's being so disinherited of all their spiritual and eternal privileges; and their being liable to such a state of misery, by Adam's sin and disobedience; whatever temporal calamities they might in justice and reason be exposed to by it; I would prove the reasonableness of the doctrine I am chiefly insisting upon, from principles which they must unavoidably grant, if they are not lost to all the common sense of mankind. You must own, that all mankind, except infants, have actually sinned, whether you own it to be the effect of Adam's sinning or not. "All have sinned, and come short of the glory of God," That it is so, in fact, is too notorious to be denied. Yea, you must own that mankind are naturally inclined to sin, and have a strong bias and propension that way. These things you must confess, account for them how you will; and I am apt to think, the scripture account, resolving the universal depravity and sinful propensions of the human nature, into the transgression of our first parent, as the cause, will answer full as well as any you can give. It will be as satisfactory as either Plato's pre-existent state in the stars, or the eternal evil principle of the Manichees; or yet the imitation and example of Pelagius. However, that mankind are so universally guilty of sin, let it come how it will, is but too manifest. Moreover, you must grant that they justly deserve punishment for their sin, from the sovereign Lawgiver of the rational world; to say otherwise, is to say that sin is not sin; sin must be as good as obedience and duty, if the sinner deserves no worse for it; which is an absurdity a little too big to swallow, that takes away all distinction between moral good and evil, and destroys all the notions of justice in the world. You must also grant, that God, from all eternity, certainly foresaw all the sins of all men, unless you have a God like yourself, who knows now, what he did not know before, by information from others. Now lay these things together, and then see, if it does not follow, by an unavoidable, logical necessity, that God might justly have decreed, and purposed from everlasting, to punish the sinful, disobedient children of men, and not to save any of them out of their guilty state. For if God from everlasting foresaw that they would deserve to be thus cast off and punished, then he might justly determine to deal so by them; unless you will say, it was unjust for him to determine to do what was just to do. And is the justness of his determining to punish a part of them only, according to the rules of governing justice, less conceivable, while he determines to save the rest in a way agreeable to the glory of his majesty and government, through the mediation and redemption of his eternal Son? Thus you may see, the denying of original sin does not overthrow the doctrine of predestination; all that is gained by it, is a certainty that all such as die in their infancy, were elected to eternal life; but then, they were not chosen in Christ, a Redeemer, nor are they brought to happiness through his redemption; which is a notion that does not chime very well with the scriptures, which everywhere represent the atonement of Christ, as the only way of eternal happiness, to any of the human progeny; which, I think, is a farther evident proof of original sin. And thus, I think, I have sufficiently cleared the first proposition.

2. In the next place, is there anything so horrid in the second article, viz: that God's decree and purpose, to save any of the fallen, apostate race, was not founded upon his foresight of their good works, and diligent endeavours, as the cause of it; but was purely owing to his own sovereign pleasure and grace? This is a sentiment so far from being unreasonable, that I think the contrary is plainly so, absolutely considered, viz: that the imperfect, corrupted, and altogether selfish endeavours of rebellious, guilty creatures, should be of such high price with God, as necessarily to determine him to save them; so that he would be unjust, if he did not thereupon design and effectuate their salvation. Is this a notion, either so very reasonable in itself, or honourable to God? And yet this is the principle that must be maintained, if the doctrine I am defending, be charged with being in itself unreasonable. To manifest a little the unreasonableness of such a notion, I would ask, if an entire and perfect obedience to the law of God, without the least defect, would be any more than our duty to him, as he is such a glorious Being, and we his creatures? If it would not, and no man in his right wits will say otherwise, then how can the very imperfect, the every way corrupt, and contemptible obedience, that is performed by guilty sinners, make it so necessary for God to pardon their past disobedience, as that he would be unreasonable and unjust, if he did not? According to this principle, pardon would not properly be pardon; it would not be an act of mere grace, and of rich mercy, but of just debt. But who is there, that has the front to demand it, as such, for all the good works that ever he did? I believe you would find hard work of it to bring the notion into practice, and very formally tell the great God, that "though you had sinned against him, and contemned his authority; yet you had done so well since, that you would not now be beholden to him for pardon, you claimed it as your due, on the score of his essential equity, which, he would be unjust, if he refused." It is, moreover, a notion that entirely supersedes and takes away all necessity of Christ's atonement and satisfaction. What need of such a propitiation and ransom, if anything that guilty sinners could do, could render it unjust in God, not to save them? And now, seeing these things are plainly so, it as plainly and necessarily follows, that it was no way unreasonable, nor unbecoming any of the divine perfections, for God to make his own sovereign, absolute good-will and pleasure, the rule of his determinations, of dispensing his saving mercies to any fallen, guilty sinners; and not their works or endeavours. Yea, I will add, it is highly presumable from reason itself, and seems to be its very dictates, that this was actually the way of God's proceeding in the case; as what was most suitable to his independent sovereignty, for the maintaining, and illustration of his exalted glory; and to abase the pride of all flesh, that none should glory in his presence; but, as it is written, "he that glorieth, should glory in the Lord alone:" that his redeemed and saved people should for ever ascribe the whole glory and praise to his sovereign, free, distinguishing grace. This method, in the case, was proceeding like a God; as becomes the Supreme Jehovah; exalts both his own glory, and the happiness of saved sinners, to the highest; while they are ever sensible, that as he might justly have saved none, so they have nothing to ascribe to themselves in the matter, why he saved them more than any others. Hence their hearts beat high with the tenderest, sweetest resentments of love and wonder, with the highest ascriptions of glory and praise, to him that sits upon the throne, and to the Lamb, for ever and ever. So that, I believe, this doctrine suits best with the language of heaven, however it be relished on earth. If we consider the hateful, horrid, and criminal nature of sin, what can there be in any sinner to engage to him the love and favour of a God of infinite holiness and incomprehensible majesty; in whose sight the heavens are not clean; who "charges his angels with folly?" Now, though all these considerations make it plainly appear, that it is every way reasonable, yea, most becoming the adorable majesty of God, that the reason of his appointing any fallen sinners, in particular, more than others, to eternal life, should be wholly resolved into his sovereign pleasure; that it should be entirely founded in himself, and not at all in them; yet I am apprehensive that here lies the main ground of the quarrel, for though sin had made man extremely poor, it has not made him humble, but much to the contrary. The unbroken pride and haughtiness of sinners' hearts will not allow it to be right or equitable at all, that it should be altogether at the free, sovereign pleasure of God, whether to save them or not. Unless they have it in their own hands, they will quarrel with God himself, although they deserve not so much as the least ground for hope that ever he will save them. It would "surely better become such hell-deserving rebels as we, to be so humbly sensible of our vile iniquities, as to

acknowledge God's sovereign right to dispose of us as he sees fit; that if he should abandon us to misery for ever, it would be but just and right, notwithstanding all that ever we could do; and if he saves us, it will be an instance of the most glorious, free, sovereign grace and mercy, which he might righteously have denied. But these things may suffice, here, to show that this part of the doctrine also stands free of all unreasonable absurdity, and unbecoming reflections on God. And if you would have the whole evidence again in a narrow compass, you may take it thus: God, the great Creator and Upholder of all things, is the rightful Lawgiver and moral Governor of the reasonable world. Considering the infinite, boundless glory and perfections of his nature, and his right in and over us, as his creatures, our obligations of love and duty to him are inconceivably great and infinite: hence sin and disobedience against such infinite majesty and obligations, is infinitely evil, deserving the sinner's everlasting rejection from God, with a superadded positive punishment. All mankind, through the sin and disobedience of their first parent, are become destitute of original righteousness, and all right to the life and happiness promised in the first covenant; and all such as are preserved to years in the world, have sinned actually in their own persons, and that far beyond what was absolutely unavoidable from their original depravity; whence they in justice deserve a far greater punishment. God had as clear and certain a knowledge of all this apostasy and sin of mankind, from all eternity, as after it actually came to pass; so that in his decrees concerning them, he considered them as in such a fallen, guilty state, deserving the execution of his vindictive justice; and altogether insufficient to do anything that might in the least satisfy its demands, for the averting of the stroke. And so, from the whole, it clearly appears, that God had as absolute, just, and great a sovereignty over them, to appoint any part of them for life or death, according to his own pleasure, as the "potter has over his clay, of the same lump, to make one vessel to honour, and another to dishonour."

And now, after all these things, what can reasonably be said against the third and last of the propositions, which is, that God determined to leave a part of these guilty sinners, (viz: those whom he did not choose to salvation,) in their fallen, guilty state, and to execute justice upon them for their sins? To say that this is unjust, &c., is to say that justice is injustice, &c. All that I shall farther observe here upon it, is, how injurious and unfair treatment it is, to give out, as too many who oppose the doctrine do, as though we maintained that God doomed men to everlasting perdition, without any respect to, or consideration had of, their sin! We say, that the reason why God chose some and rejected others, that is, these rather than those, was not because of the greater goodness of the one part, and greater sinfulness of the other, for all were "clay from the same lump," without any difference of this kind among them, amounting to such value, but "because it so seemed good in his sight." We assert, that none are doomed to everlasting perdition, but for their sin; but then, it is not the reason of the difference that is made between them and those that are chosen to everlasting life.

Now, though what has been already hitherto said, in explaining and vindicating the doctrine of predestination, might sufficiently furnish a careful, understanding reader with satisfactory answers to the objections that are usually supposed to be deduced from reason against it; yet, for the more full satisfaction of all, I shall a little consider them particularly.

One objection, that makes a mighty noise in the world, is, that it makes God the author of sin; but it is as easy for me to deny this, as for the objector to assert it; and asserting is all he can do, if he obliges himself to urge it against the doctrine, only as I have represented and explained it in the preceding pages. Let such objectors show us what part of it is justly liable to such a charge, and how it contains or infers any such blasphemy. Does it make God the author of sin, to say, that he decreed to suffer Adam to sin, when, in the meantime, we assert that he gave him sufficient power not to sin; and only suffered him, without any compulsion, to abuse his liberty? How ridiculous and senseless is such a charge for this! Such objectors seem to think, or else to be willing to have it thought, that we maintain, that God either did not afford Adam sufficient ability to preserve, or that by his superior power he forced him to sin; but let their slander die with them. Yet, I think, I have met with an author that pretends to prove this vile absurdity, consequent upon the score of bare permission. This, indeed, would be a rare art, could he make it do, to free the whole world of the blame of sin all at once; for if God cannot so much as permit sin, without being the author of it himself, then I think we are pretty clear, and all the devils too. He proves it by a simile: suppose a man to be standing on the top of a very high wall, holding a child over it by the arm; well, he does not press it down or force it to fall, but only lets it go, and suffers it to fall (if it will, I suppose); and then the demand is, whether the man was not the author of that child's fall and death? I think it is no great difficulty to answer the question. I believe none would pretend to vindicate such a gross murder; but then, I would demand if the cases were any way like one another? If this simile is supposed to be parallel to the case it is brought to illustrate, then our opinion must be, that God at first so upheld Adam by the hand of his power, as that it was impossible for him to sin; and then withdrew his hand from him, so as that it was impossible for him not to sin; whereas we assert the direct contrary of both. Before the simile can be made in any tolerable degree similar to the case, many other things must be supposed in it; particularly, that the child is endowed with such a power as that it is as easy for it to stand in the air as to fall to the ground; that the man has a rightful sovereignty and authority over it, to put it in such a situation, and make it its indispensable duty to stand where he has put it; that it has a clear knowledge of its duty, and warning of its danger, and the like. These suppositions, I believe, will pretty much alter the case.

Another objection brought against the doctrine is, that it makes God chargeable with the most unjust cruelty and sovereign tyranny; but I have already sufficiently vindicated it from this awful charge; unless it be unjust cruelty to decree justice, which is a contradiction in express terms. Was it not just in God to make man free, as well as perfectly holy and upright—to appoint Adam the covenant head and representative of his offspring, as it has been explained—to permit him to act according to his original freedom and liberty—to permit all men to sin as they do, and to punish some of them, whom he pleases, for all the sin they are guilty of? If these things are all righteous and just enough, was it unjust in God to fore-appoint and determine them? Would those, who oppose the doctrine of predestination, but fairly represent it, and speak to it still as it is, they would surely be ashamed to offer such a charge as this against it: and of this themselves seem to be sensible; and, therefore, they commonly so manage the objection, as grossly to misrepresent the doctrine, as though it contained in it that God, in his eternal purpose, doomed a number of mankind to destruction without any consideration at all had of their sin, whereby they would justly deserve it; or that he purposed, by his irresistible power, to compel them to sin, that so he might damn them with some colour of justice; whereas we disclaim both the one and the other with the utmost abhorrence.

Again, it is objected that this doctrine makes God partial and a respecter of persons, which is justly reputed a very ill character in men, and, therefore, cannot, in the least, belong to God. This argument seems to be much depended on among the more ignorant; but those who make so much of it, ought to consider what that respecting of persons is, which is so criminal in men. It is their making such a difference between persons, in their temper and conduct towards them, as is contrary to right and equity, on account of some accidental things or circumstances, wherein they may differ from one another: such as, nation, worldly dignity, relation, gifts, bribes, or the like; and I really own, that partiality and respect of persons, in this sense, is very far from God. "He accepts not the persons of princes, nor regards the rich more than the poor." Job xxxiv. 19, He is not only far from doing injustice to any, but he makes no account at all of the little differences among them, of nation, worldly state and condition, or the like, as a reason of any of his dealings towards them; and it is in this sense that respecting of persons is always taken in the Scripture, wherever it is condemned in men, or denied concerning God. And, sure, the doctrine I am defending is so far from inferring any such respect of persons in God, that it is, at the first view, directly contrary to it. Yet, farther, I would observe, there may be among men a favouring of one more than another, which you may call respecting of persons, or if you will, partiality, or by what name you please; but it carries no ill idea in it. Such, for instance, as our Lord speaks of (Matt. xx.), where the lord of the vineyard gave to some of his labourers an undeserved bounty, while he gave to others only what justice necessarily required. And this is brought in by our Lord Jesus himself, for this very case (see ver. 16.), to vindicate God's making such a difference among guilty sinners, against such as make this objection; and God's defence here is unanswerable against all the murmurings of such as he has not chosen to salvation, Friend, I do thee no wrong, whatsoever good I do to others; is it not lawful for me to do what I will with mine own? Is thine eye evil, because I am good?

It is farther objected, that, according to this doctrine, it is God's fault, and not theirs, that any perish; inasmuch as it was ever impossible for them to be saved, seeing they were under an irreversible appointment to destruction, before ever they had a being. But what has been said already, will easily answer all the difficulty that may seem to be in this argument, viz: that God appointed them to be punished only for their sins, whereby they in justice deserve it. And, surely, their sinning is not any fault in God; nor yet his appointing them to deserved punishment for it; but seeing all their punishment will be only according to the demerit of their sin, their whole destruction will properly be of themselves, and their own fault. But if any should yet foolishly think, that the mere necessity or infallible certainty of the event would render sinners free of all the blame of their destruction, because it was always certain, that so it would be in the end, let them try any other scheme they please, and see whether they can rid themselves of the difficulty; for whatsoever at any time is, was always infallibly certain to be, whether you allow a decree concerning it or not; so that you must either deny that it is so much as possible for any creature to perish justly at all, or you must own that the bare certainty of the event, that they will perish, does not free them from being the proper blamable causes of their own perdition; and its being certain by a divine appointment, makes them no more clear of the blame, because the decree only is, to punish them for, and according to, the demerit of their sins; which sins, it lays no forcible constraint or compulsion upon them, to be guilty of.

Again, it is said, "that if this doctrine be true, then it follows, that God creates men to damn them." This seems to be a ready-hand argument, almost in every one's mouth that denies the doctrine.

Before we speak to any words or propositions, we ought to understand what is meant by them. Now all the meaning I can conceive in this sentence, [God creates men to damn them,] consistent with the propriety of speech, is, that their damnation is God's end in creating them; the final cause and reason of his bringing them into being. And this imports in it that God loves and delights in the punishment and misery of creatures, merely as such, and for its own sake; which is a thing most blasphemous to suppose of him. To suppose, that the misery of any creature, strictly and abstractly in itself, without any other consideration, is agreeable and pleasing to God; yea, so agreeable, that he makes them for this very end that he may have the pleasure of punishing them; is, indeed, to represent him like the very worst of beings. But then I would ask, Does God's decreeing to punish men for their sin, as they deserve, for maintaining the dignity of his government, and the showing forth of his infinite holiness, justice, and rightful authority; does this, I say, bear in it any such thing, as that he delights barely in the misery of creatures, so as to create them for the sake of it? How irrational is such a consequence! But if any will yet insist on it as a just consequence, I desire them to consider a little how they will free their own scheme of it; which is every whit as liable to the charge. Unless they have stupid ignorance and blasphemous presumption enough to deny God's infinite understanding and fore-knowledge of all things, it is just as reasonable to bring this objection against the Arminians, as the Calvinists; and say, God creates men to damn them, if he knows beforehand that he will damn them; if he foreknew that they would die impenitent, in unbelief; and thereupon has decreed their damnation before he has created them. The truth of the matter is this, God decreed to create all men for the manifestation of his own glory, which is his end in all his works; and looking upon mankind in their apostasy and sin, he decreed to leave a particular part of them in that state, and to punish them according to their sin, for the manifestation of the glory of his sovereignty, holiness, and justice, and the right and infinite obligations of his authority, as a lawgiver over his reasonable creatures. This view of the case gives no ground for the charge contained in the objection. Though God foresees that mankind will sin against him, cannot he, notwithstanding, create them, and determine to punish them, or any part of them, as their sin deserves, for the illustration of his glory aforesaid, without being chargeable with creating them just that he might damn them? To say so, is the same thing as to say, that the sin and default of the creature must bind up God's hands from doing that which is in itself every way reasonable and right; and, in short, to say that right is wrong.

But I presume I have been long enough on the first method proposed for defending and confirming this doctrine; and that, from what has been said, it sufficiently appears, at least, that it is a doctrine free from all unreasonable absurdity in itself, and no way dishonourable to God; so that reason has nothing to say, why it may not be so. And if, in the next place, we find that God's infallible word of truth declares that it is so, this ought to put a final conclusion to the debate, and fully determine the controversy. If there is nothing in the doctrine absurd, or contrary to reason, why it may not be so; then, when a passage of Scripture is brought to prove that it is so, we must not be put off any more with this answer, that "whatever the Scripture means, it cannot mean predestination." A great asserter of the Arminian doctrine, I think, as good as owns the reasonableness of the Calvinist doctrine. I mean Bishop Burnet, when he says, "It is one of the points wherein all agree, that God might have condemned every man to have perished for his own sins." (Expos, xxxix. Art., page 167, Fol. This great man manages the debate with the greatest candour and temper of any I have met with of the Arminian side; and yet even he is far from dealing so fairly as ho ought, especially when he represents the maintainers of absolute predestination, as maintaining that the decree lays a compulsory force on the creature to sin. On this misrepresentation much of his arguing for the Arminiana proceeds. He lays hold on the Supralapsarian Scheme for it, and, without sufficient evidence, pretends that the Sublapsarian scheme ultimately resolves and terminates in the same, as so represented.) If God might have condemned all men to perdition for their sins, then, surely, much more a part of them only. But farther, reason not only readily allows, that God might have formed his eternal purposes and decrees, concerning fallen man, according to this doctrine; but, if duly attended to, without selfish prejudice, it seems, as has been already hinted, powerfully to persuade us that so the case really is, as being most becoming God's independent sovereignty; and most expressive of the absolute freeness, and glorious riches of his grace to those that are saved; whereby the whole glory of it is secured to himself, and no ground afforded to the hell-deserving sinner for anything contrary to those humble acknowledgements of his own wretchedness, that well become him; whereas the contrary doctrine leaves room to the sinner to trust to something in himself, and ascribe something to himself, in the matter of his salvation. It sets too high a value upon the despicable, religious endeavours of corrupted sinners, when it maintains, that God is thereby induced to receive the sinner to favour, notwithstanding all his rebellions; and by thus representing the God, whom by disobedience we have contemned and dishonoured, as so readily and surely reconciled to us on such terms, it depreciates his injured honours, and takes off from the infinite malignity and due horror of sin. If sin against God is looked upon as a thing that is so easily compensated, and the breach occasioned by it, so readily made up on such low conditions: what mean, unworthy conceptions are we likely to entertain of God's infinite perfections and adorable attributes, when the contempt of them by sin is reckoned such a small matter? But,

2. I proceed, with more express evidence and certainty, to prove and confirm the doctrine from the divine oracles, and infallible scriptures of truth. And here I shall first prove, that God has appointed and chosen some of fallen mankind to eternal life and salvation; and that merely of his own sovereign grace and good pleasure, and not upon the foresight of any goodness of theirs, whereby they would distinguish themselves from others, as the reason of it. Next, I shall prove that the rest of mankind, not thus chosen to life, God has appointed to leave in their sins, and to punish them for them, according to their deserts: and then I shall answer such objections as are supposed to be in the scriptures against this doctrine, and give the true meaning of such scripture passages consistent with it.

The first place of scripture I shall adduce for the proof of absolute election, is Acts xiii. 48, where, after an account of the opposition made to the apostles Paul and Barnabas, at Antioch, and the strong endeavours used by some, to prejudice the people against the doctrine which they preached, it is said, that "as many as were ordained to eternal life believed." The plain sense of these words is, that notwithstanding all the means used in that place, to hinder the people from believing the apostles' doctrine, yet a considerable number did believe; because God had ordained them to eternal life, and so gave them faith to believe, in spite of all the arts of men used with them to the contrary; and therefore it was impossible for the enemies of Christianity to keep them in unbelief. And this is perfectly agreeable to the sense of our blessed Lord, when he says, that "false Christs and false prophets should arise, showing such signs and wonders, that if it were possible, they would deceive the very elect;" (Matt. xxiv. 24;) clearly implying, that God had elected some to everlasting salvation, and the necessary means of it; whom it is therefore utterly impossible for false teachers, with all their powers, finally to deceive and keep from believing in the true Redeemer. If any should say, that the reason why these were ordained to eternal life, and had grace given them to believe, was, because they were more righteously disposed, and better than the rest; this is not only contrary to the scope of the place, and the mode of expressing the matter in the text, but we find in the next verse but one, that there were some of the most religious that believed not; we are told that these opposers stirred up the devout (that is, the religious) and honourable women, as well as the chief men of the city, to persecute the apostles; but they could not have the same influence upon those whom God had ordained to eternal life; it was impossible for them to deceive the elect.

Another very clear, and most express passage to our purpose, is in Rom. xi. 5–7. "Even so then, at this present time also, there is a remnant, according to the election of grace. And if by grace, then it is no more of works; otherwise grace is no more grace. But if it be of works, then it is no more grace. What then? Israel hath not obtained that which he seeketh for; but the election hath obtained it, and the rest were blinded." Here the apostle observes, that as in the time of the greatest defection of the people of Israel, in Elijah's days, God had reserved to himself a remnant of seven thousand; even so, at that present time, when the greater body of the Jewish nation had rejected Christ, there was also a remnant, according to the election of grace, that did believe. This believing remnant of the Jewish nation, were those who were elected and chosen out of it, to faith and salvation: and this election, whereby they were thus chosen, was an election of grace. Well, you will say, perhaps, you own all this, that God had elected a remnant of the Jews to faith in Christ, and salvation by him; but then the reason of God's electing them was their good works; whereby he foresaw they would render themselves more worthy of his choice than the rest. But don't you see, that the apostle expressly bars against such an imagination, when he says, "It is an election of grace; and that if it be of grace, then it is no more of works; or else grace is not grace?" He tells you, that the election of works, which you contend for, is not the election of grace, which he asserts: if it be of works, it is no more grace. An election of works and grace both, is a downright inconsistency, if we allow St. Paul to be the judge. "Israel has not obtained that which he seeketh for." There were many of Israel who were left to unbelief, that were seeking for righteousness and life as much as the others, that were, notwithstanding, sanctified by faith. Though they were thus equal among themselves, yet there was an election among them that obtained it, "when the rest were blinded," that is, left to their own blindness. I cannot see how the doctrine of absolute election can well be asserted in more strong, plain, and express terms, than the apostle uses for it in these verses. It cannot be said, that all he means by the "election of this remnant," was only God's purpose of affording them the privilege of the gospel, and outward means of grace; for all the rest had the advantages afforded them, as well as they, according to the words of our Lord, "Many were called, but few (i.e., a remnant of them only) were chosen;" (Matt. xx. 16;) which manifestly shows, that they were elected to the saving benefit of those means, in consequence of which, they actually did obtain it: when the rest, who had the same advantage of these outward means, and were seeking for justification and life as well as they, did not obtain it; but were left in their blindness and unbelief. To conclude this argument, the apostle here asserts an election of some, out of others, to eternal life; and asserts it to be an election of grace, in such a full sense, as that it cannot be of works in any sense. So that you may see here a flat contradiction between the inspired apostle and the Arminians. They say, "Election is on the account of works foreseen;" he says, "It is not of works, but wholly of grace." They say, "It may be of works and grace both;" he says, "It cannot, without destroying the nature of both."

For another proof, you may look as far back as Rom. viii. 28–30:—"All things work together for good to them that love God, to them who are the called according to his purpose. For whom he did foreknow, he also did predestinate to be conformed to the image of his Son. Moreover, whom he did predestinate, them he also called; and whom he called, them he also justified; and whom he justified, them he also glorified." Those whom the apostle terms "the called, according to God's purpose," he tells us, ver. 28, are those "that love God;" and, ver. 30, they are those who are justified, and, in the end, will be as surely glorified. So that by calling here, the apostle means being called effectually to faith and holiness by the Spirit of God, or saving conversion; and he tells us, that those who are thus effectually called and converted by God in time, are so called by him in pursuance of his preceding purpose and decree concerning them; for they are called according to his purpose. He predestinated, or foreappointed them to be conformed to the image of his Son, to be made like Christen holiness; and as this purpose and fore-appointment of God made their sanctification and justification infallibly certain, so it equally secures their final glorification. For whom he did predestinate, them he called, justified, and glorified. And those who are predestinated, and fore-appointed of God to holiness and happiness, are said to be those whom he foreknew. By God's foreknowing them, we are not to understand his having a bare speculative foreknowledge of them, and of what they would be before their effectual calling; for in this sense he foreknew all others as well as them; but his having had a special love to them, and gracious design to do them good, beyond the rest of mankind; or it signifies his foreknowing them as his own, as those whom he had chosen and distinguished for himself, in his eternal purpose, according to what is said, "The Lord knoweth them that are his." 2 Tim. ii. 19. Thus you see, this place is a clear proof of an election and predestination to grace and salvation; and that represented so sovereign and entirely of God, as not to be founded on any qualification in the creature; insuring both the sinner's true conversion to holiness, and his final perseverance to the heavenly glory: and all this according to God's purpose, and not their own management or behaviour.

The ninth chapter of this epistle is very plain and express on this argument. In the beginning of it, the apostle speaks with reference to the unbelief of the general part of the Jewish nation: their rejection of the true

Messiah; declaring his great grief on that account. And then, in the sixth verse, he comes to speak to a difficulty which seemed to occur, concerning God's leaving the main body of the Jews to unbelief, and so casting them off from being any longer his people, taken from his word of promise to Abraham, and often afterwards, that "he would be a God to him, and his seed after him for ever." It would seem, at that time, when God had cast off that people, all to a very small remnant, and removed his church to the Gentiles, as if he had broken his word, and his promise had not been fulfilled, or taken effect. To this the apostle answers, that that was no argument that the word of God had taken no effect; and he clears it up by showing that the word of promise peculiarly respected those of Abraham's offspring who belonged to the election of grace; saying, "they are not all Israel which are of Israel;" that is, they are not all that Israel which God had principally in his eye in the promise, who belong to Israel by natural relation, or external visible union. The peculiar Israel," or children of promise, were those whom the Lord had elected and chosen among them to everlasting life; and to these the promise was always made good, whether they were more or fewer. The promise, indeed, being a plain intimation that a large number belonging to the election of grace should be of Abraham's progeny, was the foundation of a visible church among them, and gave them all a right to the visible privileges of it, till they made a forfeiture themselves. But the promise, in the full import of it, by way of engagement on God, related only to those whom he had chosen among them. That this is the apostle's meaning here, appears plainly from all that follows. For the illustration and confirmation of this case, he shows that God put a great limitation upon that seed of Abraham to which he particularly designed the promise in his words to Abraham himself, saying, "In Isaac shall thy seed be called."

Hereby the Lord signified to him, that there was a greater number of the election to be of his posterity in Isaac's line than in the line of Ishmael, or of any of his other sons that he should ever have, as he had several by a second marriage; and, therefore, God would take a more special care of Isaac's offspring. And, indeed, no other account can be given of his distinguishing concerns about them more than the rest of Abraham's posterity; or for his affording greater advantages to one nation than another at this day, but because of a much greater number of his elect ones being among them, because he knows whom he has chosen. And then the apostle comes to give another instance of the same kind, viz: the distinction which God made between the two branches of Isaac's offspring in the tenth and following verses, "And not only this, but when Rebecca also had conceived by one, even by our father Isaac; for the children being not yet born, neither having done any good or evil, that the purpose of God according to election might stand, not of works but of him that calleth, it was said unto her, the elder shall serve the younger." Here the apostle shows, that though God had said, that the seed of Abraham, which he chiefly intended in the promise of being their God, was to be in Isaac's line, yet he intended one part of Isaac's seed more than the other; which he intimated to Rebecca before her twin-children were born, when he said, "The elder shall serve the younger." And thus he observes, there was a distinguishing purpose and decree of God concerning them, (before they had done any good or evil,) according to election; which purpose of election is not of works, "but of him that calleth," according to his own sovereign pleasure. The apostle's meaning is plainly this, that God's choosing Jacob, and a great number of his posterity, more than Esau or his posterity, was not on account of any good works to be performed by any of them, more than by the others, as the reason of it; any more than it was on account of good works already done, before they were born, when neither of them had done neither good or evil; so, though the apostle's words very likely refer to the respective posterities of those two brothers, as well as to their own persons, yet they respect their spiritual interest more than their temporal, and signify that God had many more of his elect in the posterity of Jacob than of Esau, at least, while they continued two visibly distinct bodies; and, therefore, he took more care of Jacob's posterity, taking them into, and keeping them in, a visible church relation to himself, while he suffered the posterity of Esau to degenerate into heathenism and pagan idolatry; so calling them off from so much as any visible relation to him, as his church. And this directly answers the apostle's purpose, which is, to show that God had a peculiar elect seed among the seed of Abraham and of Isaac, which he principally designed, and referred to, in the promise; and, therefore, it was no argument that the word of God had failed, or taken no effect, though great bodies of their natural seed were neglected, and separated from his church; and it was as reasonable to suppose the same thing of Jacob's seed. This election, he asserts, was not of works, but purely of him that calleth, as he pleases. And so, ver. 14, and seq., lie goes on to answer the grand objection which he saw would readily be laid against the doctrine, viz: that it makes God unjust, cruel, partial, and all what not. "What shall we say then?" says he; "Is there unrighteousness with God? God forbid. For he saith to Moses, I will have mercy on whom I will have mercy, and I will have compassion on whom I will have compassion." He observes, that God had sufficiently answered the objection himself in these words to Moses, Exodus xxxiii. 19, which clearly signify that all had sinned, and justly deserved the execution of his wrath; and so were become objects of mere mercy, which he might bestow or withhold, according to his own sovereign pleasure, without any unrighteousness. And, indeed, this is the answer that will stand for ever; and wherewith God will one day silence all the quarrelings of haughty creatures. And in these words he declares, that as he justly might, so he really has reserved this royal sovereignty to himself, of bestowing mercy to guilty creatures, just as himself pleases; that he will have mercy and compassion on whom he will. From whence the apostle clearly infers, ver. 16, "So then, it is not of him that willeth, nor of him that runneth, but of God that showeth mercy;" i.e., the election of any sinners is not at all of themselves, as being better inclined and behaved than others, but altogether of God, who bestows mercy as he pleases; "who will have mercy on whom he will have mercy; and will have compassion on whom he will have compassion." But I presume I need prosecute the argument no farther from this chapter; it is fully clear already, beyond all reasonable contradiction, that it maintains the very doctrine I have undertaken to prove.

And it is no less clearly maintained in the first chapter to the Ephesians: "According as he hath chosen us in him (viz: Christ) before the foundation of the world, that we should be holy, and without blame before him, in love. Having predestinated us unto the adoption of children, by Jesus Christ, to himself, according to the good pleasure of his will." Vers. 4, 5. The election which the apostle here speaks of, was more than a choosing of them to external church privileges, even an election to eternal salvation; for he says, "God had predestinated them to the adoption of children by Jesus Christ to himself." "And, (as he says, Rom. viii. 17,) if children, then heirs; heirs of God, and joint heirs with Christ." Moreover, he describes them as those that were in a state of saving grace, (ver. 3,) saying, "God hath blessed us with all spiritual blessings, in heavenly places, in Christ Jesus." And then immediately adds, "according as he hath chosen us in him, before the foundation of the world, that we should be holy." Their "being blessed with all spiritual blessings in Christ," was according to God's foregoing choice of them; it was the fruit of a gracious and eternal purpose to that end; and they were chosen, not because they would be holy, but that they should be holy; their goodness was not the cause, but the effect of their election. And, (ver. 5,) they were predestinated, or fore-appointed, to be the children of God, not according to their good works, or dispositions, but according to the good pleasure of his will; not to their own praise, but to the praise of the glory of his grace; as it follows (ver. 6). And very expressly, to the same purpose, he says, (ver. 11,) "In whom also we have obtained an inheritance, being predestinated according to the purpose of him who worketh all things after the counsel of his own will." We are not predestinated to the heavenly inheritance, says he, according to the purpose of one who proceeds according to the will and behaviour of others; but "according to the purpose of him who does all things after the counsel of his own will."

Another place of scripture, very expressly asserting an absolute election, you may see in 2 Tim. i. 9. "God hath saved us, and called us with an holy calling, not according to our works, but according to his own purpose and grace, which was given us in Christ Jesus before the world began." The plain meaning of these words, if they can be made plainer, is, as if the apostle had said, "God hath saved us, and effectually called us, out of a state of sin to holiness; and this is not to be ascribed to any works or endeavours of ours, as the reason of it, but to his own sovereign purpose and grace, or free favour; which grace was made sure to us in Christ, by the Father's engagement to him in the eternal covenant of redemption before the world began." This is a natural and easy paraphrase upon the words, though indeed they do not need any; I am very sure, if they were found anywhere else but in the Bible, every one would readily acknowledge they contained the Calvinistic doctrine of election. See also 2 Thess. ii. 13, 14, 1 Pet. 1, 2, John xv. 16, with many other places of scripture, which it is needless to mention.

But besides these direct and immediate testimonies of scripture to the doctrine, it may be farther clearly proved from such scripture passages as declare the absoluteness and sovereignty of God's proceeding in the effectual calling and conversion of sinners to himself. If God, in the regeneration and conversion of sinners, proceeds in an absolute sovereign way, calling whom he will, without regarding their previous motion and behaviour, as the reason of his proceeding, on which it is suspended; then his choosing of them must be absolute, and sovereign too; for actual renovation in time is just the fruit and execution of the eternal purpose; and therefore the one must exactly answer to the other. Many are the places of scripture which plainly teach us that God's renewing and converting of any sinners is wholly owing to his sovereign, distinguishing favour and mercy, and not to any distinguishing goodness of their own. I shall just only select a few. What can be more express to this purpose than these words? "For we ourselves also were sometimes foolish, disobedient, deceived, serving divers lusts and pleasures, living in malice and envy, hateful, and hating one another. But after that the kindness and love of God our Saviour toward man appeared, not by works of righteousness which we have done, but according to his mercy, he saved us, by the washing of regeneration and renewing of the Holy Ghost." Tit. iii. 3–5. In the same manner, the apostle speaks in the second chapter to the Ephesians: "And you hath he quickened, who were dead in trespasses and sins; wherein, in time past, ye walked according to the course of this world, according to the prince of the power of the air, the spirit that now worketh in the children of disobedience. Among whom also we all had our conversation in times past, in the lusts of our flesh, fulfilling the decrees of the flesh and the mind; and were by nature the children of wrath, even as others. But God, who is rich in mercy, for his great love wherewith he loved us, even when we were dead in sins, hath quickened us together with Christ, by grace ye are saved." Oh, sirs, thousands that are now in heaven, would have been in hell, had God waited for their good works, or preparing themselves for his grace, before he had laid hold of them by converting power. And what great excellency is there in all the good works, falsely so called, of an unregenerate sinner, when he has done them, to engage God to save him? How clearly is the free, absolute sovereignty of God in the effectual calling, declared (1 Cor. i. 26–30). "For ye see your calling, brethren, how that not many wise men after the flesh, not many mighty, not many noble, are called. But God hath chosen the foolish things of this world, to confound the wise; and God hath chosen the weak things of the world, to confound the things which are mighty; and base things of the world, and things which are despised, hath God chosen; yea, and things which are not, to bring to nought things that are; that no flesh should glory in his presence." Here you see, God calls just whom he will, among the guilty children of men. Some of the high and mighty of the world; but more generally he has ordered it that those whom he designs to call, shall be poor and mean in all worldly respects; and the general reason is, to dash down all human pride, that no flesh should glory in his presence; but that he that glorieth, should glory only in the Lord, ver. 31. And it is remarkable how the apostle alters the term; after he had begun with "calling," he puts in "choosing" in the place of it; because temporal vocation exactly corresponds to eternal election, as the certain consequence and evidence of it; and the one is as free and absolute as the other, so that it was equal which of the terms he used. Numbers of Scripture instances prove this truth. What good works of obedience to Christ had Paul done? Or what good dispositions had he towards Him, before He reached him by his powerful grace, to induce the Lord to choose and call him? Were not great numbers of his nation, as good as he, left to perish in unbelief? What were the good works and dispositions of Abraham, more than others, when God called him, as he was serving other gods on the other side of the flood, with the rest of his father's house? (Josh. xxiv. 2) of whom the Lord says, (Isa. li. 2,) "I called him alone, and blessed him." This argument is so clear and certain in all its parts, that I think it would be quite superfluous to bestow any more pains upon it.

Again, the doctrine of absolute election appears from the only way of fallen sinners' salvation, as it is laid down and declared in the gospel, viz: the way of believing only and entirely in the merit and righteousness of the Lord Jesus for actual reconciliation with God. The argument here may be thus formed: that doctrine which leaves no room for guilty sinners to rest and depend on anything but the merit and atonement of Jesus Christ only, for the reconciled favour of God, and their acceptance with him; the contrary of which does give room to sinners to rest, and depend also, on something else for reconciliation and acceptance with God, must be true, and its contrary false, according to the Scriptures. But the doctrine of absolute election leaves no room for guilty sinners to rest and depend on anything for the reconciled favour of God, and their acceptance with him, but the merit and atonement of Jesus Christ only; and the contrary doctrine does give them room to rest, and depend also, on something else for it, viz: something in them, or done by them; therefore, the doctrine of absolute election is true, and the contrary doctrine false, according to the Scriptures.

The Scripture clearly teaches us to look only to the merit and atonement of Christ's obedience and sufferings for actual justification before God, and reconciliation with him; and it is as clear, that the doctrine of sinners being chosen in Christ, and fore-appointed to justification and eternal life through him, of God's mere, sovereign, free grace, agrees well with this; it cuts all the sinews of self-dependence, and leaves the sinner no other foundation to cast himself upon, but the sovereign mercy of God, through a redeeming Saviour. And I think it is as clear again, on the other hand, that the opposite doctrine of a conditional election, founded either upon the actual existence of some good in, or done by the sinner, or upon the foresight of it to be in him, or done by him, lays a foundation for self-dependence, and so tends to keep undone sinners from closing with Christ in the way of the gospel. This delusive opinion makes poor creatures swell very big with a conceit of themselves, and what they do. When they imagine their qualifications and doings are of such price with God, it makes them halve the procurement of their salvation between Christ's righteousness and their own, which he will never bear. It makes them patch their filthy rags and menstruous cloaths to his complete, un-spotted robe, for a joint recommendation of them to God's acceptance. Indeed, I cannot see a material difference between Arminian Protestants and the Papists, about the doctrine of justification. And I find two great bishops, one of each sort, of my mind. Says Bishop Burnet, in his Exposition (more properly, perversion) of the thirty-nine articles of the Church of England, page 126, "This matter was so stated by many of the writers of the Church of Rome, after the Reformation, that, as to the main of it, we have no just exception to it." The bishop of Meaux, in his Exposition of the doctrine of the Catholic Church, page 93, after he has been explaining their sense and justification, and merit of good works, says, "And, indeed, we must acknowledge, that the learned of their party (meaning the Reformed) do not contend so much of late about this subject, as they did formerly; and there are but few who do not; there ought not to have been a breach on this point. But if this important difficulty about justification, upon winch their first authors laid all their stress, be not looked upon now as essential by the wisest persons among them, we leave them to think what they ought to judge of their separation; and what hopes there would be of a union, if they would but overcome their prejudice, and quit the spirit of contention." Thus we see Protestants and Papists cordially shaking hands, and agreeing again in one of the most material matters of difference. And all the contest remaining is, which side has made the approach to the other. The one says, "You have come to us;" the other says, "No; but you have come to us." And this, I believe, will be judged but a small matter for brethren to fall out about. However, I think I might venture, in a court of equity, to undertake to obtain sentence, upon this plea, in favour of the Romish gentleman.

The last argument I shall offer, for confirmation of this doctrine, shall be taken from the declared scope and design of God in the gospel, which is, as it is highly reasonable, to secure the whole glory of sinners' salvation to himself, and for ever hide pride from man. He assures us, he has so concerted the scheme and laid the plan, that the saved sinner shall not have the least ground to boast, or glory; which evidently proves, that election is not conditional, founded on sinners' good works or dispositions; but absolute, founded on God's good pleasure. For upon the conditional scheme, the justified, converted person has it to ascribe to himself, that he, more than another, is in such a happy state. The reason cannot be God's distinguishing love and grace to him, beyond others, but his own distinguishing goodness; for the others are supposed to have had as much love and kindness from God as he. Whence, then, came the difference that is between them? Not from God, for he made no difference; but from himself. And does not this give some ground for boasting in the case—to arrogate some glory and praise to himself? But the true gospel-way of salvation will not, in the least, admit of any such thing. It is cross to God's declared view and design in it. "For by grace ye are saved, through faith; and that not of yourselves: it is the gift of God. Not of works, lest any man should boast." Eph. ii. 8, 9. The way which God has laid for sinners' salvation, is such, that it precludes and bars against all boasting in those that are saved; and, therefore, it is not of works, but through faith, which is a soul-humbling, self-emptying grace, and a gift of God's royal bounty, which he bestows at pleasure. Rom. iii. 27. After the apostle has clearly laid down the true gospel way of guilty sinners' justification and salvation, through the alone righteousness of Christ, imputed in a way of believing, he asks, "Where is boasting then?" and answers, "It is excluded; not by the law of works, but by the law of faith." All boasting is entirely excluded by that method which God has established; and hence, we may, with abundant evidence, conclude that that doctrine which affords any room for glorying and boasting is not of God, being directly contrary to the plan and design of the gospel.

Having now, I think, with great clearness, from God's word of truth, proved the doctrine of absolute, unconditional election, I proceed, in the next place, to prove, that those of guilty mankind, whom God did not thus choose to everlasting life and salvation through Christ, he determined to leave in their guilty state, and inflict upon them their deserved punishment. And upon this branch of predestination I need be but short, because it is abundantly proven already by the proof of the former; for the one is a necessary consequence of the other. If God determined to deal with guilty mankind in such a sovereign way as has been proved, making his own righteous, sovereign pleasure, the only rule of procedure towards them, then it necessarily follows, that such as he did not ordain to life, he did ordain to deserved death. To suppose an absolute and certain election of a part of guilty sinners to be redeemed and saved, and yet, that the rest are not reprobated or rejected, are very inconsistent notions; for, seeing all mankind were looked upon and considered by God, in his decrees, as under a righteous sentence of condemnation to punishment for their sin, then, sure, such as he did not determine to deliver out of that condemnation and ruin, were left in it, to suffer the law. To say, "that they were all elected conditionally, though the others were absolutely," is as contrary to those scriptures which have been adduced, as to deny an absolute election altogether; for they assert election to be universally absolute, contrary to such a distinction of a two-fold election. It is a notion, especially contrary to those passages which declare the absoluteness of effectual calling in all those that are so called; and those passages which declare, that all that are saved, are saved in such a way as excludes all self-glorying and self-depending. But I proceed to offer a few other proofs from the scripture, for the confirmation of this head. And, first, I argue thus: those who are not given in charge by the Father to Jesus Christ, to be redeemed and saved by him, were left in their sins, and ordained to suffer the law for them themselves.

But those who were not certainly elected to salvation, were not given in charge by the Father to Jesus Christ, to be redeemed and saved by him: therefore, they were left in their sins, and ordained to suffer the law for them themselves. That those, who were not certainly elected to salvation, were not given in charge by the Father to Jesus Christ, to be redeemed and saved by him, is plain from this, that all those who were given in charge to Jesus Christ, to be redeemed and saved by him, shall certainly be saved by him; and were certainly and infallibly ordained to be so. This is clearly proved from the words of Christ: "For I came down from heaven, not to do mine own will, but the will of him that sent me. And this is the Father's will which hath sent me, that of all which he hath given me, I should lose nothing, but should raise it up again at the last day." John vi. 38, 39. These words, I think, plainly say, that all such as are not in the end actually saved by Jesus Christ, if he be faithful to his trust, were not committed to his charge, to be redeemed by him, and consequently they were left under the condemnatory sentence of the law.

Another proof, that those whom God has not absolutely elected to salvation, he has left to perish, and abandoned from his saving care, you have in Rom. xi. 7, where, after the apostle has said, that the remnant of Israel, which God had reserved to himself, according to the election of grace, had obtained righteousness and life; he adds, "and the rest were blinded." Very full and express to the same purpose are those words, "Christ is a stone of stumbling, and a rock of offence, even to them which stumble at the word, being disobedient, whereunto also they were appointed." 2 Pet. ii. 8. God appointed to leave them to blindness, stumbling, and disobedience; which things are always consequent upon God's leaving any to themselves.

This doctrine of sinners' rejection or reprobation in the eternal purpose of God, is indeed, I acknowledge, a very awful and solemn one; especially to those who do not find in them the comfortable evidences of election; and might reasonably excite in them a deep concern about the great concerns of their souls, and stir them up to take no peaceful rest, till they find in themselves the hopeful tokens of God's electing love, in a supernatural work of renewing, sanctifying grace in their souls. But then let us take care, that we do not charge God foolishly and wickedly in the case, as if he were cruel and unrighteous. What, if God was willing to show his wrath, and to make his power known, upon the vessels of wrath fitted to destruction, and worthy of death, who can justly find fault with him? What, if he had reprobated all apostate mankind, as well as all apostate angels, who could say, he had done wrong?

Every mouth must have been stopped, all the world being guilty before him.

But I come to speak to the objections, commonly urged from the scriptures against the foregoing doctrine, in both its branches. And here I shall first take notice of the method which those on the other side of the question, put a main confidence in, for the overthrowing of this doctrine, by going about to prove a universal redemption; that Christ died equally for all, and every individual of mankind; for one as much as another. This, they think, they can very easily prove from such places of scripture, as speak of his dying "for all men; for all the world; for the whole world; for every man;" and the like. But these universal expressions of scripture will not amount to sufficient proof of what they bring them for, for all so plain as they think they are for them. If such universal terms of scripture must of necessity be understood in such a large extent as they might seem to carry in them, we shall then as easily prove many other things from scripture which no man of common sense will believe to be intended in it. For instance, as readily and plainly as they will prove that Christ laid down his life for every individual person of Adam's race; as plainly, I say will I prove that every individual person of Adam's race will have praise from God at the day of Judgment; from 1 Cor. iv. 5, where the apostle says, "Then shall every man have praise of God." As plainly and fully will I prove, that after John the Baptist's preaching every individual of mankind pressed into the kingdom of God from Luke xvi. 16, "Since that time the kingdom of God is preached, and every man presseth into it." And by the same rule you may have it proved that every human creature spoke of the faith of the Christians at Rome. "Your faith is spoken of throughout the whole world." Rom. i. 8. These few examples, instead of great numbers which might be produced, are sufficient to show that such universal terms in scripture must be often understood under very great restrictions; and quite in another sense than our opponents will allow, when they are used concerning the death of Christ. Some of those places of scripture, where such universal terms are used, concerning Christ's death, and the effect of it, only signify the virtue and efficacy of it, to those who partake of the benefits of it. Some others signify that his death was designed promiscuously for some of all nations, and all ranks and conditions of men, as not confined to any one particular nation, or degree of mankind. Others again only mean, that Christ is the only Saviour, that none are saved but through his death. In the first sense, we are to understand Rom. v. 18. The design of that whole chapter is to show that Christ's death and satisfaction is of sufficient virtue for the justifying and saving of the most guilty sinners. For this purpose the apostle observes the efficacy of Adam's sin, and breaking the law, to the condemning of those to whom it was charged and imputed, declaring that much more is Christ's fulfilling the law effectual to the complete justification of those to whom it is imputed, notwithstanding their former condemnation. And so, when he says, that "as by the offence of one, judgment came upon all men to condemnation: even so, by the righteousness of one, the free gift came upon all men to justification of life," his meaning is, that as the offence and disobedience of Adam prevailed to the condemning of those to whom it reached, and was imputed, even so the righteousness of Christ was sufficiently effectual to the full justification of those to whom it was imputed, from the guilt of that offence, and all others, so as to entitle them again to eternal life. So that the apostle's design is not at all to run a parallel between Adam's offence and Christ's righteousness, in the extent of their influence and effects; but to compare the one with the other, as to the efficacy of their influence; in respect of which he observes that Christ's righteousness is much superior, as it justifies to life, even after Adam's sin has condemned to death. And thus the phrase, "all men," in both parts of the verse, is to be understood with this limitation, viz: all men on whom it came. In the first part of the verse, judgment came upon all men, on whom it came, to condemnation; i.e., so as to condemn them. In the latter part, the free gift came upon all men, on whom it came, to justification of life; i.e., so as to justify them to life. I presume, if every man had been in the text, instead of all men, the Universalists would have thought it every whit as strong for their purpose as they do now. And you may see how that this phrase must be understood the same way, Mark viii. 25, (I accomodate myself here to those who understand only the English translation. The term in the original is in the plural number, all men as well as in Rom. v. 18. But it is as equal to the sense, which of the ways it is rendered) where it is said of the man that had been blind, to whom Jesus Christ gave sight, that he saw every man clearly; which cannot be understood of the extent of his sight, that he saw every man that was in the world; but of the strength and efficacy of his sight, that he saw every man, whom he did see, clearly. It is indeed true, that by the offence of Adam, judgment came upon every individual of his posterity, except the human nature of Jesus Christ, to condemnation; and this verse is a clear and certain proof of it. But then, I conceive it is not the universality of the term here that proves it; it is as fully proved from the next verse as from this, where it is only said, that by his disobedience many were made sinners; because the imputation of his sin at all, is evidence enough that it is imputed to all and every one that descends from him in the ordinary way of generation; seeing his relation was the same to all, as the natural and common parent of the human race. But, farther, there is this plain reason, evincing that the universal term here must be understood in this limited sense, viz: because if it be understood in the large, extensive sense in which the Arminians will have it, it will prove a great deal too much for them, not a universal, conditional, redemption which they contend for, but a universal, absolute redemption and salvation. It will then prove that every individual of the human race is actually justified to eternal life, by the righteousness of Christ; and we are sure, that whom he justified, them he also glorified, (Rom. viii. 30.) Thus you see the true sense of this text, and manifest design of the whole context, destroy all foundation of an argument for universal redemption.

The proper import and design of those words, (1 John ii. 2,) "He is the propitiation for our sins, and not for ours only, but also for the sins of the whole world," is, that the death of Christ was a propitiation, or atonement, not only for people among the Jews, or for those who were then believers in those parts of the world, but also for some, be they more or less, in all parts and ages of the world; for he was to be God's salvation unto the ends of the earth.

When the apostle says, (1 Tim. ii. 6,) that "Christ gave himself a ransom for all," it appears from the context, that he means persons of all ranks and degrees; for he brings it in as an argument to enforce his exhortation to pray for kings, and all that are in authority. The same universal term he manifestly intends in the same sense, in the first verse, when he says, "I exhort, therefore, that first of all, supplications, prayers, intercessions, and giving of thanks, be made for all men." He cannot mean, sure, that they should pray for the millions of men that were dead, and gone to their own place before that time. Neither can he intend, that they should pray for such as the apostle John excludes from an interest in our prayers, (1 John v. 16): "There is a sin unto death: I do not say, that a man shall pray for it;" that is, for such as are guilty of it. But he explains his meaning to be for men of all stations and degrees, the high as well as the low, adding, "for kings, and all that are in authority." When the apostle says, (Heb. ii. 9,) that "Christ tasted death for every man," the meaning is, for every man that is saved; to signify, that none are saved but through Christ's death, that his death is the only purchase of salvation for any man. In the same limited manner we must understand the same term, (Col. i. 28,) "We preach Christ, warning every man, and teaching every man," that is, warning and teaching every man to whom we have an opportunity to preach. So, (1 Cor. iv. 5,) "When the Lord comes to judgment, every man shall have praise of God;" that is, every man that is saved, or has been truly godly. Another place of scripture, which is brought in to serve the cause of universal redemption, is, (2 Pet. ii. 1,) where the apostle speaks of some who should privily bring in damnable heresies, even denying the Lord that bought them, and bring upon themselves swift destruction. But the apostle only speaks of the Lord's having bought them, as what might have been hoped concerning them as well as others. The gospel revelation of a Saviour that died to redeem sinners, affords ground to all to whom it comes, to hope that his death might have been designed for them as well as others, (though it was not intended for all and every one alike,) seeing it does not point out the persons, in particular, for whom he did not intend the benefits of his death. And so, concerning these persons here, the apostle mentions it as a high aggravation of their crime, that they should deny that Redeemer, of whom they had no reason to conclude to the contrary but that he had bought and redeemed them, when they had the same ground of hope this way that any others had, before they had the special evidences of it in renewing grace.

Thus I have considered some of the most material passages of Scripture which are advanced in favour of universal redemption; and I think any considerate person might see, from what has been said, that they come far short of answering the design they are advanced for; and any other passages of the like strain are to be understood the same way. I have already mentioned a place of Scripture, (John vi. 89,) which proves that all those who were given to Christ to redeem, he will surely save, and finally glorify, unless it may be said he was unfaithful to his charge; for it was "the will of him that sent him, that he should lose none of them, but raise them up again at the last day," and so put the finishing stroke to their full glorification; which confirms a particular redemption, in opposition to a universal. In the tenth chapter of John our Lord speaks of a peculiar people, which he had both among the Jews and Gentiles, whom he calls his sheep; for whom, he says, he laid down his life. And, (John xvii,) he speaks of those whom the Father had given him, as distinct from the rest of mankind. For these, he says, he prays, and not for the world, ver. 9; and, ver. 19, he says, "For their sakes I sanctify myself;" that is, it is for their sakes that I set myself apart to the office and charge of a Redeemer, and devote myself to be a sacrifice.

I shall only farther point out, as briefly as may be, some absurdities attending the doctrine of universal redemption, and so dismiss it. If God sent his Son to die for sinners, with an equal view and design to save them all by it, intending as much the salvation of one as another, without any difference, then it will follow, that those who are saved are no more beholden or obliged to God than those who perish; and it was not from him that they were saved any more than others, but from themselves; and so he shall not have the glory of it; nay, he is rather beholden to them, for letting him have his end. Again, it will follow, that God, in a great measure, comes short of obtaining his end and design, and that in the greatest affair that ever he undertook, so far as we are acquainted; an end which he was so intent upon, that he spared not his own Son, but delivered him up to the death, that he might obtain it. The end which he was intently set upon, was the salvation of all the human race; and yet he is greatly disappointed of it, for great numbers for ever perish. Now, how can any man reasonably persuade himself, that God really proposed to himself, and intended such an end, and yet did not make it sure, and ascertain the attainment of it? Was it not easy to his power to do it? Has he not the hearts of all men in his hands? Would it have done them any injustice to have persuaded them by almighty power, and made them willing to be happy? But seeing he has not done so, it is plain that the salvation of all was not the end and design he had in view in sending his Son into the world to die. Would he have left a design he had so much at heart, upon the precarious bottom (to say the best of it that they can say) of the free-will of corrupted creatures, that were no way well affected toward him, but awfully disaffected? Nay, farther, it will follow, that it might have so happened as that he would have entirely lost his end altogether; for all so seriously as he intended it, and was set upon it, yet it seems he did not make it certain; no, not as to the salvation of any one soul, but left it altogether to themselves. One would think by this, that he was not very intent upon it, for all the great pretences of some, by this doctrine, to magnify his love and good-will to men. And it may be considered which doctrine magnifies the love of God most—that which renders the salvation of a considerable number infallibly certain, or that which leaves it altogether uncertain as to any, leaving it entirely to the good pleasure of their depraved wills? I believe it will be found that more will be saved in that way, than would have been in this; for, I think, upon this score, none at all would be saved. However, it is plain that great multitudes do finally oppose and contradict this supposed intention of God; and what hinders but all the rest might do so too, according to the universal scheme; and not so much as one be saved after all? for all are alike opposite to the way of salvation by nature. But you will say, perhaps, there was no danger of such a disappointment and frustration of God's end as this, for he foreknew who would comply with the gospel, and be saved, and so knew that he would not altogether fail of his design. But this is so far from clearing the doctrine, that it introduces a new absurdity; for how can it be conceived that God could really intend and design the death of Christ, and the benefit of it, for those who he infallibly knew would never be partakers of it? Is it not an absurdity, may not I say impossibility, in the very nature of the thing? To what purpose was the death of Christ designed for them, or for what advantage? Not to save them, for that the Lord knew would never be. And every designing of an end includes in it some degree of expectation, which could not be in this case. Was it to purchase sufficient grace for them, that so they might be saved if they would? Well, but the Lord knew that they would not make the saving use of it; and why then was it intentionally purchased for them? Sure, you will not say it was to make their guilt and punishment the greater. Let the admirers of universal redemption consider a little, how they will digest and solve these things. But to proceed.

The opposers of the doctrine of absolute decrees argue farther against it, from some places of scripture, which they suppose declare a general will and desire in God of the conversion and salvation of all sinners, and how much he would be pleased with it; which they suppose is contrary to his having purposed not to give to some the grace necessary and sufficient for their conversion, but to leave them to perish in their sins. I shall a little consider the principal passages which they advance to this purpose, and shew that they intend nothing contrary to this doctrine. One of them is (1 Tim. ii. 4,) "God will have all men to be saved, and to come unto the knowledge of the truth."

If all men, here be understood for every individual man in the world, then God's willing them to be saved, cannot mean his having willed and purposed that they shall be saved; for then they all would be saved, because he can easily fulfill all his purposes, and surely will do so. "For his counsel shall stand, and he will do all his pleasure." Isa. xlvi. 10. "The counsel of the Lord standeth for ever, and the thoughts of his heart to all generations." Psa. xxxiii. 11. But if the words be taken in this unlimited sense, the meaning of the place must only be, that the salvation of all men, in the way of faith and holiness, would be a thing very agreeable to the approving and preceptive will of God, as he delights in holiness, and the happiness which is connected with it; and that sin, for which it is that any perish, is disagreeable and hateful to his holy nature; and yet, all this is no way inconsistent with his determining to punish sinners for their sin. But I think it is plain, from the context, that by all men here, we are to understand, men of all characters and degrees; for the words are brought in as an argument to encourage Christians to pray for kings, and for all that are in authority. And in the same sense, the term all men is intended in the first verse, as I have made appear before.

Another place is (2 Pet. iii. 9), "The Lord is not slack concerning his promise; but is long suffering to us-ward, not willing that any should perish, but that all should come to repentance." I think it is pretty manifest, that the persons the apostle speaks of here, are the elect of God; the persons to whom he writes these epistles, are considered under that character. In his first epistle, (chap. i. 2,) he calls them "elect, according to the foreknowledge of God the Father, through the sanctification of the Spirit unto obedience, and to the sprinkling of the blood of Jesus Christ." And in the first verse of this chapter we are informed that he writes this second epistle to the same, or same sort of persons; and of the same he speaks in the verse under our present consideration, joining himself, as being also an elect person with them; saying, "The Lord is long suffering to us-ward;" i.e., towards us, the election of his grace, not willing that any, viz: of us, should perish, but that we all should come to repentance, and be called in. The apostle's design, in the words, is to show the reason of God's delaying to put an end to the present state of this world, and bring on the general judgment; in answer to the scoffers, that he says should be in the last days, saying, "Where is the promise of his coming? For since the fathers fell asleep, all things continue as they were from the beginning of the creation." Ver. 3, 4. In answer, I say, to these atheistical scoffs, he observes that God had done as great, unlikely, and unexpected things already, as the shutting up the scene of this world in such a solemn manner, though they wilfully neglected to take notice of them. He had not only, by the word of his power, created the heavens and the earth out of nothing at first, but a long time after had destroyed the earth and its ungodly inhabitants by a flood of water; and so it was no incredible, nor unlikely thing, that he should, at last, burn it with fire at the day of judgment and perdition of ungodly men; and notwithstanding it had stood so long, in much the same state, after the people of God had spoke of this, as what would surely be, he observes that a long space of time with us is but little with God; and then says, "the Lord is not slack concerning his promise, (as some men count slackness,) but is long suffering to us-ward, &c.;" that is, the Lord's deferring the end of the world and last judgment so long, is not through forgetfulness or careless neglect of his promise to that purpose; but the true reason of it is, that all his elect may be brought in, not being willing that any of them should perish, but that all should come to repentance, be converted and saved; and therefore he will not come to judgment at a time when there are any of them on the earth unconverted, nor until the last of the whole number is fitted for glory.

There is another scripture that is always brought in upon this head of argument, (Ezek. xxxiii. 11,) where the Lord declares, with the solemnity of an oath, "As I live, saith the Lord, I have no pleasure in the death of the wicked, but that the wicked turn from his way, and live." When the Lord says he has no pleasure in the death of the wicked, the plain sense of the words is, that the death and misery of sinners is not a pleasure to him in itself, or for its own sake, merely as it is a misery to the creature. But this does not say, but that their death and punishment may be agreeable and pleasing to him under other considerations; as it is an execution of justice, and manifestation of his own glory. If it were not so, would he inflict punishment upon any of them? Would he displease and make himself uneasy? And when he says that it is a pleasure to him, that the wicked turn from his way, and live, the meaning is, that righteousness and holiness in his creatures, and the happiness consequent upon it, is the object of his approbation and liking, a thing in itself agreeable and pleasing to his holy nature. But this, sure, is no proof that he equally and alike designed the sanctification and salvation of all sinners. If it proved anything this way, it would prove that he designed it certainly for them all, if his power could effect it.

The words of our Lord, (Matt, xxiii. 37,) are often brought in upon this head, where he says of Jerusalem, "How often would I have gathered thy children, even as a hen gathereth her chickens under her wings, and ye would not!" If we understand the Lord Jesus to speak here of his willingness to have gathered them, with reference to his divine nature, as God, the words only prove, that sinners' compliance with the gospel, and turning to holiness, is a thing in itself agreeable and pleasing to God's holy nature: holiness being the object of his love and complacence; that his dealings with that people, in the course of his ministry among them, tended in their own nature to bring them thus to duty; and that their unbelief and impenitency was owing to the perverseness and corruption of their own wills, as the cause of it. But if we suppose him to speak of his willingness merely as man, in his human nature, then I see no inconvenience in allowing that it might signify an intense and passionate desire in him of their conversion and happiness. But, surely, no such passions, or uneasy long desires, and especially for things which will never be effected, are to be ascribed to the divine nature. For my part, I cannot apprehend what sort of a will and desire for the conversion and salvation of all men, it is, which those who deny absolute predestination, suppose to be in God, any way consistent with his perfections. They suppose it includes much more than that the holiness and happiness of his creatures is a thing in itself lovely and agreeable to him; that it is his preceptive and approving will that they should be holy, and consequently happy: which is very consistent with the doctrine they oppose, from this topic of a general will; and they cannot allow it to include so much as a real purpose that all shall be sanctified and saved; because then all would be so, which is contrary to fact, or else God's purpose would be frustrated, and he would come short of what he certainly intended would come to pass, which is highly absurd. But they seem to fancy a sort of an uneasy wishing and longing desire in God for that which, notwithstanding, will never be; and if this be not to make God such a one as ourselves, I know not what is. Does it not argue God to be subject to the weaknesses of creatures? And not only so, but that he suffers himself to be made uneasy, and to be crossed in his desires by that which he could easily prevent, which is what no wise man would allow in himself; and, therefore, though God may sometimes condescend to speak to sinners in such language as they use to one another, when they would express the greatness and ardency of their desire for anything, yet we are not hence to imagine that there are any such human passions and creature-weaknesses in him. The design of such modes of speaking in God, is only to signify how desirable and excellent a thing it is in itself, for creatures to love, to obey and honour him, and how much it is both their interest and duty to do so. And the reason why this is expressed in such a manner as imports weak passions in men when they speak so, is because it is the most suitable way of dealing with such creatures as we are, best adapted to our capacity and condition; it is a method that has the most suitable tendency in itself to work upon and prevail with rational creatures, expressing best to their capacity the excellency and necessity of holiness, and the horrid, hateful nature of sin; for, though it is the supernatural power of God's Spirit that prevails with any sinners to be holy, yet, as a wise agent, he makes use of the most suitable and best adapted means for that purpose, dealing with men in a way suited to their rational nature and human capacities. Thus it is we are to understand the various expostulations and entreaties of God in the scriptures.

As another topic of argument against the doctrine of God's decrees, the opposers of it seem to think that all men have sufficient power to do that which is required as necessary to salvation, and with which salvation is certainly connected; or, at least, that they have sufficient power to ensure to themselves such supernatural power as is necessary for that purpose; and this is what is commonly called universal, sufficient grace. For the support of this opinion they refer to such passages of scripture, in which God commands all men where the gospel comes, to be holy as lie is holy, to repent and believe in Jesus Christ, to make themselves new hearts, &c. Hence they argue that all have power some way to do these things, because, they say, it would be unjust for God to require more of men than they can perform. To this I answer, that these men seem entirely to overlook, in this way of reasoning, the ruin brought upon the human offspring by the fall and apostasy of Adam, the covenant-head and representative of all mankind. He, indeed, until he sinned, was furnished with sufficient ability to do whatsoever God did or ever should require of him; at least, had he not sinned, his ability would always have been increased equally with his obligations; there was a full proportion between his power and the law he was under. And so it would have been with all his posterity, had he fulfilled the conditions of the covenant; but as, by his transgression, they lost all right and title to that happiness, and life of communion with God, which was secured to them in the covenant, upon his obedience, so they lost God's moral image, and the power of holy obedience; and it was at God's free, sovereign pleasure to confer happiness again, and the grace necessary to it, as he pleased. And as God then was under no obligation to afford strength answerable to the law, so neither was he obliged to bring down the requirements of his law to the level and capacity of the fallen, ruined creature. Though man, by his own default, has lost his power of obedience, that is no argument that God must lose his right and claim; the creature's sin and wretchedness thereby, cannot dissolve his obligations of duty to God; God's law must still remain the same, as a perfect and eternal rule of righteousness, let creatures change and alter as they will. If it be asked, for what end the law of God is set before us, and his commandments laid upon us in his word, if we have not ability to fulfil? I answer, for various ends; to teach us what is our duty to God; what we ought to be aiming at, and endeavouring after; to show us our sins and transgressions, "for by the law is the knowledge of sin," (Rom. iii. 20,) as the crookedness of a line is discovered by laying it to a straight one; to teach us our utter inability to fulfil the law, and obtain life for our obedience; for which purpose our Saviour referred one to the keeping of the commandments, (Matt. xix. 17,) whom he found big with the conceit that he could do much; that so we may see our necessity of getting righteousness and strength from Christ, a mediator; and thus the law is given as a schoolmaster to bring us to Christ. It is a means whereby the Lord brings in his elect to the Redeemer by faith; and it is given as a rule of life to the renewed children of God, to direct them how they are to honour and glorify him.

If it be objected to the above account of sinners' inability to do what is now required of them under the dispensation of the new covenant, that Adam had not the power of believing in a Redeemer, or repenting and renewing his heart, as having no need of it, and the exercise of it being inconsistent with his state of innocence; and therefore we cannot be said to have lost it in him, seeing it was not given him while he stood in the character of our representative—to this it may be easily replied. that though he had not his power for such acts and purposes as these, in his innocent state; yet, had we, in our guilty state, that power restored which he had, we would be able to believe in the Redeemer, to repent, &c. The impossibility of his putting forth such acts, was not from the want of inherent power, but the inconsistency of them with his condition. It was inconsistent with his state of innocence, to have any occasion for administering physic, to recover his health; yet this is no argument that he had not sufficient ability for it.

I would just farther refer it to the consideration of those who offer this argument against God's decrees, and yet, in the meantime, acknowledge that no man in this life can fulfil the law of God perfectly, how they are consistent with themselves: for herein themselves acknowledge that God requires more of men than they can now perform, since the fall; and, sure, they will not own it is so, and say it is unjust too.

For further proof of this universal power, or grace, they urge the invitations of the gospel to believe in Christ, and its promises to such as do believe. Such as (Isa. xiv. 22), "Look unto me, and be ye saved, all the ends of the earth:" and (Rev. iii. 20), "Behold, I stand at the door, and knock; if any man hear my voice and open the door, I will come in to him," &c. Such invitations, they think, infer that there is a power in man to comply with them, otherwise they would be vain and needless. But this is a vain argument. For, though sinners are without strength, through the darkness of their minds, and obstinacy of their wills; yet such invitations are needful, to show them their duty, and the only way in which they can ever be happy; and to afford them a ground and warrant for believing in Jesus Christ, and resting their souls upon him for salvation. By these invitations, and promises to believing, the Holy Spirit 'encourages and persuades convinced souls to close with Christ, as their Saviour, and cast themselves upon his mediation and atonement, with humble, joyful confidence. The Spirit of God, by his power, brings a sinner to believe in Christ, in a way agreeable to his nature, as a reasonable creature; and so make use of the offers and promises of the gospel, as the soul's warrant for laying claim to Christ, as his Saviour, and believing in him for his salvation. Likewise, these invitations and promises are of great use for the comfort of true believers, showing there is a sure connection between believing and salvation. When Moses tells the people of Israel (Deut. xxx. 19), "that he had set life and death before them, blessing and cursing, and bids them choose life;" the words may be easily understood in the same sense with the fore-mentioned passages, to signify that there is a certain and inseparable connection between true holiness and eternal life, though this holiness is the effect of a supernatural divine power, exerted only in whom the Lord pleases: and the Lord proposes this holiness, which is connected with happiness, to sinners' choice, to import the reasonableness and necessity of their choosing it; and that he may deal with them in a way agreeable to the nature of reasonable beings. But yet, I think it is plain from the context, that the life and death there spoken of was temporal prosperity and adversity; which life was promised to that people, upon their strict adherence to the outward prescriptions of the law that was given them: and it will be readily owned that they might thus choose and perform obedience without special renewing grace: and, in this sense, righteousness and life are to be frequently understood in the Old Testament.

It is farther argued, for this universal grace, from the parable of the talents (Matt, xxv.) But we are not to understand by these talents, universal, sufficient grace, whereby all men are enabled to convert themselves, if they will, and savingly to renew and change their wills; but other gifts and bounties of divine Providence, such as natural endowments of mind, good education, health, worldly goods, outward gospel privileges, and the like, which God distributes to mankind in various measures, as he pleases. Those who made such improvement of their talents, signify the truly godly, who are effectually renewed by God's power, according to his purpose. The person that made no improvement, signifies unconverted sinners who do not sincerely love and honour God. The account taken of these servants at their Lord's return, and his different retributions to them, according to their past conduct, are designed to teach us that the Lord Jesus will surely come at last to judgment, that we must all appear before his judgment-seat, to give an account of the deeds done in this life, and that our past behaviour here, both in heart and outward practice, will be the rule according to "which the sentence of judgment will pass upon us.

Though the reward of happiness to the godly will not be given them for their godliness, as the cause of it; yet it will be given to them only, who have been thus qualified and fore-prepared by the Lord for it; and that in different degrees, according to their different degrees of care, zeal, and diligence in the ways of God, after their conversion. On the other hand, all the ungodly shall be condemned to punishment according to the demerit of their works; and to different degrees of punishment, according to their deserts. And thus, the works, the dispositions, and conduct of men in this life, will be the rule according to which the final awards will be made at the last day to all mankind, though not the meritorious or procuring cause of them to all, but only to the wicked. These things I take to be the very scope and design of the parable; and so the universal men have no service at all to their cause from it. It is mere trifling to ask, as some do, if the servant that was punished, had made as good use of his talent, as the rest did of theirs, would he not have been as well accepted? That is, whether finally impenitent sinners would not have been accepted by Jesus Christ, as well as true believers, and sincerely godly persons, had they been true believers, and sincerely godly as well as they? I am free enough to answer in the affirmative. Had they been such, it would have been a certain evidence that they had been elected to holiness and salvation, as well as the others; for true justifying and sanctifying faith is not of ourselves, it is the gift of God, given according to his purpose and grace, which was made sure to all believers in Christ Jesus, before the world began." But then the question does not at all touch the matter in debate, viz: whether unrenewed sinners have had a sufficient inward grace given them to be true believers and godly persons, as those who are really such. Considering that sinners' impotency consists chiefly in their enmity, their inability, in the opposition of their wills to God's will, I think it is plain that no grace is sufficient, but that which is actually effectual. Their wills are not just in equilibrio, in an even balance between holiness and sin, as much inclined to the one side as the other, so as that they might bring their wills to a compliance with, and complacence in, the ways of God, by their own reason; or by the help of some divine assistances, which they might also reject: but their wills are strongly set against the new covenant way of salvation, and the holy law of God, in its spiritual nature and extent; and therefore, "no man can come unto Christ, except the Father draw him." John vi. 44.

Again, they argue in another method from the general calls, invitations, and offers of the gospel, reasoning after this manner. It would, say they, be the highest instance of dissembling and deceit for God to call sinners to repent and turn from their evil ways, with such appearance of real sincerity and earnestness, if he had before infallibly decreed that a great many of them should not repent and turn (not to communicate the grace of conversion and repentance to many, it should be). And what greater insincerity and illusion, say they, can well be imagined than for God to make such a general, unlimited offer of Christ, and salvation through him, as (Rev. xxii. 17), "Whosoever will, let him take the water of life freely;" when he has already purposed not to give salvation to many? How can such an open declaration agree with such a secret purpose? Would there not be a direct opposition between his outward expressions and inward sentiments, which is downright falsifying and hypocrisy?

But all this plausible reasoning, on which some of the greatest patrons of the Arminian scheme bestow a great deal of eloquence, is grounded upon a mistaken apprehension of the nature and true import of these calls and gospel offers. God's calls to sinners to repent and turn to him, to believe in Christ, &c., are only so many significations of what is sinners' duty, and what is agreeable to God's holy nature, pleasing and approvable in his sight. The calls do not signify what is God's purpose concerning men, but what is their duty to him, and that he loves holiness in his creatures, that the righteous Lord loves righteousness. And so, in all such calls and commands, there is an entire agreement between God's words and his will signified by them; for he does, indeed, will these things, as the matter of sinners' duty, and loves them as agreeable to his own holy law. This just view of the many calls of God in the scripture to sinners, for their repentance and conversion to holiness, destroys all the force of the argument taken from them, as though they were inconsistent with God's secret will and purpose to leave many in their sins without converting grace, for they import nothing in their true design contrary to it. And when God condescends to use arguments and expostulations with sinners about what he requires, it is that he may deal with them as reasonable beings, and convert his elect in a way agreeable to their rational nature.

As to the offers of Christ made to all where the gospel comes, and promises of salvation, through him, to all such as truly believe in him. It is most certain, that God does will and purpose to save all such as truly accept of his Son Jesus Christ, and believe in him, as he is proposed and set forth in the gospel revelation of him, for he declares that all such shall be saved. But then, we are to consider this faith in Christ as the gift of God, according to Eph. ii. 8, and a grace of his powerful operation or working, (Col. ii. 12, Eph. i. 19, 2 Thess. i. 11,) bestowed only upon, and wrought only in those whom he has chosen, and, therefore, called the faith of God's elect, (Tit. i. 1.) And thus, the promises of the gospel run exactly parallel with the election of grace, and do not import anything contrary to it. Indeed, to say that God does not really design to save all who shall believe in Christ, notwithstanding; he has declared that he will, were to impute the grossest falsehood and deceit to him; but there is no such thing in the doctrine which the argument is brought against. It is true, the offer of Christ as a Saviour is made to all, to be accepted and believed in, for their salvation in particular, wherever the news of the gospel-salvation is sent. But then, this offer does not signify or import that God designed him and the saving benefits of his death equally for all, but that, inasmuch as all have equal need of him, and God has not revealed or any way pointed out who they are whom he has not chosen to salvation through him, so as they might be known either to themselves or others, it is the great duty of all to accept of him with all their hearts, according to the declarations concerning him in the gospel, freely and willingly to comply with the way of salvation through his atonement, casting a fiducial dependence upon him, and him only, for their eternal life; for which faith the infallible promise of salvation to all such as so receive him, is sufficient warrant and encouragement. And it was necessary that the offer should be thus universal, when it was not revealed who, in particular, was elected to salvation through him, that so the elect might be brought to believe in him, upon a rational ground and foundation; for they could not know that they were chosen to life through him, more than any others, before their believing, and, therefore, could not have had a ground for faith to go upon, were it not for the promise to whosoever believes, and the declarations that it is every one's duty cordially to comply, and be pleased with that way of salvation, through an atoning Mediator; and, upon the encouragement of this promise, to cast a reliance, and the whole dependence of their souls for salvation upon him. In this manner it is that the offers of Christ in the gospel are general and universal, not importing that he died alike for all, or that he was equally designed for all, in the purpose of God; but that, seeing none have any reason certainly to conclude against themselves that they were rejected in the divine purpose; and, seeing acceptance and eternal life, through Christ, is promised to all that believe, it is the duty of all, with their whole hearts, to embrace him as he is proposed, and believe in him; and yet none will so believe in him but the chosen of God, who are called according to his purpose. And thus, as God is entirely consistent with himself in the case, so are the ministers of the gospel consistent with themselves in maintaining God's absolute decrees, and yet making such general offers of Christ, as a Saviour, to all that hear them, calling upon them to accept of and believe in him, using arguments with them for that purpose, and promising life and salvation, in his name, to all that truly comply with the gospel and believe in him. And though they do not know the elect of God among their hearers, he does and will apply this gospel to their hearts, so as to bring them to believe in Christ, and become truly godly. These considerations, if duly weighed and attended to, I think may be abundantly satisfactory in this case.

There is another argument, commonly insisted on by those on the other side of the question, taken from God's appointment of a gospel ministry, ordinances of worship, and means of grace in his church, as if they were altogether vain and useless, on supposition of such eternal decrees. According to the Calvinist doctrine of predestination, say they, "It is quite needless for ministers to preach, and as needless for people to hear, or to perform any religious duty whatsoever; and the reason is, because they cannot alter the purpose of God concerning them, whatever it be, do they well or ill; they will fare as well, let them live as they list, as if they did ever so well; and so they had even as good take their swing: nay, it had been much better for all the reprobate, that they had never had the privileges of the gospel; because, according to the scripture, the condemnation and misery of those that perish, will be much aggravated by it."

This is an awful charge, indeed; and if it be just, the doctrine is certainly most unsufferable, which takes off all restraints from the most profligate course of life, farther than what proceed from our temporal interest in this world; and arguments from private temporal interest do often sway more to the most inhuman crimes than moral honesty. But I hope to make it appear that the objection is most false and groundless. And to this purpose let these few things be considered:

First, Supposing there were no arguments for a pious, godly life, to be had from our own eternal interest; yet there are reasons of another nature, of sufficient weight and force in themselves, to induce us to it, and engage us to endeavour after it. Is not the great God, who is infinitely good and glorious, worthy of the greatest esteem, profoundest subjection, and highest adoration of all the rational creation? And has he not an inviolable right and claim to these things from us, as our Creator and Preserver? And is not conformity to God, and to obey and honour him, the greatest honour and glory of a created being? These arguments, I know, have little weight with apostate creatures whose understandings are darkened, and all their other faculties wholly corrupted; but that is not for want of sufficient weight in their own nature: nothing can ever dissolve God's title to the homage and obedience of his creatures.

Secondly, I would have two or three particulars considered and weighed together: First, that the elect are elected to salvation, "through the sanctification of the Spirit;" "whom he did predestinate, them he also called." And this effectual calling, and sanctifying grace, wrought in the heart by the Holy Spirit, is the certain fruit and evidence of eternal election; whereby those who are the partakers of this grace, may, and frequently do, come to a comfortable satisfaction, as to their election of God.

Again, you are to observe, that the elect themselves, before their conversion and effectual calling, have no notices or evidences at all of their being elected, more than others; which must needs be a very uneasy and distressing condition, when the Spirit of God touches the conscience. And then, in the next place, let it be considered, that God has appointed the preaching of the gospel, and other religious exercises, such as reading the holy scriptures, and other good books, prayer, &c., to be the means whereby he ordinarily converts and sanctifies his elect, and affords them the comfortable tokens of his electing love. He has appointed these ordinances and means as the ordinary channels wherein to communicate his special grace to those whom he has chosen. Now if these things be duly adverted to, I think, it will be clear, that there is use, and great use too, for the preaching of the gospel, and other exercises of religion, in a consistency with God's absolute decrees: and that there are sufficient reasons to engage persons to a very careful observance of them, and of all the commands of God; for the ordinances of God are the means which he sees fit, in his wisdom, to make use of for the conversion and sanctification of his elect, which work of grace is the only evidence of our belonging to God, as his elect people: and therefore one can hardly think that any but such as are stupidly unconcerned about their soul's everlasting states, could reason in earnest in the strain of the objection I am now upon. Surely, one that is any way duly thoughtful about a matter of such vast moment as his eternal well-being, would readily think with himself to this purpose; "Oh! what would I not give to have some comfortable, distinguishing evidences of being chosen of God, and appointed to life; well, his ways and ordinances are the means he uses for this purpose; the channels in which he is wont to communicate his special grace to those he designs to save. I must wait upon and look to him in that way of hope, and keep at the pool where he uses to come and heal diseased souls; it may be he will some time meet with me, in his own way, which he has appointed for visiting his chosen, and fulfil in me all the good pleasure of his goodness, and the work of faith with power, and cause me to rejoice in his love. These ways of religion are not only the ways in which alone there is reasonable ground of hope to meet with such blessings, but they are the commands and institutions of God, recommended with his awful authority; and therefore, to disregard and neglect them, will be to disobey and contemn God still more, and also will expose me to a more awful punishment." Consider now, if this be not a just and right way of reasoning in the case: nay, I am convinced that the Calvinist doctrine, rightly understood, and really believed, will make people much more careful, serious, and diligent observers of the ways of God, than the contrary doctrine will; for it tends much more to bring them to a solemn, solicitous concern of heart about their eternal state, and consequently to make them more earnest in all the most hopeful, probable ways of meeting with satisfaction about it.

Thirdly, Though it be true, that such as are rejected in the purpose of God will never be converted in the use of all the means of grace, yet, seeing they do not know the secret purpose of God concerning them, but have the same reason to entertain hopes that they may be chosen to life that any other unconverted persons have, it would be a high and provoking contempt of God for them to neglect the ordinances which he has appointed as means for the communicating special grace and sweet consolation to his elect, and which he, therefore, by his sovereign authority, requires all who have the opportunity, to attend upon; and they shall find it, if guilty of it, brought into the account against them at the great day, when every man shall be judged according to his works, and they shall receive, proportionally, the greater punishment.

Fourthly, As to the elect converted, their hearts are so renewed, as to love God above all, and to make obedience to his will their hearty choice. Believing in Jesus Christ, his love is shed abroad in their hearts, and sweetly constrains them to serve and honour him to whom they are under such endearing engagements. The consideration of God's having elected them to eternal glory, when he might justly have rejected them as well as others; the hope and prospect of that eternal glory with him, and the consideration of his having sent his Son to answer the law for them, and suffer in their room, that they might be delivered from deserved misery and made happy in the enjoyment of himself for ever; their apprehensions of his glory and excellency in himself, and his right in and over them as his creatures; all these things are powerful arguments with them to love and praise God; it is their desire and delight to glorify and honour him. Moreover, the Lord Jesus takes them for his peculiar charge; it is a part of his office as mediator, to bring them safe to glory through all dangers; accordingly, his Holy Spirit dwells in them as a sanctifier and comforter; thus they are engaged to God in the way of holiness by the most inviolable cords and loving bands; so that the doctrine of absolute election is far from destroying holiness of life; it is a strong excitement to it, in all the renewed children of God, who love him when they are enabled to see the hopeful evidences of their own election. And, therefore, such as say (as some, no less wickedly than foolishly, do) that, "if they were persuaded of the truth of the doctrine of predestination, they would never be at any pains or care to serve God more," had just as good say plainly, they have no love to God, and that they are entire strangers to the nature of true goodness.

Fifthly, Consider the method of reasoning in the objection is such as you would not allow to be just in other cases of the like nature. Can you think it would have been just reasoning in kind Hezekiah to say, that because the Lord had ordained he should live fifteen years longer, (2 Kings XX. 6,) he had no more need of either food or physic? The prophet Isaiah was of another mind, when he ordered a lump of figs to be laid to the boil, (ver. 7.)

This shows us that God brings about his purposes in the use of suitable means, and that it is therefore necessary for us to observe them. Was ever anything more absolutely and positively fixed in the purpose of God than the time and manner of Christ's death? (John vii. 30, and viii. 59, Luke iv. 29, 30, John xi. 53, 54.) Was Paul so inconsistent with himself when, though God had told him that both he and all that were in the ship with him should be saved through all the hazards of the voyage, yet, when the shipmen were about to go off in a boat and leave the rest in the distress, he said to them, "Except these abide in the ship, ye cannot be saved?" Acts xxvii. In a like manner, it may be as truly and reasonably said, that except the elect be converted and sanctified, they cannot be saved from hell, because of the certain connection God has made between the means and the end. And none have any reason to expect converting grace while they profanely neglect the means of grace.

As to the latter clause of the objection, that the non-elect who have had the opportunity of the gospel will be more miserable than if they had not, I answer, it is very likely it will be so with the most of them. But then, I think if they improved the gospel as they might do, though they would not be converted and saved by it, yet they would not be the more, but, perhaps, the less miserable for it. If it be inquired, for what end the gospel is sent to such as God has not proposed to save, I answer, it is chiefly for the elect's sake that are among them, that thereby they may be brought in to Christ, and prepared for the heavenly glory.

I shall now conclude the answer to the whole objection, with a general remark or two. Seeing the doctrine in itself does not take away our obligations to a religious life, but affords sufficient motives and arguments for it, then it is no argument against the truth of the doctrine, though some ungodly men should abuse it to liberty to sin. Other doctrines of the gospel are liable to the same abuse as well as this. Thus, Paul observes, that some might be ready to infer from the gospel doctrine of justification, as he laid it down, that they might continue in sin that grace might abound (Rom. vi. 1); that some would be ready to object against him, that he made Christ the minister of sin, i.e., one that gave liberty and encouragement to sin (Gal. ii. 17); and that some did actually affirm that he said, "Let us do evil that good may come," (Rom. iii. 8.) Again, the Lord Jesus who came to destroy the works of the devil, and purchase to himself a peculiar people, zealous of good works, will have his end, though some men of corrupt minds should abuse his truth, to the awful aggravation of their guilt in the day of his appearing. And I think we have little encouragement to go to the Arminian scheme for the advancement of true practical religion, if we consider what advancement this way it has produced since it came in fashion.

What is farther brought as an objection by some, I think, is hardly worth taking notice of, viz: that some will be apt to take occasion, from the doctrine of predestination, to live in a slothful negligence and security, from a presumption that they are elected, and so cannot miss of salvation: and others will be apt to fall into despair, from a fearful apprehension that they are not elected. As I hinted already, we are to distinguish between the abuse unreasonably made of a doctrine, and its natural tendency in itself. And what is there in this doctrine that leads to either of these wide extremes? How can it lead any to a groundless presumption and slothful negligence, when, according to it, none have reason to persuade themselves they are elected, until they are renewed and sanctified. And then they cannot be careless about the honour and obedience due to God? "How shall they that are dead to sin, live any longer therein?" Rom. vi. 2. All the gospel arguments to a life of holiness, and this, of their election, among the rest, do then effectually engage their hearts to it. Indeed, if they knew their election before their conversion, before they believed in Christ and loved God, no doubt they would abuse it to sloth and licentiousness, till God changed their hearts: but they have no sure evidence of their election till they are brought to a better disposition. And how can it bring any to desperation, when they cannot know that they are not elected? For persons to conclude positively that they are appointed to destruction, is to conclude without reason, and a pretending to know the unrevealed secrets of God's breast.

Some think the words of the Lord Jesus, (Luke xix. 42,) are contrary to this doctrine; where he says of Jerusalem, "If thou hadst known, in this thy day, the things that belong to thy peace! but now they are hid from thine eyes." Which words, they suppose, import that the inhabitants of that city had, before that time, had such inward assistance from God, as put it in their power to convert themselves; but which were then for ever withdrawn from them, for their abuse of them, so that their case was then beyond all hope. And in this same sense they suppose that all men have a day of grace, in some part of their life; or, as they rather choose to term it, a day of visitation. But this opinion is without any foundation in the text. How can the words signify that their day there spoken of, was a time in which they had sufficient inward grace, when they clearly imply that they did not so much as know the things that belonged to their peace in that day? The true import of our Lord's words is, that they had had, in that day of his public ministry among them, sufficient outward means of conviction that he was the true Messiah; sufficient to prevail with them, as rational creatures, to acknowledge and own him as such; notwithstanding of which they rejected and persecuted him and would in a little time put him to death; for which they should before long be punished with utter ruin, both of their city and nation, as it follows in the next words. And so the words also signify, that there was less probability and reasonable hope of their being converted to God, after all such means had been so long quite lost upon them, than there was before, according to God's ordinary way of working.

And now I have gone through all the contrary arguments and objections of any consequence that I know of, and, upon the whole, must desire the careful reader seriously to look back and consider if the doctrine of absolute predestination, as it has been stated and represented, be not entirely agreeable to reason, clearly founded on scripture, and perfectly consistent with every part of it, and, consequently, a most certain truth of God. Let us not be wilfully resolved against admitting reasonable evidence, but quit ourselves like men, and use our understanding, with humble application to God, on whom all creatures are dependent, for a right judgment and a sound mind. Do not say you will not believe it, just because you do not like it. That is both the shame and crime of a reasonable being, and the greatest folly in the world; for if it be a truth, it will be so, whether you like it and believe it or not. And let us also consider what is the proper use and native tendency of the doctrine. And so, let us humbly lie low, as guilty criminals, before the footstool of God's sovereignty, acknowledging his right to dispose of us, for life or death, as he pleases. Let us not be stupidly easy in our minds, without the experience of supernatural, sanctifying grace in our hearts, the only evidence of our election and means of solid comfort, "without which no man shall see the Lord." Let us seek and long for it in all the ways of God's commands and ordinances, where it is most likely to be found, and not treasure up greater loads of wrath to ourselves against the day of wrath, by disobedience to the great Lawgiver's authority. Let such of us as God has given the tokens of his special love unto, in our sanctification, give the glory and praise to him alone, and still endeavour to live answerable to the obligations of such wonderful, distinguishing love and grace. Let us give up all confidence in our own ability, and dependence on our own righteousness and good doings to entitle us to happiness, casting ourselves only on the mediation and atonement of the Son of God as he is revealed and proposed in the gospel, seeking for that living faith in him that brings joy and peace to the soul, that works by love and the freest obedience. Such as these are the things which this doctrine naturally leads to; and so it agrees to the great design of God in the new covenant, the illustration of the greatest glory of his free grace in the salvation of guilty sinners; whereas, the contrary scheme defaces and sinks it down. But God will have the glory, and it is fit he should: the whole glory, from first to last, he has secured to himself. As he laid the foundation of sinners' salvation in pure, free, and rich grace, so, at the last day, he will bring forth the head-stone thereof with shouting, crying Grace, Grace unto it, (Zech. iv. 7.).

JOHN BLAIR.

The Rev. John Blair was a younger brother of the Rev. Samuel Blair. He was an alumnus of the Log College, and as a theologian, was not inferior to any man in the Presbyterian church, in his day. He was first settled in Pennsylvania, at Big Spring, (now Newville,) in the Cumberland valley, in the vicinity of Carlisle; but by reason of the hostile incursions of the Indians, his people were obliged to leave their rude habitations on the frontier, and to retreat into the more densely populated part of the colony. Mr. Blair, it would seem, never returned to the place whence he had been driven by the invasion of the savages, but upon the decease of his brother Samuel, he received and accepted a call to be his successor at Fagg's Manor, and that not only as pastor of the church, but also as teacher of the school which his brother had instituted in that place. In this important station he continued for nine years, and though not equal to his brother as an impressive preacher, as a scholar and as a theologian he was not inferior.

After the death of Dr. Finley, Mr. Blair was elected professor of theology, in the College of New Jersey, which appointment he accepted, and was at the same time elected vice-president, and until the arrival of Dr. Witherspoon, performed all the duties of president. The funds of the college not being adequate to support a professor of theology, distinct from the president; and it being known that Dr. Witherspoon was an orthodox and eminent theologian, who could consistently with his other duties teach theology, Mr. Blair judged it would be expedient for him to resign. Upon this, he received a call to settle as pastor of a Presbyterian congregation in Wallkill, Orange Co., New York. Here he continued to labour in the duties of the ministry, until he was called away from the field by death, which occurred Dec. 8, 1771, when he was not more than fifty-one or fifty two years of age.

"John Blair was a judicious and persuasive preacher, and through his exertions, sinners were converted and the children of God edified. Fully convinced of the truth of the doctrine of grace, he addressed immortal souls with that warmth and power, which left a witness in every bosom. Though he sometimes wrote his sermons in full, yet his common mode of preaching, was by short notes, comprising the general outlines. His labours were too abundant to admit of more, and no more was necessary to a mind so richly stored with the great truths of religion. For his large family he amassed no fortune, but he left them what was infinitely better, a religious education, a holy example, and prayers which have been remarkably answered His disposition was uncommonly patient, placid, benevolent, disinterested and cheerful. He was too mild to indulge bitterness or severity, and he thought that the truth required little else but to be fairly stated and properly understood. Those who could not relish the savour of his piety, loved him as an amiable, and revered him as a great man. Though no bigot, he firmly believed that the Presbyterian form of government is most scriptural, and the most favourable to religion and happiness.

"In his last sickness, he imparted his advice to the congregation, and represented to his family the necessity of an interest in Christ. A few nights before he died, he said, 'Directly, I am going to glory! My Master calls me, I must be gone.'"

OBSERVATIONS ON REGENERATION.

BY THE REV. JOHN BLAIR.

As no truth is more interesting and important, so none has been more frequently and fully treated in a practical view, by pious writers, than the doctrine of regeneration. Many have, in this way, very excellently and largely described the happy change, which, by virtue of the supernatural work of the Holy Spirit, takes place in the whole man. I have therefore no design at present to enter upon a full consideration of the subject, but shall only beg leave to make a few very brief observations; some of which have not been so particularly considered in practical treatises, but yet perhaps, may be of some use to assist in the right apprehension of, and tend to prevent mistakes about a doctrine, which lies so much at the foundation of all true religion.

Observation 1. Regeneration is the communication of a principle of spiritual life to the soul of a sinner, naturally dead in trespasses and sins, by the agency of the Holy Spirit.

I call it a principle, not only because it is a beginning of spiritual life, but especially, because it denotes a settled determination of the mind, to right activity towards spiritual objects, under a moral consideration of them, whence results every right exercise of heart about divine things. It is the determination of the soul to a holy activity about God and divine things, or to such a kind of action, not from the impulsion of an external force, but an internal active principle, and therefore is justly called life—life of the most excellent kind. It is the life of life.

(There is some distinction between a natural and a moral principle of action; the former lies in the very essence of the being to which it belongs, or is a determination to some particular kind of action resulting from its frame or constitution. Thus, self-activity, or natural life, which is essential to the soul, is a principle of action in general. A determination to particular kinds of natural action, such as we call instinct in brutes, or reason in man, arises immediately from the existence of natural faculties, or something in the frame or constitution of creatures respectively. But a moral principle is a determination to some particular kind of action, arising from some settled judgment or sentiment, in which the will acquiesces. Thus a principle of holy action is the fixed impression of some spiritual truth or truths upon the heart.)

But as our apostasy from God has fixed in us, by nature, a very contrary determination, to a course of sinful action, therefore, while that continues (which will be till some power subdues it), there can be no tendency in the soul to an holy temper. The power of the soul to any activity lies formally in the will. Hence its whole power, by nature, is to sin, and to reject God. For "the carnal mind is enmity against God." Rom. viii. 7. Consequently some other power must be exerted in order to break this evil determination, and reduce the rebellious creature to a right temper. And that must be a power that has dominion over the will. This new determination, therefore, is from the almighty agency of the Holy Spirit; it is he that communicates this new principle of life. Accordingly, it is everywhere ascribed to him in scripture. (John iii. 3–5, John vi. 63, Tit. iii. 5).

Observation 2. This principle of spiritual life and the manner of its communication are not immediately in themselves perceptible.

As Adam did not perceive when God breathed into his nostrils the breath of natural life, but perceived its existence and nature from its activity and effects, so the existence and nature of spiritual life are known only by the experience the Christian has of its exercise and efficacy. In this view our Lord observes, "The wind bloweth where it listeth, and thou hearest the sound thereof, but canst not tell whence it cometh nor whither it goeth; so is every one that is born of the Spirit." John iii. 8. There are, indeed, those who greatly abuse this passage, thence flattering themselves that they may be the subjects of regeneration, without perceiving any great change in their hearts and lives. But this is not only foreign to the sense of the place, but contradictory to it, for the wind is very sensibly perceived. The design of our Lord seems to be to remove the surprise of Nicodemus at the mysteriousness of the doctrine, by showing him it is a supernatural work performed by the Holy Spirit, as a gracious Sovereign, to which the sinner himself is so far from contributing anything, that he is not so much as sensible of the article of communication, nor perceives the manner of the Holy Spirit's operation; q. d. there are mysteries in nature which you cannot account for. You cannot immediately perceive the origin of the wind, nor account for its ceasing when once in motion, or perceive the reason why it continually, and often very suddenly, changes its direction. You hear the sound and feel the effects, but it is only by observations on these sensations, either made by yourself, or suggested by others, that you can infer any conclusions about its nature or causes. Why then should you be surprised to find mysteries in the manner of divine operations, when performing works of grace? In this new birth, a man can only perceive the exercises of divine life in his heart, and by scriptural observations on these, infer what sort of life he lives, or form conclusions about its nature and principle. For any one, therefore, to pretend to tell what the principle of divine life is, antecedent to all exercises of life in the heart, and undertake from thence to demonstrate and explain those exercises, is a vain attempt. When he distinguishes this life from all its exercises, and goes about to tell us what it is antecedent to them all, he must talk in the dark about a certain something, of which he has no idea. To give it a name, to call it, for instance, a new temper or taste, is not to tell us what it is. Let any man explain what he means by a new or holy temper, without including some exercises of life in heart, if he can.

Observation 3. Regeneration and conversion, strictly taken, are not distinct things; but these different denominations express the same thing under different views. I say conversion strictly taken; for largely taken, it includes the first exercises of the several graces of the Holy Spirit which are but the various modifications of the same principle of spiritual life, such as a justifying faith, hope, joy, zeal, sorrow for sin, &c. From which, regeneration (though the term is often also used in the same latitude, yet) is so distinct in a strict sense, as to be altogether antecedent, not only in the order of nature, but of time too. But strictly taken, conversion is the actual submission or turning of a soul to God in the most simple motion of it. This may be, perhaps, in the soul's submitting itself into the hands of divine sovereignty, as most fitly having a right to do with him as he pleases, or in a supreme regard to God as a most glorious Being and rightful Lord. Now this, when considered as the effect of the Holy Spirit's agency, enabling or causing the soul to turn to God, is called regeneration; but when considered as an activity essential to spiritual life, and formally as the soul's act, is called conversion; but these are only different views and respects of the same thing. For regeneration undoubtedly denotes a moral effect produced by the Spirit of God. But this effect which he produced, is the soul's turning to God. Surely, nothing short of this can be called the new birth. Regeneration is the implantation of holiness in the heart. Now, certainly, there can be no real holiness without turning to God; the soul that has not turned to God is still, without controversy, unregenerate. Hence it follows

Observation 4. That this principle wrought in the soul in regeneration is not something antecedent to every act and exercise of holiness, but includes in it, or Is a first act or exercise of holiness, of the same nature with all the exercises of holiness that follow after through the course of life.

To cause life, is to cause action; for activity is essential to the idea of life. When the Holy Spirit regenerates a sinner, he communicates an active principle, otherwise it were not life. But to talk of an active principle existing in the soul absolutely without action, would be a contradiction; now this action must be cleaving to God. Hence arises,

Observation 5. Viz: that this principle of spiritual life consists in, or includes some new view of the mind, and determination or approbation of the will. This must be the case, because it is a moral principle; otherwise it would not be the principle of a course of moral action. When therefore a principle of spiritual life is implanted, a moral effect is produced; but that effect which includes no acts of the understanding and will, but is absolutely antecedent to them, must be a mere physical, and not a moral effect, and then to regenerate would be to create in a physical, not a moral sense.

I think the sacred scriptures set the matter in the same light with the above observations. Sometimes this happy change is expressed by the term "light." "Ye were sometimes darkness, but now are ye light in the Lord." Eph. V. 8. Sometimes it is represented under the notion of being made willing. "Thy people shall be willing in the day of thy power." Ps. ex. 3. Either of these expressions includes the other Thus when the regenerate are called light, the matter is not confined to the understanding only, but includes the approbation of the will, and to be willing, certainly includes the view of the understanding; for there can be no act of the will without it; sometimes both are set in view together, as: "To open their eyes, and to turn them from darkness to light, and from the power of Satan to God." Acts xxvi. 18. Certainly to open the eyes and turn from darkness to light is to enlighten the understanding; and to turn to God is the act of the will. To the same purpose is, "For God hath shined into our hearts, to give the light of the knowledge of the glory of God in the face of Jesus Christ." 2 Cor. iv. 6. To see the glory of God must include both the view of the understanding, and the approbation of the will. It is no objection to this, to say, these scriptures speak of this change largely taken. For admitting that, yet it is not by way of contradistinction from, or exclusive of, the first instance; but the first existence of life comes under the same predicament. Thus they, who were sometimes darkness, are not said to be enlightened only, but to be light. God, in the new creation, shines into the heart, in a manner analogous to his shining in the natural world, when he created light in it. It is very easy to say, that in regeneration, a holy temper is produced whence this knowledge and volition arises; but perhaps it would not be so easy to tell, in that connection, what we are to understand by that temper. Surely we are not to conceive of a moral, in the same manner as of a natural temper. In the latter, we take into the consideration such a certain, yet various construction of the human frame, as is apt to produce such and such passions, and feelings of nature. Now if we have any idea of the former, any thing like this, we must then consider it only as a new faculty created in the soul, which has nothing moral in it, any more than the understanding or will considered as natural faculties. But if we conceive of it as a moral determination of the soul towards God, then we must consider it as including some apprehension of God in the understanding, and an act of the will embracing him, which brings the matter to what I have said. Thus, we are, as it were, insensibly led to some apprehension of what this divine principle is, or wherein it consists, though we cannot comprehend the manner of the Holy Spirit's operation in producing it, or explain how it exists. It is an experimental, practical knowledge of God, or it is a new view of the infinite perfections of God, with the approbation of them in the will as most excellent; or, which is indeed the same thing under its proper denomination, it is a supreme love to God. Supreme love to God is the very essence of true religion; hence it is called "the fulfilling of the law." Rom. xiii. 10. Our Lord mentions love to God and our neighbour, as the sum and substance of the whole law. Matt. xxii. 37–40. No action can be called true obedience, if it do not flow from love to God, and every exercise of true grace may be reduced to this as its principle.

Observation 6. The Holy Spirit makes use of the word of God as a means in the work of regeneration, which lie renders irresistibly efficacious for that purpose. I am far from thinking with the Arminians, that the only influence of the Holy Spirit in this matter lies in what they call moral suasion; that is, as I understand it, the Holy Spirit having set before us the arguments and motives of the gospel in the word, both by his providence and an influence upon the mind, excites its attention to these things, and assists the natural faculties in weighing those arguments and motives, and thus strives to persuade the sinner to a compliance with gospel overtures, but still leaves it with himself to yield to or reject those arguments by a sovereign act of his own will. According to this, it is only an objective light that is set before the mind, as contained in the word; a representation of objects, as yet at a distance, of which the mind has no knowledge, but by the report and description of the word; and, perhaps, the most, if not all the light, which is usually called common illumination, may be obtained this way.

Nor can I agree with some, even eminent Calvinistic divines, that there is only a gradual difference between common and saving illumination. I believe there is a specific difference; there is in regeneration a subjective light created in the soul, which, though it is the knowledge of a glorious object presented to the mind, yet may fitly be called subjective in respect of the manner of its communication, as contradistinguished from, though not opposed to, the mere objective light of the word before described. It is an immediate intuitive sense or knowledge of the moral perfections and character of God, not gained by way of conclusion from premises, or by argumentation, but arising from the approach of God to the soul by the way of gracious presence. He thus takes possession of the heart, and fills it with a sense of himself by his presence in a peculiar manner. And this is a way of knowing, very different from that received merely by description and report of the word, and, therefore, a different kind of knowledge, viz: by way of spiritual sense and experience. Though we cannot perceive or experience the manner of the divine presence or access to the soul, yet the fact is abundantly witnessed by the experience of God's people. Notwithstanding they have an habitual spiritual knowledge of God and divine truth, yet, at one season, they are distressed with darkness, and cannot get any proper views of God; at another, they shall be full of light, and astonished with the view of divine glory: now, what is the reason of this last difference? Surely, not from any difference in the objective light of the word, or their capacity to meditate upon it. But the reason of it is, the absence of God in the one case, and his glorious presence in the other; therefore, their first such knowledge of God was from such an approach to the soul, or divine presence in it. And for the reality of the experience of God's people, I refer to the account the sacred scriptures give us sometimes of their bitter complaints of God's hiding himself, and panting for him as the hart for the water-brooks; at other times, at their rejoicing in his beauty and glory, with which they are, as it were, transported; and I think these words of Job, "I have heard of thee by the hearing of the ear, but now mine eye seeth thee," (Job xiii. 5,) fully justify this distinction of objective and subjective knowledge. For admit that the design of the word is to represent the very lively views he had of the divine excellency, so that, comparatively speaking, all his former, even experimental views were but like report; yet by a parity of reason, there is a vast difference between experience in the lowest degree and report; and he goes upon this principle, that report, or by the hearing of the ear, is a very languid and imperfect way of knowing, compared with sight and intimate acquaintance. These are very different kinds of knowledge; as different as the knowledge a man has of a country from an historical account and map of it, or the report of travellers, and that he has from travelling through, and seeing it himself. Thus then, by this presence of God in the soul, it has a knowledge of him, which it could not possibly have without it, by the most animated descriptions and representations of the word. It was thus, even innocent Adam knew the moral character and excellency of God, not only by objective evidence from without, but also by subjective evidence from his experience of the divine presence.

But all this does not exclude moral influence by way of argument, the argument contained in the word; but rather accounts for their irresistible efficacy. Though mere moral suasion will not do the business, yet it is not excluded; it is a moral effect that is to be produced; therefore, it is natural enough to expect that the power producing it should be exerted in a moral way; and, consequently, a moral mean with great propriety be admitted.

That this matter may be better apprehended, I beg leave to observe, that the blessed God must be exhibited to the mind as an object of contemplation, in order to any act of the will towards him. The will approves him as most fit and worthy to be chosen, which must be founded upon the contemplation of him in the mind. Length of time is not, indeed, necessary for this purpose. The operations of the mind are very quick. Were we to suppose an adult, who had no opportunity of the word, to be regenerated, no doubt a reflection upon his own intuitive perceptions would exhibit the blessed God to the mind, as an object of contemplation. For it is absurd to suppose a new heart to exist in an adult person without any ideas of God and divine things in the understanding; for that is to suppose a person regenerated, and yet altogether ignorant of God; to turn to God without any knowledge of him, which I think is a contradiction, and the same thing as to say a man is changed without any alteration. The thief on the cross seems to be an instance to the contrary; though he lived in the land of Judea, and had opportunity of the word of God, it is not probable a man of his abandoned character sought any considerable acquaintance with it; yet his speech to his fellow-criminal, and his address to Jesus Christ, showed very considerable discoveries of God, and the character of his Saviour.

But let it be considered, that with respect to sinners who live under the means of grace, and enjoy the word of God, though, by reason of their estrangement from God, they have no proper views of divine truths, yet their understandings are possessed of some general speculative knowledge of them. Yea, convinced sinners have more; they have such an experimental knowledge of the law convincing them of sin, as is effectual to arouse them out of their fatal security, and confute their false notions, and awaken them to a very solemn attention to the word of God. Now in regeneration, the intuitive views impressed on the mind by the divine presence, are exactly the same with the descriptions and delineations of the divine character in the word. The mind therefore, instead of reflecting immediately upon its own perceptions, looks forward to the word. Now the man's eyes are opened, and he understands the scripture in a manner he never could before. There he sees this glorious object represented as in a glass; from thence the reflection is so strong and lively as irresistibly, though in a moral way, to determine the will; for surely it is very apprehensible that the views of the mind may be so experimental, strong and full of evidence, that it is impossible for a rational being to withold the approbation and consent of the will; and thus this divine temper is formed in the heart. In this point of light, I think the apostle sets the matter, "But we all with open face, beholding, as in a glass, the glory of the Lord, are changed into the same image, from glory to glory, even as by the Spirit of the Lord." 2 Cor. iii. 18. Though these words comprehend the gradual perfecting the image of God, in the progress of the work of grace; yet, certainly, the first step of the process is in the same way with all the subsequent, in the whole series. Nor does the use of the glass at all derogate from the efficacy of the Spirit, in causing and conducting this whole matter. And indeed there is as really an immediate agency of the Spirit upon the soul, in every progressive perfecting of the image of God, and every instance of the quickening grace in believers, (when yet the concurring instrumentality of the word, notwithstanding, is acknowledged,) as there is in the first begetting of the divine life.

Here I would take notice, how very different this view of divine illumination is from the wild conceits of enthusiasts. Their pretended extraordinary discoveries and inspirations consist in unaccountable impulses without the word, the warm flights of imagination, and agitation of their passions; in all this they either have no reference to the word of God, but rather set light by it in comparison of their own great light; or else in pretending to the word, put inconsistent, ridiculous constructions upon it. But these intuitive views of God, I mentioned as primarily arising from his presence in the soul, are but the impression of such truths as the word of God describes; they lead to the scriptures, and give a rational, consistent view of them; this light is tried and judged by the word of God. "To the law and to the testimony; if they speak not according to this word, it is because there is no light in them." Isa. viii. 20.

I cannot but think the instrumentality of the word in regeneration, in the view I have given of it, is once and again asserted in the sacred scriptures; thus, "being born again, not of corruptible seed, but of incorruptible, by the word of God which liveth and abideth for ever." 1 Pet. i. 23. The word, here rendered "born again," is the same which is used John iii. 3, of which new birth the word is declared to be an instrument or mean. In the same view, the same apostle tells the Christians to whom he wrote, that "by great and precious promises, they were made partakers of the divine nature;" (2 Pet. i. 4;) and to be made partakers of the divine nature is to be regenerated. Another passage is, "Of his own will begat he us with (or by) the word of truth." James i. 18. The word here used cannot with any propriety, I think, be understood of any thing else than the first infusion or begetting of spiritual life. When this is said to be done with or by the word, it must intend that it is used as an instrument or mean: in this view this blessed change is expressed by "putting God's law in the inward parts, and writing it in the heart." Jer. xxxi. 33.

Doubtless the Holy Spirit could as easily accomplish this great work without using any means; yet, as it appears very plain he has chosen to do otherwise, we may not only suppose, but readily see, great propriety in his making use of the word in this matter. This change is to be tried and judged of by the word; therefore, must answer to the descriptions and characters there given, as the impression on the wax answers to the characters of the seal. The views of God in the mind must be such as exactly agree to the descriptions and representations of him in the word. It was, consequently, very fit that these characters of the word should be impressed upon the soul, as a medium of determining the will in regeneration.

When the Holy Spirit takes the sinner in hand, in order to bring him home to God, the first step he ordinarily takes is to convince him of sin, confute his false notions, and slay his legal hopes; in this he makes use of the law as a mean, as all acknowledge. Yet in order to this effectual access of the law to the conscience, there is as really an immediate exertion of power and influence upon the soul, as there is also in regeneration; and though this conviction does not make the sinner more worthy of the grace of God, yet the great design of it is to prepare the way for the opening of divine truths upon the mind, with the brighter evidence, in its passing this saving change; which reflects the image of this glory upon the beholding soul, and determines the will. (2 Cor. iii. 18, Ps. ex. 8.)

Observation 7. From this new view of the mind, and determination of the will, or supreme regard to God, result the various exercises of heart, which are called the graces of the Holy Spirit, and distinguished by particular names, as their proper principle.

From this view of the divine character in the enlightened mind, naturally arises a discovery of the necessity of Christ's satisfaction to divine justice, and the fitness and glory of that way of reconciliation with God; hence faith in Christ. The plan of mercy still more illustrates the glory of the divine character, for it shines in the face of Jesus Christ; by these views of faith, spiritual affections are excited, sorrow for, and hatred against sin raised; hence an habitual watchfulness against sin and opposition to it, and delight in the service of God; and all this infers

A great and permanent change in the whole course of life and action; but practical writers have abundantly explained and described these things, to whom I refer my readers, and shall insist no further upon them here.

I therefore conclude with this general remark, viz: that it is of vastly more importance and concernment of us, to inquire into the reality of a gracious change, as discovered by the alteration, and holy exercises which the regenerate experience, than spend our time and zeal in disputing about the principle of spiritual life, wherein it consists, or what it is, antecedent to all exercises thereof. While we are warmly interested in deciding the speculative dispute, we are apt to forget the practical consideration of the important subject, and the application of it to ourselves; and those who attend to us, are led to treat the matter in the same manner; by this means, the interests of vital piety languish. While we justly lament the low state of experimental religion, to devote ourselves to these speculative refinements will not be found the way to revive it. Experience will always show, that to keep up a practical view of divine truths, and the solemn application of them in serious, pungent addresses to the conscience, is the best calculated for that purpose. Besides, if we lay down, by way of hypothesis, a certain something, of which we can have no idea, (as of a principle of life, antecedent to all exercises of life, we cannot; nor can we infer any conclusions about its nature from any exercises of the heart, if it include neither idea nor volition, but is something absolutely antecedent to both,) then we shall be in danger of a superstructure as unintelligible as the basis upon which we build. Thus some have wildly dreamed, that the principle of spiritual life may exist in the soul without any act or exercise of life, as a taste, which lies dormant until a proper object be applied to it; and if it may exist one moment, why not two? And if two, why not a minute? And so on, till they bring the supposition to hours, days, months, and years; and so a regenerate person may still continue an unbeliever, and of consequence, in an unjustified state. And I see not why it would not be as easy to continue the supposition till death, and to send him to hell, with his dormant principle along with him. Thus the cause of vital religion is greatly disserved. But if we attend to the plain, practical views the scriptures give us of this matter, consider the exercises of divine life which discover the happy change produced in regeneration, and trace these to their first principle, which, from the nature of these exercises, we conclude to be something of the same nature with them—to be a first act of the series of acts or exercises that follow after, which the Holy Spirit causes the soul to exert, (i.e., causes it to live,) we are in no danger of any fatal mistake. In this way, the heart will be more likely to feel itself interested; and thus people become more solemn and exercised in examining and judging the state of their own souls. And that this may be more extensively the case among professors, may God of his infinite mercy grant for Christ's sake! Amen.

AN ESSAY ON THE MEANS OF GRACE.

BY THE REV. JOHN BIAIR.

I. The great God stands in no need of means in order to accomplish his purposes. He could, if he pleased, cause all events he sees meet to effect, to come to pass in the same way he caused the world at first to exist, viz: by the word of his power or sovereign act of his will; yet it does not at all derogate from his efficiency, but rather serves to illustrate his power, to use means, and appoint a connection between them and the end in view, both in the natural and moral world: yet such a connection as always depends upon the divine pleasure. Means are effectual or ineffectual, as he affords or withholds his concurrence—particularly, in the administration of his moral government, he deals with the subjects thereof in a way suited to their rational natures, and uses means of a moral nature in carrying on the interests of religion in our degenerate world. To this purpose, he has given his holy word, appointed a gospel ministry and ordinances of worship, such as the sacraments of the New Testament, praise and prayer.

II. These, divines commonly call means, not of Instruction only, but of grace; the reason Is, because it is in the use of these means, the Holy Spirit ordinarily communicates or bestows grace on sinners, and builds up his children in holiness, until he brings them safe home to glory. Now, whatever can be considered as a mean in reference to an end, must have some tendency to, and, in its own way, have influence upon, or concur in attaining it; for that which has no such tendency or influence, has no manner of connection with the existence or accomplishment of the end, and, consequently, is no means of it at all. If, therefore, these ordinances are means of grace, they must have a tendency to, and, in the hand of the Holy Spirit, concurrence in, the regeneration and conversion of sinners, and thence forward, in carrying on the work of grace in them. As all ordinances of worship are but various manners of administrating the word of God, it is especially to be considered as a mean for these purposes.

III. That we may see with what propriety these are called means of grace, let us attend to what we find ascribed to, or predicated of, the word In the Bible; which only can be said of it considered as an instrument or means, and not as an efficient cause, which It cannot be. The conviction of sinners Is ascribed to it, "By the law is the knowledge of sin." Rom. iii. 20. Peter's hearers, upon hearing his discourse, wherein he proved from the scriptures of the

Old Testament, that Jesus whom they had crucified was the true Messiah, "were pricked in their hearts." Acts ii. 37. By this, God distinguishes his word delivered by the true prophets, from that delivered by the false, viz: this, that his "word is like a fire, and like a hammer, that breaketh the rock in pieces." Jer. xxiii. 29. "The word of God is quick and powerful, and sharper than any two-edged sword, piercing even to the dividing asunder of soul and spirit, and of the joints and marrow, and is a discerner of the thoughts and intents of the heart." Heb. iv. 12. It kills the legal pride of sinners, "I through the law am dead to the law, that I might live unto God." Gal. ii. 19. I have already taken notice in my observations on regeneration, that Christians are said to be "born again," "begotten," and "made partakers of the divine nature,"(l Pet. i. 23, James i. 18, 2 Pet. i. 4,) by the word of God; to which I would add Ps. xix. 7, 8, where the word under the terms "Law," "Testimony," "Commandments," is said "to convert the soul," "make wise the simple," and "enlighten the eyes;" all which terms plainly express the saving change wrought in regeneration. This change is an inscription of the divine law upon the heart. Jer. xxxi. 33. All these expressions signify much more than merely instructing the speculative understanding. They must import the concurrence of the word as a mean or instrument in the hand of the Holy Spirit, both in the preparatory work of conviction, and also in effecting the saving change in regeneration. It is unnecessary to recite the many passages which represent the word and ordinances as means of quickening, supporting, comforting, sanctifying, perfecting and strengthening of God's people. I would only observe, that the efficacy of the word for these purposes, depends upon the presence and immediate agency of the Holy Spirit in the heart; which as really takes place in these instances, as in the regeneration of a sinner, and the latter as easily admits the use of means as the former.

IV. The efficacy of the means of grace lies not in any intrinsic virtue in themselves, nor depends upon the power or will of those who attend upon them; for the effect to be produced is supernatural, to which sinners are by nature entirely averse, and destitute of a true discernment of the excellency of the truths and weight of the arguments proposed in the word; but they are rendered effectual to the attainment of the end by the blessing of the Holy Spirit upon them, and his energy in them; they are means in the Spirit's hand, rather than the creature's. And sinners are to attend upon them in that view, that they may be in the way in which the Spirit meets with such and works upon them, like the poor impotent people who lay at the pool, waiting for the descent of the angel to trouble the waters. John iii. 4. With respect to creature agents, the application or use of means depends upon them; but the causality itself, or energy of means in order to the end, is not in their power, nor depends upon their will. Hence, they often fail of success in the use of the best adapted means; but when this divine agent condescends to use means, he causes their efficacy, and makes them effectual when, and with respect to whom, he pleases. I say, condescends to use means; for the very circumstance I have mentioned shows he needs them not; he could do immediately whatsoever he pleases; when, therefore, he is pleased to make use of means, it is in order to the more easy discovery of himself to his creatures. Hence it follows, that the great God is not the less an efficient for his using means, nor the less displays his power in accomplishing the end by them.

V. Yet, notwithstanding, there is an aptness and tendency in the means in order to the end in view, otherwise they would not be properly means. Those things which have no aptness or tendency to the attainment of the end can have no sort of influence upon it; the existence of the end has no kind of connection with them, and, consequently, they are no means at all of its existence. Now, the aptness or tendency of the word of God to reduce sinners to the obedience of Christ lies in, 1st. The clearness of representation, whereby divine truths are set before the mind. Divine truths are clothed in the most plain and intelligible language their sublime nature will allow of; they are descriptively expressed, so as not only to declare their nature, but also to describe their true influence, and the impressions they should make upon the heart. They are also illustrated by the most familiar similitudes. 2d. In the interesting manner in which these sacred truths are urged, or the weight of the arguments with which they are pressed home. 3d. In the awful authority and great majesty with which they are delivered, whence they bind and affect the conscience; they are set before us with a "thus saith the Lord or Jehovah," our rightful Sovereign, with whom is terrible majesty, "and your God," who has a covenant claim upon his professing people. Hence, then, when the Holy Spirit takes the word in his hand, and makes application of it to the heart, it is most apt and fit as a mean to instruct the mind and inform the conscience, and thus to convince and awaken the sinner; to lay restraints upon men, and repress, or in some measure restrain, even the natural enmity of the awakened sinner: and when the Holy Spirit effectually opens the sinner's eyes, and makes him understand divine truths as they are represented in the word, they have a most apt tendency, by way of argument, to persuade and determine the will, and to promote the life and exercise of all the graces of the Holy Spirit in true Christians.(I would here refer the reader to what I have said in the sixth Observation on Regeneration, concerning the instrumentality of the word therein.)

I have said that when the word is so effectually applied to the conscience as to convince the sinner, it is a means of repressing or restraining his natural enmity. As this will probably in a particular manner be called in question, I beg leave to offer a few thoughts further upon it. I do not at all suppose the sinner's enmity is in this case subdued; for then he would be regenerated, which is contrary to the supposition. The wickedness of men may be, yea, in many instances is, restrained, when its governing power is not all broken. Hence, those who were clean escaped from them who live in error, and escaped the pollutions of the world through the knowledge of the Lord and Saviour Jesus Christ, may be allured through the lusts of the flesh, and much wantonness, and be again entangled; yea, it too often proves to be the case, that, "according to the true proverb, the dog is turned to his own vomit again, and the sow that is washed, to her wallowing in the mire." 2 Pet. ii. 18–22. The acting of the sinner's enmity is, indeed, more direct against God and spiritual objects, thus brought near and set in view before him by conviction, and this, no doubt, is a great aggravation of those exercises of enmity; yet it will by no means follow that enmity, as an evil principle in the heart, is more prevalent, or has, in this case, acquired a greater degree of power. The power of this, as well as every other evil habit, lies in the sway and dominion it has in the heart. Enmity reigns in the heart ever while it is destitute of true love to God; but yet the more peaceably it possesses the heart, and the more fully it has its consent, the more powerful it is. While the sinner is in a state of security, though he does not feel so explicit opposition to God in his heart, as being more out of view; yet it is the same principle of enmity that carries him on in casting God's law behind his back, in neglecting the divine service, and giving a loose rein to his corruptions, while he despises, and perhaps derides, strict religion. His enmity lords it over him without control, and hardens his heart against reproof and conviction. It is unmolested in its sway, and carries the sinner headlong whichever way it directs; and he justifies himself in all this, and refuses to take blame to himself; but the awakened sinner, while conviction is borne home upon the conscience, confesses the just authority over him, that he has most unjustly trampled upon it, and violated his law. Though he has no holy acquiescence in, or choice of, the divine government, yet he has a rational conviction that it is rightful, and that he deserves punishment for contradicting it; that he feels his heart averse, greatly alarms him, and convinces him of the existence of enmity in his heart. Instead of spurning at his convictions, trampling them under foot, and casting them off, which would be the case if enmity acquired strength in proportion to his convictions, he cherishes them, and is afraid of falling back into security again. Though he feels risings of heart, yea, some sinners make some attempts to shake off their convictions, with whom they are too powerful, and are increased till they break their stout spirits, as they give up their struggles to stifle them, and become afraid lest they should leave them again to fall into a hardened state; yet this is so far from proving the increase of enmity as to strength or prevalence, that, in reality, it proves the restraint of it by the authority of God's law in the conscience, and convincing influences of the Holy Spirit. Upon a discovery of the exceeding depravity and wickedness of his heart, the sinner, upon some principle, wishes his heart was changed. True, he does not choose holiness or turning to God in itself considered, for that he does not, is one main thing that fills his conscience with so much guilt; yet he earnestly desires there was such a heart in him, as did see the beauty of holiness, and truly choose it. He desires this, indeed, upon no higher principle, than a regard to his own happiness. This, where there is no higher, is not a holy principle, nor is this sort of desire of grace such as denotes true grace in the heart; yet it is not, in itself, a wicked principle. That this respect to his own happiness does not regard holiness as an ingredient in it, and is not subordinate to, and under the influence of, a higher and more noble principle, is his crime; but that it is in him, and has influence upon him, is not. Surely, the sinner's enmity is not as prevalent and unrestrained, when he is thus anxiously solicitous to obtain heart-changing grace, even on this principle, as when he utterly disregarded the matter, and justified himself in refusing to return.

When it is said, that the awakened sinner still continues to reject Christ, and hate God with all his heart, the meaning must either be, that, under all his convictions, the sinner exerts himself to the utmost with all his might in opposition to them; that he the more pours contempt on the gospel, and stoutly resolves to reject Jesus Christ, that he casts about to find out how he may bear himself up in a determined opposition to the gospel overtures of salvation, and the more he is convinced, the more maliciously does he oppose, and impudently justify himself in refusing, Christ and his redemption, like the Scribes and Pharisees of old, which would argue the increase of enmity with a witness; and then, the proposition is not true, yea, notoriously contrary to fact. Or else the meaning must only be, that notwithstanding all his convictions, and increase of light, his enmity is not at all subdued, but if present restraints were removed, it would return to its old stubborn stoutness in the way of sin; and all the faculties and powers of the soul are still under the reigning power of that hateful principle; and then I have no controversy with any man about it. But this is no way inconsistent with what I have said, unless we say, that to lay restraint upon the lusts and corruptions of men, is inconsistent with their dominion in the heart; or else, that they have as great a degree of power under restraints, as when most unrestrained; neither of which will any man in the due use of his reason assert, for that would destroy all ideas of different degrees of wickedness. The sinner's convictions awaken his attention to those glorious objects, God, and his Son Jesus Christ, and the way of salvation through him; and thereby the actings of his natural enmity are more direct and explicit, which doubtless more aggravates them as particular acts, and exposes the malignity of that hateful principle. Yet that very discovery, and the sinner's condemning himself for it, and cries to God for deliverance from it, show that it has not as quiet possession of the heart, and as prevalent energy in it as formerly. Now it is from the principles, good or bad, which have the governing prevalence in the heart, that persons have their character, especially in the eye of the heart searching God; if, then, under solemn convictions by the authority of God's law, and the convincing influences of the Holy Spirit, the sinner's natural enmity be restrained, it will follow, that the awakened sinner's character is not, on the whole, rendered more vile and odious in the sight of God, than it was in the days of his security and contented course of sin against him. (It will by no means follow, that awakened sinners are, in a degree, accepted of God, on account of their being less sinful than they were in the days of their security; for the divine law still condemns them as falling short, infinitely short of its demands; and their less sinfulness makes no atonement for the smallest past transgression. It only follows that, in their present case, they merit a less degree of disapprobation and punishment; i.e., they are less offensive; and this we must admit, or else deny different degrees of wickedness; or assert that the lowest degree of wickedness is as offensive, and disapproved in as high a degree, as the greatest.) Can it be imagined, that the sinner's enmity has as strong an energy in him, "when brought to break off from his course of external sins, as when he pursued them with greediness? When he earnestly attends to the duties of religion, as when he neglected them with scorn and contempt, or trifled with them in a listless formality? And when he eagerly seeks the company of God's people, asking their advice, as when he hated to be near them, could not bear their conversation, but took delight in the company of the profane and ungodly? But to return.

That the means of grace have a tendency to the conviction and conversion of sinners, as well as the edification of God's people, appears by the expostulations God uses with them in his word, as utterly inexcusable and perverse in continuing impenitents after all the pains he has taken upon them, and means used with them. In the fifth chapter of Isaiah from the beginning, the Lord represents the abundant provision he had made for their fruitfulness, in point of means and advantages which he had afforded them. "What could have been done to my vineyard that I have not done in it? Wherefore when I looked that it should bring forth grapes, brought it forth wild grapes?" Isa. V. 4. "But this thing commanded I them, saying, Obey my voice and I will be your God, and ye shall be my people: and walk ye in all the ways that I have commanded you, that it may be well unto you; but they hearkened not, nor inclined their ear, but walked in the counsels and imaginations of their evil heart, and went backward and not forward. Since the day that your fathers came forth of the land of Egypt unto this day, I have even sent you all my servants the prophets, daily rising up early and sending them. Yet they hearkened not unto me, nor inclined their ear, but hardened their neck; they did worse than their fathers. Therefore, thou shalt speak all these words unto them, but they will not hearken unto thee; thou shalt also call unto them, but they will not answer thee; but thou shalt say unto them, This is a nation that obeyeth not the voice of the Lord their God, nor receiveth correction. Truth is perished and cut off from their mouth. Cut off thine hair, Jerusalem, and cast it away, and take up a lamentation on high places, for the Lord hath rejected and forsaken the generation of his wrath." Jer. vii. 23–29. Here we see their disobedience to, and abuse of, the means he had used with them, was the reason why they were so peculiarly the people of God's wrath, and of the sad issue of their case. If it be said, the instruction they got from the word is sufficient to render impenitent sinners inexcusable, I answer, either this light and instruction has a tendency to their conversion, (and if this be admitted, the matter is fairly given up,) or it has no such tendency at all; and then how does it at all render them inexcusable in continuing impenitent and unconverted?

The conversion of sinners to God is the great scope of the means of grace; this the word of God calls for at their hands, commands and presses it with the greatest importunity. It is needless to recite authorities for this to such as are acquainted with their Bible, since we might quote a greater part of that sacred book to this purpose. Therefore it is, that the gospel ministry is called the ministry of reconciliation, and it is the business of gospel ministers to pray sinners in Christ's stead to be reconciled to God. Yet,

VI. There is no certain or infallible connection between the most diligent and earnest attendance on the means of grace that unregenerate sinners are capable of, and their obtaining the saving grace of God. This issue of the matter is entirely from the sovereign mercy of God. If we suppose a certain necessary connection in this case, it must arise either from the nature of the thing, viz: some constitution or law of nature, or from some promise and positive appointment of God to that purpose; but in the case before us, there is no such connection in either way. Not the former; for the means of grace are positive institutions, and don't fall under the laws of nature; nor do they operate by way of influence upon God to move him to show mercy, but are means whereby the blessed God deals with sinners, and works effectually on whom he pleases; their efficacy depends upon his blessing and energy. In this view he has appointed means, and requires fallen man to attend upon them. Guilty sinners lie at mercy upon which they have no claim, but it lies in the breast of God as a Sovereign, of his own grace, to show mercy or not as he pleases; and, therefore, according to his sovereign pleasure, he renders the means of grace effectual or not; and as to the latter part of connection, viz: by promise or positive appointment, there is not the smallest evidence of it in the word of God; if there be, let any one show it who thinks he can. I must confess I have not met with one such promise in all the book of God. As to such passages as Luke xi. 9 and Matt. vii. 7, "Ask and it shall be given you; seek and ye shall find; knock and it shall be opened unto you," there the conduct of God as Father towards his children is plainly spoken of; and, therefore, asking, seeking, and knocking in faith, asking, &c., in a gracious manner is intended; and they are the children of God who are spoken of. So the moral efficacy of the means of grace terminated on God to move him to give grace, (the very mention of which shows the absurdity of the supposition,) or the sinner's use of them were at all the ground or reason of his showing mercy; then, indeed, the very appointment of means would imply a promise of success, or something equal to it, in the required use of them; but this is so far from being the case, that, on the contrary, the tendency of the means to the end lies in their moral influence upon the consciences and hearts of sinners. Yet whatever aptness to such an influence there is in the means of grace, such is the blindness, deadness, enmity and prejudice of poor sinners, that until the Holy Spirit accompany them with his presence and energy, no such influence will effectually take place in their hearts. Now, he works in or by these means as a Sovereign; hence, he strives with many only in such a way as that he suffers them still to resist, until in just resentment he forsakes them. But with respect to the vessels of mercy, he prosecutes his gracious design, until by the "rod of his strength" (the word of his grace), he irresistibly conquers, "and rules in the midst of his enemies." Psa. ex. 2.

Therefore sinners are to use the means of grace as creatures lying at mercy, seeking pure grace, which depends on the mighty energy of the Holy Spirit; but they can found no claim to grace on their most diligent use of said means. It is enough to engage sinners to the use of means, that God has appointed them as such, has required their attendance upon them; there is an aptness in the means themselves and a proper tendency, and it is by these means the Holy Spirit works; in this way he meets with perishing creatures in mercy, and they cannot expect the grace of God in the neglect of his institutions. While there is a "may be the Lord will be gracious," (Amos v. 15,) or, "who knoweth if the Lord will return, and repent, and leave a blessing behind him?" (Joel ii. 14,) sinners will be utterly inexcusable in neglecting them, and justly charged with choosing their own destruction.

VII. From what has been said it will follow, as a conclusion on the whole, that all sinners, when the gospel comes, are under the most indispensable obligations to attend the means of grace. The design of their institution, as mediums of the Spirit's dealing with their souls about their eternal interests, lays them under bonds of gratitude. For why, shall the offended majesty of heaven thus seek after rebellious sinners? Would it not then be the basest ingratitude to treat him with neglect? The gracious authority of God binds their consciences; he requires their attendance upon his ordinances; their very institution implies such a requisition, and it will be a disobedience, highly criminal, to neglect them.

We also hence see what grounds of encouragement sinners have, for their attendance on the means of grace; they have not the assurance of a promise that they shall be successful; the great God has come under no such engagement; they have no ground of present peace and security from their most diligent and earnest use of them. Such apprehensions would lead to, and support, a self-righteous spirit, and be an abuse of the means of grace. They have great reason of deepest anxiety lest they fail of the grace of God, and provoke the Holy Spirit to forsake them. Yet they have sufficient motives from the aforesaid design of their institution; their moral aptness and tendency, whereby they are adapted to our rational natures and the Spirit's operations, and suited to affect the hearts of men in a moral way. It is the stated way of the Spirit's dealing with the souls of men; by his word and ordinances he strives with sinners, and by the same means he accomplishes his special work of grace; and in this way there is the only probability of meeting with mercy. In the continued neglect of God's ordinances there is certain destruction, but in waiting on God in this way there is a peradventure the Lord may have mercy. The Holy Spirit has rendered the means of grace effectual to multitudes, and how knows each sinner but, of his rich grace, he may effectually reach him?

Hence, also, we may see that ministers of the gospel not only may, with safety and propriety, but are bound, in duty, to urge unregenerate sinners, as well as others, to a diligent use and improvement of the means of grace, and in that way to seek unto God for regenerating grace. If the preceding view of the matter be kept up, such exhortations can have no tendency to settle people in a legal dependence on the means, nor promote security nor carnal confidence. Yea, it is highly incumbent on the ministers of Christ to give particular directions to poor sinners in order to their improvement of the means, in such a manner as has the most likely tendency, and wherewith it is most probable the Holy Spirit may concur for their conversion to God. Certainly, a mere external attendance upon the administration of ordinances, while the heart is secure and careless, is not likely to answer any good end. Undoubtedly, such have need to be directed so to attend to the word of God as to compare themselves therewith, to examine themselves, and enter into a serious consideration of their own state and character, and lay to heart the danger they are in. Awakened sinners are inclined to seek shelter in the duties of religion, and to expect healing and relief to their consciences from their earnest use of means. These need to be warned of that dangerous rock, and be directed to such a view of God's law as may more deeply convince them of their utter depravity, and slay them dead to the law. Gal. ii. 19. Their attention to the overtures of the gospel should be urged. Our safe path lies between two dangerous extremes, viz: of those who only try to convince men of their unregenerate state, call upon them to embrace Jesus Christ, and then leave them under all their perplexing exercises and distresses, without any counsel or direction; and thus their various temptations, discouragements, and despondencies are overlooked, and no assistance is administered when they most need it. It is a matter of great consequence into what hands poor, convinced sinners fall; an unskilful treatment of them is vastly injurious. The other extreme is of those who direct sinners to duties and attendance on the means of grace in such a legal manner as to encourage their dependence upon them; such lead poor creatures to think they can do something to recommend themselves to God; their utter insufficiency in themselves is never fairly opened up. On the contrary, they are told if they will do their part, God will do his; and thus they are made to believe there is a certain connection between their own best endeavours and the saving grace of God; that if they do what they can, God will do the rest. Thus the nature and design of the means is misrepresented. They are considered as means which sinners use with God in order to prevail with him, rather than means whereby he deals with them, in order to call them back again to himself, and renders them irresistibly efficacious for that purpose when he pleases. The first of these extremes tends to make sinners neglect all attempts to perform the duties of religion, or if they give their presence at ordinances, yet make no essay to strive with their own hearts, as being altogether in vain, without any tendency to promote their good, and not required of them in their present circumstances. While this doctrine is believed, Satan is not much afraid of damage to his interest from all their convictions of being in an unregenerate state; for the consequence is, they quench the Spirit. If convictions startle them, they, upon this principle, make no attempt to cherish their convictions, easily fall asleep again, and lie still in careless indolence. By the latter extreme, the striving of sinners is turned into a wrong channel, and they are directed to the use of means upon principles entirely wrong. The directions they get, send them to the law for life, and settle them upon a righteousness of their own. Both the extremes are injurious to the interests of religion, and destructive to the souls of men. Both are to be avoided; the ministers of the gospel are to endeavour the conviction and awakening of sinners, and when there are any awakenings they are to attend and cherish them, and by prudent, seasonable and evangelical counsel to direct their way, and point out the method of salvation to them. They have sufficient encouragement to such a conduct upon this principle, that however dead, miserable and helpless sinners arc, yet it is by such views and impressions as evangelical counsels and directions tend to, that the Holy Spirit carries on his work in the souls of men; and therefore, when he concurs, they shall be rendered effectual. May the God of all grace teach his servants how to negotiate the treaty of peace and reconciliation, and make them abundantly wise to win souls to Jesus Christ! Amen.

WILLIAM TENNENT, JR.

The Rev. "William Tennent, Jr., was the second son of William Tennent, Sen., and was born on the 5th day of Jan., 1705, in the County of Armagh, in Ireland, and was just turned of thirteen years when he came to this country. Being a youth of zeal and industry, he made great proficiency in the languages, particularly in the Latin. Being early impressed with a deep sense of divine things, he soon determined to follow the example of his father and elder brother, by devoting himself to the service of God in the ministry of the gospel. Having completed his classical course, he commenced the study of theology with his brother Gilbert, in New Brunswick, and after going through a regular course, was preparing for his examination by the Presbytery as a candidate for the gospel ministry. By intense application, his health was affected and he appeared to be going into a decline. It was at this point in his history, that he fell into that remarkable death-like trance, which is fully recorded in his life in the "Log College." On recovery from this trance, he was found to be totally ignorant of every transaction of his life previous to his sickness. He could not read a single word, neither did he seem to have any idea of what it meant. As soon as he became capable of attention, he was taught to read and write, as children are usually taught; and afterwards began to learn the Latin language under the tuition of his brother. One day, as he was reciting a lesson, he suddenly started, clapped his hand to his head, as if something had hurt him, and made a pause. His brother asked him what was the matter; he said that he felt a sudden shock in his head, and it now seemed to him as if he had read that book before. By degrees his recollection was restored, and he could speak the Latin as fluently as before his sickness. His memory so completely revived, that he gained a perfect knowledge of the past transactions of his life, as if no difficulty had previously occurred. As soon as circumstances would permit, Mr. Tennent was licensed and began to preach the everlasting gospel with great zeal and success. la Oct., 1733, Mr. Tennent was regularly ordained the pastor of the Freehold Church, as successor to his brother John, where he continued through the whole of a pretty long life, one of the best proofs of ministerial fidelity.

Mr. Tennent was rather more than six feet high, of a spare, thin visage, and of an erect carriage. He had bright, piercing eyes, a long sharp nose, and a long face. His general countenance was grave and solemn, but at all times cheerful and pleasant with his friends. It may be said of him, with peculiar propriety, that he appeared, in an extraordinary manner, to live above the world and all its allurements. He seemed habitually to have such clear views of spiritual and heavenly things, as afforded him much of the fore-taste and enjoyment of them. His faith was, really and experimentally, "the substance of things hoped for, and the evidence of things unseen." Literally his daily walk was with God, and he lived "as seeing him who is invisible." The divine presence with him was frequently manifested in his public ministrations and in his private conduct.

About the latter end of Feb., 1777, Mr. Tennent was suddenly seized with a fever, attended by violent symptoms. During his whole sickness he continued perfectly resigned to the divine will, until death was swallowed up in victory, on the 8th of March, 1777. He was buried in his own church at Freehold.

GOD'S SOVEREIGNTY, NO OBJECTION TO THE SINNER'S STRIVING.

A SERMON BY THE REV. WILLIAM TENNENT, JR., PREACHED TO THE MEMBERS OF THE ENGLISH PRESBYTERIAN CHURCH, NEW YORK, JAN. 20, 1765.

"Strive to enter in at the strait gate."
—Luke xiii. 24.

Such doctrines as Christ taught, his disciples need not fear to teach; such admonitions as the infallible Saviour of the world hath given, we are warranted to give, and need not fear their consequence. When, therefore, we behold sinners, in gay and numerous multitudes, gliding carelessly down the broad way that leadeth to destruction, while a solitary few struggle in the narrow path of virtue, what though some arise and cavil? What though some endeavour to bewilder the pious mind with difficulties? We may safely warn them, as did our Divine Master; we need not fear his displeasure, as some pretend, if we persuade them to stop their career, to strive and struggle, that they may enter the strait gate. But that you may ascertain the meaning of our great Lord in the text, I beg leave to direct your attention to two things.

1. By the strait gate is undoubtedly intended, the terms of Christianity, or the conditions upon which our salvation is suspended.

To be assured of this, we need only reflect upon the figure made use of in the text; this is more largely and particularly inserted in Matt. vii. 13. Both of the evangelists, without doubt, refer to the same expression of our Saviour; both give the same idea, but one more fully than the other, as in many other instances besides the present; by consulting both, we shall therefore get the true and full idea which Christ designed to convey. Matthew only says, "enter the strait gate." Luke says, "strive to enter." Matthew gives the meaning, but Luke more fully; that Luke gives the very words of our Lord, in this part of the sentence, we may reasonably suppose. Tor first, if he does not, he certainly conveys an idea more than was ever intended by Christ. A struggle towards entering is certainly more than simply entering. It appears, in the second place, perfectly agreeable to the latter part of the figure, where the narrowness of the gate implies the necessity of striving to enter it. Matthew mentions one reason for the direction, viz: "for strait is the gate, and narrow is the way that leadeth to life;" with this addition by way of alarm, "and few there be who find it." Luke does not mention this, but another as alarming; "that many shall seek to enter and shall not be able." By taking both together, you find our Lord's direction at large, which is this: "Strive—struggle—be in great earnest to enter the strait gate; for wide is the gate, and broad is the way that leadeth to destruction, and many go in thereat; but strait is the gate, and narrow is the way that leadeth to life, and few there are who find it; and let this your strife be without delay; for many, when it is too late, shall seek to enter in and shall not be able.

Whence, it is easy to perceive, that man, since the fall, is represented as by nature travelling in pursuit of happiness, but in a mistaken path; travelling in a way which, though broad, descending and easy, yet leads unerring to the abode of death. Our Divine Master represents himself as one, who, filled with compassion, at the sight of this numerous throng, gaily moving on to ruin, hath in his gospel opened a narrow gate for their reception, which, with most disinterested pity, he persuades them to strive to enter. The way you are in, says he, is confessedly broad, and you are kept in countenance by the multitude; but, I warn you, eternal death hath his dwelling there. This way is narrow and difficult; but life and happiness dwell here. Strive and struggle then to enter.

By the strait gate, is therefore intended the terms of Christianity, or the conditions of the gospel. And what are these, but repentance and faith? By the narrow way, the continuance in these terms, or the progress of the Christian. Those are termed strait and narrow, because of the natural corruption and evil propensities of the soul, which make the duties of Christianity difficult and mortifying. To enter the strait gate, then, means neither more nor less, than to begin to be a Christian: to submit to the terms of the gospel, or to enter a state of grace. Remark this, my brethren, for it will be the foundation of our discourse.

2. But to whom is this direction given? A second particular, which you will please to attend to. Is it to the saints? To those who are already in a state of favour with God, and are already treading the rugged paths of virtue? No, it would be an absurdity, that those who have already entered, should be persuaded to enter. They are not desired to continue, but to begin; it is to sinners that the words are addressed; it is to those who are in the broad way of sin, which corrupt nature makes easy, and throngs with a multitude.

And what direction doth he give them? What advice

flows from his divine, infallible lips? What direction, of consequence, is fit and proper to be given to all such poor wanderers by nature? What direction are his ministers herefrom warranted to give to the numbers whom they behold treading the same downward road? Why, "Strive to enter the strait gate." Let me remark, my brethren, there is more emphasis in the original word, translated "strive," than can be crowded into one English term: *agonizesthe*, let your strife be most intense and earnest; not only strive but struggle, as one who would force through a narrow pass. It signifies a struggling with a mere agony; I would render it agonize and bow every power of the soul in the earnest attempt as one who would save an immortal soul

What difference—what immense difference is there between this advice, and the opinion of certain modern reformers of doctrine, who insist that sinners ought not to be put upon striving for the salvation of their souls; that they ought not to be directed to seek for faith, or an entrance into this strait gate, into these mortifying conditions of the gospel; and who brand all attempts to enter upon the narrow way of Jesus, with the foulest names!

Our Lord commands, and, therefore, there must be certain strivings, not only lawful, but the absolute duty of the unconverted, that they may enter the strait gate.

But because this notion is supposed by some to be inconsistent with God's sovereign disposal of grace, let me take up a little of your time,

I. In reconciling the notion of the sinner's striving, with that of the unmoved bestowment of grace. And in the

II place, Let me answer the objections offered to the doctrine.

I. In order to the first, let me lay down a few plain propositions or considerations, which being attended to, the difficulties vanish, and the truths appear reconciled of themselves.

1. God, in the bestowment of his grace or sanctifying the soul, treats man not as he would a stone, in the new modelling its form, but as a reasonable being; by his divine power making use of motives and means in changing his disposition.

Such rational means and motives as are in themselves fitted to influence the mind, infinite power makes use of as the instruments in converting the mind. To what other end are all the rational and persuasive calls to sinners in the gospel, if they are not to be the means in the hand of God for their conversion? To what end are such glorious prospects set before them to awaken their hopes? Why such awful terror to alarm their fears—such powerful motives to their gratitude—such afflictive providences—such instances of mercy and goodness which (the apostle expressly asserts) lead to repentance? Are these only sent to vex and disquiet them, without any tendency to bring them to God? Why do we preach and you hear?

Why do we persuade and you listen? Is the whole intent, the only design of this, to condemn and make miserable? God forbid that we should harbour such a thought! To suppose that God would lay and execute such a plan, the whole design of which is to condemn and render more wretched, is a thought highly injurious to the great fountain of happiness.

Now, although we can conceive of God's implanting a principle of holiness into the soul by his immediate power, without the interposition of any instruments, yet we have no reason to think that this is his ordinary method. Though by a single fiat the whole creation might have come into its present existence and order, yet he chose to do it in days, and by distinct commands; he saw fit that his Spirit, or his winds, should move on the face of the water, although he might have caused the whole human race to be in a moment, by a single command; yet he sees proper to make use of instruments in its production. As in the world of nature, so in the world of grace, he uses his word and ordinances; they are the instruments in the hands of infinite power to produce the change; but they are only instruments which, without that power, would never effect it, more than the naked, inactive tools would frame a house, without the workman's strength and wisdom. Hence, God is said to "beget us by his word."

But here it is replied. What is this to our striving? Is there no distinction between the means which God uses with us, and those which we use with ourselves?

2. We answer by our second proposition, which is, that as our souls are rational, and to be changed by the interposition of certain motives and arguments in the hand, and set home by the power, of God; so it is necessary, that we, somehow or other, attend to these motives and arguments. If this is not the case, the pagans in Africa are in as fair a way to be converted by the gospel, as we who have it in our hands. If there is not a necessity that we diligently attend to it, there can be no benefit in having it. If we never hear, if we never attend to these motives and arguments, how can they be the instruments of our conversion? If we never hear, if we never read, if we never meditate on the word of God at all, how can that word be the means of begetting us again? In this sense, undoubtedly, faith is said to come by hearing, and hearing by the word of God. Now says the apostle, "How shall they

hear unless there is a preacher, and how shall he preach, unless he be sent?" Upon the apostle's plan, there must be a preacher—he must preach—we must hear, attend and consider, or else we cannot have faith. Here you see, we must be active in the matter. Now, as this is the ordinary way in which it hath pleased God to communicate faith, is not he very absurd, who dreams of getting faith, without such attendance and reflection, and all those other things which are consequent upon, and necessarily connected with it? And is not this reason enough for us to persuade mankind to go and hear the word preached, to attend with all their might, to strive by reflection to see and feel its force, and so on as to other duties? This kind of striving, you see, is absolutely necessary to faith and holiness, in the ordinary course of God's dealing with sinners. And we can see no reason, why this notion should be objected to, because there seems to be something done in the matter, which God hath not immediately done: for if it may be his sovereign pleasure, to make use of the instrumentality of others towards my conversion, I see not why he may not also make, use of the instrumentality of my own thoughts and reflections, to bring about that desirable end. And if we may call the dealings of God with us, by the instrumentality of others, the means of grace, I can see no reason, why we may not also term his dealing with us, by our own instrumentality, the means of grace likewise.

Now, my brethren, though some loudly exclaim against our calling these means, the way in which God usually confers his grace, because Christ hath, by way of eminence, stiled himself the way, that is, the foundation or procuring cause of salvation; yet there is an evident distinction between the way, or manner in which, and the procuring cause of which; and inasmuch as we always use it in the former sense, when we speak on this subject, I can see no reason to change the term, a term so expressive, until our great reformer of Christianity shall furnish us with a better.

To conclude this section, although the salvation of a sinner, from first to last, may, in a sound and theological sense, be termed a miracle, and is begun and accomplished "according to the working of God's mighty power, which he wrought in Christ when he raised him from the dead;" (Eph. i. 19;) yet, as it has pleased God to subject his works in nature to the instrumentality of second causes, and the ways of his providence and grace, in their ordinary dispensation, to the rational use of means, we are not to expect our salvation, or even the common blessings of this life, without using the means appointed to obtain them. There is a wide difference between what God can do, and sometimes does in an extraordinary way, and what we, as reasonable creatures, ought to do. And we leave it to our hearers to judge, whether, according to the instituted method of divine grace, revealed in the holy scriptures, and confirmed by the experience of the saints, it is not as reasonable to hope, that God will overset nature, and extinguish the sun by a miracle, for our salvation, as to expert it without striving; and in all seasons, whether ordinary or extraordinary, which have happened in the Church of God, the first evidence we have of a sinner's return is, after diligent use of appointed means, and previous earnest striving. St. Paul's conversion was very sudden, and as miraculous as any who read of; yet the first notice we have of it, is, "behold he prayeth." Acts ix. 11. The conversion of the three thousand, on the day of Pentecost, was in the way of an anxious concern for salvation; and we read, that from the days of John the Baptist, the kingdom of heaven suffered violence, and the violent took it by force. Matt. xi. 12. And we have no reason to suppose, that salvation can be obtained upon easier terms at this day.

Objection. But if his striving is so necessary, may he not make a merit of it, and thus the bestowment of grace not appear wholly free? See here the principal objection to this scheme, which gives occasion to our third proposition.

3. There is a wide difference between the way or manner in which God chooses to bestow his grace, and the procuring, meritorious cause for which. You may exemplify this in the case even of the saints. How are saints appointed to get more grace? Are they to be idle, and carelessly wait to see whether a sovereign God will bestow it? No; they are to cry for it, and act like babes; according to Paul, they are eagerly to "desire the sincere milk of the word that they may grow thereby." Now, their eager desires, their praying and crying, were it prolonged to eternity, cannot be esteemed an equivalent for one smile of their God. Their desires and prayers are not the procuring cause, or the merit for which God bestows more grace: they do not move him to do it by way of desert; and yet he hath appointed this as the way in which, for Christ's sake, they may expect it. These ordinances are the means he makes use of in conveying it;

Christ, and Christ alone, is the meritorious and procuring cause. Thus you see, there is an undeniable distinction between the way in which God, as a Sovereign, chooses to confer, and the procuring cause for which. And if the saint who obtains fresh supplies of grace in this way, hath no cause, and will never find cause to boast of his having deserved, or moved God to it by his prayers, much less will the poor sinner, whose attendance upon the means of grace is so much more imperfect. "Boasting is therefore wholly excluded."

If we consider matters strictly, we shall find that our diligence to eternity is not a sufficient payment for a morsel of bread. The smallest mercy of God cannot be repaid by an eternity of our little services, much less can the unspeakable blessing of a new heart, a blessing that extends its happy influence through perpetual ages! I say, much less can this be purchased by a poor worm's listening, or praying, or crying. What! hath it ever entered the heart of a rational man to suppose that a few sighs, a few tears, a few moments' attendance to the proposals of the gospel, is the price to purchase a forfeited, happy eternity? God, therefore, being under no obligation to our merit, even after we have done all, need not bestow his grace. And this scheme represents him as sovereign in his gifts as sovereignty itself, or as the opposers of our doctrine can wish. You can conceive of nothing more sovereign and free, than that which is bestowed without any foundation of merit in the subject, but against merit. It is necessary that we should attend in that way, but the necessity of our so attending doth not argue any desert in it, or that God is brought under any obligation; it only argues that God is sovereign in choosing the way of his bestowment, and even when we attend in that way, he is sovereign in bestowing, or not bestowing, as he pleases. We, therefore, cannot see any cause our opponents have to cry out against the doctrine, as tending to lead sinners to expect justification in part by their striving, and to leave only part of their justification to Christ. In this argument we have nothing to do with justification; and so much as to bring it in, by way of objection, is a gross impertinency, and only calculated to blind the unwary. Justification can only be founded on merit, and in this affair we plead for no merit at all; we insist there is none.

It is true, the sinner who is thus active, is less guilty than he who lives in rebellious contempt. But a bare absence of guilt, my being not so wicked, for instance, as Beelzebub, is no reason God should bestow peculiar favours on me; it is no positive merit, but only a reason why I should not be punished equally to another.

But, say our opposers, "Suppose the man who hath thus attended and sought for mercy, to meet with his miserable friend in eternity, who had neglected thus to seek, and died in his sins, would he not have a right to accost him thus, ' thou miserable wretch! why didst thou not strive as I did, and have obtained mercy?' "hinting, that his seeking had in some degree deserved the favour. We answer, through rich grace, the saints have a prospect of better judgments, than to be liable to the absurd mistake. The triumphant happy spirit would necessarily see, that although he had attended in the way which his Sovereign had made necessary to his salvation; yet his so attending (although it rendered him, as far as it went, less guilty) had no procuring merit in it; and far from ascribing the praise to himself, his Redeemer, who procured the blessing, would be all his song.

Only reason with yourselves, and you will find that the glorified saint, who sits upon a throne of more exalted eminence in the world above, will have just as much reason to exult over his inferior friend, as the saint will have over the sinner. For God is as sovereign, in the bestowment of superior degrees of grace, in the use of means, upon saints, as he is in giving grace to sinners at all. Our opponents cannot deny this, consistent with their own sentiments. And do you think that the most exalted spirit above will have an opportunity to boast over the inferior? You need not allege, that God hath bound himself by promise to his people, and therefore there is a difference; they may strive and obtain more grace. God never acts, God never promises under the gospel, but upon the footing of equity and merit. If he hath promised, it is not upon the footing of desert in them, but only in Christ, and that in their attendance upon the means of his institution. The saint cannot deserve the mercy by his doings, more than the sinner. The favour conferred on him is therefore as free grace, as that on the sinner; and if the sovereignty and freedom of grace is an argument against endeavouring to obtain it, it was as much against the saint's endeavours, as against those of the sinner.

Thus "we see, a proper attention to the plain distinction between the way in which, and the meritorious cause for which, entirely removes all the difficulty about boasting.

But you will say, "There is a wide difference; the saint can do actions that are spiritually good; the sinner can not, for he is represented as spiritually dead." We answer, this doth not at all alter the case, as to the sovereignty of God's bestowment, unless it be supposed that the spirituality of these actions does really merit such a bestowment; but this our opponents cannot allow, upon their own principles. And if their spiritual actions do not justify, or merit, they are as much the subjects of pure mercy, as the sinner. This brings us to our fourth proposition.

4. Though the unconverted can do nothing that is

spiritually good, yet they can do what is materially good; nor is this distinction vain. The matter and the form of duty are most obviously distinct. Praying is the matter of a duty—with faith is the form of it. Hearing is the matter of a duty—with love is the form; doing alms is the matter; from a principle of divine charity is the form. Where these good dispositions are wanting, the form of the duty is bad, though the performer is, nevertheless, not so guilty as he who ' neglects matter and form both. Now the sinner can pray, he can hear, he can do alms, he can do things materially good, though not formally so. The performance of these duties, as a natural man can perform them, is the way in which God usually confers his grace, for Christ's sake, although they do not merit it; and such performance leaves him less guilty, than if he did not perform them at all. The one is only an improper compliance, the other an open, affronting denial. If this is not a truth, then you can make no difference, as to guilt, between the most profligate, and him who is only outwardly moral. It is as absurd, therefore, as it is shocking, that some oppose the use of any means by men in their natural estate, under the notion that they only render themselves more guilty than they would be without them. It is not only contrary to reason, and sides with the cursed suggestions of the wicked heart, but opens a door to all licentiousness.

Objection. "But will God ever reward duties sinfully performed?" It is not a reward that we look for in the present case; it is not a reward that we would have sinners expect. They are only to attend upon God in the way in which he ordinarily takes notice of sinners, hoping that sovereign pity will deign to light on them, and confessing that they may with justice be abandoned after all.

5. Our fifth and last proposition is founded on the rest, viz: the man who carefully attends upon the means of grace, and seeks for the renewing influences of the Holy Spirit, hath all the encouragement which fallen, sinful creatures should dare to ask; but those who live in the avowed neglect of the gospel have no encouragement at all.

As for the former, he is encouraged from the gospel scheme. He knows that Christ has died to make it possible for such to come to God. He knows that he hath purchased the Holy Spirit for that very purpose; he knows that faith cometh by hearing, and that God ordinarily bestows his grace by the instrumentality of these means. And is not this a sufficient encouragement to make them attend upon them?

As to those who live in the avowed neglect of the gospel, they have no encouragement to hope for grace at all.

When they look at the general course of his proceeding, they cannot hope from that. As to the motives and means in the gospel, they withdraw themselves from them. And to hope that God will convert them in an extraordinary and miraculous way, is as absurd as to hope that he will change the course of nature. What if he hath done it in a few instances? So he hath caused the sun to stand still, but is it to be expected that he will always do so, and especially, that he will make thee a signal instance, when thou, presuming on that, dost make it a foundation to abuse him?

But of all, methinks there can be no idea more detestable to our rational nature, than that propagated by some, viz: that the most presumptuous, heaven-daring sinner, is in as fair a way to meet with God's favour, as he who is seeking for grace as a natural man may seek. Nay, say some, he is in a fairer way, for publicans and harlots should enter the kingdom of heaven, sooner than the self-righteous Pharisees.

Those publicans and harlots, who came to our Lord, and sought for his favour, it is true, were in a more likely way to obtain it, than those self-conceited men, the whited sepulchres, Who denied him, and despised the only Saviour of mankind. But to suppose that publicans and harlots, in general, have a fairer prospect than the moral seeker, not only contradicts all our notions of God's working on the heart, by the means and motives of the gospel, which cannot be in the case of him who never attends to them; but it casts a most horrible reflection upon the very nature of God, as if he were inclined most to mercy, where the most abominable guilt is, and therefore the more accursed our crimes, the nearer to heaven. Oh, infernal blasphemy! Upon this plan—go on, ye profane! Laugh at heaven, despise the terrors of God, blaspheme the awful name, excel hell itself, and cause the damned to shudder at superior crimes! The more execrable, the more to be exalted! And ye infidels, ye atheists of every name, ye who most disbelieve and most contemn the gospel, ye have the fairest prospects of salvation by it!

It is in vain that you attempt to excuse the blasphemous insinuation, by saying that it gives more glory to the grace of God. Is it giving more glory to his grace to say, that it is readier to alight on a greater transgressor than on a small one? that the more guilty, the more fit objects for his mercy? Does this give a lovely idea of the best of beings? We do not deny that he can, and does make some examples of his grace among the most profligate, to show the happy extent of his gospel: to show that Christ is able to save even them. But to argue from hence, that it is more agreeable to his nature, than to let his mercy fall upon smaller transgressors, is blasphemous and false; and even to say that he makes as many instances of grace, among the former as among the latter, is also false. The least vicious have no claim to his favour by that, as it is no virtue or real merit in me, that I am not so bad as the devil. Yet to say that the vicious are not farther off from God, and of consequence that their salvation is not more improbable, implies blasphemy. And if the gospel, my beloved brethren, gives you any such notion of God; if it renders the salvation of the greatest sinner only as probable as that of the least, oh, be terrified! the gospel encourages the presumptuous sinner, and you ought not to receive it. Reject, then, that impious book, that gives so false an idea of infinite perfection, and serves to poison the already poisoned souls of mankind. But rather blast the wretched pen, which would palm on inspiration, doctrines of which this is the plain consequence; and thus, under the guise of friendship, betray the cause like Judas!

But to sum up the whole. If God ordinarily bestows his grace in the use and by the instrumentality of certain means, and thereby hath rendered our attendance upon those means necessary; if our attendance upon those means infers no obligation upon God by way of merit, but leaves him still sovereign in his bestowment; if he who strives hath sufficient encouragement, and he who does not hath none; what shall we conclude? What, but that it is reasonable and warrantable to urge home the advice of my text upon sinners? Strive to enter the strait gate.

II. A few objections remain to be answered.

1. "The essence of true religion," say some, "seems to consist in an entire willingness to return to God through Christ. Now, it appears absurd to suppose that a man can make himself willing; for it is to be supposed that we are willing already when we strive."

We answer, common experience may contradict this, for who knows not, that often our rational judgment and our practical judgment contradict each other? "What I would, that do I not, and what I would not, that do I," could an apostle say. In my depraved state, I often find myself unwilling to do what my reason dictates. And when I am convinced that the ways of holiness are best in themselves, and lead to life; when my conscience approves them, and yet I find my heart reluctant, may I not sit down and calmly strive to reason myself into willingness? Are not the people of God often obliged to do this when they find reluctance within? Why, then, may not the sinner use this means, and many others? And how know you that God will not render them effectual to that end? So that you see we may be unwilling and yet strive.

2. Objection. "The apostle gave no such direction to the trembling jailer, who asked what he should do to be saved. We find his reply is only, 'Believe.'"

The apostle answered according to the question, which proceeded from pagan ignorance of the terms of salvation. And such also should be our answer, when a blind heathen is solicitous what is required of him, as a suspending term of salvation. But if we are asked what is the most probable way to have this faith implanted, the question is different, and we must answer as in our text.

3. "But is not this setting up a new law of works?" Yes, if we made our doings the procuring cause for which, or the means of our justification. But when we exclude them from having the least share in it, and only admit them as the most probable way to get faith, we are not afraid of this imputation.

4. But it is objected, in the fourth place, that "sinners are already so prone to depend upon these attempts, to recommend them to God, that it is dangerous to direct them." And if they are prone to turn good into evil, shall we not therefore insist upon their duty? All that can follow from this argument is, that we should be extremely careful to show them, that no dependence is to be placed upon anything but Christ for justification.

5. "Who then maketh us to differ? If the first step towards this is our own, may we not claim a share in the event?" No more than the lifeless, impotent tool of the carver can claim a share in the excellency of a fine performance in carving. If the preacher can claim no share in the conversion of that soul, which, without the energy of the Divine Spirit, had remained in the chains of sin, sure the hearer must be silent. Suppose I laboured under a dangerous disease, and by the order of my physician, it became necessary that I should wait upon him in a certain place; suppose me in effect cured by his prescriptions, should not I be laughed at, if I assumed to myself any praise of the cure, because I had complied with that order? Hearer, apply it.

6. As to those objections brought against us by a certain sophistical and splenetic pen, (with which popularity seems to be the greatest crime,) drawn from the popularity of this doctrine, they are insufficient and false.

Insufficient, inasmuch as although we confess that many of the distinguishing doctrines of the gospel are disgusting to the carnal mind, yet we cannot thence infer, that every doctrine which is not so is not a Christian doctrine. For many of the doctrines of Christianity are so self evident and really pleasing to the rational mind, that they do not disgust even the wicked; and the case hath been known when even a pagan emperor desired of an august assembly that the man Jesus should be enrolled among their gods, on account of some of his doctrines. But the objection to our plan is

2. *False.* It is far from pleasing the carnal taste. The carnal mind ever hates the divine sovereignty, and we represent the deity, first, sovereign in designing to bestow grace at all; secondly, sovereign in his conditions; thirdly, sovereign in his choice of the way or manner in which sinners must attend; and at last he is sovereign in bestowing or not bestowing at all, even after we strive to obtain it. And this idea of the divine sovereignty is, at least, as mortifying to the carnal mind, as that opinion of our opponents, who represent the most base of mankind as near to heaven as the moral seeker after divine grace. Let none of us, therefore, my brethren, give into that specious trap, and suppose, that, because the promulgator of such pernicious doctrines meets with deserved contempt, they, therefore, must be genuine Christianity.

Our discourse concludes with a few remarks upon the pernicious tendency of the doctrine we oppose, and with a short application to such as our text is addressed to in particular.

1. The doctrine we oppose, in the first place, tends to give an unlovely idea of the nature of God, as being equally inclined to have mercy upon the most abhorred, as upon the least so. And here, be not afraid that it can be replied, that we represent the sovereign majesty as actuated by a view of real merit in the least vicious, which is not in him which is more so. We have already observed, and it is evident to common sense, that the not being so wicked is no positive claim to peculiar favours. An absence of guilt can only procure an absence of punishment, but not positive blessings.

2. The contrary doctrine represents all the means which are used with sinners, under the gospel, as useless; and thus all those calls, those motives, those tender arguments addressed to sinners—arguments in which all the bowels of heaven seem to sound—are to be esteemed as useless lumber. For unless they are to be attended to, of what use are they? If they are necessary and useful, must it not be the duty of sinners to attend to them? And if so, what is the guilt of those who would prevail with sinners to contemn their duty, and to omit, alas! what they are too much inclined to omit already.

3. But, what is most shocking, they who would discourage the strivings of the unconverted, only join with the reluctant wicked heart, and join with the enemy of God and man, to encourage a continuance in sin. It is well known that the carnal heart is only to be worked upon by motives of profit and fear, that are present. If, therefore, their present prospects, as to the favour of God, are wholly the same, whether they serve their abandoned lusts to the utmost or not; whether they seek for divine mercy in the abstinence from gross sins, or wholly give themselves up to wickedness; then what single motive have we to restrain them? It is vain to tell them that they will be more miserable hereafter—hereafter never affects them as the present. They are void of that faith, which is the evidence of things not seen; and unless they have the prospect of some present advantage, they will not abstain. "We can but be damned," say they; "then let us fill up our measure, since it is as probable that in this way we shall meet with favour as in any other." This is the conclusion the wicked are apt to draw, in spite of all our endeavours to the contrary; this is the excuse they plead, and methinks there is little need to confirm it. We dare appeal to every wicked heart here present, and it must confess, that it frequently brings our opponents' doctrine as a plea for its licentiousness; and we now call to witness the effects, the sad and horrible effects, which have followed wherever the fatal doctrine hath been preached. Only let it be proclaimed from this desk, that the most vicious are in as likely a way to obtain divine grace, as he who is seeking it in a moral life, and you will directly hear it in the mouth of every impious debauchee, as a justifying argument. The secure sinner makes it a reason for his carelessness, and contempt of every ordinance. The duties of the family and the closet are neglected; and those who have been baptized, lead the life of pagans. Well did you collect your household churches, ye faithful servants of the Most High! Well did you warn your sons and daughters to turn a deaf ear to the preacher, and to avoid the fatal rock. (We have understood, that some worthy persons have found themselves obliged, upon hearing such doctrines, to call their families together and warn them against it.)

O my beloved brethren! it is painful to see the consequences which have followed, and which must follow, in places where the infernal scheme hath been broached. Let me conclude by earnestly entreating the secure and careless, that they will not suffer themselves to be deceived, either by the suggestions of a wicked heart, by the enemy of God and man, or even by this—what shall I name it?—infernal machination. Ye who are in the broad road to destruction, who are unwilling to struggle in the narrow paths of virtue and life, oh, reflect, where do those gay and sprightly ways conduct you? Doth not eternal death hold his domain before you? Why, for a few moments' guilty pleasure, would you abandon yourself to eternal pains? The gay mob, it is true, is with you; but why should that encourage you? Oh, learn to look upon them only as oxen, who, though trimmed with garlands, and playing down an easy passage, are devoted to slaughter.

The Saviour of mankind hath opened a safe retreat from death. The Saviour of mankind, out of disinterested compassion, invites you to "strive to enter the strait gate." Your souls, your eternity join in the important demand; and all that should influence a rational being urges home the proposal. In this, it is true, you will be opposed by the world, with all its scorn and malice, the flesh with all its corrupt inclinations, and by the devil with every art his long practised cunning can invent; and, therefore, striving, struggling, nay, agonizing will be necessary. That careless, indolent life will never do. But remember, a whole immortality—the love of Jehovah himself is the prize.

And let it not discourage you, that God, and God alone, must be the great efficient. Were it to be performed by a man, or even by an angel, you would have some room for discouragement; but infinite benevolence, the eternal fountain of goodness and grace, is He to whom your suit is directed.

Let me, therefore, conclude with the apostle's exhortation to this purpose, "Work out your salvation with fear and trembling." For why? "Knowing that it is God who worketh in us to will and to do," and that it is of his own "good pleasure." Amen.

JOHN TENNENT.

The Rev. John Tennent, the third son of the Rev. William Tennent, Sen., was born in the County of Armagh, in Ireland, the 12th of Nov., 1707. The whole of his education he obtained under the paternal roof and in the Log College.

We have a most interesting narrative of his conversion, from the pen of his brother Gilbert, showing the fearful nature of his convictions of sin, danger, and misery; from which, after an agony almost uninterrupted for four days and nights, he was signally relieved and filled with joy and praise.

When he had finished his preparatory studies in the Log College, he presented himself to the Presbytery of Philadelphia; and after passing with credit the usual trials, he was licensed to preach the gospel. Soon after his licensure, he visited the congregation of Freehold, in the County of Monmouth, New Jersey, which was now without a pastor. Being a young man of uncommon modesty and humility, he was very reluctant to go, and even after he had consented to visit them, he regretted the engagement very much; for it seemed to him that they were a people whom God had given up for the abuse of the gospel. But though he went under this cloud of discouragement, his first labours among this people were remarkably blessed. On his first visit, he preached four or five Sabbaths, and found among the people a serious disposition to attend to the concerns of their souls, and to search the scriptures, to see whether the things they heard from the pulpit were so. And he was assisted to preach with so much freedom, that he told his brother William, that he was fully persuaded that Christ Jesus had a large harvest to bring home there; and though they were a poor broken people, yet, if they called him, he would go to them though he should be under the necessity of begging his bread. On the 15th of April, 1730, they assembled and gave him a unanimous call, which he accepted, and was ordained Nov. 19th, of the same year.

His labours in this congregation, according to his brother Gilbert, were attended with three notable qualities: prudence, diligence, and success. Though the time was short which he was permitted to remain among them, yet his labours were abundant. His race was swift and vehement, and his heart was so fixed on the work of God, that he could not be persuaded to desist from his public labours, even when his body was emaciated and debilitated by a consumptive disease; and when, in the judgment of physicians, it was prejudicial to his broken constitution. As his death drew near, his love for hi8 people and concern for their welfare increased, and he would often express himself in such language as the following: "I am grieved for my people, for I fear they will be left to wander as sheep without a shepherd, or get one that will pull down what I have poorly endeavoured to build up." His brother who watched with him in his sickness, has frequently overheard him in the deep silence of the night wrestling with God by prayer, with sobs and tears, for his people.

His last words were like those of some of the old martyrs. A few minutes before he expired, holding his brother William by the hand, he broke out into the following rapturous expressions: "Farewell, my brethren, farewell, father and mother; farewell, world with all thy vain delights. Welcome, God and Father—welcome, sweet Lord Jesus—welcome, death—welcome, eternity. Amen." Then with a loud voice he said, "Lord Jesus, come, Lord Jesus." And so he fell asleep in Christ. His death occurred on the 23d of April, 1732, in the twenty-fifth year of his age.

REGENERATION OPENED.

A SERMON BY THE REV. JOHN TENNENT.

"Jesus answered and said unto him, Verily, verily, I say unto thee, Except a man be born again, he cannot see the kingdom of God." John iii. 3.

These words are part of a remarkable dialogue between Christ and Nicodemus, in which Nicodemus's fear, ignorance, and willingness to be taught are principally bewrayed. He was one of the Pharisees, as we are informed from the first verse of this chapter, who in general were stated enemies against Christ and his gospel. These Pharisees were proud separatists, who, upon the opinion of their own righteousness, despised all others.

As to his station, he was a ruler, as the word *archón* signifies. This man, being in a high and eminent station, through fear of incurring the anger or displeasure of the Jewish Sanhedrim by openly professing Christ, came to him by night, verse 2. Thus we see what clogs, hindrances, and impediments, honour, grandeur, and greatness are in the way of the profession and practice of truth and holiness; yet it is evident from the words of Nicodemus in the second verse, notwithstanding his fears to acknowledge openly the truth of Christ's mission from the Father, that he had a well grounded persuasion of it from the miracles the blessed Jesus had wrought. "Rabbi, we know that thou art a teacher come from God: for no man can do those miracles that thou doest, except God be with him." But certainly, it is of vast consequence and importance, that the gross ignorance and strange stupidity of this learned man, a teacher in Israel, concerning the vital part of piety, are so perspicuously detected in our text and context. "Jesus answered and said unto him, Verily."—In the words are three things remarkable, I. A proposition. II. An asseveration. III. The implicit occasion of them both.

I. The proposition in these words, "Except a man be born again, he cannot see the kingdom of God." In it there are two things, 1. The subject, a man. 2. The predicate, or that which is spoken concerning the subject, "be born again."

1. As to the subject, a man. This indefinite expression (the matter so requiring as the present case is) is equipollent, or equivalent to a universal. It is as much as if he had said, every one, of whatsoever order, or character, or age, or nation, great or small, rich or poor, noble or ignoble, learned or unlearned, young or old, Jew or Gentile, bond or free, male or female, must be born again, or they cannot see the kingdom of God. Gal. vi. 15. Heb. xii. 14. 1 Pet. i. 23. 2 John i. 13. John iii. 7. 1 John ii. 29. iii. 9. V. 4.

2. The predicate, which being complex, treats of two things, viz: 1. Of happiness under that term the "kingdom of God." 2. The qualification universally necessary to obtain it, which is "being born again;" *ean me tis gennethe anothen.* The Greek word *anothen* is generally rendered *superne*, from above, but the tenor of our context, especially Nicodemus's answer to Christ, "How can a man enter the second time?" (ver. 4.) sufficiently proves that it signifies as much here as *deuteron*, or again, *ouk dunatai idein ten basileian tou Theou*; "he cannot see the kingdom of God. "By seeing here, I understand possessing, according to that phrase of the Romans, *Hereditatem cernere*. A proof of this we have in our Lord's sermon on the Mount, (Matt. v. 8,) "Blessed are the pure in heart: for they shall see God," i.e., they shall see him to their comfort, see him so as to enjoy him, see him as a Friend and Father, and possess him as a satisfying portion. "Cannot—"an unregenerate man is under a threefold impotency in regard of the enjoyment of God's kingdom.

1. Natural. He must take this kingdom by main force, out of the hands of a just and infinite God, if he gets it at all, while he remains in this state. Now what power has a guilty worm to do this, whose foundation is in the dust, and who is crushed before the moth? Job iv. 19.

2. Moral. He is a subject utterly unqualified for the pure pleasures that kingdom affords, being universally corrupt, and subject to the government of sin and sense.

3. Judicial. He is disseized of, and separated from, this inheritance, by the sentence of Christ, the judge of quick and dead; which no power in heaven or earth can reverse; for he that liveth and was dead, carries the keys of hell and death at his girdle. Rev. i. 18.

An unregenerate person, as such, neither can, nor shall see the kingdom of heaven, so as to inherit it, if there be power enough in God and Christ to keep him out; for this Christ gives his word in pawn, which he will surely accomplish. Now there is a threefold kingdom made mention of in the holy scriptures.

1. A kingdom of God's providence, established upon the basis of God's uncontrollable power, and unsearchable wisdom. 1 Chron. xxix. 11. Jacob's God has the reins of government on his shoulders, he wields the eternal sceptre, and sits at the sacred helm.

2. The kingdom of God's grace in the church; built upon Christ, the golden foundation, the chief corner

stone; this kingdom is given to the Branch by God the Father, as the inspired evangelist testifies. Luke i. 32.

3. A kingdom of glory and blessedness: "Come ye blessed of my Father, inherit the kingdom prepared for you." Matt. xxv. 34. This last mentioned I take to be the kingdom designed by Jesus in the text, viz; that triumphant choir in which the saints and angels sing eternal hallelujahs to the everlasting King. Heaven is called a kingdom, because in it God rules his sons and subjects. God's kingdom is where he reigns: now he reigns in righteousness.

1 "Thy throne, God, is for ever and ever! a sceptre of righteousness is the sceptre of thy kingdom." Heb. i. 8. II. The asseveration. Verily, verily. This asseveration is a conspicuous confirmation of the truth of the proposition, tending clearly to manifest the great momentousness and importance of it. There are two things in the asseveration which serve to establish inviolably the veracity or truth of the proposition, viz: 1. The repetition of the particle "amen." 2. The dignity of the speaker. The word "amen," rendered "verily" in the text, is twofold, either prefixed or affixed; when it is prefixed, or put before a pro-position, it is the note of a certain and earnest affirmation, as in the words of our text, Verily, verily. When it is affixed? or subsequent to a proposition, it notes two things: either 1. The assent of the mind, will, affections, as at the conclusion of the creed and the Lord's prayer. Or 2. An asseveration, or certain affirmation, as the word amen, at the end of the Lord's prayer, signifies not only our assent to, but assurance of, the reality and certainty of the things therein contained. Now the repetition of this particle in our text, like the redoubling of Pharaoh's dream, (Gen. xli. 32,) shows us at once the undeniable certainty and great weight of the thing spoken of.

2. The dignity of the speaker: who is it that speaks thus? The blessed and holy Jesus, as our text informs us; which name some derive from *iemi*, a word that signifies to send, because the Lord Jesus is the bright angel, the faithful messenger of the everlasting covenant. Mai. iii. 1. Heb. iii. 2. Others, from *iao*, a word that signifies to heal, because the Lord Jesus was the true physician. Matt. ix. 12, Mark ii. 17. Basil and Cyril among the ancients are of this opinion.

But the angel explains the true derivation of it. "And thou shalt call his name Jesus, for he shall save his people from their sins." Matt. i. 21. And that not only typically, as Moses and Joshua, and others, hut really and truly. Nor 2. only temporally, as those before mentioned, just from bodily miseries, but from spiritual and eternal, from sin and death. Heb. ii. 14. 1 Cor. xv. 55–57. 1 John iii. 8. 3. Neither did he only free his people from misery, as Moses did Israel out of Egypt; no, but as his type Joshua led Israel into Canaan, so does the blessed Jesus, the antitype, introduce his people into a state of endless, uninterrupted, and unspeakably ravishing delight, in the imperial paradise, of which the earthly Canaan was but a dark figure. Now, I say the dignity of the person speaking in our text, gives great weight and confirmation to the truth spoken. Will he, who is truth itself, lie? Will he, who is the great prophet of his people, co-equal and co-eternal with his Father, the brightness of his glory, the express image of his person, (Heb. xiii. 4, 8,) deceive us? I say unto you: I, who am the Alpha and Omega, the first and the last: the King of kings, and Lord of lords, and Prince of the kings of the earth.

As to the third particular, the ground or occasion of the words of our text, implied in that phrase, "Jesus answered:" it is difficult to find out what were the words Nicodemus spake, to which Jesus gave answer; there is a diversity of opinions about it. Some think that Christ's words are a direct answer to those words of Nicodemus mentioned in the second verse, as if Christ had said. Thou lookest upon me as a prophet only, thou canst do no otherwise unless thou wert regenerated. Others think, and that more probably, that from the good opinion Nicodemus had of Christ, he asked the way to salvation, and that our text is an answer to that question.

From the words thus briefly explained, there arise these two doctrinal observations, the one implied, and the other expressed.

Observation I. That man from his very birth is depraved.

Observation II. That regeneration is absolutely necessary in order to obtain eternal salvation.

As to the first of these which is this. That man from his very birth is depraved.

The method I design to follow in prosecuting this doctrine is

1. To prove the truth of it.
2. Explain the nature of it.
3. To improve it. And,

1. I am to consider the truth of the doctrine. This is plain from the text, for if the first birth was not vitiated, what need would there be of a second? The royal prophet Isaiah upbraids Israel with this, "And was called a transgressor from the womb." Isa. xlviii. 8. The psalmist gives testimony to the same truth, (Psa. li. 5,) "I was shapen in sin," not only corrupted with sin as soon as born, but

before, even in our formation. Job confirms this in the fourteenth chapter of his book, verse 4, "Who can bring a clean thing out of an unclean? not one." Yea, the blessed Jesus makes this the ground of the necessity of a change in the seventh verse of our context, "That which is born of the flesh is flesh:" as if Christ should say, You need not wonder, Nicodemus, at my inculcation of the necessity of this inward change or new birth; because men are corrupted from their first birth. This original depravity is conveyed to all the sons of Adam by generation, unless prevented by a miracle, as in Christ. The sickness and death of infants are a plain and unanswerable proof of this; "For the wages of sin is death." Rom. vi. 23. Also the baptismal laver shows this hereditary contagion and infection. But,

2. I am to explain the nature of this depravity, which consists chiefly in these three things, viz:

1. In a privation of good.
2. In an antipathy to God.
3. In a propensity to evil.

1. Then, in every unregenerate soul there is a privation of all good. There is no spark or signature of that pristine, beautiful image engraven at first on the soul by God; no relics of man's primitive righteousness, neither in habit or in act, in inclination or motion, that is spiritually good; "In my flesh," i.e., in my nature considered as corrupted, "there dwells no good thing." Rom. vii. 18. The soul is deprived of its ancient ornaments and furniture; it is left poor without spiritual riches, blind without saving knowledge, naked without spiritual raiment. Rev. iii. 17. And,

2. There is an antipathy to God, his ways, his people, his image. "The carnal mind is enmity to God." Rom. viii. 7. This is evident from the speech and practice of wicked people, their embittered jeers, and satirical invectives against God's people. A Cain hated an Abel, and an Ishmael an Isaac, and an Esau a Jacob, and that because of their goodness. 1 John iii. 12. Now, this hellish spite is to be found in all natural, unregenerate people, till removed by the supernatural change, of which I design to speak afterwards. I now proceed to the,

3d Particular contained in this depravity, which is the propensity that is in all unconverted people to every evil. "Foolishness is bound in the heart of a child." Prov. xxii. 15. Indeed, there is not an equal propensity in all, to every sin; no, for some by reason of their natural temperament, manner of education, or custom, are inclined to one sin more than some others; yet all men by nature are virtually disposed to every sin; for we are prone to evil, as the sparks fly upward. Job v. 7. Every sin is formed in our nature; they want only time, opportunity, temptation, and the removal of restraining grace, to bring them forth into action.

Use. Hence we are informed 1, of man's miserable and deplorable state by nature, which affords us sufficient matter for the deepest humiliation, and most doleful lamentation. It is on this account that we are rendered obnoxious to the vindictive justice of a terrible and holy God. Eph. ii. 3. This is it, that makes our lives so corrupted, and all our religious services so defective and depraved.

2. This informs us of the absolute necessity of a universal change, of heart as well as practice, in order to obtain fellowship and communion with a holy sin-hating God here, (1 John i. 6,) or the more full enjoyment of him in the life to come. How can there be a sweet communion, and full enjoyment, without love? And how can there be love without likeness? And pray what likeness or resemblance is there between an infinitely pure God, and an unconverted sinner, who is a very mass of pollution and defilement? How can that God who is glorious in holiness, fix his complacential love upon that which is the object of his eternal abhorrence? And how can an unrenewed sinner, who is filled with enmity against God, (Rom. viii. 7,) fix his highest love upon one he hates with an implacable hatred? All which considered, complexly shows us the absolute necessity of a universal change; which naturally leads me to the second observation, which is,

That regeneration is absolutely necessary in order to obtain eternal salvation.

This is evident from the words of our text. Except a man be born again, he cannot see the kingdom of God. Also from Gal. vi. 15; "For in Christ Jesus neither circumcision nor uncircumcision avails any thing, but a new creature. Therefore if any man be in Christ Jesus, he is a new creature; old things are passed away, and all things are become new." "Without holiness, no man shall see the Lord." Heb. xii. 14. "And there shall in no wise enter into it, any thing that defileth, neither whatsoever worketh abomination, or maketh a lie, but they which are written in the Lamb's book of life." Rev. xxi. 27.

In prosecuting this doctrine, I shall endeavour to observe the following method.

I. Show negatively what regeneration is not.
II. Positively show what it is
III. Propose those reasons that urge the necessity of it.
IV. Improve it.

As to the first proposed, which was to show what regeneration is not. And,

1. It is not what Nicodemus grossly conceived, a re-entry into the womb of our mother. It is surprising that a man of so polite literature as we have reason to believe Nicodemus was: a master, a teacher in Israel; acquainted with the law and word of God, where doubtless he had read frequently such passages as those, (Ezek. xxxvi. 26,) should have such gross conceptions of this work of God; but hereby are these sayings of God verified, (1 Cor. i. 21, & ii. 14,) "For in the wisdom of God the world by wisdom knew not God; but the natural man receiveth not the things of the Spirit of God, for they are foolishness unto him; neither can he know them, because they are spiritually discerned." Such is the inherent hereditary contagion of our apostatized nature, that were we born a thousand times in a natural way, it would not remedy that malady. This the blessed and holy Jesus plainly and clearly confirms in the sixth verse of our context, That which is born of the flesh, is flesh, i.e., it is corrupted and contaminated.

Hence it appears to be a prodigy of incomparable folly for any to boast of, and glory in, the grandeur of their descent and lineage, seeing that whatsoever is born of the flesh is flesh, and without outward cultivation, and inward renovation, must be the subjects of indelible misery. Neither,

2. Is regeneration a change of the essence, or being of the soul (*hæc semper eadem physicè manet*): the soul is not made new as to its being or substance (*aut quoad esse physicum*,) other ways a new soul must be infused, which we read not of; but as to its qualities (*aut quoad esse morale*), new qualities or principles of action are infused into the soul by God, by which it is inclined and swayed after another manner, and to another scope, than formerly. Some do talk strangely of this affair, that the substance of the soul is changed. It is true, the scripture calls this gracious change a participation of the divine nature. 2 Pet. i. 4. But this is only to show 1. the reality and fixedness of this work of grace, that it is no notion or fancy, but a solid reality; 2. the resemblance it bears to the divine perfections. Such persons are renewed after God's image, in knowledge, righteousness and holiness; they have a divine temper and disposition of soul; the principal bias of their hearts is towards God and his service. But though they are thus born after God, and of God, yet they are not thereby made God. That which is by way of substance or essence in him, is only by way of accident in us. Neither,

3. Doth it consist in an outward profession of Christ or his ways. The foolish virgins had large lamps, but no oil. Matt. XXV. A man may be reformed from Paganism or Popery to the profession of true Christianity, and yet be a stranger to this work of God. Nor

4. In the enjoyment of outward privileges, such as baptism, the Lord's Supper, and others of the like nature. The Jews of old depended upon these outward privileges and prerogatives. Jer. vii. 4. Rom. x. 3. And so do many of the gospelized world now; but the divinely inspired Jeremiah pungently inculcates the invalidity of outward ordinances, without the thing signified by them, to obtain bliss and glory; therefore, he puts the circumcised Jews, who were uncircumcised in heart, in a parallel case with Edom, Ammon, and Moab, heathenish nations. Jer. ix. 25. Yea, Christ himself had a controversy with the Jews upon the same account; he endeavoured to destroy their fond hopes of heaven, grounded upon their outward privileges, and for his plain dealing he received abusive treatment. John viii. The apostle Paul very plainly showeth the insufficiency of these things without an inward renovation. Gal. vi. 15. Neither,

5. Doth it consist in an external conformity to the law of God: for this is something inward, the workmanship of God in the heart. A man may pray, read, hear outwardly, keep the Sabbath, be faithful to his word, and just in his dealings, and yet be a stranger to this work of God in the soul: for such were some of the Pharisees of old. Phil. iii. 6. Mark x. 20. And yet our ascended Lord and Saviour positively avers, that unless our righteousness exceed the righteousness of the Scribes and Pharisees, we shall in no wise enter into the kingdom of heaven. Matt. v. 20. Nor

6. In a restraint of the old man. God restrains many whom he never renews. So he did Abimelech, a heathen. Gen, XX. 6. One that is not renewed may avoid gross sins, through fear, shame, or the absence of opportunities and temptations, or through the influence of nature's light, the precepts of morality, the doctrines of the gospel, and the civil laws of the land. The apostle Peter speaks of some that had escaped the pollutions of the world through the knowledge of the Lord Christ, and yet were again entangled in them. 2 Pet. ii. 20–22. Restraining grace keeps only from the outward acts of sin, through slavish fear, or some selfish motives; but saving grace subdues sin at the root, and raises an irreconcilable hatred in the soul against it. 2 Cor. vii. 11. Nor,

7. In common gifts or motions of the Holy Spirit, which are without distinction conferred on both the elect and reprobate. It is not a gift of prayer, tongues, utter-

ance, or a faculty of unfolding scripture difficulties. Judas had all or most of these, yet was he not born again, but a son of perdition. John xvii. 12. "It is not with men as with trees," as one observes, "for every bud, blossom, or leaf, argues some life in the tree; but every ability to preach or to pray, does not prove this supernatural life in us." Neither does it consist in the common motions of the Holy Spirit, such as some sight of sin, some grief for it, and wishes after amendment. Personal afflictions, a prospect of eternity in sickness, or other such alarming occurrences may cause such like workings. Herod delighted to hear John the Baptist. Mark vi. 20. Felix trembled when he heard Paul preach. Acts xxiv. 25. And Agrippa was almost persuaded; *en oligo*, which compared with Paul's answer, ver. 29, Acts xxvi. 28, may be justly rendered "all to a little." And even wicked Balaam could wish for a happy death, though he did not so well relish a holy life. "Let me die the death of the righteous, and let my last end be like his." Num. xxiii. 10. 2 Pet. ii. 15. Nor,

8. Does regeneration consist in a partial change of the soul, or of some of its faculties only; but it is a total change of the soul in all its powers. There may be strange changes in some of the faculties, and yet no true conversion to God; as particularly, 1. There may be great light and knowledge of divine truths, with an assent to, and persuasion of, their veracity, in the mind. "And though I have the gift of prophecy, and understand all mysteries, and all knowledge; and though I have all faith, so that I could remove mountains, and have no charity (or love, for so the word agape signifies), I am nothing." 1 Cor. xiii. 2. Also, "For it is impossible for those who were once enlightened," Heb. vi. 4. Rom. ii. 17, 18. Here we see the understanding, the directive power, may be so illuminated by the Spirit of God, as to perceive divine truths with a more clear and affecting view than before, without a saving change. Also the will, which is a cardinal faculty of man's soul, may be much bowed, and almost persuaded in some of the unregenerate. Acts xxvi. 28. Again, the conscience, another power, or as some say, a reflex act of the mind, may be much awakened by the terror of God upon the account of sin. Gen. iv. 13, 14. Acts xxiv. 25. Also the passions may be in some measure changed in the unregenerate: they may have great sorrow for sin. 1 Kings xxi. 27. Matt, xxvii. 4, 5; joy and delight from divine objects; Heb. vi. 4; Matt, xiii. 20; and in attendance upon divine ordinances; John v. 35. Isa. lviii. 2; desires after Christ; Mai. iii. 2. John vi. 34; after grace; Matt. xxv. 8; after heaven; Num. xxiii. 10; some hatred against sin; Rom. ii. 22. 2 Kings x. 26–28; some purposes to forsake it; Num. xxii. 17, 18; some love to God; Jer. ii. 2. Deut. ix. 6, 24; compared with Christ; Matt. x. 37; to the people of God in general; this, the parable of the wise and foolish virgins proves; Matt, xxv; for it is probable that the foolish would not have associated and dwelt with the wise so as they did, unless they had loved them; Gal. iv. 7; to faithful, soul-searching ministers in particular; Mark vi. 20; some fear of God; James ii. 19; Jonah i. 10, 16; some zeal for God; 2 Kings x. 6. Phil. 3, 6. Rom. X. 2; some faith in God; Acts viii. 13. Job ii. 23, 24; some dependence and reliance upon God; Mic. iii. 11. 2 Chron. xiii. 5–13 & 18, compared with Deut. ix. 6, 24 & 1 Kings xv. 3; some confident persuasion of their interest in his special favour and friendship; Matt. xxv. 7, 11. Job viii. 38. 2 Chron. xiii. 10. Num. xxii. 18. All these things I have mentioned under this head, people may have, and yet want regenerating grace, and so be damned at last. But I proceed to consider the 2d thing proposed, which was to show positively what regeneration is. And,

I. More generally, it may be said to be a restoration of God's defaced image in man, to some degree of its primitive beauty and lustre. Our first parents were made after God's image, in knowledge, righteousness and true holiness, with dominion over the creatures. Ecc. vii. 29. Gen. i. 27. Psa. viii. 5. This image of God consisted in a universal rectitude of the whole soul, with all its faculties, powers and affections; the understanding being the guide and governor of the soul's faculties, had clear perceptions of the mind and will of God; the will was subject to the understanding's directions, having an inherent inclination to will that which the mind by its native light showed to be good. The whole train of passions freely followed the guidance of these superior powers, without the least reluctance. Thus there was a universal harmony at first among all the soul's faculties established by the God of order, but sin has introduced a confusion and chaos among these faculties, it has darkened the understanding, rendered the will obstinate, and misplaced the affections upon diametrically opposite objects, hardened the heart, stupefied the conscience. Now the blind will, which was before a subject, usurps the empire, and hurries the other powers to a compliance with its inordinate dictates. Now regeneration is a renewing that gracious image of God in us, which we have lost; for by it, the blind understanding is in some measure enlightened; Acts xxvi. 18; the stony heart mollified; Ezek. xxxvi. 26; the disordered affections rectified and fixed upon the most suitable and noble objects, God himself as their chief good and last end. But more particularly,

A law work generally precedes this change; hence the law is said to be a schoolmaster to lead us to Christ; Gal. iii. 24; which I apprehend is wrought in the following manner.

1. There is a discovery of sin, which the Lord effects by the law and by the Spirit. "I had not known sin, but by the law." Rom. vii. 7. Before this, Christless sinners are secure, like Peter sleeping in his chains. Acts xii. 6. The Spirit of God concurs with the law. This is one of his first works with unconverted sinners; as is evident from Job xvi. 8. Before he convinces them of righteousness, he convinces them of sin; their eyes are opened. Acts xxvi. 18. Now they see sin in its loathsome nature, deplorable circumstances, and dreadful consequences; they begin to see the holiness of God, the spiritual latitude of his law, and their own corrupt nature; then are they apt to cry out, Who can stand before this great and dreadful God? Now, though this discovery of sin begins at a particular evil, as with the Jews, (Acts ii. 37,) yet it proceeds to more; as Ezekiel was led to divers parts of the temple to see greater and greater abominations. Ezek. viii. 6–13.

2. There is an application of the merit of sin. God convinces the sinner that all the threatenings belong to him; yea, he particularly applies them to himself, as Nathan his parabolical discourse to David, (2 Sam. xii. 7,) I am the man that these curses are directed against. He hears his condemnation sounded by the trumpet of the word; he sees and feels that he is in the utmost distress, environed with dangers, and can at present see no way of escape opened. Luke xv. 17. He is in the case of the afflicted, pursued Israelites at the Red Sea. Ex. xiv. 14, 15. This is that spirit of bondage to fear, which ordinarily precedes the spirit of adoption. Rom. viii. 15.

3. Compunction, or sharp anguish for sin. The sight of sin and wrath wounds the soul, as though it were stabbed with a sword. Acts ii. 37. They have such acute pains as if a sharp spear lanced their hearts. It is elsewhere called the "rending of the heart." Joel ii. 14. When we are greatly grieved in soul for sin, so that it even cuts us to the heart to think how we have dishonoured God, and disparaged ourselves by it; when we conceive an aversion to sin, and earnestly desire and endeavour to get clear of the principles of it, and never to return to the practice of it, then we rend our hearts for it, and then will God rend the heavens, and come down to us with mercy. Also, this compunction I am treating of is called breaking up of the fallow ground. "Break up your fallow ground, and sow not among thorns;" (Jer. iv. 3.) which represents both the necessity and difficulty of it. "An unconvinced heart," says one, "is like fallow ground, untilled, unfenced, unfruitful of any thing besides thorns, which is the natural produce of the soil; which we are bound to get ploughed up by the word of God, (Heb. iv. 12,) otherwise they will choke our attempts, and blast our hopes," Hos. X. 11. It is also compared to a taking away the fore-skin of the heart. "Circumcise yourselves to the Lord, and take away the fore-skins of your heart, ye men of Judah, and inhabitants of Jerusalem: lest my fury come forth like fire, and burn that none can quench it, because of the evil of your doings;" (Jer. iv. 4;) {. e., saith Mr. Poole, "take away that brawniness and obstinacy that is upon your hearts, having to do with God that hath respect unto the heart, (Deut. X. 16. Ezek. xliv. 9. Acts vii. 51,) lest you proceed so far in your obstinacy, that I will not be appeased." Jer. xxi. 12. Amos v. 6.

4. Enquiry. When the apostle Peter's preaching, accompanied with divine energy, had wounded the Jews, this was the necessary effect of it, "What shall we do?" Acts ii. 37.

Thus I thought it necessary, to prevent mistakes, to speak first of that which is previous and preparatory to this change. Now I come to speak somewhat briefly of the change itself in the several faculties of man's soul. And,

1. The understanding is renewed in its several powers or acts; a light from on high shines into it, whereby its natural darkness is in some measure dissipated, so that it hath new apprehensions of things. As natural light was one of the first things produced in the old creation, "And God said, Let there be light, and there was light;" (Gen. i. 3;) so spiritual light is one of the first in the new. 2 Cor. iv. 6. Formerly, the face of Christ was veiled from the soul, as the face of Moses from the Israelites; but now he sees something of his peerless beauty, and transcendent excellency. Christ is to him as the apple tree among the trees of the woods, as the rose of Sharon, and the lily of the valley. Cant. ii. 1–3. His very name is as fragrant ointment poured forth, and aromatic spices. Cant. i. 3. All other enjoyments are as dross in comparison of him, in the enlightened sinner's esteem. Phil. iii. 8. Now he sees the loathsome and abominable nature of sin. Rom. vii. 13. Now he sees, and experience tells him, that there is no true solace, contentment, or satisfaction to be had in any sublunary trifles; he sees that such earthly enjoyments are empty of solid good, transient, unsatisfying, and bewitching; contrary to his former apprehension. Isa. lv. 2. 1 Cor. vii. 31. Psa. vi. 1 Tim. vi. 9, 10. They can find no more nourishment in them for their hungering souls, than a starving man would do in gravel-stones,

wind, husks, ashes. Prov. xx. 17. Hos. xii. 1. Luke xv. 16. Isa. xliv. 20. That heart-holiness, and circumspection of life, which he was apt formerly to ridicule and deride, as needless preciseness, affected and foolish singularity, (Cant. v. 9. 1 Pet. iv. 4,) he sees not only necessary, but desirable and lovely. Cant. vi. 1. Zech. viii. 23. Mai. iii. 16, 17. Now he sees clearly that that good heart, those good words, good deeds, good meanings, for which he thought God would spare and reward him, deserve nothing less than the revengeful strokes of God's direful justice. Isa. lxiv. 6. Phil. iii. 7.

2. He has a new assent, his understanding being enlightened to perceive the precious truths of Christ; he assents to them with a kind of plerophory, in a lively, sensible manner. Luke i. 1. His assent is not grounded upon opinion, conjecture, or historical credit, as formerly; and therefore, is not light and superficial, but firm and real. The natural atheism of his heart is in some measure cured, so that he does not so staggeringly assent to divine truths as before.

3. His judgment is changed. Formerly it was an absurd paradox to him, if he had all the honours, profits, and pleasures his heart could desire, that he should not be happy then; but now he judges by experience, that these things can no more satisfy an enlightened soul, than an adamant stone, or a puff of wind, would satisfy a hungry person. Formerly he used to think that the new birth was but a fancy, a whim, a fiction, introduced by some hypocondriac, silly, precise people, that imposed upon themselves and others, with dreams and notions, the effects of melancholy blood, a sickly constitution, or a disordered brain; but now he sees and feels an absolute necessity of it, and that he must be damned unless he obtains it, according to the solemn, redoubled asseveration of the Lord Christ, in our text. In short, he used to judge of things by their appearance, but now he judges of them according to what they are in reality.

4. His estimate of things is changed. He was wont to think highly of the world and the things of it, however contrarily he might speak, these had the throne of his heart; but now he prefers even the reproach of Christ before them. Heb. xi. 26. Thus his estimate is changed in respect of honours, pleasures, companions, gifts, parts, privileges, performances, which would take up more time than can be well spared at present to explain and illustrate. I proceed therefore to another particular.

5. His purposes are changed, he has vastly different designs from those he was wont to entertain and indulge before his new birth. While he was in a state of security, his principal scope was to get the world, if possible; to this end, he would be frequently, almost continually, framing the most artful and suitable schemes, and if these did not answer as he would have them, then perhaps his sleep would be broken, and his thoughts disturbed, and he put upon a rack of impatient pain. In short, his purposes were for sin and self, but now they are for God and his soul, now he strives as much daily to get his heart and affections deadened to the world, as he did before to secure and advance his interest in it. Now his anxious mind is often contriving, what measures he should take to glorify the blessed God, to subdue abominable sin, and advance the despised interest of his dear Lord Jesus.

6. His reasonings are changed. He was wont in his state of sin and security, to argue for sin and the world, against Christ and holiness; from the mercy and goodness of God, to liberty (so called, but it is really the basest bondage), in sinning against him, but now it is the greatest motive to holiness, and circumspection.

7. The will is changed. It has got a new bias and centre of its actings; in his unconverted state, himself or the world was the centre, in reality (notwithstanding his fair and false flams and flourishes of empty talk to the contrary), to which he moved, for which he acted with a furious natural proneness. Psa. iv. 6. 2 Tim. iii, 2. But now God in Christ is the centre to which all his actions, whether natural, civil, or sacred, do bend and terminate.

He aims at God's glory in all his actions universally, and singly? the inclinations of his will bend towards God freely from an inward and powerful principle of life. 1 Cor. x. 31. Grace is in him as a well of water springing up to eternal life. John iv. 14. His will has an unconstrained motion. Some, under the views of a vast eternity, or some afflictive dispensation, have weak motions of heart towards God. Psa. lxxviii. 34. But when the prospect of danger is removed, the motions cease, (Psa. lxxviii. 57,) like the motion of a clock when the spring is removed; but the motions of a believer's heart are constant, even when outward enforcements are taken away, (Psa. cxix. 112,) because they flow from an inward and vital cause.

Furthermore, his will has new enjoyments. In his state of unregeneracy, his life was only a vexatious wandering from vanity to vanity; all the contentment he had, was in some worldly accommodations, or outward performances, Psa. xlvi. Amos. vi. 1, 3–6. Rom. x. 3. But now they are as husks to him, he cannot be satisfied without the children's bread. Psa. cxix. 37. & cvi. 4. It was an observable saying of Augustine, "*Tu fecisti eor nostrum, et irrequietum est donec ad te revertatur,*" i.e., "Thou hast made our heart, and it is restless till it returns to thee." The sinner in his security would be contented with the husk and shell of duties, but now nothing will satisfy him but the presence of Jesus in them; a sight of the king's face, a sense of his special love. But the cardinal acts of the will are assent and dissent, these are the very hinges upon which it exerts its receptive and exclusive faculties, suitable to its love or dislike to the object proposed. John I. 12 & V. 40. When Christ is offered to the soul appended to the pole of the gospel, on his own terms of self denial, and taking up the cross, the new-born person is willing to want all, that he may have Him, to lose all, that he may gain Him. 8. The affections of the soul are changed, such as desire, delight, fear, hatred, joy, and love. New-born persons have frequent and vehement desires after communion with, and conformity to, God in Christ here, and the full enjoyment of him hereafter, arising from a sight of his beauty and excellency. "As the hart panteth after the water brooks, so panteth my soul after thee, God. My soul thirsteth for God, for the living God; when shall I come and appear before God?" Psa. xlii. 1, 2. "My flesh longeth for thee in a dry and thirsty land where no water is; to see thy power and thy glory—because thy loving kindness is better than life—my soul followeth hard after thee." Psa. lxiii. 1–3, 8. "How amiable are thy tabernacles, Lord of hosts! My soul longeth, yea, even fainteth for the courts of the Lord: my heart and my flesh crieth out for the living God." Psa. lxxxiv. 1, 2. "Let him kiss me with the kisses of his mouth: for thy love is better than wine." Cant. i. 2. "Whom have I in heaven but thee? and there is none upon earth that I desire besides thee." Psa. lxxiii. 25. "that my ways were directed to keep thy statutes! I have longed for thy salvation, Lord, and thy law is my delight." Psa. cxix. 5, 174. "He which testifieth these things saith, Surely I come quickly. Amen, even so, come Lord Jesus." Rev. xxii. 20. And as their desires are after Christ, so their delight is in him. "The king hath brought me into his chambers: we will be glad and rejoice in thee, we will remember thy love more than wine." Cant. i. 4. "A bundle of myrrh is my well beloved unto me; he shall lie all night betwixt my breasts." Cant. i. 13. "As the apple tree among the trees of the wood, so is my beloved among the sons. I sat down under his shadow with great delight, and his fruit was sweet to my taste." Cant. ii. 3. "His mouth is most sweet; {i.e., the communications of his love by his word are most delightful,) yea, he is altogether lovely. This is my beloved, and this is my friend, daughters of Jerusalem." Cant. v. 16. And as they delight in him, so they fear to offend him, and that even in the least things. 1 Thess. v. 22. They are apt to cry out when they are tempted, as Joseph, "How shall I do this great wickedness and sin against God?" Gen. xxxix. 9. They see the baseness and feel the bitterness of sin, and, therefore, fear it. Lam. iii. Having in remembrance the wormwood and the gall, they feel a sense of the divine goodness, and, therefore, fear sinning against it. "Afterward shall the children of Israel return, and seek the Lord their God, and shall fear the Lord and his goodness in the latter days." Hos. iii. 5. Rom. ii. 4. And as they fear sin, so they hate it universally and irreconcilably, (Psa. cxix. 104,) and cannot at any time fall in love with it as formerly. 1 John iii. 3–10. Again, the objects of their love are changed. God's people, his laws, his image, his ordinances are the objects to which their affections freely flow. Now, the new born person loves sincerely and fervently those whom he once despised, and pities those whom he once loved and admired, and disdains their society, their scoffs and threatenings, as well as their destructive gains, and perishing, insipid pleasures. Psa. xv. 4 & cxix. 115. 2 Kings iii. 14. Psa. ii. 1, 4 & lii. 6, 7. Isa. xxxiii. 15. Psa. cxli. 4. Heb. xi. 24. Now he sees that the people of God are the most excellent persons on earth, as much preferable to others as jewels, the stones of a crown, refined gold, a royal diadem, are to common pebbles, dross, and rubbish. Mai. iii. 17. Zech. ix. 16. Lam. iv. 2. Isa. lxii. 3. Psa. xvi. 3. As much excelling others, as wheat does chaff (Matt. xiii. 30. Psa. i. 4); light, darkness (Matt. v. 14. Eph. v. 8); cedars and myrtle trees, the tares and thorns. Psa. xcii. 12. Isa. lv. 13. Matt. xiii. 38. Cant, ii. 2. As much as the most potent kings, the basest slaves. Rev. i. 6. Acts viii. 23. Isa. lxi. 1. As much as lambs and doves are preferable in their qualities to goats, swine, dogs, and foxes (Hos. iv. 14. Matt. X. 16 & XXV. 33 & vii. 6. 2 Pet. ii. 22. Luke xiii. 32); and vipers. Matt. iii. 7. Therefore, the new born person resorts to God's people, covets their company, (which he before shunned,) that with them he may seek Jesus. Acts iv. 23. Cant. i. 7 & vi, 1. When the blinded jailor came to have his eyes opened, he soon washed the wounds he had made before by many and cruel stripes. Acts xvi. 23, 33. Their love is fixed on God in Jesus, as their highest good and last end, as their complete, satisfying and everlasting portion; (Lam. iii. 24. Psa. xvi. 5. & lxxiii. 26); which shows it in lively, warm, vigorous actings, so that the whole soul feels sometimes the sweet pains, and refreshful qualms of a love-sickness after Christ. Cant. v. 8. All the waters of affliction cannot quench this love, but make it burn more brightly, as oil cast into the fire. "Set me as a seal upon thy heart, as a seal upon thine arm: for love is strong as death." Cant. viii. 6. Their sorrow is also changed as to its objects; they were wont, in their carnal and secure state, to mourn principally about worldly losses and disappointments, (Psa. iv. 6. 2 Cor. vii. 10,) that either they could not amass and obtain, or retain such a quantity of worldly pelf, as their greedy desires longed for; or their trouble principally centred upon the loss of their relations or friends, or their credit and worldly comfort. Gen. xxvii. 38. 1 Sam. xv. 30. But now they mourn chiefly over their sins against God, (Psa. li. 4,) that they are so many, so heinous, that they have continued in sin so long; (Rom. vi. 21); that they are so inwardly and universally corrupted by it; (Rom. vii. 21); and they do not only grieve that they themselves have sinned against such a good God, but that others, also, do grievously reproach the Almighty, and affront his majesty, by contemning his authority, profaning his sacred name, violating his sabbath, slighting his word and ordinances, opposing his truths, and abusing his people. Ezek. ix. 4. 2 Pet. ii. 7, 8. Psa. cxix. 136. Lam. iv. 2. They also mourn an absent God! The withdrawing of his comfortable presence from them distresses their spirits. Psa. xlii. 5. Cant. iii. 1–3. & v. 6, 8. The numerous crowds of wicked people, the smallness of the number of those that are truly godly, and the little success of the gospel of Christ, affords matter of great sorrow to new born persons. Matt. vii. 13 & xx. 16 & xxii. 14. Nahum vii. 1, 2. Psa. iii. 1. Isa. liii. 1.

9. The conscience is changed. As before it was not able to perform its offices, or functions, viz: to apply, convince, or tremble at the word, but now, when the soul feels the regenerating influences of the Holy Spirit, what a tender sense fills the renewed conscience! For what small things will it smite, rebuke and check the sinner! How strongly will it bind to duty, and bar against sin! The consciences of the most of ungodly people are large, secure, and mostly silent; if it be not when they commit gross and notorious crimes. Tit. i. 15. But the consciences of regenerate persons, being purged from dead works, (Heb. ix. 14,) do wake and rebuke sharply for small offences, (1 Sam. xxiv. 5,) and put the sinner into distress and anguish. Gen. xliii. 21. Now it is the continued labour of the new born person to get and keep a good conscience. 2 Cor. i. 12. Acts xxiv. 16.

10. The memory; now it is more apt to embrace and retain divine things than formerly. Cant. i. 4. Psa. ciii. 18 & cxix. 11. The regenerate person endeavours to lay up the sayings of Jesus in the cabinet of his memory. Matt. xxvi. 75. I confess that regenerating grace does not change the natural imperfections of the human constitution, only the moral. If a person has naturally a weak memory, it cannot be reasonably expected that grace will strengthen the natural faculty, for its design is not to heal the body but the soul, it only turns the vein of the thoughts and affections on divine subjects, and helps to perceive better, fundamental truths, (1 John ii. 20, 27,) and makes a person the more desirous to retain them, but it does not enlarge or strengthen the faculty itself ordinarily; a person may be a strong Christian, have an affectionate heart, and a holy humble practice, and yet have but a weak memory; but, in the meantime, it is surely the practice of new-born persons to pore much upon divine things. Psa. i. 2 & civ. 34 & cxix. 97, 99. Therefore when they forget precious truths they have heard explained, (their affections being fixed upon them,) they are grieved. But,

11. Their conversation is changed. They were wont to be like moles grovelling in the earth, now their mind and conversation are in heaven; Phil. iii. 20. Heb. xiii. 14; they are ashamed and blush at their former conversation. Rom. vi. 21. They have changed their former masters, sin, Satan, and the world, and broken their detestable league with them and death. Rom. vi. 14, 16–23. Isa. xxviii. 15, 18. "And they that are Christ's have crucified the flesh, with the affections and lusts." Gal. v. 24. The new born person maintains a continual conflict with sin. Gal. V. 17. Rom. vii. 23. Now he does not only endeavour to restrain the outward act, but to crucify the root of his inward corruption. Psa. li. Not only to cut off some branches, but all; even that sin which has the strongest seat in his constitution. Psa. xviii. 23. He endeavours to repress the first motions of sin, and to flee the appearance of evil, being diffident of his own strength, and afraid to offend his God. 1 Thess. v. 22.

But I proceed to the third thing proposed.

III. To offer reasons urging the necessity of regeneration. And

1. The universal corruption of our nature shows the indispensable necessity of renewing grace, as in the sixth verse of our context. "For without holiness no man shall see the Lord." Heb. xii. 14. Rom. viii. 13. Is it reasonable to suppose that such a holy God as Jehovah is, who cannot look on sin but with abhorrence, should receive such polluted wretches as unconverted sinners are, into his complacential embraces?

2. Because while unconverted the law condemns us; Gal. iii. 10. Rom. iii. 19; which sentence cannot be removed any other ways but by faith in Christ (Mark xvi.

16. John iii. 18), which no unconverted person has; for if he had, it would change his heart and practice. Gal. v. 6. 2 Thess. i. 11. James ii. 14. He may, indeed, have a historical or temporary faith, but that will not do for salvation. James ii. 19, 20.

3. Because of the stability and firmness of God's word. He who cannot lie hath spoken it, and heaven and earth may, and shall pass away, but not one tittle that God hath spoken, shall pass away unaccomplished. Matt. xxiv. 35. Therefore regeneration is necessary to salvation.

4. The consideration of the nature of the happiness of heaven, with the respect that regeneration hath to it, plainly manifests the necessity of it. Surely the nature of future happiness is pure and spiritual, consisting in the vision and fruition of a holy God, who is a Spirit, (1 Cor. xiii. 12,) and in the society and social worship of saints and angels, and such pleasures and employments as the beauty of the objects and other circumstances of the place, may be supposed to imply. Now what suitableness is there between a carnal, unrenewed mind, and the spiritual and pure pleasures of heaven? Does not pleasure spring from the suitableness between the object and the faculty? What pleasure then can be expected by the unregenerate in heaven itself, if they were carried there in their present condition (though they may be sure, in the meantime, that while such, they will never have the trial. Rev. xxi. 27 & xxii. 15)? There is such a discord between their present dispositions and the temper, and entertainments, and employments of heaven, for these are holy and spiritual, but they are carnal and sensual. This Dr. Scott expresses beautifully, "For alas (if we consider the matter rightly), how could souls of their relish and complexion find a proper employment for themselves in the regions of bliss? There are no wanton amours among those heavenly lovers; no rivers of wine, among their rivers of pleasure, to gratify their boundless sensuality; no parasite to flatter their lofty pride; no miseries to feed their meagre envy; no mischiefs to tickle their devilish revenge; but all the felicities with which that state abounds (viz: praise, love, contemplation), are such that they would loath and nauseate them, as too pure and refined for their depraved appetites; and not improbably (if they had their own option), desire to fly to hell for shelter, to spirits of their own depravity, rather than stay to be tormented in a heaven so incongruous to their nature." So that if these men would be happy, they must either find out a new heaven, or get new hearts.

Bishop Beveridge expresses himself thus upon this head: "Supposing it should please God to take us all up immediately into the highest heavens, and there place us around our blessed Saviour; all such as are real saints among us, as love God above all things, and have prepared their minds for spiritual enjoyments, how glad would they be to see their Redeemer, shining in all his glory! How suddenly would they strike up with the choir of heaven, in singing the praises of Him that brought them thither! What infinite pleasure would they take in the place, employment, company, and every thing they see there! But as for others who are still in their sins, and mind only earthly things, how sad and disconsolate would they be! They would wonder to see the saints so pleasant and joyful; for, as for their parts, they would see nothing there to take delight in; in the midst of light they would be still in darkness, and in sorrow in the midst of joys, they would not hear the heavenly music, or if they did, it would sound harsh, and be all discords to them; they could not taste these spiritual dainties, or if they did, they could not relish or find any sweetness in them; they could not see the face of God, or if they did, they would not be pleased, but terrified and confounded at it; and all this for the want of a true principle of grace and holiness, without which a blind man may as well delight in pictures, the deaf man in music, or a brute beast in metaphysics, as men of such tempers either in heaven, or God himself."

Again, regeneration hath such a relation to our salvation, that it is indeed a part and beginning of it. *Gratia, est aurora gloriae*, grace is the very dawn of glory, differing only in degree and duration from the happiness of heaven. "The truth is," saith Stanhope, "God in his wisdom hath so ordered the matter, so admirably contrived our nature and our duty, that virtue and happiness, grace and glory, are one and the same thing, differing only in the circumstances and several prospects we view them under. The good man begins his heaven upon earth, and finishes there what is imperfect here; for the more he masters his sensual appetites, and gets above the world, the more he is spiritualized, and made meet to be a partaker with the saints in light."

Pray consider seriously that precious, but awful place of holy scripture, Gal. vi. 15. It is observable here, that the apostle was speaking of some who desired to make a fair show in the flesh, and, therefore, urged the necessity of circumcision, whom the apostle informed and assured that in Christ Jesus neither circumcision nor uncircumcision availed anything, i.e., to salvation, but the new creature. Circumcision was certainly an ordinance of God's own appointment, a seal of the covenant between

God and his people, (Rom. iv, 11,) a badge of distinction between them and the infidel nations, (Rom. iii. 2,) a sign of their original pravity, and of the necessity of inward sanctity. Jer. iv. 4. Col. ii. 13. Yet the apostle informs those who thought they were bound to observe it, that without an internal change, these supposed privileges would avail nothing, and by a parity of reason, (as Dr. Edwards justly observes,) "he must be interpreted to speak to us, that our sacramental washing in baptism, our spiritual gifts and endowments, our profound knowledge and learning, our observation of the ordinances of Christ, and our outward acts of religious worship, will all avail us nothing, unless we have a new principle implanted in us, such as influences our lives and produces evangelical obedience." But I proceed to the,

IVth thing proposed, which was to improve the doctrine. And,

Use 1. It informs us that the way to be made a member of the invisible church is by regeneration; "For there shall in no wise enter into it any thing that defileth, neither whatsoever worketh abomination, or maketh a lie; but they which are written in the Lamb's book of life." Rev. xxi. 27.

2. It informs us of the love of God in revealing that way to us (Hos. viii. 12); which should strike our admiration and awake our gratitude.

3. It informs us of the love of Christ in purchasing, after such a painful manner, that life for his people, to which this way leads. "For ye know the grace of our Lord Jesus Christ, that though he was rich, yet for our sakes he became poor, that ye through his poverty might be rich." 2 Cor. viii. 9. "Who hath abolished death and hath brought life and immortality to light through the gospel." 2 Tim. i. 10. That having your affections dead to, and weaned from, all enjoyments here, "your life may be hid with Christ in God; that when he who is your life appears, you may appear with him." Col. iii. 4.

4. It informs us of the emptiness and insufficiency of all outward and legal performances to obtain an actual interest in the purchased happiness, without good principles of action, such as a new heart, and transcendent love to the divine majesty. "For a good tree bringeth not forth corrupt fruit: neither doth a corrupt tree bring forth good fruit." Luke vi. 43. Therefore, according to the words of Jesus, "If you would have the fruit good, you must make the tree good." Matt. xii. 33. For God is a Spirit, and, therefore, will not accept of, or be pleased with, any worship but that which is agreeable to his nature. John iv. 24.

Use 2. Of examination. Now that you may know your present state and condition, I shall propose some characters of regeneration.

Now, the first property of regeneration is divine life. As natural life is the natural product of generation, so is a spiritual life, of regeneration. Gal. ii. 20. 2 Cor. iv. 10. Now, this divine life has these following properties, by which it may be known, analogous or agreeable to the properties of a natural life.

1. Food. Without this a natural life would soon expire. Psa. civ. 29. Thus it is with the spiritual, "As new born babes desire the sincere milk of the word." 1 Pet. ii. 2. Some render the original words (*logicon gala*) rational milk, such as is fit for the nourishment, not of the body, but of the mind. A true convert desires the sincere milk, the pure word of God, not blended or diluted with adulterating, depraving, and debasing mixtures. It is the natural property of every kind of life to desire food suited to its nature, without which it cannot subsist. Now, as the natural man chiefly longs after the enjoyments of this world, (Psa. iv. 6,) so does the new born person after heavenly enjoyments. Col. iii. 1.

2. Sense. As a natural life feels what opposeth it, grapples with its enemy, and if stronger, proves victorious, so it is eminently in the divine life, which having such supernatural assistances, proves too hard for its opponents. Gal. V. 17. 1 John v. 4, 18 & iii. 9.

3. Growth. It is natural for children to grow fast, if some uncommon accident does not prevent it, and that not in the head only, for indeed such are distempered with the rickets, but in all other parts proportionally; so do babes in Christ grow fast, if not distempered (2 Thess. i. 3), and that not only in knowledge, but in faith, love, holiness. 2 Pet. iii. 18. "When I was a child I spake as a child, I thought as a child, when I became a man, I put away childish things." 1 Cor. xiii. 11. So it is with a growing Christian, he puts away childish things; and this among the rest, viz: entertaining a fond imagination, that he shall be always dandled on his Father's knee, or in his Lord's lap, or always embraced in his Husband's arms: when he was but a babe in Jesus, he was apt to conclude his Father had quite abandoned him, if he lost sight of his face but for a little; if he wanted the sweet sense of his love he was peevish and dejected; but now he knows better, that he is not to live by sense but by faith. Gal. ii. 20. Though he retains still an earnest desire after communion with God, yet it is more discreet, believing and submissive; and when they cannot perceive any growth in themselves after some time, they grieve and mourn. A child of God not only weeps at its birth but afterwards.

Mr. Burkett has a very good observation upon this: "that as natural children come crying into the world, so no spiritual child is still-born," or born dumb. Acts ix. 11. We may justly reckon those graceless and unrenewed persons, who do not earnestly long and labour after growth, or mourn not for their little proficiency. Heb. vi. 1. Phil, iii. 14. They that are contented with stinted measures of supposed grace, in reality have no saving grace at all. 1 Cor. XV. 8. Eph. iii. 18.

4. Motion. This is an inseparable property of a natural life. Acts xvii. 28. When we see any thing stand stock still for a considerable time without the least motion, we know it is dead; e.g., when we observe a statue void of motion, with its eyes fixed for some space of time, we are soon convinced, for all its fair face, that it has no life; so when we behold professors of Christianity having but an empty form, without the powerful and progressive practice of piety, (2 Tim. iii. 5,) may not we judge them, and should not they judge themselves to be (notwithstanding of their fair pretences) dead idols in a spiritual sense, void of the life of Jesus?

5. A generative faculty, when grown to maturity: so those that have a divine life labour to communicate it to others. John iv. 28, 29. Luke xxii. 32. Here we may apply justly that of the poet: *Nascitur indigne, per quem non nascitur alter.* "He is unworthy of life himself, who is not the cause of it to another."

6. Likeness. The father begets a son in his own likeness; so did the first Adam, (Gen. v. 3,) and so does the second. John iii. 6. The image of the first is of the earth earthy. 1 Cor. xv. 47–49. "For that which is born of the flesh is flesh;" (John iii. 6;) i.e., exceedingly corrupt and sinful; not only fleshly but flesh; abstracts denote great degrees of what is spoken. Eph. v. 8. Man, by a sinful indulgence of his appetite, (Gen. iii. 6,) prostituted the dominion of his soul to the tyranny of sense; so that now before conversion he is quite sunk in sensuality; instead of deserving the honourable character of a living soul as formerly, (Gen. ii. 7,) he now incurs that just, but sarcastical one of flesh! His reason and all his noble powers are so degraded, unhinged and corrupted; he acts with such indifference about eternal, and with such vigour about temporal things, as if he had no soul, but was wholly flesh: a mere master-beast. But the image of the second Adam is heavenly and spiritual. 1 Cor. xv. 47–49. "For that which is born of the Spirit is spirit;" (John iii. 6;) i.e., his soul has recovered its just, though lost, empire over the senses and brutish appetites, and is now guided and governed by the influence and direction of the Holy Spirit. Rom. viii. 1, 4. As the natural parent communicates of his nature to the child, go those that are born of God are said to partake of the divine nature; (2 Pet. i. 4;) i.e., they have a certain resemblance of the moral, communicable perfections of the Deity, wrought in them: "They are holy as he is holy." 1 Pet. i. 15, 16. "Merciful as their Father is merciful." Luke vi. 36. "Perfect as their Father in heaven is perfect;" (Matt. v. 48;) i.e., they endeavour earnestly after perfection of degrees as well as of parts. Phil. iii. 13, 14. Eph. v. 1, 2. So long as men are contrary to God in their generally prevailing dispositions, and course of action, we may tell them as our Lord the perverse Jews: "Ye are of your father the devil, and the lusts of your father ye will do." John viii. 44,

7. Love. A child hath a love to his father and brethren, which the law of nature teaches, and the likeness that is between them confirms. He is a very monster in nature that is void of this affection! Thus the new-born Christian hath,

1. A predominant love to God in Christ. Psa. lxxv. 25. Matt. X. 37.

2. A permanent love. John xv. 9, 10.

3. A panting, longing love. Psa. lxxxiv. 1, 2.

4. An operative and efficacious love. 2 Cor. v. 14. John xiv. 21. Rom. vi. 4, 5. And so he has a real, effectual, universal, and well grounded affection to the children of God, as his brethren in Christ. His affection does not consist in windy words (1 John iii. 17, 18); neither is his love limited to a party of his own denomination, temper, or sentiments. No, no! that is too narrow a circle for truly Christian love, (such a confined affection is but a natural, selfish, party zeal, which does not deserve the name of love,) which extends itself to all that carry the image of the holy God, and speak in the language of Canaan, of whatever nation they be, or denomination they bear; and as he loves all Christians for what of God he sees in them, so consequently his affection is carried forth with a greater degree of ardour towards such as excel others in holiness, humility, and circumspection; and that not with a fearful but complacential respect. Psa. xvi. 3. 1 John iv.

8. The 8th Character is that change of the practice which I described in the doctrinal part of this discourse; which I think is rather an effect of the new birth than a part of it. It is observable that, in every generation, there is a great change in the old creation, to which this work of God is for many and weighty reasons compared. Eph. ii. 10. There was an admirable alteration, when the present most beautiful and regular system of things was produced by the agency of the infinite Spirit of God (who moved

upon the face of the waters), out of the former disorder, dark mass, and confused chaos. So is there not an admirable change, when a profane, ignorant, sottish creature is turned into a sober, holy, heavenly Christian? "Give me," says Lactantius, "a man as profane and abusive, as lewd and lascivious, as can be imagined, and with a few instructions of God, I will make him as meek and innocent as a lamb. Could ever any of the philosophers do this?" Lib. 2. In short, such a change deserves our admiration more than if a clod of earth were turned into a star of heaven. This is no less a change than from darkness to light, from death to life. Eph. V. 8.

And now, brethren, I pray you, for Christ's sake, examine yourselves, whether you have had the experience of these things; it is easy to be mistaken in this matter, and a mistake is dangerous. Jer. xvii, 9. Prov. xiv. 12. I shall propose a few questions to your consciences, from what I have been treating of, and I beg you would answer them impartially as in the presence of God. And,

Quest. 1. Has sin been discovered, and applied to your consciences with power, both in respect of its vile nature, and dreadful effects, by the law of God, and the Spirit of God, as I before described?

Q. 2. Have you been made to see your lost and deplorable state by nature, so as to be exceedingly distressed, and put to a soul-afflicting plunge and loss, about obtaining deliverance out of it, and shut up to Christ as the only door of hope? Acts ii. 37 & xiv. 27. John x. 7.

Q. 3. Hast thou, sinner, been made to inquire after, and seek for relief, with anguish of soul? Acts ix.

Q. 4. Has the Lord Jesus been discovered by his word and Spirit to your inquiring, burdened, anxious soul, in his mediatorial excellency and sufficiency? Matt. xi. 21. Gal. i. 16.

Q. 5. And have you, with deliberation and resolution, unreservedly closed with the offered Redeemer, upon the terms of discipleship he has specified, viz: of taking up his cross, denying yourselves and following him? John i. 12. Luke ix. 23 & xiv. 26. That is, have you been, and are you willing, and heartily resolved, to quit freely and cheerfully your dearest natural and civil interests, your friends, relations, estates, lives, liberties, respectively, if called to it, for the defence of truth, and readily embrace shame, solitude, poverty and death? Are you willing also to abandon your own righteousness, all your religious performances in point of dependence, and absolutely, immediately, and freely, forsake all your darling lusts, and embrace strict holiness? What sayest thou, sinner? How is it with thee in these respects, willing or not? What! does that man say, It is hard—I cannot now? Wretched soul! As the Lord lives, thou art a dead man.

Q. 6. Are old things passed away? 2 Cor. v. 17. As particularly,

1. Is thy old blindness removed? 1 Pet. i. 4.

2. Thy old security disturbed? Luke xi. 21.

3. Thy old hope sapped at the foundation? Rom. vii. 9.

4. Thy old enmity against God's people subdued? Cant. vi. 1.

5. Thy old, carnal, worldly thoughts, affections and practice altered, or are they still as they were? Why then, I may say to thee, as the apostle Peter to Simon Magus, "Thou hast neither part nor lot in this matter, for thy heart is not right in the sight of God. I perceive thou art in the gall of bitterness, and in the bond of iniquity." Acts. viii. 21, 23.

Q. 7. Are all things made new? 2 Cor. v. 17. As particularly,

1. Hast thou that new light in the understanding? Acts xxvi. 18.

2. That pliableness in the will? Psa. ex. 3. Acts ix. 6.

3. That proneness in the affections Godward and heaven-ward, which I before described? Col. iii. 2.

4. That tenderness of conscience?

5. That tenaciousness of memory respecting divine things? Psa. cxix. 98.

6. That reformation in practice, which was before described?

Q. 8. Have you had that life of God, that likeness to God, that love for God and his people, which was before spoken of?

Q. 9. Is your obedience evangelical, universal, continual?

But I proceed to,

Use 3. which is of conviction and terror to those that are not born again; but who are they, and what may afford them necessary terror?

1. More generally, you are they who cannot, with a good conscience, say yea in answer to the nine questions I proposed before. But, more particularly,

1. May persons make a strict profession of piety, and be admitted to, and enjoy religious privileges, and so pass for Christians, and yet be unconverted? How far, then, are you from this blessed change, who even scorn to profess Christ and piety, who disdain and disclaim the very name saint, as a term of reproach, a badge of dishonour, and grin and show your teeth (silly souls!) when the very word is but mentioned in your hearing? Remember, for this you shall gnash your teeth in hell, except ye repent. I

suppose you think to be saved without the new birth, in a way of your own contrivance, (0 blind moles!) ay, but then, the devil, your dear father, and your brethren, the sons of Belial, the whole crew of profane, unclean rebels and venomous vermin the burdened earth now bears, or hell contains, must be saved along with you, and a pretty company you would make all together, would you not? A fine heaven, indeed! How can you expect that Christ will own you hereafter, when you will not own him here?

2. May people be convinced of sin, and of their lost and deplorable condition because of sin, so as to be in great distress about it, without being new born? Alas, then! What will become of you who are yet secure and asleep in sin?

3. May persons be restrained from gross impieties and yet be in a state of death, estranged from this divine birth? Oh! what will then become of you who give a loose to profaneness, swearing, sabbath-breaking, drunkenness, uncleanness, fraud, and the derision of what is good? Are not burnings, burnings from God, burnings hotter than Sodom's flame, likely to be your portion?

4. May persons attain the form of piety, and be externally regular in the performance of all religious duties, and yet not be new born? Then, wretched sinners! how far are you from this divine birth, who profane God's name, slight his word and ordinances by neglecting to attend upon the one, and to seek preparation for the other, who, as fearlessly as profanely, violate his holy sabbaths, and neglect many positive duties of religion? Read that passage of God's word, and blush and tremble. Matt. v. 20.

5. May people have great gifts and good motions, and want this new birth I have been treating upon? Then what will become of you, ignorant souls, especially such of you as are willingly ignorant? how far are you from a sound conversion to God, which begins in light and knowledge! 1 Cor. iv. 6. And how far will you be at last from obtaining that inheritance conversion qualifies persons for? Isa. xxvii. 11. 2 Thess. i. 7, 8.

6. May persons have a partial alteration upon some or all the powers of their souls, and be almost persuaded to be real Christians, and yet be void of the new birth? What will become of you, hardened wretches, every of whose faculties is perhaps altered for the worse, whose necks are as an iron sinew, and whose brow is brass? Pharisees, heathens and devils outdo you in what is good. The Pharisees in most or in all the outward duties of religion. Phil, iii. The heathens in their morality (perhaps), e.g., the Turks or some of them, have had a greater concern about their souls than thou hast. Remember trembling Felix, and be ashamed of thy horrible stupidity! Yea, the very devils tremble, and yet thou art senseless! man! Is thy breast adamant, or thy bowels iron, that thou thus slightest the terrors of the Almighty, which set themselves in battle array against thee? Canst thou imagine that thou art new born, or shalt be saved in this condition? No, no: be not deceived, the devil himself would find as easy an admission into heaven as thou in thy present condition, as our text demonstrates.

7. May persons have a zeal for religion as Jehu and others, and yet be unconverted? Oh then! What will become of you, lifeless, listless, careless Gallios in religious affairs, who do not care a straw whether religion prospers or not? If you can but get worldly prosperity, if you can but with Gehazi get the changes of raiment, with Judas carry the bag, or with cursed Achan get the wedges of gold, you care not, perhaps, though for it you should betray Christ's cause, and bring judgments upon others. But will not such lukewarm, selfish wretches be spued out of Christ's mouth? Rev. iii. 16. How far are ye, poor souls, from this divine birth?

8. May unconverted persons come so far as to love God's people, associate with them, and delight in hearing of God's word, and attending upon his ordinances? How far then are those from regeneration, or the way to it, who do not come half so far as hypocrites in this? Instead of associating with God's people, they carefully avoid their company, deride them, and spitefully abuse them, and most contemptuously neglect opportunities of hearing God's word, instead of delighting in it, and that, forsooth, because the preacher will not be false to God and souls, and preach smooth things according to their fancy. Will not Herod, that heard John the Baptist gladly, rise up in judgment at last, and condemn the haughty and contemptuous wretches of this generation?

9. May persons be brought to mourn for sin with bitterness and anguish, and yet be strangers to the new birth, as Ahab and Judas? How far, then, are those monsters in nature from conversion, who, instead of mourning for their impieties, boast of them, and so glory in their shame?

But what are the miseries of those and all other kinds of unconverted sinners?

Ans. 1. Ye are blind men. Acts xxvi. 18. Ye see not the beauty of holiness, of Christ and heaven, otherwise ye would not live as ye do. John iv. 10.

2. Poor men, however you swell and strut in worldly wealth and grandeur. Rev. iii. 17.

3. Mad men, Psalm xiv. 1, compared with x. 1. Luke XV. 17. You act like distracted men in preferring sin to holiness, perishing, sensual gratifications to the pure, sinless, and everlasting delights that are at God's right hand. Do you not act like fools in preferring your lusts to God and Christ—your worldly gain, which lasts but for a moment, to an immortal crown of life? And does not your folly and madness eminently appear in your daring to affront such a sovereign, infinite Majesty, whom you can neither overcome, deceive nor avoid, whose loving-kindness is better than life, but whose anger is worse than death, and you will find it so in a little time, when you shall wish for death as a sanctuary from it, but shall not obtain your desire?

4. Dead men, wholly void of divine life. Eph. ii. 1.

5. Darkened men, or men under the power of darkness. Eph. V. 8. Col. i. 13. By which metaphor the Scriptures express all kinds of misery. Psa. xxiii. 4. Matt. xxii. 13. Isa. 1. 10.

6. Possessed men, under the power and government, and in the possession, of the devil, his slaves, his vassals. Luke xi. 21. 1 John iii. 8, 10. 2 Tim. ii. 26.

7. You arc cursed men, cursed by the God that made you, which none can revoke but himself, and who has declared he will not unless ye repent. Gal. iii. 10. Luke xiii. 3.

8. You are condemned men. John iii. 18.

9. Guilty men. Mark iv. 12. And remember, God has said he will "by no means clear the guilty." Num. xiv. 18.

10. You are bereaved men, secluded from, and bereaved of, all the notices and sweet intimations of God's peculiar favour and friendship, in this world or the next. You are without God in the world, and what can be worse than, this? Eph. ii. 12. And as you are justly deprived of his love, so you are continually exposed to his wrath. John iii. 36. You are the very children of the devil by imitation and possession, the seed of the serpent. Gen. iii. 13. 1 John iii. 9, 10, John viii. 44.

11. Miserable men; you are not only void of true light, life, comfort in this world, but of any interest in the inheritance of God's chosen in the next, as our text asserts, and are entitled to a very contrary portion. Eph. ii. 3.

12. Murdering men, cruel murderers, self-murderers, soul-murderers. Ezek. xviii. 31, 32 & xxxiii. 11.

13. Inexcusable men; your eternal damnation is but the natural and necessary fruits of your own wickedness and obstinacy, in rejecting, against your own souls, God's repeated warnings and invitations; and therefore it is but justice, and that not owing to any rigorous severity of God, but entirely to your own cruelty and barbarity, against yourselves, that you should perish. Hos. xiii. 9. Acts xili. 46. And this you will be forced to own at last to God's honour, and your own shame. Matt. xxii. 11, 12. For you have slighted the remedy provided with infinite cost for sin; this will make your sin inexcusable, your damnation unavoidable, and yourselves unworthy of pity, because your misery is a voluntary misery, but the fruits of your own choice. Psa. xcv. 8, 11. Matt. xxii. 3, 5 & xxviii. 37. Prov. xxix. 1. What unspeakable pain will your reflections upon these things cause in your consciences to eternity! Mark ix. 44. Isa. Ixvi. 24. Oh! think of these things and apply them to heart before it is too late, and never rest until you get converting grace.

ROBERT SMITH, D. D.

The Rev. Robert Smith was born in Ireland, and was descended from a Scottish family which had taken refuge in that country, and had settled in Londonderry. About the year 1730, his parents emigrated to North America, and brought their son Robert, then a child, with them. His ancestors, both by his father's and mother's side, were substantial farmers, and had for several generations been distinguished for a vein of good sense, and for prudent deportment, and, what is better still, for fervent piety.

The residence of Dr. Smith's parents was on the head waters of the Brandywine, about forty miles from the city of Philadelphia, where he was brought up in the pursuit of agriculture. At the age of fifteen or sixteen, he became a subject of divine grace, under the preaching of Mr. Whitefield, who spent some time in his father's neighbourhood on his first visit to America. As soon as young Mr. Smith had experienced the power of religion in his own soul, he felt a strong desire to become a preacher, that he might make known the precious truths of the gospel to his fellow men. In this desire, his pious parents readily concurred, and with their permission, he placed himself under the tuition of the Rev. Samuel Blair, at his school in Faggs Manor. Here, for several years, he pursued his classical, and then his theological studies.

In the year 1750, he was licensed to preach the gospel, and was married to a younger sister of his venerated preceptor. In the year 1751, the next after his licensure, he was ordained and installed pastor of the Presbyterian church in Pequea, in the county of Lancaster, Pa., in which situation he continued to labour faithfully to the time of his death. lie was ordained by the Presbytery of New Castle, within the jurisdiction of which his church lay.

In the year 1784, Mr. Smith received from the College of New Jersey the honorary degree of Doctor of Divinity, and seldom has that degree been more judiciously conferred; for Mr. Smith was a sound and well-informed theologian, of which he gave evidence in several productions of his pen. He also excelled as a preacher. His discourses were instructive, evangelical, and deeply impressive.

Shortly after his settlement at Pequea, Mr. Smith established a school, with a special view to the gospel ministry, where the Latin, Greek, and Hebrew languages were taught. In this school, Mr. Smith was assisted by respectable and able teachers; and a large number of young men were here prepared for entering the ministry, before any college existed within the limits of the Presbyterian church; and after the erection of the College of New Jersey at Princeton, young men were fitted to enter that institution, of which Dr. Smith was one of the early and zealous friends.

Beloved and esteemed by all who knew him, he was held in high estimation through a large extent of country, and was looked up to as a father by the churches in Pennsylvania and the neighbouring states. In the year 1790, he was chosen the moderator of the General Assembly; and in 1791, was again a member, and preached before that body at its opening, with uncommon ardour and elevation of mind.

The last public act of his life, was that of attending a meeting of the trustees of the College of New Jersey, at the distance of a hundred miles from home. At this time his bodily health was much reduced, and the effect of this fatiguing journey was to exhaust and debilitate him exceedingly. When he had nearly reached his home, he found it necessary to call at the house of a friend to obtain a little rest and refreshment. He met the family with his wonted benignity and affection, and requested the opportunity of retiring for a short time to a private chamber; and there in a few minutes, without a struggle or a groan, "he calmly and sweetly breathed out his soul;" and the same smile, with which he entered this friend's house, seemed to be imprinted on his countenance after death. He died in the 63d year of his age.

THE PRINCIPLE OF SIN AND HOLINESS.

BY THE REV. ROBERT SMITH, D. D.

"But I see another law in my members, warring against the law of my mind, and bringing me into captivity to the law of sin which is in my members."—Rom. vii. 23.

The gracious heart is a seat of conflict, the greatest, and most important! a conflict between the flesh and the spirit. Nor does the highest degree of grace raise its subject above the necessity of engaging in this debate. A pregnant instance of this we find in the eminently holy apostle Paul, who, after all his advancement in the spiritual life, "sees a law in his members warring against the law of his mind."

In this engagement, we may, first, observe the combatants, viz: "the law of the members, and the law of the mind;" i.e., grace, and indwelling sin (that the apostle does not speak in this passage of the operations of the soul before its conversion, as some suppose, and that, therefore, the opponents in this debate are sin and holiness, and not conscience and reason only contending with depraved appetites and passions, will plainly appear by consulting the context, where he speaks in the strongest terms of his hatred to sin, and delight in the law of God; characters which can never be predicated of the unregenerate, whose hearts are unyielding enmity against God.), which mutually engage each other, and warmly contend for victory. These have displayed their banners under their respective sovereigns: Jesus, the Prince of peace, and Satan, the prince of darkness. The generals of the field are, "the beloved lust," which most easily besets us, on the side of sin; and on the side of grace, faith, to which, among all the graces, the preeminence is given in the spiritual warfare. And while those opposite principles resist each other, as contending parties of different aims and interests, they respectively operate upon the heart, like laws of different tendencies.(We have here, as is usual in scripture, an assemblage of metaphors, viz: war, and law, to illustrate the same subject. For such is the sublimity of divine truths, and the imperfection of the things of nature, that no allusion drawn from them, can fully illustrate any one point; therefore a number of these are frequently used, that one may help to supply the deficiency of the other.)

Secondly, we may take notice of what is sometimes the sad event with respect to the better side, which is overcome so far, that the believer is brought "into captivity to the law of sin." The law of sin is the same as the law of the members, mentioned in the former clause. To be brought into captivity to it, is to be brought under its power. Now, doleful as this event is, there is something in it, which pleads the spiritual soldier's loyalty to his Sovereign; he does not capitulate, or come to terms of agreement with sin; but is overcome, and taken as a reluctant and mournful captive. The engagement often appears dubious, now on one side, now another, seeming to overcome, as Israel and Amalek of old. When Moses let down his hands, Amalek prevailed: Israel prevailed when he held them up. So sin prevails, when Christ withholds the aids of his Spirit; when he grants them, grace prevails. Yet, in general, grace has the ascendency, and shall finally obtain a glorious victory.

A mistake about this warfare proves fatal to many carnal professors, who fondly imagine that they are pious, mistaking the reproaches of a natural conscience for the spiritual conflict: a conflict, of which they never had any experience, and, infatuated with this delusion, they rest secure in a graceless state. On the other hand, their fears that all their debates with sin are only some stings of conscience, and, consequently, that they are yet children of wrath, frequently obstruct both the duty and comfort of the saints. Therefore, that I may afford conviction to the one, and relief to the other, I shall attempt in the following pages to explain:

I. The nature of grace, and show the reasons why it is called a law of the mind.

II. The nature of indwelling sin, and the reasons why it is called the law of the members.

III. The nature of the conflict between these opposite principles, and give some marks by which it may be distinguished from the uneasiness arising in the breasts of unbelievers.

I. I am to explain the nature of grace, and show the reasons why it is called a law of the mind.

Now, grace is a principle of spiritual life infused into the soul by the Holy Ghost. This divine principle receives various denominations in the word of God, as "being born again," "regeneration," "a new heart," "a new creature," "God's workmanship created anew:" all which phrases, with many others, plainly evince, that grace is a new, a spiritual, a holy nature; nay, it is called a "divine nature," (2 Pet. i. 4,) because it is the impress of God's moral glories upon the soul. I shall not enter into the dispute, whether this principle precisely consists in divine light let into the mind, or in a holy affection. I think it is most safe and proper to describe it as consisting of both. For grace is a restoration of what we lost by the fall, viz: of the divine image, consisting in knowledge, righteousness, and holiness. Eph. iv. 24. Col. iii. 10. Righteousness is seated in the will, holiness in the affections. The affections are sundry vigorous operations of the will, attended with sensible commotions of the animal spirits. It follows, then, that holiness in the affections is the vigorous operation of righteousness in the will. But the will has a respect to objects as eligible, and the ground of its choice is the apprehended goodness of its objects, by which an affection for them is excited. Love to their objects is, for the same reason, necessarily supposed in the affections. This is evident in all the religious affections. Sorrow for sin is affliction of the mind for wrongs done to a beloved object. The soul's expectation of a future good, undoubtedly, supposeth her love to the object of her hope. Desire is the aspiration of love, and joy in its triumph. On the whole, it appears, that an affection for divine objects is the very essence of righteousness and holiness; and that this affection, and knowledge, the other part of the divine image, are the very constituents of a gracious principle, or the new-nature. On this account grace is called, "the law of God written upon the heart," (Jer. xxxi. 33,) a phrase of equal import with the law of the mind, and plainly implies a sanctifying knowledge of the objects exhibited in the law, and a hearty regard for them impressed upon the heart by the Spirit of God.

1. Then a leading ingredient of true grace consists in a view of the transcendent beauty of divine objects. The principal object viewed is the glory of God's moral perfections displayed in the salvation of lost sinners. This necessarily supposeth a view of Christ's willingness and ability to save; for it is in his face alone, that we can obtain "the light of the knowledge of the glory of God," (2 Cor. iv. 6,) a view of the extent, the spirituality, and purity of God's law, which is a transcript of his glory, and the means by which we are convinced of the need of Christ—a view of the fulness and amazing glory of the new covenant plan of life, in its nature, privileges, and precious promises—and, in short, it supposeth a just view of the various foundation-doctrines of the gospel, particularly of the necessity and beauty of holiness in its several branches. Of these things, true believers obtain views different in their nature and effects from the views of any graceless persons. The graceless, as rational creatures, may discern the meaning of words and propositions, the connection of sentences, and the propriety of conclusions drawn from rational premises. But there is a spiritual and holy beauty in divine objects which, being morally blind and vitiated, they cannot discern nor relish; therefore, they have no just idea of the objects at all. Sin has spread a veil of darkness over their hearts, exceeding the midnight shades, and adding fresh gloom to hell itself. They understand gospel doctrines no otherwise than a logician understands a system of logic, viz: by the mere strength of natural powers. With devils, they may confess that Jesus is the Son of God; they may, with them, believe there is one God; nay, they may believe and tremble, without the least true discovery of, or the least affection for, his holy, transcendent beauties. Some may brand this doctrine with the odious name of enthusiasm; but I shall rest safely under the censure while divine testimony assures me, "that the natural man receiveth not the things of the Spirit of God: for they are foolishness unto him; neither can he know them, because they are spiritually discerned." 1 Cor. ii. 14. They are spiritually discerned, but he has not a spiritual eye to discern them.

Graceless sinners quite mistake the nature of divine objects. At one time, they conceive of God as all mercy; at another, as all justice; and again, will not conceive of him either as merciful or as just; but only think of him, as an idle, unconcerned spectator of the universe, "saying in their hearts. The Lord will not do good, neither will he do evil." Zeph. i. 12. Before I proceed farther, I beg your patience, while I suggest an argument or two in proof of this point. 1st. It appears from their dependence upon themselves for salvation, of which they are all guilty, whatever may be their profession to the contrary, or to whatsoever degree of knowledge they may have attained. But what false ideas must this suppose of the rectitude of Jehovah, the perfection of his law, and the awful malignity of sin! and what unbelief, as well as ignorance of the whole gospel scheme of life through Jesus Christ! 2d. Seeing the nature of the human soul is such, that it immediately makes choice of that which appears most excellent, and best for it in its present circumstances, their giving their preference to sin and the world, is a plain evidence that they do not understand nor relish the superior glory of divine things. How splendid soever their profession of religion may be, they do not believe what they profess, but are infidels in heart. They may, indeed, yield their assent to this truth, that religion is the best choice, and may resolve to be religious hereafter, but for the present they see more beauty in creatures, and taste more sweetness in creature enjoyments, than in holiness; nor would they ever resolve to be religious in any future period, nor ever desire any other than a Mahometan paradise, did they not fear the wrath of God. Corrupt affections spread a veil over their hearts, and provoke Jehovah, in just resentment, to conceal his glory in a cloud of vengeance. Therefore, though they may sometimes be struck with awful apprehensions of his awful majesty, yet they do not discover the amiable glory and beauty of his perfections, till it pleases God to make them shine upon their hearts in the face of Jesus Christ, by whose atonement the human offence was removed, and a way opened, in which he could, consistent with his glory, grant saving manifestations of himself to a lost and sinning world. But when the Holy Ghost rends the veil from their hearts, he discovers to them the transcendent beauties of Jehovah with such irresistible efficacy, and brightness of spiritual evidence, as transforms them into the same likeness; "for with open face beholding as in a glass the glory of the Lord, they are changed into the same image, from glory to glory, even as by the Spirit of the Lord." 2 Cor. iii. 16–18. By that very influence which reveals the glory of God to them, the Holy Spirit forms in their hearts a supreme regard for his glory, which brings me to observe,

2. That a principle of grace necessarily includes a supreme affection for God. This affection is the very essence of holiness. For to view objects in their own nature, and to acquiesce in, and esteem them in proportion to their worth, is, doubtless, most fit and becoming. Now as God knows no equal, he cannot but view and acquiesce in his own glory as supreme; consequently, he cannot but have an infinite complacency, in a supreme affection for his glory, and an infinite displacency in the least disaffection thereto, in the reasonable creatures. This is his holiness, or the rectitude of his nature, and is the foundation and pattern of all moral excellency. But grace being the impression of God's moral image upon the soul, by which it bears a conformity to his holiness, there is necessarily contained in its very essence a transcendent love for his glory.

It is the nature of sin to draw our affections off from God, and fix them upon the creatures; and it is the nature of grace to place them again upon God; "for they who are after the flesh, mind the things of the flesh; but they who are after the Spirit, the things of the Spirit." Rom. viii. 5. The saints esteem God as an object worthy of all their affections, and earnestly desire the enjoyment of him as the greatest good. They see a transcendent beauty in all his glories, and love him for them all—for his justice and holiness, as well as for his goodness. And because they love God, they love his image, in whomsoever they behold it, and every mean in which he affords them true communion with himself. The saints they esteem as "the excellent of the earth," and choose them as companions in their way to heaven. Psa. xiv. 2. They delight in the law of God as the transcript of his glory; and in the gospel, as the brightest glass by which his beauties are reflected. In one word, they take delight in the most spiritual sermons, books, and conversation, and in all the ordinances and duties of religion, because these are the means through which he displays his glory, and affords them the sweetest sensations of his love.

By this time, you may easily perceive, that the grand constituents of the new man are faith and love in their simple nature, i.e., existing as principles of grace in the soul. In believers' views of divine objects, is implied such clear objective certainty, as obtains the firmest assent of their minds to their reality and importance. This is faith in the understanding, in which sense faith is called, "the knowledge of God's will in all spiritual wisdom and understanding," (Col. i. 2,) "and the full assurance of the understanding." Col. ii. 2. And in this sense the gospel is said to have come to the Thessalonians "in much assurance." (Faith, in this view of it, is a necessary prerequisite to faith as seated in the will, which is the soul's choice of the object as good, the truth of which is apprehended by the understanding. Or, in other words, the soul's view of the truth and excellency of an object, necessarily precedes her embracing that object as good. But it is her choice of the object, which is the justifying act of faith; for this is that act, by which we accept of, and are united to, Christ. Nor is saving faith distinguished from the faith of hypocrites, only by the soul's embracing Christ, but also by her assent to his suitableness to save; for, as I have already observed, graceless persons never obtain a just view of divine objects; therefore, they never make choice of them.) 1 Thess. i. 5. Love being the sum of the divine law "written upon the heart of our first parents, was an original affection of nature. This heaven-born beauty, which was lost by sin, is the glorious image drawn by the Holy Spirit, when he writes the law upon our hearts. Love is therefore the sum of religion. It was the reigning affection in innocence. It is the reigning affection in grace. And it will reign triumphant in glory, when the other graces shall for ever cease. The other graces, which only become necessary by our apostasy, and not from our original make, are evidences of love, and flow from it as their source.

(Love, being a principle of grace, is a necessary ingredient of all the graces, [which are specifically distinguished from each other, by their acts and motives], and only differs from the acts of love, considered as a distinct grace, as a fountain differs from the streams which issue from it.)

From what has been said, we see with what propriety divines have called faith and love radical graces, and gracious principles. For, in their simple nature, they are holy principles, from whence all the graces grow up, as so many fruitful branches of holiness; they are the foundation of all those spiritual exercises of heart and practice, which are the native acts and evidences of a spiritual life. (God has implanted in nature, a principle of action suited to the various operations which arise from it. And can we suppose he will be less liberal in dispensing his special favours? Or that we can perform truly holy actions without a spiritual principle? As well may we expect streams without a fountain, or living actions from a dead carcase. "Being dead in trespasses and sins," we cannot exert the acts of a spiritual life, till animated from above with a living principle. While we continue in a state of nature, the ends, the motives, and the principles of our actions being merely selfish, they are morally evil, though the nature of them be good; therefore are they, in a spiritual sense, dead works. Yet we are not to suppose, that believers without the immediate concurrence of the Holy Spirit, can exert the acts of a spiritual life, by virtue of a principle of holiness disposing them thereto. For as it is by almighty power upholding the frame of nature, and keeping all its springs in tune, that we are enabled to perform natural actions; so it is only by the Holy Spirit's maintaining and exciting the principle of grace implanted in us, that we can perform spiritual actions. Therefore says Christ to his disciples, "Without me, ye can do nothing.") If we are "God's workmanship created anew, it is to good works." Eph. ii. 10. God "takes away the stony heart out of our flesh, and gives us an heart of flesh, that we may walk in his statutes to do them" (Ezek. xxxix. 26, 27); viz: in that spiritual and holy manner, which is congruous to his holiness and the spirituality of his nature.

Our way is now prepared to show why grace is called "a law of the mind." Like a law, it has a prevailing influence over all the powers and operations, aims and pursuits of the mind. Laws are made for the government of their subjects, and for that purpose, afford light to direct, and motives to influence their conduct. But grace is a principle of light and love in the minds of believers; "light which shines brighter and brighter to the perfect day." Prov. iv. 18. The more they view divine objects, the more beauties they discover in them, and consequently, the more ardent is the flame of their love towards them.

Love is a very powerful passion, which, by its sweetness, strongly impels the mind to desire, and endeavour to obtain, the enjoyment of its object; especially when its object is viewed as most amiable. Believers have, therefore, the most prevailing motives, both from within and without, to excite them to every pious exercise of heart and life. The incomparable beauty of divine objects, and the inexpressible sweetness of love to them, inflame their soul with strong desires to obtain the fullest enjoyment of them. Time would fail to mention the powerful motives to repentance and universal obedience, to every grace and every duty, arising from the personal, uncreated glories of Jehovah; from creating, preserving and redeeming goodness; from the fulness and excellent frame of the new covenant; from the endless glories and happiness of heaven; and from the necessity, reasonableness, sweetness and importance of religion in its various branches. But none are stronger or sweeter than those drawn from the cross of Christ.

The invincible charms of his love, the riches of his pardoning mercy, and the amazing stoops of his condescension therein displayed, sweetly open the springs of all the affections, and irresistibly captivate the whole soul.

Conscious of the comforts arising from spiritual views and affections, believers languish when they lose their frame, and with the solicitous spouse, Importunately seek their Lord, until he is pleased to restore to them a sense of his love. And the more they drink of this fountain, the stronger they thirst. Their enjoyments only excite their desires. It Is a natural and invincible property of the human mind, to desire not only a repetition, but higher degrees of those enjoyments, in which it finds a transcendent satisfaction. When the Lord condescended "to speak to Moses, face to face, as a man speaketh to his friend," the pleasure of this sweet Interview excites him to put up this ardent prayer, "I beseech thee, show me thy glory." Ex. xxx. 11, 18. So insatiable was his desire, that, had his request been granted in its full extent, it would have proved fatal to his mortal frame; therefore the Lord says to him, "Thou canst not see my face; for there shall no man see me and live." Ex. xxxlii. 20. A love to the end, reconciles them to the means of obtaining the end. Because they delight in communion with God, they delight in all his ordinances and commands, the means of communion with him. They desire to "remain in the house of the Lord, to behold his beauty, and be satisfied with marrow and fatness." Psa. xxvii. 4. lxii. 1, 5. "Delighting in the law of God after the inward man," they perform the duties required in it, not of constraint, but with a ready mind, for their obedience is the willing offering of love. Rom. vii. 22. John xiv. 15. The most difficult as well as the most easy duties are their choice. And as holy objects have command of their hearts, they perform duty with fervency, when the edge of their affections is not blunted with temptation and sin. In one word, grace overcomes temptation, resists sin, excites believers to war a good warfare, and run with patience the race that is set before them, until they obtain the glorious prize at the end of their race. Thus does it powerfully prevail in the heart like a law. And, Oh! happy, inexpressibly happy for believers, were this the only principle which has influence upon their actions. But alas! another principle, the direct reverse of this, often disturbs their peace, and brings them into captivity to the law of sin. But this leads us, in the,

II. place, to explain the nature of indwelling sin, and show why it is called a law of the members. Though believers are sanctified in every part, they are perfectly sanctified in none; a sinful principle remains in them which, like a law, operates in their members, and wars against the law of their minds. This principle is original corruption, and it is represented by the members of the body.

1. Because as the body is but one entire frame consisting of many members, so original sin is one mass of impurity, which defiles the whole man, and, therefore, consists of many branches. It is darkness in the understanding, aversion to divine things in the will, filthiness in all the affections, baseness and irregularity in all the sensual appetites.

2. The principal reason why it is thus represented is, because it exerts itself chiefly in and by the members of the natural body. Sin altering the temperament of our bodies, has introduced into the animal frame such a strength and irregularity of sensual appetites, as powerfully attach our souls to sensible objects. By virtue of the law of union between our souls and bodies, they have a mutual influence upon each other: carnal appetites are corrected or excited by the views of the mind; the mind is subjected to carnal appetites. Sensitive propensities exciting fancy to sport with sensible flesh, pleasing objects, and these, in their turn, striking the fancy through the avenues of the senses, kindle an impure flame in the affections, and strongly attract them to forbidden objects, or fix them excessively on lawful ones. But so far as our affections for creatures exceed due bounds, so far they are taken off from God, and set in opposition to his glory.

From the carnal tendencies of the heart arise the most filthy scenes of drunkenness, uncleanness, gluttony, thefts, robberies, unlawful and excessive gambling, and frolicking of every kind. Besides these lusts that have their seat more immediately in the flesh, vices of the mind (such as pride, malice, envy, hatred, wrath) are called carnal lusts, and lusts of the flesh; not only because they are part of carnal men's characters, but also because they are excited and strengthened by the propensities of the flesh. All the wild irregularities of fancy and passion are influenced by the irregularities which sin has introduced into the animal frame. Occasions to sin lie much in our flesh and blood. The enjoyments of sensible things, being agreeable to the flesh, are the object of carnal desires. The riches, the luxuries, the pomp, and the various gayeties of this life, are the gods of ungodly sinners, and temptations to the saints themselves. Fine clothes, fine houses, glittering equipages, and high sounding titles, strike the mind with their fancied beauty. Relishing dishes and flowing bowls please voluptuous palates. The adulterer's heart is caught by delusive charms. Large treasures and large estates are snares for the covetous. By Bathsheba's beauty, David's lust is inflamed, and Achan's covetous desire, by a wedge of gold. The glory of his kingdom swells the pride of Nebuchadnezzar's heart; and an unbounded thirst for unrivalled military honours, prompts Joab to jealousy and murder.

By this time it may easily appear, that indwelling sin is called a law of the members, because of the powerful influence it has upon the whole man. It clouds the understanding, bewitches the fancy, debauches the affections, sets the will in opposition to God, and turns all the members of the body into instruments of unrighteousness. The unregenerate are wholly under its power. They are carried away with "the lusts of the flesh, the lust of the eye and the pride of life." Being "after the flesh, they only mind the things of the flesh," i.e., for these only they have a relish. Now every person's taste has a governing influence upon his actions; nor will anything appear beautiful to the mind, for which it has no relish. But carnal men not only have no relish for the glory of God, but an unreconcilable enmity against it, as being contrary to their sensual inclinations; therefore they can see no beauty, nor taste any sweetness, in moral excellency. Their pursuits, aims, and desires, are altogether carnal. "What shall we eat? What shall we drink? Wherewithal shall we be clothed?" are their leading queries; as if they were born only to pamper the flesh, and feed themselves up as oxen for the slaughter. Nor is there any species of wickedness into which they would not run with greater eagerness, than ever the horse rushed into the battle, were it not for the restraints laid upon them by Providence, conscience, education, and fear of divine wrath.

But grace obtaining the predominancy in the hearts of believers, they are happily delivered from the "dominion of sin." Rom. vi. 14. They have new thoughts, new hopes, new inclinations and designs; and the chief objects of their pursuits are spiritual. Yet are they afflicted with some of the carnal lusts which were born with them. Some of the former root of bitterness remaining in them, sprouts up, and, when divine influences are withdrawn, and they are off" their guard, it will prevail. They are not all spirit. Faith's views are not yet perfect, nor their affections perfectly refined: though grace has subdued and regulated their appetites and passions, yet, while they live in a world of sense, sensible objects will sometimes entangle their affections and lead them into mournful captivity. This is one chief source of their falls and sorrows. Satan, apprehensive that the most likely way to prevail against our first parents, even when their minds were under no sinful bias, was by objects pleasing to their senses, presented to them the beauty and goodness of the forbidden fruit, by which means they were seduced to break the divine command. The same game he attempted to play with our Saviour, when he painted before him "all the kingdoms of the world with the glory of them," and promised him all these, "if he would fall down and worship him." Matt. iv. 8, 9. No wonder then, if, in this manner, he solicits, and sometimes beguiles the sons of grace into sinful compliances, in whom there is corruption to catch at his temptations, as powder to catch at the spark.

Some of the saints find a much greater difficulty in mortifying the deeds of the body, than others, and are much more easily overcome by them. This flows, no doubt, from the much greater strength of their passions, and irregularity of their fluids. From the very contexture of their frame, some of them are more passionate, or proud, or peevish, or malicious, or wanton, than others of their fellow saints; while others, again, are sunk in despondency, and almost perpetually deluged with distressing sorrows. It was said of a great man of God, he had "grace enough for ten men, but had not half enough for himself, because his natural constitution was so violent and passionate." Peter was rash and hot-headed. Thomas seems to have been sour and unbelieving. But John, highly favoured in nature as well as grace, lived in love.

But though the saints are sometimes overcome by the temptations of Satan joining with the corruption of their hearts, yet grace shall usually prevail, and finally triumph in victory. Of this, our Lord assures them, when he promises, that "the water which he shall give them, shall be in them a well of water, springing up to everlasting life," (John iv. 14,) i.e., the influences of the Holy Ghost, which first infused grace into their hearts, shall continue therein as a vital fountain, ever sending forth the salutary streams of holiness, till spiritual life shall be perfected in eternal life and glory. By the continued union of the Holy Spirit with their spirits, the principle of grace is preserved, strengthened, and excited to its various exercises, "till they come to the measure of the stature of perfect men in Christ Jesus." Eph. iv. 13. Yet while they are in the body, "the flesh will lust against the Spirit, and the Spirit against the flesh, and these being contrary, the one to the other," (Gal. v. 17,) you may see in them, "as it were the company of two armies." Cant. vi. 13.

From what has been said, we learn, that the believer is indeed a mystery, the greatest in our lower world. He is both a sinner and a saint; he has in him both the old nature and the new—a love to God, and enmity against him. He is black, yet comely; carnal, yet spiritual; earthly, yet has set his affections upon things above. He is a mixture of the most opposite qualities, represented by the most opposite things in nature—the poison of the serpent and innocence of the dove; the sublimity of the eagle, and meanness of the crawling worm! Nay, he is a mixture of heaven, earth and hell! In sin, he resembles devils; angels, in holiness; and in his animal nature, he is akin to the beasts that perish!

Again, if occasions to sin lie much in your flesh, it ought to be much of your care, with the apostle Paul, "to keep your bodies under, and bring them into subjection." 1 Cor. ix. 27. You must guard all the avenues of sense. I "made a covenant with mine eyes," said Job, "that I should not look upon a maid." Avoid as much as possible every means of provoking sensual lusts and appetites. If you place your happiness in the gratification of these, what are you better than the brutes? These are the only pleasures they know, or are capable of knowing. But you are capable of pleasures more refined—pleasures arising from intellectual views, and the enjoyment of eternal, invisible glories. If you do not fix your affections on those glories, you forfeit the rational character, and degrade yourselves to the level of mere animals. Endeavour to obtain clear views of the superior glories of spiritual objects, the beauty and sweetness of which will deaden your affections to the things of time and sense. With Solomon, learn this lesson, that every thing below the sun is vanity.

Especially let those of affluent circumstances learn it; for in treasuring up riches, you treasure up fuel to feed the flame of lust. This is a powerful argument to excite the poor to be contented with their condition, and bless God for what they enjoy. If he withholds this world's goods from you, he only withholds the snares that prove the destruction of multitudes.

Because the allurements of sense are enemies to religion, God, in infinite wisdom and goodness, has so ordered matters concerning his people, that those who are rich in faith, are generally poor in this world. Riches, in themselves, are the blessings of providence, and God will give to a number of his people such a portion of them, as he sees needful to enable them to support the external interests of his kingdom. Yet, if we may credit infinite veracity, they are great temptations to a degenerate world. "How hardly," says Christ, "shall they that have riches enter into the kingdom of God! It is easier for a camel to go through the eye of a needle, than for a rich man to enter into the kingdom of God." Mark x. 23, 25. The splendour of a crown, the glitter of external pomp, and the soothing enchantments of an affluent fortune, are delusive baits to sensual hearts.

THE SPIRITUAL CONFLICT.

BY THE REV. ROBERT SMITH, D. D.

"But I see another law in my members, warring against the law of my mind, and bringing me into captivity to the law of sin which is in my members."—Rom. vii. 23.

Having, in the preceding discourse treated of the principle of sin and holiness, I proceed, in the III. Place, to explain the conflict between these in the hearts of believers, and give some marks by which it may be distinguished from the uneasiness arising in the breasts of unbelievers.

1. The cause of the strife, is the irreconcilable contrariety of those jarring principles, the one to the other. The essence of holiness, as has been manifested in the preceding sermon, consists in love to God. Sin is unyielding enmity against him. But love and hatred being very powerful, and directly opposite in their operation, a warm debate necessarily arises between them, and will subsist so long as there are any remains of sin to oppose the operations of grace. The question therefore to be resolved, for the assistance of solicitous enquirers about their spiritual state, are not whether they have no love to sin, and no hatred to holiness; but whether there is in their hearts a real principle of holiness, resisting the operations of sin; and what is the ground of this opposition? Believers being conformed to God in affections and views, the reason of their regard to holiness, and, consequently, of their opposition to sin, must be the same with his, viz: the intrinsic beauty of the one, and deformity of the other. They see a beauty, and taste a sweetness, in holiness, inconceivably surpassing the beauty and sweetness of all earthly enjoyments. By this, they are enabled to glorify God, by this, they enjoy the comfort of communion with him, and the perfection of this they wait and long for as the very perfection of happiness. Doubtless, souls of a mould so heavenly cannot but resent the hostile invasions, when sin, as a bold usurper, assumes the throne. They hate it, because it is hateful to God, and rises in opposition to his glory. "Against thee, thee only have I sinned," says David, "and done this evil in thy sight!" Psa. li. 4. What! Had not David sinned against his own soul V Against Bathsheba? Against Uriah? Against his whole kingdom? Against all these, no doubt; but this single thought, the dishonour his sin had done to God, overwhelms his impressions of all its other evils. Saint Paul speaks the language of every Christian, when he laments his wretchedness by reason of

sin, and earnestly wrestles for deliverance from it, as a vile, an oppressive, body of death. Rom. vii. 24. But unbelievers' debate with sin arises only from conscience and reason declaiming against the indulgence of vicious inclinations, as subjecting them to the wrath of God. They do not oppose it from any dislike to it, or any love to holiness. Give them their carnal pleasures, and they desire no other heaven. They hate the holiness of God, and did they not fear his justice, they would not attempt the obedience of his commands in one single instance, nor refrain from any vice to which their degenerate natures are inclined. There are persons, indeed, who, without either virtue or grace, may not have a propensity to some particular vices: they may, from their natural constitution, be averse to drunkenness, and yet be wretched, covetous worldlings. One sin may also contend with another. Prodigality opposes avarice, and avarice prodigality. Yet this is only a debate between the flesh and the flesh. But grace is ever uniform, all the graces being united in perfect harmony, and materially aiding to each other.

2. This conflict, as to its nature, resembles both a foreign and domestic war. Carnal reasoning in the understanding, and spiritual desires in the will, mutually oppose each other, as do also faith in the understanding, and carnal desires in the will. Carnal reason pleads for the indulgence of the flesh; spiritual desires resist the flesh, and give the preference to holiness. Sensual inclinations reject the cross of Christ as too heavy; faith endures, "as seeing him who is invisible." Nor does the debate subsist only between the different powers of the soul, but is also in the very same powers; by which means each of them seems to be set in opposition to itself. In the same understanding faith and carnal reason contend with each other, and the desires of the flesh and spirit in the same will. It is sweet to carnal desires to fulfil the lusts of the flesh; spiritual desires prefer communion with Christ, as much sweeter. Carnal reason says. To trim with the times may be useful to ourselves and the Church of Christ; faith bids us strictly follow the path of duty, and commit events to God, "whose counsel shall stand fast, and he will do all his pleasure." But as there is no spiritual light in the minds of graceless sinners to resist the dictates of carnal reason, nor holiness in their affections to resist the lustings of the flesh, their contest with sin is wholly of the foreign kind. They are altogether unacquainted with the vigorous efforts of faith and love, and their victories over carnal reasoning and affections.

3. True believers have "respect to all God's commandments, and hate every false way," and, therefore, maintain a war with every sin. Sensible of the deceitfulness and desperate wickedness of their hearts, they fight not only with outward evils, but with their inbred corruptions, and with secret as well as open sins; with sins of lesser aggravations, as well as those of greater; with sins which promise worldly honour, interest and safety, as well as those which threaten the contrary. Secrecy, respect, interest, importunity, and almost every temptation conspired to persuade Joseph to comply with the solicitations of his wanton mistress; but the respect he paid to the honour and approbation of an all-seeing God had greater influence upon his conduct, than any selfish motives whatsoever. "How (says he) shall I do this great wickedness and sin against God?" Gen. xxxix. 9. Deeply affected with the depravity of their natures, they enter into the secret recesses of their hearts, and bewail those iniquities of which God and their own souls are conscious. David most heartily confesses, and prays to be cleansed from, his original corruption, as the filthy source of all his actual transgressions. "I was shapen in iniquity, and in sin did my mother conceive me. Create in me a clean heart, God, and renew a right spirit within me." Psa. 1. 5, 10.

But in nothing is the honesty of their hearts more fully evinced, than in their keeping themselves from the iniquity, which is by nature and habit their most beloved lust. Psa. xviii. With this they are willing to part, though naturally dear and pleasant to them, as a "right hand or a right eye." Against this divine grace has fixed their firmest resolutions. This is the cause of their greatest sorrows, and to obtain victory over this, affords them the greatest pleasure. But when the unconverted make any resistance at all against sin, it is generally against those sins which expose them to shame and punishment in this world; against atrocious crimes, which are most apt to affect conscience: or against some particular crimes, to the commission of which they have not a strong temptation in the flesh; or of which, through custom and education, they may have contracted a kind of abhorrence. These they may part with to pacify conscience, and retain their beloved lusts with greater ease. But they are very little, if at all, attentive to the wickedness of their hearts, except when seized with affliction, or a pang of conscience, and even then, their sensations are soon lost, and all their resolutions soon forgotten. They pray for the destruction of sin, while they desire to indulge it; and, Felix-like, defer any proper vigorous attempts to obtain their request, till a more convenient season; or as Augustine, who in the days of his vanity, prayed to be made chaste, his heart in the meantime repeating, "Not too soon, Lord, not too soon." Oh that the youth in this assembly, would treasure up this sentence in their hearts!

4. We proceed to take notice of the manner in which spiritual soldiers carry on a war with sin. Possessed with an irreconcilable hatred to the camp of the enemy, they resolve to give no quarter, and admit of no correspondence with them, nor any cessation of arms. Therefore do they engage warmly, with a fixed determination not to yield. They strive for victory, and take the kingdom of heaven by holy violence; others make a feint of fighting, but they exert all their strength and policy. Nothing short of complete victory will afford them satisfaction. Jealous of the fair promises and alluring baits of sin and the world, they are fully resolved to reject all their deceitful enticements. In an unguarded moment, indeed, they may be surprised by a violent onset; or, by stratagem, may be taken captive for a season. Yet will not their hearts ever be reconciled to the camp and interest of the enemy. They cannot usually take pleasure in meditating upon sin, nor commit it with the same complacence and peace of mind as graceless sinners do. Conscious of its baseness, and the comforts of which it deprives them, their pleasure is lessened in the very act. And when dragged into captivity by it, languishing after their former sweet spiritual liberties, they cannot enjoy themselves, nor be contented, until they return to the camp of Christ. Therefore exerting themselves to the utmost to shake off the bonds of their captivity, they rally again, and renew the attack with greater vigour than before. By the searchless wisdom and goodness of God, their foils are improved to the destruction of their sins, and become a means of their standing more sure. For by these being taught the strength and policy of their enemies, their own weakness, and their daily need of divine aid, they are excited to greater watchfulness, take the field with firmer resolution than ever, and cease not, until they obtain an eternal triumph.

But as there is not that antipathy between sin and natural reason, as there is between sin and holiness, graceless folks soon drop the arms they seemed to have taken up against sin. It is too powerful for the strongest and best refined reason. To whatsoever degrees of improvement the natural man may attain, he has still a hearty affection for sin; therefore, a truce with it is very pleasing to him. Ready to hearken to the cravings of the flesh, and receive for truth the false colouring which Satan and a depraved fancy put upon the dalliance of his heart with sin, temptations to the commission of it easily obtain his consent. His debate with it is like that of the wind with the tide, which may presently tack about, and go in the same direction with the tide. The hypocrite will not always call upon God. His goodness is like the morning cloud and early dew, it goeth away. Hos. vii. 4. He will either plague the church with false zeal, or degenerate into dry formality, or, abandoning religion entirely, he will fall into the most pernicious errors in principle, in practice, or in both. The unclean spirit returning with seven other spirits more wicked than himself, they enter into him, and his last state is worse than the first. Matt. xii. 43–45. Such persons in every age have given the greatest wound to religion.

5. Spiritual warriors make use of the whole armour of God. Truth or sincerity of heart and conversation is the guide of their lives. For a breast-plate, they put on the exercise of universal righteousness and holiness. Their feet are shod with the preparation of the gospel of peace, i.e., all their conduct and pursuits are influenced by gospel principles and motives. For an helmet they take the hope of salvation, which bears up their spirits amidst every danger, and fortifies them against every furious attack. Above all, they take the shield of faith, wherewith they are enabled to quench all the fiery darts of the wicked. Through faith they receive of Christ's fulness, and grace for grace—grace to resist and overcome every temptation, and every sin: so clear, so sweet, and so glorious are its views, that they kindle in their hearts the warmest affection for its objects, while they disengage them from the pursuit of carnal pleasures. By this, they see that spiritual objects infinitely transcend the value of every thing below the sun. By this, they take a distant prospect of heaven, and converse with invisible glories far beyond the reach of sense. And by this, their eye is steadily fixed on the crown of life promised to those who overcome. This, therefore, is the very spring of all the strength, courage, and vigour necessary for the spiritual warfare.

In the hand of faith they carry the sword of the Spirit, which is the word of God. This is a piece of armour, which never fails them—armour with which, after the example of the Captain of their salvation, they overcome the tempter. Soon as they present to the devil the sword of the Spirit, like a coward he flies off. Are they, in a gloomy hour, tempted to think their sins are so heinous, they cannot be pardoned? The word of God informs them, that, "where sin abounded, grace much more abounds." Does Satan take the advantage of their spiritual pride, to excite them to trust their own strength and goodness? This informs them, that "all their own righteousnesses are as filthy rags," and that "Christ alone is the Lord, their righteousness and strength." In a long night of desertion, they are supported with the promise, that "the vision will speak, though it seem to tarry." And as an encouragement to prayer, the Holy Ghost is promised to be in them, as "a Spirit of grace and supplication." Nor are they called to perform any duty, resist any temptation, endure any suffering, nor is there any circumstance they can be in whatsoever, but there is still something in God's word suited to that very case. It Is therefore a noble mean to assist them in the spiritual warfare. And as often as they forget their sword, or fail in the proper use of it, so often their adversary obtains an advantage of them.

Finally, sensible of their own utter insufficiency for their duty, they constantly wait at the throne of grace, in all sorts of earnest addresses to God, for skill to use their armour, and strength to vanquish all their enemies. Jacob-like, they wrestle with God, until they obtain a blessing, the Holy Ghost helping their infirmities, and enabling them to make known their requests, with groans which cannot be uttered. But carnal persons use carnal weapons, or spiritual weapons in a carnal manner. They consult carnal reason more than the word of God; and instead of a dependence upon Christ, they trust their own goodness, strength, and wisdom; careless about holiness of heart, they rest in their outward reformations, and duties, or in some common, superficial impressions made by the Holy Spirit upon their minds. As the Jews followed Christ for the loaves, they sometimes make a show of following him only from worldly views. They profess religion to obtain character and interest among men, or gain the favour of particular persons, upon whom they have a dependence. But let the hopes of their gain be over, and their care about religion is over. Slavish fears of hell, and mercenary hopes of heaven, are their highest inducements to perform any duty, or resist any sin. The sweetness and intrinsic excellence of the exercise have no influence at all upon them.

The Improvement.

I. What has been said saps the foundation of the hypocrite's hope, and may afford assistance in solving a case of conscience, which often perplexes doubting Christians. They are puzzled to reconcile the prevalence of sin, which they sometimes feel in their own hearts, with their interest in the divine promise that it "shall not have dominion over them." Rom. vi. 14. But it is the allowed and usual sway of sin, against which the promise affords them security. Now it may, at times, bring them into captivity, though it does not generally rule in them, nor will they live in friendship with it by any means. When the Holy Spirit withdraws, in just resentment for their untenderness, they may apprehend that they feel in their hearts the workings of blasphemous thoughts, unbelief, self-righteousness, and various carnal propensities, almost in their full strength. They may also be so far left of God, as to fall into very heinous crimes. At such seasons conscience may be exceedingly benumbed; and though they do not entirely cast off a regard to religion, yet their desires after Christ are very languid; and when they attempt to seek him like the spouse upon her bed, they do it in a careless, trifling manner. Yet they cannot be easy while at a distance from him. They are sold under sin, and this is their burden. Rom. vii. 14, 24. All the while they live in it, they do that which they allow not; that which they hate. Rom. vii. 15. Their spark of spiritual life, however smothered, is not wholly extinguished. Though they sleep, their hearts wake, and they know the voice of their Beloved when he knocks for entrance. Cant. V. 2. His endearing voice, speaking to them in reproofs, directions, invitations, and promises, revives their decaying graces, and excites them to seek Christ with carefulness and importunity until they find him, and are enabled to say, "My Beloved is mine and I am his." Cant. v. & vi. 3. And when enlarged by divine grace, they are most watchful against every sin, especially against a relapse into their former backslidings. They are daily subject to invincible human infirmities; nor shall they ever in this life obtain a perfect freedom from the body of death; yet they are scarcely, if at all, guilty of repeating the same gross offences. We hear of Noah's drunkenness but once, and but once of David's adultery. They may, indeed, repeat the same offence, before they are restored by actual repentance: as Peter thrice denied his Lord; but we read of his denying him no more after he went out, and wept bitterly.

But to be repeatedly guilty of the same crimes; to live in the constant practice of sin; to roll it as a sweet morsel under your tongue, or to allow it the peaceable possession of your hearts, is inconsistent with a state of grace. "Whosoever is born of God, cannot sin (in this sense); for his seed remaineth in him." 1 John iii. 9. And though you may sometimes attempt to resist its operations, yet has it the full consent of your souls, if arguments drawn from shame and punishment have greater influence to restrain you from it, than those drawn from the love of Christ, the beauties of holiness, and the intrinsic vileness of sin itself.

2. This subject points out your duty, who have enlisted in the spiritual warfare. Be diligent, faithful, and coura-

geous in fighting "the good fight of faith." In order to this, it will be of great advantage to be well acquainted with the motions, the strength, the stratagems of your enemies. You wrestle not only with flesh and blood, but with principalities, and powers, and spiritual wickednesses. Eph. vi. 12. All the embattled troops of hell conspire with the world and your own wicked hearts to plot your ruin. Sometimes the devil succeeds in his hellish designs by crafty wiles, and sometimes by violent assaults. It is one of his crafty wiles to paint sin as duty, and duty as sin. Under the notion of greater purity, he persuades people to refrain from ordinances purely administered. When offended with fellow professors, he slily insinuates that resentment is a Christian duty. But whatsoever varnish he puts upon it, a desire of revenge is generally at the bottom, rather than the glory of God, the interest of the church, or the good of an offending brother. Sometimes he persuades them, that they may please their imaginations without much danger, by indulging them in painting a fanciful scene, whereby their affections are ensnared before they are aware, and they are inclined to the commission of some base iniquity, contrary to their first design or expectation. Now he fills them with great disquietude, by painting their difficulties in the strongest colours; now, leading them into the fools' paradise, he so tickles their minds with scenes of vanity, that they forget the evil day till it comes upon them with double distress. One while he would seem to turn advocate for heaven, persuading them their sins are so heinous that they cannot be forgiven consistent with the divine honour; at another time, concealing the turpitude of sin, and fixing their minds intensely on their good affections and good deeds, he excites in them spiritual pride and self-confidence. When he cannot seduce them by crafty wiles, he attempts to overcome them by storm, before they have time to fortify themselves against his violent assaults. Taking the advantage of a critical juncture to raise their fears, he suddenly hurries them into sin in order to screen themselves, or escape an apprehended danger, as in the case of Peter, when he denied his Lord with oaths and cursing. He plays upon them with all his fiery darts, such as blasphemous injections, temptations to part with Christ, or question the reality of religion; fiery darts, indeed, and most painful, the poison whereof seems to drink up their exhausted spirits. By such means as these, Satan will try to gain ground upon you; to prevent which, you ought to learn the nature of his temptations, and the means by which they may be repelled. Learn your weak side, and guard it well, for on this quarter the attacks of the enemy are most likely to succeed. Be constantly careful to mortify all the deeds of the body, especially your constitutional sin. In this, nature affords the tempter a double advantage against you; this has the command of other lusts. Take the leader, then, and the whole band will be easily routed. In order to assist you in finding it out, I shall give you some of its leading characters. It is that sin, which you have most frequently wished were no sin; that on account of which you have been enabled to endure the greatest difficulties; that for which conscience is most apt to accuse you, and for which invention is most ready to find out excuses; it is that sin which disturbs you most in your secret retirements, crowds first upon your thoughts in the morning, employs them most in the silent watches of the night, and most easily carries away your heart at any time.

Watch against and resist the very first motions of sin. Lay restraint upon the first sallies of corrupt affections and wandering thoughts. Whenever you find imagination begin to be pleased with tempting baits, to devise excuses for the indulgence of the flesh, or for the neglect or careless performance of duty, then you may be assured you are falling into temptation, and that it is high time for you to be upon your guard. Immediately check the dalliance of your hearts with forbidden objects, and hold not the least correspondence with the enemy. Want of care, in this point, was the source of the numerous train of miseries, into which the whole human race are plunged.

Take unto you the whole armour of God. Be skilful, be constant, be active in the use of every part of the spiritual armour. It is a shame for a soldier to loiter, or suffer his arms to lie by him rusty. If you quit your arms, or turn your backs, you will, doubtless, fall a prey to your enemies. Armour is provided for every part except your back, to teach you that you must maintain the war with courage, and persevering constancy. There is no discharge in this warfare, while you are in your enemies' country, or any of them infest your borders; but thousands of them every moment besiege your hearts. The Christian life is a life of progress, in order to which the continued exercise of grace is necessary, especially of faith, which is the life of every grace. The various ordinances are conduits for the communication of divine influences to mortify your corruptions and quicken your graces. These are appointed as means to lead your minds away from the world, and fix them upon spiritual objects, the beauty of which kindles in the heart a growing affection for them; but a growing affection for spiritual objects is the life and increase of holiness, and the increase of holiness is the destruction of sin, your mortal enemy. If, then, you neglect to stir up the gift of grace God has bestowed upon you, by neglecting the means appointed for that purpose, you will decay in spiritual strength, and your enemies will prevail against you.

Finally, follow the directions and example of your Leader, and keep close by his standard. A brave general is the life of war. But in Christ you have the most glorious example to influence all your conduct, and aid for the performance of all your duty—an example of diligence, watchfulness, zeal, courage, wisdom, and faithfulness in fulfilling all righteousness and resisting every temptation. Continually imitate this worthy pattern, and look to the Captain of your salvation for all the succours you need. He has every supply to give, and you have an oath and promise that "as your day is so shall your strength be." Keep close by the camp of Christ, for if you carelessly wander from it, you will fall into the hands of your enemies. Follow "the footsteps of the flock." Spiritual example and spiritual conversation are noble means of promoting the spiritual life. It is an unspeakable advantage to have brave assistants in the field of battle; their heroism inspires their fellows to noble actions. But those who are with our Lord "are called, and faithful, and chosen;" whose faith follow, and imitate them as far as they imitate Christ. Tread in the steps of those worthy heroes, who have trod the paths of virtue and grace before you, and having distinguished themselves by their noble achievements, now gloriously triumph before the throne.

Did you need motives to excite you to duties so necessary and so noble, I might observe to you the glory of the cause which you have espoused. You have enlisted to fight the battles of the King of glory. The royalties of heaven have been invaded, and you are called to resist the bold invader. Consider also the dignity of your character—a brave soldier has been a glorious character in every age; but what is the glory of the Alexanders, the Scipios, and all the renowned heroes of antiquity, to the glory of the spiritual soldier—a soldier under the Lord of hosts! To subdue one corruption is greater glory than to conquer a kingdom—a world! Yes, greater glory than to conquer ten thousand worlds! How great the glory, then, to obtain victory over your innumerable lusts, the countless temptations of an ensnaring world, and the prince of darkness himself, with all his furious, infernal forces! Besides, you go not a warfare at your own charge. Your armour is provided, and everything you need for the warfare. Take a view of what it is for which you fight—not for a spot of earth—not for a temporal throne or kingdom—not for a crown of yellow dust—No! but for an everlasting kingdom! for a crown of glory which fadeth not away! Nor is it for another you fight, but for yourselves. Every spiritual soldier shall reign for ever as a king. "To him that overcometh," saith Christ, "will I grant to sit with me in my throne, even as I also overcame, and am set down with my Father in his throne." Rev. iii. 23. And the more valiant you are for the Lord of hosts, your crown will shine with the more distinguished brightness. Oh, the dignity of the martyrs' crown! the glory of their reward, who have gone to heaven through a sea of blood! The eternal weight of glory you have in prospect as a reward of victory, is sufficient to awaken all your strength, to rouse all your resolution, and inflame all the ardour of your breasts. Nor do you proceed upon uncertainties; the Captain of your salvation has secured to you the victory. Upon the cross he triumphed over all his enemies, and yours. In dying he conquered death, and him that has the power of death; and now he is exalted to his eternal throne, he holds the keys of hell and death. Courage, then, Christians! courage—You shall be more than conquerors through him that loved you, and washed you in his own blood! To arms! to arms! A few strokes more, and you win the crown for ever!

3. I shall finish this discourse with an address to graceless sinners—to you who still continue in Satan's interests! Each of you I address under this character, who live in the practice of any known sin of heart or life; who live in the neglect of any known duty to God or man; who take pleasure in the service of Satan, and in the conversation of those who join with him in his conspiracy against heaven; who never felt the arrows of conviction stick fast in your hearts, nor ever have dropped the weapons of your rebellion; who have never by faith enlisted with Christ, nor ever engaged in the spiritual warfare. You are enemies to Christ, and join in confederacy with his bitterest enemies. Christ has set up a standard in our guilty world, and by the offers of the gospel invites your flight to it. Satan has also set up a standard in opposition to Christ, and by the various corruptions of your nature, the allurements of the world, and his sly insinuations, he binds you to his interest. His promises are fair but false. He makes large promises of much comfort in the world and in the indulgence of your filthy lusts. He persuades you that there is no great danger, nor any necessity for so much earnestness about religion as ministers urge you to: there is enough time to repent, God is merciful, and will not be severe to mark small offences against you. True, God is merciful, blessed be his name! but he is just as well

as merciful; and never, never will he exercise mercy to the prejudice of his justice! If you continue in your sins, you shall perish. If you expect to be happy, you must renounce all your lusts, and all the vanities of this deluding world. You must enlist in the spiritual warfare, put on the armour of Christ and wear his livery. You must have common friends, common enemies, and common interests with him. And can all this be done by a few lazy wishes, and ineffectual resolutions? No! to obtain true religion, is not so easy to corrupt nature as some imagine. Indolent souls have no claim to it. "The kingdom of heaven suffereth violence, and the violent take it by force." You must deny yourselves, take up your cross and follow Christ, if you expect to enter into heaven. You must strive, you must wrestle, you must fight, for the crown. Rouse, then, sinner! rouse from your fatal security! an hour's delay may cost you an eternity of sufferings!

Your present warfare is most base, dangerous, and unreasonable. You commit hostilities against the "Lord of lords and King of kings;" his royalties you have invaded, his authority contemned, trampled upon his laws, and cut off your allegiance to him. You have revolted from his government, turned enemies to his crown; and, were it possible, would not only dethrone Jehovah, but destroy his being: for "the fool hath said in his heart, There is no God." Oh, your horrid ingratitude against the parent of your being—the God of all your mercies! By his power you live, and every moment of your life you receive countless favours from the unwasted treasures of his goodness; and yet you join against him with cursed demons who, for their base revolt, were damned to the bottomless pit. And this is all the wages you shall receive, if you persevere in your present warfare.

Your conduct is not only wicked, but weak, and the consequences of it will be terrible to your souls if persisted in. You rebel against Him, who in one moment can dash you in pieces as a potter's sherd. The pillars of heaven totter, and the everlasting hills bow before him! If he look on the mountains, they smoke, and the most obdurate devils in hell tremble at his presence! How, then, shall worms of the dust bear up under the weight of his wrath? Why should you attempt the unequal war? Are you a match for Jehovah? Can you thunder with a voice like his? Can you bear the lightning of his glittering spear? He has levelled all the artillery of heaven against you! prepared his instruments of death! fixed his arrows upon the string! whet his sword—his sword edged with all the flaming vengeance of God! Harness yourselves for the battle, ye rebels! Clothe you with all your hellish armour, your hardness of heart, your presumption, your atheism and infidelity, your horrid oaths and imprecations, and try if they will be any defence in the day of his anger, in the day when he shall come forth to avenge the injuries of insulted majesty! Oh, what language, what idea can paint the displeasure of incensed Deity! Indignation and wrath, tribulation and anguish is its mildest voice! But to all this punishment you are exposed, my poor, thoughtless, deluded fellow mortals! If you turn not from the evil of your ways, the tempest of his fury shall beat upon your naked souls, in one eternal, unremitted storm.

Drop, then, guilty sinners! drop the weapons of your rebellion! submit to the Lord Jesus Christ! Touch his peaceful sceptre, lest he break you in pieces with his iron rod! The flag of mercy held out in the gospel invites you over to the camp of Christ; the glory of the cause in which you are called to engage invites you; and all the rewards of victory invite you—rewards the most glorious and most certain. If you enlist in the spiritual warfare, you shall overcome through the blood of the Lamb and the word of his testimony. You shall triumphantly enter the new Jerusalem with palms of everlasting victory.

SAMUEL FINLEY, D. D.

Dr. Finley was born in the County of Armagh, in Ireland, in the year 1715, and was one of seven sons, who were all esteemed pious.

The parents of Dr. Finley were of Scotch descent, and were distinguished for their piety. Finding their son to be of a quick capacity, and fond of learning, they resolved to give him the best education which their circumstances would admit; and after he had obtained the rudiments of an English education, he was sent abroad some distance from home, to prosecute his studies. In this school, he distinguished himself by his assiduity and his proficiency in learning.

When he was in his nineteenth year, he emigrated to America. He arrived in Philadelphia, on the 28th of September, in the year 1734. He appears to have become a subject of divine grace, at a very early age. Upon his coming to America, he steadily pursued his studies with a view to the holy ministry. And as he arrived in Philadelphia at the very time when Mr. Tennent's school was flourishing at Neshaminy, and as there was then no other institution in the Presbyterian Church where young men were trained for the ministry, there is the strongest probability that he was a student at the Log College. This probability is strengthened by the fact that he put himself under the care of the New Brunswick Presbytery, most of the members of which were educated in this school. His licensure took place on the 5th of August, in the year 1740. Having received authority to preach, he itinerated extensively; and, as his pulpit talents were of a high order of excellence, he was eminently useful.

His labours were greatly blessed in West Jersey;—in Deerfield, Greenwich, and Cape May. He preached also for six months, with great acceptance, in the congregation to which Gilbert Tennent was afterwards called, in Philadelphia. His ordination took place on the 13th of October, in the year 1742. He was probably ordained as an evangelist, and continued to visit the places destitute of the stated means of grace, for several years; and all accounts agree in ascribing much success to his itinerant labours. It is probably during this period, while preaching in a congregation in New Haven, on account of the rigid laws of the land, he was seized as a vagrant, and carried beyond the limits of the colony. He does not appear to have been permanently settled as a pastor, until June, 1744, when he accepted a call from Nottingham, Maryland. In this place he remained for seventeen years. It was here, also, he established an academy, with the view, chiefly, of preparing young men for the ministry.

Dr. Finley was elected president of the College of New Jersey in the year 1761, and immediately entered upon the duties of his office, and the trustees were not disappointed in their expectations of his wisdom and efficiency. As he was permitted to remain five years in office, he had the opportunity of carrying into effect plans for the improvement of the institution, so that its reputation was greatly extended.

The disease of which he died was brought on by too great assiduity in his studies, and too constant occupation in the public duties of his office. He did not die at home, but in the city of Philadelphia, whither he had gone to consult physicians respecting his disease. His death occurred on the 16th day of July, 1766, in the fifty-first year of his age.

His death-bed experience was most remarkable, which can be seen in his biography in the "Log College."

THE MADNESS OF MANKIND.

A SERMON BY THE REV. SAMUEL FINLEY, PREACHED IN THE "NEW PRESBYTERIAN CHURCH," PHILADELPHIA, JUNE 9TH, 1754.

"And madness is in their heart while they live, and after that they go to the dead."—Eccl. ix. 3.

Whoever seriously views and wisely considers the manners of mankind, and brings them to the test of right reason, will be forced to receive the same melancholy idea of them represented in this text. The words are Solomon's, who was not only an indefatigable student of nature, but an accurate observer of divine providence, of the conduct of men, and the several consequences of actions, divine and human. He here tells us the result of his researches respecting these. As to providence, that though God has a special regard to the holy and good, yet in external things he makes no difference, but "all things come alike to all." As to mankind, that they take occasion from these promiscuous dispensations to commit wickedness without reserve. "Their heart is full of evil;" for they observe, that "such as work wickedness are set up; and they who tempt God are even delivered." Mai. iii. 15.

This has sometimes been puzzling to the pious, but has struck the ungodly with madness. Hence it comes, that "madness is in their heart while they live."

Madness is a state of irregularity and discomposure. The person affected with it is not fixed in his purpose; is not influenced in his conduct by the most engaging motives; pays no regard to the dictates of right reason; nor is careful about what is decorous, disadvantageous, or dangerous. Now, we are assured by unerring truth, that this is the state of the "sons of men." It is true, they make high pretences to wisdom, and have a show of it; but "the wisdom of this world is foolishness with God." 1 Cor. iii. 19. If madness were concealed in the heart, we could not discover it; but "out of the abundance of the heart the mouth speaketh" (Matt. xii. 34); and so by mens' words and actions we come to know what is in their hearts. Hence, a course of life contrary to right reason, and just rules of conduct, will evidence heart-madness.

In treating this subject, I am naturally led to show wherein the madness of human hearts discovers itself. This cannot be done but by mentioning particular instances of human conduct. And as I apprehend that the method of such a narration is in a great measure arbitrary, I shall not attempt a nice arrangement of the general heads in natural order, but propose them as they occur.

I. Precipitant conclusions concerning persons, things, or opinions, formed without evidence, and often in defiance of demonstration to the contrary, discover a degree of madness. The crowd of mankind determine the most important points, without weighing the reasons on both sides of the question. In their own imagination they quickly penetrate matters, which to the more judicious are abstruse and intricate. If they embrace truth, it is by accident. They contend for religion not because they see its proper evidence, but because they have been accustomed to it. And thus they may be orthodox and regular Christians, from no better principles than those from which the Turks are Mohammedans. Nay, they form their judgment of religion, the highest concern of all, with more indifference than of the small affairs of this life. From hence arise the many sottish opinions, wild reveries, and destructive heresies, that pass for pure religion with their respective votaries, divide the christianized world into so many opposite parties, are contended for with a peremptoriness that knows not to yield to argument, and promoted frequently with a bitter, sometimes with a bloody zeal. What intelligent Christian is there, who, without a mixture of pity and contempt, can observe the professors of wisdom become fools (Rom. i. 22); hear the dictates of eternal wisdom pronounced folly, with a supercilious air, and fanciful chimeras substituted in its room? It would seem as though the faculty of reasoning was, to many, given in vain; while one asserts the uselessness of it in religion, another, its sufficiency in our lapsed state. This denies the necessity of any divine revelation; that asserts, every circumstance must be immediately revealed. One thinks saving grace consists in moral honesty; another places it in the observance of invented forms. One is a libertine, who fancies lie serves God while he gratifies his lusts; another is superstitious, and thinks to please him by monkish austerities. One is content with a dead faith, which neither "purifies the heart," nor "works by love;" another is persuaded he shall be saved by his good works, though imperfect, without faith in the righteousness of Christ. This lays the whole stress on orthodox principles; that thinks it indifferent what we believe. Some doubt not their safety, because they are of such a particular religious denomination; others are of opinion that all denominations stand alike fair for salvation. Here is a bigot, who esteems every circumstance in religion to be essential, and whatever he believes to be right and true must be a term of communion; there is a latitudinarian whose religion has little or nothing in it that is important, or worthy to be earnestly contended for. Here unaffecting speculation is triumphant; there ignorance is the mother of devotion. Here religion is dressed in gaudy attire, with Jewish, worldly pomp, insomuch that its first institution is hardly at all discernible; there the pure, external ordinances of God himself are rejected with scorn, from a swollen conceit of spirituality. Now all these contradictory parties will be equally stiff and positive in their notions; yet are all equally extravagant and monstrous, all opposite to divine revelation and the reason of things. And are all these, my soul! are all these the rational sons of men? Are all these sure they are wise? Can truth, divine truth, be a system—a system did I say?—a heap of dotages? Can reason, strict reason, approve contradictions? or rather, must we not assuredly conclude, "that madness is in their heart while they live?"

Nor shall we find more wisdom in their judgment of men, than of things. They conclude of characters in the lump; can hardly see anything amiable and good, when some things displease; nor are blemishes apt to be disgustful, when some good qualities shine. Superficial defects hide substantial excellencies from the vulgar eye; whilst the absence of all valuable accomplishments is easily supplied by mere sound, and empty show. Wisdom and virtue, meanly clothed, are despised; whilst ignorance and vice, dressed in purple, are honoured. An easy air, and genteel address, often recommend nonsense, and make flattery appear sincere; but an uncouth mode will cause the same persons to disrelish undissembled regard, and solid discretion. Even learned critics do sometimes defend the very absurdities of a favourite author, and censure what is truly sublime in another. Whole communities, nay, whole nations lie under the censure which belongs only to a part, and perhaps a small part of them. Thus mankind judge as though reason taught them to make the conclusion universal, when the premises are only particular.

II. Men judge not more precipitantly, than speak and act inconsiderately. How frequently may we see proper and improper confused—no respect had to time, or place, or persons; nor a thought of the obvious and unavoidable consequences! How many live as if there was no need of caution, no possible danger of missing the right, nor any extreme to be feared—as if nothing could follow from any course of conduct, and a necessary cause would not produce its genuine effect—as if prudence and circumspection were names, and no power of deliberation had ever been given! They live at random, and seem to consider right and wrong with absolute indifference. In the religious life some are offensive, others stumble and fall, and some take offence when none is given. In the civil life, many ruin themselves in their worldly affairs, and others too, by indiscretion. Some live above their ability, engage in matters too high for them, and fall by those means by which they thought to rise. The imprudent pursuit of grandeur brings others into contempt, whilst they industriously seek to obtain a character which they cannot support; and climb to a pinnacle, where their brains are turned and they cannot stand. Many in a devout qualm engage in a course of strict religion, without a rational sense of its importance, or "counting the cost." Luke xiv. 28. They think not what offences and stumbling blocks are in the way—what artifices of Satan—what allurements of the flesh, and what terrors of the world are combined to turn them aside—how "strait the gate," how "narrow the path," (Matt. vii. 14,) how arduous the ascent, and how deceitful and impotent their souls—what self-denial, what humbleness of mind, what watchfulness and care, and what courage and determined resolution, are requisite for the purpose. They assure themselves that they will stand firm against all assaults, though they were at no pains to dig deep, and found themselves on a rock. Hence, when the rain descends, when the floods come, and the winds blow and beat upon them, they fall, (Matt. vii. 26, 27,) and are carried headlong down the stream. Hence their goodness is as a morning cloud, and vanishes like the early dew. Hos. vi. 4. They either become profane, or are taken in the snare of some delusive opinion or heresy. "They turn away their ears from the truth, and are turned unto fables," (2 Tim. iv. 4,) and thus ends their religion.

III. Many appear to have false views of what is advantageous or hurtful, and draw false inferences from actions and events. In how strange a light do they look on strict piety, who disdain it as mean, or avoid it as unpleasant; and how come the paths of sin to appear honourable and blissful? Religious persons and spiritual conversation are by many shunned, as though they were dangerous, while the loose and profane are chosen for companions, as though they were most safe. They are not afraid to violate the laws of God, yet they dread his threatened vengeance. Hell is their terror, sin their sport and entertainment. They tremble at the effect, yet delight in its proper cause. But how absurd is it, mentally to separate misery from sin, when they can never be separated in fact? The eternal reason of things has made their connection inviolable. What false apprehension have many of their own cases! The aged and infirm think of years to come, and hence defer their intended preparations for death. The drunkard never knows his capacity, but thinks he may safely venture to take the other glass; nor does the covetous miser ever judge truly of his necessity, and therefore lives poor in the midst of plenty.

Every occurrence is perverted. The goodness of God, which would seem sufficient to melt hard hearts, and form them according to his will, becomes a mean of hardening them against him. If he gives to some abundance of worldly wealth, they use it as though it were a license given them to indulge wantonness, excess of riot, luxury, and all those sensual pleasures, which to others are forbidden. If honour and power are conferred on them, they act as though they were advanced above a scrupulous regard to the divine commands. They seem to say, "Who is the Lord that we should obey him?" Ex. v. 2. Because the wicked prosper, they conclude that it is quite safe to follow their ways: "and because sentence against an evil work is not speedily executed" (Eccl. viii. 11), they are bold in impiety, presuming on perpetual impunity. They see men despise piety, and even sit in the scorner's chair, yet no visible evil befalls them; hence some are tempted to think divine threats are but bug-bears, and religion but a fancy. On the contrary, pious people are distressed, often severely reproached and run down, and no visible regard manifested for all their care to please God. Upon this, others readily determine, that "it is vain to serve him!" Mai. iii. 14. Some, who made a plausible profession of strict religion, fall away, and prove themselves, by their after conduct, to have been but hypocrites; therefore, others carefully avoid any appearance of piety, that they may avoid hypocrisy. They expect to be accounted honest and upright, when they are openly wicked and glory in their shame.

IV. There are numbers who do not so much as attempt to form their judgment or regulate their practice, by reason. They follow the vogue without scruple. They seek no other test of truth, than that it is said by the great or the many; nor any other proof of the propriety and goodness of their behaviour, but that it is modish. Custom is to them instead of reason, and influences them much more powerfully, than the authority of God himself. Let their conduct be irrational, let it be wicked too, provided only it be fashionable. Has it a multitude to patronize it? Then it is no matter though it cannot stand the test of scripture; no, nor of common sense. The crowd, like a torrent, carries them along, and they lose themselves in it. Their weak minds are confused with the tumult, and made giddy with the glare of giddy pomp. Sedate thought and calm reason, by means of numberless airy vanities, lose their weight, and are resolved into fume and vapour. In this plight, it is no wonder that they esteem those contemptibly weak who choose rather to expose themselves to the censure of the world, than to offend God. They judge of religion itself by the fashion. By that they determine which of the divine commands it is proper to obey; and which of them, for the sake of decency, is to be laid aside. If religious discourse is reckoned impolite, a serious expression will shock a gay company, and a few would go near to disperse them. Though it is the will of God that sin should be reproved, and the sinner made ashamed, yet we would offend against modern politeness, should we discover even a calm disapprobation of what is wickedly spoken or acted In company. They who would be quite acceptable to this world, must at least seam to approve what God condemns, that so none may ever be made uneasy by their presence. They must "say to every one that despises the Lord, and that walks after the imagination of his heart, Ye shall have peace, and no evil shall come upon you." Jer. xxiii. 17. "But, surely, the friendship of the world is enmity to God." James iv. 4. But let us proceed further, and take a view of men who mistake not their duty; who acknowledge the things "that are excellent, being instructed out of the law," and we cannot but conclude that they exceed in madness: for

V. Multitudes continually counteract their judgment and conscience when rightly informed. They own the soul to be more excellent than the body, yet are most anxious to provide for the latter. They spare not cost and pains to cure a bodily distemper, while the immortal spirit, all disordered, is quite neglected. Remedies are carefully sought for a headache, but none for a hard heart. A fever is deplored, irregular and distorted passions are indulged. The body is gorgeously clothed and delicately fed, while the soul is naked, without righteousness, and no bread of life sought after for its nourishment. It is of more value than the "whole world," yet is bartered away for a very small part of it, for vanity, for songs, for trifles. That heaven is infinitely preferable to this earth, eternal glory to temporal felicity, is not disputed; yet sinners choose to live here always. They are conscious to themselves, that they would desire no other kind of blessedness than this world affords, could they but still enjoy it, and enjoy it fully, and, hence, grasp the present regardless of the future. They acknowledge that they should make it the very business of their life to please God, and that his favour is more valuable than the favour of all mankind;

yet they gratify their appetites and humours, when they know they displease him in so doing; and if they stand fair in the opinion of men, are quite careless about his approbation. They commend virtue, but practise vice; and while they own that wickedness is the way to hell, walk boldly on in it at all adventures. They confess that reason should guide, and the passions should be governed by its dictates; yet when their passions become clamorous, the voice of reason is drowned, and its loudest remonstrances no more heard. The covetous man is drawn into absurdities by the love of money, the voluptuous hurries on in pursuit of ruining pleasures, and thirst of praise carries the ambitious headlong.

They make no suitable improvement of their own experiences, nor correct past follies by after observation. The world and its evil customs are infectious; they have been often caught in the same snare, yet never learn to be guarded and circumspect. The review of past scenes of guilty pleasures gives griping remorse, the present do not satisfy, yet many trials convince them not that the future will surely disappoint them. After drinking to excess, the heart is thirsty; and hunger succeeds the most plenteous repast. "In the midst of laughter the heart is sorrowful, and the end of that mirth is heaviness." Prov. xiv. 13. For oftentimes reason is debauched, the conscience seared, the passions inflamed, the constitution broken, the estate ruined, and the person despised. Guilt is contracted, time wasted, and the spirits flag by means of an immoderate elevation. Sensual joys clog and surfeit, but do not content: they gratify the brute, but starve the man, and frequently ruin the Christian. Yet we see multitudes of mortals eagerly fluttering to grasp joys which, like airy phantoms, still elude their embraces, and are hardly the shadows of realities! Disappointed, they nevertheless still pursue, still go the tiresome road, and tread the same beaten path in vain! In fine, after numberless experiments, they neither learn the emptiness of earthly things, nor the deceitfulness of their own hearts.

VI. It is well known that madness hurries persons, who are affected with it, into most desperate courses: and this is the case of mankind. "They know the judgment of God, that they who commit such things are worthy of death" (Rom. ii. 4); yet they do those, and delight in them. They sin against plainest precepts, guarded with most awful threatenings. In the very sight of Sinai's burning mount, amidst the thunders of offended Jehovah, hardy rebels durst form a god of gold. Sinners are still the same. They sin against shocking terrors, felt by themselves; and disregard alluring offers of pardon, and charming promises of eternal salvation. They sin, while they are receiving tender mercies, never considering, "that the goodness of God should lead them to repentance" (Rom. ii. 4), and while they suffer the infliction of severe judgments. Examples of despair, the fearful ends of wretched offenders, deter them not; nor are they persuaded to be religious by the death-bed joys of pure and living piety. Let their dearest friends, and the most learned and godly ministers, convince and beseech them, yet will they not yield themselves to God. Solomon, with all his wisdom, the royal authority, joined with the sublimest strains of the "sweet singer of Israel," the persuasive oratory of Apollos, with Peter's burning zeal, could not turn sinners from their course. Let miracles be wrought, the mountains removed, the dead raised, the deaf made to hear, and the blind to see; even these things will not have the force of argument with them. "Uncover destruction, make hell naked" before them, with open eyes they rush into those flames. Let angels come from heaven, and fiends from the infernals; let eternal raptures, and endless horrors, be presented lively to their view, and they will hardly so much as make a pause. Tell them, nay, show them, how sottish and foolish their way is, yet they will not be ashamed. Conscience speaks, but it is not heard; commands, but is not obeyed. What shall I say more? They "rush on God himself, on the thick bosses of his buckler"(Job xv. 26)—they provoke incensed Omnipotence to unequal engagement; defy his power, despise his truth, and like leviathans, "laugh at the shaking of his spear." Job xii. 29. They cannot successfully contend, nor is it possible to escape, yet they will not submit—will be broken rather than bow, and "dashed in pieces like a potter's vessel,"(Psa. xi. 9,) rather than comply with the confessedly righteous will of God. They are told that eternal damnation cannot be avoided, nor eternal glory obtained, but only by the merits of Jesus Christ; yet many, (could it have been thought?) many make light even of a Saviour! despise the Redeemer! most horrid, most desperate thought! His exquisite agonies, his exceeding sorrowful soul, his bloody sweat, the soldiers' scourges, the crown of thorns, the cruel mockings, the painful and accursed death he endured for sin, instead of affecting them with reverence and love to his person, are the matter of their scorn; or, at best, received with cold indifference. "my soul, come not thou into their secret; unto their assembly, mine honour, be not thou united." Gen. xlix. 6. "Be astonished, ye heavens," at the madness, the daring impiety, of guilty mortals! "be horribly afraid, be ye very desolate." Jer. ii. 12.

VII. Madness discovers itself in absurd and unreasonable hopes. Earthly-minded and sensual persons hope to content their lustful appetites by gratifying them to the full; whereas it is plain, that all vicious passions, like the dropsy, increase by indulgence. Endeavours to satisfy them, and by that means to get rid of their importunate cravings, is the same as heaping fuel on fire in order to extinguish it, which yet only serves to heighten and perpetuate the flame. There is no mean that has a proper tendency to quell irregular desires, but only self-denial. Some hope to obtain heaven without holiness; "to be glorious in the eyes of the Lord," though quite unlike him; to dwell for ever in his presence, though "enemies in their minds by wicked works;" and to enjoy spiritual blessedness, while they carnalize their affections, and more and more indispose themselves to relish it. Thus they separate what God has joined together, while they expect the end without the appointed means. They hope to be pardoned without a heart-purifying faith, and accepted of God without the imputed righteousness of Christ—to be embraced by that mercy which they grossly abuse, and spared by that patience which they continue to provoke. Nay, they propose, what is obviously impossible, to live with the wicked, the worldly, and debauched, and yet to die with the holy and self-denied; to be followers of the meek and humble Jesus, and yet indulge wrath and ambition; and to be happy without friendly intercourse with the Father of their spirits, and fountain of bliss; and hence, live contented, without "having fellowship with the Father and his Son Jesus Christ." 1 John i. 3. Though all fallible and prone to deceive, they nevertheless depend more firmly on each other's word, than on the promise and oath of God, "who cannot lie." Tit. i. 2. They hope to get victory over sin by slothful wishes, without striving earnestly against it, and to become somehow good, without ever "exercising themselves unto godliness." 1 Tim. iv. 7. Oh, what shocking disappointments they meet with! The higher they rise, the more dreadful their fall. They will be "cut down like a tree," (Job xix. 10,) and end in certain despair.

VIII. Madness appears in the precarious fickleness of human hearts. Mankind are blown hither and thither, like withered leaves in autumn, or like chaff, the sport of winds. They are not only contradictory to each other, but the same individual is discordant with himself. One thing is approved in the morning, the contrary in the evening. Now love is predominant, but the next pulse beats disaffection to the same object. This hour the sinner, disturbed in mind, rejects a favourite lust with abhorrence; the next, he calls and embraces it. He now resolves to be religious in earnest, but presently defers it till to-morrow; and when the morrow is come, he has forgotten the whole.

Now the judgment is clear, and things appear in comely order; now it is covered with clouds, and what was order becomes confusion. Now the heart is calm, easy and pliant; now a tempest ruffles the bosom, and obstinacy that cannot bend takes place. Now mercy and kindness sweeten the temper, which is presently soured by revenge and moroseness. Now he steers a steady course this way, but turns to a different point with the next veering gale. Excellent sentiments are quickly blotted, and the last impressions razed out by the next succeeding. A determinate and fixed resolve but mocks the observer, and seems more like the effect of chance, than of judgment and deliberation.

How ludicrous are the quick changes of customs and fashions! yet each of them approved, and each of them censured in its turn by the very same persons! Now it pleases; now it gives disgust; and now it pleases again. The gay and fashionable, and they who live in affluent circumstances, are busied too, and even perplexed in the variety of vanity, and wearied in the giddy chase—and though many of them are, in some lesser points, more polished than others, yet they afford us a prospect not more rational, nor less wild, than those they despise. Worldly prosperity, perverted from its use by human depravity, makes their passions impetuous, their impatience violent, and their judgment weak. This being the character, though not of all, yet of the greater part who glory in high life, what can follow from it but a wild inconstancy? my soul! how evanid are human thoughts and human things! how delusive the scenes of mortal pleasure! and how little reason is there to depend on the power, or wisdom, or fidelity of the fallen human race! "Trust not in princes themselves, nor in the son of man, in whom there is no help," (Psa. cxlvi. 3,) but rather "cease from man, whose breath is in his nostrils; for wherein is he to be accounted of?" Isa. ii. 22. These characters are no fictions, nor exaggerations of the truth, but are all taken from the life. And though the half is not told, yet in what a shocking point of light do even these rough and imperfect sketches set mankind!

But what aggravates this madness to the highest degree is, that "after all they go to the dead." Solemn consideration! The gay and jovial, the rich, the great, the poor and mean, the sorrowful and afflicted—all depart hence, and are seen no more among the living! See whole ages swept away by the "besom of destruction!" noisy and bustling millions silent in the dust! and all their mortal honours, their sensual joys, and earthly cares, are for ever departed with them! What authority or empire have Alexander the Great, Cyrus, or Caesar now? Where are their favourites, their friends, their flatterers, and their subjects? Who fears their frowns, trembles at their threats, or courts their favour in the house of silence? And what do their triumphs and spoils avail them now? Implacable enemies are hushed into everlasting peace. Are these the men that "made the earth tremble, that shook kingdoms?" Isa. xiv. 16. They are become weak as the meanest; their pomp is brought down to the grave; the worm is spread under them, and the worms cover them. Isa. xiv. 10, 11. Thus mankind in every age bustle and die. Like bubbles they are blown up, and glitter and break; like flowers they spring, bloom, and are cut down, and like "shadows they pass away," and "continue not." Job xiv. 2. But whither do they pass? Where shall our curious or rather solicitous thoughts follow them? Is death the end of their existence? No; "after that comes the judgment." They are summoned to appear before the august, the impartial, and sovereign Judge; they stand at his bar, and hear an irrevocable doom. What doom! Can we bear to contemplate the state of those, who madly provoked their Judge, and perished impenitent? Does not the heart recoil, the imagination startle, at the direful thought of a horrible gloom—regions of eternal despair—the steam of sulphur mixed with unquenchable fire—the torturing gripes, the relentless lashings of a guilty conscience, that gnawing, never-dying-vulture—the insufferable impression of almighty wrath, and the hideous shrieks of damned souls? And are the bare thoughts of these things shocking? what, then, will it be to endure them? And can we judge those to be sober, and in their right minds, who are in continual danger of plunging into these miseries, and yet are secure and careless about any endeavour to escape from the wrath to come? What an amazing scene do the sons and daughters of pleasure exhibit to us! They are daily exposed to a thousand deaths; are easily broken by numberless unforeseen accidents; and if they die impenitent, they are for ever undone: yet are no more alarmed than if they were immortal. All thoughtless, all volatile, hating serious things, and lectures of death, which, therefore, surprises them, finds them unprovided, hurries them away, and pushes them reluctant down the dreadful precipice—from time into eternity. the hardy adventure! to take a leap in the dark into an endless, unalterable state! Merry company, balls, assemblies, and plays, amuse them so, that they forget they are mortal, till they die, and see not their danger till they are beyond relief. They live in jest, "and after that they go to the dead" in earnest. What degree of folly is it to catch a feather, and let go a crown! to gain a toy, and lose a kingdom! for a morsel, to barter a birth-right! and for a moment's pleasure, to part with everlasting joys, and suffer eternal woes! Are these your men of sense, who look indignant on those who are so weak as to be deeply concerned about such important affairs? "Vain man, forsooth, would be wise, though he is born like a wild ass's colt." Job xi. 12. It is an inexpressible absurdity, that temporal things, whether riches, honour, or pleasure, should engross the intensest thoughts of beings bound for eternity. And it is an eternal solecism in religion, to be engaged about the concerns of it in a cold and indifferent manner. "The kingdom of heaven suffereth violence, and the violent take it by force." Matt. xi. 12.

After considering all these things, will it seem an abuse of mankind, if I compare this world to a great bedlam, filled with persons strangely and variously distracted? Some are so desperate as to refuse all salutary medicines; and the habit so inveterate, as to non-plus the physician's skill, and make him almost despair of their cure. Some appear hopeful for awhile, but relapse, and their case is more dangerous than before. And some are actually recovered in a less, some in a greater degree; but not so much as one perfectly well. My text will warrant the comparison; and I may not flatter mankind by soothing expressions, when their case requires plain dealing; nor be so polite as not to learn of God how to speak, when I deliver his message.

From the whole we are taught,

1. How little reason any one has to be puffed up with popular applause, or dispirited when he does not obtain it. For, consider, who are the judges? Are they all persons of sound mind, whose conclusions are according to truth? Far from it. It is true, all fancy themselves mighty good judges of merit; but I speak charitably, when I say, perhaps one in a hundred can distinguish. That soul, therefore, is lighter than vanity that is tossed hither and thither, according to the ebbing and flowing tides of inconstant affections. The favourable opinion of mankind is chiefly to be valued as it gives an opportunity to serve their best interests more successfully.

2. How much reason there is in that divine exhortation, "Be not conformed to this world." Rom. xii. 2. Do not act upon its principles, nor accommodate yourselves to its evil customs and modes. For this world is at variance

with God, and "no man can serve two masters." Matt. vi. 24. It is here modish to make light of religion, and treat it, if treated at all, with an air of the most absolute indifference and unconcern. Nay, with many it is polite, to sneer at solemn devotion, and make a mock of sin. He appears big, who dares trample on sacred and inviolable authority, and laugh at divine threatenings; and wise, who can ridicule the mysteries of the gospel. He who is a companion of such fools shall be destroyed. Prov. xiii. 20.

Lastly. Let the follies of others be a motive to engage your more earnest pursuit of saving wisdom. "Seek her as silver, search for her as for hidden treasure." Prov. ii. 4. "Happy is the man that finds her, for she is more precious than silver, than fine gold and rubies—her ways are ways of pleasantness, and all her paths are peace. Prov. iii. 13–15 and 17. If any of you lack this spiritual wisdom, ask it of God, who gives liberally and upbraids not; and let it ever be a small matter with you, to be judged weak and foolish, by a mad world, provided always that you are wise to salvation.

THE END.

Freedom of the Will

A Careful and Strict Enquiry Into the Modern Prevailing Notions of that Freedom of Will, which Is Supposed to Be Essential to Moral Agency, Virtue and Vice, Reward and Punishment, Praise and Blame.

By Jonathan Edwards, A. M., Pastor of the Church in Stockbridge.

Rom. ix. 16. It is not of him that willeth—

[NOTE REGARDING THIS EDITION: Brackets throughout represent historical corrections implemented after the addressing of a list of errors, both printed and noted by studiers of Edwards' works, from the earliest editions; some brackets contain additional citation references. Several of the lengthy footnoted quotations from Edwards' works have been adjusted from their original location and replaced in appropriate order as run-in or block quotations within the text to avoid confusion in the modern column layout.]

AUTHOR'S PREFACE

Many find much fault with the calling professing Christians, that differ one from another in some matters of opinion, by distinct names; especially calling them by the names of particular men, who have distinguished themselves as maintainers and promoters of those opinions: as the calling some professing Christians "Arminians," from Arminius; others "Arians," from Arius; others "Socinians," from Socinus, and the like. They think it unjust in itself; as it seems to suppose and suggest, that the persons marked out by these names, received those doctrines which they entertain, out of regard to, and reliance on those men after whom they are named; as though they made them their rule: in the same manner, as the followers of Christ are called "Christians"; after his name, whom they regard and depend upon, as their great Head and Rule. Whereas, this is an unjust and groundless imputation on those that go under the forementioned denominations. Thus (say they) there is not the least ground to suppose, that the chief divines, who embrace the scheme of doctrine which is by many called Arminianism, believe it the more because Arminius believed it: and that there is no reason to think any other, than that they sincerely and impartially study the Holy Scriptures, and inquire after the mind of Christ, with as much judgment and sincerity, as any of those that call them by these names; that they seek after truth, and are not careful whether they think exactly as Arminius did; yea, that in some things they actually differ from him. This practice is also esteemed actually injurious on this account, that it is supposed naturally to lead the multitude to imagine the difference between persons thus named and others, to be greater than it is; yea, as though it were so great, that they must be as it were another species of beings. And they object against it as arising from an uncharitable, narrow, contracted spirit; which, they say, commonly inclines persons to confine all that is good to themselves and their own party, and to make a wide distinction between themselves and others, and stigmatize those that differ from them with odious names. They say moreover, that the keeping up such a distinction of names has a direct tendency to uphold distance and disaffection, and keep alive mutual hatred among Christians, who ought all to be united in friendship and charity, however they can't in all things think alike.

I confess, these things are very plausible. And I will not deny, that there are some unhappy consequences of this distinction of names, and that men's infirmities and evil dispositions often make an ill improvement of it. But yet I humbly conceive, these objections are carried far beyond reason. The generality of mankind are disposed enough, and a great deal too much, to uncharitableness, and to be censorious and bitter towards those that differ from them in religious opinions: which evil temper of mind will take occasion to exert itself, from many things in themselves innocent, useful and necessary. But yet there is no necessity to suppose, that the thus distinguishing persons of different opinions by different names, arises mainly from an uncharitable spirit. It may arise from the disposition there is in mankind (whom God has distinguished with an ability and inclination for speech) to improve the benefit of language, in the proper use and design of names, given to things which they have often occasion to speak of, or signify their minds about; which is to enable them to express their ideas with ease and expedition, without being incumbered with an obscure and difficult circumlocution. And the thus distinguishing persons of different opinions in religious matters, may not imply, nor infer any more than that there is a difference, and that the difference is such as we find we have often occasion to take notice of, and make mention of. That which we have frequent occasion to speak of (whatever it be, that gives the occasion) this wants a name: and 'tis always a defect in language, in such cases, to be obliged to make use of a description, instead of a name. Thus we have often occasion to speak of those who are the descendants of the ancient inhabitants of France, who were subjects or heads of the government of that land, and spake the language peculiar to it; in distinction from the descendants of the inhabitants of Spain, who belonged to that community, and spake the language of that country. And therefore we find the great need of distinct names to signify these different sorts of people, and the great convenience of those distinguishing words, "French" and "Spaniards"; by which the signification of our minds is quick and easy, and our speech is delivered from the burden of a continual reiteration of diffuse descriptions, with which it must otherwise be embarrassed.

That the difference of the opinions of those, who in their general scheme of divinity agree with these two noted men, Calvin, and Arminius, is a thing there is often occasion to speak of, is what the practice of the latter, itself confesses; who are often, in their discourses and writings, taking notice of the supposed absurd and pernicious opinions of the former sort. And therefore the making use of different names in this case can't reasonably be objected against, or condemned, as a thing which must come from so bad a cause as they assign. It is easy to be accounted for, without supposing it to arise from any other source, than the exigence and natural tendency of the state of things; considering the faculty and disposition God has given mankind, to express things which they have frequent occasion to mention, by certain distinguishing names. It is an effect that is similar to what we see arise, in innumerable cases which are parallel, where the cause is not at all blameworthy.

Nevertheless, at first I had thoughts of carefully avoiding the use of the appellation "Arminian" in this treatise. But I soon found I should be put to great difficulty by it; and that my discourse would be so encumbered with an often repeated circumlocution, instead of a name, which would express the thing intended, as well and better, that I altered my purpose. And therefore I must ask the excuse of such as are apt to be offended with things of this nature, that I have so freely used the term "Arminian" in the following discourse. I profess it to be without any design, to stigmatize persons of any sort with a name of reproach, or at all to make them appear more odious. If when I had occasion to speak of those divines who are commonly called by this name, I had, instead of styling them Arminians, called them "these men," as Dr. Whitby does Calvinistic divines; it probably would not have been taken any better, or thought to show a better temper, or more good manners. I have done as I would be done by, in this matter. However the term "Calvinist" is in these days, among most, a term of greater reproach than the term "Arminian"; yet I should not take it at all amiss, to be called a Calvinist, for distinction's sake: though I utterly disclaim a dependence on Calvin, or believing the doctrines which I hold, because he believed and taught them; and cannot justly be charged with believing in everything just as he taught.

But lest I should really be an occasion of injury to some persons, I would here give notice, that though I generally speak of that doctrine, concerning free will and moral agency, which I oppose, as an Arminian doctrine; yet I would not be understood, that every divine or author whom I have occasion to mention as maintaining that doctrine, was properly an Arminian, or one of that sort which is commonly called by that name. Some of them went far beyond the Arminians: and I would by no means charge Arminians in general with all the corrupt doctrine, which these maintained. Thus for instance, it would be very injurious, if I should rank Arminian divines in general, with such authors as Mr. Chubb. I doubt not, many of them have some of his doctrines in abhorrence; though he agrees, for the most part, with Arminians, in his notion of the freedom of the will. And on the other hand, though I suppose this notion to be a leading article in the Arminian scheme, that which, if pursued in its consequences, will truly infer, or naturally lead to all the rest; yet I don't charge all that have held this doctrine, with being Arminians. For whatever may be the consequences of the doctrine really, yet some that hold this doctrine, may not own nor see these consequences; and it would be unjust, in many instances, to charge every author with believing and maintaining all the real consequences of his avowed doctrines. And I desire it may be particularly noted, that though I have occasion in the following discourse, often to mention the author of the book entitled, An Essay on the Freedom of the Will, in God and the Creature, as holding that notion of freedom of will, which I oppose; yet I don't mean to call him an Arminian: however in that doctrine he agrees with Arminians, and departs from the current and general opinion of Calvinists. If the author of that essay be the same as it is commonly ascribed to, he doubtless was not one that ought to bear that name. But however good a divine he was in many respects, yet that particular Arminian doctrine which he maintained, is never the better for being held by such an one: nor is there less need of opposing it on that account; but rather is there the more need of it; as it will be likely to have the more pernicious influence, for being taught by a divine of his name and character; supposing the doctrine to be wrong, and in itself to be of an ill tendency.

I have nothing further to say by way of preface; but only to bespeak the reader's candor, and calm attention to what I have written.

The subject is of such importance, as to demand attention, and the most thorough consideration. Of all kinds of knowledge that we can ever obtain, the knowledge of God, and the knowledge of ourselves, are the most important. As religion is the great business, for which we are created, and on which our happiness depends; and as religion consists in an intercourse between ourselves and our Maker; and so has its foundation in God's nature and ours, and in the relation that God and we stand in to each other; therefore a true knowledge of both must be needful in order to true religion. But the knowledge of ourselves consists chiefly in right apprehensions concerning those two chief faculties of our nature, the understanding and will. Both are very important: yet the science of the latter must be confessed to be of greatest moment; inasmuch as all virtue and religion have their seat more immediately in the will, consisting more especially in right acts and habits of this faculty. And the grand question about the freedom of the will, is the main point that belongs to the science of the will. Therefore I say, the importance of this subject greatly demands the attention of Christians, and especially of divines. But as to my manner of handling the subject, I will be far from presuming to say, that it is such as demands the attention of the reader to what I have written. I am ready to own, that in this matter I depend on the reader's courtesy. But only thus far I may have some color for putting in a claim; that if the reader be disposed to pass his censure on what I have written, I may be fully and patiently heard, and well attended to, before I am condemned. However, this is what I would humbly ask of my readers; together with the prayers of all sincere lovers of truth, that I may have much of that Spirit which Christ promised his disciples, which guides into all truth; and that the blessed and powerful influences of this Spirit would make truth victorious in the world.

PART ONE

Wherein Are Explained and Stated Various Terms and Things Belonging to the Subject of the Ensuing Discourse

SECTION 1.

CONCERNING THE NATURE OF THE WILL

It may possibly be thought, that there is no great need of going about to define or describe the "will"; this word being generally as well understood as any other words we can use to explain it: and so perhaps it would be, had not philosophers, metaphysicians and polemic divines brought the matter into obscurity by the things they have said of it. But since it is so, I think it may be of some use, and will tend to the greater clearness in the following discourse, to say a few things concerning it.

And therefore I observe, that the will (without any metaphysical refining) is plainly, that by which the mind chooses anything. The faculty of the will is that faculty or power or principle of mind by which it is capable of choosing: an act of the will is the same as an act of choosing or choice.

If any think is a more perfect definition of the will, to say, that it is that by which the soul either chooses or refuses; I am content with it: though I think that 'tis enough to say, it's that by which the soul chooses: for in every act of will whatsoever, the mind chooses one thing rather than another; it chooses something rather than the contrary, or rather than the want or nonexistence of that thing. So in every act of refusal, the mind chooses the absence of the thing refused; the positive and the negative are set before the mind for its choice, and it chooses the negative; and the mind's making its choice in that case is properly the act of the will: the will's determining between the two is a voluntary determining; but that is the same thing as making a choice. So that whatever names we call the act of the will by—choosing, refusing, approving, disapproving, liking, disliking, embracing, rejecting, determining, directing, commanding, forbidding, inclining or being averse, a being pleased or displeased with—all may be reduced to this of choosing. For the soul to act voluntarily, is evermore to act electively.

Mr. Locke [John Locke, An Essay Concerning Human Understanding (1690), Bk. II, ch. 21, no. 17; ed. A. C. Frazer (2 vols. Oxford, 1894), 1, 321. JE cites the 7th ed. London, 1716] says, "The will signifies nothing but a power or ability to prefer or choose." And in the foregoing page says, "The word 'preferring' seems best to express the act of volition"; but adds, that "it does it not precisely; for (says he) though a man would prefer flying to walking, yet who can say he ever wills it?" [Ibid., no. 15; p. 320.] But the instance he mentions don't prove that there is anything else in "willing" but merely "preferring": for it should be considered what is the next and immediate object of the will, with respect to a man's walking, or any other external action; which is not his being removed from one place to another; on the earth, or through the air; these are remoter objects of preference; but such or such an immediate exertion of himself. The thing nextly chosen or preferred when a man wills to walk, is not his being removed to such a place where he would be, but such an exertion and motion of his legs and feet, etc. in order to it. And his willing such an alteration in his body in the present moment, is nothing else but his choosing or preferring such an alteration in his body at such a moment, or his liking it better than the forbearance of it. And God has so made and established the human nature, the soul being united to a body in proper state, that the soul preferring or choosing such an immediate exertion or alteration of the body, such an alteration instantaneously follows. There is nothing else in the actings of my mind, that I am conscious of while I walk, but only my preferring or choosing, through successive moments, that there should be such alterations of my external sensations and motions; together with a concurring habitual expectation that it will be so; having ever found by experience, that on such an immediate preference, such sensations and motions do actually instantaneously, and constantly arise. But it is not so in the case of flying: though a man may be said remotely to choose or prefer flying; yet he don't choose or prefer, incline to or desire, under circumstances in view, any immediate exertion of the members of his body in order to it; because he has no expectation that he should obtain the desired end by any such exertion; and he don't prefer or incline to any bodily exertion or effort under this apprehended circumstance, of its being wholly in vain. So that if we carefully distinguish the proper objects of the several acts of the will, it will not appear by this, and suchlike instances, that there is any difference between "volition" and "preference"; or that a man's choosing, liking best, or being best pleased with a thing, are not the same with his willing that thing; as they seem to be according to those general and more natural notions of men, according to which language is formed. Thus an act of the will is commonly expressed by its pleasing a man to do thus or thus; and a man's doing as he wills, and doing as he pleases, are the same thing in common speech.

Mr. Locke says, "The will is perfectly distinguished from desire; which in the very same action may have a quite contrary tendency from that which our wills set us upon. A man (says he) whom I cannot deny, may oblige me to use persuasions to another, which, at the same time I am speaking, I may wish may not prevail on him. In this case 'tis plain the will and desire run counter" [Ibid., no. 30; p. 332]. I don't suppose, that "will" and "desire" are words of precisely the same signification: "will" seems to be a word of a more general signification, extending to things present and absent. "Desire" respects something absent. I may prefer my present situation and posture, suppose sitting still, or having my eyes open, and so may will it. But yet I can't think they are so entirely distinct, that they can ever be properly said to run counter. A man never, in any instance, wills anything contrary to his desires, or desires anything contrary to his will. The forementioned instance, which Mr. Locke produces, don't prove that he ever does. He may, on some consideration or other, will to utter speeches which have a tendency to persuade another, and still may desire that they may not persuade him: but yet his will and desire don't run counter at all: the thing which he wills, the very same he desires; and he don't will a thing, and desire the contrary in any particular. In this instance, it is not carefully observed, what is the thing willed, and what is the thing desired: if it were, it would be found that will and desire don't clash in the least. The thing willed on some consideration, is to utter such words; and certainly, the same consideration so influences him, that he don't desire the contrary; all things considered, he chooses to utter such words, and don't desire not to utter 'em. And so as to the thing which Mr. Locke speaks of as desired, viz. that the words, though they tend to persuade, should not be effectual to that end, his will is not contrary to this; he don't will that they should be effectual, but rather wills that they should not, as he desires. In order to prove that the will and desire may run counter, it should be shown that they may be contrary one to the other in the same thing, or with respect to the very same object of will or desire: but here the objects are two; and in each, taken by themselves, the will and desire agree. And 'tis no wonder that they should not agree in different things, however little distinguished they are in their nature. The will may not agree with the will, nor desire agree with desire, in different things. As in this very instance which Mr. Locke mentions, a person may, on some consideration, desire to use persuasions, and at the same time may desire they may not prevail; but yet nobody will say, that desire runs counter to desire; or that this proves that desire is perfectly a distinct thing from desire. The like might be observed of the other instance Mr. Locke produces, of a man's desiring to be eased of pain and so forth.

But not to dwell any longer on this, whether desire and will, and whether preference and volition be precisely the same things or no; yet, I trust it will be allowed by all, that in every act of will there is an act of choice; that in every volition there is a preference, or a prevailing inclination of the soul, whereby the soul, at that instant, is out of a state of perfect indifference, with respect to the direct object of the volition. So that in every act, or going forth of the will, there is some preponderation of the mind or inclination, one way rather than another; and the soul had rather have or do one thing than another, or than not to have or do that thing; and that there, where there is absolutely no preferring or choosing, but a perfect continuing equilibrium, there is no volition.

SECTION 2.

CONCERNING THE DETERMINATION OF THE WILL

By "determining the will," if the phrase be used with any meaning, must be intended, causing that the act of the will or choice should be thus, and not otherwise: and the will is said to be determined, when, in consequence of some action, or influence, its choice is directed to, and fixed upon a particular object. As when we speak of the determination of motion, we mean causing the motion of the body to be such a way, or in such a direction, rather than another.

To talk of the determination of the will, supposes an effect, which must have a cause. If the will be determined, there is a determiner. This must be supposed to be intended even by them that say, the will determines itself. If it be so, the will is both determiner and determined; it is a cause that acts and produces effects upon itself, and is the object of its own influence and action.

With respect to that grand inquiry, what determines the will, it would be very tedious and unnecessary at present to enumerate and examine all the various opinions, which have been advanced concerning this matter; nor is it needful that I should enter into a particular disquisition of all points debated in disputes on that question, whether the will always follows the last dictate of the understanding. It is sufficient to my present purpose to say, it is that motive, which, as it stands in the view of the mind, is the strongest, that determines the will.—But it may be necessary that I should a little explain my meaning in this.

By "motive," I mean the whole of that which moves, excites or invites the mind to volition, whether that be one thing singly, or many things conjunctly. Many particular things may concur and unite their strength to induce the mind; and when it is so, all together are as it were one complex motive. And when I speak of the "strongest motive," I have respect to the strength of the whole that operates to induce to a particular act of volition, whether that be the strength of one thing alone, or of many together.

Whatever is a motive, in this sense, must be something that is extant in the view or apprehension of the understanding, or perceiving faculty. Nothing can induce or invite the mind to will or act anything, any further than it is perceived, or is some way or other in the mind's view; for what is wholly unperceived, and perfectly out of the mind's view, can't affect the mind at all. 'Tis most evident, that nothing is in the mind, or reaches it, or takes any hold of it, any otherwise than as it is perceived or thought of.

And I think it must also be allowed by all, that everything that is properly called a motive, excitement or inducement to a perceiving willing agent, has some sort and degree of tendency, or advantage to move or excite the will, previous to the effect, or to the act of the will excited. This previous tendency of the motive is what I call the "strength" of the motive. That motive which has a less degree of previous advantage or tendency to move the will, or that appears less inviting, as it stands in the view of the mind, is what I call a "weaker motive." On the contrary, that which appears most inviting, and has, by what appears concerning it to the understanding or apprehension, the greatest degree of previous tendency to excite and induce the choice, is what I call the "strongest motive." And in this sense, I suppose the will is always determined by the strongest motive.

Things that exist in the view of the mind, have their strength, tendency or advantage to move or excite its will, from many things appertaining to the nature and circumstances of the thing viewed, the nature and circumstances of the mind that views, and the degree and manner of its view; which it would perhaps be hard to make a perfect enumeration of. But so much I think may be determined in general, without room for controversy, that whatever is perceived or apprehended by an intelligent and voluntary agent, which has the nature and influence of a motive to volition or choice, is considered or viewed as good; nor has it any tendency to invite or engage the election of the soul in any further degree than it appears such. For to say otherwise, would be to say, that things that appear have a tendency by the appearance they make, to engage the mind to elect them, some other way than by their appearing eligible to it; which is absurd. And therefore it must be true, in some sense, that the will always is as the greatest apparent good is. But only, for the right understanding of this, two things must be well and distinctly observed.

1. It must be observed in what sense I use the term "good"; namely, as of the same import with "agreeable." To appear good to the mind, as I use the phrase, is the same as to appear agreeable, or seem pleasing to the mind. Certainly, nothing appears inviting and eligible to the mind, or tending to engage its inclination and choice, considered as evil or disagreeable; nor indeed, as indifferent, and neither agreeable nor disagreeable. But if it tends to draw the inclination, and move the will, it must be under the notion of that which suits the mind. And therefore that must have the greatest tendency to attract and engage it, which, as it stands in the mind's view, suits it best, and pleases it most; and in that sense, is the greatest apparent good: to say otherwise, is little, if anything, short of a direct and plain contradiction.

The word "good," in this sense, includes in its signification, the removal or avoiding of evil, or of that which is disagreeable and uneasy. 'Tis agreeable and pleasing, to avoid what is disagreeable and displeasing, and to have uneasiness removed. So that here is in eluded what Mr. Locke supposes determines the will. For when he speaks of uneasiness as determining the will, he must be understood as supposing that the end or aim which governs in the volition or act of preference, is the avoiding or removal of that uneasiness; and that is the same thing as choosing and seeking what is more easy and agreeable.

2. When I say, the will is as the greatest apparent good is, or (as I have explained it) that volition has always for its object the thing which appears most agreeable; it must be carefully observed, to avoid confusion and needless objection, that I speak of the direct and immediate object of the act of volition; and not some object that the act of will has not an immediate, but only an indirect and remote respect to. Many acts of volition have some

remote relation to an object, that is different from the thing most immediately willed and chosen. Thus, when a drunkard has his liquor before him, and he has to choose whether to drink it, or no; the proper and immediate objects, about which his present volition is conversant, and between which his choice now decides, are his own acts, in drinking the liquor, or letting it alone; and this will certainly be done according to what, in the present view of his mind, taken in the whole of it, is most agreeable to him. If he chooses or wills to drink it, and not to let it alone; then this action, as it stands in the view of his mind, with all that belongs to its appearance there, is more agreeable and pleasing than letting it alone.

But the objects to which this act of volition may relate more remotely, and between which his choice may determine more indirectly, are the present pleasure the man expects by drinking, and the future misery which he judges will be the consequence of it: he may judge that this future misery, when it comes, will be more disagreeable and unpleasant, than refraining from drinking now would be. But these two things are not the proper objects that the act of volition spoken of is nextly conversant about. For the act of will spoken of is concerning present drinking or forbearing to drink. If he wills to drink, then drinking is the proper object of the act of his will; and drinking, on some account or other, now appears most agreeable to him, and suits him best. If he chooses to refrain, then refraining is the immediate object of his will, and is most pleasing to him. If in the choice he makes in the case, he prefers a present pleasure to a future advantage, which he judges will be greater when it comes; then a lesser present pleasure appears more agreeable to him than a greater advantage at a distance. If on the contrary a future advantage is preferred, then that appears most agreeable, and suits him best. And so still the present volition is as the greatest apparent good at present is.

I have rather chosen to express myself thus, that the will always is as the greatest apparent good, or as what appears most agreeable, is, than to say that the will is determined by the greatest apparent good, or by what seems most agreeable; because an appearing most agreeable or pleasing to the mind, and the mind's preferring and choosing, seem hardly to be properly and perfectly distinct. If strict propriety of speech be insisted on, it may more properly be said, that the voluntary action which is the immediate consequence and fruit of the mind's volition or choice, is determined by that which appears most agreeable, than the preference or choice itself; but that the act of volition itself is always determined by that in or about the mind's view of the object, which causes it to appear most agreeable. I say, in or about the mind's view of the object, because what has influence to render an object in view agreeable, is not only what appears in the object viewed, but also the manner of the view, and the state and circumstances of the mind that views.—Particularly to enumerate all things pertaining to the mind's view of the objects of volition, which have influence in their appearing agreeable to the mind, would be a matter of no small difficulty, and might require a treatise by itself, and is not necessary to my present purpose. I shall therefore only mention some things in general.

I. One thing that makes an object proposed to choice agreeable, is the apparent nature and circumstances of the object. And there are various things of this sort, that have an hand in rendering the object more or less agreeable; as,

1. That which appears in the object, which renders it beautiful and pleasant, or deformed and irksome to the mind; viewing it as it is in itself.

2. The apparent degree of pleasure or trouble attending the object, or the consequence of it. Such concomitants and consequents being viewed as circumstances of the object, are to be considered as belonging to it, and as it were parts of it; as it stands in the mind's view, as a proposed object of choice.

3. The apparent state of the pleasure or trouble that appears, with respect to distance of time; being either nearer or farther off. 'Tis a thing in itself agreeable to the mind, to have pleasure speedily; and disagreeable, to have it delayed: so that if there be two equal degrees of pleasure set in the mind's view, and all other things are equal, but only one is beheld as near, and the other far off; the nearer will appear most agreeable, and so will be chosen. Because, though the agreeableness of the objects be exactly equal, as viewed in themselves, yet not as viewed in their circumstances; one of them having the additional agreeableness of the circumstance of nearness.

II. Another thing that contributes to the agreeableness of an object of choice, as it stands in the mind's view, is the manner of the view. If the object be something which appears connected with future pleasure, not only will the degree of apparent pleasure have influence, but also the manner of the view, especially in two respects.

1. With respect to the degree of judgment, or firmness of assent, with which the mind judges the pleasure to be future. Because it is more agreeable to have a certain happiness, than an uncertain one; and a pleasure viewed as more

probable, all other things being equal, is more agreeable to the mind, than that which is viewed as less probable.

2. With respect to the degree of the idea of the future pleasure. With regard to things which are the subject of our thoughts, either past, present or future, we have much more of an idea or apprehension of some things than others; that is, our idea is much more clear, lively and strong. Thus, the ideas we have of sensible things by immediate sensation, are usually much more lively than those we have by mere imagination, or by contemplation of them when absent. My idea of the sun, when I look upon it, is more vivid, than when I only think of it. Our idea of the sweet relish of a delicious fruit is usually stronger when we taste it, than when we only imagine it. And sometimes, the ideas we have of things by contemplation, are much stronger and clearer, than at other times. Thus, a man at one time has a much stronger idea of the pleasure which is to be enjoyed in eating some sort of food that he loves, than at another. Now the degree, or strength of the idea or sense that men have of future good or evil, is one thing that has great influence on their minds to excite choice or volition. When of two kinds of future pleasure, which the mind considers of, and are presented for choice, both are supposed exactly equal by the judgment, and both equally certain, and all other things are equal, but only one of them is what the mind has a far more lively sense of, than of the other; this has the greatest advantage by far to affect and attract the mind, and move the will. 'Tis now more agreeable to the mind, to take the pleasure it has a strong and lively sense of, than that which it has only a faint idea of. The view of the former is attended with the strongest appetite, and the greatest uneasiness attends the want of it; and 'tis agreeable to the mind, to have uneasiness removed, and its appetite gratified. And if several future enjoyments are presented together, as competitors for the choice of the mind, some of them judged to be greater, and others less; the mind also having a greater sense and more lively idea of the good of some of them, and of others a less; and some are viewed as of greater certainty or probability than others; and those enjoyments that appear most agreeable in one of these respects, appear least so in others: in this case, all other things being equal, the agreeableness of a proposed object of choice will be in a degree some way compounded of the degree of good supposed by the judgment, the degree of apparent probability or certainty of that good, and the degree of the view or sense, or liveliness of the idea the mind has, of that good; because all together concur to constitute the degree in which the object appears at present agreeable; and accordingly volition will be determined.

I might further observe, the state of the mind that views a proposed object of choice, is another thing that contributes to the agreeableness or disagreeableness of that object; the particular temper which the mind has by nature, or that has been introduced and established by education, example, custom, or some other means; or the frame or state that the mind is in on a particular occasion. That object which appears agreeable to one, does not so to another. And the same object don't always appear alike agreeable to the same person, at different times. It is most agreeable to some men, to follow their reason; and to others, to follow their appetites: to some men, it is more agreeable to deny a vicious inclination, than to gratify it; others it suits best to gratify the vilest appetites. 'Tis more disagreeable to some men than others, to counteract a former resolution. In these respects, and many others which might be mentioned, different things will be most agreeable to different persons; and not only so, but to the same persons at different times.

But possibly 'tis needless and improper, to mention the frame and state of the mind, as a distinct ground of the agreeableness of objects from the other two mentioned before; viz. the apparent nature and circumstances of the objects viewed, and the manner of the view: perhaps if we strictly consider the matter, the different temper and state of the mind makes no alteration as to the agreeableness of objects, any other way, than as it makes the objects themselves appear differently beautiful or deformed, having apparent pleasure or pain attending them: and as it occasions the manner of the view to be different, causes the idea of beauty or deformity, pleasure or uneasiness to be more or less lively.

However, I think so much is certain, that volition, in no one instance that can be mentioned, is otherwise than the greatest apparent good is, in the manner which has been explained. The choice of the mind never departs from that which, at that time, and with respect to the direct and immediate objects of that decision of the mind, appears most agreeable and pleasing, all things considered. If the immediate objects of the will are a man's own actions, then those actions which appear most agreeable to him he wills. If it be now most agreeable to him, all things considered, to walk, then he now wills to walk. If it be now, upon the whole of what at present appears to him, most agreeable to speak, then he chooses to speak: if it suits him best to keep silence, then he chooses to keep silence. There is scarcely a plainer and more universal dictate of the sense and experience of mankind, than that, when men act voluntarily, and do what they please, then they do what suits them best, or what is most agreeable to them. To say, that they do what they please, or what pleases them, but yet don't do what is agreeable to them, is the same thing as to say, they do what they please, but don't act their pleasure; and that is to say, that they do what they please, and yet don't do what they please.

It appears from these things, that in some sense, the will always follows the last dictate of the understanding. But then the understanding must be taken in a large sense, as including the whole faculty of perception or apprehension, and not merely what is called reason or judgment. If by the dictate of the understanding is meant what reason declares to be best or most for the person's happiness, taking in the whole of his duration, it is not true, that the will always follows the last dictate of the understanding. Such a dictate of reason is quite a different matter from things appearing now most agreeable; all things being put together which pertain to the mind's present perceptions, apprehensions or ideas, in any respect. Although that dictate of reason, when it takes place, is one thing that is put into the scales and is to be considered as a thing that has concern in the compound influence which moves and induces the will; and is one thing that is to be considered in estimating the degree of that appearance of good which the will always follows; either as having its influence added to other things, or subducted from them. When it concurs with other things, then its weight is added to them, as put into the same scale; but when it is against them, it is as a weight in the opposite scale, where it resists the influence of other things: yet its resistance is often overcome by their greater weight, and so the act of the will is determined in opposition to it.

The things which I have said may, I hope, serve, in some measure, to illustrate and confirm the position I laid down in the beginning of this section, viz. that the will is always determined by the strongest motive, or by that view of the mind which has the greatest degree of previous tendency to excite volition. But whether I have been so happy as rightly to explain the thing wherein consists the strength of motives, or not, yet my failing in this will not overthrow the position itself; which carries much of its own evidence with it, and is the thing of chief importance to the purpose of the ensuing discourse: and the truth of it, I hope, will appear with greater clearness, before I have finished what I have to say on the subject of human liberty.

SECTION 3.

CONCERNING THE MEANING OF THE TERMS NECESSITY, IMPOSSIBILITY, INABILITY, ETC.; AND OF CONTINGENCE

The words "necessary," "impossible," etc. are abundantly used in controversies about free will and moral agency; and therefore the sense in which they are used, should be clearly understood.

Here I might say, that a thing is then said to be necessary, when it must be, and cannot be otherwise. But this would not properly be a definition of necessity, or an explanation of the word, any more than if I explained the word "must" by there being a necessity. The words "must," "can," and "cannot" need explication as much as the words "necessary" and "impossible"; excepting that the former are words that children commonly use, and know something of the meaning of earlier than the latter.

The word "necessary," as used in common speech, is a relative term; and relates to some supposed opposition made to the existence of the thing spoken of, which is overcome, or proves in vain to hinder or alter it. That is necessary, in the original and proper sense of the word, which is, or will be, notwithstanding all supposable opposition. To say, that a thing is necessary, is the same thing as to say, that it is impossible [it] should not be: but the word "impossible" is manifestly a relative term, and has reference to supposed power exerted to bring a thing to pass, which is insufficient for the effect; as the word "unable" is relative, and has relation to ability or endeavor which is insufficient; and as the word "irresistible" is relative, and has always reference to resistance which is made, or may be made to some force or power tending to an effect, and is insufficient to withstand the power, or hinder the effect. The common notion of necessity and impossibility implies something that frustrates endeavor or desire.

Here several things are to be noted.

1. Things are said to be necessary in general, which are or will be notwithstanding any supposable opposition from us or others, or from whatever quarter. But things are said to be necessary to us, which are or will be notwithstanding all opposition supposable in the case from us. The same may be observed of the word "impossible" and other suchlike terms.

2. These terms "necessary," "impossible," "irresistible," etc. do especially belong to the controversy about liberty and moral agency, as used in the latter of the two senses

now mentioned, viz. as necessary or impossible to us, and with relation to any supposable opposition or endeavor of ours.

3. As the word "necessity," in its vulgar and common use, is relative, and has always reference to some supposable insufficient opposition; so when we speak of anything as necessary to us, it is with relation to some supposable opposition of our wills, or some voluntary exertion or effort of ours to the contrary. For we don't properly make opposition to an event, any otherwise than as we voluntarily oppose it. Things are said to be what must be, or necessarily are, as to us, when they are, or will be, though we desire or endeavor the contrary, or try to prevent or remove their existence: but such opposition of ours always either consists in, or implies opposition of our wills.

'Tis manifest that all suchlike words and phrases, as vulgarly used, are used and accepted in this manner. A thing is said to be necessary, when we can't help it, let us do what we will. So anything is said to be impossible to us, when we would do it, or would have it brought to pass, and endeavor it; or at least may be supposed to desire and seek it; but all our desires and endeavors are, or would be vain. And that is said to be irresistible, which overcomes all our opposition, resistance, and endeavor to the contrary. And we are to be said unable to do a thing, when our supposable desires and endeavors to do it are insufficient.

We are accustomed, in the common use of language, to apply and understand these phrases in this sense: we grow up with such a habit; which by the daily use of these terms, in such a sense, from our childhood, becomes fixed and settled; so that the idea of a relation to a supposed will, desire and endeavor of ours, is strongly connected with these terms, and naturally excited in our minds, whenever we hear the words used. Such ideas, and these words, are so united and associated, that they unavoidably go together; one suggests the other, and carries the other with it, and never can be separated as long as we live. And if we use the words, as terms of art, in another sense, yet, unless we are exceeding circumspect and wary, we shall insensibly slide into the vulgar use of them, and so apply the words in a very inconsistent manner: this habitual connection of ideas will deceive and confound us in our reasonings and discourses, wherein we pretend to use these terms in that manner, as terms of art.

4. It follows from what has been observed, that when these terms "necessary," "impossible," "irresistible," "unable," etc. are used in cases wherein no opposition, or insufficient will or endeavor, is supposed, or can be supposed, but the very nature of the supposed case itself excludes and denies any such opposition, will or endeavor; these terms are then not used in their proper signification, but quite beside their use in common speech. The reason is manifest; namely, that in such cases, we can't use the words with reference to a supposable opposition, will or endeavor. And therefore if any man uses these terms in such cases, he either uses them nonsensically, or in some new sense, diverse from their original and proper meaning. As for instance; if a man should affirm after this manner, that it is necessary for a man, and what must be, that a man should choose virtue rather than vice, during the time that he prefers virtue to vice; and that it is a thing impossible and irresistible, that it should be otherwise than that he should have this choice, so long as this choice continues; such a man would use these terms "must," "irresistible," etc. with perfect insignificance and nonsense, or in some new sense, diverse from their common use; which is with reference, as has been observed, to supposable opposition, unwillingness and resistance; whereas, here, the very supposition excludes and denies any such thing: for the case supposed is that of being willing, and choosing.

5. It appears from what has been said, that these terms "necessary," "impossible," etc. are often used by philosophers and metaphysicians in a sense quite diverse from their common use and original signification: for they apply them to many cases in which no opposition is supposed or supposable. Thus they use them with respect to God's existence before the creation of the world, when there was no other being but he: so with regard to many of the dispositions and acts of the divine Being, such as his loving himself, his loving righteousness, hating sin, etc. So they apply these terms to many cases of the inclinations and actions of created intelligent beings, angels and men; wherein all opposition of the will is shut out and denied, in the very supposition of the case.

Metaphysical or philosophical necessity is nothing different from certainty. I speak not now of the certainty of knowledge, but the certainty that is in things themselves, which is the foundation of the certainty of the knowledge of them; or that wherein lies the ground of the infallibility of the proposition which affirms them.

What is sometimes given as the definition of philosophical necessity, namely, that by which a thing cannot but be, or whereby it cannot be otherwise, fails of being a proper explanation of it, on two accounts: first, the words "can" or "cannot" need explanation as much as the word "necessity"; and the former may as well be explained by the latter, as the latter by the former. Thus, if anyone asked us what we mean, when we say, a thing cannot but be, we might explain ourselves by saying, we mean, it must necessarily be so; as well as explain necessity, by saying, it is that by which a thing cannot but be. And secondly, this definition is liable to the forementioned great inconvenience: the words "cannot" or "unable" are properly relative, and have relation to power exerted, or that may be exerted, in order to the thing spoken of; to which, as I have now observed, the word "necessity," as used by philosophers, has no reference.

Philosophical necessity is really nothing else than the full and fixed connection between the things signified by the subject and predicate of a proposition, which affirms something to be true. When there is such a connection, then the thing affirmed in the proposition is necessary, in a philosophical sense; whether any opposition, or contrary effort be supposed, or supposable in the case, or no. When the subject and predicate of the proposition, which affirms the existence of anything, either substance, quality, act or circumstance, have a full and certain connection, then the existence or being of that thing is said to be necessary in a metaphysical sense. And in this sense I use the word "necessity," in the following discourse, when I endeavor to prove that necessity is not inconsistent with liberty.

The subject and predicate of a proposition, which affirms existence of something, may have a full, fixed, and certain connection several ways.

(1) They may have a full and perfect connection in and of themselves; because it may imply a contradiction, or gross absurdity, to suppose them not connected. Thus many things are necessary in their own nature. So the eternal existence of being generally considered, is necessary in itself: because it would be in itself the greatest absurdity, to deny the existence of being in general, or to say there was absolute and universal nothing; and is as it were the sum of all contradictions; as might be shewn, if this were a proper place for it. So

God's infinity, and other attributes are necessary. So it is necessary in its own nature, that two and two should be four; and it is necessary, that all right lines drawn from the center of a circle to the circumference should be equal. It is necessary, fit and suitable, that men should do to others, as they would that they should do to them. So innumerable metaphysical and mathematical truths are necessary in themselves; the subject and predicate of the proposition which affirms them, are perfectly connected of themselves.

(2) The connection of the subject and predicate of a proposition, which affirms the existence of something, may be fixed and made certain, because the existence of that thing is already come to pass; and either now is, or has been; and so has as it were made sure of existence. And therefore, the proposition which affirms present and past existence of it, may by this means be made certain, and necessarily and unalterably true; the past event has fixed and decided the matter, as to its existence; and has made it impossible but that existence should be truly predicated of it. Thus the existence of whatever is already come to pass, is now become necessary; 'tis become impossible it should be otherwise than true, that such a thing has been.

(3) The subject and predicate of a proposition which affirms something to be, may have a real and certain connection consequentially; and so the existence of the thing may be consequentially necessary; as it may be surely and firmly connected with something else, that is necessary in one of the former respects: as it is either fully and thoroughly connected with that which is absolutely necessary in its own nature, or with something which has already received and made sure of existence. This necessity lies in, or may be explained by the connection of two or more propositions one with another. Things which are perfectly connected with other things that are necessary, are necessary themselves, by a necessity of consequence.

And here it may be observed, that all things which are future, or which will hereafter begin to be, which can be said to be necessary, are necessary only in this last way. Their existence is not necessary in itself; for if so, they always would have existed. Nor is their existence become necessary by being made sure, by being already come to pass. Therefore, the only way that anything that is to come to pass hereafter, is or can be necessary, is by a connection with something that is necessary in its own nature, or something that already is, or has been; so that the one being supposed, the other certainly follows. And this also is the only way that all things past, excepting those which were from eternity, could be necessary before they came to pass, or could come to pass necessarily; and therefore the only way in which any effect or event, or anything whatsoever that ever has had, or will have a beginning, has come into being necessarily, or will hereafter necessarily exist. And therefore this is the necessity which especially belongs to controversies about the acts of the will.

It may be of some use in these controversies, further to observe concerning metaphysical necessity, that (agreeable to the distinction before observed of necessity, as vulgarly understood) things that exist may be said to be necessary, either with a general or particular necessity. The existence of a thing may be said to be necessary with a general necessity, when all things whatsoever being considered, there is a foundation for certainty of its existence; or when in the most general and universal view of things, the subject and predicate of the proposition, which affirms its existence, would appear with an infallible connection.

An event, or the existence of a thing, may be said to be necessary with a particular necessity, or with regard to a particular person, thing or time, when nothing that can be taken into consideration, in or about that person, thing or time, alters the case at all, as to the certainty of that event, or the existence of that thing; or can be of any account at all, in determining the infallibility of the connection of the subject and predicate in the proposition which affirms the existence of the thing; so that it is all one, as to that person, or thing, at least, at that time, as if the existence were necessary with a necessity that is most universal and absolute. Thus there are many things that happen to particular persons, which they have no hand in, and in the existence of which no will of theirs has any concern, at least, at that time; which, whether they are necessary or not, with regard to things in general, yet are necessary to them, and with regard to any volition of theirs at that time; as they prevent all acts of the will about the affair. I shall have occasion to apply this observation to particular instances in the following discourse. Whether the same things that are necessary with a particular necessity, be not also necessary with a general necessity, may be a matter of future consideration.

Let that be as it will, it alters not the case, as to the use of this distinction of the kinds of necessity.

These things may be sufficient for the explaining of the terms "necessary" and "necessity," as terms of art, and as often used by metaphysicians, and controversial writers in divinity, in a sense diverse from, and more extensive than their original meaning, in common language, which was before explained.

What has been said to shew the meaning of the terms "necessary" and "necessity," may be sufficient for the explaining of the opposite terms, "impossible" and "impossibility." For there is no difference, but only the latter are negative, and the former positive. Impossibility is the same as negative necessity, or a necessity that a thing should not be. And it is used as a term of art in a like diversity from the original and vulgar meaning, with necessity.

The same may be observed concerning the words "unable" and "inability." It has been observed, that these terms, in their original and common use, have relation to will and endeavor, as supposable in the case, and as insufficient for the bringing to pass the thing willed and endeavored. But as these terms are often used by philosophers and divines, especially writers on controversies about free will, they are used in a quite different, and far more extensive sense; and are applied to many cases wherein no will or endeavor for the bringing of the thing to pass, is or can be supposed, but is actually denied and excluded in the nature of the case.

As the words "necessary," "impossible," "unable," etc. are used by polemic writers, in a sense diverse from their common signification, the like has happened to the term "contingent." Anything is said to be contingent, or to come to pass by chance or accident, in the original meaning of such words, when its connection with its causes or antecedents, according to the established course of things, is not discerned; and so is what we have no means of the foresight of. And especially is anything said to be contingent or accidental with regard to us, when anything comes to pass that we are concerned in, as occasions or subjects, without our foreknowledge, and beside our design and scope.

But the word "contingent" is abundantly used in a very different sense; not for that whose connection with the series of things we can't discern, so as to foresee the event; but for something which has absolutely no previous ground or reason, with which its existence has any fixed and certain connection.

SECTION 4.

OF THE DISTINCTION OF NATURAL AND MORAL NECESSITY, AND INABILITY

That necessity which has been explained, consisting in an infallible connection of the things signified by the subject and predicate of a proposition, as intelligent beings are the subjects of it, is distinguished into moral and natural necessity.

I shall not now stand to inquire whether this distinction be a proper and perfect distinction; but shall only explain how these two sorts of necessity are understood, as the terms are sometimes used, and as they are used in the following discourse.

The phrase "moral necessity" is used variously: sometimes 'tis used for a necessity of moral obligation. So we say, a man is under necessity, when he is under bonds of duty and conscience, which he can't be discharged from. So the word "necessity" is often used for great obligation in point of interest. Sometimes by "moral necessity" is meant that apparent connection of things, which is the ground of moral evidence; and so is distinguished from absolute necessity, or that sure connection of things, that is a foundation for infallible certainty. In this sense, "moral necessity" signifies much the same as that high degree of probability, which is ordinarily sufficient to satisfy, and be relied upon by mankind, in their conduct and behavior in the world, as they would consult their own safety and interest, and treat others properly as members of society. And sometimes by "moral necessity" is meant that necessity of connection and consequence, which arises from such moral causes, as the strength of inclination, or motives, and the connection which there is in many cases between these, and such certain volitions and actions. And it is in this sense, that I use the phrase "moral necessity" in the following discourse.

By "natural necessity," as applied to men, I mean such necessity as men are under through the force of natural causes; as distinguished from what are called moral causes, such as habits and dispositions of the heart, and moral motives and inducements. Thus men placed in certain circumstances, are the subjects of particular sensations by necessity: they feel pain when their bodies are wounded; they see the objects presented before them in a clear light, when their eyes are opened: so they assent to the truth of certain propositions, as soon as the terms are understood; as that two and two make four, that black is not white, that two parallel lines can never cross one another: so by a natural necessity men's bodies move downwards, when there is nothing to support them.

But here several things may be noted concerning these two kinds of necessity.

1. Moral necessity may be as absolute, as natural necessity. That is, the effect may be as perfectly connected with its moral cause, as a naturally necessary effect is with its natural cause. Whether the will in every case is necessarily determined by the strongest motive, or whether the will ever makes any resistance to such a motive, or can ever oppose the strongest present inclination, or not; if that matter should be controverted, yet I suppose none will deny, but that, in some cases, a previous bias and inclination, or the motive presented, may be so powerful, that the act of the will may be certainly and indissolubly connected therewith. When motives or previous bias are very strong, all will allow that there is some difficulty in going against them. And if they were yet stronger, the difficulty would be still greater. And therefore, if more were still added to their strength, to a certain degree, it would make the difficulty so great, that it would be wholly impossible to surmount it; for this plain reason, because whatever power men may be supposed to have to surmount difficulties, yet that power is not infinite; and so goes not beyond certain limits. If a man can surmount ten degrees of difficulty of this kind, with twenty degrees of strength, because the degrees of strength are beyond the degrees of difficulty; yet if the difficulty be increased to thirty, or an hundred, or a thousand degrees, and his strength not also increased, his strength will be wholly insufficient to surmount the difficulty. As therefore it must be allowed, that there may be such a thing as a sure and perfect connection between moral causes and effects; so this only is what I call by the name of "moral necessity."

2. When I use this distinction of moral and natural necessity, I would not be understood to suppose, that if anything comes to pass by the former kind of necessity, the nature of things is not concerned in it, as well as in the latter. I don't mean to determine, that when a moral habit or motive is so strong, that the act of the will infallibly follows, this is not owing to the nature of things. But these are the names that these two kinds of necessity have usually been called by; and they must be distinguished by some names or other; for there is a distinction or difference between them, that is very important in its consequences: which difference does not lie so much in the nature of the connection, as in the two terms connected. The cause with which the effect is connected, is of a particular kind; viz. that which is of a moral nature; either some previous habitual disposition, or some motive exhibited to the understanding. And the effect is also of a particular kind; being likewise of a moral nature; consisting in some inclination or volition of the soul, or voluntary action.

I suppose, that necessity which is called natural, in distinction from moral necessity, is so called, because "mere nature," as the word is vulgarly used, is concerned, without anything of choice. The word "nature" is often used in opposition to "choice"; not because nature has indeed never any hand in our choice; but this probably comes to pass by means that we first get our notion of nature from that discernible and obvious course of events, which we observe in many things that our choice has no concern in; and especially in the material world; which, in very many parts of it, we easily perceive to be in a settled course; the stated order and manner of succession being very apparent. But where we don't readily discern the rule and connection (though there be a connection, according to an established law, truly taking place), we signify the manner of event by some other name. Even in many things which are seen in the material and inanimate world, which don't discernibly and obviously come to pass according to any settled course, men don't call the manner of the event by the name of nature, but by such names as "accident," "chance," "contingence," etc. So men make a distinction between "nature" and "choice"; as though they were completely and universally distinct. Whereas, I suppose none will deny but that choice, in many cases, arises from nature, as truly as other events. But the dependence and connection between acts of volition or choice, and their causes, according to established laws, is not so sensible and obvious. And we observe that choice is as it were a new principle of motion and action, different from that established law and order of things which is most obvious, that is seen especially in corporeal and sensible things; and also that choice often interposes, interrupts and alters the chain of events in these external objects, and causes 'em to proceed otherwise than they would do, if let alone, and left to go on according to the laws of motion among themselves. Hence it is spoken of, as if it were a principle of motion entirely distinct from nature, and properly set in opposition to it—names being commonly given to things, according to what is most obvious, and is suggested by what appears to the senses without reflection and research.

3. It must be observed, that in what has been explained, as signified by the name of "moral necessity," the word "necessity" is not used according to the original design and meaning of the word: for, as was observed before, such terms "necessary," "impossible," "irresistible," etc. in common speech, and their most proper sense, are always relative; having reference to some supposable voluntary opposition or endeavor, that is insufficient. But no such opposition, or contrary will and endeavor, is supposable in the case of moral necessity; which is a certainty of the inclination and will itself; which does not admit of the supposition of a will to oppose and resist it. For 'tis absurd, to suppose the same individual will to oppose itself, in its present act; or the present choice to be opposite to, and resisting present choice: as absurd as it is to talk of two contrary motions, in the same moving body, at the same time. And therefore the very case supposed never admits of any trial, whether an opposing or resisting will can overcome this necessity.

What has been said of natural and moral necessity, may serve to explain what is intended by natural and moral inability. We are said to be naturally unable to do a thing, when we can't do it if we will, because what is most commonly called nature don't allow of it, or because of some impeding defect or obstacle that is extrinsic to the will; either in the faculty of understanding, constitution of body, or external objects. Moral inability consists not in any of these things; but either in the want of inclination; or the strength of a contrary inclination; or the want of sufficient motives in view, to induce and excite the act of the will, or the strength of apparent motives to the contrary. Or both these may be resolved into one; and it may be said in one word, that moral inability consists in the opposition or want of inclination. For when a person is unable to will or choose such a thing, through a defect of motives, or prevalence of contrary motives, 'tis the same thing as his being unable through the want of an inclination, or the prevalence of a contrary inclination, in such circumstances, and under the influence of such views.

To give some instances of this moral inability: A woman of great honor and chastity may have a moral inability to prostitute herself to her slave. A child of great love and duty to his parents, may be unable to be willing to kill his father. A very lascivious man, in case of certain opportunities and temptations, and in the absence of such and such restraints, may be unable to forbear gratifying his lust. A drunkard, under such and such circumstances, may be unable to forbear taking of strong drink. A very malicious man may be unable to exert benevolent acts to an enemy, or to desire his prosperity: yea, some may be so under the power of a vile disposition, that they may be unable to love those who are most worthy of their esteem and affection. A strong habit of virtue and great degree of holiness may cause a moral inability to love wickedness in general, may render a man unable to take complacence in wicked persons or things; or to choose a wicked life, and prefer it to a virtuous life. And on the other hand, a great degree of habitual wickedness may lay a man under an inability to love and choose holiness; and render him utterly unable to love an infinitely holy Being, or to choose and cleave to him as his chief good.

Here it may be of use to observe this distinction of moral inability, viz. of that which is general and habitual, and that which is particular and occasional. By a general and habitual moral inability, I mean an inability in the heart to all exercises or acts of will of that nature or kind, through a fixed and habitual inclination, or an habitual and stated defect, or want of a certain kind of inclination. Thus a very ill-natured man may be unable to exert such acts of benevolence, as another, who is full of good nature, commonly exerts; and a man, whose heart is habitually void of gratitude, may be unable to exert such and such grateful acts, through that stated defect of a grateful inclination. By particular and occasional moral inability, I mean an inability of the will or heart to a particular act, through the strength or defect of present motives, or of inducements presented to the view of the understanding, on this occasion. If it be so, that the will is always determined by the strongest motive, then it must always have an inability, in this latter sense, to act otherwise than it does; it not being possible, in any case, that the will should, at present, go against the motive which has now, all things considered, the greatest strength and advantage to excite and induce it. The former of these kinds of moral inability, consisting in that which is stated habitual and general, is most commonly called by the name of "inability"; because the word "inability," in its most proper and original signification, has respect to some stated defect. And this especially obtains the name of "inability" also upon another account: I before observed, that the word "inability" in its original and most common use, is a relative term; and has respect to will and endeavor, as supposable in the case, and as insufficient to bring to pass the thing desired and endeavored. Now there may be more of an appearance and shadow of this, with respect to the acts which arise from a fixed and strong habit, than others that arise only from transient occasions and causes. Indeed will and endeavor against, or diverse from present acts of the will, are in no case supposable, whether those acts be occasional or habitual; for that would be to suppose the will, at present, to be otherwise than, at present, it is. But yet there may be will and endeavor against future acts of the will, or volitions that are likely to take place, as viewed at a distance. 'Tis no contradiction, to suppose that the acts of the will at one time, may be against the acts of the will at another time; and there may be desires and endeavors to prevent or excite future acts of the will; but such desires and endeavors are, in many cases, rendered insufficient and vain, through fixedness of habit: when the occasion returns, the strength of habit overcomes, and baffles all such opposition. In this respect, a man may be in miserable slavery and bondage to a strong habit. But it may be comparatively easy to make an alteration with respect to such future acts, as are only occasional and transient; because the occasion or transient cause, if foreseen, may often easily be prevented or avoided. On this account, the moral inability that attends fixed habits, especially obtains the name of "inability." And then, as the will may remotely and indirectly resist itself, and do it in vain, in the case of strong habits; so reason may resist present acts of the will, and its resistance be insufficient; and this is more commonly the case also, when the acts arise from strong habit.

But it must be observed [concerning] moral inability, in each kind of it, that the word "inability" is used in a sense very diverse from its original import. The word signifies only a natural inability, in the proper use of it; and is applied to such cases only wherein a present will or inclination to the thing, with respect to which a person is said to be unable, is supposable. It can't be truly said, according to the ordinary use of language, that a malicious man, let him be never so malicious, can't hold his hand from striking, or that he is not able to shew his neighbor kindness; or that a drunkard, let his appetite be never so strong, can't keep the cup from his mouth. In the strictest propriety of speech, a man has a thing in his power, if he has it in his choice, or at his election: and a man can't be truly said to be unable to do a thing, when he can do it if he will. 'Tis improperly said, that a person can't perform those external actions, which are dependent on the act of the will, and which would be easily performed, if the act of the will were present. And if it be improperly said, that he cannot perform those external voluntary actions, which depend on the will, 'tis in some respect more improperly said, that he is unable to exert the acts of the will themselves; because it is more evidently false, with respect to these, that he can't if he will: for to say so, is a downright contradiction: it is to say, he can't will, if he does will. And in this case, not only is it true, that it is easy for a man to do the thing if he will, but the very willing is the doing; when once he has willed, the thing is performed; and nothing else remains to be done. Therefore, in these things to ascribe a nonperformance to the want of power or ability, is not just; because the thing wanting is not a being able, but a being willing. There are faculties of mind, and capacity of nature, and everything else, sufficient, but a disposition: nothing is wanting but a will.

SECTION 5.

CONCERNING THE NOTION OF LIBERTY, AND OF MORAL AGENCY

The plain and obvious meaning of the words "freedom" and "liberty," in common speech, is power, opportunity, or advantage, that anyone has, to do as he pleases. Or in other words, his being free from hindrance or impediment in the way of doing, or conducting in any respect, as he wills. (I say not only "doing," but "conducting"; because a voluntary forbearing to do, sitting still, keeping silence, etc. are instances of persons' conduct, about which liberty is exercised; though they are not properly called "doing.") And the contrary to liberty, whatever name we call that by, is a person's being hindered or unable to conduct as he will, or being necessitated to do otherwise.

If this which I have mentioned be the meaning of the word "liberty," in the ordinary use of language; as I trust that none that has ever learned to talk, and is unprejudiced, will deny; then it will follow, that in propriety of speech, neither liberty, nor its contrary, can properly be ascribed to any being or thing, but that which has such a faculty, power or property, as is called "will." For that which is possessed of no such thing as will, can't have any power or opportunity of doing according to its will, nor be necessitated to act contrary to its will, nor be restrained from acting agreeably to it. And therefore to talk of liberty, or the contrary, as belonging to the very will itself, is not to speak good sense; if we judge of sense, and nonsense, by the original and proper signification of words. For the will itself is not an agent that has a will: the power of choosing, itself, has not a power of choosing. That which has the power of volition or choice is the man or the soul, and not the power of volition itself. And he that has the liberty of doing according to his will, is the agent or doer who is possessed of the will; and not the will which he is possessed of. We say with propriety, that a bird let loose has power and liberty to fly; but not that the bird's power of flying has a power and liberty of flying. To be free is the property of an agent, who is possessed of powers and faculties, as much as to be cunning, valiant, bountiful, or zealous. But these qualities are the properties of men or persons; and not the properties of properties.

There are two things that are contrary to this which is called liberty in common speech. One is constraint; the same is otherwise called force, compulsion, and coaction; which is a person's being necessitated to do a thing contrary to his will. The other is restraint; which is his being hindered, and not having power to do according to his will. But that which has no will, can't be the subject of these things.—I need say the less on this head, Mr. Locke having set the same thing forth, with so great clearness, in his Essay on the Human Understanding. [Locke, Essay, Bk. II, ch. 21, nos. 14–21; 1, 319–24.]

But one thing more I would observe concerning what is vulgarly called liberty; namely, that power and opportunity for one to do and conduct as he will, or according to his choice, is all that is meant by it; without taking into the meaning of the word, anything of the cause or original of that choice; or at all considering how the person came to have such a volition; whether it was caused by some external motive, or internal habitual bias; whether it was determined by some internal antecedent volition, or whether it happened without a cause; whether it was necessarily connected with something foregoing, or not connected. Let the person come by his volition or choice how he will, yet, if he is able, and there is nothing in the way to hinder his pursuing and executing his will, the man is fully and perfectly free, according to the primary and common notion of freedom.

What has been said may be sufficient to shew what is meant by liberty, according to the common notions of mankind, and in the usual and primary acceptation of the word: but the word, as used by Arminians, Pelagians and others, who oppose the Calvinists, has an entirely different signification. These several things belong to their notion of liberty: 1. That it consists in a self-determining power in the will, or a certain sovereignty the will has over itself, and its own acts, whereby it determines its own volitions; so as not to be dependent in its determinations, on any cause without itself, nor determined by anything prior to its own acts. 2. Indifference belongs to liberty in their notion of it, or that the mind, previous to the act of volition be, *in equilibrio*. 3. Contingence is another thing that belongs and is essential to it; not in the common acceptation of the word, as that has been already explained, but as opposed to all necessity, or any fixed and certain connection with some previous ground or reason of its existence. They suppose the essence of liberty so much to consist in these things, that unless the will of man be free in this sense, he has no real freedom, how much soever he may be at liberty to act according to his will.

A moral agent is a being that is capable of those actions that have a moral quality, and which can properly be denominated good or evil in a moral sense, virtuous or vicious, commendable or faulty. To moral agency belongs a moral faculty, or sense of moral good and evil, or of such a thing as desert or worthiness of praise or blame, reward or punishment; and a capacity which an agent has of being influenced in his actions by moral inducements or motives, exhibited to the view of understanding and reason, to engage to a conduct agreeable to the moral faculty.

The sun is very excellent and beneficial in its action

and influence on the earth, in warming it, and causing it to bring forth its fruits; but it is not a moral agent: its action, though good, is not virtuous or meritorious. Fire that breaks out in a city, and consumes great part of it, is very mischievous in its operation; but is not a moral agent: what it does is not faulty or sinful, or deserving of any punishment. The brute creatures are not moral agents: the actions of some of 'em are very profitable and pleasant; others are very hurtful: yet, seeing they have no moral faculty, or sense of desert, and don't act from choice guided by understanding, or with a capacity of reasoning and reflecting, but only from instinct, and are not capable of being influenced by moral inducements, their actions are not properly sinful or virtuous; nor are they properly the subjects of any such moral treatment for what they do, as moral agents are for their faults or good deeds.

Here it may be noted, that there is a circumstantial difference between the moral agency of a ruler and a subject. I call it circumstantial, because it lies only in the difference of moral inducements they are capable of being influenced by, arising from the difference of circumstances. A ruler acting in that capacity only, is not capable of being influenced by a moral law, and its sanctions of threatenings and promises, rewards and punishments, as the subject is; though both may be influenced by a knowledge of moral good and evil. And therefore the moral agency of the supreme Being, who acts only in the capacity of a ruler towards his creatures, and never as a subject, differs in that respect from the moral agency of created intelligent beings. God's actions, and particularly those which he exerts as a moral governor, have moral qualifications, are morally good in the highest degree. They are most perfectly holy and righteous; and we must conceive of him as influenced in the highest degree, by that which, above all others, is properly a moral inducement; viz. the moral good which he sees in such and such things: and therefore he is, in the most proper sense, a moral agent, the source of all moral ability and agency, the fountain and rule of all virtue and moral good; though by reason of his being supreme over all, 'tis not possible he should be under the influence of law or command, promises or threatenings, rewards or punishments, counsels or warnings. The essential qualities of a moral agent are in God, in the greatest possible perfection; such as understanding, to perceive the difference between moral good and evil; a capacity of discerning that moral worthiness and demerit, by which some things are praiseworthy, others deserving of blame and punishment; and also a capacity of choice, and choice guided by understanding, and a power of acting according to his choice or pleasure, and being capable of doing those things which are in the highest sense praiseworthy. And herein does very much consist that image of God wherein he made man (which we read of Gen. 1:26, 27 and ch. 9:6), by which God distinguished man from the beasts, viz. in those faculties and principles of nature, whereby he is capable of moral agency. Herein very much consists the natural image of God; as his spiritual and moral image, wherein man was made at first, consisted in that moral excellency, that he was endowed with.

PART TWO

Wherein it Is Considered Whether There Is or Can Be Any Such Sort of Freedom of Will, as that Wherein Arminians Place the Essence of the Liberty of All Moral Agents; and Whether Any Such Thing Ever Was or Can Be Conceived Of

SECTION 1.

SHEWING THE MANIFEST INCONSISTENCE OF THE ARMINIAN NOTION OF LIBERTY OF WILL, CONSISTING IN THE WILL'S SELF-DETERMINING POWER

Having taken notice of those things which may be necessary to be observed, concerning the meaning of the principal terms and phrases made use of in controversies concerning human liberty, and particularly observed what liberty is, according to the common language, and general apprehension of mankind, and what it is as understood and maintained by Arminians; I proceed to consider the Arminian notion of the freedom of the will, and the supposed necessity of it in order to moral agency, or in order to anyone's being capable of virtue or vice, and properly the subject of command or counsel, praise or blame, promises or threatenings, rewards or punishments; or whether that which has been described, as the thing meant by liberty in common speech, be not sufficient, and the only liberty, which makes, or can make anyone a moral agent, and so properly the subject of these things. In this part, I shall consider whether any such thing be possible or conceivable, as that freedom of will which Arminians insist on; and shall inquire whether any such sort of liberty be necessary to moral agency, etc. in the next part.

And first of all, I shall consider the notion of a self-determining power in the will: wherein, according to the Arminians, does most essentially consist the will's freedom; and shall particularly inquire, whether it be not plainly absurd, and a manifest inconsistence, to suppose that the will itself determines all the free acts of the will.

Here I shall not insist on the great impropriety of such phrases, and ways of speaking, as "the will's determining itself"; because actions are to be ascribed to agents, and not properly to the powers of agents; which improper way of speaking leads to many mistakes, and much confusion, as Mr. Locke observes. But I shall suppose that the Arminians, when they speak of the will's determining itself, do by the will mean "the soul willing." I shall take it for granted, that when they speak of the will, as the determiner, they mean the soul in the exercise of a power of willing, or acting voluntarily. I shall suppose this to be their meaning, because nothing else can be meant, without the grossest and plainest absurdity. In all cases, when we speak of the powers or principles of acting, as doing such things, we mean that the agents which have these powers of acting, do them, in the exercise of those powers. So when we say, valor fights courageously, we mean, the man who is under the influence of valor fights courageously. When we say, love seeks the object loved, we mean, the person loving seeks that object. When we say, the understanding discerns, we mean the soul in the exercise of that faculty. So when it is said, the will decides or determines, the meaning must be, that the person in the exercise of a power of willing and choosing, or the soul acting voluntarily, determines.

Therefore, if the will determines all its own free acts, the soul determines all the free acts of the will in the exercise of a power of willing and choosing; or, which is the same thing, it determines them of choice; it determines its own acts by choosing its own acts. If the will determines the will, then choice orders and determines the choice: and acts of choice are subject to the decision, and follow the conduct of other acts of choice. And therefore if the will determines all its own free acts, then every free act of choice is determined by a preceding act of choice, choosing that act. And if that preceding act of the will or choice be also a free act, then by these principles, in this act too, the will is self-determined; that is, this, in like manner, is an act that the soul voluntarily chooses; or which is the same thing, it is an act determined still by a preceding act of the will, choosing that. And the like may again be observed of the last mentioned act. Which brings us directly to a contradiction: for it supposes an act of the will preceding the first act in the whole train, directing and determining the rest; or a free act of the will, before the first free act of the will. Or else we must come at last to an act of the will, determining the consequent acts, wherein the will is not self-determined, and so is not a free act, in this notion of freedom: but if the first act in the train, determining and fixing the rest, be not free, none of them all can be free; as is manifest at first view, but shall be demonstrated presently.

If the will, which we find governs the members of the body, and determines and commands their motions and actions, does also govern itself, and determine its own motions and acts, it doubtless determines them the same way, even by antecedent volitions. The will determines which way the hands and feet shall move, by an act of volition or choice: and there is no other way of the will's determining, directing or commanding anything at all. Whatsoever the will commands, it commands by an act of the will. And if it has itself under its command, and determines itself in its own actions, it doubtless does it the same way that it determines other things which are under its command. So that if the freedom of the will consists in this, that it has itself and its own actions under its command and direction, and its own volitions are determined by itself, it will follow, that every free volition arises from another antecedent volition, directing and commanding that: and if that directing volition be also free, in that also the will is determined; that is to say, that directing volition is determined by another going before that; and so on, till we come to the first volition in the whole series: and if that first volition be free, and the will self-determined in it, then that is determined by another volition preceding that. Which is a contradiction; because by the supposition, it can have none before it, to direct or determine it, being the first in the train. But if that first volition is not determined by any preceding act of the will, then that act is not determined by the will, and so is not free, in the Arminian notion of freedom, which consists in the will's self-determination. And if that first act of the will, which determines and fixes the subsequent acts, be not free, none of the following acts, which are determined by it, can be free. If we suppose there are five acts in the train, the fifth and last determined by the fourth, and the fourth by the third, the third by the second, and the second by the first; if the first is not determined by the will, and so not free, then none of them are truly determined by the will: that is, that each of them are as they are, and not otherwise, is not first owing to the will, but to the determination of the first in the series, which is not dependent on the will, and is that which the will has no hand in the determination of. And this being that which decides what the rest shall be, and determines their existence; therefore the first determination of their existence is not from the will. The case is just the same, if instead of a chain of five acts of the will, we should suppose a succession of ten, or an hundred, or ten thousand. If the first act be not free, being determined by something out of the will, and this determines the next to be agreeable to itself, and that the next, and so on; they are none of them free, but all originally depend on, and are determined by some cause out of the will: and so all freedom in the case is excluded, and no act of the will can be free, according to this notion of freedom. If we should suppose a long chain, of ten thousand links, so connected, that if the first link moves, it will move the next, and that the next; and so the whole chain must be determined to motion, and in the direction of its motion, by the motion of the first link; and that is moved by something else: in this case, though all the links, but one, are moved by other parts of the same chain; yet it appears that the motion of no one, nor the direction of its motion, is from any self-moving or self-determining power in the chain, any more than if every link were immediately moved by something that did not belong to the chain. If the will be not free in the first act, which causes the next, then neither is it free in the next, which is caused by that first act: for though indeed the will caused it, yet it did not cause it freely; because the preceding act, by which it was caused, was not free. And again, if the will ben't free in the second act, so neither can it be in the third, which is caused by that; because, in like manner, that third was determined by an act of the will that was not free. And so we may go on to the next act, and from that to the next; and how long soever the succession of acts is, it is all one; if the first on which the whole chain depends, and which determines all the rest, ben't a free act, the will is not free in causing or determining any one of those acts; because the act by which it determines them all, is not a free act; and therefore the will is no more free in determining them, than if it did not cause them at all. Thus, this Arminian notion of liberty of the will, consisting in the will's self-determination, is repugnant to itself, and shuts itself wholly out of the world.

SECTION 2. SEVERAL SUPPOSED WAYS OF EVADING THE FOREGOING REASONING, CONSIDERED

If to evade the force of what has been observed, it should be said, that when the Arminians speak of the will's determining its own acts, they don't mean that the will determines its acts by any preceding act, or that one act of the will determines another; but only that the faculty or power of will, or the soul in the use of that power, determines its own volitions; and that it does it without any act going before the act determined; such an evasion would be full of the most gross absurdity. I confess, it is an evasion of my own inventing; and I don't know but I should wrong the Arminians, in supposing that any of them would make use of it. But it being as good a one as I can invent, I would observe upon it a few things.

First, if the faculty or power of the will determines an act of volition, or the soul in the use or exercise of that power, determines it, that is the same thing as for the soul to determine volition by an act of will. For an exercise of the power of will, and an act of that power, are the same thing. Therefore to say, that the power of will, or the soul in the use or exercise of that power, determines volition, without an act of will preceding the volition determined, is a contradiction.

Secondly, if a power of will determines the act of the will, then a power of choosing determines it. For, as was before observed, in every act of will, there is choice, and a power of willing is a power of choosing. But if a power of choosing determines the act of volition, it determines it by choosing it. For 'tis most absurd to say, that a power of choosing determines one thing rather than another, without choosing anything. But if a power of choosing determines volition by choosing it, then here is the act of volition determined by an antecedent choice, choosing that volition.

Thirdly, to say, the faculty, or the soul, determines its own volition, but not by any act, is a contradiction. Because for the soul to direct, decide, or determine anything, is to act; and this is supposed; for the soul is here spoken of as being a cause in this affair, bringing something to pass, or doing something; or, which is the same thing, exerting itself in order to an effect, which effect is the determination of volition, or the particular kind and manner of an act of will. But certainly, this exertion or action is not the same with the effect, in order to the production of which it is exerted; but must be something prior to it.

Again, the advocates for this notion of the freedom of the will, speak of a certain sovereignty in the will, whereby it has power to determine its own volitions. And therefore the determination of volition must itself be an act of the will; for otherwise it can be no exercise of that supposed power and sovereignty.

Again, if the will determines itself, then either the will is active in determining its volitions, or it is not. If it be active in it, then the determination is an act of the will; and so there is one act of the will determining another. But if the will is not active in the determination, then how does it exercise any liberty in it? These gentlemen suppose that the thing wherein the will exercises liberty, is in its determining its own acts. But how can this be, if it ben't active in determining? Certainly the will, or the soul, can't exercise any liberty in that wherein it don't act, or wherein it don't exercise itself. So that if either part of this dilemma be taken, this scheme of liberty, consisting in self-determining power, is overthrown. If there be an act of the will in determining all its own free acts, then one free act of the will is determined by another; and so we have the absurdity of every free act, even the very first, determined by a foregoing free act. But if there be no act or exercise of the will in determining its own acts, then no liberty is exercised in determining them. From whence it follows, that no liberty consists in the will's power to determine its own acts: or, which is the same thing, that there is no such thing as liberty consisting in a self-determining power of the will.

If it should be said, that although it be true, if the soul determines its own volitions, it must be active in so doing, and the determination itself must be an act; yet there is no need of supposing this act to be prior to the volition determined; but the will or soul determines the act of the will in willing; it determines its own volition, in the very act of volition; it directs and limits the act of the will, causing it to be so and not otherwise, in exerting the act, without any preceding act to [excite] that. If any should say after this manner, they must mean one of these three things: either (1) that the determining act, though it be before the act determined in the order of nature, yet is not before it in the order of time. Or (2) that the determining act is not before the act determined, either in the order of time or nature, nor is truly distinct from it; but that the soul's determining the act of volition is the same thing with its exerting the act of volition: the mind's exerting such a particular act, is its causing and determining the act. Or (3) that volition has no cause, and is no effect; but comes into existence, with such a particular determination, without any ground or reason of its existence and determination. I shall consider these distinctly.

(1) If all that is meant, be, that the determining act is not before the act determined in order of time, it will not help the case at all, though it should be allowed. If it be before the determined act in the order of nature, being the cause or ground of its existence, this as much proves it to be distinct from it, and independent on it, as if it were before in the order of time. As the cause of the particular motion of a natural body in a certain direction, may have no distance as to time, yet can't be the same with the motion effected by it, but must be as distinct from it, as any other cause, that is before its effect in the order of time: as the architect is distinct from the house which he builds, or the father distinct from the son which he begets. And if the act of the will determining be distinct from the act determined, and before it in the order of nature, then we can go back from one to another, till we come to the first in the series, which has no act of the will before it in the order of nature, determining it; and consequently is an act not determined by the will, and so not a free act, in this notion of freedom. And this being the act which determines all the rest, none of them are free acts. As when there is a chain of many links, the first of which only is taken hold of and drawn by hand; all the rest may follow and be moved at the same instant, without any distance of time; but yet the motion of one link is before that of another in the order of nature; the last is moved by the next, and that by the next, and so till we come to the first; which not being moved by any other, but by something distinct from the whole chain, this as much proves that no part is moved by any self-moving power in the chain, as if the motion of one link followed that of another in the order of time.

(2) If any should say, that the determining act is not before the determined act, either in the order of time, or of nature, nor is distinct from it; but that the exertion of the act is the determination of the act; that for the soul to exert a particular volition, is for it to cause and determine that act of volition: I would on this observe, that the thing in question seems to be forgotten, or kept out of sight, in a darkness and unintelligibleness of speech; unless such an objector would mean to contradict himself. The very act of volition itself is doubtless a determination of mind; i.e. it is the mind's drawing up a conclusion, or coming to a choice between two things, or more, proposed to it. But determining among external objects of choice, is not the same with determining the

act of choice itself, among various possible acts of choice. The question is, what influences, directs, or determines the mind or will to come to such a conclusion or choice as it does? or what is the cause, ground or reason, why it concludes thus, and not otherwise? Now it must be answered, according to the Arminian notion of freedom, that the will influences, orders and determines itself thus to act. And if it does, I say, it must be by some antecedent act. To say, it is caused, influenced and determined by something, and yet not determined by anything antecedent, either in order of time or nature, is a contradiction. For that is what is meant by a thing's being prior in the order of nature, that it is some way the cause or reason of the thing, with respect to which it is said to be prior.

If the particular act or exertion of will, which comes into existence, be anything properly determined at all, then it has some cause of its existing, and of its existing in such a particular determinate manner, and not another; some cause, whose influence decides the matter: which cause is distinct from the effect, and prior to it. But to say, that the will or mind orders, influences and determines itself to exert such an act as it does, by the very exertion itself, is to make the exertion both cause and effect; or the exerting such an act, to be a cause of the exertion of such an act. For the question is, what is the cause and reason of the soul's exerting such an act? To which the answer is, the soul exerts such an act, and that is the cause of it. And so, by this, the exertion must be prior in the order of nature to itself, and distinct from itself.

(3) If the meaning be, that the soul's exertion of such a particular act of will, is a thing that comes to pass of itself, without any cause; and that there is absolutely no ground or reason of the soul's being determined to exert such a volition, and make such a choice, rather than another; I say, if this be the meaning of Arminians, when they contend so earnestly for the will's determining its own acts, and for liberty of will consisting in self-determining power; they do nothing but confound themselves and others with words without a meaning. In the question, what determines the will? and in their answer, that the will determines itself, and in all the dispute about it, it seems to be taken for granted, that something determines the will; and the controversy on this head is not, whether anything at all determines it, or whether its determination has any cause or foundation at all: but where the foundation of it is, whether in the will itself, or somewhere else. But if the thing intended be what is above mentioned, then all comes to this, that nothing at all determines the will; volition having absolutely no cause or foundation of its existence, either within, or without. There is a great noise made about self-determining power, as the source of all free acts of the will: but when the matter comes to be explained, the meaning is, that no power at all is the source of these acts, neither self-determining power, nor any other, but they arise from nothing; no cause, no power, no influence, being at all concerned in the matter.

However, this very thing, even that the free acts of the will are events which come to pass without a cause, is certainly implied in the Arminian notion of liberty of will; though it be very inconsistent with many other things in their scheme, and repugnant to some things implied in their notion of liberty. Their opinion implies, that the particular determination of volition is without any cause; because they hold the free acts of the will to be contingent events; and contingence is essential to freedom in their notion of it. But certainly, those things which have a prior ground and reason of their particular existence, a cause which antecedently determines them to be, and determines them to be just as they are, don't happen contingently. If something foregoing, by a causal influence and connection, determines and fixes precisely their coming to pass, and the manner of it, then it don't remain a contingent thing whether they shall come to pass or no.

And because it is a question, in many respects, very important in this controversy about the freedom of will, whether the free acts of the will are events which come to pass without a cause? I shall be particular in examining this point in the two following sections.

SECTION 3.

WHETHER ANY EVENT WHATSOEVER, AND VOLITION IN PARTICULAR, CAN COME TO PASS WITHOUT A CAUSE OF ITS EXISTENCE

Before I enter on any argument on this subject, I would explain how I would be understood, when I use the word "cause" in this discourse: since, for want of a better word, I shall have occasion to use it in a sense which is more extensive, than that in which it is sometimes used. The word is often used in so restrained a sense as to signify only that which has a positive efficiency or influence to produce a thing, or bring it to pass. But there are many things which have no such positive productive influence; which yet are causes in that respect, that they have truly the nature of a ground or reason why some things are, rather than others; or why they are as they are, rather than otherwise. Thus the absence of the sun in the night, is not the cause of the falling of the dew at that time, in the same manner as its beams are the cause of the ascending of the vapors in the daytime; and its withdrawment in the winter, is not in the same manner the cause of the freezing of the waters, as its approach in the spring is the cause of their thawing. But yet the withdrawment or absence of the sun is an antecedent, with which these effects in the night and winter are connected, and on which they depend; and is one thing that belongs to the ground and reason why they come to pass at that time, rather than at other times; though the absence of the sun is nothing positive, nor has any positive influence.

It may be further observed, that when I speak of connection of causes and effects, I have respect to moral causes, as well as those that are called natural in distinction from 'em. Moral causes may be causes in as proper a sense, as any causes whatsoever; may have as real an influence, and may as truly be the ground and reason of an event's coming to pass.

Therefore I sometimes use the word "cause," in this inquiry, to signify any antecedent, either natural or moral, positive or negative, on which an event, either a thing, or the manner and circumstance of a thing, so depends, that it is the ground and reason, either in whole, or in part, why it is, rather than not; or why it is as it is, rather than otherwise; or, in other words, any antecedent with which a consequent event is so connected, that it truly belongs to the reason why the proposition which affirms that event, is true; whether it has any positive influence, or not. And in an agreeableness to this, I sometimes use the word "effect" for the consequence of another thing, which is perhaps rather an occasion than a cause, most properly speaking.

I am the more careful thus to explain my meaning, that I may cut off occasion, from any that might seek occasion to cavil and object against some things which I may say concerning the dependence of all things which come to pass, on some cause, and their connection with their cause.

Having thus explained what I mean by cause, I assert, that nothing ever comes to pass without a cause. What is self-existent must be from eternity, and must be unchangeable: but as to all things that begin to be, they are not self-existent, and therefore must have some foundation of their existence without themselves. That whatsoever begins to be, which before was not, must have a cause why it then begins to exist, seems to be the first dictate of the common and natural sense which God hath implanted in the minds of all mankind, and the main foundation of all our reasonings about the existence of things, past, present, or to come.

And this dictate of common sense equally respects substances and modes, or things and the manner and circumstances of things. Thus, if we see a body which has hitherto been at rest, start out of a state of rest, and begin to move, we do as naturally and necessarily suppose there is some cause or reason of this new mode of existence, as of the existence of a body itself which had hitherto not existed. And so if a body, which had hitherto moved in a certain direction, should suddenly change the direction of its motion; or if it should put off its old figure, and take a new one; or change its color: the beginning of these new modes is a new event, and the mind of mankind necessarily supposes that there is some cause or reason of them.

If this grand principle of common sense be taken away, all arguing from effects to causes ceaseth, and so all knowledge of any existence, besides what we have by the most direct and immediate intuition. Particularly all our proof of the being of God ceases: we argue his being from our own being, and the being of other things, which we are sensible once were not, but have begun to be; and from the being of the world, with all its constituent parts, and the manner of their existence; all which we see plainly are not necessary in their own nature, and so not self-existent, and therefore must have a cause. But if things, not in themselves necessary, may begin to be without a cause, all this arguing is vain.

Indeed, I will not affirm, that there is in the nature of things no foundation for the knowledge of the being of God without any evidence of it from his works. I do suppose there is a great absurdity, in the nature of things simply considered, in supposing that there should be no God, or in denying being in general, and supposing an eternal, absolute, universal nothing: and therefore that here would be foundation of intuitive evidence that it cannot be, and that eternal infinite most perfect Being must be; if we had strength and comprehension of mind sufficient, to have a clear idea of general and universal being, or, which is the same thing, of the infinite, eternal, most perfect divine Nature and Essence. But then we should not properly come to the knowledge of the being of God by arguing; but our evidence would be intuitive: we should see it, as we see other things that are necessary in themselves, the contraries of which are in their own nature absurd and contradictory; as we see that twice two is four; and as we see that a circle has no angles. If we had as clear an idea of universal infinite entity, as we have of these other things, I suppose we should most intuitively see the absurdity of supposing such being not to be; should immediately see there is no room for the question, whether it is possible that being, in the most general abstracted notion of it, should not be. But we have not that strength and extent of mind, to know this certainly in this intuitive independent manner: but the way that mankind come to the knowledge of the being of God, is that which the Apostle speaks of (Rom. 1:20), "The invisible things of Him, from the creation of the world, are clearly seen; being understood by the things that are made; even his eternal power and Godhead." We first ascend, and prove a posteriori, or from effects, that there must be an eternal cause; and then secondly, prove by argumentation, not intuition, that this being must be necessarily existent; and then thirdly, from the proved necessity of his existence, we may descend, and prove many of his perfections a priori.

But if once this grand principle of common sense be given up, that what is not necessary in itself, must have a cause; and we begin to maintain, that things may come into existence, and begin to be, which heretofore have not been, of themselves, without any cause; all our means of ascending in our arguing from the creature to the Creator, and all our evidence of the being of God, is cut off at one blow. In this case, we can't prove that there is a God, either from the being of the world, and the creatures in it, or from the manner of their being, their order, beauty and use. For if things may come into existence without any cause at all, then they doubtless may without any cause answerable to the effect. Our minds do alike naturally suppose and determine both these things; namely, that what begins to be has a cause, and also that it has a cause proportionable and agreeable to the effect. The same principle which leads us to determine, that there cannot be anything coming to pass without a cause, leads us to determine that there cannot be more in the effect than in the cause.

Yea, if once it should be allowed, that things may come to pass without a cause, we should not only have no proof of the being of God, but we should be without evidence of the existence of anything whatsoever, but our own immediately present ideas and consciousness. For we have no way to prove anything else, but by arguing from effects to causes: from the ideas now immediately in view, we argue other things not immediately in view: from sensations now excited in us, we infer the existence of things without us, as the causes of these sensations: and from the existence of these things, we argue other things, which they depend on, as effects on causes. We infer the past existence of ourselves, or anything else, by memory; only as we argue, that the ideas, which are now in our minds, are the consequences of past ideas and sensations. We immediately perceive nothing else but the ideas which are this moment extant in our minds. We perceive or know other things only by means of these, as necessarily connected with others, and dependent on them. But if things may be without causes, all this necessary connection and dependence is dissolved, and so all means of our knowledge is gone. If there be no absurdity or difficulty in supposing one thing to start out of non-existence, into being, of itself without a cause; then there is no absurdity or difficulty in supposing the same of millions of millions. For nothing, or no difficulty multiplied, still is nothing, or no difficulty: nothing multiplied by nothing don't increase the sum.

And indeed, according to the hypothesis I am opposing, of the acts of the will coming to pass without a cause, it is the case in fact, that millions of millions of events are continually coming into existence contingently, without any cause or reason why they do so, all over the world, every day and hour, through all ages. So it is in a constant succession, in every moral agent. This contingency, this efficient Nothing, this effectual No-Cause, is always ready at hand, to produce this sort of effects, as long as the agent exists, and as often as he has occasion.

If it were so, that things only of one kind, viz. acts of the will, seemed to come to pass of themselves; but those of this sort in general came into being thus; and it were an event that was continual, and that happened in a course, wherever were capable subjects of such events; this very thing would demonstrate that there was some cause of them, which made such a difference between this event and others, and that they did not really happen contingently. For contingence is blind, and does not pick and choose for a particular sort of events. Nothing has no choice. This No-Cause, which causes no existence, can't cause the existence which comes to pass, to be of one particular sort only, distinguished from all others. Thus, that only one sort of matter drops out of the heavens, even water, and that this comes so often, so constantly and plentifully, all over the world, in all ages, shows that there is some cause or reason of the falling of water out of the heavens; and that something besides mere contingence has a hand in the matter.

If we should suppose Nonentity to be about to bring

forth; and things were coming into existence, without any cause or antecedent, on which the existence, or kind or manner of existence depends; or which could at all determine whether the things should be; stones, or stars, or beasts, or angels, or human bodies, or souls, or only some new motion or figure in natural bodies, or some new sensations in animals, or new ideas in the human understanding, or new volitions in the will; or anything else of all the infinite number of possibles; then certainly it would not be expected, although many millions of millions of things are coming into existence in this manner, all over the face of the earth, that they should all be only of one particular kind, and that it should be thus in all ages, and that this sort of existences should never fail to come to pass where there is room for them, or a subject capable of them, and that constantly, whenever there is occasion for them.

If any should imagine, there is something in the sort of event that renders it possible for it to come into existence without a cause; and should say, that the free acts of the will are existences of an exceeding different nature from other things; by reason of which they may come into existence without any previous ground or reason of it, though other things cannot; if they make this objection in good earnest, it would be an evidence of their strangely forgetting themselves: for they would be giving an account of some ground of the existence of a thing, when at the same time they would maintain there is no ground of its existence. Therefore I would observe, that the particular nature of existence, be it never so diverse from others, can lay no foundation for that thing's coming into existence without a cause; because to suppose this, would be to suppose the particular nature of existence to be a thing prior to the existence; and so a thing which makes way for existence, with such a circumstance, namely without a cause or reason of existence. But that which in any respect makes way for a thing's coming into being, or for any manner or circumstance of its first existence, must be prior to the existence. The distinguished nature of the effect, which is something belonging to the effect, can't have influence backward, to act before it is. The peculiar nature of that thing called volition, can do nothing, can have no influence, while it is not. And afterwards it is too late for its influence: for then the thing has made sure of existence already, without its help.

So that it is indeed as repugnant to reason, to suppose that an act of the will should come into existence without a cause, as to suppose the human soul, or an angel, or the globe of the earth, or the whole universe, should come into existence without a cause. And if once we allow, that such a sort of effect as a volition may come to pass without a cause, how do we know but that many other sorts of effects may do so too? 'Tis not the particular kind of effect that makes the absurdity of supposing it has being without a cause, but something which is common to all things that ever begin to be, viz. that they are not self-existent, or necessary in the nature of things.

SECTION 4.

WHETHER VOLITION CAN ARISE WITHOUT A CAUSE, THROUGH THE ACTIVITY OF THE NATURE OF THE SOUL

The author of the *Essay on the Freedom of the Will in God and the Creatures*, in answer to that objection against his doctrine of a self-determining power in the will (pp. 68, 69), "that nothing is, or comes to pass, without a sufficient reason why it is, and why it is in this manner rather than another," allows that it is thus in corporeal things, "which are properly and philosophically speaking passive beings"; but denies that it is thus in "spirits, which are beings of an active nature, who have the spring of action within themselves, and can determine themselves." [Isaac Watts, *An Essay on Freedom of Will in God and in Creatures*, (London, 1732) Sec. 6, obj. 2 and ans.; in The Works of the Reverend and Learned Isaac Watts, D.D., ed. Jennings and Doddridge; 1st ed. 1753; 6 vols. London, 1811), 6, 265.] By which it is plainly supposed, that such an event as an act of the will, may come to pass in a spirit, without a sufficient reason why it comes to pass, or why it is after this manner, rather than another; by reason of the activity of the nature of a spirit. But certainly this author, in this matter, must be very unwary and inadvertent. For,

1. The objection or difficulty proposed by this author, seems to be forgotten in his answer or solution. The very difficulty, as he himself proposes it, is this: how an event can "come to pass without a sufficient reason why it is, or why it is in this manner rather than another"? Instead of solving this difficulty, or answering this question with regard to volition, as he proposes, he forgets himself, and answers another question quite diverse, and wholly inconsistent with this, viz. what is a sufficient reason why it is, and why it is in this manner rather than another? And he assigns the active being's own determination as the cause, and a cause sufficient for the effect; and leaves all the difficulty unresolved, and the question unanswered, which yet returns, even, how the soul's own

determination, which he speaks of, came to exist, and to be what it was without a cause? The activity of the soul may enable it to be the cause of effects; but it don't at all enable or help it to be the subject of effects which have no cause; which is the thing this author supposes concerning acts of the will. Activity of nature will no more enable a being to produce effects, and determine the manner of their existence, within itself, without a cause, than out of itself, in some other being. But if an active being should, through its activity, produce and determine an effect in some external object, how absurd would it be to say, that the effect was produced without a cause!

2. The question is not so much, how a spirit endowed with activity comes to act, as why it exerts such an act, and not another; or why it acts with such a particular determination? If activity of nature be the cause why a spirit (the soul of man for instance) acts, and don't lie still; yet that alone is not the cause why its action is thus and thus limited, directed and determined. Active nature is a general thing; 'tis an ability or tendency of nature to action, generally taken; which may be a cause why the soul acts as occasion or reason is given; but this alone can't be a sufficient cause why the soul exerts such a particular act, at such a time, rather than others. In order to this, there must be something besides a general tendency to action; there must also be a particular tendency to that individual action. If it should be asked, why the soul of man uses its activity in such a manner as it does; and it should be answered, that the soul uses its activity thus, rather than otherwise, because it has activity; would such an answer satisfy a rational man? Would it not rather be looked upon as a very impertinent one?

3. An active being can bring no effects to pass by his activity, but what are consequent upon his acting: he produces nothing by his activity, any other way than by the exercise of his activity, and so nothing but the fruits of its exercise: he brings nothing to pass by a dormant activity. But the exercise of his activity is action; and so his action, or exercise of his activity, must be prior to the effects of his activity. If an active being produces an effect in another being, about which his activity is conversant, the effect being the fruit of his activity, his activity must be first exercised or exerted, and the effect of it must follow. So it must be, with equal reason, if the active being is his own object, and his activity is conversant about himself, to produce and determine some effect in himself; still the exercise of his activity must go before the effect, which he brings to pass and determines by it. And therefore his activity can't be the cause of the determination of the first action, or exercise of activity itself, whence the effects of activity arise; for that would imply a contradiction; it would be to say, the first exercise of activity is before the first exercise of activity, and is the cause of it.

4. That the soul, though an active substance, can't diversify its own acts, but by first acting; or be a determining cause of different acts, or any different effects, sometimes of one kind, and sometimes of another, any other way than in consequence of its own diverse acts, is manifest by this; that if so, then the same cause, the same causal power, force or influence, without variation in any respect, would produce different effects at different times. For the same substance of the soul before it acts, and the same active nature of the soul before it is exerted (i.e. before in the order of nature) would be the cause of different effects, viz. different volitions at different times. But the substance of the soul before it acts, and its active nature before it is exerted, are the same without variation. For 'tis some act that makes the first variation in the cause, as to any causal exertion, force or influence. But if it be so, that the soul has no different causality, or diverse causal force or influence, in producing these diverse effects; then 'tis evident, that the soul has no influence, no hand in the diversity of the effect; and that the difference of the effect can't be owing to anything in the soul; or which is the same thing, the soul don't determine the diversity of the effect; which is contrary to the supposition. 'Tis true, the substance of the soul before it acts, and before there is any difference in that respect, may be in a different state and circumstances: but those whom I oppose, will not allow the different circumstances of the soul to be the determining causes of the acts of the will; as being contrary to their notion of self-determination and self-motion.

5. Let us suppose, as these divines do, that there are no acts of the soul, strictly speaking, but free volitions; then it will follow, that the soul is an active being in nothing further than it is a voluntary or elective being; and whenever it produces effects actively, it produces effects voluntarily and electively. But to produce effects thus, is the same thing as to produce effects in consequence of, and according to its own choice. And if so, then surely the soul don't by its activity produce all its own acts of will or choice themselves: for this, by the supposition, is to produce all its free acts of choice voluntarily and electively, or in consequence of its own free acts of choice, which brings the matter directly to the forementioned contradiction, of a free act of choice before the first free act of choice. According to these gentlemen's own notion of action, if there arises in the mind a volition without a

free act of the will or choice to determine and produce it, the mind is not the active voluntary cause of that volition; because it don't arise from, nor is regulated by choice or design. And therefore it can't be, that the mind should be the active, voluntary, determining cause of the first and leading volition that relates to the affair. The mind's being a designing cause, only enables it to produce effects in consequence of its design; it will not enable it to be the designing cause of all its own designs. The mind's being an elective cause, will only enable it to produce effects in consequence of its elections, and according to them; but can't enable it to be the elective cause of all its own elections; because that supposes an election before the first election. So the mind's being an active cause enables it to produce effects in consequence of its own acts, but can't enable it to be the determining cause of all its own acts; for that is still in the same manner a contradiction; as it supposes a determining act conversant about the first act, and prior to it, having a causal influence on its existence, and manner of existence.

I can conceive of nothing else that can be meant by the soul's having power to cause and determine its own volitions, as a being to whom God has given a power of action, but this; that God has given power to the soul, sometimes at least, to excite volitions at its pleasure, or according as it chooses. And this certainly supposes, in all such cases, a choice preceding all volitions which are thus caused, even the very first of them. Which runs into the foremention'd great absurdity.

Therefore the activity of the nature of the soul affords no relief from the difficulties which the notion of a self-determining power in the will is attended with, nor will it help, in the least, its absurdities and inconsistencies.

SECTION 5.

SHEWING, THAT IF THE THINGS ASSERTED IN THESE EVASIONS SHOULD BE SUPPOSED TO BE TRUE, THEY ARE ALTOGETHER IMPERTINENT, AND CAN'T HELP THE CAUSE OF ARMINIAN LIBERTY; AND HOW (THIS BEING THE STATE OF THE CASE) ARMINIAN WRITERS ARE OBLIGED TO TALK INCONSISTENTLY

What was last observed in the preceding section may shew, not only that the active nature of the soul can't be a reason why any act of the will is, or why it is in this manner, rather than another; but also that if it could be so, and it could be proved that volitions are contingent events, in that sense, that their being and manner of being is not fixed or determined by any cause, or anything antecedent; it would not at all serve the purpose of Arminians, to establish the freedom of the will, according to their notion of its freedom, as consisting in the will's determination of itself; which supposes every free act of the will to be determined by some act of the will going before to determine it; inasmuch as for the will to determine a thing, is the same as for the soul to determine a thing by *willing*; and there is no way that the will can determine an act of the will, than by willing that act of the will, or, which is the same thing, choosing it. So that here must be two acts of the will in the case, one going before another, one conversant about the other, and the latter the object of the former, and chosen by the former. If the will don't cause and determine the act by choice, it don't cause or determine it at all; for that which is not determined by choice, is not determined voluntarily or willingly: and to say, that the will determines something which the soul don't determine willingly, is as much as to say, that something is done by the will, which the soul don't do with its will.

So that if Arminian liberty of will, consisting in the will's determining its own acts, be maintained, the old absurdity and contradiction must be maintained, that every free act of will is caused and determined by a foregoing free act of will. Which don't consist with the free act's arising without any cause, and being so contingent, as not be fixed by anything foregoing. So that this evasion must be given up, as not at all relieving, and as that which, instead of supporting this sort of liberty, directly destroys it.

And if it should be supposed, that the soul determines its own acts of will some other way, than by a foregoing act of will; still it will not help the cause of their liberty of will. If it determines them by an act of the understanding, or some other power, then the will don't determine itself; and so the self-determining power of the will is given up. And what liberty is there exercised, according to their own opinion of liberty, by the soul's being determined by something besides its own choice? The acts of the will, it is true, may be directed, and effectually determined and fixed; but it is not done by the soul's own will and pleasure: there is no exercise at all of choice or will in producing the effect: and if will and choice are not exercised in it, how is the liberty of the will exercised in it?

So that let Arminians turn which way they please with

their notion of liberty, consisting in the will's determining its own acts, their notion destroys itself. If they hold every free act of will to be determined by the soul's own free choice, or foregoing free act of will; foregoing, either in the order of time, or nature; it implies that gross contradiction, that the first free act belonging to the affair, is determined by a free act which is before it. Or if they say that the free acts of the will are determined by some other act of the soul, and not an act of will or choice, this also destroys their notion of liberty, consisting in the acts of the will being determined by the will itself; or if they hold that the acts of the will are determined by nothing at all that is prior to them, but that they are contingent in that sense, that they are determined and fixed by no cause at all; this also destroys their notion of liberty, consisting in the will's determining its own acts.

This being the true state of the Arminian notion of liberty, it hence comes to pass, that the writers that defend it are forced into gross inconsistencies, in what they say upon this subject. To instance in Dr. Whitby; he in his "Discourse on the Freedom of the Will," [Daniel Whitby, A Discourse concerning… Dis. IV, ch. 4 (2d ed. London, 1735), pp. 350, 351, 352] opposes the opinion of the Calvinists, who place man's liberty "only in a power of doing what he will," as that wherein they plainly agree with Mr. Hobbes. And yet he himself mentions the very same notion of liberty, as the dictate of "the sense and common reason of mankind, and a rule laid down by the light of nature"; viz. that "liberty is a power of acting from ourselves, or doing what we will" (Dis. IV, ch. 1; ibid., pp. 325 f).This is indeed, as he says, a thing agreeable to "the sense and common reason of mankind"; and therefore 'tis not so much to be wondered at, that he unawares acknowledges it against himself: for if liberty don't consist in this, what else can be devised that it should consist in? If it be said, as Dr. Whitby elsewhere insists, that it don't only consist in liberty of "doing what we will," but also a liberty of willing without necessity; still the question returns, what does that liberty of willing without necessity consist in, but in a power of willing as we please, without being impeded by a contrary necessity? or in other words, a liberty for the soul in its willing to act according to its own choice? Yea, this very thing the same author seems to allow, and suppose again and again, in the use he makes of sayings of the fathers, whom he quotes as his vouchers. Thus he cites these words of Origen, which he produces as a testimony on his side: "The soul acts by her own choice, and it is free for her to incline to whatever part she will" (Dis. IV, ch. 2; ibid., p. 342). And those words of Justin Martyr: "The doctrine of the Christians is this, that nothing is done or suffered according to fate, but that every man doth good or evil according to his own free choice" (Dis. IV, ch. 4; ibid., p. 360). And from Eusebius, these words: "If fate be established, philosophy and piety are overthrown ... all these things depending upon the necessity introduced by the stars, and not upon meditation and exercise proceeding from our own free choice" (Dis. IV, ch. 4; ibid., p. 363). And again, the words of Macarius, "God, to preserve the liberty of man's will, suffered their bodies to die, that it might be in their choice to turn to good or evil…They who are acted by the Holy Spirit, are not held under any necessity, but have liberty to turn themselves, and do what they will in this life" (Dis. IV, ch. 5; ibid., pp. 369, 370).

Thus, the Doctor in effect comes into that very notion of liberty, which the Calvinists have; which he at the same time condemns, as agreeing with the opinion of Mr. Hobbes, namely, the soul's acting by its own choice, men's doing good or evil according to their own free choice, their being in that exercise which proceeds from their own free choice, having it in their choice to turn to good or evil, and doing what they will. So that if men exercise this liberty in the acts of the will themselves, it must be in exerting acts of will as they will, or "according to their own free choice"; or exerting acts of will "that proceed from their choice." And if it be so, then let everyone judge whether this don't suppose a free choice going before the free act of will, or whether an act of choice don't go before that act of the will which proceeds from it. And if it be thus with all free acts of the will, then let everyone judge, whether it won't follow that there is a free choice or will going before the first free act of the will exerted in the case. And then let everyone judge, whether this be not a contradiction. And finally, let everyone judge whether in the scheme of these writers there be any possibility of avoiding these absurdities.

If liberty consists, as Dr. Whitby himself says, in a man's "doing what he will"; and a man exercises this liberty, not only in external actions, but in the acts of the will themselves; then so far as liberty is exercised in the latter, it consists in willing what he wills: and if any say so, one of these two things must be meant, either (1) that a man has power to will, as he does will; because what he wills, he wills; and therefore has power to will what he has power to will. If this be their meaning, then all this mighty controversy about freedom of the will and self-determining power, comes wholly to nothing; all that is contended for being no more than this, that the mind of man does what it does, and is the subject of what it is the subject of, or that what is, is; wherein none has any controversy with them. Or (2) the meaning must be, that a man has power to will as he pleases or chooses to will: that is, he has power by one act of choice, to choose another; by an antecedent act of will to choose a consequent act; and therein to execute his own choice. And if this be their meaning, it is nothing but shuffling with those they dispute with, and baffling their own reason. For still the question returns, wherein lies man's liberty in that antecedent act of will which chose the consequent act? The answer according to the same principles must be, that his liberty in this also lies in his willing as he would, or as he chose, or agreeable to another act of choice preceding that. And so the question returns in infinitum, and the like answer must be made in infinitum: in order to support their opinion, there must be no beginning, but free acts of will must have been chosen by foregoing free acts of will, in the soul of every man, without beginning; and so before he had a being, from all eternity.

SECTION 6.

CONCERNING THE WILL'S DETERMINING IN THINGS WHICH ARE PERFECTLY INDIFFERENT, IN THE VIEW OF THE MIND

A great argument for self-determining power, is the supposed experience we universally have of an ability to determine our wills, in cases wherein no prevailing motive is presented: the will (as is supposed) has its choice to make between two or more things, that are perfectly equal in the view of the mind; and the will is apparently altogether indifferent; and yet we find no difficulty in coming to a choice; the will can instantly determine itself to one, by a sovereign power which it has over itself, without being moved by any preponderating inducement.

Thus the forementioned author of an Essay on the Freedom of the Will, etc. (pp. 25, 26, 27) [Watts, Essay, Sec. 2; in Works, 6, 250], supposes,

> that there are many instances, wherein the will is determined neither by present uneasiness, nor by the greatest apparent good, nor by the last dictate of the understanding, nor by anything else, but merely by itself, as a sovereign self-determining power of the soul; and that the soul does not will this or that action, in some cases, by any other influence, but because it will. Thus (says he) I can turn my face to the south, or the north; I can point with my finger upward, or downward. And thus, in some cases, the will determines itself in a very sovereign manner, because it will, without a reason borrowed from the understanding: and hereby it discovers its own perfect power of choice, rising from within itself, and free from all influence or restraint of any kind.

And in pages 66, 70, and 73, 74 [Ibid., Sec. 6, obj. 2, 3; in Works, 6, 265–7], this author very expressly supposes the will in many cases to be determined by "no motive at all, and acts altogether without motive, or ground of preference."—Here I would observe,

1. The very supposition which is here made, directly contradicts and overthrows itself. For the thing supposed, wherein this grand argument consists, is, that among several things the will actually chooses one before another, at the same time that it is perfectly indifferent; which is the very same thing as to say, the mind has a preference, at the same time that it has no preference. What is meant can't be, that the mind is indifferent before it comes to have a choice, or till it has a preference; or, which is the same thing, that the mind is indifferent until it comes to be not indifferent. For certainly this author did not suppose he had a controversy with any person in supposing this. And then it is nothing to his purpose, that the mind which chooses, was indifferent once; unless it chooses, remaining indifferent; for otherwise, it don't choose at all in that case of indifference, concerning which is all the question. Besides, it appears in fact, that the thing which this author supposes, is not that the will chooses one thing before another, concerning which it is indifferent before it chooses; but also is indifferent when it chooses; and that its being otherwise than indifferent is not till afterwards, in consequence of its choice; that the chosen thing's appearing preferable and more agreeable than another, arises from its choice already made. His words are (p. 30) [Ibid., Sec. 3, prop. 3; in Works, 6, 251]:

> Where the objects which are proposed, appear equally fit or good, the will is left without a guide or director; and therefore must make its own choice, by its own determination; it being properly a self-determining power. And in such cases the will does as it were make a good to itself by its own choice, i.e. creates its own pleasure or delight

in this self-chosen good. Even as a man by seizing upon a spot of unoccupied land, in an uninhabited country, makes it his own possession and property, and as such rejoices in it. Where things were indifferent before, the will finds nothing to make them more agreeable, considered merely in themselves; but the pleasure it feels arising from its own choice, and its perseverance therein. We love many things which we have chosen, and purely because we chose them.

This is as much as to say, that we first begin to prefer many things, now ceasing any longer to be indifferent with respect to them, purely because we have preferred and chosen them before. These things must needs be spoken inconsiderately by this author. Choice or preference can't be before itself, in the same instance, either in the order of time or nature: it can't be the foundation of itself, or the fruit or consequence of itself. The very act of choosing one thing rather than another, is preferring that thing, and that is setting a higher value on that thing. But that the mind sets an higher value on one thing than another, is not, in the first place, the fruit of its setting a higher value on that thing.

This author says (p. 36) [Ibid., Sec. 3, prop. 8; in Works, 6, 253], "The will may be perfectly indifferent, and yet the will may determine itself to choose one or the other." And again in the same page, "I am entirely indifferent to either; and yet my will may determine itself to choose." And again, "Which I shall choose must be determined by the mere act of my will." If the choice is determined by a mere act of will, then the choice is determined by a mere act of choice. And concerning this matter, viz. that the act of the will itself is determined by an act of choice, this writer is express, in p. 72 [Ibid., Sec. 6, obj. 3, ans. 2; in Works, 6, 267]. Speaking of the case, where there is no superior fitness in objects presented, he has these words: "There it must act by its own choice, and determine itself as it pleases." Where it is supposed that the very determination, which is the ground and spring of the will's act, is an act of choice and pleasure, wherein one act is more agreeable, and the mind better pleased in it than another; and this preference, and superior pleasedness is the ground of all it does in the case. And if so, the mind is not indifferent when it determines itself, but had rather do one thing than another, had rather determine itself one way than another. And therefore the will don't act at all in indifference; not so much as in the first step it takes, or the first rise and beginning of its acting. If it be possible for the understanding to act in indifference, yet to be sure the will never does; because the will's beginning to act is the very same thing as its beginning to choose or prefer. And if in the very first act of the will, the mind prefers something, then the idea of that thing preferred, does at that time preponderate, or prevail in the mind; or, which is the same thing, the idea of it has a prevailing influence on the will. So that this wholly destroys the thing supposed, viz. that the mind can by a sovereign power choose one of two or more things, which in the view of the mind are, in every respect, perfectly equal, one of which does not at all preponderate, nor has any prevailing influence on the mind above another.

So that this author, in his grand argument for the ability of the will to choose one of two, or more things, concerning which it is perfectly indifferent, does at the same time, in effect, deny the thing he supposes, and allows and asserts the point he endeavors to overthrow; even that the will, in choosing, is subject to no prevailing influence of the idea, or view of the thing chosen. And indeed it is impossible to offer this argument without overthrowing it; the thing supposed in it being inconsistent with itself, and that which denies itself. To suppose the will to act at all in a state of perfect indifference, either to determine itself, or to do anything else, is to assert that the mind chooses without choosing. To say that when it is indifferent, it can do as it pleases, is to say that it can follow its pleasure, when it has no pleasure to follow. And therefore if there be any difficulty in the instances of two cakes, or two eggs, etc. which are exactly alike, one as good as another; concerning which this author supposes the mind in fact has a choice [Ibid., Sec. 3, prop. 8; in Works, 6, 253–4], and so in effect supposes that it has a preference; it as much concerned himself to solve the difficulty, as it does those whom he opposes. For if these instances prove anything to his purpose, they prove that a man chooses without choice. And yet this is not to his purpose; because if this is what he asserts, his own words are as much against him, and do as much contradict him, as the words of those he disputes against can do.

2. There is no great difficulty in shewing, in such instances as are alleged, not only that it must needs he so, that the mind must be influenced in its choice by something that has a preponderating influence upon it, but also how it is so. A little attention to our own experience, and a distinct consideration of the acts of our own minds in such cases, will be sufficient to clear up the matter.

Thus, supposing I have a chessboard before me; and because I am required by a superior, or desired by a friend, or to make some experiment concerning my own ability and liberty, or on some other consideration, I am determined to touch some one of the spots or squares on the board with my finger; not being limited or directed in the first proposal, or my own first purpose, which is general, to any one in particular; and there being nothing in the squares in themselves considered, that recommends any one of all the sixty-four, more than another: in this case, my mind determines to give itself up to what is vulgarly called accident (I have elsewhere observed [p. 155] what that is which is vulgarly called "accident"; that it is nothing akin to the Arminian metaphysical notion of "contingence," something not connected with anything foregoing; but that it is something that comes to pass in the course of things, in some affair that men are concerned in, unforeseen, and not owing to their design), by determining to touch that square which happens to be most in view, which my eye is especially upon at that moment, or which happens to be then most in my mind, or which I shall be directed to by some other suchlike accident. Here are several steps of the mind's proceeding (though all may be done as it were in a moment): the first step is its general determination that it will touch one of the squares. The next step is another general determination to give itself up to accident, in some certain way; as to touch that which shall be most in the eye or mind at that time, or to some other suchlike accident. The third and last step is a particular determination to touch a certain individual spot, even that square, which, by that sort of accident the mind has pitched upon, has actually offered itself beyond others. Now 'tis apparent that in none of these several steps does the mind proceed in absolute indifference, but in each of them is influenced by a preponderating inducement. So it is in the first step; the mind's general determination to touch one of the sixty-four spots: the mind is not absolutely indifferent whether it does so or no: it is induced to it, for the sake of making some experiment, or by the desire of a friend, or some other motive that prevails. So it is in the second step, the mind's determining to give itself up to accident, by touching that which shall be most in the eye, or the idea of which shall be most prevalent in the mind, etc. The mind is not absolutely indifferent whether it proceeds by this rule or no; but chooses it, because it appears at that time a convenient and requisite expedient in order to fulfill the general purpose aforesaid. And so it is in the third and last step, its determining to touch that individual spot which actually does prevail in the mind's view. The mind is not indifferent concerning this; but is influenced by a prevailing inducement and reason; which is, that this is a prosecution of the preceding determination, which appeared requisite, and was fixed before in the second step.

Accident will ever serve a man, without hindering him a moment, in such a case. It will always be so among a number of objects in view, one will prevail in the eye, or in idea beyond others. When we have our eyes open in the clear sunshine, many objects strike the eye at once, and innumerable images may be at once painted in it by the rays of light; but the attention of the mind is not equal to several of them at once; or if it be, it don't continue so for any time. And so it is with respect to the ideas of the mind in general: several ideas are not in equal strength in the mind's view and notice at once; or at least, don't remain so for any sensible continuance. There is nothing in the world more constantly varying, than the ideas of the mind: they don't remain precisely in the same state for the least perceivable space of time: as is evident by this, that all perceivable time is judged and perceived by the mind only by the succession or the successive changes of its own ideas. Therefore while the views or perceptions of the mind remain precisely in the same state, there is no perceivable space or length of time, because no sensible succession at all.

As the acts of the will, in each step of the forementioned procedure, don't come to pass without a particular cause, every act is owing to a prevailing inducement; so the accident, as I have called it, or that which happens in the unsearchable course of things, to which the mind yields itself, and by which it is guided, is not anything that comes to pass without a cause; and the mind in determining to be guided by it, is not determined by something that has no cause; any more than if it determined to be guided by a lot, or the casting of a die. For though the die's falling in such a manner be accidental to him that casts it, yet none will suppose that there is no cause why it falls as it does. The involuntary changes in the succession of our ideas, though the cause may not be observed, have as much a cause, as the changeable motions of the motes that float in the air, or the continual, infinitely various, successive changes of the unevennesses on the surface of the water.

There are two things especially, which are probably the occasions of confusion in the minds of them who insist upon it, that the will acts in a proper indifference, and without being moved by any inducement, in its determinations in such cases as have been mentioned.

1. They seem to mistake the point in question, or at least not to keep it distinctly in view. The question

they dispute about, is, whether the mind be indifferent about the objects presented, one of which is to be taken, touched, pointed to, etc., as two eggs, two cakes, which appear equally good. Whereas the question to be considered, is, whether the person be indifferent with respect to his own actions; whether he don't, on some consideration or other, prefer one act with respect to these objects before another. The mind in its determination and choice, in these cases, is not most immediately and directly conversant about the objects presented; but the acts to be done concerning these objects. The objects may appear equal, and the mind may never properly make any choice between them: but the next act of the will being about the external actions to be performed, taking, touching, etc., these may not appear equal, and one action may properly be chosen before another. In each step of the mind's progress, the determination is not about the objects, unless indirectly and improperly, but about the actions, which it chooses for other reasons than any preference of the objects, and for reasons not taken at all from the objects.

There is no necessity of supposing, that the mind does ever at all properly choose one of the objects before another; either before it has taken, or afterwards. Indeed the man chooses to take or touch one rather than another; but not because it chooses the thing taken, or touched; but from foreign considerations. The case may be so, that of two things offered, a man may, for certain reasons, choose and prefer the taking of that which he undervalues, and choose to neglect to take that which his mind prefers. In such a case, choosing the thing taken, and choosing to take, are diverse: and so they are in a case where the things presented are equal in the mind's esteem, and neither of them preferred. All that fact and experience make evident, is, that the mind chooses one action rather than another. And therefore the arguments which they bring, in order to be to their purpose, ought to be to prove that the mind chooses the action in perfect indifference, with respect to that action; and not to prove that the mind chooses the action in perfect indifference with respect to the object; which is very possible, and yet the will not act at all without prevalent inducement, and proper preponderation.

2. Another reason of confusion and difficulty in this matter, seems to be, not distinguishing between a general indifference, or an indifference with respect to what is to be done in a more distant and general view of it, and a particular indifference, or an indifference with respect to the next immediate act, viewed with its particular and present circumstances. A man may be perfectly indifferent with respect to his own actions, in the former respect; and yet not in the latter. Thus, in the foregoing instance of touching one of the squares of a chessboard; when 'tis first proposed that I should touch one of them, I may be perfectly indifferent which I touch; because as yet I view the matter remotely and generally, being but in the first step of the mind's progress in the affair. But yet, when I am actually come to the last step, and the very next thing to be determined is, which is to be touched, having already determined that I will touch that which happens to be most in my eye or mind, and my mind being now fixed on a particular one, the act of touching that, considered thus immediately, and in these particular present circumstances, is not what my mind is absolutely indifferent about.

SECTION 7.

CONCERNING THE NOTION OF LIBERTY OF WILL CONSISTING IN INDIFFERENCE

What has been said in the foregoing section, has a tendency in some measure to evince the absurdity of the opinion of such as place liberty in indifference, or in that equilibrium whereby the will is without all antecedent determination or bias, and left hitherto free from any prepossessing inclination to one side or the other; that the determination of the will to either side may be entirely from itself, and that it may be owing only to its own power, and that sovereignty which it has over itself, that it goes this way rather than that. (Dr. Whitby, and some other Arminians, make a distinction of different kinds of freedom; one of God, and perfect spirits above; another of persons in a state of trial. The former Dr. Whitby allows to consist with necessity; the latter he holds to be without necessity; and this latter he supposes to be requisite to our being the subjects of praise or dispraise, rewards or punishments, precepts and prohibitions, promises and threats, exhortations and dehortations, and a covenant treaty. And to this freedom he supposes indifference to be requisite. In his Discourse on the Five Points, [Dis. IV, ch. 1] pp. 299, 300, he says: "It is a freedom, speaking of a freedom not only from coaction, but from necessity, requisite, as we conceive, to render us capable to trial or probation, and to render our actions worthy of praise or dispraise, and our persons of rewards or punishments." And in the next page, speaking of the same matter, he says, "Excellent to this purpose, are the words of Mr. Thorndike: 'We say not, that indifference is requisite to all freedom, but to the freedom of man alone in this state of travail and proficience; the ground of which is God's tender of a treaty, and conditions of peace and reconcilement to fallen man, together with those precepts and prohibitions, those promises and threats, those exhortations and dehortations, it is enforced with.'") But inasmuch as this has been of such long standing, and has been so generally received, and so much insisted on by Pelagians, semi-Pelagians, Jesuits, Socinians, Arminians, and others, it may deserve a more full consideration. And therefore I shall now proceed to a more particular and thorough inquiry into this notion.

Now lest some should suppose that I don't understand those that place liberty in indifference, or should charge me with misrepresenting their opinion, I would signify, that I am sensible, there are some, who when they talk of the liberty of the will as consisting in indifference, express themselves as though they would not be understood of the indifference of the inclination or tendency of the will, but of, I know not what, indifference of the soul's power of willing; or that the will, with respect to its power or ability to choose, is indifferent, can go either way indifferently, either to the right hand or left, either act or forbear to act, one as well as the other. Though this seems to be a refining only of some particular writers, and newly invented, and which will by no means consist with the manner of expression used by the defenders of liberty of indifference in general. And I wish such refiners would thoroughly consider, whether they distinctly know their own meaning, when they make a distinction between indifference of the soul as to its power or ability of willing or choosing, and the soul's indifference as to the preference or choice itself; and whether they don't deceive themselves in imagining that they have any distinct meaning at all. The indifference of the soul as to its ability or power to will, must be the same thing as the indifference of the state of the power or faculty of the will, or the indifference of the state which the soul itself, which has that power or faculty, hitherto remains in, as to the exercise of that power, in the choice it shall by and by make.

But not to insist any longer on the abstruseness and inexplicableness of this distinction; let what will be supposed concerning the meaning of them that make use of it, thus much must at least be intended by Arminians, when they talk of indifference as essential to liberty of will, if they intend anything, in any respect to their purpose, viz. that it is such an indifference as leaves the will not determined already; but free from actual possession, and vacant of predetermination, so far, that there may be room for the exercise of the self-determining power of the will; and that the will's freedom consists in, or depends upon this vacancy and opportunity that is left for the will itself to be the determiner of the act that is to be the free act.

And here I would observe in the first place, that to make out this scheme of liberty, the indifference must be perfect and absolute; there must be a perfect freedom from all antecedent preponderation or inclination. Because if the will be already inclined, before it exerts its own sovereign power on itself, then its inclination is not wholly owing to itself: if when two opposites are proposed to the soul for its choice, the proposal don't find the soul wholly in a state of indifference, then it is not found in a state of liberty for mere self-determination. The least degree of antecedent bias must be inconsistent with their notion of liberty. For so long as prior inclination possesses the will, and is not removed, it binds the will, so that it is utterly impossible that the will should act otherwise than agreeably to it. Surely the will can't act or choose contrary to a remaining prevailing inclination of the will. To suppose otherwise, would be the same thing as to suppose, that the will is inclined contrary to its present prevailing inclination, or contrary to what it is inclined to. That which the will chooses and prefers, that, all things considered, it preponderates and inclines to. It is equally impossible for the will to choose contrary to its own remaining and present preponderating inclination, as 'tis to prefer contrary to its own present preference, or choose contrary to its own present choice. The will therefore, so long as it is under the influence of an old preponderating inclination, is not at liberty for a new free act, or any act that shall now be an act of self-determination. The act which is a self-determined free act, must be an act which the will determines in the possession and use of such a liberty, as consists in a freedom from everything, which, if it were there, would make it impossible that the will, at that time, should be otherwise than that way to which it tends.

If anyone should say, there is no need that the indifference should be perfect; but although a former inclination and preference still remains, yet, if it ben't very strong and violent, possibly the strength of the will may oppose and overcome it—

This is grossly absurd; for the strength of the will, let it be never so great, does not at all enable it to act one way, [and act the contrary way], both at the same time. It gives it no such sovereignty and command, as to cause itself to prefer and not to prefer at the same time, or to choose contrary to its own present choice.

Therefore, if there be the least degree of antecedent preponderation of the will, it must be perfectly abolished, before the will can be at liberty to determine itself the contrary way. And if the will determines itself the same way, it was not a free determination, because the will is not wholly at liberty in so doing: its determination is not altogether from itself, but it was partly determined before, in its prior inclination: and all the freedom the will exercises in the case, is in an increase of inclination, which it gives itself, over and above what it had by foregoing bias; so much is from itself, and so much is from perfect indifference. For though the will had a previous tendency that way, yet as to that additional degree of inclination, it had no tendency. Therefore the previous tendency is of no consideration, with respect to the act wherein the will is free. So that it comes to the same thing which was said at first, that as to the act of the will, wherein the will is free, there must be perfect indifference, or equilibrium.

To illustrate this; if we should suppose a sovereign self-moving power in a natural body: but that the body is in motion already, by an antecedent bias; for instance, gravitation towards the center of the earth; and has one degree of motion already, by virtue of that previous tendency; but by its self-moving power it adds one degree more to its motion, and moves so much more swiftly towards the center of the earth than it would do by its gravity only: it is evident, that all that is owing to a self-moving power in this case, is the additional degree of motion; and that the other degree of motion which it had from gravity, is of no consideration in the case, don't help the effect of the free self-moving power in the least; the effect is just the same, as if the body had received from itself one degree of motion from a state of perfect rest. So if we should suppose a self-moving power given to the scale of a balance, which has a weight of one degree beyond the opposite scale; and we ascribe to it an ability to add to itself another degree of force the same way, by its self-moving power; this is just the same thing as to ascribe to it a power to give itself one degree of preponderation from a perfect equilibrium; and so much power as the scale has to give itself an overbalance from a perfect equipoise, so much self-moving self-preponderating power it has, and no more. So that its free power this way is always to be measured from perfect equilibrium.

I need say no more to prove, that, if indifference be essential to liberty, it must be perfect indifference; and that so far as the will is destitute of this, so far it is destitute of that freedom by which it is its own master, and in a capacity of being its own determiner, without being at all passive, or subject to the power and sway of something else, in its motions and determinations.

Having observed these things, let us now try whether this notion of the liberty of will consisting in indifference and equilibrium, and the will's self-determination in such a state, be not absurd and inconsistent.

And here I would lay down this as an axiom of undoubted truth; that every free act is done in a state of freedom, and not only after such a state. If an act of the will be an act wherein the soul is free, it must be exerted in a state of freedom, and in the time of freedom. It will not suffice, that the act immediately follows a state of liberty; but liberty must yet continue, and coexist with the act; the soul remaining in possession of liberty. Because that is the notion of a free act of the soul, even an act wherein the soul uses or exercises liberty. But if the soul is not, in the very time of the act, in the possession of liberty, it can't at that time be in the use of it.

Now the question is, whether ever the soul of man puts forth any act of will, while it yet remains in a state of liberty, in that notion of a state of liberty, viz. as implying a state of indifference; or whether the soul ever exerts an act of choice or preference, while at that very time the will is in a perfect equilibrium, not inclining one way more than another. The very putting of the question is sufficient to show the absurdity of the affirmative answer: for how ridiculous would it be for anybody to insist, that the soul chooses one thing before another, when at the very same instant it is perfectly indifferent with respect to each! This is the same thing as to say, the soul prefers one thing to another, at the very same time that it has no preference. Choice and preference can no more be in a state of indifference, than motion can be in a state of rest, or than the preponderation of the scale of a balance can be in a state of equilibrium. Motion may be the next moment after rest; but can't coexist with it, in any, even the least part of it. So choice may be immediately after a state of indifference, but has no coexistence with it: even the very beginning of it is not in a state of indifference. And therefore if this be liberty, no act of the will, in any degree, is ever performed in a state of liberty, or in the time of liberty. Volition and liberty are so far from agreeing together, and being essential one to another, that they are contrary one to another, and one excludes and destroys the other, as much as motion and rest, light and darkness, or life and death. So that the will acts not at all, does not so much as begin to act in the time of such liberty: freedom is perfectly at an end, and has ceased to be, at the first moment of action; and therefore liberty can't reach the action, to affect, or qualify it, or give it a denomination, or any part of it, any more than if it had ceased to be twenty years before the action began. The moment that liberty ceases to be, it ceases to be a qualification of anything. If light and darkness succeed one another instantaneously, light qualifies nothing after it is gone out, to make anything lightsome or bright, any more at the first moment of perfect darkness, than months or years after. Life denominates nothing vital at the first moment of perfect death. So freedom, if it consists in, or implies indifference, can denominate nothing free, at the first moment of preference or preponderation. Therefore 'tis manifest, that no liberty which the soul is possessed of, or ever uses, in any of its acts of volition, consists in indifference; and that the opinion of such as suppose, that indifference belongs to the very essence of liberty, is to the highest degree absurd and contradictory.

If anyone should imagine, that this manner of arguing is nothing but trick and delusion; and to evade the reasoning, should say, that the thing wherein the will exercises its liberty, is not in the act of choice or preponderation itself, but in determining itself to a certain choice or preference; that the act of the will wherein it is free, and uses its own sovereignty, consists in its causing or determining the change or transition from a state of indifference to a certain preference, or determining to give a certain turn to the balance, which has hitherto been even; and that this act the will exerts in a state of liberty, or while the will yet remains in equilibrium, and perfect master of itself; I say, if anyone chooses to express his notion of liberty after this, or some such manner, let us see if he can make out his matters any better than before.

What is asserted is, that the will, while it yet remains in perfect equilibrium, without preference, determines to change itself from that state, and excite in itself a certain choice or preference. Now let us see whether this don't come to the same absurdity we had before. If it be so, that the will, while it yet remains perfectly indifferent, determines to put itself out of that state, and give itself a certain preponderation; then I would inquire, whether the soul don't determine this of choice; or whether the will's coming to a determination to do so, be not the same thing as the soul's coming to a choice to do so. If the soul don't determine this of choice, or in the exercise of choice, then it don't determine it voluntarily. And if the soul don't determine it voluntarily, or of its own will, then in what sense does its will determine it? And if the will don't determine it, then how is the liberty of the will exercised in the determination? What sort of liberty is exercised by the soul in those determinations, wherein there is no exercise of choice, which are not voluntary, and wherein the will is not concerned? But if it be allowed, that this determination is an act of choice, and it be insisted on, that the soul, while it yet remains in a state of perfect indifference, chooses to put itself out of that state, and to turn itself one way; then the soul is already come to a choice, and chooses that way. And so we have the very same absurdity which we had before. Here is the soul in a state of choice, and in a state of equilibrium, both at the same time: the soul already choosing one way, while it remains in a state of perfect indifference, and has no choice of one way more than the other. And indeed this manner of talking, though it may a little hide the absurdity, in the obscurity of expression, is more nonsensical, and increases the inconsistence. To say, the free act of the will, or the act which the will exerts in a state of freedom and indifference, does not imply preference in it, but is what the will does in order to causing or producing a preference, is as much as to say, the soul chooses (for to will and to choose are the same thing) without choice, and prefers without preference, in order to cause or produce the beginning of a preference, or the first choice. And that is, that the first choice is exerted without choice, in order to produce itself.

If any, to evade these things, should own, that a state of liberty, and a state of indifference are not the same, and that the former may be without the latter; but should say, that indifference is still essential to the freedom of an act of will, in some sort, namely, as 'tis necessary to go immediately before it; it being essential to the freedom of an act of will that it should directly and immediately arise out of a state of indifference: still this will not help the cause of Arminian liberty, or make it consistent with itself. For if the act springs immediately out of a state of indifference, then it does not arise from antecedent choice or preference. But if the act arises directly out of a state of indifference, without any intervening choice to choose and determine it, then the act not being determined by choice, is not determined by the will; the mind exercises no free choice in the affair, and free choice and free will have no hand in the determination of the act. Which is entirely inconsistent with their notion of the freedom of volition.

If any should suppose, that these difficulties and absurdities may be avoided, by saying, that the liberty of the mind consists in a power to suspend the act of the will, and so to keep it in a state of indifference, till there has been opportunity for consideration; and so shall say, that however indifference is not essential to liberty in such a manner, that the mind must make its choice in a state of indifference, which is an inconsistency, or that the act of will must spring immediately out of indifference; yet indifference may be essential to the liberty of acts of the will in this respect; viz. that liberty consists in a power of the mind to forbear or suspend the act of volition, and keep the mind in a state of indifference for the present, till there has been opportunity for proper deliberation: I say, if anyone imagines that this helps the matter, it is a great mistake: it reconciles no inconsistency, and relieves no difficulty which the affair is attended with. For here the following things must be observed,

1. That this suspending of volition, if there be properly any such thing, is itself an act of volition. If the mind determines to suspend its act, it determines it voluntarily; it chooses, on some consideration, to suspend it. And this choice or determination, is an act of the will: and indeed it is supposed to be so in the very hypothesis; for 'tis supposed, that the liberty of the will consists in its power to do thus, and that its doing it is the very thing wherein the will exercises its liberty. But how can the will exercise liberty in it, if it ben't an act of the will? The liberty of the will is not exercised in anything but what the will does.

2. This determining to suspend acting is not only an act of the will, but 'tis supposed to be the only free act of the will; because it is said, that this is the thing wherein the liberty of the will consists. Now if this be so, then this is all the act of will that we have to consider in this controversy, about the liberty of will, and in our inquiries, wherein the liberty of man consists. And now the forementioned difficulties remain: the former question returns upon us; viz. wherein consists the freedom of the will in those acts wherein it is free? And if this act of determining a suspension be the only act in which the will is free, then wherein consists the will's freedom with respect to this act of suspension? And how is indifference essential to this act? The answer must be, according to what is supposed in the evasion under consideration, that the liberty of the will in this act of suspension, consists in a power to suspend even this act, till there has been opportunity for thorough deliberation. But this will be to plunge directly into the grossest nonsense: for 'tis the act of suspension itself that we are speaking of; and there is no room for a space of deliberation and suspension, in order to determine whether we will suspend or no.

For that supposes, that even suspension itself may be deferred: which is absurd; for the very deferring the determination of suspension, to consider whether we will suspend or no, will be actually suspending. For during the space of suspension, to consider whether to suspend, the act is ipso facto suspended. There is no medium between suspending to act, and immediately acting; and therefore no possibility of avoiding either the one or the other one moment; and so no room for deliberation before we do either of them.

And besides, this is attended with ridiculous absurdity another way: for now it is come to that, that liberty consists wholly in the mind's having power to suspend its determination whether to suspend or no; that there may be time for consideration, whether it be best to suspend. And if liberty consists in this only, then this is the liberty under consideration: we have to inquire now, how liberty with respect to this act of suspending a determination of suspension, consists in indifference, or how indifference is essential to it. The answer, according to the hypothesis we are upon, must be, that it consists in a power of suspending even this last mentioned act, to have time to consider whether to suspend that. And then the same difficulties and inquiries return over again with respect to that; and so on forever. Which, if it would shew anything, would shew only that there is no such thing as a free act. It drives the exercise of freedom back in infinitum; and that is to drive it out of the world.

And besides all this, there is a delusion, and a latent gross contradiction in the affair another way; inasmuch as in explaining how, or in what respect the will is free with regard to a particular act of volition, 'tis said, that its liberty consists in a power to determine to suspend that act, which places liberty not in that act of volition which the inquiry is about, but altogether in another antecedent act. Which contradicts the thing supposed in both the question and answer. The question is, wherein consists the mind's liberty in any particular act of volition? And the answer, in pretending to shew wherein lies the mind's liberty in that act, in effect says, it don't lie in that act at all, but in another, viz. a volition to suspend that act. And therefore the answer is both contradictory, and altogether impertinent and beside the purpose. For it don't shew wherein the liberty of the will consists in the act in question; instead of that, it supposes it don't consist in that act at all, but in another distinct from it, even a volition to suspend that act, and take time to consider of it. And no account is pretended to be given wherein the mind is free with respect to that act, wherein this answer supposes the liberty of the mind indeed consists, viz. the act of suspension, or of determining the suspension.

On the whole, 'tis exceeding manifest, that the liberty of the mind does not consist in indifference, and that indifference is not essential or necessary to it, or at all belonging to it, as the Arminians suppose; that opinion being full of nothing but absurdity and self-contradiction.

SECTION 8.

CONCERNING THE SUPPOSED LIBERTY OF THE WILL, AS OPPOSITE TO ALL NECESSITY

'Tis a thing chiefly insisted on by Arminians, in this controversy, as a thing most important and essential in human liberty, that volitions, or the acts of the will, are contingent events; understanding contingence as opposite, not only to constraint, but to all necessity. Therefore I would particularly consider this matter. And

1. I would inquire, whether there is, or can be any such thing, as a volition which is contingent in such a sense, as not only to come to pass without any necessity of constraint or coaction, but also without a necessity of consequence, or an infallible connection with anything foregoing.

2. Whether, if it were so, this would at all help the cause of liberty.

I. I would consider whether volition is a thing that e'er does, or can come to pass, in this manner, contingently.

And here it must be remembered, that it has been already shown, that nothing can ever come to pass without a cause, or reason why it exists in this manner rather than another; and the evidence of this has been particularly applied to the acts of the will. Now if this be so, it will demonstrably follow, that the acts of the will are never contingent, or without necessity, in the sense spoken of; inasmuch as those things which have a cause, or reason of their existence, must be connected with their cause. This appears by the following considerations.

1. For an event to have a cause and ground of its existence, and yet not to be connected with its cause, is an inconsistence. For if the event ben't connected with the cause, it is not dependent on the cause; its existence is as it were loose from its influence, and may attend it, or may not; it being a mere contingence, whether it follows or attends the influence of the cause, or not: and that is the same thing as not to be dependent on it. And to say, the event is not dependent on its cause, is absurd: 'tis the same thing as to say, it is not its cause, nor the event the effect of it: for dependence on the influence of a cause, is the very notion of an effect. If there be no such relation between one thing and another, consisting in the connection and dependence of one thing on the influence of another, then it is certain there is no such relation between them as is signified by the terms "cause" and "effect." So far as an event is dependent on a cause, and connected with it, so much causality is there in the case, and no more. The cause does, or brings to pass no more in any event, than is dependent on it. If we say, the connection and dependence is not total, but partial, and that the effect, though it has some connection and dependence, yet is not entirely dependent on it; that is the same thing as to say, that not all that is in the event is an effect of that cause, but that only part of it arises from thence, and part some other way.

2. If there are some events which are not necessarily connected with their causes, then it will follow, that there are some things which come to pass without any cause, contrary to the supposition. For if there be any event which was not necessarily connected with the influence of the cause under such circumstances, then it was contingent whether it would attend or follow the influence of the cause, or no; it might have followed, and it might not, when the cause was the same, its influence the same, and under the same circumstances. And if so, why did it follow, rather than not follow? There is no cause or reason of this. Therefore here is something without any cause or reason why it is, viz. the following of the effect on the influence of the cause, with which it was not necessarily connected. If there be [not] a necessary connection of the effect on anything antecedent, then we may suppose that sometimes the event will follow the cause, and sometimes not, when the cause is the same, and in every respect in the same state and circumstances. And what can be the cause and reason of this strange phenomenon, even this diversity, that in one instance, the effect should follow, in another not? 'Tis evident by the supposition, that this is wholly without any cause or ground. Here is something in the present manner of the existence of things, and state of the world, that is absolutely without a cause. Which is contrary to the supposition, and contrary to what has been before demonstrated.

3. To suppose there are some events which have a cause and ground of their existence, that yet are not necessarily

connected with their cause, is to suppose that they have a cause which is not their cause. Thus, if the effect be not necessarily connected with the cause, with its influence, and influential circumstances; then, as I observed before, 'tis a thing possible and supposable, that the cause may sometimes exert the same influence, under the same circumstances, and yet the effect not follow. And if this actually happens in any instance, this instance is a proof, in fact, that the influence of the cause is not sufficient to produce the effect. For if it had been sufficient, it would have done it. And yet, by the supposition, in another instance, the same cause, with perfectly the same influence, and when all circumstances which have any influence, are the same, it was followed with the effect. By which it is manifest, that the effect in this last instance was not owing to the influence of the cause, but must come to pass some other way. For it was proved before, that the influence of the cause was not sufficient to produce the effect. And if it was not sufficient to produce it, then the production of it could not be owing to that influence, but must be owing to something else, or owing to nothing. And if the effect be not owing to the influence of the cause, then it is not the cause. Which brings us to the contradiction, of a cause, and no cause, that which is the ground and reason of the existence of a thing, and at the same time is not the ground and reason of its existence, nor is sufficient to be so.

If the matter be not already so plain as to render any further reasoning upon it impertinent, I would say, that that which seems to be the cause in the supposed case, can be no cause; its power and influence having, on a full trial, proved insufficient to produce such an effect: and if it be not sufficient to produce it, then it don't produce it. To say otherwise, is to say, there is power to do that which there is not power to do. If there be in a cause sufficient power exerted, and in circumstances sufficient to produce an effect, and so the effect be actually produced at one time; these things all concurring, will produce the effect at all times. And so we may turn it the other way; that which proves not sufficient at one time, cannot be sufficient at another, with precisely the same influential circumstances. And therefore if the effect follows, it is not owing to that cause; unless the different time be a circumstance which has influence: but that is contrary to the supposition; for 'tis supposed that all circumstances that have influence, are the same. And besides, this would be to suppose the time to be the cause; which is contrary to the supposition of the other thing's being the cause. But if merely diversity of time has no influence, then 'tis evident that it is as much of an absurdity to say, the cause was sufficient to produce the effect at one time, and not at another; as to say, that it is sufficient to produce the effect at a certain time, and yet not sufficient to produce the same effect at that same time.

On the whole, it is clearly manifest, that every effect has a necessary connection with its cause, or with that which is the true ground and reason of its existence. And therefore if there be no event without a cause, as was proved before, then no event whatsoever is contingent in the manner that Arminians suppose the free acts of the will to be contingent.

SECTION 9.

OF THE CONNECTION OF THE ACTS OF THE WILL WITH THE DICTATES OF THE UNDERSTANDING

It is manifest, that the acts of the will are none of them contingent in such a sense as to be without all necessity, or so as not to be necessary with a necessity of consequence and connection; because every act of the will is some way connected with the understanding, and is as the greatest apparent good is, in the manner which has already been explained; namely, that the soul always wills or chooses that which, in the present view of the mind, considered in the whole of that view, and all that belongs to it, appears most agreeable. Because, as was observed before, nothing is more evident than that, when men act voluntarily, and do what they please, then they do what appears most agreeable to them; and to say otherwise, would be as much as to affirm, that men don't choose what appears to suit them best, or what seems most pleasing to them; or that they don't choose what they prefer. Which brings the matter to a contradiction.

As 'tis very evident in itself, that the acts of the will have some connection with the dictates or views of the understanding, so this is allowed by some of the chief of the Arminian writers: particularly by Dr. Whitby and Dr. Samuel Clarke. Dr. Turnbull, though a great enemy to the doctrine of necessity, allows the same thing. In his Christian Philosophy (p. 196) he with much approbation cites another philosopher, as of the same mind, in these words:

No man (says an excellent philosopher) sets himself about anything, but upon some view or other, which serves him for a reason for what he does; and whatsoever faculties he employs, the understanding, with such light as it has, well or ill informed, constantly leads; and by that light, true or false, all her operative powers are directed. The will itself, how absolute and incontrollable soever it may be thought, never fails in its obedience to the dictates of the understanding. Temples have their sacred images; and we see what influence they have always had over a great part of mankind; but in truth, the ideas and images in men's minds are the invisible powers that constantly govern them; and to these they all pay universally a ready submission. [George Turnbull, *The Principles of Moral and Christian Philosophy* (2 vols. London, 1740), 2 (containing Christian Philosophy), 196]

But whether this be in a just consistence with themselves, and their own notions of liberty, I desire may now be impartially considered.

Dr. Whitby plainly supposes, that the acts and determinations of the will always follow the understanding's apprehension or view of the greatest good to be obtained, or evil to be avoided; or in other words, that the determinations of the will constantly and infallibly follow these two things in the understanding.

1. The degree of good to be obtained, and evil to be avoided, proposed to the understanding, and apprehended, viewed, and taken notice of by it.

2. The degree of the understanding's view, notice or apprehension of that good or evil; which is increased by attention and consideration. That this is an opinion he is exceeding peremptory in (as he is in every opinion which he maintains in his controversy with the Calvinists), with disdain of the contrary opinion, as absurd and self-contradictory, will appear by the following words of his, in his Discourse on the Five Points.

Now, 'tis certain, that what naturally makes the understanding to perceive, is evidence proposed, and apprehended, considered or adverted to: for nothing else can be requisite to make us come to the knowledge of the truth....Again, what makes the will choose, is something approved by the understanding; and consequently appearing to the soul as good. And whatsoever it refuseth, is something represented by the understanding, and so appearing to the will, as evil. Whence all that God requires of us is, and can be only this; to refuse the evil, and choose the good. Wherefore, to say that evidence proposed, apprehended and considered, is not sufficient to make the understanding approve; or that the greatest good proposed, the greatest evil threatened, when equally believed and reflected on, is not sufficient to engage the will to choose the good and refuse the evil, is in effect to say, that which alone doth move the will to choose or to refuse, is not sufficient to engage it so to do; which being contradictory to itself, must of necessity be false. Be it then so, that we naturally have an aversation to the truths proposed to us in the gospel; that only can make us indisposed to attend to them, but cannot hinder our conviction, when we do apprehend them, and attend to them. ... Be it, that there is in us also a renitency to the good we are to choose; that only can indispose us to believe it is, and to approve it as our chiefest good. Be it, that we are prone to the evil that we should decline; that only can render it the more difficult for us to believe it is the worst of evils. But yet, what we do really believe to be our chiefest good, will still be chosen; and what we apprehend to be the worst of evils, will, whilst we do continue under that conviction, be refused by us. It therefore can be only requisite, in order to these ends, that the good Spirit should so illuminate our understandings, that we attending to, and considering what lies before us, should apprehend, and be convinced of our duty; and that the blessings of the gospel should be so propounded to us, as that we may discern them to be our chiefest good; and the miseries it threateneth, so as we may be convinced they are the worst of evils; that we may choose the one, and refuse the other. (Whitby, *Discourse on the Five Points*, pp. 211, 212, 213; Dis. III, ch. 1.)

Here let it be observed, how plainly and peremptorily it is asserted, that the greatest good proposed, and the greatest evil threatened, when equally believed and reflected on, is sufficient to engage the will to choose the good, and refuse the evil, and is that alone which doth move the will to choose or to refuse; and that it is contradictory to itself, to suppose otherwise; and therefore must of necessity be false; and then what we do really believe to be our chiefest good will still be chosen, and what we apprehend to be the worst of evils, will, whilst we continue under that conviction, be refused by us. Nothing could have been said more to the purpose, fully to signify and declare, that the determinations of the will must evermore follow the illumination, conviction and notice of the understanding, with regard to the greatest good and evil proposed, reckoning both the degree of good and evil understood, and the degree of understanding, notice and conviction of that proposed good and evil; and that it is thus necessarily, and can be otherwise in no instance: because it is asserted, that it implies a contradiction, to suppose it ever to be otherwise.

I am sensible, the Doctor's aim in these assertions is against the Calvinists; to shew, in opposition to them, that there is no need of any physical operation of the Spirit of God on the will, to change and determine that to a good choice, but that God's operation and assistance is only moral, suggesting ideas to the understanding; which he supposes to be enough, if those ideas are attended to, infallibly to obtain the end. But whatever his design was, nothing can more directly and fully prove, that every determination of the will, in choosing and refusing, is necessary; directly contrary to his own notion of the liberty of the will. For if the determination of the will, evermore, in this manner, follows the light, conviction and view of the understanding, concerning the greatest good and evil, and this be that alone which moves the will, and it be a contradiction to suppose otherwise; then it is necessarily so, the will necessarily follows this light or view of the understanding, not only in some of its acts, but in every act of choosing and refusing. So that the will don't determine itself in any one of its own acts; but all its acts, every act of choice and refusal, depends on, and is necessarily connected with some antecedent cause; which cause is not the will itself, nor any act of its own, nor anything pertaining to that faculty, but something belonging to another faculty, whose acts go before the will, in all its acts, and govern and determine them every one.

Here, if it should be replied, that although it be true, that according to the Doctor, the final determination of the will always depends upon, and is infallibly connected with the understanding's conviction, and notice of the greatest good; yet the acts of the will are not necessary; because that conviction and notice of the understanding is first dependent on a preceding act of the will, in determining to attend to, and take notice of the evidence exhibited; by which means the mind obtains that degree of conviction which is sufficient and effectual to determine the consequent and ultimate choice of the will; and that the will with regard to that preceding act, whereby it determines whether to attend or no, is not necessary; and that in this, the liberty of the will consists, that when God holds forth sufficient objective light, the will is at liberty whether to command the attention of the mind to it—

Nothing can be more weak and inconsiderate than such a reply as this. For that preceding act of the will, in determining to attend and consider, still is an act of the will (it is so to be sure, if the liberty of the will consists in it, as is supposed); and if it be an act of the will, it is an act of choice or refusal. And therefore, if what the Doctor asserts be true, it is determined by some antecedent light in the understanding concerning the greatest apparent good or evil. For he asserts, it is that light "which alone doth move the will to choose or refuse." And therefore the will must be moved by that in choosing to attend to the objective light offered, in order to another consequent act of choice: so that this act is no less necessary than the other. And if we suppose another act of the will, still preceding both these mentioned, to determine both, still that also must be an act of the will, and an act of choice; and so must, by the same principles, be infallibly determined by some certain degree of light in the understanding concerning the greatest good. And let us suppose as many acts of the will, one preceding another, as we please, yet they are everyone of them necessarily determined by a certain degree of light in the understanding, concerning the greatest and most eligible good in that case; and so, not one of them free according to Dr. Whitby's notion of freedom. And if it be said, the reason why men don't attend to light held forth, is because of ill habits contracted by evil acts committed before, whereby their minds are indisposed to attend to, and consider of the truth held forth to them by God, the difficulty is not at all avoided: still the question returns, what determined the will in those preceding evil acts? It must, by Dr. Whitby's principles, still be the view of the understanding concerning the greatest good and evil. If this view of the understanding be "that alone which doth move the will to choose or refuse," as the Doctor asserts, then every act of choice or refusal, from a man's first existence, is moved and determined by this view; and this view of the understanding exciting and governing the act, must be before the act: and therefore the will is necessarily determined, in everyone of its acts, from a man's first existence, by a cause beside the will, and a cause that don't proceed from, or depend on any act of the will at all. Which at once utterly abolishes the Doctor's whole scheme of liberty of will; and he, at one stroke, has cut the sinews of all his arguments from the goodness, righteousness, faithfulness and sincerity of God, in his commands, promises, threatenings, calls, invitations, expostulations; which he makes use of, under the heads of reprobation, election, universal redemption, sufficient and effectual grace, and the freedom of the will of man; and has enervated and made vain all those exclamations against the doctrine of the Calvinists, as charging God with manifest unrighteousness, unfaithfulness, hypocrisy, fallaciousness, and cruelty; which he has over, and over, and over again, numberless times in his book.

Dr. Samuel Clarke, in his Demonstration of the Being and Attributes of God [Sixth ed. (London, 1725), p. 93] to evade the argument to prove the necessity of volition, from its necessary connection with the last dictate of the understanding, supposes the latter not to be diverse from the act of the will itself. But if it be so, it will not alter the case as to the evidence of the necessity of the act of the will. If the dictate of the understanding be the very same with the determination of the will or choice, as Dr. Clarke supposes, then this determination is no fruit or effect of choice: and if so, no liberty of choice has any hand in it: as to volition or choice, it is necessary; that is, choice can't prevent it. If the last dictate of the understanding be the same with the determination of volition itself, then the existence of that determination must be necessary as to volition; inasmuch as volition can have no opportunity to determine whether it shall exist or no, it having existence already before volition has opportunity to determine anything. It is itself the very rise and existence of volition. But a thing, after it exists, has no opportunity to determine as to its own existence; it is too late for that.

If liberty consists in that which Arminians suppose, viz. in the will's determining its own acts, having free opportunity, and being without all necessity; this is the same as to say, that liberty consists in the soul's having power and opportunity to have what determinations of the will it pleases or chooses. And if the determinations of the will, and the last dictates of the understanding be the same thing, then liberty consists in the mind's having power to have what dictates of the understanding it pleases, having opportunity to choose its own dictates of understanding. But this is absurd; for it is to make the determination of choice prior to the dictate of understanding, and the ground of it; which can't consist with the dictate of understanding's being the determination of choice itself.

Here is no way to do in this case, but only to recur to the old absurdity, of one determination before another, and the cause of it; and another before that, determining that; and so on in infinitum. If the last dictate of the understanding be the determination of the will itself, and the soul be free with regard to that dictate, in the Arminian notion of freedom; then the soul, before that dictate of its understanding exists, voluntarily and according to its own choice determines, in every case, what that dictate of the understanding shall be; otherwise that dictate, as to the will, is necessary; and the acts determined by it, must also be necessary. So that here is a determination of the mind prior to that dictate of the understanding, an act of choice going before it, choosing and determining what that dictate of the understanding shall be: and this preceding act of choice, being a free act of will, must also be the same with another last dictate of the understanding: and if the mind also be free in that dictate of understanding, that must be determined still by another; and so on forever.

Besides, if the dictate of the understanding, and determination of the will be the same, this confounds the understanding and will, and makes them the same. Whether they be the same or no, I will not now dispute; but only would observe, that if it be so, and the Arminian notion of [liberty be just, then all] liberty consists in a self-determining power in the understanding, free of all necessity; being independent, undetermined by anything prior to its own acts and determinations; and the more the understanding is thus independent, and sovereign over its own determinations, the more free. By this therefore the freedom of the soul, as a moral agent, must consist in the independence of the understanding on any evidence or appearance of things, or anything whatsoever that stands forth to the view of the mind, prior to the understanding's determination. And what a sort of liberty is this! consisting in an ability, freedom and easiness of judging, either according to evidence, or against it; having a sovereign command over itself at all times, to judge, either agreeably or disagreeably to what is plainly exhibited to its own view. Certainly, 'tis no liberty that renders persons the proper subjects of persuasive reasoning, arguments, expostulations, and suchlike moral means and inducements. The use of which with mankind, is a main argument of the Arminians, to defend their notion of liberty without all necessity. For according to this, the more free men are, the less they are under the government of such means, less subject to the power of evidence and reason, and more independent on their influence, in their determinations.

And whether the understanding and will are the same

or no, as Dr. Clarke seems to suppose, yet in order to maintain the Arminian notion of liberty without necessity, the free will is not determined by the understanding, nor necessarily connected with the understanding; and the further from such connection, the greater the freedom. And when the liberty is full and complete, the determinations of the will have no connection at all with the dictates of the understanding. And if so, in vain are all applications to the understanding, in order to induce to any free virtuous act; and so in vain are all instructions, counsels, invitations, expostulations, and all arguments and persuasives whatsoever: for these are but applications to the understanding, and a clear and lively exhibition of the objects of choice to the mind's view. But if, after all, the will must be self-determined, and independent on the understanding, to what purpose are things thus represented to the understanding, in order to determine the choice?

SECTION 10.

VOLITION NECESSARILY CONNECTED WITH THE INFLUENCE OF MOTIVES; WITH PARTICULAR OBSERVATIONS ON THE GREAT INCONSISTENCE OF MR. CHUBB'S ASSERTIONS AND REASONINGS, ABOUT THE FREEDOM OF THE WILL

That every act of the will has some cause, and consequently (by what has been already proved) has a necessary connection with its cause, and so is necessary by a necessity of connection and consequence, is evident by this, that every act of the will whatsoever, is excited by some motive: which is manifest, because, if the will or mind, in willing and choosing after the manner that it does, is excited so to do by no motive or inducement, then it has no end which it proposes to itself, or pursues in so doing; it aims at nothing, and seeks nothing. And if it seeks nothing, then it don't go after anything, or exert any inclination or preference towards anything. Which brings the matter to a contradiction; because for the mind to will something, and for it to go after something by an act of preference and inclination, are the same thing.

But if every act of the will is excited by a motive, then that motive is the cause of the act of the will. If the acts of the will are excited by motives, then motives are the causes of their being excited; or, which is the same thing, the cause of their being put forth into act and existence. And if so, the existence of the acts of the will is properly the effect of their motives. Motives do nothing as motives or inducements, but by their influence; and so much as is done by their influence, is the effect of them. For that is the notion of an effect, something that is brought to pass by the influence of another thing.

And if volitions are properly the effects of their motives, then they are necessarily connected with their motives. Every effect and event being, as was proved before, necessarily connected with that which is the proper ground and reason of its existence. Thus it is manifest, that volition is necessary, and is not from any self-determining power in the will: the volition which is caused by previous motive and inducement, is not caused by the will exercising a sovereign power over itself, to determine, cause and excite volitions in itself. This is not consistent with the will's acting in a state of indifference and equilibrium, to determine itself to a preference; for the way in which motives operate, is by biasing the will, and giving it a certain inclination or preponderance one way.

Here it may be proper to observe, that Mr. Chubb, in his collection of Tracts on Various Subjects [Thomas Chubb, A Collection of Tracts on Various Subjects, London, 1730], has advanced a scheme of liberty, which is greatly divided against itself, and thoroughly subversive of itself; and that many ways.

I. He is abundant in asserting, that the will, in all its acts, is influenced by motive and excitement; and that this is the previous ground and reason of all its acts, and that it is never otherwise in any instance. He says (p. 262), "No action can take place without some motive to excite it." And in p. 263: "Volition cannot take place without some previous reason or motive to induce it." And in p. 310: "Action would not take place without some reason or motive to induce it; it being absurd to suppose, that the active faculty would be exerted without some previous reason to dispose the mind to action." So also p. 257. And he speaks of these things as what we may be absolutely certain of, and which are the foundation, the only foundation we have of a certainty of the moral perfections of God (pp. 252, 253, 254, 255, 261, 262, 263, 264).

And yet at the same time, by his scheme, the influence of motives upon us to excite to action, and to be actually a ground of volition, is consequent on the volition or choice of the mind. For he very greatly insists upon it, that in all free actions, before the mind is the subject of those volitions which motives excite, it chooses to be so. It chooses whether it will comply with the motive, which presents itself in view, or not; and when various motives are presented, it chooses which it will yield to, and which it will reject. So p. 256: "Every man has power to act, or to refrain from acting agreeably with, or contrary to, any motive that presents." P. 257: "Every man is at liberty to act, or refrain from acting agreeably with, or contrary to, what each of these motives, considered singly, would excite him to....Man has power, and is as much at liberty to reject the motive that does prevail, as he has power, and is at liberty to reject those motives that do not." And so pp. 310, 311: "In order to constitute a moral agent, it is necessary, that he should have power to act, or to refrain from acting, upon such moral motives as he pleases." And to the like purpose in many other places. According to these things, the will acts first, and chooses or refuses to comply with the motive that is presented, before it falls under its prevailing influence: and 'tis first determined by the mind's pleasure or choice, what motives it will be induced by, before it is induced by them.

Now, how can these things hang together? How can the mind first act, and by its act of volition and choice determine what motives shall be the ground and reason of its volition and choice? For this supposes, the choice is already made, before the motive has its effect; and that the volition is already exerted, before the motive prevails, so as actually to be the ground of the volition; and makes the prevailing of the motive, the consequence of the volition, which yet it is the ground of. If the mind has already chosen to comply with a motive, and to yield to its excitement, it don't need to yield to it after this: for the thing is effected already, that the motive would excite to, and the will is beforehand with the excitement; and the excitement comes in too late, and is needless and in vain afterwards. If the mind has already chosen to yield to a motive which invites to a thing, that implies and in fact is a choosing the thing invited to; and the very act of choice is before the influence of the motive which induces, and is the ground of the choice; the son is beforehand with the father that begets him: the choice is supposed to be the ground of that influence of the motive, which very influence is supposed to be the ground of the choice. And so vice versa, the choice is supposed to be the consequence of the influence of the motive, which influence of the motive is the consequence of that very choice.

And besides, if the will acts first towards the motive before it falls under its influence, and the prevailing of the motive upon it to induce it to act and choose, be the fruit and consequence of its act and choice, then how is the motive "a previous ground and reason of the act and choice," so that "in the nature of the things, volition cannot take place without some previous reason and motive to induce it"; and that this act is consequent upon, and follows the motive? Which things Mr. Chubb often asserts, as of certain and undoubted truth. So that the very same motive is both previous and consequent, both before and after, both the ground and fruit of the very same thing!

II. Agreeable to the forementioned inconsistent notion of the will's first acting towards the motive, choosing whether it will comply with it, in order to its becoming a ground of the will's acting, before any act of volition can take place, Mr. Chubb frequently calls motives and excitements to the action of the will, "the passive ground or reason of that action" [Tracts, pp. 257, 258, 263, 264]. Which is a remarkable phrase; than which I presume there is none more unintelligible, and void of distinct and consistent meaning, in all the writings of Duns Scotus, or Thomas Aquinas. When he represents the motive to action or volition as passive, he must mean—passive in that affair, or passive with respect to that action which he speaks of; otherwise it is nothing to his purpose, or relating to the design of his argument: he must mean (if that can be called a meaning) that the motive to volition is first acted upon or towards by the volition, choosing to yield to it, making it a ground of action, or determining to fetch its influence from thence; and so to make it a previous ground of its own excitation and existence. Which is the same absurdity, as if one should say, that the soul of man, or any other thing should, previous to its existing, choose what cause it would come into existence by, and should act upon its cause, to fetch influence from thence, to bring it into being; and so its cause should be a passive ground of its existence!

Mr. Chubb does very plainly suppose motive or excitement to be the ground of the being of volition. He speaks of it as the ground or reason of the exertion of an act of the will (pp. 391 and 392); and expressly says, that "volition cannot take place without some previous ground or motive to induce it" (p. 263). And he speaks of the act as from the motive, and from the influence of the motive (p. 352); and from the influence that the motive has on the man, for the production of an action (p. 317). Certainly, there is no need of multiplying words about this; 'tis easily judged, whether motive can be the ground of volition's being exerted and taking place, so that the very production of it is from the influence of the motive, and yet the motive, before it becomes the ground of the volition, is passive, or acted upon by the volition. But this I will say, that a man who insists so much on clearness of meaning in others, and is so much in blaming their confusion and inconsistence, ought, if he was able, to have explained his meaning in this phrase of "passive ground of action," so as to show it not to be confused and inconsistent.

If any should suppose, that Mr. Chubb, when he speaks of motive as a "passive ground of action," don't mean passive with regard to that volition which it is the ground of, but some other antecedent volition (though his purpose and argument, and whole discourse, will by no means allow of such a supposition) yet it would not help the matter in the least. For (1) if we suppose there to be an act of volition or choice, by which the soul chooses to yield to the invitation of a motive to another volition, by which the soul chooses something else; both these supposed volitions are in effect the very same. A volition, or choosing to yield to the force of a motive inviting to choose something, comes to just the same thing as choosing the thing which the motive invites to, as I observed before. So that here can be no room to help the matter, by a distinction of two volitions. (2) If the motive be passive with respect, not to the same volition that the motive excites to, but one truly distinct and prior; yet, by Mr. Chubb, that prior volition can't take place, without a motive or excitement, as a "previous ground" of its existence. For he insists, that "it is absurd to suppose any volition should take place without some previous motive to induce it." So that at last it comes to just the same absurdity: for if every volition must have a previous motive, then the very first in the whole series must be excited by a previous motive; and yet the motive to that first volition is passive; but can't be passive with regard to another antecedent volition, because, by the supposition, it is the very first: therefore if it be passive with respect to any volition, it must be so with regard to that very volition that it is the ground of, and that is excited by it.

III. Though Mr. Chubb asserts, as above, that every volition has some motive, and that, "in the nature of the thing, no volition can take place without some motive to induce it"; yet he asserts, that volition does not always follow the strongest motive; or in other words, is not governed by any superior strength of the motive that is followed, beyond motives to the contrary, previous to the volition itself. His own words, p. 258, are as follows: "Though with regard to physical causes, that which is strongest always prevails, yet it is otherwise with regard to moral causes. Of these, sometimes the stronger, sometimes the weaker, prevails. And the ground of this difference is evident, namely, that what we call moral causes, strictly speaking, are no causes at all, but barely passive reasons of, or excitements to the action, or to the refraining from acting: which excitements we have power, or are at liberty to comply with or reject, as I have shewed above." And so throughout the paragraph, he, in a variety of phrases, insists, that the will is not always determined by the strongest motive, unless by strongest we preposterously mean actually prevailing in the event; which is not in the motive, but in the will; but that the will is not always determined by the motive which is strongest, by any strength previous to the volition itself. And he elsewhere does abundantly assert, that the will is determined by no superior strength or advantage that motives have, from any constitution or state of things, or any circumstances whatsoever, previous to the actual determination of the will. And indeed his whole discourse on human liberty implies it, his whole scheme is founded upon it.

But these things cannot stand together. There is such a thing as a diversity of strength in motives to choice, previous to the choice itself. Mr. Chubb himself supposes, that they do "previously invite," "induce," "excite" and "dispose the mind to action." This implies, that they have something in themselves that is inviting, some tendency to induce and dispose to volition, previous to volition itself. And if they have in themselves this nature and tendency, doubtless they have it in certain limited degrees, which are capable of diversity; and some have it in greater degrees, others in less; and they that have most of this tendency, considered with all their nature and circumstances, previous to volition, they are the strongest motives; and those that have least, are the weakest motives.

Now if volition sometimes don't follow the motive which is strongest, or has most previous tendency or advantage, all things considered, to induce or excite it, but follows the weakest, or that which as it stands previously in the mind's view, has least tendency to induce it; herein the will apparently acts wholly without motive, without any previous reason to dispose the mind to it, contrary to what the same author supposes. The act wherein the will must proceed without previous motive to induce it, is the act of preferring the weakest motive. For how absurd is it to say, the mind sees previous reason in the motive, to prefer that motive before the other; and at the same time to suppose, that there is nothing in the motive, in its nature, state, or any circumstances of it whatsoever, as it stands in the previous view of the mind, that gives it any preference; but on the contrary, the other motive that stands in competition with it, in all these respects, has most belonging to it, that is inviting and moving, and has most of a tendency to choice and preference? This is certainly as much as to say, there is previous ground and reason in the motive for the act of preference, and yet no previous reason for it. By the supposition, as to all that is in the two rival motives which tends to preference, previous to the act of preference, it is not in that which is preferred, but wholly in the other: because appearing superior strength, and all appearing preferableness is in that; and yet Mr. Chubb supposes, that the act of preference is from "previous ground and reason" in the motive which is preferred. But are these things consistent? Can there be previous ground in a thing for an event that takes place, and yet no previous tendency in it to that event? If one thing follows another, without any previous tendency to its following, then I should think it very plain, that it follows it without any manner of previous reason why it should follow.

Yea, in this case, Mr. Chubb supposes, that the event follows an antecedent or a previous thing, as the ground of its existence, not only that has no tendency to it, but a contrary tendency. The event is the preference which the mind gives to that motive which is weaker, as it stands in the previous view of the mind; the immediate antecedent is the view the mind has of the two rival motives conjunctly; in which previous view of the mind, all the preferableness, or previous tendency to preference, is supposed to be on the other side, or in the contrary motive; and all the unworthiness of preference, and so previous tendency to comparative neglect, rejection or undervaluing, is on that side which is preferred: and yet in this view of the mind is supposed to be the "previous ground or reason" of this act of preference, "exciting it, and disposing the mind to it." Which, I leave the reader to judge, whether it be absurd or not. If it be not, then it is not absurd to say, that the previous tendency of an antecedent to a consequent, is the ground and reason why that consequent does not follow; and the want of a previous tendency to an event, yea, a tendency to the contrary, is the true ground and reason why that event does follow.

An act of choice or preference is a comparative act, wherein the mind acts with reference to two or more things that are compared, and stand in competition in the mind's view. If the mind, in this comparative act, prefers that which appears inferior in the comparison, then the mind herein acts absolutely without motive, or inducement, or any temptation whatsoever. [Thus], if a hungry man has the offer of two sorts of food, both which he finds an appetite to, but has a stronger appetite to one than the other; and there be no circumstances or excitements whatsoever in the case to induce him to take either one or the other, but merely his appetite: if in the choice he makes between them, he chooses that which he has least appetite to, and refuses that to which he has the strongest appetite, this is a choice made absolutely without previous motive, excitement, reason or temptation, as much as if he were perfectly without all appetite to either: because his volition in this case is a comparative act, attending and following a comparative view of the food which he chooses, viewing it as related to, and compared with the other sort of food, in which view his preference has absolutely no previous ground, yea, is against all previous ground and motive. And if there be any principle in man from whence an act of choice may arise after this manner, from the same principle volition may arise wholly without motive on either side. If the mind in its volition can go beyond motive, then it can go without motive: for when it is beyond the motive, it is out of the reach of the motive, out of the limits of its influence, and so without motive. If volition goes beyond the strength and tendency of motive, and especially if it goes against its tendency, this demonstrates the independence of volition [on] motive. And if so, no reason can be given for what Mr. Chubb so often asserts, even that "in the nature of things volition cannot take place without a motive to induce it."

If the most High should endow a balance with agency or activity of nature, in such a manner, that when unequal weights are put into the scales, its agency could enable it to cause that scale to descend which has the least weight, and so to raise the greater weight; this would clearly demonstrate, that the motion of the balance does not depend on weights in the scales, at least as much, as if the balance should move itself, when there is no weight in either scale. And the activity of the balance which is sufficient to move itself against the greater weight, must certainly be more than sufficient to move it when there is no weight at all.

Mr. Chubb supposes, that the will can't stir at all without some motive; and also supposes, that if there be a motive to one thing, and none to the contrary, volition will infallibly follow that motive. This is virtually to suppose an entire dependence of the will on motives: if it were not wholly dependent on them, it could surely help itself a little without them, or help itself a little against a motive, without help from the strength and weight of a contrary motive. And yet his supposing that the will, when it has before it various opposite motives, can use them as it pleases, and choose its own influence from them, and neglect the strongest, and follow the weakest, supposes it to be wholly independent on motives.

It further appears, on Mr. Chubb's supposition, that volition must be without any previous ground in any motive, thus: if it be as he supposes, that the will is not determined by any previous superior strength of the motive, but determines and chooses its own motive, then, when the rival motives are exactly equal in strength and tendency to induce, in all respects, it may follow either; and may in such a case, sometimes follow one, sometimes the other. And if so, this diversity which appears between the acts of the will, is plainly without previous ground in either of the motives; for all that is previously in the motives, is supposed precisely and perfectly the same, without any diversity whatsoever. Now perfect identity, as to all that is previous in the antecedent, can't be the ground and reason of diversity in the consequent. Perfect identity in the ground can't be a reason why it is not followed with the same consequence. And therefore the source of this diversity of consequence must be sought for elsewhere.

And lastly, it may be observed, that however Mr. Chubb does much insist that no volition can take place without some motive to induce it, which previously disposes the mind to it; yet, as he also insists that the mind without reference to any previous superior strength of motives, picks and chooses for its motive to follow; he himself herein plainly supposes, that with regard to the mind's preference of one motive before another, it is not the motive that disposes the will, but the will disposes itself to follow the motive.

IV. Mr. Chubb supposes necessity to be utterly inconsistent with agency; and that to suppose a being to be an agent in that which is necessary, is a plain contradiction (p. 311). And throughout his discourses on the subject of liberty, he supposes, that necessity cannot consist with agency or freedom; and that to suppose otherwise, is to make liberty and necessity, action and passion, the same thing. And so he seems to suppose, that there is no action strictly speaking, but volition; and that as to the effects of volition in body or mind, in themselves considered, being necessary, they are said to be free, only as they are the effects of an act that is not necessary.

And yet, according to him, volition itself is the effect of volition; yea, every act of free volition: and therefore every act of free volition must, by what has now been observed from him, be necessary. That every act of free volition is itself the effect of volition, is abundantly supposed by him. In p. 341, he says, "If a man is such a creature as I have above proved him to be, that is, if he has in him a power or liberty of doing either good or evil, and either of these is the subject of his own free choice, so that he might, if he had pleased, have chosen and done the contrary." Here he supposes, all that is good or evil in man is the effect of his choice; and so that his good or evil choice itself is the effect of his pleasure or choice, in these words, "he might if he had pleased, have chosen the contrary." So in p. [386]: "Though it be highly reasonable, that a man should always choose the greater good… yet he may, if he please, choose otherwise." Which is the same thing as if he had said, he may, if he chooses, choose otherwise. And then he goes on, "that is, he may, if he pleases, choose what is good for himself, etc." And again in the same page, "The will is not confined by the understanding to any particular sort of good, whether greater or less; but is at liberty to choose what kind of good it pleases." If there be any meaning in these last words, the meaning must be this, that the will is at liberty to choose what kind of good it chooses to choose; supposing the act of choice itself determined by an antecedent choice. The liberty Mr. Chubb speaks of, is not only a man's having power to move his body agreeably to an antecedent act of choice, but to use or exert the faculties of his soul. Thus, in p. 379, speaking of the faculties of his mind, he says, "Man has power, and is at liberty to neglect these faculties, to use them aright, or to abuse them, as he pleases." And that he supposes an act of choice, or exercise of pleasure, properly distinct from, and antecedent to those acts thus chosen, directing, commanding and producing the chosen acts, and even the acts of choice themselves, is very plain in p. 283, "He can command his actions; and herein consists his liberty; he can give or deny himself that pleasure as he pleases." And p. 377: "If the actions of men…are not the produce of a free choice, or election, but spring from a necessity of nature…he cannot in reason be the object of reward or punishment on their account. Whereas, if action in man, whether good or evil, is the produce of will or free choice; so that a man in either case, had it in his power, and was at liberty to have chosen the contrary, he is the proper object of reward or punishment, according as he chooses to behave himself." Here in these last words, he speaks of liberty of choosing, according as he chooses. So that the behavior which he speaks of as subject to his choice, is his choosing itself, as well as his external conduct consequent upon it. And therefore 'tis evident, he means not only external actions, but the acts of choice themselves, when he speaks of "all free actions, as the produce of free choice." And this is abundantly evident in what he says in pp. 372, and 373.

Now these things imply a twofold great absurdity and inconsistence.

1. To suppose, as Mr. Chubb plainly does, that every free act of choice is "commanded by," and is the "produce of free choice," is to suppose the first free act of choice belonging to the case, yea, the first free act of choice that ever man exerted, to be "the produce" of an antecedent act of choice. But I hope I need not labor at all to convince my readers, that 'tis an absurdity to say, the very first act is the produce of another act that went before it.

2. If it were both possible and real, as Mr. Chubb insists, that every free act of choice were the produce or the effect of a free act of choice; yet even then, according to his principles, no one act of choice would be free, but everyone necessary; because, every act of choice being the effect of a foregoing act, every act would be necessarily connected with that foregoing cause. For Mr. Chubb himself says (p. 389), "When the self-moving power is exerted, it becomes the necessary cause of its effects." So that his notion of a free act, that is rewardable or punishable, is a heap of contradictions. It is a free act, and yet, by his own notion of freedom, is necessary; and therefore by him it is a contradiction, to suppose it to be free. According to him, every free act is the produce of a free act; so that there must be an infinite number of free acts in succession, without any beginning, in an agent that has a beginning. And therefore here is an infinite number of free acts, everyone of them free; and yet not any one of them free, but every act in the whole infinite chain a necessary effect. All the acts are rewardable or punishable, and yet the agent cannot, in reason, be the object of reward or punishment, on account of any one of these actions. He is active in them all, and passive in none; yet active in none, but passive in all, etc.

V. Mr. Chubb does most strenuously deny, that motives are "causes" of the acts of the will; or that the moving principle in man is "moved," or "caused to be exerted" by motives. His words (p. 388) are, "If the moving principle in man is moved, or caused to be exerted, by something external to man, which all motives are, then it would not be a self-moving principle, seeing it would be moved by a principle external to itself. And to say, that a self-moving principle is moved, or caused to be exerted, by a cause external to itself, is absurd and a contradiction, etc." And in the next page, 'tis particularly and largely insisted, that motives are causes in no case, that "they are merely passive in the production of action, and have no causality in the production of it ... no causality, to be the cause of the exertion of the will."

Now I desire it may be considered, how this can possibly consist with what he says in other places. Let it be noted here,

1. Mr. Chubb abundantly speaks of motives as "excitements of the acts of the will"; and says, that "motives do excite volition, and induce it," and that they are necessary to this end; that "in the reason and nature of things, volition cannot take place without motives to excite it." But now if motives excite the will, they move it; and yet he says, 'tis absurd to say, the will is moved by motives. And again (if language is of any significance at all) if motives excite volition, then they are the cause of its being excited; and to cause volition to be excited, is to cause it to be put forth or exerted. Yea, Mr. Chubb says himself (p. 317), motive is necessary to the "exertion" of the active faculty. To excite, is positively to do something; and certainly that which does something, is the cause of the thing done by it. To create, is to cause to be created; to make, is to cause to be made; to kill, is to cause to be killed; to quicken, is to cause to be quickened; and to excite, is to cause to be excited. To excite, is to be a cause, in the most proper sense, not merely a negative occasion, but a ground of existence by positive influence. The notion of exciting, is exerting influence to cause the effect to arise or come forth into existence.

2. Mr. Chubb himself (p. 317) speaks of motives as the ground and reason of action by "influence," and by "prevailing influence." Now, what can be meant by a cause, but something that is the ground and reason of a thing by its influence, an influence that is prevalent and so effectual?

3. This author not only speaks of motives as the ground and reason of action, by prevailing influence; but expressly of their "influence as prevailing for the production of an action," in the same p. 317: which makes the inconsistency still more palpable and notorious. The production of an effect is certainly the causing of an effect; and productive influence is causal influence, if anything is; and that which has this influence prevalently, so as thereby to become the ground of another thing, is a cause of that thing, if there be any such thing as a cause. This influence, Mr. Chubb says, motives have to produce an action; and yet he says, 'tis absurd and a contradiction, to say they are causes.

4. In the same page, he once and again speaks of motives as "disposing" the agent to action, "by their influence." His words are these:

> As motive, which takes place in the understanding, and is the product of intelligence, is necessary to action, that is, to the exertion of the active faculty, because that faculty would not be exerted without some previous reason to dispose the mind to action; so from hence it plainly appears, that when a man is said to be disposed to one action rather than another, this properly signifies the prevailing influence that one motive has upon a man for the production of an action, or for the being at rest, before all other motives, for the production of the contrary. For as motive is the ground and reason of any action, so the motive that prevails, disposes the agent to the performance of that action.

Now, if motives dispose the mind to action, then they cause the mind to be disposed; and to cause the mind to be disposed, is to cause it to be willing; and to cause it to be willing, is to cause it to will; and that is the same thing as to be the cause of an act of the will. And yet this same Mr. Chubb holds it to be absurd, to suppose motive to be a cause of the act of the will.

And if we compare these things together, we have here again a whole heap of inconsistencies. "Motives are the previous ground and reason" of the acts of the will; yea, the "necessary" ground and reason of "their exertion, without which they will not be exerted, and cannot in the nature of things take place"; and they do "excite" these acts of the will, and do this by a "prevailing influence"; yea, "an influence which prevails for the production of the act" of the will, and for "the disposing of the mind to it": and yet 'tis "absurd," to suppose "motive to be a cause" of an act of the will, or that "a principle of will is moved or caused to be exerted by it," or that it has "any causality in the production of it, or any causality to be the cause of the exertion of the will."

A due consideration of these things which Mr. Chubb has advanced, the strange inconsistencies which the notion of liberty consisting in the will's power of self-determination void of all necessity, united with that dictate of common sense, that there can be no volition without a motive, drove him into, may be sufficient to convince us, that it is utterly impossible ever to make that notion of liberty consistent with the influence of motives in volition. And as it is in a manner self-evident, that there can be no act of will, choice or preference of the mind, without some motive or inducement, something in the mind's view, which it aims at, seeks, inclines to, and goes after; so 'tis most manifest, there is no such liberty in the universe as Arminians insist on; nor any such thing possible, or conceivable.

SECTION 11.

THE EVIDENCE OF GOD'S CERTAIN FOREKNOWLEDGE OF THE VOLITIONS OF MORAL AGENTS

That the acts of the wills of moral agents are not contingent events, in that sense, as to be without all necessity, appears by God's certain foreknowledge of such events.

In handling this argument, I would in the first place prove, that God has a certain foreknowledge of the voluntary acts of moral agents; and secondly, show the consequence, or how it follows from hence, that the volitions of moral agents are not contingent, so as to be without necessity of connection and consequence.

First, I am to prove, that God has an absolute and certain foreknowledge of the free actions of moral agents.

One would think, it should be wholly needless to enter on such an argument with any that profess themselves Christians: but so it is; God's certain foreknowledge of the free acts of moral agents, is denied by some that pretend to believe the Scriptures to be the Word of God; and especially of late. I therefore shall consider the evidence of such a prescience in the most High, as fully as the designed limits of this essay will admit of; supposing myself herein to have to do with such as own the truth of the Bible.

Arg. I. My first argument shall be taken from God's prediction of such events. Here I would in the first place lay down these two things as axioms.

(1) If God don't foreknow, he can't foretell such events; that is, he can't peremptorily and certainly foretell them. If God has no more than an uncertain guess concerning events of this kind, then he can declare no more than an uncertain guess. Positively to foretell, is to profess to foreknow, or to declare positive foreknowledge.

(2) If God don't certainly foreknow the future volitions of moral agents, then neither can he certainly foreknow those events which are consequent and dependent on these volitions. The existence of the one depending on the existence of the other, the knowledge of the existence

of the one depends on the knowledge of the existence of the other; and the one can't be more certain than the other.

Therefore, how many, how great, and how extensive soever the consequences of the volitions of moral agents may be; though they should extend to an alteration of the state of things through the universe, and should be continued in a series of successive events to all eternity, and should in the progress of things branch forth into an infinite number of series, each of them going on in an endless line or chain of events; God must be as ignorant of all these consequences, as he is of the volition whence they first take their rise: all these events, and the whole state of things depending on them, how important, extensive and vast soever, must be hid from him.

These positions being such as I suppose none will deny, I now proceed to observe the following things.

1. Men's moral conduct and qualities, their virtues and vices, their wickedness and good practice, things rewardable and punishable, have often been foretold by God. Pharaoh's moral conduct, in refusing to obey God's command, in letting his people go, was foretold. God says to Moses (Ex. 3:19), "I am sure, that the king of Egypt will not let you go." Here God professes not only to guess at, but to know Pharaoh's future disobedience. In ch. 7:4, God says, "But Pharaoh shall not hearken unto you; that I may lay mine hand upon Egypt," etc. And ch. 9:30: Moses says to Pharaoh, "As for thee, and thy servants, I know that ye will not fear the Lord." See also ch. 9:9. The moral conduct of Josiah, by name, in his zealously exerting himself in opposition to idolatry, in particular acts of his, was foretold above three hundred years before he was born, and the prophecy sealed by a miracle, and renewed and confirmed by the words of a second prophet, as what surely would not fail (I Kgs. 13:1–6, 32). This prophecy was also in effect a prediction of the moral conduct of the people, in upholding their schismatical and idolatrous worship till that time, and the idolatry of those priests of the high places, which it is foretold Josiah should offer upon that altar of Bethel. Micaiah foretold the foolish and sinful conduct of Ahab, in refusing to hearken to the word of the Lord by him, and choosing rather to hearken to the false prophets, in going to Ramoth-Gilead to his ruin (I Kgs. 21:20–22). The moral conduct of Hazael was foretold, in that cruelty he should be guilty of; on which Hazael says, "What, is thy servant a dog, that he should do this thing!" [II Kgs. 8:13.] The prophet speaks of the event as what he knew, and not what he conjectured. II Kgs. 8:12: "I know the evil thou wilt do unto the children of Israel: thou wilt dash their children, and rip up their women with child." The moral conduct of Cyrus is foretold, long before he had a being, in his mercy to God's people, and regard to the true God, in turning the captivity of the Jews, and promoting the building of the Temple (Is. 44:28 and 45: 13; compare II Chron. 36:22, 23 and Ezra 1:1–4). How many instances of the moral conduct of the kings of the north and south, particular instances of the wicked behavior of the kings of Syria and Egypt, are foretold in the eleventh chapter of Daniel? Their corruption, violence, robbery, treachery, and lies. And particularly, how much is foretold of the horrid wickedness of Antiochus Epiphanes, called there a "vile person," instead of "Epiphanes," or illustrious. In that chapter, and also in 8:9–14, 23, to the end, are foretold his flattery, deceit and lies, his having "his heart set to do mischief," and set "against the holy Covenant," his "destroying and treading under foot the holy people," in a marvelous manner, his "having indignation against the holy Covenant, setting his heart against it," and "conspiring against it," his "polluting the sanctuary of strength, treading it under foot, taking away the daily sacrifice, and placing the abomination that maketh desolate"; his great pride, "magnifying himself against God," and "uttering marvellous blasphemies against Him," till God in "indignation should destroy him." Withal the moral conduct of the Jews, on occasion of his persecution, is predicted. 'Tis foretold, that "he should corrupt many by flatteries" (11:32–34). But that others should behave with a glorious constancy and fortitude, in opposition to him (ver. 32). And that some good men should fall, and repent (ver. 35). Christ foretold Peter's sin, in denying his Lord, with its circumstances, in a peremptory manner. And so, that great sin of Judas, in betraying his master, and its dreadful and eternal punishment in hell, was foretold in the like positive manner (Matt. 26:21–25 and parallel places in the other Evangelists).

2. Many events have been foretold by God, which were consequent and dependent on the moral conduct of particular persons, and were accomplished, either by their virtuous or vicious actions. Thus, the children of Israel's going down into Egypt to dwell there, was foretold to Abraham (Gen. 15), which was brought about by the wickedness of Joseph's brethren in selling him, and the wickedness of Joseph's mistress, and his own signal virtue in resisting her temptation. The accomplishment of the thing prefigured in Joseph's dream, depended on the same moral conduct. Jotham's parable and prophecy (Judg. 9:15–20), was accomplished by the wicked

conduct of Abimelech, and the men of Shechem. The prophecies against the house of Eli (I Sam. 2, 3) were accomplished by the wickedness of Doeg the Edomite, in accusing the priests; and the great impiety, and extreme cruelty of Saul in destroying the priests at Nob (I Sam. 22). Nathan's prophecy against David (II Sam. 12:11, 12) was fulfilled by the horrible wickedness of Absalom, in rebelling against his father, seeking his life, and lying with his concubines in the sight of the sun. The prophecy against Solomon (I Kgs. 11:11–13) was fulfilled by Jeroboam's rebellion and usurpation, which are spoken of as his wickedness (II Chron. 13:5, 6; compare ver. 18). The prophecy against Jeroboam's family (I Kgs. 14) was fulfilled by the conspiracy, treason, and cruel murders of Baasha (I Kgs. 15:27, etc.). The predictions of the prophet Jehu against the house of Baasha (I Kgs. 16 at the beginning) were fulfilled by the treason and parricide of Zimri (I Kgs. 16:9–13, 20).

3. How often has God foretold the future moral conduct of nations and peoples, of numbers, bodies, and successions of men; with God's judicial proceedings, and many other events consequent and dependent on their virtues and vices; which could not be foreknown, if the volitions of men, wherein they acted as moral agents, had not been foreseen? The future cruelty of the Egyptians in oppressing Israel, and God's judging and punishing them for it, was foretold long before it came to pass (Gen. 15:13, 14). The continuance of the iniquity of the Amorites, and the increase of it until it "should be full," and they ripe for destruction, was foretold above four hundred years beforehand (Gen. 15:16; Acts 7:6, 7). The prophecies of the destruction of Jerusalem, and the land of Judah, were absolute (II Kgs. 20:17–19; ch. 22:15 to the end). It was foretold in Hezekiah's time, and was abundantly insisted on in the book of the prophet Isaiah, who wrote nothing after Hezekiah's days. It was foretold in Josiah's time, in the beginning of a great reformation (II Kgs. 22). And it is manifest by innumerable things in the predictions of the prophets, relating to this event, its time, its circumstances, its continuance and end; the return from the captivity, the restoration of the Temple, city and land, and many circumstances, and consequences of that; I say, these shew plainly, that the prophecies of this great event were absolute. And yet this event was connected with, and dependent on two things in men's moral conduct: first, the injurious rapine and violence of the king of Babylon and his people, as the efficient cause; which God often speaks of as what he highly resented, and would severely punish; and secondly, the final obstinacy of the Jews. That great event is often spoken of as suspended on this (Jer. 4:1; 5:1; 7:1–7; 11:1–6; 17:24 to the end; 25:1–7; 26:1–8, 13; and 38:17, 18). Therefore this destruction and captivity could not be foreknown, unless such a moral conduct of the Chaldeans and Jews had been foreknown. And then it was foretold, that the people "should be finally obstinate," to the destruction and utter desolation of the city and land (Is. 6:9–11; Jer. 1:18, 19; 7:27–29; Ezek. 3:7; and 24:13, 14).

The final obstinacy of those Jews who were left in the land of Israel, and who afterwards went down into Egypt, in their idolatry and rejection of the true God, was foretold by God, and the prediction confirmed with an oath (Jer. 44:26, 27). And God tells the people (Is. 48:3, 4–8) that he had predicted those things which should be consequent on their treachery and obstinacy, because he knew they would be obstinate; and that he had declared these things beforehand, for their conviction of his being the only true God, etc.

The destruction of Babylon, with many of the circumstances of it, was foretold, as the judgment of God for the exceeding pride and haughtiness of the heads of that monarchy, Nebuchadnezzar, and his successors, and their wickedly destroying other nations, and particularly for their exalting themselves against the true God and his people, before any of these monarchs had a being (Is. chs. 13, 14, 47; compare Hab. 2:5 to the end, and Jer. 50 and 51). That Babylon's destruction was to be a recompense, according to the works of their own hands, appears by Jer. 25:14. The immorality which the people of Babylon, and particularly her princes and great men, were guilty of, that very night that the city was destroyed, their reveling and drunkenness at Belshazzar's idolatrous feast, was foretold (Jer. 51:39,

The return of the Jews from the Babylonish captivity is often very particularly foretold, with many circumstances, and the promises of it are very peremptory (Jer. 31:35–40; and 32:6–15, 41–44; and 33:24–26). And the very time of their return was prefixed (Jer. 25:11, 12; and 29:10, 11; II Chron. 36:21; Ezek. 4:5, 6; and Dan. 9:2). And yet the prophecies represent their return as consequent on their repentance. And their repentance itself is very expressly and particularly foretold (Jer. 29:12, 13, 14; 31:8, 9, 18–31; 33:8; 50:4, 5; Ezek. 6:8, 9, 10; 7:16; 14:22, 23; and 20:43, 44).

It was foretold under the Old Testament, that the Messiah should suffer greatly through the malice and cruelty of men; as is largely and fully set forth (Ps. 22, applied to Christ in the New Testament, Matt. 27:35, 43; Luke 23:34; John 19:24; Heb. 2:12). And likewise in Ps. 69, which, it is also evident by the New Testament, is spoken of Christ (John 15:25; 7:5, etc.; and 2:17; Rom. 15:3; Matt. 27:34, 48; Mark 15:23; John 19:29). The same thing is also foretold, Is. 53 and 50:6; and Mic. 5:1. This cruelty of men was their sin, and what they acted as moral agents. It was foretold, that there should be an union of heathen and Jewish rulers against Christ (Ps. 2:1, 2, compared with Acts 4:25–28). It was foretold, that the Jews should generally reject and despise the Messiah (Is. 49:5, 6, 7 and 53: 1–3; Ps. 22:6, 7 and 69:4, 8, 19, 20). And it was foretold, that the body of that nation should be rejected in the Messiah's days, from being God's people, for their obstinacy in sin (Is. 49:4–7 and 8:14, 15, 16, compared with Rom. 10:19; and Is. 65 at the beginning, compared with Rom. 10:20, 21). It was foretold, that Christ should be rejected by the chief priests and rulers among the Jews (Ps. 1 18:22, compared with Matt. 21:42; Acts 4:11; I Pet. 2:4, 7).

Christ himself foretold his being delivered into the hands of the elders, chief priests and scribes, and his being cruelly treated by them, and condemned to death; and that he by them should be delivered to the Gentiles; and that he should be mocked, and scourged, and crucified (Matt. 16:21 and 20:17–19; Luke 9:22; John 8:28), and that the people should be concerned in and consenting to his death (Luke 20:13–18), especially the inhabitants of Jerusalem (Luke 13:33–35). He foretold, that the disciples should all be offended because of him that night that he was betrayed, and should forsake him (Matt. 26:31; John 16:32). He foretold that he should be rejected of that generation, even the body of the people, and that they should continue obstinate, to their ruin (Matt. 12:45; 21:33–42; and 22:1–7; Luke 13:25–35; 17:25; 19:14, 27, 41–44; 20:13–18; and 23: 34–39).

As it was foretold in both Old Testament and New, that the Jews should reject the Messiah, so it was foretold that the Gentiles should receive him, and so be admitted to the privileges of God's people; in places too many to be now particularly mentioned. It was foretold in the Old Testament, that the Jews should envy the Gentiles on this account (Deut. 32:21 compared with Rom. 10:19). Christ himself often foretold, that the Gentiles would embrace the true religion, and become his followers and people (Matt. 8:10, 11, 12; 21:41–43; and 22:8–10; Luke 13:28; 14:16–24; and 20:16; John 10:16). He also foretold the Jews' envy of the Gentiles on this occasion (Matt. 20:12–16; Luke 15:26 to the end). He foretold, that they should continue in this opposition and envy, and should manifest it in cruel persecutions of his followers, to their utter destruction (Matt. 21:33–42; 22:6; and 23:34–39; Luke 11:49–51). The Jews' obstinacy is also foretold (Acts 22:18). Christ often foretold the great persecutions his followers should meet with, both from Jews and Gentiles (Matt. 10:16–18, 21, 22, 34–36; and 24:9; Mark 13:9; Luke 10:3; 12:11, 49–53; and 21:12, 16, 17; John 15:18–21; and 16:1–4, 20–22, 33). He foretold the martyrdom of particular persons (Matt. 20:23; John 13:36; and 21:18, 19, 22). He foretold the great success of the gospel in the city of Samaria, as near approaching; which afterwards was fulfilled by the preaching of Philip (John 4:35–38). He foretold the rising of many deceivers, after his departure (Matt. 24:4, 5, 11), and the apostasy of many of his professed followers (Matt. 24: 10–12).

The persecutions, which the Apostle Paul was to meet with in the world, were foretold (Acts 9:16–20:23; and 21:11). The Apostle says to the Christian Ephesians (Acts 20:29, 30), "I know, that after my departure shall grievous wolves enter in among you, not sparing the flock: also of your own selves shall men arise, speaking perverse things, to draw away disciples after them." The Apostle says, he knew this; but he did not know it, if God did not know the future actions of moral agents.

4. Unless God foreknows the future acts of moral agents, all the prophecies we have in Scripture concerning the great Antichristian apostasy; the rise, reign, wicked qualities and deeds of the Man of Sin, and his instruments and adherents; the extent and long continuance of his dominion, his influence on the minds of princes and others, to corrupt them, and draw them away to idolatry, and other foul vices; his great and cruel persecutions; the behavior of the saints under these great temptations, etc.: I say, unless the volitions of moral agents are foreseen, all these prophecies are uttered without knowing the things foretold.

The predictions relating to this great apostasy are all of a moral nature, relating to men's virtues and vices, and their exercises, fruits and consequences, and events depending on them; and are very particular; and most of them often repeated, with many precise characteristics, descriptions, and limitations of qualities, conduct, influence, effects, extent, duration, periods, circumstances, final issue, etc. which it would be very long to mention particularly. And to suppose, all these are predicted by God without any certain knowledge of the future moral behavior of free agents, would be to the utmost degree absurd.

5. Unless God foreknows the future acts of men's wills, and their behavior as moral agents, all those great things which are foretold in both Old Testament and New concerning the erection, establishment, and universal extent of the kingdom of the Messiah, were predicted and promised while God was in ignorance whether any of these things would come to pass or no, and did but guess at them. For that kingdom is not of this world, it don't consist in things external, but is within men, and consists in the dominion of virtue in their hearts, in righteousness, and peace, and joy in the Holy Ghost; and in these things made manifest in practice, to the praise and glory of God. The Messiah came to save men from their sins, and deliver them from their spiritual enemies; that they might serve him in righteousness and holiness before him: he gave himself for us, that he might redeem us from all iniquity, and purify unto himself a peculiar people, zealous of good works. And therefore his success consists in gaining men's hearts to virtue, in their being made God's willing people in the day of his power. His conquest of his enemies consists in his victory over men's corruptions and vices. And such success, such victory, and such a reign and dominion is often expressly foretold: that his kingdom shall fill the earth; that all people, nations and languages should serve and obey him; and so, that all nations should go up to the mountain of the house of the Lord, that he might teach them his ways, and that they might walk in his paths: and that all men should be drawn to Christ, and the earth be full of the knowledge of the Lord (by which, in the style of Scripture, is meant true virtue and religion) as the waters cover the seas; that God's law should be put into men's inward parts, and written in their hearts; and that God's people should be all righteous, etc., etc.

A very great part of the prophecies of the Old Testament is taken up in such predictions as these. And here I would observe, that the prophecies of the universal prevalence of the kingdom of the Messiah, and true religion of Jesus Christ, are delivered in the most peremptory manner, and confirmed by the oath of God. Is. 45:22 to the end: "Look to me, and be ye saved, all the ends of the earth; for I am God, and there is none else. I have sworn by myself, the word is gone out of my mouth in righteousness, and shall not return, that unto me every knee shall bow; and every tongue shall swear. Surely, shall one say, in the Lord have I righteousness and strength: even to him shall men come," etc. But here this peremptory declaration, and great oath of the most High, are delivered with such mighty solemnity, to things which God did not know, if he did not certainly foresee the volitions of moral agents.

And all the predictions of Christ and his apostles, to the like purpose, must be without knowledge: as those of our Saviour comparing the kingdom of God to a grain of mustard seed, growing exceeding great, from a small beginning; and to leaven, hid in three measures of meal, till the whole was leavened, etc. And the prophecies in the Epistles concerning the restoration of the nation of the Jews to the true church of God, and the bringing in the fulness of the Gentiles; and the prophecies in all the Revelation concerning the glorious change in the moral state of the world of mankind, attending the destruction of Antichrist, the kingdoms of the world becoming the kingdoms of our Lord and of his Christ; and its being granted to the Church to be arrayed in that fine linen, white and clean, which is the righteousness of saints, etc.

Corol. 1. Hence that great promise and oath of God to Abraham, Isaac and Jacob, so much celebrated in Scripture, both in the Old Testament and New, namely, that in their seed all the nations and families of the earth should be blessed, must be made on uncertainties, if God don't certainly foreknow the volitions of moral agents. For the fulfillment of this promise consists in that success of Christ in the work of redemption, and that setting up of his spiritual kingdom over the nations of the world, which has been spoken of. Men are blessed in Christ no otherwise than as they are brought to acknowledge him, trust in him, love and serve him, as is represented

and predicted in Ps. 72:11: "All kings shall fall down before him; all nations shall serve him." With ver. 17: "Men shall be blessed in him; all nations shall call him Blessed." This oath to Jacob and Abraham is fulfilled in subduing men's iniquities; as is implied in that of the prophet Micah (Mic. 7:19, 20).

Corol. 2. Hence also it appears, that first gospel promise that ever was made to mankind, that great prediction of the salvation of the Messiah, and his victory over Satan, made to our first parents (Gen. 3:15), if there be no certain prescience of the volitions of moral agents, must have no better foundation than conjecture. For Christ's victory over Satan consists in men's being saved from sin, and in the victory of virtue and holiness, over that vice and wickedness, which Satan by his temptation has introduced, and wherein his kingdom consists.

6. If it be so, that God has not a prescience of the future actions of moral agents, it will follow, that the prophecies of Scripture in general are without foreknowledge. For Scripture prophecies, almost all of them, if not universally

without any exception, are either predictions of the actings and behaviors of moral agents, or of events depending on them, or some way connected with them; judicial dispensations, judgments on men for their wickedness, or rewards of virtue and righteousness, remarkable manifestations of favor to the righteous, or manifestations of sovereign mercy to sinners, forgiving their iniquities, and magnifying the riches of divine grace; or dispensations of providence, in some respect or other, relating to the conduct of the subjects of God's moral government, wisely adapted thereto; either providing for what should be in a future state of things, through the volitions and voluntary actions of moral agents, or consequent upon them, and regulated and ordered according to them. So that all events that are foretold, are either moral events, or other events which are connected with, and accommodated to moral events.

That the predictions of Scripture in general must be without knowledge, if God don't foresee the volitions of men, will further appear, if it be considered, that almost all events belonging to the future state of the world of mankind, the changes and revolutions which come to pass in empires, kingdoms, and nations, and all societies, depend innumerable ways on the acts of men's wills; yea, on an innumerable multitude of millions of millions of volitions of mankind. Such is the state and course of things in the world of mankind, that one single event, which appears in itself exceeding inconsiderable, may in the progress and series of things, occasion a succession of the greatest and most important and extensive events; causing the state of mankind to be vastly different from what it would otherwise have been, for all succeeding generations.

For instance, the coming into existence of those particular men, who have been the great conquerors of the world, which under God have had the main hand in all the consequent state of the world, in all after ages; such as Nebuchadnezzar, Cyrus, Alexander, Pompey, Julius Caesar, etc.; undoubtedly depended on many millions of acts of the will, which followed, and were occasioned one by another, in their parents. And perhaps most of these volitions depended on millions of volitions of hundreds and thousands of others, their contemporaries of the same generation; and most of these on millions of millions of volitions of others in preceding generations. As we go back, still the number of volitions, which were some way the occasion of the event, multiply as the branches of a river, till they come at last, as it were, to an infinite number. This will not seem strange, to anyone who well considers the matter; if we recollect what philosophers tell us of the innumerable multitudes of those things which are as it were the principia, or stamina vitae, concerned in generation; the *animalcida in semine musculo*, and the ova in the womb of the female; the impregnation, or animating of one of these in distinction from all the rest, must depend on things infinitely minute, relating to the time and circumstances of the act of the parents, the state of their bodies, etc. which must depend on innumerable foregoing circumstances and occurrences; which must depend, infinite ways, on foregoing acts of their wills; which are occasioned by innumerable things that happen in the course of their lives, in which their own, and their neighbor's behavior, must have a hand, an infinite number of ways. And as the volitions of others must be so many ways concerned in the conception and birth of such men; so, no less, in their preservation, and circumstances of life, their particular determinations and actions, on which the great revolutions they were the occasions of, depended. As for instance, when the conspirators in Persia, against the Magi, were consulting about a succession to the empire, it came into the mind of one of them, to propose, that he whose horse neighed first, when they came together the next morning, should be king. Now such a thing's coming into his mind, might depend on innumerable incidents, wherein the volitions of mankind had been concerned. But in consequence of this accident, Darius, the son of Histaspes, was king. And if this had not been, probably his successor would not have been the same, and all the circumstances of the Persian empire might have been far otherwise. And then perhaps Alexander might never have conquered that empire. And then probably the circumstances of the world in all succeeding ages, might have been vastly otherwise. I might further instance in many other occurrences; such as those on which depended Alexander's preservation, in the many critical junctures of his life, wherein a small trifle would have turned the scale against him; and the preservation and success of the Roman people, in the infancy of their kingdom and commonwealth, and afterwards; which all the succeeding changes in their state, and the mighty revolutions that afterwards came to pass in the habitable world, depended upon. But these hints may be sufficient for every discerning considerate person, to convince him, that the whole state of the world of mankind, in all ages, and the very being of every person who has ever lived in it, in every age, since the times of the ancient prophets, has depended on more volitions, or acts of the wills of men, than there are sands on the seashore.

And therefore, unless God does most exactly and perfectly foresee the future acts of men's wills, all the predictions which he ever uttered concerning David, Hezekiah, Josiah, Nebuchadnezzar, Cyrus, Alexander; concerning the four monarchies, and the revolutions in them; and concerning all the wars, commotions, victories, prosperities and calamities, of any of the kingdoms, nations, or communities of the world, have all been without knowledge.

So that, according to this notion of God's not foreseeing the volitions and free actions of men, God could foresee nothing pertaining to the state of the world of mankind in future ages; not so much as the being of one person that should live in it; and could foreknow no events, but only such as he would bring to pass himself by the extraordinary interposition of his immediate power; or things which should come to pass in the natural material world, by the laws of motion, and course of nature, wherein that is independent on the actions or works of mankind: that is, as he might, like a very able mathematician and astronomer, with great exactness calculate the revolutions of the heavenly bodies, and the greater wheels of the machine of the external creation.

And if we closely consider the matter, there will appear reason to convince us, that he could not with any absolute certainty foresee even these. As to the first, namely things done by the immediate and extraordinary interposition of God's power, these can't be foreseen, unless it can be foreseen when there shall be occasion for such extraordinary interposition. And that can't be foreseen, unless the state of the moral world can be foreseen. For whenever God thus interposes, it is with regard to the state of the moral world, requiring such divine interposition. Thus God could not certainly foresee the universal deluge, the calling of Abraham, the destruction of Sodom and Gomorrah, the plagues on Egypt, and Israel's redemption out of it, the expelling the seven nations of Canaan, and the bringing Israel into that land; for these all are represented as connected with things belonging to the state of the moral world. Nor can God foreknow the most proper and convenient time of the day of judgment, and general conflagration; for that chiefly depends on the course and state of things in the moral world.

Nor, secondly, can we on this supposition reasonably think, that God can certainly foresee what things shall come to pass, in the course of things, in the natural and material world, even those which in an ordinary state of things might be calculated by a good astronomer. For the moral world is the end of the natural world; and the course of things [in the latter, is undoubtedly subordinate to God's designs with respect to the former]. Therefore he has seen cause, from regard to the state of things in the moral world, extraordinarily to interpose, to interrupt and lay an arrest on the course of things in the natural world; and even in the greater wheels of its motion; even so as to stop the sun in its course. And unless he can foresee the volitions of men, and so know something of the future state of the moral world, he can't know but that he may still have as great occasion to interpose in this manner, as ever he had: nor can he foresee how, or when, he shall have occasion thus to interpose.

Corol. 1. It appears from the things which have been observed, that unless God foresees the volitions of moral agents, that cannot be true which is observed by the Apostle James, Acts 15:18: "Known unto God are all his works from the beginning of the world."

Corol. 2. It appears from what has been observed, that unless God foreknows the volitions of moral agents, all the prophecies of Scripture have no better foundation than mere conjecture; and that, in most instances, a conjecture which must have the utmost uncertainty; depending on an innumerable, and as it were infinite, multitude of volitions, which are all, even to God, uncertain events: however, these prophecies are delivered as absolute predictions, and very many of them in the most positive manner, with asseverations; and some of them with the most solemn oaths.

Corol. 3. It also follows from what has been observed, that if this notion of God's ignorance of future volitions be true, in vain did Christ say (after uttering many great and important predictions, concerning God's moral kingdom, and things depending on men's moral actions, Matt. 24:35): "Heaven and earth shall pass away; but my words shall not pass away."

Corol. 4. From the same notion of God's ignorance, it would follow, that in vain has God himself often spoken of the predictions of his Word, as evidences of his foreknowledge; and so as evidences of that which is his prerogative as God, and his peculiar glory, greatly distinguishing him from all other beings; as in Is. 41:22–26; 43:9, 10; 44:8; 45:21; 46:10; and 48:14.

Arg. II. If God don't foreknow the volitions of moral agents, then he did not foreknow the fall of man, nor of angels, and so could not foreknow the great things which are consequent on these events; such as his sending his Son into the world to die for sinners, and all things pertaining to the great work of redemption; all the things which were done for four thousand years before Christ came, to prepare the way for it; and the incarnation, life, death, resurrection and ascension of Christ; and the setting him at the head of the universe, as king of heaven and earth, angels and men; and the setting up his church and kingdom in this world, and appointing him the judge of the world; and all that Satan should do in the world in opposition to the kingdom of Christ: and the great transactions of the day of judgment, that men and devils shall be the subjects of, and angels concerned in; they are all what God was ignorant of before the fall. And if so, the following scriptures, and others like them, must be without any meaning, or contrary to truth: Eph. 1:4: "According as he hath chosen us in him before the foundation of the world." I Pet. 1:20: "Who verily was foreordained before the foundation of the world."

II Tim. 1:9: "Who hath saved us, and called us with an holy calling; not according to our works, but according to his own purpose, and grace, which was given us in Christ Jesus before the world began." So, Eph. 3:11 (speaking of the wisdom of God in the work of redemption): "According to the eternal purpose which he purposed in Christ Jesus." Titus 1:2: "In hope of eternal life, which God, that cannot lie, promised before the world began." Rom. 8:29: "Whom he did foreknow, them he also did predestinate," etc. I Pet. 1:2: "Elect, according to the foreknowledge of God the Father." If God did not foreknow the fall of man, nor the redemption by Jesus Christ, nor the volitions of man since the fall; then he did not foreknow the saints in any sense; neither as particular persons, nor as societies or nations; either by election, or mere foresight of their virtue or good works; or any foresight of anything about them relating to their salvation; or any benefit they have by Christ, or any manner of concern of theirs with a Redeemer.

Arg. III. On the supposition of God's ignorance of the future volitions of free agents, it will follow, that God must in many cases truly repent what he has done, so as properly to wish he had done otherwise: by reason that the event of things, in those affairs which are most important, viz. the affairs of his moral kingdom, being uncertain and contingent, often happens quite otherwise than he was aware beforehand. And there would be reason to understand that, in the most literal sense, in Gen. 6:6: "It repented the Lord, that he had made man on the earth, and it grieved him at his heart." And that, I Sam. 15:11, contrary to that, Num. 23:19: "God is not the son of man, that he should repent." And, I Sam. 15:15, 29: "Also the Strength of Israel will not lie, nor repent: for he is not a man that he should repent." Yea, from this notion it would follow, that God is liable to repent and be grieved at his heart, in a literal sense, continually; and is always exposed to an infinite number of real disappointments, in his governing the world; and to manifold, constant, great perplexity and vexation: but this is not very consistent with his title of "God over all, blessed for evermore"; which represents him as possessed of perfect, constant and uninterrupted tranquillity and felicity, as God over the universe, and in his management of the affairs of the world, as supreme and universal ruler. See Rom. 1:25; 9:5; II Cor. 11:31; I Tim. 6:15.

Arg. IV. It will also follow from this notion, that as God is liable to be continually repenting what he has done; so he must be exposed to be constantly changing his mind and intentions, as to his future conduct; altering his measures, relinquishing his old designs, and forming new schemes and projections. For his purposes, even as to the main parts of his scheme, namely, such as belong to the state of his moral kingdom, must be always liable to be broken, through want of foresight; and he must be continually putting his system to rights, as it gets out of order, through the contingence of the actions of moral agents: he must be a being, who, instead of being absolutely immutable, must necessarily be the subject of infinitely the most numerous acts of repentance, and changes of intention, of any being whatsoever; for this plain reason, that his vastly extensive charge comprehends an infinitely greater number of those things which are to him contingent and uncertain. In such a situation, he must have little else to do, but to mend broken links as well as he can, and be rectifying his disjointed frame and disordered movements, in the best manner the case will allow. The supreme Lord of all things must needs be under great and miserable disadvantages, in governing the world which he has made, and has the care of, through his being utterly unable to find out things of chief importance, which hereafter shall befall his system; which if he did but know, he might make seasonable provision for. In many cases, there may be very great necessity that he should make provision, in the manner of his ordering and disposing things, for some great events which are to happen, of vast and extensive influence, and endless consequence to the universe; which he may see afterwards, when it is too late, and may wish in vain that he had known beforehand, that he might have ordered his affairs accordingly. And it is in the power of man, on these principles, by his devices, purposes and actions, thus to disappoint God, break his measures, make him continually to change his mind, subject him to vexation, and bring him into confusion.

But how do these things consist with reason, or with the Word of God? Which represents, that all God's works, all that he has ever to do, the whole scheme and series of his operations, are from the beginning perfectly in his view; and declares, that whatever "devices" and designs "are in the hearts of men, the counsel of the Lord is that which shall stand," and "the thoughts of his heart to all generations" (Prov. 19:21; Ps. 33:10, 11). "And that which the Lord of Hosts hath purposed, none shall disannul" (Is. 14:27). And that he cannot be frustrated "in one design or thought" (Job 42:2). "And that what God doth, it shall be forever, that nothing can be put to it, or taken from it" (Eccles. 3:14). The stability and perpetuity of God's counsels are expressly spoken of as connected with the foreknowledge of God (Is. 46:10), "Declaring the end from the beginning, and from ancient times the things that are not yet done; saying, my counsel shall stand, and I will do all my pleasure." And how are these things consistent with what the Scripture says of God's immutability, which represents him as "without variableness, or shadow of turning"; and speaks of him most particularly as unchangeable with regard to his purposes. Mal. 3:6: "I am the Lord; I change not; therefore ye sons of Jacob are not consumed." Ex. 3:14: "I am that I am." Job 23:13, 14: "He is in one mind; and who can turn him? And what his soul desireth, even that he doth: for he performeth the thing that is appointed for me."

Arg. V. If this notion of God's ignorance of the future volitions of moral agents be thoroughly considered in its consequences, it will appear to follow from it, that God, after he had made the world, was liable to be wholly frustrated of his end in the creation of it; and so has been in like manner liable to be frustrated of his end in all the great works he hath wrought. 'Tis manifest, the moral world is the end of the natural: the rest of the creation is but an house which God hath built, with furniture, for moral agents: and the good or bad state of the moral world depends on the improvement they make of their [moral] agency, and so depends on their volitions. And therefore, if these can't be foreseen by God, because they are contingent, and subject to no kind of necessity, then the affairs of the moral world are liable to go wrong, to any assignable degree; yea, liable to be utterly ruined. As on this scheme, it may well be supposed to be literally said, when mankind, by the abuse of their moral agency, became very corrupt before the flood, "that the Lord repented that he had made man on the earth, and it grieved him at his heart" [Gen. 6:6]; so, when he made the universe, he did not know but that he might be so disappointed in it, that it might grieve him at his heart that he had made it. It actually proved, that all mankind became sinful, and a very great part of the angels apostatized: and how could God know beforehand, that all of them would not? And how could God know but that all mankind, notwithstanding means used to reclaim them, being still left to the freedom of their own will, would continue in their apostasy, and grow worse and worse, as they of the old world before the flood did?

According to the scheme I am endeavoring to confute, neither the fall of men nor angels, could be foreseen, and God must be greatly disappointed in these events; and so the grand scheme and contrivance for our redemption, and destroying the works of the devil, by the Messiah, and all the great things God has done in the prosecution of these designs, must be only the fruits of his own disappointment, and contrivances of his to mend and patch up, as well as he could, his system, which originally was all very good, and perfectly beautiful; but was marred, broken and confounded by the free will of angels and men. And still he must be liable to be totally disappointed a second time: he could not know, that he should have his desired success, in the incarnation, life, death, resurrection and exaltation of his only begotten Son, and other great works accomplished to restore the state of things: he could not know after all, whether there would actually be any tolerable measure of restoration; for this depended on the free will of man. There has been a general great apostasy of almost all the Christian world, to that which was worse than heathenism; which continued for many ages. And how could God, without foreseeing men's volitions, know whether ever Christendom would return from this apostasy? And which way could he tell beforehand how soon it would begin? The Apostle says, it began to work in his time; and how could it be known how far it would proceed in that age? Yea, how could it be known that the gospel, which was not effectual for the reformation of the Jews, would ever be effectual for the turning of the heathen nations from their heathen apostasy, which they had been confirmed in for so many ages?

'Tis represented often in Scripture, that God who made the world for himself, and created it for his pleasure, would infallibly obtain his end in the creation, and in all his works; that as all things are of him, so they would all be to him; and that in the final issue of things, it would appear that he is the first, and the last. Rev. 21:6: "And he said unto me, it is done. I am Alpha and Omega, the beginning and the end, the first and the last." But these things are not consistent with God's being so liable to be disappointed in all his works, nor indeed with his failing of his end in anything that he has undertaken, or done.

SECTION 12.

GOD'S CERTAIN FOREKNOWLEDGE OF THE FUTURE VOLITIONS OF MORAL AGENTS, INCONSISTENT WITH SUCH A CONTINGENCE OF THOSE VOLITIONS, AS IS WITHOUT ALL NECESSITY

Having proved, that God has a certain and infallible prescience of the acts of the will of moral agents, I come now, in the second place, to shew the consequence; to shew how it follows from hence, that these events are necessary, with a necessity of connection or consequence.

The chief Arminian divines, so far as I have had opportunity to observe, deny this consequence; and affirm, that if such foreknowledge be allowed, 'tis no evidence of any necessity of the event foreknown. Now I desire, that this matter may be particularly and thoroughly inquired into. I cannot but think, that on particular and full consideration, it may be perfectly determined, whether it be indeed so, or not.

In order to a proper consideration of this matter, I would observe the following things.

I. 'Tis very evident, with regard to a thing whose existence is infallibly and indissolubly connected with something which already hath, or has had existence, the existence of that thing is necessary. Here may be noted,

1. I observed before, in explaining the nature of necessity, that in things which are past, their past existence is now necessary: having already made sure of existence, 'tis too late for any possibility of alteration in that respect: 'tis now impossible, that it should be otherwise than true, that that thing has existed.

2. If there be any such thing as a divine foreknowledge of the volitions of free agents, that foreknowledge, by the supposition, is a thing which already has, and long ago had existence; and so, now its existence is necessary; it is now utterly impossible to be otherwise, than that this foreknowledge should be, or should have been.

3. 'Tis also very manifest, that those things which are indissolubly connected with other things that are necessary, are themselves necessary. As that proposition whose truth is necessarily connected with another proposition, which is necessarily true, is itself necessarily true. To say otherwise, would be a contradiction; it would be in effect to say, that the connection was indissoluble, and yet was not so, but might be broken. If that, whose existence is indissolubly connected with something whose existence is now necessary, is itself not necessary, then it may possibly not exist, notwithstanding that indissoluble connection of its existence. Whether the absurdity ben't glaring, let the reader judge.

4. 'Tis no less evident, that if there be a full, certain and infallible foreknowledge of the future existence of the volitions of moral agents, then there is a certain infallible and indissoluble connection between those events and that foreknowledge; and that therefore, by the preceding observations, those events are necessary events; being infallibly and indissolubly connected with that whose existence already is, and so is now necessary, and can't but have been.

To say, the foreknowledge is certain and infallible, and yet the connection of the event with that foreknowledge is not indissoluble, but dissoluble and fallible, is very absurd. To affirm it, would be the same thing as to affirm, that there is no necessary connection between a proposition's being infallibly known to be true, and its being true indeed. So that it is perfectly demonstrable, that if there be any infallible knowledge of future volitions, the event is necessary; or, in other words, that it is impossible but the event should come to pass. For if it ben't impossible but that it may be otherwise, then it is not impossible but that the proposition which affirms its future coming to pass, may not now be true. But how absurd is that, on the supposition that there is now an infallible knowledge (i.e. knowledge which it is impossible should fail) that it is true. There is this absurdity in it, that it is not impossible but that there now should be no truth in that proposition, which is now infallibly known to be true.

II. That no future event can be certainly foreknown, whose existence is contingent, and without all necessity, may be proved thus; 'tis impossible for a thing to be certainly known to any intellect without evidence. To suppose otherwise, implies a contradiction: because for a thing to be certainly known to any understanding, is for it to be evident to that understanding: and for a thing to be evident to any understanding, is the same thing, as for that understanding to see evidence of it: but no understanding, created or increated, can see evidence where there is none: for that is the same thing, as to see that to be, which is not. And therefore, if there be any truth which is absolutely without evidence, that truth is absolutely unknowable, insomuch that it implies a contradiction to suppose that it is known.

But if there be any future event, whose existence is contingent, without all necessity, the future existence of that event is absolutely without evidence. If there be any evidence of it, it must be one of these two sorts, either self-evidence, or proof; for there can be no other sort of evidence but one of these two; an evident thing must be either evident in itself, or evident in something else; that is, evident by connection with something else. But a future thing, whose existence is without all necessity, can have neither of these sorts of evidence. It can't be self-evident: for if it be, it may be now known by what is now to be seen in the thing itself; either its present existence, or the necessity of its nature: but both these are contrary to the supposition. It is supposed, both that the thing has no present existence to be seen; and also that it is not of such a nature as to be necessarily existent for the future: so that its future existence is not self-evident. And secondly, neither is there any proof, or evidence in anything else, or evidence of connection with something else that is evident; for this also is contrary to the supposition. 'Tis supposed, that there is now nothing existent, with which the future existence of the contingent event is connected. For such a connection destroys its contingence, and supposes necessity. Thus 'tis demonstrated, that there is in the nature of things absolutely no evidence at all of the future existence of that event, which is contingent, without all necessity (if any such event there be); neither self-evidence nor proof. And therefore the thing in reality is not evident; and so can't be seen to be evident, or, which is the same thing, can't be known.

Let us consider this in an example. Suppose that five thousand seven hundred and sixty years ago, there was no other being but the divine Being; and then this world, or some particular body or spirit, all at once starts out of nothing into being, and takes on itself a particular nature and form; all in absolute contingence, without any concern of God, or any other cause, in the matter; without any manner of ground or reason of its existence; or any dependence upon, or connection at all with anything foregoing: I say, that if this be supposed, there was no evidence of that event beforehand. There was no evidence of it to be seen in the thing itself; for the thing itself, as yet, was not. And there was no evidence of it to be seen in anything else; for evidence in something else, is connection with something else: but such connection is contrary to the supposition. There was no evidence before, that this thing would happen; for by the supposition, there was no reason why it should happen, rather than something else, or rather than nothing. And if so, then all things before were exactly equal, and the same, with respect to that and other possible things; there was no preponderation, no superior weight or value; and therefore nothing that could be of any weight or value to determine any understanding. The thing was absolutely without evidence, and absolutely unknowable. An increase of understanding, or of the capacity of discerning, has no tendency, and makes no advance, to a discerning any signs or evidences of it, let it be increased never so much; yea, if it be increased infinitely. The increase of the strength of sight may have a tendency to enable to discern the evidence which is far off, and very much hid, and deeply involved in clouds and darkness; but it has no tendency to enable to discern evidence where there is none. If the sight be infinitely strong, and the capacity of discerning infinitely great, it will enable [a being] to see all that there is, and to see it perfectly, and with ease; yet it has no tendency at all to enable a being to discern that evidence which is not; but on the contrary, it has a tendency to enable to discern with great certainty that there is none.

III. To suppose the future volitions of moral agents not to be necessary events; or, which is the same thing, events which it is not impossible but that they may not come to pass; and yet to suppose that God certainly foreknows them, and knows all things; is to suppose God's knowledge to be inconsistent with itself. For to say, that God certainly, and without all conjecture, knows that a thing will infallibly be, which at the same time he knows to be so contingent, that it may possibly not be, is to suppose his knowledge inconsistent with itself; or that one thing that he knows is utterly inconsistent with another thing that he knows. 'Tis the same thing as to say, he now knows a proposition to be of certain infallible truth, which he knows to be of contingent uncertain truth. If a future volition is so without all necessity, that there is nothing hinders but that it may not be, then the proposition which asserts its future existence, is so uncertain, that there is nothing hinders but that the truth of it may entirely fail. And if God knows all things, he knows this proposition to be thus uncertain. And that is inconsistent with his knowing that it is infallibly true; and so inconsistent with his infallibly knowing that it is true. If the thing be indeed contingent, God views it so, and judges it to be contingent, if he views things as they are. If the event be not necessary, then it is possible it may never be: and if it be possible it may never be, God knows it may possibly never be; and that is to know that the proposition which affirms its existence, may possibly not be true; and that is to know that the truth of it is uncertain; which surely is inconsistent with his knowing it as a certain truth. If volitions are in themselves contingent events, without all necessity, then 'tis no argument of perfection of knowledge in any being to determine peremptorily that they will be; but on the contrary, an argument of ignorance and mistake: because it would argue, that he supposes that proposition to be certain, which in its own nature, and all things considered, is uncertain and contingent. To say in such a case, that God may have ways of knowing contingent events which we can't conceive of, is ridiculous; as much so, as to say, that God may know contradictions to be true, for ought we know, or that he may know a thing to be certain, and at the same time know it not to be certain, though we can't conceive how; because he has ways of knowing, which we can't comprehend.

Corol. 1. From what has been observed it is evident, that the absolute decrees of God are no more inconsistent with human liberty, on account of any necessity of the event which follows from such decrees, than the absolute foreknowledge of God. Because the connection between the event and certain foreknowledge, is as infallible and indissoluble, as between the event and an absolute decree. That is, 'tis no more impossible that the event and decree should not agree together, than that the event and absolute knowledge should disagree. The connection between the event and foreknowledge is absolutely perfect, by the supposition: because it is supposed, that the certainty and infallibility of the knowledge is absolutely perfect. And it being so, the certainty can't be increased; and therefore the connection between the knowledge and thing known, can't be increased; so that if a decree be added to the foreknowledge, it don't at all increase the connection, or make it more infallible and indissoluble. If it were not so, the certainty of knowledge might be increased by the addition of a decree; which is contrary to the supposition, which is, that the knowledge is absolutely perfect, or perfect to the highest possible degree.

There is as much of an impossibility but that the things which are infallibly foreknown, should be, or (which is the same thing) as great a necessity of their future existence, as if the event were already written down, and was known and read by all mankind, through all preceding ages, and there were the most indissoluble and perfect connection possible, between the writing, and the thing written. In such a case, it would be as impossible the event should fail of existence, as if it had existed already; and a decree can't make an event surer or more necessary than this.

And therefore, if there be any such foreknowledge, as it has been proved there is, then necessity of connection and consequence, is not at all inconsistent with any liberty which man, or any other creature enjoys. And from hence it may be inferred, that absolute decrees of God, which don't at all increase the necessity, are not at all inconsistent with the liberty which man enjoys, on any such account, as that they make the event decreed necessary, and render it utterly impossible but that it should come to pass. Therefore if absolute decrees are inconsistent with man's liberty as a moral agent, or his liberty in a state of probation, or any liberty whatsoever that he enjoys, it is not on account of any necessity which absolute decrees infer.

Dr. Whitby supposes, there is a great difference between God's foreknowledge, and his decrees, with regard to necessity of future events. In his Discourse on the Five Points, p. 474, etc. [Whitby, Discourse on the Five Points, Dis. VI, ch. 1; pp. 474–5] he says, "God's prescience has no influence at all on our actions.... Should God (says he) by immediate revelation, give me the knowledge of the event of any man's state or actions, would my knowledge of them have any influence upon his actions? Surely none at all....Our knowledge doth not affect the things we know, to make them more certain, or more future, than they would be without it. Now foreknowledge in God is knowledge. As therefore knowledge has no influence on things that are, so neither has foreknowledge on things that shall be. And consequently, the foreknowledge of any action that would be otherwise free, cannot alter or diminish that freedom. Whereas God's decree of election is powerful and active, and comprehends the preparation and exhibition of such means, as shall unfrustrably produce the end....Hence God's prescience renders no actions necessary." And to this purpose (p. 473), he cites Origen, where he says, "God's prescience is not the cause of things future, but their being future is the cause of God's prescience that they will be": and Le Blanc, where he says, "This is the truest resolution of this difficulty, that prescience is not the cause that things are future; but their being future is the cause they are foreseen." In like manner Dr. Clarke, in his Demonstration of the Being and Attributes of God (pp. 95–99). And the author of The Freedom of Will, in God and the Creature, speaking to the like purpose with Dr. Whitby, represents "foreknowledge as having no more influence on things known, to make them necessary," than "after-knowledge," or to that purpose.

To all which I would say; that what is said about knowledge, its not having influence on the thing known to make it necessary, is nothing to the purpose, nor does it in the least affect the foregoing reasoning. Whether prescience be the thing that makes the event necessary or no, it alters not the case. Infallible foreknowledge may prove the necessity of the event foreknown, and yet not be the thing which causes the necessity. If the foreknowledge be absolute, this proves the event known to be necessary, or proves that 'tis impossible but that the event should be, by some means or other, either by a decree, or some other way, if there be any other way: because, as was said before, 'tis absurd to say, that a proposition is known to be certainly and infallibly true, which yet may possibly prove not true.

The whole of the seeming force of this evasion lies in this; that, inasmuch as certain foreknowledge don't cause an event to be necessary, as a decree does; therefore it don't prove it to be necessary, as a decree does. But there is no force in this arguing: for it is built wholly on this supposition, that nothing can prove, or be an evidence of a thing's being necessary, but that which has a causal influence to make it so. But this can never be maintained. If certain foreknowledge of the future existing of an event, be not the thing which first makes it impossible that it should fail of existence; yet it may, and certainly does demonstrate, that it is impossible it should fail of it, however that impossibility comes. If foreknowledge be not the cause, but the effect of this impossibility, it may prove that there is such an impossibility, as much as if it were the cause. It is as strong arguing from the effect to the cause, as from the cause to the effect. 'Tis enough, that an existence which is infallibly foreknown, cannot fail, whether that impossibility arises from the foreknowledge, or is prior to it. 'Tis as evident, as 'tis possible anything should be, that it is impossible a thing which is infallibly known to be true, should prove not to be true: therefore there is a necessity that it should [not] be otherwise; whether the knowledge be the cause of this necessity, or the necessity the cause of the knowledge.

All certain knowledge, whether it be foreknowledge or after-knowledge, or concomitant knowledge, proves the thing known now to be necessary, by some means or other; or proves that it is impossible it should now be otherwise than true. I freely allow, that foreknowledge don't prove a thing to be necessary any more than after-knowledge: but then after-knowledge which is certain and infallible, proves that 'tis now become impossible but that the proposition known should be true. Certain after-knowledge proves that it is now, in the time of the knowledge, by some means or other, become impossible but that the proposition which predicates past existence on the event, should be true. And so does certain foreknowledge prove, that now, in the time of the knowledge, it is by some means or other, become impossible but that the proposition which predicates future existence on the event, should be true. The necessity of the truth of the propositions, consisting in the present impossibility of the nonexistence of the event affirmed, in both cases, is the immediate ground of the certainty of the knowledge; there can be no certainty of knowledge without it.

There must be a certainty in things themselves, before they are certainly known, or (which is the same thing) known to be certain. For certainty of knowledge is nothing else but knowing or discerning the certainty there is in the things themselves which are known. Therefore there must be a certainty in things to be a ground of certainty of knowledge, and to render things capable of being known to be certain. And this is nothing but the necessity of the truth known, or its being impossible but that it should be true; or, in other words, the firm and infallible connection between the subject and predicate of the proposition that contains that truth. All certainty of knowledge consists in the view of the firmness of that connection. So God's certain foreknowledge of the future existence of any event, is his view of the firm and indissoluble connection of the subject and predicate of the proposition that affirms its future existence. The subject is that possible event; the predicate is its future existing: but if future existence be firmly and indissolubly connected with that event, then the future existence of that event is necessary. If God certainly knows the future existence of an event which is wholly contingent, and may possibly never be, then he sees a firm connection between a subject and predicate that are not firmly connected; which is a contradiction.

I allow what Dr. Whitby says to be true, "that mere knowledge don't affect the thing known, to make it more certain or more future." But yet, I say, it supposes and proves the thing to be already, both future, and certain; i.e. necessarily future. Knowledge of futurity, supposes futurity; and a certain knowledge of futurity, supposes certain futurity, antecedent to that certain knowledge. But there is no other certain futurity of a thing, antecedent to certainty of knowledge, than a prior impossibility but that the thing should prove true; or (which is the same thing) the necessity of the event.

I would observe one thing further concerning this matter, and it is this; that if it be as those forementioned writers suppose, that God's foreknowledge is not the cause, but the effect of the existence of the event foreknown; this is so far from shewing that this foreknowledge don't infer the necessity of the existence of that event, that it rather shews the contrary the more plainly. Because it shews the existence of the event to be so settled and firm, that it is as if it had already been; inasmuch as in effect it actually exists already; its future existence has already had actual influence and efficiency, and has produced an effect, viz. prescience: the effect exists already; and as the effect supposes the cause, is connected with the cause, and depends entirely upon it, therefore it is as if the future event, which is the cause, had existed already. The effect is firm as possible, it having already the possession of existence, and has made sure of it. But the effect can't be more firm and stable than its cause, ground and reason. The build-ins can't be firmer than the foundation.

To illustrate this matter, let us suppose the appearances and images of things in a glass; for instance, a reflecting telescope, to be the real effects of heavenly bodies (at a distance, and out of sight) which they resemble: if it be so, then, as these images in the telescope have had a past actual existence, and it is become utterly impossible now that it should be otherwise than that they have existed; so they being the true effects of the heavenly bodies they resemble, this proves the existing of those heavenly bodies to be as real, infallible, firm and necessary, as the existing of these effects; the one being connected with, and wholly depending on the other. Now let us suppose future existences some way or other to have influence back, to produce effects beforehand, and cause exact and perfect images of themselves in a glass, a thousand years before they exist, yea, in all preceding ages; but yet that these images are real effects of these future existences, perfectly dependent on, and connected with their cause; these effects and images, having already had actual existence, rendering that matter of their existing perfectly firm and stable, and utterly impossible to be otherwise; this proves in like manner as in the other instance, that the existence of the things which are their causes, is also equally sure, firm and necessary; and that it is alike impossible but that they should be, as if they had been already, as their effects have. And if instead of images in a glass, we suppose the antecedent effects to be perfect ideas of them in the divine mind, which have existed there from all eternity, which are as properly effects, as truly and properly connected with their cause, the case is not altered.

Another thing which has been said by some Arminians, to take off the force of what is urged from God's prescience, against the contingence of the volitions of moral agents, is to this purpose; "that when we talk of foreknowledge in God, there is no strict propriety in our so speaking; and that although it be true, that there is in God the most perfect knowledge of all events from eternity to eternity, yet there is no such thing as before and after in God, but he sees all things by one perfect unchangeable view, without any succession." To this I answer,

1. It has been already shewn, that all certain knowledge proves the necessity of the truth known; whether it be before, after, or at the same time. Though it be true, that there is no succession in God's knowledge, and the manner of his knowledge is to us inconceivable, yet thus much we know concerning it, that there is no event, past, present, or to come, that God is ever uncertain of; he never is, never was, and never will be without infallible knowledge of it; he always sees the existence of it to be certain and infallible. And as he always sees things just as they are in truth; hence there never is in reality anything contingent in such a sense, as that possibly it may happen never to exist. If, strictly speaking, there is no foreknowledge in God, 'tis because those things which are future to us, are as present to God, as if they already had existence: and that is as much as to say, that future events are always in God's view as evident, clear, sure and necessary, as if they already were. If there never is a time wherein the existence of the event is not present with God, then there never is a time wherein it is not as much impossible for it to fail of existence, as if its existence were present, and were already come to pass.

God's viewing things so perfectly and unchangeably as that there is no succession in his ideas or judgment, don't hinder but that there is properly now, in the mind of God, a certain and perfect knowledge of the moral actions of men, which to us are an hundred years hence: yea, the objection supposes this; and therefore it certainly don't hinder but that, by the foregoing arguments, it is now impossible these moral actions should not come to pass.

We know, that God knows the future voluntary actions of men in such a sense beforehand, as that he is able particularly to declare, and foretell them, and write them, or cause them to be written down in a Book, as he often has done; and that therefore the necessary connection which there is between God's knowledge and the event known, does as much prove the event to be necessary beforehand, as if the divine knowledge were in the same sense before the event, as the prediction or writing is. If the knowledge be infallible, then the expression of it in the written prediction is infallible; that is, there is an infallible connection between that written prediction and the event. And if so, then it is impossible it should ever be otherwise, than that that prediction and the event should agree: and this is the same thing as to say, 'tis impossible but that the event should come to pass: and this is the same as to say, that its coming to pass is necessary. So that it is manifest, that there being no proper succession in God's mind, makes no alteration as to the necessity of the existence of the events which God knows. Yea,

2. This is so far from weakening the proof, which has been given of the impossibility of the not coming to pass of future events known, as that it establishes that wherein the strength of the foregoing arguments consists, and shews the clearness of the evidence. For,

(1) The very reason why God's knowledge is without succession, is, because it is absolutely perfect, to the highest possible degree of clearness and certainty: all things, whether past, present or to come, being viewed with equal evidence and fullness; future things being seen with as much clearness, as if they were present; the view is always in absolute perfection; and absolute constant perfection admits of no alteration, and so no succession; the actual existence of the thing known, don't at all increase, or add to the clearness or certainty of the thing known: God calls the things that are not, as though they were; they are all one to him as if they had already existed. But herein consists the strength of the demonstration before given, of the impossibility of the not existing of those things whose existence God knows; that it is as impossible they should fail of existence, as if they existed already. This objection, instead of weakening this argument, sets it in the clearest and strongest light; for it supposes it to be so indeed, that the existence of future events is in God's view so much as if it already had been, that when they come actually to exist, it makes not the least alteration or variation in his view or knowledge of them.

(2) The objection is founded on the immutability of God's knowledge: for 'tis the immutability of knowledge makes his knowledge to be without succession. But this most directly and plainly demonstrates the thing I insist on, viz. that 'tis utterly impossible the known events should fail of existence. For if that were possible, then it would be possible for there to be a change in God's knowledge and view of things. For if the known event should fail of existence, and not come into being, as God expected, then God would see it, and so would change his mind, and see his former mistake; and thus there would be change and succession in his knowledge. But as God is immutable, and so it is utterly and infinitely impossible that his view should be changed; so 'Tis, for the same reason, just so impossible that the foreknown event should not exist: and that is to be impossible in the highest degree: and therefore the contrary is necessary. Nothing is more impossible than that the immutable God should be changed, by the succession of time; who comprehends all things, from eternity to eternity, in one, most perfect, and unalterable view; so that his whole eternal duration is *vitae interminabilis, tota, simul,* and *perfecta possessio.*

On the whole, I need not fear to say, that there is no geometrical theorem or proposition whatsoever, more capable of strict demonstration, than that God's certain prescience of the volitions of moral agents is inconsistent with such a contingence of these events, as is without all necessity; and so is inconsistent with the Arminian notion of liberty.

Corol. 2. Hence the doctrine of the Calvinists, concerning the absolute decrees of God, does not at all infer any more fatality in things, than will demonstrably follow from the doctrine of most Arminian divines, who acknowledge God's omniscience, and universal prescience. Therefore all objections they make against the doctrine of the Calvinists, as implying Hobbes' doctrine of necessity, or the Stoical doctrine of fate, lie no more against the doctrine of Calvinists, than their own doctrine: and therefore it don't become those divines, to raise such an outcry against the Calvinists, on this account.

Corol. 3. Hence all arguing from necessity, against the doctrine of the inability of unregenerate men to perform the conditions of salvation, and the commands of God requiring spiritual duties, and against the Calvinistic doctrine of efficacious grace; I say, all arguings of Arminians (such of 'em as own God's omniscience) against these things, on this ground, that these doctrines, though they don't suppose men to be under any constraint or coaction, yet suppose 'em under necessity, with respect to their moral actions, and those things which are required of 'em in order to their acceptance with God; and their arguing against the necessity of men's volitions, taken from the reasonableness of God's commands, promises, and threatenings, and the sincerity of his counsels and invitations; and all objections against any doctrines of the Calvinists as being inconsistent with human liberty, because they infer necessity; I say, all these arguments and objections must fall to the ground, and be justly esteemed vain and frivolous, as coming from them; being maintained in an inconsistence with themselves, and in like manner leveled against their own doctrine, as against the doctrine of the Calvinists.

SECTION 13.

WHETHER WE SUPPOSE THE VOLITIONS OF MORAL AGENTS TO BE CONNECTED WITH ANYTHING ANTECEDENT, OR NOT, YET THEY MUST BE NECESSARY IN SUCH A SENSE AS TO OVERTHROW ARMINIAN LIBERTY

Every act of the will has a cause, or it has not. If it has a cause, then, according to what has already been demonstrated, it is not contingent, but necessary; the effect being necessarily dependent and consequent on its cause; and that, let the cause be what it will. If the cause is the will itself, by antecedent acts choosing and determining; still the determined and caused act must be a necessary effect. The act that is the determined effect of the foregoing act which is its cause, can't prevent the efficiency of its cause; but must be wholly subject to its determination and command, as much as the motions of the hands and feet: the consequent commanded acts of the will are as passive and as necessary, with respect to the antecedent determining acts, as the parts of the body are to the volitions which determine and command them. And therefore, if all the free acts of the will are thus, if they are all determined effects, determined by the will itself, that is, determined by antecedent choice, then they are all necessary; they are all subject to, and decisively fixed by the foregoing act, which is their cause: yea, even the determining act itself; for that must be determined and fixed by another act, preceding that, if it be a free and voluntary act; and so must be necessary. So that by this all the free acts of the will are necessary, and can't be free unless they are necessary: because they can't be free, according to the Arminian notion of freedom, unless they are determined by the will; which is to be determined by antecedent choice; which being their cause, proves 'em necessary. And yet they say, necessity is utterly inconsistent with liberty. So that, by their scheme, the acts of the will can't be free unless they are necessary, and yet cannot be free [if they be necessary]! But if the other part of the dilemma be taken, and it be affirmed that the free acts of the will have no cause, and are connected with nothing whatsoever that goes before them and determines them, in order to maintain their proper and absolute contingence, and this should be allowed to be possible; still it will not serve their turn. For if the volition comes to pass by perfect contingence, and without any cause at all, then it is certain, no act of the will, no prior act of the soul was the cause, no determination or choice of the soul, had any hand in it. The will, or the soul, was indeed the subject of what happened to it accidentally, but was not the cause. The will is not active in causing or determining, but purely the passive subject; at least according to their notion of action and passion. In this case, contingence does as much to prevent the determination of the will, as a proper cause; and as to the will, it was necessary, and could be no otherwise. For to suppose that it could have been otherwise, if the will or soul had pleased, is to suppose that the act is dependent on some prior act of choice or pleasure; contrary to what now is supposed: it is to suppose that it might have been otherwise, if its cause had made it or ordered it otherwise. But this don't agree to its having no cause or orderer at all. That must be necessary as to the soul, which is dependent on no free act of the soul: but that which is without a cause, is dependent on no free act of the soul: because, by the supposition, it is dependent on nothing, and is connected with nothing. In such a case, the soul is necessarily subjected to what accident brings to pass, from time to time, as much as the earth, that is inactive, is necessarily subjected to what falls upon it. But this don't consist with the Arminian notion of liberty, which is the will's power of determining itself in its own acts, and being wholly active in it, without passiveness, and without being subject to necessity. Thus, contingence belongs to the Arminian notion of liberty, and yet is inconsistent with it.

I would here observe, that the author of the Essay on the Freedom of Will, in God and the Creature (pp. 76, 77) [Watts, Essay, Sec. 6, ans. to obj. 5; in Works, 6, 268] says as follows, "The word 'chance' always means something done without design. Chance and design stand in direct opposition to each other: and chance can never be properly applied to the acts of the will, which is the spring of all design, and which designs to choose whatsoever it doth choose, whether there be any superior fitness in the thing which it chooses, or no; and it designs to determine itself to one thing, where two things perfectly equal are proposed, merely because it will." But herein appears a very great inadvertence in this author. For if "the will be the spring of all design," as he says, then certainly it is not always the effect of design; and the acts of the will themselves must sometimes come to pass when they don't spring from design; and consequently come to pass by chance, according to his own definition of chance. And if "the will designs to choose whatsoever it does choose, and designs to determine itself," as he says, then it designs to determine all its designs. Which carries us back from one design to a foregoing design determining that, and to another determining that; and so on in infinitum. The very first design must be the effect of foregoing design, or else it must be by chance, in his notion of it. Here another alternative may be proposed, relating to the connection of the acts of the will with something foregoing that is their cause, not much unlike to the other; which is this: either human liberty is such that it may well stand with volitions being necessarily connected with the views of the understanding, and so is consistent with necessity; or it is inconsistent with, and contrary to such a connection and necessity. The former is directly subversive of the Arminian notion of liberty, consisting in freedom from all necessity. And if the latter be chosen, and it be said, that liberty is inconsistent with any such necessary connection of volition with foregoing views of the understanding, it consisting in freedom from any such necessity of the will as that would imply; then the liberty of the soul consists (in part at least) in the freedom from restraint, limitation and government, in its actings, by the understanding, and in liberty and liableness to act contrary to the understanding's views and dictates: and consequently the more the soul has of this disengagedness, in its acting, the more liberty. Now let it be considered what this brings the noble principle of human liberty to, particularly when it is possessed and enjoyed in its perfection, viz. a full and perfect freedom and liableness to act altogether at random, without the least connection with, or restraint or government by, any dictate of reason, or anything whatsoever apprehended, considered or viewed by the understanding; as being inconsistent with the full and perfect sovereignty of the will over its own determinations. The notion mankind have conceived of liberty, is some dignity or privilege, something worth claiming. But what dignity or privilege is there, in being given up to such a wild contingence as this, to be perfectly and constantly liable to act unintelligently and unreasonably, and as much without the guidance of understanding, as if we had none, or were as destitute of perception as the smoke that is driven by the wind!

PART THREE

Wherein Is Inquired, Whether Any Such Liberty of Will as Arminians Hold, Be Necessary to Moral Agency, Virtue and Vice, Praise, and Dispraise, etc.

SECTION 1.

GOD'S MORAL EXCELLENCY NECESSARY, YET VIRTUOUS AND PRAISEWORTHY

Having considered the first thing that was proposed to be inquired into, relating to that freedom of will which Arminians maintain; namely, whether any such thing does, ever did, or ever can exist, or be conceived of; I come now to the second thing proposed to be the subject of inquiry, viz. whether any such kind of liberty be requisite to moral agency, virtue and vice, praise and blame, reward and punishment, etc.

I shall begin with some consideration of the virtue and agency of the supreme moral Agent, and fountain of all agency and virtue.

Dr. Whitby, in his Discourse on the Five Points (p. 14) [Whitby, Discourse on the Five Points, Dis. I, ch. 1; p. 14], says, "If all human actions are necessary, virtue and vice must be empty names; we being capable of nothing that is blameworthy, or deserveth praise; for who can blame a person for doing only what he could not help, or judge that he deserveth praise only for what he could not avoid?" To the like purpose he speaks in places innumerable; especially in his discourse on the freedom of the will; constantly maintaining, that a "freedom not only from coaction, but [from] necessity," is absolutely requisite, in order to actions being either worthy of blame, or deserving of praise [Ibid., Dis. I, ch. 1; p. 328]. And to this agrees, as is well known, the current doctrine of Arminian writers; who in general hold, that there is no virtue or vice, reward or punishment, nothing to be commended or blamed, without this freedom. And yet Dr. Whitby, p. 300, allows, that God is without this freedom; and Arminians, so far as I have had opportunity to observe, generally acknowledge, that God is necessarily holy, and his will necessarily determined to that which is good.

So that, putting these things together, the infinitely holy God, who always used to be esteemed by God's people, not only virtuous, but a being in whom is all possible virtue, and every virtue in the most absolute purity and perfection, and in infinitely greater brightness and amiableness than in any creature; the most perfect pattern of virtue, and the fountain from whom all others' virtue is but as beams from the sun; and who has been supposed to be, on the account of his virtue and holiness, infinitely more worthy to be esteemed, loved, honored, admired, commended, extolled and praised, than any creature; and he who is thus everywhere represented in Scripture; I say, this being, according to this notion of Dr. Whitby, and other Arminians, has no virtue at all; virtue, when ascribed to him, is but "an empty name"; and he is deserving of no commendation or praise; because he is under necessity, he can't avoid being holy and good as he is; therefore no thanks to him for it. It seems, the holiness, justice, faithfulness, etc. of the most High, must not be accounted to be of the nature of that which is virtuous and praiseworthy. They will not deny, that these things in God are good; but then we must understand them, that they are no more virtuous, or of the nature of anything commendable, than the good that is in any other being that is not a moral agent; as the brightness of the sun, and the fertility of the earth are good, but not virtuous, because these properties are necessary to these bodies, and not the fruit of self-determining power.

There needs no other confutation of this notion of God's not being virtuous or praiseworthy, to Christians acquainted with the Bible, but only stating and particularly representing of it. To bring texts of Scripture, wherein God is represented as in every respect, in the highest manner virtuous, and supremely praiseworthy, would be endless, and is altogether needless to such as have been brought up under the light of the gospel.

It were to be wished, that Dr. Whitby, and other divines of the same sort, had explained themselves, when they have asserted that that which is necessary, is "not deserving of praise"; at the same time that they have owned God's perfection to be necessary, and so in effect represented God as not deserving praise. Certainly, if their words have any meaning at all, by "praise," they must mean the exercise or testimony of some sort of esteem, respect, or honorable regard. And will they then say, that men are worthy of that esteem, respect, and honor for their virtue, small and imperfect as it is, which yet God is not worthy of, for his infinite righteousness, holiness, and goodness? If so, it must be because of some sort of peculiar excellency in the virtuous man, which is his prerogative, wherein he really has the preference; some dignity, that is entirely distinguished from any excellency, amiableness or honorableness in God; not in imperfection and dependence, but in pre-eminence; which therefore he don't receive from God, nor is God the fountain or pattern of it; nor can God, in that respect, stand in competition with him, as the object of honor and regard; but man may claim a peculiar esteem, commendation and glory, that God can have no pretension to. Yea, God has no right, by virtue of his necessary holiness, to intermeddle with that grateful respect and praise, due to the virtuous man, who chooses virtue, in the exercise of a freedom *ad utrumque*; any more than a precious stone, which can't avoid being hard and beautiful.

And if it be so, let it be explained what that peculiar respect is, that is due to the virtuous man, which differs in nature and kind, in some way of pre-eminence, from all that is due to God. What is the name or description of that peculiar affection? Is it esteem, love, admiration, honor, praise, or gratitude? The Scripture everywhere represents God as the highest object of all these: there we read of the "soul's magnifying the Lord," or "loving him with all the heart, with all the soul, with all the mind, and with all the strength"; admiring him, and his righteous acts, or greatly regarding them as marvellous and wonderful; honoring, glorifying, exalting, extolling, blessing, thanking, and praising him; "giving unto him all the glory" of the good which is done or received, rather than unto men; "that no flesh should glory in his presence"; but that he should be regarded as the being to whom all glory is due. What then is that respect? What passion, affection, or exercise is it, that Arminians call "praise," diverse from all these things, which men are worthy of for their virtue, and which God is not worthy of, in any degree?

If that necessity which attends God's moral perfections and actions, be as inconsistent with a being worthy of praise, as a necessity of coaction; as is plainly implied in or inferred from Dr. Whitby's discourse; then why should we thank God for his goodness, any more than if he were forced to be good, or any more than we should thank one of our fellow creatures who did us good, not freely, and of good will, or from any kindness of heart, but from mere compulsion, or extrinsical necessity? Arminians suppose, that God is necessarily a good and gracious being: for this they make the ground of some of their main arguments against many doctrines maintained by Calvinists: they say, these are "certainly" false, and it is "impossible" they should be true, because they are not consistent with the goodness of God. This supposes, that it is impossible but that God should be good: for if it be possible that he should be otherwise, then that impossibility of the truth of these doctrines ceases, according to their own argument.

That virtue in God is not, in the most proper sense, rewardable, is not for want of merit in his moral perfections and actions, sufficient to deserve rewards from his creatures; but because he is infinitely above all capacity of receiving any reward or benefit from the creature: he is already infinitely and unchangeably happy, and we can't be profitable unto him. But still he is worthy of our supreme benevolence for his virtue; and would be worthy of our beneficence, which is the fruit and expression of benevolence, if our goodness could extend to him. If God deserves to be thanked and praised for his goodness, he would for the same reason, deserve that we should also requite his kindness, if that were possible. "What shall I render to the Lord for all his benefits?" [Ps. 116:12] is the natural language of thankfulness: and so far as in us lies, it is our duty to recompense God's goodness, and render again according to benefits received. And that we might have opportunity for so natural an expression of our gratitude to God, as beneficence, notwithstanding his being infinitely above our reach; he has appointed others to be his receivers, and to stand in his stead, as the objects of our beneficence; such are especially our indigent brethren.

SECTION 2.

THE ACTS OF THE WILL OF THE HUMAN SOUL OF JESUS CHRIST NECESSARILY HOLY, YET TRULY VIRTUOUS, PRAISEWORTHY, REWARDABLE, ETC.

I have already considered how Dr. Whitby insists upon it, that a freedom, not only from coaction, but necessity, is "requisite to either virtue or vice, praise or dispraise, reward or punishment." He also insists on the same freedom as absolutely requisite to a person's being the subject of a law, of precepts or prohibitions; in the book before mentioned (pp. 301, 314, 328, 339, 340, 341, 342, 347, 361, 373, 410). And of promises and threatenings (pp. 298, 301, 305, 311, 339, 340, 363). And as requisite to a state of trial (p. 297, etc.).

Now therefore, with an eye to these things, I would inquire into the moral conduct and practice of our Lord Jesus Christ, which he exhibited in his human nature here, in his state of humiliation. And first, I would show, that his holy behavior was necessary; or that it was impossible it should be otherwise, than that he should behave himself holily, and that he should be perfectly holy in each individual act of his life. And secondly, that his holy behavior was properly of the nature of virtue, and was worthy of praise; and that he was the subject of law, precepts or commands, promises and rewards; and that he was in a state of trial.

I. It was impossible, that the acts of the will of the human soul of Christ should, in any instance, degree or circumstance, be otherwise than holy, and agreeable to God's nature and will. The following things make this evident.

1. God had promised so effectually to preserve and uphold him by his Spirit, under all his temptations, that he should not fail of reaching the end for which he came into the world; which he would have failed of, had he fallen into sin. We have such a promise (Is. 42:1, 2, 3, 4), "Behold my servant, whom I uphold; mine elect, in whom my soul delighteth: I have put my Spirit upon him: he shall bring forth judgment to the Gentiles: he shall not cry, nor lift up, nor cause his voice to be heard in the street…He shall bring forth judgment unto truth. He shall not fail, nor be discouraged, till he have set judgment in the earth; and the isles shall wait for his law." This promise of Christ's having God's Spirit put upon him, and his not crying and lifting up his voice, etc. relates to the time of Christ's appearance on earth; as is manifest from the nature of the promise, and also the application of it in the New Testament (Matt. 12:18). And the words imply a promise of his being so upheld by God's Spirit, that he should be preserved from sin; particularly from pride and vainglory, and from being overcome by any of the temptations he should be under to affect the glory of this world; the pomp of an earthly prince, or the applause and praise of men: and that he should be so upheld, that he should by no means fail of obtaining the end of his coming into the world, of bringing forth judgment unto victory, and establishing his kingdom of grace in the earth. And in the following verses, this promise is confirmed, with the greatest imaginable solemnity: "Thus saith the Lord, he that created the heavens, and stretched them out; he that spread forth the earth, and that which cometh out of it; he that giveth breath unto the people upon it, and spirit to them that walk therein: I the Lord have called thee in righteousness, and will hold thine hand; and will keep thee, and give thee for a covenant of the people, for a light of the Gentiles, to open the blind eyes, to bring out the prisoners from the prison, and them that sit in darkness out of the prison-house. I am Jehovah, that is my name," etc. [Is. 42:5–8].

Very parallel with these promises is that (Is. 49:7, 8, 9) which also has an apparent respect to the time of Christ's humiliation on earth: "Thus saith the Lord, the Redeemer of Israel, and his holy One, to him whom man despiseth, to him whom the nation abhorreth, to a servant of rulers; kings shall see and arise, princes also shall worship; because of the Lord that is faithful, and the holy One of Israel, and he shall choose thee. Thus saith the Lord, in an acceptable time have I heard thee; in a day of salvation have I helped thee; and I will preserve thee, and give thee for a covenant of the people, to establish the earth," etc.

And in Is. 50:5–9, we have the Messiah expressing his assurance, that God would help him, by so opening his ear, or inclining his heart to God's commandments, that he should not be rebellious, but should persevere, and not apostatize, or turn his back: that through God's help, he should be immovable, in a way of obedience, under the great trials of reproach and suffering he should meet with; setting his face like a flint: so that he knew he should not be ashamed, or frustrated in his design; and finally should be approved and justified, as having done his work faithfully: "The Lord hath opened mine ear; so that I was not rebellious, neither turned away my back: I gave my back to the smiters, and my cheeks to them that plucked off the hair; I hid not my face from shame and spitting. For the Lord God will help me; therefore shall I not be confounded: therefore have I set my face as a flint, and I know that I shall not be ashamed. He is near that justifieth me: who will contend with me? Let us stand together. Who is mine adversary? Let him come near to me. Behold the Lord God will help me: who is he that shall condemn me? Lo, they shall all wax old as a garment, the moth shall eat them up."

2. The same thing is evident from all the promises which God made to the Messiah, of his future glory, kingdom and success, in his office and character of a mediator: which glory could not have been obtained, if his holiness had failed, and he had been guilty of sin. God's absolute promise of any things makes the things promised necessary, and their failing to take place absolutely impossible: and in like manner it makes those things necessary, on which the thing promised depends, and without which it can't take effect. Therefore it appears, that it was utterly impossible that Christ's holiness should fail, from such absolute promises as those (Ps. 110:4), "The Lord hath sworn, and will not repent, thou art a priest forever, after the order of Melchizedek." And from every other promise in that psalm, contained in each verse of it. And Ps. 2:6, 7, "I will declare the decree: the Lord hath said unto me, thou art my Son, this day have I begotten thee: ask of me, and I will give thee the heathen for thine inheritance," etc. Ps. 45:3, 4, etc.: "Gird thy sword on thy thigh, O most mighty, with thy glory and thy majesty; and in thy majesty ride prosperously." And so everything that is said from thence to the end of the psalm. And those promises, Is. 52:13, 14, 15; and 53:10, 11, 12. And all those promises which God makes to the Messiah, of success, dominion and glory in the character of redeemer, in Is. ch. 49.

3. It was often promised to the church of God of old, for their comfort, that God would give them a righteous, sinless Saviour. Jer. 23:5, 6: "Behold, the days come, saith the Lord, that I will raise up unto David a righteous branch; and a king shall reign and prosper, and shall execute judgment and justice in the earth. In his days shall Judah be saved, and Israel shall dwell safely. And this is the name whereby he shall be called, the Lord our Righteousness." So, Jer. 33:15: "I will cause the branch of righteousness to grow up unto David; and he shall execute judgment and righteousness in the land." Is. 9:6, 7: "For unto us a child is born…upon the throne of David and of his kingdom, to order it, and to establish it with judgment and justice, from henceforth, even forever: the zeal of the Lord of hosts will do this." Ch. 11, at the beginning: "There shall come forth a rod out of the stem of Jesse, and a branch shall grow out of his roots; and the Spirit of the Lord shall rest upon him… the spirit of knowledge, and of the fear of the Lord… with righteousness shall he judge the poor, and reprove with equity…righteousness shall be the girdle of his loins, and faithfulness the girdle of his reins." Ch. 52:13: "My servant shall deal prudently." Ch. 53:9: "Because he had done no violence, neither was guile found in his mouth." If it be impossible, that these promises should fail, and it be easier for heaven and earth to pass away, than for one jot or tittle of these promises of God to pass away, then it was impossible that Christ should commit any sin. Christ himself signified, that it was impossible but that the things which were spoken concerning him should be fulfilled. Luke 24:44: "That all things must be fulfilled, which were written in the law of Moses, and in the prophets, and in the Psalms concerning me." Matt. 26:54: "But how then shall the Scripture be fulfilled, that thus it must be?" Mark 14:49: "But the Scriptures must be fulfilled." And so the Apostle, Acts 1:16, 17: "This Scripture must needs have been fulfilled."

4. All the promises which were made to the church of old, of the Messiah as a future Saviour, from that made

to our first parents in paradise, to that which was delivered by the prophet Malachi, show it to be impossible that Christ should not have persevered in perfect holiness. The ancient predictions given to God's church, of the Messiah as a Saviour, were of the nature of promises; as is evident by the predictions themselves, and the manner of delivering them. But they are expressly, and very often called promises in the New Testament; as in Luke 1:54, 55, 72, 73; Acts 13:32, 33; Rom. 1:1, 2, 3; and ch. 15:8; Heb. 6:13, etc. These promises were often made with great solemnity, and confirmed with an oath; as in Gen. 22:16, 17, "By myself have I sworn, saith the Lord, that in blessing, I will bless thee, and in multiplying, I will multiply thy seed, as the stars of heaven, and as the sand which is upon the seashore:...and in thy seed shall all the nations of the earth be blessed." Compare Luke 1:72, 73 and Gal. 3:8, 15, 16. The Apostle in Heb. 6:17, 18 speaking of this promise to Abraham, says, "Wherein God willing more abundantly to shew to the heirs of promise the immutability of his counsel, confirmed it by an oath; that by two immutable things, in which it was impossible for God to lie, [we] might have strong consolation." In which words, the necessity of the accomplishment, or (which is the same thing) the impossibility of the contrary, is fully declared. So God confirmed the promise of the great salvation of the Messiah, made to David, by an oath (Ps. 89:3, 4), "I have made a covenant with my chosen, I have sworn unto David my servant; thy seed will I establish forever, and build up thy throne to all generations." There is nothing that is so abundantly set forth in Scripture, as sure and irrefragable, as this promise and oath to David. See Ps. 89:34, 35, 36; II Sam. 23:5; Is. 55:3; Acts 2:29, 30; and 13:34. The Scripture expressly speaks of it as utterly impossible that this promise and oath to David, concerning the everlasting dominion of the Messiah of his seed, should fail. Jer. 33: 15, etc.: "In those days, and at that time, I will cause the branch of righteousness to grow up unto David....For thus saith the Lord, David shall never want a man to sit upon the throne of the house of Israel." Ver. 20, 21: "If you can break my covenant of the day, and my covenant of the night, and that there should not be day and night in their season; then may also my covenant be broken with David my servant, that he should not have a son to reign upon his throne." So in ver. 25, 26. Thus abundant is the Scripture in representing how impossible it was, that the promises made of old concerning the great salvation and kingdom of the Messiah should fail: which implies, that it was impossible that this Messiah, the second Adam, the promised seed of Abraham, and of David, should fall from his integrity, as the first Adam did.

5. All the promises that were made to the church of God under the Old Testament, of the great enlargement of the church, and advancement of her glory, in the days of the gospel, after the coming of the Messiah; the increase of her light, liberty, holiness, joy, triumph over her enemies, etc. of which so great a part of the Old Testament consists; which are repeated so often, are so variously exhibited, so frequently introduced with great pomp and solemnity, and are so abundantly sealed with typical and symbolical representations; I say, all these promises imply, that the Messiah should perfect the work of redemption; and this implies, that he should persevere in the work which the Father had appointed him, being in all things conformed to his will. These promises were often confirmed by an oath (see Is. 54:9 with the context; ch. 62:8). And it is represented as utterly impossible that these promises should fail (Is. 49:15 with the context; ch. 54:10 with the context; ch. 51:4–8; ch. 40:8 with the context). And therefore it was impossible, that the Messiah should fail, or commit sin.

6. It was impossible, that the Messiah should fail of persevering in integrity and holiness, as the first Adam did, because this would have been inconsistent with the promises which God made to the blessed Virgin, his mother, and to her husband; implying, that "he should save his people from their sins," that "God would give him the throne of his father David," that "he should reign over the house of Jacob forever"; and that "of his kingdom there should be no end" [Matt. 1:21; Luke 1:32, 33]. These promises were sure, and it was impossible they should fail. And therefore the Virgin Mary, in trusting fully to them, acted reasonably, having an immovable foundation of her faith; as Elizabeth observes, [Luke 1:] ver. 45, "And blessed is she that believeth; for there shall be a performance of those things which were told her from the Lord."

7. That it should have been possible that Christ should sin, and so fail in the work of our redemption, does not consist with the eternal purpose and decree of God, revealed in the Scriptures, that he would provide salvation for fallen man in and by Jesus Christ, and that salvation should be offered to sinners through the preaching of the gospel. Such an absolute decree as this Arminians don't deny. Thus much at least (out of all controversy) is implied in such Scriptures, as I Cor. 2:7; Eph. 1:4, 5 and ch. 3:9, 10, 11; I Pet. 1:19, 20. Such an absolute decree as this, Arminians allow to be signified in these texts.

And the Arminians' election of nations and societies, and general election of the Christian church, and conditional election of particular persons, imply this. God could not decree before the foundation of the world, to save all that should believe in, and obey Christ, unless he had absolutely decreed that salvation should be provided, and effectually wrought out by Christ. And since (as the Arminians themselves strenuously maintain) a decree of God infers necessity; hence it became necessary that Christ should persevere, and actually work out salvation for us, and that he should not fail by the commission of sin.

8. That it should have been possible for Christ's holiness to fail, is not consistent with what God promised to his Son before all ages. For, that salvation should be offered to men through Christ, and bestowed on all his faithful followers, is what is at least implied in that certain and infallible promise spoken of by the Apostle (Titus 1:2), "In hope of eternal life; which God, that cannot lie, promised before the world began." This don't seem to be controverted by Arminians. (See Dr. Whitby Discourse on the Five Points, Dis. I, ch. 3; pp. 48 ff.)

9. That it should be possible for Christ to fail of doing his Father's will, is inconsistent with the promise made to the Father by the Son, by the Logos that was with the Father from the beginning, before he took the human nature: as may be seen in Ps. 40:6, 7, 8 (compared with the Apostle's interpretation, Heb. 10:5–9), "Sacrifice and offering thou didst not desire: mine ears hast thou opened (or bored); burnt-offering and sin-offering thou hast not required. Then said I, Lo, I come: in the Volume of the Book it is written of me, I delight to do thy will, O my God, and thy law is within my heart." Where is a manifest allusion to the covenant which the willing servant, who loved his master's service, made with his master, to be his servant forever, on the day wherein he had his ear bored; which covenant was probably inserted in the public records, called the "Volume of the Book," by the judges, who were called to take cognizance of the transaction (Ex. 21). If the Logos, who was with the Father, before the world, and who made the world, thus engaged in covenant to do the will of the Father in the human nature, and the promise, was as it were recorded, that it might be made sure, doubtless it was impossible that it should fail; and so it was impossible that Christ should fail of doing the will of the Father in the human nature.

10. If it was possible for Christ to have failed of doing the will of his Father, and so to have failed of effectually working out redemption for sinners, then the salvation of all the saints, who were saved from the beginning of the world, to the death of Christ, was not built on a firm foundation. The Messiah, and the redemption which he was to work out by his obedience unto death, was the foundation of the salvation of all the posterity of fallen man, that ever were saved. Therefore, if when the Old Testament saints had the pardon of their sins, and the favor of God promised them, and salvation bestowed upon them, still it was possible that the Messiah, when he came, might commit sin, then all this was on a foundation that was not firm and stable, but liable to fail; something which it was possible might never be. God did as it were trust to what his Son had engaged and promised to do in future time; and depended so much upon it, that he proceeded actually to save men on the account of it, as though it had been already done. But this trust and dependence of God, on the supposition of Christ's being liable to fail of doing his will, was leaning on a staff that was weak, and might possibly break. The saints of old trusted on the promises of a future redemption to be wrought out and completed by the Messiah, and built their comfort upon it: Abraham saw Christ's day and rejoiced; and he and the other patriarchs died in the faith of the promise of it (Heb. 11:13). But on this supposition, their faith and their comfort, and their salvation, was built on a movable fallible foundation; Christ was not to them a tried stone, a sure foundation; as in Is. 28:16. David entirely rested on the covenant of God with him, concerning the future glorious dominion and salvation of the Messiah, of his seed; says, it was "all his salvation, and all his desire"; and comforts himself that this covenant was an "everlasting covenant, ordered in all things and sure" (II Sam. 23:5). But if Christ's virtue might fail, he was mistaken: his great comfort was not built so sure, as he thought it was, being founded entirely on the determinations of the free will of Christ's human soul; which was subject to no necessity, and might be determined either one way or the other. Also the dependence of those who looked for redemption in Jerusalem, and waited for the consolation of Israel (Luke 2:25 and 38), and the confidence of the disciples of Jesus, who forsook all and followed him, that they might enjoy the benefits of his future kingdom, was built on a sandy foundation.

11. The man Christ Jesus, before he had finished his course of obedience, and while in the midst of temptations and trials, was abundant in positively predicting his own future glory in his kingdom, and the enlargement of his church, the salvation of the Gentiles through him, etc. and in promises of blessings he would bestow on his

true disciples in his future kingdom; on which promises he required the full dependence of his disciples (John 14). But the disciples world have had no ground for such dependence, if Christ had been liable to fail in his work: and Christ himself would have been guilty of presumption, in so abounding in peremptory promises of great things, which depended on a mere contingence; viz. the determinations of his free will, consisting in a freedom *ad utrumque*, to either sin or holiness, standing in indifference, and incident, in thousands of future instances, to go either one way or the other.

Thus it is evident, that it was impossible that the acts of the will of the human soul of Christ should be otherwise than holy, and conformed to the will of the Father; or, in other words, they were necessarily so conformed.

I have been the longer in the proof of this matter, it being a thing denied by some of the greatest Arminians, by Episcopius in particular; and because I look upon it as a point clearly and absolutely determining the controversy between Calvinists and Arminians, concerning the necessity of such a freedom of will as is insisted on by the latter, in order to moral agency, virtue, command or prohibition, promise or threatening, reward or punishment, praise or dispraise, merit or demerit. I now therefore proceed,

II. To consider whether Christ, in his holy behavior on earth, was not thus a moral agent, subject to commands, promises, etc.:

Dr. Whitby very often speaks of what he calls a freedom *ad utrumlibet* without necessity, as requisite to law and commands; and speaks of necessity as entirely inconsistent with injunctions and prohibitions. But yet we read of Christ's being the subject of the commands of his Father (John 10:18; and 15:10). And Christ tells us, that everything that he said, or did, was in compliance with commandments he had received of the Father (John 12:49, 50; and 14:31). And we often read of Christ's obedience to his Father's commands (Rom. 5:19; Phil. 2:8; Heb. 5:8).

The forementioned writer represents promises offered as motives to persons to do their duty, or a being moved and induced by promises, as utterly inconsistent with a state wherein persons have not a liberty *ad utrumlibet*, but are necessarily determined to one. (See particularly, pp. 298 and 311). But the thing which this writer asserts, is demonstrably false, if the Christian religion be true. If there be any truth in Christianity or the holy Scriptures, the man Christ Jesus had his will infallibly, unalterably and unfrustrably determined to good, and that alone; but yet he had promises of glorious rewards made to him, on condition of his persevering in, and perfecting the work which God had appointed him (Is. 53: 10, 11, 12; Ps. 2 and 110; Is. 49:7, 8, g). In Luke 22:28, 29, Christ says to his disciples, "Ye are they which have continued with me in my temptations; and I appoint unto you a kingdom, as my Father hath appointed unto me." The word most properly signifies to appoint by covenant, or promise. The plain meaning of Christ's words is this: "As you have partook of my temptations and trials, and have been steadfast, and have overcome; I promise to make you partakers of my reward, and to give you a kingdom; as the Father has promised me a kingdom for continuing steadfast, and overcoming in those trials." And the words are well explained by those in Rev. 3:21, "To him that overcometh, will I grant to sit with me in my throne; even as I also overcame, and am set down with my Father in his throne." And Christ had not only promises of glorious success and rewards made to his obedience and sufferings, but the Scriptures plainly represent him as using these promises for motives and inducements to obey and suffer; and particularly that promise of a kingdom which the Father had appointed him, or sitting with the Father on his throne; as in Heb. 12:1, 2, "Let us lay aside every weight, and the sin which doth easily beset us, and let us run with patience the race that is set before us, looking unto Jesus, the author and finisher of our faith; who for the joy that was set before him, endured the cross, despising the shame, and is set down on the right hand of the throne of God."

And how strange would it be to hear any Christian assert, that the holy and excellent temper and behavior of Jesus Christ, and that obedience which he performed under such great trials, was not virtuous or praiseworthy; because his will was not free *ad utrumque*, to either holiness or sin, but was unalterably determined to one; that upon this account, there is no virtue at all, in all Christ's humility, meekness, patience, charity, forgiveness of enemies, contempt of the world, heavenly-mindedness, submission to the will of God, perfect obedience to his commands (though he was obedient unto death, even the death of the cross), his great compassion to the afflicted, his unparalleled love to mankind, his faithfulness to God and man, under such great trials; his praying for his enemies, even when nailing him to the cross; that "virtue," when applied to these things, "is but an empty name"; that there was no merit in any of these things; that is, that Christ was "worthy" of nothing at all on the account of them, worthy of no reward, no praise, no honor or respect from God or man; because his will was not indifferent, and free either to these things, or the contrary; but under such a strong inclination or bias to the things that were excellent, as made it impossible that he should choose the contrary; that upon this account (to use Dr. Whitby's language) "it would be sensibly unreasonable" that the human nature should be rewarded for any of these things! [Discourse on the Five Points, Dis. I, ch. 1, no. 3; p. 15.]

According to this doctrine, that Creature who is evidently set forth in Scripture as the "first born of every creature," as having "in all things the preeminence" [Col. 1:15, 18], and as the highest of all creatures in virtue, honor, and worthiness of esteem, praise and glory, on the account of his virtue, is less worthy of reward or praise, than the very least of saints; yea, no more worthy than a clock or mere machine, that is purely passive, and moved by natural necessity.

If we judge by scriptural representations of things, we have reason to suppose, that Christ took on him our nature, and dwelt with us in this world, in a suffering state, not only to satisfy for our sins; but that he, being in our nature and circumstances, and under our trials, might be our most fit and proper example, leader and captain, in the exercise of glorious and victorious virtue, and might be a visible instance of the glorious end and reward of it; that we might see in him the beauty, amiableness, and true honor and glory, and exceeding benefit of that virtue, which it is proper for us human beings to practice; and might thereby learn, and be animated, to seek the like glory and honor, and to obtain the like glorious reward. See Heb. 2:9–14, with 5:8, 9 and 12: 1, 2, 3; John 15: 10; Rom. 8: 17; II Tim. 2:11, 12; I Pet. 2:19, 20; and 4:13. But if there was nothing of any virtue or merit, or worthiness of any reward, glory, praise or commendation at all, in all that he did, because it was all necessary, and he could not help it; then how is here anything so proper to animate and incite us, free creatures, by patient continuance in well doing, to seek for honor, glory, and virtue?

God speaks of himself as peculiarly well pleased with the righteousness of this servant of his (Is. 42:21), "The Lord is well pleased for his righteousness sake." The sacrifices of old are spoken of as a sweet savor to God, but the obedience of Christ as far more acceptable than they. Ps. 40:6, 7, 8: "Sacrifice and offering thou didst not desire: mine ear hast thou opened [as thy servant performing willing obedience (Edwards' original brackets here)]; burnt-offering and sin-offering hast thou not required: then said I, Lo, I come [as a servant that cheerfully answers the calls of his master (Edwards' original brackets here)]: I delight to do thy will, O my God, and thy law is within mine heart." Matt. 17:5: "This is my beloved Son, in whom I am well pleased." And Christ tells us expressly, that the Father loves him for that wonderful instance of his obedience, his voluntarily yielding himself to death, in compliance with the Father's command. John 10:17, 18: "Therefore doth my Father love me, because I lay down my life: ... no man taketh it from me; but I lay it down of myself....This commandment received I of my Father."

And if there was no merit in Christ's obedience unto death, if it was not worthy of praise, and of the most glorious rewards, the heavenly hosts were exceedingly mistaken, by the account that is given of them, in Rev. 5:8–12, "The four beasts and the four and twenty elders fell down before the Lamb, having everyone of them harps, and golden vials full of odors...and they sung a new song, saying, thou art worthy to take the book, and to open the seals thereof; for thou wast slain...and I beheld, and I heard the voice of many angels round about the throne, and the beasts, and the elders, and the number of them was ten thousand times ten thousand, and thousands of thousands, saying with a loud voice, worthy is the Lamb that was slain, to receive power, and riches, and wisdom, and strength, and honor, and glory, and blessing."

Christ speaks of the eternal life which he was to receive, as the reward of his obedience to the Father's commandments. John 12:49, 50: "I have not spoken of myself; but the Father which sent me, he gave me a commandment what I should say, and what I should speak: and I know that his commandment is life everlasting: whatsoever I speak therefore, even as the Father said unto me, so I speak." God promises to divide him a portion with the great etc. for his being his righteous servant, for his glorious virtue under such great trials and sufferings. Is. 53:1.1, 12: "He shall see of the travail of his soul and be satisfied: by his knowledge shall my righteous servant justify many; for he shall bear their iniquities. Therefore will I divide him a portion with the great, and he shall divide the spoil with the strong, because he hath poured out his soul unto death." The Scriptures represent God as rewarding him far above all his other servants. Phil. 2:7, 8, 9: "He took on him the form of a servant, and was made in the likeness of men: and being found in fashion as a man, he humbled himself, and became obedient unto death, even the death of the cross: wherefore

God also hath highly exalted him, and given him a Name above every name." Ps. 45:7: "Thou lovest righteousness, and hatest wickedness; therefore God, thy God, hath anointed thee with the oil of gladness above thy fellows."

There is no room to pretend, that the glorious benefits bestowed in consequence of Christ's obedience, are not properly of the nature of a reward. What is a reward, in the most proper sense, but a benefit bestowed in consequence of something morally excellent in quality or behavior, in testimony of well-pleasedness in that moral excellency, and respect and favor on that account? If we consider the nature of a reward most strictly, and make the utmost of it, and add to the things contained in this description, proper merit or worthiness, and the bestowment of the benefit in consequence of a promise; still it will be found, there is nothing belonging to it, but that the Scripture is most express as to its belonging to the glory bestowed on Christ, after his sufferings; as appears from what has been already observed: there was a glorious benefit bestowed in consequence of something morally excellent, being called "righteousness" and "obedience"; there was great favor, love and well-pleasedness, for this righteousness and obedience, in the bestower; there was proper merit, or worthiness of the benefit, in the obedience; it was bestowed in fulfillment of promises, made to that obedience; and was bestowed therefore, or because he had performed that obedience.

I may add to all these things, that Jesus Christ, while here in the flesh, was manifestly in a state of trial. The last Adam, as Christ is called (I Cor. 15:45; Rom. 5:14), taking on him the human nature, and so the form of a servant, and being under the law, to stand and act for us, was put into a state of trial, as the first Adam was. Dr. Whitby mentions these three things as evidences of persons being in a state of trial (on the Five Points, pp. 298, 299): namely, their afflictions being spoken of as their trials or temptations, their being the subjects of promises, and their being exposed to Satan's temptations. But Christ was apparently the subject of each of these. Concerning promises made to him, I have spoken already. The difficulties and afflictions he met with in the course of his obedience, are called his temptations or trials (Luke 22:28), "Ye are they which have continued with me in my temptations," or trials. Heb. 2:18: "For in that he himself hath suffered, being tempted [or tried (Edwards' original brackets here)] he is able to succor them that are tempted." And ch. 4:15, "We have not an High Priest, which cannot be touched with the feeling of our infirmities; but was in all points tempted like as we are, yet without sin." And as to his being tempted by Satan, it is what none will dispute.

SECTION 3.

THE CASE OF SUCH AS ARE GIVEN UP OF GOD TO SIN, AND OF FALLEN MAN IN GENERAL, PROVES MORAL NECESSITY AND INABILITY TO BE CONSISTENT WITH BLAMEWORTHINESS

Dr. Whitby asserts freedom, not only from coaction, but necessity, to be essential to anything deserving the name of "sin," and to an action's being culpable: in these words (Discourse on Five Points edit. 3, p. 348), "If they be thus necessitated, then neither their sins of omission or commission could deserve that name; it being essential to the nature of sin, according to St. Austin's definition, that it be an action, a *quo liberum est abstinere*. Three things seem plainly necessary to make an action or omission culpable: 1. That it be in our power to perform or forbear it: for, as Origen, and all the fathers say, no man is blameworthy for not doing what he could not do." And elsewhere the Doctor insists, that when any do evil of necessity, what they do is no vice, that they are guilty of no-fault, are worthy of no blame, dispraise, or dishonor, but are unblamable.

If these things are true, in Dr. Whitby's sense of necessity, they will prove all such to be blameless, who are given up of God to sin, in what they commit after they are thus given up. That there is such a thing as men's being judicially given up to sin, is certain, if the Scripture rightly informs us; such a thing being often there spoken of: as in Ps. 81:12, "So I gave them up to their own hearts' lust, and they walked in their own counsels." Acts 7:42: "Then God turned, and gave them up to worship the host of heaven." Rom. 1:24: "Wherefore, God also gave them up to uncleanness, through the lusts of their own hearts, to dishonor their own bodies between themselves." Ver. 26: "For this cause God gave them up to vile affections." Ver. 28: "And even as they did not like to retain God in their knowledge, God gave them over to a reprobate mind, to do those things that are not convenient."

'Tis needless to stand particularly to inquire, what God's "giving men up to their own hearts' lusts" signifies: it is sufficient to observe, that hereby is certainly meant God's so ordering or disposing things, in some respect or other, either by doing or forebearing to do, as that the consequence should be men's continuing in their sins.

So much as men are given up to, so much is the consequence of their being given up; whether that be less or more. If God don't order things so, by action or permission, that sin will be the consequence, then the event proves that they are not given up to that consequence. If good be the consequence, instead of evil, then God's mercy is to be acknowledged in that good; which mercy must be contrary to God's judgment in giving up to evil. If the event must prove that they are given up to evil as the consequence, then the persons who are the subjects of this judgment, must be the subjects of such an event, and so the event is necessary.

If not only coaction, but all necessity, will prove men blameless, then Judas was blameless, after Christ had given him over, and had already declared his certain damnation, and that he should verily betray him. He was guilty of no sin in betraying his master, on this supposition; though his so doing is spoken of by Christ as the most aggravated sin, more heinous than the sin of Pilate in crucifying him. And the Jews in Egypt, in Jeremiah's time, were guilty of no sin, in their not worshipping the true God, after God had "sworn by his great Name, that his name should be no more named in the mouth of any man of Judah, in all the land of Egypt" (Jer. 44:26).

Dr. Whitby (Discourse on Five Points, pp. 302, 303) (Ibid., Dis. IV, ch. 1, no. 3) denies, that men, in this world, are ever so given up by God to sin, that their wills should be necessarily determined to evil; though he owns, that hereby it may become "exceeding difficult" for men to do good, having a strong bent, and powerful inclination to what is evil. But if we should allow the case to be just as he represents, the judgment of giving up to sin will no better agree with his notions of that liberty, which is essential to praise or blame, than if we should suppose it to render the avoiding of sin impossible. For if an impossibility of avoiding sin wholly excuses a man; then, for the same reason, its being difficult to avoid it excuses him in part; and this just in proportion to the degree of difficulty. If the influence of moral impossibility or inability be the same, to excuse persons in not doing, or not avoiding anything, as that of natural inability (which is supposed), then undoubtedly, in like manner, moral difficulty has the same influence to excuse with natural difficulty. But all allow, that natural impossibility wholly excuses, and also that natural difficulty excuses in part, and makes the act or omission less blamable, in proportion to the difficulty. All natural difficulty, according to the plainest dictates of the light of nature, excuses in some degree, so that the neglect is not so blamable, as if there had been no difficulty in the case: and so the greater the difficulty is, still the more excusable, in proportion to the increase of the difficulty. And as natural impossibility wholly excuses and excludes all blame, so the nearer the difficulty approaches to impossibility, still the nearer a person is to blamelessness, in proportion to that approach. And if the case of moral impossibility or necessity, be just the same with natural necessity or coaction, as to influence to excuse a neglect, then also, for the same reason, the case of natural difficulty don't differ in influence, to excuse a neglect, from moral difficulty, arising from a strong bias or bent to evil, such as Dr. Whitby owns in the case of those that are given up to their own hearts' lusts. So that the fault of such persons must be lessened, in proportion to the difficulty, and approach to impossibility. If ten degrees of moral difficulty make the action quite impossible, and so wholly excuse, then if there be nine degrees of difficulty, the person is in great part excused, and in nine degrees in ten, less blameworthy, than if there had been no difficulty at all; and he has but one degree of blameworthiness. The reason is plain, on Arminian principles; viz. because as difficulty, by antecedent bent and bias on the will, is increased, liberty of indifference, and self-determination in the will, is diminished: so much hindrance and impediment is there, in the way of the will's acting freely, by mere self-determination. And if ten degrees of such hindrance take away all such liberty, then nine degrees take away nine parts in ten, and leave but one degree of liberty. And therefore there is but one degree of blamableness, *caeteris paribus*, in the neglect; the man being no further blamable in what he does, or neglects, than he has liberty in that affair: for blame or praise (say they) arises wholly from a good use or abuse of liberty.

From all which it follows, that a strong bent and bias one way, and difficulty of going the contrary, never causes a person to be at all more exposed to sin, or anything blamable: because as the difficulty is increased, so much the less is required and expected. Though in one respect, exposedness to sin or fault is increased, viz. by an increase of exposedness to the evil action or omission; yet it is diminished in another respect, to balance it; namely, as the sinfulness or blamableness of the action or omission is diminished in the same proportion. So that, on the whole, the affair, as to exposedness to guilt or blame, is left just as it was.

To illustrate this, let us suppose a scale of a balance to be intelligent, and a free agent, and indued with a self-moving power, by virtue of which it could act and produce effects to a certain degree; [e.g.] to move itself up or down with a force equal to a weight of ten pounds; and that it might therefore be required of it, in ordinary circumstances, to move itself down with that force; for which it has power and full liberty, and therefore would be blameworthy if it failed of it. But then let us suppose a weight of ten pounds to be put in the opposite scale, which in force entirely counterbalances its self-moving power, and so renders it impossible for it to move down at all; and therefore wholly excuses it from any such motion. But if we suppose there to be only nine pounds in the opposite scale, this renders its motion not impossible, but yet more difficult; so that it can now only move down with the force of one pound: but however, this is all that is required of it under these circumstances; it is wholly excused from nine parts of its motion: and if the scale, under these circumstances, neglects to move, and remains at rest, all that it will be blamed for, will be its neglect of that one tenth part of its motion; which it had as much liberty and advantage for, as in usual circumstances, it has for the greater motion, which in such a case would be required. So that this new difficulty, don't at all increase its exposedness to anything blameworthy.

And thus the very supposition of difficulty in the way of a man's duty, or proclivity to sin, through a being given up to hardness of heart, or indeed by any other means whatsoever, is an inconsistence, according to Dr. Whitby's notions of liberty, virtue and vice, blame and praise. The avoiding sin and blame, and the doing what is virtuous and praiseworthy, must be always equally easy.

Dr. Whitby's notions of liberty, obligation, virtue, sin, etc. lead him into another great inconsistence. He abundantly insists, that necessity is inconsistent with the nature of sin or fault. He says in the forementioned treatise (p. 14), "Who can blame a person for doing what he could not help?" And (p. 15), "It being sensibly unjust, to punish any man for doing that which it was never in his power to avoid" [Discourse on the Five Points, Dis. I, ch. 1, no. 3]. And in p. 341 to confirm his opinion, he quotes one of the fathers, saying, "Why doth God command, if man hath not free will and power to obey?" And again in the same and the next page, "Who will not cry out, that it is folly to command him, that hath not liberty to do what is commanded; and that it is unjust to condemn him, that has it not in his power to do what is required?" [Ibid., Dis. IV, ch. 2, no. 4.] And in p. 373, he cites another saying, "A law is given to him that can turn to both parts; i.e. obey or transgress it: but no law can be against him who is bound by nature" [Ibid., Dis. IV, ch. 5, no. 2].

And yet the same Dr. Whitby asserts, that fallen man is not able to perform perfect obedience. In p. 165 he has these words, "The nature of Adam had power to continue innocent, and without sin; whereas it is certain, our nature never had so" [Ibid., Dis. II, ch. 6, no. 7]. But if we han't power to continue innocent and without sin, then sin is consistent with necessity, and we may be sinful in that which we have not power to avoid; and those things can't be true, which he asserts elsewhere, namely, "That if we be necessitated, neither sins of omission nor commission, would deserve that name" (p. 348) [Ibid., Dis. IV, ch. 3, no. 3]. If we have it not in our power to be innocent, then we have it not in our power to be blameless: and if so, we are under a necessity of being blameworthy. And how does this consist with what he so often asserts, that necessity is inconsistent with blame or praise? If we have it not in our power to perform perfect obedience to all the commands of God, then we are under a necessity of breaking some commands, in some degree; having no power to perform so much as is commanded. And if so, why does he cry out of the unreasonableness and folly of commanding beyond what men have power to do?

And Arminians in general are very inconsistent with themselves in what they say of the inability of fallen man in this respect. They strenuously maintain, that it would be unjust in God, to require anything of us beyond our present power and ability to perform; and also hold, that we are now unable to perform perfect obedience, and that Christ died to satisfy for the imperfections of our obedience, and has made way that our imperfect obedience might be accepted instead of perfect: wherein they seem insensibly to run themselves into the grossest inconsistence. For (as I have observed elsewhere), "They hold that God in mercy to mankind has abolished that rigorous constitution or law, that they were under originally; and instead of it, has introduced a more mild constitution, and put us under a new law, which requires no more than imperfect sincere obedience, in compliance with our poor infirm impotent circumstances since the fall." [This quote is from a sermon entitled, "Justification by Faith Alone," delivered 1734; published in 1738: *Sermons on Various Important Subjects*, ed., 7, 33.]

Now, how can these things be made consistent? I would ask what law these imperfections of our obedience are a breach of? If they are a breach of no law that we were ever under, then they are not sins. And if they be not sins, what need of Christ's dying to satisfy for them? But if they are sins, and the breach of some law, what law is it? They can't be a breach of their new law; for that requires no other than imperfect obedience, or obedience with imperfections: and therefore to have obedience attended with imperfections, is no breach of it; for 'tis as much as it requires. And they can't be a breach of their old law; for that, they say, is entirely abolished, and we never were under it. They say, it would not be just in God to require of us perfect obedience, because it would not be just to require more than we can perform, or to punish us for failing of it. And therefore, by their own scheme, the imperfections of our obedience don't deserve to be punished. What need therefore of Christ's dying, to satisfy for them? What need of his suffering, to satisfy for that which is no fault, and in its own nature deserves no suffering? What need of Christ's dying, to purchase, that our imperfect obedience should be accepted, when according to their scheme, it would be unjust in itself, that any other obedience than imperfect should be required? What need of Christ's dying to make way for God's accepting such an obedience, as it would be unjust in him not to accept? Is there any need of Christ's dying, to prevail with God not to do unrighteously? If it be said, that Christ died to satisfy that old law for us, that so we might not be under it, but that there might be room for our being under a more mild law; still I would inquire, what need of Christ's dying that we might not be under a law, which (by their principles) it would be in itself unjust that we should be under, whether Christ had died or no, because in our present state we are not able to keep it?

So the Arminians are inconsistent with themselves, not only in what they say of the need of Christ's satisfaction to atone for those imperfections which we cannot avoid, but also in what they say of the grace of God, granted to enable men to perform the sincere obedience of the new law. "I grant (says Dr. Stebbing, *A Treatise Concerning the Operations of the Holy Spirit, Being the Substance of the late Reverend and Learned Dr. William Clagett's Discourse upon That Subject, with Large Additions*, 1719) indeed, that by reason of original sin, we are utterly disabled for the performance of the condition, without new grace from God. But I say then, that he gives such grace to all of us, by which the performance of the condition is truly possible: and upon this ground he may, and doth most righteously require it." If Dr. Stebbing intends to speak properly, by "grace" he must mean, that assistance which is of grace, or of free favor and kindness. But yet in the same place he speaks of it as very "unreasonable, unjust and cruel," for God to require that, as the condition of pardon, that is become impossible by original sin. If it be so, what grace is there in giving assistance and ability to perform the condition of pardon? Or why is that called by the name of grace, that is an absolute debt, which God is bound to bestow, and which it would be unjust and cruel in him to withhold, seeing he requires that, as the condition of pardon, which we cannot perform without it?

SECTION 4.

COMMAND, AND OBLIGATION TO OBEDIENCE, CONSISTENT WITH MORAL INABILITY TO OBEY

It being so much insisted on by Arminian writers, that necessity is inconsistent with law or command, and particularly, that it is absurd to suppose God by his command should require that of men which they are unable to do; not allowing in this case for any difference that there is between natural and moral inability; I would therefore now particularly consider this matter.

And for the greater clearness, I would distinctly lay down the following things.

I. The will itself, and not only those actions which are the effects of the will, is the proper object of precept or command. That is, such or such a state or acts of men's wills, is in many cases, properly required of them by command; and not only those alterations in the state of their bodies or minds that are the consequences of volition. This is most manifest; for 'tis the soul only, that is properly and directly the subject of precepts or commands; that only being capable of receiving or perceiving commands. The motions or state of the body are matter of command, only as they are subject to the soul, and connected with its acts. But now the soul has no other faculty whereby it can, in the most direct and proper sense, consent, yield to, or comply with any command, but the faculty of the will; and 'tis by this faculty only, that the soul can directly disobey, or refuse compliance: for the very notions of "consenting," "yielding," 'accepting," "complying," "refusing," "rejecting," etc. are, according to the meaning of the terms, nothing but certain acts of the will. Obedience, in the primary nature of it, is the submitting and yielding of the will of one to the will of another. Disobedience is the not consenting, not complying of the will of the commanded to the manifested will of the commander. Other acts that are not the acts of the will, as certain motions of the body and alterations in the soul, are obedience or disobedience only indirectly, as they are connected with the state or actions of the will, according to an established law of nature. So that 'tis manifest, the will itself may be required: and the being of a good will is the most proper, direct and immediate subject of command; and if this can't be prescribed or required by command or precept, nothing can; for other things can be required no otherwise than as they depend upon, and are the fruits of a good will.

Corol. 1. If there be several acts of the will, or a series of acts, one following another, and one the effect of another, the first and determining act is properly the subject of command, and not only the consequent acts, which are dependent upon it. Yea, 'tis this more especially which is that which command or precept has a proper respect to; because 'tis this act that determines the whole affair: in this act the obedience or disobedience lies, in a peculiar manner; the consequent acts being all subject to it, and governed and determined by it. This determining governing act must be the proper subject of precept, or none.

Corol. 2. It also follows from what has been observed, that if there be any sort of act, or exertion of the soul, prior to all free acts of the will or acts of choice in the case, directing and determining what the acts of the will shall be; that act or exertion of the soul can't properly be subject to any command or precept, in any respect whatsoever, either directly or indirectly, immediately or remotely. Such acts can't be subject to commands directly, because they are no acts of the will; being by the supposition prior to all acts of the will, determining and giving rise to all its acts: they not being acts of the will, there can be in them no consent to, or compliance with any command. Neither can they be subject to command or precept indirectly or remotely; for they are not so much as the effects or consequences of the will, being prior to all its acts. So that if there be any obedience in that original act of the soul, determining all volitions, it is an act of obedience wherein the will has no concern at all; it preceding every act of will. And therefore, if the soul either obeys or disobeys in this act, it is wholly involuntarily; there is no willing obedience or rebellion, no compliance or opposition of the will in the affair: and what sort of obedience or rebellion is this!

And thus the Arminian notion of the freedom of the will consisting in the soul's determining its own acts of will, instead of being essential to moral agency, and to men's being the subjects of moral government, is utterly inconsistent with it. For if the soul determines all its acts of will, it is therein subject to no command or moral government, as has been now observed; because its original determining act is no act of will or choice, it being prior, by the supposition, to every act of will. And the soul can't be the subject of command in the act of the will itself, which depends on the foregoing determining act, and is determined by it; inasmuch as this is necessary, being the necessary consequence and effect of that prior determining act, which is not voluntary. Nor can the man be the subject of command or government in his external actions; because these are all necessary, being the necessary effects of the acts of the will themselves. So that mankind, according to this scheme, are subjects of command or moral government in nothing at all; and all their moral agency is entirely excluded, and no room left for virtue or vice in the world.

So that 'tis the Arminian scheme, and not the scheme of the Calvinists, that is utterly inconsistent with moral government, and with all use of laws, precepts, prohibitions, promises, or threatenings. . Neither is there any way whatsoever to make their principles consist with these things. For if it be said, that there is no prior determining act of the soul, preceding the acts of the will, but that volitions are events that come to pass by pure accident, without any determining cause, this is most palpably inconsistent with all use of laws and precepts; for nothing is more plain than that laws can be of no use to direct and regulate perfect accident; which by the supposition of its being pure accident, is in no case regulated by anything preceding; but happens this way or that perfectly by chance, without any cause or rule. The perfect uselessness of laws and precepts also follows from the Arminian notion of indifference, as essential to that liberty which is requisite to virtue or vice. For the end of laws is to bind to one side; and the end of commands is to turn the will one way: and therefore they are of no use unless they turn or bias the will that way. But if liberty consists in indifference, then their biasing the will one way only, destroys liberty; as it puts the will out of equilibrium. So that the will, having a bias, through the influence of binding law, laid upon it, is not wholly left to itself, to determine itself which way it will, without influence from without.

II. Having shown that the will itself, especially in those acts which are original, leading and determining in any case, is the proper subject of precept and command, and not only those alterations in the body, etc. which are the effects of the will; I now proceed in the second place, to observe that the very opposition or defect of the will itself, in that act which is its original and determining act in the case, I say the will's opposition in this act to a thing proposed or commanded, or its failing of compliance, implies a moral inability to that thing: or in other words, whenever a command requires a certain state or act of the will, and the person commanded, notwithstanding the command and the circumstances under which it is exhibited, still finds his will opposite or wanting, in that, belonging to its state or acts, which is original and determining in the affair, that man is morally unable to obey that command.

This is manifest from what was observed in the first part, concerning the nature of moral inability, as distinguished from natural: where it was observed, that a man may then be said to be morally unable to do a thing, when he is under the influence or prevalence of a contrary inclination, or has a want of inclination, under such circumstances and views. 'Tis also evident from what has been before proved, that the will is always, and in every individual act, necessarily determined by the strongest motive; and so is always unable to go against the motive, which all things considered, has now the greatest strength and advantage to move the will. But not further to insist on these things, the truth of the position now laid down, viz. that when the will is opposite to, or failing of a compliance with a thing in its original determining inclination or act, it is not able to comply, appears by the consideration of these two things.

1. The will in the time of that diverse or opposite leading act or inclination, and when actually under the influence of it, is not able to exert itself to the contrary, to make an alteration, in order to a compliance. The inclination is unable to change itself; and that for this plain reason, that it is unable to incline to change itself. Present choice can't at present choose to be otherwise: for that would be at present to choose something diverse from what is at present chosen. If the will, all things now considered, inclines or chooses to go that way, then it can't choose, all things now considered, to go the other way, and so can't choose to be made to go the other way. To suppose that the mind is now sincerely inclined to change itself to a different inclination, is to suppose the mind is now truly inclined otherwise than it is now inclined. The will may oppose some future remote act that it is exposed to, but not its own present act.

2. As it is impossible that the will should comply with the thing commanded with respect to its leading act, by any act of its own, in the time of that diverse or opposite leading and original act, or after it is actually come under the influence of that determining choice or inclination; so 'tis impossible it should be determined to a compliance by any foregoing act; for by the very supposition, there is no foregoing act; the opposite or noncomplying act being that act which is original and determining in the case. Therefore it must be so, that if this first determining act be found noncomplying, on the proposal of the command, the mind is morally unable to obey. For to suppose it to be able to obey, is to suppose it to be able to determine and cause its first determining act to be otherwise, and that it has power better to govern and regulate its first governing and regulating act, which is absurd; for it is to suppose a prior act of the will, determining its first determining act; that is, an act prior to the first, and leading and governing the original and governing act of all; which is a contradiction.

Here if it should be said, that although the mind has not any ability to will contrary to what it does will, in the original and leading act of the will, because there is supposed to be no prior act to determine and order it otherwise, and the will can't immediately change itself, because it can't at present incline to a change; yet the mind has an ability for the present to forbear to proceed to action, and take time for deliberation; which may be an occasion of the change of the inclination—

I answer, (1) In this objection that seems to be forgotten which was observed before, viz. that the determining to take the matter into consideration, is itself an act of the will: and if this be all the act wherein the mind exercises ability and freedom, then this, by the supposition, must be all that can be commanded or required by precept. And if this act be the commanded act, then all that has been observed concerning the commanded act of the will remains true, that the very want of it is a moral inability to exert it, etc. (2) We are speaking concerning the first and leading act of the will in the case, or about the affair; and if a determining to deliberate, or on the contrary, to proceed immediately without deliberating, be the first and leading act; or whether it be or no, if there be another act before it, which determines that; or whatever be the original and leading act; still the foregoing proof stands good, that the non-compliance of the leading act implies moral inability to comply.

If it should be objected, that these things make all moral inability equal, and suppose men morally unable to will otherwise than they actually do will, in all cases, and equally so, in every instance—

In answer to this objection, I desire two things may be observed.

First, that if by being equally unable, be meant as really unable; then so far as the inability is merely moral, 'tis true, the will, in every instance, acts by moral necessity, and is morally unable to act otherwise, as truly and properly in one case as another; as, I humbly conceive, has been perfectly and abundantly demonstrated by what has been said in the preceding part of this essay. But yet, in some respect, the inability may be said to be greater in some instances than others: though the man may be truly unable (if moral inability can truly be called inability), yet he may be further from being able to do some things than others. As it is in things which men are naturally unable to do. A person whose strength is no more than sufficient to lift the weight of one hundred pounds, is as truly and really unable to lift one hundred and one pounds, as ten thousand pounds; but yet he is further from being able to lift the latter weight than the former; and so, according to common use of speech, has a greater inability for it. So it is in moral inability. A man is truly morally unable to choose contrary to a present inclination, which in the least degree prevails; or contrary to that motive, which, all things considered, has strength and advantage now to move the will, in the least degree, superior to all other motives in view: but yet he is further from ability to resist a very strong habit, and a violent and deeply rooted inclination, or a motive vastly exceeding all others in strength. And again, the inability may in some respects be called greater, in some instances than others, as it may be more general and extensive to all acts of that kind. So men may be said to be unable in a different sense, and to be further from moral ability, who have that moral inability which is general and habitual, than they who have only that inability which is occasional and particular. (See this distinction of moral inability explained in Pt. I, Sec. 4.) Thus in cases of natural inability; he that is born blind may be said to be unable to see, in a different manner, and is in some respects further from being able to see, than he whose sight is hindered by a transient cloud or mist.

And besides, that which was observed in the first part of this discourse concerning the inability which attends a strong and settled habit, should be here remembered; viz. that fixed habit is attended with this peculiar moral inability, by which it is distinguished from occasional volition, namely, that endeavors to avoid future volitions of that kind, which are agreeable to such a habit, much more frequently and commonly prove vain and insufficient. For though it is impossible there should be any true sincere desires and endeavors against a present volition or choice, yet there may be against volitions of that kind, when viewed at a distance. A person may desire and use means to prevent future exercises of a certain inclination; and in order to it, may wish the habit might be removed; but his desires and endeavors may be ineffectual. The man may be said in some sense to be unable; yea, even as the word "unable" is a relative term, and has relation to ineffectual endeavors; yet not with regard to present, but remote endeavors.

Secondly, it must be borne in mind, according to what was observed before, that indeed no inability whatsoever which is merely moral, is properly called by the name of "inability"; and that in the strictest propriety of speech, a man may be said to have a thing in his power, if he has it at his election; and he can't be said to be unable to do a thing, when he can if he now pleases, or whenever he has a proper, direct and immediate desire for it. As to those desires and endeavors that may be against the exercises of a strong habit, with regard to which men may be said to be unable to avoid those exercises, they are remote desires and endeavors in two respects. First, as to time; they are never against present volitions, but only against volitions of such a kind, when viewed at a distance. Secondly, as to their nature; these opposite desires are not directly and properly against the habit and inclination itself, or the volitions in which it is exercised; for these, in themselves considered, are agreeable; but against something else, that attends them, or is their consequence; the opposition of the mind is leveled entirely against this; the inclination or volitions themselves are not at all opposed directly, and for their own sake; but only indirectly, and remotely on the account of something alien and foreign.

III. Though the opposition of the will itself, or the very want of will to a thing commanded, implies a moral inability to that thing; yet, if it be as has been already shown, that the being of a good state or act of will, is a thing most properly required by command; then, in some cases such a state or act of will may properly be required, which at present is not, and which may also be wanting after it is commanded. And therefore those things may properly be commanded, which men have a moral inability for.

Such a state or act of the will, may be required by command, as does not already exist. For if that volition only may be commanded to be which already is, there could be no use of precept; commands in all cases would be perfectly vain and impertinent. And not only may such a will be required as is wanting before the command is given, but also such as may possibly be wanting afterwards; such as the exhibition of the command may not be effectual to produce or excite. Otherwise, no such thing as disobedience to a proper and rightful command is possible in any case; and there is no case supposable or possible, wherein there can be an inexcusable or faulty disobedience. Which Arminians cannot affirm, consistently with their principles: for this makes obedience to just and proper commands always necessary, and disobedience impossible. And so the Arminian would overthrow himself, yielding the very point we are upon, which he so strenuously denies, viz. that law and command are consistent with necessity.

If merely that inability will excuse disobedience, which is implied in the opposition or defect of inclination, remaining after the command is exhibited, then wickedness always carries that in it which excuses it. 'Tis evermore so, that by how much the more wickedness there is in a man's heart, by so much is his inclination to evil the stronger, and by so much the more therefore has he of moral inability to the good required. His moral inability, consisting in the strength of his evil inclination, is the very thing wherein his wickedness consists; and yet according to Arminian principles, it must be a thing inconsistent with wickedness; and by how much the more he has of it, by so much is he the further from wickedness.

Therefore, on the whole, it is manifest, that moral inability alone (which consists in disinclination) never renders anything improperly the subject matter of precept or command, and never can excuse any person in disobedience, or want of conformity to a command.

Natural inability, arising from the want of natural capacity, or external hindrance (which alone is properly called inability) without doubt wholly excuses, or makes a thing improperly the matter of command. If men are excused from doing or acting any good thing, supposed to be commanded, it must be through some defect or obstacle that is not in the will itself, but extrinsic to it; either in the capacity of understanding, or body, or outward circumstances.

Here two or three things may be observed,

1. As to spiritual duties or acts, or any good thing in the state of immanent acts of the will itself, or of the affections (which are only certain modes of the exercise of the will) if persons are justly excused, it must be through want of capacity in the natural faculty of understanding. Thus the same spiritual duties, or holy affections and exercises of heart, can't be required of men, as may be of angels; the capacity of understanding being so much inferior. So men can't be required to love those amiable persons whom they have had no opportunity to see, or hear of, or come to the knowledge of, in any way agreeable to the natural state and capacity of the human understanding. But the insufficiency of motives will not excuse; unless their being insufficient arises not from the moral state of the will or inclination itself, but from the state of the natural understanding. The great kindness and generosity of another may be a motive insufficient to excite gratitude in the person that receives the kindness, through his vile and ungrateful temper: in this case, the insufficiency of the motive arises from the state of the will or inclination of heart, and don't at all excuse. But if this generosity is not sufficient to excite gratitude, being unknown, there being no means of information adequate to the state and measure of the person's faculties, this insufficiency is attended with a natural inability, which entirely excuses.

2. As to such motions of body, or exercises and alterations of mind, which don't consist in the immanent acts or state of the will itself, but are supposed to be required as effects of the will; I say, in such supposed effects of the will, in cases wherein there is no want of a capacity of understanding; that inability, and that only excuses, which consists in want of connection between them and the will. If the will fully complies, and the proposed effect don't prove, according to the laws of nature, to be connected with his volition, the man is perfectly excused; he has a natural inability to the thing required. For the will itself, as has been observed, is all that can be directly and immediately required by command; and other things only indirectly, as connected with the will. If therefore there be a full compliance of will, the person has done his duty; and if other things don't prove to be connected with his volition, that is not owing to him.

3. Both these kinds of natural inability that have been mentioned, and so all inability that excuses, may be resolved into one thing; namely, want of natural capacity or strength; either capacity of understanding, or external strength. For when there are external defects and obstacles, they would be no obstacles, were it not for the imperfection and limitations of understanding and strength.

Corol. If things for which men have a moral inability, may properly be the matter of precept or command, then they may also of invitation and counsel. Commands, and invitations come very much to the same thing; the difference is only circumstantial: commands are as much a manifestation of the will of him that speaks, as invitations, and as much testimonies of expectation of compliance. The difference between them lies in nothing that touches the affair in hand. The main difference between command and invitation consists in the enforcement of the will of him who commands or invites. In the latter it is his kindness, the goodness which his will arises from: in the former it is his authority. But whatever be the ground of the will of him that speaks, or the enforcement of what he says, yet seeing neither his will nor expectation is any more testified in the one case than the other; therefore a person's being known to be morally unable to do the thing to which he is directed by invitation, is no more an evidence of insincerity in him that directs, in manifesting either a will, or expectation which he has not, than his being known to be morally unable to do what he is directed to by command. So that all this grand objection of Arminians against the inability of fallen men to exert faith in Christ, or to perform other spiritual gospel duties, from the sincerity of God's counsels and invitations, must be without force.

SECTION 5.

THAT SINCERITY OF DESIRES AND ENDEAVORS, WHICH IS SUPPOSED TO EXCUSE IN THE NONPERFORMANCE OF THINGS IN THEMSELVES GOOD, PARTICULARLY CONSIDERED

'Tis what insisted on by many, that some men, though they are not able to perform spiritual duties, such as repentance of sin, love to God, a cordial acceptance of Christ as exhibited and offered in the gospel, etc. yet they may sincerely desire and endeavor these things; and therefore must be excused; it being unreasonable to blame 'em for the omission of those things which they sincerely desire and endeavor to do, but can't do.

Concerning this matter, the following things may be observed.

1. What is here supposed, is a great mistake, and gross absurdity; even that men may sincerely choose and desire those spiritual duties of love, acceptance, choice, rejection, etc. consisting in the exercise of the will itself, or in the disposition and inclination of the heart; and yet not be able to perform or exert them. This is absurd, because 'tis absurd to suppose that a man should directly, properly and sincerely incline to have an inclination, which at the same time is contrary to his inclination: for that is to suppose him not to be inclined to that which he is inclined to. If a man, in the state and acts of his will and inclination, does properly and directly fall in with those duties, he therein performs 'em: for the duties themselves consist in that very thing; they consist in the state and acts of the will being so formed and directed. If the soul properly and sincerely falls in with a certain proposed act of will or choice, the soul therein makes that choice its own. Even as when a moving body falls in with a proposed direction of its motion, that is the same thing as to move in that direction.

2. That which is called a "desire" and "willingness" for those inward duties, in such as don't perform them, has respect to these duties only indirectly and remotely, and is improperly represented as a willingness for them; not only because (as was observed before) it respects those good volitions only in a distant view, and with respect to future time; but also because evermore, not these things themselves, but something else, that is alien and foreign, is the object that terminates these volitions and desires.

A drunkard, who continues in his drunkenness, being under the power of a love, and violent appetite to strong drink, and without any love to virtue; but being also extremely covetous and close, and very much exercised and grieved at the diminution of his estate, and prospect of poverty, may in a sort "desire" the virtue of temperance: and though his present will is to gratify his extravagant appetite, yet he may wish he had a heart to forbear future acts of intemperance, and forsake his excesses, through an unwillingness to part with his money: but still he goes on with his drunkenness; his wishes and endeavors are insufficient and ineffectual: such a man has no proper, direct, sincere willingness to forsake this vice, and the vicious deeds which belong to it: for he acts voluntarily in continuing to drink to excess: his desire is very improperly called a willingness to be temperate; it is no true desire of that virtue; for it is not that virtue that terminates his wishes; nor have they any direct respect at all to it. 'Tis only the saving his money, and avoiding poverty, that terminates, and exhausts the whole strength of his desire. The virtue of temperance is regarded only very indirectly and improperly, even as a necessary means of gratifying the vice of covetousness.

So, a man of an exceeding corrupt and wicked heart, who has no love to God and Jesus Christ, but on the contrary, being very profanely and carnally inclined, has the greatest distaste of the things of religion, and enmity against 'em; yet being of a family, that from one generation to another, have most of 'em died in youth of an hereditary consumption; and so having little hope of living long; and having been instructed in the necessity of a supreme love to Christ, and gratitude for his death and sufferings, in order to his salvation from eternal misery; if under these circumstances he should, through fear of eternal torments, wish he had such a disposition: but his profane and carnal heart remaining, he continues still in his habitual distaste of, and enmity to God and religion, and wholly without any exercise of that love and gratitude (as doubtless the very devils themselves, notwithstanding all the devilishness of their temper, would wish for a holy heart, if by that means they could get out of hell): in this case, there is no sincere willingness to love Christ and choose him as his chief good: these holy dispositions and exercises are not at all the direct object of the will: they truly share no part of the inclination or desire of the soul; but all is terminated on deliverance from torment: and these graces and pious volitions, notwithstanding this forced consent, are looked upon [as] undesirable; as when a sick man desires a dose he greatly abhors, to save his life.—From these things it appears:

3. That this indirect willingness which has been spoken of, is not that exercise of the will which the command requires; but is entirely a different one; being a volition of a different nature, and terminated altogether on different objects; wholly falling short of that virtue of will, which the command has respect to.

4. This other volition, which has only some indirect concern with the duty required, can't excuse for the want of that good will itself, which is commanded; being not the thing which answers and fulfills the command, and being wholly destitute of the virtue which the command seeks.

Further to illustrate this matter: If a child has a most excellent father, that has ever treated him with fatherly kindness and tenderness, and has every way in the highest degree merited his love and dutiful regard, being withal very wealthy; but the son is of so vile a disposition, that he inveterately hates his father; and yet, apprehending that his hatred of him is like to prove his ruin, by bringing him finally to poverty and abject circumstances, through his father's disinheriting him, or otherwise; which is exceeding cross to his avarice and ambition; he therefore wishes it were otherwise: but yet remaining under the invincible power of his vile and malignant disposition, he continues still in his settled hatred of his father. Now if such a son's indirect willingness to have love and honor towards his father, at all acquits or excuses before God, for his failing of actually exercising these dispositions towards him which God requires, it must be on one of these two accounts. (1) Either that it answers and fulfills the command. But this it does not, by the supposition; because the thing commanded is love and honor to his worthy parent. If the command be proper and just, as is supposed, then it obliges to the thing commanded; and so nothing else but that can answer the obligation. Or (2) it must be at least because there is that virtue or goodness in his indirect willingness, that is equivalent to the virtue required; and so balances or countervails it, and makes up for the want of it. But that also is contrary to the supposition. The willingness the son has merely from a regard to money and honor, has no goodness in it, to countervail the want of the pious filial respect required.

Sincerity and reality, in that indirect willingness which has been spoken of, don't make it the better. That which is real and hearty is often called sincere; whether it be in virtue or vice. Some persons are sincerely bad; others are sincerely good; and others may be sincere and hearty in things which are in their own nature indifferent; as a man may be sincerely desirous of eating when he is hungry. But a being sincere, hearty and in good earnest, is no virtue, unless it be in a thing that is virtuous. A man may be sincere and hearty in joining a crew of pirates, or a gang of robbers. When the devils cried out, and besought Christ not to torment them, it was no mere pretence; they were very hearty in their desires not to be tormented: but this did not make their will or desires virtuous. And if men have sincere desires, which are in their kind and nature no better, it can be no excuse for the want of any required virtue.

And as a man's being sincere in such an indirect desire or willingness to do his duty, as has been mentioned, can't excuse for the want of performance; so it is with endeavors arising from such a willingness. The endeavors can have no more goodness in 'em, than the will which they are the effect and expression of. And therefore, however sincere and real, and however great a person's endeavors are; yea, though they should be to the utmost of his ability; unless the will which they proceed from be truly good and virtuous, they can be of no avail, influence or weight to any purpose whatsoever, in a moral sense or respect. That which is not truly virtuous in God's sight, is looked upon by him as good for nothing: and so can be of no value, weight or influence in his account, to recommend, satisfy, excuse or make up for any moral defect. For nothing can counterbalance evil, but good. If evil be in one scale, and we put a great deal into the other, sincere and earnest desires, and many and great endeavors; yet if there be no real goodness in all, there is no weight in it; and so it does nothing towards balancing the real weight which is in the opposite scale. 'Tis only like the substracting a thousand noughts from before a real number, which leaves the sum just as it was.

Indeed such endeavors may have a negatively good influence. Those things which have no positive virtue, have no positive moral influence; yet they may be an occasion of persons avoiding some positive evils. As if a man were in the water with a neighbor that he had ill will to, who could not swim, holding him by his hand; which neighbor was much in debt to him; and should be tempted to let him sink and drown; but should refuse to comply with the temptation; not from love to his neighbor, but from the love of money, and because by his drowning he should lose his debt; that which he does in preserving his neighbor from drowning, is nothing good in the sight of God: yet hereby he avoids the greater guilt that would have been contracted, if he had designedly let his neighbor sink and perish. But when Arminians in their disputes with Calvinists insist so much on sincere desires and endeavors, as what must excuse men, must be accepted of God, etc. 'Tis manifest they have respect to some positive moral weight or influence of those desires and endeavors. Accepting, justifying, or excusing on the account of sincere honest endeavors (as they are called) and men's doing what they can, etc. has relation to some moral value, something that is accepted as good, and as such, countervailing some defect.

But there is a great and unknown deceit, arising from the ambiguity of the phrase, "sincere endeavors." Indeed there is a vast indistinctness and unfixedness in most, or at least very many of the terms used to express things pertaining to moral and spiritual matters. Whence arise innumerable mistakes, strong prejudices, inextricable confusion, and endless controversy.

The word "sincere" is most commonly used to signify something that is good: men are habituated to understand by it the same as "honest" and "upright"; which terms excite an idea of something good in the strictest and highest sense; good in the sight of him who sees not only the outward appearance, but the heart. And therefore men think that if a person be sincere, he will certainly be accepted. If it be said that anyone is sincere in his endeavors, this suggests to men's minds as much, as that his heart and will is good, that there is no defect of duty, as to virtuous inclination; he honestly and uprightly desires and endeavors to do as he is required; and this leads 'em to suppose that it would be very hard and unreasonable to punish him, only because he is unsuccessful in his endeavors, the thing endeavored being beyond his power.—Whereas it ought to be observed, that the word "sincere" has these different significations:

1. "Sincerity," as the word is sometimes used, signifies no more than reality of will and endeavor, with respect to anything that is professed or pretended; without any consideration of the nature of the principle or aim, whence this real will and true endeavor arises. If a man has some real desire to obtain a thing, either direct or indirect, or does really endeavor after a thing, he is said sincerely to desire or endeavor it; without any consideration of the goodness or virtuousness of the principle he acts from, or any excellency or worthiness of the end he acts for. Thus a man that is kind to his neighbor's wife, who is sick and languishing, and very helpful in her case, makes a shew of desiring and endeavoring her restoration to health and vigor; and not only makes such a shew, but there is a reality in his pretense, he does heartily and earnestly desire to have her health restored, and uses his true and utmost endeavors for it; he is said sincerely to desire and endeavor it, because he does so truly or really; though perhaps the principle he acts from, is no other than a vile and scandalous passion; having lived in adultery with her, he earnestly desires to have her health and vigor restored, that he may return to his criminal pleasures with her. Or,

2. By "sincerity" is meant, not merely a reality of will and endeavor of some sort or other, and from some consideration or other, but a virtuous sincerity. That is, that in the performance of those particular acts that are the matter of virtue or duty, there be not only the matter, but the form and essence of virtue, consisting in the aim that governs the act, and the principle exercised in it. There is not only the reality of the act, that is as it were the body of the duty; but also the soul, which should properly belong to such a body. In this sense, a man is said to be sincere, when he acts with a pure intention; not from sinister views, or by-ends: he not only in reality desires and seeks the thing to be done, or qualification to be obtained, for some end or other; but he wills the thing directly and properly, as neither forced nor bribed; the virtue of the thing is properly the object of the will.

In the former sense, a man is said to be sincere, in opposition to a mere pretense, and shew of the particular thing to be done or exhibited, without any real desire or endeavor at all. In the latter sense, a man is said to be sincere, in opposition to that shew of virtue there is in merely doing the matter of duty, without the reality of the virtue itself in the soul, and the essence of it, which there is a shew of. A man may be sincere in the former sense, and yet in the latter be in the sight of God, who searches the heart, a vile hypocrite.

In the latter kind of sincerity, only, is there anything truly valuable or acceptable in the sight of God. And this is the thing which in Scripture is called sincerity, uprightness, integrity, truth in the inward parts, and a being of a perfect heart. And if there be such a sincerity, and such a degree of it as there ought to be, and there be anything further that the man is not able to perform, or which don't prove to be connected with his sincere desires and endeavors, the man is wholly excused and acquitted in the sight of God; his will shall surely be accepted for his deed: and such a sincere will and endeavor is all that in strictness is required of him, by any command of God. But as to the other kind of sincerity of desires and endeavors, it having no virtue in it (as was observed before), can be of no avail before God, in any case, to recommend, satisfy, or excuse, and has no positive moral weight or influence whatsoever.

Corol. 1. Hence it may be inferred, that nothing in the reason and nature of things appears, from the consideration of any moral weight of that former kind of sincerity, which has been spoken of, at all obliging us to believe, or leading us to suppose, that God has made any positive promises of salvation, or grace, or any saving assistance, or any spiritual benefit whatsoever, to any desires, prayers, endeavors, striving, or obedience of those, who hitherto have no true virtue or holiness in their hearts; though we should suppose all the sincerity, and the utmost degree of endeavor, that is possible to be in a person without holiness.

Some object against God's requiring, as the condition of salvation, those holy exercises, which are the result of a supernatural renovation; such as a supreme respect to Christ, love to God, loving holiness for its own sake, etc. that these inward dispositions and exercises are above men's power, as they are by nature; and therefore that we may conclude, that when men are brought to be sincere in their endeavors, and do as well as they can, they are accepted; and that this must be all that God requires in order to men's being received as the objects of his favor, and must be what God has appointed as the condition of salvation. Concerning which I would observe, that in such a manner of speaking Of men's being accepted, because they are sincere, and do as well as they can, there is evidently a supposition of some virtue, some degree of that which is truly good; though it don't go so far as were to be wished. For if men "do what they can," unless their so doing be from some good principle, disposition, or exercise of heart, some virtuous inclination or act of the will; their so doing what they can, is in some respects not a whit better than if they did nothing at all. In such a case, there is no more positive moral goodness in a man's doing what he can, than in a windmill's doing what it can; because the action does no more proceed from virtue; and there is nothing in such sincerity of endeavor, or doing what we can, that should render it any more a proper or fit recommendation to positive favor and acceptance, or the condition of any reward or actual benefit, than doing nothing; for both the one and the other are alike nothing, as to any true moral weight or value.

Corol. 2. Hence also it follows, there is nothing that appears in the reason and nature of things, which can justly lead us to determine, that God will certainly give the necessary means of salvation, or some way or other bestow true holiness and eternal life on those heathen, who are sincere (in the sense above explained) in their endeavors to find out the will of the deity, and to please him, according to their light, that they may escape his future displeasure and wrath, and obtain happiness in their future state, through his favor.

SECTION 6.

LIBERTY OF INDIFFERENCE, NOT ONLY NOT NECESSARY TO VIRTUE, BUT UTTERLY INCONSISTENT WITH IT; AND ALL, EITHER VIRTUOUS OR VICIOUS HABITS OR INCLINATIONS, INCONSISTENT WITH ARMINIAN NOTIONS OF LIBERTY AND MORAL AGENCY

To suppose such a freedom of will, as Arminians talk of, to be requisite to virtue and vice, is many ways contrary to common sense.

If indifference belongs to liberty of will, as Arminians suppose, and it be essential to a virtuous action that it be performed in a state of liberty, as they also suppose; it will follow, that it is essential to a virtuous action that it be performed in a state of indifference: and if it be performed in a state of indifference, then doubtless it must be performed in the time of indifference. And so it will follow, that in order to the virtuousness of an act, the heart must be indifferent in the time of the performance of that act, and the more indifferent and cold the heart is with relation to the act which is performed, so much the better; because the act is performed with so much the greater liberty. But is this agreeable to the light of nature? Is it agreeable to the notions which mankind, in all ages, have of virtue, that it lies in that which is contrary to indifference, even in the tendency and inclination of the heart to virtuous action; and that the stronger the inclination, and so the further from indifference, the more virtuous the heart, and so much the more praiseworthy the act which proceeds from it?

If we should suppose (contrary to what has been before demonstrated) that there may be an act of will in a state of indifference; for instance, this act, viz. the will's determining to put itself out of a state of indifference, and give itself a preponderation one way, then it would follow, on Arminian principles, that this act or determination of the will is that alone wherein virtue consists, because this only is performed while the mind remains in a state of indifference, and so in a state of liberty: for when once the mind is put out of its equilibrium, it is no longer in such a state; and therefore all the acts which follow afterwards, proceeding from bias, can have the nature neither of virtue nor vice. Or if the thing which the will can do, while yet in a state of indifference, and so of liberty, be only to suspend acting, and determine to take the matter into consideration, then this determination is that alone wherein virtue consists, and not proceeding to action after the scale is turned by consideration. So that it will follow from these principles, all that is done after the mind, by any means, is once out of its equilibrium and already possessed by an inclination, and arising from that inclination, has nothing of the nature of virtue or vice, and is worthy of neither blame nor praise. But how plainly contrary is this to the universal sense of mankind, and to the notion they have of sincerely virtuous actions? Which is, that they are actions which proceed from a heart well disposed and inclined; and the stronger, and the more fixed and determined the good disposition of the heart, the greater the sincerity of virtue, and so the more of the truth and reality of it. But if there be any acts which are done in a state of equilibrium, or spring immediately from perfect indifference and coldness of heart, they cannot arise from any good principle or disposition in the heart; and consequently, according to common sense, have no sincere goodness in 'em, having no virtue of heart in 'em. To have a virtuous heart, is to have a heart that favors virtue, and is friendly to it, and not one perfectly cold and indifferent about it.

And besides the actions that are done in a state of indifference, or that arise immediately out of such a state, can't be virtuous, because, by the supposition, they are not determined by any preceding choice. For if there be preceding choice, then choice intervenes between the act and the state of indifference; which is contrary to the supposition of the acts arising immediately out of indifference. But those acts which are not determined by preceding choice, can't be virtuous or vicious by Arminian principles, because they are not determined by the will. So that neither one way, nor the other, can any actions be virtuous or vicious according to Arminian principles. If the action be determined by a preceding act of choice it can't be virtuous; because the action is not done in a state of indifference, nor does immediately arise from such a state; and so is not done in a state of liberty. If the action be not determined by a preceding act of choice, then it can't be virtuous; because then the will is not self-determined in it. So that 'tis made certain, that neither virtue nor vice can ever find any place in the universe.

Moreover, that it is necessary to a virtuous action that it be performed in a state of indifference, under a notion of that's being a state of liberty, is contrary to common sense; as 'tis a dictate of common sense, that indifference itself, in many cases, is vicious, and so to a high degree. As if when I see my neighbor or near friend, and one who has in the highest degree merited of me, in extreme distress, and ready to perish, I find an indifference in my heart with respect to anything proposed to be done, which I can easily do, for his relief. So if it should be proposed to me, to blaspheme God, or kill my father, or to do numberless other things which might be mentioned; the being indifferent, for a moment, would be highly vicious and vile.

And it may be further observed, that to suppose this liberty of indifference is essential to virtue and vice, destroys the great difference of degrees of the guilt of different crimes, and takes away the heinousness of the most flagitious horrid iniquities; such as adultery, bestiality, murder, perjury, blasphemy, etc. For according to these principles, there is no harm at all in having the mind in a state of perfect indifference with respect to these crimes; nay, 'tis absolutely necessary in order to any virtue in avoiding them, or vice in doing them. But for the mind to be in a state of indifference with respect to 'em, is to be next door to doing them: it is then infinitely near to choosing, and so committing the fact: for equilibrium is the next step to a degree of preponderation; and one, even the least degree of preponderation (all things considered) is choice. And not only so, but for the will to be in a state of perfect equilibrium with respect to such crimes, is for the mind to be in such a state, as to be full as likely to choose 'em as to refuse 'em, to do 'em as to omit 'em. And if our minds must be in such a state wherein it is as near to choosing as refusing, and wherein it must of necessity, according to the nature of things, be as likely to commit 'em, as to refrain from 'em; where is the exceeding heinousness of choosing and committing them? If there be no harm in often being in such a state, wherein the probability of doing and forbearing are exactly equal, there being an equilibrium, and no more tendency to one than the other; then according to the nature and laws of such a contingence, it may be expected, as an inevitable consequence of such a disposition of things, that we should choose 'em as often as reject 'em: that it should generally so fall out is necessary, as equality in the effect is the natural consequence of the equal tendency of the cause, or of the antecedent state of things from which the effect arises: why then should we be so exceedingly to blame, if it does so fall out?

'Tis many ways apparent, that the Arminian scheme of liberty is utterly inconsistent with the being of any such things as either virtuous or vicious habits or dispositions. If liberty of indifference be essential to moral agency, then there can be no virtue in any habitual inclinations of the heart; which are contrary to indifference, and imply in their nature the very destruction and exclusion of it. They suppose nothing can be virtuous, in which no liberty is exercised; but how absurd is it to talk of exercising indifference under bias and preponderation!

And if self-determining power in the will be necessary to moral agency, praise, blame, etc. then nothing done by the will can be any further praise or blameworthy, than so far as the will is moved, swayed and determined by itself, and the scales turned by the sovereign power the will has over itself. And therefore the will must not be put out of its balance already, the preponderation must not be determined and effected beforehand; and so the self-determining act anticipated. Thus it appears another way, that habitual bias is inconsistent with that liberty which Arminians suppose to be necessary to virtue or vice; and so it follows, that habitual bias itself cannot be either virtuous or vicious.

The same thing follows from their doctrine concerning the inconsistence of necessity with liberty, praise, dispraise, etc. None will deny, that bias and inclination may be so strong as to be invincible, and leave no possibility of the will's determining contrary to it; and so be attended with necessity. This Dr. Whitby allows concerning the will of God, angels and glorified saints, with respect to good; and the will of devils with respect to evil. Therefore if necessity be inconsistent with liberty; then when fixed inclination is to such a degree of strength, it utterly excludes all virtue, vice, praise or blame. And if so, then the nearer habits are to this strength, the more do they impede liberty, and so diminish praise and blame. If very strong habits destroy liberty, the lesser ones proportionably hinder it, according to their degree of strength. And therefore it will follow, that then is the act most virtuous or vicious, when performed without any inclination or habitual bias at all; because it is then performed with most liberty.

Every prepossessing fixed bias on the mind brings a degree of moral inability for the contrary; because so far as the mind is biased and prepossessed, so much hindrance is there of the contrary. And therefore if moral inability be inconsistent with moral agency, or the nature of virtue and vice, then so far as there is any such thing as evil disposition of heart, or habitual depravity of inclination; whether covetousness, pride, malice, cruelty, or whatever else; so much the more excusable persons are; so much the less have their evil acts of this kind, the nature of vice. And on the contrary, whatever excellent dispositions and inclinations they have, so much are they the less virtuous.

'Tis evident, that no habitual disposition of heart, whether it be to a greater or lesser degree, can be in any degree virtuous or vicious; or the actions which proceed from them at all praise or blameworthy. Because, though we should suppose the habit not to be of such strength as wholly to take away all moral ability and self-determining power; or hinder but that, although the act be partly from bias, yet it may be in part from self-determination; yet in this case, all that is from antecedent bias must be set aside, as of no consideration; and in estimating the degree of virtue or vice, no more must be considered than what arises from self-determining power, without any influence of that bias, because liberty is exercised in no more: so that all that is the exercise of habitual inclination, is thrown away, as not belonging to the morality of the action. By which it appears, that no exercise of these habits, let 'em be stronger or weaker, can ever have anything of the nature of either virtue or vice.

Here if anyone should say, that notwithstanding all these things, there may be the nature of virtue and vice in habits of the mind; because these habits may be the effects of those acts wherein the mind exercised liberty; that however the forementioned reasons will prove that no habits which are natural, or that any are born or [created with], can be either virtuous or vicious; yet they will not prove this of habits, which have been acquired and established by repeated free acts—

To such an objector I would say, that this evasion will not at all help the matter. For if freedom of will be essential to the very nature of virtue and vice, then there is no virtue or vice but only in that very thing, wherein this liberty is exercised. If a man in one or more thing that he does, exercises liberty, and then by those acts is brought into such circumstances, that his liberty ceases, and there follows a long series of acts or events that come to pass necessarily; those consequent acts are not virtuous or vicious, rewardable or punishable; but only the free acts that established this necessity; for in them alone was the man free. The following effects that are necessary, have no more of the nature of virtue or vice, than health or sickness of body have properly the nature of virtue or vice, being the effects of a course of free acts of temperance or intemperance; or than the good qualities of a clock are of the nature of virtue, which are the effects of free acts of the artificer; or the goodness and sweetness of the fruits of a garden are moral virtues, being the effects of the free and faithful acts of the gardener. If liberty be absolutely requisite to the morality of actions, and necessity wholly inconsistent with it, as Arminians greatly insist; then no necessary effects whatsoever, let the cause be never so good or bad, can be virtuous or vicious; but the virtue or vice must be only in the free cause. Agreeably to this, Dr. Whitby supposes, the necessity that attends the good and evil habits of the saints in heaven, and damned in hell, which are the consequence of their free acts in their state of probation, [shews they] are not rewardable or punishable.

On the whole, it appears, that if the notions of Arminians concerning liberty and moral agency be true, it will follow that there is no virtue in any such habits or qualities as humility, meekness, patience, mercy, gratitude, generosity, heavenly-mindedness; nothing at all praiseworthy in loving Christ above father and mother, wife and children, or our own lives; or in delight in holiness, hungering and thirsting after righteousness, love to enemies, universal benevolence to mankind: and on the other hand, there is nothing at all vicious, or worthy of dispraise, in the most sordid, beastly, malignant, devilish dispositions; in being ungrateful, profane, habitually hating God, and things sacred and holy; or in being most treacherous, envious and cruel towards men. For all these things are dispositions and inclinations of the heart. And in short, there is no such thing as any virtuous or vicious quality of mind; no such thing as inherent virtue and holiness, or vice and sin: and the stronger those habits or dispositions are, which used to be called virtuous and vicious, the further they are from being so indeed; the more violent men's lusts are, the more fixed their pride, envy, ingratitude and maliciousness, still the further are they from being blameworthy. If there be a man that by his own repeated acts, or by any other means, is come to be of the most hellish disposition, desperately inclined to treat his neighbors with injuriousness, contempt and malignity; the further they should be from any disposition to be angry with him, or in the least to blame him. So on the other hand, if there be a person, who is of a most excellent spirit, strongly inclining him to the most amiable actions, admirably meek, benevolent, etc. so much is he further from anything rewardable or commendable. On which principles, the man Jesus Christ was very far from being praiseworthy for those acts of holiness and kindness which he performed, these propensities being so strong in his heart. And above all, the infinitely holy and gracious God, is infinitely remote from anything commendable, his good inclinations being infinitely strong, and he therefore at the utmost possible distance from being at liberty. And in all cases, the stronger the inclinations of any are to virtue, and the more they love it, the less virtuous they are; and the more they love wickedness, the less vicious. Whether these things are agreeable to Scripture, let every Christian, and every man who has read the Bible, judge: and whether they are agreeable to common sense, let everyone judge, that have human understanding in exercise.

And if we pursue these principles, we shall find that virtue and vice are wholly excluded out of the world; and that there never was, nor ever can be any such thing as one or the other; either in God, angels or men. No propensity, disposition or habit can be virtuous or vicious, as has been shewn; because they, so far as they take place, destroy the freedom of the will, the foundation of all moral agency, and exclude all capacity of either virtue or vice. And if habits and dispositions themselves be not virtuous nor vicious, neither can the exercise of these dispositions be so: for the exercise of bias is not the exercise of free self-determining will, and so there is no exercise of liberty in it. Consequently no man is virtuous or vicious, either in being well or ill disposed, nor in acting from a good or bad disposition. And whether this bias or disposition be habitual or not, if it exists but a moment before the act of will, which is the effect of it, it alters not the case, as to the necessity of the effect. Or if there be no previous disposition at all, either habitual or occasional, that determines the act, then it is not choice that determines it: it is therefore a contingence, that happens to the man, arising from nothing in him; and is necessary, as to any inclination or choice of his; and therefore can't make him either the better or worse, any more than a tree is better than other trees, because it oftener happens to be lit upon by a swan or nightingale; or a rock more vicious than other rocks, because rattlesnakes have happened oftener to crawl over it. So that there is no virtue nor vice in good or bad dispositions, either fixed or transient; nor any virtue or vice in acting from any good or bad previous inclination; nor yet any virtue or vice in acting wholly without any previous inclination. Where then shall we find room for virtue or vice?

SECTION 7.

ARMINIAN NOTIONS OF MORAL AGENCY INCONSISTENT WITH ALL INFLUENCE OF MOTIVE AND INDUCEMENT, IN EITHER VIRTUOUS OR VICIOUS ACTIONS

As Arminian notions of that liberty, which is essential to virtue or vice, are inconsistent with common sense, in their being inconsistent with all virtuous or vicious habits and dispositions; so they are no less so in their inconsistency with all influence of motives in moral actions.

'Tis equally against those notions of liberty of will, whether there be, previous to the act of choice, a preponderancy of the inclination, or a preponderancy of those circumstances, which have a tendency to move the inclination. And indeed it comes to just the same thing: to say, the circumstances of the mind are such as tend to sway and turn its inclination one way, is the same thing as to say, the inclination of the mind, as under such circumstances, tends that way.

Or if any think it most proper to say, that motives do alter the inclination, and give a new bias to the mind; it will not alter the case, as to the present argument. For if motives operate by giving the mind an inclination, then they operate by destroying the mind's indifference, and laying it under a bias. But to do this, is to destroy the Arminian freedom: it is not to leave the will to its own self-determination, but to bring it into subjection to the power of something extrinsic, which operates upon it, sways and determines it, previous to its own determination. So that what is done from motive, can't be either virtuous or vicious. And besides, if the acts of the will are excited by motives, those motives are the causes of those acts of the will: which makes the acts of the will necessary; as effects necessarily follow the efficiency of the cause. And if the influence and power of the motive causes the volition, then the influence of the motive determines volition, and volition don't determine itself; and so is not free, in the sense of Arminians (as has been largely shewn already), and consequently can be neither virtuous nor vicious.

The supposition, which has already been taken notice of as an insufficient evasion in other cases, would be in like manner impertinently alleged in this case; namely, the supposition that liberty consists in a power of suspending action for the present, in order to deliberation. If it should be said, though it be true, that the will is under a necessity of finally following the strongest motive, yet it may for the present forbear to act upon the motive presented, till there has been opportunity thoroughly to consider it, and compare its real weight with the merit of other motives. I answer, as follows:

Here again it must be remembered, that if determining thus to suspend and consider, be that act of the will wherein alone liberty is exercised, then in this all virtue and vice must consist; and the acts that follow this consideration, and are the effects of it, being necessary, are no more virtuous or vicious than some good or bad events which happen when they are fast asleep, and are the consequences of what they did when they were awake. Therefore I would here observe two things.

1. To suppose that all virtue and vice, in every case, consists in determining whether to take time for consideration, or not, is not agreeable to common sense. For according to such a supposition, the most horrid crimes, adultery, murder, buggery, blasphemy, etc. do not at all consist in the horrid nature of the things themselves, but only in the neglect of thorough consideration before they were perpetrated: which brings their viciousness to a small matter, and makes all crimes equal. [Note that the word "buggery" in this use refers to sodomy; originally "bougrerie"; derived from "Bulgarian"; see: Derrick Sherwin Bailey, *Homosexuality and the Western Christian Tradition* (New York, 1955), pp. 135–44.] If it be said, that neglect of consideration, when such heinous evils are proposed to choice, is worse than in other cases: I answer, this is inconsistent, as it supposes the very thing to be, which at the same time is supposed not to be; it supposes all moral evil, all viciousness and heinousness, does not consist merely in the want of consideration. It supposes some crimes in themselves, in their own nature, to be more heinous than others, antecedent to consideration or inconsideration, which lays the person under a previous obligation to consider in some cases more than others.

2. If it were so, that all virtue and vice, in every case,

consisted only in the act of the will, whereby it determines whether to consider or no, it would not alter the case in the least, as to the present argument. For still in this act of the will on this determination, it is induced by some motive, and necessarily follows the strongest motive; and so is necessary, even in that act wherein alone it is either virtuous or vicious.

One thing more I would observe, concerning the inconsistence of Arminian notions of moral agency with the influence of motives. I suppose none will deny, that 'tis possible for motives to be set before the mind so powerful, and exhibited in so strong a light, and under so advantageous circumstances, as to be invincible; and such as the mind cannot but yield to. In this case, Arminians will doubtless say, liberty is destroyed. And if so, then if motives are exhibited with half so much power, they hinder liberty in proportion to their strength, and go half way towards destroying it. If a thousand degrees of motive abolish all liberty, then five hundred take it half away. If one degree of the influence of motive don't at all infringe or diminish liberty, then no more do two degrees; for nothing doubled, is still nothing. And if two degrees don't diminish the will's liberty, no more do four, eight, sixteen, or six thousand. For nothing multiplied never so much, comes to but nothing. If there be nothing in the nature of motive or moral suasion, that is at all opposite to liberty, then the greatest degree of it can't hurt liberty. But if there be anything in the nature of the thing, that is against liberty, then the least degree of it hurts it in some degree; and consequently hurts and diminishes virtue. If invincible motives to that action which is good, take away all the freedom of the act, and so all the virtue of it; then the more forcible the motives are, so much the worse, so much the less virtue; and the weaker the motives are, the better for the cause of virtue; and none is best of all.

Now let it be considered, whether these things are agreeable to common sense. If it should be allowed, that there are some instances wherein the soul chooses without any motive, what virtue can there be in such a choice? I am sure, there is no prudence or wisdom in it. Such a choice is made for no good end; for it is for no end at all. If it were for any end, the view of the end would be the motive exciting to the act; and if the act be for no good end, and so from no good aim, then there is no good intention in it: and therefore, according to all our natural notions of virtue, no more virtue in it than in the motion of the smoke, which is driven to and fro by the wind, without any aim or end in the thing moved, and which knows not whither, nor why and wherefore, it is moved.

Corol. 1. By these things it appears, that the argument against the Calvinists, taken from the use of counsels, exhortations, invitations, expostulations, etc. so much insisted on by Arminians, is truly against themselves. For these things can operate no other way to any good effect, than as in them is exhibited motive and inducement, tending to excite and determine the acts of the will. But it follows on their principles, that the acts of will excited by such causes, can't be virtuous; because so far as they are from these, they are not from the will's self-determining power. Hence it will follow, that it is not worth the while to offer any arguments to persuade men to any virtuous volition or voluntary action; 'tis in vain to set before them the wisdom and amiableness of ways of virtue, or the odiousness and folly of ways of vice. This notion of liberty and moral agency frustrates all endeavors to draw men to virtue by instruction, or persuasion, precept, or example: for though these things may induce men to what is materially virtuous, yet at the same time they take away the form of virtue, because they destroy liberty; as they, by their own power, put the will out of its equilibrium, determine and turn the scale, and take the work of self-determining power out of its hands. And the clearer the instructions are that are given, the more powerful the arguments that are used, and the more moving the persuasions or examples, the more likely they are to frustrate their own design; because they have so much the greater tendency to put the will out of its balance, to hinder its freedom of self-determination; and so to exclude the very form of virtue, and the essence of whatsoever is praiseworthy.

So it clearly follows from these principles, that God has no hand in any man's virtue, nor does at all promote it, either by a physical or moral influence; that none of the moral methods he uses with men to promote virtue in the world, have tendency to the attainment of that end; that all the instructions which he has given to men, from the beginning of the world to this day, by prophets, or apostles, or by his son Jesus Christ; that all his counsels, invitations, promises, threatenings, warnings and expostulations; that all means he has used with men, in ordinances, or providences; yea, all influences of his Spirit, ordinary and extraordinary, have had no tendency at all to excite any one virtuous act of the mind, or to promote anything morally good and commendable, in any respect. For there is no way that these or any other means can promote virtue, but one of these three. Either (1) by a physical operation on the heart. But all effects that are wrought in men in this way, have no virtue in them, by the concurring voice of all Arminians. Or (2) morally, by exhibiting motives to the understanding, to excite good acts in the will. But it has been demonstrated, that volitions which are excited by motives, are necessary, and not excited by a self-moving power; and therefore, by their principles, there is no virtue in them. Or (3) by merely giving the will an opportunity to determine itself concerning the objects proposed, either to choose or reject, by its own uncaused, unmoved, uninfluenced self-determination. And if this be all, then all those means do no more to promote virtue, than vice: for they do nothing but give the will opportunity to determine itself either way, either to good or bad, without laying it under any bias to either: and so there is really as much of an opportunity given to determine in favor of evil, as of good.

Thus that horrid blasphemous consequence will certainly follow from the Arminian doctrine, which they charge on others; namely, that God acts an inconsistent part in using so many counsels, warnings, invitations, entreaties, etc. with sinners, to induce 'em to forsake sin, and turn to the ways of virtue; and that all are insincere and fallacious. It will follow from their doctrine, that God does these things when he knows at the same time, that they have no manner of tendency to promote the effect he seems to aim at; yea, knows that if they have any influence, this very influence will be inconsistent with such an effect, and will prevent it. But what an imputation of insincerity would this fix on Him who is infinitely holy and true! So that theirs is the doctrine which if pursued in its consequences, does horribly reflect on the most High, and fix on him the charge of hypocrisy; and not the doctrine of the Calvinist; according to their frequent, and vehement exclamations and invectives.

Corol. 2. From what has been observed in this section, it again appears, that Arminian principles and notions, when fairly examined, and pursued in their demonstrable consequences, do evidently shut all virtue out of the world, and make it impossible that there should ever be any such thing, in any case; or that any such thing should ever be conceived of. For by these principles, the very notion of virtue or vice implies absurdity and contradiction. For it is absurd in itself, and contrary to common sense, to suppose a virtuous act of mind without any good intention or aim; and by their principles, it is absurd to suppose a virtuous act with a good intention or aim; for to act for an end, is to act from a motive. So that if we rely on these principles, there can be no virtuous act with a good design and end; and 'tis self-evident, there can be none without: consequently there can be no virtuous act at all.

Corol. 3. 'Tis manifest, that Arminian notions of moral agency, and the being of a faculty of will, cannot consist together; and that if there be any such thing as, either a virtuous, or vicious act, it can't be an act of will; no will can be at all concerned in it. For that act which is performed without inclination, without motive, without end, must be performed without any concern of the will. To suppose an act of the will without these, implies a contradiction. If the soul in its act has no motive or end; then in that act (as was observed before) it seeks nothing, goes after nothing, exerts no inclination to anything; and this implies, that in that act it desires nothing, and chooses nothing; so that there is no act of choice in the case: and that is as much as to say, there is no act of will in the case. Which very effectually shuts out all vicious and virtuous acts out of the universe; inasmuch as, according to this, there can be no vicious or virtuous act wherein the will is concerned; and according to the plainest dictates of reason, and the light of nature, and also the principles of Arminians themselves, there can be no virtuous or vicious act wherein the will is not concerned. And therefore there is no room for any virtuous or vicious acts at all.

Corol. 4. If none of the moral actions of intelligent beings are influenced by either previous inclination or motive, another strange thing will follow; and this is, that God not only can't foreknow any of the future moral actions of his creatures, but he can make no conjecture, can give no probable guess concerning them. For, all conjecture in things of this nature, must depend on some discerning or apprehension of these two things, previous disposition, and motive; which, as has been observed, Arminian notions of moral agency, in their real consequence, altogether exclude.

PART FOUR

Wherein the Chief Grounds of the Reasonings of Arminians, in Support and Defense of the Forementioned Notions of Liberty, Moral Agency, etc. and Against the Opposite Doctrine, Are Considered

SECTION 1.

THE ESSENCE OF THE VIRTUE AND VICE OF DISPOSITIONS OF THE HEART, AND ACTS OF THE WILL, LIES NOT IN THEIR CAUSE, BUT THEIR NATURE

One main foundation of the reasons, which are brought to establish the forementioned notions of liberty, virtue, vice, etc. is a supposition, that the virtuousness of the dispositions or acts of the will consists not in the nature of these dispositions or acts, but wholly in the origin or cause of them: so that if the disposition of the mind or act of the will be never so good, yet if the cause of the disposition or act be not our virtue, there is nothing virtuous or praiseworthy in it; and on the contrary, if the will in its inclination or acts be never so bad, yet unless it arises from something that is our vice or fault, there is nothing vicious or blameworthy in it. Hence their grand objection and pretended demonstration, or self-evidence, against any virtue and commendableness, or vice and blameworthiness, of those habits or acts of the will, which are not from some virtuous or vicious determination of the will itself.

Now, if this matter be well considered, it will appear to be altogether a mistake, yea, a gross absurdity; and that it is most certain, that if there be any such things, as a virtuous, or vicious disposition, or volition of mind, the virtuousness or viciousness of them consists not in the origin or cause of these things, but in the nature of them.

If the essence of virtuousness or commendableness, and of viciousness or fault, don't lie in the nature of the dispositions or acts of mind, which are said to be our virtue or our fault, but in their cause, then it is certain it lies nowhere at all. Thus, for instance, if the vice of a vicious act of will, lies not in the nature of the act, but the cause; so that its being of a bad nature will not make it at all our fault, unless it arises from some faulty determination of ours as its cause, or something in us that is our fault; then for the same reason, neither can the viciousness of that cause lie in the nature of the thing itself, but in its cause: that evil determination of ours is not our fault, merely because it is of a bad nature, unless it arises from some cause in us that is our fault. And when we are come to this higher cause, still the reason of the thing holds good; though this cause be of a bad nature, yet we are not at all to blame on that account, unless it arises from something faulty in us. Nor yet can blameworthiness lie in the nature of this cause, but in the cause of that. And thus we must drive faultiness back from step to step, from a lower cause to a higher, in infinitum: and that is thoroughly to banish it from the world, and to allow it no possibility of existence anywhere in the universality of things. On these principles, vice or moral evil can't consist in anything that is an effect; because fault don't consist in the nature of things, but in their cause; as well as because effects are necessary, being unavoidably connected with their cause: therefore the cause only is to blame. And so it follows, that faultiness can lie only in that cause, which is a cause only, and no effect of anything. Nor yet can it lie in this; for then it must lie in the nature of the thing itself; not in its being from any determination of ours, nor anything faulty in us which is the cause, nor indeed from any cause at all, for by the supposition, it is no effect, and has no cause. And thus, he that will maintain, it is not the nature of habits or acts of will that makes them virtuous or faulty, but the cause, must immediately run himself out of his own assertion; and in maintaining it, will insensibly contradict and deny it.

This is certain, that if effects are vicious and faulty, not from their nature, or from anything inherent in them, but because they are from a bad cause, it must be on account of the badness of the cause; and so on account of the nature of the cause: a bad effect in the will must be bad, because the cause is bad, or of an evil nature, or has badness as a quality inherent in it: and a good effect in the will must be good, by reason of the goodness of the cause, or its being of a good kind and nature. And if this be what is meant, the very supposition of fault and praise lying not in the nature of the thing, but the cause, contradicts itself, and does [at last] resolve the essence of virtue and vice into the nature of things, and supposes it originally to consist in that. And if a caviller has a mind to run from the absurdity, by saying, "No, the fault of the thing which is the cause, lies not in this, that the cause itself is of an evil nature, but that the cause is evil in that sense, that it is from another bad cause." Still the absurdity will follow him; for if so, then the cause before charged is at once acquitted, and all the blame must be laid to the higher cause, and must consist in that's being evil, or of an evil nature. So now we are come again to lay the blame of the thing blameworthy, to the nature of the thing, and not to the cause. And if any is so foolish as to go higher still, and ascend from step to step, till he is come to that which is the first cause concerned in the whole affair, and will say, all the blame lies in that; then at last he must be forced to own, that the faultiness of the thing which he supposes alone blameworthy, lies wholly in the nature of the thing, and not in the original or cause of it; for the supposition is, that it has no original, it is determined by no act of ours, is caused by nothing faulty in us, being absolutely without any cause. And so the race is at an end, but the evader is taken in his flight.

'Tis agreeable to the natural notions of mankind, that moral evil, with its desert of dislike and abhorrence, and all its other ill-deservings, consists in a certain deformity in the nature of certain dispositions of the heart, and acts of the will; and not in the deformity of something else, diverse from the very thing itself, which deserves abhorrence, supposed to be the cause of it. Which would be absurd, because that would be to suppose, a thing that is innocent and not evil, is truly evil and faulty, because another thing is evil. It implies a contradiction; for it would be to suppose, the very thing which is morally evil and blameworthy, is innocent and not blameworthy; but that something else, which is its cause, is only to blame. To say, that vice don't consist in the thing which is vicious, but in its cause, is the same as to say, that vice don't consist in vice, but in that which produces it.

'Tis true, a cause may be to blame, for being the cause of vice: it may be wickedness in the cause, that it produces wickedness. But it would imply a contradiction, to suppose that these two are the same individual wickedness. The wicked act of the cause in producing wickedness, is one wickedness; and the wickedness produced, if there be any produced, is another. And therefore the wickedness of the latter don't lie in the former, but is distinct from it; and the wickedness of both lies in the evil nature of the things which are wicked.

The thing which makes sin hateful, is that by which it deserves punishment; which is but the expression of hatred. And that which renders virtue lovely, is the same with that, on the account of which, it is fit to receive praise and reward; which are but the expressions of esteem and love. But that which makes vice hateful, is its hateful nature; and that which renders virtue lovely, is its amiable nature. 'Tis a certain beauty or deformity that are inherent in that good or evil will, which is the soul of virtue and vice (and not in the occasion of it) which is their worthiness of esteem or disesteem, praise or dispraise, according to the common sense of mankind. If the cause or occasion of the rise of an hateful disposition or act of will, be also hateful; suppose another antecedent evil will; that is entirely another sin, and deserves punishment by itself, under a distinct consideration. There is worthiness of dispraise in the nature of an evil volition, and not wholly in some foregoing act which is its cause; otherwise the evil volition which is the effect, is no moral evil, any more than sickness, or some other natural calamity, which arises from a cause morally evil.

Thus for instance, ingratitude is hateful and worthy of dispraise, according to common sense; not because something as bad, or worse than ingratitude, was the cause that produced it; but because it is hateful in itself, by its own inherent deformity. So the love of virtue is amiable, and worthy of praise, not merely because something else went before this love of virtue in our minds, which caused it to take place there; for instance our own choice; we chose to love virtue, and by some method or other wrought ourselves into the love of it; but because of the amiableness and condecency of such a disposition and inclination of heart. If that w as the case, that we did choose to love virtue, and so produced that love in ourselves, this choice itself could be no otherwise amiable or praiseworthy, than as love to virtue, or some other amiable inclination, was exercised and implied in it. If that choice was amiable at all, it must be so on account of some amiable quality in the nature of the choice. If we chose to love virtue, not in love to virtue, or anything that was good, and exercised no sort of good disposition in the choice, the choice itself was not virtuous, nor worthy of any praise, according to common sense, because the choice was not of a good nature.

It may not be improper here to take notice of something said by an author, that has lately made a mighty noise in America. "A necessary holiness (says he: John Taylor: *The Scripture-Doctrine of Original Sin Proposed to Free and Candid Examination*, 3d ed. Belfast, John Hay, 1746, p. 180) is no holiness....Adam could not be originally created in righteousness and tine holiness, because he must choose to be righteous, before he could be righteous. And therefore he must exist, he must be created, yea, he must exercise thought and reflection, before he was righteous." There is much more to the same effect in that place, and also in pp. 437, 438, 439, 440. If these things are so, it will certainly follow, that the first choosing to be righteous is no righteous choice; there is no righteousness or holiness in it; because no choosing to be righteous goes before it. For he plainly speaks of choosing to be righteous, as what must go before righteousness: and that which follows the choice, being the effect of the choice, can't be righteousness or holiness: for an effect is a thing necessary, and can't prevent the influence or efficacy of its cause; and therefore is unavoidably dependent upon the cause: and he says, "a necessary holiness is no holiness." So that neither can a choice of righteousness be righteousness or holiness, nor can anything that is consequent on that choice, and the effect of it, be righteousness or holiness; nor can anything that is without choice, be righteousness or holiness. So that by his scheme, all righteousness and holiness is at once shut out of the world, and no door left open, by which it can ever possibly enter into the world.

I suppose, the way that men came to entertain this absurd inconsistent notion, with respect to internal inclinations and volitions themselves (or notions that imply it), viz. that the essence of their moral good or evil lies not in their nature, but their cause; was, that it is indeed a very plain dictate of common sense, that it is so with respect to all outward actions, and sensible motions of the body; that the moral good or evil of 'em don't lie at all in the motions themselves; which taken by themselves, are nothing of a moral nature; and the essence of all the moral good or evil that concerns them, lies in those internal dispositions and volitions which are the cause of them. Now being always used to determine this, without hesitation or dispute, concerning external actions; which are the things that in the common use of language are signified by such phrases, as men's "actions," or their "doings"; hence when they came to speak of volitions, and internal exercises of their inclinations, under the same denomination of their "actions," or what they "do," they unwarily determined the case must also be the same with these, as with external actions; not considering the vast difference in the nature of the case.

If any shall still object and say, why is it not necessary that the cause should be considered, in order to determine whether anything be worthy of blame or praise? Is it agreeable to reason and common sense, that a man is to be praised or blamed for that which he is not the cause or author of, and has no hand in?

I answer, such phrases as "being the cause," "being the author." "having a hand," and the like are ambiguous. They are most vulgarly understood for being the designing voluntary cause, or cause by antecedent choice: and it is most certain that men are not in this sense the causes or authors of the first act of their wills, in any case; as certain as anything is, or ever can be; for nothing can be more certain, than that a thing is not before it is, nor a thing of the same kind before the first thing of that kind; and so no choice before the first choice. As the phrase, "being the author," may be understood, not of being the producer by an antecedent act of will; but as a person may be said to be the author of the act of will itself, by his being the immediate agent, or the being that is acting, or in exercise in that act; if the phrase of "being the author," is used to signify this, then doubtless common sense requires men's being the authors of their own acts of will, in order to their being esteemed worthy of praise or dispraise on account of them. And common sense teaches, that they must be the authors of external actions, in the former sense, namely, their being the causes of 'em by an act of will or choice, in order to their being justly blamed or praised: but it teaches no such thing with respect to the acts of the will themselves. But this may appear more manifest by the things which will be observed in the following section.

SECTION 2.

THE FALSENESS AND INCONSISTENCE OF THAT METAPHYSICAL NOTION OF ACTION, AND AGENCY, WHICH SEEMS TO BE GENERALLY ENTERTAINED BY THE DEFENDERS OF THE ARMINIAN DOCTRINE CONCERNING LIBERTY, MORAL AGENCY, ETC.

One thing that is made very much a ground of argument and supposed demonstration by Arminians, in defense of the forementioned principles, concerning moral agency, virtue, vice, etc. is their metaphysical notion of agency and action. They say, unless the soul has a self-determining power, it has no power of "action"; if its volitions be not caused by itself, but are excited and determined by some extrinsic cause, they can't be the soul's own "acts"; and that the soul can't be "active," but must be wholly "passive," in those effects which it is the subject of necessarily, and not from its own free determination.

Mr. Chubb lays the foundation of his scheme of liberty, and of his arguments to support it, very much in this position, that man is an agent, and capable of action. Which doubtless is true: but self-determination belongs to his notion of "action," and is the very essence of it. Whence he infers that it is impossible for a man to act and be acted upon, in the same thing, at the same time; and that nothing that is an action, can be the effect of the action of another: and he insists, that a "necessary agent," or an agent that is necessarily determined to act, is a "plain contradiction" [*Tracts*, p. 311, and see above, p. 234, n. 2].

But those are a precarious sort of demonstrations, which men build on the meaning that they arbitrarily affix to a word; especially when that meaning is abstruse, inconsistent, and entirely diverse from the original sense of the word in common speech.

That the meaning of the word "action," as Mr. Chubb and many others use it, is utterly unintelligible and inconsistent, is manifest, because it belongs to their notion of an action, that 'tis something wherein is no passion or passiveness; that is (according to their sense of passiveness) it is under the power, influence or action of no cause. And this implies, that action has no cause, and is no effect: for to be an effect implies passiveness, or the being subject to the power and action of its cause. And yet they hold, that the mind's action is the effect of its own determination, yea, the mind's free and voluntary determination; which is the same with free choice. So that action is the effect of something preceding, even a preceding act of choice: and consequently, in this effect the mind is passive, subject to the power and action of the preceding cause, which is the foregoing choice, and therefore can't be active. So that here we have this contradiction, that action is always the effect of foregoing choice; and therefore can't be action; because it is passive to the power of that preceding causal choice; and the mind can't be active and passive in the same thing, at the same time. Again, they say, necessity is utterly inconsistent with action, and a necessary action is a contradiction; and so their notion of action implies contingence, and excludes all necessity. And therefore their notion of action implies, that it has no necessary dependence or connection with anything foregoing; for such a dependence or connection excludes contingence, and implies necessity. And yet their notion of action implies necessity, and supposes that it is necessary, and can't be contingent. For they suppose, that whatever is properly called action, must be determined by the will and free choice; and this is as much as to say, that it must be necessary, being dependent upon, and determined by something foregoing; namely, a foregoing act of choice. Again, it belongs to their notion of action, of that which is a proper and mere act, that it is the beginning of motion, or of exertion of power; but yet it is implied in their notion of action, that it is not the beginning of motion or exertion of power, but is consequent and dependent on a preceding exertion of power, viz. the power of will and choice: for they say there is no proper action but what is freely chosen; or, which is the same thing, determined by a foregoing act of free choice. But if any of them shall see cause to deny this, and say they hold no such thing as that every action is chosen, or determined by a foregoing choice; but that the very first exertion of will only, undetermined by any preceding act, is properly called action; then I say, such a man's notion of action implies necessity; for what the mind is the subject of without the determination of its own previous choice, it is the subject of necessarily, as to any hand that free choice has in the affair; and without any ability the mind has to prevent it, by any will or election of its own: because by the supposition it precludes all previous acts of the will or choice in the case, which might prevent it. So that it is again, in this other way, implied in their notion of act, that it is both necessary and not necessary. Again, it belongs to their notion of an "act," that it is no effect of a pre-determining bias or preponderation, but springs immediately out of indifference; and this implies that it can't be from foregoing choice, which is foregoing preponderation: if it be not habitual, but occasional, yet if it causes the act, it is truly previous, efficacious and determining. And yet, at the same time, 'tis essential to their notion of an act, that it is what the agent is the author of freely and voluntarily, and that is, by previous choice and design.

So that according to their notion of an act, considered with regard to its consequences, these following things are all essential to it; viz. that it should be necessary, and not necessary; that it should be from a cause, and no cause; that it should be the fruit of choice and design, and not the fruit of choice and design; that it should be the beginning of motion or exertion, and yet consequent on previous exertion; that it should be before it is; that it should spring immediately out of indifference and equilibrium, and yet be the effect of preponderation; that it should be self-originated, and also have its original from something else; that it is what the mind causes itself, of its own will, and can produce or prevent, according to its choice or pleasure, and yet what the mind has no power to prevent, it precluding all previous choice in the affair.

So that an act, according to their metaphysical notion of it, is something of which there is no idea; 'tis nothing but a confusion of the mind, excited by words without any distinct meaning, and is an absolute nonentity; and that in two respects: (1) there is nothing in the world that ever was, is, or can be, to answer the things which must belong to its description, according to what they suppose to be essential to it. And (2) there neither is, nor ever was, nor can be, any notion or idea to answer the word, as they use and explain it. For if we should suppose any such notion, it would many ways destroy itself. But 'tis impossible, any idea or notion should subsist in the mind, whose very nature and essence, which constitutes it, destroys it. If some learned philosopher, who had been abroad, in giving an account of the curious observations he had made in his travels, should say, he "had been in Tierra del Fuego, and there had seen an animal, which he calls by a certain name, that begat and brought forth itself, and yet had a sire and a dam distinct from itself; that it had an appetite, and was hungry before it had being; that his master, who led him, and governed him at his pleasure, was always governed by him, and driven by him as he pleased; that when he moved, he always took a step before the first step; that he went with his head first, and yet always went tail foremost; and this, though he had neither head nor tail": it would be no impudence at all, to tell such a traveler, though a learned man, that he himself had no notion or idea of such an animal as he gave an account of, and never had, nor ever would have.

As the forementioned notion of action is very inconsistent, so it is wholly diverse from the original meaning of the word. The more usual signification of it in vulgar speech, seems to be some motion or exertion of power, that is voluntary, or that is the effect of the will; and is used in the same sense as "doing": and most commonly 'tis used to signify outward actions. So thinking is often distinguished from acting; and desiring and willing, from doing.

Besides this more usual and proper signification of the word "action," there are other ways in which the word is used that are less proper, which yet have place in common speech. Oftentimes 'tis used to signify some motion or alteration in inanimate things, with relation to some object and effect. So the spring of a watch is said to act upon the chain and wheels; the sunbeams, to act upon plants and trees; and the fire, to act upon wood. Sometimes the word is used to signify motions, alterations, and exertions of power, which are seen in corporeal things, considered absolutely; especially when these motions seem to arise from some internal cause which is hidden; so that they have a greater resemblance of those motions of our bodies, which are the effects of internal volition, or invisible exertions of will. So the fermentation of liquor, the operations of the loadstone, and of electrical bodies, are called the action of these things. And sometimes the word "action" is used to signify the exercise of thought, or of will and inclination: so meditating, loving, hating, inclining, disinclining, choosing and refusing, may be sometimes called acting; though more rarely (unless it be by philosophers and metaphysicians) than in any of the other senses.

But the word is never used in vulgar speech in that sense which Arminian divines use it in, namely, for the self-determinate exercise of the will, or an exertion of the soul that arises without any necessary connection with anything foregoing. If a man does something voluntarily, or as the effect of his choice, then in the most proper sense, and as the word is most originally and commonly used, he is said to act: but whether that choice or volition be self-determined, or no, whether it be connected with foregoing habitual bias, whether it be the certain effect of the strongest motive, or some extrinsic cause, never comes into consideration in the meaning of the word.

And if the word "action" is arbitrarily used by some men otherwise, to suit some scheme of metaphysics or morality, no argument can reasonably be founded on such a use of this term, to prove anything but their own pleasure. For divines and philosophers strenuously to urge such arguments, as though they were sufficient to support and demonstrate a whole scheme of moral philosophy and divinity, is certainly to erect a mighty edifice on the sand, or rather on a shadow. And though it may now perhaps, through custom, have become natural for 'em to use the word in this sense (if that may be called a sense or meaning, which is so inconsistent with itself) yet this don't prove that it is agreeable to the natural notions men have of things, or that there can be anything in the creation that should answer such a meaning. And though they appeal to experience, yet the truth is, that men are so far from experiencing any such thing, that it is impossible for 'em to have any conception of it.

If it should be objected, that "action" and "passion" are doubtless words of a contrary signification; but to suppose that the agent, in its action, is under the power and influence of something extrinsic, is to confound action and passion, and make 'em the same thing—

I answer, that action and passion are doubtless, as they are sometimes used, words of opposite signification; but not as signifying opposite existences, but only opposite relations. The words "cause" and "effect" are terms of opposite signification; but nevertheless, if I assert that the same thing may at the same time, in different respects and relations, be both cause and effect, this will not prove that I confound the terms. The soul may be both active and passive in the same thing in different respects, active with relation to one thing, and passive with relation to another. The word "passion" when set in opposition to action or rather activeness, is merely a relative term: it signifies no effect or cause, nor any proper existence; but is the same with passiveness, or a being passive, or a being acted upon by something. Which is a mere relation of a thing to some power or force exerted by some cause, producing some effect in it, or upon it. And "action," when set properly in opposition to passion, or passiveness, is no real existence; it is not the same with "an action," but is a mere relation: 'tis the activeness of something on another thing, being the opposite relation to the other, viz. a relation of power, or force exerted by some cause, towards another thing, which is the subject of the effect of that power. Indeed the word "action" is frequently used to signify something not merely relative, but more absolute, and a real existence; as when we say "an action"; when the word is not used transitively, but absolutely, for some motion or exercise of body or mind, without any relation to any object or effect: and as used thus, it is not properly the opposite of "passion"; which ordinarily signifies nothing absolute, but merely the relation of being acted upon. And therefore if the word "action" be used in the like relative sense, then action and passion are only two contrary relations. And 'tis no absurdity to suppose, that contrary relations may belong to the same thing, at the same time, with respect to different things. So to suppose, that there are acts of the soul by which a man voluntarily moves, and acts upon objects, and produces effects, which yet themselves are effects of something else, and wherein the soul itself is the object of something acting upon, and influencing that, don't at all confound "action" and "passion." The words may nevertheless be properly of opposite signification: there may be as true and real a difference between acting and being caused to act, though we should suppose the soul to be both in the same volition, as there is between living, and being quickened, or made to live. 'Tis no more a contradiction, to suppose that action may be the effect of some other cause, besides the agent, or being that acts, than to suppose that life may be the effect of some other cause, besides the liver, or the being that lives, in whom life is caused to be.

The thing which has led men into this inconsistent notion of action, when applied to volition, as though it were essential to this internal action, that the agent should be self-determined in it, and that the will should be the cause of it, was probably this; that according to the sense of mankind, and the common use of language it is so, with respect to men's external actions; which are what originally, and according to the vulgar use and most proper sense of the word, are called "actions." Men in these are self-directed, self-determined, and their wills are the cause of the motions of their bodies, and the external things that are done; so that unless men do 'em voluntarily, and of choice, and the action be determined by their antecedent volition, it is no action or doing of theirs. Hence some metaphysicians have been led unwarily, but exceeding absurdly, to suppose the same concerning volition itself, that that also must be determined by the will; which is to be determined by antecedent volition, as the motion of the body is; not considering the contradiction it implies.

But 'tis very evident, that in the metaphysical distinction between action and passion (though long since become common and the general vogue), due care has not been taken to conform language to the nature of things, or to any distinct clear ideas. As it is in innumerable other philosophical, metaphysical terms, used in these disputes; which has occasioned inexpressible difficulty, contention, error and confusion.

And thus probably it came to be thought, that necessity was inconsistent with action, as these terms are applied to volition. First, these terms "action" and "necessity" are changed from their original meaning, as signifying external voluntary action, and constraint (in which meaning they are evidently inconsistent), to signify quite other things, viz. volition itself, and certainty of existence. And when the change of signification is made, care is not taken to make proper allowances and abatements for the difference of sense; but still the same things are unwarily attributed to "action" and "necessity," in the new meaning of the words, which plainly belonged to 'em in their first sense; and on this ground, maxims are established without any real foundation, as though they were the most certain truths, and the most evident dictates of reason.

But however strenuously it is maintained, that what is necessary can't be properly called action, and that a necessary action is a contradiction, yet 'tis probable there are few Arminian divines, who if thoroughly tried, would stand to these principles. They will allow, that God is in the highest sense an active being, and the highest fountain of life and action; and they would not probably deny, that those that are called God's acts of righteousness, holiness and faithfulness, are truly and properly God's acts, and God is really a holy agent in them: and yet I trust, they will not deny, that God necessarily acts justly and faithfully, and that it is impossible for him to act unrighteously and unholily.

SECTION 3.

THE REASONS WHY SOME THINK IT CONTRARY TO COMMON SENSE, TO SUPPOSE THOSE THINGS WHICH ARE NECESSARY, TO BE WORTHY OF EITHER PRAISE OR BLAME

'Tis abundantly affirmed and urged by Arminian writers, that it is contrary to common sense, and the natural notions and apprehensions of mankind, to suppose otherwise than that necessity (making no distinction between natural and moral necessity) is inconsistent with virtue and vice, praise and blame, reward and punishment. And their arguments from hence have been greatly triumphed in; and have been not a little perplexing to many who have been friendly to the truth, as clearly revealed in the holy Scriptures: it has seemed to them indeed difficult, to reconcile Calvinistic doctrines with the notions men commonly have of justice and equity. And the true reasons of it seem to be these that follow.

I. 'Tis indeed a very plain dictate of common sense, that natural necessity is wholly inconsistent with just praise or blame. If men do things which in themselves are very good, fit to be brought to pass, and very happy effects, properly against their wills, and can't help it; or do them from a necessity that is without their wills, or with which their wills have no concern or connection; then 'tis a plain dictate of common sense, that it's none of their virtue, nor any moral good in them; and that they are not worthy to be rewarded or praised; or at all esteemed, honored or loved on that account. And on the other hand, that if from like necessity they do those things which in themselves are very unhappy and pernicious, and do them because they can't help it; the necessity is such, that it is all one whether they will them, or no; and the reason why they are done, is from necessity only, and not from their wills; 'tis a very plain dictate of common sense that they are not at all to blame; there is no vice, fault, or moral evil at all in the effect done; nor are they who are thus necessitated, in any wise worthy to be punished, hated, or in the least disrespected, on that account.

In like manner, if things in themselves good and desirable are absolutely impossible, with a natural impossibility, the universal reason of mankind teaches, that this wholly and perfectly excuses persons in their not doing them.

And 'tis also a plain dictate of common sense, that if the doing things in themselves good, or avoiding things in themselves evil, is not absolutely impossible, with such a natural impossibility, but very difficult, with a natural difficulty; that is, a difficulty prior to, and not at all consisting in will and inclination itself, and which would remain the same, let the inclination be what it will; then a person's neglect or omission is excused in some measure, though not wholly; his sin is less aggravated, than if the thing to be done were easy. And if instead of difficulty and hindrance, there be a contrary natural propensity in the state of things, to the thing to be done, or effect to be brought to pass, abstracted from any consideration of the inclination of the heart; though the propensity be not so great as to amount to a natural necessity; yet being some approach to it, so that the doing the good thing be very much from this natural tendency in the state of things, and but little from a good inclination; then it is a dictate of common sense, that there is so much the less virtue in what is done; and so it is less praiseworthy and rewardable. The reason is easy, viz. because such a natural propensity or tendency is an approach to natural necessity; and the greater the propensity, still so much the nearer is the approach to necessity. And therefore as natural necessity takes away or shuts out all virtue, so this propensity approaches to an abolition of virtue; that is, it diminishes it. And on the other hand, natural difficulty in the state of things is an approach to natural impossibility. And as the latter, when it is complete and absolute, wholly takes away blame; so such difficulty takes away some blame, or diminishes blame; and makes the thing done to be less worthy of punishment.

II. Men in their first use of such phrases as these, "must," "can't," "can't help it," "can't avoid it," "necessary," "unable," "impossible," "unavoidable," "irresistible," etc. use them to signify a necessity of constraint or restraint, a natural necessity or impossibility; or some necessity that the will has nothing to do in; which may be, whether men will or no; and which may be supposed to be just the same, let men's inclinations and desires be what they will. Such kind of terms in their original use, I suppose among all nations, are relative; carrying in their signification (as was before observed) a reference or respect to some contrary will, desire or endeavor, which, it is supposed, is, or may be in the case. All men find, and begin to find in early childhood, that there are innumerable things that can't be done, which they desire to do; and innumerable things which they are averse to, that must be, they can't avoid them, they will be, whether they choose them or no. 'Tis to express this necessity, which men so soon and so often find, and which so greatly and so early affects them in innumerable cases, that such terms and phrases are first formed; and 'tis to signify such a necessity, that they are first used, and that they are most constantly used, in the common affairs of life; and not to signify any such metaphysical, speculative and abstract notion, as that connection in the nature or course of things, which is between the subject and predicate of a proposition, and which is the foundation of the certain truth of that proposition; to signify which, they who employ themselves in philosophical inquiries into the first origin and metaphysical relations and dependences of things, have borrowed these terms, for want of others. But we grow up from our cradles in a use of such terms and phrases, entirely different from this, and carrying a sense exceeding diverse from that in which they are commonly used in the controversy between Arminians and Calvinists. And it being, as was said before, a dictate of the universal sense of mankind, evident to us as soon as we begin to think, that the necessity signified by these terms, in the sense in which we first learn them, does excuse persons, and free them from all fault or blame; hence our ideas of excusableness or faultlessness is tied to these terms and phrases by a strong habit, which is begun in childhood as soon as we begin to speak, and grows up with us, and is strengthened by constant use and custom, the connection growing stronger and stronger.

The habitual connection which is in men's minds between blamelessness and those forementioned terms, "must," "cannot," "unable," "necessary," "impossible," "unavoidable," etc. becomes very strong; because as soon as ever men begin to use reason and speech, they have occasion to excuse themselves, from the natural necessity signified by these terms, in numerous instances. "I can't do it." "I could not help it." And all mankind have constant and daily occasion to use such phrases in this sense, to excuse themselves and others in almost all the concerns of life, with respect to disappointments, and things that happen which concern and affect us and others, that are hurtful, or disagreeable to us or them, or things desirable that we or others fail of.

That a being accustomed to an union of different ideas, from early childhood, makes the habitual connection exceeding strong, as though such connection were owing to nature, is manifest in innumerable instances. It is altogether by such an habitual connection of ideas, that men judge of the bigness or distance of the objects of sight from their appearance. Thus 'tis owing to such a connection early established, and growing up with a person, that he judges a mountain, which he sees at ten miles distance, to be bigger than his nose, or further off than the end of it. Having been used so long to join a considerable distance and magnitude with such an appearance, men imagine it is by a dictate of natural sense: whereas it would be quite otherwise with one that had his eyes newly opened, who had been born blind: he would have the same visible appearance, but natural sense would dictate no such thing concerning the magnitude or distance of what appeared.

III. When men, after they had been so habituated to connect ideas of innocency or blamelessness with such terms, that the union seems to be the effect of mere nature, come to hear the same terms used, and learn to use them themselves in the forementioned new and metaphysical sense, to signify quite another sort of necessity, which has no such kind of relation to a contrary supposable will and endeavor; the notion of plain and manifest blamelessness, by this means, is by a strong prejudice, insensibly and unwarily transferred to a case to which it by no means belongs: the change of the use of the terms, to a signification which is very diverse, not being taken notice of, or adverted to. And there are several reasons why it is not.

1. The terms, as used by philosophers, are not very distinct and clear in their meaning: few use them in a fixed determined sense. On the contrary, their meaning is very vague and confused. Which is what commonly happens to the words used to signify things intellectual and moral, and to express what Mr. Locke calls "mixed modes." If men had a clear and distinct understanding of what is intended by these metaphysical terms, they would be able more easily to compare them with their original and common sense; and so would not be so easily cheated by them. The minds of men are so easily led into delusion by no sort of terms in the world, as by words of this sort.

2. The change of the signification of the terms is the more insensible, because the things signified, though indeed very different, yet do in some generals agree. In "necessity," that which is vulgarly so called, there is a strong connection between the thing said to be necessary, and something antecedent to it, in the order of nature; so there is also in "philosophical necessity." And though in both kinds of necessity, the connection can't be called by that name, with relation to an opposite will or endeavor, to which it is superior; which is the case in vulgar necessity; yet in both, the connection is prior to will and endeavor, and so in some respect superior. In both kinds of necessity there is a foundation for some certainty of the proposition that affirms the event. The terms used being

the same, and the things signified agreeing in these and some other general circumstances, and the expressions as used by philosophers being not well defined, and so of obscure and loose signification; hence persons are not aware of the great difference; and the notions of innocence or faultlessness, which were so strongly associated with them, and were strictly united in their minds, ever since they can remember, remain united with them still, as if the union were altogether natural and necessary; and they that go about to make a separation, seem to them to do great violence even to nature itself.

IV. Another reason why it appears difficult to reconcile it with reason, that men should be blamed for that which is necessary with a moral necessity (which as was observed before is a species of philosophical necessity) is, that for want of due consideration, men inwardly entertain that apprehension, that this necessity may be against men's wills and sincere endeavors. They go away with that notion, that men may truly will and wish and strive that it may be otherwise; but that invincible necessity stands in the way. And many think thus concerning themselves: some that are wicked men think they wish that they were good, that they loved God and holiness; but yet don't find that their wishes produce the effect. The reasons why men think thus, are as follows: (1) They find what may be called an indirect willingness to have a better will, in the manner before observed. For it is impossible, and a contradiction to suppose the will to be directly and properly against itself. And they don't consider, that this indirect willingness is entirely a different thing from properly willing the thing that is the duty and virtue required; and that there is no virtue in that sort of willingness which they have. They don't consider, that the volitions which a wicked man may have that he loved God, are no acts of the will at all against the moral evil of not loving God; but only some disagreeable consequences. But the making the requisite distinction requires more care of reflection and thought than most men are used to. And men through a prejudice in their own favor, are disposed to think well of their own desires and dispositions, and to account 'em good and virtuous, though their respect to virtue be only indirect and remote, and 'tis nothing at all that is virtuous that truly excites or terminates their inclinations. (2) Another thing that insensibly leads and beguiles men into a supposition that this moral necessity or impossibility is, or may be against men's wills, and true endeavors, is the derivation and formation of the terms themselves, that are often used to express it, which is such as seems directly to point to, and hold this forth.

Such words, for instance, as "unable," "unavoidable," "impossible," "irresistible"; which carry a plain reference to a supposable power exerted, endeavors used, resistance made, in opposition to the necessity: and the persons that hear them, not considering nor suspecting but that they are used in their proper sense: that sense being therefore understood, there does naturally, and as it were necessarily arise in their minds a supposition that it may be so indeed, that true desires and endeavors may take place, but that invincible necessity stands in the way, and renders 'em vain and to no effect.

V. Another thing which makes persons more ready to suppose it to be contrary to reason, that men should be exposed to the punishments threatened to sin, for doing those things which are morally necessary, or not doing those things morally impossible, is, that imagination strengthens the argument, and adds greatly to the power and influence of the seeming; reasons against it, from the greatness of that punishment. To allow that they may be justly exposed to a small punishment, would not be so difficult. Whereas, if there were any good reason in the case, if it were truly a dictate of reason that such necessity was inconsistent with faultiness, or just punishment, the demonstration would be equally certain with respect to a small punishment, or any punishment at all, as a very great one: but it is not equally easy to the imagination. They that argue against the justice of damning men for those things that are thus necessary, seem to make their argument the stronger, by setting forth the greatness of the punishment in strong expressions: "That a man should be cast into eternal burnings, that he should be made to fry in hell to all eternity, for those things which he had no power to avoid, and was under a fatal, unfrustrable, invincible necessity of doing."

SECTION 4.

IT IS AGREEABLE TO COMMON SENSE, AND THE NATURAL NOTIONS OF MANKIND, TO SUPPOSE MORAL NECESSITY TO BE CONSISTENT WITH PRAISE AND BLAME, REWARD AND PUNISHMENT

Whether the reasons that have been given, why it appears difficult to some persons to reconcile with common sense the praising or blaming, rewarding or punishing those things which are morally necessary, are thought satisfactory, or not; yet it most evidently appears by the following things, that if this matter be rightly understood, setting aside all delusion arising from the impropriety and ambiguity of terms, this is not at all inconsistent with the natural apprehensions of mankind, and that sense of things which is found everywhere in the common people, who are furthest from having their thoughts perverted from their natural channel, by metaphysical and philosophical subtleties; but on the contrary, altogether agreeable to, and the very voice and dictate of this natural and vulgar sense.

I. This will appear if we consider what the vulgar notion of blameworthiness is. The idea which the common people through all ages and nations have of faultiness, I suppose to be plainly this; a person's being or doing wrong, with his own will and pleasure; containing these two things: 1. His doing wrong, when he does as he pleases. 2. His pleasure's being wrong. Or in other words, perhaps more intelligibly expressing their notion; a person's having his heart wrong, and doing wrong from his heart. And this is the sum total of the matter.

The common people don't ascend up in their reflections and abstractions, to the metaphysical sources, relations and dependences of things, in order to form their notion of faultiness or blameworthiness. They don't wait till they have decided by their refinings, what first determines the will; whether it be determined by something extrinsic, or intrinsic; whether volition determines volition, or whether the understanding determines the will; whether there be any such thing as metaphysicians mean by contingence (if they have any meaning); whether there be a sort of a strange unaccountable sovereignty in the will, in the exercise of which, by its own sovereign acts, it brings to pass all its own sovereign acts. They don't take any part of their notion of fault or blame from the resolution of any such questions. If this were the case, there are multitudes, yea, the far greater part of mankind, nine hundred and ninety-nine out of a thousand would live and die without having any such notion as that of fault ever entering into their heads, or without so much as once having any conception that anybody was to be either blamed or commended for anything. To be sure, it would be a long time before men came to have such notions. Whereas 'tis manifest, they are some of the first notions that appear in children; who discover as soon as they can think, or speak, or act at all as rational creatures, a sense of desert. And certainly, in forming their notion of it, they make no use of metaphysics. All the ground they go upon consists in these two things; experience, and a natural sensation of a certain fitness or agreeableness which there is in uniting such moral evil as is above described, viz. a being or doing wrong with the will, and resentment in others, and pain inflicted on the person in whom this moral evil is. Which natural sense is what we call by the name of "conscience."

'Tis true, the common people and children, in their notion of a faulty act or deed of any person, do suppose that it is the person's own act and deed. But this is all that belongs to what they understand by a thing's being a person's own deed or action; even that it is something done by him of choice. That some exercise or motion should begin of itself, don't belong to their notion of an action, or doing. If so, it would belong to their notion of it, that it is something which is the cause of its own beginning: and that is as much as to say, that it is before it begins to be. Nor is their notion of an action some motion or exercise that begins accidentally, without any cause or reason; for that is contrary to one of the prime dictates of common sense, namely, that everything that begins to be, has some cause or reason why it is.

The common people, in their notion of a faulty or praiseworthy deed or work done by anyone, do suppose that the man does it in the exercise of liberty. But then their notion of liberty is only a person's having opportunity of doing as he pleases. They have no notion of liberty consisting in the will's first acting, and so causing its own acts; and determining, and so causing its own determinations; or choosing, and so causing its own choice. Such a notion of liberty is what none have, but those that have darkened their own minds with confused metaphysical speculation, and abstruse and ambiguous terms. If a man is not restrained from acting as his will determines, or constrained to act otherwise; then he has liberty, according to common notions of liberty, without taking into the idea that grand contradiction of all the determinations of a man's free will being the effects of the determinations of his free will. Nor have men commonly any notion of freedom consisting in indifference. For if so, then it would be agreeable to their notion, that the greater indifference men act with, the more freedom they act with; whereas the reverse is true. He that in acting, proceeds with the fullest inclination, does what he does with the greatest freedom, according to common sense. And so far is it from being agreeable to common sense, that such liberty as consists in indifference is requisite to praise or blame, that on the contrary, the dictate of every man's natural sense through the world is, that the further he is from being indifferent in his acting good or evil, and the more he does either with full and strong inclination, the more is he esteemed or abhorred, commended or condemned.

II. If it were inconsistent with the common sense of mankind, that men should be either to be blamed or commended in any volitions they have or fail of, in case of moral necessity or impossibility; then it would surely also be agreeable to the same sense and reason of mankind, that the nearer the case approaches to such a moral necessity or impossibility, either through a strong antecedent moral propensity on the one hand ('tis here argued, on supposition that not all propensity implies moral necessity, but only some very high degrees; which none will deny), or a great antecedent opposition and difficulty on the other, the nearer does it approach to a being neither blamable nor commendable; so that acts exerted with such preceding propensity would be worthy of proportionably less praise; and when omitted, the act being attended with such difficulty, the omission would be worthy of the less blame. It is so, as was observed before, with natural necessity and impossibility, propensity and difficulty: as 'tis a plain dictate of the sense of all mankind, that natural necessity and impossibility takes away all blame and praise; and therefore, that the nearer the approach is to these through previous propensity or difficulty, so praise and blame are proportionably diminished. And if it were as much a dictate of common sense, that moral necessity of doing, or impossibility of avoiding, takes away all praise and blame, as that natural necessity or impossibility does this; then, by a perfect parity of reason, it would be as much the dictate of common sense, that an approach to moral necessity of doing, or impossibility of avoiding, diminishes praise and blame, as that an approach to natural necessity and impossibility does so. 'Tis equally the voice of common sense, that persons are excusable in part, in neglecting things difficult against their wills, as that they are excusable wholly in neglecting things impossible against their wills. And if it made no difference, whether the impossibility were natural and against the will, or moral, lying in the will, with regard to excusableness; so neither would it make any difference, whether the difficulty, or approach to necessity be natural against the will, or moral, lying in the propensity of the will.

But 'tis apparent, that the reverse of these things is true. If there be an approach to a moral necessity in a man's exertion of good acts of will, they being the exercise of a strong propensity to good, and a very powerful love to virtue; 'tis so far from being the dictate of common sense, that he is less virtuous, and the less to be esteemed, loved and praised; that 'tis agreeable to the natural notions of all mankind that he is so much the better man, worthy of greater respect, and higher commendation. And the stronger the inclination is, and the nearer it approaches to necessity in that respect, or to impossibility of neglecting the virtuous act, or of doing a vicious one; still the more virtuous, and worthy of higher commendation. And on the other hand, if a man exerts evil acts of mind; as for instance, acts of pride or malice, from a rooted and strong habit or principle of haughtiness and maliciousness, and a violent propensity of heart to such acts; according to the natural sense of all men, he is so far from being the less hateful and blamable on that account, that he is so much the more worthy to be detested and condemned by all that observe him.

Moreover, 'tis manifest that it is no part of the notion which mankind commonly have of a blamable or praise-worthy act of the will, that it is an act which is not determined by an antecedent bias or motive, but by the sovereign power of the will itself; because if so, the greater hand such causes have in determining any acts of the will, so much the less virtuous or vicious would they be accounted; and the less hand, the more virtuous or vicious. Whereas the reverse is true: men don't think a good act to be the less praiseworthy, for the agent's being much determined in it by a good inclination or a good motive; but the more. And if good inclination or motive has but little influence in determining the agent, they don't think his act so much the more virtuous, but the less. And so concerning evil acts, which are determined by evil motives or inclinations.

Yea, if it be supposed that good or evil dispositions are implanted in the hearts of men by nature itself (which, it is certain, is vulgarly supposed in innumerable cases) yet it is not commonly supposed that men are worthy of no praise or dispraise for such dispositions; although what is natural is undoubtedly necessary, nature being prior to all acts of the will whatsoever. Thus for instance, if a man appears to be of a very haughty or malicious disposition, and is supposed to be so by his natural temper, 'tis no vulgar notion, no dictate of the common sense and apprehension of men, that such dispositions are no vices or moral evils, or that such persons are not worthy of disesteem, odium and dishonor; or that the proud or malicious acts which flow from such natural dispositions, are worthy of no resentment. Yea, such vile natural dispositions, and the strength of 'em, will commonly be mentioned rather as an aggravation of the wicked acts that come from such a fountain, than an extenuation of 'em. Its being natural for men to act thus, is often observed by men in the height of their indignation: they will say, "'Tis his very nature: he is of a vile natural temper; 'tis as natural to him to act so, as it is to breathe; he can't help serving the devil," etc. But it is not thus with regard to hurtful mischievous things that any are the subjects or occasions of by natural necessity, against their inclinations. In such a case, the necessity, by the common voice of mankind, will be spoken of as a full excuse. Thus 'tis very plain, that common sense makes a vast difference between these two kinds of necessity, as to the judgment it makes of their influence on the moral quality and desert of men's actions.

And these dictates of men's minds are so natural and necessary, that it may be very much doubted whether the Arminians themselves have ever got rid of 'em; yea, their greatest doctors, that have gone furthest in defense of their metaphysical notions of liberty, and have brought their arguments to their greatest strength, and as they suppose to a demonstration, against the consistence of virtue and vice with any necessity: 'tis to be questioned, whether there is so much as one of them, but that if he suffered very much from the injurious acts of a man under the power of an invincible haughtiness and malignancy of temper, would not, from the forementioned natural sense of mind, resent it far otherwise, than if as great sufferings came upon him from the wind that blows, and fire that burns by natural necessity; and otherwise than he would, if he suffered as much from the conduct of a man perfectly delirious; yea, though he first brought his distraction upon him some way by his own fault.

Some seem to disdain the distinction that we make between natural and moral necessity, as though it were altogether impertinent in this controversy: "That which is necessary (say they) is necessary; it is that which must be, and can't be prevented. And that which is impossible, is impossible, and can't be done: and therefore none can be to blame for not doing it." And such comparisons are made use of, as the commanding of a man to walk who has lost his legs, and condemning and punishing him for not obeying; inviting and calling upon a man, who is shut up in a strong prison, to come forth, etc. But in these things Arminians are very unreasonable. Let common sense determine whether there be not a great difference between those two cases; the one, that of a man who has offended his prince, and is cast into prison; and after he has lain there a while, the king comes to him, calls him to come forth to him; and tells him that if he will do so, and will fall down before him, and humbly beg his pardon, he shall be forgiven, and set at liberty, and also be greatly enriched, and advanced to honor: the prisoner heartily repents of the folly and wickedness of his offense against his prince, is thoroughly disposed to abase himself, and accept of the king's offer; but is confined by strong walls, with gates of brass, and bars of iron. The other case is, that of a man who is of a very unreasonable spirit, of a haughty, ungrateful, willful disposition; and moreover, has been brought up in traitorous principles; and has his heart possessed with an extreme and inveterate enmity to his lawful sovereign; and for his rebellion is cast into prison, and lies long there, loaden with heavy chains, and in miserable circumstances. At length the compassionate prince comes to the prison, orders his chains to be knocked off, and his prison doors to be set wide open; calls to him, and tells him, if he will come forth to him, and fall down before him, acknowledge that he has treated him unworthily, and ask his forgiveness; he shall be forgiven, set at liberty, and set in a place of great dignity and profit in his court. But he is so stout and stomachful, and full of haughty malignity, that he can't be willing to accept the offer: his rooted strong pride and malice have perfect power over him, and as it were bind him, by binding his heart: the opposition of his heart has the mastery over him, having an influence on his mind far superior to the king's grace and condescension, and to all his kind offers and promises. Now, is it agreeable to common sense, to assert and stand to it, that there is no difference between these two cases, as to any worthiness of blame in the prisoners; because, forsooth, there is a necessity in both, and the required act in each case is impossible? 'Tis true, a man's evil dispositions may be as strong and immovable as the bars of a castle. But who can't see, that when a man, in the latter case, is said to be "unable" to obey the command, the expression is used improperly, and not in the sense it has originally and in common speech? And that it may properly be said to be in the rebel's power to come out of prison, seeing he can easily do it if he pleases; though by reason of his vile temper of heart which is fixed and rooted, 'tis impossible that it should please him?

Upon the whole, I presume there is no person of good understanding, who impartially considers the things which have been observed, but will allow that 'tis not evident from the dictates of the common sense, or natural notions of mankind, that moral necessity is inconsistent with praise and blame. And therefore, if the Arminians would prove any such inconsistency, it must be by some philosophical and metaphysical arguments, and not common sense.

There is a grand illusion in the pretended demonstration of Arminians from common sense. The main strength of all these demonstrations, lies in that prejudice that arises through the insensible change of the use and meaning of such terms as "liberty," "able," "unable," "necessary," "impossible," "unavoidable," "invincible," "action," etc. from their original and vulgar sense, to a metaphysical sense entirely diverse; and the strong connection of the ideas of blamelessness, etc. with some of these terms, by an habit contracted and established, while these terms were used in their first meaning. This prejudice and delusion is the foundation of all those positions they lay down as maxims, by which most of the scriptures, which they allege in this controversy, are interpreted, and on which all their pompous demonstrations from Scripture and reason depend. From this secret delusion and prejudice they have almost all their advantages: 'tis the strength of their bulwarks, and the edge of their weapons. And this is the main ground of all the right they have to treat their neighbors in so assuming a manner, and to insult others, perhaps as wise and good as themselves, as weak bigots, men that dwell in the dark caves of superstition, perversely set, obstinately shutting their eyes against the noonday light, enemies to common sense, maintaining the first-born of absurdities, etc. But perhaps an impartial consideration of the things which have been observed in the preceding parts of this inquiry, may enable the lovers of truth better to judge, whose doctrine is indeed absurd, abstruse, self-contradictory, and inconsistent with common sense, and many ways repugnant to the universal dictates of the reason of mankind.

Corol. From things which have been observed, it will follow, that it is agreeable to common sense to suppose, that the glorified saints have not their freedom at all diminished, in any respect; and that God himself has the highest possible freedom, according to the true and proper meaning of the term; and that he is in the highest possible respect an agent, and active in the exercise of his infinite holiness; though he acts therein in the highest degree necessarily: and his actions of this kind are in the highest, most absolutely perfect manner virtuous and praiseworthy; and are so, for that very reason, because they are most perfectly necessary.

SECTION 5.

CONCERNING THOSE OBJECTIONS, THAT THIS SCHEME OF NECESSITY RENDERS ALL MEANS AND ENDEAVORS FOR THE AVOIDING OF SIN, OR THE OBTAINING VIRTUE AND HOLINESS, VAIN, AND TO NO PURPOSE; AND THAT IT MAKES MEN NO MORE THAN MERE MACHINES IN AFFAIRS OF MORALITY AND RELIGION

Arminians say, if it be so, that sin and virtue come to pass by a necessity consisting in a sure connection of causes and effects, antecedents and consequents, it can never be worth the while to use any means or endeavors to obtain the one, and avoid the other; seeing no endeavors can alter the futurity of the event, which is become necessary by a connection already established.

But I desire, that this matter may be fully considered; and that it may be examined with a thorough strictness, whether it will follow that endeavors and means, in order to avoid or obtain any future thing, must be more in vain, on the supposition of such a connection of antecedents and consequents, than if the contrary be supposed.

For endeavors to be in vain, is for 'em not to be successful; that is to say, for 'em not eventually to be the means of the thing aimed at, which can't be, but in one of these two ways; either, first, that although the means are used, yet the event aimed at don't follow: or, secondly, if the event does follow, it is not because of the means, or from any connection or dependence of the event on the means, the event would have come to pass, as well without the means, as with them. If either of these two things are the case, then the means are not properly successful, and are truly in vain. The successfulness or unsuccessfulness of means, in order to an effect, or their being in vain or not in vain, consists in those means being connected, or not connected, with the effect, in such a manner as this, viz. that the effect is with the means, and not without them; or, that the being of the effect is, on the one hand, connected with the means, and the want of the effect, on the other hand, is connected with the want of the means. If there be such a connection as this between means and end, the means are not in vain: the more there is of such a connection, the further they are from being in vain; and the less of such a connection, the more are they in vain.

Now therefore the question to be answered (in order

to determine, whether it follows from this doctrine of the necessary connection between foregoing things and consequent ones, that means used in order to any effect, are more in vain than they would be otherwise) is, whether it follows from it, that there is less of the forementioned connection between means and effect; that is, whether on the supposition of there being a real and true connection between antecedent things and consequent ones, there must be less of a connection between means and effect, than on the supposition of there being no fixed connection between antecedent things and consequent ones: and the very stating of this question is sufficient to answer it. It must appear to everyone that will open his eyes, that this question can't be affirmed, without the grossest absurdity and inconsistence. Means are foregoing things, and effects are following things: and if there were no connection between foregoing things, and following ones, there could be no connection between means and end; and so all means would be wholly vain and fruitless. For 'tis by virtue of some connection only, that they become successful: 'tis some connection observed, or revealed, or otherwise known, between antecedent things and following ones, that is what directs in the choice of means. And if there were no such thing as an established connection, there could be no choice, as to means; one thing would have no more tendency to an effect, than another; there would be no such thing as tendency in the case. All those things which are successful means of other things, do therein prove connected antecedents of them: and therefore to assert, that a fixed connection between antecedents and consequents makes means vain and useless, or stands in the way to hinder the connection between means and end, is just so ridiculous, as to say, that a connection between antecedents and consequents stands in the way to hinder a connection between antecedents and consequents.

Nor can any supposed connection of the succession or train of antecedents and consequents, from the very beginning of all things, the connection being made already sure and necessary, either by established laws of nature, or by these together with a decree of sovereign immediate interpositions of divine power, on such and such occasions, or any other way (if any other there be); I say, no such necessary connection of a series of antecedents and consequents can in the least tend to hinder, but that the means we use may belong to the series; and so may be some of those antecedents which are connected with the consequents we aim at, in the established course of things. Endeavors which we use, are things that exist; and therefore they belong to the general chain of events; all the parts of which chain are supposed to be connected: and so endeavors are supposed to be connected with some effects, or some consequent things, or other. And certainly this don't hinder but that the events they are connected with, may be those which we aim at, and which we choose, because we judge 'em most likely to have a connection with those events, from the established order and course of things which we observe, or from something in divine revelation.

Let us suppose a real and sure connection between a man's having his eyes open in the clear daylight, with good organs of sight, and seeing; so that seeing is connected with his opening his eyes, and not seeing with his not opening his eyes; and also the like connection between such a man's attempting to open his eyes, and his actually doing it: the supposed established connection between these antecedents and consequents, let the connection be never so sure and necessary, certainly don't prove that it is in vain, for a man in such circumstances to attempt to open his eyes, in order to seeing: his aiming at that event, and the use of the means, being the effect of his will, don't break the connection, or hinder the success.

So that the objection we are upon, don't lie against the doctrine of the necessity of events by a certainty of connection and consequence: on the contrary, it is truly forcible against the Arminian doctrine of contingence and self-determination; which is inconsistent with such a connection. If there be no connection between those events wherein virtue and vice consist, and anything antecedent; then there is no connection between these events and any means or endeavors used in order to them: and if so, then those means must be in vain. The less there is of connection between foregoing things and following ones, so much the less there is between means and end, endeavors and success; and in the same proportion are means and endeavors ineffectual and in vain.

It will follow from Arminian principles, that there is no degree of connection between virtue or vice, and any foregoing event or thing: or in other words, that the determination of the existence of virtue or vice don't in the least depend on the influence of anything that comes to pass antecedently, from which the determination of its existence is, as its cause, means, or ground; because, so far as it is so, it is not from self-determination: and therefore, so far there is nothing of the nature of virtue or vice. And so it follows, that virtue and vice are not at all, in any degree, dependent upon, or connected with any foregoing event or existence, as its cause, ground, or means. And if so, then all foregoing means must be totally in vain.

Hence it follows, that there cannot, in any consistence with the Arminian scheme, be any reasonable ground of so much as a conjecture concerning the consequence of any means and endeavors, in order to escaping vice or obtaining virtue, or any choice or preference of means, as having a greater probability of success by some than others; either from any natural connection or dependence of the end on the means, or through any divine constitution, or revealed way of God's bestowing or bringing to pass these things, in consequence of any means, endeavors, prayers or deeds. Conjecture in this latter case depends on a supposition that God himself is the giver, or determining cause of the events sought: but if they depend on self-determination, then God is not the determining or disposing author of them: and if these things are not of his disposal, then no conjecture can be made from any revelation he has given concerning any way or method of his disposal of them.

Yea, on these principles, it will not only follow that men can't have any reasonable ground of judgment or conjecture, that their means and endeavors to obtain virtue or avoid vice, will be successful, but they may be sure they will not; they may be certain, that they will be in vain; and that if ever the thing which they seek comes to pass, it will not be at all owing to the means they use. For means and endeavors can have no effect at all, in order to obtain the end, but in one of these two ways; either (1) through a natural tendency and influence, to prepare and dispose the mind more to virtuous acts, either by causing the disposition of the heart to be more in favor of such acts, or by bringing the mind more into the view of powerful motives and inducements: or (2) by putting persons more in the way of God's bestowment of the benefit. But neither of these can be the case. Not the latter; for as has been just now observed, it don't consist with the Arminian notion of self-determination, which they suppose essential to virtue, that God should be the bestower, or (which is the same thing) the determining, disposing author of virtue. Not the former; for natural influence and tendency supposes causality and connection; and that supposes necessity of event, which is inconsistent with Arminian liberty. A tendency of means, by biasing the heart in favor of virtue, or by bringing the will under the influence and power of motives in its determinations, are both inconsistent with Arminian liberty of will, consisting in indifference, and sovereign self-determination, as has been largely demonstrated.

But for the more full removal of this prejudice against that doctrine of necessity which has been maintained, as though it tended to encourage a total neglect of all endeavors as vain; the following things may be considered.

The question is not, whether men may not thus improve this doctrine: we know that many true and wholesome doctrines are abused: but, whether the doctrine gives any just occasion for such an improvement; or whether, on the supposition of the truth of the doctrine, such a use of it would not be unreasonable? If any shall affirm, that it would not, but that the very nature of the doctrine is such as gives just occasion for it, it must be on this supposition; namely, that such an invariable necessity of all things already settled, must render the interposition of all means, endeavors, conclusions or actions of ours, in order to the obtaining any future end whatsoever, perfectly insignificant; because they can't in the least alter or vary the course and series of things, in any event or circumstance; all being already fixed unalterably by necessity: and that therefore 'tis folly, for men to use any means for any end; but their wisdom, to save themselves the trouble of endeavors, and take their ease. No person can draw such an inference from this doctrine, and come to such a conclusion, without contradicting himself, and going counter to the very principles he pretends to act upon: for he comes to a conclusion, and takes a course, in order to an end, even his ease, or the saving himself from trouble; he seeks something future, and uses means in order to a future thing, even in his drawing up that conclusion, that he will seek nothing, and use no means in order to anything future; he seeks his future ease, and the benefit and comfort of indolence. If prior necessity that determines all things, makes vain all actions or conclusions of ours, in order to anything future; then it makes vain all conclusions and conduct of ours, in order to our future ease. The measure of our ease, with the time, manner and every circumstance of it, is already fixed, by all-determining necessity, as much as anything else. If he says within himself, "What future happiness or misery I shall have, is already in effect determined by the necessary course and connection of things; therefore I will save myself the trouble of labor and diligence, which can't add to my determined degree of happiness, or diminish my misery; but will take my ease, and will enjoy the comfort of sloth and negligence." Such a man contradicts himself: he says, the measure of his future happiness and misery is already fixed, and he won't try to diminish the one, nor add to the other: but yet in his very conclusion, he contradicts this; for he takes up this conclusion, to add to his future happiness, by the ease and comfort of his negligence; and to diminish his future trouble and misery, by saving himself the trouble of using means and taking pains.

Therefore persons can't reasonably make this improvement of the doctrine of necessity, that they will go into a voluntary negligence of means for their own happiness. For the principles they must go upon, in order to this, are inconsistent with their making any improvement at all of the doctrine: for to make some improvement of it, is to be influenced by it, to come to some voluntary conclusion, in regard to their own conduct, with some view or aim: but this, as has been shown, is inconsistent with the principles they pretend to act upon. In short, the principles are such as cannot be acted upon at all, or in any respect, consistently. And therefore in every pretence of acting upon them, or making any improvement at all of them, there is a self-contradiction.

As to that objection against the doctrine which I have endeavored to prove, that it makes men no more than mere machines; I would say, that notwithstanding this doctrine, man is entirely, perfectly and unspeakably different from a mere machine, in that he has reason and understanding, and has a faculty of will, and so is capable of volition and choice; and in that, his will is guided by the dictates or views of his understanding; and in that his external actions and behavior, and in many respect also his thoughts, and the exercises of his mind, are subject to his will; so that he has liberty to act according to his choice, and do what he pleases; and by means of these things, is capable of moral habits and moral acts, such inclinations and actions as according to the common sense of mankind, are worthy of praise, esteem, love and reward; or on the contrary, of disesteem, detestation, indignation and punishment.

In these things is all the difference from mere machines, as to liberty and agency, that would be any perfection, dignity or privilege, in any respect: all the difference that can be desired, and all that can be conceived of; and indeed all that the pretensions of the Arminians themselves come to, as they are forced often to explain themselves (though their explications overthrow and abolish the things asserted, and pretended to be explained). For they are forced to explain a self-determining power of will, by a power in the soul, to determine as it chooses or wills; which comes to no more than this, that a man has a power of choosing, and in many instances, can do as he chooses. Which is quite a different thing from that contradiction, his having power of choosing his first act of choice in the case.

Or if their scheme makes any other difference than this, between men and machines, it is for the worse: it is so far from supposing men to have a dignity and privilege above machines, that it makes the manner of their being determined still more unhappy. Whereas machines are guided by an understanding cause, by the skillful hand of the workman or owner; the will of man is left to the guidance of nothing, but absolute blind contingence.

SECTION 6.

CONCERNING THAT OBJECTION AGAINST THE DOCTRINE WHICH HAS BEEN MAINTAINED, THAT IT AGREES WITH THE STOICAL DOCTRINE OF FATE, AND THE OPINIONS OF MR. HOBBES

When Calvinists oppose the Arminian notion of the freedom of will, and contingence of volition, and insist that there are no acts of the will, nor any other events whatsoever, but what are attended with some kind of necessity; their opposers cry out of them, as agreeing with the ancient Stoics in their doctrine of fate, and with Mr. Hobbes in his opinion of necessity.

It would not be worth while, to take notice of so impertinent an objection, had it not been urged by some of the chief Arminian writers. There were many important truths maintained by the ancient Greek and Roman philosophers, and especially the Stoics, that are never the worse for being held by them. The Stoic philosophers, by the general agreement of Christian divines, and even Arminian divines, were the greatest, wisest and most virtuous of all the heathen philosophers; and in their doctrine and practice came the nearest to Christianity of any of their sects. How frequently are the sayings of these philosophers, in many of the writings and sermons, even of Arminian divines, produced, not as arguments of the falseness of the doctrines which they delivered, but as a confirmation of some of the greatest truths of the Christian religion, relating to the unity and perfections of the Godhead, a future state, the duty and happiness of mankind, etc. as observing how the light of nature and reason in the wisest and best of the heathen, harmonized with, and confirms the gospel of Jesus Christ.

And it is very remarkable concerning Dr. Whitby, that although he alleges the agreement of the Stoics with us, wherein he supposes they maintained the like doctrine with us, as an argument against the truth of our doctrine; yet this very Dr. Whitby alleges the agreement of the Stoics with the Arminians, wherein he supposes they taught the same doctrine with them, as an argument for the truth of their doctrine (*Discourse on the Five Points*, Dis. IV, ch. 1, no. 8; pp. 325, 326, 327). So that when the Stoics agree with them, this (it seems) is a confirmation of their doctrine, and a confutation of ours, as shewing that our opinions are contrary to the natural sense and common reason of mankind: nevertheless, when the Stoics agree with us, it argues no such thing in our favor; but on the contrary, is a great argument against us, and shews our doctrine to be heathenish.

It is observed by some Calvinistic writers, that the Arminians symbolize with the Stoics, in some of those doctrines wherein they are opposed by the Calvinists; particularly in their denying an original, innate, total corruption and depravity of heart; and in what they held of man's ability to make himself truly virtuous and conformed to God; and in some other doctrines.

It may be further observed, 'tis certainly no better objection against our doctrine, that it agrees in some respects with the doctrine of the ancient Stoic philosophers, than it is against theirs, wherein they differ from us, that it agrees in some respects with the opinion of the very worst of the heathen philosophers, the followers of Epicurus, that father of atheism and licentiousness, and with the doctrine of the Sadducees and Jesuits.

I am not much concerned to know precisely what the ancient Stoic philosophers held concerning fate, in order to determine what is truth; as though it were a sure way to be in the right, to take good heed to differ from them. It seems that they differed among themselves; and probably the doctrine of fate, as maintained by most of 'em, was in some respects erroneous. But whatever their doctrine was, if any of 'em held such a fate, as is repugnant to any liberty consisting in our doing as we please, I utterly deny such a fate. If they held any such fate, as is not consistent with the common and universal notions that mankind have of liberty, activity, moral agency, virtue and vice; I disclaim any such thing, and think I have demonstrated that the scheme I maintain is no such scheme. If the Stoics by fate meant anything of such a nature, as can be supposed to stand in the way of the advantage and benefit of the use of means and endeavors, or makes it less worth the while for men to desire, and seek after anything wherein their virtue and happiness consists; I hold no doctrine that is clogged with any such inconvenience, any more than any other scheme whatsoever; and by no means so much as the Arminian scheme of contingence; as has been shewn. If they held any such doctrine of universal fatality, as is inconsistent with any kind of liberty, that is or can be any perfection, dignity, privilege or benefit, or anything desirable, in any respect, for any intelligent creature, or indeed with any liberty that is possible or conceivable; I embrace no such doctrine. If they held any such doctrine of fate as is inconsistent with the world's being in all things subject to the disposal of an intelligent wise agent, that presides, not as the soul of the world, but as the sovereign Lord of the universe, governing all things by proper will, choice and design, in the exercise of the most perfect liberty conceivable, without subjection to any constraint, or being properly under the power or influence of anything before, above or without himself; I wholly renounce any such doctrine.

As to Mr. Hobbes' maintaining the same doctrine concerning necessity; I confess, it happens I never read Mr. Hobbes. Let his opinion be what it will, we need not reject all truth which is demonstrated by clear evidence, merely because it was once held by some bad man. This great truth, that Jesus is the Son of God, was not spoiled because it was once and again proclaimed with a loud voice by the devil. If truth is so defiled because it is spoken by the mouth, or written by the pen of some ill-minded mischievous man, that it must never be received, we shall never know when we hold any of the most precious and evident truths by a sure tenure. And if Mr. Hobbes has made a bad use of this truth, that is to be lamented: but the truth is not to be thought worthy of rejection on that account. 'Tis common for the corruptions of the hearts of evil men, to abuse the best things to vile purposes.

I might also take notice of its having been observed, that the Arminians agree with Mr. Hobbes (Dr. Gill, in his answer to Dr. Whitby [John Gill, *The Cause of God and Truth, Being a Confutation of the Arguments from Reason Used by the Arminians; and Particularly by Dr. Whitby, in His Discourse on the Five Points*, ch. 5, sec. 11, nos. 6 f. (London, 1737), Pt. III, pp. 183 ff]) in many more things than the Calvinists. As, in what he is said to hold concerning original sin, in denying the necessity of supernatural illumination, in denying infused grace, in denying the doctrine of justification by faith alone; and other things.

SECTION 7.

CONCERNING THE NECESSITY OF THE DIVINE WILL

Some may possibly object against what has been supposed of the absurdity and inconsistence of a self-determining power in the will, and the impossibility of its being otherwise, than that the will should be determined in every case by some motive, and by a motive which (as it stands in the view of the understanding) is of superior strength to any appearing on the other side; that if these things are true, it will follow, that not only the will of created minds, but the will of God himself is necessary in all its determinations. Concerning which says the author of the Essay on the Freedom of Will in God and in the Creature (p. 85, 86) [Watts, *Essay*, Sec. 7, dif. 1; in *Works*, 6, 272],

> What strange doctrine is this, contrary to all our ideas of the dominion of God? Does it not destroy the glory of his liberty of choice, and take away from the creator and governor and benefactor of the world, that most free and sovereign agent, all the glory of this sort of freedom? Does it not seem to make him a kind of mechanical medium of fate, and introduce Mr. Hobbes's doctrine of fatality and necessity, into all things that God hath to do with? Does it not seem to represent the blessed God, as a being of vast understanding, as well as power and efficiency, but still to leave him without a will to choose among all the objects within his view? In short, it seems to make the blessed God a sort of almighty minister of fate, under its universal and supreme influence; as it was the professed sentiment of some of the ancients, that fate was above the gods.

This is declaiming, rather than arguing; and an application to men's imaginations and prejudices, rather than to mere reason. But I would calmly endeavor to consider whether there be any reason in this frightful representation. But before I enter upon a particular consideration of the matter, I would observe this: that 'tis reasonable to suppose, it should be much more difficult to express or conceive things according to exact metaphysical truth, relating to the nature and manner of the existence of things in the divine understanding and will, and the operation of these faculties (if I may so call them) of the divine mind, than in the human mind; which is infinitely more within our view, and nearer to a proportion to the measure of our comprehension, and more commensurate to the use and import of human speech. Language is indeed very deficient, in regard of terms to express precise truth concerning our own minds, and their faculties and operations. Words were first formed to express external things; and those that are applied to express things internal and spiritual, are almost all borrowed, and used in a sort of figurative sense. Whence they are most of 'em attended with a great deal of ambiguity and unfixedness in their signification, occasioning innumerable doubts, difficulties and confusions in inquiries and controversies about things of this nature. But language is much less adapted to express things in the mind of the incomprehensible Deity, precisely as they are.

We find a great deal of difficulty in conceiving exactly of the nature of our own souls. And notwithstanding all the progress which has been made in past and present ages, in this kind of knowledge, whereby our metaphysics, as it relates to these things, is brought to greater perfection than once it was; yet here is still work enough left for future inquiries and researches, and room for progress still to be made, for many ages and generations. But we had need to be infinitely able metaphysicians, to conceive with clearness, according to strict, proper and perfect truth, concerning the nature of the divine essence, and the modes of the action and operation of the powers of the divine mind.

And it may be noted particularly, that though we are obliged to conceive of some things in God as consequent and dependent on others, and of some things pertaining to the divine nature and will as the foundation of others, and so before others in the order of nature: as, we must conceive of the knowledge and holiness of God as prior in the order of nature to his happiness; the perfection of his understanding, as the foundation of his wise purposes and decrees; the holiness of his nature, as the cause and reason of his holy determinations. And yet when we speak of cause and effect, antecedent and consequent, fundamental and dependent, determining and determined, in the first Being, who is self-existent, independent, of perfect and absolute simplicity and immutability, and the first cause of all things; doubtless there must be less propriety in such representations, than when we speak of derived dependent beings, who are compounded, and liable to perpetual mutation and succession.

Having premised this, I proceed to observe concerning

the forementioned author's exclamation, about the necessary determination of God's will, in all things, by what he sees to be fittest and best.

That all the seeming force of such objections and exclamations must arise from an imagination, that there is some sort of privilege or dignity in being without such a moral necessity, as will make it impossible to do any other, than always choose what is wisest and best; as though there were some disadvantage, meanness and subjection, in such a necessity; a thing by which the will was confined, kept under, and held in servitude by something, which, as it were, maintained a strong and invincible power and dominion over it, by bonds that held him fast, and that he could by no means deliver himself from. Whereas, this must be all mere imagination and delusion. 'Tis no disadvantage or dishonor to a being, necessarily to act in the most excellent and happy manner, from the necessary perfection of his own nature. This argues no imperfection, inferiority or dependence, nor any want of dignity, privilege or ascendancy.

It might have been objected with much more plausibleness, that the supreme cause cannot be free, because he must needs do always what is best in the whole. But this would not at all serve Spinoza's purpose: for this is a necessity, not of nature and fate, but of fitness and wisdom; a necessity consistent with the greatest freedom, and most perfect choice. For the only foundation of this necessity is such an unalterable rectitude of will, and perfection of wisdom, as makes it impossible for a wise being to act foolishly." Samuel Clarke, Demonstration of the Being and Attributes of God [6th ed. London, 1725], p. 64.

Though God is a most perfectly free agent, yet he cannot but do always what is best and wisest in the whole. The reason is evident; because perfect wisdom and goodness are as steady and certain principles of action, as necessity itself; and an infinitely wise and good being, indued with the most perfect liberty, can no more choose to act in contradiction to wisdom and goodness, than a necessary agent can act contrary to the necessity by which it is acted; it being as great an absurdity and impossibility in choice, for infinite wisdom to choose to act unwisely, or infinite goodness to choose what is not good, as it would be in nature, for absolute necessity to fail of producing its necessary effect. There was indeed no necessity in nature, that God should at first create such beings as he has created, or indeed any being at all; because he is in himself infinitely happy and all-sufficient. There was also no necessity in nature, that he should preserve and continue things in being, after they were created; because he would be self-sufficient without their continuance, as he was before their creation. But it was fit and wise and good, that infinite wisdom should manifest, and infinite goodness communicate itself; and therefore it was necessary, in the sense of necessity I am now speaking of, that things should be made at such a time, and continued so long, and indeed with various perfections in such degrees, as infinite wisdom and goodness saw it wisest and best that they should." Ibid., pp. 112 f.

'Tis not a fault, but a perfection of our nature, to desire, will and act, according to the last result of a fair examination.

This is so far from being a restraint or diminution of freedom, that it is the very improvement and benefit of it: 'tis not an abridgment, 'tis the end and use of our liberty; and the further we are removed from such a determination, the nearer we are to misery and slavery. A perfect indifference in the mind, not determinable by its last judgment of the good or evil that is thought to attend its choice, would be so far from being an advantage and excellency of any intellectual nature, that it would be as great an imperfection as the want of indifferency to act, or not to act, till determined by the will, would be an imperfection on the other side.... 'Tis as much a perfection, that desire or the power of preferring should be determined by good, as that the power of acting should be determined by the will: and the certainer such determination is, the greater the perfection. Nay, were we determined by anything but the last result of our own minds, judging of the good or evil of any action, we were not free. The very end of our freedom being, that we might attain the good we choose; and therefore every man is brought under a necessity by his constitution, as an intelligent being, to be determined in willing by his own thought and judgment, what is best for him to do; also he would be under the determination of some other than himself, which is want of liberty. And to deny that a man's will, in every determination, follows his own judgment, is to say, that a man wills and acts for an end that he would not have, at the same time that he wills and acts for it. For if he prefers it in his present thoughts, before any other, 'tis plain he then thinks better of it, and would have it before any other; unless he can have, and not have it; will, and not will it, at the same time; a contradiction too manifest to be admitted.

If we look upon those superior beings above us, who enjoy perfect happiness, we shall have reason to judge, that they are more steadily determined in their choice of good than we; and yet we have no reason to think they are less happy, or less free, than we are. And if it were fit for such poor finite creatures as we are, to pronounce what infinite wisdom and goodness could do, I think we might say, that God himself cannot choose what is not good. The freedom of the Almighty hinders not his being determined by what is best.

But to give a right view of this mistaken part of liberty, let me ask, would anyone be a changeling, because he is less determined by wise determinations [Locke has "considerations"], than a wise man? Is it worth the name of freedom, to be at liberty to play the fool, and draw shame and misery upon a man's self? If to break loose from the conduct of reason, and to want that restraint of examination and judgment, that keeps us from doing or choosing the worse, be liberty, true liberty, mad men and fools are the only free men. Yet I think nobody would choose to be mad, for the sake of such liberty, but he that is mad already." Locke, *Essay*, Bk. II, ch. 21, nos. 48–51; 1, 345–7.

This Being having all things always necessarily in view, must always, and eternally will, according to his infinite comprehension of things; that is, must will all things that are wisest and best to be done. There is no getting free of this consequence. If it can will at all, it must will this way. To be capable of knowing, and not capable of willing, is not to be understood. And to be capable of willing otherwise than what is wisest and best, contradicts that knowledge which is infinite. Infinite knowledge must direct the will without error. Here then is the origin of moral necessity; and that is really, of freedom.... Perhaps it may be said, when the divine will is determined, from the consideration of the eternal aptitudes of things, it is as necessarily determined, as if it were physically impelled, if that were possible. But it is unskillfulness, to suppose this an objection. The great principle is once established, vis. that the divine will is determined by the eternal reason and aptitudes of things, instead of being physically impelled; and after that, the more strong and necessary this determination is, the more perfect the Deity must be allowed to be: it is this that makes him an amiable and adorable being, whose will and power are constantly, immutably determined, by the consideration of what is wisest and best; instead of a surd being, with power, but without discerning and reason. It is the beauty of this necessity, that it is strong as fate itself, with all the advantage of reason and goodness. ... It is strange, to see men contend, that the Deity is not free, because he is necessarily rational, immutably good and wise; when a man is allowed still the perfecter being, the more fixedly and constantly his will is determined by reason and truth." Andrew Baxter, *An Enquiry into the Nature of the Human Soul, Wherein the Immateriality of the Soul is Evinced from the Principles of Reason and Philosophy*, 3d ed., 2, 403 f.

'Tis not inconsistent with the absolute, and most perfect sovereignty of God. The sovereignty of God is his ability and authority to do whatever pleases him; whereby "he doth according to his will in the armies of heaven, and amongst the inhabitants of the earth, and none can stay his hand, or say unto him, what dost thou?" [Dan. 4:35]. The following things belong to the sovereignty of God; viz. (1) supreme, universal, and infinite power; whereby he is able to do what he pleases, without control, without any confinement of that power, without any subjection in the least measure to any other power; and so without any hindrance or restraint, that it should be either impossible, or at all difficult, for him to accomplish his will; and without any dependence of his power on any other power, from whence it should be derived, or which it should stand in any need of: so far from this, that all other power is derived from him, and is absolutely dependent on him. (2) That he has supreme authority; absolute and most perfect right to do what he wills, without subjection to any superior authority, or any derivation of authority from any other, or limitation by any distinct independent authority, either superior, equal, or inferior; he being the head of all dominion, and fountain of all authority; and also without restraint by any obligation, implying either subjection, derivation, or dependence, or proper limitation. (3) That his will is supreme, underived, and independent on anything without himself; being in everything determined by his own counsel, having no other rule but his own wisdom; his will not being subject to, or restrained by the will of any other, and others' wills being perfectly subject to his. (4) That his wisdom, which determines his will, is supreme, perfect, underived, self-sufficient, and independent; so that it may be said as in Is. 40:14, "With whom took he counsel? And who instructed him and taught him in the path of judgment, and taught him knowledge, and showed him the way of understanding?" —There is no other divine sovereignty but this: and this is properly absolute sovereignty: no other is desirable; nor would any other be honorable, or happy: and indeed there is no other conceivable or possible. 'Tis the glory and greatness of the divine sovereignty, that God's will is determined by his own infinite all-sufficient wisdom in everything; and in nothing at all is either directed by any inferior wisdom, or by no wisdom; whereby it would become senseless arbitrariness, determining and acting without reason, design or end.

If God's will is steadily and surely determined in everything by supreme wisdom, then it is in everything necessarily determined to that which is most wise. And certainly it would be a disadvantage and indignity, to be otherwise. For if the divine will was not necessarily determined to that which in every case is wisest and best, it must be subject to some degree of undesigning contingence; and so in the same degree liable to evil. To suppose the divine will liable to be carried hither and thither at random, by the uncertain wind of blind contingence, which is guided by no wisdom, no motive, no intelligent dictate whatsoever (if any such thing were possible), would certainly argue a great degree of imperfection and meanness, infinitely unworthy of the deity. If it be a disadvantage, for the divine will to be attended with this moral necessity, then the more free from it, and the more left at random, the greater dignity and advantage. And consequently to be perfectly free from the direction of understanding, and universally and entirely left to senseless unmeaning contingence, to act absolutely at random, would be the supreme glory.

It no more argues any dependence of God's will, that his supremely wise volition is necessary, than it argues a dependence of his being, that his existence is necessary. If it be something too low, for the supreme Being to have his will determined by moral necessity, so as necessarily, in every case, to will in the highest degree holily and happily; then why is it not also something too low, for him to have his existence, and the infinite perfection of his nature, and his infinite happiness determined by necessity? It is no more to God's dishonor, to be necessarily wise, than to be necessarily holy. And if neither of them be to his dishonor, then it is not to his dishonor necessarily to act holily and wisely. And if it be not dishonorable, to be necessarily holy and wise, in the highest possible degree, no more is it mean or dishonorable, necessarily to act holily and wisely in the highest possible degree; or (which is the same thing) to do that, in every case, which above all other things is wisest and best.

The reason why it is not dishonorable, to be necessarily most holy, is, because holiness in itself is an excellent and honorable thing. For the same reason, it is no dishonor to be necessarily most wise, and in every case to act most wisely, or do the thing which is the wisest of all; for wisdom is also in itself excellent and honorable.

The forementioned author of the Essay on the Freedom of Will, etc., as has been observed, represents that doctrine of the divine will's being in everything necessarily determined by superior fitness, as making the blessed God a kind of almighty minister and mechanical medium of fate: and he insists (pp. 93, 94) [Watts, Essay, Sec. 7, dif. 3; in *Works*, 6, 275.], that this moral necessity and impossibility is in effect the same thing with physical and natural necessity and impossibility: and in pp. 54, 55 [Ibid., Sec. 5, adv. 4; in *Works*, 6, 260] he says,

> The scheme which determines the will always and certainly by the understanding, and the understanding by the appearance of things, seems to take away the true nature of vice and virtue. For the sublimest of virtues, and the vilest of vices, seem rather to be matters of fate and necessity, flowing naturally and necessarily from the existence, the circumstances, and present situation of persons and things: for this existence and situation necessarily makes such an appearance to the mind; from this appearance flows a necessary perception and judgment, concerning these things; this judgment necessarily determines the will: and thus by this chain of necessary causes, virtue and vice would lose their nature, and become

natural ideas, and necessary things, instead of moral and free actions.

And yet this same author allows (pp. 30, 31) [Ibid., Sec. 3, prop. 4; in *Works*, 6, 251], that a perfectly wise being will constantly and certainly choose what is most fit; and says (pp. 102, 103) [Ibid., Sec. 7, dif. 6; in *Works*, 6, 278], "I grant, and always have granted, that wheresoever there is such an antecedent superior fitness of things, God acts according to it, so as never to contradict it; and particularly, in all his judicial proceedings, as a governor, and distributer of rewards and punishments." Yea, he says expressly (p. 42) [Ibid., Sec. 4, prop. 11; in *Works*, 6, 255], "That it is not possible for God to act otherwise, than according to this fitness and goodness in things."

So that according to this author, putting these several passages of his Essay together, there is no virtue, nor anything of a moral nature, in the most sublime and glorious acts and exercises of God's holiness, justice, and faithfulness; and he never does anything which is in itself supremely worthy, and above all other things fit and excellent, but only as a kind of mechanical medium of fate; and in what he does as the judge, and moral governor of the world, he exercises no moral excellency; exercising no freedom in these things, because he acts by moral necessity, which is in effect the same with physical or natural necessity; and therefore he only acts by an Hobbistical fatality; as "a being indeed of vast understanding, as well as power and efficiency (as he said before) but without a will to choose, being a kind of almighty minister of fate, acting under its supreme influence." For he allows, that in all these things God's will is determined constantly and certainly by a superior fitness, and that it is not possible for him to act otherwise. And if these things are so, what glory or praise belongs to God for doing holily and justly, or taking the most fit, holy, wise and excellent course, in any one instance? Whereas, according to the Scriptures, and also the common sense of mankind, it don't in the least derogate from the honor of any being, that through the moral perfection of his nature, he necessarily acts with supreme wisdom and holiness: but on the contrary, his praise is the greater: herein consists the height of his glory.

The same author (p. 56) [*Essay*, Sec. 5, adv. 5; in *Works*, 6, 260] supposes, that herein appears the excellent "character of a wise and good man, that though he can choose contrary to the fitness of things, yet he does not; but suffers himself to be directed by fitness"; and that in this conduct "he imitates the blessed God." And yet he supposes 'tis contrariwise with the blessed God; not that he suffers himself to be directed by fitness, when he can choose contrary to the fitness of things, but that "he cannot choose contrary to the fitness of things"; as he says (p. 42), "That it is not possible for God to act otherwise, than according to this fitness, where there is any fitness or goodness in things": yea, he supposes (p. 31) [Ibid., Sec. 3, prop. 4; in *Works*, 6, 251] that if a man "were perfectly wise and good, he could not do otherwise than be constantly and certainly determined by the fitness of things."

One thing more I would observe, before I conclude this section; and that is, that if it derogates nothing from the glory of God, to be necessarily determined by superior fitness in some things, then neither does it to be thus determined in all things; from anything in the nature of such necessity, as at all detracting from God's freedom, independence, absolute supremacy, or any dignity or glory of his nature, state, or manner of acting; or as implying any infirmity, restraint, or subjection. And if the thing be such as well consists with God's glory, and has nothing tending at all to detract from it; then we need not be afraid of ascribing it to God in too many things, lest thereby we should detract from God's glory too much.

SECTION 8.

SOME FURTHER OBJECTIONS AGAINST THE MORAL NECESSITY OF GOD'S VOLITIONS CONSIDERED

The author last cited, as has been observed, owns that God, being perfectly wise, will constantly and certainly choose what appears most fit, where there is a superior fitness and goodness in things; and that it is not possible for him to do otherwise. So that it is in effect confessed, that in those things where there is any real preferableness, 'tis no dishonor, nothing in any respect unworthy of God, for him to act from necessity; notwithstanding all that can be objected from the agreement of such a necessity, with the fate of the Stoics, and the necessity maintained by Mr. Hobbes. From which it will follow, that if it were so, that in all the different things, among which God chooses, there were evermore a superior fitness or preferableness on one side, then it would be no dishonor, or anything, in any respect, unworthy, or unbecoming of God, for his will to be necessarily determined in everything. And if this be allowed, it is a giving up entirely the argument, from the unsuitableness of such a necessity to the liberty, supremacy, independence and glory of the divine Being; and a resting the whole weight of the affair on the decision of another point wholly diverse; viz. whether it be so indeed, that in all the various possible things which are in God's view, and may be considered as capable objects of his choice, there is not evermore a preferableness in one thing above another. This is denied by this author; who supposes, that in many instances, between two or more possible things, which come within the view of the divine mind, there is a perfect indifference and equality as to fitness, or tendency to attain any good end which God can have in view, or to answer any of his designs. Now therefore I would consider whether this be evident.

The arguments brought to prove this, are of two kinds. (1) It is urged, that in many instances we must suppose there is absolutely no difference between various possible objects of choice, which God has in view: and (2) that the difference between many things is so inconsiderable, or of such a nature, that it would be unreasonable to suppose it to be of any consequence; or to suppose that any of God's wise designs would not be answered in one way as well as the other.

Therefore,

I. The first thing to be considered is, whether there are any instances wherein there is a perfect likeness, and absolutely no difference, between different objects of choice, that are proposed to the divine understanding?

And here in the first place, it may be worthy to be considered, whether the contradiction there is in the terms of the question proposed, don't give reason to suspect that there is an inconsistence in the thing supposed. 'Tis inquired, whether different objects of choice mayn't be absolutely without difference? If they are absolutely without difference, then how are they different objects of choice? If there be absolutely no difference in any respect, then there is no variety or distinction: for distinction is only by some difference. And if there be no variety among proposed objects of choice, then there is no opportunity for variety of choice, or difference of determination. For that determination of a thing which is not different in any respect, is not a different determination, but the same. That this is no quibble, may appear more fully anon.

The arguments, to prove that the most High, in some instances, chooses to do one thing rather than another, where the things themselves are perfectly without difference, are two.

1. That the various parts of infinite time and space, absolutely considered, are perfectly alike, and don't differ at all one from another: and that therefore, when God determined to create the world in such a part of infinite duration and space, rather than others, he determined and preferred among various objects, between which there was no preferableness, and absolutely no difference.

Answer. This objection supposes an infinite length of time before the world was created, distinguished by successive parts, properly and truly so; or a succession of limited and [measurable] periods of time, following one another, in an infinitely long series: which must needs be a groundless imagination. The eternal duration which was before the world, being only the eternity of God's existence; which is nothing else but his immediate, perfect and invariable possession of the whole of his unlimited life, together and at once; *vitæ interminabilis, iota, simul et perfecta possessio*. Which is so generally allowed, that I need not stand to demonstrate it.

If all created beings were taken away, all possibility of any mutation or succession of one thing to another would appear to be also removed. Abstract succession in eternity is scarce to be understood. What is it that succeeds? One minute to another perhaps, *velut unda supervenit undam*. But when we imagine this, we fancy that the minutes are things separately existing. This is the common notion; and yet it is a manifest prejudice. Time is nothing but the existence of created successive beings, and eternity the necessary existence of the Deity. Therefore, if this necessary Being hath no change or succession in his nature, his existence must of course be unsuccessive. We seem to commit a double oversight in this case; first, we find succession in the necessary nature and existence of the Deity himself: which is wrong, if the reasoning above be conclusive. And then we ascribe this succession to eternity, considered abstractedly from the eternal Being; and suppose it, one knows not what, a thing subsisting by itself, and flowing, one minute after another. This is the work of pure imagination, and contrary to the reality of things. Hence the common metaphorical expressions: 'time runs apace' 'let us lay hold on the present minute,' and the like. The philosophers themselves mislead us by their illustrations; they compare eternity to the motion of a point running on forever, and making a traceless infinite line. Here the point is supposed a thing actually subsisting, representing the present minute; and then they ascribe motion or succession to it: that is, they ascribe motion to a mere non-entity, to illustrate to us a successive eternity made up of finite successive parts. ... If once we allow an all-perfect Mind, which hath an eternal immutable and infinite comprehension of all things, always (and allow it we must) the distinction of past and future vanishes with respect to such a mind. ... In a word, if we proceed step by step, as above, the eternity or existence of the Deity will appear to be *vita interminabilis, tota, simul et perfecta possessio*; how much soever this may have been a paradox hitherto." (Baxter, 3d ed. 2, 409 ff.) [1st ed., pp. 375–6; 2d ed. 2, 438–9.]

So this objection supposes an extent of space beyond the limits of the creation, of an infinite length, breadth and depth, truly and properly distinguished into different measurable parts, limited at certain stages, one beyond another, in an infinite series. Which notion of absolute and infinite space is doubtless as unreasonable, as that now mentioned, of absolute and infinite duration. 'Tis as improper, to imagine that the immensity and omnipresence of God is distinguished by a series of miles and leagues, one beyond another; as that the infinite duration of God is distinguished by months and years, one after another. A diversity and order of distinct parts, limited by certain periods, is as conceivable, and does as naturally obtrude itself on our imagination, in one case as the other; and there is equal reason in each case, to suppose that our imagination deceives us. 'Tis equally improper, to talk of months and years of the divine existence, and mile-squares of deity: and we equally deceive ourselves, when we talk of the world's being differently fixed with respect to either of these sorts of measures. I think, we know not what we mean, if we say, the world might have been differently placed from what it is, in the broad expanse of infinity; or, that it might have been differently fixed in the long line of eternity: and all arguments and objections which are built on the imaginations we are apt to have of infinite extension or duration, are buildings founded on shadows, or castles in the air.

2. The second argument, to prove that the most High wills one thing rather than another, without any superior fitness or preferableness in the thing preferred, is God's actually placing in different parts of the world, particles or atoms of matter that are perfectly equal and alike. The forementioned author says (p. 78, etc.) [Watts, *Essay*, Sec. 6, ans. to obj. 6; in *Works*, 6, 269], "If one would descend to the minute specific particles, of which different bodies are composed, we should see abundant reason to believe that there are thousands of such little particles or atoms of matter, which are perfectly equal and alike, and could give no distinct determination to the will of God, where to place them." He there instances in particles of water, of which there are such immense numbers, which compose the rivers and oceans of this world; and the infinite myriads of the luminous and fiery particles, which compose the body of the sun; so many, that it would be very unreasonable to suppose no two of them should be exactly equal and alike.

Answer (1). To this I answer: that as we must suppose matter to be infinitely divisible, 'tis very unlikely that any two of all these particles are exactly equal and alike; so unlikely, that it is a thousand to one, yea, an infinite number to one, but it is otherwise: and that although we should allow a great similarity between the different particles of water and fire, as to their general nature and figure; and however small we suppose those particles to be, 'tis infinitely unlikely, that any two of them should be exactly equal in dimensions and quantity of matter. If we should suppose a great many globes of the same nature with the globe of the earth, it would be very strange, if there were any two of them that had exactly the same number of particles of dust and water in them. But infinitely less strange, than that two particles of light should have just the same quantity of matter. For a particle of light (according to the doctrine of the infinite divisibility of matter) is composed of infinitely more assignable parts, than there are particles of dust and water in the globe of the earth. And as it is infinitely unlikely, that any two of these particles should be equal; so it is, that they should be alike in other respects: to instance, in the configuration of their surfaces. If there were very many globes, of the nature of the earth, it would be very unlikely that any two should have exactly the same number of particles of dust, water and stone, in their surfaces, and all posited exactly alike, one with respect to another, without any difference, in any part discernible either by the naked eye or microscope; but infinitely less strange, than that two particles of light should be perfectly of the same figure. For there are infinitely more assignable real parts on the surface of a particle of light, than there are particles of dust, water and stone, on the surface of the terrestrial globe.

Answer (2). But then, supposing that there are two particles or atoms of matter perfectly equal and alike, which

God has placed in different parts of the creation; as I will not deny it to be possible for God to make two bodies perfectly alike, and put them in different places; yet it will not follow, that two different or distinct acts or effects of the divine power have exactly the same fitness for the same ends. For these two different bodies are not different or distinct, in any other respects than those wherein they differ: they are two in no other respects than those wherein there is a difference. If they are perfectly equal and alike in themselves, then they can be distinguished, or be distinct, only in those things which are called circumstances; as, place, time, rest, motion, or some other present or past circumstances or relations. For 'tis difference only, that constitutes distinction. If God makes two bodies in themselves every way equal and alike, and agreeing perfectly in all other circumstances and relations, but only their place; then in this only is there any distinction or duplicity. The figure is the same, the measure is the same, the solidity and resistance are the same, and everything the same, but only the place. Therefore what the will of God determines, is this, namely, that there should be the same figure, the same extension, the same resistance, etc. in two different places. And for this determination he has some reason. There is some end, for which such a determination and act has a peculiar fitness, above all other acts. Here is no one thing determined without an end, and no one thing without a fitness for that end, superior to anything else. If it be the pleasure of God to cause the same resistance, and the same figure, to be in two different places and situations, we can no more justly argue from it, that here must be some determination or act of God's will, that is wholly without motive or end, [than] we can argue that whenever, in any case, it is a man's will to speak the same words, or make the same sounds at two different times; there must be some determination or act of his will, without any motive or end. The difference of place, in the former case, proves no more than the difference of time does in the other. If any-one should say with regard to the former case, that there must be something determined without an end; viz. that of those two similar bodies, this in particular should be made in this place, and the other in the other, and should inquire why the creator did not make them in a transposition, when both are alike, and each would equally have suited either place? The inquiry supposes something that is not true; namely, that the two bodies differ and are distinct in other respects besides their place. So that with this distinction, inherent in them, they might in their first creation have been transposed, and each might have begun its existence in the place of the other.

Let us for clearness' sake suppose, that God had at the beginning made two globes, each of an inch diameter, both perfect spheres, and perfectly solid without pores, and perfectly alike in every respect, and placed them near one to another, one towards the right hand, and the other towards the left, without any difference as to time, motion or rest, past or present, or any circumstance, but only their place; and the question should be asked, Why God in their creation placed 'em so? Why that which is made on the right hand, was not made on the left, and vice versa? Let it be well considered, whether there be any sense in such a question; and whether the inquiry don't suppose something false and absurd. Let it be considered, what the creator must have done otherwise than he did, what different act of will or power he must have exerted, in order to the thing proposed. All that could have been done, would have been to have made two spheres, perfectly alike, in the same places where he has made them, without any difference of the things made, either in themselves, or in any circumstance; so that the whole effect would have been without any difference, and therefore just the same. By the supposition, the two spheres are different in no other respect but their place; and therefore in other respects they are the same. Each has the same roundness: it is not a distinct rotundity, in any other respect but its situation. There are also the same dimensions, differing in nothing but their place. And so of their resistance, and everything else that belongs to them.

Here if any chooses to say, "that there is a difference in another respect, viz. that they are not numerically the same: that it is thus with all the qualities that belong to them: that it is confessed they are in some respects the same; that is, they are both exactly alike; but yet numerically they differ. Thus the roundness of one is not the same numerical, individual roundness with that of the other." Let this be supposed; then the question about the determination of the divine will in the affair, is, why did God will, that this individual roundness should be at the right hand, and the other individual roundness at the left? Why did not he make them in a contrary position? Let any rational person consider, whether such questions be not words without a meaning; as much as if God should see fit for some ends to cause the same sounds to be repeated, or made at two different times; the sounds being perfectly the same in every other respect, but only one was a minute after the other; and it should be asked upon it, why God caused these sounds, numerically different, to succeed one the other in such a manner? why he did not make that individual sound which was in the first minute, to be in the second? and the individual sound of the last minute to be in the first? Which inquiries would be even ridiculous; as I think every person must see at once, in the case proposed of two sounds, being only the same repeated, absolutely without any difference, but that one circumstance of time. If the most High sees it will answer some good end, that the same sound should be made by lightning at two distinct times, and therefore wills that it should be so, must it needs therefore be, that herein there is some act of God's will without any motive or end? God saw fit often, at distinct times, and on different occasions, to say the very same words to Moses; namely those, "I am Jehovah." And would it not be unreasonable, to infer as a certain consequence from this, that here must be some act or acts of the divine will, in determining and disposing these words exactly alike at different times, wholly without aim or inducement? But it would be no more unreasonable than to say, that there must be an act of God's without any inducement, if he sees it best, and for some reason, determines that there shall be the same resistance, the same dimensions, and the same figure, in several distinct places.

If in the instance of the two spheres, perfectly alike, it be supposed possible that God might have made them in a contrary position; that which is made at the right hand, being made at the left; then I ask, whether it is not evidently equally possible, if God had made but one of them, and that in the place of the right-hand globe, that he might have made that numerically different from what it is, and numerically different from what he did make it; though perfectly alike, and in the same place; and at the same time, and in every respect, in the same circumstances and relations? Namely, whether he might not have made it numerically the same with that which he has now made at the left hand; and so have left that which is now created at the right hand, in a state of nonexistence? And if so, whether it would not have been possible to have made one in that place, perfectly like these, and yet numerically differing from both? And let it be considered, whether from this notion of a numerical difference in bodies, perfectly equal and alike, which numerical difference is something inherent in the bodies themselves, and diverse from the difference of place or time, or any circumstance whatsoever; it will not follow, that there is an infinite number of numerically different possible bodies, perfectly alike, among which God chooses, by a self-determining power, when he goes about to create bodies.

Therefore let us put the case thus: supposing that God in the beginning had created but one perfectly solid sphere, in a certain place; and it should be inquired, why God created that individual sphere, in that place, at that time? And why he did not create another sphere perfectly like it, but numerically different, in the same place, at the same time? Or why he chose to bring into being there, that very body, rather than any of the infinite number of other bodies, perfectly like it; either of which he could have made there as well, and would have answered his end as well? Why he caused to exist, at that place and time, that individual roundness, rather than any other of the infinite number of individual rotundities, just like it? Why that individual resistance, rather than any other of the infinite number of possible resistances just like it? And it might as reasonably be asked, why, when God first caused it to thunder, he caused that individual sound then to be made, and not another just like it? Why did he make choice of this very sound, and reject all the infinite number of other possible sounds just like it, but numerically differing from it, and all differing one from another? I think, everybody must be sensible of the absurdity and nonsense of what is supposed in such inquiries. And if we calmly attend to the matter, we shall be convinced, that all such kind of objections as I am answering, are founded on nothing but the imperfection of our manner of conceiving of things, and the obscureness of language, and great want of clearness and precision in the signification of terms.

If any shall find fault with this reasoning, that it is going a great length into metaphysical niceties and subtleties; I answer, the objection which they are in reply to, is a metaphysical subtlety, and must be treated according to the nature of it. "For men to have recourse to subtleties, in raising difficulties, and then complain, that they should be taken off by minutely examining these subtleties, is a strange kind of procedure" (Baxter, 2, 331) [1st ed., p. 340–1; 2d ed., 2, 355–6].

II. Another thing alleged is, that innumerable things which are determined by the divine will, and chosen and done by God rather than others, differ from those that are not chosen in so inconsiderable a manner, that it would be unreasonable to suppose the difference to be of any consequence, or that there is any superior fitness or goodness, that God can have respect to in the determination.

To which I answer; it is impossible for us to determine with any certainty or evidence, that because the difference is very small, and appears to us of no consideration, therefore there is absolutely no superior goodness, and no valuable end which can be proposed by the creator and governor of the world, in ordering such a difference. The forementioned author mentions many instances. One is, there being one atom in the whole universe more, or less. But I think it would be unreasonable to suppose, that God made one atom in vain, or without any end or motive. He made not one atom but what was a work of his almighty power, as much as the whole globe of the earth, and requires as much of a constant exertion of almighty power to uphold it; and was made and is upheld understanding, and on design, as much as if no other had been made but that. And it would be as unreasonable to suppose, that he made it without anything really aimed at in so doing, as much as to suppose that he made the planet Jupiter without aim or design.

'Tis possible, that the most minute effects of the creator's power, the smallest assignable differences between the things which God has made, may be attended, in the whole series of events, and the whole compass and extent of their influence, with very great and important consequences. If the laws of motion and gravitation, laid down by Sir Isaac Newton, hold universally, there is not one atom, nor the least assignable part of an atom, but what has influence, every moment, throughout the whole material universe, to cause every part to be otherwise than it would be, if it were not for that particular corporeal existence. And however the effect is insensible for the present, yet it may in length of time become great and important.

To illustrate this, let us suppose two bodies moving the same way, in straight lines, perfectly parallel one to another; but to be diverted from this parallel course, and drawn one from another, as much as might be by the attraction of an atom, at the distance of one of the furthest of the fixed stars from the earth; these bodies being turned out of the lines of their parallel motion, will, by degrees, get further and further distant, one from the other; and though the distance may be imperceptible for a long time, yet at length it may become very great. So the revolution of a planet round the sun being retarded or accelerated, and the orbit of its revolution made greater or less, and more or less elliptical, and so its periodical time longer or shorter, no more than may be by the influence of the least atom, might in length of time perform a whole revolution sooner or later than otherwise it would have done; which might make a vast alteration with regard to millions of important events. So the influence of the least particle may, for ought we know, have such effect on something in the constitution of some human body, as to cause another thought to arise in the mind at a certain time, than otherwise would have been; which in length of time (yea, and that not very great) might occasion a vast alteration through the whole world of mankind. And so innumerable other ways might be mentioned, wherein the least assignable alteration may possibly be attended with great consequences.

Another argument, which the forementioned author brings against a necessary determination of the divine will by a superior fitness, is, that such doctrine derogates from the freeness of God's grace and goodness, in choosing the objects of his favor and bounty, and from the obligation upon men to thankfulness for special benefits (p. 89 etc.) [Watts, Essay, Sec. 5, adv. 8; in Works, 6, 262. See above, Intro., Pt. 5, no. 17].In answer to this objection, I would observe,

1. That it derogates no more from the goodness of God, to suppose the exercise of the benevolence of his nature to be determined by wisdom, than to suppose it determined by chance, and that his favors are bestowed altogether at random, his will being determined by nothing but perfect accident, without any end or design whatsoever; which must be the case, as has been demonstrated, if volition be not determined by a prevailing motive. That which is owing to perfect contingence, wherein neither previous inducement, nor antecedent choice has any hand, is not owing more to goodness or benevolence, than that which is owing to the influence of a wise end.

2. 'Tis acknowledged, that if the motive that determines the will of God, in the choice of the objects of his favors , be any moral quality in the object, recommending that object to his benevolence above others, his choosing that object is not so great a manifestation of the freeness and sovereignty of his grace, as if it were otherwise. But there is no necessity of supposing this, in order to our supposing that he has some wise end in view, in determining to bestow his favors on one person rather than another. We are to distinguish between the merit of the object of God's favor, or a moral qualification of the object attracting that favor and recommending to it, and the natural fitness of such a determination of the act of God's goodness, to answer some wise design of his own, some end in the view of God's omniscience. 'Tis God's own act, that is the proper and immediate object of his volition.

3. I suppose that none will deny, but that in some instances, God acts from wise design in determining the particular subjects of his favors: none will say, I presume, that when God distinguishes by his bounty particular societies or persons, he never, in any instance, exercises any wisdom in so doing, aiming at some happy consequence. And if it be not denied to be so in some instances, then I would inquire, whether in these instances God's goodness is less manifested, than in those wherein God has no aim or end at all? And whether the subjects have less cause of thankfulness? And if so, who shall be thankful for the bestowment of distinguishing mercy, with that enhancing circumstance of the distinction's being made without an end? How shall it be known when God is influenced by some wise aim, and when not? It is very manifest with respect to the Apostle Paul, that God had wise ends in choosing him to be a Christian and an apostle, who had been a persecutor, etc. The Apostle himself mentions one end. I Tim. 1:15, 16: "Christ Jesus came into the world to save sinners, of whom I am chief. Howbeit, for this cause I obtained mercy, that in me first, Jesus Christ might show forth all long-suffering, for a pattern to them who should hereafter believe on him to life everlasting." But yet the Apostle never looked on it as a diminution of the freedom and riches of divine grace in his election, which he so often and so greatly magnifies. This brings me to observe,

4. Our supposing such a moral necessity in the acts of God's will as has been spoken of, is so far from necessarily derogating from the riches of God's grace to such as are the chosen objects of his favor, that in many instances, this moral necessity may arise from goodness, and from the great degree of it. God may choose this object rather than another, as having a superior fitness to answer the ends, designs and inclinations of his goodness; being more sinful, and so more miserable and necessitous than others; the inclinations of infinite mercy and benevolence may be more gratified, and the gracious design of God's sending his Son into the world may be more abundantly answered, in the exercises of mercy towards such an object, rather than another.

One thing more I would observe, before I finish what I have to say on the head of the necessity of the acts of God's will; and that is, that something much more like a servile subjection of the divine being to fatal necessity, will follow from Arminian principles, than from the doctrines which they oppose. For they (at least most of them) suppose, with respect to all events that happen in the moral world depending on the volitions of moral agents, which are the most important events of the universe, to which all others are subordinate; I say, they suppose with respect to these, that God has a certain foreknowledge of them, antecedent to any purposes or decrees of his about them. And if so, they have a fixed certain futurity, prior to any designs or volitions of his, and independent on them, and to which his volitions must be subject, as he would wisely accommodate his affairs to this fixed futurity of the state of things in the moral world. So that here, instead of a moral necessity of God's will, arising from or consisting in the infinite perfection and blessedness of the divine Being, we have a fixed unalterable state of things, properly distinct from the perfect nature of the divine mind, and the state of the divine will and design, and entirely independent on these things, and which they have no hand in, because they are prior to them; and which God's will is truly subject to, being obliged to conform or accommodate himself to it, in all his purposes and decrees, and in everything he does in his disposals and government of the world; the moral world being the end of the natural; so that all is in vain, that is not accommodated to that state of the moral world, which consists in, or depends upon the acts and state of the wills of moral agents, which had a fixed futurition from eternity. Such a subjection to necessity as this, would truly argue an inferiority and servitude, that would be unworthy of the supreme Being; and is much more agreeable to the notion which many of the heathen had of fate, as above the gods, than that moral necessity of fitness and wisdom which has been spoken of; and is truly repugnant to the absolute sovereignty of God, and inconsistent with the supremacy of his will; and really subjects the will of the most High to the will of his creatures, and brings him into dependence upon them.

SECTION 9.

CONCERNING THAT OBJECTION AGAINST THE DOCTRINE WHICH HAS BEEN MAINTAINED, THAT IT MAKES GOD THE AUTHOR OF SIN

'Tis urged by Arminians, that the doctrine of the necessity of men's volitions, or their necessary connection with antecedent events and circumstances, makes the first cause, and supreme orderer of all things, the author of sin; in that he has so constituted the state and course of things, that sinful volitions become necessary, in consequence of his disposal. Dr. Whitby, in his "Discourse on the Freedom of the Will" (Dis. IV, ch. 4, no. 3; p. 361) cites one of the ancients, as on his side, declaring that this opinion of the necessity of the will "absolves sinners, as doing nothing of their own accord which was evil, and would cast all the blame of all the wickedness committed in the world, upon God, and upon his providence, if that were admitted by the asserters of this fate; whether he himself did necessitate them to do these things, or ordered matters so that they should be constrained to do them by some other cause." And the Doctor says in another place (Ibid., Dis. VI, ch. 1, no. 4; p. 486), "In the nature of the thing, and in the opinion of philosophers, *causa deficiens, in rebus necessariis, ad causam per se efficientem reducenda est.* In things necessary, the deficient cause must be reduced to the efficient. And in this case the reason is evident; because the not doing what is required, or not avoiding what is forbidden, being a defect, must follow from the position of the necessary cause of that deficiency."

Concerning this, I would observe the following things.

1. If there be any difficulty in this matter, 'tis nothing peculiar to this scheme; 'tis no difficulty or disadvantage wherein it is distinguished from the scheme of Arminians; and therefore not reasonably objected by them.

Dr. Whitby supposes, that if sin necessarily follows from God's withholding assistance, or if that assistance be not given which is absolutely necessary to the avoiding of evil; then in the nature of the thing, God must be as properly the author of that evil, as if he were the efficient cause of it. From whence, according to what he himself says of the devils and damned spirits, God must be the proper author of their perfect unrestrained wickedness: he must be the efficient cause of the great pride of the devils, and of their perfect malignity against God, Christ, his saints, and all that is good, and of the insatiable cruelty of their disposition. For he allows, that God has so forsaken them, and does so withhold his assistance from them, that they are incapacitated from doing good, and determined only to evil [Ibid., Dis. IV, ch. 1, no. 3; pp. 302, 305]. Our doctrine, in its consequence, makes God the author of men's sin in this world, no more, and in no other sense, than his doctrine, in its consequence, makes God the author of the hellish pride and malice of the devils. And doubtless the latter is as odious an effect as the former.

Again, if it will follow at all, that God is the author of sin, from what has been supposed of a sure and infallible connection between antecedents and consequents, it will follow because of this, viz. that for God to be the author or orderer of those things which he knows beforehand, will infallibly be attended with such a consequence, is the same thing in effect, as for him to be the author of that consequence. But if this be so, this is a difficulty which equally attends the doctrine of Arminians themselves; at least, of those of them who allow God's certain foreknowledge of all events. For on the supposition of such a foreknowledge, this is the case with respect to every sin that is committed: God knew, that if he ordered and brought to pass such and such events, such sins would infallibly follow. As for instance, God certainly foreknew, long before Judas was born, that if he ordered things so, that there should be such a man born, at such a time, and at such a place, and that his life should be preserved, and that he should, in divine providence, be led into acquaintance with Jesus; and that his heart should be so influenced by God's spirit or providence, as to be inclined to be a follower of Christ; and that he should be one of those twelve, which should be chosen constantly to attend him as his family; and that his health should be preserved so that he should go up to Jerusalem, at the last Passover in Christ's life; and it should be so ordered that Judas should see Christ's kind treatment of the woman which anointed him at Bethany, and have that reproof from Christ, which he had at that time, and see and hear other things, which excited his enmity against his master, and other circumstances should be ordered, as they were ordered; it would be what would most certainly and infallibly follow, that Judas would betray his Lord, and would soon after hang himself, and die impenitent, and be sent to hell, for his horrid wickedness.

Therefore this supposed difficulty ought not to be brought as an objection against the scheme which has been maintained, as disagreeing with the Arminian scheme, seeing 'tis no difficulty owing to such a disagreement; but a difficulty wherein the Arminians share with us. That must be unreasonably made an objection against our differing from them, which we should not escape or avoid at all by agreeing with them.

And therefore I would observe,

II. They who object, that this doctrine makes God the author of sin, ought distinctly to explain what they mean by that phrase, "the author of sin." I know, the phrase, as it is commonly used, signifies something very ill. If by "the author of sin," be meant the sinner, the agent, or actor of sin, or the doer of a wicked thing; so it would be a reproach and blasphemy, to suppose God to be the author of sin. In this sense, I utterly deny God to be the author of sin; rejecting such an imputation on the most

High, as what is infinitely to be abhorred; and deny any such thing to be the consequence of what I have laid down. But if by "the author of sin," is meant the permitter, or not a hinderer of sin; and at the same time, a disposer of the state of events, in such a manner, for wise, holy and most excellent ends and purposes, that sin, if it be permitted or not hindered, will most certainly and infallibly follow: I say, if this be all that is meant, by being the author of sin, I don't deny that God is the author of sin (though I dislike and reject the phrase, as that which by use and custom is apt to carry another sense), it is no reproach for the most High to be thus the author of sin. This is not to be the actor of sin, but on the contrary, of holiness. What God doth herein, is holy; and a glorious exercise of the infinite excellency of his nature. And I don't deny, that God's being thus the author of sin, follows from what I have laid down; and I assert, that it equally follows from the doctrine which is maintained by most of the Arminian divines.

That it is most certainly so, that God is in such a manner the disposer and orderer of sin, is evident, if any credit is to be given to the Scripture; as well as because it is impossible in the nature of things to be otherwise. In such a manner God ordered the obstinacy of Pharaoh, in his refusing to obey God's commands, to let the people go. Ex. 4:21: "I will harden his heart, and he shall not let the people go." Ch. 7:2–5: "Aaron thy brother shall speak unto Pharaoh, that he send the children of Israel out of his land. And I will harden Pharaoh's heart, and multiply my signs and my wonders in the land of Egypt. But Pharaoh shall not hearken unto you; that I may lay mine hand upon Egypt, by great judgments," etc. Ch. 9:12: "And the Lord hardened the heart of Pharaoh, and he hearkened not unto them, as the Lord had spoken unto Moses." Ch. 10:1, 2: "And the Lord said unto Moses, go in unto Pharaoh; for I have hardened his heart, and the heart of his servants, that I might shew these my signs before him, and that thou mayst tell it in the ears of thy son, and thy son's son, what things I have wrought in Egypt, and my signs which I have done amongst them, that ye may know that I am the Lord." Ch. 14:4: "And I will harden Pharaoh's heart, that he shall follow after them: and I will be honored upon Pharaoh, and upon all his host." Ver. 8: "And the Lord hardened the heart of Pharaoh King of Egypt, and he pursued after the children of Israel." And it is certain that in such a manner, God for wise and good ends, ordered that event, Joseph's being sold into Egypt by his brethren. Gen. 45:5: "Now therefore be not grieved, nor angry with yourselves, that ye sold me hither; for God did send me before you to preserve life." Ver. 7, 8: "God did send me before you to preserve a posterity in the earth, and to save your lives by a great deliverance: so that now it was not you, that sent me hither, but God." Ps. 105:17: "He sent a man before them, even Joseph, who was sold for a servant." 'Tis certain, that thus God ordered the sin and folly of Sihon King of the Amorites, in refusing to let the people of Israel pass by him peaceably. Deut. 2:30: "But Sihon King of Heshbon would not let us pass by him; for the Lord thy God hardened his spirit, and made his heart obstinate, that he might deliver him into thine hand." 'Tis certain, that God thus ordered the sin and folly of the kings of Canaan, that they attempted not to make peace with Israel, but with a stupid boldness and obstinacy, set themselves violently to oppose them and their God. Josh. 11:20: "For it was of the Lord, to harden their hearts, that they should come against Israel in battle, that he might destroy them utterly, and that they might have no favor; but that he might destroy them, as the Lord commanded Moses." 'Tis evident, that thus God ordered the treacherous rebellion of Zedekiah, against the King of Babylon. Jer. 52:3: "For through the anger of the Lord it came to pass in Jerusalem, and Judah, till he had cast them out from his presence, that Zedekiah rebelled against the King of Babylon." So II Kgs. 24:20. And 'tis exceeding manifest, that God thus ordered the rapine and unrighteous ravages of Nebuchadnezzar, in spoiling and ruining the nations round about. Jer. 25:9: "Behold, I will send and take all the families of the north, saith the Lord, and Nebuchadnezzar my servant, and will bring them against this land, and against all the nations round about; and will utterly destroy them, and make them an astonishment, and an hissing, and perpetual desolations." Ch. 43:10, 11: "I will send and take Nebuchadnezzar the King of Babylon, my servant; and I will set his throne upon these stones that I have hid, and he shall spread his royal pavilion over them. And when he cometh, he shall smite the land of Egypt, and deliver such as are for death to death, and such as are for captivity to captivity, and such as are for the sword to the sword." Thus God represents himself as sending for Nebuchadnezzar, and taking of him and his armies, and bringing him against the nations which were to be destroyed by him, to that very end, that he might utterly destroy them, and make them desolate; and as appointing the work that he should do, so particularly, that the very persons were designed, that he should kill with the sword; and those that should be killed with famine and pestilence, and those that should be carried into captivity; and that in doing all these things, he should act as his servant: by which, less can't be intended, than that he should serve his purposes and designs. And in Jer. 27:4, 5, 6, God declares how he would cause him thus to serve his designs, viz. by bringing this to pass in his sovereign disposals, as the great possessor and governor of the universe, that disposes all things just as pleases him: "Thus saith the Lord of Hosts, the God of Israel; I have made the earth, the man and the beast that are upon the ground, by my great power, and my stretched out arm, and have given it unto whom it seemed meet unto me: and now I have given all these lands into the hands of Nebuchadnezzar my servant, and the beasts of the field have I given also to serve him." And Nebuchadnezzar is spoken of as doing these things, by having his "arms strengthened" by God, and having "God's sword put into his hands, for this end" (Ezek. 30:24, 25, 26). Yea, God speaks of his terribly ravaging and wasting the nations, and cruelly destroying all sorts, without distinction of sex or age, as the weapon in God's hand, and the instrument of his indignation, which God makes use of to fulfill his own purposes, and execute his own vengeance. Jer. 51:20, etc.: "Thou art my battle-axe, and weapons of war. For with thee will I break in pieces the nations, and with thee I will destroy kingdoms, and with thee I will break in pieces the horse and his rider, and with thee I will break in pieces the chariot and his rider; with thee also will I break in pieces man and woman; and with thee will I break in pieces old and young; and with thee will I break in pieces the young man and the maid," etc. 'Tis represented, that the designs of Nebuchadnezzar, and those that destroyed Jerusalem, never could have been accomplished, had not God determined them, as well as they; Lam. 3:37, "Who is he that saith, and it cometh to pass, and the Lord commandeth it not?" And yet the King of Babylon's thus destroying the nations, and especially the Jews, is spoken of as his great wickedness, for which God finally destroyed him (Is. 14:4, 5, 6, 12; Hab. 2:5–12; and Jer. ch. 50 and 51). 'Tis most manifest, that God, to serve his own designs, providentially ordered Shimei's cursing David. II Sam. 16:10, 11: "The Lord hath said unto him, curse David....Let him curse, for the Lord hath bidden him." 'Tis certain, that God thus, for excellent, holy, gracious and glorious ends, ordered the fact which they committed, who were concerned in Christ's death; and that therein they did but fulfill God's designs. As, I trust, no Christian will deny it was the design of God, that Christ should be crucified, and that for this end, he came into the world. 'Tis very manifest by many scriptures, that the whole affair of Christ's crucifixion, with its circumstances, and the treachery of Judas, that made way for it, was ordered in God's providence, in pursuance of his purpose; notwithstanding the violence that is used with those plain Scriptures, to obscure and pervert the sense of 'em. Acts 2:23: "Him being delivered, by the determinate counsel and foreknowledge of God, ye have taken, and with wicked hands, have crucified and slain." Luke 22:21, 22: "But behold the hand of him that betrayeth me, is with me on the table: and truly the Son of man goeth, as it was determined." Acts 4:27, 28: "For of a truth, against thy holy child Jesus, whom thou hast anointed, both Herod, and Pontius Pilate, with the Gentiles, and the people of Israel, were gathered together, for to do whatsoever thy hand and thy counsel determined before to be done." Acts 3:17, 18: "And now brethren, I wot that through ignorance ye did it, as did also your rulers: but these things, which God before had showed by the mouth of all his prophets, that Christ should suffer, he hath so fulfilled." So that what these murderers of Christ did, is spoken of as what God brought to pass or ordered, and that by which he fulfilled his own word.

In Rev. 17:17, "the agreeing of the kings of the earth to give their kingdom to the beast," though it was a very wicked thing in them, is spoken of as "a fulfilling God's will," and what "God had put it into their hearts to do." 'Tis manifest, that God sometimes permits sin to be committed, and at the same time orders things so, that if he permits the fact, it will come to pass, because on some accounts he sees it needful and of importance that it should come to pass. Matt. 18:7: "It must needs be, that offences come; but woe to that man by whom the offence cometh." With I Cor. 11:19, "For there must also be heresies among you, that they which are approved, may be made manifest among you."

Thus it is certain and demonstrable, from the holy Scriptures, as well as the nature of things, and the principles of Arminians, that God permits sin; and at the same time, so orders things, in his providence, that it certainly and infallibly will come to pass, in consequence of his permission.

I proceed to observe in the next place,

III. That there is a great difference between God's being concerned thus, by his permission, in an event and act, which in the inherent subject and agent of it, is sin (though the event will certainly follow on his permission), and his being concerned in it by producing it and exerting the act of sin; or between his being the orderer of its certain existence, by not hindering it, under certain circumstances, and his being the proper actor or author of it, by a positive agency or efficiency. And this, notwithstanding what Dr. Whitby offers about a saying of philosophers, that *causa deficiens, in rebus necessariis, ad causam per se efficientem reducenda est.* As there is a vast difference between the sun's being the cause of the lightsomeness and warmth of the atmosphere, and brightness of gold and diamonds, by its presence and positive influence; and its being the occasion of darkness and frost, in the night, by its motion, whereby it descends below the horizon. The motion of the sun is the occasion of the latter kind of events; but it is not the proper cause, efficient or producer of them; though they are necessarily consequent on that motion, under such circumstances: no more is any action of the divine Being the cause of the evil of men's wills. If the sun were the proper cause of cold and darkness, it would be the fountain of these things, as it is the fountain of light and heat: and then something might be argued from the nature of cold and darkness, to a likeness of nature in the sun; and it might be justly inferred, that the sun itself is dark and cold, and that his beams are black and frosty. But from its being the cause no otherwise than by its departure, no such thing can be inferred, but the contrary; it may justly be argued, that the sun is a bright and hot body, if cold and darkness are found to be the consequence of its withdrawment; and the more constantly and necessarily these effects are connected with, and confined to its absence, the more strongly does it argue the sun to be the fountain of light and heat. So, inasmuch as sin is not the fruit of any positive agency or influence of the most High, but on the contrary, arises from the withholding of his action and energy, and under certain circumstances, necessarily follows on the want of his influence; this is no argument that he is sinful, or his operation evil, or has anything of the nature of evil; but on the contrary, that he, and his agency, are altogether good and holy, and that he is the fountain of all holiness. It would be strange arguing indeed, because men never commit sin, but only when God leaves 'em to themselves, and necessarily sin, when he does so, that therefore their sin is not from themselves, but from God; and so, that God must be a sinful being: as strange as it would be to argue, because it is always dark when the sun is gone, and never dark when the sun is present, that therefore all darkness is from the sun, and that his disk and beams must needs be black.

IV. It properly belongs to the supreme and absolute Governor of the universe, to order all important events within his dominion, by his wisdom: but the events in the moral world are of the most important kind; such as the moral actions of intelligent creatures, and their consequences.

These events will be ordered by something. They will either be disposed by wisdom, or they will be disposed by chance; that is, they will be disposed by blind and undesigning causes, if that were possible, and could be called a disposal. Is it not better, that the good and evil which happens in God's world, should be ordered, regulated, bounded and determined by the good pleasure of an infinitely wise Being, who perfectly comprehends within his understanding and constant view, the universality of things, in all their extent and duration, and sees all the influence of every event, with respect to every individual thing and circumstance, throughout the grand system, and the whole of the eternal series of consequences; than to leave these things to fall out by chance, and to be determined by those causes which have no understanding or aim? Doubtless, in these important events, there is a better and a worse, as to the time, subject, place, manner and circumstances of their coming to pass, with regard to their influence on the state and course of things. And if there be, 'tis certainly best that they should be determined to that time, place, etc. which is best. And therefore 'tis in its own nature fit, that wisdom, and not chance, should order these things. So that it belongs to the Being, who is the possessor of infinite wisdom, and is the creator and owner of the whole system of created existences, and has the care of all; I say, it belongs to him, to take care of this matter; and he would not do what is proper for him, if he should neglect it. And it is so far from being unholy in him, to undertake this affair, that it would rather have been unholy to neglect it; as it would have been a neglecting what fitly appertains to him; and so it would have been a very unfit and unsuitable neglect.

Therefore the sovereignty of God doubtless extends to this matter; especially considering, that if it should be supposed to be otherwise, and God should leave men's volitions, and all moral events, to the determination and disposition of blind and unmeaning causes, or they should be left to happen perfectly without a cause; this would be no more consistent with liberty, in any notion of it, and particularly not in the Arminian notion of it, than if these events were subject to the disposal of divine providence, and the will of man were determined by circumstances which are ordered and disposed by divine wisdom; as appears by what has been already observed. But 'tis evident, that such a providential disposing and determining men's moral actions, though it infers a moral necessity of those actions, yet it does not in the least infringe the real liberty of mankind; the only liberty that common sense teaches to be necessary to moral agency, which, as has been demonstrated, is not inconsistent with such necessity.

On the whole, it is manifest, that God may be, in the manner which has been described, the orderer and disposer of that event, which in the inherent subject and agent is moral evil; and yet his so doing may be no moral evil. He may will the disposal of such an event, and its coming to pass for good ends, and his will not be an immoral or sinful will, but a perfectly holy will. And he may actually in his providence so dispose and permit things, that the event may be certainly and infallibly connected with such disposal and permission, and his act therein not be an immoral or unholy, but a perfectly holy act. Sin may be an evil thing, and yet that there should be such a disposal and permission, as that it should come to pass, may be a good thing. This is no contradiction, or inconsistence. Joseph's brethren's selling him into Egypt, consider it only as it was acted by them, and with respect to their views and aims which were evil, was a very bad thing; but it was a good thing, as it was an event of God's ordering, and considered with respect to his views and aims which were good. Gen. 50:20: "As for you, ye thought evil against me; but God meant it unto good." So the crucifixion of Christ, if we consider only those things which belong to the event as it proceeded from his murderers, and are comprehended within the compass of the affair considered as their act, their principles, dispositions, views and aims; so it was one of the most heinous things that ever was done; in many respects the most horrid of all acts: but consider it, as it was willed and ordered of God, in the extent of his designs and views, it was the most admirable and glorious of all events; and God's willing the event was the most holy volition of God, that ever was made known to men; and God's act in ordering it, was a divine act, which above all others, manifests the moral excellency of the divine Being.

The consideration of these things may help us to a sufficient answer to the cavils of Arminians concerning what has been supposed by many Calvinists, of a distinction between a secret and revealed will of God, and their diversity one from the other; supposing, that the Calvinists herein ascribe inconsistent wills to the most High: which is without any foundation. God's secret and revealed will, or in other words, his disposing and preceptive will may be diverse, and exercised in dissimilar acts, the one in disapproving and opposing, the other in willing and determining, without any inconsistence. Because, although these dissimilar exercises of the divine will may in some respects relate to the same things, yet in strictness they have different and contrary objects, the one evil and the other good. Thus for instance, the crucifixion of Christ was a thing contrary to the revealed or preceptive will of God; because, as it was viewed and done by his malignant murderers, it was a thing infinitely contrary to the holy nature of God, and so necessarily contrary to the holy inclination of his heart revealed in his Law. Yet this don't at all hinder but that the crucifixion of Christ, considered with all those glorious consequences, which were within the view of the divine omniscience, might be indeed, and therefore might appear to God to be, a glorious event; and consequently be agreeable to his will, though this will may be secret, i.e. not revealed in God's Law. And thus considered, the crucifixion of Christ was not evil, but good. If the secret exercises of God's will were of a kind that is dissimilar and contrary to his revealed will, respecting the same, or like objects; if the objects of both were good, or both evil; then indeed to ascribe contrary kinds of volition or inclination to God, respecting these objects, would be to ascribe an inconsistent will to God: but to ascribe to him different and opposite exercises of heart, respecting different objects, and objects contrary one to another, is so far from supposing God's will to be *inconsistent* with itself, that it can't be supposed consistent with itself any other way. For any being to have a will of choice respecting good, and at the same time a will of rejection and refusal respecting evil, is to be very consistent: but the contrary, viz. to have the same will towards these contrary objects, and to choose and love both good and evil at the same time, is to be very inconsistent.

There is no inconsistence in supposing, that God may hate a thing as it is in itself, and considered simply as evil, and yet that it may be his will it should come to pass, considering all consequences. I believe, there is no person of good understanding, who will venture to say, he is certain that it is impossible it should be best, taking in the whole compass and extent of existence, and all consequences in the endless series of events, that there should be such a thing as moral evil in the world.

(Here are worthy to be observed some passages of a late noted writer, of our nation, that nobody who is acquainted with him will suspect to be very favorable to Calvinism.) "It is difficult (says he) to handle the necessity of evil in such a manner, as not to stumble such as are not above being alarmed at propositions which have an uncommon sound. But if philosophers will but reflect calmly on the matter, they will find, that consistently with the unlimited power of the supreme Cause, it may be said, that in the best ordered system, evils must have place." George Turnbull, The Principles of Moral Philosophy, an Enquiry into the Wise and Good Government of the Moral World (London, 1740), pp. 327 f. in the footnote. He is there speaking of moral evils, as may be seen. [It may also be seen that Turnbull justifies the existence of moral evil not only by considering all the consequences which God may have in his view, but by himself viewing moral evil as an unavoidable result and risk of freedom, which great good everyone may witness along with the evil, or else phrase as follows his "complaint against nature": "Nature hath dealt unkindly by us in making our happiness depend in any measure on ourselves, and in making us capable of the pleasures of knowledge, foresight, self-direction, and good management" (p. 326; italics mine).]

Again the same author [George Turnbull], in his second volume entitled, Christian Philosophy, [The Principles of Moral and Christian Philosophy (2 vols. London, 1740), 2], 35, has these words: "If the Author and Governor of all things be infinitely perfect, then whatever is, is right; of all possible systems he hath chosen the best: and consequently there is no absolute evil in the universe.... This being the case, all the seeming imperfections or evils in it are such only in a partial view; and with respect to the whole system, they are goods." Ibid., p. 37:

"Whence then comes evil, is the question that hath in all ages been reckoned the Gordian knot in philosophy. And indeed, if we own the existence of evil in the world in an absolute sense, we diametrically contradict what hath been just now proved of God. For if there be any evil in the system, that is not good with respect to the whole, then is the whole not good, but evil: or at best, very imperfect: and an author must be as his workmanship is; as is the effect, such is the cause. But the solution of this difficulty is at hand; that there is no evil in the universe. What! Are there no pains, no imperfections? Is there no misery, no vice in the world? Or are not these evils? Evils indeed they are; that is, those of one sort are hurtful, and those of the other sort are equally hurtful and abominable: but they are not evil or mischievous with respect to the whole."

Ibid., p. 42:

"But He is at the same time said to create evil, darkness, confusion; and yet to do no evil, but to be the author of good only. He is called the 'Father of lights,' the Author of every perfect and good gift, with whom there is no variableness nor shadow of turning, who tempteth no man, but giveth to all men liberally, and upbraideth not. And yet by the prophet Isaias he is introduced saying of himself, 'I form light, and create darkness; I make peace, and create evil: I the Lord do all these things.' What is the meaning, the plain language of all this, but that the Lord delighteth in goodness, and (as the Scripture speaks) evil is his strange work? He intends and pursues the universal good of his creation: and the evil which happens is not permitted for its own sake, or through any pleasure in evil, but because it is requisite to the greater good pursued."

And if so, it will certainly follow, that an infinitely wise Being, who always chooses what is best, must choose that there should be such a thing. And if so, then such a choice is not an evil, but a wise and holy choice. And if so, then that providence which is agreeable to such a choice, is a wise and holy providence. Men do will sin as sin, and so are the authors and actors of it: they love it as sin, and for evil ends and purposes. God don't will sin as sin, or for the sake of anything evil; though it be his pleasure so to order things, that he permitting, sin will come to pass; for the sake of the great good that by his disposal shall be the consequence. His willing to order things so that evil should come to pass, for the sake of the contrary good, is no argument that he don't hate evil, as evil: and if so, then it is no reason why he mayn't reasonably forbid evil as evil, and punish it as such.

The Arminians themselves must be obliged, whether they will or no, to allow a distinction of God's will, amounting to just the same thing that Calvinists intend by their distinction of a secret and revealed will. They must allow a distinction of those things which God thinks best should be, considering all circumstances and consequences, and so are agreeable to his disposing will, and those things which he loves, and are agreeable to his nature, in themselves considered. Who is there that will dare to say, that the hellish pride, malice and cruelty of devils, are agreeable to God, and what he likes and approves? And yet, I trust, there is no Christian divine but what will allow, that 'tis agreeable to God's will so to order and dispose things concerning them, so to leave them to themselves, and give them up to their own wickedness, that this perfect wickedness should be a necessary consequence. Be sure Dr. Whitby's words do plainly suppose and allow it [*Discourse on the Five Points*, Dis. IV, ch. 1, nos. 1, 2, 5; pp. 300, 305, 309].

These following things may be laid down as maxims of plain truth, and indisputable evidence.

1. That God is a perfectly happy Being, in the most absolute and highest sense possible.

2. That it will follow from hence, that God is free from every thing that is contrary to happiness; and so, that in strict propriety of speech, there is no such thing as any pain, grief or trouble in God.

3. When any intelligent being is really crossed and disappointed, and things are contrary to what he truly desires, he is the less pleased, or has less pleasure, his pleasure and happiness is diminished, and he suffers what is disagreeable to him, or is the subject of something that is of a nature contrary to joy and happiness, even pain and grief. (Certainly 'tis not less absurd and unreasonable, to talk of God's will and desire's being truly and properly crossed, without his suffering any uneasiness, or anything grievous or disagreeable, than it is to talk of something that may be called a revealed will, which may in some respect be different from a secret purpose; which purpose may be fulfilled, when the other is opposed.)

From this last axiom it follows, that if no distinction is to be admitted between God's hatred of sin, and his will with respect to the event and the existence of sin, as the all-wise determiner of all events, under the view of all consequences through the whole compass and series of things; I say, then it certainly follows, that the coming to pass of every individual act of sin is truly, all things considered, contrary to his will, and that his will is really crossed in it; and this in proportion as he hates it. And as God's hatred of sin is infinite, by reason of the infinite contrariety of his holy nature to sin; so his will is infinitely crossed, in every act of sin that happens. Which is as much as to say, he endures that which is infinitely disagreeable to him, by means of every act of sin that he sees committed. And therefore, as appears by the preceding positions, he endures truly and really, infinite grief or pain from every sin. And so he must be infinitely crossed, and suffer infinite pain, every day, in millions of millions of instances: he must continually be the subject of an immense number of real, and truly infinitely great crosses and vexations. Which would be to make him infinitely the most miserable of all beings.

If any objector should say; all that these things amount to, is, that God may do evil that good may come; which is justly esteemed immoral and sinful in men; and therefore may be justly esteemed inconsistent with the moral perfections of God. I answer, that for God to dispose and permit evil, in the manner that has been spoken of, is not to do evil that good may come; for it is not to do evil at all. In order to a thing's being morally evil, there must be one of these things belonging to it: either it must be a thing unfit and unsuitable in its own nature; or it must have a bad tendency; or it must proceed from an evil disposition, and be done for an evil end. But neither of these things can be attributed to God's ordering and permitting such events, as the immoral acts of creatures, for good ends, (i) It is not unfit in its own nature, that he should do so. For it is in its own nature fit, that infinite wisdom, and not blind chance, should dispose moral good and evil in the world. And 'tis fit, that the Being who has infinite wisdom, and is the maker, owner, and supreme governor of the world, should take care of that matter. And therefore there is no unfitness, or unsuitableness in his doing it. It may be unfit, and so immoral, for any other beings to go about to order this affair; because they are not possessed of a wisdom, that in any manner fits them for it; and in other respects they are not fit to be trusted with this affair; nor does it belong to them, they not being the owners and lords of the universe.

We need not be afraid to affirm, that if a wise and good man knew with absolute certainty, it would be best, all things considered, that there should be such a thing as moral evil in the world, it would not be contrary to his wisdom and goodness, for him to choose that it should be so. 'Tis no evil desire, to desire good, and to desire that which, all things considered, is best. And it is no unwise choice, to choose that that should be, which it is best should be; and to choose the existence of that thing concerning which this is known, viz. that it is best it should be, and so is known in the whole to be most worthy to be chosen. On the contrary, it would be a plain defect in wisdom and goodness, for him not to choose it. And the reason why he might not order it, if he were able, would not be because he might not desire it, but only the ordering of that matter don't belong to him. But it is no harm for him who is by right, and in the greatest propriety, the supreme orderer of all things, to order everything in such a manner, as it would be a point of wisdom in him to choose that they should be ordered. If it would be a plain defect of wisdom and goodness in a being, not to choose that that should be, which he certainly knows it would, all things considered, be best should be (as was but now observed) then it must be impossible for a being who has no defect of wisdom and goodness, to do otherwise than choose it should be; and that, for this very reason, because he is perfectly wise and good. And if it be agreeable to perfect wisdom and goodness for him to choose that it should be, and the ordering of all things supremely and perfectly belongs to him, it must be agreeable to infinite wisdom and goodness, to order that it should be. If the choice is good, the ordering and disposing things according to that choice must also be good. It can be no harm in one to whom it belongs "to do his will in the armies of heaven, and amongst the inhabitants of the earth," to execute a good volition. If his will be good, and the object of his will be, all things considered, good and best, then the choosing or willing it is not willing evil that good may come. And if so, then his ordering according to that will is not doing evil, that good may come.

2. 'Tis not of a bad tendency, for the supreme Being thus to order and permit that moral evil to be, which it is best should come to pass. For that it is of good tendency, is the very thing supposed in the point now in question. Christ's crucifixion, though a most horrid fact in them that perpetrated it, was of most glorious tendency as permitted and ordered of God.

3. Nor is there any need of supposing, it proceeds from any evil disposition or aim: for by the supposition, what is aimed at is good, and good is the actual issue, in the final result of things.

SECTION 10.

CONCERNING SIN'S FIRST ENTRANCE INTO THE WORLD

The things which have already been offered, may serve to obviate or clear many of the objections which might be raised concerning sin's first coming into the world; as though it would follow from the doctrine maintained, that God must be the author of the first sin, through his so disposing things, that it should necessarily follow from his permission, that the sinful act should be committed, etc. I need not therefore stand to repeat what has been said already, about such a necessity's not proving God to be the author of sin, in any ill sense, or in any such sense as to infringe any liberty of man, concerned in his moral agency, or capacity of blame, guilt and punishment.

But if it should nevertheless be said, supposing the case so, that God, when he had made man, might so order his circumstances, that from these circumstances, together with his withholding further assistance and divine influence, his sin would infallibly follow, why might not God as well have first made man with a fixed prevailing principle of sin in his heart?

I answer, 1. It was meet, if sin did come into existence, and appear in the world, it should arise from the imperfection which properly belongs to a creature, as such, and should appear so to do, that it might appear not to be from God as the efficient or fountain. But this could not have been, if man had been made at first with sin in his heart; nor unless the abiding principle and habit of sin were first introduced by an evil act of the creature. If sin had not arose from the imperfection of the creature, it would not have been so visible, that it did not arise from God, as the positive cause, and real source of it.—But it would require room that can't be here allowed, fully to consider all the difficulties which have been started, concerning the first entrance of sin into the world.

And therefore,

2. I would observe, that objections against the doctrine that has been laid down, in opposition to the Arminian notion of liberty, from these difficulties, are altogether impertinent; because no additional difficulty is incurred, by adhering to a scheme in this manner differing from theirs, and none would be removed or avoided, by agreeing with, and maintaining theirs. Nothing that the Arminians say, about the contingence, or self-determining power of man's will, can serve to explain with less difficulty, how the first sinful volition of mankind could take place, and man be justly charged with the blame of it. To say, the will was self-determined, or determined by free choice, in that sinful volition; which is to say, that the first sinful volition was determined by a foregoing sinful volition; is no solution of the difficulty. It is an odd way of solving difficulties, to advance greater, in order to it. To say, two and two makes nine; or, that a child begat his father, solves no difficulty: no more does it, to say, the first sinful act of choice was before the first sinful act of choice, and chose and determined it, and brought it to pass. Nor is it any better solution, to say, the first sinful volition chose, determined and produced itself;

which is to say, it was before it was. Nor will it go any further towards helping us over the difficulty, to say, the first sinful volition arose accidentally, without any cause at all; any more than it will solve that difficult question, How the world could be made out of nothing? to say, it came into being out of nothing, without any cause; as has been already observed. And if we should allow that that could be, that the first evil volition should arise by perfect accident, without any cause, it would relieve no difficulty, about God's laying the blame of it to man. For how was man to blame for perfect accident, which had no cause, and which therefore, he (to be sure) was not the cause of, any more than if it came by some external cause? Such kind of solutions are no better, than if some person, going about to solve some of the strange mathematical paradoxes, about infinitely great and small quantities; as, that some infinitely great quantities are infinitely greater than some other infinitely great quantities; and also that some infinitely small quantities are infinitely less than others, which yet are infinitely little; in order to a solution, should say, that mankind have been under a mistake, in supposing a greater quantity to exceed a smaller; and that a hundred multiplied by ten, makes but a single unit.

SECTION 11.

OF A SUPPOSED INCONSISTENCE OF THESE PRINCIPLES, WITH GOD'S MORAL CHARACTER

The things which have been already observed, may be sufficient to answer most of the objections, and silence the great exclamations of Arminians against the Calvinists, from the supposed inconsistence of Calvinistic principles with the moral perfections of God, as exercised in his government of mankind. The consistence of such a doctrine of necessity as has been maintained, with the fitness and reasonableness of God's commands, promises and threatenings, rewards and punishments, has been particularly considered: the cavils of our opponents, as though our doctrine of necessity made God the author of sin, have been answered; and also their objection against these principles, as inconsistent with God's sincerity, in his counsels, invitations and persuasions, has been already obviated, in what has been observed, respecting the consistence of what Calvinists suppose concerning the secret and revealed will of God: by that it appears, there is no repugnance in supposing it may be the secret will of God, that his ordination and permission of events should be such that it shall be a certain consequence, that a thing never will come to pass; which yet it is man's duty to do, and so God's preceptive will, that he should do; and this is the same thing as to say, God may sincerely command and require him to do it. And if he may be sincere in commanding him, he may for the same reason be sincere in counseling, inviting and using persuasions with him to do it. Counsels and invitations are manifestations of God's preceptive will, or of what God loves, and what is in itself, and as man's act, agreeable to his heart; and not of his disposing will, and what he chooses as a part of his own infinite scheme of things. It has been particularly shown (Pt. Ill, Sec. 4) that such a necessity as has been maintained, is not inconsistent with the propriety and fitness of divine commands; and for the same reason, not inconsistent with the sincerity of invitations and counsels, in the corollary at the end of that section. Yea, it hath been shewn (Pt. Ill, Sec. 7, Corol. 1) that this objection of Arminians, concerning the sincerity and use of divine exhortations, invitations and counsels, is demonstrably against themselves.

Notwithstanding, I would further observe, that the difficulty of reconciling the sincerity of counsels, invitations and persuasions, with such an antecedent known fixedness of all events, as has been supposed, is not peculiar to this scheme, as distinguished from that of the generality of Arminians, which acknowledge the absolute foreknowledge of God: and therefore, it would be unreasonably brought as an objection against my differing from them. The main seeming difficulty in the case is this: that God in counseling, inviting and persuading, makes a shew of aiming at, seeking and using endeavors for the thing exhorted and persuaded to; whereas, 'tis impossible for any intelligent being truly to seek, or use endeavors for a thing, which he at the same time knows most perfectly will not come to pass; and that it is absurd to suppose, he makes the obtaining of a thing his end, in his calls and counsels, which he at the same time infallibly knows will not be obtained by these means. Now, if God knows this, in the utmost certainty and perfection, the way by which he comes by this knowledge makes no difference. If he knows it by the necessity which he sees in things, or by some other means; it alters not the case. But it is in effect allowed by Arminians themselves, that God's inviting and persuading men to do things, which he at the same time certainly knows will not be done, is no evidence of insincerity; because they allow, that God has a certain foreknowledge of all men's sinful actions and omissions. And as this is thus implicitly allowed by most Arminians, so all that pretend to own the Scriptures to be the Word of God, must be constrained to allow it. God commanded and counseled Pharaoh to let his people go, and used arguments and persuasions to induce him to it; he laid before him arguments taken from his infinite greatness and almighty power (Ex. 7:16) and forewarned him of the fatal consequences of his refusal, from time to time (Ch. 8:1, 2, 20, 21; Ch. 9:1–5, 13–17; and 10:3, 6). He commanded Moses, and the elders of Israel, to go and beseech Pharaoh to let the people go; and at the same time told 'em, he knew surely that he would not comply to it. Ex. 3:18, 19: "And thou shalt come, thou and the elders of Israel, unto the king of Egypt, and you shall say unto him; the Lord God of the Hebrews hath met with us; and now let us go, we beseech thee, three days' journey into the wilderness, that we may sacrifice unto the Lord our God": and, "I am sure that the king of Egypt will not let you go." So our blessed Saviour, the evening wherein he was betrayed, knew that Peter would shamefully deny him, before the morning; for he declares it to him with asseverations, to shew the certainty of it; and tells the disciples, that all of them should be offended because of him that night (Matt. 26:31–35; John 13: 38; Luke 22:31–34; John 16:32). And yet it was their duty to avoid these things; they were very sinful things, which God had forbidden, and which it was their duty to watch and pray against; and they were obliged to do so from the counsels and persuasions Christ used with them, at that very time, so to do (Matt. 26:41), "Watch and pray, that ye enter not into temptation." So that whatever difficulty there can be in this matter, it can be no objection against any principles which have been maintained in opposition to the principles of Arminians; nor does it any more concern me to remove the difficulty, than it does them, or indeed all that call themselves Christians, and acknowledge the divine authority of the Scriptures. Nevertheless, this matter may possibly (God allowing) be more particularly and largely considered, in some future discourse, on the doctrine of predestination.

But I would here observe, that however the defenders of that notion of liberty of will, which I have opposed, exclaim against the doctrine of Calvinists, as tending to bring men into doubts, concerning the moral perfections of God; it is their scheme, and not the scheme of Calvinists, that indeed is justly chargeable with this. For 'tis one of the most fundamental points of their scheme of things, that a freedom of will, consisting in self-determination, without all necessity, is essential to moral agency.

This is the same thing as to say, that such a determination of the will without all necessity, must be in all intelligent beings, in those things, wherein they are moral agents, or in their moral acts: and from this it will follow, that God's will is not necessarily determined, in anything he does, as a moral agent, or in any of his acts that are of a moral nature. So that in all things, wherein he acts holily, justly and truly, he don't act necessarily; or his will is not necessarily determined to act holily and justly; because if it were necessarily determined, he would not be a moral agent in thus acting: his will would be attended with necessity; which they say is inconsistent with moral agency: "He can act no otherwise; he is at no liberty in the affair; he is determined by unavoidable invincible necessity: therefore such agency is no moral agency; yea, no agency at all, properly speaking: a necessary agent is no agent: he being passive, and subject to necessity, what he does is no act of his, but an effect of a necessity prior to any act of his." This is agreeable to their manner of arguing. Now then what is become of all our proof of the moral perfections of God? How can we prove, that God certainly will in any one instance do that which is just and holy; seeing his will is determined in the matter by no necessity? We have no other way of proving that anything certainly will be, but only by the necessity of the event. Where we can see no necessity, but that the thing may be, or may not be, there we are unavoidably left at a loss. We have no other way properly and truly to demonstrate the moral perfections of God, but the way that Mr. Chubb proves them, in pp. 252, 261, 262, 263 of his *Tracts*; viz. that God must necessarily perfectly know what is most worthy and valuable in itself, which in the nature of things is best and fittest to be done. And as this is most eligible in itself, he being omniscient, must see it to be so; and being both omniscient and self-sufficient, cannot have any temptation to reject it; and so must necessarily will that which is best. And thus, by this necessity of the determination of God's will to what is good and best, we demonstrably establish God's moral character.

Corol. From things which have been observed, it appears, that most of the arguments from Scripture, which Arminians make use of to support their scheme, are no other than begging the question. For in these their arguments they determine in the first place, that without such a freedom of will as they hold, men can't be proper moral agents, nor the subjects of command, counsel, persuasion, invitation, promises, threatenings, expostulations, rewards and punishments; and that without such a freedom 'tis to no purpose for men to take any care, or use any diligence, endeavors or means, in order to their avoiding sin, or becoming holy, escaping punishment or obtaining happiness: and having supposed these things, which are grand things in question in the debate, then they heap up scriptures containing commands, counsels, calls, warnings, persuasions, expostulations, promises and threatenings (as doubtless they may find enough such; the Bible is confessedly full of them, from the beginning to the end); and then they glory, how full the Scripture is on their side, how many more texts there are that evidently favor their scheme, than such as seem to favor the contrary. But let them first make manifest the things in question, which they suppose and take for granted, and shew them to be consistent with themselves, and produce clear evidence of their truth; and they have gained their point, as all will confess, without bringing one scripture. For none denies, that there are commands, counsels, promises, threatenings, etc. in the Bible. But unless they do these things, their multiplying such texts of Scripture is insignificant and vain.

It may further be observed, that such scriptures as they bring, are really against them, and not for them. As it has been demonstrated, that 'tis their scheme, and not ours, that is inconsistent with the use of motives and persuasives, or any moral means whatsoever, to induce men to the practice of virtue, or abstaining from wickedness: their principles, and not ours, are repugnant to moral agency, and inconsistent with moral government, with law or precept, with the nature of virtue or vice, reward or punishment, and with everything whatsoever of a moral nature, either on the part of the moral Governor, or in the state, actions, or conduct of the subject.

SECTION 12.

OF A SUPPOSED TENDENCY OF THESE PRINCIPLES TO ATHEISM AND LICENTIOUSNESS

If any object against what has been maintained, that it tends to atheism; I know not on what grounds such an objection can be raised, unless it be that some atheists have held a doctrine of necessity which they suppose to be like this. But if it be so, I am persuaded the Arminians would not look upon it just, that their notion of freedom and contingence should be charged with a tendency to all the errors that ever any embraced, who have held such opinions. The Stoic philosophers, whom the Calvinists are charged with agreeing with, were no atheists, but the greatest theists, and nearest akin to Christians in their opinions concerning the unity and the perfections of the Godhead, of all the heathen philosophers. And Epicurus, that chief father of atheism, maintained no such doctrine of necessity, but was the greatest maintainer of contingence.

The doctrine of necessity, which supposes a necessary connection of all events, on some antecedent ground and reason of their existence, is the only medium we have to prove the being of God. And the contrary doctrine of contingence, even as maintained by Arminians (which certainly implies or infers, that events may come into existence, or begin to be, without dependence on anything foregoing, as their cause, ground or reason) takes away all proof of the being of God; which proof is summarily expressed by the Apostle, in Rom. 1:20. And this is a tendency to atheism with a witness. So that indeed it is the doctrine of Arminians, and not of the Calvinists, that is justly charged with a tendency to atheism; it being built on a foundation that is the utter subversion of every demonstrative argument for the proof of a deity; as has been shewn (Pt. II, Sec. 3).

And whereas it has often been said, that the Calvinistic doctrine of necessity, saps the foundations of all religion and virtue, and tends to the greatest licentiousness of practice: this objection is built on the pretense, that our doctrine renders vain all means and endeavors, in order to be virtuous and religious. Which pretense has been already particularly considered in the 5th section of this part; where it has been demonstrated, that this doctrine has no such tendency; but that such a tendency is truly to be charged on the contrary doctrine: inasmuch as the notion of contingence, which their doctrine implies, in its certain consequences, overthrows all connection, in every degree, between endeavor and event, means and end.

And besides, if many other things which have been observed to belong to the Arminian doctrine, or to be plain consequences of it, be considered, there will appear just reason to suppose that it is that, which must rather tend to licentiousness. Their doctrine excuses all evil inclinations, which men find to be natural; because in such inclinations, they are not self-determined, as such inclinations are not owing to any choice or determination of their own wills. Which leads men wholly to justify themselves in all their wicked actions, so far as natural inclination has had a hand in determining their wills, to the commission of 'em. Yea, these notions which suppose moral necessity and inability to be inconsistent with blame or moral obligation, will directly lead men to justify the vilest acts and practices, from the strength of their wicked inclinations of all sorts; strong inclinations inducing a moral necessity; yea, to excuse every degree of evil inclination, so far as this has evidently prevailed, and been the thing which has determined their wills: because, so far as antecedent inclination determined the will, so far the will was without liberty of indifference and self-determination. Which at last will come to this, that men will justify themselves in all the wickedness they commit. It has been observed already, that this scheme of things does exceedingly diminish the guilt of sin, and the difference between the greatest and smallest offences (Part III, Sec. 6): and if it be pursued in its real consequences, it leaves room for no such thing, as either virtue or vice, blame or praise in the world (Pt. Ill, Sees. 6, 7; Pt. IV, Sec. 1; Pt. Ill, Sec. 3, corol. 1 after the first Head). And then again, how naturally does this notion of the sovereign self-determining power of the will, in all things, virtuous or vicious, and whatsoever deserves either reward or punishment, tend to encourage men to put off the work of religion and virtue, and turning from sin to God; it being that which they have a sovereign power to determine themselves to, just when they please; or if not, they are wholly excusable in going on in sin, because of their inability to do any other.

If it should be said, that the tendency of this doctrine of necessity, to licentiousness, appears by the improvement many at this day actually make of it, to justify themselves in their dissolute courses; I will not deny that some men do unreasonably abuse this doctrine, as they do many other things which are true and excellent in their own nature: but I deny that this proves, the doctrine itself has any tendency to licentiousness. I think, the tendency of doctrines, by what now appears in the world, and in our nation in particular, may much more justly be argued from the general effect which has been seen to attend the prevailing of the principles of Arminians, and the contrary principles; as both have had their turn of general prevalence in our nation. If it be indeed, as is pretended, that Calvinistic doctrines undermine the very foundation of all religion and morality, and enervate and disannul all rational motives, to holy and virtuous practice; and that the contrary doctrines give the inducements to virtue and goodness their proper force, and exhibit religion in a rational light, tending to recommend it to the reason of mankind, and enforce it in a manner that is agreeable to their natural notions of things: I say, if it be thus, 'tis remarkable, that virtue and religious practice should prevail most, when the former doctrines, so inconsistent with it, prevailed almost universally: and that ever since the latter doctrines, so happily agreeing with it, and of so proper and excellent a tendency to promote it, have been gradually prevailing, vice, profaneness, luxury and wickedness of all sorts, and contempt of all religion, and of every kind of seriousness and strictness of conversation, should proportionably prevail; and that these things should thus accompany one another, and rise and prevail one with another, now for a whole age together. 'Tis remarkable, that this happy remedy (discovered by the free inquiries, and superior sense and wisdom of this age) against the pernicious effects of Calvinism, so inconsistent with religion, and tending so much to banish all virtue from the earth, should on so long a trial, be attended with no good effect; but that the consequence should be the reverse of amendment; that in proportion, as the remedy takes place, and is thoroughly applied, so the disease should prevail; and the very same dismal effect take place, to the highest degree, which Calvinistic doctrines are supposed to have so great a tendency to; even the banishing of religion and virtue, and the prevailing of unbounded licentiousness of manners. If these things are truly so, they are very remarkable, and matter of very curious speculation!

SECTION 13.

CONCERNING THAT OBJECTION AGAINST THE REASONING, BY WHICH THE CALVINISTIC DOCTRINE IS SUPPORTED, THAT IT IS METAPHYSICAL AND ABSTRUSE

It has often been objected against the defenders of Calvinistic principles, that in their reasonings, they run into nice scholastic distinctions, and abstruse metaphysical subtleties, and set these in opposition to common sense. And 'tis possible, that after the former manner it may be alleged against the reasoning by which I have endeavored to confute the Arminian scheme of liberty and moral agency, that it is very abstracted and metaphysical. Concerning this, I would observe the following things.

I. If that be made an objection against the foregoing reasoning, that it is metaphysical, or may properly be reduced to the science of metaphysics, it is a very impertinent objection; whether it be so or no, is not worthy of any dispute or controversy. If the reasoning be good, 'tis as frivolous to inquire what science it is properly reduced to, as what language it is delivered in: and for a man to go about to confute the arguments of his opponent, by telling him, his arguments are "metaphysical" would be as weak as to tell him, his arguments could not be substantial, because they were written in French or Latin. The question is not, whether what is said be metaphysics, physics, logic, or mathematics, Latin, French, English, or Mohawk [tribe]? but, whether the reasoning be good, and the arguments truly conclusive? The foregoing arguments are no more metaphysical, than those which we use against the Papists, to disprove their doctrine of transubstantiation; alleging, it is inconsistent with the notion of corporeal identity, that it should be in ten thousand places at the same time. 'Tis by metaphysical arguments only we are able to prove, that the rational soul is not corporeal; that lead or sand can't think; that thoughts are not square or round, or don't weigh a pound. The arguments by which we prove the being of God, if handled closely and distinctly, so as to shew their clear and demonstrative evidence, must be metaphysically treated. 'Tis by metaphysics only, that w 7 e can demonstrate, that God is not limited to a place, or is not mutable; that he is not ignorant, or forgetful; that it is impossible for him to lie, or be unjust; and that there is one God only, and not hundreds or thousands. And indeed we have no strict demonstration of anything, excepting mathematical truths, but by metaphysics. We can have no proof, that is properly demonstrative, of any one proposition, relating to the being and nature of God, his creation of the world, the dependence of all things on him, the nature of bodies or spirits, the nature of our own souls, or any of the great truths of morality and natural religion, but what is metaphysical. I am willing, my arguments should be brought to the test of the strictest and justest reason, and that a clear, distinct and determinate meaning of the terms I use, should be insisted on; but let not the whole be rejected, as if all were confuted, by fixing on it the epithet "metaphysical."

II. If the reasoning which has been made use of, be in some sense metaphysical, it will not follow, that therefore it must needs be abstruse, unintelligible, and akin to the jargon of the schools. I humbly conceive, the foregoing reasoning, at least as to those things which are most material belonging to it, depends on no abstruse definitions or distinctions, or terms without a meaning, or of very ambiguous and undetermined signification, or any points of such abstraction and subtlety, as tend to involve the attentive understanding in clouds and darkness. There is no high degree of refinement and abstruse speculation, in determining, that a thing is not before it is, and so can't be the cause of itself; or that the first act of free choice, has not another act of free choice going before that, to excite or direct it; or in determining, that no choice is made, while the mind remains in a state of absolute indifference; that preference and equilibrium never coexist; and that therefore no choice is made in a state of liberty, consisting in indifference: and that so far as the will is determined by motives, exhibited and operating previous to the act of the will, so far it is not determined by the act of the will itself; that nothing can begin to be, which before was not, without a cause, or some antecedent ground or reason, why it then begins to be; that effects depend on their causes, and are connected with them; that virtue is not the worse, nor sin the better, for the strength of inclination, with which it is practiced, and the difficulty which thence arises of doing otherwise; that when it is already infallibly known, that a thing will be, it is not a thing contingent whether it will ever be or no; or that it can be truly said, notwithstanding, that it is not necessary it should be, but it either may be, or may not be. And the like might be observed of many other things which belong to the foregoing reasoning.

If any shall still stand to it, that the foregoing reasoning is nothing but metaphysical sophistry; and that it must be so, that the seeming force of the arguments all depends on some fallacy and wile that is hid in the obscurity, which always attends a great degree of metaphysical abstraction and refinement; and shall be ready to say, "Here is indeed something that tends to confound the mind, but not to satisfy it: for who can ever be truly satisfied in it, that men are fitly blamed or commended, punished or rewarded, for those volitions which are not from themselves, and of whose existence they are not the causes. Men may refine, as much as they please, and advance their abstract notions, and make out a thousand seeming contradictions, to puzzle our understandings; yet there can be no satisfaction in such doctrine as this: the natural sense of the mind of man will always resist it."

(A certain noted author, of the present age, says, the arguments for necessity are nothing but "quibbling, or logomachy, using words without a meaning, or begging the question." I don't know what kind of necessity any authors he may have reference to, are advocates for; or whether they have managed their arguments well, or ill. As to the arguments I have made use of, if they are "quibbles," they may be shewn to be so: such knots are capable of being untied, and the trick and cheat may be detected and plainly laid open. If this be fairly done, with respect to the grounds and reasons I have relied upon, I shall have just occasion for the future to be silent, if not to be ashamed of my argumentations. I am willing, my proofs should be thoroughly examined; and if there be nothing but "begging the question," or mere "logomachy," or dispute of words, let it be made manifest, and shewn how the seeming strength of the argument depends on my "using words without a meaning," or arises from the ambiguity of terms, or my making use of words in an indeterminate and unsteady manner; and that the weight of my reasons rest mainly on such a foundation; and then, I shall either be ready to retract what I have urged, and thank the man that has done the kind part, or shall be justly exposed for my obstinacy. The same author is abundant in appealing, in this affair, from what he calls "logomachy and sophistry," to "experience." A person can experience only what passes in his own mind. But yet, as we may well suppose, that all men have the same human faculties; so a man may well argue from his own experience to that of others, in things that shew the nature of those faculties, and the manner of their operation. But then one has as good right to allege his experience, as another. As to my own experience, I find, that in innumerable things I can do as I will; that the motions of my body, in many respects, instantaneously follow the acts of my will concerning those motions; and that my will has some command of my thoughts; and that the acts of my will are my own, i.e. that they are acts of my will, the volitions of my own mind; or in other words, that what I will, I will. Which, I presume, is the sum of what others experience in this affair. But as to finding by experience, that my will is originally determined by itself; or that my will first choosing what volition there shall be, the chosen volition accordingly follows; and that this is the first rise of the determination of my will in any affair; or that any volition arises in my mind contingently; I declare, I know nothing in myself, by experience, of this nature; and nothing that ever I experienced, carries the least appearance or shadow of any such thing, or gives me any more reason to suppose or suspect any such thing, than to suppose that my volitions existed twenty years before they existed. 'Tis true, I find myself possessed of my volitions before I can see the effectual power of any cause to produce them (for the power and efficacy of the cause is not seen but by the effect) and this, for ought I know, may make some imagine, that volition has no cause, or that it produces itself. But I have no more reason from hence to determine any such thing, than I have to determine that I gave myself my own being, or that I came into being accidentally without a cause, because I first found myself possessed of being, before I had knowledge of a cause of my being.)

I humbly conceive, that such an objector, if he has capacity and humility and calmness of spirit, sufficient impartially and thoroughly to examine himself, will find that he knows not really what he would be at; and that indeed his difficulty is nothing but a mere prejudice, from an inadvertent customary use of words, in a meaning that is not clearly understood, nor carefully reflected upon. Let the objector reflect again, if he has candor and patience enough, and don't scorn to be at the trouble of close attention in the affair. He would have a man's volition be from himself. Let it be from himself, most primarily and originally of any way conceivable; that is, from his own choice: how will that help the matter, as to his being justly blamed or praised, unless that choice itself be blame or praiseworthy? And how is the choice itself (an ill choice, for instance) blameworthy, according to these principles, unless that be from himself too, in the same manner; that is, from his own choice? But the original and first determining choice in the affair is not from his choice: his choice is not the cause of it. And if it be from himself some other way, and not from his choice, surely that will not help the matter: if it ben't from himself of choice, then it is not from himself voluntarily; and if so, he is surely no more to blame, than if it were not from himself at all. It is a vanity, to pretend it is a sufficient answer to this, to say, that it is nothing but metaphysical refinement and subtlety, and so attended with obscurity and uncertainty.

If it be the natural sense of our minds, that what is blameworthy in a man must be from himself, then it doubtless is also, that it must be from something bad in himself, a bad choice, or bad disposition. But then our natural sense is, that this bad choice or disposition is evil in itself, and the man blameworthy for it, on its own account, without taking into our notion of its blameworthiness, another bad choice, or disposition going before this, from whence this arises; for that is a ridiculous absurdity, running us into an immediate contradiction, which our natural sense of blameworthiness has nothing to do with, and never comes into the mind, nor is supposed in the judgment we naturally make of the affair. As was demonstrated before, natural sense don't place the moral evil of volitions and dispositions in the cause of them, but the nature of them. An evil thing's being "from" a man, or from something antecedent in him, is not essential to the original notion we have of blameworthiness: but 'tis its being the choice of the heart; as appears by this, that if a thing be "from" us, and not from our choice, it has not the nature of blameworthiness or ill desert, according to our natural sense. When a thing is from a man, in that sense, that it is from his will or choice, he is to blame for it, because his will is in it: so far as the will is in it, blame is in it, and no further. Neither do we go any further in our notion of blame, to inquire whether the bad will be "from" a bad will: there is no consideration of the original of that bad will; because according to our natural apprehension, blame originally consists in it. Therefore a thing's being "from" a man, is a secondary consideration, in the notion of blame or ill-desert. Because those things in our external actions, are most properly said to be from us, which are from our choice; and no other external actions but those that are from us in this sense, have the nature of blame; and they indeed, not so properly because they are from us, as because we are in them, i.e. our wills are in them; not so much because they are from some property of ours, as because they are our properties.

However, all these external actions being truly from us, as their cause; and we being so used, in ordinary speech, and in the common affairs of life, to speak of men's actions and conduct that we see, and that affect human society, as deserving ill or well, as worthy of blame or praise; hence it is come to pass, that philosophers have incautiously taken all their measures of good and evil, praise and blame, from the dictates of common sense, about these overt acts of men; to the running of everything into the most lamentable and dreadful confusion. And therefore I observe,

III. 'Tis so far from being true (whatever may be pretended) that the proof of the doctrine which has been maintained, depends on certain abstruse, unintelligible, metaphysical terms and notions; and that the Arminian scheme, without needing such clouds and darkness, for its defense, is supported by the plain dictates of common sense; that the very reverse is most certainly true, and that to a great degree. 'Tis fact, that they, and not we, have confounded things with metaphysical, unintelligible notions and phrases, and have drawn them from the light of plain truth, into the gross darkness of abstruse metaphysical propositions, and words without a meaning. Their pretended demonstrations depend very much on such unintelligible, metaphysical phrases, as "self-determination" and "sovereignty of the will"; and the metaphysical sense they put on such terms, as "necessary," "contingency," "action," "agency," etc. quite diverse from their meaning as used in common speech; and which, as they use them, are without any consistent meaning, or any manner of distinct consistent ideas; as far from it as any of the abstruse terms and perplexed phrases of the peripatetic philosophers, or the most unintelligible jargon of the schools, or the cant of the wildest fanatics. Yea, we may be bold to say, these metaphysical terms, on which they build so much, are what they use without knowing what they mean themselves; they are pure metaphysical sounds, without any ideas whatsoever in their minds to answer them; inasmuch as it has been demonstrated, that there cannot be any notion in the mind consistent with these expressions, as they pretend to explain them; because their explanations destroy themselves. No such notions as imply self-contradiction, and self-abolition, and this a great many ways, can subsist in the mind; as there can be no idea of a whole which is less than any of its parts, or of solid extension without dimensions, or of an effect which is before its cause. Arminians improve these terms, as terms of art, and in their metaphysical meaning, to advance and establish those things which are contrary to common sense, in a high degree. Thus, instead of the plain vulgar notion of liberty, which all mankind, in every part of the face of the earth, and in all ages, have; consisting in opportunity to do as one pleases; they have introduced a new strange liberty, consisting in indifference, contingence, and self-determination; by which they involve themselves and others in great obscurity, and manifold gross inconsistence. So, instead of placing virtue and vice, as common sense places them very much, in fixed bias and inclination, and greater virtue and vice in stronger and more established inclination; these, through their refinings and abstruse notions, suppose a liberty consisting in indifference, to be essential to all virtue and vice. So they have reasoned themselves, not by metaphysical distinctions, but metaphysical confusion, into many principles about moral agency, blame, praise, reward and punishment, which are, as has been shewn, exceeding contrary to the common sense of mankind; and perhaps to their own sense, which governs them in common life.

THE CONCLUSION

Whether the things which have been alleged, are liable to any tolerable answer in the ways of calm, intelligible and strict reasoning, I must leave others to judge: but I am sensible they are liable to one sort of answer. 'Tis not unlikely, that some who value themselves on the supposed rational and generous principles of the modern fashionable divinity, will have their indignation and disdain raised at the sight of this discourse, and on perceiving what things are pretended to be proved in it. And if they think it worthy of being read, or of so much notice as to say much about it, they may probably renew the usual exclamations, with additional vehemence and contempt, about the "fate" of the heathen, "Hobbes' necessity," and "making men mere machines"; accumulating the terrible epithets of "fatal," "unfrustrable," "inevitable," "irresistible," etc. and it may be, with the addition of "horrid" and "blasphemous"; and perhaps much skill may be used to set forth things which have been said, in colors which shall be shocking to the imaginations, and moving to the passions of those who have either too little capacity, or too much confidence of the opinions they have imbibed, and contempt of the contrary, to try the matter by any serious and circumspect examination.

(A writer of the present age, whom I have several times had occasion to mention, speaks once and again of those who hold the doctrine of necessity, as scarcely worthy of the name of "philosophers." I don't know, whether he has respect to any particular notion of necessity, that some may have maintained; and if so, what doctrine of necessity it is that he means. Whether I am worthy of the name of a philosopher, or not, would be a question little to the present purpose. If any, and ever so many, should deny it, I should not think it worth the while to enter into a dispute on that question; though at the same time I might expect, some better answer should be given to the arguments brought for the truth of the doctrine I maintain; and I might further reasonably desire, that it might be considered, whether it don't become those who are truly worthy of the name of philosophers, to be sensible, that there is a difference between argument and contempt; yea, and a difference between the contemptibleness of the person that argues, and the inconclusiveness of the arguments he offers.)

Or difficulties may be started and insisted on which don't belong to the controversy; because, let them be more or less real, and hard to be resolved, they are not what are owing to anything distinguishing of this scheme from that of the Arminians, and would not be removed nor diminished by renouncing the former, and adhering to the latter. Or some particular things may be picked out, which they may think will sound harshest in the ears of the generality; and these may be glossed and descanted on, with tart and contemptuous words; and from thence, the whole treated with triumph and insult.

'Tis easy to see how the decision of most of the points in controversy, between Calvinists and Arminians, depends on the determination of this grand article concerning the freedom of the will requisite to moral agency; and that by clearing and establishing the Calvinistic doctrine in this point, the chief arguments are obviated, by which Arminian doctrines in general are supported, and the contrary doctrines demonstratively confirmed. Hereby it becomes manifest, that God's moral government over mankind, his treating them as moral agents, making them the objects of his commands, counsels, calls, warnings, expostulations, promises, threatenings, rewards and punishments, is not inconsistent with a determining disposal of all events, of every kind, throughout the universe, in his providence; either by positive efficiency, or permission. Indeed such an universal, determining providence, infers some kind of necessity of all events; 1 such a necessity as implies an infallible previous fixedness of the futurity of the event: but no other necessity of moral events, or volitions of intelligent agents, is needful in order to this, than moral necessity; which does as much ascertain the futurity of the event, as any other necessity. But, as has been demonstrated, such a necessity is not at all repugnant to moral agency, and the reasonable use of commands, calls, rewards, punishments, etc. Yea, not only are objections of this kind against the doctrine of an universal determining providence, removed by what has been said; but the truth of such a doctrine is demonstrated. As it has been demonstrated, that the futurity of all future events is established by previous necessity, either natural or moral; so 'tis manifest, that the sovereign Creator and Disposer of the world has ordered this necessity, by ordering his own conduct, either in designedly acting, or forbearing to act. For, as the being of the world is from God, so the circumstances in which it had its being at first, both negative and positive, must be ordered by him, in one of these ways; and all the necessary consequences of these circumstances, must be ordered by him. And God's active and positive interpositions, after the world was created, and the consequences of these interpositions; also every instance of his forbearing to interpose, and the sure consequences of this forbearance, must all be determined according to his pleasure. And therefore every event which is the consequence of anything whatsoever, or that is connected with any foregoing thing or circumstance, either positive or negative, as the ground or reason of its existence, must be ordered of God; either by a designed efficiency and interposition, or a designed forbearing to operate or interpose. But, as has been proved, all events whatsoever are necessarily connected with something foregoing, either positive or negative, which is the ground of its existence. It follows therefore, that the whole series of events is thus connected with something in the state of things, either positive or negative, which is original in the series; i.e. something which is connected with nothing preceding that, but God's own immediate conduct, either his acting or forbearing to act. From whence it follows, that as God designedly orders his own conduct, and its connected consequences, it must necessarily be, that he designedly orders all things.

The things which have been said, obviate some of the chief objections of Arminians against the Calvinistic doctrine of the total depravity and corruption of man's nature^ whereby his heart is wholly under the power of sin, and he is utterly unable, without the inter-position of sovereign grace, savingly to love God, believe in Christ, or do anything that is truly good and acceptable in God's sight. For the main objection against this doctrine is, that it is inconsistent with the freedom of man's will, consisting in indifference and self-determining power; because it supposes man to be under a necessity of sinning, and that God requires things of him, in order to his avoiding eternal damnation, which he is unable to do; and that this doctrine is wholly inconsistent with the sincerity of counsels, invitations, etc. Now this doctrine supposes no other necessity of sinning, than a moral necessity; which, as has been shewn, don't at all excuse sin; and supposes no other inability to obey any command, or perform any duty, even the most spiritual and exalted, but a moral inability, which, as has been proved, don't excuse persons in the nonperformance of any good thing, or make 'em not to be the proper objects of commands, counsels and invitations. And moreover, it has been shewn, that there is not, and never can be, either in existence, or so much as in idea, any such freedom of will, consisting in indifference and self-determination, for the sake of which, this doctrine of original sin is cast out; and that no such freedom is necessary, in order to the nature of sin, and a just desert of punishment.

The things which have been observed, do also take off the main objections of Arminians against the doctrine of efficacious grace; and at the same time, prove the grace of God in a sinner's conversion (if there be any grace or divine influence in the affair) to be efficacious, yea, and irresistible too, if by irresistible is meant, that which is attended with a moral necessity, which it is impossible should ever be violated by any resistance. The main objection of Arminians against this doctrine is, that it is inconsistent with their self-determining freedom of will; and that it is repugnant to the nature of virtue, that it should be wrought in the heart by the determining efficacy and power of another, instead of its being owing to a self-moving power; that in that case, the good which is wrought, would not be our virtue, but rather God's virtue; because it is not the person in whom it is wrought, that is the determining author of it, but God that wrought it in him. But the things which are the foundation of these objections, have been considered; and it has been demonstrated, that the liberty of moral agents does not consist in self-determining power; and that there is no need of any such liberty, in order to the nature of virtue; nor does it at all hinder, but that the state or act of the will may be the virtue of the subject, though it be not from self-determination, but the determination of an extrinsic cause; even so as to cause the event to be morally necessary to the subject of it. And as it has been proved, that nothing in the state or acts of the will of man is contingent; but that on the contrary, every event of this kind is necessary, by a moral necessity; and has also been now demonstrated, that the doctrine of an universal determining providence, follows from that doctrine of necessity, which was proved before: and so, that God does decisively, in his providence, order all the volitions of moral agents, either by positive influence or permission: and it being allowed on all hands, that what God does in the affair of man's virtuous volitions, whether it be more or less, is by some positive influence, and not by mere permission, as in the affair of a sinful volition: if we put these things together, it will follow, that God's assistance or influence, must be determining and decisive, or must be attended with a moral necessity of the event; and so, that God gives virtue, holiness and conversion to sinners, by an influence which determines the effect, in such a manner, that the effect will infallibly follow by a moral necessity; which is what Calvinists mean by efficacious and irresistible grace.

The things which have been said, do likewise answer the chief objections against the doctrine of God's universal and absolute decree, and afford infallible proof of that doctrine; and of the doctrine of absolute, eternal, personal election in particular. The main objections against these doctrines are, that they infer a necessity of the volitions of moral agents, and of the future moral state and acts of men; and so are not consistent with those eternal rewards and punishments, which are connected with conversion and impenitence; nor can be made to agree with the reasonableness and sincerity of the precepts, calls, counsels, warnings and expostulations of the Word of God; or with the various methods and means of grace, which God uses with sinners, to bring 'em to repentance; and the whole of that moral government, which God exercises towards mankind: and that they infer an inconsistence between the secret and revealed will of God; and make God the author of sin. But all these things have been obviated in the preceding discourse. And the certain truth of these doctrines, concerning God's eternal purposes, will follow from what was just now observed concerning God's universal providence; how it infallibly follows from what has been proved, that God orders all events, and the volitions of moral agents amongst others, by such a decisive disposal, that the events are infallibly connected with his disposal. For if God disposes all events, so that the infallible existence of the events is decided by his providence, then he doubtless thus orders and decides things knowingly, and on design. God don't do what he does, nor order what he orders, accidentally and unawares; either without, or beside his intention. And if there be a foregoing design of doing and ordering as he does, this is the same with a purpose or decree. And as it has been shewn, that nothing is new to God, in any respect, but all things are perfectly and equally in his view from eternity; hence it will follow, that his designs or purposes are not things formed anew, founded on any new views or appearances, but are all eternal purposes. And as it has been now shewn, how the doctrine of determining efficacious grace certainly follows from things proved in the foregoing discourse; hence will necessarily follow the doctrine of particular, eternal, absolute election. For if men are made true saints, no otherwise than as God makes 'em so, and distinguishes 'em from others, by an efficacious power and influence of his, that decides and fixes the event; and God thus makes some saints, and not others, on design or purpose, and (as has been now observed) no designs of God are new; it follows, that God thus distinguished from others, all that ever become true saints, by his eternal design or decree. I might also shew, how God's certain foreknowledge must suppose an absolute decree, and how such a decree can be proved to a demonstration from it: but that this discourse mayn't be lengthened out too much, that must be omitted for the present.

From these things it will inevitably follow, that however Christ in some sense may be said to die for all, and to redeem all visible Christians, yea, the whole world by his death; yet there must be something particular in the design of his death, with respect to such as he intended should actually be saved thereby. As appears by what has been now shewn, God has the actual salvation or redemption of a certain number in his proper absolute design, and of a certain number only; and therefore such a design only can be prosecuted in anything God does, in order to the salvation of men. God pursues a proper design of the salvation of the elect in giving Christ to die, and prosecutes such a design with respect to no other, most strictly speaking; for 'tis impossible, that God should prosecute any other design than only such as he has: he certainly don't, in the highest propriety and strictness of speech, pursue a design that he has not. And indeed such a particularity and limitation of redemption will as infallibly follow from the doctrine of God's foreknowledge, as from that of the decree. For 'tis as impossible, in strictness of speech, that God should prosecute a design or aim at a thing, which he at the same time most perfectly knows will not be accomplished, as that he should use endeavors for that which is beside his decree.

By the things which have been proved, are obviated some of the main objections against the doctrine of the infallible and necessary perseverance of saints, and some of the main foundations of this doctrine are established. The main prejudices of Arminians against this doctrine seem to be these; they suppose such a necessary, infallible perseverance to be repugnant to the freedom of the Will; that it must be owing to man's own self-determining power, that he first becomes virtuous and holy; and so in like manner, it must be left a thing contingent, to be determined by the same freedom of will, whether he will persevere in virtue and holiness; and that otherwise his continuing steadfast in faith and obedience would not be his virtue, or at all praiseworthy and rewardable; nor could his perseverance be properly the matter of divine commands, counsels and promises, nor his apostasy be properly threatened, and men warned against it. Whereas we find all these things in Scripture: there we find steadfastness and perseverance in true Christianity, represented as the virtue of the saints, spoken of as praiseworthy in them, and glorious rewards promised to it; and also find, that God makes it the subject of his commands, counsels and promises; and the contrary, of threatenings and warnings. But the foundation of these objections has been removed, in its being shewn that moral necessity and infallible certainty of events is not inconsistent with these things; and that, as to freedom of will lying in the power of the will to determine itself, there neither is any such thing, nor any need of it, in order to virtue, reward, commands, counsels, etc.

And as the doctrines of efficacious grace and absolute election do certainly follow from things which have been proved in the preceding discourse; so some of the main foundations of the doctrine of perseverance are thereby established. If the beginning of true faith and holiness, and a man's becoming a true saint at first, don't depend on the self-determining power of the will, but on the determining efficacious grace of God; it may well be argued, that it is so also with respect to men's being continued saints, or persevering in faith and holiness. The conversion of a sinner being not owing to a man's self-determination, but to God's determination, and eternal election, which is absolute, and depending on the sovereign will of God, and not on the free will of man; as is evident from what has been said: and it being very evident from the Scriptures, that the eternal election which there is of saints to faith and holiness, is also an election of them to eternal salvation; hence their appointment to salvation must also be absolute, and not depending on their contingent, self-determining will. From all which it follows, that it is absolutely fixed in God's decree, that all true saints shall persevere to actual eternal salvation.

But I must leave all these things to the consideration of the fair and impartial reader; and when he has maturely weighed them, I would propose it to his consideration, whether many of the first Reformers, and others that succeeded them, whom God in their day made the chief pillars of his church, and greatest instruments of their deliverance from error and darkness, and of the support of the cause of piety among them, have not been injured, in the contempt with which they have been treated by many late writers, for their teaching and maintaining such doctrines as are commonly called Calvinistic. Indeed some of these new writers, at the same time that they have represented the doctrines of these ancient and eminent divines, as in the highest degree ridiculous, and contrary to common sense, in an ostentation of a very generous charity, have allowed that they were honest well-meaning men: yea, it may be some of them, as though it were in great condescension and compassion to them, have allowed that they did pretty well for the day which they lived in, and considering the great disadvantages they labored under: when at the same time, their manner of speaking has naturally and plainly suggested to the minds of their readers, that they were persons, who through the lowness of their genius, and greatness of the bigotry, with which their minds were shackled, and thoughts confined, living in the gloomy caves of superstition, fondly embraced, and demurely and zealously taught the most absurd, silly and monstrous opinions, worthy of the greatest contempt of gentlemen possessed of that noble and generous freedom of thought, which happily prevails in this age of light and inquiry. When indeed such is the case, that we might, if so disposed, speak as big words as they, and on far better grounds. And really all the Arminians on earth might be challenged without arrogance or vanity, to make these principles of theirs wherein they mainly differ from their fathers, whom they so much despise, consistent with common sense; yea, and perhaps to produce any doctrine ever embraced by the blindest bigot of the church of Rome, or the most ignorant Mussulman, or extravagant enthusiast, that might be reduced to more, and more demonstrable inconsistencies, and repugnancies to common sense, and to themselves; though their inconsistencies indeed may not lie so deep, or be so artfully veiled by a deceitful ambiguity of words, and an indeterminate signification of phrases. I will not deny, that these gentlemen, many of them, are men of great abilities, and have been helped to higher attainments in philosophy, than those ancient divines, and have done great service to the church of God in some respects: but I humbly conceive, that their differing from their fathers with such magisterial assurance, in these points in divinity, must be owing to some other cause than superior wisdom.

It may also be worthy of consideration, whether the great alteration which has been made in the state of things in our nation, and some other parts of the Protestant world, in this and the past age, by the exploding so generally Calvinistic doctrines, that is so often spoken of as worthy to be greatly rejoiced in by the friends of truth, learning and virtue, as an instance of the great increase of light in the Christian Church; I say, it may be worthy to be considered, whether this be indeed a happy change, owing to any such cause as an increase of true knowledge and understanding in things of religion; or whether there is not reason to fear, that it may be owing to some worse cause.

And I desire it may be considered, whether the boldness of some writers may not be worthy to be reflected on, who have not scrupled to say, that if these and those things are true (which yet appear to be the demonstrable dictates of reason, as well as the certain dictates of the mouth of the most High) then God is unjust and cruel, and guilty of manifest deceit and double-dealing, and the like. Yea, some have gone so far, as confidently to assert, that if any book which pretends to be Scripture, teaches such doctrines, that alone is sufficient warrant for mankind to reject it, as what cannot be the Word of God.

Some who have not gone so far, have said, that if the Scripture seems to teach any such doctrines, so contrary to reason, we are obliged to find out some other interpretation of those texts, where such doctrines seem to be exhibited. Others express themselves yet more modestly: they express a tenderness and religious fear, lest they should receive and teach anything that should seem to reflect on God's moral character, or be a disparagement to his methods of administration, in his moral government; and therefore express themselves as not daring to embrace some doctrines, though they seem to be delivered in Scripture, according to the more obvious and natural construction of the words. But indeed it would shew a truer modesty and humility, if they would more entirely rely on God's wisdom and discerning, who knows infinitely better than we, what is agreeable to his own perfections, and never intended to leave these matters to the decision of the wisdom and discerning of men; but by his own unerring instruction, to determine for us what the truth is; knowing how little our judgment is to be depended on, and how extremely prone, vain and blind men are, to err in such matters.

The truth of the case is, that if the Scripture plainly taught the opposite doctrines, to those that are so much stumbled at, viz. the Arminian doctrine of free will, and others depending thereon, it would be the greatest of all difficulties that attend the Scriptures, incomparably greater than its containing any, even the most mysterious of those doctrines of the first Reformers, which our late free thinkers have so superciliously exploded. Indeed it is a glorious argument of the divinity of the holy Scriptures, that they teach such doctrines, which in one age and another, through the blindness of men's minds, and strong prejudices of their hearts, are rejected, as most absurd and unreasonable, by the wise and great men of the world; which yet, when they are most carefully and strictly examined, appear to be exactly agreeable to the most demonstrable, certain, and natural dictates of reason. By such things it appears, that the "foolishness of God is wiser than men," and God does as is said in I Cor. 1:19, 20: "For it is written, I will destroy the wisdom of the wise; I will bring to nothing the understanding of the prudent. Where is the wise! Where is the Scribe! Where is the disputer of this world! Hath not God made foolish the wisdom of this world?" And as it used to be in time past, so it is probable it will be in time to come, as it is there written, in ver. 27, 28, 29, "But God hath chosen the foolish things of the world, to confound the wise: and God hath chosen the weak things of the world, to confound the things that are mighty: and base things of the world, and things which are despised, hath God chosen: yea, and things which are not, to bring to nought things that are; that no flesh should glory in his presence." Amen.

Sermons of George Whitefield

1. The Seed of the Woman, and the Seed of the Serpent

Genesis 3:15—"And I will put Enmity between thee and the Woman, and between thy Seed and her Seed, it shall bruise thy Head, and thou shalt bruise his Head."

On reading to you these words, I may address you in the language of the holy angels to the shepherds, that were watching their flocks by night: "Behold, I bring you glad tidings of great joy." For this is the first promise that was made of a Savior to the apostate race of Adam. We generally look for Christ only in the New Testament; but Christianity, in one sense, is very near as old as the creation. It is wonderful to observe how gradually God revealed his Son to mankind. He began with the promise in the text, and this the elect lived upon, till the time of Abraham. To him, God made further discoveries of his eternal council concerning man's redemption. Afterwards, at sundry times, and in divers manners, God spoke to the fathers by the prophets, till at length the Lord Jesus himself was manifested in flesh, and came and tabernacled amongst us.

This first promise must certainly be but dark to our first parents, in comparison of that great light which we enjoy: And yet, dark as it was, we may assure ourselves they built upon it their hopes of everlasting salvation, and by that faith were saved.

How they came to stand in need of this promise, and what is the extent and meaning of it, I intend, God willing, to make the subject-matter of your present meditation.

The fall of man is written in too legible characters not to be understood: Those that deny it, by their denying, prove it. The very heathens confessed, and bewailed it: They could see the streams of corruption running through the whole race of mankind, but could not trace them to the fountain-head. Before God gave a revelation of his Son, man was a riddle to himself. And Moses unfolds more, in this one chapter (out of which the text is taken) than all mankind could have been capable of finding out of themselves, though they had studied to all eternity.

In the preceding chapter he had given us a full account, how God spoke the world into being; and especially how he formed man of the dust of the earth, and breathed into him the breath of life, so that he became a living soul. A council of the Trinity was called concerning the formation of this lovely creature. The result of that council was, "Let us make man in our image, after our likeness. So God created man in his own image, in the image of God created he him." Moses remarkably repeats these words, that we might take particular notice of our divine Original. Never was so much expressed in so few words: None but a man inspired could have done so. But it is remarkable, that though Moses mentions our being made in the image of God, yet he mentions it but twice, and that in a transient manner; as though he would have said, "man was made in honor, God make him upright, 'in the image of God, male and female created he them.'" But man so soon fell, and became like the beasts that perish, nay, like the devil himself, that it is scarce worth mentioning."

How soon man fell after he was created, is not told us; and therefore, to fix any time, is to be wise above what is written. And, I think, they who suppose that man fell the same day in which he was made, have no sufficient ground for their opinion. The many things which are crowded together in the former chapter, such as the formation of Adam's wife, his giving names to the beasts, and his being put into the garden which God had planted, I think require a longer space of time than a day to be transacted in. However, all agree in this, "man stood not long." How long, or how short a while, I will not take upon me to determine. It more concerns us to inquire, how he came to fall from his steadfastness, and what was the rise and progress of the temptation which prevailed over him. The account given us in this chapter concerning it, is very full; and it may do us much service, under God, to make some remarks upon it.

"Now the serpent (says the sacred historian) was more subtle than any beast of the field which the Lord God had made, and he said unto the woman, Yes, hath God said, ye shall not eat of every tree of the garden?"

Though this was a real serpent, yet he that spoke was no other than the devil; from hence, perhaps, called the old serpent, because he took possession of the serpent when he came to beguile our first parents. The devil envied the happiness of man, who was made, as some think, to supply the place of the fallen angels. God made man upright, and with full power to stand if he would: He was just, therefore, in suffering him to be tempted. If he fell, he had no one to blame except himself. But how must Satan effect his fall? He cannot do it by his power, he attempts it therefore by policy: he takes possession of a serpent, which was more subtle than all the beasts of the field, which the Lord God had made; so that men who are full of subtlety, but have no piety, are only machines for the devil to work upon, just as he pleases.

"And he said unto the woman." Here is an instance of his subtlety. He says unto the woman, the weaker vessel, and when she was alone from her husband, and therefore was more liable to be overcome; "Yes, hath God said, ye shall not eat of every tree of the garden?" These words are certainly spoken in answer to something which the devil either saw or heard. In all probability, the woman was now near the tree of knowledge of good and evil; (for we shall find her, by and by, plucking an apple from it) perhaps she might be looking at, and wondering what tree was in that tree more than the others, that she and her husband should be forbidden to take of it. Satan seeing this, and coveting to draw her into a parley with him, (for if the devil can persuade us not to resist, but to commune with him, he hath gained a great point) he says, "Yea, hath God said, ye shall not eat of every tree in the garden?" The first thing he does is to persuade he, if possible to entertain hard thoughts of God; this is his general way of dealing with God's children: "Yea, hath God said, ye shall not eat of every tree of the garden? What! Hath God planted a garden, and placed you in the midst of it, only to tease and perplex you? Hath he planted a garden, and yet forbid you making use of any of the fruits of it at all?" It was impossible for him to ask a more ensnaring question, in order to gain his end: For Eve was here seemingly obliged to answer, and vindicate God's goodness. And therefore,—

Verses Genesis 3:2, and Genesis 3:3, The woman said unto the serpent, "We may eat of the fruit of the trees of the garden: But of the fruit of the tree which is in the midst of the garden, God hath said, ye shall not eat of it, neither shall ye touch it, lest ye die."

The former part of the answer was good, "We may eat of the fruit of the trees of the garden, God has not forbid us eating of every tree of the garden. No; we may eat of the fruit of the trees in the garden (and, it should seem, even of the tree of life, which was as a sacrament to man in the state of innocence) there is only one tree in the midst of the garden, of which God hath said, ye shall not eat of it, neither shall ye touch it, lest ye die." Here she begins to warp, and sin begins to conceive I her heart. Already she has contracted some of the serpent's poison, by talking with him, which she ought not to have done at all. For she might easily suppose, that it could be no good being that could put such a question unto her, and insinuate such dishonorable thoughts of God. She should therefore have fled from him, and not stood to have parleyed with him at all. Immediately the ill effects of it appear, she begins to soften the divine threatening. God had said, "the day thou eatest thereof, thou shalt surely die;" or, dying thou shalt die. But Eve says, "Ye shall not eat of it, neither shall ye touch it, lest ye die." We may be assured we are fallen into, and begin to fall by temptations, when we begin to think God will not be as good as his word, in respect to the execution of his threatenings denounced against sin. Satan knew this, and therefore artfully

"Said unto the woman, (ver. Genesis 3:4, Ye shall not surely die," in an insinuating manner, "Ye shall not surely die. Surely; God will not be so cruel as to damn you only for eating an apple, it cannot be." Alas! How many does Satan lead captive at his will, by flattering them, that they shall not surely die; that hell torments will not be eternal; that God is all mercy; that he therefore will not punish a few years sin with an eternity of misery? But Eve found God as good as his word; and so will all they who go on in sin, under a false hope that they shall not surely die.

We may also understand the words spoken positively, and this is agreeable to what follows; You shall not surely die; "It is all a delusion, a mere bugbear, to keep you in a servile subjection."

For ver. Genesis 3:5, "God doth know, that in the day ye eat thereof, then shall your eyes be opened, and ye shall be as gods, knowing good and evil."

What child of God can expect to escape slander, when God himself was thus slandered even in paradise? Surely the understanding of Eve must have been, in some measure, blinded, or she would not have suffered the tempter to speak such perverse things. In what odious colors is God here represented! "God doth know, that in the day ye eat thereof, ye shall be as gods," (equal with God.) So that the grand temptation was, that they should be hereafter under no control, equal, if not superior, to God that made them, knowing good and evil. Eve could not tell what Satan meant by this; but, to be sure, she understood it of some great privilege which they were to enjoy. And thus Satan now points out a way which seems right to sinners, but does not tell them the end of that way is death.

To give strength and force to this temptation, in all probability, Satan, or the serpent, at this time plucked an apple from the tree, and ate it before Eve; by which Eve might be induced to think, that the sagacity and power of speech, which the serpent had above the other beasts, must be owing, in a great measure, to his eating that fruit; and, therefore, if he received so much improvement, she might also expect a like benefit from it. All this, I think, is clear; for, otherwise, I do not see with what propriety it could be said, "When the woman saw that it was good for food." How could she know it was good for food, unless she had seen the serpent feed upon it?

Satan now begins to get ground space. Lust had conceived in Eve's heart; shortly it will bring forth sin. Sin being conceived, brings forth death. Verse Genesis 3:6, "And when the woman saw that the tree was good for food, and that it was pleasant to the eyes, and a tree to be desired to make one wise, she took of the fruit thereof, and did eat, and gave also unto her husband, and he did eat."

Our senses are the landing ports of our spiritual enemies. How needful is that resolution of holy Job, "I have made a covenant with mine eyes!" When Eve began to gaze on the forbidden fruit with her eyes, she soon began to long after it with her heart. When she saw that it was good for food, and pleasant to the eyes, (here was the lust of the flesh, and lust of the eye) but, above all, a tree to be desired to make one wise, wiser than God would have her be, nay, as wise as God himself; she took of the fruit thereof, and gave also unto her husband with her, and he did eat. As soon as ever she sinned herself, she turned tempter to her husband. It is dreadful, when those, who should be help-meets for each other in the great work of their salvation, are only promoters of each other's damnation: but thus it is. If we ourselves are good, we shall excite others to goodness; if we do evil, we shall entice others to do evil also. There is a close connection between doing and teaching. How needful then is it for us all to take heed that we do not sin any way ourselves, lest we should become factors for the devil, and ensnare, perhaps, our nearest and dearest relatives? "she gave also unto her husband with her, and he did eat."

Alas! What a complication of crimes was there in this one single act of sin! Here is an utter disbelief of God's threatening; the utmost ingratitude to their Maker, who had so lately planted this garden, and placed them in it, with such a glorious and comprehensive charter. And, the utmost neglect of their posterity, who they knew were to stand or fall with them. Here was the utmost pride of heart: they wanted to be equal with God. Here's the utmost contempt put upon his threatening and his law: the devil is credited and obeyed before him, and all this only to satisfy their sensual appetite. Never was a crime of such a complicated nature committed by any here below: Nothing but the devil's apostasy and rebellion could equal it.

And what are the consequences of their disobedience? Are their eyes opened? Yes, their eyes are opened; but, alas! It is only to see their own nakedness. For we are told ver. Genesis 3:7,"That the eyes of them both were opened; and they knew that they were naked." Naked of God, naked of every thing that was holy and good, and destitute of the divine image, which they before enjoyed. They might rightly now be termed Ichabod; for the glory of the Lord departed from them. O how low did these sons of the morning then fall! Out of God, into themselves; from being partakers of the divine nature, into the nature of the devil and the beast. Well, therefore, might they know that they were naked, not only in body, but in soul.

And how do they behave now they are naked? Do they flee to God for pardon? Do they seek to God for a robe to cover their nakedness? No, they were now dead to God, and became earthly, sensual, devilish: therefore, instead of applying to God for mercy, "they sewed or platted fig-leaves together, and made themselves aprons, "or things to gird about them. This is a lively representation of all natural man: we see that we are naked: we, in some measure, confess it; but, instead of looking up to God for succor, we patch up a righteousness of our own (as our first parents platted fig-leaves together) hoping to cover our nakedness by that. But our righteousness will not stand the severity of God's judgment: it will do us no more service than the fig-leaves did Adam and Eve, that is, none at all.

For ver. Genesis 3:8,"They heard the voice of the Lord God walking in the trees of the garden, in the cool of the day; and Adam and his wife (notwithstanding their fig-leaves) hid themselves from the presence of the Lord God, among the trees of the garden."

They heard the voice of the Lord God, or the Word of the Lord God, even the Lord Jesus Christ, who is "the word that was with God, and the word that was God." They heard him walking in the trees of the garden, in the cool of the day. A season, perhaps, when Adam and Eve used to go, in a n especial manner, and offer up an evening sacrifice of praise and thanksgiving. The cool of the day. Perhaps the sin was committed early in the morning, or at noon; but God would not come upon them immediately, he staid till the cool of the day. And if we would effectually reprove others, we should not do it when they are warmed with passion, but wait till the cool of the day.

But what an alteration is here! Instead of rejoicing at the voice of their beloved, instead of meeting him with open arms and enlarged hearts, as before, they now hide themselves in the trees of the garden. Alas, what a foolish attempt was this? Surely they must be naked, otherwise how could they think of hiding themselves from God? Whither could they flee from his presence? But, by their fall, they had contracted an enmity against God: they now hated, and were afraid to converse with God their Maker. And is not this our case by nature? Assuredly it is. We labor to cover our nakedness with the fig-leaves of our own righteousness: We hide ourselves from God as long as we can, and will not come, and never should come, did not the Father prevent, draw, and sweetly constrain us by his grace, as he here prevented Adam.

Verse Genesis 3:9, "And the Lord God called unto Adam, and said unto him, Adam, where art thou?"

"The Lord God called unto Adam." (for otherwise Adam would never have called unto the Lord God) and said, "Adam, where art thou? How is it that thou comest not to pay thy devotions as usual?" Christians, remember the Lord keeps an account when you fail coming to worship. Whenever therefore you are tempted to withhold your attendance, let each of you fancy you heard the Lord calling unto you, and saying, "O man, O woman, where art thou? It may be understood in another and better sense; "Adam, where art thou?" What a condition is thy poor soul in? This is the first thing the Lord asks and convinces a sinner of; when he prevents and calls him effectually by his grace; he also calls him by name; for unless God speaks to us in particular, and we know where we are, how poor, how miserable, how blind, how naked, we shall never value the redemption wrought out for us by the death and obedience of the dear Lord Jesus. "Adam, where art thou?"

Verse Genesis 3:10, "And he said, I heard thy voice in the garden, and I was afraid." See what cowards sin makes us. If we knew no sin, we should know no fear. "Because I was naked, and I hid myself." Ver. Genesis 3:11, "And he said, who told thee that thou was naked? Hast thou eaten of the tree, whereof I (thy Maker and Law-giver) commanded thee, that thou shouldest not eat?"

God knew very well that Adam was naked, and that he had eaten of the forbidden fruit, But God would know it from Adam's own mouth. Thus God knows all our necessities before we ask, but yet insists upon our asking for his grace, and confessing our sins. For, by such acts, we acknowledge our dependence upon God, take shame to ourselves, and thereby give glory to his great name.

Verse Genesis 3:12, "And the man said, the woman which thou gavest to be with me, she gave me of the tree, and I did eat."

Never was nature more lively delineated. See what pride Adam contracted by the fall! How unwilling he is to lay the blame upon, or take shame to himself. This answer is full of insolence towards God, enmity against his wife, and disingenuity in respect to himself. For herein he tacitly reflects upon God. "The woman that thou gavest to be with me." As much as to say, if thou hadst not given me that woman, I had not eaten the forbidden fruit. Thus, when men sin, they lay the fault upon their passions; then blame and reflect upon God for giving them those passions. Their language is, "the appetites that thou gavest us, they deceived us; and therefore we sinned against thee." But, as God, notwithstanding, punished Adam for hearkening to the voice of his wife, so he will punish those who hearken to the dictates of their corrupt inclinations. For God compels no man to sin. Adam might have withstood the solicitations of his wife, if he would. And so, if we look up to God, we should find grace to help in the time of need. The devil and our own hearts tempt, but they cannot force us to consent, without the concurrence of our own wills. So that our damnation is of ourselves, as it will evidently appear at the great day, notwithstanding all men's present impudent replies against God. As Adam speaks insolently in respect to God, so he speaks with enmity against his wife; the woman, or this woman, she gave me. He lays all the fault upon her, and speaks of her with much contempt. He does not say, my wife, my dear wife; but, *this woman*. Sin disunites the most united hearts: It is, the bane of holy fellowship. Those who have been companions in sin here, if they die without repentance, will both hate and condemn one another hereafter. All damned souls are accusers of their brethren. Thus it is, in some degree, on this side of the grave. "The woman whom thou gavest to be with me, she gave me of the tree, and I did eat." What a disingenuous [deceitful] speech was here! He makes use of no less than fifteen words to excuse himself, and but one or two (in the original) to confess his fault, if it may be called a confession at all. "The woman which thou gavest to be with me, she gave me of the tree;" here are fifteen words; "and I did eat." With what reluctance do these last words come out? How soon are they uttered are they uttered? "And I did eat." But thus it is with an unhumbled, unregenerate heart; It will be laying the fault upon the dearest friend in the world, nay, upon God himself, rather than take shame to itself. This pride we are all subject to by the fall; and, till our hearts are broken, and made contrite by the spirit of our Lord Jesus Christ, we shall be always charging God foolishly. "Against thee, and thee only, have I sinned, that thou mightest be justified in thy saying, and clear when thou art judged," is the language of none but those, who, like David, are willing to confess their faults, and are truly sorry for their sins. This was not the case of Adam; his heart was not broken; and therefore he lays the fault of his disobedience upon his wife and God, and not upon himself; "The woman which thou gavest to be with me, she gave me of the tree, and I did eat."

Verse Genesis 3:13, "And the Lord God said, What is this that thou hast done?" What a wonderful concern does God express in this expostulation! "What a deluge of misery hast thou brought upon thyself, thy husband, and thy posterity? What is this that thou has done? Disobeyed thy God, obeyed the devil, and ruined thy husband, for whom I made thee to be an help-meet! What is this that thou hast done?" God would here awaken her to a sense of her crime and danger, and therefore, as it were, thunders in her ears: for the law must be preached to self-righteous sinners. We must take care of healing before we see sinners wounded, lest we should say, Peace, peace, where there is no peace. Secure sinners must hear the thunderings of mount Sinai, before we bring them to mount Zion. They who never preach up the law, it is to be feared, are unskillful in delivering the glad tidings of the gospel. Every minister should be a Boanerges, a son of thunder, as well as a Barnabus, a son of consolation. There was an earthquake and a whirlwind, before the small still voice came to Elijah: We must first show people they are condemned, and then show them how they must be saved. But how and when to preach the law, and when to apply the promises of the gospel, wisdom is profitable to direct. "And the Lord God said unto the woman, What is this that thou has done?"

"And the woman said, The serpent beguiled me, and I did eat." She does not make use of so many words to excuse herself, as her husband; but her heart is as unhumbled as his. What is this, says God, that thou hast done? God here charges her with doing it. She dares not deny the fact, or say, I have not done it; but she takes all the blame off herself, and lays it upon the serpent; "The serpent beguiled me, and I did eat." She does not say, "Lord, I was to blame for talking with the serpent; Lord, I did wrong, in not hastening to my husband, when he put the first question to me; Lord, I plead guilty, I only am to blame, O let not my poor husband suffer for my wickedness!" This would have been the language of her heart had she now been a true penitent. But both were now alike proud; therefore neither will lay the blame upon themselves; "The serpent beguiled me, and I did eat. The woman which thou gavest to be with me, she gave me of the tree, and I did eat."

I have been the more particular in remarking this part of their behavior, because it tends so much to the magnifying of Free-grace, and plainly shows us, that salvation cometh only from the Lord. Let us take a short view of the miserable circumstances our first parents were now in: They were legally and spiritually dead, children of wrath, and heirs of hell. They had eaten the fruit, of which God had commanded them, that they should not eat; and when arraigned before God, notwithstanding their crime was so complicated, they could not be brought to confess it. What reason can be given, why sentence of death should not be pronounced against the prisoners at the bar? All must own they are worthy to die. Nay, how can God, consistently with his justice, possibly forgive them? He had threatened, that they day wherein they eat of the forbidden fruit, they should "surely die;" and, if he did not execute this threatening, the devil might then slander the Almighty indeed. And yet mercy cries, spare these sinners, spare the work of thine own hands. Behold, then, wisdom contrives a scheme how God may be just, and yet be merciful; be faithful to his threatening, punish the offense, and at the same time spare the offender. An amazing scene of divine love here opens to our view, which had been from all eternity hid in the heart of God! Notwithstanding Adam and Eve were thus unhumbled, and did not so much as put up on single petition for pardon, God immediately passes sentence upon the serpent, and reveals to them a Savior.

Verse Genesis 3:14, "And the Lord God said unto the serpent, because thou hast done this, thou art accursed above all cattle, and above every beast of the field; upon thy belly shalt thou go, and dust shalt thou eat all the days of thy life;" i.e. he should be in subjection, and his power should always be limited and restrained. "His enemies shall lick the very dust," says the Psalmist. (Verse Genesis 3:15,"And I will put enmity between thee and the woman, and between thy seed and her seed: it shall bruise thy head, and thou shalt bruise his heel."

Before I proceed to the explanation of this verse, I cannot but take notice of one great mistake which the author of the *whole duty of man* is guilty of, in making this verse contain a covenant between God and Adam, as though God now personally treated with Adam, as before the fall. For, talking of the second covenant in his preface, concerning caring for the soul, says he, "This second covenant was made with Adam, and us in him, presently after the fall, and is briefly contained in these words, Genesis 3:15, where God declares, 'The seed of the woman shall break the serpent's head; and this was made up, as the first was, of some mercies to be afforded by God, and some duties to be performed by us." This is exceeding false divinity: for those words are not spoken to Adam; they are directed only to the serpent. Adam and Eve stood by as criminals, and God could not treat with them, because they had broken his covenant. And it is so far from being a covenant wherein "some mercies are to be afforded by God, and some duties to be performed by us," that here is not a word looking that way; it is only a declaration of a free gift of salvation through Jesus Christ our Lord. God the Father and God the Son had entered into a covenant concerning the salvation of the elect from all eternity, wherein God the Father promised, That, if the Son would offer his soul a sacrifice for sin, he should see his seed. Now this is an open revelation of this secret covenant, and therefore God speaks in the most positive terms, "It shall bruise thy head, and thou shalt bruise his heal." The first Adam, God had treated with before; he proved false: God therefore, to secure the second covenant from being broken, puts it into the hands of the second Adam, the Lord from heaven. Adam, after the fall, stood no longer as our representative; he and Eve were only private persons, as we are, and were only to lay hold on the declaration of mercy contained in this promise by faith, (as they really did) and by that they were saved. I do not say but we are to believe and obey, if we are everlastingly saved. Faith and obedience are conditions, if we only mean that they in order go before our salvation, but I deny that these are proposed by God to Adam, or that God treats with him in this promise, as he did before the fall under the covenant of works. For how could that be, when Adam and Eve were now prisoners at the bar, without strength to perform any conditions at all? The truth is this: God, as a reward of Christ's sufferings, promised to give the elect faith and repentance, in order to bring them to eternal life; and both these, and every thing else necessary for their everlasting happiness, and infallibly secured to them in this promise; as Mr. Rastan, an excellent Scots divine, clearly shows, in a book entitled, "A view of the covenant of grace."

This is by no means an unnecessary distinction; it is a matter of great importance: for want of knowing this, people have been so long misled, They have been taught that they must do so and so, and though they were under a covenant of works, and then for *doing* this, they should be saved. Whereas, on the contrary, people should be taught, That the Lord Jesus was the second Adam, with whom the Father entered into covenant for fallen man; That they can now do nothing of or for themselves, and should therefore come to God, beseeching him to give them faith, by which they shall be enabled to lay hold on the righteousness of Christ; and that faith they will then show forth by their works, out of love and gratitude to the ever blessed Jesus, their most glorious Redeemer, for what he has done for their souls. This is a consistent scriptural scheme; without holding this, we must run into one of those two bad extremes; I mean Antinomianism on the one hand, or Arminianism on the other: from both which may the good Lord deliver us!

But to proceed: By the seed of the woman, we are here

to understand the Lord Jesus Christ, who, though very God of very God, was, for us men and our salvation, to have a body prepared for him by the Holy Ghost, and to be born of a woman who never knew man, and by his obedience and death make an atonement for man's transgression, and bring in an everlasting righteousness, work in them a new nature, and thereby bruise the serpent's head, i.e. destroy his power and dominion over them. By the serpent's seed, we are to understand the devil and all his children, who are permitted by God to tempt and sift his children. But, blessed be God, he can reach no further than our heel.

It is to be doubted but Adam and Eve understood this promise in this sense; for it is plain, in the latter part of the chapter, sacrifices were instituted. From whence should those skins come, but from beasts slain for sacrifice, of which God made them coats? We find Abel, as well as Cain, offering sacrifice in the next chapter: and the Apostle tells us, he did it by faith, no doubt in this promise. And Eve, when Cain was born, said, "I have gotten a man from the Lord," or, (as Mr. Henry observes, it may be rendered) "I have gotten a man,—the Lord,—the promised Messiah." Some further suppose, that Eve was the first believer; and therefore they translate it thus, "The seed, (not of the, but) of this woman:" which magnifies the grace of God so much the more, that she, who was first in the transgression, should be the first partaker of redemption. Adam believed also, and was saved: for unto Adam and his wife did the Lord God make coats of skins, and clothed them: which was a remarkable type of their being clothed with the righteousness of our Lord Jesus Christ.

This promise was literally fulfilled in the person of our Lord Jesus Christ. Satan bruised his heel, when he tempted him for forty days together in the wilderness: he bruised his heel, when he raised up strong persecution against him during the time of his public ministry: he in an especial manner bruised his heel, when our Lord complained, that his soul was exceeding sorrowful, even unto death, and he sweat great drops of blood falling upon the ground, in the garden; He bruised his heel, when he put it into the heart of Judas to betray him: ad he bruised him yet most of all, when his emissaries nailed him to an accursed tree, and our Lord cried out, "My God, my God, why hast thou forsaken me?" Yet, in all this, the blessed Jesus, the seed of the woman, bruised Satan's accursed head; for, in that he was tempted, he was able to succor those that are tempted. By his stripes we are healed. The chastisement of our peace was upon him.

By dying, he destroyed him that had the power of death, that is, the devil. He thereby spoiled principalities and powers, and made a show of them openly, triumphing over them upon the cross.

This promise has been fulfilled in the elect of God, considered collectively, as well before, as since the coming of our Lord in the flesh: for they may be called, the seed of the woman. Marvel not, that all who will live godly in Christ Jesus, must suffer persecution. In this promise, there is an eternal enmity put between the seed of the woman, and the seed of the serpent; so that those that are born after the flesh, cannot but persecute those that are born after the spirit. This enmity showed itself, soon after this promise was revealed, in Cain's bruising the heel of Abel: it continued in the church through all ages before Christ came in the flesh, as the history of the Bible, and the 11th chapter of the Hebrews, plainly show. It raged exceedingly after our Lord's ascension; witness the Acts of the Apostles, and the History of the Primitive Christians. It now rages, and will continue to rage and show itself, in a greater or less degree, to the end of time. But let not this dismay us; for in all this, the seed of the woman is more than conqueror, and bruises the serpent's head. Thus the Israelites, the more they were oppressed, the more they increased. Thus it was with the Apostles; thus it was with their immediate followers. So that Tertullian compares the church in his time to a mowed field; the more frequently it is cut, the more it grows. The blood of the martyrs was always the seed of the church. And I have often sat down with wonder and delight, and admired how God has made the very schemes which his enemies contrived, in order to hinder, become the most effectual means to propagate his gospel. The devil has had so little success in persecution, that if I did not know that he and his children, according to this verse, could not but persecute, I should think he would count it his strength to sit still. What did he get by persecuting the martyrs in Queen Mary's time? Was not the grace of God exceedingly glorified in their support? What did he get by persecuting the good old Puritans? Did it not prove the peopling of New-England? Or, to come nearer our own times, what has he got by putting us out of the synagogues? Hath not the word of God, since that, mightily prevailed? My dear hearers, you must excuse me for enlarging on this head; God fills my soul generally, when I come to this topic. I can say with Luther, "If it were not for persecution, I should not understand the scripture." If Satan should be yet suffered to bruise my heel further, and his servants should thrust me into prison, I doubt not, but even that would only tend to the more effectual bruising of his head. I remember a saying the then Lord Chancellor to the pious Bradford: "Thou hast done more hurt, said he, by thy exhortations in private in prison, than thou didst in preaching before thou was put in," or words to this effect. The promise of the text is my daily support: "I will put enmity between thy seed and her seed; it shall bruise thy head, and thou shalt bruise his heel."

Further: this promise is also fulfilled, not only in the church in general, but in every individual believer in particular. In every believer there are two seeds, the seed of the woman, and the seed of the serpent; the flesh lusting against the spirit, and the spirit against the flesh. It is with the believer, when quickened with grace in his heart, as it was with Rebekah, when she had conceived Esau and Jacob in her womb; she felt a struggling, and began to be uneasy; "If it be so says she, why am I thus?" Gen. 25:22, Thus grace and nature struggle (if I may so speak) in the womb of a believers heart: but, as it was there said, "The elder shall serve the younger;" so it is here,—grace in the end shall get the better of nature; the seed of the woman shall bruise the serpent's head. Many of you that have believed in Christ, perhaps may find some particular corruption yet strong, so strong, that you are sometimes ready to cry out with David, "I shall fall one day by the hand of Saul." But, fear not, the promise in the text insures the perseverance and victory of believers over sin, Satan, death, and hell. What if indwelling corruption does yet remain, and the seed of the serpent bruise your heel, in vexing and disturbing your righteous souls? Fear not, though faint, yet pursue: you shall yet bruise the serpent's head. Christ hath died for you, and yet a little while, and he will send death to destroy the very being of sin in you. Which brings me

To show the most extensive manner in which the promise of the text shall be fulfilled, vis. at the final judgment, when the Lord Jesus shall present the elect to his Father, without spot or wrinkle, or any such thing, glorified both in body and soul.

Then shall the seed of the woman give the last and fatal blow, in bruising the serpent's head. Satan, the accuser of the brethren, and all his accursed seed, shall then be cast out, and never suffered to disturb the seed of the woman any more. Then shall the righteous shine as the sun in the kingdom of their Father, and sit with Christ on thrones in majesty on high.

Let us, therefore, not be weary of well-doing; for we shall reap an eternal harvest of comfort, if we faint not. Dare, dare, my dear brethren in Christ, to follow the Captain of your salvation, who was made perfect through sufferings. The seed of the woman shall bruise the serpent's head. Fear not men. Be not too much cast down at the deceitfulness of your hearts. Fear not devils; you shall get the victory even over them. The Lord Jesus has engaged to make you more than conquerors over all. Plead with you Savior, plead: plead the promise in the tent. Wrestle, wrestle with God in prayer. If it has been given you to believe, fear not if it should also be given you to suffer. Be not any wise terrified by your adversaries; the king of the church has them all in a chain: be kind to them, pray for them; but fear them not. The Lord will yet bring back his ark; though at present driven into the wilderness; and Satan like lightening shall fall from heaven.

Are there any enemies of God here? The promise of the text encourages me to bid you defiance: the seed of the woman, the ever-blessed Jesus, shall bruise the serpent's head. What signifies all your malice? You are only raging waves of the sea, foaming out your own shame. For you, without repentance, is reserved the blackness of darkness for ever. The Lord Jesus sits in heaven, ruling over all, and causing all things to work for his children's good: he laughs you to scorn: he hath you in the utmost derision, and therefore so will I. Who are you that persecute the children of the ever blessed God? Though a poor stripling, the Lord Jesus, the seed of the woman, will enable me to bruise your heads.

My brethren in Christ, I think I do not speak thus in my own strength, but in the strength of my Redeemer. I know in whom I have believed; I am persuaded he will keep that safe, which I have committed unto him. He is faithful who hath promised, that the seed of the woman shall bruise the serpent's head. May we all experience a daily completion of this promise, both in the church and in our hearts, till we come to the church of the first-born, the spirits of just men made perfect, in the presence and actual fruition of the great God our heavenly Father!

To whom, with the Son, and the Holy Ghost, be ascribed all honor, power, might, majesty, and dominion, now and for evermore. Amen.

2. Walking with God

Genesis 5:24—"And Enoch walked with God: and he was not; for God took him."

Various are the pleas and arguments which men of corrupt minds frequently urge against yielding obedience to the just and holy commands of God. But, perhaps, one of the most common objections that they make is this, that our Lord's commands are not practicable, because contrary to flesh and blood; and consequently, that he is 'an hard master, reaping where he has not sown, and gathering where he has not strewed'. These we find were the sentiments entertained by that wicked and slothful servant mentioned in the 25th of St. Matthew; and are undoubtedly the same with many which are maintained in the present wicked and adulterous generation. The Holy Ghost foreseeing this, hath taken care to inspire holy men of old, to record the examples of many holy men and women; who, even under the Old Testament dispensation, were enabled cheerfully to take Christ's yoke upon them, and counted his service perfect freedom. The large catalogue of saints, confessors, and martyrs, drawn up in the 11th chapter to the Hebrews, abundantly evidences the truth of this observation. What a great cloud of witnesses have we there presented to our view? All eminent for their faith, but some shining with a greater degree of luster than do others. The proto-martyr Abel leads the van. And next to him we find Enoch mentioned, not only because he was next in order of time, but also on account of his exalted piety; he is spoken of in the words of the text in a very extraordinary manner. We have here a short but very full and glorious account, both of his behavior in this world, and the triumphant manner of his entry into the next. The former is contained in these words, 'And Enoch walked with God'. The latter in these, 'and he was not: for God took him'. He was not; that is, he was not found, he was not taken away in the common manner, he did not see death; for God had translated him. (Heb. 11:5.) Who this Enoch was, does not appear so plainly. To me, he seems to have been a person of public character; I suppose, like Noah, a preacher of righteousness. And, if we may credit the apostle Jude, he was a flaming preacher. For he quotes one of his prophecies, wherein he saith, 'Behold, the Lord cometh with ten thousands of his saints, to execute judgment upon all, and to convince all that are ungodly among them, of all their ungodly deeds which they have ungodly committed, and of all their hard speeches, which ungodly sinners have spoken against him'. But whether a public or private person, he has a noble testimony given him in the lively oracles. The author of the epistle to the Hebrews saith, that before his translation he had this testimony, 'that he pleased God'; and his being translated, was a proof of it beyond all doubt. And I would observe, that it was wonderful wisdom in God to translate Enoch and Elijah under the Old Testament dispensation, that hereafter, when it should be asserted that the Lord Jesus was carried into heaven, it might not seem a thing altogether incredible to the Jews; since they themselves confessed that two of their own prophets had been translated several hundred hears before. But it is not my design to detain you any longer, by enlarging, or making observations, on Enoch's short but comprehensive character: the thing I have in view being to give a discourse, as the Lord shall enable, upon a weighty and a very important subject; I mean, *walking with God*. 'And Enoch walked with God.' If so much as this can be truly said of you and me after our decease, we shall not have any reason to complain that we have lived in vain.

In handling my intended subject, I shall,

First, Endeavor to show what is implied in these words, *walked with God*.

Secondly, I shall prescribe some means, upon the due observance of which, believers may keep up and maintain their *walk with God*. And,

Thirdly, Offer some motives to stir us up, if we never walked with God before, to come and walk with God now. The whole shall be closed with a word or two of application.

First, I am to show what is implied in these words, 'walked with God'; or, in other words, what we are to understand by *walking with God*.

And *First*, *walking with God* implies, that the prevailing power of the enmity of a person's heart be taken away by the blessed Spirit of God. Perhaps it may seem a hard saying to some, but our own experience daily proves what the scriptures in many places assert, that the carnal mind, the mind of the unconverted natural man, nay, the mind of the regenerate, so far as any part of him remains unrenewed, is enmity, not only an enemy, but enmity itself, against God; so that it is not subject to the law of God, neither indeed can it be. Indeed, one may well wonder that any creature, especially that lovely creature man, made after his Maker's own image, should ever have any enmity, much less a prevailing enmity, against that very God in whom he lives, and moves, and hath his being. But alas! so it is. Our first parents contracted it when they fell from God by eating the forbidden fruit, and the bitter and malignant contagion of it hath descended to, and quite overspread, their whole posterity. This enmity discovered itself in Adam's endeavoring to hide himself in the trees of the garden. When he heard the voice of the Lord God, instead of running with an open heart, saying Here I am; alas! he now wanted no communion with God; and still more discovered his lately contracted enmity, by the excuse he made to the Most High: 'The woman (or, this woman) thou gavest to be with me, she gave me of the tree, and I did eat'. By saying thus, he in effect lays all the fault upon God; as though he had said, If thou hadst not given me this woman, I had not sinned against thee, so thou mayest thank thyself for my transgression. In the same manner this enmity works in the hearts of Adam's children. They now and again find something rising against God, and saying even unto God, What doest thou? 'It scorns any meaner competitor (says the learned Dr. Owen, in his excellent treatise on indwelling sin) than God himself.' Its command is like that of the Assyrians in respect to Ahab—shoot only at the king. And it strikes against every thing that has the appearance of real piety, as the Assyrians shot at Jehoshaphat in his royal clothes. But the opposition ceases when it finds that it is only an appearance, as the Assyrians left off shooting at Jehoshaphat, when they perceived it was not Ahab they were shooting at. This enmity discovered itself in accursed Cain; he hated and slew his brother Abel, because Abel loved, and was peculiarly favored by, his God. And this same enmity rules and prevails in every man that is naturally engendered of the offspring of Adam. Hence that a averseness to prayer and holy duties which we find in children, and very often in grown persons, who have notwithstanding been blessed with a religious education. And all that open sin and wickedness, which like a deluge has overflowed the world, are only so many streams running from this dreadful contagious fountain; I mean a enmity of man's desperately wicked and deceitful heart. He that cannot set his seal to this, knows nothing yet, in a saving manner, of the Holy Scriptures, or of the power of God. And all that do know this, will readily acknowledge, that before a person can be said to walk with God, the prevailing power of this heart-enmity must be destroyed: for persons do not use to walk and keep company together, who entertain an irreconcilable enmity and hatred against one another. Observe me, I say, the prevailing power of this enmity must be taken away; for the in-being of it will never be totally removed, till we bow down our heads, and give up the ghost. The apostle Paul, no doubt, speaks of himself, and that, too, not when he was a Pharisee, but a real Christian; when he complains, 'that when he would do good, evil was present with him'; not having dominion over him, but opposing and resisting his good intentions and actions, so that he could not do the things which he would, in that perfection which the new man desired. This is what he calls sin dwelling in him. 'And this is that phronhma sarko", which (to use the words of the ninth article of our church,) some do expound the wisdom, some sensuality, some the affectation, some the desire, of the flesh, which doth remain, yea, in them that are regenerated.' But as for its prevailing power, it is destroyed in every soul that is truly born of God, and gradually more and more weakened as the believer grows in grace, and the Spirit of God gains a greater and greater ascendancy in the heart.

But *Secondly*, Walking with God not only implies, that the prevailing power of the enmity of a man's heart be taken away, but also that a person is actually reconciled to God the Father, in and through the all-sufficient righteousness and atonement of his dear Son. 'Can two walk together, (says Solomon, [actually Amos 3:3]) unless they are agreed?' Jesus is our peace as well as our peace-maker. When we are justified by faith in Christ, then, but not till then, we have peace with God; and consequently cannot be said till then to walk with him, walking with a person being a sign and token that we are friends to that person, or at least, though we have been at variance, yet that now we are reconciled and become friends again. This is the great errand that gospel ministers are sent out upon. To us is committed the ministry of reconciliation; as ambassadors for God, we are to beseech sinners, in Christ's stead, to be reconciled unto God, and when they comply with the gracious invitation, and are actually by faith brought into a state of reconciliation with God, then, and not till then, may they be said so much as to begin to walk with God.

Further, *Thirdly*, Walking with God implies a settled abiding communion and fellowship with God, or what in scripture is called, 'The Holy Ghost dwelling in us'. This is what our Lord promised when he told his disciples that 'the Holy Spirit would be in and with them'; not to be like wayfaring man, to say only for a night, but to reside and make his abode in their hearts. This, I am apt to believe, is what the apostle John would have us understand, when he talks of a person 'abiding in him, in Christ, and walking as he himself also walked'. And this is what is particularly meant in the words of our text. 'And Enoch walked with God', that is, he kept up and maintained a holy, settled, habitual, though undoubtedly not altogether uninterrupted communion and fellowship with God, in and through Christ Jesus. So that to sum up what has been said on this part of the first general head, *walking with God* consists especially in the fixed habitual bent of the will for God, in an habitual dependence upon his power and promise, in an habitual voluntary dedication of our all to his glory, in an habitual eyeing of his precept in all we do, and in an habitual complacence in his pleasure in all we suffer.

Fourthly, walking with God implies our making progress or advances in the divine life. *Walking*, in the very first idea of the word, seems to suppose a progressive motion. A person that walks, though he move slowly, yet he goes forward, and does not continue in one place. And so it is with those that walk with God. They go on, as the Psalmist says, 'from strength to strength'; or, in the language of the apostle Paul, 'they pass from glory to glory, even by the Spirit of the Lord'. Indeed, in one sense, the divine life admits of neither increase nor decrease. When a soul is born of God, to all intents and purposes he is a child of God; and though he should live to the age of Methuselah, yet he would then be only a child of God after all. But in another sense, the divine life admits of decays and additions. Hence it is, that we find the people of God charged with backslidings and losing their first love. And hence it is that we hear of babes, young men, and fathers in Christ. And upon this account it is that the apostle exhorts Timothy, 'to let his progress be made known to all men'. And what is here required of Timothy in particular, by St. Peter is enjoined on all Christians in general. 'But grow in grace, (says he), and in the knowledge of our Lord and Savior Jesus Christ'. For the new creature increases in spiritual stature; and though a person can but be a new creature, yet there are some that are more conformed to the divine image than others, and will after death be admitted to a greater degree of blessedness. For want of observing this distinction, even some gracious souls, that have better hearts than heads, (as well as men of corrupt minds, reprobates concerning the faith) have unawares run into downright Antinomian principles, denying all growth of grace in a believer, or any marks of grace to be laid down in the scriptures of truth. From such principles, and more especially from practices naturally consequent on such principles, may the Lord of all lords deliver us!

From what then has been said, we may now know what is implied in the words, 'walked with God', viz. Our having the prevailing enmity of our hearts taken away by the power of the Spirit of God; our being actually reconciled and united to him by faith in Jesus Christ; our having and keeping up a settled communion and fellowship with him; and our making a daily progress in this fellowship, so as to be conformed to the divine image more and more.

How this is done, or, in other words, by what means believers keep up and maintain their walk with God, comes to be considered under our second general head.

And, *First*, Believers keep up and maintain their walk with God by reading of his holy word. 'Search the scriptures', says our blessed Lord, 'for these are they that testify of me'. And the royal Psalmist tells us 'that God's word was a light unto his feet, and a lantern unto his paths'; and he makes it one property of a good man, 'that his delight is in the law of the Lord, and that he exercises himself therein day and night'. 'Give thyself to reading', (says Paul to Timothy); 'And this book of the law, (says God to Joshua) shall not go out of thy mouth'. For whatsoever was written aforetime was written for our learning. And the word of God is profitable for reproof, for correction, and for instruction in righteousness, and every way sufficient to make every true child of God thoroughly furnished unto every good work. If we once get above our Bibles, and cease making the written word of God our sole rule both as to faith and practice, we shall soon lie open to all manner of delusion, and be in great danger of making shipwreck of faith and a good conscience. Our blessed Lord, though he had the Spirit of God without measure, yet always was governed by, and fought the devil with, 'It is written'. This the apostle calls the 'sword of the Spirit'. We may say of it, as David said of Goliath's sword, 'None like this'. The scriptures are called the lively oracles of God: not only because they are generally made use of to beget in us a new life, but also to keep up and increase it in the soul. The apostle Peter, in his second epistle, prefers it even to seeing Christ transfigured upon the mount. For after he had said, chap. 1:18. 'This voice which came from heaven we heard, when we were with him in the holy mount'; he adds, 'We have also a more sure word of prophecy; whereunto ye do well that ye take heed, as unto a light shining in a dark place, until the day dawn, and the day-star arise in your hearts': that is, till we shake off these bodies, and see Jesus face to face. Till then we must see and converse with him through the glass of his word. We must make his testimonies our counselors, and daily, with Mary, sit at Jesus' feet, by faith hearing his word. We shall then by happy experience find, that they are spirit and life, meat indeed and drink indeed, to our souls.

Secondly, Believers keep up and maintain their walk with God by secret prayer. The spirit of grace is always accompanied with the spirit of supplication. It is the very breath of the new creature, the fan of the divine life, whereby the spark of holy fire, kindled in the soul by God, is not only kept in, but raised into a flame. A neglect of secret prayer has been frequently an inlet to many spiritual diseases, and has been attended with fatal consequences. Origen observed, "that the day he offered incense to an idol, he went out of his closet without making use of secret prayer." It is one of the most noble parts of the believers' spiritual armor. 'Praying always', says the apostle, 'with all manner of supplication.' 'Watch and pray', says our Lord, 'that ye enter not into temptation.' And he spake a parable, that his disciples should pray, and not faint. Not that our Lord would have us always upon our knees, or in our closets, to the neglect of our other relative duties. But he means, that our souls should be kept in a praying frame, so that we might be able to say, as a good man in Scotland once said to his friends on his death-bed, 'Could these curtains, or could these walls speak, they would tell you what sweet communion I have had with my God here'. O prayer! Prayer! It brings and keeps God and man together. It raises man up to God, and brings God down to man. If you would there, O believers, keep up your walk with God; pray, pray without ceasing. Be much in secret, set prayer. And when you are about the common business of life, be much in ejaculatory prayer, and send, from time to time, short letters post to heaven upon the wings of faith. They will reach the very heart of God, and return to you again loaded with spiritual blessings.

Thirdly, Holy and frequent meditation is another blessed means of keeping up a believer's walk with God. 'Prayer, reading, temptation, and meditation', says Luther, make a minister.' And they also make and perfect a Christian. Meditation to the soul, is the same as digestion to the body. Holy David found it so, and therefore he was frequently employed in meditation, even in the night season. We read also of Isaac's going out into the fields to meditate in the evening; or, as it is in the margin, to pray. For meditation is a kind of silent prayer, whereby the soul is frequently as it were carried out of itself to God, and in a degree made like unto those blessed spirits, who by a kind of immediate intuition always behold the face of our heavenly Father. None but those happy souls that have been accustomed to this divine employ, can tell what a blessed promoter of the divine life, meditation is. 'Whilst I was musing', says David, 'the fire kindled.' And whilst the believer is musing on the works and word of God, especially that work of works, that wonder of wonders, that mystery of godliness, 'God manifest in the flesh', the Lamb of God slain for the sins of the world, he frequently feels the fire of divine love kindle, so that he is obliged to speak with his tongue, and tell of the loving-kindness of the Lord to his soul. Be frequent therefore in meditation, all ye that desire to keep up and maintain a close and uniform walk with the most high God.

Fourthly, Believers keep up their walk with God, by watching and noting his providential dealings with them. If we believe the scriptures, we must believe what our Lord hath declared therein, 'That the very hairs of his disciples' heads are all numbered; and that a sparrow does not fall to the ground, (either to pick up a grain of corn, or when shot by a fowler), without the knowledge of our heavenly Father'. Every cross has a call in it, and every particular dispensation of divine providence has some particular end to answer in those to whom it is sent. If it be of an afflictive nature, God does thereby say, 'My son, keep thyself from idols': if prosperous, he does, as it were by a small still voice, say, 'My son, give me thy heart'. If believers, therefore, would keep up their walk with God, they must from time to time hear what the Lord has to say concerning them in the voice of his providence. Thus we find that Abraham's servant, when he went to fetch a wife for his master Isaac, eyed and watched the providence of God, and by that means found out the person that was designed for his master's wife. 'For a little hint from providence', says pious Bishop Hall, 'is enough for faith to feed upon.' And as I believe it will be one part of our happiness in heaven, to take a view of, and look back upon, the various links of the golden chain which drew us there; so those that enjoy most of heaven below, I believe, will be the most minute in remarking God's various dealings with them, in respect to his providential dispensations here on earth.

Fifthly, In order to walk closely with God, his children must not only watch the motions of God's providence without them, but the motions also of his blessed Spirit in their hearts. 'As many as are the sons of God, are led by the Spirit of God', and give up themselves to be guided by the Holy Ghost, as a little child gives its hand to be led by a nurse or parent. It is no doubt in this sense that we are to be converted, and become like little children. And though it is the quintessence of enthusiasm, to pretend to be guided by the Spirit without the written word; yet it is every Christian's bounden duty to be guided by the Spirit in conjunction with the written word of God. Watch, therefore, I pray you, O believers, the motions of God's blessed Spirit in your souls, and always try the suggestions or impressions that you may at any time feel, by the unerring rule of God's most holy word: and if they are not found to be agreeable to that, reject them as diabolical and delusive. By observing this caution, you will steer a middle course between the two dangerous extremes many of this generation are in danger of running into; I mean, *enthusiasm*, on the one hand, and *deism*, and *downright infidelity*, on the other.

Sixthly, They that would maintain a holy walk with God, must walk with him in ordinances as well as providences, etc. It is therefore recorded of Zachary and Elizabeth, that 'they walked in all God's ordinances, as well as commandments, blameless'. And all rightly informed Christians, will look upon ordinances, not as beggarly elements, but as so many conduit-pipes, whereby the infinitely condescending Jehovah conveys his grace to their souls. They will look upon them as children's bread, and as their highest privileges. Consequently they will be glad when they hear others say, 'Come, let us go up to the house of the Lord'. They will delight to visit the place where God's honor dwelleth, and be very eager to embrace all opportunities to show forth the Lord Christ's death till he come.

Seventhly and *Lastly*, If you would walk with God, you will associate and keep company with those that do walk with him. 'My delight', says holy David, 'is in them that do excel' in virtue. They were, in his sight, the excellent ones of the earth. And the primitive Christians, no doubt, kept up their vigor and first love, by continuing in fellowship one with another. The apostle Paul knew this full well, and therefore exhorts the Christians to see to it, that they did not forsake the assembling of themselves together. For how can one be warm alone? And has not the wisest of men told us, that 'As iron sharpeneth iron, so doth the countenance of a man his friend?' If we look, therefore, into church history, or make a just observation of our own times, I believe we shall find, that as the power of God prevails, Christian societies, and fellowship meetings prevail proportionably. And as one decays, the other has insensibly decayed and dwindled away at the same time. So necessary is it for those that would walk with God, and keep up the life of religion, to meet together as they have opportunity, in order to provoke one another to love and good works.

Proceed we now to the third general thing proposed: to offer some motives to excite all to come and walk with God.

And, *First*, walking with God is a very honorable thing. This generally is a prevailing motive to persons of all ranks, to stir them up to any important undertaking. O that it may have its due weight and influence with you in respect to the matter now before us! I suppose you would all think it a very high honor to be admitted into an earthly prince's privy council, to be trusted with his secrets, and to have his ear at all times and at all seasons. It seems Haman thought it so when he boasted, Esther 5:11, that besides his being 'advanced above the princes and servants of the king; yea, moreover, Esther the queen did let no man come in with the king unto the banquet that she had prepared, but myself; and tomorrow am I invited unto her also with the king'. And when afterwards a question was put to this same Haman, Chap. 6:6. 'What shall be done unto the man whom the king delighteth to honor?' he answered, verse 8. 'Let the royal apparel be brought which the king used to wear, and the horse that the king rideth upon, and the crown royal which is set upon his head; and let this apparel and horse be delivered to the hand of one of the king's most noble princes, that they may array the man withal whom the king delighteth to honor, and bring him on horseback through the street of the city and proclaim before him, Thus shall it be done to the man whom the king delighteth to honor.' This was all, then, it seems, that an ambitious Haman could ask, and the most valuable thing that he thought Ahasuerus, the greatest monarch upon earth, could give. But, alas, what is this honor in comparison of that which the meanest of those enjoy, that walk with God! Think ye it a small thing, sirs, to have the secret of the Lord of lords with you, and to be called the friends of God? And such honor have all God's saints. The secret of the Lord is with them that fear him: and 'Henceforth(says the blessed Jesus) call I you no longer servants, but friends; for the servant knoweth not the will of his master'. Whatever you may think of it, holy David was so sensible of the honor attending a walk with God that he declares, 'he had rather be a door-keeper in his house, than to dwell even in the tents of ungodliness'. O that all were like-minded with him!

But, *Secondly*, As it is an honorable, so it is a pleasing thing, to walk with God. The wisest of men has told us, that 'wisdom's ways are ways of pleasantness, and all her paths peace'. And I remember pious Mr. Henry, when he was about to expire, said to a friend, 'You have heard many men's dying words, and these are mine: A life spent in communion with God, is the pleasantest life in the world'. I am sure I can set to my seal that this is true. Indeed, I have been listed under Jesus' banner only for a few years; but I have enjoyed more solid pleasure in one moment's communion with my god, than I should or could have enjoyed in the ways of sin, though I had continued to have gone on in them for thousands of years.

And may I not appeal to all you that fear and walk with God, for the truth of this? Has not one day in the Lord's courts been better to you than a thousand? In keeping God's commandments, have you not found a present, and very great reward? Has not his word been sweeter to you than the honey or the honeycomb? O what have you felt, when, Jacob-like, you have been wrestling with your God? Has not Jesus often met you when meditating in the fields, and been made known to you over and over again in breaking of bread? Has not the Holy Ghost frequently shed the divine love abroad in your hearts abundantly, and filled you with joy unspeakable, even joy that is full of glory? I know you will answer all these questions in the affirmative, and freely acknowledge the yoke of Christ to be easy, and his burden light; or (to use the words of one of our collects), 'His service is perfect freedom'. And what need we then any further motive to excite us to walk with God?

But methinks I hear some among you say, 'How can these things be? For, if walking with God, as you say, is such an honorable and pleasant thing, whence is it that the name of the people of this way is cast out as evil, and every where spoken against? How comes it to pass that they are frequently afflicted, tempted, destitute, and tormented? Is this the honor, this the pleasure, that you speak of?' I answer, Yes. Stop a while; be not over hasty. Judge not according to appearance, but judge righteous judgment, and all will be well. It is true, we acknowledge the 'people of this way', as you, and Paul before you, when a persecutor, called them, have their names cast out as evil, and are a sect every where spoken against. But by whom? Even by the enemies of the most high God. And do you think it is disgrace to be spoken evil of by them? Blessed be God, we have not so learned Christ. Our royal Master has pronounced those 'blessed, who are persecuted, and have all manner of evil spoken against them falsely'. He has commanded them 'to rejoice and be exceeding glad', for it is the privilege of their discipleship, and that their reward will be great in heaven. He himself was thus treated. And can there be a greater honor put upon a creature, than to be conformed to the ever-blessed Son of God? And further, it is equally true that the people of this way are frequently afflicted, tempted, destitute, and tormented. But what of all this? Does this destroy the pleasure of walking with God? No, in no wise; for those that walk with God are enabled, through Christ strengthening them, to joy even in tribulation, and to rejoice when they fall into divers temptations. And I believe I may appeal to the experience of all true and close walkers with God, whether or not their suffering times have not frequently been their sweetest times, and that they enjoyed most of God when most cast out and despised by men? This we find was the case of Christ's primitive servants, when threatened by the Jewish sanhedrin, and commanded to preach no more in the name of Jesus; they rejoiced that they were accounted worthy to suffer shame for the sake of Jesus. Paul and Silas sang praises even in a dungeon; and the face of Stephen, that glorious proto-martyr of the Christian church, shone like the face of an angel. And Jesus is the same now as he was then, and takes care so to sweeten sufferings and afflictions with his love, that his disciples find, by happy experience, that as afflictions abound, consolations do much more abound. And therefore these objections, instead of destroying, do only enforce the motives before urged, to excite you to walk with God.

But supposing the objections were just, and walkers with God were as despicable and unhappy as you would represent them to be; yet I have a third motive to offer, which if weighed in the balance of the sanctuary, will over-weigh all objections, viz. That there is a heaven at the end of this walk. For, to use the words of pious bishop Beveridge, 'Though the way be narrow, yet it is not long: and though the gate be strait, yet it opens into everlasting life'. Enoch found it so. He walked with God on earth, and God took him to sit down with him for ever in the kingdom of heaven. Not that we are to expect to be taken away as he was: no, I suppose we shall all die the common death of all men. But after death, the spirits of those who have walked with God shall return to God that gave them; and at the morning of the resurrection, soul and body shall be for ever with the Lord; their bodies shall be fashioned like unto Christ's glorious body, and their souls filled with all the fullness of God. They shall sit on thrones; they shall judge angels. They shall be enabled to sustain an exceeding and eternal weight of glory, even that glory which Jesus Christ enjoyed with the Father before the world began. 'O gloriam quantam et qualem', said the learned and pious Arndt, just before he bowed down his head, and gave up the ghost. The very thought of it is enough to make us 'wish to leap our seventy years', as good Dr. Watts expresses himself, and to make us break out into the earnest language of the royal Psalmist, 'My soul is athirst for God, yea, for the living God. When shall I come to appear in the presence of my God?' I wonder not that a sense of this, when under a more than ordinary irradiation and influx of divine life and love, causes some persons to faint away, and even for a time lose the power of their senses. A less sight than this, even the sight of Solomon's glory, made Sheba's queen astonished; and a still lesser sight than that, even a sight of Joseph's wagons, made holy Jacob faint, and for a while, as it were, die away. Daniel, when admitted to a distant view of this excellent glory, fell down at the feet of the angel as one dead. And if a distant view of this glory be so excellent, what must the actual possession of it be? If the first fruits are so glorious, how infinitely must the harvest exceed in glory?

And now, what shall I, or, indeed, what can I well say more to excite you, even you that are yet strangers to Christ, to come and walk with God? If you love honor, pleasure, and a crown of glory, come, seek it where alone it can be found. Come, put ye on the Lord Jesus. Come, haste ye away and walk with God, and make no longer provision for the flesh, to fulfill the lust thereof. Stop, stop, O sinner! Turn ye, turn ye, O ye unconverted men, for the end of that way you are now walking in, however right it may seem in your blinded eyes, will be death, even eternal destruction both of body and soul. Make no longer tarrying, I say: at your peril I charge you, step not one step further on in your present walk. For how knowest thou, O man, but the next step thou takest may be into hell? Death may seize thee, judgment find thee, and then the great gulf will be fixed between thee and endless glory for ever and ever. O think of these things, all ye that are unwilling to walk with God. Lay them to heart. Show yourselves men, and in the strength of Jesus say, Farewell, lust of the flesh, I will no more walk with thee! Farewell, lust of the eye, and pride of life! Farewell, carnal acquaintance and enemies of the cross, I will no more walk and be intimate with you! Welcome Jesus, welcome thy word, welcome thy ordinances, welcome thy Spirit, welcome thy people, I will henceforth walk with you. O that there may be in you such a mind! God will set his almighty fiat to it, and seal it with the broad seal of heaven, even the signet of his holy Spirit. Yes, he will, though you have been walking with, and following after, the devices and desires of your desperately wicked hearts ever since you have been born. 'I, the high and lofty One', says the great Jehovah, 'that inhabiteth eternity, will dwell with the humble and contrite heart, even with the man that trembleth at my word.' The blood, even the precious blood of Jesus Christ, if you come to the Father in and through him, shall cleanse you from all sin.

But the text leads me to speak to you that are saints as well as to you that are open and unconverted sinners. I need not tell you, that walking with God is not honorable, but pleasant and profitable also; for ye know it by happy experience, and will find it more and more so every day. Only give me leave to stir up your pure minds by way of remembrance, and to beseech you by the mercies of God in Christ Jesus, to take heed to yourselves, and walk closer with your God than you have in days past: for the nearer you walk with God, the more you will enjoy of him whose presence is life, and be the better prepared for being placed at his right hand, where are pleasures for evermore. O do not follow Jesus afar off! O be not so formal, so dead and stupid in your attendance on holy ordinances! Do not so shamefully forsake the assembling yourselves together, or be so niggardly or indifferent about the things of God. Remember what Jesus says of the church of Laodicea, 'Because thou art neither hot nor cold, I will spew thee out of my mouth'. Think of the love of Jesus, and let that love constrain you to keep near unto him; and though you die for him, do not deny him, do not keep at a distance from him in any wise.

One word to my brethren in the ministry that are here present, and I have done. You see, my brethren, my heart is full; I could almost say it is too big to speak, and yet too big to be silent, without dropping a word to you. For does not the text speak in a particular manner to those who have the honor of being styled the ambassadors of Christ, and stewards of the mysteries of God. I observed at the beginning of this discourse, that Enoch in all probability was a public person, and a flaming preacher. Though he be dead, does he not yet speak to us, to quicken our zeal, and make us more active in the service of our glorious and ever-blessed Master? How did Enoch preach! How did Enoch walk with God, though he lived in a wicked and adulterous generation! Let us then follow him, as he followed Jesus Christ, and ere long, where he is there shall we be also. He is not entered into his rest: yet a little while and we shall enter into ours, and that too much sooner than he did. He sojourned here below three hundred years; but blessed be God, the days of man are now shortened, and in a few days our walk will be over. The Judge is before the door: he that cometh will come, and will not tarry: his reward is with him. And we shall all (if we are zealous for the Lord of hosts) ere long shine as the stars in the firmament, in the kingdom of our heavenly Father, for ever and ever. To Him, the blessed Jesus, and eternal Spirit, be all honor and glory, now, and to all eternity. Amen, and Amen.

3. Abraham's Offering Up His Son Isaac

Genesis 22:12—"And he said, Lay not thine hand upon the lad, neither do thou any thing unto him, for now I know that thou fearest God, seeing thou hast not withheld thy Son, thine only Son from me."

The great Apostle Paul, in one of his epistles, informs us, that "whatsoever was written aforetime was written for our learning, that we through patience and comfort of the holy scripture might have hope." And as without faith it is impossible to please God, or be accepted in Jesus, the Son of his love; we may be assured, that whatever instances of a more than common faith are recorded in the book of God, they were more immediately designed by the Holy Spirit for our learning and imitation, upon whom the ends of the world are come. For this reason, the author of the epistle to the Hebrews, in the 11th chapter, mentions such a noble catalogue of Old Testament saints and martyrs, "who subdued kingdoms, wrought righteousness, stopped the mouths of lions, etc. and are gone before us to inherit the promises." A sufficient confutation, I think, of their error, who lightly esteem the Old Testament saints, and would not have them mentioned to Christians, as persons whose faith and patience we are called upon more immediately to follow. If this was true, the apostle would never have produced such a cloud of witnesses out of the Old Testament, to excite the Christians of the first, and consequently purest age of the church, to continue steadfast and unmoveable in the profession of their faith. Amidst this catalogue of saints, methinks the patriarch Abraham shines the brightest, and differs from the others, as one star differeth from another star in glory; for he shone with such distinguished luster, that he was called the "friend of God," the "father of the faithful;" and those who believe on Christ, are said to be "sons and daughters of, and to be blessed with, faithful Abraham." Many trials of his faith did God send this great and good man, after he had commanded him to get out from his country, and from his kindred, unto a land which he should show him; but the last was the most sever of all, I mean, that of offering up his only son. This, by the divine assistance, I propose to make the subject of your present meditation, and, by way of conclusion, to draw some practical inferences, as God shall enable me, from this instructive story.

The sacred penman begins the narrative thus; Genesis 22:1, "And it came to pass, after these things, God did tempt Abraham." After these things, that it, after he had underwent many severe trials before, after he was old, full of days, and might flatter himself perhaps that the troubles and toils of life were now finished; "after these things, God did tempt Abraham." Christians, you know not what trials you may meet with before you die: notwithstanding you may have suffered, and been tried much already, yet, it may be, a greater measure is still behind, which you are to fill up. "Be not high-minded, but fear." Our last trials, in all probability, will be the greatest: and we can never say our warfare is accomplished, or our trials finished, till we bow down our heads, and give up the ghost. "And it came to pass, after these things, that God did tempt Abraham."

"God did tempt Abraham." But can the scripture contradict itself? Does not the apostle James tell us, "that God tempts no man;" and God does tempt no man to evil, or on purpose to draw him into sin; for, when a man is thus tempted, he is drawn away of his own heart's lust, and enticed. But in another sense, God may be said to tempt, I mean, to try his servants; and in this sense we are to understand that passage of Matthew, where we are told, that, "Jesus was led up by the Spirit (the good Spirit) into the wilderness, to be tempted of the devil." And our Lord, in that excellent form of prayer which he has been pleased to give us, does not require us to pray that we may not absolutely be led into temptation, but delivered from the evil of it; whence we may plainly infer, that God sees it fit sometimes to lead us into temptation, that is, to bring us into such circumstances as will try our faith and other Christian graces. In this sense we are to understand the expression before us; "God did tempt or try Abraham."

How God was pleased to reveal his will at this time to his faithful servant, whether by the Sheckinah, or divine appearance, or by a small still voice, as he spoke to Elijah, or by a whisper, like that of the Spirit to Philip, when he commanded him to join himself to the eunuch's chariot, we are not told, nor is it material to inquire. It is enough that we are informed, God said unto him, Abraham; and that Abraham knew it was the voice of God: for he said, "Behold, here I am." O what a holy familiarity (if I may so speak) is there between God and those holy souls that are united to him by faith in Christ Jesus! God says, Abraham; and Abraham said (it should seem without the least surprise) Behold, here I am. Being reconciled to God by the death and obedience of Christ, which he rejoiced in, and saw by faith afar off; he did not, like guilty Adam, seed the trees of the garden to hide himself from, but takes pleasure in conversing with God, and talketh with him, as a man talketh with his friend. O that Christless sinners knew what it is to have fellowship with the Father and the Son! They would envy the happiness of saints, and count it all joy to be termed enthusiasts and fools for Christ's sake.

But what does God say to Abraham? Genesis 22:2, "Take now thy son, thine only son Isaac, whom thou lovest, and get thee into the land of Moriah, and offer him there for a burnt-offering upon one of the mountains which I shall tell thee of."

Every word deserves our particular observation. Whatever he was to do, he must do it now, immediately, without conferring with flesh and blood. But what must he do? "Take now thy son." Had God said, take now a firstling, or choicest lamb or beast of thy flock, and offer it up for a burnt-offering, it would not have appeared so ghastly; but for God to say, "take now thy son, and offer him up for a burnt-offering," one would imagine, was enough to stagger the strongest faith. But this is not all: it must not only be a son, but "thine only son Isaac, whom thou lovest." If it must be a son, and not a beast, that must be offered, why will not Ishmael do, the son of the bond-woman? No, it must be his only son, the heir of all, his Isaac, by interpretation laughter, the son of his old age, in whom his soul delighted, "whom thou lovest," says God, in whose life his own was wrapped up: and this son, this only son, this Isaac, the son of his love, must be taken now, even now, without delay, and be offered up by his own father, for a burnt offering, upon one of the mountains of the which God would tell him.

Well might the apostle, speaking of this man of God, say, that "against hope he believed in hope, and, being strong in faith, gave glory to God." For, had he not been blesses with faith which man never before had, he must have refused to comply with this severe command. For now many arguments might nature suggest, to prove that such a command could never come from God, or to excuse himself from obeying it? "What! (might the good man have said) butcher my own child! It is contrary to the very law of nature: much more to butcher my dear son Isaac, in whose seed God himself has assured me of a numerous posterity. But supposing I could give up my own affections, and be willing to part with him, though I love him so dearly, yet, if I murder him, what will become of God's promise? Besides, I am now like a city built upon a hill; I shine as a light in the world, in the midst of a crooked and perverse generation: How then shall I cause God's name to be blasphemed, how shall I become a by-word among the heathen, if they hear that I have committed a crime which they abhor! But, above all, what will Sarah my wife say? How can I ever return to her again, after I have imbrued (to wet or stain) my hands in my dear child's blood? O that God would pardon me in this thing, or take my life in the place of my son's!" Thus, I say, Abraham might have argued, and that too seemingly with great reason, against complying with the divine command. But as before by faith he considered not the deadness of Sarah's womb, when she was past age, but believed on him, who said, "Sarah thy wife shall bear thee a son indeed;" so now, being convinced that the same God spoke to and commanded him to offer up that son, and knowing that God was able to raise him from the dead, without delay he obeys the heavenly call.

O that unbelievers would learn of faithful Abraham, and believe whatever is revealed from God, though they cannot fully comprehend it! Abraham knew God commanded him to offer up his son, and therefore believed, notwithstanding carnal reasoning might suggest may objections. We have sufficient testimony, that God has spoken to us by his son; why should we not also believe, though many things in the New Testament are above our reason? For, where reason ends, faith begins. And, however infidels may stile themselves reasoners, of all men they are the most unreasonable: For, is it not contrary to all reason, to measure an infinite by a finite understanding, or think to find out the mysteries of godliness to perfection?

But to return to the patriarch Abraham: We observed before what plausible objections he might have made; but he answered not a single word: no, without replying against his Maker, we are told in, Genesis 22:3, that "Abraham rose up early in the morning, and saddled his ass, and took two of his young men with him, and Isaac his son, and clave the wood for the burnt-offering, and rose up and went unto the place of which God had told him."

From this verse we may gather, that God spoke to Abraham in a dream, or vision of the night: For it is said, he rose up early. Perhaps it was near the fourth watch of the night, just before break of day, when God said, Take now thy son; and Abraham rises up early to do so; as I doubt not but he used to ruse early to offer up his morning-sacrifice of praise and thanksgiving. It is often remarked of people in the Old Testament, that they rose early in the morning; and particularly of our Lord in the

New, that he rose a great while before day to pray. The morning befriends devotion; and, if people cannot use so much self-denial as to rise early to pray, I know not how they will be able to die at a stake (if called to it) for Jesus Christ.

The humility as well as the piety of the patriarch is observable: he saddled his own ass (great men should be humble) and to show the sincerity, though he took two of his young men with him, and Isaac his son, yet he keeps his design as a secret from them all: nay, he does not so much as tell Sarah his wife; for he knew not but she might be a snare unto him in this affair; and, as Rebekah afterwards, on another occasion, advised Jacob to flee, so Sarah also might persuade Isaac to hide himself; or the young men, had they known of it, might have forced him away, as in after-ages the soldiers rescued Jonathan out of the hands of Saul. But Abraham fought no such evasion, and therefore, like an Israelite indeed, in whom there was no guile, he himself resolutely "clave the wood for the burnt-offering, rose up and went unto the place of which God had told him." In the second verse God commanded him to offer up his son upon one of the mountains which he would tell him of. He commanded him to offer his son up, but would not then directly tell him the place where: this was to keep him dependent and watching unto prayer: for there is nothing like being kept waiting upon God; and, if we do, assuredly God will reveal himself unto us yet further in his own time. Let us practice what we know, follow providence so far as we can see already; and what we know not, what we see not as yet, let us only be found in the way of duty, and the Lord will reveal even that unto us. Abraham knew not directly where he was to offer up his son; but he rises up and sets forward, and behold now God shows him: "And he went to the place of which God had told him." Let us go and do likewise.

Verse Genesis 22:4, "Then on the third day Abraham lifted up his eyes, and saw the place afar off."

So that the place, of which God had told him, was no less than three days journey distant from the place where God first appeared to him, and commanded him to take his son. Was not this to try his faith, and to let him see that what he did, was not merely from a sudden pang of devotion, but a matter of choice of deliberation? But who can tell what the aged patriarch felt during these three days? Strong as he was in faith, I am persuaded his bowels often yearned over his dear son Isaac. Methinks I see the good old man walking with his dear child in his hand, and now and then looking upon him, loving him, and then turning aside to weep. And perhaps, sometimes he stays a little behind to pour out his heart before God, for he had no mortal to tell his case to. Then, methinks, I see him join his son and servants again, and talking to them of the things pertaining to the kingdom of God, as they walked by the way. At length, "on the third day, he lifts up his eyes, and saw the place afar off." And, to show that he was yet sincerely resolved to do whatsoever the Lord requested of him, he even how will not discover his design to his servants, but "said, verse, Genesis 22:5, To his young men," (as we should say to our worldly thoughts, when about to tread the courts of the Lord's house) "Abide you here with the ass; and I and the lad will go up yonder and worship, and come again to you." This was a sufficient reason for their staying behind; and, it being their master's custom to go frequently to worship, they could have no suspicion of what he was going about. And by Abraham's saying, that he and the lad would come again, I am apt to think he believed God would raise him from the dead, if so be he permitted him to offer his child up for a burnt-offering. However that be, he is yet resolved to obey God to the uttermost; and therefore,

Verse Genesis 22:6, "Abraham took the wood of the burnt-offering, and laid it upon Isaac his son; and he took the fire in his hand, and a knife, and they went both of them together." Little did Isaac think that he was to be offered on that very wood which he was carrying upon his shoulders; and therefore Isaac innocently, and with a holy freedom (for good men should not keep their children at too great a distance) "spake unto Abraham his father, and said, My father; and he (with equal affection and holy condescension) said, Here am I, my son." And to show how careful Abraham had been (as all Christian parents ought to do) to instruct his Isaac how to sacrifice to God, like a youth trained up in the way wherein he should go; Isaac said, "Behold the fire and the wood; but where is the lamb for a burnt-offering?" How beautiful is early piety! How amiable, to hear young people ask questions about sacrificing to God in an acceptable way! Isaac knew very well that a lamb was wanting, and that a lamb was necessary for a proper sacrifice: "Behold the fire and the wood; but where is the lamb for a burnt-offering?" Young men and maidens, learn of him.

Hitherto, it is plain, Isaac knew nothing of his father's design: but I believe, by what his father said in answer to his question, that now was the time Abraham revealed it unto him.

Verse Genesis 22:8, "And Abraham said, My son,

God will provide himself a Lamb for a burnt-offering." Some think, that Abraham by faith saw the Lord Jesus afar off, and here spoke prophetically of that Lamb of God already slain in decree, and hereafter to be actually offered up for sinners. This was a lamb of God's providing indeed (we dared not have thought of it) to satisfy his own justice, and to render him just in justifying the ungodly. What is all our fire and wood, the best preparations and performances we can make or present, unless God had provided himself this Lamb for a burnt-offering? He could not away with them. The words will well bear this interpretation. But, whatever Abraham might intend, I cannot but think he here made an application, and acquainted his son, of God's dealing with his soul; and at length, with tears in his eyes, and the utmost affection in his heart, cried out, "Thou art to be the lamb, my Son;" God has commanded me to provide thee for a burnt-offering, and to offer thee upon the mountain which we are now ascending. And, as it appears from a subsequent verse, Isaac, convinced that it was the divine will, made no resistance at all; For it is said, "They went both of them together;" and again, when we are told, that Abraham bound Isaac, we do not hear of his complaining, or endeavoring to escape, which he might have done, being (as some think) near thirty years of age, and, it is plain, capable of carrying wood enough for a burnt-offering. But he was partaker of the like precious faith with his aged father, and therefore is as willing to be offered, as Abraham is to offer him: And "so they went both of them together."

Ver. Genesis 22:9, At length "they came to the place of which God had told Abraham. He built an altar there, and laid the wood in order, and bound Isaac his son, and laid him on the altar upon the wood."

And here let us pause a while, and by faith take a view of the place where the father has laid him. I doubt not but that blessed angels hovered round the altar, and sang. "Glory be to God in the highest," for giving such faith to man. Come, all ye tender hearted parents, who know what it is to look over a dying child: fancy that you saw the altar erected before you, and the wood laid in order, and the beloved Isaac bound upon it: fancy that you saw the aged parent standing by weeping. (For, why may we not suppose that Abraham wept, since Jesus himself wept at the grave of Lazarus?) O what pious, endearing expressions passed now alternately between the father and the son! Joseph records a pathetic speech made by each, whether genuine I now not: but methinks I see the tears trickle down the Patriarch Abraham's cheeks; and out of the abundance of the heart, he cries, Adieu, adieu, my son; the Lord gave thee to me, and the Lord calls thee away; blessed be the name of the Lord: adieu, my Isaac, my only son, whom I love as my own soul; adieu, adieu. I see Isaac at the same time meekly resigning himself into his heavenly Father's hands, and praying to the most High to strengthen his earthly parent to strike the stroke. But why do I attempt to describe what either son or father felt? It is impossible: we may indeed form some faint idea of, but shall never full comprehend it, till we come and sit down with them in the kingdom of heaven, and hear them tell the pleasing story over again. Hasten, O Lord, that blessed time! O let thy kingdom come!

And now, the fatal blow is going to be given. "And Abraham stretched forth his hand, and took the knife to slay his son." But do you not think he intended to turn away his head, when he gave the blow? Nay, why may we not suppose he sometimes drew his hand in, after it was stretched out, willing to take another last farewell of his beloved Isaac, and desirous to defer it a little, though resolved at last to strike home? Be that is it will, his arm is now stretched out, the knife is in his hand, and he is about to put it to his dear son's throat.

But sing, O heavens! and rejoice, O earth! Man's extremity is God's opportunity: for behold, just as the knife, in all probability, was near his throat, ver. Genesis 22:11, "the angel of the Lord, (or rather the Lord of angels, Jesus Christ, the angel of the everlasting covenant) called unto him, (probably in a very audible manner) from heaven, and said, Abraham, Abraham. (The word is doubled, to engage his attention; and perhaps the suddenness of the call made him draw back his hand, just as he was going to strike his son.) And Abraham said, Here am I."

"And he said, Lay not thine hand upon the lad, neither do thou any thing unto him: for now know I that thou fearest God, seeing thou hast not withheld thy son, thine only son from me."

Here then it was that Abraham received his son Isaac from the dead in a figure. He was in effect offered upon the altar, and God looked upon him as offered and given unto him. Now it was that Abraham's faith, being tried, was found more precious than gold purified seven times in the fire. Now as a reward of grace, though not of debt, for this signal act of obedience, by an oath, God gives and confirms the promise, "that in his seed all the nations of the earth should be blessed," ver. Genesis 22:17, and Genesis 22:18, With what comfort may we suppose the good old man and his son went down from the mount, and returned unto the young men! With what joy may we imagine he went home, and related all that had passed to Sarah! And above all, with what triumph is he now exulting in the paradise of God, and adoring rich, free, distinguishing, electing, everlasting love, which alone made him to differ from the rest of mankind, and rendered him worthy of that title which he will have so long as the sun and the moon endure, "The Father of the faithful!"

But let us now draw our eyes from the creature, and do what Abraham, if he was present, would direct to; I mean, fix them on the Creator, God blessed for evermore.

I see your hearts affected, I see your eyes weep. (And indeed, who can refrain weeping at the relation of such a story?) But, behold, I show you a mystery, hid under the sacrifice of Abraham's only son, which, unless your hearts are hardened, must cause you to weep tears of love, and that plentifully too. I would willingly hope you even prevent me here, and are ready to say, "It is the love of God, in giving Jesus Christ to die for our sins." Yes; that is it. And yet perhaps you find your hearts, at the mentioning of this, not so much affected. Let this convince you, that we are all fallen creatures, and that we do not love God or Christ as we ought to do: for, if you admire Abraham offering up his Isaac, how much more ought you to extol, magnify and adore the love of God, who so loved the world, as to give his only begotten Son Christ Jesus our Lord, "that whosoever believeth on Him should not perish, but have everlasting life?" May we not well cry out, Now know we, O Lord, that thou hast loved us, since thou hast not withheld thy Son, thine only Son from us! Abraham was God's creature (and God was Abraham's friend) and therefore under the highest obligation to surrender up his Isaac. But O stupendous love! Whilst we were his enemies, God sent forth his Son, made of a woman, made under the law, that he might become a curse for us. O the freeness, as well as the infinity, of the love of God our Father! It is unsearchable: I am lost in contemplating it; it is past finding out. Think, O believers, think of the love of God, in giving Jesus Christ to be a propitiation for our sins. And when you hear how Abraham built an altar, and laid the wood in order, and bound Isaac his son, and laid him on the altar upon the wood; think how your heavenly Father bound Jesus Christ his only Son, and offered him upon the altar of his justice, and laid upon him the iniquities of us all. When you read of Abraham's stretching forth his hand to slay his son, Think, O think, how God actually suffered his Son to be slain, that we might live for evermore. Do you read of Isaac carrying the wood upon his shoulders, upon which he was to be offered? Let this lead you to mount Calvary (this very mount of Moriah where Isaac was offered, as some think) and take a view of the antitype Jesus Christ, the Son of God, bearing and ready to sink under the weight of that cross, on which he was to hang for us. Do you admire Isaac so freely consenting to die, though a creature, and therefore obliged to go when God called? O do not forget to admire infinitely more the dear Lord Jesus, that promised seed, who willingly said, "Lo, I come," though under no obligation so to do, "to do thy will," to obey and die for men, "O God!" Did you weep just now, when I bid you fancy you saw the altar, and the wood laid in order, and Isaac laid bound on the altar? Look by faith, behold the blessed Jesus, our all-glorious Emmanuel, not bound, but nailed on a accursed tree: see how he hangs crowned with thorns, and had in derision of all that are round about him: see how the thorns pierce him, and how the blood in purple streams trickle down his sacred temples! Hark how the God of nature groans! See how he bows his head, and at length humanity gives up the ghost! Isaac is saved, but Jesus, the God of Isaac, dies; A ram is offered up in Isaac's room, but Jesus has no substitute; Jesus must bleed, Jesus must die; God the Father provided this Lamb for himself from all eternity. He must be offered in time, or man must be damned for evermore. And now, where are your tears? Shall I say, refrain your voice from weeping? No; rather let me exhort you to look to him whom you have pierced, and mourn, as a woman mourneth for her first-born: for we have been the betrayers, we have been the murderers of this Lord of glory; and shall we not bewail those sins, which brought the blessed Jesus to the accursed tree? Having so much done, so much suffered for us, so much forgiven, shall we not love much! O! let us love Him with all our hearts, and minds, and strength, and glorify him in our souls and bodies, for they are his. Which leads me to a second inference I shall draw from the foregoing discourse.

From hence we may learn the nature of true, justifying faith. Whoever understands and preaches the truth, as it is in Jesus, must acknowledge, that salvation is God's free gift, and that we are saved, not by any or all the works of righteousness which we have done or can do: no; we can neither wholly nor in part justify ourselves in the light of God. The Lord Jesus Christ is our righteousness; and if we are accepted with God, it must be only in and through the personal righteousness, the active and passive obedience, of Jesus Christ his beloved Son. This righteousness must be imputed, or counted over to us, and applied by faith to our hearts, or else we can in no wise be justified in God's sight: and that very moment a sinner is enabled to lay hold on Christ's righteousness by faith, he is freely justified from all his sins, and shall never enter into condemnation, notwithstanding he was a fire-brand of hell before. Thus is was that Abraham was justified before he did any good work: he was enabled to believe on the Lord Christ; it was accounted to him for righteousness; that is, Christ's righteousness was made over to him, and so accounted his. This, this is the gospel; this is the only was of finding acceptance with God: good works have nothing to do with our justification in his sight. We are justified by faith alone, as saith the article of our church; agreeable to which the apostle Paul says, "By grace ye are saved, through faith; and that not of yourselves; it is the gift of God." Notwithstanding, good works have their proper place: they justify our faith, though not our persons; they follow it, and evidence our justification in the sight of men. Hence it is that the apostle James asks, was not Abraham justified by works? (alluding no doubt to the story on which we have been discoursing) that is, did he not prove he was in a justified state, because his faith was productive of good works? This declarative justification in the sight of men, is what is directly to be understood in the words of the text; "Now know I, says God, that thou fearest me, since thou hast not withheld thy son, thine only son from me." Not but that God knew it before; but this is spoken in condescension to our weak capacities, and plainly shows, that his offering up his son was accepted with God, as an evidence of the sincerity of his faith, and for this, was left on record to future ages. Hence then you may learn, whether you are blessed with, and are sons and daughters of, faithful Abraham. You say you believe; you talk of free grace and free justification: you do well; the devils also believe and tremble. But has the faith, which you pretend to, influenced your hearts, renewed your souls, and, like Abraham's, worked by love? Are you affections, like his, set on things above? Are you heavenly-minded, and like him, do you confess yourselves strangers and pilgrims on the earth? In short, has your faith enabled you to overcome the world, and strengthened you to give up your Isaacs, your laughter, your most beloved lusts, friends, pleasures, and profits for God? If so, take the comfort of it; for justly may you say, "We know assuredly, that we do fear and love God, or rather are loved of him." But if you are only talking believers, have only a faith of the head, and never felt the power of it in your hearts, however you may bolster yourselves up, and say, "We have Abraham for our father, or Christ is our Savior," unless you get a faith of the heart, a faith working by love, you shall never sit with Abraham, Isaac, Jacob, or Jesus Christ, in the kingdom of heaven.

But I must draw one more inference, and with that I shall conclude.

Learn, O saints! From what has been said, to sit loose to all your worldly comforts; and stand ready prepared to part with everything, when God shall require it at your hand. Some of you perhaps may have friends, who are to you as your own souls; and others may have children, in whose lives your own lives are bound up: all I believe have their Isaacs, their particular delights of some kind or other. Labor, for Christ's sake, labor, ye sons and daughters of Abraham, to resign them daily in affection to God, that, when he shall require you really to sacrifice them, you may not confer with flesh and blood, any more than the blessed patriarch now before us. And as for you that have been in any measure tried like unto him, let his example encourage and comfort you. Remember, Abraham your father was tried so before you: think, O think of the happiness he now enjoys, and how he is incessantly thanking God for tempting and trying him when here below. Look up often by the eye of faith, and see him sitting with his dearly beloved Issac in the world of spirits. Remember, it will be but a little while, and you shall sit with them also, and tell one another what God has done for your souls. There I hope to sit with you, and hear this story of his offering up his Son from his own mouth, and to praise the Lamb that sitteth upon the throne, for what he hath done for all or souls, for ever and ever.

4. The Great Duty of Family Religion

Joshua 24:15—"As for me and my house, we will serve the Lord."

These words contain the holy resolution of pious Joshua, who having in a most moving, affectionate discourse recounted to the Israelites what great things God had done for them, in the verse immediately preceding the text, comes to draw a proper inference from what he had been delivering; and acquaints them, in the most pressing terms, that since God had been so exceeding gracious unto them, they could do not less, than out of gratitude for such uncommon favors and mercies, dedicate both themselves and families to his service. "Now therefore, fear the Lord, and serve him in sincerity and truth, and put away the Gods which your fathers served on the other side of the flood." And by the same engaging motive does the prophet Samuel afterwards enforce their obedience to the commandments of God, 1 Sam. 12:24, "Only fear the Lord, and serve him in truth, with all your heart; for consider how great things he hath done for you." But then, that they might not excuse themselves (as too many might be apt to do) by his giving them a bad example, or think he was laying heavy burdens upon them, whilst he himself touched them not with one of his fingers, he tells them in the text, that whatever regard they might pay to the doctrine he had been preaching, yet he (as all ministers ought to do) was resolved to live up to and practice it himself: "Choose you therefore, whom you will serve, whether the Gods which your fathers served, or the Gods of the Amorites, in whose land ye dwell: but as for me and my house, we will serve the Lord."

A resolution this, worthy of Joshua, and no less becoming, no less necessary for every true son of Joshua, that is entrusted with the care and government of a family in our day: and, if it was ever seasonable for ministers to preach up, or people to put in practice family-religion, it was never more so than in the present age; since it is greatly to be feared, that out of those many households that call themselves Christians, there are but few that serve God in their respective families as they ought.

It is true indeed, visit our churches, and you may perhaps see something of the form of godliness still subsisting amongst us; but even that is scarcely to be met with in private houses. So that were the blessed angels to come, as in the patriarchal age, and observe our spiritual oeconomy [meaning not in dictionary, but oecumenical=ecumenical, so oeconomy may be same as economy] at home, would they not be tempted to say as Abraham to Abimilech, "Surely, the fear of God is not in this place?" Gen. 20:11".

How such a general neglect of family-religion first began to overspread the Christian world, is difficult to determine. As for the primitive Christians, I am positive it was not so with them: No, they had not so learned Christ, as falsely to imagine religion was to be confined solely to their assemblies for public worship; but, on the contrary, behaved with such piety and exemplary holiness in their private families, that St. Paul often styles their house a church: "Salute such a one, says he, and the church which is in his house." And, I believe, we must for ever despair of seeing a primitive spirit of piety revived in the world, till we are so happy as to see a revival of primitive family religion; and persons unanimously resolving with good old Joshua, in the words of the text, "As for me and my house, we will serve the Lord."

From which words, I shall beg leave to insist on these three things.

I. First, That it is the duty of every governor of a family to take care, that not only he himself, but also that those committed to his charge, "serve the Lord."

II. Secondly, I shall endeavor to show after what manner a governor and his household ought to serve the Lord. And,

III. Thirdly, I shall offer some motives, in order to excite all governors, with their respective households, to serve the Lord in the manner that shall be recommended.

And First, I am to show that it is the duty of every governor of a family to take care, that not only he himself, but also that those committed to his charge, should serve the Lord.

And this will appear, if we consider that every governor of a family ought to look upon himself as obliged to act in three capacities as a prophet, to instruct: as a priest, to pray for and with; as a king, to govern, direct, and provide for them. It is true indeed, the latter of these, their kingly office, they are not so frequently deficient in, (nay in this they are generally too solicitous) but as for the two former, their priestly and prophetic office, like Gallio, they care for no such things. But however indifferent some governors may be about it, they may be assured, that God will require a due discharge of these offices at their hands. For if, as the apostle argues, "He that does not provide for his own house," in temporal things, has denied the faith, and is worse than an infidel;" to what greater degree of apostasy must he have arrived, who takes no thought to provide for the spiritual welfare of his family!

But farther, persons are generally very liberal of their invectives against the clergy, and think they justly blame the conduct of that minister who does not take heed to and watch over the flock, of which the Holy Ghost has made him overseer: but may not every governor of a family, be in a lower degree liable to the same censure, who takes no thought for those souls that are committed too his charge? For every house is as it were a little parish, every governor (as was before observed) a priest, every family a flock; and if any of them perish through the governor's neglect, their blood will God require at their hands.

Was a minister to disregard teaching his people publicly, and from house to house, and to excuse himself by saying, that he had enough to do to work out his own salvation with fear and trembling, without concerning himself with that of others; would you not be apt to think such a minister, to be like the unjust judge, "One that neither feared God, nor regarded man?" And yet, odious as such a character would be, it is no worse than that governor of a family deserves, who thinks himself obliged only to have his own soul, without paying any regard to the souls of his household. For (as was above hinted) every house is as it were a parish, and every master is concerned to secure, as much as in him lies, the spiritual prosperity of every one under his roof, as any minister whatever is obliged to look to the spiritual welfare of every individual person under his charge.

What precedents men who neglect their duty in this particular, can plead for such omission, I cannot tell. Doubtless not the example of holy Job, who was so far from imagining that he had no concern, as governor of a family, with any one's soul but his own, that the scripture acquaints us, "When the days of his children's feasting were gone about, that Job sent and sanctified them, and offered burnt-offerings, according to the number of them all; for Job said, It may be that my sons have sinned and cursed God in their hearts: thus did Job continually." Nor can they plead the practice of good old Joshua, whom, in the text, we find as much concerned for his household's welfare, as his own. Nor lastly, that of Cornelius, who feared God, not only himself, but with all his house: and were Christians but of the same spirit of Job, Joshua, and the Gentile centurion, they would act as Job, Joshua, and Cornelius did.

But alas! If this be the case, and all governors of families ought not only to serve the Lord themselves, but likewise to see that their respective households do so too; what will then become of those who not only neglect serving God themselves, but also make it their business to ridicule and scoff at any of their house that do? Who are not content with "not entering into the kingdom of heaven themselves; but those also that are willing to enter in, they hinder." Surely such men are factors for the devil indeed. Surely their damnation slumbereth not: for although God, is in his good providence, may suffer such stumbling-blocks to be put in his children's way, and suffer their greatest enemies to be those of their own households, for a trial of their sincerity, and improvement of their faith; yet we cannot but pronounce a woe against those masters by whom such offenses come. For if those that only take care of their own souls, can scarcely be saved, where will such monstrous profane and wicked governors appear?

But hoping there are but few of this unhappy stamp, proceed we now to the

Second thing proposed: To show after what manner a governor and his household ought to serve the Lord.

1. And the first thing I shall mention, is *reading the Word of God*. This is a duty incumbent on every private person. "Search the scriptures, for in them ye think ye have eternal life," is a precept given by our blessed Lord indifferently to all: but much more so, ought every governor of a family to think it in a peculiar manner spoken to himself, because (as hath been already proved) he ought to look upon himself as a prophet, and therefore agreeably to such a character, bound to instruct those under his charge in the knowledge of the word of God.

This we find was the order God gave to his peculiar people Israel: for thus speaks his representative Moses, Deut. 6:6–7, "These words," that is, the scripture words, "which I command thee this day, shall be in thy heart, and thou shalt teach them diligently unto thy children," that is, as it is generally explained, servants, as well as children, "and shalt talk of them when thou sittest in thy house." From whence we may infer, that the only reason, why so many neglect to read the words of scripture diligently to their children is, because the words of scripture are not in their hearts: for if they were, out of the abundance of the heart their mouth would speak.

Besides, servants as well as children, are, for the generality, very ignorant, and mere novices in the laws of God: and how shall they know, unless some one teach them? And what more proper to teach them by, than the lively oracles of God, "which are able to make them wise unto salvation?" And who more proper to instruct them by these lively oracles, than parents and masters, who (as hath been more than once observed) are as much concerned to feed them with spiritual, as with bodily bread, day by day.

But if these things be so, what a miserable condition are those unhappy governors in, who are so far from feeding those committed to their care with the sincere milk of the word, to the intent they may grow thereby, that they neither search the scriptures themselves, nor are careful to explain them to others? Such families must be in a happy way indeed to do their Master's will, who take such prodigious pains to know it! Would not one imagine that they had turned converts to the Church of Rome, that they thought ignorance to be the mother of devotion; and that those were to be condemned as heretics who read their Bibles? And yet how few families are there amongst us, who do not act after this unseemly manner! But shall I praise them in this? I praise them not; Brethren, this thing ought not so to be.

2. Pass we on now to the second means whereby every governor and his household ought to serve the Lord, *Family-Prayer*.

This is a duty, though as much neglected, yet as absolutely necessary as the former. Reading is a good preparative for prayer, as prayer is an excellent means to render reading effectual. And the reason why every governor of a family should join both these exercises together, is plain, because a governor of a family cannot perform his priestly office (which we before observed he is in some degree invested with) without performing this duty of family prayer.

We find it therefore remarked, when mention is made of Can and Abel's offering sacrifices, that they brought them. But to whom did they bring them? Why, in all probability, to their father Adam, who, as priest of the family, was to offer sacrifice in their names. And so ought every spiritual son of the second Adam, who is entrusted with the care of an household, to offer up the spiritual sacrifices of supplications and thanksgivings, acceptable to God through Jesus Christ, in the presence and name of all who wait upon, or eat meat at his table.

Thus we read our blessed Lord behaved, when he tabernacled amongst us: for it is said often, that he prayed with his twelve disciples, which was then his little family. And he himself has promised a particular blessing to joint supplications: "Wheresoever two or three are gathered together in my name, there am I in the midst of them." And again, "If two or three are agreed touching any thing they shall ask, it shall be given them." Add to this, that we are commanded by the Apostle to "pray always, with all manner of supplication," which doubtless includes family prayer. And holy Joshua, when he set up the good resolution in the text, that he and his household would serve the Lord, certainly resolved to pray with his family, which is one of the best testimonies they could give of their serving him.

Besides, there are no families but what have some common blessings, of which they have been all partakers, to give thanks for; some common crosses and afflictions, which they are to pray against; some common sins, which they are all to lament and bewail: but how this can be done, without joining together in one common act of humiliation, supplication, and thanksgiving, is difficult to devise.

From all which considerations put together, it is evident, that family prayer is a great and necessary duty; and consequently, those governors that neglect it, are certainly without excuse. And it is much to be feared, if they live without family prayer, they live without God in the world.

And yet, such an hateful character as this is, it is to be feared, that was God to send out an angel to destroy us, as he did once to destroy the Egyptian first-born, and withal give him a commission, as then, to spare no houses but where they saw the blood of the lintel, sprinkled on the door-post, so now, to let no families escape, but those that called upon him in morning and evening prayer; few would remain unhurt by his avenging sword. Shall I term such families Christians or heathens? Doubtless they deserve not the name of Christians; and heathens will rise up in judgment against such profane families of this generation: for they had always their household gods, whom they worshipped and whose assistance they frequently invoked. And a pretty pass those families surely are arrived at, who must be sent to school to pagans. But will not the Lord be avenged on such profane households as these? Will he not pour out his fury upon those that call not upon his name?

3. But it is time for me to hasten to the third and last means I shall recommend, whereby every governor ought with his household to serve the Lord, *catechizing andinstructing* their children and servants, and bringing them up in the nurture and admonition of the Lord.

That this, as well as the two former, is a duty incumbent on every governor of an house, appears from that famous encomium or commendation God gives of Abraham: "I know that he will command his children and his household after him, to keep the way of the Lord, to do justice and judgment." And indeed scarce any thing is more frequently pressed upon us in holy writ, than this duty of catechizing. Thus, says God in a passage before cited, "Thou shalt teach these words diligently unto thy children." And parents are commanded in the New Testament, to "bring up their children in the nurture and admonition of the Lord." The holy Psalmist acquaints us, that one great end why God did such great wonders for his people, was, "to the intent that when they grew up, they should show their children, or servants, the same." And in Deut. 6 at the 20th and following verses, God strictly commands his people to instruct their children in the true nature of the ceremonial worship, when they should inquire about it, as he supposed they would do, in time to come. And if servants and children were to be instructed in the nature of Jewish rites, much more ought they now to be initiated and grounded in the doctrines and first principles of the gospel of Christ: not only, because it is a revelation, which has brought life and immortality to a fuller and clearer light, but also, because many seducers are gone abroad into the world, who do their utmost endeavor to destroy not only the superstructure, but likewise to sap the very foundation of our most holy religion.

Would then the present generation have their posterity be true lovers and honorers of God; masters and parents must take Solomon's good advice, and train up and catechize their respective households in the way wherein they should go.

I am aware but of one objection, that can, with any show of reason, be urged against what has been advanced; which is, that such a procedure as this will take up too much time, and hinder families too long from their worldly business. But it is much to be questioned, whether persons that start such an abjection, are not of the same hypocritical spirit as the traitor Judas, who had indignation against devout Mary, for being so profuse of her ointment, in anointing our blessed Lord, and asked why it might not be sold for two hundred pence, and given to the poor. For has God given us so much time to work for ourselves, and shall we not allow some small pittance of it, morning and evening, to be devoted to his more immediate worship and service? Have not people read, that it is God who gives men power to get wealth, and therefore that the best way to prosper in the world, is to secure his favor? And has not our blessed Lord himself promised, that if we seek first the kingdom of God and his righteousness, all outward necessaries shall be added unto us?

Abraham, no doubt, was a man of as great business as such objectors may be; but yet he would find time to command his household to serve the Lord. Nay, David was a king, and consequently had a great deal of business upon his hands; yet notwithstanding, he professes that he would walk in his house with a perfect heart. And, to instance but one more, holy Joshua was a person certainly engaged very much in temporal affairs; and yet he solemnly declares before all Israel, that as for him and his household, they would serve the Lord. And did persons but redeem their time, as Abraham, David, or Joshua did, they would no longer complain, that family duties kept them too long from the business of the world.

III. But my Third and Last general head, under which I was to offer some motives, in order to excite all governors, with their respective households, to serve the Lord in the manner before recommended, I hope, will serve instead of a thousand arguments, to prove the weakness and folly of any such objection.

1. And the first motive I shall mention is the duty of *gratitude*, which you that are governors of families owe to God. Your lot, every one must confess, is cast in a fair ground: providence hath given you a goodly heritage, above many of your fellow-creatures, and therefore, bout of a principle of gratitude, you ought to endeavor, as much as in you lies, to make every person of your respective households to call upon him as long as they live: not to mention, that the authority, with which God has invested you as parents and governors of families, is a talent committed to your trust, and which you are bound to improve to your Master's honor. In other things we find governors and parents can exercise lordship over their children and servants readily, and frequently enough can say to one, Go, and he goeth; and to another, Come, and he cometh; to a third, Do this, and he doeth it. And shall this power be so often employed in your own affairs, and never exerted in the things of God? Be astonished, O heavens, at this!

Thus did not faithful Abraham; no, God says, that he knew Abraham would command his servants and children after him. Thus did not Joshua: no, he was resolved not only to walk with God himself, but to improve his authority in making all about him do so too: "As for me and my household, we will serve the Lord." Let us go and do likewise.

2. But Secondly, If gratitude to God will not, methinks *love and pity to your children* should move you, with your respective families, to serve the Lord.

Most people express a great fondness for their children: nay so great, that very often their own lives are wrapped up in those of their offspring. "Can a woman forget her sucking child, that she should not have compassion on the son of her womb?" says God by his Prophet Isaiah. He speaks of it as a monstrous thing, and scarce credible; but the words immediately following, affirm it to be possible, "Yes, they may forget" and experience also assures us they may. Father and mother may both forsake their children: for what greater degree of forgetfulness can they express towards them, than to neglect the improvement of their better part, and not bring them up in the knowledge and fear of God?

It is true indeed, parents seldom forget to provide for their children's bodies, (though, it is to be feared, some men are so far sunk beneath the beasts that perish, as to neglect even that) but then how often do they forget, or rather, when do they remember, to secure the salvation of their immortal souls? But is this their way of expressing their fondness for the fruit of their bodies? Is this the best testimony they can give of their affection to the darling of their hearts? Then was Delilah fond of Samson, when she delivered him up into the hands of the Philistines? Then were those ruffians well affected to Daniel, when they threw him into a den of lions?

3. But Thirdly, If neither gratitude to God, nor love and pity to your children, will prevail on you; yet let a principle of *common honesty and justice* move you to set up the holy resolution in the text.

This is a principle which all men would be thought to act upon. But certainly, if any may be truly censured for their injustice, none can be more liable to such censure, than those who think themselves injured if their servants withdraw themselves from their bodily work, and yet they in return take no care of their inestimable souls. For is it just that servants should spend their time and strength in their master's service, and masters not at the same time give them what is just and equal for their service?

It is true, some men may think they have done enough when they give unto their servants food and raiment, and say, "Did not I bargain with thee for so much a year?" But if they give them no other reward than this, whet do they less for their very beasts? But are not servants better than they? Doubtless they are: and however masters may put off their convictions for the present, they will find a time will come, when they shall know they ought to have given them some spiritual as well as temporal wages; and the cry of those that have mowed down their fields, will enter into the ears of the Lord of Sabaoth.

4. But Fourthly, If neither gratitude to God, pity to children, nor a principle for common justice to servants, are sufficient to balance all objections; yet let that darling, that prevailing motive of *self-interest* turn the scale, and engage you with your respective households to serve the Lord.

This weighs greatly with you in other matters: be then persuaded to let it have a due and full influence on you in this: and if it has, if you have but faith as a grain of mustard-seed, how can you avoid believing, that promoting family-religion, will be the best means to promote your own temporal, as well as eternal welfare? For "Godliness has the promise of the life that now is, as well as that which is to come."

Besides, you all, doubtless wish for honest servants, and pious children: and to have them prove otherwise, would be as great a grief to you, as it was to Elisha to have a treacherous Gehazi, or David to be troubled with a rebellious Absolom. But how can it be expected they should learn their duty, except those set over them, take care to teach it to them? Is it not as reasonable to expect you should reap where had not sewn, or gather where you had not strawed?

Did Christianity, indeed, give any countenance to children and servants to disregard their parents and masters according to the flesh, or represent their duty to them, as inconsistent with their entire obedience to their father and master who is in heaven, there might then be some pretense to neglect instructing them in the principles of such a religion. But since the precepts of this pure and undefiled religion, are all of them holy, just, and good; and the more they are taught their duty to God, the better they will perform their duties to you; methinks, to neglect the improvement of their souls, out of a dread of spending too much time in religious duties, is acting quite contrary to your own interest as well as duty.

5. Fifthly and Lastly, If neither gratitude to God, love to your children, common justice to your servants, nor even that most prevailing motive self-interest, will excite; yet let a consideration of the terrors of the Lord persuade you to put in practice the pious resolution in the text. Remember, the time will come, and that perhaps very shortly, when we must all appear before the judgment-seat of Christ; where we must give a solemn and strict account how we have had our conversation, in our respective families in this world. How will you endure to see your children and servants (who ought to be your joy and crown of rejoicing in the day of our Lord Jesus Christ) coming out as so many swift witnesses against you; cursing the father that begot them, the womb that bare them, the paps which they have sucked, and the day they ever entered into your houses? Think you not, the damnation which men must endure for their own sins, will be sufficient, that they need load themselves with the additional guilt of being accessory to the damnation of others also? O consider this, all ye that forget to serve the Lord with your respective households, "lest he pluck you away, and there be none to deliver you!"

But God forbid, brethren, that any such evil should befall you: no, rather will I hope, that you have been in some measure convinced by what has been said of the great importance of *family-religion*; and therefore are ready to cry out in the words immediately following the text, "God forbid that we should forsake the Lord;" and again, ver. 21, "Nay, but we will (with our several households) serve the Lord."

And that there may be always such a heart in you, let

me exhort all governors of families, in the name of our Lord Jesus Christ, often to reflect on the inestimable worth of their own souls, and the infinite ransom, even the precious blood of Jesus Christ, which has been paid down for them. Remember, I beseech you to remember, that you are fallen creatures; that you are by nature lost and estranged from God; and that you can never be restored to your primitive happiness, till by being born again of the Holy Ghost, you arrive at your primitive state of purity, have the image of God restamped upon your souls, and are thereby made meet to be partakers of the inheritance with the saints in light. Do, I say, but seriously and frequently reflect on, and act as persons that believe such important truths, and you will no more neglect your family's spiritual welfare than your own. No, the love of God, which will then be shed abroad in your hearts, will constrain you to do your utmost to preserve them: and the deep sense of God's free grace in Christ Jesus, (which you will then have) in calling you, will excite you to do your utmost to save others, especially those of your own household. And though, after all your pious endeavors, some may continue unreformed; yet you will have this comfortable reflection to make, that you did what you could to make your families religious: and therefore may rest assured of sitting down in the kingdom of heaven, with Abraham, Joshua, and Cornelius, and all the godly householders, who in their several generations shone forth as so many lights in their respective households upon earth. Amen.

5. Christ the Best Husband

This psalm is called the song of loves, the most pure and spiritual, the most ear and delightful loves; namely, those which are between Christ the beloved, and his church, which is his spouse; wherein is set forth, first, the Lord Jesus Christ in regard of his majesty, power, and divinity, his truth, meekness and equity: And then the spouse is set forth, in regard of her ornaments, companions, attendants and posterity; and both in regard of their comeliness and beauty. After the description of Christ, an invitation to his espousals, is given the children of men, called by the name of daughter; and therefore, particularly applicable unto you, my dear sisters, as being the daughters of men, yet not so as excluding the sons of men.

I shall now, therefore, consider the words, as spoken to you in particular, and containing this doctrine;

That the Lord Jesus Christ doth invite the daughters of men to be his spouse; and is exceeding desirous of their beauty; who, forgetting their people and father's house, do hearken, consider and incline to his invitation, and join themselves to him in this relation.

I shall show,

I. How Christ doth espouse himself unto the children, but, more especially, unto the daughters of men.

The Lord Jesus Christ, doth espouse himself unto the children of men, in the world, but the public solemnization of the marriage, is reserved until the last day; when his spouse shall be brought forth to him, in white robes, and a raiment of perfect righteousness, more rich and curious, my dear sisters, than any of your needle-work; and the marriage feast will be kept in his Father's house, in heaven, when they shall be received into the nearest and closest embraces of his love. The marriage knot is tied here, in which are included four things:

First; Mutual Choice,
Secondly, Mutual Affection,
Thirdly, Mutual Union,
Fourthly, Mutual Obligation.

First, my dear sisters, there is a *mutual choice*, which is not only in Christ, as Mediator, but also by Christ as the eternal Son of God, yea, God himself; notwithstanding all that the polite Arians and Socinians say to the contrary. The Lord Jesus Christ, my dear sisters, doth choose you merely by his free grace; it is freely of his own mercy, that he brings you into the marriage covenant: You, who have so grievously offended him, yet, the Lord Jesus Christ hath chosen you; you did not, you would not have chosen him; but when once, my dear sisters, he hath chosen you, then, and not till then, you make choice of him for your Lord and Husband.

The Lord Jesus Christ when he first comes to you, finds you full of sin and pollution; you are deformed, defiled, enslaved, poor, miserable and wretched, very despicable and loathsome, by reason of sin; and he maketh choice of you, not because of your holiness, nor of your beauty, nor of your being qualified for them; no, the Lord Jesus Christ puts these qualifications upon you, as may make you meet for his embrace; and you are drawn to make choice of the Lord Jesus Christ because he first chose you.

Secondly, In this espousal of yours, my dear sisters, there is a *mutual affection*; this doth accompany the choice. Your hearts are drawn out after Christ; your souls pant and long for him; you cannot be at rest until you are engaged to this Jesus: You are ready to cry out continually, none but Christ, none but Christ: this is the language of your hearts, if you are truly sensible of your need of him. The more acquaintance you have of this Lord Jesus, the more pleased you are with your choice, and the more your affections are drawn towards him. And where can you place your affections better than upon that Jesus who shed his blood for your sakes? Surely he deserves both your loves and affections: Go on, go on, my dear sisters, that your affections may grow stronger and stronger.

Thirdly, There is not only mutual choice, and mutual affection, but likewise *mutual union*: And here doth the marriage lie chiefly, in this union; Christ and souls are contracted, and the knot is tied so fast, that neither men on earth, how great soever they be, nor devils in hell, though they should combine all their wrath and rage together, still they cannot dissolve, they cannot untie it; no, my dear sisters, it is indissolvable, for the union is, by the spirit, on Christ's part, and by faith on yours: By the spirit, Christ doth lay hold on you; and by faith, you do lay hold on him; and thus the match is made; Christ becomes yours, his person, portion, and all his benefits are yours; and you become Christ's, your persons, your hearts, and all that you have is resigned up unto him, and O that they may be so more and more.

Fourthly, There is a *mutual obligation* between Christ and his spouse. Christ obliges himself to love you here, he will not, indeed he never will leave you, he will protect you from the malice of the Pharisees of this generation, he will provide for you in all difficulties; he will live with you here, and at last he will take you to himself, to live with him forever. And you are engaged to him to be loving, loyal, faithful, obedient; and you are to stick close to him as long as you live; and then you will find yourselves to be married to the best advantage, both for soul and body, for time and for eternity.

II. Christ doth invite all of you to be his spouse.

And it on this account that he sends forth his ministers to preach. It is this, that makes me thus come among you; that you would accept of this invitation, to which, in the name of the Lord Jesus Christ, I do call and entreat you to take him, on his own terms. He calls all of you, my sisters, whether elder or younger, whether married or unmarried, of higher degree, or of the meanest quality, the poorest servants, yea, the rabble of this world, as the world calls you, who are willing to be espoused unto the Lord Jesus Christ. I say, the poor are as welcome to be Christ's spouse as those that are rich. He regardeth not the rich more than the poor; he chose a mean virgin, espoused to a carpenter, to be his mother; and he chooseth and calleth all such to be his spouse; then be not discouraged at your being despised in the world; for if you are but loved by Christ, and espoused to him, it will be an over-sufficiency for all the trouble that you have met with here.

III. Those who would be espoused unto Christ, must hearken, consider, and incline to his invitation, and forget even their father's house.

Such as would be espoused unto Christ must hearken. "Hearken, O daughter." Many amongst you, my sisters, stop their ears against the calls of the gospel; they shut their ears like the deaf adder, which will not hearken unto the voice of the charmer, though he charm never so wisely. You will not hearken unto the invitations of Christ; you can hearken unto the vanities of the world, and be delighted with the espousals of the world, but never think or are delighted with the espousals of Christ.

It was by the ear, that the temptation of sin was received by the first man, when he departed from God; and by the ear, the invitation to be Christ's spouse must be received, before the heart will be opened to receive Jesus Christ in this conjugal relation.

If you would, my dear sisters, be espoused to Christ, you must consider Christ's invitation. It is not a slight or bare hearing of Christ's invitation, which will be of any service to you, or make up the match between Christ and your souls; no, you must receive Christ in the heart; you must consider the thing itself, the advantages of it, the difference between Christ's invitations and the devil's temptations, or any of the world's proffers.

Those who would be espoused to Christ, must be inclined to accept of Christ's invitation. "Hearken, O daughter, consider and incline thine ear." This is to incline your hearts: You must consent with your wills; there must be a compliance to the motion of Christ, and you must have desires after Christ, and then your hearts will say, "Lord, let us be thy spouse, and be thou our beloved."

You must likewise forget your father's house. "Hearken, O daughter, and consider, and forget thy father's house." You are not here to cast off all affections unto natural relations; but you must forget all relations, so as to be ready to forgo all their favor, when it standeth in competition with that of the Lord Jesus Christ: and do not let your carnal friends and relations hinder you from closing with, and espousing the Lord Jesus. I earnestly beseech you to suffer the loss of any thing, rather than to lose his favors; you must indeed forget your own people, that is, you must forget all your evil customs which you have learned in your father's house, and forsake all your vain conversation, your reading of plays, novels, or romances; and you must keep from learning to sing the songs of the drunkard; for Christ, if you are his spouse, hath redeem you.

Such of you, my dear sisters, as are espoused to the Lord Jesus Christ are very beautiful. I do not mean in respect of your bodies; you may have less of external comeliness than others, in respect of your bodies, but as to your souls you will exceed in beauty, not so much in the eyes of man, as n the eyes of God; such have the most beautiful image of God stamped upon them; none n the world beside them, have the least spark of spiritual beauty. Such as are not married to Christ, are unregenerated, they are not born again, nor brought from sin unto God, which must be done before you be espoused to Christ.

And the Lord Jesus Christ desireth to see this beauty in his spouse, for he cries out, "O my dove, thou are in the clefts of the rock, in the secret places of the stairs, let me see thy countenance, let me hear thy voice, for sweet is thy voice, and thy countenance is comely." He calleth his spouse his love, being the dear object of his love; and he admireth her loveliness; he repeats it twice in one verse, "Behold thou art fair, my love, behold thou art fair." Thus you see he describes their beauty. And then, my sisters, we have wonderful expression of Christ to his spouse, "Thou hast ravished my heart, my sister, my spouse, thou hast ravished my heart with one of thine eyes, with one chain of thy neck." Thus you see how pleased the Lord Jesus Christ is with his spouse; and will not you, therefore, be espoused unto the Lord Jesus? I offer Jesus Christ to all of you; if you have been never so notorious for sin, if you have been as great a harlot as Mary Magdalen was, when once you are espoused to Christ, you shall be forgiven. Therefore be not discouraged, at whatever slights and contempts the world may pass upon you, but come and join yourselves to the Lord Jesus Christ, and all your sins shall be washed away in his blood; and when once you are espoused to Jesus, you are disjoined from sin, you are born again. You are now, as it were, espoused unto sin; sin is your husband, and you are too fond of it, but when once you are married to Christ, when you are born again, then you may be said to die unto sin; but till then, sin liveth in your affections; therefore, my sisters, give sin its death-wound in your hearts; you have been called by the word time after time, and it has had no effect upon you; but when you are espoused unto the Lord Jesus Christ, then you will be brought to him by his Spirit: You will then lay hold on him by faith, his Spirit will draw you unto himself; he will make you to be willing in the day of his power; he will give you faith in him. Faith is the hand of the soul which layeth hold on Christ; therefore do not rest contented till you have this grace of faith wrought in you with power; do not be contented till you have received the Lord Jesus Christ.

Embrace Christ in the arms of your dearest love; then you love the Lord Jesus Christ with sincerity, when you love and esteem him before father, mother, or all the delights and pleasures of this life, but if you do delight in any thing that this world can produce, more than in the Lord Jesus Christ, you have not true love to him.

If you are espoused to Christ, you have acquaintance and converse with him; you will endeavor to promote his interest, and advance his name in the world; when others are going to the polite and fashionable diversions of life, you will be laboring to bring honor to the Lord Jesus Christ; you will commend your beloved above all other beloveds, and endeavor to bring others into love to him. Can you, my dear sisters, who are now assembled to worship God, show such evidence of your espousals unto the Lord Jesus Christ? O! how joyful, how comfortable an estate is this! Surely this is a marriage worth seeking after; this is the only desirable marriage, and the Lord Jesus Christ is the only lover that is worth seeking after.

Now, my dear sisters, I shall speak a few words to those of you who have not yet espoused yourselves to the Lord Jesus. It is a great sin, and surely you highly affront the Lord that bought you. It is likewise your folly to refuse and neglect the gracious proffers of being the spouse of Christ; hereby you forfeit all that love which he would bestow upon you; hereby you choose rags before robes, dross before gold, pebbles before jewels, built before a pardon, wounds before healing, defilement before cleansing, deformity before comeliness, trouble before peace, slavery before liberty, the service of the devil before the service of Christ. Hereby you choose dishonor before a crown, death before life, hell before heaven, eternal misery and torment before everlasting joy and glory. And need there a further evidence of your folly and madness, in refusing and neglecting Christ to be your spouse.

My dear sisters, I should exceed the limits of your time, should I particularize all the advantages which you would obtain by being espoused to the Lord Jesus. This is your wisdom; they are foolish virgins who refuse; but you are the wise virgins who have accepted of the Lord Jesus Christ, and have disposed of yourselves to him; you have made the wisest choice; and however the blind world may deem you fools, and despise you as being methodically mad, yet you are wise in the esteem of God, and will, one day, appear so in the esteem of them that now despise you. It is your glory that you are espoused unto the Lord Jesus; and therefore glory is your espousal; glory not in yourselves, but in the Lord who hath thus freely and graciously bestowed these favors upon you. It is your safety to be espoused unto the Lord Jesus Christ, he will protect and defend you even from sin and Satan, and eternal ruin; and therefore thus far you are safe; he hath a regard for you in times of danger from men, and these times of danger seem to be hastening; it is now arising as a black cloud no bigger than a man's hand, and by and by it will overspread the heavens, and when it is full it will burst; but if you are espoused to Christ, you are safe.

Now, my dear sisters, I shall conclude with an earnest exhortation to high and low, rich and poor, one with another, to be espoused unto Christ.

Let me speak unto you, young women, who are not yet espoused unto Christ, in an especial manner. It may be to satisfy your curiosity, has brought many of you here; though, perhaps, this may be the time when you shall be brought home to embrace the Lord Jesus, and be espoused to him. And O, that I may persuade you, by his Spirit, to espouse yourselves unto the Lord of life.

And if you are but brought to close with the Lord Jesus Christ, I shall attain my end, and then both you and I shall rejoice that I preached this sermon to you.

Come virgins, will you give me leave to be a suitor unto you, not in my own name, but in the name of the Lord? O! that I may prevail with you for your affections, and persuade you to give them unto Christ! May I be instrumental of bringing your souls unto Christ! May I be instrumental to join you and Christ together this day!

Be not coy (bashful, shy; showing reluctance to make a definite commitment), as some of you possibly are in other loves: modesty and the virgin blush may very well come you, when proposals of another kind are made unto you; but here coyness is filly, and backwardness to accept of this motion, is shame: you have ten thousand times more reason to blush at the refusal of Christ for your beloved, than at the acceptance; when otherwise the devil and sin would ravish your virgin affections. Never had you a better motion made to you; never was such a match proffered to you as this, of being matched and espoused unto the Lord Jesus Christ.

Consider who the Lord Jesus is, whom you are invited to espouse yourselves unto; he is the best husband; there is none comparable to Jesus Christ.

Do you desire one that is great? He is of the highest dignity, he is the glory of heaven, the darling of eternity, admired by angels, dreaded by devils, and adored by saints. For you to be espoused to so great a king, what honor will you have by this espousal?

Do you desire one that is rich? None is comparable to Christ, the fullness of the earth belongs to him. If you be espoused to Christ, you shall share in his unsearchable riches; you shall receive of his fullness, even grace for grace here, and you shall hereafter be admitted to glory, and shall live with this Jesus to all eternity.

Do you desire one that is wise? There is none comparable to Christ for wisdom. His knowledge is infinite, and his wisdom is correspondent thereto. And if you are espoused to Christ, he will guide and counsel you, and make you wise unto salvation.

Do you desire one that is potent, who may defend you against your enemies, and all the insults and reproaches of the Pharisees of this generation? There is none that can equal Christ in power; for the Lord Jesus Christ hath all power.

Do you desire one that is good? There is none like unto Christ in this regard; others may have some goodness, but it is imperfect; Christ's goodness is complete and perfect, he is full of goodness and in him dwelleth no evil.

Do you desire one that is beautiful? His eyes are most sparkling, his looks and glances of love are ravishing, his smiles are most delightful and refreshing unto the soul: Christ is the most lovely person of all others in the world.

Do you desire one that can love you? None can love you like Christ: His love, my dear sisters, is incomprehensible; his love passeth all other loves: The love of the Lord Jesus is first, without beginning; his love is free without any motive; his love is great without any measure; his love is constant without any change, and his love is everlasting.

It was the love of the Lord Jesus Christ, my dear sisters, which brought him down from heaven; and which veiled his divinity in a human soul and body; for he is God over all blessed for ever: It was love that made him subject to hunger, thirst and sorrow; he was humbled, even unto death for you; for you who are espoused to him, he underwent the painful, shameful and ignominious death of the cross: and can you, my sisters, hear this, and not be concerned to think that the blessed Jesus underwent all this for such sinful creatures as you and I are? And when out of love he had finished the redemption on earth, as to what was needful for satisfaction; it was his love that carried him back to heaven, where he was before, that he might make application of what he had purchased, that there he might make intercession for those whom he had redeemed, and prepare a place for them, even glorious mansions with himself, in the house not made with hands, which is eternal in the heavens. It is out of love that he sendeth such tokens to his people from heaven to earth, which he conveyeth through his ordinances, by his Spirit unto them. Surely then none is so deserving as the Lord Jesus Christ for you to espouse yourselves unto: if you be espoused unto Christ he is yours, all that he is, all that he hath; you shall have his heart, and share in the choicest expressions of his dearest love.

The Lord Jesus Christ, my dear sisters, doth beseech you to be his spouse. We ministers have a commission from the Lord Jesus Christ to invite you, in his name, unto this very thing; and Christ's invitations are real; general; frequent; earnest; free.

Christ's invitations of you, to be his spouse, are *real*: and as the thing is real, so you, my dear sisters, are really invited unto it. The Lord doth not mock and dissemble with you, as some pretending lovers, who dissemble love unto virgins, until they have gained their affections, and then falsely and basely relinquish them, never really intending either to espouse, or marry them: but the Lord doth really intend the thing, in his invitations of you; he never cast off any whose consent and affections he had gained. Again,

Christ's invitations of you, my dear sisters, are *general*. All of you are invited, none of you are excluded; all sorts of sinners are invited; the most vile and abominable sinners, the most notorious transgressors are invited to be Christ's spouse, and shall be as welcome as any unto the embraces of his love.

Christ's invitations of you are *frequent*: Jesus Christ calls on you frequently; he hath waited on you time after time, one year after another; and he doth now invite you, by me this day, to come unto Him. Do not slight this invitation, but receive it with joy and thankfulness. Come, I beseech you, to this Jesus, who thus, invites you to be his spouse. Again,

Christ's invitations to be his spouse are *earnest*: he doth call upon you, and not only call, but call earnestly too; yea, he useth many arguments with you; he will press you to come unto him; he is loth (loathe) to take any denial from you: he knocks, and knocks hard at the door of your hearts for entertainment; and surely you will not deny the Lord of life and glory who died for you, and gave himself for you: O my dear sisters, let this be the evening of your espousals to the Lord Jesus Christ.

He invites you *freely* to be his spouse, for all his invitations are free; he doth not expect a portion with you, as worldly lovers do; He wants nothing of you: nay, you must have nothing, if you be espoused unto the Lord Jesus Christ. If you be poor, miserable, blind, naked, Jesus Christ will supply all these defects of his own free mercy; he will fill and supply you with all things out of his treasury; he will make you meet for himself; he will prepare you to live with him for ever.

Consider, if you be once espoused unto Christ, if once joined in this relation, you shall never be separated from him; neither men nor devils shall be able to separate you: none, none, shall disjoin you; and when death doth break all other bonds, it shall not break the conjugal bond between you and Christ, but bring you unto the most full and everlasting possession of your beloved.

And what do you now say, young women? Shall I have a grant for my master, or be sent away with a repulse and refusal; no, I cannot carry such a message to my master; I hope better things of you, my sisters, and things which accompany salvation: methinks by this time ye should begin to have a mind unto Jesus Christ; you look as if you did desire; you hearken as if you would consent. What do you say? Shall the match be made up this evening between Christ and your souls? O that I may be instrumental in joining your hands, or rather your hearts together: O that I may be instrumental to tie that knot, which never can be unloosed.

Some marry in haste, and repent at leisure; but if you were once espoused unto Jesus Christ, you would never repent; nothing would grieve you, but that you were not joined to him sooner; and you would not be disjoined again for all the world.

Shall this be the day of your espousals? Some of you have stayed a long time; and will you defer any longer? If you will not now, perhaps you may never have another opportunity; this may be the last time of asking; and therefore it is dangerous to refuse; some of you are very young, too young for other espousals; but none of you, by dear sisters, are too young to be espoused unto the Lord Jesus Christ: in other espousals, you must have the consent of your parents; but in this you are at your own disposal; you may give, and ought to match yourselves to Christ, whether parents do consent or not.

But if any of you should ask, what you must do that you may be espoused unto Christ? You must be sensible of your need of being espoused to him, and until you are sensible of your need of the Lord Jesus Christ, you cannot be espoused to him: You must have desires after this Jesus, and seek unto him for an interest in him, you must cry nightly unto him to espouse you to himself; put off the filthiness of sin and all its defilements; and then, my sisters, put on the white raiment, and clean garments, which Christ hath provided for you, the robes of his righteousness; in these garments you shall be beautiful; and in these garments you shall be accepted: you must have the wedding garment on; you must put off all your own good works, for they will be but a means to keep you from Christ; no, you must come as not having your own righteousness, which is of the law, but you must have the righteousness of Christ. Therefore, come unto the Lord Jesus Christ, and he will give it to you; he will not send you away without it. Receive him upon his own terms, and he is yours forever: O devote yourselves to him, soul and body, and all, to be his for ever; and Christ will be yours and then happy, happy you, that ever you were born! But if any of you die before this espousal unto the Lord Jesus Christ, then woe, woe, unto you, that ever you had a being in life; but if you go to Christ you shall be espoused unto the Lord Jesus: though your sins have been never so great, yea, the blood of Christ will cleanse you from them; the marriage covenant between Christ and your souls will dissolve all your sins; you will then be weary of your old ways, for all things will become new in your souls.

Now, my dear sisters, I shall conclude by just speaking a word or two to those of you, who are already espoused unto the Lord Jesus Christ.

O admire, admire the rich and free grace, which hath brought you to this relation: Is not this an instance of the greatest of love, that you should be the spouse of the Lord Jesus Christ? You that had no beauty, you that had no comeliness, that was full of sin, that He should embrace such as you and I are; that we should be taken into the embrace of this Lord Jesus. O infinite condescending kindness! O amazing love! Reverence, reverence, I beseech you, this Lord Jesus Christ.

He is you Lord, and you must reverence him, love and be faithful unto him, be subject to him, and careful to please him in every thing; endeavor to keep up a daily communion with him; look, long and prepare for Christ's second appearance, when the nuptials between you shall be solemnized, and you live with him in mansions of everlasting joys, where you shall love and live with this king of glory for ever and ever.

I know not how to conclude; methinks I could speak to you till midnight, if it would bring you unto the Lord Jesus Christ, and make you be espoused to him, for indeed, that will be the espousal which will turn to the greatest advantage, as you will find by experience, if you will but make the trial; and that you may do so, my prayers and my constant endeavor shall be used.

I will, my dear sisters, spend and be spent for you, and by the assistance of God, will persevere in this that I have begun; and as many of you may have opportunity some evening in the week, without breaking in on the business of life; I shall therefore, my sisters, either be here, or where you shall be publicly acquainted with: I will not mind being reproached or despised: the men of this world may use what language the please; they may say I am a Methodist. Indeed, my sisters, I am resolved, by the grace of God, to use all methods I can, to pluck you from Satan, that you may be as brands plucked from the burning fire: this shall be my method, which I hope will be the means of effectually having your precious and immortal souls.

And if I am the instrument of this, I shall rejoice, yea, and I will rejoice in spite of what men, or devils, can say or do to the contrary: and may the Lord Jesus Christ direct, and assist me at all times, to act what will be most for is glory, and the welfare of your souls: and may you all say a hearty Amen thereto.

"Now the Lord Jesus Christ, who is God over all, blessed for ever, assist and watch over you, keep you from all evil and sin here, and present you before his Father faultless at the great day of account! To this Lord Jesus Christ, the Father , and the blessed Spirit, three persons and but one eternal and invisible God, be ascribed all honor, power, glory, might, majesty and dominion, now, henceforth, and for ever more. Amen, Amen."

"The grace of our Lord Jesus Christ, the love of God, and the fellowship of the Holy Ghost be with you all, to comfort under, and deliver you from tribulation; to preserve you to your respective place of abode; and when there, to keep you in his fear, that you may live to his glory; that to live may be Christ's, and to die by your eternal gain; so that you may live with him through eternal ages, and sing Hallelujahs to him for ever. Amen."

6. Britain's Mercies, and Britain's Duty

Psalm 55:45—"That they might observe his statutes and keep his laws."

Men, brethren, and fathers, and all ye to whom I am about to preach the kingdom of God, I suppose you need not be informed, that being indispensably obliged to be absent on your late thanksgiving day, I could not show my obedience to the governor's proclamation, as my own inclination led me, or as might justly be expected from, and demanded of me. But as the occasion of that day's thanksgiving is yet, and I trust ever will be, fresh in our memory, I cannot think that a discourse on that subject can even now be altogether unseasonable. I take it for granted, further, that you need not be informed, that among the various motives which are generally urged to enforce obedience to the divine commands, that of love is the most powerful and cogent. The terrors of the law ma affright and awe, but love dissolves and melts the heart. "The love of Christ," says the great apostle of the Gentiles, "constraineth us." Nay, love is so absolutely necessary for those that name the name of Christ, that without it, their obedience cannot truly be stiled evangelical, or be acceptable in the sight of God. "Although, (says the apostle) I bestow all my goods to feed the poor, and though I give my body to be burnt, and have not charity," (i.e. unless unfeigned love to God, and to mankind for his great name's sake, be the principle of such actions, howsoever it may benefit others) it profiteth me nothing." This is the constant language of the lively oracles of God. And, from them it is equally plain, that nothing has a greater tendency to beget and excite such an obediential love in us, than a serious and frequent consideration of the manifold mercies we receive time after time from the bands of our heavenly Father. The royal psalmist, who had the honor of being stiled, "the man after God's own heart," had an abundant experience of this. Hence it is, that whilst he is musing on the divine goodness, the fire of divine love kindles in his soul; and, out of the abundance of his heart, his mouth speaketh such grateful and ecstatic language as this, "What shall I render unto the Lord for all his mercies? Bless the Lord, O my soul, and all that is within me, bless his holy name." And why? "who forgiveth all thine iniquities, who healeth all thy diseases, who redeemeth thy life from destruction, who crowneth thee with loving kindness and tender mercies." And when the same holy man of God had a mind to stir up the people of the Jews to set about a national reformation, as the most weighty and prevailing argument he could make use of for that purpose, he lays before them, as it were, in a draught, many national mercies, and distinguishing deliverances, which have been conferred upon and wrought out for them, by the most high God. The psalm to which the words of our text belong, is a pregnant proof of this; it being a kind of epitome or compendium of the whole Jewish history: at least it contains an enumeration of man signal and extraordinary blessings the Israelites had received from God, and also the improvement they were in duty bound to make of them, "Observe his statues and keep his laws."

To run through all the particulars of the psalm, or draw a parallel (which might with great ease and justice be done) between God's dealings with us and the Israelites of old; To enumerate all the national mercies bestowed upon, and remarkable deliverances wrought out for the kingdoms of Great Britain and Ireland, from the infant state of William the Norman to their present manhood, and more than Augustan, under the auspicious reign of our rightful Sovereign King George the second; howsoever pleasing and profitable it might be at any other time, would, at this juncture, prove, if not an irksome, yet an unreasonable undertaking.

The occasion of the late solemnity, I mean the suppression of a most horrid and unnatural rebellion, will afford more than sufficient matter for a discourse of this nature, and furnish us with abundant motives to love and obey that glorious Jehovah, who giveth salvation unto kings, and delivers his people from the hurtful sword.

Need I make an apology, before this auditory, if, in order to see the greatness of our late deliverance, I should remind you of the many unspeakable blessings which we have for a course of years enjoyed, during the reign of his present Majesty, and the gentle, mile administration under which we live? Without justly incurring the censure of giving flattering titles, I believe all who have eyes to see, and ears to hear, and are but a little acquainted with our public affairs, must acknowledge, that we have one of the best of Kings. It is now above nineteen years since he began to reign over us. And yet, was he seated on a royal throne, and were all his subjects placed before him, was he to address them as Samuel once addressed the Israelites, "Behold here I am, old and gray-headed, witness against me before the Lord, whose ox have I taken? Or whose ass have I taken? Or whom have I defrauded? Whom have I oppressed?" They must, if they would do him justice, make the same answer as was given to Samuel, "Thou hast not defrauded us, nor oppressed us." What Tertulius, by way of flattery, said to Felix, may with the strictest justice be applied to our sovereign, "By thee we enjoy great quietness, and very worthy deeds have been done unto our nation by thy providence." He has been indeed Peter Patria, a father to our country, and though old and gray-headed, has jeopardized his precious life for us in the high places of the field. Nor has he less deserved the great and glorious title, which the Lord promises, that kings should sustain in the latter days, I mean, "a nursing father of the church." For not only the Church of

England, as by law established, but all denominations of Christians whatsoever, have enjoyed their religious as well as civil liberties. As there has been no authorized oppression in the state, so there has been no publicly allowed persecution in the church. We breathe indeed in free air? As free (if not better) both as to temporals and spirituals, as any nation under heaven. Nor is the prospect likely to terminate in his majesty's death, which I pray God to defer. Our princesses are disposed of to Protestant powers. And we have great reason to be assured, that the present heir apparent, and his consort, are like minded with their royal father. And I cannot help thinking, that it is a peculiar blessing vouchsafed us by the King of kings, that his present Majesty has been continued so long among us. For now, his immediate successor (though his present situation obliges him, as it were, to lie dormant) has great and glorious opportunities, which we have reason to think he daily improves, of observing and weighing the national affairs, considering the various steps and turns of government, and consequently of laying in a large fund of experience, to make him a wise and great prince, if ever God should call him to sway the British scepter. Happy art thou, O England! Happy art thou, O America, who on every side art thus highly favored!

But, alas! How soon would this happy scene have shifted, and a melancholy gloomy prospect have succeeded in its room, had the revels gained their point, and a popish abjured pretender been forced upon the British throne! For, supposing his birth not to be spurious, (as we have great reason to think it really was) what could we expect from one, descended from a father, who, when Duke of York, put all Scotland into confusion; and afterwards, when crowned King of England, for his arbitrary and tyrannical government, both in church and state, was justly obliged to abdicate the throne, by the assertors of British liberty? Or, supposing the horrid plot, first hatched in hell, and afterwards nursed at Rome, had taken place? Supposing, I say, the old Pretender should have obtained the triple crown, and have transferred his pretended title (as it is reported he has done) to his eldest son, what was all this for, but that, by being advanced to the popedom, he might rule both son and subjects with less control, and by their united interest, keep the three kingdoms of England, Scotland, and Ireland, in greater vassalage to the see of Rome? Ever since this unnatural rebellion broke out, I have looked upon the young Pretender as the phaeton (vehicle) of the present age. He is ambitiously and presumptuously aiming to seat himself in the throne of our rightful sovereign King George, which he is no more capable of keeping, than Phaetan was to guide the chariot of the sun; and had he succeeded in his attempt, like him, would only have set the world on fire. It is true, to do him justice, he has deserved well of the Church of Rome, and, in all probability, will hereafter be canonized amongst the noble order of their fictitious saints. But, with what an iron rod we might expect to have been bruised, had his troops been victorious, may easily be gathered from these cruel orders said to be found in the pockets of some of his officers, "Give no quarters to the Elector's troops." Add to this, that there was great reason to suspect, that, upon the first news of the success of the rebels, a general massacre was intended. So that if the Lord had not been on our side, Great Britain, not to say America, would, in a few weeks or months, have been an Akeldama, a field of blood.

Besides, was a Popish pretender to rule over us, instead of being represented by a free parliament, and governed by laws made by their consent, as we now are; we should shortly have had only the shadow of one, and it may be no parliament at all. This is the native product of a Popish government, and what the unhappy family, from which this young adventurer pretends he descended, has always aimed at. Arbitrary principles he has sucked in with his mother's milk, and if he had been so honest, instead of that immature motto upon his standard, Tandem triumphant, only to have put, Sret pro ratient Vahmitat, he had given us a short, but true portrait of the nature of his intended, but blessed be God, now defeated reign. And why should I mention, that the sinking of the national debt, or rending away the funded property of the people, and the dissolution of the present happy union between the two kingdoms, would have been the immediate consequences of his success, as he himself declares in his second manifesto, dated from Holy-read House? These are evils, and great ones too; but then they are only evils of a temporary nature. They chiefly concern the body, and must necessarily terminate in the grave.

But, alas! What an inundation of spiritual mischiefs, would soon have overflowed the Church, and what unspeakable danger should we and our posterity have been reduced to in respect to our better parts, our precious and immortal souls? How soon would whole swarms of monks, dominicans and friars, like so many locusts, have overspread and plagued the nation; with what winged speed would foreign titular bishops have posted over, in order to take possession of their respective fees? How quickly would our universities have been filled with youths who have been sent abroad by their Popish parents, in order to drink in all the superstitions of the church of Rome? What a speedy period would have been put to societies of all kinds, for promoting Christian knowledge, and propagating the gospel in foreign parts? How soon would have our pulpits have every where been filled with these old antichristian doctrines, free-will, meriting by works, transubstantiation, purgatory, works of supererogation, passive-obedience, non-resistance, and all the other abominations of the whore of Babylon? How soon would our Protestant charity schools in England, Scotland and Ireland, have been pulled down, our Bibles forcibly taken from us, and ignorance every where set up as the mother of devotion? How soon should we have been deprived of that invaluable blessing, liberty of conscience, and been obliged to commence (what they falsely call) catholics, or submit to all the tortures which a bigoted zeal, guided by the most cruel principles, could possibly invent? How soon would that mother of harlots have made herself once more drunk with the blood of the saints? And the whole tribe even of free-thinkers themselves, been brought to this dilemma, either to die martyrs for (although I never yet heard of one that did so) or, contrary to all their most avowed principles, renounce their great Diana, unassisted, unenlightened reason? But I must have done, lest while I am speaking against antichrist, I should unawares fall myself, and lead my hearers into an antichristian spirit. True and undefiled religion will regulate our zeal, and teach us to treat even the man of sin with no harsher language than that which the angel gave to his grand employer Satan, "The Lord rebuke thee."

Glory be to God's great name! The Lord has rebuked him; and that too at a time when we had little reason to expect such a blessing at God's hands. My dear hearers, neither the present frame of my heart, nor the occasion of your late solemn meeting, lead me to give you a detail of our public vices. Though, alas! They are so many, so notorious, and withal of such a crimson-dye, that a gospel minister would not be altogether inexcusable, was he, even on such a joyful occasion, to lift up his voice like a trumpet, to show the British nation their transgression, and the people of America their sin. However, though I would not cast a dismal shade upon the pleasing picture the cause of our late rejoicings set before us; yet thus much may, and ought to be said, that as God has not dealt so bountifully with any people as with us, so no nation under heaven has dealt more ungratefully with Him. We have been like Capernaum, lifted up to heaven in privileges, and for the abuse of them, like her, have deserved to be thrust down into hell. How well soever it may be with us, in respect to our civil and ecclesiastical constitution, yet in regard to our morals, Isaiah's description of the Jewish polity is too applicable, "The whole head is sick, the whole heart is faint; from the crown of the head to the sole of our feet, we are full of wounds and bruises, and putrifying sores." We have, Jeshurun-like, waxed fat and kicked. *We* have played the harlot against God, both in regard to principles and practices. "Our gold is become dim, and our fine gold changed." We have crucified the Son of God afresh, and put him to an open shame. Nay, Christ has been wounded in the house of his friends. And every thing long ago seemed to threaten an immediate storm. But, O the long-suffering and goodness of God to us-ward! When all things seemed ripe for destruction, and matters were come to such a crisis, that God's praying people began to think, that though Noah, Daniel and Job, were living, they would only deliver their own souls; yet then in the midst of judgment the Most High remembered mercy, and when a popish enemy was breaking in upon us like a flood, the Lord himself graciously lifted up a standard.

This to me does not seem to be one of the most unfavorable circumstances which have attended this mighty deliverance; nor do I think you will look upon it as a circumstance altogether unworthy your observation. Had this cockatrice indeed been crushed in the egg, and the young Pretender driven back upon his first arrival, it would undoubtedly have been a great blessing. But not so great as that for which you lately assembled to give God thanks; for then his Majesty would not have had so good an opportunity of knowing his enemies, or trying his friends. The British subjects would in a manner have lost the fairest occasion that ever offered to express their loyalty and gratitude to the rightful sovereign. France would not have been so greatly humbled; nor such an effectual stop have been put, as we trust there now is, to any such further Popish plot, to rob us of all that is near and dear to us. "Out of the eater therefore hath come forth meat, and out of the strong hath come forth sweetness." The Pretender's eldest son is suffered not only to land in the North-West Highlands in Scotland, but in a little while he becomes a great band. This for a time is not believed, but treated as a thing altogether incredible. The friends of the government in those parts, not for want of loyalty, but of sufficient authority to take up arms, could not resist him. He is permitted to pass on with his terrible banditti, and, like the comet that was lately seen, spreads his baleful influences all around him. He is likewise permitted to gain a short-lived triumph by a victory over a body of our troops at Prestan-Pans, and to take a temporary possession of the metropolis of Scotland. Of this he makes his boast, and informs the public, that "Providence had hitherto favored him with wonderful success, led him in the way to victory, and to the capital of the ancient kingdom, though he came without foreign aid." Nay, he is further permitted to press into the very heart of England. But now the Almighty interposes. Hitherto he was to go, and no further. Here were his malicious designs to be staid. His troops of s sudden are driven back. Away they post to the Highlands, and there they are suffered not only to increase, but also to collect themselves into a large body, that having, as it were, what Caligula once wished Rome had, but one neck, they might be cut off with one blow.

This time, manner, and instruments of this victory, deserves our notice. It was on a general fast-day, when the clergy and good people of Scotland were lamenting the disloyalty of their persidious countrymen, and, like Moses, lifting up their hands, that Amalek might not prevail. The victory was total and decisive. Little blood was spilt on the side of the Royalists. And, to crown all, Duke William, his Majesty's youngest son, has the honor of first driving back, and then defeating the rebel-army. A prince, who in his infancy and youth, gave early proofs of an uncommon bravery and nobleness of mind; a prince, whose courage has increased with his years. Who returned wounded from the battle of Dettingen, behaved with surprising bravery at Fontenoy, and now, by a conduct and magnanimity becoming the high office he sustains, like his glorious predecessor the Prince of Orange, has delivered three kingdoms from the dread of popish cruelty, and arbitrary power. What renders it still more remarkable is, The day on which his Highness gained this victory, was the day after his birthday, when he was entering on the 26th year of his age; and when Sullivan, one of the Pretender's privy-council, like another Abitaphel, advised the rebels to give our soldiers battle, presuming they were surfeited and over-charged with their yesterday's rejoicings, and consequently unfit to make any great stand against them. But, glory be to God, who catches the wise in their own craftiness! His counsel, like Ahitaphel's, proves abortive. Both General and soldiers were prepared to meet them. "God taught their hands to war, and their fingers to fight," and brought the Duke, after a deserved slaughter of some thousands of the rebels, with most of his brave soldiers, victorious from the field.

If we then take a distinct view of this notable transaction, and trace it in all the particular circumstances that have attended it, I believe we must with one heart and voice confess, that if it be a mercy for a state to be delivered from a worse than a Catiline's conspiracy, or a church to be rescued from a hotter than a Dioclestan persecution; if it be a mercy to be delivered from a religion that turns plough-shares into swords, and pruning-hooks into spears, and makes it meritorious to shed Protestant blood; if it be a mercy to have all our present invaluable privileges, both in church and state secured to us more than ever; if it be a mercy to have these great things done for us, at a season, when for our crying sins, both church and state justly deserved to be overturned; and if it be a mercy to have all this brought about for us, under God, by one of the blood-royal, a prince acting with an experience far above his years; if any, or all of these are mercies, then have you lately commemorated one of the greatest mercies that ever the glorious God vouchsafed to the British nation.

And shall we not rejoice and give thanks? Should we refuse, would not the stones cry out against us? Rejoice then we may and ought: but, O let our rejoicing be in the Lord, and run in a religious channel. This, we find, has been the practice of God's people in all ages. When he was pleased, with a mighty hand, and out-stretched arm to lead the Israelites through the Red Sea, as on dry ground, "Then sang Moses and the children of Israel; and Miriam the prophetess, the sister of Aaron, took a timbrel in her hand, and all the women went out after her. And Miriam answered them, Sing ye to the Lord; for he hath triumphed gloriously." When God subdued Jabin, the King of Canaan, before the children of Israel, "then sang Deborah and Barak on that day, saying, "Praise ye the Lord for the avenging of Israel." When the ark was brought back out of the hands of the Philistines, David, though a king, danced before it. And, to mention but one instance more, which may serve as a general directory to us on this and such-like occasions: when the great Head of the church had rescued his people from the general massacre intended to be executed upon them by a cruel and ambitious Haman, "Mordecai sent letters unto all the Jews that were in all the provinces of the King Ahaserus, both nigh and far, to establish among them, that they should keep the fourteenth day of the month Adar, and the fifteenth day of the same yearly, as the days wherein the Jews rested from their enemies, and the month which was turned unto them from sorrow unto joy, and from mourning into a good day: that they should make them days of feasting and joy, and of sending portions one to another, and gifts to the poor." And why should wee not to and do likewise?

And shall we not also, on such an occasion, express our gratitude to, and make honorable mention of, those worthies who have signalized themselves, and been ready to sacrifice both lives and fortunes at this critical juncture?

This would be to act the part of those ungrateful Israelites, who are branded in the book of God, for not showing kindness to the house of "Jerub-Baal, namely Gideon, according to all the goodness which he showed unto Israel." Even a Pharaoh could prefer a deserving Joseph, Ahasuerus a Mordecai, and Nebuchadnezzar a Daniel, when made instruments of signal service to themselves and people. "My heart, says Deborah, is towards (i.e. I have a particular veneration and regard for) the Governors of Israel that offered themselves willingly. And blessed above women shall Jael the wife of Heber the Kenite be; for she put her hand to the nail, and her right hand to the workman's hammer, and with the hammer she smote Sisera, she smote off his head, when she had pierced and stricken through his temples." And shall we not say, "Blessed above men let his Royal Highness the Duke of Cumberland be; for through his instrumentality, the great and glorious Jehovah hath brought might things to pass?" Should not our hearts be towards the worthy Archbishop of Tirk, the Royal Hunters, and those other English heroes who offered themselves so willingly? Let the names of Blakeney, Bland and Rea, and all those who waxed valiant in fight on this important occasion, live for ever in the British annals. And let the name of that great, that incomparable brave soldier of the King, and a good soldier of Jesus Christ, Colonel Gardiner, (excuse me if I here drop a tear; he was my intimate friend) let his name, I say, be had in everlasting remembrance.

But, after all, is there not an infinitely greater debt of gratitude and praise due from us, on this occasion, to Him that is higher than the highest, even the King of kings and Lord of Lords, the blessed and only Potentate? Is not his arm, his strong and mighty arm, (what instruments soever may have been made use of) that hath brought us this salvation? And may I not therefore address you, in the exulting language of the beginning of this psalm, from which we have taken our text? "O give thanks unto the Lord, call upon his name, make known his deeds among the people. Sing unto Him; sing psalms unto him; talk ye of all his wondrous works; glory ye in his holy name; remember his marvelous work which he hath done."

But shall we put off our good and gracious benefactor with mere lip-service? God forbid. Your worthy Governor has honored God in his late excellent proclamation, and God will honor him. But shall our thanks terminate with the day? No, in no wise. Our text reminds us of a more noble sacrifice, and points out to us the great end the Almighty Jehovah proposes, in bestowing such signal favors upon a people, "That they should observe his statutes, and keep his laws."

This is the return we are all taught to pray, that we may make to the Most High God, the Father of mercies, in the daily office or our church, "That our hearts may be unfeignedly thankful, and that we may show forth his praise, not only with our lips, but in our lives, by giving up ourselves to his service, and by walking before him in holiness and righteousness all our days." O that these words were the real language of all the use them! O that these were in us such a mind! How soon would our enemies then flee before us? And God, even our own God, would yet give us more abundant blessings!

And why should not we "observe God's statutes, and keep his laws?" Dare we say, that any of his commands are grievous? Is not Christ's yoke, to a renewed soul, as far as renewed, easy; and his burden comparatively light? May I not appeal to the most refined reasoner whether the religion of Jesus Christ be not a social religion? Whether the Moral Law, as explained by the Lord Jesus in the gospel, has not a natural tendency to promote the present good and happiness of a whole commonwealth, supposing they were obedient to them, as well as the happiness of every individual? From when come wars and fighting amongst us? From what fountain do all those evil, which the present and past ages have groaned under, flow, but from a neglect of the laws and statues of our great and all-wise law-giver Jesus of Nazareth? Tell me, ye men of letters, whether Lycurgus or Solon, Pythagoras or Plato, Aristotle, Seneca, Cicero, or all the ancient lawgivers and heathen moralists, put them all together, ever published a system of ethics, any way worthy to be compared with the glorious system laid down in that much despised book, (to use Sir Richard Steel's expression) emphatically called, the Scriptures? Is not the divine image and superscription written upon every precept of the gospel? Do they not shine with a native intrinsic luster? And, though many things in them are above, yet, is there any thing contrary to the strictest laws of right reason? Is not Jesus Christ, in scripture, stiled the Word, the Logos, the Reason? And is not his service a reasonable service? What if there be mysteries in his religion? Are they not without all controversy great and glorious? Are they not mysteries of godliness, and worthy of that God who reveals them? Nay, is it not the greatest mystery, that men, who pretend to reason, and call themselves philosophers, who search into the arcana natura, and consequently find a mystery in every blade of grass, should yet be so irrational as to decry all mysteries in religion? Where is the scribe? Where is the wise? Where is the disputer against the Christian revelation? Does not every thing without and within us, conspire to prove its divine original? And would not self-interest, if there was no other motive, excite us to observe God's statutes, and keep his laws?

Besides, considered as a Protestant people, do we not lie under the greatest obligations of any nation under heaven, to pay a cheerful, unanimous, universal, persevering obedience to the divine commands.

The wonderful and surprising manner of God's bringing about a Reformation, in the reign of King Henry the Eighth; his carrying it on in the blessed reign of King Edward the Sixth; his delivering us out of the bloody hands of Queen Mary, and destroying the Spanish invincible armada, under her immediate Protestant successor Queen Elizabeth, his discovery of the popish plot under King James; the glorious revolution by King William, and, to come nearer to our own times, his driving away four thousand five hundred Spaniards, from a weak (though important) frontier colony, when they had, in a manner, actually taken possession of it; his giving us Louisbourg, one of the strongest fortresses of our enemies, contrary to all human probability, but the other day, into our hands: these, I say, with the victory which you have lately been commemorating, are such national mercies, not to mention any more, as will render us utterly inexcusable, if they do not produce a national Reformation, and incite us all, with one heart, to keep God's statutes, and observe his laws.

Need I remind you further, in order to excite in you a greater diligence to comply with the intent of the text, that though the storm, in a great measure, is abated by his Royal Highness's late success, yet we dare not say, it is altogether blown over?

The clouds may again return after the rain; and the few surviving rebels (which I pray God avert) may yet be suffered to make head against us. We are still engaged in a bloody, and, in all probability, a tedious war, with two of the most inveterate enemies to the interests of Great-Britain. And, though I cannot help thinking, that their present intentions are so iniquitous, their conduct so persidious, and their schemes so directly derogatory to the honor of the Most High God, that he will certainly humble them in the end, yet, as all things in this life happen alike to all, they may for a time, be dreadful instruments of scourging us. If not, God has other arrows in his quiver to smite us with, besides the French King, his Catholic Majesty, or an abjured Pretender. Not only the sword, but plague, pestilence, and famine, are under the divine command. Who knows but he may say to them all, "Pass through these lands?" A fatal murrain has lately swept away abundance of cattle at home and abroad. A like epidemical disease may have a commission to seize our persons as well as our beasts. Thus God dealt with the Egyptians: who dare say, he will not deal so with us? Has he not already given some symptoms of it? What great numbers upon the continent have been lately taken off by the bloody-flux, small-pox, and yellow-fever? Who can tell what further judgments are yet in store? However, this is certain, the rod is yet hanging over us: and I believe it will be granted on all sides, that if such various dispensations of mercy and judgment do not teach the inhabitants of any land to learn righteousness, they will only ripen them for a greater ruin. Give my leave, therefore, to dismiss you at this time with that solemn awful warning and exhortation, with which the venerable Samuel, on a public occasion, took leave of the people of Israel: "Only fear the Lord, and serve him in truth, with all your heart: for consider how great things he hath done for you. But if ye shall still do wickedly, [I will not say as the Prophet did, You shall be consumed; but] ye know not but you may provoke the Lord Almighty to consume both you and your king." Which God of his infinite mercy prevent, for the sake of Jesus Christ: to whom, with the Father, and the Holy Ghost, three persons, but one God, be all honor and glory, now and for evermore. Amen, Amen.

7. Thankfulness for Mercies Received, a Necessary Duty

Numberless marks does man bear in his soul, that he is fallen and estranged from God; but nothing gives a greater proof thereof, than that backwardness, which every one finds within himself, to the duty of praise and thanksgiving.

When God placed the first man in paradise, his soul no doubt was so filled with a sense of the riches of the divine love, that he was continually employing that breath of life, which the Almighty had not long before breathed into him, in blessing and magnifying that all-bountiful, all gracious God, in whom he lived, moved, and had his being.

And the brightest idea we can form of the angelical hierarchy above, and the spirits of just men made perfect, is, that they are continually standing round the throne of God, and cease not day and night, saying, "Worthy art thou, O Lamb that wast slain, to receive power and riches, and wisdom, and strength, and honor, and glory, and blessing." Rev. 5:12.

That then, which was man's perfection when time first began, and will be his employment when death is swallowed up in victory, and time shall be no more, without controversy, is part of our perfection, and ought to be our frequent exercise on earth: and I doubt not but those blessed spirits, who are sent forth to minister to them who shall be heirs of salvation, often stand astonished when they encamp around us, or find our hearts so rarely enlarged, and our mouths so seldom opened, to show forth the loving-kindness of the Lord, or to speak of all his praise.

Matter for praise and adoration, can never be wanting to creatures redeemed by the blood of the Son of God; and who have such continual scenes of his infinite goodness presented to their view, that were their souls duly affected with a sense of his universal love, they could not but be continually calling on heaven and earth, men and angels, to join with them in praising and blessing that "high and lofty one, who inhabiteth eternity, who maketh his sun to shine on the evil and on the good," and daily pours down his blessings on the whole race of mankind.,

But few are arrived to such a degree of charity or love, as to rejoice with those that do rejoice, and to be as thankful for other mercies, as their own. This part of Christian perfection, though begun on earth, will be consummated only in heaven; where our hearts will glow with such fervent love towards God and one another, that every fresh degree of glory communicated to our neighbor, will also communicate to us a fresh topic of thankfulness and joy.

That which has the greatest tendency to excite the generality of fallen men to praise and thanksgiving, is a sense of God's private mercies, and particular benefits bestowed upon ourselves. For as these come nearer our own hearts, so they must be more affecting: and as they are peculiar proofs, whereby we may know, that God does in a more especial manner favor us above others, so they cannot but sensibly touch us; and if our hearts are not quite frozen, like coals of a refiner's fire, they must melt us down into thankfulness and love. It was a consideration of the distinguishing favor God had shown to his chosen people Israel, and the frequent and remarkable deliverance wrought by him in behalf of "hose who go down to the Sea in ships, and occupy their business in great matters," that made the holy Psalmist break out so frequently as he does in this psalm, into this moving, pathetical exclamation, "that men would therefore praise the Lord for his goodness, and declare the wonders that he doeth for the children of men!"

His expressing himself in so fervent a manner, implies both the importance and neglect of the duty. As when Moses in another occasion cried out, "O that they were wise, that they understood this, that they would practically consider their latter end!" Deut. 32:29.

I say, importance and neglect of the duty; for out of those man thousands that receive blessings from the Lord, how few give thanks in remembrance of his holiness? The account given us of the ungrateful lepers, is but too lively a representation of the ingratitude of mankind in general; who like them, when under any humbling providence, can cry, "Jesus, Master, have mercy on us!" Luke 17:13. But when healed of their sickness, or delivered from their distress, scarce one in ten can be found "returning to give thanks to God."

And yet as common as this sin of ingratitude is, there is nothing we ought more earnestly to pray against. For what is more absolutely condemned in holy scripture than ingratitude? Or what more peremptorily (absolutely, emphatically) required than the contrary temper? Thus says the Apostle, "Rejoice evermore; in every thing give thanks," 1 Thes. 5:16, "Be careful for nothing; but in every thing by prayer and supplication, with thanksgiving, let your requests be made known unto God," Phil. 4:6.

On the contrary, the Apostle mentions it as one of the highest crimes of the Gentiles, that they were not thankful. "Neither were they thankful," Rom. 1:21. As also in another place, he numbers the "unthankful," Tim. 3:2 amongst those unholy, profane person, who are to have their portion in the lake of fire and brimstone.

As for our sins, God puts them behind his back; but his mercies he will have acknowledged, "There is virtue gone out of me," says Jesus Christ, Luke 8:46 and the woman who was cured of her bloody issue, must confess it. And we generally find, when God sent any remarkable punishment upon a particular person, he reminded him of the favors he had received, as so many aggravations of his ingratitude. Thus when God was about to visit Eli's house, he thus expostulates with him by his prophet: "Did I plainly appear unto the house of thy fathers, when they were in Egypt, in Pharaoh's house? And did I choose him out of all the tribes of Israel, to be my priest, to offer upon mine altar, to burn incense, and to wear an ephod before me? Wherefore kick ye at my sacrifice, and at mine offering, which I have commanded in my habitation, and honorest thy sons above me; so make yourselves fat with the chiefest of all the offerings of Israel my people? Wherefore the Lord God of Israel saith, I said indeed, that thy house, and the house of thy father, should walk before me for ever; but now the Lord saith, Be it far from me, for them that honor me will I honor, and they that despise me shall be lightly esteemed" 2 Sam. 2:27–30.

It was this and such like instances of God's severity against the unthankful, that inclined me to choose the words of the text, as the most proper subject I could discourse on at this time.

Four months, my good friends, we have now been upon the sea in this ship, and "have occupied our business in the great waters." At God Almighty's word, we have seen "the stormy wind arise, which hath lifted up the waves thereof. We have been carried up to the heaven, and down again to the deep, and some of our souls melted away because of the trouble; but I trust we cried earnestly unto the Lord, and he delivered us out of our distress. For he made the storm to cease; so that the waves thereof were still. And now we are glad, because we are at rest, for God hath brought us to the haven where we would be. O that you would therefore praise the Lord for his goodness, and declare the wonders that he hath done for us, the unworthiest of the sons of men."

Thus Moses, thus Joshua behaved. For when they were about to take their leave of the children of Israel, they recounted to them what great things God had done for them, as the best arguments and motives they could urge to engage them to obedience. And how can I copy after better examples? What fitter, what more noble motives, to holiness and purity of living, can I lay before you, than they did?

Indeed, I cannot say, that we have seen the "pillar of a cloud by day, or a pillar of fire by night," going visibly before us to guide our course; but this I can say, that the same God who was in that pillar of a cloud, and pillar of fire, which departed not from the Israelites, and who has made the sun to rule the day, and the moon to rule the night, has, by his good providence, directed us in our right way, or else the pilot had steered us in vain.

Neither can I say, That we have seen the "sun stand still," as the children of Israel did in the days of Joshua. But surely God, during part of our voyage, has caused it to withhold some of that heat, which it usually sends forth in these warmer climates, or else it had not failed, but some of you must have perished in the sickness that has been, and does yet continue among us.

We have not seen the waters stand purposely on an heap, that we might pass through, neither have we been pursued by Pharaoh and his host, and delivered out of their hands; but we have been led through the sea as through a wilderness, and were once remarkably preserved from being run down by another ship; which had God permitted, the waters, in all probability, would immediately have overwhelmed us, and like Pharaoh and his host, we should have sunk, as stones, into the sea.

We may, indeed, atheist like, ascribe all these things to natural causes, and say, "Our own skill and foresight has brought us hither in safety." But as certainly as Jesus Christ, the angel of the covenant, in the days of his flesh, walked upon the water, and said to his sinking disciples, "Be not afraid, it is I," so surely has the same everlasting I AM, "who decketh himself with light as with a garment, who spreadeth out the heavens like a curtain, who claspeth the winds in his fist, who holdeth the waters in the hollow of his hands," and guided the wise men by a star in the east; so surely, I say, has he spoken, and at his command the winds have blown us where we are not arrived. For his providence ruleth all things; "Wind and storms obey his word:" he saith to it at one time, Go, and it goeth; at another, Come, and it cometh; and at a third time, Blow this way, and it bloweth.

It is he, my brethren; and not we ourselves, that has of late sent us such prosperous gales, and made us to ride, as it were, on the wings of the wind, into the haven where we would be.

"O that you would therefore praise the Lord for his goodness," and by your lives declare, that you are truly thankful for the wonders he had shown to us; who are less than the least of the sons of men.

I say, declare it by your lives. For to give him thanks, barely with your lips; while your hearts are far from him, is but a mock sacrifice, nay, an abomination unto the Lord.

This was the end, the royal Psalmist says, God had in view, when he showed such wonders, from time to time, to the people of Israel, "That they might keep his statutes, and observe his laws," Psalm 105:44 and this, my good friends, is the end God would have accomplished in us, and the only return he desires us to make him, for all the benefits he hath conferred upon us.

O then, let me beseech you, give to God your hearts, your whole hearts; and suffer yourselves to be drawn by the cords of infinite love, to honor and obey him.

Assure yourselves you can never serve a better master; for his service is perfect freedom, his yoke, when worn a little while, is exceeding easy, his burden light, and in keeping his commandments there is great reward; love, peace, joy in the Holy Ghost here, and a crown of glory that fadeth not away, hereafter.

You may, indeed, let other lords have dominion over you, and Satan may promise to give you all the kingdoms of the world, and the glory of them, if you will fall down and worship him; but he is a liar, and was so from the beginning; he has not so much to give you, as you may tread on with the soul of your foot; or could he give you the whole world, yea, that could not make you happy without God. It is God alone, my brethren, whose we are, in whose name I now speak, and who has of late showed us such mercies in the deep, that can give solid lasting happiness to your souls; and he for this reason only desires your hearts, because without him you must be miserable.

Suffer me not then to go away without my errand; as it is the last time I shall speak to you, let me not speak in vain; but let a sense of the divine goodness lead you to repentance.

Even Saul, that abandoned wretch, when David showed him his skirt, which he had cut off, when he might have also taken his life, was so melted down with his kindness, that he lifted up his voice and wept. And we must have hearts harder than Saul's, nay, harder than the nether millstone, if a sense of God's late loving kindnesses, notwithstanding he might so often have destroyed us, does not even compel us to lay down our arms against him, and become his faithful servants and soldiers unto our lives end.

If they have not this effect upon us, we shall, of all men, be most miserable; for God is just, as well as merciful; and the more blessings we have received here, the greater damnation, if we do not improve them, shall we incur hereafter.

But God forbid that any of those should ever suffer the vengeance of eternal fire, amongst whom, I have, for these four months, been preaching the gospel of Christ; but yet thus must it be, if you do not improve the divine mercies: and instead of your being my crown of rejoicing in the day of our Lord Jesus Christ, I must appear as a swift witness against you.

But, brethren, I am persuaded better things of you, and things that accompany salvation, though I thus speak.

Blessed be God, some marks of a partial reformation at least, have been visible amongst all you that are soldiers. And my weak, though sincere endeavors, to build you up in the knowledge and fear of God, have not been altogether in vain in the Lord.

Swearing, I hope is, in a great measure, abated with you; and God, I trust, has blessed his late visitations, by making them the means of awakening your consciences, to a more solicitous inquiry about the things which belong to your everlasting peace.

Fulfill you then my joy, by continuing thus minded, and labor to go on to perfection. For I shall have no greater pleasure than to see, or hear, that you walk in the truth.

Consider, my good friends, you are now, as it were, entering on a new world, where you will be surrounded with multitudes of heathens; and if you take not heed to "have your conversation honest amongst them," and to "walk worthy of the holy vocation wherewith you are called," you will act the hellish part of Herod's soldiers over again; and cause Christ's religion, as they did his person, to be had in derision of those that are round about you.

Consider further, what peculiar privileges you have enjoyed, above many others that are entering on the same land. They have had, as it were, a famine of the word, but you have rather been in danger of being surfeited with your spiritual manna. And, therefore, as more instructions have been given you, so from you, men will most justly expect the greater improvement in goodness.

Indeed, I cannot say, I have discharged my duty towards you as I ought. No, I am sensible of many faults in my ministerial office, and for which I have not failed, nor, I hope, ever shall fail, to humble myself in secret before God. However, this I can say, that except a few days that have been spent necessarily on other persons, whom God immediately called me to write and minister unto, and the two last weeks wherein I have been confined by sickness; all the while I have been aboard, I have been either actually engaged in, or preparing myself for instructing you. And though you are now to be committed to the care of another (whose labors I heartily beseech God to bless amongst you) yet I trust I shall, at all seasons, if need be, willingly spend, and be spent, for the good of your souls, though the more abundantly I love you, the less I should be loved.

As for your military affairs, I have nothing to do with them. Fear God, and you must honor the King. Nor am I well acquainted with the nature of that land which you are now come over to protect; only this I may venture to affirm in the general, that you must necessarily expect upon your arrival at a new colony, to meet with many difficulties. But your very profession teaches you to endure hardship; "be not, therefore, faint-hearted, but quit yourselves like men, and be strong," Numb. 14. Be not like those cowardly persons, who were affrighted at the report of the false spies, that came and said, that there were people tall as the Anakims to be grappled with, but be ye like unto Caleb and Joshua, all heart; and say, we will act valiantly, for we shall be more than conquerors over all difficulties through Jesus Christ that loved us. Above all things, my brethren, take heed, and beware of murmuring, like the perverse Israelites, against those that are set over you; and "learn, whatsoever state you shall be in, therewith to be content," Phil. 4:11.

As I have spoken to you, I hope your wives also will suffer the word of exhortation,

Your behavior on shipboard especially the first part of the voyage, I choose to throw a cloak over; for to use them mildest terms, it was not such as became the gospel of our Lord Jesus Christ. However, of late, blessed be God, you have taken more heed to your ways, and some of you have walked all the while, as became "women professing godliness." Let those accept my hearty thanks, and permit me to entreat you all in general, as you are all now married, to remember the solemn vow you made at your entrance into the marriage state, and see that you be subject to your own husbands, in every lawful thing: Beg of God to keep the door of your lips, that you offend not with your tongues; and walk in love, that your prayers be not hindered. You that have children, let it be your chief concern to breed them up in the nurture and admonition of the Lord. And live all of you so holy and unblameable, that you may not so much as be suspected to be unchaste; and as some of you have imitated Mary Magdalen in her sin, strive to imitate her also in her repentance.

As for you, sailors, what shall I say? How shall I address myself to you? How shall I do that which I so much long to do; touch your hearts? Gratitude obliges me to wish thus well to you. For you have often taught me many instructive lessons, and reminded me to put up many prayers to God for you, that you might receive your spiritual sight.

When I have seen you preparing for a storm, and reefing [could also be reesing] your sails to guard against it; how have I wished that you and I were as careful to avoid that storm of God's wrath, which will certainly, without repentance, quickly overtake us? When I have observed you catch at ever fair gale, how I secretly cried, O that we were as careful to know the things that belong to our peace, before they are forever hid from our eyes! And when I have taken notice, how steadily you eyed your compass in order to steer aright, how have I wished, that we as steadily eyed the word of God, which alone can preserve us from "making shipwreck of faith, and a good conscience!" In short, there is scarce anything you do, which has not been a lesson of instruction to me; and, therefore, it would me ungrateful in me, did I not take this opportunity of exhorting you in the name of our Lord Jesus Christ, to be as wise in the things which concern you soul, as I have observed you to be in the affairs belonging to your ship.

I am sensible, that the sea is reckoned but an ill school to learn Christ in: and to see a devout sailor, is esteemed an uncommon a thing, as to see a Saul amongst the prophets. But whence this wondering? Whence this looking upon a godly sailor, as a man to be wondered at, as a speckled bird in the creation? I am sure, for the little time I have come in and out amongst you, and as far as I can judge from the little experience I have had of things, I scarce know any way of life, that is capable of greater improvements than yours.

The continual danger you are in of being overwhelmed by the great waters; the many opportunities you have of beholding God's wonders in the deep; the happy retirement you enjoy from worldly temptations; and the daily occasions that are offered you, to endure hardships, are such noble means of promoting the spiritual life, that were your hearts bent towards God, you would account it your happiest, that his providence has called you, to "go down to the sea in ships, and to occupy your business in the great waters."

The royal Psalmist knew this, and, therefore, in the words of the text, calls more especially on men of your employ, to "praise the Lord for his goodness, and declare the wonders he doeth for the children of men."

And O that you would be wise in time, and hearken to his voice today, "whilst it is called to-day!" For ye yourselves know how little is to be done on a sick bed. God has, in an especial manner, of late, invited you to repentance: two of your crew he has taken off by death, and most of you he has mercifully visited with a grievous sickness. The terrors of the Lord have been upon you, and when burnt with a scorching fever, some of you have cried out, "What shall we do to be saved?" Remember then the resolutions you made, when you thought God was about to take away your souls; and see that according to your promises, you show forth your thankfulness, not only with your lips, but in your lives. For though God may bear long, he will not forbear always; and if these signal mercies and judgments do not lead you to repentance, assure yourselves there will at last come a fiery tempest, from the presence of the Lord, which will sweep away you, and all other adversaries of God.

I am positive, neither you nor the soldiers have wanted, nor will want any manner of encouragement to piety and holiness of living, from those two persons who have here the government over you; for they have been such helps to me in my ministry, and have so readily concurred in every thing for your good, that they may justly demand a public acknowledgment of thanks both from you and me.

Permit me, my honored friends, in the name of both classes of your people, to return you hearty thanks for the ears and tenderness you have expressed for the welfare of their better parts.

As for the private favors you have shown to my person, I hope so deep a sense of them is imprinted on my heart, that I shall plead them before God in prayer, as long as I live.

But I have still stronger obligations to intercede in your behalf. For God, ever adored be his free grace in Christ Jesus! Has set his seal to my ministry in your hearts. Some distant pangs of the new birth I have observed to come upon you; and God forbid that I should sin against the Lord, by ceasing to pray, that the good work begun in your souls, may be carried on till the day of our Lord Jesus Christ.

The time of our departure from each other is not at hand, and you are going out into a world of temptations. But though absent in body, let us be present with each other in spirit; and God, I trust, will enable you to be singularly good, to be ready to be accounted fools for Christ's sake; and then we shall meet never to part again in the kingdom of our Father which is in heaven.

To you, my companions and familiar friends, who came over with me to sojourn in a strange land, do I in the next place address myself. For you I especially fear, as well as for myself, because as we take sweet counsel together oftner than others, and as you are let into a more intimate friendship with me in private life, the eyes of all men will be upon you to note even the minutest miscarriage; and, therefore, it highly concerns you to "walk circumspectly towards those that are without," I hope, that nothing but a single eye to God's glory and the salvation of your own souls, brought you from your native country. Remember than the end of your coming hither, and you can never do amiss. Be patterns of industry, as well as of piety, to those who shall be around you; and above all things let us have such fervent charity amongst ourselves, that it may be said of us, as of the primitive Christians, "See how the Christians love one another."

And now I have been speaking to others particularly, I have one general request to make to all, and that with reference to myself.

You have heard, my dear friends, how I have been exhorting every one of you to show forth your thankfulness for the divine goodness, not only with your lips, but in your lives. But "physician heal thyself," may justly be retorted on me. For (without any false pretenses to humility) I find my own heart so little inclined to this duty of thanksgiving for the benefits I have received, that I had need fear sharing Hezekiah's fate, who because he was lifted up by, and not thankful enough for, the great things God had done for him, was given up a prey to the pride of his own heart.

I need, therefore, and beg your most importunate petitions at the throne of grace, that no such evil may befall me; that the more Go exalts me, the more I may debase myself; and that after I have preached to others, I myself may not be cast away.

And now, brethren, into God's hands I commend your spirits, who, I trust, through his infinite mercies in Christ Jesus, will preserve you blameless, till his second coming to judge the world.

Excuse my detaining you for long; perhaps it is the last time I shall speak to you: my heart is full, and out of the abundance of it, I could continue my discourse until midnight. But I must away to your new world; may God give you new hearts, and enable you to put in practice what you have heard from time to time, to by your duty, and I need not wish you anything better. For then God will so bless you, that "you will build you cities to dwell in; then will you sow your lands and plant vineyards, which will yield you fruits of increase,"

"To which blessed rest, God of his infinite mercy bring us all, through Jesus Christ our Lord! To whom with the Father and Holy Ghost be all honor and glory, might, majesty, and dominion, now, henceforth, and forevermore. Amen, Amen."

8. The Necessity and Benefits of Religious Society

> Eccles. 4:9–12—"Two are better than one, because they have a good reward for their labor. For if they fall, the one will lift up his fellow: but woe be to him that is alone when he falleth; for he hath not another to help him up. Again, if two lie together, then they have heat; but how can one be warm alone? And if one prevail against him, two shall withstand him; and a threefold cord is not quickly broken."

Among the many reasons assignable for the sad decay of true Christianity, perhaps the neglecting to assemble ourselves together, in religious societies, may not be one of the least. That I may therefore do my endeavor towards promoting so excellent a means of piety, I have selected a passage of scripture drawn from the experience of the wisest of men, which being a little enlarged on and illustrated, will fully answer my present design; being to show, in the best manner I can, the necessity and benefits of society in general, and of religious society in particular.

"Two are better than one."

From which words I shall take occasion to prove,

First, The truth of the wise man's assertion, "Two are better than one," and that in reference to society in general, and religious society in particular.

Secondly, To assign some reasons why two are better than one, especially as to the last particular. 1. Because men can raise up one another when they chance to slip: "For if they fall, the one will lift up his fellow." 2. Because they can impart heat to each other: "Again, if tow lie together, then they have heat, but how can one be warm alone?" 3. Because they can secure each other from those that do oppose them: "And if one prevail against him, two shall withstand him; and a threefold cord is not quickly broken." From hence,

Thirdly, I shall take occasion to show the duty incumbent on every member of a religious society.

And *Fourthly*, I shall draw an inference or two from what may be said; and then conclude with a word or two of exhortation.

First, I am to prove the truth of the wise man's assertion, that "two are better than one," and that in reference to society in general, and religious societies in particular.

And how can this be done better, than by showing that it is absolutely necessary for the welfare both of the bodies and souls of men? Indeed, if we look upon man as he came out of the hands of his Maker, we imagine him to be perfect, entire, lacking nothing. But God, whose thoughts are not as our thoughts, saw something still wanting to make Adam happy. And what was that? Why, and help meet for him. For thus speaketh the scripture: "And the Lord God said, It is not good that the man should be alone, I will make an help meet for him."

Observe, God said, "It is not good," thereby implying that the creation would have been imperfect, in some sort, unless an help was found out meet for Adam. And if this was the case of man before the fall; if an help was meet for him in a state of perfection; surely since the fall, when we come naked and helpless out of our mother's womb, when our wants increase with our years, and we can scarcely subsist a day without the mutual assistance of each other, well may we say, "It is not good for man to be alone."

Society then, we see, is absolutely necessary in respect to our bodily and personal wants. If we carry our view farther, and consider mankind as divided into different cities, countries, and nations, the necessity of it will appear yet more evident. For how can communities be kept up, or commerce carried on, without society? Certainly not at all, since providence seems wisely to have assigned a particular product to almost each particular country, on purpose, as it were, to oblige us to be social; and hath so admirably mingled the parts of the whole body of mankind together, "that the eye cannot say to the hand, I have no need of thee; nor again, the hand to the foot, I have no need of thee."

Many other instances might be given of the necessity of society, in reference to our bodily, personal, and national wants. But what are all these when weighed in the balance of the sanctuary, in comparison of the infinite greater need of it, with respect to the soul? It was chiefly in regard to this better part, no doubt, that God said, "It is not good for the man to be alone." For, let us suppose Adam to be as happy as may be, placed as the Lord of the creation in the paradise of God, and spending all his hours in adoring and praising the blessed Author of his being; yet as his soul was the very copy of the divine nature, whose peculiar property it is to be communicative, without the divine all sufficiency he could not be completely happy, because he was alone and incommunicative, nor even content in paradise, for want of a partner in his joys. God knew this, and therefore said, "It is not good that the man shall be alone, I will make a help meet for him."

And though this proved a fatal means of his falling; yet that was not owing to any natural consequence of society; but partly to that cursed apostate, who craftily lies in wait to deceive; partly to Adam's own folly, in rather choosing to be miserable with one he loved, than trust in God to raise him up another spouse.

If we reflect indeed on that familiar intercourse, our first parent could carry on with heaven, in a state of innocence, we shall be apt to think he had as little need of society, as to his soul, as before we supposed him to have, in respect to his body. But yet, as God and the holy angels were so far above him on the one hand, and the beasts so far beneath him on the other, there was nothing like having one to converse with, who was "bone of his bone, and flesh of his flesh."

Man, then, could not be fully happy, we see, even in paradise, without a companion of his own species, much less now he is driven out. For, let us view him a little in his natural estate now, since the fall, as "having his understanding darkened, his mind alienated from the life of God;" as no more able to see his way wherein he should go, than a blind man to describe the sun: that notwithstanding this, he must receive his sight ere he can see God: and that if he never sees him, he never can be happy. Let us view him in this light (or rather than darkness) and deny the necessity of society if we can. A divine revelation we find is absolutely necessary, we being by nature as unable to know, as we are to do our duty. And how shall we learn except one teach us? But was God to do this himself, how should we, but with Moses, exceedingly quake and fear? Nor would the ministry of angels in this affair, be without too much terror. It is necessary, therefore (at least God's dealing with us hath showed it to be so) that we should be drawn with the cords of a man. And that a divine revelation being granted, we should use one another's assistance, under God, to instruct each other in the knowledge, and to exhort one another to the practice of those things which belong to our everlasting peace. This is undoubtedly the great end of society intended by God since the fall, and a strong argument it is, why "two are better than one," and why we should "not forsake the assembling ourselves together."

But further, let us consider ourselves as Christians, as having this natural veil, in some measure, taken off from our eyes by the assistance of God's Holy Spirit, and so enabled to see what he requires of us. Let us suppose ourselves in some degree to have tasted the good word of life, and to have felt the powers of the world to come, influencing and molding our souls into a religious frame: to be fully and heartily convinced that we are soldiers lifted under the banner of Christ, and to have proclaimed open war at our baptism, against the world, the flesh, and the devil; and have, perhaps, frequently renewed our obligations so to do, by partaking of the Lord's supper: that we are surrounded with millions of foes without, and infected with a legion of enemies within: that we are commanded to shine as lights in the world, in the midst of a crooked and perverse generation: that we are traveling to a long eternity, and need all imaginable helps to show, and encourage us in our way thither. Let us, I say, reflect on all this, and then how shall each of us cry out, brethren, what a necessary thing it is to meet together in religious societies?

The primitive Christians were fully sensible of this, and therefore we find them continually keeping up communion with each other: for what says the scripture? They continued steadfastly in the apostle's doctrine and fellowship, Acts 2:42. Peter and John were no sooner dismissed by the great council, than they haste away to their companions. "And being set at liberty they came to their own, and told them all these things which the high priest had said unto them," Acts 4:23. Paul, as soon as converted, "tarried three days with the disciples that were at Damascus." Acts 9:19. And Peter afterwards, when released from prison, immediately goes to the house of Mary, where there were "great multitudes assembled, praying," Acts 12:12. And it is reported of the Christians in after ages, that they used to assemble together before day-light, to sing a psalm to Christ as God. So precious was the Communion of Saints in those days.

If it be asked, what advantages we shall reap from such a procedure now? I answer, much every way. "Two are better than one, because they have a good reward for their labor: for if they fall, the one will lift up his fellow; but woe be to him that is alone when he falleth, for he hath not another to help him up. Again, if two lie together, then they have heat; but how can one be warm alone? And if one prevail against him, two shall withstand him; and a threefold cord is not quickly broken."

Which directly leads me to my *Second* general head, under which I was to assign some reasons why "two are better than one," especially in Religious Society.

1. As man in his present condition cannot always stand upright, but by reason of the frailty of his nature cannot but fall; one eminent reason why two are better than one, or, in other words, one great advantage of religious society is, "That when they fall, the one will lift up his fellow."

And an excellent reason this, indeed! For alas! When we reflect how prone we are to be drawn into error in our judgments, and into vice in our practice; and how unable, at least how very unwilling, to espy or correct our own miscarriages; when we consider how apt the world is to flatter us in our faults, and how few there are so kind as to tell us the truth; what an inestimable privilege must it be to have a set of true, judicious, hearty friends about us, continually watching over our souls, to inform us where we have fallen, and to warn us that we fall not again for the future. Surely it is such a privilege, that (to use the words of an eminent Christian) we shall never know the value thereof, till we come to glory.

But this is not all; for supposing that we could always stand upright, yet whosoever reflects on the difficulties of religion in general, and his own propensity to lukewarmness and indifference in particular, will find that he must be zealous as well as steady, if ever he expects to enter the kingdom of heaven. Here, then, the wise man points out to us another excellent reason why two are better than one. "Again, if two lie together, then they have heat; but how can one be warm alone?" Which was the next thing to be considered.

2. A Second reason why two are better than one, is because they can impart heat to each other.

It is an observation no less true than common, that kindled coals, if placed asunder, soon go out, but if heaped together, quicken and enliven each other, and afford a lasting heat. The same will hold good in the case now before us. If Christians kindled by the grace of God, unite, they will quicken and enliven each other; but if they separate and keep asunder, no marvel if they soon grow cool or tepid. If two are three meet together in Christ's name, they will have heat: but how can one be warm alone?

Observe, "How can one be warm alone?" The wise man's expressing himself by way of question, implies an impossibility, at least a very great difficulty, to be warm in religion without company, where it may be had. Behold here, then, another excellent benefit flowing from religious society; it will keep us zealous, as well as steady, in the way of godliness.

But to illustrate this a little farther by a comparison or two. Let us look upon ourselves (as was above hinted) as soldiers listed under Christ's banner; as going out with "ten thousand, to meet one that cometh against us with twenty thousand;" as persons that are to "wrestle not only with flesh and blood, but against principalities, against powers, and spiritual wickednesses in high places." And then tell me, all ye that fear God, if it be not an invaluable privilege to have a company of fellow soldiers continually about us, animating and exhorting each other to stand our ground, to keep our ranks, and manfully to follow the captain of our salvation, though it be through a sea of blood?

Let us consider ourselves in another view before mentioned, as persons traveling to a long eternity; as rescued by the free grace of God, in some measure, from our natural Egyptian bondage, and marching under the conduct of our spiritual Joshua, through the wilderness of this world, to the land of our heavenly Canaan. Let us farther reflect how apt we are to startle at every difficulty; to cry, "There are lions! There are lions in the way! There are the sons of Anak" to be grappled with, ere we can possess the promised land. How prone we are, with Lot's wife, to look wishfully back on our spiritual Sodom, or, with the foolish Israelites, to long again for the flesh-pots of Egypt; and to return to our former natural state of bondage and slavery. Consider this, my brethren, and see what a blessed privilege it will be to have a set of Israelites indeed about us, always reminding us of the folly of any such cowardly design, and of the intolerable misery we shall run into, if we fall in the least short of the promised land.

More might be said on this particular, did not the limits of a discourse of this nature oblige me to hasten,

3. To give a third reason, mentioned by the wise man in the text, why two are better than one; because they can secure each other from enemies without. "And if one prevail against him, yet two shall withstand him: and a threefold cord is not quickly broken."

Hitherto we have considered the advantages of religious societies, as a great preservative against falling (at least dangerously falling) into sin and lukewarmness, and that too from our own corruptions. But what says the wise son of Sirach? "My son, when thou goest to serve the Lord, prepare thy soul for temptation:" and that not only from inward, but outward foes; particularly from those two grand adversaries, the world and the devil: for no sooner will thine eye be bent heavenward, but the former will be immediately diverting it another way, telling thee thou needest not be singular in order to be religious; that you may be a Christian without going so much out of the common road.

Nor will the devil be wanting in his artful insinuations, or impious suggestions, to divert or terrify thee from pressing forwards, "that thou mayst lay hold on the crown of life." And if he cannot prevail this way, he will try another; and, in order to make his temptation the more undiscerned, but withal more successful, he will employ, perhaps, some of thy nearest relatives, or most powerful friends, (as he set Peter on our blessed Master) who will always be bidding thee to spare thyself; telling thee thou needest not take so much pain; that it is not so difficult a matter to get to heaven as some people would make of it, nor the way so narrow as others imagine it to be.

But see here the advantage of religious company; for supposing thou findest thyself thus surrounded on every side, and unable to withstand such horrid (though seemingly friendly) counsels, haste away to thy companions, and they will teach thee a truer and better lesson; they will tell thee, that thou must be singular if thou wilt be religious; and that it is as impossible for a Christian, as for a city set upon a hill, to be hidden: that if thou wilt be an almost Christian (and as good be none at all) thou mayest live in the same idle, indifferent manner as thou seest most other people do: but if thou wilt be not only almost, but altogether a Christian, they will inform thee thou must go a great deal farther: that thou must not only faintly seek, but "earnestly strive to enter in at the strait gate:" that there is but one way now to heaven as formerly, even through the narrow passage of a sound conversion: and that in order to bring about this mighty work, thou must undergo a constant, but necessary discipline of fasting, watching, and prayer. And therefore, the only reason why those friends give thee such advice, is, because they are not willing to take to much pains themselves; or, as our Savior told Peter on a like occasion, because they "savor not the things that be of God, but the things that be of men."

This then, is another excellent blessing arising from religious society, that friends can hereby secure each other from those who oppose them. The devil is fully sensible of this, and therefore he has always done his utmost to suppress, and put a stop to the communion of saints. This was his grand artifice at the first planting of the gospel; to persecute the professors of it, in order to separate them. Which, though God, as he always will, over-ruled for the better; yet, it shows, what an enmity he has against Christians assembling themselves together. Nor has he yet left off his old stratagem; it being his usual way to entice us by ourselves, in order to tempt us; where, by being destitute of one another's help, he hopes to lead us captive at his will.

But, on the contrary, knowing his own interest is strengthened by society, he would first persuade us to neglect the communion of saints, and then bid us "stand in the way of sinners," hoping thereby to put us into the seat of the scornful. Judas and Peter are melancholy instances of this. The former had no sooner left his company at supper, but he went out and betrayed his master: and the dismal downfall of the latter, when he would venture himself amongst a company of enemies, plainly shows us what the devil will endeavor to, when he gets us by ourselves. Had Peter kept his own company, he might have kept his integrity; but a single cord, alas! how quickly was it broken? Our blessed Savior knew this full well, and therefore it is very observable, that he always sent out his disciples "two by two."

And now, after so many advantages to be reaped from religious society, may we not very justly cry out with the wise man in my text, "Woe be to him that is alone; for when he falleth, he hath not another to lift him up!" When he is cold, he hath not a friend to warm him; when he is assaulted, he hath not a second to help him to withstand his enemy.

III. I now come to my third general head, under which was to be shown the sever duties incumbent on every member of a religious society, as such, which are three. 1. Mutual reproof; 2. Mutual exhortation; 3. Mutual assisting and defending each other.

1. Mutual reproof. "Two are better than one; for when they fall, the one will lift up his fellow."

Now, reproof may be taken either in a more extensive sense, and then it signifies our raising a brother by the gentlest means, when he falls into sin and error; or in a more restrained signification, as reaching no farther than whose miscarriages, which unavoidably happen in the most holy men living.

The wise man, in the text supposes all of us subject to both: "For when they fall (thereby implying that each of us may fall) the one will lift up his fellow." From whence we may infer, that "when any brother is overtaken with a fault, he that is spiritual (that is, regenerate, and knows the corruption and weakness of human nature) ought to restore such a one in the spirit of meekness." And why he should do so, the apostle subjoins a reason "considering thyself, lest thou also be tempted;" i.e. considering thy own frailty, lest thou also fall by the like temptation.

We are all frail unstable creatures; and it is merely owing to the free grace and good providence of God that we run not into the same excess of riot with other men. Every offending brother, therefore, claims our pity rather than our resentment; and each member should strive to be the most forward, as well as most gentle, in restoring him to his former state.

But supposing a person not to be overtaken, but to fall willfully into a crime; yet who art thou that deniest forgiveness to thy offending brother? "Let him that standeth take heed lest he fall." Take ye, brethren, the holy apostles as eminent examples for you to learn by, how you ought to behave in this matter. Consider how quickly they joined the right hand of fellowship with Peter, who had so willfully denied his master: for we find John and him together but two days after, John 20:2. And ver. John 20:19, we find him assembled with the rest. So soon did they forgive, so soon associate with their sinful, yet relenting brother. "Let us go and do likewise."

But there is another kind of reproof incumbent on every member of a religious society; namely, a gentle rebuke for some miscarriage or other, which though not actually sinful, yet may become the occasion of sin. This indeed seems a more easy, but perhaps will be found a more difficult point than the former: for when a person has really sinned, he cannot but own his brethren's reproof to be just; whereas, when it was only for some little misconduct, the pride that is in our natures will scarce suffer us to brook (endure, tolerate) it. But however ungrateful this pill may be to our brother, yet if we have any concern for his welfare, it must be administered by some friendly hand or other. By all means then let it be applied; only, like a skillful physician, gild over the ungrateful pill, and endeavor, if possible, to deceive thy brother into health and soundness. "Let all bitterness, and wrath, and malice, and evil speaking, be put away" from it. Let the patient know, his recovery is the only thing aimed at, and that thou delightest not causelessly to grieve thy brother; then thou canst not want success.

2. Mutual exhortation is the second duty resulting from the words of the text. "Again, if two lie together, then they have heat."

Observe, the wise man supposes it as impossible for religious persons to meet together, and not to be the warmer for each other's company, as for two persons to lie in the same bed, and yet freeze with cold. But now, how is it possible to communicate heat to each other, without mutually stirring up the gift of God which is in us, by brotherly exhortation? Let every member then of a religious society write that zealous apostle's advice on the tables of his heart; "See that ye exhort, and provoke one another to love, and to good works; and so much the more, as you see the day of the Lord approaching." Believe me, brethren, we have need of exhortation to rouse up our sleepy souls, to set us upon our watch against the temptations of the world, the flesh, and the devil; to excite us to renounce ourselves, to take up our crosses, and follow our blessed master, and the glorious company of saints and martyrs, "who through faith have fought the good fight, and are gone before us to inherit the promises." A third part, therefore, of the time wherein a religious society meets, seems necessary to be spent in this important duty: for what avails it to have our understandings enlightened by pious reading, unless our wills are at the same time inclined, and inflamed by mutual exhortation, to put it in practice? Add also, that this is the best way both to receive and impart light, and the only means to preserve and increase that warmth and heat which each person first brought with him; God so ordering this, as all other spiritual gifts, that "to him that hath, i.e. improves and communicates what he hath, shall be given; but from him that hath not, or does not improve the heat he hath, shall be taken away even that which he seemed to have." So needful, so essentially necessary, is exhortation to the good of society.

3. Thirdly, The text points out another duty incumbent on every member of a religious society, to defend each other from those that do oppose them. "And if one prevail against him, yet two shall withstand him; and a threefold cord is not quickly broken."

Here the wise man takes it for granted, that offenses will come, nay , and that they may prevail too. And this is not more than our blessed master has long since told us. Not, indeed, that there is any thing in Christianity itself that has the least tendency to give rise to, or promote such offenses: No, on the contrary, it breathes nothing but unity and love.

But so it is, that ever since the fatal sentence pronounced by God, after our first parents fall, "I will put enmity between thy seed and her seed;" he that is born after the flesh, the unregenerate unconverted sinner, has in all ages "persecuted him that is born after the spirit:" and so it always will be. Accordingly we find an early proof given of this in the instance of Cain and Abel; of Ishmael and Isaac; and of Jacob and Esau. And, indeed, the whole Bible contains little else but an history of the great and continued opposition between the children of this world, and the children of God. The first Christians were remarkable examples of this; and though those troublesome time, blessed be God, are now over, yet the apostle has laid it down as a general rule, and all who are sincere experimentally prove the truth of it; that "they that will live godly in Christ Jesus, must (to the end of the world, in some degree or other) suffer persecution." That therefore this may not make us desert our blessed master's cause, every member should unite their forces in order to stand against it. And for the better effecting this, each would do well, from time to time, to communicate his experiences, grievances, and temptations, and beg his companions (first asking God's assistance, without which all is nothing) to administer reproof, exhortation, or comfort, as his case requires: so that "if one cannot prevail against it, yet two shall withstand it; and a three-fold (much less a many-fold) cord will not be quickly broken."

IV. But it is time for me to proceed to the fourth general thing proposed, to draw an inference or two from what has been said.

1. And first, if "two are better than one," and the advantages of religious society are so many and so great; then it is the duty of every true Christian to set on foot, establish and promote, as much as in him lies, societies of this nature. And I believe we may venture to affirm, that if ever a spirit of true Christianity is revived in the world, it must be brought about by some such means as this. Motive, surely, cannot be wanting, to stir us up to the commendable and necessary undertaking: for, granting all hitherto advanced to be of no force, yet methinks the single consideration, that great part of our happiness in heaven will consist in the Communion of Saints; or that the interest as well as piety of those who differ from us, is strengthened and supported by nothing more than their frequent meetings; either of these considerations, I say, one would think, should induce us to do our utmost to copy after their good example, and settle a lasting and pious communion of the saints on earth. Add to this, that we find the kingdom of darkness established daily by such like means; and shall not the kingdom of Christ be set in opposition against it? Shall the children of Belial assemble and strengthen each other in wickedness; and shall not the children of God unite, and strengthen themselves in piety? Shall societies on societies be countenanced for midnight revellings, and the promoting of vice, and scarcely one be found intended for the propagation of virtue? Be astonished, O heavens at this!

2. But this leads me to a second inference; namely, to warn persons of the great danger those are in, who either by their subscriptions, presence, or approbation, promote societies of a quite opposite nature to religion.

And here I would not be understood, to mean only those public meetings which are designed manifestly for nothing else but revellings and banquetings, for chambering and wantonness, and at which a modest heathen would blush to be present; but also those seemingly innocent entertainments and meetings, which the politer part of the world are so very fond of, and spend so much time in: but which, notwithstanding, keep as many persons from a sense of true religion, as doth intemperance, debauchery, or any other crimes whatever. Indeed, whilst we are in this world, we must have proper relaxations, to fit us both for the business of our profession, and religion. But then, for persons who call themselves Christians, that have solemnly vowed at their baptism, to renounce the vanities of this sinful world; that are commanded in scripture "to abstain from all appearance of evil, and to have their conversation in heaven:" for such persons as these to support meetings, which (to say no worse of them) are vain and trifling, and have a natural tendency to draw off our minds from God, is absurd, ridiculous, and sinful. Surely two are not better than one in this case: No; it is to be wished there was not one to be found concerned in it. The sooner we forsake the assembling ourselves together in such a manner, the better; and no matte how quickly the cord that hold such societies (was it a thousand-fold) is broken.

But you, brethren, have not so learned Christ: but, on the contrary, like true disciples of your Lord and Master, have by the blessing of God (as this evening's solemnity abundantly testifies) happily formed yourselves into such societies, which, if duly attended on, and improved, cannot but strengthen you in your Christian warfare, and "make you fruitful in every good word and work."

What remains for me, but, as was proposed, in the first place, to close what has been said, in a word or two, by way of exhortation, and to beseech you, in the name of our Lord Jesus Christ, to go on in the way you have begun; and by a constant conscientious attendance on your respective societies, to discountenance vice, encourage virtue, and build each other up in the knowledge and fear of God.

Only permit me to "stir up your pure minds, by way of remembrance," and to exhort you, "if there be any consolation in Christ, any fellowship of the spirit," again and again to consider, that as all Christians in general, so all members of religious societies in particular, are in an especial manner, as houses built upon an hill; and that therefore it highly concerns you to walk circumspectly towards those that are without, and to take heed to yourselves, that your conversation, in common life, be as becometh such an open and peculiar profession of the gospel of Christ: knowing that the eyes of all men are upon you, narrowly to inspect every circumstance of your behavior: and that every notorious willful miscarriage of any single member will, in some measure, redound to the scandal and dishonor of your whole fraternity.

Labor, therefore, my beloved brethren, to let your practice correspond to your profession: and think not that it will be sufficient for you to plead at the last day, Lord have we not assembled ourselves together in thy name, and enlivened each other, by singing psalms, and hymns, and spiritual songs? For verily, I say unto you, notwithstanding this, our blessed Lord will bid you depart from him; nay, you shall receive a great damnation, if, in the mists of these great pretensions, you are found to be workers of iniquity.

But God forbid that any such evil should befall you; that there should be ever a Judas, a traitor, amongst such distinguished followers of our common master. No, on the contrary, the excellency of your rule, the regularity of your meetings, and more especially your pious zeal in assembling in such a public and solemn manner so frequently in the year, persuade me to think, that you are willing, not barely to seem, but to be in reality, Christians; and hope to be found at the last day, what you would be esteemed now, holy, sincere disciples of a crucified Redeemer.

Oh, may you always continue thus minded! And make it your daily, constant endeavor, both by precept and example, to turn all your converse with, more especially those of your own societies, into the same most blessed spirit and temper. Thus will you adorn the gospel of our Lord Jesus Christ in all things: Thus will you anticipate the happiness of a future state; and by attending on, and improving the communion of stints on earth, be made meet to join the communion and fellowship of the spirits of just men made perfect, of the holy angels, nay, of the ever blessed and eternal God in heaven.

Which God of his infinite mercy grant through Jesus Christ our Lord; to whom with the Father and the Holy Ghost, three persons and one God, be ascribed, as is most due, all honor and praise, might, majesty and dominion, now and for ever. Amen.

9. The Folly and Danger of Being Not Righteous Enough

Ecclesiastes 7:16—"Be not righteous overmuch, neither make thyself over-wise: why shouldst thou destroy thyself?"

Nothing is more frequent, than while people are living in a course of sin, and after the fashion and manner of the world, there is not notice taken of them; neither are their ways displeasing to their companions and carnal relations: but if they set their faces Zion-ward, and begin to feel the power of God on their hearts; they then are surrounded with temptations from their friends, who thus act the devil's part. The enemies, the greatest enemies a young convert meets with, my dear brethren, are those of his own house. They that will be godly, must suffer persecution; so it was in Christ" time, and so it was in the Apostles time too; for our Lord came not to send peace, but a sword. Our relations would not have us sit in the scorner's chair; they would not have us be prodigals, consuming our substance upon harlots; neither would they have us rakes (a dissolute [loose in morals or conduct] person) or libertines, but they would have us be contented with an almost Christianity. To keep up our reputation by going to church, and adhering to the outward forms of religion, saying our prayers, reading the word of God, and taking the sacraments; this, they imagine, is all that is necessary for to be Christians indeed; and when we go one step farther than this, their mouths are open against us, as Peter's was to Christ: "Spare thyself, do thyself no harm."

And of this nature are the words of the text. They are not the words of Solomon himself, but the words of an infidel speaking to him, whom he introduces in several parts of this book; for Solomon had been showing the misfortunes which attended the truly good, as in the verse before our text.

Upon this the infidel says, "Be not righteous overmuch, neither be thou over-wise; why shouldst thou destroy thyself?" i.e. Why shouldst thou bring these misfortunes upon thyself, by being over strict? Be not righteous over-much; eat, drink, and be merry, live as the world lives, and then you will avoid those misfortunes which may attend you, by being righteous over-much.

This text has another meaning; but take it which way you will, by brethren, it was spoken by an unbeliever; therefore it was no credit for the person who lately preached upon this text, to take it for granted, that these were the words of Solomon: the words of an infidel was not a proper text to a Christian congregation. But as David came out against Goliath, not armed as the champion was, with sword and spear, but with a sling and stone, and then cut off his head with his own sword; so I come out against these letter-learned men, in the strength of the Lord Jesus Christ; and, my dear brethren, I trust he will direct me to use my sling, so that our enemies may not gainsay us; and by the sword of God's word, cut off the heads of our Redeemer's enemies.

But though they are not the words of Solomon, yet we will take them in the same manner the late writer did; and, from the words, shall,

First, Show you what it is, not to be righteous over-much, that we may not destroy ourselves.

Secondly, I shall let you see what it is to be righteous over-much. And then,

Thirdly, Conclude with an exhortation to all of you, high and low, rich and poor, one with another, to come to the Lord Jesus Christ.

First, The first thing proposed, is to show you what it is not to be righteous over-much. And here,

It is by no means to be righteous over-much, to affirm we must have the same Spirit of God as the first Apostles had, and must feel that Spirit upon our hearts.

By receiving the Spirit of God, is not to be understood, that we are to be inspired to show outward signs and wonders, to raise dead bodies, to cure leprous persons, or to give sight to the blind: these miracles were only of use in the first ages of the church; and therefore Christians (nominal Christians, for we have little else but the name) may have all the gifts of the Spirit, and yet none of the graces of it. Thou, O man, mayest be enabled by faith to remove mountains; thou, by the power of God, mayest cast out devils; thou, by that power, mayest speak with the tongues of men and angels; yes, thou mayest, by that power, hold up thy finger and stop the sun in the firmament; and if all these are unsanctified by the Spirit of God, they would be of no service to thee, but would hurry thee to hell with the greater solemnity. Saul received the spirit of prophesying, and had another heart, yet Saul was probably a cast-away. We must receive the Spirit of God in its sanctifying graces upon our souls; for Christ says, "Unless a man be born again, he cannot see the kingdom of God." We are all by nature born in sin, and at as great a distance from God, as the devils themselves. I have told you often, and now tell you again, that you are by nature a motley mixture of the beast and devil, and we cannot recover ourselves from the state wherein we have fallen, therefore must be renewed by the Holy Ghost. By the Holy Ghost, I mean, the third Person of the ever blessed Trinity, co-equal, co-essential, co-eternal, and consubstantial with the Father and the Son; and therefore, when we are baptized, it is into the nature of the Father, into the nature of the Son, and into the nature of the Holy Ghost: and we are not true Christians, till we are sanctified by the Spirit of God.

Though our modern preachers do not actually deny the Spirit of God, yet they say, "Christians must not feel him;" which is in effect to deny him. When Nicodemus came to Christ, and the Lord Jesus was instructing him, concerning the new birth, says he to our Lord, "How can these things be?" Nicodemus, though a master of Israel, acts just as our learned Rabbi's do now. The answer that Christ gave him should stop the mouths of our letter-learned Pharisees: "The wind bloweth where it listeth, and we hear the sound thereof, but cannot tell whence it cometh, nor whither it goeth." Now till the Spirit of God is felt on our souls as the wind on our bodies, indeed, my dear brethren, you have no interest in him: religion consists not in external performance, it must be in the heart, or else it is only a name, which cannot profit us, a name to live whilst we are dead.

A late preacher upon this text, seems to laugh at us, for talking of the Spirit in a sensible manner, and talks to us as the Jews did to Christ: They said, "How can this man give us his flesh to eat?" So he asks, "What sign or proof do we give of it?" We do not imagine, that God must appear to us, and give it us: no; but there may be, and is, a frequent receiving, when no seeing of it; and it is as plainly felt in the soul, as any impression is, or can be, upon the body. To what a damnable condition should we bring poor sinners, if they could not be sensible of the Spirit of God; namely, a reprobate mind and past feeling?

"What proof do they give?" says the writer. What sign would they have? Do they expect us to raise the dead, to give sight to the blind, to cure lepers, to make the lame to walk, and the deaf to hear? If these are what they expect, I speak with humility, God, by us, hath done greater things than these: many, who were dead in sin, are raised to scripture-life: those, who were leprous by nature, are cleansed by the Spirit of God; those, who were lame in duty, not run in God's commands; those, who were deaf, their ears are unstopped to hear his discipline, and hearken to his advice; and the poor have the gospel preached to them. No wonder people talk at this rate, when they can tell us, "That the Spirit of God, is a good conscience, consequent thereupon." My dear brethren, Seneca, Cicera, Plato, or any of the heathen philosophers, would have given as good a definition as this. It means no more, than reflecting that we have done well. This, this is only Deism refined: Deists laugh at us, when we pretend to be against notions, and yet these men use no other reason for our differing from them, than what is agreeable to Deists principles.

This writer tell us, "It is against common-sense to talk of the feeling of the Spirit of God." Common-sense, my brethren, was never allowed to be a judge; yea, it is above its comprehension, neither are, nor can the ways of God be known by common-sense. We should never have known the things of God at all by our common sense: no; it is the revelation of God which is to be our judge; it is that we appeal to, and not to our weak and shallow conceptions of things. Thus we may see, it is by no means to be righteous over-much, to affirm we must have the Spirit of God as the Apostles had. Nor,

Secondly, Is it to be righteous over-much to frequent religious assemblies.

The preacher, upon this text, aims at putting aside all the religious societies that are in the kingdom: Indeed, he says, "You may go to church as often as opportunity serves, and on Sundays; say your prayers, read the word of God; and, in his opinion, every thing else had better be let alone: and as for the Spirit of God upon your souls, you are to look upon it as useless and unnecessary." If this, my brethren, is the doctrine we have now preached, Christianity is at a low ebb indeed; but God forbid you should thus learn Jesus Christ. Do you not forbear the frequenting of religious assemblies; for as nothing helps to build up the devil's kingdom more than the societies of wicked men, nothing would be more for pulling of it down, than the people of God meeting to strengthen each others hands; and as the devil has so many friends, will none of you be friends to the blessed Jesus? Yes, I hope many of you will be of the Lord's side, and build each other up in Christian love and fellowship. This is what the primitive Christians delighted in; and shall not we follow so excellent an example? My brethren, till Christian conversation is more agreeable to us, we cannot expect to see the gospel of Christ run and be glorified. Thus it is by no means to be righteous over-much, to frequent religious assemblies. Nor,

Thirdly, Is it to be righteous over-much, to abstain from the diversions and entertainments of the age.

We are commanded to "abstain from the appearance of evil," and that "whatsoever we do, whether we eat or drink, we shall do all to the glory of God." The writer upon this text tells us, "That it will be accounted unlawful to smell to a rose:" no, my dear brethren, you man smell to a pink and rose too if you please, but take care to avoid the appearance of sin. They talk of innocent diversions and recreations; for my part, I know of no diversion, but that of doing good: if you can find any diversion which is not contrary to your baptismal vow, of renouncing the pomps and vanities of this wicked world; if you can find any diversion which tends to the glory of God; if you can find any diversion, which you would be willing to be found at by the Lord Jesus Christ, I give you free license to go to them and welcome; but if, on the contrary, they are found to keep sinners from coming to the Lord Jesus Christ; if they are a means to harden the heart, and such as you would not willingly be found in when you come to die, then, my dear brethren, keep from them: for, indeed, the diversions of this age are contrary to Christianity. Many of you may think I have gone too far, but I shall go a great deal farther yet: I will attack the devil in his strongest holds, and bear my testimony against our fashionable and polite entertainments. What satisfaction can it be, what pleasure is there in spending several hours at cards? Strange! That even people who are grown old, can spend whole nights in this diversion: perhaps many of you will cry out, "What harm is there in it?" My dear brethren, whatsoever is not of faith, or for the glory of God, is a sin. Now does cards tend to promote this? Is it not misspending your precious time, which should be employed in working out your salvation with fear and trembling? Do play-houses, horse-racing, balls and assemblies, tend to promote the glory of God? Would you be willing to have your soul demanded of you, while you are at one of those places? Many of these are, (I must speak, I cannot forbear to speak against these entertainments; come what will, I will declare against them) many, I say, of these are kept up by public authority; the play-houses are supported by a public fund, and our newspapers are full of horse-races all through the kingdom: these things are sinful; indeed they are exceeding sinful. What good can come from a horse-race; from abusing God Almighty's creatures, and putting them to that use he never designed for them: the play-houses, are they not nurseries of debauchery in the age? And the supporters and patrons of them, are encouragers and promoters of all the evil that is done by them; they are the bane of the age, and will be the destruction of those who frequent them. Is it not high time for the true ministers of Jesus Christ, who have been partakers of the heavenly gift, to lift up their voices as a trumpet, and cry aloud against these diversions of the age? Are they not earthly, sensual, devilish? If you have tasted of the love of God, and have felt his power upon your souls, you would no more go to a play, than you would run your head into a furnace.

And what occasions these place to be so much frequented, is the clergy's making no scruple to be at these polite places: they frequent play-houses, they go to horse-races, they go to balls and assemblies, they frequent taverns, and follow all the entertainments that the age affords; and yet these are the persons who should advise their hearers to refrain from them; but instead thereof, they encourage them by their example. Persons are too apt to rely upon, and believe their pastors, rather than the scriptures; they think that there is no crime in going to plays or horse-races, to balls and assemblies; for if there were, they think those persons, who are their ministers, would not frequent them: but, my dear brethren, observe they always go disguised, the ministers are afraid of being seen in their gowns and cassocks; the reason thereof is plain, their consciences inform them, that it is not an example fit for the ministers of the gospel to set; thus, they are the means of giving that offense to the people of God, which I would not for ten thousand worlds: they lay a stumbling-block in the way of their weak brethren, which they will not remove, though it is a stumbling-block of offense. "Woe unto the world because of offenses, but woe unto that man by whom the offense cometh." The polite gentlemen of the age, spend their time in following those diversions, because the love of God is not in their hearts; they are void of Christ, and destitute of the Spirit of God; and not being acquainted with the delight there is in God and his ways, being strangers to these things, they run to the devil for diversions, and are pleased and delighted with the silly ones he shows them.

My dear brethren, I speak of these things, these innocent diversions, as the polite part of the world calls them, by experience; perhaps none, for my age, hath read or seen more plays than I have: I took delight in, and was pleased with them. It is true, I went to church frequently, received the sacrament, and was diligent in the use of the forms of religion, but I was all this while ignorant of the power of God on my heart, and unacquainted with the work of grace; but when God was pleased to shine with power upon my soul, I could no longer be contented to feed on husks, or what the swine die eat; the Bible then was my food; there, and there only I took delight: and till you feel this same power, you will not abstain from the earthly delights of this age, you will take no comfort in God's ways, nor receive any comfort from him; for you are void of the love of God, having only the form of godliness, while you are denying the power of it; you are nominal Christians, when you have not the power of Christianity.

The polite gentlemen say, "Are we to be always upon our knees? Would you have us be always at prayer, and reading or hearing the word of God?"

My dear brethren, the fashionable ones, who take delight in hunting, are not tired of being continually on horseback after their hounds; and when once you are renewed by the Spirit of God, it will be a continua pleasure to be walking with, and talking of God, and telling what great things Jesus Christ hath done for your souls; and till you can find as much pleasure in conversing with God, as these men do of their hounds, you have no share in him; but when you have tasted how good the Lord is, you will show forth his praise; out of the abundance of your heart your mouth will speak.

This brings me to the second thing proposed, which is an extreme that very seldom happens:

Secondly, To show what it is to be righteous over-much, And here,

First, When we confine the Spirit of God to this or that particular church; and are not willing to converse with any but those of the same communion; this is to be righteous over-much with a witness: and so it is, to confine our communion within church-walls, and to think that Jesus could not preach in a field as well as on consecrated ground; this is judaism, this is bigotry: this is like Peter, who would not go to preach the gospel to the Gentiles, till he had a vision from God: and when his conduct was blamed by the disciples, he could not satisfy them till he had acquainted them with the vision he had seen. And, therefore, we may justly infer, the Spirit of God is the center of unity; and wherever I see the image of my Master, I never inquire of them their opinions; I ask them not what they are, so they love Jesus Christ in sincerity and truth, but embrace them as my brother, my sister, and my spouse: and this is the spirit of Christianity. Many persons, who are bigots to this or that opinion, when one of a different way of thinking hath come where they were, have left the room or place on the account: this is the spirit of the devil; and if it was possible that these persons could be admitted into heaven with such tempers, that very place would be hell to them. Christianity will never flourish, till we are all of one heart and of one mind; and this would be the only means of seeing the gospel of Jesus to flourish, more than ever it will by persecuting those who differ from us.

This may be esteemed as enthusiasm and madness, and as a design to undermine the established church: No; God is my judge, I should rejoice to see all the world adhere to her articles; I should rejoice to see the ministers of the Church of England, preach up those very articles they have subscribed to; but those ministers who do preach up the articles, are esteemed as madmen, enthusiasts, schismatics, and underminers of the established church: and though they say these things of me, blessed be God, they are without foundation. My dear brethren,

I am a friend to her articles, I am a friend to her homilies, I am a friend to her liturgy; and, if they did not thrust me out of their churches, I would read them every day; but I do not confine the Spirit of God there; for I say it again, I love all that love the Lord Jesus Christ, and esteem him my brother, my friend, my spouse; aye, my very soul is knit to that person. The spirit of persecution will never, indeed it will never make any to love Jesus Christ. The Pharisees make this to be madness, so much as to mention persecution in a Christian country; but there is as much of the spirit of persecution now in the world, as ever there was; their will is as great, but blessed be God, they want the power; otherwise, how soon would the send me to prison, make my feet fast in the stocks, yea, would think they did God service in killing me, and would rejoice to take away my life.

This is not the Spirit of Christ, my dear brethren; I had not come to have thus preached; I had not come into the highways and hedges; I had not exposed myself to the ill treatment of these letter-learned men, but for the sake of your souls: indeed, I had no other reason, but your salvation; and for that (I speak the truth in Christ, I lie not) I would be content to go to prison; yea, I would rejoice to die for you, so I could but be a means to bring some of you to Jesus: I could not bear to see so many in the highway to destruction, and not show them their danger: I could not bear, my brethren, to see you more willing to learn, than the teachers are to instruct you: and if any of them were to come and preach to you, I should not envy them, I should not call them enthusiasts or madmen; I should rejoice to hear they had ten thousand times more success than I have met with; I would give them the right hand of fellowship; I would advise them to go on; I would wish them good luck in the name of the Lord, and say as Christ did, when the disciples informed him of some casting out devils in his name, and were for rebuking of them, "Forbid them not, for they that are not against us are for us;" or as St. Paul says, "Some preach Christ of envy, and some of good-will; notwithstanding, so Christ is but preached, I rejoice; yea, and will rejoice." The gospel of Jesus, is the gospel of peace. Thus you may see, that to be righteous over-much, is to be uncharitable, censorious, and to persecute persons for differing from us in religion.

Secondly, Persons are righteous over-much, when they spend so much time in religious assemblies, as to neglect their families. There is no license given by the blessed Jesus, for idleness; for in the very infancy of the world, idleness was not allowed of. In paradise, Adam and Eve dressed the garden, Cain was a tiller of the ground, and Abel was a keeper of sheep; and there is a proverb amongst the Jews, "That he who brings his son up without a business, brings him up to be a thief:" and therefore our Savior was a carpenter; "Is not this the carpenter's son," said the Jews: and St. Paul, though brought up at the feet of Gamaliel, was a tent-maker. Labor, my brethren, is imposed on all mankind as part of the divine curse; and you are called to be useful in the society to which you belong: take care first for the kingdom of God, and all things necessary shall be added. To labor for the meat that perisheth, is your duty; only take care, that you do not neglect getting the meat for the soul: that is the greatest consequence, for this plain reason, the things of this life are temporal, but those of the next are eternal. I would have rich men to work as well as poor; it is owing to their idleness, that the devil hurries them to his diversions; they can be in their beds all the morning, and spend the afternoon and evening in dressing, visiting, and at balls, plays, or assemblies, when they should be working out their salvation with fear and trembling. Such a life as this, occasions a spiritual numbness in the soul; and if Jesus Christ was not to stop those who thus spend their time, they would be hurried into eternity, without once thinking of their immortal souls. But Jesus Christ has compassion upon many of them, and while they are in their blood, he bids them "live." And though I preach this doctrine to you, yet I do not bid you be idle; no, they that do not work should not eat. You have two callings, a general one, and a special one: as we are to regard the one in respect of our bodies, so we are to regard the other on account of our souls. Take heed, my brethren, I beseech you, take heed, lest you labor so for the meat that perisheth, as to forget that meat which endureth for ever. Seek the things of God first; look well to obtain oil in your lamps, grace in your hearts. I am not persuading you to take no care about the things of the world, but only not to be encumbered with them, so as to neglect your duty towards God, and a proper concern for your souls. It is meet, it is right, it is your bounden duty, to mind the calling wherein God hath placed you; and you may be said to be righteous over-much not to regard them. This brings me,

Thirdly, To give you another sign of being righteous over-much; and that is, when we fast and use corporal authorities, so as to unfit us for the service of God.

This, my brethren, you may think there is no occasion at all to caution you against, and indeed there is not a great necessity for it; however, many persons, upon their first being awakened to a sense of their sin, are tempted to use authorities to that excess which is sinful. It is our duty to fast, it is our duty to fast often, and it is what we are directed to by Jesus Christ himself; but then we are to take care to do it in a proper manner: to bring our bodies under for the service of God, is that which we are commanded by our Lord Jesus Christ.

The late preacher upon this text, runs into great extremes, and charges us with saying and acting things of which we never thought; but I do not regard what he said of me: I do not mind his bitter invectives against my ministry; I do not mind his despising my youth, and calling me novice and enthusiast; I forgive him from my very heart: but when he reflects on my Master; when he speaks against my Redeemer; when Jesus Christ is spoken against, I must speak, (I must speak indeed, or I should burst:) when he gives liberty to persons to take a cheerful glass, and alledges Christ for an example, as in the marriage-feast, saying, "Christ turned water into wine, when it is plain there had been more drank than was necessary before;" what is this, but to charge Christ with encouraging drunkenness? It is true, the Governor says, "Every man in the beginning sets forth good wine, and when men have well drank, that which is worse; but thou hast kept the good wine until now:" but it does not at all follow, that it was not necessary, or that there had been a sufficient quantity before: I would not speak thus slightingly of one of my Master's miracles, for the whole world. And we may observe, that as Christ chiefly visited poor people, they might not have wherewithal to buy a sufficient quantity of wine; for having more guests than were expected, the wine was expended sooner than they thought; then the Mother of Jesus tells him, "They have no wine;" he answers, "Woman, what have I to do with thee? My hour is not yet come." After this he commanded them to fill the water-pots with water, and they filled them to the brim, and this water he turned into wine: now it does not follow, that there was more drank than was necessary; neither would the Lord Jesus Christ have continued in the house if there had. But we have an excellent lesson to learn from this miracle: by the water-pots being empty, we may understand, the heart of man being by nature destitute of his grace, his speaking and commanding to fill them, shows, that when Christ speaks, the heart that was empty of grace before, shall be filled; and the water pots being filled to the brim, shows, that Christ will fill believers hearts brim full of the Holy Ghost: and from the Governor's observing, that the last wine was the best, learn, that a believer's best comforts, shall be the last and greatest, for they shall come with the greatest power upon the soul, and continue longest there: this, this my dear brethren, is the lesson we may learn from this miracle.

But one great inconsistency I cannot avoid taking notice of in this late learned preacher. In the beginning of his sermon, he charges us with "laying heavy burdens upon people, which they are not able to bear;" in the latter part he charges us with being Antinomians, whose tenets are, "So you say you believe in the Lord Jesus Christ, you may live the life of devils." Now, he charges us with being too strict, and by and by with being too loose. Which side, my brethren, will you take? Thus you see, when persons forsake Christ, they make strange mistakes; for here can be no greater opposition of sentiments than this letter-learned writer has made: as opposite as light and darkness, good and evil, sweet and bitter. And, on this account, to find out these lettered-learned gentlemens notions of the new-birth, I put a paragraph in my Journal; and, blessed be God, I have obtained my desires, and have plainly perceived, that the persons who have lately written concerning the new-birth, know no more of it than a blind man does of colors, nor can they have any more notion of it, (by all their learning, falsely so called) than the blind man, who was to give an account what the sun was, and, after a considerable time allowed for study, he said, "It was like the sound of a trumpet." And till they are taught of God, they will be unacquainted with the new-birth; therefore, if you have a mind to know what the devil has to say against us, read Dr. Trapp's sermons.

It is with grief I speak these things, and were not the welfare of your souls, and my Redeemer's honor at stake, I would not now open my mouth, yes I would willingly die (God is my judge) for the person who wrote such bitter things against me, so it would be a means of saving his soul. If he had only spoken against me, I would not have answered him; but, on his making my Redeemer a pattern of vice, if I was not to speak, the very stones would cry out; therefore, the honor of my Redeemer, and love to you, constrains me to speak. It is of necessity that I speak, when the divinity of Jesus Christ is spoken against, it is the duty of ministers to cry aloud, and spare not. I cannot forbear, come what will; for I know not what kind of divinity we have not among us: we must have a righteousness of our own, and do our best endeavors, and then Christ will make up the deficiency; that is, you must be your own Savior, in part. This is not the doctrine of the gospel; this not the doctrine of Jesus: no; Christ is all in all; Jesus Christ must be your whole wisdom; Jesus Christ must be your whole righteousness. Jesus Christ must be your whole sanctification; or Jesus Christ will never be your eternal redemption and sanctification. Inward holiness is looked on, by some, as the effect of enthusiasm and madness; and preachers of the necessity of the new-birth, are esteemed as persons fit for Bedlam. Our polite and fashionable doctrine, is, "That there is a fitness in man, and that God, seeing you a good creature, bestows upon you his grace." God forbid, my dear brethren, you should thus learn Jesus Christ!

This is not the doctrine I preach to you: I say, salvation is the free gift of God. It is God' free grace, I preach unto you, not of works, lest any one should boast. Jesus Christ justifies the ungodly; Jesus Christ passed by, and saw you polluted with your blood, and bid you live. It is not of works, it is of faith: we are not justified for our faith, for faith is the instrument, but by your faith, the active as well as the passive obedience of Christ, must be applied to you. Jesus Christ hath fulfilled the law, he hath made it honorable; Jesus Christ hath made satisfaction to his Father's justice, full satisfaction; and it is as complete as it is full, and God will not demand it again. Jesus Christ is the way; Jesus Christ is the truth; and Jesus Christ is the life. The righteousness of Jesus Christ, my brethren, must be imputed to you, or you can never have any interest in the blood of Jesus; your own works are but as filthy rags, for you are justified before God, without any respect to your works past, present, or to come. This doctrine is denied by the learned rabbi's; but if they deny these truths of the gospel, they must not offended, though a child dare speak to a doctor; and, in vindication of the cause of Jesus Christ, a child, a boy, by the Spirit of God, can speak to the learned clergy of this age.

If I had a voice so great, and could speak so loud, as that the whole world could hear me, I would cry, "Be not righteous over-much," by bringing your righteousness to Christ, and by being righteous in your own eyes. Man must be abased, that God may be exalted.

The imputed righteousness of Jesus Christ is a comfortable doctrine to all real Christians; and you sinners, who ask what you must do to be saved? How uncomfortable would it be, to tell you by good works, when, perhaps, you have never done one good work in all your life: this would be driving you to despair, indeed: no; "Believe in the Lord Jesus Christ, and you shall be saved:" therefore none of you need go away despairing. Come to the Lord Jesus by faith, and he shall receive you. You have no righteousness of your own to depend on. If you are saved, it is by the righteousness of Christ, through his atonement, his making a sacrifice for sin: his righteousness must be imputed to you, otherwise you cannot be saved. There is no difference between you, by nature, and the greatest malefactor that ever was executed at Tyburn: the difference made, is all owing to the free, the rich, the undeserved grace of God; this has made the difference. It is true, talking at this rate, will offend the Pharisees, who do not like this leveling doctrine, (as they call it); but if ever you are brought to Jesus Christ by faith, you will experience the truth of it. Come by faith to Jesus Christ; do not come, Pharisee-like, telling God what you have done, how often you have gone to church, how often you have received the sacrament, fasted, prayed, or the like: no; come to Christ as poor, lost, undone, damned sinners; come to him in this manner, and he will accept of you: do not be rich in spirit, proud and exalted, for there is no blessing attends such; but be ye poor in spirit, for theirs is the kingdom of God; they shall be made members of his mystical body here, and shall be so of the church triumphant hereafter. Acknowledge yourselves as nothing at all, and when you have done all, say, "You are unprofitable servants." There is no salvation but by Jesus Christ; there is no other name given under heaven amongst men, whereby we may be saved, but that of the Lord Jesus. God, out of Christ, is a consuming fire; therefore strive for an interest in his Son the Lord Jesus Christ; take him on the terms offered to you in the gospel; accept of him in God's own way, lay hold on him by faith.

Do not think you are Christians; do not flatter yourselves with being righteous enough, and good enough, because you lead moral decent lives, do no one any harm, go to church, and attend upon the outward means of grace; no, my brethren, you may do this, and a great deal more, and yet be very far from having a saving, experimental knowledge of Jesus Christ.

Beg of Christ to strike home upon your hearts, that you may feel the power of religion. Indeed, you must feel the power of God here, or the wrath of God hereafter. These are truths of the utmost consequence; therefore, do not go contradicting, do not go blaspheming away. Blessed be God, you are not such cowards to run away for a little rain. I hope good things of you; I hope you have felt the power of God; and if God should bring any of you to himself through this foolishness of preaching, you will have no reason to complain it was done by a youth, by a child; no; if I could be made an instrument to bring you to God, they may call me novice, enthusiast, or what they please, I should rejoice; yea, and I would rejoice.

O that some sinner might be brought to Jesus Christ! Do not say I preach despair; I despair of no one, when I consider God had mercy on such a wretch as I, who was running in a full career to hell: I was hastening thither, but Jesus Christ passed by and stopped me; Jesus Christ passed by me while I was in my blood, when I was polluted with filth; he passed by me, and bid me live. Thus I am a monument of God's free grace; and therefore, my brethren, I despair of none of you, when I consider, I say, what a wretch I was. I am not speaking now out of a false humility, a pretended sanctity, as the Pharisees call it: no, the truth in Christ I speak, and therefore, men and devils do your worst; I have a gracious Master will protect me; it is his work I am engaged in, and Jesus Christ will carry me above their rage.

Those who are come here this night out of curiosity to hear what the babbler says; those who come to spend an idle hour to find something for an evening-conversation at a coffee-house; or you who have stopped in your coaches as you passed by, remember that you have had Jesus Christ offered to you; I offer Jesus Christ to every one of you: perhaps you may not regard it because it is in a field. But Jesus Christ is wherever his people meet in sincerity and truth to worship him: he is not confined to church walls: he has met us here; many, very many of you know he has; and therefore you may believe on him with greater confidence.

Can you bear to think of a bleeding, panting, dying Jesus, offering himself up for sinners, and you will not accept of him? Do not say, you are poor, and therefore are ashamed to go to church, for God has sent the gospel out unto you. Do not harden your hearts: oppose not the will of Jesus.

O that I could speak to your hearts, that my words would center there. My heart is full of love to you. I would speak, till I could speak no more, so I could but bring you to Christ. I may never meet you all, perhaps, any more. The cloud of God's providence seems to be moving. God calls me by his providence away from you, for a while. God knows whether we shall ever see each other in the flesh. At the day of judgment we shall all meet again. I earnestly desire your prayers. Pray that I may not only begin, John-like, I the spirit, but that I may continue in it. Pray that I may not fall away, that I may not decline suffering for you, if I should be called to it. Be earnest, O be earnest with God in my behalf, that while I am preaching to others, I may not be a cast-away. Put up your prayers for me, I beseech you. Go not to the throne of grace, without carrying me upon your heart; for you know not what influence your prayers may have. As for you, my dear brethren, God knows my heart. I continually bear you on my mind, when I go in and out before the Lord; and it is my earnest desire, you may not perish for lack of knowledge, but that he would send out more ministers to water what his own right-hand hath planted. May the Ancient of Days come forth upon his white horse, and may all opposition fall to the ground. As we have begun to bruise the serpent's head, we must expect he will bruise our heel. The devil will not let his kingdom fall without raging horribly. He will not suffer the ministers of Christ to go on, without bringing his power to stop them. But fear not, my dear brethren, David, though a stripling, encountered the great Goliath; and if we pray, God will give us strength against all our spiritual enemies. Show your faith by your works. Give the world the lye. Press forward. Do not stop, do not linger in your journey, but strive for the mark set before you. Fight the good fight of faith, and God will give you spiritual mercies. I hope we shall all meet at the right-hand of God. Strive, strive to enter in at the strait gate, that we may be born to Abraham's bosom, where sin and sorrow shall cease. No scoffer will be there, but we shall see Jesus, who died for us; and not only see him, but live with him forever.

Which God, of his infinite mercy.

10. A Preservative Against Unsettled Notions, and Want of Principles, in Regard to Righteousness and Christian Perfection

Ecclesiastes 7:16—"Be not righteous over much; neither make thyself over wise: why shouldest thou destroy thyself?"

To all the Members of Christ's Holy Church.

Dear Fellow Christians,

The great, and indeed the only motive which prompted me to publish this sermon, was the desire of providing for your security from error, at a time when the deviators from, and false pretenders to truth, are so numerous, that the most discerning find it a matter of the greatest difficulty to avoid being led astray by one or by other into downright falsehood. There is no running divisions upon truth; like a mathematical point, it will neither admit of subtraction nor addition: And as it is indivisible in its nature, there is no splitting the difference, where truth is concerned. Irreligion and enthusiasm are diametrical opposites, and true piety between both, like the center of an infinite line, is at an equal infinite distance from the one and the other, and therefore can never admit of a coalition with either. The one erring by defect, the other by excess. But whether we err by defect, or excess, is of little importance, if we are equally wide of the mark, as we certainly are in either case. For whatever is less than truth, cannot be truth; and whatever is more than true must be false.

Wherefore, as the whole of this great nation seams now more than ever in danger of being hurried into one or the other of these equally pernicious extremes, irreligion or fanaticism, I thought myself more than ordinarily obliged to rouse your, perhaps drowsy vigilance, by warning you of the nearness of your peril; cautioning you from leaning towards either side, though but to peep at the slippery precipice; and stepping between you and error, before it comes nigh enough to grapple with you. The happy medium of true Christian piety, in which it has pleased the mercy of God to establish you, is built on a firm rock, "and the gates of hell shall never prevail against it." While then you stand steadily upright in the fullness of the faith, falsehood and sin shall labor in vain to approach you; whereas, the least familiarity with error, will make you giddy, and if once you stagger in principles, your ruin is almost inevitable.

But not I have cautioned you of the danger you are in from the enemies who threaten your subversion, I hope your own watchfulness will be sufficient to guard you from any surprise. And from their own assaults you have nothing to fear, since while you persist in the firm resolution, through God's grace, to keep them out, irreligion and enthusiasm, falsehood and vice, impiety and false piety, will combine in vain to force an entrance into your hearts.

Take then, my dearly beloved fellow members of Christ's mystical body, take the friendly caution I give you in good part, and endeavor to profit by it: attend wholly to the saving truths I here deliver to you, and per persuaded, that they are uttered by one who has your eternal salvation as much at heart as his own.

"And thou, O Lord Jesus Christ, fountain of all truth, whence all wisdom flows, open the understandings of thy people to the light of thy true faith, and touch their hearts with thy grace, that they may both be able to see, and willing to perform what thou requirest of them. Drive away from us every cloud of error and perversity; guard us alike from irreligion and false pretensions to piety; and lead us on perpetually towards that perfection to which thou hast taught us to aspire; that keeping us here in a constant imitation of thee, and peaceful union which each other, thou mayest at length bring us to that everlasting glory, which thou hast promised to all such as shall endeavor to be perfect, even as the Father who is in heaven is perfect, who with thee and the Holy Ghost lives and reigns one God, world without end! Amen, Amen.

Ecclesiastes 7:16, "Be not righteous over much; neither make thyself over wise: why shouldest thou destroy thyself?"

Righteousness over-much! May one say; Is there any danger of that? Is it even possible? Can we be too good? If we give any credit to the express word of God, we cannot be too good, we cannot be righteous over-much. The injunction given by God to Abraham is very strong: "Walk before me, and be thou perfect." The same he again lays upon all Israel, in the eighteenth of Deuteronomy: "Thou shalt be perfect, and without blemish, with the Lord thy God." And lest any should think to excuse themselves from this obligation, by saying, it ceased when the old law was abolished, our blessed Savior ratified and explained it: "Be ye, therefore, perfect, even as your Father who is in heaven is perfect." So that until our perfection surpasses that of our heavenly Father, we can never be too good nor righteous over-much; and as it is impossible we should ever surpass, or even come up to him in the perfection of goodness and righteousness, it follows in course that we never can be good or righteous in excess. Nevertheless Doctor Trapp has found out that we may be righteous over-much, and has taken no small pains, with much agitation of spirit, to prove that it is a great folly and weakness, nay, a great sin. "O Lord! Rebuke thou his spirit, and grant that this false doctrine may not be published to his confusion in the day of judgment!"

But if what this hasty, this deluded man advances had been true, could there be any occasion, however, of warning against it in these times, "when the danger (as he himself to his confusion owns) is on the contrary extreme; when all manner of vice and wickedness abounds to a degree almost unheard of?" I answer for the present, that "there must be heresies amongst you, that they who are approved may be made manifest."

However, this earthly-minded minister of a new gospel, has taken a text which seems to favor his naughty purpose, of weaning the well-disposed little ones of Christ from that perfect purity of heart and spirit, which is necessary to all such as mean to live to our Lord Jesus. O Lord, what shall become of thy flock, when their shepherds betray them into the hands of the ravenous wolf!

When a minister of thy word perverts it to overthrow thy kingdom, and to destroy scripture with scripture!

Solomon, in the person of a desponding, ignorant, indolent liver (resident), says to the man of righteousness: "Be not righteous over-much, neither make thyself overwise: Why shouldest thou destroy thyself?" But must my angry, over-sighted brother Trapp, therefore, personate a character so unbecoming his function, merely to overthrow the express injunction of the Lord to us; which obliges us never to give over pursuing and thirsting after the perfect righteousness of Christ, until we rest in him? Father, forgive him, for he knows not what he says!

What advantage might not Satan gain over the elect, if the false construction, put upon this text by that unseeing teacher, should prevail! Yet though he blushes not to assist Satan to bruise our heel, I shall endeavor to bruise the heads of both, by showing,

I. *First*, The genuine sense of the text in question.

II. The character of the persons, who are to be supposed speaking here: And

III. The character of the persons spoken to.

From whence will naturally result these consequences.

First, That the Doctor was grossly (Lord grant he was not maliciously) mistaken in his explanatory sermon on this text, as well as in the application of it.

Secondly, That he is a teacher and approver of worldly maxims.

Thirdly, That he is of course an enemy to perfect righteousness in men, through Christ Jesus, and, therefore, no friend to Christ: And therefore, that no one ought to be deluded by the false doctrine he advances, to beguile the innocent, and deceive, if possible, even the elect.

I. To come at the true sense of the text in question, it will be necessary to look back, to the preceding verse, where the wise man, reflecting on the vanities of his youth, puts on for a moment his former character. "All things, have I seen in the days of my vanity: (and among the rest) there is a just man that perisheth in his righteousness, and there is a wicked man who prolongeth his life in his wickedness." Now it is very plain, that he is not here talking of a man, who is righteous over-much, in the Doctor's manner of understanding the words, that is, "faulty, and criminal by excess." For on one side he commends him for being a just man, and full of righteousness, and yet on the other tells us, that his righteousness is the shortening of his life. Whereas, had he looked upon his perishing in righteousness to be an over-righteousness, he would never have called him a just man. Neither by a wicked man, can he mean a man given up to the utmost excess of wickedness, since he tells us, that he prolongeth his life in (or by) his wickedness. Who does not know, that the excess of almost every kind of vice, is of itself a shortener of life. So that the whole opposition and contrast lies between a good man, and a bad man. A good man whose goodness shortens his life, and bad man whose iniquity lengthens his life, or at least is not excessive enough to shorten the thread of it. Solomon, absorbed in these reflections, speaks here by way of prosopopeia, not the sense of Solomon, the experienced, the learned, the wise; but of the former Solomon, a vain young fellow, full of self-love, and the strong desires of life. In the quality of such a one then, he looks with the same eye upon the righteous man, who perishes in his righteousness, as he would on a wicked one, who should perish in his wickedness. For it is neither the righteousness of the one, nor the wickedness of the other, that offends him, but the superlative degrees of both; which tending equally to shorten life, he looks upon them as equally opposite to the self-love he fondles within him. And, therefore, he deems an excess of debauchery as great an enemy to the lasting enjoyment of the pleasures of life, as an extraordinary righteousness would be. Well then might he say to the latter, in this character, "Be not over-much wicked, neither be thou foolish; why shouldst thou die before thy time?" And to the former: "Be not righteous over-much, neither make thyself over-wise: Why shouldst thou destroy thyself?"

What wonder then, that a youth of sprightliness and sense, but led away by self-love to be fond of the pleasures and enjoyments of life, when attained without hurry, and possessed without risk; what wonder, I say, that such a youth should conceive an equal dislike to the superlative degrees of virtue and vice, and, therefore, advise such of his companions as give into the excess of debauchery, to refrain from it: as it must infallibly tend to clog their understandings, stupify their senses, and entail upon their constitutions a train of infirmities, which cannot but debilitate their natural vigor, and shorten their days? "Be not over-much wicked, neither be thou foolish: Why shouldst thou die before thy time?" What wonder, that the same self-love should prompt him to dissuade such of his friends or acquaintance, as he wishes to have for companions, and countenancers of his worldly-minded pursuits, from pursuing righteousness and wisdom to a degree that must destroy in them all taste of earthly pleasures, and may possibly impair their constitutions, and forward their end? "Be not righteous over-much, neither make thyself overwise: Why shouldst thou destroy thyself?"

This is the sense in which Solomon (placing himself in the state of vanity of his youth) speaks to the one, and the other: to the righteous, and to the ungodly. This is the true, genuine sense of the letter; and every other sense put upon it, is false and groundless, and wrested rather to pervert than explain the truth of the text. O Christian simplicity, whither art thou fled? Why will not the clergy speak truth? And why must this false prophet suffer thy people, O Lord, to believe a lie? They have held the truth in unrighteousness. Raise up, I beseech thee, O Lord, some true pastors, who may acquaint them with the nature and necessity of perfect righteousness, and lead them to that love of Christian perfection which the angry-minded, pleasure-taking Doctor Trapp, labors to divert them from, by teaching, that "all Christians must have to do with some vanities."

Is not the meaning of this text plain to the weakest capacity? I have here given it to you, as I have it from the mouth of the royal preacher himself. I have made use of no "philosophy and vain deceit after the tradition of men, after the rudiments of the world, and not after Christ," to impose a fleshly sense upon you, for the sense of the word of God. No, I have given you a natural exposition obvious from the very words themselves. Hence you may see, my fellow-strugglers in righteousness, how grossly our angry adversary is mistaken in his explanation of this text. Lord! Open his eyes, and touch his heart; and convert him, and all those erring ministers, who have seen vain and foolish things for thy people, and have not discovered their iniquity, to turn away thy captivity. For they have erred through wine, and through strong drink are out of the way! The priest and the prophet have erred through strong drink, they are swallowed up of wine, they are out of the way through strong drink, they err in vision, they stumble in judgment.

It is plain from the words of the text, that the royal Preacher was speaking in the person of a vain worldling, when he said, "Be not righteous over-much;" whereby he meant to exhort the truly righteous not to be dismayed, terrified, or disturbed from their constant pursuit of greater and greater perfection of righteousness, until they rest in Christ; notwithstanding the derision, fleshly persuasion, ill-treatment and persecution of worldly men: Who, one day, repenting and groaning for anguish of spirit, shall say within themselves, "These were they whom we had sometimes in derision, and a proverb of reproach. We fools, accounted their lives madness; and their end to be without honor. How are they numbered among the children of God, and their lot is among the saints!"

How blind then is the application (not to say perverse) which this self-wise clergyman makes from the text, to such as, following the advice of the apostle, Coloss. 3:2, "set their affections on things above, not on things on the earth." Must hastiness in anger get the better of sense and truth? Must the people be misled because the pastor cannot, or will not see? Or must the injunction of Christ, "Be perfect, even as your Father, who is in heaven, is perfect," give place to the maxim of the heathen Tully: The greatest reproach to a philosopher, is to confute his doctrine by his practice; if this be the case, alas, what a deplorable, unspeakably deplorable condition is that of some Christians? Wherefore, "thus saith the Lord concerning the prophets who make his people to err, that bite with their teeth and cry peace; and he that putteth not into their mouths, they even prepare war against him: therefore night shall be unto you, that ye shall not have a vision, and it shall be dark unto you, that ye shall not divine, and the sun shall go down over the prophets, and the day shall be dark over them.

But I will leave these lovers of darkness, and turn to you, O beloved, elect of God! I beseech you, by the bowels of Christ, suffer not yourselves to be deceived by their flattering, sin-soothing speeches. "Be not of that rebellious people, lying children, children who will not hear the law of the Lord: who say to the seers, see not; and to the prophets, prophesy not unto us right things, speak unto us smooth things, prophesy deceits." Follow not those, who flatter you in the vanities they practice themselves. O may you never be of the number of those, in the person of whom Solomon here says, "Be not righteous over-much;" for their character is the character of the beast.

II. The character of the persons, who are to be supposed speaking here in the text, is in a word the same with the character of those whom Solomon here personates: who, as is already shown, are a vain set of men, neither righteous enough to have an habitual desire of improving virtue to its perfection, nor quite so flagitious [sinful, unlawful, wicked] as to give into self-destroying vices: in a word, they are self-lovers, the sole end of whose pursuits, whether indifferent, bad, or laudable in themselves, is self-enjoyment. Insomuch that they look upon virtue and vice, righteousness and wickedness, with the same eye, and their fondness of aversion for both is alike, as their different degrees appear to be the means to enhance and prolong the enjoyment of pleasure, or to lessen and shorten those pleasures. Thus any virtue, while it is kept within such bounds as may render it subservient to the pleasurable degrees of vice, will meet with no opposition from them; on the contrary, they will even commend it. But the moment it becomes a restraint to vice in moderation (if I may be allowed to make use of terms adequate to their system) from that moment it gives offense, and they put it in their caveat, "Be not righteous over-much." In like manner, vice, while confined to certain limits, which rather improve than obstruct pleasures ,is with them a desirable good; but no sooner does it launch out into any depth, sufficient to drown and diminish the relish of those pleasures, than they declare open war against it; "Be not over-much wicked." And the reason they assign for their opposition in both cases, is the same: "why shouldst thou destroy thyself? Why shouldst thou die before thy time?" Such is the prudence of the world, the flesh, and the devil. Such the maxims of these refined libertines, so much that more dangerous as they are less obvious; so much the more insinuating, as they are removed from certain extra-vagancies capable of shocking every man who has the least sense and delicacy. O Lord, how true is it, that the sons of darkness are wiser in their generation than the sons of light!

You are not then, beloved in the Lord, to imagine that your greatest opposition, in struggling for perfect righteousness, is to come from profligates, from men whose enormous vices create horror even to themselves: no, your most dangerous, most formidable enemies, are the kind of men I have painted to you, who render vice relishable with a mixture of apparent virtue, and clothe wickedness in the apparel of righteousness; "Beware of them, for they come to you in the clothing of sheep, but inwardly are ravenous wolves."

This perverse generation will ensnare you into ungodliness, by seeming oppositions to vice, and allow you to swallow the seemings of virtue and righteousness like an emetic, only to puke forth the reality of them. They paint black, white, and the white they convert into black. Not content with seeming what they are not, they labor to make you, what they are. Righteousness and wickedness they interweave in an artful tissue, capable of deceiving the very elect, and difficult for the most discerning among them to unravel; as almsgiving and avarice, pride and humility, temperance and luxury, are dexterously blended together; while as mutual curbs to each other, they combine to stem the tide of impediments to worldly enjoyment, which might flow from extraordinary degrees on either side. Thus "Almsgiving (you are told) is very excellent," and you believe the proposition, without knowing the particular sense it is spoken in, which is, that alms-giving is an excellent curb upon avarice, by preserving a rich man from such a superlative love of money as deprives him of the self-enjoyment of it. And upon the strength of this belief, the worldly-minded man, who labors to deceive you, gains credit enough with you to establish this maxim, that all superlative degrees of alms-giving, are *great sins*, and that a man must never sell all he has and give it to the poor, because some may have families of their own, and ought to make sufficient provision for them, according to that proverb, "Charity begins at home;" when no one, at least scarce any one, is wise enough to know, when he has a sufficiency. O Lord, which are we to believe, these worldlings, or thee? If thou dost deceive us, why dost thou threaten us with punishments, if we do not heed thee? And if the world is deceitful, shall we not flee from it to cleave to thee?

"Pride is a great sin" even with these worldlings, inasmuch as the external excesses of it, may obstruct the way to many ambitious terminations of view, and its internal agitations are the destruction of that peace, to which even self-love aspires; besides, the frequent extravagancy of its motions may not only be prejudicial to health, but a shortner of life. And, therefore, no wonder they should object against it, "Be not over much wicked: why shouldst thou die before thy time?" For this reason, they look upon a little mixture of humility to be not only commendable, but even necessary to cub the extravagant follies of an overbearing pride. But then a superlative degree of humility, that is, humility free from the least tincture of pride or vanity, which is the same with them, as "an over-strained humility, is a fault as well as folly;" because, forsooth, it is an expediment to the self-enjoyment of the world and its pleasures; "All Christians must have to do with some vanities, or else they must needs go out of the world indeed; for the world itself is all over vanity." 'Tis nothing, therefore, surprising, my brethren, to see a man of this cast of mind making a vain ostentation (act of display, show) of his little superficial acquaintance, with the ancient Greeks and Romans. What is this but acting conformably to his own principle, that "all Christians must have to do with some vanities?" And shall we wonder to hear such a one prefer their writings, to those of an apostle; or be astonished to see him wound the apostle with raillery, (good-natured ridicule) through your sides, for wishing to know nothing but Jesus Christ, and him crucified? No, with him it is consistency to laugh and reprove you out of the perfection of righteousness, which, however he may play with terms, is with him the same as being righteousness over-much; but with you it would be inconsistency, who ought to know no difference between being righteous, and living in a perpetual, habitual desire of being superlatively so. It is no more than, than you ought to expect to hear such advocates for the world cry out to you, "Be not righteous over-much: why should you destroy yourselves?" But, O Lord, surely this is not the same voice which tells us, that unless we humble ourselves like unto children, we shall not enter into the kingdom of heaven, and that he is greatest there, who humbles himself the most like a child! But what will not men advance who are drunk with passion, and intoxicated with self-love?

"The vice of intemperance in eating, and drinking, is plain to everybody," they own. And, therefore, they give it up as an excess which cannot but tend to the impairing of health, and shortening of life: nay, it drowns the very relish of pleasure in actual eating and drinking. Hence will every refined debauchee exclaim against it with Dr. Trapp: "Be not over much wicked: why shouldst thou destroy thyself?" Little sobriety, say they, is requisite to give a zest to luxury and worldly pleasures. But too much of it is too much, "to eat nothing but bread and herbs, and drink nothing but water, unless there be a particular reason for it (such perhaps as Doctor Cheyne may assign) is folly at best (that is, even though it be done for Christ's sake) therefore no virtue:" "Be not then righteous over-much, why shouldst thou destroy thyself?" And if you should answer those carnally-minded men with the words of the apostle, Rom. 8, "We are debtors, not to the flesh, to live after the flesh; For if we live after the flesh, we shall die: but if we, through the spirit, do mortify the deeds of the flesh, we shall live." If you answer them thus, they will tell you, this is teaching for doctrines the commandments of men." And it will be to as little purpose to answer them, with what St. Paul says elsewhere (Rom. 14:17) "The kingdom of God is not meat and drink, but righteousness, and peace, and joy in the Holy Ghost:" They will not blush to tell you, that "our blessed Savior came eating and drinking, nay worked a miracle to make wind (at an entertainment) when it is plain there had been more drank than was necessary." To such lengths does the love of the world hurry these self-fond, merry-making worldlings! Tell them of self-denial, they will not hear you, it is an encroachment upon the pleasures of life, and may shorten it of a few days, which you are never sure of possessing; it is being "righteous over-much: why shouldst thou destroy thyself?" Jesus, you will say, tells us (John 12:25) "He that loveth his life shall lose it, and he that hateth his life in this world, shall keep it unto life eternal." But this and the like, they will inform you, "are hyperbolical phrases." Now what signifies minding Jesus, when he speaks hyperbolically, that is, speaks more than is strictly true. Yet, O Lord Jesus, grant us to mind thee, whatever these worldlings may say; remind us, that if any man will come after thee, he must deny himself, and take up his cross, and follow thee! O how enlarging is it to the soul, to take up the cross of Christ and follow him!

But you are charged, ye beloved lovers of perfect righteousness, with extravagances. You allow of "no sort of recreation or diversion; nothing but an universal mortification and self-denial; no pleasure but from religion only:" you teach "that the bodily appetites must not be in the least degree gratified, any farther than is absolutely necessary to keep body and soul together, and mankind in being: No allowances are to be made for melancholy misfortunes, or human infirmity: grief must be cured only by prayer;" (a horrid grievance this, to such as think prayer burdensome at best) "To divert it by worldly amusements is carnal." A heavy charge this: but left it should seem so only to those carnal persons, who are resolved to give way to their carnal appetites; what you look upon as advisable only, these perverters of truth insinuate to be looked upon by you as indispensable duties. And lest prevarication should fail, downright falsehoods must be placed to your account, "so that to taste an agreeable fruit, or smell to a rose, must be unlawful with you," however you disown it. But O, my beloved Christians, be not discouraged from the pursuit of perfect righteousness by these or such vile misrepresentations. For "blessed are ye when men shall revile you, and shall say all manner of evil against you falsely for the sake of Christ Jesus. Rejoice, and be exceeding glad: For great is your reward in heaven: for so persecuted they the prophets who were before you."

Thus far, then, may suffice to show clearly with what dangerous views the worldly-minded men, whom Solomon personates in the text before us, lay siege to your souls in fair speeches. What I have said, is enough to convince you, that their character is that of the beast, whom St. John, in the Revelations, "saw coming up from the sea (that is, the flagitious [sinful, unlawful, wicked] world) with seven heads." And what shall we say of a man, a clergyman, who teaches, and is an advocate for their perverse doctrines? May we not, nay, must we not, for the glory of God, and your good, inform you, that he is a "Teacher and approver of worldly maxims." May I not, nay, must I not, give you this caution with the royal preacher: "When he speaketh fair, believer him not, for there are seven abominations in his heart?" But how different is the character I have given you, from the character of the persons to whom the text under consideration is spoken! That is, the character of all such, as, like you, are resolved never to rest, 'till they rest in Christ Jesus. To show this, I shall now pass to my third point.

III. To what sort of persons does Solomon in the character of a worldling address himself, when he says, "Be not righteous over-much, neither make thyself over-wise: why shouldst thou destroy thyself?" Not to the wicked, 'tis plain; for besides that it would have been an unnecessary precaution, he turns to these in the next verse with another kind of warning, which however has some analogy with this. "Be not over-much wicked, neither be thou foolish, why shouldst thou die before thy time?" Was it then to the righteous, in a common way; that is, to such as content themselves with the observance of the absolute essentials of God's laws? Surely our adversaries will not allow this, unless they be of opinion, that to be righteous at all, is to be righteous over-much. And yet it cannot possibly be supposed that the persons spoken to, are men perfectly righteous; since, as I proved to you, in the introduction of this discourse, till we come up to the perfection of our heavenly father, we can never be righteous enough, much less perfectly righteous: wherefore, as in this life, men cannot attain to the perfection of their heavenly father, it follows in course that the persons here spoken to, cannot be men perfectly righteous, there being no such men existing; for as St. John saith, "If we say that we have no sin, we deceive ourselves, and the truth is not in us." Alas, O Lord, when shall we be delivered from the body of this death?

It remains, that the persons spoken to, in the text, are such only, as persisting steadfastly in a firm adherence to all the essential laws of God, content not themselves with the practice of common virtues in a common degree, but live in a perpetual habitude of desires, struggles, and yearnings towards an intimate union with Christ, the perfection of righteousness. They are not of the number of those righteous with indifference, who would fain blend the service of God and mammon, would fain have Christ and the world for their masters, and halting between two, like the children of Israel of old, with their faces to heaven, and their hearts to the earth, are neither hot nor cold. Alas, would they were cold or hot! But "because they are luke-warm, and neither cold nor hot, the Lord shall spew the out of his mouth."

Not so the persons spoken to in my text; not so you, O beloved in God, who having shaken off the world and worldly affection; to run the more swiftly after righteousness, hate your own lives for the sake of Christ. Happy, happy are all you, who put on our Lord Jesus, and with him the new man! "You are the true circumcision which worship God in spirit, and rejoice in Christ Jesus, and have no confidence in the flesh."

What wonder then, Christians! To you I speak, all ye lovers and strugglers after the perfect righteousness of your divine Master Christ; what wonder is it, that you should be charged with enthusiasm, with folly, with fanaticism and madness? Were not the apostles so before you, when they preached Christ Jesus? Nay were they not reputed drunk with wine? Can you be amazed at it in an age, "when all manner of vice abounds to a degree almost unheard of," when the land is full of adulterers, and because of swearing the land mourneth. O how is the faithful city become an harlot! My heart within me is broken, because of the clergy, all my bones shake? I am like a drunken man, and like a man whom wine hath overcome; because of the Lord, and because of the words of his holiness, perverted by this deluded clergyman.

When the clergy, whom Christ has appointed to teach his people "to walk before him and be perfect," become teachers of worldly maxims, what can be expected from the laity? It is notorious, that for the moralizing iniquity of the priest, the land mourns. They have preached and lived many sincere persons out of the church of England. They endeavor to make you vain: (as the prophets did in the day of Jeremiah) they speak a vision out of their own mouth, and not out of the mouth of the Lord. In a word, "both prophet and priest are profane, and do wickedness in the very house of the Lord." Nay, they say still to them who despise the Lord, The Lord hath said, Ye shall have peace; and they say to every one who walketh after the imagination of his own heart, No evil shall come upon you.

Such is the language, my beloved lovers of Christian perfection, which the indolent, earthly-minded, pleasure-taking clergy of the church of England, use to strengthen the hands of evil-doers, that none may return from his wickedness. Such is the doctrine of the letter-learned divine, who has dipped his pen in gall, to decry perfect righteousness, and to delude you from it, with a false application of that text so greatly misunderstood by him: "Be not righteous over-much, neither be thou over-wise: why shouldst thou destroy thyself?" But suffer not yourselves, my fellow-Christians, to be deluded by him. For as I have already shown to you, he is grossly (Lord grant he was not maliciously) mistaken in his manner of explaining this text; and so far from making a right application of it according to the wise, the experienced Solomon's intention, he acts the character of a vain libertine, full of self-love, and earthly desires, whom Solomon but personates, to ridicule. But the doctor by realizing that character is himself, becomes the teacher and approver of worldly maxims, which he applies to you, on purpose to destroy in you the yearnings after perfect righteousness in Christ. May I not then, nay, must I not warn you, my beloved, that this man is an enemy to perfect righteousness in men through Christ Jesus, and, therefore, no friend to Christ? O that my head was an ocean, and my eyes fountains of tears, to weep night and day for this poor creature, this hood-winked member of the clergy.

Pray you, O true Christians, pray and sigh mightily to the Lord; importune him in the behalf of this erring pastor; pray that he would vouchsafe to open the eyes, and touch the stubborn heart of this scribe, that he may become better instructed. Otherwise, as the Lord said by the mouth of his true prophet Jeremiah, "Behold, I will feed him with wormwood, and make him drink the water of gall; for from him is profaneness gone forth into all the land."

This good, however, hath he done by attempting to show the folly, sin, and danger of that which he miscalls being righteous over-much, that is, being superlatively righteous, in desire and habitual struggles; he has thereby given me the occasion to show you, brethren, in the course of this sermon, the great and real folly, sin, and danger of not being righteous enough; which, perhaps, I should never have thought of doing, had not this false doctrine pointed out to me the necessity of doing it. Thus does the all-wise providence of God, make use of the very vices of men to draw good out of evil; and choose their very errors to confound falsehood and make way for truth. Though this should be more than our angry adversary intended, yet, Lord, reward him according to his works: and suffer him no longer to be hasty in his words, that we may have room to entertain better hopes of him for the future.

Blessed be God for sending you better guides! I am convinced it was his divine will: our dear fellow-creature, Doctor Trapp, falling to such errors, has given so great a shock to the sound religion of Christian perfection, that unless I had opposed him, I verily believe the whole flock who listened to his doctrine, would have been scattered abroad like sheep having no shepherd. "But woe to you scribes and Pharisees! Woe be unto the pastors that destroy and scatter the sheep of my pasture, saith the Lord."

Full well I know that this sermon will not be pleasing to my poor peevish adversary; but correction is not to pleasure but to profit: few children can be brought willingly to kiss the rod which rebuketh them; though, when they become of riper understanding, they will bless the hand that guided them. Thus shall this angry man, I trust, thank me one day for reproving him, when his reason shall be restored to him by the light of the Holy Spirit. O Lord, grant thou this light unto him, and suffer him to see with what bowels of pity and tenderness I love him in thee, even while I chasten him.

Neither am I insensible, brethren, how offensive my words will be to worldlings in general, who loving falsehood better than truth, and the flesh before the spirit will still prefer the doctor's sin-soothing doctrines to the plain gospel verities preached by me. O how my soul pities them. But I have done my duty, I wash my hands, and am innocent of the blood of all. I have not fought to please my hearers, but have spoken plain truth though it should offend. For what things were gain to me, those I counted loss for Christ; and hope I shall ever do so. Not that I presume to think myself already perfect. But "I press towards the mark, for the prize of the high calling of God in Christ Jesus."

None of us, as I before told you, can boast of having attained the summit of perfection; though, he is the nearest to it, who is widest from the appetites of the flesh, and he stands the highest, who is the lowliest in his own esteem: wherefore, as many of us as have made any advances towards Christ and his kingdom, "whereto we have already attained, let us walk by the same rule, let us mind the same thing."

Walk not then, brethren, according to the ways of the world: but be followers of Christ together with me. And if any, even an angel of light, should presume to teach you any other gospel than that which I have here taught you, let him be accursed. "For you will find many walking, like such of whom I have told you already, and now tell you weeping, that they are the enemies of the cross of Christ: whose end is destruction, whose God is their belly: and whose glory is in their shame, for they mind worldly things. But your conversation is in heaven, from whence also you look for the Savior, the Lord Jesus Christ: who shall change your vile bodies, that they may be fashioned like unto his glorious body, according to the working whereby he is able to subdue even all things unto himself," even the stubborn heart of our perverse adversary.

Which God of his infinite mercy grant.

11. The Benefits of an Early Piety

The amiableness of religion in itself, and the innumerable advantages that flow from it to society in general, as well as to each sincere professor in particular, cannot but recommend it to the choice of every considerate person, and make, even wicked men, as they wish to die the death, so in their more sober intervals, to envy the life of the righteous. And, indeed, we must do the world so much justice, as to confess, that the question about religion does not usually arise from a dispute whether it be necessary or not (for most men see the necessity of doing something for the salvation of their souls;) but when is the best time to set about it. Persons are convinced by universal experience, that the first essays or endeavors towards the attainment of religion, are attended with some difficulty and trouble, and therefore they would willingly defer the beginning of such a seemingly ungrateful work, as long as they can. The wanton prodigal, who is spending his substance in riotous living, cries, a little more pleasure, a little more sensuality, and then I will be sober in earnest. The covetous worldling, that employs all his care and pains in "heaping up riches, though he cannot tell who shall gather them," does not flatter himself that this will do always; but hopes with the rich fool in the gospel, to lay up goods for a few more years on earth, and then he will begin to lay up treasures in heaven. And, in short, thus it is that most people are convinced of the necessity of being religious some time or another; but then, like Felix, they put off the acting suitably to their convictions, 'till, what they imagine, a more convenient season: whereas, would we be so humble as to be guided by the experience and counsel of the wisest men, we should learn that youth is the fittest season for religion; "Remember now thy creator, (says Solomon) in the days of thy youth." By the word remember, we are not to understand a bare speculative remembrance, or calling to mind, (for that, like a dead faith, will profit us nothing,) but such a remembrance as will constrain us to obedience, and oblige us out of gratitude, to perform all that the Lord our God shall require of us. For as the forgetting God in scripture language, implies a total neglect of our duty, in like manner remembering him signifies a perfect performance of it: so that, when Solomon says, "Remember thy Creator in the days of thy youth,: it is the same as if he had said, keep God's commandments; or, in other words, be religious in the days of thy youth, thereby implying, that youth is the most proper season for it.

I shall in the following discourse,

First, Endeavor to make good the wise man's proposition, implied in the words of the text, and to show that youth is the fittest season for religion.

Secondly, By way of motive, I shall consider the many unspeakable advantages that will arise from, "Remembering our Creator in the days of our youth." And,

Thirdly, I shall conclude with a word or two of exhortation to the younger part of this audience.

First, I am to make good the wise man's proposition, implied in the words of the text, and to show that youth is the fittest season for religion: "Remember now thy Creator in the days of thy youth." But to proceed more clearly in this argument, it may not be improper, first, to explain what I mean by the word religion. By this term, then, I would not be understood to mean a bare outward profession or naming the name of Christ; for we are told, that many who have even prophesied in his name, and in his name cast out devils, shall notwithstanding be rejected by him at the last day: nor would I understand by it, barely being admitted into Christ's church by baptism; for then Simon Magus, Arius, and the heresiarchs [heresies, maybe arch-heresies] of old, might pass for religious persons; for these were baptized: nor yet the receiving the other seal of the covenant, for then Judas himself might be canonized for a saint; nor indeed do I mean any or all of these together, considered by themselves; but a thorough, real, inward change of nature, wrought in us by the powerful operations of the Holy Ghost, conveyed to and nourished in our hearts, by a constant use of all the means of grace, evidenced by a good life, and bringing forth the fruits of the spirit.

The attaining this real, inward religion, is a work of so great difficulty, that Nicodemus, a learned doctor and teacher in Israel, thought it altogether impossible, and therefore ignorantly asked our blessed Lord, "How this thing could be?" And, truly, to rectify a disordered nature, to mortify our corrupt passions, to turn darkness to light, to put off the old man, and put on the new, and thereby to have the image of God reinstamped upon the soul, or, in one word, "to be born again," however light some may make of it, must, after all our endeavors, be owned by man to be impossible. It is true, indeed, Christ's yoke is said to be an easy or a gracious yoke, and his burden light; but then it is to those only to whom grace has been given to bear and draw in it. For, as the wise son of Sirach observes, "At first wisdom walked with her children in crooked ways, and bring them into fear, and torments them with her discipline, and does not turn to comfort and rejoice them, 'till she has tried them and d proved their judgment." No, we must not flatter ourselves that we shall walk in wisdom's pleasant ways, unless we first submit to a great many difficulties. The spiritual birth is attended with its pangs, as well as the natural: for they that have experienced it (an they only are the proper judges,) can acquaint you, that in all things that are dear to corrupt nature, we must deny ourselves, lest, after all, when w come to the birth, we should want strength to bring forth.

But if these things are so; if there are difficulties and pangs attending our being born again; if we must deny ourselves, what season more proper than that of youth? When, if ever, our bodies are robust and vigorous, and our minds active and courageous; and, consequently, we are then best qualified to endure hardness, as good soldiers of Jesus Christ.

We find, in secular matters, people commonly observe this method, and send their children abroad among the toils and fatigues of business, in their younger years, as well knowing they are then fittest to undergo them. And why do they not act with the same consistency in the grand affair of religion? Because, as our Savior has told us, "The children of this world are wiser in their generation than the children of light."

But, *Secondly*, If pure and undefiled religion consists in the renewal of our corrupted natures, then it is not only a work of difficulty, but, the perfection of it, of time.

And if this be the case, then it highly concerns every one to set about it betimes, and to "work their work while it is day, before the night cometh, when no man can work."

Could we, indeed, live to the age of Methuselah, and had but little business to employ ourselves in, we might then be more excusable, if we made no other use of this world, than what too many do, take our pastime therein: but since our lives are so very short, and we are called to work our salvation with fear and trembling, we have no room left for trifling, lest we should be snatched away while our lamps are untrimmed, and we are entirely unprepared to meet the Bridegroom.

Did we know a friend or neighbor, who had a long journey of the utmost importance to make, and yet should stand all the day idle, neglecting to set out till the sun was about to go down, we could not but pity and condemn his egregious folly. And yet it is to be feared most men are just such fools; they have a long journey to take, nay, a journey to eternity, a journey of infinite importance, and which they are obliged to dispatch before the sun of their natural life be gone down; and yet they loiter away the time allotted them to perform their journey in, till sickness or death surprises them; and then they cry out, "What shall we do to inherit eternal life?" But leaving such to the mercies of God in Christ, who can call at the eleventh hour, I pass on to

The *Second* general thing proposed, To show the advantages that will arise from remembering our Creator in the days of our youth; which may serve as so many motives to excite and quicken all persons immediately to set about it.

And the *First* benefit resulting from thence is, that it will bring most honor and glory to God. This, I suppose, every serious person will grant, ought to be the point in which our actions should center; for to this end were we born, and to this end were we redeemed by the precious blood of Jesus Christ, that we should promote God's eternal glory. And as the glory of God is most advanced by paying obedience to his precepts, they that begin soonest to walk in his ways, act most to his glory. The common objection against the divine laws in general, and the doctrines of the gospel in particular, is, they are not practicable; that they are contrary to flesh and blood; and that all those precepts concerning self-denial, renunciation of and deadness to the world, are but so many arbitrary restraints imposed upon human nature: but when we see mere striplings not only practicing, but delighting in such religious duties, and in the days of their youth, when, if ever, they have a relish for sensual pleasures, subduing and despising the lust of the flesh, the lust of the eyes and the pride of life; this, this is pleasing to God; this vindicates his injured honor; this shows that his service is perfect freedom, "that his yoke is easy, and his burden light."

But, *Secondly*, as an early piety redounds most to the honor o God, so it will bring most honor to ourselves: for those that honor God, God will honor. We find it, therefore, remarked to the praise of Obadiah, that he served the Lord from his youth: of Samuel, that he stood, when young, before God in a linen ephod: of Timothy, that from a child he had known the holy scriptures: of St. John, that he was the youngest and most beloved disciple: and of our blessed Lord himself, that at twelve years old he went up to the temple, and sat among the doctors, both hearing and asking them questions.

Nor, *Thirdly*, will an early piety afford us less comfort than honor, not only because it renders religion habitual to us, but also because it gives us a well-grounded assurance of the sincerity of our profession. Was there no other argument against a death-bed repentance, but the unsatisfactoriness and anxiety of such a state, that should be sufficient to deter all thinking persons from deferring the most important business of their life to such a dreadful period of it. For supposing a man to be sincere in his profession of repentance on a death-bed (which, in most cases, is very much to be doubted) yet, he is often afraid lest his convictions and remorse proceed not from a true sorrow for sin, but a servile fear of punishment. But one, who is a young saint, need fear no such perplexity; he knows that he loves God for his own sake, and is not driven to him by a dread of impending evil; he does not decline the gratifications of sense, because he can no longer "hear the voice of singing men and singing women;" but willingly takes up his cross, and follows his blessed Master in his youth, and therefore has reason to expect greater confidence of his sincerity towards God. But further, as an early piety assures the heart of its sincerity, so, likewise, it brings its present reward with it, as it renders religion and its duties habitual and easy. A young saint, were you to ask him, would joyfully tell you the unspeakable comfort of beginning to be religious betimes: as for his part, he knows not what men mean by talking of mortification, self-denial, and retirement, as hard and rigorous duties; for he has so accustomed himself to them, that, by the grace of God, they are now become even natural, and he takes infinitely more pleasure in practicing the severest precepts of the gospel, than a luxurious Dives in a bed of state, or an ambitious Haman at a royal banquet. And O how happy must that youth be, whose duty is become a second nature, and to whom those things, which seem terrible to others, are grown both easy and delightful!

But the greatest advantage of an early piety is still behind, *Fourthly*, It lays in the best provision of comfort and support against such time as we shall stand most in need thereof, viz. All times of our tribulation, and in particular, against the time of old age, the hour of death, and the day of judgment.

This is the argument the wise man makes use of in the words immediately following the text: "Remember now your Creator in the days of thy youth, while the evil days come not, nor the years draw nigh, wherein thou shalt say, I have no pleasure in them." Observe, the time of old age, is an evil time, years wherein there is no pleasure: and ask those that are grown old, and they will inform you so. Cordials surely, then, must be exceeding proper to support our drooping spirits: and O what cordial comparable to the recollection of early piety, depending wholly on the righteousness of Christ? When the eyes, like Isaac's, are grown dim with age; when "the keepers of the house, the hands, shall tremble," as the wise man goes on to describe the infirmities of old age; when "the strong men bow themselves," or the legs grow feeble; and the "grinders," the tooth, shall cease to do their proper office, because they are few; for a person then to hear the precepts of the gospel read over to him, and to be able to lay his hand on his heart, and to say sincerely, notwithstanding a consciousness of numberless short-comings, "All these have I endeavored, through grace, to keep from my youth:" this must give him, through Christ who worketh all, comfort that I want words to express and thoughts to conceive. But, supposing it was possible for us to escape the inconveniences of old age, yet still death is a debt, since the fall, we all must pay; and, what is worse, it generally comes attended with such dreadful circumstances, that it will make even a Felix to tremble. But as for the godly, that have been enabled to serve the Lord from their youth, it is not usually so with them; no, they have faith given them to look upon death, not as a king of terrors, but as a welcome messenger, that is come to conduct them to their wished-for home. All the days of their appointed time have they waited, and it has been the business of their whole lives to study to prepare themselves for the coming of their great change; and, therefore, they rejoice to hear they are called to meet the heavenly Bridegroom. Thus dies the early pious, whose "path has been as the shining light, that shineth more and more unto the perfect day." But follow him beyond the grave, and see with what an holy triumph he enters into his Master's joy; with what an humble boldness he stands at the dreadful tribunal of Jesus Christ; and can you then forbear to cry out, "Let me die the death of the righteous, and let my latter end, and future state, be like his?"

Need I then, after having shown so many advantages to arise from an early piety, use any more arguments to persuade the younger part of this audience, to whom, in the *Third* and last place, I address myself, to "remember their Creator in the days of their youth?"

What! Will not all the arguments I have mentioned, prevail with them to leave their husks, and return home to eat of the fatted calf? What! Will they thus requite our Savior's love? That be far from them! Did he come down and shed his precious blood to deliver them from the power of sin; and will they spend their youthful strength and vigor in the service of it, and then think to serve Christ, when they can follow their lusts no longer? Is it fit, that many, who are endowed with excellent gifts, and are thereby qualified to be supports and ornaments of our sinking church, should, notwithstanding, forget the God who gave them, and employ them in things that will not profit? O why will they not arise, and, like so many Phineas's, be zealous for the Lord of Hosts? Doubtless, when death overtakes them, they will wish they had: and what hinders them, but that they begin now? Think you that any one yet ever repented that he began to be religious too soon? But how many, on the contrary, have repented that they began when almost too late? May we not well imagine, that young Samuel now rejoices that he waited so soon at the tabernacle of the Lord? Or young Timothy, that from a child he knew the holy scriptures? And if you wish to be partakers of their joy, let me persuade you to be partakers of their piety.

I could still go on to fill my mouth with arguments; but the circumstances and piety of those amongst whom I am now preaching "the kingdom of God," remind me to change my style; and, instead of urging any more dissuasives from sin, to fill up what is behind of this discourse, with encouragements to persevere in holiness.

Blessed, for ever blessed be the God and the Father of our Lord Jesus Christ, I am not speaking to persons inflamed with youthful lusts, but to a multitude of young professors, who by frequently assembling together, and forming themselves into religious societies, are, I hope on good ground, in a ready way to be of the number of those "young men, who have overcome the wicked-one."

Believe me, it gladdens my very soul, to see so many of your faces set heaven-wards, and the visible happy effects of your uniting together, cannot but rejoice the hearts of all sincere Christians, and oblige them to wish you good luck in the name of the Lord. The many souls who are nourished weekly with the spiritual body and blood of Jesus Christ, by your means; the weekly and monthly lectures that are preached by your contributions; the daily incense of thanksgiving and prayer which is publicly sent up to the throne of grace by your subscriptions; the many children which are trained up "in the nurture and admonition of the Lord," by your charities; and, lastly, the commendable and pious zeal you exert in promoting and encouraging divine psalmody, are such plain and apparent proofs of the benefit of your religious societies, that they call for a public acknowledgment of praise and thanksgiving to our blessed Master, who has not only put into your hearts such good designs, but enabled you also to bring the same to good effect.

It is true it has been object, "That young men forming themselves into religious societies, has a tendency to make them spiritually proud, and to think more highly of themselves than they ought to think." And, perhaps, the imprudent, imperious behavior of some novices in religion, who, "though they went out from you, were not of you," may have given too much occasion for such as aspersion.

But you, brethren, have not so learned Christ. Far, far be it from you to look upon yourselves, as righteous, and despise others, because you often assemble yourselves together. No; this, instead of creating pride, ought to beget an holy fear in your hearts, lest your practice should not correspond with your profession, and that, after you have benefited and edified others, you yourselves should become cast-aways.

Worldly-mindedness, my brethren, is another rock against which we are in danger of splitting. For, if other sins have slain their thousands of professing Christians, this has slain its ten thousands. I need not appeal to past ages; your own experience, no doubt, has furnished you with many unhappy instances of young men, who, "after (as one would have imagined) they had escaped the pollutions which are in the world through lust," and "had tasted the good word of life," and endured for a season, whilst under the tuition and inspection of others; yet, when they have come to be their own masters, through a want of faith, and through too great an earnestness in "laboring for the meat which perisheth," have cast off their first love, been again entangled with the world, and "returned like the dog to his vomit, and like the sow that was washed, to her wallowing in the mire." You would, therefore, do well, my brethren, frequently to remind each other of this dangerous snare, and to exhort one another to begin, pursue, and end your Christian warfare, in a thorough renunciation of the world, and worldly tempers; so that, when you are obliged by Providence to provide for yourselves, and those of your respective households, you may continue to walk by faith, and still "seek first the kingdom of God, and his righteousness;" not doubting, but all other things, upon your honest industry and endeavors, shall be added unto you.

And now, what shall I say more? To speak unto you, fathers, who have been in Christ so many years before me, and know the malignity of worldly-mindedness, and pride in the spiritual life, would be altogether needless. To you, therefore, O young men, (for whom I am distressed, for whom I fear as well as for myself) do I once more address myself, in the words of the beloved disciple, "Look to yourselves, that we lose not those things which we have wrought, but receive a full reward." Be ever mindful, then, of the words that have been spoken to us by the apostles of the Lord and Savior, "Give diligence to make your calling and election sure. Beware, lest ye also being led away by the error of the wicked, fall from your own steadfastness. Let him that thinketh he standeth, take heed lest he fall. Be not high-minded, but fear. But we are persuaded better things of you, and things that accompany salvation, though we thus speak. For God is not unrighteous, to forget your works and labor of love. And we desire that every one of you do show the same diligence, to the full assurance of hope unto the end: that ye be not slothful, but followers of them, who through faith and patience inherit the promises." It is true, we have many difficulties to encounter, many powerful enemies to overcome, ere we can get possession of the promised land. We have an artful devil, and ensnaring world, and above all, the treachery of our own hearts, to withstand and strive against. "For straight is the gate, and narrow is the way that leadeth unto eternal life." But wherefore should we fear, since he that is with us is far more powerful, than all who are against us? Have we not already experienced his almighty power, in enabling us to conquer some difficulties which seemed as insurmountable then, as those we struggle with now? And cannot he, who delivered us out of the paws of those bears and lions, preserve us also from being hurt by the strongest Goliath?

"Be steadfast therefore, my brethren, be immovable." Be not "ashamed of the gospel of Christ: for it is the power of God unto salvation." Fear not man; fear not the contempt and revilings which you must meet with in the way of duty; for one of you shall chase a thousand; and two of you put ten thousand of your enemies to flight. And if you will be contented, through grace, to suffer for a short time here; I speak the truth in Christ, I lie not; then may ye hope, according to the blessed word of promise, that ye shall be exalted to sit down with the Son of Man, when he shall come in the glory of his Father, with his holy angels, to judgment hereafter. May Almighty God give every one of us such a measure of his grace, that we may not be of the number of those that draw back unto perdition, but of them that believe and endure unto the end, to the saving of our souls, through our Lord Jesus Christ.

Which God.

12. Christ the Believer's Husband

Isaiah 54:5—"For thy Maker is thy Husband."

Although believers by nature, are far from God, and children of wrath, even as others, yet it is amazing to think how nigh they are brought to him again by the blood of Jesus Christ. Eye hath not seen, nor ear heard, neither hath it entered into the heart of any man living, fully to conceive, the nearness and dearness of that relation, in which they stand to their common head. He is not ashamed to call them brethren. Behold, says the blessed Jesus in the days of his flesh, "my mother and my brethren." And again after his resurrection, "go tell my brethren." Nay sometimes he is pleased to term believers his friends. "Henceforth call I you no longer servants, but friends." "Our friend Lazarus sleepeth." And what is a friend? Why there is a friend that is nearer than a brother, nay as near as one's own soul. And "thy friend, (says God in the book of Deuteronomy) which is as thy own soul." Kind and endearing applications these, that undoubtedly bespeak a very near and ineffably intimate union between the Lord Jesus and the true living members of his mystical body! But, methinks, the words of our text point out to us a relation, which not only comprehends, but in respect to nearness and dearness, exceeds all other relations whatsoever. I mean that of a Husband, "For thy Maker is thy husband; the Lord of Hosts is his name; and thy Redeemer the Holy One of Israel, the God of the whole earth shall he be called."

These words were originally spoken to the people of the Jews, considered collectively as a peculiar people, whom our Lord had betrothed and married to himself; and they seem to be spoken, when religion was on the decline among their churches; when they had, in a great measure, lost that life and power, which they once experienced; and their enemies began to insult them with a "where is now your God?" Such a state of things must undoubtedly be very afflicting to the true mourners in Zion; and put them upon crying unto the Lord, in this their deep distress. He hears their prayer, his bowels yearn towards them; and in the preceding verse, he assures them, that though the enemy had broken in upon them like a flood, yet their extremity should be his opportunity to lift up a standard against him. "Fear not, (says the great Head and King of his church) for thou shalt not be ashamed (finally or totally); neither be thou confounded, (dissipated or dejected, giving up all for gone, as though thou never shouldst see better days, or another revival of religion) for thou shalt not (entirely) be put to shame;" though for a while, for thy humiliation, and the greater confusion of thy adversaries, I suffer them to triumph over thee: "For thou shalt forget the shame of thy youth, and shalt not remember the reproach of thy widow-hood any more;" i.e. I will vouchsafe you such another glorious gale of my blessed Spirit, that you shall quite forget your former troubled widow-state, and give your enemies no more occasion to insult you, on account of your infant-condition, but rather to envy you, and gnash their teeth, and melt away at the sight of your un-thought-of glory and prosperity. And why will the infinitely great and condescending Jesus deal thus with his people? Because the church is his spouse; "For, (as in the words just now read to you) thy Maker is thy husband; thy Redeemer, the Holy One of Israel;" and therefore he loves them too well, to let thy enemies always trample thee under foot. "The Lord of Hosts is his name, the God of the whole earth shall he be called;" and therefore he is armed with sufficient power to relieve his oppressed people, and over come and avenge himself of all their haughty and insulting foes.

This seems to be the prime and genuine interpretation of the text and context, especially if we add, that they may have a further view to the latter-day glory, and that blesses state of the church, which the people of God have been looking for in all ages, and the speedy approach of which, we undoubtedly pray for, when we put up that petition of our Lord's, "thy kingdom come."

But, though the words were originally spoken to the Jews, yet they are undoubtedly applicable to all believers in all ages, and, when enlarged on in a proper manner, will afford us suitable matter of discourse both for sinners and for saints; for such as know God, as well as for such who know him not; and likewise for those, who once walked in the light of his blessed countenance, but are now backslidden from him, have their harps hung upon the willows, and are afraid that their beloved is gone, and will return to their souls no more. Accordingly, without prefacing this discourse any further, as I suppose that a mixed multitude of saints, unconverted sinners, and backsliders, are present here this day, I shall endeavor to speak from the words of the text, that each may have a proper portion, and none be went empty away.

In prosecuting this design, I will,

I. Endeavor to show, what must pass between Jesus Christ and our souls before we can say, "that our Maker is our husband."

II. The duties of love which they owe to our Lord, who stand in so near a relation to him,

III. The miserable condition of such as cannot yet say "their Maker is their husband." And

IV. I shall conclude with a general exhortation to all such unhappy souls, to come and match with the dear Lord Jesus. And O! may that God who blessed Abraham's servant, when he went out to seek a wife for his son Isaac, bless me, even me also, now I am come, I trust, relying on divine strength, to invite poor sinners, and recall backsliders, to my Master Jesus!

And *First*, I am to show, what must pass between Jesus Christ and our souls before we can say, "Our Maker is our husband."

But before I proceed to this, it may not be improper to observe, that if any of you, amongst whom I am now preaching the kingdom of God, are enemies to inward religion, and explode the doctrine of inward feelings, as enthusiasm, cant and nonsense, I shall not be surprised, if your hearts rise against me whilst I am preaching; for I am about to discourse on true, vital, internal piety; and an inspired apostle hath told us, "that the natural man discerneth not the things of the spirit, because they are spiritually discerned." But, however, be noble as the Bereans were; search the Scriptures as they did; lay aside prejudice; hear like Nathaniel, with a true Israelitish ear; be willing to do the will of God; and then you shall according to the promise of our dearest Lord, "know of the doctrine, whether it be of God, or whether I speak of myself."

I would further observe, that if any here do expect fine preaching from me this day, they will, in all probability, go away disappointed. For I came not here to shoot over people's heads; but, if the Lord shall be pleased to bless me, to reach their hearts. Accordingly, I shall endeavor to clothe my ideas in such plain language, that the meanest negro or servant, if God is pleased to give a hearing ear, may understand me; for I am certain, if the poor and unlearned can comprehend, the learned and rich must.

This being premised, proceed we to show what must pass between Jesus Christ and our souls, before we can say, "our Maker is our husband."

Now, that we may discourse more pertinently and intelligibly upon this point, it may not be amiss to consider, what is necessary to be done, before a marriage between two parties amongst ourselves, can be said to be valid in the sight of God and men. And that will lead us in a familiar way, to show what must be done, or what must pass between us and Jesus Christ, before we can say, "our Maker is our husband."

And *First*, in all lawful marriages, it is absolutely necessary, that the parties to be joined together in that holy and honorable estate, are actually and legally freed from all pre-engagements whatsoever. "A woman is bound to her husband, (saith the apostle) so long as her husband liveth." The same law holds good in respect to the man. And so likewise, if either party be betrothed and promised, though not actually married to another, the marriage is not lawful, till that pre-engagement and promise be fairly and mutually dissolved. Now, it is just thus between us and the Lord Jesus. For, we are all by nature born under, and wedded to the law, as a covenant of works. Hence it is that we are so fond of, and artfully go about, in order to establish a righteousness o four own. It is as natural for us to do this, as it is to breathe. Our first parents, Adam and Eve, even after the covenant of grace was revealed to them in that promise, "the seed of the woman shall bruise the serpent's head," reached out their hands, and would again have taken hold of the tree of life, which they had forfeited, had not God drove them our of paradise, and compelled them, as it were, to be saved by grace. And thus all their descendants naturally run to, and want to be saved, partly at least, if not wholly, by their works. And even gracious souls, who are inwardly renewed, so far as the old man abides in them, find a strong propensity this way. Hence it is, that natural men are generally so fond of Arminian principles. "Do and live," is the native language of a proud, self-righteous heart. But before we can say, "our Maker is our husband," we must be delivered from our old husband the law; we must renounce our own righteousness, our own doings and performances, in point of dependence, whether in whole or part, as dung and dross, for the excellency of the knowledge of Christ Jesus our Lord. For thus speaks the apostle Paul to the Romans, chapter 7:4, "Ye also are become dead to the law (as a covenant of works) by the body of Christ, that ye should be married to another, even to him, who is raised from the dead." As he also speaketh in another place, "I have espoused you, as a chaste virgin to Jesus Christ." This was the apostle's own case. Whilst he depended on his being a Hebrew of the Hebrews, and thought himself secure, because, as to the outward observation of the law, he was blameless; he was an entire stranger to the divine life: but when he began to experience the power of Jesus Christ's resurrection, we find him, in his epistle to the Philippians, absolutely renouncing all his external privileges, and all his Pharisaical righteousness; "Yes, doubtless, and I count all things but loss, nay but dung, that I may win Christ, and be found in him, not having mine own righteousness, which is of the law, but that which is through the faith of Jesus Christ, the righteousness which is of God by faith." And thus it must be with is. Ere we can say, "our Maker is our husband." Though we may not be wrought upon in that extraordinary way in which the apostle was, yet we must be dead to the law, we must be espoused as chaste virgins to Jesus Christ, and count all external privileges, and our most splendid performances (as was before observed) only "ad dung and dross, for the excellency of the knowledge of Jesus Christ our Lord."

But further; before a marriage among us can stand good in law, both parties must not only be freed from all pre-engagements, but there must be a mutual consent on both sides. We are not used to marry people against their wills. This is what the Jews called betrothing, or espousing, a thing previous to the solemnity of marriage. Thus we find, the Virgin Mary is said to be espoused to Joseph, before they actually came together, Matt. 1:18, And thus it is among us. Both parties are previously agreed, and, as it were, espoused to each other, before we publish, what we call the banns of marriage concerning them. And so it will be in the spiritual marriage, between Jesus Christ and our souls. Before we are actually married or united to him by faith; or, to keep to the terms of the text, before we assuredly can say, that "our Maker is our husband," we must be made willing people in the day of God's power, we must be sweetly and effectually persuaded by the Holy Spirit of God, that the glorious Emanuel is willing to accept of us, just as we are, and also that we are willing to accept of him upon his own terms, yea, upon any terms. And when once it comes to this, the spiritual marriage goes on apace, and there is but one thing lacking to make it complete. And what is that? An actual union.

From what has been delivered, may not the poorest and most illiterate person here present easily know whether or not he is really married to Jesus Christ. Some indeed, I am afraid, are so presumptuous as to affirm, as least to insinuate, that there is no such thing as knowing, or being fully assured, whilst here below, whether we are in Christ or not. Or at least, if there be such a thing, it is very rare, or was only the privilege of the primitive believers. Part of this is true, and part of this absolutely false. That this glorious privilege of a full assurance is very rare, is too, too true. And so it is equally too true, that real Christians, comparatively speaking, are very rare also. But that there is no such thing, or that this was only the privilege of the first followers of our blessed Lord, is directly opposite to the word of God. "We know (says St. John, speaking of believers in general) that we are his, by the spirit which he hath given us;" and, "He that believeth hath the witness of himself;" "because you are sons (saith St. Paul) God hath sent forth his Spirit into your hearts, even the spirit of adoption, whereby we cry, Abba, Father." Not that I dare affirm, that there is no real Christian, but what has this full assurance of faith, and clearly knows, that his Maker is his husband. In speaking thus, I should undoubtedly condemn some of the generation of God's dear children, who through the prevalence of unbelief, indwelling sin, spiritual sloth, or it may be, for want of being informed of the privileges of believers, may walk in darkness, and see no light; therefore, though I dare not affirm, that a full assurance of faith is absolutely necessary for the very being, yet I dare assert, that it is absolutely necessary, for the well being of a Christian. And for my own part, I cannot conceive, how any persons, that pretend to Christianity, can rest satisfied or contented without it. This is stopping short, on this side Jordan, with a witness. And gives others too much reason to suspect, that such persons, however high their profession may be, have, as yet, no true saving grace at all.

Men, whose hearts are set on this world's goods, or, to use our Lord's language, "the children of this world," act not so. I suppose there is scarce a single merchant in this great congregation, especially in these troublous times, that will venture out either his ship or cargo, without first insuring, both against the violence of an enemy, or a storm. And I suppose there is scarce a single house, of any considerable value, in any populous town or city, but the owner has taken out a policy from the fire-office, to unsure it, in case of fire. And can I be so irrational as to think, that there is such a thing as securing my goods, and my house, and that there is no such thing as insuring, what is infinitely more valuable, my precious and immortal soul? Or if there be such a thing, as undoubtedly there is, what foolishness of folly must it needs be in men, that pretend to be men of parts, of good sense, and solid reasoning, to be so anxious to secure their ships against a storm, and their houses against a fire, and at the same time, not to be unspeakably more solicitous, to take a policy out of the assurance-office of heaven; even the soul and witness of the blessed Spirit of God, to insure their souls against that storm of divine wrath, and that vengeance of eternal fire, which will at the last decisive day come upon all those, who know not God, and have not obeyed his gracious gospel? To affirm therefore, that there is no such thing as knowing, that "our Maker is our husband;" or that it was a privilege peculiar to the first Christians, to speak in the mildest terms, is both irrational and unscriptural. Not that all who can say, their Maker is their husband, can give the same clear and distinct account of the time, manner and means of their being spiritually united and married by faith, to the blessed bridegroom of the church. Some there may be now, as well as formerly, sanctified from the womb. And others in their infancy and non-age, as it were silently converted. Such perhaps may say, with a little Scotch maiden, now with God, when I asked her, whether Jesus Christ had taken away her old heart, and given her a new one? "Sir, it may be, (said she,) I cannot directly tell you the time and place, but this I know, it is done." And indeed it is not so very material, though no doubt it is very satisfactory, if we cannot relate all the minute and particular circumstances, that attended our conversion; if so be we are truly converted now, and can say, the work is done, and that, "our Maker is our husband." And I question, whether there is one single adult believer, now on earth, who lived before conversion, either in a course of secret or open sin, but can, in a good degree, give an account of the beginning and progress of a work of grace in his heart.

What think ye? Need I tell my married persons in this congregation, that they must go to the university, and learn the languages, before they can tell whether they are married or not? Or, if their marriage was to be doubted, could they not, think you, bring their certificates, to certify the time and place of their marriage; and the minister that joined them together in that holy state? And if you are adult, and are indeed married to Jesus Christ, though you may be unlearned, and what the world terms illiterate men, cannot you tell me the rise and progress, and consummation of the spiritual marriage, between Jesus Christ and your souls? Know you not the time, when you were first under the drawings of the Father, and Jesus began to woo you for himself? Tell me, O man, tell me, O woman, knowest thou not the time, or at least, knowest thou not, that there was a time, when the blessed Spirit of God stripped thee of the fig-leaves of thy own righteousness, hunted thee out of the trees of the garden of they performances, forced thee from the embraces of thy old husband the law, and made thee to abhor thy own righteousness, as so many filthy rags? Canst thou not remember, when, after a long struggle with unbelief, Jesus appeared to thee, as altogether lovely, mighty and willing to save? And canst thou not reflect upon a season, when thy own stubborn heart was made to bend; and thou wast made willing to embrace him, as freely offered to thee in the everlasting gospel? And canst thou not, with pleasure unspeakable, reflect on some happy period, some certain point of time, in which a sacred something (perhaps thou could it not then well tell what) did captivate, and fill thy heart, so that thou could say, in a rapture of holy surprise, and ecstasy of divine love, "My Lord and my God! My beloved is mine, and I am his; I know that my Redeemer liveth;" or, to keep to the words of our text, "My Maker is my husband." Surely, amidst this great and solemn assembly, there are many that can answer these questions in the affirmative. For these are transactions, not easily to be forgotten; and the day of our espousals is, generally, a very remarkable day; a day to be had in everlasting remembrance.

And can any of you indeed, upon good grounds say, that your Maker is your husband? May I not then (as it is customary to wish persons joy who are just entered into the marriage state) congratulate you upon your happy change, and wish you joy, with all my heart? Sure am I that there was joy in heaven on the day of your espousals: and why should not the blessed news occasion joy on earth? May I not address you in the language of our Lord to the women that came to visit his sepulcher, "All hail!" for ye are highly favored. Blessed are ye among men, blessed are ye among women! All generations shall call you blessed. What! "is your Maker your husband? The holy on of Israel your Redeemer?" Sing, O heavens, and rejoice, O earth! What an amazing stoop is this! What a new thing has God created on the earth! Do not your hearts, O believers, burn within you, when meditating on this unspeakable condescension of the high and lofty one that inhabiteth eternity? Whilst you are musing, does not the sacred fire of divine love kindle in your souls? And, out of the abundance of your hearts, do you not often speak with your tongues, and call upon all that is within you, to laud and magnify your Redeemer's holy name? Is not that God-exalting, self-abasing expression frequently in your mouths, "Why me, Lord, why me?" And are you not often constrained to break out into that devout exclamation of Solomon, when the glory of the Lord filled the temple, "And will God indeed dwell with man?" ungrateful, rebellious, ill, and hell-deserving man! O, my brethren, my heart is enlarged towards you! Tears, while I am speaking, are ready to gush out. But they are tears of love and joy. How shall I give it vent? How shall I set forth thy happiness, O believer, thou bride of God! And is thy Maker thy husband? Is his name "The Lord of hosts?" Whom then shouldst thou fear? And is thy Redeemer the holy one of Israel? The God of the whole earth should he be called! Of whom then shouldst thou be afraid? He that toucheth thee, toucheth the very apple of God's eye. "The very hairs of thy head are all numbered;" and "it is better that a man should have a millstone tied round his neck, and be drowned in the sea, than that he should justly offend thee."

All hail, (I must again repeat it) thou Lamb's bride! For thou art all glorious within, and comely, through the comeliness thy heavenly bridegroom hath put upon thee. Thy garment is indeed of wrought gold; and, ere long, the King shall bring thee forth with a raiment of needle-work, and present thee blameless before his Father, without spot, or wrinkle, or any such thing. In the mean while, well shall it be with you, and happy shall you be, who are married to Jesus Christ: for all that Christ has, is yours. "He is made of God to you, wisdom, righteousness, sanctification, and eternal redemption." "Whether Paul, or Cephas, or the world, or life, or death, or things present, or things to come; all are yours." All his attributes are engaged for your preservation, and all things shall work together for your good, who love God, and, by being thus married to the Lord Jesus, give an evident proof that you are called according to his purpose. What say you? When you meditate on these things, are you not frequently ready to cry out, What shall we render unto the Lord for all these mercies, which, of his free unmerited grace, he hath been pleased to bestow upon us? For, though you are dead to the law, as a covenant of works, yet you are alive to the law as a rule of life, and are in, or under the law (for either expression seems to denote the same thing) to your glorious husband, Jesus Christ.

Pass we on therefore to the

Second general head, under which I was to show, what duties of love they owe to Jesus Christ, who are so happy as to be able to say, "My Maker is my husband."

I say, duties of love. For being now married to Jesus Christ, you work not for life, but from life. The love of God constrains you, so that, if there was no written law, or supposing Jesus would set you at liberty from his yoke, so far as grace prevails in your hearts, you would say, we love our blessed bridegroom, and will not go from him.

And what does the Lord require of you? That we may speak on this head as plainly as may be, we shall pursue the method we began with; and, by carrying on the allegory, and examining what is required of truly Christian wives, under the gospel, infer what our Lord may justly demand of those who are united to him by faith, and can therefore say, "our Maker is our husband."

And here let us go to the law and to the testimony. What says the scripture? "Let the wife see that she *reverence* her "husband." It is, no doubt, the duty of married women to think highly of their husbands. From whom may husbands justly command respect, if not from their wives? The apostle's expression is emphatic. "Let the wife see that she reverence her husband;" thereby implying, that women, some of them at least, are too prone to disrespect their husbands; as Michal, Saul's daughter, despised David in her heart, when she tauntingly said, 2 Sam. 6:20, "How glorious was the king of Israel to-day, who uncovered himself to-day in the eyes of the handmaids of his servants, as one of the vain fellows shamelessly uncovereth himself."

This is a source and fountain, from whence many domestic evils frequently flow. Women should remember the character that husbands sustain in scripture. They are to them, what Christ is to the church. And it is mentioned to the honor of Sarah, that she called Abraham "Lord." "Shall I have a child who am old, my Lord being old also?" It is remarkable, there are but two good words in that whole sentence, "my Lord," (for all the others are the language of unbelief) and yet those two words the Holy Ghost mentions to her eternal honor, and buries, as it were, the rest in oblivion. "Even as Sarah (says St. Peter) obeyed Abraham, calling him Lord." An evident proof how pleasing it is in the sight of God, for women in the married state to reverence and respect their husbands. Not that husbands therefore should lord it over their wives, or require too much respect at their hands. This would be unchristian, as well as ungenerous, indeed. They ought rather, as God has taken such care to keep up their authority, commanding their wives to reverence and respect them; they ought, I say, to be doubly careful, that they live so holy and unblameable, as to lay their wives under no temptation to despise them. But to return from this digression. Does the apostle say, "Let the wife see that she reverence her husband?" May I not pertinently apply this caution to you who are married to Jesus Christ? See to it that you reverence and respect your husband. I say, *see to it*. For the devil will be often suggesting to you hard and mean thoughts against your husband. It was thus he beset our mother Eve, even in a state of innocence. He would fain persuade her to entertain hard thoughts of her glorious benefactor, "What, has God said, ye shall not eat of the trees of the garden?" Has he been so cruel to put you here in a beautiful garden only to vex and tease you? This he made use of as an inlet to all his succeeding insinuations. And this trade he is still pursuing, and will be pursuing to the very end of time. Besides, in the eyes of the world, Jesus Christ has no form or comeliness that they should desire him; and therefore, unless you "watch and pray," you will be led into temptation, and not keep up such high thoughts of your blessed Jesus as he justly deserves. In this you can never exceed. Women, perhaps may sometimes think too highly of, and, through excess of love, idolize their earthly comforts. But it is impossible for you to think too highly of your heavenly husband, Jesus Christ.

Farther, what says the apostle in his epistle to the Ephesians? Speaking of the marriage state, he says, "The wife is the glory of her husband;" as though he had said, a Christian wife should so behave, and so walk, as to be a credit to her husband. As Abigail was an honor to Nubal, and by her sweet deportment made up, in some degree, for her husband's churlishness. This is to be a help-meet indeed. Such a woman will be praised in the gate; and her husband get glory, and meet with respect on her account. And ought a woman to be the glory of her husband? How much more ought you, that are the Lamb's bride, so to live, and so to walk, as to bring glory, and gain respect, to the cause and interest of your husband Jesus? This is what the apostle everywhere supposes, when he would draw a parallel between a temporal and spiritual marriage. "The woman, is the glory of her husband, even as the church is the glory of Christ." Agreeable to this, he tells the Corinthians, "Whether you eat or drink, or whatsoever you do, do all to the glory of God;" and as he also speaks to the Thessalonians, 1 Thess. 2:11–12, "As you know how we exhorted, and comforted, and charged every one of you (as a father doth his children) that you would walk worthy of God who hath called you to his kingdom, and his glory." What an expression is here! "That you would walk worthy of God." O! how ought this, and such like texts, to stir up your pure minds, O believers, so to have your conversation in this world, that you may be what the apostle says some particular persons were, even "the glory of Christ." You are his glory; he rejoices over you with singing; and you should so walk, that all who know and hear of you, may glorify Christ in you.

Subjection, is another duty, that is enjoined married women, in the word of God. They are to "be subject to their own husbands in every thing." Every lawful thing: "For, the husband is the head of the wife, even as Christ is the head of the church." And knowing how inapt some base minds would be to submit to the husband's authority, he takes care to enforce this duty of subjection by many cogent and powerful arguments." "For Adam was first made, and not Eve. Neither was the man made for the woman, but the woman for the man." And again, "The man was not first in the transgression, but the woman." Upon which accounts, subjection was imposed on her as part of her punishment. "Thy desire (says God) shall be to thy husband, and he shall rule (though not tyrannize) over thee." So then, to use the words of pious Mr. Henry, those who attempt to usurp authority over their husbands, not only contradict a divine command, but thwart a divine curse. And if women are to be subject to their own husbands in every thing, how much more ought believers, whether men or women, to be subject to Jesus Christ: for he is the head of the church. He has bought her by his blood. Believers therefore are not their own, but are under the highest obligations to glorify and obey Jesus Christ, in their bodies and their souls, which are his. Add to this, that his service, as it is admirably expressed in one of our collects, is perfect freedom. His commandments holy, just, and good. And therefore it is your highest privilege, O believers, to submit to, and obey them. Earthly husbands may be so mean as to impose some things upon their wives, merely to show their authority; but it is not so with Jesus Christ. He can and does impose nothing, but what immediately conduces to our present, as well as future good. In doing, nay, in suffering for Jesus Christ, there is a present unspeakable reward. And therefore I may say to believers, as the blessed Virgin said to the servants at the marriage in Cana, "Whatsoever he says unto you, do it." "For his yoke is easy, and his burden is light." And I believe it might easily be proved in a few minutes, that all the disorders which are now in the world, whether in church or state, are owing to a want of being universally, unanimously, cheerfully, and perseveringly conformed to the laws and example of our Lord and Savior Jesus Christ.

Again, *faithfulness* in the marriage state, is strictly enjoined in the scriptures of truth. "Marriage is honorable in all, and the bed undefiled. But whoremongers and adulterers God will judge." Nay, adultery is an iniquity to be punished by the earthly judges; it dissolves the marriage relation. "For the man has not power over his own body, but the woman; neither has the woman power over her own body, but the man." The heathens themselves have been taught this by the light of nature; and adultery, among some of them, is punished with immediate death. And ought married persons to be thus careful to keep the marriage-bed undefiled, how carefully then ought believers to keep their souls chaste, pure, and undefiled, now they are espoused to Jesus Christ? For there is such a thing as spiritual adultery; "O ye adulterers and adulteresses," saith St. James. And God frequently complains of his people's playing the harlot. Hence it is, that St. John, in the most endearing manner, exhorts believers to "keep themselves from idols." For the lust of the eye, the lust of the flesh, and pride of life, are always ready to steal away our hearts from Jesus Christ. And every time we place our affections upon any thing more than Christ, we do undoubtedly commit spiritual adultery. For we admit a creature to rival the Creator, who is God over all, blessed for evermore. "Little children, therefore, keep yourselves from idols."

But it is time for me to draw towards the close of this head. *Fruitfulness* was a blessing promised by God to the first happy pair; "Increase and multiply, and replenish the earth." "Lo, children, and the fruit of the womb, (says the Psalmist) are a gift and heritage, which cometh of the Lord." And so, if we are married to Jesus Christ, we must be fruitful. In what? In every good word and work: for this speaks the Apostle, in his epistle to the Romans: "Wherefore, my brethren, ye also are become dead to the law, by the body of Christ, that ye should be married to another, even to him who is raised from the dead." What follows? "That we should bring forth fruit unto God." Glorious words, and proper to be considered in a peculiar manner, by such who would explode the doctrine of free justification, as an Antinomian doctrine, and as though it destroyed good works. No; it establishes, and lays a solid foundation, whereon to build the superstructure of good works. Titus is therefore commanded to "exhort believers to be careful to maintain good works." And "herein (says our Lord) is my Father glorified, that ye bring forth much fruit. Let your light so shine before men, that they may see your good works, and glorify your Father which is in heaven;" with a multitude of passages to the same purpose.

Moreover, it is required of wives, that they not only love and reverence their husbands, but that they also love and respect their *husband's friends*. And if we are married to Jesus Christ, we shall not only reverence the bridegroom, but we shall also love and honor the bridegroom's friends. "By this, shall all men know that ye are my disciples, if ye love one another." "By this we know, (says the beloved disciple) that we have passed from death to life because we love the brethren." Observe, the brethren, indefinitely; of whatever denomination. And this love must be "without dissimulation, and with a pure heart fervently." This was the case of the primitive Christians. They were all of one heart, and of one mind. It was said of them

(O that it could be said of us!) "See how these Christians love one another!" They were of the same spirit as a good woman of Scotland was, who, when she saw a great multitude, as is customary in the country, coming from various parts to receive the blessed sacrament, saluted them with a "Come in, ye blessed of the Lord, I have an house that will hold an hundred of you, and a heart that will hold ten thousand." Let us go and do likewise.

Once more. Persons that are married, take one another *for better or for worse*, for richer or for poorer, to love and to cherish each other in sickness and in health. And if we are married to Jesus Christ, we shall be willing to bear his *cross*, as well as to wear his *crown*. "If any man will come after me, let him deny himself, take up his cross, and follow me." Neither will they be compelled to do this, as Simon of Cyrene was, but they will be volunteers in his service; they will cry out, Crown him, crown him, when others are crying out, "Crucify him, crucify him." They will never leave or forsake him, but willingly follow the Captain of their salvation, though it be through a sea of blood.

I might run the parallel still further, and also enlarge upon the hints already given; but I fear I have said enough already to reproach most believers; I am sure I have said more than enough to abash and upbraid myself. For alas! how vilely, treacherously, and ungratefully have we behaved towards our spiritual husband, the dear Lord Jesus, ever since the day of our espousals? Had our friends, or even the wives of our own bosoms, behaved to us as we have behaved to our great and best friend, our glorious husband, we should have broken off our friendship, and sued for a bill of divorcement long ago. Under our first love, what promises did we make to him? But how frowardly have we behaved ourselves in this covenant? How little have we reverenced him? How often has our Beloved been no more to us than another beloved? How little have we lived to his glory? Have we not been a shame and reproach to his gospel? Have we not crucified him afresh, and has he not been sorely wounded in the house of his friends? Nay, has not his holy name been blasphemed through our means? For alas! how little have we obeyed him? How careless and indifferent have we been, whether we pleased him or not? We have often said, indeed, when commanded by him to go work in his vineyard, We go, Lord; but alas! we went not. Or if we did go, with what reluctance has it been? How unwilling to watch with our dear Lord and Master, only one hour? And of his sabbaths, how often have we said, What weariness is this? As for our adulteries, and spiritual fornications, how frequent, how aggravated have they been? Have not idols of all sorts, been suffered to fill up the room of the ever-blessed Jesus in our hearts? You that love him in sincerity, will not be offended if I tell you, that the 16th chapter of Ezekiel gives, in my opinion, a lively description of our behavior towards our Lord. We were, like base-born children, cast out in the field to the loathing of our persons: no eye pitied or had compassion on us. Jesus passed by, saw us polluted in our own blood, and said unto us, "Live," i.e. preserved us, even in our natural state, from death. And when his time of love was come, he spread the skirt of his imputed righteousness over us, and covered the nakedness of our souls, entered into covenant with us, and we became his. He washed us also with water, even in the laver of regeneration, and thoroughly washed us by his precious blood, from the guild of all our sins. He clothed us also with broidered work, and decked us with ornaments, even with righteousness, and peace, and joy in the Holy Ghost. We did eat fine flour and honey at his ordinances, and we fed on Jesus Christ in our hearts by faith, with thanksgiving. In short, we were made exceeding beautiful, and the kingdom of God was erected in our hearts. We were renowned among our neighbors for our love to God, and all that know us took knowledge of us, that we had been with Jesus. But alas! how have we fallen, who were once sons of the morning! How have we trusted in our own beauty, have grown spiritually proud, and provoked our patient and unspeakably long-suffering Lord to anger? Where is that ardent love we spoke of, when we told him, that, though we should die for him, we would not deny him in any wise? How desperately wicked, and deceitful above all things, have we proved our hearts to be, since we have done all these things, even the work of an imperious woman? These are great and numerous charges; but great and numerous as they are, there is not a single believer here present, but, if he knows his own heart, may plead guilty to some, or all of them. But this is a tender point: I see you concerned: your tears, O believers, are a proof of the anguish of your souls. And can any of us give any reason, why Jesus Christ should not give us a bill of divorcement, and put us away? May he not justly speak to us as he did to his adulteress Israel, in the aforementioned 16th of Ezekiel, "Wherefore, O harlot, hear the word of the Lord; I will judge thee as women that break wedlock, and shed blood, are judged. I will give thee blood in fury and jealousy, because thou hast not remembered the days of thy youth, but hast fretted me in all these things. Behold, therefore, I also will recompense thy way upon thy head. I will even deal with thee as thou hast done, who hast despised the oath, in breaking the covenant, the marriage contract that was between us." This, I am persuaded, you will confess to be the treatment which we all most justly deserve. But be not overwhelmed with over-much sorrow: for though the Lord our God is a jealous God, and will certainly visit our offenses with a rod, and our backslidings with a spiritual scourge, yet his loving-kindness will he not utterly take from us, nor suffer his truth to fail. Though we have changed, yet he changeth not: He abideth faithful: his loving-kindness abideth for evermore. Hark! how sweetly he speaks to his backsliding people of old; "O Israel, thou hast destroyed thyself, but in me is thy help. I will heal their backsliding, and love them freely." And in the verses immediately following the words of the text, how comfortably does he address his espoused people! "In a little wrath, I hid my face from thee for a moment; but with everlasting kindness will I have mercy on thee, saith the Lord thy Redeemer. For this is as the waters of Noah unto me; for as I have sworn, that the waters of Noah should no more go over the earth; so have I sworn, that I would not be wroth with thee, nor rebuke thee. For the mountains shall depart, and the hills be removed, but my kindness shall not depart from thee, neither shall the covenant of my peace be removed, saith the Lord that hath mercy on thee." O that this goodness may lead us to repentance! O that this unparalleled, infinite, unchangeable love, may constrain us to an universal, uniform, cheerful, unanimous, persevering obedience to all the commands of God!

Brethren, my heart is enlarged towards you, and I could dwell a long while upon the many great and precious invitations that are made to backsliders, to return to their first love, and do their first works: but it is high time for me, if, as was proposed,

III. I give to every one their proper portion; to speak to those poor souls, who know nothing of this blessed Bridegroom of the church, and consequently cannot say, "My Maker is my husband."

Ah! I pity you from my inmost soul; I could weep over, and for you, though perhaps you will not weep for yourselves. But surely you would weep, and howl too, did you know the miserable condition those are in, who are not married to Jesus Christ. Will you give me leave (I think I speak it in much love) to inform you, that if you are not married to Jesus Christ, you are married to the law, the world, the flesh, and the devil, neither of which can make you happy; but all, on the contrary, concur to make you miserable. Hear ye not, ye that are married to the law, and seek to be justified in the sight of God, partly, at least, if not wholly, by your own works, what the law saith to those that are under it, as a covenant of works? "Cursed is every one that continueth not in all things that are written in the book of the law, to do them." Every word breathes threatening and slaughter to poor fallen creatures. Cursed, both here and hereafter, be this man, and every one, naturally engendered of the offspring of Adam, without exception, that continueth not, even to the very end of life, in all things; not only in some, or many, but in all things, that are written in the book of the law, to do them, in the utmost perfection; for "he that offendeth in one point, is guilty of all." So that, according to the tenor of the covenant of works, whosoever is guilty of one wicked thought, word, or action, is under the curse of an angry sin-avenging God. "For as many as are under the law, are under the curse." And do you know what it is to be under the curse of God, and to have the wrath of God abide upon you? If you did, I believe you would not be so unwilling to be divorced from the law, and be espoused, as chaste virgins, to Jesus Christ.

And why are ye so wedded to the world? Did it ever prove faithful or satisfactory to any of its votaries? Has not Solomon reckoned up the sum total of worldly happiness? And what does it amount to? "Vanity, vanity, saith the preacher, all is vanity," nay he adds, "and vexation of spirit." And has not a greater than Solomon informed us, that a man's life, the happiness of a man's life, doth not consist in the things which he possesseth? Besides, "know ye not that the friendship of this world is enmity with God; so that whosoever will be a friend to the world, (to the corrupt customs and vices of it) is an enemy of God?" And what better reasons can you give for being wedded to your lusts? Might not the poor slaves in the galleys, as reasonably be wedded to their chains? For do not your lusts fetter down your souls from God? Do they not lord it, and have they not dominion over you? Do not they say, Come, and ye come; Go, and ye go; Do this, and ye do it? And is not he or she that liveth in pleasure, dead, whilst he liveth? And above all, how can ye bear the thoughts of being wedded to the devil, as every natural man is: for thus speaks the scripture, "He now ruleth in the children of disobedience." And how can ye bear to be ruled by one, who is such a professed open enemy to the most high and holy God? Who will make a drudge of you, whilst you live, and be your companion in endless and extreme torment, after you are dead? For thus will our Lord say to those on the left hand, "Depart from me, ye cursed, into everlasting fire, prepared for the devil and his angels." But,

IV. Will you permit me, O sinners, that I may draw towards a close of this discourse, to propose a better match to your souls. This is a part of the discourse which I long to come to, it being my heart's desire, and earnest prayer to God, that your souls may be saved. "And now, O Lord God Almighty, thou Father of mercies, and God of all consolations, thou God and Father of our Lord Jesus Christ, who hast promised to give thy Son the heathen for his inheritance, and the uttermost parts of the earth for his possession, send me good speed this day. O Lord, send me now prosperity. Behold, I stand here without the camp, bearing a little of thy dear Son's sacred reproach! Hear me, O Lord, hear me, and according to thy word, let thy dear, thine only begotten Son, see of the travail of his soul, and be satisfied! O help me so to speak, that many may believe on, and cleave unto thy blessed, thine holy child Jesus!

But who am I, that I should undertake to recommend the blessed Jesus to others, who am myself altogether unworthy to take his sacred name into my polluted lips? Indeed, my brethren, I do not count myself worthy of such an honor; but since it has pleased him, in whom all fullness dwells, to count me worthy, and put me into the ministry, the very stones would cry out against me, did I not attempt, at least, to lisp out his praise, and earnestly recommend the ever-blessed Jesus to the choice of all.

Thus Abraham's faithful servant behaved, when sent out to fetch a wife for his master Isaac. He spake of the riches and honors, which God had conferred on him; but what infinitely greater honors and riches, has the God and Father of our Lord Jesus, conferred on his only Son, to whom I now invite every Christless sinner! To you, therefore, I call, O ye sons of men, assuring you, there is everything in Jesus that your hearts can desire, or hunger and thirst after. Do people in disposing of themselves or their children in marriage, generally covet to be matched with *persons of great names*? Let this consideration serve as a motive to stir you up to match with Jesus. For God the Father has given him a name above every name; he has upon his vesture, and upon his thigh, a name written, "The King of kings, and the Lord of lords;" and herein the text we are told, "The Lord of Hosts is his name." Nor has he an empty title, but power equivalent; for he is a prince, as well as savior. "All power is given unto him, both in heaven and on earth;" "The God of the while earth, (says our text) he shall be called." The government of men, of the church, and of devils, is put upon his shoulders: "Thrones, principalities and powers, are made subject unto him; by him kings reign, and princes decree justice; he setteth up one, and putteth down another: and of his kingdom there shall be no end." Will *riches* be an inducement unto you to come and match with Jesus? Why then, I can tell you, the riches of Jesus are infinite: for unto me, who am less than the least of all saints, is this grace given, that I should preach to poor sinners, the unsearchable riches of Jesus Christ. I appeal to you that are his saints, whether you have not found this true, by happy experience; and though some of you, may have been acquainted with him thirty, forty, fifty years ago, do you not find his riches are yet unsearchable, and as much past finding out, as they were the very first moment in which you gave him your hearts?

Would you match with a *wise husband*? Haste then, sinners, come away to Jesus: He is the fountain of wisdom, and makes all that come unto him, wise unto salvation: "He is the wisdom of the Father: the Lord possessed him in the beginning of his way, before his works of old. When he prepared the heavens, he was there; when he appointed the foundations of the earth, then was he with him, as one brought up with him; he was daily his delight, rejoicing always before him." As he is wise, so is he *holy*; and therefore, in the words of our text, he is stiled, "The Redeemer, the Holy One of Israel:" and by the angel Gabriel, "That holy Thing." The apostles, addressing God the Father, stile him his "holy child Jesus:" and the spirits of just men made perfect, and the angels in heaven, cease not day or night, saying, "Holy, holy, holy." Nor is his *beauty* inferior to his wisdom or holiness; the seraphs veil their faces, when they appear before him: "He is the chiefest among ten thousand, nay, he is altogether lovely." And, as he is altogether lovely, so is he altogether *loving*: his name and his nature is Love. God, God in Christ is love: love in the abstract. And in this has he manifested his love, in that, whilst we were yet sinners, may open enemies, Jesus, in his own due time, died for the ungodly. He loved us so as to give himself for us. O what manner of love is this! What was Jacob's love to Rachel, in comparison of the love which Jesus bore to a perishing world! He became a curse for us. For it is written, "Cursed is every man that hangeth upon a tree." What Zipporah said to her husband improperly, Jesus may say properly to his spouse the church, "A bloody wife hast thou been to me, because of the crucifixion." For he has purchased her with his own blood. And having once loved his people, he loves them unto the end. His love, like himself, is from everlasting to everlasting.

He hates putting away: though we change, yet he changeth not: he abideth faithful. When we are married here, there comes in that shocking clause, t use the words of holy Mr. Boston, "Till death us doth part:" but death itself shall not separate a true believer from the love of God, which is in Christ Jesus his Lord: for he will never cease loving his Bride, till he has loved her to heaven, and presented her before his Father, without spot or wrinkle, or any such thing. Nay, his love will, as it were, but be beginning, through the endless ages of eternity.

And now, Sirs, what say you? Shall I put that question to you, which Rebecca's relations, upon a proposal of marriage, put to her? "Will ye go with the man?" With the God-man, this infinitely great, this infinitely powerful, this all-wise, all-holy, altogether lovely, ever-loving Jesus? What objection have you to make against such a gracious offer? One would imagine, you had not a single one; but it is to be feared, through the prevalency of unbelief, and the corruption of your desperately wicked deceitful hearts, you are ready to urge several. Methinks I hear some of you say within yourselves, "We like the proposal, but alas! we are poor." Are you so? If that be all, you may, notwithstanding, be welcome to Jesus: "For has not God chosen the poor of this world, to make them rich in faith, and heirs of his everlasting kingdom?" And what says that Savior, to whom I am now inviting you? "Blessed are the poor in Spirit, for there is the kingdom of heaven." And what says his Apostle concerning him? "Though he was rich, yet for our sakes he became poor, that we through his poverty might be made rich. But say you, "We are not only poor, but we are in debt; we owe God ten thousand talents, and have nothing to pay;" but that need not keep you back: for God the Father, from the Lord Jesus, his dearly beloved Son, has received double for all believers sins: the blood of Jesus cleanseth from them all. But you are blind, and miserable, and naked; to whom then should you fly for succor, but to Jesus, who came to open the eyes of the blind, to seek and save the miserable and lost, and clothe the naked with his perfect and spotless righteousness. And now, what can hinder your espousals with the dear and ever-blessed Lamb of God? I know but of one thing, that dreadful sin of unbelief. But this is my comfort, Jesus died for unbelief, as well as for other sins, and has promised to send down the Holy Spirit to convince the world of this sin in particular: "If I go not away, the Comforter will not come unto you; but if I go away, I will send the Comforter, and he will convince the world of son." What sin? of unbelief; "because they believe not on me." O that this promise may be so fulfilled in your hearts, and Jesus may so become the author of divine faith in your souls, that you may be able to send me the same message as a good woman in Scotland, on her dying bed, sent me by a friend: "Tell him, (says she) for his comfort, that at such a time he married me to the Lord Jesus." This would be comfort indeed. Not that we can marry you to Christ: No; the Holy Ghost must tie the marriage knot. But such honor have all God's ministers; under him they espouse poor sinners to Jesus Christ. "I have espoused you (says St. Paul) as a chaste virgin to Jesus Christ." O that you may say, We will go with the man; then will I bow my head, as Abraham's servant did, and go with joy and tell my Master, that he has not left his poor servant destitute this day: then shall I rejoice in your felicity. For I know, my Master will take you into the banqueting-house of his ordinances, and his banner over you shall be love. That this may be the happy case of you all, may the glorious God grant, for the sake of Jesus his dearly beloved Son, the glorious bridegroom of his church, to whom, with the Father, and the Holy Spirit, be all honor and glory, now and for evermore. Amen, and Amen.

13. The Potter and the Clay

> **Jeremiah 18:1–6—"The word which came to Jeremiah from the Lord, saying, Arise, and go down to the potter's house, and there I will cause thee to hear my words. Then I went down to the potter's house, and, behold, he wrought a work on the wheels. And the vessel that he made of clay was marred in the hand of the potter: so he made it again another vessel, as seemed good to the potter to make [it]. Then the word of the Lord came to me, saying, O house of Israel, cannot I do with you as this potter? saith the Lord. Behold, as the clay [is] in the potter's hand, so [are] ye in mine hand, O house of Israel."**

At sundry times, and in diverse manners, God was pleased to speak to our fathers by the prophets, before he spoke to us in these last days by his Son. To Elijah, he revealed himself by a small still voice. To Jacob, by a dream. To Moses, he spoke face to face. Sometimes he was pleased to send a favorite prophet on some especial errand; and whilst he was thus employed, vouchsafed to give him a particular message, which he was ordered to deliver without reserve to all the inhabitants of the land. A very instructive instance of this kind we have recorded in the passage now read to you. The first verse informs us that it was a word, or message, which came immediately from the Lord to the prophet Jeremiah. At what time, or how the prophet was employed when it came, we are not told. Perhaps, whilst he was praying for those who would not pray for themselves. Perhaps, near the morning, when he was slumbering or musing on his bed. For the word came to him, saying, "Arise." And what must he do when risen? He must "go down to the potter's house" (the prophet knew where to find it) "and there (says the great Jehovah) I will cause thee to hear my words." Jeremiah does not confer with flesh and blood, he does not object that it was dark or cold, or desire that he might have his message given him there, but without the least hesitation is immediately obedient to the heavenly vision. "Then (says he) I went down to the potter's house, and behold he wrought a work upon the wheels." Just as he was entering into the house or workshop, the potter, it seems, had a vessel upon his wheel. And was there any thing so extraordinary in this, that it should be ushered in with the word Behold? What a dreaming visionary, or superstitious enthusiast, would this Jeremiah be accounted, even by many who read his prophecies with seeming respect, was he alive now? But this was not the first time Jeremiah had heard from heaven in this manner. He therefore willingly obeyed; and had you or I accompanied him to the potter's house, I believe we should have seen him silently, but intensely waiting upon his great and all-wise Commander, to know wherefore he sent him thither. Methinks I see him all attention. He takes notice, that "the vessel was of clay;" but as he held it in his hand, and turned round the wheel, in order to work it into some particular form, "it was marred in the hands of the potter," and consequently unfit for the use he before intended to put it to. And what becomes of this marred vessel? Being thus marred, I suppose, the potter, without the least imputation of injustice, might have thrown it aside, and taken up another piece of clay in its room. But he did not. "He made it again another vessel." And does the potter call a council of his domestics, to inquire of them what kind of vessel they would advise him to make of it? No, in no wise. "He made it again another vessel, as seemed good to the potter to make it."

"Then," adds Jeremiah, whilst he was in the way of duty—then—whilst he was mentally crying, Lord what wouldst thou have me to do? "Then the word of the Lord came unto me, saying, O house of Israel, cannot I do with you as this potter? Saith the Lord. Behold, as the clay is in the hands of the potter (marred, and unfit for the first designed purpose) so are ye in mine hand, O house of Israel." At length, then, Jeremiah hath his sermon given to him: short, but popular. It was to be delivered to the whole house of Israel, princes, priests, and people: short, but pungent, even sharper than a two-edged sword. What! says the sovereign Lord of heaven and earth, must I be denied the privilege of a common potter? May I not do what I will with my own? "Behold, as the clay is in the potter's hands, so are ye in mine hands, O house of Israel. I made and formed you into a people, and blessed you above any other nation under heaven: but, O Israel, thou by thy backslidings hast destroyed thyself. As the potter therefore might justly have thrown aside his marred clay, so may I justly unchurch and unpeople you. But what if I should come over the mountains of your guilt, heal your backslidings, revive my work in the midst of the years, and cause your latter end greatly to increase? Behold, as the clay is in the hands of the potter, lying at his disposal, either to be destroyed or formed into another vessel, so are ye in my hands, O house of Israel: I may either reject, and thereby ruin you, or I may revisit and revive you according to my own sovereign good will and pleasure, and who shall say unto me, what dost thou?"

This seems to be the genuine interpretation, and primary intention of this beautiful part of holy writ. But waving all further inquiries about its primary design or meaning, I shall now proceed to show, that what the glorious Jehovah here says of the house of Israel in general, is applicable to every individual of mankind in particular. And as I presume this may be done, without either wire-drawing scripture on the one hand, or wrestling it from its original meaning on the other, not to detain you any longer, I shall, from the passage thus explained and paraphrased, deduce, and endeavor to enlarge on these two general heads.

First, I shall undertake to prove, that every man naturally engendered of the offspring of Adam, is in the sight of the all-seeing, heart-searching God, only as a "piece of marred clay."

Secondly, That being thus marred, he must necessarily be renewed: and under this head, we shall likewise point out by whose agency this mighty change is to be brought about.

These particulars being discussed, way will naturally be made for a short word of application.

First, To prove that every man naturally engendered of the offspring of Adam, is in the sight of an all-seeing, heart-searching God, only as a piece of marred clay.

Be pleased to observe, that we say every man *naturally* engendered of the offspring of Adam, or every man since the fall: for if we consider man as he first came out of the hands of his Maker, he was far from being in such melancholy circumstances. No; he was originally made upright; or as Moses, that sacred penman, declares, "God made him after his own image." Surely never was so much expressed in so few words; which hath often made me wonder how that great critic Longinus, who so justly admires the dignity and grandeur of Moses's account of the creation, and "God said, Let there be light, and there was light;" I say I have often wondered why he did not read a little further, and bestow as just an encomium [praise, approval, acclaim] upon this short, but withal inexpressibly august [noble, elegant, superb] and comprehensive description of the formation of man, "so God created man in his own image." Struck with a deep sense of such amazing goodness, and that he might impress yet a deeper sense of it upon our minds too, he immediately adds, "in the image of God made he him." A council of the most adorable Trinity was called on this important occasion: God did not say, Let there be a man, and there was a man, but God said, "Let us make man in our image, after our likeness." This is the account which the lively oracles of God do give us of man in his first estate; but it is very remarkable, that the transition from the account of his creation to that of his misery, is very quick, and why? For a very good reason, because he soon fell from his primeval dignity; and by that fall, the divine image is so defaced, that he is now to be valued only as antiquarians value an ancient medal, merely for the sake of the image and superscription once stamped upon it; or of a second divine impress, which, through grace, it may yet receive.

Let us take a more particular survey of him, and see whether these things are so or not: and first, as to his *understanding*. As man was created originally "after God in knowledge," as well as righteousness and true holiness, we may rationally infer, that his understanding, in respect to things natural, as well as divine, was of a prodigious extent: for he was make but a little lower than the angels, and consequently being like them, excellent in his understanding, he knew much of God, of himself, and all about him; and in this as well as every other respect, was, as Mr. Golter expresses it in one of his essays, a perfect major: but this is far from being our case now. For in respect to *natural things*, our understandings are evidently darkened. It is but little that we can know, and even that little knowledge which we can acquire, is with much weariness of the flesh, and we are doomed to gain it as we do our daily bread, I mean by the sweat of our brows.

Men of low and narrow minds soon commence wise in their own conceits: and having acquired a little smattering of the learned languages, and made some small proficiency in the dry sciences, are easily tempted to look upon themselves as a head taller than their fellow mortals, and accordingly too, too often put forth great swelling words of vanity. But persons of a more exalted, and extensive reach of thought, dare not boast. No: they know that the greatest scholars are in the dark, in respect to many even of the minutest things in life: and after all their painful researches into the Arcana Natura, they find such an immense void, such an unmeasurable expanse yet to be traveled over, that they are obliged at last to conclude, almost with respect to every thing, "that they know nothing yet as they ought to know." This consideration, no doubt, led Socrates, when he was asked by one of his scholars, why the oracle pronounced him the wisest man on earth, to give him this judicious answer, "Perhaps it is, because I am most sensible of my own ignorance." Would to God, that all who call themselves Christians, had learned so much as this heathen! We should then no longer hear so many learned men, falsely so called, betray their ignorance by boasting of the extent of their shallow understanding, nor by professing themselves so wise, prove themselves such arrant pedantic fools.

If we view our understandings in respect to spiritual things, we shall find that they are not only darkened, but become darkness itself, even "darkness that may be felt" by all who are not past feeling. And how should it be otherwise, since the infallible word of God assures us, that they are alienated from the light of life of God, and thereby naturally as incapable to judge of divine and spiritual things, comparatively speaking, as a man born blind is incapacitated to distinguish the various colors of the rainbow. "The natural man, (says on inspired apostle) discerneth not the things of the Spirit of God;" so far from it, "they are foolishness unto him;" and why? Because they are only to be "spiritually discerned." Hence it was, that Nicodemus, who was blessed with an outward and divine revelation, who was a ruler of the Jews, nay a master of Israel, when our Lord told him, "he must be born again;" appeared to be quite grappled. "How (says he) can a man be born when he is old? Can he enter a second time into his mother's womb and be born? How can these things be?" Were three more absurd questions ever proposed by the most ignorant man alive? Or can there be a clearer proof of the blindness of man's understanding, in respect to divine, as well as natural things? Is not man then a piece of marred clay?

This will appear yet more evident, if we consider the *perverse bent of his will*. Being made in the very image of God; undoubtedly before the fall, man had no other will but his Maker's. God's will, and Adam's, were than like unisons in music. There was not the least disunion, or discord between them. But now he hath a will, as directly contrary to the will of God, as light is contrary to darkness, or heaven to hell. We all bring into the world with us a carnal mind, which is not only an enemy to God, but "enmity itself, and which is therefore not subject unto the law of God, neither indeed can it be." A great many show much zeal in talking against the man of sin, and loudly (and indeed very justly) exclaim against the Pope for sitting in the temple, I mean the church of Christ, and "exalting himself above all that is called God." But say not within thyself, who shall go to Rome, to pull down this spiritual antichrist? As though there was no antichrist but what is without us. For know, O man, whoever thou art, an infinitely more dangerous antichrist, because less discerned, even *self-will*, fits daily in the temple of thy heart, exalting itself, above all that is called God, and obliging all its votaries to say of Christ himself, that Prince of peace, "we will not have this man to reign over us." God's people, whose spiritual senses, are exercised about spiritual things, and whose eyes are opened to see the abominations that are in their hearts, frequently feel this to their sorrow. Whether they will or not, this enmity from time to time bubbles up, and in spite of all their watchfulness and care, when they are under the pressure of some sharp affliction, a long desertion, or tedious night of temptation, they often find something within rising in rebellion against the all-wise disposals of divine Providence, and saying unto God their heavenly Father, "what dost thou?" This makes them to cry (and no wonder, since it constrained one of the greatest saints and apostles first to introduce the expression) "O wretched man that I am, who shall deliver me from the body of this death?" The spiritual and renewed soul groans thus, being burdened; but as for the natural and unawakened man, it is not so with him; self-will, as well as every other evil, either in a more latent or discernible manner, reigns in his unrenewed soul, and proves him, even to a demonstration to others, whether he knows, or will confess it himself or not, that in respect to the disorders of his will, as well as his understanding, man is only a piece of marred clay.

A transient view of fallen man's *affections* will yet more firmly corroborate this melancholy truth, These, at his being first placed in the paradise of God, were always kept within proper bounds, fixed upon their proper objects, and, like so many gentle rivers, sweetly, spontaneously and habitually glided into their ocean, God. But now the scene is changed. For we are not naturally full of vile affections, which like a mighty and impetuous torrent carry all before them. We love what we should hate, and hate what we should love; we fear what we should hope for, and hope for what we should fear; nay, to such an ungovernable height do our affections sometimes rise, that though our judgments are convinced to the contrary, yet we will gratify our passions though it be at the expense of our present and eternal welfare. We feel a war of our affections, warring against the law of our minds, and bringing us into captivity to the law of sin and death. So that video meliora proboque, deteriora foquor [latin phrase], I approve of better things but follow worse, is too, too often the practice of us all.

I am sensible, that many are offended, when mankind are compared to beasts and devils. And they might have some shadow of reason for being so, if we asserted in a physical sense, that they were really beasts and really devils. For then, as I once heard a very learned prelate, who was objecting against this comparison, observe, "a man being a beast would be incapable, and being a devil, would be under an impossibility of being saved." But when we make use of such shocking comparisons, as he was pleased to term them, we would be understood only in a moral sense; and in so doing, we assert no more than some of the most holy men of God have said of themselves, and others, in the lively oracles many ages ago. Holy David, the man after God's own heart, speaking of himself, says, "so foolish was I, and as a beast before thee." And holy Job, speaking of man in general, says, that "he is born as a wild ass's colt," or take away the expletive, which as some think ought to be done, and then he positively asserts, that man is a wild ass's colt. And what says our Lord, "Ye are of your father the devil;" and "the whole world is said to lie in him, the wicked one, who now rules in the children of disobedience," that is, in all unrenewed souls. Our stupidity, proneness to fix our affections on the things of the earth, and our eagerness to make provision for the flesh, to fulfill the lusts thereof, evidence us to be earthly and brutes!; and our mental passions, anger, hatred, malice, envy, and such like, prove with equal strength, that we are also devilish. Both together conspire to evince, that in respect to his affections, as well as his understanding and will, man deservedly may be termed a piece of marred clay.

The present *blindness of natural conscience* makes this appear in a yet more glaring light; in the soul of the first man Adam, conscience was no doubt the candle of the Lord, and enabled him rightly and instantaneously to discern between good and evil, right and wrong. And, blessed be God! Some remains of this are yet left; but alas, how dimly does it burn, and how easily and quickly is it covered, or put out and extinguished. I need not send you to the heathen world, to learn the truth of this; you all know it by experience. Was there no other evidence, your own consciences are instead of a thousand witnesses, that man, as to his natural conscience, as well as understanding, will and affections, is much marred clay.

Nor does that great and boasted Diana, I mean *unassisted unenlightened reason*, less demonstrate the justness of such an assertion. Far be it from me to decry or exclaim against human reason. Christ himself is called the "*Logos, the Reason;*" and I believe it would not require much learning, or take up much time to prove, that so far and no farther than as we act agreeably to the laws of Christ Jesus, are we any way conformable to the laws of right reason. His service is therefore called "a reasonable service." And however his servants and followers may now be looked upon as fools and madmen; yet there will come a time, when those who despise and set themselves to oppose divine revelation, will find, that what they now call reason, is only *reasondepraved*, and an utterly incapable, of itself, to guide us into the way of peace, or show the way of salvation, as the men of Sodom were to find Lot's door after they were struck with blindness by the angels, who came to lead him out of the city. The horrid and dreadful mistakes, which the most refined reasoners in the heathen world ran into, both as to the object, as well as manner of divine worship, have sufficiently demonstrated the weakness and depravity of human reason: nor do our modern boasters afford us any better proofs of the greatness of its strength, since the best improvement they generally make of it, is only to reason themselves into downright willful infidelity, and thereby reason themselves out of eternal salvation. Need we now any further witness, that man, fallen man, is altogether a piece of marred clay?

But this is not all, we have yet more evidence to call; for do the blindness of our understandings, the perverseness of our will, the rebellion of our affections, the corruption our consciences, the depravity of our reason prove this charge; and does not present *disordered frame and constitution of our bodes* confirm the same also? Doubtless in this respect, man, in the most literal sense of the word, is a piece of marred clay. For God originally made him of the "dust of the earth." So that notwithstanding our boasting of our high pedigrees, and different descent, we were all originally upon a level, and a little red earth was the common substratum out of which we were all formed. Clay indeed it was, but clay wonderfully modified, even by the immediate hands of the Creator of heaven and earth. One therefore hath observed, that it is said "God built the man;" he did not form him rashly or hastily, but built and finished him according to the plan before laid down in his own eternal mind. And though, as the great God is without body, parts, or passions, we cannot suppose when it is said "God made man after his own image," that it has any reference to his body, yet I cannot help thinking (with Doctor South) that as the eternal Logos was hereafter to appear, God manifest in the flesh, infinite wisdom was undoubtedly exerted in forming a casket into which so invaluable a pearl was in the fullness of time to be deposited. Some of the ancients are said to have asserted, that man at the first, had what we call a glory shining round him; but without attempting to be wise above what is written, we may venture to affirm, that he had a glorious body, which knowing no sin, knew neither sickness nor pain. But now on this, as well as other accounts, he may justly be called Ichabod; for its primitive strength and glory are sadly departed from it, and like the ruins of some ancient and stately fabric, only so much less as to give us some faint idea of what it was when it first appeared in its original and perfect beauty. The apostle Paul, therefore, who knew how to call things by their proper names, as well as any man living, does not scruple to term the human body, though in its original constitution fearfully and wonderfully made, a "vile body;" vile indeed! Since it is subject to such vile diseases, put to such vile, yea very vile uses, and at length is to come to so vile an end. "For dust we are, and to dust we must return." This among other considerations, we may well suppose, caused the blessed Jesus to weep at the grave of Lazarus. He wept, not only because his friend Lazarus was dead, but he wept to see human nature, through man's own default, thus laid in ruins, by being subject unto such a dissolution, made like unto the beasts that perish.

Let us here pause a while, and with our sympathizing Lord, see if we cannot shed a few silent tears at least, upon the same sorrowful occasion. Who, who is there amongst us, that upon such a melancholy review of man' present, real, and most deplorable depravity both in body and soul, can refrain from weeping over such a piece of marred clay? Who, who can help adopting holy David's lamentation over Saul and Jonathan? "How are the mighty fallen! How are they slain in their high places!" Originally it was not so. No, "God made man after his own image; in the image of God made he man." Never was there so much expressed in so few words. He was created after God in righteousness and true holiness.

This is the account, which the sacred volume gives us of this interesting point. This, this is that blessed book, that book of books, from whence, together with an appeal to the experience of our own hearts, and the testimonies of all past ages, we have thought proper to fetch our proofs. For, after all, we must be obliged to divine revelation, to know what we were, what we are, and what we are to be. In these, as in a true glass, we may see our real and proper likeness. And from these only can we trace the source and fountain of all those innumerable evils, which like a deluge have overflowed the natural and moral world. If any should object against the authenticity of this revelation, and consequently against the doctrine this day drawn from thence, they do in my opinion thereby very much confirm it. For unless a man was very much disordered indeed, as to his understanding, will, affections, natural conscience, and his power of reasoning, he could never possibly deny such a revelation, which is founded on a multiplicity of infallible external evidences, hath so many internal evidences of a divine stamp in every page, is so suited to the common exigencies of all mankind, so agreeable to the experience of all men, and which hath been so wonderfully handed and preserved to us, hath been so instrumental to the convicting, converting, and comforting so many millions of souls, and hath stood the test of the most severe scrutinies, and exact criticisms of the most subtle and refined, as well as the most malicious and persecuting enemies, that ever lived, even from the beginning of time to this very day. Persons of such a turn of mind, I think, are rather to be prayed for, than disputed with, if so be this perverse wickedness of their hearts may be forgiven them: "They are in the very gall of bitterness, and must have their consciences seared as it were with a red-hot iron," and must have their eyes "blinded by the god of this world," otherwise they could not but see, and feel, and assent to the truth of this doctrine, of man's being universally depraved; which not only in one or two, but in one or two thousands, in every page, I could almost say, is written, in such legible characters, that runs may read. Indeed, revelation itself is founded upon the doctrine of the fall. Had we kept our original integrity, the law of God would have yet been written in our hearts, and thereby the want of a divine revelation, at least such as ours, would have been superseded; but being fallen, instead of rising in rebellion against God, we ought to be filled with unspeakable thankfulness to our all bountiful Creator, who by a few lines in his own books hath discovered more to us, than all the philosophers and most learned men in the world could, or would, have discovered, though they had studied to all eternity.

I am well aware, that some who pretend to own the validity of divine revelation, are notwithstanding enemies to the doctrine that hath this day been delivered; and would fain elude the force of the proofs generally urged in defense of it, by saying, they only bespeak the corruption of particular persons, or have reference only to the heathen world: but such persons err, not knowing their own hearts, or the power of Jesus Christ: for by nature there is no difference between Jew or Gentile, Greek or Barbarian, bond or free. We are altogether equally become abominable in God's sight, all equally fallen short of the glory of God, and consequently all alike so many pieces of marred clay.

How God came to suffer man to fall? how long man stood before he fell? And how the corruption contracted by the fall, is propagated to every individual of his species are questions of such an abstruse and critical nature, that should I undertake to answer them, would be only gratifying a sinful curiosity, and tempting you, as Satan tempted dour first parents, to eat forbidden fruit. It will much better answer the design of this present discourse, which is practical, to pass on

II. To the next thing proposed, and point out to you the absolute necessity there is of this fallen nature's being renewed.

This I have had all along in my eye, and on account of this, have purposely been so explicit on the first general head: for has Archimedes once said, "Give me a place where I may fix my foot, and I will move the world;" so without the least imputation of arrogance, with which, perhaps, he was justly chargeable, we may venture to say, grant the foregoing doctrine to be true, and then deny the necessity of man's being renewed who can.

I suppose, I may take it for granted, that all of you amongst whom I am now preaching the kingdom of God, hope after death to go to a place which we call Heaven. And my heart's desire and prayer to God for you is, that you all may have mansions prepared for you there. But give me leave to tell you, were you now to see these heavens opened, and the angel (to use the words of the seraphic Hervey clothed with all his heavenly drapery, with one foot upon the earth, and another upon the sea; nay, were you to see and hear the angel of the everlasting covenant, Jesus Christ himself, proclaiming "time shall be no more," and giving you all an invitation immediately to come to heaven; heaven would be no heaven to you, nay it would be a hell to your souls, unless you were first prepared for a proper enjoyment of it here on earth. "For what communion hath light with darkness?" Or what fellowship could unrenewed sons of Belial possibly keep up with the pure and immaculate Jesus?

The generality of people form strange ideas of heaven. And because the scriptures, in condescension to the weakness of our capacities, describe it by images taken from earthly delights and human grandeur, therefore they are apt to carry their thoughts no higher, and at the best only form to themselves a kind of Mahomitan paradise. But permit me to tell you, and God grant it may sink deep into your hearts! Heaven is rather a state than a place; and consequently, unless you are previously disposed by a suitable state of mind, you could not be happy even in heaven itself. For what is grace but glory militant? What is glory but grace triumphant? This consideration made a pious author say, that "holiness, happiness, and heaven, were only three different words for one and the self-same thing." And this made the great Preston, when he was about to die, turn to his friends, saying, "I am changing my place, but not my company." He had conversed with God and good men on earth; he was going to keep up the same, and infinitely more refined communion with God, his holy angels, and the spirits of just men made perfect, in heaven.

To make us meet to be blissful partakers of such heavenly company, this "marred clay," I mean, these depraved natures of ours, must necessarily undergo an universal moral change; our understandings must be enlightened; our wills, reason, and consciences, must be renewed; our affections must be drawn toward, and fixed upon things above; and because flesh and blood cannot inherit the kingdom of heaven, this corruptible must put on incorruption, this mortal must put on immortality. And thus old things must literally pass away, and behold all things, even the body as well as the faculties of the soul, must become new.

This moral change is what some call, repentance, some, conversion, some, regeneration; choose what name you please, I only pray God, that we all may have the thing. The scriptures call it holiness, sanctification, the new creature, and our Lord calls it a "New birth, or being born again, or born from above." These are not barely figurative expressions, or the flights of eastern language, nor do they barely denote a relative change of state conferred on all those who are admitted into Christ's church by baptism; but they denote a real, moral change of heart and life, a real participation of the divine life in the soul of man. Some indeed content themselves with a figurative interpretation; but unless they are made to experience the power and efficacy thereof, by a solid living experience in their own souls, all their learning, all their labored criticism, will not exempt them from a real damnation. Christ hath said it, and Christ will stand, "Unless a man," learned or unlearned, high or low, though he be a master of Israel as Nicodemus was, unless he "be born again, he cannot see, he cannot enter into the kingdom of God."

If it be inquired, who is to be the potter? And by whose agency this marred clay is to be formed into another vessel? Or in other words, if it be asked, how this great and mighty change is to be effected? I answer, not by the mere dint and force of moral suasion [persuasion]. This is good in its place. And I am so far from thinking, that Christian preachers should not make use of rational arguments and motives in their sermons, that I cannot think they are fit to preach at all, who either cannot, or will not use them. We have the example of the great God himself for such a practice; "Come (says he) and let us reason together." And St. Paul, that prince of preachers, "reasoned of temperance, and righteousness, and a judgment to come." And it is remarkable, "that whilst he was reasoning of these things, Felix trembled." Nor are the most persuasive strains of holy rhetoric less needful for a scribe ready instructed to the kingdom of God. The scriptures both of the Old and New Testament, every where abound with them. And when can they be more properly employed, and brought forth, than when we are acting as ambassadors or heaven, and beseeching poor sinners, as in Christ's stead, to be reconciled unto God. All this we readily grant. But at the same time, I would as soon go to yonder church-yard, and attempt to raise the dead carcasses, with a "come forth," as to preach to dead souls, did I not hope for some superior power to make the word effectual to the designed end. I should only be like a sounding brass for any saving purpose, or as a tinkling cymbal. Neither is this change to be wrought by the power of our own free-will. This is an idol every where set up, but we dare not fall down and worship it. "No man (says Christ) can come to me, unless the Father draw him." Our own free-will, if improved, may restrain us from the commission of many evils, and put us in the way of conversion; but, after exerting our utmost efforts (and we are bound in duty to exert them) we shall find the words of our own church article to be true, that "man since the fall hath no power to turn to God." No, we might as soon attempt to stop the ebbing and flowing of the tide, and calm the most tempestuous sea, as to imagine that we can subdue, or bring under proper regulations, our own unruly wills and affections by any strength inherent in ourselves.

And therefore, that I may keep you no longer in suspense, I inform you, that this heavenly potter, this blessed agent, is the Almighty Spirit of God, the Holy Ghost, the third person in the most adorable Trinity, coessential with the Father and the Son. This is that Spirit, which at the beginning of time moved on the face of the waters, when nature lay in one universal chaos. This was the Spirit that overshadowed the Holy Virgin, before that holy thing was born of her: and this same Spirit must come, and move upon the chaos of our souls, before we can properly be called the sons of God. This is what John the Baptist calls "being baptized with the Holy Ghost," without which, his and all other baptisms, whether infant or adult, avail nothing. This is that fire, which our Lord came to send into our earthly hearts, and which I pray the Lord of all lords to kindle in every unrenewed one this day.

As for the extraordinary operations of the Holy Ghost, such as working of miracles, or speaking with divers kinds of tongues, they are long since ceased. But as for this miracle of miracles, turning the soul to God by the more ordinary operations of the Holy Ghost, this abides yet, and will abide till time itself shall be no more. For it is he that sanctifieth us, and all the elect people of God. On this account, true believers are said to be "born from above, to be born not of blood, nor of the will of the flesh, nor of the will of man, but of God." Their second, as well as their first creation, is truly and purely divine. It is, therefore, called "a creation;" but put ye on (says the apostle) the new man which is created"—And how? Even as the first man was, "after God in righteousness and true holiness."

These, these are the precious truths, which a scoffing world would fain rally or ridicule us out of. To produce this glorious change, this new creation, the glorious Jesus left his Father's bosom. For this he led a persecuted life; for this he died an ignominious and accursed death; for this he rose again; and for this he now sitteth at the right hand of his Father. All the precepts of his gospel, all his ordinances, all his providences, whether of an afflictive or prosperous nature, all divine revelation from the beginning to the end, all center in these two points, to show us how we are fallen, and to begin, early on, and complete a glorious and blessed change in our souls. This is an end worthy of the coming of so divine a personage. To deliver a multitude of souls of every nation, language and tongue, from so many moral evils, and to reinstate them in an incomparably more excellent condition than that from whence they are fallen, is an end worthy the shedding of such precious blood. What system of religion is there now, or was there ever exhibited to the world, any way to be compared to this? Can the deistical scheme pretend in any degree to come up to it? Is it not noble, rational, and truly divine? And why then will not all that hitherto are strangers to this blessed restoration of their fallen natures, (for my heart is too full to abstain any longer from an application) why will you any longer dispute or stand out against it? Why will you not rather bring your clay to this heavenly Potter, and say from your inmost souls, "Turn us, O good Lord, and so shall we be turned?" This, you may and can do: and if you go thus far, who knows but that this very day, yea this very hour, the heavenly Potter may take you in hand, and make you vessels of honor fit for the Redeemer's use? Others that were once as far from the kingdom of God as you are, have been partakers of this blessedness. What a wretched creature was Mary Magdalene? And yet out of her Jesus Christ cast seven devils. Nay, he appeared to her first, after he rose from the dead, and she became as it were an apostle to the very apostles. What a covetous creature was Zaccheus? He was a griping cheating publican; and yet, perhaps, in one quarter of an hour's time, his heart is enlarged, and he made quite willing to give half of his goods to feed the poor. And to mention no more, what a cruel person was Paul. He was a persecutor, a blasphemer, injurious; one that breathed out threatenings against the disciples of the Lord, and made havoc of the church of Christ. And yet what a wonderful turn did he meet with, as he was journeying to Damascus? From a persecutor, he became a preacher; was afterwards made a spiritual father to thousands, and now probably sits nearest the Lord Jesus Christ in glory. And why all this? That he might be made an example to them that should hereafter believe. O then believe, repent; I beseech you, believe the gospel. Indeed, it is glad tidings, even tidings of great joy. You will then no longer have any thing to say against the doctrine of Original Sin; or charge the Almighty foolishly, for suffering our first parents to be prevailed on to eat such sour grapes, and permitting thereby their children's teeth to be set on edge. You will then no longer cry out against the doctrine of the New Birth, as enthusiasm, or brand the assertors of such blessed truths with the opprobrious names of fools and madmen. Having felt, you will then believe; having believed, you will therefore speak; and instead of being vessels of wrath, and growing harder and harder in hell fire, like vessels in a potter's oven, you will be made vessels of honor, and be presented at the great day by Jesus, to his heavenly Father, and be translated to live with him as monuments of rich, free, distinguishing and sovereign grace, for ever and ever.

You, that have in some degree experienced the quickening influence (for I must not conclude without dropping a word or two to God's children) you know how to pity, and therefore, I beseech you also to pray for those, to whose circumstances this discourse is peculiarly adapted. But will you be content in praying for them? Will you not see reason to pray for yourselves also? Yes, doubtless, for yourselves also. For you, and you only know, how much there is yet lacking in your faith, and how far you are from being partakers in that degree, which you desire to be, of the whole mind that was in Christ Jesus. You know what a body of sin and death you carry about with you, and that you must necessarily expect many turns of God's providence and grace, before you will be wholly delivered form it. But thanks be to God, we are in safe hands. He that has been the author, will also be the finisher of our faith. Yet a little while, and we like him shall say "It is finished;" we shall bow down our heads an give up the ghost. Till then, (for to thee, O Lord, will we now direct our prayer) help us, O Almighty Father, in patience to posses our souls. Behold, we are the clay, and thou art the Potter. Let not the thing formed say to him that formed it, whatever the dispensations of thy future Will concerning us may be, Why dost thou deal with us thus? Behold, we put ourselves as blanks in thine hands, deal with us as seemeth good in thy sight, only let every cross, ever affliction, every temptation, be overruled to the stamping thy blessed image in more lively characters on our hearts; that so passing from glory to glory, by the powerful operations of the blessed Spirit, we may be made thereby more and more meet for, and at last be translated to a full, perfect, endless, and uninterrupted enjoyment of glory hereafter, with thee O Father, thee O Son, and thee O blessed Spirit; to whom, three persons but one God, be ascribed, as is most due, all honor, power, might, majesty and dominion, now and to all eternity. Amen and Amen.

14. The Lord Our Righteousness

Jeremiah 23:6—"The Lord our Righteousness."

Whoever is acquainted with the nature of mankind in general, or the propensity of his own heart in particular, must acknowledge, that self-righteousness is the last idol that is rooted out of the heart: being once born under a covenant of works, it is natural for us all to have recourse to a covenant of works, for our everlasting salvation. And we have contracted such devilish pride, by our fall from God, that we would, if not wholly, yet in part at least, glory in being the cause of our own salvation. We cry out against popery, and that very justly; but we are all Papists, at least, I am sure, we are all Arminians by nature; and therefore no wonder so many natural men embrace that scheme. It is true, we disclaim the doctrine of merit, are ashamed directly to say we deserve any good at the hands of God; therefore, as the Apostle excellently well observes, "we go about," we fetch a circuit, "to establish a righteousness of our own, and," like the Pharisees of old, "will not wholly submit to that righteousness which is of God through Jesus Christ our Lord."

This is the sorest, though, alas! the most common evil that was ever yet seen under the sun. An evil, that in any age, especially in these dregs of time wherein we live, cannot sufficiently be inveighed against. For as it is with the people, so it is with the priests; and it is to be feared, even in those places, where once the truth as it is in Jesus was eminently preached, many ministers are so sadly degenerated from their pious ancestors, that the doctrines of grace, especially the personal, *All-Sufficient Righteousness* of Jesus, is but too seldom, too slightly mentioned. Hence the love of many waxeth cold; and I have often thought, was it possible, that this single consideration would be sufficient to raise our venerable forefathers again from their graves; who would thunder in their ears their fatal error.

The righteousness of Jesus Christ is one of those great mysteries, which the angels desire to look into, and seems to be one of the first lessons that God taught men after the fall. For, what were the coats that God made to put on our first parents, but types of the application of the merits of righteousness of Jesus Christ to believers hearts? We are told, that those coats were made of skins of beasts; and, as beasts were not then food for men, we may fairly infer, that those beasts were slain in sacrifice, in commemoration of the great sacrifice, Jesus Christ, thereafter to be offered. And the skins of the beasts thus slain, being put on Adam and Eve, they were hereby taught how their nakedness was to be covered with the righteousness of the Lamb of God.

This is it which is meant, when we are told, "Abraham believed on the Lord, and it was accounted to him for righteousness." In short, this is it of which both the law and the prophets have spoken, especially Jeremiah in the words of the text, "The Lord our righteousness."

I propose, through divine grace,

I. To consider who we are to understand by the word Lord.

II. How the Lord is man's righteousness.

III. I will consider some of the chief objections that are generally urged against this doctrine.

IV. I shall show some very ill consequences that flow naturally from denying this doctrine.

V. Shall conclude with an exhortation to all to come to Christ by faith, that they may be enabled to say with the prophet in the text, "The Lord our righteousness."

I. I am to consider who we are to understand by the word Lord. The Lord our righteousness.

If any Arians of Socinians are drawn by curiosity to hear what the babbler has to say, let them be ashamed of denying the divinity of that Lord, who has bought poor sinners with his precious blood. For the person mentioned in the text, under the character of the Lord, is Jesus Christ. Jeremiah 23:5, "Behold, the days come, saith the Lord, that I will raise unto David a righteous branch, a king shall reign and prosper, and shall execute judgment and justice in the earth. In his days, Jeremiah 23:6, "Judah shall be saved, and Israel shall dwell safely; and this is his name whereby he shall be called, The Lord our righteousness." By the righteous branch, all agree, that we are to understand Jesus Christ. He it is that is called the Lord in our text. If so, if there were no other text in the Bible to prove the divinity of Christ, this is sufficient: for if the word Lord may properly belong to Jesus Christ, he must be God. And, as you have it in the margin of your Bibles, the word Lord is in the original Jehovah, which is the essential title of God himself. Come then, ye Arians, kiss the son of God, bow down before him, and honor him, even as ye honor the Father. Learn of the angels, those morning-stars, and worship him as truly God: for otherwise you are as much idolaters, as those that worship the Virgin Mary. And as for you Socinians, who say Christ was a mere man, and yet profess that he was your Savior, according to your own principles you are accursed: for, if Christ be a mere man, then he is only an arm of flesh: and it is written, "Cursed is he that trusteth on an arm of flesh." But I would hope, there are no such monsters here; at least, that, after these considerations, they would be ashamed of broaching such monstrous absurdities any more. For it is plain, that, by the word Lord, we are to understand the Lord Jesus Christ, who here takes to himself the title Jehovah, and therefore must be very God of very God; or, as the Apostle devoutly expresses it, "God blessed for evermore."

II. How the Lord is to be man's righteousness, comes next to be considered.

And that is, in one word, by *Imputation*. For it pleased God, after he had made all things by the word of his power, to create man after his own image. And so infinite was the condescension of the high and lofty One, who inhabiteth eternity, that, although he might have insisted on the everlasting obedience of him and his posterity; yet he was pleased to oblige himself, by a covenant or agreement made with his own creatures, upon condition of an unsinning obedience, to give them immortality and eternal life. For when it is said, "The day thou eatest thereof, thou shalt surely die;" we may fairly infer, so long as he continued obedient, and did not eat thereof, he should surely live. The 3rd of Genesis gives us a full, but mournful account, how our first parents broke this covenant, and thereby stood in need of a better righteousness than their own, in order to procure their future acceptance with God. For what must they do? They were as much under a covenant of works as ever. And though, after their disobedience, they were without strength; yet they were obliged not only to do, but continue to do all things, and that too in the most perfect manner, which the Lord had required of them: and not only so, but to make satisfaction to God's infinitely offended justice, for the breach they had already been guilty of. Here then opens the amazing scene of *Divine Philanthropy*; I mean, God's love to man. For behold, what man could not do, Jesus Christ, the son of his Father's love, undertakes to do for him. And that God might be just in justifying the ungodly, though "he was in the form of God, and therefore thought it no robbery to be equal with God; yet he took upon him the form of a servant," even human nature. In that nature he obeyed, and thereby fulfilled the whole moral law in our stead; and also died a painful death upon the cross, and thereby became a curse for, or instead of, those whom the Father had given to him. As God, he satisfied, at the same time that he obeyed and suffered as man; and, being God and man in one person, he wrought out a full, perfect, and sufficient righteousness for all to whom it was to be imputed.

Here then we see the meaning of the word righteousness. It implies the active as well as passive obedience of the Lord Jesus Christ. We generally, when talking of the merits of Christ, only mention the latter,—his death; whereas, the former,—his life and active obedience, is equally necessary. Christ is not such a Savior as becomes us, unless we join both together. Christ not only died, but lived, not only suffered, but obeyed for, or instead of, poor sinners. And both these jointly make up that complete righteousness, which is to be imputed to us, as the disobedience of our first parents was made ours by imputation. In this sense, and no other, are we to understand that parallel which the apostle Paul draws, in the 5th of the Romans, between the first and second Adam. This is what he elsewhere terms, "our being made the righteousness of God in him." This is the sense wherein the Prophet would have us to understand the words of the text; therefore, Jer. 33:16, "She (i.e. the church itself) shall be called, (having this righteousness imputed to her) The Lord our righteousness." A passage, I think, worthy of the profoundest meditation of all the sons and daughters of Abraham.

Many are the objections which the proud hearts of fallen men are continually urging against this wholesome, this divine, this soul saving doctrine. I come now,

III. To answer some few of those which I think the most considerable.

And, *First*, they say, because they would appear friends to morality, "That the doctrine of an imputed righteousness is "destructive of good works, and leads to licentiousness."

And who, pray, are the persons that generally urge this objection? Are they men full of faith, and men really concerned for good works? No; whatever few exceptions there may be, if there be any at all, it is notorious, they are generally men of corrupt minds, reprobate concerning the faith. The best title I can give them is, that of *profane moralists*, or moralists false so called. For I appeal to the experience of the present as well as past ages, if iniquity did and does not most abound, where the doctrine of Christ's whole personal righteousness is most cried down, and most seldom mentioned. Arminian being antichristian principles, always did, and always will lead to antichristian practices. And never was there a reformation brought about in the church, but by the preaching the doctrine of an imputed righteousness. This, as the man of God, Luther, calls it, is "Artienlus statntis out cedentis Eichlesin," the article by which the Church stands or falls. And though the preachers of this doctrine are generally branded by those on the other side, with the opprobrious names of Antinomians, deceivers, and what not; yet, I believe, if the truth of the doctrine on both sides was to be judged of by the lives of the preachers of professors of it, on our side the question would have the advantage every way.

It is true, this, as well as every other doctrine of grace, may be abused. And perhaps the unchristian walk of some, who have talked of Christ's imputed righteousness, justification by faith, and the like, and yet never felt it imputed to their own souls, has given the enemies of the Lord thus cause to blaspheme. But this is a very unsafe, as well as a very unfair way of arguing. The only question should be, Whether or not this doctrine of an imputed righteousness, does in itself cut off the occasion of good works, or lean to licentiousness? To this we may boldly answer, In no wise. It excludes works, indeed, from being any cause of our justification in the sight of God; but it requires good works as a proof of our having this righteousness imputed to us, and as a declarative evidence of our justification in the sight of men. And then, how can the doctrine of an imputed righteousness be a doctrine leading to licentiousness?

It is all calumny. The apostle Paul introduceth an infidel making this objection, in his epistle to the Romans; and none but infidels, that never felt the power of Christ's resurrection upon their souls, will urge it over again. And therefore, notwithstanding this objection, with the Prophet in the text, we may boldly say, "The Lord is our righteousness."

But Satan (and no wonder that his servants imitate him) often transforms himself into an angel of light; and therefore, (such perverse things will infidelity and Arminianism make men speak) in order to dress their objections in the best colors, some urge, "That our Savior preached no such doctrine; that in his sermon on the mount, he mentions only morality:" and consequently the doctrine of an imputed righteousness falls wholly to the ground.

But surely the men, who urge this objection, either never read, or never understood, our Lord's blessed discourse, wherein the doctrine of an imputed righteousness is so plainly taught, that he who runs, If he has eyes that see, may read.

Indeed our Lord does recommend morality and good works, (as all faithful ministers will do) and clears the moral law from many corrupt glosses put upon it by the letter-learned Pharisees. But then, before he comes to this, 'tis remarkable, he talks of inward piety, such as poverty of spirit, meekness, holy mourning, purity of heart, especially hungering and thirsting after righteousness; and then recommends good works, as an evidence of our having his righteousness imputed to us, and these graces and divine tempers wrought in our hearts. "Let your light (that is, the divine light I before have been mentioning) shine before men, in a holy life; that they, seeing your good works, may glorify your father which is in heaven." And then he immediately adds, "Think not that I am come to destroy the moral law: I came not to destroy, (to take away the force of it as a rule of life) but to fulfill, (to obey it in its whole latitude, and give the complete sense of it.") And then he goes on to show how exceeding broad the moral law is. So that our Lord, instead of setting aside an imputed righteousness in his sermon upon the mount, not only confirms it, but also answers the foregoing objection urged against it, by making good works a proof and evidence of its being imputed to our souls. He, therefore, that hath ears to hear, let him hear what the Prophet says in the words of the text, "The Lord our righteousness."

But as Satan not only quoted scripture, but backed one temptation after another with it, when he attacked Christ in the wilderness; so his children generally take the same method in treating his doctrine. And, therefore, they urge another objection against the doctrine of an imputed righteousness, from the example of the young man in the gospel.

We may state it thus: "The Evangelist Mark, say they, chapter, Mark 10, mentions a young man that came to Christ, running, and asking him what he should do to inherit eternal life? Christ referred him to the commandments, to know what he must do to inherit eternal life. It is plain, therefore, works were to be, partly at least, the cause of his justification; and consequently the doctrine of an imputed righteousness is unscriptural." This is the objection in its full strength: and little strength in all its fullness. For, was I to prove the necessity of an imputed righteousness, I scarce know how I could bring a better instance to make it good.

Let us take a nearer view of this young man, and of our Lord's behavior towards him, Mark 10:17, the Evangelist tells us, "That when Christ was gone forth into the way, there came one running (it should seem it was some nobleman; a rarity indeed to see such a one running to Christ!) and not only so, but he kneeled to him, (perhaps many of his rank now, scarce know the time when they kneeled to Christ) and asked him, saying, Good Master, what shall I do that I may inherit eternal life?" Then Jesus, to see whether or not he believed him to be what he really was, truly and properly God, said unto him, "Why callest thou me good? There is none good but one, that is God." And, that he might directly answer his question, says he, "Thou knowest the commandments: do not commit adultery, do not bear false witness, defraud not, honor thy father and thy mother." This was a direct answer to his question; namely, That eternal life was not to be attained by his doings. For our Lord, by referring him to the commandments, did not (as the objectors insinuate) in the least hint, that his morality would recommend him to the favor and mercy of God; but he intended thereby, to make the law his schoolmaster to bring him to himself; that the young man, seeing how he had broken every one of these commandments, might thereby be convinced of the insufficiency of his own, and consequently of the absolute necessity of looking out for a better righteousness, whereon he might depend for eternal life.

This was what our Lord designed. The young man being self-righteous, and willing to justify himself, said, "All these have I observed from my youth;" but had he known himself, he would have confessed, all these have I broken from my youth. For, supposing he had not actually committed adultery, had he never lusted after a woman in his heart? What, if he had not really killed another, had he never been angry without a cause, or spoken unadvisedly with his lips? If so, by breaking one of the least commandments in the least degree, he became liable to the curse of God: for "cursed is he (saith the law) that continueth not to do all things that are written in this book." And therefore, as observed before, our Lord was so far from speaking against, that he treated the young man in that manner, on purpose to convince him of the necessity of an imputed righteousness.

But perhaps they will reply, it is said, "Jesus beholding him, loved him." And what then? This he might do with a human love, and at the same time this young man have no interest in his blood. Thus Christ is said to wonder, to weep over Jerusalem, and say, "O that thou hadst known, Me." But such like passages are to be referred only to his human nature. And there is a great deal of difference between the love wherewith Christ loved this young man, and that wherewith he loved Mary, Lazarus, and their sister Martha. To illustrate this by comparison: A minister of the Lord Jesus Christ seeing many amiable dispositions, such as a readiness to hear the word, a decent behavior at public worship, and a life outwardly spotless in many, cannot but so far love them; but then there is much difference betwixt the love which a minister feels for such, and that divine love, that union and sympathy of soul, which he feels for those that he is satisfied are really born again of God. Apply this to our Lord's case, as a faint illustration of it. Consider what has been said upon the young man's case in general, and then, if before you were fond of this objection, instead of triumphing, like him you will go sorrowful away. Our Savior's reply to him more and more convinces us of the truth of the prophet's assertion in the text, that "the Lord is our righteousness."

But there is a fourth, and a grand objection yet behind, which is taken from the 25th chapter of Matthew, "where our Lord is described as rewarding people with eternal life, because they fed the hungry, clothed the naked, and such-like. Their works therefore were a cause of their justification, consequently the doctrine of imputed righteousness is not agreeable to scripture."

This, I confess, is the most plausible objection that is brought against the doctrine insisted on from the text; and that we may answer it in as clear and brief a manner as may be, we confess, with the Article of the Church of England, "That albeit good works do not justify us, yet they will follow after justification, as fruits of it; and though they spring from faith in Christ, and a renewed soul, they shall receive a reward of grace, though not of debt; and consequently the more we abound in such good works, the greater will be our reward when Jesus Christ shall come to judgment."

Take these consideration along with us, and they will help us much to answer the objection now before us. For thus saith Matthew, "Then shall the King say to them on his right hand, Come, ye blessed children of my Father, inherit the kingdom prepared for you from the foundation of the world. For I was an hungered, and ye gave me meat; I was thirsty, and ye gave me drink; I was a stranger, and ye took me in; naked, and ye clothed me; I was sick, and ye visited me; I was in prison, and ye came unto me. I will therefore reward you, because you have done these things out of love to me, and hereby have evidenced yourselves to be my true disciples." And that the people did not depend on these good actions for their justification in the sight of God, is evident. "For when saw we thee an hungered, say they, and fed thee? Or thirsty, and gave thee drink? When saw we thee a stranger, and took thee in, or naked, and clothed thee? Or when saw we thee sick, or in prison, and came unto thee?" Language, and questions, quite improper for persons relying on their own righteousness, for acceptance and acquittance in the sight of God.

But then they reply against thee: "In the latter part of the chapter, it is plain that Jesus Christ rejects and damns the others for not doing these things. And therefore, if he damns these for not doing, he saves those for doing; and consequently the doctrine of an imputed righteousness is good for nothing."

But that is no consequence at all; for God may justly damn any man for omitting the least duty of the moral law, and yet in himself is not obliged to give to any one any reward, supposing he has done all that he can. We are unprofitable servants; we have not done near so much as it was our duty to do, must be the language of the most holy souls living; and therefore, from or in ourselves, cannot be justified in the sight of God. This was the frame of the devout souls just now referred to. Sensible of this, they were so far from depending on their works for justification in the sight of God, that they were filled, as it were, with a holy blushing, to think our Lord should condescend to mention, much more to reward them for, their poor works of faith and labors of love. I am persuaded their hearts would rise with a holy indignation against those who urge this passage, as an objection to the assertion of the prophet, that "the Lord is our righteousness."

Thus, I think, we have fairly answered these grand objections, which are generally urged against the doctrine of an *imputed righteousness*. Was I to stop here, I think I may say, "We are made more than conquerors through him that loved us." But there is a way of arguing which I have always admired, because I have thought it always very convincing, by showing the *absurdities* that will follow from denying any particular proposition in dispute.

IV. This is the next thing that was proposed. And never did greater or more absurdities flow from the denying any doctrine, than will flow from denying the doctrine of Christ's imputed righteousness.

And *First*, if we deny this doctrine, we turn the truth, I mean the word of God, as much as we can, into a lie, and utterly subvert all those places of scripture which say that we are saved by grace; that it is not of works, lest any man should boast, that salvation is God's free gift, and that he who glorieth, must glory only in the Lord. For, if the whole personal righteousness of Jesus Christ be not the sole cause of my acceptance with God, if any work done by or foreseen in me, was in the least to be joined with it, or looked upon by God an in inducing, impulsive cause of acquitting my soul from guilt, then I have somewhat whereof I may glory in myself. Not boasting is excluded in the great work of our redemption; but that cannot be, if we are enemies to the doctrine of an imputed righteousness. It would be endless to enumerate how many texts of scripture must be false, if this doctrine be not true. Let it suffice to affirm in the general, that if we deny an imputed righteousness, we may as well deny a divine revelation all at once; for it is the alpha and omega, the beginning and the end of the book of God. We must either disbelieve that, or believe what the prophet has spoken in the text, "that the Lord is our righteousness."

But further: I observed at the beginning of this discourse, that we are all Arminians and Papists by nature; for as one says, "Arminianism is the back way to popery." And here I venture further to affirming that if we deny the doctrine of an imputed righteousness, whatever we may stile ourselves, we are really Papists in our hearts; and deserve no other title from men.

Sirs, what think you? Suppose I was to come and tell you that you must intercede with saints, for them to intercede with God for you; would you not say, I was justly reputed a papist missionary by some, and deservedly thrust out of thy synagogues by others? I suppose you would. And why? Because, you would say, the intercession of Jesus Christ was sufficient of itself, without the intercession of saints, and that it was blasphemous to join theirs with his, as though he was sufficient.

Suppose I went a little more round about, and told you that the death of Christ was not sufficient, without our death being added to it; that you must die as well as Christ, join your death with his, and then it would be sufficient. Might you not then, with a holy indignation, throw dust in the air, and justly call me a "setter forth of strange doctrines?" And how then, if it be not only absurd, but blasphemous to join the intercession of saints with the intercession of Christ, as though his intercession was not sufficient; or our death with the death of Christ, as though his death was not sufficient: judge ye, if it be not equally absurd, equally blasphemous, to join our obedience, either wholly or in part, with the obedience of Christ, as if that was not sufficient. And if so, what absurdities will follow the denying that the Lord, both as to his active and passive obedience, is our righteousness?

One more absurdity I shall mention, as following the denying this doctrine, and I have done.

I remember a story of a certain prelate, who, after many arguments in vain urged to convince the Earl of Rochester of the invisible realities of another world, took his leave of his lordship with some such words as these: "Well, my lord, if there be no hell, I am safe; but if there should be such a thing as hell, what will become of you?" I apply this so those that oppose the doctrine now insisted on. If there be no such thing as the doctrine of an imputed righteousness, those who hold it, and bring forth fruit unto holiness, are safe; but if there be such a thing (as there certainly is) what will become of you that deny it? It is no difficult matter to determine. Your portion must be in the lake of fire and brimstone for ever and ever. Since you will rely upon your works, by your works you shall be judged. They shall be weighed in the balance of the sanctuary; and they will be found wanting. By your works therefore shall you be condemned; and you, being out of Christ, shall find God, to your poor wretched souls, a consuming fire.

The great Stoddard or Northampton in New England, has therefore well entitled a book which he wrote (and which I would take this opportunity to recommend) "The Safety of appearing in the Righteousness of Christ." For why should I lean upon a broken reed, when I can have the rock of ages to stand upon, that never can be moved?

And now, before I come to a more particular application, give me leave, in the apostle's language, triumphantly to cry out, "Where is the scribe, where the disputer?" Where is the reasoning infidel of this generation? Can any thing appear more reasonable, even according to your own way of arguing, than the doctrine here laid down? Have you not felt a convincing power go along with the word? Why then will you not believe on the Lord Jesus Christ, that so he may become the Lord your righteousness?

But it is time for me to come a little closer to your consciences.

Brethren, though some may be offended at this doctrine, and may account it foolishness; yet, to many of you, I doubt not but it is precious, it being agreeable to the form of sound words, which from your infancy has been delivered to you; and, coming from a quarter, you would least have expected, may be received with more pleasure and satisfaction. But give me leave to ask you one question; Can you say, the Lord our righteousness? I say, the Lord *our* righteousness. For entertaining this doctrine in your heads, without receiving the Lord Jesus Christ savingly by a lively faith into your hearts, will but increase your damnation. As I have often told you, so I tell you again, an unapplied Christ is no Christ at all. Can you then, with believing Thomas, cry our, "My Lord and my God?" Is Christ your sanctification, as well as your outward righteousness? For the word righteousness, in the text, not only implies Christ's personal righteousness imputed to us, but also holiness wrought in us. These two, God has joined together. He never did, he never dies, he never will put them asunder. If you are justified by the blood, you are also sanctified by the Spirit of our Lord. Can you then in this sense say, The Lord our righteousness? Were you ever made to abhor yourselves for your actual and original sins, and to loathe your own righteousness; for, as the prophet beautifully expresses it, "your righteousness is as filthy rags? Were you ever made to see and admire the all-sufficiency of Christ's righteousness, and excited by the Spirit of God to hunger and thirst after it? Could you ever say, my soul is athirst for Christ, yea, even for the righteousness of Christ? O when shall I come to appear before the presence of my God in the righteousness of Christ! Nothing but Christ! Nothing but Christ! Give me Christ, O god, and I am satisfied! My soul shall praise thee for ever.

Was this ever the language of your hearts? And, after these inward conflicts, were you ever enabled to reach out the arm of faith, and embrace the blessed Jesus in your souls, so that you could say, "my beloved is mine, and I am his?" If so, fear not, whoever you are. Hail, all hail, you happy souls! The Lord, the Lord Christ, the everlasting God, is your righteousness. Christ has justified you, who is he that condemneth you? Christ has died for you, nay rather is risen again, and ever liveth to make intercession for you. Being now justified by his grace, you have peace with God, and shall, ere long, be with Jesus in glory, reaping everlasting and unspeakable fruits both in body and soul. For there is no condemnation to those that are really in Christ Jesus. "Whether Paul or Apollos, or life or death, all is yours if you are Christ's, for Christ is God's. My brethren, my heart is enlarged towards you! O think of the love of Christ in dying for you! If the Lord be your righteousness, let the righteousness of your Lord be continually in your mouth. Talk of, O talk of, and recommend the righteousness of Christ, when you lie down, and when you rise up, at your going out and coming in! Think of the greatness of the gift, as well as the giver! Show to all the world, in whom you have believed! Let all by your fruits know, that the Lord is your righteousness, and that you are waiting for your Lord from heaven! O study to be holy, even as he who has called you, and washed you in his own blood, is holy! Let not the righteousness of the Lord be evil spoken of through you. Let not Jesus be wounded in the house of his friends, but grow in grace, and in the knowledge of our Lord and Savior Jesus Christ, day by day. O think of his dying love! Let that love constrain you to obedience! Having much forgiven, love much. Be always asking, What shall I do, to express my gratitude to the Lord, for giving me his righteousness? Let that self-abasing, God-exalting question be always in your mouths; "Why me, Lord? Why me?" why am I taken, and others left? Why is the Lord my righteousness? Why is he become my salvation, who have so often deserved damnation at his hands?

My friends, I trust I feel somewhat of a sense of God's distinguishing love upon my heart; therefore I must divert a little from congratulating you, to invite poor Christless sinners to come to him, and accept of his righteousness, that they may have life.

Alas, my heart almost bleeds! What a multitude of precious souls are now before me! How shortly must all be ushered into eternity! And yet, O cutting thought! Was God now to require all your souls, how few, comparatively speaking, could really say, the Lord our righteousness!

And think you, O sinner, that you will be able to stand in the day of judgment, if Christ be not your righteousness? No, that alone is the wedding garment in which you must appear. O Christless sinners, I am distressed for you! The desires of my soul are enlarged. O that this may be an accepted time! That the Lord may be your righteousness! For whither would you flee, if death should fine you naked? Indeed there is no hiding yourselves from his presence. The pitiful fig-leaves of your own righteousness will not cover your nakedness, when God shall call you to stand before him. Adam found them ineffectual, and so will you. O think of death! O think of judgment! Yet a little while, and time shall be no more; and then what will become of you, if the Lord be not your righteousness? Think you that Christ will spare you? No, he that formed you, will have no mercy on you. If you are not of Christ, if Christ be not your righteousness, Christ himself shall pronounce you damned. And can you bear to think of being damned by Christ? Can you bear to hear the Lord Jesus say to you, "Depart from me, ye cursed, into everlasting fire, prepared for the devil and his angels." Can you live, think you, in everlasting burnings? Is your flesh brass, and your bones iron? What if they are? Hell-fire, that fire prepared for the devil and his angels, will heat them through and through. And can you bear to depart from Christ? O that heart-piercing thought! Ask those holy souls, who are at any time bewailing an absent God, who walk in darkness, and see no light, though but a few days or hours; ask them, what it is to lose a light and presence of Christ? See how they seek him sorrowing, and go mourning after him all the day long! And, if it is so dreadful to lose the sensible presence of Christ only for a day, what must it be to be banished from him to all eternity!

But thus it must be, if Christ be not your righteousness. For God's justice must be satisfied; and, unless Christ's righteousness is imputed and applied to you here, you must hereafter be satisfying the divine justice in hell-torments eternally; nay, Christ himself shall condemn you to that place of torment. And how cutting is that thought! Methinks I see poor, trembling, Christless wretches, standing before the bar of god, crying out, Lord, if we must be damned, let some angel, or some archangel, pronounce the damnatory sentence: but all in vain. Christ himself shall pronounce the irrevocable sentence. Knowing therefore the terrors of the Lord, let me persuade you to close with Christ, and never rest till you can say, "the Lord our righteousness." Who knows but the Lord may have mercy on, may, abundantly pardon you? Beg of God to give you faith; and, if the Lord gives you that, you will by it receive Christ, with his righteousness, and his All. You need not fear the greatness or number of your sins. For are you sinners? So am I. Are you the chief of sinners? So am I. Are you backsliding sinners? So am I. And yet the Lord (for ever adored be his rich, free and sovereign grace) the Lord is my righteousness. Come then, O young man, who (as I acted once myself) are playing the prodigal, and wandering away afar off from your heavenly Father's house, come home, come home, and leave your swines trough. Feed no longer on the husks of sensual delights: for Christ's sake arise, and come home! Your heavenly Father now calls you. See yonder the best robe, even the righteousness of his dear Son, awaits you. See it, view it again and again. Consider at how dear a rate it was purchased, even by the blood of God. Consider what great need you have of it. You are lost, undone, damned for ever, without it. Come then, poor, guilty prodigals, come home: indeed, I will not, like the elder brother in the gospel, be angry; no, I will rejoice with the angels in heaven. And O that God would now bow the heavens, and come down! Descend, O Son of God, descend; and, as thou hast shown in me such mercy, O let thy blessed Spirit apply thy righteousness to some young prodigals now before thee, and clothe their naked souls with thy best robe!

But I must speak a word to you, young maidens, as well as young men. I see many of you adorned, as to your bodies, but are not your souls naked? Which of you can say, the Lord is my righteousness? Which of you was ever solicitous to be dressed in this robe of invaluable price, and without which you are no better than whited sepulchers in the sight of God? Let not then so many of you, young maidens, any longer forget your chief and only ornament. O seek for the Lord to be your righteousness, or otherwise burning will soon be upon you, instead of beauty!

And what shall I say to you of a middle age, you busy merchants, you cumbered Martha's, who, with all your gettings, have not yet gotten the Lord to be your righteousness? Alas! what profit will there be of all your labor under the sun, if you do not secure this pearl of invaluable price? This one thing, so absolutely needful, that it only can stand you in stead, when all other things shall be taken from you. Labor therefore no longer so anxiously for the meat which perisheth, but henceforward seek for the Lord to be your righteousness, a righteousness that will entitle you to life everlasting. I see also many hoary heads here, and perhaps the most of them cannot say, the Lord is my righteousness. O gray-headed sinner, I could weep over you! Your gray hairs, which ought to be your crown, and in which perhaps you glory, are now your shame. You know not that the Lord is your righteousness: O haste then, haste ye, aged sinners, and seek an interest in redeeming love! Alas, you have one foot already in the grave, your glass is just run out, your sun is just going down, and it will set and leave you in an eternal darkness, unless the Lord be your righteousness! Flee then, O flee for your lives! Be not afraid. All things are possible with God. If you come, though it be at the eleventh hour, Christ Jesus will in no wise cast you out. Seek then for the Lord to be your righteousness, and beseech him to let you know, how it is that a man may be born again when he is old! But I must not forget the lambs of the flock. To feed them was one of my Lord's last commands. I know he will be angry with me, if I do not tell them, that the Lord may be their righteousness; and that of such is the kingdom of heaven. Come then, ye little children, come to Christ; the Lord Christ shall be your righteousness. Do not think, that you are too young to be converted. Perhaps many of you may be nine or ten years old, and yet cannot say, the Lord is our righteousness: which many have said, though younger than you. Come then, while you are young. Perhaps you may not live to be old. Do not stay for other people. If your fathers and mothers will not come to Christ, do you come without them. Let children lead them, and show them how the Lord may be their righteousness. Our Lord Jesus Christ loved little children. You are his lambs; he bids me feed you. I pray God make you willing betimes to take the Lord for your righteousness.

Here then I could conclude; but I must not forget the poor negroes; no, I must not. Jesus Christ had died for them, as well as for others. Nor do I mention you last, because I despise your souls; but because I would have what I shall say, make the deeper impression upon your hearts. O that you would seek the Lord to be your righteousness! Who knows but he may be found of you? For in Jesus Christ there is neither male nor female, bond nor free; even you may be the children of God, if you believe in Jesus. Did you never read of the eunuch belonging to the queen of Candace? A negro like yourselves. He believed. The Lord was his righteousness. He was baptized. Do you also believe, and you shall be saved. Christ Jesus is the same now as he was yesterday, and will wash you in his own blood. Go home then, turn the words of the text into a prayer, and entreat the Lord to be your righteousness. Even so, come Lord Jesus, come quickly, into all our souls! Amen, Lord Jesus, Amen and Amen!

15. The Righteousness of Christ, an Everlasting Righteousness

Daniel 9:24—"And to bring everlasting Righteousness."

On reading these words, I cannot help addressing you in the language of the angels to the poor shepherds, who kept watch over their flocks by night, "Behold, I bring you glad tidings of great joy," such tidings, that if we have ears to hear, if we have eyes to see, and if our hearts have indeed experienced the grace of God, must cause us to cry out with the Virgin Mary, "My soul doth magnify the Lord, and my spirit doth rejoice in God my Savior." The words which I have read to you, are part of one of the most explicit revelations that was given of Jesus Christ, before he made his public entrance into this our world. It has been observed by some, and very properly too, that it is one mark of the divine goodness to his creatures, that he is pleased to let light come in gradually upon the natural world. If the sun from midnight darkness, was immediately to shine forth in his full meridian blaze, his great splendor would be apt to dazzle our eyes, and strike us blind again: but God is pleased to make light come gradually in, and by that means we are prepared to receive it. And as God is pleased to deal with the natural, so he has dealt with the moral, with the spiritual world. The Lord Jesus Christ did not appear in his full glory all at once, but as the sun rises gradually, so did the Lord Jesus, the Sun of righteousness, rise gradually upon men, with healing under his wings. Hence it was, that our first parents had nothing to fix their faith upon, but that first promise, "The seed of the woman shall bruise the serpent's head." And in future ages, at sundry times, and after divers manners, God was pleased to speak to our fathers by the prophets, before he spake to us in these last days by his Son; and the prophets that were more peculiarly dear to God, it should seem had more peculiar and extraordinary revelations vouchsafed to them, concerning Jesus Christ.

It is plain from the accounts we have in Scripture, that the Prophet Daniel was one of these; he is stiled by the angel, not only a "man that was beloved," but a "man that was greatly beloved," or as it is in the margin of your bibles, "he was a man of desires," of large and extensive desires to promote the glory of God; he was a desirable man, a man that did much good in his generation, and therefore his life was much to be desired by those who loved God. The words which I have chosen for the subject of our present meditation, contain part of a revelation made to this man. If you look back to the beginning of this chapter, you will find how the good man was employed, when God was pleased to give him this revelation; verse Daniel 9:2, "In the first year of Darius's reign, I Daniel understood by books the number of the years, whereof the word of the Lord came to Jeremiah the prophet, that he would accomplish seventy years in the desolations of Jerusalem." Daniel was a great man, and withal a good man; great as he was, it seems he was not above reading his Bible; he made the Bible his constant study; for it is the Bible we are to understand by what is here termed books, and elsewhere, the scriptures of truth. He found, that the time for God's people being delivered from the captivity, was now at hand. Well, one would have thought, that therefore Daniel needed not to pray; but this, instead of retarding, quickened him in his prayers: and therefore we are told in the third verse, "I set my face unto the Lord God, to seek by prayer and supplications, with fasting and sackcloth, and ashes." It is beautifully expressed: "he set his face," as though he was resolved never to let his eye go off God, till God was pleased to give him an answer; he was resolved, Jacob-like, to wrestle with the Lord God, until God should be pleased to give him the desired blessing. We are told in the fourth verse, that "he prayed unto the Lord, and made confession," not only of his own sins, but the sins of his people. And when ye retire hence to your houses, before ye go to bed, I would recommend to you the reading of this prayer; every word of it bespeaks his exceeding concern for the public good. It would take me up too much time, was I to make such observations as indeed the prayer deserved; to bring you sooner to the words of the text, let us go forward to the twentieth verse, and there you will find the success that Daniel met with, when praying. Says he, "And whiles I [was] speaking, and praying, and confessing my sin and the sin of my people Israel, and presenting my supplication before the *Lord* my God for the holy mountain of my God; Yea, whiles I [was] speaking in prayer, even the man Gabriel, whom I had seen in the vision at the beginning, being caused to fly swiftly, touched me about the time of the evening oblation. The manner in which Daniel expressed himself, is very emphatical: "While I was speaking in prayer;" implying, that God suffers us, when we draw near to him by faith in prayer, to lay all our complaints before him; he suffers us to speak unto, and talk with him, as a man talketh with his friend. Daniel at this time too was making confession one part of his prayer; for we are never, never in a better frame to receive answers from above, than when we are humbling ourselves before the Lord. He was not only confessing his own sins, but he was confessing the sins of his people; he was praying for those, who perhaps seldom prayed for themselves; "while I was speaking in prayer, the man Gabriel:" which word, by interpretation, signifies the strength of God; a very proper name, says Bishop Hall, for that angel who was to come and bring the news to the world, of the God of strength, the Lord Jesus Christ. This angel is here represented as flying, and as flying swiftly; to show us how willing, how unspeakably willing those blessed spirits are, to bring good news to men. And it is upon this account, I suppose, that we are taught by our Lord to pray, "that God's will may be done by us on earth, as it is done in heaven," that we may imitate a little of that alacrity and vigor, which angels employ, when they are sent on errands for God.

Well, here is not only mention made of the angel's flying swiftly, but there is mention made of the time that he came; "He came and touched me, about the time of the evening oblations," that is, about three o'clock in the afternoon; at this time there was a sacrifice made to God, and this sacrifice was in a peculiar manner a type of the Lord Jesus, who in the evening of the world was to become a sacrifice for sinners. We are told in the Daniel 9:22, verse, what message this angel delivered, "He informed me, and talked with me, and said, O Daniel, I am now come forth to give thee skill and understanding; at the beginning of thy supplication, the commandment came forth, and I am come to show thee, for thou art greatly beloved, therefore understand the matter, and consider the vision." This passage, with such like passages of scripture, hath often comforted my soul, and may comfort the hearts of all God's people. There are a great many of you, perhaps, have prayed, and prayed again to God, and probably you do not find any answer given you: you pray for an enlarged heart, you pray for comfort, you pray for deliverance; God is pleased to withhold it for a while; then the devil strikes in, and says, God has shut out your prayers, God will never hear, God will never regard you, therefore pray no more. But, my dear friends, this is a mistake; a thousand years are with God as one day; and the Lord Jesus had bid us, "to pray always, and not faint." You may have had your prayers heard, the very moment they went out of your lips, though it may not please your God, (and it may not be proper for you) to let you know that they are heard. "At the beginning of thy supplication, the commandment went forth;" and this very angel some hundred years after, told Zecharias, that his prayer was heard;" a prayer for what? A prayer for a child: it could not be supposed that at the very time Zecharias was praying for a child; but his prayer he had put up forty years before, God was pleased to answer so long afterwards.

But to proceed with Gabriel's declaration, ver. Daniel 9:24, Seventy years are determined upon thy people, and upon thy holy city, to finish transgression, to make an end of sins, and to make reconciliation for iniquity, and to bring in everlasting righteousness." I do not intend to trouble you about the critical exposition of these seventy weeks; commentators are divided exceedingly upon this subject; some of them explain them one way, and some another, and perhaps we shall never know till the day of judgment, till the glorious day spoken of in the New Testament, which are right. My intention is to dwell upon this particular part of the angel's message, that some one person was to do something unspeakable for God's people, even "to bring in an everlasting righteousness."

If you want to know who was the person that was to do this, look to the 26th verse, and you will find the person mentioned, the Lord Jesus Christ: "after threescore and two weeks shall the Messiah be cut off, but not for himself:" he is the person spoken of, he was "to put an end to sin, to make reconciliation for iniquity, and to bring in everlasting righteousness."

From these important words, I shall endeavor,

First, To show you what we are to understand by the word, "Righteousness."

Secondly, I shall endeavor to show you, upon what account it lay that the righteousness mentioned in the text, is called an "everlasting righteousness."

Thirdly, I shall show, what we are to understand by "bringing it in." And,

Then speak a word to saints and sinners. And while I am speaking to your ears, may God, for the Lord Jesus Christ's sake, speak to your hearts!

First, To explain what we are to understand by the word, "righteousness." If I was to ask some people what we are to understand by the word, righteousness; if the person was an Arminian, or an enemy to the doctrine of free grace, he would answer me, it signifies what we commonly call moral honesty, or doing justice between man and man. And, indeed, in various passages of scripture, the word righteousness has no other meaning, at least, it bears that meaning. I suppose, we are to understand it in this sense, when we are told, that Paul, preaching before Felix, "reasoned of temperance, of righteousness, and of a judgment to come." Felix had been a very unrighteous and unjust man, and therefore, to convince him of his wickedness, to alarm his conscience, to put him upon seeking help in the Lord Jesus, Paul preached not only of temperance, (for Felix had been a very intemperate man) but he preached to him of righteousness, of the necessity of doing justice because he had been an unjust man; and he puts before him the judgment to come, in order to make him fly to Jesus Christ for deliverance from the bad consequences of that judgment; and there are other places of scripture, where the word righteousness may be understood in this sense.

It likewise signifies inward holiness, wrought in us by the blessed Spirit of God. But, I believe, the word righteousness in my text signifies, what, I trust most, I should be glad if I could say, all who attend this night, will be glad to hear of: What is that? It is what all reformed divines, that have clear heads and clean hearts, call an imputed righteousness, or the righteousness of the Lord Jesus Christ to be imputed to poor sinners upon their believing: and, if you ask me, what I mean by an imputed righteousness, not to shoot over you heads, but rather, if God shall be pleased to make me, to reach your hearts, I will tell you by the word "righteousness," I understand all that Christ hat done, and all that Christ hath suffered: or, to make use of the term generally made use of by sound divines, "Christ's active, and Christ's passive obedience;" put those two together, and they make up the righteousness of the Lord Jesus Christ. My dear friends, thus stood the case between God and man: at first God made man upright. Moses gives us a short, but never was so full a description of the origin and nature of man given by any other but himself. "In the image of God made he man, says the sacred historian, being inspired by the Spirit of God. God said, and it was done; God commanded, and the world arose before him; "Let there be light," and instantaneously behold light appeared: but when that lovely, that divine, that blessed creature Man, the Lord of the creation, God's vicegerent was to be made; God calls a council, and says, "Let us make man after our own image." Now, this image is to be understood, no doubt, in respect of man's soul; for God being no corporeal substance, man could not be made after his image that way. Well, in this condition God made man. Adam stood as our representative. Adam and Eve had but one name originally, "God made man, and called their name Adam. God left Adam to his own free will; he was pleased to enter into a covenant with him, which, indeed, is an amazing instance of God's condescension. God might have ordered man to do so and so, and not made him any promise of a reward: but the great Creator was pleased to promise him, that if he performed an unsinning obedience, if he abstained from eating a particular tree, that he and his posterity should live forever; but if he broke that command, in the day that he ate thereof, he and all his prosperity were to die. Now, I verily believe, had you and I been there present, however some people may object against God's severity, in imputing Adam's sin to us; yet I believe, if you and I, and all the world had been present, we should have heartily come into this agreement. Supposing God had called the whole creation together, and had said, "Ye, my creatures, I have made here a man after my own image, I have breathed into him the breath of life, I have caused him to become a living soul, I have filled him with righteousness and true holiness; he has not the least propensity to sin, only he is a fallible and mutable creature; all that I desire of this man is, that he abstain from yonder tree; I have given to him all the trees of the garden, I have made him, and planted for him a garden with mine own right hand, I desire he may abstain from plucking yonder fruit! Will ye stand or fall by this m an, will ye let him be your representative, will ye be content that his obedience or disobedience be imputed to you?" If we had been all there, every one of us would have said, "Lord God, we will let him be our representative;" the terms were so easy, the improbability of his falling was so exceeding great; that I believe every one of us should have all put our hand to the covenant. And supposing us alive, and that we had agreed to that covenant, who is that man or woman that could find fault with God's imputing Adam's sin to us. Well, my friends, God made man in this condition; the devil envied his happiness; it is supposed by some, that man was made to supply the places of the fallen angels. But the devil envied man, and had leave to tempt him; Eve soon reached out her hand and plucked of the forbidden fruit, and afterwards Adam transgressed also; and from that very moment, to make use of Mr. Beston's words, "Man's name was Ichabod," the glory of the Lord departed from him. Adam and Eve then fell; you, and I, and all their posterity (whom they represented) fell in them. Mankind had but one neck; and God might have served mankind, as Caligula would have served Rome, according to his own words, "I wish it had but one neck, and I would cut it off with one blow." God, if he pleased, might have sent us all to hell. Here Calvin represents God's attributes as struggling one with another; Justice saying to God, seeing Justice had framed the sanction, "Is the law broken, damn the offender, and send him to hell." The mercy of God, his darling attribute, cries out, "Spare him, spare him." The wisdom of God contrives a way, that justice might be satisfied, and yet mercy be triumphant still. How was that? The Lord Jesus interposes, the days-man, the dear Redeemer! He saw God wielding his flaming sword, and his hand taking hold of vengeance; the Lord Jesus Christ saw the sword ready to be sheathed in the blood of the offender; when no eye could pity, when no angel or archangel could rescue, just as God was, as it were, about to give the fatal blow, just as the knife was put to the throat of the offender, the Son of God, the eternal Logos, says, "Father, spare the sinner; let him not die; Father, Father, O hold thy hand, withdraw thy sword, for I come to do thy will; man has broken thy law, and violated thy covenant: I do not deny but man deserves to be damned forever; but, Father, what Adam could not do, it thou wilt prepare me a body, I in the fullness of time will go, and die for him; he has broken thy law, but I will go and keep it, that thy law may be honored; I will give a perfect unsinning obedience to all thy commandments; and that thou mayst justify ungodly creatures, I will not only go down and obey thy law, but I will go down and bleed; I will go down and die: here I am; I will step in between thee and sinners, and be glad to have thy sword sheathed in my heart's blood for them."

In the fullness of time descends the eternal Logos, "In the fullness of time God sent forth his Son made of a woman, made under the law, to redeem them that are under the law from the curse of it, being made a curse for us." The Lord Jesus Christ being clothed in human nature, fulfilled all righteousness; he submitted to every institution of God, and was pleased to obey the whole moral law; and afterwards, O can we think of it, O can you hear of it, without a heart leaping with joy, at last the Lord Jesus bled and died! And when he was just expiring, just as he was about to bow down his head, and give up the ghost, what do ye think he said? He said, "It is finished!" As much as to say, "Now the arduous work, the difficult task I had undertaken, blessed be God, is not completely over; all the demands of the law are finished; now God's justice is satisfied; now a new and living way is opened by my blood to the holiest of all for poor sinners."

So that when Christ's righteousness is here spoken of, we are to understand "Christ's obedience and death," all that Christ has done, and all that Christ has suffered for an elect world, for all that will believe on him. And blessed be God for this righteousness! Blessed be God for the epithet which in the text is put to this righteousness; it might be called a blessed righteousness, it might be called a glorious righteousness, it might be called an invaluable righteousness; but the angel calls it an everlasting righteousness: God give you to take the comfort of it!

Secondly, I am to show, on what account, this righteousness is here called an everlasting righteousness; and pray why do you think is Christ's righteousness called an everlasting righteousness?

I suppose it is called an everlasting righteousness,

First, Because Christ's righteousness was intended by the great God to extend to mankind even from eternity. All of you know, that old love is the best love. When we have an old acquaintance, a friend, that has loved us for many years, indeed that love is sweet: though we may love new friends, yet when an old friend and a new friend meet together, we may say, that the old is better. Now this should endear God to us, to think that from all the ages of eternity God had thoughts of you; God intended the Lord Jesus Christ to save your souls and mine: hence it is, that God, to endear Jeremiah to him, tells him, I have love thee with an everlasting love. Hence it is, that the Lord Jesus when he calls his elect people up to heaven, says, "Come, ye blessed of my Father;" what follows? "receive the kingdom prepared for you;" how long? "from the foundation of the world." All that we receive in time; all the streams that come to our souls, are but so many steams flowing from that inexhaustible fountain, God's electing, God's sovereign, God's distinguishing, God's everlasting love; and, therefore, the righteousness of Jesus Christ may properly be called an everlasting righteousness, because God intended it from everlasting.

Secondly, It is called an everlasting righteousness, because the efficacy of Christ's death took place immediately upon Adam's fall. Christianity, in one sense, is as old as the creation. Great Professor Franck, of Germany, says, "That Christ is the sum and substance of all righteousness." Mr. Henry observes, "That the Lord Jesus Christ is the treasure hid in the field of the Old Testament, under the types and shadows of the Mosaic dispensation." We have the Sun of Righteousness shining in his full meridian in the New Testament dispensation." We have the Sun of Righteousness shining in his full meridian in the New Testament dispensation. Now the righteousness of Jesus Christ, may be called an everlasting righteousness, because all the saints that have been saved, or that ever will be saved, are all saved by the righteousness of Christ. A great many censorious people are mighty inquisitive to know, what will become of the heathens, that never heard of Jesus Christ. I would say to such persons, as the Lord Jesus Christ did to another curious inquirer, "What is that to thee? Follow thou me." Pray, for what should you and I trouble ourselves about the heathens? Are not we heathens? It is too true, that we have too much of a heathens temper and practice with us. But why should we lost our time in inquiring about what will become of the heathen, and not rather inquire what will become of our own souls? We may be sure God will deal with heathens according to their light: if he has given them no revelation, they will not be judged by a revelation; if they have not had a law, they will be judged without law. But as for the Jews and Gentiles, who have the gospel revealed to them, however Deists may argue contrary to it; however they may set up reason in opposition to divine revelation; we may be sure none were ever saved, or will be saved, but by the righteousness of Christ. It was through faith in him, that Abel was saved; it was through the sacrifice of Jesus Christ, that Abraham was accepted, and that all the prophets of old were accepted; and there is none other name given under heaven, whereby we can be saved, but that of Christ. And therefore, since persons under the law, and under the gospel, are to be saved only through Christ; therefore, Christ's righteousness may properly be called an everlasting righteousness. But this is not all.

Thirdly, The righteousness of Jesus Christ, is not only to be called an everlasting righteousness, because that all persons under the law and all persons under the gospel, are saved by it; but because the efficacy thereof, blessed be God for it! Is to continue till time shall be no more. Blessed be God for Jesus Christ! The efficacy of whose blood, death, and atonement, is as great and as effectual now to the salvation of poor sinners, as when he bowed his blessed head, and gave up the ghost: "Jesus Christ is the same yesterday, today, and forever;" and whosoever believes on him, now, whosoever comes to, and accepts of him, shall now see his power, shall taste of his grace, and shall be actually saved by him, the save as if he had been in company with those who saw him expiring.

Fourthly, Christ's righteousness may be called an everlasting righteousness, because the benefit of it is to endure to everlasting life. Indeed, some people tell us, that a person may be in Christ today, and go to the devil tomorrow: but, blessed be God, ye have not so learned Christ! No, my dear friends, thanks be to God for that divine text, "There is now no condemnation to them that are in Christ Jesus." Though God's people may fall foully; and though many are full of doubts and fears, and say, "One day I shall fall by the hands of Saul;" however your poor souls may be harassed, yet no wicked devil, nor your own depraved heart, shall be able to separate you from the love of God: God has loved you, God has fixed his heart upon you, and having loved his own, he loves them unto the end. The Lord of life and of glory, the blessed Jesus, will never cease loving you, till he hath loved and brought you to heaven; when he will rejoice, and say, "Behold me, O my Father, and the dear children that thou hast given me; thou gavest them me; thine they were, I have bought them with my blood, I have won them with my sword and with my bow, and I now will wear them as so many jewels of my crown." Therefore, Jesus Christ's righteousness may be called an everlasting righteousness, because those who once take hold of, and are interested in it, shall be saved everlastingly by Christ: "It is God that justifies us, (says St. Paul) who is he that condemneth? It is Christ that died, yea rather that is risen again." He gives devils the challenge, "O death, where is thy sting, O grave, where is thy victory? Who shall separate us from the love of God? I am persuaded that neither death nor life, neither principalities nor powers, nor any other creature, shall ever be able to separate us from the love of God, which is in Christ Jesus our Lord." Those whom God justifies, he also glorifies. And because Christ lives, blessed be God, we shall live also. I know not what you may say; but though I trust I have felt the grace of Christ every day for fresh strength as if I had never believed before: and if I was to depend upon my own faithfulness, and not the faithfulness of the Son of God, I am sure I should soon desert the Lord Jesus Christ. But glory be to God, he is faithful that hath promised! Glory be to God, our salvation depends not upon our own free will, but upon God's free grace! Here is a sure bottom; the believer may build upon it; let the storms blow as long and as high as they please, they may make the poor creature tremble, but blessed be God, they never shall be able to take him off the foundation; though they may shake him, they shall only shake off his corruption: and I believe all that fear God, will be glad to part with it. *On* all these accounts, Christ's righteousness may be called an everlasting righteousness.

III. It is said, in my text, that Jesus was to bring it in. What are we to understand by his bringing it in? Our Lord's promulgating and proclaiming it to the world. Indeed, it was brought in under the law, but then it was brought in under types and shadows, and most of the Jews looked no further. But Jesus Christ brought life and immortality to light by the gospel. The light of Moses was only twilight; the light of the gospel, is like the sun at noon-day, shining in his full meridian. Therefore, Jesus Christ may be said to bring in this everlasting righteousness, because he proclaimed it to the world, and commanded it to be preached, that God sent his Son into the world, that the world through him might be saved.

Again, The Lord Jesus Christ brought in this righteousness, as he wrought it out for sinners upon the cross. Some Antinomians, for want of a proper distinction, run into a grievous error, telling us, Because God intended to justify by the righteousness of Jesus Christ, therefore man is justified from all eternity: which is absurd: a person cannot be justified, till he is actually existing; therefore, though man is justified, as it lies in God's mind from all eternity, yet it was not actually brought in till the Lord Jesus Christ pronounced those blessed words, "It is finished;" the grand consummation! Then Jesus brought it in. A new and a living way was to be opened to the Holy of Holies, for poor sinners, by the blood of Christ. But I do not think that the expression, brought in, is to be limited to this sense, though I suppose it is the primary one; it implies not only Christ's bringing it into the world, as promulgating, and having it written in the word of God, and as having wrought it out for sinners in his life, and on the cross; but he brings it in, in a manner, which, I pray God may take place this night; I mean, bringing it, by his blessed Spirit, into poor believers hearts. All that Christ hath done, all that Christ hat suffered, all Christ's active obedience, all Christ's passive obedience, will do us no good, unless by the Spirit of God, it is brought into our souls. As one expresses it, "An unapplied Christ is no Christ at all." To hear of a Christ dying for sinners, will only increase your damnation, will only sink you deeper into hell, unless we have ground to say, by a work of grace wrought in our hearts, that the Lord Jesus hath brought this home to us. Hence it is, that the Apostle, speaking of Christ, says, "Who love me, and gave himself for me." O that dear, that great, that little, but important word, me. Happy they, who can adopt the Apostle's language! Happy they that can apply it to their own heart; and when they hear that Christ has brought in an everlasting righteousness, can say, Blessed be God, it is brought in by the blessed Spirit to my soul!

Are there any here that can go along with me on this doctrine? But why do I ask this question, when preaching to numbers, who, I hope, have tasted of the grace of God long ago? I do not know, I cannot distinguish you; you are just like other people, as to your looks and habits; but if I do not, and if your neighbors cannot know you, that great God, in whose presence you are, knows you; He, before whose tribunal we are shortly to appear, knows you. If Christ Jesus hath brought his everlasting righteousness into your heart; if it is applied by the Spirit of God to your soul, what shall I say to you? I will say as the Angel to John, "Come up hither," thou child of God! Come up hither, thou son, thou daughter of Abraham! Come and join with me, in calling upon angels and archangels, in calling upon the spirits of just men made perfect, to help thee to praise that loving Redeemer, that has brought in an everlasting righteousness. O was ever love like this! When Abraham was about to offer up his son, God said, "Now I know that thou lovest me, since thou hast not withheld thy son, thine only son from me." Now may each child of God say, "Now, O God, I know that thou hast loved me, since thou hast not withheld thy Son, thy dear Son, the Lord Jesus Christ, from dying for me." If thou hast got Christ brought into thy soul by faith, O look forward, look towards a happy eternity; O look towards those everlasting mansions, into which God will bring thee after death. My dear friends, I could say much from this text to comfort God's people: But

I must address myself to you, poor souls, who cannot say, that this righteousness has been brought home to your souls; but if it was never brought home before, may God, for the Lord Jesus Christ's sake, bring it home now! Are any of you depending upon a righteousness of your own? Do any of you here, think to save yourselves by your own doings? I say to you, as the Apostle said to one that offered money for a power to confer the gift of the Holy Ghost, your righteousness shall perish with you. Poor miserable creatures! What is there in your tears? What in your prayers? What in your performances, to appease the wrath of an angry God? Away from the trees of the garden; come, ye guilty wretches, come as poor, lost, undone, and wretched creatures, and accept of a better righteousness than your own. As I said before, so I tell you again, the righteousness of Jesus Christ is an everlasting righteousness: it is wrought out for the very chief of sinners. Ho, every one that thirsteth, let him come and drink of this water of life freely. Are any of you wounded by sin? Do any of you feel you have no righteousness of your own? Are any of you perishing for hunger? Are any of you afraid ye will perish forever? Come, dear souls, in all your rags; come, thou poor man; come, thou poor, distressed woman; you, who think God will never forgive you, and that your sins are too great to be forgiven; come, thou doubting creature, who art afraid thou wilt never get comfort; arise, take comfort, the Lord Jesus Christ, the Lord of life, the Lord of glory, calls for thee: through his righteousness there is hope for the chief of sinners, for the worst of creatures. What if thou hadst committed all the sins in the world? What if thou hadst committed the sins of a thousand, what if thou hadst committed the sins of a million of worlds? Christ's righteousness will cover, the blood of the Lord Jesus Christ will cleanse, thee from the guilt of them all. O let not one poor soul stand at a distance from the Savior. My dear friends, could my voice hold out, was my strength equal to my will, I would wrestle with you; I would strive with arguments, till you came and washed in this blood of the Lamb; till you came and accepted of this everlasting righteousness. O come, come! Now, since it is brought into the world by Christ, so in the name, in the strength, and by the assistance of the great God, I bring it now to the pulpit; I now offer this righteousness, this free, this imputed, this everlasting righteousness to all poor sinners that will accept of it. For God's sake accept it this night: you do not know but ye may die before tomorrow. How do he know, but while I am speaking, a fit of the apoplexy may seize, and death arrest you? O my dear friends, where can ye go? Where will ye appear? How will ye stand before an angry God, without the righteousness of the Lord Jesus Christ put upon your souls? Can ye stand in your own rags? Will ye dare to appear before a heart-searching God, without the apparel of your elder brother? If ye do, I know your doom: Christ will frown you into hell: "Depart, depart, ye cursed, into everlasting fire," shall be your portion. Think, I pray you, therefore, on these things; go home, go home, go home, pray over the text, and say, "Lord God, thou hast brought an everlasting righteousness into the world by the Lord Jesus Christ; by the blessed Spirit bring it into my heart!" then, die when ye will, ye are safe; if it be tomorrow, ye shall be immediately translated into the presence of the everlasting God: that will be sweet! Happy they who have got this robe on; happy they that can say, "My God hath loved me, and I shall be loved by him with an everlasting love!" That every one of you may be able to say so, may God grant, for the sake of Jesus Christ, the dear Redeemer; to whom be glory for ever. Amen.

16. The Observation of the Birth of Christ

Matthew 1:21—"And she shall bring forth a Son, and then shalt call his Name Jesus: For he shall save his People from their Sins."

The celebration of the birth of Christ hath been esteemed a duty by most who profess Christianity. When we consider the condescension and love of the Lord Jesus Christ, in submitting to be born of a virgin, a poor sinful creature; and especially as he knew how he was to be treated in this world; that he was to be despised, scoffed at, and at last to die a painful, shameful, and ignominious death; that he should be treated as though he was the off-scouring of all mankind; used, not like the son of man, and, therefore, not at all like the Son of God; the consideration of these things should make us to admire the love of the Lord Jesus Christ, who was so willing to offer himself as a ransom for the sins of the people, that when the fullness of time was come, Christ came, made of a woman, made under the law: he came according to the eternal counsel of the Father; he came, not in glory or in splendor, not like him who brought all salvation with him: no, he was born in a stable, and laid in a manger; oxen were his companions. O amazing condescension of the Lord Jesus Christ, to stoop to such low and poor things for our sake. What love is this, what great and wonderful love was here, that the Son of God should come into our world in so mean a condition, to deliver us from the sin and misery in which we were involved by our fall in our first parents! And as all that proceeded from the springs must be muddy, because the fountain was so, the Lord Jesus Christ came to take our natures upon him, to die a shameful, a painful, and an accursed death for our sakes; he died for our sins, and to bring us to God: he cleansed us by his blood from the guilt of sin, he satisfied for our imperfections; and now, my brethren, we have access unto him with boldness; he is a mediator between us and his offended Father.

Therefore, if we do but consider into what state, and at how great a distance from God we are fallen; how vile our natures were; what a depravity, and how incapable to restore that image of God to our souls, which we lost in our first parents: when I consider these things, my brethren, and that the Lord Jesus Christ came to restore us to that favor with God which we had lost, and that Christ not only came down with an intent to do it, but actually accomplished all that was in his heart towards us; that he raised and brought us into favor with God, that we might find kindness and mercy in his sight; surely this calls for some return of thanks on our part to our dear Redeemer, for this love and kindness to our souls. How just would it have been of him, to have left us in that deplorable state wherein we, by our guilt, had involved ourselves? For God could not, nor can receive any additional good by our salvation; but it was love, mere love; it was free love that brought the Lord Jesus Christ into our world about 1700 years ago. What, shall we not remember the birth of our Jesus? Shall we yearly celebrate the birth of our temporal king, and shall that of the King of kings be quite forgotten? Shall that only, which ought to be had chiefly in remembrance, be quite forgotten? God forbid! No, my dear brethren, let us celebrate and keep this festival of our church, with joy in our hearts: let the birth of a Redeemer, which redeemed us from sin, from wrath, from death, from hell, be always remembered; may this Savior's love never be forgotten! But may we sing forth all his love and glory as long as life shall last here, and through an endless eternity in the world above! May we chant forth the wonders of redeeming love, and the riches of free grace, amidst angels and archangels, cherubim and seraphim, without intermission, for ever and ever! And as, my brethren, the time for keeping this festival is approaching, let us consider our duty in the true observation thereof, of the right way for the glory of God, and the good of immortal souls, to celebrate the birth of our Lord Jesus Christ; an event which ought to be had in eternal remembrance.

It is my design to lay down rules for the true keeping of that time of Christmas, which is now approaching.

I. I shall show you when you may be said, not to observe this festival aright.

II. I shall show you, when your observation and celebrating of this festival is done according to the glory of God, and to the true manner of keeping of it.

III. Shall conclude with an exhortation to all of you, high and low, rich and poor, one with another, to have a regard to your behavior at all times, but more especially, my dear brethren, on this solemn occasion.

I. My brethren, I am to show when your celebration of this festival is not of the right kind.

And *First*, you do not celebrate this aright, when you spend most of your time in cards, dice, or gaming of any sort.

This is a season, for which there is no more allowance for wasting of your precious time in those unlawful entertainments, than any other. Persons are apt to flatter themselves that they are free and at liberty to spend whole evenings now at cards, at dice, or any diversion whatsoever, to pass away, as they call it, a tedious evening. They can do any thing now to pass away that, which is hastening as fast as thought: time is always upon the wing; it is no sooner present but it is past, and no sooner come but it is gone. And have we so much to do, and so little time to do it in, and yet complain of time lying heavy upon our hands? Have we not the devil and the beast to get our of our souls? Are not our natures to be changed, our corruptions to be subdued, our wills to be brought over to God, or hard hearts to be softened, all old things to be done away, and all things to become new in our souls? Is there not all this to be done? And yet we have too much time upon our hands! It is well, that instead of having too much time, it be not found that we have got too little, when we come to die: then we shall wish, my brethren, that we had made more account of our time, that we had improved it for the glory of God, and the welfare of our immortal souls.

Good God! How amazing is the consideration, that many can go to church in the morning, and take the Sacrament, and come home and spend the afternoon and evening in cards. Is this, my brethren, discerning the Lord's body? Is this taking the sacrament according to its institution? Is not this a pollution thereof, and making the blood of the covenant an unholy thing.

Therefore, those of you who have made this your practice in times past, let me beseech you, in the bowels of mercy, not to do so any more; for, indeed, it is earthly, it is sensual, it is devilish. Consider what is said of those who eat and drink at the Lord's table unworthily, that they eat and drink their own damnation: And can they, my brethren, be said to eat and drink any otherwise, who no sooner go from the table of the Lord, but run to the diversions of the devil? Indeed this is exceeding sinful, and displeasing unto the Lord; then forbear those diversions which are so evil in themselves: O be not found in those exercises, and in that pleasure, which you would not be found in when you come to die. Thus, my brethren, you see it is not a right celebration of the birth of the Lord Jesus, to spend it in cards, dice, or any other diversions, which proceed so directly from the devil, and are destructive to all true goodness.

Secondly, They cannot be said truly to celebrate this time, who spend their time in eating and drinking to excess.

This is a season when persons are apt to indulge themselves in all manner of luxury: iniquity now abounds apace; nothing is scarcely to be seen but things of the greatest extravagance imaginable; not only for the necessities of the body, but to pamper it in lust, to feed its vices, to make it go on in sin, to be a means for gratifying our carnal appetite; and this is a means to make us forget the Lord of glory. This makes us only fit to do such drudgery, as the devil shall set us about; this is only preparing to run wheresoever the devil sends: this, instead of denying ourselves, is indulging ourselves, this is not, nor cannot be called, a celebration of the birth of our Lord Jesus Christ, when we are making ourselves worst than the beasts that perish.

I am not speaking against eating and drinking of the good things of life, but against the eating and drinking of them to excess, because, thus they unqualify us for the service of God; and to our fellow-creatures they make us unsociable, and may occasion us to be guilty of saying and acting those things, which we should be ashamed to think of, if we had only ate or drank with moderation.

Therefore, my dear brethren, let me beseech you to set a watch over yourselves; be careful that you do not run into that company which may tempt you to evil, for would a man run himself into danger on purpose? Would a man enter himself into that company, where, before he goes, he knows he shall be exposed to great temptations; and therefore, if you have any reason to think that the company you are going into will be a temptation, I beseech you, by the mercies of God in Christ Jesus, that you would not run into it.

How can you say, "Lead us not into temptation," when you are resolved to lead yourselves into it, by running into the occasions of sins. You are commanded to keep from the appearance of evil; and do you do that, by running into the place and company where it is like to be committed? No, this is so far from avoiding, and shunning it, that it is a plain proof to the contrary; therefore, if you are for observing this time, this festival of our church, let it not be done by running to excess; for you plainly see, that those who are guilty thereof, cannot be said properly to celebrate it.

Thirdly, Nor can they, my brethren, be said to keep, or rightly observe the commemoration of the birth of our Redeemer, the Lord Jesus Christ, who neglect their worldly callings to follow pleasures and diversions.

Alas! many, instead of keeping this time as it ought to be, run into sin with greediness; instead of devoting their time to the Lord, it is only devoted to the devil and their own lusts. How many who thus mispend their time, at this season, lay by the work of their callings for a considerable time, with no other view, but to follow earthly, sensual, and devilish pleasures. If they should go to hear a sermon, or to a society, my brethren, the mouths of all the Pharisees at once are open against them, that they are not only a going to be ruined themselves, but are going to ruin their families too; they think it needless to make so much ado; this is being righteous over-much; but you may be as wicked as you please, and they will not cry out; however, when you are wicked over-much, by serving the devil and your own pleasures for a week or a month together, then, my brethren, with them you are only taking a little recreation, spending your time in innocent diversions; no one cries out against you, there is no outcry that you are going to be ruined. Again, if you give never so small a matter among the poor people of God for their relief, then you are robbing your families, then you are going to turn madmen! And in a few days will be to methodistically mad, that you are not fit for a polite gentleman's conversation; but if you spend one hundred times the money in playhouses, &c. on your lusts and pleasures, then you are liked and esteemed as a good friend and companion; but, my dear brethren, these good companions in the world's account, are never so in the Lord Jesus Christ's. You cannot serve God and mammon; you must either lost your lusts, your pleasures, and your delights, or you cannot expect to find favor with God; for indeed, and indeed, the ways that too many follow at this time, are sinful, yea, they are exceeding sinful. You see they cannot be said to celebrate this holy time, who thus mispend their precious time to the neglect of their families; such are destroying themselves with a witness.

Thus, my dear brethren, I have shown you who they are who do not observe this holy festival.

II. I come now, in the second place, to show you, who they are who do rightly observe, and truly celebrate the birth of our Redeemer.

And I shall show you who they are in two particulars, directly opposite to the others; and then, my brethren, take your choice: you must choose the one or the other, there is no medium, you must either serve the Lord or Baal; and, therefore, my dear brethren, let me beg of you to consider,

First, That those spend their time aright, and truly observe this festival, who spend their hours in reading, praying, and religious conversation.

What can we do to employ our time to a more noble purpose, than reading of what our dear Redeemer has done and suffered; to read, that the King of kings, and the Lord of lords, came from his throne and took upon him the form of the meanest of his servants; and what great things he underwent. This, this is an history worth reading, this is worth employing our time about: and surely, when we read of the sufferings of our Savior, it should excite us to prayer, that we might have an interest in the Lord Jesus Christ; that the blood which he spilt upon mount Calvary, and his death and crucifixion, might make an atonement for our sins, that we might be made holy; that we might be enabled to put off the old man with his deeds, and put on the new man, even the Lord Jesus Christ; that we may throw away the heavy yoke of sin, and put on the yoke of the Lord Jesus Christ. Indeed, my brethren, these things call for prayer, and for earnest prayer too; and O do be earnest with God, that you may have an interest in this Redeemer, and that you may put on his righteousness, so that you may not come before him in your filthy rags, nor be found not having on the wedding garment. O do not, I beseech you, trust unto yourselves for justification; you cannot, indeed, you cannot be justified by the works of the law. I entreat that your time may be thus spent; and if you are in company, let your time be spent in that conversation which profiteth: let it not be about your dressing, your plays, your profits, or your worldly concerns, but let it be the wonders of redeeming love: O tell, tell to each other, what great things the Lord has done for your souls; declare unto one another, how you were delivered from the hands of your common enemy, Satan, and how the Lord has brought your feet from the clay, and has set them upon the rock of ages, the Lord Jesus Christ; there, my brethren, is no slipping; other conversation, by often repeating, you become fully acquainted with, but of Christ there is always something new to raise your thoughts; you can never want matter when the love of the Lord Jesus Chris is the subject: then let Jesus be the subject, my brethren, of all your conversation.

Let your time be spent on him: O this, this is an employ, which if you belong to Jesus, will last you to all eternity. Let others enjoy their cards, their dice, and gaming hours; do you, my brethren, let your time be spent in reading, praying, and religious conversations. Which will stand the trial best at the last day? Which do you think will bring most comfort, most peace, in a dying hour? O live and spend your time now, as you will wish to have done, when you come to die.

Secondly, Let the good things of life, you enjoy, be used with moderation.

I am not, as the scoffers of this day tell you, against eating and drinking the good things of life; no, my brethren, I am only against their being used to an excess; therefore, let me beseech you to avoid those great indiscretions, those sinful actions, which will give the enemies of God room to blaspheme. Let me beseech you, to have a regard, a particular regard to your behavior, at this time; for indeed the eyes of all are upon you, and they would rejoice much to find any reason to complain of you. They can say things against us without a cause; and how would they rejoice if there was wherewith they might blame us? Then they would triumph and rejoice indeed; and all your little slips, my dear brethren, are, and would be charged upon me. O at this time, when the eyes of so many are upon you, be upon your guard; and if you use the good things of this life with moderation, you do then celebrate this festival in the manner which the institution calls for.

And instead of running into excess, let that money, which you might expend to pamper your own bodies, be given to feed the poor; now, my brethren, is the season, in which they commonly require relief; and sure you cannot act more agreeable, either to the season, to the time, or for the glory of God, than in relieving his poor distressed servants. Therefore, if any of you have poor friends, or acquaintance, who are in distress, I beseech you to assist them; and not only those of your acquaintance, but the poor in general. O my dear brethren, that will turn to a better account another day, than all you have expended to please the lust of the flesh, the lust of the eye, or the pride of life. Consider, Christ was always willing to relieve the distressed; it is his command also; and can you better commemorate the birth of your king, your Savior, the Lord Jesus Christ, than in obeying one of his commands?

Do not, my dear brethren, be forgetful of the poor of the world; consider, if providence has smiled upon you, and blessed you with abundance of the things of this life, God calls for some returns of gratitude from you; be ye mindful of the poor, and when you are so, then you may be said to have a true regard for that time which is now approaching; if you would truly observe this festival, let it be done with moderation, and a regard to the poor of this world.

Thirdly, Let me beg of you not to alienate too much of your time from the worldly business of this life, but have a proper regard thereunto, and then you may be said rightly to observe this festival.

God allows none to be idle: in all ages business was commended; and therefore do not think that any season will excuse us in our callings; we are not, my brethren, to labor for the things of this life inordinately, but we are to labor for them will all moderation: we are not to neglect our callings; no, we are to regard those places and stations of life, which God in his providence has thought convenient for us; and therefore, when you neglect your business of the hurt of your families, whatever pretense you thereby make for so doing, you are guilty of sin; you are not acting according to the doctrine of the gospel, but are breaking the commands of the Lord Jesus Christ, both according to his word, and to his own practice.

At this festival, persons are apt to take a little more liberty than usual; and if that time from our vocations is not prejudicial to ourselves or families, and is spent in the service of God, and the good of immortal souls, then I do not thing it sinful; but there is too much reason to fear, that the time spent upon our own lusts, and then it is exceeding sinful, it is against our own souls, and it is against the good of our families, and instead of commemorating the birth of our dear Redeemer, we are dishonoring him in the greatest degree possibly we can.

Therefore, inquire strictly into your end and design in spending your time; see, my brethren, whether it proceeds from a true love to your Redeemer, or whether there is not some worldly pleasure or advantage at the bottom: if there is, our end is not right; but if it proceed entirely from love to him that died, and gave himself for us, our actions will be a proof thereof; then our time will be spent, not in the polite pleasures of life, but according to the doctrine and commands of the blessed Jesus; then our conversation will be in heaven; and O that this might be found to be the end of each of you, who now hear me; then we should truly observe this festival, and have a true regard to the occasion thereof, that of Christ's coming to redeem the souls of those which were lost.

Let me now conclude, my dear brethren, with a few words of exhortation, beseeching you to think of the love of the Lord Jesus Christ. Did Jesus come into the world to save us from death, and shall we spend no part of our time in conversing about our dear Jesus; shall we pay no regard to the birth of him, who came to redeem us from the worst of slavery, from that of sin, and the devil; and shall this Jesus not only be born on our account, but likewise die in our stead, and yet shall we be unmindful of him? Shall we spend our time in those things which are offensive to him? Shall we not rather do all we can to promote his glory, and act according to his command? O my dear brethren, be found in the ways of God; let us not disturb our dear Redeemer by any irregular proceedings; and let me beseech you to strive to love, fear, honor and obey him, more than ever you have done yet; let not the devil engross your time, and that dear Savior who came into the world on your accounts, have so little. O be not so ungrateful to him who has been so kind to you! What could the Lord Jesus Christ have done for you more than he has? Then do not abuse his mercy, but let your time be spent in thinking and talking of the love of Jesus, who was incarnate for us, who was born of a woman, and made under the law, to redeem us from the wrath to come.

Now to God the Father, God the Son.

17. THE TEMPTATION OF CHRIST

Matthew 4:1–11—"Then was Jesus led up of the Spirit into the wilderness to be tempted of the devil. And when he had fasted forty days and forty nights, he was afterward an hungered. And when the tempter came to him, he said, If thou be the Son of God, command that these stones be made bread. But he answered and said, It is written, Man shall not live by bread alone, but by every word that proceedeth out of the mouth of God. Then the devil taketh him up into the holy city, and setteth him on a pinnacle of the temple, And saith unto him, If thou be the Son of God, cast thyself down: for it is written, He shall give his angels charge concerning thee: and in [their] hands they shall bear thee up, lest at any time thou dash thy foot against a stone. Jesus said unto him, It is written again, Thou shalt not tempt the Lord thy God. Again, the devil taketh him up into an exceeding high mountain, and sheweth him all the kingdoms of the world, and the glory of them; And saith unto him, All these things will I give thee, if thou wilt fall down and worship me. Then saith Jesus unto him, Get thee hence, Satan: for it is written, Thou shalt worship the Lord thy God, and him only shalt thou serve. Then the devil leaveth him, and, behold, angels came and ministered unto him."

Dearly beloved, today you are invited to take a walk into the wilderness, to behold, sympathize with, and get instruction and comfort from a Savior tempted. In the conflict, he approves himself to be God's beloved Son; and the Father gives demonstrable evidence, that with, and in him he is indeed well pleased. Let us with serious attention consider when, where, and how, our great Michael fought with and overcame the dragon. The Evangelist Matthew is very particular in relating the preparations for, the beginning, process, and issue of this glorious and important combat.

"Then was Jesus led up of the spirit into the wilderness, to be tempted of the devil." In the close of the foregoing chapter we are told, that the blessed Jesus had been publicly baptized, and was also solemnly inaugurated in his mediatorial office, by the opening of the heavens, by the Spirit of God descending on him like a dove, and by a voice from heaven, saying, "This is my beloved Son, in whom I am well pleased;" and then it was, when he came from the solemn ordinance of baptism; when he was about to show himself openly unto Israel; when he was full of the Holy Ghost Luke 4:1, even then was he led, with a holy unconstrained violence, as a champion into the field, to engage an enemy, whom he was sure to conquer. But whither is this conqueror led? Into a lonesome, wide, howling wilderness; probably, says Mr. Henry, into the great wilderness of Sinai; a wilderness, not only lonesome, but inhabited by wild beasts, Mark 1:13. Hither was our Lord led, not only that he might prepare himself by retirement and prayer, but also that he might be alone, and thereby give Satan all the advantages he could desire. In this combat, as well as that of his last agony, "of the people, there was to be none with him." Neither does he content himself with praying, but he fasts also, and that "forty days and forty nights," (verse Matthew 4:9,): as Moses and Elias had done, many years before, it may be, in the very same place. All these fasts were miraculous; and therefore, though we are taught hereby, that fasting is a Christian duty, yet, to pretend, in an ordinary way, to imitate them, by fasting for so long a term together, in no doubt superstitious, presumptuous, and sinful; but few people, I believe, need such a caution.

During these forty days, we may suppose, our Lord felt no hunger; converse with heaven, to him was instead of meat and drink; but "afterwards he was an hungered:" exceedingly so, no doubt. And now, the important fight begins. For, then "the tempted," emphatically so called, because he first tempted our first parents to sin, and hath ever since been unwearied in tempting their descendants; then the tempter, who in an invisible manner had been attacking our blessed Lord all the whole forty days, when he saw him hungering, and in such distressing circumstances, came to him, as it should seem, in a visible shape, and probably transformed into the appearance of an angel of light. And what does he tempt him to? To nothing less, than to doubt of his being the Son of God." "If thou be the Son of God." What! Put an if to this, Satan, after the glorious Jesus had been proved to be God's son, and repeatedly too in such a glorious manner? Surely, thou thyself couldst not but see the heavens opened, and the Spirit descending; surely, thou didst hear the voice that came to him from heaven, immediately after his baptism, saying, "This is my beloved Son:" And dost thou now say unto him, "If thou be the Son of God." Yes; but Satan knew, and believed he was full well; but he wanted to make our Lord to doubt of it. And why? Because he was in such a melancholy situation. As though he had said, "If God was thy father, he would never suffer thee to starve to death in a howling wilderness, among wild beasts. Surely, the voice thou lately didst hear, was only a delusion. If thou wast the Son of God, especially his beloved Son, in whom he was so pleased, thou wouldst be taken more care of by him." Thus he attacked our first parents, by suggesting to them hard thoughts of their all-bountiful Creator: "Yea, hath God said, Ye shall not eat of every tree in the garden?" "Hath he placed you amidst such a variety of delicious fruits, only to tease and make you miserable?" And how artfully now does he labor to insinuate himself into our Lord's affections, as he then did to ingratiate himself with our first parents. "If thou be the Son of God, says he, come, prove it, by commanding these stones (a heap of which, probably, lay very near) to be made bread: this will demonstrate thy divinity, and relieve thy pressing necessity at the same time." Thus, as in all his other temptations, Satan would fain appear to be his very kind friend; but the holy Jesus saw through the disguised enmity of his antagonist; and scorning either to distrust his righteous Father on the one hand, or to work a miracle to please and gratify the devil on the other, although he had the Spirit of God without measure, and might have made use of a thousand other ways, yet answers him with a text of scripture: "It is written, that man shall not live by bread alone, but by every word that proceedeth out of the mouth of God." This is a quotation from Deuteronomy 8:3, and contains a reason given by the great God, why he chose to feed the Israelites with manna; that they might learn thereby, man doth not live by bread alone, but by every word that proceedeth out of the mouth of God. This our blessed Lord here applies to himself; and his being in the wilderness, made the application of it still more pertinent. Israel was God's son: out of Egypt was he called to sojourn in the wilderness, where he was miraculously supported. And therefore our Lord, knowing that he was typified by this Israel, and that, like them, he was now in a wilderness, quotes this scripture as a reason why he should not, at Satan's suggestion, either despair of receiving help from his Father in his present circumstances, or distrust the validity of his late manifestations, or make use of any unwarrantable means for his present relief. For as God was his father, he would, therefore, either in an ordinary way spread a table for him in the wilderness, or support and sustain him, as he did his Israel of old, in some extraordinary way or other without it: "For man shall not live by bread alone, but by every word that proceedeth out of the mouth of God."

Thus is the tempter foiled in the first onset; but he hath other arrows in his quiver, with which he will farther strive to wound the immaculate Lamb of God. Since he cannot draw him in either to distrust, or despair, he will not try if he cannot prevail on him to presume. In order to effect this, "He taketh the blessed Jesus up into the Holy City," or Jerusalem, called by our Savior, the city of the Great King, and here called holy, because the holy temple was in it, and, we would hope, many holy people. This was a populous place, and therefore, would greatly befriend the devil's design. And not only so, but "he setteth him on a pinnacle," a battlement or wing, "of the temple," the top of which was so very high, that, as Josephus observes, it would make a man's head run giddy to look down from it. And some think this was done at the time of public worship. How the holy Jesus suffered himself to be taken hither; whether he was transported through the air, or whether he followed Satan on foot, is uncertain; but certainly it was an instance of amazing condescension in our Lord, that he would permit so foul a fiend, to carry or lead his holy body about in this manner. Well! Satan hath now gotten him upon the pinnacle of the temple, and still harping upon this old string, "If thou be the Son of God, (says he) cast thyself down," and thereby show to this large worshipping assembly, (who will assuredly then believe) that thou art God's beloved Son, under the special protection of heaven, and art the Messiah, "who was to come into the world." This was artful, very artful. But he seems to improve in cunning: for he brings his Bible with him, and backs his temptation with a text of scripture; "For it is written, (says he) he shall give his angels charge concerning thee, and in their hands they shall bear thee up, lest at any time thou dash thy foot against a stone." But is Saul also among the prophets? Does the devil quote scripture, yea, and seemingly such a very apposite [appropriate] one too? I suspect some design, without doubt: for herein, he would mimic our Lord, who, he perceived, intended to fight him with this weapon; and not liking the sharp edge of it, he thought that if he quoted scripture, the Lord Jesus would not employ it against him any more. "It is written, (therefore said he) he shall give his angels charge concerning thee, and in their hands they shall bear thee up, lest at any time thou dash thy foot against a stone: and therefore, since thou art sure of such protection, thou needst not fear to cast thyself down." This was plausible, and by the length of it, one would be apt to imagine, it was a fair quotation; but Satan takes care, not only to misapply, but also to maim it, purposely omitting these important words, "in all thy ways." It is true, God had given charge to his angels, concerning his children in general, and his beloved Son in particular, that they should keep him in all his ways; but, if our Lord had at this time, at the devil's request, and to gratify pride, thrown himself down from the pinnacle, and thereby unnecessarily presumed on his Father's protection, he would not have been in God's way, and therefore, would have had no right to the promised protection at all. Satan was aware of this, and therefore fitly left out what he knew would not suit his purpose. But is scripture the worse, for being abused or perverted by the devil, or his emissaries? No, in no wise. Our Lord, therefore, lets him know, that he should not throw aside this important weapon upon this account, but puts by this home thrust, with another scripture: "It is written again, Thou shalt not tempt the Lord thy God." Still our Lord quotes something out of the book of Deuteronomy, and hath his eye upon Israel in his wilderness state. Originally these words were directed to the Israelites in general, and accordingly are in the plural number; but here our Lord, as before, makes a particular application of them to himself: Satan bids him cast himself down, assuring him, God had promised in his word, to order his angels to take care of him. Now, says our Lord, "It is written in another part of his word, that the Israelites should not tempt the Lord their God, by distrusting his goodness on the one hand, or presuming on his protection on the other. And, therefore, as I would not command the stones to be made bread, needlessly and distrustfully set up to provide for myself; neither will I now presume unnecessarily upon God's power, by casting myself down, though placed by thee in such a dangerous situation.

Thus our great Michael comes off conqueror in the second assault. And doth not the serpent feel his head bruised enough yet? Not at all: on the contrary, being more and more enraged at such unusual opposition, and want of success, "He again taketh him up into an exceeding high mountain, (what mountain is not very material) and showeth him all the kingdoms of the world, and the glory of them," St. Luke adds, "in a moment of time:" which confirms the common conjecture, that Satan did not show our Lord really the kingdoms of the world, (for that must have taken up more time) but only took him up into an exceeding high mountain to humor the thing, and by exerting his utmost art, impressed on our Lord's imagination all at once, a very strong, and to any but innocence itself, a very striking prospect of the kingdoms of the world, and the glory of them; not the cares: that would not serve Satan's turn. He showed our Savior crowns, but never told him those crowns were gilded [inlaid] with thorns; "He showed him, (says Mr. Henry, my favorite commentator) as in a landscape, or airy representation in a cloud, such as that great deceiver could easily frame and put together, the glorious and splendid appearance of princes, their robes and retinue, their equipage and lifeguards; the pomps of thrones and courts, and stately palaces; the sumptuous buildings in cities; the gardens and fields about the country feats, with the various instances of their wealth, pleasure, and gaiety; so as might be most likely to strike the fancy, and excite the admiration and affection. Such was this show." Our Savior very well knew it, only lets Satan go to the full length of his string, that his victory over him might be the more illustrious. And now, says the devil, "All these things (a mighty all indeed; a mere imaginary bubble!) will I give thee, if thou wilt fall down and worship me. He would fain have it taken for granted, that he had succeeded in the two preceding temptations: "Come, thou seest thou art not the Son of God, or if thou art, thou seest what an unkind Father he is; thou art here in a starving condition, therefore take my advice, disown thy relation to him, set up for thyself, call me father, ask of me blessings, and all these will I give thee; while all that I desire in return, is but a bow, only fall down and worship me." Here Satan discovers himself with a witness: this was a desperate parting stroke, indeed. It is not high time for thee, O thou enemy of souls, to be commanded to depart! Filled with a holy resentment at such hellish treatment, and impatient of the very thought of settling up for himself, or alienating the least part of his heart and affections from his Father, or dividing them between his God and the world; "Then said Jesus unto him, Get thee hence, Satan, (I know thee who thou art, under all thy disguises) get thee hence, thou grand adversary; for it is written, Thou shalt worship the Lord thy God, and him only shalt thou serve; this is the great commandment of the law; this is the commandment my Father gave unto his Israel of old, and wouldst thou have me, who came to fulfill the law and the prophets, thus shamefully be a transgressor of it? Get thee hence, I will bear thy insolence no longer: thy other temptations were hellish, like thyself, but this intolerably so; get thee therefore hence, Satan: my heavenly Father is the Lord my God, and him only will I serve."

And now the battle is over; the important combat is ended; Jesus hath won the field: Satan is routed and totally put to flight. "Then," when the devil found that Jesus could withstand even the golden bait, the lust of the eye and pride of life, in the two last, as well as the lust of the flesh in the first temptation, despairing of the least success, and quite stunned with that all-powerful *get thee hence, Satan*, "he leaveth him."

Hell, we may well suppose, like the Philistines of old, was confounded, and gave a horrible groan, when they saw their great Goliath, in whom they had so long trusted, thus shamefully and totally defeated in no less than three pitched battles. The first Adam was attacked but once, and was conquered; but the second Adam, though thus repeatedly assaulted, comes off without the least sin, not only conqueror, but more than conqueror. Think you not, that there was joy, joy unspeakable in heaven, upon this glorious occasion? Think you not that the angels, those sons of God, and the multitude of the heavenly host, who shouted so loud at our Lord's birth, did not repeat, if possible, with yet greater ecstasy, that heavenly anthem, "Glory be to God in the highest." For a while they were only spectators, orders, we may suppose, being issued out, that they should only wait around, but not relieve their praying, fasting, tempted Lord; but now the restraint is removed: Satan departs, and "behold, angels came and ministered unto him;" they came to administer to his bodily necessities, and to congratulate him upon the glorious and complete victory which he had gained: some of them, it may be, had done this kind office for Elijah long ago; and with unspeakably greater joy, they repeat it to the Lord of Elijah now. His Father sends him bread from heaven; and by this lets him know, that notwithstanding the horrid temptations with which he had been attacked, he is his own beloved son, in and with whom he was well pleased.

And was there joy in heaven on this happy occasion?

What equal, and if possible, what infinitely greater joy ought there to be among the children of God here on earth? For we should do well to remember, that our blessed Lord in this great fight with, and conquest over the dragon, acted as a public person, as a federal head of his mystical body the church, even the common representative of all believers. We may therefore from this blessed passage gather strong consolations; since by our Lord's conquest over Satan, we are thereby assured of our own, and in the mean while can apply to him as a compassionate High Priest, who was in all things tempted as we are, that he might experimentally be enabled to succor us when we are tempted.

Who, who after hearing of or reading this, can think themselves hardly used, or utterly cast off by God, because they are tempted to self-murder, blasphemy, or any other horrid and shocking crimes? Who can wonder at wave being permitted to come upon wave, and one trial to follow upon the back of another? Who can admire, that Satan follows them to holy ordinances, and tempts them to doubt of the reality of all their manifestations, and of their being God's children, even after they have enjoyed the most intimate and delightful communion with their heavenly Father? Was not our Lord treated thus? And "shall the servant be above his Lord, or the disciple above his Master?" No, it is sufficient that the servant be as his Lord, and the disciple as his Master.

But not to dwell on a general improvement, let us see what particular lessons may be learned from this affecting portion of holy writ.

And *First*, was our Lord thus violently beset in the wilderness? Then we may learn, that however profitable solitude and retirement may be, when used in due season, yet when carried to an extreme is hurtful, and rather befriends than prevents temptation. Woe be to him that is thus always alone; for he hath not another to lift him up when he falleth, or to advise with when he is tempted. As a hermit in America once told me, when I asked him whether he found that way of life lessened his temptations: "Dost not thou know, friend, (said he) that a tree which grows by itself, is more exposed to winds and storms than another that stands surrounded with other trees in the woods?" Our Lord knew this, and therefore he was *led by the Spirit* into the wilderness to be tempted of the devil. Lord, keep us from leading ourselves into this temptation, and succor and support us whenever led by thy providence into it! Then, and then only, shall we be safe amidst the fiery darts of the grand enemy of our souls.

Secondly, Did our Lord by prayer, fasting, and temptation, prepare himself for his public ministry? Surely then, all those who profess to be inwardly moved by the Holy Ghost to take upon them the office and administration of the church, should be prepared in the same manner. For though the knowledge of books and men, are good in their places, yet without a knowledge of Satan's devices be superadded, a minister will be only like a physician, that undertakes to prescribe to sick people, without having studied the nature of herbs. And hence, it is to be feared, many heavy laden and afflicted souls have been sent by certain ministers, to surgeons, to be blooded in the arm, instead of being directed to apply to the blood of Christ to cleanse their hearts. Hence, conviction is looked upon as a delirium, and violent temptations censured as downright madness. Hence, souls that are truly and earnestly repenting of their sins, and as earnestly seeking after rest in Christ, have been directed to plays, novels, romances, and merry company, to divert them from being righteous over-much. Miserable comforters are such blind guides! Surely, they deserve not better titles than that of murderers of souls! They go not into the kingdom of heaven themselves, and those who are entering in they would by this means hinder. Go not after them, all ye young men who would be able ministers of the New Testament; but on the contrary, if you would be useful in binding up the broken hearted, and pouring the oil of consolation into wounded souls, prepare yourselves for manifold temptations. For as Luther says, "prayer and meditation, reading and temptation, make a minister." If now exercised with spiritual conflicts, be not disheartened, it is a good sign that our Lord intends to make use of you. Being thus tempted like unto your brethren, you will be the better enabled to succor and advise those who shall apply to you under their temptations. What says the apostle Paul? "If we are afflicted, it is for your sake." And if you are afflicted, it is only that you may save your own souls, and help to save the souls of those who shall be committed to your charge. Be strong therefore in the grace which is in Christ Jesus, and learn to endure hardness, like good soldiers, that are hereafter to instruct others how they must fight the good fight of faith.

Thirdly, Did the tempter come to Christ when he saw him an hungered? Let those of you that are reduced to a low estate, from hence learn, that an hour of poverty is an hour of temptation, not only to murmuring and doubting of our sonship and the divine favor, but also to help ourselves by unlawful means. "If thou be the Son of God, said Satan, command that these stones may be made bread." This is what Agur dreaded, "lest I be poor and steal." Learn, ye godly poor, to be upon your guard, and remember that poverty and temptations are no marks of your being cast off by God. Your Lord was an hungered; your Lord was tempted on this account to doubt his sonship, before you. Learn of him not to distrust, but rather to trust in your heavenly Father. Angels came and ministered unto Christ; and he who is Lord of the angels, will send some kind messenger or another to relieve your wants. Your extremity shall be the Redeemer's opportunity to help you. Make your wants known unto him, he careth for you. Though in a desart [desert?], though no visible means appear at present, yet you shall in God's due time find a table spread for you and yours; "For man doth not live by bread alone, but by every word that proceedeth out of the mouth of God."

And may not such among you, who are exalted, as well as those who are brought low, from Satan's taking the Lord Jesus, and placing him upon a pinnacle of the temple, learn also a lesson of holy watchfulness and caution. High places are slippery places, and are apt to make even the strongest heads and most devout hearts to turn giddy. How necessary therefore is that excellent petition in our Litany, "in all time of our wealth, (as well as in all time of our tribulation) good Lord deliver us!" Agreeably to this, Agur prays as much against riches as poverty; if he was poor, he feared he should be tempted to steal, if rich, that he should trust in uncertain riches; and say, who is the Lord?

I charge, therefore, all of you, who are rich and high in this world, to watch and pray, lest ye fall by Satan's temptation. Those especially of you, that are placed as on the pinnacle of the temple, exalted above your fellows in the church of God, take heed in an especial manner unto yourselves, lest by spiritual pride, vanity, or any other sin that doth most easily beset persons in such eminent stations, ye cast yourselves down. This is what Satan aims at. He strives to make us destroyers of ourselves. And he hath a particular enmity against such as you; he knows, that your name is Legion; and that if you cast yourselves down, he shall gain a great advantage over many others; you cannot fall alone. O that it may be said of us, as the papists use to say of Luther, "That German beast doth not love gold." May the fire of divine love burn up all the love of this present evil world, and pride of life, out of your hearts! This, Satan reserved for his last, as thinking it was the most powerful and prevailing temptation, "He took our Lord up into an exceeding high mountain, and showed him all the kingdoms of the world and the glory of them." He cares not how high he exalts us, or how high he is obliged to bid, so he can but get our hearts divided between God and the world. All this will he offer to give us, if we will only fall down and worship him. Arm us, dear Lord Jesus, with thy Spirit, and help us under all such circumstances, to learn of thee, and say unto the tempter, "Get thee hence, Satan; for it is written, thou shalt worship the Lord thy God, and him only shalt thou serve."

Fourthly, Whether beset with this or any other temptation, let all us learn of our Lord to fight the devil with the sword of the Spirit, which is the word of God. Though he had the Spirit without measure, yet he always made use of this. We pray say of it, as David did of Goliath's sword, "none like this," none like this. And supposing Satan should be permitted to transform himself into an angel of light, and by false impressions, and delusive applications of misquoted texts, attempt to turn this weapon upon us against ourselves; let us not therefore be prevailed on to let go, but by comparing spiritual things with spiritual, as our Lord did, find out God's mind and our duty. Had Christ's children and ministers only observed this one lesson, how much strange fire would quickly have been extinguished? How much real enthusiasm been easily stopped? How may imaginary revelations have been detected? How many triumphs of Satan and his emissaries been prevented? And how much more would the comforts of Christ's people and ministers been continued and increased, not only in this present, but also in every age of the Christian church? But let us not be discouraged or think worse of Christ, his cause, or his word, because through Satan's subtlety, any of us, or others, may have been drawn in to make some wrong applications of it; others have been thus tempted and mistaken before us. However, let us be humbled before God and man, and be excited by our past ignorance of Satan's devices, to adhere more closely to the written word, and to pray more earnestly for God's holy Spirit to give us direction by it. "Then will it still be a lantern unto our feet, and a light unto our path;" we shall yet be enabled to behave more skillfully under all our future trials. Many we must yet expect; nay, perhaps our severest temptations are yet to come; Satan left our Lord, after his attacking him in the wilderness, "only for a season," as St. Luke has it, until the season of his death and passion. And thus he may be permitted to deal with us. We are not yet come to our complete rest; the King of terrors is yet to be grappled with, and the valley of the shadow of death to be passed through; long before that, we may be called to endure many a fiery trial, and be beset with manifold temptations, under which we may be as ignorant how to behave, as under those with which we have already been visited. Alas! we know not what remaining corruptions are in our hearts, which time and temptation may draw out and discover. Perhaps Satan hath not yet attacked us on our weakest side; when he does, if left to ourselves, how weak shall we be? It is said of Achilles, that he was invulnerable, except in the heel, and by a wound in that, at last he died. Let not him, therefore, that putteth on the harness, boast as though he had put it off." Neither, on the other hand, let us be faint-hearted or dismayed. Satan may tempt, but cannot force; he may sift, but Christ will pray. He who hath helped us already, will help us to the end. He who conquered for us in the wilderness, will ere long make us also more than conquerors over all trials and temptations, inward and outward, and over death and hell itself, through his almighty, everlasting and never-failing love. We now sow in tears; in a very little time, and we shall reap with joy; we may now go on our way weeping, by reason of the enemy oppressing us; but, ere long, angels shall be sent, not to minister to us in this wilderness, but to carry us to an heavenly Canaan, even to Abraham's bosom. Then shall we see this accuser and tempter of our Lord, of our brethren, and of ourselves, cast out: this wicked one, as well as the wicked world, and wicked heart, will no more be permitted to vex, disturb or annoy us.

"But woe unto you that laugh now; for you shall then lament and weep." Woe unto you, who either believer there is no devil, or never felt any of his temptations. Woe unto you that are at ease in Zion, and instead of staying to be tempted by the devil, by idleness, self-indulgence, and making continual provision for the flesh, even tempt the devil to tempt you. Woe unto you, who not content with sinning yourselves, turn factors for hell, and make a trade of tempting others to sin. Woe unto you, who either deny divine revelation, or never make use of it but to serve a bad turn. Woe unto you who sell your consciences, and pawn your souls for a little worldly wealth or honor. Woe unto you who climb up to high places, when in church or state, by corruption, bribery, extortion, cringing, flattery, or bowing down to, and soothing the vices of those by whom you expect to rise. Woe unto you! For whether you will own the relation or not, surely you are of your father the devil; for the works of your father you will do; I tremble for you. How can you escape the damnation of hell?

But I have not time to follow such as you any farther. This discourse, and the present frame of my mind, lead me rather to speak to those, who by feeling Satan's fiery darts, know assuredly that there is a devil. Comfort thou, comfort thou, these afflicted ones, O Lord. O thou all-merciful and all-bountiful God, and thou compassionate High-Priest, thou once tempted, but now triumphant Savior, as thou once didst not disdain to be ministered unto by angels, bless we pray thou this discourse, to the support and strengthening of thy tempted people, though delivered by the meanest messenger thou didst ever yet employ in thy church!

I add no more. The Lord bless you and keep you! The Lord lift up the light of his countenance, stablish, strengthen, and settle you, and bring you to his eternal kingdom!

18. The Heinous Sin of Profane Cursing and Swearing

Matthew 5:34—"But I say unto you, Swear not at all."

Among the many heinous sins for which this nation is grown infamous, perhaps there is no one more crying, but withal more common, than the abominable custom of profane swearing and cursing. Our streets abound with persons of all degrees and qualities, who are continually provoking the holy one of Israel to anger, by their detestable oaths and blasphemies: and our very children, "out of whose mouths," the psalmist observes in his days, "was perfected praise," are now grown remarkable for the quite opposite ill quality of cursing and swearing. This cannot but be a melancholy prospect, for every sincere and honest minister of Jesus Christ, to view his fellow-creatures in; and such as will put him on contriving some means to prevent the spreading at least of so growing an evil; knowing that the Lord (without repentance) will assuredly visit for these things. But alas! what can he do? Public animadversions are so neglected amongst us, that we seldom find a common swearer punished as the laws direct. And as for private admonition, men are now so hardened through the deceitfulness of sin, that to give them sober and pious advice, and to show them the evil of their doings, is but like "casting pearls before swine; they only turn again and rend you." Since matters then are come to this pass, all that we can do is, that as we are appointed watchmen and ambassadors of the Lord, it our duty from time to time to show the people their transgression, and warn them of their sin; so that whether they will hear, or whether they will forbear, we however may deliver our own souls. That I therefore may discharge my duty in this particular, give me leave, in the name of God, humbly to offer to your most serious consideration, some few observations on the words of the text, in order to show the heinousness of profane cursing and swearing.

But, before I proceed directly to the prosecution of this point, it will be proper to clear this precept of our Lord from a misrepresentation that has been put on it by some, who infer from hence, that our Savior prohibits swearing before a magistrate, when required on a solemn and proper occasion. But that all swearing is not absolutely unlawful for a Christian, is evident from the writings of St. Paul, whom we often find upon some solemn occasions using several forms of imprecation, as, "I call God as witness;" "God is my judge;" "By your rejoicing in Christ Jesus," and suchlike. And that our savior does by no means forbid swearing before a magistrate, in the words now before us, is plain, if we consider the sense and design he had in view, when he gave his disciples this command. Permit me to observe to you then, that our blessed master had set himself, from the 27th verse of the chapter, out of which the text is taken, to vindicate and clear the moral law from the corrupt glosses and misconstruction of the Pharisees, who then sat in Moses's chair, but were notoriously faulty in adhering too closely to the literal expression of the law, without ever considering the due extent and spiritual meaning of it. Accordingly they imagined, that because God had said, "Thou shalt not commit adultery," that therefore, supposing a person was not guilty of the very act of adultery, he was not chargeable with the breach of the seventh commandment. And likewise in the matter of swearing, because God had forbidden his people, in the books of Exodus and Deuteronomy, "to take his name in vain," or to swear falsely by his name; they therefore judged it lawful to swear by any creature in common discourse, supposing they did not directly mention the name of God. Our blessed Savior therefore, in the words now before us, rectifies this their mistake about swearing, as he had done in the verses immediately forgoing, concerning adultery, and tells the people, that whatever allowances the Pharisees might give to swear by any creature, yet he pronounced it absolutely unlawful for any of his followers to do so. "You have heard, that it has been said by them of old time," (namely, by the Pharisees and teachers of the Jewish law) "Thou shalt not forswear thyself, but perform unto the Lord thine oaths; but I say unto you," (I who am appointed by the Father to be the great prophet and true law-giver of his church) "Swear not at all, (in your common conversation) neither by heaven for it is God's throne; (and therefore to swear by that, is to swear by Him that sits thereon) neither by the earth, for it is his foot-stool; nor by Jerusalem, for it is the city of the great King; neither shalt thou swear by thy head, because thou canst not make one hair white or black: but let your communications (which plainly shows that Christ is here speaking of swearing, not before a magistrate, but in common conversation) let your communication be yea, yea; nay, nay, (a strong affirmation or negation at the most); for whatsoever is more than this, cometh of evil;" that is, cometh from an evil principle, from the evil one, the devil, the author of all evil.

Which by the way, methinks, should be a caution to all such persons, who, though not guilty of swearing in the gross sense of the word, yet attest the truth of what they are speaking of, though ever so trifling, by saying, Upon my life,—as I live,—by my faith,—by the heavens, and such like: which expressions, however harmless and innocent they may be esteemed by some sorts of people, yet are the very oaths which our blessed Lord condemns in the words immediately following the text; and persons who use such unwarrantable forms of speaking, must expect to be convicted and condemned as swearers, at our Savior's second coming to judge the world.

But to return: It appears then from the whole tenor of our Savior's discourse, that in the words of the text he does by no means disannul or forbid swearing before a magistrate (which, as might easily be shown, is both lawful and necessary) but only profane swearing in common conversation; the heinousness and sinfulness of which I come now, more immediately to lay before you.

And here, not to mention that it is a direct breach of our blessed master's and great law-giver's command in the words of the text, as likewise of the third commandment, wherein God positively declares, "he will not hold him guiltless (that is, will assuredly punish him) that taketh his name in vain:" not to mention that it is the greatest abuse of that noble faculty of speech, whereby we are distinguished from the brute creation; or the great hazard the common swearer runs, of being perjured some time or other: not to mention those reasons against it, which of themselves would abundantly prove the folly and sinfulness of swearing: I shall at this time content myself with instancing four particulars, which highly aggravate the crime of profane swearing, and those are such as follow:

I. *First*, Because there is no temptation in nature to this sin, nor does the commission of it afford the offender the least pleasure or satisfaction.

II. *Secondly*, Because it is a sin which may be so often repeated.

III. *Thirdly*, Because it hardens infidels against the Christian religion, and must give great offense, and occasion much sorrow and concern to every true disciple of Jesus Christ.

IV. *Fourthly*, Because it is an extremity of sin, which can only be matched in hell.

I. The first reason then, why swearing in common conversation is so heinous in God's sight, and why we should not swear at all, is, because it has no temptation in nature, nor does the commission of it, unless a man be a devil incarnate, afford the offender the least pleasure or satisfaction.

Now here, I presume, we may lay it down as a maxim universally agreed on, that the guilt of any crime is increased or lessened in proportion to the weakness or strength of the temptation, by which a person is carried to the commission of it. It was this consideration that extenuated and diminished the guilt of Saul's taking upon him to offer sacrifice before the Prophet Samuel came; and of Uzza's touching the ark, because it was in danger of falling: as, on the contrary, what so highly aggravated the disobedience of our first parents, and of Lot's wife, was, because the former had so little reason to eat the forbidden fruit, and the latter so small a temptation to look back on Sodom.

And now if this be granted, surely the common swearer must of all sinners be the most without excuse, since there is no manner of temptation in nature to commission of his crime. In most of the other commands, persons, perhaps, may plead the force of natural inclination in excuse for the breach of them: one, for instance, may alledge his string propensity to anger, to excuse his breaking of the sixth; another, his proneness to lust, for his violation of the seventh. But surely the common swearer has nothing of this kind to urge in his behalf; for though he may have a natural inclination to this or that crime, yet no man, it is to be presumed, can say, he is born with a swearing constitution.

But further, As there is no temptation to it, so there is no pleasure or profit to be reaped from the commission of it. Ask the drunkard why he rises up early to follow strong drink, and he will tell you, because it affords his sensual appetite some kind of pleasure and gratification, though it be no higher than that of a brute. Inquire of the covetous worldling, why he defrauds and over-reaches his neighbor, and he has an answer ready; to enrich himself, and lay up goods for many years. But it must certainly puzzle the profane swearer himself, to inform you what pleasure he reaps from swearing: for alas! it is a fruitless tasteless thing that he sells his soul for. But indeed he does not sell it at all: in this case he prodigally gives it away (without repentance) to the devil; and parts with a blessed eternity, and runs into everlasting torment, merely for nothing.

II. But *Secondly*, what increases the heinousness of profane swearing, is, that it is a sin which may so often be repeated.

This is another consideration which always serves to lessen or increase the guilt and malignity of any sin. It was some excuse for the drunkenness of Noah, and the adultery of David, that they committed these crimes but once; as, on the contrary, of the patriarch Abraham's distrust of God, that he repeated the dissembling [deception] of Sarah to be his wife, two several times. And if this be admitted as an aggravation of other profane crimes, surely much more so of the guilt of common swearing, because it is a sin which may be, and is for the generality often repeated. In many other gross sins it cannot be so: if a man be overcome in drink, there must be a considerable time ere he can recover his debauch, and return to his cups again: or if he be accustomed to profane the sabbath, he cannot do it every day, but only one in seven. But alas! the profane swearer is ready for another oath, almost before the sound of the first is out of our ears; yea, some double and treble them in one sentence, even so as to confound the sense of what they say, by an horrid din of blasphemy! Now if the great and terrible Jehovah has expressly declared that he will not hold him guiltless, that is, will assuredly punish him, that taketh his name but once in vain; what a vast heap of these heinous sins lies at every common swearer's door? It would be apt to sink him into an intolerable despair, did he but see the whole sum of them. And O what a seared conscience must that wretch have, that does not feel this prodigious weight!

III. But *Thirdly*, what makes the sin of profane swearing appear yet more exceeding sinful, is, that it hardens infidels against the Christian religion.

It is the Apostle Peter's advice to the married persons of his time, that they should walk as became the gospel of Christ, that those who were without, might be won to embrace the Christian religion, by seeing and observing their pious conversation coupled together with fear. And what the Apostle presses on married persons, we find elsewhere enjoined on each particular member of the church. Accordingly we are commanded by our blessed Lord, to "let our light to shine before men, that they may see our good works, and glorify our Father which is in heaven;" And the Apostle Paul bids us "walk circumspectly towards them that are without, redeeming the time;" that is, embracing all opportunities to do them good, "because the days are evil." But alas! in what a direct contradiction does the profane swearer live to this and such-like precepts, who, instead of gaining proselytes to Christ from the unbelieving part of the world, does all he can to oppose it! For how can it be expected, that infidels should honor God, when Christians themselves despise him; or that any should embrace our religion, when professors of it themselves make so light of one of its strictest commands? No; to our grief and shame be it spoken, it is by reason of such impieties as these, that our holy religion (the best and purest in itself) is become a by-word among the heathen; that the sacred authority of the holy Jesus and his doctrine is despised; and "God's name (as it is written) blasphemed among the Gentiles."

These cannot but be sad stumbling-blocks and offenses in the way of our brethren's conversion; "But woe be to those men by whom such offenses come." We may say of them, as our blessed Lord did of Judas, "It had been better for such men, that they had never been born;" or, as he threatens in another place, "It shall be more tolerable for Sodom and Gomorrah in the day of judgment, than for such sinners."

But this is not all; As profane swearing must undoubtedly harden those in their infidelity, that are without, so must it no less grieve and give great offense to those hones and sincere persons that are within the church. We hear of David's complaining and crying out, "Woe is me, that I am constrained to dwell with Mesech, and to have my habitation amongst the tents of Kedar;" that is, that he was obliged to live and converse with a people exceedingly wicked and profane. And St. Peter tells us, that "Lot's righteous soul was grieved day by day, whilst he saw and observed the ungodly conversation of the wicked." And no doubt it was one great part of our blessed Master's sufferings whilst on earth, that he was compelled to converse with a wicked and perverse generation, and to hear his heavenly Father's sacred name profaned and scoffed at by unrighteous and wicked men. And surely it cannot but pierce the heart of every true and sincere Christian, of every one that does in any measure partake of the spirit of his master, to hear the multitude of oaths and curses which proceed daily and hourly out of the mouths of many people, and those too, whose liberal education, and seeming regard for the welfare of religion, one would think, should teach them a more becoming behavior. To hear the great and terrible name of God polluted by men, which is adored by angels; and to consider how often that sacred name is profaned in common discourse, which we are not worthy to mention in our prayers; this, I say, cannot but make each of them cry out with holy David, "Woe is me, that I am constrained to dwell with Mesech, and to have my habitation amongst the tents of Kedar." And though the blasphemous and profane discourses of others, will not be imputed to sincere persons for sin, so long as they "have no fellowship with such hellish fruits of darkness, but rather reprove them;" yet it will greatly enhance the present guilt, and sadly increase the future punishment of every profane swearer, by whom such offenses come. For if, as our Savior tells us, "it had been better for a man to have a mill-stone tied around his neck, than that he should offend one of his little once, (that is, the weakest of his disciples) how much sorer punishment will they be thought worthy of," who not only cause God's name to be blasphemed among the Gentiles, and the religion of our dear Redeemer to be abhorred; but who make his saints to weep and mourn, and vex their righteous souls from day to day, by their ungodly, profane, and blasphemous conversation? Surely, as God will put the tears of the one into his bottle, so it will be just in him to punish the other with eternal sorrow, for all their ungodly and hard speeches, and cast them into a lake of fire and brimstone, where they shall be glad of a drop of water to cool those tongues, with which they have so often blasphemed the Lord of Hosts, and grieved the people of our God.

IV. But it is time for me to proceed to give my *Fourth* and last reason, why common swearing is so exceeding sinful; and that is, Because it is such an extremity of sin, that can only be matched in hell, where all are desperate, and without hope of mercy.

The damned devils, and damned souls of men in hell, may be supposed to rave and blaspheme in their torments, because they know that the chains wherein they are held, can never be knocked off; but for men that swim in the river of God's goodness, whose mercies are renewed to them every morning, and who are visited with fresh tokens of his infinite unmerited loving-kindness every moment; for these favorite creatures to set their mouths against heaven, and to blaspheme a gracious, patient, all-bountiful God; is a height of sin which exceeds the blackness and impiety of devils and hell itself.

And now, after what has been here offered, to show

the heinousness of profane cursing and swearing in common conversation, may I not very justly address myself to you in the words of the text, "Therefore I say unto you, Swear not at all;" since it is a sin that has no temptation in nature, nor brings any pleasure or profit to the committer of it; since it hardens infidels in their infidelity, and affords sad causes of grief and lamentation to every honest Christian; since it is a sin that generally grows into a habit, and lastly, such a sin that can only be matched in hell.

1. And first then, if these things be so, and the sin of profane swearing, as hath been in some measure shown, is so exceeding sinful, what shall we say to such unhappy men, who think it not only allowable, but fashionable and polite, to "take the name of God in vain;" who imagine that swearing makes them look big among their companions, and really think it a piece of honor to abound in it? But alas! little do they think that such a behavior argues the greatest degeneracy of mind and fool-hardiness, that can possibly be thought of. For what can be more base, than one hour to pretend to adore God in public worship, and the very next moment to blaspheme his name; indeed, such a behavior, from persons who deny the being of a God, (if any such fools there be) is not altogether too much to be wondered at; but for men, who not only subscribe to the belief of a Deity, but likewise acknowledge him to be a God of infinite majesty and power; for such men to blaspheme his holy name, by profane cursing and swearing, and at the same time confess, that this very God has expressly declared, he will not hold him guiltless, but will certainly and eternally punish (without repentance) him that taketh his name in vain; is such an instance of fool-hardiness, as well as baseness, that can scarcely be paralleled. This is what they presume not to do in other cases of less danger: they dare not revile a general at the head of his army, nor rouse a sleeping lion when within reach of his paw. And is the Almighty God, the great Jehovah, the everlasting King, who can consume them by the breath of his nostrils, and frown them to hell in an instant; is he the only contemptible being in their account, that may be provoked without fear, and offended without punishment? No; though God hear long, he will not bear always; the time will come, and that too, perhaps, much sooner than such persons may expect, when God will vindicate his injured honor, when he will lay bare his almighty arm, and make those wretches feel the eternal smart of his justice, show power and name they have so often vilified and blasphemed. Alas! what will become of all their bravery then? Will they then wantonly sport with the name of their Maker, and call upon the King of all the earth to damn them any more in jest? No; their note will then be changed: indeed, they shall call, but it will be for "the rocks to fall on them, and the hills to cover them from the wrath of him that sitteth upon the throne, and from the Lamb for ever." It is true, time was when they prayed, though without thought, perhaps, for damnation both for themselves and others; and now they will find their prayers answered. "They delighted in cursing, therefore shalt it happen unto them; they loved not blessing, therefore shall it be far from them; they clothed themselves with cursing like as with a garment, and it shall come into their bowels like water, and like oil into their bones."

2. But further, if the sin of swearing is so exceeding heinous, and withal so common, then it is every particular person's duty, especially those that are in authority, to do their utmost towards discountenancing and suppressing so malignant a crime. The duty we owe both to God and our neighbor, requires this at our hands; by the one we are obliged to assert our Maker's honor; by the other to prevent our neighbor's ruin; and it is but doing as we would be done by, and as we ourselves act in cases of lesser consequence. Were we to hear either our own or our friend's good name vilified [slandered, maligned] and traduced [slandered, maligned], we should think it our bounden duty to vindicate the wronged reputation of each; and shall the great, terrible, and holy name of our best and only friend, our king, our father, nay our God: shall this be daily, nay every moment, defied and blasphemed; and will no one dare to stand up in defense of his honor and holiness? Be astonished, O heavens, at this! No; let us scorn all such base and treacherous treatment; let us resolve to support the cause of religion, and with a becoming prudent courage manifest our zeal for the honor of the Lord of Hosts. Men in authority have double the advantages of ordinary Christians; their very office shows they are intended for the punishment of evil doers. And such is the degeneracy of mankind, that the generality of them will be more influenced by the power of persons in authority, than by the most labored exhortations from the pulpit. To such, therefore, if there are any here present, I humbly address myself, beseeching them, in the name of our Lord Jesus Christ, to do their utmost to put a stop to, and restrain profane cursing and swearing. And though it must be confessed, that this is a work which requires a great deal of courage and pains, yet they would do well to consider, it is for God they undertake it, who certainly will support and bear them out in a

due execution of their office here, and reward them with an exceeding and eternal weight of glory hereafter. But it is time to draw towards a conclusion.

3. Let me, therefore, once more address myself to every person here present, in the name of our Lord Jesus Christ; and if any amongst them have been any way guilty of this notorious sin of swearing, let me entreat them by all that is near and dear to them, that they would neither give the magistrate the trouble to punish, nor their friends any reason for the future to warn them against committing the crime; but keep a constant and careful watch over the door of their lips, and withal implore the divine assistance (without which all is nothing) that they offend no more so scandalously with their tongues. Let them seriously lay to heart, what with great plainness and simplicity has here been delivered: and if they have any regard for themselves as men, or their reputation as Christians; if they would not be a public scandal to their profession, or a grief to all that know or converse with them: in short, if they would not be devils incarnate here, and provoke God to punish them eternally hereafter; I say unto them in the name of our Lord Jesus Christ, "Swear not at all."

19. Christ the Support of the Tempted

Matthew 6:13—"Lead us not into temptation."

The great and important duty which is incumbent on Christians, is to guard against all appearance of evil; to watch against the first risings in the heart to evil; and to have a guard upon our actions, that they may not be sinful, or so much as seem to be so. It is true, the devil is tempting us continually, and our own evil hearts are ready to join with the tempter, to make us fall into sins, that he thereby may obtain a victory over us, and that we, my brethren, may be his subjects, his servants, his slaves; and then by-and-by he will pay us our wages, which will be death temporal, and death eternal. Our Lord Jesus Christ saw how his people would be tempted; and that the great enemy of their souls would lay hold of every opportunity, so he could but be a means of keeping poor sinners from coming to the Lord Jesus Christ; hurrying you with temptation, to drive you to some great sins; and then if he cannot gain you over, sell it to a smaller, and suit his temptations time after time; and when he finds none of these things will do, often transform himself into an angel of light, and by that means make the soul fall into sin, to the dishonor of God, and the wounding of itself; the Lord Jesus, I say, seeing how liable his disciples, and all others, would be to be overcome by temptation, therefore advises them, when they pray, to beg that they might not be led into temptation. It is so dangerous to engage so subtle and powerful an enemy as Satan is, that we shall be overcome as often as we engage, unless the Lord is on our side. My brethren, if you were left to yourselves, you would be overcome by every temptation with which you are beset.

These words are part of the prayer which Christ taught his disciples; and I shall, therefore, make no doubt, but that you all believe them to be true, since they are spoken by one who cannot lie. I shall,

I. Show you who it is that tempts you.

II. Shall show, my brethren, why he tempts you.

III. Mention some of the ways and means he makes use of, to draw you over to his temptations.

IV. Let you see how earnest you ought to be to the Lord, that he may preserve you from being led into temptation.

V. I shall make some application by way of entreaty unto you, to come unto Christ, that he, my brethren, may deliver you from being tempted.

I. *First*, We are to consider who it is that tempts us.

And the tempter is Satan, the prince of the power of the air, he that now ruleth in the children of disobedience; he is an enemy to God and goodness, he is a hater of all truth. Why else did he slander God in paradise? Why did he tell Eve, "You shall not surely die?" He is full of malice, envy, and revenge; for what reasons else could induce him to molest innocent man in paradise? The person that tempts ye, my brethren, is remarkable for his subtlety; for having not power given him from above, he is obliged to wait for opportunities to betray us, and to catch us by guile; he, therefore, made use of the serpent to tempt our first parents; and to lie in wait to deceive, is another part of his character. And though this character is given of the devil, if we were to examine our own hearts, we should find many of the tempter's characters legible in us.

Do not many of you love to make a lie? And if it is done in your trade; you therefore look on it as excusable; but whether you believe it or not, it is sinful, it is exceedingly sinful. Though you may value yourselves as fine rational creatures, and that you are noble beings; and you were so, as you first came out of God's hands; but now you are fallen, there is nothing lovely, nothing desirable in man; his heart is a sink of pollution, full of sin and uncleanness: Yet, though a man's own heart is so desperately wicked, he is told by our modern polite preachers, that there is a fitness in men, and that God seeing you a good creature, gives you his grace; but this, though it is a modern, polite, and fashionable way of talking, is very unscriptural; it is very contrary to the doctrines of the Reformation, and to our own Articles. But however contrary to the doctrines of the Church of England, yet our pulpits ring of nothing more, than doing no one any harm, living honestly, loving your neighbor as yourselves, and do what you can, and then Christ is to make up the deficiency: this is making Christ to be half a savior, and man the other part; but I say, Christ will be your whole righteousness, your whole wisdom, your whole sanctification, or else he will never be your whole redemption. How amazing is it, that the ministers of the church of England should speak quite contrary to what they have subscribed! Good God! If these are the guides of the ignorant, and esteemed to be the true ministers of Jesus, because they have a great share of letter-learning; when at the same time they are only the blind leaders of the blind; and without a special Providence, they both will fall into the ditch.

No wonder at people's talking of the fitness and unfitness of things, when they can tell us, that the Spirit of God, is a good conscience, and the comforts of the Holy Ghost are consequent thereupon. But this is wrong; for it should be said, the Spirit of God, are the comforts of the Holy Ghost, and a good conscience consequent thereupon. Seneca, Cicero, Plato, or any of the heathen philosophers, would have given as good a definition as this; it means no more than reflecting we have done well.

But let these modern, polite gentlemen, and let my letter-learned brethren, paint man in as lovely colors as they please, I will not do it; I dare not make him better than the word of God does. If I was to paint man in his proper colors, I must go to the kingdom of hell for a copy; for man is by nature full of pride, subtlety, malice, envy, revenge, and all uncharitableness; and what are these but the temper of the devil? And lust, sensuality, pleasure, these are the tempers of the beast. Thus, my brethren, man is half a beast, and half a devil, a motley mixture of the beast and devil. And this is the creature, who has made himself so obnoxious to the wrath of God, and open to his indignation, that is told, that he must be part his own savior, by doing good works, and what he cannot do Christ will do for him.

This is giving the tempter great room to come in with his temptation; he may press a soul to follow moral duties, to go to church, take the sacrament, read, pray, meditate; the devil is well content you should do all these; but if they are done in your own strength, or if you go no farther than here, you are only going a smoother way to hell.

Thus, my brethren, you may see who it is that tempts us. But

II. Why he tempts you, is the second thing I am to show you.

It is our of envy to you, and to the Lord Jesus Christ, he endeavors to keep you from closing with Jesus; and if he can but keep you from laying hold by faith on Christ, he knows he has you safe enough; and the more temptations you are under, and according to their nature and greatness, you are more hurried in your minds; and the more unsettled your thoughts and affections are, the more apt you are to conclude, that if you were to go to Christ, at present, in all that hurry of mind, he would not receive you; but this is a policy of the tempter, to make you have low and dishonorable thoughts of the blessed Jesus; and so by degrees he works upon your minds, that you are careless and indifferent about Christ. This, this, my brethren, is the design of the tempter. Nothing will please him more, than to see you ruined and lost forever. He tempts you for that end, that you may lose your interest in Jesus Christ, and that you may dwell with him and apostate spirits to all eternity. He knows that Jesus Christ died for sinners, yet he would fain keep souls from seeking to this city of refuge for shelter, and from going to Gilead for the true balm.

It is he that rules in thy heart, O scoffer, O Pharisee; the devil reigns there, and endeavors to blind your eyes, that you shall not see what danger you are in, and how much evil there is in those hearts of yours; and as long as he can keep you easy and unconcerned about having your hearts changed, he will be easy; though if he can, he will tempt you to sin against him, until you are hardened in your iniquity. O, my brethren, do not give the devil a handle wherewith he may lay hold on you; alas! it is not wonder that the devil tempts you, when he finds you at a play, a ball, or masquerade; if you are doing the devil's work, it is no wonder if he presses you in the continuation thereof; and how can any say, "Lead us not into temptation," in the morning, when they are resolved to run into it at night? Good God! Are these persons members of the church of England? Alas, when you have gone to church, and read over the prayers, it is offering no more than the sacrifice of fools; you say Amen to them with your lips, when in your hearts you are either unconcerned at what you are about, or else you think that the bare saying of your prayers is sufficient, and that then God and you have balanced accounts.

But, my dear brethren, do not deceive yourselves, God is not to be mocked. You are only ruining yourselves for time and eternity. You pray, "lead us not into temptation," when you are tempting the devil to come and tempt you.

III. I shall now point out some of the ways and means, he makes use of to draw you to himself.

But this is a field so large, and I have but just begun to be a soldier of Jesus Christ, that I cannot name many unto you. I shall therefore be very short on this head.

1. He endeavors to make you think sin is not so great as it is; that there is no occasion of being so over-strict, and that you are righteous over-much; that you are ostentatious [showy, pompous, egotistical], and will do yourself harm by it; and that you will destroy yourselves. He shows you, by brethren, the bait, but he hides the hook; he shows you the pleasure, profits, and advantages, that attend abundance of this world's goods; but he does not show you crosses, losses and vexations that you may have while you are in the enjoyment of the blessings of this world.

2. When he finds he cannot allure you by flattery, he will try you by frowns, and the terrors of this world; he will stir up people to point at you, and cry, "Here comes another troop of his followers;" He will stir them up to jeer, scoff, backbite, and hate you; but if he still finds this will not do, then he throws doubts, my brethren, and discouragement in your mind, whether the way you are in is the true way or not; or else he will suggest, What! Do you expect to be saved by Christ? Also, He did not die for you; you have been too great a sinner; you have lived in sin so long, and committed such sins against Christ, which he will not forgive. Thus he hurries poor sinners almost into despair.

And very often, when the people of God are met to worship him, he sends his agents, the scoffers, to disturb them. We saw an instance of their rage just now; they would fain have disturb us; but the Lord was on our side, and so prevented all the attempts of wicked and designing men, to disturb and disquiet us. Lord Jesus, forgive them who are thus persecuting thy truth! Jesus, show them that they are fighting against thee, and that it is hard for them to kick against the pricks! These, my brethren, are some of the ways Satan takes, in is temptations, to bring you from Christ. Many more might be named; but these are sufficient, I hope, to keep you on your guard, against all that the enemy can do to hinder you from coming to Christ.

IV. I come to show you, how earnest you ought to be with Jesus Christ, either not to suffer you to be led into temptations, or to preserve you under them.

And here, my dear brethren, let me beseech you to go to Jesus Christ; tell him, how you are assaulted by the evil one, who lies in wait for your souls; tell him, you are not able to master him, in your own strength; beg his assistance, and you shall find him ready to help you; ready to assist you, and to be your Guide, your Comforter, your Savior, your All; He will give you strength to resist the fiery darts of the devil; and, therefore, you can no where find one so proper to relieve you, as Jesus Christ; he knows what it is to be tempted; he was tempted by Satan in the wilderness, and he will give you the assistance of his Spirit, to resist the evil one, and then he will fly from you. In Christ Jesus you shall have the strength you stand in need of, the devil shall have no power; therefore fear not, for in the name of the Lord we shall overcome all our spiritual Amalekites. Let the devil and his agents rage, let them breathe out threatenings, yes, let them breathe out slaughters, yet we can rejoice in this, that Jesus Christ hath them in his power, they shall go no farther than he permits them; they may rage, they may rage horribly, but they can go no farther, until they have got more power from on high.

If they could do us what mischief they would, very few of us should be permitted to see our habitations any more; but, blessed be God, we can commit ourselves to his protection; he has been our protector hitherto, he will be so still. Then earnestly entreat of the Lord to support you under those temptations, which the devil may assault you with; he is a powerful adversary, he is a cunning one too; he would be too hard for us, unless we have the strength of Christ to be with us. But let us be looking up unto Jesus, that he would send his Spirit into our hearts, and keep us from falling. O my dear brethren in Christ Jesus, how stands it now between God and your souls? Is Jesus altogether lovely to your souls? Is he precious unto you? I am sure, if you have not gone back from Christ, he will not from you; he will root out the accursed things of this world, and dwell in your hearts. You are candidates for heaven; and will you mind earth ? What are all the pleasures of earth, without an interest in the Lord Jesus Christ? And one smile from him is more to be desired than rubies, yea more than the whole world.

O you who have found Jesus Christ assisting you, and supporting you under all the temptations of this life, will you forsake him? Have you not found him a gracious master? Is he not the chiefest of ten thousand, and altogether lovely? Now you see a form and comeliness in Christ, which you never saw before. O! how do you and I wish we had known Jesus sooner, and that we had more of his love; it is condescending love, it is amazing, it is forgiving love, it is dying love, it is exalted and interceding love, and it is glorified love. Methinks when I am talking of the love of Jesus Christ, who loved me before I love him; he saw us polluted in blood, full of sores, a slave to sin, to death and hell, running to destruction, then he passed by me, and said unto my soul, "Live;" he snatched me as a brand plucked from the burning. It was love that saved me, it was all of the free grace of God, and that only. The little experience I have had of this love, makes me amazed at the condescension, the love, and mercifulness of the blessed Jesus, that he should have mercy upon such a wretch. O, my brethren, the kingdom of God is within me, and this fills me so full of love, that I would not be in my natural state again, not for millions of millions of worlds; I long to be with Jesus, to live with the Lord that bought me, to live forever with the Lamb that was slain, and to sing Hallelujah's unto him. Eternity itself will be too short to set forth the love of the Lord Jesus Christ. I cannot, indeed I cannot forbear speaking again, and again, and again, of the Lord Jesus.

And if there are any here who are strangers to this love of the Lord Jesus Christ, do not despair; come, come unto Christ, and he will have mercy upon you, he will pardon all your sins, he will heal all your backslidings, he will love you freely, and take you to be with himself.. Come therefore, O my guilty brethren, unto Jesus, and you shall find rest for your souls. You need not fear, you need not despair, when God has had mercy upon such a wretch as I; and he will save you also, if you will come unto him by faith.

Why do ye delay? What! Do you say, you are poor, and therefore ashamed to come? It is not your poverty that Christ mindeth; come in all your rags, in all your pollution, and he will save you. Do not depend upon any thing but the blood of Jesus Christ; do not stand out an hour longer, but give your hearts to Christ, give him the firstlings of the flock; come unto him now, lest he should cut you off before you are prepared, and your soul be sent to that pit from whence there is no redemption.

Do not waver, but give him that which he desires, your hearts; it is the heart the Lord Jesus Christ wanteth; and when you have an inward principle wrought in your hearts by this same Jesus, then you will feel the sweetness and pleasure of communion with God. O consider, my brethren, the love of the Lord Jesus Christ, in dying for you; and are you resolved to slight his dying love? Your sins brought Christ from heaven, and I humbly pray to the Lord that they may not be a means of sending you to hell. What language will make you leave your sins and come to Christ? O that I did but know! And that it lay in my power to give you this grace; not one of you, not the greatest scoffer here should go hence before he was changed from a natural to a spiritual life; then, then we would rejoice and take sweet council together; but all this is not in my power; but I tell you where you may have it, even of the Lord Jesus; he will give it to you, if you ask it of him, for he has told us, "Ask, and you shall receive;" therefore ask of him, and if you are repulsed again and again, entreat him more, and he will be unto you as he was to the poor Syrophoenician woman, who came to Christ on account of her daughter; and is she was so importunate to him for a body, how much more should we be solicitous for our souls? If you seek to him in faith, his answer will be to you as it was to her, "Thy faith hath saved thee, be it as thou wouldest have it."

O, do not forsake the seeking of the Lord; do not, I beseech you, neglect the opportunities which may be offered to you, for the salvation of your souls; forsake not the assembling of yourselves together, to build up and confirm and strengthen those who are weak in faith; to convince sinners, that they may feel the power of God pricking them in their hearts, and make them cry out, "What must we do to be saved?"

The devil and his agents have their clubs of reveling, and their societies of drunkenness; they are not ashamed to be seen and heard doing the devil their master's works; they are not ashamed to proclaim him; and sure you are not ashamed of the Lord Jesus Christ; you dare proclaim that Jesus, who died that you might live, and who will own you before his Father and all the holy angels; Therefore, dare to be singularly good; be not afraid of the face of man; let not all the threats of the men of this world move you; what is the loss of all the grandeur, or pleasure, or reputation of this life, compared to the loss of heaven, of Christ and of your souls? And as for the reproaches of the world, do not mind them; when they revile you, never, never revile again; do not answer railing with railing; but let love, kindness, meekness, patience, long-suffering, be found in you, as they were in the blessed Jesus; therefore, I beseech you, do not neglect the frequent coming together, and telling each other, what great things Jesus Christ hath done for your souls.

I do not now, as the Pharisees say I do, encourage you to leave your lawful callings, and your business, in which God, by his providence, hath placed you; for you have two callings, the one a general, and the other a special one; it is your duty to regard your families, and if you neglect them out of any pretense whatever, as going to church or in societies, you are out of the way of your duty, and offering that to God which he commanded you not. But then, my brethren, you are to take care that the things of this life do not hinder the preparing for that which is to come; let not the business of the world make you unmindful of your souls; but in all your moral actions, in the business of life, let all be done with a view to the glory of God, and the salvation of your souls.

The nigh draws on, and obliges me to hasten to a conclusion; though, methinks, I could speak until my tongue clave to the roof of my mouth, yes, until I could speak no more, if it was to save your souls from the paws of him who seeketh to devour you.

Therefore let me beseech you, in all love and compassion; Consider, you, who are Pharisees; you, who will not come to Christ, but are trusting to yourselves for righteousness; who think, because you lead civil, honest, decent lives, all will go well at last; but let me tell you, O ye Pharisees, that harlots, murderers, and thieves, shall enter the kingdom of God before you. Do not flatter yourselves of being in the way to heaven, when you are in the broad way to hell; but if you will throw away your righteousness and come to Christ, and be contented to let Jesus Christ do all for you, and in you, then Christ is willing to be your Savior; but if you bring your good works with you, and think to be justified on the account of them, you may seek to be justified by them forever, and never be justified; no, it is only the blood of Jesus Christ that cleanseth us from the filth and pollution of all our sins; and you must be sanctified before you are justified. As for good works, we are justified before God without any respect to them, either past, present, or to come: when w are justified, good works will follow our justification, for we can do no good works, until we are cleansed of our pollution, by the sanctification of the Spirit of God.

O ye scoffers, come and see this Jesus, this Lord of glory whom you have despised; and if you will but come to Christ, he will be willing to receive you, notwithstanding all the persecution you have used towards his members; However, if you are resolved to persist in your obstinacy, remember, salvation was offered to you, that Christ and free grace were proposed; but you refused to accept of either, and therefore your blood will be required at your own hands.

I shall only say this unto you, that however you may despise either me or my ministry, I shall not regard it, but shall frequently show you your danger, and propose to you the remedy; and shall earnestly pity and pray for you, that God would show you your error, and bring you home into his sheepfold, that you, from ravenous lions, may become peaceful lambs.

And as for you, O my brethren, who desire to choose Christ for you Lord, and to experience his power upon your souls, and as you do not find your desires and prayers answered; go on, and Christ will manifest himself unto you, as he does not unto the world; you shall be made to see and feel this love of Jesus upon your souls; you shall have a witness in your own breast, that you are the Lord's; therefore, do not fear, the Lord Jesus Christ will gather you with his elect, when he comes at that great day of accounts, to judge every one according to the deeds done in the body, whether they be good, or whether they be evil; and, O that the thought of answering to God for all our actions, would make us more mindful about the consequences that will attend it.

And now let me address all of you, high and low, rich and poor, one with another, to accept of mercy and grace while it is offered to you; Now is the accepted time, now is the day of salvation; and will you not accept it, now it is offered unto you? Do not stand out one moment longer; but come and accept of Jesus Christ in his own way, and then you shall be taken up at the last day, and be with him forever and ever; and sure this should make you desirous of being with that Jesus who has done so much for you, and is not interceding for you, and preparing mansions for you; where may we all arrive and sit down with Jesus to all eternity!

Which God of his infinite mercy grant.

20. Worldly Business No Plea for the Neglect of Religion

Matthew 8:22—"Let the dead bury their dead."

St. Paul preaching at Athens, tells them, that as he passed by and beheld their devotions, he perceived they were in all things too superstitious. But was this apostle to rise, can come publishing the glad tidings of salvation in any of our populous cities, he would see no reason why he should charge the inhabitants with this; but rather as he passed by and observed the tenor of their life, say, I perceive in all things ye are two worldly-minded; ye are too eagerly bent on pursuing your lawful business; so eagerly, as either wholly to neglect, or at least too heedlessly to attend on the one thing needful.

There cannot then be a greater charity shown to the Christian world, than to sound an alarm in their ears, and to warn them of the inexpressible danger, of continually grasping after the things of this life, without being equally, nay a thousand times more concerned for their well-being in a future state.

And there is still the more occasion for such an alarm, because worldly-mindedness so easily and craftily besets the hearts of men. For out of a specious pretense of serving God in laboring for the meat which perisheth, they are insensibly lulled into such a spiritual slumber, as scarce to perceive their neglect to secure that which endureth to everlasting life.

The words of the text, if not at first view, yet when examined and explained, will be found applicable to this case, as containing an admirable caution not to pursue the affairs of this world, at the expense of our happiness in the next.

They are the words of Jesus Christ himself: the occasion of their being spoken was this; As he was conversing with those that were gathered round about him, he gave one of them an immediate summons to follow him: but he, either afraid to go after such a persecuted master, or rather loving this present world, says, "Suffer me first to go home and bury my father," or, as most explain it, let me first go and dispatch some important business I have now in hand. But Jesus said unto him, "Let the dead bury their dead;" leave worldly business to worldly men, let thy secular business be left undone, rather than thou shouldst neglect to follow me.

Whether this person did as he was commanded, I know not; but this I know, that what Christ said here is person, he has often whispered with the small still voice of his holy Spirit, and said to many here present, that rise up early and late take rest, and eat the bread of carefulness, Come draw off your affections from the things of this life; take up your cross and follow me. But they, willing to justify themselves, make answer, Lord, suffer us first to bury our fathers, or dispatch our secular affairs. I say unto all such, "Let the dead bury their dead," let your worldly business be left undone, rather than you should neglect to follow him.

From the words thus explained, naturally arises this proposition, that no business, though ever so important, can justify a neglect of true religion.

The truth of which I shall first show, and then make an application of it.

I. *First* then, I am to prove, that no temporal business, though ever so important, can justify a neglect of true religion.

By the word religion, I do not mean any set of moral virtues, any partial amendment of ourselves, or formal attendance on any outward duties whatsoever: but an application of Christ's whole and personal righteousness, made by faith to our hearts; a thorough real change of nature wrought in us by the invisible, yet powerful operation of the Holy Ghost, preserved and nourished in our souls by a constant use of all the means of grace, evidenced by a good life, and bringing forth the fruits of the Spirit.

This is true and undefiled religion, and for the perfecting this good work in our hearts, the eternal Son of God came down and shed his precious blood; for this end were we made, and sent into the world, and by this alone can we become the sons of God. Were we indeed to judge by the common practice of the world, we might think we were sent into it for no other purpose, than to care and toil for the uncertain riches of this life: but if we consult the lively oracles, they will inform us, that we were born for nobler ends, even to be born again from above, to be restored to the divine likeness by Jesus Christ, our second Adam, and thereby be made meet to inherit the kingdom of heaven; and consequently, there is an obligation laid upon all, even the most busy people, to secure this end; it being an undeniable truth, that all creatures ought to answer the end for which they were created.

Some indeed are for confining religion to the clergy, and think it only belongs to those who serve at the altar; but what a fatal mistake is this, seeing all persons are indifferently called by God to the same state of inward holiness. As we are all corrupt in our nature, so must we all be renewed and sanctified. And though it must be granted, that the clergy lie under double obligations to be examples to believers, in faith, zeal, charity, and whatever else s commendable and of good report, as being more immediately dedicated to the service of God; yet as we have been all baptized with one baptism into the death of Christ, we are all under the necessity of performing our baptismal covenant, and perfecting holiness in the fear of God: for the holy scriptures point out to us but one way of admission into the kingdom of Christ, through the narrow gate of a sound conversion: And he that does not enter into the sheepfold, whether clergy or lay-men, by this door, will find, to his everlasting confusion, there is no climbing up another way.

Besides, what a gross ignorance of the nature of true

religion, as well as of our own happiness, does such a distinction discover? For what does our Savior, by willing us to be religious, require of us? But to subdue our corrupt passions, to root out ill habits, to engraft the heavenly graces of God's most holy Spirit in their room; and, in one word, to fill us with all the fullness of God.

And will men be so much their own enemies, as to affirm this belongs only to those who minister in holy things? Does it not equally concern the most active man living? Is it the end of religion to make men happy, and is it not every one's privilege to be as happy as he can? Do persons in business find the corruptions of their nature, and disorder of their passions, so pleasing, that they care not whether they ever regulate or root them out? Or will they consent that ministers shall be alone partakers of the inheritance of the saints in light? If not, as they desire the same end, why will they not make use of the same means? Do they think that God will create a new thing upon the earth, and, contrary to the purity of his nature, and immutability of his counsel, admit them into heaven in their natural state, because they have been encumbered about many worldly things? Search the scriptures, and see if they give any room for such a groundless hope.

But farther, one would imagine there was something of the highest concern and utmost importance in our temporal affairs, that they should divert so many from purifying their hearts by faith which is in Christ Jesus.

A covetous miser, who neglects religion by being continually intent on seeking great things for himself and those of his own household, flatters himself he herein acts most wisely; and at the same time will censure and condemn a young prodigal, who has no time to be devout, because he is so perpetually engaged in wasting his substance by riotous living and following of harlots. But yet a little while, and men will be convinced, that they are as much without excuse who lost their souls by hunting after riches, as those who lose them by hunting after sensual pleasures. For though business may assume an air of importance, when compared with other trifling amusements, yet when put in the balance with the loss of our precious and immortal souls, it is equally frivolous, according to that of our Savior, "What shall it profit a man, if he shall gain the whole world, and lost his own soul; or what shall a man give in exchange for his soul?"

And now what need we any further proof? We have heard the decision out of Christ's own mouth. But because it is so difficult to convince such of this important truth, whose hearts are blinded by the deceitfulness of riches, that we had need cry out to them in the language of the prophet, "O earth, earth, hear the word of the Lord," I shall lay before you one passage of scripture more, which I could wish were written on the tables of all our hearts. In the 14th of St. Luke, the 18th and following verses, our blessed Lord puts forth this parable, "A certain man made a great supper, and bade many, and sent his servant at supper-time, to call them that were bidden: but they all, with one consent, began to make excuse. The one said, I have bought a piece of ground, and I must needs go and see it, I pray thee have me excused. And another said, I have bought a yoke of oxen, and I must needs go and prove them, I pray thee therefore have me excused. So the servant returned, and showed his master all these things." And what follows? Did the master accept of their excuses? No, the text tells us the good man was angry, and said, "that none of those which were bidden, should taste of his supper." And what does this parable teach, but that the most lawful callings cannot justify our neglect; nay, that they are no longer lawful when they in any wise interfere with the great concerns of religion? For the marriage supper here spoken of, means the gospel; the master of the house is Christ; the servants sent out, are his ministers, whose duty it is, from time to time, to call the people to this marriage-feast, or, in other words, to be religious. Now we find those that were bidden, were very well and honestly employed. There was no harm in buying or seeing a piece of ground, or in going to prove a yoke of oxen; but here lay their faults, they were doing those things, when they were invited to come to the marriage feast.

Without doubt, persons may very honestly and commendably be employed in following their respective callings; but yet, if they are engaged so deeply in these, as to hinder their working out their salvation with fear and trembling, they must expect the same sentence with their predecessors in the parable, that none of them shall taste of Christ's supper: for our particular calling, as of this or that profession, must never interfere with our general and precious calling, as Christians. Not that Christianity calls us entirely out of the world, the holy scriptures warrant no such doctrine.

It is very remarkable, that in the book of life, we find some almost of all kinds of occupations, who notwithstanding served God in their respective generations, and shone as so many lights in the world. Thus we hear of a good centurion in the evangelists, and a devout Cornelius in the Acts; a pious lawyer; and some that walked with God, even of Nero's household, in the epistles; and our divine master himself, in his check to Martha, does not condemn her for minding, but for being cumbered or perplexed about many things.

No, you may, nay, you must labor, our of obedience to God, even for the meat which perisheth.

But I come, in the *Second* place, to apply what has been said.

I beseech you, by the mercies of God in Christ Jesus, let not your concern for the meat which perisheth be at the expense of that which endureth to everlasting life; for, to repeat our blessed Savior's words, "What shall it profit a man, if he shall gain the whole world, and lose his own soul; or, what shall a man give in exchange for his soul?"

Were we always to live in the world, then worldly wisdom would be our highest wisdom: but forasmuch as we have here no continuing city, and were only sent into this world to have our natures changed, and to fit ourselves for that which is to come; then to neglect this important work for a little worldly gain, what is it but, with profane Esau, to sell our birth-right for a mess of pottage.

Alas! how unlike are Christians to Christianity! They are commanded to "seek first the kingdom of God and his righteousness," and all other real necessaries shall be added unto them; but they are fearful (O men of little faith!) that if they should do so, all other necessaries would be taken from them: they are strictly forbidden to be careful for the morrow, and yet they rest not night or day, but are continually heaping up riches for many years, though they know not who shall gather them. Is this acting like persons that are strangers and pilgrims upon earth? Is this keeping their baptismal vow? Or rather, is it not directly apostatizing from it, and deserting the service of Jesus Christ, to list themselves under the banner of mammon?

But what will be the hope of such worldlings, when God shall take away their souls? What if the almighty should say to each of them, as he did to the rich fool in the gospel, "this night shall thy soul be required of thee;" O then, what would all those things profit them, which they are now so busy in providing?

Was eternal life, that free gift of God in Christ Jesus, to be purchased with money; or could men carry their flocks beyond the grave, to buy oil for their lamps, i.e. grace for their hearts, when they should be called to meet the bridegroom, there might be some reason why God might well bear with them: but since their money is to perish with them; since it is certain, as they brought nothing into the world, so they can carry nothing out; or supposing they could, since there is no oil to be bought, no grace to be purchased when once the lamp of their natural life is gone out; would it not be much more prudent to spend the short time they have here allotted them, in buying oil while it may be had, and not for fear of having a little less of that which will quickly be another man's, eternally lose the true riches?

What think you? Is it to be supposed, it grieved that covetous worldling before mentioned, when his sprung into the world of spirits, that he could not stay here till he had pulled down his barns and built greater? Or think you not that all things here below seemed equally little to him then, and he only repented that he had not employed more time in pulling down every high thought that exalted itself against the Almighty, and building up his soul in the knowledge and fear of God?

And thus it will be with all unhappy men, who like him are disquieting themselves in a vain pursuit after worldly riches, and at the same time are not rich towards God.

They may, for a season, seem excellently well employed in being solicitously careful about the important concerns of this life; but when once their eyes are opened by death, and their souls launched into eternity, they will then see the littleness of all sublunary cares, and wonder they should be so besotted [intoxicated, loaded] to the things of another life, while they were, it may be, applauded for their great wisdom and profound sagacity in the affairs of this world.

Alas! how will they bemoan themselves for acting like the unjust steward, so very wisely in their temporal concerns, in calling their respective debtors so carefully, and asking how much every one owes to them, and yet never remembering to call themselves to an account, or inquire how much they owed to their own great Lord and master?

And now what shall I say more? The God of this world, and the inordinate desire of other things, must have wholly stifled the conscience of that man, who does not see the force of these plain reasonings.

Permit me only to add a word or two to the rich, and to persons that are freed from the business of this life.

But here I must pause a while, for I am sensible that it is but an ungrateful, and as some may imagine, an assuming thing, for such a novice in religion to take upon him to instruct men in high stations, and who perhaps would disdain to set me with the dogs of their flock.

But however, since St. Paul, who knew what best became a young preacher, commanded Timothy, young as he was, to exhort and charge the rich with all authority; I hope none here that are so, will be offended, if with humility I beg leave to remind them, though they once knew this, that if persons in the most busy employs are indispensably obliged to "work out their salvation with fear and trembling," much more ought they to do so, who are free from the toils and encumbrance of a lower way of life, and consequently have greater opportunities to leisure to prepare themselves for a future state.

But is this really the case? Or do we not find, by fatal experience, that too many of those whom God has exalted above their brethren, who are "clothed in purple and fine linen, and fare sumptuously every day," by a sad abuse of God's great bounty towards them, think that their stations set them above religion, and so let the poor, who live by the sweat of their brows, attend more constantly on the means of grace than do they?

But woe unto such rich men! For they have received their consolation. Happy had it been if they had never been born: for if the careless irreligious tradesman cannot be saved, where will luxurious and wicked gentlemen appear?

Let me therefore, by way of conclusion, exhort all persons, high and low, rich and poor, one with another, to make the renewal of their fallen nature, the one business of their lives; and to let no worldly profit, no worldly pleasure, divert them from the thoughts of it. Let this cry, "Behold the bridegroom cometh," be ever sounding in our ears; and let us live as creatures that are every moment liable to be hurried away by death to judgment: let us remember, that this life is a state of infinite importance, a point between two eternities, and that after these few days are ended, there will remain no more sacrifice for sin; let us be often asking ourselves, how we shall wish we had lived when we leave the world? And then we shall always live in such a state, as we shall never fear to die in. Whether we live, we shall live unto the Lord; or whether we die, we shall die unto the Lord; so that living or dying we may be the Lord's.

To which end, let us beseech God, the protector of all them that put their trust in him, without whom nothing is string, nothing is holy, to increase and multiply upon us his mercy, that he being our ruler and guide, we may so pass through things temporal, that we finally lose not the things eternal; though Jesus Christ our Lord.

21. Christ the Only Rest for the Weary and Heavy-Laden

Matthew 11:28—"Come unto me, all ye that are weary and heavy laden, and I will give you rest."

Nothing is more generally known than our duties which belong to Christianity; and yet, how amazing is it, nothing is less practiced? There is much of it in name and show, but little of it in the heart and conversation; indeed, if going to church, and to the sacrament, or, if our being called after the name of Christ, and being baptized into that name; if that will make us Christians, I believe all of us would have a claim thereto: but if it consists in the heart, that there must be an inward principle wrought in us by faith; that there must be a change of the whole nature, a putting off the old man with his deeds, a turning from sin unto God, a cleaving only unto the Son of Righteousness; and that there must be a new birth, and we experience the pangs thereof; and that you must feel yourselves weary and heavy laden with your sins, before you will seek for deliverance from them; if this is to be the case, if there is so much in being children of God, alas! how many who please themselves with an outside show, a name to live whilst they are dead; and how few that have any share in this spiritual state, in this true and living name? How few are they who are weary and heavy laden with their sins, and seek to Christ for rest? They say, in a formal customary manner, we are sinners, and there is no health in us; but how few feel themselves sinners, and are so oppressed in their own spirits, that they have no quiet nor rest in them, because of the burden of their sins, and the weight that is fallen and lays on their minds?

Under these burdens, these heavy burdens, they are at a loss what to do whereby they may obtain rest; they fly to their works, they go to a minister, and he tells them to read, to pray, and meditate, and take the sacrament: thus they go away, and read, and pray, and meditate almost without ceasing, and never neglect the sacrament whenever there is an opportunity for the taking of it. Well, when the poor soul has done all this, it still finds no ease, there is yet no relief. Well, what must you do then? To lie still under the burden they cannot, and to get rid of it then cannot. O what must the burdened soul do! Why, goes to the clergyman again, and tells him the case, and what it has done, and that it is no better. Well, he asks, have you given alms to the poor? Why no. Then go and do that, and you will find rest. Thus the poor sinner is hurried from duty to duty, and still finds no rest: all things are uneasy and disquiet within, and there remains no rest in the soul. And if it was to go through all the duties of religion, and read over a thousand manuals of prayers, none would ever give the soul any rest; nothing will, until it goes to the Lord Jesus Christ, for there is the only true rest; that is the rest which abideth, and will continue for ever. It is not in your own works, nor in your endeavors: no; when Christ comes into your souls, he pardons you, without any respect to your works, either past, present, or to come.

From the words, my brethren, I have now read, I shall
I. Show you who are the weary and heavy laden.
II. Inquire what is meant by coming to Christ. And,
III. Conclude with exhorting you to accept of the invitation which the Lord Jesus Christ gives unto you to come unto him, with the assurance of finding rest.

First, I am to show you, who are the weary and heavy-laden.

And here it will be necessary to consider who are not; and then, to consider who they are that are really so.

1. Those who think themselves good enough, and are pleased that they are not so bad as others, these are not weary or heavy laden.

No, these Pharisees are not thus troubled; they laugh and jest at those who talk of feeling their sins, and think there is no occasion to make so much ado about religion: it is to be righteous over-much, and the means to destroy yourselves. They think if they do but mean well, and say their prayers, as they call them, it is sufficient: though they may say a prayer, yea, thousands of prayers, and all the while be only offering up the sacrifice of fools. They may call God, Father, every day, when it is only mocking of God, and offering up false fire unto him; and it would be just for him to serve them, as he did Nadab and Abihu, destroy them, cut them off from the face of the earth: but he is waiting to be gracious, and willing to try a little longer, whether you will bring forth any thing more than the leaven of an outward profession, which is not all that the Lord requires; no, he wants the heart; and unless you honor him with that, he does not regard your mouths, when the other is far from him. You may say over your prayers all your lives, and yet you may never pray over one: therefore, while you flatter yourselves you are good enough, and that you are in a state of salvation, you are only deceiving you own souls, and hastening on your own destruction. Come unto him, not as being good enough, but as vile sinners, as poor, and blind, and naked, and miserable, and then Jesus will have compassion.

O ye Pharisees, what fruits do ye bring forth? Why, you are moral, polite creatures; you do your endeavors, you do what you can, and so Jesus is to make up the rest. You esteem yourselves fine, rational, and polite beings, and think it is too unfashionable to pray; it is not polite enough: perhaps you have read some prayers, but knew not how to pray from your hearts; no, by no means: that was being righteous over-much indeed.

But when once you are sensible of your being lost, damned creatures, and see hell gaping ready to receive you: if God was but to cut the thread of life, O then, then you would cry earnestly unto the Lord to receive you, to open the door of mercy unto you; your bones would then be changed, you would no more flatter yourselves with your abilities and good wishes; no, you would see how unable you were, how incapable to save yourselves; that there is no fitness, no free will in you; no fitness, but for eternal damnation, no free will but that of doing evil; and that when you would do good, evil is present with you, and the thing that ye would not, that do ye. He knows the secret intent of every heart; and this is a pleasure to you, my dear brethren, who come on purpose to meet with him, though it be a field. And, however some may esteem me a mountebank, and an enthusiast, one that is only going to make you methodically mad; they may breathe out their invectives against me, yet Christ knows all; he takes notice of it, and I shall leave it to him to plead my cause, for he is a gracious Master: I have already found him so, and am sure he will continue so. Vengeance is his, and he will repay it. Let them revile me; let them cast me out of their synagogues, and have my name in reproach, I shall not answer them by reviling again, or in speaking evil against them: no, that is not the Spirit of Christ, but meekness, patience, long-suffering, kindness, &c.

Ye Pharisees, who are going about to establish your own righteousness; you, who are too polite to follow the Lord Jesus Christ in sincerity and truth; you, who are all for a little show, a little outside work; who lead moral, civil, decent lives, Christ will not know you at the great day, but will say unto you, O ye Pharisees, was there any place for me in your love? Alas! you are full of anger and malice, and self-will; yet you pretended to love and serve me, and to be my people: but, however, I despise you; I, who am God, and knoweth the secret of all hearts; I, who am truth itself, the faithful and true witness, say unto you, "Depart from me, ye workers of iniquity, into that place of torment, prepared for the devil and his angels." Good God! And must these discreet polite creatures, who never did any one harm, but led such civil, decent lives, must they suffer the vengeance of eternal fire? Cannot their righteous souls be saved? Where then must the sinner and the ungodly appear? Where wilt thou, O Sabbath-breaker, appear, thou, who canst take thy pleasure, thy recreation, on the Lord's-day, who refuseth to hear the word of God, who wilt not come to church to be instructed in the ways of the Lord? Where will you, O ye adulterers, fornicators, and such-like of this generation appear? Whoremongers and adulterers God will judge, and them he will condemn. Then you will not call these tricks of youth: no, but you will call on the rocks and the mountains to fall on you, to hide you from the fury and anger of the Lord. Where wilt thou, O man, appear, that takes pleasure in making a mock of sin, who despiseth all reproof, who throws about thy jests as a madman does fire, and asks whether thou art not in sport? Where wilt thou, O man, appear, that makes it thy business to preach against the children of the Most High; thou, who art inventing methods in order to stop the progress of the gospel, and using thy utmost power to quash [squash] the preaching thereof; who art raising of evil reports against the disciple of Christ, and esteemest them madmen, fools, schismatics, and a parcel of rabble? Thou, O man, with all thy letter-learning, wilt surely see the judgment seat of Christ, though, perhaps, sorely against your will; to be cast by him into eternal fire, a place prepared for the devil and his angels. There is a burning tophet kindled by the fury of an avenging God, which will never, never be quenched. The devil longs to embrace you in his hellish arms, whenever the sentence is past, where you must for ever bear the weight of your sin: there is no redemption then; the day of grace is past; the door of hope is shut; mercy will be no more offered, but you must be shut out from God for ever. O who can dwell with everlasting burnings!

However you may think of hell, indeed it is not a painted fire; it is not an imagination to keep people in awe: then, then you will feel the power of the almighty arm. If you will not lay hold on his golden scepter, he will break you with his iron rod. O ye Pharisees, who are now so good, so much better than others, how will ye stand before Christ, when dressed in his glory as judge? You Arians, may now despise his divinity; then you shall have a proof of it; he will show, that he has all power, and that he was no subordinate God; he will show you that he has all power in heaven and earth; that he was King of kings, and Lord of lords; that he was the mighty God, the everlasting Father; and this power that he has, he will exercise in preserving you to no other end, but to punish you forever. Thus you, who please yourselves with being good enough now, who are not weary and heavy laden with a sense of your sins here, will be weary and heavy laden with a sense of your punishment hereafter.

2. Those, my brethren, are not weary and heavy laden with a sense of their sins, who can delight themselves in the polite entertainments of the age, and follow the sinful diversion of life.

Now they can go to balls and assemblies, play-houses and horse-racing; they have no thought of their sins; they know not what it is to weep for sin, or humble themselves under the mighty hand of God; they can laugh away their sorrows, and sing away their cares, and drive away these melancholy thoughts: they are too polite to entertain any sad thoughts; the talk of death and judgment is irksome to them, because it damps their mirth; they could not endure to think of their sin and danger; they could not go to a play, and think of hell; they could not go quietly to a masquerade, and think of their danger; they could not go to a ball or an assembly in peace, if they thought of their sins.

And so it is proved, even to a demonstration, that these are not weary and heavy laden: for if they are not thoughtful about their sins, they will never be weary and heavy laden of them. But at the day of judgment all will be over; they shall lose all their carnal mirth, all their pleasure, all their delight will be gone forever.

They will say then of their laughter, it is mad; and of mirth, What dost thou? Their merry conceits, and witty jests against the poor despised people of God, are then over. Their mirth was but as the crackling of thorns under a pot; it made a great blaze and unseemly noise for a while, but it was presently gone, and will return no more.

They think now, that if they were to fast or to pray, and meditate and mourn, they should be righteous overmuch, and destroy themselves; their lives would be a continual trouble, and it would make them run mad. Alas, my brethren, what misery must that life be, where there is no more pleasant days, no more balls or plays, no cards or dice, those wasters of precious time, no horse-racing and cock-fighting, from whence no good ever came, unless abusing God Almighty's creatures, and putting them to that use which he never designed them, can be called so. How miserable will your life be, when all your joys are over, when your pleasures are all past, and no more mirth or pastime? Do you think there is one merry heart in hell? One pleasing countenance? Or jesting, scoffing, swearing tongue? A sermon now is irksome; the offer of salvation, by the blood of Jesus Christ, is now termed enthusiasm; but then you would give thousands of worlds, if in your power, for one tender of mercy, for one offer of grace, which now you so much despise.

Now, you are not weary of your diversions, nor are you heavy laden with the sins, with which they are accompanied; but then you will be weary of your punishment, and the aggravation which attends it. Your cards and dice, your hawks and hounds, and bowls, and your pleasant sports, will then be over. What mirth will you have in remembering your sports and diversions? I would not have you mistake me, and say, I am only preaching death and damnation to you; I am only showing you what will be the consequence of continuing in these sinful pleasures; and if the devil does not hurry you away with half a sermon, I shall show you how to avoid these dangers, which I now preach up as the effect of sin unrepented of. I mention this, lest you should be hurried away by the devil: but be not offended, if I point our unto you more of the terrors which will attend your following these polite and fashionable entertainments of the present age, and of not being weary and heavy laden with a sense of your sins.

They who delight in drinking wine to excess, and who are drunkards, what bitter draughts will they have instead of wine and ale? The heat of lust will be then also abated; they will no more sing the song of the drunkard; no more spend their time in courting their mistresses, in lascivious discourse, in amorous songs, in wanton dalliances, in brutish defilements: no, these are all over; and it will but prick each other to the heart to look one another in the face. Then they will wish, that instead of sinning together, they had prayed together; had frequented religious societies; had stirred up each other to love and holiness, and endeavored to convince each other of the evil of sin, and how obnoxious they are to the wrath of God; and the necessity of being weary and heavy laden with a sense thereof; that they might have escaped the punishment which they suffer, by their following the sinful an polite diversions of the age they fell into. But as it was against God himself they had sinned, so no less than God will punish them for their offenses: he hath prepared those torments for his enemies; his continual anger will still be devouring of them; his breath of indignation will kindle the flame; his wrath will be a continual burden to their souls. Woe be to him who falls under the stroke of the Almighty!

Thus they are not weary and heavy laden with their sins, who can follow the polite and fashionable entertainments of the age. But,

Secondly, I am to show you what it is to be weary and heavy laden with sins. And

1. You may be said, my brethren, to be weary and heavy laden, when your sins are grievous unto you, and it is with grief and trouble you commit them.

You, who are awakened unto a sense of your sins, who see how hateful they are to God, and how they lay you open to his wrath and indignation, and would willingly avoid them; who hate yourselves for committing them; when you are thus convinced of sin, when you see the terrors of the law, and are afraid of his judgments; then you may be said to be weary of your sins. And O how terrible do they appear when you are first awakened to a sense of them; when you see nothing but the wrath of God ready to fall upon you, and you are afraid of his judgments! O how heavy is your sin to you then! Then you feel the weight thereof, and that it is grievous to be born.

2. When you are obliged to cry out under the burden of your sins, and know not what to do for relief; when this is your case, you are weary of your sins. It does not consist in a weariness all of a sudden; no, it is the continual burden of your soul, it is your grief and concern that you cannot live without offending God, and sinning against him; and these sins are so many and so great, that you fear they will not be forgiven.

I come, *Secondly*, to show you what is meant by coming to Christ.

It is not, my brethren, coming with your own works: no, you must come in full dependence upon the Lord Jesus Christ, looking on him as the Lord who died to save sinners: Go to him, tell him you are lost, undone, miserable sinners, and that you deserve nothing but hell; and when you thus go to the Lord Jesus Christ out of yourself, in full dependence on the Lord Jesus Christ, you will find him an able and a willing savior; he is pleased to see sinners coming to him in a sense of their own unworthiness; and when their case seems to be most dangerous, most distressed, then the Lord in his mercy steps in and gives you his grace; he puts his Spirit within you, takes away your heart of stone, and gives you a heart of flesh. Stand not out then against this Lord, but go unto him, not in your own strength, but in the strength of Jesus Christ.

And this brings me, *Thirdly*, to consider the exhortation Christ gives unto all of you, high and low, rich and poor, one with another, to come unto him that you may have rest. And if Jesus Christ gives you rest, you may be sure it will be a rest indeed; it will be such a rest as your soul wants; it will be a rest which the world can neither give nor take away. O come all of ye this night, and you shall find rest: Jesus Christ hath promised it. Here is a gracious invitation, and do not let a little rain hurry you away from the hearing of it; do but consider what the devil and damned spirits would give to have the offer of mercy, and to accept of Christ, that they may be delivered from the torments they labor under, and must do so forever; or, how pleasing would this rain be to them to cool their parched tongues; but they are denied both, while you have mercy offered to you; free and rich mercy to come to Christ; here is food for your souls, and the rain is to bring forth the fruits of the earth, as food for you bodies. Here is mercy upon mercy.

Let me beseech you to come unto Christ, and he will give you rest; you shall find rest unto your souls. O you, my weary, burdened brethren, do but go to Christ in this manner, and though you go to him weary, you shall find rest before you come from him: let not anything short of the Lord Jesus Christ be your rest; for wherever you seek you will be disappointed; but if you do but seek unto the Lord Jesus Christ, there you will find a fullness of every thing which your weary soul wants. Go to him this night; here is an invitation to all you who are weary souls. He does not call you, O Pharisees; not, it is only you weary sinners; and sure you will not stay from him, but accept of his invitation; do not delay; one moment may be dangerous: death may take you off suddenly. You know not but that a fit of the apoplexy may hurry you from time into eternity; therefore, be not for staying till you have something to bring; come in all your rags, in all your filthiness, in all your distresses, and you will soon find Jesus Christ ready to help, and to relieve you; he loves you as well in your rags, as in your best garments; he regards not your dress; no, do but come unto him, and you shall soon find rest for your souls.

What say you? Shall I tell my Master you will come unto him, and that you will accept him on his own terms. Let me, my brethren, beseech you to take Jesus without anything of your own righteousness: for if you expect to mix anything of yourself with Christ, you build upon a sandy foundation; but if you take Christ for your rest, he will be that unto you. Let me beseech you to build upon this rock of ages. O my brethren, think of the gracious invitation, "Come unto me," to Jesus Christ; it is he that calls you; And will you not go?

Come, come unto him. If your souls were not immortal, and you in danger of losing them, I would not thus speak unto you; but the love of your souls constrains me to speak: methinks this would constrain me to speak unto you forever. Come then by faith, and lay hold of the Lord Jesus; though he be in heaven, he now calleth thee. Come, all ye drunkards, swearers, Sabbath-breakers, adulterers, fornicators; come, all ye scoffers, harlots, thieves, and murderers, and Jesus Christ will save you; he will give you rest, if you are weary of your sins. O come lay hold upon him. Had I less love for your souls, I might speak less; but that love of God, which is shed abroad in my heart, will not permit me to leave you, till I see whether you will come to Christ or no. O for your life receive him, for fear he may never call you any more. Behold, the Bridegroom cometh; it may be this night the cry may be made. Now would you hear this, if you were sure to die before the morning light? God grant you may begin to live, that when the king of terrors shall come, you may have nothing to do but to commit your souls into the hands of a faithful Redeemer.

Now to God the Father, God the Son, and God the Holy Ghost, be all honor, praises, dominion, and power, henceforth and for evermore. Amen, Amen.

22. The Folly and Danger of Parting with Christ for the Pleasures and Profits of Life

Matthew 8:23–34—"And when he was entered into a ship, his disciples followed him. And, behold, there arose a great tempest in the sea, insomuch that the ship was covered with the waves: but he was asleep. And his disciples came to [him], and awoke him, saying, Lord, save us: we perish. And he saith unto them, Why are ye fearful, O ye of little faith? Then he arose, and rebuked the winds and the sea; and there was a great calm. But the men marveled, saying, What manner of man is this, that even the winds and the sea obey him! And when he was come to the other side into the country of the Gergesenes, there met him two possessed with devils, coming out of the tombs, exceeding fierce, so that no man might pass by that way. And, behold, they cried out, saying, What have we to do with thee, Jesus, thou Son of God? art thou come hither to torment us before the time? And there was a good way off from them an herd of many swine feeding. So the devils besought him, saying, If thou cast us out, suffer us to go away into the herd of swine. And he said unto them, Go. And when they were come out, they went into the herd of swine: and, behold, the whole herd of swine ran violently down a steep place into the sea, and perished in the waters. And they that kept them fled, and went their ways into the city, and told every thing, and what was befallen to the

> **possessed of the devils. And, behold, the whole city came out to meet Jesus: and when they saw him, they besought [him] that he would depart out of their coasts."**

If we were but sensible of the great necessity there is, in this our day, of being real Christians, sure we should not be contented with being nominal ones; but we are sunk into I know not what; we are no better than baptized heathen. And how amazing is it, that we should profess the name of Christ, and yet so little converse about him; surely, this name whereby we are called, should be the theme of our discourse here, and of our eternal Hallelujahs in a world to come. But is it not more amazing, to consider, that instead of the name of Jesus, whereby we are to have salvation, we are taught to look for it in ourselves, and that there must be a fitness in us before God bestows his grace and favor upon us. But what doctrine is this? Not the doctrine of the scripture, not the doctrine of Jesus, not that of the primitive Christians, not that of the reformation, nor that of the articles of the church of England. No, it is the doctrine of the devil; this is making Christ but half a Savior, and driving man into an error of the greatest consequence, in making him go to Jesus in his own strength, and not in the name of the Lord Jesus Christ. But, my brethren, unless you go in the strength of Jesus Christ; unless you depend only upon him for salvation; unless he is your wisdom, righteousness and sanctification, he will never be your redemption. Our salvation is the free gift of God; it is owing to his free love, and the free grace of Jesus Christ, that ever you are saved.

Do not flatter yourselves of being good enough, because you are morally so; because you go to church, say the prayers, and take the sacrament, therefore you think no more is required; alas, you are deceiving your own souls; and if God, in his free grace and mercy, does not show you your error, it will only be leading you a softer way to your eternal ruin; but God forbid that any of you, to whom I am now speaking, should imagine this; no, you must be abased, and God must be exalted, or you will never begin at the right end, you will never see Jesus with comfort or satisfaction, unless you go to him only on the account of what he has done and suffered.

Is it not plain to a demonstration, that we are acting the part of the Gergesenes, who came and desired Jesus to depart from them? Let us consider the words, and then we shall see how exactly we are performing the part of these men over again.

And when he was entered into a ship his disciples followed him.

Christ had been working of many miracles, as we may read a few verses before; and as he continually went about doing good, so now he was going to the country of the Gergesenes to dispossess two, who were possessed with devils; and his disciples followed him; No doubt they were reproached and pointed at, for following such a babbler, as the Scribes and Pharisees esteemed the Lord Jesus Christ. Doubtless they were pointed at, jeered, scoffed, and esteemed madmen, enthusiasts, and a parcel of rabble; but still they followed the Lord Jesus Christ, they did not mind a little reproach; no, they loved their Master too well to forbear following him for the sake of a little persecution. And if you do but love the Lord Jesus Christ, love him above all, you will follow him in spite of the malice of all the Scribes and Pharisees of this generation.

And behold there arose a great tempest on the sea.

The presence of Christ in the ship, did not preserve the disciples from fears and troubles; they were filled with uneasiness, although Christ was with them: this was only for a trial of their faith, to see if they would stand fast for the Lord in a persecuting time. My dear brethren, if the Lord is trying of you, do not give out; no, stand fast in all that the Lord may call you to suffer: It is easy to follow Christ when all things are safe: but your love to Jesus Christ would be seen more, if you must lose your lives, or deny your Jesus; it would be a trial of your love, when fire and faggot was before you, if you would rush into that, rather than flee from the truth as it is in Jesus. Though all things are calm now, the storm is gathering, and by and by it will break; it is at present no bigger than a man's hand; but when it is full it will break, and then you will see whether you are found Christians or not. Persecution would scatter the hypocrites, and make nominal Christians afraid to worship God; they would then soon turn unto the world and the things of it.

And his disciples came to [him], and awoke him, saying, Lord, save us: we perish. And he saith unto them, Why are ye fearful, O ye of little faith? Then he arose, and rebuked the winds and the sea; and there was a great calm. But the men marveled, saying, What manner of man is this, that even the winds and the sea obey him!

Here we may see the great compassion of the Lord Jesus Christ; no sooner had the disciples awakened him, and he saw their danger, but he rebuked the winds and seas, and all things were calm. Thus it was in a natural way, and will be so in a spiritual one; for no sooner does

Jesus Christ speak peace to a troubled soul, but all is calm and quiet. Now none but God could have performed this great miracle, and therefore it is no wonder that his disciples and the men of the ship were amazed to see the wonders he performed; and they could not forbear to express their sense thereof, by inquiring, "What manner of man is this!"

And when he was come to the other side into the country of the Gergesenes, there met him two possessed with devils, coming out of the tombs, exceeding fierce, so that no man might pass by that way. And, behold, they cried out, saying, What have we to do with thee, Jesus, thou Son of God? art thou come hither to torment us before the time?

Two men, who were possessed bodily with that evil one who is going about seeking whom he may devour, met Jesus; as soon as they saw him they were afraid, and cried out: though they made every one afraid of them, yet they no sooner saw Christ, but their power left them, and they cried out, "What have we to do with thee, Jesus, thou Son of God?" We know that thou are God; we do not want thee, we have no power over thee, but thou hast over us, and we fear thou art come to torment us before our time; we know that we are to be brought to judgment, and therefore we would not be tormented until that time come.

And there was a good way off from them an herd of many swine feeding. So the devils besought him, saying, If thou cast us out, suffer us to go away into the herd of swine.

The evil spirits were sensible that Christ was come to dispossess them, and that their time was now come, when they must leave the bodies of these two men; for when Christ comes, who is stronger than the strong man armed, all must fall before him; they could not stand against the power of Christ. And here we may observe, that though the devil is an enemy, yet he is a chained one; he cannot hurt a poor swine until he has power given him from above: and we may likewise see the malice of the devil, that he would hurt a poor swine rather than do no mischief; and the devil would, if in his power, destroy each of your souls, but Christ, by his mighty power, prevents him.

And he said unto them, Go. And when they were come out, they went into the herd of swine: and, behold, the whole herd of swine ran violently down a steep place into the sea, and perished in the waters. And they that kept them fled, and went their ways into the city, and told every thing, and what was befallen to the possessed of the devils. And, behold, the whole city came out to meet Jesus: and when they saw him, they besought [him] that he would depart out of their coasts.

Here observe, that no sooner had Christ given the devils permission to enter the swine, but they did, and their malice was so great, that the swine ran violently down a steep place into the sea, and were drowned.

What poor spite was here, that the devil should disturb poor swine! And the city, therefore, was so grieved for the loss of a little wealth, that they came and besought Christ to depart; they did not want his company; they preferred a few poor swine before the company of Christ; and few worldly good, a little pleasure, or any thing rather than Christ, part with Christ before any thing; but one, who is sensible of the love of Christ, will part with all, rather than with the Lord Jesus Christ.

Thus far the letter of the story goes; perhaps you think there is nothing to be learned herefrom, and that this is all you are to understand by it; but if so, my brethren, you are much mistaken; for here is an excellent lesson to be learned, and that you will see, by considering the words again, in a spiritual sense.

And, behold, there arose a great tempest in the sea, insomuch that the ship was covered with the waves: but he was asleep.

And do not you frequently experience great tempests in this world? Does not the sea of temptation beat over your souls? You are afraid lest you should be overcome by them; you can see no way to escape, for your souls are covered with waves, and you expect to be swallowed up in the tempest; you are afraid lest you should fall into the hands of the evil one. O do not fear, for Jesus Christ, though he may be asleep to your thinking, yet will keep you, he will preserve you from the raging of the men, of the Pharisees of this world; they may rage and spit forth all their venom against you, still Christ will deliver, preserve and protect you; if you but seek unto him in a sense of your own helplessness and unworthiness, you will soon find he is a God ready to pardon and forgive. O that all that hear me would be persuaded to bow their knee, and their hearts, as soon as they go home: but alas, how many of our Christians go to God, day by day, and call him, Father, which is but mocking of God, when the devil is their father. None have a right to call him father, but those who have received the spirit of adoption, whereby they have a right to call him, "Abba, Father." Could the brute beasts speak, they might call God father as well as some of you; for hi is their Creator to whom they owe their being; but this will not entitle you to call

God father, in a spiritual sense; no, you must be born again of God; however you may flatter yourselves, you must have an inward principle wrought in your hearts by faith. This you must experience, this, this you must feel before you are Christians indeed.

The Lord Jesus Christ takes notice of each of you, you may think the Lord does not take notice of us, because we are in a field, and out of church walls; but he does observe with what view you came this evening to hear his word; he knows whether it was to satisfy your curiosity, or to find out wherewith you might ridicule the preacher. The thoughts and intentions of all your hearts are not hidden from Jesus Christ; though he may seem to be asleep, because you are, at present, insensible of his workings upon your heart, and he may not seem to take notice of you, and regard you, no more than he did the Syrophoenician woman; yet he will turn to you and behold you with live; the Lord will be mindful of you in due time, and speak peace to your troubled soul, though the sea of troubles is beating over you, though the Pharisees of this day are scoffing at you, yet, when Christ rebukes, then they shall cease.

Do not depend on yourself; say unto him, "Save us, Lord, or we perish!" beseech him to be your guide, and your salvation: I beseech you, by the tender mercies of God, which are in Christ Jesus, that you present yourselves to him, as your reasonable service.

Awake, you that sleep, and arise from the dead, from the death of sin, and Christ then will give you the light of his righteousness. Come to Christ and you shall be welcome; O come unto this blessed Jesus, come notwithstanding your vileness; for if you come not you will perish. If Christ does not save you, your own good meaning, your own good intentions cannot; no, as you are in your blood, so you must perish in your blood; but if you come to Christ you will find mercy, you shall not perish. You cannot find salvation in any other but in Christ; if the disciples could have saved themselves, they would not have awoken Jesus Christ; but they were sensible that no one could save them but him; and therefore they cried out unto him; and so you, who are under the sense of sin, who are in fear of hell, if you seek unto your own works, you only seek your own death; for there is no fitness in you. I speak the truth in Christ Jesus, I lie not, there is not fitness in you, but a fitness for eternal damnation; for what are you by nature, but children of wrath, and your hearts are Satan's garrison. Because you have gone to church, said the prayers, gone to the sacrament, and done o one any harm, you speak peace to your souls; and all is in peace you think, and your case is good enough; but indeed, all is a false peace, and if you have no other peace than this, you must shortly lie down in everlasting flames; this is an ungrounded, self-created peace, and if you trust to this peace you will perish.

But do as the disciples did when they were in distress; they go to Christ and say to him, "Lord, save us, we perish." I offer you salvation this day; the door of mercy is not yet shut, there does yet remain a sacrifice for sins, for all that will accept of the Lord Jesus Christ; he only knows the inmost thoughts of thy heart, he will embrace you in the arms of his love; he sees the first risings of grace in you, and would willingly encourage it: the angels long for your being in the love and favor of God; they will rejoice to see you turn from sin unto him. All the ministers of the blessed Jesus would be glad to be instruments to turn you from darkness to light, and from the power of Satan unto God.

And he saith to them, why are ye fearful, O ye of little faith?

And so, my brethren, I may say to you; why are you fearful to leave you sins and turn to God? O turn to him, turn in a sense of your own unworthiness; tell him how polluted you are, how vile, and be not faithless, but believe; do not go in your own strength, and then you need not fear. Why fear ye that the Lord Jesus Christ will not accept of you? Your sins will be no hindrance, your unworthiness will be no hindrance; if your own corrupt hearts do not keep you back, or if your own good works do not hinder you from coming, nothing will hinder Christ from receiving of you: he loves to see poor sinners coming to him, he is pleased to see them lie at his feet pleading his promises: and if you thus come to Christ, he will not send you away without his Spirit; no, but will receive and bless you.

O do not put a slight on infinite love; what would you have Christ do more? Is it not enough for him to come on purpose to save? Will you not serve God in your souls, as well as with your bodies? If not, you are only deceiving yourselves; and mocking of God; he must have the heart. O ye of little faith, why are ye fearful lest he should not accept of you? If you will not believe me, sure you will believe the Lord Jesus Christ; he has told thee that he will receive you; then why tarry ye, and do not go to him directly? Does he desire impossibilities? It is only, "Give me thy heart;" or, does he want your heart only for the same end as the devil does, to make you miserable? No, he only wants you to believe on him, that you might be saved. This, this, is all the dear Savior desires, to make you happy, that you may leave your sins, to sit down eternally with him, at the marriage supper of the Lamb.

Then he arose and rebuked the winds and the sea, and there was a great calm.

Thus, you see, it was only to the power of Christ to stop the raging of the sea; he rebuked it; the disciples might have spoken for ever, and it would not have ceased; so it is with the word preached; I may preach to you while I live; I may speak till I can speak no more; but the doctrines of Christ will never do you good, unless he impress them upon your hearts; O then, in all thy troubles look up to Christ, that he may rebuke them; and if he speaks the word, then they shall cease. If the Pharisees of this generation scoff and jeer you, if they say all manner of evil against you, do not answer them; leave it unto Christ to rebuke them; for all you can say will be of no more signification, than the disciples speaking to the sea; but when Christ speaks the word, then they shall cease; let it not discourage you, for if you will live godly in Christ Jesus, you must suffer persecution.

It is true, that those who are sincerely good, are set up for marks for every one to shoot at. There is a continual enmity between the seed of the woman and the seed of the serpent; if you were of the world, the world would love its own; but because Christ hath chosen you out of the world, therefore it hateth you.

Do not think of following Christ into glory, unless you go through the press here. Look forward, my brethren, into eternity, and behold Christ coming, and his reward with him, to give a kind recompense for all the temptations and difficulties of this present life.

But the men marveled, saying, What manner of man is this, that even the winds and the seas obey him!

The men of the ship were amazed to see the miracle that Jesus Christ wrought only by his word; they thought he was something more than a man. And have not we as much reason to admire, that when we are overwhelmed with troubles, from within and without, that Jesus Christ, only by the word of his power, should speak peace, and then there is peace indeed. When God first awakens us with a sense of sin, and sets his terrors in array against us, then there are troubles and tempests; for Satan having got possession, before he will give place, he will fight and strive hard to keep the soul from closing with Jesus. But when Christ comes, he storms the heart, he breaks the peace, he giveth it most terrible alarms of judgment and hell, he sets all in a combustion of fear and sorrow, 'till he hath forced it to yield to his mere mercy, and take him for its governor; then Satan is cast out; then the storm is rebuked, and he establishes a firm and lasting peace.

Can the sea be still while the wind is raging? No, it is impossible; so it is that there can be no peace in the soul, while it is at enmity with Christ; indeed, it may flatter itself and speak peace, but there can be no true peace; though thou, O Pharisee, may harden and fortify thy heart against fear, grief, and trouble, yet, as sure as God is true, they will batter down thy proud and fortified spirit, and seize upon it, and drive thee to amazement. This will be done here, or hereafter; here in mercy, or hereafter in wrath and judgment.

O my brethren, consider what Christ hath done, and you will be astonished that he has done so much for such wicked wretches as you and I are. If you are easy under the storm and tempest of sin, and do not cry to Christ for salvation, thou art in a dangerous condition; and it is a wonder to consider, how a man that is not sure of having made his peace with God, can eat, or drink, or live in peace; that thou art not afraid, when thou liest down, that thou should'st awake in hell: but if Christ speak peace unto thy soul, who can then speak trouble? None; no, not men or devils. Therefore, lie down at the feet of Christ whom you have resisted, and say, Lord, what wouldst thou have me to do? And he will rebuke the winds and seas of thy troubled mind, and all things will be calm.

And when he was come to the other side into the country of the Gergesenes, there met him two possesses with devils, coming out of the tombs, exceeding fierce, so that no man might pass by that way.

The Lord Jesus Christ, who went about doing good continually, very well knew, that he should meet two poor men in this country of the Gergesenes, who were possessed with devils; and Jesus Christ went on purpose that way, that he might relieve them. The devil, where he has the power, never wants will; but as I said before, so I say again, though the devil is an enemy, yet he is a chained one; he could not destroy these two poor men, he could not hurt the people that passed that way, he could only terrify them; and thus it is with you; the devil tries his utmost skill and power to frighten you from coming to the Lord Jesus; he uses the utmost of his endeavors to keep poor sick and weary sinners from coming to Jesus; if he can but make you lose your souls, it is the end he aims at.

And how many souls does he keep from Christ, for fear of reproach? Many thousands would willingly see Christ in his glory, in the world to come, and would be happy with him there, but they are afraid of being now laughed at, and of hearing the Pharisees say, here is another of his followers; they are afraid of losing their worldly business, or of being counted methodistically mad and fit for bedlam. I doubt not but many are kept from Jesus Christ, for fear of a little of inconveniency.

What will such say, when the Lord Jesus Christ shall appear in his glory? Would you be glad to be confessed by him then, you must now not be ashamed of confessing him before men; let not the fierceness of the devil keep you back from Christ, for fear of being counted fools; for the time will come, when it will be found who are truly wise, and who are truly mad.

Are you afraid to stand up for the cause of Christ in the world? Dare not you be singularly good? Are you afraid of being members of Jesus Christ? I tell you, such persons would crucify him afresh were he in the world. But do not you, my brethren, so learn Christ; let not the temptations of the devil keep you from coming to the Lord Jesus Christ; he may be fierce, he may hurry you from place to place, but strive with him, so that he may not drive you from Christ; and if you seek unto Christ, he will so help you that you shall resist the devil, and then he will fly from you; Christ will dispossess him, be not afraid therefore to meet Jesus Christ; tell him all that your souls want, and he will give it to you; and you shall not be any longer troubled with the fierce outrages of the devil.

And they cried out, saying, what have we to do with thee, Jesus, thou Son of God? Art thou come to torment us before the time?

As soon as the devils observed Jesus coming near, then they were afraid, lest he was come to punish them before that day of accounts, when all must be brought to judgment.

The devils themselves are enough to convince all our polite Arians and Socinians. They here own the Lord Jesus Christ to be God blessed for ever; they feel his power, and are assured of his being the God who must condemn them at the great day of accounts; and they were afraid lest the Lord Jesus Christ was come to punish them now. But though the devils believe the divinity of Christ, yet the world swarms with Arians and Socinians.

The Arians make Christ no more than a titular God, a subordinate deity, one who was more than a man, and yet less than God; that he was a prophet sent from God they own, but deny him to be equal with the Father. But I hope, my brethren, he is to you, what our creed makes him, God of God, very God of very God, co-eternal and consubstantial with the Father; that as there was not a moment of time in which God the Father was not, so there is not a moment of time in which God the Son was not. For he says himself, "All things were made by him;" and if they were made by him, he must be God; and whoever reads but the word of God, will find divine homage is paid to him, "and that he thought it no robbery to be equal with God;" he is "the Alpha and Omega." These and a great many more places might be brought to prove the divinity of the Lord Jesus Christ; he could never have made satisfaction for our sins if he had not been God as well as Man. As Man he suffered; as God he satisfied; so was God and man in one person; he took our nature upon him, and was offered upon the cross for the sins of all those who come unto him, which if he had not been God he could never have satisfied for. It may be proved, even to a demonstration, that the Lord Jesus Christ is God, and that he is equal with the Father.

The Socinians do not go so far as the others; they look on Christ to be no more than a good man, who told the people their duty, and died in defense of the doctrines which he delivered unto them.

But I hope there are none such here, that have so low and dishonorable thoughts of the blessed Jesus, and that thus despise the divinity of the Lord who bought them. No, I hope better things of you, and things that accompany salvation. Think you, that any one who denies the deity of Christ can ever be saved by him, living and dying in that state? Surely, the time will come, when they who have denied his Deity, shall feel the power of it hereafter; they shall feel that he is God as well as man; then he will be owned as God by all those who now dare to deny his truths; but God forbid it should go undetermined till then! Woe unto the polite infidels of this generation, for the devils will rise up in judgment against them.

If any such are here, consider what you are doing of, before it is too late; return, return ye unto the Lord, and he will have mercy upon you, and to Jesus Christ, and he will abundantly pardon. O my friends, let me beseech you to consider what you are about, lest you fall into hell, and there be none to deliver you.

And the devils besought him, saying, If thou cast us out, suffer us to go away into the herd of swine. And he said unto them, Go. And when they were come out, they went into the herd of swine: and, behold, the whole herd of swine ran violently down a steep place into the sea, and perished in the waters.

Here we may see, that no sooner had the devil power, but he puts it into execution; thus, if the devil has but power to tempt, or to hurry a soul, O how grievous a tyrant he is, hurrying from one temptation to another, from one sin unto another, and would, if it were possible, hurry you all into hell with as much violence, as he did the poor swine into the sea; but Christ by his grace prevents it. Jesus Christ died for souls, and therefore the devil cannot do with them as he will; he may have the will, but he cannot get the power. It is plain, that when the devil himself, or persecuting men, get the power, they will harass the poor Christians; everything is goo good for them, and they are not worthy to be set with the dogs of the flock. My brethren, how joyful would many be, if the laws of our land would permit them to destroy us; how would the Pharisees hurry us to prison and to death; but, blessed be God, he does not say to them, as to the devil, "Go." No, he bids them stay, he hedges their way up with thorns that they cannot stir to hurt us; they would fain, but they dare not destroy us; nothing withholds them but the power of the blessed Jesus. And therefore, be not afraid of their wrath though it is cruel, and of their anger though it be fierce; let them shoot their arrows, even bitter words, against us, blessed be God, the shield of faith will be a preservative against them all.

And when you are thus preserved, it will be the occasion of joy in the Holy Ghost; though many look on the joy of the Holy Ghost as enthusiasm and madness, and say that there is no such thing; but well do I know there is, it carries its own evidence along with it. Plead therefore with God, in the name of Jesus Christ; continue to wrestle with him, until he bestows the blessing upon you, and gives you a feeling of that joy which the world intermeddles not with, and which they are strangers to; indeed the devil may stir up his agents to hurry us from one trouble to another; but it will not signify, for the Lord Jesus Christ will not suffer him to hurry us into hell; no, but will give us his Spirit, which will be a preservative against all the assaults of the devil. Now see what followed this miracle, which Jesus had wrought, by permitting the devil to enter into the herd of swine.

And they that kept them fled, and went their ways into the city, and told every thing, and what was befallen to the possessed of the devils.

The people were so amazed to see the power that Christ had, and the malice with which the devil was possessed, that they were afraid, and told all that had befallen the possessed of the devils; and so, when the spirit of God has been at work on your souls, and you are brought to feel the power of God upon your hearts, you will be so overjoyed that you will tell to every one what great things God has done for your souls; you will be so full of joy, that you will declare the whole working of God on your hearts, and you will declare how you have been enabled to overcome Satan, and how you were affected at such a sermon, in such a place, and at such a time.

You will then love to talk of Jesus; no conversation will be so pleasing as that of the Lord Jesus Christ; no, he will be altogether lovely unto you, when you have once tasted of his love, and felt the power of his grace upon your hearts.

And, behold, the whole city came out to meet Jesus: and when they saw him, they besought [him] that he would depart out of their coasts.

The whole city came to meet Jesus, not to worship, nor to thank him for the releasing of the two poor men who were possessed; no, but to beseech him to go from them; they valued their swine more than the Lord Jesus Christ, and had rather part from him, than them; and have we not among us, thousands who call themselves Christians, who had rather part with Christ than their pleasures? A play, a ball, or an assembly is far more agreeable to them than the company and presence of the Lord Jesus Christ: if they can but indulge their sensual appetite, please and pamper their bellies, satisfy the lust of the eye, the lust of the flesh, and the pride of life, they regard no more, but rest contented, as if they were to live here always. O my dear brethren, I hope none of you can rest contented with such proceedings as these, but that you like the company of the Lord Jesus too well to part with him for a few delights of this life: and are there not many, who part with Christ for their own good works, and think they can go to heaven, if they do but go to church and say their prayers and take the sacrament? But alas! they will be much deceived, for if they were in any thing short of the Lord Jesus, if they do not make him the chief corner-stone, they will fall infinitely short of what they flattered themselves to attain unto.

I would speak a few words to you before I part from you this evening, by way of application. Let me beseech you to come to Jesus Christ; I invite you all to come to him and receive him as your Lord and Savior; he is ready to receive you; if you are afraid to go because you are in a lost condition, he came to save such; and to such as were weary and heavy laden, such as feel the weight and burden of their sins, he has promised he will give rest: such as feel the weight and burden of their sins on their souls, a burden too heavy for them to bear, are weary of it, and know not how to obtain deliverance of it, in the name of my Lord and master, I invite you to come to him, that you may find rest for your souls.

If you will but come unto him he will not reproach

you, as justly he might; he will not reflect upon you for not coming sooner unto him; no, my dear brethren, he will rejoice and be glad, and will say unto you, "Son, daughter, be of good cheer, your sins are forgiven you:" these words he said to others; and if you will but come unto him, by faith in his blood, he is ready to say the same unto you now, as he did to them formerly, for "he is the same to-day, yesterday and for ever:" though he suffered on the cross seventeen hundred years ago, yet he is the same in goodness and power as ever he was.

He calls you, by his ministers; O come unto him, beg of him to break your stubborn hearts, that you may be willing to be brought to him in his own way, to be made poor in spirit, and entitled to an inheritance among them that are sanctified.

O come and drink of the water of life; you may buy without money and without price; he is laboring to bring you back from sin, and from Satan unto himself: open the door of your hearts, and the King of glory shall enter in.

But if you are strangers to this doctrine, and account it foolishness; or, if you think you have enough of your own to recommend you to the favor of God, however you may go to church, or receive the sacrament, you have no true love to the Lord Jesus Christ; you are strangers to the truth of grace in your hearts, and are unacquainted with the new-birth; you do not know what it is to have your natures changed; and 'till you do experience these things, you never can enter into the kingdom of God.

What shall I say, my brethren, unto you? My heart is full, it is quite full, and I must speak, or I shall burst. What, do you think your souls of no value? Do you esteem them as not worth saving? Are your pleasures worth more than your souls? Had you rather regard the diversions of this life, than the salvation of your souls? If so, you will never be partakers with him in glory; but if you come unto him, he will give you a new nature, supply you with his grace here, and bring you to glory hereafter; and there you may sing praises and hallelujahs o the Lamb forever.

And may this be the happy end of all who hear me! may the Lord guide you by his counsel, until he comes to fetch you to heaven, and make you partakers of his glory!

May he direct you in his ways, and lead you in those paths which lead to everlasting life! May you be holy here, and happy hereafter: may your lives answer the profession you make, that we may all be found at the right hand of the Lord Jesus Christ, when he shall come to judge the world according to our works, whether they be good or evil! And that we then may be presented faultless before the presence of his glory with exceeding joy, God of his infinite mercy grant.

23. Marks of a True Conversion

Matthew 18:3—"Verily, I say unto you, except ye be converted, and become as little children, ye shall not enter into the kingdom of heaven."

I suppose I may take it for granted, that all of you, among whom I am now about to preach the kingdom of God, are fully convinced, that it is appointed for all men once to die, and that ye all really believe that after death comes the judgment, and that the consequences of that judgment will be, that ye must be doomed to dwell in the blackness of darkness, or ascend to dwell with the blessed God, for ever and ever. I may take it for granted also, that whatever your practice in common life may be, there is not one, though ever so profligate and abandoned, but hopes to go to that place, which the scriptures call Heaven, when he dies. And, I think, if I know any thing of mine own heart, my heart's desire, as well as my prayer to God, for you all, is, that I may see you sitting down in the kingdom of our heavenly Father. But then, though we all hope to go to heaven when we die, yet, if we may judge by people's lives, and our Lord says, "that by their fruits we may know them," I am afraid it will be found, that thousands, and ten thousands, who hope to go to this blessed place after death, are not now in the way to it while they live. Though we call ourselves Christians, and would consider it as an affront put upon us, for any one to doubt whether we were Christians or not; yet there are a great many, who bear the name of Christ, that yet do not so much as know what real Christianity is. Hence it is, that if you ask a great many, upon what their hopes of heaven are founded, they will tell you, that they belong to this, or that, or the other denomination, and part of Christians, into which Christendom is now unhappily divided. If you ask others, upon what foundation they have built their hope of heaven, they will tell you, that they have been baptized, that their fathers and mothers, presented them to the Lord Jesus Christ in their infancy; and though, instead of fighting under Christ's banner, they have been fighting against him, almost ever since they were baptized, yet because they have been admitted to church, and their names are in the Register book of the parish, therefore they will make us believe, that their names are also written in the book of life. But a great many, who will not build their hopes of salvation upon such a sorry rotten foundation as this, yet if they are, what we generally call, negatively good people; if they live so as their neighbors cannot say that they do anybody harm, they do not doubt but they shall be happy when they die; nay, I have found many such die, as the scripture speaks, "without any hands in their death." And if a person is what the world calls an honest moral man, if he does justly, and, what the world calls, love a little mercy, is not and then good-natured, reacheth out his hand to the poor, receives the sacrament once or twice a year, and is outwardly sober and honest; the world looks upon such an one as a Christian indeed, and doubtless we are to judge charitably of every such person. There are many likewise, who go on in a round of duties, a model of performances, that think they shall go to heaven; but if you examine them, though they have a Christ in their heads, they have no Christ in their hearts.

The Lord Jesus Christ knew this full well; he knew how desperately wicked and deceitful men's hearts were; he knew very well how many would go to hell even by the very gates of heaven, how many would climb up even to the door, and go so near as to knock at it, and yet after all be dismissed with a "verily I know you not." The Lord, therefore, plainly tells us, what great change must be wrought in us, and what must be done for us, before we can have any well grounded hopes of entering into the kingdom of heaven. Hence, he tells Nicodemus, "that unless a man be born again, and from above, and unless a man be born of water and of the Spirit, he cannot enter into the kingdom of God." And of all the solemn declarations of our Lord, I mean with respect to this, perhaps the words of the text are one of the most solemn, "except, (says Christ) ye be converted, and become as little children, ye shall not enter into the kingdom of heaven." The words, if you look back to the context, are plainly directed to the disciples; for we are told, "that at the same time came the disciples unto Jesus." And I think it is plain from many parts of Scripture, that these disciples, to whom our Lord addressed himself at this time, were in some degree converted before. If we take the words strictly, they are applicable only to those, that have already gotten some, though but weak, faith in Christ. Our Lord means, that though they had already tasted the grace of God, yet there was so much of the old man, so much indwelling sin, and corruption, yet remaining in their hearts, that unless they were more converted than they were, unless a greater change past upon their souls, and sanctification was still carried on, they could give but very little evidence of their belonging to his kingdom, which was not to be set up in outward grandeur, as they supposed, but was to be a spiritual kingdom, begun here, but completed in the kingdom of God hereafter. But though the words had a peculiar reference to our Lord's disciples; yet as our Lord makes such a declaration as this in other places of Scripture, especially in the discourse to Nicodemus, I believe the words may be justly applied to saints and sinners; and as I suppose there are two sorts of people here, some who know Christ, and some of you that do not know him, some that are converted, and some that are strangers to conversion, I shall endeavor so to speak, that if God shall be pleased to assist me, and to give you an hearing ear and an obedient heart, both saints and sinners may have their portion.

First, I shall endeavor to show you in what respects we are to understand this assertion of our Lord's, "that we must be converted and become like little children." I shall then,

Secondly, Speak to those who profess a little of this child-like temper,

And *Lastly*, shall speak to you, who have no reason to think that this change has ever past upon your souls. And

First, I shall endeavor to show you, what we are to understand by our Lord's saying, "Except ye be converted and become as little children." But I think, before I speak to this point, it may be proper to premise one or two particulars.

1. I think, that the words plainly imply, that before you or I can have any well-grounded, scriptural hope, of being happy in a future state, there must be some great, some notable, and amazing change pass upon our souls. I believe, there is not one adult person in the congregation, but will readily confess, that a great change hath past upon their bodies, since they came first into the world, and were infants dandled upon their mother's knees. It is true, ye have no more members than ye had then, but how are these altered! Though you are in one respect the same ye were, for the number of your limbs, and as to the shape of your body, yet if a person that knew you when ye were in your cradle, had been absent from you for some years, and saw you when grown up, then thousand to one if he would know you at all, ye are so altered, so different from what ye were, when ye were little ones. And as the words plainly imply, that there has a great change past upon our bodies since we were children, so before we can go to heaven, there must as great a change pass upon our souls. Our souls considered in a physical sense are still the same, there is to be no philosophical change wrought on them. But then, as for our temper, habit and conduct, we

must be so changed and altered, that those who knew us the other day, when in a state of sin, and before we knew Christ, and are acquainted with us now, must see such an alteration, that they may stand as much amazed at it, as a person at the alteration wrought on any person he has not seen for twenty years from his infancy.

2. But I think it proper to premise something farther, because this text is the grand strong-hold of Arminians, and others. They learn of the devil to bring texts to propagate bad principles: when the devil had a mind to tempt Jesus Christ, because Christ quoted scripture, therefore Satan did so too. And such persons, that their doctrine and bad principles may go down the better, would fain persuade unwary and unstable souls, that they are founded upon the word of God. Though the doctrine of original sin, is a doctrine written in such legible characters in the word of God, that he who runs may read it; and though, I think, everything without us, and everything within us, plainly proclaims that we are fallen creatures; though the very heathens, who had no other light, but the dim light of unassisted reason, complained of this, for they felt the wound, and discovered the disease, but were ignorant of the cause of it; yet there are too many persons of those who have been baptized in the name of Christ, that dare to speak against the doctrine of original sin, and are angry with those ill-natured ministers, who paint man in such black colors. Say they, "It cannot be that children come into the world with the guild of Adam's sin lying upon them." Why? Desire them to prove it from Scripture, and they will urge this very text, our Lord tells us, "Except ye be converted, and become as little children, ye shall not enter into the kingdom of heaven." Now their argument runs thus, "It is implied in the words of the text, that little children are innocent, and that they come into the world like a mere blank piece of white paper, otherwise our Lord must argue absurdly, for he could never pretend to say, that we must be converted, and be made like wicked creatures; that would be no conversion." But, my dear friends, this is to make Jesus Christ speak what he never intended, and what cannot be deduced from his words. That little children are guilty, I mean, that they are conceived and born in sin, is plain from the whole tenor of the book of God. David was a man after God's own heart, yet, says he, "I was conceived in sin." Jeremiah speaking of every one's heart, says, "the heart of man is deceitful and desperately wicked above all things." God's servants unanimously declare, (and Paul cites it from one of them) "that we are altogether now become abominable, altogether gone out of the way of original righteousness, there is not one of us that doeth good (by nature), no not one." And I appeal to any of you that are mothers and fathers, if ye do not discern original sin or corruption in your children, as soon as they come into the world; and as they grow up, if ye do not discover self-will, and an aversion to goodness. What is the reason your children are so averse to instruction, but because they bring enmity into the world with them, against a good and gracious God? So then, it is plain from scripture and fact, that children are born in sin, and consequently that they are children of wrath. And for my part, I think, that the death of every child is a plain proof of original sin; sickness and death came into the world by sin, and it seems not consistent with God's goodness and justice, to let a little child be sick or die, unless Adam's first sin was imputed to him. If any charge God with injustice for imputing Adam's sin to a little child, behold we have gotten a second Adam, to bring our children to him. Therefore, when our Lord says, "unless ye are converted, and become as little children," we are not to understand, as though our Lord would insinuate, that little children are perfectly innocent; but in a comparative, and as I shall show you by and by, in a rational sense. Little children are innocent, compare them with grown people; but take them as they are, and as they come into the world, they have hearts that are sensual, and minds which are carnal. And I mention this with the greatest concern, because I verily believe, unless parents are convinced of this, they will never take proper care of their children's education. If parents were convinced, that children's hearts were so bad as they are, you would never be fond of letting them go to balls, assemblies, and plays, the natural tendency of which is to debauch their minds, and make them the children of the devil. If parents were convinced of this, I believe they would pray more, when they bring their children to be baptized, and would not make it a mere matter of form. And I believe, if they really were convinced, that their children were conceived in sin, they would always put up that petition, before their children came into the world, which I have heard that a good woman always did put up, "Lord Jesus, let me never bear a child for hell or the devil." O! is it not to be feared, that thousands of children will appear, at the great day, before God, and in presence of angels and men will say, Father and mother, next to the wickedness of mine own heart, I owe my damnation to your bad education of me.

Having premised these two particulars, I now proceed to show in what sense we are really to understand the words, that we must be converted and become like little children. The Evangelist tell us, "that the disciples at this time came unto Jesus, saying, Who is the greatest in the kingdom of heaven?" These disciples had imbibed the common prevailing notion, that the Lord Jesus Christ was to be a temporal prince; they dreamed of nothing but being ministers of state, of sitting on Christ' right hand in his kingdom, and lording it over God's people; they thought themselves qualified for state offices, as generally ignorant people are apt to conceive of themselves. Well, say they, "Who is the greatest in the kingdom of heaven?" Which of us shall have the chief management of public affairs? A pretty question for a few poor fishermen, who scarcely knew how to drag their nets to shore, much less how to govern a kingdom. Our Lord, therefore, in the 2nd verse, to mortify them, calls a little child, and sets him in the midst of them. This action was as much as if our Lord had said, "Poor creatures! Your imaginations are very towering; you dispute who shall be greatest in the kingdom of heaven; I will make this little child preach to you, or I will preach to you by him. Verily I say unto you, (I who am truth itself, I know in what manner my subjects are to enter into my kingdom; I say unto you, ye are so far from being in a right temper for my kingdom, that) except ye be converted, and become as this little child, ye shall not enter into the kingdom of heaven, (unless ye are, comparatively speaking, as loose to the world, as loose to crowns, scepters, and kingdoms, and earthly things, as this poor little child I have in my hand) ye shall not enter into my kingdom." So that what our Lord is speaking of, is not the innocency of little children, if you consider the relation they stand in to God, and as they are in themselves, when brought into the world; but what our Lord means is, that as to ambition and lust after the world, we must in this sense become as little children. Is there never a little boy or girl in this congregation? Ask a poor little child, that can just speak, about a crown, scepter, or kingdom, the poor creature has no notion about it: give a little boy or girl a small thing to play with, it will leave the world to other people. Now in this sense we must be converted, and become as little children; that is, we must be as loose to the world, comparatively speaking, as a little child.

Do not mistake me, I am not going to persuade you to shut up your shops, or leave your business; I am not going to persuade you, that if ye will be Christians, ye must turn hermits, and retire out of the world; ye cannot leave your wicked hearts behind you, when you leave the world; for I find when I am alone, my wicked heart has followed me, go where I will. No, the religion of Jesus is a social religion. But though Jesus Christ does not call us to go out of the world, shut up our shops, and leave our children to be provided for by miracles; yet this must be said to the honor Christianity, if we are really converted, we shall be loose from the world. Though we are engaged in it, and are obliged to work for our children; though we are obliged to follow trades and merchandise, and to be serviceable to the commonwealth, yet if we are real Christians, we shall be loose to the world; though I will not pretend to say that all real Christians have attained to the same degree of spiritual-mindedness. This is the primary meaning of these words, that we must be converted and become as little children; nevertheless, I suppose the words are to be understood in other senses.

When our Lord says, we must be converted and become as little children, I suppose he means also, that we must be sensible of our weakness, comparatively speaking, as a little child. Every one looks upon a little child, as a poor weak creature; as one that ought to go to school and learn some new lesson every day; and as simple and artless; one without guile, having not learned the abominable art, called dissimulation. Now in all these senses, I believe we are to understand the words of the text.—Are little children sensible of their weakness? Must they be led by the hand? Must we take hold of them or they will fall? So, if we are converted, if the grace of God be really in our hearts, my dear friends, however we may have thought of ourselves once, whatever were our former high exalted imaginations; yet we shall now be sensible of our weakness; we shall no more say, "We are rich and increased with goods, and lack nothing;" we shall be inwardly poor; we shall feel "that we are poor, miserable, blind, and naked." And as a little child gives up its hand to be guided by a parent or a nurse, so those who are truly converted, and are real Christians, will give up the heart, their understandings, their wills, their affections, to be guided by the word, providence, and the Spirit of the Lord. Hence it is, that the Apostle, speaking of the sons of God, says, "As many as are led by the Spirit of God, they are (and to be sure he means they only are) the sons of God."

And as little children look upon themselves to be ignorant creatures, so those that are converted, do look upon themselves as ignorant too. Hence it is, that John, speaking to Christians, calls them little children; "I have written unto you, little children." And Christ's flock is called a little flock, not only because little in number, but also because those who are members of his flock, are indeed little in their own eyes. Hence that great man, that great apostle of the Gentiles, that spiritual father of so many thousands of souls, that man, who in the opinion of Dr. Goodwin, "fits nearest the God-man, the Lord Jesus Christ, in glory," that chosen vessel, the Apostle Paul, when he speaks of himself, says, "Unto me, who am less than the least of all saints, is this grace given, that I should preach among the Gentiles the unsearchable riches of Christ." Perhaps some of you, when you read these words, will be apt to think that Paul did not speak true, that he did not really feel what he said; because you judge Paul's heart by your own proud hearts: but the more ye get of the grace of God, and the more ye are partakers of the divine life, the more will ye see your own meanness and vileness, and be less in your own eyes. Hence it is, that Mr. Flavel, in his book called, *Husbandry Spiritualized*, compares young Christians to green corn; which before it is ripe, shoots up very high, but there is little solidity in it: whereas, an old Christian is like ripe corn; it doth not lift up its head so much, but then it is more weighty, and fit to be cut down, and put into the farmer's barn. Young Christians are also like little rivulets; ye know rivulets are shallow, yet make great noise; but an old Christian, he makes not much noise, he goes on sweetly, like a deep river sliding into the ocean.

And as a little child is looked upon as an harmless creature, and generally speaks true; so, if we are converted, and become as little children, we shall be guileless as well as harmless. What said the dear Redeemer when he saw Nathaniel? As though it was a rare sight he gazed upon, and would have others gaze upon it; "Behold an Israelite indeed:" Why so? "In whom is no guile." Do not mistake me; I am not saying, that Christians ought not to be prudent; they ought exceedingly to pray to God for prudence, otherwise they may follow the delusions of the devil, and by their imprudence give wrong touches to the ark of God. It was the lamentation of a great man, "God has given me many gifts, but God has not given me prudence." Therefore, when I say, a Christian must be guileless, I do not mean, he should expose himself, and lie open to every one's assault: we should pray for the wisdom of the serpent, though we shall generally learn this wisdom by our blunders and imprudence: and we must make some advance in Christianity, before we know our imprudence. A person really converted, can say, as it is reported of a philosopher, "I wish there was a window in my breast, that every one may see the uprightness of my heart and intentions:" And though there is too much of the old man in us, yet, if we are really converted, there will be in us no allowed guile, we shall be harmless. And that is the reason why the poor Christian is too often imposed upon; he judgeth other people by himself; having an honest heart, he thinks every one as honest as himself, and therefore is a prey to every one. I might enlarge upon each of these points, it is a copious and important truth; but I do not intend to multiply many marks and heads.

And therefore, as I have something to say by way of personal application, give me leave therefore, with the utmost tenderness, and at the same time with faithfulness, to call upon you, my dear friends. My text is introduced in an awful manner, "Verily I say unto you;" and what Jesus said then, he says now to you, to me, and to as many as sit under a preached gospel, and to as many as the Lord our God shall call. Let me exhort you to see whether ye are converted; whether such a great and almighty change has passed upon any of your souls. As I told you before, so I tell you again, ye all hope to go to heaven, and I pray God Almighty ye may be all there: when I see such a congregation as this, if my heart is in a proper frame, I feel myself ready to lay down my life, to be instrumental only to save one soul. It makes my heart bleed within me, it makes me sometimes most unwilling to preach, lest that word that I hope will do good, may increase the damnation of any, and perhaps of a great part of the auditory, through their own unbelief. Give me leave to deal faithfully with your souls. I have your dead warrant in my hand: Christ has said it, Jesus will stand to it, it is like the laws of the Medes and Persians, it altereth not. Hark, O man! Hark, O woman! He that hath ears to hear, let him hear what the Lord Jesus Christ says, "Verily I say unto you, except ye be converted, and become as little children, ye shall not enter into the kingdom of heaven." Though this is Saturday night, and ye are now preparing for the Sabbath, for what you know, you may yet never live to see the Sabbath. You have had awful proofs of this lately; a woman died but yesterday, a man died the day before, another was killed by something that fell from a house, and it may be in twenty-four hours more, many of you may be carried into an unalterable state. Now then, for God's sake, for your own souls sake, if ye have a mind to dwell with God, and cannot bear the thought of dwelling in everlasting burning, before I go any further, silently put up one prayer, or say Amen to the prayer I would put in your mouths; "Lord, search me and try me, Lord, examine my heart, and let my conscience speak; O let me know whether I am converted or not!" What say ye, my dear hearers? What say ye, my fellow-sinners? What say ye, my guilty brethren? Has God by his blessed Spirit wrought such a change in your hearts? I do not ask you, whether God has made you angels? That I know will never be; I only ask you, Whether ye have any well-grounded hope to think that God has made you new creatures in Christ Jesus? So renewed and changed your natures, that you can say, I humbly hope, that as to the habitual temper and tendency of my mind, that my heart is free from wickedness; I have a husband, I have a wife, I have also children, I keep a shop, I mind my business; but I love these creatures for God' sake, and do every thing for Christ: and if God was now to call me away, according to the habitual temper of my mind, I can say, Lord, I am ready; and however I love the creatures, I hope I can say, Whom have I in heaven but thee? Whom have I in heaven, O my God and my dear Redeemer, that I desire in comparison of thee? Can you thank God for the creatures, and say at the same time, these are not my Christ? I speak in plain language, you know my way of preaching: I do not want to play the orator, I do not want to be counted a scholar; I want to speak so as I may reach poor people's hearts. What say ye, my dear hearers? Are ye sensible of your weakness? Do ye feel that ye are poor, miserable, blind, and naked by nature? Do ye give up your hearts, your affections, your wills, your understanding to be guided by the Spirit of God, as a little child gives up its hand to be guided by its parent? Are ye little in your own eyes? Do ye think meanly of yourselves? And do you want to learn something new every day? I mention these marks, because I am apt to believe they are more adapted to a great many of your capacities. A great many of you have not that showing of affection ye sometimes had, therefore ye are for giving up all your evidences, and making way for the devil's coming into your heart. You are not brought up to the mount as ye used to be, therefore ye conclude ye have no grace at all. But if the Lord Jesus Christ has emptied thee, and humbled thee, if he is giving thee to se and know that thou art nothing; though thou are not growing upward, thou art growing downward; and though thou hast not so much joy, yet thy heart is emptying to be more abundantly replenished by and by. Can any of you follow me? Then, give God thanks, and take the comfort of it.

If thou art thus converted, and become a little child, I welcome thee, in the name of the Lord Jesus, into God's dear family; I welcome thee, in the name of the dear Redeemer, into the company of God's children. O ye dear souls, though the world sees nothing in you, though there be no outward difference between you and others, yet I look upon you in another light, even as so many kings sons and daughters: all hail! In the name of God, I wish every one of you joy from my soul, ye sons and daughters of the King of kings. Will not you henceforth exercise a child-like temper? Will not such a thought melt down your hearts, when I tell you, that the great God, who might have frowned you to hell for your secret sins, that nobody knew of but God and your own souls, and who might have damned you times without number, hath cast the mantle of his love over you; his voice hath been, Let that man, that woman live, for I have found a ransom. O will ye not cry out, Why me, Lord? Was King George to send for any of your children, and were you to hear they were to be his adopted sons, how highly honored would you think your children to be? What great condescension was it for Pharaoh's daughter to take up Moses, a poor child exposed in an ark of bulrushes, and bred him up for her child? But what is that happiness in comparison of thine, who was the other day a child of the devil, but now by converting grace art become a child of God? Are ye converted? Are ye become like little children? Then what must ye do? My dear hearers, be obedient to God, remember God is your father; and as every one of you must know what a dreadful cross it is to have a wicked, disobedient child; if ye do not want your children to be disobedient to you, for Christ's sake be not disobedient to your heavenly parent. If God be your father, obey him: if God be your father, serve him; love him with all your heart, love him with all your might, with all your soul, and with all your strength. If God be your father, fly from everything that may displease him; and walk worthy of that God, who has called you to his kingdom and glory. If ye are converted and become like little children, then behave as little children: they long for the breast, and with it will be contented. Are ye new-born babes? Then desire the sincere milk of the word, that ye may grow thereby. I do not want that Arminian husks should go down with you; ye are kings sons and daughters, and have a more refined taste; you must have the doctrines of grace; and blessed be God that you dwell in a country, where the sincere word is so plainly preached. Are ye children? Then grow in grace, and in the knowledge of your Lord and Savior Jesus Christ. Have any of you children that do not grow? Do not ye lament these children, and cry over them; do not ye say, my child will never be fit for anything in the world? Well, doth it grieve you to see a child that will not grow; how much must it grieve the heart of Christ to see you grow so little? Will ye be always children? Will ye be always learning the first principles of Christianity, and never press forward toward the mark, for the prize of the high calling of God in Christ Jesus?

God forbid. Let the language of your heart be, "Lord Jesus help me to grow, help me to learn more, learn me to live so as my progress may be known to all!"

Are ye God's children? Are ye converted, and become like little children? Then deal with God as your little children do with you; as soon as ever they want any thing, or if any body hurt them, I appeal to yourselves if they do not directly run to their parent. Well, are ye God's children? Doth the devil trouble you? Doth the world trouble you? Go tell your father of it, go directly and complain to God. Perhaps you may say, I cannot utter fine words: but do any of you expect fine words from your children? If they come crying, and can speak but half words, do not your hearts yearn over them? And has not God unspeakably more pity to you? If ye can only make signs to him; "As a father pitieth his children, so will the Lord pity them that fear him." I pray you therefore be gold with your Father, saying, "Abba, Father," Satan troubles me, the world troubles me, my own mother's children are angry with me; heavenly Father, plead my cause! The Lord will then speak for you some way or other.

Are ye converted, and become as little children, have ye entered into God's family? Then assure yourselves, that your heavenly father will chasten you now and then: "for what son is there whom the father chasteneth not: if ye are without chastisement, of which all are partakers, then are ye bastards and not sons." It is recorded of bishop Latimer, that in the house where he came to lodge, he overheard the master of the house say, I thank God I never had a cross in my life: O said he, then I will not stay here. I believe there is not a child of God, when in a good frame, but has prayed for great humility; they have prayed for great faith, they have prayed for great love, they have prayed for all the graces of the Spirit: Do ye know, when ye put us these prayers, that ye did also say, Lord send us great trials: for how is it possible to know ye have great faith, humility and love, unless God put you into great trials, that ye may know whether ye have them or not. I mention this, because a great many of the children of God (I am sure it has been a temptation to me many times, when I have been under God's smarting rod) when they have great trials, think God is giving them over. If therefore ye are God's children; if ye are converted and become as little children; do not expect that God will be like a foolish parent; no, he is a jealous God, he loves his child too well to spare his rod. How did he correct Miriam? How did he correct Moses? How hath God in all ages corrected his dearest children? Therefore if ye are converted, and become as little children, if God hath taken away a child, or your substance, if God suffers friends to forsake you, and if you are forsaken as it were both by God and man, say, Lord I thank thee! I am a perverse child, or God would not strike me so often and so hard. Do not blame your heavenly Father, but blame yourselves; he is a loving God, and a tender Father, "he is afflicted in all our afflictions:" therefore when God spake to Moses, he spake out of the bush, as much as to say, "Moses, this bush represents my people; as this bush is burning with fire, so are my children to burn with affliction; but I am in the bush; if the bush burns, I will burn with it, I will be with them in the furnace, I will be with them in the water, and though the water come over them, it shall not overflow them."

Are ye God's children? Are ye converted and become as little children? Then will ye not long to go home and see your Father? O happy they that have gotten home before you; happy they that are up yonder, happy they who have ascended above this field of conflict. I know not what you may think of it, but since I heard that some, whose hearts God was pleased to work upon, are gone to glory, I am sometimes filled with grief, that God is not pleased to let me go home too. How can you see so much coldness among God's people? How can ye see God's people like the moon, waxing and waning? Who can but desire to be forever with the Lord? Thanks be to God, the time is soon coming; thanks be to God, he will come and will not tarry. Do not be impatient, God in his own time will fetch you home. And though ye may be brought to short allowance now, though some of you may be narrow in your circumstances, yet do not repine; a God, and the gospel of Christ, with brown bread, are great riches. In thy Father's house there is bread enough and to spare; though thou are now tormented, yet by and by thou shalt be comforted; the angels will look upon it as an honor to convey thee to Abraham's bosom, though thou are but a Lazarus here. By the frame of my heart, I am much inclined to speak comfortably to God's people.

But I only mention one thing more, and that is, if ye are converted, and become as little children, then for God's sake take care of doing what children often do; they are too apt to quarrel one with another. O love one another; "he that dwells in love dwells in God, and God in him." Joseph knew that his brethren were in danger of falling out, therefore when he left them, says he, "fall not out by the way." Ye are all children of the same Father, ye are all going to the same place; why should ye differ? The world has enough against us, the devil has enough against us, without our quarreling with each other; O walk in love. If I could preach no more, if I was not able to hold out to the end of my sermon, I would say as John did, when he was grown old and could not preach, "Little children, love one another:" if ye are God's children, then love one another. There is nothing grieves me more, than the differences amongst God's people. O hasten that time, when we shall either go to heaven, or never quarrel any more!

Would to God I could speak to all of you in this comfortable language; but my master tells me, I must "not give that which is holy to dogs, I must not cast pearls before swine;" therefore, though I have been speaking comfortably, yet what I have been saying, especially in this latter part of the discourse, belongs to children; it is children's bread, it belongs to God's people. If any of you are graceless, Christless, unconverted creatures, I charge you not to touch it, I fence it in the name of God; here is a flaming sword turning every way to keep you from this bread of life, till ye are turned to Jesus Christ. And therefore, as I suppose many of you are unconverted, and graceless, go home! And away to your closets, and down with your stubborn hearts before God; if ye have not done it before, let this be the night. Or, do not stay till ye go home; begin now, while standing here; pray to God, and let the language of thy heart be, Lord convert me! Lord make me a little child, Lord Jesus let me not be banished from thy kingdom! My dear friends, there is a great deal more implied in the words, than is expressed: when Christ says, "Ye shall not enter into the kingdom of heaven," it is as much to say, "ye shall certainly go to hell, ye shall certainly be damned, and dwell in the blackness of darkness for ever, ye shall go where the worm dies not, and where the fire is not quenched." The Lord God impress it upon your souls! May an arrow (as one lately wrote me in a letter) dipped in the blood of Christ, reach every unconverted sinner's heart! May God fulfill the text to every one of your souls! It is he alone that can do it. If ye confess your sins, and leave them, and lay hold on the Lord Jesus Christ, the Spirit of God shall be given you; if you will go and say, turn me, O my God! Thou knowest not, O man, what the return of God may be to thee. Did I think that preaching would be to the purpose, did I think that arguments would induce you to come, I would continue my discourse till midnight. And however some of you may hate me without a cause, would to God every one in this congregation was as much concerned for himself, as at present (blessed be God) I feel myself concerned for him. O that my head were waters, O that mine eyes were a fountain of tears, that I might weep over an unconverted, graceless, wicked, and adulterous generation. Precious souls, for God's sake think what will become of you when ye die, if you die without being converted; if ye go hence without the wedding garment, God will strike you speechless, and ye shall be banished from his presence for ever and ever. I know ye cannot dwell with everlasting burnings; behold then I show you a way of escape; Jesus is the way, Jesus is the truth, the Lord Jesus Christ is the resurrection and the live. It is his Spirit must convert you, come to Christ, and ye shall have it; and may God for Christ's sake give it to you all, and convert you, that we may all meet, never to part again, in his heavenly kingdom; even so Lord Jesus, Amen and Amen.

24. What Think Ye of Christ?

Matthew 22:42—"What think ye of Christ?"

When it pleased the eternal Son of God to tabernacle among us, and preach the glad tidings of salvation to a fallen world, different opinions were entertained by different parties concerning him. As to his person, some said he was Moses; others that he was Elias, Jeremias, or one of the ancient prophets; few acknowledged him to be what he really was, God blessed for evermore. And as to his doctrine, though the common people, being free from prejudice, were persuaded of the heavenly tendency of his going about to do good, and for the generality, heard him gladly, and said he was a good man; yet the envious, worldly-minded, self-righteous governors and teachers of the Jewish church, being grieved at his success on the one hand, and unable (having never been taught of God) to understand the purity of his doctrine, on the other; notwithstanding our Lord spake as never man spake, and did such miracles which no man could possibly do, unless God was with him; yet they not only were so infatuated, as to say, that he deceived the people; but also were so blasphemous as to affirm, that he was in league with the devil himself, and cast out devils by Beeluzbul, the prince of devils. Nay, our Lord's own brethren and kinsmen, according to the flesh, were so blinded by prejudices and unbelief, that on a certain day; when he went out to teach the multitudes in the fields, they sent to take hold of him, urging this as a reason for their conduct, "That he was besides himself."

Thus was the King and the Lord of glory judged by man's judgment, when manifest in flesh: far be it from any of his ministers to expect better treatment. No, if we come in the spirit and power of our Master, in this, as in every other part of his sufferings, we must follow his steps. The like reproaches which were cast on him, will be thrown on us also. Those that received our Lord and his doctrine, will receive and hear us for his name's sake. The poor, blessed be God, as our present meeting abundantly testifies, receive the gospel, and the common people hear us gladly; whilst those who are sitting in Moses' chair, and love to wear long robes, being ignorant of the righteousness which is of God by faith in Christ Jesus, and having never felt the power of God upon their hearts, will be continually crying our against us, as madmen, deceivers of the people, and as acting under the influence of evil spirits.

But he is unworthy the name of a minister of the gospel of peace, who is unwilling, not only to have his name cast out as evil, but also to die for the truths of the Lord Jesus. It is the character of hirelings and false prophets, who care not for the sheep, to have all men speak well of them. "Blessed are you, (says our Lord to his first apostles, and in them to all succeeding ministers) when men speak all manner of evil against you falsely for my name's sake." And indeed it is impossible but such offenses must come; for men will always judge of others, according to the principles from which they act themselves. And if they care not to yield obedience to the doctrines which we deliver, they must necessarily, in self-defense, speak against the preachers, lest they should be asked that question, which the Pharisees of old feared to have retorted on them, if they confessed that John was a prophet, "Why then did you not believe on him?" In all such cases, we have nothing to do but to search our own hearts, and if we can assure our consciences, before God, that we act with a single eye to his glory, we are cheerfully to go on in our work, and not in the least to regard what men or devils can say against, or do unto us.

But to return. You have heard what various thoughts there were concerning Jesus Christ, whilst here on earth; nor is he otherwise treated, even now he is exalted to sit down at the right hand of his Father in heaven. A stranger to Christianity, were he to hear, that we all profess to hold one Lord, would naturally infer, that we all thought and spoke one and the same thing about him. But alas! to our shame be it mentioned, though Christ be not divided in himself, yet professors are sadly divided in their thoughts about him; and that not only as to the circumstances of his religion, but also of those essential truths which must necessarily be believed and received by us, if ever we hope to be heirs of eternal salvation.

Some, and I fear a multitude which no man can easily number, there are amongst us, who call themselves Christians, and yet seldom or never seriously think of Jesus Christ at all. They can think of their shops and their farms, their plays, their balls, their assemblies, and horse-races (entertainments which directly tend to exclude religion out of the world); but as for Christ, the author and finisher of faith, the Lord who has bought poor sinners with his precious blood, and who is the only thing worth thinking of, alas! he is not in all, or at most in very few of their thoughts. But believe me, O ye earthly, sensual, carnally-minded professors, however little you may think of Christ now, or however industriously you may strive to keep him out of your thoughts, by pursuing the lust of the eye, the lust of the flesh, and the pride of life, yet there is a time coming, when you will wish you had thought of Christ more, and of your profits and pleasures less. For the gay, the polite, the rich also must die as well as others, and leave their pomps and vanities, and all their wealth behind them. And O! what thoughts will you entertain concerning Jesus Christ, in that hour?

But I must not purpose these reflections: they would carry me too far from the main design of this discourse, which is to show, what those who are truly desirous to know how to worship God in spirit and in truth, ought to think concerning Jesus Christ, whom God hath sent to be the end of the law for righteousness to all them that shall believe.

I trust, my brethren, you are more noble than to think me too strict or scrupulous, in thus attempting to regulate your thoughts about Jesus Christ: for by our thoughts, as well as our words and actions, are we to be judged at the great day. And in vain do we hope to believe in, or worship Christ aright, unless our principles, on which our faith and practice are founded, are agreeable to the form of sound words delivered to us in the scriptures of truth.

Besides, many deceivers are gone abroad into the world. Mere heathen morality, and not Jesus Christ, is preached in most of our churches. And how should people think rightly of Christ, of whom they have scarcely heard? Bear with me a little then, whilst, to inform your consciences, I ask you a few questions concerning Jesus Christ. For there is no other name given under heaven, whereby we can be saved, but his.

First, What think you about the person of Christ? "Whose Son is he?" This is the question our Lord put to the Pharisees in the words following the text; and never was it more necessary to repeat this question than in these last days. For numbers that are called after the name of Christ, and I fear, many that pretend to preach him, are so far advanced in the blasphemous chair, as openly to deny his being really, truly, and properly God. But no one that ever was partaker of his Spirit, will speak thus lightly of him. No; if they are asked, as Peter and his brethren were, "But whom say ye that I am?" they will reply without hesitation, "Thou art Christ the Son of the ever-living God." For the confession of our Lord's divinity, is the rock upon which he builds his church. Was it possible to take this away, the gates of hell would quickly prevail against it. My brethren, if Jesus Christ be not very God of very God, I would never preach the gospel of Christ again. For it would not be gospel; it would be only a system of moral ethics. Seneca, Cicero, or any of the Gentile philosophers, would be as good a Savior as Jesus of Nazareth. It is the divinity of our Lord that gives a sanction to his death, and makes him such a high-priest as became us, one who by the infinite mercies of his suffering could make a full, perfect sufficient sacrifice, satisfaction and oblation to infinitely offended justice. And whatsoever minister of the church of England, makes use of her forms, and eats of her bread, and yes holds not this doctrine (as I fear too many such are crept in amongst us) such a one belongs only to the synagogue of Satan. He is not a child or minister of God: no; he is a wolf in sheep's clothing; he is a child and minister of that wicked one the devil.

Many will think these hard sayings; but I think it no breach of charity to affirm, that an Arian or Socinian cannot be a Christian. The one would make us believe Jesus Christ is only a created God, which is a self-contradiction: and the other would have us look on him only as a good man; and instead of owning his death to be an atonement for the sins of the world, would persuade us, that Christ died only to seal the truth of hid doctrine with his blood. But if Jesus Christ be no more than a mere man, if he be not truly God, he was the vilest sinner that ever appeared in the world. For he accepted of divine adoration from the man who had been born blind, as we read John 9:38, "And he said, Lord I believe, and he worshipped him." Besides, if Christ be not properly God, our faith is vain, we are yet in our sins: for no created being, though of the highest order, could possibly merit anything at God's hands; it was our Lord's divinity, that alone qualified him to take away the sins of the world; and therefore we hear St. John pronouncing so positively, that "the Word (Jesus Christ) was not only with God, but was God." For the like reason, St. Paul says, "that he was in the form of God: That in him dwelt all the fullness of the godhead bodily." Nay, Jesus Christ assumed the title which God gave to himself, when he sent Moses to deliver his people Israel. "Before Abraham was, I AM." And again, "I and my father are one." Which last words, though our modern infidels would evade and wrest, as they do other scriptures, to their own damnation, yet it is evident that the Jews understood our Lord, when he spoke thus, as making himself equal with God; otherwise, why did they stone him as a blasphemer? And now, why should it be thought a breach of charity, to affirm, that those who deny the divinity of Jesus Christ, in the strictest sense of the word, cannot be Christians? For they are greater infidels than the devils themselves, who confessed that they knew who he was, "even the holy one of God." They not only believe, but, which is more than the unbelievers of this generation do, they tremble. And was it possible for arch-heretics, to be released from their chains of darkness, under which (unless they altered their principles before they died) they are now reserved to the judgment of the great day, I am persuaded they would inform us, how hell had convinced them of the divinity of Jesus Christ, and that they would advise their followers to abhor their principles, lest they should come into the same place, and thereby increase each others torments.

But, *Secondly*, What think you of the manhood or incarnation of Jesus Christ? For Christ was not only God, but he was God and man in one person. Thus runs the text and context, "When the Pharisees were gathered together, Jesus asked them, saying, What think ye of Christ? Whose Son is he? They say unto him, The Son of David. How then, says our divine master, does David in spirit call him Lord?" From which passage it is evident, that we do not think rightly of the person of Jesus Christ, unless we believe him to be perfect God and perfect man, or a reasonable soul and human flesh subsisting.

For it is on this account that he is called Christ, or the anointed one, who through his own voluntary offer was set apart by the father, and strengthened and qualified by the anointing or communication of the Holy Ghost, to be a mediator between Him and offending man.

The reason why the Son of God took upon him our nature, was, the fall of our first parents. I hope there is no one present so atheistical, as to think, that man made himself; no, it was God that made us, and not we ourselves. And I would willingly think, that no one is so blasphemous as to suppose, that if God did make us, he made us such creatures as we now find ourselves to be. For this would be giving God's word the lie, which tells us, that "in the image of God (not in the image which we now bear on our souls) made he man." As God made man, so God made him perfect. He placed him in the garden of Eden, and condescended to enter into a covenant with him, promising him eternal life, upon condition of unsinning obedience; and threatening eternal death, if he broke his law, and did eat the forbidden fruit.

Man did eat; and herein acting as our representative, thereby involved both himself and us in that curse, which God, the righteous judge, had said should be the consequence of his disobedience. But here begins that mystery of godliness, God manifested in the flesh. For (sing, O heavens, and rejoice, O earth!) the eternal Father, foreseeing how Satan would bruise the heel of man, had in his eternal counsel provided a means whereby he might bruise that accursed Serpent's head. Man is permitted to fall, and become subject to death; but Jesus, the only begotten Son of God, begotten of the Father before all worlds, Light of light, very God of very God, offers to die to make an atonement for his transgression, and to fulfill all righteousness in his stead. And because it was impossible for him to do this as he was God, and yet since man had offended, it was necessary it should be done in the person of man; rather than we should perish, this everlasting God, this Prince of Peace, this Ancient of Days, in the fullness of time, had a body prepared for him by the Holy Ghost, and became an infant. In this body he performed a complete obedience to the law of God; whereby he, in our stead, fulfilled the covenant of works, and at last became subject to death, even death upon the cross; that as God he might satisfy, as man he might obey and suffer; and being God and man in one person, might once more procure a union between God and our souls.

And now, What think you of this love of Christ? Do not you think it was wondrous great? Especially when you consider, that we were Christ's bitter enemies, and that he would have been infinitely happy in himself, notwithstanding we had perished forever. Whatever you may think of it, I know the blessed angels, who are not so much concerned in this mystery of godliness as we, think most highly of it. They do, they will desire to look into, and admire it, through all eternity. Why, why O ye sinners, will you not think of this love of Christ? Surely it must melt down the most hardened heart. Whilst I am speaking, the thought of this infinite and condescending love fires and warms my soul. I could dwell on it for ever. But it is expedient for you, that I should ask you another question concerning Jesus Christ.

Thirdly, What think you about being justified by Christ? I believe I can answer for some of you; for many, I fear, think to be justified or looked upon as righteous in God's sight, without Jesus Christ. But such will find themselves dreadfully mistaken; for out of Christ, "God is a consuming fire." Others satisfy themselves, with believing that Christ was God and man, and that he came into the world to save sinners in general; whereas, their chief concern ought to be, how they may be assured that Jesus Christ came into the world to save them in particular. "The life that I now live in the flesh, (says the Apostle) is by faith of the Son of God, who loved me, and gave himself for me." Observe, *for me*: it is this immediate application of Jesus Christ to our own hearts; and that they can be justified in God's sight, only in or through him: but then they make him only in part a savior. They are for doing what they can themselves, and then Jesus Christ is to make up the deficiencies of their righteousness. This is the sum and substance of our modern divinity. And was it possible for me to know the thoughts of most that hear me this day, I believe they would tell me, this was the scheme they had laid, and perhaps depended on for some years, for their eternal salvation. Is it not then high time, my brethren, for you to entertain quite different thoughts concerning justification by Jesus Christ? For if you think thus, you are in the case of those unhappy Jews, who went about to establish their own righteousness, and would not submit to, and consequently missed of that righteousness which is of God by faith in Christ Jesus our Lord. What think you then, if I tell you, that you are to be justified freely through faith in Jesus Christ, without any regard to any work or fitness foreseen in us at all? For salvation is the free gift of God, I know no fitness in man, but a fitness to be cast into the lake of fire and brimstone for ever. Our righteousnesses, in God's sight, are but as filthy rags; he cannot away with them. Our holiness, if we have any, is not the cause, but the effect of our justification in God's sight. "We love God, because he first loved us." We must not come to God as the proud Pharisee did, bringing in as it were a reckoning of our services; we must come in the temper and language of the poor Publican, smiting upon our breasts, and saying, "God be merciful to me a sinner;" for Jesus Christ justifies us whilst we are ungodly. He came not to call the righteous, but sinners to repentance. The poor in spirit only, they who are willing to go out of themselves, and rely wholly on the righteousness of another, are so blessed as to be members of his kingdom. The righteousness, the whole righteousness of Jesus Christ, is to be imputed to us, instead of our own: "or we are not under the law, but under grace; and to as many as walk after this rule, peace be on them;" for they, and they only are the true Israel of God. In the great work of man" redemption, boasting is entirely excluded; which could not be, if only one of our works was to be joined with the merits of Christ. Our salvation is all of God, from the beginning to the end; it is not of works, lest any man should boast; man has no hand in it: it is Christ who is to be made to us of God the Father, wisdom, righteousness, sanctification, and eternal redemption. His active as well as his passive obedience, is to be applied to poor sinners. He has fulfilled all righteousness in our stead, that we might become the righteousness of God in him. All we have to do, is to lay hold on this righteousness by faith; and the very moment we do apprehend it by a lively faith, that very moment we may be assured, that the blood of Jesus Christ has cleansed us from all sin. "For the promise is to us and to our children, and to as many as the Lord our God shall call." If we and our whole houses believe, we shall be saved as well as the jailer and his house; for the righteousness of Jesus Christ is an everlasting, as well as a perfect righteousness. It is as effectual to all who believe in him now, as formerly; and so it will be, till time shall be no more. Search the scriptures, as the Bereans did, and see whether these things are not so. Search St. Paul's epistles to the Romans and Galatians, and there you will find this doctrine so plainly taught you, that unless you have eyes and see not, he that runs may read. Search the Eleventh Article of our Church: "We are accounted righteous before God, only for the merits of our Lord and Savior Jesus Christ by faith, and not for our own works or deservings."

This doctrine of our free justification by faith in Christ Jesus, however censured and evil spoken of by our present Masters of Israel, was highly esteemed by our wise fore-fathers; for in the subsequent words of the aforementioned article, it is called a most *wholesome doctrine*, and very full of comfort; and so it is to all that are weary and heavy laden, and are truly willing to find rest in Jesus Christ.

This is gospel, this is glad tidings of great joy to all that feel themselves poor, lost, undone, damned sinners. "Ho, every one that thirsteth, come unto the waters of life, and drink freely; come and buy without money and without price." Behold a fountain opened in your Savior's side, for sin and for all uncleanness. "Look unto him whom you have pierced;" look unto him by faith, and verily you shall be saved, though you came here only to ridicule and blaspheme, and never thought of God or of Christ before.

Not that you must think God will save you because, or on account of your faith; for faith is a work, and then you would be justified for your works; but when I tell you, we are to be justified by faith, I mean that faith is the instrument whereby the sinner applies or brings home the redemption of Jesus Christ to his heart. And to whomsoever God gives such a faith, (for it is the free gift of God) he may lift up his head with boldness, he need not fear; he is a spiritual son of our spiritual David; he is passed from death to life, he shall never come into condemnation. This is the gospel which we preach. If any man or angel preach any other gospel, than this of our being freely justified through faith in Christ Jesus, we have the authority of the greatest Apostle, to pronounce him accursed.

And now, my brethren, what think you of this foolishness of preaching? To you that have tasted the good word of life, who have been enlightened to see the riches of God's free grace in Christ Jesus, I am persuaded it is precious, and has distilled like the dew into your souls. And O that all were like-minded! But I am afraid, numbers are ready to go away contradicting and blaspheming. Tell me, are there not many of you saying within yourselves, "This is a licentious doctrine; this preacher is opening a door for encouragement in sin." But this does not surprise me at all, it is a stale, antiquated objection, as old as the doctrine of justification itself; and (which by the way is not much to the credit of those who urge it now) it was made by an infidel. St. Paul, in his epistle to the Romans, after he had, in the first five chapters, demonstrably proved the doctrine of justification by faith alone; in the sixth, brings in an unbeliever saying, "Shall we continue in sin then, that grace may abound?" But as he rejected such an inference with a "God forbid!" so do I: for the faith which we preach, is not a dead speculative faith, an assenting to things credible, as credible, as it is commonly defined: it is not a faith of the head only, but a faith of the heart. It is a living principle wrought in the soul, by the Spirit of the ever-living God, convincing the sinner of his lost, undone condition by nature; enabling him to apply and lay hold on the perfect righteousness of Jesus Christ, freely offered him in the gospel, and continually exciting him, out of a principle of love and gratitude, to show forth that faith, by abounding in every good word and work. This is the sum and substance of the doctrine that has been delivered. And if this be a licentious doctrine, judge ye. No, my brethren, this is not destroying, but teaching you how to do good works, from a proper principle. For to use the words of our Church in another of her Articles, "Works done before the grace of Christ, and the inspiration of the Spirit, are not pleasant to God, forasmuch as they spring not of faith in Jesus Christ; rather, for that they are not done as God has willed and commanded them to be done, we doubt not but they have the nature of sin." So that they who bid you do, and then live, are just as wise as those who would persuade you to build a beautiful magnificent house, without laying a foundation.

It is true, the doctrine of our free justification by faith in Christ Jesus, like other gospel truths, may and will be abused by men of corrupt minds, reprobates concerning the faith; but they who receive the truth of God in the love if it, will always be showing their faith by their works. For this reason, St. Paul, after he had told the Ephesians, "By grace they were saved through faith, not of works, lest any man should boast," immediately adds, "For we are his workmanship, created in Christ Jesus unto good works." And in his epistle to Titus, having given him directions to tell the people they were justified by grace, directly subjoins, Titus 3:8, "I will that you affirm constantly, that they who have believed in God might be careful to maintain good works." Agreeable to this, we are told in our Twelfth Article, "That albeit good works, which are the fruits of faith, and follow after justification, cannot put away our sins, and endure the severity of God's judgment; yet are they pleasing and acceptable to God in Christ; and do spring necessarily out of a true and lively faith, insomuch, that a lively faith may be as evidently known by them, as a tree discerned by the fruit."

What would I give, that this Article was duly understood and preached by all that have subscribed to it! The ark of the Lord would not then be driven into the wilderness, nor would so many persons dissent from the Church of England. For I am fully persuaded, that it is not so much on account of rites and ceremonies, as our not preaching the truth as it is in Jesus, that so many have been obliged to go and seek for food elsewhere. Did not we fall from our established doctrines, few, comparatively speaking, would fall from the Established Church. Where Christ is preached, though it be in a church or on a common, dissenters of all denominations have, and do must freely come. But if our clergy will preach only the law, and not show the way of salvation by faith in Christ, the charge of schism at the day of judgment, I fear, will chiefly lie at their door. The true sheep of Christ know the voice of Christ's true shepherds, and strangers they will not hear.

Observe, my dear brethren, the words of the Article, "Good works are the fruits of faith, and follow after justification." How then can they precede, or be any way the cause of it? Our persons must be justified, before our performances can be accepted. God had respect to Abel before he had respect to his offering; and therefore the righteousness of Jesus Christ must be freely imputed to, and apprehended by us through faith, before we can offer an acceptable sacrifice to God: for out of Christ, as I hinted before, God is a consuming fire: and whatsoever is not of faith in Christ, is sin.

That people mistake the doctrine of free justification, I believe, is partly owing to their not rightly considering the different persons to whom St. Paul and St. James wrote in their epistles; as also the different kind of justification each of them writes about. The former affects in line upon line, argument upon argument, "That we are justified by faith alone:" The latter put this question, "Was not Abraham justified by works?" From whence many, not considering the different views of these holy men, and the different persons they wrote to, have blended and joined faith and works, in order to justify us in the sight of God. But this is a capital mistake; for St. Paul was writing to the Jewish proselytes, who sought righteousness by the works, not of the ceremonial only, but of the moral law. In contradistinction to that, he tells them, they were to look for justification in God's sight, only by the perfect righteousness of Jesus Christ apprehended by faith. St. James had a different set of people to deal with; such who abused the doctrines of free justification, and thought they should be saved (as numbers among us do now) upon their barely professing to believe on Jesus Christ. These the holy Apostle endeavors wisely to convince, that such a faith was only a dead and false faith; and therefore, it behooved all who would be blessed with faithful Abraham, to show forth their faith by their works, as he did. "For was not Abraham justified by works?" Did he not prove that his faith was a true justifying faith, by its being productive of good works? From whence it is plain, that St. James is talking of a declarative justification before men; show me, demonstrate, evidence to me, that thou hast a true faith, by thy works. Whereas, St. Paul is talking only of our being justified in the sight of God; and thus he proves, that Abraham, as we also are to be, was justified before ever the moral or ceremonial law was given to the Jews, for it is written, "Abraham believed in the Lord, and it was accounted to him for righteousness."

Take the substance of what has been said on this head, in the few following words. Every man that is saved, is justified three ways: *First, meritoriously,* by the death of

Jesus Christ: "It is the blood of Jesus Christ alone that cleanses us from all sin." *Secondly, instrumentally*, by faith; faith is the means or instrument whereby the merits of Jesus Christ are applied to the sinner's heart: "Ye are all the children of God by faith in Christ Jesus." *Thirdly*, we are justified *declaratively*; namely, by good works; good works declare and prove to the world, that our faith is a true saving faith. "Was not Abraham justified by works?" And again, "Show me thy faith by thy works."

It may not be improper to illustrate this doctrine by an example or two. I suppose no one will pretend to say, that there was any fitness for salvation in Zaccheus the publican, when he came to see Jesus out of no better principle, than that whereby perhaps thousands are led to hear me preach; I mean, curiosity: but Jesus Christ prevented and called him by his free grace, and sweetly, but irresistibly inclined him to obey that call; as, I pray God, he may influence all you that come only to see who the preacher is. Zaccheus received our Lord joyfully into his house, and at the same time by faith received him into his heart; Zaccheus was then freely justified in the sight of God. But behold the immediate fruits of that justification! He stands forth in the midst and as before he had believed in his heart, he now makes confession with his mouth to salvation: "Behold, Lord, the half of my goods I give unto the poor; and if I have taken any thing from any man by false accusation, I restore him four-fold." And thus it will be with thee, O believer, as soon as ever God's dear Son is revealed in thee by a living faith; thou wilt have no rest in thy spirit, till out of love and gratitude for what God has done for thy soul, thou showest forth thy faith by thy works.

Again, I suppose every body will grant there was no fitness for salvation in the persecutor Saul; no more than there is in those persecuting zealots of these last days, who are already breathing out threatenings, and, if in their power, would breathe out slaughter also, against the disciples of the Lord.

Now our Lord, we know, freely prevented him by his grace, (and O that he would thus effectually call the persecutors of this generation) and by a light from heaven struck him to the ground. At the same time, by his Spirit, he pricked him to the heart, convinced him of sin, and caused him to cry out, "Who art thou, Lord?" Christ replies, "I am Jesus whom thou persecutest." Faith then was instantaneously given to him, and behold, immediately Saul cries out, "Lord, what wouldst thou have me to do?" And so will every poor soul that believes on the Lord Jesus with his whole heart. He will be always asking, Lord, what shall I do for thee? Lord, what wouldst thou have me to do? Not to justify himself, but only to evidence the sincerity of his love and thankfulness to his all-merciful High-priest, for plucking him as a firebrand out of the fire.

Perhaps many self-righteous persons amongst you, may flatter yourselves, that you are not so wicked as either Zaccheus or Saul was, and consequently there is a greater fitness for salvation in you than in them. But if you think thus, indeed you think more highly of yourselves than you ought to think: for by nature we are all alike, all equally fallen short of the glory of God, all equally dead in trespasses and sins, and there needs the same almighty power to be exerted in converting any one of the most sober, good-natured, moral persons here present, as there was in converting the publican Zaccheus, or that notorious persecutor Saul. And was it possible for you to ascend into the highest heaven, and to inquire of the spirits of just men made perfect, I am persuaded they would tell you this doctrine is from God. But we have a more sure word of prophecy, to which we do well to give heed, as unto a light shining in a dark place. My brethren, the word is nigh you; search the scriptures; beg of God to make you willing to be saved in this day of his power; for it is not flesh and blood, but the Spirit of Jesus Christ, that alone can reveal these things unto you.

Fourthly and *Lastly*, What think you of Jesus Christ being formed within you? For whom Christ justifies, them he also sanctifies. Although he finds, yet he does not leave us unholy. A true Christian may not so properly be said to live, as Jesus Christ to live in him. For they only that are led by the Spirit of Christ, are the true sons of God.

As I observed before, so I tell you again, the faith which we preach is not a dead, but a lively active faith wrought in the soul, working a thorough change, by the power of the Holy Ghost, in the whole man; and unless Christ be thus in you, notwithstanding you may be orthodox as to the foregoing principles, notwithstanding you may have good desires, and attend constantly on the means of grace; yet, in St. Paul's opinion, you are out of a state of salvation. "Know you not, (says that Apostle to the Corinthians, a church famous for its gifts above any church under heaven) that Christ is in you, (by his Spirit) unless you are reprobates?"

For Christ came not only to save us from the guilt, but from the power of our sins; till he has done this, however he may be a Savior to others, we can have no assurance of well-grounded hope, that he has saved us; for it is by receiving his blessed Spirit into our hearts, and feeling him witnessing with our spirits, that we are the sons of God, that we can be certified of our being sealed to the day of redemption.

This is a great mystery; but I speak of Christ and the new-birth. Marvel not at my asking you, what you think about Christ being formed within you? For either God must change his nature, or we ours. For as in Adam we all have spiritually died, so all that are effectually saved by Christ, must in Christ be spiritually made alive. His only end in and rising again, and interceding for us now in heaven, is to redeem us from the misery of our fallen nature, and, by the operation of his blessed Spirit, to make us meet to be partakers of the heavenly inheritance with the saints in light. None but those that thus are changed by his grace here, shall appear with him in glory hereafter.

Examine yourselves, therefore, my brethren, whether you are in the faith; prove yourselves; and think it not sufficient to say in your creed, I believe in Jesus Christ; many say so, who do not believe, who are reprobates, and yet in a state of death. You take God's name in vain, when you call him Father, and your prayers are turned into sin, unless you believe in Christ, so as to have your life hid with him in God, and to receive life and nourishment from him, as branches do from the vine.

I know, indeed, the men of this generation deny there is any such thing as feeling Christ within them; but alas! to what a dreadful condition would such reduce us, even to the state of the abandoned heathen, who, St. Paul tells us, "were past feeling." The Apostle prays, that the Ephesians may abound in all knowledge and spiritual understanding, or as it might be rendered, spiritual sensation. And in the office for the visitation of the sick, the minister prays, that the Lord may make the sick person know and feel, that there is no other name under heaven given unto men, in whom and through whom they may receive health and salvation, but only the name of our Lord Jesus. For there is a spiritual, as well as a corporeal feeling; and though this is not communicated to us in a sensible manner, as outward objects affect our senses, yet it is as real as any sensible or visible sensation, and may be as truly felt and discerned by the soul, as any impression from without can be felt by the body. All who are born again of God, know that I lie not.

What think you, Sirs, did Naaman feel, when he was cured of his leprosy? Did the woman feel virtue coming out of Jesus Christ, when she touched the hem of his garment, and was cured of her bloody issue? So surely mayst thou feel, O believer, when Jesus Christ dwelleth in thy heart. I pray God to make you all know and feel this, ere you depart hence.

O my brethren, my heart is enlarge towards you. I trust I feel something of that hidden, but powerful presence of Christ, whilst I am preaching to you. Indeed it is sweet, it is exceedingly comfortable. All the harm I wish you, who without cause are my enemies, is, that you felt the like. Believe me, though it would be hell to my soul, to return to a natural state again, yet I would willingly change status with you for a little while, that you might know what it is to have Christ dwelling in your hearts by faith. Do not turn your backs; do not let the devil hurry you away; be not afraid of convictions; do not think worse of the doctrine, because preached without the church walls. Our Lord, I the days of his flesh, preached on a mount, in a ship, and a field; and I am persuaded, many have felt his gracious presence here. Indeed we speak what we know. Do not reject the kingdom of God against yourselves; be so wise as to receive our witness. I cannot, I will not let you go; stay a little, let us reason together. However lightly you may esteem your souls, I know our Lord has set an unspeakable value on them. He thought them worthy of his most precious blood. I beseech you, therefore, O sinners, be ye reconciled to God. I hope you do not fear being accepted in the beloved. Behold, he calleth you; behold, he prevents and follows you with his mercy, and hath sent forth his servants unto the highways and hedges, to compel you to come in. Remember then, that at such an hour of such a day, in such a year, in this place, you were all told what you ought to think concerning Jesus Christ. If you now perish, it will not be for lack of knowledge: I am free from the blood of you all. You cannot say I have been preaching damnation to you; you cannot say I have, like legal preachers, been requiring you to make brick without straw. I have not bidden you to make yourselves saints, and then come to God; but I have offered you salvation on as cheap terms as you can desire. I have offered you Christ's whole wisdom, Christ's whole righteousness, Christ's whole sanctification and eternal redemption, if you will but believe on him. If you say, you cannot believe, you say right; for faith, as well as every other blessing, is the gift of God; but then wait upon God, and who knows but he may have mercy on thee? Why do we not entertain more loving thoughts of Christ? Or do you think he will have mercy on others, and not on you? But are you not sinners? And did not Jesus Christ come into the world to save sinners? If you say you are the chief of sinners, I answer, that will be no hindrance to your salvation, indeed it will not, if you lay hold on him by faith. Read the Evangelists, and see how kindly he behaved to his disciples who fled from and denied him: "Go tell my brethren," says he. He did not say, Go tell those traitors; but, "Go tell my brethren in general, and poor Peter in particular, "that I am risen;" O comfort his poor drooping heart, tell him am reconciled to him; bit him weep no more so bitterly: for though with and curses he thrice denied me, yet I have died for his sins, I am risen again for his justification: I freely forgive him all. Thus slow to anger, and of great kindness, was our all-merciful High-priest. And do you think he has changed his nature, and forgets poor sinners; now he is exalted to the right hand of God? No, he is the same yesterday, today, and forever, and sitteth there only to make intercession for us. Come then, ye harlots, come ye publicans, come ye most abandoned of sinners, come and believe on Jesus Christ. Though the whole world despise you and cast you out, yet he will not disdain to take you up. O amazing, O infinitely condescending love! even you, he will not be ashamed to call his brethren. How will you escape if you neglect such a glorious offer of salvation? What would the damned spirits, now in the prison of hell, give, if Christ was so freely offered to their souls? And why are not we lifting up our eyes in torments? Does any one out of this great multitude dare say, he does not deserve damnation? If not, why are we left, and others taken away by death? What is this but an instance of God's free grace, and a sign of his good will towards us? Let God's goodness lead us to repentance! O let there be joy in heaven over some of you repenting! Though we are in a field, I am persuaded the blessed angels are hovering now around us, and do long, "as the hart panteth after the water-brooks," to sing an anthem at your conversion. Blessed be God, I hope their joy will be fulfilled. An awful silence appears amongst us. I have good hope that the words which the Lord has enabled me to speak in your ears this day, have not altogether fallen to the ground. Your tears and deep attention, are an evidence, that the Lord God is amongst us of a truth. Come, ye Pharisees, come and see, in spite of your satanical rage and fury, the Lord Jesus is getting himself the victory. And brethren, I speak the truth in Christ, I lie not, if one soul of you, by the blessing of God, be brought to think savingly of Jesus Christ this day, I care not if my enemies were permitted to carry me to prison, and put my feet fast in the stocks, as soon as I have delivered this sermon. Brethren, my heart's desire and prayer to God is, that you may be saved. For this cause I follow my Master without the camp. I care not how much of his sacred reproach I bear, so that some of you be converted from the errors of your ways. I rejoice, yea and I will rejoice. Ye men, ye devils, do your worst: the Lord who sent, will support me. And when Christ, who is our life, and whom I have now been preaching, shall appear, I also, together with his despised little ones, shall appear with him in glory. And then, what will you think of Christ? I know what you will think of him. You will then think him to be the fairest among ten thousand: You will then think and feel him to be a just and sin-avenging judge. Be ye then persuaded to kiss him lest he be angry, and so you be banished for ever from the presence of the Lord. Behold, I come to you as the angel did to Lot. Flee, flee, for your lives; haste, linger no longer in your spiritual Sodom, for otherwise you will be eternally destroyed. Numbers, no doubt, there are amongst you, that may regard me no more than Lot's sons-in-law regarded him. I am persuaded I seem t some of you as one that mocketh: but I speak the truth in Christ, I lie not; as sure as fire and brimstone was rained from the Lord out of heaven, to destroy Sodom and Gomorrah, so surely, at the great day, shall the vials of God's wrath be poured on you. If you do not think seriously of, and act agreeable to the gospel of the Lord's Christ. Behold, I have told you before; and I pray God, all you that forget him may seriously think of what has been said, before he pluck you away, and there be none to deliver you.

Now to God the Father.

25. The Wise and Foolish Virgins

Matthew 25:13—"Watch therefore, for ye know neither the day nor the hour in which the Son of man cometh." (Text is actually Matt. 25:1–13)

The apostle Paul, in his epistle to the Hebrews, informs us, "That it is appointed for all men once to die; after that is the judgment." And I think, if any consideration be sufficient to awaken a sleeping drowsy world, it must be this, That there will be a day wherein these heavens shall be wrapped up like a scroll, this element melt with fervent heat, the earth and all things therein be burnt up, and every soul, of every nation and language, summoned to appear before the dreadful tribunal of the righteous Judge of quick and dead, to receive rewards and punishments, according to the deeds done in their bodies. The great apostle just mentioned, when brought before Felix, could think of no better means to convert that sinful man, than to reason to temperance, righteousness, and more especially of a judgment to come. The first might in some measure affect, but, I am persuaded, it was the last consideration, a judgment to come, that made him to tremble: and so bad as the world is now grown, yet there are few have their consciences so far seared, as to deny that there will be a reckoning hereafter. The promiscuous dispensations of providence in this life, wherein we see good men afflicted, destitute, tormented, and the wicked permitted triumphantly to ride over their heads, has been always looked upon as an indisputable argument, by the generality of men, that there will be a day in which God will judge the world in righteousness, and administer equity unto his people. Some indeed are so bold as to deny it, while they are engaged in the pursuit of the lust of the eye, and the pride of life. But follow them to their death bed, ask them, when their souls are ready to launch into eternity, what they then think of a judgment to come and they will tell you, they dare not give their consciences the lie any longer. They feel a fearful looking for of judgment and fiery indignation in their hearts. Since then these things are so, does it not highly concern each of us, my brethren, before we come on a bed of sickness, seriously to examine how the account stands between God and our souls, and how it will fare with us in that day? As for the openly profane, the drunkard, the whoremonger, the adulterer, and such-like, there is no doubt of what will become of them; without repentance they shall never enter into the kingdom of God and his Christ: no; their damnation slumbereth not; a burning fiery Tophet, kindled by the fury of God's eternal wrath, is prepared for their reception, wherein they must suffer the vengeance of eternal fire. Nor is there the least doubt of the state of true believers. For though they are despised and rejected of natural men, yet being born again of God, they are heirs of God, and joint heirs with Christ. They have the earnest of the promised inheritance in their hearts, and are assured that a new and living way is made open for them, into the holy of holies, by the blood of Jesus Christ, into which an abundant entrance shall be administered to them at the great day of account. The only question is, what will become of the *Almost Christian*, one that is content to go, as he thinks, in a middle way to heaven, without being profane on the one hand, or, as he falsely imagines, righteous over-much on the other? Many there are in every congregation, and consequently some here present, of this stamp. And what is worst of all, it is more easy to convince the most notorious publicans and sinners of their being out of a state of salvation, than any of these. Notwithstanding, if Jesus Christ may be our judge, they shall as certainly be rejected and disowned by him at the last day, as though they lived in open defiance of all his laws. For what says our Lord in the parable of which the words of the text are a conclusion, and which I intend to make the subject of my present discourse. "Then," at the day of judgment, which he had been discoursing of in the foregoing, and prosecutes in this chapter, "shall the kingdom of heaven, (the state of professors in the gospel church) be likened unto ten virgins, who took their lamps, and went forth to meet the bridegroom." In which words, is a manifest allusion to a custom prevailing in our Lord's time among the Jews, at marriage solemnities, which were generally at night, and at which it was customary for the persons of the bride-chamber to go out in procession, with many lights, to meet the bridegroom. By the bridegroom, you are here to understand Jesus Christ. The church, i.e. true believers, are his Israel; he is united to them by one spirit, even in this life; but the solemnizing of their sacred nuptials, is reserved till the day of judgment, when he shall come to take them home to himself, and present them before men and angels, as his purchase, to his Father, without spot or wrinkle, or any such thing. By the ten virgins we are to understand, the professors of Christianity in general. All are called virgins, because all are called to be saints. Whosoever names the name of Christ, is obliged by that profession to depart from all iniquity. But the pure and chaste in heart, are the only persons that will be blessed as to see God. As Christ was born of a virgin, so he can dwell in none but virgins souls, made pure and holy by the cohabitation of his holy Spirit. What says the apostle? "All are not Israel that are of Israel," all are not Christians that are called after the name of Christ: No, says our Lord, in the 2nd verse, "Five of those virgins were wise," true believers, "and five were foolish," formal hypocrites. But why are five said to be wise, and the other five foolish? Hear what our Lord says in the following verses; "They that were foolish took their lamps, and took no oil with them: but the wise took oil in their vessels with their lamps." They that were foolish took their lamps of an outward profession. They would go to church, say over several manuals of prayers, come perhaps into a field to hear a sermon, give at a collection, and receive the sacrament constantly, nay, oftener than once a month. But then here lay the mistake; they had no oil in their lamps, no principle of grace, no living faith in their hearts, without which, though we should give all our goods to feed the poor, and our bodies to be burnt, it would profit us nothing. In short, they were exact, nay, superstitious bigots as to the form, but all the while they were strangers to, and, in effect, denied the power of godliness in their hearts. They would go to church, but at the same time, think it no harm to go to a ball or an assembly, notwithstanding they promised at their baptism, to renounce the pomps and vanities of this wicked world. They were so exceedingly fearful of being righteous overmuch, that they would even persecute those that were truly devout, if they attempted to go a step farther than themselves. In one word, they never effectually felt the power of the world to come. They thought they might be Christians without so much inward feeling, and therefore, notwithstanding their high pretensions, had only a name of live.

And now, Sirs, let pause a while, and in the name of God, whom I endeavor to serve in the gospel of his dear Son, give me leave to ask one question. Whilst I have been drawing, though in miniature, the character of these foolish virgins, have not many of your consciences made the application, and with a small, still, though articulate voice, said, Thou man, thou woman, art one of those foolish virgins, for thy sentiments and practice agree thereto? Stifle not, but rather encourage these convictions; and who knows, but that Lord who is rich in mercy to all that call upon him faithfully, may so work upon you even by this foolishness of preaching, as to make you wise virgins before you return home?

What they were you shall know immediately: "But the wise took oil in their vessels with their lamps." Observe, the wise, the true believers, had their lamps as well as the foolish virgins; for Christianity does not require us to cast off all outward forms; we may use forms, and yet not be formal: for instance, it is possible to worship God in a set form of prayer, and yet worship him in spirit and in truth. And therefore, brethren, let us not judge one another. The wise virgins had their lamps; herein did not lie the difference between them and the foolish, that one worshipped God with a form, and the other did not: No: as the Pharisee and Publican went up to the temple to pray, so these wise and foolish virgins might go to the same place of worship, and sit under the same ministry; but then the wise took oil in their vessels with their lamps; they kept up the form, but did not rest in it; their words in prayer were the language of their hearts, and they were no strangers to inward feelings; they were not afraid of searching doctrines, nor affronted when ministers told them they deserved to be damned; they were not self-righteous, but were willing that Jesus Christ should have all the glory of their salvation; they were convinced that the merits of Jesus Christ were to be apprehended only by faith; but yet were they as careful to maintain good works, as though they were to be justified by them: in short, their obedience flowed from love and gratitude, and was cheerful, constant, uniform, universal, like that obedience which the holy angels pay our Father in heaven.

Here then let me exhort you to pause again; and if any of you can faithfully apply these characters to your hearts, give God the glory, and take the comfort to your own souls; you are not false but true believers. Jesus Christ has been made of God to you wisdom, even that wisdom, whereby you shall be made wise unto salvation. God sees a difference between you and foolish virgins, if natural men will not. You need not be uneasy, though one chance and fate in this may happen to you both. I say, once chance and fate; for, ver. Matthew 25:5, "while the bridegroom tarried," in the space of time which passed between our Lord's ascension and his coming again to judgment, "they all slumbered and slept." The wise as well as foolish died, for dust we are, and to dust we must return. It is no reflection at all upon the divine goodness, that believers, as well as hypocrites, must pass through the valley of the shadow of death; for Christ has taken away the sting of death, so that we need fear no evil. It is to them a passage to everlasting life: death is only terrible to those who have no hope, because they live without faith in the world. Whosoever there are amongst you, that have received the first-fruits of the spirit, I am persuaded you are ready to cry out, we would not live here always, we long to be dissolved, that we may be with Jesus Christ; and though worms must destroy our bodies as well as others, yet we are content, being assured that our Redeemer liveth, that he will stand at the latter days upon the earth, and that in our flesh we shall see God.

But it is not so with hypocrites and unbelievers beyond the grave; for what says our Lord? "And at midnight:" observe, at midnight, when all was hushed and quiet, and no one dreaming of any such thing, "a cry was made;" the voice of the arch-angel and the trump of God was heard sounding this general alarm; to things in heaven, to things in earth, and to things in the waters under the earth, "Behold!" mark how this awful summons is ushered in with the word *behold*, to engage our attention? "Behold the bridegroom cometh!" even Jesus Christ, the desire of nations, the bridegroom of his spouse the church: Because he tarried for a while to exercise the faith of saints, and give sinners space to repent, scoffers were apt to cry out, "Where is the promise of his coming? But the Lord is not slack concerning his promise, as these men account slackness." For behold, he that was to come, now cometh, and will not tarry any longer: he cometh to be glorified in his saints, and to take vengeance on them that know not God, and have not obeyed his gospel: he cometh not as a poor despised Galilean; not be laid in a stinking manger; not to be despised and rejected of men; not to be blindfolded, spit upon, and buffeted; not to be nailed to an accursed tree; he cometh not as the Son of man, but as he really was, the eternal Son of the eternal God: He cometh riding on the wings of the wind, in the glory of the Father and his holy angels, and to be had in everlasting reverence of all that shall be round about him. 'Go ye forth to meet him;" arise, ye dead, ye foolish, as well as wise virgin, arise and come to judgment. Multitudes, no doubt, that hear this awakening cry, would rejoice if the rocks might fall on, and the hills cover them from the presence of the Lamb: what would they give, if as they lived as beasts, they might now die like the beasts that perish? How would they rejoice, if those same excuses which they made on this side eternity for not attending on holy ordinances, would serve to keep them from appearing before the heavenly bridegroom! But as Adam, notwithstanding his fig-leaves, and the trees of the garden, could not hide himself from God, when arrested with an "Adam, where art thou?" So now the decree is gone forth, and the trump of God has given its last sound; all tongues, people, nations, and languages, both wise and foolish virgins, must come into his presence, and bow beneath his footstool; even Pontius Pilate, Annas and Caiaphas; even the proud persecuting high-priests and Pharisees of this generation, must appear before him: for says our Lord, "then, (when the cry was made, Behold, the bridegroom cometh!) in a moment, in the twinkling of an eye, the graves were opened, the sea gave up its dead, and "all those virgins, both wise and foolish, arose and trimmed their lamp," or endeavored to put themselves in a proper posture to meet the bridegroom.

But how may we imagine the foolish virgins were surprised, when, notwithstanding their high thoughts and proud imaginations of their security, they now find themselves wholly naked, and void of that inward holiness and purity of heart, without which no man living at that day shall comfortably meet the Lord! I doubt not, but many of these foolish virgins, whilst in this world, were clothed in purple and fine linen, fared sumptuously every day, and disdained [1. To consider unworthy of one's regard or notice; treat with contempt or scorn: to disdain a coward. 2. To consider unworthy of one's position or character; refuse scornfully: to disdain to beg for food.—n. A feeling or attitude of superiority and dislike; proud contempt.] to set the wise virgins, some of whom might be as poor as Lazarus, even with the dogs of their flock. These were looked upon by them as enthusiasts and madmen, as persons that were righteous over-much, and who intended to turn the world upside down: but now death hath opened their eyes, and convinced them, to their eternal sorrow, that he is not a true Christian, who is only one outwardly. Now they find (though, alas! too late) they, and not the wise virgins, had been beside themselves. Now their proud hearts are made to stoop, their lofty looks are brought low; and as Dives entreated that Lazarus might dip the tip of his finger in water, and be sent to cool his tongue, so these foolish virgins, these formal hypocrites, are obliged to turn beggars to those whom they once despised: "Give us of your oil;" O! impart to us a little of that grace and holy spirit, for the insisting on which we fools accounted your lives madness; for alas! "our lamps are gone out;" we had only the form of godliness; we were whited sepulchers; we were heart-hypocrites; we contented ourselves with desiring to be good; and though confident of salvation whilst we lived, yet our hope is entirely gone, now God has taken away our souls: Give us therefore, O! give us, though we once despised you, give us of your oil, for our lamps of an outward profession, and transient convictions, are quite gone out. "Comfort ye, comfort ye, my people, saith the Lord." My brethren in Christ, hear what the foolish say to the wise virgins, and learn in patience to possess your souls. If you are true followers of the lowly Jesus, I am persuaded you have your names cast out, and all manner of evil spoken falsely against you, for his name's sake; for no one ever did or will live godly in Christ Jesus, without suffering persecution; nay, I doubt not but your chief foes are those of your own household: tell me, do not your carnal relations and friends vex your tender souls day by day, in bidding you spare yourselves, and take heed lest you go too far: And as you passed along to come and hear the word of God, have you not heard many a Pharisee cry out, Here comes another troop of his followers! Brethren, be not surprised, Christ's servants were always the world's fools; you know it hated him before it hated you. Rejoice and be exceeding glad. Yet a little while, and behold the bridegroom cometh, and then shall you hear these formal scoffing Pharisees saying unto you, "Give us of your oil, for our lamps are gone out." When you are reviled, revile not again: when you suffer, threaten not; commit your souls into the hands of him that judgeth righteously: for behold the day cometh, when the children of God shall speak for themselves.

The wise virgins, in the parable, no doubt endured the same cruel mockings as you may do, but as the lamb before the shearers is dumb, so in this life opened they not their mouths; but now we find they can give their enemies an answer: "Not so, lest there be not enough for us and you; but go ye rather to them that sell, and buy for yourselves." These words are not to be understood as though they were spoken in an insulting manner; for true charity teaches us to use the worst of sinners, and our most bitter enemies, with the meekness and gentleness of Christ: Though Dives was in hell, yet Abraham does not say, Thou villain, but only, "Son, remember:" and I am persuaded, had it been in the power of these wise virgins, they would have dealt with the foolish virgins, as God knows, I would willingly deal with my most inveterate [firmly established by long continuance] enemies, not only give them of their oil, but also exalt them to the right hand of God. It was not then for want of love, but the fear of wanting a sufficiency for themselves, that made them return this answer, "Not so, lest there be not enough for us and you:" For they that have most grace, have none to spare; none but self-righteous, foolish virgins think they are good enough, or have already attained. Those who are truly wise are always most distrustful of themselves, pressing forwards to the things that are before, and think it well if after they have done all, they can make their calling and election sure. "Not so, lest there be not enough for us and you; but go ye rather to them that sell, and buy for yourselves." These words indeed seem to be spoken in a triumphant, but certainly they were uttered in the most compassionate manner; "go ye to them that sell, and buy for yourselves;" unhappy virgins! you accounted our lives folly; whilst with you in the body, how often have you condemned us for our zeal in running to hear the word of God, and looked upon us as enthusiasts, for talking and affirming, that we must be led by the spirit, and walk by the spirit, and feel the spirit of God witnessing with our spirits, that we are his children? But now you would be glad to be partakers of this privilege, but it is not ours to give. You contented yourselves with seeking, when you should have been striving to enter in at the strait gate. And now go to them that sell, if you can, and buy for yourselves.

And what say you to this, ye foolish formal professors? For I doubt not but curiosity and novelty hath brought many such, even to this despised place, to hear a sermon. Can you hear this reply to the foolish virgins, and yet not tremble? Why, yet a little while, and thus it shall be done to you. Rejoice and bolster yourselves up in your duties and forms; endeavor to cover your nakedness with the fig-leaves of an outward profession and a legal righteousness, and despise the true servants of Christ as much as you please, yet know, that all your hopes will fail you when God brings you into judgment. For not he who commendeth himself is justified, but he whom the Lord commendeth.

But to return; we do not hear of any reply the foolish virgins make: No, their consciences condemned them; like the person without a wedding-garment, they are struck dumb, and are now filled with anxious thoughts how they shall buy oil, that they may lift up their heads before the bridegroom. "But whilst they went to buy," ver. Matthew 25:10, whilst they were thinking what they should do, the bridegroom, the Lord Jesus, the king, the husband of his spouse the church, cometh, attended with thousands and twenty times then thousands of saints and angels, publicly to count up his jewels; "and they that were ready," the wise virgins who had oil in their lamp, and were sealed by his spirit to the day of redemption, these having on the wedding garment of an imputed righteousness, and a new nature, "went in with him to the marriage."

But who can express the transports that these wise virgins felt, when they were thus admitted, in holy triumph, into the presence and full enjoyment of him, whom their souls hungered and thirsted after! No doubt they had tasted of his love, and by faith had often fed on him in their hearts, when sitting down to commemorate his last supper here on earth; but how full may we think their hearts and tongues were of his praises, when they see themselves seated together to eat bread in his heavenly kingdom. And what was best of all, "the door was shut, and shut them in, to enjoy the ever blessed God, and the company of angels and the spirits of just men made perfect, without interruption for evermore. I say, without interruption; for in this life, their eyes often gushed out with water, because men kept not God's law; and they could never come to appear before the Lord, or to hear his word, but Satan and his emissaries would come also to disturb them; but now "the door is shut," now there is a perfect communion of saints, which they in vain longed for in this lower world; not tares no longer grow up with the wheat; not one single hypocrite or unbeliever can screen himself amongst them. "Now the wicked cease from troubling, and now their weary souls enjoy an everlasting rest."

Once more, O believers, let me exhort you in patience to possess your souls. God, if he has freely justified you by faith in his son, and given you his spirit, has sealed you to be his; and has secured you, as surely as he secured Noah, when he locked him in the ark. But though heirs of God, and joint heirs with Christ, and neither men nor devils can pluck you out of your heavenly Father's hand, yet you must be tossed about with manifold temptations; however, lift up your heads, the day of your perfect, complete redemption draweth nigh. Behold the bridegroom cometh to take you to himself, the door shall be shut, and you shall be for ever with the Lord.

But I even tremble to tell you, O nominal Christians, that the door will be shut, I mean the door of mercy, never, never to be opened to give you admission, though you should continue knocking to all eternity. For thus speaks our Lord, v. Matthew 25:11, "Afterwards," after those that were ready went in, and the door was shut; after they had, to their sorrow, found that no oil was to be bought, no grace to be procured, "came also the other virgins;" and as Esau, after Jacob had gotten the blessing, cried with an exceeding bitter cry, "Bless me, even me also, O my father;" so they came saying, "Lord, Lord, open to us." Observe the importunity of these foolish virgins, implied in the words, "Lord, Lord." Whilst in the body, I suppose they only read, did not pray over their prayers. If you now tell them, they should "pray without ceasing," they should pray from their hearts, and feel the want of what they pray for; they would answer, they could not tell what you mean by inward feelings; that God did not require us to be always on our knees, but if a man did justly, and loved mercy, and did as the church forms required him, it was as much as the Lord required at his hands.

I fear, sirs, too many among us are of this mind: nay, I fear there are many so polite, so void of the love of God, as to think it too great a piece of self-denial, to rise early to offer up a sacrifice of praise and thanksgiving acceptable to God through Jesus Christ. If any such, by the good providence of God, are brought hither this morning, I beseech you to consider your ways, and remember, if you are not awakened out of your spiritual lethargy, and live a life of prayer here, you shall but in vain cry out with the foolish virgins, "Lord, Lord, open unto us," hereafter. Observe farther, the impudence, as well as importunity of these other virgins; "Lord, Lord," say they, as though they were intimately acquainted with the holy Jesus. Like numbers among us, who because they go to church, repeat their creeds, and receive the blessed sacrament, think they have a right to call Jesus their Savior, and dare call God their Father, when they put up the Lord's prayer.

But Jesus is not your Savior. The devil, not God, is your father, unless your hearts are purified by faith, and you are born again from above. It is not merely being baptized by water, but being born again of the Holy Ghost that must qualify you for salvation; and it will do you no service at the great day, to say unto Christ, Lord, my name is in the register of such and such a parish. I am persuaded, the foolish virgins could say this and more; but what answer did Jesus make? He answered and said, ver. Matthew 25:12, "Verily, I say unto you:" He puts the *verily*, to assure them he was in earnest. "I say unto you," I who am truth itself, I whom you have owned in words, but in works denied, "verily, I say unto you, I know you not." These words must not be understood literally; for whatever Arians and Socinians may say to the contrary, yet we affirm, that Jesus Christ is God, God blessed for ever, and therefore knoweth all things. He saw Nathaniel, when under the fig-tree: he sees, and is not looking down from heaven his dwelling-place, upon us, to see how we behave in these fields. Brethren, I know nothing of the thoughts and intents of your hearts, in coming hither; but Jesus Christ knows who came like new-born babes, desirous to be fed with the sincere milk of the word; and he knows who came to hear what the babbler says, and to run away with part of a broken sentence, that they may have whereof to accuse him. This expression then, "I know you not," must not be understood literally; no, it implies a knowledge of approbation, as though Christ has said, "You call me, Lord, Lord, but you have not done the things that I have said; you desire me to open the door, but how can you come in hither not having on a wedding garment? Alas, you are naked! Where is my outward righteousness imputed to you? Where is my divine image stamped upon your souls? How dare you call me Lord, Lord, when you have not received the Holy Ghost, whereby I seal all that are truly mine? "Verily, I know you not; depart from me, ye cursed, into everlasting fire, prepared for the devil and his angels."

And now, he that hath ears to hear, let him hear what manner of persons these were, whom Jesus Christ dismissed with this answer. Remember, I entreat you, remember they are not sent away for being fornicators, swearers, Sabbath-breakers, or prodigals. No, in all probability, as I observed before, they were, touching the outward observance of the moral law, blameless; they were constant as to the form of religion; and if they did no good, yet no one could say, they did any one any harm. The only thing for which they were condemned, and eternally banished from the presence of the Lord, (for so much is implied in "I know you not") was this, they had no oil in their lamps, no principle of a true living faith and holiness in their hearts. And if persons may go to church, receive the sacrament, lead honest moral lives, and yet be sent to hell at the last day, as they certainly will be if they advance no farther, Where wilt thou, O drunkard? Where wilt thou, O swearer? Where wilt thou, O Sabbath-breaker? Where wilt thou that deniest divine revelation, and even the form of godliness? Where wilt you, and such like sinners appear? I know very well. You must appear before the dreadful tribunal of Jesus Christ; however you may, like Felix, put off the prosecution of your convictions, yet you, as well as others, must arise after death, and appear in judgment; you will then find, to your eternal sorrow, what I just hinted at in the beginning of this discourse, that your damnation slumbereth not: sin has blinded your hearts, and hardened your foreheads now, but yet a little while, and our Lord will ease him of his adversaries. Methinks, by faith, I see the heavens opened, and the holy Jesus coming, with his face brighter than ten thousand suns, darting fury upon you from his eyes! Methinks I see you rising from your graves, trembling and astonished, and crying out, who can abide this day of his coming!

And now what inference shall I draw from what has been delivered? Our Lord, in the words of the text, has drawn one for me; "Watch therefore, for ye know neither the day nor the hour wherein the Son of man cometh."

"Watch," that is, be upon your guard, and keep your graces in continual exercise. For as when we are commanded to watch unto prayer, it signifies that we should continue instant in that duty; so when we are required to watch in general, it means that we should put on the whole armor of God, and live every day as though it was our last. And O that the Lord may now enable me to lift up my voice like a trumpet! For had I a thousand tongues, or could I speak so loud that the whole world might hear me, I could not sound a more useful alarm than that which is contained in the text. Watch therefore, my brethren, I beseech you by the mercies of God in Christ Jesus, watch; be upon your guard; awake, ye that sleep in the dust: for ye know neither the day nor the hour wherein the Son of man cometh. Perhaps today, perhaps this midnight, the cry may be made: "for in a moment, in the twinkling of an eye, the trump is to sound." However, supposing the final day of judgment may yet be a great way off, the day of death is certainly near at hand: for what is our life? "It is but a vapor," but a span long, soon passeth it away, and we are gone.

Blessed be God, we are all here well; but who, out of this great multitude, dares say, I shall go home to my house in safety? Who knows, but whilst I am speaking, God may commission his ministering spirits immediately to call some of you away by a sudden stroke, to give an account with what attention you have heard this sermon. You know, my brethren, some such instances we have lately had. And what angel or spirit hath assured us, that some of you shall not be the next? "Watch therefore, for ye know neither the day nor the hour wherein the Son of man will come;" And it is chiefly for this reason, that God has hidden the day of our deaths from us. For since I know not but I may die to morrow, why, O my soul, may each of us say, wilt thou not watch to day? Since I know not but I may die the next moment, why wilt thou not prepare for dying this? Many such reflections as these, my brethren, crowd in upon my mind. At present, blessed be the Lord, who delights to magnify his strength in a poor worm's weakness, I am at a stand, not so much about what I shall say, as what I shall leave unsaid. My belly, like Elihu's, is, as it were, full of new wines; "out of the abundance of my heart my mouth speaketh." The seeing so great a multitude standing before me; a sense of the infinite majesty of that God in whose name I preach, and before whom I as well as you must appear, to give an account, and the uncertainty there is whether I shall live another day, to speak to you any more: these considerations, especially the presence of God, which I feel upon my soul, furnishes me with so much matter, that I scarce know where to begin, or where to end my application. However, for method-sake, by the divine assistance, I will branch it into three particulars.

And *First*, I would remind you that are notoriously ungodly, of what our Lord says in the text: For though I have said that your damnation slumbereth no, whilst you continue in an impenitent state; yet that was only to set you upon your watch, to convince you of your danger, and excite you to cry out, "What shall we do to be saved?" I appeal to all that hear me, whether I have said, the door of mercy should be shut against you, if you believe on Jesus Christ: No, if you are the chief of sinners; if you are murderers of fathers, and murderers of mothers; if you are emphatically the dung and offscouring of all things; yet if you believe on Jesus Christ, and cry unto him with the same faith as the expiring thief, "Lord, remember me, now thou art in thy kingdom;" I will pawn my eternal salvation upon it, if he does not shortly translate you to his heavenly paradise. Wonder not at my speaking with so much assurance: For I know "it is a faithful and true saying, and worthy of all acceptation, that Jesus Christ came into the world to save (all truly affected and believing) sinners: Nay, so great is his love, that I am persuaded, was it necessary, he would come again into the world, and die a second time for them on the cross. But, blessed be God, when our Lord bowed down his head, and gave up the ghost, our redemption was finished. It is not our sins, but our want of a lively faith in his blood, that will prove our condemnation: if you draw near to him by faith, though ye are the worst of sinners, yet he will not say unto you, "Verily I know you not." No, a door of mercy shall be opened to you. Look then, look then, by an eye of faith, to that God-man whom ye have pierced. Behold him bleeding, panting, dying upon the cross, with arms stretched out ready to embrace you all. Hark! How he groans! See how all nature is in agony! The rocks rend, the graves open; the sun withdraws its light, ashamed as it were to see the God of nature suffer; and all this to usher in man's great redemption. Nay, the Holy Jesus, in the very agonies and pangs of death, prays for his very murderers; "Father, forgive them, for they know not what they do." If then you have crucified the Son of God afresh, and put him to an open shame, yet do not despair, only believe, and even this shall be forgiven. You have read, at least you have heard, no doubt, how three thousand were converted at St. Peter's preaching one single sermon, after our Lord's ascension into heaven; and many of those who crucified the Lord of glory undoubtedly were amongst them, and why should you despair? For "Jesus Christ is the same yesterday, today, and for ever." The Holy Ghost shall be sent down on you, as well as on them, if you do but believe; for Christ ascended up on high to receive this gift even for the vilest of men. Come then, all ye that are weary and heavy laden with the sense of your sins, lay hold on Christ by faith, and he will give you rest; for salvation is the free gift of God to all them that believe. And though you may think this too good news to be true, yet I speak the truth in Christ, I lie not, this is the gospel, this is the glad tidings which we are commissioned to preach to every creature. Be not faithless then, but believing. Let not the devil lead you captive at his will any longer; for all the wages he gives his servants is death, death often in this life, death everlasting in the next: But the free gift of God, is eternal life to all that believe in Jesus Christ. Pharisees are and will be offended at my coming here, and offering you salvation on such cheap terms; but the more they bid me hold my peace, the more will I cry out and proclaim to convicted sinners, that Jesus, David's Son according to the flesh, but David's Lord as he was God, will have mercy upon all that by a living faith truly turn to him. If this is to be vile, I pray God, I may be more vile. If they will not let me preach Christ crucified, and offer salvation to poor sinners in a church, I will preach him in the lanes, streets, highways and hedges; and nothing pleases me better, than to think I am now in one of the devil's strongest holds. Surely, the Lord has not sent me and all you hither for nothing; no, blessed be God, the fields are white ready unto harvest, and many souls I hope will be gathered into his heavenly garner. It is true, it is the midnight of the church, especially the poor church of England, but God has lately sent forth his servants to cry, "Behold the bridegroom cometh:" I beseech you, O sinners, hearken unto the voice! Let me espouse you by faith to my dear master; and henceforward "watch and pray," that you may be ready to go forth to meet him.

Secondly, I would apply myself to those amongst you, that are not openly profane, but by depending on a formal round of duties, deceive your own souls, and are only foolish virgins. But I must speak to your conviction, rather than your comfort. My dear brethren, do not deceive your own souls. You have heard how far the foolish virgins went, and yet were answered with "Verily I know you not." The reason is, because none but such who have a living faith in Jesus Christ, and are truly born again, can possibly enter into the kingdom of heaven. You may, perhaps, live honest and outwardly moral lives, but if you depend on that morality, or join your works with your faith, in order to justify you before God, you have no lot or share in Christ's redemption: For what is this but to deny the Lord that has bought you? What is this but making yourselves your own Saviors? Taking the crown from Jesus Christ, and putting it on your own heads? The crime of the devil, some have supposed, consisted in this, that he would not bow to Jesus Christ, when the Father commanded all the angels to worship him; and what do you less? You will not own and submit to his righteousness; and though you pretend to worship him with your lips, yet your hearts are far from him; besides you, in effect, deny the operations of his blessed spirit, you mistake common for effectual grace; you hope to be saved, because you have good desires, and a few short convictions; and what is this, but to give God, his word, and all his saints, the lie? A Jew, a Turk, has equally as good grounds whereon to build his hopes of salvation. Need I not then to cry out to you, ye foolish virgins, watch. Beg of God to convince you of your self-righteousness, and the secret unbelief of your hearts; or otherwise, whensoever the cry shall be made, "Behold the bridegroom cometh," you will find yourselves utterly unprepared to go forth to meet him: You may cry "Lord, Lord;" but the answer will be, "Verily, I know you not."

Thirdly, I would speak a word or two by way of exhortation to those who are wise virgins, and are assured that they have on a wedding garment. That there are many such amongst you, who by grace have renounced your own righteousness, and know that the righteousness of the Lord Jesus is imputed to you, I make no doubts. God has his secret ones in the worst of times; and I am persuaded he has not let so loud a gospel cry to be made amongst his people, as of late has been heard, for nothing. No, I am confident, the Holy Ghost has been given to many at the preaching of faith, and has powerfully fallen upon many, whilst they have been hearing the word. You are now then no longer foolish, but wise virgins; notwithstanding, I beseech you also to suffer the word of exhortation, for wise virgins are too apt, whilst the bridegroom tarries, to slumber and sleep. Watch therefore, my dear brethren, watch and pray, at this time especially; for perhaps a time of suffering is at hand. The ark of the Lord begins already to be driven into the wilderness. Be ye therefore upon your watch, and still persevere in following your Lord, even without the camp, bearing his reproach; the cry that has been lately made, has awakened the devil and his servants; they begin to rage horribly; and well they may; for I hope their kingdom is in danger. Watch therefore, for if we are not always upon our guard, a time of trial may overtake us unawares; and instead of owning, like Peter we may be tempted to deny our master. Set death and eternity often before you. Look unto Jesus, the author and finisher of your faith, and consider how little a while it will be, ere he comes to judgment; and then our reproach shall be wiped away; the accusers of us and our brethren shall be cast down, and we all shall be lodged in heaven for ever, with our dear Lord Jesus.

Lastly, what I say unto you, I say unto all, watch; high and low, rich and poor, young and old, one with another, I beseech you, by the mercies of Jesus, to be upon your guard: fly, fly to Jesus Christ, that heavenly bridegroom; behold he desires to take you to himself, miserable, poor, blind and naked as you are; he is willing to clothe you with his everlasting righteousness, and make you partakers of that glory, which he enjoyed with the Father before the world began. Do not turn a deaf ear to me; do not reject the message on account of the meanness of the messenger. I am a child; but the Lord has chosen me, that the glory might be all his own. Had he sent to invite you by a learned rabbi, you might have been tempted to think the man had done something; but now God has sent a child, that the excellency of the power may be seen not to be of man, but of God. Let the learned Pharisees then despise my youth: I care not how vile I appear in the sight of such men; I glory in it. And I am persuaded, if any of you should be married to Christ by this preaching, you will have no reason to repent, when you come to heaven, that God sent a child to cry, "Behold the bridegroom cometh!" O! my brethren, the thought of being instrumental in bringing one of you to glory, fills me with fresh zeal. Once more I entreat you, "Watch, watch and pray:" For the Lord Jesus will receive all that call upon him faithfully. Let that cry, "Behold the bridegroom cometh," be continually sounding in your ears; and begin now to live, as though you were assured, this night you were to "go forth to meet him." I could say more, but the other business and duties of the day oblige me o stop. May the Lord give you all an hearing ear, and obedient heart, and so closely unite you to himself by one spirit, that when he shall come in terrible majesty, to judge mankind, you may be found having on a wedding garment, and ready to go in with him to the marriage.

Grant this, O Lord, for thy dear Son's sake!

26. "The Eternity of Hell-Torments"

Matthew 25:46—"These shall go away into everlasting punishment."

To the *Inhabitants* of Savannah in Georgia.

My dear Friends,

Though the following sermon has been preached elsewhere, yet as the occasion of my preaching it among you was particular, as you seemed to give an uncommon attention to it in public, and afterwards expressed your satisfaction in it to me, when I came to visit you in your own houses, I thought proper to offer it to you.

And here I cannot but bless God for the general dislike of heretical principles that I have found among you; as also for your zeal and approbation of my conduct, when the glory of God and your welfare, have obliged me to resent and publicly declare against the antichristian tenets of some lately under my charge.

I need only exhort you to beg of God to give you a true faith, and to add to your faith virtue, that you may adorn the gospel of our Lord Jesus Christ in all things.

Your constant daily attendance upon public worship,

the gladness wherewith you have received me into your houses, the mildness wherewith you have submitted to my reproofs, more especially the great (though unmerited) concern you showed at my departure, induce me to hope this will be your endeavor.

How long God of his good providence will keep me from you, I know not. However, you may assure yourselves I will return according to my promise, as soon as I have received imposition of hands, and completed the other business that called me hither.

In the mean while, accept of this, as a pledge of the undissembled love of

Your affectionate though unworthy pastor,

George Whitefield, London, 1738

The excellency of the gospel dispensation, is greatly evidenced by those sanctions of rewards and punishments, which it offers to the choice of all its hearers, in order to engage them to be obedient to its precepts. For it promises no less than eternal happiness to the good, and denounces no slighter a punishment than everlasting misery against the wicked: On the one hand, It is a favor of life unto life," on the other, "A favor of death unto death." And though one would imagine, the bare mentioning of the former would be sufficient to draw men to their duty, yet ministers in all ages have found it necessary, frequently to remind their people of the latter, and to set before them the terrors of the Lord, as so many powerful dissuasives from sin.

But whence is it that men are so disingenuous [insincere, deceitful]? The reason seems to be this: The promise of eternal happiness is so agreeable to the inclinations and wishes of mankind, that all who call themselves Christians, universally and willingly subscribe to the belief of it: but then there is something so shocking in the consideration of eternal torments, and seemingly such an infinite disproportion between an endless duration of pain, and short life spent in pleasure, that men (some at least of them) can scarcely be brought to confess it as an article of their faith, that an eternity of misery awaits the wicked in a future state.

I shall therefore at this time, beg leave to insist on the proof of this part of one of the Articles of our Creed; and endeavor to make good what our blessed Lord has here threatened in the words of the text, "These (that is, the wicked) shall go away into everlasting punishment."

Accordingly, without considering the words as they stand in relation to the context; I shall resolve all I have to say, into this one general proposition, "That the torments reserved for the wicked hereafter, are eternal."

But before I proceed to make good this, I must inform you that I take it for granted,

All present do steadfastly believe, They have something within them, which we call a soul, and which is capable of surviving the dissolution of the body, and of being miserable or happy to all eternity.

I take it for granted farther, That you believe a divine revelation; that those books, emphatically called the Scriptures, were written by the inspiration of God, and that the things therein contained, are founded upon eternal truth.

I take it for granted, That you believe, that the Son of God came down to die for sinners; and that there is but one Mediator between God and man, even the man Christ Jesus.

These things being granted, (and they were necessary to be premised) proceed we now to make good the one general proposition asserted in the text, That the torments reserved for the wicked hereafter are eternal. "These shall go away into everlasting punishment." The

First argument I shall advance to prove that the torments reserved for the wicked hereafter, are eternal, is, That the word of God himself assures us, in line upon line, that it will be so.

To quote all the texts that might be produced in proof of this, would be endless. Let it suffice to instance only in a few. In the Old Testament, in the book of Daniel 12:2, we are told, that "some shall wake to everlasting life, and others to everlasting contempt." In the book of Isaiah, it is said, that "the worm of those that have transgressed God's law, and die impenitently, shall not die, nor their fire be quenched." And in another place the holy Prophet , struck, no doubt, with astonishment and horror at the prospect of the continuance of the torments of the damned, breaks out into this moving expostulation, "Who can dwell with everlasting burnings?"

The New Testament is still fuller as to this point, it being a revelation which brought this and such-like particulars to a clear light. The Apostle Jude tells us of the profane despisers of dignities in his days, that "for them was reserved the blackness of darkness forever." And in the book of the Revelation, it is written, that "the smoke of the torments of the wicked ascendeth for ever and ever." And if we believe the witness of men inspired, the witness of the Son of God, who had the Spirit given him, as Mediator, without measure, is still far greater: and in St. Mark's gospel, He repeats this solemn declaration three several times, It is better for thee to enter into life maimed;" that is, it is better to forego the gratification of thy lust, or incur the displeasure of a friend, which may be as dear to thee as a hand, or as useful as a foot, "than having two hands and feet, (that is, for indulging the one, or disobeying God to oblige the other) to be cast into hell, where the worm dieth not, and the fire is not quenched."

And here again, in the words of the text, "These (the wicked) shall go away into everlasting punishment."

I know it has been objected by some who have denied the eternity of hell-torments, That the words everlasting and ever and ever, are often used in the Holy Scriptures (especially in the Old Testament) when they signify not an endless duration, but a limited term of time.

And this we readily grant: but then we reply, That when the words are used with this limitation, they either manifestly appear to be used so from the context; or are put in opposition to occasional types which God gave his people on some special occasions, as when it is said, "It shall be a perpetual or everlasting statute," or, "a statute for ever;" that is, a standing type, and not merely transient or occasional, as was the pillar of cloud, the manna, and such-like. Or, lastly, they have a relation to that covenant, God made with his spiritual Israel; which, if understood in a spiritual sense, will be everlasting, though the ceremonial dispensation be abolished.

Besides, it ought to be observed, that some of the passages just now referred to, have neither of these words so much as mentioned in them, and cannot possibly be interpreted, so as to denote only a limited term of years.

But let that be as it will, it is evident even to a demonstration, that the words of the text will not admit of such a restrained signification, as appears from their being directly opposed to the words immediately following, "That the righteous shall go into life eternal." From which words, all are ready to grant, that the life promised to the righteous will be eternal. And why the punishment threatened to the wicked should not be understood to be eternal likewise, when the very same word in the original, is used to express the duration of each, no shadow of a reason can be given.

But, Secondly, There cannot be one argument urged, why God should reward his saints with everlasting happiness, which will not equally prove that he ought to punish sinners with eternal misery.

For, since we know nothing (at least for a certainty) how he will deal with either but by a Diving Revelation; and since, as was proved by the foregoing argument, he hath as positively threatened eternally to punish the wicked, as to reward the good; it follows, that his truth will be as much impeached and called in question, did he not inflict his punishments, as it would be, if he did not confer his rewards.

To this also it has been objected, That though God is obliged by promise to give his rewards, yet his veracity could not be called in question, supposing he should not execute his threatenings, as he actually did not in the case of Nineveh; which God expressly declared by his Prophet Jonah, "should be destroyed in forty days:" notwithstanding the sequel of the story informs us, that Nineveh was spared.

But in answer to this objection we affirm, that God's threatenings, as well as promises, are without repentance; and for this reason, because they are both founded on the eternal laws of right reason. Accordingly we always find, that where the conditions were not performed, on the non-performance of which the threatenings were denounced, God always executed the punishment threatened. The driving Adam out of Eden, the destruction of the old world by a deluge of water, and the overthrow of Sodom and Gomorrah, are, and will be always so many standing monuments of God's executing his threatenings when denounced, though to our weak apprehensions, the punishment may seem far to exceed the crime.

It is true, God did spare Nineveh, and that because the inhabitants did actually repent, and therefore performed the conditions upon which it was supposed, by the Prophet's being sent to warn them, the threatened punishment should be withheld.

And so in respect to gospel threatenings. If men will so far consult their own welfare, as to comply with the gospel, God certainly will not punish them, but on the contrary, confer upon them his rewards. But to affirm that he will not punish, and that eternally to, impenitent, obstinate sinners, according as he hath threatened; what is it, in effect, but to make God like a man, that he should lie, or the son of man, that he should repent?

But the absurdity of such an opinion will appear still more evident from

The Third argument I shall offer to prove, that the torments reserved for the wicked hereafter are eternal, From the nature of the Christian covenant.

And here I must again observe, that it was taken for granted at the beginning of this discourse, that you believe the Son of God came down to save sinners; and that there is but one Mediator between God and men, even the Man Christ Jesus.

And here I take it for granted farther, (unless you believe

the absurd and unwarrantable doctrine of purgatory) that you are fully persuaded, this life is the only time allotted by Almighty God for working out our salvation, and that after a few years are passed over, there will remain no more sacrifice for sin.

And if this be granted (and who dares deny it?) it follows, that if the wicked man dieth in his wickedness, and under the wrath of God, he must continue in that state to all eternity. For, since there is no possibility of their being delivered out of such a condition, but by and through Christ; and since, at the hour of death, the time of Christ's mediation and intercession for him is irrecoverably gone; the same reason that may be given, why God should punish a sinner that dieth under the guilt of his sins for a single day, will equally hold good, why he should continue to punish him for a year, an age, nay all eternity.

But I hasten to the Fourth and last argument, to prove, That the torments reserved for the wicked hereafter are eternal, Because the devil's punishment is to be so.

That there is such a being whom we call the devil; that he was once an angel of light, but for his pride and rebellion against God, was cast down from heaven, and is now permitted, with the rest of the spiritual wickednesses, to walk to and fro, seeking whom they may devour; that there is a place of torment reserved for them, or, to use the Apostle's words, "That they are reserved in everlasting chains under darkness unto the judgment of the great day;" are truths all here present were supposed to be convinced of, at the beginning of the discourse, you believing the Holy Scriptures to be written by the inspiration of God, wherein these truths are delivered.

But then if we allow all this, and think it no injustice in God to punish those once glorious spirits for their rebellion; how can we think it unjust in him, to punish wicked men for their impenitency to all eternity?

You will say, perhaps, that they have sinned against greater light, and therefore deserve a greater punishment. And so we grant that the punishment of the fallen angels may be greater as to degree, than that of wicked men; but then we affirm, it will be equal as to the eternal duration of it: for in that day, as the lively oracles of God inform us, shall the Son of Man say to them on his left hand, "Depart from me, ye cursed, into everlasting fire, prepared for the devil and his angels." Where we find that impenitent sinners are to be cast into the same everlasting fire, with the devil and his angels; and that too very justly. For though they may have sinned against greater light, yet Christians sin against greater mercy. Since Christ took not hold of, did not die for, the fallen angels, but for men and for our salvation. So that if God spared not those excellent beings, assure thyself, O obstinate sinner, whoever thou art, he will by no means spare thee.

From what then has been said it plainly appears, that verily the torments reserved for the wicked hereafter, war eternal. And if so, brethren, how ought we to fly to Jesus Christ for refuge; how holy ought we to be in all manner of conversation and godliness, that we may be accounted worthy to escape this wrath to come!

But before I proceed to a practical exhortation, permit me to draw an inference or two from what has been said.

And First, If the torments reserved for the wicked hereafter are eternal, what shall we say to those, who make an open profession in their creed to believe a life everlasting, a life of misery as well as happiness, and yet dare to live in the actual commission of those sins which will unavoidably, without repentance, bring them into that place of torment? Thou believest that the punishments of the impenitently wicked in another life, are eternal: "Thou dost well, the devils also believe and tremble." But know O vain man, unless this belief doth influence thy practice, and makes thee bid adieu to thy sins, every time thou repeatest thy creed, thou doest in effect say, I believe I shall be undone for ever.

But, Secondly, If the torments reserved for the wicked hereafter are eternal, then let this serve as a caution to such persons, (and it is to be feared there are some such) who go about to dissuade others from the belief of such an important truth: There being no surer way, in all probability, to encourage and promote infidelity and profaneness, than the broaching or maintaining so unwarrantable a doctrine. For if the positive threats of God concerning the eternity of hell-torments, are already found insufficient to deter men from sin, what a higher pitch of wickedness may w imagine they will quickly arrive at, when they are taught to entertain any hopes of a future recovery out of them; or, what is still worse, that their souls are hereafter to be annihilated, and become like the beasts that perish? But woe unto such blind leaders of the blind. No wonder if they both fall into that ditch. And let such corrupters of God's word know, that I testify unto every man that heareth me this day, "That if any one shall add unto, or take away from the words that are written in the book of God, God shall take his part out of the book of life, an shall add unto him all the plagues that are in that book."

Thirdly and Lastly, If the torments reserved for the wicked hereafter are eternal, then this may serve as a reproof for those who quarrel with God, and say it is inconsistent with his justice, to punish a person to all eternity, only for enjoying the pleasures of sin for a season. But such persons must be told, that it is not their thinking or calling God unjust, will make him so, no more than a condemned prisoner's saying the law or judge is unjust, will render either duly chargeable with such an imputation. But knowest thou, O worm, what blasphemy thou are guilty of, in charging God with injustice? "Shall the thing formed say to him that formed it, why hast thou made me thus?" Wilt thou presume to arraign the Almighty at the bar of thy shallow reasoning? And call him unjust, for punishing thee eternally, only because thou wishest it may not be so? But hath God said it, and shall he not do it? He hath said it: and let God be true, though every man be a liar. "Shall not the judge of all the earth do right?" Assuredly he will. And if sinners will not own his justice in his threatenings here, they will be compelled ere long to own and feel them, when tormented by him hereafter.

But to come to a more practical application of what has been delivered.

You have heard, brethren, the eternity of hell-torments plainly proved, from the express declarations of holy scriptures, and consequences naturally drawn from them. And now there seems to need no great art of rhetoric to persuade any understanding person to avoid and abhor those sins, which without repentance will certainly plunge him into this eternal gulf. The disproportion between the pleasure and the pain (if there be any pleasure in sin) is so infinitely great, that supposing it was only possible, though not certain, that the wicked would be everlastingly punished, no one that has the reason of a man, for the enjoying a little momentary pleasure, would, one might imagine, run the hazard of enduring eternal pain. But since the torments of the damned are not only possible, but certain (since God himself, who cannot lie, has told us so) for men, notwithstanding, to persist in their disobedience, and then flatter themselves, that God will not make good his threatenings, is a most egregious [gross, excessive] instance of folly and presumption.

Dives himself supposed, that if one rose from the dead, his brethren would amend their lives, but Christians, it seems, will not repent, though the Son of God died and rose again, and told them what they must expect, if they continue obstinate in evil-doing.

Would we now and then draw off our thoughts from sensible objects, and by faith meditate a while on the miseries of the damned, I doubt not but we should, as it were, hear many an unhappy soul venting his fruitless sorrows, in some such piteous moans as these.

"O wretched man that I am, who shall deliver me from this body of death!" O foolish mortal that I was, thus to bring myself into these never-ceasing tortures, for the transitory enjoyment of a few short-lived pleasures, which scarcely afforded me any satisfaction, even when I most indulged myself in them. Alas! Are these the wages, these the effects of sin? O damned apostate! First to delude me with pretended promises of happiness, and after several years drudgery in his service, thus to involve me in eternal woe. O that I had never hearkened to his beguiling insinuations! O that I had rejected his very first suggestions with the utmost detestation and abhorrence! O that I had taken up my cross and followed Christ! O that I had never ridiculed serious godliness; and out of a false politeness, condemned the truly pious as too severe, enthusiastic, or superstitious! For I then had been happy indeed, happy beyond expression, happy to all eternity, yonder in those blessed regions where they fit, clothed with unspeakable glory, and chanting forth their seraphic hallelujahs to the Lamb that sitteth upon the throne for ever. But, alas! These reflections come now too late; these wishes now are vain and fruitless. I have not suffered, and therefore must not reign with them. I have in effect denied the Lord that bought me, and therefore justly am I now denied by him. But must I live for ever tormented in these flames? Must this body of mine, which not long since lay in state, was clothed in purple and fine linen, and fared sumptuously every day, must it be here eternally confined, and made the mockery of insulting devils? O eternity! That thought fills me with despair: I must be miserable for ever."

Come then, all ye self-deluding, self-deluded sinners, and imagine yourselves for once in the place of that truly wretched man I have been here describing. Think, I beseech you by the mercies of God in Christ Jesus, think with yourselves, how racking, how unsupportable the never-dying worm of a self-condemning conscience will hereafter be to you. Think how impossible it will be for you to dwell with everlasting burnings.

Come, all ye Christians of a lukewarm, Laodicean spirit, ye Gallie's in religion, who care a little, but not enough for the things of God; O think, think with yourselves, how deplorable it will be to lose the enjoyment of heaven, and run into endless torments, merely because you will be content to be almost, and will not strive to be altogether Christians. Consider, I beseech you consider, how you will rave and curse that fatal stupidity which made you believe any thing less than true faith in Jesus, productive of a life of strict piety, self-denial, and mortification, can keep you from those torments, the eternity of which I have been endeavoring to prove.

But I can no more. These thoughts are too melancholy for me to dwell on, as well as for you to hear; and God knows, as punishing is his strange work, so denouncing his threatenings is mine. But if the bare mentioning the torments of the damned is so shocking, how terrible must the enduring of them be!

And now, are not some of you ready to cry out, "These are hard sayings, who can bear them?"

But let not sincere Christians be in the least terrified at what has been delivered: No, for you is reserved a crown, a kingdom, an eternal and exceeding weight of glory. Christ never said that the righteous, the believing, the upright, the sincere, but the wicked, merciless, negatively good professors before described, shall go into everlasting punishment. For you, who love him in sincerity, a new and living way is laid open into the Holy of Holies by the blood of Jesus Christ: and an abundant entrance will be administered unto you, at the great day of account, into eternal life. Take heed, therefore, and beware that there be not in any of you a root of bitterness springing up of unbelief: but on the contrary, steadfastly and heartily rely on the many precious promises reached out to you in the gospel, knowing that he who hath promised is faithful, and therefore will perform.

But let no obstinately wicked professors dare to apply any of the divine promises to themselves: "For it is not meet to take the children's meat and give it unto dogs:" No, to such the terrors of the Lord only belong. And as certainly as Christ will say to his true followers, "Come, ye blessed children of my Father, receive the kingdom prepared for you from the beginning of the world;" so he will unalterably pronounce this dreadful sentence against all that die in their sins, "Depart from me, ye cursed, into everlasting fire, prepared for the devil and his angels."

From which unhappy state, may God of his infinite mercy deliver us all through Jesus Christ; to whom, with thee O Father, and thee O Holy Ghost, three Persons and one eternal God, be ascribed, as is most due, all honor, power, might, majesty, and dominion, now and for ever more.

27. Blind Bartimeus

Mark 10:52,—"And Jesus said unto him,
Go thy way; thy faith hath made thee whole.
And immediately he received his sight,
and followed Jesus in the way."

When the apostle Peter was recommending Jesus of Nazareth, in one of his sermons to the Jews, he gave him a short, but withal a glorious and exalted character, "That we went about doing good." He went about, he sought occasions of doing good; it was his meat and drink to do the works of him that sent him, whilst the day of his public administration lasted. Justly was he stiled by the prophet, the sun of righteousness. For, as the sun in the natural firmament diffuses his quickening and reviving beams through the universe, so, wherever this sun of righteousness, the blessed Jesus arose, he arose with healing under his wings. He was indeed a prophet like unto Moses, and proved that he was the Messiah which was to come into the world, by the miracles which he wrought; though with this material difference, the miracles of Moses, agreeable to the Old Testament dispensation, were miracles of judgment; the miracles of Jesus, who came to bear our sicknesses and heal our infirmities, were miracles of mercy, and were wrought, not only for the cure of people's bodies, but also for the conversion of their precious and immortal souls. Sometimes, one and the same person was the subject of both these mercies. A glorious proof of this, we have in the miraculous cure wrought upon a poor blind beggar, named Bartimeus, who is to be the subject of the following discourse, and to whom the words of the text refer. "Jesus said unto him, Go thy way, thy faith hath made thee whole. And immediately he received his sight, and followed Jesus in the way."

My design is, *First*, to make some observations on the matter of fact, as recorded by the evangelists. And then,

Secondly, To point out the improvement that may be made thereof. May Jesus so bless this following discourse, that every spiritually blind hearer may receive his sight, and, after the example of Bartimeus, "follow Jesus in the way!"

If we would take a view of the whole story, we must go back to the 46th verse of this chapter, "And they (our Lord and his disciples, who, we find by the context, had been conversing together) came to Jericho," a place devoted by Joshua to the curse of God; and yet, even this place yields converts to Jesus; Zaccheus had been called there formerly; and Bartimeus, as we shall hear by-and-by, in all probability, was called now. For some good may come even out of Nazareth. Christ himself was born there, and his sovereign grace can reach and overcome the worst of people, in the very worst of places. Jesus came to Jericho. Let not his ministers, if providence points out their way, shun going to seemingly the most unlikely places to do good, some chosen vessels may be therein. Jesus and his disciples came to Jericho. They were itinerants; and, as I have frequently observed, seldom stayed long in a place; not that this is any argument against the stated settlement of particular pastors over particular parishes. But however, our Lord's practice, in this respect, gives a kind of a sanction to itinerant preaching, when persons are properly called to, and qualified for, such an employ. And I believe we may venture to affirm (though we would by no means prescribe or dictate to the Holy One of Israel) that, whenever there shall be a general revival of religion in any country, itinerant preaching will be more in vogue. And it is to be feared, that those who condemn it now, merely on account of the meanness of its appearances, would have joined with the self-righteous Scribes and Pharisees, in condemning even the Son of God himself, for such a practice.

"And as he went out of Jericho with his disciples, and a great number of people;" *oclou ikanou'* a great number of mob, or rabble, as the High-priests of that generation termed them; for these were the constant followers of Jesus of Nazareth; it was the poor that received his gospel, the common people heard him gladly, and followed him from place to place. Not that all who followed him, were his true disciples. No, some followed him only for his loaves, others out of curiosity; though some undoubtedly followed to hear, and be edified by the gracious words that proceeded out of his mouth. Jesus knew this, and was also sensible how displeasing this crowding after him was to some of the rulers of the Jewish church, who, upon every occasion, were ready to say, "Have any of the Scribes and Pharisees believed on him?" But, notwithstanding, I do not hear of our blessed Lord's sending them home but once; and that was, after they had been with him three days, and had nothing left to eat, he saw they were as sheep having no shepherd, and therefore had compassion on them, and taught them. A sufficient warrant this for gospel-ministers to preach to poor souls that follow to hear the word, whatever principle their coming may proceed from. At the same time, they should caution people against thinking themselves Christians, because they follow Christ's ministers. This our Lord frequently did, For there are many that followed Jesus, and not follow his ministers, and hear them gladly; nay, perhaps do many things, as Herod did, who, it is to be feared, will never follow them into the kingdom of heaven. Much people followed Jesus out of Jericho, but how many of them were offended in him; and afterwards, it may be, cried out, "Crucify him, crucify him." Who would depend on popularity? It is like the morning cloud, or early dew, that passeth away. But what a press, and seemingly continued hurry of business did the blessed Jesus live in! He could not be hid; go where he would, much people followed him. He had scarce time to eat bread. Happy is it for such who are called to act in a public station in the church, and to be more abundant in labors, that their Jesus has trodden in this dangerous path before them. Popularity is a fiery furnace, and no one, but he who kept the three children amidst Nebuchadnezzar's flames, can preserve popular ministers from being hurt by it. But we can do all things through Christ strengthening us. And I have often thought, that there is one consideration sufficient to extinguish, or moderate at least, any excess of joy and self-complacence, which the most popular preacher may feel, when followed even by the greatest multitudes; and that is this, "How many of these hearers will go "away, without receiving any saving benefit by my preaching; nay, how many, it may be, will only have their damnation increased by it!" As we find many will say at the great day, "hast thou not taught in our streets;" to whom Jesus shall answer, "Verily, I know you not."

But to proceed, "As our Lord went out of Jericho with his disciples, and a great number of people, blind Bartimeus, (the son of Timeus) sat by the highway-side begging." It should seem that he was a noted, though by no means what we commonly call, a sturdy beggar; having no other way, as he had lost his sight, to get his bread; his case was still the more pitiable, if he was, as some think the name imports, the blind son of a blind father. It may be, her begged for his father and himself too; and if so, then this may give us light into that passage of Matthew 20:22, where we are told, that "two men spake to Jesus." It might be father and son, though only one is mentioned here, because he only followed Jesus in the way. Thus that holy, judicious, and practical expositor of holy writ, Mr. Henry. But however this be, he is not blamed for begging, neither should we discomment others for so doing, when providence calls to it. It was the unjust steward that said, "To beg I am ashamed." It is our pride that often makes us unwilling to be beholden; Jesus was not thus minded, he lived, as it were, upon alms; the women that followed him, ministered to him of their substance. Bartimeus, not being able to dig, begs for his living; and, in order to make a better trade of it, sat by the highway-side, in all probability, without, or near the gate of the city, where people must necessarily pass in and out. But though he had lost his sight, he had his hearing perfect; and it should comfort us, if we have lost one sense, that we have the use of another, and that we are not deprived of the benefit of all. Happy was it for Bartimeus that he could hear, though not see. For in all probability, upon hearing the noise and clamor of the much people that followed after our Lord, his curiosity set him upon inquiring into the cause of it, and some one or another told him, "that Jesus of Nazareth was passing by;" Jesus of Nazareth, called so, because he was bred there, or out of contempt; Nazareth being either a very mean, or very wicked place, or both, which made guileless Nathaniel say, "Can any good come out of Nazareth?" And what does Bartimeus do when he hears of Jesus? We are told, ver. Mark 10:47, "And when he heard that it was Jesus of Nazareth, he began to cry out." This plainly denotes, that though the eyes of his body were shut, yet the eyes of his mind were, in some degree, opened, so that he saw, perhaps, more than most of the multitude that followed after Jesus; for, as soon as he heard of him, he began to cry out; which he would not have done, had he not heard of him before, and believed also, that he was both able and willing to restore sight to the blind. "He began to cry out." This implies, that he had a deep sense of his own misery, and the need which he had of a cure; his prayers did not freeze as they went out of his lips; he began to cry out, that Jesus might hear him, notwithstanding the noise of the throng; and he began to cry out, as soon as he heard he was passing by, not knowing whether he might ever enjoy such an opportunity any more. "He began to cry out, Jesus, thou Son of David, have mercy upon me." The people called him Jesus of Nazareth. Bartimeus stiles him, "Jesus, thou Son of David." Thereby evidencing, that he believed him to be the Messiah who was to come into the world, unto whom the Lord God was to give the throne of his father David, and of whose kingdom there was to be no end. "Jesus, thou Son of David;" or, as it is in the parallel place of St. Matthew 20:30, "O Lord, thou son of David;" of whom it had been long foretold, Isaiah 35, that when he should come, "the eyes of the blind should be opened." "Have mercy upon me," the natural language of a soul brought to lie down at the feet of a sovereign God. Here is no laying claim to a cure by way of merit; no proud, self-righteous, God I thank thee that I am not as other men are: not bringing in a reckoning of performances, nor any doubting of Jesus' power or willingness to heal him, but out of the abundance of the heart, his mouth speaketh, and, in the language of the poor, broken-hearted publican, he cries out, "Jesus, thou Son of David, have mercy on me." Jesus, thou friend of sinners, thou Savior, who, though thou be the true God, wast pleased to become the Son of David, and to be made man, that thou mightest seek and save those that were lost, have mercy upon me; let thy bowels yearn towards a poor, miserable, blind beggar?

One would have thought that such a moving petition as this would have melted the whole multitude, that heard his piteous cry, into compassion, and induced some at least to turn suitors in his behalf, or help to carry him to the blessed Jesus. But instead of that, we are told, ver. Mark 10:48, that "many charged him." The word in the original seems to imply a charge, attended with threatening, and spoken in an angry manner. They charged him "to hold his peace;" and it may be, threatened to beat him if he did not. They looked upon him beneath the notice of Jesus of Nazareth, and were ready enough to ask, whether he thought Jesus Christ had nothing else to do but to wait upon him. This was, no doubt, very discouraging to blind Bartimeus. For opposition comes closest when it proceeds from those who are esteemed followers of the Lamb. The spouse complains as of something peculiarly afflicting, that her own mother's children were angry with her. But opposition only serves to whet the edge of true devotion, and therefore Bartimeus, instead of being silenced by their charges and threatenings, "cried out the more a great deal, thou Son of David, have mercy on me." Still he breaks out into the same humble language, and, if Jesus, the Son of David, will have mercy on him, he cares not much what some of his peevish followers said of, or did unto him. This was not a vain repetition, but a devout reiteration of his request. We may sometimes repeat the same words, and yet not be guilty of that battalogia, or vain speaking, which our Lord condemns. For our Lord himself prayed in his agony, and said twice the same words; "Father, if it be possible, let this cup pass from me." Thus Bartimeus, "Jesus, thou Son of David, have mercy upon me." And how does the Son of David treat him? Does he join issue with the multitude, and charge him to hold his peace? Or does he go on, thinking him beneath his notice? no; for, says St. Mark, ver.

Mark 10:49," And Jesus stood still," though he was on a journey, and it may be in haste (for it is not losing time to stop now and then on a journey to do a good office by the way) "and commanded him to be called:" why so? To teach us to be condescending and kind even to poor, if real beggars, and tacitly to reprove the blind, misguided zeal of those who had charged him to hold his peace. By this also our Lord prepares the multitude the better to take the more notice of the blind man's faith, and of his own mercy and power exerted in the healing of him. For there are times and seasons when we are called to perform acts of charity in the most public manner, and that too very consistently with the injunction of our Savior, "not to let our right hand know what our left hand doeth." For there is a great deal of difference between giving alms, and exercising acts of charity, that are seen of men, and doing them, that they may be seen; the one is always sinful, the other often becomes our duty. Jesus commanded Bartimeus to be called, "and they called him." Who called him? It may be, those who a little before charged him t hold his peace. For it often happens, that our opposers and discouragers, afterwards become our friends, "When a man's ways please the Lord, he makes his enemies be at peace with him." And it is to be wished, that all who have charged poor souls, that are crying after Jesus, to hold their peace, and to spare themselves, and not be righteous over-much, would imitate the people here, and encourage those they once persecuted and maligned. "They call the blind man, saying unto him, Be of good comfort, ruse, he calleth thee." The words, and manner of speaking them, implies haste, and a kind of solicitude for the blind man's relief. O! that we might hereby learn to be patient and long-suffering, towards opposers. For it may be, that many may oppose awakened souls, not out of enmity, but through prejudice and misinformation, through ignorance and unbelief, and a real, though perhaps false, persuasion, that their relations are going in a wrong way. By and by they may be convinced, that Christ is indeed calling them, and then they may become real and open friends to the cause and work of God; if not, it is our duty to behave with meekness towards all, and not to render railing for railing, but contrary-wise blessing, knowing that we are thereunto called, that we may inherit a blessing; Jesus did not break out into harsh language against these opposers, neither did Bartimeus. "Our Lord stood still, and commanded him to be called; and they call the blind man; saying unto him, Be of good comfort, rise, he calleth thee; and he, casting away his garment, rose and came to Jesus." Had Bartimeus not been in earnest when he cried, "Jesus, thou Son of David, have mercy upon me," he might have said, why do you mock me? why bid ye me arise; rise indeed I can, but after I am risen, how can I, being blind, find my way unto him? If he will come to me, it is well; if not, all you r calling availeth nothing, it being impossible for me to find my way. Thus thousands now-a-days object to evangelical preachers, saying, Why do you bid us come to, and believe on Jesus Christ, when you tell us it is impossible of ourselves to turn to God, or to do good works; and that no one can come unto him, unless the Father draw him. Is not this like the people's calling upon Bartimeus, to arise and come to Jesus, when he could not possibly see his way before him? true, it is so; and would to God that all who make this objection, would imitate Bartimeus, and put forth the strength they have! What if we do call you to come, and to believe on the Lord Jesus Christ, that you may be saved? Does this imply, that you have a power in yourselves to do so? No, in no wise, no more than Jesus saying unto Lazarus' dead and stinking carcass, "Come forth," implied, that Lazarus had a power to raise himself from the grave. We call to you, being commanded to preach the gospel to every creature, hoping and praying, that Christ's power may accompany the word, and make it effectual to the quickening and raising of your dead souls. We also call to you to believe, upon the same account as Jesus said unto the lawyer, "do this, and thou shalt live;" that you seeing your utter inability to come, might thereby be convinced of your unbelief, and be led to ask for faith of him, whose gift it is, and who is therefore in scripture emphatically stiled the Author, as well as Finisher, of our faith. Add to this, that it is your duty to wait at the pool, or to make us of the strength you have, in the earnest and steady performance of all commanded duty. For though you cannot do what is spiritually good, because you want spiritual principles of action, yet ye may do what is morally and materially good, inasmuch as ye are reasonable creatures; and though doing your duty as you can, no ways deserves mercy, or entitles you to it, yet it is the way in which you are required to walk, and the way in which God us usually found. While you are attempting to stretch out your withered arm, peradventure it may be restored; and who knows but Jesus may work faith in you, by his almighty power?

Bartimeus has set before such objectors an example; O that they would once submit to be taught by a poor blind beggar! For he, casting away his garment, rose, and blind as he was, came to Jesus; "casting away his garment." This seems to be a large coat or cloak, that he wore to screen himself from the rain and cold; undoubtedly, it was the most necessary and valuable vestment he had, and one would have thought, that he should have taken this along with him; but he knew very well, that if he did so, it might hang about his heels, and thereby his reaching Jesus be retarded at least, if not prevented entirely. Valuable therefore as it was to him, he cast it away. The word implies, that he threw it from off his shoulders, with great precipitancy and resolution, knowing that if he got a cure, which he now hoped for, by Christ's calling him, he should never want his garment again. And thus will all do that are in earnest about coming to Jesus here, or seeing and enjoying him in his kingdom eternally hereafter. They will cut off a right hand, they will pluck out a right eye, they will leave father and mother, husband and wife, yes, and their own lives also, rather than not be his disciples. The apostle Paul, therefore, exhorts Christians, to "lay aside every weight, and the sin that doth most easily beset them," or hand about their heels, as the word in the original imports; alluding to the custom of the Romans, who wore long garments. Such a one was this, which Bartimeus had wrapped round him. But he, to show that he sincerely desired to recover his sight, casting it away, arose and came to Jesus. And what treatment did Jesus give him? did he say, come not nigh me, thou impudent noisy beggar? No, "he answered and said unto him, What wilt thou, that I should do unto thee?" an odd question this, seemingly. For did not our Lord know what he wanted? Yes, he did; but the Lord Jesus dealt with him, as he deals with us. He will make us acknowledge our wants ourselves, that we thereby may confess our dependence upon him, and be made more sensible of the need we stand in, of his divine assistance. The blind man immediately replies, "Lord, (thereby intimating his belief of Christ's divinity) that I might receive my sight." Methinks, I see the poor creature listening to the voice of our Savior, and with looks and gestures bespeaking the inward earnestness of his soul, he cries out, "Lord, that I may receive my sight." As though he had said, I believe thou are that Messiah who was to come into the world. I have heard of thy fame, O Jesus! And hearing the long-wished-for glad tidings of thy coming this way, I cry unto thee, asking not for silver and gold, but what thou, thou alone canst give me, Lord, that I might receive my sight. No sooner does he ask, but he receives. For, verse Mark 10:52, "Jesus said unto him, Go thy way, thy faith hath made thee whole; and immediately he received his sight." With the word there went a power; and he that spake light out of darkness, saying, "Let there be light, and there was light," commanded light into this poor blind beggar's eyes, and behold there was light. The miracle was instantaneous; immediately he received his sight. And next to a miracle it was, that by breaking into open light all at once, he was not struck blind again: but he that gave the sight, preserved it when given. O! happy Bartimeus! Thy eyes are now opened, and the very first object thou dost behold, is the ever-loving, altogether-lovely Jesus. Methinks I see thee transported with wonder and admiration, and all the disciples, and the multitude, gazing around thee! And now, having received thy sight, why dost thou not obey the Lord's command, and go thy way? Why doest thou not haste to fetch thy garment, that thou just now in a hurry didst cast away? No, no! with his bodily eyes, I believe he received also a fresh addition of spiritual sight, and though others saw no form or comeliness in the blessed Jesus, that they should desire him; yet he by an eye of faith discovered such transcendent excellencies in his royal person, and felt at the same time such a divine attraction towards his all-bountiful benefactor, that instead of going his way to fetch his garment, "he followed Jesus in the way;" and by his actions, says with faithful, honest-hearted Ruth, "entreat me not to leave thee; for whither thou goest, I will go; where thou lodgest, I will lodge; thy people shall be my people; and thy God, my God." He followed Jesus in the way; the narrow way, the way of the cross; and I doubt not but long since he has followed him to his crown, and is at this time sitting with him at the right hand of his Father.

And now, my dear hearers, how find you your hearts affected at the relation of this notable miracle which Jesus wrought? Are you not ready to break out into the language of the song of Moses, and to say, "Who is like unto thee O Lord, glorious in holiness, fearful in praises, continually doing wonders!" Marvelous are thy works, O Jesus, and that our souls know right well! But we must not stop here, in admiring what the Lord did for Bartimeus; this, no doubt, as well as other parts of Scripture, was written for our learning, upon whom the ends of the world are come; consequently, as was proposed in the

Second place, we should see what spiritual improvement can be made of this history, upon which we have already been making some remarks.

A natural man, indeed, goes no further than the outward court of the Scripture, and reads this, and the other miracles of our blessed Savior, just in the same manner as he reads Homer's battles, or the exploits of Alexander. But God forbid, that we should rest in only hearing this matter of fact. For I tell thee, O man, I tell thee, O woman, whoever thou art, that sittest this day under a preached gospel, that if thou art in a natural state, thou art as blind in thy soul, as Bartimeus was in his body; a blind child of a blind father, even of thy father Adam, who lost his sight when he lost his innocence, and entailed his blindness, justly inflicted, upon thee, and me, and his whole posterity. Some think indeed, that thy see; but alas! such talk only like men in their sleep, like persons beside themselves; the scriptures every where represent fallen man, not only as spiritually blind, but dead also; and we no more know, by nature, savingly the way of salvation by Jesus Christ, than Bartimeus, when he was blind, knew the colors of the rainbow. This, I trust, some of you begin to feel, I see you concerned, I see you weeping, and, was I to ask some of you, what you want to have done unto you? I know your answer would be, that we may receive our sight. And God forbid, that I should charge you to hold your peace, as though Jesus would not regard you! No, your being made sensible of your natural blindness, and crying thus earnestly after Jesus, is a sign at least, that you are awakened by his holy Spirit (though it is possible, that you may cry with an exceeding bitter cry, as Esau did, and be lost at last); however, Christian charity induces me to believe and hope the best; I will therefore, in the language of those who afterwards encouraged Bartimeus, say unto you, Arise, take comfort for, I trust, Jesus is calling you; follow therefore the example of Bartimeus; cast away your garment; lay aside every weight, and the sin which doth most easily beset you, arise, and come to Jesus. He commands me, by his written word, to call to you, and say, "Come unto him, all ye that are weary, and heavy laden, and he will refresh you, he will give you rest." Be not afraid, ye seek Jesus of Nazareth; behold, he comes forth to meet you; ye are now on the highway side, and Jesus, I trust, is passing by; I feel his presence, I hope many of you feel it too; O then, cry mightily to him, who is mighty and willing to save you; lay yourselves at the feet of sovereign grace, say unto him, "Jesus, thou Son of David, have mercy on me," in the same frame as Bartimeus did, and Jesus will answer you, he will not cast out your prayer; according to your faith, so shall it be done unto you. Blind as you are, you shall notwithstanding, receive your sight; Satan, indeed, and unbelief, will suggest many objections to you, your carnal relations will also join issue with them, and charge you to hold your peace; one will tell you, that your blindness is too inveterate to be cured; another, that it is too late; a third, that though Jesus can, yet he will not have mercy upon such poor, blind, despicable beggars, as ye are; but, the more they charge you to hold your peace, do you cry out so much the more a great deal, "Jesus, thou Son of David, have mercy on us." Jesus, thou Savior, thou friend of sinners, thou Son of David, and therefore a Son of man! Gracious words! Endearing appellations! Be encouraged by them, to draw nigh unto him. Though David's Lord, yet he is become David's Son, after the flesh, that ye through him may be made the sons of God: no matter what thou art, O woman, what thou art, O man; though thou art literally a poor beggar, think not thy condition too mean for Jesus to take notice of; he came into the highways and hedges, to call such poor beggars in; or, if you are rich, think not yourselves too high to stoop to Jesus; for his is the King of kings; and you never will be truly rich, until you are made rich in Jesus; fear not being despised, or losing a little worldly honor: one sight of Jesus will make amends for all: you will find something so inviting, so attracting, so satisfying, in the altogether lovely Lamb of God, that every sublunary enjoyment will sicken, and die, and vanish before you; and you will o more desire your former vain and trifling amusements, than Bartimeus, after he had received his sight, desired to go back again and fetch his garment. O that there may be many such blind beggars among you this day!

Here is a great multitude of people following me, a poor worm, this day. I rejoice to see the fields thus white, ready unto harvest, and to spread the gospel-net amidst so many; but alas! I shall return home with a heavy heart, unless some of you will arise and come to my Jesus; I desire to preach Him, and not myself; rest not in hearing and following me. Behold, believe on, and follow the Lamb of God, who came to take away the sins of the world. Indeed, I do not despair of any of you, neither am I discouraged, on account of my preaching in the highways and hedges; Jesus called Zaccheus; Jesus called Bartimeus, as he passed through Jericho; that cursed, that devoted place; and why may he not call some of you, out of these despised fields? Is his arm shortened, that he cannot save? Is he not as mighty now, and as willing to save, even to the uttermost, all that come to the father through him, as he was seventeen hundred years ago? Assuredly he is; he hath said, and he also will do it, "Whosoever cometh to me, I will in no wise cast out." In no wise, or by no means. O encouraging words! Sinners, believe ye this? arise then, be of good comfort, for Jesus is indeed calling you. Some of you, I trust, have obeyed this invitation, and have had a sight of him long ago; I know then, you will bless and love him; and if he should say unto you, as he did unto Bartimeus, go you your way; your answer would be, we love our master, and will not go from him. But suffer ye the word of exhortation:

Suffer me to stir up your pure minds by way of remembrance, show that you have indeed seen him, and that you do indeed love him, by following him in the way; I mean, in the way of the cross, the way of his ordinances, and in the way of his holy commandments; for alas! the love of many waxeth cold, and few there are that follow Jesus rightly in the way; few there are that cast away their garments so heartily as they should; some idol or another hangs about us, and hinders us in running the race that is set before us. Awake therefore, ye sleepy, though, it may be, wise virgins. Awake, awake, put on strength; shake yourselves from the dust; arise and follow Jesus more closely in the way, than ever you did yet. Lift up the hands that hang down, and strengthen the feeble knees. Provide right paths for your feet, lest that which is lame be turned out of the way, but rather be ye healed. For though the way be narrow, yet it is not long; "though the gate be straight, (to use the words of pious bishop Beveridge) yet it opens into everlasting life." O that ye may get a fresh sight of him again this day! That would be like oil to the wheels of your graces, and make your souls like the chariots of Aminadab. It is only owing to your losing sight of him, that you go so heavily from day to day. A sight of Jesus, like the sun rising in the morning, dispels the darkness and gloominess that lies upon the soul. Take therefore a fresh view of him, O believers, and never rest until you are translated to see him as he is, and to live with him for evermore, in the kingdom of heaven. Even so, Lord Jesus, Amen and Amen!

28. Directions How to Hear Sermons

Luke 8:18—"Take heed, therefore, how ye hear."

The occasion of our Lord's giving this caution, was this: Perceiving that much people were gathered together to hear him out of every city, and knowing (for he is God, and knoweth all things) that many, if not most of them, would be hearers only, and not doers of the word; he spake to them by a parable, wherein, under the similitude of a sower that went out to sow his seed, he plainly intimated, how few there were amongst them, who would receive any saving benefit from his doctrine, or bring forth fruit unto perfection.

The application one would imagine should have been plain and obvious; but the disciples, as yet unenlightened in any great degree by the Holy Spirit, and therefore unable to see into the hidden mysteries of the kingdom of God, dealt with our Savior, as people ought to deal with their ministers; they discoursed with him privately about the meaning of what he had taught them in public; and with a sincere desire of doing their duty, asked for an interpretation of the parable.

Our blessed Lord, as he always was willing to instruct those that were teachable, (herein setting his ministers an example to be courteous and easy of access) freely told them the signification. And withal, to make them more cautious and more attentive to his doctrine for the future, he tells them, that they were in an especial manner to be the light of the world, and were to proclaim on the house-top whatsoever he told them in secret: and as their improving the knowledge already imparted, was the only condition upon which more was to be given them, it therefore highly concerned them to "take heed how they heard."

From the context then it appears, that the words were primarily spoken to the Apostles themselves. But as it is to be feared, out of those many thousands that flock to hear sermons, but few, comparatively speaking, are effectually influenced by them, I cannot but think it very necessary to remind you of the caution given by our Lord to his disciples, and to exhort you with the utmost earnestness, to "take heed how you hear."

In prosecution of which design I shall,

First, Prove that every one ought to take all opportunities of hearing sermons. And,

Secondly, I shall lay down some cautions and directions, in order to your hearing with profit and advantage.

First, I am to prove, that every one ought to take all opportunities of hearing sermons.

That there have always been particular persons set apart by God to instruct and exhort his people to practice what he should require of them, is evident from many passages of scripture. St. Jude tells us, that "Enoch, the seventh from Adam, prophesied (or preached) concerning the Lord's coming with ten thousand of his saints to judgment." And Noah, who lived not long after, is stiled by St. Peter, "a preacher of righteousness." And though in all the intermediate space between the flood and giving of the law, we hear but of few preachers, yet we may reasonably conclude, that God never left himself without witness, but at sundry times, and after diverse manners, spoke to our fathers by the patriarchs and prophets.

But however it was before, we are assured that after the delivery of the law, God constantly separated to himself a certain order of men to preach to, as well as pray for his people; and commanded them to inquire their duty at the priests mouths. And thought the Jews were frequently led into captivity, and for their sins scattered abroad on the face of the earth, yet he never utterly forsook his church, but still kept up a remnant of prophets and preachers, as Ezekiel, Jeremiah, Daniel, and others, to reprove, instruct, and call them to repentance.

Thus was it under the law. Nor has the church been worse, but infinitely better provided for under the gospel. For when Jesus Christ, that great High-priest, had through the eternal Spirit offered himself, as a full, perfect, sufficient sacrifice and satisfaction for the sins of the whole world, and after his resurrection had all power committed to him, both in heaven and earth, he gave commission to his Apostles, and in them to all succeeding ministers, to "go and preach his gospel to every creature;" promising to "to be with them, to guide, assist, strengthen, and comfort them always, even to the end of the world."

But if it be the duty of ministers to preach, (and woe be to them if they do not preach the gospel, for a necessity is laid upon them) no doubt, the people are obliged to attend to them; for otherwise, wherefore are ministers sent?

And how can we here avoid admiring the love and tender care which our dear Redeemer has expressed for his spouse the church? Who, because he could not be always with us in person, on account it was expedient he should go away, and as our forerunner take possession of that glory he had purchased by his precious blood, yet would not leave us comfortless, but first settled a sufficient number of pastors and teachers; and afterwards, according to his promise, actually did and will continue to sent down the Holy Ghost, to furnish them and their successors with proper gifts and graces "for the work of the ministry, for the perfecting of the saints, for the edifying of his body in love, till we all come in the unity of the spirit, to the fullness of the measure of the stature of Christ."

O how insensible are those persons of this unspeakable gift, who do despite to the Spirit of grace, who crucify the Son of God afresh, and put him to an open shame, by willfully refusing to attend on so great a means of salvation? How dreadful will the end of such men be? How aggravating, that light should come into the world, that the glad tidings of salvation should be so very frequently proclaimed in this populous city, and that so many should loath this spiritual manna, this angels food, and call it light bread? How much more tolerable will it be for Tyre and Sidon, for Sodom and Gomorrah, than for such sinners? Better, that men had never heard of a Savior being born, than after they have heard, not to give heed to the ministry of those, who are employed as his ambassadors, to transact affairs between God and their souls.

We may, though at a distance, without a spirit of prophesy, foretell the deplorable condition of such men; behold them cast into hell, lifting up their eyes, being in torment, and crying out, How often would our ministers have gathered us, as a hen gathereth her chickens under her wings? But we would not. O that we had known in that our day, the things that belonged to our everlasting peace! But now they are for ever hid from our eyes.

Thus wretched, thus inconceivably miserable, will such be as slight and make a mock at the public preaching of the gospel. But taking it for granted, there are but few, if any, of this unhappy stamp, who think it worth their while to tread the courts of the Lord's house, I pass on not to the

Second general thing proposed, to lay down some cautions and directions, in order to your hearing sermons with profit and advantage.

And here, if we reflect on what has been already delivered, and consider that preaching is an ordinance of God, a means appointed by Jesus Christ himself for promoting his kingdom amongst men, you cannot reasonably be offended, if, in order that you may hear sermons with profit and advantage, I

1. Direct or entreat you to come to hear them, not out of curiosity, but from a sincere desire to know and do your duty.

Formality and hypocrisy in any religious exercise, is an abomination unto the Lord. And to enter his house merely to have our ears entertained, and not our hearts reformed, must certainly be highly displeasing to the Most High God, as well as unprofitable to ourselves.

Hence it is, that so many remain unconverted, yea, unaffected with the most evangelical preaching; so that like St. Paul's companions, before his conversion, they only hear the preacher's voice with their outward ears, but do not experience the power of it inwardly in their hearts. Or, like the ground near Gideon's fleece, they remain untouched; whilst others, who came to be fed with the sincere milk of the word, like the fleece itself, are watered by the dew of God's heavenly blessing, and grow thereby.

Flee therefore, my brethren, flee curiosity, and prepare your hearts by a humble disposition, to receive with meekness the engrafted word, and then it will be a means, under God, to quicken, build up, purify, and save your souls.

2. A second direction I shall lay down for the same purpose, is, not only to prepare your hearts before you hear, but also to give diligent heed to the things that are spoken from the word of God.

If an earthly king was to issue out a royal proclamation, on performing or not performing the conditions therein contained, the life or death of his subjects entirely depended, how solicitous would they be to hear what those conditions were? And shall not we pay the same respect to the King of kings, and Lord of lords, and lend an attentive ear to his ministers, when they are declaring, in his name, how our pardon, peace, and happiness may be secured?

When God descended on mount Sinai in terrible majesty, to give unto his people the law, how attentive were they to his servant Moses? And if they were so earnest to hear the thunderings or threatenings of the law, shall not we be as solicitous to hear from the ministers of Christ, the glad tidings of the gospel?

Whilst Christ was himself on earth, it is said, that the people hung upon him to hear the gracious words that proceeded out of his mouth. And if we looked on ministers as we ought, as the sent of Jesus Christ, we should hang upon them to hear their words also.

Besides, the sacred truths that gospel ministers deliver, are not dry insipid lectures on moral philosophy, intended only to amuse us for a while; but the great mysteries of godliness, which, therefore, we are bound studiously to liken to, left through our negligence we should either not understand them, or by any other means let them slip.

But how regardless are those of this direction, who, instead of hanging on the preacher to hear him, doze or sleep whilst he is speaking to them from God? Unhappy men! Can they not watch with our blessed Lord one hour? What! Have they never read how Eutychus fell down as he was sleeping, when St. Paul continued like discourse till midnight, and was taken up dead?

But to return. Though you may prepare your hearts, as you may think, by a teachable disposition, and be attentive whilst discourses are delivering, yet this will profit you little, unless you observe a

3. A third direction, Not to entertain any the least prejudice against the minister.

For could a preacher speak with the tongue of men and angels, if his audience was prejudiced against him, he would be but as sounding brass, or tinkling cymbal.

That was the reason why Jesus Christ himself, the Eternal Word, could not do many mighty works, nor preach to any great effect among those of his own country; for they were offended at him: And was this same Jesus, this God incarnate, again to bow the heavens, and to come down speaking as never man spake, yet, if we were prejudiced against him, as the Jews were, we should harden our hearts as the Jews did theirs.

Take heed therefore, my brethren, and beware of entertaining any dislike against those whom the Holy Ghost has made overseers over you. Consider that the clergy are men of lie passions with yourselves: and though we should even hear a person teaching others to do, what he has not learned himself; yet, that is no sufficient reason for rejecting his doctrine: for ministers speak not in their own, but Christ's name. And we know who commanded the people to do whatsoever the Scribes and Pharisees should say unto them, though they said but did not. But

4. Fourthly, As you ought not to be prejudiced against, so you should be careful not to depend too much on a preacher, or think more highly of him than you ought to think. For though this be an extreme that people seldom run into, yet preferring one teacher in apposition to another, has often been of ill consequence to the church of God. It was a fault which the great Apostle of the Gentiles condemned in the Corinthians. For whereas one said, "I am of Paul; another, I am of Apollos: are ye not carnal," says he? "For who is Paul, and who is Apollos, but instruments in God's hands by whom you believed?" And are not all ministers sent forth to be ministering ambassadors to those who shall be heirs of salvation? And are they not all therefore greatly to be esteemed for their work's sake.

The Apostle, it is true, commands us to pay double honor to those who labor in the word and doctrine: but then to prefer one minister at the expense of another, (perhaps, to such a degree, as when you have actually entered a church, to come out again because he does not preach) is earthly, sensual, devilish.

Not to mention that popularity and applause cannot but be exceedingly dangerous, even to a rightly informed mind; and must necessarily fill any thinking man with a holy jealousy, lest he should take that honor to himself, which is due only to God, who alone qualifies him for his ministerial labors, and from whom alone every good and perfect gift cometh.

5. A Fifth direction I would recommend is, to make a particular application of every thing that is delivered to your own hearts.

When our Savior was discoursing at the last supper

with his beloved disciples, and foretold that one of them should betray him, each of them immediately applied it to his own heart, and said, "Lord, is it I?" And would persons, in like manner, when preachers are dissuading from any sin, or persuading to any duty, instead of crying, this was designed against such and such a one, turn their thoughts inwardly, and say, Lord, is it I? How far more beneficial should we find discourses to be, than now they generally are?

But we are apt to wander too much abroad; always looking at the mote with is in our neighbor's eye, rather than at the beam which is in our own. Haste we now to the

6. Sixth and last direction: If you would receive a blessing from the Lord, when you hear his word preached, pray to him, both before, in, and after every sermon, to endue the minister with power to speak, and to grant you a will and ability to put in practice, what he shall show from the book of God to be your duty.

This would be an excellent means to render the word preached effectual to the enlightening and enflaming your hearts; and without this, all the other means before prescribed will be in vain.

No doubt it was this consideration that made St. Paul so earnestly entreat his beloved Ephesians to intercede with God for him: "Praying always, with all manner of prayer and supplication in the spirit, and for me also, that I may open my mouth with boldness, to make known the mysteries of the gospel." And if so great an Apostle as St. Paul, needed the prayers of his people, much more do those ministers, who have only the ordinary gifts of the Holy Spirit.

Besides, this would be a good proof that you sincerely desired to do, as well as to know the will of God. And it must highly profit both ministers and people; because God, through your prayers, will give them a double portion of his Holy Spirit, whereby they will be enabled to instruct you more fully in the things which pertain to the kingdom of God.

And O that all who hear me this day, would seriously apply their hearts to practice what has now been told them! How would ministers see Satan, like lightning, fall from heaven, and people find the word preached sharper than a two-edged sword, and mighty, through God, to the pulling down of the devil's strong holds!

The Holy Ghost would then fall on all them that hear the word, as when St. Peter preached; the gospel of Christ would have free course, run very swiftly, and thousands again be converted by a sermon.

For "Jesus Christ is the same yesterday, today, and for ever." He has promised to be with his ministers always, even unto the end of the world. And the reason why we do not receive larger effusions of the blessed Spirit of God, is not because our all-powerful Redeemer's hand is shortened, but because we do not expect them, and confine them to the primitive times.

It does indeed sometimes happen, that God, to magnify his free grace in Christ Jesus, is found of them that sought him not; a notorious sinner is forcibly worked upon by a public sermon, and plucked as a firebrand out of the fire. But this is not God's ordinary way of acting; No, for the generality, he only visits those with the power of his word, who humbly wait to know what he would have them to do; and sends unqualified hearers not only empty, but hardened away.

Take heed, therefore, ye careless, curious professors, if any such be here present, how you hear. Remember, that whether we think of it or not, "we must all appear before the judgment seat of Christ;" where ministers must give a strict account of the doctrine they have delivered, and you as strict a one, how you have improved under it. And, good God! How will you be able to stand at the bar of an angry, sin-avenging judge, and see so many discourses you have despised, so many ministers, who once longed and labored for the salvation of your precious and immortal souls, brought out as so many swift witnesses against you? Will it be sufficient then, think you, to alledge, that you went to hear them only out of curiosity, to pass away an idle hour, to admire the oratory, or ridicule the simplicity of the preacher? No; God will then let you know, that you ought to have come out of better principles; that every sermon has been put down to your account, and that you must then be justly punished for not improving by them.

But fear not, you little flock, who with meekness receive the ingrafted word, and bring forth the peaceable fruits of righteousness; for it shall not be so with you. No, you will be your minister's joy, and their crown of rejoicing in the day of our Lord Jesus: And they will present you in a holy triumph, faultless, and unblameable, to our common Redeemer, saying, "Behold us, O Lord, and the children which thou hast given us."

But still take heed how you hear: for upon your improving the grace you have, more shall be given, and you shall have abundance. "He is faithful that he promised, who also will do it." Nay, God from out of Zion, shall so bless you, that every sermon you hear shall communicate to you a fresh supply of spiritual knowledge.

The word of God shall dwell in you richly; you shall go on from strength to strength, from one degree of grace unto another, till being grown up to be perfect men in Christ Jesus, and filled with all the fullness of God, you shall be translated by death to see him as he is, and to sing praises before his throne with angels and archangels, cherubim and seraphim, and the general assembly of the first-born, whose names are written in heaven, for ever and ever.

Which God.

29. The Extent and Reasonableness of Self-Denial

Luke 9:23—"And he said unto them all, if any man will come after me, let him deny himself."

Whoever reads the gospel with a single eye, and sincere intentions, will find, that our blessed Lord took all opportunities of reminding his disciples that his kingdom was not of this world; that his doctrine was a doctrine of the cross; and that their professing themselves to be his followers, would call them to a constant state of voluntary suffering and self-denial.

The words of the text afford us one instance, among many, of our savior's behavior in this matter: for having in the preceding verses revealed himself to Peter, and the other apostles, to be "The Christ of God;" lest they should be too much elated with such a peculiar discovery of his deity, or think that their relation to so great a personage would be attended with nothing but pomp and grandeur, he tells then, in the 22nd verse, that "the son of man was to suffer many things," in this world, though he was to be crowned with eternal glory and honor in the next: and that if any of them or their posterity would share in the same honor, they must bear a part with him in his self-denial and sufferings. For "He said unto them all, if any man will come after me, let him deny himself."

From which words I shall consider these three things:

I. *First*, The nature of the self-denial recommended in the text; and in how many respects we must deny ourselves, in order to come after Jesus Christ.

II. *Secondly*, I shall endeavor to prove the universality and reasonableness of this duty of self-denial.

III. *Thirdly*, I shall offer some considerations, which may serve as so man motives to reconcile us to, and quicken us in, the practice of this self-denial.

I. *First*, I am to show you the nature of the self-denial recommended in the text; or in how many respects we must deny ourselves in order to follow Jesus Christ.

Now as the faculties of the soul are distinguished by the understanding, will and affections; so in all these must each of us deny himself. We must not lean to our own understanding, being wise in our own eyes, and prudent in our own sight; but we must submit our short-sighted reason to the light of divine revelation. There are mysteries in religion, which are above, though not contrary to our natural reason: and therefore we shall never become Christians unless we call down imaginations, "and every high thing that exalteth itself against the knowledge of God, and bring into captivity every thought to the obedience of Christ." It is in this respect, as well as others, that we must become fools for Christ's sake, and acknowledge we know nothing without revelation, as we ought to know. We must, with all humility and reverence, embrace the truths revealed to us in the holy scriptures; for thus only can we become truly wise, even "Wise unto salvation." It was matter of our blessed Lord's thanksgiving to his heavenly father, that he had "hidden these things from the wise and prudent, and had revealed them unto babes." And in this respect also we must "be converted and become as little children," teachable, and willing to follow the Lamb into whatsoever mysteries he shall be pleased to lead us; and believe and practice all divine truths, not because we can demonstrate them, but because God, "who cannot lie," has revealed them to us.

Hence then we may trace infidelity to its fountain head; for it is nothing else, but a pride of the understanding, an unwillingness to submit to the truths of God, that makes so many, professing themselves wise, to become such fools as to deny the Lord, who has so dearly bought them; and dispute the divinity of that eternal Word, "in whom they live, and move, and have their being;" Whereby it is justly to be feared, they will bring upon themselves sure, if not swift destruction.

But, as we must deny ourselves in our understandings, so must we deny, or, as it might be more properly rendered, renounce our wills; that is, we must make our own wills no principle of action, but "whether we eat or drink, or whatsoever we do, we must do all, (not merely to please ourselves, but) to the glory of God." Not that we are therefore to imagine we are to have no pleasure in any thing we do: "Wisdom's ways are ways of pleasantness;" but pleasing ourselves must not be the principal, but only the subordinate end of our actions.

And I cannot but particularly press this doctrine upon you, because it is the grand secret of our holy religion. It is this, my brethren, that distinguishes the true Christian from the mere moralist and formal professor; and without which none of our actions are acceptable in God's sight: For "if thine eye be single," says our blessed Lord, Matthew 6:22, that is, if thou aimest simply to please God, without any regard to thy own will, "thy whole body, (or all thy actions) will be full of light;" agreeable to the gospel, which is called light: "But if thine eye be evil, (if thine intention be diverted any other way) thy whole body, (all thy actions) will be full of darkness," sinful and unprofitable, we must not only do the will of God, but do it because it is his will; since we pray that "God's will may be done on earth as it is in heaven." And no doubt, the blessed angels not only do every thing that God willeth, but do it cheerfully, out of this principle, because God willeth it: And if we would live as we pray, we must go and do likewise.

But farther, as we must renounce our wills in doing, so likewise must we renounce them in suffering the will of God. Whatsoever befalls us, we must say with good old Eli, "It is the Lord, let him do what seemeth him good;": or with one that was infinitely greater than Eli, "Father, not my will, but thine be done." O Jesus, thine was an innocent will, and yet thou renouncedst it. Teach us, even us also, O our Savior! To submit our wills to thine, in all the evils which shall be brought upon us; and in every thing enable us to give thanks, since it is thy blessed will concerning us!

Thirdly, we must deny ourselves, as in our understandings and wills, so likewise in our affections. More particularly, we must deny ourselves the pleasurable indulgence and self-enjoyment of riches: "If any man will come after me, he must forsake all and follow me." And again (to show the utter inconsistency of the love of the things of this world with the love of the Father) he tells us, "unless a man forsake all that he hath, he cannot be my disciple."

Far be it from me to think that these texts are to be taken in a literal sense; as though they obliged rich persons to go sell all that they have and give to the poor, (for that would put it out of their power to be serviceable to the poor for the future) but however, they certainly imply thus much, that we are to sit loose to, sell and forsake all in affection, and be willing to part with every thing, when God shall require it at our hands: that is, as the apostle observes, we must "use the world as though we used it not;" and though we are in the world, we must not be of it. We must look upon ourselves as stewards, and not proprietors, of the manifold gifts of God; provide first what is necessary for ourselves and for our households, and expend the rest, not in indulgencies and superfluous ornaments, forbidden by the apostle, but in clothing, feeding, and relieving the naked, hungry, distressed disciples of Jesus Christ. This is what our blessed Lord would have us understand by forsaking all, and in this sense must each of us deny himself.

I am sensible that this will seem an hard saying to may, who will be offended because they are covetous, and "lovers of pleasure more than lovers of God;" but if I yet pleased such men, I should not be the servant of Christ. No, we must not, like Ahab's false prophets, have a lying spirit in our mouths, but declare faithfully the whole will of God; and like honest Micajah out of pity and compassion, tell men the truth, though they may falsely think we prophecy not good but evil concerning them.

But to proceed: As we must renounce our affection for riches, so likewise our affections for relations, when they stand in opposition to our love of, and duty to God: For thus saith the Savior of the world: "If any man will come after me, and hateth not his father and mother, his children, and brethren, and sisters, yea and his own life also, he cannot be my disciple." Strange doctrine this! What, hate our own flesh! What, hate the father that begat us, the mother that bare us! How can these things be? Can God contradict himself? Has he not bid us to honor our father and mother? And yet we are here commanded to hate them. How can these truths be reconciled? By interpreting the word hate, not in a rigorous and absolute sense, but comparatively: not as implying a total alienation, but a less degree of affection. For thus our blessed Savior himself (the best and purest expositor of his own meaning) explains it in a parallel text, Matthew 10:37, "He that loveth father or mother more than me, is not worthy of me; He that loveth son or daughter more than me, is not worthy of me." So that when the persuasions of our friends (as for our trial they may be permitted to be) are contrary to the will of God, we must say with Levi, "we have not know them;" or, agreeably to our blessed Lord's rebuke to Peter, "Get you behind me, my adversaries; for you favor not the things that be of God, but the things that be of man."

Farther, we must deny ourselves in things indifferent; for it might easily be shown, that as many, if not more, perish by an immoderate use of things in themselves indifferent, as by any gross sin whatever. A prudent Christian therefore, will consider not only what is lawful, but what is expedient also: not so much what degrees of self-denial best suit his inclinations here, as what will most effectually break his will, and fit him for greater degrees of glory hereafter.

Lastly, To conclude this head, we must renounce our own righteousness: For, though we should give all our goods to feed the poor, and our bodies to be burned, yet, if we in the least depend on that, and do not wholly rely on the perfect all sufficient righteousness of Jesus Christ, it will profit us nothing. "Christ is the end of the law for righteousness to every one that believeth." We are complete in him, and him only. Our own righteousnesses are but as filthy rags. We must count all things but dung and dross, so that we may be found in him, not having our own righteousness, but the righteousness which is of God, through Jesus Christ our Lord.

And is this the doctrine of Christianity? Is not the Christian world then asleep? If not, whence so much self-righteousness, whence the self-indulgence, whence the reigning love of riches which we every where meet with? Above all, whence that predominant greediness after sensual pleasure, that has so over-run this sinful nation, that was a pious stranger to come amongst us, he would be tempted to think some heathen Venus was worshipped here, and that temples were dedicated to her service. But we have the authority of an inspired apostle to affirm, that they who live in a round of pleasure, "are dead while they live." Wherefore, as the Holy Ghost saith, "Awake thou that sleepeth, and arise from the dead, and Christ shall give thee light." But the power of raising the spiritually dead belongeth only unto God. Do thou therefore, O Holy Jesus, who by thy almighty word commandest Lazarus to come forth, though he had lain in the grave some days, speak also as effectually to these spiritually dead souls, whom Satan for many years hath so fast bound by sensual pleasures, that they are not so much as able to lift up their eyes or hearts to heaven.

II. But I pass on to the second general thing proposed, to consider the universal obligation and reasonableness of this doctrine of self-denial.

When our blessed master had been discoursing publicly concerning the watchfulness of the faithful and wise steward, his disciples asked him, "Speakest thou this parable to all, or only to us?" The same question I am aware has been, and will be put concerning the foregoing doctrine: for too many, unwilling to take Christ's easy yoke upon them, in order to evade the force of the gospel precepts, would pretend that all those commands concerning self-denial, and renouncing ourselves and the world, belonged to our Lord's first and immediate followers, and not to us or to our children. But such persons greatly err, not knowing the scriptures, nor the power of godliness in their hearts. For the doctrine of Jesus Christ, like his blesses self, is "the same yesterday, today, and for ever." What he said unto one, he said unto all, even unto the ends of the world; "If any man will come after me, let him deny himself:" and in the text it is particularly mentioned that he said it unto them *all*. And lest we should still absurdly imagine that this word *all* was to be confined to his apostles, with whom he was then discoursing, it is said in another place, that Jesus turned unto the multitude and said, "If any man will come after me, and hateth not his father and mother, yea and his own life also, he cannot be my disciple." When our blessed Lord had spoken a certain parable, it is said, "the scribes and Pharisees were offended, for they knew the parable was spoken against them:" and if Christians can now read these plain and positive texts of scripture, and at the same time not think they are spoken of them, they are more hardened than Jews, and more insincere than Pharisees.

In the former part of this discourse I observed, that the precepts concerning forsaking and selling all, did not oblige us in a literal sense, because the state of the church does not demand it of us, as it did of the primitive Christians; but still the same deadness to the world, the same abstemious use of, and readiness to part with or goods for Christ's sake, is as absolutely necessary for, and as obligatory on us, as it was on them. For though the church may differ as to the outward state of it, in different ages, yet as to the purity of its inward state, it was, is, and always will be invariably the same. And all the commands which we meet with in the epistles about "mortifying our members which are upon the earth, of setting our affections on things above, and of not being conformed to this world;" are but so many incontestable proofs that the same holiness, heavenly-mindedness, and deadness to the world, is as necessary for us, as for our Lord's immediate followers.

But farther, as such an objection argues an ignorance of the scriptures, so it is a manifest proof, that such as make it are strangers to the power of godliness in their hearts. For since the form and substance of religion consists in recovery from our fallen estate in Adam, by a new birth in Christ Jesus, there is an absolute necessity for us to embrace and practice the self-denial before spoken of. If we are alive unto God, we shall be dead to ourselves and the world. If all things belonging to the spirit live and grow in us, all things belonging to the old man must die in us. We must mourn before we are comforted, and receive the spirit of bondage before we are blessed with the unspeakable privilege of the spirit of adoption, and with a full assurance of faith can say, "Abba, Father."

Were we indeed in a state of innocence, and had we, like Adam before his fall, the divine image fully stamped upon our souls, we then should have no need of self-denial; but since we are fallen, sickly, disordered, self-righteous creatures, we must necessarily deny ourselves (and count it our privilege to do so) ere we can follow Jesus Christ to glory. To reject such a salutary practice on account of the difficulty attending it at first, is but too like the obstinacy of a perverse sick child, who nauseates and refuses the portion reached out to it by a skillful physician or a tender parent, because it is a little ungrateful to the taste.

Had any of us seen Lazarus when he lay full of sores at the rich man's gate; or Job when he was smitten with ulcers, from the crown of his head to the sole of his foot: And had we at the same time prescribed to them some healing medicines, which, because they might put them to pain, they would not apply to their wounds, should we not most justly think, that they were either fond of a distempered body, or were not sensible of their distempers? But our souls, by nature, are in an infinitely more deplorable condition than the bodies of Job or Lazarus, when full of ulcers and boils: for, alas! "our whole head is sick, and our whole heart faint, from the crown of the head to the sold of the foot, we are full of wounds and bruises and putrifying sores, and there is no health in us." And if we are unwilling to deny ourselves, and come after Jesus Christ in order to be cured, it is a sign we are not sensible of the wretchedness of our state, and that we are not truly made whole.

Even Naaman's servants could say, when he refused (pursuant to Elisha's orders) to wash in the river Jordan, that he might cure his leprosy, "Father, if the prophet had bid thee do some great thing, wouldst thou not have done it? How much rather then, when he saith to thee, wash and be clean?" And may not I very properly address myself to you in the same manner, my brethren? If Jesus Christ, our great prophet, had bid you to do some far more difficult thing, would you not have done it? Much more then should you do it, when he only bids you deny yourselves what would certainly hurt you if indulged in, and he will give you a crown of life.

But to illustrate this by another comparison: In the 12th chapter of the Acts, we read, that "St. Peter was kept in prison, and was sleeping between two soldiers, bound with two chains. And behold an angel of the Lord came upon him, and smote Peter on the side, saying, arise up quickly. And his chains fell off from his hands." But had this great apostle, instead of rising up quickly, and doing as the blessed angel commanded him, hugged his chains and begged that they might not be let fall from his hands, would not any one think that he was in love with slavery, and deserved to be executed next morning? And does not the person who refuses to deny himself, act as inconsistently, as this apostle would have done if he had neglected the means of his deliverance? For our souls, by nature, are in a spiritual dungeon, sleeping and fast bound between the world, the flesh, and the devil, not with two but ten thousand chains of lusts and corruptions. Now Jesus Christ, like St. Peter's good angel, by the power of his gospel comes and opens the prison door, and bids us "deny ourselves and follow him." But if we do not arise, gird up the loins of our mind and follow him, are we not in love with bondage, and to we not deserve never to be delivered from it?

Indeed, I will not affirm that this doctrine of self-denial appears in this just light to every one. No, I am sensible that to the natural man it is foolishness, and to the young convert an hard saying. But what says our Savior? "If any man will do my will, he shall know the doctrine, whether it be of God, or whether I speak of myself." This, my dear friends, is the best, the only way of conviction. Let us up and be doing; let us arise quickly, and deny ourselves, and the Lord Jesus will remove those scales from the eyes of our minds, which now, like so many veils, hinder us from seeing clearly the reasonableness, necessity, and inexpressible advantage of the doctrine that has been delivered. Let us but once thus show ourselves men, and then the spirit of God will move on the face of our souls, as he did once upon the face of the great deep; and cause them to emerge out of that confused chaos, in which they are most certainly now involved, if we are strangers and enemies to self-denial and the cross of Christ.

III. Proceed we therefore now to the third and last general thing proposed, to offer some considerations, which may serve as so many motives to reconcile us to, and quicken us in, the practice of this duty of self-denial.

1. And the first means I shall recommend to you, in order to reconcile you to this doctrine, is, to meditate frequently on the life of our blessed Lord and Master Jesus Christ. Follow him from his cradle to the cross, and see what a self-denying life he led! And shall not we drink of the cup that he drank of, and be baptized with the baptism that he was baptized with? Or think we, that Jesus Christ did and suffered everything in order to have us excused and exempted from sufferings? No, far be it

from any sincere Christian to judge after this manner: for St. Peter tells us, "He suffered for us, leaving us an example that we should follow his steps." Had Christ, indeed, like those that sat in Moses' chair, laid heavy burdens of self-denial upon us, (supposing they were heavy, which they are not) and refused to touch them himself with one of his fingers; we might have had some pretense to complain: But since he has enjoined us nothing, but what he first put in practice himself, thou art inexcusable, O disciple, whoever thou art, who wouldst be above thy persecuted self-denying master: And thou art no good and faithful servant, who art unwilling to suffer and sympathize with thy mortified, heavenly-minded Lord.

2. Next to the pattern of our blessed master, think often on the lives of the glorious company of the apostles, the goodly fellowship of the prophets, and the noble army of martyrs; who by a constant looking to the author and finisher of our faith, have fought the good fight, and are gone before us to inherit the promises. View again and again, how holily, how self-denyingly, how unblameably they lived: And if self-denial was necessary for them, why not for us also? Are we not men of lie passions with them? Do we not live in the same wicked world as they did? Have we not the same good spirit to assist, support, and purify us, as they had? And is not the same eternal inheritance reached out to us, as was to them? And if we have the same nature to change, the same wicked world to withstand, the same good spirit to help, and the same eternal crown at the end; why should not we lead the same lives as they did? Do we think they did works of supererogation? If not, why do not we do as they did? Or why does your own church set apart festivals to commemorate the deaths and sufferings of the saints, but in order to excite you to follow them as they did Christ.

3. Thirdly, Think often on the pains of hell; consider, whether it is not better to cut off a right hand or foot, and pull out a right eye, if they offend us (our cause us to sin) "rather than to be cast into hell, where the worm dieth not, and the fire is not quenched." Think how many thousands there are now reserved with damned spirits in chains of darkness unto the judgment of the great day. And think withal, that this, this must be our case shortly, unless we are wise in time, deny ourselves, and follow Jesus Christ. Think you, they now imagine Jesus Christ to be an hard master; or rather think you not, they would give ten thousand times ten thousand worlds, could they but return to life again, and take Christ's easy yoke upon them? And can we dwell with everlasting burnings more than they? No, if we cannot bear this precept, deny yourselves, take up your crosses; how shall we bear the irrevocable sentence, "Depart from me, ye cursed, into everlasting fire, prepared for the devil and his angels?" But I hope those, amongst whom I am now preaching the kingdom of God, are not so disingenuous as to need to be driven to their duty by the terrors of the Lord, but rather desire to be drawn by the cords of love.

Lastly, Therefore, often meditate on the joys of heaven: think, think with what unspeakable glory those happy souls are now encircled, who when on earth were called to deny themselves as well as we, and were not disobedient to that call: Lift up your hearts frequently towards the mansions of eternal bliss, and with an eye of faith, like Stephen, see the heavens opened, and the Son of man with his glorious retinue of departed saints, sitting and solacing themselves in eternal joys. Hark! Methinks I hear them chanting forth their everlasting Hallelujahs, and echoing triumphant songs of joy. And do you not long, my brethren, to join this heavenly choir? Do not your hearts burn within you? As the hart panteth after the water brooks, do not your souls so long after the blessed company of these sons of God? Behold then a heavenly ladder reached down to you, by which you may climb to this holy hill. Let us believe on the Lord Jesus Christ, and deny ourselves! By this alone, every saint that ever lived ascended into the joy of their Lord. And then, we, even we also shall ere long be lifted up into the same most blissful regions, there to enjoy an eternal rest with the people of God, and join with them in singing doxologies and songs of praise, to the everlasting, blessed, all-glorious, most adorable Trinity, for ever and ever.

Which God of his infinite mercy grant.

30. Christ's Transfiguration

Luke 9:28–36—"And it came to pass about an eight days after these sayings, he took Peter and John and James, and went up into a mountain to pray. And as he prayed, the fashion of his countenance was altered, and his raiment [was] white [and] glistering. And, behold, there talked with him two men, which were Moses and Elias: Who appeared in glory, and spake of his decease which he should accomplish at Jerusalem. But Peter and they that were with him were heavy with sleep: and when they were awake, they saw his glory, and the two men that stood with him. And it came to pass, as they departed from him,

Peter said unto Jesus, Master, it is good for us to be here: and let us make three tabernacles; one for thee, and one for Moses, and one for Elias: not knowing what he said. While he thus spake, there came a cloud, and overshadowed them: and they feared as they entered into the cloud. And there came a voice out of the cloud, saying, This is my beloved Son: hear him. And when the voice was past, Jesus was found alone. And they kept [it] close, and told no man in those days any of those things which they had seen."

When the angel was sent to the Redeemer's beloved disciple John, we are told that the angel said unto him, "Come up hither." He was to be exalted, to be brought nearer heaven, that his mind might be better prepared for those great manifestations, which an infinitely great and condescending God intended to vouchsafe him. And on reading the verse that you have just now heard, when I also see such a great and serious assembly convened in the presence of God, I think I must address you, as the angel addressed John, and say unto you, "Come up hither;" leave your worldly thoughts, for a time forget the earth. And as it is the Lord's day, a time in which we ought more particularly to think of heaven, I must desire you to pray to God, that ye may get up on Pisgah's mount, and take a view of the promised land. It is true, indeed, eye hath not seen, ear hath not heard, nor hath it entered into the heart of any man to conceive the great and good things, which God hath prepared for his people here; much less, those infinitely greater and more glorious things, that he hath laid up for them that fear him, in the eternal world: but, blessed be God! Though we are not yet in heaven, unless to be in Christ may properly be termed heaven, and then all real Christians are there already; yet, but blessed Jesus has been pleased to leave upon record some account of himself, of what happened to him in the days of his flesh, and of some manifestations he was pleased to grant to a few of his disciples; that from what happened to them here below, we may form some faint, though but a faint idea of that happiness that awaits his people in his kingdom above. If any of you inquire, in what part of our Lord's life those instances are recorded, I have an answer ready: One of these instances, and that a very remarkable one, is recorded in the verses that I have now chosen for the subject of your meditation.

The verses give us an account of what is generally called our Lord's Transfiguration; his being wonderfully changed, and his being wonderfully owned by his Father upon the mount. Some think that this was done upon a Sabbath-day; and the particular occasion of our blessed Lord's condescending to let his servants have such a sight as this, we may gather from the Luke 9:27, It seems our blessed Lord had been promising a great reward to those who should not be ashamed of him: "Whosoever shall be ashamed of me and of my words, of him shall the Son of Man be ashamed, when he shall come in his own glory, and of his Father, and of the holy angels." In this threatening is implied, a reward to those who should not be ashamed of him: "But, (adds he) I tell you of a truth, there be some standing here, who shall not taste of death, till they see the kingdom of God." As much as to say, There will be a day, when I will come in the glory of my Father and of his holy angels; but I tell you there are some of my favorites; I tell you of a truth, though you may think it too good news, there are some of you that shall not taste of death, till ye shall see the kingdom of God. Some divines think, that this promise has reference to our Lord's creating a gospel church; and if we take it in this sense, it means that the Apostles, who were then present, some of them at least, should not die, till they saw Satan's kingdom in a great measure pulled down, and the Redeemer's gospel kingdom erected. Some think it has a peculiar reference to John, who it seems survived all the other Apostles, and lived till Christ came; that is, till he came to destroy Jerusalem. But it is the opinion of Mr. Henry, of Bishop Hall, of Burkit, and others, who have written upon this passage, that our blessed Lord has a peculiar reference to the transfiguration upon the mount: "There be some of you here, that shall not taste of death, till ye see my transfiguration upon the mount; till ye see some glorified saint come down from heaven and pay me a visit, and consequently see a little of that kingdom of God, which ye shall have a full sight of when ye come to glory." This seems to be the right interpretation. If you will look to the margin of your Bibles, you will see the parallel place in Matthew, where the account of our Lord's transfiguration is given, and there you will find it immediately follows upon this promise of our Lord.

Well, as Christ had told them, that they should not taste of death, till they had seen the kingdom of God, why the Evangelist, at the Luke 9:28, tells us, "It came to pass about an eight days after these sayings, he took Peter, and John, and James, and went up into a mountain to pray." About an eight days; that is, as Bishop Hall thinks, upon the Sabbath-day; or, according to some, the first day of the week, which was hereafter to be the Christian Sabbath; our blessed Lord takes Peter, John, and James:

Why did not the Lord Jesus Christ take more of his disciples? Why three, and these three? And why three only? Our blessed Lord was pleased to take three and no more, to show us that he is a sovereign agent; to show us, that though he loved all his disciples, yet there are some to whom he is pleased to allow peculiar visits. He loved Peter, and all the other disciples; yet John was the disciple that he peculiarly loved. And he took three rather than one, because three were sufficient to testify the truth of his being transfigured: "Out of the mouth of two or three witnesses every word shall be established." And he took no more than three, because these three were enough. And he took these three, Peter, John, and James, in particular, because these very persons that were not to see Christ transfigured, were hereafter to see him agonizing in the garden, sweating great drops of blood falling unto the ground. And had not these three disciples seen Christ upon the mount, the seeing him afterwards in the garden, might have staggered them exceedingly: they might have doubted whether it was possible for the Son of God to be in such doleful circumstances. Well, our Lord takes these three "up into a mountain." Why so? Because Christ Jesus was to be like Moses, who was taken up into a mountain, when God intended to deliver unto him the moral law: And our blessed Lord went up into a mountain, because a mountain befriended devotion. When he had a mind to retire to pray to his Father, he went to such places where he could be most secret, and give the greatest vent to his heart. Thus we are told, that once when Peter prayed, it was upon the house-top. And if we have a mind to be near God, we should choose such places as are freest from ostentation, and that most befriend our communion with God. And what doth Christ, when he got up into a mountain? We are told, he went up into a mountain "to pray." Christ had no corruption to confess, and he had but few wants of his own to be relieved; yet we hear of Christ being much in prayer; we hear of his going up to a mountain to pray; of his rising up a great while before it was day to pray; and of his spending a whole night in prayer to God.

In the passage Luke 9:20, you have an account of the effect of our Lord's praying: "As he prayed, the fashion of his countenance was altered, and his raiment was white and glittering." I would have you take notice, that our Lord was not changed in respect of his body, while he was going up to the mount, but when he got upon the mount, and while engaged in prayer. It is sufficient that way for our souls to be transformed: the time we are more particularly to expect the influences of God's Spirit, is, when we are engaged in prayer. There seems to be a very great propriety in our Lord's being transfigured or changed upon the mount. I hope I need inform none of you, that when Moses went up to the mount of God, God was pleased to speak to him face to face; and when he came down from the mount, the people of Israel observed that Moses' face shone so, that he was obliged to have a veil put upon his face. Now the shining of Moses' face, was a proof to the people, that Moses had been conversing with God. And Moses told the people, "That the Lord would raise up unto them a prophet like unto him, whom the people were to hear." God the Father, in order to give his Son (considering him as man) a testimony that he was a prophet, was pleased not only to let his face glitter or shine; but to show that he was a prophet far superior to Moses, he was pleased to let his garment be white and glittering, and "his countenance (as we are told by another Evangelist) did shine as the sun." What change was here! What a sight! Methinks I see Peter, James, and John surprised; and, indeed, well might the Evangelist, considering what happened, usher in the following part of the story with the word Behold; "Behold, there talked with him two men, Moses and Elias:" And in the passage Luke 9:31, you have an account of their dress, "They appeared in glory;" and of their discourse, "They spake of his decease which he should accomplish at Jerusalem."

"Behold, two men, which were Moses and Elias;" these were two very proper persons to come upon this embassy to the Son of God. Moses was the great lawgiver, Elias was the great restorer of the law: The body of Moses was hidden and never found, Elias' body was translated immediately, and carried up in a fiery chariot to heaven: And it may be that this was done particularly, because these two were hereafter to have the honor of waiting upon the Son of God. "They appeared in glory;" that is, their bodies were not in that glorious habit, in which the bodies of believers are to be at the morning of the resurrection. Christ was, as it were, now fitting in his royal robes; and as it is usual for ambassadors, when they are to be admitted into the king's presence, on bringing a message from one king to another, to appear in all their grandeur, to make the message more solemn; so here, these heavenly messengers being to wait upon the Lord Jesus Christ, are invested as with royal dignity, they appeared in glory, and "they spake of his decease which he should accomplish at Jerusalem," they came to tell the Redeemer of his sufferings, and of the place of his sufferings, and to acquaint him, that his sufferings, however great, however bitter, were to be accomplished; that there was o be an end put to them, as our Lord himself speaks, "The things concerning me are to have an end." What other particulars they spoke to our Lord, we are not told. But what effect this had upon the disciples, you may learn from Luke 9:32, "Peter, and they that were with him, were heavy with sleep."

We are not to suppose, that Peter, James and John, were now asleep in a literal sense; no, if we compare this, with another passage of holy writ, I mean the account given us of Daniel's being impressed and overcome, when he saw the angel of the Lord, you will find that this sleep implies what we call a swoon. They were overcome with the sight of the glory of Christ's garments, the glittering of his body, and the glory in Moses and Elias appeared: these quite overcame them, sunk them down, and, like the Queen of Sheba, when she saw Solomon's glory, they had no life in them. But they recovered themselves: "when they were awake," that is, when they had recovered their strength, when God had put strength into them, as the angel put strength into Daniel, "they saw his glory, and the two men that stood with him." And how do you think they gazed upon Christ? How may we suppose they fixed their eyes upon Moses and Elias? Peter, who was always the first speaker, out of the abundance of his heart, spoke upon this occasion. Verse Luke 9:33, "And it came to pass as they departed from him, Peter said unto Jesus, Master, it is good for us to be here; and let us make three tabernacles, one for thee, and one for Moses, and one for Elias, not knowing what he said." Peter, when he had drank a little of Christ's new wine, speaks like a person intoxicated; he was overpowered with the brightness of the manifestation. "Let us make three tabernacles, one for thee, and one for Moses, and one for Elias." It is well added, "not knowing what he said." That he should cry out, "Master, it is good for us to be here," in such good company, and in so glorious a condition, is no wonder; which of us all would not have been apt to have done the same? But to talk of building tabernacles, and one for Christ, and one for Moses, and one for Elias, was saying something for which Peter himself must stand reproved. Surely, Peter, thou wast not quite awake! Thou talkest like one I a dream: If thy Lord had taken thee at thy word, what a poor tabernacle wouldst thou have had, in comparison of that house not made with hands, eternal in the heavens, in which thou hast long since dwelt, now the earthly house of the tabernacle of thy body is dissolved? What! Build tabernacles below, and have the crown, before thou hast borne the cross? O Peter, Peter! "Master, spare thyself," sticks too closely to thee: And why so selfish, Peter? Carest thou not for thy fellow disciples that are below, who came not up with thee to the mount? Carest thou not for the precious souls, that are as sheep having no shepherd, and must perish for ever, unless thy Master descends from the mount to teach, and to die for them? Wouldst thou thus eat thy spiritual morsels alone? Besides, if thou art for building tabernacles, why must there be three of them, one for Christ, and one for Moses, and one for Elias? Are Christ and the prophets divided? Do they not sweetly harmonize and agree in one? Did they not prophesy concerning the sufferings of thy Lord, as well as of the glory that should follow? Alas, how unlike is their conversation to thine? Moses and Elias came down to talk of suffering, and thou are dreaming of building I know not what tabernacles. Surely, Peter, thou art so high upon the mount, that thy head runs giddy.

However, in the midst of these infirmities, there was something that bespoke the honesty and integrity of his heart. Though he knew not very well what he said, yet he was not so stupid as his pretended successor at Rome. He does not fall down and worship these two departed saints, neither do I hear him say to either , Ora prosobis; he had not so learnt Christ; no, he applies himself directly to the head, "he said unto Jesus, Master, it is good for us to be here." And though he was for building, yet he would not build without his Master's leave. "Master, let us build," or, as St. Mark words it, "wilt thou that we build three tabernacles, one for thee, and one for Moses, and one for Elias?" I do not hear him add, and one for James, and one for John, and one for Peter. No, he would willingly stay out with them upon the mount, though it was in the cold and dark night, so that Christ and his heavenly attendants were taken care of. The sweetness of such a heavenly vision, would more than compensate for any bodily suffering that might be the consequence of their longer abode there: nay farther, he does not desire that either Christ, or Moses, or Elias, should have any trouble in building; neither does he say, let my curates, James and John, build, whilst I sit idle and lord it over my brethren; but he says, "let us build;" he will work as hard, if not harder than either of them, and desire to be distinguished only by his activity, enduring hardness, and his zeal to promote the welfare of their common Lord and Master.

Doubtless, Peter had read how the glory of the Lord filled the tabernacle, and the temple of old; and now Jesus is transfigured, and Moses and Elias appear in glory, he thinks it right that new tabernacles shall be erected for them. Such a mixture of nature and grace, of shortsightedness and infirmity, is there in the most ardent and well-meant zeal of the very best of men, when nearest the throne of grace, or even upon the mount with God. Perfection in any grace must be looked for, or expected, only among the spirits of just men made perfect in heaven. Those who talk of any such thing on earth, like Peter, they know not what they say.

But how came Peter so readily to distinguish which was Moses, and which was Elias? He seems to speak without the least hesitation, "Let us build three tabernacles, one for thee, and one for Moses, and one for Elias," as though he was very well acquainted with them, whereas they had both been dead, long, long before Peter was born. Was there, do you imagine, any thing distinguishing in their apparel? Or any thing in their conversation that discovered them? Or rather, did he not know them here on the mount, as we may from hence infer, that departed saints do, and will know each other in heaven, even by intuition and immediate revelation? But alas! how transient are our views of heaven, during our sojourning here on earth: Verse Luke 9:34, "Whilst he thus spake," whilst Peter was talking of building tabernacles, whilst he was saying, "it is good for us to be here," whilst he was dreaming that his mountain was s strong that it never could be moved, "there came a cloud and overshadowed them." St. Matthew observes, it was a bright cloud, not dark like that on mount Sinai, but bright, because the gospel opens to us a far more bright dispensation than that of the law. This overshadowed, and thereby not only filled them with an holy awe, but also screened them, in some measure, from the brightness of that glory with which they were now surrounded, and which otherwise would have been insupportable. This cloud was like the veil thrown on the face of Moses, and prepared them for the voice which they were soon to hear coming out of it. I am not much surprised at being informed by St. Matthew, that they feared as they entered into the cloud, or by St. Mark that "they were sore afraid." For since the fall, there is such a consciousness in us all of deserved wrath, that we cannot help fearing when we enter into a cloud, even though Jesus Christ himself be in the midst of it. Ah Peter, where is thy talk of building tabernacles now? Is thy strong mountain so quickly removed? What, come down so soon? why do we not now hear thee saying, "It is good for us to be here?" Alas! he and his fellow disciples are quite struck dumb; see how they tremble, and, like Moses upon another occasion, exceedingly quake and fear. But how quickly are those fears dispelled, how soon is the tumult of their minds hushed and calmed, with that soul-reviving voice that came from the excellent glory, verse Luke 9:35, "This is my beloved Son, hear him."

St. Mark and St. Matthew add "in whom I am well pleased." The same testimony that God the Father gave to the blessed Jesus at his baptism, before he entered upon his temptation, is now repeated, in order to strengthen and prepare him for his impending agony in the garden. Probably, it was a small still though articulate voice, attended neither with thunder nor lightning, nor the sound of a trumpet, but, agreeable to the blessed news which it contained, ushered in with tokens of unspeakable complacency and love. God the Father, hereby gives Moses and Elias a solemn discharge, as though they were sent from heaven on purpose to give up their commission to their rightful Lord, and like the morning star, disappear when the Sun of Righteousness himself arises to bring in a gospel day. "This is my beloved Son, hear Him." But the emphasis upon the word *this*; this Son of Man, this Jesus, whom you are shortly to see in a bloody sweat, blindfolded, spit upon, buffeted, scourged, and at length hanging upon a tree, I am not ashamed to own to be my Son, my only begotten Son, who was with me before the heavens were made, or the foundations of the earth were laid; my beloved Son, in whom I am well pleased, in whom my soul delighteth, and whom I do by these presents, publicly constitute and appoint to be the king, priest, and prophet of the church. "Hear ye Him." No longer look to Moses or Elias, no longer expect to be saved by the works of the law; but by the preaching and application of the ever-blessed gospel. Hear ye him, so as to believe on, love, serve, obey, and, if needs be, to die and lay down your very lives for him. "Hear him;" hear what he hath to say, for he comes with a commission from above. Hear his doctrine; hear him, so as to obey him; hear him, so as to put in practice his precepts, and copy after his good example.

In the 36th verse, we have the close of his heavenly feast; "When the voice was past, Jesus was found alone; and they kept it close, and told no man in those days, any of those things which they had seen." If we compare this, with the account which the other Evangelists give of our blessed Lord's transfiguration, you will find this was done by Christ's order: Peter, James, and John, would otherwise have gone down and told the whole world, that they had seen the Lord Christ upon the mount of transfiguration; but our Lord ordered them to keep it silent. Why so? If they had gone down from the mount, and told it to the other disciples, it might have raised ill blood in the others; they might have said, Why did our Master single out Peter, James, and John? Why might not we have had the privilege of going up to the mount as well as they? Had they said, that their Lord was transfigured, people would not have believed them; they would have thought, that Peter, James, and John were only enthusiasts; but if they kept it till after his resurrection, and he had broken the gates of death, for them then to say, that they saw him upon the mount transfigured, would corroborate the evidence.

I have thus paraphrased the words for your better understanding the account the Evangelist gives of our blessed Lord's transfiguration; but I have not yet done; I have been speaking to your heads; the practical part is yet to come. O that God may reach your hearts! And though, according to order, I ought to begin with the practical inferences that might be drawn from the first part; yet, I think it best to show you, who are the people of God, especially you young converts, that have honesty, but not much prudence, what instructions our Lord would here have you to learn.

"When the voice was past, Jesus was found alone, and they kept it close, and told no man in those days any of those things which they had seen." There is nothing more common, when God vouchsafes communications to a poor soul, than for the person that enjoys them, to go and tell all that he has seen and felt, and often at improper seasons and to improper persons. I remember that Mr. Henry observes, "Joseph had more honesty than he had policy, or else he would never have told his brethren of his dreams." Young Christians are too apt to blunder thus: I am sure it is a fault of which I have been exceedingly guilty, speaking of things, which, perhaps, had better been concealed; which is a fault God's people are too apt to fall into. Though it is good for those that have seen Christ, and that have felt his love, to tell others what God hath done for their souls; yet, however you may think of it now, when you come down from the mount, and know yourselves a little, ye will find reason often to hold your tongue. Young Christians are like children, to whom if you give a little money in their pocket, they cannot be quiet till they have spent it upon something or other: young Christians, when they get a little of God, are ready to talk too much of it. They should therefore beware, and know when to speak, and when to be silent.

But, my dear friends, did our Lord Jesus Christ take Peter, James, and John into a mountain to pray? Are any of you fathers, mothers, masters and mistresses of families? Learn then from hence to take your children, your servants, and those that belong to you, from the world, at certain times, and not only pray for them, but pray with them. If Christ did thus, who had few wants of his own to be supplied, and nothing to confess and lament over; if Christ was such a lover of prayer, surely, you and I, who have so many wants to be supplied, so many corruptions to mourn over; you and I should spend much time in prayer. I do not say that you are to lock yourselves up in your closets, and not mind your shops or farms, or worldly business; I only say, that you should take care to husband all your time: and if you are God's children, you will frequently retire from the world, and seek a visit from your God.

Was the Lord Jesus transformed or transfigured, while he was praying? Learn hence, to be much in spiritual prayer. The way to have the soul transformed, changed into, and make like unto God, is frequently to converse with God. We say, a man is as his company. Persons by conversing together, frequently catch each others tempers: and if you have a mind to imbibe the divine temper, pray much. And as Christ's garments became white and glittering, so shall your souls get a little of God's light to shine upon them.

Did Moses and Elias appear in glory? Are there any old saints here? I doubt not but there are a considerable number. And are any of you afraid of death? Do any of you carry about with you a body that weighs down your immortal soul? I am sure a poor creature is preaching to you, that every day drags a crazy load along. But come, believers, come, ye children of God, come, ye aged decrepit saints, come and trample upon that monster death. As thou goest over yonder church-yard, do as I know an old excellent Christian in Maryland did; go, sit upon the grave, and meditate on thine own dissolution. Thou mayest, perhaps, have a natural fear of dying: the body and the soul do not care to part without a little sympathy and a groan; but O look yonder, loon up to heaven, see there thy Jesus, thy Redeemer, and learn, that thy body is to be fashioned here-after like unto Christ's most glorious body; that poor body which is not subject to gout and gravel, and that thou canst scarce drag along; that poor body, which hinders thee so much in the spiritual life, will ere long hinder thee no more; it shall be put into the grave; but though it be sown in corruption, it shall be raised in incorruption; though it is sown in dishonor, it shall be raised again in glory. This consideration made blessed Paul to cry out, "O death, where is thy sting! O grave, where is thy victory!" Thy soul and body shall be united together again, and thou shalt be "forever with the Lord." Those knees of thine, which perhaps are hard by kneeling in prayer; that tongue of thine, which hath sung hymns to Christ; those hands of thine, which have wrought for God; those feet, which have ran to Christ's ordinances; shall all, in the twinkling of an eye, be changed; and thou shalt be able to stand under an exceeding and an eternal weight of glory. Come then, ye believers in Christ, look beyond the grave; come, ye dear children of God, and however weak and sickly ye are now, say, Blessed be God, I shall soon have a body strong, full of vigor and of glory.

But as this speaks comfort to saints, it speaks terror to sinners, to all persons that live and die out of Christ. It is the opinion of Archbishop Usher, that as the bodies of the saints shall be glorified, so the bodies of the damned shall be deformed. And if this be true, alas! what a poor figure will the fine ladies cut, who die without a Christ! What a poor figure will the fine gentleman cut in the morning of the resurrection, that now dresses up his body, and at the same time neglects to secure an interest in Christ and eternal happiness! It is the opinion, likewise of Archbishop Usher, that damned souls will lose all the good tempers they had here; so that though God gave unregenerate people a constitutional meekness, good nature, and courage, for the benefit of the commonwealth; yet, the use of those blessings being over, and they having died without Christ, and it being impossible there will be an appearance of good in hell, their good tempers will be forever lost. If this be so, it is an awful consideration; and I think persons who love their bodies, should also hence take care to secure the welfare of their souls.

Did Peter know which was Moses and which Elias? Then I think, and God be praised for it, it is plain from this and other passages of scripture, that we shall know one another when we come to heaven. Dives knew Lazarus: "Father Abraham, send Lazarus:" And we are told, "he saw Lazarus sitting in Abraham's bosom." Adam knew his wife Eve; though cast into a deep sleep when God made her out of his rib, yes, by a kind of intuition he says, "This is bone of my bone, and flesh of my flesh." And it is on this account, that the Apostle, speaking to the Philippians, says, "Ye are my joy and crown of rejoicing, in the day of the Lord." What comfort will this be to a spiritual father! Says one, Here is the man, O Lord Jesus, that brought my soul to taste of thy love; says another, This is the man, that at such a time, and with such words, struck my heart: thou, O Lord knowest it. Then the spiritual father will rejoice over his children. You that have met and have prayed together, sighted and sympathized together, and told your temptations to one another, shall be forever with the Lord and with each other. There we shall see Abraham, Isaac, and Jacob sitting, with all the redeemed company; and we shall know the names of every one mentioned in the book of God. O blessed prospect! O blessed time! Who that thinks of this, of seeing the Lamb sitting upon the throne, with all God's people about him, but must desire to go to heaven, and be forever, forever with the Lord. And if there is such comfort for believers to know one another in heaven, with what comfort may any of you, that have lost fathers, mothers, or friends, think of them: we are parted for a little while, but we shall see them again. My father died in Christ, my mother died in the Lord, my husband, my wife, was a follower of Jesus; I shall see them, though not now; I shall go to them, but they shall not return to me! This may keep you from sorrowing as persons without hope; and keep you from being so cruel, as to wish them to come down to this evil world.

But O what a dreadful consideration is this for damned souls! I believe, that as glorified spirits will know one another, so will damned souls know one another too. And as the company of the blessed increases the happiness of heaven, so the company of the damned will increase their torments. What made Dives to put up that petition? "I have five brethren; send somebody to my father's house to testify unto them, lest they also come into this place of torment." One would imagine at first reading, that hell had made Dives charitable, and that though he was ill natured on earth, yet he had acquired some good nature in hell. No, no, there is not a spark of good nature in the place of torment. But Dives knew, if his five brethren came there, they might say, We may thank you, next to an evil heart, for coming hither; you made us drink healths, till we were drunk; you taught us to game, to curse, to swear, &c. He knew very well, that his five brethren being brought to hell by his example, hell would be heated five times hotter to torment his soul. One will cry out, Cursed be the day that ever I was companions with such an one in sin; cursed be the day that ever we hearkened to one another's advice, and were allured by each other's example to sin against God!

But did a cloud overshadow Peter, James, and John?

Were heavenly and divine visits here but short? Then wonder not, ye people of God, if ye are upon the mount one hour, and down in the valley of the shadow of death the next. There is nothing in the world more common, after you have been in a good frame, than for a cloud to overshadow you. We generally say, "It is good to be here," and often make a Christ of our graces; and therefore the Lord sends a cloud to overshadow us. But never fear; God shall speak to you out of the cloud; God will reveal himself to you; this cloud shall soon be gone; ere long we shall be in heaven, and in that glory where no cloud can possibly reach us.

I can now only mention one thing more, and that is, Did the Father say, "This is my beloved Son, hear him?" then let every one of our hearts echo to this testimony give of Christ, "This is my beloved Savior." Did God so love the world, as to send his only begotten Son, his well beloved Son to preach to us? Then, my dear friends, *hear Him.* What God said seventeen hundred years ago, immediately by a voice from heaven, concerning his Son upon the mount, that same thing God says to you immediately by his word, "Hear him." If ye never heard him before, hear him now. Hear him so as to take him to be your prophet, priest, and your king; hear him, so as to take him to be your God and your all. Hear him today, ye youth, while it is called today; hear him now, lest God should cut you off before you have another invitation to hear him; hear him while he cries, "Come unto me;" hear him while he opens his hand and his heart; hear him while he knocks at the door of your souls, lest you should hear him saying, "Depart, depart, ye cursed, into everlasting fire, prepared for the devil and his angels." Hear him, ye old and gray-headed, hear him, ye that have one foot in the grave; hear him, I say; and if ye are dull of hearing, beg of God to open the ears of your hearts, and your blind eyes; beg of God that you may have an enlarged and a believing heart, and that ye may know what the Lord God saith concerning you. God will resent it, he will avenge himself on his adversaries, if you do not hear a blessed Savior. He is God's son, he is God's beloved son; he came upon a great errand, even to shed his precious blood for sinners; he came to cleanse you from all sin, and to save you with an everlasting salvation. Ye who have heard him, hear him again; still go on, believe in and obey him, and by-and-by you shall hear him saying, "Come, ye blessed of my Father, receive the kingdom prepared for you from the foundation of the world." May God grant it to you all, for the Lord Jesus Christ's sake. Amen, and Amen.

31. The Care of the Soul Urged as the One Thing Needful

Luke 10:42—"But one thing is needful."

It was the amiable character of our blessed Redeemer, that "he went about doing good," this great motive, which animated all his actions, brought him to the house of his friend Lazarus, at Bethany, and directed his behavior there. Though it was a season of recess from public labor, our Lord brought the sentiments and the pious cares of a preacher of righteousness into the parlor of a friend; and there his doctrine dropped as the rain, and distilled as the dew, as the little happy circle that were then surrounding him. Mary, the sister of Lazarus, with great delight made one amongst them; she seated herself at the feet of Jesus, in the posture of an humble disciple; and we have a great deal of reason to believe, that Martha, his other sister, would gladly have been with her there; but domestic cares pressed hard upon her, and "she was cumbered with much serving," being, perhaps, too solicitous to prepare a sumptuous entertainment for her heavenly master and the train that attended him. Happy are they, who in a crowd of business do not lose something of the spirituality of their minds, and of the composure and sweetness of their tempers. This good woman comes to our Lord with too impatient a complaint; insinuating some little reflection, not only on Mary, but on himself too. "Lord, dost thou not care that my sister hath left me to serve alone? Bid her, therefore, that she help me." Our Lord, willing to take all opportunities of suggesting useful thoughts, answers her in these words, of which the text is a part, "Martha, Martha, thou art careful and troubled about many things, but one thing is needful; and Mary, has chosen that good part, which shall not be taken away from her." Alas, Martha! The concerns of the soul are of so much greater importance than those of the body, that I cannot blame your sister on this occasion: I rather recommend her to your imitation, and caution you, and all my other friends, to be much on your guard, that in the midst of your worldly cares, you do not lose sight of what much better deserves your attention.

I shall consider these words, "One thing is needful," as a kind of aphorism, or wise and weighty sentence, which dropped from the mouth of our blessed Redeemer, and is evidently worthy of our most serious regard. I shall,

I. Consider what we are to understand by "The one thing" here spoken of.

II. Show you what is intended, when it is said to be the one thing *needful*.

III. I will show how justly it may be so represented, or prove that it is, indeed, the one thing needful. And then conclude with some reflections.

My friends, the words which are now before us, are to this day, as true, as they were seventeen hundred years ago. Set your hearts to attend to them. O that you may, by divine grace, be awakened to hear them with a due regard, and be so impressed with the plain and serious things which are now to be spoken, as you probably would, if I were speaking by your dying beds, and you had the near and lively view of eternity!

First, I am to consider, what we are to understand by the "one thing needful."

Now in a few words, it is the "Care of the soul," opposed, as you see in the text, to the care, the excessive care of the body; to which Martha was gently admonished by our Lord. This is a general answer, and it comprehends a variety of important particulars, which is the business of our ministry often to open to you at large: The care of the soul, implies a readiness to hear the words of Christ, to seat ourselves with Mary at his feet, and to receive both the law and the gospel from his mouth. It supposes, that we learn from this divine teacher the worth of our souls, their danger, and their remedy; and that we become above all things solicitous about their salvation. That, heartily repenting of all our sins, and cordially believing the everlasting gospel, we receive the Lord Jesus Christ for righteousness and life, resting our souls on the value of his atonement, and the efficacy of his grace. It imports, the sincere dedication of ourselves to the service of God, and a faithful adherence to it, notwithstanding all oppositions arising from inward corruptions, or outward temptations; and a resolute perseverance in the way of gospel dependence, 'till we receive the end of our faith in our complete salvation. This is the "one thing needful," represented indeed in various scriptures by various names. Sometimes it is called "Regeneration," or "the new creature," because it is the blessed work of God's efficacious grace. Sometimes the "Fear of God," and sometimes "his love, and the keeping his commandments;" and very frequently in the new testament it is called "faith," or "receiving Christ, and believing on him," which therefore is represented as the "great work of God," John 6:20, the great thing which God in his glorious gospel requires, as well as by his spirit produces in us: each of these, if rightly understood and explained, comprehends all that I have said on this head. On the whole, we may say, that, as the body is one, though it has many members, and the soul is one, though it has many faculties, so in the present case, this real vital religion is "one thing," one sacred principle of divine life, bringing us to attend to the care of our souls, as of our greatest treasure. It is one thing, notwithstanding all the variety of views in which it may be considered, and of characters under which it may be described. I proceed,

Secondly, To consider what may be intended in the representation which is here made of it, as the "one thing *needful*."

Now I think it naturally includes these three particulars: it is a matter of universal concern; of the highest importance; and of so comprehensive a nature, that every thing which is truly worthy of our regard, may be considered as included in, or subservient to it. Let me a little illustrate each of these particulars.

1. The care of the soul may be called the "one thing needful," as it is matter of universal concern.

Our Lord, you see, speaks of it as needful in the general. He says not, for this or that particular person; or for those of such an age, station, or circumstance in life, but needful for all. And indeed, when discoursing on such a subject, one might properly introduce it with those solemn words of the psalmist, "Give ear, all ye people, hear, all ye inhabitants of the earth, both high and low, rich and poor, together," Psalms 49:1, Psalms 49:2, For it is the concern of all, from the king that sits upon the throne, to the servant that grindeth at the mill, or the beggar that lieth upon the dunghill. It is needful for us that are *ministers*, for our own salvation is concerned: and woe, insupportable woe will be to our souls, if we think it enough to recommend it to others, and to talk of it in a warm, or an awful manner, in public assemblies, or in our private converse, while it does not penetrate our hearts, as our own greatest care. Our case will then be like that of the Israelitish lord in Samaria, 2 Kings 7:2, who was employed to distribute the corn when the siege was raised; though we see it with our eyes, and dispense it with our hands, we shall ourselves die miserably, without tasting the blessings we impart. It is needful to all you that are our *hearers*, without the exception of one single person. It is needful to you that are *rich*, though it may on some accounts be peculiarly difficult for you, even as difficult, comparatively speaking, as for a "Camel to go through the eye of a needle," Matthew 19:24, yet if it be neglected, you are poor in the midst of all your wealth, and miserable in all your abundance; a wretch starving for hunger, in a magnificent palace and a rich dress, would be less the object of compassion than you. It is needful for you that are *poor*; though you are distressed with so many anxious cares, "what you shall eat, and what you shall drink, and wherewithal you shall be clothed." Matthew 6:31, The nature that makes you capable of such anxieties as these, argues your much greater concern in the "bread which endures to eternal life, John 6:27, than in that by which this mortal body must be supported. It is needful for you that are *advanced in years*; though your strength be impaired so that the "grasshopper is a burthen, Ecclesiastes 12:5, and though you have by your long continuance in sin, rendered this great work so hard, that were it less important, one would in pity let you alone without reminding you of it; yes, late as it is, it must be done, or your hoary heads will be brought down to the grave with wrath, and sink under a curse aggravated by every year and by every day of your lives. It is needful to you that are *young*, though solicited by so many gay vanities, to neglect it, though it may be represented as an unseasonable care at present, yet I repeat it, it is needful to you; immediately needful, unless you who walk so frequently over the dust of your brethren and companions, that died in the bloom and vigor of their days, have made some secret covenant with the grave for yourselves, and found out some wonderful method, hitherto unknown, or securing this precarious life, and of answering for days and months to come, while others cannot answer for one single moment.

2. The care of the soul is "a matter of the highest importance;" beyond any thing which can be brought into comparison with it.

As Solomon says of wisdom, that "it is more precious than rubies, and that all things which can be desired are not to be compared with her, Proverbs 3:15, So I may properly say of this great and most important branch of wisdom; whatever can be laid in the balance wit it, will be found altogether lighter than vanity. This is strongly implied when it is said in the text, "one thing is needful;" one thing, and *one thing alone* is so. Just as the blessed God is said to be "only wise," 1Timothy 1:17, and "only holy, Revelation 15:4, Because the wisdom and holiness of angels and men is as nothing, when compared with his. What seems most great and most important in life, what kings and senates, what the wisest and greatest of this world are employing their time, their councils, their pens, their labors upon, are trifles, when compared with this one thing. A man may subsist, he may in some considerable measure be happy, without learning, without riches, without titles, without health, without liberty, without friends, nay, though "the life be more than meat, and the body than raiment, Matthew 6:25, yet may he be happy, unspeakably happy, without the body itself. But he cannot be so, in the neglect of the one thing needful. I must therefore bespeak your regard to it in the words of Moses, "it is not a light thing, but it is your life, Deuteronomy 32:47,

3. The care of the soul is of so comprehensive a nature, that "every thing truly worthy of our regard may be considered as included in it, or subservient to it.

As David observes, that "the commandment of God is exceeding broad, Psalms 119:96, so we may say of this one thing needful; or as Solomon very justly and emphatically expresses it, "to fear God and to keep his commandments is the whole duty of man, Ecclesiastes 12:13, His whole duty, and his whole interest; and every thing which is wise and rational does in its proper place and connection make a part of it. We should judge very ill concerning the nature of this care, if we imagined, that it consisted merely in acts of devotion, or religious contemplation; it comprehends all the lovely and harmonious band of social and human virtues. It requires a care of society, a care of our bodies, and of our temporal concerns; but then all is to be regulated, directed, and animated by proper regards to God, Christ, and immortality. Our food and our rest, our trades and our labors, are to be attended to, and all the offices of humanity performed in obedience to the will of God, for the glory of Christ, and in a view of improving the mind in a growing meekness for a state of complete perfection. Name anything which has not reference at all to his, and you name a worthless trifle, however it may be gilded to allure the eye, or however it may be sweetened to gratify the taste. Name a thing, which, instead of thus improving the soul, has a tendency to debase and pollute, to enslave and endanger it, and you name what is most unprofitable and mischievous, be the wages of iniquity ever so great; most foul and deformed, be it in the eyes of men ever so honorable, or in their customs ever so fashionable. Thus I have endeavored to show you what we may suppose implied in the expression of "one thing being needful." I am now,

Thirdly, To show you with how much propriety the care of the soul may be represented under this character, as the one thing needful, or as a matter of universal and most serious concern, to which every thing else is to be considered as subservient, if at all worthy of our care and pursuit.

There let me appeal to the sentiments of those who must be allowed most capable of judging, and to the evident reason of the case itself, as it must appear to every unprejudiced mind.

1. Let me argue "from the opinions of those who must be allowed most capable of judging in such an affair," and we shall quickly see that the care of the soul appears to them, the one thing needful.

Is the judgment of the blessed God "according to truth," how evidently and how solemnly is that judgment declared? I will not say merely in this or the other particular passage of his word, but in the whole series of his revelations to the children of men, and the whole tenor of his addresses to them. Is not this the language of all, from the early days of Job and Moses to the conclusion of the canon of scripture. Job 28:21, Job 28:23, Job 28:28, "If wisdom be hid from the eyes of all the living, surely God understandeth the way thereof, he knoweth the place thereof;" and if he does, it is plainly pointed out, for "unto man he still saith, behold, the fear of the Lord, that is wisdom, and to depart from evil, that is understanding." By Moses he declared to the Israelites, that "to do the commandments of the Lord would be their wisdom and their understanding in the sight of the nations, who should hear his statutes, and say, surely this is a wise and an understanding people," Deuteronomy 4:6, When he had raised up one man on the throne of Israel, with the character of the wisest that ever lived upon the face of the earth, he chose to make him eminently a teacher of this great truth. And though now all that he spoke on the curious and less concerning subjects of natural philosophy is lost, "though he spoke of trees from the cedar to the hyssop, and of beasts, and of fowls, and of creeping things, and of fishes, 1 Kings 4:33, that saying is preserved in which he testifies, that "the fear of the Lord is the beginning of wisdom," Proverbs 1:7, Proverbs 1:9, Proverbs 1:10, and those Proverbs, in almost every line of which, they who neglect God and their own souls, are spoken of as fools, as if that were the most proper signification of the word, while the religious alone are honored with the title of wise. But in this respect, as attesting this truth in the name of God and in his own, "a greater than Solomon is here."

For if we inquire what it was that our Lord Jesus Christ judged to be the one thing needful, the words of the text contain as full an answer as can be imagined; and the sense of them is repeated in a very lively and emphatical manner, in that remarkable passage wherein our Lord not only declares his own judgment, but seems to appeal to the conscience of all, as obliged by their own secret convictions to subscribe to the truth of it. "What is a man profited, is he gain the whole world, and lost his own soul; or what shall a man give in exchange for his soul?" Matthew 16:26, If it were once lost, what would he not be willing to give to redeem it? But it depends not on the words of Christ alone. Let his actions, his sufferings, his blood, his death, speak what a value he set on the souls of men. Is it to be imagined, that he would have relinquished heaven, have dwelt upon earth, have labored by night and by day, and at last have expired on the cross, for a matter of light importance? Or can we think that he, in whom "dwell all the treasures of wisdom and knowledge, and all the fullness of the Godhead bodily," Colossians 2:3, Colossians 2:9, was mistaken in judgment so deliberately formed, and so solemnly declared?

If after this, there were room to mention human judgment and testimonies, how easy would it be to produce a cloud of witnesses in such a cause, and to show that the wisest and best of men in all ages of the world have agreed in this point, that amidst all the diversities of opinion and profession, which succeeding generations have produced, this has been the unanimous judgment, this the common and most solicitous care of those whose characters are most truly valuable, to secure the salvation of their own souls, and to promote the salvation of others.

And let me beseech you seriously to reflect, what are the characters of those who have taken the liberty, most boldly and freely to declare their judgment on the contrary side? The number of such is comparatively few; and when you compare what you have observed of their temper and conduct, I will not say with what you read of holy men of old, but with what you have yourselves seen in the faithful, active, and zealous servants of Christ, in these latter ages, with whom you have conversed; do you on the whole find, that the rejecters and deriders of the gospel, are in other respects so much more prudent and judicious, so much wiser for themselves, and for others, that are influenced by them, as that you can be in reason obliged to pay any great deference to the authority of a few such names as these, in opposition to those to whom they are here opposed?

But you will say, and you will say it too truly, Though but a few may venture in words to declare for the neglect of the soul and its eternal interest, that the greater part of mankind do it in their actions. But are the greater part of mankind so wise, and so good, as implicitly to be followed in matters of the highest importance? And do not multitudes of these declare themselves on the other side, in their most serious moments? When the intoxications of worldly business and pleasures are over, and some languishing sickness forces men to solitude and retirement; what have you generally observed to be the affect of such a circumstance? Have they not then declared themselves convinced of the truth we are now laboring to establish? Nay, do we not sometimes see, that a distemper which seizes the mind with violence, yet does not utterly destroy its reasoning faculties, fixes this conviction on the soul in a few hours, nay, sometimes in a few moments? Have you never seen a gay, thoughtless creature, surprised in the giddy round of pleasures and amusements, and presently brought not only to seriousness, but terror and trembling, by the near views of death? Have you never seen the man of business and care interrupted, like the rich fool in the parable, in the midst of his schemes for the present world? And have you not heard one and the other of them owning the vanity of those pleasures and cares, which but a few days ago were every thing to them? Confessing that religion was the one thing needful, and recommending it to others with an earnestness, as if they hoped thereby to atone for their own former neglect? We that are ministers, frequently are witnesses to such things as these, and I believe few of our hearers are entire strangers to them.

Once more, what if to the testimony of the dying, we could add that of the dead? What if God were to turn aside the veil between us and the invisible world, and permit the most careless sinner in the assembly to converse for a few moments with the inhabitants of it? If you were to apply yourself to a happy Spirit, that trod the most thorny road to paradise, or passed through the most fiery trial, and to ask him, "was it worth your while to labor so much, and to endure so much for what you now possess?" Surely if the blessed in heaven were capable of indignation, it would move them to hear that it should be made a question. And, on the other hand, if you could inquire of one tormented in that flame below, though he might once be "clothed in purple and fine linen, and fare sumptuously every day," Luke 16:19, If you could ask him, "whether his former enjoyments were an equivalent for his present sufferings and despair?" What answer do you suppose he would return? Perhaps an answer of so much horror and rage, as you would not be able so much as to endure. Or if the malignity of his nature should prevent him from returning any answer at all, surely there would be a language even in that silence, a language in the darkness, and flames, and groans of that infernal prison, which would speak to your very soul what the word of God is with equal certainty, though less forcible conviction, speaking to your ear, that "one thing is needful."

You see it is so in the judgment of God the Father, and the Lord Jesus Christ, of the wisest and best of men, of many, who seemed to judge most differently of it, when they come to more deliberate and serious thought, and not only of the dying, but of the dead too, of those who have experimentally known both worlds, and most surely know what is to be preferred. But I will not rest the whole argument here; therefore,

2. I appeal to the evident reason of the case itself, as it must appear to every unprejudiced mind, that the care of the soul is indeed the one thing needful.

I still consider myself as speaking not to atheists, or to deists, but to those who not only believe the existence and providence of God, and a future state of happiness and misery, but likewise who credit the truth of the Christian revelation, as many undoubtedly do, who live in a fatal neglect of God, and their own souls. Now on these principles, a little reflection may be sufficient to convince you, that it is needful to the present repose of your own mind; needful, if ever you would secure eternal happiness, and avoid eternal misery, which will be aggravated, rather than alleviated by all your present enjoyments.

1. The care of the soul is the one thing needful, because, "without it you cannot secure the peace of your own mind, nor avoid the upbraidings of your conscience."

That noble faculty is indeed the vicegerent of God in the soul. It is sensible of the dignity and worth of an immortal spirit, and will sometimes cry out of the violence that is offered to it, and cry so loud, as to compel the sinner to hear, whether he will or not. Do you not sometimes find it yourselves? When you labor most to forget the concerns of your soul, do they not sometimes force themselves on your remembrance? You are afraid of the reflections of your own mind, but with all your artifice and all your resolution can you entirely avoid them? Does not conscience follow you to your beds, even if denied the opportunity of meeting you in your closets, and, though with an unwelcome voice, there warn you, "that your soul is neglected, and will quickly be lost." Does it not follow you to your shops and your fields, when you are busiest there? Nay, I will add, does it not sometimes follow you to the feast, to the club, to the dance, and perhaps, amidst all resistance, to the theater too? Does, it not sometimes mingle your sweetest draughts with wormwood, and your gayest scenes with horror? So that you are like a tradesman, who, suspecting his affairs to be in a bad posture, lays by his books and his papers, yet sometimes they will come accidentally in his way. He hardly dares to look abroad for fear of meeting a creditor or an arrest: and if he labors to forget his cares and his dangers, in a course of luxury at home, the remembrance is sometimes awakened, and the alarm increased, by those very extravagancies in which he is attempting to lose it. Such probably is the case of your minds, and it is a very painful state; and while things are thus within, external circumstances can no more make you happy, than a fine dress could relieve you under a violent fit of the stone. Whereas, if this great affair were secured, you might delight in reflection, as much as you now dread it; and conscience, of your bitterest enemy, would become a delightful friend, and the testimony of it your greatest rejoicing.

2. The care of the soul is the one thing needful, "because without this your eternal happiness will be lost."

A crown of everlasting glory is not surely such a trifle as to be thrown away on a careless creature, that will not in good earnest pursue it. God doth not ordinarily deal thus, even with the bounties of his common providence, which are comparatively of little value. As to these, the hand of the diligent generally makes rich, and he would be thought distracted, rather than prudent, who should expect to get an estate merely by wishing for it, or without some resolute and continued application to a proper course of action for that purpose. Now, that we may not foolishly dream of obtaining heaven, in the midst of a course of indolence and sloth; we are expressly told in the word of God, that "the kingdom of heaven suffers violence, and the violent take it by force," Matthew 11:12, and are therefore exhorted to "strive," with the greatest intenseness, and eagerness of mind, as the word properly signifies, "to enter in at the strait gate," for this great and important reason, "because many shall another day seek to enter in, and shall not be able, Luke 13:24, Nay, when our Lord makes the most gracious promises to the humble petitioner, he does it in such a manner as to exclude the hopes of those who are careless and indifferent. "Ask, and it shall be given you; seek, and you shall find; knock, and it shall be opened unto you, Matthew 7:7,. If, therefore, you do not ask, seek, and knock, the door of mercy will not be opened, and eternal happiness will be lost. Not that heaven is to be obtained by our own good works: no, no; for having done all, we must account ourselves unprofitable servants.

And surely if I could say no more as to the fatal consequences of your neglect, than this, that eternal happiness will be lost, I should say enough to impress every mind, that considers what *eternity* means. To fall into a state of everlasting forgetfulness, might indeed appear a refuge to a mind filled with the apprehension of future misery. But O how dreadful a refuge is it! Surely it is such a refuge, as a vast precipice, (from which a man falling would be dashed to pieces in a moment) might appear to a person, pursued by the officers of justice, that he might be brought out to a painful and lingering execution. If an extravagant youth would have reason to look round with anguish, on some fair and ample paternal inheritance, which he had sold or forfeited merely for the riot of a few days: how much more melancholy would it be for a rational mind to think that its eternal happiness is lost for any earthly consideration whatever? Tormenting thought! "Had I attended to that one thing which I have neglected, I might have been, through the grace of God in Christ Jesus, great and happy beyond expression, beyond conception: not merely for the little span of ten thousand thousand ages, for ever. A line reaching even to the remotest star would not have been able to contain the number of ages, nor would millions of years have been sufficient to figure them down; this is eternity, but I have lost it, and am now on the verge of being. This lamp, which might have outlasted those of the firmament, will presently be extinguished, and I blotted out from amongst the works of God, and cut off from all the bounties of his hand." Would not this be a very miserable case, if this were all? And would it not be sufficient to prove this to be the better part, which, as our Lord observes, can "never be taken away?" But God forbid that we should be so unfaithful to him, and to the souls of men, as to rest in such a representation alone. I therefore add once more,

3. The care of the soul is the one thing needful, because "without it, you cannot avoid a state of eternal misery, which will be aggravated, rather than alleviated by all your present enjoyments."

Nothing can be more evident from the word of the God of truth. It there plainly appears to be a determined case, which leaves no room for a more favorable conjecture or hope. "The wicked shall be turned into hell, even all the nations that forget God," Psalms 9:17, "They shall go away into everlasting punishment, Matthew 25:46, into a state where they shall in vain seek death, and death shall flee from them. Oh! brethren, it is a certain, but an awful truth, that your souls will be thinking and immortal beings, even in spite of themselves. They may indeed torment, but they cannot destroy themselves. They can no more suspend their power of thought and perception, than a mirror its property of reflecting rays that fall off its surface. Do you suspect the contrary? Make the trial immediately. Command your minds to create from thinking but for one quarter of an hour, or for half that time, and exclude every idea and every reflection. Can you succeed in that attempt? Or rather, does not thought press in with a more sensible violence on that resistance; as an anxious desire to sleep, makes us so much the more wakeful. Thus will thought follow you beyond the grave, thus will it, as an unwelcome guest, force itself upon you, when it can serve only to perplex and distress the mind. It will for ever upbraid you, that notwithstanding all the kind expostulations of God and man, notwithstanding all the keen remonstrances of conscience, and the pleadings of the blood of Christ, you have gone on in your folly, till heaven is lost, and damnation incurred; and all, for what for a shadow and a dream?

Oh think not, sinners, that the remembrance of your past pleasures, and of your success in your other cares, whilst that of the one thing needful was forgotten, think not that this will ease you minds. It will rather torment them the more. "Son, remember that thou in thy lifetime receivedst thy good things." Bitter remembrance! Well might the heathen poets represent the unhappy spirits in the shades below, as eagerly catching at the water of forgetfulness, yet unable to reach it. Your present comforts will only serve to give you a livelier sense of your misery, as having tasted such degrees of enjoyment; and to inflame the reckoning, as you have misimproved those talents lodged in your hands for better purposes. Surely, if these things were believed, and seriously considered, the sinner would have no more heart to rejoice in his present prosperity, than a man would have to amuse himself with the curiosities of a fine garden, through which he was led to be broken upon the rack.

But I will enlarge no farther on these things. Would to God that the unaccountable stupidity of men's minds, and their fatal attachment to the pleasures and cares of the present life, did not make it necessary to insist on them so frequently and so copiously!

I now proceed to the reflections which naturally arise from hence, and shall only mention two.

1. How much reason have we to lament the follow of mankind in neglecting the one thing needful.

If religion be indeed the truest wisdom, then surely we have the justest reason to say with Solomon, "the folly and madness is in men's hearts, Ecclesiastes 9:3, Is it the one thing needful? Look on the conduct of the generality of mankind, and you would imagine they thought it the one thing needless: the vainest dream, and the idlest amusement of the mind. God is admonishing them by ordinances, and providences, sometimes by such as are most awful, to lay it to heart;" he speaks once, yea twice, (yes a multitude of times) but man regards not, Job 33:14, They profess perhaps to believe all that I have been saying, but act as if the contrary were self-evident; they will risk their fouls and eternity for a thing of nought, for that, for the sake of which they would not risk so much as a hand, or a finger, or a joint, no, nor perhaps a toy that adorns it. Surely this is the wonder of angels, and perhaps of devils too, unless the observation of so many ages may have rendered it familiar to both. And can we, my Christian brethren, behold such a scene with indifference? If some epidemical madness had seized our country, or the places where we live, so that as we went from one place to another, we every where met with lunatics, and saw amongst the rest, some perhaps of the finest genius, in the most eminent stations in life, amusing themselves with others; surely were we ever so secure from the danger of infection or assault, the fight would cut us to the heart. A good-natured man would hardly be able to go abroad, or even be desirous to live, if it must be amongst so many sad spectacles. Yet these poor creatures might, notwithstanding this, be the children of God, and the higher their frenzy rose, the nearer might their complete happiness be. But alas! the greater part of mankind are seized with a worse kind of madness, in which they are ruining their souls; and can we behold it with indifference? The Lord awaken our compassion, our prayers, and our endeavors, in dependence on divine grace, that we may be instrumental in bringing them to their mind, and making them wise indeed, that is, wise to salvation!

2. How necessary is it that we should seriously inquire, how this one thing needful is regarded by us!

Let me entreat you to remember your own concern in it, and inquire—Have I thought seriously of it? Have I seen the importance of it? Ha it lain with a due and abiding weight on my mind? Has it brought me to Christ, that I might lay the stress of these great eternal interests on him? And am I acting in the main of my life, as one that has these convictions? Am I willing, in fact, to give up other things, my interests, my pleasures, my passions to this? Am I conversing with God and with man, as one that believes these things; as one that has deliberately chosen the better part, and is determined to abide by that choice?

Observe the answer which conscience returns to these inquiries, and you will know your own part in that more particular application, with which I shall conclude.

1. Let me address those that are entirely unconcerned about the one thing needful.

Brethren, I have been stating the case at large, and now I appeal to your consciences, are these things so, or are they not? God and your own hearts best know for what the care of your soul is neglected; but be it what it will, the difference between one grain of sand and another, is not great, when it comes to be weighed against a talent of gold. Whatever it is, you had need to examine it carefully. You had need to view that commodity on all sides, of which you do in effect say, For this will I sell my soul; for this will I give up heaven, and venture hell, be heaven and hell whatever they may. In the name of God, brethren, is this the part of a man, of a rational creature? To go on with your eyes open towards a pit of eternal ruin, because there are a few gay flowers in the way: or what if you shut your eyes, will that prevent your fall? It signifies little to say, I will not think of these things, I will not consider them: God has said, "In the last days they shall consider it perfectly, Jeremiah 23:20, The revels of a drunken malefactor will not prevent nor respite his execution. Pardon my plainness; if it were a fable or a tale, I would endeavor to amuse you with words, but I cannot do it where souls are at stake.

2. I would apply to those who are, in some sense, convinced of the importance of their souls, and yet are inclined to defer that care of them a little longer, which, in the general, they see to be necessary.

I know you that are young, are under peculiar temptations to do this; though it is strange that the death of so many of your companions, should not be an answer to some of the most specious and dangerous of those temptations. Methinks, if these were the least degree of uncertainty, the importance is too weighty to put matters to the venture. But here the uncertainty is great and apparent. You must surely know, that there are critical seasons of life for managing the concerns of it, which are of such a nature, that if once left, they may never return: here is a critical season: "Now is the accepted time, now is the day of salvation," 1 Corinthians 6:2, "today, if ye will hear his voice, harden not your hearts," Hebrews 3:7, Hebrews 3:8, This language may not be spoken tomorrow. Talk not of a more convenient season; none can be more convenient; and that to which you would probably refer it, is least of all so, a dying time. You would not choose then to have any important business in hand; and will you of choice refer the greatest business of all to that languishing, hurrying, amazing hour? If a friend were then to come to you with the balance of an intricate account, or a view of a title to an estate, you would shake your fainting head, and lift up your pale trembling hand, and say, perhaps, with a feeble voice, "Alas, is this a time for these things?" And is it a time for so much greater things than these? I wish you knew, and would consider, into what a strait, we that are minister are sometime brought, when we are called to the dying beds of those who have spent their lives in the neglect of the one thing needful. On the one hand, we fear, lest if we palliate [sugarcoat] matters, and speak smooth things, we shall betray and ruin their souls; and on the other, that if we use a becoming plainness and seriousness, in warning them of their danger, we shall quite overwhelm them, and hasten the dying moments, which is advancing by such swift steps. O let me entreat you for our sakes, and much more for your own, that you do not drive us to such sad extremities; but if you are convinced, as I hope some of you may now be, that the care of the soul is that needful thing we have represented, let the conviction work, let it drive you immediately to the throne of grace; from thence you may derive that wisdom and strength, which will direct you in all the intricacies which entangle you, and animate you in the midst of difficulty an discouragement.

3. I would in the last place address myself to those happy souls, who have in good earnest attended to the one thing needful.

I hope, that when you see how commonly it is neglected, neglected indeed, by many, whose natural capacities, improvements, and circumstances in life, appear to you superior to your own; you will humbly acknowledge, that it was distinguishing grace which brought you into this happy state, and formed you to this most necessary care. Bless the Lord, therefore, who hath given you that counsel, in virtue of which you can say, "He is your portion." Rejoice in the thought, that the great concern is secured: as it is natural for us to do, when some important affair is dispatched, which has long lain before us, and which we have been inclined to put off from one day to another, but have at length strenuously and successfully attended. Remember still to endeavor to continue acting on these great principles, which at first determined your choice; and seriously consider, that those who desire their life may at last be given them for a prey, must continue on their guard, in all stages of their journey through a wilderness, where daily dangers are still surrounding them. Being enabled to secure the great concern, make yourselves easy as to others of smaller importance. You have chosen the kingdom of God, and his righteousness; other things, therefore, shall be added unto you: and if any which you desire should, not be added, comfort yourselves with this thought, that you have the good part, which can never be taken away. And, not to enlarge on these obvious hints, which must often occur, be very solicitous that others may be brought to a care about the one thing needful. If it be needful for you, it is so for your children, your friends, your servants. Let them, therefore, see your concern in this respect for them, as well as for yourselves. Let parents especially attend to this exhortation; whose care for their offspring often exceeds in other respects, and falls in this. Remember that your children may never live to enjoy the effects of your labor and concern to get them estates and portions: the charges of their funerals may, perhaps, be all their share of what you are so anxiously careful to lay up for them. And O think what a sword would pierce through your very heart, if you should stand by the corpse of a beloved child with this reflection: "This poor creature has done with life, before it learnt its great business in it; and is gone to eternity, which I have seldom been warning it to prepare for, and which, perhaps, it learned of me to forget."

On the whole, may this grand care be awakened in those by whom it has been hitherto neglected: may it be revived in each of our minds. And that you may be encouraged to pursue it with greater cheerfulness, let me conclude with this comfortable thought, that in proportion to the necessity of the case, through the merits of Christ Jesus, is the provision which divine grace has made for our assistance. If you are disposed to sit down at Christ's feet, he will teach you by his word and Spirit. If you commit this precious jewel, which is your eternal all, into his hand, he will preserve it unto that day, and will then produce it richly adorned, and gloriously improved to his own honor, and to your everlasting joy.

Which God of his infinite mercy grant.

32. A Penitent Heart, the Best New Year's Gift

Luke 13:3—"Except ye repent, ye shall all likewise perish."

When we consider how heinous and aggravating our offenses are, in the sight of a just and holy God, that they bring down his wrath upon our heads, and occasion us to live under his indignation; how ought we thereby to be deterred from evil, or at least engaged to study to repent thereof, and not commit the same again; but man is so thoughtless of an eternal state, and has so little consideration of the welfare of his immortal soul, that he can sin without any thought that he must give an account of his actions at the day of judgment; or if he, at times, has any reflections on his behavior, they do not drive him to true repentance: he may, for a short time, refrain from falling into some gross sins which he had lately committed; but then, when the temptation comes again with power, he is carried away with the lust; and thus he goes on promising and resolving, and in breaking both his resolutions and his promises, as fast almost as he has made them. This is highly offensive to God, it is mocking of him. My brethren, when grace is given us to repent truly, we shall turn wholly unto God; and let me beseech you to repent of your sins, for the time is hastening when you will have neither time nor call to repent; there is none in the grave, whither we are going; but do not be afraid, for God often receives the greatest sinner to mercy through the merits of Christ Jesus; this magnifies the riches of his free grace; and should be an encouragement for you, who are great and notorious sinners, to repent, for he shall have mercy upon you, if you through Christ return unto him.

St. Paul was an eminent instance of this; he speaks of himself as "the chief of sinners," and he declareth how God showed mercy unto him. Christ loves to show mercy unto sinners, and if you repent, he will have mercy upon you. But as no word is more mistaken than that of repentance, I shall

I. Show you what the nature of repentance is.

II. Consider the several parts and causes of repentance.

III. I shall give you some reasons, why repentance is necessary to salvation. And

IV. Exhort all of you, high and low, rich and poor, one with another, to endeavor after repentance.

I. Repentance, my brethren, in the first place, as to its nature, is the carnal and corrupt disposition of men being changed into a renewed and sanctified disposition. A man that has truly repented, is truly regenerated: it is a different word for one and the same thing; the motley mixture of the beast and devil is gone; there is, as it were, a new creation wrought in your hearts. If your repentance is true, you are renewed throughout, both in soul and body; your understandings are enlightened with the knowledge of God, and of the Lord Jesus Christ; and your wills, which were stubborn, obstinate, and hated all good, are obedient and comformable to the will of God. Indeed, our deists tell us, that man now has a free will to do good, to love God, and to repent when he will; but indeed, there is no free will in any of you, but to sin; nay, your free-will leads you so far, that you would, if possible, pull God from is throne. This may, perhaps, offend the Pharisees; but (it is the truth in Christ which I speak, I lie not) every man by his own natural will hates God; but when he is turned unto the Lord, by evangelical repentance, then his will is changed; then your consciences, nor hardened and benumbed, shall be quickened and awakened; then your had hearts shall be melted, and your unruly affections shall be crucified. Thus, by that repentance, the whole soul will be changed, you will have new inclinations, new desires, and new habits.

You may see how vile we are by nature, that it requires so great a change to be made upon us, to recover us from this state of sin, and therefore the consideration of our dreadful state should make us earnest with God to change our condition, and that change, true repentance implies; therefore, my brethren, consider how hateful your ways are to God, while you continue in sin; how abominable you are unto him, while you run into evil: you cannot be said to be Christians while you are hating Christ, and his people; true repentance will entirely change you, the bias of your souls will be changed, then you will delight in God, in Christ, in his law, and in his people; you will then believe that there is such a thing as inward feeling, though now you may esteem it madness and enthusiasm; you will not then be ashamed of becoming fools for Christ's sake; you will not regard being scoffed at; it is not then their pointing after you and crying, "Here comes another troop of his followers," will dismay you; no, your soul will abhor such proceedings, the ways of Christ and his people will be your whole delight.

It is the nature of such repentance to make a change, and the greatest change as can be made here in the soul. Thus you see what repentance implies in its own nature; it denotes an abhorrence of all evil, and a forsaking of it. I shall now proceed

Secondly, To show you the parts of it, and the causes concurring thereto.

The parts are, sorrow, hatred, and an entire forsaking of sin.

Our sorrow and grief for sin, must not spring merely from a fear of wrath; for if we have no other ground but that, it proceeds from self-love, and not from any love to God; and if love to God is not the chief motive of your repentance, your repentance is in vain, and not to be esteemed true.

Many, in our days, think their crying, God forgive me! or, Lord have mercy upon me! or, I am sorry for it! Is repentance, and that God will esteem it as such; but, indeed, they are mistaken; it is not the drawing near to God with our lips, while our hearts are far from him, which he regards. Repentance does not come by fits and starts; no, it is one continued act of our lives; for as we daily commit sin, so we need a daily repentance before God, to obtain forgiveness for those sins we commit.

It is not your confessing yourselves to be sinners, it is not knowing your condition to be sad and deplorable, so long as you continue in your sins; your care and endeavors should be, to get the heart thoroughly affected therewith, that you may feel yourselves to be lost and undone creatures, for Christ came to save such as are lost; and if you are enabled to groan under the weight and burden of your sins, then Christ will ease you and give you rest.

And till you are thus sensible of your misery and lost condition, you are a servant to sin and to your lusts, under the bondage and command of Satan, doing his drudgery: thou are under the curse of God, and liable to his judgment. Consider how dreadful thy state will be at death, and after the day of judgment, when thou wilt be exposed to such miseries which the ear hath not heard, neither can the heart conceive, and that to all eternity, if you die impenitent.

But I hope better things of you, my brethren, though I thus speak, and things which accompany salvation; go to God in prayer, and be earnest with him, that by his Spirit he would convince you of your miserable condition by nature, and make you truly sensible thereof. O be humbled, be humbled, I beseech you, for your sins. Having spent so many years in sinning, what canst thou do less, than be concerned to spend some hours in mourning and sorrowing for the same, and be humbled before God.

Look back into your lives, call to mind thy sins, as many as possible thou canst, the sins of thy youth, as well as of thy riper years; see how you have departed from a gracious Father, and wandered in the way of wickedness, in which you have lost yourselves, the favor of God, the comforts of his Spirit, and the peace of your own consciences; then go and beg pardon of the Lord, through the blood of the Lamb, for the evil thou hast committed, and for the good thou hast omitted. Consider, likewise, the heinousness of thy sins; see what very aggravating circumstances thy sins are attended with, how you have abused the patience of God, which should have led you to repentance; and when thou findest thy heart hard, beg of God to soften it, cry mightily unto him, and he will take away thy stony heart, and give thee a heart of flesh.

Resolve to leave all thy sinful lusts and pleasures; renounce, forsake, and abhor thy old sinful course of life, and serve God in holiness and righteousness all the remaining part of life. If you lament and bewail past sins, and do not forsake them, your repentance is in vain, you are mocking of God, and deceiving your own soul; you must put off the old man with his deeds, before you can put on the new man, Christ Jesus.

You, therefore, who have been swearers and cursers, you, who have been harlots and drunkards, you, who have been thieves and robbers, you, who have hitherto followed the sinful pleasures and diversions of life, let me beseech you, by the mercies of God in Christ Jesus, that you would no longer continue therein, but that you would forsake your evil ways, and turn unto the Lord, for he waiteth to be gracious unto you, he is ready, he is willing to pardon you of all your sins; but do not expect Christ to pardon you of sin, when you run into it, and will not abstain from complying with the temptations; but if you will be persuaded to abstain from evil and choose the good, to return unto the Lord, and repent of your wickedness, he hath promised he will abundantly pardon you, he will heal your back-slidings, and will love you freely. Resolve now this day to have done with your sins for ever; let your old ways and you be separated; you must resolve against it, for there can be no true repentance without a resolution to forsake it. Resolve for Christ, resolve against the devil and his works, and go on fighting the Lord's battles against the devil and his emissaries; attack him in the strongest holds he has, fight him as men, as Christians, and you will soon find him to be a coward; resist him and he will fly from you. Resolve, through grace, to do this, and your repentance is half done; but then take care that you do not ground your resolutions on your own strength, but in the strength of the Lord Jesus Christ; he is the way, he is the truth, and he is the life; without his assistance you can do nothing, but through his grace strengthening thee, thou wilt be enabled to do all things; and the more ready Christ will be to help thee; and what can all the men of the world do to thee when Christ is for thee? Thou wilt not regard what they say against thee, for you will have the testimony of a good conscience.

Resolve to cast thyself at the feet of Christ in subjection to him, and throw thyself into the arms of Christ for salvation by him. Consider, my dear brethren, the many invitations he has given you to come unto him, to be saved by him; "God has laid on him the iniquity of us all." O let me prevail with you, above all things, to make choice of the Lord Jesus Christ; resign yourselves unto him, take him, O take him, upon his own terms, and whosoever thou art, how great a sinner soever you have been, this evening, in the name of the great God, do I offer Jesus Christ unto thee; as thou valuest thy life and soul refuse him not, but stir up thyself to accept of the Lord Jesus, take him wholly as he is, for he will be applied wholly unto you, or else not at all. Jesus Christ must be your whole wisdom, Jesus Christ must be your whole righteousness, Jesus Christ must be your whole sanctification, or he will never be your eternal redemption.

What though you have been ever so wicked and profligate, yet, if you will not abandon your sins, and turn unto the Lord Jesus Christ, thou shalt have him given to thee, and all thy sins shall be freely forgiven. O why will you neglect the great work of your repentance? Do not defer the doing of it one day longer, but today, even now, take that Christ who is freely offered to you.

Now as to the causes hereof, the first cause is God; he is the author, "we are born of God," God hath begotten us, even God, the Father of our Lord Jesus Christ; it is he that stirs us up to will and to do of his own good pleasure: and another cause is, God's free grace; it is owing to the "riches of his free grace," my brethren, that we have been prevented from going down to hell long ago; it is because the compassions of the Lord fail not, they are new every morning, and fresh every evening.

Sometimes the instruments are very unlikely: a poor despised minister, or member of Jesus Christ, may, by the power of God, be made an instrument in the hands of God, of bringing you to true evangelical repentance; and this may be done to show, that the power is not in men, but that it is entirely owing to the good pleasure of God; and if there has been any good done among many of you, by preaching the word, as I trust there has, though it was preached in a field, if God has met and owned us, and blessed his word, though preached by an enthusiastic babbler, a boy, a madman; I do rejoice, yea, and will rejoice, let foes say what they will. I shall now

Thirdly, Show the reasons why repentance is necessary to salvation.

And this, my brethren, is plainly revealed to us in the word of God, "The soul that does not repent and turn unto the Lord, shall die in its sins, and their blood shall be required at their own heads." It is necessary, as we have sinned, we should repent; for a holy God could not, nor ever can, or will, admit any thing that is unholy into his presence: this is the beginning of grace in the soul; there must be a change in heart and life, before there can be a dwelling with a holy God. You cannot love sin and God too, you cannot love God and mammon; no unclean person can stand in the presence of God, it is contrary to the holiness of his nature; there is a contrariety between the holy nature of God, and the unholy nature of carnal and unregenerate men.

What communication can there be between a sinless God, and creatures full of sin, between a pure God and impure creatures? If you were to be admitted into heaven with your present tempers, in your impenitent condition, heaven itself would be a hell to you; the songs of angels would be as enthusiasm, and would be intolerable to you; therefore you must have these tempers changed, you must be holy, as God is: he must be your God here, and you must be his people, or you will never dwell together to all eternity. If you hate the ways of God, and cannot spend an hour in his service, how will you think to be easy, to all eternity, in singing praises to him that sits upon the throne, and to the Lamb for ever.

And this is to be the employment, my brethren, of all those who are admitted into this glorious place, where neither sin nor sinner is admitted, where no scoffer ever can come, without repentance from his evil ways, a turning unto God, and a cleaving unto him: this must be done, before any can be admitted into the glorious mansions of God, which are prepared for all that love the Lord Jesus Christ in sincerity and truth: repent ye then of all your sins. O my dear brethren, it makes my blood run cold, in thinking that any of you should not be admitted into the glorious mansions above. O that it was in my power, I would place all of you, yea, you my scoffing brethren, and the greatest enemy I have on earth, at the right hand of Jesus; but this I cannot do: however, I advise and exhort you, with all love and tenderness, to make Jesus your refuge; fly to him for relief; Jesus died to save such as you; he is full of compassion; and if you go to him, as poor, lost, undone sinners, Jesus will give you his spirit; you shall live and reign, and reign and live, you shall love and live, and live and love with this Jesus to all eternity.

I am, *Fourthly*, to exhort all of you, high and low, rich and poor, one with another, to repent of all your sins, and turn unto the Lord.

And I shall speak to each of you; for you have either repented, or you have not, you are believers in Christ Jesus, or unbelievers.

And first, you who never have truly repented of your sins, and never have truly forsaken your lusts, be not offended if I speak plain to you; for it is love, love to your souls, that constrains me to speak: I shall lay before you your danger, and the misery to which you are exposed, while you remain impenitent in sin. And O that this may be a means of making you fly to Christ for pardon and forgiveness.

While thy sins are not repented of, thou art in danger of death, and if you should die, you would perish for ever. There is no hope of any who live and die in their sins, but that they will dwell with devils and damned spirits to all eternity. And how do we know we shall live much longer: we are not sure of seeing our own habitations this night in safety. What mean ye then being at ease and pleasure while your sins are not pardoned. As sure as ever the word of God is true, if you die in that condition, you are shut out of all hope and mercy for ever, and shall pass into ceaseless and endless misery.

What is all thy pleasures and diversions worth? They last but for a moment, they are of no worth, and but of short continuance. And sure it must be gross folly, eagerly to pursue those sinful lusts and pleasures, which war against the soul, which tend to harden the heart, and keep us from closing with the Lord Jesus; indeed, these are destructive o four peace here, and without repentance, will be of our peace hereafter.

O the folly and madness of this sensual world; sure if there were nothing in sin but present slavery, it would keep an ingenuous spirit from it. But to do the devils drudgery! And if we do that, we shall have his wages, which is eternal death and condemnation; O consider this, my guilty brethren, you that think it no crime to swear, whore, drink, or scoff and jeer at the people of God; consider how your voices will then be changed, and you that counted their lives madness, and their end without honor, shall howl and lament at your own madness and filly, that should bring you to so much woe and distress. Then you will lament and bemoan your own dreadful condition; but it will be of no signification: for he that is not your merciful Savior, will then become your inexorable Judge. Now he is easy to be entreated; but then, all your tears and prayers will be in vain: for God hath allotted to every man a day of grace, a time of repentance, which if he doth not improve, nut neglects and despises the means which are offered to him, he cannot be saved.

Consider, therefore, while you are going on in a course of sin and unrighteousness, I beseech you, my brethren, to think of the consequence that will attend your thus mispending your precious time; your souls are worth being concerned about: for if you can enjoy all the pleasures and diversions of life, at death you must leave them; that will put an end to all your worldly concerns. And will it not be very deplorable, to have your good things here, all your earthly, sensual, devilish pleasures, which you have been so much taken up with, all over: and the thought for how trifling a concern thou hast lost eternal welfare, will gnaw thy very soul.

Thy wealth and grandeur will stand in no stead; thou canst carry nothing of it into the other world: then the consideration of thy uncharitableness to the poor, and the ways thou didst take to obtain thy wealth, will be a very hell unto thee.

Now you enjoy the means of grace, as the preaching of his word, prayer, and sacraments; and God has sent his ministers out into the fields and highways, to invite, to woo you to come in; but they are tiresome to thee, thou hadst rather be at thy pleasures: ere long, my brethren, they will be over, and you will be no more troubled with them; but then thou wouldst give ten thousand worlds for one moment of that merciful time of grace which thou hast abused; then you will cry for a drop of that precious blood which now you trample under your feet; then you will wish for one more offer of mercy, for Christ and his free grace to be offered to you again; but your crying will be in vain: for as you would not repent here, God will not give you an opportunity to repent hereafter: if you would not in Christ's time, you shall not in your own. In what a dreadful condition will you then be? What horror and astonishment will possess your souls? Then all thy lies and oaths, thy scoffs and jeers at the people of God, all thy filthy and unclean thoughts and actions, thy mispent time in balls, plays, and assemblies, thy spending whole evenings at cards, dice, and masquerades, thy frequenting of taverns and alehouses, thy worldliness, covetousness, and thy uncharitableness, will be brought at once to thy remembrance, and at once charged upon thy guilty soul. And how can you bear the thoughts of these things? Indeed I am full of compassion towards you, to think that this should be the portion of any who now hear me. These are truths, though awful ones; my brethren, these are the truths of the gospel; and if there was not a necessity for thus speaking, I would willingly forbear: for it is no pleasing subject to me, any more than it is to you; but it is my duty to show you the dreadful consequences of continuing in sin. I am only now acting the part of a skillful surgeon, that searches a wound before he heals it: I would show you your danger first, that deliverance may be the more readily accepted by you.

Consider, that however you may be for putting the evil day away from you, and are now striving to hide your sins, at the day of judgment there shall be a full discovery of all; hidden things on that day shall be brought to light; and after all thy sins have been revealed to the whole world, then you must depart into everlasting fire in hell, which will not be quenched night and day; it will be without intermission, without end. O then, what stupidity and senselessness hath possessed your hearts, that you are not frighted from your sins. The fear of Nebuchadnezzar's fiery furnace, made men do any thing to avoid it; and shall not an everlasting fire make men, make you, do any thing to avoid it?

O that this would awaken and cause you to humble yourselves for your sins, and to beg pardon for them, that you might find mercy in the Lord.

Do not go away, let not the devil hurry you away before the sermon is over; but stay, and you shall have a Jesus offered to you, who has made full satisfaction for all your sins.

Let me beseech you to cast away your transgressions, to strive against sin, to watch against it, and to beg power and strength from Christ, to keep down the power of those lusts that hurry you on in your sinful ways.

But if you will not do any of these things, if you are resolved to sin on, you must expect eternal death to be the consequence; you must expect to be seized with horror and trembling, with horror and amazement, to hear the dreadful sentence of condemnation pronounced against you: and then you will run and call upon the mountains to fall on you, to hide you from the Lord, and from the fierce anger of his wrath.

Had you now a heart to turn from your sins unto the living God, by true and unfeigned repentance, and to pray unto him for mercy, in and through the merits of Jesus Christ, there were hope; but at the day of judgment, thy prayers and tears will be of no signification; they will be of no service to thee, the Judge will not be entreated by thee: as you would not hearken to him when he called unto thee, but despised both him and his ministers, and would not leave your iniquities; therefore, on that day he will not be entreated, notwithstanding all thy cries and tears; for God himself hath said, "Because I have called, and you refused; I have stretched out my hand, and no man regarded, but ye have set at nought all my counsel, and would have one of my reproof; I will also laugh at your calamity, and mock when your fear cometh as desolation, and your destruction cometh as a whirlwind; when distress and anguish cometh upon you, then shall they call upon me, but I will not answer, they shall seek me early, but they shall not find me."

Now you may call this enthusiasm and madness; but at that great day, if you repent not of your sins here, you will find, by woeful experience, that your own ways were madness indeed; but God forbid it should be left undone till then: seek after the Lord while he is to be found; call upon him while he is near, and you shall find mercy:

repent this hour, and Christ will joyfully receive you.

What say you? Must I go to my Master, and tell him you will not come unto him, and will have none of his counsels? No; do not send me on so unhappy an errand: I cannot, I will not tell him any such thing. Shall not I rather tell him, you are willing to repent and to be converted, to become new men, and take up a new course of life: this is the only wise resolution you can make. Let me tell my Master, that you will come unto, and will wait upon him: for if you do not, it will be your ruin in time, and to eternity.

You will at death wish you had lived the life of the righteous, that you might have died his death. Be advised then; consider what is before you, Christ and the world, holiness and sin, life and death: choose now for yourselves; let your choice be made immediately, and let that choice be your dying choice.

If you would not choose to die in your sins, to die drunkards, to die adulterers, to die swearers and scoffers, &c. live not out this night in the dreadful condition you are in. Some of you, it may be, may say, You have not power, you have no strength: but have not you been wanting to yourselves in such things that were within your power? Have you not as much power to go to hear a sermon, as to go into a playhouse, or to a ball, or masquerade? You have as much power to read the Bible, as to read plays, novels, and romances; and you can associate as well with the godly, as with the wicked and profane: this is but an idle excuse, my brethren, to go on in your sins: and if you will be found in the means of grace, Christ hath promised he will give you strength. While Peter was preaching, the Holy Ghost fell on all that heard the word: how then should you be found in the way of your duty? Jesus Christ will then give thee strength; he will put his Spirit within thee; thou shalt find he will be thy wisdom, thy righteousness, thy sanctification, and thy redemption. Do but try what a gracious, a kind, and loving Master he is; he will be a help to thee in all thy burdens: and if the burden of sin is on thy soul, go to him as weary and heavy laden, and thou shalt find rest.

Do not say, that your sins are too many and too great to expect to find mercy! No, be they ever so many, or ever so great, the blood of the Lord Jesus Christ will cleanse you from all sins. God's grace, my brethren, is free, rich, and sovereign. Manassah was a great sinner, and yet he was pardoned; Zaccheus was gone far from God, and went out to see Christ, with no other view but to satisfy his curiosity; and yet Jesus met him, and brought salvation to his house. Manassah was an idolater and murderer, yet her received mercy; the other was an oppressor and extortioner, who had gotten riches by fraud and deceit, and by grinding the faces of the poor: so did Matthew too, and yet they found mercy.

Have you been blasphemers and persecutors of the saints and servants of God? So was St. Paul, yet her received mercy: Have you been common harlots, filthy and unclean persons? So was Mary Magdalene, and yet she received mercy. Hast thou been a thief? The thief upon the cross found mercy. I despair of none of you, however vile and profligate you have been; I say, I despair of none of you, especially when God has had mercy on such a wretch as I am.

Remember the poor Publican, how he found favor with God, when the proud, self-conceited Pharisee, who, puffed up with his own righteousness, was rejected. And if you will go to Jesus, as the poor Publican did, under a sense of your own unworthiness, you shall find favor as he did: there is virtue enough in the blood of Jesus, to pardon greater sinners than he has yet pardoned. Then be not discouraged, but come unto Jesus, and you will find him ready to help in all thy distresses, to lead thee into all truth, to bring thee from darkness to light, and from the power of Satan to God.

Do not let the devil deceive you, by telling you, that then all your delights and pleasures will be over: No; this is so far from depriving you of all pleasure, that it is an inlet unto unspeakable delights, peculiar to all who are truly regenerated. The new birth is the very beginning of a life of peace and comfort; and the greatest pleasantness is to be found in the ways of holiness.

Solomon, who had experience of all other pleasures, yet saith of the ways of godliness, "That all her ways are ways of pleasantness, and all her paths are paths of peace." Then sure you will not let the devil deceive you; it is all he wants, it is that he aims at, to make religion appear to be melancholy, miserable, and enthusiastic: but let him say what he will, give not ear to him, regard him not, for he always was and will be a liar.

What words, what entreaties shall I use, to make you come unto the Lord Jesus Christ? The little love I have experienced since I have been brought from sin to God, is so great, that I would not be in a natural state for ten thousand worlds; and what I have felt is but little to what I hope to feel; but that little love which I have experienced, is a sufficient buoy against all the storms and tempests of this boisterous world: and let men and devils do their worst, I rejoice in the Lord Jesus, yea, and I will rejoice.

And O if you repent and come to Jesus, I would rejoice on your accounts too; and we should rejoice together to all eternity, when once passed on the other side of the grave. O come to Jesus. The arms of Jesus Christ will embrace you; he will sash away all your sins in his blood, and will love you freely.

Come, I beseech you to come unto Jesus Christ. O that my words would pierce to the very soul! O that Jesus Christ was formed in you! O that you would turn to the Lord Jesus Christ, that he might have mercy upon you! I would speak till midnight, yea, I would speak till I could speak no more, so it might be a means to bring you to Jesus; let the Lord Jesus but enter your souls, and you shall find peace which the world can neither give nor take away. There is mercy for the greatest sinner amongst you; go unto the Lord as sinners, helpless and undone without it, and then you shall find comfort in your souls, and be admitted at last amongst those who sing praises unto the Lord to all eternity.

Now, my brethren, let me speak a word of exhortation to those of you, who are already brought to the Lord Jesus, who are born again, who do belong to God, to whom it has been given to repent of your sins, and are cleansed from their guilt; and that is, be thankful to God for his mercies towards you. O admire the grace of God, and bless his name forever! Are you made alive in Christ Jesus? Is the life of God begun in your souls, and have you the evidence thereof? Be thankful for this unspeakable mercy to you: never forget to speak of his mercy. And as your life was formerly devoted to sin, and to the pleasures of the world, let it now be spent wholly in the ways of God; and O embrace every opportunity of doing and of receiving good. Whatsoever opportunity you have, do it vigorously, do it speedily, do not defer it. If thou seest one hurrying on to destruction, use the utmost of thy endeavor to stop him in his course; show him the need he has of repentance, and that without it he is lost for ever; do not regard his despising of you; still go on to show him his danger: and if thy friends mock and despise, do not let that discourage you; hold on, hold out to the end, so you shall have a crown which is immutable, and that fadeth not away.

Let the love of Jesus to you, keep you also humble; do not be high-minded, keep close unto the Lord, observe the rules which the Lord Jesus Christ has given in his word, and let not the instructions be lost which you which you are capable of giving. O consider what reason you have to be thankful to the Lord Jesus Christ for giving you that repentance you yourselves had need of: a repentance which worketh by love. Now you find more pleasure in walking with God one hour, than in all your former carnal delights, and all the pleasures of sin. O! the joy you feel in your own souls, which all the men of the world, and all the devils in hell, though they were to combine together, could not destroy. Then fear not their wrath or malice, for through many tribulations we must enter into glory.

A few days, or weeks, or years more, and then you will be beyond their reach, you will be in the heavenly Jerusalem; there is all harmony and love, there is all joy and delight; there the weary soul is at rest.

Now we have many enemies, but at death they are all lost; they cannot follow us beyond the grave: and this is a great encouragement to us not to regard the scoffs and jeers of the men of this world.

O let the love of Jesus be in your thoughts continually. It was his dying that brought you life; it was his crucifixion that paid the satisfaction for your sins; his death, burial, and resurrection that completed the work; and he is now in heaven, interceding for you at the right hand of his Father. And can you do too much for the Lord Jesus Christ, who has done so much for you? His love to you is unfathomable. O the height, the depth, the length and breadth of this love, that brought the King of glory from his throne, to die for such rebels as we are, when we had acted so unkindly against him, and deserved nothing but eternal damnation. He came down and took our nature upon him; he was made of flesh and dwelt among us; he was put to death on our account; he paid our ransom: surely this should make us rejoice in him, and not do as too many do, and as we ourselves have too often, crucify this Jesus afresh. Let us do all we can, my dear brethren, to honor him.

Come, all of you, come, and behold him stretched out for you; see his hands and feet nailed to the cross. O come, come, my brethren, and nail your sins thereto; come, come and see his side pierced; there is a fountain open for sin, and for uncleanness: O wash, wash and be clean: come and see his head crowned with thorns, and all for you. Can you think of a panting, bleeding, dying Jesus, and not be filled with pity towards him? He underwent all this for you. Come unto him by faith; lay hold on him: there is mercy for every soul of you that will come unto him. Then do not delay; fly unto the arms of this Jesus, and you shall be made clean in his blood.

O what shall I say unto you to make you come to Jesus: I have showed you the dreadful consequence of not repenting of your sins: and if after all I have said, you are resolved to persist, your blood will be required at your own heads; but I hope better things of you, and things that accompany salvation. Let me beg of you to pray in good earnest for the grace of repentance. I may never see your faces again; but at the day of judgment I will meet you: there you will either bless God that ever you were moved to repentance; or else this sermon, though in a field, will be as a swift witness against you. Repent, repent therefore, my dear brethren, as John the Baptist, and as our blessed Redeemer himself earnestly exhorted, and turn from your evil ways, and the Lord will have mercy on you.

Show them, O Father, wherein they have offended thee; make them to see their own vileness, and that they are lost and undone without true repentance; and O give them that repentance, we beseech of thee, that they may turn from sin unto thee the living and true God. These things, and whatever else thou seest needful for us, we entreat that thou wouldst bestow upon us, on account of what the dear Jesus Christ has done and suffered; to whom, with Thyself, and holy Spirit, three persons, and one God, be ascribed, as is most due, all power, glory, might, majesty, and dominion, now, henceforth, and for evermore. Amen.

33. The Gospel Supper

Luke 14:22–24—"And the servant said, Lord, it is done as thou hast commanded, and yet there is room. And the lord said unto the servant, Go out into the high-ways, and hedges, and compel them to come in, that my house may be filled.

For I say unto you, that none of those men which were bidden, shall taste of my supper."

Though here is a large and solemn assembly, yet I suppose you are all convinced, that you are not to live in this world always. May I not take it for granted, that even the most profane amongst you, do in your hearts believe, what the sacred oracles have most clearly revealed, "That as it is appointed for all men once to die, so after death comes the judgment?" Yes, I know you believe, that nothing is more certain, than that we are to "appear before the judgment-seat of Christ, to be rewarded according to the deeds done in the body, whether they have been good, or whether they have been evil." And, however hard the saying may seem to you at the first hearing, yet I cannot help informing you, that I am thoroughly persuaded, as many will be driven from that judgment-seat, with a "Depart ye cursed into everlasting fire," for pursuing things in themselves lawful, out of a wrong principle, and in too intense a degree; as for drunkenness, adultery, fornication, or any other gross enormity [atrocity, outrage, depravity] whatsoever. Bas as the world is, blessed be God, there are great numbers yet left amongst us, who either through the restraints of a religious education, or self-love, and outward reputation, abstain from gross sin themselves, and look with detestation and abhorrence upon others, who indulge themselves in it. But then, through an over-eager pursuit after the things of sense and time, their souls are insensibly lulled into a spiritual slumber, and by degrees become as dead to God, and as deaf to all the gracious invitations of the gospel, as the most abandoned prodigals. It is remarkable, therefore, that our Savior, knowing how desperately wicked and treacherous the heart of man was, in this, as well as other respects, after he had cautioned his disciples, and us in them, to "take heed that their hearts were not at any time overcharged with surfeiting and drunkenness," immediately adds, "and the cares (the immoderate anxious cares) of this life." For they are of a distracting, intoxicating nature, and soon overcharge and weigh down the hearts of the children of men. To prevent or remedy this evil, our Lord, during the time of his tabernacling here below, spake many parables, but not one more pertinent, not one, in which the freeness of the gospel-call, and the frivolous pretenses men frame to excuse themselves from embracing it, and the dreadful doom they incur by so doing, are more displayed, or set off in livelier colors, than that to which the words of the text refer. "And the lord said unto the servant, Go out into the highways and hedges, and compel them to come in, that my house may be filled: For I say unto you, that none of those that were bidden shall taste of my supper."

In order to have a clear view of the occasion, scope, and contents of the parable, to which these words belong, it is necessary for us to look back to the very beginning of this chapter. "And it came to pass, as he went into the house of one of the chief Pharisees to eat bread, on the Sabbath day, that they watched him." The person here spoken of, as going into this Pharisee's house, is our blessed Savior. For as he came eating and drinking, agreeable to his character, he was free, courteous and affable [friendly, good-natured] to all; and therefore though it was on a Sabbath-day, he accepted an invitation, and went into the house of one of the chief Pharisees to eat bread, notwithstanding he knew the Pharisees were his professed enemies, and that they watched him, hoping to find some occasion to upbraid him, either for his discourse or behavior. If the Pharisee into whose house our

Lord went, was one of this stamp, his invitation bespeaks him to be a very ill man, and may serve to teach us, that much rancor and heart-enmity against Jesus Christ, may be concealed and cloaked under a great and blazing profession of religion. However, our Savior was more than a match for all his enemies, and by accepting this invitation, hath warranted his ministers and disciples, to comply with the like invitations, and converse freely about the things of God, though those who invite them, may not have real religion at heart. For how knowest thou, O man, but thou mayest drop something, that may benefit their souls, and make them religious indeed? And supposing they should watch thee, watch thou unto prayer, whilst thou art in their company, and that same Jesus, who went into this Pharisee's house, and was so faithful and edifying in his conversation when there, will enable thee to go and do likewise.

That our Lord's conversation was not trifling, but such as tended to the use of edifying, and that he behaved among the guests as a faithful physician, rather than as a careless, indifferent companion, is evident from the 7th verse of this chapter, where we are told, that "he marked how they chose the chief rooms;" or, to speak in our common way, were desirous of sitting at the upper end of the table. And whether we think of it or not, the Lord Jesus takes notice of our behavior, even when we are going to sit down only at our common meals. Would to God, all that make a profession of real Christianity, considered this well! Religion then would not be so much confined to church, or meeting, but be brought home to our private houses, and many needless unchristian compliments be prevented. For (with grief I speak it) is it not too true, that abundance of professors love, and are too fond of the uppermost places in houses, as well as synagogues? This was what our Lord blamed in the guests where he now was. He marked, he took notice, he looked before he spake (as we should always do, if we would speak to the purpose) how they chose out the chief rooms. Therefore, though they were rich in this world's goods, and were none of his guests, yet unwilling to suffer the least sin upon them, or lost any opportunity of giving instruction, he gave them a lecture upon humility, saying unto them, or directing his discourse to all in general, though probably he spake to one in particular, who sat near him, and whom, it may be, he took notice of, as more than ordinarily solicitous in choosing a chief room, or couch, on which they lay at meals, after the custom of the Romans; "When thou art bidden of any man to a wedding (which seems to intimate that this was a wedding-feast) sit not down in the highest room, lest a more honorable man than thou be bidden of him; and he that bade thee and him come and say to thee, Give this man place; and thou begin with shame to take the lowest room. But when thou are bidden, go and sit down in the lowest room; that when he that bade thee cometh, he may say unto thee, Friend, go up higher: then shalt thou have worship (or respect) in the presence of them who sit at meat with thee." O glorious example of faithfulness and love to souls! How ought ministers especially, to copy after their blessed Master, and, with simplicity an godly sincerity, mildly and opportunely rebuke the faults of the company they are in, though superior to them in outward circumstances? What rightly informed person, after reading this passage, can think they teach right and agreeable to the word of God in this respect, who say, we must not, at least need not, reprove natural men? Surely such doctrine cometh not from above! For are we not commanded, in any wise, to reprove our neighbor (whether he be a child of God or no) and not to suffer sin upon him? Is it not more than probable, that all these guests were natural men? And yet our Lord reproved them. Help us then, O Savior, in this and every other instance of thy moral conduct, to walk as thou hast set us an example!

Neither did our Lord stop here; but observing that none but the rich, the mighty, and the noble, were called to the feast, he took occasion also from thence, to give even his host (for the best return we make our friends for their kindness, is to be faithful to their souls) one of the chief Pharisees, a wholesome piece of advice. "Then said he also to him that bade him, when thou makest a dinner or a supper, call not thy friends, nor thy brethren, neither thy kinsmen nor thy rich neighbors, lest they also bid thee again, and a recompense be made thee. But when thou makest a feast, call the poor, the maimed, the lame, the blind, and thou shalt be blessed; for they cannot recompense thee. For thou shalt be recompensed at the resurrection of the just!" Thus did our Lord entertain the company. Words spoken in such due season, how good are they! Would Christ's followers thus exert themselves, and, when in company, begin some useful discourse for their great master, they know not what good they might do, and how many might be influenced, by their good example, to second them in it.

An instance of this we have in the 14th verse: "And when one of them that sat at meat with him heard these things, he said unto him, Blessed is he that shall eat bread in the kingdom of God." Happy they who shall be recompensed at that resurrection of the just, which thou hast been speaking of. A very pertinent saying this! every way suitable to persons sitting down to eat bread on earth, which we should never do, without talking of, and longing for that time, when we shall sit down and eat bread in the kingdom of heaven. This opened to our Lord a fresh topic of conversation, and occasioned the parable, which is to be the more immediate subject of your present meditation. As though he had said to the person that spoke last, Thou sayest right: blessed are they indeed, who shall sit down to eat bread in the kingdom of God: But alas! most men, especially you Pharisees, act as if you did not believe this; and therefore he said unto him, "A certain man made a great supper, and bade many;" by the certain man making a great supper, we are to understand God the Father, who has made provision for perishing souls, by the obedience and death of his beloved Son Christ Jesus. This provision is here represented under the character of a supper, because the Caena or supper, among the ancients, was their grand meal: Men could never have made such provision for themselves, or angels for them. No, our salvation is all from God, from the beginning to the end. He made it, and not we ourselves; and it is wholly owing to the divine wisdom, and not our own, that we are become God's people, and the sheep of his pasture. This provision for perishing souls, may be justly called *great*, because there is rich and ample provision made in the gospel for a great many souls. For however Christ's flock may be but a little flock, when asunder, yet when they come all together, they will be a multitude which no man can number. And it is especially called *great*, because it was purchased at so great a price, the price of Christ's most precious blood. And therefore, when the apostle would exhort the Christians to glorify God in their souls and bodies, he makes use of this glorious motive, "That they were bought with a price." He does not say what price, but barely a *price*, emphatically so called; as though all the prices in the world were nothing (as indeed they are not) when compared to this price of Christ's most precious blood.

For these reasons, Jesus said in the parable, "A certain man made a great supper, and bade many, and sent his servant at supper-time, to say to them that were bidden, Come, for all things are now ready." He bade many; the eternal God took the Jews for his peculiar people, under the Mosaic dispensation; and by types, shadows, and prophesies of the Old Testament, invited them to partake of the glorious privileges of the gospel. "But at supper-time," in the fullness of time, which God the Father had decreed from eternity, in the evening of the world (for which reason the gospel times are called the last times) "he sent his servant," Christ his Son, here called his servant, because acting as Mediator he was inferior to the Father; therefore says the prophet Isaiah, "Behold my servant whom I have chosen:" "to say to them that were bidden," to the professing Jews, called by St. John, "his own," that is, his peculiar professing people—with this message, "Come;" repent and believe the gospel. Nothing is required on man's part, but to come, or accept of the gospel offer. It is not according to the old covenant, "Do and live;" but only "come, believe, and thou shalt be saved." All things are ready. Nothing is wanting on God's part. "All things are now ready." There seems to be a particular emphasis to be put upon *now*, implying, this was an especial season of grace, and God was now exerting his last efforts, to save lost man. Well then, if the great God be at so great an expense, to make so great a supper, for perishing creatures, and sends so great a person as his own Son, in the form of a servant, to invite them to come to it; one would imagine, that all who heard these glad tidings, should readily say, Lord, lo we come. But instead of this, we are told, "They all, (the greatest part of the Jews) with one consent began to make excuse." Conscience told them they ought to come, and in all probability they had some faint desire to come; and they had nothing, as we hear of, to object either against the person who prepared the supper, or the person that invited them, or the entertainment itself; neither do we hear that they treated either with contempt, as is the custom of too many in the days wherein we live. In all probability, they acknowledged all was very good, and that it was kind in that certain man, to send them such an invitation. But being very busy, and as they thought very lawfully engaged, they begun to make excuse.

But the excuses they made, rendered their refusal inexcusable. "The first said unto him, I have bought a piece of ground, and I must needs go and see it." Thou fool, buy a piece of ground, and then go see it! A prudent man would have gone and seen the ground first, and bought it afterwards. Why must he needs go? At least, why must he needs go *now*? The land was his own, could he not therefore have accepted the invitation today, and gone and seen his estate, or plantation, on the morrow? As he had bought it, he need not fear losing his bargain, by another's buying it from him. But notwithstanding all this, there is a needs must for his going, and therefore says he, "I pray thee, have me excused," and improve thy interest with thy master in my behalf. This was a bad excuse.

The second was rather worse. For what says the evangelist, verse Luke 14:19, "And another said, I have bought five yoke of oxen, and I go to prove them:" One, it seems, had been buying an estate; another, cattle, to stock an estate already bought; and both equally foolish in making their bargains. For this second had bought five yoke of oxen, which must needs cost them a considerable sum, perhaps all he had in the world, and now he must go and prove them. A wise dealer would have proved the oxen first, and bought them afterwards: But our Savior speaks this, to show us, that we will trust one another, nay I may add, the devil himself, more than we will trust God.

The excuse which the third makes, is worst of all. "I have married a wife, and therefore I cannot come." Had he said, I will not come, he had spoken the real sentiments of his heart: for it is not so much men's impotency, as their want of a will, and inclination, that keeps them from the gospel-feast. But why cannot he come? He has "married a wife." Has he so? Why then, by all means he should come. For the supper to which he was invited, as it should seem, was a wedding-supper, and would have saved him the trouble of a nuptial entertainment. It was a great supper, and consequently there was provision enough for him, and his bride too. And it was made by a great man, who sent out his servant to bid many, so that he need not have doubted of meeting with a hearty welcome, though he should bring his wife with him. Or supposing his wife was unwilling to come, yet as the husband is the head of the wife, he ought to have laid his commands on her, to accompany him. For we cannot do better for our yoke-fellows, than to bring them to the gospel-feast. Or, supposing after all, she would not be prevailed upon, he ought to have gone without her: for "those that have wives, must be as though they had none;" and we must not let carnal affection get such an ascendancy over us, as to be kept thereby from spiritual entertainments. Adam paid dear for hearkening to the voice of his wife: and sometimes, unless we forsake wives, as well as houses and lands, we cannot be the Lord's disciples.

This then was the reception the servant met with, and such were the excuses, and answers, that were sent back. And what was the consequence? "So that servant came (no doubt with a sorrowful heart) and showed his Lord these things." However little it be thought of, yet ministers must show the Lord, what success their ministry meets with. We must how it to our Lord here. We must spread the case before him in prayer. We must show it to our Lord hereafter, before the general assembly of the whole world. But how dreadful is it, when ministers are obliged to go upon their knees, crying, "O! my leanness, my leanness!" and Elias-like, to intercede as it were against those, to whom they would not only have imparted the gospel, but even their own lives. It is a heart-breaking consideration. But thus it must be; "The servant came and showed the Lord these things;" so must we. Well, and what says the Lord? We are told, verse 21st, that "the master of the house was angry?" Not with the servant: for though Israel be not gathered, yet shall Christ be glorious; and faithful ministers shall be rewarded, whether people obey the gospel or not. "We are a sweet savor unto God, whether the world be a savor of life unto life, or a savor of death unto death." The master of the house therefore was angry, not with the servant, but with these worldly-minded, pleasure-taking refusers of his gracious invitation; who, in all probability, went to see and stock their estates, and attend upon their brides, not doubting, but their excuses would be taken, because they were lawfully employed. And, indeed, in one sense, their excuses were accepted. For I do not hear that they were ever invited any more. God took them at their word, though they would not take him at his. They begged to be excused, and they were excused, as we shall see in the sequel of this parable. Let us not therefore harden our hearts, as in the day of provocation; "Now is the accepted time, now is the day of salvation." But must the feast want guests? No, if they cannot, or will not come, others shall, and will. The master of the house therefore being angry, sent the servant upon a second errand. "Go out quickly into the streets, and lanes of the city, and bring in hither the poor, and the maimed, and the halt, and the blind." Every word bespeaks a spirit of resentment and importunity. Go out quickly, make no delay, dread no attempt or danger, into the streets and lanes of the city, and bring in hither, not only call them, but bring them in (for the master here, to encourage the servant, assures him of success) the poor, and the maimed, and the halt, and the blind. This was fulfilled, when Jesus Christ, after the gospel was rejected by the Jews, went and invited the Gentiles, and when the publicans and harlots took the kingdom of God by a holy violence, whilst the self-righteous scribes and Pharisees rejected the kingdom of God against themselves. This was also a home reproof of the rich Pharisee, at whose house the Lord Jesus was, as well as a cutting lesson to the other guests. For our Savior would hereby show them, that God took a quite different method from his host, and was not above receiving the poor, and halt, and blind, and maimed, to the gospel supper, though he had called none such to sit down at his table. Whether the guests resented it or not, we are not told. But if they were not quite blind, both host and guests might easily see that the parable was spoken against them. But to proceed,

The servant again returns, but with a more pleasing answer than before, "Lord, it is done as thou hast commanded, and yet there is room." The words bespeak the servant to be full of joy at the thoughts of the success he had met with. None can tell, but those who experience it, what comfort ministers have in seeing their labors blest. "Now I live, (says the apostle) if you stand fast in the Lord. Ye are our joy and crown of rejoicing in the day of the Lord Jesus." "Lord, it is done as thou hast commanded. The poor, and maimed, and halt, and blind, have been called, and have obeyed the summons, and I have brought them with me; yet, Lord, thy house, and thy supper is so great, there is room for more. Hereby he insinuated that he wanted to be employed again, in calling more souls; and the more we do, the more may we do for God: "To him that hath, shall be given;" and present success is a great encouragement to future diligence. Such hints are pleasing to our Savior. He delights to see his ministers ready for new work, and waiting for fresh orders. "The Lord, therefore, we are told, ver. Luke 14:23, said unto his servant, (the same servant,) Go out into the highways and hedges, and compel them to come in, that my house may be filled; Luke 14:24, For I say unto you, that none of those who are bidden, shall taste of my supper." O cutting words to those that sat at meat, if they had hearts to make the application! But glad tidings of great joy to the publicans, harlots, and Gentiles, who were rejected by the proud Pharisees, as aliens to the commonwealth of Israel, and strangers to the covenant of promise! This was fulfilled, when our Lord sent the apostles, not only into the streets and lanes of the city, and places bordering upon Jerusalem and Judea; but when he gave them a commission to go out into all the world, and preach the gospel to every creature, Gentile as well a Jew; and not only gave them a command, but blessed their labors with such success, that three thousand were converted in one day. And I am not without hopes that it will be still further fulfilled, by the calling of some of you home this day. For however this parable was spoken originally to the Jews, and upon a particular occasion, as at a feast, yet it is applicable to us, and to our children, and to as many as are afar off; yea, to as many as the Lord our God shall call. It gives a sanction, methinks, to preaching in the fields, and other places besides the synagogues; and points out the reception the gospel meets with in these days, in such a lively manner, that one would think it had a particular reference to the perfect age. For is it not too, too plain, that the gospel-offers, and gospel-grace, have been slighted, and made light of, by many professors of this generation? We have been in the churches, telling them, again and again, that God has made a great supper (and has invited many, even them) and sent us by his providence and his spirit, "to say unto them that were bidden, Come, for all things are now ready. Believe on the Lord Jesus, and you shall be saved." But the generality of the laity have made light of it, they have given us the hearing, but are too busy in their farms and their merchandises, their marrying and giving in marriage, to come and be blessed in the Lord of life. We have told them, again and again, that we do not want them to hide themselves from the world, but to teach them how they may live in, and yet not be of it. But all will not do. Many of the clergy also (like the letter-learned Scribes and Pharisees in our Savior's time) reject the kingdom of God against themselves, and deny us the use of the pulpits, for no other reason but because we preach the doctrine of justification in the sight of God by faith alone, and invite sinners to come and taste of the gospel feast freely, without money and without price.

Whatever they may think, we are persuaded, the great master of the house is angry with them, for being angry with us without a cause. He therefore now, by his providence, bids us "Go out quickly into the streets and lanes of the city, and bring in the poor, and the maimed, and the halt, and the blind," or call in the publicans and harlots, the common cursers and swearers, and Sabbath-breakers, and adulterers, who, perhaps, never entered a church door, or heard that Jesus Christ died for such sinners as they are. We, through grace, have obeyed the command, we have gone out, though exposed to such contempt for so doing, and, blessed be God, our labor has not been in vain in the Lord. For many have been made willing in the day of God's power; and, we would speak it with humility, we can go cheerfully to our Savior, and say, "It is done, Lord, as thou hast commanded, and yet there is room." He is therefore pleased, in spite of all opposition from men or devils, to continue, and renew, and enlarge our commission; he hath sent us literally into the highways and hedges; and, I trust, has given us a commission to compel sinners to come. For, could we speak with the tongues of men and angels, yet if the Lord did not attend the word with his power, and sweetly inclined men's wills to comply with the gospel-call, we should be as a sounding brass, or a tinkling cymbal. But this we believe our Savior will do, for his house must be filled: every soul for whom he has shed his blood, shall finally be saved, "and all that the Father hath given him, shall come unto him, and whosoever cometh unto him he will in no wise cast out." This comforted our Lord, when his gospel was rejected by the Jews. As though he had said, Well, tho' you despise the offers of my grace, yet I shall not shed my blood in vain; for all that the Father hath given me shall come unto me.

Supported by this consideration, I am not ashamed to come out this day into the highways and hedges, and to confess that my business is to call the poor, and the maimed, and the halt, and the blind, self-condemned, helpless sinners, to the marriage-feast of the supper of the Lamb. My cry is, Come, believe on the Lord Jesus; throw yourselves at the footstool of his mercy, and you shall be saved; for all things are now ready. God the Father is ready, God the Son is ready, God the Holy Ghost is ready; the blessed angels above are ready, and the blessed saints below are ready, to welcome you to the gospel-feast. A perfect and everlasting righteousness is now wrought out by Jesus Christ. God, now, upon honorable terms, can acquit the guilty. God can now be just, and yet justify the ungodly. "For he hath made Christ to be sin for us, who knew no sin, that we might be made the righteousness of God in him." The fatted calf is now killed, and "Christ, our Passover, is sacrificed for us." Come, sinners, and feed upon him in your hearts by faith, with thanksgiving. For Jesus Christ's sake, do not with one consent begin to make excuse. Do not let a piece of ground, five yoke of oxen, or even a wife, keep you from this great supper. These you may enjoy, as the gifts of God, and make use of them for the Mediator's glory, and yet be present at the gospel feast. True and undefiled religion does not take away, but rather greatly enhances the comforts of life; and our Lord did not pray that we should be taken out of the world, but "that we should be delivered from the evil of it." O then that you would all, with one consent, say, Lo! we come. Assure yourselves here is provision enough. For it is a great supper. In our Father's house there is bread enough and to spare. And though a great God makes the supper, yet he is as good and condescending as he is great. Though he be the high and lofty one that inhabiteth eternity, yet he will dwell with the humble and contrite heart, even with the man that trembleth at his word. Neither can you complain for want of room; "for yet there is room. In our Father's house are many mansions." If it was not so, our Savior would have told us. The grace of Christ is as rich, as free, and as powerful as ever. He is "the same yesterday, today, and for ever." He is full of grace and truth, and out of his fullness, all that come to him may receive grace for grace. He giveth liberally, and upbraideth not. He willeth not the death of a sinner, but rather that he should believe and live. Come then, all ye halt, poor, maimed, and blind sinners; take comfort, the Lord Jesus has sent his servant to call you. It is now supper-time, and a day of uncommon grace. The day may be far spent. Haste, therefore, and away to the supper of the Lamb. If you do not come, I know the master will be angry. And who can stand before him when he is angry? "Harden not therefore your hearts, as in the day of provocation, as in the day of temptation in the wilderness." Do not provoke the Lord to say, "None of those that were bidden shall taste of my supper." O dreadful words! Much more is implied in them than is expressed. It is the same with that in the psalms, "I sware in my wrath, that they should not enter into my rest." And if you do not enter into God's rest, nor taste of Christ's supper, you must lift up your eyes in torments, where you will have no rest, and must sup with the damned devils for ever more.

Knowing therefore the terrors of the Lord, we persuade you to haste away, and make no more frivolous excuses. For there is no excuse against believing. Perhaps you say, You call to the halt, and maimed, and blind, and poor. But if we are halt, and maimed, how can we come?: if we are blind, how can we see our way? If we are poor, how can we expect admission to so great a table? Ah! Happy are ye, if you are sensible, that you are halt and maimed. For if you feel yourselves so, and are lamenting it, who knows but whilst I am speaking, God may send his Spirit with the word, and fetch you home? Though you are blind, Jesus has eye salve to anoint you. Though you are poor, yet you are welcome to this rich feast. It cost Jesus Christ a great price, but you shall have it gratis. For such as you was it designed: "Blessed are the poor in spirit, for theirs is the kingdom of heaven." Rich, self-righteous, self-sufficient sinners, I know, will scorn both the feast and its great provider. They have done so already, therefore the Lord has sent us into the highways and hedges, to bring such poor souls as you are in. Venture then, my dear friends, and honor God, by taking him at his word. Come to the marriage-feast. Believe me, you will there partake of most delicious fare.

Tell me, ye that have been made to taste that the Lord is gracious, will you not recommend this feast to all? Are you not; whilst I am speaking, ready to cry out, Come all ye that are without, come ye, obey the call, for we have sat under the Redeemer's shadow with great delight, and his fruit has been pleasant to our taste. Whilst I am speaking, does not the fire kindle, do not your hearts burn with a desire that others may come and be blessed too? If you are Christians indeed, I know you will be thus minded, and the language of your hearts will be, Lord, whilst he is calling, let thy Spirit compel them to come in. O that the Lord may say, Amen! And why should we doubt? Surely our Savior will not let me complain this day that I have labored in vain, and spent my strength for nought. Methinks I see many desiring to come. O how shall I compel you to come forwards. I will not use fire or sword, as the Papists do, by terribly perverting this text of scripture. But I will tell you of the love of God, the love of God in Christ, and surely that must compel you, that must constrain you, whether you will or not. Sinners, my heart is enlarged towards you. I could fill my mouth with arguments. Consider the greatness of the God who makes the supper. Consider the greatness of the price, wherewith it was purchased. Consider the greatness of the provision made for you. What would you have more? Consider God's infinite condescension, in calling you now, when you might have been in hell, "where the worm dieth not, and the fire is not quenched." And that you might be without excuse, he has sent his servant into the highways and hedges to invite you there. O that you tasted what I do now! I am sure you would not want arguments to induce you to come in: No, you would fly to the gospel-feast, as doves to the windows.

But, poor souls! many of you, perhaps, are not hungry. You do not feel yourselves halt, or maimed, or blind, and therefore you have no relish for this spiritual entertainment. Well, be not angry with me for calling you; be not offended if I weep over you, because you know not the day of your visitation. If I must appear in judgment as a swift witness against you, I must. But that thought chills my blood! I cannot bear it; I feel that I could lay down my life for you. But I am not willing to go without you. What say you, my dear friends? I would put the question to you once more, Will you taste of Christ's supper, or will you not? You shall all be welcome. There is milk at this feast for babes, as well as meat for strong men, and for persons of riper years. There is room and provision for high and low, rich and poor, one with another; and our Savior will thank you for coming. Amazing condescension! Astonishing love! The thought of it quite overcomes me. Help me, help me, O believers, to bless and praise him.

And O! that this love may excite us to come afresh to him, as though we had never come before! For, though we have been often feasted, yet our souls will starve, unless we renew our acts of faith, and throw ourselves, as lost, undone sinners, continually at the feet of Christ. Feeding upon past experiences will not satisfy our souls, any more than what we did eat yesterday will sustain our bodies to day. No, believers must look for fresh influences of divine grace, and beg of the Lord to water them every moment. The parable therefore speaks to saints as well as sinners. Come ye to the marriage-feast; you are as welcome now as ever. And may God set your souls a longing for that time when we shall sit down and eat bread in the kingdom of heaven! There we shall have full draughts of divine love, and enjoy the glorious Emanuel for ever more. Even so, Lord Jesus, Amen.

34. The Pharisee and Publican

Luke 18:14—"I tell you, this man went down to his house justified rather than the other: For every one that exalteth himself, shall be abased; and he that humbleth himself, shall be exalted."

Though there be some who dare to deny the Lord Jesus, and disbelieve the revelation he has been pleased to give us, and thereby bring upon themselves swift destruction; yet I would charitably hope there are but few if any such among you, to whom I am now to preach the kingdom of God. Was I to ask you, how you expect to be justified in the sight of an offended God? I suppose you would answer, only for the sake of our Lord Jesus Christ. But, was I to come more home to your consciences, I fear that most would make the Lord Jesus but in part their Savior, and go about, as it were, to establish a righteousness of their own. And this is not thinking contrary to the rules of Christian charity: for we are all self-righteous by nature; it is as natural for us to turn to a covenant of works, as for the sparks to fly upwards. We have had so many legal and so few free-grace preachers, for these many years, that most professors now seem to be settled upon their lees [residue, remains, grounds, settlings], and rather deserve the title of Pharisees than Christians.

Thus it was with the generality of the people during the time of our Lord's public ministration: and therefore, in almost all his discourses, he preached the gospel to poor sinners, and denounced terrible woes against proud self-justiciaries. The parable, to which the words of the text belong, looks both these ways: For the evangelist informs us (ver. Luke 18:9) that our Lord "spake it unto certain who trusted in themselves that they were righteous, and despised others." And a notable parable it is; a parable worthy of your most serious attention. "He that hath ears to hear, let him hear," what Jesus Christ speaks to all visible professors in it.

Ver. Luke 18:10, "Two men went up to the temple to pray (and never two men of more opposite characters) the one a Pharisee and the other a Publican." The Pharisees were the strictest sect among the Jews. "I was of the strictest sect, of the Pharisees," says Paul. They prayed often; not only so, but they made long prayers; and, that they might appear extraordinary devout, they would pray at the corners of the street, where two ways met, that people going or coming, both ways, might see them. "They made broad (as our Lord informs us) the borders of their phylacteries," they had pieces of parchment sown to their long robes, on which some parts of the Scripture were written, that people might from thence infer, that they were lovers of the law of God. They were so very punctual and exact in outward purifications, that they washed at their going out and coming in. They held the washing of pots, brazen vessels and tables, and many other such-like things they did. They were very zealous for the traditions of the fathers, and for the observation of the rites and ceremonies of the church, notwithstanding they frequently made void the law of God by their traditions. And they were so exceedingly exact in the outward observation of the Sabbath, that they condemned our Lord for making a little clay with his spittle; and called him a sinner, and said, he was not of God, because he had given sight to a man born blind, on the Sabbath-day. For these reasons they were had in high veneration among the people, who were sadly misled by these blind guides: they had the uppermost places in the synagogues, and greetings in the market-places (which they loved dearly) and were called of men, Rabbi; in short, they had such a reputation for piety, that it became a proverb among the Jews, that, if there were but two men saved, the one of them must be a Pharisee.

As for the Publicans, it was not so with them. It seems they were sometimes Jews, or at least proselytes of the gate; for we find one here coming up to the temple; but for the generality, I am apt to think they were Gentiles; for they were gatherers of the Roman taxes, and used to amass much wealth (as appears by the confession of Zaccheus, one of the chief of them) by wronging men with false accusations. They were so universally infamous, that our Lord himself tells his disciples, "the excommunicated man should be to them as a heathen man, or a Publican." And the Pharisees thought it a sufficient impeachment of our Lord's character, that he was a friend to Publicans and sinners, and went to sit down with them at meat.

But, however they disagreed in other things, they agreed in this, that public worship is a duty incumbent upon all: for they both came up to the temple. The very heathens were observers of temple-worship. We have very early notice of men's sacrificing to, and calling upon the name of the Lord, in the Old Testament; and I find it no where contradicted in the New. Our Lord, and his apostles, went up to the temple; and we are commanded by the apostle, "not to forsake the assembling ourselves together," as the manner of too many is in our days; and such too, as would have us think well of them, though they seldom or never tread the courts of the Lord's house. But, though our devotions begin in our closets, they must not end there. And, if people never show their devotions abroad, I must suspect they have little or none at home. "Two men went up to the temple." And what went they thither for? Not (as multitudes amongst us do) to make the house of God a house of merchandise, or turn it into a den of thieves; much less to ridicule the preacher, or disturb the congregation; no, they came to the temple, says our Lord, "to pray." Thither should the tribes of God's spiritual Israel go up, to talk with, and pour out their hearts before the mighty God of Jacob.

"Two men went up to the temple to pray." I fear one of them forgot his errand. I have often been at a loss what to call the Pharisee's address; it certainly does not deserve the name of a prayer: he may rather be said to come to the temple to boast, than to pray; for I do not find one word of confession of his original guilt; not one single petition for pardon of his past actual sins, or for grace to help and assist him for the time to come: he only brings to God, as it were, a reckoning of his performances; and does that, which no flesh can justly do, I mean, glory in his presence.

Ver. "The Pharisee stood, and prayed thus with himself; God, I thank thee that I am not as other men are, extortioners, unjust, adulterers, or even as this Publican."

Our Lord first takes notice of his posture; "the Pharisee *stood*," he is not to be condemned for that; for standing, as well as kneeling, is a proper posture for prayer. "When you stand praying," says our Lord; though sometimes our Lord kneeled, nay, lay flat on his face upon the ground; his apostles also kneeled, as we read in the Acts, which has made me wonder at some, who are so bigoted to standing in family, as well as public prayer, that they will not kneel, notwithstanding all kneel that are around them. I fear there is something of the Pharisee in this conduct. Kneeling and standing are indifferent, if the knee of the soul be bent, and the heart upright towards

God. We should study not to be particular in indifferent things, lest we offend weak minds. What the Pharisee is remarked for, is his "standing by himself:" for the words may be rendered, he stood by himself, upon some eminent place, at the upper part of the temple, near the Holy of holies, that the congregation might see what a devout man he was: or it may be understood as we read it, he prayed by himself, or of himself, out of his own heart; he did not pray by form; it was an extempore prayer: for there are many Pharisees that pray and preach too, extempore. I do not see why these may not be acquired, as well as other arts and sciences. A man, with a good elocution [articulation, oratory, speech], ready turn of thought, and good memory, may repeat his own or other men's sermons, and, by the help of Wilkins or Henry, may pray seemingly excellently well, and yet not have the least grain of true grace in his heart; I speak this, not to cry down extempore prayer, or to discourage those dear souls who really pray by the spirit; I only would hereby give a word of reproof to those who are so bigoted to extempore prayer, that they condemn, as least judge, all that use forms, as though not so holy and heavenly, as others who pray without them. Alas! this is wrong. Not every one that prays extempore is a spiritual, nor every one that prays with a form, a formal man. Let us not judge one another; let not him that uses a form, judge him that prays extempore, on that account; and let not him that prays extempore, despise him who uses a form.

"The Pharisee stood, and prayed thus by himself." Which may signify also praying inwardly in his heart; for there is a way (and that an excellent one too) of praying when we cannot speak; thus Anna prayed, when she spoke not aloud, only her lips moved. Thus God says to Moses, "Why criest thou?" when, it is plain, he did not speak a word. This is what the apostle means by the "spirit making intercession (for believers) with groanings which cannot be uttered." For there are times when the soul is too big to speak; when God fills it as it were, and overshadows it with his presence, so that it can only fall down, worship, adore, and lie in the dust before the Lord. Again, there is a time when the soul is benumbed, barren and dry, and the believer has not a word to say to his heavenly Father; and then the heart only can speak. And I mention this for the encouragement of weak Christians, who think they never are accepted but when they have a flow of words, and fancy they do not please God at the bottom, for no other reason but because they do not please themselves. Such would do well to consider, that God knows the language of the heart, and the mind of the spirit; and that we make use of words, not to inform God, but to affect ourselves. Whenever therefore any of you find yourselves in such a frame, be not discouraged: offer yourselves up in silence before God, as clay in the hands of the potter, for him t write and stamp his own divine image upon your souls. But I believe the Pharisee knew nothing of this way of prayer: he was self-righteous, a stranger to the divine life; and therefore either of the former explanations may be best put upon these words.

"He stood, and prayed thus with himself; God, I thank thee that I am not as other men are, extortioners, unjust, adulterer, or even as this Publican." Here is some appearance of devotion, but it is only in appearance. To thank God that we are not extortioners, unjust, adulterers, and as wicked in our practices as other men are, is certainly meet, right, and our bounden duty: for whatever degrees of goodness there may be in us, more than in others, it is owing to God's restraining, preventing, and assisting grace. We are all equally conceived and born in sin; all are fallen short of the glory of God, and liable to all the curses and maledictions of the law; so that "he who glorieth, must glory only in the Lord." For none of us have any thing which we did not receive; and whatever we have received, we did not in the least merit it, nor could we lay the least claim to it on any account whatever: we are wholly indebted to free grace for all. Had the Pharisee thought thus, when he said, "God, I thank thee that I am not as other men are," it would have been an excellent introduction to his prayer: but he was a free-willer, as well as self-righteous (for he that is one must be the other) and thought by his own power and strength, he had kept himself from these vices. And yet I do not see what reason he had to trust in himself that he was righteous, merely because he had to trust in himself that he was righteous, merely because he was not an extortioner, unjust, adulterer; for all this while he might be, as he certainly was (as is also every self-righteous person) as proud as the devil. But he not only boasts, but lies before God (as all self-justiciaries will be found liars here or hereafter.) He thanks God that he was not unjust: but is it not an act of the highest injustice to rob God of his prerogative? is it not an act of injustice to judge our neighbor? and yet of both these crimes this self-righteous vaunter is guilty. "Even as this Publican!" He seems to speak with the utmost disdain; this Publican! Perhaps he pointed at the poor man, that others might treat him with the like contempt. Thou proud, confident boaster, what hadst thou to do with that poor Publican? supposing other Publicans were unjust, and extortioners, did it therefore follow that he must be so? or, if he had been such a sinner, how knowest thou but he has repented of those sins? His coming up to the temple to pray, is one good sign of a reformation at least. Thou art therefore inexcusable, O Pharisee, who thus judgest the Publican: for thou that judgest him to be unjust, art, in the very act of judging, unjust thyself: thy sacrifice is only the sacrifice of a fool.

We have seen what the Pharisee's negative goodness comes to; I think, nothing at all. Let us see how far his positive goodness extends; for, if we are truly religious, we shall not only eschew evil, but also do good: "I fast twice in the week, I give tithes of all that I possess."

The Pharisee is not here condemned for his fasting, for fasting is a Christian duty; "when you fast," says our Lord, thereby taking it for granted that his disciples would fast. And "when the bridegroom shall be taken away, then shall they fast in those days." "In fasting often," says the apostle. And all that would not be cast-aways, will take care, as their privilege, without legal constraint, to "keep their bodies under, and bring them into subjection." The Pharisee is only condemned for making a righteousness of his fasting, and thinking that God would accept him, or that he was any better than his neighbors, merely on account of his fasting, and thinking that God would accept him, or that he was any better than his neighbors, merely on account of his fasting: this is what he was blamed for. The Pharisee was not to be discommended for fasting twice in a week; I wish some Christians would imitate him more in this: but to depend on fasting in the least, for his justification in the sight of God, was really abominable. "I give tithes of all that I possess." He might as well have said, I pay tithes. But self-righteous people (whatever they may say to the contrary) think they give something to God. "I give tithes of all that I possess:" I make conscience of giving tithes, not only of all that the law requires, but of my mint, annise, and cummin, of all things whatsoever I possess; this was well; but to boast of such things, or of fasting, is pharisaical and devilish. Now then let us sum up all the righteousness of this boasting Pharisee, and see what little reason he had to trust in himself, that he was righteous, or to despise others. He is not unjust (but we have only his bare word for that, I think I have proved the contrary;) he is no adulterer, no extortioner; he fasts twice in the week, and gives tithes of all that he possesses; and all this he might do, and a great deal more, and yet be a child of the devil: for here is no mention made of his loving the Lord his God with all his heart, which was the "first and great commandment of the law;" here is not a single syllable of inward religion; and he was not a true Jew, who was only one outwardly. It is only an outside piety at the best; inwardly he is full of pride, self-justification, free-will and great uncharitableness.

Were not the Pharisees, do you think, highly offended at this character? for they might easily know it was spoken against them. And though, perhaps, some of you may be offended at me, yet, out of love, I must tell you, I fear this parable is spoken against many of you: for are there not many of you, who go up to the temple to pray, with no better spirit than this Pharisee did? And because you fast, it may be in the Lent, or every Friday, and because you do no body any harm, receive the sacrament, pay tithes, and give an alms now and then; you think that you are safe, and trust in yourselves that you are righteous, and inwardly despise those, who do not come up to you in these outward duties? this, I am persuaded, is the case of many of you, though, alas! it is a desperate one, as I shall endeavor to show at the close of this discourse.

Let us now take a view of the Publican, ver. Luke 18:13, "And the Publican standing afar off, would not lift up so much as his eyes unto heaven, but smote upon his breast, saying, God be merciful to me a sinner."

"The Publican standing afar off." Perhaps in the outward court of the temple, conscious to himself that he was not worthy to approach the Holy of holies; so conscious and so weighed down with a sense of his own unworthiness, that he would not so much as lift up his eyes unto heaven, which he knew was God's throne. Poor heart! what did he feel at this time! none but returning publicans, like himself, can tell. Methinks I see him standing afar off, pensive, oppressed, and even overwhelmed with sorrow; sometimes he attempts to look up; but then, thinks he, the heavens are unclean in God's sight, and the very angels are charged with folly; how then shall such a wretch as I dare to lift up my guilty head! And to show that his heart was full of holy self-resentment, and that he sorrowed after a godly sort, he smote upon his breast; the word in the original implies, that he struck hard upon his breast: he will lay the blame upon none but his own wicked heart. He will not, like unhumbled Adam, tacitly lay the fault of his vileness upon God, and say, The passions which thou gavest me, they deceived me, and I sinned: he is too penitent thus to reproach his Maker; he smites upon his breast, his treacherous, ungrateful, desperately wicked breast; a breast now ready to burst: and at length, out of the abundance of his heart, I doubt not, with many tears, he as last cries out, "God be merciful to me a sinner." Not, God be merciful to yonder proud

Pharisee: he found enough in himself to vent his resentment against, without looking abroad upon others. Not, God be merciful to me a saint; for he knew "all his righteousnesses were but filthy rags." Not, God be merciful to such or such a one; but, God be merciful to me, even to me a sinner, a sinner by birth, a sinner in thought, word, and deed; a sinner as to my person, a sinner as to all my performances; a sinner in whom is no health, in whom dwelleth no good thing, a sinner, poor, miserable, blind and naked, from the crown of the head to the sole of the feet, full of wounds, and bruises, and putrefying sores; a self-accused, self-condemned sinner. What think you? would this Publican have been offended if any minister had told him that he deserved to be damned? would he have been angry, if any one had told him, that by nature he was half a devil and half a beast? No: he would have confessed a thousand hells to have been his due, and that he was an earthly, devilish sinner. He felt now what a dreadful thing it was to depart from the living God: he felt that he was inexcusable every way; that he could in nowise, upon account of any thing in himself, be justified in the sight of God; and therefore lays himself at the feet of sovereign mercy. "God be merciful to me a sinner." Here is no confidence in the flesh, no plea fetched from fasting, paying tithes, or the performance of any other duty; here is no boasting that he was not an extortioner, unjust, or an adulterer. Perhaps he had been guilty of all these crimes, at least he knew he would have been guilty of all these, had he been left to follow the devices and desires of his own heart; and therefore, with a broken and contrite spirit, he cries out, "God be merciful to me a sinner."

This man came up to the temple to pray, and he prayed indeed. And a broken and contrite heart God will not despise. "I tell you," says our Lord, I who lay in the bosom of the Father from all eternity; I who am God, and therefore know all things; I who can neither deceive, nor be deceived, whose judgment is according to right; I tell you, whatever you may think of it, or think of me for telling you so, "this man," this Publican, this despised, sinful, but broken-hearted man, "went down to his house justified (acquitted, and looked upon as righteous in the sight of God) rather than the other."

Let Pharisees take heed that they do not pervert this text: for when it is said, "This man went down to his house justified rather than the other," our Lord does not mean that both were justified, and that the Publican had rather more justification than the Pharisee: but it implies, either that the Publican was actually justified, but the Pharisee was not; or, that the Publican was in a better way to receive justification, than the Pharisee; according to our Lord's saying, "The Publicans and Harlots enter the kingdom of heaven before you." That the Pharisee was not justified is certain, for "God resisteth the proud;" and that the Publican was at this time actually justified (and perhaps went home with a sense of it in his heart) we have great reason to infer from the latter part of the text, "For every one that exalteth himself shall be abased, and he that humbleth himself shall be exalted."

The parable therefore now speaks to all who hear me this day: for that our Lord intended it for our learning, is evident, from his making such a general application: "For every one that exalteth himself shall be abased, and he that humbleth himself shall be exalted."

The parable of the Publican and Pharisee, is but as it were a glass, wherein we may see the different disposition of all mankind; for all mankind may be divided into two general classes. Either they trust wholly in themselves, or in part, that they are righteous, and then they are Pharisees; or they have no confidence in the flesh, are self-condemned sinners, and then they come under the character of the Publican just now described. And we may add also, that the different reception these men meet with, points out to us in lively colors, the different treatment the self-justiciary and self-condemned criminal will meet with at the terrible day of judgment: "Every one that exalts himself shall be abased, but he that humbleth himself shall be exalted."

"Every one," without exception, young or old, high or low, rich or poor (for God is no respecter of persons) "every one," whosoever he be, that exalteth himself, and not free-grace; every one that trusteth in himself that he is righteous, that rests in his duties, or thinks to join them with the righteousness of Jesus Christ, for justification in the sight of God, though he be no adulterer, not extortioner, though he be not outwardly unjust, nay, though he fast twice in the week, and gives tithes of all that he possess; yet shall he be abased in the sight of all good men who know him here, and before men and angels, and God himself, when Jesus Christ comes to appear in judgment hereafter. How low, none but the almighty God can tell. He shall be abased to live with devils, and make his abode in the lowest hell for evermore.

Hear this, all ye self-justiciaries, tremble, and behold your doom! a dreadful doom, more dreadful than words can express, or thought conceive! If you refuse to humble yourselves, after hearing this parable, I call heaven and earth to witness against you this day, that God shall visit you with all his storms, and pour all the vials of his wrath upon your rebellious heads; you exalted yourselves here, and God shall abase you hereafter; you are as proud as the devil, and with devils shall you dwell to all eternity. "Be not deceived, God is not mocked;" he sees your hearts, he knows all things. And, notwithstanding you may come up to the temple to pray, your prayers are turned into sin, and you go down to your houses unjustified, if you are self-justiciaries; and do you know what it is to be unjustified? why, if you are unjustified, the wrath of God abideth upon you; you are in your blood; all the curses of the law belong to you: cursed are you when you go out, cursed are you when you come in; cursed are your thoughts, cursed are your words, cursed are your deeds; every thing you do, say, or think, from morning to night is only one continued series of sin. However highly you may be esteemed in the sight of men, however you may be honored with the uppermost seats in the synagogues, in the church militant, you will have no place in the church triumphant. "Humble yourselves therefore under the mighty hand of God:" pull down every self-righteous thought, and every proud imagination, that now exalteth itself against the perfect, personal, imputed righteousness of the dear Lord Jesus: "For he (and he alone) that humbleth himself shall be exalted."

He that humbleth himself, whatever be he: if, instead of fasting twice in the week, he has been drunk twice in the week; if, instead of giving tithes of all that he possesses, he has cheated the minister of his tithes, and the king of his taxes; notwithstanding he be unjust, an extortioner, an adulterer, nay, notwithstanding the sins of all mankind center and unite in him; yet, if through grace, like the Publican, he is enabled to humble himself, he shall be exalted; not in a temporal manner; for Christians must rather expect to be abased, and to have their names cast out as evil, and to lay down their lives for Christ Jesus in this world: but he shall be exalted in a spiritual sense; he shall be freely justified from all his sins by the blood of Jesus; he shall have peace with God, a peace which passeth all understanding; not only peace, but joy in believing; he shall be translated from the kingdom of Satan, to the kingdom of God's dear Son: he shall dwell in Christ, and Christ in him: he shall be one with Christ, and Christ one with him: he shall drink of divine pleasures, as out of a river: he shall be sanctified throughout in spirit, soul and body; in one word, he shall be filled with all the fullness of God. Thus shall the man that humbleth himself be exalted here; but O, how high shall he be exalted hereafter! as high as the highest heavens, even to the right-hand of God: there he shall sit, happy both in soul and body, and judge angels; high, out of the reach of all sin and trouble, eternally secure from all danger of falling. O sinners, did you but know how highly God intends to exalt those who humble themselves, and believe in Jesus, surely you would humble yourselves, at least beg of God to humble you; for it is he that must strike the rock of your hearts, and cause floods of contrite tears to flow therefrom. O that God would give this sermon such a commission, as he once gave to the rod of Moses! I would strike you through and through with the rod of his word, until each of you was brought to cry out with the poor Publican, "God be merciful to me a sinner." What pleasant language would this be in the ears of the Lord of Sabbaoth!

Are there no poor sinners among you? what, are you all Pharisees? Surely, you cannot bear the thoughts of returning home unjustified; can you? what if a fit of the apoplexy should seize you, and your souls be hurried away before the awful Judge of quick and dead? what will you do without Christ's righteousness? if you go out of the world unjustified, you must remain so for ever. O that you would humble yourselves! then would the Lord exalt you; it may be, that, whilst I am speaking, the Lord might justify you freely by his grace. I observed, that perhaps the Publican had a sense of his justification before he went from the temple, and knew that his pardon was sealed in heaven: and who knows but you may be thus exalted before you go home, if you humble yourselves? O what peace, love and joy, would you then feel in your hearts! you would have a heaven upon earth. O that I could hear any of you say (as I once heard a poor sinner, under my preaching, cry out) He is come, He is come! How would you then, like him, extol a precious, a free-hearted Christ! how would you magnify him for being such a friend to Publicans and sinners? greater love can no man show, than to lay down his life for a friend; but Christ laid down his life for his enemies, even for you, if you are enabled to humble yourselves, as the Publican did. Sinners, I know not how to leave off talking with you; I would fill my mouth with arguments, I would plead with you. "Come, let us reason together;" though your sins be as scarlet, yet, if you humble yourselves, they shall be as white as snow. One act of true faith in Christ, justifies you for ever and ever; he has not promised you what he cannot perform; he is able to exalt you: for God hath exalted, and given him a name above every name; that at the name of Jesus every knee shall bow; nay, God hath exalted him to be not only a Prince, but a Savior.

May he be a Savior to you! and then I shall have reason to rejoice; in the day of judgment, that I have not preached in vain, not labored in vain.

35. The Marriage of Cana

John 2:11—"This beginning of miracles did Jesus in Cana of Galilee, and manifested forth his glory; and his disciples believed on him."

I have more than once had occasion to observe, that the chief end St. John had in view, when he wrote his gospel, was to prove the divinity of Jesus Christ, [that Word, who not only was from everlasting with God, but also was really God blessed for evermore] against those archheretics Ebion and Cerinthus, whose pernicious principles too many follow in these last days. For this purpose, you may take notice, that he is more particular than any other Evangelist, in relating our Lord's divine discourses, and also the glorious miracles which he wrought, not by a power derived from another, like Moses, and other prophets, but from a power inherent in himself.

The words of the text have a reference to a notable miracle which Christ performed, and thereby gave proof of his eternal power and Godhead. "This beginning of miracles did Jesus in Cana of Galilee, and manifested forth his glory; and his disciples believed on him."

The miracle here spoken of, is that of our Lord's turning water into wine at a marriage feast. I design, at present, by God's help, to make some observations on the circumstances and certainty of the miracle, and then conclude with some practical instructions; that you, by hearing how Jesus Christ has showed forth his glory, may, by the operation of God's Spirit upon your hearts, with the disciples mentioned in the text, be brought to believe on him.

First, then, I would make some observations on the miracle itself.

Verse John 2:1, and John 2:2, "And the third day there was a marriage in Cana of Galilee; and the mother of Jesus was there. And both Jesus was called, and his disciples, to the marriage." By our Lord's being at a feast we may learn, that feasting upon solemn occasions is not absolutely unlawful: but then we must be exceeding careful at such seasons, that the occasion be solemn, and that we go not for the sake of eating and drinking, but to edify one another in love. Feasting in any other manner, I think absolutely unlawful for the followers of Jesus Christ: because if we eat and drink out of any other view, it cannot be to the glory of God. The Son of man, we know, "came eating and drinking." If a Pharisee asked him to come to his house, our Lord went, and sat down with him. But then we find his discourse was always such as tended to the use of edifying. We may then, no doubt, go and do likewise.

We may observe farther, that if our Lord was present at a marriage feast, then, to deny marriage to any order of men, is certainly a "doctrine of devils." "Marriage (says the Apostle) is honorable in all." Our Lord graced a marriage feast with his first public miracle. It was an institution of God himself, even in paradise: and therefore, no doubt, lawful for all Christians, even for those who are made perfect in holiness through the faith of Jesus Christ. But then, we may learn the reason why we have so many unhappy marriages in the world; it is because the parties concerned do not call Jesus Christ by prayer, nor ask the advice of his true disciples when they are about to marry. No; Christ and religion are the last things that are consulted; and no wonder then if matches of the devil's making (as all such are, which are contracted only on account of outward beauty, or for filthy lucre's sake) prove most miserable, and grievous to be borne.

I cannot but dwell a little on this particular, because I am persuaded the devil cannot lay a greater snare for young Christians, than to tempt them unequally to yoke themselves with unbelievers; as are all who are not born again of God. This was the snare wherein the sons of God were entangled before the flood, and one great cause why God brought that flood upon the world. For what says Moses, Genesis 6:2, Genesis 6:3, "The sons of God (the posterity of pious Seth) saw the daughters of men, (or the posterity of wicked Cain) that they were fair, (not that they were pious) and they took them wives of all which they chose:" not which God chose for them. What follows? "And the Lord saith, My spirit shall not always strive with man, for that he also is flesh;" that is, even the few righteous souls being now grown carnal by their ungodly marriages, the whole world was altogether become abominable, and had made themselves vessels of wrath fitted for destruction. I might instance farther, the care the ancient patriarchs took to choose wives for their children out of their own religious families, and it was one great mark of Esau's rebellion against his father, that he took unto himself wives of the daughters of the Canaanites, who were strangers to the covenant of promise made unto his fathers. But I forbear. Time will not permit me to enlarge here. Let it suffice to advise all, whenever they enter into a marriage state, to imitate the people of Cana in Galilee, to call Christ to the marriage; He certainly will hear and choose for you; and you will always find his choice to be the best. He then will direct you to such yoke-fellows as shall be helps meet for you in the great work of your salvation, and then he will also enable you to serve him without distraction, and cause you to walk, as Zachary and Elizabeth, in all his commandments and ordinances blameless.

But to proceed. Who these persons were that called our Lord and his disciples to the marriage, is not certain. Some (because it is said, that the mother of Jesus was there) have supposed that they were related to the Virgin, and that therefore our Lord and his disciples were invited on her account. However that be, it should seem they were not very rich, (for what had rich folks to do with a despised Jesus of Nazareth, and his mean followers?) because we find they were unfurnished with a sufficient quantity of wine for a large company, and therefore, "when they wanted wind, the mother of Jesus," having, as it should seem by her applying to him so readily on this occasion, even in his private life, seen some instances of his miraculous power, "saith unto him, They have no wine." She thought is sufficient only to inform him of the wants of the host, knowing that he was as ready to give as she to ask. In this light the blessed Virgin's request appears to us at the first view; but if we examine our Lord's answer, we shall have reason to think there was something which was not right; for Jesus saith unto her, ver. John 2:4, "Woman, what have I to do with thee?" Observe, he calls her woman, not mother; to show her, that though she was his mother, as he was man, yet she was his creature, as he was God. "What have I to do with thee?" Think you that I must work miracles at your bidding? Some have thought that she spoke as though she had an authority over him, which was a proud motion, and our Lord therefore checks her for it, And if Jesus Christ would not turn a little water into wine, whilst he was here on earth, at her command, how idolatrous is that church, and how justly do we separate from her, which prescribes forms, wherein the Virgin is desired to command her Son to have compassion on us!

But notwithstanding the holy Virgin was blamable in this respect, yet she hath herein set rich and poor an example which it is your duty to follow. You that are rich, and live in cieled houses, learn of her to go into the cottages of the poor; your Lord was not above it, and why should you? And when you do visit them, like the virgin-mother, examine their wants; and when you see they have no wine, and are ready to perish with hunger, shut not up your bowels of compassion, but bless the Lord for putting it in your power to administer to their necessities. Believe me, such visits would do you good. You would learn then to be thankful that God has given you bread enough, and to spare. And I am persuaded, every mite that you bestow on feeding the hungry and clothing the naked disciples of Jesus Christ, will afford you more satisfaction at the hour of death, and in the day of judgment, than all the thousands squandered away in balls and assemblies, and such like entertainments.

You that are poor in this world's goods, and thereby are disabled from helping, yet you may learn from the Virgin, to pray for one another. She could not turn the water into wine, but she could entreat her son to do it: and so may you; and doubt not of the Lord's hearing you; for God has chosen the poor in this world, rich in faith: and by your servant prayers, you may draw down many a blessing on your poor fellow creatures. O that I may ever be remembered by you before the throne of our dear Lord Jesus! But what shall we say? Will our Lord entirely disregard this motion of his mother? No; though he check her with, "Woman, what have I to do with thee?" yet he intimates that he would do as she desired by-and-by; "Mine hour is not yet come." As though he had said, The wine is almost, but not quite out; when they are come to an extremity, and sensible of the want of my assistance, then will I show forth my glory, that they may behold it, and believe on me.

Thus, Sirs, hath our Lord been frequently pleased to deal with me, and, I doubt not, with many of you also. Often, often when I have found his presence as it were hidden from my soul, and his comforts well nigh gone, I have went unto him complaining that I had no visit and token of his love, as usual. Sometimes he has seemed to turn a deaf ear to my request, and as it were said, "What have I to do with thee?" which has made me go sorrowing all the day long; so foolish was I, and faithless before him: for I have always found he loved me notwithstanding, as he did Lazarus, though he stayed two days after he heard he was sick. But when my hour of extremity has been come, and my will broken, then hath he lifted up the light of his blessed countenance afresh; he has showed forth his glory, and made me ashamed for disbelieving him, who often hath turned my water into wine. Be not then discouraged, if the Lord does not immediately seem to regard the voice of your prayer, when you cry unto him. The holy Virgin we find was not; no, she was convinced his time was the best time, and therefore, verse

John 2:5, "saith unto the servants, (O that we could follow her advice!) whatsoever he saith unto you, do it."

And now, behold the hour is come, when the eternal Son of God will show forth his glory. The circumstance of the miracle is very remarkable; ver. John 2:6, "And there were set six water-pots of water, after the manner of the purifying of the Jews, containing two or three firkins a-piece." The manner of this purifying we have an account of in the other Evangelist, especially St. Mark, who informs us, that the Pharisees, and all the Jews, except they wash their hands oft, eat not; and when they come from the market, except they wash they eat not. This was a superstitious custom; but, however, we may learn from it, whenever we come in from conversing with those that are without, to purify our hearts by self-examination and prayer; for it is hard to go through the world, and to be kept unspotted from it.

Observe further, verse John 2:7, "Jesus saith unto them," not to his own disciples, but unto the servants of the house, who were strangers to the holy Jesus, and whom the virgin had before charged to do whatsoever he said unto them; "Fill the water-pots with water. And they filled them to the brim. And he saith unto them, draw out now, and bear to the governor of the feast. And they bear it." How our Lord turned the water into wine we are not told. What have we to do with that? Why should we desire to be wise above what is written? It is sufficient for the manifestation of his glorious godhead, that we are assured he did do it. For we are told, verse John 2:9, John 2:10, "When the ruler of the feast had tasted the water that was made wine, and knew not whence it was (but the servants that drew the water knew) the governor of the feast called the bridegroom, and saith unto him, every man at the beginning doth set forth good wine, and when they have well drank, that which is worse; but thou hast kept the good wine until now."

To explain this passage, you must observe, it was the custom of the Jews, nay even of the heathens themselves, (to the shame of our Christian baptized heathens be it spoken) at their public feasts to choose a governor, who was to ever see and regulate the behavior of the guests, and to take care that all things were carried on with decency and order. To this person then did the servants bear the wine; and we may judge how rich it was by his commendation of it, "Every man at the beginning, &c." Judge ye then, whether Jesus did not show forth his glory, and whether you have not good reason, like the disciple here mentioned, to believe on him?

Thus, my brethren, I have endeavored to make some observations on the miracle itself. But alas! this is only the outward court thereof, the veil is yet before our eyes; turn that aside, and we shall see such mysteries under it, as will make our hearts to dance for joy, and fill our mouths with praise for evermore!

But here I cannot help remarking what a sad inference one of our masters of Israel, in a printed sermon, has lately drawn from this commendation of the bridegroom. His words are these. "Our blessed Savior came eating and drinking, was present at weddings, and other entertainments, (though I hear of his being only at one;) nay, at one of them (which I suppose is that of which I am now discoursing) worked a miracle to make wine, when it is plain there had been more drank than was absolutely necessary for the support of nature, and consequently something had been indulged to pleasure and cheerfulness."

I am sorry such words should come from the mouth and pen of a dignified clergyman of the Church of England. Alas! how is she fallen! or at least, in what danger must her tottering ark be, when such unhallowed hands are stretched out to support it! Well may I bear patiently to be stiled a blasphemer, and a setter forth of strange doctrine, when my dear Lord Jesus is thus traduced; and when those who pretend to preach in his name, urge this example to patronize licentiousness and excess. It is true (as I observed at the beginning of this discourse) our blessed Savior did come eating and drinking; he was present at a wedding, and other entertainments; nay, at one of them worked a miracle to make wine, (you see I have been making some observations on it) but then it is not plain there had been more wine drank than was absolutely necessary for the support of nature; much less does it appear, that something had been indulged to pleasure and cheerfulness.

The governor does indeed say, "When men have well drunken," but it no where appears that they were the men. Is it to be supposed, that the most holy and unspotted Lamb of God, who was manifested to destroy the works of the devil, and who, when at a Pharisee's house, took notice of even the gestures of those with whom he sat at meat; is it to be supposed, that our dear Redeemer, whose constant practice it was to tell people they must deny themselves, and take up their crosses daily; who bid his disciples to take heed, lest at any time their hearts might be over-charged with surfeiting and drunkenness; can it be supposed, that such a self-denying Jesus should now turn six large water-pots of water into the richest wine, to encourage excess and drunkenness in persons, who, according to this writer, had indulged to pleasure and cheerfulness already? Had our Lord sat by, and seen them indulge, without telling them of it, would it not be a sin? But to insinuate he not only did this, but also turned water into wine, to increase that indulgence; this is making Christ a minister of sin indeed. What is this, but using him like the Pharisees of old, who called him a glutton, and a wine-bibber? Alas! how may we expect our dear Lord's enemies will treat him, when he is thus wounded in the house of his seeming friends? Sirs, if you follow such doctrine as this, you will not be righteous, but I am persuaded you will be wicked over-much.

But God forbid you should think our Lord behaved so much unlike himself in this matter. No, he had nobler ends in view, when he wrought this miracle. One, the evangelist mentions in the words of the text, "to show forth his glory," or to give a proof of his eternal power and godhead.

Here seems to be an allusion to the appearance of God in the tabernacle, which this same evangelist takes notice of in his first chapter, where he says, "The Word (Jesus Christ) was made flesh, and dwelt (or, as it is rendered in the margin, tabernacled) amongst us." Our dear Lord, though very God of very God, and also most perfect and glorious in himself as man, was pleased to throw a veil of flesh over this his great glory, when he came to make his soul an offering for sin. And that the world might know and believe in him as the Savior of all men, he performed many miracles, and this in particular; for thus speaks the evangelist, "This first," &c.

This then was the chief design of our Lord's turning the water into wine. But there are more which our Lord may be supposed to have had in view, some of which I shall proceed to mention.

Secondly, he might do this to reward the hose for calling him and his disciples to the marriage. Jesus Christ will not be behind-hand with those who receive him or his followers, for his name's sake. Those who thus honor him, he will honor. A cup of cold water given in the name of a disciple, shall in no wise lose its reward. He will turn water into wine. Though those who abound in alms-deeds, out of a true faith in, and love for Jesus, may seem as it were to throw their bread upon the waters, yet they shall find it again after many days. For they who give to the poor out of this principle, lend unto the Lord; and look, whatsoever they lay out, it shall be repaid them again. Even in this life, God often orders good measure pressed down and running over, to be returned into his servants bosoms. It is the same in spirituals. To him that hath, and improves what he hath, for the sake of Christ and his disciples, shall be given, and he shall have abundance. Brethren, I would not boast; but, to my master's honor and free grace be it spoken, I can prove this to be true by happy experience. When I have considered that I am a child, and cannot speak, and have seen so many of you come out into the wilderness to be fed, I have often said within myself, what can I do with my little stock of grace and knowledge among so great a multitude? But, at my Lord's command, I have given you to eat of such spiritual food as I had, and before I have done speaking, have had my soul richly fed with the bread which cometh down from heaven. Thus shall it be done to all such who are willing to spend and be spent for Christ or his disciples; for there is no respect of persons with God.

Thirdly, Our Lord's turning the water, which was poured out so plentifully, into wine, is a sign of the plentiful pouring out of his Spirit into the hearts of believers. The holy Spirit is in scripture compared unto wine; and therefore the prophet calls us to buy wine as well as milk, that is, the spirit of love, which fills and gladdens the soul as it were with new wine. The apostle alludes to this, when he bids the Ephesians "not to be drunk with wine, wherein is excess, but be filled with the Spirit." And our Lord shows us thus much by choosing wine; to show forth the strength and refreshment of his blood, in the blessed sacrament. I know these terms are unintelligible to natural men, they can no more understand me, than if I spoke to them in an unknown tongue, for they are only to be spiritually discerned. To you then that are spiritual do I speak, to you who are justified by faith, and feel the blessed Spirit of Jesus Christ working upon your hearts, you can judge of what I say; you have already (I am persuaded) been as it were filled with new wine by the inspiration of his Holy Spirit. But alas! you have not yet had half your portion; thee are only earnests, and in comparison but shadows of good things to come; our Lord keeps his best wine for you till the last; and though you have drank deep of it already, yet he intends to give you more: He will not leave you, till he has filled you to the brim, till you are ready to cry out, Lord, stay thine hand, thy poor creatures can hold no more! Be not straitened in your own bowels, since Jesus Christ is not straitened in his. Open your hearts as wide as ever you will, the Spirit of the Lord shall fill them. Christ deals with true believers, as Elijah did with the poor woman, whose oil increased, to pay her husband's debts; as long as she brought pitchers, the oil continued. It did not cease till she ceased bringing vessels to contain it. My brethren, our hearts are like those pitchers; open them freely by faith, and the oil of God's free gift, the oil of gladness, the love of God through Christ, shall be continually pouring in; for believers are to be filled with all the fullness of God.

Fourthly, Our Lord's turning water into wine, and keeping the best until last, may show forth the glory of the latter days of his marriage feast with his church. Great things God has done already, whereat millions of saints have rejoiced, and do yet rejoice. Great things God is doing now, but yet, my brethren, we shall see greater things than these. It is meet, right, and our bounden duty, to give thanks unto God, even the Father; for many righteous men have desired to see the things which we see, and have not seen them; and to hear the things which we hear, and have not heard them. But still there are more excellent things behind. Glorious things are spoken of these times, "when the earth shall be filled with the knowledge of the Lord, as the waters cover the sea." There is a general expectation among the people of God, when the partition-wall between Jew and Gentile shall be broken down, and all Israel be saved. Happy those who live when God does this. They shall see Satan, like lightning, fall from heaven. They shall not weep, as the Jews did at the building of the second temple. No, they shall rejoice with exceeding great joy. For all the former glory of the Christian church shall be nothing in comparison of that glory which shall excel. Then shall they cry out with the governor of the feast, "thou hast kept thy good wine until now!"

Fifthly, and lastly, This shows us the happiness of that blessed state, when we shall all sit together at the marriage supper of the Lamb, and drink of the new wine in his eternal and glorious kingdom!

The rewards which Jesus Christ confers on his faithful servants, and the comforts of his love wherewith he comforts them, whilst pilgrims here on earth, are often so exceeding great, that was it not promised, it were almost presumption for them to hope for any reward hereafter. But, my brethren, all the manifestations of God that we can possibly be favored with here, when compared with the glory that is to be revealed in us, are no more than a drop of water when compared with an unbounded ocean. Though Christ frequently fills his saints even to the brim, yet their corruptible bodies weigh down their souls, and cause them to cry, "Who shall deliver us from these bodies of death?" These earthly tabernacles can hold no more: But, blessed be God, these earthly tabernacles are to be dissolved; this corruptible is to put on incorruption; this mortal is to put on immortality: and when God shall cause all his glory to pass before us, then shall we cry out, Lord, thou hast kept thy good wine until now. We have drank deeply of thy spirit; we have heard glorious things spoken of this thy city, O God! but we now find, that not the half, not the thousandth part hath been told us. O the invisible realities of the world of faith! Eye hath not seen, ear hath not heard, neither hath it entered into the heart of the greatest saint to conceive how Christ will show forth his glory there! St. Paul, who was carried up into the third heavens, could give us little or no account of it. And well he might not—for he heard and saw such things as is not possible for a man clothed with flesh and blood to utter. Whilst I am thinking, and only speaking of those things unto you, I am almost carried beyond myself. Methinks, I now receive some little foretastes of that new wine which I hope to drink with you in the heavenly kingdom for ever and ever.

And wherefore do you think I have been saying these things? Many, perhaps, may be ready to say, To manifest thy own vain-glory. But it is a small matter with me to be judged of man's judgment. He that judgeth me is the Lord. He knows that I have spoken of his miracle, only for the same end for which he at first performed it, and which I at first proposed, that is, "to show forth his glory," that you also may be brought to believe on him.

Did I come to preach myself, and not Christ Jesus my Lord, I would come to you, not in this plainness of speech, but with the enticing words of man's wisdom. Did I desire to please natural men, I need not preach here in the wilderness. I hope my heart aims at nothing else, than what our Lord's great fore-runner aimed at, and which ought to be the business of every gospel minister, that is, to point out to you the God-man Christ Jesus. "Behold then (by faith behold) the Lamb of God, who taketh away the sins of the world." Look unto him, and be saved. You have heard how he manifested, and will yet manifest his glory to true believers; and why then, O sinners, will you not believe in him? I say, O sinners, for now I have spoken to the saints, I have many things to say to you. And may God give you all an hearing ear, and an obedient heart!

The Lord Jesus who showed forth his glory above 1700 years ago, has made a marriage feast, and offers to espouse all sinners to himself, and to make them flesh of his flesh, and bone of his bone. He is willing to be united to you by one spirit. In every age, at sundry times, and after divers manners, he hath sent forth his servants, and they had bidden many, but yet, my brethren, there is room. The Lord therefore now has given a commission in these last days to others of his servants, even to compel poor sinners by the cords of love to come in. For our master's house must and shall be filled. He will not shed his gracious blood in vain. Come then, come to the marriage. Let this be the day of your espousals with Jesus Christ, he is willing to receive you, though other lords have had dominion over you. Come then to the marriage. Behold the oxen and fatlings are killed, and all things are ready; let me hear you say, as Rebecca did, when they asked her, whether she would go and be a wife to Isaac; O let me hear you say, we will come. Indeed you will not repent it. The Lord shall turn your water into wine. He shall fill your souls with marrow and fatness, and cause you to praise him with joyful lips.

Do not say, you are miserable, and poor, and blind, and naked, and therefore ashamed to come, for it is to such that this invitation is not sent. The polite, the rich, the busy, self-righteous Pharisees of this generation have been bidden already, but they have rejected the counsel of God against themselves. They are too deeply engaged in going, one to his country house, another to his merchandise. They are so deeply wedded to the pomps and vanities of this wicked world, that they, as it were with one consent, have made excuse. And though they have been often called in their own synagogues, yet all the return they make, is to thrust us out, and thereby in effect say, they will not come. But God forbid, my brethren, that you should learn of them; no, since our Lord condescends to call first, (because if left to yourselves you would never call after him) let me beseech you to answer him, as he answered for you, when called upon by infinite offended justice to die for you sins, "Lo! I come to do thy will, O God!" What if you are miserable, and poor, and blind, and naked, that is no excuse; faith is the only wedding garment which Christ requires; he does not call you because you already are, but because he intends to make you saints. It pities him to see you naked. He wants to cover you with his righteousness. In short, he desires to show forth his glory, that is, his free love through your faith in him. Not but that he will be glorified, whether you believe in him or not; for the infinitely free love of Jesus Christ will be ever the same, whether you believe it, or so receive it, or the contrary. But our Lord will not always send out his servants in vain, to call you; the time will come when he will say, None of those which were bidden, and would not come, shall taste of my supper. Our Lord is a God of justice, as well as of love; and if sinners will not take hold of his golden scepter, verily he will bruise them with his iron rod. It is for your sakes,

O sinners, and not his own, that he thus condescends to invite you: suffer him then to show forth his glory, even the glory of the exceeding riches of his free grace, by believing on him, "For we are saved by grace through faith." It was grace, free grace, that moved the Father so to love the world, as to "give his only begotten Son, that whosoever believeth in him should not perish, but have everlasting life!" It was grace, that made the Son to come down and die. It was grace, free grace, that moved the Holy Ghost to undertake to sanctify the elect people of God: and it was grace, free grace, that moved our Lord Jesus Christ to send forth his ministers to call poor sinners this day. Let me not then, my brethren, go without my errand. Why will you not believe in him? Will the devil do such great and good things for you as Christ will? No indeed, he will not. Perhaps, he may give you to drink at first of a little brutish pleasure; but what will he give you to drink as last? a cup of fury and of trembling; a never-dying worm, a self-condemning conscience, and the bitter pains of eternal death. But as for the servants of Jesus Christ, it is not so with them. No, he keeps his best wine till the last. And though he may cause you to drink of the brook in the way to heaven, and of the cup of affliction, yet he sweetens it with a sense of his goodness, and makes it pleasant drink, such as their souls do love. I appeal to the experience of any saint here present, (as I doubt not but there are many such in this field) whether Christ has not proved faithful, ever since you have been espoused to him? Has he not showed forth his glory, ever since you have believed on him?

And now, sinners, what have you to object? I see you are all silent, and well you may. For if you will not be drawn by the cords of infinite and everlasting love, what will draw you? I could urge many terrors of the Lord to persuade you; but if the love of Jesus Christ will not constrain you, your case is desperate. Remember then this day I have invited all, even the worst of sinners, to be married to the Lord Jesus. If you perish, remember you do not perish for lack of invitation. You yourselves shall stand forth at the last day, and I here give you a summons to meet me at the judgment seat of Christ, and to clear both my master and me. Would weeping, would tears prevail on you, I could wish my head were waters, and my eyes fountains of tears, that I might weep out every argument, and melt you into love. Would any thing I could do or suffer, influence your hearts, I think I could bear to pluck out my eyes, or even to lay down my life for your sakes. Or was I sure to prevail on you by importunity, I could continue my discourse till midnight, I would wrestle with you even till the morning watch, as Jacob did with the angel, and would not go away till I had overcome. But such power belongeth only unto the Lord, I can only invite; it is He only can work in you both to will and to do after his good pleasure; it is his property to take away the heart of stone, and give you a heart of flesh; it is his spirit that must convince you of unbelief, and of the everlasting righteousness of his dear Son; it is He alone must give faith to apply his righteousness to your hearts; it is He alone can give you a wedding garment, and bring you to sit down and drink new wine in his kingdom. As to spirituals we are quite dead, and have no more power to turn to God of ourselves, than Lazarus had to raise himself, after he had lain stinking in the grave four days. If thou canst go, O man, and breathe upon all the dry bones that lie in the graves, and bid them live; if thou canst take thy mantle and divide yonder river, as Elijah did the river Jordan; then will we believe thou hast a power to turn to God of thyself: But as thou must despair of the one, so thou must despair of the other, without Christ's quickening grace; in him is thy only help; fly to him then by faith; say unto him, as the poor leper did, "Lord, if thou wilt," thou canst make me willing; and he will stretch forth the right-hand of his power to assist and relieve you: He will sweetly guide you by his wisdom on earth, and afterwards take you up to partake of his glory in heaven.

To his mercy therefore, and Almighty protection, do I earnestly, humbly, and most affectionately commit you: the Lord bless you and keep you; the Lord lift up the light of his blessed countenance upon you, and give you all peace and joy in believing, now and for evermore!

36. The Duty of Searching the Scriptures

John 5:39—"Search the Scriptures."

When the Sadducees came to our blessed Lord, and put to him the question, "whose wife that woman should be in the next life, who had seven husbands in this," he told them "they erred, not knowing the scriptures." And if we would know whence all the errors, that have over-spread the church of Christ, first arose, we should find that, in a great measure, they flowed from the same fountain, ignorance of the word of God.

Our blessed Lord, though he was the eternal God, yet as man, he made the scriptures his constant rule and guide. And therefore, when he was asked by the lawyer, which was the great commandment of the law, he referred him to his Bible for an answer, "What readest thou?" And thus, when led by the Spirit to be tempted by the devil, he repelled all his assaults, with "it is written."

A sufficient confutation this, of their opinion, who say, "the Spirit only, and not the Spirit by the Word, is to be our rule of action." If so, our Savior, who had the Spirit without measure, needed not always have referred to the written word.

But how few copy after the example of Christ? How many are there who do not regard the word of God at all, but throw the sacred oracles aside, as an antiquated book, fit only for illiterate men?

Such do greatly err, not knowing what the scriptures are, I shall, therefore,

First, Show, that it is every one's duty to search them.

And *Secondly*, Lay down some directions for you to search them with advantage.

I. I am to show, that it is every person's duty to search the Scriptures.

By the Scriptures, I understand the law and the prophets, and those books which have in all ages been accounted canonical, and which make up that volume commonly called the Bible.

These are emphatically stiled the Scriptures, and, in one place, the "Scriptures of Truth," as though no other books deserved the name of true writings or scripture in comparison of them.

They are not of any private interpretation, authority, or invention, but holy men of old wrote them, as they were moved by the Holy Ghost.

The fountain of God's revealing himself thus to mankind, was our fall in Adam, and the necessity of our new birth in Christ Jesus. And if we search the scriptures as we ought, we shall find the sum and substance, the Alpha and Omega, the beginning and end of them, is to lead us to a knowledge of these two great truths.

All the threats, promises and precepts, all the exhortations and doctrines contained therein, all the rites, ceremonies and sacrifices appointed under the Jewish law; nay, almost all the historical parts of holy scripture, suppose our being fallen in Adam, and either point out to us a Mediator to come, or speak of him as already come in the flesh.

Had man continued in a state of innocence, he would not have needed an outward revelation, because the law of God was so deeply written in the tables of his heart. But having eaten the forbidden fruit, he incurred the displeasure of God, and lost the divine image, and, therefore, without an external revelation, could never tell how

God would be reconciled unto him, or how he should be saved from the misery and darkness of his fallen nature.

That these truths are so, I need not refer you to any other book, than your own hearts.

For unless we are fallen creatures, whence those abominable corruptions which daily arise in our hearts? We could not come thus corrupt out of the hands of our Maker, because he being goodness itself could make nothing but what is like himself, holy, just, and good. And that we want to be delivered from these disorders of our nature, is evident, because we find an unwillingness within ourselves to own we are thus depraved, and are always striving to appear to others of a quite different frame and temper of mind than what we are.

I appeal to the experience of the most learned disputer against divine revelation, whether he does not find in himself, that he is naturally proud, angry, revengeful, and full of other passions contrary to the purity, holiness, and long suffering of God. And is not this a demonstration that some way or other he is fallen from God? And I appeal also, whether at the same time that he finds these hurtful lusts in his heart, he does not strive to seem amiable, courteous, kind and affable [friendly, good-natured, easy-going]; and is not this a manifest proof, that he is sensible he is miserable, and wants, he knows not how, to be redeemed or delivered from it?

Here then, God by his word steps in, and opens to his view such a scene of divine love, and infinite goodness in the holy scriptures, that none but men, of such corrupt and reprobate minds as our modern deists, would shut their eyes against it.

What does God in his written word do more or less, than show thee, O man, how thou art fallen into that blindness, darkness, and misery, of which thou feelest and complainest? And, at the same time, he points out the way to what thou desirest, even how thou mayest be redeemed out of it by believing in, and copying after the Son of his love.

As I told you before, so I tell you again, upon these two truths rest all divine revelation. It being given us for no other end, but to show our misery, and our happiness; our fall and recovery; or, in one word, after what manner we died in Adam, and how in Christ we may again be made alive.

Hence, then arises the necessity of searching the scriptures: for since they are nothing else but the grand charter of our salvation, the revelation of a covenant made by God with men in Christ, and a light to guide us into the way of peace; it follows, that all are obliged to read and search them, because all are equally fallen from God, all equally stand in need of being informed how they must be restored to, and again united with him.

How foolishly then do the disputing infidels of this generation act, who are continually either calling for signs from heaven, or seeking for outward evidence to prove the truth of divine revelation? Whereas, what they so earnestly seek for is nigh unto, nay, within them. For let them but consult their own hearts, they cannot but feel what they want. Let them but consult the lively oracles of God, and they cannot but see a remedy revealed for all their wants, and that the written word does as exactly answer the wants and desires of their hearts, as face answers to face in the water. Where then is the scribe, where is the wise, where is the solidity of the reasoning of the disputers of this world? Has not God revealed himself unto them, as plain as their own hearts could wish? And yet they require a sign: but there shall no other sign be given them. For if they believe not a revelation which is every way so suited to their wants, neither will they be persuaded though on should rise from the dead.

But this discourse is not designed so much for them that believe not, as for them, who both know and believe that the scriptures contain a revelation which came from God, and that it is their duty, as being chief parties concerned, not only to read but search them also.

I pass on, therefore, in the

Second place, to lay down some directions, how you may search them with advantage.

First, Have always in view, the end for which the scriptures were written, even to show us the way of salvation, by Jesus Christ.

"Search the scriptures," says our blessed Lord, "for they are they that testify of me." Look, therefore, always for Christ in the scripture. He is the treasure hid in the field, both of the Old and New Testament. In the Old, you will find him under prophesies, types, sacrifices, and shadows; in the New, manifested in the flesh, to become a propitiation for our sins as a Priest, and as a Prophet to reveal the whole will of his heavenly Father.

Have Christ, then, always in view when you are reading the word of God, and this, like the star in the east, will guide you to the Messiah, will serve as a key to every thing that is obscure, and unlock to you the wisdom and riches of all the mysteries of the kingdom of God.

Secondly, Search the scriptures with an humble child-like disposition.

For whosoever does not read them with this temper, shall in no wise enter into the knowledge of the things contained in them. For God hides the sense of them, from those that are wise and prudent in their own eyes, and reveals them only to babes in Christ: who think they know nothing yet as they ought to know; who hunger and thirst after righteousness, and humbly desire to be fed with the sincere milk of the word, that they may grow thereby.

Fancy yourselves, therefore, when you are searching the scriptures, especially when you are reading the New Testament, to be with Mary sitting at the feet of the holy Jesus; and be as willing to learn what God shall teach you, as Samuel was, when he said, "Speak, Lord, for thy servant heareth."

Oh that the unbelievers would pull down every high thought and imagination that exalts itself against the revealed will of God! O that they would, like new-born babes, desire to be fed with the pure milk of the word! Then we should have them no longer scoffing at Divine revelation, nor would they read the Bible any more with the same intend the Philistines brought our Samson, to make sport at it; but they would see the divine image and superscription written upon every line. They would hear God speaking unto their souls by it, and, consequently, be built up in the knowledge and fear of him, who is the Author thereof.

Thirdly, Search the scriptures, with a sincere intention to put in practice what you read.

A desire to do the will of God is the only way to know it; if any man will do my will, says Jesus Christ, "He shall know of my doctrine, whether it be of God, or whether I speak of myself." As he also speaks in another place to his disciples, "To you, (who are willing to practice your duty) it is given to know the mysteries of the kingdom of God, but to those that are without (who only want to raise cavils against my doctrine) all these things are spoken in parables, that seeing they may see and not understand, and hearing they may hear and not perceive."

For it is but just in God to send those strong delusions, that they may believe a lie, and to conceal the knowledge of himself from all such as do not seek him with a single intention.

Jesus Christ is the same now, as formerly, to those who desire to know from his word, who he is that they may believe on, and live by; and to him he will reveal himself as clearly as he did to the woman of Samaria, when he said, "I that speak to thee am he," or as he did to the man that was born blind, whom the Jews had cast out for his name's sake, "He that talketh with thee, is he." But to those who consult his word with a desire neither to know him, nor keep his commandments, but either merely for their entertainment, or to scoff at the simplicity of the manner in which he is revealed, to those, I say, he never will reveal himself, though they should search the scriptures to all eternity. As he never would tell those whether he was the Messiah or not, who put that question to him either out of curiosity, or that they might have whereof to accuse him.

Fourthly, In order to search the scriptures still more effectually, make an application of every thing you read to your own hearts.

For whatever was written in the book of God, was written for our learning. And what Christ said unto those aforetime, we must look upon as spoken to us also: for since the holy scriptures are nothing but a revelation from God, how fallen man is to be restored by Jesus Christ: all the precepts, threats, and promises, belong to us and to our children, as well as to those, to whom they were immediately made known.

Thus the Apostle, when he tells us that he lived by the faith of the Son of God, adds, "who died and gave himself for me." It is this application of Jesus Christ to our hearts, that makes his redemption effectual to each of us.

And it is this application of all the doctrinal and historical parts of scripture, when we are reading them over, that must render them profitable to us, as they were designed for reproof, for correction, for instruction in righteousness, and to make every child of God perfect, thoroughly furnished to every good work.

I dare appeal to the experience of every spiritual reader of holy writ, whether or not, if he consulted the word of God in this manner, he was not at all times and at all seasons, as plainly directed how to act, as though he had consulted the Urim and Thummim, which was upon the high-priest's breast. For this is the way God now reveals himself to man: not by making new revelations, but by applying general things that are revealed already to every sincere reader's heart.

And this, by the way, answers an objection made by those who say, "The word of God is not a perfect rule of action, because it cannot direct us how to act or how to determine in particular cases, or what place to go to, when we are in doubt, and therefore, the Spirit, and not the word, is to be our rule of action."

But this I deny, and affirm on the contrary, that God at all times, circumstances, and places, though never so minute, never so particular, will, if we diligently seek the assistance of his Holy Spirit, apply general things to our hearts, and thereby, to use the words of the holy Jesus, will lead us into all truth, and give us the particular assistance we want. But this leads me to a

Fifth direction how to search the scriptures with profit: Labor to attain that Spirit by which they were written.

For the natural man discerneth not the words of the Spirit of God, because they are spiritually discerned; the words that Christ hath spoken, they are spirit, and they are life, and can be no more understood as to the true sense and meaning of them, by the mere natural man, than a person who never had learned a language can understand another speaking in it. The scriptures, therefore, have not unfitly been compared, by some, to the cloud which went before the Israelites, they are dark and hard to be understood by the natural man, as the cloud appeared dark to the Egyptians; but they are light, they are life to Christians indeed, as that same cloud which seemed dark to Pharaoh and his house, appeared bright and altogether glorious to the Israel of God.

It was the want of the assistance of this Spirit, that made Nicodemus, a teacher of Israel, and a ruler of the Jews, so utterly ignorant in the doctrine of regeneration: for being only a natural man, he could not tell how that thing could be; it was the want of this Spirit that made our Savior's disciples, though he so frequently conversed with them, daily mistake the nature of the doctrines he delivered; and it is because the natural veil is not taken off from their hearts, that so many who now pretend to search the scriptures, yet see no farther than into the bare letter of them, and continue entire strangers to the spiritual meaning couched under every parable, and contained in almost all the precepts of the book of God.

Indeed, how should it be otherwise, for God being a spirit, he cannot communicate himself any otherwise than in a spiritual manner to the hearts of men; and consequently if we are strangers to his Spirit, we must continue strangers to his word, because it is altogether like himself, spiritual. Labor, therefore, earnestly for to attain this blessed Spirit; otherwise, your understandings will never be opened to understand the scriptures aright: and remember, prayer is one of the most immediate means to get this Holy Spirit. Therefore,

Sixthly, Let me advise you, before you read the scriptures, to pray, that Christ, according to his promise, would send his Spirit to guide you into all truth; intersperse short ejaculations whilst you are engaged in reading; pray over every word and verse, if possible; and when you close up the book, most earnestly beseech God, that the words which you have read, may be inwardly engrafted into your hearts, and bring forth in you the fruits of a good life.

Do this, and you will, with a holy violence, draw down God's Holy Spirit into your hearts; you will experience his gracious influence, and feel him enlightening, quickening, and inflaming your souls by the word of God; you will then not only read, but mark, learn, and inwardly digest what you read: and the word of God will be meat indeed, and drink indeed unto your souls; you then will be as Apollos was, powerful in the scriptures; be scribes ready instructed to the kingdom of God, and bring out of the good treasures of your heart, things both from the Old and New Testament, to entertain all you converse with. One

Direction more, which shall be the last, *Seventhly*, Read the scripture constantly, or, to use our Savior's expression in the text, "search the scriptures;" dig in them as for hid treasure; for here is a manifest allusion to those who dig in mines; and our Savior would thereby teach us, that we must take as much pains in constantly reading his word, if we would grow wise thereby, as those who dig for gold and silver. The scriptures contain the deep things of God, and therefore, can never be sufficiently searched into by a careless, superficial, cursory way of reading them, but by an industrious, close, and humble application.

The Psalmist makes it the characteristic of a good man, that he "meditates on God's law day and night." And "this book of the law, (says God to Joshua) shall not go out of thy mouth, but thou shalt meditate therein day and night;" for then thou shalt make thy way prosperous, and thou shalt have good success. Search, therefore, the scriptures, not only devoutly but daily, for in them are the words of eternal life; wait constantly at wisdom's gate, and she will then, and not till then, display and lay open to you her heavenly treasures. You that are rich, are without excuse if you do not; and you that are poor, ought to take heed and improve that little time you have: for by the scriptures you are to be acquitted, and by the scriptures you are to be condemned at the last day.

But perhaps you have no taste for this despised book; perhaps plays, romances, and books of polite entertainment, suit your taste better: if this be your case, give me leave to tell you, your taste is vitiated [corrupted, depraved], and unless corrected by the Spirit and word of God, you shall never enter into his heavenly kingdom: for unless you delight in God here, how will you be made meet to dwell with him hereafter. Is it a sin then, you will say, to read useless impertinent books; I answer, Yes. And that for the same reason, as it is a sin to indulge useless conversation, because both immediately tend to grieve and quench that Spirit, by which alone we can be sealed to the day of redemption. You may reply, How shall we know this? Why, put in practice the precept in the text; search the scripture in the manner that has been recommended, and then you will be convinced of the danger, sinfulness, and unsatisfacteriness of reading any others than the book of God, or such as are wrote in the same spirit. You will then say, when I was a child, and ignorant of the excellency of the word of God, I read what the world calls harmless books, as other children in knowledge, though old in years, have done, and still do; but now I have tasted the good word of life, and am come to a more perfect knowledge of Christ Jesus my Lord, I put away these childish, trifling things, and am determined to read no other books but what lead me to a knowledge of myself and of Christ Jesus.

Search, therefore, the scriptures, my dear brethren; taste and see how good the word of God is, and then you will never leave that heavenly manna, that angel's food, to feed on dry husks, that light bread, those trifling, sinful compositions, in which men of false taste delight themselves: no, you will then disdain such poor entertainment, and blush that yourselves once were fond of it. The word of God will then be sweeter to you than honey, and the honey-comb, and dearer than gold and silver; your souls by reading it, will be filled as it were, with marrow and fatness, and your hearts insensibly molded into the spirit of its blessed Author. In short, you will be guided by God's wisdom here, and conducted by the light of his divine word into glory hereafter.

37. The Indwelling of the Spirit, the Common Privilege of All Believers

John 7:37–39—"In the last day, that great [day] of the feast, Jesus stood and cried, saying, If any man thirst, let him come unto me, and drink. He that believeth on me, as the scripture hath said, out of his belly shall flow rivers of living water. (But this spake he of the Spirit, which they that believe on him should receive."

Nothing has rendered the cross of Christ of less effect; nothing has been a greater stumbling-block and rock of offense to weak minds, that a supposition, now current among us, that most of what is contained in the gospel of Jesus Christ, was designed only for our Lord's first and immediate followers, and consequently calculated but for one or two hundred years. Accordingly, many now read the life, sufferings, death, and resurrection of Jesus Christ, in the same manner as Caesar's Commentaries, or the Conquests of Alexander are read: as things rather intended to afford matter for speculation, than to be acted over again in and by us.

As this is true of the doctrines of the gospel in general, so it is of the operation of God's Spirit upon the hearts of believers in particular; for we no sooner mention the necessity of our receiving the Holy Ghost in these last days, as well as formerly, but we are looked upon by some, as enthusiasts and madmen; and by others, represented as willfully deceiving the people, and undermining the established constitution of the church.

Judge ye then, whether it is not high time for the true ministers of Jesus, who have been made partakers of this heavenly gift, to lift up their voices like a trumpet; and if they would not have those souls perish, for which the Lord Jesus has shed his precious blood, to declare, with all boldness, that the Holy Spirit is the common privilege and portion of all believers in all ages; and that we as well as the first Christians, must receive the Holy Ghost, before we can be truly called the children of God.

For this reason, (and also that I might answer the design of our church in appointing the present festival [Whitsuntide]) I have chosen the words of the text.

They were spoken by Jesus Christ, when he was at the feast of tabernacles. Our Lord attended on the temple-service in general, and the festivals of the Jewish church in particular. The festival at which he was now present, was that of the feast of tabernacles, which the Jews observed according to God's appointment in commemoration of their living in tents. At the last day of this feast, it was customary for many pious people to fetch water from a certain place, and bring it on their heads, singing this anthem out of Isaiah, "And with joy shall they draw water out of the wells of salvation." Our Lord observing this, and it being his constant practice to spiritualize every thing he met with, cries out, "If any man thirst, let him come unto me, (rather than unto that well) and drink. He that believeth on me, as the scripture hath spoken, (where it is said, God will make water to spring out of a dry rock, and such-like) out of his belly shall flow rivers of living water." And that we might know what our Savior meant by this living water, the Evangelist immediately adds, "But this spake he of the Spirit, which they that believe on him should receive."

The last words I shall chiefly insist on in the ensuing discourse: And

First, I shall briefly show, what is meant by the word Spirit.

Secondly, That this Spirit is the common privilege of all believers.

Thirdly, I shall show the reason on which this doctrine is founded. And

Lastly, Conclude with a general exhortation to believe on Jesus Christ, whereby alone we can receive the Spirit.

First, I am to show, what is meant by the word Spirit.

By the Spirit, is evidently to be understood the Holy Ghost, the third person in the ever-blessed Trinity, con-substantial and co-eternal with the Father and the Son, proceeding from, yet equal to them both. For, to use the words of our Church in this day's office, that which we believe of the glory of the Father, the same we believe of the Son, and of the Holy Ghost, without any difference or inequality.

Thus, says St. John, in his first epistle, 1 John 5:7, "There are three that bear record in heaven, the Father, the Word, and the Holy Ghost, and these three are one." And our Lord, when he gave his Apostles commission to go and teach all nations, commanded them to baptize in the name of the Holy Ghost, as well as of the Father and the Son. And St. Peter, Acts 5:3, said to Ananias, "Why hath Satan filled thine heart to lie to the Holy Ghost?" And ver. Acts 5:4, he says, "Thou hast not lied unto men, but unto God." From all which passages, it is plain, that the Holy Ghost, is truly and properly God, as well as the Father and the Son. This is an unspeakable mystery, but a mystery of God's revealing, and, therefore, to be assented to with our whole hearts: seeing God is not a man that he should lie, nor the son of man that he should deceive. I proceed,

Secondly, To prove that the Holy Ghost is the common privilege of all believers.

But, here I would not be understood of to receiving the Holy Ghost, as to enable us to work miracles, or show outward signs and wonders. I allow our adversaries, that to pretend to be inspired, in this sense, is being wise above what is written. Perhaps it cannot be proved, that God ever interposed in this extraordinary manner, but when some new revelation was to be established, as at the first settling of the Mosaic and gospel dispensation: and as for my own part, I cannot but suspect the spirit of those who insist upon a repetition of such miracles at this time. For the world being now become nominally Christian, (though, God knows, little of the power is left among us) there need not outward miracles, but only an inward co-operation of the Holy Spirit with the word, to prove that Jesus is the Messiah which was to come into the world.

Besides, if it was possible for thee, O man, to have faith, so as to be able to remove mountains, or cast out devils; nay, couldst thou speak with the tongue of men and angels, yea, and bid the sun stand still in the midst of heaven; what would all these gifts of the Spirit avail thee, without being made partaker of his sanctifying graces? Saul had the spirit of government for a while, so as to become another man, and yet probably was a cast-away. And many, who cast out devils, in Christ's name, at the last will be disowned by him. If therefore, thou hadst only the gifts, and was destitute of the graces of the Holy Ghost, they would only serve to lead thee with so much the more solemnity to hell.

Here then we join issue with our adversaries, and will readily grant, that we are not in this sense to be inspired, as were our Lord's first Apostles. But unless men have eyes which see not, and ears that hear not, how can they read the latter part of the text, and not confess that the Holy Spirit, in another sense, is the common privilege of all believers, even to the end of the world? "This spake he of the Spirit, which they that believe on him should receive." Observe, he does not say, they that believe on him for one or two ages, but they that believe on him in general, or, at all times, and in all places. So that, unless we can prove, that St. John was under a delusion when he wrote thee words, we must believe that even we also, shall receive the Holy Ghost, if we believe on the Lord Jesus with our whole hearts.

Again, our Lord, just before his bitter passion, when he was about to offer up his soul an offering for the sins of the elect world; when his heart was most enlarged and he would undoubtedly demand the most excellent gift for his disciples, prays, "That they all may be one, as thou, Father, art in me, and I in thee; that they also may be one in us, I in them, and thou in me; that they may be made perfect in one;" that is, that all his true followers might be united to him by his holy Spirit, by as real, vital, and mystical an union, as there was between Jesus Christ and the Father. I say all his true followers; for it is evident, from our Lord's own words, that he had us, and all believers, in view, when he put up this prayer; "Neither pray I for these alone, but for them also which shall believe on me through their word;" so that, unless we treat our Lord as the high priests did, and count him a blasphemer, we must confess, that all who believe in Jesus Christ, through the word, or ministration of his servants, are to be joined to Jesus Christ, by being made partakers of the Holy Spirit.

A great noise hath been made of late, about the word enthusiast, and it has been cast upon the preachers of the gospel, as a term of reproach; but every Christian, in the proper sense of the word, must be an enthusiast; that is, must be inspired of God or have God, by his Spirit, in him. St. Peter tells us, "we have many great and precious promises, that we may be made partakers of the divine nature;" our Lord prays, "that we may be one, as the Father and he are one;" and our own church, in conformity to these texts of Scripture, in her excellent communion-office, tells us, that those who receive the sacrament worthily, "dwell in Christ, and Christ in them; that they are one with Christ, and Christ with them." And yet, Christians must have their names cast out as evil, and ministers in particular, must be looked upon as deceivers of the people, for affirming, that we must be really united to God, by receiving the Holy Ghost. Be astonished, O heavens, at this!

Indeed, I will not say, all our letter-learned preachers deny this doctrine in express words; but however, they do in effect; for they talk professedly against inward feelings, and say, we may have God's Spirit without feeling it, which is in reality to deny the thing itself. And had I a mind to hinder the progress of the gospel, and to establish the kingdom of darkness, I would go about, telling people, they might have the Spirit of God, and yet not feel it.

But to return: When our Lord was about to ascend to his Father and our Father, to his God and our God he gave his apostles this commission, "Go and teach all nations, baptizing them in the name of the Father, and of the Son, and of the Holy Ghost." And accordingly, by authority of this commission, we do teach and baptize in this, and every age of the church. And though we translate the words, "baptizing them in the name;" yet, as the name of God, in the Lord's prayer, and several other places, signifies his nature, they might as well be translated thus, "baptizing them into the nature of the Father, into the nature of the Son, and into the nature of the Holy Ghost." Consequently, if we are all to be baptized into the nature of the Holy Ghost, before our baptism be effectual to salvation, it is evident, that we all must actually receive the Holy Ghost, and ere we can say, we truly believe in Jesus Christ. For no one can say, that Jesus is my Lord, but he that has thus received the Holy Ghost.

Numbers of other texts might be quoted to make this doctrine, if possible, still more plain; but I am astonished, that any who call themselves members; much more, that many, who are preachers in the church of England, should dare so much as to open their lips against it. And yet, with grief I speak it, God is my Judge, persons of the established church seem more generally to be ignorant of it, than any dissenters whatsoever.

But, my dear brethren, what have you been doing? How often have your hearts given your lips the lie how often have you offered to God the sacrifice of fools, and had your prayers turned into sin, if you approve of, and use our church-liturgy, and yet deny the Holy Spirit to be the portion of all believers? In the daily absolution, the minister exhorts the people to pray, that "God would grant them repentance, and his Holy Spirit:" in the Collect for Christmas day, we beseech God, "that he would daily renew us by his Holy Spirit;" in the last week's Collect, we prayed that "we may evermore rejoice in the comforts of the Holy Ghost;" and in the concluding prayer, which we put up every day, we pray, not only that the grace of our Lord Jesus Christ, and the love of God, but that "the fellowship of the Holy Ghost" may be with us all evermore.

But further, a solemn season, to some, is not approaching; I mean the Easter-days, at the end of which, all that are to be ordained to the office of a deacon, are in the sight of God, and in the presence of the congregation, to declare, that "they trust they are inwardly moved by the Holy Ghost, to take upon them that administration;" and to those, who are to be ordained priests, the bishop is to repeat these solemn words, "Receive thou the Holy Ghost, now committed unto them, by the imposition of our hands." And yet, O that I had no reason to speak it, many that use our forms, and many who have witnessed this good confession, yet dare to both talk and preach against the necessity of receiving the Holy Ghost now; and not only so, but cry out against those, who do insist upon it, as madmen, enthusiasts, schismatics, and underminers of the established constitution.

But you are the schismatics, you are the bane of the church of England, who are always crying out, "the temple of the Lord, the temple of the Lord;" and yet starve the people out of our communion, by feeding them only with the dry husks of dead morality, and not bringing out to them the fatted calf; I mean, the doctrines of the operations of the blessed Spirit of God. But here is the misfortune; many of us are not led by, and therefore no wonder that we cannot talk feelingly of, the Holy Ghost; we subscribe to our articles, and make them serve for a key to get into church-preferment, and then preach contrary to those very articles to which we have subscribed.

Far be it from me, to charge all the clergy with this hateful hypocrisy; no, blessed be God, there are some left among us, who dare maintain the doctrines of the Reformation, and preach the truth as it is in Jesus. But I speak the truth in Christ, I lie not; the generality of the clergy are fallen from our articles, and do not speak agreeable to them, or to the form of sound words delivered in the Scriptures; woe be unto such blind leaders of the blind! How can you escape the damnation of hell? It is not all your learning (falsely so called) it is not all your preferments can keep you from the just judgment of God. Yet a little while, and we shall all appear before the tribunal of Christ; there, there will I meet you; there Jesus Christ, the great Shepherd and Bishop of souls, shall determine who are the false prophets; who are the wolves in sheep's clothing. Those who say, that we must now receive and feel the Holy Ghost, or those who exclaim against it, as the doctrine of devils.

But I can no more; it is an unpleasing talk to censure any order of men, especially those who are in the ministry; nor would any thing excuse it but necessity: that necessity which extorted from our Lord himself so many woes against the Scribes and Pharisees, the letter-learned rulers and teachers of the Jewish church; and surely, if I could bear to see people perish for lack of knowledge, and yet be silent towards those who keep from them the key of true knowledge, the very stones would cry out.

Would we restore the church to its primitive dignity, the only way is to live and preach the doctrine of Christ, and the articles to which we have subscribed; then we shall find the number of dissenters will daily decrease, and the church of England become the joy of the whole earth.

I am, in the *Third* place, to show the reasonableness of this doctrine.

I say, the reasonableness of this doctrine; for however it may seem foolishness to the natural man, yet to those, who have tasted of the good word of life, and have felt the power of the world to come, it will appear to be founded on the highest reason; and is capable, to those who have eyes to see, even of a demonstration; I say of demonstration: for it stands on this self-evident truth, that we are fallen creatures, or, to use the scripture-expression, "have all died in Adam."

I know indeed, it is now no uncommon thing amongst us, to deny the doctrine of original sin, as well as the divinity of Jesus Christ; but it is incumbent on those who deny it, first to disprove the authority of the holy Scriptures; if thou canst prove, thou unbeliever, that the book, which we call The Bible, does not contain the lively oracles of God; if thou canst show, that holy men of old, did not write this book, as they were inwardly moved by the Holy Ghost, then will we give up the doctrine of original sin; but unless thou canst do this, we must insist upon it, that we are all conceived and born in sin; if for no other, yet for this one reason, because that God, who cannot lie, has told us so.

But what has light to do with darkness, or polite infidels with the Bible? Alas! as they are strangers to the power, so they are generally as great strangers to the word of God. And therefore, if we will preach to them, we must preach to and from the heart: for talking in the language of scripture, to them, is but like talking in an unknown tongue. Tell me then, O man, whosoever thou art, that deniest the doctrine of original sin, if thy conscience be not seared as with a hot iron! Tell me, if thou dost not find thyself, by nature, to be a mostly mixture of brute and devil? I know these terms will stir up the whole Pharisee in thy heart; but let not Satan hurry thee hence; stop a little, and let us reason together; dost thou not find, that by nature thou art prone to pride? Otherwise, wherefore art thou now offended? Again, dost not thou find in thyself the seeds of malice, revenge, and all uncharitableness? And what are these but the very tempers of the devil? Again, do we not all by nature follow, and suffer ourselves to be led by our natural appetites, always looking downwards, never looking upwards to that God, in whom we live, move, and have our being? And what is this but the very nature of the beasts that perish? Out of thy own heart, therefore, will I oblige thee to confess, what an inspired apostle has long since told us, that "the whole world (by nature) lies in the wicked one;" we are no better than those whom St. Jude calls "brute beasts;" for we have tempers in us all by nature, that prove to a demonstration, that we are earthly, sensual, devilish.

And this will serve as another argument, to prove the reality of the operations of the blessed Spirit on the hearts of believers, against those false professors, who deny there is any such thing as influences of the Holy Spirit, that may be felt. For if they will grant that the devil worketh, and so as to be felt in the hearts of the children of disobedience (which they must grant, unless they will give an apostle the lie) where is the wonder that the good Spirit should have the same power over those who are truly obedient to the faith of Jesus Christ?

If it be true then; that we are all by nature, since the

fall, a mixture of brute an devil, it is evident, that we all must receive the Holy Ghost, ere we can dwell with and enjoy God.

When you read, how the prodigal, in the gospel, was reduced to so low a condition, as to eat husks with swine, and how Nebuchadnezzar was turned out, to graze with oxen; I am confident, you pity their unhappy state. And when you hear, how Jesus Christ will say, at the last day, to all that are not born again of God, "Depart from me, ye cursed, into everlasting fire, prepared for the devil and his angels," do not your hearts shrink within you, with a secret horror? And if creatures, with only our degree of goodness, cannot bear even the thoughts of dwelling with beasts or devils, to whose nature we are so nearly allied, how do we imagine God, who is infinite goodness, and purity itself, can dwell with us, while we are partakers of both their natures? We might as well think to reconcile heaven and hell.

When Adam had eaten the forbidden fruit, he fled and hid himself from God; why? Because he was naked; he was alienated from the life of God, the due punishment of his disobedience. Now, we are all by nature naked and void of God, as he was at that time, and consequently, until we are changed, renewed, and clothed with a divine nature again, we must fly from God also.

Hence then appears the reasonableness of our being obliged to receive the Spirit of God. It is founded on the doctrine of original sin: and, therefore, you will always find, that those who talk against feeling the operations of the Holy Ghost, very rarely, or slightly at least, mention our fall in Adam; no, they refer St. Paul's account of the depravity of unbelievers, only to those of old time. Whereas it is obvious, on the contrary, that we are all equally included under the guilt and consequences of our first parent's sin, even as others; and to use the language of our own church-article, "bring into the world with us, a corruption, which renders us liable to God's wrath, and eternal damnation."

Should I preach to you any other doctrine, I should wrong my own soul; I should be found a false witness towards God and you; and he that preaches any other doctrine, howsoever dignified and distinguished, shall bear his punishment, whosoever he be.

From this plain reason then appears the necessity why we, as well as the first apostles, in this sense, must receive the Spirit of God.

For the great work of sanctification, or making us holy, is particularly reserved to the Holy Ghost; therefore, our Lord says, "Unless a man be born of the Spirit, he cannot enter into the kingdom of God."

Jesus Christ came down to save us, not only from the guilt, but also from the power of sin: and however often we have repeated our creed, and told God we believe in the Holy Ghost, yet, if we have not believed in him, so as to be really united to Jesus Christ by him, we have no more concord with Jesus Christ than Belial himself.

And now, my brethren, what shall I say more? Tell me, are not many of you offended at what has been said already? Do not some of you think, though I mean well, yet I have carried the point a little too far? Are not others ready to cry out, if this be true, who then can be saved? Is not this driving people into despair?

Yes, I ingenuously confess it is; but into what despair? A despair of mercy through Christ? No, God forbid; but a despair of living with God without receiving the Holy Ghost. And I would to God, that not only all you that hear me this day, but that the whole world was filled with this despair. Believe me, I have been doing no more than you allow your bodily physicians to do every day: if you have a wound, and are in earnest about a cure, you bid the surgeon probe it to the very bottom; and shall not the physician of your souls be allowed the same freedom? What have I been doing but searching your natural wounds, that I might convince you of your danger, and put you upon applying to Jesus Christ for a remedy? Indeed I have dealt with you as gently as I could; and now I have wounded, I will attempt to heal you. For I was in the

Last place, to exhort you all to come to Jesus Christ by faith, whereby you, even you also, shall receive the Holy Ghost. "For this spake he of the Spirit, which they that believe on him should receive."

This, this is what I long to come to. Hitherto I have been preaching only the law; but behold I bring you glad tidings of great joy. If I have wounded you, be not afraid; behold, I now bring a remedy for all your wounds. Notwithstanding you are sunk into the nature of the beast and devil, yet, if you truly believe on Jesus Christ, you shall receive the quickening Spirit promised in the text, and be restored to the glorious liberties of the sons of God; I say, if you believe on Jesus Christ. "For by faith we are saved; it is not of works, lest any one should boast." And, however some men may say, there is a fitness required in the creature, and that we must have a righteousness of our own, before we can lay hold on the righteousness of Christ; yet , if we believe the scripture, salvation is the free gift of God, in Christ Jesus our Lord;

and whosoever believeth on him with his whole heart, though his soul be as black as hell itself, shall receive the gift of the Holy Ghost. Behold then, I stand up, and cry out in this great day of the feast, let every one that thirsteth come unto Jesus Christ and drink. "He that believeth on him, out of his belly shall flow (not only streams of rivulets, but whole) rivers of living water." This I speak of the Spirit, which they that believe on Jesus shall certainly receive. For Jesus Christ is the same yesterday, today, and for ever; he is the way, the truth, the resurrection, and the life; "whosoever believeth on him, though he were dead, yet shall he live." There is no respect of persons with Jesus Christ; high and low, rich and poor, one with another, may come to him with an humble confidence, if they draw near by faith; from him we may all receive grace upon grace; for Jesus Christ is full of grace and truth, and ready to save to the uttermost, all that by a true faith turn unto him. Indeed, the poor generally receive the gospel, and "God has chosen the poor in this world, rich in faith." But though not may mighty, not many noble are called; and though it be easier for a camel to go through the eye of a needle, than for a rich man to enter into the kingdom of God, yet, even to you that are rich, do I now freely offer salvation, by Jesus Christ, if you will renounce yourselves, and come to Jesus Christ as poor sinners; I say, as poor sinners; for the "poor in spirit" are only so blessed, as to have a right to the kingdom of God. And Jesus Christ calls none to him, but those who thirst after his righteousness, and feel themselves weary, and heavy laden with the burden of their sins. Jesus Christ justifies the ungodly; he came not to call the righteous, but sinners to repentance.

Do not then say you are unworthy, for this is a faithful and true saying, and worthy of all men to be received, "that Jesus Christ came into the world to save sinners;" and if you are the chief of sinners, if you feel yourselves such, verily Jesus Christ came into the world chiefly to save you. When Joseph was called out of the prison-house to Pharaoh's court, we are told, that he stayed some time to prepare himself; but do you come with all your prison clothes about you; come poor, and miserable, and blind, and naked, as you are, and God the Father shall receive you with open arms, as was the returning prodigal. He shall cover you nakedness with the best robe of his dear Son's righteousness, shall seal you with the signet of his Spirit, and feed you with the fatted calf, even with the comforts of the Holy Ghost. O, let there then be joy in heaven over some of you, as believing; let me not go back to my Master, and say, Lord, they will not believe my report. Harden no longer your hearts, but open them wide, and let the King of glory enter in; believe me, I am willing to go to prison or death for you; but I am not willing to go to heaven without you. The love of Jesus Christ constrains me to lift up my voice like a trumpet. My heart is not fill; out of the abundance of the love which I have for your precious and immortal souls, my mouth now speaketh; and I could now not only continue my discourse until midnight, but I could speak until I could speak no more. And why should I despair of any? No, I can despair of no one, when I consider Jesus Christ has had mercy on such a wretch as I am; but the free grace of Christ prevented me; he saw me in my blood, he passed by me, and said unto me, Live; and the same grace which we sufficient for me, is sufficient for you also; behold, the same blessed Spirit is ready to breathe on all your dry bones, if you will believe on Jesus Christ, whom God has sent; indeed, you can never believe on, or serve a better master, one that is more mighty, or more willing to save; I can say, the Lord Christ is gracious, his yoke is easy, his burden exceeding light; after you have served him many years, like the servants under the law, was he willing to discharge you, you would say, we love our Master, and will not go from him. Come then, my guilty brethren, come and believe on the Lord that bought you with his precious blood; look up by faith, and see him whom you have pierced; behold him bleeding, panting, dying! Behold him with arms stretched out ready to receive you all; cry unto him as the penitent thief did, Lord, remember us now thou art in thy kingdom, and he shall say to your souls, shortly shall you be with me in paradise. For those whom Christ justified, them he also glorifies, even with that glory which he enjoyed with the Father, before the world began. Do not say, I have bought a piece of ground, and must needs go see it; or I have bought a yoke of oxen, and must needs go prove them; or I have married a wife, I am engaged in an eager pursuit after the lust of the eye, and the pride of life, that therefore cannot come. Do not fear having your name cast out as evil, or being accounted a fool for Christ's sake; yet a little while, and you shall shine like the stars in the firmament for ever. Only believe, and Jesus Christ shall be to you wisdom, righteousness, sanctification, and eternal redemption; your bodies shall be fashioned like unto his glorious body, and your souls be partakers of all the fullness of God.

Which God of his infinite mercy.

38. The Resurrection of Lazarus

John 11:43–44—"And when he thus had spoken, he cried with a loud voice, Lazarus, come forth. And he that was dead came forth, bound hand and foot with grave clothes: and his face was bound about with a napkin. Jesus saith unto them, Loose him, and let him go."

When Jesus Christ, the eternal Word, was pleased to make all things by the word of his power, his last works were the best. When he looked back upon, and beheld the first products of his almighty power, he pronounced them "good;" but when that last, that lovely creature man, was formed, he pronounced them "very good." So, the same Jesus, when he came to tabernacle among us, and to begin and carry on a new and second creation, though all his works were miracles of wonder, and manifested forth the glory of his eternal Godhead, yet the nearer he came to the end of his public ministrations, the greater and more noble did the miracles which he wrought appear. The resurrection of Lazarus, that is to be the subject of the following discourse, I think, is a sufficient proof of this. To an eye of sense, it seems to be one of the greatest, if not the very greatest miracle of all which our blessed Lord performed. When our Savior bid John's disciple go and tell their Maser what things they had seen and heard, he commands them to inform him, that by his divine power "the dead were raised;" alluding no doubt to the Ruler's daughter, who was raised immediately after her decease; and the Widow's son, who at the command of Jesus, rose out of his coffin, as they were carrying his corpse to the burial. These were pregnant proofs, that Jesus was indeed the Messiah that was to come into the world. But his raising of Lazarus from the dead, after he had lain four days dead, and saw corruption, is still, if possible, a greater miracle; and consequently a stronger proof of his being the Anointed, the Christ of God. The evangelist John is very particular in giving us an account of this miracle; even so particular, as to spend a whole chapter in relating the circumstances which preceded, attended, and followed after it. And as he was undoubtedly directed herein by the all-wise, unerring Spirit of God, does it not point out unto us, that this miracle, with all its respective circumstances, calls for our particular and most serious meditation? It appears to me in this light; and therefore, as the Lord shall be pleased to assist, I shall go back to the beginning of this chapter, follow the evangelist step by step, and consider the particulars of this wondrous miracle, make some practical observations as I go along, and conclude with some suitable instructions and exhortations, which will naturally arise from the body of the discourse.

The evangelist in the first verse, makes mention of the sickness of Lazarus. "Now, a certain man was sick, named Lazarus of Bethany, the town of Mary, and her sister Martha." Some think these sisters were very wealthy, so as to own good part of the town, or, as the original word seems to imply, the village. But then it is probably the evangelist would have said the town of Lazarus, estates usually descending, as with us, in the male line: it means therefore no more, than that Martha and Mary lived in Bethany. The Holy Ghost pointing out to us hereby, that nothing makes a town so worthy of a gracious soul's remark of esteem, as its having many of God's dear children for its inhabitants. Bethany, though a little place, is more famous because it was the town of Martha and Mary, than if Alexander had fought in it one of his greatest battles. Both these women loved Jesus in sincerity, and were as good as they were great. But Mary, though the younger sister, seems to be the most eminent: for the evangelist in the second verse, speaks of her in a very distinguishing manner. "It was that Mary (that never-to-be-forgotten Mary) which anointed the Lord with ointment (expensive as it was) and wiped his feed, (after she had washed them with tears of love with her hair," even the hair of her head. What notice is taken of this action! With what an eulogy, and in what a high strain of commendation is it here spoken of? And such are the honors of all God's saints. Though all our good works are not recorded as Mary's are, yet God is not unmindful, that he should forget our works of faith, and labors which have proceeded of love. Every tear we shed, every sigh we fetch, every alms we give, though it be only a cup of cold water, are all recorded in the Lamb's book of remembrance, and shall be produced to our eternal honor, and rewarded with a reward of grace, though not of debt, at the great and terrible day of the Lord. "I was an hungered, and ye gave me meat, I was thirsty, and ye gave me drink, naked, and ye clothed me, sick and in prison, and ye came unto me." What reason have we then to be "steadfast and unmovable, always abounding in the work of the Lord, forasmuch as we are assured, that our labors will not be in vain or forgotten by the Lord!" It was that Mary that anointed the Lord with ointment, and wiped his feet with her hair. And what follows? "Whose brother Lazarus was sick." So that being related to Christ, or his disciples, will not exempt persons from sickness. In this life, time and chance happens to all, only with this material difference, those afflictions which harden the obstinately impenitent, soften and purify the heart of a true believer. "My son, therefore despise not the chastening of the Lord (on one hand), nor faint when thou art rebuked of him (on the other): for whom the Lord loveth he chasteneth, and scourgeth every son whom he receiveth."

Verse John 11:5, that "Jesus loved Martha and her sister, and Lazarus." Oh happy family! Three in it beloved of Jesus, with a peculiar, everlasting love. "Very often it so happens, (to use the words of the pious Bishop Beveridge) that there "is but one in a city, and two in a country of this stamp." But here are two sisters and a brother, all lovers of, and beloved by the glorious Jesus. What shall we say to these things? Why, that our savior's grace is free and sovereign, and he may do what he will with his own. They who are thus so highly favored as to have so many converted in one house, ought to be doubly thankful! Such a blessing have not all his saints. No; many, very many, go mourning over their perverse and graceless relations all their lives long; and find, even to their dying day, that their greatest foes are those of their own household. Surely these three relations lived a heaven upon earth. For what can they want, what could make them miserable, who are assured of Jesus' love? But surely if Jesus loves this dear little family, the next news one might think we should hear, would be, that he went immediately and healed Lazarus; or at least cured him at a distance. But instead of that, we are told, verse John 11:6, "When he had heard that he was sick, he abode two days still in the same place where he was." A strange way this, in the eye of natural reason, of expressing love; but not so strange in the eye of faith: for the Lord Jesus very often showeth his love, by deferring to give immediate answers to our prayers. Hereby he tries our faith and patience, and exercises all our passive graces. We have a proof of this in the Syrophonecian woman, upon whom the blessed Jesus frowned, and spake roughly to at first, only that he might afterwards turn unto her and say, "O woman, great is thy faith." Let not those then who believe, make too much haste; or immediately in their hearts repine against the Lord, because he may not answer their requests, in their own time and way. God's time and way is best. And we shall find it to be so in the end. Martha and Mary experienced the truth of this, though undoubtedly our Lord's seeming delay, to come and heal their brother, cost them great searchings of heart. But will the Lord Jesus forget his dear Lazarus, whom his soul loveth? "Can a woman forget her sucking child?" Indeed she may; but the Lord never faileth those that fear him. Neither is he slack concerning his promise, as some men count slackness: for his very delays are answers. The vision is for an appointed time; in the end it will speak and not lie.

Though our Lord abode two days where he was, to try the faith of these sisters, yet after this, he said unto his disciples, verse John 11:7, "Let us go into Judea again." With what a holy familiarity does Jesus converse with his dear children! Our Savior seems to speak to his disciples, as though he was only their brother, and as it were upon a level with them; "Let us go into Judea again." How gently, according to what was predicted of him, does he lead those that are with young! Jesus very well knew the weakness of his disciples, and also what a dangerous place Judea was: how gradually therefore does he make known unto them, his design of going thither! And how does he admit his disciples to expostulate with him on this account! "Master, say they, the Jews of late sought to stone thee, and goest thou thither again?" They were amazed at our Lord's boldness, and were ready to call it presumption; as we generally are prone to censure and condemn other zealous and enterprising persons, as carrying matters too far; it may be for no other reason, if we examine the bottom of our hearts, but because they go before, and excel ourselves. The disciples, no doubt, thought that they spoke out of love to their Lord, and assuredly they did; but what a deal of self-love was there mixed and blended with it? They seem much concerned for their Master, but they were more concerned for themselves. However Jesus overlooks their weakness, and mildly replies, verse John 11:9, and John 11:10, "Are there not twelve hours in the day? If any man walk in the day, he stumbleth not, because he seeth the light of the world; but if any man walk in the night, he stumbleth, because there is no light in him." As though our Lord had said, My dear disciples, I thank you for your care and concern for me. Judea is a dangerous place, and what you say of the treatment I met with from its inhabitants, is just and true: but be not afraid of going there upon my account. For as a man walketh safely twelve hours of the day, because he walketh in the light: so as long as the time appointed by my Father for my public administration lasts, I shall be as secure from the hands of my enemies, as a man that walks in broad-day is secure from falling. But as a man stumbleth if he walketh in the night, so when the night of my passion cometh, then, but not till then, shall I be given up into the hands of my spiteful foes. Oh what comfort have these words, by the blessing of God, frequently brought to my soul! How may all

Christ's ministers strengthen themselves with this consideration, that so long as God hath work for them to do, they are immortal! And if after our work is over, our Lord should call us to lay down our lives for the brethren, and to seal the truth of our doctrine with our blood, it would certainly be the highest honor that can be put upon us. "To you it is given not only to believe, but also to suffer," says the apostle to the Philippians.

"These things the evangelist tells us, ver. John 11:11, said Jesus, and after that, (to satisfy them that he was not going into Judea without a proper call) he saith unto them, Our friend Lazarus sleepeth." Our friend. Amazing! For what is a friend? As one's own soul. How dear then, and near are true believers to the most adorable Jesus! "Our friend *Lazarus*." Still more amazing! Here is condescension, here is unparalleled familiarity indeed. And what of him? "He sleepeth." A figurative way of expression. For what is death to the lovers of Jesus Christ, but a sleep, and a refreshing one too? Thus it is said of Stephan when he died, that "he fell asleep." Christ indeed died, but believers only sleep. And "those that sleep in Jesus, (says the scripture) will God bring with him." "Our friend Lazarus sleepeth." For though he be dead, I shall raise him from the grave so soon, that his dying will be only like a person's taking a short sleep. "Our friend Lazarus sleepeth, but I go that I may awake him out of sleep." By this time, one would imagine, our Lord's disciples should have understood him: But how unwilling are we to believe anything that we do not like. "Then said his disciples, Lord, if he sleep he shall do well." Oh fearful, and slow of heart to believe! How fain would they excuse themselves from going into Judea, for fear of a few stones! By this way of talking, how do they in effect impeach their blessed Master's conduct, and under a pretense of preserving his person, foster, and as it were plead for their own (though perhaps undiscerned) cowardice and unbelief? That charity, which hopeth and believeth all things for the best, teacheth us to judge thus favorably of them. For, "Howbeit Jesus spake of his death: they thought that he had spoken of taking rest in sleep." The great and compassionate High priest knowing and remembering they were but dust, throws a veil of love over their infirmity; and at length, verse John 11:14, "Saith unto them plainly (for if we wait on Jesus, we shall know his will plainly, one way or another) Lazarus is dead." And even then, lest they should be swallowed up with overmuch sorrow, he immediately adds, verse John 11:15, "And I am glad for your sakes that I was not there, to the intent ye may believe," or have more faith, or have that faith which you already possess increased and confirmed. A plain proof this, that all Jesus' delays to answer prayer, are only to strengthen our faith.

"Nevertheless, says our Lord, let us go unto him." This was a sufficient hint, if they knew how to improve it, that he intended to do something extraordinary, though he would not tell them directly what he intended. For the Lord Jesus will keep those whom he loves, at his foot, and dependent on him. "Let us go unto him." He still speaks as though they were his equals. Oh that Christians in general, Oh that ministers in particular, would learn of him their great exemplar, to condescend to men of low degree! Well, the secret is now out. Jesus has said unto them plainly, Lazarus is dead. And what reception does this melancholy news meet with? With great condolence, especially from Thomas; for verse John 11:16, "Then said Thomas, who is called Didymus, unto his fellow disciples, let us also go and die with him;" i.e. according to some, with Lazarus, with whom, it may be Thomas had contracted an intimate acquaintance. But granting it was so; shall I commend him for this passionate expression? I commend him not. Surely he spake unadvisedly with his lips; "Let us also go and die with him." As though there was no comfort henceforward to be expected in the world, now his friend Lazarus was gone. This was a great fault, and yet a fault that many of God's children run into daily, by mourning for their deceased relations overmuch, like persons that have no hope. But this infirmity ought not to be indulged. For if our friends and dear relatives are dead, Jesus, that friend of sinners, is not dead. He will be better to us than seven sons, and will abundantly supply the place of all creature-comforts. But I am more inclined to think that the word *Him*, refers to Jesus his dear Master; and if so, he is so far from being blamed, that he spake like a good soldier of Jesus Christ. Let us also go, that we may die with him. If our dear master will go into Judea, and hazard his precious life, let us not any longer make such frivolous excuses, but let us manfully accompany him; and if the Jews should not only be permitted to stone, but also to kill him, let us also go and die with him, we cannot die in a better cause. This was a speech worthy of a Christian hero, and Thomas herein hath set us an example, that we should follow his steps, by exciting and provoking one another closely to adhere to the blessed Jesus, especially when his cause and interest is in any immediate danger. This exhortation, it seems, had a proper effect. They all went, and as far as we know, cheerfully accompanied their glorious Master.

How their thoughts were exercised on the road, we are

not told. But I am apt to believe they were a little discouraged when they came to Bethany. For "When Jesus came, he found that Lazarus had been in the grave for four days already." And what would it avail them, to come so many miles only to see a dead man's tomb? But how wisely were all things ordered by the blessed Jesus, to manifest his glory in the most extraordinary manner, that not only his disciples might have their faiths confirmed, but many also of the Jews might believe on him. This Bethany, it seems, verse John 11:18, "was nigh unto Jerusalem, about fifteen furlongs off;" or about two miles; and Martha and Mary, being what we may call people of fashion, and devout likewise; many of the devout, and we may suppose many of the wealthy Jews came from the metropolis, as well as other adjacent places, verse John 11:19, to Martha and Mary; not to pay an idle, trifling, but a serious, profitable visit, "to comfort them concerning their brother." This was kind and neighborly. To weep with those that weep, and to visit the afflicted in their distresses, is one essential branch of true and undefiled religion. And O how sweet is it when we visit surviving friends, that we have reason to think that their departed relations died in the Lord! And we can therefore give them comfort concerning them. For "blessed are the dead, that die in the Lord, even so saith the Spirit, for they rest from their labors." This and such-like arguments, no doubt, these visitors made use of, to comfort Martha and Mary. And indeed they stood in much need of consolation. For we have reason to suppose, from our Lord" answer, "This sickness is not unto death, but the glory of God;" that they had entertained thoughts of the recovery of their brother. But who can tell what these two holy souls must feel, when they found their brother did not recover, but was dead, laid out, and now stinking in the silent grave! What hard thoughts, without judging them, may we suppose they entertained concerning Jesus! Think you not that they were ready to cry out in the language of the prophet, "Thou hast deceived us, and we are deceived?" But man's extremity is Jesus' opportunity. In the multitude of the sorrows that they had in their hearts, the news of Christ's coming refreshes their souls. Somebody or another, commendably officious [direct, forceful, forward], privately informs Martha of it. "Who, as soon as she heart that Jesus was come (without making any apology to the company for her rudeness) went and met him. But Mary sat still in the house." But why so, Mary? I thought thou hadst been most forward to attend on Jesus, and thy sister Martha more prone to be cumbered about the many things of this life. Why sittest thou still? It may be the news was brought only privately to Martha (for it is plain from verse 31st, that the Jews who were in the house knew not of it;) and Martha knowing how our Lord had chid her once, was resolved he should have no reason on the same account to chide her anymore; therefore when the news was brought, she would not so much as stay to inform her sister, but went out to see whether it were true or not, and if so, as the eldest sister, she would invite the blessed Jesus in. How happy is it, when Christ's reproofs for past neglects, excite our future zeal to come out and meet him! Such reproofs are an excellent oil. Or, it may be, the news reached Mary's ears, as well as Martha's, but being overcome with sorrow, the thought is too good news to be true, and therefore sat still in the house. O how careful ought believers to be, to cherish and maintain, even in the midst of tribulation, a holy confidence and joy in God! For the joy of the Lord is a believer's strength. Whereas giving way to melancholy and unbelief, raises gloom and vapors in the mind, clouds the understanding, clogs us in the way of duty, and gives the enemy, who loves to fish in troubled waters, a very great advantage over us.

Mary, perhaps, through the prevalence of this, and being also naturally of a sedentary disposition, "sat still in the house," while her sister Martha got the start of her, and went out to meet Jesus. And how does she accost him? Why, in a language bespeaking the distress of a burdened and disordered mind. For she said unto Jesus, verse John 11:21, "Lord, if thou hadst been here, my brother had not died." Here is a mixture of faith and unbelief. Faith made her say, "Lord, if thou hadst been here, my brother had not died." But unbelief made her confine Christ's power to his bodily presence. Besides, here was a tacit accusation of the blessed Jesus of unkindness, for not coming when they sent unto him the message, "Lord, he whom thou lovest is sick." Once she charged Jesus with want of care; "Lord, carest thou not, that my sister hath left me to serve alone?" Now she taxes him with want of kindness. "If thou hadst been here;" as much as to say, if thou hadst been so kind as to have come when we sent for thee," "my brother had not died;" and by saying thus, she does as it were lay her brother's death to Jesus Christ. O how apt are even those whom Jesus loves in a peculiar manner, to charge him foolishly! How often does the enmity of our desperately wicked hearts rise against Christ, when we are under the afflicting hand of his providence! And not the very best of us frequently tempted, in such circumstances, to say within ourselves at least, Why does God thus cruelly deal with us? Why did not he keep off this stroke, seeing it was in his power to have prevented it? How should we be ashamed and confounded before him upon this account? How should we pray and labor to be delivered from this remaining enmity of the heart, and long for that time, when mortality shall be swallowed up of life, and we shall never feel one single rising of heart, against a good and gracious, and all-wise and glorious Redeemer, any more? However, to do Martha justice, she pretty well recovers herself, verse John 11:22, "But I know, that even now, whatsoever thou wilt ask of God, God will give it to thee." Whether these words imply an actual belief of our Lord's divinity, is not certain. To me they do; because we shall presently find, that she did believe our Lord was the Son of God, and the Messiah which was to come into the world. Therefore when she said, she knew that whatsoever he asked of God, God would give it to him, she may be understood as referring to God the Father, under whom the Lord Jesus acted as Mediator, though equal to him in respect to his eternal glory and godhead. This mystery we may well suppose her acquainted with, because Jesus had been frequently preaching at her house, and consequently, had opened that mystery unto her. O what a blessed thing must it be to have such a Mediator! Such an high-priest and intercessor at the Father's right-hand, that whatever he asks the father in our behalf, he will give unto us! Jesus takes this kindly at Martha's hand, and passes over her infirmity. For if the Lord was exact to mark every thing that we say or do amiss, alas! who could abide? He only calmly says unto her, verse John 11:23, "Thy brother shall rise again."

Glad tidings these of great joy. This should comfort us concerning our deceased, pious relations, that ere long they shall rise again, and soul and body be for ever with the Lord. Howbeit Jesus spake here of an immediate resurrection, though he did not speak plainly: For Christ loves to exercise the faith and patience of his disciples, and frequently leaves them to find out his meaning by degrees. It is best for us in our present state, that it should be so. In heaven it will be otherwise. "Thy brother, (says Christ to Martha) shall rise again." She might immediately have replied, When, Lord? But she fetches a circuit as it were, and labors to find out the mind of Jesus by degree. "I know, says she, that he shall rise again at the resurrection of the last day." These words seem to imply, that she had some distant thought of our Lord's design to raise her brother now, and that she spoke thus only to draw our Savior to speak, and tell her plainly whether he meant to do so or not. Those who are acquainted with Jesus, are taught an holy art by the blessed Spirit, in dealing with their blessed master. "I know, says she, he shall rise again at the resurrection of the last day," (a notable proof this, by the way, that the pious Jews believed the resurrection of the body). It is just the same as though she had said, Lord, dost thou mean that my brother shall rise again before that time? Our savior wisely keeps off from giving her a direct answer, but chooses rather to preach to her heart. "Jesus said unto her, I am the resurrection and the life: He that believeth in me, though he were dead, yet shall he live." On this Martha's faith, if in exercise, might take hold. O glorious words! How encouraging to you poor sinners lying in your blood! Though you are dead in trespasses and sins, and might justly be condemned to die the second death, yet if you believe on the Lord Jesus you shall live. He adds, "And whosoever believeth in me shall never die;" never die as to their souls, never die eternally, and consequently never finally fall away from God. This is an encouraging soul-comforting declaration for you, O believers, who are thus kept, as it were, in a garrison, by the mighty power of God, through faith, unto salvation! "Believest thou this?" says Christ to Martha, verse John 11:26 What avail all the many great and precious promises of the gospel, unless they are applied and brought home in particular to each of our souls? The word does not profit unless it is mixed with faith. We therefore do well, when we are reading Christ's words, to put this question to ourselves; O my soul, believest thou this? And well would it be for us, if upon putting this question to ourselves, we could with the same holy confidence, and in the same delightful frame, say with Martha, verse John 11:27, "Yea, Lord: I believe that thou art the Christ, the Son of God, which should come into the world." This I think is a direct confession of our Lord's divinity. How full was her heart when she spoke these words! I am persuaded it burnt within her. What a divine warmth had she contracted by talking with Jesus! How does she long that her sister might share in her holy joy! For when she had so said, verse John 11:28, "she went away;" full of love, no doubt, and called Mary her sister, as all will labor to call their near relations, who have felt the Lord Jesus to be the resurrection and the life themselves. But Martha took care, in the midst of her zeal (as we should always do) to behave with prudence; and therefore "she called her sister secretly, saying, The master is come, and calleth for thee." The master is come. She need say no more; Mary knew very well whom she meant. For holy souls easily understand one another when talking of their master Jesus. The divine Herbert used to delight (when speaking of Jesus) to say, "My Master;" perhaps he learned if of Martha, who said here, "The Master is come, and calleth for thee? Surely a woman of thy exalted piety will not tell a deliberate lie, and in order to induce thy sister to come to Jesus, acquaint her that Jesus called her, when indeed he did not. Thou needest not put thyself to such an expense, or do so much evil, that good may come of it. Only mention Jesus to Mary, and let her know for a certainty that the Master id indeed come, and I am persuaded she will sit no longer. Martha no doubt knew, and therefore I cannot judge her as some do, as though in her haste she said what was not true. For Jesus might bid her to call her sister, though it be not directly mentioned in this chapter. And it is very probably, that our Lord did inquire after Mary, because she used to take such great delight in sitting at his feet, and hearing the gracious words that proceeded our of his mouth. "The Master is come (saith Martha to her sister) and calleth for thee." And so say I to all poor sinners. Jesus, your Lord and Master, your Prince and Savior, is come, come unto this lower world, and is come this day in his word, and by me, who am less than the least of all his servants, and calleth for you. O that he may also come in the demonstration of the Spirit, and by his mighty power bow your stubborn hearts and wills to obey the call, as holy Mary did.

For we are told, verse John 11:29, "When she heard that, she rose quickly, and came to Jesus." Sinners, when will you do so? Or why do you not do so? How know you whether Jesus will call for you any more, before he calls you by death to judgment? Linger, O linger no longer. Fly, fly for your lives. Arise quickly, and with Mary come to Jesus. She obeyed the call so very speedily, that her haste was taken notice of by her visitors. "The Jews then, who were with her in the house, and comforted her, when they saw Mary that she rose up hastily (without any ceremony at all) and went out, followed her, saying, she goeth to the grave, to weep there." How wisely does our Lord permit and order all this, to bring the Jews out to behold the wonderful miracle that he was about to perform! Little did Mary and the Jews think for what end they were thus providentially led out. But when Jesus hath work to be done, he will bring souls to the place where he intends to call them, in spite of men or devils. But how does Mary behave when she comes to Jesus? We may be assured, not without great humility. No wonder then we are told, verse John 11:32, that "when she saw him, she immediately fell down at his feet (a place Mary had been used to, and in an agony of grief, says, as her sister had done before her) Lord, if thou hadst been here, my brother had not died." Poor Mary! Her concern was great indeed. Though she was a holy woman, she could not well bear the loss of her brother. She knew very well, that the world would miss him, and no doubt he had been a kind and tender brother to her. But I am afraid she was sinfully overcome with overmuch sorrow. However, had we been there, the sight must have affected us. It seems to have affected the visitors, especially the blessed Jesus. He, instead of blaming her, for her tacitly accusing him of unkindness, and for not coming to her brother's relief, pities and sympathizes both with Mary and her weeping friends! "When Jesus saw her weep, and the Jews also weeping, he groaned in his Spirit, and was troubled." Troubled: Not with any sinful perturbation we may be assured: nothing of that nature could possibly be in his sinless soul. And, therefore, some have judiciously enough compared the trouble our Lord now felt, to some crystal water shaken in a glass or bottle; you may shake it, but there will be no sediment: it will be crystal water still. "He groaned in is spirit." I do not see why this may not be understood of his praying in the spirit, which maketh intercession for the saints, with *ajlalhvtoi stenagmoi'*, "groanings that cannot be uttered." Romans 8:26," Methinks I see the immaculate Lamb of God, secretly, but powerfully agonizing with his Father; his heart is big with sympathy! At length, out of the fullness of it, he said, ver. John 11:34, "Where have ye laid him? They (I suppose Mary and Martha) say unto him, Lord, come and see." He came, he say, "He wept," ver. John 11:35, It is put in a verse by itself, that we might pause a while, and ask, why Jesus wept?

He wept, to show us, that is was no sin to shed a tear of love and resignation at the grave of a deceased friend; he wept, so see what havoc sin had made in the world, and how it had reduced man, who was originally little lower than the angels, (by making him subject to death) to a level with the beasts that perish: but above all, he wept at the foresight of the people's unbelief; he wept, to think how many then present, would not only not believe on, but would be hardened, and have their prejudices increased more and more against him, though he should raise Lazarus from the dead before their eyes. Well then may ministers be excused, who, whilst they are preaching, now and then drop a few tears, at the consideration of their sermons being, through the perverseness and unbelief of many of their audience, a savor of death unto death, instead of a savor of life unto life. Upon a like occasion Jesus wept. What an affecting sight was here!

Let us for a while suppose ourselves placed amidst these holy mourners; let us imagine that we see the sepulcher just before us, and the Jews, and Mary, and the blessed Jesus weeping round it. Surely, the most obdurate of us all must drop a tear, or at least be affected with the sight; we find that it affected those who were really by-standers: for then said the Jews, ver. John 11:36, "Behold, how he loved him." And did they say, Behold, how he loved him, when Jesus only shed a few tears over the grave of his departed Lazarus? Come then, O sinners, and view Christ dying and pouring out his precious heart's blood for you upon an accursed tree, and then surely you must needs cry out, Behold, how he loved us!

But alas, though all were affected, yet, it seems, all were not well affected at seeing Jesus weep! For we are told, ver. John 11:37, that some of them said, "Could not this man, who opened the eyes of the blind, have caused that even this man should not have died?" One would imagine, that Satan himself could scarce have uttered a more perverse speech: every word is full of spite and rancor. Could not this man, this fellow, this deceiver, who pretends to say, that he opened the eyes of the blind, have caused that this man, whom he seems to love so, should not have died? Is not this a sufficient proof that he is a cheat? Have we catched him at last? Is it likely that he really helped others, when he could not help his own friend?—O how patient ought the servants of our Lord to be! And how may they expect to be censured, and have their good deeds questioned, and lessened, when their blessed Master has been thus treated before them! However, Jesus will do good, notwithstanding all these slights put upon him; and therefore, again groaning in himself, "he cometh to the grave; it was a cave, (or vault, as is customary in great families) and a stone lay upon it; Jesus said, ver. John 11:39, "Take ye away the stone." How gradually does our Lord proceed, in order to engage the people's attention the more! Methinks I see them all eye, all ear, and eagerly waiting to see the issue of this affair. But Martha now returning with the rest of the company, seems to have lost that good frame which she was in when she went to call her sister; "She saith unto him, ver. John 11:39," Lord, by this time he stinketh: for he hath been either dead or buried for four days." O the dismal effects of carnal reasoning! How naturally do we fall into doubts and fears, when we have not our eye simply directed to the blessed Jesus! Martha, instead of looking up to him, looks down into the grace, and poring upon her brother's stinking corpse, falls into a fit of unbelief: "By this time he stinketh;" and, therefore,

a sight of him will only be offensive. Perhaps she might think our Lord only wanted to take a view of her brother Lazarus; Jesus therefore, to give her yet a further hint, that he intended to do something extraordinary, saith unto her, ver. John 11:40, "Said I not unto thee, that if thou wouldst believe, thou shouldst see the glory of God?" Our Lord speaks here with some degree of warmth: for nothing displeases him more than the unbelief of his own disciples. "Said I not unto thee, if thou wouldst believe, thou shouldst see the glory of God?" When Christ first spoke these words unto her, we are not told; it might be, this was part of their conversation upon another occasion some time before: however, he checks her openly for her unbelief now: for those whom Jesus loves, must expect to be rebuked sharply by him, whenever they dishonor him by unbelief. The reproof is taken.

Without making any more objections, "They took away the stone from the place where the dead was laid." And now behold with what solemnity the holy Jesus prepares himself to execute his gracious design! "And Jesus lift up his eyes, and said, Father, I thank thee that thou hast heard me; and I knew that thou hearest me always: but because of the people which stand by, I said it, that they may believe that thou hast sent me." Who can express with what fervor and intenseness of spirit, our glorious High-priest uttered these words! They are a thanksgiving arising from an assurance that his father had heard him: for Christ, as Mediator, was inferior to the Father. "I knew that thou hearest me always (and so may every believer in his degree say so); but because of the people which stand by, I said it."—Said what? We do not hear that Jesus said any thing by way of prayer before; and that is true, if we mean vocally, but mentally he did say something, even when he groaned in the spirit once and again, and was troubled. There is a way of praying, even when we do not, and cannot speak. "Why cryest thou," said God to Moses; though we do not hear that he spoke one single word: but he cried in his heart. And I observe this for the comfort of some weak, but real Christians, who think they never pray, unless they can have a great flow of words; but this is a great mistake: for we often pray best, when we can speak least. There are times when the heart is too big to speak: and the spirit itself maketh intercession for the saints, and that too according to the will of God, with groanings that cannot be uttered. Such was Hannah's prayer for a son, "She spake not, only her lips moved:" and such was our Lord's way of praying at this time. And perhaps the soul is never in a better frame, than when in a holy stillness, and unspeakable serenity, it can put itself as a blank in Jesus' hand, for him to stamp on it just what he pleases.

And now the hour of our Savior's performing this long-expected miracle, is come. Ver. John 11:43, "When he thus had spoken, he cried with a loud voice, Lazarus, come forth." With the word there went an irresistible power: he spake, and it was done: he cried, and behold, "He that was dead came forth bound hand and foot with grave clothes; and his face was bound about with a napkin." What sight was here! Methinks I see surprise sit upon each spectator's face: as the body rises, their wonder rises too. See how they gaze! See how their looks bespeak the language of astonished hearts; and all with a kind of silent, but expressive oratory, ready to say, What manner of man is this? Surely this is the Messiah that was to come into the world. How did the hearts of Martha and Mary, as we may very well suppose, leap for joy! How were they ashamed of themselves, for charging Jesus foolishly, and taxing him with unkindness, for not coming to prevent their brother's dying! It is true, Christ suffered him to die, but behold he is not alive again! Jesus never denies us one thing, but he intends to give us something better in the stead of it. Think you not that Martha and Mary were not the most officious to obey our blessed Lord's command, "Loose him, and let him go?" That same power that raised Lazarus from the dead, might have also taken the grave-clothes from him: but Jesus Christ never did, and never will work a needless miracle. Others could unloose his grave-clothes, but Jesus could unloose the bands of death.

And now, perhaps, some may be ready to ask, What news hath Lazarus brought from the other world! But stop, O man, thy vain curiosity! It is forbidden, and therefore useless knowledge. The scriptures are silent concerning it. Why should we desire to be wise above what is written? It becomes us rather to be wholly employed in adoring the gracious hand of that mighty Redeemer who raised him from the dead, and to see (now we have heard the history) what improvement we can make of such a remarkable and instructive transaction.

Would to God that my preaching upon the resurrection of Lazarus today, may have the same blessed effects upon you, as the sight of it had upon some of the standers-by. For we are told, ver. John 11:45, "Then many of the Jews who came to Mary, and had seen the things which Jesus did, believed on him." A profitable visit this! the best, no doubt, that they ever paid in their lives. And this was in answer to our Savior's prayer, "But because of the people who stand by, I said it, that they may believe, that thou hast sent me." One would imagine, that all who saw this miracle, were induced thereby, really to believe on him: But alas! I could almost say, that I can tell you of a greater miracle than raising Lazarus from the dead. And what is that? Why, that some of these very persons who were on the spot, instead of believing on him, "went their way to the Pharisees, and told them what Jesus had done." Ver. John 11:46, It was so far from convincing them, that it only excited their envy, stirred up the whole hell of their self-righteous hearts, and made them, from that day forward, "take counsel together," to execute what they had long before designed, to put the innocent Jesus to death. See how busy they are, ver John 11:47, "Then gathered the chief priests and the Pharisees a council, and said, What do we? For this man doeth many miracles." Envy itself, it seems, could not deny that. And need they say then, "What do we," or what should we do? Believe in, to be sure, and submit to him; take up the cross, and follow him. No; on the contrary, say they, ver John 11:48, "If we let him this alone, (which they would not have done so long, had not God put a hook in the Leviathan's jaws) all men will believe on him." And suppose they did? Then all men would be blessed indeed, and have a title to true happiness. No, say they, "then the Romans shall come and take away both our place and nation." But were not the Romans come already? Were they not at this time tributaries to Caesar? But they were afraid of the church as well as the state: "They will come and take away our place," our place of worship: and consequently, they look upon Jesus Christ and his proceedings, and adherents, as dangerous both to church and state.

This hath been always the method of Pharisees and high-priests, when they have been taking counsel against the Lord Jesus, and his dear anointed ones. But they need not have been afraid on this account: for our Savior's kingdom neither was, nor is of this world; and the only way to have preserved their place and nation, was to have countenanced, and as much as in them lay, caused all to believe on Jesus. How miserably were they out in their politics! The death of Jesus, which they thought would save, was the grand cause of the utter destruction both of their place and nation: And so will all politics formed against Christ and his gospel end at last in the destruction of those who contrived them.

O the desperate wickedness and treachery of man's deceitful heart! Where are the scribes, where are the infidels, where are the letter-learned disputers of this world, who are daily calling for a repetition of miracles, in order to confirm and evidence the truth of the Christian religion? Surely if they believe not Moses and the prophets, neither would they believe, though one rose from the dead. Here was one raised from the dead before many witnesses, and yet all those witnesses did by no means believe on Jesus. For divine faith is not wrought in the heart by moral persuasion (though moral suasion is very often made use of as a means to convey it); faith is the peculiar gift of God: no one can come to Jesus unless the Father draw him: and, therefore, that I may draw near the close of this discourse, let me shut up all with a word of exhortation.

Come, ye dead, Christless, unconverted sinners, come and see the place where they laid the body of the deceased Lazarus; behold him laid out, bound hand and foot with grave-clothes, locked up and stinking in a dark cave, with a great stone placed on the top of it! View him again and again; go nearer to him; be not afraid; smell him, ah! How he stinketh. Stop there now, pause a while; and whilst thou art gazing upon the corpse of Lazarus, give me leave to tell thee with great plainness, but greater love, that this dead, bound, entombed, stinking carcass, is but a faint representation of thy poor soul in its natural state: for, whether thou believest it or not, thy spirit which thou bearest about with thee, sepulchered in flesh and blood, is as literally dead to God, and as truly dead in trespasses and sins, as the body of Lazarus was in the cave. Was he bound hand and foot with grave-clothes? So art thou bound hand and foot with thy corruptions: and as a stone was laid on the sepulcher, so is there a stone of unbelief upon thy stupid heart. Perhaps thou hast lain in this state, not only four days, but many years, stinking in God's nostrils. And; what is still more affecting, thou art as unable to raise thyself out of this loathsome, dead state, to a life of righteousness and true holiness, as ever Lazarus was to raise himself from the cave in which he lay so long. Thou mayest try the power of thy own boasted free-will, and the force and energy of moral persuasion and rational arguments (which, without all doubt, have their proper place in religion); but all thy efforts, exerted with never so much vigor, will prove quite fruitless and abortive, till that same Jesus, who said, "Take away the stone," and cried, "Lazarus, come forth," comes by his mighty power, removes the stone of unbelief, speaks life to thy dead soul, looses thee from the fetters of thy sins and corruptions, and by the influences of his blessed Spirit, enables thee to arise, and to walk in the way of his holy commandments. And O that he would now rend the heavens, and come down amongst you! O that there may be a stirring among the dry bones this day! O that whilst I am speaking, and saying, "Dead sinners, come forth," a power, an almighty power might accompany the word, and cause you to emerge into new life!

If the Lord should vouchsafe me such a mercy, and but one single soul in this great congregation, should arise and shake himself from the dust of his natural state; according to the present frame of my heart, I should not care if preaching this sermon here in the fields, was an occasion of hastening my death, as raising Lazarus hastened the death of my blessed Master. For methinks death, in some respects, is more tolerable, than to see poor sinners day by day lying sepulchered, dead and stinking in sin. O that you saw how loathsome you are in the sight of God, whilst you continue in your natural state! I believe you would not so contentedly hug your chains, and refuse to be set at liberty.

Methinks I see some of you affected at this part of my discourse. What say you? Are there not some ready to complain, alas! we have some relations present, who are so notoriously wicked, that they not only hug their chains, but make a mock of sin, and stink not only in the sight of God, but man. Dear souls! You are ready to urge this, as a reason why Jesus will not raise them; and think it hard, perhaps, that Jesus does not come, in answer to your repeated groans and prayers, to convert and save them. But what Jesus said unto Martha, I say unto you, "Believe, and you shall see the glory of God." Think it not a thing incredible, that God should raise their dead souls. Think not hard of Jesus for delaying an answer to your prayers: assure yourselves he heareth you always. And who knows, but this day Jesus may visit some of your dear relations hearts, upon whose account you have traveled [travailed] in birth till Christ be formed in them? You have already sympathized with Martha and Mary, in their doubts and fears; who knows but you may also be partakers of that joy which their souls experienced, when they received their risen brother into their longing arms.

O Christless souls, you do not know what grief your continuance in sin occasions to your godly relations! You do not know how you grieve the heart of Jesus. I beseech you give him no fresh cause to weep over you upon account of your unbelief: let him not again groan in his spirit and be troubled. Behold how he has loved you, even so as to lay down his life for you. What could he do more? I pray you, therefore, dead sinners, come forth; arise and sup with Jesus. This was an honor conferred on Lazarus, and the same honor awaits you. Not that you shall sit down with him personally in this life, as

Lazarus did, but you shall sit down with him at the table of his ordinances, especially at the table of the Lord's supper, and ere long sit down with him in the kingdom of heaven.

Happy, thrice happy ye, who are already raised from spiritual death, and have an earnest of an infinitely better and more glorious resurrection in your hearts. You know a little, how delightful it must have been to Martha and Mary and Lazarus, to sit down with the blessed Jesus here below; but how infinitely more delightful will it be, to sit down, not only with Mary and Martha, but with Abraham, Isaac, and Jacob, and all your other dear brethren and sisters, in the kingdom of heaven. Do you not long for that time, when Jesus shall say unto you, "Come up hither?" Well! Blessed be God, yet a little while, and that same Jesus, who cried with a loud voice, "Lazarus, come forth;" shall with the same voice, and with the same power, speak unto all that are in their graves, and they shall come forth. That all who hear me this day may be then enabled to lift up their heads and rejoice, that the day of their complete redemption is indeed fully come, may Jesus Christ grant, for his infinite mercy's sake. Amen, and Amen.

39. The Holy Spirit Convincing the World of Sin, Righteousness, and Judgment

John 16:8—"And when he is come, he will reprove the world of sin, and of righteousness, and of judgment."

These words contain part of a gracious promise, which the blessed Jesus was pleased to make to his weeping and sorrowful disciples. The time was now drawing near, in which the Son of man was first to be lifted up on the cross, and afterwards to heaven. Kind, wondrous kind! Had this merciful High-priest been to his disciples, during the time of his tabernacling amongst them. He had compassion on their infirmities, answered for them when assaulted by their enemies, and set them right when out of the way, either in principle or practice. He neither called nor used them as servants, but as friends; and he revealed his secrets to them from time to time. He opened their understandings, that they might understand the scriptures; explained to them the hidden mysteries of the kingdom of God, when he spoke to others in parables: nay, he became the servant of them all, and even condescended to wash their feet. The thoughts of parting with so dear and loving a Master as this, especially for a long season, must needs affect them much. When on a certain occasion he intended to be absent from them only for a night, we are told, he was obliged to constrain them to leave him; no wonder then, that when he now informed them he must entirely go away, and that the Pharisees in his absence should put them out of their synagogues, and excommunicate them; yea, that the time should come, that whosoever killed them, would think they did God service (a prophecy, one would imagine, in an especial manner designed for the suffering ministers of this generation); no wonder, I say, considering all this, that we are told, John 16:6, Sorrow had filled their hearts: "Because I have said these things unto you, sorrow hath filled your hearts." The expression is very emphatical; their hearts were so full of concern, that they were ready to burst. In order, therefore, to reconcile them to this mournful dispensation, our dear and compassionate Redeemer shows them the necessity he lay under to leave them; "Nevertheless I tell you the truth; it is expedient for you that I go away:" As though he had said, Think not, my dear disciples, that I leave you out of anger: no, it is for your sakes, for your profit, that I go away: for if I go not away, if I die not upon the cross for your sins, and rise again for your justification, and ascend into heaven to make intercession, and plead my merits before my Father's throne; the Comforter, the Holy Ghost, will not, cannot come unto you; but if I depart, I will send him unto you. And that they might know what he was to do, "When he is come, he will reprove the world of sin, and of righteousness, and of judgment."

The person referred to in the words of the text, is plainly the Comforter, the Holy Ghost; and the promise was first made to our Lord's apostles. But though it was primarily made to them, and was literally and remarkably fulfilled at the day of Pentecost, when the Holy Ghost came down as a mighty rushing wind, and also when three thousand were pricked to the heart by Peter's preaching; yet, as the Apostles were the representatives of the whole body of believers, we must infer, that this promise must be looked upon as spoken to us, and to our children, and to as many as the Lord our God shall call.

My design from these words, is to show the manner in which the Holy Ghost generally works upon the hearts of those, who, through grace, are made vessels of mercy, and translated from the kingdom of darkness into the kingdom of God's dear Son.

I say, *generally*: For, as God is a sovereign agent, his sacred Spirit bloweth not only on whom, but when and how it listeth. Therefore, far be it from me to confine the Almighty to one way of acting, or say, that all undergo an equal degree of conviction: no, there is a holy variety in God's methods of calling home his elect. But this we may affirm assuredly, that, wherever there is a work of true conviction and conversion wrought upon a sinner's heart, the Holy Ghost, whether by a greater or less degree of inward soul-trouble, does that which our Lord Jesus told the disciples, in the words of the text, that he should do when he came.

If any of you ridicule inward-religion, or think there is no such thing as our feeling or receiving the Holy Ghost, I fear my preaching will be quite foolishness to you, and that you will understand me no more than if I spoke to you in an unknown tongue. But as the promise in the text, is made to the world, and as I know it will be fulfilling till time shall be no more, I shall proceed to explain the general way whereby the Holy Ghost works upon every converted sinner's heart; and I hope that the Lord, even whilst I am speaking, will be pleased to fulfill it in many of your hearts. "And when he is come, he will reprove the world of sin, or righteousness, and of judgment."

The word, which we translate reprove, ought to be rendered convince; and in the original it implies a conviction by way of argumentation, and coming with a power upon the mind equal to a demonstration. A great many scoffers of these last days, will ask such as they term pretenders to the Spirit, how they feel the Spirit, and how they know the Spirit? They might as well ask, how they know, and how they feel the sun when it shines upon the body? For with equal power and demonstration does the Spirit of God work upon and convince the soul. And,

First, It convinces of sin; and generally of some enormous sin, the worst perhaps the convicted person ever was guilty of. Thus, when our Lord was conversing with the woman of Samaria, he convinced her first of her adultery: "Woman, go call thy husband. The woman answered, and said, I have no husband. Jesus said unto her, Thou hast well said, I have no husband: for thou hast had five husbands, and he whom thou now hast, is not thy husband: in this saidst thou truly." With this there went such a powerful conviction of all her other actual sins, that soon after, "she left her water-pot, and went her way into the city, and saith to the men, Come, and see a man that told me all things that ever I did: is not this the Christ?" Thus our Lord also dealt with the persecutor Saul: he convinced him first of the horrid sin of persecution; "Saul, Saul, why persecutest thou me?" Such a sense of all his other sins, probably at the same time revived in his mind, that immediately he died; that is, died to all his false confidences, and was thrown into such an agony of soul, that he continued three days, and neither did eat nor drink. This is the method the Spirit of God generally takes in dealing with sinners; he first convinces them of some heinous actual sin, and at the same time brings all their other sins into remembrance, and as it were sets them in battle-array before them: "When he is come, he will reprove the world of sin.

And was it ever thus with you, my dear hearers? (For I must question you as I go along, because I intend, by the Divine help, to preach not only to your heads, but your hearts). Did the Spirit of God ever bring all your sins thus to remembrance, and make you cry out to God, "Thou writest bitter things against me?" Did your actual sins ever appear before you, as though drawn in a map? If not, you have great reason (unless you were sanctified from the womb) to suspect that you are not convicted, much more not converted, and that the promise of the text was never yet fulfilled in your hearts.

Farther: When the Comforter comes into a sinner's heart, though it generally convinces the sinner of his actual sin first, yet it leads him to see and bewail his original sin, the fountain from which all these polluted streams do flow.

Though every thing in the earth, air, and water; every thing both without and within, concur to prove the truth of that assertion in the scripture, "in Adam we all have died;" yet most are so hardened through the deceitfulness of sin, that notwithstanding they may give an assent, to the truth of the proposition in their heads, yet they never felt it really in their hearts. Nay, some in words professedly deny it, though their works too, too plainly prove them to be degenerate sons of a degenerate father. But when the Comforter, the Spirit of God, arrests a sinner, and convinces him of sin, all carnal reasoning against original corruption, every proud and high imagination, which exalteth itself against that doctrine, is immediately thrown down; and he is made to cry out, "Who shall deliver me from the body of this death?" He now finds that concupiscence is sin; and does not so much bewail his actual sins, as the inward perverseness of his heart, which he now finds not only to be an enemy to, but also direct enmity against God.

And did the Comforter, my dear friends, ever come with such a convincing power as this unto your hearts? Were you ever made to see and feel, that in your flesh dwelleth no good thing; that you are conceived and born in sin; that you are by nature children of wrath; that God would be just if he damned you, though you never committed an actual sin in your lives? So often as you have been at church and sacrament, did you ever feelingly confess, that there was no health in you; that the remembrance of your original and actual sins was grievous unto you, and the burden of them intolerable? If not, you have been only offering to God vain oblations; you never yet prayed in your lives; the Comforter never yet came effectually into your souls: consequently you are not in the faith properly so called; no, you are at present in a state of death and damnation.

Again, the Comforter, when he comes effectually to work upon a sinner, not only convinces him of the sin of his nature, and the sin of his life, but also of the sin of his duties.

We all naturally are Legalists, thinking to be justified by the works of the law. When somewhat awakened by the terrors of the Lord, we immediately, like the Pharisees of old, go about to establish our own righteousness, and think we shall find acceptance with God, if we seek it with tears: finding ourselves damned by nature and our actual sins, we then think to recommend ourselves to God by our duties, and hope, by our doings of one kind or another, to inherit eternal life. But, whenever the Comforter comes into the heart, it convinces the soul of these false rests, and makes the sinner so see that all his righteousnesses are but filthy rags; and that, for the;most pompous services, he deserves no better a doom than that of the unprofitable servant, "to be thrown into outer darkness, where is weeping, and wailing, and gnashing of teeth."

And was this degree of conviction ever wrought in any of your souls? Did the Comforter ever come into your hearts, so as to make you sick of your duties, as well as your sins? Were you ever, with the great Apostle of the Gentiles, made to abhor your own righteousness which is by the law, and acknowledge that you deserve to be damned, though you should give all your goods to feed the poor? Were you made to feel, that your very repentance needed to be repented of, and that every thing in yourselves is but dung and dross? And that all the arguments you can fetch for mercy, must be out of the heart and pure unmerited love of God? Were you ever made to lie at the feet of sovereign Grace, and to say, Lord, if thou wilt, thou mayest save me; if not, thou mayest justly damn me; I have nothing to plead, I can in no wise justify myself in thy sight; my best performances, I see, will condemn me; and all I have to depend upon is thy free grace? What say you? Was this ever, or is this now, the habitual language of your hearts? You have been frequently at the temple; but did you ever approach it in the temper of the poor Publican, and, after you have done all, acknowledge that you have done nothing; and, upon a feeling experimental sense of your own unworthiness and sinfulness every way, smite upon your breasts, and say, "God be merciful to us sinners?" If you never were thus minded, the Comforter never yet effectually came into your souls, you are out of Christ; and if God should require your souls in that condition, he would be no better to you than a consuming fire.

But there is a fourth sin, of which the Comforter, when he comes, convinces the soul, and which alone (it is very remarkable) our Lord mentions, as though it was the only sin worth mentioning; for indeed it is the root of all other sins whatsoever: it is the reigning as well as the damning sin of the world. And what now do you imagine that sin may be? It is that cursed sin, that root of all other evils, I mean the sin of unbelief. Says our Lord, John 16:9, "Of sin, because they believe not on me."

But does the Christian world, or any of you that hear me this day, want the Holy Ghost to convince you of unbelief? Are there any infidels here? Yes, (O that I had not too great reason to think so!) I fear most are such: not indeed such infidels as professedly deny the Lord that bought us (though I fear too many even of such monsters are in every country); but I mean such unbelievers, that have no more faith than the devils themselves. Perhaps you may think you believe, because you repeat the Creed, or subscribe to a Confession of Faith; because you go to church or meeting, receive the sacrament, and are taken into full communion. These are blessed privileges; but all this may be done, without our being true believers. And I know not how to detect your false hypocritical faith better, than by putting to you this question: How long have you believed? Would not most of you say, as long as we can remember; we never did disbelieve? Then this is a certain sign that you have no true faith at all; no, not so much as a grain of mustard-seed: for, if you believe now, unless you were sanctified from your infancy, which is the case of some) you must know that there was a time in which you did not believe on the Lord Jesus Christ; and the Holy Ghost, if ever you received it, convinced you of this. Eternal truth has declared, "When he is come, he will convince the world of sin, because they believe not on me."

None of us believe by nature: but after the Holy Ghost has convinced us of the sin of our natures, and the sin of our lives and duties, in order to convince us of our utter inability to save ourselves, and that we must be beholden to God, as for every thing else, so for faith (without which it is impossible to please, or be saved by Christ) he convinces us also, that we have no faith. "Dost thou believe on the Son of God?" is the grand question which the Holy Ghost now puts to the soul: at the same time he works with such power and demonstration, that the soul sees, and is obliged to confess, that it has no faith.

This is a thing little thought of by most who call themselves believers. They dream they are Christians, because they live in a Christian country: If they were born Turks, they would believe on Mohammed; for what is that which men commonly call faith, but an outward consent to the established religion? But do not you thus deceive your own selves; true faith is quite another thing. Ask yourselves, therefore, whether or not the Holy Ghost ever powerfully convinced you of the sin of unbelief? You are perhaps so devout (you may imagine) as to get a catalogue of sins; which you look over, and confess in a formal manner, as often as you go to the holy sacrament: but among all your suns, did you ever once confess and bewail that damning sin of unbelief? Were you ever made to cry out, "Lord, give me faith; Lord, give me to believe on thee; O that I had faith! O that I could believe!" If you never were thus distressed, at least, if you never saw and felt that you had no faith, it is a certain sign that the Holy Ghost, the Comforter, never came into and worked savingly upon your souls.

But is it not odd, that the Holy Ghost should be called a Comforter, when it is plain, by the experience of all God's children, that this work of conviction is usually attended with sore inward conflicts, and a great deal of soul-trouble? I answer, The Holy Ghost may well be termed a Comforter, even in this work; because it is the only way to, and ends in, true solid comfort. Blessed are they that are thus convicted by him, for they shall be comforted. Nay, not only so, but there is present comfort, even in the midst of these convictions: the soul secretly rejoices in the sight of its own misery, blesses God for bringing it out of darkness into light, and looks forward with a comfortable prospect of future deliverances, knowing, that, "though sorrow may endure for a night, joy will come in the morning."

Thus it is that the Holy Ghost convinces the soul of sin. And, if so, how wretchedly are they mistaken, that blend the light of the Spirit with the light of conscience, as all such do, who say, that Christ lighteth every man that cometh into the world, and that light, if improved, will bring us to Jesus Christ? If such doctrine be true, the promise in the text was needless: our Lord's apostles had already that light; the world hereafter to be convinced, had that light; and, if that was sufficient to bring them to Christ, why was it expedient that Christ should go away to heaven, to send down the Holy Ghost to do this for them! Alas! all have not this Spirit: it is the special gift of God, and, without this special gift, we can never come to Christ.

The light of conscience will accuse or convince us of any common sin; but the light of natural conscience never did, never will, and never can, convince of unbelief. If it could, how comes it to pass, that not one of the heathens, who improved the light of nature in such an eminent degree, was ever convinced of unbelief? No, natural conscience cannot effect this; it is the peculiar property of the Holy Ghost the Comforter: "When he is come, he will reprove (or convince) the world of sin, or righteousness, and judgment."

We have heard how he convinces of sin: we come not to show,

Secondly, What is the righteousness, of which the Comforter convinces the world.

By the word righteousness, in some places of scripture, we are to understand that common justice which we ought to practice between man and man; as when Paul is said to reason of temperance and righteousness before a trembling Felix. But here (as in a multitude of other places in holy writ) we are to understand by the word righteousness, the active and passive obedience of the dear Lord Jesus; even that perfect, personal, all-sufficient righteousness, which he has wrought out for that world which the Spirit is to convince. "Of righteousness, (says our Lord) because I go to the Father, and ye see me no more." This is one argument that the Holy Spirit makes use of to prove Christ's righteousness, because he is gone to the Father, and we see him no more. For, had he not wrought out a sufficient righteousness, the Father would have sent him back, as not having done what he undertook; and we should have seen him again.

O the righteousness of Christ! It so comforts my soul, that I must be excused if I mention it in almost all my discourses. I would not, if I could help it, have one sermon without it. Whatever infidels may object, or Arminians sophistically argue against an imputed righteousness; yet whoever know themselves and God, must acknowledge, that "Jesus Christ is the end of the law for righteousness, (and perfect justification in the sight of God) to every one that believeth," and that we are to be made the righteousness of God in him. This, and this only, a poor sinner can lay hold of, as a sure anchor of his hope. Whatever other scheme of salvation men may lay, I acknowledge I can see no other foundation whereon to build my hopes of salvation, but on the rock of Christ's personal righteousness, imputed to my soul.

Many, I believe, have a rational conviction of, and agree with me in this: but rational convictions, if rested in, avail but little; it must be a spiritual, experimental conviction of the truth, which is saving. And therefore our Lord says, when the Holy Ghost comes in the day of his power, it convinces of this righteousness, of the reality, completeness, and sufficiency of it, to save a poor sinner.

We have seen how the Holy Ghost convinces the sinner of the sin of his nature, life, duties, and of the sin of unbelief; and what then must the poor creature do? He must, he must inevitably despair, if there be no hope but in himself. When therefore the Spirit has hunted the sinner out of all his false rests and hiding-places, taken off the pitiful fig-leaves of his own works, and driven him out of the trees of the garden (his outward reformations) and place him naked before the bar of a sovereign, holy, just, and sin-avenging God; then, then it is, when the soul, having the sentence of death within itself because of unbelief, has a sweet display of Christ's righteousness made to it by the Holy Spirit of God. Here it is, that he begins more immediately to act in the quality of a Comforter, and convinces the soul so powerfully of the reality and all-sufficiency of Christ's righteousness, that the soul is immediately set a hungering and thirsting after it. Now the sinner begins to see, that though he has destroyed himself, yet in Christ is his help; that, though he has no righteousness of his own to recommend him, there is a fullness of grace, a fullness of truth, a fullness of righteousness in the dear Lord Jesus, which, if once imputed to him, will make him happy for ever and ever.

None can tell, but those happy souls who have experienced it, with what demonstration of the Spirit this conviction comes. O how amiable, as well as all-sufficient, does the blessed Jesus now appear! With what new eyes does the soul now see the Lord its righteousness! Brethren, it is unutterable. If you were never thus convinced of Christ's righteousness in your own souls, though you may believe it doctrinally, it will avail you nothing, if the Comforter never came savingly into your souls, then you are comfortless indeed. But

What will this righteousness avail, if the soul has it not in possession?

Thirdly, The next thing therefore the Comforter, when he comes, convinces the soul of, is judgment.

By the word judgment, I understand that well-grounded peace, that settled judgment, which the soul forms of itself, when it is enabled by the Spirit of God to lay hold on Christ's righteousness, which I believe it always does, when convinced in the matter before-mentioned. "Of judgment (says our Lord) because the Prince of this world is judged;" the soul, being enabled to lay hold on Christ's perfect righteousness by a lively faith, has a conviction wrought in it by the Holy Spirit, that the Prince of this world is judged. The soul being now justified by faith, has peace with God through our Lord Jesus Christ, and can triumphantly say, It is Christ that justifies me, who is he that condemns me? The strong man armed is now cast out; my soul is in a true peace; the Prince of this world will come and accuse, but he has now no share in me: the blessed Spirit which I have received, and whereby I am enabled to apply Christ's righteousness to my poor soul, powerfully convinces me of this: why should I fear? Or of what shall I be afraid, since God's Spirit witnesses with my spirit, that I am a child of God? The Lord is ascended up on high; he has led captivity captive; he has received the Holy Ghost the Comforter, that best of gifts for men: and that Comforter is come into my heart: he is faithful that hath promised: I, even I, am powerfully, rationally, spiritually convicted of sin, righteousness and judgment. By this I know the Prince of this world is judged.

Thus, I say, may we suppose that soul to triumph, in which the promise of the text is happily fulfilled. And though, at the beginning of this discourse, I said, most had never experienced any thing of this, and that therefore this preaching must be foolishness to such; yet I doubt not but there are some few happy souls, who, through grace, have been enabled to follow me step by step; and notwithstanding the Holy Ghost might not directly work in the same order as I have described, and perhaps they cannot exactly say the time when, yet they have a well-grounded confidence that the work is done, and that they have really been convinced of sin, righteousness and judgment in some way, or at some time or another.

And now, what shall I say to you? O thank God, thank the Lord Jesus, thank the ever-blessed Trinity, for this unspeakable gift: for you would never have been thus highly favored, had not he who first spoke darkness into light, loved you with an everlasting love, and enlightened you by his Holy Spirit, and that too, not on account of any good thing foreseen in you, but for his own name's sake.

Be humble therefore, O believers, be humble: look to the rock from whence you have been hewn: extol free grace; admire electing love, which alone has made you to differ from the rest of your brethren. Has God brought you into light? Walk as becometh children of light. Provoke not the Holy Spirit to depart from you: for though he hath sealed you to the day of redemption, and you know that the Prince of this world is judged; yet if you backslide, grow luke-warm, or forget your first love, the Lord will visit your offenses with the rod of affliction, and your sin with spiritual scourges. Be not therefore high-minded, but fear. Rejoice, but let it be with trembling. As the elect of God, put on, not only humbleness of mind, but bowels of compassion; and pray, O pray for your unconverted brethren! Help me, help me now, O children of God, and hold up my hands, as Aaron and Hur once held up the hands of Moses. Pray, whilst I am preaching, that the Lord may enable me to say, This day is the promise in the text fulfilled in some poor sinners hearts. Cry mightily to God, and, with the cords of holy violence, pull down blessings on your neighbors heads. Christ yet lives and reigns in heaven: the residue of the Spirit is yet in his hand, and a plentiful effusion of it is promises in the latter days of the church. And O that the Holy Ghost, the blessed Comforter, would now come down, and convince those that are Christless amongst you, of sin, of righteousness, and of judgment! O that you were once made willing to be convinced!

But perhaps you had rather be filled with wine than with the Spirit, and are daily chasing that Holy Ghost from your souls. What shall I say for you to God? "Father, forgive them, for they know not what they do." What shall I say from God to you? Why? That "God was in Christ reconciling the world unto himself." Therefore I beseech you, as in Christ's stead, be ye reconciled to God. Do not go away contradicting and blaspheming. I know Satan would have you be gone. Many of you may be uneasy, and are ready to cry out, "What a weariness is this!" But I will not let you go: I have wrestled with God for my hearers in private, and I must wrestle with you here in public. Though of myself I can do nothing, and you can no more by your own power come to and believe on Christ, than Lazarus could come forth from the grave; yet who knows but God may beget some of you again to a lively hope by this foolishness of preaching, and that you may be some of that world, which the Comforter is to convince of sin, or righteousness, and of judgment? Poor Christless souls! Do you know what a condition you are in? Why, you are lying in the wicked one, the devil; he rules in you, he walks and dwells in you, unless you dwell in Christ, and the Comforter is come into your hearts. And will you contentedly lie in that wicked one that devil? What wages will he give you? Eternal death. O that you would come to Christ! The free gift of God through him is eternal life. He will accept of you even now, if you will believe in him. The Comforter may yet come into your hearts, even yours. All that are now his living temples, were once lying in the wicked one, as well as you. This blessed gift, this Holy Ghost, the blessed Jesus received even for the rebellious.

I see many of you affected: but are your passions only a little wrought upon, or are your souls really touched with a lively sense of the heinousness of your sins, your want of faith, and the preciousness of the righteousness of Jesus Christ? If so, I hope the Lord has been gracious, and that the Comforter is coming into your hearts. Do not stifle these convictions! Do not go away, and straightway forget what manner of doctrine you have heard, and thereby show that these are only common workings of a few transient convictions, floating upon the surface of your hearts. Beg of God that you may be sincere (for he alone can make you so) and that you may indeed desire the promise of the text to be fulfilled in your souls. Who knows but the Lord may be gracious? Remember you have no plea but sovereign mercy; but, for your encouragement also, remember it is the world, such as you are, to whom the Comforter is to come, and whom he is to convince: wait therefore at wisdom's gates. The bare probability of having a door of mercy opened, is enough to keep you striving. Christ Jesus came into the world to save sinners, the chief of them: you know not but he came to save you. Do not go and quarrel with God's decrees, and say, if I am a reprobate, I shall be damned; if I am elected, I shall be saved; and therefore I will do nothing. What have you to do with God's decrees? Secret things belong to him; it is you business to "give all diligence to make your calling and election sure." If there are but few who find the way that leads to life, do you strive to be some of them: you know not but you may be in the number of those few, and that your striving may be the means which God intends to bless, to give you an entrance in. If you do not act thus, you are not sincere; and, if you do, who knows but you may find mercy? For though, after you have done all that you can, God may justly cut you off, yet never was a single person damned who did all that he could. Though therefore your hands are withered, stretch them out; though you are impotent, sick, and lame, come, lie at the pool. Who knows but by and by the Lord Jesus may have compassion on you, and send the Comforter to convince you of sin, righteousness, and of judgment? He is a God full of compassion and long-suffering, otherwise you and I had been long since lifted up our eyes in torments. But still he is patient with us!

O Christless sinners, you are alive, and who knows but God intends to bring you to repentance? Could my prayers or tears affect it, you should have vollies of the one, and floods of the other. My heart is touched with a sense of your condition: May our merciful High-priest now send down the Comforter, and make you sensible of it also! O the love of Christ! It constrains me yet to beseech you to come to him; what do you reject, if you reject Christ, the Lord of glory! Sinners, give the dear Redeemer a lodging in your souls. Do not be Bethshemites; give Christ your hearts, your whole hearts. Indeed he is worthy. He made you, and not you yourselves. You are not your own; give Christ then your bodies and souls, which are his! Is it not enough to melt you down, to think that the high and lofty One, who inhabiteth eternity, should condescend to invite you by his ministers? How soon can he frown you to hell? And how know you, but he may, this very instant, if you do not hear his voice? Did any yet harden their hearts against Christ, and prosper? Come then, do not send me sorrowful away: do not let me have reason to cry out, O my leanness, my leanness! Do not let me go weeping into my closet, and say, "Lord, they will not believe my report; Lord, I have called them, and they will not answer; I am unto them as a very pleasant song, and as one that plays upon a pleasant instrument; but their hearts are running after the lust of the eye, the lust of the flesh, and the pride of life." Would you be willing that I should give such an account of you, or make such a prayer before God? And yet I must not only do so here, but appear in judgment against you hereafter, unless you will come to Christ. Once more therefore I entreat you to come. What objections have you to make? Behold, I stand here in the name of God, to answer all that you can offer. But I know no one can come, unless the Father draw him: I will therefore address one to my God, and intercede with him to send the Comforter into your hearts.

O blessed Jesus, who art a God whose compassions fail not, and in whom all the promises are yea and amen; thou that sittest between the cherubims, show thyself amongst us. Let us now see thy outgoings! O let us now taste that thou art gracious, and reveal thy almighty arm! Get thyself the victory in these poor sinners hearts. Let not the word spoken prove like water spilt upon the ground. Send down, send down, O great High-priest, the Holy Spirit, to convince the world of sin, of righteousness, and of judgment. So will we give thanks and praise to thee, O Father, thee O Son, and thee O blessed Spirit; to whom, as three Persons, but one God, be ascribed by angels and archangels, by cherubims and seraphims, and all the heavenly hosts, all possible power, might, majesty, and dominion, now and for evermore. Amen, Amen, Amen.

40. The Conversion of Zaccheus

Luke 19:9–10—"And Jesus said unto him, This day is salvation come to this house; forasmuch as he also is the Son of Abraham. For the Son of man is come to seek and to save that which was lost."

Salvation, every where through the whole scripture, is said to be the free gift of God, through Jesus Christ our Lord. Not only free, because God is a sovereign agent, and therefore may withhold it from, or confer it on, whom he pleaseth; but free, because there is nothing to be found in man, that can any way induce God to be merciful unto him. The righteousness of Jesus Christ is the sole cause of our finding favor in God's sight: this righteousness apprehended by faith (which is also the gift of God) makes it our own; and this faith, if true, will work by love.

These are parts of those glad tidings which are published in the gospel; and of the certainty of them, next to the express word of God, the experience of all such as have been saved, is the best, and, as I take it, the most undoubted proof. That God might teach us every way, he has been pleased to leave upon record many instances of the power of his grace exerted in the salvation of several persons, that we, hearing how he dealt with them, might from thence infer the manner we must expect to be dealt with ourselves, and learn in what way we must look for salvation, if we truly desire to be made partakers of the inheritance with the saints in light.

The conversion of the person referred to in the text, I think, will be of no small service to us in this matter, if rightly improved. I would hope, most of you know who the person is, to whom the Lord Jesus speaks; it is the publican Zaccheus, to whose house the blessed Jesus said, salvation came, and whom he pronounces a Son of Abraham.

It is my design (God helping) to make some remarks upon his conversion recorded at large in the preceding verses, and then to enforce the latter part of the text, as an encouragement to poor undone sinners to come to Jesus Christ. "For the Son of man is come, to seek and to save that which was lost."

The evangelist Luke introduces the account of this man's conversion thus, verse Luke 19:1, "And Jesus entered and passed through Jericho." The holy Jesus made it his business to go about doing good. As the sun in the firmament is continually spreading his benign, quickening, and cheering influences over the natural; so the Son of righteousness arose with healing under his wings, and was daily and hourly diffusing his gracious influences over the moral world. The preceding chapter acquaints us of a notable miracle wrought by the holy Jesus, on poor blind Bartimeus; and in this, a greater presents itself to our consideration. The evangelist would have us take particular notice of it; for he introduces it with the word "behold:" "and behold, there was a man named Zaccheus, who was the chief among the Publicans, and he was rich."

Well might the evangelist usher in the relation of this man's conversion with the word "behold!" For, according to human judgment, how many insurmountable obstacles lay in the way of it! Surely no one will say there was any fitness in Zaccheus for salvation; for we are told that he was a Publican, and therefore in all probability a notorious sinner. The Publicans were gatherers of the Roman taxes; they were infamous for their abominable extortion; their very name therefore became so odious, that we find the Pharisees often reproached our Lord, as very wicked, because he was a friend unto and sat down to meat with them. Zaccheus then, being a Publican, was no doubt a sinner; and, being chief among the Publicans, consequently was chief among sinners. Nay, "he was rich." One inspired apostle has told us, that "not many mighty, not many noble are called." Another saith, "God has chosen the poor of this world, rich in faith." And he who was the Maker and Redeemer of the apostles, assures us, "that it is easier for a camel, (or cable-rope) to go through the eye of a needle, than for a rich man to enter into the kingdom of God." Let not therefore the rich glory in the multitude of their riches.

But rich as he was, we are told, verse Luke 19:3," that "he sought to see Jesus." A wonder indeed! The common people heard our Lord gladly, and the poor received the gospel. The multitude, the *oclos*, the mob, the people that know not the law, as the proud high-priests called them, used to follow him on foot into the country, and sometimes stayed with him three days together to hear him preach. But did the rich believe or attend on him? No. Our Lord preached up the doctrine of the cross; he preached too searching for them, and therefore they counted him their enemy, persecuted and spoke all manner of evil against him falsely. Let not the ministers of Christ marvel, if they meet with the like treatment from the rich men of this wicked and adulterous generation. I should think it no scandal (supposing it true) to hear it affirmed, that none but the poor attended my ministry. Their souls are as precious to our Lord Jesus Christ, as the souls of the greatest men. They were the poor that attended him in the days of his flesh: these are they whom he hath chosen to rich in faith, and to be the greatest in the kingdom of heaven. Were the rich in this world's goods generally to speak well of me, woe be unto me; I should think it a dreadful sign that I was only a wolf in sheep's clothing, that I spoke peace, peace, when there was no peace, and prophesied smoother things than the gospel would allow of. Hear ye this, O ye rich. Let who will dare to do it, God forbid that I should despise the poor; in doing so, I should reproach my Maker. The poor are dear to my soul; I rejoice to see them fly to the doctrine of Christ, like the doves to their windows. I only pray, that the poor who attend, may be evangelized, and turned into the spirit of the gospel: if so, "Blessed are ye; for yours is the kingdom of heaven."

But we must return to Zaccheus. "He sought to see Jesus." That is good news. I heartily wish I could say, it was out of a good principle: but, without speaking contrary to that charity which hopes and believeth all things for the best, we may say, that the same principle drew him after Christ, which now draws multitudes (to speak plainly, it may be multitudes of you) to hear a particular preacher, even curiosity: for we are told, that he came not to hear his doctrine, but to view his person, or, to use the words of the evangelist, "to see who he was." Our Lord's fame was now spread abroad through all Jerusalem, and all the country round about: some said he was a good man; others, "Nay, but he deceiveth the people." And therefore curiosity drew out this rich Publican Zaccheus, to see who this person was, of whom he had heard such various accounts. But it seems he could not conveniently get a sight of him for the press, and because he was little of stature. Alas! how many are kept from seeing Christ in glory, by reason of the press! I mean, how many are ashamed of being singularly good, and therefore follow a multitude to do evil, because they have a press or throng of polite acquaintance! And, for fear of being set an nought by those with whom they used to sit at meat, they deny the Lord of glory, and are ashamed to confess him before men. This base, this servile fear of man, is the bane of true Christianity; it brings a dreadful snare upon the soul, and is the ruin of ten thousands: for I am fully persuaded, numbers are rationally convicted of gospel-truths; but, not being able to brook contempt, they will not prosecute their convictions, nor reduce them to practice. Happy those, who in this respect, like Zaccheus, are resolved to overcome all impediments that lie in their way to a sight of Christ; for, finding he could not see Christ because of the press and the littleness of his natural stature, he did not smite upon his breast, and depart, saying, "It is in vain to seek after a sight of him any longer, I can never attain unto it." No, finding he could not see Christ, if he continued in the midst of, "he ran before the multitude, and climbed up into a sycamore-tree, to see him; for he was to pass that way."

There is no seeing Christ in Glory, unless we run before the multitude, and are willing to be in the number of those despised few, who take the kingdom of God by violence. The broad way, in which so many go, can never be that strait and narrow way which leads to life. Our Lord's flock was, and always will be, comparatively a little one; and unless we dare to run before the multitude in a holy singularity, and can rejoice in being accounted fools for Christ's sake, we shall never see Jesus with comfort, when he appears in glory. From mentioning the sycamore-tree, and considering the difficulty with which Zaccheus must climb it, we may farther learn, that those who would see Christ, must undergo other difficulties and hardships, besides contempt. Zaccheus, without doubt, went through both. Did not many, think you, laugh at him as he ran along, and in the language of Michal, Saul's daughter, cry out, "How glorious did the rich Zaccheus look today, when, forgetting the greatness of his station, he ran before a pitiful, giddy mob, and climbed up a sycamore-tree, to see an enthusiastic preacher!" But Zaccheus cares not for all that; his curiosity was strong: if he could but see who Jesus was, he did not value what scoffers said of him. Thus, and much more will it be with all those who have an effectual desire to see Jesus in heaven: they will go on from strength to strength, break through every difficulty lying in their way, and care not what men or devils say of or do unto them. May the Lord make us all thus minded, for his dear Son's sake!

At length, after taking much pains, and going (as we may well suppose) through much contempt, Zaccheus has climbed the tree; and there he sits, as he thinks, hid in the leaves of it, and watching when he should see Jesus pass by: "For he was to pass by that way."

But sing, O heavens, and rejoice, O earth! Praise, magnify, and adore sovereign, electing, free, preventing love; Jesus the everlasting God, the Prince of peace, who saw Nathanael under the fig-tree, and Zaccheus from eternity, now sees him in the sycamore-tree, and calls him in time.

Verse Luke 19:5, "And when Jesus came to the place, he looked up, and saw him, and said unto him, Zaccheus, make haste and come down; for this day I must abide at thy house." Amazing love! Well might Luke usher in the account with "behold!" It is worthy of our highest admiration. When Zaccheus thought of no such thing, nay, thought that Christ Jesus did not know him; behold, Christ does what we never hear he did before or after, I mean, invite himself to the house of Zaccheus, saying, "Zaccheus, make haste and come down; for this day I must abide at thy house." Not pray let me abide, but I must abide this day at thy house. He also calls him by name, as though he was well acquainted with him: and indeed well he might; for his name was written in the book of life, he was one of those whom the Father had given him from all eternity: therefore he must abide at his house that day. "For whom he did predestinate, them he also called."

Here then, as through a glass, we may see the doctrine of free grace evidently exemplified before us. Here was not fitness in Zaccheus. He was a Publican, chief among the Publicans; not only so, but rich, and came to see Christ only out of curiosity: but sovereign grace triumphs over all. And if we do God justice, and are effectually wrought upon, we must acknowledge there was no more fitness in us than in Zaccheus; and, had not Christ prevented us by his call, we had remained dead in trespasses and sins, and alienated from the divine life, even as others. "Jesus looked up, and saw him, and said unto him, Zaccheus, make haste and come down; for this day I must abide at thy house."

With what different emotions of heart may we suppose Zaccheus received this invitation? Think you not that he was surprised to hear Jesus Christ call him by name, and not only so, but invite himself to his house? Surely, thinks Zaccheus, I dream: it cannot be; how should he know me? I never saw him before: besides, I shall undergo much contempt, if I receive him under my rood. Thus,

I say, we may suppose Zaccheus thought within himself. But what saith the scripture? "I will make a willing people in the day of my power." With this outward call, there went an efficacious power from God, which sweetly overruled his natural will: and therefore, verse Luke 19:6, "He made haste, and came down, and received him joyfully;" not only into his house, but also into his heart.

Thus it is the great God brings home his children. He calls them by name, by his word or providence; he speaks to them also by his spirit. Hereby they are enabled to open their hearts, and are made willing to receive the King of glory. For Zaccheus's sake, let us not entirely condemn people that come under the word, out of no better principle than curiosity. Who knows but God may call them? It is good to be where the Lord is passing by. May all who are now present out of this principle, hear the voice of the Son of God speaking to their souls, and so hear that they may live! Not that men ought therefore to take encouragement to come out of curiosity. For perhaps a thousand more, at other times, came to see Christ out of curiosity, as well as Zaccheus, who were not effectually called by his grace. I only mention this for the encouragement of my own soul, and the consolation of God's children, who are too apt to be angry with those who do not attend on the word out of love to God: but let them alone. Brethren, pray for them. How do you know but Jesus Christ may speak to their hearts! A few words from Christ, applied by his spirit, will save their souls. "Zaccheus, says Christ, make haste and come down. And he made haste, and came down, and received him joyfully."

I have observed, in holy scripture, how particularly it is remarked, that persons rejoiced upon believing in Christ. Thus the converted Eunuch went on his way rejoicing; thus the jailer rejoiced with his whole house; thus Zaccheus received Christ joyfully. And well may those rejoice who receive Jesus Christ; for with him they receive righteousness, sanctification, and eternal redemption. Many have brought up an ill report upon our good land, and would fain persuade people that religion will make them melancholy mad. So far from it, that joy is one ingredient of the kingdom of God in the heart of a believer; "The kingdom of God is righteousness, peace, and joy in the Holy Ghost." To rejoice in the Lord, is a gospel-duty. "Rejoice in the Lord always, and again I say, rejoice." And who can be so joyful, as those who know that their pardon is sealed before they go hence and are no more seen? The godly may, but I cannot see how any ungodly men can, rejoice: they cannot be truly cheerful. What if wicked men may sometimes have laughter amongst them? It is only the laughter of fools; in the midst of it there is heaviness; At the best, it is but like the cracking of thorns under a pot; it makes a blaze, but soon goes out. But, as for the godly, it is not so with them; their joy is solid and lasting. As it is a joy that a stranger intermeddleth not with, so it is a joy that no man taketh from them: it is a joy in God, a "joy unspeakable and full of glory."

It should seem that Zaccheus was under soul-distress but a little while; perhaps (says Guthrie, in his book entitled, *The Trial Concerning A Saving Interest In Christ*) not above a quarter of an hour. I add, perhaps not so long: for, as one observes, sometimes the Lord Jesus delights to deliver speedily. God is a sovereign agent, and works upon his children in their effectual calling, according to the counsel of his eternal will. It is with the spiritual, as natural birth: all women have not the like pangs; all Christians have not the like degree of conviction. But all agree in this, that all have Jesus Christ formed in their hearts: and those who have not so many trials at first, may be visited with the greater conflicts hereafter; though they never come into bondage again, after they have once received the spirit of adoption. "We have not, (says Paul) received the spirit of bondage again unto fear." We know not what Zaccheus underwent before he died: however, this one thing I know, he now believed in Christ, and was justified, or acquitted, and looked upon as righteous in God's sight, though a Publican, chief among the Publicans, not many moments before. And thus it is with all, that, like Zaccheus, receive Jesus Christ by faith into their hearts: the very moment they find rest in him, they are freely justified from all things from which they could not be justified by the law of Moses; "for by grace are we saved, through faith, and that not of ourselves, it is the gift of God."

Say not within yourselves, this is a licentious Antinomian doctrine; for this faith, if true, will work by love, and be productive of the fruits of holiness. See an instance in this convert Zaccheus; no sooner had he received Jesus Christ by faith into his heart, but he evidences it by his works; for, ver. Luke 19:8, we are told, "Zaccheus stood forth, and said unto the Lord, Behold, Lord, the half of my goods I give unto the poor; and if I have taken any thing from any man by false accusation, I restore him four-fold."

Having believed on Jesus in his heart, he now makes confession of him with his mouth to salvation. "Zaccheus stood forth;" he was not ashamed, but stood forth before his brother Publicans; for true faith casts out all servile, sinful fear of man; "and said, Behold, Lord." It is remarkable, how readily people in scripture have owned the divinity of Christ immediately upon their conversion. Thus the woman at Jacob's well; "Is not this the Christ?" Thus the man born blind; "Lord, I believe; and worshipped him." Thus Zaccheus, "Behold, Lord." An incontestable proof this to me, that those who deny our Lord's divinity, never effectually felt his power: if they had, they would not speak so lightly of him: they would scorn to deny his eternal power and Godhead. "Zaccheus stood forth, and said, Behold, Lord, the half of m goods I give to the poor; and if I have taken any thing from any man by false accusation, I restore him four-fold." Noble fruits of a true living faith in the Lord Jesus! Every word calls for our notice. Not some small, not the tenth part, but the *half*. Of what? My goods; things that were valuable. *My* goods, his own, not another's. I give: not, I will give when I die, when I can keep them no longer; but, I give now, even now. Zaccheus would be his own executor. For whilst we have time we should do good. But to whom would he give half of his goods? Not to the rich, not to those who were already clothed in purple and fine linen, of whom he might be recompensed again; but to the poor, the maimed, the halt, the blind, from which he could expect no recompense till the resurrection of the dead. "I give to the poor." But knowing that he must be just before he could be charitable, and conscious to himself that in his public administrations he had wronged many persons, he adds, "And if I have taken any thing from any man by false accusation, I restore him four-fold." Hear ye this, all ye that make no conscience of cheating the king of his taxes, or of buying or selling run goods. If ever God gives you true faith, you will never rest, till, like Zaccheus, you have made restitution to the utmost of your power. I suppose, before his conversion, he thought it no harm to cheat thus, no more than you may do now, and pleased himself frequently, to be sure, that he got rich by doing so: but now he is grieved for it at his heart; he confesses his injustice before men, and promises to make ample restitution. Go ye cheating Publicans, learn of Zaccheus; go away and do likewise. If you do not make restitution here, the Lord Jesus shall make you confess your sins before men and angels, and condemn you for it, when he comes in the glory of his Father to judgment hereafter.

After all this, with good reason might our Lord say unto him, "This day is salvation come to this house; forasmuch as he also is the son of Abraham;" not so much by a natural as by a spiritual birth. He was made partaker of like precious faith with Abraham: like Abraham he believed on the Lord, and it was accounted to him for righteousness: his faith, like Abraham's, worked by love; and I doubt not, but he has been long since sitting in Abraham's harbor.

And now, are you not ashamed of yourselves, who speak against the doctrines of grace, especially that doctrine of being justified by faith alone, as though it leaded to licentiousness? What can be more unjust than such a charge? Is not the instance of Zaccheus, a sufficient proof to the contrary? Have I strained it to serve my own turn? God forbid. To the best of my knowledge I have spoken the truth in sincerity, and the truth as it is in Jesus. I do affirm that we are saved by grace, and that we are justified by faith alone: but I do also affirm, that faith must be evidenced by good works, where there is an opportunity of performing them.

What therefore has been said of Zaccheus, may serve as a rule, whereby all may judge whether they have faith or not. You say you have faith; but how do you prove it? Did you ever hear the Lord Jesus call you by name? Were you ever made to obey the call? Did you ever, like Zaccheus, receive Jesus Christ joyfully into your hearts? Are you influenced by the faith you say you have, to stand up and confess the Lord Jesus before men? Were you ever made willing to own, and humble yourselves for, your past offenses? Does your faith work by love, so that you conscientiously lay up, according as God has prospered you, for the support of the poor? Do you give alms of all things that you possess? And have you made due restitution to those you have wronged? If so, happy are ye; salvation is come to your souls, you are sons, you are daughters of, you shall shortly be everlastingly blessed with, faithful Abraham. But, if you are not thus minded, do not deceive your own souls. Though you may talk of justification by faith, like angels, it will do you no good; it will only increase your damnation. You hold the truth, but it is in unrighteousness: your faith being without works, is dead: you have the devil, not Abraham, for your father. Unless you get a faith of the heart, a faith working by love, with devils and damned spirits shall you dwell for evermore.

But it is time now to enforce the latter part of the text; "For the Son of man is come to seek and to save that which was lost." These words are spoken by our savior in answer to some self-righteous Pharisees, who, instead of rejoicing with the angels in heaven, at the conversion of such a sinner, murmured, "That he was gone to be a guest with a man that was a sinner." To vindicate his conduct, he tells them, that this was an act agreeable to the design of his coming: "For the Son of Man is come to seek and to save that which was lost." He might have said, the Son of God. But O the wonderful condescension of our Redeemer! He delights to stile himself the Son of man. He came not only to save, but to seek and to save that which was lost. He came to Jericho to seek and save Zaccheus; for otherwise Zaccheus would never have been saved by him. But from whence came he? Even from heaven, his dwelling-place, to this lower earth, this vale of tears, to seek and save that which was lost; or all that feel themselves lost, and are willing, like Zaccheus, to receive him into their hearts to save them; with how great a salvation? Even from the guilt, and also from the power of their sins; to make them heirs of God, and joint heirs with himself, and partakers of that glory which he enjoyed with the Father before the world began. Thus will the Son of man save that which is lost. He was made the son of man, on purpose that he might save them. He had no other end but this in leaving his father's throne, in obeying the moral law, and hanging upon the cross: all that was done and suffered, merely to satisfy, and procure a righteousness for poor, lost, undone sinners, and that too without respect of persons. "That which was lost;" all of every nation and language, that feel, bewail, and are truly desirous of being delivered from their lost state, did the Son of man come down to seek and to save: for he is mighty, not only so, but willing, to save to the uttermost all that come to God through him. He will in no wise cast out: for he is the same today, as he was yesterday. He comes now to sinners, as well as formerly; and, I hope, hath sent me out this day to seek, and, under him, to bring home some of you, the lost sheep of the house of Israel.

What say you? Shall I go home rejoicing, saying, That many like sheep have went astray, but they have now believed on Jesus Christ, and so returned home to the great Shepherd and Bishop of their souls? If the Lord would be pleased thus to prosper my handy-work, I care not how many legalists and self-righteous Pharisees murmur against me, for offering salvation to the worst of sinners: for I know the Son of man came to seek and to save them; and the Lord Jesus will now be a guest to the worst Publican, the vilest sinner that is amongst you, if he does but believe on him. Make haste then, O sinners, make haste, and come by faith to Christ. Then, this day, even this hour, nay, this moment, if you believe, Jesus Christ shall come and make his eternal abode in your hearts. Which of you is made willing to receive the King of glory? Which of you obeys his call, as Zaccheus did?

Alas! why do you stand still? How know you, whether Jesus Christ may ever call you again? Come then, poor, guilty sinners; come away, poor, lost, undone publicans: make haste, I say, and come away to Jesus Christ. The Lord condescends to invite himself to come under the filthy roofs of the houses of your souls. Do not be afraid of entertaining him; he will fill you with all peace and joy in believing. Do not be ashamed to run before the multitude, and to have all manner of evil spoke against you falsely for his sake: one sight of Christ will make amends for all. Zaccheus was laughed at; and all that will live godly in Christ Jesus, shall suffer persecution. But what of that? Zaccheus is now crowned in glory; as you also shall shortly be, if you believe on, and are reproached for Christ's sake. Do not, therefore, put me off with frivolous excuses: there's no excuse can be given for your not coming to Christ. You are lost, undone, without him; and if he is not glorified in your salvation, he will be glorified in your destruction; if he does not come and make his abode in your hearts, you must take up an eternal abode with the devil and his angels. O that the Lord would be pleased to pass by some of you at this time! O that he may call you by his Spirit, and make you a willing people in this day of his power! For I know my calling will not do, unless he, by his efficacious grace, compel you to come in. O that you once felt what it is to receive Jesus Christ into your hearts! You would soon, like Zaccheus, give him everything. You do not love Christ, because you do not know him; you do not come to him, because you do not feel your want of him: you are whole, and not broken hearted; you are not sick, at least not sensible of your sickness; and, therefore, no wonder you do not apply to Jesus Christ, that great, that almighty physician. You do not feel yourselves lost, and therefore do not seek to be found in Christ. O that God would wound you with the sword of his Spirit, and cause his arrows of conviction to stick deep in your hearts! O that he would dart a ray of divine light into your souls! For if you do not feel yourselves lost without Christ, you are of all men most miserable: your souls are dead; you are not only an image of hell, but in some degree hell itself: you carry hell about with you, and you know it not. O that I could see some of you sensible of this, and hear you cry out, "Lord, break this hard heart; Lord, deliver me from the body of this death; draw me, Lord, make me willing to come after thee; I am lost; Lord, save me, or I perish!" Was this your case, how soon would the Lord stretch forth his almighty hand, and say, Be of good cheer, it is I; be not afraid? What a wonderful calm would then possess your troubled souls! Your fellowship would then be with the Father and the Son: your life would be hid with Christ in God.

Some of you, I hope, have experienced this, and can say, I was lost, but I am found; I was dead, but am alive again: the Son of man came and sought me in the day of his power, and saved my sinful soul. And do you repent that you came to Christ? Has he not been a good master? Is not his presence sweet to your souls? Has he not been faithful to his promise? And have you not found, that even in doing and suffering for him, there is an exceeding present great reward? I am persuaded you will answer, Yes. O then, ye saints, recommend and talk of the love of Christ to others, and tell them, O tell them what great things the Lord has done for you! This may encourage others to come unto him. And who knows but the Lord may make you fishers of men? The story of Zaccheus was left on record for this purpose. No truly convicted soul, after such an instance of divine grace has been laid before him, need despair of mercy. What if you are Publicans? Was not Zaccheus a Publican? What if you are chief among the Publicans? Was not Zaccheus likewise? What if you are rich? Was not Zaccheus rich also? And yet almighty grace made him more than conqueror over all these hindrances. All things are possible to Jesus Christ; nothing is too hard for him: he is the Lord almighty. Our mountains of sins must all fall before this great Zerubbabel. On him God the Father has laid the iniquities of all that shall believe on him; and in his own body he bare them on the tree. There, there, by faith, O mourners in Zion, may you see your Savior hanging with arms stretched out, and hear him, as it were, thus speaking to your souls; "Behold how I have loved you! Behold my hands and my feed! Look, look into my wounded side, and see a heart flaming with love: love stronger than death. Come into my arms, O sinners, come wash your spotted souls in my heart's blood. See here is a fountain opened for all sin and all uncleanness! See, O guilty souls, how the wrath of God is now abiding upon you: come, haste away, and hide yourselves in the clefts of my wounds; for I am wounded for your transgressions; I am dying that you may live for evermore. Behold, as Moses lifted up the serpent in the wilderness, so am I here lifted up upon a tree. See how I am become a curse for you: the chastisement of your peace is upon me. I am thus scourged, thus wounded, thus crucified, that you by my stripes may be healed. O look unto me, all ye trembling sinners, even to the ends of the earth! Look unto me by faith, and you shall be saved: for I came thus to be obedient even unto death, that I might save that which was lost."

And what say you to this, O sinners? Suppose you saw the King of glory dying, and thus speaking to you; would you believe on him? No, you would not, unless you believe on him now: for though he is dead, he yet speaketh all this in the scripture; nay, in effect, says all this in the words of the text, "The Son of man is come to seek and to save that which is lost." Do not therefore any longer crucify the Lord of glory. Bring those rebels, your sins, which will not have him to reign over them, bring them out to him: though you cannot slay them yourselves, yet he will slay them for you. The power of his death and resurrection is as great now as formerly. Make haste therefore, make haste, O ye publicans and sinners, and give the dear Lord Jesus your hearts, your whole hearts. If you refuse to hearken to this call of the Lord, remember your damnation will be just: I am free from the blood of you all: you must acquit my Master and me at the terrible day of judgment. O that you may know the things that belong to your everlasting peace, before they are eternally hid from your eyes! Let all that love the Lord Jesus Christ in sincerity say, Amen.

41. Saul's Conversion

Acts 9:22—"But Saul increased the more in strength, and confounded the Jews which dwelt at Damascus, proving that this is very Christ."

It is an undoubted truth, however paradoxical it may seem to natural men, that "whosoever will live godly in Christ Jesus, shall suffer persecution." And therefore it is very remarkable, that our blessed Lord, in his glorious sermon on the mount, after he had been pronouncing those blessed, who were poor in spirit, meek, pure in heart, and such like, immediately adds (and spends no less than three verses in this beatitude "Blessed are they who are persecuted for righteousness sake." No one ever was, or ever will be endowed with the forementioned graces in any degree, but he will be persuaded for it in a measure. There is an irreconcilable enmity between the seed of the woman, and the seed of the serpent. And if we are not of the world, but show by our fruits that we are of the number of those whom Jesus Christ has chosen out of this world, for that very reason the world will hate us. As this is true of every particular Christian, so it is true of every Christian church in general. For some years past we have heard but little of a public persecution: Why? Because but little of the power of godliness has prevailed amongst all denominations. The strong man armed has had full possession of most professors hearts, and therefore he has let them rest in a false peace. But we may assure ourselves, when Jesus Christ begins to gather in his elect in any remarkable manner, and opens an effectual door for preaching the everlasting gospel, persecution will flame out, and Satan and his emissaries will do their utmost (though all in vain) to stop the work of God. Thus it was in the first ages, thus it is in our days, and thus it will be, till time shall be no more.

Christians and Christian churches must then expect enemies. Our chief concern should be, to learn how to behave towards them in a Christian manner: For, unless we make good heed to ourselves, we shall embitter our spirits, and act unbecoming the followers of that Lord, "who, when he was reviled, reviled not again; when he suffered, threatened not; and, as a lamb before his shearers is dumb, so opened he not his mouth." But what motive shall we make use of to bring ourselves to this blessed lamb-like temper? Next to the immediate operation of the Holy Spirit upon our hearts, I know of no consideration more conducive to teach us long-suffering towards our most bitter persecutors, than this, "That, for all we know to the contrary, some of those very persons, who are now persecuting, may be chosen from all eternity by God, and hereafter called in time, to edify and build up the church of Christ."

The persecutor Saul, mentioned in the words of the text, (and whose conversion, God willing, I propose to treat on in the following discourse) is a noble instance of this kind.

I say, a persecutor, and that a bloody one. For see how he is introduced in the beginning of this chapter; "And Saul yet breathing out threatenings and slaughter against the disciples of our Lord, went unto the high priest, and desired of him letters to Damascus to the synagogues, that if he found any of this way, whether they were men or women, he might bring them bound to Jerusalem."

"And Saul yet breathing out." This implies that he had been a persecutor before. To prove which, we need only look back to the 7th chapter, where we shall find him so very remarkably active at Stephen's death, that "the witnesses laid down their clothes at a young man's feet, whose name was Saul." He seems, though young, to be in some authority. Perhaps, for his seal against the Christians, he was preferred in the church, and was allowed to sit in the great council or Sanhedrin: For we are told, Acts 8:1," That Saul was consenting unto his death;" and again, at Acts 8:3, he is brought in as exceeding all in his opposition; for thus speaks the evangelist, "As for Saul, he made havoc of the church, entering into every house, and haling men and women, committed them to prison." One would have imagined, that this should have satisfied, at least abated the fury of this young zealot. No: being exceedingly mad against them, as he himself informs Agrippa, and having made havoc of all in Jerusalem, he now is resolved to persecute the disciples of the Lord, even to strange cities; and therefore yet breathing out threatenings. "Breathing out." The words are very emphatical, and expressive of his bitter enmity. It was as natural to him now to threaten the Christians, as it was for him to breathe: he could scarce speak, but it was some threatenings against them. Nay, he not only breathed out threatenings, but slaughters also (and those who threaten, would also slaughter, if it were in their power) against the disciples of the Lord. Insatiable therefore as hell, finding he could not confute or stop the Christians by force of argument, he is resolved to do it by force of arms; and therefore went to the high priest (for there never was a persecution yet without a high priest at the head of it) and desired of him letters, issued out of his spiritual court, to the synagogues or ecclesiastical courts at Damascus, giving him authority, "that if he found any of this way, whether they were men or women, he might bring them bound unto Jerusalem," I suppose, there to be arraigned and condemned in the high priest's court. Observe how he speaks of the Christians. Luke, who wrote the Acts, calls them "disciples of the Lord," and Saul stiles them "Men and women of this way." I doubt not but he represented them as a company of upstart enthusiasts, that had lately gotten into a new method or way of living; that would not be content with the temple-service, but they must be righteous over-much, and have their private meetings or conventicles, and break bread, as they called it, from house to house, to the great disturbance of the established clergy, and to the utter subversion of all order and decency. I do not hear that the high priest makes any objection: no, he was as willing to grant letters, as Saul was to ask them; and wonderfully pleased within himself, to find he had such an active zealot to employ against the Christians.

Well then, a judicial process is immediately issued out, with the high priest's seal affixed to it. And now methinks I see the young persecutor finely equipped, and pleasing himself with thoughts, how triumphantly he should ride back with the "men and women of this way," dragging them after him to Jerusalem.

What a condition may we imagine the poor disciples at Damascus were in at this time! No doubt they had heard of Saul's imprisoning and making havoc of the saints at Jerusalem, and we may well suppose they were apprised of his design against them. I am persuaded this was a growing, because a trying time with these dear people. O how did they wrestle with God in prayer, beseeching him either to deliver them from, or give them grace sufficient to enable them to bear up under, the fury of their persecutors? The high priest doubtless with the rest of his reverend brethren, flattered themselves, that they should now put an effectual stop to this growing heresy, and waited with impatience for Saul's return.

But "He that sitteth in heaven laughs them to scorn, the Lord has them in derision." And therefore, Acts 8:3,"As Saul journeyed, and came even near unto Damascus," perhaps to the very gates, (our Lord permitting this, to try the faith of his disciples, and more conspicuously to baffle the designs of his enemies) "suddenly (at mid-day, as he acquaints Agrippa) there shined round about him a light from heaven," a light brighter than the sun; "and he fell to the earth (why not into hell?) and heard a voice saying unto him, Saul, Saul, why persecutest thou me/" The word is doubled, "Saul, Saul:" Like that of our Lord to Martha: "Martha, Martha;" or the prophet, O earth, earth, earth!" Perhaps these words came like thunder to his soul. That they were spoken audibly, we are assured from Acts 8:7,"His companions heard the voice." Our Lord now arrests the persecuting zealot, calling him by name; for the word never does us good, till we find it spoken to us in particular. "Saul, Saul, Why persecutest thou Me?" Put the emphasis upon the word *why*, what evil have I done? Put it upon the word *persecutest*, why persecutest? I suppose Saul thought he was not persecuting; no, he was only putting the laws of the ecclesiastical court into execution; but Jesus, whose eyes are as a flame of fire, saw through the hypocrisy of his heart, that, notwithstanding his specious pretenses, all this proceeded from a persecuting spirit, and secret enmity of heart against God; and therefore says, "Why persecutest thou me?" Put the emphasis upon the word *me*, why persecutest thou me? alas! Saul was not persecuting Christ, was he? He was only taking care to prevent innovations in the church, and bringing a company of enthusiasts to justice, who otherwise would overturn the established constitution. But Jesus says, "Why persecutest thou me?" For what is done to Christ's disciples, he takes as done to himself, whether it be good, or whether it be evil. He that touches Christ's disciples, touches the apple of his eye; and they who persecute the followers of our Lord, would persecute our Lord himself, was he again to come and tabernacle amongst us.

I do not find that Saul gives any reason why he did persecute; no, he was struck dumb; as every persecutor will be, when Jesus Christ puts this same question to them at the terrible day of judgment. But being pricked at the heart, no doubt with a sense not only of this, but of all his other offenses against the great God, he said, Acts 8:5, "Who art thou, Lord?" See how soon God can change the heart and voice of his most bitter enemies. Not many days ago, Saul was not only blaspheming Christ himself, but, as much as in him lay, compelling others to blaspheme also: but not, he, who before was an impostor; is called Lord; "Who art thou; Lord?" This admirably points out the way in which God's Spirit works upon the heart: it first powerfully convinces of sin, and of our damnable state; and then puts us upon inquiring after Jesus Christ. Saul being struck to the ground, or pricked to the heart, cries out after Jesus, "Who art thou, Lord?" As many of you that were never so far made sensible of your damnable state, as to be made feelingly to seek after Jesus Christ, were never yet truly convicted by, much less converted to, God. May the Lord, who struck Saul, effectually now strike all my Christless hearers, and set them upon inquiring after Jesus, as their all in all! Saul said, "Who art thou, Lord? And the Lord said, I am Jesus, whom thou persecutest." Never did any one inquire truly after Jesus Christ, but Christ made a saving discovery of himself, to his soul. It should seem, our Lord appeared to him in person; for Ananias, afterwards, says, "The Lord who appeared to thee in the way which thou camest;" though this may only imply Christ's meeting him in the way; it is not much matter: it is plain Christ here speaks to him, and says, "I am Jesus, whom thou persecutest." It is remarkable, how our Lord takes to himself the name of Jesus; for it is a name in which he delights: I am Jesus, a Savior of my people, both from the guilt and power of their sins; "a Jesus, whom thou persecutest." This seems to be spoken to convince Saul more and more of his sin; and I doubt not, but every word was sharper than a two-edged sword, and came like so many daggers to his heart; O how did these words affect him! a Jesus! A Savior! And yet I am persecuting him! this strikes him with horror; but then the word Jesus, though he was a persecutor, might give him some hope. However, our dear Lord, to convince Saul that he was to be saved by grace, and that he was not afraid of his power and enmity, tells him, "It is hard for thee to kick against the pricks." As much as to say, though he was persecuting, yet he could not overthrow the church of Christ: for he would sit as King upon his holy hill of Zion; the malice of men or devils should never be able to prevail against him.

Acts 8:6,"And he, trembling and astonished, said, Lord, what wilt thou have me to do?" Those, who think Saul had a discovery of Jesus made to his heart before, think that this question is the result of his faith, and that he now desires to know what he shall do, out of gratitude, for what the Lord had done for his soul; in this sense it may be understood; "and I have made use of it as an instance to prove, that faith will work by love; but perhaps it may be more agreeable to the context, if we suppose, that Saul had only some distant discovery of Christ made to him, and not o full assurance of faith: for we are told, "he trembling and astonished," trembling at the thoughts of his persecuting a Jesus, and astonished at his own vileness, and the infinite condescension of this Jesus, cries out, "Lord, what wilt thou have me to do?" Persons under soul-trouble, and sore conviction, would be glad to do any thing, or comply on any terms, to get peace with God. "Arise, (says our Lord) and go into the city, and it shall be told thee what thou shalt do."

And here we will leave Saul a while, and see what is become of his companions. But what shall we say? God is a sovereign agent; his sacred Spirit bloweth when and where it listeth; "he will have mercy on whom he will have mercy." Saul is taken, but, as far as we know to the contrary, his fellow-travelers are left to perish in their sins: for we are told, Acts 8:7, "That the men who journeyed with him stood, indeed, speechless, and hearing a confused voice;" I say, a confused voice, for so the word signifies, and must be so interpreted, in order to reconcile it with Acts 22:9, where Saul, giving an account of these men, tells Agrippa, "They heard not the voice of him that spake to me." They heard a voice, a confused noise, but not the articulate voice of him that spake to Saul, and therefore remained unconverted. For what are all ordinances, all, even the;most extraordinary dispensations of providence, without Christ speaks to the soul in them? Thus it is now under the word preached: many, like Saul's companions, are sometimes so struck with the outgoings of God appearing in the sanctuary, that they even stand speechless; they hear the preacher's voice, but not the voice of the Son of God, who, perhaps, at the same time is speaking effectually to many other hearts; this I have known often; and what shall we say to these things? O the depth of the sovereignty of God! It is past finding out. Lord, I desire to adore what I cannot comprehend. "Even so, Father, for so it seemeth good in thy sight!"

But to return to Saul: the Lord bids him, "arise and go into the city;" and we are told, Acts 8:8, that "Saul arose from the earth; and when his eyes were opened, (he was so overpowered with the greatness of the light that shone upon them, that) he saw no man; but they led him by the hand, and brought him into Damascus," that very city which was to be the place of his executing or imprisoning the disciples of the Lord. "And he was three days without sight, and neither did eat nor drink." But who can tell what horrors of conscience, what convulsions of soul, what deep and pungent convictions of sin he underwent during these three long days? It was this took away his appetite (for who can eat or drink when under a sense of the wrath of God for sin?) and, being to be greatly employed hereafter, he must be greatly humbled now; therefore, the Lord leaves him three days groaning under the spirit of bondage, and buffeted, no doubt, with the fiery darts of the devil, that, being tempted like unto his brethren, he might be able hereafter to succor those that were tempted. Had Saul applied to any of the blind guides of the Jewish church, under these circumstances, they would have said, he was mad, or going besides himself; as many carnal teachers and blind Pharisees now deal with, and so more and more distress, poor souls laboring under awakening convictions of their damnable state. But God often at our first awakenings, visits us with sore trials, especially those who are, like Saul, to shine in the church, and to be used as instruments in bringing many sons to glory: those who are to be highly exalted, must first be deeply humbled; and this I speak for the comfort of such, who may be now groaning under the spirit of bondage, and perhaps, like Saul, can neither eat nor drink; for I have generally observed, that those who have had the deepest convictions, have afterwards been favored with the most precious communications, and enjoyed most of the divine presence in their souls. This was after wards remarkably exemplified in Saul, who was three days without sight, and neither did eat nor drink.

But will the Lord leave his poor servant in this distress? No; his Jesus (though Saul persecuted him) promised (and he will perform) that "it should be told him what he must do. And there was a certain disciple at Damascus, named Ananias; and unto him, said the Lord, in a vision, Ananias; and he said, Behold, I am here, Lord." What a holy familiarity is there between Jesus Christ and regenerate souls! Ananias had been used to such love-visits, and therefore knew the voice of his beloved. The Lord says, "Ananias;" Ananias says, "Behold, I am here, Lord." Thus it is that Christ now, as well as formerly, often talks with his children at sundry times and after divers manners, as a man talketh with his friend. But what has the Lord to say to Ananias?

Acts 8:11, "And the Lord said unto him, Arise, and go into the street, which is called Straight, and inquire in the house of Judas, for one called Saul of Tarsus;" (See here for your comfort, O children of the most high God, what notice Jesus Christ takes of the street and the hose where his own dear servants lodge) "for behold, he prayeth;" but why is this ushered in with the word behold? What, was it such a wonder, to hear that Saul was praying? Why, Saul was a Pharisee, and therefore, no doubt, tasted and made long prayers: and, since we are told that he profited above many of his equals, I doubt not but he was taken notice of for his gift in prayer; and yet it seems, that before these three days, Saul never prayed in his life; and why? Because, before these three days, he never felt himself a condemned creature: he was alive in his own opinion, because without a knowledge of the spiritual meaning of the law; he felt not a want of, and therefore, before now, cried not after a Jesus; and consequently, though he might have said or made a prayer (as many Pharisees do now a-days) he never prayed a prayer; but now, "behold! He prayed indeed;" and this was urged as one reason why he was converted. None of God's children, as one observes, comes into the world still-born; prayer is the very breath of the new creature: and therefore, if we are prayerless, we are Christless; if we never had the spirit of supplication, it is a sad sign that we never had the spirit of grace in our souls: and you may be assured you never did pray, unless you have felt yourselves sinners, and seen the want of Jesus to be your Savior. May the Lord, whom I serve in the gospel of his dear Son, prick you all to the heart, and may it be said of you all, as it was of Saul, behold, they pray!

The Lord goes on to encourage Ananias to go to Saul: says he, Acts 8:12, "For he hath seen in a vision a man named Ananias, coming in, and putting his hand on him, that he might receive his sight." So that though Christ converted Saul immediately by himself, yet he will carry on the work, thus begun, by a minister. Happy they, who under soul-troubles have such experienced guides, and as well acquainted with Jesus Christ as Ananias was; you that have such, make much of and be thankful for them; and you who have them not, trust in God; he will carry on his own work without them.

Doubtless, Ananias was a good man; but shall I commend him for his answer to our Lord? I commend him not: for says he, Acts 8:13, "Lord, I have heard by many of this man, how much evil he hath done to the saints at Jerusalem: And here, he hath authority from the chief priests to bind all that call upon thy name." I fear this answer proceeded from some relics of self-righteousness, as well as infidelity, that lay undiscovered in the heart of Ananias. "Arise, (said our Lord) and go into the street, which is called Straight, and inquire in the hose of Judas, for one called Saul of Tarsus; for behold, he prayeth!" One would think this was sufficient to satisfy him; but says Ananias, "Lord, I have heart by many of this man (he seems to speak of him with much contempt; for even good men are apt to think too contemptuously of those who are yet in their sins) how much evil he hath done to thy saints in Jerusalem: And here, he hath authority from the chief priests to bind all that call upon Christ's name, should bind him also, if he went unto him; but the Lord silences all objections, with a "Go thy way, for he is a chosen vessel unto me, to bear my name before the Gentiles, and kings, and the children of Israel. For I will show him how great things he must suffer for my name's sake." Here God stops his mouth immediately, by asserting his sovereignty, and preaching to him the doctrine of election. And the frequent conversion of notorious sinners to God, to me is one great proof, amongst a thousand others, of that precious, but too much exploded and sadly misrepresented, doctrine of God's electing love; for whence is it that such are taken, whilst thousands, not near so vile, die senseless and stupid? All the answer that can be given, is, they are chosen vessels; "Go thy way, (says God) for he is a chosen vessel unto me, to bear my name before the Gentiles, and kings, and the children of Israel: For I will show him how great things he must suffer for my name's sake." Observe what a close connection there is between doing and suffering for Christ. If any of my brethren in the ministry are present, let them bear what preferment we must expect, if we are called out to work remarkably for God: not great prebendaries or bishopricks, but great sufferings for our Lord's name sake; these are the fruits of our labor: and he that will not contentedly suffer great things for preaching Christ, is not worthy of him. Suffering will be found to be the best preferment, when w are called to give an account of our ministry at the great day.

I do not hear, that Ananias quarreled with God concerning the doctrine of election; no, (O that all good men would, in this, learn of him!) "He went his way, and entered into the house; and put his hands on him, and said, Brother Saul;" just now, it was *this man*; now it is *brother Saul*: it is not matter what a man has been, if he be now a Christian; the same should be our brother, our sister and mother; God blots our every convert's transgressions as with a thick cloud, and so should we; the more vile a man has been, the more should we love him when believing in Christ, because Christ will be more glorified on his behalf. I doubt not, but Ananias was wonderfully delighted to hear that so remarkable a persecutor was brought home to God: I am persuaded he felt his soul immediately united to him by love, and therefore addresses him not with, thou persecutor, thou murderer, that camest to butcher me and my friends; but, "brother Saul." It is remarkable that the primitive Christians much used the word brother and brethren; I know it is a term now much in reproach; but those who despise it, I believe, would be glad to be of our brotherhood, when they see us sitting at the right-hand of the Majesty on high. "Brother Saul, the Lord (even Jesus that appeared unto thee in the way as thou camest) hath sent me, that thou mightest receive thy sight, and be filled with the Holy Ghost." At this time, we may suppose, he laid his hands upon him. See the consequences.

The scales are now removed from the eyes of Saul's mind; Ananias has done that for him, under God: he must now do another office, baptize him, and so receive him into the visible church of Christ; a good proof to me of the necessity of baptism where it may be had: for I find here, as well as elsewhere, that baptism is administered even to those who had received the Holy Ghost; Saul was convinced of this, and therefore arose and was baptized; and now it is time for him to recruit the outward man, which, by three days abstinence and spiritual conflicts, had been much impaired; we are therefore told, Acts 8:19, "when he had received meat, he was strengthened."

But O, with what comfort did the apostle now eat his food? I am sure it was with singleness, I am persuaded also with gladness of heart; and why? He knew that he was reconciled to God; and, for my own part, did I not know how blind and flinty our hearts are by nature, I should wonder how any one could eat even his common food with any satisfaction, who has not some well-grounded hope of his being reconciled to God. Our Lord intimates thus much to us: for in his glorious prayer, after he has taught us to pray for our daily bread, immediately adds that petition, "Forgive us our trespasses;" as though our daily bread would do us no service, unless we were sensible of having the forgiveness of our sins.

To proceed; Saul hath received meat, and is strengthened; and whither will he go now? To see the brethren; "then was Saul certain days with the disciples that were at Damascus." If we know and love Christ, we shall also love and desire to be acquainted with the brethren of Christ: we may generally know a man by his company. And though all are not saints that associate with saints, (for tares will be always springing up amongst the wheat till the time of harvest) yet, if we never keep company, but are shy and ashamed of the despised children of God, it is a certain sign we have not yet experimentally learned Jesus, or received him into our hearts. My dear friends, be not deceived; if we are friends to the Bridegroom, we shall be friends to the children of the Bridegroom. Saul, as soon as he was filled with the Holy Ghost, "was certain days with the disciples that were at Damascus."

But who can tell what joy these disciples felt when Saul came amongst them! I suppose holy Ananias introduced him. Methinks I see the once persecuting zealot, when they came to salute him with a holy kiss, throwing himself upon each of their necks, weeping over them with floods of tears, and saying, "" my brother, O my sister, Can you forgive me? Can you give such a wretch as I the right-hand of fellowship, who intended to drag you behind me bound unto Jerusalem!" Thus, I say, we may suppose Saul addressed himself to his fellow-disciples; and I doubt not but they were as ready to forgive and forget as Ananias was, and saluted him with the endearing title of "brother Saul." Lovely was this meeting; so lovely, that it seemed Saul continued certain days with them, to communicate experiences, and to learn the way of God more perfectly; to pray for a blessing on his future ministry, and to praise Christ Jesus for what he had done for their souls. Saul, perhaps, had sat certain years at the feet of Gamaliel, but undoubtedly learned more these certain days, than he had learned before in all his life. It pleases me to think how this great scholar is transformed by the renewing of his mind. What a mighty change was here! That so great a man as Saul was, both as to his station in life, and internal qualifications, and such a bitter enemy to the Christians; for him, I say, to go and be certain days with the people of *this* mad way, and to sit quietly, and be taught of illiterate men, as many of these disciples we may be sure were; what a substantial proof was this of the reality of his conversion!

What a hurry and confusion may we suppose the chief priests were now in! I warrant they were ready to cry out, What! Is he also deceived? As for the common people, who knew not the law, and are accursed, for them to be carried away, is no such wonder; but for a man bred up at the feet of Gamaliel, for such a scholar, such an enemy to the cause as Saul; for him to be led away with a company of silly, deceived men and women, surely it is impossible: we cannot believe it. But Saul soon convinces them of the reality of his becoming a fool for Christ's sake: for straightway, instead of going to deliver the letters from the high priests, as they expected, in order to bring the disciples that were at Damascus bound to Jerusalem, "he preached Christ n the synagogues, that he is the Son of God." This is another proof of his being converted. He not only conversed with Christians in private, but he preached Christ publicly in the synagogues; especially, he insisted on the divinity of our Lord, proving, notwithstanding his state of humiliation, that he was really the Son of God.

But why did Saul preach Christ thus? Because he had felt the power of Christ upon his own soul. And here is the reason why Christ is so seldom preached, and his divinity so slightly insisted on in our synagogues: because the generality of those that pretend to preach him, never felt a saving work of conversion upon their own souls. How can they preach, unless they are first taught of, and then sent by God? Saul did not preach Christ before he knew him; no more should any one else. An unconverted minister, though he could speak with the tongues of men and angels, will be but as a sounding brass and tinkling cymbal to those whose senses are exercised to discern spiritual things. Ministers that are unconverted, may talk and declaim of Christ, and prove from books that he is the Son of God; but they cannot preach with the demonstration of the Spirit and with power, unless they preach from experience, and have had a proof of his divinity, by a work of grace wrought upon their own souls. God forgive those, who lay hands on an unconverted man, knowing that he is such: I would not do it for a thousand worlds, Lord Jesus, keep thy own faithful servants pure, and let them not be partakers of other men's sins!

Such an instance as was Saul's conversion, we may be assured, must make a great deal of noise; and, therefore, no wonder we are told, Acts 8:21 "But all that heard him were amazed, and said, Is not this he that destroyed them who called on this name in Jerusalem, and came hither for that intent, that he might bring them bound to the chief priests."

Thus it will be with all that appear publicly for Jesus Christ; and it is as impossible for a true Christian to be hid, as a city built upon a hill. Brethren, if you are faithful to, you must be reproached and have remarks made on you for Christ; especially of you have been remarkably wicked before your conversion. Your friends will say, is not this he, or she, who a little while ago would run to as great an excess of riot and vanity as the worst of us all? What has turned your brain?—Or if you have been close, false, formal hypocrites, as Saul was, they will wonder that you should be so deceived, as to think you were not in a safe state before. No doubt, numbers were surprised to hear Saul, who was touching the law blameless, affirm that he was in a damnable condition (as in all probability he did) a few days before.

Brethren, you must expect to meet with many such difficulties as these. The scourge of the tongue, is generally the first cross we are called to bear for the sake of Christ. Let not, therefore, this move you: It did not intimidate, no, it rather encouraged Saul: says the text, "But Saul increased the more in strength, and confounded the Jews who dwelt at Damascus, proving that this is very Christ." Opposition never yet did, or ever will hurt a sincere convert: Nothing like opposition to make the man of God perfect. None but a hireling, who careth not for the sheep, will be affrighted at the approach or barking of wolves. Christ's ministers are as bold as lions: it is not for such men as they to flee.

And therefore (that I may draw towards a conclusion() let the ministers and disciples of Christ learn from Saul, not to fear men or their revilings; but, like him, increase in strength, the more wicked men endeavor to weaken their hands. We cannot be Christians without being opposed: no; disciples in general must suffer; ministers in particular must suffer great things. But let not this move any of us from our steadfastness in the gospel: He that stood by and strengthened Saul, will also stand by and strengthen us: He is a God mighty to save all that put their trust in him. If we look up with an eye of faith, we, as well as the first martyr Stephen, may see Jesus standing at the right hand of God, ready to assist and protect us. Though the Lord' seat is in heaven, yet he has respect to his saints in an especial manner, when suffering here on earth: then the Spirit of Christ and of glory rests upon their souls. And, if I may speak my own experience, I never enjoy more rich communications from God than when despised and rejected of men for the sake of Jesus Christ." However little they may design it, my enemies are my greatest friends. What I most fear, is a calm; but the enmity which is in the hearts of natural men against Christ, will not suffer them to be quiet long; No; as I hope the work of God will increase, so the rags of men and devils will increase also. Let us put on, therefore, the whole armor of God: let us not fear the face of men: "Let us fear him only, who can destroy both body and soul in hell." I say unto you let us fear him alone. You see how soon God can stop the fury of his enemies.

You have just now heard of a proud, powerful zealot stopped in his full career, struck down to the earth with a light from heaven, converted by the almighty power of efficacious grace, and thereupon zealously promoting, nay, resolutely suffering for, the faith, which once with threatenings and slaughters he endeavored to destroy. Let his teach us to pity and pray for our Lord's most inveterate enemies. Who knows, but in answer thereunto, our Lord may give them repentance unto life? Most think, that Christ had respect to Stephen's prayer, when he converted Saul. Perhaps for this reason God suffers his adversaries to go on, that his goodness and power may shine more bright in their conversion.,

But let not the persecutors of Christ take encouragement from this to continue in their opposition. Remember, though Saul was converted, yet the high-priest, and Saul's companions, were left dead in trespasses and sins. And, if this should be your case, you will of all men be most miserable: for persecutors have the lowest place in hell. And, if Saul was struck to the earth by a light from heaven, how will you be able to stand before Jesus Christ, when he comes in terrible majesty to take vengeance on all those who have persecuted his gospel? Then the question, "Why persecutest thou me?" will cut you through and through. The secret enmity of your hearts shall be then detected before men and angels, and you shall be doomed to dwell in the blackness of darkness for evermore. Kiss the Son, therefore, lest he be angry: for even you may yet find mercy, if you believe on the Son of God: though you persecute him, yet he will be your Jesus. I cannot despair of any of you, when I find a Saul among the disciples at Damascus. What though your sins are as scarlet, the blood of Christ shall wash them as white as snow. Having much to be forgiven, despair not; only believe, and like Saul, of whom I have now been speaking, love much. He counted himself the chiefest sinner of all, and therefore labored more abundantly than all.

Who is there among you fearing the Lord? Whose hearts hath the Lord now opened to hearken to the voice of his poor unworthy servant? Surely, the Lord will not let me preach in vain. Who is the happy soul that is this day to be washed in the blood of the Lamb? Will no poor sinner take encouragement from Saul to come to Jesus Christ? You are all thronging round, but which of you will touch the Lord Jesus? What a comfort will it be to Saul, and to your own souls, when you meet him in heaven, to tell him, that hearing of his, was a means, under God, of your conversion! Doubtless it was written for the encouragement of all poor, returning sinners; he himself tells us so: for "in me God showed all long-suffering, that I might be an example to them that should hereafter believe." Was Saul here himself, he would tell you so, indeed he would; but being dead, by this account of his conversion he yet speaketh. O that God may speak by it to your hearts! O that the arrows of God might this day stick fast in your souls, and you made to cry out, "Who art thou, Lord?" Are there any such amongst you? Methinks I feel something of what this Saul felt, when he said, "I travail in birth again for you, till Christ be formed again in your hearts." O come, come away to Jesus, in whom Saul believed; and then I care not if the high-priests issue out never so many writs, or injuriously drag me to a prison. The thoughts of being instrumental in saving you, will make me sing praises even at midnight. And I know you will be my joy and crown of rejoicing, when I am delivered from this earthly prison, and meet you in the kingdom of God hereafter.

Now to God.

42. Marks of Having Received the Holy Ghost

Acts 19:2—"Have ye received the Holy Ghost since ye believed?"

Two different significations have been given of these words. Some have supposed, that the question here put, is, Whether these disciples, whom St. Paul found at Ephesus, had received the Holy Ghost by imposition of hands at confirmation? Others think, these disciples had been already baptized into John's baptism; which not being attended with an immediate effusion of the Holy Spirit, the Apostle here asks them, Whether they had received the Holy Ghost by being baptized into Jesus Christ? And upon their answering in the negative, he first baptized, and then confirmed them in the name of the Lord Jesus.

Which of these interpretations is the most true, is neither easy nor very necessary to determine. However, as the words contain a most important inquiry, without any reference to the context, I shall from them,

First, Show who the Holy Ghost here spoken of, is; and that we must all receive him, before we can be stiled true believers.

Secondly, I shall lay down some scripture marks whereby we may know, whether we have thus received the Holy Ghost or not. And

Thirdly, By way of conclusion, address myself to several distinct classes of professors, concerning the doctrine that shall have been delivered.

First, I am to show who the Holy Ghost spoken of in the text, is; and that we must all receive him before we can be stiled true believers.

By the Holy Ghost is plainly signified the Holy Spirit, the third Person in the ever-blessed Trinity, consubstantial and co-eternal with the Father and the Son, proceeding from, yet equal to them both. He is emphatically called Holy, because infinitely holy in himself, and the author and finisher of all holiness in us.

This blessed Spirit, who once moved on the face of the great deep; who over-shadowed the blessed Virgin before that holy child was born of her; who descended in a bodily shape, like a dove, on our blessed Lord, when he came up out of the water at his baptism; and afterwards came down in fiery tongues on the heads of all his Apostles at the day of Pentecost: this is the Holy Ghost, who must move on the faces of our souls; this power of the Most High, must come upon us, and we must be baptized with his baptism and refining fire, before we can be stiled true members of Christ" mystical body.

Thus says the Apostle Paul, "Know ye not that Jesus Christ is in you, (that is, by his Spirit) unless you are reprobates?" And, "If any man hath not the Spirit of Christ, he is none of his," And again, says St. John, "We know that we are his, by the Spirit that he hath given us."

It is not, indeed, necessary that we should have the Spirit now given in that miraculous manner, in which he was at first given to our Lord's Apostles, by signs and wonders, but it is absolutely necessary, that we should receive the Holy Ghost in his sanctifying graces, as really as they did: and so will it continue to be till the end of the world.

For this stands the case between God and man: God at first made man upright, or as the sacred Penman expresses it, "In the image of God made he man;" that is, his soul was the very copy, the transcript of the divine nature. He, who before, by his almighty fiat, spoke the world into being, breathed into man the breath of spiritual life, and his soul was adorned with a resemblance of the perfections of Deity. This was the finishing stroke of the creation: the perfection both of the moral and material world. And so near did man resemble his divine Original, that God could not but rejoice and take pleasure in his own likeness: And therefore we read, that when God had finished the inanimate and brutish part of the creation, he looked upon it, and beheld it was good; but when that lovely, God-like creature man was made, behold it was very good.

Happy, unspeakably happy must man needs be, when thus a partaker of the divine nature. And thus might he have still continued, had he continued holy. But God placed him in a state of probation, with a free grant to eat of every tree in the garden of Eden, except the tree of knowledge of good and evil: the day he should eat thereof, he was surely to die; that is, not only to be subject to temporal, but spiritual death; and consequently, to lose that divine image, that spiritual life God had not long since breathed into him, and which was as much his happiness as his glory.

These, one would imagine, were easy conditions for a finite creature's happiness to depend on. But man, unhappy man, being seduced by the devil, and desiring, like him, to be equal with his Maker, did eat of the forbidden fruit; and thereby became liable to that curse, which the eternal God, who cannot lie, had denounced against his disobedience.

Accordingly we read, that soon after Adam had fallen, he complained that he was naked; naked, not only as to his body, but naked and destitute of those divine graces which, before decked and beautified his soul. The unhappy mutiny, and disorder which the visible creation fell into, the briars and thorns which not sprung up and overspread the earth, were but poor emblems, lifeless representations of that confusion and rebellion, and those divers lusts and passions which sprung up in, and quite overwhelmed the soul of man immediately after the fall. Alas! he was now no longer the image of the invisible God; but as he had imitated the devil's sin, he became as it were a partaker of the devil's nature, and from an union with, sunk into a state of direct enmity against God.

Now in this dreadful disordered condition, are all of us brought into the world: for as the root is, such must the branches be. Accordingly we are told, "That Adam beget a son in his own likeness;" or, with the same corrupt nature which he himself had, after he had eaten the forbidden fruit. And experience as well as scripture proves, that we also are altogether born in sin and corruption; and therefore incapable, whilst in such a state, to hole communion with God. For as light cannot have communion with darkness, so God can have no communion with such polluted sons of Belial.

Here then appears the end and design why Christ was manifest in the flesh; to put an end to these disorders, and to restore us to that primitive dignity in which we were at first created. Accordingly he shed his precious blood to satisfy his Father's justice for our sins; and thereby also he procured for us the Holy Ghost, who should once more re-instamp the divine image upon our hearts, and make us capable of living with and enjoying the blessed God.

This was the great end of our Lord's coming into the world; nay, this is the only end why the world itself is now kept in being. For as soon as a sufficient number are sanctified out of it, the heavens shall be wrapped up like a scroll, the elements shall melt with fervent heat, the earth, and all that therein is, shall be burnt up.

This sanctification of the Spirit, is that new birth mentioned by our blessed Lord to Nicodemus, "without which we cannot see the kingdom of God." This is what St. Paul calls being "renewed in the spirit of our minds;" and it is the spring of that holiness, without which no man shall see the Lord.

Thus then, it is undeniably certain, we must receive the Holy Ghost ere we can be stiled true members of Christ's mystical body.

I come in the *Second* place to lay down some scriptural marks, whereby we may easily judge, whether we have thus received the Holy Ghost or not.

And the *First* I shall mention, is, our having received a spirit of prayer and supplication; for that always accompanies the spirit of grace. No sooner was Paul converted, but "behold he prayeth." And this was urged as an argument, to convince Ananias that he was converted. And God's elect are also said to "cry to him day and night."

And since one great work of the Holy Spirit is to convince us of sin, and to set us upon seeking pardon and renewing grace, through the all-sufficient merits of a crucified Redeemer, whosoever has felt the power of the world to come, awakening him from his spiritual lethargy, cannot but be always crying out, "Lord, what wouldst thou have me to do?" Or, in the language of the importunate blind Bartimeus, "Jesus, thou Son of David, have mercy upon me."

The blessed Jesus, as he received the Holy Ghost without measure, so he evidenced it by nothing more, than his frequent addresses at the throne of grace. Accordingly we read, that he was often alone on the mountain praying; that he rose a great while before day to pray: nay, that he spent whole nights in prayer. And whosoever is made partaker of the same Spirit which the holy Jesus, will be of the same mind, and delight in nothing so much, as to "draw nigh unto God," and lift up holy hands and hearts in frequent and devout prayer.

It must be confessed, indeed, that this spirit of supplication is often as it were sensibly lost, and decays, for some time, even in those who have actually received the Holy Ghost. Through spiritual dryness and barrenness of soul, they find in themselves a listlessness and backwardness to this duty of prayer; but then they esteem it as their cross, and still persevere in seeking Jesus, though it be sorrowing: and their hearts, notwithstanding, are fixed upon God, though they cannot exert their affections so strongly as usual, on account of that spiritual deadness, which God, for wise reasons, has suffered to benumb their souls.

But as for the formal believer, it is not so with him: no; he either prays not at all, or if he does enter into his closet, it is with reluctance, out of custom, or to satisfy the checks of his conscience. Whereas, the true believer can no more live without prayer, than without food day by day. And he finds his soul as really and perceptibly fed by the one, as his body is nourished and supported by the other.

A *Second* scripture mark of our having received the Holy Ghost, is, Not committing sin.

"Whosoever is born of God, (says St. John) sinneth not, neither can he sin, because his seed remaineth in him." Neither can he sin. This expression does not imply the impossibility of a Christian's sinning: for we are told, that "in many things we offend all:" It only means thus much: that a man who is really born again of God, doth not willfully commit sin, much less live in the habitual practice of it. For how shall he that is dead to sin, as every converted person is, live any longer therein?

It is true, a man that is born again of God, may, through surprise, or the violence of a temptation, fall into an act of sin: witness the adultery of David, and Peter's denial of his Master. But then, like them, he quickly rises again, goes out from the world, and weeps bitterly; washes the guilt of sin away by the tears of sincere repentance, joined with faith in the blood of Jesus Christ; takes double heed to his ways for the future, and perfects holiness in the fear of God.

The meaning of this expression of the Apostle, that "a man who is born of God, cannot commit sin," has been fitly illustrated, by the example of a covetous worldling, to the general bent of whose inclinations, liberality and profuseness are directly opposite: but if, upon some unexpected, sudden occasion, he does play the prodigal, he immediately repents him of his fault, and returns with double care to his niggardliness again. And so is every one that is born again: to commit sin, is as contrary to the habitual frame and tendency of his mind, as generosity is to the inclinations of a miser; but if at any time, he is drawn into sin, he immediately, with double zeal, returns to his duty, and brings forth fruits meet for repentance. Whereas, the unconverted sinner is quite dead in trespasses and sins: or if he does abstain from gross acts of it, through worldly selfish motives, yet, there is some right eye he will not pluck out; some right-hand which he will not cut off; some specious Agag that he will not sacrifice for God; and thereby he is convinced that he is but a mere Saul: and consequently, whatever pretensions he may make to the contrary, he has not yet received the Holy Ghost.

A *Third* mark whereby we may know, whether or not we have received the Holy Ghost, is, Our conquest over the world.

"For whosoever is born of God, (says the Apostle) overcometh the world." By the world, we are to understand, as St. John expressed it, "all that is in the world, the lust of the eye, the lust of the flesh, and the pride of life:" And by overcoming of it, is meant, our renouncing these, so as not to follow or be led by them: for whosoever is born from above, has his affections set on things above: he feels a divine attraction in his soul, which forcibly draws his mind heavenwards; and as the hart panteth after the water-brooks, so doth it make his soul so long after the enjoyment of his God.

Not that he is so taken up with the affairs of another life, as to neglect the business of this: No; a truly spiritual man dares not stand any day idle; but then he takes care, though he laboreth for the meat which perisheth, first to secure that which endureth to everlasting life. Or, if God has exalted him above his brethren, yet, like Moses, Joseph, and Daniel, he, notwithstanding, looks upon himself as a stranger and pilgrim upon earth: having received a principle of new life, he walks by faith and not by sight; and his hopes being full of immortality, he can look on all things here below as vanity and vexation of spirit: In short, though he is in, yet he is not of the world; and as he was made for the enjoyment of God, so nothing but God can satisfy his soul.

The ever-blessed Jesus was a perfect instance of overcoming the world. For though he went about continually doing good, and always lived as in a press and throng; yet, wherever he was, his conversation tended heavenwards. In like manner, he that is joined to the Lord in one spirit, will so order his thoughts, words, and actions, that he will evidence to all, that his conversation is in heaven.

On the contrary, an unconverted man being of the earth, is earthy; and having no spiritual eye to discern spiritual things, he is always seeking for happiness in this life, where it never was, will, or can be found. Being not born again from above, he is bowed down by a spirit of natural infirmity: the serpent's curse becomes his choice, and he eats of the dust of the earth all the days of his life.

A *Fourth* scripture mark of our having received the Holy Ghost, is, Our loving one another.

"We know (says St. John) we are passed from death unto life, because we love the brethren." "And by this (says Christ himself) shall all men know that ye are my disciples, if ye have love one towards another." Love is the fulfilling of the gospel, as well as of the law: for "God is love; and whosoever dwelleth in love, dwelleth in God."

But by this love we are not to understand a softness and tenderness of mere nature, or a love founded on worldly motives (for this a natural man may have); but a love of our brethren, proceeding from love towards God: loving all men in general, because to their relation to God; and loving good men in particular, for the grace we see in them, and because they love our Lord Jesus in sincerity.

This is Christian charity, and that new commandment which Chris gave to his disciples. *New*, not in its object, but in the motive and example whereon it is founded, even Jesus Christ. This is that love which the primitive Christians were so renowned for, that it became a proverb, *see how these Christians love one another*. And without this love, though we should give all our goods to feed the poor, and our bodies to be burnt, it would profit us nothing.

Further, this love is not confined to any particular set of men, but is impartial and catholic: A love that embraces God's image wherever it beholds it, and that delights in nothing so much as to see Christ's kingdom come.

This is the love wherewith Jesus Christ loved mankind: He loved all, even the worst of men, as appears by his weeping over the obstinately perverse; but wherever he saw the least appearance of the divine likeness, that soul he loved in particular. Thus we read, that when he heard the young man say, "All these things have I kept from my youth," that so far he loved him. And when he saw any noble instance of faith, though in a Centurion and a Syrophonecian, aliens to the commonwealth of Israel, how is he said to marvel at, to rejoice in, speak of, and commend it? So every spiritual disciple of Jesus Christ will cordially embrace all who worship God in spirit and in truth, however they may differ as to the appendages of religion, and in things not essentially necessary to salvation.

I confess, indeed, that the heart of a natural man is not thus enlarged all at once; and a person may really have received the Holy Ghost, (as Peter, no doubt, had when he was unwilling to go to Cornelius) though he be not arrived to this: but then, where a person is truly in Christ, all narrowness of spirit decreases in him daily; the partition wall of bigotry and party zeal is broken down more and more; and the nearer he comes to heaven, the more his heart is enlarged with that love, which there will make no difference between any people, nation, or language, but we shall all, with one heart, and one voice, sing praises to him that sitteth upon the throne for ever.

But I hasten to a *Fifth* scripture mark, Loving our enemies.

"I say unto you, (says Jesus Christ) Love your enemies, bless them that curse you, do good to those that hate you, and pray for them that despitefully use you and persecute you." And this duty of loving your enemies is so necessary, that without it, our righteousness does not exceed the righteousness of the Scribes and Pharisees, or even of Publicans and sinners: "For if you do good to them only, who do good to you, what do you more than others?" What do you extraordinary? "Do not even the Publicans the same?" And these precepts our Lord confirmed by his own example; when he wept over the bloody city; when he suffered himself to be led as a sheep to the slaughter; when he made that mile reply to the traitor Judas, "Judas, betrayest thou the Son of man with a kiss?" and more especially, when in the agonies and pangs of death, he prayed for his very murderers, "Father, forgive them, for they know not what they do."

This is a difficult duty to the natural man; but whosoever is made partaker of the promise of the Spirit, will find it practicable and easy: for if we are born again of God, we must be like him, and consequently delight to be perfect in this duty of doing good to our worst enemies in the same manner, though not in the same degree as he is perfect: He sends his rain on the evil and the good; causeth his sun to shine on the just and unjust; and more especially commended his love towards us, that whilst we were his enemies, he sent forth his Son, born of a woman, made under the law, that he might become a curse for us.

Many other marks are scattered up and down the scriptures, whereby we may know whether or not we have received the Holy Ghost: such as, "to be carnally minded, is death, but to be spiritually minded is life and peace." "Now the fruits of the Spirit are joy, peace, long-suffering, meekness," with a multitude of texts to the same purpose. But as most, if not all of them, are comprehended in the duties already laid down, I dare affirm, whosoever upon an impartial examination, can find the aforesaid marks on his soul, may be as certain, as though an angel was to tell him, that his pardon is sealed in heaven.

As for my own part, I had rather see these divine graces, and this heavenly temper stamped upon my soul, than to hear an angel from heaven saying unto me, Son, be of good cheer, thy sins are forgiven thee.

These are infallible witnesses; these are Emmanuel, God with and in us; these make up that white stone, which none knoweth, saving he who hath receiveth it; these are the earnests of the heavenly inheritance in our hearts: In short, these are glory begun, and are that good thing, that better part, and which if you continue to stir up this gift of God, neither men nor devils shall ever be able to take from us.

I proceed, as was proposed, in the *Third* place, to make an application of the doctrine delivered, to several distinct classes of professors. And

First, I shall address myself to those who are dead in trespasses and sins. And, O how could I weep over you, as our Lord wept over Jerusalem? For, alas! how distant must you be from God? What a prodigious work have you to finish, who, instead of praying day and night, seldom or never pray at all? And, instead of being born again of God, so as not to commit sin, are so deeply sunk into the nature of devils, as to make a mock at it? Or, instead of overcoming the world, so as not to follow or be led by it, are continually making provision for the flesh, to fulfill the lusts thereof. And, instead of being endued with the god-like disposition of loving all men, even your enemies, have your hearts full of hatred, malice, and revenge, and deride those who are the sincere followers of the lowly Jesus. But think you, O sinners, that God will admit such polluted wretches into his sight? Or should he admit you, do you imagine you could take any pleasure in him? No; heaven itself would be no heaven to you; the devilish dispositions which are in your hearts, would render all the spiritual enjoyments of those blessed mansions, ineffectual to make you happy. To qualify you to be blissful partakers of that heavenly inheritance with the saints in light, there is a meekness required: to attain which, ought to be the chief business of your lives.

It is true, you, as well as the righteous, in one sense, shall see God; (for we must all appear before the judgment-seat of Christ) but you must see him once, never to see him more. For as you carry about in you the devil's image, with devils you must dwell: being of the same nature, you must share the same doom. "Repent, therefore, and be converted, that your sins may be blotted out." See that you receive the Holy Ghost, before you go hence: for otherwise, how can you escape the damnation of hell?

Secondly, Let me apply myself to those who deceive themselves with false hopes of salvation. Some, through the influence of a good education, or other providential restraints, have not run into the same excess of riot with other men, and they think they have no need to receive the Holy Ghost, but flatter themselves that they are really born again.

But do you show it by bringing forth the fruits of the Spirit? Do you pray without ceasing? Do you not commit sin? Have you overcome the world? And do you love your enemies, and all mankind, in the same manner, as Jesus Christ loved them?

If these things, brethren, be in you and abound, then may you have confidence towards God; but if not, although you may be civilized, yet you are not converted: no, you are yet in your sins. The nature of the old Adam still reigneth in your souls; and unless the nature of the second Adam be grafted in its room, you can never see God.

Think not, therefore, to dress yourselves up in the ornaments of a good nature, and civil education, and say with Agag, "surely the bitterness of death is past;" For God's justice, notwithstanding that, like Samuel, shall hew you to pieces. However you may be highly esteemed in the sight of men, yet, in the sight of God, you are but like the apples of Sodom, dunghills covered over with snow, mere whited sepulchers, appearing a little beautiful without, but inwardly full of corruption and of all uncleanness: and consequently will be dismissed at the last day with a "Verily, I know you not."

But the word of God is profitable for comfort as well as correction.

Thirdly, Therefore I address myself to those who are under the drawings of the Father, and are exercised with the Spirit of bondage, and not finding the marks before mentioned, are crying out, Who shall deliver us from the body of this death?

But fear not, little flock; for notwithstanding your present infant state of grace, it shall be your father's good pleasure to give you the kingdom. The grace of God, through Jesus Christ, shall deliver you, and give you what you thirst after: He hath promised, he will also do it. Ye shall receive the spirit of adoption, that promise of the Father, if you faint not: only persevere in seeking it; and determine not to be at rest in your soul, till you know and feel that you are thus born again from above, and God's Spirit witnesseth with your spirits that you are the children of God.

Fourthly and *Lastly*, I address myself to those who have received the Holy Ghost in all his sanctifying graces, and are almost ripe for glory.

Hail, happy saints! For your heaven is begun on earth: you have already received the first fruits of the Spirit, and are patiently waiting till that blessed change come, when your harvest shall be complete. I see and admire you, though, alas! at so great a distance from you: your life, I know, is hid with Christ in God. You have comforts, you have meat to eat, which a sinful, carnal, ridiculing world knows nothing of. Christ's yoke is not become easy to you, and his burden light. You have passed through the pangs of the new birth, and now rejoice that Christ Jesus is spiritually formed in your hearts. You know what it is to dwell in Christ, and Christ in you. Like Jacob's ladder, although your bodies are on earth, yet your souls and hearts are in heaven: and by your faith and constant recollection, like the blessed angels, you do always behold the face of your Father which is in heaven.

I need not exhort you to press forward, for you know that in walking in the Spirit there is a great reward. Rather will I exhort you, in patience to possess your souls yet a little while, and Jesus Christ will deliver you from the burden of the flesh, and an abundant entrance shall be administered to you, into the eternal joy and uninterrupted felicity of his heavenly kingdom.

Which God of his infinite mercy grant, through Jesus Christ our Lord: To whom, with the Father, and the Holy Ghost, three Persons and one God, be ascribed all honor, power, and glory, for ever and ever.

43. THE ALMOST CHRISTIAN

Acts 26:28—"Almost thou persuadest me to be a Christian."

The chapter, out of which the text is taken, contains an admirable account which the great St. Paul gave of his wonderful conversion from Judaism to Christianity, when he was called to make his defense before Festus a Gentile governor, and king Agrippa. Our blessed Lord had long since foretold, that when the Son of man should be lifted up, "his disciples should be brought before kings and rulers, for his name's sake, for a testimony unto them." And very good was the design of infinite wisdom in thus ordaining it; for Christianity being, from the beginning, a doctrine of the Cross, the princes and rulers of the earth thought themselves too high to be instructed by such mean teachers, or too happy to be disturbed b such unwelcome truths; and therefore would have always continued strangers to Jesus Christ, and him crucified, had not the apostles, by being arraigned before them, gained opportunities of preaching to them "Jesus and the resurrection." St. Paul knew full well that this was the main reason, why his blessed Master permitted his enemies at this time to arraign him at a public bar; and therefore, in compliance with the divine will, thinks it not sufficient, barely to make his defense, but endeavors at the same time to convert his judges. And this he did with such demonstration of the spirit, and of power, that Festus, unwilling to be convinced by the strongest evidence, cries out with a loud voice, "Paul, much earning doth make thee mad." To which the brave apostle (like a true follower of the holy Jesus) meekly replies, I am not mad, most noble Festus, but speak forth the words of truth and soberness." But in all probability, seeing king Agrippa more affected with his discourse, and observing in him an inclination to know the truth, he applies himself more particularly to him. "The king knoweth of these things; before whom also I speak freely; for I am persuaded that none of these things are hidden from him." And then, that if possible he might complete his wished-for conversion, he with an inimitable strain of oratory, addresses himself still more closely, "King Agrippa, believest thou the prophets? I know that thou believest them." At which the passions of the king began to work so strongly, that he was obliged in open court, to own himself affected by the prisoner's preaching, and ingenuously to cry out, "Paul, almost thou persuadest me to be a Christian."

Which words, taken with the context, afford us a lively representation of the different reception, which the doctrine of Christ's ministers, who come in the power and spirit of St. Paul, meets with now-a-days in the minds of men. For notwithstanding they, like this great apostle, "speak forth the words of truth and soberness;" and with such energy and power, that all their adversaries cannot justly gainsay or resist; yet, too many, with the noble Festus before-mentioned, being like him, either too proud to be taught, or too sensual, too careless, or too worldly-minded to live up to the doctrine, in order to excuse themselves, cry out, that "much learning, much study, or, what is more unaccountable, much piety, hath made them mad." And though, blessed be God! All do not thus disbelieve our report; yet amongst those who gladly receive the word, and confess that we speak the words of truth and soberness, there are so few, who arrive at any higher degree of piety than that of Agrippa, or are any farther persuaded than to be almost Christians, that I cannot but think it highly necessary to warn my dear hearers of the danger of such a state. And therefore, from the words of the text, shall endeavor to show these three things:

First, What is meant by an almost-Christian.

Secondly, What are the chief reasons, why so many are no more than almost Christians.

Thirdly, I shall consider the ineffectualness, danger, absurdity, and uneasiness which attends those who are but almost Christians; and then conclude with a general exhortation, to set all upon striving not only be almost, but altogether Christians.

I. And, *First*, I am to consider what is meant by an almost Christians.

An almost Christian, if we consider him in respect to his duty to God, is one that halts between two opinions; that wavers between Christ and the world; that would reconcile God and Mammon, light and darkness, Christ and Belial. It is true, he has an inclination to religion, but then he is very cautious how he goes too far in it: his false heart is always crying out, Spare thyself, do thyself no harm. He prays indeed, that "God's will may be done on earth, as it is in heaven." But notwithstanding, he is very partial in his obedience, and fondly hopes that God will not be extreme to mark every thing that he willfully does amiss; though an inspired apostle has told him, that "he who offends in one point is guilty of all." But chiefly, he is one that depends much on outward ordinances, and on that account looks upon himself as righteous, and despises others; though at the same time he is as great a stranger to the divine life as any other person whatsoever. In short, he is fond of the form, but never experiences the power of godliness in his heart. He goes on year after year, attending on the means of grace, but then, like Pharaoh's lean kine [cow?], he is never the better, but rather the worse for them.

If you consider him in respect to his neighbor, he is one that is strictly just to all; but then this does not proceed from any love to God or regard to man, but only through a principle of self-love: because he knows dishonesty will spoil his reputation, and consequently hinder his thriving in the world.

He is one that depends much upon being negatively good, and contents himself with the consciousness of having done no one any harm; though he reads in the gospel, that "the unprofitable servant was cast into outer darkness," and the barren fig-tree was cursed and dried up from the roots, not for bearing bad, but no fruit.

He is no enemy to charitable contributions in public, if not too frequently recommended: but then he is unacquainted with the kind offices of visiting the sick and imprisoned, clothing the naked, and relieving the hungry in a private manner. He thinks that these things belong only to the clergy, though his own false heart tells him, that nothing but pride keeps him from exercising these acts of humility; and that Jesus Christ, in the 25th chapter of St. Matthew, condemns persons to everlasting punishment, not merely for being fornicators, drunkards, or extortioners, but for neglecting these charitable offices, "When the Son of man shall come in his glory, he shall set the sheep on his right-hand, and the goats on his left. And then shall he say unto them on his left hand, depart from me, ye cursed, into everlasting fire prepared for the devil and his angels: for I was an hungered, and ye gave me no meat; I was thirsty, and ye gave me no drink; I was a stranger, and ye took me not in; naked, and ye clothed me not; sick and in prison, and ye visited me not. Then shall they also say, Lord, when saw we thee an hungered, or a-thirst, or a stranger, or naked, or sick, or in prison, and did not minister unto thee? Then shall he answer them, Verily I say unto you, inasmuch as ye have not done it unto one of the least of these my brethren, ye did it not unto me: and these shall go away into everlasting punishment unto me: and these shall go away into everlasting punishment." I thought proper to give you this whole passage of scripture at large, because our Savior lays such a particular stress upon it; and yet it is so little regarded, that were we to judge by the practice of Christians, one should be tempted to think there were no such verses in the Bible.

But to proceed in the character of an *Almost Christian*: If we consider him in respect of himself; as we said he was strictly honest to his neighbor, so he is likewise strictly sober in himself: but then both his honesty and sobriety proceed from the same principle of a false self-love. It is true, he runs not into the same excess of riot with other men; but then it is not out of obedience to the laws of God, but either because his constitution will not away with intemperance; or rather because he is cautious of forfeiting his reputation, or unfitting himself for temporal business. But though he is so prudent as to avoid intemperance and excess, for the reasons before-mentioned; yet he always goes to the extremity of what is lawful. It is true, he is no drunkard; but then he has no *Christian self-denial*. He cannot think our Savior to be so austere a Master, as to deny us to indulge ourselves in some particulars: and so by this means he is destitute of a sense of true religion, as much as if he lived in debauchery, or any other crime whatever. As to settling his principles as well as practice, he is guided more by the world, than by the word of God: for his part, he cannot think the way to heaven so narrow as some would make it; and therefore considers not so much what scripture requires, as what such and such a good man does, or what will best suit his own corrupt inclinations. Upon this account, he is not only very cautious himself, but likewise very careful of young converts, whose faces are set heavenward; and therefore is always acting the devil's part, and bidding them spare themselves, though they are doing no more than what the scripture strictly requires them to do: The consequence of which is, that "he suffers not himself to enter into the kingdom of God, and those that are entering in he hinders."

Thus lives the almost Christian: not that I can say, I have fully described him to you; but from these outlines and sketches of his character, if your consciences have done their proper office, and made a particular application of what has been said to your own hearts, I cannot but fear that some of you may observe some features in his picture, odious as it is, to near resembling your own; and therefore I cannot but hope, that you will join with the apostle in the words immediately following the text, and wish yourselves "to be not only almost, but altogether Christians."

II. I proceed to the second general thing proposed; to consider the reasons why so many are no more than almost Christians.

1. And the first reason I shall mention is, because so many set out with false notions of religion; though they live in a Christian country, yet they know not what Christianity is. This perhaps may be esteemed a hard saying, but experience sadly evinces the truth of it; for some place religion in being of this or that communion; more in morality; most in a round of duties, and a model of performances; and few, very few acknowledge it to be, what it really is, a thorough inward change of nature, a divine life, a vital participation of Jesus Christ, an union of the soul with God; which the apostle expresses by saying, "He that is joined to the Lord is one spirit." Hence it happens, that so many, even of the most knowing professors, when you come to converse with them concerning the essence, the life, the soul of religion, I mean our new birth in Jesus Christ, confess themselves quite ignorant of the matter, and cry out with Nicodemus, "How can

this thing be?" And no wonder then, that so many are only almost Christians, when so many know not what Christianity is: no marvel, that so many take up with the form, when they are quite strangers to the power of godliness; or content themselves with the shadow, when they know so little about the substance of it. And this is one cause why so many are almost, and so few are altogether Christians.

2. A second reason that may be assigned why so many are no more than almost Christians, is a servile fear of man: multitudes there are and have been, who, though awakened to a sense of the divine life, and have tasted and felt the powers of the world to come; yet out of a base sinful fear of being counted singular, or contemned by men, have suffered all those good impressions to wear off. It is true, they have some esteem for Jesus Christ; but then, like Nicodemus, they would come to him only by night: they are willing to serve him; but then they would do it secretly, for fear of the Jews: they have a mind to see Jesus, but then they cannot come to him because of the press, and for fear of being laughed at, and ridiculed by those with whom they used to sit at meat. But well did our Savior prophesy of such persons, "How can ye love me, who receive honor one of another?" Alas! have they never read, that "the friendship of this world is enmity with God;" and that our Lord himself has threatened, "Whosoever shall be ashamed of me or of my words, in this wicked and adulterous generation, of him shall the Son of man be ashamed, when he cometh in the glory of his Father and of his holy angels?" No wonder that so many are no more than almost Christians, since so many "love the praise of men more than the honor which cometh of God."

3. A third reason why so many are no more than almost Christians, is a reigning love of money. This was the pitiable case of that forward young man in the gospel, who came running to our blessed Lord, and kneeling before him, inquired "what he must do to inherit eternal life;" to whom our blessed Master replied, "Thou knowest the commandments, Do not kill, Do not commit adultery, Do not steal:" To which the young man replied, "All these have I kept from my youth." But when our Lord proceeded to tell him, "Yet lackest thou one thing; Go sell all that thou hast, and give to the poor; he was grieved at that saying, and went away sorrowful, for he had great possessions!" Poor youth! He had a good mind to be a Christian, and to inherit eternal life, but thought it too dear, if it could be purchased at no less an expense than of his estate! And thus many, both young and old, now-a-days, come running to worship our blessed Lord in public, and kneel before him in private, and inquire at his gospel, what they must do to inherit eternal life: but when they find they must renounce the self-enjoyment of riches, and forsake all in affection to follow him, they cry, "The Lord pardon us in this thing! We pray thee, have us excused."

But is heaven so small a trifle in men's esteem, as not to be worth a little gilded earth? Is eternal life so mean a purchase, as not to deserve the temporary renunciation of a few transitory riches? Surely it is. But however inconsistent such a behavior may be, this inordinate love of money is too evidently the common and fatal cause, why so many are no more than almost Christians.

4. Nor is the love of pleasure a less uncommon, or a less fatal cause why so many are no more than almost Christians. Thousands and ten thousands there are, who despise riches, and would willingly be true disciples of Jesus Christ, if parting with their money would make them so; but when they are told that our blessed Lord has said, "Whosoever will come after him must deny himself;" like the pitiable young man before-mentioned, "they go away sorrowful"" for they have too great a love for sensual pleasures. They will perhaps send for the ministers of Christ, as Herod did for John, and hear them gladly: but touch them in their Herodias, tell them they must part with such or such a darling pleasure; and with wicked Ahab they cry out, "Hast thou found us, O our enemy?" Tell them of the necessity of mortification and self-denial, and it is as difficult for them to hear, as if you was to bid them "cut off a right-hand, or pluck out a right-eye." They cannot think our blessed Lord requires so much at their hands, though an inspired apostle has commanded us to "mortify our members which are upon earth." And who himself, even after he had converted thousands, and was very near arrived to the end of his race, yet professed that it was his daily practice to "keep under his body, and bring it into subjection, lest after he had preached to others, he himself should be a cast-away!"

But some men would be wiser than this great apostle, and chalk out to us what they falsely imagine an easier way to happiness. They would flatter us, we may go to heaven without offering violence to our sensual appetites; and enter into the strait gate without striving against our carnal inclinations. And this is another reason why so many are only almost, and not altogether Christians.

5. The fifth and last reason I shall assign why so many are only almost Christians, is a fickleness and instability of temper.

It has been, no doubt, a misfortune that many a minister and sincere Christian has met with, to weep and wail over numbers of promising converts, who seemingly began in the Spirit, but after a while fell away, and basely ended in the flesh; and this not for want of right notions in religion, nor out of a servile fear of man, nor from the love of money, or of sensual pleasure, but through an instability and fickleness of temper. They looked upon religion merely for novelty, as something which pleased them for a while; but after their curiosity was satisfied, they laid it aside again: like the young man that came to see Jesus with a linen cloth about his naked body, they have followed him for a season, but when temptations came to take hold on them, for want of a little more resolution, they have been stripped of all their good intentions, and fled away naked. They at first, like a tree planted by the water-side, grew up and flourished for a while; but having no root in themselves, no inward principle of holiness and piety, like Jonah's gourd, they were soon dried up and withered. Their good intentions are too like the violent motions of the animal spirits of a body newly beheaded, which, though impetuous, are not lasting. In short, they set out well in their journey to heaven, but finding the way either narrower or longer than they expected, through an unsteadiness of temper, they have made an eternal halt, and so "returned like the dog to his vomit, or like the sow that was washed to her wallowing in the more!"

But I tremble to pronounce the fate of such unstable professors, who having put their hands to the plough, for want of a little more resolution, shamefully look back. How shall I repeat to them that dreadful threatening, "If any man draw back, my soul shall have no pleasure in him:" And again, "It is impossible (that is, exceeding difficult at least) for those that have been once enlightened, and have tasted of the heavenly gift, and the powers of the world to come, if they should fall away, to be renewed again unto repentance." But notwithstanding the gospel is so severe against apostates, yet many that begun well, through a fickleness of temper, (O that none of us here present may ever be such) have been by this means of the number of those that turn back unto perdition. And this is the fifth, and the last reason I shall give, why so many are only almost, and not altogether Christians.

III. Proceed we now to the general thing proposed, namely, to consider the folly of being no more than an almost Christian.

1. And the *First* proof I shall give of the folly of such a proceeding is, that it is ineffectual to salvation. It is true, such men are almost good; but almost to hit the mark, is really to miss it. God requires us "to love him with all our hearts, with all our souls, and with all our strength." He loves us too well to admit any rival; because, so far as our hearts are empty of God, so far must they be unhappy. The devil, indeed, like the false mother that came before Solomon, would have our hearts divided, as she would have had the child; but God, like the true mother, will have all or none. "My Son, give me thy heart," thy whole heart, is the general call to all: and if this be not done, we never can expect the divine mercy.

Persons may play the hypocrite; but God at the great day will strike them dead, (as he did Ananias and Sapphira by the mouth of his servant Peter) for pretending to offer him all their hearts, when they keep back from him the greatest part. They may perhaps impose upon their fellow-creatures for a while; but he that enabled Elijah to cry out, "Come in thou wife of Jeroboam," when she came disguised to inquire about the sick son, will also discover them through their most artful dissimulations; and if their hearts are not wholly with him, appoint them their portion with hypocrites and unbelievers.

2. But, *Secondly*, What renders an half-way-piety more inexcusable is, that it is not only insufficient to our own salvation, but also very prejudicial to that of others.

An almost Christian is one of the most hurtful creatures in the world; he is a wolf in sheep's clothing: he is one of those false prophets, our blessed Lord bids us beware of in his sermon on the mount, who would persuade men, that the way to heaven is broader than it really is; and thereby, as it was observed before, "enter not into the kingdom of God themselves, and those that are entering in they hinder." These, these are the men that turn the world into a luke-warm Laodicean spirit; that hang out false lights, and so shipwreck unthinking benighted souls in their voyage to the haven of eternity. These are they who are greater enemies to the cross of Christ, than infidels themselves: for of an unbeliever every one will be aware; but an almost Christian, through his subtle hypocrisy, draws away many after him; and therefore must expect to receive the greater damnation.

3. But, *Thirdly*, As it is most prejudicial to ourselves and hurtful to others, so it is the greatest instance of ingratitude we can express towards our Lord and Master Jesus Christ. For did he come down from heaven, and shed his precious blood, to purchase these hearts of ours, and shall we only give him half of them? O how can we say we love him, when our hearts are not wholly with him? How can we call him our Savior, when we will not

endeavor sincerely to approve ourselves to him, and so let him see the travail of his soul, and be satisfied!

Had any of us purchased a slave at a most expensive rate, and who was before involved in the utmost miseries and torments, and so must have continued for ever, had we shut up our bowels of compassion from him; and was this slave afterwards to grow rebellious, or deny giving us but half his service; how, how should we exclaim against his base ingratitude! And yet this base ungrateful slave thou art, O man, who acknowledgest thyself to be redeemed from infinite unavoidable misery and punishment by the death of Jesus Christ, and yet wilt not give thyself wholly to him. But shall we deal with God our Maker in a manner we would not be dealt with by a man like ourselves? God forbid! No. Suffer me, therefore,

To add a word or two of exhortation to you, to excite you to be not only almost, but altogether Christians. O let us scorn all base and treacherous treatment of our King and Savior, of our God and Creator. Let us not take some pains all our lives to go to haven, and yet plunge ourselves into hell as last. Let us give to God our whole hearts, and no longer halt between two opinions: if the world be God, let us serve that; if pleasure be a God, let us serve that; but if the Lord he be God, let us, O let us serve him alone. Alas! why, why should we stand out any longer? Why should we be so in love with slavery, as not wholly to renounce the world, the flesh, and the devil, which, like so many spiritual chains, bind down our souls, and hinder them from flying up to God. Alas! what are we afraid of? Is not God able to reward our entire obedience? If he is, as the almost Christian's lame way of serving him, seems to grant, why then will we not serve him entirely? For the same reason we do so much, why do we not do more? Or do you think that being only half religious will make you happy, but that going farther, will render you miserable and uneasy? Alas! this, my brethren, is delusion all over: for what is it but this half piety, this wavering between God and the world, that makes so many, that are seemingly well disposed, such utter strangers to the comforts of religion? They choose just so much of religion as will disturb them in their lusts, and follow their lusts so far as to deprive themselves of the comforts of religion. Whereas on the contrary, would they sincerely leave all in affection, and give their hearts wholly to God, they would then (and they cannot till then) experience the unspeakable pleasure of having a mind at unity with itself, and enjoy such a peace of God, which even in this life passes all understanding, and which they were entire strangers to before. It is true, it we will devote ourselves entirely to God, we must meet with contempt; but then it is because contempt is necessary to heal our pride. We must renounce some sensual pleasures, but then it is because those unfit us for spiritual ones, which are infinitely better. We must renounce the love of the world; but then it is that we may be filled with the love of God: and when that has once enlarged our hearts, we shall, like Jacob when he served for his beloved Rachel, think nothing too difficult to undergo, no hardships too tedious to endure, because of the love we shall then have for our dear Redeemer. Thus easy, thus delightful will be the ways of God even in this life: but when once we throw off these bodies, and our souls are filled with all the fullness of God, O! what heart can conceive, what tongue can express, with what unspeakable joy and consolation shall we then look back on our past sincere and hearty services. Think you then, my dear hearers, we shall repent we had done too much; or rather think you not, we shall be ashamed that we did no more; and blush we were so backward to give up all to God; when he intended hereafter to give us himself?

Let me therefore, to conclude, exhort you, my brethren, to have always before you the unspeakable happiness of enjoying God. And think withal, that every degree of holiness you neglect, every act of piety you omit, is a jewel taken out of your crown, a degree of blessedness lost in the vision of God. O! do but always think and act thus, and you will no longer be laboring to compound matters between God and the world; but, on the contrary, be daily endeavoring to give up yourselves more and more unto him; you will be always watching, always praying, always aspiring after farther degrees of purity and love, and consequently always preparing yourselves for a fuller sight and enjoyment of that God, in whose presence there is fullness of joy, and at whose right-hand there are pleasures for ever more. Amen! Amen!

44. Christ, the Believer's Wisdom, Righteousness, Sanctification and Redemption

Of all the verses in the book of God, this which I have now read to you, is, I believe, one of the most comprehensive: what glad tidings does it bring to believers! What precious privileges are they herein invested with! How are they here led to the fountain of them all, I mean, the love, the everlasting love of God the Father! 'Of him are ye in Christ Jesus, who of God is made unto us wisdom, righteousness, sanctification, and redemption.'

Without referring you to the context, I shall from the words,

First, Point out to you the fountain, from which all those blessings flow, that the elect of God partake of in Jesus Christ, "Who of God is made unto'. And,

Secondly, I shall consider what these blessings are, 'Wisdom, righteousness, sanctification, and redemption'.

First, I would point out to you the fountain, from which all those blessings flow, that the elect of God partake of in Jesus, 'who of God is made unto us', the father he it is who is spoken of here. Not as though Jesus Christ was not God also; but God the Father is the fountain of the Deity; and if we consider Jesus Christ acting as Mediator, God the Father is greater than he; there was an eternal contract between the Father and the Son: "I have made a covenant with my chosen, and I have sworn unto David my servant'; now David was a type of Christ, with whom the Father made a covenant, that if he would obey and suffer, and make himself a sacrifice for sin, he should 'see his seed, he should prolong his days, and the pleasure of the Lord should prosper in his hands'. This compact our Lord refers to, in that glorious prayer recorded in the 17th chapter of John; and therefore he prays for, or rather demands with a full assurance, all that were given to him by the Father: 'Father, I will that they also whom thou hast given me, be with me where I am.' For this same reason, the apostle breaks out into praises of God, even the Father of our Lord Jesus Christ; for he loved the elect with an everlasting love, or, as our Lord expresses it, 'before the foundation of the world'; and, therefore, to show them to whom they were beholden for their salvation, our Lord, in the 25th of Matthew, represents himself saying, 'Come, ye blessed children of my Father, receive the kingdom prepared for you from the foundation of the world'. And thus, in reply to the mother of Zebedee's children, he says, 'It is not mine to give, but it shall be given to them for whom it is prepared of the Father'. The apostle therefore, when here speaking of the Christian's privileges, lest they should sacrifice to their own drag, or think their salvation was owing to their own faithfulness, or improvement of their own free-will, reminds them to look back on the everlasting love of God the Father; 'who of God is made unto us', etc.

Would to God this point of doctrine was considered more, and people were more studious of the covenant of redemption between the Father and the Son! We should not then have so much disputing against the doctrine of election, or hear it condemned (even by good men) as a doctrine of devils. For my own part, I cannot see how true humbleness of mind can be attained without a knowledge of it; and though I will not say, that every one who denies election is a bad man, yet I will say, with that sweet singer, Mr. Trail, it is a very bad sign: such a one, whoever he be, I think cannot truly know himself; for, if we deny election, we must, partly at least, glory in ourselves; but our redemption is so ordered that no flesh should glory in the Divine presence; and hence it is, that the pride of man opposes this doctrine, because, according to this doctrine, and no other, 'he that glories, must glory only in the Lord'. But what shall I say? Election is a mystery that shines with such resplendent brightness, that, to make use of the words of one who has drunk deeply of electing love, it dazzles the weak eyes even of some of God's dear children; however, though they know it not, all the blessings they receive, all the privileges they do or ill enjoy, through Jesus Christ, flow from the everlasting love of God the Father: 'But of him are you in Christ Jesus, who of God is made unto us, wisdom, righteousness, sanctification, and redemption.'

Secondly, I come to show what these blessings are, which are here, through Christ, made over to the elect. And,

1: *First*, Christ is made to them *wisdom*; but wherein does true wisdom consist? Were I to ask some of you, perhaps you would say, in indulging the lust of the flesh, and saying to your souls, eat, drink, and be merry: but this is only the wisdom of brutes; they have as good a gust and relish for sensual pleasures, as the greatest epicure on earth. Others would tell me, true wisdom consisted in adding house to house, and field to field, and calling lands after their own names: but this cannot be true wisdom; for riches often take to themselves wings, and fly away, like an eagle towards heaven. Even wisdom itself assures us, 'that a man's life doth not consist in the abundance of the things which he possesses'; vanity, vanity, all these things are vanity; for, if riches leave not the owner, the owners must soon leave them; 'for rich men must also die, and leave their riches for others'; their riches cannot procure them redemption from the grave, whither we are all hastening apace.

But perhaps you despise riches and pleasure, and therefore place wisdom in the knowledge of books: but it is possible for you to tell the numbers of the stars, and call them all by their names, and yet be mere fools; learned men are not always wise; nay, our common learning, so much cried up, makes men only so many accomplished fools; to keep you therefore no longer in suspense, and withal to humble you, I will send you to a heathen to school, to learn what true wisdom is: 'Know thyself', was a saying of one of the wise men of Greece; this is certainly true wisdom, and this is that wisdom spoken of in the text, and which Jesus Christ is made to all elect sinners—they are made to know themselves, so as not to think more highly of themselves than they ought to think. Before, they were darkness; now, they are light in the Lord; and in that light they see their own darkness; they now bewail themselves as fallen creatures by nature, dead in trespasses and sins, sons and heirs of hell, and children of wrath; they now see that all their righteousnesses are but as filthy rags; that there is no health in their souls; that they are poor and miserable, blind and naked; and that there is no name given under heaven, whereby they can be saved, but that of Jesus Christ. They see the necessity of closing with a Savior, and behold the wisdom of God in appointing him to be a Savior; they are also made willing to accept of salvation upon our Lord's own terms, and receive him as their all in all; thus Christ is made to them wisdom.

2. *Secondly, righteousness*, 'Who of God is made unto us, wisdom, righteousness': Christ's whole personal righteousness is made over to, and accounted theirs. They are enabled to lay hold on Christ by faith, and God the Father blots out their transgressions, as with a thick cloud: their sins and their iniquities he remembers no more; they are made the righteousness of God in Christ Jesus, 'who is the end of the law for righteousness to every one that believeth'. In one sense, God now sees no sin in them; the whole covenant of works is fulfilled in them; they are actually justified, acquitted, and looked upon as righteous in the sight of God; they are perfectly accepted in the beloved; they are complete in him; the flaming sword of God's wrath, which before moved every way, is not removed, and free access given to the tree of life; they are enabled to reach out the arm of faith, and pluck, and live for evermore. Hence it is that the apostle, under a sense of this blessed privilege, breaks out into this triumphant language; 'It is Christ that justifies, who is he that condemns?' Does sin condemn? Christ's righteousness delivers believers from the guilt of it: Christ is their Savior, and is become a propitiation for their sins: who therefore shall lay any thing to the charge of God's elect? Does the law condemn? By having Christ's righteousness imputed to them, they are dead to the law, as a covenant of works; Christ has fulfilled it for them, and in their stead. Does death threaten them? They need not fear: the sting of death is sin, the strength of sin is the law; but God has given them the victory by imputing to them the righteousness of the Lord Jesus.

And what a privilege is here! Well might the angels at the birth of Christ say to the humble shepherds, 'Behold, I bring you glad tidings of great joy'; unto you that believe in Christ 'a Savior is born'. And well may angels rejoice at the conversion of poor sinners; for the Lord is their righteousness; they have peace with God through faith in Christ's blood, and shall never enter into condemnation. O believers! (for this discourse is intended in a special manner for you) lift up your heads; 'rejoice in the Lord always; again I say, rejoice'. Christ is mad to you, of God, righteousness, what then should you fear? You are made the righteousness of God in him; you may be called, 'The Lord our righteousness'. Of what then should you be afraid? What shall separate you henceforward from the love of Christ? 'Shall tribulation, or distress, or persecution, or famine, or nakedness, or peril, or sword? No, I am persuaded, neither death, nor life, nor angels, nor principalities, nor powers, nor things present, nor things to come, nor height, nor depth, nor any other creature, shall be able to separate you from the love of God, which is in Christ Jesus our Lord', who of God is made unto you righteousness.

This is a glorious privilege, but this is only the beginning of the happiness of believers: For,

3: *Thirdly*, Christ is not only made to them righteousness, but sanctification; by sanctification, I do not mean a bare hypocritical attendance on outward ordinances, though rightly informed Christians will think it their duty and privilege constantly to attend on all outward ordinances. Nor do I mean by sanctification a bare outward reformation, and a few transient convictions, or a little legal sorrow; for all this an unsanctified man may have; but, by sanctification I mean a total renovation of the whole man: by the righteousness of Christ, believers come legally, by sanctification they are made spiritually, alive; by the one they are entitled to, by the other they are made meet for, glory. They are sanctified, therefore, throughout, in spirit, soul, and body.

Their understandings, which were dark before, now become light in the Lord; and their wills, before contrary to, now become one with the will of God; their affections are now set on things above; their memory is now filled with divine things; their natural consciences are now enlightened; their members, which were before instruments of uncleanness, and of iniquity into iniquity, are now new creatures; 'old things are passed away, all things are become new', in their hearts: sin has now no longer dominion over them; they are freed from the power, though not the indwelling of being, of it; they are holy both in heart and life, in all manner of conversation: they are made partakers of a divine nature, and from Jesus Christ, they receive grace; and every grace that is in Christ, is copied and transcribed into their souls; they are transformed into his likeness; he is formed within them; they dwell in him, and he in them; they are led by the Spirit, and bring forth the fruits thereof; they know that Chris is their Emmanuel, God with and in them; they are living temples of the Holy Ghost. And therefore, being a holy habitation unto the Lord, the whole Trinity dwells and walks in them; even here, they sit together with Christ in heavenly places, and are vitally united to him, their Head, by a living faith; their Redeemer, their Maker, is their husband; they are flesh of his flesh, bone of his bone; they talk, they walk with him, as a man talketh and walketh with his friend; in short, they are one with Christ, even as Jesus Christ and the Father are one.

Thus is Christ made to believers sanctification. And O what a privilege is this! to be changed from beasts into saints, and from a devilish, to be made partakers of a divine nature; to be translated from the kingdom of Satan, into the kingdom of God's dear Son! To put off the old man, which is corrupt, and to put on the new man, which is created after God, in righteousness and true holiness! O what an unspeakable blessing is this! I almost stand amazed at the contemplation thereof. Well might the apostle exhort believers to rejoice in the Lord; indeed they have reason always to rejoice, yea, to rejoice on a dying bed; for the kingdom of God is in them; they are changed from glory to glory, even by the Spirit of the Lord: well may this be a mystery to the natural, for it is a mystery even to the spiritual man himself, a mystery which he cannot fathom. Does it not often dazzle your eyes, O ye children of God, to look at your own brightness, when the candle of the Lord shines out, and your redeemer lifts up the light of his blessed countenance upon your souls? Are not you astonished, when you feel the love of God shed abroad in your hearts by the Holy Ghost, and God holds out the golden scepter of his mercy, and bids you ask what you will, and it shall be given you? Does not that peace of God, which keeps and rules your hearts, surpass the utmost limits of your understandings? And is not the joy you feel unspeakable? Is it not full of glory? I am persuaded it is; and in your secret communion, when the Lord's love flows in upon your souls, you are as it were swallowed up in, or, to use the apostle's phrase, 'filled with all the fullness of God'. Are not you ready to cry out with Solomon, 'And will the Lord, indeed, dwell thus with men!' How is it that we should be thus thy sons and daughters, O Lord God Almighty!

If you are children of God, and know what it is to have fellowship with the Father and the Son; if you walk by faith, and not by sight; I am assured this is frequently the language of your hearts.

But look forward, and see an unbounded prospect of eternal happiness lying before thee, O believer! what thou hast already received are only the first-fruits, like the cluster of grapes brought out of the land of Canaan; only an earnest and pledge of yet infinitely better things to come: the harvest is to follow; thy grace is hereafter to be swallowed up in glory. Thy great Joshua, and merciful High-Priest, shall administer an abundant entrance to thee into the land of promise, that rest which awaits the children of God: for Christ is not only made to believers wisdom, righteousness, and sanctification, but also *redemption*.

But, before we enter upon the explanation and contemplation of this privilege,

Firstly, Learn hence the great mistake of those writers and clergy, who, notwithstanding they talk of sanctification and inward holiness, (as indeed sometimes they do, though in a very loose and superficial manner,) yet they generally make it the *cause*, whereas they should consider it as the *effect*, of our justification. 'Of him are ye in Christ Jesus, who of God is made unto us, wisdom, righteousness, (and then) sanctification.' For Christ's righteousness, or that which Christ has done in our stead without us, is the sole cause of our acceptance in the sight of God, and of all holiness wrought in us: to this, and not to the light within, or any thing wrought within, should poor sinners seek for justification in the sight of God: for the sake of Christ's righteousness alone, and not any thing wrought in us, does God look favorably upon us; our sanctification at best, in this life, is not complete: though we be delivered from the power, we are not freed from the in-being of sin; but not only the dominion, but the in-being of sin, is forbidden, by the perfect law of God: for it is not said, thou shalt not give way to lust, but 'thou shalt not lust'. So that whilst the principle of lust remains in the least degree in our hearts, though we are otherwise never so holy, yet we cannot, on account of that, hope for acceptance with God. We must first, therefore, look for a righteousness without us, even the righteousness of our Lord Jesus Christ: for this reason the apostle mentions it, and puts it before sanctification, in the words of the text. And whosoever teacheth any other doctrine, doth not preach the truth as it is in Jesus.

Secondly, From hence also, the Antinomians and formal hypocrites may be confuted, who talk of Christ without, but know nothing, experimentally, of a work of sanctification wrought within them. Whatever they may pretend to, since Christ is not in them, the Lord is not their righteousness, and they have no well-grounded hope of glory: for though sanctification is not the cause, yet it is the effect of our acceptance with God; 'Who of God is made unto us righteousness and sanctification'. He, therefore, that is really in Christ, is a new creature; it is not going back to a covenant of works, to look into our hearts, and, seeing that they are changed and renewed, from thence form a comfortable and well grounded assurance of the safety of our states: no, but this I what we are directed to in scripture; by our bringing forth the fruits, we are to judge whether or not we ever did truly partake of the Spirit of God. 'We know (says John) that we are passed from death unto life, because we love the brethren.' And however we may talk of Christ's righteousness, and exclaim against legal preachers, yet, if we be not holy in heart and life, if we be not sanctified and renewed by the Spirit in our minds, we are self-deceivers, we are only formal hypocrites: for we must not put asunder what God has joined together; we must keep the medium between the two extremes; not insist so much on the one hand upon Christ without, as to exclude Christ within, as an evidence of our being his, and as a preparation for future happiness; nor, on the other hand, so depend on inherent righteousness or holiness wrought in us, as to exclude the righteousness of Jesus Christ without us. But,

4: *Fourthly*, Let us now go on, and take a view of the other link, or rather the end, of the believer's golden chain or privileges, *redemption*. But we must look very high; for the top of it, like Jacob's ladder, reaches heaven, where all believers will ascend, and be placed at the right hand of God. 'Who of God is made unto us, wisdom, righteousness, sanctification, and *redemption*.'

This is a golden chain indeed! and, what is best of all, not one link can ever be broken asunder from another. Was there no other text in the book of God, this single one sufficiently proves the final perseverance of true believers: or never did God yet justify a man, whom he did not sanctify; nor sanctify one, whom he did not completely redeem and glorify: no! as for God, his way, his works, is perfect; he always carried on and finished the work he begun; thus it was in the first, so it is in the new creation; when God says, 'Let there be light', there is light, that shines more and more unto the perfect day, when believers enter into their eternal rest, as God entered into his. Those whom God has justified, he has in effect glorified: for as a man's worthiness was not the cause of God's giving him Christ's righteousness; so neither shall his unworthiness be a cause of his taking it away; God's gifts and callings are without repentance: and I cannot think they are clear in the notion of Christ's righteousness, who deny the final perseverance of the saints; I fear they understand justification in that low sense, which I understood it in a few years ago, as implying no more than remission of sins: but it not only signifies remission of sins past, but also a *federal right* to all good things to come. If God has given us his only Son, how shall he not with him freely give us all things? Therefore, the apostle, after he says, 'Who of God is made unto us righteousness', does not say, perhaps he may be made to us sanctification and redemption: but, 'he is made': for there is an eternal, indissoluble connection between these blessed privileges. As the obedience of Christ is imputed to believers, so his perseverance in that obedience is to be imputed to them also; and it argues great ignorance of the covenant of grace and redemption, to object against it.

By the word *redemption*, we are to understand, not only a complete deliverance from all evil, but also a full enjoyment of all good both in body and soul: I say, both in body and soul; for the Lord is also for the body; the bodies of the saints in this life are temples of the Holy Ghost; God makes a covenant with the dust of believers; after death, though worms destroy them, yet, even in their flesh shall they see God. I fear, indeed, there are some Sadducees in our days, or at least heretics, who say, either, that there is no resurrection of the body, or that the resurrection is past already, namely, in our regeneration: Hence it is, that our Lord's coming in the flesh, at the day of judgment, is denied; and consequently, we must throw aside the sacrament of the Lord's supper. For why should we remember the Lord's death until he come to judgment, when he is already come to judge our hearts, and will not come a second time? But all this is only the reasoning of unlearned, unstable men, who certainly know not what they say, nor whereof they affirm. That we must follow our Lord in the regeneration, be partakers of a new birth, and that Christ must come into our hearts, we freely confess; and we hope, when speaking of these things, we speak no more than what we know and feel: but then it is plain, that Jesus Christ will come, hereafter, to judgment, and that he ascended into heaven with the body which he had here on earth; for says he, after his resurrection, 'Handle me, and see; a spirit has not flesh and bones, as you see me have'. And it is plain, that Christ's resurrection was an earnest of ours: for says the apostle, 'Christ is risen from the dead, and become the first-fruits of them that sleep; and as in Adam all die, and are subject to mortality; so all that are in Christ, the second Adam, who represented believers as their federal head, shall certainly be made alive, or rise again with their bodies at the last day'.

Here then, O believers! is one, though the lowest, degree of that redemption which you are to be partakers of hereafter; I mean, the redemption of your bodies: for this corruptible must put on incorruption, this mortal must put on immortality. Your bodies, as well as souls, were given to Jesus Christ by the Father; they have been companions in watching, and fasting, and praying: your bodies, therefore, as well as souls, shall Jesus Christ raise up at the last day. Fear not, therefore, O believers, to look into the grave: for to you it is not other than a consecrated dormitory, where your bodies shall sleep quietly until the morning of the resurrection; when the voice of the archangel shall sound, and the trump of God given the general alarm, 'Arise, ye dead, and come to judgment'; earth, air, fire, water, shall give up your scattered atoms, and both in body and soul shall you be ever with the Lord. I doubt not, but many of you are groaning under crazy bodies, and complain often that the mortal body weighs down the immortal soul; at least this is my case; but let us have a little patience, and we shall be delivered from our earthly prisons; ere long, these tabernacles of clay shall be dissolved, and we shall be clothed with our house which is from heaven; hereafter, our bodies shall be spiritualized, and shall be so far from hindering our souls through weakness, that they shall become string; so strong, as to bear up under an exceeding and eternal weight of glory; others again may have deformed bodies, emaciated also with sickness, and worn out with labor at age; but wait a little, until your blessed change by death comes; then your bodies shall be renewed and made glorious, like unto Christ's glorious body: of which we may form some faint idea, from the account given us of our Lord's transfiguration on the mount, when it is said, 'His raiment became bright and glistening, and his face brighter than the sun'. Well then may a believer break out in the apostle's triumphant language, 'O death, where is thy sting! O grave, where is thy victory!'

But what is the redemption of the body, in comparison of the redemption of the better part, our souls? I must, therefore say to you believers, as the angel said to John, 'Come up higher'; and let us take as clear a view as we can, at such a distance, of the redemption Christ has purchased for, and will shortly put you in actual possession of. Already you are justified, already you are sanctified, and thereby freed from the guilt and dominion of sin: but, as I have observed, the being and indwelling of sin yet remains in you; God sees it proper to leave some Amalekites in the land, to keep his Israel in action. The most perfect Christian, I am persuaded, must agree, according to one of our Articles, 'That the corruption of nature remains even in the regenerate; that the flesh lusteth always against the spirit, and the spirit against the flesh'. So that believers cannot do things for God with that perfection they desire; this grieves their righteous souls day by day, and, with the holy apostle, makes them cry out, 'Who shall deliver us from the body of this death!' I thank God, our Lord Jesus Christ will, but not completely before the day of our dissolution; they will the very being of sin be destroyed, and an eternal stop put to inbred, indwelling corruption. And is not this a great redemption? I am sure believers esteem it o: for there is nothing grieves the heart of a child of God so much, as the remains of indwelling sin. Again, believers are often in heaviness through manifold temptations; God sees that it is needful and good for them so to be; and though they may be highly favored, and wrapt up in communion with God, even to the third heavens; yet a messenger of Satan is often sent to buffet them, lest they should be puffed up with the abundance of revelations. But be not weary, be not faint in your minds: the time of your complete redemption draweth nigh. In heaven the wicked one shall cease from troubling you, and your weary souls shall enjoy an everlasting rest; his fiery darts cannot reach those blissful regions: Satan will never come any more to appear with, disturb, or accuse the sons of God, when once the Lord Jesus Christ shuts the door. Your righteous souls are now grieved, day by day, at the ungodly conversation of the wicked; tares now grow up among the wheat; wolves come in sheep's clothing: but the redemption spoken of in the text, will free your souls from all anxiety on these accounts; hereafter you shall enjoy a perfect communion of saints; nothing that is unholy or unsanctified shall enter into the holy of holies, which is prepared for you above: this, and all manner of evil whatsoever, you shall be delivered from, when your redemption is hereafter made complete in heaven; not only so, but you shall enter into the full enjoyment of all good. It is true, all saints will not have the same degree of happiness, but all will be as happy as their hearts can desire. Believers, you shall judge the evil, and familiarly converse with good, angels: you shall sit down with Abraham, Isaac, Jacob, and all the spirits of just men made perfect; and, to sum up all your happiness in one word, you shall see God the Father, Son, and Holy Ghost; and, by seeing God, be more and more like unto him, and pass from glory to glory, even to all eternity.

But I must stop the glories of the upper world crowd in so fast upon my soul, that I am lost in the contemplation of them. Brethren, the redemption spoken of is unutterable; we cannot here find it out; eye hath not seen, nor ear heard, nor has it entered into the hearts of the most holy men living to conceive, how great it is. Were I to entertain you whole ages with an account of it, when you come to heaven, you must say, with the queen of Sheba, 'Not half, no, not one thousandth part was told us'. All we can do here, is to go upon mount Pisgah, and, by the eye of faith, take a distant view of the promised land: we may see it, as Abraham did Christ, afar off, and rejoice in it; but here we only know in part. Blessed be God, there is a time coming, when we shall know God, even as we are known, and God be all in all. Lord Jesus, accomplish the number of thine elect! Lord Jesus, hasten thy kingdom!

And now, where are the scoffers of these last days, who count the lives of Christians to be madness, and their end to be without honor? Unhappy men! you know not what you do. Were your eyes open, and had you senses to discern spiritual things, you would not speak all manner of evil against the children of God, but you would esteem them as the excellent ones of the earth, and envy their happiness: your souls would hunger and thirst after it: you also would become fools for Christ's sake. You boast of wisdom; so did the philosophers of Corinth: but your wisdom is the foolishness of folly in the sight of God. What will your wisdom avail you, if it does not make you wise unto salvation? Can you, with all your wisdom, propose a more consistent scheme to build you hopes of salvation on, than what has been now laid before you? Can you, with all the strength of natural reason, find out a better way of acceptance with God, than by the righteousness of the Lord Jesus Christ? Is it right to think your own works can in any measure deserve or procure it? If not, why will you not believe in him? Why will you not submit to his righteousness? Can you deny that you are fallen creatures? Do not you find that you are full of disorders, and that these disorders make you unhappy? Do not you find that you cannot change your own hearts? Have you not resolved many and many a time, and have not your corruptions yet dominion over you? Are you not bondslaves to your lusts, and led captive by the devil at his will? Why then will you not come to Christ for sanctification? Do you not desire to die the death of the righteous, and that your future state may be like theirs; I am persuaded you cannot bear the thoughts of being annihilated, much less of being miserable for ever. Whatever you may pretend, if you speak truth, you must confess, that conscience breaks in upon you in more sober intervals whether you will or not, and even constrains you to believe that hell is no painted fire. And why then will you not come to Christ? He alone can procure you everlasting redemption. Haste, haste away to him, poor beguiled sinners. You lack wisdom; ask it of Christ. Who knows but he may give it you? He is able: for he is the wisdom of the Father; he is that wisdom which was from everlasting. You have no righteousness; away, therefore, to Christ: 'He is the end of the law for righteousness to every one that believeth.' You are unholy: flee to the Lord Jesus: He is full of grace and truth;;and of his fullness all may receive that believe in him. You are afraid to die; let this drive you to Christ: he has the keys of death and hell: in him is plenteous redemption; he alone can open the door which leads to everlasting life.

Let not, therefore, the deceived reasoner boast any longer of his pretended reason. Whatever you may think, it is the most unreasonable thing in the world not to believe on Jesus Christ, whom God has sent. Why, why will you die? Why will you not come unto him, that you may have life? 'Ho! every one that thirsteth, come unto the waters of life, and drink freely: come, buy without money and without price.' Were these blessed privileges in the text to be purchased with money, you might say, we are poor, and cannot buy: or, were they to be conferred only on sinners of such a rank or degree, then you might say, how can such sinners as we, expect to be so highly favored? But they are to be freely given of God to the worst of sinners. 'To us', says the apostle, to me a persecutor, to you Corinthians, who were 'unclean, drunkards, covetous persons, idolaters.' Therefore, each poor sinner may say then, why not unto me? Has Christ but one blessing? What if he has blessed millions already, by turning them away from their iniquities; yet he still continues the same: he lives for ever to make intercession, and therefore will bless you, even you also. Though, Esau-like, you have been profane, and hitherto despised your heavenly Father's birth-right; even now, if you believe, 'Christ will be made to you of God, wisdom, righteousness, sanctification, and redemption'.

But I must turn again to believers, for whose instruction, as I observed before, this discourse was particularly intended. You see, brethren, partakers of the heavenly calling, what great blessings are treasured up for you in Jesus Christ your Head, and what you are entitled to by believing on his name. Take heed, therefore, that ye walk worthy of the vocation wherewith ye are called. Think often how highly you are favored; and remember, you have not chosen Christ, but Christ has chosen you. Put on (as the elect of God) humbleness of mind, and glory, but let it be only in the Lord; for you have nothing but what you have received of God. By nature ye were foolish, as legal, as unholy, and in as damnable a condition, as others. Be pitiful, therefore, be courteous; and, as sanctification is a progressive work, beware of thinking you have already attained. Let him that is holy be holy still; knowing, that he who is most pure in heart, shall hereafter enjoy the clearest vision of God. Let indwelling sin be your daily burden; and not only bewail and lament, but see that you subdue it daily by the power of divine grace; and look up to Jesus continually to be the finisher, as well as author, of your faith. Build not on your own faithfulness, but on God's unchangeableness. Take heed of thinking you stand by the power of your own free will. The everlasting love of God the Father, must be your only hope and consolation; let this support you under all trials. Remember that God's gifts and callings are without repentance; that Christ having once loved you, will love you to the end. Let this constrain you to obedience, and make you long and look for that blessed time, when he shall not only be your wisdom, and righteousness, and sanctification, but also complete and everlasting redemption.

Glory be to God in the highest!

45. The Knowledge of Jesus Christ the Best Knowledge

The persons to whom these words were written, were the members of the church of Corinth; who, as appears by the foregoing chapter, were not only divided into different sects, by one saying, "I am of Paul, and another, I am of Apollos;" but also had man amongst them, who were so full of the wisdom of this world, and so wise in their own eyes, that they set at nought the simplicity of the gospel, and accounted the Apostle's preaching foolishness.

Never had the Apostle more need of the wisdom of the serpent, mingled with the innocency of the dove, than now. What is the sum of all his wisdom? He tells them, in the words of the text, "I determined not to know any thing amongst you, save Jesus Christ, and him crucified."

A resolution this, worthy of the great St. Paul; and no less worthy, no less necessary for every minister, and every disciple of Christ, to make always, even unto the end of the world.

In the following discourse, I shall,

First, Explain what is meant by "not knowing any thing, save Jesus Christ, and him crucified."

Secondly, Give some reasons why every Christian should determine not to know any thing else. And

Thirdly, Conclude with a general exhortation to put this determination into practice.

First, I am to explain what is meant by "not knowing any thing, save Jesus Christ, and him crucified."

By Jesus Christ, we are to understand the eternal Son of God. He is called Jesus, a Savior, because he was to save us from the guilt and power of our sins; and, like Joshua, by whom he was remarkably typified, to lead God's spiritual Israel through the wilderness of this world, to the heavenly Canaan, the promised inheritance of the children of God.

He is called *Christ*, which signifies anointed, because he was anointed by the Holy Ghost at his baptism, to be a prophet to instruct, a priest to make an atonement for, and a king to govern and protect his church. And he was crucified, or hung (O stupendous love!) till he was dead upon the cross, that he might become a curse for us: for it is written, "Cursed is every man that hangeth upon a tree."

The foundation or first cause of his suffering, was our fall in Adam; in whom, as the living oracles of God declare, "We all died;" his sin was imputed to us all. It pleased God, after he had spoken the world into being, to create man after his own divine image, to breathe into him the breath of life, and to place him as our representative in the garden of Eden.

But he being left to his own free will, did eat of the forbidden fruit, notwithstanding God had told him, "The day in which he eat thereof, he should surely die;" and thereby he, with his whole posterity, in whose name he acted, became liable to the wrath of God, and sunk into a spiritual death.

But behold the goodness, as well as the severity of God! For no sooner had man been convicted as a sinner, but lo! A Savior is revealed to him, under the character of the seed of the woman: the merits of whose sacrifice were then immediately to take place, and who should, in the fullness of time, by suffering death, satisfy for the guilt we had contracted; by obeying the whole moral law, work out for us an everlasting righteousness; and by becoming a principle of new life in us, destroy the power of the devil, and thereby restore us to a better state than that in which we were at first created.

This is the plain scriptural account of that mystery of godliness, God manifested in the flesh; and to this our own hearts, unless blinded by the god of this world, cannot but yield an immediate assent.

For, let us but search our own hearts, and ask ourselves, if we could create our own children, whether or not we would not create them with a less mixture of good and evil, than we find in ourselves? Supposing God then only to have our goodness, he could not, at first, make us so sinful, so polluted as we are. But supposing him to be as he is, infinitely good, or goodness itself, then it is absolutely impossible that he should create any thing but what is like himself, perfect, entire, lacking nothing. Man then could not come out of the hands of his Maker, so miserably blind and naked, with such a mixture of the beast and devil, as he finds now in himself, but must have fallen from what he was; and as it does not suit with the goodness and justness of God, to punish the whole race of mankind with these disorders merely for nothing; and since men bring these disorders into the world with them; it follows, that as they could not sin themselves, being yet unborn, some other man's sin must have been imputed to them; from whence, as from a fountain, all these evils flow.

I know this doctrine of our *original sin*, or fall in Adam, is esteemed foolishness by the wise disputer of this world, who will reply, How does it suit the goodness of God, to impute one man's sin to an innocent posterity? But has it not been proved to a demonstration, that it is so? And therefore, supposing we cannot reconcile it to our shallow comprehensions, that is no argument at all: for if it appears that God has done a thing, we may be sure it is right, whether we can see the reasons for it or not.

But this is entirely cleared up by what was said before, that no sooner was the sin imputed, but a Christ was revealed; and this Christ, this God incarnate, who was conceived by the Holy Ghost, that he might be freed from the guilt of our original sin; who was born of the Virgin Mary, that he might be the seed of the woman only; who suffered under Pontius Pilate, a Gentile governor, to fulfill these prophecies, which signified what death he should die: This same Jesus, who was crucified in weakness, but raised in power, is that divine person, that Emmanuel, that God with us, whom we preach, in whom ye believe, and whom alone the Apostle, in the text, was determined to know.

By which word *know*, we are not to understand a bare historical knowledge; for to know that Christ was crucified by his enemies at Jerusalem, in this manner only, will do us no more service, than to know that Caesar was butchered by his friends at Rome; but the work *know*, means to know, so as to approve of him; as when Christ says, "Verily, I know you not;" I know you not, so as to approve of you. It signifies to know him, so as to embrace him in all his offices; to take him to be our prophet, priest, and king; so as to give up ourselves wholly to be instructed, saved, and governed by him. It implies an experimental knowledge of his crucifixion, so as to feel the power of it, and to be crucified unto the world, as the Apostle explains himself in the epistle to the Philippians, where he says, "I count all things but dung and dross, that I may know him, and the power of his resurrection."

This knowledge the Apostle was so swallowed up in, that he was determined not to know any thing else; he was resolved to make that his only study, the governing principle of his life, the point and end in which all his thoughts, words, and actions, should center.

Secondly, I pass on to give some reasons why every Christian should, with the Apostle, determine "not to know any thing, save Jesus Christ, and him crucified."

First, Without this, our persons will not be accepted in the sight of God. "This (and consequently this only) is life eternal, to know thee, the only true God, and Jesus Christ, whom thou has sent." As also St. Peter says, "There is now no other name given under heaven, whereby we can be saved, but that of Jesus Christ."

Some, indeed, ma please themselves in knowing the world, others boast themselves in the knowledge of a multitude of languages; but could we speak with the tongue of men and angels, or did we know the number of the stars, and could call them all by their names, yet, without this experimental knowledge of Jesus Christ, and him crucified, it would profit us nothing.

The former, indeed, may procure us a little honor, which cometh of man; but the latter only can render us acceptable in the sight of God: for, if we are ignorant of Christ, God will be to us a consuming fire.

Christ is the way, the truth, and the life; "No one cometh to the Father, but through him;" "He is the Lamb slain from the foundation of the world;" and none ever were, or ever will be received up into glory, but by an experimental application of his merits to their hearts.

We might as well think to rebuild the tower of Babel, or reach heaven with our hands, as to imagine we could enter therein by any other door, than that of the knowledge of Jesus Christ. Other knowledge may make you wise in your own eyes, and puff you up; but this alone edifieth, and maketh wise unto salvation.

As the meanest Christian, if he knows but this, though he know nothing else, will be accepted; so the greatest master in Israel, the most letter-learned teacher, without this, will be rejected. His philosophy is mere nonsense, his wisdom mere foolishness in the sight of God.

The author of the word now before us, was a remarkable instance of this; never, perhaps, was a greater scholar, in all what the world calls fine learning, than he: for he was bred up at the feet of Gamaliel, and profited in the knowledge of books, as well as in the Jewish religion, above many of his equals, as appears by the language, rhetoric, and spirit of his writings; and yet, when he came to know what it was to be a Christian, "He accounted all things but loss, so he might win Christ." And, though he was now at Corinth, that seat of polite learning, yet he was absolutely determined not to know any thing, or to make nothing his study, but what taught him to know Jesus Christ, and him crucified.

Hence then, appears the folly of those who spend their whole lives in heaping up other knowledge; and, instead of searching the scriptures, which testify of Jesus Christ, and are alone able to make them wise unto salvation, disquiet themselves in a pursuit after the knowledge of such things, as when known, concern them no more, than to know that a bird dropped a feather upon one of the Pyrenean mountains.

Hence it is, that so many, who profess themselves wise, because they can dispute of the causes and effects, the moral fitness and unfitness of things, appear mere fools in the things of God; so that when you come to converse with them about the great work of redemption wrought out for us by Jesus Christ, and of his being a propitiation for our sins, a fulfiller of the covenant of works, and a principle of new life to our souls, they are quite ignorant of the whole matter; and prove, to a demonstration, that, with all their learning, they know nothing yet, as they ought to know.

But, alas! how must it surprise a man, when the Most High is about to take away his soul, to think that he has passed for a wise-man, and a learned disputer in this world, and yet is left destitute of that knowledge which alone can make him appear with boldness before the judgment-seat of Jesus Christ? How must it grieve him, in a future state, to see others, whom he despised as illiterate men, because they experimentally knew Christ, and him crucified, exalted to the right-hand of God; and himself, with all his fine accomplishments, because he knew every thing, perhaps, but Christ, thrust down into hell?

Well might the Apostle, in a holy triumph, cry out, "Where is the wise? Where is the scribe? Where is the disputer of this world?" For, God will then make foolish the wisdom of this world, and bring to nought the wisdom of those who were so knowing in their own eyes.

I have made this digression from the main point before us, not to condemn or decry human literature, but to show, that it ought to be used only in subordination to divine; and that a Christian, if the Holy Spirit guided the pen of the Apostle, when he wrote this epistle, ought to study no books, but such as lead him to a farther knowledge of Jesus Christ, and him crucified.

And there is the more reason for this, because of the great mischief the contrary practice has done to the church of God: for, what was it but this learning, or rather this ignorance, that kept so many of the Scribes and Pharisees from the saving knowledge of Jesus Christ? And what is it, but this human wisdom, this science, false so called, that blinds the understanding, and corrupts the hearts of so many modern unbelievers, and makes them unwilling to submit to the righteousness which is of God by faith in Christ Jesus? But,

Secondly, Without this knowledge our performances, as well as persons will not be acceptable in the sight of God.

"Through faith," says the Apostle, that is, through a lively faith in a Mediator to come, "Abel offered a more acceptable sacrifice than Cain." And it is through a like faith, or an experimental knowledge of the same divine Mediator, that our sacrifices of prayer, praise, and thanksgivings, come up as an incense before he throne of grace.

Two persons may go up to the temple to pray; but he only will return home justified, who, in the language of our collects, sincerely offers up his prayers through Jesus Christ our Lord.

For it is this great atonement, this all-sufficient sacrifice, which alone can give us boldness to approach with our prayers o the Holy of Holies: and he that presumes to go without this, acts Korah's crime over again; offers unto God strange fire, and, consequently, will be rejected by him.

Farther, as our devotions to God will not, so neither, without this knowledge of Jesus Christ, will our acts of charity to men be accepted by him. For did we give all our goods to feed the poor, and yet were destitute of this knowledge, it would profit us nothing.

This our blessed Lord himself intimates in the 25th of Matthew, where he tells those who had been rich in good works, "That inasmuch as they did it unto one of the least of his brethren, they did it unto him." From whence we may plainly infer, that it is seeing Christ in his members, and doing good to them out of an experimental knowledge of his love to us, that alone will render our alms-deeds rewardable at the last day.

Lastly, As neither our acts of piety nor charity, so neither will our civil nor moral actions be acceptable to God, without this experimental knowledge of Jesus Christ.

Our modern pretenders to reason, indeed, set up another principle to act from; they talk, I know not what, Of doing moral an civil duties of life, from the moral fitness and unfitness of things. But such men are blind, however they may pretend to see; and going thus about to establish their own righteousness, are utterly ignorant of the righteousness which is of God by faith in Christ Jesus.

For though we grant that morality is a substantial part of Christianity, and that Christ came not to destroy, or take off the moral law, as a rule of action, but to explain, and so fulfill it; yet we affirm, that our moral and civil actions are now no farther acceptable in the sight of God the Father, than as they proceed from the principle of a new nature, and as experimental knowledge of, or vital faith in his dear Son.

The death of Jesus Christ has turned our whole lives into one continued sacrifice; and whether we eat or drink, whether we pray to God, or do any thing to man, it must all be done out of a love for, and knowledge of him who died and rose again, to render all, even our most ordinary deeds, acceptable in the sight of God.

If we live by this principle, if Christ be the Alpha and Omega of all our actions, then our least are acceptable sacrifices; but if this principle be wanting, our most pompous services avail nothing: we are but spiritual idolater; we sacrifice to our own net; we make an idol of ourselves, by making ourselves, and not Christ, the end of our actions: and, therefore, such actions are so far from being accepted by God, that, according to the language of one of the Articles of our Church, "We doubt not but they have the nature of sin, because they spring not from an experimental faith in, and knowledge of Jesus Christ."

Were we not fallen creatures, we might then act, perhaps, from other principles; but since we are fallen from God in Adam, and are restored again only by the obedience and death of Jesus Christ, the face of things I entirely changed, and all we think, speak, or do, is only accepted in and through him.

Justly, therefore, may I, in the

Third and *Last* places, Exhort you to put the Apostle's resolution in practice, and beseech you, with him to determine, Not to know any thing, save Jesus Christ, and him crucified."

I say, *determine*; for unless you sit down first, and count the cost, and from a well-grounded conviction of the excellency of this ,above all other knowledge whatsoever, resolve to make this your chief study, your only end, your one thing needful, every frivolous temptation will draw you aside from the pursuit after it.

Your friends and carnal acquaintance, and, above all, your grand adversary the devil, will be persuading you to determine not to know any thing, but how to lay up goods for many years, and to get a knowledge and taste of the pomps and vanities of this wicked world; but do you determine not to follow, or be led by them; and the more they persuade you to know other things, the more do you "determine not to know any thing, save Jesus Christ, and him crucified." For, this knowledge never faileth; but whether they be riches, they shall fail; whether they be pomps, they shall cease; whether they be vanities, they shall fade away: but the knowledge of Jesus Christ, and him crucified, abideth for ever.

Whatever, therefore, you are ignorant of, be not ignorant of this. If you know Christ, and him crucified, you know enough to make you happy, supposing you know nothing else; and without this, all your other knowledge cannot keep you from being everlastingly miserable.

Value not then, the contempt of friends, which you must necessarily meet with upon your open profession to act according to this determination. For your Master, whose you are, was despised before you; and all that will know nothing else but Jesus Christ, and him crucified, must, in some degree or other, suffer persecution.

It is necessary that offenses should come, to try what is in our hearts, and whether we will be faithful soldiers of Jesus Christ or not.

Dare ye then to confess our blessed Master before men, and to shine as lights in the world, amidst a crooked and perverse generation? Let us not be content with following him afar off; for then we shall, as Peter did, soon deny him; but let us be altogether Christians, and let our speech, and all our actions declare to the world whose disciples we are, and that we have indeed "determined not to know any thing, save Jesus Christ, and him crucified." Then, well will it be with us, and happy, unspeakably happy shall we be, even here; and what is infinitely better, when others that despised us, shall be calling for the mountains to fall on them, and the hills to cover them, we shall be exalted to sit down on the right-hand of God, and shine as the sun in the firmament, in the kingdom of our most adorable Redeemer, for ever and ever.

Which God of his infinite mercy grant .

46. Of Justification by Christ

It has been objected by some, who dissent from, nay, I may add, by others also, who actually are friends to the present ecclesiastical establishment, that the ministers of the Church of England preach themselves, and not Christ Jesus the Lord; that they entertain their people with lectures of mere morality, without declaring to them the glad tidings of salvation by Jesus Christ. How well grounded such an objection may be, is not my business to inquire: All I shall say at present to the point is, that whenever such a grand objection is urged against the whole body of the clergy in general, every honest minister of Jesus Christ should do his utmost to cut off all manner of occasion, from those who desire an occasion to take offense at us; that so by hearing us continually sounding forth the word of truth, and declaring with all boldness and assurance of faith, "that there is no other name given under heaven, whereby they can be saved, but that of Jesus Christ," they may be ashamed of this their same confident boasting against us.

It was an eye to this objection, joined with the agreeableness and delightfulness of the subject (for who can but delight to talk of that which the blessed angels desire to look into?) that induces me to discourse a little on that great and fundamental article of our faith; namely, our being freely justified by the precious blood of Jesus Christ. "But ye are washed, but ye are sanctified, but ye are justified, in the name of our Lord Jesus Christ, and by the Spirit of our God."

The words beginning with the particle *but*, have plainly a reference to something before; it may not therefore be improper, before I descend to particulars, to consider the words as they stand in relation to the context. The apostle, in the verses immediately foregoing, had been reckoning up many notorious sins, drunkenness, adultery, fornication, and such like, the commission of which, without a true and hearty repentance, he tells the Corinthians, would entirely shut them out of the kingdom of God. But then, lest they should, on the one hand, grow spiritually proud by seeing themselves differ from their unconverted brethren, and therefore be tempted to set them at nought, and say with the self-conceited hypocrite in the prophet, "Come not nigh me, for I am holier than thou;" or, on the other hand, by looking back on the multitude of their past offenses, should be apt to think their sins were too many and grievous to be forgiven: he first, in order to keep them humble, reminds them of their sad state before conversion, telling them in plain terms, "such (or as it might be read, these things) were some of you;" not only one, but all that sad catalogue of vices I have been drawing up, some of you were once guilty of; but then, at the same time, to preserve them from despair, behold he brings them glad tidings of great joy: "But ye are washed; but ye are sanctified, but ye are justified in the name of our Lord Jesus Christ, and by the Spirit of our God."

The former part of this text, our being sanctified, I have in some measure treated of already; I would not enlarge on our being freely justified by the precious obedience and death of Jesus Christ: "But ye are justified in the name of our Lord Jesus Christ."

From which words I shall consider three things:

First, What is meant by the word justified.

Secondly, I shall endeavor to prove that all mankind in general, and every individual person in particular, stands in need of being justified.

Thirdly, That there is no possibility of obtaining this justification, which we so much want, but by the all-perfect obedience, and precious death of Jesus Christ.

First, I am to consider what is meant by the word justified.

"But ye are justified," says the apostle; which is, as though he had said, you have your sins forgiven, and are looked upon by God as though you never had offended him at all: for that is the meaning of the word justified, in almost all the passages of holy scripture where this word is mentioned. Thus, when this same apostle writes to the Romans, he tells them, that "whom God called, those he also justified:" And that this word justified, implies a blotting out of all our transgressions, is manifest from what follows, "them he also glorified," which could not be if a justified person was not looked upon by God, as though he never had offended him at all. And again, speaking of Abraham's faith, he tells them, that "Abraham believed on Him that justifies the ungodly," who acquits and clears the ungodly man; for it is a law-term, and alludes to a judge acquitting an accused criminal of the thing laid to his charge. Which expression the apostle himself explains by a quotation out of the Psalms: "Blessed is the man to whom the Lord imputeth no sin." From all which proofs, and many others that might be urged, it is evident, that by being justified, we are to understand, being so acquitted in the sight of God as to be looked upon as though we never had offended him at all. And in this sense we are to understand that article, which we profess to believe in our creed, when each of us declare in his own person, I believe the forgiveness of sins. This leads me to the

Second thing proposed, to prove that all mankind in general, and every individual person in particular, stands in need of being justified.

And indeed the apostle supposes this in the words of the text: "But ye are justified," thereby implying that the Corinthians (and consequently all mankind, there being no difference, as will be shown hereafter) stood in need of being justified.

But not to rest in bare suppositions, in my farther enlargement on this head, I shall endeavor to prove, that we all stand in need of being justified on account of the sin of our natures, and the sin of our lives.

1. *First*, I affirm that we all stand in need of being justified, on account of the sin of our natures: for we are all chargeable with original sin, or the sin of our first parents. Which, though a proposition that may be denied by a self-justifying infidel, who "will not come to Christ that he may have life;" yet can never be denied by any one who believes that St. Paul's epistles were written by divine inspiration; where we are told, that "in Adam all died;" that is, Adam's sin was imputed to all; and lest we should forget to make a particular application, it is added in another place, "that there is none that doeth good (that is, by nature) no, not one: That we are all gone out of the way, (of original righteousness) and are by nature the children of wrath." And even David, who was a man after God's own heart, and, if any one could, might surely plead an exemption from this universal corruption, yet he confesses, that "he was shapen in iniquity, and that in sin did his mother conceive him." And, to mention but one text more, as immediately applicable to the present purpose, St. Paul, in his epistle to the Romans, says, that "Death came upon all men, for the disobedience of one, namely, of Adam, even upon those, (that is, little children) who had not sinned after the similitude of Adam's transgression;" who had not been guilty of actual sin, and therefore could not be punished with temporal death (which came into the world, as this same apostle elsewhere informs us, only by sin) had not the disobedience of our first parents been imputed to them. So that what has been said in this point seems to be excellently summed up in that article of our church, where she declares that "Original sin standeth not in the following of Adam, but it is the fault and corruption of every man, that naturally is engendered of the offspring of Adam; whereby man is very far gone from original righteousness, and is of his own nature inclined to evil, so that the flesh lusteth always contrary to the spirit; and the therefore in every person born into this world, it deserveth God's wrath and damnation."

I have been more particular in treating of this point, because it is the very foundation of the Christian religion: For I am verily persuaded, that it is nothing but a want of being well grounded in the doctrine of original sin, and of the helpless, nay, I may say, damnable condition, each of us comes into the world in, that makes so many infidels oppose, and so many who call themselves Christians, so very lukewarm in their love and affections to Jesus Christ. It is this, and I could almost say, this only, that makes infidelity abound among us so much as it does. For, alas! we are mistaken if we imagine that men now commence or continue infidels, and set up corrupted reason in opposition to divine revelation merely for want of evidence, (for I believe it might easily be proved, that a modern unbeliever is the most credulous creature living;) no, it is only for want of an humble mind, of a sense of their original depravity, and a willingness to own themselves so depraved, that makes them so obstinately shut their eyes against the light of the glorious gospel of Christ. Whereas, on the contrary, were they but once pricked to the heart with a due and lively sense of their natural corruption and liableness to condemnation, we should have them no more scoffing at divine revelation, and looking on it as an idle tale; but they would cry out with the trembling jailer, "What shall I do to be saved?" It was an error in this fundamental point, that made so many resist the evidence the Son of God himself gave of his divine mission, when he tabernacled amongst us. Every word he spake, every action he did, every miracle he wrought, proved that he came from God. And why then did so many harden their hearts, and would not believe his report? Why, he himself informs us, "They will not come unto me that they may have life:" They will obstinately stand out against those means God had appointed for their salvation: And St. Paul tells us, "that if the gospel be hid, it is hid to them that are lost; in whom the God of this world hath blinded the eyes of them which believe not, lest the light of the glorious gospel of Christ, who is the image of God, should shine upon them." 2 Cor. 4:3–4.

If it be asked, how it suits with the divine goodness, to impute the guilt of one man's sin, to an innocent posterity? I should think it sufficient to make use of the apostle's words: "Nay, but O man, who art thou that repliest against God? Shall the thing formed say to him that formed it, why hast thou made me thus?" But to come to a more direct reply: Persons would do well to consider that in the first covenant God made with man, Adam acted as a public person, as the common representative of all mankind, and consequently we must stand or fall with him. Had he continued in his obedience, and not eaten the forbidden fruit, the benefits of that obedience would doubtless have been imputed to us: But since he did not persist in it, but broke the covenant made with him, and us in him; who dares charge the righteous Judge of all the earth with injustice for imputing that to us also? I proceed,

Secondly, To prove that we stand in need of being justified, on account of the sin of our lives.

That God, as he made man, has a right to demand his obedience, I suppose is a truth no one will deny: that he hath also given us both a natural and a written law, whereby we are to be judged, cannot be questioned by any one who believes St. Paul's epistle to the Romans to be of divine authority: For in it we are told of a law written in the heart, and a law given by Moses; and that each of us hath broken these laws, is too evident from our sad and frequent experience. Accordingly the holy scriptures inform us that "there is no man which liveth and sinneth not;" that "in many things we offend all;" that "if we say we have no sin we deceive ourselves," and such like. And if we are thus offenders against God, it follows, that we stand in need of forgiveness for thus offending Him; unless we suppose God to enact laws, and at the same time not care whether they are obeyed or no; which is as absurd as to suppose that a prince should establish laws for the proper government of his country, and yet let every violator of them come off with impunity. But God has not dealt so foolishly with his creatures: no, as he gave us a law, he demands our obedience to that law, and has obliged us universally and perseveringly to obey it, under no less a penalty than incurring his curse and eternal death for every breach of it: For thus speaks the scripture; "Cursed is he that continueth not in all things that are written in the law to do them;" as the scripture also speaketh in another place, "The soul that sinneth, it shall die." Now it has already been proved, that we have all of us sinned; and therefore, unless some means can be found to satisfy God's justice, we must perish eternally.

Let us then stand a while, and see in what a deplorable condition each of us comes into the world, and still continues, till we are translated into a state of grace. For surely nothing can well be supposed more deplorable, than to be born under the curse of God; to be charged with original guilt; and not only so, but to be convicted as actual breakers of God's law, the least breach of which justly deserves eternal damnation. Surely this can be but a melancholy prospect to view ourselves in, and must put us upon contriving some means whereby we may satisfy and appease our offended judge. But what must those means be? Shall we repent? Alas! there is not one word of repentance mentioned in the first covenant: "The day that thou eatest thereof, thou shalt surely die." So that, if God be true, unless there be some way found out to satisfy divine justice, we must perish; and there is no room left for us to expect a change of mind in God, though we should seek it with tears. Well then, if repentance will not do, shall we plead the law of works? Alas! "By the law shall no man living be justified: for by the law comes the knowledge of sin." It is that which convicts and condemns, and therefore can by no means justify us; and "all our righteousnesses (says the prophet) are but as filthy rags." Wherewith then shall we come before the Lord, and bow down before the most high God? Shall we come before Him with calves of a year old, with thousands of rams, or ten thousands of rivers of oil? Alas! God has showed thee, O man, that this will not avail: For he hath declared, "I will take no bullock out of thy house, nor he-goat out of thy fold: for all the beasts of the forests are mine, and so are the cattle upon a thousand hills." Will the Lord then be pleased to accept our first-born for our transgression, the fruit of our bodies for the sin of our souls? Even this will not purchase our pardon: for he hath declared that "the children shall not bear the iniquities of their parents." Besides, they are sinners, and therefore, being under the same condemnation, equally stand in need of forgiveness with ourselves. They are impure, and will the Lord accept the blind and lame for sacrifice? Shall some angel then, or archangel, undertake to fulfill the covenant which we have broken, and make atonement for us? Alas! they are only creatures, though creatures of the highest order; and therefore are obliged to obey God as well as we; and after they have done all, must say they have done no more than what was their duty to do. And supposing it was possible for them to die, yet how could the death of a finite creature satisfy an infinitely offended justice? O wretched men that we are! Who shall deliver us? I thank God, our Lord Jesus Christ. Which naturally leads me to the

Third thing proposed, which was to endeavor to prove, that there is no possibility of obtaining this justification, which we so much want, but by the all-perfect obedience and precious death of Jesus Christ, "But ye are justified in the name of our Lord Jesus Christ."

But this having been in some measure proved by what has been said under the foregoing head, wherein I have shown that neither our repentance, righteousness, nor sacrifice, no not the obedience and death of angels, themselves, could possibly procure justification for us, nothing remains for me to do under this head, but to show that Jesus Christ has procured it for us.

And here I shall still have recourse "to the law and to the testimony." For after all the most subtle disputations on either side, nothing but the lively oracles of God can give us any satisfaction in this momentous point: it being such an inconceivable mystery, that the eternal only-begotten Son of God should die for sinful man, that we durst not have presumed so much as to have thought of it, had not God revealed it in his holy word. It is true, reason may show us the wound, but revelation only can lead us to the means of our cure. And though the method God has been pleased to take to make us happy, may be to the infidel a stumbling-block, and to the wise opiniator and disputer of this world, foolishness; yet wisdom, that is, the dispensation of our redemption, will be justified, approved of, and submitted to, by all her truly wise and holy children, by every sincere and upright Christian.

But to come more directly to the point before us. Two things, as was before observed, we wanted, in order to be at peace with God.

1. To be freed from the guilt of the sin of our nature.
2. From the sin of our lives.

And both these (thanks be to God for this unspeakable gift) are secured to believers by the obedience and death of Jesus Christ. For what says the scripture?

1. As to the *first*, it informs us, that "as by the disobedience of one man, (or by one transgression, namely, that of Adam) many were made sinners; so by the obedience of one, Jesus Christ (therein including his passive as well as active obedience) many were made righteous." And again, "As by the disobedience of one man, judgment came upon all men unto condemnation;" or all men were condemned on having Adam's sin imputed to them; "so by the obedience of one, that is, Jesus Christ, the free gift of pardon and peace came upon all men, (all sorts of men) unto justification of life." I say all sorts of men; for the apostle in this chapter is only drawing a parallel between the first and second Adam in this respect, that they acted both as representatives; and as the posterity of Adam had his sin imputed to them, so those for whom Christ died, and whose representative he is, shall have his merits imputed to them also. Whoever run the parallel farther, in order to prove universal redemption (whatever arguments they may draw for the proof of it from other passages of scripture,) if they would draw one from this for that purpose, I think they stretch their line of interpretation beyond the limits of scripture.

2. Pardon for the sin of our lives was another thing, which we wanted to have secured to us, before we could be at peace with God.

And this the holy scriptures inform us, is abundantly done by the death of Jesus Christ. The evangelical prophet foretold that the promised Redeemer should be "wounded for our transgressions, and bruised for our iniquities; that the chastisement of our peace should be upon him; and that by his stripes we should be healed," Isaiah 53:6. The angels at his birth said, that he should "save his people from their sins." And St. Paul declares, that "this is a faithful saying, and worthy of all acceptation, that Jesus Christ came into the world to save sinners." And here in the words of the text, "Such (or, as I observed before, these things) were some of you; but ye are washed, &c." and again, "Jesus Christ is the end of the law for righteousness to every one that believeth." And, to show us that none but Jesus Christ can do all this, the apostle St. Peter says, "Neither is their salvation in any other; for there is no other name under heaven given among men, whereby we must be saved, but the name of Jesus Christ.

How God will be pleased to deal with the Gentiles, who yet sit in darkness and under the shadow of death, and upon whom the sun of righteousness never yet arose, is not for us to inquire. "What have we to do to judge those that are without?" To God's mercy let us recommend them, and wait for a solution of this and every other difficult point, till the great day of accounts, when all God's dispensations, both of providence and grace, will be fully cleared up by methods to us, as yet unknown, because unrevealed. However, this we know, that the judge of all the earth will, most assuredly, do right.

But it is time for me to draw a conclusion.

I have now, brethren, by the blessings of God, discoursed on the words of the text in the method I proposed. Many useful inferences might be drawn from what has been delivered; but as I have detained you, I fear, too long already, permit me only to make a reflection or two on what has been said, and I have done.

If then we are freely justified by the death and obedience of Jesus Christ, let us here pause a while; and as before we have reflected on the misery of a fallen, let us now turn aside and see the happiness of the believing, soul. But alas! how am I lost to think that God the Father, when we were in a state of enmity and rebellion against Him, should notwithstanding yearn in his bowels towards us his fallen, his apostate creatures: And because nothing but an infinite ransom could satisfy an infinitely offended justice, that should send his only and dear Son Jesus Christ (who is God, blessed for ever, and who had lain in his bosom from all eternity) to fulfill the covenant of works, and die a cursed, painful, ignominious death, for us and for our salvation! who can avoid crying out, at the consideration of his mystery of godliness. "Oh the depth of the riches of God's love" to us his wretched, miserable and undone creatures! "How unsearchable is his mercy, and his ways past finding out!" Now know we of a truth, O God, that thou hast loved us, "since thou hast not with-held thy Son, thine only Son Jesus Christ," from thus doing and dying for us.

But as we admire the Father sending, let us likewise humbly and thankfully adore the Son coming, when sent to die for man. But O! what thoughts can conceive, what words express the infinite greatness of that unparalleled love, which engaged the Son of God to come down from the mansions of his Father's glory to obey and die for sinful man! The Jews, when he only shed a tear at poor Lazarus' funeral, said, "Behold how he loved him." How much more justly then may we cry out, Behold how he loved us! When he not only fulfilled the whole moral law, but did not spare to shed his own most precious blood for us.

And can any poor truly-convicted sinner, after this, despair of mercy? What, can they see their Savior hanging on a tree, with arms stretched out ready to embrace them, and yet, on their truly believing on him, doubt of finding acceptance with him? No, away with all such dishonorable, desponding thoughts. Look on his hands, bored with pins of iron; look on his side, pierced with a cruel spear, to let loose the sluices of his blood, and open a fountain for sin, and for all uncleanness; and then despair of mercy if you can! No, only believe in Him, and then, though you have crucified him afresh, yet will he abundantly pardon you; "though your sins be as scarlet, yet shall they be as wool; though deeper than crimson, yet shall they be whiter than snow."

Which God of his infinite mercy grant.

47. The Great Duty of Charity Recommended

1 Corinthians 13:8, "Charity never faileth."

Nothing is more valuable and commendable, and yet, not one duty is less practiced, than that of charity. We often pretend concern and pity for the misery and distress of our fellow-creatures, but yet we seldom commiserate their condition so much as to relieve them according to our abilities; but unless we assist them with what they may stand in need of, for the body, as well as for the soul, all our wishes are no more than words of no value or regard, and are not to be esteemed or regarded: for when we hear of any deplorable circumstance, in which our fellow-creatures are involved, be they friends or enemies; it is our duty, as Christians, to assist them to the utmost of our power.

Indeed, we are not, my brethren, to hurt ourselves or our families; this is not that charity which is so much recommended by St. Paul; no, but if we are any ways capable of relieving them without injuring either ourselves, or families, then it is our duty to do it; and this never faileth, where it proceeds from a right end, and with a right view.

St. Paul had been showing, in the preceding chapter, that spiritual gifts were divers; that God had disposed of one blessing to one, and another to another; and though there was a diversity of blessings, God did not bestow them to one person, but gave to one a blessing which he denied to another, and gave a blessing, or a gift to the other which might make him as eminent in one way, as the other's gift made him so in another: but though there are these divers spiritual gifts, they are all given for some wise end, even to profit withal, and to that end they are thus diversely bestowed. We are not, on the one hand, to hide those gifts which God has given us: neither are we, on the other, to be so lavish of them, as to spend them upon our lusts and pleasures, to satisfy our sensual appetites, but they are to be used for the glory of God, and the good of immortal souls. After he had particularly illustrated this, he comes to show, that all gifts, however great they may be in themselves, are of no value unless we have charity, as you may see particularly, by considering from the beginning of this chapter.

But before I go any further, I shall inform you what the apostle means by charity; and that it, Love; if there is true love, there will be charity; there will be an endeavor to assist, help, and relieve according to that ability wherewith God has blessed us: and, since this is so much recommended by the apostle, let us see how valuable this charity is, and how commendable in all those who pursue it. I shall,

I. Consider this blessing as relation to the bodies of men.

II. I shall show how much more valuable it is, when relating to the souls of men.

III. Shall show you when your charity is of the right kind.

IV. Why this charity, or the grace of love, never faileth.

V. Shall conclude all, with an exhortation to high and low, rich and poor, one with another, to be found in the constant practice of this valuable and commendable duty.

First, I shall consider this duty, as relating to the bodies of men. And,

1. O that the rich would consider how praise-worthy this duty is, in helping their fellow-creatures! We were created to be a help to each other; God has made no one so independent as not to need the assistance of another; the richest and most powerful man upon the face of this earth, needs the help and assistance of those who are around him; and though he may be great today, a thousand accidents may make him as low tomorrow; he that is rolling in plenty today, may be in as much scarcity tomorrow. If our rich men would be more charitable to their poor friends and neighbors, it would be a means of recommending them to the savor of others, if Providence should frown upon them; but alas, our great men had much rather spend their money in a playhouse, at a ball, an assembly, or a masquerade, than relieve a poor distressed servant of Jesus Christ. They had rather spend their estates on their hawks and hounds, on their whores, and earthly, sensual, devilish pleasures, than comfort, nourish, or relieve one of their distressed fellow-creatures. What difference is there between the king on the throne, and the beggar on the dunghill, when God demands their breaths? There is no difference, my brethren, in the grave, nor will there be any at the day of judgment. You will not be excused because you have had a great estate, a fine house, and lived in all the pleasures that earth could afford you; no, these things will be one means of your condemnation; neither will you be judged according to the largeness of your estate, but according to the use you have made of it.

Now, you may think nothing but of your pleasures and delights, of living in ease and plenty, and never consider how many thousands of your fellow-creatures would rejoice at what you are making waste of, and setting no account by. Let me beseech you, my rich brethren, to consider the poor of the world, and how commendable and praise-worthy it is to relieve those who are distressed. Consider, how pleasing this is to God, how delightful it is to man, and how many prayers you will have put up for your welfare, by those persons whom you relieve; and let this be a consideration to spare a little out of the abundance wherewith God has blessed you, or the relief of his poor. He could have placed you in their low condition, and they in your high state; it is only his good pleasure that has thus made the difference, and shall not this make you remember your distressed fellow-creatures?

Let me beseech you to consider, which will stand you best at the day of judgment, so much money expended at a horse-race, or a cockpit, at a play or masquerade, or so much given for the relief of your fellow-creatures, and for the distressed members of Jesus Christ.

I beseech you, that you would consider how valuable and commendable this duty is: do not be angry at my thus exhorting you to that duty, which is so much recommended by Jesus Christ himself, and by all his apostles: I speak particularly to you, my rich brethren, to entreat you to consider those that are poor in this world, and help them from time to time, as their necessity calls for it. Consider, that there is a curse denounced against the riches of those, who do not thus do good with them; namely, "Go to now you rich men, weep and howl for your miseries that shall come upon you; your riches are corrupted, your garments are moth-eaten, your gold and silver is cankered, and the rust of them shall be a witness against you, and shall eat your flesh, as it were fire; ye have heaped your treasure together for the last day." You see the dreadful woe pronounced against all those who hoard up the abundance of the things of this life, without relieving the distresses of those who are in want thereof: and the apostle James goes on also to speak against those who have acquired estates by fraud, as too many have in these days. "Behold the hire of the laborers, which have reaped down your fields, which is by you kept back by fraud, crieth; and the cries of them who have reaped, are entered into the ears of the Lord God of Sabbaoth. Ye have lived in pleasure on the earth, and been wanton; ye have nourished your hearts, as in the day of slaughter." Thus, if you go on to live after the lust of the flesh, to pamper your bellies, and make them a God, while the poor all around you are starving, God will make these things a witness against you, which shall be as a worm to your souls, and gnaw your consciences to all eternity; therefore, let me once more recommend charity unto the bodies of men, and beseech you to remember what a blessed Lord Jesus Christ has promised unto those who thus love his members, that "as they have done it to the least of his members, they have done it unto him."

I am not now speaking for myself; I am not recommending my little flock in Georgia to you; then you might say, as many wantonly do, that I wanted the money for myself; no, my brethren, I am now recommending the poor of this land to you, your poor neighbors, poor friends, yea, your poor enemies; they are whom I am now speaking for; and when I see so many starving in the streets, and almost naked, my bowels are moved with pity and concern, to consider, that many in whose power it is, to lend their assisting hand, should shut up their bowels of compassion, and will not relieve their fellow-creatures, though in the most deplorable condition for the want thereof.

As I have thus recommended charity particularly to the rich among you; so now I would,

2. *Secondly*, Recommend this to another set of people among us, who, instead of being the most forward in acts of charity, are commonly the most backward; I mean the clergy of this land.

Good God! How amazing is the consideration, that those, whom God has called out to labor in spiritual things, should be so backward in this duty, as fatal experience teacheth. Our clergy (that is the generality thereof) are only seeking after preferment, running up and down, to obtain one benefice after another; and to heap up an estate, either to spend on the pleasures of life, or to gratify their sensual appetites, while the poor of their flock are forgotten; nay, worse, they are scorned, hated, and disdained.

I am not now, my brethren, speaking of all the clergy; no, blessed be God, there are some among them, who abhor such proceedings, and are willing to relieve the necessitous; but God knows, these are but very few, while many take no thought of the poor among them.

They can visit the rich and the great, but the poor they cannot bear in their sight; they are forgetful, willfully forgetful of the poor members of Jesus Christ.

They have gone out of the old paths, and turned into a new polite way, but which is not warranted in the word of God: they are sunk into a fine way of acting; but as fine as it is, it was not the practice of the apostles, or of the Christians in any age of the church: for they visited and relieved the poor among them; but how rare is this among us, how seldom do we find charity in a clergyman?

It is with grief I speak these things, but woeful experience is a witness to the truth thereof: and if all the clergy of this land were here, I would tell them boldly, that they did not keep in the ways of charity, but were remiss in their duty; instead of "selling all and giving to the poor," they will not sell any thing, nor give at all to the poor.

3. *Thirdly*, I would exhort you who are poor, to be charitable to one another.

Though you may not have money, or the things of this life, to bestow upon one another; yet you may assist them, by comforting, and advising them not to be discouraged though they are low in the world; or in sickness you may help them according as you have time or ability: do not be unkind to one another: do not grieve, or vex, or be angry with each other; for this is giving the world an advantage over you.

And if God stirs up any to relieve you, do not make an ill use of what his providence, by the hands of some Christian, hath bestowed upon you: be always humble and wait on God; do not murmur or repine, if you see any relieved and you are not; still wait on the Lord, and help one another, according to your abilities, from time to time.

Having showed you how valuable this is to the bodies of men, I now proceed,

Secondly, To show you how much more valuable this charity is, when it extends to the souls of men.

And is not the soul more valuable than the body? It would be of no advantage, but an infinite disadvantage, to obtain all the world, if we were to lose our souls. The soul is of infinite value, and of infinite concern, and, therefore, we should extend our charity whenever we see it needful, and likewise should reprove, rebuke, and exhort with all godliness and love.

We should, my dear brethren, use all means and opportunities for the salvation of our own souls, and of the souls of others. We may have a great deal of charity and concern for the bodies of our fellow-creatures, when we have no thought, or concern, for their immortal souls: But O how sad is it, to have thought for a mortal, but not for the immortal part; to have charity for the body of our fellow-creatures, while we have no concern for their immortal souls; it may be, we help them to ruin them, but have no concern in the saving of them.

You may love to spend a merry evening, to go to a play, or a horse-race, with them; but on the other hand, you cannot bear the thoughts of going to a sermon, or a religious society, with them; no, you would sing the songs of the drunkard, but you will not sing hymns, with them; this is not polite enough, this is unbecoming a gentleman of taste, unfashionable, and only practiced among a parcel of enthusiasts and madmen.

Thus, you will be so uncharitable as to join hand in hand with those who are hastening to their own damnation, while you will not be so charitable as to assist them in being brought from darkness t light, and from the power of Satan unto God. But this, this, my dear brethren, is the greatest charity, as can be, to save a soul from death: this is of far greater advantage, than relieving the body of a fellow-creature: for the most miserable object as could be, death would deliver it from all. But death, to those who are not born again, would be so far from being a release from all misery, that it would be an inlet to all torment, and that to all eternity. Therefore, we should assist, as much as possible, to keep a soul from falling into the hands of Satan: for he is the grand enemy of souls. How should this excite you to watch over your own and others souls? For unless you are earnest with God, Satan will be too hard for you. Surely, it is the greatest charity to watch over one another's words and actions, that we may forewarn each other when danger is nigh, or when the enemy of souls approaches.

And if you have once known the value of your own souls, and know what it is to be snatched as brands out of the burning fire, you will be solicitous that others may be brought out of the same state. It is not the leading of a moral life, being honest, and paying every man his just due; this is not a proof of your being in a state of grace, or of being born again, and renewed in the spirit of your minds: No, you may die honest, just, charitable, and yet not be in a state of salvation.

It is not the preaching of that morality, which most of our pulpits now bring forth, that is sufficient to bring you from sin unto God. I saw you willing to learn, and yet were ignorant of the necessity of being born again, regenerated, of having all old things done away, and all things becoming new in your souls: I could not bear, my brethren, to see you in the highway to destruction, and none to bring you back. It was love to your souls, it was a desire to see Christ formed in you, which brought me into the fields, the highways, and hedges, to preach unto you Jesus, a crucified Jesus as dying for you. It was charity, indeed it was charity to your souls, which has exposed me to the present ill treatment of my letter-learned brethren.

Therefore, let me advise you to be charitable to the souls of one another; that is, by advising them with all love and tenderness, to follow after Christ, and the things which belong to their immortal peace, before they be forever hid from their eyes.

I now proceed, in the *Third* place, to show when your charity is of the right kind.

And here, my brethren, I shall show, *First*, When it is not; and, *Secondly*, When it is of the right kind.

1. *First*, Your charity is not of the right kind, when it proceeds from worldly views or ends.

If it is to be seen of men, to receive any advantage from them, to be esteemed, or to gain a reputation in the world; or if you have any pride in it, and expect to reap benefit from God merely for it; if all, or each of these is the end of your charity, then it is all in vain; your charity does not proceed from a right end, but you are hereby deceiving your own souls. If you give an alms purely to be observed by man, or as expecting favor from God, merely on the account thereof, then you have not the glory of God, or the benefit of your fellow-creatures at heart, but merely yourself: this, this is not charity. Nor,

Secondly, Is that true charity, when we give any thing to our fellow-creatures purely to indulge them in vice: this is so far from being charity, that it is a sin, both against God, and against our fellow-creatures. And yet, this is a common, as it is sinful, to carry our friends, under a specious pretense of charity, to one or the other entertainment, with no other view, but to make them guilty of excess. Hereby you are guilty of a double sin: we are not to sin ourselves, much less should we endeavor to make another sin likewise. But,

Thirdly, Our charity comes from a right end, when it proceeds from love to God, and for the welfare both of the body and soul of our fellow-creatures.

When this is the sole end of relieving our distressed fellow-creatures, then our charity comes from a right end, and we may expect to reap advantage by it: this is the charity which is pleasing to God. God is well pleased, when all our actions proceed from love, love to himself, and love to immortal souls.

Consider, my dear brethren, that it was love for souls, that brought the blessed Jesus down from the bosom of his Father; that made him, who was equal in power and glory, to come and take upon him our nature; that caused the Lord of life to die the painful, ignominious, and accursed death of the cross. It was love to immortal souls, that brought this blessed Jesus among us. And O that we might hence consider how great the value of souls was and is: it was that which made Jesus to bled, pant, and die. And surely souls must be of infinite worth, which made the Lamb of God to die so shameful a death.

And shall not this make you have a true value for souls? It is of the greatest worth: and this, this is the greatest charity, when it comes from love to God, and from love to souls. This will be a charity, the satisfaction of which will last to all eternity. O that this may make you have so much regard for the value of souls, as not to neglect all opportunities for the doing of them good: here is something worth having charity for, because they remain to all eternity. Therefore, let me earnestly beseech you both to consider the worth of immortal souls, and let your charity extend to them, that by your advice and admonition, you may be an instrument, in the hands of God, in bringing souls to the Lord Jesus.

I am in the next place to consider, *Fourthly*, Why this charity, or grace of love never faileth.

And it never faileth in respect of its proceeding from an unchangeable God. We are not to understand, that our charity is always the same: No, there may, and frequently are, ebbs and flowings; but still it never totally faileth: No, the grace of love remaineth for ever. There is, and will be, a charity to all who have erred and run astray from God. We cannot be easy to see souls in the highway to destruction, and not use our utmost endeavor to bring them back from sin, and show them the dreadful consequence of running into evil. Christians cannot bear to see those souls for whom Christ died, perish for want of knowledge: and if they see any of the bodies of their fellow-creatures in want, they will do the utmost in their power to relieve them.

Charity will never fail, among those who have a true love to the Lord Jesus, and know the value of souls: they will be charitable to those who are in distress. And thus you see, that true charity, if it proceeds from a right end, never faileth.

I now proceed, my brethren, in the *Last* place, to exhort all of you, high and low, rich and poor, one with another, to practice this valuable and commendable duty of charity.

It is not rolling in your coaches, taking your pleasure, and not considering the miseries of your fellow-creatures, that is commendable or praise-worthy; but the relieving your distressed poor fellow-creatures, is valuable and praise-worthy wherever it is found. But alas! how very few of our gay and polite gentlemen consider their poor friends; rather they despise, and do not regard them. They can indulge themselves in the follies of life, and had much rather spend their estates in lusts and pleasures, while the poor all round them are not thought worthy to be set with the dogs of their flock. If you have an abundance of the things of this world, then you are esteemed as companions for the polite and gay in life; but if you are poor, then you must not expect to find any favor, but be hated, or not thought fit for company or conversation: and if you have an abundance of the things of this life, and do not want any assistance, then you have many ready to help you. My dear brethren, I do not doubt but your own experience is a proof of my assertions; as also, that if any come into distress, then those, who promised to give relief, quite forget what they promise, and will despise, because Providence has frowned. But this is not acting like those who are bound for the heavenly Jerusalem; thus our hearts and our actions give our lips the lie: for if we profess the name of Christ, and do not depart from all iniquity, we are not those, who are worthy of being esteemed Christians indeed.

For, if we have not charity, we are not Christians: charity is the great duty of Christians: and where is our Christianity, if we want charity? Therefore, let me beseech you to exercise charity to your distressed fellow-creatures. Indeed, my dear brethren, this is truly commendable, truly valuable; and therefore, I beseech you, in the bowels of tender mercy to Christ, to consider his poor distressed members; exercise, exercise, I beseech you, this charity: if you have no compassion, you are not true disciples of the Lord Jesus Christ. I humbly beg you to consider those who want relief, and are really destitute, and relieve them according to your abilities. Consider, that the more favorable Providence has been to you, it should make you the more earnest and solicitous to relieve those whom you may find in distress: it is of the utmost consequence, what is well pleasing to your fellow-creatures, and doing your duty to God.

When you are called from hence, then all riches and grandeur will be over; the grave will make no distinction; great estates will be of no signification in the other world; and if you have made a bad use of the talent which God hath put into your hands, it will be only an aggravation of your condemnation at the great day of account, when God shall come to demand your souls, and to call you to an account, for the use to which you have put the abundance of the things of this life.

To conclude, let me once more beseech each of you to act according to the circumstances of life, which God, in his rich and free mercy, has given you.

If you were sensible of the great consequences which would attend your acting in this charitable manner, and considered it as a proof of your love to God, the loving his members; you could not be uncharitable in your tempers, nor fail to relieve any of your distressed fellow creatures.

Consider how easy it is for many of you, by putting your mites together, to help one who is in distress; and how can you tell, but that the little you give, may be the means of bringing one from distress into flourishing circumstances; and then, if there is a true spirit of a Christian in them, they can never be sufficiently thankful to God the author, and to you as the instrument, in being so great a friend to them in their melancholy circumstances: consider also, once more, how much better your account will be at the day of judgment, and what peace of conscience you will enjoy. How satisfactory must be the thought of having relieved the widow and the fatherless? This is recommended by the Lord Jesus Christ, and has been practiced in all ages of the church: and therefore, my brethren, be ye now found in the practice of this duty.

I have been the larger upon this, because our enemies say we deny all moral actions; but, blessed be God, they speak against us without cause: we highly value them; but we say, that faith in Christ, the love of God, and being born again, are of infinite more worth; but you cannot be true Christians without having charity to your fellow-creatures, be they friends or enemies, if in distress. And, therefore, exert yourselves in this duty, as is commanded by the blessed Jesus: and if you have true charity, you shall live and reign with him for ever.

Now to God the Father, God the Son, and God the Holy Ghost, be all honor, power, glory, might, majesty, and dominion, both now and for evermore. Amen.

48. Satan's Devices

The occasion of these words was as follows: In the church of Corinth there was an unhappy person, who had committed such incest, as was not so much as named among the Gentiles, in taking his father's wife; but either on account of his wealth, power, or some such reasons, like many notorious offenders now-a-days, he had not been exposed to the censures of the church. St. Paul, therefore, in his first epistle, severely chides them for this neglect of discipline, and commands them, "in the name of our Lord Jesus Christ, when they were gathered together, to deliver such a one, whoever he was, to Satan, for the destruction of the flesh, that his Spirit might be saved in the day of the Lord;" that is, they should solemnly excommunicate him; which was then commonly attended with some bodily disease. The Corinthians, being obedient to the Apostle, as dear children, no sooner received this reproof, but they submitted to it, and cast the offending party out of the church. But whilst they were endeavoring to amend one fault, they unhappily ran into another; and as they formerly had been too mild and remiss, so now they behaved towards him with too much severity and resentment. The Apostle, therefore, in this chapter, reproves this, and tells them, that "sufficient to the offender's shame, was the punishment which had been inflicted of many:" that he had now suffered enough; and that, therefore, lest he should be tempted to say with Cain, "My punishment is greater than I can bear;" or to use the Apostle's own words, "Lest he should be swallowed up with overmuch sorrow;" they ought, now he had given proof of his repentance, to forgive him, to confirm their love towards him, and to restore him in the spirit of meekness; "Lest Satan, (to whose buffetings he was now given, by tempting him to despair) should get an advantage over us:" and so, by representing you as merciless and cruel, cause that holy name to be blasphemed, by which you are called; "for we are not ignorant of his devices:" we know very well how many subtle ways he has to draw aside and beguile unguarded unthinking men.

Thus then, stand the words in relation to the context; but as Satan has many devices, and as his quiver is full of other poisonous darts, besides those which he shoots at us to drive us to despair, I shall, in the following discourse,

First, Briefly observe who we are to understand by Satan. And,

Secondly, Point out to you, what are the chief devices he generally makes use of to draw off converts from Christ, and also prescribe some remedies against them.

First, Who are we to understand by Satan?

The word Satan, in its original signification, meant an adversary; and in its general acceptation, is made use of, to point out to us the chief of the devils, who, for striving to be as God, was cast down from heaven, and is now permitted, "with the rest of his spiritual wickednesses in high places, to walk up and down, seeking whom he may devour." We hear of him immediately after the creation, when in the shape of a serpent, he lay in wait to deceive our first parents. He is called Satan, in the book of Job, where we are told, that "when the sons of God came to present themselves before the Lord, Satan also came amongst them." As the scripture also speaketh in the book of Chronicles; "and Satan moved David to number the people." In the New Testament he goes under different denominations; sometimes he is called the evil One, because he is evil in himself, and tempts us to evil. Sometimes, "the Prince of the power of the air;" and, "the Spirit that now ruleth in the children of disobedience;" because he resides chiefly in the air, and through the whole world: and all that are not born of God, are said to lie in him.

He is an enemy to God and goodness; he is a hater of all truth. Why else did he slander God in paradise? Why did he tell Eve, "You shall not surely die?" And why did he promise to give all the kingdoms of the world, and the glories of them, to Jesus Christ, if he would fall down and worship him?

He is full of malice, envy, and revenge: For what other

motives could induce him to molest innocent man in paradise? And why is he still so restless in his attempts to destroy us, who have done him no wrong?

He is a being of great power, as appears in his being able to act on the imagination of our blessed Lord, so as to represent to him all the kingdoms of the world, and the glories of them, in a moment of time. As also in carrying his sacred body through the air up to a pinnacle of the temple; and his driving a herd of swine so furiously into the deep. Nay, so great is his might, that, I doubt not, was God to let him use his full strength, but he could turn the earth upside down, or pull the sun from its orb.

But what he is most remarkable for is, his subtlety: for not having power given him from above, to take us by force, he is obliged to wait for opportunities to betray us, and to catch us by guile. He, therefore, made use of the serpent, which was subtle above all the beasts of the field, in order to tempt our first parents; and accordingly he is said, in the New Testament, "To lie in wait to deceive;" and, in the words of the text, the Apostle says, "We are not ignorant of his devices:" thereby implying, that we are more in danger of being seduced by his policy, than over-borne by his power.

From this short description of Satan, we may easily judge whose children they are, who love to make a lie, who speak evil of, and slander their neighbor, and whose hearts are full of pride, subtlety, malice, envy, revenge, and all uncharitableness. Surely they have Satan for their father: for the tempers of Satan they know, and the works of Satan they do. But were they to see either themselves, or Satan as he is, they could not but be terrified at their own likeness, and abhor themselves in dust and ashes.

But, the justice of God in suffering us to be tempted, is vindicated from the following considerations: That we are here in a state of disorder; That he has promised not to suffer us to be tempted above what we are able to bear; and not only so, but to him that overcometh he will give a crown of life.

The holy angels themselves, it should seem, were once put to a trial whether they would be faithful or not. The first Adam was tempted, even in paradise. And Jesus Christ, that second Adam, though he was a son, yet was carried, as our representative, by the Holy Spirit, into the wilderness, to be tempted of the devil. And there is not one single saint in paradise, amongst the goodly fellowship of the prophets, the glorious company of the apostles, the noble army of martyrs, and the spirits of just men made perfect, who, when on earth, was not assaulted by the fiery darts of that wicked one, the devil.

What then has been the common lot of all God's children, and of the angels, nay, of the eternal Son of God himself, we must not think to be exempted from: No, it is sufficient if we are made perfect through temptations, as they were. And, therefore, since we cannot but be tempted, unless we could unmake human nature, instead of repining at our condition, we should rather be inquiring, at what time of our lives Satan most violently assaults us? And what those devices are, which he commonly makes use of, in order to "get an advantage over us?"

As to the first question, what time of life? I answer, we must expect to be tempted by him, in some degree or other, all our lives long.—For this life being a continual warfare, we must never expect to have rest from our spiritual adversary the devil, or to say, our combat with him is finished, 'till, with our blessed master, we bow down our heads, and give up the ghost.

But since the time of our conversion, or first entering upon the spiritual life, is the most critical time at which he, for the most part, violently besets us, as well knowing, if he can prevent our setting out, he can lead us captive at his will; and since the wise son of Sirach particularly warns us, when we are going to serve the Lord, to prepare our souls for temptation, I shall, in answer to the other question, pass on to the

Second general thing proposed; and point out those devices, which Satan generally makes use of at our first conversion, in order to get an advantage over us.

But let me observe to you, that whatsoever shall be delivered in the following discourse is only designed for such as have actually entered upon the divine life; and not for carnal almost Christians, who have the form of godliness, but never yet felt the power of it in their hearts.

This being premised, The *First* device I shall mention, which Satan makes use of, is, to drive us to despair.

When God the Father awakens a sinner by the terrors of the law, and by his Holy Spirit convinceth him of sin, in order to lead him to Christ, and show him the necessity of a Redeemer; then Satan generally strikes in, and aggravates those convictions to such a degree, as to make the sinner doubt of finding mercy thro' the Mediator.

Thus, in all his temptations of the Holy Jesus, he chiefly aimed to make him question, whether he was the Son of God? "If thou be the Son of God," do so and so. With many such desponding thoughts, no doubt, he filled the heart of the great St. Paul, when he continued three days, neither eating bread nor drinking water; and therefore he speaks by experience, when he says, in the words of the text, "We are not ignorant of his devices," that he would endeavor to drive the incestuous person to despair.

But let not any of you be influenced by him, to despair of finding mercy. For it is not the greatness or number of our crimes, but impenitence and unbelief, that will prove our ruin: No, were our sins more in number than the hairs of our head, or of a deeper die than the brightest scarlet; yet the merits of the death of Jesus Chris are infinitely greater, and faith in his blood shall make them white as snow.

Answer always, therefore, his despairing suggestions, as your Blessed Lord did, with an "It is written." Tell him, you know that your Redeemer liveth, ever to make intercession for you; that the Lord hath received from him double for all your crimes: And tho' you have sinned much, that is no reason why you should despair, but only why you should love much, having so much forgiven.

A *Second* device that Satan generally makes use of, to get an advantage over young converts, is, to tempt them to presume, or to think more highly of themselves than they ought to think.

When a person ha for some little time tasted the good word of life, and felt the powers of the world to come, he is commonly (as indeed well he may) most highly transported with that sudden change he finds in himself. But then, Satan will not be wanting, at such a time, to puff him up with a high conceit of his own attainments as if he was some great person; and will tempt him to set at nought his brethren, as though he was holier than they.

Take heed therefore, and let us beware of this device of our spiritual adversary; for as before honor is humility, so a haughty spirit generally goes before a fall; and God is obliged, when under such circumstances, to send us some humbling visitation, or permit us to fall, as he did Peter into some grievous sin, that we may learn not to be too high minded.

To check therefore all suggestions to spiritual pride, let us consider, that we did not apprehend Christ, but were apprehended of him. That we have nothing but what we have received. That the free grace of God has alone made the difference between us and others; and, was God to leave us to the deceitfulness of our own hearts but one moment, we should become weak and wicked, like other men. We should farther consider, that being proud of grace, is the most ready way to lose it. "For God resisteth the proud, and giveth more grace only to the humble." And were we endowed with the perfections of the seraphim; yet if we were proud of those perfections, they would but render us more accomplished devils. Above all, we should pray earnestly to Almighty God, that we may learn of Jesus Christ, to be lowly in heart. That his grace, through the subtlety and deceivableness of Satan, may not be our poison. But that we may always think soberly of ourselves, as we ought to think.

A *Third* device I shall mention, which Satan generally makes use of, "to get an advantage over us," is to tempt us to uneasiness, and to have hard thoughts of God, when we are dead and barren in prayer.

Though this is a term not understood by the natural man, yet, whosoever there are amongst you, who have passed through the pangs of the new birth, they know full well what I mean, when I talk of deadness and dryness in prayer. And, I doubt not, but many of you, amongst whom I am not preaching the kingdom of God, are at this very time laboring under it.

For, when persons are first awakened to the divine life, because grace is weak and nature strong, God is often pleased to vouchsafe them some extraordinary illuminations of his Holy Spirit; but when they are grown to be more perfect men in Christ, then he frequently seems to leave them to themselves; and not only so, but permits a horrible deadness and dread to overwhelm them; at which times Satan will not be wanting to vex and tempt them to impatience, to the great discomfort of their souls.

But be not afraid; for this is no more than your blessed Redeemer, that spotless Lamb of God, has undergone before you: witness his bitter agony in the garden, when his soul was exceeding sorrowful, even unto death. When he sweat great drops of blood, falling on the ground; when the sense of the Divinity was drawn from him; and Satan, in all probability, was permitted to set all his terrors in array before him.

Rejoice, therefore, my brethren, when you fall into the like circumstances; as knowing, that you are therein partakers of the sufferings of Jesus Christ. Consider, that it is necessary such inward trials should come, to wean us from the immoderate love of sensible devotion, and teach us to follow Christ, not merely for his loaves, but out of a principle of love and obedience. In patience, therefore, possess your souls, and be not terrified by Satan's suggestions. Still persevere in seeking Jesus in the use of means, though it be sorrowing; and though through barrenness of soul, you may go mourning all the day long. Consider that the spouse is with you, though behind the curtain; as he was with Mary, at the sepulcher, though she knew it not. That he was withdrawn but for a little while, to make his next visit more welcome. That though he may now seem to frown and look back on you, as he did on the Syrophonecian woman; yet if you, like her, or blind Bartimeus, cry out so much the more earnestly, "Jesus, thou Son of David, have mercy on us;" he will be made known unto you again, either in the temple, by breaking of bread, or some other way.

But amongst all the devices that Satan makes use of, "to get an advantage over us," there is none in which he is more successful, or by which he grieves the children of God worse, than a

Fourth device I am going to mention, his troubling you with blasphemous, profane, unbelieving thoughts; and sometimes to such a degree, that they are as tormenting as the rack.

Some indeed are apt to impute all such evil thoughts to a disorder of body. But those who know any thing of the spiritual life, can inform you, with greater certainty, that for the generality, they proceed from that wicked one, the devil; who, no doubt, has power given him from above, as well now as formerly, to disorder the body, as he did Job's, that he may, with the more secrecy and success, work upon, ruffle and torment the soul.

You that have felt his fiery darts, can subscribe to the truth of this, and by fatal experience can tell, how often he has bid you, "curse God and die," and darted into your thoughts a thousand blasphemous suggestions, even in your most secret and solemn retirements; the bar looking back on which makes your very hearts to tremble.

I appeal to your own consciences; Have not some of you, when you have been lifting up holy hands in prayer, been pestered with such a crowd of the most horrid insinuations, that you have been often tempted to rise off from your knees, and been made to believe your prayers were an abomination to the Lord? Nay, when, with the rest of your Christian brethren, you have crowded round the holy table, and taken the sacred symbols of Christ's most blessed body and blood into your hands, instead of remembering the death of your Savior, have you not employed in driving out evil thoughts, as Abraham was in driving away the birds, that came to devour his sacrifice; and thereby have been terrified, lest you have eat and drank your own damnation?

But marvel not, as though some strange thing happened unto you; for this has been the common lot of all God's children. We read, even in Job's time, "That when the sons of God came to appear before their Maker, (at public worship) Satan also came amongst them," to disturb their devotions.

And think not that God is angry with you for these distracting, though ever so blasphemous thoughts: No, he knows it is not you, but Satan working in you; and therefore, notwithstanding he may be displeased with, and certainly will punish him; yet he will both pity and reward you. And though it be difficult to make persons in your circumstances to believe so; yet I doubt not but you are more acceptable to God, when performing your holy duties in the midst of such involuntary distractions, than when you are wrapped up by devotion, as it were, into the third heavens; for you are then suffering, as well as doing the will of God at the same time; and, like Nehemiah's servants at the building of the temple, are holding a trowel in one hand, and a sword in the other. Be not driven from the use of any ordinance whatever, on account of those abominable suggestions; for then you let Satan get his desired advantage over you; it being his chief design, by these thoughts, to make you fall out with the means of grace; and to tempt you to believe, you do not please God, for no other reason, than because you do not please yourselves. Rather persevere in the use of the holy communion especially, and all other means whatever; and when these temptations have wrought that resignation in you, for which they were permitted, God will visit you with fresh tokens of his love, as he met Abraham, when he returned from the slaughter of the five kings; and will send an angel from heaven, as he did to his Son, on purpose to strengthen you.

Hitherto we have only observed such devices as Satan makes use of immediately by himself; but there is a

Fifth I shall mention, which is not the least, tempting us by our carnal friends and relatives.

This is one of the most common, as well as most artful devices he makes use of, to draw young converts from God; for when he cannot prevail over them by himself, he will try what he can do by the influence and mediation of others.

Thus he tempted Eve, that she might tempt Adam. Thus he stirred up Job's wife, to bid him "Curse God and die." And thus he made use of Peter's tongue, to persuade our blessed Lord "to spare himself," and thereby decline those sufferings, by which alone we could be preserved from suffering the vengeance of eternal fire. And thus, in these last days, he often stirs up our most powerful friends and dearest intimates, to dissuade us from going in that narrow way, which alone leadeth unto life eternal.

But our blessed Lord has furnished us with a sufficient answer to all such suggestions. "Get you behind me, my adversaries;" for otherwise they will be an offense unto you; and the only reason why they give such advice is, because they "favor not the things that be of God, but the things that be of men."

Whoever, therefore, among you are resolved to serve the Lord, prepare your souls for many such temptations as these; for it is necessary that such offenses should come, to try your sincerity, to teach us to cease from man, and to see if we will forsake all to follow Christ.

Indeed our modernisers of Christianity would persuade us, that the gospel was calculated only for about two hundred years; and that now there is no need of hating father and mother, or of being persecuted for the sake of Christ and his gospel.

But such persons err, not knowing the scriptures, and the power of godliness in their hearts; for whosoever receives the love of God in the truth of it, will find, that Christ came to send not peace, but a sword upon earth, as much now as ever. That the father-in-law shall be against the daughter-in-law, in these latter, as well as in the primitive times; and that if we will live godly in Christ Jesus, we must, as then, so now, from carnal friends and relations, suffer persecution. But the devil hath a

Sixth device, which is as dangerous as any of the former, by not tempting us at all, or rather, by withdrawing himself for a while, in order to come upon us at an hour when we think not of it.

Thus it is said, that he left Jesus Christ only for a season; and our blessed Lord has bid us to watch and pray always, that we enter not into temptation; thereby implying, that Satan, whether we think of it or not, is always seeking how he may devour us.

If we would therefore behave like good soldiers of Jesus Christ, we must be always upon our guard, and never pretend to lay down our spiritual weapons of prayer and watching, till our warfare is accomplished by death; for if we do, our spiritual Amalek will quickly prevail against us. What if he has left us? It is only for a season; yet a little while, and, like a roaring lion, with double fury, he will break out upon us again. So great a coward as the devil is, he seldom leaves us at the first onset. As he followed our blessed Lord with one temptation after another, so will he treat his servants. And the reason why he does not renew his attacks, is sometimes, because God knows we are yet weak and unable to bear them, sometimes, because our grand adversary thinks to beset us at a more convenient season.

Watch carefully over thy heart, O Christian; and whenever thou perceivest thyself to be falling into a spiritual slumber, say to it, as Christ to his disciples, "Arise (my soul) why sleepest thou?" Awake, awake; put on strength, watch and pray, or otherwise the Philistines will be upon thee, and lead thee whither thou wouldst not. Alas! Is this life a time to lie down and slumber in? Arise, and call upon thy God; thy spiritual enemy is not dead, but lurketh in some secret place, seeking a convenient opportunity how he may betray thee. If thou ceasest to strive with him, thou ceasest to be a friend of God; thou ceasest to go in that narrow way which leadeth unto life.

Thus have I endeavored to point out to you some of those devices, that Satan generally makes use of "to get an advantage over us;" many others there are, no doubt, which he often uses.

But these, on account of my youth and want of experience, I cannot yet apprise you of; they who have been listed for many years in their master's service, and fought under his banner against our spiritual Amalek, are able to discover more of his artifices; and, being tempted in all things, like unto their brethren, can, in all things, advise and succor those that are tempted.

In the mean while, let me exhort my young fellow-soldiers, who, like myself, are but just entering the field, and for whose sake this was written, not to be discouraged at the fiery trial wherewith they must be tried, if they would be found faithful servants of Jesus Christ. You see, my dearly beloved brethren, by what has been delivered, that our way through the wilderness of this world to the heavenly Canaan, is beset with thorns, and that there are sons of Anak to be grappled with, ere you can possess the promised land. But let not these, like so many false spies, discourage you from going up to fight the Lord's battles, but say with Caleb and Joshua, "Nay, but we will go up, for we are able to conquer them." Jesus Christ, that great captain of our salvation, has in our stead, and as our representative, baffled the grand enemy of mankind, and we have nothing to do, but manfully to fight under his banner, and to go on from conquering to conquer. Our glory does not consist in being exempted from, but in enduring temptations. "Blessed is the man, (says the apostle) that endureth temptation;": and again, "Brethren, count it all joy, when you fall into divers temptations:" And in that perfect form our blessed Lord has prescribed to us, we are taught to pray, not so much to be delivered from all temptation, as "from the evil" of it. Whilst we are on this side eternity, it must needs be that temptations come; and, no doubt, "Satan has desired to have all of us, to sift us as wheat." But wherefore should we fear? For he that is for us, is by far more powerful, than all that are against us.

Jesus Christ, our great High-priest, is exalted to the right hand of God, and there sitteth to make intercession for us, that our faith fail not.

Since then Christ is praying, whom should we fear? And since he has promised to make us more than conquerors, of whom should we be afraid? No, though an hose of devils are set in array against us, let us not be afraid; though there should rise up the hottest persecution against us, yet let us put our trust in God. What though Satan, and the rest of his apostate spirits, are powerful, when compared with us; yet, if put in competition with the Almighty, they are as weak as the meanest worms. God has them all reserved in chains of darkness unto the judgment of the great day. So far as he permits them, they shall go, but no farther; and where he pleases, there shall their proud malicious designs be stayed. We read in the gospel, that though a legion of them possessed one man, yet they could not destroy him; nor could they so much as enter into a swine, without first having leave given them from above. It is true, we often find they foil us, when we are assaulted by them; but let us be strong, and very courageous; for, though they bruise our heels, we shall, at length, bruise their heads. Yet a little while, and he that shall come, will come; and then we shall see all our spiritual enemies put under our feet. What f they do come out against us, like so many great Goliaths; yet, if we can go forth, as the stripling David, in the name and strength of the Lord of hosts, we may say, O Satan, where is thy power? O fallen spirits, where is your victory?

Once more therefore, and to conclude; let us be strong, and very courageous, and let us put on the whole armor of God, that we may be able to stand against the fiery darts of the wicked one. Let us renounce ourselves, and the world, and then we shall take away the armor in which he trusteth, and he will find nothing in us for his temptations to work upon. We shall then prevent his malicious designs; and being willing to suffer ourselves, shall need less sufferings to be sent us from above. Let us have our loins girt about with truth; and for an helmet, the hope of salvation; "praying always with all manner of supplication." Above all things, "Let us take the sword of the spirit, which is the word of God," and "the shield of faith," looking always to Jesus, the author and finisher of our faith, who for the joy that was set before him, endured the cross, despising the shame, and is now sat down at the right hand of God.

To which happy place, may God of his infinite mercy translate us all, through our Lord Jesus Christ.

To whom, with the Father, and the Holy Ghost, three persons and one eternal God, be all honor and glory, now and for evermore. Amen.

49. On Regeneration

The doctrine of our regeneration, or new birth in Christ Jesus, though one of the most fundamental doctrines of our holy religion; though so plainly and often pressed on us in sacred writ, "that he who runs may read;" nay though it is the very hinge on which the salvation of each of us turns, and a point too in which all sincere Christians, of every denomination, agree; yet it is so seldom considered, and so little experimentally understood by the generality of professors, that were we to judge of the truth of it, by the experience of most who call themselves Christians, we should be apt to imagine they had "not so much as heard" whether there be any such thing as regeneration or not. It is true, men for the most part are orthodox in the common articles of their creed; they believe "there is but one God, and one Mediator between God and men, even the man Christ Jesus;" and that there is no other name given under heaven, whereby they can be saved, besides his: But then tell them, they must be regenerated, they must be born again, they must be renewed in the very spirit, in the inmost faculties of their minds, ere they can truly call Christ, "Lord, Lord," or have an evidence that they have any share in the merits of his precious blood; and they are ready to cry out with Nicodemus, "How can these things be?" Or with the Athenians, on another occasion, "What wilt this bumbler say? He seemeth to be a setter-forth of strange doctrines;" because we preach unto them Christ, and the new-birth.

That I may therefore contribute my mite towards curing the fatal mistake of such persons, who would thus put asunder what God has inseparably joined together, and vainly think they are justified by Christ, or have their sins forgiven, and his perfect obedience imputed to them, when they are not sanctified, have not their natures changed, and made holy, I shall beg leave to enlarge on the words of the text in the following manner:

First, I shall endeavor to explain what is meant by being in Christ: "If any man be in Christ."

Secondly, What we are to understand by being a new creature: "If any man be in Christ he is a new creature."

Thirdly, I shall produce some arguments to make good the apostle's assertion. And

Fourthly, I shall draw some inferences from what may

be delivered, and then conclude with a word or two of exhortation.

First, I am to endeavor to explain what is meant by this expression in the text, "If any man be in Christ."

Now a person may be said to be in Christ two ways.

First, Only by an outward profession. And in this sense, every one that is called a Christian, or baptized into Christ's church, may be said to be in Christ. But that this is not the sole meaning of the apostle's phrase before us, is evident, because then, every one that names the name of Christ, or is baptized into his visible church, would be a new creature. Which is notoriously false, it being too plain, beyond all contradiction, that comparatively but few of those that are "born of water," are "born of the Spirit" likewise; to use another spiritual way of speaking, many are baptized with water, which were never baptized with the Holy Ghost.

To be in Christ therefore, in the full import of the word, must certainly mean something more than a bare outward profession, or being called after his name. For, as this same apostle tells us, "All are not Israelites that are of Israel," so when applied to Christianity, all are not real Christians that are nominally such. Nay, this is so far from being the case, that our blessed Lord himself informs us, that many who have prophesied or preached in his name, and in his name cast out devils, and done many wonderful works, shall notwithstanding be dismissed at the last day, with "depart from me, I know you not, ye workers of iniquity."

It remains therefore, that this expression, "if any man be in Christ," must be understood in a

Second and closer signification, to be in him so as to partake of the benefits of his sufferings. To be in him not only by an outward profession, but by an inward change and purity of heart, and cohabitation of his Holy Spirit. To be in him, so as to be mystically united to him by a true and lively faith, and thereby to receive spiritual virtue from him, as the members of the natural body do from the head, or the branches from the vine. To be in him in such a manner as the apostle, speaking of himself, acquaints us he knew a person was, "I knew man in Christ," a true Christian; or, as he himself desires to be in Christ, when he wishes, in his epistle to the Philippians, that he might be found in him.

This is undoubtedly the proper meaning of the apostle's expression in the words of the text; so that what he says in his epistle to the Romans about circumcision, may very well be applied to the present subject; that he is not a real Christian who is only one outwardly; nor is that true baptism, which is only outward in the flesh. But he is a true Christian, who is one inwardly, whose baptism is that of the heart, in the spirit, and not merely in the water, whose praise is not of man but of God. Or, as he speaketh in another place, "Neither circumcision nor uncircumcision availeth any thing (of itself) but a new creature." Which amounts to what he here declares in the verse now under consideration, that if any man be truly and properly in Christ, he is a new creature. Which brings me to show,

Secondly, What we are to understand by being a new creature.

And here it is evident at the first view, that this expression is not to be so explained as though there was a physical change required to be made in us; or as though we were to be reduced to our primitive nothings, and then created and formed again. For, supposing we were, as Nicodemus ignorantly imagined, to enter a "second time into our mother's womb, and be born," alas! what would it contribute towards rendering us spiritually new creatures? Since "that which was born of the flesh would be flesh still;" we should be the same carnal persons as ever, being derived from carnal parents, and consequently receiving the seeds of all manner of sin and corruption from them. No, it only means, that we must be so altered as to the qualities and tempers of our minds, that we must entirely forget what manner of persons we once were. As it may be said of a piece of gold, that was once in the ore, after it has been cleansed, purified and polished, that it is a new piece of gold; as it may be said of a bright glass that has been covered over with filth, when it is wiped, and so become transparent and clear, that it is a new glass: Or, as it might be said of Naaman, when he recovered of his leprosy, and his flesh returned unto him like the flesh of a young child, that he was a new man; so our souls, though still the same as to offense, yet are so purged, purified and cleansed from their natural dross, filth and leprosy, by the blessed influences of the Holy Spirit, that they may be properly said to be made anew.

How this glorious change is wrought in the soul, cannot easily be explained: For no one knows the ways of the Spirit save the Spirit of God himself. Not that this ought to be any argument against this doctrine; for, as our blessed Lord observed to Nicodemus, when he was discoursing on this very subject, "The wind bloweth where it listeth, and thou hearest the sound thereof, but knowest not whence it cometh, and whither it goeth;" and if we are told of natural things, and we understand them not, how much less ought we to wonder, if we cannot immediately account for the invisible workings of the Holy Spirit? The truth of the matter is this: the doctrine of our regeneration, or new birth in Christ Jesus, is hard to be understood by the natural man. But that there is really such a thing, and that each of us must be spiritually born again, I shall endeavor to show under my

Third general head, in which I was to produce some arguments to make good the apostle's assertion.

And here one would think it sufficient to affirm,

First, That God himself, in his holy word, hath told us so. Many texts might be produced out of the Old Testament to prove this point, and indeed, one would wonder how Nicodemus, who was a teacher in Israel, and who was therefore to instruct the people n the spiritual meaning of the law, should be so ignorant of this grand article, as we find he really was, by his asking our blessed Lord, when he was pressing on him this topic, How can these things be? Surely, he could not forget how often the Psalmist had begged of God, to make him "a new heart," and "to renew a right spirit within him;" as likewise, how frequently the prophets had warned the people to make them "new hearts," and new minds, and so turn unto the Lord their God. But not to mention these and such like texts out of the Old Testament, this doctrine is so often and plainly repeated in the New, that, as I observed before, he who runs may read. For what says the great Prophet and Instructor of the world himself: "Except a man (every one that is naturally the offspring of Adam) be born again of water and the Spirit, he cannot enter into the kingdom of God." And lest we should be apt to slight this assertion, and Nicodemus-like, reject the doctrine, because we cannot immediately explain "How this thing can be;" our blessed Master therefore affirms it, as it were, by an oath, "Verily, verily, I say unto you," or, as it may be read, I the Amen; I who am truth itself, say unto you, that it is the unalterable appointment of my heavenly Father, that "unless a man be born again, he cannot enter into the kingdom of God."

Agreeable to this, are those many passages we meet with in the epistles, where we are commanded to be "renewed in the Spirit," or, which was before explained, in the inmost faculties of our minds; to "put off the Old Man, which is corrupt; and to put on the New Man, which is created after God, in righteousness and true holiness;" that "old things must pass away, and that all things must become new;" that we are to be "saved by the washing of regeneration, and the renewing of the Holy Ghost." Or, methinks, was there no other passage to be produced besides the words of the text, it would be full enough, since the apostle therein positively affirms, that "If any man be in Christ, he is a new creature."

Multitudes of other texts might be produced to confirm this same truth; but those already quoted are so plain and convincing, that one would imagine no one should deny it; were we not told, there are some, "who having eyes, see not, and ears, hear not, and that will not understand with their hearts, or hear with their ears, lest they should be converted, and Christ should heal them.

But I proceed to a

Second argument; and that shall be taken from the purity of God, and the present corrupt and polluted state of man.

God is described in holy scripture (and I speak to those who profess to know the scripture) as a Spirit; as a being of such infinite sanctity, as to be of "purer eyes than to behold iniquity;" as to be so transcendently holy, that it is said "the very heavens are not clean in his sight; and the angels themselves he chargeth with folly." On the other hand, man is described (and every regenerate person will find it true by his own experience) as a creature altogether "conceived and born in sin;" as having "no good thing dwelling in him;" as being "carnal, sold under sin;" nay, as having "a mind which is at enmity with God," and such-like. And since there is such an infinite disparity, can any one conceive how a filthy, corrupted, polluted wretch can dwell with an infinitely pure and holy God, before he is changed, and rendered, in some measure, like him? Can he, who is of purer eyes than to behold iniquity, dwell with it? Can he, in whose sight the heavens are not clean, delight to dwell with uncleanness itself? No, we might as well suppose light to have communion with darkness, or Christ to have concord with Belial. But I pass on to a

Third argument, which shall be founded on the consideration of the nature of that happiness God has prepared for those that unfeignedly love him.

To enter indeed on a minute and particular description of heaven, would be vain and presumptuous, since we are told that "eye hath not seen, nor ear heard, neither hath in entered into the heart of man to conceive, the things that are there prepared" for the sincere followers of the holy Jesus, even in this life, much less in that which is to come. However, this we may venture to affirm in general, that as God is a Spirit, so the happiness he has laid up for his people is spiritual likewise; and consequently, unless our carnal minds are changed, and spiritualized, we can never be made meet to partake of that inheritance with the saints in light.

It is, doubtless, for this reason, that the apostle declares it to be the irrevocable decree of the Almighty, that "without holiness, (without being made pure by regeneration, and having the image of God thereby reinstamped upon the soul) no may shall see the Lord." And it is very observable, that our divine Master, in the famous passage before referred to, concerning the absolute necessity of regeneration, does not say, Unless a man be born again, he *shall not*, but "unless a man be born again, he *cannot* enter into the kingdom of God." It is founded in the very nature of things, that unless we have dispositions wrought in us suitable to the objects that are to entertain us, we can take no manner of complacency or satisfaction in them. For instance; what delight can the most harmonious music afford to a deaf, or what pleasure can the most excellent picture give to a blind man? Can a tasteless palate relish the richest dainties, or a filthy swine be pleased with the finest garden of flowers? No: and what reason can be assigned for it? An answer is ready; because they have neither of them any tempers of mind correspondent or agreeable to what they are to be diverted with. And thus it is with the soul hereafter; for death makes no more alteration in the soul, than as it enlarges its faculties, and makes it capable of receiving deeper impressions either of pleasure or pain. If it delighted to converse with God here, it will be transported with the sight of his glorious Majesty hereafter. If it was pleased with the communion of saints on earth, it will be infinitely more so with the communion and society of holy angels, and the spirits of just men made perfect in heaven. But if the opposite of all this be true, we may assure ourselves the soul could not be happy, was God himself to admit it (which he never will do) into the regions of the blessed. But it is time for me to hasten to the

Fourth argument, because Christ's redemption will not be complete in us, unless we are new creatures.

If we reflect indeed on the first and chief end of our blessed Lord's coming, we shall find it was to be a propitiation for our sins, to give his life a ransom for many. But then, if the benefits of our dear Redeemer's death were to extend no farther than barely to procure forgiveness of our sins, we should have as little reason to rejoice in it, as a poor condemned criminal that is ready to perish by some fatal disease, would have in receiving a pardon from his judge. For Christians would do well to consider, that there is not only a legal hindrance to our happiness, as we are breakers of God's law, but also a moral impurity in our natures, which renders us incapable of enjoying heaven (as hath been already proved) till some mighty change have been wrought in us. It is necessary therefore, in order to make Christ's redemption complete, that we should have a grant of God's Holy Spirit to change our natures, and so prepare us for the enjoyment of that happiness our Savior has purchased by his precious blood.

Accordingly the holy scriptures inform us, that whom Christ justifies, or whose sins he forgives, and to whom he imputes his perfect obedience, those he also sanctifies, purifies and cleanses, and totally changeth their corrupted natures. As the scripture also speaketh in another place, "Christ is to us justification, sanctification, and then redemption." But,

Fourthly, Proceed we now to the next general thing proposed, to draw some inferences from what has been delivered, And,

First, If he that is in Christ be a new creature, this may serve as a reproof for those who rest in a bare performance of outward duties, without perceiving any real inward change of heart.

We may observe a great many persons to be very punctual in the regular returns of public and private prayer, as likewise of receiving the holy communion, and perhaps now and then too in keeping a fast. But here is the misfortune, they rest barely in the use of the means, and think all is over, when they have thus complied with those sacred institutions; whereas, were they rightly informed, they would consider, that all the instituted means of grace, as prayer, fasting, hearing and reading the word of God, receiving the blessed sacrament, and such-like, are no farther serviceable to us, than as they are found to make us inwardly better, and to carry on the spiritual life in the soul.

It is true, they are means; but then they are only means; they are part, but not the whole of religion: for if so, who more religious than the Pharisee? He fasted twice in the week, and gave tithes of all that he possessed, and yet was not justified, as our Savior himself informs us, in the sight of God.

You perhaps, like the Pharisee, may fast often, and make long prayers; you may, with Herod, hear good sermons gladly. But yet, if you continue vain and trifling, immoral or worldly-minded, and differ from the rest of your neighbors barely in going to church, or in complying with some outward performances, are you better than they? No, in no wise; you are by far much worse: for if you use them, and at the same time abuse them, you thereby encourage others to think there is nothing in them and therefore must expect to receive the greater damnation. But,

Secondly, If he that is in Christ be a new creature, then this may check the groundless presumption of another class of professors, who rest in the attainment of some moral virtues, and falsely imagine they are good Christians, if they are just in their dealings, temperate in their diet, and do not hurt or violence to any man.

But if this was all that is requisite to make us Christians, why might not the heathens of old be good Christians, who were remarkable for these virtues? Or St. Paul before his conversion, who tells us, that he lived in all good conscience? But we find he renounces all dependence on works of this nature, and only desires to be found in Christ, and to know the power of his resurrection, or have an experimental proof of receiving the Holy Ghost, purchased for him by the death, and ensured and applied to him by the resurrection of Jesus Christ.

The sum of the matter is this: Christianity includes morality, as grace does reason; but if we are only mere Moralists, if we are not inwardly wrought upon, and changed by the powerful operations of the Holy Spirit, and our moral actions, proceed from a principle of a new nature, however we may call ourselves Christians, we shall be found naked at the great day, and in the number of those, who have neither Christ's righteousness imputed to them for their justification in the sight, nor holiness enough in their souls as the consequence of that, in order to make them meet for the enjoyment, of God. Nor,

Thirdly, Will this doctrine less condemn those, who rest in a partial amendment of themselves, without experiencing a thorough, real, inward change of heart.

A little acquaintance with the world will furnish us with instances, of no small number of persons, who, perhaps, were before openly profane; but seeing the ill consequences of their vices, and the many worldly inconveniencies it has reduced them to, on a sudden, as it were, grow civilized; and thereupon flatter themselves that they are very religious, because they differ a little from their former selves, and are not so scandalously wicked as once they were: whereas, at the same time, they shall have some secret darling sin or other, some beloved Delilah or Herodias, which they will no part with; some hidden lust, which they will not mortify; some vicious habit, which they will not take pains to root out. But wouldst thou know, O vain man! Whoever thou art, what the Lord thy God requires of thee? Thou must be informed, that nothing short of a thorough sound conversion will fit thee for the kingdom of heaven. It is not enough to turn from profaneness to civility; but thou must turn from civility to godliness. Not only some, but "all things must become new" in thy soul. It will profit thee but little to do many things, if yet some one thing thou lackest. In short, thou must not only be an almost, but altogether a new creature, or in vain thou boasteth that thou art a Christian.

Fourthly, If he that is in Christ be a new creature, then this may be prescribed as an infallible rule for every person of whatever denomination, age, degree or quality, to judge himself by; this being the only solid foundation, whereon we can build a well-grounded assurance of pardon, peace, and happiness.

We may indeed depend on the broken reed of an external profession; we may think we are good enough, if we lead such sober, honest, moral lives, as many heathens did. We may imagine we are in a safe condition, if we attend on the public offices of religion, and are constant in the duties of our closets. But unless all these tend to reform our lives, and change our hearts, and are only used as so many channels of divine grace; as I told you before, so I tell you again, Christianity will profit you nothing.

Let each of us therefore seriously put this question to our hearts: Have we received the Holy Ghost since we believed? Are we new creatures in Christ, or no? At least, if we are not so yet, is it our daily endeavor to become such? Do we constantly and conscientiously use all the means of grace required thereto? Do we fast, watch and pray? Do we, not lazily seek, but laboriously strive to enter in at the strait gate? In short, do we renounce our own righteousness, take up our crosses and follow Christ? If so, we are in that narrow way which leads to life; the good seed is sown in our hearts, and will, if duly watered and nourished by a regular persevering use of all the means of grace, grow up to eternal life. But on the contrary, if we have only heard, and know not experimentally, whether there be any Holy Ghost; if we are strangers to fasting, watching and prayer, and all the other spiritual exercises of devotion; if we are content to go in the broad way, merely because we see most other people do so, without once reflecting whether it be the right one or not; in short, if we are strangers, nay enemies to the cross of Christ, by lives of worldly-mindedness, and sensual pleasure, and thereby make others think, that Christianity is but an empty name, a bare formal profession; if this be the case, I say, Christ is as yet dead in vain, to us; we are under the guilt of our sins; and are unacquainted with a true and thorough conversion.

But beloved, I am persuaded better things of you, and things that accompany salvation, though I thus speak; I would humbly hope that you are sincerely persuaded, that he who hath not the Spirit of Christ is none of his; and that, unless the Spirit, which raised Jesus from the dead, dwell in you here, neither will your mortal bodies be quickened by the same Spirit to dwell with him hereafter.

Let me therefore (as was proposed in the *last* place) earnestly exhort you, in the name of our Lord Jesus Christ, to act suitable to those convictions, and to live as Christians, that are commanded in holy writ, to "put off their former conversation concerning the Old Man, and to put on the New Man, which is created after God in righteousness and true holiness."

It must be owned indeed, that this is a great and difficult work; but, blessed be God, it is not impossible. Many thousands of happy souls have been assisted by a divine power to bring it about, and why should we despair of success? Is God's hand shortened, that it cannot save? Was he the God of our Fathers, is he not the God of their children also? Yes, doubtless, of their children also. It is a task likewise, that will put us to some pain; it will oblige us to part with some lust, to break with some friend, to mortify some beloved passion, which may be exceeding dear to us, and perhaps as hard to leave, as to cut off a right-hand, or pluck out a right-eye. But what of all this? Will not the being made a real living member of Christ, a child of God, and an inheritor of the kingdom of heaven, abundantly make amends for all this trouble? Undoubtedly it will.

The setting about and carrying on the great and necessary work, perhaps may, nay assuredly will expose us also to the ridicule of the unthinking part of mankind, who will wonder, that we run not into the same excess of riot with themselves; and because we deny our sinful appetites, and are not conformed to this world, being commanded in scripture to do the one, and to have our conversation in heaven, in opposition to the other, they may count our lives folly, and our end to be without honor. But will not the being numbered among the saints, and shining as the stars for ever and ever, be a more than sufficient recompense for all the ridicule, calumny, or reproach, we can possibly meet with here?

Indeed, was there no other reward attended a thorough conversion, but that peace of God, which is the unavoidable consequence of it, and which, even in this life, "passeth all understanding," we should have great reason to rejoice. But when we consider, that this is the least of those mercies God has prepared for those that are in Christ, and become new creatures; that, this is but the beginning of an eternal succession of pleasures; that the day of our deaths, which the unconverted, unrenewed sinner must so much dread, will be, as it were, but the first day of our new births, and open to us an everlasting scene of happiness and comfort; in short, if we remember, that they who are regenerate and born again, have a real title to all the glorious promises of the gospel, and are infallibly certain of being as happy, both here and hereafter, as an all-wise, all-gracious, all-powerful God can make them; methinks, every one that has but the least concern for the salvation of his precious and immortal soul, having such promises, such an hope, such an eternity of happiness set before him, should never cease watching, praying, and striving, till he find a real, inward, saving change wrought in his heart, and thereby doth know of a truth, that he dwells in Christ, and Christ in him; that he is a new creature, therefore a child of God; that he is already an inheritor, and will ere long be an actual possessor of the kingdom of heaven.

Which God of his infinite mercy grant, through Jesus Christ our Lord.

50. Christians, Temples of the Living God

Isaiah, speaking of the glory of gospel days, said, "Men have not heard nor perceived by the ear, neither hath the eye seen, O God, besides thee, what he hath prepared for him that waiteth for him." Chap. 64:4. Could a world lying in the wicked one, be really convinced of this, they would need no other motive to induce them to renounce themselves, take up their cross, and follow Jesus Christ. And had believers this truth always deeply impressed upon their souls, they could not but abstain from every evil, be continually aspiring after every good; and in a word, use all diligence to walk worthy of Him who hath called them to his kingdom and glory. If I mistake not, that is the end purposed by the apostle Paul, in the words of the text, "Ye are the temple of the living God." Words originally directed to the church of Corinth, but which equally belong to us, and to our children, and to as many as the Lord our God shall call. To give you the true meaning of, and then practically to improve them, shall be my endeavor in the following discourse.

It is thus that Christians are "the temple of the living God," of Father, Son, and Holy Ghost; they who once held a consultation to create, are all equally concerned in making preparations for, and effectually bringing about the redemption of man. The Father creates, the Son redeems, and the Holy Ghost sanctifies all the elect people of God. Being loved from eternity, they are effectually called in time, they are chosen out of the world, and not only by an external formal dedication at baptism, or at the Lord's supper, but by a free, voluntary, unconstrained oblation, they devote themselves, spirit, soul, and body, to the entire service of Him, who hath loved and given himself for them.

This is true and undefiled religion before God our heavenly Father: This is the real Christian's reasonable service, or, as some think the word imports, this is the service required of us in the word of God. It implies no less than a total renunciation of the world; in short, turns the Christian's whole life into one continued sacrifice of love to God; so that, "whether he eats or drinks, he does all to his glory." Not that I would hereby insinuate, that to be Christians, or to keep to the words of our text, in order to be temples of the living God, we must become hermits, or shut ourselves up in nunneries or cloysters; this be far from me! No. The religion, which this bible in my hand prescribes, is a social religion, a religion equally practicable by high and low, rich and poor, and which absolutely requires a due discharge of all relative duties, in whatsoever state of life God shall be pleased to place and continue us.

That some, in all ages of the church, have literally separated themselves from the world, and from a sincere desire to save their souls, and attain higher degrees of Christian perfection, have wholly devoted themselves to solitude and retirement, is what I make no doubt of. But then such a zeal is in no wise according to knowledge; for private Christians, as well as ministers, are said to be "the salt of the earth, and the lights of the world, and are commanded to "let their light shine before men." But how can this be done, if we shut ourselves up, and thereby entirely exclude ourselves from all manner of conversation with the world? Or supposing we could take the wings of the morning, and fly into the most distant and desolate parts of the earth, what would this avail us, unless we could agree with a wicked heart and wicked tempter not to pursue and molest us there?

So far should we be from thus getting ease and comfort, that I believe we should on the contrary soon find by our experience the truth of what a hermit himself once told me, that a tree which stands by itself, is most exposed and liable to the strongest blasts. When our Savior was to be tempted by the devil, he was led by the Spirit into the wilderness. How contrary this to their practice, who go into a wilderness to avoid temptation! Surely such are unmindful of the petition put up for us by our blessed Lord, "Father, I pray not that thou wouldst take them out of the world, but that thou wouldst keep them from the evil." This then is to be a Christian indeed; to be in the world, and yet not of it; to have our hands, according to our respective stations in life, employed on earth, and our hearts at the same time fixed on things above. Then, indeed, are we "temples of the living God," when with a humble boldness, we can say with a great and good soldier of Jesus Christ, we are the same in the parlor, as we are in the closet; and can at night throw off our cares, as we throw off our clothes; and being at peace with the world, ourselves, and God, are indifferent whether we sleep or die.

Farther, the Jewish temple was a house of prayer. "My house (says the Great God) shall be called a house of prayer:" and implies that the hearts of true believers are the seats of prayer. For this end was it built, and adorned with such furniture. Solomon, in that admirable prayer which he put up to God at the dedication of the temple, saith, "Hearken therefore unto the supplication of thy servant, and of the people Israel, which they shall make towards this place." And hence I suppose it was that Daniel, that man greatly beloved, in the time of captivity, "prayed as aforetime three times a day with his face towards the temple." And what was said of the first, our Lord applies to the second temple, "My house shall be called a house of prayer." On this account also, true believers may be stiled, "the temple of the living God." For being wholly devoted and dedicated to God, even a God in Christ, their heart becomes the seats of prayer, from whence, as to many living altars, a perpetual sacrifice of prayer and praise (like unto, tho' infinitely superior to the perpetual oblation under the Mosaic dispensation) is continually ascending, and offered up, to the Father of Mercies, the God of all Consolations. Such, and such only, who thus worship God in the temple of their hearts, can truly be said to be made priests unto God, or be stiled a royal priesthood; such, and such only, can truly be stiled, "the temple of the living God," because such only pray to him, as one expresses it, in the temple of their hearts, and consequently worship him in spirit and in truth.

Let no one say that such a devotion is impracticable, or at least only practicable by a few, and those such who have nothing to do with the common affairs of life; for this is the common duty and privilege of all true Christians. "To pray without ceasing," and "to rejoice in the Lord always," are precepts equally obligatory on all that name the name of Christ. And though it must be owned, that it is hard for persons that are immersed in the world, to serve the Lord without distraction; and though we must confess, that the lamp of devotion, even in the best of saints, sometimes burns too dimly, yet those who are the temple of the living God, find prayer to be their very element: And when those who make this objection, once come to love prayer, as some unhappy men love swearing, they will find no more difficulty in praying to, and praising God always, than these unhappy creatures do in cursing and swearing always. What hath been advanced, is far from being a state peculiar to persons wholly retired from the world.

My brethren, the love of God is all in all. When once possessed of this, as we certainly must be, if e are "the temple of the loving God," meditation, prayer, praise, and other spiritual exercises, become habitual and delightful. When once touched with this divine magnet, for ever after the soul feels a divine attraction, and continually turns to its center, God; and if diverted therefrom, by any sudden or violent temptation, yet when that obstruction is removed, like as a needle touched by a lodestone when your finger is taken away, turns to its rest, ins center, its God, it's All, again.

The Jewish temple was also a place where the Great Jehovah was pleased in a more immediate manner to reside. Hence, he is said to put and record his name there, and to sit or dwell between the cherubims; and when Solomon first dedicated it, we are told, "the house was filled with a cloud, so that the priests could not stand to minister by reason of the cloud, for the glory of the Lord had filled the house." And wherefore all this amazing manifestation of the Divine Glory? Even for this, O man, to show thee how the High and Lofty One that inhabiteth eternity, would make believers hearts his living temple, and dwell and make his abode in all those that tremble at his word.

To this, the apostle more particularly alludes in the words immediately following our text; for having called the Corinthians "the temple of the living God," he adds, "as God hath said, I will dwell in them, and I will walk in them, and I will be their God, and they shall be my people." Strange and string expressions these! But strange and strong as they are, must be experienced by all who are indeed "the temple of the loving God." For they are said, to be "chosen to be a holy habitation through the Spirit; to dwell in God and God in them; to have the witness in themselves, and to have God's Spirit witnessing with their spirits that they are the children of God." Which expressions import no more or less, than that prayer of our Lord which he put up for his church and people a little before his bitter passion, "That they may be one, even as we are one, I in them, and thou in me, that they may be made perfect in one:" This glorious passage our church adopts in her excellent communion office, and is so far from thinking that this was only the privilege of apostles, that she asserts in the strongest terms, that it is the privilege of every worthy communicant. For then (says she) if we receive the sacrament worthily, we are one with Christ, and Christ is one with us; we dwell in Christ, and Christ in us. And what is it, but that inspiration of the Holy Spirit, which we pray for in the beginning of that office, and that fellowship of the Holy Ghost, which the minister, in the conclusion of every day's public prayer, entreats the Lord to be with us all evermore?

Brethren, the time would fail me to mention all the scriptures, and the various branches of our liturgy, articles, and homilies, that speak of this inestimable blessing, the indwelling of the blessed Spirit, whereby we do indeed become, "the temples of the living God." If you have eyes that see, or ears that hear, you may view it almost in every page of the lively oracles, and every part of those offices, which some of you daily use, and hear read to you, in the public worship of Almighty God. In asserting therefore this doctrine, we do not vent the whimsies of a disordered brain, and heated imagination; neither do we broach any new doctrines, or set up the peculiar opinions of any particular sect or denomination of Christians whatsoever; but we speak the words of truth and soberness, we show you the right and good old way, even that, in which the articles of all the reformed churches, and all sincere Christians of all parties, however differing in other respects, do universally agree. We are now insisting upon a point, which may properly be termed the Christian shibboleth, something which is the grand criterion of our most holy religion; and on account of which, the holy Ignatius, one of the first fathers of the church, was used to stile himself a bearer of God, and the people to whom he wrote, bearers of God: For this, as it is recorded of him, he was arraigned before Trajan, who imperiously said, Where is this man, that says, he carries God about with him. With an humble boldness he answered, I am he, and then quoted the passage in the text, "Ye are the temple of the living God; as God hath said, I will dwell in them, and walk in them, and I will be their God, and they shall be my people." Upon this, to cure him of his enthusiast, he was condemned to be devoured by lions.

Blessed be God! We are not in danger of being called before such persecuting Trajans now: under our present mild and happy administration, the scourge of the tongue is all that they can legally lash us with. But if permitted to go farther, we need not be ashamed of witnessing this good confession. Suffering grace will be given for suffering times; and if, like Ignatius, we are bearers of God, we also shall be enabled to say with him, when led to the devouring lions, Now I begin to be a disciple of Christ.

But it is time for me,

Secondly, To make some practical improvement of what has been delivered. You have heard in what sense it is that real Christians are "the temple of the living God." Shall I ask, Believe ye these things? I know and am persuaded that some of you do indeed believe them, not because I have told you, but because you yourselves have experienced the same.

I congratulate you from my inmost soul. O that your hearts may be in tune this day to "magnify the Lord," and your spirits prepared to "rejoice in God your Savior." Like the Virgin Mary, you are highly favored, and from henceforth all the generations of God's people shall call you blessed. You can call Christ, Lord, by the Holy Ghost, and thereby have an internal, as well as external evidence of the divinity, both of his person, and of his holy word. You can now prove that despised book, emphatically called The Scriptures, doth contain the perfect and acceptable will of God. You have found the second Adam to be a quickening spirit; He hath raised you from death to life. And being thus taught, and born of God, however unlearned in other respects, you can say, "Is not this the Christ?" O ineffable blessing! Inconceivable privilege! God's spirit witnesseth with your spirits, that you are the children of God. When you think of this, are you not ready to cry out with the beloved disciple, "What manner of love is this, that we should be called the children of God!" I believe that holy man was in an ecstasy when he wrote these words; and tho' he has been in heaven so long, yet his ecstatic surprise is but now beginning, and will be but as beginning through the ages of eternity. Thus shall it be with all you likewise, whom the high and lofty One, that inhabiteth eternity, hath made his living temples. For He hath sealed you to the day of redemption, and hath given you the earnest of your future inheritance. His eyes and heart shall therefore be upon you continually: and in spite of all opposition from men or devils, the top-stone of this spiritual building shall be brought forth, and you shall shout Grace, grace unto it: your bodies shall be fashioned like unto the Redeemer's glorious body, and your souls, in which (O infinite condescension!) He now delights to dwell, shall be filled with all the fullness of God. You shall then go no more out; you shall then no more need the light of the sun or the light of the moon, for the Lord himself will be your temple, and the Lamb in the midst thereof shall be your glory. Dearly beloved in the Lord, what say you to these things? Do not your hearts burn within you whilst thinking of these deep, but glorious truths of God. Whilst I am musing, and speaking of them, methinks a fire kindles even in this cold, icy heart of mine: O what shall we render unto the Lord for all these mercies? Surely He hath done great things for us: How great is his goodness, and his bounty! O the height, the depth, the length, and the breadth of the love of God! Surely it passeth knowledge. O for humility! And a soul-abasing, God-exalting sense of these things! When the blessed virgin went into the hill country, to pay a visit to her cousin Elizabeth, amazed at such a favor, she cried out, "Whence is it that the mother of my Lord vouchsafes to come to me?" And when the great Jehovah filled the temple with his glory, out of the abundance of his heart, king Solomon burst forth into this pathetic exclamation, "But will God in very deed dwell with men on the earth?" With how much greater astonishment ought we to say, And will the Lord himself in very deed come to us? Will the high and lofty One that inhabiteth eternity, dwell in, and make our earthly hearts his living temples? My brethren, whence is this? From any fitness in us foreseen? No, I know you disclaim such an unbecoming thought. Was it then from the improvement of our own free-will? No, I am persuaded you will not thus debase the riches of God's free grace. Are you not all ready to say, Not unto us, not unto us, but unto thy free, thy unmerited, thy sovereign, distinguishing love and mercy, O Lord, be all the glory. It is this, and this alone, hath made the difference between us and others. We have nothing but what is freely given us from above: if we love God, it is because God first loved us. Let us look then unto the rock from whence we have been hewn, and the hole of the pit from whence we have been digged. And if there be any consolation in Christ, if any comfort of love, if any fellowship of the spirit, if any bowels and mercies, let us study and strive to walk as becometh those who are made the temples of the loving God, or, as the apostle elsewhere expresseth himself, "a holy temple unto the Lord." What manner of persons ought such to be in all holy conversation and godliness? How holily and how purely should we live! As our apostle argues in another place, "For what fellowship hath righteousness and unrighteousness? What communion hath light with darkness? Or what concord hath Christ with Belial?" Shall those who are temples of the living

God, suffer themselves to be dens of thieves and cages of unclean birds? Shall vain unchaste thoughts be suffered to dwell within them? Much less shall any thing that is impure be conceived or acted by them? Shall we provoke the Lord to jealousy? God forbid! We all know with what distinguished ardor our blessed Redeemer purged an earthly temple; a zeal for his father's house even eat him up: with what a holy vehemence did he overturn the tables of the money-changers, and scourge the buyers and sellers out before him! Why? They made his father's house a house of merchandise: they had turned the house of prayer into a den of thieves.

O my brethren, how often have you and I been guilty of this great evil? How often have the lust of the flesh, the lust of the eye, and the pride of life, insensibly stolen away our hearts from God? Once they were indeed houses of prayer; faith, hope, love, peace, joy, and all the other fruits of the blessed Spirit lodged within them; but now, O now, it may be, thieves and robbers. *Hinc illa lachryma*. Hence those hidings of God's face, that dryness, and deadness, and barrenness of soul, those wearisome nights and days, which many of us have felt from time to time, and have been made to groan under. Hence those dolorous and heart-breaking complaints, "O that I knew where I might find him! O that it was with me as in days of old, when the candle of the Lord shone bright upon my soul!" Hence those domestic trials, those personal losses and disappointments: and to this perhaps some of us may add, hence all those public rebukes with which we have been visited: they are all only as so many scourges of small cords in the loving Redeemer's hands, to scourge the buyers and sellers out of the temple of our hearts. O that we may know the rod and who hath appointed it! He hath chastised us with whips: may we be wise, and by a more close and circumspect walk prevent his chastising us in time to come with scorpions! But who is sufficient for this thing? None but thou, O Lord, to whom alone all hearts are open, all desires known, and from whom no secrets are hidden! Cleanse thou therefore the thoughts of our hearts by the inspiration of thy blessed Spirit, that henceforward we may more perfectly love thee and more worthily magnify thy holy name!

But are not some of you ready to object, and to fear, that the Lord hath forgotten to be gracious, that he hath shut up his loving kindness in displeasure, and that he will be no more entreated? Thus the psalmist once thought, when visited for his backslidings with God's heave hand. But he acknowledged this to be his infirmity; and whether you think of it or no, I tell you, this is your infirmity. O ye dejected, desponding, distrustful souls, hear ye the word of the Lord, and call to mind his wonderful declarations of old to his people. "I, even I am He that blotteth out thy transgressions: for a small moment have I forsaken thee, but with everlasting mercies will I gather thee. Can a woman forget her sucking child? Yes she may, but the Lord will not forget you, O ye of little faith. For as a father pitieth his own children, so doth the Lord pity them that fear him. How shall I give thee up, O Ephraim? How shall I make thee as Admah? How shall I set thee as Zeboim?" And what is the result of all these interrogations? "My repentings are kindled together: I will not return to execute the fierceness of my anger against Ephraim: For I am God, and not man." And is not the language of all these endearing passages, like that of Joseph to his self-convicted, troubled brethren? "Come near to me." O that it may be said of you, as it is said of them, "And they came near unto him." Then should you find by happy experience, that the Lord, the Lord God, merciful ad gracious, is indeed slow to anger and of great kindness, and repenteth him of the evil. Who knows but he may come down this day, this hour, nay this moment, and suddenly revisit the temple of your hearts? Who knows but he may revive his work in your precious souls, cause you to return to your first love, help you to do your first works, and even exceed your hopes, and cause the glory of this second visitation even to surpass that glory which filled your hearts, in that happy, never to be forgotten day, in which he first vouchsafed to make you his living temples? Even so, Father, let it seem good in thy sight!

But the improvement of our subject must not end here. Hitherto I have been giving bread to the children; and it is my meat and drink so to do: but must nothing be said to those of you who are without? I mean to such who cannot yet say, that they are "the temple of the living God." And O how great, put you all together, may the number of you be: by far, in all probability, the greatest part of this auditory. Say not I am uncharitable; the God of truth, hath said it, "Strait is the gate, and narrow is the way, which leadeth unto life, and few there be that find it." Suffer me to speak plainly to you, my brethren; you have heard what has been said upon the words of our text, and what must be wrought in us, ere we can truly say that we are "the temple of the loving God." Is it so with you? Are ye separated from the world and worldly tempers? Are your hearts become houses of prayer? Doth the Spirit of God dwell in your souls? And whether you eat or drink, or whatsoever you do, as to the habitual bent of your minds, do you do all to the glory of God? These are short, but plain, and let me tell you very important questions. What answer can you make to them? Say not, "Go thy way, and at a more convenient season I will call for thee." I will not, I must not suffer you to put me off so; I demand an answer in the name of the Lord of Hosts. What say ye? Methinks, I hear you say, We have been dedicated to God in baptism, we go to church or meeting, we say our prayers, repeat our creeds, or have subscribed the articles, and the confession of faith; we are quite orthodox, and great friends to the doctrines of grace; we do no body any harm, we are honest moral people, we are church-members, we keep up family-prayer, and constantly go to the table of the Lord." All these things are good in their places. But thus far, nay much farther may you go, and yet be far from the kingdom of God. The unprofitable servant did no one any harm; and the foolish virgins had a lamp of an outward profession, and went up even to heaven's gate, calling Christ, "Lord, Lord." These things may make you whited sepulchers, but not "the temples of the loving God." Alas! Alas! one thing you yet lack, the one chief thing, and without which all is nothing; I mean the indwelling of God's blessed Spirit, without which you can never become "the temples of the loving God."

Awake therefore, ye deceived formalists, awake; who, vainly puffed up with your model of performances, boastingly cry out, "The temple of the Lord, the temple of the Lord, the temple of the Lord we are." Awake, ye outward-court worshippers: ye are building on a sandy foundation: take heed lest you also go to hell by the very door of heaven. Behold, and remember, I have told you before.

And as for you who have done none of these things, who instead of making an outward profession of religion, have as it were renounced your baptism, proclaim your sin like Sodom, and willfully and daringly live a without God in the world; I ask you, how can you think to escape, if you persist in neglecting such a great salvation. Verily, I should utterly despair of your ever attaining the blessed privilege of being temples of the living God, did I not hear of thousands, who through the grace of God have been translated from a like state of darkness into his marvelous light. Such, says the apostle Paul, writing to these very Corinthians who were now God's living temples, (drunkards, whoremongers, adulterers, and such like) "such were some of you. But ye are washed, but ye are sanctified, but ye are justified in the name of the Lord Jesus, and by the Spirit of our God." O that the same blessed Spirit may this day vouchsafe to come and pluck you also as brands out of the burning! Behold, I warn you to flee from the wrath to come. Go home, and meditate on these things; and think whether it is not infinitely better, even here, to be temples of the living God, than to be bondslaves to every brutish lust, and to be led captive by the devil at his will. The Lord Jesus can, and if you fly to him for refuge, he will set your souls at liberty. He hath led captivity captive, he hath ascended up on high, on purpose to receive this gift of the blessed Spirit of God for men, "even for the rebellious," that he might dwell in your hearts by faith here, and thereby prepare you to dwell with Him and all the heavenly host in his kingdom hereafter.

That this may be the happy lot of you all, may God of his infinite mercy grant, for the sake of his dear Son Christ Jesus our Lord; to whom with the father, and the blessed Spirit, three persons, but one God, be ascribed all power, might, majesty, and dominion, now and for evermore. Amen! And Amen!

51. Christ the Only Preservative Against a Reprobate Spirit

The doctrines of the gospel are doctrines of peace, and they bring comfort to all who believe in them; they are not like the law given by Moses, which consisted of troublesome and painful ceremonies; neither do they carry with them that terror which the law did; as, "cursed is every one who continueth not to do all things which are written in the book of the law:" If you were to keep the whole law, and break but in one point, you are guilty of the breach of all. The law denounces threatenings against all who do not conform to her strict commands; but the gospel is a declaration of grace, peace and mercy; here you have an account of the blood of Christ, blood which speaketh better things than that of Abel; for Abel's blood cried aloud from vengeance, vengeance. But Jesus Christ's crieth mercy, mercy, mercy upon the guilty sinner. If he comes to Christ, confesses and forsakes his sin, then Jesus will have mercy upon him: And if, my brethren, you are but sensible of your sins, convinced of your iniquities, and feel yourselves lost, undone sinners, and come and tell Christ of your lost condition, you will soon find how ready he is to help you; he will give you his spirit; and if you have his spirit you cannot be reprobates: you will find his spirit to be quickening and refreshing; not like the spirit of the world, a spirit of reproach, envy, and all uncharitableness.

Most of your own experiences will confirm the truth

hereof; for are not you reproached and slandered, and does not the world say all manner of evil against you, merely because you follow Jesus Christ; because you will not go to the same excess of riot with them? While they are singing the songs of the drunkard, you are singing psalms and hymns: while they are at a playhouse, you are hearing a sermon: while they are drinking, reveling and misspending their precious time, and hastening on their own destruction, you are reading, praying, meditating, and working out your salvation with fear and trembling. This is matter enough for a world to reproach you; you are not polite and fashionable enough for them. If you will live godly, you must suffer persecution; you must not expect to go through this world without being persecuted and reviled. If you were of the world, the world would love you; for it always loves its own; but if you are not of the world, it will hate you; it has done so in all ages, it never loved any but those who were pleased with its vanities and allurements. It has been the death of many a lover of Jesus, merely because they have loved him: And, therefore, my brethren, do not be surprised if you meet with a fiery trial, for all those things will be a means of sending you to your master the sooner.

The spirit of the world is hatred; that of Christ is love; the spirit of the world is vexation; that of Christ is pleasure: the spirit of the world is sorrow; that of Christ is joy: the spirit of the world is evil, and that of Christ is good: the spirit of the world will never satisfy us, but Christ's spirit is all satisfaction: the spirit of the world is misery; that of Christ is ease. In one word, the spirit of the world has nothing lasting; but the spirit of Christ is durable, and will last through an eternity of ages: the spirit of Christ will remove every difficulty, satisfy every doubt, and be a means of bringing you to himself, to live with him for ever and ever.

From the words of my text, I shall show you,

I. The necessity of receiving the spirit of Christ.

II. Who Christ is, whose spirit you are to receive. And then

Shall conclude with an exhortation to all of you, high and low, rich and poor, to come unto the Lord Jesus Christ; and to beg that you may receive his spirit, so that you may not be reprobates.

First, I am to show you the necessity there is of receiving the spirit of Christ.

And here, my brethren, it will be necessary to consider you as in your first state; that is, when God first created Adam, and placed him in the garden of Eden, and gave him a privilege of eating of all the trees in the garden, except the tree of knowledge of good and evil, which stood in the midst thereof. Our first parents had not been long in this state of innocence, before they fell from it, they broke the divine commands, and involved all their posterity in guilt; for as Adam was our representative, so we were to stand or fall in him; and as he was our federal head, his falling involved all our race under the power of death, for death came into the world by sin; and we all became liable to the eternal punishment due from God, for man's disobedience to the divine command.

Now as man had sinned, and a satisfaction was demanded, it was impossible for a finite creature to satisfy him, who was a God of so strict purity as not to behold iniquity: And man by the justice of God would have been sent down into the pit, which was prepared of old for the devil and his angels; but when justice was going to pass the irrevocable sentence, then the Lord Jesus Christ came and offered himself a ransom for poor sinners. Here was admirable condescension of the Lord Jesus Christ! That he who was in the bosom of his father, should come down from all that glory, to die for such rebels as you and I are, who if it lay in our power, would pull the Almighty from his throne: Now can you think that if there was no need of Christ's death, can you think that if there could have been any other ransom found, whereby poor sinners might have been saved, God would not have spared his only begotten Son, and not have delivered him up for all that believe in him?

This, my brethren, I think proves to a demonstration, that it was necessary for Christ to die: But consider, it will be of no service to know that Christ died for sinners, if you do not accept of his spirit, that you may be sanctified, and fitted for the reception of that Jesus, who died for all those who believe in him. The sin of your nature, your original sin, is sufficient to sink you into torments, of which there will be no end; therefore unless you receive the spirit of Christ you are reprobates, and you cannot be saved: Nothing short of the blood of Jesus applied to your souls, will make you happy to all eternity: Then, seeing this is so absolutely necessary, that you cannot be saved without having received the spirit of Christ, but that ye are reprobates, do not rest contented 'till you have good hopes, through grace, that the good work is begun in your souls; that you have received a pardon for your sins; that Christ came down from heaven, died, and made satisfaction for your sins. Don't flatter yourselves that a little morality will be sufficient to save you; that going to church, or prayers, and sacrament, and doing all the duties of religion in an external manner, will ever carry you to heaven; no, you must have grace in your hearts; there must be a change of the whole man.

You must be born again, and become new creatures, and have the spirit of Christ within you: And until you have that spirit of Christ, however you may think to the contrary, and please yourselves in your own imagination, I say, you are no better than reprobates. You may content yourselves with leading civil, outward decent lives, but what will that avail you, unless you have the spirit of the Lord Jesus Christ in your hearts: His kingdom must be set up in your souls; there must be the life of God in the soul of man, else you belong not to the Lord Jesus Christ; and until you belong to him, you are reprobates.

This may seem as enthusiasm to some of you, but if it is so, it is what the apostle Paul taught; and therefore, my brethren, they are the words of truth. I beseech you, in the mercies of God in Christ Jesus, not to despise these words, as if they do not concern you, but were only calculated for the first ages of Christianity, and, therefore, of no signification: If you think thus, you are wronging your own souls; for whatever is written, was written for you in these times, as well as for the Christians in the first ages of the church.

For the case stands thus between God and man: God, at first, made man upright, or, as the sacred penman expresses it, "In the image of God made he man;" his soul was the very copy, the transcript of the divine nature. He who had, by his almighty power, spoken the world into being, breathed into man the breath of spiritual life; and his soul became adorned with purity and perfection. This was the finishing stroke of the creation; the perfection both of the moral and material world; and it so resembled the divine Original, that God could not but rejoice and take pleasure in his own likeness: Therefore, we read, that when God had finished the inanimate and brutish part of the creation, "he looked, and behold it was good." But when that lovely, god-like creature man was made, "behold it was very good."

Happy, unspeakably happy, to be thus partaker of a divine Nature; and thus man might have continued still, had he continued holy; but God placed him in a state of probation, with a free grant to eat of every tree in the garden, except the tree of knowledge of good and evil. The day he did eat thereof he was not only to become subject to temporal, but spiritual death; and so lost that divine image, that spiritual life which God had breathed into him, and which was as much his happiness as his glory.

But man, unhappy man, being seduced by the devil, did eat of the forbidden fruit, and thereby became liable to that curse which the eternal God had pronounced on him for his disobedience. And we read, that soon after Adam was fallen, he complained that he was naked; naked, not only as to his body, but naked and destitute of those divine graces which before beautified his soul.

An unhappy mutiny and disorder then fell upon this world; those briars and thorns which now spring up and overspread the earth, were but poor emblems, lifeless representations of that confusion and rebellion which sprung up in, and overwhelmed, the soul of man, immediately after the fall. He now sunk into the temper of a beast and devil.

In this dreadful and disordered condition are all of us brought into the world: We are told, my brethren, that "Adam had a son in his own likeness," or with the same corrupt nature which he himself had sunk into, after eating the forbidden fruit: And experience, as well as scripture, proves, that we are altogether born in sin, and, therefore, incapable, whilst in such a state, to have communion with God.

For as light cannot have communion with darkness, so God can have no communion with such polluted sons of Belial. Here, here, appears the great and glorious end, why Christ was manifest in the flesh, to put an end to these disorders, and to restore us unto the savor of God. He came down from heaven and shed his precious blood upon the cross, to satisfy the divine justice of his Father, for our sins; and so, he purchased this Holy Ghost, who must once more re-stamp the divine image on our hearts, and make us capable of living with, and enjoying of God. We must be renewed by the spirit of God; he must dwell in us before we can be new creatures, and be freed from a reprobate spirit: the spirit of Christ must bring us home unto that fold where all his sheep are, and implant his grace in our hearts, and take from us that spirit of sin which reigns in us: And till this is rooted out of our hearts, however we may flatter ourselves with being good Christians, because we are good moralists, and lead civil, moral, decent lives, yet if we live and die, my brethren, in this way, we are only flattering ourselves into hell.

I think I have proved, to a demonstration, the necessity there is of receiving the spirit of Christ. I now come to show you,

Secondly, Who Christ is, whose spirit you are to receive.

My brethren, (Jesus Christ is coequal, coessential, coeternal, and consubstantial with the Father, very God of very God; and as there was not a moment of time in which God the Father was not, so there was not a moment of time in which God the Son was not.

Arians and Socinians deny this godhead of Christ, and esteem him only as a creature: The Arians look on him as a titular Deity, as a created and subordinate God; but, if they would humbly search the scriptures they would find divine homage paid to Christ. He is called God in scripture, particularly when the great evangelical Prophet says, "He shall be called the mighty God, the everlasting Father, and the government shall be upon his shoulders:" And Jesus Christ himself says, that he is the Alpha and Omega;" and that "the world was made by him:" But though this be ever so plain, our gay airy sparks of this age will not believe the Lord Jesus Chris to be equal with his Father, and that for no other reason, but because it is a fashionable and polite doctrine to deny his divinity, and esteem him only as a created God.

Our Socinians do not go so far they look upon Christ only to be a good man sent from God, to show the people the way they should go, on their forsaking of Judaism; that he was to be also an example to the world, and that his death was only to prove the truth of his doctrines.

Many of those who call themselves members, yea, teachers of the church of England, have got into this polite scheme. Good God! My very soul shudders at the thoughts of the consequence that will attend such a belief. O my brethren, do not think so dishonorably of the Lord who bought you; of the Jesus who dies for you: he must be all in all unto your souls, if ever you are saved by him: Christ must be your active, as well as passive obedience; his righteousness must be imputed to you. The doctrine of Christ's righteousness being imputed, is a comfortable, a desirable doctrine to all real Christians: And to you, sinners, who are inquiring what you must do to be saved? How uncomfortable would it be to tell you, by your own good works, when, perhaps, you have never done one good work in all your lives: This would be driving you to despair indeed; no, "believe in the Lord Jesus Christ and you shall be saved;" come to the Lord Jesus by faith, and he shall receive you. He is able and willing to save you.

This second person in the Trinity, who is God-man, the mediator of the new covenant; he, my brethren, hath virtue enough, in his blood, to atone for the sins of millions of worlds. As man he died, he was crucified, nailed to, and pierced on the accursed tree: This was the love of the Lord Jesus Christ for you; and will you then have low and dishonorable thoughts of Jesus Christ, after his having done so much for you? O my dear brethren, don't be so polite as to deny the Deity of Christ; though you may be counted fools in the eye of the world, yet in God's account, you shall be esteemed wise, wise for salvation.

You may now be looked upon as fools and madmen, as a parcel of rabble, and, in a short time, fit for Bedlam. They may say you are going to undermine the established church; but God knows the secrets of all hearts, knows our innocency; and I speak the truth in Christ, I lie not, I should rejoice to see all the world adhere to her articles; I should rejoice to see the teachers, the ministers of the church of England, preach up those very articles they have subscribed to; but those ministers who do preach them up, they esteem as madmen, and look on them as the off-scouring of the earth, unfit for company and conversation.

The evil things they say of me, blessed be God, are without foundation; I am a friend to the church homilies; I am a friend to her liturgy, and if they did not thrust me out of their churches, I would read it every day.

My brethren, I am not for limiting the spirit of God, but am for uniting all in the bonds of love; I love all that love the Lord Jesus Christ: This will make more Christians, than will the spirit of persecution.

The Pharisees may think it madness to mention persecution in a Christian country, but the spirit of persecution resides in many: their will is as great, but blessed be God, they want the power; if they had that, my brethren, fire and faggot is what we must expect, for the devil's temple is shaken. Many are coming unto Jesus, I hope many of you are already come, and many more coming; this must make Satan rage, to see his kingdom weakened; he will stir up all his malice against the people of God. We must expect, that a suffering time will certainly come; it is now hastening on, it is ripening a-pace; then it will be proved, to a demonstration, whether you are hypocrites or not; for suffering times are always trying times. O my brethren, do not be afraid of a little reproach, but look on it as a fore-runner of what will be the attendant upon it: Therefore let me, by way of application,

Exhort all of you, high and low, rich and poor, one with another, to come unto the Lord Jesus Christ, that he may give you strength to undergo whatsoever he, in his wisdom, calls you to. Come, come, my brethren, to Jesus Christ, and he will give you grace, which will make you willing and ready to suffer all things for Jesus Christ.

It is not being pointed at; it is not being despised and looked on as mad, and a deluded people: Alas! what does this signify to a soul who has Jesus Christ? Do not be afraid to confess the blessed Jesus; dare to be singularly good: Don't be afraid of singing of hymns, or of meeting together to build each other up in the ways of the Lord:

Shine ye as lights in the world amidst a crooked and perverse generation.

It is necessary that offenses should come, to try what is in our hearts, and whether we will be faithful soldiers of Jesus Christ or not: Be not content with following Christ afar off, for then we shall, as Peter did, soon deny him; but let us be altogether Christians. Let our speech and all our actions declare to the whole world, whose disciples we are, and that we have determined to know nothing but Jesus Christ, and him crucified. O then, then, will it be well with us, happy, unspeakably happy, shall we be, even here; and what is infinitely better, when others that despised us shall be calling for the mountains to fall on them, and the hills to cover them, we shall be exalted to sit down on the right hand of God, and shine as the sun in the firmament, and live for ever with our Redeemer. And will not this be a sufficient recompense for all the sufferings you have undergone here? Therefore, do not strive to have the greatness, the riches, the honor, and pleasures of this world, but strive to have Jesus Christ.

Your friends and carnal acquaintance, and, above all, your grand adversary the devil, will be persuading you not to have Christ until you are grown old; he would have you lay up goods for many years; to see plays, play at cards; go to balls, and masquerades; and to make you the more willing, to draw you in, he calls sinful pleasures, innocent diversions.

A late learned Rabbi of our church, told the people, in a sermon, which I myself heart, that if people went to church of a Sunday, and said the prayers while there, that it was no harm, neither would God count it a sin, to take their recreation, after the service of the church was over: But I say, my brethren, and the command of God says so too, that the whole Sabbath must be kept holy; and that as God has allowed you six days for yourselves, to do the duties in those several stations wherein Providence has place you, he expects you should give him one day to himself; and will you waste that Sabbath which should be spent in gathering provisions for your souls? God forbid!

You had ten thousand times better be ignorant of all the polite diversions of the age, than to be ignorant of the spirit of Christ's being within you, and that it must be, before you are new creatures, and are in Christ; and if you have not an interest in Christ, you are lost, your damnation is hastening on. "He that believeth shall be saved, and he that believeth not shall be damned."

If you stand out against Christ, you are fighting against yourselves. O come unto him, do not stay to bring good works with you, for they will be of no service; all your works will never carry you to heaven, they will never pardon one sin, nor give you the least comfort in a dying hour; if you have nothing more than your own works to recommend you to God, they will not prevent your sinking in that eternal abyss, where there is no bottom.

But come unto Christ, and he will give you that righteousness which will stand you in good account at the great day of the Lord, when he shall come to take notice of them that love him, and of those who have the wedding garment on.

Let all your actions spring from the love of Jesus; let him be the Alpha and Omega of all your actions; then, my brethren, our indifferent ones are acceptable sacrifices; but if this principle be wanting, our most pompous services avail nothing; we are only spiritual idolaters; we sacrifice to our own net, and make an idol of ourselves, by making ourselves and not Christ, the spring of our actions; and therefore, my brethren, such actions are so far from being accepted by God, that according to the language of one of the articles of our church, "We doubt not but that they have the nature of sin, because they spring not from an experimental faith in, and knowledge of Jesus Christ.

Were we not fallen creatures, we might then act upon other principles; but since we are fallen in Adam, and are restored again only by the death of Jesus Christ, the face of things in entirely changed, and all we think, speak, or do, is only accepted in and through him.

Therefore, my brethren, I beseech you, in the bowels of love and compassion, that you would come unto Jesus: Do not go away scoffing, offended, or blaspheming. Indeed, all I say is in love to your souls; and if I could be but an instrument of bringing you to Jesus Christ, if you were to be never so much exalted, I should not envy, but rejoice in your happiness: If I was to make up the last of the train of the companions of the blessed Jesus, it would rejoice me to see you above me in glory. I do not speak out of a false humility, a pretended sanctity; no, God is my judge, I speak the truth in Christ, I lie not, I would willingly go to prison, or to death for you, so I could but bring one soul from the devil's strong holds, into the salvation which is by Christ Jesus.

Come then unto Christ every one that hears me this night; I offer Jesus Christ, pardon, and salvation to all you, who will accept thereof. Come, O ye drunkards, lay aside your cups, drink no more to excess; come and drink of the water which Christ will give you, and then you will thirst no more: come, O ye thieves; let him that has stolen, steal no more, but fly unto Christ and he will receive you. Come unto him, O ye harlots; lay aside your lusts and turn unto the Lord, and he will have mercy upon you, he will cleanse you of all your sins, and wash you in his blood. Come, all ye liars; come, all ye Pharisees; come, all ye fornicators, adulterers, swearers, and blasphemers, come to Christ, and he will take away all your filth, he will cleanse you from your pollution, and your sins shall be done away. Come, come, my guilty brethren; I beseech you for Christ's sake, and for your immortal soul's sake, to come unto Christ: Do not let me knock at the door of your hearts in vain, but open and let the King of Glory in, and he will dwell with you, he will come and sup with you this night; this hour, this moment he is ready to receive you, therefore come unto him.

Do not consult with flesh and blood, let not the world hinder you from coming to the Lord of life: What are a few transitory pleasures of this life worth? They are not worth your having, but Jesus Christ is a pearl of great price, he is worth the laying out all you have, to buy.

And if you are under afflictions, fly not to company to divert you, neither read what the world calls harmless books; they only tend to harden the heart, and to keep you from closing with the Lord Jesus Christ.

When I was a child, yea, when I came to riper years, God knows, it is with grief I speak it, when ignorant of the excellency of the word of God, I read as many of these harmless books as any one; but now I have tasted the good word of life, and am come to a more perfect knowledge of Christ Jesus my Lord; I put away these childish, trifling things, and am determined to read no other books but what lead me to a knowledge of myself, and Jesus Christ.

Methinks I could speak till midnight unto you, my brethren; I am full of love towards you; let me beseech you to fly to Christ for succor: "Now is the accepted time, now is the day of salvation;" therefore delay not, but strive to enter in at the strait gate; do not go the broad way of the polite world, but choose to suffer affliction with the people of God, rather than to enjoy the pleasures of sin for a season: You will have a reward afterwards, that will make amends for all the taunts, jeers, and calamities you may undergo here.

And will not the presence of Christ be a sufficient reward for all you have suffered for his name's sake? Why will you not accept of the Lord of glory? Do not say you have not heard of Christ, for he is now offered to you, and you will not accept of him; do not blame my master, he is willing to save you, if you will but lay hold on him by faith; and if you do not, your blood will be required of your own heads.

But I hope that you will not let the blood of Jesus be shed in vain, and that you will not let my preaching be of no signification. Would you have me go and tell my master, you will not come, and that I have spent my strength in vain; I cannot bear to carry so unpleasing a message unto him, I would not, indeed, I would not be a swift witness against any of you at the great day of accounts; but if you will refuse these gracious invitations, and not accept of them, I must do it: and will it not move your tender hearts to see your friends taken up into heaven, and you yourselves thrust down into hell? But I hope better things of most of you, even that you will turn unto the Lord of love, the Jesus who died for you, that in the day when he shall come to take his people to the mansions of everlasting rest, you may hear his voice, "Come, ye blessed of my Father, enter into the kingdom prepared for you before the foundation of the world." And that we may all enter into that glory, do thou, O Jesus, prepare us, by thy grace; give us thy spirit; and may our hearts be united to thee: May the word that has now been spoken, take deep root in thy people's hearts, that it may spring up and bring forth fruit, in some thirty, in some forty, and in some an hundred fold; do thou preserve them while in this life from all evil, and keep them from falling, and at last present them faultless before thy Father, when thou comest to judge the world, that where thou art, they may be also. Grant this, O Lord Jesus Christ, with whatever else thou seest needful for us, both at this time and for evermore.

Now to God the Father, God the Son, and God the Holy Ghost, be ascribed all honor, power, glory, might, majesty and dominion, both now and for evermore, Amen.

52. The Heinous Sin of Drunkenness

Ephesians 5:18—"Be not drunk with Wine, wherein is Excess; but be filled with the Spirit."

The persons to whom these words were written, were the inhabitants of Ephesus, as we are told in the Acts, had been worshippers of the great goddess Diana, and, in all probability, worshipped the God Baccbus also; at the celebration of whose festivals, it was always customary, nay, part of their religion, to get drunk; as though there was no other way to please their God, but by turning themselves into brutes.

The apostle therefore in this chapter, amongst many other precepts more especially applicable to them, lays down this in the text; and exhorts them, as they had now, by the free grace of God, been turned from heathenish darkness to the light of the gospel, to walk as children of light, and no longer make it part of their religion or practice to be "drunk with wine, wherein is excess;" but, on the contrary, strive to "be filled with the Spirit" of that Savior, after whose name they were called, and whose religion taught them to abstain from a filthy sin, and to live soberly as they ought to live.

The world being now Christian, and the doctrines of the gospel every where received, one would imagine, there should be no reason for repeating the precept now before us. But alas, Christians! I mean Christians falsely so called, are led captive by all sin in general, and by this or drunkenness in particular; that was St. Paul to rise again from the dead, he might be tempted to think most of us were turned back to the worship of dumb idols; had set up temples in honor of Baccbus; and made it part of our religion, as the Ephesians did of theirs, "to be drunk with wine, wherein is excess."

Some of our civil magistrates have not been wanting to use the power given them from above, for the punishment and restraint of such evil doings; and I wish it could be said this plague of drinking, by what they have done, had been stayed amongst us. But alas! though their labor, we trust, has not been altogether in vain in the Lord, yet thousands, and I could almost say ten thousands, fall daily at our right-hand, by this sin of drunkenness, in our streets; nay, men seem to have made a covenant with hell, and though the power of the civil magistrate is exerted against them, nay, though they cannot but daily see the companions of their riot hourly, by this sin, brought to the grave, yet "they will rise up early to follow strong drink, and cry, To-morrow shall be as today, and so much the more abundantly; when we awake, we will seek it yet again."

It is high time therefore, for thy ministers, O God, to lift up their voices like a trumpet; and since human threats cannot prevail, to set before them the terrors of the Lord, and try if these will not persuade them to cease from the evil of their doings.

But alas! how shall I address myself to them? I fear excess of drinking has made them such mere Nabals, that there is no speaking to them. And many of God's servants have toiled all their life-time in dissuading them from this sin of drunkenness, yet they will not forbear. However, at thy command, I will speak also, though they be a rebellious house. Magnify thy strength, O Lord, in my weakness, and grant that I may speak with such demonstration of the Spirit, and power, that from henceforward they may cease to act so unwisely, and this sin of drunkenness may not be their ruin.

Believe me, ye unhappy men of Belial, (for such, alas! this sin has made you) it is not without the strongest reasons, as well as utmost concern for your precious and immortal souls, that I now conjure you, in the Apostle's words, "Not to be drunk with wine, or any other liquor, wherein is excess." For,

First, Drunkenness is a sin which must be highly displeasing to God; because it is an abuse of his good creatures.

When God first made man, and had breathed into him the breath of life, he gave him dominion over the works of his hands; and every herb bearing seed, and every tree, in which was the fruit of a tree yielding seed, to him was given for meat: but when Adam had tasted the forbidden fruit, which was the only restraint laid upon him, he forfeited this privilege, and had no right, after he had disobeyed his Creator, to the use of any one of the creatures.

But, blessed be God, this charter, as well as all other privileges, is restored to us by the death of the second Adam, our Lord and Master Jesus Christ. Of every beast of the field, every fish of the sea, and whatsoever flieth in the air, or moveth on the face of the earth, that is fit for food, "we may freely eat," without scruple take and eat; but then, with this limitation, that we use them moderately. For God, by the death of Jesus, has given no man license to be intemperate; but, on the contrary, has laid us under the strongest obligations to live soberly, as well as godly, in this present world.

But the drunkard, despising the goodness and bounty of God, in restoring to us what we had so justly forfeited, turns his grace into wantonness; and as though the creature was not of itself enough subject to vanity, by being cursed for our sake, he abuses it still more, by making it administer to his lusts; and turns that wine which was intended to make glad his heart, into a deadly poison.

But thinkest thou, O drunkard, whosoever thou art, thou shalt escape the righteous judgment of God? No, the time will shortly come that thou must be no longer steward, and then the Sovereign Lord of all the earth will reckon with thee for thus wasting his goods. Alas! wilt thou then wrest scripture any longer to thy own damnation? And because Jesus Christ turned water into wine at the marriage-feast, to supply the wants of his indigent host, say, that it is therefore meet to make merry, and be drunken. No, thou shalt be silent before him; and know, that though thou hast encouraged thyself in drunkenness by such-like arguments, yet for all these things God will bring thee into judgment. But,

Secondly, What makes drunkenness more exceedingly sinful, is, that a man, by falling into it, sinneth against his own body.

When the apostle would dissuade the Corinthians from fornication, he urges this as an argument, "Flee fornication, brethren; for he that committeth fornication, sinneth against his own body." And may not I as justly cry out, Flee drunkenness, my brethren, since he that committeth that crime, sinneth against his own body? For, from whence come so many diseases and distempers in your bodies? Come they not from hence, even from your intemperance in drinking? Who hath pains in the head? Who hath rottenness in the bones? Who hath redness of eyes? He that tarries long at the wine, he that rises early to seek new wine. How many walking skeletons have you seen, whose bodies were once exceeding fair to look upon, fat and well-favored; but, by this sin of drinking, how has their beauty departed from them, and how have they been permitted to walk to and fro upon the earth, as though God intended to set them up, as he did Lot's wife, for monuments of his justice, that others might learn not to get drunk? Nay, I appeal to yourselves: are not many, for this cause, even now sickly among you? And have not many of your companions, whom you once saw so flourishing, like green bay trees, been brought by it with sorrow to their graves?

We might, perhaps, think ourselves hardly dealt with by God, was he to send us, as he did the royal Psalmist, to choose one plague out of three, whereby we should be destroyed. But had the Almighty decreed to cut off man from the face of the earth, and to shorten his days, he could not well send a more effectual plague, than to permit men, as they pleased, to over-charge themselves with drunkenness; for though it be a slot, yet it is a certain poison. And if the sword has slain its thousands, drunkenness has slain its ten thousands.

And will not this alarm you, O ye transgressors? Will not this persuade you to spare yourselves, and to do your bodies no harm? What, have you lost the first principles of human nature, the fundamental law of self-preservation? You seem to have a great fondness for your bodies; why, otherwise, to gratify the inordinate appetites, do you drink to excess? But surely, if you truly loved them, you would not thus destroy them; and was there no other argument to be urged against drunkenness, the consideration that it will destroy those live you are so fond of, one would imagine, should be sufficient.

I know, indeed, that it is a common answer, which drunkards make to those, who, out of love, would pull them as firebrands out of the fire, we are no body's enemy but our own. But this, instead of being an excuse for, is an aggravation of their guilt: for (not to mention that the drunkenness of one man has clothes many a family with rags, and that it is scarce possible for a person to be drunk, without tempting his neighbor also) not to mention these, and many other ill consequences, which would prove such an excuse to be entirely false: yet what is dearer to a man than himself? And if he himself be lost, what would all the whole world avail him? But how wilt thou stand, O man, before the judgment-seat of Christ, and make such an excuse, when thou shalt be arraigned before him as a self-murderer? Will it then be sufficient, thinkest thou, to say, I was no man's enemy but my own? No; God will then tell thee, that thou oughtest to have glorified him with thy spirit, and with thy body, which were his; and since thou hast, by intemperance, destroyed thy body, he will destroy both thy body and soul in hell. But,

Thirdly, What renders drunkenness more inexcusable, is, that it robs a man of his reason.

Reason is the glory of a man; the chief thing whereby God has made us to differ from the brute creation. And our modern unbelievers have exalted it to such a high degree, as even to set it in opposition to revelation, and so deny the Lord that bought them. But though, in doing this, they greatly err, and whilst they profess themselves wise, become real fools; yet we must acknowledge, that reason is the candle of the Lord, and whosoever puts it out, shall bear his punishment, whosoever he be.

But yet, this the drunkard does. Nebuchadnezzar's curse he makes his choice, his reason departeth from him; and then what is he better than a brute?

The very heathen kings were so sensible of this, that, in order to deter their young princes from drinking, they used to make their slaves get drunk, and be exposed before them. And didst thou but see thine own picture, O drunkard, when, after having drowned thy reason, thou staggerest to and fro, like one of the fools in Israel, and seest thy very companions making songs upon thee, surely thou wouldst not return to thy vomit again, but abhor thyself in dust and ashes!

When David, in a holy ecstasy, was dancing before the ark, Michal, Saul's daughter, despised him in her heart; and when he came home, she said, "How glorious was the king of Israel today, who uncovered himself today in the eyes of the hand-maids of his servants, as one of the vain fellows shamelessly uncovereth himself." But may not every one that meets a drunkard, more justly say, How glorious does he, that was made a little lower than the angels, look today, when, unmindful of his dignity, he has by drinking robbed himself of his reason, and reduced himself to a level with the beasts that perish.

But what if God, in the midst of one of these drunken fits, should arrest thee by death, and say unto thee, "Thou fool, this moment shall thy soul be required of thee." O! how shouldst thou appear in those filthy garments before that God, in whose sight the heavens are not clean. And how knowest thou, O man, but this may be thy lit? Hast thou not known many summoned at such an unguarded hour? And what assurance hast thou, that thou shalt not be the next? Because God has forborn thee so long, thinkest thou he will forbear always? No, this is rather a sign that he will come at an hour thou lookest not for him; and since his goodness and long-suffering has not led thee to repentance, he will cut thee down, and not permit thee to cumber the ground any longer. Consider this then, all ye that count it a pleasure to turn yourselves into brutes, lest God pluck you away by a sudden death, and there be none to deliver you.

Fourthly, There is a farther aggravation of this crime, that it is an inlet to, and forerunner of many other sins; for it seldom comes alone.

We may say of drunkenness, as Solomon does in strife, that it is like the letting out of water; for we know not what will be the end thereof. Its name is Legion; behold a troop of sins cometh after it. And, for my own part, when I see a drunkard, with the holy Prophet, when he looked in Hazael's face, I can hardly forbear weeping, to consider how many vices he may fall into, ere he comes to himself again.

What horrid incest did righteous Lot commit with his own daughters, when they had made him drunk? And, I doubt not, but there are many amongst you, who have committed such crimes when you have deprived yourselves of your reason by drinking, that were you to hear of them, your heart, like Nabal's, after he was told how he had abused David when he was drunk, would die within you. And, had any one told you, when you were sober, that you would have been guilty of such crimes, you would have cried out, with Hazael before-mentioned, "Are thy servants so many dogs, that they should do that?"

But no marvel that drunkards commit such crimes; for drunkenness drives the Holy Spirit from them; they become mere machines for the devil to work up to what he pleases; he enters into them, as he entered into the herd of swine; and no wonder if they then commit all uncleanness, and any other crime, with greediness. But this leads me to a

Fifth consideration, which highly aggravates the sin of drunkenness, it separates the Holy Spirit from us.

It is to be hoped, that no one here present need be informed, that before we can be assured we are Christians indeed, we must receive the Holy Ghost, must be born again from above, and have the Spirit of God witnessing with our spirits, that we are the sons of God. This, this alone is true Christianity; and without the cohabitation of this blessed Spirit in our hearts, our righteousness does not exceed the righteousness of the Scribes and Pharisees, and we shall in no wise enter into the kingdom of God.

But now, drunkards do in effect bid this blessed Spirit to depart from them: for what has he to do with such filthy swine? They have no log of share in the Spirit of the Son of David. They have chased him out of their hearts, by defiling his temple; I mean their bodies. And he can no more hold communion with them, than light can have communion with darkness, or Christ have concord with Belial.

The apostle, therefore, in the words of the text, exhorts the Ephesians, "not to be drunk with wine, wherein is excess, but to be filled with the Spirit;" thereby implying, that drunkenness and the Spirit of God could never dwell in the same heart. And in another epistle, he bids them to avoid unprofitable conversation, as a thing which grieved the Holy Spirit: whereby alone they could be sealed to the day of redemption. And if unprofitable conversation grieves the Holy Spirit, at what an infinite distance must drunkenness drive him from the hearts of men?

O that you were wise! That you would consider what a dreadful thing it is to have the Spirit of the loving God depart from you! For, assure yourselves, if you live without him, you will live without God in the world. You are in the same miserable forlorn condition as Saul was, when an evil spirit of the Lord came upon him; and you are only so many vessels of wrath fitted for destruction. But this brings me to a

Sixth reason against the sin of drunkenness; it absolutely unfits a man for the enjoyment of God in heaven, and exposes him to his eternal wrath.

To see and enjoy God, and to be like the blessed angels, always beholding the face of our heavenly Father, in the glories of his kingdom, is such an unspeakable happiness, that even wicked men, though they will not live the life of the righteous, cannot but wish their future state to be like his.

But think you, O ye drunkards, that you shall ever be

partakers of this inheritance with the saints in light? Do you flatter yourselves, that you, who have made them often the subject of your drunken songs, shall now be exalted to sing with them the heavenly songs of Zion? No, as by drunkenness you have made your hearts cages of unclean birds, with impure and unclean spirits must you dwell.

A burning Tophet, kindled by God's wrath, is prepared for you reception, where you must suffer the vengeance of eternal fire, and in vain cry out for a drop of water to cool your tongues. Indeed you shall drink, but it shall be a cup of God's fury: for in the hand of the Lord there will be a cup of fury, it will be full mixed, and as for the dregs thereof, all the drunkards of the land shall suck them out.

But perhaps you may not believe this report. These words may be looked upon by you as idle tales, and I may seem to you as Lot did to his sons-in-law, when he came to warn them to get up out of Sodom, "as one that mocketh." But if you believe not me, believe eternal truth itself, which has positively declared, that no drunkard shall ever enter into his kingdom.

And I call heaven and earth to witness against you this day, that as surely as the Lord rained fire and brimstone, as soon as Lot went out of Sodom, so surely will God cast you into a lake of fire and brimstone, when he shall come to take vengeance on them that know not God, and have not obeyed the gospel of our Lord Jesus Christ.

Behold then I have told you before; remember, that you this day were informed what the end of drunkenness would be. And I summon you, in the name of that God whom I serve, to meet me at the judgment-seat of Christ, that you may acquit both my Master and me; and confess, with your own mouths, that your damnation was of yourselves, and that we are free from the blood of you all.

But, Lord, has no one believed our report? Wilt thou suffer so many words to be spoken in vain, if it be yet in vain? No, methinks I see some pricked to the heart, and ready to cry out, in the language of David to Abigail, "Blessed be the Lord God of Israel, which sent thee this day to speak unto us." For surely, unless he had sent thee, this sin of drunkenness had been our ruin: but now, since we find whither it will lead us, we are resolved to drink no liquor to excess while the world stands, lest we should be tormented in the flames of hell.

But alas! how shall we be delivered from the power of this sin? Can the Ethiopian change his skin, or the leopard his spots? So hard, almost, will it be for you who have been accustomed to be intemperate, to learn to live sober.

But do not despair; for what is impossible with man, is possible with God. Of whom then should you seek for succor, but of him your Lord? Who, though for this sin of drunkenness, he might justly turn away his face from you; yet observe,

First, If you pour out your hearts before him in *daily prayer*, and ask assistance from above, it may be God will endue you with power from on high, and make you more than conquerors through Jesus Christ. Had you kept up communion with him in prayer, you would not so long, by drunkenness, have had communion with devils. But, like the Prodigal, you have desired to be your own masters; you have lived without prayer, depended on your own strength; and now see, alas! on what a broken reed you have leaned. How soon have you made yourselves like the beasts that have no understanding? But turn ye, turn ye from your evil ways. Come to him with the repenting Prodigal saying, "Father we have sinned;" we beseech thee, let not this sin of drunkenness have any longer dominion over us. Lay hold on Christ by faith, and lo! It shall happen to you even as you will. A

Second means I would recommend to you, in order to get the better or drunkenness, is to *avoid evil company*. For it is the evil communication of wicked men, that has drawn many thousands into this sin, and so corrupted their good manners.

But you may say, If I leave my companions, I must expect contempt: for they will certainly despise me for being singular. And thinkest thou, O man, ever to enter in at the strait gate by a true conversion, without being had in derision of them that are round about thee? No; though thou mayst be despised, and not go to heaven, yet thou canst not go to heaven without being despised: "For the friendship of the world is enmity with God." And they that are born after the flesh, will persecute those that are born after the Spirit. Let not, therefore, a servile fear of being despised by a man that shall die, hinder thy turning unto the living God. For what is a little contempt? It is but a vapor which vanisheth away, and cometh not again. Better be derided by a few companions here, than be made ashamed before men and angels hereafter. Better be the song of a few drunkards on earth, than dwell with them, where they will be eternally reproaching and cursing each other in hell. Yet a little while, and they themselves shall praise thy doings, and shall say, We, fools, counted his leaving us to be folly, and his end to be without honor: but how is he numbered among the sons of God, and his lot among the saints!

But I hasten to lay down a

Third means for those who would overcome the sin of

drunkenness, to enter upon a life of *strict self-denial* and mortification: for this kind of sin goeth not forth but by prayer and fasting. It is true, this may seem a difficult task; but then, we must thank ourselves for it; for had we begun sooner, our work would have been the easier. And even now, if you will but strive, the yoke of mortification will grow lighter and lighter every day.

And now, by way of conclusion, I cannot but exhort all persons, high and low, rich and poor, to practice a strict self-denial in eating and drinking. For though "the kingdom of God consists not in meats and drinks," yet an abstemious [moderate, sober, temperate] use of God's good creatures, greatly promotes the spiritual life. And perhaps there are more destroyed by living in a regular sensuality, than even by the very sin I have been warning you of. I know indeed, that many, who are only almost Christians, and who seek, but do not strive to enter into the kingdom of God, urge a text of scripture to justify their indulgence, saying, that "it is not what entereth into the man defileth the man." And so we grant, when taken moderately; but then they should consider, that it is possible, nay, it is proved by daily experience, that a person may eat and drink so much as not to hurt his body, and yet do infinite prejudice to his soul: for self-indulgence lulls the soul into a spiritual slumber, as well as direct intemperance; and though the latter may expose us to more contempt among men, yet the former, if continued in, will as certainly shut us out from the presence of God. St. Paul knew this full well; and therefore, though he was the spiritual father of thousands, and was near upon finishing his course, yet he says, it was his daily practice to "keep his body under, and bring it into subjection, lest after he had preached to others, he himself should be a cast-away," or disapproved of, or do something that might make him an offense or stumbling-block to any of God's children: for of his own, and all other saints final perseverance, he makes no doubt, as is evident from many of his epistles; and the word *ajdovkimo* bears this sense, 2 Cor. 13:5 and sundry other places. But why urge I the apostle's example, to excite you to a strict temperance in eating and drinking? Rather let me exhort you only to put in practice the latter part of the text, to labor to "be filled with the Spirit of God," and then you will no longer search the scriptures to find arguments for self-indulgence; but you will seal sincerely with yourselves, and eat and drink no more at any time, than what is consistent with the strictest precepts of the gospel. O beg of God, that you may see, how you are fallen in Adam, and the necessity of being renewed, ere you can be happy, by the Spirit of Jesus Christ! Let us beseech him to enlighten us to see the treachery of our corrupt hearts, and how pure and holy these bodies ought to be, that they ought to be living temples of the Holy Ghost, and then we shall show ourselves men. And being made temples of the Holy Ghost, by his dwelling in our bodies here, though after death, worms may destroy them, yet shall they be raised by the same Spirit at the general resurrection of the last day, to be fashioned like unto Christ's glorious body hereafter.

Which God of his infinite mercy grant.

53. The Power of Christ's Resurrection

Philippians 3:10—"That I may know Him, and the power of his resurrection."

The apostle, in the verses before the text, had been cautioning the Philippians to "beware of the concision," Judaizing teachers, who endeavored to subvert them from the simplicity of the gospel, by telling them, they still ought to be subject to circumcision, and all the other ordinances of Moses. And that they might not think he spoke out of prejudice, and condemned their tenets, because he himself was a stranger to the Jewish dispensation, he acquaints them, that if any other man thought he had whereof he might trust in the flesh, or seek to be justified by the outward privileges of the Jews, he had more: For he was "circumcised the eighth day; of the stock of Israel (not a proselyte, but a native Israelite); of the tribe of Benjamin (the tribe which adhered to Judah when the others revolted); an Hebrew of the Hebrews (a Jew both on the father's and mother's side); and as touching the law, a Pharisee," the strictest sect amongst all Israel. To show that he was no Gallio in religion, through his great, though misguided zeal, he had persecuted the church of Christ; and "as touching the righteousness of the law (as far as the Pharisees exposition of it went, he was) blameless," and had kept it from his youth. But, when it pleased God, who separated him from his mother's womb, to reveal his Son in him, "What things were gain to me," (he says) those privileges I boasted myself in, and sought to be justified by, "I counted loss for Christ." And that they might not think he repented that he had done so, he tells them, he was now more confirmed than ever in his judgment. For, says he, "yea doubtless (the expression in the original rises with a holy triumph) and I do count all things but loss for the excellency of the knowledge of Christ Jesus my Lord." And that they might not object that he said, and did not, he acquaints them, he had given proofs of the sincerity of these professions, because for the sake of them, he had suffered the loss of all his worldly things, and still was willing to do more; for, "I count them but dung (no more than offals thrown out to dogs) so that I may win, (or have a saving interest in) Christ, and be found in him (as the manslayer in the city of refuge) not having my own righteousness which is of the law, (not depending on having Abraham for my father, or on any works of righteousness which I have done, either to atone or serve as a balance for my evil deeds) but that which is through the faith of Christ, the righteousness which is of God by faith," a righteousness of God's appointing, and which will be imputed to me, if I believe in Christ, "that I may know him, and the power of his resurrection;" that I may have an experimental knowledge of the efficacy of his resurrection, by feeling the influences of his blessed Spirit on my soul. In which words two things are implied.

First, That Jesus Christ did rise from the dead.

Secondly, That it highly concerns us to know the power of his rising again.

Accordingly, in the following discourse I shall endeavor to show,

First, That Christ is risen indeed from the dead; and that it was necessary for him so to do; and,

Secondly, That it highly concerns us to know and experience the power of his resurrection.

First, Christ is indeed risen.

That Jesus should rise from the dead was absolutely necessary;

1. *First*, On his own account. He had often appealed to this as the last and most convincing proof he would give them that the was the Messiah, "There shall no other sign be given you, than the sign of the prophet Jonas." And again, "Destroy this temple of my body, and in three days I will build it up." Which words his enemies remembered, and urged it as an argument, to induce Pilate to grant them a watch, to prevent his being stolen out of the grave. "We know that deceiver said, whilst he was yet alive, after three days I will rise again." So that had he not risen again, they might have justly said, we know that this man was an impostor.

2. *Secondly*, It was necessary on our account. "He rose again" (says the apostle) for our justification;" or that the debt we owed to God for our sins, might be fully satisfied and discharged.

It had pleased the Father (for ever adored be his infinite love and free grace) to wound his only Son for our transgressions, and to arrest and confine him in the prison of the grave, as our surety for the guilt we had contracted by setting at nought his commandments. Now had Christ continued always in the grave, we could have had no more assurance that our sins were satisfied for, than any common debtor can have of his creditor's being satisfied, whilst his surety is kept confined. But he being released from the power of death, we are thereby assured, that with his sacrifice God was well pleased, that our atonement was finished on the cross, and that he hath made a full, perfect, and sufficient sacrifice, oblation, and satisfaction for the sins of the world.

3. *Thirdly*, It was necessary that our Lord Jesus should rise again from the dead, to assure us of the certainty of the resurrection of our own bodies.

The doctrine of the resurrection of the body was entirely exploded and set at nought among the Gentiles, as appears from the Athenians mocking at, and calling St. Paul "a babbler and a setter forth of strange doctrines," when he preached to them Jesus, and the resurrection. And though it was believed by most of the Jews, as is evident from many passages of scripture, yet not by all; the whole sect of the Sadducees denied it. But the resurrection of Jesus Christ put it out of dispute. For as he acted as our representative, if he our head be risen, then must we also, who are his members, rise with him. And as in the first Adam we all died, even so in him our second Adam we must all, in this sense, be made alive.

As it was necessary, upon these accounts, that our blessed Lord should rise from the dead; so it is plain beyond contradiction, that he did. Never was any matter of fact better attested; never were more precautions made use of to prevent a cheat. He was buried in a sepulcher, hewn out of a rock, so that it could not be said that any digged under, and conveyed him away. It was a sepulcher also wherein never man before was laid; so that if any body did rise from thence, it must be the body of Jesus of Nazareth. Besides, the sepulcher was sealed; a great stone rolled over the mouth of it; and a band of soldiers (consisting not of friends, but of his professed enemies) was set to guard it. And as for his disciples coming by night and stealing him away, it was altogether improbable: For it was not long since, that they had all forsaken him, and they were the most backward in believing his resurrection. And supposing it was true, that they came whilst the soldiers slept; yet the soldiers must be cast into a deep sleep indeed, that the rolling away so great a stone did not awake some of them.

And our blessed Lord's afterwards appearing at sundry

times, and in divers manners, to his disciples, as when they were assembled together, when they were walking to Emmaus, when they were fishing: nay, and condescending to show them his hands and feet, and his appearing to above five hundred brethren at once, put the truth of his resurrection out of all dispute.

Indeed, there is one objection that may be made against what has been said, that the books wherein these facts are recorded were written by his disciples.

And who more proper persons than those who were eye-witnesses of what they related, and eat and drank with him after his resurrection? "But they were illiterate and ignorant men." Yet as good witnesses of a plain matter of fact, as the most learned masters in Israel. Nay, this rendered them more proper witnesses. For being plain men, they were therefore less to be suspected of telling or making a lie, particularly, since they laid down their lives for a testimony of the truth of it. We read indeed of Jacob's telling a lie, though he was a plain man, in order to get his father's blessing. But it was never heard since the world began, that any man, much less a whole set of men, died martyrs, for the sake of an untruth, when they themselves were to reap no advantage from it.

No, this single circumstance proves them to Israelites indeed, in whom was no guile. And the wonderful success God gave to their ministry afterwards, when three thousand were converted by one sermon; and twelve poor fishermen, in a very short time enabled to be more than conquerors over all the opposition men or devils could make, was as plain a demonstration, that Christ was risen, according to their gospel, as that a divine power, at the sound of a few ram's horns, causes the walls of Jericho to fall down.

But what need we any farther witnesses? Believe you the resurrection of our blessed Lord? I know that you believe it, as your gathering together on this first day of the week in the courts of the Lord's house abundantly testifies.

What concerns us most to be assured of, and which is the

Second thin I was to speak to, is, Whether we have experimentally known the power of his resurrection; that is, Whether or not we have received the Holy Ghost, and by his powerful operations on our hearts have been raised from the death of sin, to a life of righteousness and true holiness.

It was this, the great apostle was chiefly desirous to know. The resurrection of Christ's body he was satisfied would avail him nothing, unless he experienced the power of it in raising his dead soul.

For another, and that a chief end of our blessed Lord's rising from the dead, was to enter heaven as our representative, and to send down the Holy Ghost to apply that redemption he had finished on the cross, to our hearts, by working an entire change in them.

Without this, Christ would have died in vain. For it would have done us no service to have had his outward righteousness imputed to us, unless we had an inward inherent righteousness wrought in us. Because, being altogether conceived and born in sin, and consequently unfit to hold communion with an infinitely pure and holy God, we cannot possibly be made meet to see or enjoy him, till a thorough renovation has passed upon our hearts.

Without this, we leave out the Holy Ghost in the great work of our redemption. But as we were made by the joint concurrence and consultation of the blessed trinity; and as we were baptized in their name, so must all of them concur in our salvation: As the Father made, and the Son redeemed, so must the Holy Ghost sanctify and seal us, or otherwise we have believed in vain.

This then is what the apostle means by the "Power of Christ's resurrection," and this is what we are as much concerned experimentally to know, as that He rose at all.

Without this, though we may be moralists, though we may be civilized, good-natured people, yet we are no Christians. For he is not a true Christian, who is only one outwardly; nor have we therefore a right, because we daily profess to believe that Christ rose again the third day from the dead. But he is a true Christian who is one inwardly; and then only can we be stiled true believers, when we not only profess to believe, but have felt the power of our blessed Lord's rising from the dead, by being quickened and raised by his Spirit, when dead in trespasses and sins, to a thorough newness both of heart and life.

The devils themselves cannot but believe the doctrine of the resurrection, and tremble; but yet they continue devils, because the benefits of this resurrection have not been applied to them, nor have they received a renovating power from it, to change and put off their diabolical nature. And so, unless we not only profess to know, but also feel that Christ is risen indeed, by being born again from above, we shall be as far from the kingdom of God as they: our faith will be as ineffectual as the faith of devils.

Nothing has done more harm to the Christian world, nothing has rendered the cross of Christ of less effect, than a vain supposition, that religion is something without us. Whereas we should consider, that every thing that

Christ did outwardly, must be done over again in our souls; or otherwise, the believing there was such a divine person once on earth, who triumphed over hell and the grave, will profit us no more, than believing there was once such a person as Alexander, who conquered the world.

As Christ was born of the Virgin's womb, so must he be spiritually formed in our hearts. As he died for sin, so must we die to sin. And as he rose again from the dead, so must we also rise to a divine life.

None but those who have followed him in this regeneration, or new-birth, shall sit on thrones as approvers of his sentence, when he shall come in terrible majesty to judge the twelve tribes of Israel.

It is true, as for the outward work of our redemption, it was a transient act, and was certainly finished on the cross, but the application of that redemption to our hearts, is a work that will continue always, even unto the end of the world.

So long as there is an elect man breathing on the earth, who is naturally engendered of the offspring of the first Adam, so long must the quickening spirit, which was purchased by the resurrection of the second Adam, that Lord from heaven, be breathing upon his soul.

For though we may exist by Christ, yet we cannot be said to exist in him, till we are united to him by one spirit, and enter into a new state of things, as certainly as he entered into a new state of things, after that he rose from the dead.

We may throng and crowd about Christ, and call him "Lord, Lord," when we come to worship before his footstool; but we have not effectually touched him, till by a lively faith in his resurrection, we perceive a divine virtue coming out of him, to renew and purify our souls.

How greatly then do they err who rest in a bare historical faith of our Savior's resurrection, and look only for external proofs to evidence it? Whereas were we the most learned disputers of this world, and could speak of the certainty of this fact with the tongue of men and angels, yet without this inward testimony of it in our hearts, though we might convince others, yet we should never be saved by it ourselves.

For we are but dead men, we are like so many carcasses wrapt up in grave clothes, till that same Jesus who called Lazarus from his tomb, and at whose own resurrection many that slept arose, doth raise us also by his quickening Spirit from our natural death, in which we have so long lain, to a holy and heavenly life.

We might think ourselves happy, if we had seen the Holy Jesus after He was risen from the dead, and our hands had handled that Lord of life. But more happy are they who have not seen him, and yet having felt the power of his resurrection, therefore believe in him. For many saw our divine master, who were not saved by him; but whosoever has thus felt the power of his resurrection, has the earnest of his inheritance in his heart, he has passed from death to life, and shall never fall into final condemnation.

I am very sensible that this is foolishness to the natural man, as were many such like truths to our Lord's own disciples, when only weak in faith, before he rose again. But when these natural men, like them, have fully felt the power of his resurrection, they will then own that this doctrine is from God, and say with the Samaritans, "Now we believe not because of thy saying," for we ourselves have experienced it in our hearts.

And O that all unbelievers, all letter-learned masters of Israel, who now look upon the doctrine of the power of Christ's resurrection, or our new birth, as an idle tale, and condemn the preachers of it as enthusiasts and madmen, did but thus feel the power of it in their souls, they would no longer ask, how this thing could be? But they would be convinced of it, as much as Thomas was, when he saw the Lord's Christ; and like him, when Jesus bud him reach out his hands and thrust them into his side, in a holy confession they would cry out, "My Lord and my God!"

But how shall an unbeliever, how shall the formal Christian come thus to "know Christ, and the power of his resurrection?" God, who cannot lie, has told us, "I am the resurrection and the life, whosoever liveth and believeth in me, though he were dead, yet shall he live." Again, says the apostle, "By faith we are saved, and that not of ourselves, it is the gift of God."

This, this is the way, walk in it. Believe, and you shall live in Christ, and Christ in you; you shall be one with Christ, and Christ one with you. But without this, your outward goodness and professions will avail you nothing.

But then, by this faith we are not to understand a dead speculative faith, a faith in the head; but a living principle wrought in the heart by the powerful operations of the Holy Ghost, a faith that will enable us to overcome the world, and forsake all the affection for Jesus Christ. For thus speaks our blessed Master, "Unless a man forsake all that he hath, he cannot be my disciple."

And so the apostle, in the words immediately following the text, says, "being made conformable to his death;" thereby implying, that we cannot know the power of

Christ's resurrection, unless we are made conformable to him in his death.

If we can reconcile light and darkness, heaven and hell, then we may hope to know the power of Christ's resurrection without dying to ourselves and the world. But till we can do this, we might as well expect that Christ will have concord with Belial.

For there is such a contrariety between the spirit of this world, and the Spirit of Jesus Christ, that he who will be at friendship with the one, must be at enmity with the other: "We cannot serve God and mammon."

This may, indeed, seem a hard saying; and many, with the young man in the gospel, may be tempted to go away sorrowful. But wherefore should this offend them? For what is all that is in the world, the lust of the eye, the lust of the flesh, and the pride of life, but vanity and vexation of spirit?

God is love; and therefore, could our own wills, or the world, have made us happy, he never would have sent his own dear Son Jesus Christ to die and rise again, to deliver us from the power of them. But because they only torment, and cannot satisfy, therefore God bids us to renounce them.

Had any one persuaded profane Esau not to lose so glorious a privilege, merely for the sake of gratifying a present corrupt inclination, when he saw him about to sell his birth-right for a little red pottage, would not one think that man to have been Esau's friend? And just thus stands the case between God and us. By the death and resurrection of Jesus Christ, we are new-born to an heavenly inheritance amongst all them which are sanctified; but our own corrupt wills, would tempt us to sell this glorious birth-right for the vanities of the world, which, like Esau's red pottage, may please us for a while, but will soon be taken away from us. God knows this, and therefore rather bids us renounce them for a reason, than for the short enjoyment of them lost the privilege of that glorious birth-right, to which, by knowing the power of the resurrection of Jesus Christ, we are entitled.

O the depth of the riches and excellency of Christianity! Well might the great St. Paul count all things but dung and dross for the excellency of the knowledge of it. Well might he desire so ardently to know Jesus, and the power of his resurrection. For even on this side eternity it raises us above the world, and makes us to sit in heavenly places in Christ Jesus.

Well might that glorious company of worthies, recorded in the Holy scriptures, supported with a deep sense of their heavenly calling, despise the pleasures and profits of this life, and wander about in sheep-skins, and goat-skins, in dens and caves of the earth, being destitute, afflicted, tormented.

And O that we were all like minded! That we felt the power of Christ's resurrection as they did! How should we then "count all things as dung and dross for the excellency of the knowledge of Christ Jesus our Lord!" How should we then recover our primitive dignity, trample the earth under our feet, and with our souls be continually gasping after God?

And what hinders but we may be thus minded? Is Jesus Christ, our great High Priest, altered from what he was? No, "he is the same yesterday, today, and for ever." And though he is exalted to the right hand of God, yet he is not ashamed to call us brethren. The power of his resurrection is as great now as formerly, and the Holy Spirit, which was assured to us by his resurrection, as ready and able to quicken us who are dead in trespasses and sins, as any saint that ever lived. Let us but cry, and that instantly, to Him that is mighty and able to save; let us, in sincerity and truth, without secretly keeping back the least part, renounce ourselves and the world; then we shall be Christians indeed. And though the world may cast us out, and separate from our company, yet Jesus Christ will walk with, and abide in us. And at the general resurrection of the last day, when the voice of the archangel and trump of God shall bid the sea and the graves to give up their dead, and all nations shall appear before him, then will he confess us before his Father and the holy angels, and we shall receive that invitation which he shall then pronounce to all who love and fear him, "Come, ye blessed children of my Father, inherit the kingdom prepared for you from the beginning of the world.

Grant this, O Father, for thy dear Son's sake, Jesus Christ our Lord; to whom, with Thee and the Holy Ghost.

54. Intercession Every Christian's Duty

If we inquire, why there is so little love to be found amongst Christians, why the very characteristic, by which every one should know that we are disciples of the holy Jesus, is almost banished out of the Christian world, we shall find it, in a great measure, owing to a neglect or superficial performance of that excellent part of prayer, *intercession*, or imploring the divine grace and mercy in behalf of others.

Some forget this duty of praying for others, because they seldom remember to pray for themselves: and even those who are constant in praying to their Father who is in heaven, are often so selfish in their addresses to the throne of grace, that they do not enlarge their petitions for the welfare of their fellow Christians as they ought; and thereby fall short of attaining that Christian charity, that unfeigned love to their brethren, which their sacred profession obliges them to aspire after, and without which, though they should bestow all their goods to feed the poor, and even give their bodies to be burned, yet it would profit them nothing.

Since these things are so, I shall from the words of the text (though originally intended to be more confined) endeavor, to show,

I. *First*, That it is every Christian's duty to pray for others as well as for himself.

II. *Secondly*, Show, whom we ought to pray for, and in what manner we should do it. And,

III. *Thirdly*, I shall offer some motives to excite all Christians to abound in this great duty of intercession.

I. *First*, I shall endeavor to show, That it is every Christian's duty to pray for others, as well as for himself.

Now *Prayer* is a duty founded on natural religion; the very heathens never neglected it, though many Christian heathens amongst us do: and it is so essential to Christianity, that you might as reasonably expect to find a living man without breath, as a true Christian without the spirit of prayer and supplication. Thus, no sooner was St. Paul converted, but "behold he prayeth," saith the Lord Almighty. And thus will it be with every child of God, as soon as he becomes such: prayer being truly called, The natural cry of the new-born soul.

For in the heart of every true believer there is a heavenly tendency, a divine attraction, which as sensibly draws him to converse with God, as the lodestone attracts the needle.

A deep sense of their own weakness, and of Christ's fullness; a strong conviction of their natural corruption, and of the necessity of renewing grace; will not let them rest from crying day and night to their Almighty Redeemer, that the divine image, which they lost in Adam, may through his all-powerful mediation, and the sanctifying operation of his blessed spirit, be begun, carried on, and fully perfected both in their souls and bodies.

Thus earnest, thus importunate, are all sincere Christians in praying for themselves: but then, not having so lively, lasting, and deep a sense of the wants of their Christian brethren, they are for the most part too remiss and defective in their prayers for them. Whereas, was the love of God shed abroad in our hearts, and did we love our neighbor in that manner, in which the Son of God our savior loved us, and according to his command and example, we could not but be as importunate for their spiritual and temporal welfare, as for our own; and as earnestly desire and endeavor that others should share in the benefits of the death and passion of Jesus Christ, as we ourselves.

Let not any one think, that this is an uncommon degree of charity; an high pitch of perfection, to which not every one can attain: for, if we are all commanded to "love our neighbor (that is every man) even as ourselves," nay to "lay down our lives for the brethren;" then, it is the duty of all to pray for their neighbors as much as for themselves, and by all possible acts and expressions of love and affection towards them, at all times, to show their readiness even to lay down their lives for them, if ever it should please God to call them to it.

Our blessed Savior, as "he hath set us an example, that we should follow his steps" in every thing else, so hath he more especially in this: for in that divine, that perfect and inimitable prayer (recorded in the 17th of St. John) which he put up just before his passion, we find but few petitions for his own, though many for his disciples welfare: and in that perfect form which he has been pleased to prescribe us, we are taught to say, not *my*, but "*our* Father," thereby to put us in mind, that, whenever we approach the throne of grace, we ought to pray not for ourselves alone, but for all our brethren in Christ.

Intercession then is certainly a duty incumbent upon all Christians.

II. Whom we are to intercede for, and how this duty is to be performed, comes next to be considered.

1. And first, our intercession must be *Universal*. "I will, (says the apostle) that prayers, supplications and intercessions be made for all men." For as God's mercy is over all his works, as Jesus Christ died to redeem a people out of all nations and languages; so we should pray, that "all men may come to the knowledge of the truth, and be saved." Many precious promises are made in holy writ, that the gospel shall be published through the whole world, that "the earth shall be covered with the knowledge of the Lord, as the waters cover the sea:" and therefore it is our duty not to confine our petitions to our own nation, but to pray that all those nations, who now sit in darkness and in the shadow of death, may have the glorious gospel shine out upon them, as well as upon us. But you need not that any man should teach you this, since ye yourselves are taught of God, and of Jesus Christ himself, to

pray, that his kingdom may come; part of the meaning of which petition is, that "God's ways may be known upon earth, and his saving health among all nations."

2. Next to the praying for all men, we should, according to St. Paul's rule, pray for *Kings*; particularly for our present sovereign King George, and all that are put in authority under him: that we may lead quiet lives, in all godliness and honesty. For, if we consider how heavy the burden of government is, and how much the welfare of any people depends on the zeal and godly conversation of those that have the rule over them: if we set before us the many dangers and difficulties, to which governors by their station are exposed, and the continual temptations they be under to luxury and self-indulgence; we shall not only pity, but pray for them: that he who preserved Esther, David, and Josiah, "unspotted from the world," amidst the grandeur of a court, and gave success to their designs, would also preserve them holy and unblameable, and prosper all the works of their hands upon them. But

3. *Thirdly*, you ought, in a more especial manner, to pray for those, whom "the Holy Ghost hath made *Overseers* over you." This is what St. Paul begs, again and again, of the churches to whom he writes: Says he in the text, "Brethren, pray for us;" and again, in his epistle to the Ephesians, "praying always, with all manner of supplication; and for me also, that I may open my mouth boldly, to declare the mystery of the gospel." And in another place, to express his earnestness in this request, and the great importance of their prayers for him, he bids the church "strive, (or, as the original word signifies, be in a agony) together with him in their prayers." And surely, if the great St. Paul, that chosen vessel, that favorite of heaven, needed the most importunate prayers of his Christian converts; much more do the ordinary ministers of the gospel stand in need of the intercession of their respective flocks.

And I cannot but in a more especial manner insist upon this branch of your duty, because it is a matter of such importance: for, no doubt, much good is frequently withheld from many, by reason of their neglecting to pray for their ministers, and which they would have received, had they prayed for them as they ought. Not to mention, that people often complain of the want of diligent and faithful pastors. But how do they deserve good pastors, who will not earnestly pray to God for such? If we will not pray to the Lord of the harvest, can it be expected he will send forth laborers into his harvest?

Besides, what ingratitude is it, not to pray for your ministers! For shall they watch and labor in the word and doctrine for you, and your salvation, and shall not you pray for them in return? If any bestow favors on your bodies, you think it right, meet, and your bounden duty, to pray for them; and shall not they be remembered in your prayers, who daily feed and nourish your souls? Add to all this, that praying for your ministers, will be a manifest proof of your believing, that though Paul plant, and Apollos water, yet it is God alone who giveth the increase. And you will also find it the best means you can use, to promote your own welfare; because God, in answer to your prayers, may impart a double portion of his Holy Spirit to them, whereby they will be qualified to deal out to you larger measures of knowledge in spiritual things, and be enabled more skillfully to divide the word of truth.

Would men but constantly observe this direction, and when their ministers are praying in their name to God, humbly beseech him to perform all their petitions: or, when they are speaking in God's name to them, pray that the Holy Ghost may fall on all them that hear the word; we should find a more visible good effect of their doctrine, and a greater mutual love between ministers and their people. For ministers hands would then be hold up by the people's intercessions, and the people will never dare to villify or traduce those who are the constant subjects of their prayers.

4. Next to our ministers, *Our Friends* claim a place in our intercessions; but then we should not content ourselves with praying in general terms for them, but suit our prayers to their particular circumstances. When Miriam was afflicted with a leprosy from God, Moses cried and said, "Lord, heal her." And when the nobleman came to apply to Jesus Christ, in behalf of his child, he said, "Lord, my little daughter lieth at the point of death, I pray thee to come and heal her." In like manner, when our friends are under any afflicting circumstances, we should endeavor to pray for them, with a particular regard to those circumstances. For instance, is a friend sick? We should pray, that if it be God's good pleasure, it may not be unto death; but is otherwise, that he would give him grace so to take his visitation, that, after this painful life ended, he may dwell with him in life everlasting. Is a friend in doubt in an important matter? We should lay his case before God, as Moses did that of the daughters of Zelophehad, and pray, that God's Holy Spirit may lead him into all truth, and give all seasonable direction. Is he in want? We should pray, that his

faith may never fail, and that in God's due time he may be relieved. And in all other cases, we should not pray for our friends only in generals, but suit our petitions to their particular sufferings and afflictions; for otherwise, we may never ask perhaps for the things our friends most want.

It must be confessed, that such a procedure will oblige some often to break from the forms they use; but if we accustom ourselves to it, and have a deep sense of what we ask for, the most illiterate will want proper words to express themselves.

We have many noble instances in holy scripture of the success of this kind of particular intercession; but none more remarkable than that of Abraham's servant, in the book of Genesis, who being sent to seek a wife for his son Isaac, prayed in a most particular manner in his behalf. And the sequel of the story informs us, how remarkably his prayer as answered. And did Christians now pray for their friends in the same particular manner, and with the same faith as Abraham's servant did for his master; they would, no doubt, in many instances, receive as visible answers, and have as much reason to bless God for them, as he had. But

5. As we ought thus to intercede for our friends, so in like manner must we also pray for *Our Enemies*. "Bless them that curse you, (says Jesus Christ) and pray for them that despitefully use you, and persecute you." Which commands he enforced in the strongest manner by his own example: in the very agonies and pangs of death, he prayed even for his murderers, "Father, forgive them, for they know not what they do!" This, it must needs be confessed, is a difficult duty, yet not impracticable, to those who have renounced the things of this present life, (from an inordinate love of which all enmities arise) and who knowing the terrible woes denounced against those who offend Christ's little ones, can, out of real pity, and a sense of their danger, pray for those by whom such offenses come.

6. Lastly, and to conclude this head, we should intercede for all that are any ways *afflicted* in mind, body, or estate; for all who desire, and stand in need of our prayers, and for all who do not pray for themselves.

And Oh! That all who hear me, would set apart some time every day for the due performance of this most necessary duty! In order to which,

I shall now proceed,

III. To show the advantages, and offer some considerations to excite you to the practice of daily intercession. And

1. *First*, It will fill your hearts with love one to another. He that every day heartily intercedes at the throne of grace for all mankind, cannot but in a short time be filled with love and charity to all: and the frequent exercise of his love in this manner, will insensibly enlarge his heart, and make him partaker of that exceeding abundance of it which is in Christ Jesus our Lord! Envy, malice, revenge, and such like hellish tempers, can never long harbor in a gracious intercessor's breast; but he will be filled with joy, peace, meekness, long-suffering, and all other graces of the Holy Spirit. By frequently laying his neighbor's wants before God, he will be touched with a fellow-feeling of them; he will rejoice with those that do rejoice, and weep with those that weep. Every blessing bestowed on others, instead of exciting envy in him, will be looked on as an answer to his particular intercession, and fill his soul with joy unspeakable and full of glory.

Abound therefore in acts of general and particular intercessions; and when you hear of your neighbor's faults, instead of relating them to, and exposing them before others, lay them in secret before God, and beg of him to correct and amend them. When you hear of a notorious sinner, instead of thinking you do well to be angry, beg of Jesus Christ to convert, and make him a monument of his free grace; you cannot imagine what a blessed alteration this practice will make in your heart, and how much you will increase day by day in the spirit of love and meekness towards all mankind!

But farther, to excite you to the constant practice of this duty of intercession, consider the many instances in holy scripture, of the power and efficacy of it. Great and excellent things are there recorded as the effects of this divine employ. It has stopped plagues, it has opened and shut heaven; and has frequently turned away God's fury from his people. How was Abimelech's house freed from the disease God sent amongst them, at the intercession of Abraham! When "Phineas stood up and prayed," how soon did the plague cease! When Daniel humbled and afflicted his soul, and interceded for the Lord's inheritance, how quickly was an angel dispatched to tell him, "his prayer was heard!" And, to mention but one instance more, how does God own himself as it were overcome with the importunity of Moses, when he was interceding for his idolatrous people, "Let me alone," says God!

This sufficiently shows, I could almost say, the omnipotency of intercession, and how we may, like Jacob, wrestle with God, and by an holy violence prevail both for ourselves and others. And no doubt it is owing to the secret and prevailing intercessions of the few righteous souls who still remain among us, that God has yet spared this miserably sinful nation: for were there not some such faithful ones, like Moses, left to stand in the gap, we should soon be destroyed, even as was Sodom, and reduced to ashes like unto Gomorrah.

But, to stir you up yet farther to this exercise of intercession, consider, that in all probability, it is the frequent employment even of the glorified saints: for though they are delivered from the burden of the flesh, and restored to the glorious liberty of the sons of God, yet as their happiness cannot be perfectly consummated till the resurrection of the last day, when all their brethren will be glorified with them, we cannot but think they are often importunate in beseeching our heavenly Father, shortly to accomplish the number of his elect, and to hasten his kingdom. And shall now we, who are on earth, be often exercised in this divine employ with the glorious company of the spirits of just men made perfect? Since our happiness is so much to consist in the communion of saints in the church triumphant above, shall we not frequently intercede for the church militant here below; and earnestly beg, that we may all be one, even as the Holy Jesus and his Father are one, that we may also be made perfect in one?

To provoke you to this great work and labor of love, remember, that it is the never ceasing employment of the holy and highly exalted Jesus himself, who sits at the right hand of God, to hear all our prayers, and to make continual intercession for us! So that he who is constantly employed in interceding for others, is doing that on earth, which the eternal Son of God is always doing in heaven.

Imagine therefore, when you are lifting up holy hands in prayer for one another, that you see the heavens opened, and the Son of God in all his glory, as the great high-priest of your salvation, pleading for you the all-sufficient merit of his sacrifice before the throne of his heavenly Father! Join then your intercessions with his, and beseech him, that they may, through him, come up as incense, and be received as a sweet-smelling favor, acceptable in the sight of God! This imagination will strengthen your faith, excite a holy earnestness in your prayers, and make you wrestle with God, as Jacob did, when he saw him face to face, and his life was preserved; as Abraham, when he pleaded for Sodom; and as Jesus Christ himself, when he prayed, being in an agony, so much the more earnestly the night before his bitter passion.

And now, brethren, what shall I say more, since you are taught of Jesus Christ himself, to abound in love, and in this good work of praying one for another. Though ever so mean, though as poor as Lazarus, you will then become benefactors to all mankind; thousands, and twenty times ten thousands, will then be blessed for your sakes! And after you have employed a few years in this divine exercise here, you will be translated to that happy place, where you have so often wished others might be advanced; and be exalted to sit at the right hand of our All-powerful, All-prevailing Intercessor, in the kingdom of his heavenly Father hereafter.

However, I cannot but in an especial manner press this upon you now, because all ye, amongst whom I have now been preaching, in all probability will see me no more: for I am now going (I trust under the conduct of God's most Holy Spirit) from you, knowing not what shall befall me: I need therefore your most importunate intercessions, that nothing may move me from my duty, and that I may not "count even my life dear unto myself, so that I may finish my course with joy, and the ministry I have received of the Lord Jesus, to testify the gospel of the grace of God!"

Whilst I have been here, to the best of my knowledge, I have not failed to declare unto you the whole will of God: and though my preaching may have been a savor of death unto death to some; yet I trust it has been also a savor of life unto life to others; and therefore I earnestly hope that those will not fail to remember me in their prayers. As for my own part, the many unmerited kindnesses I have received from you, will not suffer me to forget you: out of the deep, therefore, I trust shall my cry come unto God; and whilst the winds and storms are blowing over me, unto the Lord will I make my supplication for you. For it is but a little while, and "we must all appear before the judgment seat of Christ;" where I must give a strict account of the doctrine I have preached, and you of your improvement under it. And O that I may never be called out as a swift witness, against any of those, for whose salvation I have sincerely, though too faintly, longed and labored!

It is true, I have been censured by some as acting out of sinister and selfish views; "but it is a small matter with me to be judged by man's judgment; I hope my eye is single; but I beseech you, brethren, by the mercies of God in Christ Jesus, pray that it may be more so! And that I may increase with the increase of grace in the knowledge and love of God through Jesus Christ our Lord.

And now, brethren, what shall I say more? I could wish to continue my discourse much longer; for I can never fully express the desire of my soul towards you! Finally, therefore, brethren, "whatsoever things are holy, whatsoever things are pure, whatsoever things are honest, whatsoever things are of good report: if there be any consolation in Christ, if any fellowship of the spirit," if any hopes of our appearing to the comfort of each other at the awful tribunal of Jesus Christ, "think of the things that you have heard," and of those which your pastors have declared, and will yet declare unto you; and continue under their ministry to "work out your own salvation with fear and trembling:" so that whether I should never see you any more, or whether it shall please God to bring me back again at any time, I may always have the satisfaction of knowing that your conversation is such "as becometh the gospel of Christ."

I almost persuade myself, that I could willingly suffer all things, so that it might any ways promote the salvation of your precious and immortal souls; and I beseech you, as my last request, "obey them that have the rule over you in the Lord;" and be always ready to attend on their ministry, as it is your bounden duty. Think not that I desire to have myself exalted at the expense of another's character; but rather think this, not to have any man's person too much in admiration; but esteem all your ministers highly in love, as they justly deserve for their work's sake.

And now, "brethren, I commend you to god, and to the word of his grace, which is able to build you up, and give you an inheritance amongst all them that are sanctified." May God reward you for all your works of faith, and labors of love, and make you to abound more and more in every good word and work towards all men. May he truly convert all that have been convinced, and awaken all that are dead in trespasses and sins! May he confirm all that are wavering! And may you all go on from one degree of grace unto another, till you arrive unto the measure of the stature of the fullness of Christ; and thereby be made meet to stand before that God, "in whose presence is the fullness of joy, and at whose right-hand there are pleasures for evermore!" Amen! Amen!

55. Persecution Every Christian's Lot

When our Lord was pleased to take upon himself the form of a servant, and to go about preaching the kingdom of God; he took all opportunities in public, and more especially in private, to caution his disciples against seeking great things for themselves, and also to forewarn them of the many distresses, afflictions and persecutions, which they must expect to endure for his name's sake. The great apostle Paul therefore, the author of this epistle, in this, as in all other things, following the steps of his blessed Master, takes particular care, among other apostolical admonitions, to warn young Timothy of the difficulties he must expect to meet with in the course of his ministry: "This know also, that in the last days perilous times shall come. For men shall be lovers of their ownselves, covetous, proud, blasphemers, disobedient to parents, unthankful, unholy, without natural affection, truce-breakers, false accusers, incontinent, fierce, despisers of those that are good, traitors, heady, highminded, lovers of pleasure more than lovers of God; having a form of godliness, but denying the power thereof: from such turn away. For of this sort are they who creep into houses, and lead captive silly women laden with sins, led away with divers lusts, ever learning, and never able to come to the knowledge of the truth. Now, as Jannes and Jambres (two of the Egyptian magicians) withstood Moses (by working sham miracles) so do they also resist the truth; and (notwithstanding they keep up the form of religion) are men of corrupt minds, reprobate concerning the faith." But, in order to keep him from sinking under their opposition, he tells him, that though God, for wise ends, permitted these false teachers, as he did the magicians, to oppose for some time, yet they should now proceed no farther: "For their folly (says he) shall be made manifest unto all men, as theirs (the Magicians) also was," when they could not stand before Moses because of the boil; for the boil was upon the Magicians, as well as upon all the Egyptians. And then, to encourage Timothy yet the more, he propounds to him his own example; "But thou hast fully known my doctrine, manner of life, purpose, faith, long-suffering, charity, patience, persecutions, afflictions, which came unto me at Antioch, at Iconium, at Lystra; what persecutions I endured; but out of them all the Lord delivered me." And then, lest Timothy might think that this was only the particular case of Paul, says he, in the words of the text, "Yea, and all that will live godly in Christ Jesus, shall suffer persecution."

The words, without considering them as they stand in relation to the context, contain an important truth, that persecution is the common lot of every godly man. This is a hard saying, How few can bear it? I trust God, in the following discourse, will enable me to make it good, by showing,

I. What it is to live godly in Christ Jesus.

II. The different kinds of persecution to which they, who live godly, are exposed.

III. Why it is, that godly men must expect to suffer persecution.

Lastly, We shall apply the whole.

1. *First*, Let us consider what it is to live godly in Christ Jesus. This supposes, that we are made the righteousness of God in Christ, that we are born again, and are one with Christ by a living faith, and a vital union, even as Jesus Christ and the Father are One. Unless we are thus converted, and transformed by the renewing of our minds, we cannot properly be said to be in Christ, much less to live godly in him. To be in Christ merely by baptism, and an outward profession, is not to be in Him in the strict sense of the word: no; "They that are in Christ, are new creatures; old things are passed away, and all things are become new" in their hearts. Their life is hid with Christ in God; their souls daily feed on the invisible realities of another world. To "live godly in Christ," is to make the divine will, and not our own, the sole principle of all our thoughts, words, and actions; so that, "whether we eat or drink, or whatsoever we do, we do all to the glory of God." Those who live godly in Christ, may not so much be said to live, as Christ to live in them: He is their Alpha and Omega, their first and last, their beginning and end. They are led by his Spirit, as a child is led by the hand of its father; and are willing to follow the Lamb withersoever he leads them. They hear, know, and obey his voice. Their affections are set on things above; their hopes are full of immortality; their citizenship is in heaven. Being born again of God, they habitually live to, and daily walk with, God. They are pure in heart; and, from a principle of faith in Christ, are holy in all manner of conversation and godliness.

This is to "live godly in Christ Jesus:" and hence we may easily learn, why so few suffer persecution? Because, so few live godly in Christ Jesus. You may live formally in Christ, you may attend on outward duties; you may live morally in Christ, you may (as they term it) do no one any harm, and avoid persecution: but they "that will live godly in Christ Jesus, shall suffer persecution."

2. *Secondly*, What is the meaning of the word Persecution, and how many kinds there are of it, I come now to consider.

The word Persecution, is derived from a Greek word signifying to pursue, and generally implies pursuing a person for the sake of his goodness, or God's good-will to him. The

First kind of it, is that of the *Heart*. We have an early example of this in the wicked one Cain, who, because the Lord had respect to Abel and his offering, and not to him and his offering, was very wroth, his countenance fell, and at length he cruelly slew his envied brother. Thus the Pharisees hated and persecuted our Lord long before they laid hold on him: and our Lord mentions being inwardly hated of men, as one kind of Persecution his disciples were to undergo. This heart-enmity (if I may so term it) is the root of all other kinds of Persecution, and is, in some degree or other, to be found in the soul of every unregenerated man; and numbers are guilty of this persecution, who never have it in their power to persecute any other way. Nay, numbers would actually put in practice all other degrees of persecution, was not the name of Persecution become odious amongst mankind, and did they not hereby run the hazard of losing their reputation. Alas! how many at the great day, whom we know not now, will be convicted and condemned, that all their life harbored a secret evil-will against Zion! They may now screen it before men; but God seeth the enmity of their hearts, and will judge them as Persecutors at the great and terrible day of judgment.

Second degree of Persecution is that of the tongue; "out of the abundance of the heart, the mouth speaketh." Many, I suppose, think it no harm to shoot out arrows, even bitter words, against the disciples of the Lord: they scatter their firebrands, arrows and death, saying, "Are we not in sport?" But, however they may esteem it, in God's account evil-speaking is a high degree of Persecution. Thus Ishmael's mocking Isaac, is termed persecuting him. "Blessed are ye (says out Lord) when men shall revile you and persecute you, and shall say all manner of evil against you falsely for my name's sake." From whence we may gather, that reviling, and speaking all manner of evil for Christ's sake, is a high degree of persecution. For "a good name, says the wise man) is better than precious ointment," and, to many, is dearer than life itself. It is a great breach of the sixth commandment, to slander any one; but to speak evil of and slander the disciples of Christ, merely because they are his disciples, must be highly provoking in the sight of God; and such who are guilty of it (without repentance) will find that Jesus Christ will call them to an account, and punish them for all their ungodly and hard speeches in a lake of fire and brimstone. This shall be their portion to drink. The

Third and *Last* kind of Persecution, is that which expresses itself in *Actions*: as when wicked men separate the children of God from their company; "Blessed are ye, (says our Lord) when they shall separate you from their company:" or expose them to church-censures. "They shall put you out of their synagogues;" threatening and prohibiting them from making an open profession of his religion or worship; or interdicting ministers for preaching his word, as the high-priests threatened the apostles, and "forbad them any more to speak in the name of Jesus;" and Paul breathed out threatenings and slaughters against the disciples of the Lord: or when they call them into courts; "You shall be called before governors," says our Lord: or when they fine, imprison, or punish them, by confiscation of goods, cruel scourging, and, lastly, death itself.

It would be impossible to enumerate in what various shapes persecution has appeared. It is a many-headed monster, cruel as the grave, insatiable as hell; and, what is worse, it generally appears under the cloak of religion. But, cruel, insatiable, and horrid as it is, they that live godly in Christ Jesus, must expect to suffer and encounter with it in all its forms.

This is what we are to make good under our next general head.

3. *Thirdly*, Why is it that godly men must expect to suffer persecution? And,

First, This appears from the whole tenor of our Lord's doctrine. We will begin with his divine sermon on the mount. "Blessed are they who are persecuted for righteousness sake; for theirs is the kingdom of heaven." So that, if our Lord spoke truth, we are not so blessed as to have an interest in the kingdom of heaven, unless we are or have been persecuted for righteousness sake. Nay, our Lord (it is remarkable) employs three verses in this beatitude, and only one in each of the others; not only to show that it was a thing which men (as men) are unwilling to believe, but also the necessary consequence of it upon our being Christians. This is likewise evident from all those passages, wherein our Lord informs us, that he came upon the earth, "not to send peace, but a sword;" and that the father-in-law should be against the mother-in-law, and a man's foes should be those of his own household. Passages, which though confined by false prophets to the first, I am persuaded will be verified by the experience of all true Christians in this, and every age of the church. It would be endless to recount all the places, wherein our Lord forewarns his disciples, that they should be called before rulers, and thrust out of synagogues, nay, that the time would come, wherein men should think they did God service to kill them.

For this reason he so frequently declared, that "unless a man forsake all that he had, and even hated life itself, he could not be his disciple." And therefore it is worthy our observation, that in the remarkable passage, wherein our Lord makes such an extensive promise to those who left all for him, he cautiously inserts persecution. "And Jesus answered and said, Verily I say unto you, there is no man that hath left house, or brethren, or sisters, or father, or mother, or wife, or children, or lands, for my sake and the gospel's, but he shall receive an hundred-fold now in this time; houses and brethren, and sisters and mothers, and children and lands, with persecutions; (the word is in the plural number, including all kinds of persecution) and in the world to come eternal life." He that hath ears to hear, let him hear what Christ says in all these passages, and then confess, that all who will godly in Christ Jesus shall suffer persecution.

As this is proved from our Lord's doctrine, so it is no less evident from his life. Follow him from the manger to the cross, and see whether any persecution was like that which the Son of God, the Lord of glory, underwent whilst here on earth. How was he hated by wicked men? How often would that hatred have excited them to lay hold of him, had it not been for fear of the people? How was he reviled, counted and called a Blasphemer, a Winebibber, a Samaritan, nay, a Devil, and, in one word, had all manner of evil spoken against him falsely? What contradiction of sinners did he endure against himself? How did men separate from his company, and were ashamed to walk with him openly? Insomuch that he once said to his own disciples, "Will you also go away?" Again, How was he stoned, thrust out of the synagogues, arraigned as a deceiver of the people, a seditious and pestilent fellow, an enemy of Caesar, and as such scourged, blind-folded, spit upon, and at length condemned, and nailed to an accursed tree? Thus was the Master persecuted, thus did the Lord suffer; and the servant is not above his Master, nor the disciple above his Lord: "If they have persecuted me, they will also persecute you," says the blessed Jesus. And again, "Every man that is perfect (a true Christian) must be as his Master," or suffer as he did. For in all these things our Lord has set us an example, that we should follow his steps: and therefore, far be it that any, who live godly in Christ Jesus, should henceforward expect to escape suffering persecution.

But farther: not only our Lord's example, but the example of all the saints that ever lived, evidently demonstrates the truth of the apostle's assertion in the text. How soon was Abel made a martyr for his religion? How was Isaac mocked by the son of the bond-woman? And what a large catalogue of suffering Old Testament saints, have we recorded in the 11th chapter of the Hebrews! Read the Acts of the Apostles, and see how the first Christians were threatened, stoned, imprisoned, scourged, and persecuted even unto death. Examine Church History in after-ages, and you will find the murder of the innocents by Herod, was but an earnest of the innocent blood which should be shed for the sake of Jesus. Examine the experience of saints now living on earth; and, if it were possible to consult the spirits of just men made perfect, I am persuaded each would concur with the apostle in asserting, that "all who will live godly in Christ Jesus, shall suffer persecution."

How can it be otherwise in the very nature of things? Ever since the fall, there has been a irreconcilable enmity between the seed of the woman and the seed of the serpent. Wicked men hat God, and therefore cannot but hate those who are like him: they hate to be reformed, and therefore must hate and persecute those, who, by a contrary behavior, testify of them, that their deeds are evil. Besides, pride of heart leads men to persecute the servants of Jesus Christ. If they commend them, they are afraid of being asked, Why do not you follow them? And therefore because they dare not imitate, though they may sometimes be even forced to approve their way, yet pride and envy make them turn persecutors. Hence it is, that as it was formerly, so it is now, and so will it be to the end of time; "He that is born after the flesh, (the natural man, does and) will persecute him that is born after the Spirit," the regenerate man. Because Christians are not of the world, but Christ hath chosen them out of the world, therefore the world will hate them. If it be objected against this doctrine, that we now live in a Christian world, and therefore must not expect such persecution as formerly; I answer, All are not Christians that are called so; and, till the heart is changed, the enmity against God (which is the root of all persecution) remains: and consequently Christians, falsely so called, will persecute as well as others. I observed therefore, in the beginning of this discourse, that Paul mentions those that had a form of religion, as persons of whom Timothy had need be chiefly aware: for, as our Lord and his apostles were mostly persecuted by their countrymen the Jews, so we must expect the like usage from the Formalists of our own nation, the Pharisees, who seem to be religious. The most horrid and barbarous persecutions have been carried on by those who have called themselves Christians; witness the days of queen Mary; and the fines, banishments and imprisonments of the children of God in the last century, and the bitter, irreconcilable hatred that appears in thousands who call themselves Christians, even in the present days wherein we live.

Persons, who argue against persecution, are not sufficiently sensible of the bitter enmity of the heart of every unregenerate man against God. For my own part, I am so far from wondering that Christians are persecuted, that I wonder our streets do not run with the blood of the saints: was mens power equal to their wills, such a horrid spectacle would soon appear. But,

Persecution is necessary in respect to the godly themselves. If we have not all manner of evil spoken of us, how can we know whether we seek only that honor which cometh from above? If we have no persecutors, how can our passive graces be kept in exercise? How can many Christian precepts be put into practice? How can we love; pray for; and do good to; those who despitefully use us? How can we overcome evil with good? In short, how can we know we love God better than life itself? Paul was sensible of all this, and therefore so positively and peremptorily asserts, that "all who live godly in Christ Jesus, shall suffer persecution."

Not that I affirm, all are persecuted in a like degree. No: this would be contrary both to scripture and experience. But though all Christians are not really called to suffer every kind of persecution, yet all Christians are liable thereto: and notwithstanding some may live in more peaceful times of the church than others, yet all Christians, in all ages, will find by their own experience, that, whether they act in a private or public capacity, they must, in some degree or other, suffer persecution.

Here then I would pause, and, *Lastly*, by way of application, exhort all persons,

First, To stand a while and examine themselves. For, by what has been said, you may gather one mark, whereby you may judge whether you are Christians or not. Were you ever persecuted for righteousness sake? If not, you never yet lived godly in Christ our Lord. Whatever you may say to the contrary, the inspired apostle, in the words of the text (the truth of which, I think, I have sufficiently proved) positively asserts, that all who will live godly in Him, shall suffer persecution. Not that all who are persecuted are real Christians; for many sometimes suffer, and are persecuted, on other accounts than for righteousness sake. The great question therefore is, Whether you were ever persecuted for living godly? You may boast of your great prudence and sagacity (and indeed these are excellent things) and glory because you have not run such lengths, and made yourselves so singular, and liable to such contempt, as some others have. But, alas! this is not a mark of your being of a Christian, but of a Laodicean spirit, neither how nor cold, and sit only to be spewed out of the mouth of God. That which you call prudence, is often, only cowardice, dreadful hypocrisy, pride of heart, which makes you dread contempt, and afraid to give up your reputation for God. You are ashamed of Christ and his gospel; and in all probability, was he to appear a second time upon earth, in words, as well as works, you would deny him. Awake therefore, all ye that live only formally in Christ Jesus, and no longer seek that honor which cometh of man. I do not desire to court you, but I entreat you to live godly, and fear not contempt for the sake of Jesus Christ. Beg of God to give you his Holy Spirit, that you may see through, and discover the latent hypocrisy of your hearts, and no longer deceive your own souls. Remember you cannot reconcile two irreconcilable differences, God and Mammon, the friendship of this world with the favor of God. Know you not who hath told you, that "the friendship of this world is enmity with God?" If therefore you are in friendship with the world, notwithstanding all your specious pretenses to piety, you are at enmity with God: you are only heart-hypocrites; and, "What is the hope of the hypocrite, when God shall take away his soul?" Let the words of the text sound an alarm in your ears; O let them sink deep into your hearts; "Yea, and all that will live godly in Christ Jesus, shall suffer persecution."

Secondly, From the words of the text, I would take occasion to speak to those, who are about to list themselves under the banner of Christ's cross. What say you? Are you resolved to live godly in Christ Jesus, notwithstanding the consequence will be, that you must suffer persecution? You are beginning to build; but have you taken our Lord's advice, to "sit down first and count the cost?" Have you well weighed with yourselves that weighty declaration, "He that loveth father or mother more than Me, is not worthy of Me;" and again, "Unless a man forsake all that he hath he cannot be my disciple?" Perhaps some of you have great possessions; will not you go away sorrowful, if Christ should require you to sell all that you have! Others of you again may be kinsmen, or some way related, or under obligations, to the high-priests, or other great personages, who may be persecuting the church of Christ: What say you? Will you, with Moses, "rather choose to suffer affliction with the people of God, than enjoy the pleasures of sin for a season?" Perhaps you may say, my friends will not oppose me. That is more than you know: in all probability your chief enemies will be those of your own household. If therefore they should oppose you, are you willing naked to follow a naked Christ? And to wander about in sheep-skins and goats-skins, in dens and caves of the earth; being afflicted, destitute, tormented, rather than not be Christ's disciples? You are now all following with zeal, as Ruth and Orpah did Naomi, and may weep under the word; but are not your tears crocodiles tears? And, when difficulties come, will you not go back form following your Lord, as Orpah departed form following Naomi? Have you really the root of grace in your hearts? Or, are you only stony-ground hearers? You receive the word with joy; but, when persecution arises because of the word, will you not be immediately offended? Be not angry with me for putting these questions to you. I am jealous over you, but it is with a godly jealousy: for, alas! how many have put their hands to the plough, and afterwards have shamefully looked back? I only deal with you, as our Lord did with the person that said, "Lord, I will follow thee withersoever thou wilt. The foxes have holes, and the birds of the air have nests, but the son of man, (says he) hath not where to lay his head." What say you? Are you willing to endure hardness, and thereby approve yourselves good soldiers of Jesus Christ? You now come on foot out of the towns and villages to hear the word, and receive me as a messenger of God: but will you not by and by cry out, Away with him, away with him; it is not fit such a fellow should live upon the earth? Perhaps some of you, like Hazael, may say, "Are we dogs, that we should do this?" But, alas! I have met with many unhappy souls, who have drawn back unto perdition, and have afterwards accounted me their enemy, for dealing faithfully with them; though once, if it were possible, they would have plucked out their own eyes, and have given them unto me. Sit down therefore, I beseech you, and seriously count the cost, and ask yourselves again and again, whether you count all things but dung and dross, and are willing to suffer the loss of all things, so that you may win Christ, and be found in him: for you may assure yourselves, the apostle hath not spoken in vain, "All that will live godly in Christ Jesus, shall suffer persecution."

Thirdly, The text speaks to you that are patiently suffering for the truth's sake: "Rejoice, and be exceeding glad; great shall be your reward in heaven." For to you it is given, not only to believe, but also to suffer, and perhaps remarkably too, for the sake of Jesus! This is a mark of your discipleship, an evidence that you do live godly in Christ Jesus. Fear not, therefore, neither be dismayed. O be not weary and faint in your minds! Jesus, your Lord, your life, cometh, and his reward is with him. Though all men forsake you, yet will not he: no; the Spirit of Christ and of glory shall rest upon you. In patience therefore possess your souls. Sanctify the Lord God in your hearts. Be in nothing terrified by your adversaries: on their part Christ is evil spoken of; on your part his is glorified. Be not ashamed of your glory, since others can glory in their shame. Think it not strange concerning the fiery trial, wherewith you are or may be tried. The Devil rages, knowing that he hath but a short time to reign. He or his emissaries have no more power than what is given them from above: God sets them their bounds, which they cannot pass; and the very hairs of your head are all numbered. Fear not; no one shall set upon you to hurt you, without your heavenly Father's knowledge. Do your earthly friends and parents forsake you? Are you cast out of the synagogues? The Lord shall reveal himself to you, as to the man that was born blind. Jesus Christ shall take you up. If they carry you to prison, and load you with chains, so that the iron enter into your souls, even there shall Chris send an angel from heaven to strengthen you, and enable you, with Paul and Silas, to "sing praises at midnight." Are you threatened to be thrown into a den of lions, or cast into a burning fiery furnace, because you will not bow down and worship the beast? Fear not; the God, whom you serve, is able to deliver you: or, if he should suffer the flames to devour your bodies, they would only serve, as so many fiery chariots, to carry your souls to God. Thus it was with the martyrs of old; so that once, when he was burning, cried out, "Come, you Papists, if you want a miracle, here, behold one! This bed of flames is to me a bed of down." Thus it was with almost all that suffered in former times: for Jesus, notwithstanding he withdrew his own divinity from himself, yet has always lifted up the light of his countenance upon the souls of suffering saints. "Fear not therefore those that can kill the body, and after that have no more that they can do; but fear Him only, who is able to destroy both body and soul in hell." Dare, dare to live godly in Christ Jesus, though you suffer all manner of persecution. But,

Fourthly, Are there any true ministers of Jesus Christ here? You will not be offended if I tell you, that the words of the text are, in an especial manner, applicable to you. Paul wrote them to Timothy; and we, of all men, that live godly in Christ Jesus, must expect to suffer the severest persecution. Satan will endeavor to bruise our heels, let who will escape: and it has been the general way of God's providence, in times of persecution, to permit the shepherds first to be smitten, before the sheep are scattered. Let us not therefore show that we are only hirelings, who care not for the sheep; but, like the great Shepherd and Bishop of souls, let us readily lay down our lives for the sheep. Whilst others are boasting of their great performents, let us rather glory in our great afflictions and persecutions for the sake of Christ. Paul rejoiced that he suffered afflictions and persecutions at Iconium and Lystra: out of all, the Lord delivered him; out of all, the Lord will deliver us, and cause us hereafter to sit down with him on thrones, when he comes to judge the twelve tribes of Israel.

I could proceed; but I am conscious, in this part of my discourse, I ought more particularly to speak to myself, knowing that Satan has desired to have me, that he may sift me as wheat. Without a spirit of prophecy, we may easily discern the signs of the times. Persecutions even at the doors: the tabernacle of the Lord is already driven into the wilderness: the ark of the Lord is fallen into the unhallowed hands of uncircumcised Philistines. They have long since put us out of their synagogues, and high-priests have been calling on civil magistrates to exert their authority against the disciples of the Lord. Men in power have been breathing out threatenings: we may easily guess what will follow, imprisonment and slaughter. The storm has been gathering some time; it must break shortly. Perhaps it may fall on me first.

Brethren therefore, whether in the ministry or not, I beseech you, "pray for me," that I may never suffer justly, as an evil-doer, but only for righteousness sake. O pray that I may not deny my Lord in any wise, but that I may joyfully follow him, both to prison and to death, if he is pleased to call me to seal his truths with my blood. Be not ashamed of Christ, or of his gospel, though I should become a prisoner of the Lord. Though I am bound, the word of God will not be bound: no; an open, an effectual door is opened for preaching the everlasting gospel, and men or devils shall never be able to prevail against it. Only pray, that, whether it be in life or death, Christ may be glorified in me: then I shall rejoice, yea, and will rejoice.

And now, to whom shall I address myself next?

Fifthly, To those, who persecute their neighbors for living godly in Christ Jesus. But, what shall I say to you? Howl and weep for the miseries that shall come upon you; for a little while the Lord permits you to ride over the heads of his people; but, by and by, death will arrest you, judgment will find you, and Jesus Christ shall put a question to you, which will strike you dumb, *why perse-*

cuted you me? You may plead your laws and your canons, and pretend what you do is out of zeal for God; but God shall discover the cursed hypocrisy and serpentine enmity of your hearts, and give you over to the tormentors. It is well, if in this life God does not send some mark upon you. He pleaded the cause of Naboth, when innocently condemned for blaspheming God and the king; and our Lord sent forth his armies, and destroyed the city of those who killed the prophets, and stoned them that were sent unto them. If you have a mind therefore to fill up the measure of your iniquities, go on, persecute and despise the disciples of the Lord: but know, "that for all these things, God shall bring you to judgment." Nay, those you now persecute, shall be in part your judges, and sit on the right-hand of the Majesty on high, whilst you are dragged by infernal spirits into a lake that burneth with fire and brimstone, and the smoke of your torment shall be ascending up for ever and ever. Lay down therefore, ye rebels, your arms against the most high God, and no longer persecute those who live godly in Christ Jesus. The Lord will plead, the Lord will avenge, their cause. You may be permitted to bruise their heels, yet in the end they shall bruise your accursed heads. I speak not this, as though I were afraid of you; for I know in whom I have believed: only out of pure love I warn you, and because I know not but Jesus Christ may make some of you vessels of mercy, and snatch you, even you persecutors, as firebrands out of the fire. Jesus Christ came into the world to save sinners, even persecutors, the worst of sinners: his righteousness is sufficient for them; his Spirit is able to purify and change their hearts. He once converted Saul: may the same God magnify his power, in converting all those who are causing the godly in Christ Jesus, as much as in them lies, to suffer persecution! The Lord be with you all. Amen.

56. An Exhortation to the People of God Not to Be Discouraged

Hebrews 4:9—"There remaineth therefore a rest to the people of God."

When we consider the persecutions they are exposed to, who live righteously and godly in this present world; it is amazing to consider, that the people of this generation should be so fond of a name to live, while they are in effect dead. The people of God are to expect little else but troubles and trials while they are in this world; common experience is a contradiction to my text, that there is a rest to the people of God; but the author of the Hebrews, when speaking of this rest, did not mean that they should have a rest here. No; he too well knew that the people of God, all who would seek and serve the Lord Jesus, must be despised, hated, scoffed, slandered, and evil entreated; but the time was hastening when they should have a perfect rest: there is a rest laid up for them, and this is an encouragement for you, my brethren, to hold on, and hold out your way rejoicing; after death there will be a rest for ever; at judgment, you shall be taken up to dwell with the Lord Jesus Christ; and there, you shall be for ever exempted from sin; you shall rest from all manner of sorrow, and be no more troubled with the temptations of Satan. Now, you can set about nothing for the glory of God, or for your own soul's welfare, but the devil is dissuading you from it, or distracting you in it, or discouraging you after it. Here we are scoffed and derided; as the world hated the Lord Jesus Christ, so will it hate you: but be not discouraged, though we are here the scorn and offscouring of all things; and are as a gazing stock to men and angels. Though they put us out of their synagogues, cast out our name as evil, and look on us as persons unfit for their company; yet, in that rest which is prepared for you, my brethren, we shall then be gazed at for our glory, and they shut out of the assembly of the saints, and separated from us, whether they will or no; unless the Lord Jesus Christ, by his free, rich, and sovereign grace, brings them unto himself.

The letter-learned Scribes and Pharisees of this day, look on us as madmen and enthusiasts; but though they make so much noise about the world enthusiast, it means no more than this, one in God; and what Christian can say, he is not in God, and God in him? And if this is to be an enthusiast, God grant I may be more and more so; if we being in Christ, and Christ in us, makes us enthusiasts. I would to God we were all more and more enthusiasts. They now think it strange, that we run not with them into all excess of riot, and because we will not go to the devil's diversions with them, therefore they speak evil of us. We cannot now go along the street, but every one is pointing out his finger with scorn, and cries, Here comes another of his followers; what! You are become one of his disciples too! But there is a rest which will be a complete deliverance for you. Let none of these things move you; for, though you are thus treated here, consider, you shall in heaven have no discouraging company, nor any but what will be an assistance to you; you will have no scoffer there, all will be ready to join with heart and voice in your everlasting joy and praises. You will not be counted enthusiasts, madmen, and rabble, in that rest which remaineth for the people of God. Therefore, possess your souls in patience; account it matter of joy when you fall into tribulation; God, in his own time, will deliver us; let not their hindering us from preaching in the church, be any discouragement; do not shrink, and draw back, because of opposition; be not ashamed of your work or master; but hold fast your integrity. You must expect to go through evil report, and good report; fear not the violence of unreasonable men; let them hate you, and cast you out for the Lord's sake, behold he shall appear to your joy, and they shall be ashamed: therefore hold on, and hold out to the end. Be steadfast and patient, and bear the troubles of the world; if you are the people of God, there is a rest provided for you, which you shall certainly obtain.

I shall not speak unto you, Pharisees, this morning, nor to any, except to you who have experienced the pangs of the new-birth, or are at present under them, and who know what it is to love the Lord Jesus in sincerity and truth: do not be discouraged, or think hard of the ways of God, my dear brethren, because you are not loved by the men of this world; if you were of the world it would love you; it would then be pleased with your company; it would not thrust you from a tavern, or an alehouse; it would not dislike you for singing the songs of the drunkard, or for going to plays, balls, or other polite and fashionable entertainments, as they are called; no, these the children of the world like; but if you will sing hymns and psalms, and go to hear what God hath to say unto your souls, and spend your time in reading, praying, and frequenting religious assemblies, then it is that they dislike you, and thrust you out of their company, as unworthy thereof; but let none of these things move you, for the rest which Jesus Christ hath prepared for you, is an ample recompense for all you may meet with here.

This rest is the fruit of the blood of the Lord Jesus Christ: O how will it fill our souls with love, to think that through the streams of this blood, we have overcome the violence of the world, and the snares of the devil. My dear brethren, be not discouraged at the treatment you meet with here, but let it be a means to stir you up to advance in the love of the Lord Jesus Christ, who hath prepared a rest for you. Can you consider, what Christ has done and suffered for you, and have your hearts stupefied with vile and senseless pleasures? Can you hear of a panting, bleeding, dying Jesus, and yet be dull and unaffected? Was there any sorrow like unto his sorrow? And all this, he underwent to save you, who were vile, and polluted, and by nature, since the fall, a motley mixture of the beast and devil. Jesus Christ, by dying upon the cross, intended to take away the devil and beast from your heart, and to prepare it for himself to dwell in. Think of the love of this your Jesus, and then, will a little reproach and scorn move you? Sure it will not. I hope better things of you, and things that accompany salvation.

O think with what pleasing astonishment you will see the Lord Jesus Christ, when he comes to take you to his rest: now his heart is open to us; but our hearts are shut against him; then, then, his heart shall be open, and ours shall be so too. O my brethren, how will your love be increased? With what raptures will you see the Lord Jesus Christ? Therefore, undergo a few reproaches here patiently, and revile not again. Let them say what they please of me, the reproaches, scorns, and contempt of this world, will no ways hurt me, but will recoil upon their own heads; leave it to the Lord, who knows what is best for you and me: do not question his love; he will be with you; only do you, who have tasted the Lord to be gracious, follow hard after him.

And now, let me speak a word unto you, who have not yet experienced the love of Christ to your souls, but are waiting for his appearance. I shall be but very short, because I would not break in upon the duties of the day.

I shall speak unto you a word of invitation; even, to wait still on the Lord; do not forsake him, though he may not answer your petitions at once or twice seeking unto him; hold on, do not leave seeking him, and you shall have an answer of peace; remember the poor man who was lame, and had lain at the pool of Bethesda thirty-eight years for relief, yet at last he found that it was worth waiting for, he obtained his desire.

And if you are but zealous for the Lord, and seek unto Jesus, if your zeal be according to godliness, and you pray unto him for his Spirit, you shall certainly have an answer of peace; you shall find it is good to seek unto the Lord, you will be adopted into his family, and by his spirit be enabled to cry, "Abba, Father." O then do not leave, but be continually waiting at wisdom's gate, and you shall find all her ways to be ways of pleasantness, and all her paths are peace; then, you shall find that it is worth waiting on the Lord Jesus; and when you have got his Spirit within you, all the power of men or devils cannot make you forsake the ways of the Lord Jesus Christ.

If you do but once taste of his pardoning love, it will be so delightful unto you, that you will cry for more and more thereof; you will be as full as you can hold, and still not be satisfied; you will desire more and more of this love of Jesus, you will hunger and thirst, and hunger and thirst again, and never be satisfied till you come to that rest which is prepared for the people of God, where all hungering and thirsting will cease, and will be turned into songs and hallelujahs, and that for ever and ever.

As many of you as design to partake of the emblems of the body and blood of our dying Lord, examine well yourselves, lest by eating and drinking unworthily, you eat and drink damnation unto yourselves: remember the dying love of your dying Lord, and eat and drink in commemoration thereof; do not let the world keep you from partaking hereof; and when you have eaten and drank, do not go away and run into the world; let the world see that you have been with Jesus; give them no room to speak unseemly, they do that enough without occasion; but how would they rejoice if they had just reason.

Look well then unto your paths, that you do not slip; remember that all your faults are magnified, and that all your little slips are laid upon me; therefore, look well unto your ways, your words, your actions, that they may silence gainsayers; let them see that we have the presence of God with us, and that there has been good done by field preaching.

Let me exhort you once more to consider the love of the Lord Jesus Christ. O do not forget this love. Consider, I beseech you, how great it has been unto you, and do not slight this his grace, the riches, the love, the kindness of your dear Redeemer, the Lord Jesus Christ, who hath prepared this eternal rest for you; he also laid down his life for your sakes: what great love was here! that while you were enemies to the Lord of glory, he died for you, to redeem you from sin, from hell and wrath, that you might live and reign with him, world without end.

The Lamb that died, and was buried, is now risen and exalted, and sits on the right-hand of God the Father; and when he shall come to judge all the world, then, my brethren, it will be seen whether we have deserved the usage the world has given us; then it will be known who are the true followers of the Lord Jesus, and who are madmen and fools; but, may it be determined in this world, that we and our present enemies may enter into that rest which God hath prepared for those that love him.

Which God of his infinite mercy grant!

My brethren, let not these few words of exhortation be forgotten, but lay them up in your hearts, and remember they must be called over another day. I should have enlarged, but the duties of the day obliged me to forbear.

Now, to God the Father, Son, and Holy Ghost, be all power.

57. Preached Before the Governor, and Council, and the House of Assembly, in Georgia, on January 28, 1770

Zech. 4:10—"For who hath despised the Day of small things?"

Men, brethren, and fathers, at sundry times and in diverse manners, God spake to the fathers by the prophets, before he spoke to us in these last days by his Son. And as God is a sovereign agent, and his sacred Spirit bloweth when and where it listeth, surely he may reveal and make known his will to his creatures, when, where, and how he pleaseth; "and who shall say unto him, what doest thou?" Indeed, this seems to be one reason, to display his sovereignty, why he chose, before the canon of scripture was settled, to make known his mind in such various methods, and to such a variety of his servants and messengers.

Hence it is, that we hear, he talked with Abraham as "a man talketh with a friend." To Moses he spoke "face to face." To others by "dreams in the night," or by "visions" impressed strongly on their imaginations. This seems to be frequently the happy lot of the favorite evangelical prophet Zechariah, I call him evangelical prophet, because his predictions, however they pointed at some approaching or immediate event, ultimately terminated in Him, who is the Alpha and Omega, the beginning and the end of all the lively oracles of God. The chapter from which our text is selected, among many other passages, is a striking proof of this: An angel, that had been more than once sent to him on former occasions, appears again to him, and by way of vision, and "waked him, (to use his own words) as a man that is wakened out of his sleep." Prophets, and the greatest servants of God, need waking sometimes out of their drowsy frames.

Methinks I see this man of God starting out of his sleep, and being all attention: the angle asked him, "what seest thou?" He answers, "I have looked, and behold, a candle-stick all of gold," an emblem of the church of God, "with a bowl upon the top of it, and seven lamps thereon, and seven pipes to the seven lamps, which were upon the top thereof;" implying, that the church, however reduced to the lowest ebb, should be preserved, be kept supplied, and shining, through the invisible, but not less real, because invisible aids and operations of the blessed Spirit of God. The occasion of such an extraordinary vision, if we compare this passage with the second chapter of the Prophecy of the prophet Haggai, seems to be this: It was now near eighteen years since the Jewish people had been delivered from their long and grievous Babylonian captivity; and being so lone deprived of their temple and its worship, which fabric had been rased even to the ground, one would have imagined, that immediately upon their return, they should have postponed all private works, and with their united strength have first set about rebuilding that once stately and magnificent structure. But they, like too many Christians of a like lukewarm stamp, though all acknowledged that this church-work was a necessary work, yet put themselves and others off, with this godly pretense, "The time is not come, the time that the Lord's house should be built." The time is not come! What, not in eighteen years! For so long had they now been returned from their state of bondage: and pray, why was not the time come? The prophet Haggai tells them; their whole time was so taken up building for an habitation for their great and glorious Benefactor, the mighty God of Jacob.

This ingratitude must not be passed by unpunished. Omniscience observes, Omnipotence resents it! And that they might read their sin in their punishment, as they thought it best to get rich, and secure houses and lands and estates for themselves, before they set about unnecessary church-work, the prophet tells them, "You have sown much, but bring in little: ye eat, but ye have not enough: ye drink, but ye are not filled with drink: ye clothe you, but there is none warm: and he that earneth wages, earneth wages to put it into a bag with holes." Still he goes on thundering and lightening, "Ye looked for much, and lo it came to little: wand when ye brought it home, (pleasing yourselves with your fine crops) I did blow upon it: why? Saith the Lord of Hosts; because of mine house that is waste, and ye run every man unto his own house." A thundering sermon this! delivered not only to the common people, but also unto, and in the presence of "Zerubbabel, the son of Shealtiel, and Joshua, the son of Josedech the high-priest. The prophet's report is believed; and the arm of the Lord was revealed. Zerubbabel, the son of Shealtiel, and Joshua, the son of Josedech (O happy times when church and state are thus combined) with all the remnant of the people, obeyed the voice of the Lord their God, and the words of Haggai the prophets."

The spirit of Zerubbabel, and of Joshua, and the spirits of all the remnant of the people were stirred up, and they immediately came, disregarding, as it were, their own private buildings, "and did work in the house of the Lord of Hosts their God." For a while, they proceeded with vigor; the foundation of the house is laid, and the superstructure raised to some considerable height: but whether this fit of hot zeal soon cooled, as is too common, or the people were discouraged by the false representations of their enemies, which perhaps met with too favorable a reception as the court of Darius; it so happened, that the hearts of the magistrates and ministers of the people waxed faint; and an awful chasm intervened, between the finishing and laying the foundation of this promising and glorious work.

Upon this, another prophet, even Zechariah, (who with Haggai had been joint sufferer in the captivity) is sent to lift up the hands that hang down, to strengthen the feeble knees, and by the foregoing instructive vision, to reanimate Joshua and the people in general, and the heart of Zerubbabel, the son of Shealtiel, in particular, maugre all discouragements, either from inveterate enemies, or from timid unstable friends, or all other obstacles whatsoever. If Haggai thunders, Zechariah's message is as lightening. "This is the word of the Lord unto Zerubbabel, saying, Not by might, not by power, (not by barely human power or policy) but by my spirit, saith the Lord of Hosts: Who art thou, O great mountain? (thou Sanballat and thy associates, who have been so long crying out, what mean these feeble Jews? However great, formidable, and seemingly insurmountable) before Zerubbabel thou shalt (not only be lowered and rendered more accessible, but) become a plain;" thy very opposition shall, in the end, promote the work, and help to expedite that very building, which thou intendest to put a stop to, and destroy.

And lest Zerubbabel, through unbelief and outward opposition, or for want of more bodily strength, should think this would be a work of time, and that he should not live to see it completed in his days, "The word of the Lord came to Zechariah, saying, The hands of Zerubbabel have laid the foundation of this house; his hands also shall finish it, and he shall bring forth the headstone thereof with shoutings, crying, Grace, grace unto it." Grace! Grace! Unto it: a double acclamation, to show, that out of the abundance of their hearts, their mouth spake; and this with shoutings and crying from all quarters. Even their enemies should see the hand and providence of God in the beginning, continuance, and ending of this seemingly improbable and impracticable work; so that they should be constrained to cry, "Grace unto it," and wish both the work and the builders much prosperity: But as for its friends, they should be so transported with heart-felt joy in the reflection upon the signal providences which had attended them through the whole process, that they would shout and cry, "Grace, grace unto it:" or, This is nothing but the Lord's doing; God prosper and bless this work more and more, and make it a place where his free grace and glory may be abundantly displayed. Then by a beautiful and pungent sarcasm, turning to the insulting enemies, he utters the spirited interrogation in my text, "Who hath despised the day of small things?" Who are you, that vauntingly said, what can these feeble Jews do, pretending to lay the foundation of a house which they never will have money, or strength, or power to finish? Or, who are you, O timorous, short-sighted, doubting, though well-meaning people, who, through unbelief, were discouraged at the small beginnings and feebleness of the attempt to build a second temple? And, because you thought it could not come up to the magnificence of the first, therefore were discouraged from so much as beginning to build a second at all?

A close instructive question this; a question, implying, that whenever God intends to bring about any great thing, he generally begins with a day of small things.

As a proof of this, I will not lead you so far back, as to the beginning of time, when the Everlasting "I AM" spoke all things into existence, by his almighty fiat; and out of a confused chaos, "without form and void," produced a world worthy of a God to create, and of his favorite creature man, his vicegerent and representative here below, to inhabit, and enjoy in it both himself and his God. And yet, though the heavens declare his glory, and the firmament showeth his handy work, though there is o speech nor language where their voice is not heard, and their line is gone out through all the earth: and by a dumb, yet persuasive language, proves the hand that made them to be divine; yet there have been, and are now, such fools in the world, as to "say in their hearts, There is no God;" or so wise, as by their wisdom, not to know God, or own his divine image to be stamped on that book, wherein these grand things are recorded, and that in such legible characters, that he who runs may read.

Neither will I divert your attention, honored fathers, to the histories of Greece and Rome, or any of the great kingdoms and renowned monarchies, which constitute so great a part of ancient history; but whose beginnings were very small, (witness Romulus's ditch) their progress as remarkably great, and their declension and downfall, when arrived at their appointed zenith, as sudden, unexpected, and marvelous. These make the chief subjects of the learning of our schools; though they make but a mean figure in sacred history, and would not perhaps have been mentioned at all, had they not been, in some measure, connected with the history of God's people, which is the grand subject of that much despised book, emphatically called, The Scriptures. Whoever hath a mind to inform himself of the one, may read Rollin's Ancient History, and whoever would see the connection with the other, may consult the learned Prideaux's admirable and judicious connection. Books which, I hope, will be strenuously recommended, and carefully studied, when this present infant institution gathers more strength, and grows up into a seat of learning. I can hardly forbear mentioning the final beginnings of Great Britain, now so distinguished for liberty, opulence and renown; and the rise and rapid progress of the American colonies, which promises to be one of the most opulent and powerful empires in the world. But my present views, and the honors done this infant institution this day, and the words of my text, as well as the feelings of my own heart, and I trust, of the hearts of all that hear me, lead me to confine your meditations to the history of God's own peculiar people, which for the simplicity and sublimity of its language, the veracity of its author, and the importance and wonders of the facts therein recorded, if weighed in a proper balance, hath not its equal under the sun. And yet, though God himself hath become an author among us, we will not condescend to give his book one thorough reading. Be astonished, O heavens, at this!

Who would have thought that from once, even from Abraham, and from so small a beginning, as the emigration of a single private family, called out of a land wholly given to idolatry, to be sojourners and pilgrims in a strange land; who would have thought, that from a man, who for a long season was written childless, a man whose first possession in this strange land, was by purchasing a burying place for his wife, and in whose grave one might have imagined he would have buried all future expectations; who would have thought, that from this very man and woman, according to the course of nature, both as good as dead, should descend a numerous offspring like unto the stars of heaven for multitude, and as the sand which is upon the sea shore innumerable? Nay, who would have imagined, that against all probability, and in all human appearance impossible, a kingdom should arise? Behold a poor captive stave, even Joseph, who was cruelly separated from his brethren, became second in Pharaoh's kingdom: he was sent before to work out a great deliverance, and to introduce a family which should take root, deep root downwards and bear fruit upwards, and fill the land. How could it enter into the heart of man to conceive, that when oppressed by a king, who knew not Joseph, though they were the best, most loyal, industrious subjects this king had, when an edict was issued forth as impolitic as cruel, (since the safety and glory of all kingdoms chiefly consist in the number of its inhabitants) that an outcast, helpless infant should be taken, and bred up in all the learning of the Egyptians, and in that very court from which, and by that very tyrant from whom the edict came, and that the deliverer should be nurtured to be king in Jeshurun?

But time as well as strength would fail me, was I to give you a detail of all the important particulars respecting God's peculiar people; as their miraculous support in the wilderness, the events which took place while they were under a divine theocracy, and during their settlement in Canaan to the time of their return from Babylon, and from thence to the destruction of their second temple, &c. by the Romans. Indeed, considering to whom I am speaking, persons conversant in the sacred and profane history, I have mentioned these things only to stir up your minds by way of remembrance.

But if we descend from the Jewish, to the Christian era, we shall find, that its commencement was, in the eyes of the world, a "day of small things" indeed. Our blessed Lord compares the beginning of its progress in the world, to a grain of mustard-seed, which though the smallest of all seeds when sown, soon becomes a great tree, and so spread, that the "birds of the air," or a multitude of every nation, language and tongue, came and lodged in its branches: and its inward progress in the believers heart, Christ likens to a little leaven which a woman hid in three measures of meal. How both the Jewish and Christian dispensations have been, and even to this day are despised, by the wise disputers of this world, on this very account, is manifest to all who read the lively oracles with a becoming attention. What ridicule, obloquy, and inveterate opposition Christianity meets with, in this our day, not only from the open deist, but from formal professors, is too evident to every truly pious soul.

And what opposition the kingdom of grace meets with in the heart, is well known by all those who are experimentally acquainted with their hearts: they know, to their sorrow, what the great apostle of the Gentiles means, by "the Spirit striving against the flesh, and the flesh against the Spirit."

But the sacred Oracles, and the histories of all ages acquaint us, that God brings about the greatest thing, not only by small and unlikely means, but by ways and means directly opposite to the carnal reasonings of unthinking men: he chooses things that be not, to bring to nought those which are. How did Christianity spread and flourish, by one, who was despised and rejected of men, a man of sorrows, and acquainted with grief, and who expired on a cross? He was despised and rejected, not merely by the vulgar and illiterate, but the Rabbis and Masters of Israel, the Scribes and Pharisees, who by the Jewish churchmen were held too in so high a reputation for their outward sanctity, that it became a common proverb, "if only two went to heaven, the one would be a Scribe, and the other a Pharisee." Yet there were they who endeavored to silence the voice of all his miracles and heavenly doctrine with, "Is not this the Carpenter's son?" Nay, "He is mad, why hear you him? he hath a devil, and casteth out devils by Beelzebub the prince of the devils." And their despite not only followed him to, but after death, and when in the grave. "We remember (said they) that this deceiver said, after three days I will rise again; command therefore that the sepulcher be made sure;" but, maugre all your impotent precautions, in sealing the stone, and setting a watch, he burst the bars of death asunder, and, according to his repeated predictions, proved himself to be the Son of God with power, by rising the third day from the dead. And afterwards, in pretense of great multitudes, was he received up into glory; as a proof thereof, he sent down the Holy Ghost, (on the mission of whom he pawned all his credit with his disciples) in such an instantaneous, amazing manner, as one would imagine, should have forced and compelled all who saw it to own, that this was indeed the finger of God.

And yet how was this grand transaction treated? With the utmost contempt: when instantaneously the apostles commenced orators and linguists, and with a divine profusion spoke of the wonderful things of God; "these men (said some) are full of new wine." And yet by these men, mean fishermen, illiterate men, idiots, in the opinion of the Scribes and Pharisees, and notwithstanding all the opposition of earth and hell, and that too only by the foolishness of preaching, did this grain of mustard-seed grow up, till thousands, ten thousands of thousands, a multitude which no man can number, out of every nation, language and people, came and lodged under the branches of it.

Neither shall it rest here; whatever dark parenthesis may intervene, we are assured, that being still watered by the same divine hand, it shall take deeper and deeper root downward, and bear more and more fruit upward, till the whole earth be filled with the knowledge of the Lord, as the waters cover the sea. Who shall live when God doth this? Hasten O Lord that blessed time! O let this thy kingdom come! Come, not only by the external preaching of the gospel in the world, but by its renovating, heart-renewing, soul-transforming power, to awakened sinners! For want of this, alas! alas! though we understood all mysteries, could speak with the tongues of men and angels, we should be only like sounding brass, or so many tinkling cymbals.

And yet, what a "day of small things" is the first implantation of the seed of divine life in the soul of man? Well might our Lord, who alone is the author and finisher of our faith, compare it to a little leaven, which a woman took, and hid in three measures of meal, till the whole was leavened. Low similes, mean comparisons these, in the eyes of those, who having eyes, see not; who having ears, hear not; whose heart, being waxed gross, cannot, will not understand! To such, it is despicable, mysterious, and unintelligible in its description; and, if possible, infinitely more so, when made effectual by the power of God, to the salvation of any individual soul. For the wisdom of God will always be foolishness to natural men. As it was formerly, so it is now; they who are born after the flesh, will persecute those that are born after the spirit: the disciple must be as his master: they that will live godly in him; they that live most godly in him, must, shall suffer persecution. This is so interwoven in the very nature and existence of the gospel, that our Lord makes it one part of the beatitudes, in that blessed sermon which he preached, when, to use the words of my old familiar friend the seraphic Hervey, a mount was his pulpit, and the heavens his sounding board. A part, which, like others of the same nature, I believe, will be little relished by such who are always clamoring against those few highly favored souls, who dare stand up and preach the doctrine of *justification by faith alone* in the imputed righteousness of Jesus Christ, and are reproached with not preaching, like their master, Morality, as they term it, in his glorious sermon on the mount; for did we more preach, and more live it, we should soon find all manner of evil would be spoken against us for Christ's sake.

But shall this hinder the progress, the growth, and consummation? And shall the Christian therefore be dismayed and discouraged? God forbid! On the contrary, the weakest believer may, and ought, to rejoice and be exceeding glad. And why? For a very good reason; because, he that hath begun the good work, hath engaged also to finish it; though Christ found him as black as hell, he shall present him, and every individual purchased with his blood, without spot or wrinkle, or any such-thing, before the Divine Presence. O glorious prospect! How will the saints triumph, and the sons of God then shout for joy? If they shouted when God said, "Let there be light, and there was light;" and if there is joy in heaven over one sinner only that repenteth, how will the heavenly arches echo and rebound with praise, when all the redeemed of the Lord shall appear together, and the Son of God shall say, "of all these that thou hast given to me, have I lost nothing." On the contrary, what weeping, wailing, and gnashing of teeth will there be, not only amongst the devil and his angels, but amongst the fearful and unbelieving, when they see that all the hellish temptations and devices, instead of destroying, were over-ruled to the furtherance of the gospel in general, and to the increase and growth of grace in every individual believer in particular. And how will despisers then behold and wonder and perish, when they shall be obliged to say, "we fools counted their lives madness, and their end to be without honor; but how are they numbered among the children of God, and how happy is their lot among the saints!"

But whither am I going? Pardon me, my dear hearers, if you think this to be a digression from my main point. It is true, whilst I am musing, the fire begins to kindle: I am flying, but not so high, I trust, as to lose sight of my main subject. And yet, after meditating and talking of the rise and progress of the gospel of the kingdom, I shall find it somewhat difficult to descend so low, as to entertain you with the small beginnings of this infant colony, and of the Orphan-house, in which I am now preaching. But I should judge myself inexcusable on this occasion, if I did not detain you a little longer, in taking a transient view of the traces of divine Providence, in the rise and progress of the colony in general, and the institution of this Orphan-house in particular. Children yet unborn, I trust, will have occasion to bless God for both.

The very design of this settlement, as charity inclines us to hope all things, was, that it might be an Asylum, and a place of business, for as many as were in distress; for foreigners, as well as natives; for Jews and Gentiles. On February 1, a day, the memory of which, I think, should still be perpetuated, the first embarkation was made with forty-five English families; men, who had once lived well in their native country, and who, with many persecuted Saltzburghers, headed by a good old soldier of Jesus lately deceased, the Rev. Mr. Boltzius, came to find a refuge here. They came, they saw, they labored, and endeavored to settle; but by an essential, though well-meant defect, in the very beginning of the settlement, too well known by some now present, and too long, and too much felt to bear repeating, prohibiting the importation and use of Negroes, &c. their numbers gradually diminished, and matters were brought to so low an ebb, that the whole colony became a proverb of reproach.

About this time, in the year 1737, being previously stirred up thereto by a strong impulse, which I could by no means resist, I came here, after the example of my worthy and reverend friends, Messieurs John and Charles Wesley, and Mr. Ingham, who, with the most disinterested views, had come hither to serve the colony, by endeavoring to convert the Indians. I came rejoicing to serve the colony also, and to become your willing servant for Christ's sake. My friend and father, good Bishop Bensen, encouraged me, though my brethren and kinsmen after the flesh, as well as religious friends, opposed it. I came, and I saw (you will not be offended with me to speak the truth) the nakedness of the land. Gladly did I distribute about the four hundred pounds sterling, which I had collected in England, among my poor parishioners. The necessity and propriety of erecting an Orphan-house, was mentioned and recommended before my first embarkation. But thinking it a matter of too great importance to be set about unwarily, I deferred the farther prosecution for this laudable design till my return to England in the year 1738, for to have priests orders.

Miserable was the condition of many grown persons, as well as children, whom I left behind. Their cause I endeavored to plead, immediately upon my arrival; but being denied the churches, in which I had the year before collected many hundreds for the London charity-schools, I endeavored to plead their cause in the fields. The people threw in their mites most willingly; once or twice, I think, twenty-two pounds were collected in copper; the alms were accompanied with many prayers, and which, as I told them, laid, I am persuaded, a blessed foundation to the future charitable superstructure. In a short time, though plucked as it were out of the fire, the collections and charitable contributions amounted to more than a one thousand pounds sterling.

With that I reimbarked, taking Philadelphia in my way, and upon my second arrival, found the spot fixed upon; but, alas! who can describe the low estate to which it was reduced! The whole country almost was left desolate, and the metropolis Savannah, was but like a cottage in a vineyard, or as a lodge in a garden of cucumbers. Many orphans, whose parents had been taken from them by the distresses that naturally attend new settlements, were dispersed here and there in a very forlorn helpless condition; my bowels yearned towards them, and, animated by the example of the great professor Franck, previous to bringing them here, I hired a house, furnished an infirmary, employed all that were capable of employment, and in a few weeks walked to the house of God with a large family of above sixty orphans, and others in as bad a condition.

On March 25, 1740, in full assurance of faith, I laid the foundation of this house; and in the year following, brought in my orphan family, who, with the workmen, now made up the number of one hundred and fifty: by the money which was expended on these, the remaining few were kept in the colony, and were enabled to pay the debts they owed; so that in a representation made to the House of Commons, by some, who for very good reasons wanted the constitution of the colony altered; they declared, that the very existence of the colony was in a great measure, if not totally, owing to the building and supporting of the Orphan House.

Finding the care of such a family, incompatible with the care due to a parish, upon giving previous warning to the then trustees, I gave up the living of Savannah, which without fee or reward I had voluntarily taken upon me: I then ranged through the northern colonies, and afterwards once more returned home. What calumny, what loads of reproach, I for many years was called to undergo, in thus turning beggars for a family, few here present need to be informed; a family, utterly unconnected by any ties of nature; a family, not only to be maintained with food, but clothed and educated also, and that too in the dearest part of his Majesty's dominions, on a pine barren, and in a colony where the use of Negroes was totally denied; this appeared so very improbable, that all beholders looked daily for its decline and annihilation.

But, blessed be God, the building advanced and flourished, and the wished-for period is now come, after having supported the family for thirty-two years, by a change of constitution and the smiles of government, with liberal donations from the northern, and especially the adjacent provinces, the same hands that laid the foundation, are now called to finish it, by making an addition of a seat of learning, the whole products and profits of which, are to go towards the increase of the fund, as at the beginning, for destitute orphans, or such youths as may be called of God to the sacred ministry of his Gospel. I need not call on any here, to cry, "Grace, grace, unto it." For on the utmost scrutiny of the intention of those employed, and considering the various exercises they have been called to undergo, and the opposition the building hath every where met with, we may justly say, "not by might, nor by power, but by thy Spirit, O Lord," hath this work been carried on thus far; it is his doing, let it be marvelous in our eyes. With humble gratitude, therefore, would we now set up our Ebenezer, and say, "Hitherto thou, Lord, hast helped us;" and wherefore should we doubt, but that he, who hath thus far helped, will continue to help, when the weary heads of the first founders and present helpers, are laid in the silent grave.

I am very well aware, what an invidious task it must be to a person in my circumstances, thus to speak on an affair in which he hath been so much concerned. Some may perhaps think, I am become a fool in thus glorying. But as I am now, blessed be God, in the decline of life, and as, in all probability, I shall never be present to celebrate another anniversary, I thought it best to be a little more explicit, that if I have spoken any thing but truth, I may be confronted; and if not, that future ages, and future successors, may see with what a purity of intention, and what various interpositions of Providence, the work was begun, and hath been carried on to its present height.

It was the reading of a like account, written by the late Professor Franck, that encouraged me: who knows but hereafter, the reading something of a similar nature, may encourage others to begin and carry on a like work elsewhere? I have said its present height, for I would humbly hope, that this is, comparatively speaking, only a "day of small things," only the dawn of brighter scenes. Private genius's and individuals, as well as collective bodies, have, like the human body, the nonage, puerile, juvenile estate, before they arrive at their zenith, and their lives as gradually they decline. But yet I would hope, that both the province and Bethesda, are but in their puerile or juvenile state. And long, long may they increase, and make large strides, till they arrive at a glorious zenith! I mean not merely in trade, merchandise, and opulence, (though I would be far from secluding them from the province, and would be thankful for the advances it hath already made) but a zenith of glorious gospel blessings, without which, all outward emoluments are less than nothing, or as the small dust of the balance: "For what shall it profit a man, if he shall gain the whole world and lost his own soul."

Who can imagine, that the prophet Zechariah would be sent to strengthen the hands of Zerubbabel, in building and laying the foundation of the temple, if that temple was not to be frequented with worshippers that worshipped the Father in spirit and truth. The most gaudy fabrics, stately temples, new moon Sabbaths, and solemn assemblies, are only solemn mockeries God cannot away with. This God hath shown by the destruction of both the first and second temples. What is become of the seven churches of Asia? How are all their golden candlesticks overthrown? "God is a Spirit, and they who worship him must worship him in spirit and truth." And no longer do I expect that this house will flourish, than when the power of religion is encouraged and promoted, and the persons educated here, prosecute their studies, not only to be great scholars, but good saints.

Blessed be God! I can say with Professor Franck, that it is in a great measure owing to the disinterested spirit of my first fellow-helpers, as well as those who are now employed, that the building hath reached to its present height. This I am bound to speak, not only in honor to those who are now with God, but those at present before me. Nor dare I conclude, without offering to

Your Excellency, our pepper corn of acknowledgment for the countenance you have always shown Bethesda's institution, and the honor you did us last year, inlaying the first brick of yonder wings: in thus doing, you have honored Bethesda's God. May he long delight to honor you here on earth! And after a life spent to his glory, and your country's good, may he honor you to all eternity, in placing you as Christ's right-hand in the kingdom above!

Next to your Excellency, my dear Mr. President, I must beg your acceptance both of thanks and congratulation on the annual return of this festival. For you was not only my dear familiar friend, and first fellow-traveler in this infant province; but you was directed by Providence to this spot, laid the second brick of this house, watched, prayed, and wrought for the family's good: A witness of innumerable trials, partner of my joys and griefs; you will have now the pleasure of seeing the Orphan-house a fruitful bough, its branches running over the wall. For this, no doubt, God hath smiled upon and blessed you, in a manner we could not expect, much less design; and may he continue to bless you with all spiritual blessings in heavenly places in Christ Jesus. Look to the rock from whence you have been hewn, and may your children never be ashamed, that their father left his native country, and married a real Christian, born again under this roof. May Bethesda's Good grant this may be the happy portion of your children, and children's children!

Gentlemen of his Majesty's council,

Mr. Speaker, and you members of the General Assembly, many thanks are owing to you, for your late address to his Excellency in favor of Bethesda. Your joint recommendation of it, when I was last here, which, though in some measure through the bigotry of some, for the present is rendered abortive, by their wanting to have it confined to a party, yet I trust the event will prove that every thing shall be over-ruled to the furtherance of the work. Here I repeat, what I have often declared, that as far as lies in my power before and after my decease, Bethesda shall be always on a broad bottom. All denominations have freely given; all denominations, all the continent, God being my helper, shall receive benefit from it. May Bethesda's God bless you all! In your private as well as public capacity; and as you are honored to be the representatives of a now flourishing increasing people: may you be directed in all your ways! May truth, justice, religion, and piety be established amongst you through all generations!

Lastly, My reverend brethren, and you inhabitants of the colony, accept unfeigned thanks for the honor done me, in letting us see you at Bethesda this day. You, Sir, for the sermon preached here last year. Tell it in Germany, tell my great, good friend, Professor Franck, that Bethesda's God, is a God whose mercy endureth for ever. O let us have your earnest prayers! Encourage your people not to "despise the day of small things." What hath God wrought? From its infancy, this colony hath been blessed with many faithful gospel ministers: O that this may be a nursery to many more! This hath been the case of the New England College for almost a century, and why not the Orphan-house Academy at Georgia?

Men, brethren, fathers, as many of you, whether inhabitants or strangers, who have honored this day with your presence, give us the additional blessings of your prayers. And O that Bethesda's God may make this day, though but a day of small things, productive of great things to the souls of all amongst whom I have been now preaching the kingdom of God. A great and good day will it be indeed, if Jesus Christ, our great Zerubbabel, should, by the power of the eternal Spirit, bless any thing that hath now been said, to cause every mountain of difficulty, that lies in the way of your conversion, to become a plain. And what art thou, O great mountain, whether the lust of the flesh, the lust of the eye, or the pride of life, sin, or self-righteousness? Before our Bethesda's God, thou shalt become a plain.

Brethren, my heart is enlarged towards you: it is written, blessed be God that it is written, "In the name of Jesus every knee shall bow, whether things in heaven, or things in earth, or things under the earth." O that we may be made a willing people in the day of his power! Look, look unto him, all ye that are placed in these ends of the earth. This house hath often been an house of God, a gate of heaven, to some of your fathers. May it be a house of God, a gate of heaven, to the children also! Come unto him, all ye that are weary and heavy laden, he will give you rest; rest from the guilt, rest from the power, rest from the punishment of sin; rest from the fear of divine judgments here, rest with himself eternally hereafter. Fear not, though the beginnings are but small, Christ will not despise the day of small things. A bruised reed will he not break, and the smoking flax will he not quench, until he bring forth judgment unto victory. His hands that laid the foundation, also shall finish it: yet a little while and the top-stone shall be brought forth with shouting, and men and angels join in crying "Grace! Grace! Unto it." That all present may be in this happy number, may God of his infinite mercy grant, through Jesus our Lord.

58. The Method of Grace

Jeremiah 6:14—"They have healed also the hurt of the daughter of my people slightly, saying, Peace, peace, when there is no peace."

As God can send a nation or people no greater blessing than to give them faithful, sincere, and upright ministers, so the greatest curse that God can possibly send upon a people in this world, is to give them over to blind, unregenerate, carnal, lukewarm, and unskilled guides. And yet, in all ages, we find that there have been many wolves in sheep's clothing, many that daubed with untempered mortar, that prophesied smoother things than God did allow. As it was formerly, so it is now; there are many that corrupt the Word of God and deal deceitfully with it. It was so in a special manner in the prophet Jeremiah's time; and he, faithful to his Lord, faithful to that God who employed him, did not fail from time to time to open his mouth against them, and to bear a noble testimony to the honor of that God in whose name he from time to time spake. If you will read this prophecy, you will find that none spake more against such ministers than Jeremiah, and here especially in the chapter out of which the text is taken, he speaks very severely against them—he charges them with several crimes; particularly, he charges them with covetousness: says he in the 13th verse, 'from the least of them even to the greatest of them, every one is given to covetousness; and from the prophet even unto the priest, every one dealeth false.' And then, in the words of the text, in a more special manner, he exemplifies how they had dealt falsely, how they had behaved treacherously to poor souls: says he, 'They have healed also the hurt of the daughter of my people slightly, saying, Peace, peace, when there is no peace.' The prophet, in the name of God, had been denouncing war against the people, he had been telling them that their house should be left desolate, and that the Lord would certainly visit the land with war. 'Therefore,' says he, in the 11th verse, 'I am full of the fury of the Lord; I am weary with holding in; I will pour it out upon the children abroad, and upon the assembly of young men together; for even the husband with the wife shall be taken, the aged with him that is full of days. And their houses shall be turned unto others, with their fields and wives together; for I will stretch out my hand upon the inhabitants of the land, saith the Lord.' The prophet gives a thundering message, that they might be terrified and have some convictions and inclinations to repent; but it seems that the false prophets, the false priests, went about stifling people's convictions, and when they were hurt or a little terrified, they were for daubing over the wound, telling them that Jeremiah was but an enthusiastic preacher, that there could be no such thing as war among them, and saying to people, Peace, peace, be still, when the prophet told them there was no peace. The words, then, refer primarily unto outward things, but I verily believe have also a further reference to the soul, and are to be referred to those false teachers, who, when people were under conviction of sin, when people were beginning to look towards heaven, were for stifling their convictions and telling them they were good enough before. And, indeed, people generally love to have it so; our hearts are exceedingly deceitful, and desperately wicked; none but the eternal God knows how treacherous they are. How many of us cry, Peace, peace, to our souls, when there is no peace! How many are there who are now settled upon their lees, that now think they are Christians, that now flatter themselves that they have an interest in Jesus Christ; whereas if we come to examine their experiences, we shall find that their peace is but a peace of the devil's making—it is not a peace of God's giving—it is not a peace that passeth human understanding. It is matter, therefore, of great importance, my dear hearers, to know whether we may speak peace to our hearts. We are all desirous of peace; peace is an unspeakable blessing; how can we live without peace? And, therefore, people from time to time must be taught how far they must go, and what must be wrought in them, before they can speak peace to their hearts. This is what I design at present, that I may deliver my soul, that I may be free from the blood of those to whom I preach—that I may not fail to declare the whole counsel of God. I shall, from the words of the text, endeavor to show you what you must undergo, and what must be wrought in you before you can speak peace to your hearts.

But before I come directly to this, give me leave to premise a caution or two. And the first is, that I take it for granted you believe religion to be an inward thing; you believe it to be a work in the heart, a work wrought in the soul by the power of the Spirit of God. If you do not believe this, you do not believe your Bibles. If you do not believe this, though you have got your Bibles in your hand, you hate the Lord Jesus Christ in your heart; for religion is everywhere represented in Scripture as the work of God in the heart. 'The kingdom of God is within us,' says our Lord; and, 'He is not a Christian who is one outwardly; but he is a Christian who is one inwardly.' If any of you place religion in outward things, I shall not perhaps please you this morning; you will understand me no more when I speak of the work of God upon a poor sinner's heart, than if I were talking in an unknown tongue. I would further premise a caution, that I would by no means confine God to one way of acting. I would by no means say, that all persons, before they come to have a settled peace in their hearts, are obliged to undergo the same degrees of conviction. No; God has various ways of bringing his children home; his sacred Spirit bloweth when, and where, and how it listeth. But, however, I will venture to affirm this, that before ever you can speak peace to your heart, whether by shorter or longer continuance of your convictions, whether in a more pungent or in a more gentle way, you must undergo what I shall hereafter lay down in the following discourse.

First, then, before you can speak peace to your hearts, you must be made to see, made to feel, made to weep over, made to bewail, your actual transgressions against the law of God. According to the covenant of works, 'The soul that sinneth it shall die;' cursed is that man, be he what he may, that continueth not in all things that are written in the book of the law to do them. We are not only to do some things, but we are to do all things, and we are to continue so to do; so that the least deviation from the moral law, according to the covenant of works, whether in thought, word, or deed, deserves eternal death at the hand of God. And if one evil thought, if one evil word, if one evil action, deserves eternal damnation, how many hells, my friends, do every one of us deserve, whose whole lives have been one continued rebellion against God! Before ever, therefore, you can speak peace to your hearts, you must be brought to see, brought to believe, what a dreadful thing it is to depart from the living God.

And now, my dear friends, examine your hearts, for I hope you came hither with a design to have your souls made better. Give me leave to ask you, in the presence of God, whether you know the time, and if you do not know exactly the time, do you know there was a time, when God wrote bitter things against you, when the arrows of the Almighty were within you? Was ever the remembrance of your sins grievous to you? Was the burden of your sins intolerable to your thoughts? Did you ever see that God's wrath might justly fall upon you, on account of your actual transgressions against God? Were you ever in all your life sorry for your sins? Could you ever say, My sins are gone over my head as a burden too heavy for me to bear? Did you ever experience any such thing as this? Did ever any such thing as this pass between God and your soul? If not, for Jesus Christ's sake, do not call yourselves Christians; you may speak peace to your hearts, but there is no peace. May the Lord awaken you, may the Lord convert you, may the Lord give you peace, if it be his will, before you go home!

But further: you may be convinced of your actual sins, so as to be made to tremble, and yet you may be strangers to Jesus Christ, you may have no true work of grace upon your hearts. Before ever, therefore, you can speak peace to your hearts, conviction must go deeper; you must not only be convinced of your actual transgressions against the law of God, but likewise of the foundation of all your transgressions. And what is that? I mean original sin, that original corruption each of us brings into the world with us, which renders us liable to God's wrath and damnation. There are many poor souls that think themselves fine reasoners, yet they pretend to say there is no such thing as original sin; they will charge God with injustice in imputing Adam's sin to us; although we have got the mark of the beast and of the devil upon us, yet they tell us we are not born in sin. Let them look abroad into the world and see the disorders in it, and think, if they can, if this is the paradise in which God did put man. No! everything in the world is out of order. I have often thought, when I was abroad, that if there were no other argument to prove original sin, the rising of wolves and tigers against man, nay, the barking of a dog against us, is a proof of original sin. Tigers and lions durst not rise against us, if it were not for Adam's first sin; for when the creatures rise up against us, it is as much as to say, You have sinned against God, and we take up our Master's quarrel. If we look inwardly, we shall see enough of lusts, and man's temper contrary to the temper of God. There is pride, malice, and revenge, in all our hearts; and this temper cannot come from God; it comes from our first parent, Adam, who, after he fell from God, fell out of God into the devil. However, therefore, some people may deny this, yet when conviction comes, all carnal reasonings are battered down immediately and the poor soul begins to feel and see the fountain from which all the polluted streams do flow. When the sinner is first awakened, he begins to wonder—How came I to be so wicked? The Spirit of God then strikes in, and shows that he has no good thing in him by nature; then he sees that he is altogether gone out of the way, that he is altogether become abominable, and the poor creature is made to live down at the foot of the throne of God, and to acknowledge that God would be just to damn him, just to cut him off, though he never had committed one actual sin in his life. Did you ever feel and experience this, any of you—to justify God in your damnation—to own that you are by nature children of wrath, and that God may justly cut you off, though you never actually had offended him in all your life? If you were ever truly convicted, if your hearts were ever truly cut, if self were truly taken out of you, you would be made to see and feel this. And if you have never felt the weight of original sin, do not call yourselves Christians. I am verily persuaded original sin is the greatest burden of a true convert; this ever grieves the regenerate soul, the sanctified soul. The indwelling of sin in the heart is the burden of a converted person; it is the burden of a true Christian. He continually cries out, "O! who will deliver me from this body of death,' this indwelling corruption in my heart? This is that which disturbs a poor soul most. And, therefore, if you never felt this inward corruption, if you never saw that God might justly curse you for it, indeed, my dear friends, you may speak peace to your hearts, but I fear, nay, I know, there is no true peace.

Further: before you can speak peace to your hearts, you must not only be troubled for the sins of your life, the sin of your nature, but likewise for the sins of your best duties and performances. When a poor soul is somewhat awakened by the terrors of the Lord, then the poor creature, being born under the covenant of works, flies directly to a covenant of works again. And as Adam and Eve hid themselves among the trees of the garden, and sewed fig leaves together to cover their nakedness, so the poor sinner, when awakened, flies to his duties and to his performances, to hide himself from God, and goes to patch up a righteousness of his own. Says he, I will be mighty good now—I will reform—I will do all I can; and then certainly Jesus Christ will have mercy on me.

But before you can speak peace to your heart, you must be brought to see that God may damn you for the best prayer you ever put up; you must be brought to see that all your duties—all your righteousness—as the prophet elegantly expresses it—put them all together, are so far from recommending you to God, are so far from being any motive and inducement to God to have mercy on your poor soul, that he will see them to be filthy rags, a menstruous cloth—that God hates them, and cannot away with them, if you bring them to him in order to recommend you to his favor. My dear friends, what is there in our performances to recommend us unto God? Our persons are in an unjustified state by nature, we deserve to be damned ten thousand times over; and what must our performances be? We can do no good thing by nature: 'They that are in the flesh cannot please God.' You may do many things materially good, but you cannot do a thing formally and rightly good; because nature cannot act above itself. It is impossible that a man who is unconverted can act for the glory of God; he cannot do anything in faith, and 'whatsoever is not of faith is sin.' After we are renewed, yet we are renewed but in part, indwelling sin continues in us, there is a mixture of corruption in every one of our duties; so that after we are converted, were Jesus Christ only to accept us according to our works, our works would damn us, for we cannot put up a prayer but it is far from that perfection which the moral law requireth. I do not know what you may think, but I can say that I cannot pray but I sin—I cannot preach to you or any others but I sin—I can do nothing without sin; and, as one expresseth it, my repentance wants to be repented of, and my tears to be washed in the precious blood of my dear Redeemer. Our best duties are as so many splendid sins. Before you can speak peace in your heart, you must not only be made sick of your original and actual sin, but you must be made sick of your righteousness, of all your duties and performances. There must be a deep conviction before you can be brought out of your self-righteousness; it is the last idol taken out of our heart. The pride of our heart will not let us submit to the righteousness of Jesus Christ. But if you never felt that you had o righteousness of your own, if you never felt the deficiency of your own righteousness, you cannot come to Jesus Christ. There are a great many now who may say, Well, we believe all this; but there is a great difference betwixt talking and feeling. Did you ever feel the want of a dear Redeemer? Did you ever feel the want of Jesus Christ, upon the account of the deficiency of your own righteousness? And can you now say from your heart, Lord, thou mayst justly damn me for the best duties that ever I did perform? If you are not thus brought out of self, you may speak peace to yourselves, but yet there is no peace.

But then, before you can speak peace to your souls, there is one particular sin you must be greatly troubled for, and yet I fear there are few of you think what it is; it is the reigning, the damning sin of the Christian world, and yet the Christian world seldom or never think of it. And pray what is that? It is what most of you think you are not guilty of—and that is, the sin of unbelief. Before you can speak peace to your heart, you must be troubled for the unbelief of your heart. But, can it be supposed that any of you are unbelievers here in this church-yard, that are born in Scotland, in a reformed country, that go to church every Sabbath? Can any of you that receive the sacrament once a year—O that it were administered oftener!—can it be supposed that you who had tokens for the sacrament, that you who keep up family prayer, that any of you do not believe in the Lord Jesus Christ? I appeal to your own hearts, if you would not think me uncharitable, if I doubted whether any of you believed in Christ; and yet, I fear upon examination, we should find that most of you have not so much faith in the Lord Jesus Christ as the devil himself. I am persuaded the devil believes more of the Bible than most of us do. He believes the divinity of Jesus Christ; that is more than many who call themselves Christians do; nay, he believes and trembles, and that is more than thousands amongst us do. My friends, we mistake a historical faith for a true faith, wrought in the heart by the Spirit of God. You fancy you believe, because you believe there is such a book as we call the Bible—because you go to church; all this you may do, and have no true faith in Christ. Merely to believe there was such a person as Christ, merely to believe there is a book called the Bible, will do you no good, more than to believe there was such a man a Caesar or Alexander the Great. The Bible is a sacred depository. What thanks have we to give to God for these lively oracles! But yet we may have these, and not believe in the Lord Jesus Christ. My dear friends, there must be a principle wrought in the heart by the Spirit of the living God. Did I ask you how long it is since you believed in Jesus Christ, I suppose most of you would tell me, you believed in Jesus Christ as long as ever you remember—you never did misbelieve. Then, you could not give me a better proof that you never yet believed in Jesus Christ, unless you were sanctified early, as from the womb; for, they that otherwise believer in Christ know there was a time when they did not believe in Jesus Christ. You say you love God with all your heart, soul, and strength. If I were to ask you how long it is since you loved God, you would say, As long as you can remember; you never hated God, you know no time when there was enmity in your heart against God. Then, unless you were sanctified very early, you never loved God in your life. My dear friends, I am more particular in this, because it is a most deceitful delusion, whereby so many people are carried away, that they believe already. Therefore, it is remarked of Mr. Marshall, giving account of his experiences, that he had been working for life, and he had ranged all his sins under the ten commandments, and then coming to a minister, asked him the reason why he could not get peace. The minister looked at his catalogue, Away, says he, I do not find one word of the sin of unbelief in all your catalogue. It is the peculiar work of the Spirit of God to convince us of our unbelief—that we have got no faith. Says Jesus Christ, of the sin of unbelief; 'of sin,' says Christ, 'because they believe not on me.' Now, my dear friends, did God ever show you that you had no faith? Were you ever made to bewail a hard heart of unbelief? Was it ever the language of your heart, Lord, give me faith; Lord, enable me to lay hold on thee; Lord, enable me to call thee *my* Lord and *my* God? Did Jesus Christ ever convince you in this manner? Did he ever convince you of your inability to close with Christ, and make you to cry out to God to give you faith? If not, do not speak peace to your heart. May the Lord awaken you, and give you true, solid peace before you go hence and be no more!

Once more then: before you can speak peace to your heart, you must not only be convinced of your actual and original sin, the sins of your own righteousness, the sin of unbelief, but you must be enabled to lay hold upon the perfect righteousness, the all-sufficient righteousness, of the Lord Jesus Christ; you must lay hold by faith on the righteousness of Jesus Christ, and then you shall have peace. 'Come,' says Jesus, 'unto me, all ye that are weary and heavy laden, and I will give you rest.' This speaks encouragement to all that are weary and heavy laden; but the promise of rest is made to them only upon their coming and believing, and taking him to be their God and their all. Before we can ever have peace with God, we must be justified by faith through our Lord Jesus Christ, we must be enabled to apply Christ to our hearts, we must have Christ brought home to our souls, so as his righteousness may be made our righteousness, so as his merits may be imputed to our souls. My dear friends, were you ever married to Jesus Christ? Did Jesus Christ ever give himself to you? Did you ever close with Christ by a lively faith, so as to feel Christ in your hearts, so as to hear him speaking peace to your souls? Did peace ever flow in upon your hearts like a river? Did you ever feel that peace that Christ spoke to his disciples? I pray God he may come and speak peace to you. These things you must experience. I am not talking of the invisible realities of another world, of inward religion, of the work of God upon a poor sinner's heart. I am not talking of a matte of great importance, my dear hearers; you are all concerned in it, your souls are concerned in it, your eternal salvation is concerned in it. You may be all at peace, but perhaps the devil has lulled you asleep into a carnal lethargy and security, and will endeavor to keep you there, till he get you to hell, and there you will be awakened; but it will be dreadful to be awakened and find yourselves so fearfully mistaken, when the great gulf is fixed, when you will be calling to all eternity for a drop of water to cool your tongue, and shall not obtain it.

Give me leave, then, to address myself to several sorts of persons; and O may God, of his infinite mercy, bless the application! There are some of you perhaps can say, Through grace we can go along with you. Blessed be God, we have been convinced of our actual sins, we have been convinced of original sin, we have been convinced of self-righteousness, we have felt the bitterness of unbelief, and through grace we have closed with Jesus Christ; we can speak peace to our hearts, because God hath spoken peace to us. Can you say so? Then I will salute you, as the angels did the women the first day of the week, All hail! Fear not ye, my dear brethren, you are happy souls; you may lie down and be at peace indeed, for God hath given you peace; you may be content under all the dispensations of providence, for nothing can happen to you now, but what shall be the effect of God's love to your soul; you need not fear what sightings may be without, seeing there is peace within. Have you closed with Christ? Is God your friend? Is Christ your friend? Then, look up with comfort; all is yours, and you are Christ's, and Christ is God's. Everything shall work together for your good; the very hairs of your head are numbered; he that toucheth you, toucheth the apple of God's eye. But then, my dear friends, beware of resting on your first conversion. You that are young believers in Christ, you should be looking out for fresh discoveries of the Lord Jesus Christ every moment; you must not build upon your past experiences, you must not build upon a work within you, but always come out of yourselves to the righteousness of Jesus Christ without you; you must be always coming as poor sinners to draw water out of the wells of salvation; you must be forgetting the things that are behind, and be continually pressing forward to the things that are before. My dear friends, you must keep u a tender, close walk with the Lord Jesus Christ. There are many of us who lose our peace by our untender walk; something or other gets in betwixt Christ and us, and we fall into darkness; something or other steals our hearts from God, and this grieves the Holy Ghost, and the Holy Ghost leaves us to ourselves. Let me, therefore, exhort you that have got peace with God, to take care that you do not lose this peace. It is true, if you are once in Christ, you cannot finally fall from God: 'There is no condemnation to them that are in Christ Jesus;' but if you cannot fall finally, you may fall foully, and may go with broken bones all your days. Take care of backslidings; for Jesus Christ's sake, do not grieve the Holy Ghost you may never recover your comfort while you live. O take care of going a gadding and wandering from God, after you have closed with Jesus Christ. My dear friends, I have paid dear for backsliding. Our hearts are so cursedly wicked, that if you take not care, if you do not keep up a constant watch, your wicked hearts will deceive you, and draw you aside. It will be sad to be under the scourge of a correcting Father; witness the visitation of Job, David, and other saints in Scripture. Let me, therefore, exhort you that have got peace to keep a close walk with Christ. I am grieved with the loose walk of those that are Christians, that have had discoveries of Jesus Christ; there is so little difference betwixt them and other people, that I scarce know which is the true Christian. Christians are afraid to speak of God—they run down with the stream; if they come into worldly company, they will talk of the world as if they were in their element; this you would not do when you had the first discoveries of Christ's love; you could talk then of Christ's love for ever, when the candle of the Lord shined upon your soul. That time has been when you had something to say for your dear Lord; but now you can go into company and hear others speaking about the world bold enough, and you are afraid of being laughed at if you speak for Jesus Christ. A great many people have grown conformists now in the worst sense of the word; they will cry out against the ceremonies of the church, as they may justly do; but then you are mighty fond of ceremonies in your behavior; you will conform to the world, which is a great deal worse. Many will stay till the devil bring up new fashions. Take care, then, not to be conformed to the world. What have Christians to do with the world? Christians should be singularly good, bold for their Lord, that all who are with you may take notice that you have been with Jesus. I would exhort you to come to a settlement in Jesus Christ, so as to have a continual abiding of God in your heart. We go a-building on our faith of adherence, and lost our comfort; but we should be growing up to a faith of assurance, to know that we are God's, and so walk in the comfort of the Holy Ghost and be edified. Jesus Christ is now much wounded in the house of his friends. Excuse me in being particular; for, my friends, it grieves me more that Jesus Christ should be wounded by his friends than by his enemies. We cannot expect anything else from Deists; but for such as have felt his power, to fall away, for them not to walk agreeably to the vocation wherewith they are called—by these means we bring our Lord's religion into contempt, to be a byword among the heathen. For Christ's sake, if you know Christ keep close by him; if God have spoken peace, O keep that peace by looking up to Jesus Christ every moment. Such as have got peace with God, if you are under trials, fear not, all things shall work for your good; if you are under temptations, fear not, if he has spoken peace to your hearts, all these things shall be for your good.

But what shall I say to you that have got o peace with God?—and these are, perhaps, the most of this congregation: it makes me weep to think of it. Most of you, if you examine your hearts, must confess that God never yet spoke peace to you; you are children of the devil, if Christ is not in you, if God has not spoken peace to your heart. Poor soul! What a cursed condition are you in. I would not be in your case for ten thousand, thousand worlds. Why? You are just hanging over hell. What peace can you have when God is your enemy, when the wrath of God is abiding upon your poor soul? Awake, then, you that are sleeping in a false peace, awake, ye carnal professors, ye hypocrites that go to church, receive the sacrament, read your Bibles, and never felt the power of God upon your hearts; you that are formal professors, you that are baptized heathens; awake, awake, and do not rest on a false bottom. Blame me not for addressing myself to you; indeed, it is out of love to your souls. I see you are lingering in your Sodom, and wanting to stay there; but I come to you as the angel did to Lot, to take you by the hand. Come away, my dear brethren—fly, fly, fly for your lives to Jesus Christ, fly to a bleeding God, fly to a throne of grace; and beg of God to break your hearts, beg of God to convince you of your actual sins, beg of God to convince you of your original sin, beg of God to convince you of your self-righteousness—beg of God to give you faith, and to enable you to close with Jesus Christ. O you that are secure, I must be a son of thunder to you, and O that God may awaken you, though it be with thunder; it is out of love, indeed, that I speak to you. I know by sad experience what it is to be lulled asleep with a false peace; long was I lulled asleep, long did I think myself a Christian, when I knew nothing of the Lord Jesus Christ. I went perhaps farther than many of you do; I used to fast twice a-week, I used to pray sometimes none times a-day, I used to receive the sacrament constantly every Lord's-day; and yet I knew nothing of Jesus Christ in my heart, I knew not that I must be a new creature—I knew nothing of inward religion in my soul. And perhaps, many of you may be deceived as I, poor creature, was; and, therefore, it is out of love to you indeed, that I speak to you. O if you do not take care, a form of religion will destroy your soul; you will rest in it, and will not come to Jesus Christ at all; whereas, these things are only the means, and not the end of religion; Christ is the end of the law for righteousness to all that believe. O, then, awake, you that are settled on your lees; awake you Church professors; awake you that have got a name to live, that are rich and think you want nothing, not considering that you are poor, and blind, and naked; I counsel you to come and buy of Jesus Christ gold, white raiment, and eye-salve. But I hope there are some that are a little wounded; I hope God does not intend to let me preach in vain; I hope God will reach some of your precious souls, and awaken some of you out of your carnal security; I hope there are some who are willing to come to Christ, and beginning to think that they have been building upon a false foundation. Perhaps the devil may strike in, and bid you despair of mercy; but fear not, what I have been speaking to you is only out of love to you—is only to awaken you, and let you see your danger. If any of you are willing to be reconciled to God, God the Father, Son, and Holy Ghost, is willing to be reconciled to you. O then, though you have no peace as yet, come away to Jesus Christ; he is our peace, he is our peace-maker—he has made peace betwixt God and offending man. Would you have peace with God? Away, then, to God through Jesus Christ, who has purchased peace; the Lord Jesus has shed his heart's blood for this. He died for this; he rose again for this; he ascended into the highest heaven, and is now interceding at the right hand of God. Perhaps you think there will be no peace for you. Why so? Because you are sinners? Because you have crucified Christ—you have put him to open shame—you have trampled under foot the blood of the Son of God? What of all this? Yet there is peace for you. Pray, what did Jesus Christ say of his disciples, when he came to them the first day of the week? The first word he said was, he showed them his hands and his side, and said, 'Peace be unto you.' It is as much as if he had said, Fear not, my disciples; see my hands and my feet how they have been pierced for your sake; therefore fear not. How did Chris speak to his disciples? 'Go tell my brethren, and tell broken-hearted Peter in particular, that Christ is risen, that he is ascended unto his Father and your Father, to his God and your God.' And after Christ rose from the dead, he came preaching peace, with an olive branch of peace, like Noah's dove; 'My peace I leave with you.' Who were they? They were enemies of Christ as well as we, they were deniers of Christ once as well as we. Perhaps some of you have backslidden and lost your peace, and you think you deserve no peace; and no more you do. But, then, God will heal your backslidings, he will love you freely. As for you that are wounded, if you are made willing to come to Christ, come away. Perhaps some of you want to dress yourselves in your duties, that are but rotten rags. No, you had better come naked as you are, for you must throw aside your rags, and come in your blood. Some of you may say, We would come, but we have got a hard heart. But you will never get it made soft till ye come to Christ; he will take away the heart of stone, and give you an heart of flesh; he will speak peace to your souls; though ye have betrayed him, yet he will be your peace. Shall I prevail upon any of you this morning to come to Jesus Christ? There is a great multitude of souls here; how shortly must you all die, and go to judgment! Even before night, or to-morrow's night, some of you may be laid out for this kirk-yard. And how will you do if you be not at peace with God—if the Lord Jesus Christ has not spoken peace to your heart? If God speak not peace to you here, you will be damned for ever. I must not flatter you, my dear friends; I will deal sincerely with your souls. Some of you may think I carry things too far. But, indeed, when you come to judgment, you will find what I say is true, either to your eternal damnation or comfort. May God influence your hearts to come to him! I am not willing to go away without persuading you. I cannot be persuaded but God may make use of me as a means of persuading some of you to come to the Lord Jesus Christ. O did you but feel the peace which they have that love the Lord Jesus Christ! 'Great peace have they,' say the psalmist, 'that love they law; nothing shall offend them.' But there is no peace to the wicked. I know what it is to live a life of sin; I was obliged to sin in order to stifle conviction. And I am sure this is the way many of you take; If you get into company, you drive off conviction. But you had better go to the bottom at once; it must be done—your wound must be searched, or you must be damned. If it were a matter of indifference, I would not speak one word about it. But you will be damned without Christ. He is the way, he is the truth, and the life. I cannot think you should go to hell without Christ. How can you dwell with everlasting burnings? How can you abide the thought of living with the devil for ever? Is it not better to have some soul-trouble here, than to be sent to hell by Jesus Christ hereafter? What is hell, but to be absent from Christ? If there were no other hell, that would be hell enough. It will be hell to be tormented with the devil for ever. Get acquaintance with God, then, and be at peace. I beseech you, as a poor worthless ambassador of Jesus Christ, that you would be reconciled to God. My business this morning, the first day of the week, is to tell you that Christ is willing to be reconciled to you. Will any of you be reconciled to Jesus Christ? Then, he will forgive you all your sins, he will blot out all your transgressions. But if you will go on and rebel against Christ, and stab him daily—if you will go on and abuse Jesus Christ, the wrath of God you must expect will fall upon you. God will not be mocked; that which a man soweth, that shall he also reap. And if you will not be at peace with God, God will not be at peace with you. Who can stand before God when he is angry? It is a dreadful thing to fall into the hands of an angry God. When the people came to apprehend Christ, they fell to the ground when Jesus said, 'I am he.' And if they could not bear the sight of Christ when clothed with the rags of mortality, how will they hear the sight of him when he is on his Father's throne? Methinks I see the poor wretches dragged out of their graves by the devil; methinks I see them trembling, crying out to the hills and rocks to cover them. But the devil will say, Come, I will take you away; and then they shall stand trembling before the judgment-seat of Christ. They shall appear before him to see him once, and hear him pronounce that irrevocable sentence, 'Depart from me, ye cursed.' Methinks I hear the poor creatures saying, Lord, if we must be damned, let some angel pronounce the sentence. No, the God of love, Jesus Christ, will pronounce it. Will ye not believe this? Do not think I am talking at random, but agreeably to the Scriptures of truth. If you do not, then show yourselves men, and this morning go away with full resolution, in the strength of God, to cleave to Christ. And may you have no rest in your souls till you rest in Jesus Christ! I could still go on, for it is sweet to talk of Christ. Do you not long for the time when you shall have new bodies—when they shall be immortal, and made like Christ's glorious body? And then they will talk of Jesus Christ for evermore. But it is time, perhaps, for you to go and prepare for your respective worship, and I would not hinder any of you. My design is, to bring poor sinners to Jesus Christ. O that God may bring some of you to himself! May the Lord Jesus now dismiss you with his blessing, and may the dear Redeemer convince you that are unawakened, and turn the wicked from the evil of their way! And may the love of God, that passeth all understanding, fill your hearts. Grant this, O Father, for Christ's sake; to whom, with thee and the blessed Spirit, be all honor and glory, now and for evermore. Amen.

59. The Good Shepherd: A Farewell Sermon

John 10:27–28—"My sheep hear my voice, and I know them, and they follow me. And I give unto them eternal life, and they shall never perish, neither shall any pluck them out of my hand."

It is a common, and I believe, generally speaking, my dear hearers, a true saying, that bad manners beget good laws. Whether this will hold good in every particular, in respect to the affairs of this world, I am persuaded the observation is very pertinent in respect to the things of another: I mean bad manners, bad treatment, bad words, have been overruled by the sovereign grace of God, to produce, and to be the cause of, the best sermons that were ever delivered from the mouth of the God-man, Christ Jesus.

One would have imagined, that as he came clothed with divine efficience, as he came with divine credentials, as he speak as never man spake, no one should have been able to have resisted the wisdom with which he spake; one would imagine, they should have been so struck with the demonstration of the Spirit, that with one consent they should all own that he was 'that prophet that was to be raised up like unto Moses.' But you seldom find our Lord preaching a sermon, but something or other that he said was cavilled at; nay, their enmity frequently broke through all good manners. They often, therefore, interrupted him whilst he was preaching, which shows the enmity of their hearts long before God permitted it to be in their power to shed his innocent blood. If we look no further than this chapter, where he presents himself as a good shepherd, one that laid down his life for his sheep; we see the best return he had, was to be looked upon as possessed or distracted; for we are told, that there was a division therefore again among the Jews for these sayings, and many of them said, 'He hath a devil, and is mad; why hear ye him?' If the master of the house was served so, pray what are the servants to expect? Others, a little more sober-minded, said, 'These are not the words of him that hath a devil;' the devil never used to preach or act in this way; 'Can a devil open the eyes of the blind?' So he had some friends among these rabble. This did not discourage our Lord; he goes on in his work; and we shall never, never go on with the work of God, till, like our Master, we are willing to go through good and through evil report; and let the devil see we are not so complaisant as to stop one moment for his barking at us as we go along.

We are told, that our Lord was at Jerusalem at the feast of the dedication, and it was winter; the feast of dedication held, I think, seven or eight days, for the commemoration of the restoration of the temple and altar, after its profanation by Antiochus. Now this was certainly a mere human institution, and had no divine image, had no divine superscription upon it; and yet I do not find that our blessed Lord and Master preached against it; I do not find that he spent his time about this; his heart was too big with superior things; and I believe when we, like him, are filled with the Holy Ghost, we shall not entertain our audiences with disputes about rites and ceremonies, but shall treat upon the essentials of the gospel, and then rites and ceremonies will appear with more indifference. Our Lord does not say, that he would not go up to the feast, for, on the contrary, he did go there, not so much as to keep the feast, as to have an opportunity to spread the gospel-net; and that should be our method, not to follow disputing; and it is the glory of the Methodists, that we have been now forty years, and, I thank God, there has not been one single pamphlet written by any of our preachers, about the non-essentials of religion.

Our Lord always made the best of every opportunity; and we are told, 'he walked in the temple in Solomon's porch.' One would have thought the scribes and Pharisees would have put him in one of their stalls, and have complimented him with desiring him to preach: no, they let him walk in Solomon's porch. Some think he walked by himself, no body choosing to keep company with him. Methinks I see him walking and looking at the temple, and foreseeing within himself how soon it would be destroyed; he walked pensive, to see the dreadful calamities that would come upon the land, for not knowing the day of its visitation; and it was to let the world see he was not afraid to appear in public: he walked, as much as to say, Have any of you any thing to say to me? and he put himself in their way, that if they had any things to ask him, he was ready to resolve them; and to show them, that though they had treated him so ill, yet he was ready to preach salvation to them.

In the 24th verse we are told, 'Then came the Jews round about him, and said unto him, How long dost thou make us doubt?' They came round about him when they saw him walking in Solomon's porch; now, say they, we will have him, now we will attack him. And now was fulfilled that passage in the Psalms, 'they compassed me about like bees,' to sting me, or rather like wasps. Now, say they, we will get him in the middle of us, and see what sort of a man he is; we will see whether we cannot conquer him; they came to him, and they say, 'How long dost thou make us to doubt?' Now this seems a plausible question, 'How long dost thou make us to doubt?' Pray how long, sir, do you intend to keep us in suspense? Some think the words will bear this interpretation; Pray, sir, how long do you intend thus to steal away our hearts? They would represent him to be a designing man, like Absalom, to get the people on his side, and then set up himself for the Messiah; thus carnal minds always interpret good men's actions. But the meaning seems to be this, they were doubting concerning Christ; doubting Christians may think it is God's fault that they doubt, but, God knows, it is all their own. 'How long dost thou make us to doubt?' I wish you would speak a little plainer, sir, and not let us have any more of your parables. Pray let us know who you are, let us have it from your own mouth; 'if thou be the Christ, tell us plainly;' and I do not doubt, but they put on a very sanctified face, and looked very demure; 'if thou be the Christ, tell us plainly,' intending to catch him: if he do not say he is the Christ, we will say he is ashamed of his own cause; if he tells us plainly that he is the Christ, then we will impeach him to the governor, we will go and tell the governor that this man says he is the Messiah; now we know of no Messiah, but what is to jostle Caesar out of his throne.—The devil always wants to make it believed that God's people, who are the most loyal people in the world, are rebels to the government under which they live; 'If thou be the Christ, tell us plainly.' Our Lord does not let them wait long for an answer; honesty can soon speak: 'I told you, and ye believed not; the works that I do in my Father's name, they bear witness of me.' Had our Lord said, I am the Messiah, they would have taken him up; he knew that, and therefore he joined 'the wisdom of the serpent' with 'the innocence of the dove;' says he, I appeal to my works and doctrine, and if you will not infer from them that I am the Messiah, I have no further argument. 'But,' he adds, 'ye believe not, because ye are not of my sheep.' He complains twice; for their unbelief was the greatest grief of heart to Christ: then he goes on in the words of our text, 'My sheep hear my voice, and I know them, and they follow me. And I give unto them eternal life, and they shall never perish, neither shall any pluck them out of my hand.' My sheep hear my voice; you think to puzzle me, you think to chagrin me with this kind of conduct, but you are mistaken; you do not believe on me, because you are not of my sheep. The great Mr. Stoddard of New England, (and no place under heaven produces greater divines than New England), preached once from these words, 'But ye believe not, because ye are not of my sheep;' a very strange text to preach upon, to convince a congregation! Yet God so blessed it, that two of three hundred souls were awakened by that sermon: God grant such success to attend the labors of all his faithful ministers.

'My sheep hear my voice, and they follow me.' It is very remarkable, there are but two sorts of people mentioned in scripture: it does not say that the Baptists and Independents, nor the Methodists and Presbyterians; no, Jesus Christ divides the whole world into but two classes, sheep and goats: the Lord give us to see this morning to which of these classes we belong.

But it is observable, believers are always compared to something that is good and profitable, and unbelievers are always described by something that is bad, and good for little or nothing.

If you ask me why Christ's people are called sheep, as God shall enable me, I will give you a short, and I hope it will be to you an answer of peace. Sheep, you know, generally love to be together; we say a flock of sheep, we do not say a herd of sheep; sheep are little creatures, and Christ's people may be called sheep, because they are little in the eyes of the world, and they are yet less in their own eyes. O, some people think, if the great men were on our side, if we had king, lords, and commons on our side, I mean if they were all true believers, O if we had all the kings upon the earth on our side! Suppose you had: alas! alas! do you think the church would go on the better? Why, if it were fashionable to be a Methodist at court, if it were fashionable to be a Methodist abroad, they would go with a Bible or a hymn-book, instead of a novel; but religion never thrives under too much sun-shine. 'Not many mighty, not many noble, are called, but God hath chosen the foolish things of the world to confound the wise, and God hath chosen the weak things of the world to confound the things which are mighty.' Dr. Watts says, Here and there I see a king, and here and there a great man, in heaven, but their number is but small.

Sheep are looked upon to be the most harmless, quiet creatures that God hath made: O may God, of his infinite mercy, give us to know that we are his sheep, by our having this blessed temper infused into our hearts by the Holy Ghost. 'Learn of me,' saith our blessed Lord; what to do? To work miracles? No; 'Learn of me, for I am meek and lowly in heart.' A very good man, now living, said once, if there be any particular temper I desire more than another, it is the grace of *meekness*, quietly to bear bad treatment, to forget and to forgive: and at the same time that I am sensible I am injured, not to be overcome of evil, but to have grace given me to overcome evil with good. To the honor of Moses, it is declared, that he was the meekest man upon earth. Meekness is necessary for people in power; a man that is passionate is dangerous. Every governor should have a warm temper, but a man of an unrelenting, unforgiving temper, is no more fit for government than Phaethon to drive the chariot of the sun; he only sets the world on fire.

You all know, that sheep of all creatures in the world are the most apt to stray and be lost; Christ's people may justly, in that respect, be compared to sheep; therefore, in the introduction to our morning service, we say, 'We have erred and strayed from thy ways like lost sheep.' Turn out a horse, or a dog, and they will find their way home, but a sheep wanders about; he bleats here and there, as much as to day, Dear stranger, show me my way home again; thus Christ's sheep are too apt to wander from the fold; having their eye off the great Shepherd, they go into this field and that field, over this hedge and that, and often return home with the loss of their wool.

But at the same time sheep are the most useful creatures in the world; they manure the land, and thereby prepare it for the seed; they clothe our bodies with wool, and there is not the least part of a sheep but is useful to man: O my brethren, God grant that you and I may, in this respect, answer the character of sheep. The world says, because we preach faith we deny good works; this is the usual objection against the doctrine of imputed righteousness, but it is a slander, an impudent slander. It was a maxim in the first reformers' time, that though the *Arminians* preached up good works, you must go to the *Calvinists for them*. Christ's sheep study to be useful, and to clothe all they can; we should labor with our hands, that we may have to give to all those that need.

Believers consider Christ's property in them; he says, 'my sheep:' O blessed be God for that little, dear, great word *My*. We are his eternal election: "the sheep which thou hast given me," says Christ. They were given by God the Father to Christ Jesus, in the covenant made between the Father and the Son from all eternity. They that are not led to see this, I wish them better heads; though, I believe, numbers that are against it have got better hearts: the Lord help us to bear with one another where there is an honest heart.

He calls them 'My sheep;' they are his by purchase. O sinner, sinner, you are come this morning to hear a poor creature take 'his last farewell:' but I want you to forget the creature that is preaching, I want to lead you further than the Tabernacle: Where do you want to lead us? Why, to mount Calvary, there to see at what an expense of blood Christ purchased those whom he calls his own; he redeemed them with his own blood, so that they are not only his by eternal election, but also by actual redemption in time; and they were given to him by the Father, upon condition that he should redeem them by his heart's blood. It was a hard bargain, but Christ was willing to strike the bargain, that you and I might not be damned for ever.

They are his, because they are enabled in a day of God's power voluntarily to give themselves up unto him; Christ says of these sheep, especially, 'that they hear his voice, and that they follow him.' Will you be so good as to mind that! Here is an allusion to a shepherd; now in some places in scripture, the shepherd is represented as going after his sheep; Sam 7:8, Ps 78:71. That is our way in England; but in the Eastern nations, the shepherds generally went before; they held up their crook, and they had a particular call that the sheep understood. Now, says Christ, 'My sheep hear my voice.' 'This is my beloved Son,' saith God, 'hear ye him.' And again, 'The dead shall hear the voice of the Son of God, and live:' now the question is, what do we understand by hearing Christ's voice?

First, we hare Moses' voice, we hear the voice of the law; there is no going to Mount Zion but by the way of mount Sinai; that is the right straight road. I know some say, they do not know when they were converted; those are, I believe, very few: generally, nay, I may say almost always, God deals otherwise. Some are, indeed, called sooner by the Lord than others, but before they are made to see the glory of God, they must hear the voice of the law; so you must hear the voice of the law before ever you will be savingly called unto God. You never throw off your cloak in a storm, but you hug it the closer; so the law makes a man hug close his corruptions, (Rom 7:7, but when the gospel of the Son of God shines into your souls, then they throw off the corruptions which they have hugged so closely; they hear his voice saying, Son, daughter, be of good cheer, thy sins, which are many, are all forgiven thee. 'They hear his voice;' that bespeaks the habitual temper of their minds: the wicked hear the voice of the devil, the lusts of the flesh, the lusts of the eye, and the pride of life; and Christ's sheep themselves attended to it before conversion; but when called afterwards by God, they hear the voice of a Redeemer's blood speaking peace unto them, they hear the voice of his word and of his Spirit.

The consequence of hearing his voice, and the proof that we do hear his voice, will be—to follow him. Jesus said unto his disciples, 'If any man will come after me, let him deny himself, and take up his cross and follow me.' And it is said of the saints in glory, that 'they followed the Lamb whithersoever he went.' Wherever the shepherd turns his crook, and the sheep hear his voice, they follow him; they often tread upon one another, and hurt one another, they are in such haste in their way to heaven. Following Christ means following him through life, following him in every word and gesture, following him out of one clime into another. 'Bid me come to thee upon the water,' said Peter: and if we are commanded to go over the water for Christ, God, of his infinite mercy, follow us! We must first be sure that the great Shepherd points his crook for us: but this is the character of a true servant of Christ, that he endeavors to follow Christ in thought, word, and work.

Now, my brethren, before we go further, as this is the last opportunity I shall have of speaking to you for some months, if we live; some of you, I suppose, do not choose, in general, to rise so soon as you have this morning; now I hope the world did not get into your hearts before you left your beds; now you are here, do let me entreat you to inquire whether you belong to Christ's sheep, or no. Man, woman, sinner, put thy hand to thy heart, and answer me. Didst thou ever hear Christ's voice so as to follow him, to give up thyself without reserve to him? I verily do believe from my inmost soul, (and that is my comfort, now I am about to take my leave of you,) that I am preaching to a vast body, a multitude of dear, precious souls, who, if it were proper for you to speak, would say, Thanks be unto God, that we can follow Jesus in the character of sheep, though we are ashamed to think how often we wander from him, and what little fruit we bring unto him; if that is the language of your hearts, I wish you joy; welcome, welcome, dear soul, to Christ. O blessed be God for his rich grace, his distinguishing, sovereign, electing love, by which he as distinguished you and me. And if he has been pleased to let you hear his voice, though the ministration of a poor miserable sinner, a poor, but happy pilgrim, may the Lord Jesus Christ have all the glory.

If you belong to Jesus Christ, he is speaking of you; for, says he, 'I know my sheep.' 'I know them;' what does that mean? Why, he knows their number, he knows their names, he knows every one for whom he died; and if there were to be one missing for whom Christ died, God the Father would send him down again from heaven to fetch him. 'Of all,' saith he, 'that thou hast given me, have I lost none.' Christ knows his sheep; he not only knows their number, but the words speak the peculiar knowledge and notice he takes of them; he takes as much care of each of them, as if there were but that one single sheep in the world. To the hypocrite he saith, 'Verily, I know you not;' but he knows his saints, he is acquainted with all their sorrows, their trials, and temptations. He bottles up all their tears, he knows their domestic trials, he knows their inward corruptions, he knows all their wanderings, and he takes care to fetch them back again. I remember, I heard good Dr. Marryat, who was a good market-language preacher, once say at Pinner's hall, (I hope that pulpit will be always filled with such preachers), 'God has got a great dog to fetch his sheep back,' says he. Do not you know, that when the sheep wander, the shepherd sends his dog after them, to fetch them back again? So when Christ's sheep wander, he lets the devil go after them, and suffers him to bark at them, who, instead of driving them farther off, is made a means to bring them back again to Christ's fold.

There is a precious word I would have you take notice of, 'I know them,' that may comfort you under all your trials. We sometimes think that Christ does not hear our prayers, that he does not know us; we are ready to suspect that he has forgotten to be gracious; but what a mercy it is that he does know us. We accuse one another, we turn devils to one another, are accusers of the brethren; and what will support two of God's people when judged by one another but this, Lord, thou knowest my integrity, thou knowest how matters are with me?

But, my brethren, here is something better, here is good news for you; what is that? Say you: why, 'I give unto them eternal life, and they shall never perish, neither shall any pluck them out of my hand.' O that the words may come to your hearts with as much warmth and power as they did to mine thirty-five years ago. I never prayed against any corruption I had in my life, so much as I did against going into holy orders so soon as my friends were for having me go: and bishop Benson was pleased to honor me with peculiar friendship, so as to offer me preferment, or do any thing for me. My friends wanted me to mount the church betimes, they wanted me to knock my head against the pulpit too young; but how some young men stand up here and there and preach, I do not know how it may be to them; but God knows how deep a concern entering into the ministry and preaching, was to me; I have prayed a thousand times, till the sweat has dropped from my face like rain, that God, of his infinite mercy, would not let me enter the church before he called me to, and thrust me forth in, his work. I remember once in Gloucester (I know the room, I look up at the window when I am there and walk along the street; I know the window, the bedside, and the floor, upon which I have lain prostrate) I said, Lord, I cannot go, I shall be puffed up with pride, and fall into the condemnation of the devil; Lord, do not let me go yet; I pleaded to be at Oxford two or three years more; I intended to make an hundred and fifty sermons, and thought I would set up with a good stock in trade but I remember praying, wrestling, and striving with God; I said, I am undone, I am unfit to preach in thy great name, send me not, pray, Lord, send me not yet. I wrote to all my friends in town and country, to pray against the bishop's solicitations, but they insisted I should go into orders before I was twenty-two. After all the solicitations, these words came into my mind, 'My sheep hear my voice, and none shall pluck them out of my hand.' O may the words be blessed to you, my dear friends, that I am parting with, as they were to me when they came warm upon my heart; then, and not till then, I said, Lord, I will go, send me when thou wilt. I remember when I was in a place called Dover-Island, near Georgia, we put in with bad winds; I had an hundred and fifty in family to maintain, and not a single farthing to do it with, in the dearest part of the king's dominions; I remember, I told a minister of Christ, now in heaven, I had these words once, sir, "Nothing shall pluck you out of my hand." 'O', says he, 'take comfort from them, you may be sure God will be as good as his word, if he never tells you so again.' And our Lord knew his poor sheep would be always doubting they should never reach heaven, therefore says he, 'I give to them eternal life, and they shall never perish.'

Here are in our text three blessed declarations, or promises:

First. *I know them.*

Second. *They shall never perish*; though they often think they shall perish by the hand of their lusts and corruptions; they think they shall perish by the deceitfulness of their hearts; but Christ says, 'They shall never perish.' I have brought them out of the world to myself, and do you think I will let them go to hell after that? 'I give to them eternal life;' pray mind that; not, I will, but I do. Some talk of being justified at the day of judgment; that is nonsense; if we are not justified here, we shall not be justified there. He gives them eternal life, that is, the earnest, the pledge, and assurance of it. The indwelling of the Spirit of God here, is the earnest of glory hereafter.

Third. *Neither shall any pluck them out of My hand.* He holds them in his hand, that is, he holds them by his power; none shall pluck them thence. There is always something plucking at Christ's sheep; the devil, the lust of the flesh, the lust of the eye, and the pride of life, all try to pluck them out of Christ's hand. O my brethren, they need not pluck us, yet we help all three to pluck ourselves out of the hand of Jesus; but 'none shall pluck them out of my hand,' says Christ. 'I give to them eternal life. I am going to heaven to prepare a place for them, and there they shall be.' O my brethren, if it were not for keeping you too long, and too much exhausting my own spirits, I could call upon you to leap for you; there is not a more blessed text to support the final perseverance of the saints; and I am astonished any poor souls, and good people I hope too, can fight against the doctrine of the perseverance of the saints: What if a person say they should persevere in wickedness? Ah! That is an abuse of the doctrine; what, because some people spoil good food, are we never to eat it? But, my brethren, upon this text I can leave my cares, and all my friends, and all Christ's sheep, to the protection of Christ Jesus' never-failing love.

I thought this morning, when I came here, riding from the other end of the town, it was to me like coming to be executed publicly; and when the carriage turned just at the end of the walk, and I saw you running here, O, thinks I, it is like a person now coming just to the place where he is to be executed. When I went up to put on my gown, I thought it was just like dressing myself to be made a public spectacle to shed my blood for Christ. I take all heaven and earth to witness, and God and the holy angels to witness, that though I had preferment enough offered me, that though the bishop took me in his arms, and offered me two parishes before I was two-and-twenty, and always took me to his table; though I had preferment enough offered me when I was ordained, thou, O God, knowest, that when the bishop put his hand upon my head, I looked for no other preferment than publicly to suffer for the Lamb of God: in this spirit I came out, in this spirit I came up to this metropolis. I was thinking, when I read of Jacob's going over the brook with a staff, that I could not say I had so much as a staff, but I came up without a friend, I went to Oxford without a friend, I had not a servant, I had not a single person to introduce me; but God, by his Holy Spirit, was pleased to raise me up to preach for his great name's sake: through his divine Spirit I continue to this day, and feel my affections are as strong as ever towards the work and the people of the living God. The congregations at both ends of the town are dear to me: God has honored me to build this and the other place; and, blessed be his name, when he called me to Georgia at first, and I left all London affairs to God's care, when I had most of the churches in London open to me, and had twelve or fourteen constables to keep the doors, that people might not crowd too much; I had offers of hundreds then to settle in London, yet I gave it all up to turn pilgrim for God, to go into a foreign clime; and I hope with that same single intention I am going now—

Now I must come to the hardest part I have to act; I was afraid when I came out from home, that I could not bear the shock, but I hope the Lord Jesus Christ will help me to bear it, and help you to give me up to the blessed God, let him do with me what he will. This is the thirteenth time of my crossing the mighty waters; it is a little difficult at this time of life; and though my spirits are improved in some degree, yet weakness is the best of my strength: but I am clear as light in my call and God fills me with a peace that is unutterable, which a stranger intermeddles not with: into his hands I commend my spirit; and I beg that this may be the language of your hearts: Lord, keep him, let nothing pluck him out of thy hands. I expect many a trial while I am on board, Satan always meets me there; but that God who has kept me, I believe will keep me. I thank God, I have the honor of leaving every thing quite well and easy at both ends of the town; and, my dear hearers, my prayers to God shall be, that nothing may pluck you out of Christ's hands. Witness against me, if I ever set up a party for myself. Did ever any minister, or could any minister in the world say, that I ever spoke against any one going to any dear minister? I thank God, that he has enabled me to be always strengthening the hands of all, though some have afterwards been ashamed to own me. I declare to you, that I believe God will be with me, and will strengthen me; and I believe it is in answer to your prayers that God is pleased to revive my spirits: may the Lord help you to pray on. If I am drowned in the waves, I will say, while I am drowning, Lord, take care of my London, take care of my English friends, let nothing pluck them out of thy hands.

And as Christ has given us eternal life, O my brethren, some of you, I doubt not, will be gone to him before my return; but, my dear brethren, my dear hearers, never mind that; we shall part, but it will be to meet again for ever. I dare not meet you now, I cannot bear your coming to me, to part from me; it cuts me to the heart, and quite overcomes me, but by and by all parting will be over, and all tears shall be wiped away from our eyes. God grant that none that weep now at my parting, may weep at our meeting at the day of judgment; and if you never were among Christ's sheep before, may Christ Jesus bring you now. O come, come, see what it is to have eternal life; do not refuse it; haste, sinner, haste away: may the great, the good Shepherd, draw your souls. Oh! If you never heard his voice before, God grant you may hear it now; that I may have this comfort when I am gone, that I had the last time of my leaving you, that some souls are awakened at the parting sermon. O that it may be a farewell sermon to you; that it may be a means of your taking a farewell of the world, the lust of the flesh, the lust of the eye, and the pride of life. O come! Come! Come! To the Lord Jesus Christ; to him I leave you.

And you, dear sheep, that are already in his hands, O may God keep you from wandering; God keep you near Christ's feet; I do not care what shepherds keep you, so as you are kept near the great Shepherd and Bishop of souls. The Lord God keep you, lift up the light of his countenance upon you, and give you peace. Amen.

Sermons of Reverend Charles Haddon Spurgeon

A Caution to the Presumptuous

A Sermon (No. 22) Delivered on Sabbath Morning, May 13, 1855, by the REV. C. H. SPURGEON At Exeter Hall, Strand.

"Let him that thinketh he standeth take heed lest he fall."—1 Corinthians 10:12.

It is a singular fact, but nevertheless most certain, that the vices are the counterfeits of virtues. Whenever God sends from the mint of heaven a precious coin of genuine metal, Satan will imitate the impress, and utter a vile production of no value. God gives love; it is his nature and his essence. Satan also fashioneth a thing which he calls love, but it is lust. God bestows courage; and it is a good thing to be able to look one's fellow in the face, fearless of all men in doing our duty. Satan inspires fool-hardiness, styles it courage, and bids the man rush to the cannon's mouth for "bubble reputation." God creates in man holy fear. Satan gives him unbelief, and we often mistake the one for the other. So with the best of virtues, the saving grace of faith, when it comes to its perfection it ripens into confidence, and there is nothing so comfortable and so desirable to the Christian, as the full assurance of faith. Hence, we find Satan, when he sees this good coin, at once takes the metal of the bottomless pit, imitates the heavenly image and superscription of assurance, and palms upon us the vice of presumption.

We are astonished, perhaps, as Calvinistic Christians, to find Paul saying, "Let him that thinketh he standeth take heed lest he fall;" but we need not be astonished, for though we have a great right to believe that we stand, if we think we stand through the power of God—though we cannot be too confident of the might of the Most High, there is a thing so near akin to true confidence, that unless you use the greatest discernment you cannot tell the difference. Unholy presumption—it is against that which I am to speak this morning. Let me not be misunderstood. I shall not utter one word against the strongest faith. I wish all Little-Faiths were Strong-Faiths, that all Fearings were made Valiants-for-Truth, and the Ready-to-Halts Asahel's Nimble-of-Foot, that they might all run in their Master's work. I speak not against strong faith or full assurance; God giveth it to us; it is the holiest, happiest thing that a Christian can have, and there is no state so desirable as that of being able to say, "I know whom I have believed, and am persuaded that he is able to keep that which I have committed unto him." It is not against that I speak, but I warn you against that evil thing, a false confidence and presumption which creepeth over a Christian, like the cold death-sleep on the mountain-top, from which, if he is not awakened, as God will see that he shall be, death will be the inevitable consequence. "Let him that thinketh he standeth take heed lest he fall." I shall this morning attempt first, to find out the character; secondly, to show the danger; and thirdly, to give the counsel. The character is, the man who thinks he stands; the danger is, that he may fall; and the counsel is, "let him take heed.

I. My first business shall be to FIND OUT THE CHARACTER intended by the presumptuous man, the man who thinks he stands. I could find a multitude of such if I might search the wide world o'er. I could find men in business filled with an arrogant hardihood, who, because they have in one speculation been successful will wade far out into the stormy sea of this contending life, risk their all—and lose it too. I might mention others who, presuming upon their health, are spending their years in sin and their lives in iniquity, because they think their bones iron and their nerves steel, and "all men mortal but themselves." I might speak of men who will venture into the midst of temptation, confident in their boasted power, exclaiming with self-complacency, "Do you think I am so weak as to sin? Oh! no; I shall stand. Give me the glass; I shall never be a drunkard. Give me the song; you will not find me a midnight reveller. I can drink a little and then I can stop." Such are presumptuous men. But I am not about to find them there; my business this morning is with God's church. The fanning must begin with the floor; the winnowing must try the wheat. So we are to winnow the church this morning to discover the presumptuous. We need not go far to find them. There are in every Christian church men who think they stand, men who vaunt themselves in fancied might and power, children of nature finely dressed, but not the living children of the living God; they have not been humbled or broken in spirit, or if they have, they have fostered carnal security until it has grown to a giant and trampled the sweet flower of humility under its foot. They think they stand. I speak now of real Christians, who, notwithstanding, have grown presumptuous, and indulge in a fleshly security. May my Master arouse such, while in preaching I endeavour to go to the core and root of the matter. For a little while I will expatiate upon the frequent causes of presumption in a Christian.

1. And first, a very common cause, is continued worldly prosperity. Moab is settled on his lees, he hath not been emptied from vessel to vessel. Give a man wealth; let his ships bring home continually rich freights; let the winds and waves appear to be his servants to bear his vessels across the bosom of the mighty deep; let his lands yield abundantly; let the weather be propitious to his crops, and the skies smile pleasantly upon his enterprise; let the bands of Orion be loosed for him; let the sweet influence of the Pleiades descend upon him; let uninterrupted success attend him; let him stand among men as a successful merchant, as a princely Dives, as a man who is heaping up riches to a large extent, who is always prospering: or, if not wealth, let him enjoy continued health; let him know no sickness; allow him with braced nerve and brilliant eye, to march through the world, and live happily; give him the buoyant spirit; let him have the song perpetually on his lips, and his eye be ever sparkling with joy:—the happy, happy man who laughs at care, and cries, "Begone, dull care, I prithee begone from me." I say the consequence of such a state to a man, let him be the best Christian who ever breathed, will be presumption; and he will say, "I stand." "In my prosperity," says David, "I said, I shall never be moved." And we are not much better than David, nor half as good. If God should always rock us in the cradle of prosperity—if we were always dandled on the knees of fortune—if we had not some stain on the alabaster pillar, if there were not a few clouds in the sky, some specks in our sunshine—if we had not some bitter drops in the wine of this life, we should become intoxicated with pleasure, we should dream "we stand;" and stand we should, but it would be upon a pinnacle; stand we might, but hike the man asleep upon the mast, each moment we should be in jeopardy. We bless God, then, for our afflictions; we thank him for our depressions of spirit; we extol his name for the losses of our property; for we feel that had it not so happened to us, had he not chastened us every morning, and vexed us every evening, we might have become too secure. Continued worldly prosperity is a fiery trial. If it be so with any of you, apply this proverb to your own state, "As the fining pot for silver, and the furnace for gold: so is a man to his praise."

2. Again, light thoughts of sin will engender presumption. When we are first converted, our conscience is so very tender, that we are afraid of the slightest sin. I have known young converts almost afraid to proceed a step, lest they should put their feet in the wrong direction. They will ask advice of their minister, and difficult cases of moral casuistry will they bring before us, such as we hardly know how to answer. They have a holy timidity, a godly fear, lest they should offend against God. But alas! very soon the fine bloom upon these first ripe fruits is removed by the rough handling of the surrounding world. The sensitive plant of young piety turns into a willow in after life, too pliant, too easily yielding. It is sadly true, that even a Christian will grow by degrees so callous, that the sin which once startled him and made his blood run cold, does not alarm him in the least. I can speak from my own experience. When first I heard an oath, I stood aghast, and knew not where to hide myself; yet now I can hear an imprecation or blasphemy against God, and though a shudder still runs through my veins,

there is not that solemn feeling, that intense anguish, which I felt when first I heard such evil utterances. By degrees we get familiar with sin. The ear in which the cannon has been booming will not notice slight sounds. The men who work in those huge vessels, the hammering of which causes immense noise, cannot at first sleep, for the continual din in their ears; but by-and-by, they, when they are used to it, think nothing of it. So with sin. First, a little sin doth startle us. Soon we say, "Is it not a little one?" like Lot did of Zoar. Then there comes another, larger, and then another, until by degrees we begin to regard it as but a little ill; and then you know, there comes an unholy presumption, and we think we stand. "We have not fallen," say we, "we only did such a little thing; we have not gone astray. True, we tripped a little, but we stood upright in the main. We might have uttered one unholy word, but as for the most of our conversation, it was consistent." So we palliate sin; we throw a gloss over it, we try to hide it. Christian, beware! when thou thinkest lightly of sin, then thou hast become presumptuous. Take heed, lest thou shouldst fall. Sin—a little thing! Is it not a poison! Who knows its deadliness? Sin—a little thing! Do not the little foxes spoil the vines? Sin—a little thing! Doth not the tiny coral insect build a rock that wrecks a navy? Do not little strokes fell lofty oaks? Will not continual droppings wear away stones? Sin—a little thing! It girded his head with thorns that now is crowned with glory. Sin—a little thing! It made him suffer anguish, bitterness, and woe, till he endured "All that incarnate God could bear, with strength enough, and none to spare." It is not a little thing, sirs. Could you weigh it in the scales of eternity, you would fly from it as from a serpent, and abhor the least appearance of evil. But alas! loose thoughts of sin often beget a presumptuous spirit, and we think we stand.

3. A third reason often is, low thoughts of the value of religion. We none of us value religion enough. Religious furor, as it is called, is laughed at everywhere; but I do not believe there is such a thing as religious furor at all. If a man could be so enthusiastic as to give his body to be burned at the stake, could he pour out his drops of blood and turn each drop into a life, and then let that life be slaughtered in perpetual martyrdom, he would not love his God too much. Oh, no! when we think that this world is but a narrow space; that time will soon be gone, and we shall be in the for-ever of eternity; when we consider we must be either in hell or in heaven throughout a never-ending state of immortality, how sirs, can we love too much? how can we set too high a value on the immortal soul? Can we ask too great a price for heaven? Can we think we do too much to serve that God who gave himself for our sins? Ah! no; and yet my friends, most of us do not sufficiently regard the value of religion. We cannot any of us estimate the soul rightly; we have nothing with which to compare it. Gold is sordid dust; diamonds are but small lumps of congealed air that can be made to melt away. We have nought with which to compare the soul; therefore we cannot tell its value. It is because we do not know this, that we presume. Doth the miser who loves his gold let it be scattered on the floor that his servant may steal it? Doth he not hide it in some secret place where no eye shall behold it? Day after day, night after night, he counteth out his treasure because he loves it. Doth the mother trust her babe by the riverside? Doth she not in her sleep think of it? and when it is sick, will she leave it to the care of some poor nurse, who may suffer it to die? Oh! no; what we love, we will not wantonly throw away; what we esteem most precious, we will guard with the most anxious care. So, if Christians knew the value of their souls, if they estimated religion at its proper rate, they never would presume; but low thoughts of Christ, low thoughts of God, mean thoughts of our souls' eternal state—these things tend to make us carelessly secure. Take heed, therefore, of low ideas of the gospel, lest ye be overtaken by the evil one.

4. But again, this presumption often springs from ignorance of what we are, and where we stand. Many Christians have not yet learned what they are. It is true, the first teaching of God is to shew us our own state, but we do not know that thoroughly till many year s after we have known Jesus Christ. The fountains of the great deep within our hearts are not broken up all at once; the corruption of our soul is not developed in an hour. "Son of man," said the angel of Ezekiel, "I will show thee the abominations of Israel." He then took him in at one door, where he saw abominable things, and stood aghast. "Son of man, I will show thee greater abominations than these;" then he takes him into another chamber, and Ezekiel says, "Surely I have now seen the worst." "No," says the angel, "I will show thee greater things than these." So, all our life long the Holy Spirit reveals to us the horrid abomination of our hearts. I know there are some here who do not think anything about it; they think they are good-hearted creatures. Good hearts, have you? Good hearts! Jeremiah had a better heart than you, yet he said, "The heart is deceitful above all things, and desperately wicked; who can know it?" No; the black lesson cannot be learned in a night. God alone knows the evil of

the heart; and Young says, "God spares all eyes but his own that awful sight—the vision of a human heart." If we could but see it, we should stand aghast. Well, it is ignorance of this that makes us presume. We say, "I have a good nature, I have a noble disposition; I have none of those hot and angry passions that some have; I can stand secure; I have not that dry, tindery heart that is on fire in a moment; my passions are weakened; my powers for evil are somewhat taken down, and I may stand safely." Ah! ye little know that it is when ye talk like this, that ye presume. O worm of the dust, thou art not yet free from an evil nature, for sin and corruption remain in the heart even of the regenerate; and it is strangely true, though it appears a paradox, as Ralph Erskine said, that a Christian sometimes thinks himself "To good and evil equal bent And both a devil and a saint." There is such corruption in a Christian, that while he is a saint in his life, and justified through Christ, he seems a devil sometimes in imagination, and a demon in the wishes and corruptions of his soul. Take heed, Christian, thou hast need to be upon the watch tower; thou hast a heart of unbelief; therefore watch thou both night and day.

5. But to finish this delineation of a presumptuous man—Pride is the most pregnant cause of presumption. In all its various shapes it is the fountain of carnal security. Sometimes it is pride of talent. God has endowed a man with gifts; he is able to stand before the multitude, or to write for the many; he has a discerning mind, he has a judgment, and such like things. Then says he, " As for the ignorant, those who have no talent, they may fall; my brother ought to take care: but look at me. How am I wrapped in grandeur!" And thus in his self-complacency he thinks he stands. Ah! those are the men that fall. How many that flamed like comets in the sky of the religious world have rushed into space and been quenched in darkness! How many a man who has stood like a prophet before his fellows, and who would exclaim as he wrapped himself in his conceit, "I, only I am alive, I am the only prophet of God;" and yet that only prophet fell; his lamp was quenched, and his light put out in darkness. How many have boasted of their might and dignity, and have said, "I have built this mighty Babylon," but then they thought they stood, and they fell at once. "Let him that thinketh he standeth," with the proudest talents, "take heed lest he fall."

Others have the pride of grace. That is a curious fact; but there is such a thing as being proud of grace. A man says, "I have great faith, I shall not fall; poor little faith may, but I never shall." " I have fervent love," says another man, "I can stand, there is no danger of my going astray; as for my brother over there, he is so cold and slow, he will fall, I dare say." Says another, "I have a most burning hope of heaven, and that hope will triumph; it will purge my soul from sense and sin, as Christ the Lord is pure. I am safe." He who boasts of grace, has little grace to boast of. But there are some who do that, who think their graces can keep them, knowing not that the stream must flow constantly from the fountain head, else the bed of the brook shall soon be dry, and ye shall see the pebbles at the bottom. If a continuous stream of oil come not to the lamp, though it burn brightly to-day, it shall smoke to-morrow, and noxous will be the scent thereof. Take heed that thou neither gloriest in thy talents nor in thy graces.

Many are worse still; they think they shall not fall because of their privileges. "I take the sacrament, I have been baptized in an orthodox manner, as written in God's word; I attend such and such a ministry; I am well fed; I am fat and flourishing in the courts of my God. If I were one of those starved creatures who hear a false gospel, possibly I might sin; but oh! our minister is the model of perfection; we are constantly fed and made fat; surely we shall stand." Thus in the complacency of their priviledges they run down others, exclaiming, "My mountain standeth firm, I shall never be moved." Take heed, presumption, take heed. Pride cometh before a fall; and a haughty spirit is the usher of destruction. Take heed; watch thy footsteps; for where pride creepeth in, it is the worm at the root of the gourd, causing it to wither and die. "Let him that thinketh he standeth," because of pride of talent, or grace, or privilege, "take heed lest he fall."

I hope I have touched some here; I trust the lancet has been sharp; I have taken the scalpel, and I hope I have discovered something. O ye presumptuous ones, I speak to you; and I shall do so while next I warn you of your danger.

II. I shall be more brief on the second point—THE DANGER. He who thinks he stands is in danger of a fall. The true Christian cannot possibly suffer a final fall, but he is very much disposed to a foul fall. Though the Christian shall not stumble so as to destroy his life, he may break his limb. Though God has given his angels charge over him, to keep him in all his ways, yet there is no commission to keep him when he goes astray; and when he is astray he may thrust himself through with many sorrows.

1. I must now try and give you the reason why a man who thinks he stands is more exposed to the danger of falling than any other. First, because such a man in the

midst of temptation will be sure to be more or less careless. Make a man believe he is very strong, and what will he do? The fight is thickening around him; yet he has his sword in his scabbard. "Oh," saith he, " my arm is nimble and strong; I can draw it out and strike home." So perhaps he lies down in the field, or sloth-fully sleeps in his tent; "for," saith he, "when I hear enemies approaching, such is my prowess and such my might, that I can mow them down by thousands. Ye sentinels watch the weak; go to the Ready-to-halts and the Fearings, and arouse them. But I am a giant; and let me once get this old Toledo blade in my hand, it will cut through body and soul. Whenever I meet my enemies I shall be more than conqueror." The man is careless in battle. He lifteth up his helmet, as it is said Goliath did, and then a stone pierceth his forehead; he throws away his shield, and then an arrow penetrateth his flesh; he will put his sword into his scabbard, then the enemy smiteth him, and he is ill prepared to resist. The man who thinks he is strong, is off his guard; he is not ready to parry the stroke of the evil one, and then the poignard entereth his soul.

2. Again, the man who thinks he stands will not be careful to keep out of the way of temptation, but rather will run into it. I remember seeing a man who was going to a place of worldly amusement—he was a professor of religion—and I called to him, "What doest thou there, Elijah?" "Why do you ask me such a question as that?" said he. I said, "What doest thou here, Elijah? Thou art going there." "Yes," he replied, with some sort of blush, "but I can do that with impunity." "I could not," said I; "if I were there I know I should commit sin. I should not care what people said about it; I always do as I like, so far as I believe it to be right; I leave the saying to anybody who likes to talk about me. But it is a place of danger, and I could not go there with impunity." "Ah!" said he, "I could; I have been before, and I have had some sweet thoughts there. I find it enlarges the intellect. You are narrow-minded; you do not get these good things. It is a rich treat I assure you. I would go if I were you." "No," I said, "it would be dangerous for me: from what I hear, the name of Jesus is profaned there; and there is much said that is altogether contrary to the religion we believe. The persons who attend there are none of the best, and it will surely be said that birds of a feather flock together." "Ah, well," he replied, "perhaps you young men had better keep away; I am a strong man, I can go;" and off he went to the place of amusement. That man, sirs, was an apple of Sodom. He was a professor of religion. I guessed there was something rotten at the core from that very fact; and I found it so by experience, for the man was a downright sensualist even then. He wore a mask, he was a hypocrite, and had none of the grace of God in his heart. Presumptuous men will say they can go into sin, they are so full of moral strength; but when a man tells you he is so good, always read his words backwards, and understand him to mean that he is as bad as he can be. The self-confident man is in danger of falling because he will even run into temptation in the confidence that he is strong, and able to make his escape.

3. Another reason is, that these strong men sometimes will not use the means of grace, and therefore they fall. There are some persons here, who never attend a place of worship very likely; they do not profess to be religious; but I am sure they would be astonished if I were to tell them, that I know some professedly religious people who are accepted in some churches as being true children of God, who yet make it a habit of stopping away from the house of God, because they conceive they are so advanced that they do not want it. You smile at such a thing as that. They boast such deep experience within; they have a volume of sweet sermons at home, and they will stop and read them; they need not go to the house of God, for they are fat and flourishing. They conceit themselves that they have received food enough seven years ago to last them the next ten years. They imagine that old food will feed their souls now. These are your presumptuous men. They are not to be found at the Lord's table, eating the body and drinking the blood of Christ, in the holy emblems of bread and wine. You do not see them in their closets; you do not find them searching the Scriptures with holy curiosity. They think they stand—they shall never be moved; they fancy that means are intended for weaker Christians; and leaving those means, they fall. They will not have the shoe to put upon the foot, and therefore the flint cutteth them; they will not put on the armour, and therefore the enemy wounds them—sometimes well-nigh unto death. In this deep quagmire of neglect of the means, many a haughty professor has been smothered.

4. Once more, the man who is self-confident runs a fearful hazard, because God's Spirit always leaves the proud. The gracious Spirit delights to dwell in the low places. The holy dove came to Jordan; we read not that it ever rested on Bashan. The man upon the white horse rode among the myrtle trees, not among the cedars. The myrtle trees grew at the foot of the mountains; the cedars on the summit thereof. God loves humility. He who walks with fear and trembling, fearing lest he should go astray, that man the Spirit loves; but when once pride

creeps in, and the man declares, "Now I am in no danger," away goes the dove; it flies to heaven and will have nought to do with him. Proud souls, ye quench the Spirit. Ye arrogant men, ye grieve the Holy Ghost. He leaves every heart where pride dwelleth; that evil spirit of Lucifer he abhors; he will not rest with it; he will not tarry in its company. Here is your greatest danger, ye proud ones—that the Spirit leaves those who deny their entire dependence on him.

III. The third point is THE COUNSEL. I have been expounding the text; now I want to enforce it. I would, if my Lord would allow me, speak home to your souls, and so picture the danger of a presumptuous man, that I would make you all cry out to heaven that sooner might you die than presume; that sooner might you be found amongst those who lie prostrate at the foot of Christ, trembling all their lives, than amongst those who think they stand, and therefore fall. Christian men, the counsel of Scripture is—"Take heed."

1. First, take heed, because so many have fallen. My brother, could I take thee into the wards of that hospital where lie sick and wounded Christians, I could make you tremble. I would show you one, who, by a sin that occupied him not a single moment, is so sore broken, that his life is one continued scene of misery. I could show you another one, a brilliant genius, who served his God with energy, who is now—not a priest of the devil it is true, but almost that—sitting down in despair, because of his sin. I could point you to another person, who once stood in the church, pious and consistent, but who now comes up to the same house of prayer as if he were ashamed of himself, sits in some remote corner, and is no longer treated with the kindness he formerly received, the brethren themselves being suspicious, because he so greatly deceived them, and brought such dishonor upon the cause of Christ. Oh! did ye know the sad pain which those endure who fall. Could ye tell how many have fallen, (and have not perished, it is true,) but still have dragged themselves along, in misery, throughout their entire existence, I am sure ye would take heed. Come with me to the foot of the mountain of presumption. See there the maimed and writhing forms of many who once soared with Icarian wings in the airy regions of self-confidence; yet there they lie with their bones broken, and their peace destroyed. There lies one who had immortal life within him; see how full of pain he appears, and he looks a mass of helpless matter. He is alive, it is true, but just alive. Ye know not how some of those enter heaven who are saved, "so as by fire." One man walks to heaven; he keeps consistent; God is with him, and he is happy all his journey through. Another says, "I am strong, I shall not fall." He runs aside to pluck a flower; he sees something which the devil has laid in his way; he is caught first in this gin, and then in that trap; and when he comes near the river, instead of finding before him that stream of nectar of which the dying Christian drinks, he sees fire through which he has to pass, blazing upon the surface of the water. The river is on fire, and as he enters it he is scorched and burned. The hand of God is lifted up saying, "Come on, come on;" but as he dips his foot in the stream, he finds the fire kindling around him, and though the hand clutches him by the hair of the head, and drags him through, he stands upon the shore of heaven, and cries, " I am a monument of divine mercy, for I have been saved so as by fire." Oh! do you want to be saved by fire, Christians? Would ye no rather enter heaven, singing songs of praises? Would ye not glorify him on earth, and then give your last testimony with, "Victory, victory, victory, unto him that loved us;" then shut your eyes on earth, and open them in heaven? If you would do so, presume not. "Let him that thinketh he standeth take heed lest he fall."

2. Once more, my brother, take heed, because a fall will so much damage the cause of Christ. Nothing has hurt religion one-half, or one thousandth part, so much as the fall of God's people. Ah! when a true believer sins, how will the world point at him. "That man was a deacon, but he knows how to charge exorbitantly. That man was a professor, but he can cheat as well as his neighbours. That man is a minister, and he lives in sin." Oh! when the mighty fall—it is rejoice fir tree, for the cedar has fallen—how does the world exult! They chuckle over our sin; they rejoice over our faults; they fly around us, and if they can see one point where we are vulnerable, how will they say, "See these holy people are no better than they should be." Because there is one hypocrite, men set down all the rest the same. I heard one man say, a little while ago, that he did not believe there was a true Christian living, because he had found out so many hypocrites. I reminded him that there could be no hypocrites if there were no genuine ones. No one would try to forge bank notes if there were no genuine ones. No one would think of passing a bad sovereign if there were no sterling coin. So the fact of their being some hypocrites proves that there are some genuine characters. But let those who are so, take heed; let them always, in their conduct, have the ring of true gold. Let your conversation be such as to become the gospel of Christ, lest by any means the

enemy get the advantage over us, and slander the name of Jesus.

And especially is this incumbent upon the members of our own denomination, for it is often said that the doctrines we believe have a tendency to lead us to sin. I have heard it asserted most positively, that those high doctrines which we love and which we find in the Scriptures, are licentious ones. I do not know who has the hardihood to make that assertion, when they consider that the holiest of men have been believers in them. I ask the man who dares to say that Calvinism is a licentious religion, what he thinks of the character of Augustine, or Calvin, or Whitfield, who in successive ages were the great exponents of the system of grace; or what will he say of those Puritans, whose works are full of them? Had a man been an Arminian in those days, he would have been accounted the vilest heretic breathing; but now we are looked upon as the heretics, and they the orthodox. We have gone back to the old school; we can trace our descent from the Apostles. It is that vein of free grace running through the sermonising of Baptists, which has saved us as a denomination. Were it not for that, we should not stand where we are. We can run a golden link from hence up to Jesus Christ himself, through a holy succession of mighty fathers, who all held these glorious truths; and we can say of them, where will you find holier and better men in the world? We are not ashamed to say of ourselves, that however much we may be maligned and slandered, ye will not find a people who will live closer to God than those who believe that they are saved not by their works, but by free grace alone. But, oh! ye believers in free grace, be careful. Our enemies hate the doctrine; and if one falls, "Ah there," say they, "see the tendency of your principles." Nay, we might reply, see what is the tendency of your doctrine. The exception in our case proves the rule is true, that after all, our gospel does lead us to holiness. Of all men, those have the most disinterested piety, the sublimest reverence, the most ardent devotion, who believe that they are saved by grace, without works, through faith, and that not of themselves, it is the gift of God. Christian take heed, lest by any means Christ should be crucified afresh, and should be put unto an open shame.

And now what more can I say? Oh ye, my beloved, ye my brethren, think not that ye stand, lest ye should fall. Oh ye fellow heirs of everlasting life and glory, we are marching along through this weary pilgrimage; and I, whom God hath called to preach to you, would turn affectionately to you little ones, and say, take heed lest ye fall. My brother, stumble not. There lieth the gin, there the snare. I am come to gather the stones out of the road, and take away the stumbling blocks. But what can I do unless, with due care and caution, ye yourselves walk guardedly. Oh, my brethren; be much more in prayer than ever. Spend more time in pious adoration. Read the Scriptures more earnestly and constantly. Watch your lives more carefully. Live nearer to God. Take the best examples for your pattern. Let your conversation be redolent of heaven. Let your hearts be perfumed with affection for men's souls. So live that men may take knowledge of you that you have been with Jesus, and have learned of him; and when that happy day shall come when he whom you love shall say, "Come up higher," let it be your happiness to hear him say, "Come my beloved, thou hast fought a good fight, thou hast finished thy course, and henceforth there is laid up for thee a crown of righteousness that fadeth not away". On, Christian, with care and caution! On, with holy fear and trembling! On yet, with faith and confidence, for thou shalt not fall. Read the next verse of this very chapter: "He will not suffer you to be tempted above that which ye are able to bear, but will, with the temptation, also make a way to escape." But I have some here, perhaps, who may never hear my voice again; and I will not let my congregation go, God helping me, without telling them the way of salvation. Sirs, there are some of you who know ye have not believed in Christ. If ye were to die where ye now sit ye have no hope that ye would rise amongst the glorified in bliss. How many are there here who if their hearts could speak, must testify that they are without God, without Christ, and strangers from the common-wealth of Israel. Oh, let me tell you then, what ye must do to be saved. Does your heart beat high? Do ye grieve over your sins? Do ye repent of your iniquities? Will ye turn unto the living God? If so, this is the way of salvation; "Whosoever believeth and is baptised shall be saved." I cannot reverse my Master's order—he says, "believeth," and then "baptised;" and he tells me that "he that believeth not shall be damned." Oh, my hearers, your works cannot save you. Though I have spoken to Christians, and exhorted them to live in good works, I talk not so to you. I ask ye not to get the flower before ye have the seed. I will not bid you get the roof of your house before ye lay the foundation. Believe on the name of the Lord Jesus Christ, and ye shall be saved. Whosoever here will now cast himself as a guilty worm flat on Jesus—whoever will throw himself into the arms of everlasting love, that man shall be accepted; he shall go from that door justified and forgiven, with his soul as safe as if he were in heaven, without the danger of its ever being lost. All this is through belief in Christ.

Surely ye need no argument. If I thought ye did I would use it. I would stand and weep till ye came to Christ. If I thought I was strong enough to fetch a soul to Jesus, if I thought that moral suasion could win you, I would go round to each of your seats and beg of you in God's name to repent. But since I cannot do that, I have done my duty when I have prophesied to the dry bones. Remember we shall meet again. I boast of neither eloquence nor talent, and I cannot understand why ye come here; I only speak right on, and tell you what I feel; but mark me, when we meet before God's bar, however ill I may have spoken, I shall be able to say, that I said to you, "Believe on the name of Jesus, and ye shall be saved." Why will ye die, O house of Israel? Is hell so sweet, is everlasting torment so much to be desired, that therefore ye can let go the glories of heaven, the bliss of eternity? Men, are ye to live for ever? or, are ye to die like brutes? "Live!" say you, Well, then, are you not desirous to live in a state of bliss? Oh, may God grant you grace to turn to him with full purpose of heart! Come, guilty sinner, come! God help you to come, and I shall be well repaid, if but one soul be added to the visible fold of Jesus, through aught I may have said.

All Joy in All Trials

A Sermon (No. 1704) Delivered on Lord's Day Morning, February 4th, 1883, by C. H. SPURGEON, At the Metropolitan Tabernacle, Newington.

"My brethren, count it all joy when ye fall into divers temptations; knowing this, that the trying of your faith worketh patience. But let patience have her perfect work, that ye may be perfect and entire, wanting nothing."—James 1:2–4.

James calls the converted among the twelve tribes his brethren. Christianity has a great uniting power: it both discovers and creates relationships among the sons of men. It reminds us of the ties of nature, and binds us with the bonds of grace. Every one that is born of the Spirit of God is brother to every other that is born of the same Spirit. Well may we be called brethren, for we are redeemed by one blood; we are partakers of the same life; we feed upon the same heavenly food; we are united to the same living head; we seek the same ends; we love the same Father: we are heirs of the same promises; and we shall dwell for ever together in the same heaven. Wherefore, let brotherly love continue; let us love one another with a pure heart fervently, and manifest that love, not in word only, but in deed and in truth. Whatever brotherhood may be a sham, let the brotherhood of believers be the most real thing beneath the stars.

Beginning with this word "brethren," James shows a true brotherly sympathy with believers in their trials, and this is a main part of Christian fellowship. "Bear ye one another's burdens, and so fulfil the law of Christ." If we are not tempted ourselves at this moment, others are: let us remember them in our prayers; for in due time our turn will come, and we shall be put into the crucible. As we would desire to receive sympathy and help in our hour of need, let us render it freely to those who are now enduring trial. Let us remember those that are in bonds, as bound with them, and those that suffer affliction as being ourselves in the body. Remembering the trials of his brethren, James tries to cheer them, and therefore he says, "My brethren, count it all joy when ye fall into divers trials." It is a part of our high calling to rise ourselves into confidence; and it is also our duty to see that none of our brethren despond, much less despair. The whole tendency of our holy faith is to elevate and to encourage. Grace breeds no sorrow, except the healthy sorrow which comes with saving repentance and leads to the joy of pardon: it comes not to make men miserable, but to wipe all tears from their eyes. Our dream is not of devils descending a dreary staircase to hell, but of angels ascending and descending upon a ladder, the top of which leads to the shining throne of God. The message of the gospel is one of joy and gladness, and were it universally understood and received this world would be no longer a wilderness, but it would rejoice and blossom as the rose. Let grace reign in all hearts, and this earth will become a temple filled with perpetual song; and even the trials of life will become causes of the highest joy, so beautifully described by James as "all joy," as if every possible delight were crowded into it. Blessed be God, it is our work, not to upbraid, but to cheer all the brotherhood: we walk in a light which glorifies everything upon which it falls, and turns losses into gains. We are able in sober earnest to speak with the afflicted, and bid them be patient under the chastening hand of God; yea, to count it all joy when they fall into divers trials because those trials will work out for them such signal, such lasting good. They may be well content to sow in tears since they are sure to reap in joy.

Without further preface we will come at once to the text; and observe that in speaking about affliction, for that is the subject of the text, the apostle notes, first, the essential point which is assailed by temptation, namely, your faith. Your faith is the target that all the arrows are shot at; the furnace is kindled for the trial of your faith. Notice, secondly, the invaluable blessing which is thus gained, namely, the proving of your faith, discovering whether it be the right faith or no. This proof of our faith is a blessing of which I cannot speak too highly. Then, thirdly, we may not overlook the priceless virtue which is produced by this process of testing, namely, patience; for the proving of your faith produces patience, and this is the soul's surest enrichment. Lastly, in connection with that patience we shall note the spiritual completeness which is thus promoted:—"That ye may be perfect and entire, lacking nothing." Perhaps you have noticed that little variations I have made in the text; but I am now following the Revised Version, which gives an admirable rendering. I will read it. "Count it all joy, my brethren, when ye fall into manifold temptations; knowing that the proof of your faith worketh patience. And let patience have its perfect work, that ye may be perfect and entire, lacking in nothing."

I. First, let us think a little upon THE ESSENTIAL POINT WHICH IS ASSAILED by temptation or trial. It is your faith which is tried. It is supposed that you have that faith. You are not the people of God, you are not truly brethren unless you are believers. It is this faith of yours which is peculiarly obnoxious to Satan and to the world which lieth in the wicked one. If you had not faith they would not be enemies of yours; but faith is the mark of the chosen of God, and therefore his foes become the foes of all the faithful, spitting their venom specially upon their faith. God Himself hath put enmity between the serpent and the woman, between the serpent's seed and the woman's seed; and that enmity must show itself. The serpent bites at the heel of the true seed: hence mockings, persecutions, temptations, and trials are sure to beset the pathway to faith. The hand of faith is against all evil, and all evil is against faith. Faith is that blessed grace which is most pleasing to God, and hence it is the most displeasing to the devil. By faith God is greatly glorified, and hence by faith Satan is greatly annoyed. He rages at faith because he sees therein his own defeat and the victory of grace.

Because the trial of your faith brings honour to the Lord, therefore the Lord Himself is sure to try it that out of its trial praise may come to his grace by which faith is sustained. Our chief end is to glorify God, and if our trials enable us more fully to answer the end of our being it is well that they should happen unto us. So early in our discourse we see reason to count it all joy when we fall into manifold trials.

It is by our faith that we are saved, justified, and brought near to God, and therefore it is no marvel that it is attacked. It is by believing in Christ that we are delivered from the reigning power of sin, and receive power to become the sons of God. Faith is as vital to salvation as the heart is vital to the body: hence the javelins of the enemy are mainly aimed at this essential grace. Faith is the standard bearer, and the object of the enemy is to strike him down that the battle may be gained. If the foundations be removed what can the righteous do? If the cable can be snapped whither will the vessel drift? All the powers of darkness which are opposed to right and truth are sure to fight against our faith, and manifold temptations will march in their legions against our confidence in God.

It is by our faith that we live; we began to live by it, and continue to live by it, for "the just shall live by faith." Once let faith go and our life is gone; and hence it is that the powers which war against us make their main assault upon this royal castle, this key of the whole position. Faith is your jewel, your joy, your glory; and the thieves who haunt the pilgrim way are all in league to tear it from you. Hold fast, therefore, this your choice treasure.

It is by faith, too, that Christians perform exploits. If men of old wrought daring and heroic deeds it was by faith. Faith is the fighting principle and the conquering principle: therefore it is Satan's policy to slay it even as Pharaoh sought to kill the male children when Israel dwelt in Egypt. Rob a Christian of his faith and he will be like Samson when his locks were cut away: the Philistines will be upon him and the Lord will have departed from him. Marvel not if the full force of the current shall beat upon your faith, for it is the foundation of your spiritual house. Oh that your faith may abide steadfast and unmovable in all present trials, that so it may be found true in the hour of death and in the day of judgment. Woe unto that man whose faith fails him in this land of peace, for what will he do in the swelling of Jordan?

Now, think of how faith is tried. According to the text we are said to fall into "manifold temptations" or into "divers temptations"—that is to say, we may expect very many and very different troubles. In any case these trials will be most real. The twelve tribes to whom this epistle was written were a specially tried people, for in the first place they were, as Jews, greatly persecuted by all other nations, and when they became Christians they were cruelly persecuted by their own people. A Gentile convert was somewhat less in peril than a Jewish Christian, for the latter was crushed between the upper and nether millstones of Paganism and Judaism. The Israelitish Christian was usually so persecuted by his own kith and kin that he had to flee from them, and whither could he go, for all other people abhorred the Jews? We are not in such a plight, but God's people even to this day will find that trial is no sham word. The rod in God's house is no toy to play with. The furnace, believe me, is no mere place of extra warmth to which you may soon accustom yourself: it is often heated seven times hotter, like the furnace of Nebuchadnezzar and God's children are made to know that the fire burns and devours. Our temptations are no inventions of nervousness nor hobgoblins of dreamy fear. Ye have heard of the patience of Job—his was real patience, for his afflictions were real. Could each tried believer among us tell his own story I do not doubt we would convince all who heard us that the troubles and temptations which we have endured are no fictions of romance, but must be ranked among the stern realities of actual life.

Ay, and note too, that the trials of Christians are such as would in themselves lead us into sin, for I take it that our translators would not have placed the word "temptation" in the text, and the Revisionists would not have retained it, if they had not felt that there was a colouring of temptation in its meaning, and that "trial" was hardly the word. The natural tendency of trouble is not to sanctify, but to induce sin. A man is very apt to become unbelieving under affliction: that is a sin. He is apt to murmur against God under it: that is a sin. He is apt to put forth his hand to some ill way of escaping from his difficulty: and that would be sin. Hence we are taught to pray, "Lead us not into temptation; because trial has in itself a measure of temptation"; and if it were not neutralized by abundant grace it would bear us towards sin. I suppose that every test must have in it a measure of temptation. The Lord cannot be tempted of evil, neither tempteth he any man; but this is to be understood of his end and design. He entices no man to do evil; but yet He tries the sincerity and faithfulness of men by placing them where sin comes in their way, and does its best or its worst to ensnare them: His design being that the uprightness of His servants may thus be proved, both to themselves and others. We are not taken out of this world of temptation, but we are kept in it for our good. Because our nature is depraved it makes occasions for sin, both out of our joys and our trials, but by grace we overcome the tendency of nature, and so derive benefit from tribulation. Do I not speak to many here who at times feel strong impulses towards evil, especially in the darksome hour when the spirit of evil walks abroad? Have you not been made to tremble for yourselves in season of fierce trial, for your feet were almost gone, your steps had well-nigh slipped. Is there any virtue that has not been weather-beaten? Is there any love that has not at times been so tried that it threatened to curdle into hate? Is there any good thing this side heaven which has marched all the way in silver slippers? Did ever a flower of grace blossom in this wretched clime without being tried with frost or blight? Our way is up the river; we have to stem the current, and struggle against a flood which would readily bear us to destruction. Thus, not only trials, but black temptations assail the Christian's faith.

As to what shape they take, we may say this much: the trial or temptation of each man is distinct from that of every other. When God did tempt Abraham he was bidden to take his son, his only son, and offer him upon a mountain for a sacrifice. Nobody here was ever tried in that way: nobody ever will be. We may have the trial of losing our child, but certainly not the trial of having a command to offer him in sacrifice. That was a trial peculiar to Abraham: necessary and useful to him, though never proposed to us. In the case of the young man in the gospels, our Lord Jesus tried him with, "If thou wouldest be perfect, go and sell that thou hast, and give to the poor, and thou shalt have treasure in heaven." Some have dreamed that it must therefore be the duty of everybody to part with their possessions: but this is idle. It would not be the duty of any man to offer up his only son; and it is not the duty of every man to part with all his goods. These were tests to particular persons; and others equally special and searching have been applied in other cases. We are not to try ourselves, nor to desire other men's trials; it will be well if we endure those which the Lord appoints for us, for they will be wisely chosen. That which would most severely test me would perhaps be no trial to you; and that which tries you might be no temptation to me. This is one reason why we often judge one another so severely, because feeling ourselves to be strong in that particular point we argue that the fallen one must have been strong in that point too, and therefore must have willfully and earnestly have determined to do wrong. This may be a cruel supposition. We hastily conclude that the temptation must have been as feeble in his case as it would have been in our own; which is a great mistake, for a temptation which to you or to me would be no temptation at all, may be to another individual, of a peculiar constitution and under singular circumstances, a most fierce and terrible blast from the adversary, before which he falls mournfully, but not with malice aforethought. Divers trials, says the apostle, and he knew what he said.

And, dear friends, sometimes these divers trials derive great force from their seemingly surrounding us, and cutting off escape: James says,—"Ye fall into divers temptations": like men who fall into a pit, and do not know how to get out; or like soldiers who fall into an ambuscade; or travellers in the good old times when two or three footpaths surrounded them and made them feel that they had fallen into bad hands. The tempted see not which way to turn; they appear to be hemmed in; they are as a bird that is taken in the fowler's snare. This it is that makes calamity of our manifold temptations, that they hedge up our way, and unless faith finds the clue we wander in a thorny maze.

At times temptation comes suddenly upon us, and so we fall into it. When we were at rest, and were quiet, suddenly the evil came, like a lion leaping from the thicket. When Job's children were eating and drinking in their elder brother's house, then suddenly a wind came from the wilderness, and the patriarch was bereaved: the cattle were ploughing, the sheep were grazing, the camels were at their service, and in a moment, by fire from heaven, and by robber bands, the whole of these possessions vanished. One messenger had not told his story before another followed at his heels; Job had no breathing time, the blows fell thick and fast. The trial of our faith is most severe when divers trials happen to us when we look not for them. It is not strange in the light of these things that James should say, "Count it all joy when ye fall into divers trials"?

Those were the days of tumults, imprisonment, crucifixion, sword, and fire. Then the amphitheatre devoured Christians by thousands. The general cry was "The Christians to the lions!" Do you wonder if sometimes the bravest were made to say, Is our faith really true? This faith which is abhorred of all mankind, can it be divine? Has it come from God? Why, then, does He not interpose and deliver His people? Shall we apostatise? Shall we deny Christ and live, or shall we go on with our confession through innumerable torments even to a bloody death? Will fidelity answer after all? Is there a crown of glory? is there an eternity of bliss? Is there in very deed a resurrection of the dead? These questions came into men's minds then, and were fairly faced: the faith of martyrs was not taken up at second hand, or borrowed from their parents; they believed for themselves in downright earnest. Men and women in those days believed in such a way that they never flinched nor started aside from fear of death; indeed, they pressed forward to confess their faith in Jesus in such crowds that at last the heathen cried, "There must be something in it: it must be a religion of God, or how could these men so gladly bear their troubles?" This was the faith of God's elect, the work of the Holy Ghost.

You see, then, the main point of attack is our faith, and happy is the man whose shield can catch and quench all the fiery darts of the enemy.

II. That we may make the text more clear we shall next notice THE INVALUABLE BLESSING WHICH IS GAINED BY THE TRIAL OF OUR FAITH. The blessing gained is this, that our faith is tried and proved. Two Sabbaths ago I addressed you upon the man whose bad foundations led to the overthrow of his house; and I know that many said after the sermon:—"God grant that we may not be like him: may we have a firm foundation for our soul to rest on." Then you went home, and you sat down and said, "Have I this sure foundation?" You began to question, argue, reason, and so on, and your design was a good one. But I do not reckon that much came of it; our own looking within seldom yields solid comfort. Actual trial is far more satisfactory; but you must not try yourself. The effectual proof is by trials of God's sending. The way of trying whether you are a good soldier is to go down to the battle: the way to try whether a ship is well built is, not merely to order the surveyor to examine her, but to send her to sea: a storm will be the best test of her staunchness. They have built a new lighthouse upon the Eddystone: how do we know that it will stand? We judge by certain laws and principles, and feel tolerably safe about the structure; but, after all, we shall know best if after-years when a thousand tempests have beaten upon the lighthouse in vain. We need trials as a test as much as we need divine truth as our food. Admire the ancient types placed in the ark of the covenant of old: two things were laid close together,—the pot of manna and the rod. See how heavenly food and heavenly rule go together: how our sustenance and our chastening are equally provided for! A Christian cannot live without the manna nor without the rod. The two must go together. I mean this, that it is as great a mercy to have your salvation proved to you under trial as it is to have it sustained in you by the consolations of the Spirit of God. Sanctified tribulations work the proof of our faith, and this is more precious than that of gold which perisheth, though it be tried by fire.

Now, when we are able to bear it without starting aside, the trial proves our sincerity. Coming out of a trouble the Christian says to himself, "Yes, I held fast mine integrity, and did not let it go. Blessed be God, I was not afraid of threatening; I was not crushed by losses; I was kept true to God under pressure. Now, I am sure that my religion is not a mere profession, but a real consecration to God. It has endured the fire, being kept by the power of God."

Next, it proves the truthfulness of our doctrinal belief. Oh, yes, you may say, "I have heard Mr. Spurgeon expound the doctrines, and I have believed them." This is poor work; but if you have been sick, and found a comfort in those doctrines, then you are assured of their truth. If you have been on the borders of the grave, and the gospel has given you joy and gladness, then you know how true it is. Experimental knowledge is the best and surest. If you have seen others pass through death itself triumphantly you have said, "This is proof to me: my faith is no guess-work: I have seen for myself." Is not this assurance cheaply purchased at any price? May we not count it all joy when the Lord puts us in the way of getting it? It seems to me that doubt is worse than trial. I had sooner suffer any affliction than be left to question the gospel or my own interest in it. Certainly it is a jewel worth purchasing even with our heart's blood.

Next, your own faith in God is proved when you can cling to Him under temptation. Not only your sincerity, but the divinity of your faith is proved; for a faith that is never tried, how can you depend upon it? But if in the darkest hour you have still said, "I cast my burden upon the Lord, and He will sustain me," and you find He does sustain you, then is your faith that of God's elect. If in temptation you cry to God in prayer that you may keep your garment unspotted, and He helps you to do so, then also are you sure that yours is the faith which the Spirit begets in the soul. After a great fight of affliction, when I come forth a conqueror, I know that I do believe in God, and I know that this faith makes me a partaker of covenant blessings; from this I may fairly argue that my faith is of the right kind.

I find it especially sweet to learn the great strength of the Lord in my own weakness. We find out under trial where we are most weak, and just then in answer to prayer strength is given answerable to the need. The Lord suits the help to the hindrance, and puts the plaster on the wound. In the very hour when it is needed the needed grace is given. Does this not tend to breed assurance of faith?

It is a splendid thing to be able to prove even to Satan the purity of your motives. That was the great gain of Job. There was no question about his outward conduct, but the question was about his motive. "Ah," says the devil, "he serves God for what he gets out of Him. Hast Thou not set a hedge about him and all that he has? His is cupboard love: he cares nothing for God Himself, he only cares for the reward of his virtue." Well, he is tried, and everything is taken away, and when he cries, "Though He slay me, yet will I trust in Him," when he blesses the taking as well as the giving God, then the devil himself could not have the prudence to accuse him again. As to Job's own conscience, it would be quite settled and confirmed as to his pure love to God. My brethren, I reckon that the endurance of every imaginable suffering and trial would be a small price to pay for a settled assurance, which would for ever prevent the possibility of doubt. Never mind the waves if they wash you upon this rock. Therefore, when you are tempted, "Count it all joy" that you are tried, because you will thus receive a proof of your love, a proof of your faith, a proof of your being the true-born children of God.

James says, "Count it." A man requires to be trained to be a good accountant; it is an art which needs to be learned. What muddles some of us would make if we had to settle accounts and manage disbursements and incomings without the aid of a clerk! How we should get entangled with balances and deficits! We could much easier spend money than count it. But when a man once knows the science of book-keeping, and gets into the way of it, he readily arrives at the true position of affairs. He has learned to count, and no error escapes his eye. James gives us a ready reckoner, and teaches us in our troubles how to count. He sets before us a different kind of measure from that which carnal reason would use: the shekel of the sanctuary was very different from the shekel in common commerce, and so is the counting of faith far other than that of human judgment. He bids us take our pen and sit down quickly and write at his correct dictation. You are going to write down, "Manifold temptations;" that would be so much on the wrong side: but instead thereof he bids you set down the proving of your faith, and this one asset transforms the transaction into a substantial gain. Trials are like a fire; they burn up nothing in us but the dross, and they make the gold all the purer. Put down the testing process as a clear gain, and, instead of being sorry about it, count it all joy when ye fall into divers trials, for this bestows upon you a proof of your faith. So far there is sufficient ground for counting all trials joy. Now, let us go a little further.

III. Let us think of THE PRICELESS VIRTUE WHICH IS PRODUCED BY TRIAL, namely, patience; for the proof of your "faith worketh patience." Patience! We all have a large stock of it—until we need it, and then we have none. The man who truly possesses patience is the man that has been tried. What kind of patience does he get by the grace of God? First, he obtains a patience that accepts the trials as from God without a murmur. Calm resignation does not come all at once; often long years of physical pain, or mental depression, or disappointment in business, or multiplied bereavements, are needed to bring the soul into full submission to the will of the Lord. After much crying the child is weaned; after much chastening the son is made obedient to his Father's will. By degrees we learn to end our quarrel with God, and to desire that there may not be two wills between God and ourselves, but that God's will may be our will. Oh, brother, if your troubles work you to that, you are a gainer, I am sure, and you may count them all joy.

The next kind of patience is when experience enables a man to bear ill-treatment, slander, and injury without resentment. He feels it keenly, but he bears it meekly. Like his Master, he opens not his mouth to reply, and refuses to return railing for railing. Contrariwise he gives blessing in return for cursing; like the sandal-wood tree which perfumes the axe which cuts it. Blessed is that holy charity which hopeth all things, endureth all things, and is not easily provoked. Ah, friend, if the grace of God by trial shall work in you the quiet patience which never grows angry, and never ceases to love, you may have lost a trifle of comfort, but you have gained a solid weight of character.

The patience which God works in us by tribulation also takes another form, namely, that of acting without undue haste. Before wisdom has balanced our zeal we are eager to serve God all in a hurry, with a rush and a spurt, as if everything must be done within the hour or nothing would ever be accomplished. We set about holy service with somewhat more of preparedness of heart after we have been drilled in the school of trial. We go steadily and resolutely about work for Jesus, knowing what poor creatures we are, and what a glorious Master we serve. The Lord our God is in no hurry because He is strong and wise. In proportion as we grow like the Lord Jesus we shall cast aside disturbance of mind and fury of spirit. His was a grand life-work, but He never seemed to be confused, excited, worried, or hurried, as certain of His people are. He did not strive nor cry, nor cause His voice to be heard in the streets. He knew His hour was not yet come, and there were so many days in which He could work, and therefore He went steadily on till He had finished the work which His Father had given Him to do. That kind of patience is a jewel more to be desired than the gem which glitters on the imperial brow. Sometimes we blunder into a deal of mischief, making more haste than speed; and we are sure to do so when we forget to pray, and fail to commit our matters into the Divine hands. We may run with such vehemence that we may stumble, or lose our breath: there may be in our random efforts as much undoing as doing, for want of possessing our souls in patience.

That is a grand kind of patience, too, when we can wait without unbelief. Two little words are good for every Christian to learn and to practise—pray and stay. Waiting on the Lord implies both praying and staying. What if the world is not converted this year! What if the Lord Jesus does not come to-morrow! What if still our tribulations are lengthened out! What if the conflict is continued! He that has been tried and by grace has obtained the true profit of his trials, both quietly waits and joyfully hopes for the salvation of God. Patience, brother! Is this high virtue scarce with thee? The Holy Spirit shall bestow it upon thee through suffering.

This patience also takes the shape of believing without wavering, in the very teeth of strange providences and singular statements, and perhaps inward misgivings. The established Christian says, "I believe my God, and therefore if the vision tarry I will wait for it. My time is not yet come. I am to have my worst things first and my best things afterwards, and so I sit me down at Jesus' feet and tarry his leisure."

Brothers and sisters, if, in a word, we learn endurance we have taken a high degree. You look at the weather-beaten sailor, the man who is at home on the sea: he has a bronzed face and mahogany-coloured flesh, he looks as tough as heart of oak, and as hardy as if he were made of iron. How different from us poor landsmen. How did the man become so inured to hardship, so able to breast the storm, so that he does not care whether the wind blows south-west or north-west? He can go out to sea in any kind of weather; he has his sea legs on: how did he come to this strength? By doing business in great waters. He could not have become a hardy seaman by tarrying on shore. Now, trial works in the saints that spiritual hardihood which cannot be learned in ease. You may go to school for ever, but you cannot learn endurance there: you may colour your cheek with paint, but you cannot give it that ingrained brown which comes of stormy seas and howling winds. Strong faith and brave patience come of trouble, and a few men in the church who have thus been prepared are worth anything in times of tempest. To reach that condition of firm endurance and sacred hardihood is worth all the expense of all the heaped-up troubles that ever come upon us from above or from beneath. When trial worketh patience we are incalculably enriched. The Lord give us more of this choice grace. As Peter's fish had the money in its mouth, so have sanctified trials spiritual riches for those who endure them graciously.

IV. Lastly, all this works something better still, and this is our fourth head: THE SPIRITUAL COMPLETENESS PROMOTED. "That ye may be perfect and entire, wanting nothing." Brethren, the most valuable thing a man can get in this world is that which has most to do with his truest self. A man gets a good house; well, that is something: but suppose he is in bad health, what is the good of his fine mansion? A man is well clothed and well fed: that is something: but suppose he shivers with ague, and has no appetite through indigestion. That spoils it all. If a man is in robust health this is a far more valuable boon. Health is far more to be prized than wealth, or honour, or learning: we all allow that, but then suppose that a man's innermost self is diseased while his body is healthy, so that he is disgraced by vice or fevered with passion, he is in a poor plight, notwithstanding that he has such a robust frame? The very best thing is that which will make the man himself a better man; make him right, and true, and pure, and holy. When the man himself is better, he has made an unquestionable gain. So, if our afflictions tend, by trying our faith, to breed patience, and that patience tends to make us into perfect men in Christ Jesus, then we may be glad of trials. Afflictions by God's grace make us all-around men, developing every spiritual faculty, and therefore they are our friends, our helpers, and should be welcomed with "all joy."

Afflictions find out our weak points, and this makes us attend to them. Being tried, we discover our failures, and then going to God about those failures we are helped to be perfect and entire, wanting nothing.

Moreover, our trials, when blessed of God to make us patient, ripen us. I do not know how to explain what I mean by ripening, but there is a sort of mellowness about believers who have endured a great deal of affliction that you never meet in other people. It cannot be mistaken or imitated. A certain measure of sunlight is wanted to bring out the real flavour of fruits, and when a fruit has felt its measure of burning sun it develops a lusciousness which we all delight in. So is it in men and women: a certain amount of trouble appears to be needful to create a certain sugar of graciousness in them, so that they may contain the rich, ripe juice of a gracious character. You must have known such men and such women, and have said to yourselves, "I wish I could be like them, so calm, so quiet, so self-contained, so happy, and when not happy, yet so content not to be happy; so mature in judgment, so spiritual in conversation, so truly ripe." This only comes to those in whom the proof of their faith works experience, and then experience brings forth the fruits of the Spirit. Dear brothers and sisters, there is a certain all-roundness of spiritual manhood which never comes to us except by manifold temptations. Let me attempt to show you what I mean. Sanctified trials produce a chastened spirit. Some of us by nature are rough and untender; but after awhile friends notice that the roughness is departing, and they are quite glad to be more gently handled. Ah, that sick chamber did the polishing; under God's grace, that depression of spirit, that loss, that cross, that bereavement,—these softened the natural ruggedness, and made the man meek and lowly, like his Lord. Sanctified trouble has a great tendency to breed sympathy, and sympathy is to the church as oil to machinery. A man that has never suffered feels very awkward when he tries to sympathize with a tried child of God. He kindly does his best, but he does not know how to go to work at it; but those repeated blows from the rod make us feel for others who are smarting, and by degrees we are recognized as being the Lord's anointed comforters, made meet by temptation to succour those who are tempted.

Have you never noticed how tried men, too, when their trouble is thoroughly sanctified, become cautious and humble? They cannot speak quite so fast as they used to do: they do not talk of being absolutely perfect, though they are the very men who are Scripturally perfect; they say little about their doings, and much about the tender mercy of the Lord. They recollect the whipping they had behind the door from their Father's hands, and they speak gently to other erring ones. Affliction is the stone which our Lord Jesus throws at the brow of our giant pride, and patience is the sword which cuts off its head.

Those, too, are the kind of people who are most grateful. I have known what it is to praise God for the power to move one leg in bed. It may not seem much to you, but it was a great blessing to me. They that are heavily afflicted come to bless God for everything. I am sure that woman who took a piece of bread and a cup of water for her breakfast, and said, "What, all this, and Christ too!" must have been a tried woman, or she would not have exhibited so much gratitude. And that old Puritan minister was surely a tried man, for when his family had only a herring and a few potatoes for dinner, he said, "Lord, we bless Thee that Thou hast ransacked sea and land to find food for us this day." If he had not been a tried man, he might have turned up his nose at the meal, as many do at much more sumptuous fare. Troubled men get to be grateful men, and that is no small thing.

As a rule, where God's grace works, these come to be hopeful men. Where others think the storm will destroy the vessel, they can remember storms equally fierce which did not destroy it, and so they are so calm that their courage keeps others from despair.

These men, too, become unworldly men. They have had too much trouble to think that they can ever build their nest in this black forest. There are too many thorns in their nest for them to reckon that this can be their home. These birds of paradise take to their wings, and are ready to fly away to the land of unfading flowers.

And these much-tempted ones are frequently the most spiritual men, and out of this spirituality comes usefulness. Mr. Greatheart, who led the band of pilgrims up to the celestial city, was a man of many trials, or he would not have been fit to lead so many to their heavenly rest; and you, dear brother, if ever you are to be a leader and a helper, as you would wish to be, in the church of God, it must be by such means as this that you must be prepared for it. Do you not wish to have every virtue developed? Do you not wish to become a perfect man in Christ Jesus? If so, welcome with all joy divers trials and temptations; fly to God with them; bless Him for having sent them: ask Him to help you to bear them with patience, and then let that patience have its perfect work, and so by the Spirit of God you shall become "perfect and entire, lacking in nothing." May the Comforter bless this word to your hearts, for Jesus Christ's sake. Amen.

An Earnest Warning about Lukewarmness

A Sermon (No. 1185) Delivered on Lord's-Day Morning, July 26th, 1874, by C. H. SPURGEON, At the Metropolitan Tabernacle, Newington.

"Unto the angel of the church of the Laodiceans write; These things saith the Amen, the faithful and true witness, the beginning of the creation of God; I know thy works, that thou art neither cold nor hot: I would thou wert cold or hot. So then because thou art lukewarm, and neither cold nor hot, I will spue thee out of my mouth. Because thou sayest, I am rich, and increased with goods, and have need of nothing; and knowest not that thou art wretched, and miserable, and poor, and blind, and naked: I counsel thee to buy of me gold tried in the fire, that thou mayest be rich; and white raiment, that thou mayest be clothed, and [that] the shame of thy nakedness do not appear; and anoint thine eyes with eyesalve, that thou mayest see. As many as I love, I rebuke and chasten: be zealous therefore, and repent. Behold, I stand at the door, and knock: if any man hear my voice, and open the door, I will come in to him, and will sup with him, and he with me. To him that overcometh will I grant to sit with me in my throne, even as I also overcame, and am set down with my Father in his throne."
—Revelation 3:14–21.

No Scripture ever wears out. The epistle to the church of Laodicea is not an old letter which may be put into the waste basket and be forgotten; upon its page still glow the words, "He that hath an ear, let him hear what the Spirit saith unto the churches." This Scripture was not meant to instruct the Laodiceans only, it has a wider aim. The actual church of Laodicea has passed away, but other Laodiceas still exist—indeed, they are sadly multiplied in our day, and it has ever been the tendency of human nature, however inflamed with the love of God, gradually to chill into lukewarmness. The letter to the Laodiceans is above all others the epistle for the present times.

I should judge that the church at Laodicea was once in a very fervent and healthy condition. Paul wrote a letter to it which did not claim inspiration, and therefore its loss does not render the Scriptures incomplete, for Paul may have written scores of other letters besides. Paul also mentions the church at Laodicea in his letter to the church at Colosse; he was, therefore, well acquainted with it, and as he does not utter a word of censure with regard to it, we may infer that the church was at that time in a sound state. In process of time it degenerated, and cooling down from its former ardour it became careless, lax, and indifferent. Perhaps its best men were dead, perhaps its wealth seduced it into worldliness, possibly its freedom from persecution engendered carnal ease, or neglect of prayer made it gradually backslide; but in any case it declined till it was neither cold nor hot. Lest we should ever get into such a state, and lest we should be in that state now, I pray that my discourse may come with power to the hearts of all present, but especially to the consciences of the members of my own church. May God grant that it may tend to the arousing of us all.

I. My first point will be THE STATE INTO WHICH CHURCHES ARE VERY APT TO FALL. A church may fall into a condition for other than that for which it has a repute. It may be famous for zeal and yet be lethargic. The address of our Lord begins, "I know thy works," as much as to say, "Nobody else knows you. Men think better of you than you deserve. You do not know yourselves, you think your works to be excellent; but I know them to be very different." Jesus views with searching eyes all the works of his church. The public can only read reports, but Jesus sees for himself. He knows what is done, and how it is done, and why it is done. He judges a church not merely by her external activities, but by her internal pieties; he searches the heart, and tries the reins of the children of men. He is not deceived by glitter; he tests all things, and values only that gold which will endure the fire. Our opinion of ourselves and Christ's opinion of us may be very different, and it is a very sad thing when it is so. It will be melancholy indeed if we stand out as a church notable for earnestness and distinguished for success, and yet are not really fervent in spirit, or eager in soul-winning. A lack of vital energy where there seems to be most strength put forth, a lack of real love to Jesus where apparently there is the greatest devotedness to him, are sad signs of fearful degeneracy. Churches are very apt to put the best goods into the window, very apt to make a fair show in the flesh, and like men of the world, they try to make a fine figure upon a very slender estate. Great reputations have often but slender foundations, and lovers of the truth lament that it should be so. Not only is it true of churches, but of every one of us as individuals, that often our reputation is in advance of our deserts. Men often live on their former credit, and trade upon their past characters, having still a name to live, though they are indeed dead. To be slandered is a dire affliction, but it is, upon the whole, a less evil than to be thought better than we are; in the one case we have a promise to comfort us, in the second we are in danger of self-conceit. I speak as unto wise men, judge ye how far this may apply to us.

The condition described in our text is, secondly, one of mournful indifference and carelessness. They were not cold, but they were not hot; they were not infidels, yet they were not earnest believers; they did not oppose the gospel, neither did they defend it; they were not working mischief, neither were they doing any great good; they were not disreputable in moral character, but they were not distinguished for holiness; they were not irreligious, but they were not enthusiastic in piety nor eminent for zeal: they were what the world calls "Moderates," they were of the Broad-church school, they were neither bigots nor Puritans, they were prudent and avoided fanaticism, respectable and averse to excitement. Good things were maintained among them, but they did not make too much of them; they had prayer-meetings, but there were few present, for they liked quiet evenings at home: when more attended the meetings they were still very dull, for they did their praying very deliberately and were afraid of being too excited. They were content to have all things done decently and in order, but vigour and zeal they considered to be vulgar. Such churches have schools, Bible-classes, preaching rooms, and all sorts of agencies; but they might as well be without them, for no energy is displayed and no good comes of them. They have deacons and elders who are excellent pillars of the church, if the chief quality of pillars be to stand still, and exhibit no motion or emotion. They have ministers who may be the angels of the churches, but if so, they have their wings closely clipped, for they do not fly very far in preaching the everlasting gospel, and they certainly are not flames of fire: they may be shining lights of eloquence, but they certainly are not burning lights of grace, setting men's hearts on fire. In such communities everything is done in a half-hearted, listless, dead-and-alive way, as if it did not matter much whether it was done or not. It makes one's flesh creep to see how sluggishly they move: I long for a knife to cut their red tape to pieces, and for a whip to lay about their shoulders to make them bestir themselves. Things are respectably done, the rich families are not offended, the sceptical party is conciliated, and the good people are not quite alienated: things are made pleasant all round. The right things are done, but as to doing them with all your might, and soul, and strength, a Laodicean church has no notion of what that means. They are not so cold as to abandon their work, or to give up their meetings for prayer, or to reject the gospel; if they did so, then they could be convinced of their error and brought to repentance; but on the other hand they are neither hot for the truth, nor hot for conversions, nor hot for holiness, they are not fiery enough to burn the stubble of sin, nor zealous enough to make Satan angry, nor fervent enough to make a living sacrifice of themselves upon the altar of their God. They are "neither cold not hot."

This is a horrible state, because it is one which in a church wearing a good repute renders that reputation a lie. When other churches are saying, "See how they prosper! see what they do for God!" Jesus sees that the church is doing his work in a slovenly, make-believe manner, and he considers justly that it is deceiving its friends. If the world recognizes such a people as being very distinctly an old-fashioned puritanic church, and yet there is unholy living among them, and careless walking, and a deficiency of real piety, prayer, liberality, and zeal, then the world itself is being deceived, and that too in the worst way, because it is led to judge falsely concerning Christianity, for it lays all these faults upon the back of religion, and cries out, "It is all a farce! The thing is a mere pretence! Christians are all hypocrites!" I fear there are churches of this sort. God grant we may not be numbered with them!

In this state of the church there is much self-glorification, for Laodicea said, "I am rich and increased with goods, and have need of nothing." The members say, "Everything goes on well, what more do we want? All is right with us." This makes such a condition very hopeless, because reproofs and rebukes fall without power, where the party rebuked can reply, "We do not deserve your censures, such warnings are not meant for us." If you stand up in the pulpit and talk to sleepy churches, as I pretty frequently do, and speak very plainly, they often have the honesty to say, "There is a good deal of truth in what the man has said": but if I speak to another church, which really is half asleep, but which thinks itself to be quite a model of diligence, then the rebuke glides off like oil down a slab of marble, and no result comes of it. Men are less likely to repent when they are in the middle passage between hot and cold, than if they were in the worst extremes of sin. If they were like Saul of Tarsus, enemies of God, they might be converted; but if, like Gamaliel, they are neither opposed nor favouring, they will probably remain as they are till they die. The gospel converts a sincerely superstitious Luther, but Erasmus, with his pliant spirit, flippant, and full of levity, remains unmoved. There is more hope of warning the cold than the lukewarm.

When churches get into the condition of half-hearted faith, tolerating the gospel, but having a sweet tooth for error, they do far more mischief to their age than downright heretics.

It is harder a great deal to work for Jesus with a church which is lukewarm than it would be to begin without a church. Give me a dozen earnest spirits and put me down anywhere in London, and by God's good help we will soon cause the wilderness and the solitary place to rejoice; but give me the whole lot of you, half-hearted, undecided, and unconcerned, what can I do? You will only be a drag upon a man's zeal and earnestness. Five thousand members of a church all lukewarm will be five thousand impediments, but a dozen earnest, passionate spirits, determined that Christ shall be glorified and souls won, must be more than conquerors; in their very weakness and fewness will reside capacities for being the more largely blessed of God. Better nothing than lukewarmness.

Alas, this state of lukewarmness is so congenial with human nature that it is hard to fetch men from it. Cold makes us shiver, and great heat causes us pain, but a tepid bath is comfort itself. Such a temperature suits human nature. The world is always at peace with a lukewarm church, and such a church is always pleased with itself. Not too worldly,—no! We have our limits! There are certain amusements which of course a Christian must give up, but we will go quite up to the line, for why are we to be miserable? We are not to be so greedy as to be called miserly, but we will give as little as we can to the cause. We will not be altogether absent from the house of God, but we will go as seldom as we can. We will not altogether forsake the poor people to whom we belong, but we will also go to the world's church, so as to get admission into better society, and find fashionable friends for our children. How much of this there is abroad! Compromise is the order of the day. Thousands try to hold with the hare and run with the hounds, they are for God and Mammon, Christ and Belial, truth and error, and so are "neither hot nor cold." Do I speak somewhat strongly? Not so strongly as my Master, for he says, "I will spue thee out of my mouth." He is nauseated with such conduct, it sickens him, and he will not endure it. In an earnest, honest, fervent heart nausea is created when we fall in with men who dare not give up their profession, and yet will not live up to it; who cannot altogether forsake the work of God, but yet do it in a sluggard's manner, trifling with that which ought to be done in the best style for so good a Lord and so gracious a Saviour. Many a church has fallen into a condition of indifference, and when it does so it generally becomes the haunt of worldly professors, a refuge for people who want an easy religion, which enables them to enjoy the pleasures of sin and the honours of piety at the same time; where things are free and easy, where you are not expected to do much, or give much, or pray much, or to be very religious; where the minister is not so precise as the old school divines, a more liberal people, of broad views, free-thinking and free-acting, where there is full tolerance for sin, and no demand for vital godliness. Such churches applaud cleverness in a preacher; as for his doctrine, that is of small consequence, and his love to Christ and zeal for souls are very secondary. He is a clever fellow, and can speak well, and that suffices. This style of things is all too common, yet we are expected to hold our tongue, for the people are very respectable. The Lord grant that we may be kept clear of such respectability!

We have already said that this condition of indifference is attended with perfect self-complacency. The people who ought to be mourning are rejoicing, and where they should hang out signals of distress they are flaunting the banners of triumph. "We are rich, we are adding to our numbers, enlarging our schools, and growing on all sides; we have need of nothing. What can a church require that we have not in abundance?" Yet their spiritual needs are terrible. This is a sad state for a church to be in. Spiritually poor and proud. A church crying out to God because it feels itself in a backsliding state; a church mourning its deficiency, a church pining and panting to do more for Christ, a church burning with zeal for God, and therefore quite discontented with what it has been able to do; this is the church which God will bless: but that which writes itself down as a model for others, is very probably grossly mistaken and is in a sad plight. This church, which was so rich in its own esteem, was utterly bankrupt in the sight of the Lord. It had no real joy in the Lord; it had mistaken its joy in itself for that. It had no real beauty of holiness upon it; it had mistaken its formal worship and fine building and harmonious singing for that. It had no deep understanding of the truth and no wealth of vital godliness, it had mistaken carnal wisdom and outward profession for those precious things. It was poor in secret prayer, which is the strength of any church; it was destitute of communion with Christ, which is the very life blood of religion; but it had the outward semblance of these blessings, and walked in a vain show. There are churches which are poor as Lazarus as to true religion, and yet are clothed in scarlet and fare sumptuously every day upon the mere form of godliness. Spiritual leanness exists side by side with vain-glory. Contentment as to worldly goods makes men rich, but contentment with our spiritual condition is the index of poverty.

Once more, this church of Laodicea had fallen into a condition which had chased away its Lord. The text tells us that Jesus said, "I stand at the door and knock." That is not the position which our Lord occupies in reference to a truly flourishing church. If we are walking aright with him, he is in the midst of the church, dwelling there, and revealing himself to his people. His presence makes our worship to be full of spirituality and life; he meets his servants at the table, and there spreads them a feast upon his body and his blood; it is he who puts power and energy into all our church-action, and causes the word to sound out from our midst. True saints abide in Jesus and he in them. Oh, brethren, when the Lord is in a church, it is a happy church, a holy church, a mighty church, and a triumphant church; but we may grieve him till he will say, "I will go and return to my place, until they acknowledge their offence and seek my face." Oh, you that know my Lord, and have power with him, entreat him not to go away from us. He can see much about us as a people which grieves his Holy Spirit, much about any one of us to provoke him to anger. Hold him, I pray you, and do not let him go, or if he be gone, bring him again to his mother's house, into the chamber of her that bare him, where, with holy violence, we will detain him and say, "Abide with us, for thou art life and joy, and all in all to us as a church. Ichabod is written across our house if thou be gone, for thy presence is our glory and thy absence will be our shame." Churches may become like the temple when the glory of the Lord had left the holy place, because the image of jealousy was set up and the house was defiled. What a solemn warning is that which is contained in Jeremiah 7:12–15, "But go ye now unto my place which was in Shiloh, where I set my name at the first, and see what I did to it for the wickedness of my people Israel. And now, because ye have done all these works, saith the Lord, and I spake unto you, rising up early and speaking, but ye heard not; and I called you, but ye answered not; therefore I will do unto this house, which is called by my name, wherein ye trust, and unto the place which I gave to you and to your fathers, as I have done to Shiloh. And

I will cast you out of my sight, as I have cast out all your brethren, even the whole seed of Ephraim."

II. Now let us consider, secondly, THE DANGER OF SUCH A STATE. The great danger is, first, to be rejected of Christ. He puts it, "I will spue thee out of my mouth,"—as disgusting him, and causing him nausea. Then the church must first be in his mouth, or else it could not be spued from it. What does this mean? Churches are in Christ's mouth in several ways, they are used by him as his testimony to the world; he speaks to the world through their lives and ministries. He does as good as say, "O sinners, if ye would see what my religion can do, see here a godly people banded together in my fear and love, walking in peace and holiness." He speaks powerfully by them, and makes the world see and know that there is a true power in the gospel of the grace of God. But when the church becomes neither cold nor hot he does not speak by her, she is no witness for him. When God is with a church the minister's words come out of Christ's mouth. "Out of his mouth went a two-edged sword," says John in the Revelation, and that "two-edged sword" is the gospel which we preach. When God is with a people they speak with divine power to the world, but if we grow lukewarm Christ says, "Their teachers shall not profit, for I have not sent them, neither am I with them. Their word shall be as water spilt on the ground, or as the whistling of the wind." This is a dreadful thing. Better far for me to die than to be spued out of Christ's mouth.

Then he also ceases to plead for such a church. Christ's special intercession is not for all men, for he says of his people, "I pray for them: I pray not for the world, but for them which thou hast given me." I do not think Christ ever prays for the church of Rome—what would he pray for, but her total overthrow? Other churches are nearing the same fate; they are not clear in his truth or honest in obedience to his word: they follow their own devices, they are lukewarm. But there are churches for which he is pleading, for he has said, "For Zion's sake will I not hold my peace, and for Jerusalem's sake I will not rest, until the righteousness thereof go forth as brightness, and the salvation thereof as a lamp that burneth." Mighty are his pleadings for those he really loves, and countless are the blessings which comes in consequence. It will be an evil day when he casts a church out of that interceding mouth, and leaves her unrepresented before the throne because he is none of his. Do you not tremble at such a prospect? Will you not ask for grace to return to your first love? I know that the Lord Jesus will never leave off praying for his own elect, but for churches as corporate bodies he may cease to pray, because they become anti-Christian, or are mere human gatherings, but not elect assemblies, such as the church of God ought to be. Now this is the danger of any church if it declines from its first ardour and becomes lukewarm. "Remember therefore from whence thou art fallen, and repent, and do thy first works; or else I will come unto thee quickly, and will remove thy candlestick out of his place, except thou repent."

What is the other danger? This first comprehends all, but another evil is hinted at,—such a church will be left to its fallen condition, to become wretched,—that is to say, miserable, unhappy, divided, without the presence of God, and so without delight in the ways of God, lifeless, spiritless, dreary, desolate, full of schisms, devoid of grace, and I know not what beside, that may come under the term "wretched." Then the next word is "miserable," which might better be rendered "pitiable." Churches which once were a glory shall become a shame. Whereas men said, "The Lord has done great things for them," they shall now say, "see how low they have fallen! What a change has come over the place! What emptiness and wretchedness! What a blessing rested there for so many years, but what a contrast now!" Pity will take the place of congratulation, and scorn will follow upon admiration. Then it will be "poor" in membership, poor in effort, poor in prayer, poor in gifts and graces, poor in everything. Perhaps some rich people will be left to keep up the semblance of prosperity, but all will be empty, vain, void, Christless, lifeless. Philosophy will fill the pulpit with chaff, the church will be a mass of worldliness, the congregation an assembly of vanity. Next, they will become blind, they will not see themselves as they are, they will have no eye upon the neighborhood to do it good, no eye to the coming of Christ, no eye for his glory. They will say, "We see," and yet be blind as bats. Ultimately they will become "naked," their shame will be seen by all, they will be a proverb in everybody's mouth. "Call that a church!" says one. "Is that a church of Jesus Christ?" cries a second. Those dogs that dared not open their mouths against Israel when the Lord was there will begin to howl when he is gone, and everywhere will the sound be heard, "How are the mighty fallen, how are the weapons of war broken."

In such a case as that the church will fail of overcoming, for it is "to him that overcometh" that a seat upon Christ's throne is promised; but that church will come short of victory. It shall be written concerning it even as of the children of Ephraim, that being armed and carrying bows they turned their backs in the day of battle.

"Ye did run well," says Paul to the Galatians, "what did hinder you that ye should not obey the truth?" Such a church had a grand opportunity, but it was not equal to the occasion, its members were born for a great work, but inasmuch as they were unfaithful, God put them aside and used other means. He raised up in their midst a flaming testimony for the gospel, and the light thereof was cast athwart the ocean, and gladdened the nations, but the people were not worthy of it, or true to it, and therefore he took the candlestick out of its place, and left them in darkness. May God prevent such an evil from coming upon us: but such is the danger to all churches if they degenerate into listless indifference.

III. Thirdly, I have to speak of THE REMEDIES WHICH THE LORD EMPLOYS. I do earnestly pray that what I say may come home to all here, especially to every one of the members of this church, for it has come very much home to me, and caused great searching of heart in my own soul, and yet I do not think I am the least zealous among you. I beseech you to judge yourselves, that you be not judged. Do not ask me if I mean anything personal. I am personal in the most emphatic sense. I speak of you and to you in the plainest way. Some of you show plain symptoms of being lukewarm, and God forbid that I should flatter you, or be unfaithful to you. I am aiming at personality, and I earnestly want each beloved brother and sister here to take home each affectionate rebuke. And you who come from other churches, whether in America or elsewhere, you want arousing quite as much as we do, your churches are not better than ours, some of them are not so good, and I speak to you also, for you need to be stirred up to nobler things.

Note, then, the first remedy. Jesus gives a clear discovery as to the church's true state. He says to it—"Thou are lukewarm, thou art wretched and miserable, and poor, and blind, and naked." I rejoice to see people willing to know the truth, but most men do not wish to know it, and this is an ill sign. When a man tells you that he has not looked at his ledger, or day-book, or held a stock-taking for this twelvemonths, you know whereabouts he is, and you say to your manager, "Have you an account with him? Then keep it as close as you can." When a man dares not know the worst about his case, it is certainly a bad one, but he that is right before God is thankful to be told what he is and where he is. Now, some of you know the faults of other people, and in watching this church you have observed weak points in many places,—have you wept over them? Have you prayed over them? If not, you have not watched as you should do for the good of your brethren and sisters, and, perhaps, have allowed evils to grow which ought to have been rooted up: you have been silent when you should have kindly and earnestly spoken to the offenders, or made your own example a warning to them. Do not judge your brother, but judge yourself: if you have any severity, use it on your own conduct and heart. We must pray the Lord to use this remedy, and make us know just where we are. We shall never get right as long as we are confident that we are so already. Self-complacency is the death of repentance.

Our Lord's next remedy is gracious counsel. He says, "I counsel thee to buy of me gold tried in the fire." Does not that strike you as being very like the passage in Isaiah, "Come ye, buy, and eat; yea, come, buy wine and milk without money and without price?" It is so, and it teaches us that one remedy for lukewarmness is to begin again just as we began at first. We were at a high temperature at our first conversion. What joy, what peace, what delight, what comfort, what enthusiasm we had when first we knew the Lord! We bought gold of him then for nothing, let us go and buy again at the same price.

If religion has not been genuine with us till now, or if we have been adding to it great lumps of shining stuff which we thought was gold and was not, let us now go to the heavenly mint and buy gold tried in the fire, that we may be really rich. Come, let us begin again, each one of us. Inasmuch as we may have thought we were clothed and yet we were naked, let us hasten to him again, and at his own price, which is no price, procure the robe which he has wrought of his own righteousness, and that goodly raiment of his Spirit, which will clothe us with the beauty of the Lord. If, moreover, we have come to be rather dim in the eye, and no longer look up to God and see his face, and have no bright vision of the glory to be revealed, and cannot look on sinners with weeping eyes, as we once did, let us go to Jesus for the eye-salve, just as we went when we were stone blind at first, and the Lord will open our eyes again, and we shall behold him in clear vision as in days gone by. The word from Jesus is, "Come near to me, I pray you, my brethren. If you have wandered from me, return; if you have been cold to me I am not cold to you, my heart is the same to you as ever, come back to me, my brethren. Confess your evil deeds, receive my forgiveness, and henceforth let your hearts burn towards me, for I love you still and will supply all your needs." That is good counsel, let us take it.

Now comes a third remedy, sharp and cutting, but sent in love, namely, rebukes and chastenings. Christ will have his favoured church walk with great care, and if she will not follow him fully by being shown wherein she has erred, and will not repent when kindly counselled, he then betakes himself to some sharper means. "As many as I love I rebuke and chasten." The word here used for "love" is a very choice one; it is one which signifies an intense personal affection. Now, there are some churches which Christ loves very specially, favouring them above others, doing more for them than for others, and giving them more prosperity; they are the darlings of his heart, his Benjamins. Now, it is a very solemn thing to be dearly loved by God. It is a privilege to be coveted, but mark you, the man who is so honoured occupies a position of great delicacy. The Lord thy God is a jealous God, and he is most jealous where he shows most love. The Lord lets some men escape scot free for awhile after doing many evil things, but if they had been his own elect he would have visited them with stripes long before. He is very jealous of those whom he has chosen to lean upon his bosom and to be his familiar friends. Your servant may do many things which could not be thought of by your child or your wife; and so is it with many who profess to be servants of God—they live a very lax life, and they do not seem to be chastened for it, but if they were the Lord's own peculiarly beloved ones he would not endure such conduct from them. Now mark this, if the Lord exalts a church, and gives it a special blessing, he expects more of it, more care of his honour, and more zeal for his glory than he does of any other church; and when he does not find it, what will happen? Why, because of his very love he will rebuke it with hard sermons, sharp words, and sore smitings of conscience. If these do not arouse it he will take down the rod and deal out chastenings. Do you know how the Lord chastens churches? Paul says, "For this cause some are sickly among you, and many sleep." Bodily sickness is often sent in discipline upon churches, and losses, and crosses, and troubles are sent among the members, and sometimes leanness in the pulpit, breakings out of heresy and divisions in the pew, and lack of success in all church work. All these are smitings with the rod. It is very sad, but sometimes that rod does not fall on that part of the church which does the wrong. Sometimes God may take the best in the church, and chasten them for the wrong of others. You say, "How can that be right?" Why, because they are the kind of people who will be most benefited by it. If a vine wants the knife, it is not the branch that bears very little fruit which is trimmed, but the branch which bears much fruit is purged because it is worth purging. In their case the chastening is a blessing and a token of love. Sorrow is often brought upon Christians by the sins of their fellow-members, and many an aching heart there is in this world that I know of, of brethren and sisters who love the Lord and want to see souls converted, but they can only sigh and cry because nothing is done. Perhaps they have a minister who does not believe the gospel, and they have fellow-members who do not care whether the minister believes it or not, they are all asleep together except those few zealous souls who besiege the throne of grace day and night, and they are the ones who bear the burden of the lukewarm church. Oh, if the chastening comes here, whoever bears it, may the whole body be the better for it, and may we never rest till the church begins to glow with the sacred fire of God, and boil with enthusiastic desire for his glory.

The last remedy, however, is the best of all to my mind. I love it best and desire to make it my food when it is not my medicine. The best remedy for backsliding churches is more communion with Christ. "Behold," saith he, "I stand at the door and knock." I have known this text preached upon to sinners numbers of times as though Christ knocked at their door and they had to open it, and so on. The preacher has never managed to keep to free grace for this reason, that the text was not meant to be so used, and if men will ride a text the wrong way, it will not go. This text belongs to the church of God, not to the unconverted. It is addressed to the Laodicean church. There is Christ outside the church, driven there by her unkindness, but he has not gone far away, he loves his church too much to leave her altogether, he longs to come back, and therefore he waits at the doorpost. He knows that the church will never be restored till he comes back, and he desires to bless her, and so he stands waiting, knocking and knocking, again and again; he does not merely knock once, but he stands knocking by earnest sermons, by providences, by impressions upon the conscience, by the quickenings of his Holy Spirit; and while he knocks he speaks, he uses all means to awaken his church. Most condescendingly and graciously does he do this, for having threatened to spue her out of his mouth, he might have said, "I will get me gone; and I will never come back again to thee," that would have been natural and just; but how gracious he is when, having expressed his disgust he says, "Disgusted as I am with your condition, I do not wish to leave you; I have taken my presence from you, but I love you, and therefore I knock at your door, and wish to be received into your heart. I will not force myself upon you, I want you voluntarily to open the door to me." Christ's presence in a church is always a very tender thing. He never is there against the will of the church, it cannot be, for he lives in his people's wills and hearts, and "worketh in them to will and to do of his own good pleasure." He does not break bolt and bar and come in as he often does into a sinner's heart, carrying the soul by storm, because the man is dead in sin, and Christ must do it all, or the sinner will perish; but he is here speaking to living men and women, who ought also to be loving men and women, and he says, "I wish to be among you, open the door to me." We ought to open the door at once, and say, "Come in, good Lord, we grieve to think we should ever have put thee outside that door at all."

And then see what promises he gives. He says he will come and sup with us. Now, in the East, the supper was the best meal of the day, it was the same as our dinner; so that we may say that Christ will come and dine with us. He will give us a rich feast, for he himself is the daintiest and most plenteous of all feasts for perishing souls. He will come and sup with us, that is, we shall be the host and entertain him: but then he adds, "and he with me," that is, he will be the host and guest by turns. We will give him of our best, but poor fare is that, too poor for him, and yet he will partake of it. Then he shall be host, and we will be guest, and oh, how we will feast on what he gives! Christ comes, and brings the supper with him, and all we do is to find the room. The Master says to us, "Where is the guest chamber?" and then he makes ready and spreads his royal table. Now, if these be the terms on which we are to have a feast together, we will most willingly fling open the doors of our hearts and say, "Come in, good Lord." He says to you, "Children, have you any meat?" and if you are obliged to say, "No, Lord," he will come in unto you none the less readily, for there are the fish, the net is ready to break, it is so full, and here are more upon the coals ready. I warrant you, if we sup with him, we shall be lukewarm no longer. The men who live where Jesus is soon feel their hearts burning. It is said of a piece of scented clay by the old Persian moralist that the clay was taken up and questioned. "How camest thou to smell so sweetly, being nothing but common clay?" and it replied, "I laid for many a year in the sweet society of a rose, until at last I drank in its perfume"; and we may say to every warm-hearted Christian, "How camest thou so warm?" and his answer will be, "My heart bubbleth up with a good matter, for I speak of the things which I have made touching the King. I have been with Jesus, and I have learned of him."

Now, brethren and sisters, what can I say to move you to take this last medicine? I can only say, take it, not only because of the good it will do you, but because of the sweetness of it. I have heard say of some persons that they were pledged not to take wine except as a medicine, but then they were very pleased when they were ill: and so if this be the medicine, "I will come and sup with him, and he with me," we may willingly confess our need of so delicious a remedy. Need I press it on you? May I not rather urge each brother as soon as he gets home today to see whether he cannot enter into fellowship with Jesus? and may the Spirit of God help him!

This is my closing word, there is something for us to do in this matter. We must examine ourselves, and we must confess the fault if we have declined in grace. An then we must not talk about setting the church right, we must pray for grace each one for himself, for the text does not say, "If the church will open the door," but "If any man hear my voice and open the door." It must be done by individuals: the church will only get right by each man getting right. Oh, that we might get back into an earnest zeal for our Lord's love and service, and we shall only do so by listening to his rebukes, and then falling into his arms, clasping him once again, and saying, "My Lord and my God." That healed Thomas, did it not? Putting his fingers into the print of the nails, putting his hand into the side, that cured him. Poor, unbelieving, staggering Thomas only had to do that and he became one of the strongest of believers, and said, "My Lord and my God." You will love your Lord till your soul is as coals of juniper if you will daily commune with him. Come close to him, and once getting close to him, never go away from him any more. The Lord bless you, dear brethren, the Lord bless you in this thing. PORTION OF SCRIPTURE READ BEFORE SERMON—Revelation 3. HYMNS FROM "OUR OWN HYMN BOOK"—184, 787, 992.

Christ Is All

A Sermon (No. 3446) Published on Thursday, February 18th, 1915. Delivered by C. H. SPURGEON, At the Metropolitan Tabernacle, Newington.

"Christ is all"—Colossians 3:11.

My text is so very short that you cannot forget it; and, I am quite certain, if you are Christians at all, you will be sure to agree with it. What a multitude of religions there is in this poor wicked world of ours! Men have taken it into their heads to invent various systems of religion and if you look round the world, you will see scores of different sects; but it is a great fact that, while there is a multitude of false religions, there is but one that is true. While there are many falsehoods, there can be but one truth; real religion is, therefore, one. There is but one gospel—the gospel of our Lord Jesus Christ. What a wonderful thing it is that Jesus Christ, the Son of God, should be born of humble parents, and live as a poor man in this world, for the purpose of our salvation! He lived a life of suffering and trial, and at length, through the malignity of his enemies, was crucified on Calvary as an outcast of society. "Now," said they, "there is an end of his religion; now it will be such a contemptible thing, that nobody will ever call himself a Christian; it will be discreditable to have anything to do with the name of the man Jesus, the prophet of Nazareth." But it is a wonderful fact that this religion has not only lived, but is at this hour as strong as ever. Yes! the religion he founded still exists, and is still powerful, and constantly extending. While other religions have sunk into the darkness of the past, and the idols have been cast to the moles and to the bats, the name of Jesus is still mighty; and it shall continue to be a blessed power so long as the universe shall endure.

The religion of Jesus is the religion of God; hence, notwithstanding all the obloquy and persecution which it has had to encounter, it still exists, and still flourishes. It is this religion which I shall attempt to preach to you—the one gospel of our Lord and Saviour, Jesus Christ—and the text embraces it all in the most comprehensive manner, "Christ is all."

I shall use it, first as a test to try you, and, afterwards, as a motive to encourage you. I want, first, to sift you, to see how many of you are the people of God, and how many are not. I shall make my text a great sieve, and put you in it to see which is wheat and which is chaff. We must consider this passage in two or three senses in order, first, to use it as:—

I. A TEST TO TRY YOU.

Christ must be all, as your Great Master and Teacher. There are some who set up a certain man as their authority; they regard him as their master, they look up to him as their teacher, and whatever he says is right; it is the truth, and is not to be disputed. Or, perhaps, they have taken a certain book, other than the Bible, and say, "We will judge all things by this book"; and if the preacher does not teach exactly the creed written in that book, he is set down as not sound in the faith, and this they do not hesitate to say at once, because he does not come up to the standard of their little book! We meet with many people in this world who make their creed, their one little narrow creed, everything, and they measure everything and everybody by that. But, my friends, I must have you say that "Christ is all," and not any man, however good or great, before I can allow that you are Christians. We have not to follow men. Our faith stands not in the wisdom of man, but in the power of God. We are to follow no man, except so far as he follows Christ, who alone is our Master. Be not deceived; submit not yourselves to creeds, to books, or to men; give yourselves to the study of God's Word, derive your creed and the doctrines of your faith from it alone, and then you will be able to say:—

Should all the forms that men devise
    Assault my faith with treacherous art,
I'd call them vanity and lies,
And bind the gospel to my heart.

Let Christ be your only Master, and say, in the words of our text, "Christ is all." Now can you say this, or are you boasting, "The Baptists are all"—"The Wesleyans are all"—"The Church of England is all"? As the Lord lives, if you are saying that, you do not know his truth; because you are not testifying that "Christ is all," but simply uttering the Shibboleth of your little party. I should like to see the word party blotted out from the vocabulary of the Christian Church. I thank God that I have no sympathy whatever with that which is merely sectarian, and have grace given me to protest against it, and to exclaim:—

Let party names no more
    The Christian world o'erspread;
since:—
    Gentile and Jew, and bond and free,
Are one in Christ, their Head.

If "Christ is all" to you, you are Christians; and I, for one, am ready to give you the right hand of brotherhood. I do not mind what place of worship you attend, or by what distinctive name you may call yourselves, we are brethren; and I think, therefore, that we should love one another. If, my friends, you cannot embrace all who love the Lord Jesus Christ, no matter to what denomination they may belong, and as belonging to the universal Church, you have not hearts large enough to go to heaven; because, if such be your contracted views, you cannot possibly say, "Christ is all."

Next, Christ must be all, as your principal object in life—your chief good. Your great aim must be to glorify

Christ on the earth, in the hope and expectation of enjoying him for ever above. But as it regards some of you, Christ is not your all. You think more of your shop than you do of him. You are up early in the morning looking at your ledgers, and all day long toiling at your business. Do not mistake me: I dislike lazy people, who let the grass grow over their shoes; and God disapproves of them too. We want no lazy gospellers. The true Christian will say, "I know that I am bound to be diligent in business; but I want to work for eternity as well as for time. I need something besides earthly riches; I want an inheritance not made with hands, a mansion not built by man, a possession in the skies." Are you making this world you all? Poor souls, if you are, the world and the fashion thereof are passing away; your all will soon be gone. I fancy I see a rich man, one whose gold is his all, when he gets into the next world, looking for his gold, and wondering where it is, and being at length compelled to exclaim, in despair, "Oh! my all is gone!" But if you can say that Christ is your all, then your treasure will never be gone; for he will never leave you, nor forsake you. Not only in this world, but also in that which is to come, you shall be happy and blessed, for you shall be crowned with glory, and made to sit with Christ on his throne for ever.

"Well," says some easy-going gentleman, "I do not make business my all, I assure you; not I: my maxim is, let us enjoy this life, let us fill the glass to the brim, and live in pleasure while we may." I have a word also for you Do you think that such a course of conduct will fit you for heaven, for the enjoyments of eternity? Do you imagine that, when you come to die, it will be any pleasure for you to think of your drunkenness? When you are lying on a sick bed, will your oaths bring you any peace, as they reverberate upon your conscience, just as I hear my voice, at this moment, echoing back to my ears the words I am saying? I think I see you starting up as you hear your blasphemies against God thus returning upon you, while, with a mind oppressed with anguish, and eyes starting from their sockets, you exclaim in your terror, "I hear my own oaths again! God is coming to call me to judgment; to demand of me why I dare blaspheme his name!" and the Judge will say, "You, with oaths and curses, profaned my holy name; you asked me to curse your soul, and now I will do it; you prayed in your profane moments that you might be lost, and now you shall be." How horrible that would be! You who say pleasure is all, let me warn you that you will have to drink the bitter dregs of the cup of pleasure to all eternity, no matter how sweet the draught may now be to your taste.

But there are some more moderate people, who are by no means extravagant in their pleasures, and are great sticklers for religion; they go to church or chapel every Sunday, and believe themselves to be very good sort of people, and such as will be accepted at the last day, and placed on the right hand of the throne. Again I put the question, can you say, "Christ is all"? No; you cannot say that. Many of you make the externals of religion your all, resting in the letter, but knowing or caring nothing for the spirit. This will not do; and you are not such Christians as Christ will own if you are making anything your all but himself. Religion is not to be stowed away in the dark garret of the brain. Christianity is a heart religion, and if you cannot say, from the very depths of your being, "Christ is all," you have neither part nor lot in the blessings and privileges of the gospel, and your end will be destruction, everlasting banishment from the presence of the Lord. God grant it may not be so; but that in both your lives and mine we may each be enabled to say of a truth, "Christ is all"; and that we may meet again around the eternal throne!

Next, Christ will be all, as the source of your joy. Some people seem to think that Christians are a very melancholy sort of folk, that they have no real happiness. I know something about religion, and I will not admit that I stand second to any man in respect of being happy. So far as I know religion, I have found it to be a very happy thing. "I would not change my blest estate, For all that earth calls good or great."

I used to think that a religious man must never smile; but, on the contrary, I find that religion will make a man's eye bright, and cover his face with smiles, and impart comfort and consolation to his soul, even in the deepest of his earthly tribulations. In illustration of this, I might tell you the story of a poor man who lives in one of the courts in Holborn, who experiences great joy in religion, even in the midst of the deepest poverty. A Christian visitor, going up into the poor man's room at the top of the house, said, "My friend, how long have you been in this place?"

"I have not been downstairs, nor walked across the room, these twelve months."

"Have you anything to depend upon?"

"Nothing," he replied; but recollecting himself, he added, "I have a good Father up in heaven, and I depend upon him entirely, and he never lets me want. Some kind Christian friends are sure to call, and they never go away without leaving me something; and I get enough to live on and pay my rent, and I am very happy. I would not change places with anybody in the world, for I have Jesus Christ with me, and my heavenly Father will take me home by-and-bye, and then I shall be as rich as any of them—shall I not, sir? Sometimes I get very low, and Satan tells me that I am not a child of God, and that I had better give up all as lost; but I tell him that he is a great coward to come and meddle with a poor weak creature like me; and I show him the blood, sir; and I tell him the blood of Jesus Christ cleanseth from all sin; and when I show Satan the precious blood, sir, he leaves off tempting me, and flees directly, for he cannot bear the sight of the Saviour's blood."

Thus we see that true religion can cheer the sick man's couch, can make the poor man feel that he is rich, and bid him be joyful in the Lord. Well did the old man say that the devil cannot bear the sight of the Saviour's blood; and if, beloved friends, you can take Christ's blood, and put it on your conscience, however sinful you may have been, you will be able to sing of Christ as all your hope, all your joy, and all your support. I ask you who love Jesus, does religion ever make you unhappy? Does love to Jesus distress you, and make you miserable? It may bring you into trouble sometimes, and cause you to endure persecution for his name's sake. If you are a child of God, you will have to suffer tribulation; but all the afflictions which you may be called upon to endure for him will work for your good, and are not worthy to be compared with the glory which is to be revealed hereafter.

Now, then, let me ask, could you go with me while I have been speaking? Can you now say that Christ is your only Master, your chief good, your only joy? "Oh! yes; I do love Jesus, because he first loved me." Then, welcome, brother; you are one with Jesus, and we are one with each other. But if you cannot say it, how terrible it shall be with some of you, when you shall find your gourds wither, the props whereon you now lean struck down at a blow, your false refuges swept away, and, deprived of all your feathers and finery, your soul will appear before God in its true character! May it not be so with any of you, but may you be united to Christ by living faith, which works by love, and purifies the heart! Secondly, I shall now consider the text as:—

II. A MOTIVE TO ENCOURAGE YOU.

"Christ is all." My beloved friends, in what is he all? Christ is all in the entire work of salvation. Let me just take you back to the period before this world was made. There was a time when this great world, the sun, the moon, the stars, and all which now exist throughout the whole of the vast universe, lay in the mind of God, like unborn forests in an acorn cup. There was a time when the Great Creator lived alone, and yet he could foresee that he would make a world, and that men would be born to people it; and in that vast eternity a great scheme was devised, whereby he might save a fallen race. Do you know who devised it? God planned it from first to last. Neither Gabriel nor any of the holy angels had anything to do with it. I question whether they were even told how God might be just, and yet save the transgressors. God was all in the drawing up of the scheme, and Christ was all in carrying it out. There was a dark and doleful night! Jesus was in the garden, sweating great drops of blood, which fell to the ground; nobody then came to bear the load that had been laid upon him. An angel stood there to strengthen him, but not to bear the sentence. The cup was put into his hands, and Jesus said, "Father, must I drink it?" and his Father replied, "If thou dost not drink, sinners cannot be saved"; and he took the cup and drained it to its very dregs. No man helped him. And when he hung upon that accursed tree of Calvary, when his precious hands were pierced, when:—

> From his head, his hands, his feet,
> Sorrow and love flowed mingled down,
>   there was nobody to help him. He was "all" in
>   the work of salvation.

And, my friends, if any of you shall be saved, it must be by Christ alone. There must be no patchwork; Christ did it all, and will not be helped in the matter. Christ will not allow you, as some say, to do what you can, and leave him to make up the rest. What can you do that is not sinful? Christ has done all for us; the work of redemption is all finished. Christ planned it all, and worked out all; and we, therefore, preach a full salvation through Jesus Christ.

What could we poor mortals do towards saving ourselves? Our best works are but mean and worthless to that great end; I am sure I could not do it. My preaching—I am ashamed of that, and there are a thousand faults in my prayers. God wants nothing of us by way of "making up" Christ's work; but he cancels all the sins, and blots out all the transgressions of everyone who trusts to his Son's death.

If I have found Christ, I have found all. "I have not strong faith," say you. Never mind; Christ is all. "I do not feel my sins sufficiently"; but Christ is all. Many people think they must feel a load of repentance before they may hope Christ will receive them. I know every child of God will repent; but we are not all brought to the cross by the terrors of the law. It is not your feelings, my friends, that will save you; but Christ only, Christ standing in your stead, Christ being your Substitute. If, feeling your need of his grace to pardon you, and his righteousness to justify you before God, you can but just look to Christ, though you have nothing good about you, you will have done all that is necessary to carry you to heaven; because it is not your act that can save you, but the act of Christ alone. A little while ago, I had a conversation with an Irishman, who had been to hear me preach. He had come to ask me, he said, the way of salvation. "What troubles me," said he, "is this: God says that he will condemn the sinner, and punish him; then how can God forgive, because he must punish if he would keep his word?" I placed before him the Scriptural view of the atonement, in the substitution of Christ for the sinner; and the poor man was astonished and delighted beyond measure, never having understood the beauty and simplicity of the gospel way of salvation before. "Is it really so?" said he. "It is in the Bible," I replied. "Then the Bible must be true," said he, "for nobody but God could have thought it." If Jesus Christ is our Surety, friends, we are safe from the demands of the law. If Christ is our Substitute, we shall not suffer the penalty due to sin; for God will never punish the same sin twice. If I have nothing but Christ, I do not want anything else, for Christ is all. If Christ is your all, you will not want anything to help you, either in living or in dying. Now for two thoughts before I close.

1. If a man has Christ, then what does he want else? If a man has Christ, he has everything. If I want perfection, and I have Christ, I have absolute perfection in him. If I want righteousness, I shall find in him my beauty and my glorious dress. I want pardon, and if I have Christ, I am pardoned. I want heaven, and if I have Christ, I have the Prince of heaven, and shall be there by-and-bye, to live with Christ, and to dwell in his blessed embrace for ever. If you have Christ, you have all. Do not be desponding, do not give ear to the whisperings of Satan that you are not the children of God; for if you have Christ, you are his people, and other things will come by-and-bye. Christ makes you complete in himself; as the apostle says, "Ye are complete in him." I think of poor Mary Magdalene; she would have nothing to bring of her own; she would remember that she had been a harlot; but when she comes to heaven's gates, she will say, "I have Christ," and the command will go forth, "Let her in, Gabriel; let her in." Here comes a poor squalid wretch, what has he been doing? He has never learned to write, he scarcely went even to a Ragged-school, but he has Christ in his heart. "Gabriel, let him in." Next comes a rich bad man, with rings on his fingers, and fine clothes upon his person; but the command is, "Shut the gates, Gabriel; he has no business here." Then comes a fine flaing professor of the gospel; but he never knew Christ in his heart. "Shut the gate, Gabriel." If a man has Christ, he has all for eternity; and if he has not Christ, he is poor, and blind, and naked, and will be miserable for ever. Will not you, then, who are listening to me now, resolve, in the strength of the Lord, to seek him at once, and make him your Friend? No matter what may be your state or condition, you are invited to come to him.

Ye blind, ye lame, who are far from Christ, come to him, and receive your sight, and obtain strength! He is made your all; you need bring nothing in your hand to come to him. "Ah!" says one, "I am not good enough yet." Beggars do not talk thus: they consider that, the more needy they are, the more likely are they to obtain that for which they ask. The worse the dress, the better for begging. It is the same with respect to the gospel; and you are invited to come to Christ just as you are, naked and miserable, that he may clothe and comfort you.

2. My last thought is this: How poor is that man who is destitute of Christ! If I were to say to some one of you that you are poor, you would reply, "I am not poor; I have 250 pounds a year coming in, a decent house, and an excellent situation." And yet, if you have not Christ, you are a poor man indeed. Look at that poor worldling with a load of 10,000 pounds upon his back, a quantity of stocks and annuities in one hand, policies and railway scrip in the other; but he is wretched with all his wealth, though he can hardly carry it. There is a poor beggar-woman, who says to him, "Let me take a part of your burden"; but the miserable man refuses all assistance, and resolves to carry all his load himself. But by-and-bye he comes to a great gulf, and, instead of finding these riches help him, they hang around his neck like millstones, and weigh him down. Yet there are some who would do anything for gold. If there be one man more miserable than another in hell, it must be the man who robbed his neighbours to feather his own nest; such feathers will help the flight of the arrows which shall pierce his soul to all eternity. No matter what your wealth, if you have not Christ, you are miserably poor; but with Christ, you are rich to all eternity.

Methinks I see one of you ungodly ones in your last moments; someone stands by your bedside, and watches your face; the death-sweat comes over you, and the big drops stand on your brow; the strong man is bowed down, and the mighty one falls; and now the eye closes, and the hand falls powerless—life is fled. Ah! but the soul never dies! Up it flies to appear at God's bar. How will it appear there? Oh! the poor soul without Christ! It will be a naked soul; it will have no garment to cover it—it will be a perishing soul, no salvation for it. Mercy cannot be secured then; it will be in vain to pray then, because the lamp will be put out in eternal darkness. And the Judge will say, in tones that will pierce you to the quick, "Depart from me, ye cursed."

May God give all of you grace to repent, and to embrace the salvation which is revealed in the gospel! Every sin-sick soul may have Christ; but as for you who are Pharisees, and trusting in yourselves that you are righteous, if you know nothing about sin, you can know nothing about Christ. The way to be saved is to believe on the Lord Jesus Christ. "But what is it to believe?" you say. I have heard of a captain who had a little son, and this little boy was very fond of climbing aloft. One day he climbed to the mast-head, and the father saw that, if the boy attempted to return, he would be dashed to pieces; he, therefore, shouted to him not to look down, but to drop into the sea. The poor boy kept fast hold of the mast; but the father saw it was his only chance of safety, and he shouted once more, "Boy, the next time the ship lurches, drop, or I will shoot you." The boy is gone; he drops into the sea, and is saved. Had he not dropped, he must have perished. This is just your condition: so long as you cling to works and ceremonies, you are in the utmost peril; but when you give yourselves up entirely to the mercy of Christ, you are safe. Try it, sinner; try it, that is all. "He that believeth and is baptized shall be saved," is Christ's promise, and it shall never fail you. The invitation is to all who thirst. "The Spirit and the bride say, Come. And let him that heareth say, Come. And let him that is athirst come, and take the water of life freely." I have heard that, in the deserts where they can only get water at long intervals, they send a man on a camel in search of it; when he sees a pool, he springs off his beast, and before he himself drinks he calls out, "Come," and there is another man at a little distance, and he shouts, "Come," and one further away still repeats the word, "Come," until the whole desert resounds with the cry, "Come," and they come rushing to the water to drink. Now I do not make the gospel invitation wider than the declaration of the Word of God, "Whosoever will, let him take the water of life freely." Whosoever you are, and whatsoever you may have been, if you feel your need of Christ, "Come," and he will receive you, and give you to drink of the water of life freely.

Colossians 3; 4:1–4. Psalm 28:1–6.

Verse 1. If ye then be risen with Christ, seek those things which are above, where Christ sitteth on the right hand of God. Oh! how often we need to be called to this, for the flesh is grovelling, and it holds down the spirit; and very often we are seeking the things below as if we had not yet attained to the new life, and did not know anything about the resurrection power of Christ within the soul. Now, if it be that you, believers, have risen with Christ, do not live as if you had never done so, but "seek those things which are above, where Christ sitteth on the right hand of God."

2. Set your affection.

Not "your affections." Tie them up into one bundle. Make one of them.

2. On things above, not on things on the earth. You say that you were dead with Christ, and that you have risen with Christ. Live, then, the risen life, and not the life of those who have never undergone this matchless process. Live above.

3. For ye are dead, and your life is hid with Christ in God. The old life is dead. You are dead to it. You will not be consumed by it: you cannot be controlled by it. You have a newer and higher life. Let it have full scope.

4. When Christ, who is our life, shall appear, then shall ye also appear with him in glory. Christ was hidden while he was here. The world knew him not. So is your life. But there is to be a glorious manifestation. When Christ is made manifest, so shall you be. Wait for him.

5. Mortify therefore your members which are upon the earth; fornication, uncleanness, inordinate affection, evil concupiscence, and covetousness, which is idolatry: Since you are dead, let all the lusts of the flesh be put to death. Kill those. They were once a part of you. Your nature lusted this way. Mortify them. Do not merely restrain them and try to keep them under. These things you are to have nothing to do with.

6, 7. For which things sake the wrath of God cometh on the children of disobedience: In the which ye also walked some time, when ye lived in them." When ye lived in them" But now you do not live in them. You are dead to them. If it should ever come to pass that you fall into any of these things, you will loathe yourself with bitterest repentance that you could find comfort, satisfaction, life in them. You are dead to them.

8–10. But now ye also put off all these; anger, wrath,

malice, blasphemy, filthy communication out of your mouth. Lie not one to another, seeing that ye have put off the old man with his deeds: And have put on the new man, which is renewed in knowledge after the image of him that created him: No lies. Such communications are filthy. But you put these things away through your union with Christ in his risen life. Therefore, abhor them. Avoid the very appearance of them, and cry for grace to be kept from them, for you have been "renewed in knowledge after the image of him that created him."

11. Where there is neither Greek nor Jew, circumcision nor uncircumcision, Barbarian, Scythian, bond nor free: but Christ is all, and in all. In the new life there is no distinction of race and nationality. We are born into one family; we become members of Christ's body; and this is the one thing we have got to keep up—separation from all the world beside: no separations in the church, no disunion, nothing that would cause it, for we are one in Christ, and Christ is all. Now, as we have to put off these things, that is the negative side: that is the law's side, for the law says, "Thou shalt not"—"Thou shalt not." But now look at the positive side.

12. Put on therefore, as the elect of God, holy and beloved, bowels of mercies, kindness, humbleness of mind, meekness, longsuffering: This is what you have got to wear, even on the outside—to put it on; not to have a latent kindness in your heart, and a degree of humbleness deep down in your soul if you could get at it; but you are to put it on. It is to be the very dress you wear. These are the sacred vestments of your daily priesthood.

Put them on.

13. Forbearing one another, and forgiving one another, if any man have a quarrel against any: even as Christ forgave you, so also do ye. Just as readily, just as freely, just as heartily, just as completely.

14–15. And above all these things put on charity, which is the bond of perfectness. And let the peace of God rule in your hearts. For that is the great foundation of every godly fruit. We are in such a hurry, in such dreadful haste, so selfish, so discontented, so impetuous, and the major part of our sins spring from that condition of mind. But if we were godly, restful, peaceful, how many sins we should avoid! "Let the peace of God rule in your hearts."

15. To the which also ye are called in one body; and be ye thankful. It looks like a very small virtue to be thankful. Yet, dear friends, the absence of it is one of the grossest of vices. To be ungrateful is a mean thing: to be ungrateful to God is a base thing. And yet how many may accuse themselves of it! Who among us is as grateful as he should be? Be thankful.

16. Let the word of Christ dwell in you.

Alexander had a casket of gold studded with gems to carry Homer's works. Let your own heart be a casket for the command of Christ. "Let the word of Christ dwell in you."

16–18. Richly in all wisdom; teaching and admonishing one another in psalms and hymns and spiritual songs, singing with grace in your hearts to the Lord. And whatsoever ye do in word or deed, do all in the name of the Lord Jesus, giving thanks to God and the Father by him. Wives submit yourselves unto your own husbands, as it is fit in the Lord. See how our being Christians does not relax the bonds of our Christian relationship, but it calls us to the higher exercise of the responsibilities and duties connected therewith.

19. Husbands love your wives, and be not bitter against them. Oh! there are some spirits that are very bitter. A little thing puts them out, and they would take delight in a taunt which grieves the Spirit. I pity the poor woman who has such bitterness where she ought to have sweetness: yet there be some such husbands.

20–21. Children, obey your parents in all things: for this is well pleasing unto the Lord. Fathers, provoke not your children to anger, lest they be discouraged. The duties are mutual. Scripture maintains an equilibrium. It does not lay down commands for one class, and then leave the other to exercise whatever tyrannical oppression it may please. The child is to obey, but the father must not provoke.

22. Servants, obey in all things your masters according to the flesh; not with eyeservice, as menpleasers; How much there is of that! How quickly the hands go when the master's eye looks on! But the Christian servant remembers God's eye, and is diligent always. "Not with eye service as men-pleasers."

22. Chap. 4:2 But in singleness of heart, fearing God: And whatsoever ye do, do it heartily, as to the Lord, and not unto men; Knowing that of the Lord ye shall receive the reward of the inheritance: for ye serve the Lord Christ. But he that doeth wrong shall receive for the wrong which he hath done; and there is no respect of persons. Masters, give unto your servants that which is just and equal; knowing that ye also have a Master in heaven. Continue in prayer, and watch in the same with thanksgiving. See how he keeps putting that in—"Be ye thankful"—"with thanksgiving." Why, that is the oil that makes the machinery go round without its causing

obstruction. May we have much of that thanksgiving.

3, 4. Withal praying also for us, that God would open unto us a door of utterance, to speak the mystery of Christ, for which I am also in bonds: that I may make it manifest, as I ought to speak. So the preacher of the gospel asks your prayers: and it is a part of the duties arising out of the relationship between Christian men that those who are taught should pray for those who teach God's Word.

Christ Precious to Believers

A Sermon (No. 242) Delivered on Sabbath Morning, March 13th, 1859, by the REV. C. H. SPURGEON at the Music Hall, Royal Surrey Gardens.

"Unto you therefore which believe he is precious."—1 Peter 2:7.

This text calls to my recollection the opening of my ministry. It is about eight years since as a lad of sixteen, I stood up for the first time in my life to preach the gospel in a cottage to a handful of poor people, who had come together for worship. I felt my own inability to preach, but I ventured to take this text, "Unto you therefore which believe he is precious." I do not think I could have said anything upon any other text, but Christ was precious to my soul and I was in the flush of my youthful love, and I could not be silent when a precious Jesus was the subject. I had but just escaped from the bondage of Egypt, I had not forgotten the broken fetter; still did I recollect those flames which seemed to burn about my path, and that devouring gulf which opened its mouth as if ready to devour me. With all these things fresh in my youthful heart, I could speak of his preciousness who had been my Saviour, and had plucked me as a brand from the burning, and set me upon a rock, and put a new song in my mouth, and established my goings. And now, at this time what shall I say? "What hath God wrought?" How hath the little one become a thousand, and the small one a great people? And what shall I say concerning this text, but that if the Lord Jesus was precious then, he is as precious now? And if I could declare then, that Jesus was the object of my soul's desire, that for him I hoped to live, and for him I would be prepared to die, can I not say, God being my witness, that he is more precious to me this day than ever he was? In the recollection of his unparalleled mercy towards the chief of sinners, I must anew devote myself to him, and afresh surrender my heart to him who is Lord and King.

This remark is uttered by way of introduction, it may seem egotistical, but that I cannot help. I must give glory to God in the midst of the great congregation, and pay my vows to the Lord now in the midst of all his saints, in the midst of thee, O Jerusalem.

My text states a positive fact, namely, that Christ is precious to believers. This shall be the first part of our discourse; then in the second we will try to answer the question, why is Jesus Christ so precious to his believing people? And conclude by declaring the test whereby you may try yourselves whether you are believers or not; for if you be believers in Christ, then Christ is precious to you, and if you think little of him, then rest assured you have not a true and saving faith in him.

I. First, this is a positive fact, that UNTO BELIEVERS JESUS CHRIST IS PRECIOUS. In himself he is of inestimable preciousness, for he is the very God of very God. He is moreover, perfect man without sin. The precious gopher wood of his humanity is overlaid with the pure gold of his divinity. He is a mine of jewels, and a mountain of gems. He is altogether lovely, but, alas! this blind world seeth not his beauty. The painted harlotries of that which, Madam Bubble, the world can see, and all men wonder after her. This life, its joy, its lust, its gains, its honours,—these have beauty in the eye of the unregenerate man, but in Christ he sees nothing which he can admire. He hears his name as a common word, and looks upon his cross as a thing in which he has no interest, neglects his gospel, despises his Word, and, perhaps, vents fierce spite upon his people. But not so the believer. The man who has been brought to know that Christ is the only foundation upon which the soul can build its eternal home, he who has been taught that Jesus Christ is the first and the last, the Alpha and the Omega, the author and the finisher of faith, thinks not lightly of Christ. He calls him all his salvation and all his desire; the only glorious and lovely one.

Now, this is a fact which has been proved in all ages of the world. Look at the beginning of Christ's appearance upon earth. Nay, we might go farther back and mark how Christ was precious in prospect to those who lived before his incarnation; but, I say, since he has come into the world, what abundant proofs have we that he is precious to his people! There were men found who were not unwilling to part with houses, and lands, and wife, and children, and country, and reputation, and honour, and wealth, nay, with life itself, for Christ's sake. Such was the charm that Christ had for ancient Christians, that if they must renounce their patrimony and their earthly wealth for his sake, they did it cheerfully and without a murmur. Nay, they could say, that what things were gain they counted but loss for Christ's sake, and did esteem them but as dross and dung if they could win Christ and be found in him.

We talk lightly of these things, but these were no mean sacrifices. For a man to leave the partner of his bosom, to be despised by her who ought to honour him, to be spit upon by his own children, to be driven out by his countrymen, and have his name mentioned as a hissing, and a reproach, and a bye-word; this is no easy matter to bear; and yet the Christians in the first ages took up this cross, and not only carried it patiently, but carried it joyfully; rejoicing in tribulations, if those tribulations fell upon them for Christ's sake and the gospel. Nay, more than this, Satan has been permitted to put forth his hand and touch Christ's people, not only in their goods and in their families, but in their bone and in their flesh. And mark how Christ's disciples have reckoned nothing to be a loss, so that they might win Christ. Stretched upon the rack, their strained nerves have only made them sing the louder, as though they were harp strings, only put in tune when they were drawn out to their extreme length. They have been tortured with hot irons and with the pincers; their backs have been ploughed with scourges, but when have you found any of the true followers of Christ flinch in the hour of pain? They have borne all this, and challenged their persecutors to do more, and invent fresh arts and devices, fresh cruelties, and try them. Christ was so precious, that all the pain of the body could not make them deny him, and when at last they have been taken forth to a shameful death—let the axe and the block, let the cross of crucifixion, let the spear, let the fire and the stake, let the wild horse and the desert testify that the believer has always been a man, who would suffer all this, and vastly more, but who would never renounce his confidence in Christ. Look at Polycarp before the lions, when he is brought into the midst of the assembly, and it is demanded of him that he will deny his God. Thousands of savage eyes look down upon him, and there he stands, a feeble man, alone in the arena, but he tells them that "he has known his Lord these many years and he never did him a displeasure, and he will not deny him at the last." "To the lions!" they cry, "To the lions!" and the lions rush upon him, and he is speedily devoured; but all this he would have borne at the mouths of a thousand lions, if he had a thousand lives, rather than he would have thought anything amiss against the Majesty of Jesus of Nazareth. The whole history of the ancient church of Christ, proves that Jesus has been an object of his peoples' highest veneration; that they set nothing in rivalry with him, but cheerfully and readily, without a murmur, or a thought, gave up all for Jesus Christ, and rejoiced to do so.

And this is just as true to-day as it was then. If to-morrow the stake could be set in Smithfield, Christian people are prepared to be fuel for the flame. If once more the block fixed on Tower hill, and the axe were brought forth from its hiding place, the heads of Christ's people would be cheerfully given, if they might but crown the head of Jesus and vindicate his cause. Those who declare that the ancient valour of the church is departed, know not what they say. The professing church may have lost its masculine vigour; the professors of this day may be but effeminate dwarfs, the offspring of glorious fathers; but the true church, the elect out of the professing church, the remnant whom God hath chosen, are as much in love with Jesus as his saints of yore, and are as ready to suffer and to die. We challenge hell and its incarnate representative, old Rome herself; let her build her dungeons, let her revive her inquisitions, let her once more get power in the state to cut, and mangle, and burn; we are still able to possess our souls in patience. We sometimes feel it were a good thing if persecuting days should come again, to try the church once more, and drive away the chaff, and make her like a goodly heap of wheat, all pure and clean. The rotten branches of the forest may tremble at the hurricane, for they shall be swept away, but those that have sap within them tremble not. Our roots are intertwisted with the Rock of Ages, and the sap of Christ flows within us and we are branches of the living vine, and nothing shall sever us from him. We know that not persecution, nor famine, nor nakedness, nor peril, nor sword, shall divide us from the love of Christ, for in all these things we shall be as the church has been, more than conquerors through him that loved us.

Does any one think that I exaggerate? Mark, then, if what I have said be not true, then Christ has no church at all; for the church that is not prepared to suffer, and bleed and die for Christ, is not Christ's church. For what does he say? "He that loveth father and mother more than me is not worthy of me; and he that taketh not his cross, and followeth after me, is not worthy of me."—Matthew, 10:37–38. Albeit that Christ may not put us fully to the test, yet, if we be true, we must be ready for the ordeal; and if we be sincere, though we may tremble at the thought of it, we shall not tremble in the endurance of it. Many a man who says in his heart, "I have not a martyr's faith," has really that noble virtue; and let him but once come to the push, and the world shall see the grace that has been hidden, rising a giant from his slumbers. The faith which endures the relaxing of the world's sunshine, would endure the cutting frost of the world's persecution. We need not fear; if we be true to-day, we shall be true always.

This is not mere fiction, many are the proofs that Christ is still precious. Shall I tell you of the silent sufferers for Christ, who at this day suffer a martyrdom of which we hear not, but which is true and real? How many a young girl there is who follows Christ in the midst of an ungodly family; her father upbraids her, laughs at her, makes a scoff of her holiness, and pierces her through the heart with his sarcasm! Her brothers and her sisters call her "Puritan," "Methodist," and the like, and she is annoyed day by day with what the apostle calls, "Trial of cruel mockings." But she bears all this, and though the tear is sometimes forced by it from her eye, yet though she should weep blood she would "resist unto blood, striving against sin." These sufferers are unrecorded, they are not put into a Book of Martyrs. We have no Fox to write their martyrology, they have not the flesh-contenting knowledge that they shall be publicly honoured; but they suffer alone and unheard of, still praying for those who laugh at them: bowing themselves before God on their knees in agony, not on account of the persecution, but in agony of soul for the persecutors themselves, that they may be saved. How many there are of such young men in workshops, employed in large establishments, who bend their knee at night by the bed-side, in a large room where there are many scoffers. Some of us have known this in our youthful days, and have had to endure it; but Christ is precious to the silent sufferings of his people; these unhonoured martyrdoms prove that his church has not ceased to love him, not to esteem him precious.

How many there are, too—how many thousands of unseen and unknown labourers for Christ, whose names cannot be here declared. They toil from morning till night all through the week, and the Sabbath day should be a day of rest to them; but they work more on the Sabbath day than on any other day. They are visiting the beds of the sick; their feet are weary, and nature says rest, but they go into the lowest dens and haunts of the city to speak to the ignorant, and endeavour to spread the name and honour of Jesus where it has not been known. There are many such who are working hard for Christ, though the church scarce knows of it. And how many, too, there are who prove that they love Christ by the continual liberality of their offerings. Many are the poor people I have discovered, who have denied themselves of this and that, because they would serve Christ's cause. And many there are, too—every now and then we find them out—in the middle ranks of society, who give a hundred times as much to the cause of Christ as many of the rich and wealthy; and if you knew to what little trials they are put, to what shifts they are driven in order to serve Christ, you would say, "The man that can do this proves clearly that Christ is precious to him." And mark this, the reason why the church is not more laborious, not more generous in its gifts to the offertory of the Saviour, is just this, because the church of the day is not the church of Christ in its mass and bulk. There is a church of Christ within it, but the visible church, as it stands before you, is not to be considered the church of Christ; we must pass it through the fire, and bring the third part through the flame; for this is the day when the dross is mingled with gold. How hath the much fine gold become dim; how hath the glory departed. Zion is under a cloud. But mark, though you see it not, there is a church, a hidden church; an unmoving centre amidst the growing of profession, there is a life within this outward fungus of a growing Christianity; there is a life that is within, and to that hidden host, that chosen company, Christ is precious—they are proving it every day by their patient sufferings, by their laborious efforts, by their constant offerings to the church of Christ. "Unto you therefore which believe he is precious."

I will tell you one thing that proves—proves to a demonstration, that Christ is still precious to his people, and it is this:—send one of Christ's people to hear the most noted preacher of the age, whoever that may be; he preaches a very learned sermon, very fine and magnificent, but there is not a word about Christ in that sermon. Suppose that to be the case, and the Christian man will go out and say, "I did not care a farthing for that man's discourse." Why? "Because they have taken away my Lord, and I know not where they have laid him. I heard nothing about Christ." Send that man on the Sabbath morning to hear some hedge and ditch preacher, some one who cuts the king's English about never so badly, but who preaches Jesus Christ—you will see the tears rolling down that man's face, and when he comes out he will say, "I do not like that man's bad grammar; I do not like the many mistakes he has made, but oh! it has done my heart good, for he spoke about Christ." That, after all, is the main thing for the Christian; he wants to hear about his Lord, and if he hears him magnified he will overlook a hundred faults. In fact, you will find that Christians are all agreed, that the best sermon is that which is fullest of Christ. They never like to hear a sermon unless there is something of Christ in it. A Welsh minister who was preaching last Sabbath at the chapel of my dear brother, Jonathan George, was saying, that Christ was the sum and substance of the gospel, and he broke out into this story:—A young man had been preaching in the presence of a venerable divine, and after he had done he went to the old minister, and said, "What do you think of my sermon?"

"A very poor sermon indeed," said he.

"A poor sermon?" said the young man, "it took me a long time to study it."

"Ay, no doubt of it."

"Why, did you not think my explanation of the text a very good one?"

"Oh, yes," said the old preacher, "very good indeed."

"Well, then, why do you say it is a poor sermon? Didn't you think the metaphors were appropriate and the arguments conclusive?"

"Yes, they were very good as far as that goes, but still it was a very poor sermon."

"Will you tell me why you think it a poor sermon?"

"Because," said he, "there was no Christ in it."

"Well," said the young man, "Christ was not in the text; we are not to be preaching Christ always, we must preach what is in the text."

So the old man said, "Don't you know young man that from every town, and every village, and every little hamlet in England, wherever it may be, there is a road to London?"

"Yes," said the young man.

"Ah!" said the old divine, "and so form every text in Scripture, there is a road to the metropolis of the Scriptures, that is Christ. And my dear brother, your business in when you get to a text, to say, 'Now what is the road to Christ?' and then preach a sermon, running along the road towards the great metropolis—Christ. And," said he, "I have never yet found a text that had not got a road to Christ in it, and if I ever do find one that has not a road to Christ in it, I will make one; I will go over hedge and ditch but I would get at my Master, for the sermon cannot do any good unless there is a savour of Christ in it." Now since you say amen to that, and declare that what you want to hear is Jesus Christ, the text is proved—"Unto you therefore which believe he is precious."

But if you want to try this again and prove it, go and see some of our sick and dying friends; go and talk to them about the Reform Bill, and they will look you in the face and say, "Oh, I am going from this time-state: it is a very small matter to me whether the Reform Bill will be carried or not." You will not find them much interested in that matter. Well, then, sit down and talk to them about the weather, and how the crops are getting on—"Well, it is a good prospect for wheat this year." They will say, "Ah, my harvest is ripening in glory." Introduce the most interesting topic you can, and a believer, who is lying on the verge of eternity, will find nothing precious in it; but sit down by the bedside of this man, and he may be very near gone, almost unconscious, and begin to talk about Jesus—mention that precious soul-reviving, soul-strengthening name Jesus, and you will see his eye glisten, and the blanched cheek will be flushed once more—"Ah," he will say, "Precious Jesus, that is the name which calms my fears, and bids my sorrows cease." You will see that you have given the man a strong tonic, and that his whole frame is braced up for the moment. Even when he dies, the thought of Jesus Christ and the prospect of seeing him shall make him living in the midst of death, strong in the midst of weakness, and fearless in the midst of trembling. And this proves, by the experience of God's people, that with those who believe in him, Christ is and ever must be a precious Christ.

II. The second thing is, WHY IS CHRIST PRECIOUS TO THE BELIEVER? I observe—and I shall run over those particulars very briefly, though they would be worthy of a long, long sermon—Jesus Christ is precious to the believer, because he is intrinsically precious. But here let me take you through an exercise in grammar; here is an adjective, let us go through it. He is precious positively; he is more precious than anything comparatively; he is most precious of all things, and most precious even if all things were rolled into one and put into competition with him; he is thus precious superlatively. Now, there are few things you can thus deal with. You say, a man is a good man, he is good positively, and you say he is a great deal better than many other people; he is good comparatively: but you can never truly say to any man that he is good superlatively, because there he would still be found short of perfection. But Christ is good positively, comparatively, and superlatively.

Is he good positively? Election is a good thing; to be chosen of God, and precious; but we are elect in Christ Jesus. Adoption is a good thing; to be adopted into the family of God is a good thing—ah, but we are adopted in Christ Jesus and made joint-heirs with him. Pardon is a good thing—who will not say so?—ay, but we are pardoned through the precious blood of Jesus. Justification—is not that a noble thing, to be robed about with a perfect righteousness?—ay, but we are justified in Jesus. To be preserved—is not that a precious thing?—ay; but we are preserved in Christ Jesus, and kept by his power even to the end. Perfection—who shall say that this is not precious? Well, but we are perfect in Christ Jesus. Resurrection, is not that glorious? We are risen with him. To ascend up on high, is not that precious? But he hath raised us up and made us sit together with him in heavenly places in Jesus Christ—so that Christ must be good positively, for he is all the best things in one. And if all these be good, surely he must be good in whom, and by whom, and to whom, and through are all these precious things.

But Christ is good comparatively. Bring anything here and compare with him. One of the brightest jewels we can have is liberty. If I be not free, let me die. Put the halter to my neck but put not the fetter to my wrist—a free man I must be while I live. Will not the patriot say that he would give his blood to buy liberty, and think it a cheap price? Ay, but put liberty side by side with Christ, and I would wear the fetter for Christ and rejoice in the chain. The apostle Paul himself could say, "I would that ye were altogether such I am,"—and he might add, "except these bonds," but though he excepted bonds for others, he did not except them for himself, for he rejoiced in the chain and counted it as a mark of honor. Besides liberty, what a precious thing is life! "Skin for skin, yea, all that a man hath, will he give for his life." But let a Christian—a true Christian, once have the choice between life and Christ,—"No," says he, "I can die, but I cannot deny; I can burn, but I cannot turn. I confess Christ and perish in the flame; but I cannot deny Christ, even though you exalt me to a throne." There would be no choice between the two. And then whatever earthly good there may be in comparison with Christ, the believer's testimony goes to prove that Christ is precious comparatively, for there is nothing that can match with him.

And then to go higher still—Christ is good superlatively. The superlative of all things is heaven, and if it could be possible to put Christ in competition with heaven, the Christian would not stop a moment in his choice; he would sooner be on earth with Christ than be in heaven without him. Nay, I do not know whether he would not go almost as far as Rutherford, who said, "Lord, I would sooner be in hell with thee than in heaven without thee; for if I were in heaven without thee it would be a hell to me, and if I were in hell with thee it would be a heaven to me." We may put it so, and every Christian will subscribe to it. Now, come ye messengers of the world and take on your shoulders all its treasures. Cësar, pour out thy gold in one glittering pile; Cësar, lay down thine honours here in one gaudy heap; here, Tiberius, bring all the joys of Capri's lust and vice; Solomon, bring here all the treasures of wisdom; Alexander, bring all thy triumphs; Napoleon, bring thy wide-spread empire and thy fame, put them all here, all that earth calls good; and now come, thou bleeding Lamb of God, thou marred and matchless Saviour, come here and tread these beneath thy feet, for what are all these compared with thee? I pour contempt on them all. Now am I dead to all the world, and all the world is dead to me. The whole realm of nature is small in comparison with thee, as a drop in the bucket when compared with a boundless ocean. Jesus Christ, then, is precious superlatively.

2. What more can we say? Still to answer this question again: Why is Christ precious to the believer more than to any other man? Why it is the believer's want that makes Christ precious to him. That is one answer. We have been having a small shower of rain lately, and I dare say there are very few of you who felt grateful for it; since it gave you a little wetting coming here. But suppose that shower of rain could have fallen on the desert of Arabia, what a precious thing it would have been. Yea, every rain drop would have been worth a pearl; and as for the shower, though it had rained gold dust, the rich deposit would not have been comparable to the flood when it descended from on high. But what is the reason that water is so precious there? Simply because it is so rare. Suppose I am in England; there is abundance of water and I cannot sell it; water is so common, and therefore so cheap. But put a man in the desert and let the water-skin be dried up, let him come to the well wherein he expected to find water, and it has failed him; can you not conceive that that small drop of water might be worth a king's ransom? Nay, that a man might hoard it up, and conceal it from all his comrades, because on that small drop of water depended his life? The way to prize water is to value it with a tongue like a firebrand, and with a mouth like an oven. Then can I estimate its value when I know its want. So with Christ. The worldling does not care for Christ, because he has never hungered and thirsted after him; but the Christian is athirst for Christ; he is in a dry and thirsty land, where not water is, and his heart and his flesh pant after God, yea for the living God; and as the thirsty soul dying, cries

out water, water, water, so the Christian cries out Christ, Christ, Christ! This is the one thing needful for me, and if I have it not, this thirst must destroy me.

Mark, too, that the believer may be found in many aspects, and you will always find that his needs will endear Christ to him. Here is a man about to be tried for his life. Before he had committed the wrong, he used to say, "Lawyers, attorneys, pleaders, away with them, what is the good of them?" Now he has got into prison he thinks very differently. He says, "I wish I could get a good special pleader to plead my cause;" and he runs over the roll to see the best man to plead for him. At last he says, "Here is a man, if he could plead my cause I might hope to escape, but I have no money with which to engage him;" and he says to his wife—"Wife, we must sell our house;" or, "We must get money somehow, for I am on trial for my life, and I must have an advocate." And what will not a woman do to get an advocate for her husband? Why, she will pledge the last rag she has to get one. Now, does not the believer feel himself to be in just such a position? He is a poor sinner on trial for his life, and he wants an advocate; and every time he looks on Christ pleading his cause before the Father's throne, he says, "O what a precious Christ he is to a poor sin-destroyed sinner, for he pleads his cause before the throne."

But suppose another case; that of a man drawn for a soldier. In such times men always look out for substitutes. I remember when the ballot was coming for the militia, how every man joined a substitute club in order that if he were drawn he might not go himself. Now suppose a man had been drawn, how valuable would a substitute have been—for no man in his senses likes to be food for powder—he would rather a man without brains go and do such work as that, but as for him he estimates himself at too high a price. But suppose he is not only drawn for a soldier, but condemned to die. See yon poor wretch coming up the gallows stairs; some one whispers to him, "What would you give for a substitute now? What would you give for some one to come and bear this punishment?" See his eye rolls madness at the thought. "A substitute," says he, "I could not buy one for the whole world. Who would be a substitute for me, to swing into eternity amidst the yellings of a crowd?" But suppose—and we are only supposing what has actually occurred—suppose this man saw not only the gallows and the drop, but hell fire before him, and it were said to him, "You must burn in that for ever unless you find a substitute," would not that be a precious one? Now, mark, that is just our position. The Christian feels that hell is before him, if it were not that he has a glorious substitute. Jesus came forward, and said, "I will bear that punishment; pour hell on me, my Father let me drink damnation dry;" and he did it; he endured all those pains, or an equivalent for them; he suffered in the rebel's stead; and now, through him the substitute, we are absolved and free. Oh, must not he be a precious Christ?

But think of Christ again, and then think of the believer's wants. I will try and run over a number of them. The believer is a silly sheep. What a precious thing is a shepherd, and how precious are green pastures and still waters. The believer is like a desolate woman. What a precious thing is a husband who shall provide for her, and shall console and cherish her. The believer is a pilgrim, and the hot sun beats on him. What a precious thing is the shadow of a great rock in a weary land. The believer is a bond-slave by nature. What a precious thing is the trump of jubilee, and the ransom-price that sets him free. The believer, by nature, is a sinking, drowning man. How precious to him is that plank of free-grace, the cross of Christ, on which he puts his poor trembling hand and secures glory. But what more shall I say? Time would fail me to tell of all the wants of the believer, and of the all-abounding and ever-flowing streams of love that flow from Christ, the fountain that fills the believer to the brim. O say, ye children of God, is he not while ye are in these lowlands of want and suffering, inconceivably, unutterably, superlatively precious to you?

3. But once more. Look at the believer not only in his wants, but in his highest earthly state. The believer is a man that was once blind and now sees. And what a precious thing is light to a man that sees. If I, as a believer, have an eye, how much I need the sun to shine. If I have no light my eye becomes a torture, and I might as well have been blind. And when Christ gives sight to the blind he makes his people a seeing people. It is then that they find what a precious thing is the sight, and how pleasant a thing it is for a man to behold the sun. The believer is a man that is quickened. A dead corpse wants no clothing, for it feels no cold. Let a man once be quickened and he finds himself naked, and wants clothing. From the very fact that the Christian is a quickened man, he values the robe of righteousness that is put about him. Christ touches his people's ears and opens them; but it were better for man to be deaf than to hear for ever doleful groans and hissings. But such must he have been, ever hearing it if it were not for Christ playing sweet music to him every

day, and pouring streams of melody into his ears through his promises. Yes, I say, the very new-born powers of the Christian would be very channels for misery if it were not for Christ. Even in his highest estate the Christian must feel that Christ is necessary unto him, and then he must conclude that Christ is precious to him.

But believer, how precious is Christ to thee in the hour of conviction of sin, when he says, "Thy sins which are many, are all forgiven thee." How precious to thee in the hour of sickness, when he comes to thee and says, "I will make all thy bed in thy sickness." How precious to thee in the day of trial, when he says, "All things work together for thy good." How precious when friends are buried, for he says, "I am the resurrection and the life." How precious in thy grey old age, "even in old age I am with thee, and to hoary hairs will I carry you." How precious in the lone chamber of death, for "I will fear no evil, thou art with me, thy rod and thy staff comfort me." But, last of all, how precious will Christ be when we see him as he is. All we know of Christ here is as nothing compared with what we shall know hereafter. Believer, when thou seest Christ's face now, thou only seest if through a veil—Christ is so glorious, that like Moses he is compelled to put a veil upon his face, for his poor people while they are here are so feeble that they could not behold him face to face. And if he be lovely here, when he is marred and spit upon, how lovely must he be when he is adored and worshipped. If he is precious on his cross, how much more precious when he sits on his throne. If I can weep before him, and love him, and live to him, when I see him as the despised man of Nazareth; Oh, how shall my spirit be knit to him, how shall my heart be absorbed with love to him, when I see his face and behold his crown of glory, when I mark the harpings of the never-ceasing harpers who harp his praise. Wait awhile, Christian. If he is precious to the believer now, when faith is turned to sight he will be more precious still. Go out of this hall, and cry, "O Lord Jesus, I must love thee, I must serve thee better, I must live for thee; I must be ready to die for thee—for 'Thou art precious to my soul, My transport and my trust.'" This brings me to conclude—and here I want your solemn and earnest attention while each one for himself shall answer this question—my hearer, is Christ precious to you? My young brother, you of the same age as myself, is Jesus precious to you in your youth? Wherewithal shall a young man cleanse his way? only by taking heed thereto according to Christ's word, and by walking in his footsteps. Ye men and women of middle age, is Christ precious to you?

Remember that this world is but a dream, and if you have not something more satisfactory than that, you will be disappointed, even though you succeed beyond your highest wishes. And ye grey headed men, who are going tottering to your graves, whose life is like a candle-snuff, almost expiring, like a lamp whose oil is spent. Is Christ precious to you, ye with the bald head, and with the hoary lock, is Jesus precious to your soul? Remember, on your answer to this question depends your condition. You believe, if he is precious to you, but if he is not precious, then you are not believers, and you are condemned already because you believe not on the Son of God. Now, which is it? Oh, methinks some of you feel as if you could spring from your seats, and say, "Yes, he is precious to me, I cannot deny it." Once there was a good minister who was catechising his class, and he said to the young people, "The question which I am about to ask is such that I want none of you to answer but those who can answer from your heart." The congregation was gathered together, and he put this question to them concerning Christ—"Suppose Christ was here, and should say, 'Lovest thou me?' what would be your reply?" He looked around, and glanced upon all the young men and the young women, and said, "Jesus speaks to you the first time, and says, 'Lovest thou me?' He speaks a second time, and he says, 'Lovest thou me?'" There was a solemn pause and no one answered; and the congregation looked at the class, and at last the minister said once more, "Jesus speaks by me a third time, and says, 'Lovest thou me?'" Up rose a young woman, who could keep her seat no longer, and, bursting into tears, said, "Yea, Lord, thou knowest all things, thou knowest that I love thee." Now, how many are there here who could say that? Could not you now, if this were the time—although you might be bashful in the midst of so many—could you not, if Christ asked you the question, boldly say, though in the midst of enemies—"Yea, Lord, thou knowest all things, thou knowest that I love thee." Well, if you can give such an answer as that, go home and pray that others may be brought to love him, for you yourselves are saved; but if you are compelled to be silent to such a question as that, O may God lead you to seek Christ, may you too be driven to the cross, may you there see his dear bleeding wounds, may you behold his open side, and falling at his feet, may you say, "I trust thee, I rely upon thee, I depend upon thee," and he will say, "I have saved thee;" and then will you spring to your feet, and say, "Lord I love thee, because thou hast first loved me." May such be the end of this sermon, and to God be all the glory.

CHRIST CRUCIFIED

A Sermon (No. 7–8) Delivered on Sabbath Morning, February 11, 1855, by the REV. C. H. SPURGEON At Exeter Hall, Strand.

"But we preach Christ crucified, unto the Jews a stumblingblock, and unto the Greeks foolishness; but unto them which are called, both Jews and Greeks, Christ the power of God, and the wisdom of God."—1 Corinthians 1:23–24.

What contempt hath God poured upon the wisdom of this world! How hath he brought it to nought, and made it appear as nothing. He has allowed it to word out its own conclusions, and prove its own folly. Men boasted that they were wise; they said that they could find out God to perfection; and in order that their folly might be refuted once and forever, God gave them the opportunity of so doing. He said, "Worldly wisdom, I will try thee. Thou sayest that thou art mighty, that thine intellect is vast and comprehensive, that thine eye is keen, and thou canst find all secrets; now, behold, I try thee; I give thee one great problem to solve. Here is the universe; stars make its canopy, fields and flowers adorn it, and the floods roll o'er its surface; my name is written therein; the invisible things of God may be clearly seen in the things which are made. Philosophy, I give thee this problem—find me out. Here are my works—find me out. Discover in the wondrous world which I have made, the way to worship me acceptably. I give thee space enough to do it—there are data enough. Behold the clouds, the earth, and the stars. I give thee time enough; I will give thee four thousand years, and I will not interfere; but thou shalt do as thou wilt with thine own world. I will give thee men enough; for I will make great minds and vast, whom thou shalt call lords of earth; thou shalt have orators, thou shalt have philosophers. Find me out, O reason; find me out, O wisdom; find me out, if thou canst; find me out unto perfection; and if thou canst not, then shut thy mouth forever, and then will I teach thee that the wisdom of God is wiser than the wisdom of man; yea, that the foolishness of God is wiser than men." And how did the wisdom of man work out the problem? How did wisdom perform her feat? Look upon the heathen nations; there you see the result of wisdom's researches. In the time of Jesus Christ, you might have beheld the earth covered with the slime of pollution, a Sodom on a large scale—corrupt, filthy, depraved; indulging in vices which we dare not mention; revelling in lust too abominable even for our imagination to dwell upon for a moment. We find the men prostrating themselves before blocks of wood and stone, adoring ten thousand gods more vicious than themselves. We find, in fact, that reason wrote out her lines with a finger covered with blood and filth, and that she forever cut herself out from all her glory by the vile deeds she did. She would not worship God. She would not bow down to him who is "clearly seen," but she worshipped any creature—the reptile that crawled, the viper—everything might be a god; but not, forsooth, the God of heaven. Vice might be made into a ceremony, the greatest crime might be exalted into a religion; but true worship she knew nothing of. Poor reason! poor wisdom! how art thou fallen from heaven; like Lucifer—thou son of the morning—thou art lost; thou hast written out thy conclusion, but a conclusion of consummate folly. "After that in the wisdom of God, the world by wisdom knew not God, it pleased God by the foolishness of preaching to save them that believe."

Wisdom had had its time, and time enough; it had done its all, and that was little enough; it had made the world worse than it was before it stepped upon it, and "now," says God, "Foolishness shall overcome wisdom; now ignorance, as ye call it, shall sweep away science; now, humble, child-like faith shall crumble to the dust all the colossal systems your hands have piled." He calls his armies. Christ puts his trumpet to his mouth, and up come the warriors, clad in fishermen's garb, with the brogue of the lake of Galilee—poor humble mariners. Here are the warriors, O wisdom, that are to confound thee; these are the heroes who shall overcome thy proud philosophers; these men are to plant their standard upon thy ruined walls, and bid them to fall forever; these men and their successors are to exalt a gospel in the world which ye may laugh at as absurd, which ye may sneer at as folly, but which shall be exalted above the hills, and shall be glorious even to the highest heavens. Since that day, God has always raised up successors of the apostles; not by any lineal descent, but because I have the same roll and charter as any apostle, and am as much called to preach the gospel as Paul himself; if not as much owned by the conversion of sinners, yet, in a measure, blessed of God; and, therefore, here I stand, foolish as Paul might be, foolish as Peter, or any of those fishermen; but still with the might of God I grasp the sword of truth, coming here to "preach Christ and him crucified, unto the Jews a stumblingblock, and unto the Greeks foolishness;

but unto them which are called, both Jews and Greeks, Christ the power of God, and the wisdom of God."

Before I enter upon our text, let me very briefly tell you what I believe preaching Christ and him crucified is. My friends, I do not believe it is preaching Christ and him crucified, to give people a batch of philosophy every Sunday morning and evening, and neglect the truths of this Holy Book. I do not believe it is preaching Christ and him crucified, to leave out the main cardinal doctrines of the Word of God, and preach a religion which is all a mist and a haze, without any definite truths whatever. I take it that man does not preach Christ and him crucified, who can get through a sermon without mentioning Christ's name once; nor does that man preach Christ and him crucified, who leaves out the Holy Spirit's work, who never says a word about the Holy Ghost, so that indeed the hearers might say, "We do not so much as know whether there be a Holy Ghost." And I have my own private opinion, that there is no such thing as preaching Christ and him crucified, unless you preach what now-a-days is called Calvinism. I have my own ideas, and those I always state boldly. It is a nickname to call it Calvinism. Calvinism is the gospel, and nothing else. I do not believe we can preach the gospel, if we do not preach justification by faith without works; not unless we preach the sovereignty of God in his dispensation of grace; nor unless we exalt the electing, unchangeable, eternal, immutable, conquering love of Jehovah; nor, I think, can we preach the gospel, unless we base it upon the peculiar redemption which Christ made for his elect and chosen people; nor can I comprehend a gospel which lets saints fall away after they are called, and suffers the children of God to be burned in the fires of damnation, after having believed. Such a gospel I abhor. The gospel of the Bible is not such a gospel as that. We preach Christ and him crucified in a different fashion, and to all gainsayers we reply, "We have not so learned Christ."

There are three things in the text: first, a gospel rejected, "Christ crucified, to the Jews a stumblingblock, and to the Greeks foolishness"; secondly, a gospel triumphant, "unto those who are called, both Jews and Greeks"; and thirdly, a gospel admired; it is to them who are called "the power of God and the wisdom of God."

I. First, we have here A GOSPEL REJECTED. One would have imagined that, when God sent his gospel to men, all men would meekly listen, and humbly receive its truths. We should have thought that God's ministers had but to proclaim that life is brought to light by the gospel, and that Christ is come to save sinners, and every ear would be attentive, every eye would be fixed, and every heart would be wide open to receive the truth. We should have said, judging favorably of our fellow-creatures, that there would not exist in the world a monster so vile, so depraved, so polluted, as to put so much as a stone in the way of the progress of truth; we could not have conceived such a thing; yet that conception is the truth. When the gospel was preached, instead of being accepted and admired, one universal hiss went up to heaven; men could not bear it; its first preacher they dragged to the brow of the hill, and would have sent him down headlong; yea, they did more—they nailed him to the cross, and there they let him languish out his dying life in agony such as no man hath borne since. All his chosen ministers have been hated and abhorred by worldlings; instead of being listened to they have been scoffed at; treated as if they were the offscouring of all things, and the very scum of mankind. Look at the holy men in the old times, how they were driven from city to city, persecuted, afflicted, tormented, stoned to death, wherever the enemy had power to do so. Those friends of men, those real philanthropists, who came with hearts big with love, and hands full of mercy, and lips pregnant with celestial fire, and souls that burned with holy influence; those men were treated as if they were spies in the camp, as if they were deserters from the common cause of mankind; as if they were enemies, and not, as they truly were, the best of friends. Do not suppose, my friends, that men like the gospel any better now than they did then. There is an idea that you are growing better. I do not believe it. You are growing worse. In many respects men may be better—outwardly better; the heart within is still the same. The human heart of today dissected, would be like the human heart a thousand years ago; the gall of bitterness within that breast of yours, is just as bitter as the gall of bitterness in that of Simon of old. We have in our hearts the same latent opposition to the truth of God; and hence we find men, even as of old, who scorn the gospel.

I shall, in speaking of the gospel rejected, endeavour to point out the two classes of persons who equally despise truth. The Jews make it a stumblingblock, and the Greeks account it foolishness. Now these two very respectable gentlemen—the Jew and the Greek—I am not going to make these ancient individuals the object of my condemnation, but I look upon them as members of a great parliament, representatives of a great constituency, and I shall attempt to show that, if all the race of Jews were cut off, there would be still a great number in the world who would answer to the name of Jews, to whom Christ is a stumblingblock; and that if Greece were swallowed up by some earthquake, and ceased to be a nation, there would still be the Greek unto whom the gospel would be foolishness. I shall simply introduce the Jew and the Greek, and let them speak a moment to you, in order that you may see the gentlemen who represent you; the representative men; the persons who stand for many of you, who as yet are not called by divine grace.

The first is a Jew; to him the gospel is a stumblingblock. A respectable man the Jew was in his day; all formal religion was concentrated in his person; he went up to the temple very devoutly; he tithed all he had, even to the mint and the cummin. You would see him fast twice in the week, with a face all marked with sadness and sorrow. If you looked at him, he had the law between his eyes; there was the phylactery, and the borders of his garments of amazing width, that he might never be supposed to be a Gentile dog; that no one might ever conceive that he was not an Hebrew of pure descent. He had a holy ancestry; he came of a pious family; a right good man was he. He could not like those Sadducees at all, who had no religion. He was thoroughly a religious man; he stood up for his synagogue; he would not have that temple on Mount Gerizim; he could not bear the Samaritans, he had no dealings with them; he was a religionist of the first order, a man of the very finest kind; a specimen of a man who is a moralist, and who loves the ceremonies of the law. Accordingly, when he heard about Christ, he asked who Christ was. "The Son of a Carpenter." Ah! "The son of a carpenter, and his mothers's name was Mary, and his father's name was Joseph." "That of itself is presumption enough," said he; "positive proof, in fact, that he cannot be the Messiah." And what does he say? Why, he says, "Woe unto you, Scribes and Pharisees, hypocrites." "That won't do." Moreover, he says, "It is not by the works of the flesh that any man can enter into the kingdom of heaven." The Jew tied a double knot in his phylactery at once; he thought he would have the borders of his garment made twice as broad. He bow to the Nazarene! No, no; and if so much as a disciple crossed the street, he thought the place polluted, and would not tread in his steps. Do you think he would give up his old father's religion, the religion which came from Mount Sinai, that old religion that lay in the ark and the overshadowing cherubim? He give that up! not he. A vile imposter—that is all Christ was in his eyes. He thought so. "A stumblingblock to me; I cannot hear about it; I will not listen to it." Accordingly, he turned a deaf ear to all the preacher's eloquence, and listened not at all. Farewell, old Jew! Thou sleepest with thy fathers, and thy generation is a wandering race, still walking the earth. Farewell! I have done with thee. Alas! poor wretch, that Christ, who was thy stumbling-block, shall be thy judge, and on thy head shall be that loud curse. "His blood be on us and on our children." But I am going to find out Mr. Jew here in Exeter Hall—persons who answer to his description—to whom Jesus Christ is a stumblingblock. Let me introduce you to yourselves, some of you. You were of a pious family too, were you not? Yes. And you have a religion which you love; you love it so far as the chrysalis of it goes, the outside, the covering, the husk. You would not have one rubric altered, nor one of those dear old arches taken down, nor the stained glass removed, for all the world; and any man who should say a word against such things, you would set down as a heretic at once. Or, perhaps, you do not go to such a place of worship, but you love some plain old meeting-house, where your forefathers worshipped, called a dissenting chapel. Ah! it is a beautiful plain place; you love it, you love its ordinances, you love its exterior; and if any one spoke against the place, how vexed you would feel. You think that what they do there, they ought to do everywhere; in fact, your church is a model one; the place where you go is exactly the sort of place for everybody; and if I were to ask you why you hope to go to heaven, you would perhaps say, "Because I am a Baptist," or, "Because I am an Episcopalian," or whatever other sect you belong to. There is yourself; I know Jesus Christ will be to you a stumblingblock. If I come and tell you, that all your going to the house of God is good for nothing; if I tell you that all those many times you have been singing and praying, all pass for nothing in the sight of God, because you are a hypocrite and a formalist. If I tell you that your heart is not right with God, and that unless it is so, all the external is good for nothing, I know what you will say,—"I shan't hear that young man again." It is a stumblingblock. If you had stepped in anywhere where you had heard formalism exalted: if you had been told "this must you do, and this other must you do, and then you will be saved," you would highly approve of it. But how many are there externally religious, with whose characters you could find no fault, but who have never had the regenerating influence of the Holy Ghost; who never were made to lie prostrate on their face before Calvary's cross; who never turned a wistful eye to yonder Saviour crucified; who never put their trust in him that was slain for the sons of men. They love a superficial religion, but when a man talks deeper than that, they set it down for cant. You may love all that is external about religion, just as you may love a man for his clothes—caring nothing for the man himself. If so, I know you are one of those who reject the gospel. You will hear me preach; and while I speak about the externals, you will hear me with attention; whilst I plead for morality, and argue against drunkenness, or show the heinousness of Sabbath-breaking, but if once I say, "Except ye be converted, and become as little children, ye can in no wise enter into the kingdom of God"; if once I tell you that you must be elected of God: that you must be purchased with the Saviour's blood—that you must be converted by the Holy Ghost—you say, "He is a fanatic! Away with him, away with him! We do not want to hear that any more." Christ crucified, is to the Jew—the ceremonialist—a stumblingblock.

But there is another specimen of this Jew to be found. He is thoroughly orthodox in his sentiments. As for forms and ceremonies, he thinks nothing about them. He goes to a place of worship where he learns sound doctrine. He will hear nothing but what is true. He likes that we should have good works and morality. He is a good man, and no one can find fault with him. Here he is, regular in his Sunday pew. In the market he walks before men in all honesty—so you would imagine. Ask him about any doctrine, and he can give you a disquisition upon it. In fact, he could write a treatise upon anything in the Bible, and a great many things besides. He knows almost everything: and here, up in this dark attic of the head, his religion has taken up its abode; he has a best parlor down in his heart, but his religion never goes there—that is shut against it. He has money in there—Mammon, worldliness; or he has something else—self-love, pride. Perhaps he loves to hear experimental preaching; he admires it all; in fact, he loves anything that is sound. But then, he has not any sound in himself; or rather, it is all sound and there is no substance. He likes to hear true doctrine; but it never penetrates his inner man. You never see him weep. Preach to him about Christ crucified, a glorious subject, and you never see a tear roll down his cheek; tell him of the mighty influence of the Holy Ghost—he admires you for it, but he never had the hand of the Holy Spirit on his soul; tell him about communion with God, plunging in Godhead's deepest sea, and being lost in its immensity—the man loves to hear, but he never experiences, he has never communed with Christ; and accordingly, when you once begin to strike home; when you lay him on the table, take out your dissecting knife, begin to cut him up, and show him his own heart, let him see what it is by nature, and what it must become by grace—the man starts, he cannot stand that; he wants none of that—Christ received in the heart, and accepted. Albeit that he loves it enough in the head, 'tis to him a stumblingblock, and he casts it away. Do you see yourselves here, my friends? See yourselves as God sees you? For so it is, here be many to whom Christ is as much a stumblingblock now as ever he was. O ye formalists! I speak to you; O ye who have the nutshell, but abhor the kernel; O ye who like the trappings and the dress, but care not for that fair virgin who is clothed therewith; O ye who like the paint and the tinsel, but abhor the solid gold, I speak to you; I ask you, does your religion give you solid comfort? Can you stare death in the face with it, and say, "I know that my Redeemer liveth?" Can you close your eyes at night, singing as your vesper song—"I to the end must endure as sure as the earnest is given"?

Can you bless God for affliction? Can you plunge in, accounted as ye are, and swim through all the floods of trial? Can you march triumphant through the lion's den, laugh at affliction, and bid defiance to hell? Can you? No! Your gospel is an effeminate thing—a thing of words and sounds, and not of power. Cast it from you, I beseech you; it is not worth your keeping; and when you come before the throne of God, you will find it will fail you, and fail you so that you shall never find another; for lost, ruined, destroyed, ye shall find that Christ, who is now "a stumblingblock," will be your Judge.

I have found out the Jew, and I have now to discover the Greek. He is a person of quite a different exterior to the Jew. As to the phylactery, to him it is all rubbish; and as to the broad hemmed garment, he despises it. He does not care for the forms of religion; he has an intense aversion, in fact, to broad-brimmed hats, or to everything which looks like outward show. He likes eloquence; he admires a smart saying; he loves a quaint expression; he likes to read the last new book; he is a Greek, and to him the gospel is foolishness. The Greek is a gentleman found everywhere, now-a-days; manufactured sometimes in colleges, constantly made in schools, produced everywhere. He is on the exchange, in the market; he keeps a shop, rides in a carriage; he is noble, a gentleman; he is everywhere, even in court. He is thoroughly wise. Ask him anything, and he knows it. Ask for a quotation from any of the old poets, or any one else, and he can give it you. If you are a Mohammedan, and plead the claims of your religion, he will hear you very patiently. But if you are a Christian, and talk to him of Jesus Christ, "Stop your cant," he says, "I don't want to hear anything about that." This Grecian gentleman believes all philosophy except the true one; he studies all wisdom except the wisdom of God; he likes all learning except spiritual learning; he loves everything except that which God approves; he likes everything which man makes, and nothing which comes from God; it is foolishness to him, confounded foolishness. You have only to discourse about one doctrine in the Bible, and he shuts his ears; he wishes no longer for your company—it is foolishness. I have met this gentleman a great many times. Once, when I saw him, he told me he did not believe in any religion at all; and when I said I did, and had a hope that when I died I should go to heaven, he said he dared say it was very comfortable, but he did not believe in religion, and that he was sure it was best to live as nature dictated. Another time he spoke well of all religions, and believed they were very good in their place, and all true; and he had no doubt that, if a man were sincere in any kind of religion, he would be alright at last. I told him I did not think so, and that I believed there was but one religion revealed of God—the religion of God's elect, the religion which is the gift of Jesus. He then said I was a begot, and wished me good morning. It was to him foolishness. He had nothing to do with me at all. He either liked no religion, or every religion. Another time I held him by the coat button, and I discussed with him a little about faith. He said, "It is all very well, I believe that is true Protestant doctrine." But presently I said something about election, and he said, "I don't like that; many people have preached that and turned it to bad account." I then hinted something about free grace; but that he could not endure, it was to him foolishness. He was a polished Greek, and thought that if he were not chosen, he ought to be. He never liked that passage, "God hath chosen the foolish things of this world to confound the wise, and the things which are not, to bring to nought things that are." He thought it was very discreditable to the Bible and when the book was revised, he had no doubt it would be cut out. To such a man—for he is here this morning, very likely come to hear this reed shaken of the wind—I have to say this: Ah! thou wise man, full of worldly wisdom; thy wisdom will stand thee here, but what wilt thou do in the swellings of Jordan? Philosophy may do well for thee to learn upon whilst thou walkest through this world; but the river is deep, and thou wilt want something more than that. If thou hast not the arm of the Most High to hold thee up in the flood and cheer thee with promises, thou wilt sink, man; with all thy philosophy, thou wilt sink; with all thy learning, thou shalt sink, and be washed into that awful ocean of eternal torment, where thou shalt be forever. Ah! Greeks, it may be foolishness to you, but ye shall see the man your judge, and then shall ye rue the day that e'er ye said that God's gospel was foolishness.

II. Having spoken thus far upon the gospel rejected, I shall now briefly speak upon the GOSPEL TRIUMPHANT. "Unto us who are called, both Jews and Greeks, it is the power of God, and the wisdom of God." Yonder man rejects the gospel, despises grace, and laughs at it as a delusion. Here is another man who laughed at it, too; but God will fetch him down upon his knees. Christ shall not die for nothing. The Holy Ghost shall not strive in vain. God hath said, "My word shall not return unto me void, but it shall accomplish that which I please, and it shall prosper in the thing whereto I sent it." "He shall see of the travail of his soul, and shall be abundantly satisfied." If one sinner is not saved, another shall be. The Jew and the Greek shall never depopulate heaven. The choirs of glory shall not lose a single songster by all the opposition of Jews and Greeks; for God hath said it; some shall be called; some shall be saved; some shall be rescued. "Perish the virtue, as it ought, abhorred, And the fool with it, who insults his Lord. The atonement a Redeemer's love has wrought Is not for you—the righteous need it not. See'st thou yon harlot wooing all she meets, The worn-out nuisance of the public streets Herself from morn till night, from night to morn, Her own abhorrence, and as much your scorn: The gracious shower, unlimited and free, Shall fall on her, when heaven denies it thee. Of all that wisdom dictates, this the drift, That man is dead in sin, and life a gift." If the righteous and good are not saved, if they reject the gospel, there are others who are to be called, others who shall be rescued; for Christ will not lose the merits of his agonies, or the purchase of his blood.

"Unto us who are called." I received a note this week asking me to explain that word "called"; because in one passage it says, "Many are called but few are chosen," while in another it appears that all who are called must be chosen. Now, let me observe that there are two calls. As my old friend, John Bunyan, says, the hen has two calls, the common cluck, which she gives daily and hourly, and the special one, which she means for her little chickens. So there is a general call, a call made to every man; every man hears it. Many are called by it; all you are called this morning in that sense, but very few are chosen. The other is a special call, the children's call. You know how the bell sounds over the workshop, to call the men to work—that is a general call. A father goes to the door and calls out, "John, it is dinner time"—that is the special call. Many are called with the general call, but they are not chosen; the special call is for the children only, and that is what is meant in the text, "Unto us who are called, both Jews and Greeks, the power of God and the wisdom of God." That call is always a special one. While I stand here and call men, nobody comes; while I preach to sinners universally, no good is done; it is like the sheet lightning you sometimes see on the summer's evening, beautiful, grand; but whoever heard of anything being struck by it? But the special call is the forked flash from heaven; it strikes somewhere; it is the arrow sent in between the joints of the harness. The call which saves is like that of Jesus, when he said "Mary," and she said unto him "Rabonni." Do you know anything about that special call, my beloved? Did Jesus ever call you by name? Canst thou recollect the hour when he whispered thy name in thine ear, when he said, "Come to me"? If so, you will grant the truth of what I am going to say next about it—that it is an effectual call; there is no resisting it. When God calls with his special call, there is no standing out. Ah! I know I laughed at religion; I despised, I abhorred it; but that call! Oh, I would not come. But God said, "Thou shalt come. All that the Father giveth to me shall come." "Lord, I will not." "But thou shalt," said God. And I have gone up to God's house sometimes almost with a resolution that I would not listen, but listen I must. Oh, how the word came into my soul! Was there a power of resistance? No; I was thrown down; each bone seemed to be broken; I was saved by effectual grace. I appeal to your experience, my friends. When God took you in hand, could you withstand him? You stood against your minister times enough. Sickness did not break you down; disease did not bring you to God's feet; eloquence did not convince you; but when God puts his hand to the work, ah! then what a change. Like Saul, with his horses going to Damascus, that voice from heaven said, "I am Jesus whom thou persecutest." "Saul, Saul, why persecutest thou me?" There was no going further then. That was an effectual call. Like that, again, which Jesus gave to Zaccheus, when he was up in the tree; stepping under the tree, he said, "Zaccheus, come down, today I must abide in thy house." Zaccheus was taken in the net; he heard his own name; the call sank into his soul; he could not stop up in the tree, for an almighty impulse drew him down. And I could tell you some singular instances of persons going to the house of God and having their characters described, limned out to perfection, so that they have said, "He is painting me, he is painting me." Just as I might say to that young man here, who stole his master's gloves yesterday, that Jesus calls him to repentance. It may be that there is such a person here; and when the call comes to a peculiar character, it generally comes with a special power. God gives his ministers a brush, and shows them how to use it in painting life-like portraits, and thus the sinner hears the special call. I cannot give the special call; God alone can give it, and I leave it with him. Some must be called. Jew and Greek may laugh, but still there are some who are called, both Jews and Greeks.

Then, to close up this second point, it is a great mercy that many a Jew has been made to drop his self righteousness; many a legalist has been made to drop his legalism, and come to Christ; and many a Greek has bowed his genius at the throne of God's gospel. We have a few such. As Cowper says: "We boast some rich ones whom the gospel sways, And one who wears a coronet, and prays; Like gleanings of an olive tree they show, Here and there one upon the topmost bough."

III. Now we come to our third point, A GOSPEL ADMIRED; unto us who are called of God, it is the power of God, and the wisdom of God. Now, beloved, this must be a matter of pure experience between your souls and God. If you are called of God this morning, you will know it. I know there are times when a Christian has to say,

> 'Tis a point I long to know,
>   Oft it causes anxious thought;
>   Do I love the Lord or no?
>   Am I his, or am I not?

But if a man never in his life knew himself to be a Christian, he never was a Christian. If he never had a moment of confidence, when he could say, "Now I know in whom I have believed," I think I do not utter a harsh thing when I say, that that man could not have been born again; for I do not understand how a man can be killed and then made alive again, and not know it; how a man can pass from death unto life, and not know it; how a man can be brought out of darkness into marvellous liberty without knowing it. I am sure I know it when I shout out my old verse,

> Now free from sin, I walk at large,
>   My Saviour's blood's my full discharge;
>   At his dear feet content I lay,
>   A sinner saved, and homage pay.

There are moments when the eyes glisten with joy and we can say, "We are persuaded, confident, certain."

I do not wish to distress any one who is under doubt. Often gloomy doubts will prevail; there are seasons when you fear you have not been called, when you doubt your interest in Christ. Ah! what a mercy it is that it is not your hold of Christ that saves you, but his hold of you! What a sweet fact that it is not how you grasp his hand, but his grasp of yours, that saves you. Yet I think you ought to know, sometime or other, whether you are called of God. If so, you will follow me in the next part of my discourse, which is a matter of pure experience; unto us who are saved, it is "Christ the power of God, and the wisdom of God."

The gospel is to the true believer a thing of power. It is Christ the power of God. Ay, there is a power in God's gospel beyond all description. Once, I, like Mazeppa, bound on the wild horse of my lust, bound hand and foot, incapable of resistance, was galloping on with hell's wolves behind me, howling for my body and my soul, as their just and lawful prey. There came a mighty hand which stopped that wild horse, cut my bands, set me down, and brought me into liberty. Is there power, sir? Ay, there is power, and he who has felt it must acknowledge it. There was a time when I lived in the strong old castle of my sins, and rested in my works. There came a trumpeter to the door, and bade me open it. I with anger chide him from the porch, and said he ne'er should enter. There came a goodly personage, with loving countenance; his hands were marked with scars, where nails were driven, and his feet had nail-prints too; he lifted up his cross, using it as a hammer; at the first blow the gate of my prejudice shook; at the second it trembled more; at the third down it fell, and in he came; and he said, "Arise, and stand upon thy feet, for I have loved thee with an everlasting love." A thing of power! Ah! it is a thing of power. I have felt it here, in this heart; I have the witness of the Spirit within, and know it is a thing of might, because it has conquered me; it has bowed me down. "His free grace alone, from the first to the last, Hath won my affection, and held my soul fast." The gospel to the Christian is a thing of power. What is it that makes the young man devote himself as a missionary to the cause of God, to leave father and mother, and go into distant lands? It is a thing of power that does it—it is the gospel. What is it that constrains yonder minister, in the midst of the cholera, to climb up that creaking staircase, and stand by the bed of some dying creature who has that dire disease? It must be a thing of power which leads him to venture his life; it is love of the cross of Christ which bids him do it. What is that which enables one man to stand up before a multitude of his fellows, all unprepared it may be, but determined that he will speak nothing but Christ and him crucified? What is it that enables him to cry, like the war-horse of Job in battle, Aha! and move glorious in might? It is a thing of power that does it—it is Christ crucified. And what emboldens that timid female to walk down that dark lane in the wet evening, that she may go and sit beside the victim of a contagious fever? What strengthens her to go through that den of thieves, and pass by the profligate and profane? What influences her to enter into that charnel-house of death, and there sit down and whisper words of comfort? Does gold make her do it? They are too poor to give her gold. Does fame make her do it? She shall never be known, nor written among the mighty women of this earth. What makes her do it? Is it love of merit? No; she knows she has no desert before high heaven. What impels her to it? It is the power of the gospel on her heart; it is the cross of Christ; she loves it, and she therefore says—

> Were the whole realm of nature mine.
>   That were a present far too small;
>   Love so amazing, so divine,
>   Demands my soul, my life, my all.

But I behold another scene. A martyr is going to the stake; the halberd men are around him; the crowds are mocking, but he is marching steadily on. See, they bind him, with a chain around his middle, to the stake; they heap faggots all about him; the flame is lighted up; listen to his words: "Bless the Lord, O my soul, and all that is within me, bless his holy name." The flames are kindling round his legs; the fire is burning him even to the bone; see him lift up his hands and say, "I know that my Redeemer liveth, and though the fire devour this body, yet in my flesh shall I see the Lord." Behold him clutch the stake and kiss it, as if he loved it, and hear him say, "For every chain of iron that man girdeth me with, God shall give me a chain of gold; for all these faggots, and this ignominy and shame, he shall increase the weight of my eternal glory." See all the under parts of his body are consumed; still he lives in the torture; at last he bows himself, and the upper part of his body falls over; and as he falls you hear him say, "Into thy hands I commend my Spirit." What wondrous magic was on him, sirs? What made that man strong? What helped him to bear that cruelty? What made him stand unmoved in the flames? It was the thing of power; it was the cross of Jesus crucified. For "unto us who are saved it is the power of God."

But behold another scene far different. There is no crowd there; it is a silent room. There is a poor pallet, a lonely bed: a physician standing by. There is a young girl: her face is blanched by consumption; long hath the worm eaten her cheek, and though sometimes the flush came, it was the death flush of the deceitful consumption. There she lieth, weak, pale, wan, worn, dying, yet behold a smile upon her face, as if she had seen an angel. She speaketh, and there is music in her voice. Joan of Arc of old was not half so mighty as that girl. She is wrestling with dragons on her death-bed; but see her composure, and hear her dying sonnet:

Jesus, lover of my soul,
  Let me to thy bosom fly,
  While the nearer waters roll,
  While the tempest still is high!
Hide me, O my Saviour, hide,
  Till the storm of life is past,
  Safe into the haven guide,
  O receive my soul at last!

And with a smile she shuts her eye on earth, and opens it in heaven. What enables her to die like that? It is the thing of power; it is the cross; it is Jesus crucified.

I have little time to discourse upon the other point, and it be far from me to weary you by a lengthened and prosy sermon, but we must glance at the other statement: Christ is, to the called ones, the wisdom of God as well as the power of God. To a believer, the gospel is the perfection of wisdom, and if it appear not so to the ungodly, it is because of the perversion of judgement consequent on their depravity.

An idea has long possessed the public mind, that a religious man can scarcely be a wise man. It has been the custom to talk of infidels, atheists, and deists, as men of deep thought and comprehensive intellect; and to tremble for the Christian controversialist, as if he must surely fall by the hand of his enemy. But this is purely a mistake; for the gospel is the sum of wisdom; an epitome of knowledge; a treasure-house of truth; and a revelation of mysterious secrets. In it we see how justice and mercy may be married; here we behold inexorable law entirely satisfied, and sovereign love bearing away the sinner in triumph. Our meditation upon it enlarges the mind; and as it opens to our soul in successive flashes of glory, we stand astonished at the profound wisdom manifest in it. Ah, dear friends! if ye seek wisdom, ye shall see it displayed in all its greatness; not in the balancing of the clouds, nor the firmness of earth's foundations; not in the measured march of the armies of the sky, nor in the perpetual motions of the waves of the sea; not in vegetation with all its fairy forms of beauty; nor in the animal with its marvellous tissue of nerve, and vein, and sinew: nor even in man, that last and loftiest work of the Creator. But turn aside and see this great sight!—an incarnate God upon the cross; a substitute atoning for mortal guilt; a sacrifice satisfying the vengeance of Heaven, and delivering the rebellious sinner. Here is essential wisdom; enthroned, crowned, glorified. Admire, ye men of earth, if ye be not blind; and ye who glory in your learning bend your heads in reverence, and own that all your skill could not have devised a gospel at once so just to God, so safe to man.

Remember, my friends, that while the gospel is in itself wisdom, it also confers wisdom on its students; she teaches young men wisdom and discretion, and gives understanding to the simple. A man who is a believing admirer and a hearty lover of the truth as it is in Jesus, is in a right place to follow with advantage any other branch of science. I confess I have a shelf in my head for everything now. Whatever I read I know where to put it; whatever I learn I know where to stow it away. Once when I read books, I put all my knowledge together in glorious confusion; but ever since I have known Christ, I have put Christ in the centre as my sun, and each science revolves round it like a planet, while minor sciences are satellites to these planets. Christ is to me the wisdom of God. I can learn everything now. The science of Christ crucified is the most excellent of sciences, she is to me the wisdom of God. O, young man, build thy studio on Calvary! there raise thine observatory, and scan by faith the lofty things of nature. Take thee a hermit's cell in the garden of Gethsemane, and lave thy brow with the waters of Silo. Let the Bible be thy standard classic—thy last appeal in matters of contention. Let its light be thine illumination, and thou shalt become more wise than Plato, more truly learned than the seven sages of antiquity.

And now, my dear friends, solemnly and earnestly, as in the sight of God, I appeal to you. You are gathered here this morning, I know, from different motives; some of you have come from curiosity; others of you are my regular hearers; some have come from one place and some from another. What have you heard me say this morning? I have told you of two classes of persons who reject Christ; the religionist, who has a religion of form and nothing else; and the man of the world, who calls our gospel foolishness. Now, put your hand upon your heart, and ask yourself this morning, "Am I one of these?"

If you are, then walk the earth in all your pride; then go as you came in: but know that for all this the Lord shall bring thee unto judgement; know thou that thy joys and delights shall vanish like a dream, "and, like the baseless fabric of a vision," be swept away forever. Know thou this, moreover, O man, that one day in the halls of Satan, down in hell, I perhaps may see thee amongst those myriad spirits who revolve forever in a perpetual circle with their hands upon their hearts. If thine hand be transparent, and thy flesh transparent, I shall look through thy hand and flesh, and see thy heart within. And how shall I see it? Set in a case of fire—in a case of fire! And there thou shalt revolve forever with the worm gnawing within thy heart, which ne'er shall die—a case of fire around thy never-dying, ever-tortured heart. Good God! let not these men still reject and despise Christ; but let this be the time when they shall be called.

To the rest of you who are called, I need say nothing. The longer you live, the more powerful will you find the gospel to be; the more deeply Christ-taught you are, the more you live under the constant influence of the Holy Spirit, the more you will know the gospel to be a thing of power, and the more also will you understand it to be a thing of wisdom. May every blessing rest upon you; and may God come up with us in the evening!

> Let men or angels dig the mines
>   Where nature's golden treasure shines;
>   Brought near the doctrine of the cross,
>   All nature's gold appears but dross.
> Should vile blasphemers with disdain
> Pronounce the truths of Jesus vain,
> We'll meet the scandal and the shame,
> And sing and triumph in his name.

Christ in the Covenant

A Sermon (No. 103) Delivered on Sabbath Morning, August 31, 1856, by the REV. C. H. SPURGEON At New Park Street Chapel, Southwark.

"I will give thee for a covenant of the people."—Isaiah 49:8.

We all believe that our Saviour has very much to do with the covenant of eternal salvation. We have been accustomed to regard him as the Mediator of the covenant, as the surety of the covenant, and as the scope or substance of the covenant. We have considered him to be the Mediator of the covenant, for we were certain that God could make no covenant with man unless there were a mediator—a days-man, who should stand between the both. And we have hailed him as the Mediator, who, with mercy in his hands, came down to tell to sinful man the news that grace was promised in the eternal counsel of the Most High. We have also loved our Saviour as the Surety of the covenant, who, on our behalf, undertook to pay our debts; and on his Father's behalf, undertook, also, to see that all our souls should be secure and safe, and ultimately presented unblemished and complete before him. And I doubt not, we have also rejoiced in the thought that Christ is the sum and substance of the covenant; we believe that if we would sum up all spiritual blessings, we must say, "Christ is all." He is the matter, he is the substance of it; and although much might be said concerning the glories of the covenant, yet nothing could be said which is not to be found in that one word, "Christ." But this morning I shall dwell on Christ, not as the Mediator, nor as the surety, nor as the scope of the covenant, but as one great and glorious article of the covenant which God has given to his children. It is our firm belief that Christ is ours, and is given to us of God; we know that "he freely delivered him up for us all," and we, therefore, believe that he will, "with him, freely give us all things." We can say, with the spouse, "My beloved is mine." We feel that we have a personal property in our Lord and Saviour Jesus Christ, and it will therefore delight us for a while, this morning, in the simplest manner possible, without the garnishings of eloquence or the trappings of oratory, just to mediate upon this great thought, that Jesus Christ in the covenant is the property of every believer.

First, we shall examine this property; secondly, we shall notice the purpose for which it was conveyed to us; and thirdly, we shall give one precept, which may well be affixed upon so great a blessing as this, and is indeed an inference from it.

I. In the first place, then, here is a GREAT POSSESSION—Jesus Christ by the covenant is the property of every believer. By this we must understand Jesus Christ in many different senses; and we will begin, first of all, by declaring that Jesus Christ is ours, in all his attributes. He has a double set of attributes, seeing that there are two natures joined in glorious union in one person. He has the attributes of very God, and he has the attributes of perfect man; and whatever these may be, they are each one of them the perpetual property of every believing child of God. I need not dwell on his attributes as God;

you all know how infinite is his love, how vast his grace, how firm his faithfulness, how unswerving his veracity; you know that he is omniscient; you know that he is omnipresent; you know that he is omnipotent, and it will console you if you will but think that all these great and glorious attributes which belong to God are all yours. Has he power? That power is yours—yours to support and strengthen you; yours to overcome your enemies, yours to keep you immutably secure. Has he love? Well, there is not a particle of his love in his great heart, which is not yours; all his love belongs to you; you may dive into the immense, bottomless ocean of his love, and you may say of it all, "it is mine." Hath he justice? It may seem a stern attribute; but even that is yours, for he will by his justice see to it, that all which is covenanted to you by the oath and promise of God shall be most certainly secured to you. Mention whatever you please which is a characteristic of Christ as the ever glorious Son of God, and O faithful one, thou mayest put thine hand upon it and say, "it is mine." Thine arm, O Jesus, upon which the pillars of the earth do hang, is mine. Those eyes, O Jesus, which pierce through the thick darkness and behold futurity—thine eyes are mine, to look on me with love. Those lips, O Christ, which sometimes speak words louder than ten thousand thunders, or whisper syllables sweeter than the music of the harps of the glorified—those lips are mine. And that great heart which beateth high with such disinterested, pure, and unaffected love—that heart is mine. The whole of Christ, in all his glorious nature as the Son of God, as God over all, blessed for ever, is yours, positively, actually, without metaphor, in reality yours.

1. Consider him as man too. All that he has as perfect man is yours. As a perfect man he stood before his Father, "full of grace and truth," full of favour; and accepted by God as a perfect being. O believer, God's acceptance of Christ is thine acceptance; for knowest thou not, that that love which the Father set on a perfect Christ, he sets on thee now? For all that Christ did is thine. That perfect righteousness which Jesus wrought out, when through his stainless life he kept the law and made it honorable, is thine. There is not a virtue which Christ ever had, that is not thine; there is not a holy deed which he ever did which is not thine; there is not a prayer he ever sent to heaven that is not thine; there is not one solitary thought towards God which it was his duty to think, and which he thought as man serving his God, which is not thine. All his righteousness, in its vast extent, and in all the perfection of his character, is imputed to thee. Oh! canst thou think what thou hast gotten in the word "Christ?" Come, believer, consider that word "God," and think how mighty it is; and then meditate upon that word "perfect man," for all that the Man-God, Christ, and the glorious God-man, Christ, ever had, or ever can have as the characteristic of either of his natures, all that is thine. It all belongs to thee; it is out of pure free favour, beyond the fear of revocation, passed over to thee to be thine actual property—and that for ever.

2. Then, consider believer, that not only is Christ thine in all his attributes, but he is thine in all his offices. Great and glorious these offices are; we have scarce time to mention them all. Is he a prophet? Then he is thy prophet. Is he a priest? Then he is thy priest. Is he a king? Then he is thy king. Is he a redeemer? Then he is thy redeemer. Is he an advocate? Then he is thy advocate. Is he a forerunner? Then he is thy forerunner. Is he a surety of the covenant? The he is thy surety. In every name he bears, in every crown he wears, in every vestment in which he is arrayed, he is the believer's own. Oh! child of God, if thou hadst grace to gather up this thought into thy soul it would comfort thee marvellously, to think that in all Christ is in office, he is most assuredly thine. Dost thou see him yonder, interceding before his Father, with outstretched arms? Dost thou mark his ephod—his golden mitre on his brow, inscribed with "holiness unto the Lord?" Dost see him as he lifts up his hands to pray? Hearest thou not that marvellous intercession such as man never prayed on earth; that authoritative intercession such as he himself could not use in the agonies of the garden? For "With sighs and groans, he offered up His humble suit below; But with authority he pleads, Enthroned I glory now."

Dost see how he asks, and how he received, as soon as his petition is put up? And canst thou, darest thou believe that that intercession is all thine own, that on his breast thy name is written, that in his heart thy name is stamped in marks of indelible grace, and that all the majesty of that marvellous, that surpassing intercession is thine own, and would all be expended for thee if thou didst require it; that he has not any authority with his Father, that he will not use on thy behalf, if thou dost need it; that he has no power to intercede that he would not employ for thee in all times of necessity? Come now, words cannot set this forth; it is only your thoughts that can teach you this; it is only God the Holy Spirit bringing home the truth that can set this ravishing, this transporting thought in its proper position in your heart; that Christ is yours in all he is and has. Seest thou him on earth? There he stands, the priest offering his bloody sacrifice; see him on the tree, his hands are pierced, his feet are gushing gore!

Oh! dost thou see that pallid countenance, and those languid eyes flowing with compassion? Dost thou mark that crown of thorns? Dost thou behold that mightiest of sacrifices, the sum and substance of them all? Believer, that is thine, those precious drops plead and claim thy peace with God; that open side is thy refuge, those pierced hands are thy redemption; that groan he groans for thee; that cry of a forsaken heart he utters for thee; that death he dies for thee. Come, I beseech thee, consider Christ in any one of his various offices; but when thou dost consider him lay hold of this thought, that in all these things he is THY Christ, given unto thee to be one article in the eternal covenant—thy possession for ever.

3. Then mark next, Christ is the believer's in every one of his works. Whether they be works of suffering or of duty, they are the property of the believer. As a child, he was circumcised, and is that bloody rite mine? Ay, "Circumcised in Christ." As a believer he is buried, and is that watery sign of baptism mine? Yes; "Buried with Christ in baptism unto death." Jesus' baptism I share when I lie interred with my best friend in the selfsame watery tomb. See there, he dies, and it is a master work to die. But is his death mine? Yes, I die in Christ. He rises. Mark him startling his guards, and rising from the tomb! And is that resurrection mine? Yes, we are "risen together with Christ." Mark again, he ascends up on high, and leads captivity captive. Is that ascension mine? Yes, for he hath "raised us up together." And see, he sits on his Father's throne; is that deed mine? Yes, he hath made us, "sit together in heavenly places." All he did is ours. By divine decree, there existed such an union between Christ and his people, that all Christ did his people did: and all Christ has performed, his people did perform in him, for they were in his loins when he descended to the tomb, and in his loins they have ascended up on high; with him they entered into bliss; and with him they sit in heavenly places. Represented by him, their Head, all his people even now are glorified in him—even in him who is the head over all things to his church. In all the deeds of Christ, either in his humiliation or his exaltation, recollect, O believer, thou hast a covenant interest, and all those things are thine.

4. I would for one moment hint at a sweet thought, which is this, you know that in the person of Christ "dwelleth all the fulness of the Godhead bodily." AH! believer, "and of his fulness have we received, and grace for grace." All the fulness of Christ! do you know what that is? Do you understand that phrase? I warrant you, you do not know it, and shall not do just yet. But all that fulness of Christ, the abundance of which you may guess of by your own emptiness—all that fulness is thine to supply thy multiplied necessities. All the fulness of Christ to restrain thee, to keep thee and preserve thee; all that fulness of power, of love, of purity, which is stored up in the person of the Lord Jesus Christ, is thine. Do treasure up that thought, for then thine emptiness need never be a cause of fear; how canst thou be lost whilst thou hast all fulness to fly to?

5. But I come to something sweeter than this; the very life of Christ is the property of the believer. Ah! this is a thought into which I cannot dive, and I feel I have outdone myself in only mentioning it. The life of Christ is the property of every believer. Canst thou conceive what Christ's life is? "Sure," you say, "he poured it out upon the tree." He did, and it was his life that he gave to thee then. But he took that life again; even the life of his body was restored; and the life of his great and glorious Godhead had never undergone any change, even at that time. But now, you know he has immortality: "he only hath immortality." Can you conceive what kind of life that is which Christ possesses? Can he ever die? No; far sooner may the harps of heaven be stopped, and the chorus of the redeemed cease for ever; far sooner may the glorious walls of paradise be shaken, and the foundations thereof be removed; than that Christ, the Son of God, should ever die. Immortal as his Father, now he sits, the Great Eternal One. Christian, that life of Christ is thine. Hear what he says: "Because I live ye shall live also." "Ye are dead; and your life"—where is it? It is "hid with Christ in God." The same blow which smites us dead, spiritually, must slay Christ too; the same sword which can take away the spiritual life of a regenerate man, must take away the life of the Redeemer also; for they are linked together—they are not two lives, but one. We are but the rays of the great Sun of Righteousness, our Redeemer,—sparks which must return to the great orb again. If we are indeed the true heirs of heaven, we cannot die until he from whom we take our rise dieth also. We are the stream that cannot stop till the fountain be dry; we are the rays that cannot cease until the sun doth cease to shine. We are the branches, and we cannot wither until the trunk itself shall die. "Because I live, ye shall live also." The very life of Christ is the property of every one of his brethren.

6. And best of all, the person of Jesus Christ is the property of the Christian. I am persuaded, beloved, we think a great deal more of God's gifts than we do of God; and we preach a great deal more about the Holy Spirit's influence than we do about the Holy Spirit. And

I am also assured that we talk a great deal more about the offices, and works, and attributes of Christ than we do about the person of Christ. Hence it is that there are few of us who can often understand the figures that are used in Solomon's Song, concerning the person of Christ, because we have seldom sought to see him or desired to know him. But, O believer, thou hast sometimes been able to behold thy Lord. Hast thou not seen him, who is white and ruddy, "the chief amongst ten thousand, and the altogether lovely?" Hast thou not been sometimes lost in pleasure when thou hast seen his feet, which are like much fine gold, as if they burned in a furnace? Hast thou not beheld him in the double character, the white and the red, the lily and the rose, the God yet the man, the dying yet the living; the perfect, and yet bearing about with him a body of death? Hast thou ever beheld that Lord with the nail-print in his hands, and the mark still on his side? And hast thou ever been ravished at his loving smile, and been delighted at his voice? Hast thou never had love visits from him? Has he never put his banner over thee? hast thou never walked with him to the villages and the garden of nuts? Hast thou never sat under his shadow? hast thou never found his fruit sweet unto thy taste? Yes, thou hast. His person then is thine. The wife loveth her husband; she loveth his house and his property; she loveth him for all that he giveth her, for all the bounty he confers, and all the love he bestows; but his person is the object of her affections. So with the believer: he blesses Christ for all he does and all he is. But oh! it is Christ that is everything. He does not care so much about his office, as he does about the Man Christ. See the child on his father's knee—the father is a professor in the university; he is a great man with many titles, and perhaps the child knows that these are honourable titles, and esteems him for them; but he does not care so much about the professors and his dignity, as about the person of his father. It is not the college square cap, or the gown that the child loves; ay, and if it be a loving child it will not be so much the meal the father provides, or the house in which it lives, as the father which it loves; it is his dear person that has become the object of true and hearty affection. I am sure it is so with you, if you know your Saviour; you love his mercies, you love his offices, you love his deeds, but oh! you love his person best. Reflect, then that the person of Christ is in the covenant conveyed to you: "I will give thee to be a covenant for the people."

II. Now we come to the second: FOR WHAT PURPOSE DOES GOD PUT CHRIST IN THE COVENANT?

1. Well, in the first place, Christ is in the covenant in order to comfort every coming sinner. "Oh," says the sinner who is coming to God, "I cannot lay hold on such a great covenant as that, I cannot believe that heaven is provided for me, I cannot conceive that the robe of righteousness and all these wondrous things can be intended for such a wretch as I am." Here comes in the thought that Christ is in the covenant. Sinner, canst thou lay hold on Christ? Canst thou say, "Nothing in my hand I bring, Simply to thy cross I cling?" Well, if thou hast got that, it was put in on purpose for thee to hold fast by God's covenant mercies all go together, and if thou hast laid hold on Christ, thou hast gained every blessing in the covenant. That is one reason why Christ was put there. Why, if Christ were not there, the poor sinner would say, "I dare not lay hold on that mercy. It is a God-like and a divine one, but I dare not grasp it; it is too good for me. I cannot receive it, it staggers my faith." But he sees Christ with all his great atonement in the covenant; and Christ looks so lovingly at him, and opens his arms so wide, saying, "Come unto me, all ye that labour and are heavy laden, and I will give you rest," that the sinner comes and throws his arms around Christ, and then Christ whispers, "Sinner, in laying hold of me, thou hast laid hold of all." Why, Lord, I dare not think I could have the other mercies. I dare trust thee, but I dare not take the others. Ah, sinner, but in that thou hast taken me thou hast taken all, for the mercies of the covenant are like links in the chain. This one link is an enticing one. The sinner lays hold of it; and God has purposely put it there to entice the sinner to come and receive the mercies of the covenant. For when he has once got hold of Christ—here is the comfort—he has everything that the covenant can give.

2. Christ is put also to confirm the doubting saint. Sometimes he cannot read his interest in the covenant. He cannot see his portion among them that are sanctified. He is afraid that God is not his God, that the Spirit hath no dealings with his soul; but then,

> Amid temptations, sharp and strong,
>   His soul to that dear refuge flies;
> Hope is his anchor, firm and strong,
>   When tempests blow and billows rise.

So he lays hold of Christ, and were it not for that, even the believer dare not come at all. he could not lay hold on any other mercy than that with which Christ is connected. "Ah," saith he, "I know I am a sinner, and Christ came to save sinners." So he holds fast to Christ. "I can hold fast here," he says, "my black hands will not black Christ, my filthiness will not make him unclean." So the saint holds hard by Christ, as hard as if it were the death-clutch of a drowning man. And what then? Why, he has got every mercy of the covenant in his hand. It is the wisdom of God that he has put Christ in, so that a poor sinner, who might be afraid to lay hold of another, knowing the gracious nature of Christ, is not afraid to lay hold of him, and therein he grasps the whole, but ofttimes unconsciously to himself.

3. Again, it was necessary that Christ should be in the covenant, because there are many things there that would be nought without him. Our great redemption is in the covenant, but we have no redemption except through his blood. It is true that my righteousness is in the covenant, but I can have no righteousness apart from that which Christ has wrought out, and which is imputed to me by God. It is very true that my eternal perfection is in the covenant, but the elect are only perfect in Christ. They are not perfect in themselves, nor will they ever be, until they have been washed, and sanctified, and perfected by the Holy Ghost. And even in heaven their perfection consists not so much in their sanctification, as in their justification in Christ. "Their beauty this, their glorious dress, Jesus the Lord their righteousness." In fact, if you take Christ out of the covenant, you have just done the same as if you should break the string of a necklace: all the jewels, or beads, or corals, drop off and separate from each other. Christ is the golden string whereon the mercies of the covenant are threaded, and when you lay hold of him, you have obtained the whole string of pearls. But if Christ be taken out, true there will be the pearls, but we cannot wear them, we cannot grasp them; they are separated, and poor faith can never know how to get hold of them. Oh! it is a mercy worth worlds, that Christ is in the covenant.

4. But mark once more, as I told you when preaching concerning God in the covenant, Christ is in the covenant to be used. There are some promises in the Bible which I have never yet used; but I am well assured that there will come times of trial and trouble when I shall find that that poor despised promise, which I thought was never meant for me, will be the only one on which I can float. I know that the time is coming when every believer shall know the worth of every promise in the covenant. God has not given him any part of an inheritance which he did not mean him to till. Christ is given us to use. Believer, use him! I tell thee again, as I told thee before, that thou dost not use thy Christ as thou oughtest to do. Why, man, when thou art in trouble, why dost thou not go and tell him? Has he not a sympathising heart, and can he not comfort and relieve thee? No, thou art gadding about to all thy friends save thy best friend, and telling thy tale everywhere except into the bosom of thy Lord. Oh, use him, use him. Art thou black with yesterday's sins? Here is a fountain filled with blood; use it, saint, use it. Has thy guilt returned again? Well, his power has been proved again and again; come use him! use him! Dost thou feel naked? Come hither, soul, put on the robe. Stand not staring at it; put it on. Strip, sir, strip thine own righteousness off, and thine own fears too. Put this on, and wear it, for it was meant to wear. Dost thou feel thyself sick? What, wilt thou not go and pull the night-bell of prayer, and wake up thy physician? I beseech thee go and stir him up betimes, and he will give the cordial that will revive thee. What! art thou sick, with such a physician next door to thee, a present help in time of trouble, and wilt thou not go to him? Oh, remember thou art poor, but then thou hast "a kinsman, a mighty man of wealth." What! wilt thou not go to him and ask him to give thee of his abundance, when he has given thee this promise, that as long as he has anything thou shalt go shares with him, for all he is and all he has is thine? Oh, believer, do use Christ, I beseech thee. There is nothing Christ dislikes more than for his people to make a show-thing of him and not to use him. he loves to be worked. He is a great labourer; he always was for his Father, and now he loves to be a great labourer for his brethren. The more burdens you put on his shoulders the better he will love you. Cast your burden on him. You will never know the sympathy of Christ's heart and the love of his soul so well as when you have heaved a very mountain of trouble from yourself to his shoulders, and have found that he does not stagger under the weight. Are your troubles like huge mountains of snow upon your spirit? Bid them rumble like an avalanche upon the shoulders of the Almighty Christ. He can bear them all away, and carry them into the depths of the sea. Do use thy Master, for this very purpose he was put into the covenant, that thou mightest use him whenever thou needest him.

III. Now, lastly, here is A PRECEPT, and what shall the precept be? Christ is ours; then be ye Christ's, beloved. Ye are Christ's, ye know right well. Ye are his by your Father's donation when he gave you to the Son. You are his by his bloody purchase, when he counted down the price for your redemption. You are his by dedication, for you have dedicated yourselves to him. You are his by adoption, for you are brought to him and made one of his brethren and joint-heirs with him. I beseech you, labour, dear brethren, to show the world that you are his in practice. When tempted to sin, reply, "I cannot do this great wickedness. I cannot, for I am one of Christ's." When wealth is before thee to be won by sin, touch it not; say that thou art Christ's, else thou wouldst take it; but now thou canst not. Tell Satan that you would not gain the world if you had to love Christ less. Are you exposed in the world to difficulties and dangers? Stand fast in the evil day, remembering that you are one of Christ's. Are you in a field where much is to be done, and others are sitting down idly and lazily, doing nothing? Go at your work, and when the sweat stands upon your brow and you are bidden to stay, say, "No, I cannot stop; I am one of Christ's. He had a baptism to be baptised with, and so have I, and I am straitened until it be accomplished. I am one of Christ's. If I were not one of his, and purchased by blood, I might be like Issachar, crouching between two burdens; but I am one of Christ's." When the syren song of pleasure would tempt thee from the path of right, reply, "Hush your strains, O temptress; I am one of Christ's. Thy music cannot affect me; I am not my own, I am bought with a price. When the cause of God needs thee, give thyself to it, for thou art Christ's. When the poor need thee, give thyself away, for thou art one of Christ's. When, at any time there is ought to be done for his church and for his cross, do it, remembering that thou art one of Christ's. I beseech thee, never belie thy profession. Go not where others could say of thee, "He cannot be Christ's;" but be thou ever one of those whose brogue is Christian, whose very idiom is Christ-like, whose conduct and conversation are so redolent of heaven, that all who see thee may know that thou art one of the Saviour's and may recognise in thee his features and his lovely countenance.

And now, dearly beloved hearers. I must say one word to those of you to whom I have not preached, for there are some of you who have never laid hold of the covenant. I sometimes hear it whispered, and sometimes read it, that there are men who trust to the uncovenanted mercies of God. Let me solemnly assure you that there is now no such thing in heaven as uncovenanted mercy; there is no such thing beneath God's sky or above it, as uncovenanted grace towards men. All ye can receive, and all you ever ought to hope for, must be through the covenant of free grace, and that alone.

Mayhap, poor convinced sinner thou darest not take hold of the covenant to-day. Thou canst not say the covenant is thine. Thou art afraid it never can be thine; thou art such an unworthy wretch. Hark thee; canst thou lay hold on Christ? Darest thou do that? "Oh," sayest thou, "I am too unworthy." Nay, soul, darest thou touch the hem of his garment to-day? Darest thou come up to him just so much as to touch the very skirt that is trailing on the ground? "No," sayest thou "I dare not," Why not, poor soul, why not? Canst thou not trust to Christ? "Are not his mercies rich and free? Then say, poor soul, why not for thee." "I dare not come; I am so unworthy," you say. Hear, then; my Master bids you come, and will you be afraid after that? "Come unto me, all ye that labour and are heavy laden, and I will give you rest." "This is a faithful saying, and worthy of all acceptation, that Christ Jesus came into the world to save sinners." Why dare you not come to Christ? Oh, you are afraid he will turn you away! Hark ye, then, what he saith; "Whosoever cometh unto me, I will in nowise cast out." Thou sayest, "I know he would cast me out." Come, then, and see if thou canst prove him a liar. I know thou canst not, but come and try. He has said "whosoever." "But I am the blackest." Nevertheless, he has said "whosoever:" come along, blackest of the black. "Oh, but I am filthy." Come along, filthy one, come and try him, come and prove him; recollect he has said he will cast out none that come to him by faith. Come and try him. I do not ask thee to lay hold on the whole covenant, thou shalt do that by-and-bye; but lay hold on Christ, and if thou wilt do that, then thou hast the covenant." "Oh, I cannot lay hold of him," saith one poor soul. Well, then, lie prostrate at his feet, and beg of him to lay hold of thee. Do groan one groan, and say, "Lord, have mercy on me, a sinner!" Do sigh one sigh, and say, "Lord, save, or I perish." Do let thy heart say it, if thy lips cannot. If grief, long smothered, burns like a flame within thy bones, at least let one spark out. Now prayer one prayer, and verily I say unto thee, one sincere prayer shall most assuredly prove that he will save thee. One true groan, where God has put it in the heart, is an earnest of his love; one true wish after Christ, if it be followed by sincere and earnest seeking of him, shall be accepted of God, and thou shalt be saved. Come, soul, once more. Lay hold on Christ. "Oh, but I dare not do it." Now I was about to say a foolish thing; I was going to say that I wish I was a sinner like thyself this moment, and I think I would run before, and lay hold on Christ, and then say to you, "Take hold too." But I am a sinner like thyself, and no better than thyself; I have no merits, no righteousness, no works; I shall be damned in hell unless Christ have mercy on me, and should have been there now if I had had my deserts. Here am I a sinner once as black as thou art; and yet, O Christ, these arms embrace thee. Sinner, come and take thy turn after me. Have not I embraced him? Am I not as vile as thou art? Come and let my case assure thee. How did he treat me when I first laid hold of him? Why he said to me, "I have loved thee with an everlasting love, therefore with loving-kindness have I drawn thee." Come, sinner, come and try, If Christ did not drive me away, he will never spurn you. Come along, poor soul, come along—

Venture on him, ('tis no venture,) venture wholly,
Let no other trust intrude; None but Jesus
Can do helpless sinners good.

He can do thee all the good thou wantest: oh! trust my Master, oh! trust my Master; he is a precious Lord Jesus, he is a sweet Lord Jesus, he is a loving Saviour, he is a kind and condescending forgiver of sin. Come, ye black; come, ye filthy; come, ye poor; come, ye dying; come, ye lost—ye who have been taught to feel your need of Christ, come all of you—come now for Jesus bids you come; come quickly. Lord Jesus, draw them, draw them by this Spirit! Amen.

Children Brought to Christ

A Sermon Excerpt (No. 581) Delivered on Sunday Morning, July 24th, 1864, by the Rev. C. H. SPURGEON, At the Metropolitan Tabernacle, Newington.

"And they brought young children to him, that he should touch them: and his disciples rebuked those that brought them. But when Jesus saw it, he was much displeased, and said unto them, Suffer the little children to come unto me, and forbid them not: for of such is the kingdom of God. Verily I say unto you, whosoever shall not receive the kingdom of God as a little child, he shall not enter therein. And he took them up in his arms, put his hands upon them, and blessed them"—Mark 10:13–16.

How can we bring children to Jesus Christ to be blessed? We cannot do it in a corporeal sense, for Jesus is not here, "he is risen;" but we can bring our children in a true, real, and spiritual sense. We take them up in the arms of our prayer. I hope many of us, so soon as our children saw the light, if not before, presented them to God with this anxious prayer, that they might sooner die than live to disgrace their father's God. We only desired children that we might in them live over again another life of service to God; and when we looked into their young faces, we never asked wealth for them, nor fame, nor anything else, but that they might be dear unto God, and that their names might be written in the Lamb's Book of Life. We did then bring our children to Christ as far as we could do it, by presenting them before God, by earnest prayer on their behalf. And have we ceased to bring them to Christ? Nay, I hope we seldom bow the knee without praying for our children. Our daily cry is, "O, that they might live before thee!" God knows that nothing would give us more joy than to see evidence of their conversion; our souls would almost leap out of our bodies with joy, if we should but know that they were the children of the living God. Nor has this privilege been denied to us, for there are some here who can rejoice in a converted household. Truly we can say with the apostle Paul, "I have no greater joy than this, that my children walk in the truth." We continue, therefore, to bring them to Christ by daily, constant, earnest prayer on their behalf. So soon as they become of years capable of understanding the things of God, we endeavour to bring them to Christ by teaching them the truth. Hence our Sabbath-schools, hence the use of the Bible and family prayer, and catechizing at home. Any person who shall forbid us to pray for our children, will incur Christ's high displeasure; and any who shall say, "Do not teach your children; they will be converted in God's own time if it be his purpose, therefore leave them to run wild in the streets," will certainly both "sin against the child" and the Lord Jesus. We might as well say, "If that piece of ground is to grow a harvest, it will do so if it be God's good pleasure; therefore leave it, and let the weeds spring up and cover it; do not endeavour for a moment to kill the weeds, or to sow the good seed." Why, such reasoning as this would be not only cruel to our children, but grievously displeasing to Christ. Parents! I do hope you are all endeavouring to bring your children to Christ by teaching them the things of God. Let them not be strangers to the plan of salvation. Never let it be said that a child of yours reached years in which his conscience could act, and he could judge between good and evil, without knowing the doctrine of the atonement, without understanding the great substitutionary work of Christ. Set before your child life and death, hell and heaven, judgment and mercy, his own sin, and Christ's most precious blood; and as you set these before him, labour with him, persuade him, as the apostle did his congregation, with tears and weeping, to turn unto the Lord; and your prayers and supplications shall be heard so that the Spirit of God shall bring them to Jesus...

I cannot tell you how much I owe to the solemn words of my good mother. It was the custom on Sunday evenings, while we were yet little children, for her to stay at home with us, and then we sat round the table and read verse by verse, and she explained the Scripture to us. After that was done, then came the time of pleading; there was a little piece of "Alleyn's Alarm," or of Baxter's "Call to the Unconverted," and this was read with pointed observations made to each of us as we sat round the table; and the question was asked how long it would be before we would think about our state, how long before we would seek the Lord. Then came a mother's prayer, and some of the words of a mother's prayer we shall never forget, even when our hair is grey. I remember on one occasion her praying thus: "Now, Lord, if my children go on in their sins, it will not be from ignorance that they perish, and my soul must bear a swift witness against them at the day of judgment if they lay not hold of Christ." That thought of a mother's bearing swift witness against me, pierced my conscience and stirred my heart. This pleading with them for God and with God for them is the true way to bring children to Christ. Sunday-school teachers! you have a high and noble work, press forward in it. In our schools you do not try to bring children to the baptistry for regeneration, you point them away from ceremonies; if I know the teachers of this school aright, I know you are trying to bring your classes to Christ. Let Christ be the sum and substance of your teaching in the school. Young men and young women, in your classes lift up Christ, lift him up on high; and if anybody shall say to you, "Why do you thus talk to the children?" you can say, "Because my soul yearns towards them, and I pant for their conversion;" and if any should afterwards object, you can remember that Jesus is greatly displeased with them, and not with you, for you only obey the injunction, "Feed my lambs."

Coming to Christ means laying hold upon Christ with the hand of faith; looking to him for my life, my pardon, my salvation, my everything. If there be a poor little child here who is saying in her little heart, or his little heart, "I would like to come to Christ, O that I might be pardoned while I am yet a little one"—come, little lamb; come, and welcome. Did I hear your cry? Was it this?

> Gentle Jesus, meek and mild,
>   Look upon a little child;
> Pity my simplicity,
>   Suffer me to come to thee.

Dear little one, Jesus will not despise your lispings, nor will his servant keep you back. Jesus calls you, come and receive his blessing. If any of you say a word to keep the young heart back, Jesus will be displeased with you. Now I am afraid some do that; those, for instance, who think that the gospel is not for little children. Many of my brethren, I am sorry to say, preach in such a way that there is no hope of children ever getting any good by their preaching. I cannot glory in learning or eloquence, but in this one thing I may rejoice, that there is always a number of happy children here, who are quite as attentive as any of my audience. I do love to think that the gospel is suitable to little children. There are boys and girls in many of our Sabbath-school classes down below stairs who are as truly converted to God as any of us. Nay, and if you were to speak with them about the things of God, though you should get to the knotty points of election and predestination, you would find those boys and girls well taught in the things of the kingdom: they know free will from free grace, and you cannot puzzle them when you come to talk about the work of Jesus and the work of the Spirit, for they can discern between things which differ. But a minister who preaches as though he never wanted to bring children to Christ, and shoots right over the little one's heads, I do think Jesus is displeased with him.

Then there are others who doubt whether children ever will be converted. They do not look upon it as a thing likely to happen, and whenever they hear of a believing child, they hold up their hands at the prodigy, and say, "What a wonder of grace!" It ought to be, and in those Churches where the gospel is simply preached, it is as common a thing for children to be converted as for grown-up people to be brought to Christ. Others begin to doubt the truth of juvenile conversions. They say, "They are very young, can they understand the gospel? Is it not merely an infantile emotion, a mere profession?" My brethren, you have no more right to suspect the sincerity of the young, than to mistrust the grey-headed; you ought to receive them with the same open-breasted confidence with which you receive others when they profess to have found the Saviour. Do, I pray you, whenever you see the faintest desire in your children, go down on your knees, as your servant does, when the fire is almost out, and blow the spark with your own breath—seek by prayer to fan that spark to a flame. Do not despise any godly remark the child may make. Do not puff the child up on account of the goodness of the remark, lest you make him vain and so injure him, but do encourage him; let his first little prayers be noticed by you; though you may not like to teach him a form of prayer—I shall not care if you do not—yet teach him what prayer is; tell him to express his desires in his own words, and when he does so, join ye in it and plead with God on his behalf, that your little one may speedily find true peace in a Saviour's blood. You must not, unless you would displease my Master, keep back the smallest child that longs to come to Christ.

Here let us observe that the principle is of general application; you must not hinder any awakened soul from seeking the Saviour. O my brethren and sisters, I hope we have such a love for souls, such an instinct within us to desire to see the travail of Christ's soul, that instead of putting stumbling-blocks in the way, we would do the best we could to gather out the stones. On Sabbath days I have laboured to clear up the doubts and fears which afflict coming sinners; I have entreated God the Holy Spirit to enable me so to speak, that those things which hindered you from coming to the Saviour might be removed; but how sad must be the case of those who delight themselves in putting stumbling-blocks in men's way. The doctrine of election for instance, a great and glorious truth, full of comfort to God's people; how often is that made to frighten sinners from Jesus! There is a way of preaching that with a drawn sword, and say, "You must not come unless you know you are one of God's elect." That is not the way to preach the doctrine. The true way of preaching it is, "God has a chosen people, and I hope you are one of them; come, lay hold on Jesus, put your trust in him." Then there be others who preach up frames and feelings as a preparation for Christ. They do in effect say, "Unless you have felt so much depression of spirit, or experienced a certain quantity of brokenness of heart, you must not come to Christ," instead of declaring, that whosoever will is permitted to come, and that the true way of coming to Christ is not with a qualification of frames and feeling and mental depressions, but just as you are. Oh! it is my soul's delight to preach a gospel which has an open door to it, to preach a mercy-seat which has no veil before it; the veil is rent in twain, and now the biggest sinner out of hell who desires to come, is welcome. You who are eighty years of age, and have hated Christ all the time, if now the Spirit of God makes you willing to come, Christ seems to say, "Suffer the grey-headed to come unto me, and forbid them not:" while to you little children, he stretches out his arms in the same manner, "Suffer the little children to come unto me." O my beloved, see to it that your heart longs to come to Christ, and not to ceremonies! I stand here this day to cry, "Come ye to the cross, not to the font." When I forget to lift up the Lord Jesus, and to cast down the forms of man's devising, "let my right hand forget her cunning," and "let my tongue cleave to the roof of my mouth"—None but Jesus, none but Jesus, Can do helpless sinners good;" The font is a mockery and an imposition if it be put before Christ. If you have baptism after you have come to Christ, well and good, but to point you to it either as being Christ, or as being inevitably connected with Christ, or as being the place to find Christ, is nothing better than to go back to the beggarly elements of the old Romish harlot, instead of standing in the "liberty wherewith Christ hath made us free," and bidding the sinner to come as a sinner to Christ Jesus, and to Christ Jesus alone.

III. In the third and last place, let us also gather from our text, that WHEN WE DISCOURAGE ANY, WE ALWAYS GO UPON WRONG GROUNDS. Here was the case of children. I suppose that the grounds upon which the apostles kept back the children would be one of these—either that the children could not receive a blessing, or else that they could not receive it worthily.

Did they imagine that these little children could not receive the blessing? Perhaps so, for they thought them too young. Now, brethren, that was a wrong ground to go upon, for these children could receive the blessing and they did receive it, for Jesus took them in his arms and blessed them. If I keep back a child from coming to Christ on the ground that he is too young, I do it in the face of facts; because there have been children brought to Christ at an extremely early period. You who are acquainted with Janeway's "Tokens for Children," have noticed very many beautiful instances of early conversion. Our dear friend, Mrs. Rogers, in that book of hers, "The Folded Lamb," gave a very sweet picture of a little son of hers, soon folded in the Saviour's bosom above, who, as early as two or three years of age, rejoiced and knew the Saviour. I do not doubt at all, I cannot doubt it, because one has seen such cases, that children of two or three years of age may have precocity of knowledge, and of grace; a forwardness which in almost every case has betokened early death, but which has been perfectly marvellous to those who have talked with them. The fact is that we do not all at the same age arrive at that degree of mental stature which is necessary for understanding the things of God. Children have been reported as reading Latin, Greek, and other languages, at five or six years of age. I do not know that such early scholarship is any great blessing, it is better not to reach that point so soon; but some children are all that their minds ever will be at three or four, and then they go home to heaven; and so long as the mind has been brought up to such a condition that it is capable of understanding, it is also capable of faith, if the Holy Spirit shall implant it. To suppose that he ever did give faith to an unconscious babe is ridiculous; that there can be any faith in a child that knows nothing whatever I must always take ground to doubt, for "How shall they believe without a preacher?" And yet they are brought up to make a profession in their long-clothes, when they have never heard a sermon in their lives. But those dear children to whom I have before referred, have understood the preacher, have understood the truth, have rejoiced in the truth, and their first young lispings have been as full of grace as those glorious expressions of aged saints in their triumphant departures. Children are capable, then, of receiving the grace of God. Do mark by the way, that all those champions who have come out against me so valiantly, have made a mistake; they have said that we deny that little infants may be regenerated; we do not deny that God can regenerate them if he pleases; we do not know anything about what may or may not happen to unconscious babes; but we did say that little children were not regenerated by their godparents telling lies at a font—we did say that, and we say it again, that little children are not regenerated, nor made members of Christ, nor children of God, nor inheritors of the kingdom of heaven, by solemn mockery, in which godfathers and godmothers promise to do for them what they cannot do for themselves, much less for their children. That is the point; and if they will please to meet it, we will answer them again, but till such time as that, we shall probably let them talk on till God gives them grace to know better.

The other ground upon which the apostles put back the children would be, that although the children might receive the blessing, they might not be able to receive it worthily. The Lord Jesus in effect assures them that so far from the way in which a little child enters into the kingdom of heaven being exceptional, it is the rule; and the very way in which a child enters the kingdom, is the way in which everybody must enter it. How does a child enter the kingdom of heaven? Why, its faith is very simple; it does not understand mysteries and controversies, but it believes what it is told upon the authority of God's Word, and it comes to God's Word without previous prejudice. It has its natural sinfulness, but grace overcomes it, and the child receives the Word as it finds it. You will notice in boyish and girlish conversions, a peculiar simplicity of belief: they believe just what Christ says, exactly what he says. If they pray, they believe Christ will hear them: if they talk about Jesus, it is as of a person near at hand. They do not, as we do, get into the making of these things into mysteries and shadows, but little children have a realizing power. Then they have great rejoicing. The most cheerful Christians we have are young believers; and the most cheerful old Christians are those who were converted when they were young. Why, see the joy of a child that finds a Saviour! "Mother," he says, "I have sought Jesus Christ, and I have trusted him, and I am saved." He does not say, "I hope," and "I trust," but "I am;" and then he is ready to leap for joy because he is saved. Of the many boys and girls whom we have received into Church-fellowship, I can say of them all, they have all gladdened my heart, and I have never received any with greater confidence than I have these: this I have noticed about them, they have greater joy and rejoicing than any others; and I take it, it is because they do not ask so many questions as others do, but take Jesus Christ's word as they find it, and believe in it. Well now, just the very way in which a child receives Christ, is the way in which you must receive Christ if you would be saved. You who know so much that you know too much; you who have big brains; you who are always thinking, and have tendency to criticism, and perhaps to scepticism, you must come and receive the gospel as a little child. You will never get a hold of my Lord and Master while you are wearing that quizzing cap; no, you must take it off, and by the power of the Holy Spirit you must come trusting Jesus, simply trusting him, for this is the right way to receive the kingdom.

But here, let me say, the principle which holds good in little children holds good in all other cases as well. Take for instance the case of very great sinners, men who have been gross offenders against the laws of their country. Some would say they cannot be saved; they can be for some of them have been. Others would say they never receive the truth as it is in Jesus in the right manner; ay, but they do. How do great sinners receive Christ? There are some here who have been reclaimed from drunkenness, and I know not what. My brethren, how did you receive Christ? Why in this way. You said, "All unholy, all unclean, I am nothing else but sin; but if I am saved, it will be grace, grace, grace." Why, when you and I stood up, black, and foul, and filthy, and yet dared to believe in Christ, we said, "If we are saved, we shall be prodigies of divine mercy, and we will sing of his love for ever." Well but, my dear friends, you must all receive Jesus Christ in that very way. That which would raise an objection to the salvation of the big sinner is thrown back upon you, for Christ might well say, "Except ye receive these things as the chief of sinners, ye cannot enter the kingdom." I will prove my point by the instance of the apostle Paul. He has been held by some to be an exception to the rule, but Paul did not think so, for he says that God in him showed forth all longsuffering for a pattern to them that believe, and made him as it were a type of all conversions; so that instead of being an exception his was to be the rule. You see what I am driving at. The case of the children looks exceptional, but it is not; it has, on the contrary, all the features about it which must be found in every true conversion. It is of such that the kingdom of heaven is composed, and if we are not such we cannot enter it. Let this induce all of us who love the Lord, to pray for the conversion both of children and of all sorts of men. Let our compassion expand, let us shut out none from the plea of our heart; in prayer and in faith let us bring all who come under our range, hoping and believing that some of them will be found in the election of grace, that some of them will be washed in the Saviour's blood, and that some of them will shine as stars in the firmament of God for ever. Let us, on no consideration, believe that the salvation of any man or child is beyond the range of possibility, for the Lord saveth whom he wills. Let no difficulties which seem to surround the case hinder our efforts; let us, on the contrary, push with greater eagerness forward, believing that where there seems to be some special difficulty, there will be manifested, as in the children's case, some special privilege. O labour for souls, my dear friends! I beseech you live to win souls. This is the best rampart against error, a rampart built of living stones—converted men and women. This is the way to push back the advances of Popery, by imploring the Lord to work conversions. I do not think that mere controversial preaching will do much, though it must be used; it is grace-work we want; it is bringing you to Christ, it is getting you to lay hold of him—it is this which shall put the devil to a nonplus and expand the kingdom of Christ. O that my God would bring some of you to Jesus! If he is displeased with those who would keep you back, then see how willing he is to receive you. Is there in your soul any desire towards him? Come and welcome, sinner, come. Do you feel now that you must have Christ or die? Come and have him, he is to be had for the asking. Has the Lord taught you your need of Jesus? Ye thirsty ones, come and drink; ye hungry ones, come and eat. Yea, this is the proclamation of the gospel to-day, "The Spirit and the bride say, Come. And let him that heareth say, Come. And let him that is athirst come. And whosoever will, let him take the water of life freely." I do trust there may be encouragement in this to some of you. I pray my Master make you feel it. If he be angry with those who keep you back, then he must be willing to receive you, glad to receive you; and if you come to him he will in no wise cast you out. May the Lord add his blessing on these words for Jesus' sake. Amen.

Christ Exalted

A Sermon (No. 91) Delivered on
Sabbath Morning, July 6th, 1856,
by the REV. C. H. SPURGEON
At Exeter Hall, Strand.

"This man, after he had offered on sacrifice for sins for ever, sat down on the right hand of God; From henceforth expecting till his enemies be made his footstool."—Hebrews 10:12–13.

At the Lord's table we wish to have no subject for contemplation but our blessed Lord Jesus Christ, and we have been wont generally to consider him as the crucified One, "the Man of sorrows, and acquainted with grief," while we have had before us the emblems of his broken body, and of his blood shed for many for the remission of sins; but I am not quite sure that the crucified Saviour is the only appropriate theme, although, perhaps, the most so. It is well to remember how our Saviour left us—by what road he travelled through the shadows of death; but I think it is quite as well to recollect what he is doing while he is away from us—to remember the high glories to which the crucified Saviour has attained; and it is, perhaps, as much calculated to cheer our spirits to behold him on his throne as to consider him on his cross. We have seen him one his cross, in some sense; that is to say, the eyes of men on earth did see the crucified Saviour; but we have no idea of what his glories are above; they surpass our highest thought. Yet faith can see the Saviour exalted on his throne, and surely there is no subject that can keep our expectations alive, or cheer our drooping faith better than to consider, that while our Saviour is absent, he is absent on his throne, and that when he has left his Church to sorrow for him, he has not left us comfortless—he has promised to come to us—that while he tarries he is reigning, and that while he is absent he is sitting high on his father's throne.

The Apostle shews here the superiority of Christ's sacrifice over that of every other priest. "Every priest standeth daily ministering and offering oftentimes the same sacrifices, which can never take away sins; but this man," or priest—for the word "man" is not in the original "after he had offered one sacrifice for sins," had finished his work, and for ever, he "sat down." You see the superiority of Christ's sacrifice rests in this, that the priest offered continually, and after he had slaughtered one lamb, another was needed; after one scape-goat was driven into the wilderness, a scape-goat was needed the next year, "but this man, when he had offered only one sacrifice for sins," did what thousands of scape-goats never did, and what hundreds of thousands of lambs never could effect. He perfected our salvation, and worked out an entire atonement for the sins of all his chosen ones.

We shall notice, in the first place, this morning, the completeness of the Saviour's work of atonement—he has done it: we shall gather that from the context: secondly, the glory which the Saviour has assumed; and thirdly, the triumph which he expects. We shall dwell very briefly on each point, and endeavour to pack our thoughts as closely together as we can.

I. We are taught here in the first place, THE COMPLETENESS OF THE SAVIOUR'S WORK. He has done all that was necessary to be done, to make an atonement and an end of sin. He has done so much, that it will never be needful for him again to be crucified. His side, once opened, has sent forth a stream deep, deep enough, and precious enough, to wash away all sin; and he needs not again that his side should be opened, or, that any more his hands should be nailed to the cross. I infer that his work is finished, from the fact that he is described here as sitting down. Christ would not sit down in heaven if he had more work to do. Sitting down is the posture of rest. Seldom he sat down on earth; he said, "I must be about my Father's business." Journey after journey, labour after labour, preaching after preaching, followed each other in quick succession. His was a life of incessant toil. Rest was a word which Jesus never spelled. he may sit for a moment on the well; but even there he preaches to the woman of Samaria. He goes into the wilderness, but not to sleep; he goes there to pray. His midnights are spent in labours as hard as those of the day—labours of agonising prayer, wrestling with his Father for the souls of men. His was a life of continual bodily, mental, and spiritual labour; his whole man was exercised. But now he rests; there is no more toil for him now; here is no more sweat of blood, no more the weary foot, no more the aching head. No more has he to do. He sits still. But do you think my Saviour would sit still if he had not done all his work? Oh! no beloved; he said once, "For Zion's sake I will not rest until her glory goeth forth like a lamp that burneth." And sure I am he would not rest, or be sitting still, unless the great work of our atonement were fully accomplished. Sit still, blessed Jesus, while there is a fear of thy people being lost? Sit still, while their salvation is at hazard? No; alike thy truthfulness and thy compassion tell us, that thou wouldst still labour if the work were still undone. Oh! if the last thread had not been woven in the great garment of our righteousness, he would be spinning it now; if the last particle of our debt had not been paid, he would be counting it down now; and if all were not finished and complete, he would never rest, until, like a wise builder, he had laid the top-stone of the temple of our salvation. No; the very fact that he sits still, and rests, and is at ease, proves that his work is finished and is complete.

And then note again, that his sitting at the right hand of God implies, that he enjoys pleasure; for at God's right hand "there are pleasures for evermore." Now, I think, that the fact that Christ enjoys infinite pleasure has in it some degree of proof that he must have finished his work. It is true, he had pleasure with his Father ere that work was begun; but I cannot conceive that if, after having been incarnate, his work was still unfinished, he would rest. He might rest before he began the work, but as soon as ever he had begun it, you will remember, he said he had a baptism wherewith he must be baptised, and he appeared to be hastening to receive the whole of the direful baptism of agony. He never rested on earth till the whole work was finished; scarcely a smile passed his brow till the whole work was done. He was "a man of sorrows and acquainted with grief," until he could say, "it is finished;" and I could scarcely conceive the Saviour happy on his throne if there were any more to do. Surely, living as he was on that great throne of his, there would be anxiety in his breast if he had not secured the meanest lamb of his fold, and if he had not rendered the eternal salvation of every blood-bought one as sacred as his own throne. The highest pleasure of Christ is derived from the fact, that he has become the "head over all things to his Church," and has saved that Church. He has joys as God;

but as the man-God, his joys spring from the salvation of the souls of men. That is his joy, which is full, in the thought that he has finished his work and has cut it short in righteousness. I think there is some degree of proof, although not perhaps positive proof there, that Jesus must have finished his work.

But now, something else. The fact that it is said he has sat down for ever proves that he must have done it. Christ has undertaken to save all the souls of the elect. If he has not already saved them, he is bound to do something that will save them, fir he has given solemn oath and promise to his Father, that he will bring many souls unto glory, and that he will make them perfect through his own righteousness. He has promised to present our souls unblemished and complete,—

Before the glory of his face
  With joys divinely great.

Well, if he has not done enough to do that, then he must come again to do it; but from the fact that he is to sit there for ever, that he is to wear no more the thorny crown, that he is never again to leave his throne, to cease to be king any more, that he is still to be girded by his grandeur and his glory, and sit for ever there, is proof that he has accomplished the great work of propitiation. It is certain that he must have done all, from the fact that he is to sit there for ever, to sit on his throne throughout all ages, more visibly in the ages to come, but never to leave it, again to suffer and again to die.

Yet, the best proof is, that Christ sits at his Father's right hand at all. For the very fact that Christ is in heaven, accepted by his Father proves that his work must be done. Why, beloved, as long as an ambassador from our country is at a foreign court, there must be peace; and as long as Jesus Christ our Saviour is at his Father's court, it shows that there is real peace between his people and his Father. Well, as he will be there for ever, that shows that our peace must be continual, and like the waves of the sea, shall never cease. But that peace could not have been continual, unless the atonement had been wholly made, unless justice had been entirely satisfied; and, therefore, from that very fact it becomes certain that the work of Christ must be done. What! Christ enter heaven—Christ sit on his Father's right hand before all the guilt of his people was rolled away? AH! no; he was the sinner's substitute; and unless he paid the sinner's doom, and died the sinner's death, there was no heaven in view for me. He stood in the sinner's place, and the guilt of all his elect was imputed to him. God accounted him as a sinner, and as a sinner, he could not enter heaven until he had washed all that sin away in a crimson flood of his own gore—unless his own righteousness had covered up the sins which he had taken on himself, and unless his own atonement had taken away those sins which had become his by imputation; and the fact that the Father allowed him to ascend up on high—that he gave him leave, as it were, to enter heaven, and that he said, "Sit thou on my right hand," proves that he must have perfected his Father's work, and that his Father must have accepted his sacrifice. But he could not have accepted it if it had been imperfect. Thus, therefore, we prove that the work must have been finished, since God the Father accepted it. Oh! glorious doctrine! This Man has done it; this Man has finished it: this Man has completed it. He was the Author, he is the Finisher; he was the Alpha, he is the Omega. Salvation is finished, complete; otherwise, he would not has ascended up on high, nor would he also sit at the right hand of God. Christian! rejoice! Thy salvation is a finished salvation; atonement is wholly made; neither stick nor stone of thine is wanted; not one stitch is required to that glorious garment of his—not one patch to that glorious robe that he has finished. 'Tis done—'tis done perfectly; thou art accepted perfectly in his righteousness; thou art purged in his blood. "By one offering he hath perfected for ever them that are sanctified."

II. And now, our second point—THE GLORY WHICH HE HAS ASSUMED. "After he has offered one sacrifice for sins for ever, sat down on the right hand of God"—the glory which Christ has assumed.

Now, by this you are to understand the complex person of Christ; for Christ, as God, always was on his Father's throne; he always was God; and even when on earth he was still in heaven. The Son of God did not cease to be omnipotent and omnipresent, when he came wrapped in the garments of clay. He was still on his Father's throne; he never left it, never came down from heaven in that sense; he was still there, "God over all, blessed for ever." As he has said, "The Son of Man who came down from heaven, who, also," at that very moment, was "in heaven." But Jesus Christ, as the Man-God, has assumed glories and honors which once he had not; for as man, he did not at one time sit on his Father's throne; he was a man, a suffering man, a man full of pains and groans, more than mortals have ever known: but as God-man, he has assumed a dignity next to God; he sits at the right hand of God: at the right hand of the glorious Trinity, Father, Son, and Holy Ghost, sits the person of the man

Jesus Christ, exalted at the right hand of the Majesty on High. From this we gather, that the dignity which Christ now enjoys is surpassing dignity. There is no honor, there is no dignity to be compared to that of Christ. No angel flies higher than he does. Save only the great Three-One God, there is none to be found in heaven who can be called superior to the person of the man Christ Jesus. He sits on the right hand of God, "Far above all angels, and principalities, and powers, and every name that is named." His Father "hath highly exalted him, and given him a name which is above every name, that at the name of Jesus every knee should bow, of things in heaven, and of things on earth, and of things under the earth." No dignity can shine like his. The sons of righteousness that have turned many to God, are but as stars compared with him, the brightest of the suns there. As for angels, they are but flashes of his own brightness, emanations from his own glorious self. He sits there, the great masterpiece of Deity.

God, in the person of his Son,
Hath all his mightiest works outdone.

That glorious man, taken into union with Deity, that mighty Man-God, surpasses everything in the glory of his majestic person. Christian! remember, thy Master has unsurpassed dignity.

In the next place, Christ has real dignity. Some persons have mere empty titles, which confer but little power and little authority. But the Man-Christ Jesus, while he has many crowns and many titles, has not one tinsel crown or one empty title. While he sits there he sits not there pro forma; he does not sit there to have nominal honor done to him; but he has real honor and real glory. That Man-Christ, who once walked the streets of Jerusalem, now sits in heaven, and angels bow before him. That Man-Christ, who once hung on Calvary, and there expired in agonies the most acute, now, on his Father's throne exalted sins, and sways the sceptre of heaven—nay, devils at his presence tremble, the whole earth owns the sway of his providence, and on his shoulders the pillars of the universe rest. "He upholdeth all things by the word of his power." He overruleth all mortal things, making the evil work a good, and the good produce a better, and a better still, in infinite progression. The power of the God-Man Christ is infinite; you cannot tell how great it is. He is "able to save unto the uttermost them that come unto God by him." He is "able to keep us from falling, and to present us spotless before his presence." He is able to make "all things work together for good." He is "able to subdue all things unto himself." He is able to conquer even death, for he hath the power of death, and he hath the power of Satan, who once had power over death; yea, he is Lord over all things, for his Father hath made him so. The glorious dignity of our Saviour! I cannot talk of it in words, beloved: all I can say to you must be simple repetition. I can only repeat the statements of Scripture. There is no room for flights; we must just keep where we ever have been, telling out the story that his Father hath exalted him to real honors and real dignities.

And once more: this honor that Christ hath now received (I mean the Man-God Christ, not the God-Christ, for he already had that, and never lost it, and therefore could never obtain it; he was Man-God, and as such he was exalted;) was deserved honor; that dignity which his Father gave him he well deserved. I have sometimes thought, if all the holy spirits in the universe had been asked what should be done for the man whom the King delighteth to honor, they would have said, Christ must be the man whom God delighteth to honor, and he must sit on his Father's right hand. Why, if I might use such a phrase, I can almost suppose his mighty Father putting it to the vote of heaven as to whether Christ should be exalted, and that they carried it by acclamation, "Worthy is the Lamb that was slain, to receive honor and glory for ever and ever." His Father gave him that; but still the suffrages of all the saints, and of all the holy angels, said to it, amen; and this thing I am certain of, that every heart here—every Christian heart, says amen to it. Ah, beloved, we would exalt him, we would crown him, "crown him Lord of all;" not only will his Father crown him, but we, ourselves, would exalt him if we had the power; and when we shall have power to do it, we will cast our crowns beneath his feet, and crown him Lord of all. It is deserved honor. No other being in heaven deserves to be there; even the angels are kept there, and God "chargeth his angels with folly," and gives them grace, whereby he keeps them; and none of his saints deserve it; they feel that hell was their desert. But Christ's exaltation was a deserved exaltation. His father might say to him, "Well done, my Son, well done; thou hast finished the work which I had given thee to do; sit thou for ever first of all men, glorified by union with the person of the Son. My glorious co-equal Son, sit thou on my right hand, till I make thine enemies thy foot-stool."

One more illustration, and we have done with this. We must consider the exaltation of Christ in heaven as being in some degree a representative exaltation. Christ

Jesus exalted at the Father's right hand, though he has eminent glories, in which the saints must not expect to share, essentially he is the express image of the person of God, and the brightness of his Father's glory, yet, to a very great degree, the honors which Christ has in heaven he has as our representative there. Ah! brethren it is sweet to reflect, how blessedly Christ lives with his people. Ye all know that we were

> One, when he died, one, when he rose,
>   One, when he triumphed o'er his foes;
>   One, when in heaven he took his seat,
>   And angels sang all hell's defeat.

To-day you know that you are one with him, now, in his presence. We are at this moment "raised up together," and may, afterwards, "sit together in heavenly places, even in him." As I am represented in parliament, and as you are, so is ever child of God represented in heaven; but as we are not one with our parliamentary representatives, that figure fails to set forth the glorious representation of us which our forerunner, Christ, carries on in heaven, for we are actually one with him; we are members of his body, of his flesh, and of his bones, and his exaltation is our exaltation. He will give us to sit upon his throne, for as he has overcome, and is set down with his Father on his throne; he has a crown, and he will not wear his crown, unless he gives us crowns too; he has a throne, but he is not content with having a throne to himself; on his right hand there must be his bride in gold of Ophir. And he cannot be there without his bride; the Saviour cannot be content to be in heaven unless he has his Church with him, which is "the fulness of him that filleth all in all." Beloved, look up to Christ now; let the eye of your faith catch a sight of him; behold him there, with many crowns upon his head. Remember, as ye see him there, ye will one day be like him, and when ye shall see him as he is; ye shall not be as great as he is, ye shall not be as glorious in degree, but still ye shall, in a measure, share the same honors, and enjoy the same happiness and the same dignity which he possesses. Be then, content to live unknown for a little while; be content to bear the sneer, the jest, the joke, the ribald song; be content to walk your weary way, through the fields of poverty, or up the hills of affliction; by-and-bye ye shall reign with Christ, for he has "made us kings and priests unto God, and we shall reign for ever and ever." By-and-bye we shall share the glories of the Head; the oil has been poured on his head; it has not trickled down to us yet, save only in that faithful fellowship which we have; but by-and-bye that oil shall flow to the very skirts of the garments, and we, the meanest of his people, shall share a part in the glories of his house by being made kings with him, to sit on his throne, even as he sit on his Father's throne.

III. And now, in the last place, WHAT ARE CHRIST'S EXPECTATIONS? We are told, he expects that his enemies shall be made his footstool. In some sense that is already done; the foes of Christ are, in some sense, his footstool now. What is the devil but the very slave of Christ? for he doth no more than he is permitted against God's children. What is the devil, but the servant of Christ, to fetch his children to his loving arms? What are wicked men, but the servants of God's providence unwittingly to themselves? Christ has even now "power over all flesh that he may give eternal life to as many as God has given him," in order that the purposes of Christ might be carried out. Christ died for all, and all are now Christ's property. There is not a man in this world who does not belong to Christ in that sense, for he is God over him and Lord over him.

He is either Christ's brother, or else Christ's slave, his unwilling vassal, that must be dragged out in triumph, if he follow him not willingly. In that sense all things are now Christ's.

Be we expect greater things than these, beloved, at his coming, when all enemies shall be beneath Christ's feet upon earth. We are, therefore, many of us, "looking for that blessed hope; that glorious appearing of the kingdom of our Saviour Jesus Christ;" many of us are expecting that Christ will come; we cannot tell you when, we believe it to be folly to pretend to guess the time, but we are expecting that even in our life the Son of God will appear, and we know that when he shall appear he will tread his foes beneath his feet, and reign from pole to pole, and from the river even to the ends of the earth. Not long shall anti-christ sit on her seven hills; not long shall the false prophet delude his millions; not long shall idol gods mock their worshippers with eyes that cannot see, and hands that cannot handle, and ears that cannot hear—

> Lo! he comes, with clouds descending;

In the winds I see his chariot wheels; I know that he approaches and when he approaches he "breaks the bow and cuts the spear in sunder, and burns the chariot in the fire;" and Christ Jesus shall then be king over the whole world. He is king now, virtually; but he is to have another kingdom; I cannot see how it is to be a spiritual one, for that is come already; he is as much king spiritually now as he ever will be in his Church, although his kingdom will assuredly be very extensive; but the kingdom that is to come, I take it, will be something even greater than the spiritual kingdom; it will be a visible kingdom of Christ on earth. Then kings must bow their necks before his feet; then at his throne the tribes of earth shall bend; then the rich and mighty, the merchants of Tyre, and the travellers where gold is found, shall bring their spices and myrrh before him, and lay their gold and gems at his feet;

> Jesus shall reign where'er the sun,
> Does his successive journeys run;
> His kingdom stretch from shore to shore,
> Till moons shall wax and wane no more.

Once more, beloved; Christ will have all his enemies put beneath his feet, in that great day of judgment. Oh! that will be a terrible putting of his foes beneath his feet, when at that second resurrection the wicked dead shall rise; when the ungodly shall stand before his throne, and his voice shall say, "Depart, ye cursed." Oh! rebel, thou that hast despised Christ, it will be a horrible thing for thee, that that man, that gibbeted, crucified man, whom thou hast often despised, will have power enough to speak thee into hell; that the man whom thou hast scoffed and laughed at, and of whom thou hast virtually said, "If he be the Son of God, let him come down from the cross," will have power enough, in two or three short words, to damn thy soul to all eternity: "Depart from me, ye cursed, into everlasting fire, prepared for the devil and his angels." Oh! what a triumph that will be, when men, wicked men, persecutors, and all those who opposed Christ, are all cast into the lake that burneth! But, if possible, it will be a greater triumph, when he who led men astray shall be dragged forth. "Shall lift his brazen front, with thunder scarred, Receive the sentence, and begin anew his hell." Oh! when Satan shall be condemned, and when the saints shall judge angels, and the fallen spirits shall all be under the feet of Christ, "then shall be brought to pass the saying that is written, he hath put all things under him." And when death, too, shall come forth, and the "death of death and hell's destruction" shall grind his iron limbs to powder, then shall it be said, "Death is swallowed up in victory," for the great shout of "Victory, victory, victory," shall drown the shrieks of the past; shall put out the sound of the howlings of death; and hell shall be swallowed up in victory. He is exalted on high—he sitteth on his Father's right hand, "from henceforth expecting till his enemies be made his footstool."

CHRIST'S FIRST AND LAST SUBJECT

A Sermon (No. 329) Delivered on Sabbath Morning, August 19th, 1860, by the REV. C. H. SPURGEON at Exeter Hall, Strand.

"From that time Jesus began to preach, and to say, Repent: for the kingdom of heaven is at hand"—Matthew 4:17. "And that repentance and remission of sins should be preached in his name among all nations, beginning at Jerusalem"—Luke 24:47.

It seems from these two texts that repentance was the first subject upon which the Redeemer dwelt, and that it was the last, which, with his departing breath, he commended to the earnestness of his disciples. He begins his mission crying, "Repent," he ends it by saying to his successors the apostles, "Preach repentance and remission of sins among all nations, beginning at Jerusalem." This seems to me to be a very interesting fact, and not simply interesting, but instructive. Jesus Christ opens his commission by preaching repentance. What then? Did he not by this act teach us how important repentance was—so important that the very first time he opens his mouth, he shall begin with, "Repent, for the kingdom of heaven is at hand." Did he not feel that repentance was necessary to be preached before he preached faith in himself, because the soul must first repent of sin before it will seek a Saviour, or even care to know whether there is a Saviour at all? And did he not also indicate to us that as repentance was the opening lesson of the divine teaching, so, if we would be his disciples, we must begin by sitting on the stool of repentance, before we can possibly go upward to the higher forms of faith and of full assurance? Jesus at the first begins with repentance,—that repentance may be the Alpha, the first letter of the spiritual alphabet which all believers must learn; and when he concluded his divine commission with repentance, what did he say to us but this—that repentance was still of the very last importance? He preaches it with his first, he will utter it with his last breath; with this he begins, with this he will conclude. He knew that repentance was, to spiritual life, a sort of Alpha and Omega—it was the duty of the beginning, it was the duty of the end. He seemed to say to us, "Repentance, which I preached to you three years ago, when I first came into the world, as a public teacher, is as binding, as necessary for you who heard me then, and who then obeyed my voice, as it was at the very first instant, and it is equally needful that you who have been with me from the beginning, should not imagine that the theme is exhausted and out of date; you too must begin your ministry and conclude it with the same exhortation, 'Repent and be converted, for the kingdom of heaven is at hand.'" It seems to me that nothing could set forth Jesus Christ's idea of the high value of repentance, more fully and effectually than the fact that he begins with it, and that he concludes with it—that he should say, "Repent," as the key-note of his ministry, preaching this duty before he fully develops all the mystery of godliness, and that he should close his life-song as a good composer must, with his first key-note, bidding his disciples still cry, "Repentance and remission of sins are preached in Jesus' name." I feel then that I need no further apology for introducing to your solemn and serious attention, the subject of saving repentance. And oh! while we are talking of it, may God the Holy Ghost breathe into all our spirits, and may we now repent before him, and now find those blessings which he hath promised to the penitent.

With regard to repentance, these four things:—first, its origin; secondly, its essentials; thirdly, its companions; and fourthly, its excellencies.

I. Repentance—ITS ORIGIN.

When we cry, "Repent and be converted," there are some foolish men who call us legal. Now we beg to state, at the opening of this first point, that repentance is of gospel parentage. It was not born near Mount Sinai. It never was brought forth anywhere but upon Mount Zion. Of course, repentance is a duty—a natural duty—because, when man hath sinned, who is there brazen enough to say that it is not man's bounden duty to repent of having done so? It is a duty which even nature itself would teach. But gospel repentance was never yet produced as a matter of duty. It was never brought forth in the soul by demands of law, nor indeed can the law, except as the instrument in the hand of grace, even assist the soul towards saving repentance. It is a remarkable fact that the law itself makes no provision for repentance. It says, "This do, and thou shalt live; break my command, and thou shalt die." There is nothing said about penitence; there is no offer of pardon made to those that repent. The law pronounces its deadly curse upon the man that sins but once, but it offers no way of escape, no door by which the man may be restored to favour. The barren sides of Sinai have no soil in which to nourish the lovely plant of penitence. Upon Sinai the dew of mercy never fell. Its lightnings and its thunders have frightened away the angel of Mercy once for all, and there Justice sits, with sword of flame, upon its majestic throne of rugged rock, never purposing for a moment to put up its sword into the scabbard, and to forgive the offender. Read attentively the twentieth chapter of Exodus. You have the commandments there all thundered forth with trumpet voice, but there is no pause between where Mercy with her silver voice may step in and say, "But if ye break this law, God will have mercy upon you, and will shew himself gracious if ye repent." No words of repentance, I say, were ever proclaimed by the law; no promise by it made to penitents; and no assistance is by the law ever offered to those who desire to be forgiven. Repentance is a gospel grace. Christ preached it, but not Moses. Moses neither can nor will assist a soul to repent, only Jesus can use the law as a means of conviction and an argument for repentance. Jesus gives pardon to those who seek it with weeping and with tears; but Moses knows of no such thing. If repentance is ever obtained by the poor sinner, it must be found at the foot of the cross, and not where the ten commandments lie shivered at Sinai's base.

And as repentance is of gospel parentage, I make a second remark, it is also of gracious origin. Repentance was never yet produced in any man's heart apart from the grace of God. As soon may you expect the leopard to regret the blood with which its fangs are moistened,—as soon might you expect the lion of the wood to abjure his cruel tyranny over the feeble beasts of the plain, as expect the sinner to make any confession, or offer any repentance that shall be accepted of God, unless grace shall first renew the heart. Go and loose the bands of everlasting winter in the frozen north with your own feeble breath, and then hope to make tears of penitence bedew the cheek of the hardened sinner. Go ye and divide the earth, and pierce its bowels with an infant's finger, and then hope that your eloquent appeal, unassisted by divine grace, shall be able to penetrate the adamantine heart of man. Man can sin, and he can continue in it, but to leave the hateful element is a work for which he needs a power divine. As the river rushes downward with increasing fury, leaping from crag to crag in ponderous cataracts of power, so is the sinner in his sin; onward and downward, onward, yet more swiftly, more mightily, more irresistibly, in his hellish course. Nothing but divine grace can bid that cataract leap upward, or make the floods retrace the pathway which they have worn for themselves down the rocks.

Nothing, I say, but the power which made the world, and digged the foundations of the great deep, can ever make the heart of man a fountain of life from which the floods of repentance may gush forth. So then, soul, if thou shalt ever repent, it must be a repentance, not of nature, but of grace. Nature can imitate repentance; it can produce remorse; it can generate the feeble resolve; it can even lead to a partial, practical reform; but unaided nature cannot touch the vitals and new-create the soul. Nature may make the eyes weep, but it cannot make the heart bleed. Nature can bid you amend your ways, but it cannot renew your heart. No, you must look upward, sinner; you must look upward to him who is able to save unto the uttermost. You must at his hands receive the meek and tender spirit; from his finger must come the touch that shall dissolve the rock; and from his eye must dart the flash of love and light that can scatter the darkness of your impenitence. Remember, then, at the outset, that true repentance is of gospel origin, and is not the work of the law; and on the other hand, it is of gracious origin, and is not the work of the creature.

II. But to pass forward from this first point to our second head, let us notice the ESSENTIALS of true repentance. The old divines adopted various methods of explaining penitence. Some of them said it was a precious medicine, compounded of six things; but in looking over their divisions, I have felt that I might with equal success divide repentance into four different ingredients. This precious box of ointment which must be broken over the Saviour's heard before the sweet perfume of peace can ever be smelt in the soul—this precious ointment is compounded of four most rare, most costly things. God give them to us and then give us the compound itself mixed by the Master's hand. True repentance consists of illumination, humiliation, detestation, and transformation.

To take them one by one. The first part of true repentance consists of illumination. Man by nature is impenitent, because he does not know himself to be guilty. There are many acts which he commits in which he sees no sin, and even in great and egregious faults, he often knows that he is not right, but he does not perceive the depth, the horrible enormity of the sin which is involved in them. Eye-salve is one of the first medicines which the Lord uses with the soul. Jesus touches the eye of the understanding, and the man becomes guilty in his own sight, as he always was guilty in the sight of God. Crimes long forgotten start up from the grave where his forgetfulness had buried them; sins, which he thought were no sins, suddenly rise up on their true character, and acts, which he thought were perfect, now discover themselves to have been so mixed with evil motive that they were far from being acceptable with God. The eye is no more blind, and therefore the heart is no more proud, for the seeing eye will make a humble heart. If I must paint a picture of penitence in this first stage, I should portray a man with his eyes bandaged walking through a path infested with the most venomous vipers; vipers which have formed a horrible girdle about his loins, and are hanging like bracelets from his wrists. The man is so blind that he knows not where he is, nor what it is which he fancies to be a jewelled belt upon his arm. I would then in the picture touch his eyes and bid you see his horror, and his astonishment, when he discovers where he is and what he is. He looks behind him, and he sees through what broods of vipers he has walked; he looks before him, and he sees how thickly his future path is strewed with these venomous beasts. He looks about him, and in his living bosom looking out from his guilty heart, he sees the head of a vile serpent, which has twisted its coils into his very vitals. I would try, if I could, to throw into that face, horror, dismay, dread, and sorrow, a longing to escape, an anxious desire to get rid of all these things which must destroy him unless he should escape from them. And now, my dear hearers, have you ever been the subject of this divine illumination? Has God, who said to an unformed world, "Let there be light," has he said, "Let there be light" in your poor benighted soul? Have you learned that your best deeds have been vile, and that as for your sinful acts they are ten thousand times more wicked than ever you believed them to be? I will not believe that you have ever repented unless you have first received divine illumination. I cannot expect a blind eye to see the filth upon a black hand, nor can I ever believe that the understanding which has never been enlightened can detect the sin which has stained your daily life.

Next to illumination, comes humiliation. The soul having seen itself, bows before God, strips itself of all its vain boasting, and lays itself flat on its face before the throne of mercy. It could talk proudly once of merit, but now it dares not pronounce the word. Once it could boast itself before God, with "God, I thank thee that I am not as other men are"; but now it stands in the distance, and smites upon its breast, crying, "God be merciful to me a sinner." Now the haughty eye, the proud look, which God abhorreth, are cast away, and the eye, instead thereof, becomes a channel of tears—its floods are perpetual, it mourneth, it weepeth, and the soul crieth out both day and night before God, for it is vexed with itself, because it has vexed the Holy Spirit, and is grieved within itself because it hath grieved the Most High. Here if I had to depict penitence, I should borrow the picture of the men of Calais before our conquering king. There they kneel, with ropes about their necks, clad in garments of sackcloth, and ashes cast about their heads, confessing that they deserve to die; but stretching out their hands they implore mercy; and one who seems the personification of the angel of mercy—or rather, of Christ Jesus, the God of mercy—stands pleading with the king to spare their lives. Sinner, thou hast never repented unless that rope has been about thy neck after a spiritual fashion, if thou hast not felt that hell is thy just desert, and that if God banish thee for ever from himself, to the place where hope and peace can never come, he has only done with thee what thou hast richly earned. If thou hast not felt that the flames of hell are the ripe harvest which thy sins have sown, thou hast never yet repented at all. We must acknowledge the justice of the penalty as well as the guilt of the sin, or else it is but a mock repentance which we pretend to possess. Down on thy face, sinner, down on thy face; put away thine ornaments from thee, that he may know what to do with thee. No more anoint thine head and wash thy face, but fast and bow thy head and mourn. Thou hast made heaven mourn, thou hast made earth sad, thou hast digged hell for thyself. Confess thine iniquity with shame, and with confusion of face; bow down before the God of mercy and acknowledge that if he spare thee it will be his free mercy that shall do it; but if he destroy thee, thou shalt not have one word to say against the justice of the solemn sentence. Such a stripping does the Holy Spirit give, when he works this repentance, that men sometimes under it sink so low as even to long for death in order to escape from the burden which soul-humiliation has cast upon them. I do not desire that you should have that terror, but I do pray that you may have no boasting left, that you may stop your mouth and feel that if now the judgment hour were set, and the judgment day were come, you must stand speechless, even though God should say, "Depart, ye cursed, into everlasting fire in hell." Without this I say there is no genuine evangelical repentance.

The third ingredient is detestation. The soul must go a step further than mere sorrow; it must come to hate sin, to hate the very shadow of it, to hate the house where once sin and it were boon companions, to hate the bed of pleasure and all its glittering tapestries, yea, to hate the very garments spotted with the flesh. There is no repentance where a man can talk lightly of sin, much less where he can speak tenderly and lovingly of it. When sin cometh to thee delicately, like Agag, saying, "Surely the bitterness of death is past," if thou hast true repentance it will rise like Samuel and hew thy Agag in pieces before the Lord. As long as thou harbourest one idol in thy heart, God will never dwell there. Thou must break not only the images of wood and of stone, but of silver and of gold; yea, the golden calf itself, which has been thy chief idolatry, must be ground in powder and mingled in the bitter water of penitence, and thou must be made to drink thereof. There is such a loathing of sin in the soul of the true penitent that he cannot bear its name. If you were to compel him to enter its palaces he would be wretched. A penitent cannot bear himself in the house of the profane. He feels as if the house must fall upon him. In the assembly of the wicked he would be like a dove in the midst of ravenous kites. As well may the sheep lick blood with the wolf, as well may the dove be comrade at the vulture's feast of carrion, as a penitent sinner revel in sin. Through infirmity he may slide into it, but through grace he will rise out of it and abhor even his clothes in which he has fallen into the ditch (Job 9:31). The sinner unrepentant, like the sow, wallows in the mire; but the penitent sinner, like the swallow, may sometimes dip his wings in the limpid pool of iniquity, but he is aloft again, twittering forth with the chattering of the swallow most pitiful words of penitence, for he grieves that he should have so debased himself and sinned against his God. My hearer, if thou dost not so hate thy sins as to be ready to give them all up—if thou art not willing now to hang them on Haman's gallows a hundred and twenty cubits high—if thou canst not shake them off from thee as Paul did the viper from his hand, and shake it into the fire with detestation, then, I say, thou knowest not the grace of God in truth; for if thou lovest sin thou lovest neither God nor thyself, but thou choosest thine own damnation. Thou art in friendship with death and in league with hell; God deliver thee from this wretched state of heart, and bring thee to detest thy sin.

There lacks one more ingredient yet. We have had illumination, humiliation, and detestation. There must be another thing, namely, a thorough transformation, for—

Repentance is to leave
   The sins we loved before,
And show that we in earnest grieve
   By doing so no more.

The penitent man reforms his outward life. The reform is not partial, but in heart, it is universal and complete.

Infirmity may mar it, but grace will always be striving against human infirmity, and the man will hate and abandon every false way. Tell me not, deceptive tradesman, that you have repented of your sin while lying placards are still upon your goods. Tell me not, thou who wast once a drunkard, that thou hast turned to God while yet the cup is dear to thee, and thou canst still wallow in it by excess. Come not to me and say I have repented, thou avaricious wretch, whilst thou art yet grinding thine almost cent, per cent, out of some helpless tradesman whom thou hast taken like a spider in thy net. Come not to me and say thou are forgiven, when thou still harboureth revenge and malice against thy brother, and speaketh against thine own mother's son. Thou liest to thine own confusion. Thy face is as the whore's forehead that is brazen, if thou darest to say "I have repented," when thine arms are up to the elbow in the filth of thine iniquity. Nay, man, God will not forgive your lusts while you are still revelling in the bed of your uncleanness. And do you imagine he will forgive your drunken feasts while you are still sitting at the glutton's table! Shall he forgive your profanity when your tongue is still quivering with an oath? Think you that God shall forgive your daily transgressions when you repeat them again, and again, and again, wilfully plunging into the mire? He will wash thee, man, but he will not wash thee for the sake of permitting thee to plunge in again and defile thyself once more. "Well," do I hear you say, "I do feel that such a change as that has taken place in me." I am glad to hear it, my dear sir; but I must ask you a further question. Divine transformation is not merely in act but in the very soul; the new man not only does not sin as he used to do, but he does not want to sin as he used to do. The flesh-pots of Egypt sometimes send up a sweet smell in his nostrils, and when he passes by another man's house, where the leek, and garlic, and onion are steaming in the air, he half wishes to go back again to his Egyptian bondage, but in a moment he checks himself, saying, "No, no; the heavenly manna is better than this; the water out of the rock is sweeter than the waters of the Nile, and I cannot return to my old slavery under my old tyrant." There may be insinuations of Satan, but his soul rejects them, and agonizes to cast them out. His very heart longs to be free from every sin, and if he could be perfect he would. There is not one sin he would spare. If you want to give him pleasure, you need not ask him to go to your haunt of debauchery; it would be the greatest pain to him you could imagine. It is not only his customs and manners, but his nature that is changed. You have not put new leaves on the tree, but there is a new root to it. It is not merely new branches, but there is a new trunk altogether, and new sap, and there will be new fruit as the result of this newness. A glorious transformation is wrought by a gracious God. His penitence has become so real and so complete that the man is not the man he used to be. He is a new creature in Christ Jesus. If you are renewed by grace, and were to meet your old self, I am sure you would be very anxious to get out of his company. "No," say you, "no, sir, I cannot accompany you." "Why, you used to swear"! "I cannot now." "Well, but," says he, "you and I are very near companions." "Yes, I know we are, and I wish we were not. You are a deal of trouble to me every day. I wish I could be rid of you for ever." "But," says Old Self, "you used to drink very well." "Yes, I know it. I know thou didst, indeed, Old Self. Thou couldst sing a song as merrily as any one.

Thou wast ringleader in all sorts of vice, but I am no relation of thine now. Thou art of the old Adam, and I of the new Adam. Thou art of thine old father, the devil; but I have another—my Father, who is in heaven." I tell you, brethren, there is no man in the world you will hate so much as your old self, and there will be nothing you will so much long to get rid of as that old man who once was dragging you down to hell, and who will try his hand at it over and over again every day you live, and who will accomplish it yet, unless that divine grace which has made you a new man shall keep you a new man even to the end.

Good Rowland Hill, in his "Village Dialogues," gives the Christian, whom he describes in the first part of the book, the name of Thomas Newman. Ah! and everyman who goes to heaven must have the name of new-man. We must not expect to enter there unless we are created anew in Christ Jesus unto good works, which God hath before ordained that we should walk in them. I have thus, as best I could, feeling many and very sad distractions in my own mind, endeavored to explain the essentials of true repentance—illumination, humiliation, detestation, transformation. The endings of the words, though they are long words may commend them to your attention and assist you to retain them.

III. And now, with all brevity, let me notice, in the third place, the COMPANIONS of true repentance.

Her first companion is faith. There was a question once asked by the old Puritan divines—Which was first in the soul, Faith or Repentance? Some said that a man could not truly repent of sin until he believed in God, and had some sense of a Saviour's love. Others said a man could not have faith till he had repented of sin; for he must hate sin before he could trust Christ. So a good old minister who was present made the following remark: "Brethren," said he, "I don't think you can ever settle this question. It would be something like asking whether, when an infant is born, the circulation of the blood, or the beating of the pulse can be first observed"? Said he, "It seems to me that faith and repentance are simultaneous. They come at the same moment. There could be no true repentance without faith. There never was yet true faith without sincere repentance." We endorse that opinion. I believe they are like the Siamese twins; they are born together, and they could not live asunder, but must die if you attempt to separate them. Faith always walks side by side with his weeping sister, true Repentance. They are born in the same house at the same hour, and they will live in the same heart every day, and on your dying bed, while you will have faith on the one hand to draw the curtain of the next world, you will have repentance, with its tears, as it lets fall the curtain upon the world from which you are departing. You will have at the last moment to weep over your own sins, and yet you shall see through that tear the place where tears are washed away. Some say there is no faith in heaven. Perhaps there is not. If there be none, then there will be no repentance, but if there be faith there will be repentance, for where faith lives, repentance must live with it. They are so united, so married and allied together, that they never can be parted, in time or in eternity. Hast thou, then, faith in Jesus? Does thy soul look up and trust thyself in his hands? If so, then hast thou the repentance that needeth not to be repented of.

There is another sweet thing which always goes with repentance, just as Aaron went with Moses, to be spokesman for him, for you must know that Moses was slow of speech, and so is repentance. Repentance has fine eyes, but stammering lips. In fact, it usually happens that repentance speaks through her eyes and cannot speak with her lips at all, except her friend—who is a good spokesman—is near; he is called, Mr. Confession. This man is noted for his open breastedness. He knows something of himself, and he tells all that he knows before the throne of God. Confession keeps back no secrets. Repentance sighs over the sin—confession tells it out. Repentance feels the sin to be heavy within—confession plucks it forth and indicts it before the throne of God. Repentance is the soul in travail—confession delivers it. My heart is ready to burst, and there is a fire in my bones through repentance—confession gives the heavenly fire a vent, and my soul flames upward before God. Repentance, alone, hath groanings which cannot be uttered—confession is the voice which expresses the groans. Now then, hast thou made confession of thy sin—not to man, but to God? If thou hast, then believe that thy repentance cometh from him, and it is a godly sorrow that needeth not to be repented of.

Holiness is evermore the bosom friend of penitence. Fair angel, clad in pure white linen, she loves good company and will never stay in a heart where repentance is a stranger. Repentance must dig the foundations, but holiness shall erect the structure, and bring forth the topstone. Repentance is the clearing away of the rubbish of the past temple of sin; holiness builds the new temple which the Lord our God shall inherit.

Repentance and desires after holiness never can be separated.

Yet once more—wherever repentance is, there cometh also with it, peace. As Jesus walked upon the waters of Galilee, and said, "Peace, be still," so peace walks over the waters of repentance, and brings quiet and calm into the soul. If thou wouldst shake the thirst of thy soul, repentance must be the cup out of which thou shalt drink, and then sweet peace shall be the blessed effect. Sin is such a troublesome companion that it will always give thee the heartache till thou hast turned it out by repentance, and then thy heart shall rest and be still. Sin is the rough wind that tears through the forest, and sways every branch of the trees to and fro; but after penitence hath come into the soul the wind is hushed, and all is still, and the birds sing in the branches of the trees which just now creaked in the storm. Sweet peace repentance ever yields to the man who is the possessor of it. And now what sayest thou my hearer—to put each point personally to thee—hast thou had peace with God? If not, never rest till thou hast had it, and never believe thyself to be saved till thou feelest thyself to be reconciled. Be not content with the mere profession of the head, but ask that the peace of God which passeth all understanding, may keep your hearts and minds through Jesus Christ.

IV. And now I come to my fourth and last point, namely, the EXCELLENCIES of repentance.

I shall somewhat surprise you, perhaps, if I say that one of the excellencies of repentance lies in its pleasantness. "Oh"! you say, "but it is bitter"! Nay, say I, it is sweet. At least, it is bitter when it is alone, like the waters of Marah; but there is a tree called the cross, which if thou canst put into it, it will be sweet, and thou wilt love to drink of it. At a school of mutes who were both deaf and dumb, the teacher put the following question to her pupils:—

"What is the sweetest emotion"? As soon as the children comprehended the question, they took their slates and wrote their answers. One girl in a moment wrote down "Joy." As soon as the teacher saw it, she expected that all would write the same, but another girl, more thoughtful, put her hand to her brow, and she wrote "Hope." Verily, the girl was not far from the mark. But the next one, when she brought up her slate, had written "Gratitude," and this child was not wrong. Another one, when she brought up her slate, had written "Love," and I am sure she was right. But there was one other who had written in large characters,—and as she brought up her slate the tear was in her eye, showing she had written what she felt,—"Repentance is the sweetest emotion." And I think she was right. Verily, in my own case, after that long drought, perhaps longer than Elisha's three years in which the heavens poured forth no rain, when I saw but one tear of penitence coming from my hard, hard soul—it was such a joy! There have been times when you know you have done wrong, but when you could cry over it you have felt happy. As one weeps for his firstborn, so have you wept over your sin, and in that very weeping you have had your peace and your joy restored. I am a living witness that repentance is exceeding sweet when mixed with divine hope, but repentance without hope is hell. It is hell to grieve for sin with the pangs of bitter remorse, and yet to know that pardon can never come, and mercy never be vouchsafed. Repentance, with the cross before its eyes, is heaven itself; at least, if not heaven, it is so next door to it, that standing on the wet threshold I may see within the pearly portals, and sing the song of the angels who rejoice within. Repentance, then, has this excellency, that it is very sweet to the soul which is made to lie beneath its shadow.

Besides this excellency, it is specially sweet to God as well as to men. "A broken and a contrite heart, O God, thou wilt not despise." When St. Augustine lay a-dying, he had this verse always fixed upon the curtains, so that as often as he awoke, he might read it—"A broken and a contrite heart, O God, thou wilt not despise." When you despise yourselves, God honours you; but as long as you honour yourselves, God despises you. A whole heart is a scentless thing; but when it is broken and bruised, it is like that precious spice which was burned as holy incense in the ancient tabernacle. When the blood of Jesus is sprinkled on them, even the songs of the angels, and the vials full of odours sweet that smoke before the throne of the Most High, are not more agreeable to God than the sighs, and groans, and tears of the brokenhearted soul. So, then, if thou wouldest be pleasing with God, come before him with many and many a tear: "To humble souls and broken hearts God with his grace is ever nigh; Pardon and hope his love imparts, When men in deep contrition lie. He tells their tears, he counts their groans, His Son redeems their souls from death; His Spirit heals their broken bones, They in his praise employ their breath." John Bunyan, in his "Siege of Mansoul," when the defeated townsmen were seeking pardon, names Mr. Wet-eyes as the intercessor with the king. Mr. Wet-eyes—good Saxon word! I hope we know Mr. Wet-eyes, and have had him many times in our house, for if he cannot intercede with God, yet Mr. Wet-eyes is a great friend with the Lord Jesus Christ, and Christ will undertake his case, and then we shall prevail. So have I set forth, then, some, but very few, of the excellencies of repentance. And now, my dear hearers, have you repented of Sin? Oh, impenitent soul, if thou dost not weep now, thou wilt have to weep for ever. The heart that is not broken now, must be broken for ever upon the wheel of divine vengeance. Thou must now repent, or else for ever smart for it. Turn or burn—it is the Bible's only alternative. If thou repentest, the gate of mercy stands wide open. Only the Spirit of God bring thee on thy knees in self-abasement, for Christ's cross stands before thee, and he who bled upon it bids thee look at him. Oh, sinner, obey the divine bidding. But, if your heart be hard, like that of the stubborn Jews in the days of Moses, take heed, lest,—

> The Lord in vengeance dressed,
>   Shall lift his head and swear,—
>   You that despised my promised rest,
>   Shall have no portion there.

At any rate, sinner, if thou wilt not repent, there is one here who will, and that is myself. I repent that I could not preach to you with more earnestness this morning, and throw my whole soul more thoroughly into my pleading with you. the Lord God, whom I serve, is my constant witness that there is nothing I desire so much as to see your hearts broken on account of sin; and nothing has gladdened my heart so much as the many instances lately vouchsafed of the wonders God is doing in this place. There have been men who have stepped into this Hall, who had never entered a place of worship for a score years, and here the Lord has met with them, and I believe, if I could speak the word, there are hundreds who would stand up now, and say, "'Twas here the Lord met with me. I was the chief of sinners; the hammer struck my heart and broke it, and now it has been bound up again by the finger of divine mercy, and I tell it unto sinners, and tell it to this assembled congregation, there have been depths of mercy found that have been deeper than the depths of my iniquity." This day there will be a soul delivered; this morning there will be, I do not doubt, despite my weakness, a display of the energy of God, and the power of the Spirit; some drunkard shall be turned from the error of his ways; some soul, who was trembling on the very jaws of hell, shall look to him who is the sinner's hope, and find peace and pardon—ay, at this very hour. So be it, O Lord, and thine shall be the glory, world without end.

Christ Our Passover

A Sermon (No. 54) Delivered on
Sabbath Evening, December 2, 1855,
by the REV. C. H. SPURGEON
At New Park Street Chapel, Southwark.

"For even Christ our passover is sacrificed for us."
—1 Corinthians 5:7.

The more you read the Bible, and the more you meditate upon it, the more you will be astonished with it. He who is but a casual reader of the Bible, does not know the height, the depth, the length and breadth of the mighty meanings contained in its pages. There are certain times when I discover a new vein of thought, and I put my hand to my head and say in astonishment, "Oh, it is wonderful I never saw this before in the Scriptures." You will find the Scriptures enlarge as you enter them; the more you study them the less you will appear to know of them, for they widen out as we approach them. Especially will you find this the case with the typical parts of God's Word. Most of the historical books were intended to be types either of dispensations, or experiences, or offices of Jesus Christ. Study the Bible with this as a key, and you will not blame Herbert when he calls it "not only the book of God, but the God of books." One of the most interesting points of the Scriptures is their constant tendency to display Christ; and perhaps one of the most beautiful figures under which Jesus Christ is ever exhibited in sacred writ, is the Passover Paschal Lamb. It is Christ of whom we are about to speak to-night.

Israel was in Egypt, in extreme bondage; the severity of their slavery had continually increased till it was so oppressive that their incessant groans went up to heaven. God who avenges his own elect, though they cry day and night unto him, at last, determined that he would direct a fearful blow against Egypt's king and Egypt's nation, and deliver his own people. We can picture the anxieties and the anticipations of Israel, but we can scarcely sympathize with them, unless we as Christians have had the same deliverance from spiritual Egypt. Let us, brethren, go back to the day in our experience, when we abode in the land of Egypt, working in the brick-kilns of sin, toiling to make ourselves better, and finding it to be of no avail; let us recall that memorable night, the beginning of months, the commencement of a new life in our spirit, and the beginning of an altogether new era in our soul. The Word of God struck the blow at our sin; he gave us Jesus Christ our sacrifice; and in that night we went out of Egypt. Though we have passed through the wilderness since then, and have fought the Amalekites, have trodden on the fiery serpent, have been scorched by the heat and frozen by the snows, yet we have never since that time gone back to Egypt; although our hearts may sometimes have desired the leeks, the onions, and the flesh-pots of Egypt, yet we have never been brought into slavery since then. Come, let us keep the Passover this night, and think of the night when the Lord delivered us out of Egypt. Let us behold our Saviour Jesus as the Paschal Lamb on which we feed; yea, let us not only look at him as such, but let us sit down to-night at his table, let us eat of his flesh and drink of his blood; for his flesh is meat indeed, and his blood is drink indeed. In holy solemnity let our hearts approach that ancient supper; let us go back to Egypt's darkness, and by holy contemplation behold, instead of the destroying angel, the angel of the covenant, at the head of the feast,—"the Lamb of God which taketh away the sins of the world."

I shall not have time to-night to enter into the whole history and mystery of the Passover; you will not understand me to be to-night preaching concerning the whole of it; but a few prominent points therein as a part of them. It would require a dozen sermons to do so; in fact a book as large as Caryl upon Job—if we could find a divine equally prolix and equally sensible. But we shall first of all look at the Lord Jesus Christ, and show how he corresponds with the Paschal Lamb, and endeavour to bring you to the two points—of having his blood sprinkled on you, and having fed on him.

I. First, then, JESUS CHRIST IS TYPIFIED HERE UNDER THE PASCHAL LAMB; and should there be one of the seed of Abraham here who has never seen Christ to be the Messiah, I beg his special attention to that which I am to advance, when I speak of the Lord Jesus as none other than the Lamb of God slain for the deliverance of his chosen people. Follow me with your Bibles, and open first at the 12th chapter of Exodus.

We commence, first of all, with the victim—the lamb. How fine a picture of Christ. No other creature could so well have typified him who was holy, harmless, undefiled, and separate from sinners. Being also the emblem of sacrifice, it most sweetly pourtrayed our Lord and Saviour Jesus Christ. Search natural history through, and though you will find other emblems which set forth different characteristics of his nature, and admirably display him to our souls, yet there is none which seems so appropriate to the person of our beloved Lord as that of the Lamb. A child would at once perceive the likeness between a lamb and Jesus Christ, so gentle and innocent, so mild and harmless, neither hurting others, nor seeming to have the power to resent an injury. "A humble man before his foes, a weary man and full of woes." What tortures the sheepish race have received from us! how are they, though innocent, continually slaughtered for our food! Their skin is dragged from their backs, their wool is shorn to give us a garment. And so the Lord Jesus Christ, our glorious Master, doth give us his garments that we may be clothed with them; he is rent in sunder for us; his very blood is poured out for our sins; harmless and holy, a glorious sacrifice for the sins of all his children. Thus the Paschal Lamb might well convey to the pious Hebrew the person of a suffering, silent, patient, harmless Messiah.

Look further down. It was a lamb without blemish. A blemished lamb, if it had the smallest speck of disease, the least wound, would not have been allowed for a Passover. The priest would not have suffered it to be slaughtered, nor would God have accepted the sacrifice at his hands. It must be a lamb without blemish. And was not Jesus Christ even such from his birth? Unblemished, born of the pure virgin Mary, begotten of the Holy Ghost, without a taint of sin; his soul was pure, and spotless as the driven snow, white, clear, perfect; and his life was the same. In him was no sin. He took our infirmities and bore our sorrows on the cross. He was in all points tempted as we are, but there was that sweet exception, "yet without sin." A lamb without blemish. Ye who have known the Lord, who have tasted of his grace, who have held fellowship with him, doth not your heart acknowledge that he is a lamb without blemish? Can ye find any fault with your Saviour? Have you aught to lay to his charge? Hath his truthfulness departed? Have his words been broken? Have his promises failed? Has he forgotten his engagements? And, in any respect, can you find in him any blemish? Ah, no! he is the unblemished lamb, the pure, the spotless, the immaculate, "the Lamb of God who taketh away the sin of the world;" and in him there is no sin.

Go on further down the chapter. "Your lamb shall be without blemish, a male of the first year." I need not stop to consider the reason why the male was chosen; we only note that it was to be a male of the first year. Then it was in its prime then its strength was unexhausted, then its power was just ripened into maturity and perfection, God would not have an untimely fruit. God would not have that offered which had not come to maturity. And so our Lord Jesus Christ had just come to the ripeness of manhood when he was offered. At 34 years of age was he sacrificed for our sins; he was then hale and strong, although his body may have been emaciated by suffering, and his face more marred than that of any other man, yet was he then in the perfection of manhood. Methinks I see him then. His goodly beard flowing down upon his breast; I see him with his eyes full of genius, his form erect, his mien majestic, his energy entire, his whole frame in full development,—a real man, a magnificent man—fairer than the sons of men; a Lamb not only without blemish, but with all his powers fully brought out. Such was Jesus Christ—a Lamb of the first year—not a boy, not a lad, not a young man, but a full man, that he might give his soul unto us. He did not give himself to die for us when he was a youth, for he would not then have given all he was to be; he did not give himself to die for us when he was in old age, for then would he have given himself when he was in decay; but just in his maturity, in his very prime, then Jesus Christ our Passover was sacrificed for us. And, moreover, at the time of his death, Christ was full of life, for we are informed by one of the evangelists that "he cried with a loud voice and gave up the ghost." This is a sign that Jesus did not die through weakness, nor through decay of nature. His soul was strong within him; he was still the Lamb of the first year. Still was he mighty; he could, if he pleased, even on the cross, have unlocked his hands from their iron bolts; and descending from the tree of infamy, have driven his astonished foes before him, like deer scattered by a lion, yet did he meekly yield obedience unto death. My soul; canst thou not see thy Jesus here, the unblemished Lamb of the first year, strong and mighty? And, O my heart! does not then though rise up—if Jesus consecrated himself to thee when he was thus in all his strength and vigour, should not I in youth dedicate myself to him?

And if I am in manhood, how am I doubly bound to give my strength to him? And if I am in old age, still should I seek while the little remains, to consecrate that little to him. If he gave his all to me, which was much, should I not give my little all to him? Should I not feel bound to consecrate myself entirely to his service, to lay body, soul, and spirit, time, talents, all upon his altar. And though I am not an unblemished lamb, yet I am happy that as the leavened cake was accepted with the sacrifice, though never burned with it—I, though a leavened cake, may be offered on the altar with my Lord and Saviour, the Lord's burnt offering, and so, though impure, and full of leaven, I may be accepted in the beloved, an offering of a sweet savour, acceptable unto the Lord my God. Here is Jesus, beloved, a Lamb without blemish, a Lamb of the first year!

The subject now expands and the interest deepens. Let me have your very serious consideration to the next point, which has much gratified me in its discovery and which will instruct you in the relation. In the 6th verse of the 12th chapter of Exodus we are told that this lamb which should be offered at the Passover was to be selected four days before its sacrifice, and to be kept apart:—"In the tenth day of this month they shall take to them every man a lamb, according to the house of their fathers, a lamb for an house: and if the household be too little for the lamb, let him and his neighbour next unto his house take it according to the number of the souls; every man according to his eating shall make your count for the lamb." The 6th verse says, "And ye shall keep it until the fourteenth day of the same month." For four days this lamb, chosen to be offered, was taken away from the rest of the flock and kept alone by itself, for two reasons: partly that by its constant bleatings they might be put in remembrance of the solemn feast which was to be celebrated; and moreover, that during the four days they might be quite assured that it had no blemish, for during that time it was subject to constant inspection, in order that they might be certain that it had no hurt or injury that would render it unacceptable to the Lord. And now, brethren, a remarkable fact flashes before you—just as this lamb was separated four days, the ancient allegories used to say that Christ was separated four years. Four years after he left his father's house he went into the wilderness, and was tempted of the devil. Four years after his baptism he was sacrificed for us. But there is another, better than that:— About four days before his crucifixion, Jesus Christ rode in triumph through the streets of Jerusalem. He was thus openly set apart as being distinct from mankind. He, on the ass, rode up to the temple, that all might see him to be Judah's Lamb, chosen of God, and ordained from the foundation of the world. And what is more remarkable still, during those four days, you will see, if you turn to the Evangelists, at your leisure, that as much is recorded of what he did and said as through all the other part of his life. During those four days, he upbraided the fig tree, and straightway it withered; it was then that he drove the buyers and sellers from the temple; it was then that he rebuked the priests and elders, by telling them the similitude of the two sons, one of whom said he would go, and did not, and the other who said he would not go, and went; it was then that he narrated the parable of the husbandmen, who slew those who were sent to them; afterwards he gave the parable of the marriage of the king's son. Then comes his parable concerning the man who went unto the feast, not having on a wedding garment; and then also, the parable concerning the ten virgins, five of whom were very wise, and five of whom were foolish; then comes the chapter of very striking denunciations against the Pharisees:—"Woe unto you O ye blind Pharisees! cleanse first that which is within the cup and platter;" and then also comes that long chapter of prophecy concerning what should happen at the siege of Jerusalem, and an account of the dissolution of the world: "Learn a parable of the fig-tree: when his branch is yet tender and putteth forth leaves, ye know that summer is nigh.: But I will not trouble you by telling you here that at the same time he gave them that splendid description of the day of judgment, when the sheep shall be divided from the goats. In fact, the most splendid utterances of Jesus were recorded as having taken place within these four days. Just as the lamb separated from its fellows, did bleat more than ever during the four days, so did Jesus during those four days speak more; and if you want to find a choice saying of Jesus, turn to the account of the last four days' ministry to find it. There you will find that chapter, "Let not your hearts be troubled;" there also, his great prayer, "Father, I will;" and so on. The greatest things he did, he did in the last four days when he was set apart.

And there is one more thing to which I beg your particular attention, and that is, that during those four days I told you that the lamb was subject to the closest scrutiny, so, also, during those four days, it is singular to relate, that Jesus Christ was examined by all classes of persons. It was during those four days that the lawyer asked him which was the greatest commandment? and he said, "Thou shalt love the Lord thy God with all thy heart and with all thy soul, and with all thy might; and thou shalt love thy neighbour as thyself." It was then that the Herodians came and questioned him about the tribute money; it was then that the Pharisees tempted him; it was then, also, the Sadducees tried him upon the subject of the resurrection. He was tried by all classes and grades—Herodians, Pharisees, Sadducees, lawyers, and the common people. It was during these four days that he was examined: but how did he come forth? An immaculate Lamb! The officers said, "never man spake like this man." His foes found none who could even bear false witness against him, such as agreed together; and Pilate declared, "I find no fault in him." He would not have been fit for the Paschal Lamb had a single blemish have been discovered, but "I find no fault in him," was the utterance of the great chief magistrate, who thereby declared that the Lamb might be eaten at God's Passover, the symbol and the means of the deliverance of God's people. O beloved! you have only to study the Scriptures to find out wondrous things in them; you have only to search deeply, and you stand amazed at their richness. You will find God's Word to be a very precious word; the more you live by it and study it, the more will it be endeared to your minds.

But the next thing we must mark is the place where this lamb was to be killed, which peculiarly sets forth that it must be Jesus Christ. The first Passover was held in Egypt, the second Passover was held in the wilderness; but we do not read that there were more than these two Passovers celebrated until the Israelites came to Canaan. And then, if you turn to a passage in Deuteronomy, the 16th chapter, you will find that God no longer allowed them to slay the Lamb in their own houses but appointed a place for its celebration. In the wilderness, they brought their offerings to the tabernacle where the lamb was slaughtered; but at its first appointment in Egypt, of course they had no special place to which they took the lamb to be sacrificed. Afterwards, we read in the 16th of Deuteronomy, and the 5th verse, "Thou mayest not sacrifice the Passover within any of thy gates, which the Lord thy God giveth thee; but at the place which the Lord thy God shall chose to place his name in, there thou shalt sacrifice the Passover at even at the going down of the sun, at the season that thou camest forth out of Egypt." It was in Jerusalem that men ought to worship, for salvation was of the Jews; there was God's palace, there his altar smoked, and there only might the Paschal Lamb be killed. So was our blessed Lord led to Jerusalem. The infuriated throng dragged him along the city. In Jerusalem our Lamb was sacrificed for us; it was at the precise spot where God had ordained that it should be. Oh! if that mob who gathered round him at Nazareth had been able to push him headlong down the hill, then Christ could not have died at Jerusalem; but as he said, "a prophet cannot perish out of Jerusalem," so was it true that the King of all prophets could not do otherwise,—the prophecies concerning him would not have been fulfilled. "Thou shalt kill the lamb in the place the Lord thy God shall appoint." He was sacrificed in the very place. Thus, again you have an incidental proof that Jesus Christ was the Paschal Lamb for his people.

The next point is the manner of his death. I think the manner in which the lamb was to be offered so peculiarly sets forth the crucifixion of Christ, that no other kind of death could by any means have answered all the particulars set down here. First, the lamb was to be slaughtered, and its blood caught in a basin. Usually blood was caught in a golden basin. Then, as soon as it was taken, the priest standing by the altar on which the fat was burning, threw the blood on the fire or cast it at the foot of the altar. You may guess what a scene it was. Ten thousand lambs sacrificed, and the blood poured out in a purple river. Next, the lamb was to be roasted; but it was not to have a bone of its body broken. Now I do say, there is nothing but crucifixion which can answer all these three things. Crucifixion has in it the shedding of blood—the hands and feet were pierced. It has in it the idea of roasting, for roasting signifies a long torment, and as the lamb was for a long time before the fire, so Christ, in crucifixion, was for a long time exposed to a broiling sun, and all the other pains which crucifixion engenders. Moreover not a bone was broken; which could not have been the case with any other punishment. Suppose it had been possible to put Christ to death in any other way. Sometimes the Romans put criminals to death by decapitation; but by a such death the next is broken. Many martyrs were put to death by having a sword pierced through them; but, while that would have been a bloody death, and not a bone broken necessarily, the torment would not have been long enough to have been pictured by the roasting. So that, take whatever punishment you will—take hanging, which sometimes the Romans practised in the form of strangling, that mode of punishment does not involve shedding of blood, and consequently the requirements would not have been answered. And I do think, any intelligent Jew, reading through this account of the Passover, and then looking at the crucifixion, must be struck by the fact that the penalty and death of the cross by which Christ suffered, must have taken in all these three things. There was blood-shedding; the long continued suffering—the roasting of torture; and then added to that, singularly enough, by God's providence not a bone was broken, but the body was taken down from the cross intact. Some may say that burning might have answered the matter; but there would not have been a shedding of blood in that case, and the bones would have been virtually broken in the fire. Besides the body would not have been preserved entire. Crucifixion was the only death which could answer all of these three requirements. And my faith receives great strength from the fact, that I see my Saviour not only as a fulfilment of the type, but the only one. My heart rejoices to look on him whom I have pierced, and see his blood, as the lamb's blood, sprinkled on my lintel and my door-post, and see his bones unbroken, and to believe that not a bone of his spiritual body shall be broken hereafter; and rejoice, also, to see him roasted in the fire, because thereby I see that he satisfied God for that roasting which I ought to have suffered in the torment of hell for ever and ever.

Christian! I would that I had words to depict in better language; but, as it is, I give thee the undigested thoughts, which thou mayest take home and live upon during the week; for thou wilt find this Paschal Lamb to be an hourly feast, as well as supper, and thou mayest feed upon it continually, till thou comest to the mount of God, where thou shalt see him as he is, and worship him in the Lamb in the midst thereof.

II. HOW WE DERIVE BENEFIT FROM THE BLOOD OF CHRIST. Christ our Passover is slain for us. The Jew could not say that; he could say, a lamb, but "the Lamb," even "Christ our Passover," was not yet become a victim. And here are some of my hearers within these walls to-night who cannot say "Christ our Passover is slain for us." But glory be to God! some of us can. There are not a few here who have laid their hands upon the glorious Scapegoat; and now they can put their hands upon the Lamb also, and they can say, "Yes; it is true, he is not only slain, but Christ our Passover is slain for us." We derive benefit from the death of Christ in two modes: first, by having his blood sprinkled on us for our redemption; secondly, by our eating his flesh for food, regeneration and sanctification. The first aspect in which a sinner views Jesus is that of a lamb slain, whose blood is sprinkled on the door-post and on the lintel. Note the fact, that the blood was never sprinkled on the threshold. It was sprinkled on the lintel, the top of the door, on the side-post, but never on the threshold, for woe unto him who trampleth under foot the blood of the Son of God! Even the priest of Dagon trod not on the threshold of his god, much less will the Christian trample under foot the blood of the Paschal Lamb. But his blood must be on our right hand to be our constant guard, and on our left to be our continual support. We want to have Jesus Christ sprinkled on us. As I told you before, it is not alone the blood of Christ poured out on Calvary that saves a sinner; it is the blood of Christ sprinkled on the heart. Let us turn to the land of Zoan. Do you not think you behold the scene to-night! It is evening. The Egyptians are going homeward—little thinking of what is coming. But just as soon as the sun is set, a lamb is brought into every house. The Egyptian strangers passing by, say, "These Hebrews are about to keep a feast to night," and they retire to their houses utterly careless about it. The father of the Hebrew house takes his lamb, and examining it once more with anxious curiosity, looks it over from head to foot, to see if it has a blemish. He findeth none. "My son," he says to one of them, "bring hither the bason." It is held. He stabs the lamb, and the blood flows into the bason. Do you not think you see the sire, as he commands his matronly wife to roast the lamb before the fire! "Take heed," he says, "that not a bone be broken." Do you see her intense anxiety, as she puts it down to roast, lest a bone should be broken? Now, says the father, "bring a bunch of hyssop." A child brings it. The father dips it into the blood. "Come here, my children, wife and all, and see what I am about to do." He takes the hyssop in his hands, dips it in the blood, and sprinkles it across the lintel and the door-post. His children say, "What mean you by this ordinance?" He answers, "This night the Lord God will pass through to smite the Egyptians, and when he seeth the blood upon the lintel and on the two side posts, the Lord will pass over the door, and will not suffer the destroyer to come into your houses to smite you." The thing is done; the lamb is cooked; the guests are set down to it; the father of the family has supplicated a blessing; they are sitting down to feast upon it. And mark how the old man carefully divides joint from joint, lest a bone should be broken; and he is particular that the smallest child of the family should have some of it to eat, for so the Lord hath commanded. Do you not think you see him as he tells them "it is a solemn night—make haste—in another hour we shall all go out of Egypt." He looks at his hands, they are rough with labour, and clapping them, he cries, "I am not to be a slave any longer." His eldest son, perhaps, has been smarting under the lash, and he says, "Son, you have had the task-master's lash upon you this afternoon; but it is the last time you shall feel it." He looks at them all, with tears in his eyes—"This is the night the Lord God will deliver you." Do you see them with their hats on their heads, with their loins girt, and their staves in their hands? It is the dead of the night. Suddenly they hear a shriek! The father says, "Keep within doors, my children; you will know what it is in a moment." Now another shriek—another shriek—shriek succeeds shriek: they hear perpetual wailing and lamentation. "Remain within," says he, "the angel of death is flying abroad." A solemn silence is in the room, and they can almost hear the wings of the angel flap in the air as he passes their blood-marked door. "Be calm," says the sire, "that blood will save you." The shrieking increases. "Eat quickly, my children," he says again, and in a moment the Egyptians coming, say, "Get thee hence! Get thee hence! We are not for the jewels that you have borrowed. You have brought death into our houses." "Oh!" says a mother, "Go! for God's sake! go. My eldest son lies dead!" "Go!" says a father, "Go! and peace go with you. It were an ill day when your people came into Egypt, and our king began to slay your first-born, for God is punishing us for our cruelty." Ah! see them leaving the land; the shrieks are still heard; the people are busy about their dead. As they go out, a son of Pharaoh is taken away unembalmed, to be buried in one of the pyramids. Presently they see one of their task-master's sons taken away. A happy night for them—when they escape! And do you see, my hearers, a glorious parallel? They had to sprinkle the blood, and also to eat the lamb. Ah! my soul, hast thou e'er had the blood sprinkled on thee? Canst thou say that Jesus Christ is thine? It is not enough to say "he loved the world, and gave his Son," you must say, "He loved me,, and gave himself for me." There is another hour coming, dear friends, when we shall all stand before God's bar; and then God will say, "Angel of death, thou once didst smite Egypt's first born; thou knowest thy prey. Unsheath thy sword." I behold the great gathering, you and I are standing amongst them. It is a solemn moment. All men stand in suspense. There is neither hum nor murmur. The very stars cease to shine lest the light should disturb the air by its motion. All is still. God says, "Has thou sealed those that are mine?" "I have," says Gabriel; "they are sealed by blood every one of them." Then saith he next, "Sweep with thy sword of slaughter! Sweep the Earth! and send the unclothed, the unpurchased, the unwashed ones to the pit." Oh! how shall we feel beloved, when for a moment we see that angel flap his wings? He is just about to fly, "But," will the doubt cross our minds "perhaps he will come to me?" Oh! no; we shall stand and look the angel full in his face. "Bold shall I stand in that great day! For who aught to my charge shall lay? While through thy blood absolved I am From sin's tremendous curse and shame." If we have the blood on us, we shall see the angel coming, we shall smile at him; we shall dare to come even to God's face and say, "Great God! I'm clean! Through Jesus' blood, I'm clean!" But if, my hearer, thine unwashen spirit shall stand unshriven before its maker, if thy guilty soul shall appear with all its black spots upon it, unsprinkled with the purple tide, how wilt thou speak when thou seest flash from the scabbard the angel's sword swift for death, and winged for destruction, and when it shall cleave thee asunder? Methinks I see thee standing now. The angel is sweeping away a thousand there. There is one of thy pot companions. There one with whom thou didst dance and swear. There another, who after attending the same chapel like thee, was a despiser of religion. Now death comes nearer to thee. Just as when the reaper sweeps the field and the next ear trembles because its turn shall come next, I see a brother and a sister swept into the pit. Have I no blood upon me? Then, O rocks! it were kind of you to hide me. Ye have no benevolence in your arms. Mountains! let me find in your caverns some little shelter. But it is all in vain, for vengeance shall cleave the mountains and split the rocks open to find me out. Have I no blood? Have I no hope? Ah! no! he smites me. Eternal damnation is my horrible portion. The depth of the darkness of Egypt for thee, and the horrible torments of the pit from which none can escape! Ah! my dear hearers, could I preach as I could wish, could I speak to you without my lips and with my heart, then would I bid you seek that sprinkled blood, and urge you by the love of your own soul, by everything that is sacred and eternal, to labour to get this blood of Jesus sprinkled on your souls. It is the blood sprinkled that saves a sinner.

But when the Christian gets the blood sprinkled, that is not all he wants. He wants something to feed upon. And, O sweet thought! Jesus Christ is not only a Saviour for sinners, but he is food for them after they are saved. The Paschal Lamb by faith we eat. We live on it. You may tell, my hearers, whether you have the blood sprinkled on the door by this: do you eat the Lamb? Suppose for a moment that one of the old Jews had said in his heart, "I do not see the use of this feasting. It is quite right to sprinkle the blood on the lintel or else the door will not be known; but what good is all this inside? We will have the lamb prepared, and we will not break his bones; but we will not eat of it." And suppose he went and stored the lamb away. What would have been the consequence? Why, the angel of death would have smitten him as well as the rest, even if the blood had been upon him. And if, moreover, that old Jew had said, "there, we will have a little piece of it; but we will have something else to eat, we will have some unleavened bread; we will not turn the leaven out of our houses, but we will have some leavened bread." If they had not consumed the lamb, but had reserved some of it, then the sword of the angel would have found the heart out as well as that of any other man. Oh! dear hearer, you may think you have the blood sprinkled, you may think you are just; but if you do not live on Christ as well as by Christ, you will never be saved by the Paschal Lamb. "Ah!" say some, "we know nothing of this." Of course you don't. When Jesus Christ said, "except ye eat my flesh, and drink my blood, ye have no life in you," there were some that said, "This is a hard saying, who can hear it?" and many from that time went back—and walked no more with him. They could not understand him; but, Christian, dost thou not understand it? Is not Jesus Christ thy daily food? And even with the bitter herbs, is he not sweet food? Some of you, my friends, who are true Christians, live too much on your changing frames and feelings, on your experiences and evidences. Now, that is all wrong. That is just as if a worshipper had gone to the tabernacle and began eating one of the coats that were worn by the priest. When a man lives on Christ's righteousness, it is the same as eating Christ's dress. When a man lives on his frames and feelings, that is as much as if the child of God should live on some tokens that he received in the sanctuary that never were meant for food, but only to comfort him a little. What the Christian lives on is not Christ's righteousness, but Christ; he does not live on Christ's pardon, but on Christ; and on Christ he lives daily, on nearness to Christ. Oh! I do love Christ-preaching. It is not the doctrine of justification that does my heart good, it is Christ, the justifier; it is not pardon that so much makes the Christian's heart rejoice, it is Christ the pardoner; it is not election that I love half so much as my being chosen in Christ ere worlds began; ay! it is not final perseverance that I love so much as the thought that in Christ my life is hid, and that since he gives unto his sheep eternal life, they shall never perish, neither shall any man pluck them out of his hand. Take care, Christian, to eat the Paschal Lamb and nothing else. I tell thee man, if thou eatest that alone, it will be like bread to thee—thy soul's best food. If thou livest on aught else but the Saviour, thou art like one who seeks to live on some weed that grows in the desert, instead of eating the manna that comes down from heaven. Jesus is the manna. In Jesus as well as by Jesus we live. Now, dear friends, in coming to this table, we will keep the Paschal Supper. Once more, by faith, we will eat the Lamb, by holy trust we will come to a crucified Saviour, and feed on his blood, and righteousness, and atonement.

And now, in concluding, let me ask you, are you hoping to be saved my friends? One says, "Well, I don't hardly know; I hope to saved, but I do not know how." Do you know, you imagine I tell you a fiction, when I tell you that people are hoping to be saved by works, but it is not so, it is a reality. In travelling through the country I meet with all sorts of characters, but most frequently with self-righteous persons. How often do I meet with a man who thinks himself quite godly because he attends the church once on a Sunday, and who thinks himself quite righteous because he belongs to the Establishment; as a churchman said to me the other day, "I am a rigid churchman." "I am glad of that," I said to him, "because then you are a Calvinist, if you hold the 'Articles.'" He replied "I don't know about the 'Articles,' I go more by the 'Rubric.'" And so I thought he was more of a formalist than a Christian. There are many persons like that in the world. Another says, "I believe I shall be saved. I don't owe anybody anything; I have never been a bankrupt; I pay everybody twenty shillings in the pound; I never get drunk; and if I wrong anybody at any time, I try to make up for it by giving a pound a year to such-and-such a society; I am as religious as most people; and I believe I shall be saved." That will not do. It is as if some old Jew had said, "We don't want the blood on the lintel, we have got a mahogany lintel; we don't want the blood on the door-post, we have a mahogany door-post." Ah! whatever it was, the angel would have smitten it if it had not had the blood upon it. You may be as righteous as you like: if you have not the blood sprinkled, all the goodness of your door-posts and lintels will be of no avail whatever. "Yes," says another, "I am not trusting exactly there. I believe it is my duty to be as good as I can; but then I think Jesus Christ's mercy will make up the rest. I try to be as righteous as circumstances allow; and I believe that whatever deficiencies there may be, Christ will make them up." That is as if a Jew had said, "Child, bring me the blood," and then, when that was brought, he had said, "bring me a ewer of water;" and then he had taken it and mixed it together, and sprinkled the door-post with it. Why, the angel would have smitten him as well as anyone else, for it is blood, blood, blood, blood! that saves. It is not blood mixed with the water of our poor works; it is blood, blood, blood, blood! and nothing else. And the only way of salvation is by blood. For, without the shedding of blood there is no remission of sin. have precious blood sprinkled upon you, my hearers; trust in precious blood; let your hope be in a salvation sealed with an atonement of precious blood, and you are saved. But having no blood, or having blood mixed with anything else, thou art damned as thou art alive—for the angel shall slay thee, however good and righteous thou mayest be. Go home, then, and think of this: "Christ our Passover is sacrificed for us."

Christ the End of the Law

A Sermon (No. 1325) Delivered on Lord's-Day Morning, November 19th, 1876, by C. H. SPURGEON, At the Metropolitan Tabernacle, Newington.

"For Christ is the end of the law for righteousness to every one that believeth."
—Romans 10:4.

You remember we spoke last Sabbath morning of "the days of the Son of man." Oh that every Sabbath now might be a day of that kind in the most spiritual sense. I hope that we shall endeavour to make each Lord's Day as it comes round a day of the Lord, by thinking much of Jesus by rejoicing much in him, by labouring for him, and by our growingly importunate prayer, that to him may the gathering of the people be.

We may not have very many Sabbaths together, death may soon part us; but while we are able to meet as a Christian assembly, let us never forget that Christ's presence is our main necessity, and let us pray for it and entreat the Lord to vouchsafe that presence always in displays of light, life and love! I become increasingly earnest that every preaching time should be a soul-saving time. I can deeply sympathize with Paul when he said, "My heart's desire and prayer to God for Israel is that they might be saved." We have had so much preaching, but, comparatively speaking, so little believing in Jesus; and if there be no believing in him, neither the law nor the gospel has answered its end, and our labour has been utterly in vain. Some of you have heard, and heard, and heard again, but you have not believed in Jesus. If the gospel had not come to your hearing you could not have been guilty of refusing it. "Have they not heard?" says the apostle. "Yes, verily;" but still "they have not all obeyed the gospel." Up to this very moment there has been no hearing with the inner ear, and no work of faith in the heart, in the case of many whom we love. Dear friends, is it always to be so? How long is it to be so? Shall there not soon come an end of this reception of the outward means and rejection of the inward grace? Will not your soul soon close in with Christ for present salvation? Break! Break, O heavenly day, upon the benighted ones, for our hearts are breaking over them.

The reason why many do not come to Christ is not because they are not earnest, after a fashion, and thoughtful and desirous to be saved, but because they cannot brook God's way of salvation. "They have a zeal for God, but not according to knowledge," We do get them by our exhortation so far on the way that they become desirous to obtain eternal life, but "they have not submitted themselves to the righteousness of God." Mark, "submitted themselves," for it needs submission. Proud man wants to save himself, he believes he can do it, and he will not give over the task till he finds out his own helplessness by unhappy failures. Salvation by grace, to be sued for in forma pauperis, to be asked for as an undeserved boon from free, unmerited grace, this it is which the carnal mind will not come to as long as it can help it: I beseech the Lord so to work that some of you may not be able to help it. And oh, I have been praying that, while this morning I am trying to set forth Christ as the end of the law, God may bless it to some hearts, that they may see what Christ did, and may perceive it to be a great deal better than anything they can do; may see what Christ finished, and may become weary of what they themselves have laboured at so long, and have not even well commenced at this day. Perhaps it may please the Lord to enchant them with the perfection of the salvation that is in Christ Jesus. As Bunyan would say, "It may, perhaps, set their mouths a watering after it," and when a sacred appetite begins it will not be long before the feast is enjoyed. It may be that when they see the raiment of wrought gold, which Jesus so freely bestows on naked souls, they will throw away their own filthy rags which now they hug so closely.

I am going to speak about two things, this morning, as the Spirit of God shall help me: and the first is, Christ in connection with the law—he is "the end of the law for righteousness"; and secondly, ourselves in connection with Christ—"to everyone that believeth Christ is the end of the law for righteousness."

I. First, then, CHRIST IN CONNECTION WITH THE LAW. The law is that which, as sinners, we have above all things cause to dread; for the sting of death is sin, and the strength of sin is the law. Towards us the law darts forth devouring flames, for it condemns us, and in solemn terms appoints us a place among the accursed, as it is written, "Cursed is every one that continueth not in all things that are written in the book of the law to do them." Yet, strange infatuation! like the fascination which attracts the gnat to the candle which burns its wings, men by nature fly to the law for salvation, and cannot be driven from it. The law can do nothing else but reveal sin and pronounce condemnation upon the sinner, and yet we cannot get men away from it, even though we show them how sweetly Jesus stands between them and it. They are so enamoured of legal hope that they cling to it when there is nothing to cling to; they prefer Sinai to Calvary, though Sinai has nothing for them but thunders and trumpet warnings of coming judgment. O that for awhile you would listen anxiously while I set forth Jesus my Lord, that you may see the law in him.

Now, what has our Lord to do with the law? He has everything to do with it, for he is its end for the noblest object, namely, for righteousness. He is the "end of the law." What does this mean? I think it signifies three things: first, that Christ is the purpose and object of the law; secondly, that he is the fulfillment of it; and thirdly, that he is the termination of it.

First, then, our Lord Jesus Christ is the purpose and object of the law. It was given to lead us to him. The law is our schoolmaster to bring us to Christ, or rather our attendant to conduct us to the school of Jesus. The law is the great net in which the fish are enclosed that they may be drawn out of the element of sin. The law is the stormy wind which drives souls into the harbour or refuge. The law is the sheriff's office to shut men up in prison for their sin, concluding them all under condemnation in order that they may look to the free grace of God alone for deliverance. This is the object of the law: it empties that grace may fill, and wounds that mercy may heal. It has never been God's intention towards us, as fallen men, that the law should be regarded as a way to salvation to us, for a way of salvation it can never be. Had man never fallen, had his nature remained as God made it, the law would have been most helpful to him to show him the way in which he should walk: and by keeping it he would have lived, for "he that doeth these things shall live in them." But ever since man has fallen the Lord has not proposed to him a way of salvation by works, for he knows it to be impossible to a sinful creature. The law is already broken; and whatever man can do he cannot repair the damage he has already done: therefore he is out of court as to the hope of merit. The law demands perfection, but man has already fallen short of it; and therefore let him do his best. He cannot accomplish what is absolutely essential. The law is meant to lead the sinner to faith in Christ, by showing the impossibility of any other way. It is the black dog to fetch the sheep to the shepherd, the burning heat which drives the traveller to the shadow of the great rock in a weary land.

Look how the law is adapted to this; for, first of all, it shows man his sin. Read the ten commandments and tremble as you read them. Who can lay his own character down side by side with the two tablets of divine precept without at once being convinced that he has fallen far short of the standard? When the law comes home to the soul it is like light in a dark room revealing the dust and the dirt which else had been unperceived. It is the test which detects the presence of the poison of sin in the soul. "I was alive without the law once," said the apostle, "but when the commandment came sin revived and I died." Our comeliness utterly fades away when the law blows upon it. Look at the commandments, I say, and remember how sweeping they are, how spiritual, how far-reaching. They do not merely touch the outward act, but dive into the inner motive and deal with the heart, the mind, the soul. There is a deeper meaning in the commands than appears upon their surface. Gaze into their depths and see how terrible is the holiness which they require. As you understand what the law demands you will perceive how far you are from fulfilling it, and how sin abounds where you thought there was little or none of it. You thought yourself rich and increased in goods and in no need of anything, but when the broken law visits you, your spiritual bankruptcy and utter penury stare you in the face. A true balance discovers short weight, and such is the first effect of the law upon the conscience of man.

The law also shows the result and mischief of sin. Look at the types of the old Mosaic dispensation, and see how they were intended to lead men to Christ by making them see their unclean condition and their need of such cleansing as only he can give. Every type pointed to our Lord Jesus Christ. If men were put apart because of disease or uncleanness, they were made to see how sin separated them from God and from his people; and when they were brought back and purified with mystic rites in which were scarlet wool and hyssop and the like, they were made to see how they can only be restored by Jesus Christ, the great High Priest. When the bird was killed that the leper might be clean, the need of purification by the sacrifice of a life was set forth. Every morning and evening a lamb died to tell of daily need of pardon, if

God is to dwell with us. We sometimes have fault found with us for speaking too much about blood; yet under the old testament the blood seemed to be everything, and was not only spoken of but actually presented to the eye. What does the apostle tell us in the Hebrews? "Whereupon neither the first testament was dedicated without blood. For when Moses had spoken every precept to all the people according to the law, he took the blood of calves and of goats, with water, and scarlet wool, and hyssop, and sprinkled both the book, and all the people saying, this is the blood of the testament which God hath enjoined unto you. Moreover he sprinkled with blood both the tabernacle, and all the vessels of the ministry. And almost all things are by the law purged with blood; and without shedding of blood is not remission." The blood was on the veil, and on the altar, on the hangings, and on the floor of the tabernacle: no one could avoid seeing it. I resolve to make my ministry of the same character, and more and more sprinkle it with the blood of atonement. Now that abundance of the blood of old was meant to show clearly that sin has so polluted us that without an atonement God is not to be approached: we must come by the way of sacrifice or not at all. We are so unacceptable in ourselves that unless the Lord sees us with the blood of Jesus upon us he must away with us. The old law, with its emblems and figures, set forth many truths as to men's selves and the coming Saviour, intending by every one of them to preach Christ. If any stopped short of him, they missed the intent and design of the law. Moses leads up to Joshua, and the law ends at Jesus.

Turning our thoughts back again to the moral rather than the ceremonial law, it was intended to teach men their utter helplessness. It shows them how short they fall of what they ought to be, and it also shows them, when they look at it carefully, how utterly impossible it is for them to come up to the standard. Such holiness as the law demands no man can reach of himself. "Thy commandment is exceeding broad." If a man says that he can keep the law, it is because he does not know what the law is. If he fancies that he can ever climb to heaven up the quivering sides of Sinai, surely he can never have seen that burning mount at all. Keep the law! Ah, my brethren, while we are yet talking about it we are breaking it; while we are pretending that we can fulfil its letter, we are violating its spirit, for pride as much breaks the law as lust or murder. "Who can bring a clean thing out of an unclean? Not one." "How can he be clean that is born of a woman?" No, soul, thou canst not help thyself in this thing, for since only by perfection thou canst live by the law, and since that perfection is impossible, thou canst not find help in the covenant of works. In grace there is hope, but as a matter of debt there is none, for we do not merit anything but wrath. The law tells us this, and the sooner we know it to be so the better, for the sooner we shall fly to Christ.

The law also shows us our great need—our need of cleansing, cleansing with the water and with the blood. It discovers to us our filthiness, and this naturally leads us to feel that we must be washed from it if we are ever to draw near to God. So the law drives us to accept of Christ as the one only person who can cleanse us, and make us fit to stand within the veil in the presence of the Most High. The law is the surgeon's knife which cuts out the proud flesh that the wound may heal. The law by itself only sweeps and raises the dust, but the gospel sprinkles clean water upon the dust, and all is well in the chamber of the soul. The law kills, the gospel makes alive; the law strips, and then Jesus Christ comes in and robes the soul in beauty and glory. All the commandments, and all the types direct us to Christ, if we will but heed their evident intent. They wean us from self, they put us off from the false basis of self-righteousness, and bring us to know that only in Christ can our help be found. So, first of all, Christ is the end of the law, in that he is its great purpose.

And now, secondly, he is the law's fulfillment. It is impossible for any of us to be saved without righteousness. The God of heaven and earth by immutable necessity demands righteousness of all his creatures. Now, Christ has come to give to us the righteousness which the law demands, but which it never bestows. In the chapter before us we read of "the righteousness which is of faith," which is also called "God's righteousness"; and we read of those who "shall not be ashamed" because they are righteous by believing unto righteousness." What the law could not do Jesus has done. He provides the righteousness which the law asks for but cannot produce. What an amazing righteousness it must be which is as broad and deep and long and high as the law itself. The commandment is exceeding broad, but the righteousness of Christ is as broad as the commandment, and goes to the end of it. Christ did not come to make the law milder, or to render it possible for our cracked and battered obedience to be accepted as a sort of compromise. The law is not compelled to lower its terms, as though it had originally asked too much; it is holy and just and good, and ought not to be altered in one jot or tittle, nor can it be. Our Lord gives the law all it requires, not a part, for that would be an admission that it might justly have been content with less at first. The law claims complete obedience without one spot or speck, failure, or flaw, and Christ has brought in such a righteousness as that, and gives it to his people. The law demands that the righteousness should be without omission of duty and without commission of sin, and the righteousness which Christ has brought is just such an one that for its sake the great God accepts his people and counts them to be without spot or wrinkle or any such thing. The law will not be content without spiritual obedience, mere outward compliances will not satisfy. But our Lord's obedience was as deep as it was broad, for his zeal to do the will of him that sent him consumed him. He says himself, "I delight to do thy will, O my God, yea thy law is within my heart." Such righteousness he puts upon all believers. "By the obedience of one shall many be made righteous"; righteous to the full, perfect in Christ. We rejoice to wear the costly robe of fair white linen which Jesus has prepared, and we feel that we may stand arrayed in it before the majesty of heaven without a trembling thought. This is something to dwell upon, dear friends. Only as righteous ones can we be saved, but Jesus Christ makes us righteous, and therefore we are saved. He is righteous who believeth on him, even as Abraham believed God and it was counted unto him for righteousness. "There is therefore, now no condemnation to them that are in Christ Jesus," because they are made righteous in Christ. Yea, the Holy Spirit by the mouth of Paul challengeth all men, angels, and devils, to lay anything to the charge of God's elect, since Christ hath died. O law, when thou demandest of me a perfect righteousness, I, being a believer, present it to thee; for through Christ Jesus faith is accounted unto me for righteousness. The righteousness of Christ is mine, for I am one with him by faith, and this is the name wherewith he shall be called—"The Lord our righteousness."

Jesus has thus fulfilled the original demands of the law, but you know, brethren, that since we have broken the law there are other demands. For the remission of past sins something more is asked now than present and future obedience. Upon us, on account of our sins, the curse has been pronounced, and a penalty has been incurred. It is written that he "will by no means clear the guilty," but every transgression and iniquity shall have its just punishment and reward. Here, then, let us admire that the Lord Jesus Christ is the end of the law as to penalty. That curse and penalty are awful things to think upon, but Christ has ended all their evil, and thus discharged us from all the consequences of sin. As far as every believer is concerned the law demands no penalty and utters no curse. The believer can point to the Great Surety on the tree of Calvary, and say, "See there, oh law, there is the vindication of divine justice which I offer to thee. Jesus pouring out his heart's blood from his wounds and dying on my behalf is my answer to thy claims, and I know that I shall be delivered from wrath through him." The claims of the law both as broken and unbroken Christ has met: both the positive and the penal demands are satisfied in him. This was a labour worthy of a God, and lo, the incarnate God has achieved it. He has finished the transgression, made an end of sins, made reconciliation for iniquity, and brought in everlasting righteousness. All glory be to his name.

Moreover, not only has the penalty been paid, but Christ has put great and special honour upon the law in so doing. I venture to say that if the whole human race had kept the law of God and not one of them had violated it, the law would not stand in so splendid a position of honour as it does today when the man Christ Jesus, who is also the Son of God, has paid obeisance to it. God himself, incarnate, has in his life, and yet more in his death, revealed the supremacy of law; he has shown that not even love nor sovereignty can set aside justice. Who shall say a word against the law to which the Lawgiver himself submits? Who shall now say that it is too severe when he who made it submits himself to its penalties. Because he was found in fashion as a man, and was our representative, the Lord demanded from his own Son perfect obedience to the law, and the Son voluntarily bowed himself to it without a single word, taking no exception to his task. "Yea, thy law is my delight," saith he, and he proved it to be so by paying homage to it even to the full. Oh wondrous law under which even Emmanuel serves! Oh matchless law whose yoke even the Son of God does not disdain to bear, but being resolved to save his chosen was made under the law, lived under it and died under it, "obedient to death, even the death of the cross."

The law's stability also has been secured by Christ. That alone can remain which is proved to be just, and Jesus has proved the law to be so, magnifying it and making it honourable. He says, "Think not that I am come to destroy the law, or the prophets: I am not come to destroy, but to fulfill. For verily I say unto you, till heaven and earth pass, one jot or one tittle shall in no wise pass from the law, till all be fulfilled." I shall have to show you how he has made an end of the law in another sense, but as to the settlement of the eternal principles of right and wrong, Christ's life and death have achieved this forever. "Yea, we established the law." said Paul, "we do not make void the law through faith." The law is proved to be holy and just by the very gospel of faith, for the gospel which faith believes in does not alter or lower the law, but teaches us how it was to the uttermost fulfilled. Now shall the law stand fast forever and ever, since even to save elect man God will not alter it. He had a people, chosen, beloved, and ordained to life, yet he would not save them at the expense of one principle of right. They were sinful, and how could they be justified unless the law was suspended or changed? Was, then, the law changed? It seemed as if it must be so, if man was to be saved, but Jesus Christ came and showed us how the law could stand firm as a rock, and yet the redeemed could be justly saved by infinite mercy. In Christ we see both mercy and justice shining full orbed, and yet neither of them in any degree eclipsing the other. The law has all it ever asked, as it ought to have, and yet the Father of all mercies sees all his chosen saved as he determined they should be through the death of his Son. Thus I have tried to show you how Christ is the fulfillment of the law to its utmost end. May the Holy Ghost bless the teaching.

And now, thirdly, he is the end of the law in the sense that he is the termination of it. He has terminated it in two senses. First of all, his people are not under it as a covenant of life. "We are not under the law, but under grace." The old covenant as it stood with father Adam was "This do and thou shalt live": its command he did not keep, and consequently he did not live, nor do we live in him, since in Adam all died. The old covenant was broken, and we became condemned thereby, but now, having suffered death in Christ, we are no more under it, but are dead to it. Brethren, at this present moment, although we rejoice to do good works, we are not seeking life through them, we are not hoping to obtain divine favour by our own goodness, nor even to keep ourselves in the love of God by any merit of our own. Chosen, not for our works, but according to the eternal will and good pleasure of God; called, not of works, but by the Spirit of God, we desire to continue in this grace and return no more to the bondage of the old covenant. Since we have put our trust in an atonement provided and applied by grace through Christ Jesus, we are no longer slaves but children, not working to be saved, but saved already, and working because we are saved. Neither that which we do, nor even that which the Spirit of God worketh in us is to us the ground and basis of the love of God toward us, since he loved us from the first, because he would love us, unworthy though we were; and he loves us still in Christ, and looks upon us not as we are in ourselves, but as we are in him; washed in his blood and covered in his righteousness. Ye are not under the law, Christ has taken you from the servile bondage of a condemning covenant and made you to receive the adoption of children, so that now ye cry, Abba, Father.

Again, Christ is the terminator of the law, for we are no longer under its curse. The law cannot curse a believer, it does not know how to do it; it blesses him, yea, and he shall be blessed; for as the law demands righteousness and looks at the believer in Christ, and sees that Jesus has given him all the righteousness it demands, the law is bound to pronounce him blessed. "Blessed is he whose transgression is forgiven, whose sin is covered. Blessed is the man unto whom the Lord imputeth not iniquity, and in whose spirit there is no guile." Oh, the joy of being redeemed from the curse of the law by Christ, who was "made a curse for us," as it is written, "Cursed is every one that hangeth on a tree." Do ye, my brethren, understand the sweet mystery of salvation? Have you ever seen Jesus standing in your place that you may stand in his place? Christ accused and Christ condemned, and Christ led out to die, and Christ smitten of the Father, even to the death, and then you cleared, justified, delivered from the curse, because the curse has spent itself on your Redeemer. You are admitted to enjoy the blessing because the righteousness which was his is now transferred to you that you may be blessed of the Lord world without end. Do let us triumph and rejoice in this evermore. Why should we not? And yet some of God's people get under the law as to their feelings, and begin to fear that because they are conscious of sin they are not saved, whereas it is written, "he justifieth the ungodly." For myself, I love to live near a sinner's Saviour. If my standing before the Lord depended upon what I am in myself and what good works and righteousness I could bring, surely I should have to condemn myself a thousand times a day. But to get away from that and to say, "I have believed in Jesus Christ and therefore righteousness is mine," this is peace, rest, joy, and the beginning of heaven! When one attains to this experience, his love to Jesus Christ begins to flame up, and he feels that if the Redeemer has delivered him from the curse of the law he will not continue in sin, but he will endeavour to live in newness of life. We are not our own, we are bought with a price, and we would therefore glorify God in our bodies and in our spirits, which are the Lord's. Thus much upon Christ in connection with the law.

II. Now, secondly, OURSELVES IN CONNECTION WITH CHRIST—for "Christ is the end of the law to everyone that believeth." Now see the point "to everyone that believeth," there the stress lies. Come, man, woman, dost thou believe? No weightier question can be asked under heaven. "Dost thou believe on the Son of God?" And what is it to believe? It is not merely to accept a set of doctrines and to say that such and such a creed is yours, and there and then to put it on the shelf and forget it. To believe is, to trust, to confide, to depend upon, to rely upon, to rest in. Dost thou believe that Jesus Christ rose from the dead? Dost thou believe that he stood in the sinner's stead and suffered the just for the unjust? Dost thou believe that he is able to save to the uttermost them that come unto God by him? And dost thou therefore lay the whole weight and stress of thy soul's salvation upon him, yea, upon him alone? Ah then, Christ is the end of the law for righteousness to thee, and thou art righteous. In the righteousness of God thou art clothed if thou believest. It is of no use to bring forward anything else if you are not believing, for nothing will avail. If faith be absent the essential thing is wanting: sacraments, prayers, Bible reading, hearings of the gospel, you may heap them together, high as the stars, into a mountain, huge as high Olympus, but they are all mere chaff if faith be not there. It is thy believing or not believing which must settle the matter. Dost thou look away from thyself to Jesus for righteousness? If thou dost he is the end of the law to thee.

Now observe that there is no question raised about the previous character, for it is written, "Christ is the end of the law for righteousness to every one that believeth." But, Lord, this man before he believed was a persecutor and injurious, he raged and raved against the saints and haled them to prison and sought their blood. Yes, beloved friend, and that is the very man who wrote these words by the Holy Ghost, "Christ is the end of the law for righteousness to every one that believeth." So if I address one here this morning whose life has been defiled with every sin, and stained with every transgression we can conceive of, yet I say unto such, remember "all manner of sin and of blasphemy shall be forgiven unto men." If thou believest in the Lord Jesus Christ thine iniquities are blotted out, for the blood of Jesus Christ, God's dear Son, cleanseth us from all sin. This is the glory of the gospel that it is a sinner's gospel; good news of blessing not for those without sin, but for those who confess and forsake it. Jesus came into the world, not to reward the sinless, but to seek and to save that which was lost; and he, being lost and being far from God, who cometh nigh to God by Christ, and believeth in him, will find that he is able to bestow righteousness upon the guilty. He is the end of the law for righteousness to everyone that believeth, and therefore to the poor harlot that believeth, to the drunkard of many years standing that believeth, to the thief, the liar, and the scoffer who believeth, to those who have aforetime rioted in sin, but now turn from it to trust in him. But I do not know that I need mention such cases as these; to me the most wonderful fact is that Christ is the end of the law for righteousness to me, for I believe in him. I know whom I have believed, and I am persuaded that he is able to keep that which I have committed to him until that day.

Another thought arises from the text, and that is, that there is nothing said by way of qualification as to the strength of the faith. He is the end of the law for righteousness to everyone that believeth, whether he is Little Faith or Greatheart. Jesus protects the rear rank as well as the vanguard. There is no difference between one believer and another as to justification. So long as there is a connection between you and Christ the righteousness of God is yours. The link may be very like a film, a spider's line of trembling faith, but, if it runs all the way from the heart to Christ, divine grace can and will flow along the most slender thread. It is marvelous how fine the wire may be that will carry the electric flash. We may want a cable to carry a message across the sea, but that is for the protection of the wire, the wire which actually carries the message is a slender thing. If thy faith be of the mustard-seed kind, if it be only such as tremblingly touches the Saviour's garment's hem, if thou canst only say "Lord, I believe, help thou mine unbelief," if it be but the faith of sinking Peter, or weeping Mary, yet if it be faith in Christ, he will be the end of the law for righteousness to thee as well as to the chief of the apostles.

If this be so then, beloved friends, all of us who believe are righteous. Believing in the Lord Jesus Christ we have obtained the righteousness which those who follow the works of the law know nothing of. We are not completely sanctified, would God we were; we are not quit of sin in our members, though we hate it; but still for all that, in the sight of God, we are truly righteous and being qualified by faith we have peace with God. Come, look up, ye believers that are burdened with a sense of sin. While you chasten yourselves and mourn your sin, do not doubt your Saviour, nor question his righteousness. You are black, but do not stop there, go on to say as the spouse did, "I am black, but comely."

> Though in ourselves deform'd we are,
> And black as Kedar's tents appear,
> Yet, when we put Thy beauties on,
> Fair as the courts of Solomon.

Now, mark that the connection of our text assures us that being righteous we are saved; for what does it say here, "If thou shalt confess with thy mouth the Lord Jesus, and shalt believe in thine heart that God hath raised him from the dead, thou shalt be saved." He who is justified is saved, or what were the benefit of justification? Over thee, O believer, God hath pronounced the verdict "saved," and none shall reverse it. You are saved from sin and death and hell; you are saved even now, with a present salvation; "He hath saved us and called us with a holy calling." Feel the transports of it at this hour. "Beloved, now are we the sons of God."

And now I have done when I have said just this. If any one here thinks he can save himself, and that his own righteousness will suffice before God, I would affectionately beg him not to insult his Saviour. If your righteousness sufficeth, why did Christ come here to work one out? Will you for a moment compare your righteousness with the righteousness of Jesus Christ? What likeness is there between you and him? As much as between an emmet and an archangel. Nay, not so much as that: as much as between night and day, hell and heaven. Oh, if I had a righteousness of my own that no one could find fault with, I would voluntarily fling it away to have the righteousness of Christ, but as I have none of my own I do rejoice the more to have my Lord's. When Mr. Whitefield first preached at Kingswood, near Bristol, to the colliers, he could see when their hearts began to be touched by the gutters of white made by the tears as they ran down their black cheeks. He saw they were receiving the gospel, and he writes in his diary "as these poor colliers had no righteousness of their own they therefore gloried in Him who came to save publicans and sinners." Well, Mr. Whitefield, that is true of the colliers, but it is equally true of many of us here, who may not have had black faces, but we had black hearts. We can truly say that we also rejoice to cast away our own righteousness and count it dross and dung that we may win Christ, and be found in him. In him is our sole hope and only trust.

Last of all, for any of you to reject the righteousness of Christ must be to perish everlastingly, because it cannot be that God will accept you or your pretended righteousness when you have refused the real and divine righteousness which he sets before you in his Son. If you could go up to the gates of heaven, and the angel were to say to you, "What title have you to entrance here?" and you were to reply, "I have a righteousness of my own," then for you to be admitted would be to decide that your righteousness was on a par with that of Immanuel himself. Can that ever be? Do you think that God will ever allow such a lie to be sanctioned? Will he let a poor wretched sinner's counterfeit righteousness pass current side by side with the fine gold of Christ's perfection? Why was the fountain filled with blood if you need no washing? Is Christ a superfluity? Oh, it cannot be. You must have Christ's righteousness or be unrighteous, and being unrighteous you will be unsaved, and being unsaved you must remain lost forever and ever.

What! has it all come to this, then, that I am to believe in the Lord Jesus Christ for righteousness, and to be made just through faith? Yes, that is it: that is the whole of it. What! trust Christ alone and then live as I like! You cannot live in sin after you have trusted Jesus, for the act of faith brings with it a change of nature and a renewal of your soul. The Spirit of God who leads you to believe will also change your heart. You spoke of "living as you like," you will like to live very differently from what you do now. The things you loved before your conversion you will hate when you believe, and the things you hated you will love. Now, you are trying to be good, and you make great failures, because your heart is alienated from God; but when once you have received salvation through the blood of Christ, your heart will love God, and then you will keep his commandments, and they will be no longer grievous to you. A change of heart is what you want, and you will never get it except through the covenant of grace. There is not a word about conversion in the old covenant, we must look to the new covenant for that, and here it is—"Then will I sprinkle clean water upon you, and you shall be clean: from all your filthiness, and from all your idols, will I cleanse you. A new heart also will I give you, and an new spirit will I put within you: and I will take away the stony heart out of your flesh, and I will give you an heart of flesh. And I will put my spirit within you, and cause you to walk in my statutes, and ye shall keep my judgments, and do them." This is one of the greatest covenant promises, and the Holy Ghost performs it in the chosen. Oh that the Lord would sweetly persuade you to believe in the Lord Jesus Christ, and that promise and all the other covenant engagements shall be fulfilled to your soul. The Lord bless you! Spirit of God, send thy blessing on these poor words of mine for Jesus' sake. Amen.

PORTIONS OF SCCRIPTURE READ BEFORE SERMON—Romans 10. HYMNS FROM "OUR OWN HYMN BOOK"—231, 535, 647.

Christ's People—Imitators of Him

A Sermon (No. 21) Delivered on Sabbath Morning, April 29, 1855, by the REV. C. H. SPURGEON At Exeter Hall, Strand.

"Now when they saw the boldness of Peter and John, and perceived that they were unlearned and ignorant men, they marvelled; and they took knowledge of them, that they had been with Jesus."
—Acts 4:13.

Behold! what a change divine grace will work in a man, and in how short a time. That same Peter, who so lately followed his master afar off, and with oaths and curses denied that he knew his name, is now to be found side by side with the loving John, boldly declaring that there is salvation in none other name save that of Jesus Christ, and preaching the resurrection of the dead, through the sacrifice of his dying Lord. The Scribes and Pharisees soon discover the reason of his boldness. Rightly did they guess that it rested not in his learning or his talents, for neither Peter nor John had been educated; they had been trained as fishermen; their education was a knowledge of the sea—of the fisherman's craft; none other had they; their boldness could not therefore spring from the self-sufficiency of knowledge, but from the Spirit of the living God. Nor did they acquire their courage from their station; for rank will confer a sort of dignity upon a man, and make him speak with a feigned authority, even when he has no talent or genius; but these men were, as it says in the original text, idiotai, private men, who stood in no official capacity; men without rank or station. When they saw the boldness of Peter and John, and perceived that they were unlearned and private individuals, they marveled, and they came to a right conclusion as to the source of their power—they had been dwelling with Jesus. Their conversation with the Prince of light and glory, backed up, as they might also have known, by the influence of the Holy Spirit, without which even that eminently holy example would have been in vain, had made them bold for their Master's cause. Oh! my brethren, it were well if this condemnation, so forced from the lips of enemies, could also be compelled by our own example. If we could live like Peter and John; if our lives were "living epistles of God, known and read of all men;" if, whenever we were seen, men would take knowledge of us, that we had been with Jesus, it would be a happy thing for this world, and a blessed thing for us. It is concerning that I am to speak to you this morning; and as God gives me grace, I will endeavor to stir up your minds by way of remembrance, and urge you so to imitate Jesus Christ, our heavenly pattern, that men may perceive that you are disciples of the Holy Son of God.

First, then, this morning, I will tell you what a Christian should be; secondly, I will tell you when he should be so; thirdly, why he should be so; and then fourthly how he can be so.

I. As God may help us then, first of all, we will speak of WHAT A BELIEVER SHOULD BE. A Christian should be a striking likeness of Jesus Christ. You have read lives of Christ, beautifully and eloquently written, and you have admired the talent of the persons who could write so well; but the best life of Christ is his living biography, written out in the words and actions of his people. If we, my brethren, were what we profess to be; if the Spirit of the Lord were in the heart of all his children, as we could desire; and if, instead of having abundance of formal professors, we were all possessors of that vital grace, I will tell you not only what we ought to be, but what we should be: we should be pictures of Christ, yea, such striking likenesses of him that the world would not have to hold us up by the hour together, and say, "Well, it seems somewhat of a likeness;" but they would, when they once beheld us, exclaim, "He has been with Jesus; he has been taught of him; he is like him; he has caught the very idea of the holy Man of Nazareth, and he expands it out into his very life and every day actions."

In enlarging upon this point, it will be necessary to premise, that when we here affirm that men should be such and such a thing, we refer to the people of God. We do not wish to speak to them in any legal way. We are not under the law, but under grace. Christian men hold themselves bound to keep all God's precepts; but the reason why they do so is not because the law is binding upon them, but because the gospel constrains them; they believe, that having been redeemed by blood divine; having been purchased by Jesus Christ, they are more bound to keep his commands, than they would have been if they were under the law; they hold themselves to be ten thousand fold more debtors to God, than they could have been under the Mosaic dispensation. Not of force; not of compulsion; not through fear of the whip; not through legal bondage; but through pure, disinterested love and gratitude to God, they lay themselves out for his service, seeking to be Israelites indeed, in whom there is no guile. This much I have declared lest any man should think that I am preaching works as the way to salvation; I will yield to none in this, that I will ever maintain—that by grace we are saved, and not by ourselves; but equally must I testify, that where the grace of God is, it will produce fitting deeds. To these I am ever bound to exhort you, while ye are ever expected to have good works for necessary purposes. Again, I do not, when I say that a believer should be a striking likeness of Jesus, suppose that any one Christian will perfectly exhibit all the features of our Lord and Saviour Jesus Christ; yet, my brethren, the fact that perfection is beyond our reach, should not diminish the ardore of our desire after it. The artist, when he paints, knows right well that he shall not be able to excel Apelles; but that does not discourage him; he uses his brush with all the greater pains, that he may, at least in some humble measure, resemble the great master. So the sculptor, though persuaded that he will not rival Praxiteles, will hew out the marble still, and seek to be as near the model as possible. Thus so the Christian man; though he feels he never can mount to the heights of complete excellence, and perceives that he never can on earth become the exact image of Christ, still holds it up before him, and measures his own deficiencies by the distance between himself and Jesus. This will he do; forgetting all he has attained, he will press forward, crying, Excelsior! going upwards still, desiring to be conformed more and more to the image of Christ Jesus.

First, then, a Christian should be like Christ in his boldness. This is a virtue now-a-days called impudence, but the grace is equally valuable by whatever name it may be called. I suppose if the Scribes had given a definition of Peter and John, they would have called them impudent fellows.

Jesus Christ and his disciples were noted for their courage. "When they saw the boldness of Peter and John, they took knowledge of them, that they had been with Jesus." Jesus Christ never fawned upon the rich; he stooped not to the great and noble; he stood erect, a man before men—the prophet of the people; speaking out boldly and freely what he thought. Have you never admired that mighty deed of his, when going to the city where he had lived and been brought up? Knowing that a prophet had no honor in his own country, the book was put into his hands (he had but then commenced his ministry), yet without tremor he unrolled the sacred volume, and what did he take for his text? Most men, coming to their own neighborhood, would have chosen a subject adapted to the taste, in order to earn fame. But what doctrine did Jesus preach that morning? One which in our age is scorned and hated—the doctrine of election. He opened the Scriptures, and began to read thus: "Many widows were in Israel in the days of Elias, when the heaven was shut up three years and six months, when great famine was throughout all the land; but unto none of them was Elias sent, save unto Sarepta, a city of Sodom, unto a woman that was a widow. And many lepers were in Israel in the time of Eliseus, the prophet; and none of them were cleansed, saving Naaman, the Syrian." Then he began to tell, how God saveth whom he pleases, and rescues whom he chooses. Ah! how they gnashed their teeth upon him, dragged him out, and would have cast him from the brow of the hill. Do you not admire his intrepidity? He saw their teeth gnashing; he knew their hearts were hot with enmity, while their mouths foamed withe revenge and malice; still he stood like the angel who shut the lions' mouths; he feared them not; faithfully he proclaimed what he knew to be the truth of God, and still read on, despite them all. So, in his discourses. If he saw a Scribe or a Pharisee in the congregation, he did not keep back part of the price, but pointing his finger, he said, "Woe unto you, Scribes and Pharisees, hypocrites;" and when a lawyer came, saying, "Master, in speaking thus, thou condemnest us also;" he turned round and said "Woe unto you, lawyers, for ye bind heavy burdens upon men, while ye yourselves will not touch them with so much as one of your fingers." He dealt out honest truth; he never knew the fear of man; he trembled at none; he stood out God's chosen, whom he had anointed above his fellows, careless of man's esteem. My friends, be like Christ in this. Have none of the time-serving religion of the present day, which is merely exhibited in evangelical drawing-rooms,—a religion which only flourishes in a hot-bed atmosphere, a religion which is only to be perceived in good company. No; if ye are the servants of God, be like Jesus Christ, bold for your master; never blush to own your religion; your profession will never disgrace you; take care you never disgrace that. Your love to Christ will never dishonor you; it may bring some temporary slight from your friends, or slanders from your enemies; but live on, and you shall live down their calumnies; live on, and ye shall stand amongst the glorified, honored even by those who hissed you, when he shall come to be glorified by his angels, and admired by them that love him. Be like Jesus, very valiant for your God, so that when they shall see your boldness, they may say, "He has been with Jesus."

But no one feature will give a portrait of a man; so the one virtue of boldness will never make you like Christ. There have been some who have been noble men, but have carried their courage to excess; they have thus been caricatures of Christ, and not portraits of him. We must amalgamate with our boldness the loveliness of Jesus' disposition. Let courage be the brass, let love be the gold. Let us mix the two together; so shall we produce a rich Corinthian metal, fit to be manufactured into the beautiful gate of the temple. Let your love and courage be mingled together. The man who is bold may indeed accomplish wonders. John Knox did much, but he might perhaps have done more if he had had a little love. Luther was a conqueror—peace to his ashes, and honor to his name!—still, we who look upon him at a distance, think that if he had sometimes mixed a little mildness with it—if, while he had the fortitier in re, he had been also suaviter in modo, and spoken somewhat more gently, he might have done even more good than he did. So brethren, while we too are bold, let us ever imitate the loving Jesus. The child comes to him; he takes it on his knee, saying, "Suffer little children to come unto me, and forbid them not." A widow has just lost her only son; he weeps at the bier, and with a word, restores life to the dead man. He sees a paralytic, a leper, or a man long confined to his bed; he speaks, they rise, and are healed. He lived for others, not for himself. His constant labors were without any motive, except the good of those who lived in the world. And to crown all, ye know the mighty sacrifice he made, when he condescended to lay down his life for man—when on the tree, quivering with agony, and hanging in the utmost extremity of suffering, he submitted to die for our sakes, that we might be saved. Behold in Christ love consolidated! He was one mighty pillar of benevolence. As God is love, so Christ is love. Oh, ye Christians, be ye loving also. Let you love and your beneficence beam out on all men. Say not, "Be ye warmed, and be ye filled," but "give a portion to seven, and also to eight." If ye cannot imitate Howard, and unlock the prison doors—if ye cannot visit the sad house of misery, yet each in your proper sphere, speak kind words, do kind actions; live out Christ again in the kindness of your life. If there is one virtue which most commends Christians, it is that of kindness; it is to love the people of God, to love the church, to love the world, to love all. But how many have we in our churches of Crab-tree Christians, who have mixed such a vast amount of vinegar, and such a tremendous quantity of gall in their constitutions, that they can scarcely speak one good word to you: they imagine it impossible to defend religion except by passionate ebullitions; they cannot speak for their dishonored Master without being angry with their opponent; and if anything is awry, whether it be in the house, the church, or anywhere else, they conceive it to be their duty to set their faces like flint, and to defy everybody. They are like isolated icebergs, no one cares to go near them. They float about on the sea of forgetfulness, until at last they are melted and gone; and though, good souls, we shall be happy enough to meet them in heaven, we are precious glad to get rid of them from the earth. They were always so unamiable in disposition, that we would rather live an eternity with them in heaven than five minutes on earth. Be ye not thus, my brethren. Imitate Christ in your loving spirits; speak kindly, act kindly, and do kindly, that men may say of you, "He has been with Jesus."

Another great feature in the life of Christ was his deep and sincere humility; in which let us imitate him. While we will not cringe or bow3(far from it; we are the freemen whom the truth makes free; we walk through this world equal to all, inferior to none)3yet we would endeavor to be like Christ, continually humble. Oh, thou proud Christian (for though it be a paradox, there must be some, I think; I would not be so uncharitable as to say that there are not some such persons), if thou art a Christian, I bid thee look at thy Master, talking to the children, bending from the majesty of his divinity to speak to mankind on earth, tabernacling with the peasants of Galilee, and then—aye, depth of condescension unparalleled—washing his disciples' feet, and wiping them with the towel after supper. This is your Master, whom ye profess to worship; this is your Lord, whom ye adore. And ye, some of you who count yourselves Christians, cannot speak to a person who is not dressed in the same kind of clothing as yourselves, who have not exactly as much money per year as you have. In England, it is true that a sovereign will not speak to a shilling, and a shilling will not notice a sixpence, and a sixpence will sneer at a penny. But it should not be so with Christians. We ought to forget caste, degree, and rank, when we come into Christ's church. Recollect, Christian, who your Master was—a man of the poor. He lived with them; he ate with them. And will ye walk with lofty heads and stiff necks, looking with insufferable contempt upon you meaner fellow-worms? What are ye? The meanest of all, because your trickeries and adornments make you proud. Pitiful, despicable souls ye are! How small ye look in God's sight! Christ was humble; he stooped to do anything which might serve others. He had no pride; he was an humble man, a friend of publicans and sinners, living and walking with them. So, Christian, be thou like thy Master—one who can stoop; yea, be thou one who thinks it no stooping, but rather esteems others better than himself, counts it his honor to sit with the poorest of Christ's people, and says, "If my name may be but written in the obscurest part of the book of life, it is enough for me, so unworthy am I of his notice!" Be like Christ in his humility.

So might I continue, dear brethren, speaking of the various characteristics of Christ Jesus; but as you can think of them as well as I can, I shall not do so. It is easy for you to sit down and paint Jesus Christ, for you have him drawn out here in his word. I find that time would fail me if I were to give you an entire likeness of Jesus; but let me say, imitate him in his holiness. Was zealous for his master? So be you. Ever go about doing good. Let not time be wasted. It is too precious. Was he self-denying, never looking to his own interest? So be you. Was he devout? So be you fervent in your prayers. Had he deference to his Father's will? So submit yourselves to him. Was he patient? So learn to endure. And best of all, as the highest portraiture of Jesus, try to forgive your enemies as he did; and let those sublime words of you Master, "Father, forgive them, for they know not what they do," always ring in your ears. When you are prompted to revenge; when hot anger starts, bridle the steed at once, and let it not dash forward with you headlong. Remember, anger is temporary insanity. Forgive as you hope to be forgiven. Heap coals of fire on the head of your foe by your kindness to him. Good for evil, recollect, is god-like. Be god-like, then; and in all ways, and by all means, so live that your enemies may say, "He has been with Jesus."

II. Now, WHEN SHOULD CHRISTIANS BE THUS? For there is an idea in the world that persons ought to be very religious on a Sunday, but it does not matter what they are on a Monday. How many pious preachers are there on a Sabbath-day, who are very impious preachers during the rest of the week! How many are there who come up to the house of God with a solemn countenance, who join the song and profess to pray, yet have neither part nor lot in the matter, but are "in the gall of bitterness and in the bonds of iniquity!" This is true of some of you who are present here. When should a Christian, then, be like Jesus Christ? Is there a time when he may strip off his regimentals—when the warrior may unbuckle his armor, and become like other men? Oh! no; at all times and in every place let the Christian be what he professes to be. I remember talking some time ago with a person who said, "I do not like visitors who come to my house and introduce religion; I think we ought to have religion on the Sabbath-day, when we go to the house of God, but not in the drawing-room." I suggested to the individual that there would be a great deal of work for the upholsterers, if there should be no religion except in the house of God. "How is that?" was the question. "Why," I replied, "we should need to have beds fitted up in all our places of worship, for surely we need religion to die with, and consequently, every one would want to die there." Aye, we all need the consolations of God at last; but how can we expect to enjoy them unless we obey the precepts of religion during life? My brethren, let me say, be ye like Christ at all times. Imitate him in public. Most of us live in some sort of publicity; many of us are called to work before our fellow-men every day. We are watched; our words are caught; our lives are examined—taken to pieces. The eagle-eyed, argus-eyed world observes everything we do, and sharp critics are upon us. Let us live the life of Christ in public. Let us take care that we exhibit our Master, and not ourselves—so that we can say, "It is no longer I that live, but Christ that liveth in me." Take heed that you carry this into the church too, you who are church-members. Be like Christ in the church. How many there are of you like Diotrephes, seeking pre-eminence? How many are trying to have some dignity and power over their fellow Christians, instead of remembering that it is the fundamental rule of all our churches, that there all men are equal—alike brethren, alike to be received as such. Carry out the spirit of Christ, then, in your churches, wherever ye are; let your fellow members say of you, "He has been with Jesus."

But, most of all, take care to have religion in your houses. A religious house is the best proof of true piety. It is not my chapel, it is my house—it is not my minister, it is my home-companion—who can best judge me; it is the servant, the child, the wife, the friend, that can discern most of my real character. A good man will improve his household. Rowland Hill once said, he would not believe a man to be a true Christian if his wife, his children, the servants, and even the dog and cat, were not the better for it. That is being religious. If your household is not the better for your Christianity—if men cannot say, "This is a better house than others," then be not deceived—ye have nothing of the grace of God. Let not your servant, on leaving your employ, say, "Well, this is a queer sort of a religious family; there was no prayer in the morning, I began the day with my drudgery; there was no prayer at night, I was kept at home all the Sabbath-day. Once a fortnight, perhaps, I was allowed to go out in the afternoon, when there was nowhere to go where I could hear a gospel sermon. My master and mistress went to a place where of course they heard the blessed gospel of God—that was all for them; as for me, I might have the dregs and leavings of some overworked curate in the afternoon." Surely, Christian men will not act in that way. No! Carry out your godliness in your family. Let everyone say that you have practical religion. Let it be known and read in the house, as well as in the world. Take care of your character there; for what we are there, we really are. Our life abroad is often but a borrowed part, the actor's part of a great scene, but at home the wizard is removed, and men are what they seem. Take care of you home duties.

Yet again, my brethren, before I leave this point, imitate Jesus in secret. When no eye seeth you except the eye of God, when darkness covers you, when you are shut up from the observation of mortals, even then be ye like Jesus Christ. Remember his ardent piety, his secret devotion—how, after laboriously preaching the whole day, he stole away in the midnight shades to cry for help from his God. Recollect how his entire life was constantly sustained by fresh inspirations of the Holy Spirit, derived by prayer. Take care of your secret life; let it be such that you will not be ashamed to read at the last great day. Your inner life is written in the book of God, and it shall one day be open before you. If the entire life of some of you were known, it would be no life at all; it would be a death. Yea, even of some true Christians we may say it is scarce a life. It is a dragging on of an existence—one hasty prayer a day—one breathing, just enough to save their souls alive, but no more. O, my brethren, strive to be more like Jesus Christ. These are times when we want more secret prayer. I have had much fear all this week. I know not whether it is true; but when I feel such a thing I like to tell it to those of you who belong to my own church and congregation. I have trembled lest, by being away from our own place, you have ceased to pray as earnestly as you once did. I remember your earnest groans and petitions—how you would assemble together in the house of prayer in multitudes, and cry out to God to help his servant. We cannot meet in such style at present; but do you still pray in private? Have you forgotten me? Have you ceased to cry out to God? Oh! my friends, with all the entreaties that a man can use, let me appeal to you. Recollect who I am, and what I am—a child, having little education, little learning, ability or talent; and here am I called upon week after week, to preach to this crowd of people. Will ye not, my beloved, still plead for me? Has not God been pleased to hear your prayers ten thousand times? And will ye now cease, when a mighty revival is taking place in many churches? Will ye now stop your petitions? Oh! no; go to your houses, fall upon your knees, cry aloud to God to enable you still to hold up your hands like Moses on the hill, that Joshua below may fight and overcome the Amalekites. Now is the time for victory; shall we lose it? This is the high tide that will float us over the bar; now let us put out the oars; let us pull by earnest prayer, crying for God the Spirit to fill the sails! Ye who love God, of every place and every denomination, wrestle for your ministers; pray for them; for why should not God even now put out his Spirit? What is the reason why we are to be denied Pentecostal seasons? Why not this hour, as one mighty band, fall down before him and entreat him, for his Son's sake, to revive his drooping church? Then would all men discern that we are verily the disciples of Christ.

III. But now, thirdly, WHY SHOULD CHRISTIANS IMITATE CHRIST? The answer comes very naturally and easily, Christians should be like Christ, first, for their own sakes. For their honesty's sake, and for their credit's sake, let them not be found liars before God and men. For their own healthful state, if they wish to be kept from sin and preserved from going astray, let them imitate Jesus. For their own happiness' sake, if they would drink wine on the lees well refined; if they would enjoy holy and happy communion with Jesus; if they would be lifted up above the cares and troubles of this world, let them imitate Jesus Christ. Oh! my brethren, there is nothing that can so advantage you, nothing can so prosper you, so assist you, so make you walk towards heaven rapidly, so keep you head upwards towards the sky, and your eyes radiant with glory, like the imitation of Jesus Christ. It is when, by the power of the Holy Spirit, you are enabled to walk with Jesus in his very footsteps, and tread in his ways, you are most happy and you are most known to be the sons of God. For your own sake, my brethren, I say, be like Christ.

Next, for religion's sake, strive to imitate Jesus. Ah! poor religion, thou hast been sorely shot at by cruel foes, but thou hast not been wounded one-half so much by them as by thy friends. None have hurt thee, O, Christianity, so much as those who profess to be thy followers. Who have made these wounds in this fair hand of godliness? I say, the professor has done this, who has not lived up to his profession; the man who with pretences enters the fold, being naught but a wolf in sheep's clothing. Such men, sirs, injure the gospel more than others; more than the laughing infidel, more than the sneering critic, doth the man hurt our cause who professes to love it, but in his actions doth belie his love. Christian, lovest thou that cause? Is the name of the dear Redeemer precious to thee? Wouldst thou see the kingdoms of the world become the kingdoms of our Lord and his Christ? Dost thou wish to see the proud man humbled and the mighty abased? Dost thou long for the souls of perishing sinners, and art thou desirous to win them, and save their souls from the everlasting burning? Wouldst thou prevent their fall into the regions of the damned? Is it thy desire that Christ should see the travail of his soul, and be abundantly satisfied? Doth thy heart yearn over thy fellow-immortals? Dost thou long to see them forgiven? Then be consistent with thy religion. Walk before God in the land of the living. Behave as an elect man should do. Recollect what manner of people we ought to be in all holy conversation and godliness. This is the best way to convert the world; yea, such conduct would do more than even the efforts of missionary societies, excellent as they are. Let but men see that our conduct is superior to others, then they will believe there is something in our religion; but , if they see us quite the contrary to what we avow, what will they say? "These religious people are no better than others! Why should we go amongst them?" And they say quite rightly. It is but common-sense judgment. Ah! my friends, if ye love religion for her own sake, be consistent, and walk in the love of God. Follow Christ Jesus.

Then, to put it in the strongest form I can, let me say, for Christ's sake, endeavor to be like him. Oh! could I fetch the dying Jesus here, and let him speak to you! My own tongue is tied this morning, but I would make his blood, his scars, and his wounds speak. Poor dumb mouths, I bid each of them plead in his behalf. How would Jesus, standing here, show you his hands this morning! "My friends," he would say, "behold me! these hands were pierced for you; and look ye here at this my side. It was opened as the fountain of your salvation. See my feet; there entered the cruel nails. Each of these bones were dislocated for your sake. These eyes gushed with torrents of tears. This head was crowned with thorns. These cheeks were smitten; this hair was plucked; my body became the centre and focus of agony. I hung quivering in the burning sun; and all for you, my people. And will ye not love me now? I bid you be like me. Is there any fault in me? Oh! no. Ye believe that I am fairer than ten thousand fairs, and lovelier than ten thousand loves. Have I injured you? Have I not rather done all for your salvation? And do I not sit at my Father's throne, and e'en now intercede on your behalf? If ye love me,"—Christian, hear that word; let the sweet syllables ring forever in your ears, like the prolonged sounding of silver-toned bells;—"if ye love me, if ye love me, keep my commandments." Oh, Christian, let that "if" be put to thee this morning. "If ye love me." Glorious Redeemer! is it an "if" at all? Thou precious, bleeding Lamb, can there be an "if?" What, when I see thy blood gushing from thee; is it an "if?" Yes, I weep to say it is an "if." Oft my thoughts make it "if," and oft my words make it "if." But yet methinks my soul feels it is not "if," either. "Not to mine eyes is light so dear, Nor friendship half so sweet." "Yes, I love thee, I know that I love thee. Lord, thou knowest all things, thou knowest that I love thee," can the Christian say. "Well, then," says Jesus, looking down with a glance of affectionate approbation, "since thou lovest me, keep my commandments." O beloved, what mightier reason can I give than this? It is the argument of love and affection . Be like Christ, since gratitude demands obedience; so shall the world know that ye have been with Jesus.

IV. Ah! then ye wept; and I perceive ye felt the force of pity, and some of you are inquiring, "HOW CAN I IMITATE HIM?" It is my business, then, before you depart, to tell you how you can become transformed into the image of Christ.

In the first place, then, my beloved friends, in answer to your inquiry, let me say, you must know Christ as your Redeemer before you can follow him as your Exemplar. Much is said about the example of Jesus, and we scarcely find a man now who does not believe that our Lord was an excellent and holy man, much to be admired. But excellent as was his example, it would be impossible to imitate it, had he not also been our sacrifice. Do ye this morning know that his blood was shed for you? Can ye join with me in this verse,—

> O the sweet wonders of that cross,
>   Where God the Saviour lov'd and died;
> Her noblest life my spirit draws
>   From his dear wounds and bleeding side.

If so, you are in a fair way to imitate Christ. But do not seek to copy him until you are bathed in the fountain filled with blood drawn from his veins. It is not possible for you to do so; your passions will be too strong and corrupt, and you will be building without a foundation, a structure, which will be about as stable as a dream. You cannot mould your life to his pattern until you have had his spirit, till you have been clothed in his righteousness. "Well," say some, "we have proceeded so far, what next shall we do? We know we have an interest in him, but we are still sensible of manifold deficiencies." Next, then, let me entreat you to study Christ's character. This poor Bible is become an almost obsolete book, even with some Christians. There are so many magazines, periodicals, and such like ephemeral productions, that we are in danger of neglecting to search the Scriptures. Christian, wouldst thou know thy master? Look at him. There is a wondrous power about the character of Christ, for the more you regard it the more you will be conformed to it. I view myself in the glass, I go away, and forget what I was. I behold Christ, and I become like Christ. Look at him, then; study him in the evangelists, studiously examine his character. "But," say you, "we have done that, and we have proceeded but little farther." Then, in the next place, correct your poor copy every day. At night, try and recount all the actions of the twenty-four hours, scrupulously putting them under review. When I have proof-sheets sent to me of any of my writings, I have to make the corrections in the margin. I might read them over fifty times, and the printers would still put in the errors if I did not mark them. So must you do; if you find anything faulty at night, make a mark in the margin, that you may know where the fault is, and to-morrow may amend it. Do this day after day, continually noting your faults one by one, so that you may better avoid them. It was a maxim of the old philosophers, that, three times in the day, we should go over our actions. So let us do; let us not be forgetful; let us rather examine ourselves each night, and see wherin we have done amiss, that we may reform our lives.

Lastly, as the best advice I can give, seek more of the Spirit of God; for this is the way to become Christ-like. Vain are all your attempts to be like him till you have sought his spirit. Take the cold iron, and attempt to weld it if you can into a certain shape. How fruitless the effort! Lay it on the anvil, seize the blacksmith's hammer with all you might, let blow after blow fall upon it, and you shall have done nothing. Twist it, turn it, use all your implements, but you shall not be able to fashion it as you would. But put it in the fire, let it be softened and made malleable, then lay it on the anvil, and each stroke shall have a mighty effect, so that you may fashion it into any form you may desire. So take your heart, not cold as it is, not stony as it is by nature, but put it into the furnace; there let it be molten, and after that it can be turned like wax to the seal, and fashioned into the image of Jesus Christ.

Oh, my brethren, what can I say now to enforce my text, but that, if ye are like Christ on earth, ye shall be like him in heaven? If by the power of the Spirit ye become followers of Jesus, ye shall enter glory. For at heaven's gate there sits an angel, who admits no one who has not the same features as our adorable Lord. There comes a man with a crown upon his head, "Yes," he says, "thou hast a crown, it is true, but crowns are not the medium of access here." Another approaches, dressed in robes of state and the gown of learning. "Yes," says the angel, "it may be good, but gowns and learning are not the marks that shall admit you here." Another advances, fair, beautiful, and comely. "Yes," saith the angel, "that might please on earth, but beauty is not wanted here." There cometh up another, who is heralded by fame, and prefaced by the blast of the clamor of mankind; but the angel saith, "It is well with man, but thou hast no right to enter here." Then there appears another; poor he may have been; illiterate he may have been; but the angel, as he looks at him, smiles and says, "It is Christ again; a second edition of Jesus Christ is there. Come in, come in. Eternal glory thou shalt win. Thou art like Christ; in heaven thou shalt sit, because thou art like him." Oh! to be like Christ is to enter heaven; but to be unlike Christ is to descend to hell. Likes shall be gathered together at last, tares with tares, wheat with wheat. If ye have sinned with Adam and have died, ye shall lie with the spiritually dead forever, unless ye rise in Christ to newness of life; then shall we live with him throughout eternity. Wheat with wheat, tares with tares. "Be not deceived; God is not mocked: whatsoever a man soweth, that shall he also reap." Go away with this one thought, then my brethren, that you can test yourselves by Christ. If you are like Christ, you are of Christ, and shall be with Christ. If you are unlike him, you have no portion in the great inheritance. May my poor discourse help to fan the floor and reveal the chaff; yea, may it lead many of you to seek to be partakers of the inheritance of the saints in light, to the praise of his grace. To him be all honor given! Amen.

CHRIST'S PLEA FOR IGNORANT SINNERS

A Sermon (No. 2263) Intended for Reading on Lord's-Day, July 3rd, 1892, Delivered by C. H. SPURGEON, At the Metropolitan Tabernacle, Newington ON Lord's-Day Evening, October 5th, 1890.

"Then said Jesus, Father, forgive them; for they know not what they do."—Luke 23:34.

What tenderness we have here; what self-forgetfulness; what almighty love! Jesus did not say to those who crucified him, "Begone!" One such word, and they must have all fled. When they came to take him in the garden, they went backward, and fell to the ground, when he spoke but a short sentence; and now that he is on the cross, a single syllable would have made the whole company fall to the ground, or flee away in fright.

Jesus says not a word in his own defence. When he prayed to his Father, he might justly have said, "Father, note what they do to thy beloved Son. Judge them for the wrong they do to him who loves them, and who has done all he can for them." But there is no prayer against them in the words that Jesus utters. It was written of old, by the prophet Isaiah, "He made intercession for the transgressors;" and here it is fulfilled. He pleads for his murderers, "Father, forgive them."

He does not utter a single word of upbraiding. He does not say, "Why do ye this? Why pierce the hands that fed you? Why nail the feet that followed after you in mercy? Why mock the Man who loved to bless you?" No, not a word even of gentle upbraiding, much less anything like a curse. "Father, forgive them." You notice, Jesus does not say, "I forgive them," but you may read that between the lines. He says that all the more because he does not say it in words. But he had laid aside his majesty, and is fastened to the cross; and therefore he takes the humble position of a suppliant, rather than the more lofty place of one who had power to forgive. How often, when men say, "I forgive you," is there a kind of selfishness about it! At any rate, self is asserted in the very act of forgiving. Jesus take the place of a pleader, a pleader for those who were committing murder upon himself. Blessed be his name!

This word of the cross we shall use to-night, and we shall see if we cannot gather something from it for our instruction; for, though we were not there, and we did not actually put Jesus to death, yet we really caused his death, and we, too, crucified the Lord of glory; and his prayer for us was, "Father, forgive them; for they know not what they do."

I am not going to handle this text so much by way of exposition, as by way of experience. I believe there are many here, to whom these words will be very appropriate. This will be our line of thought. First, we were in measure ignorant; secondly, we confess that this ignorance is no excuse; thirdly, we bless our Lord for pleading for us; and fourthly, we now rejoice in the pardon we have obtained. May the Holy Spirit graciously help us in our meditation!

I. Looking back upon our past experience, let me say, first, that WE WERE IN MEASURE IGNORANT. We who have been forgiven, we who have been washed in the blood of the Lamb, we once sinned, in a great measure, through ignorance. Jesus says, "They know not what they do." Now, I shall appeal to you, brothers and sisters, when you lived under the dominion of Satan, and served yourselves and sin, was there not a measure of ignorance in it? You can truly say, as we said in the hymn we sang just now,—"Alas! I knew not what I did." It is true, first, that we were ignorant of the awful meaning of sin. We began to sin as children; we knew that it was wrong, but we did not know all that sin meant. We went on to sin as young men; peradventure we plunged into much wickedness. We knew it was wrong; but we did not see the end from the beginning. It did not appear to us as rebellion against God. We did not think that we were presumptuously defying God, setting at naught his wisdom, defying his power, deriding his love, spurning his holiness; yet we were doing that. There is an abysmal depth in sin. You cannot see the bottom of it. When we rolled sin under our tongue as a sweet morsel, we did not know all the terrible ingredients compounded in that deadly bittersweet. We were in a measure ignorant of the tremendous crime we committed when we dared to live in rebellion against God. So far, I think, you go with me.

We did not know, at that time, God's great love to us. I did not know that he had chosen me from before the foundation of the world; I never dreamed of that. I did not know that Christ stood for me as my Substitute, to redeem me from among men. I did not know the love of Christ, did not understand it then. You did not know that you were sinning against eternal love, against infinite compassion, against a distinguishing love such as God had fixed on you from eternity. So far, we knew not what we did.

I think, too, that we did not know all that we were doing in our rejection of Christ, and putting him to grief. He came to us in our youth; and impressed by a sermon we began to tremble, and to seek his face; but we were decoyed back to the world, and we refused Christ. Our mother's tears, our father's prayers, our teacher's admonitions, often moved us; but we were very stubborn, and we rejected Christ. We did not know that, in that rejection, we were virtually putting him away and crucifying him. We were denying his Godhead, or else we should have worshipped him. We were denying his love, or else we should have yielded to him. We were practically, in every act of sin, taking the hammer and the nails, and fastening

Christ to the cross, but we did not know it. Perhaps, if we had known it, we should not have crucified the Lord of glory. We did know we were doing wrong; but we did not know all the wrong that we were doing.

Nor did we know fully the meaning of our delays. We hesitated; we were on the verge on conversion; we went back, and turned again to our old follies. We were hardened, Christless, prayerless still; and each of us said, "Oh, I am only waiting a little while till I have fulfilled my present engagements, till I am a little older, till I have seen a little more of the world!" The fact is, we were refusing Christ, and choosing the pleasures of sin instead of him; and every hour of delay was an hour of crucifying Christ, grieving his Spirit, and choosing this harlot world in the place of the lovely and ever blessed Christ. We did not know that.

I think we may add one thing more. We did not know the meaning to our self-righteousness. We used to think, some of us, that we had a righteousness of our own. We had been to church regularly, or we had been to the meeting-house whenever it was open. We were christened; we were confirmed; or, peradventure, we rejoiced that we never had either of those things done to us. Thus, we put our confidence in ceremonies, or the absence of ceremonies. We said our prayers; we read a chapter in the bible night and morning; we did—oh, I do not know what we did not do! But there we rested; we were righteous in our own esteem. We had not any particular sin to confess, nor any reason to lie in the dust before the throne of God's majesty. We were about as good as we could be; and we did not know that we were even then perpetrating the highest insult upon Christ; for, if we were not sinners, why did Christ die; and, if we had a righteousness of our own which was good enough, why did Christ come here to work out a righteousness for us? We made out Christ to be a superfluity, by considering that we were good enough without resting in his atoning sacrifice. Ah, we did not think we were doing that! We thought we were pleasing God by our religiousness, by our outward performances, by our ecclesiastical correctness; but all the while we were setting up anti-Christ in the place of Christ. We were making out that Christ was not wanted; we were robbing him of his office and glory!

Alas! Christ would say of us, with regard to all these things, "They know not what they do." I want you to look quietly at the time past wherein you served sin, and just see whether there was not a darkness upon your mind, a blindness in your spirit, so that you did not know what you did.

II. Well now, secondly, WE CONFESS THAT THIS IGNORANCE IS NO EXCUSE. Our Lord might urge it as a plea; but we never could. We did not know what we did, and se we were not guilty to the fullest possible extent; but we were guilty enough, therefore let us own it.

For first, remember, the law never allows this as a plea. In our own English law, a man is supposed to know what the law is. If he breaks it, it is no excuse to plead that he did not know it. It may be regarded by a judge as some extenuation; but the law allows nothing of the kind. God gives us the law, and we are bound to keep it. If I erred through not knowing the law, still it was a sin. Under the Mosaic law, there were sins of ignorance, and for these there were special offerings. The ignorance did not blot out the sin. That is clear in my text; for, if ignorance rendered an action no longer sinful, they why should Christ say, "Father, forgive them"? But he does; he asks for mercy for what is sin, even though the ignorance in some measure be supposed to mitigate the criminality of it.

But, dear friends, we might have known. If we did not know, it was because we would not know. There was the preaching of the Word; but we did not care to hear it. There was this blessed Book; but we did not care to read it. If you and I had sat down, and looked at our conduct by the light of the Holy Scripture, we might have known much more of the evil of sin, and much more of the love of Christ, and much more of the ingratitude which is possible in refusing Christ, and not coming to him.

In addition to that, we did not think. "Oh, but," you say, "young people never do think!" But young people should think. If there is anybody who need not think, it is the old man, whose day is nearly over. If he does think, he has but a very short time in which to improve; but the young have all their lives before them. If I were a carpenter, and had to make a box, I should not think about it after I had made the box; I should think, before I began to cut my timber, what sort of box it was to be. In every action, a man thinks before he begins, or else he is a fool. A young man ought to think more than anybody else, for now he is, as it were, making his box. He is beginning his life-plan; he should be the most thoughtful of all men. Many of us, who are now Christ's people, would have known much more about our Lord if we had given him more careful consideration in our earlier days. A man will consider about taking a wife, he will consider about making a business, he will consider about buying a horse or a cow; but he will not consider about the claims of Christ, and the claims of the Most High God; and this renders his ignorance wilful, and inexcusable.

Beside that, dear friends, although we have confessed to ignorance, in many sins we did not know a great deal. Come, let me quicken your memories. There were times when you knew that such an action was wrong, when you started back from it. You looked at the gain it would bring you, and you sold your soul for that price, and deliberately did what you were well aware was wrong. Are there not some here, saved by Christ, who must confess that , at times, they did violence to their conscience? They did despite to the Spirit of God, quenched the light of heaven, drove the Spirit away from them, distinctly knowing what they were doing. Let us bow before God in the silence of our hearts, and own to all of this. We hear the Master say, "Father, forgive them; for they know not what they do." Let us add our own tears as we say, "And forgive us, also, because in some things we did know; in all things we might have known; but we were ignorant for want of thought, which thought was a solemn duty which we ought to have rendered to God."

One more thing I will say on this head. When a man is ignorant, and does not know what he ought to do, what should he do? Well, he should do nothing till he does know. But here is the mischief of it, that when we did not know, yet we chose to do the wrong thing. If we did not know, why did we not choose the right thing? But, being in the dark, we never turned to the right; but always blundered to the left from sin to sin. Does not this show us how depraved our hearts are?: Though we are seeking to be right, when we were let alone, we go wrong of ourselves. Leave a child alone; leave a man alone; leave a tribe alone without teaching and instruction; what comes of it? Why, the same as when you leave a field alone. It never, by any chance, produces wheat or barley. Leave it alone, and there are rank weeds, and thorns, and briars, showing that the natural set of the soil is towards producing that which is worthless. O friends, confess the inmate evil of your hearts as well as the evil of your lives, in that, when you did not know, yet, having a perverse instinct, you chose the evil, and refuse the good; and, when you did not know enough of Christ, and did not think enough of him to know whether you ought to have him or not, you would not have come unto him that you might have life. You needed light; but you shut your eyes to the sun. You were thirsty; but you would not drink of the living spring; and so your ignorance, though it was there, was a criminal ignorance, which you must confess before the Lord. Oh, come ye to the cross, ye who have been there before, and have lost your burden there! Come and confess your guilt over again; and clasp that cross afresh, and look to him who bled upon it, and praise his dear name that he once prayed for you, "Father forgive them; for they know not what they do."

Now, I am going a step further. We were in a measure ignorant; but we confess that that measurable ignorance was no excuse.

III. Now, thirdly, WE BLESS OUR LORD FOR PLEADING FOR US. So you notice when it was that Jesus pleaded? It was, while they were crucifying him. They had not just driven in the nails, they had lifted up the cross, and dished it down into its socket, and dislocated all his bones, so that he could say, "I am poured out like water, and all my bones are out of joint." Ah, dear friends, it was then that instead of a cry or groan, this dear Son of God said, "Father, forgive them; for they know not what they do." They did not ask for forgiveness for themselves, Jesus ask for forgiveness for them. Their hands were imbrued in his blood; and it was then, even then, that he prayed for them. Let us think of the great love wherewith he loved us, even while we were yet sinners, when we rioted in sin, when we drank it down as the ox drinketh down water. Even then he prayed for us. "While we were yet without strength, in due time Christ died for the ungodly." Bless his name to-night. He prayed for you when you did not pray for yourself. He prayed for you when you were crucifying him.

Then think of his plea, he pleads his Sonship. He says, "Father, forgive them." He was the Son of God, and he put his divine Sonship into the scale on our behalf. He seems to say, "Father, as I am thy Son, grant me this request, and pardon these rebels. Father, forgive them." The filial rights of Christ were very great. He was the Son of the Highest. "Light of light, very God of very God", the second Person in the Divine Trinity; and he puts that Sonship here before God and says, "Father, Father, forgive them." Oh, the power of that word from the Son's lip when he is wounded, when he is in agony, when he is dying! He says, "Father, Father, grant my one request; O Father, forgive them; for they know not what they do;" and the great Father bows his awful head, in token that the petition is granted.

Then notice, that Jesus here, silently, but really pleads his sufferings. The attitude of Christ when he prayed this prayer is very noteworthy. His hands were stretched upon the transverse beam; his feet were fastened to the upright tree; and there he pleaded. Silently his hands and feet were pleading, and his agonized body from the very sinew and muscle pleaded with God. His sacrifice was presented complete; and so it is his cross that takes up the plea, "Father, forgive them." O blessed Christ! It is thus that we have been forgiven, for his Sonship and his cross have pleaded with God, and have prevailed on our behalf.

I love this prayer, also, because of the indistinctness of it. It is "Father, forgive them." He does not say, "Father, forgive the soldiers who have nailed me here." He includes them. Neither does he say, "Father, forgive sinners in ages to come who will sin against me." But he means them. Jesus does not mention them by any accusing name: "Father, forgive my enemies. Father, forgive my murderers." No, there is no word of accusation upon those dear lips. "Father, forgive them." Now into that pronoun "them" I feel that I can crawl Can you get in there? Oh, by a humble faith, appropriate the cross of Christ by trusting in it; and get into that big little word "them"! It seems like a chariot of mercy that has come down to earth into which a man may step, and it shall bear him up to heaven. "Father, forgive them."

Notice, also, what it was that Jesus asked for; to omit that, would be to leave out the very essence of his prayer. He asked for full absolution for his enemies: "Father, forgive them. Do not punish them; forgive them. Do not remember their sin; forgive it, blot it out; throw it into the depths of the sea. Remember it not, my Father. Mention it not against them any more for ever. Father, forgive them." Oh, blessed prayer, for the forgiveness of God is broad and deep! When man forgives, he leaves the remembrance of the wrong behind; but when God pardons, he says, "I will forgive their iniquity, and I will remember their sin no more." It is this that Christ asked for you and me long before we had any repentance, or any faith; and in answer to that prayer, we were brought to feel our sin, we were brought to confess it, and to believe in him; and now, glory be to his name, we can bless him for having pleaded for us, and obtained the forgiveness of all our sins.

IV. I come now to my last remark. Which is this, WE NOW REJOICE IN THE PARDON WE HAVE OBTAINED. Have you obtained pardon? Is this your song? "Now, oh joy! My sins are pardon'd, Now I can, and do believe." I have a letter, in my pocket, from a man of education and standing, who has been an agnostic; he says that he was a sarcastic agnostic, and he writes praising God, and invoking every blessing upon my head for bringing him to the Saviour's feet. He says, "I was without happiness for this life, and without hope for the next." I believe that that is a truthful description of many an unbeliever. What hope is there for the world to come apart from the cross of Christ? The best hope such a man has is that he may die the death of a dog, and there may be an end of him. What is the hope of the Romanist, when he comes to die? I feel so sorry for many of the devout and earnest friends, for I do not know what their hope is. They do not hope to go to heaven yet, at any rate; some purgatorial pains must be endured first. Ah, this is a poor, poor faith to die on, to have such a hope as that to trouble your last thoughts. I do not know of any religion but that of Christ Jesus which tells us of sin pardoned, absolutely pardoned. Now, listen. Our teaching is not that, when you come to die, you may, perhaps, find out that it is all right, but, "Beloved, now we are the sons of God." "He that believeth on the Son hath everlasting life." He has it now, and he knows it, and he rejoices in it. So I come back to the last head of my discourse, we rejoice in the pardon Christ has obtained for us. We are pardoned. I hope that the larger portion of this audience can say, "By the grace of God, we know that the larger portion of this audience can say, "By the grace of God, we know that we are washed in the blood of the Lamb."

Pardon has come to us through Christ's plea. Our hope lies in the plea of Christ, and specially in his death. If Jesus paid my debt, and he did it if I am a believer in him, then I am out of debt. If Jesus bore the penalty of my sin, and he did it if I am a believer, then there is no penalty for me to pay, for we can say to him,—

> Complete atonement thou hast made,
>   And to the utmost farthing paid
>   Whate'er thy people owed:
> Nor can his wrath on me take place,
>   If shelter'd in thy righteousness,
>   And sprinkled with thy blood.
> "If thou hast my discharge procured,
>   And freely in my room endured
>   The whole of wrath divine:
> Payment God cannot twice demand,
>   First of my bleeding Surety's hand,
>   And then again at mine.

If Christ has borne my punishment, I shall never bear it. Oh, what joy there is in this blessed assurance! Your hope that you are pardoned lies in this, that Jesus died. Those dear wounds of his are bled for you.

We praise him for our pardon because we do know now what we did. Oh, brethren, I know not how much we ought to love Christ, because we sinned against him so grievously! Now we know that sin is "exceeding sinful." Now we know that sin crucified Christ. Now we know that we stabbed our heavenly Lover to his heart. We slew, with ignominious death, our best and dearest Friend and Benefactor. We know that now; and we could almost weep tears of blood to think that we ever treated him as we did. But, it is all forgiven, all gone. Oh, let us bless that dear Son of God, who has put away even such sins as ours! We feel them more now than ever before. We know they are forgiven, and our grief is because of the pain that the purchase of our forgiveness cost our Saviour. We never knew what our sins really were till we saw him in a bloody sweat. We never knew the crimson hue of our sins till we read our pardon written in crimson lines with his precious blood. Now, we see our sin, and yet we do not see it; for God has pardoned it, blotted it out, cast it behind his back for ever.

Henceforth ignorance, such as we have described, shall be hateful to us. Ignorance of Christ and eternal things shall be hateful to us. If, through ignorance, we have sinned, we will have done with that ignorance. We will be students of his Word. We will study that masterpiece of all the sciences, the knowledge of Christ crucified. We will ask the Holy Ghost to drive far from us the ignorance that gendereth sin. God grant that we may not fall into sins of ignorance any more; but may we be able to say, "I know whom I have believed; and henceforth I will seek more knowledge, till I comprehend, with all saints, what are the heights, and depths, and lengths, and breadths of the love of Christ, and know the love of God, which passeth knowledge"! I put in a practical word here. If you rejoice that you are pardoned, show your gratitude by your imitation of Christ. There was never before such a plea as this, "Father, forgive them; for they know not what they do." Plead like that for others. Has anybody been injuring you? Are there persons who slander you? Pray to-night, "Father, forgive them; for they know not what they do." Let us always render good for evil, blessing for cursing; and when we are called to suffer through the wrong-doing of others, let us believe that they would not act as they do if it were not because of their ignorance. Let us pray for them; and make their very ignorance the plea for their forgiveness: "Father, forgive them; for they know not what they do." I want you to think of the millions of London just now. See those miles of streets, pouring out their children this evening; but look at those public-houses with the crowds streaming in and out. God down our streets by moonlight. See what I almost blush to tell. Follow men and women, too, to their homes, and be this your prayer: "Father, forgive them; for they know not what they do." That silver bell—keep it always ringing. What did I say? That silver bell? Nay, it is the golden bell upon the priests garments. Wear it on your garments, ye priests of God, and let it always ring out its golden note, "Father, forgive them; for they know not what they do." If I can set all God's saints imitating Christ with such a prayer as this, I shall not have spoken in vain.

Brethren, I see reason for hope in the very ignorance that surrounds us. I see hope for this poor city of ours, hope for this poor country, hope for Africa, China, and India. "They know not what they do." Here is a strong argument in their favour, for they are more ignorant than we were. They know less of the evil of sin, and less of the hope of eternal life, than we do. Send up this petition, ye people of God! Heap your prayers together with cumulative power, send up this fiery shaft of prayer, straight to the heart of God, while Jesus from his throne shall add his prevalent intercession, "Father, forgive them; for they know not what they do."

If there be any unconverted people here, and I know that there are some, we will mention them in our private devotion, as well as in the public assembly; and we will pray for them in words like these, "Father, forgive them; for they know not what they do." May God bless you all, for Jesus Christ's sake! Amen.

Luke 23:33–46. John 19:25–30.

We have often read the story of our Saviour's sufferings; but we cannot read it too often. Let us, therefore, once again repair to "the place which is called Calvary." As we just now sang,—"Come, let us stand beneath the cross; So may the blood from out his side Fall gently on us drop by drop; Jesus, our Lord is crucified." We will read, first, Luke's account of our Lord's crucifixion and death.

Luke 23:33. And when they were come to the place, which is called Calvary, there they crucified him, and the malefactors, one of the right hand, and the other on the left.

They gave Jesus the place of dishonour. Reckoning him to be the worst criminal of the three, they put him between the other two. They heaped upon him the utmost scorn which they could give to a malefactor; and in so doing they unconsciously honoured him. Jesus always deserves the chief place wherever he is. In all things he must have the pre-eminence. He is King of sufferers as well as King of saints.

34. Then said Jesus, Father, forgive them; for they know not what they do.

How startled they must have been to hear such words

from one who was about to be put to death for a supposed crime! The men that drove the nails, the men that lifted up the tree, must have been started back with amazement when they heard Jesus talk to God as his Father, and pray for them: "Father, forgive them; for they know not what they do." Did ever Roman legionary hear such words before? I should say not. They were so distinctly and diametrically opposed to the whole spirit of Rome. There is was blow for blow; only in the case of Jesus they gave blows where none had been received. The crushing cruelty of the Roman must have been startled indeed at such words as these, "Father, forgive them; for they know not what they do."

34, 35. And they parted his raiment, and cast lots. And the people stood beholding.

The gambling soldiers little dreamed that they were fulfilling Scriptures while they were raffling for the raiment of the illustrious Sufferer on the cross; yet so it was. In the twenty-second Psalm, which so fully sets forth our Saviour's sufferings, and which he probably repeated while he hung on the tree, David wrote, "They parted my garments among them, and cast lots upon my vesture." "And the people stood beholding," gazing, looking on the cruel spectacle. You and I would not have done that; there is a public sentiment which has trained us to hate the sight of cruelty, especially of deadly cruelty to one of our own race; but these people thought that they did no harm when they "stood beholding." They also were thus fulfilling the Scriptures; for the seventeenth verse of the twenty-second Psalm says, "They look and stare upon me."

35. And the rulers also with them derided him, Laughed at him, made him the object of course jests.

35, 36. Saying, He saved others; let him save himself, if he be Christ, the chosen of God. And the soldiers also mocked him, coming to him, and offering him vinegar.

In mockery, not giving it to him, as they did later in mercy; but in mockery, pretending to present him with weak wine, such as they drank.

37. And saying, If thou be the king of the Jews, save thyself.

I fancy the scorn that they threw into their taunt: "If thou be the king of the Jews;" that was a bit of their own. "Save thyself;" that they borrowed from the rulers. Sometimes a scoffer or a mocker cannot exhibit all the bitterness that is in his heart except by using borrowed terms, as these soldiers did.

38. And a superscription also was written over him in the letters of Greek, and Latin, and Hebrew, THIS IS THE KING OF THE JEWS.

John tells us that Pilate wrote this title, and that the chief priests tried in vain to get him to alter it. It was written in the three current languages of the time, so that the Greek, the Roman, and the Jew might alike understand who he was who was thus put to death. Pilate did not know as much about Christ as we do, or he might have written, THIS IS THE KING OF THE JEWS, AND OF THE GENTILES, TOO.

39. And one of the malefactors which were hanged railed on him, saying, If thou be Christ, save thyself and us.

He, too, borrows this speech from the rulers who derided Christ, only putting the words "and us" as a bit of originality. "If thou be the Christ, save thyself and us."

40, 41. But the other answering rebuked him saying, Dost thou not fear God, seeing thou art in the same condemnation? And we indeed justly; for we receive the reward of our deeds: but this man hath done nothing amiss.

A fine testimony to Christ: "This man hath done nothing amiss;" nothing unbecoming, nothing out of order, nothing criminal, certainly; but nothing even "amiss." This testimony was well spoken by this dying thief.

42–46. And he said unto Jesus, Lord, remember me when thou comest into thy kingdom. And Jesus said unto him, Verily, I say unto thee, to-day shalt thou be with me in paradise. And it was about the sixth hour, and there was a darkness over all the earth until the ninth hour. And the sun was darkened, and the veil of the temple was rent in the midst. And when Jesus had cried with a loud voice, he said, Father, in the thy hands I commend my spirit: and having said thus, he gave up his ghost.

He yielded his life. He did not die, as we have to do, because our appointed time has come, but willingly the great Sacrifice parted with his life: "He gave up the ghost." He was a willing sacrifice for guilty men. Now let us see what John says concerning these hours of agony, these hours of triumph.

John 19:25. Now there stood by the cross of Jesus his mother, and his mother's sister, Mary, the wife of Cleophas, and Mary Magdalene.

Last at the cross, first at the sepulchre. No woman's lip betrayed her Lord; no woman's hand ever smote him; their eyes wept for him; they gazed upon him with pitying awe and love. God bless the Marys! When we see so many of them about the cross, we feel that we honour the very name of Mary.

26. When Jesus therefore saw his mother, and the disciple standing by, whom he loved, he saith into his mother, Woman, behold thy son!

Sad, sad spectacle! Now was fulfilled the word of Simeon, "Yes, a sword shall pierce through thine own soul also, that the thoughts of many hearts may be revealed." Did the Saviour mean, as he gave a glance to John, "Woman, thou art losing one Son; but yonder stands another, who will be a son to thee in my absence"? "Woman, behold thy son!"

27. Then saith he to the disciple, Behold thy mother!

"Take her as thy mother, stand thou in my place, care for her as I have cared for her." Those who love Christ best shall have the honour of taking care of his church and of his poor. Never say of any poor relative or friend, the widow or the fatherless, "They are a great burden to me." Oh, no! Say, "They are a great honour to me; my Lord has entrusted them to my care." John thought so; let us think so. Jesus selected the disciple he loved best to take his mother under his care. He selects those whom he loves best to-day, and puts his poor people under their wing. Take them gladly, and treat them well.

27. And from that hour that disciple took her unto his own home. You expected him to do it, did you not? He loved his Lord so well.

28. After this, Jesus knowing that all things were now accomplished, that the scripture might be fulfilled, saith, I thirst.

There was a prophecy to that effect in the Psalms, and he must needs fulfil that. Think of a dying man prayerfully going through the whole of the Scriptures and carefully fulfilling all that is there written concerning him: "That the scripture might be fulfilled, Jesus saith, I thirst."

29, 30. Now there was set a vessel full of vinegar: and they filled a sponge with vinegar, and put it upon hyssop, and put it to his mouth. When Jesus therefore had received the vinegar, For he did receive it. It was a weak kind of wine, commonly drunk by the soldiery. This is not that mixed potion which he refused, wine mingled with myrrh, which was intended to stupefy the dying in their pains: "When he had tasted thereof, he would not drink;" for he would not be stupefied. He came to suffer to the bitter end the penalty of sin; and he would not have his sorrow mitigated; but when this slight refreshment was offered to him, he received it. Having just expressed his human weakness by saying, "I thirst," he now manifests his all-sufficient strength by crying, with a loud voice as Matthew, Mark, and Luke all testify.

30. He said, It is finished:

What "it" was it that was finished? I will not attempt to expound it. It is the biggest "it" that ever was! Turn it over and you will see that it will grow, and grow, and grow, and grow, till it fills the whole earth: "It is finished."

20. And he bowed his head, and gave up the ghost.

He did not give up the ghost, and then bow his head, because he was dead; but he bowed his head as though in the act of worship, or as leaning it down upon his Father's bosom, and then gave up the ghost. Thus have we had two gospel pictures of our dying Lord. May we remember them, and learn the lessons they are intended to teach!

HYMNS FROM "OUR OWN HYMN BOOK"—561, 279, 278.

Christ's Marvellous Giving

A Sermon (No. 3513) Published on
Thursday, May 25th, 1916.
Delivered by C. H. SPURGEON,
At the Metropolitan Tabernacle, Newington.
ON Lord's-Day Evening, November 25th, 1866.

"Who gave himself for us."—Titus 2:14.

We have once more, you see, the old subject. We still have to tell the story of the love of God towards man in the person of his only begotten Son, Jesus Christ. When you come to your table you find a variety there. Sometimes there is one dish upon it, and sometimes another; but you are never at all surprised to find the bread there every time, and, perhaps, we might add that there would be a deficiency if there were not salt there every time too. So there are certain truths which cannot be repeated too often, and especially is this true of this master-truth, that "God was in Christ, reconciling the world unto himself, not imputing their trespasses unto them." Why, this is the bread of life; "God so loved the world that he gave his only-begotten Son, that whosoever believeth on him should not perish, but have everlasting life." This is the salt upon the table, and must never be forgotten, This is a faithful saying, and worthy of all acceptation, "that Jesus Christ came into the world to save sinners, even the chief."

Now we shall take the text, and use it thus: first of all we shall ask it some questions; then we shall surround it with a setting of facts; and when we have done that, we will endeavour to press out of it its very soul as we draw certain inferences from it. First then:—

I. WE WILL PUT THE TEXT INTO THE WITNESS-BOX, AND ASK IT A FEW QUESTIONS.

There are only five words in the text, and we will be

content to let it go with four questions. "Who gave himself for us" The first question we ask the text is, Who is this that is spoken of? and the text gives the answer. It is "the great God and our Saviour, Jesus Christ, who gave himself for us." We had offended God; the dignity of divine justice demanded that offenses against so good and just a law as that which God had promulgated should not be allowed to go unpunished. But the attribute of justice is not the only one in the heart of God. God is love, and is, therefore, full Of mercy. Yet, nevertheless, he never permits one quality of his Godhead to triumph over another. He could not be too merciful, and so become unjust; he would not permit mercy to put justice to an eclipse. The difficulty was solved thus: God himself stooped from his loftiness and veiled his glory in a garb of our inferior clay. The Word—that same Word without whom was not anything made that was made—became flesh, and dwelt amongst us; and his apostles, his friends, and his enemies, beheld him—the seed of the woman, but yet the Son of God, very God of very God, in all the majesty of deity, and yet man of the substance of his mother in all the weakness of our humanity, sin being the only thing which separated us from him, he being without sin, and we being full of it. It is, then, God, who "gave himself for us"; it is, then, man, who gave himself for us. It is Jesus Christ, co-equal and co-eternal with the Father, who thought it not robbery to be equal with God; who made himself of no reputation, and took upon himself the form of a servant, and was made in the likeness of sinful flesh, and, being found in fashion as a man, humbled himself and became obedient unto death, even the death of the cross. It is Christ Jesus, the man, the God, "who gave himself for us." Now I hope we shall not make any mistakes here, for mistakes here will be fatal. We may be thought uncharitable for saying it, but we should be dishonest if we did not say it, that it is essential to be right here. "Ye cannot be right in the rest Unless ye think rightly of him." You dishonour Christ if you do not believe in his deity. He will have nothing to do with you unless you accept him as being God as well as man. You must receive him as being, without any diminution, completely and wholly divine, and you must accept him as being your brother, as being a man just as you are. This, this is the person, and, relying upon him, we shall find salvation; but, rejecting his deity, he will say to us, "You know me not, and I never knew you!"

The text has answered the question "Who?" and now, putting it in the witness-box again, we ask it another question—"What? What did he do?" The answer is, "He gave himself for us." It was a gift. Christ's offering of himself for us was voluntary; he did it of his own will. He did not die because we merited that, he should love us to the death; on the contrary, we merited that he should hate us; we deserved that he should cast us from his presence obnoxious things, for we were full of sin. We were the wicked keepers of the vineyard, who devoured for our own profit the fruit which belonged to the King's Son, and he is that King's Son, whom we slew, with wicked hands ousting him out of the vineyard. But he died for us who were his enemies. Remember the words of Scripture, "Scarcely for a righteous man will one die; peradventure, for a good, a generous man, one might even dare to die; but God commendeth his love towards us, in that while we were yet sinners, Christ died for the ungodly." He gave himself. We cannot purchase the love of God. This highest expression of divine love, the gift of his own Son, was, in the nature of things, unpurchaseable. What could we have offered that God should come into this world, and be found in fashion as a man, and should die? Why, the works of all the angels in heaven put together could not have deserved one pang from Christ. If for ever the angels had continued their ceaseless songs, and if all men had remained faithful, and could have heaped up their pile of merit to add to that of the angels, and if all the creatures that ever were, or ever shall be, could each bring in their golden hemp of merit—yet could they ever deserve you cross? Could they deserve that the Son of God should hang bleeding and dying there? Impossible! It must by a gift, for it was utterly unpurchaseable; though all worlds were coined and minted, yet could they not have purchased a tear from the Redeemer; they were not worth it. It must be grace; it cannot be merit; he gave himself.

And the gift is so thoroughly a gift that no prep of any kind was brought to bear upon the Saviour. There was no necessity that he should die, except the necessity of his loving us. Ah! friends, we might have been blotted out of existence, and I do not know that there would have been any lack in God's universe if the whole race of man had disappeared. That universe is too wide and great to miss such chirping grasshoppers as we are. When one star is blotted out it may make a little difference to our midnight sky, but to an eye that sees immensity it can make no change. Know ye not that this little solar system, which we think so vast, and those distant fixed stars, and yon mighty masses of nebulae, if such they be, and yonder streaming comet, with its stupendous walk of grandeur—all these are only like a little corner in the field of God's great works? He taketh them all up as nothing, and considereth them mighty as they be, and beyond all human conception great—to be but the small dust of the balance which does not turn the scale; and if they were all gone to-morrow there would be no more loss than as if a few grains of dust were thrown to the summer's wind. But God himself must stoop, rather than we should die. Oh! what magnificence of love! And the more so because there was no need for it. In the course of nature God would have been as holy and as heavenly without us as he is with us, and the pomp of yonder skies would have been as illustrious had we been dashed into the flames of hell as it will be now. God hath gained nought, except the manifestation of a love beyond an angel's dream; a grace, the heights, and depths, and lengths, and breadths of which surpass all knowledge of all creatures. God only knows the love of God which is manifested in Jesus Christ. He gave himself. We will leave this point now, when it is fully understood that Christ's dying to save sinners, and giving himself for the ungodly, was a pure act of gratuitous mercy. There was nothing to compel God to give his Son, and nothing to lead the Son to die, except the simple might of his love to men. He would not see us die. He had a Father's love to us. He seemed to stand over our fallen race, as David stood over Absalom, and we were as bad as Absalom; and there he fled, and said, "My son, my son! Would God I had died for thee, my son, my son!" But he did more than this, for he did die for us. and all for love of Us who were his enemies! "So strange, so boundless was the love, Which pitied dying man; The Father sent his equal Son To give them life again." 'Twas all of love and of grace!

The third question is, "What did he give?" "Who gave himself for us," and here lies the glory of the text, that he gave not merely the crowns and royalties of heaven, though it was much to leave these, to come and don the humble garb of a carpenter's son; not the songs of seraphs, not the shouts of cherubim: 'twas something to leave them to come and dwell amongst the groans and tears of this poor fallen world; not the grandeur of his Father's court, though it was much to leave that to come and live with wild beasts, and men more wild than they, to fast his forty days and then to die in ignomy and shame upon the tree. No; there is little said about all this. He gave all this, it is true, but he gave himself. Mark, brethren, what a richness there is here! It is not that he gave his righteousness, though that has become our dress. It is not even that he gave his blood, though that is the fount in which we wash. It is that he gave himself—his Godhead and manhood both combined. All that that word "Christ" means he came to us and for us. He gave himself. Oh! that we could dive and plunge into—this unfathomed sea—himself! Omnipotence, Omniscience, Infinity—himself. He gave himself—purity, love, kindness, meekness, gentleness—that wonderful compound of all perfections, to make up one perfection-himself. You do not come to Christ's house and say, "He gives me this house, his church, to dwell in." You do not come to his table and merely say, "He gives me this table to feast at," but you go farther, and you take him by faith into your arms, and you say, "Who loved me, and gave himself for me." Oh! that you could get hold of that sweet word—himself! It is the love of a husband to his wife, who not only gives her all that she can wish, daily food and raiment, and all the comforts that can nourish and cherish her, and make her life glad, but who gives himself to her. So does Jesus. The body and soul of Jesus, the deity of Jesus, and all that that means, he has been pleased to give to and for his people. "Who gave himself for us."

There is another question which we shall ask the text, and that is, "For whom did Christ give himself?" Well, the text says, "For us." There be those who say that Christ has thus given himself for every man now living, or that ever did or shall live. We are not able to subscribe to the statement, though there is a truth in it, that in a certain sense he is "the Saviour of all men," but then it is added, "Specially of them that believe." At any rate, dear hearer, let me tell thee one thing that is certain. Whether atonement may be said to be particular or general, there are none who partake in its real efficacy but certain characters, and those characters are known by certain infallible signs. You must not say that he gave himself for you unless these signs are manifest in you, and the first sign is that of simple faith in the Lord Jesus. If thou believest in him, that shall be a proof to thee that he gave himself for thee. See, if he gave himself for all men alike, then he did equally for Judas and for Peter. Care you for such love as that? He died equally for those who were then in hell as for those who were then in heaven. Care you for such a doctrine as that? For my part, I desire to have a personal, peculiar, and special interest in the precious blood of Jesus; such an interest in it as shall lead me to his right hand, and enable me to say, "He hath washed me from my sins, in his blood." Now I think we have no right to conclude that we shall have any benefit from the death of Christ unless we trust him, and if we do trust him, that trust will produce the following things:—"Who gave himself for us, that he might redeem us from all iniquity"—we shall hate sin; we shall fight against it;

we shall be delivered from it—"and purify unto himself a peculiar people, zealous of good works." I have no right, therefore, to conclude that I shall be a partaker of the precious blood of Jesus unless I become in my life "zealous of good works," My good works cannot save me, cannot even help to save me; but they are evidences of my being saved, and if I am not zealous for good works, I lack the evidence of salvation, and I have no right whatever to conclude that I shall receive one jot of benefit from Christ's sufferings upon the tree. Oh! my dear hearer, I would to God that thou couldest trust the Man, the God, who died on Calvary! I would that thou couldest trust him so that thou couldest say, "He will save me; he has saved me." The gratitude which you would feel towards him would inspire you with an invincible hatred against sin. You would begin to fight against every evil way; you would conform yourselves, by his grace, to his law and his Word, and you would become a new creature in him! May God grant that you may yet be able to say, "Who gave himself for me"! I have asked the text enough questions, and there I leave them. For a few minutes only I am now going to use the text another way, namely:—

II. PUT THE TEXT INTO A SETTING OF FACTS.

There was a day before all days when there was no day but the Ancient of Days; a time when there was no time, but when Eternity was all. Then God, in the eternal purpose, decreed to save his people. If we may speak so of things too mysterious for us to know them, and which we can only set forth after the manner of men, God had determined that his people should be saved, but he foresaw that they would sin. It was necessary, therefore, that the penalty due to their sins should be borne by someone. They could not be saved except a substitute were found who would bear the penalty of sin in their place and stead. Where was such a substitute to be found? No angel offered. There was no angel, for God dwelt alone, and even if there had then been angels, they could never have dared to offer to sustain the fearful weight of human guilt. But in that solemn council-chamber, when it was deliberated who should enter into bonds of suretyship to pay all the debts of the people of God, Christ came and gave himself a bondsman and a surety for all that was due—from them, or would be due from them, to the judgment-seat of God. In that day, then, he "gave himself for us."

But Time began, and this round world had made, in the mind of God, a few revolutions. Men said the world was getting old, but to God it was but an infant. But the fulness of time was come, and suddenly, amidst the darkness of the night, there was heard sweeter singing than ere had come from mortal lips, "Glory to God in the highest; on earth peace; good will to men!" What lit up the sky with unwonted splendour and what had filled the air with chorales at the dead of night? See the Babe upon its mother's breast, there in Bethlehem's manger! "He gave himself for us." That same one who had given himself a surety has come down to earth to be a man, and to give himself for us. See him! For thirty years he toils on, amidst the drudgery of the carpenters shop! What is he doing? The law needed to be fulfilled, and he "gave himself for us," and fulfilled the law. But now the time comes when he is thirty-two or thirty-three years of age, and the law demands that the penalty shall be paid. Do you see him going to meet Judas in the garden, with confident, but solemn step? He "gave himself for us." He could with a word have driven those soldiers into hell, but they bind him—he "gave himself for us." They take him before Pilate, and Herod and Caiaphas, and they mock at him, and jeer him, and pluck his cheeks, and flagellate his shoulders! How is it that he will start at this rate? How is it that he bears so passively all the insults and indignities which they heap upon him? He gave himself for us. Our sins demanded smart; he bared his back and took the smart; he have himself for us. But do you see that dreadful procession going through the streets of Jerusalem, along the rough pavement of the Via Dolorosa? Do you see the weeping women as they mourn because of him? How is it that he is willing to be led a captive up to the hill of Calvary? Alas! they throw him on the around! They drive accursed iron through his hands and feet. They hoist him into the air! They dash the cross into its appointed place, and there he hangs, a naked spectacle of scorn and shame, derided of men, and mourned by angels. How is it that the Lord of glory, who made all worlds, and hung out the stars like lamps, should now be bleeding and dying there? He gave himself for us. Can you see the streaming fountains of the four wounds in his hands and feet' Can you trace his agony as it carves lines upon his brow and all down his emaciated frame? No you cannot see the griefs of his soul. No spirit can behold them. They were too terrible for you to know them. It seemed as though all hell were emptied into the bosom of the Son of God, and as though all the miseries of all the ages were made to meet upon him, till he bore:—"All that incarnate God, could bear, With strength enough, but none to spare." Now why is all this but that he gave himself for us till his head hung down in death, and his arms, in chill, cold death, hung down by his side, and they buried the lifeless Victor in the tomb of Joseph of Arimethea? He gave himself for us!

What more now remaineth? He lives again; on the third day he cometh from the tomb, and even then he still gave himself for us! Oh! yes, beloved, he has gone up on high but he still gives himself for us, for up there he is constantly engaged in pleading the sinner's cause. Up yonder, amidst the glories of heaven, he has not forgotten us poor sinners who are here below, but he spreads his hands, and pleads before his Father's throne and wins for us unnumbered blessings, for he gave himself for us.

And I have been thinking whether I might not use the text in another way. Christ's servants wanted a subject upon which to preach, and so he "gave himself for us," to be the constant topic of our ministry. Christ's servants wanted a sweet companion to be with them in their troubles, and he gave himself for us. Christ's people want comfort; they want spiritual food and drink, and so he gave himself for us—his flesh to be our meat, and his blood to be our spiritual drink. And we expect soon to go home to the land of the hereafter, to the realms of the blessed, and what is to be our heaven? Why, our heaven will be Christ himself, for he gave himself for Us. Oh! he is all that we want, all that we wish for! We cannot desire anything greater and better than to be with Christ, and to have Christ, to feed upon Christ, to lie in Christ's bosom, to know the kisses of his mouth, to look at the gleamings of his loving eyes, to hear his loving words, to feel him press us to his heart, and tell us that he has loved us from before the foundation of the world, and given himself for us.

I think we have put the text now into a setting of certain facts; do not forget them, but let them be your joy!

And now the last thing we have to do is to:—

III. TURN THE TEXT TO PRACTICAL ACCOUNT BY DRAWING FROM IT A FEW INFERENCES.

The first inference I draw is this—that be who gave himself for his people will cat deny them anything. This is a sweet encouragement to you who practice the art of prayer. You know how Paul puts it, "He that spared not his own Son, but delivered him up for us all, how shall he not, with him, also freely give us all things?" Christ is all. If Christ gives himself to you, he will give you your bread and your water, and he will give you a house to dwell in. If he gives you himself, he will not let you starve on the road to heaven. Jesus Christ does not Give us himself and then deny us common things. Oh! child of God, go boldly to the throne of grace! Thou hast got the major; thou shalt certainly have the minor; thou hast the greater, thou canst not be denied the less.

Now I draw another inference, namely, that if Christ has already given himself in so painful a way as I have described, since there is no need that he should suffer any more, we must believe that he is willing to give himself now unto the hearts of poor sinners. Beloved, for Christ to come to Bethlehem is a greater stoop than for him to come into your heart. Had Christ to die upon Calvary? That is all done, and he need not die again. Do you think that he who is willing to die is unwilling to apply the results of his passion? If a man leaps into the water to bring out a drowning child, after he has brought the child alive on shore, if he happens to have a piece of bread in his pocket, and the child needs it, do you think that he who rescued the child's life will deny that child so small a thing as a piece of bread? And come, dost thou think that Christ died on Calvary, and yet will not come into thy heart if thou seekest him? Dost thou believe that he who died for sinners will ever reject the prayer of a sinner? If thou believest that thou thinkest hardly of him, for his heart is very tender. He feels even a cry. You know how it is with your children; if they cry through pain, why, you would give anything for someone to come and heal them; and if you cry because your sin is painful, the great Physician will come and heal you. Ah! Jesus Christ is much more easily moved by our cries and tears than we are by the vies of our fellow-creatures. Come, poor sinner, come and put thy trust in my Master! Thou canst not think him hard-hearted. If he were, why did he die? Dost thou think him unkind? Then why did he bleed? Thou art inclined to think so hardly of him! Thou art making great cuts at his heart when thou thinkest him to be untender and ungenerous. "As I live, saith the Lord, I have no pleasure in the death of him that dieth, but rather that he would turn unto me and live." This is the voice of the God whom you look upon as so sternly just! Did Jesus Christ, the tender one, speak in even more plaintive tones, "Come unto me, all ye that labour and are heavy-laden, and I will give you rest"? You working men, you labouring men, Christ bids you come to him "all ye that labour." And you who are unhappy, you who know you have done wrong, and cannot sleep at nights because of it; you who are troubled about sin, and would fain go and hide your heads, and get:— "Anywhere, anywhere out of the world," —your Father says to you one and all, "Run not from me, but come to me, my child!" Jesus, who died, says, "Flee not from me, but come to me, for

I will accept you; I will receive you; I cast out none that come unto me. "Sinner, Jesus never did reject a coming soul yet, and he never will. Oh! try him! Try him! Now come, with thy sins about thee just as thou art, to the bleeding, dying Saviour, and he will say to thee, "I have blotted out thy sins; go and sin no more; I have forgiven thee." May God grant thee grace to put thy trust in him "who gave himself for us"!

There are many other inferences which I might draw if I had time, but if this last one we have drawn be so applied to your hearts as to be carried out, it will be enough. Now do not you go and try to do good worlds in order to merit heaven. Do not go and try to pray yourselves into heaven by the efficacy of praying. Remember, he "gave himself for us." The old proverb is that "there is nothing freer than a gift," and surely this gift of God, this eternal life, must be free, and we must have it freely, or not at all. I sometimes see put up at some of our doctors that they receive "gratis patients." That is the sort of patients my Master receives. He receives none but those who come gratis. He never did receive anything yet, and he never will, except your love and your thanks after he has saved you. But you must come to him empty-handed; came just as you are, and he will receive you now, and you shall live to sing to the praise and the glory of his grace who has accepted you in the Beloved, and "who gave himself for us" God help you to do it. Amen.

Christ's Hospital

A Sermon (No. 2260) Intended for
Reading on Lord's-Day, June 12th, 1892,
Delivered by C. H. SPURGEON,
At the Metropolitan Tabernacle, Newington.
ON Lord's-Day Evening, March 9th, 1890.

"He healeth the broken in heart, and bindeth up their wounds."—Psalm 147:3.

Often as we have read this Psalm, we can never fail to be struck with the connection in which this verse stands, especially its connection with the verse that follows. Read the two together: "He healeth the broken in heart, and bindeth up their wounds. He telleth the number of the stars; he calleth them all by their names." What condescension and grandeur! What pity and omnipotence! He who leads out yonder ponderous orbs in almost immeasurable orbits, nevertheless, is the Surgeon of men's souls, and stoops over broken hearts, and with his own tender fingers closes up the gaping wound, and binds it with the liniment of love. Think of it; and if I should not speak as well as I could desire upon the wonderful theme of his condescension, yet help me by your own thoughts to do reverence to the Maker of the stars, who is, at the same time, the Physician for broken hearts and wounded spirits.

I am equally interested in the connection of my text with the verse that goes before it: "The Lord doth build up Jerusalem: he gathereth together the outcasts of Israel." The church of God is never so well built up as when it is built up with men of broken hearts. I have prayed to God in secret many a time, of late, that he would be pleased to gather out from among us a people who have a deep experience, who should know the guilt of sin, who should be broken and ground to powder under a sense of their own inability and unworthiness; for I am persuaded that, without a deep experience of sin, there is seldom much belief in the doctrine of grace, and not much enthusiasm in praising the Saviour's name. The church needs to be built up with men who have been pulled down. Unless we know in our hearts our need of a Saviour, we shall never be worth much in preaching him. That preacher who has never been converted, what can he say about it? And he who has never been in the dungeon, who has never been in the abyss, who has never felt as if he were cast out from the sight of God, how can he comfort many who are outcasts, and who are bound with the fetters of despair? May the Lord break many hearts, and then bind them up, that with them he may build up the church, and inhabit it!

But now, leaving the connection, I come to the text itself, and I desire to speak of it so that everyone here who is troubled may derive comfort from it, God the Holy Ghost speaking through it. Consider, first, the patients and their sickness: "He healed the broken in heart." Then, consider, the Physician and his medicine, and for a while turn your eyes to him who does this healing work. Then, I shall want you to consider, the testimonial to the great Physician which we have in this verse: "He healed the broken in heart, and bindeth up their wounds." Lastly, and most practically, we will consider, what we ought to do towards him who healeth the broken in heart.

I. First, then, consider THE PATIENTS AND THEIR SICKNESS. They are broken in heart. I have heard of many who have died of a broken heart; but there are some who live with a broken heart, and who live all the better for having had their hearts broken; they live another and higher life than they lived before that blessed stroke broke their hearts in pieces.

There are many sorts of broken hearts, and Christ is good at healing them all. I am not going to lower and narrow the application of my text. The patients of the great Physician are those whose hearts are broken through sorrow. Hearts are broken through disappointment. Hearts are broken through bereavement. Hearts are broken in ten thousand ways, for this is a heart-breaking world; and Christ is good at healing all manner of heart-breaks. I would encourage every person here, even though his heart-break may not be of a spiritual kind, to make an application to him who healed the broken in heart. The text does not say, "the spiritually broken in heart", therefore I will not insert an adverb where there is none in the passage. Come hither, ye that are burdened, all ye that labour and are heavy laden; come hither, all ye that sorrow, be your sorrow what it may; come hither, all ye whose hearts are broken, be the heart-break what it may, for he healeth the broken in heart.

Still, there is a special brokenness of heart to which Christ gives the very earliest and tenderest attention. He heals those whose hearts are broken for sin. Christ heals the heart that is broken because of its sin; so that it grieves, laments, regrets, and bemoans itself, saying, "Woe is me that I have done this exceeding great evil, and brought ruin upon myself! Woe is me that I have dishonoured God, that I have cast myself away from his presence, that I have made myself liable to his everlasting wrath, and that even now his wrath abideth upon me!" If there is a man here whose heart is broken about his past life, he is the man to whom my text refers. Are you heart-broken because you have wasted forty, fifty, sixty years? Are you heart-broken at the remembrance that you have cursed the God who has blessed you, that you have denied the existence of him without whom you never would have been in existence yourself, that you have lived to train your family without godliness, without any respect to the Most High God at all? Has the Lord brought this home to you? Has he made you feel what a hideous thing it is to be blind to Christ, to refuse his love, to reject his blood, to live an enemy to your best Friend? Have you felt this? O my friend, I cannot reach across the gallery to give you my hand; but will you think that I am doing it, for I wish to do it? If there is a heart here broken on account of sin, I thank God for it, and praise the Lord that there is such a text as this: "He healeth the broken in heart." Christ also heals hearts that are broken from sin. When you and sin have quarrelled, never let the quarrel be made up again. You and sin were friends at one time; but now you hate sin, and you would be wholly rid of it if you could. You wish never to sin. You are anxious to be clear of the most darling sin that you ever indulged in, and you desire to be made as pure as God is pure. Your heart is broken away from its old moorings. That which you once loved you now hate. That which you once hated you now at least desire to love. It is well. I am glad that you are here, for to you is the text sent, "He healeth the broken in heart."

If there is a broken-hearted person anywhere about, many people despise him. "Oh," they say, "he is melancholy, he is mad, he is out of his mind through religion!" Yes, men despise the broken in heart, but such, O God, thou wilt not despise! The Lord looks after such, and heals them.

Those who do not despise them, at any rate avoid them. I know some few friends who have long been of a broken heart; and when I feel rather dull, I must confess that I do not always go their way, for they are apt to make me feel more depressed. Yet would I not get out of their way if I felt that I could help them. Still, it is the nature of men to seek the cheerful and the happy, and to avoid the broken-hearted. God does not do so; he heals the broken in heart. He goes where they are, and he reveals himself to them as the Comforter and the Healer.

In a great many cases people despair of the broken-hearted ones. "It is no use," says one, "I have tried to comfort her, but I cannot do it." "I have wasted a great many words," says another, "on such and such a friend, and I cannot help him. I despair of his ever getting out of the dark." Not so is it with God; he healeth the broken in heart. He despairs of none. He shows the greatness of his power, and the wonders of his wisdom, by fetching men and women out of the lowest dungeon, wherein despair has shut them.

As for the broken-hearted ones themselves, they do not think that they ever can be converted. Some of them are sure that they never can; they wish that they were dead, though I do not see what they would gain by that. Others of them wish that they had never been born, though that is a useless wish now. Some are ready to rush after any new thing to try to find a little comfort; while others, getting worse and worse, are sitting down in sullen despair. I wish that I knew who these were; I should like to come round, and just say to them, "Come, brother; there must be no doubting and no despair to-night, for my text is gloriously complete, and is meant for you. "He healeth the broken in heart, and bindeth up their wounds." Notice that fifth verse, "Great is our Lord, and of great power; his understanding is infinite." Consequently, he can heal the broken in heart. God is glorious at a dead lift. When a soul cannot stir, or help itself, God delights to come in with his omnipotence, and lift the great load, and set the burdened one free.

It takes great wisdom to comfort a broken heart. If any of you have ever tried it, I am sure you have not found it an easy task. I have given much of my life to this work; and I always come away from a desponding one with a consciousness of my own inability to comfort the heart-broken and cast-down. Only God can do it. Blessed be his name that he has arranged that one Person of the Sacred Trinity should undertake this office of Comforter; for no man could ever perform its duties. We might as well hope to be the Saviour as to be the Comforter of the heart-broken. Efficiently and completely to save or to comfort must be a work divine. That is why the Holy Divine Spirit, healeth the broken in heart, and bindeth up their wounds with infinite power and unfailing skill.

II. Now, secondly, we are going to consider THE PHYSICIAN AND HIS MEDICINE: "He healeth the broken in heart, and bindeth up their wounds." Who is this that healeth the broken in heart?

I answer that Jesus was anointed of God for this work. He said, "The Spirit of the Lord is upon me, because he hath anointed me to preach the gospel to the poor; he hath sent me to heal the broken-hearted." Was the Holy Spirit given to Christ in vain? That cannot be. He was given for a purpose which must be answered, and that purpose is the healing of the broken-hearted. By the very anointing of Christ by the Holy Spirit, you may be sure that our Physician will heal the broken in heart.

Further, Jesus was sent of God on purpose to do his work; "He hath sent me to heal the broken-hearted." If Christ does not heal the broken-hearted, he will not fulfill the mission for which he came from heaven. If the broken-hearted are not cheered by his glorious life and the blessings that flow out of his death, then he will have come to earth for nothing. This is the very errand on which the Lord of glory left the bosom of the Father to be veiled in human clay, that he might heal the broken in heart; and he will do it.

Our Lord was also educated for this work. He was not only anointed and sent; but he was trained for it. "How?" say you. Why, he had a broken heart himself; and there is no education for the office of comforter like being place where you yourself have need of comfort, so that you may be able to comfort others with the comfort wherewith you yourself have been comforted of God. Is your heart broken? Christ's heart was broken. He said, "Reproach hath broken my heart; and I am full of heaviness." He went as low as you have ever been, and deeper than you can ever go. "My God, my God, why hast thou forsaken me?" was his bitter cry. If that be your agonized utterance, he can interpret it by his own suffering. He can measure your grief by his grief. Broken hearts, there is no healing for you except through him who had a broken heart himself. Ye disconsolate, come to him! He can make your heart happy and joyous, by the very fact of his own sorrow, and the brokenness of his own heart. "In all our afflictions he was afflicted." He was tempted in all points like as we are", "a man of sorrows and acquainted with grief." For a broken heart, there is no physician like him.

Once more, I can strongly recommend my Lord Jesus Christ as the Healer of broken hearts, because he is so experienced in the work. Some people are afraid that the doctor will try experiments upon them; but our Physician will only do for us what he has done many times before. It is no matter of experiment with him; it is a matter of experience. If you knock to-night at my great Doctor's door, you will, perhaps say to him, "Here is the strangest patient, my Lord, that ever came to thee." He will smile as he looks at you, and he will think, "I have saved hundreds like you." Here comes one who says, "That first man's case was nothing compared with mine; I am about the worst sinner who ever lived." And the Lord Jesus Christ will say, "Yes, I saved the worst man that ever lived long ago, and I keep on saving such as he. I delight to do it." But here comes one who has a curious odd way of broken-heartedness. He is an out-of-the-way fretter. Yes, but my Lord is able to "have compassion on the ignorant, and on them that are out of the way." He can lay hold of this out-of-the-way one; for he has always been saving out-of-the-way sinners. My Lord has been healing broken hearts well nigh nineteen hundred years. Can you find a brass-plate anywhere in London telling of a physician of that age? He has been at the work longer than that; for it is not far off six thousand years since he went into this business, and he has been healing the broken in heart ever since that time.

I will tell you one thing about him that I have on good authority, that is, he never lost a case yet. There never was one who came to him with a broken heart, but he healed him. He never said to one, "You are too bad for me to heal;" but he did say, "Him that cometh to me, I will in now wise cast out." My dear hearer, he will not cast you out. You say, "You do not know me, Mr. Spurgeon." No, I do not; and you have come here to-night, and you hardly know why you are here; only you are very low and very sad. The Lord Jesus Christ loves such as you are, you poor, desponding, doubting, desolate, disconsolate one. Daughters of sorrow, sons of grief, look ye here! Jesus Christ has gone on healing broken hearts for thousands of years, and he is well up in the business. He understands it by experience, as well as by education. He is "mighty to save." Consider him; consider him; and the Lord grant you grace to come and trust him even now!

Thus I have talked to you about the Physician for broken hearts; shall I tell you what his chief medicine is? It is his own flesh and blood. There is no cure like it. When a sinner is bleeding with sin, Jesus pours his own blood into the wound; and when that wound is slow in healing, he binds his own sacrifice about it. Healing for broken hearts comes by the atonement, atonement by substitution, Christ suffering in our stead. He suffered for every one who believeth in him, and he that believeth in him is not condemned, and never can be condemned, for the condemnation due to him was laid upon Christ. He is clear before the bar of justice as well as before the throne of mercy. I remember when the Lord put that precious ointment upon my wounded spirit. Nothing ever healed me until I understood that he died in my place and stead, died that I might not die; and now, to-day, my heart would bleed itself to death were it not that I believe that he "his own self bare our sins in his own body on the tree." "With his stripes we are healed," and with no medicine but this atoning sacrifice. A wonderful heal-all is this, when the Holy Ghost applies it with his own divine power, and lets life and love come streaming into the heart that was ready to bleed to death.

III. My time flies too quickly; so, thirdly, I want you to consider THE TESTIMONIAL TO THE GREAT PHYSICIAN which is emblazoned in my text. It is God the Holy Ghost who, by the mouth of his servant David, bears testimony to this congregation to-night that the Lord Jesus heals the broken in heart, and binds up their wounds. If I said it, you need no more believe it than I need believe it if you said it. One man's word is as good as another's if we be truthful men; but this statement is found in an inspired Psalm. I believe it; I dare not doubt it, for I have proven its truth.

I understand my text to mean this: he does it effectually. As I said last Thursday night, if there is a person cast down or desponding within twenty miles, he is pretty sure to find me out. I laugh sometimes, and say, "Birds of a feather flock together;" but they come to talk to me about their despondency, and sometimes they leave me half desponding in the attempt to get them out of their sadness. I have had some very sad cases just lately, and I am afraid that, when they went out of my room, they could not say of me, "He healeth the broken in heart." I am sure that they could say, "He tried his best. He brought out all the choicest arguments he could think of to comfort me." And they have felt very grateful. They have come back sometimes to thank God that they have been a little bit encouraged; but some of them are frequent visitors; and I have been trying to cheer them up by the month together. But, when my Master undertakes the work, "He healeth the broken in heart," he not only tries to do it, he does it. He touches the secret sources of the sorrow, and takes the spring of the grief away. We try our bests; but we cannot do it. You know it is very hard to deal with the heart. The human heart needs more than human skill to cure it. When a person dies, and the doctors do not know the complaint of which he died, they say, "It was heart disease." They did not understand his malady; that is what that means. There is only one Physician who can heal the heart; but, glory be to his blessed name, "He healeth the broken in heart," he does it effectually.

As I read my text, I understand it to mean, he does it constantly. "He healeth the broken in heart." Not merely, "He did heal them years ago"; but he is doing it now. "He healeth the broken in heart, and bindeth up their wounds." What, at this minute? Ten minutes to eight? Yes, he is doing this work now. "He healeth the broken in heart," and when the service is over, and the congregation is gone, what will Jesus be doing then? Oh, he will still be healing the broken in heart! Suppose this year 1890 should run out, and the Lord does not come to judgment, what will he be doing then? He will still be healing the broken in heart. He has not used up his ointments. He has not exhausted his patience. He has not in the least degree diminished his power. He still healeth. "Oh dear!" said one, "If I had come to Christ a year ago, it would have been well with me." If you come to Christ to-night, it will be well with you, for "he healeth the broken in heart." I do not know who was the inventor of that idea of "sinning away the day of grace." If you are willing to have Christ, you may have him. If you are as old as Methuselah—and I do not suppose that you are older than he was—if you want Christ, you may have him. As long as you are out of hell, Christ is able to save you. He is going on with his old work. Because you are just past fifty, you say the die is cast; because you are past eighty, you say, "I am too old to be saved now." Nonsense! He healeth, he healeth, he is still doing it, "he healeth the broken in heart."

I go further than that, and say that he does it invariably. I have shown you that he does it effectually and constantly; but he does it invariably. There never was a broken heart brought to him that he did not heal. Do not some broken-hearted patients go out at the back door, as my Master's failures? No, not one. There never was one yet that he could not heal. Doctors are obliged, sometimes, in our hospitals to give up some persons, and say that they will never recover. Certain symptoms have proved that they are incurable. But, despairing one, in the divine hospital, of which Christ is the Physician, there never was a patient of his who was turned out as incurable. He is able to save to the uttermost. Do you know how far that is—"to the uttermost"? There is no going beyond "the uttermost", because the uttermost goes beyond everything else, to make it the uttermost. "He is able to save them to the uttermost that come unto God by him." Where are you, friend "Uttermost"? Are you here to-night? "Ah!" you say, "I wonder that I am not in hell." Well, so do I; but you are not, and you never will be, if you cast yourself on Christ. Rest in the full atonement that he has made; for he healeth always, without any failure, "he healeth the broken in heart, and bindeth up their wounds."

As I read these words, it seems to me that he glories in doing it. He said to the Psalmist, by the Holy Spirit, "Write a Psalm in which you shall begin with Hallelujah, and finish with Hallelujah, and set in the middle of the Psalm this as one of the things for which I delight to be praised, that I heal the broken in heart." None of the gods of the heathen were ever praised for this. Did you ever read a song to Jupiter, or to Mercury, or to Venus, or to any of them, in which they were praised for binding up the broken in heart? Jehovah, the God of Israel, the God of Abraham, Isaac, and Jacob, the God and Father of our Lord and Saviour Jesus Christ, is the only God who makes it his boast that he binds up the broken in heart. Come, you big, black sinner; come, you desperado; come, you that have gone beyond all measurement in sin; you can glorify God more than anybody else by believing that he can save even you! He can save you, and put you among the children. He delights to save those that seemed farthest from him.

IV. This is my last point: consider WHAT WE OUGHT TO DO.

If there is such a Physician as this, and we have broken hearts, it goes without saying that, first of all, we ought to resort to him. When people are told that they have an incurable disease, a malady that will soon bring them to their grave, they are much distressed; but if, somewhere or other, they hear that the disease may be cured after all, they say, "Where? Where?" Well, perhaps it is thousands of miles away; but they are willing to go if they can. Or the medicine may be very unpleasant or very expensive; but if they find that they can be cured, they say, "I will have it." If anyone came to their door, and said, "Here it is, it will heal you; and you can have it for nothing, and as much as you ever want of it;" there would be no difficulty in getting rid of any quantity of the medicine, so long as we found people sick. Now, if you have a broken heart to-night, you will be glad to have Christ. I had a broken heart once, and I went to him and he healed it in a moment, and made me sing for joy! Young men and women, I was about fifteen or sixteen when he healed me. I wish that you would go to him now, while you are yet young. The age of his patients does not matter. Are you younger than fifteen? Boys and girls may have broken hearts; and old men and old women may have broken hearts; but they may come to Jesus and be healed. Let them come to him tonight, and seek to be healed.

When you are about to go to Christ, possibly you ask, "How shall I go to him?" Go by prayer. One said to me, the other day, "I wish that you would write me a prayer, sir." I said, "No, I cannot do that, go and tell the Lord what you want." He replied, "Sometimes I feel such a great want that I do not know what it is I do want, and I try to pray, but I cannot. I wish that somebody would tell me what to say." "Why!" I said, "the Lord has told you what to say. This is what he has said: 'Take with you words, and turn to the Lord: say unto him, Take away all iniquity, and receive us graciously.'" Go to Christ in prayer with such words as those, or any others that you can get. If you cannot get any words, tears are just as good, and rather better; and groans and sighs and secret desires will be acceptable with God.

But add faith to them. Trust the Physician. You know that no ointment will heal you if you do not put it on the wound. Oftentimes when there is a wound, you want something with which to strap the ointment on. Faith straps on the heavenly heal-all. Go to the Lord with your broken heart, and believe that he can heal you. Believe that he alone can heal you; trust him to do it. Fall at his feet, and say, "If I perish, I will perish here. I believe that the Son of God can save me, and I will be saved by him; but I will never look anywhere else for salvation. 'Lord, I believe; help thou mine unbelief!'" If you have come as far as that, you are very near the light; the great Physician will heal your broken heart before very long. Trust him to do it now.

When you have trusted in him, and your heart is healed, and you are happy, tell others about him. I do not like my Lord to have any tongue-tied children. I do not mean that I would want you all to preach. When a whole church takes to preaching, it is as if the whole body were a mouth, and that would be a vacuum. I want you to tell others, in some way or other, what the Lord has done for you; and be earnest in endeavouring to bring others to the great Physician. You all recollect, therefore I need not tell you again, the story that we had about the doctor at one of our hospitals, a year or two ago. He healed a dog's broken leg, and the grateful animal brought other dogs to have their broken legs healed. That was a good dog; some of you are not half as good as that dog. You believe that Christ is blessing you, yet you never try to bring others to him to be saved. That must not be the case any longer. We must excel that dog in our love for our species; and it must be our intense desire that, if Christ has healed us, he should heal our wife, our child, our friend, our neighbour; and we should never rest till others are brought to him.

Then, when others are brought to Christ, or even if they will not be brought to him, be sure to praise him. If your broken heart has been healed, and you are saved, and your sins forgiven, praise him. We do not sing half enough. I do not mean in our congregations; but when we are at home. We pray every day. Do we sing every day? I think that we should. Matthew Henry used to say, about family prayer, "They that pray do well; they that read and pray do better; they that read and pray and sing do best of all." I think that Matthew Henry was right. "Well, I have no voice," says one. Have you not? Then you never grumble at your wife; your never find fault with your food; you are not one of those who make the household unhappy by your evil speeches. "Oh, I do not mean that!" No, I thought you did not mean that. Well, praise the Lord with the same voice that you have used for complaining. "But I could not lend a tune," says one. Nobody said you were to do so. You can at least sing as I do. My singing is of a very peculiar character. I find that I cannot confine myself to one tune; in the course of a verse I use half-a-dozen tunes; but the Lord, to whom I sing, never finds any fault with me.

He never blames me, because I do not keep this tune or that. I cannot help it. My voice runs away with me, and my heart too; but I keep on humming something or other by way of praising God's name. I would like you to do the same. I used to know an old Methodist; and the first thing in the morning, when he got up, he began singing a bit of a Methodist hymn; and if I met the old man during the day, he was always singing. I have seen him in his little workshop, with his lapstone on his knee, and he was always singing, and beating with his hammer. When I said to him once, "Why do you always sing, dear brother?" he replied, "Because I always have something to sing about." That is a good reason for singing. If our broken hearts have been healed, we have something to sing about in time and throughout eternity. Let us begin to do so to the praise of the glory of his grace, who "healeth the broken in heart, and bindeth up their wounds." God bless all the broken hearts that are in this congregation to-night, for Jesus' sake! Amen.

Psalm 147.

This is one of the Hallelujah Psalms; it begins and ends with "Praise ye the LORD." May our hearts be in tune, that we may praise the Lord while we read these words of praise!

Verse 1. Praise ye the LORD: It is not enough for the Psalmist to do it himself. He wants help in it, so he says, "Praise ye the LORD." Wake up, my brethren; bestir yourselves, my sisters; come, all of you, and unite in this holy exercise! "Praise ye the LORD."

1. For it is good to sing praises unto our God; for it is pleasant; and praise is comely.

When a thing is good, pleasant, and comely, you have certainly three excellent reasons for attending to it. It is not everything that is good; but here you have a happy combination of goodness, pleasantness, and comliness. It will do you good to praise God. God counts it good, and you will find it a pleasant exercise. That which is the occupation of heaven must be happy employment. "It is good to sing praises unto our God," "it is pleasant," and certainly nothing is more "comely" and beautiful, and more in accordance with the right order of things, than for creatures to praise their Creator, and the children of God to praise their Father in heaven.

2. The LORD doth build up Jerusalem:

Praise his name for that. You love his church; be glad that he builds it up. Praise him who quarries every

stone, and puts it upon the one foundation that is laid, even Jesus.

2. He gathereth together the outcasts of Israel.

Praise him for that. If you were once an outcast, and he has gathered you, give him your special personal song of thanksgiving.

3. He healeth the broken in heart, and bindeth up their wounds.

Praise him for that, ye who have had broken hearts! If he has healed you, surely you should give him great praise.

4. He telleth the number of the stars; he calleth them all by their names.

He who heals broken hearts counts the stars, and calls them by their names, as men call their servants, and send them on their way. Praise his name. Can you look up at the starry sky at night without praising him who made the stars, and leads out their host?

5. Great is our Lord, and of great power: his understanding is infinite.

Praise him, then; praise his greatness, his almightiness, his infinite wisdom. Can you do otherwise? Oh, may God reveal himself so much to your heart that you shall be constrained to pay him willing adoration!

6. The LORD lifteth up the meek:

What a lifting up it is for them, out of the very dust where they have been trodden down by the proud and the powerful! The Lord lifts them up. Praise him for that.

6. He casteth the wicked down to the ground.

Thus he puts an end to their tyranny, and delivers those who were ground beneath their cruel power. Praise ye his name for this also. Excuse me that I continue to say to you, "Praise ye the Lord," for, often as I say it, you will not praise him too much; and we need to have our hearts stirred up to this duty of praising God, which is so much neglected. After all, it is the praise of God that is the ultimatum of our religion. Prayer does but sow; praise is the harvest. Praying is the end of preaching, and praising is the end of praying. May we bring to God much of the very essence of true religion, and that will be the inward praise of the heart!

7. Sing unto the LORD with thanksgiving; sing praise upon the harp unto our God:

"Unto our God." How that possessive pronoun puts a world of endearment into the majestic word "God"! "This God is our God." Come, my hearer, can you call God your God? Is he indeed yours? If so, "Sing unto the LORD with thanksgiving; sing praise upon the harp unto our God."

8. Who covereth the heaven with clouds, who prepareth rain for the earth, who maketh grass to grow upon the mountains.

They did not talk about the "law of nature" in those days. They ascribed everything to God; let us do the same. It is a poor science that pushes God farther away from us, instead of bringing him nearer to us. HE covers the heaven with clouds, HE prepares the rain for earth, HE makes the grass to grow upon the mountains.

9. He giveth to the beast his food, and to the young ravens which cry.

Our God cares for the birds and the beasts. He is as great in little things as in great things. Praise ye his name. The gods of the heathen could not have these things said of them; but our God takes pleasure in providing for the beasts of field and the birds of the air. The commissariat of the universe is in his hand: "Thou openest thine hand, and satisfieth the desire of every living thing."

10, 11. He delighteth not in the strength of the horse: he taketh not pleasure in the legs of a man. The LORD taketh pleasure in them that fear him, in those that hope in his mercy.—

Kings of the olden times rejoiced in the thews and sinews of their soldiers and their horses; but God has no delight in mere physical strength. He takes pleasure in spiritual things, even in the weakness which makes us fear him, even that weakness which has not grown into the strength of faith, and yet hopes in his mercy. "The Lord taketh pleasure in them that fear him, in those that hope in his mercy."

12. Praise the LORD, O Jerusalem; praise thy God, O Zion.

Let whole cities join together to praise God. Shall we live to see the day when all London shall praise him? Shall we, ever, as we go down these streets, with their multitudes of inhabitants, see the people standing in the doorways, and asking, "What must we do to be saved?" Shall we ever see every house with anxious enquirers in it, saying, "Tell us, tell us, how can we be reconciled to God?" Pray that it may be so. In Cromwell's day, if your went down Cheapside at a certain hour of the morning, you would find every blind drawn down; for the inmates were all at family prayer. There is no street like that in London now. In those glorious Puritan times, there was domestic worship everywhere, and the people seemed brought to Christ's feet. Alas, it was but an appearance in many cases; and they soon turned back to their own devices! Imitating the Psalmist, let us say, "Praise the Lord, O London; praise thy God, O England!"

13. For he hath strengthened the bars of thy gates; he hath blessed thy children within thee.

As a nation, we have been greatly prospered, defended, and supplied; and the church of God has been made to stand fast against her enemies, and her children have been blessed.

14, 15. He maketh peace in thy borders, and filleth thee with the finest of the wheat. He sendeth forth his commandment upon earth: his word runneth very swiftly.

Oriental monarchs were very earnest to have good post arrangements. They sent their decrees upon swift dromedaries. They can never be compared with the swiftness of the purpose of God's decree. "His word runneth very swiftly." Oh, that the day would come when, over all the earth, God's writ should run, and God's written Word should come to be reverenced, believed, and obeyed!

16. He giveth snow like wool:

Men say, "it" snows; but what "it" is it that snows? The Psalmist rightly says of the Lord, "HE giveth snow." They say that according to the condition of the atmosphere, snow is produced; but the believer says, "He giveth snow like wool." It is not only like wool for whiteness; but it is like it for the warmth which it gives.

16. He scattereth the hoar frost like ashes.

The simile is not to be easily explained; but it will often have suggested itself to you who, in the early morning, have seen the hoar frost scattered abroad.

17. He casteth forth his ice like morsels: who can stand before his cold?

None can stand before his heat; but when he withdraws the fire, and takes away the heat, the cold is equally destructive. It burns up as fast as fire would. "Who can stand before his cold?" If God be gone, if the Spirit of God be taken away from his church, or from any of you, who can stand before his cold? The deprivation is as terrible as if it were a positive infliction. "Who can stand before his cold?"

18. He sendeth out his word, and melteth them; he causeth his wind to blow, and the waters flow.

The frozen waters were hard as iron; the south wind toucheth them, and they flow again. What can God not do? The great God of nature is our God. Let us praise him. Oh, may our hearts be in a right key to-night to make music before him!

19. He sheweth his word unto Jacob, his statutes unto Israel.

This is something greater than all his wonders in nature. The God of nature is the God of revelation. He hath not hidden his truth away from men. He hath come out of the eternal secrecies, and he hath showed his word, especially his Incarnate Word, unto his people. Let his name be praised.

20. He hath not dealt so with any nation:

Or, with any other nation. He revealed his statutes and his judgments to Israel; and since their day, the spiritual Israel has been privileged in like manner: "He hath not dealt so with any nation."

20. And as for his judgments, they have not known them.

Even to-day there are large tracts of country where God is not known. If we know him, let us praise him.

20. Praise ye the LORD.

Hallelujah! The Psalm ends upon its key-note: "Praise ye the LORD." So may all our lives end! Amen. HYMNS FROM "OUR OWN HYMN BOOK"—386, 537, 587.

Christian Conversation

A Sermon (No. 2695) Intended for
Reading on Lord's-Day, October 7th, 1900,
Delivered by C. H. SPURGEON,
At the Metropolitan Tabernacle, Newington.
ON a Lord's-Day Evening in the autumn of 1858.

"They shall speak of the glory of thy kingdom, and talk of thy power."—Psalm 145:11.

You have only to look at the preceding verse, and you will discover, in a single moment, who are the people here spoken of who shall speak of the glory of God's kingdom, and talk of his power. They are the saints: "All thy works shall praise thee, O Lord; and thy saints shall bless thee. They shall speak of the glory of thy kingdom, and talk of thy power." A saint will often be discovered by his conversation. He is a saint long before he knows it; he is a saint as being set apart unto salvation by God the Father in the covenant decree of election from all eternity; and he is a saint as being sanctified in Christ Jesus, and called. But he is more especially a saint as being sanctified by the quickening influence of the Holy Ghost, which renders him truly sanctified by making him holy, and bringing him into conformity with the image of our Lord and Saviour Jesus Christ. Yet it is not at all times easy to discern a saint except by Scriptural marks and evidences. There is nothing particular about the countenance or dress of a saint to distinguish him from his fellows. The saints have faces like other men; sometimes, they are sadly marred and furrowed by cares and troubles which worldlings do not know. They wear the same kind of garments as other men wear; they may be rich or they may be poor; but, still, there are some marks whereby we can discern them, and one of the special ways of discovering a saint is by his conversation. As I often tell you, you may know the quality of the water in a well by that which is brought up in the bucket; so may we tell a Christian by his conversation.

It is, however, much to be regretted that true children of the Lord often talk too little of him. What is the conversation of half the professors of the present day? Honesty compels us to say that, in many cases, it is a mass of froth and falsehood, and, in many more cases it is altogether objectionable; if it is not light and frivolous, it is utterly apart from the gospel, and does not minister grace unto the bearers. I consider that one of the great lacks of the Church, nowadays, is not so much Christian preaching as Christian talking,—not so much Christian prayer in the prayer-meeting, as Christian conversation in the parlour. How little do we hear concerning Christ! You might go in and out of the houses of half the professors of religion, and you would never hear of their Master at all. You might talk with them from the first of January to the last of December; and if they happened to mention their Master's name, it would be, perhaps, merely as a compliment to him, or possibly by accident. Beloved, such things ought not to be. You and I, I am sure, are guilty in this matter; we all have need to reproach ourselves that we do not sufficiently remember the words of Malachi, "Then they that feared the Lord spake often one to another: and the Lord hearkened, and heard it, and a book of remembrance was written before him for them that feared the Lord, and that thought upon his name."

Possibly some will ask, "Well, sir, how can we talk about religion? Upon what topic shall we converse? How are we to introduce it? It would not be polite, for instance, in the company with which we associate, to begin to say anything about the doctrines of grace, or about religious matters at all." Then, beloved, do not be polite; that is all I have to say in reply to such a remark as that. If it would be accounted contrary to etiquette to begin talking of the Saviour, cast etiquette to the winds, and speak about Christ somehow or other. The Christian is the aristocrat of the world; it is his place to make rules for society to obey,—not to stoop down, and conform to the regulations of society when they are contrary to the commands of his Master. He is the great Maker of laws; the King of kings, and Lord of lords; and he makes his people also to be kings. Kings make rules for ordinary men to obey; so must Christians do. They are not to submit to others; they must make others, by the worth of their principles, and the dignity of their character, submit to them. It is speaking too lightly of a Christian's dignity when we say that he dare not do the right, because it would not be fashionable. We care nothing for that, for "the fashion of this world passeth away," "but he that doeth the will of God abideth for ever."

Another says, "What could I speak of? There are so few topics that would be suitable. I must not speak upon doctrinal subjects, for it would offend one of the party. They might hold different views; one might be a Wesleyan, one might be a Baptist, one might be an Independent, one a Calvinist, one an Arminian;—how could I talk so as to please all? If I spoke of election, most of them would attack me at once; if I began to speak of redemption, we should soon differ on that subject, and I would not like to engender controversy." Beloved, engender controversy rather than have wrong conversation; better dispute over truth than agree about lies. Better, I say, is it to dispute concerning good doctrine, far more profitable is it to talk of the Word of God, even in a controversial manner, than to turn utterly away from it, and neglect it.

But, let me tell you, there is one point on which all Christians agree, and that is concerning the person, the work, and the blessed offices of our Saviour. Go where you will, professors, if they are genuine Christians, will always agree with you if you begin to talk about your Saviour; so you need not be afraid that you will provoke controversy; but supposing the mention of your Saviour's name does provoke dispute, then let it be provoked. And if your Master's truth offends the gentlemen to whom you speak of it let them be offended. His name we must confess; of his glory we will continually talk, for it is written in our text, "They shall speak of the glory of thy kingdom, and talk of thy power."

Now, then, first, here is a subject for conversation: "they shall speak of the glory of thy kingdom and talk of thy power." Secondly, we will try to find out some causes why Christians must speak concerning this blessed subject and then, thirdly, I will very briefly refer to the effect of our talking more of Christ's kingdom and power.

I. First, here is A SUBJECT FOR CONVERSATION: "They shall speak of the glory of thy kingdom, and talk of thy power." Here are two subjects; for God, when he puts grace into the heart, does not lack a subject upon which we shall converse.

First, we are to converse concerning the glory of Christ's kingdom. The glory of Christ's kingdom should ever be a subject of discourse to a Christian; he should always be speaking, not merely of Christ's priesthood or his prophesying, but also of his kingdom, which has lasted from all eternity; and especially of that glorious kingdom of grace in which we now live, and of that brighter kingdom of millennial glory, which soon shall come upon this world, to conquer all other kingdoms, and break them in pieces.

The psalmist furnishes us with some divisions of this subject, all of which illustrate the glory of Christ's kingdom. In the 12th verse he says, "To make known to the sons of men his mighty acts." The glory of a kingdom depends very much on the achievements of that kingdom; so, in speaking of the glory of Christ's kingdom, we are to make known his mighty acts. We think that the glory of Old England—at least, our historians would say so,—rests upon the great battles she has fought, and the victories she has won. We turn over the records of the past, and we see her, in one place, vanquishing thousands of Frenchmen at Agincourt; at another period, we see the fleets of the Spanish Armada scattered by the breath of God. We turn to different battles, and we trace victory after victory, dotted along the page of history, and we say that this is the glory of our kingdom. Now, Christian, when you speak of the glory of your Master's kingdom, you must tell something of his great victories;—how he routed Pharaoh, and cut the Egyptian Rahab, and wounded the dragon of the Nile; how he slew all the firstborn in one night; how, at his command, the Red Sea was divided; how the children of Israel crossed over in safety, and the chivalry of Egypt was drowned in the flood. Talk ye also of how God overcame Amalek, and smote Moab; how he utterly cut off those nations that warred against Israel, and caused them to pass away for ever. Tell how Babylon and Nineveh were made to rue the day when God smote them with his iron hand. Tell ye to the world how God hath crushed great nations and overcome proud monarchs; how Sennacherib's hosts were left dead within their camp, and how those that have risen up in rebellion against God have found his arm too mighty for their strength and prowess. Tell of the terrible acts of our Saviour's kingdom; record his victories in this world; nor cease there. Tell how our Saviour routed the devil in the wilderness when he came to tempt him. Tell how he—

> All his foes to ruin hurled,
>   Sin, Satan, earth, death, hell, the world.,
> Tell how he hath bruised the head of Satan.
> Tell how death has lost his prey.
> Tell how hell's deepest dungeons have been
>   visited,
>   and the power of the prince of darkness
>   utterly cut off.
> Tell ye how antichrist himself shall sink like a
>   millstone in the flood.
> Tell how false systems of superstition shall flee
>   away,
>   like birds of night when the sun rises too
>   brightly for their dim sight to bear.
> Tell ye all this, tell it in Askalon and in Gath;
>   tell it the wide world over,
> that the Lord of hosts is the God of battles;
> he is the conqueror of men and of devils; he is
>   Master in his own dominions.
> Tell ye the glory of his kingdom, and rehearse
>   his mighty acts.

Christian, exhaust that theme if thou canst.

Then, in speaking of the glory of Christ's kingdom, the next thing we talk of is its glorious majesty. The psalmist further says, in the 12th verse, that the saints shall not only "make known God's mighty acts, but also the glorious majesty of his kingdom." Part of the glory of England consists, not in her achievements, but in the state and majesty which surround her. In ancient times especially, monarchs were noted for the great pomp with which they were surrounded. Thousands of houses must be razed to the ground to find a site for one dwelling for a king. His palace must be gorgeous with riches; its halls must be paved with marble, and its walls set with jewels; fountains must sparkle there; there must be beds of eider on which monarchs may recline; music, such as other ears do not hear, wines from the uttermost regions of the earth, and all manner of delights, are reserved for kings; precious stones and gems adorn their crowns; and everything that is rich and rare must be brought to deck the monarch, and increase the majesty of his kingdom.

Well, Christian, when speaking of Christ's kingdom, you are to talk of its majesty. Tell of your Saviour's glorious majesty; speak of the many crowns that he wears upon his head. Tell of the crown of grace which he wears continually; tell of the crown of victory which perpetually proclaims the triumphs he has won over the foe; tell of the crown of love wherewith his Father crowned him in the day of his espousals to his Church,—the crown which he has won by ten thousand hearts which he has broken, and untold myriads of spirits which he has bound up. Tell to all mankind that the glory of your Saviour's majesty far exceeds the glories of the ancient kings of Assyria and India. Tell that, before his throne above, there stand, in glorious state, not princes, but angels; not servants in gorgeous liveries, but cherubs, with wings of fire, waiting to obey his mighty behests. Tell that his palace is floored with gold, and that he has no need of lamps, or even of the sun, to enlighten it, for he himself is the light thereof. Tell ye to the whole world what is the glorious majesty of his kingdom.

But once more, Christians, in speaking of the glory of Christ's kingdom, you must talk of its duration, for much of the honour of the kingdom depends upon the time it has lasted. In verse 13, the psalmist says, "Thy kingdom is an everlasting kingdom, and thy dominion endureth throughout all generations." If one should say to you, concerning an earthly monarch, "Our king sits upon a throne which his ancestors have occupied for many generations;" tell him that a thousand years are to your King but as one day. If another tells you that his king has crowns which were worn by kings a thousand years ago, smile in his face, and tell him that a thousand years are as nothing in Christ's sight. When they speak of the antiquity of churches, tell them that you belong to a very ancient Church. If they talk to you of the venerable character of the religion which they profess, tell them that you believe in a very venerable religion, for yours is a religion which was from everlasting. Christ's kingdom was set up long before this world was brought forth; when as yet neither sun, nor moon, nor stars, had been created, Christ's kingdom was firmly established. I wish Christians would more often talk about the glory of their Master's kingdom with regard to the time it has lasted. If you would begin to talk of the past history of God's Church, you would never have to exclaim, "I have said all that can be said about it, and I have nothing more to say." You would need eternity to keep on going back, back, back, until you came to God alone; and then you might say,—

In his mighty breast I see,
Eternal thoughts of love to me.

Then you may speak concerning the future duration of your Master's kingdom. I suppose, if you were to talk much about the second coming of Christ, you would be laughed at, you would be thought diseased in your brain; for there are so few nowadays who receive that great truth, that, if we speak of it with much enthusiasm, people turn away, and say, "Ah! we do not know much about that subject, but Mr. So-and-so has turned his brain through thinking so much about it." Men are, therefore, half-afraid to speak of such a subject; but, beloved, we are not afraid to talk of it, for Christ's kingdom is an everlasting kingdom, and we may talk of the glory of the future as well as of the past. Some say that Christ's Church is in danger. There are many churches that are in danger; and the sooner they tumble down, the better; but the Church of Christ has a future that shall never end; it has a future that shall never become dim; it has a future which shall eternally progress in glory. Her glory now is the glory of the morning twilight; it soon shall be the glory of the blazing noon. Her riches now are but the riches of the newly-opened mine; soon she shall have riches much more abundant and far more valuable than any she has at present. She is now young; by-and-by, she will come, not to her dotage, but to her maturity. She is like a fruit that is ripening, a star that is rising, a sun that is shining more and more unto the perfect day; and soon she will blaze forth in all her glory, "fair as the moon, clear as the sun and terrible as an army with banners." O Christian, here is a topic worthy of thy conversation! Talk of the glory of thy Master's kingdom. Often speak of it while others amuse themselves with stories of sieges and battles; while they are speaking of this or that or the other event in history, tell them the history of the monarchy of the King of kings; speak to them concerning the fifth great monarchy in which Jesus Christ shall reign for ever and ever.

But I must not forget briefly to hint at the other subject of the saints' conversation: "and shall talk of thy power." It is not simply of Christ's kingdom of which we are to speak, but also of his power. Here, again, the psalmist gives us something which will help us to a division of our subject. In the 14th and 15th verses, mention is made of three kinds of power of which we ought to speak: "The Lord upholdeth all that fall, and raiseth up all those that be bowed down. The eyes of all wait upon thee; and thou givest them their meat in due season."

First, the Christian should speak of Christ's upholding power. What a strange expression this is, "The Lord upholdeth all that fall"! Yet remember John Bunyan's quaint old saying,—

He that is down needs fear no fall;
  He that is low, no pride;
He that is humble, ever shall
  Have God to be his guide.

So David says, "The Lord upholdeth all that fall." What a singular expression! How can he hold up those that fall? Yet those that fall, in this sense, are the only persons that stand. It is a remarkable paradox; but it is true. The man who stands on his feet, and says, "I am mighty,—I am strong enough to stand alone;"—down he will go; but he who falls into Christ's arms, he who says,—

> But, oh! for this no power have I,
> My strength is at thy feet to lie;

—that man shall not fall. We may well talk, then, of Christ's upholding power. Tell it to Christians; tell how he kept you when your feet were going swift to hell; how, when fierce temptations did beset you, your Master drove them all away; how, when the enemy was watching, he compassed you with his mighty strength; how, when the arrows fell thickly around you, his mighty arm did hold the shield before you, and so preserved you from them all. Tell how he saved you from death, and delivered your feet from falling by making you, first of all, fall down prostrate before him.

Next, talk of his exalting power: "He raiseth up all those that be bowed down." Oh, how sweet it is, beloved, sometimes to talk of God's exalting power after we have been hewed down! I love to come into this pulpit, and talk to you as I would in my own room. I make no pretensions to preaching at all, but simply tell you what I happen to feel just now. Oh, how sweet it is to feel the praisings of God's grace when you have been bowed down! Cannot some of us tell that, when we have been bowed down beneath a load of affliction, so that we could not even move, the everlasting arms have been around us, and have lifted us up? When Satan has put his foot on our back, and we have said, "We shall never be raised up any more," the Lord has come to our rescue. If we were only to talk on that subject in our conversation with one another, no Christian need have spiritless conversation in his parlour. But, nowadays, you are so afraid to speak of your own experience, and the mercy of God to you, that you will talk any stuff and nonsense rather than that. But, I beseech you, if you would do good in the world, rehearse God's deeds of raising up those that be bowed down.

Moreover, talk of God's providing power: "The eyes of all wait upon thee; and thou givest them their meat in due season." We ought often to speak of how God provides for his creatures in providence. Why should we not tell how God has taken us out of poverty, and made us rich; or, if he has not done that for us, how he has supplied our wants day by day in an almost miraculous manner! Some persons object to such a book as Huntington's " Bank of Faith," and I have heard some respectable people call it "The Bank of Nonsense." Ah! if they had ever been brought into Huntington's condition, they would see that it was indeed a bank of faith, and not a bank of nonsense; the nonsense was in those who read it, in their unbelieving hearts, not in the book itself. And he who has been brought into many straits and trials, and has been divinely delivered out of them, would find that he could write a "Bank of Faith" as good as Huntington's if he liked to do so; for he has had as many deliverances, and he could rehearse the mighty acts of God, who has opened his hands, and supplied the wants of his needy child. Many of you have been out of a situation, and you have cried to God to furnish you with one, and you have had it. Have you not sometimes been brought so low, through painful affliction, that you could not rest? And could you not afterwards say, "I was brought low, and he helped me"? Yes; "I was brought low, and he helped me out of my distress"? Yes; I see some of you nodding your heads, as much as to say, "We are the men who have passed through that experience; we have been brought into great straits, but the Lord has delivered us out of them all." Then do not be ashamed to tell the story. Let the world hear that God provides for his people. Go, speak of your Father. Do as the child does, who, when he has a little cake given to him, will take it out, and say, "Father gave me this." Do so with all your mercies; go and tell all the world that you have a good Father, a gracious Father, a heavenly Provider; and though he gives you a hand-basket portion, and you only live from hand to mouth, yet tell how graciously he gives it, and that you would not change your blest estate for all the world calls good or great.

II. I must be brief in speaking upon THE CAUSES WHICH WILL MAKE CHRISTIANS TALK OF THE GLORY OF CHRIST'S KINGDOM AND HIS POWER.

One cause is, that it is the kingdom of their own King. We do not expect French people to talk much about the victories of the English; and I suppose there is no Russian who would pay very many compliments to the prowess of our arms; but they will all talk about their own monarchs. Well, that is the reason why a Christian should speak of the glory of his Master's kingdom, and tell of his power, because it is the kingdom of his own King. Jesus Christ may be or may not be another man's King; but, certainly he is mine; he is the Monarch to whom I yield absolute submission. I am no longer an alien and a stranger, but I am one of his subjects; and I will talk concerning him, because he is my King.

Secondly, the Christian must talk of the King's victories, because all those victories were won for him; he recollects that his Master never fought a battle for himself,—never slew an enemy for himself. He slew them all for his people. And if for me,—a poor abject worm,—my Saviour did this, shall I not talk of the glory of his kingdom, when he won all that glory for me? Will I not speak of his power, when all that power was exercised for me? It was all for me. When he died, he died for me; when he suffered, he suffered for me; and when he led captivity captive, he did it for me. Therefore, I must and will speak of his dear name. I cannot help testifying to the glory of his grace in whatever company I may be.

Again, the Christian must talk of it, because he himself has had a good share in fighting some of the battles. You know how old soldiers will "shoulder their crutch, and tell how fields were won." The soldier, home from the Crimea, when he reads the accounts of the war, says, "Ah! I know that trench; I worked in it myself. I know the Redan; I was one of the men who attacked it." He is interested because he had a share in the battle. "Quorum pars magna fui," said the old soldier, in the days of Virgil; so we, if we have had a part in the battle, like to talk concerning it. And, beloved, it is this which makes our battles dear to us; we help to fight them. Though there was one battle which our great Captain fought alone, and "of the people there was none with him," yet, in other victories, he has permitted his people to help to crush the dragon's head. Recollect that you have been a soldier in the army of the Lord; and that, in the last day, when he gives away the medals in heaven, you will have one; when he gives away the crowns, you will have one. We can talk about the battles, for we were in them; we can speak of the victories, for we helped to win them. It is to our own praise as well as to our Master's when we talk of his wondrous acts.

But the best reason why the Christian should talk of his Master is this, if he has Christ in his heart, the truth must come out; he cannot help it. The best reason in all the world is the woman's reason, who said she should do it because she would do it. So it often happens that the Christian cannot give us much reason why he must talk about his Saviour, except that he cannot help it, and he will not try to help it. It is in him, and it must come out. If God has put a fire inside a man's heart, do you think it can be kept down? If we have grace in our souls, will it never come out in conversation! God does not put his candles in lanterns through which they cannot be seen, but he sets them on candlesticks; he does not build his cities in valleys, but he puts them on hills, so that they cannot be hid. So he will not allow his grace to be concealed. A Christian man cannot help being discovered. None of you ever knew a secret believer,—a secret Christian. "Oh!" you say, "I am sure I have known such a man." But, look you, he could not have been a secret believer if you knew him, he could not be wholly secret; the fact that you knew him proves that he could not have been a secret Christian. If a man says that nobody knows a thing, and yet he knows it, he contradicts himself. You cannot, then, know a secret believer, and you never will. There may be, indeed, some who are secret for a time, but they always have to come out, like Joseph of Arimathaea, when he went and begged the body of Jesus. Ah! there are some of you sitting in your pews who fancy I shall never discover you; but I shall see you in the vestry by-and-by. Some of you keep on coming Sunday after Sunday, and you say, "Well, I must go by-and-by, and make a profession of faith." Yes, you will not be able to sit there long; if you have the grace of God within you, you will be obliged to come out, and put on the Lord Jesus Christ by being baptized in his name. Why not do so without further delay? If you love your Lord's name, come out at once, and own it.

III. Lastly, WHAT WOULD BE THE EFFECT OF OUR TALKING MORE OP CHRIST'S KINGDOM AND POWER?

The first effect would be that the world would believe us more. The world says, "What a parcel of hypocrites Christian people are!" And they are about right concerning a good many of you. The world says, "Why, just look at them! They profess a deal of religion; but if you hear them talk, they do not speak differently from other people. They sing loudly enough, it is true, when they go to church or chapel; but when do you hear them sing at home? They go to the prayer-meeting; but have they a prayer-meeting at their own family altar? Believe them to be Christians? No! Their lives give the lie to their doctrines, and we do not believe them." If we oftener talked of Christ, I am sure the world would think us to be better Christians, and they would, no doubt, say so.

Again, if our conversations were more concerning Christ, we, as Christian men, should grow faster, and be more happy. What is the reason of the bickerings and jealousies between Christians? It is this, because they do not know one another. Mr. Jay used to tell a story about a man going out, one foggy morning, and seeing something coming in the fog; he thought it was a monster. But, by-and-by, as he came nearer, he exclaimed, "Oh, dear me! that's my brother John!" So it often happens, when we see people at a distance, and hold no spiritual conversation with them, we think they are monsters. But when we begin to talk together, and get near to one another, we say, "Why, it is brother John, after all!" There are more true brethren about us than we dream of. Then, I say, let your conversation, in all companies, wherever you may be, be so seasoned with salt that a man may know you to be a Christian. In this way, you would remove bickerings better than by all the sermons that could be preached, and be promoting a true Evangelical Alliance far more excellent and efficient than all the alliances which man can form.

Again, if we oftener talked of Christ like this, how useful we might be in the salvation of souls! O beloved, how few souls have some of you won to Christ! It says, in the Canticles, "There is not one barren among them;" but are not some of you barren,—without spiritual children? It was pronounced as a curse upon one of old that he should die childless. Oh! methinks that, though the Christian is always blessed, it is half a curse to die spiritually childless. There are some of you who are childless to-night. You never were the means of the conversion of a soul in all your lives. You hardly remember having tried to win anyone for the Saviour. You are good religious people so far as your outward conduct is concerned. You go to the house of God, but you never concern yourselves about winning souls for Jesus. O my God, let me die when I can no longer be the means of saving souls! If I can be kept out of heaven a thousand years, if thou wilt give me souls as my wages, let me still speak for thee; but if there be no more sinners to be converted,—no more to be brought in by my ministry,—then let me depart, and be "with Christ, which is far better."

Oh, think of the crowns that are in heaven! "They that be wise shall shine as the brightness of the firmament; and they that turn many to righteousness as the stars for ever and ever." So many souls, so many gems! Have you ever thought what it would be to wear in heaven a starless crown? All the saints will have crowns, but those who win souls will have a star in their crown for every soul. Some of you, my friends, will wear a crown without a star; would you like that? You will be happy, you will be blessed, you will be satisfied, I know, when you will be there; but can you bear the thought of dying childless,—of having none in heaven who shall be begotten unto Christ by you,—never having travailed in birth for souls,—never having brought any to Christ? How can you bear to think of it? Then, if you would win souls, beloved, talk about Jesus. There is nothing like talking of him, to lead others to him. I read of the conversion of a servant, the other day. She was asked how she came to know the Lord, "Well," she said, "my master, at dinner, happened to make some simple observation to his sister across the table." The remark certainly was not addressed to the servant; and her master had no notion that she was listening; yet his word was blessed to her. It is well to talk behind the door that which you do not mind hearing afterwards in the street; it is good to speak that in the closet which you are not ashamed to listen to from the housetop, for you will have to listen to it from the housetop by-and-by, when God shall come and call you to account for every idle word you have spoken.

Souls are often converted through godly conversation. Simple words frequently do more good than long sermons. Disjointed, unconnected sentences are often of more use than the most finely polished periods or rounded sentences. If you would be useful, let the praises of Christ be ever on your tongue; let him live on your lips. Speak of him always; when thou walkest by the way, when thou sittest in thy house, when thou risest up, and even when thou liest down, it may be that thou hast someone to whom it is possible that thou mayest yet whisper the gospel of the grace of God. Many a sister has been brought to know the Saviour by a sister's pleadings that were only heard in the silence of the night. God give you, beloved, to fulfil our text! "They shall speak of the glory of thy kingdom, and talk of thy power." They shall do it, mark you; God will make you do it if you are his people. Go and do it willingly. Begin, from this time forth, and keep on doing it for ever. Say, concerning other conversation, "Begone far hence! avaunt! Thus shall be my constant and only theme." Be like the harp of old Anacreon, which would never sound any other note but that of love. The harpist wished to sing of Cadmus, and of mighty men of wisdom, but his harp would resound of love alone. Be, then, like Anacreon's harp,—sing of Christ alone! Christ alone! Christ alone! Jesus, Jesus only! Make him the theme of your conversation, for "they shall speak of the glory of thy kingdom, and talk of thy power." God give you grace so to do, for Christ's sake! Amen.

Christ—The Power and Wisdom of God

A Sermon (No. 132) Delivered on Sabbath Morning, May 17, 1857, by the REV. C. H. SPURGEON at the Music Hall, Royal Surrey Gardens.

"Christ the power of God, and the wisdom of God."—1 Corinthians 1:24.

Unbelief toward the gospel of Christ is the most unreasonable thing in all the world, because the reason which the unbeliever gives for his unbelief is fairly met by the character and constitution of the gospel of Christ. Notice that before this verse we read—"The Jews required a sign, the Greeks seek after wisdom." If you met the Jew who believed not on Christ in the apostle's day, he said, "I can not believe, because I want a sign;" and if you met the Greek, he said, "I can not believe, because I want a philosophic system, one that is full of wisdom." "Now," says the apostle, "both these objections are untenable and unreasonable. If you suppose that the Jew requires a sign, that sign is given him: Christ is the power of God. The miracles that Christ wrought upon earth were signs more than sufficiently abundant; and if the Jewish people had but the will to believe, they would have found abundant signs and reasons for believing in the personal acts of Christ and his apostles." And let the Greeks say, "I can not believe, because I require a wise system: O Greek, Christ is the wisdom of God. If thou wouldst but investigate the subject, thou wouldst find in it profoundness of wisdom—a depth where the most gigantic intellect might be drowned. It is no shallow gospel, but a deep, and a great deep too, a deep which passeth understanding. Thine objection is ill-founded; for Christ is the wisdom of God, and his gospel is the highest of all sciences. If thou wishest to find wisdom, thou must find it in the word of revelation."

Now, this morning, we shall try to bring out these two thoughts of the gospel; and it may be that God shall bless what we shall say to the removing of the objection of either Jew or Greek; that the one requiring a sign may see it in the power of God in Christ, and that he who requireth wisdom may behold it in the wisdom of God in Christ. We shall understand our text in a threefold manner: Christ, that is, Christ personally, is "the power of God and the wisdom of God;" Christ, that is, Christ's gospel, is "the power of God and the wisdom of God;" Christ, that is, Christ in the heart—true religion, is "the power of God and the wisdom of God."

I. First, to begin, then, with CHRIST PERSONALLY. Christ considered as God and man, the Son of God equal with his Father, and yet the man, born of the Virgin Mary. Christ, in his complex person, is "the power of God and the wisdom of God." He is the power of God from all eternity. "By his word were the heavens made, and all the host of them." "The Word was God, and the Word was with God." "All things were made by him, and without him was not any thing made that was made." The pillars of the earth were placed in their everlasting sockets by the omnipotent right hand of Christ; the curtains of the heavens were drawn upon their rings of starry light by him who was from everlasting the All-glorious Son of God. The orbs that float aloft in ether, those ponderous planets, and those mighty stars, were placed in their positions or sent rolling through space by the eternal strength of him who is "the first and the last." "the Prince of the kings of the earth." Christ is the power of God, for he is the Creator of all things, and by him all things exist.

But when he came to earth, took upon himself the fashion of a man, tabernacled in the inn, and slept in the manger, he still gave proof that he was the Son of God; not so much so when, as an infant of a span long, the immortal was the mortal and the infinite became a babe; not so much so in his youth, but afterward when he began his public ministry, he gave abundant proofs of his power and Godhead. The winds hushed by his finger uplifted, the waves calmed by his voice, so that they became solid as marble beneath his tread; the tempest, cowering at his feet, as before a conqueror whom it knew and obeyed; these things, these stormy elements, the wind, the tempest, and the water, gave full proof of his abundant power. The lame man leaping, the deaf man hearing, the dumb man singing, the dead rising, these, again, were proofs that he was, the "power of God." When the voice of Jesus startled the shades of Hades, and rent the bonds of death, with "Lazarus, come forth!" and when the carcass rotten in the tomb woke up to life, there was proof of his divine power and Godhead. A thousand other proofs he afforded; but we need not stay to mention them to you who have Bibles in your houses, and who can read them every day. At last he yielded up his life, and was buried in the tomb. Not long, however, did he sleep; for he gave another proof of his divine power and Godhead, when starting from his slumber, he affrighted the guards with the majesty of his grandeur, not being holden by the bonds of death, they being like green withes before our conquering Samson, who had meanwhile pulled up the gates of hell, and carried them on his shoulders far away.

That he is the power of God now, Scripture very positively affirmeth; for it is written, "he sitteth at the right hand of God." He hath the reins of Providence gathered in his hands; the fleet coursers of Time are driven by him who sits in the chariot of the world, and bids its wheels run round; and he shall bid them stay when it shall please him. He is the great umpire of all disputes, the great Sovereign Head of the church, the Lord of heaven, and death, and hell; and by-and-by we shall know that he shall come, "On fiery clouds and wings of wind, Appointed Judge of all mankind;" and then the quickened dead, the startled myriads, the divided firmaments, the "Depart, ye cursed," and the "Come, ye blessed," shall proclaim him to be the power of God, who hath power over all flesh, to save or to condemn, as it pleaseth him.

But he is equally "the wisdom of God." The great things that he did before all worlds were proofs of his wisdom. He planned the way of salvation; he devised the system of atonement and substitution; he laid the foundations of the great plan of salvation. There was wisdom. But he built the heavens by wisdom, and he laid the pillars of light, whereon the firmament is balanced, by his skill and wisdom. Mark the world; and learn, as ye see all its multitudinous proofs of the wisdom of God, and there you have the wisdom of Christ; for he was the creator of it. And when he became a man, he gave proofs enough of wisdom. Even in childhood, when he made the doctors sit abashed by the questions that he asked, he showed that he was more than mortal. And when the Pharisee and Sadducce and Herodian were all at last defeated, and their nets were broken, he proved again the superlative wisdom of the Son of God. And when those who came to take him, stood enchained by his eloquence, spell-bound by his marvelous oratory, there was again a proof that he was the wisdom of God, who could so enchain the minds of men. And now that he intercedeth before the throne of God, now that he is our Advocate before the throne, the pledge and surety for the blessed, now that the reins of government are in his hands, and are ever wisely directed, we have abundant proofs that the wisdom of God is in Christ, as well as the power of God. Bow before him, ye that love him; bow before him, ye that desire him! Crown him, crown him, crown him! He is worthy of it, unto him is everlasting might; unto him is unswerving wisdom: bless his name; exalt him; clap your wings, ye seraphs; cry aloud, ye cherubim; shout, shout, shout, to his praise, ye ransomed host above. And ye, O men that know his grace, extol him in your songs for ever; for he is Christ, the power of God and the wisdom of God.

II. But now Christ, that is, CHRIST'S GOSPEL, is the power and the wisdom of God.

Christ's gospel is a thing of divine power. Do you want proofs of it? Ye shall not go far. How could Christ's gospel have been established in this world as it was, if it had not in itself intrinsic might? By whom was it spread? By mitered prelates, by learned doctors, by fierce warriors, by caliphs, by prophets? No; by fishermen, untaught, unlettered; save as the Spirit gave them utterance, not knowing how to preach or speak. How did they spread it? By the bayonet, by their swords, by the keen metal of their blades? Did they drive their gospel into men at the point of the lance, and with the cimeter? Say, did myriads rush to battle, as they did when they followed the crescent of Mohammed, and did they convert men by force, by law, by might? Ah I no. Nothing but their simple words, their unvarnished eloquence, their rough declamation, their unhewn oratory; these it was, which, by the blessing of God's Spirit, carried the gospel round the world within a century after the death of its founder.

But what was this gospel which achieved so much? Was it a thing palatable to human nature? Did it offer a paradise of present happiness? Did it offer delight to the flesh and to the senses? Did it give charming prospects of wealth? Did it give licentious ideas to men? No; it was a gospel of morality most strict, it was a gospel with delights entirely spiritual—a gospel which abjured the flesh, which, unlike the coarse delusion of Joe Smith, cut off every prospect from men of delighting themselves with the joys of lust. It was a gospel holy, spotless, clean as the breath of heaven; it was pure as the wing of angel; not like that which spread of old, in the days of Mohammed, a gospel of lust, of vice, and wickedness, but pure, and consequently not palatable to human nature. And yet it spread. Why? My friends, I think the only answer I can give you is, because it has in it the power of God.

But do you want another proof? How has it been maintained since then? No easy path has the gospel had. The good bark of the church has had to plow her way through seas of blood, and those who have manned her have been bespattered with the bloody spray; yea, they have had to man her and keep her in motion, by laying down their lives unto the death. Mark the bitter persecution of the church of Christ from the time of Nero to the days of Mary, and further on, through the days of Charles the Second, and of those kings of unhappy memory, who had not as yet learned how to spell "toleration." From the dragoons of Claverhouse, right straight away to the gladiatorial shows of Rome, what a long series of persecutions has the gospel had! But, as the old divines used to say, "The blood of the martyrs" has been "the seed of the church." It has been, as the old herbalists had it, like the herb camomile, the more it is trodden on, the more it grows; and the more the church has been ill-treated, the more it has prospered. Behold the mountains where the Albigenses walk in their white garments; see the stakes of smithfield, not yet forgotten; behold ye the fields among the towering hills, where brave hands kept themselves free from despotic tyranny. Mark ye the Pilgrim Fathers, driven by a government of persecution across the briny deep. See what vitality the gospel has. Plunge her under the wave, and she rises, the purer for her washing; thrust her in the fire, and she comes out, the more bright for her burning; cut her in sunder, and each piece shall make another church; behead her, and like the hydra of old, she shall have a hundred heads for every one you cut away. She can not die, she must live; for she has the power of God within her.

Do you want another proof? I give you a better one than the last. I do not wonder that the church has outlived persecution so much as I wonder she has outlived the unfaithfulness of her professed teachers. Never was church so abused as the church of Christ has been, all through her history; from the days of Diotrephes, who sought to have the pre-eminence, even to these later times, we can read of proud, arrogant prelates, and supercilious, haughty lords over God's inheritance. Bonners, Dunstans, and men of all sorts, have come into her ranks, and done all they could to kill her; and with their lordly priestcraft they have tried to turn her aside. And what shall we say to that huge apostacy of Rome? A thousand miracles that ever the church outlived that! When her pretended head became apostate, and all her bishops disciples of hell, and she had gone far away, wonder of wonders, that she should come out, in the days of the glorious Reformation, and should still live. And, even now, when I mark the supineness of many of my brethren in the ministry-when I mark their utter and entire inefficiency of doing aught for God—when I see their waste of time, preaching now and then on the Sunday, instead of going to the highways and hedges and preaching the gospel everywhere to the poor—when I see the want of unction in the church itself, the want of prayerfulness—when I see wars and fightings, factions and disunions—when I see hot blood and pride, even in the meetings of the saints; I say it is a thousand thousand miracles that the church of God should be alive at all, after the unfaithfulness of her members, her ministers, and her bishops. She has the power of God within her, or else she would have been destroyed; for she has got enough within her own loins to work her destruction.

"But," says one, "you have not yet proved it is the power of God to my understanding." Sir, I will give you another proof There are not a few of you, who are now present, who would be ready, I know, if it were necessary, to rise in your seats and bear me witness that I speak the truth. There are some who, not many months ago, were drunkards; some who were loose livers; men who were unfaithful to every vow which should keep man to truth, and right, and chastity, and honesty, and integrity. Yes, I repeat, I have some here who look back to a life of detestable sin. You tell me, some of you, that for thirty years even (there is one such present now) you never listened to a gospel ministry, nor ever entered the house of God at all; you despised the Sabbath, you spent it in all kinds of evil pleasures, you plunged headlong into sin and vice, and your only wonder is, that God has not out you off long ago, as cumberers of the ground; and now you are here, as different as light from darkness. I know your characters, and have watched you with a father's love; for, child though I am, I am the spiritual father of some here whose years outcount mine by four times the number; and I have seen you honest who were thieves, and you sober who were drunkards. I have seen the wife's glad eye sparkling with happiness; and many a woman has grasped me by the hand, shed her tears upon me, and said, "I bless God; I am a happy woman now; my husband is reclaimed, my house is blessed; our children are brought up in the fear of the Lord." Not one or two, but scores of such are here. And, my friends, if these be not proofs that the gospel is the power of God, I say there is no proof of any thing to be had in the world, and every thing must be conjecture. Yes, and there worships with you this day (and if there be a secularist here, my friend will pardon me for alluding to him for a moment), there is in the house of God this day one who was a leader in your ranks, one who despised God, and ran very far away from right. And here he is! It is his honor this day to own himself a Christian; and I hope, when this sermon is ended, to grasp him by the hand, for he has done a valiant deed; he has bravely burned his papers in the sight of all the people, and has turned to God with full purpose of heart. I could give you proofs enough, if proofs were wanted, that the gospel has been to men the power of God and the wisdom of God. More proofs I could give, yea, thousands, one upon the other.

But we must notice the other points. Christ's gospel

is the wisdom of God. Look at the gospel itself and you will see it to be wisdom. The man who scoffs and sneers at the gospel does so for no other reason but because he does not understand it. We have two of the richest books of theology extant that were written by professed infidels—by men that were so, I mean, before they wrote the books. You may have heard the story of Lord Lyttleton and West. I believe they determined to refute Christianity; one of them took up the subject of Paul's conversion, and the other, the subject of the resurrection; they sat down, both of them, to write books to ridicule those two events, and the effect was, that in studying the subject, they, both of them, became Christians, and wrote books which are now bulwarks to the church they hoped to have overthrown. Every man who looks the gospel fairly in the face, and gives it the study it ought to have, will discover that it is no false gospel, but a gospel that is replete with wisdom, and full of the knowledge of Christ. If any man will cavil at the Bible, be must cavil. There are some men who can find no wisdom anywhere, except in their own heads. Such men, however, are no judges of wisdom. We should not set a mouse to explain the phenomena of astronomy, nor should we set a man who is so foolish as to do nothing but cavil to understand the wisdom of the gospel. It needs that a man should at least be honest, and have some share of sense, or we can not dispute with him at all. Christ's gospel, to any man who believes it, is the wisdom of God.

Allow me just to hint that to be a believer in the gospel is no dishonor to a man's intellect. While the gospel can be understood by the poorest and the most illiterate, while there are shallows in it where a lamb may wade, there are depths where leviathan may swim. The intellect of Locke found ample space in the gospel; the mind of Newton submitted to receive the truth of inspiration as a little child, and found a something in its majestic being higher than itself, unto which it could not attain. The rudest and most untaught have been enabled, by the study of the holy Scripture of God's truth to enter the kingdom; and the most erudite have said of the gospel, it surpasses thought. I was thinking the other day what a vast amount of literature must be lost if the gospel be not true. No book was ever so suggestive as the Bible. Large tomes we have in our libraries which it takes all our strength to lift, all upon holy Scripture; myriads upon myriads of smaller volumes, tens of thousands of every shape and size, all written upon the Bible; and I have thought that the very suggestiveness of Scripture, the supernatural suggestiveness of holy Writ, may be in itself a proof of its divine wisdom, since no man has ever been able to write a book which could have so many commentators and so many writers upon its text as the Bible has received, by so much as one millionth part.

III. CHRIST IN A MAN THE GOSPEL IN THE SOUL, is the power of God and the wisdom of God. We will picture the Christian from his beginning to his end. We will give a short map of his history. He begins there, in that prison-house, with huge iron bars, which he can not file; in that dark, damp cell, where pestilence and death are bred. There, in poverty and nakedness, without a pitcher to put to his thirsty lips, without a mouthful even of dry crust to satisfy his hunger, that is where be begins—in the prison chamber of conviction, powerless, lost and ruined. Between the bars I thrust my hand to him, and give to him in God's name the name of Christ to plead. Look at him; he has been filing away at these bars many and many a day, without their yielding an inch; but now he has got the name of Christ upon his lips; he puts his hands upon the bars, and one of them is gone, and another, and another; and be makes a happy escape, crying, "I am free, I am free, I am free! Christ has been the power of God to me, in bringing me out of my trouble." No sooner is he free, however, than a thousand doubts meet him. This one cries, "You are not elect;" another cries, "You are not redeemed;" another says, "You are not called;" another says, "You are not converted." "Avaunt," says he, "avaunt! Christ died;" and he just pleads the name of Christ as the power of God, and the doubts flee apace, and he walks straight on. He comes soon into the furnace of trouble; he is thrust into the innermost prison, and his feet are made fast in the stocks. God has put his hand upon him. He is in deep trouble; at midnight he begins to sing of Christ; and lo! the walls begin to totter, and the foundation of the prison to shake; and the man's chains are taken off, and he comes out free; for Christ hath delivered him from trouble. Here is a hill to climb, on the road to heaven. Wearily he pants up the side of that hill, and thinks he must die ere he can reach the summit. The name of Jesus is whispered in his ear; he leaps to his feet, and pursues his way, with fresh courage, until the summit is gained, when he cries, "Jesus Christ is the strength of my song; he also hath become my salvation." See him again. He is on a sudden beset by many enemies; how shall he resist them? With this true sword, this true Jerusalem blade, Christ, and him crucified. With this he keeps the devil at arm's length; with this he fights against temptation, and against lust, against spiritual wickedness in high places, and with this he resists. Now, he has come to his last struggle; the river Death rolls black and sullen before him; dark shapes rise upward from the flood, and howl and fright him. How shall he cross the stream? How shall he find a landing place on the other side? Dread thoughts perplex him for a moment; he is alarmed; but he remembers, Jesus died; and catching up that watchword he ventures to the flood. Before his feet the Jordan flies apace; like Israel of old, he walks through, dry shod, singing as he goes to heaven, "Christ is with me, Christ is with me, passing through the stream! Victory, victory, victory, to him that loveth me!"

To the Christian in his own experience Christ is ever the power of God. As for temptation he can meet that with Christ; as for trouble he can endure that through Christ who strengthens him, yea, he can say with Paul, "I can do all things through Christ who strengthens me." Have you never seen a Christian in trouble, a true Christian? I have read a story of a man who was converted to God by seeing the conduct of his wife in the hour of trouble. They had a lovely child, their only offspring. The father's heart doted on it perpetually, and the mother's soul was knit up in the heart of the little one. It lay sick upon its bed, and the parents watched it night and day. At last it died. The father had no God: he rent his hair, he rolled upon the floor in misery, wallowed upon the earth, cursing his being, and defying God in the utter casting down of his agony. There sat his wife, as fond of the child as ever he could be; and though tears would come, she gently said "The Lord gave, and the Lord hath taken away; blessed be the name of the Lord." "What," said he, starting to his feet, "you love that child? I thought that when that child died you would break your heart. Here am I, a strong man. I am mad: here are you, a weak woman, and yet you are strong and bold; tell me what it is possesses you?" Said she, "Christ is my Lord, I trust in him; surely I can give this child to him who gave himself for me." From that instant the man became a believer. "There must," said he, "be some truth and some power in the gospel, which could lead you to believe in such a manner, under such a trial." Christians! try to exhibit that spirit wherever you are, and prove to the worldling that in your experience at least "Christ is the power of God and the wisdom of God."

And now the last point. In the Christian's experience, Christ is wisdom, as well as power. If you want to be a thoroughly learned man the best place to begin, is to begin at the Bible, to begin at Christ. It is said that even children learn to read more quickly from the Bible than from any other book; and this I am sure of, that we, who are but grown-up children, will learn better and learn faster by beginning with Christ than we could by beginning with any thing else. I remember saying once, and as I can not say it better I will repeat it, that before I knew the gospel I gathered up a heterogeneous mass of all kinds of knowledge from here, there, and everywhere; a bit of chemistry, a bit of botany, a bit of astronomy, and a bit of this, that, and the other. I put them altogether, in one great confused chaos. When I learned the gospel, I got a shelf in my head to put every thing away upon just where it should be. It seemed to me as if, when I had discovered Christ and him crucified, I had got the center of the system, so that I could see every other science revolving around in order. From the earth, you know, the planets appear to move in a very irregular manner—they are progressive, retro grade, stationary; but if you could get upon the sun, you would see them marching round in their constant, uniform, circular motion. So with knowledge. Begin with any other science you like, and truth will seem to be awry. Begin with the science of Christ crucified, and you will begin with the sun, you will see every other science moving round it in complete harmony. The greatest mind in the world will be evolved by beginning at the right end. The old saying is, "Go from nature up to nature's God;" but it is hard work going up hill. The best thing is to go from nature's God down to nature; and if you once get to nature's God, and believe him and love him, it is surprising how easy it is to hear music in the waves, and songs in the wild whisperings of the winds; to see God everywhere, in the stones, in the rocks, in the rippling brooks, and hear him everywhere, in the lowing of cattle, in the rolling of thunder, and in the fury of tempests. Get Christ first, put him in the right place, and you will find him to be the wisdom of God in your own experience.

But wisdom is not knowledge; and we must not confound the two. Wisdom is the right use of knowledge; and Christ's gospel helps us, by teaching us the right use of knowledge. It directs us. Yon Christian has lost his way in a dark wood; but God's Word is a compass to him, and a lantern, too: he finds his way by Christ. He comes to a turn in the road. Which is right, and which is wrong? He can not tell. Christ is the great sign-post, telling him which way to go. He sees every day new straits attend; he knows not which way to steer. Christ is the great pilot who puts his hand on the tiller, and makes him wise to steer through the shoals of temptation and the rocks of sin. Get the gospel, and you are a wise man. "The fear of the

Lord is the beginning of wisdom, and right understanding have they who keep his commandments." Ah! Christian, you have had many doubts, but you have had them all unriddled, when you have come to the cross of Christ. You have had many difficulties; but they have been all explained in the light of Calvary. You have seen mysteries, when you have brought them to the face of Christ, made clear and manifest, which once you never could have known. Allow me to remark here, that some people make use of Christ's gospel to illuminate their heads, instead of making use of it to illuminate their hearts. They are like the farmer Rowland Hill once described. The farmer is sitting, by the fire with his children; the cat is purring on the hearth, and they are all in great comfort. The plowman rushes in and cries, "Thieves! thieves! thieves!" The farmer rises up in a moment, grasps the candle, holds it up to his head, rushes after the thieves, and, says Rowland Hill, "he tumbles over a wheelbarrow, because he holds the light to his head, instead of holding it to his feet." So there are many who just hold religion up to illuminate their intellect, instead of holding it down to illuminate their practice; and so they make a sad tumble of it, and cast themselves into the mire, and do more hurt to their Christian profession in one hour than they will ever be able to retrieve. Take care that you make the wisdom of God, by God's Holy Spirit, a thing of true wisdom, directing your feet into his statutes, and keeping you in his ways.

And now a practical appeal, and we have done. I have been putting my arrow on the string; and if I have used any light similes, I have but done so just as the archer tips his arrow with a feather, to make it fly the better. I know that a rough quaint saying often sticks, when another thing is entirely for-gotten. Now let us draw the bow, and send the arrow right at your hearts. Men, brethren, fathers, how many of you have felt in yourselves that Christ is the power of God, and the wisdom of God? Internal evidence is the best evidence in the world for the truth of the gospel. No Paley or Butler can prove the truth of the gospel so well as Mary, the servant girl yonder, that has got the gospel in her heart, and the power of it manifest in her life. Say, has Christ ever broken your bonds and set you free? Has he delivered you from your evil life, and from your sin? Has he given you "a good hope through grace," and can you now say, "On him I lean; on my beloved I stay myself?" If so, go away and rejoice: you are a saint; for the apostle has said, "He is unto us who are saved, Christ the power of God and the wisdom of God." But if you can not say this, allow me affectionately to warn you. If you want not this power of Christ, and this wisdom of Christ now, you will want them in a few short moments, when God shall come to judge the quick and the dead, when you shall stand before his bar, and when all the deeds that you have done shall be read before an assembled world. You will want religion then. O that you had grace to tremble now; grace to "kiss the Son, lest he be angry, and you perish from the way, when his wrath is kindled but a little." Hear ye how to be saved, and I have done. Do you feel that you are a sinner? Are you conscious that you have rebelled against God? Are you willing to acknowledge your transgressions, and do you hate and abhor them, while at the same time you feel you can do nothing to atone for them? Then hear this. Christ died for you; and if he died for you, you can not be lost. Christ died in vain for no man for whom he died. If you are a penitent and a believer, he died for you, and you are safe; go your way: rejoice "with joy unspeakable, and full of glory;" for he who has taught you your need of a Saviour, will give you that Saviour's blood to be applied to your conscience, and you shall ere long, with yonder blood-washed host, praise God and the Lamb saying, "Hallelujah, for ever, Amen!" Only do you feel that you are a sinner? If not, I have no gospel to preach to you; I can but warn you. But if you feel your lost estate, and come to Christ, come, and welcome, for he will never cast you away.

Coming Judgment of the Secrets of Men

A Sermon (No. 1849) Delivered on Lord's Day Morning, July 12th, 1885, by C. H. SPURGEON, At the Metropolitan Tabernacle, Newington.

"The day when God shall judge the secrets of men by Jesus Christ according to my gospel."
—Romans 2:16.

It is impossible for any of us to tell what it cost the apostle Paul to write the first chapter of the epistle to the Romans. It is a shame even to speak of the things which are done of the vicious in secret places; but Paul felt it was necessary to break through his shame, and to speak out concerning the hideous vices of the heathen. He has left on record an exposure of the sins of his day which crimsons the cheek of the modest when they read it, and makes both the ears of him that heareth it to tingle. Paul knew that this chapter would be read, not in his age alone, but in all ages, and that it would go into the households of the most pure and godly as long as the world should stand; and yet he deliberately wrote it, and wrote it under the guidance of the Holy Spirit. He knew that it must be written to put to shame the abominations of an age which was almost past shame. Monsters that revel in darkness must be dragged into the open, that they may be withered up by the light. After Paul has thus written in anguish he bethought himself of his chief comfort. While his pen was black with the words he had written in the first chapter, he was driven to write of his great delight. He clings to the gospel with a greater tenacity than ever. As in the verse before us he needed to mention the gospel, he did not speak of it as "the gospel," but as "my gospel." "God shall judge the secrets of men by Jesus Christ, according to my gospel." He felt he could not live in the midst of so depraved a people without holding the gospel with both hands, and grasping it as his very own. "My gospel," saith he. Not that Paul was the author of it, not that Paul had an exclusive monopoly of its blessings, but that he had so received it from Christ himself, and regarded himself as so responsibly put in trust with it, that he could not disown it even for a instant. So fully had he taken it into himself that he could not do less than call it "my gospel." In another place he speaks of "our gospel;" thus using a possessive pronoun, to show how believers identify themselves with the truth which they preach. He had a gospel, a definite form of truth, and he believed in it beyond all doubt; and therefore he spoke of it as "my gospel." Herein we hear the voice of faith, which seems to say, "Though others reject it, I am sure of it, and allow no shade of mistrust to darken my mind. To me it is glad tidings of great joy: I hail it as 'my gospel.' If I be called a fool for holding it, I am content to be a fool, and to find all my wisdom in my Lord." "Should all the forms that men devise Assult my faith with treacherous art, I'd call them vanity and lies, And bind the gospel to my heart." Is not this word "my gospel" the voice of love? Does he not by this word embrace the gospel as the only love of his soul—for the sake of which he had suffered the loss of all things, and did count them but dung—for the sake of which he was willing to stand before Nero, and proclaim, even in Caesar's palace, the message from heaven? Though each word should cost him a life, he was willing to die a thousand deaths for the holy cause. "My gospel," saith he, with a rapture of delight, as he presses to his bosom the sacred deposit of truth.

"My gospel." Does not this show his courage? As much as to say, "I am not ashamed of the gospel of Christ: for it is the power of God unto salvation to every one that believeth." He says, "my gospel," as a soldier speaks of "my colours," or of "my king." He resolves to bear this banner to victory, and to serve this royal truth even to the death.

"My gospel." There is a touch of discrimination about the expression. Paul perceives that there are other gospels, and he makes short work with them, for he saith, "Though we, or an angel from heaven, preach any other gospel unto you than that which we have preached unto you, let me be accused." The apostle was of a gentle spirit; he prayed heartily for the Jews who persecuted him, and yielded his life for the conversion of the Gentiles who maltreated him; but he had no tolerance for false gospellers. He exhibited great breadth of mind, and to save souls he became all things to all men; but when he contemplated any alteration or adulteration of the gospel of Christ, he thundered and lightninged without measure. When he feared that something else might spring up among the philosophers, or among the Judaizers, that should hide a single beam of the glorious Sun of Righteousness, he used no measured language; but cried concerning the author of such a darkening influence, "Let him be accursed." Every heart that would see men blessed whispers an "Amen" to the apostolic malediction. No greater curse can come upon mankind than the obscuration of the gospel of Jesus Christ. Paul saith of himself and his true brethren, "We are not as many, which corrupt the word of God;" and he cries to those who turned aside from the one and only gospel, "O foolish Galatians, who hath bewitched you?" Of all new doctrines he speaks as of "another gospel, which is not another; but there be some that trouble you."

As for myself, looking at the matter afresh, amidst all the filthiness which I see in the world at this day, I lay hold upon the pure and blessed Word of God, and call it all the more earnestly, my gospel,—mine in life and mine in death, mine against all comers, mine for ever, God helping me: with emphasis—"my gospel."

Now let us notice what it was that brought up this expression, "My gospel." What was Paul preaching about? Certainly not upon any of the gentle and tender themes, which we are told nowadays ought to occupy all our time; but he is speaking of the terrors of the law, and in that connection he speaks of "my gospel."Let us come at once to our text. It will need no dividing, for it divides itself. First, let us consider that on a certain day God shall judge mankind; secondly, on that day God will judge the secrets of men; thirdly, when he judges the secrets of men, it will be by Jesus Christ; and fourthly, this is according to gospel.

I. We begin with the solemn truth, that ON A CERTAIN DAY GOD WILL JUDGE MEN. A judgment is going on daily. God is continually holding court, and considering the doings of the sons of men. Every evil deed that they do is recorded in the register of doom, and each good action is remembered and laid up in store by God. That judgment is reflected in a measure in the consciences of men. Those who know the gospel, and those who know it not, alike, have a certain measure of light, by which they know right from wrong; their consciences all the while accusing or else excusing them. This session of the heavenly court continues from day to-day, like that of our local magistrates; but this does not prevent but rather necessitates the holding of an ultimate great assize.

As each man passes into another world, there is an immediate judgment passed upon him; but this is only the foreshadowing of that which will take place in the end of the world.

There is a judgment also passing upon nations, for as nations will not exist as nations in another world, they have to be judged and punished in this present state. The thoughtful reader of history will not fail to observe, how sternly this justice had dealt with empire after empire, when they have become corrupt. Colossal dominions have withered to the ground, when sentenced by the King of kings. Go ye and ask to-day, "Where is the empire of Assyria? Where are the mighty cities of Babylon? Where are the glories of the Medes and Persians? What has become of the Macedonian power? Where are the Caesars and their palaces?" These empires were forces established by cruelty, and used for oppression; they fostered luxury and licentiousness, and when they were no longer tolerable, the earth was purged from their polluting existence. Ah me! what horrors of war, bloodshed, and devastation, have come upon men as the result of their iniquities! The world is full of the monuments, both of the mercy and the justice of God: in fact the monuments of his justice, if rightly viewed, are proofs of his goodness; for it is mercy on the part of God to put an end to evil systems when, like a nightmare, they weigh heavily upon the bosom of mankind. The omnipotent, Judge has not ceased from his sovereign rule over kingdoms, and our own country may yet have to feel his chastisements. We have often laughed among ourselves at the idea of the New Zealander sitting on the broken arch of London Bridge amid the ruins of this metropolis. But is it quite so ridiculous as it looks? It is more than possible it will be realized if our iniquities continue to abound. What is there about London that it should be more enduring than Rome? Why should the palaces of our monarchs be eternal if the palaces of Koyunjik have fallen? The almost boundless power of the Pharaohs has passed away, and Egypt has become the meanest of nations; why should not England come under like condemnation? What are we? What is there about our boastful race, whether on this side of the Atlantic or the other, that we should monopolize the favour of God? If we rebel, and sin against him, he will not hold us guiltless, but will deal out impartial justice to an ungrateful race.

Still, though such judgments proceed every day, yet there is to be a day, a period of time, in which, in a more distinct, formal, public, and final manner, God will judge the sons of men. We might have guessed this by the light of nature and of reason. Even heathen peoples have had a dim notion of a day of doom; but we are not left to guess it, we are solemnly assured of it in the Holy Scripture. Accepting this Book as the revelation of God, we know beyond all doubt that a day is appointed in which the Lord will judge the secrets of men.

By judging is here meant all that concerns the proceedings of trial and award. God will judge the race of men; that is to say, first, there will be a session of majesty, and the appearing of a great white throne, surrounded with pomp of angels and glorified beings. Then a summons will be issued, bidding all men come to judgment, to give in their final account. The heralds will fly through the realms of death, and summon those who sleep in the dust: for the quick and the dead shall all appear before that judgment-seat. John says, "I saw the dead, small and great, stand before God;" and he adds, "The sea gave up the dead which were in it; and death and hell delivered up the dead which were in them." Those that have been so long buried that their dust is mingled with the soil, and has undergone a thousand transmutations, shall nevertheless be made to put in a personal appearance before the judgment-seat of Christ. What an issue will that be! You and I and all the myriad myriads of our race shall be gathered before the throne of the Son of God. Then, when all are gathered, the indictment will be read, and each one will be examined concerning things done in the body, according to that he hath done. Then the books shall be opened, and everything recorded there shall be read before the face of heaven. Every sinner shall then hear the story of his life published to his everlasting shame. The good shall ask no concealment, and the evil shall find none. Angels and men shall then see the truth of things, and the saints shall judge the world. Then the great Judge himself shall give the decision: he shall pronounce sentence upon the wicked, and execute their punishment. No partiality shall there be seen; there shall be no private conferences to secure immunity for nobles, no hushing up of matters, that great men may escape contempt for their crimes. All men shall stand before the one great judgment-bar; evidence shall be given concerning them all, and a righteous sentence shall go forth from his mouth who knows not how to flatter the great.

This will be so, and it ought to be so: God should judge the world, because he is the universal ruler and sovereign. There has been a day for sinning, there ought to be a day for punishing; a long age of rebellion has been endured, and there must be a time when justice shall assert her supremacy. We have seen an age in which reformation has been commanded, in which mercy has been presented, in which expostulation and entreaty have been used, and there ought at last to come a day in which God shall judge both the quick and the dead, and measure out to each the final result of life. It ought to be so for the sake of the righteous. They have been slandered; they have been despised and ridiculed; worse than that, they have been imprisoned and beaten, and put to death times without number: the best have had the worst of it, and there ought to be a judgment to set these things right. Besides the festering iniquities of each age cry out to God that he should deal with them. Shall such sin go unpunished? To what end is there a moral government at all, and how is its continuance to be secured, if there be not rewards and punishments and a day of account? For the display of his holiness, for the overwhelming of his adversaries, for the rewarding of those who have faithfully served him, there must be and shall be a day in which God will judge the world.

Why doth it not come at once? And when will it come? The precise day we cannot tell. Man nor angel knoweth that day, and it is idle and profane to guess at it, since even the Son of man, as such, knoweth not the time. It is sufficient for us that the Judgment Day will surely come; sufficient also to believe that it is postponed on purpose to give breathing time for mercy, and space for repentance. Why should the ungodly want to know when that day will come? What is that day to you? To you it should be darkness, and not light. It shall be your day of consuming as stubble fully dry: therefore bless the Lord that he delayeth his coming, and reckon that his longsuffering is for your salvation.

Moreover, the Lord keeps the scaffold standing till he hath built up the fabric of his church. Not yet are the elect all called out from among the guilty sons of men; not yet are all the redeemed with blood redeemed with power and brought forth out of the corruption of the age into the holiness in which they walk with God. Therefore the Lord waiteth for a while. But do not deceive yourselves. The great day of his wrath cometh on apace, and your days of reprieve are numbered. One day is with the Lord as a thousand years, and a thousand years as one day. Ye shall die, perhaps, before the appearing of the Son of man: but ye shall see his judgment-seat for all that, for ye shall rise again as surely as he rose. When the apostle addressed the Grecian sages at Athens he said, "God now commandeth all men everywhere to repent, because he hath appointed a day, in the which he will judge the world in righteousness by that man whom he hath ordained; whereof he hath given assurance unto all men, in that he hath raised him from the dead." See ye not, O ye impenitent ones, that a risen Saviour is the sign of your doom. As God hath raised Jesus from the dead, so shall he raise your bodies, that in these you may come to judgment. Before the judgment-seat shall every man and woman in this house give an account of the things done in the body, whether they be good or whether they be evil. Thus saith the Lord.

II. Now I call your attention to the fact that "GOD WILL JUDGE THE SECRETS OF MEN." This will happen to all men, of every nation, of every age, of every rank, and of every character. The Judge will, of course, judge their outward acts, but these may be said to have gone before them to judgment: their secret acts are specially mentioned, because these will make judgment to be the more searching.

By "secrets of men," the Scripture means those secret crimes which hide themselves away by their own infamy, which are too vile to be spoken of, which cause a shudder to go through a nation if they be but dragged, as they ought to be, into the daylight. Secret offences shall be brought into judgment; the deeds of the night and of the closed room, the acts which require the finger to be laid upon the lip, and a conspiracy of silence to be sworn. Revolting and shameless sins which must never be mentioned lest the man who committed them should be excluded from his fellows as an outcast, abhorred even of other sinners—all those shall be revealed. All that you have done, any of you, or are doing, if you are bearing the Christian name and yet practising secret sin, shall be laid bare before the universal gaze. If you sit here amongst the people of God, and yet where no eye sees you, if you are living in dishonesty, untruthfulness, or uncleanness, it shall all be known, and shame and confusion of face shall eternally cover you. Contempt shall be the inheritance to which you shall awake, when hypocrisy shall be no more possible. Be not deceived, God is not mocked; but he will bring the secrets of men into judgment.

Specially our text refers to the hidden motives of ever action; for a man may do that which is right from a wrong motive, and so the deed may be evil in the sight of God, though it seem right in the sight of men. Oh, think what it will be to have your motives all brought to light, to have it proven that you were godly for the sake of gain, that you were generous out of ostentation, or zealous for love of praise, that you were careful in public to maintain a religious reputation, but that all the while everything was done for self, and self only! What a strong light will that be which God shall turn upon our lives, when the darkest chambers of human desire and motive shall be as manifest as public acts! What a revelation will that be which makes manifest all thoughts, and imaginings, and lustings, and desires! All angers, and envies, and prides, and rebellions of the heart—what a disclosure will these make!

All the sensual desires and imaginings of even the best-regulated, what a foulness will these appear! What a day it will be, when the secrets of men shall be set in the full blaze of noon!

God will also reveal secrets, that were secrets even to the sinners themselves, for there is sin in us which we have never seen, and iniquity in us which we have never yet discovered.

We have managed for our own comfort's sake to blind our eyes somewhat, and we take care to avert our gaze from things which it is inconvenient to see; but we shall be compelled to see all these evils in that day, when the Lord shall judge the secrets of men. I do not wonder that when a certain Rabbi read in the book of Ecclesiastes that God shall bring every work into judgment, with every secret thing, whether it be good, or whether it be evil, he wept. It is enough to make the best men tremble. Were it not for thee, O Jesus, whose precious blood hath cleansed us from all sin, where should we be! Were it not for thy righteousness, which shall cover those who believe in thee, who among us could endure the thought of that tremendous day? In thee, O Jesus, we are made righteous, and therefore we fear not the trial-hour; but were it not for thee our hearts would fail us for fear!

Now if you ask me why God should judge, especially the secrets of men—since this is not done in human courts, and cannot be, for secret things of this kind come not under cognizance of our short-sighted tribunals—I answer it is because there is really nothing secret from God. We make a difference between secret and public sins, but he doth not; for all things are naked and open to the eyes of him with whom we have to do. All deeds are done in the immediate presence of God, who is personally present everywhere. He knows and sees all things as one upon the spot, and every secret sin is but conceived to be secret through the deluded fantasy of our ignorance. God sees more of a secret sin than a man can see of that which is done before his face. "Can any hide himself in secret places that I shall not see him? saith the Lord."

The secrets of men will be judged because often the greatest of moral acts are done in secret. The brightest deeds that God delights in are those that are done by his servants when they have shut the door and are alone with him; when they have no motive but to please him; when they studiously avoid publicity, lest they should be turned aside by the praise of men; when the right hand knoweth not what the left hand doeth, and the loving, generous heart deviseth liberal things, and doeth it behind the screen, so that it should never be discovered how the deed was done. It were a pity that such deeds should be left out at the great audit. Thus, too, secret vices are also of the very blackest kind, and to exempt them were to let the worst of sinners go unpunished. Shall it be that these polluted things shall escape because they have purchased silence with their wealth? I say solemnly "God forbid." He does forbid it: what they have done in secret, shall be proclaimed upon the house-tops.

Besides, the secret things of men enter into the very essence of their actions. An action is, after all, good or bad very much according to its motive. It may seem good, but the motive may taint it; and so, if God did not judge the secret part of the action he would not judge righteously. He will weigh our actions, and detect the design which led to them, and the spirit which prompted them.

Is it not certainly true that the secret thing is the best evidence of the man's condition? Many a man will not do in public that which would bring him shame; not because he is black-hearted enough for it, but because he is too much of a coward. That which a man does when he thinks that he is entirely by himself is the best revelation of the man. That which thou wilt not do because it would be told of thee if thou didst ill, is a poor index of thy real character. That which thou wilt do because thou wilt be praised for doing well, is an equally faint test of thy heart. Such virtue is mere self-seeking, or mean-spirited subservience to thy fellow-man; but that which thou doest out of respect to no authority but thine own conscience and thy God; that which thou doest unobserved, without regard to what man will say concerning it—that it is which reveals thee, and discovers thy real soul. Hence God lays a special stress and emphasis upon the fact that he will in that day judge "the secrets" of men by Jesus Christ.

Oh, friends, if it does not make you tremble to think of these things, it ought to do so. I feel the deep responsibility of preaching upon such matters, and I pray God of his infinite mercy to apply these truths to our hearts, that they may be forceful upon our lives. These truths ought to startle us, but I am afraid we hear them with small result; we have grown familiar with them, and they do not penetrate us as they should. We have to deal, brethren, with an omniscient God; with One who once knowing never forgets; with One to whom all things are always present; with One will conceal nothing out of fear, or favour of any man's person; with One who will shortly bring the splendour of his omniscience and the impartiality of his justice to bear upon all human lives. God help us, where'er we rove and where'er we rest, to remember that each thought, word, and act of each moment lies in that fierce light which beats upon all things from the throne of God.

III. Another solemn revelation of our text lies in this fact, that "GOD WILL JUDGE THE SECRETS OF MEN BY JESUS CHRIST." He that will sit upon the throne as the Vice-regent of God, and as a Judge, acting for God, will be Jesus Christ. What a name for a Judge! The Saviour-Anointed—Jesus Christ: he is to be the judge of all mankind. Our Redeemer will be the Umpire of our destiny.

This will be, I doubt not, first for the display of his glory. What a difference there will be then between the babe of Bethlehem's manger, hunted by Herod, carried down by night into Egypt for shelter, and the King of kings and Lord of lords, before whom every knee must bow! What a difference between the weary man and full of woes, and he that shall then be grit with glory, sitting on a throne encircled with a rainbow! From the derision of men to the throne of universal judgment, what an ascent! I am unable to convey to you my own heart's sense of the contrast between the "despised and rejected of men," and the universally-acknowledged Lord, before whom Caesars and pontiffs shall bow into the dust. He who was judged at Pilate's bar, shall summon all to his bar. What a change from the shame and spitting, from the nails and the wounds, the mockery and the thirst, and the dying anguish, to the glory in which he shall come whose eyes are as a flame of fire, and out of whose mouth there goeth a two-edged sword! He shall judge the nations, even he whom the nations abhorred. He shall break them in pieces like a potter's vessel, even those who cast him out as unworthy to live among them. Oh, how we ought to bow before him now as he reveals himself in his tender sympathy, and in his generous humiliation! Let us kiss the Son lest he be angry; let us yield to his grace, that we may not be crushed by his wrath. Ye sinners, bow before those pierced feet, which else will tread you like clusters in the wine-press. Look ye up to him with weeping, and confess your forgetfulness of him, and put your trust in him; lest he look down on you in indignation. Oh, remember that he will one day say, "But those mine enemies, which would not that I should reign over them, bring hither, and slay them before me." The holding of the judgment by the Lord Jesus will greatly enhance his glory. It will finally settle one controversy which is still upheld by certain erroneous spirits: there will be no doubt about our Lord's deity in that day: there will be no question that this same Jesus who was crucified is both Lord and God. God himself shall judge, but he shall perform the judgment in the person of his Son Jesus Christ, truly man, but nevertheless most truly God. Being God he is divinely qualified to judge the world in righteousness, and the people with his truth.

If you ask again, Why is the Son of God chosen to be the final Judge? I could give as a further answer that he receives this high office not only as a reward for all his pains, and as a manifestation of his glory, but also because men have been under his mediatorial sway, and he is their Governor and King. At the present moment we are all under the sway of the Prince Immanuel, God with us: we have been placed by an act of divine clemency, not under the immediate government of an offended God, but under the reconciling rule of the Prince of Peace. "All power is given unto him in heaven and in earth." "The Father judgeth no man, but hath committed all judgment unto the Son: that all men should honour the Son, even as they honour the Father." We are commanded to preach unto the people, and "to testify that it is he which was ordained of God to be the judge of quick and dead." (Acts 10:42) Jesus is our Lord and King, and it is meet that he should conclude his mediatorial sovereignty by rewarding his subjects to their deeds.

But I have somewhat to say unto you which ought to reach your hearts, even if other thoughts have not done so. I think that God hath chosen Christ, the man Christ Jesus, to judge the world that there may never be a cavil raised concerning that judgment. Men shall not be able to say—We were judged by a superior being who did not know our weaknesses and temptations, and therefore he judged us harshly, and without a generous consideration of our condition. No, God shall judge the secrets of men by Jesus Christ, who was tempted in all points like as we are, yet without sin. He is our brother, bone of our bone, flesh of our flesh, partaker of our humanity, and therefore understands and knows what is in men. He has shown himself to be skilful in all the surgery of mercy throughout the ages, and at last he will be found equally skilful in dissecting motives and revealing the thoughts and intents of the heart. Nobody shall ever be able to look back on that august tribunal and say that he who sat upon it was too stern, because he knew nothing of human weakness. It will be the loving Christ, whose tears, and bloody sweat, and gaping wounds, attest his brotherhood with mankind; and it will be clear to all intelligences that however dread his sentences, he could not be unmerciful. God shall judge us by Jesus Christ, that the judgment may be indisputable.

But harken well—for I speak with a great weight upon my soul—this judgment by Jesus Christ, puts beyond possibility all hope of any after-interposition. If the Saviour condemns, and such a Saviour, who can plead for us? The owner of the vineyard was about to cut down the barren tree, when the dresser of the vineyard pleaded, "Let it alone this year also;" but what can come of that tree when that vinedresser himself shall say to the master, "It must fall; I myself must cut it down!" If your Saviour shall become your judge you will be judged indeed. If he shall say, "Depart, ye cursed," who can call you back? If he that bled to save men at last comes to this conclusion, that there is no more to be done, but they must be driven from his presence, then farewell hope. To the guilty the judgment will indeed be a "Great day of dread, decision, and despair." An infinite horror shall seize upon their spirits as the words of the loving Christ shall freeze their very marrow, and fix them in the ice of eternal despair. There is, to my mind, a climax of solemnity in the fact that God shall judge the secrets of men by Jesus Christ.

Does not this also show how certain the sentence will be? for this Christ of God is too much in earnest to play with men. If he says, "Come, ye blessed," he will not fail to bring them to their inheritance. If he be driven to say, "Depart, ye cursed," he will see it done, and into the everlasting punishment they must go. Even when it cost him his life he did not draw back from doing the will of his Father, nor will he shrink in that day when he shall pronounce the sentence of doom. Oh, how evil must sin be since it constrains the tender Saviour to pronounce sentence of eternal woe! I am sure that many of us have been driven of late to an increased hatred of sin; our souls have recoiled within us because of the wickedness among which we dwell; it has made us feel as if we would fain borrow the Almighty's thunderbolts with which to smite iniquity. Such haste on our part may not be seemly, since it implies a complaint against divine long-suffering; but Christ's dealing with evil will be calm and dispassionate, and all the more crushing. Jesus, with his pierced hand, that bears the attestation of his supreme love to men, shall wave the impenitent away; and those lips which bade the weary rest in him shall solemnly say to the wicked, "Depart, ye cursed, into everlasting fire prepared for the devil and his angels." To be trampled beneath the foot which was nailed to the cross will be to be crushed indeed: yet so it is, God shall judge the secrets of men by Jesus Christ.

It seems to me as if God in this intended to give a display of the unity of all his perfections. In this same man, Christ Jesus, the Son of God, you behold justice and love, mercy and righteousness, combined in equal measure. He turns to the right, and says, "Come, ye blessed," with infinite suavity; and with the same lip, as he glances to the left, he says, "Depart, ye cursed." Men will then see at one glance how love and righteousness are one, and how they meet in equal splendour in the person of the Wellbeloved, whom God has therefore chosen to be Judge of quick and dead.

IV. I have done when you have borne with me a minute or two upon my next point, which is this: and ALL THIS IS ACCORDING TO THE GOSPEL. That is to say, there is nothing in the gospel contrary to the solemn teaching. Men gather to us, to hear us preach of infinite mercy, and tell of the love that blots out sin; and our task is joyful when we are called to deliver such a message; but oh, sirs, remember that nothing in our message makes light of sin. The gospel offers you no opportunity of going on in sin, and escaping without punishment. Its own cry is, "Except ye repent, ye shall all likewise perish." Jesus has not come into the world to make sin less terrible. Nothing in the gospel excuses sin; nothing in it affords toleration for lust or anger, or dishonesty, or falsehood. The gospel is as truly a two-edged sword against sin, as ever the law can be. There is grace for the man who quits his sin, but there is tribulation and wrath upon every man that doeth evil. "If ye turn not, he will whet his sword; he hath bent his bow, and made it ready." The gospel is all tenderness to the repenting, but all terror to the obstinate offender. It has pardon for the very chief of sinners, and mercy for the vilest of the vile, if they will forsake their sins; but it is according to our gospel that he that goeth on in his iniquity, shall be cast into hell, and he that believeth not shall be damned. With deep love to the souls of men, I bear witness to the truth that he who turns not with repentance and faith to Christ, shall go away into punishment as everlasting as the life of the righteous. This is according to our gospel: indeed, we had not needed such a gospel, if there had not been such a judgment. The background of the cross is the judgment-seat of Christ. We had not needed so great an atonement, so vast a sacrifice, if there had not been an exceeding sinfulness in sin, an exceeding justice in the judgment, and an exceeding terror in the sure rewards of transgression.

"According to my gospel," saith Paul; and he meant that the judgment is an essential part of the gospel creed. If I had to sum up the gospel I should have to tell you certain facts: Jesus, the Son of God, became man; he was born of the virgin Mary; lived a perfect life; was falsely accused of men; was crucified, dead, and buried; the third day he rose again from the dead; he ascended into heaven and sitteth on the right hand of God; from whence he shall also come to judge the quick and the dead. This is one of the elementary truths of our gospel; we believe in the resurrection of the dead, the final judgment, and the life everlasting.

The judgment is according to our gospel, and in times of righteous indignation its terrible significance seemeth a very gospel to the pure in heart. I mean this. I have read this and that concerning oppression, slavery, the treading down of the poor, and the shedding of blood, and I have rejoiced that there is a righteous Judge. I have read of secret wickednesses among the rich men of this city, and I have said within myself, "Thank God, there will be a judgment day." Thousands of men have been hanged for much less crimes than those which now disgrace gentlemen whose names are on the lips of rank and beauty. Ah me, how heavy is our heart as we think of it! It has come like a gospel to us that the Lord will be revealed in flaming fire, taking vengeance on them that know not God, and that obey not the gospel of our Lord Jesus Christ. (2 Thess. 1:8)

The secret wickedness of London cannot go on for ever. Even they that love men best, and most desire salvation for them, cannot but cry to God, "How long! How long! Great God, wilt thou for ever endure this?" God hath appointed a day in which he will judge the world, and we sigh and cry until it shall end the reign of wickedness, and give rest to the oppressed. Brethren, we must preach the coming of the Lord, and preach it somewhat more than we have done; because it is the driving power of the gospel. Too many have kept back these truths, and thus the bone has been taken out of the arm of the gospel. Its point has been broken; its edge has been blunted. The doctrine of judgment to come is the power by which men are to be aroused. There is another life; the Lord will come a second time; judgment will arrive; the wrath of God will be revealed. Where this is not preached, I am bold to say the gospel is not preached. It is absolutely necessary to the preaching of the gospel of Christ that men be warned as to what will happen if they continue in their sins. Ho, ho, sir surgeon, you are too delicate to tell the man that he is ill! You hope to heal the sick without their knowing it. You therefore flatter them; and what happens? They laugh at you; they dance upon their own graves. At last they die! Your delicacy is cruelty; your flatteries are poisons; you are a murderer. Shall we keep men in a fool's paradise? Shall we lull them into soft slumbers from which they will awake in hell? Are we to become helpers of their damnation by our smooth speeches? In the name of God we will not. It becomes every true minister of Christ to cry aloud and spare not, for God hath set a day in which he will "judge the secrets of men by Jesus Christ according to my gospel." As surely as Paul's gospel was true the judgment will come. Wherefore flee to Jesus this day, O sinners. O ye saints, come hide yourselves again beneath the crimson canopy of the atoning sacrifice, that you may be now ready to welcome your descending Lord and escort him to his judgment-seat. O my hearers, may God bless you, for Jesus' sake. Amen. Portion of Scripture read before Sermon—John 12:37–50. Hymns from "Our Own Hymn Book"—93, 12, 518.

Coming to Christ

A Sermon (No. 3509) Published on
Thursday, April 27th, 1916.
Delivered by C. H. SPURGEON,
At the Metropolitan Tabernacle, Newington.
ON Lord's-Day Evening, June 17th, 1868.

"To whom coming."—1 Peter 2:4.

In these three words you have, first of all, a blessed person mentioned, under the pronoun "whom"—"To whom coming." In the way of salvation we come alone to Jesus Christ. All comings to baptism, comings to confirmation, comings to sacrament are all null and void unless we come to Jesus Christ. That which saves the soul is not coming to a human priest, nor even attending the assemblies of God's saints; it is coming to Jesus Christ, the great exalted Saviour, once slain, but now enthroned in glory. You must get to him, or else you have virtually nothing upon which your soul can rely. "To whom coming." Peter speaks of all the saints as coming to Jesus, coming to him as unto a living stone, and being built upon him, and no other foundation can any man lay than that which is laid, and if any man say that coming anywhere but to Christ can bring salvation, he hath denied the faith and utterly departed from it. The coming mentioned in the text is a word which is sometimes explained in Scripture by hearing, at other times by trusting or believing, and quite as frequently by looking. "To whom coming." Coming to Christ does not mean coming with any natural motion of the body, for he is in heaven, and we cannot climb up to the place where he is; but it is a mental coming, a spiritual coming; it is, in one word, a trusting in and upon him. He who believes Jesus Christ to be God, and to be the appointed atonement for sin, and relies upon him as such, has come to him, and it is this coming which saves the soul. Whoever the wide world over has relied upon Jesus Christ, and is still relying upon him for the pardon of his iniquities, and for his complete salvation, is saved.

Notice one thing more in these three words, that the participle is in the present. "To whom coming," not "To whom having come," though I trust many of us have come, but the way of salvation is not to come to Christ and then forget it, but to continue coming, to be always coming. It is the very spirit of the believer to be always relying upon Christ, as much after a life of holiness as when he first commenced that life; as much when he has been blessed with much spiritual nearness of access to God, and a holy, heavenly frame of mind; as much then, I say, as when, a poor trembling penitent, he said, "God, be merciful to me a sinner." To Christ we are to be, always coming; upon him always relying, to his precious blood always looking.

So I shall take the text, then, this evening thus:—These three words describe our first salvation, describe the life of the Christian, and then describe his departure, for what even is that but to be still coming to Christ, to be in his embrace for ever? First, then, these three words describe, and very accurately too:—

I. THE FIRST SALVATION OF THE BELIEVER.

It is coming to Christ. I shall not try to speak the experience of many present; I know if it were necessary you could rise and give your "Yea, yes" to it. In describing the work of grace at the first, I may say that it was indeed a very simple thing for us to come to Christ, but simple as it was, some of us were very long in finding it out. The simplest thing in all the world is just to look to Jesus and live, to drink of the life-giving stream, and find our thirst for ever assuaged. But though it is so plain that he who runs may read, and a man needs scarce any wit to comprehend the gospel, yet we went hither and thither, and searched for years before we discovered the simplicity which is in Christ Jesus. Most of us were like Penelope, who spun by day, and then unwound her work at night. It was even so we did. We thought we were getting up a little. We had some evidence. We said, "Yes, we are in a better state; are shall yet be saved." But ere long the night of sorrow came in. We had a sight of our own sinfulness, and what we had spun, I say, by day, we unwound again quite as quickly by night. Well, there are some of you much in the same way now. You are like a foolish builder who should build a wall, and then should begin to knock down all the stones at once. You build, and then pull down. Or, like the gardener who, having put into the ground his seeds and planted his flowers, is not satisfied with them, and thinks he will have something else, and so tries again. Ah! the methods and the shifts we will be at to try and save ourselves, while, after all, Christ has done it all. We will do anything rather than be saved by Christ's charity. We do not like to bow our necks to take the mercy of God, as poor undeserving sinners. Some will attend their church or their chapel with wonderful regularity, and think that that will ease their conscience, and when they get no ease of conscience from that, then they will! try sacraments, and when no salvation comes from them, then there will be good works, Popish ceremonies, and I know not what besides.

All sorts of doings, good, bad, and indifferent, men will take to, if they may but have a finger in their own salvation, while all the while the blessed Saviour stands by, ready to save them altogether if they will but be quiet and take the salvation he has wrought. All attempts to save ourselves by our own works are but a base bargaining with God for eternal life, but he will never give eternal life at a price, nor sell it, for all that man could bring, though in each hand he should hold a star; he will give it freely to those who want it. He will dispense it without money and without price to all who come and ask for it, and, hungering and thirsting, are ready to receive it as his free gift, but:—

> Perish the virtue, as it ought, abhorred,
> And the fool with it, who insults his Lord,

by bringing in anything that he can do as a round of dependence, and putting that in the place of the blood and righteousness of the Lord Jesus Christ.

I said, dear friends, that it was very simple, and indeed it is so, a very simple thing to trust Jesus and be saved, but it cost some of us many a day to find it out. Shall I just mention some of the ways in which persons are, long before they find it out. Some ask, "What is the best way to act faith? What is the best way to get this precious believing that I hear so much spoken of?" Now the question reminds me of a madman who, standing at a table which is well spread, says to a person standing there, "Tell me what is the best way to eat. What is the philosophy of eating?" "Why," the man replies, "I cannot be long about that; I need not write a long treatise on it: the best way I know of is to eat." And when people say, "What is the best way to get faith?" I say, "Believe." "But what is the best way to believe?" Why, believe. I can tell you nothing else. Some may say to you, "Pray for faith." Well, but how can you pray without faith? Or if they tell you to read, or do, or feel, in order to get faith, that is a roundabout way. I find not such exhortations as these put down as the gospel, but our Master, when he went to heaven, bade us go into all the world and preach the gospel to every creature; and what was that gospel to me? His own words are, "He that believeth and is baptized shall be saved," and we cannot say anything clearer than that. "Believe"—that is, trust—"and be baptized," and these two things are put before you as Christ's ordained way of salvation. Now you want to philosophise, do you? Well, but why should a hungry man philosophies about the bread that it before him? Eat, sir, and philosophise afterwards. Believe in Jesus Christ, and when you get the joy and peace which faith in him will be sure to bring, then philosophize as you will.

But some are asking the question, "How shall I make myself fit to be saved?" That is similar to, a man who, being very black and filthy, coming home from a coal mine or from a forge, says, seeing the bath before him: "How shall I make myself fit to be"? You tell him at once that there cannot be any fitness for washing, except filthiness, which is the reverse of a fitness. So there can be no fitness for believing in Christ, except sinfulness, which is, indeed, the reverse of fitness. If you are hungry, you are fit to eat; if you are thirsty, you are fit to drink; if you arc naked, you are fitted to receive the garments which charity is giving to those who need them; if you are a sinner, you are fitted for Christ, and Christ for you; if you are guilty, you are fitted to be pardoned; if you are lost, you are fitted to be saved. This, is all the fitness Christ requireth, and cast every other thought of fitness far hence; yea, cast it to the winds. If thou be needy, Christ is ready to enrich thee. If thou wilt come and confess thine offences before God, the gracious Saviour is willing to pardon thee just as thou art. There is no other fitness wanted.

But then, if you have answered that, some will begin to say, "Yes, but the way of salvation is coming to Christ and I am afraid I do not come in the right way." Dear, dear, how unwise we are in the matter of salvation! We are much more foolish than little children are in common, everyday life. A mother says to her little child, "Come here, my dear, and I will give you this apple." Now I will tell you what the first thought of the child is about; it is about the apple; and the second thought off the child is about its mother; and the very last thought he has is about the way of coming. His mother told him to come, and he does not say, "Well, but I do not know whether I shall come right." He totters along as best he can, and that does not seem to occupy his thoughts at all. But when you say to a sinner, "Come to Christ, and you shall have eternal life," he thinks about nothing but his coming. He will not think about eternal life, nor yet about Jesus Christ, to whom he is bidden to come, but only about coming, when he need not think of that at all, but just do it—do what Jesus bids him—simply trust him." "What kind of coming is that," says John Bunyan, "which saves a soul?" and he answers, "Any coming in all the world if it does but come to Jesus." Some come running; at the very first sermon they hear they believe in him. Some come slowly; they are many years before they can trust him. Some come creeping; scarcely able to come, they have to be helped by others, but as long as they do but come, he has said, "Him that cometh to me I will in no wise cast out." You may have came in the most awkward way in all the world, as that man did who was let down by ropes through the ceiling into the place where Jesus was, but Christ rejects no coming sinner, and you need not be looking to your coming, but looking to Christ. Look to him as God—he can save you; as the bleeding, dying Son of Man—he is willing to save you, and flat before his cross, with all your guilt upon you, cast yourself, and believe that he will save you. Trust him to do it, and he must save you, for that is his own word, and from it he cannot depart. Oh! cease, then, that care about the calling, and look to the Saviour.

We have met with others who have said, "I Well, I understand that, that if I trust in Christ, I shall be saved, but—but—but—I do not understand that passage in the Revelation: I cannot make out that great difficulty in Ezekiel; I am a great deal troubled about predestination and free will, and I cannot believe that I shall be saved until I comprehend all this." Now, my dear friend, you are altogether on the wrong tack. When I was going from Cook's Haven to Heligoland to the North of Germany, I noticed when we were out at sea, far away from the sight of land, innumerable swarms of butterflies. I wondered whatever they could do there, and when I was at Heligoland I noticed that almost every wave that came up washed ashore large quantities of poor dead, drowned butterflies. Now do you know those butterflies were just like you? You want to go out on to the great sea of predestination, free will, and I do not know what. Now there is nothing for you there, ant you have no more business there than the butterfly has out at sea. It will drown you. How much better for you just to come and fly to this Rose of Sharon—that is the thing for you. This Lily of the Valley—come and light here. There is something here for you, but out in that dread-sounding deep, without a bottom or a shore, you will be lost, seeking after the knowledge of difficulties, which God has hidden from man, and trying to pry into the thick darkness where God conceals truth which it were better not to reveal. Come you to Jesus. If you must have the knots untied, try to untie them after you get saved, but now your first business is with Jesus; your first business is coming unto him; for if you do not, your ruin is certain, and your destruction will be irretrievable. But I must not enlarge. Coming to Christ is very simple, yet how long it takes men to find it out!

Again, we, bear our witness to-night, that nothing but coming to Christ ever did give us any peace. In my own case I was distracted, tossed with tempest, and not comforted for some years, and I never could believe my sin forgiven or have any peace by day or night until I simply trusted Jesus, and from that time my peace has been like a river. I have rejoiced in the certainty of pardon, and sung with triumph in the Lord my God, and many of you are constantly doing the same, but until you looked to Christ, you had not any peace. You searched, and searched, and searched, but your search was fruitless until you looked into the five wounds of the expiring Saviour, and there you found life from the dead.

And once more, when we did come to Christ, we came very tremblingly, but he did not cast us out. We thought he never died for us, that he could not wash our sins away. We conceived that we were not of his elect; we dreamed that our prayers could only echo upon a brazen sky, and never bring us an answer. But still we came to Christ, because we dared not stop away. We were like a timid dove that is hunted by a hawk, and is afraid. We feared we should be destroyed, but he did not say to us, "You came to me tremblingly, and I will reject you." Nay, but into the bosom of his love he received us, and blotted out our sins. When we came to Jesus, we did not come bringing anything, but we came to him for everything. We came strictly empty-handed, and we got all we wanted in Christ. There is a piece of iron, and if it were to say, "Where am I to get the power from to cling to the loadstone?" the loadstone would say, "Let me get near you, and I will supply you with that." So we sometimes think, "How can I believe? How can I hope? How can I follow Christ?" Ay, but let Christ get near us, and he finds us with all that. We do not come to Christ to bring our repentance, but to get repentance. We do not come to him with a broken heart, but for a broken heart. We do not so much even come to him with faith, as come to him for faith. "True belief and true repentance, Every grace that brings us nigh; Without money, Come to Jesus Christ, and buy." This is the first way of salvation—simply trusting and looking up to Christ for everything. But, then, we did trust. There is a difference between knowing about trust and trusting. By God's Holy Spirit, we were not left merely to talk about faith, nor to think about it, but we did believe. If the Government were to announce that there would be ten thousand acres of land in New Zealand given to a settler, I can imagine two men believing it. One believes it and forgets it; the other believes it and takes his passage to go out and get the land. Now the first kind of faith saves nobody; but the second faith, the practical faith, is that which, for the sake of seeking Christ, gives up the sins of this life, the pleasures of it—I mean the wicked pleasures of it—gives up all confidence in everything else, and casts itself into the arms of the Saviour. There is the sea of divine love; he shall be saved who plunges boldly into it, and casts himself upon its waves, hoping to be upborne. Oh! my hearer, hast thou done this? If so, thou art certainly a saved one. If thou hast not, oh! may grace enable thee to do it ere yet that setting sun has hidden himself beneath the horizon. Hast thou known this before, that a simple trust in Christ will save thee? This is the one message of this inspired Volume. This is the gospel according to Paul, the one gospel which we preach continually. Try it, and if it save thee not, we will be bondsmen for God for thee. But it must save thee, for God is true, and cannot fail, and he has declared, "He that believeth on him is not condemned, but he that believeth not is condemned already, because he hath not believed on the Son of God."

Thus I have tried to explain as clearly as I can that coming to Jesus is the first business of salvation. Now, secondly, and with brevity. This is:—

II. A GOOD DESCRIPTION OF THE ENTIRE CHRISTIAN LIFE.

The Christian is always coming to Christ. He does not look upon faith as a matter of twenty years ago, and done with, but he comes today and he will come to-morrow. He will come to Jesus Christ afresh to-night before he goes to bed. We come to Jesus daily, for Christ is like the well outside the cottager's house. The man lets down the bucket and gets the cooling draught, but he goes again to-morrow, and he will have to go again at night if he is to leave a fresh supply. He must constantly go to the same place. Fishes do not live in the water they were in yesterday; they must be in it to-day. Men do not breathe the air which they breathed a week ago; they must have fresh air into the lungs moment by moment. Nobody thinks that he can be fed upon the fact that he did have a good meal six weeks ago; he has to eat continually. So "the just shall live by faith." We come to Jesus just as we came at first, and we say to him:—

> Nothing in my hands I bring,
>   Simply to thy cross I cling;
> Naked come to thee for dress,
> Helpless, look to thee for grace;
> Foul, I to the fountain fly,
> Wash me, Saviour, or I die.

This is the daily and hourly life of the Christian.

But while we thus come daily, we come more boldly than we used to do. At first we came like cringing slaves; now we came as emancipated men. At first we came as strangers. Now we come as brethren. We still come to the cross, but it is not so much to find pardon for past sins, for these are forgiven, as to find fresh comfort from looking up to him who wrought out perfect righteousness for us.

We come, also, to Jesus Christ, more closely than we used to do. I hope, brethren and sisters, you can say that you are not at such a distance from Christ now as you once were. We ought to be always getting nearer to him. The old preachers used to illustrate nearness to Christ by the planets. They said there were Jupiter and Saturn far away, with very little light and very little heat from the sun, and then they have their satellites, their rings, their moons, and their belts to make for that. Just so they said, with some Christians. They get worldly comforts—their moons, and their belts—but they have not got much of their Master; they have got enough to save them, but oh! such little light. But, said they, when you get to Mercury, there is a planet without moons. Why, the sun is its moon, and, therefore, what does it want with moons when it has the full blaze of the sun's light and heat continually pouring upon it? And what a nimble planet it is; how it spins along in its orbit, because it is near the sun! Oh! to be like that—not to be far away from Jesus Christ, even with all the comforts of this life, but to be near him, filled with life and sacred activity through the abundance of fellowship and communion with him. It is still coming, but it is coming after a nearer sort.

And I may say, too, that it is coming of a dearer sort, for there is more love in our coming now than there used to be. We did come at first, not so much loving Christ, as venturing to trust him, thinking him, perhaps, to be a hard Master; but now we know him to be the best of friends, the dearest of husbands. We come to his bosom, and we lean our heads upon it. We come in our private devotion; we tell him all our troubles; we unburden our hearts, and get his love shed abroad in our hearts in return, and we go away with a joy that makes our heart to leap within us and to bound like a young roe over the mountain-tops. Oh! happy is that man who gets right into the wounds of Jesus, and, with Thomas, cries, "My Lord and my God!" This is no, fanaticism, but a thing of sober, sound experience with some of us. We can rejoice in him, having no confidence in the flesh. It is still coming but it is coming after a dearer fashion.

Yet, mark you, it is coming still to the same person, coming still as poor humble ones to Christ. I have often told you, my dear brethren and sisters, that when you get a little above the ground, if it is only an inch, you get too high. When you begin to think that surely you are a saint, and that you have some good thing to trust to, that rotten stuff must all be pulled to pieces. Believe me, God will not let his people wear a rag of their own spinning; they must be clothed with Christ's righteousness from head to foot. The old heathen said he wrapped himself up in his integrity, but I should think he did not know what holes there were in it, or else he would have looked for something better. But we wrap ourselves in the righteousness of Christ, and there is not a cherub before the throne that wears a vestment so right royal as the poor sinner does when he wears the righteousness of Jesus Christ. Oh! child of God, always live upon your Lord. Hang upon him, as the pitcher hangs upon the nail. Lean on your Beloved; his arm will never weary of you. Stay yourselves upon him; wash in the precious fountain always; wear his righteousness continually; and be glad in the Lord, and your gladness need never fail while you simply and wholly lean upon him. And now, not to detain you longer, I come to the last point, upon which we will only say a word or two. The text is:—

III. A VERY CORRECT DESCRIPTION OF OUR DEPARTURE.

"To whom coming." We shall soon, very soon, quit this mortal frame. I hope you have learned to think of that without any kind of shudder. Can you not sing:—

Ah! I shall soon be dying,
  Time swiftly glides away;
But on my Lord relying
  I hail the happy day.

What is there that we should wait here for? Those who have the most of this world's cods have found it paltry stuff. It perishes in the using. There is a satiety about it; it cannot satisfy the great heart of an immortal man. It is well for us that there is to be an end of this life, and especially for us to whom that end is glowing with immortality. Well, the hour of death will be to us a coming to Christ, a coming to sit upon his throne. Did you ever think of that? "To him that overcometh will I give to sit upon my throne." Lord, Lord, we would be well content to, sit at thy feet. 'Twere all the heaven we would ask if we might but creep behind the door, or stand and be manual servants, or sit, like Mordecai, in the king's court.' No; but it must not be. We must sit on his throne, and reign with him for ever and ever. This is what death will bring you—a glorious participation in the royalties of your ascended Lord.

What is the next thing? "Father, I will that they also whom thou hast given me be with me where I am, that they may behold my glory." So that we, are to be going to Christ ere long to behold his glory, and what a sight that will be! Have you ever thought of that too? What must it be to behold his glory? Some of my brethren think that when they get to heaven they shall like to behold some of the works of God in nature and so on. I must confess myself more satisfied with the idea that I shall behold his glory, the glory of the Crucified, for it seems to me that no kind of heaven but that comes up to the description of the Apostle when he saith, "Eye hath not seen, nor hath ear heard, neither hath it entered into the heart of man to conceive the things which God hath prepared for them that love him." But to see the stars, has entered into the heart of man, and to behold the works of God in nature, has been conceived of; but the joys we speak of are so spiritual that the Apostle says, "He has revealed them unto us by his Spirit," and this is what he has revealed, "That they may behold my glory." St. Augustine used to say there were two sights he would like to have seen—Rome in her splendour, and Paul preaching—the last the better sight of the two. But there is a third sight for which one might give up all, give up seeing Naples, or seeing anything, if we might but see the King his beauty. Why, even the distant glimpse which we catch of him through a glass or a telescope darkly ravishes the soul. Dr. Hawker was once waited upon by a friend, who asked him to go and see a naval review.

He said, "No, thank you; I do not want to go." "You are a loyal man, doctor, and you would like to see the defences of your country." "Thank you, I do not wish to go." "But I have got a ticket for you, and you must go." "No," he said, "thank you," and after he had been pressed hard he said, "You have pressed me till I am ashamed, and now I must tell you—mine eyes have seen the King in his beauty, and the land which is very far off, and I have not any taste now for all the pomps that this world could possibly show." And if such a distant sight of Jesus can do this, what must it be to behold his glory with what the old Scotch divines used to call "a face-to-face view"; when the veil is taken down, when the clouds are blown away, and you see him face to face? Oh! long-expected day begin, when we shall be to him coming to dwell with him.

Once more only. Recollect we shall come to Christ not only to behold his glory, but to share in it. We shall be like him, for we shall see him as he is. Whatever Christ shall be, his people shall be, in happiness, riches, and honour, and together they shall take their full share. The Church, his bride, shall sit on the same throne with him, and of all the splendours of that eternal triumph she will have her half, for Christ is no niggard to his imperial spouse, but she whom he chose before the world began, and bought with blood, and wrapped in his righteousness, and espoused to himself for ever, shall be a full partaker of all the gifts that he poses world without end. And this shall be, and this shall be, and this shall be for ever; for ever you shall be with Christ, for ever coming to him. When the miser's wealth has melted; when the honours of the conqueror have been blown away or consumed like chaff in the furnace; when sun and moon grow dim with age, and the hoary pillars of this earth begin to rock and reel with stern decay; when the angel shall have put one foot on the sea and the other on the land, and shall have sworn by him that liveth that time shall be no more; when the ocean shall be licked up with tongues of fire, and the elements shall melt with fervent heat, and the earth and all the works that are therein shall be burnt up—then, then shall you be for ever with the Lord, eternally resting, eternally feasting, eternally magnifying him; being filled with all his fulness to the utmost capacity of your enlarged being, world without end.

So God grant it to us, that we may come to Christ now, that we may continue to come to Christ, that we may come to Christ then, lest rejecting him to-night we should be rejecting him for ever; lest refusing to trust him, we should be driven from his presence to abide in misery for ever! May we come now, for Christ's sake.

Compel Them to Come In

A Sermon (No. 227) Delivered on
Sabbath Morning, December 5th, 1858,
by the REV. C. H. SPURGEON
at the Music Hall, Royal Surrey Gardens.

"Compel them to come in."—Luke 14:23.

I feel in such a haste to go out and obey this commandment this morning, by compelling those to come in who are now tarrying in the highways and hedges, that I cannot wait for an introduction, but must at once set about my business.

Hear then, O ye that are strangers to the truth as it is in Jesus—hear then the message that I have to bring you. Ye have fallen, fallen in your father Adam; ye have fallen also in yourselves, by your daily sin and your constant iniquity; you have provoked the anger of the Most High; and as assuredly as you have sinned, so certainly must God punish you if you persevere in your iniquity, for the Lord is a God of justice, and will by no means spare the guilty. But have you not heard, hath it not long been spoken in your ears, that God, in his infinite mercy, has devised a way whereby, without any infringement upon his honour, he can have mercy upon you, the guilty and the undeserving? To you I speak; and my voice is unto you, O sons of men; Jesus Christ, very God of very God, hath descended from heaven, and was made in the likeness of sinful flesh. Begotten of the Holy Ghost, he was born of the Virgin Mary; he lived in this world a life of exemplary holiness, and of the deepest suffering, till at last he gave himself up to die for our sins, "the just for the unjust, to bring us to God." And now the plan of salvation is simply declared unto you—"Whosoever believeth in the Lord Jesus Christ shall be saved." For you who have violated all the precepts of God, and have disdained his mercy and dared his vengeance, there is yet mercy proclaimed, for "whosoever calleth upon the name of the Lord shall be saved." "For this is a faithful saying and worthy of all acceptation, that Christ Jesus came into the world to save sinners, of whom I am chief;" "whosoever cometh unto him he will in no wise cast out, for he is able also to save unto the uttermost them that come unto God by him, seeing he ever liveth to make intercession for us." Now all that God asks of you—and this he gives you—is that you will simply look at his bleeding dying son, and trust your souls in the hands of him whose name alone can save from death and hell. Is it not a marvelous thing, that the proclamation of this gospel does not receive the unanimous consent of men? One would think that as soon as ever this was preached, "That whosoever believeth shall have eternal life," every one of you, "casting away every man his sins and his iniquities," would lay hold on Jesus Christ, and look alone to his cross. But alas! such is the desperate evil of our nature, such the pernicious depravity of our character, that this message is despised, the invitation to the gospel feast is rejected, and there are many of you who are this day enemies of God by wicked works, enemies to the God who preaches Christ to you to-day, enemies to him who sent his Son to give his life a ransom for many. Strange I say it is that it should be so, yet nevertheless it is the fact, and hence the necessity for the command of the text,—"Compel them to come in."

Children of God, ye who have believed, I shall have little or nothing to say to you this morning; I am going straight to my business—I am going after those that will not come—those that are in the byways and hedges, and God going with me, it is my duty now to fulfil this command, "Compel them to come in."

First, I must, find you out; secondly, I will go to work to compel you to come in.

I. First, I must FIND YOU OUT. If you read the verses that precede the text, you will find an amplification of this command: "Go out quickly into the streets and lanes of the city, and bring in hither the poor, the maimed, the halt, and the blind;" and then, afterwards, "Go out into the highways," bring in the vagrants, the highwaymen, "and into the hedges," bring in those that have no resting-place for their heads, and are lying under the hedges to rest, bring them in also, and "compel them to come in." Yes, I see you this morning, you that are poor. I am to compel you to come in. You are poor in circumstances, but this is no barrier to the kingdom of heaven, for God hath not exempted from his grace the man that shivers in rags, and who is destitute of bread. In fact, if there be any distinction made, the distinction is on your side, and for your benefit—"Unto you is the word of salvation sent"; "For the poor have the gospel preached unto them." But especially I must speak to you who are poor, spiritually. You have no faith, you have no virtue, you have no good work, you have no grace, and what is poverty worse still, you have no hope. Ah, my Master has sent you a gracious invitation. Come and welcome to the marriage feast of his love. "Whosoever will, let him come and take of the waters of life freely." Come, I must lay hold upon you, though you be defiled with foulest filth, and though you have nought but rags upon your back, though your own righteousness has become as filthy clouts, yet must I lay hold upon you, and invite you first, and even compel you to come in.

And now I see you again. You are not only poor, but you are maimed. There was a time when you thought you could work out your own salvation without God's help, when you could perform good works, attend to ceremonies, and get to heaven by yourselves; but now you are maimed, the sword of the law has cut off your hands, and now you can work no longer; you say, with bitter sorrow—

The best performance of my hands,
　Dares not appear before thy throne.

You have lost all power now to obey the law; you feel that when you would do good, evil is present with you.

You are maimed; you have given up, as a forlorn hope, all attempt to save yourself, because you are maimed and your arms are gone. But you are worse off than that, for if you could not work your way to heaven, yet you could walk your way there along the road by faith; but you are maimed in the feet as well as in the hands; you feel that you cannot believe, that you cannot repent, that you cannot obey the stipulations of the gospel.

You feel that you are utterly undone, powerless in every respect to do anything that can be pleasing to God. In fact, you are crying out—

Oh, could I but believe,
　Then all would easy be,
I would, but cannot, Lord relieve,
　My help must come from thee.

To you am I sent also. Before you am I to lift up the blood-stained banner of the cross, to you am I to preach this gospel, "Whoso calleth upon the name of the Lord shall be saved;" and unto you am I to cry, "Whosoever will, let him come and take of the water of life freely."

There is yet another class. You are halt. You are halting between two opinions. You are sometimes seriously inclined, and at another time worldly gaiety calls you away. What little progress you do make in religion is but a limp. You have a little strength, but that is so little that you make but painful progress. Ah, limping brother, to you also is the word of this salvation sent. Though you halt between two opinions, the Master sends me to you with this message: "How long halt ye between two opinions? if God be God, serve him; if Baal be God, serve him." Consider thy ways; set thine house in order, for thou shalt die and not live. Because I will do this, prepare to meet thy God, O Israel! Halt no longer, but decide for God and his truth.

And yet I see another class,—the blind. Yes, you that cannot see yourselves, that think yourselves good when you are full of evil, that put bitter for sweet and sweet for bitter, darkness for light and light for darkness; to you am I sent. You, blind souls that cannot see your lost estate, that do not believe that sin is so exceedingly sinful as it is, and who will not be persuaded to think that God is a just and righteous God, to you am I sent. To you too that cannot see the Saviour, that see no beauty in him that you should desire him; who see no excellence in virtue, no glories in religion, no happiness in serving God, no delight in being his children; to you, also, am I sent. Ay, to whom am I not sent if I take my text? For it goes further than this—it not only gives a particular description, so that each individual case may be met, but afterwards it makes a general sweep, and says, "Go into the highways and hedges." Here we bring in all ranks and conditions of men—my lord upon his horse in the highway, and the woman trudging about her business, the thief waylaying the traveller—all these are in the highway, and they are all to be compelled to come in, and there away in the hedges there lie some poor souls whose refuges of lies are swept away, and who are seeking not to find some little shelter for their weary heads, to you, also, are we sent this morning. This is the universal command—compel them to come in.

Now, I pause after having described the character, I pause to look at the herculean labour that lies before me. Well did Melanchthon say, "Old Adam was too strong for young Melanchthon." As well might a little child seek to compel a Samson, as I seek to lead a sinner to the cross of Christ. And yet my Master sends me about the errand. Lo, I see the great mountain before me of human depravity and stolid indifference, but by faith I cry, "Who art thou, O great mountain? before Zerubbabel thou shalt become a plain." Does my Master say, compel them to come in? Then, though the sinner be like Samson and I a child, I shall lead him with a thread.

If God saith do it, if I attempt it in faith it shall be done; and if with a groaning, struggling, and weeping heart, I so seek this day to compel sinners to come to Christ, the sweet compulsions of the Holy Spirit shall go with every word, and some indeed shall be compelled to come in.

II. And now to the work—directly to the work. Unconverted, unreconciled, unregenerate men and women, I am to COMPEL YOU TO COME IN. Permit me first of all to accost you in the highways of sin and tell you over again my errand. The King of heaven this morning sends a gracious invitation to you. He says, "As I live, saith the Lord, I have no pleasure in the death of him that dieth, but had rather that he should turn unto me and live:" "Come now, and let us reason together, saith the Lord, though your sins be as scarlet they shall be as wool; though they be red like crimson they shall be whiter than snow." Dear brother, it makes my heart rejoice to think that I should have such good news to tell you, and yet I confess my soul is heavy because I see you do not think it good news, but turn away from it, and do not give it due regard. Permit me to tell you what the King has done for you. He knew your guilt, he foresaw that you would ruin yourself. He knew that his justice would demand your blood, and in order that this difficulty might be escaped, that his justice might have its full due, and that you might yet be saved, Jesus Christ hath died. Will you just for a moment glance at this picture. You see that man there on his knees in the garden of Gethsemane, sweating drops of blood. You see this next: you see that miserable sufferer tied to a pillar and lashed with terrible scourges, till the shoulder bones are seen like white islands in the midst of a sea of blood. Again you see this third picture; it is the same man hanging on the cross with hands extended, and with feet nailed fast, dying, groaning, bleeding; methought the picture spoke and said, "It is finished." Now all this hath Jesus Christ of Nazareth done, in order that God might consistently with his justice pardon sin; and the message to you this morning is this—"Believe on the Lord Jesus Christ and thou shalt be saved." That is trust him, renounce thy works, and thy ways, and set thine heart alone on this man, who gave himself for sinners.

Well brother, I have told you the message, what sayest thou unto it? Do you turn away? You tell me it is nothing to you; you cannot listen to it; that you will hear me by-and-by; but you will go your way this day and attend to your farm and merchandize. Stop brother, I was not told merely to tell you and then go about my business. No; I am told to compel you to come in; and permit me to observe to you before I further go, that there is one thing I can say—and to which God is my witness this morning, that I am in earnest with you in my desire that you should comply with this command of God. You may despise your own salvation, but I do not despise it; you may go away and forget what you shall hear, but you will please to remember that the things I now say cost me many a groan ere I came here to utter them. My inmost soul is speaking out to you, my poor brother, when I beseech you by him that liveth and was dead, and is alive for evermore, consider my master's message which he bids me now address to you.

But do you spurn it? Do you still refuse it? Then I must change my tone a minute. I will not merely tell you the message, and invite you as I do with all earnestness, and sincere affection—I will go further. Sinner, in God's name I command you to repent and believe. Do you ask me whence my authority? I am an ambassador of heaven. My credentials, some of them secret, and in my own heart; and others of them open before you this day in the seals of my ministry, sitting and standing in this hall, where God has given me many souls for my hire. As God the everlasting one hath given me a commission to preach his gospel, I command you to believe in the Lord Jesus Christ; not on my own authority, but on the authority of him who said, "Go ye into all the world and preach the gospel to every creature;" and then annexed this solemn sanction, "He that believeth and is baptized shall be saved, but he that believeth not shall be damned." Reject my message, and remember "He that despised Moses's law, died without mercy under two or three witnesses: of how much sorer punishment, suppose ye, shall he be thought worthy, who hath trodden under foot the Son of God." An ambassador is not to stand below the man with whom he deals, for we stand higher. If the minister chooses to take his proper rank, girded with the omnipotence of God, and anointed with his holy unction, he is to command men, and speak with all authority compelling them to come in: "command, exhort, rebuke with all long-suffering."

But do you turn away and say you will not be commanded? Then again will I change my note. If that avails not, all other means shall be tried. My brother, I come to you simple of speech, and I exhort you to flee to Christ. O my brother, dost thou know what a loving Christ he is? Let me tell thee from my own soul what I know of him. I, too, once despised him. He knocked at the door of my heart and I refused to open it. He came to me, times without number, morning by morning, and night by night; he checked me in my conscience and spoke to me by his Spirit, and when, at last, the thunders of the law prevailed in my conscience, I thought that Christ was cruel and unkind. O I can never forgive myself that I should have thought so ill of him. But what a loving reception did I have when I went to him. I thought he would smite me, but his hand was not clenched in anger but opened wide in mercy. I thought full sure that his eyes would dart lightning-flashes of wrath upon me; but, instead thereof, they were full of tears. He fell upon my neck and kissed me; he took off my rags and did clothe me with his righteousness, and caused my soul to sing aloud for joy; while in the house of my heart and in the house of his church there was music and dancing, because his son that he had lost was found, and he that was dead was made alive. I exhort you, then, to look to Jesus Christ and to be lightened. Sinner, you will never regret,—I will be bondsman for my Master that you will never regret it,—you will have no sigh to go back to your state of condemnation; you shall go out of Egypt and shall go into the promised land and shall find it flowing with milk and honey. The trials of Christian life you shall find heavy, but you will find grace will make them light. And as for the joys and delights of being a child of God, if I lie this day you shall charge me with it in days to come. If you will taste and see that the Lord is good, I am not afraid but that you shall find that he is not only good, but better than human lips ever can describe.

I know not what arguments to use with you. I appeal to your own self-interests. Oh my poor friend, would it not be better for you to be reconciled to the God of heaven, than to be his enemy? What are you getting by opposing God? Are you the happier for being his enemy? Answer, pleasure-seeker; hast thou found delights in that cup? Answer me, self-righteous man: hast thou found rest for the sole of thy foot in all thy works? Oh thou that goest about to establish thine own righteousness, I charge thee let conscience speak. Hast thou found it to be a happy path? Ah, my friend, "Wherefore dost thou spend thy money for that which is not bread, and thy labour for that which satisfieth not; hearken diligently unto me, and eat ye that which is good, and let your soul delight itself in fatness." I exhort you by everything that is sacred and solemn, everything that is important and eternal, flee for your lives, look not behind you, stay not in all the plain, stay not until you have proved, and found an interest in the blood of Jesus Christ, that blood which cleanseth us from all sin. Are you still cold and indifferent? Will not the blind man permit me to lead him to the feast? Will not my maimed brother put his hand upon my shoulder and permit me to assist him to the banquet? Will not the poor man allow me to walk side-by-side with him? Must I use some stronger words. Must I use some other compulsion to compel you to come in? Sinners, this one thing I am resolved upon this morning, if you be not saved ye shall be without excuse. Ye, from the grey-headed down to the tender age of childhood, if ye this day lay not hold on Christ, your blood shall be on your own head. If there be power in man to bring his fellow, (as there is when man is helped by the Holy Spirit) that power shall be exercised this morning, God helping me. Come, I am not to be put off by your rebuffs; if my exhortation fails, I must come to something else. My brother, I entreat you, I entreat you stop and consider. Do you know what it is you are rejecting this morning? You are rejecting Christ, your only Saviour. "Other foundation can no man lay;" "there is none other name given among men whereby we must be saved." My brother, I cannot bear that ye should do this, for I remember what you are forgetting: the day is coming when you will want a Saviour. It is not long ere weary months shall have ended, and your strength begin to decline; your pulse shall fail you, your strength shall depart, and you and the grim monster—death, must face each other. What will you do in the swellings of Jordan without a Saviour? Death-beds are stony things without the Lord Jesus Christ. It is an awful thing to die anyhow; he that hath the best hope, and the most triumphant faith, finds that death is not a thing to laugh at. It is a terrible thing to pass from the seen to the unseen, from the mortal to the immortal, from time to eternity, and you will find it hard to go through the iron gates of death without the sweet wings of angels to conduct you to the portals of the skies. It will be a hard thing to die without Christ. I cannot help thinking of you. I see you acting the suicide this morning, and I picture myself standing at your bedside and hearing your cries, and knowing that you are dying without hope. I cannot bear that. I think I am standing by your coffin now, and looking into your clay-cold face, and saying, "This man despised Christ and neglected the great salvation." I think what bitter tears I shall weep then, if I think that I have been unfaithful to you, and how those eyes fast closed in death, shall seem to chide me and say, "Minister, I attended the music hall, but you were not in earnest with me; you amused me, you preached to me, but you did not plead with me. You did not know what Paul meant when he said, 'As though God did beseech you by us we pray you in Christ's stead, be ye reconciled to God.'"

I entreat you let this message enter your heart for another reason. I picture myself standing at the bar of God. As the Lord liveth, the day of judgment is coming. You believe that? You are not an infidel; your conscience would not permit you to doubt the Scripture. Perhaps you may have pretended to do so, but you cannot. You feel there must be a day when God shall judge the world in righteousness. I see you standing in the midst of that throng, and the eye of God is fixed on you. It seems to you that he is not looking anywhere else, but only upon you, and he summons you before him; and he reads your sins, and he cries, "Depart ye cursed into everlasting fire in hell!" My hearer, I cannot bear to think of you in that position; it seems as if every hair on my head must stand on end to think of any hearer of mine being damned. Will you picture yourselves in that position? The word has gone forth, "Depart, ye cursed." Do you see the pit as it opens to swallow you up? Do you listen to the shrieks and the yells of those who have preceded you to that eternal lake of torment? Instead of picturing the scene, I turn to you with the words of the inspired prophet, and I say, "Who among us shall dwell with the devouring fire? Who among us shall dwell with everlasting burnings?" Oh! my brother, I cannot let you put away religion thus; no, I think of what is to come after death. I should be destitute of all humanity if I should see a person about to poison himself, and did not dash away the cup; or if I saw another about to plunge from London Bridge, if I did not assist in preventing him from doing so; and I should be worse than a fiend if I did not now, with all love, and kindness, and earnestness, beseech you to "lay hold on eternal life," "to labour not for the meat that perisheth, but for the meat that endureth unto everlasting life." Some hyper-calvinist would tell me I am wrong in so doing. I cannot help it. I must do it. As I must stand before my Judge at last, I feel that I shall not make full proof of my ministry unless I entreat with many tears that ye would be saved, that ye would look unto Jesus Christ and receive his glorious salvation. But does not this avail? are all our entreaties lost upon you; do you turn a deaf ear? Then again I change my note. Sinner, I have pleaded with you as a man pleadeth with his friend, and were it for my own life I could not speak more earnestly this morning than I do speak concerning yours. I did feel earnest about my own soul, but not a whit more than I do about the souls of my congregation this morning; and therefore, if ye put away these entreaties I have something else:—I must threaten you. You shall not always have such warnings as these. A day is coming, when hushed shall be the voice of every gospel minister, at least for you; for your ear shall be cold in death. It shall not be any more threatening; it shall be the fulfillment of the threatening. There shall be no promise, no proclamations of pardon and of mercy; no peace-speaking blood, but you shall be in the land where the Sabbath is all swallowed up in everlasting nights of misery, and where the preachings of the gospel are forbidden because they would be unavailing. I charge you then, listen to this voice that now addresses your conscience; for if not, God shall speak to you in his wrath, and say unto you in his hot displeasure, "I called and ye refused; I stretched out my hand and no man regarded; therefore will I mock at your calamity; I will laugh when your fear cometh." Sinner, I threaten you again. Remember, it is but a short time you may have to hear these warnings. You imagine that your life will be long, but do you know how short it is? Have you ever tried to think how frail you are? Did you ever see a body when it has been cut in pieces by the anatomist? Did you ever see such a marvelous thing as the human frame? "Strange, a harp of a thousand strings, Should keep in tune so long." Let but one of those cords be twisted, let but a mouthful of food go in the wrong direction, and you may die. The slightest chance, as we have it, may send you swift to death, when God wills it. Strong men have been killed by the smallest and slightest accident, and so may you. In the chapel, in the house of God, men have dropped down dead. How often do we hear of men falling in our streets—rolling out of time into eternity, by some sudden stroke. And are you sure that heart of yours is quite sound? Is the blood circulating with all accuracy? Are you quite sure of that? And if it be so, how long shall it be? O, perhaps there are some of you here that shall never see Christmas-day; it may be the mandate has gone forth already, "Set thine house in order, for thou shalt die and not live." Out of this vast congregation, I might with accuracy tell how many will be dead in a year; but certain it is that the whole of us shall never meet together again in any one assembly. Some out of this vast crowd, perhaps some two or three, shall depart ere the new year shall be ushered in. I remind you, then, my brother, that either the gate of salvation may be shut, or else you may be out of the place where the gate of mercy stands. Come, then, let the threatening have power with you. I do not threaten because I would alarm without cause, but in hopes that a brother's threatening may drive you to the place where God hath prepared the feast of the gospel. And now, must I turn hopelessly away? Have I exhausted all that I can say? No, I will come to you again. Tell me what it is, my brother, that keeps you from Christ. I hear one say, "Oh, sir, it is because I feel myself too guilty." That cannot be, my friend, that cannot be. "But, sir, I am the chief of sinners." Friend, you are not. The chief of sinners died and went to heaven many years ago; his name was Saul of Tarsus, afterwards called Paul the apostle. He was the chief of sinners, I know he spoke the truth. "No," but you say still, "I am too vile." You cannot be viler than the chief of sinners. You must, at least, be second worst. Even supposing you are the worst now alive, you are second worst, for he was chief. But suppose you are the worst, is not that the very reason why you should come to Christ. The worse a man is, the more reason he should go to the hospital or physician.

The more poor you are, the more reason you should accept the charity of another. Now, Christ does not want any merits of yours. He gives freely. The worse you are, the more welcome you are. But let me ask you a question: Do you think you will ever get better by stopping away from Christ? If so, you know very little as yet of the way of salvation at all. No, sir, the longer you stay, the worse you will grow; your hope will grow weaker, your despair will become stronger; the nail with which Satan has fastened you down will be more firmly clenched, and you will be less hopeful than ever. Come, I beseech you, recollect there is nothing to be gained by delay, but by delay everything may be lost. "But," cries another, "I feel I cannot believe." No, my friend, and you never will believe if you look first at your believing. Remember, I am not come to invite you to faith, but am come to invite you to Christ. But you say, "What is the difference?" Why, just this, if you first of all say, "I want to believe a thing," you never do it. But your first inquiry must be, "What is this thing that I am to believe?" Then will faith come as the consequence of that search. Our first business has not to do with faith, but with Christ. Come, I beseech you, on Calvary's mount, and see the cross. Behold the Son of God, he who made the heavens and the earth, dying for your sins. Look to him, is there not power in him to save?

Look at his face so full of pity. Is there not love in his heart to prove him willing to save? Sure sinner, the sight of Christ will help thee to believe. Do not believe first, and then go to Christ, or else thy faith will be a worthless thing; go to Christ without any faith, and cast thyself upon him, sink or swim. But I hear another cry, "Oh sir, you do not know how often I have been invited, how long I have rejected the Lord." I do not know, and I do not want to know; all I know is that my Master has sent me, to compel you to come in; so come along with you now. You may have rejected a thousand invitations; don't make this the thousandth-and-one. You have been up to the house of God, and you have only been gospel hardened. But do I not see a tear in your eye; come, my brother, don't be hardened by this morning's sermon. O, Spirit of the living God, come and melt this heart for it has never been melted, and compel him to come in! I cannot let you go on such idle excuses as that; if you have lived so many years slighting Christ, there are so many reasons why now you should not slight him. But did I hear you whisper that this was not a convenient time? Then what must I say to you? When will that convenient time come? Shall it come when you are in hell? Will that time be convenient? Shall it come when you are on your dying bed, and the death throttle is in your throat—shall it come then? Or when the burning sweat is scalding your brow; and then again, when the cold clammy sweat is there, shall those be convenient times? When pains are racking you, and you are on the borders of the tomb?

No, sir, this morning is the convenient time. May God make it so. Remember, I have no authority to ask you to come to Christ to-morrow. The Master has given you no invitation to come to him next Tuesday. The invitation is, "To-day if ye will hear his voice, harden not your hearts as in the provocation," for the Spirit saith "to-day." "Come now and let us reason together;" why should you put it off? It may be the last warning you shall ever have. Put it off, and you may never weep again in chapel. You may never have so earnest a discourse addressed to you. You may not be pleaded with as I would plead with you now. You may go away, and God may say, "He is given unto idols, let him alone." He shall throw the reins upon your neck; and then, mark—your course is sure, but it is sure damnation and swift destruction.

And now again, is it all in vain? Will you not now come to Christ? Then what more can I do? I have but one more resort, and that shall be tried. I can be permitted to weep for you; I can be allowed to pray for you. You shall scorn the address if you like; you shall laugh at the preacher; you shall call him fanatic if you will; he will not chide you, he will bring no accusation against you to the great Judge. Your offence, so far as he is concerned, is forgiven before it is committed; but you will remember that the message that you are rejecting this morning is a message from one who loves you, and it is given to you also by the lips of one who loves you. You will recollect that you may play your soul away with the devil, that you may listlessly think it a matter of no importance; but there lives at least one who is in earnest about your soul, and one who before he came here wrestled with his God for strength to preach to you, and who when he has gone from this place will not forget his hearers of this morning. I say again, when words fail us we can give tears—for words and tears are the arms with which gospel ministers compel men to come in. You do not know, and I suppose could not believe, how anxious a man whom God has called to the ministry feels about his congregation, and especially about some of them. I heard but the other day of a young man who attended here a long time, and his father's hope was that he would be brought to Christ. He became acquainted, however, with an infidel; and now he neglects his business, and lives in a daily course of sin. I saw his father's poor wan face; I did not ask him to tell me the story himself, for I felt it was raking up a trouble and opening a sore; I fear, sometimes, that good man's grey hairs may be brought with sorrow to the grave. Young men, you do not pray for yourselves, but your mothers wrestle for you. You will not think of your own souls, but your fathers anxiety is exercised for you. I have been at prayer meetings, when I have heard children of God pray there, and they could not have prayed with more earnestness and more intensity of anguish if they had been each of them seeking their own soul's salvation. And is it not strange that we should be ready to move heaven and earth for your salvation, and that still you should have no thought for yourselves, no regard to eternal things?

Now I turn for one moment to some here. There are some of you here members of Christian churches, who make a profession of religion, but unless I be mistaken in you—and I shall be happy if I am—your profession is a lie. You do not live up to it, you dishonour it; you can live in the perpetual practice of absenting yourselves from God's house, if not in sins worse than that. Now I ask such of you who do not adorn the doctrine of God your Saviour, do you imagine that you can call me your pastor, and yet that my soul cannot tremble over you and in secret weep for you? Again, I say it may be but little concern to you how you defile the garments of your Christianity, but it is a great concern to God's hidden ones, who sigh and cry, and groan for the iniquities of the professors of Zion.

Now does anything else remain to the minister besides weeping and prayer? Yes, there is one thing else. God has given to his servants not the power of regeneration, but he has given them something akin to it. It is impossible for any man to regenerate his neighbour; and yet how are men born to God? Does not the apostle say of such an one that he was begotten by him in his bonds. Now the minister has a power given him of God, to be considered both the father and the mother of those born to God, for the apostle said he travailed in birth for souls till Christ was formed in them. What can we do then? We can now appeal to the Spirit. I know I have preached the gospel, that I have preached it earnestly; I challenge my Master to honour his own promise. He has said it shall not return unto me void, and it shall not. It is in his hands, not mine. I cannot compel you, but thou O Spirit of God who hast the key of the heart, thou canst compel. Did you ever notice in that chapter of the Revelation, where it says, "Behold I stand at the door and knock," a few verses before, the same person is described, as he who hath the key of David. So that if knocking will not avail, he has the key and can and will come in. Now if the knocking of an earnest minister prevail not with you this morning, there remains still that secret opening of the heart by the Spirit, so that you shall be compelled.

I thought it my duty to labour with you as though I must do it; now I throw it into my Master's hands. It cannot be his will that we should travail in birth, and yet not bring forth spiritual children. It is with him; he is master of the heart, and the day shall declare it, that some of you constrained by sovereign grace have become the willing captives of the all-conquering Jesus, and have bowed your hearts to him through the sermon of this morning. [Mr. Spurgeon concluded with a very interesting anecdote, but as its insertion would make the sermon too long for a penny number, the publishers have decided to print it as one of the "New Park Street Tracts."]

Confession of Sin—A Sermon With Seven Texts

A Sermon (No. 113) Delivered on Sabbath Morning, January 18, 1857, by the REV. C. H. SPURGEON At the Music Hall, Royal Surrey Gardens.

My sermon this morning will have seven texts, and yet I pledge myself that there shall be but three different words in the whole of them; for it so happens that the seven texts are all alike, occurring in seven different portions of God's holy Word. I shall require, however, to use the whole of them to exemplify different cases; and I must request those of you who have brought your Bibles with you to refer to the texts as I shall mention them.

The subject of this morning's discourse will be this—CONFESSION OF SIN. We know that this is absolutely necessary to salvation. Unless there be a true and hearty confession of our sins to God, we have no promise that we shall find mercy through the blood of the Redeemer. "Whosoever confesseth his sins and forsaketh them shall find mercy." But there is no promise in the Bible to the man who will not confess his sins. Yet, as upon every point of Scripture there is a liability of being deceived, so more especially in the matter of confession of sin. There be many who make a confession, and a confession before God, who notwithstanding, receive no blessing, because their confession has not in it certain marks which are required by God to prove it genuine and sincere, and which demonstrate it to be the work of the Holy Spirit. My text this morning consists of three words, "I have sinned." And you will see how these words, in the lips of different men, indicate very different feelings. While one says, "I have sinned," and receives forgiveness; another we shall meet with says, "I have sinned," and goes his way to blacken himself with worse crimes than before, and dive into greater depths of sin than heretofore he had discovered. The Hardened Sinner. PHARAOH—"I have sinned."—Exodus 9:27.

I. The first case I shall bring before you is that of the HARDENED SINNER, who, when under terror, says, "I have sinned." And you will find the text in the book of Exodus, the 9th chap. and 27th verse: "And Pharaoh sent, and called for Moses and Aaron, and said unto them, I have sinned this time: the Lord is righteous, and I and my people are wicked."

But why this confession from the lips of the haughty tyrant? He was not often wont to humble himself before Jehovah. Why doth the proud one bow himself? You will judge of the value of his confession when you hear the circumstances under which it was made. "And Moses stretched forth his rod toward heaven; and the Lord sent thunder and hail, and the fire ran along upon the ground; and the Lord rained hail upon the land of Egypt. So that there was hail, and fire mingled with the hail, very grievous, such as there was none like it in all the land of Egypt since it became a nation." "Now," says Pharaoh, whilst the thunder is rolling through the sky, while the lightning-flashes are setting the very ground on fire, and while the hail is descending in big lumps of ice, now, says he, "I have sinned." He is but a type and specimen of multitudes of the same class. How many a hardened rebel on shipboard, when the timbers are strained and creaking, when the mast is broken, and the ship is drifting before the gale, when the hungry waves are opening their mouths to swallow the ship up alive and quick as those that go into the pit—how many a hardened sailor has then bowed his knee, with tears in his eyes, and cried, "I have sinned!" But of what avail and of what value was his confession? The repentance that was born in the storm died in the calm; that repentance of his that was begotten amidst the thunder and the lightning, ceased so soon as all was hushed in quiet, and the man who was a pious mariner when on board ship, became the most wicked and abominable of sailors when he placed his foot on terra firma. How often, too, have we seen this in a storm of thunder and lightning? Many a man's cheek is blanched when he hears the thunder rolling; the tears start to his eyes, and he cries, "O God, I have sinned!" while the rafters of his house are shaking, and the very ground beneath him reeling at the voice of God which is full of majesty. But alas, for such a repentance! When the sun again shines, and the black clouds are withdrawn, sin comes again upon the man, and he becomes worse than before. How many of the same sort of confessions, too, have we seen in times of cholera, and fever, and pestilence! Then our churches have been crammed with hearers, who, because so many funerals have passed their doors, or so many have died in the street, could not refrain from going up to God's house to confess their sins. And under that visitation, when one, two, and three have been lying dead in the house, or next door, how many have thought they would really turn to God! But, alas! when the pestilence had done its work, conviction ceased; and when the bell had tolled the last time for a death caused by cholera, then their hearts ceased to beat with penitence, and their tears did flow no more.

Have I any such here this morning? I doubt not I have hardened persons who would scorn the very idea of religion, who would count me a cant and hypocrite if I should endeavour to press it home upon them, but who know right well that religion is true, and who feel it in their times of terror! If I have such here this morning, let me solemnly say to them, "Sirs, you have forgotten the feelings you had in your hours of alarm; but, remember, God has not forgotten the vows you then made." Sailor, you said if God would spare you to see the land again, you would be his servant; you are not so, you have lied against God, you have made him a false promise, for you have never kept the vow which your lips did utter. You said, on a bed of sickness, that if he would spare your life you would never again sin as you did before; but here you are, and this week's sins shall speak for themselves. You are no better than you were before your sickness. Couldst thou lie to thy fellow-man, and yet go unreproved? And thinkest thou that thou wilt lie against God, and yet go unpunished? No; the vow, however rashly made, is registered in heaven; and though it be a vow which man cannot perform, yet, as it is a vow which he has made himself, and made voluntarily too, he shall be punished for the non-keeping it; and God shall execute vengeance upon him at last, because he said he would turn from his ways, and then when the blow was removed he did it not. A great outcry has been raised of late against tickets-of-leave; I have no doubt there are some men here, who before high heaven stand in the same position as the ticket-of-leave men stand to our government. They were about to die, as they thought; they promised good behaviour if they might be spared, and they are here to-day on ticket-of-leave in this world: and how have they fulfilled their promise? Justice might raise the same outcry against them as they do against the burglars so constantly let loose upon us. The avenging angel might say, "O God, these men said, if they were spared they would be so much better; if anything they are worse. How have they violated their promise, and how have they brought down divine wrath upon their heads!" This is the first style of penitence; and it is a style I hope none of you will imitate, for it is utterly worthless. It is of no use for you to say, "I have sinned," merely under the influence of terror, and then to forget it afterwards. The Double-minded Man. BALAAM—"I have sinned."—Numbers 22:34.

II. Now for a second text. I beg to introduce to you another character—the double-minded man, who says, "I have sinned," and feels that he has, and feels it deeply too, but who is so worldly-minded that he "loves the wages of unrighteousness." The character I have chosen to illustrate this, is that of Balaam. Turn to the book of Numbers, the 22nd chap. and the 34th verse: "And Balaam said unto the angel of the Lord, I have sinned."

"I have sinned," said Balaam; but yet he went on with his sin afterwards. One of the strangest characters of the whole world is Balaam. I have often marvelled at that man; he seems really in another sense to have come up to the lines of Ralph Erskine—"To good and evil equal bent, And both a devil and a saint." For he did seem to be so. At times no man could speak more eloquently and more truthfully, and at other times he exhibited the most mean and sordid covetousness that could disgrace human nature. Think you see Balaam; he stands upon the brow of the hill, and there lie the multitudes of Israel at his feet; he is bidden to curse them, and he cries, "How shall I curse whom God hath not cursed?" And God opening his eyes, he begins to tell even about the coming of Christ, and he says, "I shall see him, but not now. I shall behold him, but not nigh." And then he winds up his oration by saying—"Let me die the death of the righteous, and let my last end be like his!" And ye will say of that man, he is a hopeful character. Wait till he has come off the brow of the hill, and ye will hear him give the most diabolical advice to the king of Moab which it was even possible for Satan himself to suggest. Said he to the king, "You cannot overthrow these people in battle, for God is with them; try and entice them from their God." And ye know how with wanton lusts they of Moab tried to entice the children of Israel from allegiance to Jehovah; so that this man seemed to have the voice of an angel at one time, and yet the very soul of a devil in his bowels. He was a terrible character; be was a man of two things, a man who went all the way with two things to a very great extent. I know the Scripture says, "No man can serve two masters." Now this is often misunderstood. Some read it, "No man can serve two masters." Yes he can; he can serve three or four. The way to read it is this: "No man can serve two masters," They cannot both be masters. He can serve two, but they cannot both be his master. A man can serve two who are not his masters, or twenty either; he may live for twenty different purposes, but he cannot live for more than one master purpose—there can only be one master purpose in his soul. But Balaam laboured to serve two; it was like the people of whom it was said, "They feared the Lord, and served other gods." Or like Rufus, who was a loaf of the same leaven; for you know our old king Rufus painted God on one side of his shield, and the devil on the other, and had underneath, the motto: "Ready for both; catch who can." There are many such, who are ready for both. They meet a minister, and how pious and holy they are; on the Sabbath they are the most respectable and upright people in the world, as you would think; indeed they effect a drawling in their speech, which they think to be eminently religious. But on a week day, if you want to find the greatest rogues and cheats, they are some of those men who are so sanctimonious in their piety. Now, rest assured, my hearers, that no confession of sin can be genuine, unless it be a whole hearted one. It is of no use for you to say, "I have sinned," and then keep on sinning. "I have sinned," say you, and it is a fair, fair face you show; but, alas! alas! for the sin you will go away and commit. Some men seem to be born with two characters. I remarked when in the library at Trinity College, Cambridge, a very fine statue of Lord Byron. The librarian said to me, "Stand here, sir." I looked, and I said, "What a fine intellectual countenance! What a grand genius he was!" "Come here," he said, "to the other side." "Ah! what a demon! There stands the man that could defy the deity." He seemed to have such a scowl and such a dreadful leer in his face; even as Milton would have painted Satan when he said—"Better to reign in hell than serve in heaven." I turned away and said to the librarian, "Do you think the artist designed this?" "Yes," he said, "he wished to picture the two characters—the great, the grand, the almost superhuman genius that he possessed, and yet the enormous mass of sin that was in his soul." There are some men here of the same sort. I dare say, like Balaam, they would overthrow everything in argument with their enchantments; they could work miracles; and yet at the same time there is something about them which betrays a horrid character of sin, as great as that which would appear to be their character for righteousness. Balaam, you know, offered sacrifices to God upon the altar of Baal: that was just the type of his character. So many do; they offer sacrifices to God on the shrine of Mammon; and whilst they will give to the building of a church, and distribute to the poor, they will at the other door of their counting-house grind the poor for bread, and press the very blood out of the widow, that they may enrich themselves. Ah! it is idle and useless for you to say, "I have sinned," unless you mean it from your heart. That double minded man's confession is of no avail. The Insincere Man. SAUL— I have sinned."—1 Samuel 15:24.

III. And now a third character, and a third text. In the first book of Samuel, the 15th chap. and 24th verse: "And Saul said unto Samuel, I have sinned."

Here is the insincere man—the man who is not like Balaam, to a certain extent sincere in two things; but the man who is just the opposite—who has no prominent point in his character at all, but is moulded everlastingly by the circumstances that are passing over his head. Such a man was Saul. Samuel reproved him, and he said, "I have sinned." But he did not mean what he said: for if you read the whole verse you will find him saying, "I have sinned: for I have transgressed the commandment of the Lord, and thy words; because I feared the people:" which was a lying excuse. Saul never feared anybody; he was always ready enough to do his own will—he was the despot. And just before he had pleaded another excuse, that he had saved the bullocks and lambs to offer to Jehovah, and therefore both excuses could not have been true. You remember, my friends, that the most prominent feature in the character of Saul. was his insincerity. One day he fetched David from his bed, as bethought, to put him to death in his house. Another time he declares, "God forbid that I should do aught against thee, my son David." One day, because David saved his life, he said, "Thou art more righteous than I; I will do so no more." The day before he had gone out to fight against his own son-in-law, in order to slay him. Sometimes Saul was among the prophets, easily turned into a prophet, and then afterwards among the witches; sometimes in one place, and then another, and insincere in everything. How many such we have in every Christian assembly; men who are very easily moulded! Say what you please to them, they always agree with you. They have affectionate dispositions, very likely a tender conscience; but then the conscience is so remarkably tender, that when touched it seems to give, and you are afraid to probe deeper,—it heals as soon it is wounded. I think I used the very singular comparison once before, which I must use again: there are some men who seem to have india-rubber hearts. If you do but touch them, there is an impression made at once; but then it is of no use, it soon restores itself to its original character. You may press them whatever way you wish, they are so elastic you can always effect your purpose; but then they are not fixed in their character, and soon return to be what they were before. O sirs, too many of you have done the same; you have bowed your heads in church, and said, "We have erred and strayed from thy ways;" and you did not mean what you said. You have come to your minister; you have said, "I repent of my sins;" you did not then feel you were a sinner; you only said it to please him. And now you attend the house of God; no one more impressible than you; the tear will run down your cheek in a moment, but yet. notwithstanding all that, the tear is dried as quickly as it is brought forth, and you remain to all intents and purposes the same as you were before. To say, "I have sinned," in an unmeaning manner, is worse than worthless, for it is a mockery of God thus to confess with insincerity of heart.

I have been brief upon this character; for it seemed to touch upon that of Balaam; though any thinking man will at once see there was a real contrast between Saul and Balaam, even though there is an affinity between the two. Balaam was the great bad man, great in all he did; Saul was little in everything except in stature, little in his good and little in his vice; and he was too much of a fool to be desperately bad, though too wicked to be at any time good: while Balaam was great in both: the man who could at one time defy Jehovah, and yet at another time could say, "If Balak would give me his house full of silver and gold, I cannot go beyond the word of the Lord my God, to do less or more." The Doubtful Penitent. ACHAN—"I have sinned."—Joshua 7:20.

IV. And now I have to introduce to you a very interesting case; it is the case of the doubtful penitent, the case of Achan, in the book of Joshua, the 7th chap. and the 20th verse:—"And Achan answered Joshua, indeed I have sinned."

You know that Achan stole some of the prey from the city of Jericho—that he was discovered by lot, and put to death. I have singled this case out as the representative of some whose characters are doubtful on their death beds; who do repent apparently, but of whom the most we can say is, that we hope their souls are saved at last, but indeed we cannot tell. Achan, you are aware, was stoned with stones, for defiling Israel. But I find in the Mishna, an old Jewish exposition of the Bible, these words, "Joshua said to Achan, the Lord shall trouble thee this day." And the note upon it is—He said this day, implying that he was only to be troubled in this life, by being stoned to death, but that God would have mercy on his soul, seeing that he had made a full confession of his sin." And I, too, am inclined, from reading the chapter, to concur in the idea of my venerable and now glorified predecessor, Dr. Gill, in believing that Achan really was saved, although he was put to death for the crime, as an example. For you will observe how kindly Joshua spoke to him. He said, "My son, give, I pray thee, glory to the Lord God of Israel, and make confession unto him; and tell me now what thou hast done; hide it not from me." And you find Achan making a very full confession. He says, "Indeed I have sinned against the Lord God of Israel, and thus and thus have I done. When I saw among the spoils a goodly Babylonish garment, and two hundred shekels of silver, and a wedge of gold of fifty shekels weight, then I coveted them, and took them; and, behold, they are hid in the earth in the midst of my tent, and the silver under it." It seems so full a confession, that if I might be allowed to judge, I should say, "I hope to meet Achan the sinner, before the throne of God." But I find Matthew Henry has no such opinion; and many other expositors consider that as his body was destroyed, so was his soul. I have, therefore, selected his case, as being one of doubtful repentance. Ah! dear friends, it has been my lot to stand by many a death-bed, and to see many such a repentance as this; I have seen the man, when worn to a skeleton, sustained by pillows in his bed; and he has said, when I have talked to him of judgment to come, "Sir, I feel I have been guilty, but Christ is good; I trust in him." And I have said within myself, " I believe the man's soul is safe." But I have always come away with the melancholy reflection that I had no proof of it, beyond his own words; for it needs proof in acts and in future life, in order to sustain any firm conviction of a man's salvation. You know that great fact, that a physician once kept a record of a thousand persons who thought they were dying, and whom he thought were penitents; he wrote their names down in a book as those, who, if they had died, would go to heaven; they did not die, they lived; and he says that out of the whole thousand he had not three persons who turned out well afterwards, but they returned to their sins again, and were as bad as ever. Ah! dear friends, I hope none of you will have such a death-bed repentance as that; I hope your minister or your parents will not have to stand by your bedside, and then go away and say, "Poor fellow, I hope he is saved. But alas! death-bed repentances are such flimsy things; such poor, such trivial grounds of hope, that I am afraid, after all, his soul may be lost." Oh! to die with a full assurance; oh! to die with an abundant entrance, leaving a testimony behind that we have departed this life in peace! That is a far happier way than to die in a doubtful manner, lying sick, hovering between two worlds, and neither ourselves nor yet our friends knowing to which of the two worlds we are going. May God grant us grace to give in our lives evidences of true conversion, that our case may not be doubtful! The Repentance of Despair. JUDAS—"I have sinned."—Matthew 27:4.

V. I shall not detain you too long, I trust, but I must now give you another bad case; the worst of all. It is the REPENTANCE OF DESPAIR. Will you turn to the

27th chap. of Matthew, and the 4th verse? There you have a dreadful case of the repentance of despair. You will recognize the character the moment I read the verse: "And Judas said, I have sinned." Yes, Judas the traitor, who had betrayed his Master, when he saw that his Master was condemned, "repented, and brought again the thirty pieces of silver to the chief priests and elders, saying, I have sinned, in that I have betrayed innocent blood, and cast down the pieces in the temple, and went" and what?—"and hanged himself." Here is the worst kind of repentance of all; in fact, I know not that I am justified in calling it repentance; it must be called remorse of conscience. But Judas did confess his sin, and then went and hanged himself. Oh! that dreadful, that terrible, that hideous confession of despair.

Have you never seen it? If you never have, then bless God that you never were called to see such a sight. I have seen it once in my life, I pray God I may never see it again,—the repentance of the man who sees death staring him in the face, and who says, "I have sinned." You tell him that Christ has died for sinners; and he answers, "There is no hope for me; I have cursed God to his face; I have defied him; my day of grace I know is past; my conscience is seared with a hot iron; I am dying, and I know I shall be lost!" Such a case as that happened long ago, you know, and is on record—the case of Francis Spira—the most dreadful case, perhaps, except that of Judas, which is upon record in the memory of man. Oh! my hearers, will any of you have such a repentance? If you do, it will be a beacon to all persons who sin in future; if you have such a repentance as that, it will be a warning to generations yet to come. In the life of Benjamin Keach—and he also was once of my predecessors—I find the case of a man who had been a professor of religion, but had departed from the profession, and had gone into awful sin. When he came to die, Keach, with many other friends, went to see him, but they could never stay with him above five minutes at a time; for he said, "Get ye gone; it is of no use your coming to me; I have sinned away the Holy Ghost; I am like Esau, I have sold my birthright, and though I seek it carefully with tears, I can never find it again." And then he would repeat dreadful words, like these: "My mouth is filled with gravel stones, and I drink wormwood day and night. Tell me not tell me not of Christ! I know he is a Saviour, but I hate him and he hates me. I know I must die; I know I must perish!" And then followed doleful cries, and hideous noises, such as none could bear. They returned again in his placid moments only to stir him up once more, and make him cry out in his despair, "I am lost! I am lost! It is of no use your telling me anything about it!" Ah! I there may be a man here who may have such a death as that; let me warn him, ere he come to it; and may God the Holy Spirit grant that that man may be turned unto God, and made a true penitent, and then he need not have any more fear; for he who has had his sins washed away in a Saviour's blood, need not have any remorse for his sins, for they are pardoned through the Redeemer. The Repentance of the Saint. JOB—"I have sinned."—Job 7:20

VI. And now I come into-daylight. I have been taking you through dark and dreary confessions; I shall detain you there no longer, but bring you out to the two good confessions which I have to read to you. The first is that of Job in 7th chap., at the 20th verse: "I have sinned; what shall I do unto thee, O thou preserver of men?" This is the repentance of the saint. Job was a saint, but he sinned. This is the repentance of the man who is a child of God already, an acceptable repentance before God. But as I intend to dwell upon this in the evening, I shall now leave it, for fear of wearying you. David was a specimen of this kind of repentance, and I would have you carefully study his penitential psalms, the language of which is ever full of weeping humility and earnest penitence. The Blessed Confession. THE PRODIGAL—"I have sinned."—Luke 15:18.

VII. I come now to the last instance, which I shall mention; it is the case of the prodigal. In Luke xv. 18, we find the prodigal says: "Father I have sinned." Oh, here is a blessed confession! Here is that which proves a man to be a regenerate character—"Father, I have sinned." Let me picture the scene. There is the prodigal; he has run away from a good home and a kind father, and he has spent all his money with harlots, and now he has none left. He goes to his old companions, and asks them for relief. They laugh him to scorn. "Oh," says he, "you have drunk my wine many a day; I have always stood paymaster to you in all our revelries; will you not help me?" "Get you gone" they say; and he is turned out of doors. He goes to all his friends with whom he had associated, but no man gives him anything. At last a certain citizen of the country said,—"You want something to do, do you? Well go and feed my swine." The poor prodigal, the son of a rich landowner, who had a great fortune of his own, has to go out to feed swine; and he a Jew too!—the worst employment (to his mind,) to which he could be put. See him there, in squalid rags, feeding swine; and what are his wages? Why, so little, that he "would fain have filled his belly with the husks the swine eat, but no man gave to him." Look, there he is, with the fellow commoners of the sty, in all his mire and filthiness. Suddenly a thought put there by the good Spirit, strikes his mind. "How is it," says he, "that in my father's house there is bread enough and to spare, and I perish with hunger? I will arise and go to my father, and will say unto him, Father, I have sinned against heaven and before thee, and am no more worthy to be called thy son: make me as one of thy hired servants." Off he goes. He begs his way from town to town. Sometimes he gets a lift on a coach, perhaps, but at other times he goes trudging his way up barren hills and down desolate vales, all alone. And now at last he comes to the hill outside the village, and sees his father's house down below. There it is; the old poplar tree against it, and there are the stacks round which he and his brother used to run and play; and at the sight of the old homestead all the feelings and associations of his former life rush upon him, and tears run down his cheeks, and he is almost ready to run away again. He says "I wonder whether father's dead? I dare say mother broke her heart when I went away; I always was her favorite. And if they are either of them alive, they will never see me again; they will shut the door in my face. What am I to do? I cannot go back, I am afraid to go forward." And while he was thus deliberating, his father had been walking on the housetop, looking out for his son; and though he could not see his father, his father could see him. Well, the father comes down stairs with all his might, runs up to him, and whilst he is thinking of running away, his father's arms are round his neck, and he falls-to kissing him, like a loving father indeed, and then the son begins,—"Father, I have sinned against heaven and in thy sight, and am no more worthy to be called thy son," and he was going to say, "Make me as one of thy hired servants." But his father puts his hand on his mouth. "No more of that," says he; "I forgive you all; you shall not say anything about being a hired servant—I will have none of that. Come along," says he, "come in, poor prodigal. Ho!" says he to the servants, "bring hither the best robe, and put it on him, and put shoes on his poor bleeding feet; and bring hither the fatted calf and kill it; and let us eat and be merry: For this my son was dead, and is alive again; he was lost and is found. And they began to be merry." Oh, what a precious reception for one of the chief of sinners! Good Matthew Henry says—"His father saw him, there were eyes of mercy; he ran to meet him, there were legs of mercy; he put his arms round his neck, there were arms of mercy; he kissed him, there were kisses of mercy; he said to him—there were words of mercy,—Bring hither the best robe, there were deeds of mercy, wonders of mercy—all mercy. Oh, what a God of mercy he is."

Now, prodigal, you do the same. Has God put it into your heart? There are many who have been running away a long time now. Does God say "return?" Oh, I bid you return, then, for as surely as ever thou dost return he will take thee in. There never was a poor sinner yet who came to Christ, whom Christ turned away. If he turns you away, you will be the first. Oh, if you could but try him! "Ah, sir, I am so black, so filthy, so vile." Well come along with you—you cannot be blacker than the prodigal. Come to your Father's house, and as surely as he is God he will keep his word—"Him that cometh unto me I will in no wise cast out."

Oh, if I might hear that some had come to Christ this morning, I would indeed bless God! I must tell here for the honor of God and Christ, one remarkable circumstance, and then I have done. You will remember that one morning I mentioned the case of an infidel who had been a scorner and scoffer, but who, through reading one of my printed sermons, had been brought to God's house and then to God's feet. Well, last Christmas day, the same infidel gathered together all his books, and went into the market-place at Norwich, and there made a public recantation of all his errors, and a profession of Christ, and then taking up all his books which he had written, and had in his house, on evil subjects, burned them in the sight of the people. I have blessed God for such a wonder of grace as that, and pray that there may be many more such, who, though they be born prodigal will yet return home, saying, "I have sinned"?

Consolation Proportionate to Spiritual Sufferings

A Sermon (No. 13) Delivered on Sabbath Morning, March 11, 1855, by the REV. C. H. SPURGEON At Exeter Hall, Strand.

"For as the sufferings of Christ abound in us, so our consolation also aboundeth by Christ."
—2 Corinthians 1:5.

Seek ye rest from your distresses ye children of woe and sorrow? This is the place where ye may lighten your burden, and lose your cares. Oh, son of affliction and misery, wouldst thou forget for a time thy pains and griefs? This is the Bethesda the house of mercy; this is the place where God designs to cheer thee, and to make thy distresses stay their never ceasing course; this is the spot where his children love to be found, because here they find consolation in the midst of tribulation, joy in their sorrows, and comfort in their afflictions. Even worldly men admit that there is something extremely comforting in the sacred Scriptures, and in our holy religion; I have even heard it said of some, that after they had, by their logic, as they thought, annihilated Christianity, and proved it to be untrue, they acknowledged that they had spoilt an excellently comforting delusion, and that they could almost sit down and weep to think it was not a reality. Ay, my friends, if it were not true, ye might weep. If the Bible were not the truth of God—if we could not meet together around his mercy seat, then ye might put your hands upon your loins and walk about as if ye were in travail. If ye had not something in the world beside your reason, beside the fleeting joys of earth—if ye had not something which God had given to you, some hope beyond the sky, some refuge that should be more than terrestrial, some deliverance which should be more than earthly, then ye might weep;—ah! weep your heart out at your eyes, and let your whole bodies waste away in one perpetual tear. Ye might ask the clouds to rest on your head, the rivers to roll down in streams from both your eyes, for your grief would "have need of all the watery things that nature could produce." But, blessed be God, we have consolation, we have joy in the Holy Ghost. We find it nowhere else. We have raked the earth through, but we have discovered ne'er a jewel; we have turned this dunghill-world o'er and o'er a thousand times, and we have found nought that is precious; but here, in this Bible, here in the religion of the blessed Jesus we the sons of God, have found comfort and joy; while we can truly say, "As our afflictions abound, so our consolations also abound by Christ."

There are four things in my text to which I invite your attention: the first is the sufferings to be expected—"The sufferings of Christ abound in us;" secondly, the distinction to be noticed—they are the sufferings of Christ; thirdly, a proportion to be experienced—as the sufferings of Christ abound, so our consolations abound; and fourthly, the person to be honored—"So our consolation aboundeth by CHRIST."

I. Our first division then is, THE SUFFERINGS TO BE EXCPECTED. Our holy Apostle says "The sufferings of Christ abound in us." Before we buckle on the Christian armour we ought to know what that service is which is expected of us. A recruiting sergeant often slips a shilling into the hand of some ignorant youth, and tells him that. Her Majesty's Service is a fine thing, that he has nothing to do but walk about in his flaming colors, that he will have no hard service—in fact, that he has nothing to do but to be a soldier, and go straight on to glory. But the Christian searjeant when he enlists a soldier of the cross, never deceives him like that. Jesus Christ himself said, "Count the cost." He wished to have no disciple who was not prepared to go all the way—"to bear hardness as a good soldier." I have sometimes heard religion described in such a way that its high coloring displeases me. It is true "her ways are ways of pleasantness;" but it is not true that a Christian never has sorrow or trouble. It is true that light-eyed cheerfulness, and airy-footed love, can go through the world without much depression: and tribulation: but it is not true that Christianity will shield a man from trouble; nor ought it to be so represented. In fact, we ought to speak of it in the other-way. Soldier of Christ, if thou enlisteth, thou wilt have to do hard battle. There is no bed of down for thee; there is no riding to heaven in a chariot; the rough way must be trodden; mountains must be climbed, rivers must be forded, dragons must be fought, giants must be slain, difficulties must be overcome, and great trials must be borne. It is not a smooth road to heaven, believe me; for those who have gone but a very few steps therein have found it to be a rough one. It is a pleasant one; it is the most delightful in all the world, but it is not easy in itself; it is only pleasant because of the company, because of the sweet promises on which we lean, because of our Beloved who walks with us through all the rough and thorny brakes of this vast wilderness. Christian, expect trouble: "Count it not strange concerning the fiery trial, and as though some strange thing had happened unto thee;" for as truly as thou art a child of God, thy Saviour hath left thee for his legacy,—"In the world, ye shall have tribulation; in me ye shall have peace." If I had no trouble I would not believe myself one of the family. If I never had a trial I would not think myself a heir of heaven. Children of God must not, shall not, escape the rod. Earthly parents may spoil their children but the heavenly Father never shall his. "Whom he loveth he chasteneth," and scourgeth every son whom he hath chosen. His people must suffer; therefore, expect it Christian; if thou art a child of God believe it, look for it, and when it comes, say, "Well suffering, I foresaw thee; thou art no stranger; I have looked for thee continually." You cannot tell how much it will lighten your trials, if you await them with resignation. In fact, make it a wonder if you get through a day easily. If you remain a week without persecution, think it a remarkable thing; and if you should, perchance, live a month without heaving a sigh from your inmost heart, think it a miracle of miracles. But when the trouble comes, say, "Ah! this is what I looked for; it is marked in the chart to heaven; the rock is put down; I will sail confidently by it; my Master has not deceived me." "Why should I complain of want or distress, Temptation or pain? he told me no less." But why must the Christian expect trouble? Why must he expect the sufferings of Christ to abound in him? Stand here a moment, my brother, and I will show thee four reasons wherefore thou must endure trial. First look upward, then look downward, then look around thee, and then look within thee; and thou wilt see four reasons why the sufferings of Christ should abound in thee.

Look upward. Dost thou see thy heavenly Father, a pure and holy being, spotless, just, perfect? Dost thou know that thou art one day to be like him? Thinkest thou that thou wilt easily come to be conformed to his image? Wilt thou not require much furnace work, much grinding in the mill of trouble, much breaking with the pestle in the mortar of affliction, much being broken under the wheels of agony? Thinkest thou it will be an easy thing for thy heart to become as pure as God is? Dost thou think thou canst so soon get rid of thy corruptions, and become perfect, even as thy Father which is in heaven is perfect?

Lift up thine eye again; dost thou discern those bright spirits clad in white, purer than alabaster, more chaste, more fair than Parian marble? Behold them as they stand in glory. Ask them whence their victory came. Some of them will tell you they swam through seas of blood. Behold the scars of honor on their brows; see, some of them lift up their hands and tell you they were once consumed in fire; while others were slain by the sword, rent in pieces by wild beasts; were destitute afflicted, tormented. 0 ye noble army of martyrs, ye glorious hosts of the living God. Must ye swim through seas of blood, and shall I hope to ride to heaven wrapped in furs and ermine? Did ye endure suffering, and shall I be pampered with the luxuries of this world? Did ye fight and then reign, and must I reign without a battle. Oh, no. By God's help I will expect that as ye suffered so must I, and as through much tribulation ye entered the kingdom of heaven, so shall I.

Next, Christian, turn thine eyes downward. Dost thou know what foes thou hast beneath thy feet? There are hell and its lions against thee. Thou wast once a servant of Satan and no king will willingly lose his subjects.

Dost thou think that Satan be pleased with thee? Why, thou hast changed thy country. Thou wast once a liege servant of Apollyon, but now thou art become a good soldier of Jesus Christ; and dost thou think the devil is pleased with thee? I tell thee nay. If thou hadst seen Satan the moment thou wast converted, thou wouldst have beheld a wondrous scene. As soon as thou gavest thy heart to Christ, Satan spread his bat-like-wings: down he flew into hell, and summoning all his councilors, he said "Sons of the pit, true heirs of darkness; ye who erst were clad in light, but who fell with me from high dignities, another of my servants has forsaken me; I have lost another of my family; he is gone over to the side of the Lord of Hosts. Oh ye, my compeers, ye fellow-helpers of the powers of darkness, leave no stone unturned to destroy him. I bid you all hurl all your fiercest darts at him; plague him; let hell-dogs bark at him; let fiends besiege him; give him no rest, harrass him to the death; let the fumes of our corrupt and burning lake ever rise in his nostrils; persecute him; the man is a traitor; give him no peace; since I cannot have him here to bind him in chains of adamant, since I ne'er can have him here to torment and afflict him, as long as ye can, till his dying day, I bid you howl at him; until he crosses the river, afflict him, grieve him, torment him; for the wretch has turned against me, and become a servant of the Lord." Such may have been the scene in hell, that very day when thou didst love the Lord. And dost thou think Satan loves thee better now? Ah! no. He will always be at thee, for thine enemy, "like a roaring lion, goeth about seeking whom he may devour." Expect trouble therefore, Christian, when thou lookest beneath thee.

Then, man of God, look around thee. Do not be asleep. Open thine eyes, and look around thee. Where art thou? Is that man a friend next to thee? No; thou art in an enemy's country. This is a wicked world. Half the people, I suppose, profess to be irreligious, and those who profess to be pious, often are not. "Cursed is he that trusteth in man and maketh flesh his arm."—Blessed is he that trusteth in the Lord, and whose hope the Lord is."— "As for men of low degree, they are vanity;" the voice of the crowd is not worth having; and as for "men of high degree, they are a lie," which is worse still. The world is not to be trusted in, not to be relied upon. The true Christian treads it beneath his feet, with "all that earth calls good or great." Look around thee my brother; thou wilt see some good hearts, strong and valiant; thou wilt see some true souls, sincere and honest; thou wilt see some faithful lovers of Christ; but I tell thee O child of light, that where thou meetest one sincere man, thou wilt meet twenty hypocrites; where thou wilt find one that will lead thee to heaven, thou wilt find a score who would push thee to hell. Thou art in a land of enemies, not of friends. Never believe the world is good for much. Many people have burned their fingers by taking hold of it. Many a man has been injured by putting his hand into a nest of the rattlesnake—the world; thinking that the dazzling hues of the sleeping serpent were securities from harm. O Christian! the world is not thy friend. If it is, then thou art not God's friend; for he who is the friend of the world is the enemy of God; and he who is despised of men, is often loved of Jehovah. Thou art in an enemy's country, man: therefore, expect trouble: expect that the man who "eats thy bread will lift up his heel against thee;" expect that thou shalt be estranged from those that love thee; be assured that since thou art in the land of the foe, thou shalt find foemen everywhere. When thou sleepest, think that thou sleepest on the battle-field; when thou walkest believe that there is an ambush in every hedge. Oh! take heed, take heed: this is no good world to shut thine eyes in. Look around thee, man; and when thou art upon the watch-tower, reckon surely that trouble cometh.

II. Now, secondly, there is A DISTINCTION TO BE NOTICED. Our sufferings are said to be the sufferings of Christ. Now, suffering in itself is not an evidence of Christianity. There are many people who have trials and troubles who are not children of God. I have heard some poor whining people come and say, "I know I am a child of God because I am in debt, because I am in poverty, because I am in trouble." Do you indeed? I know a great many rascals in the same condition; and I don't believe you are a child of God any the more because you happen to be in poor circumstances. There are abundance who are in trouble and distress besides God's children. It is not the peculiar lot of God's family; and if I had no other ground of my hope as a Christian, except my experience of trials, I should have but very poor ground indeed. But there is a distinction to be noticed. Are these sufferings the sufferings of Christ, or are they not? A man is dishonest, and is put in jail for it; a man is a coward and men hiss at him for it; a man is insincere, and, therefore, persons avoid him. Yet he says he is persecuted. Persecuted! Not at all; it serves him right. He deserves it. But such persons will comfort themselves with the thought, that they are "the dear people of God," because other people avoid them; when it so happens that they just deserve it. They do not live as they ought to do; therefore the world's punishment is their desert. Take heed, beloved, that your sufferings are true sufferings of Christ; be sure they are not your own sufferings; for if they are, you will get no relief. It is only when they are the sufferings of Jesus that we may take comfort.

"Well," you say, "What is meant by our sufferings being the sufferings of Christ?" You know the word "Christ" in the Bible sometimes means the whole Church with Christ, as in 1 Cor. xii.12, and several other passages which I cannot just now remember; but you will call to mind a scripture where it says, "I fill up that which is behind of the sufferings of Christ, for his body's sake, which is the Church." Now, as Christ, the head, had a certain amount of suffering to endure, so the body must also have a certain weight laid upon it. Our afflictions are the sufferings of Christ mystical, the sufferings of Christ's body, the sufferings of Christ's church; for you know that if a man could be so tall as to have his head in heaven and his feet at the bottom of the sea, it would be the same body, and the head would feel the sufferings of the feet. So, though my head is in heaven, and I am on earth, my griefs are Christ's griefs; my trials are Christ's trials, my afflictions, he suffers. "I feel at my heart all thy sighs and thy groans, For thou art most near me, my flesh and my bones; In all thy distresses, thy Head feels the pain, Yet all are most needful, not one is in vain." The trials of a true Christian are as much the sufferings of Christ, as the agonies of Calvary.

Still you say, "We want to discern whether our troubles are the trials of Christ." Well, they are the trials of Christ, if you suffer for Christ's sake. If you are called to endure hardness for the sake of the truth, then those are the sufferings of Christ. If you suffer for your own sake, it may be a punishment for your own sins; but if you endure for Christ's sake, then they are the trials of Christ. "But," say some, "is there any persecution now-a-days? Do any Christians have to suffer for Christ's sake now?" Suffer, sirs! Yes. "I could a tale unfold" this morning, if I pleased, of bigotry insufferable, of persecution well nigh as bad as that in the days of Mary; only our foes have not the power and the law on their side. I could tell you of some who, from the simple fact, that they choose to come and hear this despised young man, this ranting fellow, are to be looked upon as the offscouring of all things. Many are the persons who come to me, who have to lead a miserable and unhappy life, simply because from my lips they heard the word of truth. Still, despite of all that is said, they will hear it now. I have, I am sure, many before me, whose eyes would drop with tears, if I were to tell their history—some who have privately sent me word of how they have to suffer for Christ's sake, because they choose to hear whom they please. Why, is it not time that men should choose to do as they like. If I do not care to do just as other ministers do, have not I a right to preach as I please? If I haven't I will—that is all. And have not other parties a right to hear me if they like, without asking the lords and governors of the present day, whether the man is really clerical or not. Liberty! liberty! Let persons do as they please. But liberty—where is it? Ye say it is in Britain. It is, in a measure, but not thoroughly. However, I rejoice that there are some who say, "Well, my soul is profited: and let men say what they will, I will hold hard and fast to truth, and to the place where I hear the word to my soul's edification." So, dear hearts, go on, go on; and if ye suffer for Christ's sake, they are Christ's sufferings. If ye came here simply because ye gained anything by it, then your sufferings would be your own; but since there is nothing to gain but the profit of our own souls, still hold on; and whate'er is said, your persecution will but win you a brighter crown in glory.

Ah! Christian, this ennobles us. My brethren, this makes us proud and happy to think that our trials are the trials of Jesus. Oh! I think it must have been some honor to the old soldier, who stood by the Iron Duke in his battles, to be able to say, "We fight under the good old Duke, who has won so many battles: and when he wins, part of the honor will be ours." Christian, thou fightest side by side with Jesus; Christ is with thee; every blow is a blow aimed at Christ; every slander is a slander on Christ; the battle is the Lord's; the triumph is the Lord's, therefore, still on to victory! I remember a story of a great commander, who, having won many glorious victories, led his troops into a defile, and when there, a large body of the enemy entirely surrounded him. He knew a battle was inevitable on the morning, he therefore went round to all the tents, to hear in what condition his soldier's minds were—whether they were dispirited or not. He came to one tent, and as he listened, he heard a man say, "There is our general; he is very brave, but he is very unwise this time; he has led us into a place where we are sure to be beaten; there are so many of the enemy's cavalry, so many infantry:" and then the man counted up all the troops on their own side, and made them only so many. Then the commander, after he had heard the tale, gently drew aside a part of the tent, and said, "How many do you count me for? You have counted the infantry and cavalry; but how many do you count me for—me, your mighty captain, who have won so many victories." Now, Christian, I say, how many do you count one? He is not one, nor a thousand: he is the "chief among ten thousand." But he is more than that. Oh! put him down for a high figure; and when thou countest up thine aids and auxiliaries, put down Christ for all in all, for in him victory is certain—the triumph is secure.

III. Our third point is, A PROPORTION TO BE EXPERIENCED. As the sufferings of Christ abound in us so the consolations of Christ abound. Here is a blessed proportion. God always keeps a pair of scales—in this side he puts his people's trials and in that he puts their consolations. When the scale of trial is nearly empty, you will always find the scale of consolation in nearly the same condition; and when the scale of trials is full, you will find the scale of consolation just as heavy for as the sufferings of Christ abound in us, even so shall consolation abound by Christ. This is a matter of pure experience. Some of you do not know anything at all about it. You are not Christians, you are not born again, you are not converted; ye are unregenerate, and, therefore, ye have never realized this wonderful proportion between the sufferings and the consolations of a child of God. Oh! it is mysterious that, when the black clouds gather most, the light within us is always the brightest. When the night lowers and the tempest is coming on, the heavenly captain is always closest to his crew. It is a blessed thing, when we are most cast down, then it is that we are most lifted up by the consolations of Christ. Let me show you how.

The first reason is, because trials make more room, for consolation. There is nothing makes a man have a big heart like a great trial. I always find that little, miserable people, whose hearts are about the size of a grain of mustard-seed, never have had much to try them. I have found that those people who have no sympathy for their fellows—who never weep for the sorrows of others—very seldom have had any woes of their own. Great hearts can only be made by great troubles. The spade of trouble digs the reservoir of comfort deeper, and makes more room for consolation. God comes into our heart—he finds it full—he begins to break our comforts and to make it empty; than there is more room for grace. The humbler a man lies, the more comfort he will always have. I recollect walking with a ploughman one day—a man who was deeply taught, although he was a ploughman; and really ploughmen would make a great deal better preachers than many college gentlemen—and he said to me, "Depend upon it, my good brother, if you or I ever get one inch above the ground, we shall get just that inch too high." I believe it is true; for the lower we lie, the nearer to the ground we are—the more our troubles humble us—the more fit we are to receive comfort; and God always gives us comfort when we are most fit for it. That is one reason why consolations increase in the same ratio as our trials.

Then again, trouble exercises our graces, and the very exercise of our graces tends to make us more comfortable and happy. Where showers fall most, there the grass is greenest. I suppose the fogs and mists of Ireland make it "the Emerald Isle;" and wherever you find great fogs of trouble, and mists of sorrow, you always find emerald green hearts: full of the beautiful verdure of the comfort and love of God. O Christian, do not thou be saying, "Where are the swallows gone? they are gone: they are dead." They are not dead; they have skimmed the purple sea, and gone to a far off land; but they will be back again by-and-by. Child of God, say not the flowers are dead; say not the winter has killed them, and they are gone. Ah! no; though winter hath coated them with the ermine of its snow; they will put up their heads again, and will be alive very soon. Say not, child of God, that the sun is quenched, because the cloud hath hidden it. Ah! no; he is behind there, brewing summer for thee; for when he cometh out again, he will have made the clouds fit to drop in April showers, all of them mothers of the sweet May flowers. And oh! above all, when thy God hides his face, say not, that he has forgotten thee. He is but tarrying a little while to make thee love him better; and when he cometh, thou shalt have joy in the Lord, and. shalt rejoice with joy unspeakable. Waiting, exercises our grace; waiting, tries our faith; therefore, wait on in hope; for though the promise tarry, it can never come too late.

Another reason why we are often most happy in our troubles is this—then we have the closest dealing with God. I speak from heart knowledge and real experience. We never have such close dealings with God as when we are in tribulation. When the barn is full, man can live without God; when the purse is bursting with gold, we somehow can do without so much prayer. But once take your gourds away, you want your God; once cleanse away the idols out of the house, then you must go and honor Jehovah. Some of you do not pray half as much as you ought. If you are the children of God, you will have the whip, and when you have that whip, you will run to your Father. It is a fine day, and the child walks before its father; but there is a lion in the road, now he comes and takes his father's hand. He could run half-a-mile before him when all was fine and fair; but once bring the lion, and it is "father! father!" as close as he can be. It is even so with the Christian. Let all be well, and he forgets God. Jeshurun waxes fat, and he begins to kick against God; but take away his hopes, blast his joys, let the infant lie in the coffin, let the crops be blasted, let the herd be cut off from the stall, let the husband's broad shoulder lie in the grave, let the children be fatherless—then it is that God is a God indeed. Oh, strip me naked; take from me all I have; make me poor, a beggar, penniless, helpless: dash that cistern in pieces; crush that hope; quench the stars; put out the sun; shroud the moon in darkness, and place me all alone in space, without a friend, without a helper; still, "Out of the depths will I cry unto thee, O God." There is no cry so good as that which comes from the bottom of the mountains; no prayer half so hearty as that which comes up from the depths of the soul, through deep trials and afflictions. Hence they bring us to God, and we are happier; for that is the way to be happy—to live near to God. So that while troubles abound, they drive us to God, and then consolations abound.

Some people call troubles weights. Verily they are so. A ship that has large sails and a fair wind, needs ballast. Troubles are the ballast of a believer. The eyes are the pumps which fetch out the bilge-water of his soul, and keep him from sinking. But if trials be weights I will tell you of a happy secret. There is such a thing as making a weight lift you. If I have a weight chained to me, it keeps me down; but give me pulleys and certain appliances, and I can make it lift me up. Yes, there is such a thing as making troubles raise me towards heaven. A gentlemen once asked a friend, concerning a beautiful horse of his, feeding about in the pasture with a clog on its foot, "Why do you clog such a noble animal?" "Sir," said he, "I would a great deal sooner clog him than lose him: he is given to leap hedges." That is why God clogs his people. He would rather clog them than lose them; for if he did not clog them, they would leap the hedges and be gone. They want a tether to prevent their straying, and their God binds them with afflictions, to keep them near to him, to preserve them, and have them in his presence. Blessed fact—as our troubles abound, our consolations also abound.

IV. Now we close up with our last point; and may the Holy Ghost once more strengthen me to speak a word or two to you. THERE IS A PERSON TO BE HONOURED. It is a fact that Christians can rejoice in deep distress; it is a truth, that put them in prison, and they still will sing; like many birds, they sing best in their cages. It is true that when waves roll over them, their soul never sinks. It is true they have a buoyancy about them which keeps their heads always above the water, and helps them to sing in the dark, dark night, "God is with me still." But to whom shall we give the honor? To whom shall the glory be given? Oh! to Jesus, to Jesus; for the text says it is all by Jesus. It is not because I am a Christian that I get joy in my trouble—not necessarily so; it is not always the fact that troubles bring their consolations; but it is Christ who comes to me. I am sick in my chamber; Christ cometh up stairs, he sitteth by my bedside, and he talketh sweet words to me. I am dying; the chilly cold waters of Jordan have touched my foot, I feel my blood stagnate and freeze. I must die; Christ puts his arms around me, and says, "Fear not, beloved; to die is to be blessed; the waters of death have their fountain head in heaven; they are not bitter, they are sweet as nectar, for they flow from the throne of God." I wade in the stream, the billows gather around me, I feel that my heart and flesh fail but there is the same voice in my ears, "Fear not, I am with thee! be not dismayed; I am thy God." Now, I come to the borders of the infinite unknown, that country "from whose bourne no traveller returns;" I stand almost affrighted to enter the realm of shades; but a sweet voice says, "I will be with thee whithersoever thou goest; if thou shouldst make thy bed in Hades I will be with thee;" and I still go on, content to die, for Jesus cheers me; he is my consolation and my hope. Ah! ye who know not that matchless name, Jesus, ye have lost the sweetest note which e'er can give melody. Ah! ye who have never been entranced by the precious sonnet contained in that one word Jesu, ye who know not that Jesu means, I-ES-U, ("I ease you"); ye have lost the joy and comfort of your lives, and ye must live miserable and unhappy. But the Christian can rejoice, since Christ will never forsake him, never leave him, but will be with him.

A word or two to characters—First, I have a word with you who are expecting troubles, and are very sad because you are looking forward to them. Take the advice of the common people, and "never cross a bridge till you get to it." Follow my advice: never bring your troubles nearer than they are, for they will be sure to come down upon you soon enough. I know that many persons fret themselves about their trials before they come.

What on earth is the good of it? If you will show me any benefit in it, I will say go on; but to me it seems quite enough for the Father to lay the rod on the child without the child chastising itself. Why should you do so? You, who are afraid of trouble, why should you be so? The trial may never overtake you; and if it does come, strength will come with it. Therefore, up with thee, man, who are sitting down groaning, because of forebodings. "Religion never was designed To make our pleasures less." Out on thee! Up! up! Why wilt thou sit down and be frozen to death? When trouble comes, then fight it; with manful heart and strong, plunge into the stream, accoutred as thou art, and swim it through; but oh! do not fear it before it comes.

Then Christian in trouble, I have a word to say with thee. So my brother, thou art in trouble; thou art come into the waves of affliction, art thou? No strange thing, is it brother? Thou hast been there many times before.

"Ah," but sayest thou, "this is the worst I ever had. I have come up here this morning with a millstone round my neck; I have a mine of lead in my heart: I am miserable, I am unhappy, I am cast down exceedingly." Well, but brother, as thy troubles abound, so shall thy consolation. Brother, hast thou hung thy harp upon the willows? I am glad thou hast not broken the harp altogether. Better, to hang it on the willows than to break it; be sure not to break it. Instead of being distressed about thy trouble, rejoice in it; thou wilt then honor God, thou wilt glorify Christ, thou wilt bring sinners to Jesus, if thou wilt sing in the depths of trouble, for then they will say, "There must be something in religion after all, otherwise the man would not be so happy."

Then one word with you who are almost driven to despair. I would stretch my hands out, if I could, this morning—for I believe a preacher ought to be a Briareus, with a thousand hands to fetch out his hearers one by one, and speak to them. There is a man here quite despairing—almost every hope gone. Brother, shall I tell thee what to do? Thou hast fallen off the main deck, thou art in the sea, the floods surround thee; thou seemest to have no hope; thou catchest at straws; what shalt thou do now? Do? why lie upon the sea of trouble, and float upon it; be still, and know that God is God, and thou wilt never perish. All thy kicking and struggling will sink thee deeper; but lie still, for behold the life-boat cometh; Christ is coming to thy help; soon he will deliver thee, and fetch thee out of all thy perplexities.

Lastly, some of you have no interest in this sermon at all. I never try to deceive my hearers by making them believe that all I say belongs to all who hear me. There are different characters in God's word; it is yours to search your own hearts this day, and see whether ye are God's people, or not. As the Lord liveth, before whom I stand, there are two classes here. I do not own the distinction of aristocratic and democratic; in my sight, and in God's sight, every man is alike. We are made of one flesh and blood; we do not have china gentlemen and earthenware poor people; we are all made of the same mould of fashion. There is one distinction, and only one. Ye are all either the children of God, or children of the devil; ye are all either born again, or dead in trespasses and sins. It is yours to let the question ring in your ears: "Where am I? Is yon black tyrant, with his fiery sword, my king; or do I own Jehovah-Jesus as my strength, my shield, my Saviour?" I shall not force you to answer it; I shall not say anything to you about it. Only answer it yourselves; let your hearts speak; let your souls speak. All I can do is to propose the question. God apply it to your souls! I beseech him to send it home! and make the arrow stick fast! "Is Jesus mine! I am now prepared, To meet with what I thought most hard; Yes, let the winds of trouble blow,

And comforts melt away like snow, No blasted trees, nor failing crops, Can hinder my eternal hopes; Tho' creatures change, the Lord's the same; Then let me triumph in his name.

David's Dying Song

A Sermon (No. 19) Delivered on Sabbath Morning, April 15, 1855, by the REV. C. H. SPURGEON At Exeter Hall, Strand.

"Although my house be not so with God; yet he hath made with me an everlasting covenant, ordered in all things and sure: for this is all my salvation, and all my desire, although he make it not to grow."—2 Samuel 23:5.

These be the last words of David; so we read at the commencement of the chapter. Many have been the precious sentences which have fallen front his inspired lips; seraphic has been the music which has dropped from his fingers when they flew along the strings of his harp; but now that sweet voice is to be hushed in death, and now the son of Jesse is to sleep with his fathers. Surely it were well to press around his bed, to hear the dying monarch's last testimony; yea, we can conceive that angels themselves would for an instant check their rapid flight, that they might visit the chamber of the dying mighty one, and listen to his last death song. It is always blessed to hear the words of departing saints. How many choice thoughts have we gained in the bedchamber of the righteous, beloved? I remember one sweet idea, which I once won from a death-bed. A dying man desired to have one of the Psalms read to him, and the 17th being chosen, he stopped at the 6th verse, "Incline thine ear unto me and hear my speech," and faintly whispering, said, "Ah, Lord, I cannot speak, my voice fails me; incline thine ear, put it against my mouth, that thou mayest hear me." None but a weak and dying man, whose life was ebbing fast, could have conceived such a thought. It is well to hear saints' words when they are near heaven—when they stand upon the banks of Jordan. But here is a special case, for these be the last words of David. They are something more than human utterances; for we are told that the Spirit of the Lord spake by him, and his word was in his tongue. These were his closing accents. Ah! methinks, lisping these words he rose from earth to join the chorus of the skies. He commenced the sentence upon earth, and he finished it in heaven. He began, "Although my house be not so with God;" and as he winged his flight to heaven, he still sang, "yet hast thou made with me an everlasting covenant, ordered in all things, and sure: "and now before the throne he constantly hymns the same strain—"yet hast thou made with me an everlasting covenant, ordered in all things, and sure." I hope, my friends, there are many of us who can join in this verse this morning, and who hope to close our earthly pilgrimage with this upon our tongue.

We shall notice first, that the Psalmist had sorrow in his house—"Although my house be not so with God." Secondly, he had confidence in the covenant—"yet he hath made with me an everlasting covenant." And thirdly, he had satisfaction in his heart, for he says—"this is all my salvation, and all my desire.

I. The Psalmist says he had sorrow in his house—"Although my house be not so with God." What man is there of all our race, who, if he had to write his history, would not need to use a great many "althoughs"? If you read the biography of any man, as recorded in the Sacred Word, you will always find a "but," or an "although," before you have finished. Naaman was a mighty man of valour, and a great man with his master, but he was a leper. There is always a "but" in every condition, a crook in every lot, some dark tint upon the marble pillar, some cloud in the summer sky, some discord in the music, some alloy in the gold. So David, though a man who had been raised from the sheepfold, a mighty warrior, a conqueror of giants, a king over a great nation, yet, had his "althoughs;" and the "although" which he had, was one in his own house. Those are the worst troubles which we have in our own household. We love not an evil beast abroad, but we hate the lion most when it prowls upon our own estates, or croucheth on the floor of our dwelling. The greatest trouble with the thorn is when it lieth in our bed, and we feel it in our pillow. Civil war is always the fiercest—those are foes indeed who are of our own household. I think, perhaps David intended, when he said "Although my house be not so with God," to speak partly of his affairs. If any man else had looked at David's affairs—the government of his country—he would have said, "David's government is the mirror of excellence." His house was so rightly ordered, that few of his subjects could murmur at him; but David recollected that a greater and keener eye than that of man rested on him; and he says, speaking of his empire and his house—for you know the word "house" in Scripture often means our business, our affairs, our transactions, ("Set thine house in order, for thou must die, and not live,")—he says, although before man my house may be well swept, and garnished, yet it is not so with God as I can desire. Oh, beloved, there are some of us who can walk before our fellow-men conscious of innocence; we dare defy the gaze of our fellow-mortals; we can say, "Lord! thou knowest I am not wicked;" we are blameless before this perverse generation: we walk amongst them as lights in the world, and God has helped us, so that we are clean from the great transgression; we are not afraid of a criticism of our character, we are not fearful of being inspected by the eyes of all men, for we feel that through God's grace we have been kept from committing ourselves; he has kept us, and the evil one toucheth us not. But with all this conscious innocence—with all that dignity with which we stand before our fellows—when we go into God's sight, how changed we are! Ah, then, my friends, we say not, "Lord! thou knowest I am not wicked;" but rather, we fall prostrate, and cry, "Unclean, unclean, unclean;" and as the leper cools his heated brow with the water running in the cool sequestered brook, so do we have our body in Siloam's stream, and strive to wash ourselves clean in the water and blood from Christ's riven side. We feel that our house is "not so with God;" though in the person of Jesus we are free from sin, and white as angels are: yet when we stand before God, in our own persons, we are obliged to confess, that honest as we may be, upright as we have been, just and holy before men, yet our house is "not so with God."

But I imagine that the principal meaning of these words of David refers to his family—his children. David had many trials in his children. It has often been the lot of good men to have great troubles from their sons and daughters. True, we know some households that are the very image of peace and happiness, where the father and mother bend the knee together in family prayer, and they look upon an offspring, numerous or not, as it may be, but most of them devoting their hearts to God. I know a household which stands like a green oasis in the desert of this world. There be sons who preach God's gospel, and daughters who are growing up to fear the Lord, and to love him. Such a household is indeed a pleasant halting-place for a weary soul in its pilgrimage through this wilderness of life. Oh! happy is that family whom God hath blessed. But there are other houses where you will find the children are the trials of the parents. "Although my house be not so with God," may many an anxious father say; and ye pious mothers might lift your streaming eyes to heaven, and say, "Although my house be not so with God." That first-born son of yours, who was your pride, has now turned out your disgrace. Oh! how have the arrows of his ingratitude pierced into your soul, and how do you keenly feel at this present moment, that sooner would you have buried him in his infancy; sooner might he never have seen the light, and perished in the birth, than that he should live to have acted as he has done, to be the misery of your existence, and the sorrow of your life. O sons who are ungodly, unruly, gay, and profligate, surely ye do not know the tears of pious mothers, or ye would stop your sin. Methinks, young man, thou wouldst not willingly allow thy mother to shed tears, however dearly you may love sin. Will you not then stop at her entreaties? Can you trample upon your mother? Oh! though you are riding a steeple-chase to hell, cannot her weeping supplications induce you to stay your mad career? Will you grieve her who gave you life, and fondly cherished you at her breast? Surely you will long debate e'er you can resolve to bring her grey hairs with sorrow to the grave. Or has sin brutalized you? Are ye worse than stones? Have natural feelings become extinct? Is the evil one entirely your master? Has he dried up all the tender sympathies of your heart? Stay! young prodigal, and ponder!

But, Christian men! ye are not alone in this. If ye have family troubles, there are others who have borne the same. Remember Ephraim! Though God had promised that Ephraim should abound as a tribe with tens of thousands, yet it is recorded in 1 Chron. 7:20–22: "And the sons of Ephraim; Shuthelah and Bered his son, and Tahath his son, and Eladah his son, and Tahath his son, and Zabad his son, and Shuthelah his son, and Ezer and Elead, whom the men of Gath that were born in that land slew, because they came down to take away their cattle. And Ephraim their father mourned many days, and his brethren came to comfort him." Abraham himself had his Ishmael, and he cried to God on account thereof. Think of Eli, a man who served God as a high priest, and though he could rule the people, he could not rule his sons; and great was his grief thereat. Ah! some of you, my brethren in the gospel, may lift your hands to heaven, and ye may utter this morning these words with a deep and solemn emphasis—you may write "Although" in capitals, for it is more than true with some of you—"Although my house be not so with God."

Before we leave this point: What must I say to any of those who are thus tried and distressing in estate and family? First, let me say to you, my brethren, it is necessary that you should have an "although" in your lot, because if you had not, you know what you would do; you would build a very downy nest on earth, and there you would lie down in sleep; so God puts a thorn in your nest in order that you may sing. It is said by the old writers, that the nightingale never sang so sweetly as when she sat among thorns, since say they, the thorns prick her breast, and remind her of her song. So it may be with you. Ye, like the larks, would sleep in your nest did not some trouble pass by and affright you; then you stretch your wings, and carolling the matin song, rise to greet the sun. Trials are sent to wean you from the world; bitters are put into your drink, that ye may learn to live upon the dew of heaven: the food of earth is mingled with gall, that ye may only seek for true bread in the manna which droppeth from the sky. Your soul without trouble would be as the sea if it were without tide or motion; it would become foul and obnoxious. As Coleridge describes the sea after a wondrous calm, so would the soul breed contagion and death.

But furthermore, recollect this, O thou who art tried in thy children—that prayer can remove thy troubles. There is not a pious father or mother here, who is suffering in the family, but may have that trial taken away yet. Faith is as omnipotent as God himself, for it moves the arm which leads the stars along. Have you prayed long for your children without a result? and have ye said, "I will cease to pray, for the more I wrestle, the worse they seem to grow, and the more am I tried?" Oh! say not so, thou weary watcher. Though the promise tarrieth, it will come. Still sow the seed; and when thou sowest it, drop a tear with each grain thou puttest into the earth. Oh, steep thy seeds in the tears of anxiety, and they cannot rot under the clods, if they have been baptized in so vivifying a mixture. And what though thou diest without seeing thy sons the heirs of light? They shall be converted even after thy death; and though thy bones shall be put in the grave, and thy son may stand and curse thy memory for an hour, he shall not forget it in the cooler moments of his recollection, when he shall meditate alone. Then he shall think of thy prayers, thy tears, thy groans; he shall remember thine advice—it shall rise up, and if he live in sin, still thy words shall sound as one long voice from the realm of spirits, and either affright him in the midst of his revelry, or charm him heavenward, like angel's whispers, saying, "Follow on to glory, where thy parent is who once did pray for thee." So the Christian may say,

"Although my house be not so with God now, it may be yet;" therefore will I still wait, for there be mighty instances of conversion. Think of John Newton. He even became a slaver, yet was brought back. Hope on; never despair; faint heart never winneth the souls of men, but firm faith winneth all things; therefore watch unto prayer. "What I say unto you, I say unto all, watch." There is your trouble, a small cup filled from the same sea of tribulation as was the Psalmist's when he sung, "Although my house be not so with God."

II. But secondly: David had confidence in the covenant. Oh! how sweet it is to look from the dulness of earth to the brilliancy of heaven! How glorious it is to leap from the ever tempest-tossed bark of this world, and stand upon the terra firma of the covenant! So did David. Having done with his "Although," he then puts in a blessed "yet" Oh! it is a "yet," with jewels set: "He hath made with me an everlasting covenant, ordered in all things, and sure."

Now let us notice these words as they come. First, David rejoiced in the covenant, because it is divine in its origin. "Yet hath HE made with me an everlasting covenant." O that great word HE. Who is that? It is not my odd-father or my odd mother who has made a covenant for me—none of that nonsense. It is not a covenant man has made for me, or with me; but yet hath HE made with me an everlasting covenant." It is divine in its origin, not human. The covenant on which the Christian rests, is not the covenant of his infant sprinkling: he has altogether broken that scores of times, for he has not "renounced the pomps and vanities of this wicked world," as he should have done, nor "all the lusts of the flesh." Nor has he really become regenerate through those holy drops of water which a cassocked priest cast on his face. The covenant on which he rests and stands secure, is that covenant which God has made with him. "Yet hath HE made."

Stop, my soul. God, the everlasting Father, has positively made a covenant with thee; yes, that God, who in the thickest darkness dwells and reigns for ever in his majesty alone; that God, who spake the world into existence by a word; who holds it, like an Atlas, upon his shoulders, who poises the destiny of all creation upon his finger; that God, stooping from his majesty, takes hold of thy hand and makes a covenant with thee. Oh! is it not a deed, the stupendous condescension of which might ravish our hearts for ever if we could really understand it? Oh! the depths! "HE hath made with me a covenant." A king has not made a covenant with me—that were somewhat: an emperor has not entered into a compact with me; but the Prince of the kings of the earth, the Shaddai, the Lord of all flesh, the Jehovah of ages, the everlasting Elohim. "He hath made with me an everlasting covenant." O blessed thought! it is of divine origin.

But notice its particular application. "Yet hath he made with ME an everlasting covenant." Here lies the sweetness of it to me, as an individual. "Oh how sweet to view the flowing Of Christ's soul-redeeming blood, With divine assurance knowing, That he made my peace with God." It is nought for me that he made peace for the world; I want to know whether he made peace for me: it is little that he hath made a covenant, I want to know whether he has made a covenant with ME. David could put his hand upon his heart and say, "Yet hath he made a covenant with ME." I fear I shall not be wrong in condemning the fashionable religion of the day, for it is a religion which belongs to the crowd; and not a personal one which is enjoyed by the individual. You will hear persons say, "Well, I believe the doctrine of justification; I think that men are justified through faith." Yes, but are you justified by faith? "I believe," says another, "that we are sanctified by the Spirit." Yes, all very well, but are you sanctified by the Spirit? Mark you, if ever you talk about personal piety very much, you will always be run down as extravagant. If you really say from your heart, "I know I am forgiven; I am certain that I am a pardoned sinner;"—and every Christian will at times be able to say it, and would always, were it not for his unbelief—if you say, "I know in whom I have believed; I am confident that I have not a sin now recorded in the black roll; that I am free from sin as if I had never transgressed, through the pardoning blood of Jesus," men will say it is extravagant. Well, it is a delightful extravagance, it is the extravagance of God's Word; and I would to God more of us could indulge in that holy, blessed extravagance. For we may well be extravagant when we have an infinite sum to spend; we may well be lavish when we know we never can exhaust the treasure. Oh! how sweet it is to say, "Yet hath he made with ME an everlasting covenant. It is nought that you talk to me of my brother being saved. I am very glad that my friend should get to glory, and I shall rejoice to meet you all; but after all, the thing is, "Shall I be there?" "Shall I amongst them stand, To see his smiling face?" Now, Christian, thou canst apply this personally. The covenant is made with thee. Man, open thine eyes; there is thy name in the covenant. What is it? It is some plain English name, perhaps. It never had an M.P. nor an M.A. after it, nor a "Sir," before it. Never mind, that name is in the covenant. If you could take down your Father's family Bible in heaven, you would find your name put in the register. O blessed thought! my name—positively mine! not another's. So, then, these eyes shall see him, and not another's for me. Rejoice, Christian; it is a personal covenant. "Yet hath he made with me an everlasting covenant."Furthermore, this covenant is not only divine in its origin, but it is everlasting in its duration. I have had some very pretty letters sent me from anonymous writers who have listened to me; and being great cowards (whom I always abhor) they cannot sign their names. They may know what fate they receive; the condign punishment I appoint to them. I cut them asunder, and thrust them into the fire. I hope the authors will not have a similar fate. Some of them, however, quarrel with me, because I preach the everlasting gospel. I dare not preach another, for I would not have another if it were offered to me. An everlasting gospel is the only one which I think worthy of an everlasting God. I am sure it is the only one which can give comfort to a soul that is to live throughout eternity. Now, you know what an "everlasting covenant" signifies. It meant a covenant which had no beginning, and which shall never, never end. Some do not believe in the everlasting nature of God's love to his people. They think that God begins to love his people when they begin to love him. My Arminian friends, did you ever sing that verse in your meeting?—of course you have—"O yes, I do love Jesus, Because he first lov'd me." That is a glorious Calvinistic hymn, though we know whose hymn book it is in. Well, then, if Jesus loved you before you loved him, why cannot you believe that he always did love you? Besides, how stupid it is to talk so, when you know God does not change. There is no such thing as time with him; there is no past with him. If you say, "he loves me now," you have in fact said, "he loved me yesterday, and he will love me for ever." There is nothing but now with God. There is no such thing as past or future; and to dispute about eternal election and so on, is all of no avail; because, if God did choose his people at all—and we all admit that he chooses them now—I do not care about whether you say he did so ten thousand, thousand years ago, because there is no such thing as the past with God; with him it is all now. He sees things, past and future, as present in his eye. Only tell me that he loves me now; that word "now," in God's dictionary, means everlasting. Tell me that God has now pardoned my sins; it means, that he always has, for his acts are eternal acts. Oh how sweet to know an everlasting covenant! I would not barter my gospel for fifty thousand other gospels. I love a certain salvation; and when I first heard it preached, that if I believed, God's grace would keep me all my life long, and would never let me fall into hell, but that I should preserve my character unblemished, and walk among my fellow-creatures pure and holy, then said I, "That is the gospel for me; an everlasting gospel." As for that sandy gospel, which bets you fall away and then come back again, it is the wickedest falsehood on earth. If I believed it, I would preach the gospel and be holy on the Sunday, and fall away on the Monday, and be a Christian again on the Tuesday; and I should say, "I have fallen from grace and have got up again." But now, as a true Calvinistic Christian, I desire to have in myself, and see in others, a life of constant consistency; nor can I think it possible to fall away, and then return, after the many passages which assert the impossibility of such a thing. That is the greatest safeguard on earth—that I have something within me that never can be quenched; that I put on the regimentals of a service which I never must leave, which I cannot leave without having proved that I never was enlisted at all. Oh! that keeps me near my God. But once make me doubt that, and you will see me the vilest character living under the sun. Take from me the everlastingness of the gospel, and you have taken all. Dear old Watts Wilkinson once said to Joseph Irons, when he said, "I love you to preach the covenant everlasting nature of God's love,"—"Ah!" said the old saint, "What is there else in the gospel if you do not preach it?" Brother, what is there else? If we do not preach an everlasting gospel, the gospel is not worth twopence. You may get anything uncertain anywhere else; it is in the Bible alone that we get everlasting things. "I to the end shall endure As sure as the earnest is given; More happy, but not more secure, Are the glorified spirits in heaven."

But notice the next word, for it is a sweet one, and we must not let one portion go, " It is ordered in all things."

"Order is heaven's first law," and God has not a disorderly covenant. It is an orderly one. When he planned it, before the world began, it was in all things ordered well. He so arranged it, that justice should be fully satisfied, and yet mercy should be linked hand-in-hand with it. He so planned it that vengeance should have its utmost jot and tittle, and yet mercy should save the sinner. Jesus Christ came to confirm it, and by his atonement, he ordered it in all things; he paid every drop of his blood; he did not leave one farthing of the ransom-money for his dear people, but he ordered it in all things. And the Holy Spirit, when he sweetly applies it, always applies it in order; he orders it in all things. He makes us sometimes understand this order, but if we do not, be sure of this, that the covenant is a well-ordered covenant. I have heard of a man who bought a piece of land, and when the covenant was being made, he thought he knew more about it than the lawyer; but you know it is said that when a man is his own lawyer he has a fool for his client. In this case the man had a fool for his client; and he drew up the covenant so badly, that in a few years it was discovered to be good for nothing, and he lost his property. But our Father's covenant is drawn up according to the strictest rules of justice; and so is ordered in all things. If hell itself should search it—if it were passed round amongst a conclave of demons, they could not find a single fault with it. There are the technical terms of heaven's court; there is the great seal at the bottom, and there is the signature of Jesus, written in his own blood. So it is "ordered in all things."

That word things is not in the original, and we may read it persons, as well as things. It is ordered in all persons—all the persons whose names are in the covenant; it is ordered for them, and they shall come according to the promise: "All that the Father giveth me shall come to me; and him that cometh to me I will in no wise cast out." O my beloved Christian, stop at this promise a moment, for it is a sweet well of precious water to slake thy thirst and refresh thy weariness. It is "ordered in all things." What dost thou want more than this? Dost thou need constraining grace? It is "ordered in all things." Dost thou require more of the spirit of prayer? It is "ordered in all things." Dost thou desire more faith? It is "ordered in all things." Art thou afraid lest thou shouldst not hold out to the end? It is "ordered in all things." There is converting grace in it; pardoning grace in it; justifying grace, sanctifying grace, and persevering grace; for it is "ordered in all things, and sure." Nothing is left out; so that whene'er we come, we find all things there stored up in heavenly order.

Galen, the celebrated physician, says of the human body, that its bones are so well put together, all the parts being so beautifully ordered, that we could not change one portion of it without spoiling its harmony and beauty; and if we should attempt to draw a model man, we could not, with all our ingenuity, fashion a being more wondrous in workmanship than man as he is. It is so with regard to the covenant. If we might alter it, we could not change it for the better; all its portions are beautifully agreed. I always feel when I am preaching the gospel covenant that I am secure. If I preach any other gospel, I am vulnerable, I am open to attack; but standing upon the firm ground of God's covenant, I feel I am in a tower of strength, and so long as I hold all the truths, I am not afraid that even the devils of hell can storm my castle. So secure is the man who believes the everlasting gospel; no logic can stand against it. Only let our preachers give the everlasting gospel to the people, and they will drink it as the ox drinketh water. You will find they love God's truth. But so long as God's gospel is smothered, and the candle is put under a bushel, we cannot expect men's souls will be brought to love it. I pray God that the candle may burn the bushel up, and that the light may be manifest.

But now, to wind up our description of this covenant, it is sure. If I were a rich man, there would be but one thing I should want to make my riches all I desire, and that would be, to have them sure, for riches make to themselves wings, and fly away. Health is a great blessing, and we want but to write one word on it to make it the greatest blessing, that is the adjective "sure." We have relatives, and we love them; ah! if we could but write "sure" on them, what a blessed thing it would be. We cannot call anything "sure" on earth; the only place where we can write that word is on the covenant, which is "ordered in all things and sure." Now there is some poor brother come here this morning who has lost his covenant, as he thinks. Ah! brother, you once had peaceful hours and sweet enjoyment in the presence of God; but now you are in gloom and doubt; you have lost your roll. Well, let me tell you, though you have lost your roll, the covenant is not lost, for all that. You never had the covenant in your hands yet; you only had a copy of it, You thought you read your title clear, but you never read the title-deeds themselves; you only held a copy of the lease and you have lost it. The covenant itself; where is it? It is under the throne of God; it is in the archives of heaven, in the ark of the covenant; it is in Jesus's breast, it is on his hands, on his heart—it is there. Oh! if God were to put my salvation in my hands, I should be lost in ten minutes; but my salvation is not there—it is in Christ's hands. You have read of the celebrated dream of John Newton, which I will tell you to the best of my recollection. He thought he was out at sea, on board a vessel, when some bright angel flew down and presented him with a ring, saying, "As long as you wear this ring you shall be happy, and your soul shall be safe." He put the ring on his finger, and he felt happy to have it in his own possession. Then there came a spirit from the vasty deep, and said to him; "That ring is nought but folly;" and by cajolery and flattery the spirit at last persuaded him to slip the ring from off his finger, and he dropped it in the sea. Then there came fierce things from the deep; the mountains bellowed, and hurled upward their volcanic lava: all the earth was on fire, and his soul in the greatest trouble. By-and-bye a spirit came, and diving below, fetched up the ring, and showing it to him, said, "Now thou art safe, for I have saved the ring." Now might John Newton have said, "Let me put it on my finger again." "No, no; you cannot take care of it yourself;" and up the angel flew, carrying the ring away with him, so that then he felt himself secure, since no cajolery of hell could get it from him again, for it was up in heaven. My life is "hid with Christ in God." If I had my spiritual life in my own possession, I should be a suicide very soon; but it is not with me; and as I cannot save myself, as a Christian I cannot destroy myself, for my life is wrapped up in the covenant: it is with Christ in heaven. Oh, glorious and precious covenant!

III. Now to close our meditation. The Psalmist had a satisfaction in his heart. "This is," he said, all my salvation, and all my desire." I should ill like the task of riding till I found a satisfied worldly man. I suspect there is not a horse that would not be worn off its legs before I found him; I think I should myself grow grey with age before I had discovered the happy individual, except I went to one place—that is, the heart of a man who has a covenant made with him, "ordered in all things, and sure." Go to the palace, but there is not satisfaction there; go to the cottage, though the poet talks about sweet retirement and blest contentment, there is not satisfaction there. The only solid satisfaction—satisfying the mouth with good things—is to be found in the true believer, who is satisfied from himself, satisfied with the covenant, Behold David: he says, "As for my salvation, I am secure; as for my desire, I am gratified: for this is all my salvation, and all my desire." He is satisfied with his salvation. Bring up the moralist. He has been toiling and working in order to earn salvation. Are you confident that if you died you would enter into heaven? "Well, I have been as good as other people, and, I dare say, I shall be more religious before I die;" but he cannot answer our question. Bring up the religious man—I mean the merely outwardly religious man. Are you sure that if you were to die you would go to heaven? "Well, I regularly attend church or chapel, I cannot say that I make any pretensions to be able to say, 'He hath made with me an everlasting covenant.'" Very well, you must go. So I might introduce a score of men, and there is not one of them who can say, "This is all my salvation." They always want a little supplement, and most of you intend making that supplement a little while before you die. An old Jewish Rabbi says, that every man ought to repent at least one day before his last day; and as we do not know when our last day shall be, we ought to repent to-day. How many wish they knew when they were going to die, for then they fancy they would be sure to repent, and be converted a little while before. Why, if you had it revealed to you, that you would die at twenty minutes past twelve next Sunday, you would go on in sin up till twelve o'clock, and then you would say, "There are twenty minutes more—time enough yet;" and so until the twenty minutes past had come, when your soul would sink into eternal flames. Such is procrastination. It is the thief of time; it steals away our life; and did we know the hour of our dissolution, we should be no more prepared for it than we are now. You cannot say, can you, that you have all your salvation? But a Christian can. He can walk through the cholera and the pestilence, and feel that should the arrow smite him, death would be to him the entrance of life; he can lie down and grieve but little at the approach of dissolution, for he has all his salvation; his jewels are in his breast, gems which shall shine in heaven.

Then, the Psalmist says, he has all his desire. There is nought that can fill the heart of man except the Trinity.

God has made man's heart a triangle. Men have been for centuries trying to make the globe fill the triangle, but they cannot do it: it is the Trinity alone that can fill a triangle, as old Quarles well says. There is no way of getting satisfaction but by gaining Christ, getting heaven, winning glory, getting the covenant, for the word covenant comprises all the other things. "All my desire,"—says the Psalmist. "I nothing want on earth, above, Happy in my Saviour's love." I have not a desire; I have nothing to do but to live and be happy all my life in the company of Christ, and then to ascend to heaven, to be in his immediate presence, where "Millions of years these wondering eyes Shall o'er my Saviour's beauties rove, And endless ages I'll adore The wonders of his love."

Just one word with my friends who do not agree with me in doctrine. I am sure, my dear friends, that I wish not to anathematize any of those whose creed is the reverse of mine; only they must allow me to differ from them and to speak freely; and if they do not allow me they know very well that I shall. But I have this much to say to those dear friends who cannot bear the thought of an everlasting covenant. Now, you cannot alter it, can you? If you do not like it, there it is. "God hath made with me an everlasting covenant." And you must confess, when you read the Bible, that there are some very knotty passages for you. You might, perhaps, remove them out of your Bible; but then you cannot erase them out of divine verities. You know it is true, that God is immutable, do you not? He never changes—you must know that, for the Bible says so. It declares that when he has begun a good work, he will carry it through. Do not get reading frothy commentators any longer; take the Bible as it stands, and if you do not see everlasting love there, there is some fault in your eyes, and it is a case rather for the Ophthalmic hospital, than for me. If you cannot see everlasting, eternal security, blood-bought righteousness, there, I am hopeless altogether of your conversion to the truth, while you read it with your present prejudices. It has been my privilege to give more prominence in the religious world to those old doctrines of the gospel. I have delighted in the musty old folios which many of my brethren have kept bound in sheepskins and goatskins, on their library shelves. As for new books, I leave them to others. Oh! if we might but go back to those days when the best of men were our pastors—the days of the Puritans. Oh! for a puritanical gospel again; then we should not have the sleepy hearers, the empty chapels, the drowsy preachers, the velvet-mouthed men who cannot speak the truth; but we should have "Glory to God in the highest, on earth peace, and good-will towards men." Do go home and search. I have told you what I believe to be true; if it is not true, detect the error by reading your Bibles for yourselves, and searching out the matter. As for you, ye ungodly, who hitherto have had neither portion nor lot in this matter, recollect that God's Word speaks to you as well as to the Christian, and says," Turn ye, turn ye; why will ye die, O house of Israel?" graciously promising that whosoever cometh to Christ he will in no wise cast out. It is a free gospel, free as the air, and he who has but life to breathe it may breathe it; so that every poor soul here, who is quickened, and has a sense of his guilt, may come to Christ. "Let not conscience make you linger, Nor of fitness fondly dream." All the evidence you require is to feel your need of Christ; and recollect, if you only once come, if you do but believe, you will be safe through all eternity; and amidst the wreck of matter, the crash of worlds, the conflagration of the universe, and the destruction of all terrestrial things, your soul must still be eternally secure in the covenant of God's free grace. God enable you now to become his adopted children by faith in Jesus.

Declension from First Love

A Sermon (No. 217) Delivered on
Sabbath Evening, September 26, 1858,
by the REV. C. H. SPURGEON
At New Park Street Chapel, Southwark.

"Nevertheless I have somewhat against thee, because thou hast left thy first love."
—Revelation 2:4.

It is a great thing to have as much said in our commendation as was said concerning the church at Ephesus. Just read what "Jesus Christ, who is the faithful witness," said of them—"I know thy works, and thy labour, and thy patience, and how thou canst not bear them which are evil: and thou hast tried them which say they are apostles, and are not, and hast found them liars: and hast borne, and hast patience, and for my name's sake hast laboured, and hast not fainted." Oh, my dear brothers and sisters, we may feel devoutly thankful if we can humbly, but honestly say, that this commendation applies to us. Happy the man whose works are known and accepted of Christ. He is no idle Christian, he has practical godliness; he seeks by works of piety to obey God's whole law, by works of charity to manifest his love to the brotherhood, and by works of devotion to show his attachment to the cause of his Master. "I know thy works." Alas! some of you cannot get so far as that. Jesus Christ himself can bear no witness to your works, for you have not done any. You are Christians by profession, but you are not Christians as to your practice. I say again, happy is that man to whom Christ can say, "I know thy works." It is a commendation worth a world to have as much as that said of us. But further, Christ said, "and thy labour." This is more still. Many Christians have works, but only few Christians have labour. There were many preachers in Whitfield's day that had works, but Whitfield had labour. He toiled and travailed for souls. He was "in labours more abundant." Many were they in the apostle's days who did works for Christ; but pre-eminently the apostle Paul did labour for souls. It is not work merely, it is anxious work; it is casting forth the whole strength, and exercising all the energies for Christ. Could the Lord Jesus say as much as that of you—"I know thy labour?" No. He might say, "I know thy loitering; I know thy laziness; I know thy shirking of the work; I know thy boasting of what little thou dost; I know thine ambition to be thought something of, when thou art nothing." But ah! friends, it is more than most of us dare to hope that Christ could say, "I know thy labour."

But further, Christ says, "I know thy patience." Now there be some that labour, and they do it well. But what does hinder them? They only labour for a little season, and then they cease to work and begin to faint. But this church had laboured on for many years; it had thrown out all its energies—not in some spasmodic effort, but in a continual strain and unabated zeal for the glory of God. "I know thy patience." I say again, beloved, I tremble to think how few out of this congregation could win such praise as this. "I know thy works, and thy labour, and thy patience, and how thou canst not bear them which are evil." The thorough hatred which the church had of evil doctrine, of evil practice, and its corresponding intense love for pure truth and pure practice—in that I trust some of us can bear a part. "And thou hast tried them which say they are apostles, and are not, and hast found them liars." Here, too, I think some of us may hope to be clear. I know the difference between truth and error. Arminianism will never go down with us; the doctrine of men will not suit our taste.

The husks, the bran, and the chaff, are not things that we can feed upon. And when we listen to those who preach another gospel, a holy anger burns within us, for we love the truth as it is in Jesus; and nothing but that will satisfy us. "And hast borne, and hast patience, and for my name's sake hast laboured, and hast not fainted." They had borne persecutions, difficulties, hardships, embarrassments, and discouragements, yet had they never flagged, but always continued faithful. Who among us here present could lay claim to so much praise as this? What Sunday-school teacher have I here who could say, "I have laboured, and I have borne, and have had patience, and have not fainted." Ah, dear friends, if you can say it, it is more than I can. Often have I been ready to faint in the Master's work; and though I trust I have not been tired of it, yet there has sometimes been a longing to get from the work to the reward, and to go from the service of God, before I had fulfilled, as a hireling, my day. I am afraid we have not enough of patience, enough of labour, and enough of good works, to get even as much as this said of us. But it is in our text, I fear the mass of us must find our character. "Nevertheless I have somewhat against thee, because thou hast left thy first love." There may be a preacher here present. Did you ever hear of a minister who had to preach his own funeral sermon? What a labour that must have been, to feel that he had been condemned to die, and must preach against himself, and condemn himself! I stand here to-night, not in that capacity, but in one somewhat similar. I feel that I who preach shall this night condemn myself; and my prayer before I entered this pulpit was, that I might fearlessly discharge my duty, that I might deal honestly with my own heart, and that I might preach, knowing myself to be the chief culprit, and you each in your measure to have offended in this respect, even though none of you so grievously as I have done. I pray that God the Holy Spirit, through his renewings, may apply the word, not merely to your hearts, but to mine, that I may return to my first love, and that you may return with me.

In the first place, what was our first love? Secondly, how did we lose it? And thirdly, let me exhort you to get it again.

I. First, WHAT WAS OUR FIRST LOVE? Oh, let us go back—it is not many years with some of us. We are but youngsters in God's ways, and it is not so long with any of you that you will have very great difficulty in reckoning it. Then if you are Christians, those days were so happy that your memory will never forget them, and therefore you can easily return to that first bright spot in your history. Oh, what love was that which I had to my Saviour the first time he forgave my sins. I remember it. You remember each for yourselves, I dare say, that happy hour when the Lord appeared to us, bleeding on his cross, when he seemed to say, and did say in our hearts, "I am thy salvation; I have blotted out like a cloud thine iniquities, and like a thick cloud thy sins."

Oh, how I loved him! Passing all loves except his own was that love which I felt for him then. If beside the door of the place in which I met with him there had been a stake of blazing faggots, I would have stood upon them without chains; glad to give my flesh, and blood, and bones, to be ashes that should testify my love to him. Had he asked me then to give all my substance to the poor, I would have given all and thought myself to be amazingly rich in having beggared myself for his name's sake. Had he commanded me then to preach in the midst of all his foes, I could have said:—"There's not a lamb amongst thy flock I would disdain to feed, There's not a foe before whose face

I'd fear thy cause to plead." I could realize then the language of Rutherford, when he said, being full of love to Christ, once upon a time, in the dungeon of Aberdeen—"Oh, my Lord, if there were a broad hell betwixt me and thee, if I could not get at thee except by wading through it, I would not think twice but I would plunge through it all, if I might embrace thee and call thee mine."

Now it is that first love that you and I must confess I am afraid we have in a measure lost. Let us just see whether we have it. When we first loved the Saviour how earnest we were; there was not a single thing in the Bible, that we did not think most precious; there was not one command of his that we did not think to be like fine gold and choice silver. Never were the doors of his house open without our being there. if there were a prayer meeting at any hour in the day we were there. Some said of us that we had no patience, we would do too much and expose our bodies too frequently—but we never thought of that "Do yourself no harm," was spoken in our ears; but we would have done anything then. Why there are some of you who cannot walk to the Music Hall on a morning, it is too far. When you first joined the church, you would have walked twice as far. There are some of you who cannot be at the prayer meeting—business will not permit; yet when you were first baptized, there was never a prayer meeting from which you were absent. It is the loss of your first love that makes you seek the comfort of your bodies instead of the prosperity of your souls. Many have been the young Christians who have joined this church, and old ones too, and I have said to them, "Well, have you got a ticket for a seat?" "No, sir." "Well, what will you do? Have you got a preference ticket?" "No, I cannot get one; but I do not mind standing in the crowd an hour, or two hours. I will come at five o'clock so that I can get in. Sometimes I don't get in, sir; but even then I feel that I have done what I ought to do in attempting to get in." "Well," but I have said, "you live five miles off, and there is coming and going back twice a day—you cannot do it." "Oh, sir," they have said "I can do it; I feel so much the blessedness of the Sabbath and so much enjoyment of the presence of the Saviour." I have smiled at them; I could understand it, but I have not felt it necessary to caution them—and now their love is cool enough. That first love does not last half so long as we could wish. Some of you stand convicted even here; you have not that blazing love, that burning love, that ridiculous love as the worldling would call it, which is after all the love to be most coveted and desired. No, you have lost your first love in that respect. Again, how obedient you used to be. If you saw a commandment, that was enough for you—you did it. But now you see a commandment, and you see profit on the other side; and how often do you dally with the profit and choose the temptation, instead of yielding an unsullied obedience to Christ.

Again, how happy you used to be in the ways of God. Your love was of that happy character that you could sing all day long; but now your religion has lost its lustre, the gold has become dim; you know that when you come to the Sacramental table, you often come there without enjoying it. There was a time when every bitter thing was sweet; whenever you heard the Word, it was all precious to you. Now you can grumble at the minister. Alas! the minister has many faults, but the question is, whether there has not been a greater charge in you than there has been in him. Many are there who say, "I do not hear Mr. So-and-so as I used to,"—when the fault lies in their own ears. Oh, brethren, when we live near to Christ, and are in our first love, it is amazing what a little it takes to make a good preacher to us. Why, I confess I have heard a poor illiterate Primitive Methodist preach the gospel, and I felt as if I could jump for joy all the while I was listening to him, and yet he never gave me a new thought or a pretty expression, nor one figure that I could remember, but he talked about Christ; and even his common things were to my hungry spirit like dainty meats. And I have to acknowledge, and, perhaps, you have to acknowledge the same—that I have heard sermons from which I ought to have profited, but I have been thinking on the man's style, or some little mistakes in grammar. When I might have been holding fellowships with Christ in and through the ministry, I have, instead thereof, been getting abroad in my thoughts even to the ends of the earth. And what is the reason for this, but that I have lost my first love.

Again: when we were in our first love, what would we do for Christ; now how little will we do. Some of the actions which we performed when we were young Christians, but just converted, when we look back upon them, seem to have been wild and like idle tales. You remember when you were a lad and first came to Christ, you had a half-sovereign in your pocket; it was the only one you had, and you met with some poor saint and gave it all away. You did not regret that you had done it, your only regret was that you had not a great deal more, for you would have given all. You recollected that something was wanted for the cause of Christ. Oh! we could give anything away when we first loved the Saviour. If there was a preaching to be held five miles off, and we could walk with the lay-preacher to be a little comfort to him in the darkness, we were off. If there was a Sunday-school, however early it might be, we would be up, so that we might be present. Unheard-of feats, things that we now look back upon with surprise, we could perform them. Why cannot we do them now? Do you know there are some people who always live upon what they have been. I speak very plainly now. There is a brother in this church who may take it to himself; I hope he will. It is not very many years ago since he said to me, when I asked him why he did not do something—"Well, I have done my share; I used to do this, and I have done the other; I have done so-and-so." Oh, may the Lord deliver him, and all of us, from living on "has beens!" It will never do to say we have done a thing. Suppose, for a solitary moment, the world should say, "I have turned round; I will stand still." Let the sea say, "I have been ebbing and flowing, lo! these many years; I will ebb and flow no more." Let the sun say, "I have been shining, and I have been rising and setting so many days; I have done this enough to earn me a goodly name; I will stand still;" and let the moon wrap herself up in veils of darkness, and say, "I have illuminated many a night, and I have lighted many a weary traveller across the moors; I will shut up my lamp and be dark forever." Brethren, when you and I cease to labour, let us cease to live. God has no intention to let us live a useless life. But mark this; when we leave our first works, there is no question about having lost our first love; that is sure. If there be strength remaining, if there be still power mentally and physically, if we cease from our office, if we abstain from our labours, there is no solution of this question which an honest conscience will accept, except this, "Thou hast lost thy first love, and, therefore, thou hast neglected thy first works." Ah! we were all so very ready to make excuses for ourselves. Many a preacher has retired from the ministry, long before he had any need to do so.

He has married a rich wife. Somebody has left him a little money, and he can do without it. He was growing weak in the ways of God, or else he would have said, "My body with my charge lay down, And cease at once to work and live." And let any man here present who was a Sunday-school teacher and who has left it, who was a tract distributor and who has given it up, who was active in the way of God but is now idle, stand to-night before the bar of his conscience, and say whether he be not guilty of this charge which I bring against him, that he has lost his first love.

I need not stop to say also, that this may be detected in the closet as well as in our daily life; for when first love is lost, there is a want of that prayerfulness which we have. I remember the day I was up at three o'clock in the morning. Till six, I spent in prayer, wrestling with God. Then I had to walk some eight miles, and started off and walked to the baptism. Why, prayer was a delight to me then. My duties at that time kept me occupied pretty well from five o'clock in the morning till ten at night, and I had not a moment for retirement, yet I would be up at four o'clock to pray; and though I feel very sleepy now-a-days, and I feel that I could not be up to pray, it was not so then, when I was in my first love. Somehow or other, I never lacked time then. If I did not get it early in the morning, I got it late at night. I was compelled to have time for prayer with God; and what prayer it was! I had no need then to groan because I could not pray; for love, being fervent, I had sweet liberty at the throne of grace. But when first love departs, we begin to think that ten minutes will do for prayer, instead of an hour, and we read a verse or two in the morning, whereas we used to read a portion, but never used to go into the world without getting some marrow and fatness. Now, business has so increased, that we must get into bed as soon as we can; we have not time to pray. And then at dinner time, we used to have a little time for communion; that is dropped. And then on the Sabbath-day, we used to make it a custom to pray to God when we got home from his house, for just five minutes before dinner, so that what we heard we might profit by; that is dropped. And some of you that are present were in the habit of retiring for prayer when you went home; your wives have told that story; the messengers have heard it when they have called at your houses, when they have asked the wife—"What is your husband?" "Ah!" she has said, "he is a godly man; he cannot come home to his breakfast but he must slip upstairs alone. I know what he is doing—he is praying.

Then when he is at table, he often says—"Mary, I have had a difficulty to-day, we must go and have a word or two of prayer together." And some of you could not take a walk without prayer, you were so fond of it you could not have too much of it. Now where is it? You know more than you did; you have grown older; you have grown richer, perhaps. You have grown wiser in some respects; but you might give up all you have got, to go back to "Those peaceful hours you once enjoyed, How sweet their memory still!" Oh, what would you give if you could fill "That aching void, The world can never fill," but which only the same love that you had at first, can ever fully satisfy!

II. And now, beloved, WHERE DID YOU AND I LOSE OUR FIRST LOVE, if we have lost it? Let each one speak for himself, or rather, let me speak for each.

Have you not lost your first love in the world some of you? You used to have that little shop once, you had not very much business; well, you had enough, and a little to spare. However, there was a good turn came in business; you took two shops, and you are getting on very well. Is it not marvellous, that when you grew richer and had more business, you began to have less grace?

Oh, friends, it is a very serious thing to grow rich? Of all the temptations to which God's children are exposed it is the worst, because it is one that they do not dread, and therefore it is the more subtle temptation. You know a traveller if he is going a journey, takes a staff with him, it is a help to him; but suppose he is covetous, and says, "I will have a hundred of these sticks," that will be no help to him at all; he has only got a load to carry, and it stops his progress instead of assisting him. But I do believe there are many Christians that lived near to God, when they were living on a pound a week, that might give up their yearly incomes with the greatest joy, if they could have now the same contentment, the same peace of mind, the same nearness of access to God, that they had in times of poverty. Ah, too much of the world is a bad thing for any man! I question very much whether a man ought not sometimes to stop, and say, "There is an opportunity of doing more trade, but it will require the whole of my time, and I must give up that hour I have set apart for prayer; I will not do the trade at all; I have enough, and therefore let it go. I would rather do trade with heaven than trade with earth."Again: do you not think also that perhaps you may have lost your first love by getting too much with worldly people? When you were in your first love, no company suited you but the godly; but now you have got a young man that you talk with, who talks a great deal more about frivolity, and gives you a great deal more of the froth and scum of levity, than he ever gives you of solid godliness. Once you were surrounded by those that fear the Lord, but now you dwell in the tents of "Freedom," where you hear little but cursing. But, friends, he that carrieth coals in his bosom must be burned; and the that hath ill companions cannot but be injured.

Seek, then, to have godly friends, that thou mayest maintain thy first love.

But another reason. Do you not think that perhaps

you have forgotten how much you owe to Christ? There is one thing, that I feel from experience I am compelled to do very often, viz., to go back to where I first started:—"I, the chief of sinners am, But Jesus died for me." You and I get talking about our being saints; we know our election, we rejoice in our calling, we go on to sanctification; and we forget the hole of the pit whence we were digged. Ah, remember my brother, thou art nothing now but a sinner saved through grace; remember what thou wouldst have been, if the Lord had left thee. And surely, then, by going back continually to first principles, and to the great foundation stone, the cross of Christ, thou wilt be led to go back to thy first love.

Dost thou not think, again, that thou hast lost thy first love by neglecting communion with Christ? Now preacher, preach honestly, and preach at thyself. Has there not been, sometimes, this temptation to do a great deal for Christ, but not to live a great deal with Christ? One of my besetting sins, I feel, is this. If there is anything to be done actively for Christ, I instinctively prefer the active exercise to the passive quiet of his presence. There are some of you, perhaps, that are attending a Sunday school, who would be more profitably employed to your own souls if you were spending that hour in communion with Christ. Perhaps, too, you attend the means so often, that you have no time in secret to improve what you gain in the means. Mrs. Bury once said, that if "all the twelve apostles were preaching in a certain town, and we could have the privilege of hearing them preach, yet if they kept us out of our closets, and led us to neglect prayer, better for us never to have heard their names, than to have gone to listen to them." We shall never love Christ much except we live near to him. Love to Christ is dependent on our nearness to him. It is just like the planets and the sun. Why are some of the planets cold? Why do they move at so slow a rate? Simply because they are so far from the sun: put them where the planet Mercury is, and they will be in a boiling heat, and spin round the sun in rapid orbits. So, beloved, if we live near to Christ, we cannot help loving him: the heart that is near Jesus must be full of his love. But when we live days and weeks and months without personal intercourse, without real fellowship, how can we maintain love towards a stranger? He must be a friend, and we must stick close to him, as he sticks close to us—closer than a brother; or else, we shall never have our first love.

There are a thousand reasons that I might have given, but I leave each of you to search your hearts, to find out why you have lost, each of you, your first love.

III. Now, dear friends, just give me all your attention for a moment, while I earnestly beseech and implore of you to SEEK TO GET YOUR FIRST LOVE RESTORED. Shall I tell you why? Brother, though thou be a child of God, if thou hast lost thy first love, there is some trouble near at hand. "Whom the Lord loveth, he chasteneth," and he is sure to chasten thee when thou sinnest. It is calm with you to night, is it? Oh! but dread that calm, there is a tempest lowering. Sin is the harbinger of tempest: read the history of David. All David's life, in all his troubles, even in the rocks of the wild goats, and in the caves of Engedi, he was the happiest of men till he lost his first love; and from the day when his lustful eye was fixed upon Bathsheba, even to the last, he went with broken bones sorrowing to his grave. It was one long string of afflictions: take heed it be not so with thee. "Ah, but," you say, "I shall not sin as David did." Brother, you cannot tell: if you have lost your first love, what should hinder you but that you should lose your first purity? Love and purity go together.

He that loveth is pure; he that loveth little shall find his purity decrease, until it becomes marred and polluted. I should not like to see you, my dear friends, tried and troubled: I do weep with them that weep. If there be a child of yours sick, and I hear of it, I can say honestly, I do feel something like a father to your children, and as a father to you. If you have sufferings and afflictions, and I know them, I desire to feel for you, and spread your griefs before the throne of God. Oh, I do not want my heavenly Father to take the rod out to you all; but he will do it, if you fall from your first love. As sure as ever he is a Father, he will let you have the rod if your love cools. Bastards may escape the rod. If you are only base-born professors you may go happily along; but the true-born child of God, when his love declines, must and shall smart for it.

There is yet another thing, my dear friends, if we lose our first love—what will the world say of us if we lose our first love? I must put this, not for our name's sale, but for God's dear name's sake. O what will the world say of us? There was a time, and it is not gone yet, when men must point at this church, and say of it, "There is a church, that is like a bright oasis in the midst of a desert, a spot of light in the midst of darkness." Our prayer meetings were prayer meetings indeed, the congregations were as attentive as they were numerous. Oh, how you did drink in the words; how your eyes flashed with a living fire, whenever the name of Christ was mentioned! And what, if in a little time it shall be said, "Ah, that church is quite as sleepy as any other; look at them when the minister preaches, why they can sleep under him, they do not seem to care for the truth. Look at the Spurgeonites, they are just as cold and careless as others; they used to be called the most pugnacious people in the world, for they were always ready to defend their Master's name and their Master's truth, and they got that name in consequence, but now you may swear in their presence and they will not rebuke you: how near these people once used to live to God and his house, they were always there; look at their prayer meetings, they would fill their seats as full at a prayer meeting as at an ordinary service; now they are all gone back." "Ah," says the world, "just what I said; the fact is, it was a mere spasm, a little spiritual excitement, and it has all gone down." And the worldling says, "Ah, ah, so would I have it, so would I have it!" I was reading only the other day of an account of my ceasing to be popular; it was said my chapel was now nearly empty, that nobody went to it: and I was exceedingly amused and interested. "Well, if it come to that," I said, "I shall not grieve or cry very much; but if it is said the church has left its zeal and first love, that is enough to break any honest pastor's heart." Let the chaff go, but if the wheat remain we have comfort. Let those who are the outer-court worshippers cease to hear, what signifieth? let them turn aside, but O, ye soldiers of the Cross, if ye turn your backs in the day of battle, where shall I hide my head? what shall I say for the great name of my Master, or for the honour of his gospel? It is our boast and joy, that the old-fashioned doctrine has been revived in these days, and that the truth that Calvin preached, that Paul preached, and that Jesus preached, is still mighty to save, and far surpasses in power all the neologies and new-fangled notions of the present time.

But what will the heretic say, when he sees it is all over? "Ah," he will say, "that old truth urged on by the fanaticism of a foolish young man, did wake the people a little; but it lacked marrow and strength, and it all died away!" Will ye thus dishonour your Lord and Master, ye children of the heavenly king? I beseech you do not so—but endeavour to receive again as a rich gift of the Spirit your first love.

And now, once again, dear friends, there is a thought that ought to make each of us feel alarmed, if we have lost our first love. May not this question arise in our hearts—Was I ever a child of God at all? Oh, my God, must I ask myself this question? Yes, I will. Are there not many of whom it is said, they went out from us because they were not of us; for if they had been of us, doubtless they would have continued with us? Are there not some whose goodness is as the morning cloud and as the early dew—may that not have been my case? I am speaking for you all. Put the question—may I not have been impressed under a certain sermon, and may not that impression have been a mere carnal excitement? May it not have been that I thought I repented but did not really repent? May it not have been the case, that I got a hope somewhere but had not a right to it?

And I never had the loving faith that unites me to the Lamb of God. And may it not have been that I only thought I had love to Christ, and never had it, for if I really had love to Christ should I be as I now am? See how far I have come down! may I not keep on going down until my end shall be perdition, and the never-dying worm, and the fire unquenchable? Many have gone from heights of a profession to the depths of damnation, and may not I be the same? May it not be true of me that I am as a wandering star for whom is reserved blackness of darkness for ever? May I not have shone brightly in the midst of the church for a little while, and yet may I not be one of those poor foolish virgins who took no oil in my vessel with my lamp, and therefore my lamp will go out? Let me think, if I go on as I am, it is impossible for me to stop, if I am going downwards I may go on going downwards. And O my God, if I go on backsliding for another year—who knows where I may have backslidden to? Perhaps into some gross sin. Prevent, prevent it by thy grace!

Perhaps I may backslide totally. If I am a child of God I know I cannot do that. But still, may it not happen that I only thought I was a child of God, and may I not so far go back that at last my very name to live shall go because I always have been dead? Oh! how dreadful it is to think and to see in our church, members who turn out to be dead members! If I could weep tears of blood, they would not express the emotion that I ought to feel, and that you ought to feel, when you think there are some among us that are dead branches of a living vine. Our deacons find that there is much of unsoundness in our members. I grieve to think that because we cannot see all our members, there are many who have backslidden. There is one who says, "I joined the church, it is true, but I never was converted. I made a profession of being converted, but I was not, and now I take no delight in the things of God. I am moral, I attend the house of prayer, but I am not converted. My name may be taken off the books; I am not a godly man." There are others among you who perhaps have gone even further than that—have gone into sin, and yet I may not know it. It may not come to my ears in so large a church as this. Oh! I beseech you, my dear friends, by him that liveth and was dead, let not your good be evil spoken of, by losing your first love.

Are there some among you that are professing religion, and not possessing it? Oh, give up your profession, or else get the truth and sell it not. Go home, each of you, and cast yourselves on your faces before God, and ask him to search you, and try you, and know your ways, and see if there be any evil way in you, and pray that he may lead you in the way everlasting. And if hitherto you have only professed, but have not possessed, seek ye the Lord while he may be found, and call ye upon him while he is near. Ye are warned, each one of you; you are solemnly told to search yourselves and make short work of it. And if any of you be hypocrites, at God's great day, guilty as I may be in many respects, there is one thing I am clear of—I have not shunned to declare the whole counsel of God. I do not believe that any people in the world shall be damned more terribly than you shall if you perish; for of this thing I have not shunned to speak—the great evil of making a profession without being sound at heart. No, I have even gone so near to personality, that I could not have gone further without mentioning your names. And rest assured, God's grace being with me, neither you nor myself shall be spared in the pulpit in any personal sin that I may observe in any one of you. But oh, do let us be sincere! May the Lord sooner split this church till only a tenth of you remain, than ever suffer you to be multiplied a hundred-fold unless you be multiplied with the living in Zion, and with the holy flock that the Lord himself hath ordained, and will keep unto the end. To-morrow morning, we shall meet together and pray, that we may have our first love restored; and I hope many of you will be found there to seek again the love which you have almost lost.

And as for you that never had that love at all, the Lord breathe it upon you now for the love of Jesus. Amen.

Elijah's Appeal to the Undecided

A Sermon (No. 134) Delivered on Sabbath Morning, May 31, 1857, by the REV. C. H. SPURGEON at the Music Hall, Royal Surrey Gardens.

"How long halt ye between two opinions? If the Lord be God, follow him; if Baal, then follow him."
—1 Kings 18:21.

It was a day to be remembered, when the multitudes of Israel were assembled at the foot of Carmel and when the solitary prophet of the Lord came forth to defy the four hundred and fifty priests of the false god. We might look upon that scene with the eye of historical curiosity, and we should find it rich with interest. Instead of doing so, however, we shall look upon it with the eye of attentive consideration, and see whether we can not improve by its teachings. We have upon that hill of Carmel, and along the plain, three kinds of persons. We have first the devoted servant of Jehovah, a solitary prophet; we have, on the other hand, the decided servants of the evil one, the four hundred and fifty prophets of Baal; but the vast mass of that day belonged to a third class—they were those who had not fully determined whether fully to worship Jehovah, the God of their fathers, or Baal, the god of Jezebel. On the one hand, their ancient traditions led them to fear Jehovah, and on the other hand, their interest at court led them to bow before Baal. Many of them therefore, were secret and half-hearted followers of Jehovah, while they were the public worshipers of Baal. The whole of them at this juncture were halting between two opinions. Elijah does not address his sermon to the priests of Baal; he will have something to say to them by-and-by, he will preach them horrible sermons in deeds of blood. Nor has he aught to say to those who are the thorough servants of Jehovah, for they are not there; but his discourse is alone directed to those who are halting between two opinions.

Now, we have these three classes here this morning. We have, I hope, a very large number who are on Jehovah's side, who fear God and serve him; we have a number who are on the side of the evil one, who make no profession of religion, and do not observe even the outward symptoms of it; because they are both inwardly and outwardly the servants of the evil one. But the great mass of my hearers belong to the third class—the waverers. Like empty clouds they are driven hither and thither by the wind; like painted beauties, they lack the freshness of life; they have a name to live and are dead. Procrastinators, double-minded men, undecided persons, to you I speak this morning—"How long halt ye between two opinions?" May the question be answered by God's Spirit in your hearts, and may you be led to say, "No longer, Lord, do I halt; but this day I decide for thee, and am thy servant for ever!"

Let us proceed at once to the text. Instead of giving the divisions at the commencement, I will mention them one by one as I proceed.

I. First, you will note that the prophet insisted upon the distinction which existed between the worship Baal and the worship of Jehovah. Most of the people who were before him thought that Jehovah was God, and that Baal was God too; and that for this reason the worship of both was quite consistent. The great mass of them did not reject the God of their fathers wholly, nor did they bow before Baal wholly; but as polytheists, believing in many gods, they thought both Gods might be worshiped, and each of them have a share in their hearts. "No," said the prophet when he began, "this will not do, these are two opinions; you can never make them one, they are two contradictory things which can not be combined. I tell you that instead of combining the two, which is impossible, you are halting between the two, which makes a vast difference." "I will build in my house," said one of them, "an altar for Jehovah here, and an altar for Baal there. I am of one opinion; I believe them both to be God." "No, no," said Elijah, "it can not be so; they are two, and must be two. These things are not one opinion, but two opinions No, you can not unite them." Have I not many here who say, "I am worldly, but I am religious too; I can go to the Music Hall to worship God on Sunday; I went to the Derby races the other day: I go, on the one hand, to the place where I can serve my lusts; I am to be met with in every dancing room of every description, and yet at the same time I say my prayers most devoutly. May I not be a good churchman, or a right good dissenter, and a man of the world too? May I not, after all, hold with the hounds as well as run with the hare? May I not love God and serve the devil too—take the pleasure of each of them, and give my heart to neither? We answer—Not so, they are two opinions; you can not do it, they are distinct and separate. Mark Anthony yoked two lions to his chariot; but there are two lions no man ever yoked together yet—the Lion of the tribe of Judah and the lion of the pit. These can never go together. Two opinions you may hold in politics, perhaps, but then you will be despised by every body, unless you are of one opinion or the other, and act as an independent man. But two opinions in the matter of soul-religion you can not hold.

If God be God, serve him, and do it thoroughly; but if this world be God, serve it, and make no profession of religion. If you are a worldling, and think the things of the world the best, serve them; devote yourself to them, do not be kept back by conscience; spite your conscience, and run into sin. But remember, if the Lord be your God, you can not have Baal too; you must have one thing or else the other. "No man can serve two masters."

If God be served, he will be a master; and if the devil be served he will not be long before he will be a master; and "ye can not serve two masters." O! be wise, and think not that the two can be mingled together. How many a respectable deacon thinks that he can be covetous, and grasping in business, and grind the faces of the poor, and yet be a saint! O! liar to God and to man! He is no saint; he is the very chief of sinners! How many a very excellent woman, who is received into church fellowship among the people of God, and thinks herself one of the elect, is to be found full of wrath and bitterness, a slave of mischief and of sin, a tattler, a slanderer, a busybody; entering into other people's houses, and turning every thing like comfort out of the minds of those with whom she comes in contact—and yet she is the servant of God and of the devil too! Nay, my lady this will never answer; the two never can be served thoroughly. Serve your master, whoever he be. If you do profess to be religious, be so thoroughly; if you make any profession to be a Christian, be one; but if you are no Christian, do not pretend to be. If you love the world, then love it; but cast off the mask, and do not be a hypocrite. The double-minded man is of all men the most despicable; the follower of Janus, who wears two faces, and who can look with one eye upon the (so-called) Christian world with great delight, and give his subscription to the Tract Society, the Bible Society, and the Missionary Society, but who has another eye over there, with which he looks at the Casino, the Coal-hole, and other pleasures, which I do not care to mention, but which some of you may know more of than I wish to know. Such a man, I say, is worse than the most reprobate of men, in the opinion of any one who knows how to judge. Not worse in his open character, but worse really, because he is not honest enough to go through with that he professes. And how many such are there in London, in England; everywhere else! They try to serve both masters; but it can not be; the two things can not be reconciled; God and Mammon, Christ and Belial, these never can meet; there never can be an agreement between them, they never can be brought into unity, and why should you seek to do it? "Two opinions," said the prophet. He would not allow any of his hearers to profess to worship both. "No," said he, "these are two opinions, and you are halting between the two."

II. In the second place, the prophet calls these waverers to an account for the amount of time which they had consumed in making their choice. Some of them might have replied, "We have not had yet an opportunity of judging between God and Baal; we have not yet had time enough to make up our minds;" but the prophet puts away that objection, and he says, "How long halt ye between two opinions? How long? For three years and a half not a drop of rain has fallen at the command of Jehovah; is not that proof enough? Ye have been all this time, three years and a half expecting, till I should come, Jehovah's servant, and give you rain; and yet, though you yourselves are starving, your cattle dead, your fields parched, and your meadows covered with dust, like the very deserts, yet all this time of judgment, and trial and affliction, has not been enough for you to make up your minds. "How long then," said he, "halt ye between two opinions?"

I speak not, this morning, to the thoroughly worldly; with them I have now nothing to do; another time I may address them. But I am now speaking to you who are seeking to serve God and to serve Satan; you who are trying to be Christian worldlings, trying to be members of that extraordinary corporation, called the "religious world," which is a thing that never had an existence except in title. You are endeavoring, if you can, to make up your mind which it shall be; you know you can not serve both, and you are coming now to the period when you are saying, "Which shall it be? Shall I go thoroughly into sin, and revel in the pleasures of the earth, or become a servant of God?" Now, I say to you this morning, as the prophet did, "How long halt ye?" Some of you have been halting until your hair has grown gray; the sixtieth year of some of you is drawing nigh. Is not sixty years long enough to make up your choice? "How long halt ye?" Perhaps one of you may have tottered into this place, leaning on his staff, and you have been undecided up till now. Your eightieth year has come; you have been a religious character outwardly, but a worldling truly; you are still up to this date halting, saying, "I know not on which side to be." How long, sirs, in the name of reason, in the name of mortality, in the name of death, in the name of eternity, "How long halt ye between two opinions?" Ye middle-aged men, ye said when ye were youths, "When we are out of our apprenticeship we will become religious; let us sow our wild oats in our youth, and let us then begin to be diligent servants of the Lord." Lo! ye have come to middle age, and are waiting till that quiet villa shall be built, and ye shall retire from business, and then ye think ye will serve God. Sirs, ye said that same when ye came of age, and when your business began to increase. I therefore solemnly demand of you, "How long halt ye between two opinions?" How much time do you want? O! young man, thou saidst in thine early childhood, when a mother's prayer followed thee, "I will seek God when I come to manhood;" and thou hast passed that day; thou art a man, and more than that, and yet thou art halting still. "How long halt ye between two opinions?" How many of you have been churchgoers and chapel-goers for years! Ye have been impressed, too, many a time, but ye have wiped the tears from your eyes, and have said, "I will seek God and turn to him with full purpose of heart;" and you are now just where you were. How many sermons do you want? How many more Sundays must roll away wasted?

How many warnings, how many sicknesses, how many tollings of the bell to warn you that you must die? How many graves must be dug for your family before you will be impressed? How many plagues and pestilences must ravage this city before you will turn to God in truth? "How long halt ye between two opinions?" Would God ye could answer this question, and not allow the sands of life to drop, drop, drop from the glass saying, "When the next goes I will repent," and yet that next one findeth you impenitent. You say, "When the glass is just so low, I will turn to God." No, sir, no; it will not answer for you to talk so; for thou mayest find thy glass empty before thou thoughtest it had begun to run low, and thou mayest find thyself in eternity when thou didst but think of repenting and turning to God. How long, ye gray heads, how long, ye men of ripe years, how long, ye youths and maidens, how long will ye be in this undecided, unhappy state?

"How long halt ye between two opinions?"

Thus we have brought you so far. We have noted that there are two opinions, and we have asked the question, How long time you want to decide? One would think the question would require very little time, if time were all; if the will were not biassed to evil and contrary to good, it would require no more time than the decision of a man who has to choose a halter or life, wealth or poverty; and if we were wise, it would take no time at all; if we understood the things of God, we should not hesitate, but say at once, "Now God is my God, and that for ever."

III. But the prophet charges these people with the absurdity of their position. Some of them said, "What! prophet, may we not continue to halt between two opinions? We are not desperately irreligious, so we are better than the profane, certainly we are not thoroughly pious; but, at any rate, a little piety is better than none, and the mere profession of it keeps us decent, let us try both!" "Now," says the prophet, "how long halt ye?" or, if you like to read it so, "how long limp ye between two opinions?" (How long wriggle ye between two opinions?

would be a good word, if I might employ it.) He represents them as like a man whose legs are entirely out of joint; he first goes on one side, and then on the other, and can not go far either way. I could not describe it without putting myself into a most ludicrous posture. "How long limp ye between two opinions?" The prophet laughs at them, as it were. And is it not true, that a man who is neither one thing or another is in a most absurd position? Let him go among the worldlings; they laugh under their sleeve, and say, "This is one of the Exeter Hall saints," or, "That is one of the elect." Let him go among the Christian people, those that are saints, and they say, "How a man can be so inconsistent, how he can come into our midst one day, and the next be found in such and such society, we can not tell." Methinks even the devil himself must laugh at such a man in scorn. "There," says he, "I am every thing that is bad; I do sometimes pretend to be an angel of light, and put on that garb; but you do really excel me in every respect, for I do it to get something by it, but you do not get any thing by it. You do not have the pleasures of this world, and you do not have the pleasures of religion either; you have the fears of religion without its hopes; you are afraid to do wrong, and yet you have no hope of heaven; you have the duties of religion without the joys; you have to do just as religious people do, and yet there is no heart in the matter; you have to sit down, and see the table all spread before you, and then you have not power to eat a single morsel of the precious dainties of the gospel." It is just the same with the world; you dare not go into this or that mischief that brings joy to the wicked man's heart; you think of what society would say. We do not know what to make of you. I might describe you, if I might speak as the Americans do but I will not. Ye are half one thing, and half the other. You come into the society of the saints, and try to talk as they talk; but you are like a man who has been taught French in some day-school in England; he makes a queer sort of Frenchified English, and Englishized French, and every one laughs at him. The English laugh at him for trying to do it, and the French laugh at him for failing in it. If you spoke your own language, if you just spoke out as a sinner, if you professed to be what you are, you would at least get the respect of one side; but now you are rejected by one class, and equally rejected by the other. You come into our midst, we can not receive you; you go amongst worldlings, they reject you too; you are too good for them, and too bad for us. Where are you to be put? If there were a purgatory, that would be the place for you; where you might be tossed on the one side into ice, and on the other into the burning fire, and that for ever. But as there is no such place as purgatory, and as you really are a servant of Satan, and not a child of God, take heed, take heed, how long you stay in a position so absurdly ridiculous. At the day of judgment, wavering men will be the scoff and the laughter even of hell. The angels will look down in scorn upon the man who was ashamed to own his Master thoroughly, while hell itself will ring with laughter. When that grand hypocrite shall come there—that undecided man, they will say, "Aha! we have to drink the dregs, but above them there were sweets; you have only the dregs. You dare not go into the riotous and boisterous mirth of our youthful days, and now you have come here with us to drink the same dregs; you have the punishment without the pleasure." O! how foolish will even the damned call you, to think that you halted between two opinions! "How long limp ye, wriggle ye, walk ye in an absurd manner, between two opinions?" In adopting either opinion, you would at least be consistent; but in trying to hold both, to seek to be both one and the other, and not knowing which to decide upon, you are limping between two opinions. I think a good translation is a very different one from that of the authorized version—"How long hop ye upon two sprays?" So the Hebrew has it. Like a bird, which perpetually flies from bough to bough, and is never still. If it keeps on doing this, it will never have a nest. And so with you: you keep leaping between two boughs, from one opinion to the other; and so between the two, you get no rest for the sole of your foot, no peace, no joy, no comfort, but are just a poor miserable thing all your life long.

IV. We have brought you thus far, then; we have shown you the absurdity of this halting. Now, very briefly, the next point in my text is this. The multitude who had worshiped Jehovah and Baal, and who were now undecided, might reply, "But how do you know that we do not believe that Jehovah is God? How do you know we are not decided in opinion?" The prophet meets this objection by saying, "I know you are not decided in opinion, because you are not decided in practice. If God be God, follow him; if Baal, follow him. You are not decided in practice." Men's opinions are not such things as we imagine. It is generally said now-a-days, that all opinions are right, and if a man shall honestly hold his convictions, he is, without doubt, right. Not so; truth is not changed by our opinions; a thing is either true or false of itself, and it is neither made true nor false by our views of it. It is for us, therefore, to judge carefully, and not to think that any opinion will do. Besides, opinions have influence upon the conduct, and if a man have a wrong opinion, he will, most likely, in some way or other, have wrong conduct, for the two usually go together. "Now," said Elijah, "that you are not the servants of God, is quite evident, for you do not follow him; that you are not thoroughly servants of Baal either, is quite evident, for you do not follow him." Now I address myself to you again. Many of you are not the servants of God; you do not follow him; you follow him a certain distance in the form, but not in the spirit; you follow him on Sundays; but what do you do on Mondays? You follow him in religious company, in evangelical drawing-rooms, and so on; but what do you do in other society? You do not follow him. And, on the other hand, you do not follow Baal; you go a little way with the world, but there is a place to which you dare not go; you are too respectable to sin as others sin or to go the whole way of the world. Ye dare not go to the utmost lengths of evil. "Now," says the prophet, twithing them upon this—"if the Lord be God, follow him."

Let your conduct be consistent with your opinions; if you believe the Lord to be God, carry it out in your daily life; be holy, be prayerful, trust in Christ, be faithful, be upright, be loving; give your heart to God, and follow him. If Baal be God, then follow him; but do not pretend to follow the other." Let your conduct back up your opinion; if you really think that the follies of this world are the best, and believe that a fine fashionable life, a life of frivolity and gayety, flying from flower to flower, getting honey from none, is the most desirable, carry it out. If you think the life of the debauchee is so very desirable, if you think his end is to be much wished for, if you think his pleasures are right, follow them. Go the whole way with them. If you believe that to cheat in business is right, put it up over your door—"I sell trickery goods here;" or if you do not say it to the public, tell your conscience so; but do not deceive the public; do not call the people to prayers when you are opening a "British Bank." If you mean to be religious, follow out your determination thoroughly; but if you mean to be worldly, go the whole way with the world. Let your conduct follow out your opinions. Make your life tally with your profession. Carry out your opinions whatever they be. But you dare not; you are too cowardly to sin as others do, honestly before God's sun; your conscience will not let you do it—and yet you are just so fond of Satan, that you dare not leave him wholly and become thoroughly the servants of God. O do not let your character be like your profession; either keep up your profession, or give it up: do be one thing or the other.

V. And now the prophet cries, "If the Lord be God, follow him; if Baal, then follow him," and in so doing, he states the ground of his practical claim. Let your conduct be consistent with your opinions. There is another objection raised by the crowd. "Prophet," says one, "then comest to demand a practical proof of our affection; then sayest, Follow God. Now, if I believe God to be God, and that is my opinion, yet I do not see what claim he has to my opinions." Now, mark how the prophet puts it: he says, "If God be God, follow him." The reason why I claim that you should follow out your opinion concerning God is, that God is God; God has a claim upon you, as creatures, for your devout obedience. One person replies, "What profit should I have, if I served God thoroughly? Should I be more happy? Should I get on better in this world? Should I have more peace of mind?" Nay, nay, that is a secondary consideration. The only question for you is, "If God be God follow him."

Not if it be more advantageous to you; but, "if God be God, follow him." The secularist would plead for religion on the ground that religion might be the best for this world, and best for the world to come. Not so with the prophet; he says, "I do not put it on that ground, I insist that it is your bounden duty, if you believe in God, simply because he is God, to serve him and obey him. I do not tell you it is for your advantage—it may be, I believe it is—but that I put aside from the question; I demand of you that you follow God, if you believe him to be God. If you do not think he is God; if you really think that the devil is God, then follow him; his pretended godhead shall be your plea, and you shall be consistent; but if God be God, if he made you, I demand that you serve him; if it is he who puts the breath into your nostrils, I demand that you obey him. If God be really worthy of your worship, and you really think so, I demand that you either follow him, or else deny that he is God at all." Now, professor, if thou sayest that Christ's gospel is the gospel, if thou believest in the divinity of the gospel, and puttest thy trust in Christ, I demand of thee to follow out the gospel, not merely because it will be to thy advantage, but because the gospel is divine. If thou makest a profession of being a child of God, if thou art a believer, and thinkest and believest religion is the best, the service of God the most desirable, I do not come to plead with thee because of any advantage thou wouldst get by being holy; it is on this ground that I put it, that the Lord is God; and if he be God, it is thy business to serve him. If his gospel be true, and thou believest it to be true, it is thy duty to carry it out. If thou sayest Christ is not the Son of God, carry out thy Jewish or thy infidel convictions, and see whether it will end well. If thou dost not believe Christ to be the Son of God, if thou art a Mohammedan, be consistent, carry out thy Mohammedan convictions, and see whether it will end well. But, take heed, take heed! If, however, thou sayest God is God, and Christ the Saviour, and the gospel true; I demand of thee, only on this account, that thou carry it out.

What a strong plea some would think the prophet might have had, if he had said, "God is your fathers, God, therefore follow him!" But no, he did not come down to that; he said, "If God be God—I do not care whether he be your fathers' God or not—follow him." "Why do you go to chapel?" says one, "and not to church?"

"Because my father and grandfather were dissenters." Ask a churchman, very often, why he attends the establishment. "Well, our family were always brought up to it; that is why I go." Now, I do think that the worst of all reasons for a particular religion, is that of our being brought up to it. I never could see that at all. I have attended the house of God with my father and my grandfather; but I thought, when I read the Scriptures, that it was my business to judge for myself. I knew that my father and my grandfather took little children in their arms, and put drops of water on their faces, and they were baptized. I took up my Bible, and I could not see any thing about babes being baptized. I picked up a little Greek; and I could not discover that the word "baptized" meant to sprinkle; so I said to myself, "Suppose they are good men, they may be wrong; and though I love and revere them, yet it is no reason why I should imitate them." And therefore I left them, and became what I am to-day, a Baptist minister, so called, but I hope a great deal more a Christian than a Baptist.

It is seldom I mention it; I only do so by way of illustration here. Many a one will go to chapel, because his grandmother did. Well, she was a good old soul, but I do not see that she ought to influence your judgment.

"That does not signify," says one, "I do not like to leave the church of my fathers." No more do I; I would rather belong to the same denomination with my father; I would not willfully differ from any of my friends, or leave their sect and denomination, but let God be above our parents; though our parents are at the very top of our hearts, and we love them and reverence them, and in all other matters pay them strict obedience, yet, with regard to religion, to our own Master we stand or fall, and we claim to have the right of judging for ourselves as men, and then we think it our duty, having judged, to carry out our convictions. Now I am not going to Say,

"If God be your mother's God, serve him;" though that would be a very good argument with some of you; but with you waverers, the only plea I use is, "If God be God, serve him;" if the gospel be right, believe it; if a religious life be right, carry it out; if not, give it up. I only put my argument on Elijah's plea—"If God be God, follow him; but if Baal, then follow him." VI. And now I make my appeal to the halters and waverers, with some questions, which I pray the Lord to apply. Now I will put this question to them: "How long halt ye?" I will tell them; ye will halt between two opinions, all of you who are undecided, until God shall answer by fire.

Fire was not what these poor people wanted that were assembled there. When Elijah says, that "the God that answereth by fire let him be God," I fancy I hear some of them saying, "No; the God that answereth by water let him be God; we want rain badly enough." "No," said Elijah," if rain should come, you would say that it was the common course of providence; and that would not decide you." I tell you, all the providences that befall you undecided ones will not decide you. God may surround you with providences; he may surround you with frequent warnings from the death-bed of your fellows; but providences will never decide you. It is not the God of rain, but the God of fire that will do it. There are two ways in which you undecided ones will be decided by-and-by. You that are decided for God will want no decision; you that are decided for Satan will want no decision; you are on Satan's side, and must dwell for ever in eternal burning. But these undecided ones want something to decide them, and will have either one of the two things; they will either have the fire of God's Spirit to decide them, or else the fire of eternal judgment, and that will decide them. I may preach to you, my hearers; and all the ministers in the world may preach to you that are wavering, but you will never decide for God through the force of your own will. None of you, if left to your natural judgment, to the use of your own reason, will ever decide for God. You may decide for him merely as an outward form, but not as an inward spiritual thing, which should possess your heart as a Christian, as a believer in the doctrine of effectual grace. I know that none of you will ever decide for God's gospel, unless God decide you; and I tell you that you must either be decided by the descent of the fire of his Spirit into your hearts now, or else in the day of judgment. O! which shall it be? O! that the prayer might be put up by the thousand lips that are here: "Lord, decide me now by the fire of thy Spirit; O! let thy Spirit descend into my heart, to burn up the bullock, that I may be a whole burnt offering to God; to burn up the wood and the stones of my sin; to burn up the very dust of worldliness; ah, and to lick up the water of my impiety, which now lieth in the trenches, and my cold indifference, that seek to put out the sacrifice." "O make this heart rejoice or ache! Decide this doubt for me;

And if it be not broken, break, And heal it, if it be." "O sovereign grace, my heart subdue; I would be led in triumph too, A willing captive to my Lord, To sing the triumphs of his word." And it may be, that whilst I speak, the mighty fire, unseen by men, and unfelt by the vast majority of you, shall descend into some heart which has of old been dedicated to God by his divine election, which is now like an altar broken down, but which God, by his free grace, will this day build up. O! I pray that that influence may enter into some hearts, that there may be some go out of this place, saying, "'Tis done, the great transaction's done, I am my Lord's, and he is mine; He drew me, and I followed on, Glad to obey the voice divine." Now rest my undivided heart, fixed on this stable center, rest." O! that many may say that! But remember, if it be not so, the day is coming—dies irae, the day of wrath and anger—when ye shall be decided of God; when the firmament shall be lit up with lightnings, when the earth shall roll with drunken terror, when the pillars of the universe shall shake, and God shall sit, in the person of his Son, to judge the world in righteousness. You will not be undecided then, when, "Depart ye cursed," or "Come, ye blessed," shall be your doom. There will be no indecision then, when you shall meet him with joy or else with terror—when, "rocks hide me, mountains on me fall," shall be your doleful shriek; or else your joyful song shall be, "The Lord is come." In that day you will be decided; but till then, unless the living fire of the Holy Spirit decide you, you will go on halting between two opinions. May God grant you his Holy Spirit that you may turn unto him and be saved!

Encouragement for the Depressed

A Sermon (No. 3489) Published on
Thursday, December 9th, 1915.
Delivered by C. H. SPURGEON,
At the Metropolitan Tabernacle, Newington.
ON Lord's-Day Evening, 27th, August 1871.

"For who hath despised the day of small things?"—Zechariah 4:10.

Zechariah was engaged in the building of the temple. When its foundations were laid, it struck everybody as being a very small edifice compared with the former glorious structure of Solomon. The friends of the enterprise lamented that it should be so small; the foes of it rejoiced and uttered strong expressions of contempt. Both friends and foes doubted whether, even on that small scale, the structure would ever be completed. They might lay the foundations, and they might rear the walls a little way, but they were too feeble a folk, possessed of too little riches and too little strength, to carry out the enterprise. It was the day of small things. Friends trembled; foes jeered. But the prophet rebuked them both—rebuked the unbelief of friends, and the contempt of enemies, by this question, "Who hath despised the day of small things?" and by a subsequent prophecy which removed the fear.

Now we shall use this question at this time for the comfort of two sorts of people—first, for weak believers, and secondly, for feeble workers. Our object shall be the strengthening of the hands that hang down, and the confirming of the feeble knees. We will begin, first of all, with:—

I. WEAK BELIEVERS.

Let us describe them. It is with them a day of small things. Probably you have only been lately brought into the family of God. A few months ago you were a stranger to the divine life, and to the things of God. You have been born again, and you have the weakness of the infant. You are not strong yet, as you will be when you have grown in grace and in the knowledge of our Lord and Saviour Jesus Christ. It is the early day with you, and it is also the day of small things. Now your knowledge is small. My dear brother, you have not been a Bible student long: thank God that you know yourself a sinner, and Christ your Saviour. That is precious knowledge; but you feel now what you once would not have confessed—your own ignorance of the things of God. Especially do the deep things of God trouble you. There are some doctrines that are very simple to other believers that appear to be mysterious, and even to be depressing to you. They are high—you cannot attain to them. They are to you what hard nuts would be to children, whose teeth have not yet appeared. Well, be not at all alarmed about this. All the men in God's family have once been children too. There are some that seem to be born with knowledge—Christians that come to a height in Christ very rapidly. But these are only here and there. Israel did not produce a Samson every day. Most have to go through a long period of spiritual infancy and youth. And, alas! There are but few in the Church, even now, who might be called fathers there. Do not marvel, therefore, if you are somewhat small in your knowledge. Your discernment, too, is small. It is possible that anybody with a fluent tongue would lead you into error. You have, however, discernment, if you are a child of God, sufficient to be kept from deadly errors, for though there are some who would, if it were possible, deceive even the very elect, yet the elect cannot be deceived, for, the life of God being in them, they discern between the precious and the vile—they choose not the things of the world, but they follow after the things of God. Your discernment, however, seeming so small, need not afflict you. It is by reason of use, when the senses are exercised, that we fully discern between all that is good and all that is evil. Thank God for a little discernment—though you see men as trees walking, and your eyes are only half opened. A little light is better than none at all. Not long since you were in total darkness. Now if there be a glimmer, be thankful, for remember where a glimmer can enter the full noontide can come, yea, and shall come in due season. Therefore, despise not the time of small discernment. Of course, you, my dear brother or sister, have small experience. I trust you will not ape experience, and try to talk as if you had the experience of the veteran saints when you are as yet only a raw recruit. You have not yet done business on the great waters. The more fierce temptations of Satan have not assailed you—the wind has been tempered as yet to the shorn lamb; God has not hung heavy weights on slender threads, but hath put a small burden on a weak back. Be thankful that it is so. Thank him for the experience that you have, and do not be desponding because you have not more. It will all come in due time. "Despise not the day of small things." It is always unwise to get down a biography and say, "Oh! I cannot be right, because I have not felt all this good man did." If a child of ten years of age were to take down the diary of his grandfather and were to say, "Because I do not feel my grandfather's weakness, do not require to use his spectacles, or lean upon his staff, therefore I am not one of the same family," it would be very foolish reasoning. Your experience will ripen. As yet it is but natural that it should be green. Wait a while and bless God for what you have.

Probably this, however, does not trouble you so much as one other thing, you have but small faith, and, that faith being small, your feelings are very variable. I often hear this from young beginners in the divine life, "I was so happy a month ago, but I have lost that happiness now." Perhaps tomorrow, after they have been at the house of God, they will be as cheerful as possible, but the next day their joy is gone. Beware, my dear Christian friends, of living by feeling. John Bunyan puts down Mr. Live-by-feeling as one of the worst enemies of the town of Mansoul. I think he said he was hanged. I am afraid he, somehow or other, escaped from the executioner, for I very commonly meet him; and there is no villain that hates the souls of men and causes more sorrow to the people of God than this Mr. Live-by-feeling. He that lives by feeling will be happy today, and unhappy tomorrow; and if our salvation depended upon our feelings, we should be lost one day and saved another, for they are as fickle as the weather, and go up and down like a barometer. We live by faith, and if that faith be weak, bless God that weak faith is faith, and that weak faith is true faith. If thou believest in Christ Jesus, though thy faith be as a grain of mustard seed, it will save thee, and it will, by-and-bye, grow into something stronger. A diamond is a diamond, and the smallest scrap of it is of the same nature as the Koh-i-noor, and he that hath but little faith hath faith for all that; and it is not great faith that is essential to salvation, but faith that links the soul to Christ; and that soul is, therefore, saved. Instead of mourning so much that thy faith is not strong, bless God that thou hast any faith at all, for if he sees that thou despisest the faith he has given thee, it may be long before he gives thee more. Prize that little, and when he sees that thou art so glad and thankful for that little, then will he multiply it and increase it, and thy faith shall mount even to the full assurance of faith.

I think I hear you also add to all this the complaint that your other graces seem to be small too. "Oh," say you, "my patience is so little. If I have a little pain I begin to cry out. I was in hopes I should be able to bear it without murmuring. My courage is so little: the blush is on my cheek if anybody asks me about Christ—I think I could hardly confess him before half a dozen, much less before the world. I am very weak indeed." Ah! I don't wonder. I have known some who have been strong by reason of years, and have still been lacking in that virtue. But where faith is weak, of course, the rest will be weak. A plant that has a weak root will naturally have a weak stem and then will have but weak fruit. Your weakness of faith sends a weakness through the whole. But for all this, though you are to seek for more faith, and consequently for more grace—for stronger graces, yet do not despise what graces you have. Thank God for them, and pray that the few clusters that are now upon you, may be multiplied a thousand-fold to the praise of the glory of his grace. Thus I have tried to describe those who are passing through the day of small things.

But the text says, "Who hath despised the day of small things?" Well, some have, but there is a great comfort in this—God the Father has not. He has looked upon you—you with little grace, and little love, and little faith, and he has not despised you. No, God is always near the feeble saint. If I saw a young man crossing a common alone, I should not be at all astonished, and I should not look round for his father. But I saw today, as I went home, a very tiny little tot right out on the Common—a pretty little girl, and I thought, "The father or mother are near somewhere." And truly there was the father behind a tree, whom I had not seen. I was as good as sure that the little thing was not there all alone. And when I see a little weak child of God, I feel sure that God the Father is near, watching with wakeful eye, and tending with gracious care the feebleness of his new-born child. He does not despise you if you are resting on his promise. The humble and contrite have a word all to themselves in Scripture, that these he will not despise.

It is another sweet and consoling thought that God the Son does not despise the day of small things. Jesus Christ does not, for you remember this word, "He shall carry the lambs in his bosom." We put that which we most prize nearest our heart, and this is what Jesus does. Some of us, perhaps, have outgrown the state in which we were lambs, but to ride in that heavenly carriage of the Saviour's bosom—we might well be content to go back and be lambs again. He does not despise the day of small things.

And it is equally consolatory to reflect that the Holy Spirit does not despise the day of small things, for he it is who, having planted in the heart the grain of mustard seed, watches over it till it becomes a tree. He it is who, having seen the new-born child of grace, doth nurse, and feed, and tend it until it comes to the stature of a perfect man in Christ Jesus. The blessed Godhead despises not the weak believer. O weak believer, be consoled by this.

Who is it, then, that may despise the day of small things? Perhaps Satan has told you and whispered in your ear that such little grace as yours is not worth having, that such an insignificant plant as you are will surely be rooted up. Now let me tell you that Satan is a liar, for he himself does not despise the day of small things; and I am sure of that, because he always makes a dead set upon those who are just coming to Christ. As soon as ever he sees that the soul is a little wounded by conviction, as soon as ever he discovers that a heart begins to pray, he will assault it with fiercer temptations than ever. I have known him try to drive such a one to suicide, or to lead him into worse sin than he has ever committed before. He:—"Trembles when he sees The weakest saint upon his knees." He may tell you that the little grace in you is of no account, but he knows right well that it is the handful of corn on the top of the mountain, the fruit whereof shall shake like Lebanon. He knows it is the little grace in the heart that overthrows his kingdom there. "Ah!" say you, "but I have been greatly troubled lately because I have many friends that despise me, because though I can hardly say I am a believer, yet I have some desire towards God." What sort of friends are these? Are they worldly friends? Oh! Do not fret about what they say. It would never trouble me if I were an artist, if a blind man were to utter the sharpest criticism on my works. What does he know about it? And when an ungodly person begins to say about your piety that it is deficient and faulty, poor soul, let him say what he will—it need not affect you. "Ah!" say you, "the persons that seem to despise me, and to put me out, and tell me that I am no child of God, are, I believe, Christians." Well then, do two things: first, lay what they say to you in a measure to heart, because it may be if God's children do not see in you the mark of a child, perhaps you are not a child. Let it lead you to examination. Oh! Dear friends, it is very easy to be self-deceived, and God may employ, perhaps, one of his servants to enlighten you upon this, and deliver you from a strong delusion. But, on the other hand, if you really do trust in your Saviour, if you have begun to pray, if you have some love to God, and any Christian treats you harshly as if he thought you a hypocrite, forgive him—bear it. He has made a mistake. He would not do so if he knew you better. Say within yourself, "After all, if my brother does not know me, it is enough if my Father does. If my Father loves me, though my brother gives me the cold shoulder, I will be sorry for it, but it shall not break my heart. I will cling the closer to my Lord because his servants seem shy of me." Why, it is not much wonder, is it, that some Christians should be afraid of some of you converts, for think what you used to be a little while ago? Why, a mother hears her son say he is converted. A month or two ago she knew where he spent his evenings, and what were his habits of sin, and though she hopes it is so, she is afraid lest she should lead him to presumption, and she rejoices with trembling, and, perhaps, tells him more about her trembling than she does about her rejoicing. Why, the saints of old could not think Saul was converted at first.

He was to be brought into the church meeting and received—I will suppose the case. I should not wonder before he came, when he saw the elders, one of them would say, "Well, the young man seems to know something of the grace of God: there is certainly a change in him, but it is a remarkable thing that he should wish to join the very people he was persecuting; but, perhaps, it is a mere impulse. It may be, after all, that he will go back to his old companions." Do you wonder they should say so? Because I don't. I am not at all surprised. I am sorry when there are unjust suspicions, I am sorry when a genuine child of God is questioned; but I would not have you lay it much to heart. As I have said before, if your Father knows you, you need not be so broken in heart because your brother does not. Be glad that God does not despise the day of small things. And now let me say to you who are in this state of small things, that I earnestly trust that you will not yourselves despise the day of small things. "How can we do that?" say you. Why, you can do it by desponding. Why, I think there was a time when you would have been ready to leap for joy, if you had been told that you would have given you a little faith, and now you have got a little faith, instead of rejoicing, you are sighing, and moaning, and mourning. Do not do so. Be thankful for moonlight, and you shall get sunlight: be thankful for sunlight, and you shall get that light of heaven which is as the light of seven days. Do not despond lest you seem to despise the mercy which God has given you. A poor patient that has been very, very lame and weak, and could not rise from his bed, is at last able to walk with a stick. "Well," he says to himself, "I wish I could walk, and run, and leap as other men." Suppose he sits down and frets because he cannot. His physician might put his hand on his shoulder and say, "My good fellow, why, you ought to be thankful you can stand at all. A little while ago you know you could not stand upright. Be glad for what you have got: don't seem to despise what has been done for you." I say to every Christian here, while you long after strength, don't seem to despise the grace that God has bestowed, but rejoice and bless his name.

You can despise the day of small things, again, by not seeking after more. "That is strange," say you. Well, a man who has got a little, and does not want more—it looks as if he despised the little. He who has a little light, and does not ask for more light, does not care for light at all. You that have a little faith, and do not want more faith, do not value faith at all—you are despising it. On the one hand, do not despond because you have the day of small things, but in the next place, do not stand still and be satisfied with what you have; but prove your value of the little by earnestly seeking after more grace. Do not despise the grace that God has given you, but bless God for it: and do this in the presence of his people. If you hold your tongue about your grace, and never let anyone know, surely it must be because you do not think it is worth saying anything about. Tell your brethren, tell your sisters, and they of the Lord's household, that the Lord hath done gracious things for you; and then it will be seen that you do not despise his grace.

And now let us run over a thought or two about these small things in weak believers. Be it remembered that little faith is saving faith, and that the day of small things is a day of safe things. Be it remembered that it is natural that living things should begin small. The man is first a babe. The daylight is first of all twilight. It is by little and by little that we come unto the stature of men in Christ Jesus. The day of small things is not only natural, but promising. Small things are living things. Let them alone, and they grow. The day of small things has its beauty and its excellence. I have known some who in after years would have liked to have gone back to their first days. Oh! well do some of us remember when we would have gone over hedge and ditch to hear a sermon. We had not much knowledge, but oh! how we longed to know. We stood in the aisles then, and we never got tired. Now soft seats we need, and very comfortable places, and the atmosphere must neither be too hot nor too cold. We are getting dainty now perhaps; but in those first young days of spiritual life, what appetites we had for divine truth, and what zeal, what sacred fire was in our heart! True, some of it was wild fire, and, perhaps, the energy of the flesh mingled with the power of the spirit, but, for all that, God remembers the love of our espousals, and so do we remember it too. The mother loves her grown-up son, but sometimes she thinks she does not love him as she did when she could cuddle him in her arms. Oh! the beauty of a little child! Oh! the beauty of a lamb in the faith! I daresay, the farmer and the butcher like the sheep better than the lambs, but the lambs are best to look at, at any rate; and the rosebud—there is a charm about it that there is not in the full-blown rose. And so in the day of small things there is a special excellence that we ought not to despise. Besides, small as grace may be in the heart, it is divine—it is a spark from the ever-blazing sun. He is a partaker of the divine nature who has even a little living faith in Christ. And being divine, it is immortal.

Not all the devils in hell could quench the feeblest spark of grace that ever dropped into the heart of man. If God has given thee faith as a grain of mustard seed, it will defy all earth and hell, all time and eternity, ever to destroy it. So there is much reason why we should not despise the day of small things.

One word and I leave this point. You Christians, don't despise anybody, but specially do not despise any in whom you see even a little love to Christ. But do more—look after them, look after the little ones. I think I have heard of a shepherd who had a remarkably fine flock of sheep, and he had a secret about them. He was often asked how it was that his flocks seemed so much to excel all others. At last he told the secret—"I give my principal attention to the lambs." Now you elders of the church, and you my matronly sisters, you that know the Lord, and have known him for years, look up the lambs, search them out, and take a special care of them; and if they are well nurtured in their early days they will get a strength of spiritual constitution that will make them the joy of the Good Shepherd during the rest of their days. Now I leave that point. In the second place, I said that I would address a word or two to:—

II. FEEBLE WORKERS.

Thank God, there are many workers here tonight, and maybe they will put themselves down as feeble. May the words I utter be an encouragement to them, and to feeble workers collectively. When a church begins, it is usually small; and the day of small things is a time of considerable anxiety and fear. I may be addressing some who are members of a newly-organised church. Dear brethren, do not despise the day of small things. Rest assured that God does not save by numbers, and that results are not in the spiritual kingdom in proportion to numbers. I have been reading lately with considerable care the life of John Wesley by two or three different authors in order to get as well as I could a fair idea of the good man; but one thing I have noticed—that the beginnings of the work which has become so wonderfully large were very small indeed. Mr. Wesley and his first brethren were not rich people. Nearly all that joined him were poor. Here and there, there was a person of some standing, but the Methodists were the poor of the land. And his first preachers were not men of education. One or two were so, but the most were good outdoor preachers—head preachers, magnificent preachers as God made them by his Spirit; but they were not men who had had the benefit of college training, or who were remarkable for ability. The Methodists had neither money nor eminent men at first, and their numbers were very few. During the whole life of that good man, which was protracted for so many years, the denomination did not attain any very remarkable size. They were few, and apparently feeble; but Methodism was never so glorious as it was at first, and there never were so many conversions, I believe, as in those early days. Now I speak sorrowfully. It is a great denomination. It abounds in wealth: I am glad it does. It has mighty orators: I rejoice it has. But it has no increase, no conversion. This year and other years it remains stationary. I do not say this because that is an exceptional denomination, for almost all others have the same tale. Year by year as the statistics come in, it is just this. "No increase—hardly hold our ground." I use that as an illustration here. This church will get in precisely the same condition if we do not look out—just the same state. When we have not the means we get the blessing, and when we seem to have the might and power, then the blessing does not come. Oh! may God send us poverty; may God send us lack of means, and take away our power of speech if it must be, and help us only to stammer, if we may only thus get the blessing. Oh! I crave to be useful to souls, and all the rest may go where it will. And each church must crave the same. "Not by might, nor by power, but by my Spirit, saith the Lord." Instead of despising the day of small things, we ought to be encouraged. It is by the small things that God seems to work, but the great things he does not often use. He won't have Gideon's great host—let them go to their homes—let the mass of them go. Bring them down to the water: pick out only the men that lap, and then there is a very few. You can tell them almost on your fingers' ends—just two or three hundred men. Then Gideon shall go forth against the Midianites; and as the cake of barley bread smote the tent, and it lay along, so the sound of the sword of the Lord and of Gideon at the dead of night shall make the host to tremble, and the Lord God shall get to himself the victory. Never mind your feebleness, brethren, your fewness, your poverty, your want of ability. Throw your souls into God's cause, pray mightily, lay hold on the gates of heaven, stir heaven and earth, rather than be defeated in winning souls, and you will see results that will astonish you yet. "Who hath despised the day of small things?"

Now take the case of each Christian individually. Every one of us ought to be at work for Christ, but the great mass of us cannot do great things. Don't despise, then, the day of little things. You can only give a penny. Now then, he that sat over by the treasury did not despise the widow's two mites that made a farthing. Your little thank-offering, if given from your heart, is as acceptable as if it had been a hundred times as much. Don't, therefore, neglect to do the little. Don't despise the day of small things. You can only give away a tract in the street. Don't say, "I won't do that." Souls have been saved by the distribution of tracts and sermons. Scatter them, scatter them—they will be good seed. You know not where they may fall. You can only write a letter to a friend sometimes about Christ. Don't neglect to do it: write one tomorrow. Remember a playmate of yours; you may take liberties with him about his soul from your intimacy with him. Write to him about his state before God, and urge him to seek the Saviour. Who knows?—a sermon may miss him, but a letter from the well-known school companion will reach his heart. Mother, it is only two or three little children at home that you have an influence over. Despise not the day of small things. Take them tomorrow; put your arms around their necks as they kneel by you—pray, "God bless my boys and girls, and save them"—tell them of Christ now. Oh! How well can mothers preach to children! I can never forget my mother's teaching. On the Sunday night, when we were at home, she would have us round the table and explain the Scriptures as we read, and then pray; and one night she left an impression upon my mind that never will be erased, when she said, "I have told you, my dear children, the way of salvation, and if you perish you will perish justly. I shall have to say 'Amen' to your condemnation if you are condemned"; and I could not bear that. Anybody else might say "Amen," but not my mother. Oh! You don't know—you that have to deal with children—what you may do. Despise not these little opportunities. Put a word in edgeways for Christ—you that go about in trains, you that go into workshops and factories. If Christians were men who were all true to their colours, I think we should soon see a great change come over our great establishments. Speak up for Jesus—be not ashamed of him, and because you can say but little, don't refuse, therefore, to say that, but rather say it over twenty times, and so make the little into much. Again, and again, and again, repeat the feeble stroke, and there shall come to be as much result from it as from one tremendous blow. God accepts your little works if they are done in faith in his dear Son. God will give success to your little works: God will educate you by your little works to do greater works; and your little works may call out others who shall do greater works by far than ever you shall be able to accomplish. Evangelists, go on preaching at the street corner—you that visit the low lodging-houses, go on. Get into the room and talk of Jesus Christ there as you have done. You that go into the country towns on the Sabbath and speak on the village-greens of Christ, go on with it. I am glad to see you, but I am glad to miss you when I know you are about the Master's work. We don't want to keep the salt in the box: let it be rubbed into the putrid mass to stay the putrification. We don't want the seed forever in the corn-bin: let it be scattered and it will give us more. Oh! brethren and sisters, wake up if any of you are asleep. Don't let an ounce of strength in this church be wasted—not a single grain of ability, either in the way of doing, or praying, or giving, or holy living. Spend and be spent, for who hath despised the day of small things? The Lord encourage weak believers, and the Lord accept the efforts of feeble workers, and send to both his richest benediction for Christ's sake. Amen.

False Professors Solemnly Warned

A Sermon (No. 102) Delivered on
Sabbath Evening, August 24, 1856,
by the REV. C. H. SPURGEON
At Exeter Hall, Strand.

"For many walk, of whom I have told you often, and now tell you even weeping, that they are the enemies of the cross of Christ: Whose end is destruction, whose God is their belly, and whose glory is in their shame, who mind earthly things."—Philippians 3:18–19.

Paul was the very model of what a Christian minister should be. He was a watchful shepherd over the flock; he did not simply preach to them, and consider that he had done all his duty when he had delivered his message; but his eyes were always upon the Churches, marking their spiritual welfare, their growth in grace, or their declension in godliness. He was the unsleeping guardian of their spiritual welfare. When he was called away to other lands to proclaim the everlasting gospel, he seems always to have kept an eye upon those Christian colonies which he had founded in the midst of heathen darkness. While lighting up other lamps with the torch of truth, he did not fail to trim the lamps already burning. Here you observe he was not indifferent to the character of the little church at Philippi, for he speaks to them and warns them.

Note, too, that the apostle was a very honest pastor—when he marked anything amiss in his people, he did not blush to tell them; he was not like your modern minister, whose pride is that he never was personal in his life, and who thus glories in his shame, for had he been honest, he would have been personal, for he would have dealt out the truth of God without deceitfulness, and would have reproved men sharply, that they might be sound in the faith. "I tell you," says Paul, "because it concerns you." Paul was very honest; he did not flinch from telling the whole truth, and telling it often too, though some might think that once from the lip of Paul would be of more effect than a hundred times from any one else. "I have told you often," says he, "and I tell you yet again there are some who are the enemies of the cross of Christ." And while faithful, you will notice that the apostle was, as every true minister should be, extremely affectionate. He could not bear to think that any of the members of the churches under his care should swerve from the truth, he wept while he denounced them; he knew not how to wield the thunderbolt with a tearless eye; he did not know how to pronounce the threatening of God with a dry and husky voice. No; while he spoke terrible things the tear was in his eye, and when he reproved sharply, his heart beat so high with love, that those who heard him denounce so solemnly, were yet convinced that his harshest words were dictated by affection. "I have told you often, and I tell you, even weeping, that they are the enemies of the cross of Christ." Beloved, I have a message to deliver to-night which is to the same effect as that of the Apostle Paul, and I am afraid it is as necessary now as it was in his time. There are many now among us, as there were then, who walk in such a manner that we recognise them at once as the "enemies of the cross of Christ." I do fear that the evil, instead of having decreased, has multiplied and grown in danger. We have more profession now than there was in the age of Paul, and consequently we have more hypocrisy. It is a crying sin with our churches that there are many in their midst who never ought to be there, who would be fit members of an ale-house or any favourite resort of the gay and frivolous, but who never ought to sip the sacramental wine or eat the holy bread, the emblems of the sufferings of our Lord. We have—O Paul, how wouldst thou have said it to-night, and how wouldst thou have wept while saying it!—we have many in our midst who are the "enemies of the cross of Christ," because "their God is their belly, they mind earthly things," and their life is not consistent with the great things of God.

I shall endeavour, for a short time to-night, to tell you the reason of the apostle's extraordinary sorrow. I never read that the apostle wept when he was persecuted. Though they ploughed his back with furrows, I do believe that never a tear was seen to gush from his eye while the soldiers scourged him. Though he was cast into prison, we read of his singing, never of his groaning. I do not believe he ever wept on account of any sufferings or dangers to which he himself was exposed for Christ's sake. I call this an extraordinary sorrow, because the man who wept was no soft piece of sentiment, and seldom shed a tear even under grievous trials. He wept for three things: he wept on account of their guilt; on account of the ill effects of their conduct; and on account of their doom.

I. First, Paul wept on account of the GUILT of those persons who, having a name to live, were dead, and while uniting themselves with a Christian church, were not walking as they should do among men and before God. Notice the sin with which he charges them. He says, "Their God was their belly;" by this I understand that they were sensual persons. There were those in the early church who, after they sat at God's table, would go away and sit at the feasts of the heathen, and there indulge in gluttony and drunkenness; others indulged in lusts of the flesh, enjoying those pleasures (so miscalled) which, afterwards, bring unutterable pain even to the body itself, and are disgraceful to men, much more to professors of religion. Their God was their belly. They care more about the dress of their body than the dress of their soul; they regarded more the food of the outward carcass than the life of the inner man. Ah! my hearers; are there not many everywhere in our churches who still bow before their belly-god, and make themselves their own idols? Is it not notorious, in almost every society, that professing men can pamper themselves as much as others?—I mean not all, but some. Ay, I have heard of drunken professors; not men who positively reel through the street, who are drunken in mid-day or intoxicated before their fellow-men, but men who go to the very verge of drunkenness in their social parties; men who take so much, that while it would be an insult to their respectability to call them intoxicated, it would be equally an insult to the truth to call them sober. Have we not some men in our churches (it is idle to deny it) who are as fond of the excesses of the table and surfeit in the good things of this life as any other class of men? Have we not persons who spend a very fortune upon the dress of their bodies, adorning themselves far more than they adorn the doctrine of their Saviour; men whose perpetual business it is to take good care of their bodies, against whom flesh and blood never had any cause to complain, for they not only serve the flesh, but make a god of it? Ah! sirs, the church is not pure; the church is not perfect; we have scabbed sheep in the flock. In our own little communion, now and then, we find them out, and then comes the dread sentence of excommunication, by which they are cut off from our fellowship; but there are many of whom we are not aware, who creep like snakes along the grass, and are not discovered till they inflict a grievous wound upon religion, and do damage to our great and glorious cause. Brethren, there are some in the church (both established and dissenting)—let us say it with the deepest sorrow—"whose god is their belly."

Another of their sins was that they did mind earthly things. Beloved, the last sentence may not have touched your consciences, but this is a very sweeping assertion, and I am afraid that a very large proportion of Christ's church are verily guilty here. It is an anomaly, but it is a fact, that we hear of ambitious Christians, although Christ has told us that he who would be exalted must humble himself. There are among the professed followers of the humble Man of Galilee, men who strive to gain the topmost round of the ladder of this world; whose aim is, not to magnify Christ, but to magnify themselves at any hazard. It had been thought at one time that a Christian would be a holy, a humble, and contented man; but it is not so now-a-days. We have (Oh, shame, ye churches!) mere professors; men who are as worldly as the worldliest, and have no more of Christ's Holy Spirit in them than the most carnal who never made a profession of the truth. Again, it is a paradox, but it stares us in the face every day, that we have covetous Christians. It is an inconsistency. We might as well talk of unholy seraphim, of perfect beings subject to sin, as of covetous Christians; yet there are such men, whose purse strings were never intended to slide, at least at the cry of the poor; who call it prudence to amass wealth, and never use it in any degree in the cause of Christ. If you want men that are hard in business, that are grasping after wealth, that seize upon the poor debtor and suck the last particle of his blood; if you want the men who are grasping and grinding, that will skin the flint, and take away the very life from the orphan, you must come—I blush to say it, but it is a solemn truth—you must come sometimes to our churches to find them.

Some such there are amongst the highest of her officers, who "mind earthly things," and have none of that devotion to Christ which is the mark of pure godliness. These evils are not the fruits of religion, they are the diseases of mere profession. I rejoice that the remnant of the elect are kept pure from these, but the "mixed multitude" are sadly possessed therewith.

Another character which the Apostle gives of these men is that they gloried in their shame. A professing sinner generally glories in his shame more than any one else. In fact, he miscalls it. He labels the devil's poisons with the names of Christ's medicines. Things that he would reckon vices in any other man are virtues with himself. If he could see in another man the selfsame action which he has just performed—if another could be the looking-glass of himself, oh! how he would thunder at him! He is the very first man to notice a little inconsistency. He is the very strictest of Sabbatarians; he is the most upright of thieves; he is the most tremendously generous of misers; he is the most marvellously holy of profane men. While he can indulge in his favourite sin, he is for ever putting up his glass to his eye to magnify the faults of others. He may do as he pleases; he may sin with impunity; and if his minister should hint to him that his conduct is inconsistent, he will make a storm in the church, and say the minister was personal, and insulted him. Reproof is thrown away on him. Is he not a member of the church? Has he not been so for years? Who shall dare to say that he is unholy? O sirs, there are some of your members of churches who will one day be members of the pit. We have some united with our churches who has passed through baptism and sit at our sacramental tables, who, while they have a name to live, are dead as corpses in their graves as to anything spiritual. It is an easy thing to palm yourself off for a godly man now-a-days. There is little self-denial, little mortification of the flesh, little love to Christ wanted. Oh, no. Learn a few religious hymns; get a few cant phrases, and you will deceive the very elect; enter into the church, be called respectable, and if you cannot make all believe you, you will yet smooth your path to destruction by quieting an uneasy conscience. I am saying hard things, but I am saying true things; for my blood boils sometimes when I meet with men whom I would not own, whom I would not sit with anywhere, and who yet call me "brother." They can live in sin, and yet call a Christian "brother." God forgive them! We can feel no brotherhood with them; nor do we wish to do so until their lives are changed, and their conduct is made more consistent.

You see, then, in the Apostle's days there were some who were a disgrace to godliness, and the Apostle wept over them because he knew their guilt. Why, it is guilt enough for a man to make a God of his belly without being a professor; but how much worse for a man who knows better, who even sets up to teach other people better, still to go on and sin against God and against his conscience, by making a solemn profession, which is found in his case to be a lie. Oh! how dreadful is such a man's guilt! For him to stand up and say, "'Tis done; the great transaction's done. I am the Lord's, and he is mine," and yet to go and sin like others; to use the same conversation, to practise the same chicanery, to walk in as ungodly a manner as those who have never named the name of Christ—ah! what guilt is here! It is enough to make us weep if we have been guilty ourselves; ay, to weep tears of blood that we should so have sinned against God.

II. But the Apostle did not so much weep for them as for THE MISCHIEF THEY WERE DOING, for he says, emphatically, that they are, "The enemies of the cross of Christ." "The enemies;" as much as to say, the infidel is an enemy; the curser, the swearer, the profane man, is an enemy; Herod, yonder, the persecutor, is an enemy; but these men are the chief soldiers—the life-guards in Satan's army. "The enemies of the cross of Christ" are Pharisaic professors, bright with the whitewash of outside godliness, whilst they are rotten within. Oh! methinks there is nothing that should grieve a Christian more than to know that Christ has been wounded in the house of his friends. See, there comes my Saviour with bleeding hands and feet. O my Jesus, my Jesus, who shed that blood? Whence comes that wound? Why lookest thou so sad? He replies, "I have been wounded, but guess where I received the blow?" Why, Lord, sure thou wast wounded in the gin-palace; thou wast wounded where sinners meet, in the seat of the scornful; thou wast wounded in the infidel hall. "No, I was not," saith Christ; "I was wounded in the house of my friends; these scars were made by those who sat at my table and bore my name, and talked my language; they pierced me and crucified me afresh, and put me to an open shame." Far worst of sinners they that pierce Christ thus whilst professing to be friends. Caesar wept not until Brutus stabbed him; then it was that he was overcome, and exclaimed, "Et tu, Brute!" And thou, "Hast thou stabbed me?" So, my hearers, might Christ say to some of you. "What! thou, and thou, and thou, a professor, hast stabbed me?" Well might our Saviour muffle up his face in grief, or rather bind it in clouds of wrath, and drive the wretch away that has so injured his cause.

If I must be defeated in battle, let me be defeated by mine enemies, but let me not be betrayed by my friends. If I must yield the citadel which I am willing to defend even to the death, then let me yield it, and let my foes walk over my body; but oh! let not my friends betray me; let not the warrior who stands by my side unbar the gate and admit the foemen. That were enough to break one's heart twice—once for the defeat, and the second time at the thought of treachery.

When a small band of Protestants were striving for their liberties in Switzerland, they bravely defended a pass against an immense host. Though their dearest friends were slain, and they themselves were weary, and ready to drop with fatigue, they stood firm in the defence of the cause they had espoused. On a sudden, however, a cry was heard—a dread and terrible shriek. The enemy was winding up a steep acclivity, and when the commander turned his eye thither, O how his brow gathered with storm! He ground his teeth and stamped his foot, for he knew that some caitiff Protestant had led the blood-thirsty foe up the goat track to slay his friends.

Then turning to his friends, he said "On!" and like a lion on his prey, they rushed upon their enemies, ready now to die, for a friend had betrayed them. So feels the bold-hearted Christian, when he sees his fellow-member betraying Christ, when he beholds the citadel of Christianity given up to its foes by those who pretended to be its friends. Beloved, I would rather have a thousand devils out of the church, than have one in it. I do not care about all the adversaries outside; our greatest cause of fear is from the crafty "wolves in sheep's clothing," that devour the flock. It is against such that we would denounce in holy wrath the solemn sentence of divine indignation, and for such we would shed our bitterest tears of sorrow. They are "the enemies of the cross of Christ."

Now, for a moment, let me show you how it is that the wicked professor is the greatest enemy to Christ's church.

In the first place, he grieves the church more than any one else. It any man in the street were to pelt me with mud, I believe I should thank him for the honor, if I knew him to be a bad character, and knew that he hated me for righteousness sake. But if one who called himself a Christian should injure the cause with the filthiness of his own licentious behaviour: ah! that were more injurious than the stakes of Smithfield, or the racks of the Tower. The deepest sighs the Christian has ever heaved, have been fetched from him by carnal professors. I would not weep a tear if every man should curse me who was a hater of Christ; but when the professor forsakes Christ, and betrays his cause: ah! that indeed is grievous; and who is he that can keep back the tear on account of so vile a deed?

Again: nothing divides the church more. I have seen many divisions in journeying through the country, and

I believe almost every division may be traced to a deficiency of piety on the part of some of the members. We should be more one, if it were not for cants that creep into our midst. We should be more loving to each other, more tender-hearted, more kind, but that these men, so deceptive, coming into our midst, render us suspicious.

Moreover, they themselves find fault with those who walk worthily, in order to hide their own faults against God, and against justice. The greatest sorrows of the church have been brought upon her, not by the arrows shot by her foes, not by the discharge of the artillery of hell, but by fires lit in her own midst, by those who have crept into her in the guise of good men and true, but who were spies in the camp, and traitors to the cause.

Yet again: nothing has ever hurt poor sinners more than this. Many sinners coming to Christ would get relief far more quickly, if it were not for the ill lives of false professors. Now let me tell you a story, which I remember telling once before: it is a very solemn one; I hope to feel its power myself, and I pray that all of you may do the same. A young minister had been preaching in a country village, and the sermon apparently took deep effect on the minds of the hearers. In the congregation there was a young man who felt acutely the truth of the solemn words to which the preacher had given utterance. He sought the preacher after the service, and walked with him. On the road, the minister talked of every subject except the one that had occupied his attention in the pulpit. The poor soul was under great distress, and he asked the minister a question or two, but they were put off very coolly, as if the matter was of no great importance. Arriving at the house, several friends were gathered together, and the preached commenced very freely to crack his jokes, to utter his funny expressions, and to set the company in a roar of laughter. That, perhaps, might not have been so bad, had he not gone even farther, and uttered words which were utterly false, and verged upon the licentious. The young man suddenly rose from the table; and though he had wept under the sermon, and had been under the deepest apparent conviction, he rose up, went outside the door, and stamping his foot, said, "Religion is a lie! From this moment I abjure God, I abjure Christ; and if I am damned I will be damned, but I will lay the charge at that man's door, for he preached just now and made me weep, but now see what he is! He is a liar, and I will never hear him again." He carried out his threat; and some time afterwards, as he lay dying, he sent word to the minister that he wanted to see him. The minister had removed to a distant part, but had been brought there by providence, I believe, purposely to chasten him for the great sin he had committed. The minister stepped into the room with the Bible in his hand to do as he was accustomed—to read a chapter and to pray with the poor man. Turning his eyes on him, the man said, "Sir, I remember hearing you preach once." "Blessed be God," said the minister, "I thank God for it," thinking, no doubt, that he was a convert, and rejoicing over him. "Stop," said the man, "I do not know that there is much reason for thanking God, at any rate, on my part. Sir, do you remember preaching from such-and-such a text on such-and-such an evening?" "Yes, I do." "I trembled then, sir; I shook from head to foot; I left with the intention of bending the knee in prayer, and seeking God in Christ; but do you remember going to such-and-such a house, and what you said there!" "No," said the minister, "I cannot." "Well, then, I can tell you, and mark you! through what you said that night my soul is damned, and as true as I am a living man I will meet you at God's bar and lay it to your charge." The man then shut his eyes and died. I think you can scarcely imagine what must have been the feeling of that preacher as he retired from the bedside. He must carry with him always that horrid, that terrible incubus, that there was a soul in hell who laid his blood to his charge.

I am afraid there are some in the ranks of the church who have much guilt at their doors on this account. Many a young man has been driven from a solemn consideration of the truth by the harsh and censorious remarks of Scribes and Pharisees. Many a careful seeker has been prejudiced against sound doctrine by the evil lives of its professors. Ah! ye Scribes and Pharisees, ye enter not in yourselves, and them that would enter in ye hinder. Ye take the key of knowledge, lock up the door by your inconsistencies, and drive men away by your unholy living.

Again, they are "the enemies of the cross of Christ," because they give the devil more theme for laughter, and the enemy more cause for joy, than any other class of Christians. I do not care what all the infidel lecturers in the world like to say. They are very clever fellows, no doubt, and good need they have to be so, to prove an absurdity, and "make the worse appear the better reason;" but we care little what they say; they may say what they like against us that is false, but it is when they can say anything that is true about us that we do not like it.

It is when they can find a real inconsistency in us, and then bring it to our charge, that they have got stuff to make lectures of. If a man be an upright Christian, he never need fear what others say of him; they will get but little fun out of him if he leads a holy, blameless life; but let him be sometimes godly, and at other times ungodly, then he may grieve, for he has given the enemy cause to blaspheme by his unholy living. The devil gets much advantage over the church by the inconsistency of professors. It is when Satan makes hypocrites that he brings the great battering ram against the wall. "Your lives are not consistent"—ah! that is the greatest battering ram that Satan can use against the cause of Christ. Be particular, my dear friends, be very particular that you do not dishonour the cause you profess to love, by living in sin and walking in iniquity. And let me say a word to those of you who, like myself, are strong Calvinists. No class of persons are more maligned than we. It is commonly said that our doctrine is licentious; we are called Antinomians; we are cried down as hypers; we are reckoned the scum of creation; scarcely a minister looks on us or speaks favourably of us, because we hold strong views upon the divine sovereignty of God, and his divine electings and special love towards his own people. In many towns the legal ministers will tell you that there is a nasty nest of people there, who they say are Antinomians—such a queer set of creatures. Very likely, if a good minister enters the pulpit, when he has done his sermon, up comes some man and grasps his hand, and says, "Ah! brother, I am glad to see you down here; sixteen ounces to the pound to-day; our minister gives us nothing but milk and water." "Where do you go?" he asks. "Oh, I attend a little room where we labour to exalt free-grace alone."

"Ah! then you belong to that nasty set of Antinomians your minister was telling me of just now." Then you begin to talk with him, and you find that if he is an Antinomian you should very much like to be one yourself. Very possibly he is one of the most spiritual men in the village; he knows so much of God that he really cannot sit down under a legal ministry; he understands so much of free-grace that he is obliged to turn out or else he would be starved to death. It is common to cry down those who love God, or rather, who not only love God, but love all that God has said, and who hold the truth firmly. Let us then, not as Christians only, but as being a peculiar class of Christians, take care that we give no handle to the enemy, but that our lives are so consistent, that we do nothing to disgrace that cause which is dear to us as our lives, and which we hope to maintain faithfully unto death.

III. Lastly, Paul wept, BECAUSE HE KNEW THEIR DOOM: "Their end is destruction." Mark you, the end of a professing man who has been a hypocrite will be emphatically destruction. If there be chains in hell more heavy than others—if there be dungeons in hell more dark than others—if there be racks that shall more fearfully torment the frame—if there be fires that shall more tremendously scorch the body—if there be pangs that shall more effectually twist the soul in agonies, professing Christians must have them if they be found rotten at last, I had rather die a profligate than die a lying professor. I think I had rather die the veriest sweeping of the street than die a hypocrite. Oh, to have had a name to live, and yet to have proved insincere. The higher the soar the greater the fall. This man has soared high; how low must he tumble when he finds himself mistaken! He who thought to put to his mouth the nectared cup of heaven, finds when he quaffs the bowl, that is the very draught of hell. He who hoped to enter through the gates into the city finds the gates shut, and he himself bidden to depart as an unknown stranger. Oh! how thrilling is that sentence, "Depart from me, I never knew you!" I think I had rather hear it said to me, "Depart, accursed, among the rest of the wicked," than to be singled out, and to have it said, after exclaiming, "Lord, Lord," "Depart from me; I know you not; though you ate and drank in my courts; though you came to my sanctuary, you are a stranger to me, and I am a stranger to you." Such a doom, more horrible than hell, more direful than fate, more desperate than despair, must be the inevitable lot of those "whose god is their belly," who have "gloried in their shame," and "minded earthly things."

Now I dare say most of you will say, "Well, he has stirred the churches up to-night; if he has not spoken earnestly, he has spoken harshly, at any rate." "Ah!" says one, "I dare say it is very true; they are all a set of cants and hypocrites; I always thought so; I shall not go amongst them; none of them are genuine." Stop a bit, my friend, I did not say they were all so; I should be very wicked if I did. The very fact that there are hypocrites proves that all are not so. "How is that?" say you. Do you think there would be any bad bank notes in the world if there were no good ones? Do you think anyone would try and circulate bad sovereigns if there were no really good ones? No, I think not. It is the good bank note that makes the bad one, by prompting the wicked man to imitate it and produce a forgery. It is the very fact that there is gold in the world that makes another try to imitate the metal and so to cheat his neighbour. If there were no true Christians, there would be no hypocrites. It is the excellence of the Christian character which makes men seek after it, and because they have not the real heart of oak, they try to grain their lives to look like it. Because they have not the real solid metal, they try to gild themselves to imitate it. You must have a few brains left, and those are enough to tell you that if there be hypocrites, there must be some who are genuine. "Ah!" says another, "quite right; there are many genuine ones, and I can tell you, whatever you may think, I am genuine enough. I never had a doubt or fear. I know I was chosen of God; and though I do not exactly live as I could wish, I know if I do not go to heaven, very few will ever have a chance. Why, sir, I have been a deacon the last ten years, and a member twenty; and I am not to be shaken by anything you say. As for my neighbour there, who sits near me, I do not think he ought to be so sure; but I have never had a doubt for thirty years." Oh my dear friend, can you excuse me? I will doubt for you. If you had not doubt yourself, I begin to doubt. If you are quite so sure, I really must suspect you; for I have noticed that true Christians are the most suspicious in the world; they are always afraid of themselves. I never met with a truly good man but he always felt he was not good enough; and as you are so particularly good, you must excuse me if I cannot quite endorse your security. You may be very good, but if you will take a trifle of my advice, I recommend you to "examine yourselves, whether ye be in the faith," lest, being puffed up by your carnal fleshly mind, you fall into the snare of the wicked one. "Not too sure," is a very good motto for the Christian. "Make your calling and election sure," if you like; but do not make your opinion of yourself so sure. Take care of presumption. Many a good man in his own esteem has been a very devil in God's eyes; many a pious soul in the esteem of the church has been nothing but rottenness in the esteem of God. Let us then try ourselves. Let us say, "Search us, O God, and try our hearts; see if there be any wicked way in us, and lead us in the way everlasting." If you shall be sent home with such a thought, I shall bless God that the sermon was not altogether in vain. But there are some here who say that it does not matter whether they are in Christ or no. They intend to go on trifling still, despising God, and laughing at his name. Mark this, sinner: The cry that does for one day won't do for ever; and thou you talk of religion now as if it were a mere trifle, mark ye men, you will want it by-and-bye. You are on board ship, and you laugh at the life-boat, because there is no storm; you will be glad enough to leap into it if you are able when the storm shall come. Now you say Christ is nothing, because you do not want him, but when the storm of vengeance comes, and death lays hold upon you, mark me, you will howl after Christ, though you will not pray for him now; you will shriek after him then, though you will not call for him now. "Turn ye, turn ye; why will ye die, O house of Israel." The Lord bring you to himself, and make you his true and genuine children, that you may not know destruction, but that you may be saved now, and saved for ever!?

The tongue of the wicked has assailed Mr. SPURGEON with the most virulent abuse and lying detraction. His sentiments have been misrepresented, and his words perverted. His doctrines have been impugned as "blasphemous," "profane," and "diabolical." Nevertheless, the good hand of the Lord has been upon him, and he has not heeded the falsehoods of the ungodly.

In order that all men may know for a certainty what are the doctrines of Mr. SPURGEON, we beg to remind the readers of The New Park Street Pulpit that we have published a "CONFESSION OF FAITH," which that gentleman edited, and which he has put forth as the articles of his own creed. Price—In Paper Covers, 4d. Cloth, 8d. Roan, gilt edges, 1s. PASSMORE & ALABASTER, Publishers, 18, Paternoster Row.

Final Perseverance

A Sermon (No. 75) Delivered on
Sabbath Morning, March 23, 1856,
by the REV. C. H. SPURGEON
At New Park Street Chapel, Southwark.

"For it is impossible for those who were once enlightened, and have tasted of the heavenly gift, and were made partakers of the Holy Ghost, And have tasted the good word of God, and the powers of the world to come, If they shall fall away, to renew them again unto repentance; seeing they crucify to themselves the Son of God afresh, and put him to an open shame."
—Hebrews 6:4–6.

There are some spots in Europe which have been the scenes of frequent warfare, as for instance, the kingdom of Belgium, which might be called the battle field of Europe. War has raged over the whole of Europe, but in some unhappy spots, battle after battle has been fought. So there is scarce a passage of Scripture which has not been disputed between the enemies of truth and the upholders of it; but this passage, with one or two others, has been the special subject of attack. This is one of the texts which have been trodden under the feet of controversy; and there are opinions upon it as adverse as the poles, some asserting that it means one thing, and some declaring that it means another. We think that some of them approach somewhat near the truth; but others of them desperately err from the mind of the Spirit. We come to this passage ourselves with the intention to read it with the simplicity of a child, and whatever we find therein to state it; and if it may not seem to agree with something we have hitherto held, we are prepared to cast away every doctrine of our own, rather than one passage of Scripture.

Looking at the scope of the whole passage, it appears to us that the Apostle wished to push the disciples on. There is a tendency in the human mind to stop short of the heavenly mark. As soon as ever we have attained to the first principles of religion, have passed through baptism, and understand the resurrection of the dead, there is a tendency in us to sit still; to say, "I have passed from death unto life; here I may take my stand and rest;" whereas, the Christian life was intended not to be a sitting still, but a race, a perpetual motion. The Apostle, therefore endeavours to urge the disciples forward, and make them run with diligence the heavenly race, looking unto Jesus. He tells them that it is not enough to have on a certain day, passed through a glorious change—to have experienced at a certain time, a wonderful operation of the Spirit; but he teaches them it is absolutely necessary that they should have the Spirit all their lives—that they should, as long as they live, be progressing in the truth of God. In order to make them persevere, if possible, he shows them that if they do not, they must, most certainly be lost; for there is no other salvation but that which God has already bestowed on them, and if that does not keep them, carry them forward, and present them spotless before God, there cannot be any other. For it is impossible, he says, if ye be once enlightened, and then fall away, that ye should ever be renewed again unto repentance.

We shall, this morning, answer one or two questions. The first question will be, Who are the people here spoken? Are they true Christians or not? Secondly, What is meant by falling away? And thirdly, What is intended, when it is asserted, that it is impossible to renew them to repentance?

I. First, then, we answer the question, WHO ARE THE PEOPLE HERE SPOKEN OF? If you read Dr. Gill, Dr. Owen, and almost all the eminent Calvinistic writers, they all of them assert that these persons are not Christians. They say, that enough is said here to represent a man who is a Christian externally, but not enough to give the portrait of a true believer. Now, it strikes me they would not have said this if they had had some doctrine to uphold; for a child, reading this passage, would say, that the persons intended by it must be Christians. If the Holy Spirit intended to describe Christians, I do not see that he could have used more explicit terms than there are here. How can a man be said to be enlightened, and to taste of the heavenly gift, and to be made partaker of the Holy Ghost, without being a child of God? With all deference to these learned doctors, and I admire and love them all, I humbly conceive that they allowed their judgments to be a little warped when they said that; and I think I shall be able to show that none but true believers are here described.

First, they are spoken of as having been once enlightened. This refers to the enlightening influence of God's Spirit, poured into the soul at the time of conviction, when man is enlightened with regard to his spiritual state, shown how evil and bitter a thing it is to sin against God, made to feel how utterly powerless he is to rise from the grave of his corruption, and is further enlightened to see, that "by the deeds of the law shall no flesh living be justified," and to behold Christ on the cross, as the sinner's only hope. The first work of grace is to enlighten the soul. By nature we are entirely dark; the Spirit, like a lamp, sheds light into the dark heart, revealing its corruption, displaying its sad state of destitution, and, in due time, revealing also Jesus Christ, so that in his light we may see light. I cannot consider a man truly enlightened unless he is a child of God. Does not the term indicate a person taught of God? It is not the whole of Christian experience; but is it not a part?

Having enlightened us, as the text says, the next thing that God grants to us is a taste of the heavenly gift, by which we understand, the heavenly gift of salvation, including the pardon of sin, justification by the imputed righteousness of Jesus Christ, regeneration by the Holy Ghost, and all those gifts and graces, which in the earlier dawn of spiritual life convey salvation. All true believers have tasted of the heavenly gift. It is not enough for a man to be enlightened; the light may glare upon his eyeballs, and yet he may die; he must taste, as well as see that the Lord is good. It is not enough to see that I am corrupt; I must taste that Christ is able to remove my corruption. It is not enough for me to know that he is the only Saviour; I must taste of his flesh and of his blood, and have a vital union with him. We do think that when a man has been enlightened and has had an experience of grace, he is a Christian; and whatever those great divines might hold, we cannot think that the Holy Spirit would describe an unregenerate man as having been enlightened, and as having tasted of the heavenly gift. No, my brethren, if I have tasted of the heavenly gift, then that heavenly gift is mine; if I have had ever so short an experience of my Saviour's love, I am one of his; if he has brought me into the green pastures, and made me taste of the still waters and the tender grass, I need not fear as to whether I am really a child of God.

Then the Apostle gives a further description, a higher state of grace: sanctification by participation of the Holy Ghost. It is a peculiar privilege to believers, after their first tasting of the heavenly gift, to be made partakers of the Holy Ghost. He is an indwelling Spirit; he dwells in the hearts, and souls, and minds of men; he makes this mortal flesh his home; he makes our soul his palace, and there he rests; and we do assert (and we think, on the authority of Scripture), that no man can be a partaker of the Holy Ghost, and yet be unregenerate. Where the Holy Ghost dwells there must be life; and if I have participation with the Holy Ghost, and fellowship with him, then I may rest assured that my salvation has been purchased by the blood of the Saviour. Thou need'st not fear, beloved; if thou has the Holy Ghost, thou hast that which ensures thy salvation; if thou, by an inward communion, canst participate in his Spirit, and if by a perpetual indwelling the Holy Ghost rests in thee, thou art not only a Christian, but thou hast arrived at some maturity in and by grace. Thou hast gone beyond mere enlightenment: thou hast passed from the bare taste—thou hast attained to a positive feast, and a partaking of the Holy Ghost.

Lest there should be any mistake, however, about the persons being children of God, the Apostle goes to a further stage of grace. They "have tasted the good word of God." Now, I will venture to say there are some good Christian people here who have tasted the heavenly gift, who have never "tasted the good word of God." I mean by that, that they are really converted, have tasted the heavenly gift, but have not grown so strong in grace as to know the sweetness, the richness, and fatness of the very word that saves them. They have been saved by the word, but they have not come yet to realize, and love, and feed upon the word as many others have. It is one thing for God to work a work of grace in the soul, it is quite another thing for God to show us that work; it is one thing for the word to work in us—it is another thing for us really and habitually to relish, and taste, and rejoice in that word. Some of my hearers are true Christians; but they have not got to that stage wherein they can love election, and suck it down as a sweet morsel, wherein they can take the great doctrines of grace, and feed upon them. But these people had. They had tasted the good word of God, as well as received the good gift: they had attained to such a state, that they had loved the word, had tasted, and feasted upon it. It was the man of their right hand; they had counted it sweeter than honey—ay, sweeter than the droppings of the honeycomb. They had "tasted the good word of God." I say again, if these people be not believers—who are?

And they had gone further still. They had attained the summit of piety. They had received "the powers of the world to come." Not miraculous gifts, which are denied us in these days, but all those powers with which the Holy Ghost endows a Christian. And what are they? Why, there is the power of faith, which commands even the heavens themselves to rain, and they rain, or stops the bottles of heaven, that they rain not. There is the power of prayer, which puts a ladder between earth and heaven, and bids angels walk up and down, to convey our wants to God, and bring down blessings from above. There is the power with which God girds his servant when he speaks by inspiration, which enables him to instruct others, and lead them to Jesus; and whatever other power there may be—the power of holding communion with God, or the power of patient waiting for the Son of Man—they were possessed by these individuals. They were not simply children, but they were men; they were not merely alive, but they were endued with power; they were men, whose muscles were firmly set, whose bones were strong; they had become giants in grace, and had received not only the light, but the power also of the world to come. These, we say, whatever may be the meaning of the text, must have been, beyond a doubt, none other than true and real Christians.

II. And now we answer the second question, WHAT IS MEANT BY FALLING AWAY?

We must remind our friends, that there is a vast distinction between falling away and falling. It is nowhere said in Scripture, that if a man fall he cannot be renewed; on the contrary, "the righteous falleth seven times, but he riseth up again;" and however many times the child of God doth fall, the Lord still holdeth the righteous; yea, when our bones are broken, he bindeth up our bones again, and setteth us once more upon a rock. He saith, "Return, ye backsliding children of men; for I am married unto you;" and if the Christian do backslide ever so far, still Almighty mercy cries, "Return, return, return, and seek an injured Father's heart."

He still calls his children back again. Falling is not falling away. Let me explain the difference; for a man who falls may behave just like a man who falls away; and yet there is a great distinction between the two. I can use no better illustration than the distinction between fainting and dying. There lies a young creature; she can scarcely breathe; she cannot herself, lift up her hand, and if lifted up by any one else, it falls. She is cold and stiff; she is faint, but not dead. There is another one, just as cold and stiff as she is, but there is this difference—she is dead. The Christian may faint, and may fall down in a faint too, and some may pick him up, and say he is dead; but he is not. If he fall, God will lift him up again; but if he fall away, God himself cannot save him. For it is impossible, if the righteous fall away, "to renew them again unto repentance."

Moreover, to fall away is not to commit sin. under a temporary surprise and temptation. Abraham goes to Egypt; he is afraid that his wife will be taken away from him, and he says, "She is my sister." That was a sin under a temporary surprise—a sin, of which, by-and-by, he repented, and God forgave him. Now that is falling; but it is not falling away. Even Noah might commit a sin, which has degraded his memory even till now, and shall disgrace it to the latest time; but doubtless, Noah repented, and was saved by sovereign grace. Noah fell, but Noah did not fall away. A Christian may go astray once, and speedily return again; and though it is a sad, and woeful, and evil thing to be surprised into a sin, yet there is a great difference between this and the sin which would be occasioned by a total falling away from grace.

Nor can a man who commits a sin, which is not exactly a surprise, be said to fall away. I believe that some Christian men—(God forbid that we should say much of it!—let us cover the nakedness of our brother with a cloak.) but I do believe that there are some Christians who, for a period of time, have wandered into sin, and yet have not positively fallen away. There is that black case of David—a case which has puzzled thousands. Certainly for some months, David lived without making a public confession of his sin, but, doubtless, he had achings of heart, for grace had not ceased its work: there was a spark among the ashes that Nathan stirred up, which showed that David was not dead, or else the match which the prophet applied would not have caught light so readily. And so, beloved, you may have wandered into sin for a time, and gone far from God; and yet you are not the character here described, concerning whom it is said, that it is impossible you should be saved; but, wanderer though you be, you are your father's son still, and mercy cries, "Repent, repent; return unto your first husband, for then it was better with you than it is now. Return, O wanderer, return."

Again, falling away is not even a giving up of profession. Some will say, "Now there is So-and-so; he used to make a profession of Christianity, and now he denies it, and what is worse, he dares to curse and swear, and says that he never knew Christ at all. Surely he must be fallen away." My friend, he has fallen, fallen fearfully, and fallen woefully; but I remember a case in Scripture of a man who denied his Lord and Master before his own face. You remember his name; he is an old friend of yours—our friend Simon Peter! he denied him with oaths and curses, and said, "I say unto thee that I know not the man." And yet Jesus looked on Simon. He had fallen, but he had not fallen away; for, only two or three days after that, there was Peter at the tomb of his Master, running there to meet his Lord, to be one of the first to find him risen. Beloved, you may even have denied Christ by open profession, and yet if you repent there is mercy for you. Christ has not cast you away, you shall repent yet. You have not fallen away. If you had, I might not preach to you; for it is impossible for those who have fallen away to be renewed again unto repentance.

But some one says, "What is falling away?" Well, there never has been a case of it yet, and therefore I cannot describe it from observation; but I will tell you what I suppose it is. To fall away, would be for the Holy Spirit entirely to go out of a man—for his grace entirely to cease; not to lie dormant, but to cease to be—for God, who has begun a good work, to leave off doing it entirely—to take his hand completely and entirely away, and say, "There, man! I have half saved thee; now I will damn thee." That is what falling away is. It is not to sin temporarily. A child may sin against his father, and still be alive; but falling away is like cutting the child's head off clean. Not falling merely, for then our Father could pick us up, but being dashed down a precipice, where we are lost for ever. Falling away would involved God's grace changing its living nature. God's immutability becoming variable, God's faithfulness becoming changeable, and God, himself being undeified; for all these things falling away would necessitate.

III. But if a child of God could fall away, and grace could cease in a man's heart—now comes the third question—Paul says, IT IS IMPOSSIBLE FOR HIM TO

BE RENEWED. What did the Apostle mean? One eminent commentator says, he meant that it would be very hard. It would be very hard, indeed, for a man who fell away, to be saved. But we reply, "My dear friend, it does not say anything about its being very hard; it says it is impossible, and we say that it would be utterly impossible, if such a case as is supposed were to happen; impossible for man, and also impossible for God; for God hath purposed that he never will grant a second salvation to save those whom the first salvation hath failed to deliver. Methinks, however, I hear some one say, "It seems to me that it is possible for some such to fall away," because it says, "It is impossible, if they shall fall away, to renew them again into repentance." Well, my friend, I will grant you your theory for a moment. You are a good Christian this morning; let us apply it to yourself, and see how you will like it. You have believed in Christ, and committed your soul to God, and you think, that in some unlucky hour you may fall entirely away. Mark you, if you come to me and tell me that you have fallen away, how would you like me to say to you, "My friend, you are as much damned as the devil in hell! for it is impossible to renew you to repentance?" "Oh! no, sir," you would say, "I will repent again and join the Church." That is just the Arminian theory all over; but it is not in God's Scripture. If you once fall away, you are as damned as any man who suffereth in the gulf for ever. And yet we have heard a man talk about people being converted three, four, and five times, and regenerated over and over again. I remember a good man (I suppose he was) pointing to a man who was walking along the street, and saying, "That man has been born again three times, to my certain knowledge." I could mention the name of the individual, but I refrain from doing so. "And I believe he will fall again," said he, "he is so much addicted to drinking, that I do not believe the grace of God will do anything for him, unless he becomes a teetotaller." Now, such men cannot read the Bible; because in case their members do positively fall away, here it is stated, as a positive fact, that it is impossible to renew them again unto repentance. But I ask my Arminian friend, does he not believe that as long as there is life there is hope? "Yes," he says: "While the lamp holds out to burn, The vilest sinner may return." Well, that is not very consistent, to say this in the very next breath to that with which you tell us that there are some people who fall away, and consequently fall into such a condition, that they cannot be saved. I want to know how you make these two things fit each other; I want you to make these two doctrines agree; and until some enterprising individual will bring the north pole, and set it on the top of the south, I cannot tell how you will accomplish it.

The fact is you are quite right in saying, "While there is life there is hope;" but you are wrong in saying that any individual ever did fall into such a condition, that it was impossible for him to be saved.

We come now to do two things: first, to prove the doctrine, that if a Christian fall away, he cannot be saved; and, secondly, to improve the doctrine, or to show its use,

I. Then I am going to prove the doctrine, that if a Christian fall away—not fall, for you understand how I have explained that; but if a Christian cease to be a child of God, and if grace die out in his heart—he is then beyond the possibility of salvation, and it is impossible for him ever to be renewed. Let me show you why. First, it is utterly impossible, if you consider the work which has already broken down. When men have built bridges across streams, if they have been built of the strongest material and in the most excellent manner, and yet the foundation has been found so bad that none will stand, what do they say? Why, "We have already tried the best which engineering or architecture has taught us; the best has already failed; we know nothing that can exceed what has been tried; and we do therefore feel, that there remains no possibility of ever bridging that stream, or ever running a line of railroad across this bog, or this morass, for we have already tried what is acknowledged to be the best scheme." As the apostle says, "These people have been once enlightened; they have had once the influence of the Holy Spirit, revealing to them their sin: what now remains to be tried. They have been once convinced—is there anything superior to conviction?" Does the Bible promise that the poor sinner shall have anything over and above the conviction of his sin to make him sensible of it? Is there anything more powerful than the sword of the Spirit? That has not pierced the man's heart; is there anything else which will do it? Here is a man who has been under the hammer of God's law; but that has not broken his heart; can you find anything stronger? The lamp of God's spirit has already lit up the caverns of his soul: if that be not sufficient, where will you borrow another? Ask the sun, has he a lamp more bright than the illumination of the Spirit! Ask the stars, have they a light more brilliant than the light of the Holy Ghost?

Creation answers no. If that fails, then there is nothing else. These people, moreover, had tasted the heavenly gift; and though they had been pardoned and justified, yet pardon through Christ and justification were not enough (on this supposition) to save them. How else can they be saved? God has cast them away; after he has failed in saving them by these, what else can deliver them? Already they have tasted of the heavenly gift: is there a greater mercy for them? Is there a brighter dress than the robe of Christ's righteousness? Is there a more efficacious bath than that "fountain filled with blood?" No. All the earth echoes, "No." If the one has failed, what else does there remain?

These persons, too, have been partakers of the Holy Ghost; if that fail, what more can we give them? If, my hearer, the Holy Ghost dwells in your soul, and that Holy Ghost does not sanctify you and keep you to the end, what else can be tried? Ask the blasphemer whether he knows a being, or dares to suppose a being superior to the Holy Spirit! Is there a being greater than Omnipotence? Is there a might greater than that which dwells in the believer's new-born heart? And if already the Holy Spirit hath failed, O, heavens! tell us where we can fight aught that can excel his might? If that be ineffectual, what next is to be essayed? These people, too, had "tasted the good Word of Life;" they had loved the doctrines of grace; those doctrines had entered into their souls, and they had fed upon them. What new doctrines shall be preached to them? Prophet of ages! where whilt thou find another system of divinity? Who shall we have? Shall we raise up Moses from the tomb? shall we fetch up all the ancient seers, and bid them prophecy? If, then, there is only one doctrine that is true, and if these people have fallen away after receiving that, how can they be saved?

Again, these people, according to the text, have had "the powers of the world to come." They have had power to conquer sin—power in faith, power in prayer, power of communion; with what greater power shall they be endowed? This has already failed; what next can be done? O ye angels! answer, what next! What other means remain? What else can avail, if already the great things of salvation have been defeated? What else shall now be attempted? He hath been once saved; but yet it is supposed that he is lost. How, then, can he now be saved?

Is there a supplementary salvation? is there something that shall overtop Christ, and be a Christ where Jesus is defeated.

And then the apostle says, that the greatness of their sin which they would incur, if they did fall away, would put them beyond the bounds of mercy. Christ died, and by his death he made an atonement for his own murderers; he made an atonement for those sins which crucified him once; but do we read that Christ will ever die for those who crucify him twice? But the Apostle tells us that if believers do fall away, they will "crucify the Son of God afresh, and put him to an open shame." Where, then, would be an atonement for that? He has died for me; What! though the sins of all the world were on my shoulders, still they only crucified him once, and that one crucifixion has taken all those sins away; but if I crucified him again, where would I find pardon? Could heavens, could earth, could Christ himself, with bowels full of love, point me to another Christ, show to me a second Calvary, give me a second Gethsemane? Ah! no! the very guilt itself would put us beyond the pale of hope, if we were to fall away?

Again, beloved, think what it would necessitate to save such a man. Christ has died for him once, yet he has fallen away and is lost; the Spirit has regenerated him once, and that regenerating work has been of no use. God has given him a new heart (I am only speaking, of course, on the supposition of the Apostle), he has put his law in that heart, yet he has departed from him, contrary to the promise that he should not; he has made him "like a shining light," but he did not "shine more and more unto the perfect day," he shone only unto blackness. What next? There must be a second incarnation, a second Calvary, a second Holy Ghost, a second regeneration, a second justification, although the first was finished and complete—in fact, I know not what. It would necessitate the upsetting of the whole kingdom of nature and grace, and it would, indeed, be a world turned upside down, if after the gracious Saviour failed, he were to attempt the work again.

If you read the 7th verse, you will see that the Apostle calls nature in to his assistance. He says, "The earth which drinketh in the rain that cometh oft upon it, and bringeth forth herbs meet for them by whom it is dressed, receiveth blessing from God: But that which beareth thorns and briars is rejected, and is nigh unto cursing; whose end is to be burned." Look! there is a field; the rain comes on it, and it brings forth good fruit.

Well, then, there is God's blessing on it. But there is according to your supposition, another field, on which the same rain descends, which the same dew moistens; it has been ploughed and harrowed, as well as the other, and the husbandman has exercised all his craft upon it, and yet it is not fertile. Well, if the rain of heaven did not fertilize it, what next? Already all the arts of agriculture have been tried, every implement has been worn out on its surface, and yet it has been of no avail. What next? There remains nothing but that it shall be burnt and cursed—given up like the desert of Sahara, and resigned to destruction. So, my hearer, could it be possible that grace could work in thee, and then not affect thy salvation—that the influence of Divine grace could come down, like rain from heaven, and yet return unto God void, there could not be any hope for thee, for thou wouldst be "nigh unto cursing," and thine end would be "to be burned."

There is one idea which has occurred to us. It has struck us as a singular thing, that our friends should hold that men can be converted, made into new creatures, then fall away and be converted again. I am an old creature by nature; God creates me into a new thing, he makes me a new creature. I cannot go back into an old creature, for I cannot be uncreated. But yet, supposing that new creatureship of mine is not good enough to carry me to heaven. What is to come after that? Must there be something above a new creature—a new creature. Really, my friends, we have got into the country of Dreamland; but we were forced to follow our opponents into that region of absurdity, for we do not know how else to deal with them.

And one thought more. There is nothing in Scripture which teaches us that there is any salvation, save the one salvation of Jesus Christ—nothing that tells us of any other power, super-excellent and surpassing the power of the Holy Spirit. These things have already been tried on the man, and yet, according to the supposition, they have failed, for he has fallen away. Now, God has never revealed a supplementary salvation for men on whom one salvation has had no effect; and until we are pointed to one scripture which declares this, we will still maintain that the doctrine of the text is this: that if grace be ineffectual, if grace does not keep a man, then there is nothing left but that he must be damned. And what is that but to say, only going a little round about, that grace will do it? So that these words, instead of miltating against the Calvinistic doctrine of final perseverance, form one of the finest proofs of it that could be afforded.

And now, lastly, we come to improve this doctrine. If Christians can fall away, and cease to be Christians, they cannot be renewed again to repentance. "But," says one, "You say they cannot fall away." What is the use of putting this "if" in, like a bugbear to frighten children, or like a ghost that can have no existence? My learned friend, "Who art thou that repliest against God?" If God has put it in, he has put it in for wise reasons and for excellent purposes. Let me show you why. First, O Christian, it is put in to keep thee from falling away. God preserves his children from falling away; but he keeps them by the use of means; and one of these is, the terrors of the law, showing them what would happen if they were to fall away. There is a deep precipice: what is the best way to keep any one from going down there? Why, to tell him that if he did he would inevitably be dashed to pieces. In some old castle there is a deep cellar, where there is a vast amount of fixed air and gas, which would kill anybody who went down. What does the guide say? "If you go down you will never come up alive." Who thinks of going down? The very fact of the guide telling us what the consequences would be, keeps us from it. Our friend puts away from us a cup of arsenic; he does not want us to drink it, but he says, "If you drink it, it will kill you." Does he suppose for a moment that we should drink it. No; he tells us the consequences, and he is sure we will not do it. So God says, "My child, if you fall over this precipice you will be dashed to pieces." What does the child do? He says, "Father, keep me; hold thou me up, and I shall be safe." It leads the believer to greater dependence on God, to a holy fear and caution, because he knows that if he were to fall away he could not be renewed, and he stands far away from that great gulf, because he know that if he were to fall into it there would be no salvation for him. If I thought as the Arminian thinks, that I might fall away, and then return again, I should pretty often fall away, for sinful flesh and blood would think it very nice to fall away, and be a sinner, and go and see the play at the theatre, or get drunk, and then come back to the Church, and be received again as a dear brother who had fallen away for a little while.

No doubt the minister would say, "Our brother Charles is a little unstable at times." A little unstable! He does not know anything about grace; for grace engenders a holy caution, because we feel that if we were not preserved by Divine power we should perish. We tell our friend to put oil in his lamp, that it may continue to burn! Does that imply that it will be allowed to go out? No, God will give him oil to pour into the lamp continually. Like John Bunyan's figure; there was a fire, and he saw a man pouring water upon it. "Now," says the Preacher, "don't you see that fire would go out, that water is calculated to put it out, and if it does, it will never be lighted again;" but God does not permit that! for there is a man behind the wall who is pouring oil on the fire; and we have cause for gratitude in the fact, that if the oil were not put in by a heavenly hand, we should inevitably be driven to destruction. Take care, then Christian, for this is a caution.

II. It is to excite our gratitude. Suppose you say to your little boy, "Don't you know Tommy, if I were not to give you your dinner and your supper you would die? There is nobody else to give Tommy dinner and supper." What then? The child does not think that you are not going to give him his dinner and supper; he knows you will, and he is grateful to you for them. The chemist tells us, that if there were no oxygen mixed with the air, animals would die. Do you suppose that there will be no oxygen, and therefore we shall die? No, he only teaches you the great wisdom of God, in having mixed the gases in their proper proportions. Says one of the old astronomers, "There is great wisdom in God, that he has put the sun exactly at a right distance—not so far away that we should be frozen to death, and not so near that we should be scorched." He says, "If the sun were a million miles nearer to us we should be scorched to death." Does the man suppose that the sun will be a million miles nearer, and, therefore, we shall be scorched to death? He says, "If the sun were a million miles farther off we should be frozen to death." Does he mean that the sun will be a million miles farther off, and therefore we shall be frozen to death? Not at all. Yet it is quite a rational way of speaking, to show us how grateful we should be to God. So says the Apostle. Christian! if thou shouldst fall away, thou couldst never be renewed unto repentance. Thank thy Lord, then, that he keeps thee. "See a stone that hangs in air; see a spark in ocean live; Kept alive with death so near; I to God the glory give." There is a cup of sin which would damn thy soul, O Christian. Oh! what grace is that which holds thy arm, and will not let thee drink it? There thou art, at this hour, like the bird-catcher of St. Kilda, thou art being drawn to heaven by a single rope; if that hand which holds thee let thee go, if that rope which grasps thee do but break, thou art dashed on the rocks of damnation. Lift up thine heart to God, then, and bless him that his arm is not wearied, and is never shortened that it cannot save. Lord Kenmure, when he was dying, said to Rutherford. "Man! my name is written on Christ's hand, and I see it! that is bold talk, man, but I see it!" Then, if that be the case, his hand must be severed from his body before my name can be taken from him; and if it be engraven on his heart, his heart must be rent out before they can rend my name out.

Hold on, then, and trust believer! thou hast "an anchor of the soul, both sure and steadfast, which entereth within the veil." The winds are bellowing, the tempests howling; should the cable slip, or thine anchor break, thou art lost. See those rocks, on which myriads are driving, and thou art wrecked there if grace leave thee; see those depths, in which the skeletons of sailors sleep, and thou art there, if that anchor fail thee. It would be impossible to moor thee again, if once that anchor broke; for other anchor there is none, other salvation there can be none, and if that one fail thee, it is impossible that thou ever shouldst be saved. Therefore thank God that thou hast an anchor that cannot fail, and then loudly sing—"How can I sink with such a prop, As my eternal God, Who bears the earth's huge pillars up? And spreads the heavens abroad?" How can I die, when Jesus lives, Who rose and left the dead? Pardon and grace my soul receives, From my exalted head."

God's Word Not To Be Refused

**A Sermon (No. 3492) Published on
Thursday, December 30th, 1915.
Delivered by C. H. SPURGEON,
At the Metropolitan Tabernacle, Newington.
ON Lord's-Day Evening, 27th November, 1870.**

**"See that ye refuse not him that speaketh. For if they escaped not who refused him that spake on earth, much more shall not we escape, if we turn away from him that speaketh from heaven."
—Hebrews 12:25.**

We are not a cowering multitude gathered in trembling fear around the smoking mount of Horeb; we have come where the great central figure is the mercy of God in Christ Jesus. We have gathered virtually in the outer circle of which the saints above and holy angels make the inner ring. And now tonight Jesus speaks to us in the gospel. So far as his gospel shall be preached by us here, it shall not be the word of man, but the word of God; and although it comes to you through a feeble tongue, yet the truth itself is not feeble, nor is it any less divine than if Christ himself should speak it with his own lips. "See that ye refuse not him that speaketh."

The text contains:—

I. AN EXHORTATION OF A VERY SOLEMN, EARNEST KIND.

It does not say, "Refuse not him that speaketh," but "See that ye refuse not him that speaketh"—that is, "be very circumspect that by no means, accidental or otherwise, you do refuse the Christ of God, who now in the gospel speaks to you. Be watchful, be earnest, lest even through inadvertence ye should refuse the prophet of the gospel dispensation—Jesus Christ, the Son of God, 0who speaks in the gospel from heaven to the sons of men." It means, "Give earnest heed and careful attention, that by no means, and in no way you refuse him that speaketh." My object tonight will be to help you, beloved friends, especially you that have not laid hold on Christ, who are not the children of Zion, who are joyful in their king—to help you tonight, that you may see to it.

And to go to our point at once, we shall have many things to say, and we shall speak them in brief sentences, hoping that the thoughts as they arise may be accepted by your mind, and may, by God's Spirit, work upon your hearts and conscience. There is great need of this exhortation from many considerations not mentioned in the text. A few of these we will hint at first.

First, from the excellency of the Word of God itself. "See that ye refuse not him that speaketh." That which Jesus speaks concerns your soul, concerns your everlasting destiny; it is God's wisdom; God's way of mercy; God's plan by which you may be saved. If this were a secondary matter, ye need not be so earnest about receiving it, but of all things under heaven, nothing so concerns you as the gospel. See, then, that ye refuse not this precious Word, more precious than gold or rubies—which alone can save your souls.

See to this, again, because there is an enemy of yours who will do all he can that you may refuse him that speaketh. Satan is always busiest where the gospel is most earnestly preached. Let the sower scatter handfuls of seeds, and birds will find out the seeds and soon devour them. Let the gospel be preached, and these birds of the air, fiends of hell, will soon by some means try to remove these truths from your hearts, lest they should take root in your hearts and bring forth fruit unto repentance.

Give earnest heed, again, "that ye refuse not him that speaketh," because the tendency of your own mind will be to refuse Christ. Oh! sirs, ye are fallen through your first father, Adam, and the tendencies now of your souls are towards evil, and not towards the right, and when the Lord comes from heaven to you, you will reject him if left to yourselves. Watch, then, I say; see that ye refuse not, stir up your souls, awaken your minds, lest this delirious tendency of sin should make you angry with your best friend, and constrain you to thrust from you that which is your only hope for the hereafter. When a man knows that he has a bad tendency which may injure him, if he be wise he watches against it. So, knowing this, which God's Word tells you, watch, I pray you, lest ye refuse him that speaketh.

Bethink you well, too, that you have need to see to this, because some of you have rejected Christ long enough already. He has spoken to you from this pulpit, from other pulpits, from the Bible, from the sick-bed. He spoke to you lately in the funeral knell of your buried friend—many voices, but all with this one note, "Come to me, repent, be saved"; but until now ye have refused "him that speaketh." Will not the time past suffice to have played this mischievous game? Will not the years that have rolled into eternity bear enough witness against you? Must ye add to all this weight by again refusing? Oh! I implore you to see to it that ye do not again "refuse him that speaketh from heaven," for there is not a word of that which he speaks, but what is love to your souls. Jesus Christ, the Son of God, came not armed with terrors to work wrath among the sons of men; all was mercy, all was grace, and to those who listen to him he has nothing to speak but tenderness and loving-kindness; your sins shall be forgiven you; the time of your ignorances God will wink at; your transgressions shall be cast into the depths of the sea; for you there shall be happiness on earth, and glory hereafter. Who would not listen when it is good news to be heard? Who would not listen when the best tidings that God himself ever sent forth from the excellent glory is proclaimed by the noblest Ambassador that ever spake to men, namely, God's own Son, Jesus, the once crucified, but now exalted Saviour? For these reasons, then, at the very outset I press upon you this exhortation, "See that ye refuse not him that speaketh such precious truth", which the enemy would fain take out of your minds: truth which you yourselves have refused long enough already, and truth which is sweet, and will be exceedingly precious to your souls if you receive it.

But now the text gives us:

II. SOME FURTHER REASONS for seeing to it that we do not "refuse him that speaketh." One reason I see in the text is this: see to this because there are many ways of refusing him that speaketh, and you may have fallen into one or other of these. See to it; pass over in examination your own state and conduct, lest you may have been refusing Christ. Some refuse the Saviour by not hearing of him. In his day there were some that would not listen, and there are such now. The Sabbath days of some of you are not days of listening to the gospel. Where were you this morning? Where are you usually all the Lord's Day long? Remember, you cannot live in London, where the gospel is preached, and be without responsibility. Though you will not come to the house of God to hear of it, yet be sure of this, the kingdom of God hath come nigh unto you. You may close your ears to the invitation of the gospel, but at last you will not be able to close your ear to the denunciation of wrath. If you will not come and hear of Christ on the cross, you must one day see for yourselves Christ on his throne. "See that ye refuse not him that speaks to you from heaven" by refusing to be found where his gospel is proclaimed.

Many come to hear it, and yet refuse him that speaketh, for they hear listlessly. In many congregations—I will not judge this—a very large proportion of hearers are listless hearers. It little matters to them what is the subject in hand: they hear the sentences and phrases that come from the speaker's tongue, but these penetrate the ear only, and never reach their heart. Oh! how sad it is that this should be the case with almost all who have heard the gospel long, and who are not converted! They get used to it; no form of alarm could reach them, and perhaps no form of invitation could move them to penitence. The preacher may exhaust his art. They are like the adder that is deaf. He may know how to charm others, but these he cannot charm, charm he never so wisely.

Oh! see ye gospel hearers up yonder, and ye below here, that have been hearing Christ these many years, see that ye refuse not him that day by day during so long a time has spoken to you in the preaching of the gospel out of heaven.

But there are some who do hear, and have a very intelligent idea of what they hear, but who actually refuse to believe it. For divers reasons best known to themselves they reject the testimony of the incarnate God. They hear that God the Word was made flesh and dwelt among us, and he hath borne testimony that whosoever believeth in him is not condemned. They know but they will not believe in him. They will give you first one excuse, and then another, but all the excuses put together will never mitigate the fact that they do not believe the testimony of God concerning his Son, Jesus Christ, and so they "refuse him that speaketh." How many, how many here are by their unbelief refusing the Christ that speaks out of heaven?

Some are even offended at the gospel, as in Christ's day. When he came to a tender point in his preaching they went back and walked no more with him. Such there are to be found in our assemblies. The gospel galls them; there is some point that touches their prejudices, something that touches their favourite sin, and they are vexed and irritable. They ought to be angry—angry with their sin—but they are angry with Christ instead. They ought to denounce themselves, and patiently seek mercy, but this is not palatable to them; they would rather denounce the preacher, or denounce the preacher's Master.

Some will even hear the gospel, the very gospel of Christ to catch at words and pervert sentences to make play of the preacher's words which he uses, when they are honestly the best he can find, and, worse still, make play with the sense, too, with the very gospel—and find themes for loose jokes and profane and ribald words, even in the cross. Dicing, like the soldier at the cross-foot, with the blood falling on them, so some make merriment when the blood of Jesus is falling upon them to their condemnation. May it not be so with any here present, but there have been such who have even reviled the Saviour, and had hard words for God in human flesh—could not believe that he bore the guilt of sin, could not admire the love astounding that made him suffer for the guilt of his enemies—could not see anything admirable in the heroic sacrifice of the great Redeemer, but rather turned their heel against their benefactor, and poured forth venomous words on him that loved the sons of men and died saying, "Father, forgive them, for they know not what they do."

And some have practically shown they have refused him that speaketh, for they have begun to persecute his people; they have maltreated those that sought the glory of God, and anything that had a savour of Christ about it has been despicable and detestable to them.

Oh! dear hearers, I shall ask you, since there are all these ways of refusing Christ, to see to it that ye do not fall into any of them. The grosser forms, perhaps, you would be too shocked at, but don't fall into the others.

Do not especially fall into that indifference which has as much of insult to the Saviour almost as blasphemy. Is it nothing to you, is it nothing to you that God should come from heaven that he might be just in the salvation of men, and that, coming from heaven to be thus just, he should himself suffer that we might not suffer—the Christ of God bleed and die instead of the undeserving, hell-deserving sinners? Shall this be told you—pressed upon you—and will you refuse it? Will you refuse him who speaks himself, in his own sacrifice, and in the blood which he hath carried within the veil continues now to speak—will you, will you refuse him? Pray God you may see to it that in no form you do.

And now passing on, but keeping to the same point, striking the hammer on the head of the same nail, there are many reasons why men refuse Christ; therefore, see that for none of these reasons ye do it. Some refuse him out of perfect indifference; the great mass of men have not a thought above their meat and their drink. Like the cock that found the diamond on the dunghill, they turn it over and wish it were a grain of barley. What care they for heaven, or the pardon of sin? Their mind does not reach to that. See that ye—that ye, none of you, are so sensuous as to "refuse him that speaketh from heaven" for such a reason as this. Some reject him because of their self-righteousness: they are good enough. Jesus Christ speaks against them, they say; he does not applaud their righteousness, he ridicules them rather; he tells them that their prayers are long prayers, and their many good works are, after all, a poor ground for reliance." So as the Saviour will not patronize their righteousness, neither will they have to do with him. Oh! say not ye are rich and increased in goods; ye are naked, and poor, and miserable. Say not ye can win heaven by your merits; ye have none; your merits drag you down to hell. Yet many will refuse the Saviour because of the insanity of their self-righteousness.

Some, too, reject him because of their self-reliant wisdom. "Why," they say, "this is a very thoughtful age." And everywhere I hear it dinned into my ears, "thoughtful preaching," "thinkings," "intellectual preaching." And what a mass of rottenness before high heaven the whole lot is that is produced by these thinking preachers and these intellectual men! For my part I would rather say to them, "See that ye refuse not him that speaketh," for one word of God is better than all the thoughts of all the philosophers, and one sentence from the lip of Christ I do esteem to be more precious than the whole Alexandrian library, and the Bodleian also if you will, so much as it comes from man. Nay, it is the thinking of Christ we have to think about; otherwise our thinking may prove our curse. A man, if he is drowning, if he have a rope thrown to him, had better lay hold of it than merely be there thinking about the possibilities of salvation by some other means. While your souls are being lost, sirs, there is better employment for you than merely indulging in rhapsodies and inventions of your own supposed judgment. Take hold of this, the gospel of Jesus revealed of God, lest ye perish, and perish with a vengeance.

Some reject the Saviour from another cause: they do not like the holiness of Christ's teaching. They refuse him that speaketh because they think Christ's religion too strict, too precise, cuts off their pleasures, condemns their lusts. Yes, yes, it is so, but to reject Christ for such a reason is certainly to be most unreasonable, for it should be in every man a desire to be delivered from these passions and lusts, and because Christ can deliver us, shall we, therefore, reject him? God forbid that we should be led astray by such a reason.

Some reject him because they have a fear of the world. If they were Christians, they would probably be laughed at as Methodistic, Presbyterian, Puritanic, or some other name. And shall we lose our souls to escape the sneers of fools? He is not a man—call him by some other name—he is no man that flings away his soul because he is such a coward that he cannot bear to do and believe the right, and bear the frown of fashion.

There are others who refuse the Saviour simply out of procrastination. They have no reason for it, but they hope they shall have a more convenient season. They are young people as yet, or they are not so very old, or if they are old, yet still life will linger a little while, and so still they refuse him that speaketh.

I have not mentioned a worthy reason for refusing him that speaketh, nor do I believe there is a worthy reason. It seems to me that if it be so, that God himself has taken upon himself human form, and has come here to effect our redemption from our sin and misery, there cannot be any reason that will stand a moment's looking at for refusing him that speaketh. It must be my duty and my privilege to hear what it is that God has got to say to me: it must be my duty to lend him all my heart to try and understand what it is that he says, and then to give him all my will to do, or to be whatever he would have me to do or to be.

"But did God thus come?" says one. I always feel that the very declaration is its own proof. No heart could ever have contrived or invented this as a piece of imagination, the love, the story of the redeeming love of God in Christ Jesus. If I had no evidence but the mere statement, I think I must accept it, for it wears truth upon its very forefront. Who should conceive it? The offended God comes here to redeem his creatures from their own offence. Since he must in justice punish, he comes to bear the punishment himself, that he may be just and yet be inconceivably gracious! My soul flies into the arms of this revelation; it seems to be the best news my troubled conscience ever had—God was in Christ reconciling the world unto himself, not imputing their trespasses unto them. Oh! there cannot be a reasonable motive for rejecting the Saviour, and I, therefore, impress it upon you, since so many unreasonable motives carry men away, see that ye refuse not him that speaketh, and may the Spirit of God grant that you may not be able to refuse. But now coming to the text again, we have:—

III. A VERY HIGH MOTIVE GIVEN for seeing that we refuse not him that speaketh. It is this—because in refusing him, we shall be despising the highest possible authority. When Moses spake in God's name, it was no light thing to refuse such an ambassador. Still, Moses was but a man. Though clothed with divine authority, yet he was but a man and a servant of God. But Jesus Christ is God by nature. See that ye refuse not him who is of heavenly origin, who came from heaven, who is clothed with such divine powers, that every word he speaks is virtually spoken from heaven, and who, being now in heaven, speaks through his ever living gospel directly out of the excellent glory. Regard ye this, I pray you, and remember well the parable which Jesus gave. A certain man planted a vineyard, and let it out to husbandmen, and when the time came that he should receive the fruit he sent a servant, and they stoned him. He sent another, and they beat him. He sent another, and they maltreated him. After he had thus sent many of his servants, and the dressers of the vineyard had incurred his high displeasure by the shameful way in which they had treated the servants, he sent his own son, and he said, "They will reverence my son." It was the highest degree of guilt when they said, "This is the heir; let us kill him, that the inheritance may be ours." Then they took him and killed him, and threw him out of the vineyard. You know how the Saviour was treated by the sons of men; but here is the point I aim at; it is this: to reject Jesus Christ, to refuse him, to refuse merely his gospel, if he did not speak in it, might not be so high a misdemeanour, but to refuse him!—I don't know how it is, but my heart feels very heavy, even to sinking, at the thought that any man here should be able to refuse Christ, the Son of God, the Everlasting and the ever Blessed. But I cannot speak out what I feel. It fills my soul with horror to think that any creature should refuse his God, when his God speaks, but much more when God comes down on earth in infinite, wondrous, immeasurable love, takes upon himself the form of man, and suffers, and then turns round to his rebellious creature and says, "Listen, I am ready to forgive you; I am willing to pardon you; do but listen to me." Oh! it seems monstrous that men should refuse Christ! I don't know how you feel about it, but if you have ever measured that in your thoughts, it will have seemed to be the most monstrous of all crimes. If, in order to be saved, the terms were hard and the conditions difficult, I could understand a man saying, "It mocks me," but when the gospel is nothing but this, "Turn ye, turn ye; why will ye die?"; when it is nothing but, "Believe in the Lord Jesus Christ, and thou shalt be saved," what shall I say? I cannot fashion an excuse for any of you, and if you, after having heard the gospel, be cast into hell, I dare not think that its utmost pains will be too severe for so high an insult to such wondrous love. Ye will not be saved, sirs; ye put from you your own life; ye will not be saved when the way of salvation is plain, easy, simple, close to your hand. "What chains of vengeance they deserve, That slight the bonds of love." I cannot—I could not—conceive a punishment too severe for men who, knowing that their rejection of Christ will bring upon them everlasting punishment, yet wilfully reject him. Ye choose your own delusion. If ye drank poison and did not know it, I could pity you; if you made all your veins to swell with agony, and caused your death—but when we stand up and say, "Sirs, it is poison; see others drop and die; touch it not!"—when we give you something a thousand times better, and bid you take that, but you will not take that, but will have the poison—then if you will, you must. If, then, you would destroy your soul, it must be so; but we would plead with you yet again, "See, see that ye refuse not him that speaketh." I wish I could raise him before you tonight—even the Christ of God, and bid him stand here, and you should see his hands and his feet, and you should ask, "What are these marks we see there?" He would reply, "These are the wounds that I received when I suffered for the sons of men," and he bares his side and says, "See here, here went the spear when I died that sinners might live." In glory now, yet once, saith he, this face was defiled with spittle, and this body mangled with Pilate's scourge and Herod's rod, and I, whom angels worshipped, was treated as a menial, ay, worse, God himself forsook me, Jehovah hid his face from me, that I, bearing the punishment of sin, might really bear it, not in fiction, but in fact, and might suffer the equivalent for all the miseries that souls redeemed by me ought to have suffered had they been cast into hell. Will ye look at his wounds, and yet refuse him? Will you hear the story of his love, and yet reject him? Must he go away and say in his heart, "They have refused me; they have refused me; I told them of salvation; I showed them how I bought salvation; they have refused me; I will go my way, and they shall never see my face again till that day when they shall say, 'Mountains fall upon us; hide us from the face of him that sitteth upon the throne'"? If you will not have him in mercy, you must have him in judgment, and if the silver sceptre of God will not touch you, the Christ of God, the man of Nazareth, will come a second time on the clouds of heaven, and woe unto you in that tremendous day. Then shall the nations of the earth weep and wail because of him. They would not have him as their Saviour; they must have him as their

Judge, and out of his mouth shall the sentence come, "Depart! Depart!"

Now I have to close with the last reason that is given in the text why we should see that we "refuse not him that speaketh." It is this: that if we do:—

IV. THERE IS A DOOM TO BE FEARED, for if they escaped not who refused him that spake on earth, much more shall not we escape if we turn away from him that speaketh from heaven. You hear the din that goes up from the Red Sea when the angry billows leap over Pharaoh and his horsemen. Why is the king asleep in the midst of the waters? Why are the chivalry of Egypt cut off? They rejected Moses when he said, "Thus saith the Lord, Let my people go." If Pharaoh escaped not when he refused him that spake on earth, oh! dreadful shall be that day when the Christ who this day speaks to you, and whom you reject, shall lift up the rods of his anger, and the lake of fire, more direful than the Red Sea, shall swallow up his adversaries. See you that next sight? A number of men are standing there holding censers of incense in their hands, and there stands Moses, the servant of God, and he says, "If these die the death of common men, God hath not spoken by me," for they have rebelled against Moses. Do you see the sight? Can you picture it? If they escaped not who refused him that spake on earth, how shall we escape if we refuse him that speaketh from heaven? Go through the peninsular of the Arabian desert. See how the tribes drop, one by one, and leave graves behind them as the track of their march. Of all that came out of Egypt, not one entered into Canaan. Who slew all these? They were all slain there because they resisted the Word of God by his servant Moses, and he swore in his wrath that they should not enter into his rest. If they escaped not who refused him that spake on earth, how shall we escape if we refuse him that speaketh to us from heaven?

I might multiply instances and give you proof of how God avenged the refusal to listen to his servant Moses, but how much more will he avenge it if we listen not to Jesus Christ the Lord! "Oh!" says one, "you preach the terrors of the Lord." The terrors of the Lord!—I scarce think of them; they are too dreadful for human language; but if I speak severely, even for a moment, it is in love. I dare not play with you, sinner; I dare not tell you sin is a trifle; I dare not tell you that the world to come is a matter of no great account; I dare not come and tell you that you need not be in earnest. I shall have to answer for it to my Master. I have these words ringing in my ears, "If the watchman warns them not, they shall perish, but their blood will I require at the watchman's hands."

I cannot bear that I should have the blood of souls upon my skirts, and, therefore, do I again say to you—refuse what I say as much as you will; cast anything that is mine to the dogs; have nothing to do with it; but wherein I have spoken to you Christ's Word, and I have told you his gospel, "Believe and live," "He that believeth on him is not condemned," "He that believeth, and is baptized, shall be saved." Wherein it is Christ's gospel, it is Christ that speaks, and I again say to you, for your soul's sake, "Refuse not him that speaks from heaven to you." May his Spirit sweetly incline you to listen to Christ's Word, and may you be saved tonight.

If you don't have Christ tonight, some of you never will have him. If you are not saved tonight, some of you never will be. 'Tis now or never with you. God's Spirit strives with you, conscience is a little awakened. Catch every breeze, catch every breeze; do not let this pass by. Oh! that tonight you might seek, and that tonight you might find he Saviour. Else remember if you refuse him that speaks from heaven, he lifts his hands and swears that you shall not enter into his rest. Then are you lost, lost, lost, beyond all recall! God bless every one of you, and may we meet in heaven.

I do not know, I sometimes am afraid that there are not so many conversions as there used to be. If I thought there were no more souls to be saved by me in this place, under God, I would break away from every comfort, and go and find out a place where I could find some that God would bless. Are they all saved that will be? You seatholders, have I fished in this pond till there is no more to come? Is it to be so, that in all the ground where wheat ever will grow, wheat has grown, and there can be no more? My brethren and sisters in Christ, pray God to send his Spirit that there may be more brought to Jesus. If not, it is hard, hard work to preach in vain. Perhaps I grow stale and dull to you; I would not if I could help it. If I could learn how to preach, I would go to school. If I could find the best way to reach you I am sure I would spare no pains. I do not know what more to say, but if Christ himself shall be refused, how shall I speak for him? If his dear wounds, if his precious blood, if his dying groans, if his love to the souls of men all go for nothing, then my words cannot be anything; they may well go to the wind. But do, do turn ye to him. Cast not away your souls. Come to him; he will receive you; he waiteth to be gracious. Whosoever is heavy laden, let him come tonight. One tear, one sigh, one cry—send it up to him; he will hear you. Come and trust him; he will save you. God bless you for Christ's love's sake. Amen.

The Bible

A Sermon (No. 15) Delivered on Sabbath Evening, March 18, 1855, by the REV. C. H. SPURGEON At Exeter Hall, Strand.

> "I have written to him the great things of my law; but they were counted as a strange thing."
> —Hosea 8:12.

This is God's complaint against Ephraim. It is no mean proof of his goodness, that he stoops to rebuke his erring creatures; it is a great argument of his gracious disposition, that he bows his head to notice terrestrial affairs. He might, if he pleased, wrap himself with might as with a garment; he might put the stars around his wrist for bracelets, and bind the suns around his brow for a coronet; he might dwell alone, far, far above this world, up in the seventh heaven, and look down with calm and silent indifference upon all the doings of his creatures; he might do as the heathens supposed their Jove did, sit in perpetual silence, sometimes nodding his awful head to make the fates move as he pleased, but never taking thought of the little things of earth, disposing of them as beneath his notice, engrossed with his own being, swallowed up within himself, living alone and retired; and I, as one of his creatures, might stand by night upon a mountain-top, and look upon the silent stars and say, "Ye are the eyes of God, but ye look not down on me; your light is the gift of his omnipotence, but your rays are not smiles of love to me. God, the mighty Creator, has forgotten me; I am a despicable drop in the ocean of creation, a sear leaf in the forest of beings, an atom in the mountain of existence. He knows me not; I am alone, alone, alone." But it is not so, beloved. Our God is of another order. He notices every one of us; there is not a sparrow or a worm but is found in his decrees. There is not a person upon whom his eye is not fixed. Our most secret acts are known to him. Whatsoever we do, or bear, or suffer, the eye of God still rests upon us, and we are beneath his smile—for we are his people; or beneath his frown—for we have erred from him.

Oh! how ten-thousand-fold merciful is God, that, looking down upon the race of man, he does not smite it out of existence. We see from our text that God looks upon man; for he says of Ephraim, "I have written to him the great things of my law, but they were counted as a strange thing." But see how, when he observes the sin of man, he does not dash him away and spurn him with his foot; he does not shake him by the neck over the gulf of hell, until his brain doth reel and then drop him forever; but rather, he comes down from heaven to plead with his creatures; he argues with them; he puts himself, as it were, upon a level with the sinner—states his grievances and pleads his claim. O Ephraim, I have written unto thee the great things of my law, but they have been unto thee as a strange thing! I come here to-night in God's stead, my friends, to plead with you as God's ambassador, to charge many of you with a sin; to lay it to your hearts by the power of the Spirit, so that you may be convinced of sin, of righteousness, and of a judgment to come. The crime I charge you with is the sin of the text. God has written to you the great things of his law, but they have been unto you as a strange thing. It is concerning this blessed book, the Bible, that I mean to speak tonight. Here lies my text—this Word of God. Here is the theme of my discourse, a theme which demands more eloquence than I possess; a subject upon which a thousand orators might speak at once; a mighty, vast, and comprehensive theme, which might engross all eloquence throughout eternity, and still it would remain unexhausted.

Concerning the Bible, I have three things to say tonight, and they are all in my text. First, its author, "I have written;" secondly, its subjects—the great things of God's law; and thirdly, its common treatment—it has been accounted by most men a strange thing.

I. First, then, concerning this book: Who is the author? The text says that it is God. "I have written to him the great things of my law." Here lies my Bible—who wrote it? I open it, and find it consists of a series of tracts.

The first five tracts were written by a man called Moses; I turn on, and I find others. Sometimes I see David is the penman, at other times Solomon. Here I read Micah, then Amos, then Hosea. As I turn further on, to the more luminous pages of the New Testament, I see Matthew, Mark, Luke, and John, Paul, Peter, James, and others; but when I shut up the book; I ask myself, who is the author of it? Do these men jointly claim the authorship? Are they the compositors of this massive volume? Do they between themselves divide the honor? Our holy religion answers, No! This volume is the writing of the living God; each letter was penned with an Almighty finger; each word in it dropped from the everlasting lips; each sentence was dictated by the Holy Spirit. Albeit, that Moses was employed to write his histories with his fiery pen, God guided that pen. It may be that David touched his harp, and let sweet Psalms of melody drop from his fingers; but God moved his hands over the living strings of his golden harp. It may be that Solomon sang canticles of love, or gave forth words of consummate wisdom, but God directed his lips, and made the preacher eloquent. If I follow the thundering Nahum, when his horses plough the waters, or Habakkuk, when he sees the tents of Cushan in affliction; if I read Malachi, when the earth is burning like an oven; if I turn to the smooth page of John, who tells of love, or the rugged, fiery chapters of Peter, who speaks of fire devouring God's enemies; if I turn to Jude, who launches forth anathemas upon the foes of God, everywhere I find God speaking; it is God's voice, not man's; the words are God's words, the words of the Eternal, the Invisible, the Almighty, the Jehovah of this earth. This Bible is God's Bible, and when I see it, I seem to hear a voice springing up from it, saying, "I am the book of God; man, read me. I am God's writing; open my leaf, for I was penned by God; read it, for he is my author, and you will see him visible and manifest everywhere." "I have written to him the great things of my law."

How do you know that God wrote the book? That is just what I shall not try to prove to you. I could if I pleased, demonstrate it, for there are arguments enough, there are reasons enough, did I care to occupy your time to-night in bringing them before you; but I shall do no such thing. I might tell you, if I pleased, that the grandeur of the style is above that of an mortal writing, and that all the poets who have ever existed could not, with all their works united, give us such sublime poetry and such mighty language as is to be found in the Scriptures. I might insist upon it, that the subjects of which it treats are beyond the human intellect; that man could never have invented the grand doctrines of a Trinity in the Godhead; man could not have told us anything of the creation of the universe; he could never have been the author of the majestic idea of Providence—that all things are ordered according to the will of one great Supreme Being, and work together for good. I might enlarge upon its honesty, since it tells the faults of its writers; its unity, since it never belies itself; its master simplicity, that he who runs may read it; and I might mention a hundred more things, which would all prove, to a demonstration, that the book is of God. But I come not here to prove it. I am a Christian minister, and you are Christians, or profess to be so; and there is never any necessity for Christian ministers to make a point of bringing forward infidel arguments in order to answer them. It is the greatest folly in the world. Infidels, poor creatures, do not know their own arguments till we tell them, and then they glean their blunted shafts to shoot them at the shield of truth again. It is follow to bring forward these firebrands of hell, even if we are well prepared t quench them. Let men of the world learn error of themselves; do not let us be propagators of their falsehoods. True, there are some preachers who are short of stock, and want to fill them up; but God's own chosen men need not do that; they are taught of God, and God supplies them with matter, with language, with power. There may be some one here to-night who has come without faith, a man of reason, a freethinker. With him I have no argument at all. I profess not to stand here as a controversialist, but as a preacher of things that I know and feel. But I too, have been like him. There was an evil hour when I once shipped the anchor of my faith; I cut the cable of my belief; I no longer moored myself hard by the coasts of Revelation; I allowed my vessel to drift before the wind; I said to reason, "Be thou my captain;" I said to my own brain, "Be thou my rudder;" and I started on my mad voyage. Thank God, it is all over now; but I will tell you its brief history. It was one hurried sailing over the tempestuous ocean of free thought. I went on, and as I went, the skies began to darken; but to make up for that deficiency, the waters were brilliant with coruscations of brilliancy. I saw sparks flying upward that pleased me, and I thought, "If this be free thought, it is a happy thing." My thoughts seemed gems, and I scattered stars with both my hands; but anon, instead of these coruscations of glory, I saw grim fiends, fierce and horrible, start up from the waters, and as I dashed on, they gnashed their teeth, and grinned upon me; they seized the prow of my ship and dragged me on, while , in part, gloried at the rapidity of my motion, but yet shuddered at the terrific rate with which I passed the old landmarks of my faith. As I hurried forward, with an awful speed, I began to doubt my very existence; I doubted if there were a world, I doubted if there was such a thing as myself. I went to the very verge of the dreary realms of unbelief. I went to the very bottom of the sea of Infidelity. I doubted everything. But here the devil foiled himself: for the very extravagance of the doubt, proved its absurdity. Just when I saw the bottom of that sea, there came a voice which said, "And can this doubt be true?" At this very thought I awoke. I started from that deathdream, which, God knows might have damned my soul, and ruined this, my body, if I had not awoke. When I arose, faith took the helm; from that moment I doubted not. Faith steered me back; faith cried, "Away, away!" I cast my anchor on Calvary; I lifted my eye to God; and here I am, "alive, and out of hell."

Therefore, I speak what I do know. I have sailed that perilous voyage; I have come safe to land. Ask me again to be an infidel! No; I have tried it; it was sweet at first, but bitter afterwards. Now, lashed to God's gospel more firmly than ever, standing as on a rock of adamant, I defy the arguments of hell to move me; for "I know in whom I have believed, and am persuaded that he is able to keep that which I have committed unto him." But I shall neither plead nor argue this night. You profess to be Christian men, or else you would not be here. Your professions may be lies; what you say you are, may be the very contrary to what you really are; but still I suppose you all admit that this is the Word of God. A thought or two then upon it. "I have written to him the great things of my law." First, my friends, stand over this volume, and admire its authority. This is no common book. It is not the sayings of the sages of Greece; here are not the utterances of philosophers of past ages. If these words were written by a man, we might reject them; but O let me think the solemn thought, that this book is God's handwriting—that these words are God's! Let me look at its date; it is dated from the hills of heaven. Let me look at its letters; they flash glory on my eye. Let me read the chapters; they are big with meaning and mysteries unknown. Let me turn over the prophecies; they are pregnant with unthought-of wonders. Oh, book of books! And wast thou written by my God? Then will I bow before thee. Thou book of vast authority! thou art a proclamation from the Emperor of Heaven; far be it from me to exercise my reason in contradicting thee.

Reason, thy place is to stand and find out what this volume means, not to tell what this book ought to say. Come thou, my reason, my intellect, sit thou down and listen, for these words are the words of God. I do not know how to enlarge on this thought. Oh! if you could ever remember that this Bible was actually and really written by God. Oh! if ye had been let into the secret chambers of heaven, if ye had beheld God grasping his pen and writing down these letters—then surely ye would respect them; but they are just as much God's handwriting as if you had seen God write them. This Bible is a book of authority; it is an authorized book, for God has written it. Oh! tremble, lest any of you despise it; mark its authority, for it is the Word of God.

Then, since God wrote it, mark its truthfulness. If I had written it, there would be worms of critics who would at once swarm upon it, and would cover it with their evil spawn; Had I written it, there would be men who would pull it to pieces at once, and perhaps quite right too. But this is the Word of God; come, search, ye critics, and find a flaw; examine it, from its Genesis to its Revelation, and find an error. This is a vein of pure gold, unalloyed by quartz, or any earthly substance. This is a star without a speck; a sun without a blot; a light without darkness; a moon without its paleness; a glory without a dimness. O Bible! it cannot be said of any other book, that it is perfect and pure; but of thee we can declare all wisdom is gathered up in thee, without a particle of folly. This is the judge that ends the strife, where wit and reason fail. This is the book untainted by any error; but is pure, unalloyed, perfect truth. Why? Because God wrote it. Ah! charge God with error if ye please; tell him that his book is not what it ought to be. I have heard men, with prudish and mock-modesty, who would like to alter the Bible; and (I almost blush to say it) I have heard ministers alter God's Bible, because they were afraid of it. Have you never heard a man say, "He that believeth and is baptized, shall be saved; but he that believeth not"—what does the Bible say?—"Shall be damned." But that does not happen to be polite enough, so they say, "Shall be condemned." Gentlemen, pull the velvet out of your mouths; speak God's word; we want none of your alterations. I have heard men in prayer instead of saying, "Make your calling and election sure," say "Make your calling and salvation sure." Pity they were not born when God lived far—far back that they might have taught God how to write. Oh, impudence beyond all bounds! Oh full-blown self-conceit! To attempt to dictate to the All-wise—to teach the Omniscient and instruct the Eternal. Strange that there should be men so vile as to use the penknife of Jehoiakim to cut passages out of the word, because they are unpalatable. O ye who dislike certain portions of Holy Writ, rest assured that your taste is corrupt, and that God will not stay for you little opinion. Your dislike is the very reason why God wrote it, because you out not to be suited; you have no right to be pleased. God wrote what you do not like; he wrote the truth.

Oh! let us bend in reverence before it, for God inspired it. It is pure truth. Here from this fountain gushes aqua vitae—the water of life—without a single particle of earth; here from this sun cometh forth rays of radiance, without the mixture of darkness. Blessed Bible! thou art all truth.

Yet once more, before we leave this point, let us stop and consider the merciful nature of God, in having written us a Bible at all. Ah! he might have left us without it, to grope our dark way, as blind men seek the wall; he might have suffered us to wander on with the star of reason as our only guide. I recollect a story of Mr. Hume, who so constantly affirmed that the light of reason is abundantly sufficient. Being at a good minister's house one evening, he had been discussing the question, and declaring his firm belief in the sufficiency of the light of nature. On leaving, the minister offered to hold him a candle to light him down the steps. He said "No; the light of nature would be enough; the moon would do." It so happened that the moon was covered with a cloud, and he fell down the steps. "Ah!" said the minister, "you had better have had a little light from above, after all, Mr. Hume." So, supposing the light of nature to be sufficient, we had better have a little light from above too, and then we shall be sure to be right. Better have two lights than only one. The light of creation is a bright light. God may be seen in the stars; his name is written in gilt letters on the brow of night; you may discover his glory in the ocean waves, yea, in the trees of the field; but it is better to read it in two books than in one. You will find it here more clearly revealed; for he has written this book himself, and he has given you the key to understand it, if you have the Holy Spirit. Ah, beloved, let us thank God for this Bible; let us love it; let us count it more precious than much fine gold.

But let me say one thing, before I pass on to the second point. If this be the Word of God, what will become of some of you who have not read it for the last month? "Month, sir! I have not read it for this year." Ay, there are some of you who have not read it at all. Most people treat the Bible very politely . They have a small pocket volume, neatly bound; they put a white pocket-handkerchief round it and carry it to their places of worship; when they get home, they lay it up in a drawer till next Sunday morning; then it comes out again for a little bit of a treat, and goes to chapel; that is all the poor Bible gets in the way of an airing. That is your style of entertaining this heavenly messenger. There is dust enough on some of your Bibles to write "damnation" with your fingers. There are some of you who have not turned over your Bibles for a long, long while, and what think you? I tell you blunt words, but true words. What will God say at last? When you shall come before him, he shall say, "Did you read my Bible?" "No." "I wrote you a letter of mercy; did you read it?" "No." "Rebel! I have sent thee a letter inviting thee to me; didst thou ever read it?" "Lord, I never broke the seal; I kept it shut up." "Wretch!" says God, "then, thou deservest hell, if I sent thee a loving epistle, and thou wouldst not even break the seal; what shall I do unto thee?" Oh, let it not be so with you. Be Bible-readers.

II. Our second point is: The subjects on which the Bible treats. The words of the text are these: "I have written to him the great things of my law." The Bible treats of great things, and of great things only. there is nothing in this Bible which is unimportant. Every verse in it has a solemn meaning; and if we have not found it out yet, we hope yet to do it. You have seen mummies, wrapped round and round with folds of linen. Well, God's Bible is like that; it is a vast roll of white linen, woven in the loom of truth; so you will have to continue unwinding it, roll after roll, before you get the real meaning of it from the very depth; and when you have found, as you think, a part of the meaning, you will still need to keep on unwinding, unwinding, and all eternity you will be unwinding the words of this great volume. Yet there is nothing in the Bible but great things. Let me divide, so as to be more brief. First, all things in this Bible are great; but, secondly, some things are the greatest of all.

All things in the Bible are great. Some people think it does not matter what doctrines you believe; that it is immaterial what church you attend; that all denominations are alike. Well, I dislike Mrs. Bigotry above almost all people in the world, and I never give her any compliment or praise; but there is another woman I hate equally as much, and that is Mrs. Latitudinarianism—a well-known character, who has made the discovery that all of us are alike. Now, I believe that a man may be saved in any church. Some have been saved in the Church of Rome—a few blessed men whose names I could mention here. I know, blessed be God, what multitudes are saved in the Church of England; she has a host of pious, praying men in her midst. I think that all sections of Protestant Christians have a remnant according to the election of grace; and they had need to have, some of them, a little salt, for otherwise they would go to corruption. But when I say that, do you imagine that I think them all on a level? Are they all alike truthful? One sect says infant baptism is right; another says it is wrong; yet you say they are both right. I cannot see that. One teaches we are saved by free grace; another say us that we are not, but are saved by free will; and yet you believe they are both right. I do not understand that. One says that God loves his people, and never leaves off loving them; another says that he did not love his people before they loved him—that he often loves them, and then ceases to love them, and turns them away. They may both be right in the main; but can they both be right when one says "Yes," and the other says "No?" I must have a pair of spectacles, to enable me to look backwards and forwards at the same time, before I can see that. It cannot be, sirs, that they are both right. But some say they differ upon non-essentials. This text says, "I have written to him the great things of my law." There is nothing in God's Bible which is not great. Did ever any of you sit down to see which was the purest religion? "Oh," say you, "we never took the trouble. We went just where our father and mother went." Ah! that is a profound reason indeed. You went where you father and mother did. I thought you were sensible people; I didn't think you went where other people pulled you, but went of your own selves. I love my parents above all that breathe, and the very thought that they believe a thing to be true, helps me to think it is correct; but I have not followed them; I belong to a different denomination, and I thank God that I do. I can receive them as Christian brethren and sisters; but I never thought that, because they happened to be one thing, I was to be the same. No such thing. God gave me brains, and I will use them; and if you have any intellect, use it too. Never say it doesn't matter. Whatever God has put here is of eminent importance; he would not have written a thing that was indifferent. Whatever is here is of some value; therefore, search all questions, try all by the Word of God. I am not afraid to have what I preach tried by this book. Only give me a fair field and no favor, and this book; if I say anything contrary to it, I will withdraw it the next Sabbath-day. By this I stand, by this I fall. Search and see; but don't say, "it does not matter." If God says a thing, it always must be of importance.

But, while all things in God's word are important, all are not equally important. There are certain fundamental and vital truths which must be believed, or otherwise no man would be saved. If you want to know what you must believe, if ye would be saved, you will find the great things of God's law between these two covers; they are all contained here. As a sort of digest or summary of the great things of law, I remember an old friend of mine once saying, "Ah! you preach the three R's, and God will always bless you." I said, "What are the three R's?" and he answered, "Ruin, redemption, and regeneration." They contain the sum and substance of divinity.

R for ruin. We were all ruined in the fall; we were lost when Adam sinned, and we were all ruined by our own transgressions; we are all ruined by our own evil hearts, and our own wicked wills; and we all shall be ruined, unless grace saves us. Then there is a second R for redemption. We are ransomed by the blood of Christ, a lamb without blemish and without spot; we are rescued by his power; we are ransomed by his merits; we are redeemed by his strength. then there is R for regeneration. If we would be pardoned, we must also be regenerated; for no man can partake of redemption unless he is regenerate. Let him be as good as he pleases; let him serve God, as he imagines, as much as he likes; unless he is regenerate, and has a new heart, a new birth, he will still be in the first R, that is ruin. These things contain an epitome of the gospel. I believe there is a better epitome in the five points of Calvinism;—Election according to the foreknowledge of God; the natural depravity and sinfulness of man; particular redemption by the blood of Christ; effectual calling by the power of the Spirit; and ultimate perseverance by the efforts of God's might. I think all those need to be believed, in order to salvation; but I should not like to write a creed like the Athanasian, beginning with "Whosoever shall be saved, before all things it is necessary that he should hold the Catholic faith, which faith is this,"—when I got so far, I should stop, because I should not know what to write. I hold the Catholic faith of the Bible, the whole Bible, and nothing but the Bible. It is not for me to draw up creeds; but I ask you to search the Scriptures, for this is the word of life.

God says, "I have written to him the great things of my law." Do you doubt their greatness? Do ye think they are not worth your attention? Reflect a moment, man. Where art thou standing now? "Lo on a narrow neck of land, 'Twixt two unbounded seas I stand; An inch of time, a moment's space, May lodge me in yon heavenly place, Or shut me up in hell."

I recollect standing on a seashore once, upon a narrow neck of land, thoughtless that the tide might come up. The tide kept continually washing up on either side, and, wrapped in thoughts, I stood there, until at last there was the greatest difficulty in getting on shore. You and I stand each day on a narrow neck, and there is one wave coming up there; see, how near it is to your foot; and lo! another follows at every tick of the clock; "Our hearts, like muffled drums, are beating funeral marches to the tomb." We are always tending downwards to the grave each moment that we live. This book tells me that if I am converted, when I die, there is a heaven of joy and love to receive me; it tells me that angels' pinions shall be stretched, and I, borne by strong cherubic wings, shall out-soar the lightning, and mount beyond the stars, up to the throne of God, to dwell forever. "Far from a world of grief and sin, With God eternally shut in." Oh! it makes the hot tear start from my eye, it makes my heart too big for this my body, and my brain whirls at the thought of "Jerusalem, my happy home, Name ever dear to me." Oh! that sweet scene beyond the clouds; sweet fields arrayed in living green, and rivers of delight. Are not these great things? But then, poor unregenerate soul, the Bible says if thou are lost, thou art lost forever; it tells thee that if thou diest without Christ, without God, there is no hope for thee; that there is no place without a gleam of hope, where thou shalt read, in burning letters, "Ye knew your duty, but ye did it not;" it tells you, that ye shall be driven from his presence with a "depart, ye cursed." Are these not great things? Yes, sirs, as heaven is desirable, as hell is terrible, as time is short, as eternity is infinite, as the soul is precious, as pain is to be shunned, as heaven is to be sought, as God is eternal, and as his words are sure, these are great things, things ye ought to listen to.

III. Our last point is: The treatment which the poor Bible receives in this world; it is accounted a strange thing. What does that mean—the Bible accounted a strange thing? In the first place, it means that it is very strange to some people, because they never read it. I remember reading, on one occasion, the sacred story of David and Goliath, and there was a person present, positively grown up to years of maturity, who said to me, "Dear me! what an interesting story; what book is that in?" And I recollect a person once coming to me in private; I spoke to her about her soul, she told me how deeply she felt, how she had a desire t serve God, but she found another law in her members. I turned to a passage in Romans, and read to her, "The good that I would I do not; and the evil which I would not that I do!" She said, "Is that in the Bible? I did not know it." I did not blame her, because she had no interest in the Bible till then; but I did not wonder that there could be found persons who knew nothing about such a passage. Ah! you know more about your ledgers than your Bible; you know more about your day-books than what God has written; many of you will read a novel from beginning to end, and what have you got? A mouthful of froth when you have done. But you cannot read the Bible; that solid, lasting, substantial, and satisfying food goes uneaten, locked up in the cupboard of neglect; while anything that man writes, a catch of the day, is greedily devoured. "I have written to him the great things of my law, but they were counted as a strange thing." Ye have never read it. I bring the broad charge against you. Perhaps, ye say, I ought not to charge you with any such thing. I always think it better to have a worse opinion of you than too good an one. I charge you with this: you do not read your Bibles. Some of you have never read it through. I know I speak what your heart must say is honest truth. You are not Bible readers. You say you have the Bible in your houses; do I think you are such heathens as not to have a Bible? But when did you read it last? How do you know that your spectacles, which you have lost, have not been there for the last three years? Many people have not turned over its pages for a long time, and God might say unto them, "I have written unto you the great things of my law, but they have been accounted unto you a strange thing."

Others there be who read the Bible; but when they read it, they say it is so horribly dry. That young man over there says it is a "bore;" that is the words he uses. He says, "My mother says to me, when you go up to town, read a chapter every day. Well, I thought I would please her, and I said I would. I am sure I wish I had not. I did not read a chapter yesterday, or the day before. We were so busy, I could not help it." You do not love the Bible, do you? "No, there is nothing in it which is interesting." Ah, I thought so. But a little while ago I could not see anything in it. Do you know why? Blind men cannot see, can they? But when the Spirit touches the scales of the eyes, they fall off; and when he puts eye-salves on, the Bible becomes precious. I remember a minister who went to see an old lady, and he thought he would give her some precious promises out of the word of God. Turning to one, he saw written in the margin "P.," and he asked, "What does this mean?" "That means precious, sir." Further down, he saw "T. and P.," and he asked what the letters meant. "That," she said, "means tried and proved, for I have tried and proved it." If you have tried God's word and proved it—if it is precious to your soul. then you are Christians; but those persons who despise the Bible, have "neither part nor lot in the matter." If it is dry to you, you will be dry at last in hell. If you do not esteem it as better than your necessary food, there is no hope for you; for you lack the greatest evidence of your Christianity.

Alas! alas! the worst case is to come. There are some people who hate the Bible, as well as despise it. Is there such an one stepped in here? Some of you said, "Let us go and hear what the young preacher has to say to us." This is what he has to say to you: "Behold, ye despisers, and wonder and perish." This is what he hath to say to you: "The wicked shall be turned into hell, and all that forget God." And this, again he has to say to you: "Behold, there shall come in the last days, mockers, like yourselves, walking after your own lusts." But more: he tells you to-night that if you are saved, you must find salvation here. Therefore, despise not the Bible; but search it, read it, and come unto it. Rest thee will assured, O scorner, that thy laughs cannot alter truth, thy jests cannot avert thine inevitable doom. Though in thy hardihood thou shouldst make a league with death, and sign a covenant with hell—yet swift justice shall o'ertake thee, and strong vengeance strike the low. In vain dost thou jeer and mock, for eternal verities are mightier than thy sophistries, nor can thy smart sayings alter the divine truth of a single word of this volume of Revelation. Oh! why dost thou quarrel with thy best friend, and ill-treat thy only refuge? There yet remains hope, even for the scorner. Hope in a Saviour's veins. Hope in the Father's mercy. Hope in the Holy Spirit's omnipotent agency.

I have done when I have said one word. My friend, the philosopher, says it may be very well for me to urge people to read the Bible; but he thinks there are a great many sciences far more interesting and useful than theology. Extremely obliged to you for your opinion, sir. What science do you mean? The science of dissecting beetles and arranging butterflies? "No," you say, "certainly not." The science, then, of arranging stones, and telling us of the strata of the earth? "No, not exactly that." Which science, then? "Oh, all sciences," say you, "are better than the science of the Bible." Ah! sir, that is your opinion; and it is because you are far from God, that you say so. But the science of Jesus Christ is the most excellent of sciences. Let no one turn away from the Bible because it is not a book of learning and wisdom. It is. Would ye know astronomy? It is here: it tells you of the Sun of Righteousness and the Star of Bethlehem. Would you know of botany? It is here: it tells you of the plant of renown—the Lily of the Valley, and the rose of Sharon. Would you know geology and mineralogy? You shall learn it here: for you may read of the Rock of Ages, and the White Stone with the name engraven thereon, which no man knoweth saving he that receiveth it. Would ye study history? Here is the most ancient of all the records of the history of the human race. Whate'er your science is, come and bend o'er this book; your science is here. Come and drink out of this fair fount of knowledge and wisdom, and ye shall find yourselves made wise unto salvation. Wise and foolish, babes and men, gray-headed sires, youths and maidens—I speak to you, I plead with you, I beg of you respect your Bibles, and search them out, for in them ye think ye have eternal life, and these are they which testify of Christ.

I have done. Let us go home and practice what we have heard. I have heard of a woman, who, when she was asked what she remembered of the minister's sermon, said, "I don't recollect anything of it. It was about short weights and bad measures, and I didn't recollect anything but to go home and burn the bushel." So, if you will remember to go home and burn the bushel, if you will recollect to go home and read your Bibles, I shall have said enough. And may God, in his infinite mercy, when you read your Bibles, pour into your souls the illuminating rays of the Sun of Righteousness, by the agency of the ever-adorable Spirit; then you will read to your profit and to your soul's salvation.

We may say of THE BIBLE: "God's cabinet of revealed counsel 't is! Where weal and woe, are ordered so That every man may know which shall be his; Unless his own mistake, false application make. "It is the index to eternity. He cannot miss of endless bliss. That takes this chart to steer by, Nor can he be mistook that speaketh by this book. "It is the book of God. What if I should Say, God of books, let him that looks Angry at that expression, as too bold, His thoughts in silence smother, till he find such another."

The Ark of His Covenant

**A Sermon (No. 2427) Intended for
Reading on Lord's-day, August 25th, 1895,
Delivered by C. H. SPURGEON,
At the Metropolitan Tabernacle, Newington.
On Thursday Evening, August 18th, 1887.**

"And there were lightnings, and voices, and thunderings, and an earthquake And the temple of God was opened in heaven, and there was seen in his temple the ark of his testament [covenant– R-V.]:, and great hail."—Revelation 11:19.

I shall take the passage quite by itself. I do not fully understand its connection, whether it relates to that which goes before or that which comes afterwards; and happily, it is necessary for us to know this, for the passage stands complete in itself, and is full of valuable instruction.

Dear friends, even we who believe have as yet failed to see much of the truth of God. We know enough to save us, to comfort us, and to help us on our way to heaven; but oh, how much of the glory of divine truth has never yet been revealed to our eyes! Some of God's children do not fully know even the common truths as yet, and those who do not know them realize but little of their depth and height. From our text, it appears that there are certain things of God which as yet we have not yet seen there is need that they should be opened to us: "The temple of God was opened in heaven." When our Lord Jesus died, He rent the veil of the temple, and so He laid open the Holy of Holies but such is our dimness of sight, that we need to have the temple opened, and we need to have the Holy of Holies opened, so that we may see what is not really concealed, but what we are not ready to perceive by reason of the slowness of our understandings. The two words for "temple" here may relate not only to the temple itself, but also to the Holy of Holies, the innermost shrine. Both of these, it seems, need to be opened, or else we shall not see what there is in them. Blessed be the Holy Spirit that He does open up one truth after another to us. Our Savior's promise to His disciples was, "When he, the Spirit of truth, is come, he will guide you into all truth." If we were more teachable, if we were more anxious to be taught, and waited upon Him more, He would, doubtless, lead us into many a truth which at the present moment we have not fully enjoyed. It is a happy thing for you and for me when at any time we can say, "The temple of God was opened in heaven, so that we saw even that which was in the innermost shrine of the holy temple."

The saints in heaven doubtless behold all the glory of God so far as it can be perceived by created beings; but we who are on the right way thither behold, as in a glass darkly, the glory of the Lord. We know only in part, but the part we do know is not so great as it might be, we might know far more than we do even here. Some suppose that they can know but little, because they say that it is written, "Eye hath not seen, nor ear heard, neither have entered into the heart of man, the things which God hath prepared for them that love him." Yes, but why do you stop there? Half a text is often not true; go on to the end of the passage: "But God hath revealed them unto us by his Spirit: for the Spirit searcheth all things, yea, the deep things of God"; and that which your eye cannot see, and your ear cannot hear, and the heart of man cannot imagine, can be revealed to you by the Spirit of the Lord. Oh, that we were more conscious of the power of the Spirit, and that we waited upon Him for yet fuller instruction! Then I am persuaded that, in our measure and degree, it would be true to us, even as to the perfected ones above, "The temple of God was opened in heaven," and they saw that which was in the holiest place.

What did they see when the temple was opened? When the secret place was laid bare to them, what did they see? That is to be my subject now. "There was seen in his temple the ark of his covenant." If we could look into heaven at this moment, this is what we should see, "the ark of his covenant." O sinner, thou thinkest that thou wouldst see an angry God, but thou wouldst see the ark of His covenant! O child of God, perhaps thou dreamest of many things that might distress thee in the glory of that sight; but rest thou content, this would be the main sight that thou wouldst see, Jesus, the incarnate God, the great covenant Surety! Thou wouldst see there, where, the Godhead shines resplendent, the ark of His covenant.

I. I shall begin by noticing. first, that THE ARK OF HIS COVENANT IS ALWAYS NEAR TO GOD: "There was seen in his temple the ark of his covenant."

Of course, the outward symbol is gone; we are not now speaking of a temple made with hands, that is to say, of this building. We speak of the spiritual temple above; we speak of the spiritual Holy of Holies. If we could look in there, we should see the ark of the covenant; and we should see the covenant itself always near to God. The covenant is always there. God never forgets it; it is ever before Him: "There was seen in his temple the ark of his covenant."

Why is this? Is it not because the covenant is always standing? The Lord said concerning His people of old. "I will make with them an everlasting covenant," of which David said, "Yet hath he made with me an everlasting covenant, ordered in all things and sure." If God has made a covenant with you, it is not simply for today and tomorrow, nor merely for this life, but for the ages of ages, even forever and ever. If He has struck hands with you through the great Surety, and He has pledged Himself to you, remember, "If we believe not, yet he abideth faithful: he cannot deny himself." Jehovah hath said, "The mountains shall depart, and the hills be removed; but my kindness shall not depart from thee, neither shall the covenant of my peace be removed."

What He hath said He will stand to forever. He will keep His Word. He said to His Son, "I will preserve thee and give thee for a covenant of the people"; and He will never revoke the gift. This covenant stands secure. Though earth's old columns bow, and though my spirits sink, and flesh and heart fail me, yet this covenant shall bear me up even to the end.

The covenant of grace is forever the same, because, first, the God who made it changes not. There can be no change in God. The supposition is inconsistent with a belief in His deity. Hear what He says: "I am the Lord, I change not; therefore ye sons of Jacob are not consumed." The sun hath his changes, but the Father of lights is without variableness, or shadow of turning. "God is not a man, that he should lie; neither the son of man, that he should repent: hath he said, and shall he not do it? or hath he spoken, and shall he not make it good?" God has never to alter His purposes; why should He? Those purposes are always infinitely wise. He knoweth the end from the beginning; so His covenant, which He made with such deliberation in the councils of eternity, that covenant which is sealed with the most precious things He ever had, even with the blood of His only-begotten Son, that covenant upon which He stakes His eternal honor, for His glory and honor are wrapped up with the covenant of grace—that covenant cannot be changed because God Himself changeth not.

Then, next, the Christ who is its Surety and Substance changes not. Christ, the great Sacrifice by whose death the covenant was ratified, Christ, the Surety, who has sworn to carry out our part of the covenant, Christ, who is the very sum and substance of the covenant, never alters. "All the promises of God in him are yea, and in him Amen, unto the glory of God by us." If we had a variable Savior, brethren, we should have a changeable covenant. Look at Adam; he could change, and therefore he was a poor representative of the human race. Our first federal head soon fell because he was a mere man; but the Surety of the new covenant is the Son of God, who, like His Father, faileth not, and changeth not. Though He is of the substance of His mother, bone of our bone, and flesh of our flesh, and therefore can stand as man's Representative, yet is he Light of Light, very God of very God, and so He standeth fast and firm, like the unchanging God Himself. In this great truth we do and we will rejoice. The covenant is always before God, for Christ is always there. He, the Lamb in the midst of the throne, makes the covenant always to be close to the heart of God.

And, beloved, note you this. The covenant must always be near to God because the love which suggested it changes not. The Lord loves His people with a love which has no beginning, no end, no boundary, no change.

He says, "I have loved thee with an everlasting love: therefore with loving-Kindness have I drawn thee." When the love of God's heart goeth forth toward the believer, it is not changeful like the love of man, sometimes high and sometimes low, sometimes strong and sometimes weak; but, as it is said of our Savior, "having loved his own which were in the world, he loved them unto the end," so can it be said of the great Father that His love is evermore the same; and if the love which dictated the covenant is always in the heart of God, depend upon it that the covenant which comes of that love is always there in the secret place of the Most High.

Reflect also, beloved brethren, that the promises contained in the covenant change not. I quoted to you, just now, one passage about the promises, and that is enough: "All the promises of God in him are yea, and in him, Amen." Not one single promise of God shall ever fall to the ground unfulfilled. His Word in the form of promises, as well as in the form of the gospel, shall not return unto Him void. O souls, you may hang your whole weight upon any promise of God! You need not fear that it will break. Though all the vessels of the King's house were hung on one nail made by Him, that nail would bear them all up, as well as the fagons as the vessels of smaller measure. Heaven and earth may hang upon a single promise of God. The voice that rolls the stars along, and keeps them all in their orbits, is that voice which spoke even the least of the promises, and therefore every promise of God stands secure forever.

And once more, not only the promises, but the force and binding power of the covenant change not. All God's acts are done with a reference to His covenant, and all His covenant has a reference to His covenanted ones. Remember what Moses said of old, "When the Most High divided to the nations their inheritance, when he separated the sons of Adam, he set the bounds of the people according to the number of the children of Israel." Everything that He does follows the line and rule of His covenant. If He chastens and afflicts, it is not in anger, but in His dear covenant love. When first that covenant came into full action with the redeemed, it was all powerful; but it is just as powerful still. All that God doeth is still guided and directed by His eternal purpose and His covenant pledges to His people. Stand still, then, and when thou lookest up, if thou canst not see that temple because thine eye of faith is dim, if thou scarcely darest to look within into the secret place which is the holiest of all, yet know thou of a surety that the covenant is still there, and always there, whether thou seest it or seest it not.

I will tell thee when perhaps, thou wilt best know that the covenant is there; that is, when the storm-clouds gather the most thickly. When thou shalt see the black masses come rolling up, then remember that the Lord said to Noah, "I do set my bow in the loud, and it shall he for a token of a covenant between me and the earth." Then shalt thou know that Jehovah remembereth His covenant; thou mayest even be half glad of a black cloud, that the sun of the divine love may paint upon it the many-colored bow, that God may look on it, and remember His covenant. It is good for thee to look on it; but what must it be for Him to look on it, and to remember His covenant? Be thou glad that the covenant is always near to God, as out text declares, "And the temple of God was opened in heaven, and there was seen in his temple the ark of his covenant."

II. Now, secondly, THE COVENANT IS SEEN OF SAINTS: There was seen in his temple the ark of his covenant.

First, we see it when, by faith, we believe in Jesus as our Covenant-head.

By faith we know that God has entered into covenant with us. He that believeth in Christ Jesus is in covenant with God. "He that believeth on the Son hath everlasting life." "He that believeth on Him is not condemned."

He that believeth in Him is at peace with God, he has passed from death unto life, and shall never come into condemnation. Thou art in covenant with God, believer. Wipe thy weeping eyes, ask God to take the dust out of them, that thou mayest see that there is an unchanging covenant made with thee tonight and forever.

Next, we see this covenant when, by faith, we perceive it in God's actions toward us. Faith may see the covenant of God in all His actions. Do you not remember how the old Scotch woman blessed God for her porridge, but she blessed Him most of all because the porridge was in the covenant? God had promised bread and water, and therefore it was sure to come to her. God sent her bread to her in the form of porridge, and she blessed the Lord that it was in the covenant. Now, I thank God that food is in the covenant, and that raiment is in the covenant. It is written, "Thy shoes shall be iron and brass," so they are in the covenant Life is in the covenant and death is in the covenant: "To die is gain." Everything that is to happen to us is in the covenant; and when faith sees it so, it makes like a happy one. Am I chastened? I say to myself "Well, the rod was in the covenant, for the Lord said that, if His children disobeyed Him, He would chasten them with the rod of men.

If I never had the rod, I should be afraid I was not in the covenant." Is it not written, "In the world ye shall have tribulation?" That is a part of the covenant, you see; so that, when you get it, say to yourself, "The God who is evidently keeping this part of His covenant will keep the rest of it to me, His child."

Brethren, we get, perhaps. the best sight of the covenant when by prayer we plead it. In that hour of our wrestling, in the time of our inward craving of mercies from the hand of God, we come at last to this. "Lord, thou hast promised; do as thou hast said." I love to put my finger on a promise, and then to plead it with the Lord, saying, "This is thy Word, my Father; and I know that thou wilt not run back from it. O God, I believe in the inspiration of this Book, and I take very word of it as coming from thy lips. Wilt thou not seal it to my conscience, my heart, my experience, by proving it to be true?" Have you ever found the Lord's promises fail you? I remember one who had put in the margin of her Bible in several places, "I and P"; and when she was asked what those letters meant, she said, "That they mean, 'Tried and Proved.' As I go through life, I keep trying and proving the promises of God, and then I put a mark in the margin of my Bible against every one I have tested, that I may not forget it the next time I have to plead it." That is the way to see the covenant at the right hand of God, when you plead it in prayer.

And there are some of us, I think, who can say that our experience up till now proves that God does not forget His covenant. We have wandered, but we have been able to say, "He restoreth my soul." for He has restored us. We have needed many things, and we have gone to Him in prayer, and pleaded that word, "No good thing will he withhold from them that walk uprightly," and He has listened to the cries of His servants. He said He would do so: "Call upon me in the day of trouble: I will deliver thee, and thou shalt glorify me." He has remembered us in our low estate, for His mercy endureth forever; and some of us who are no longer young can set to our seal that God is true because of many experiences of His faithfulness. If they tell us that there is nothing in the Bible, and nothing in God, and nothing in the gospel of Christ, we laugh them to scorn. We have now for many a year lived upon the faithfulness of God, and we cannot be driven into a distrust of Him.

He is faithful, and His mercy endureth forever.

Do you not also think that, when we arrive in heaven, we shall have a wonderful retrospect, and that retrospect will all come to this: "The temple of God was opened in heaven, and there was seen in his temple the ark of his covenant?" Miss Hannah More very prettily puts it that, often, we do not see the right side of things here. She went into a carpet manufactory, and she looked at what the workmen were doing, and she could see nothing that looked like beauty of design. 'There were tags and ends hanging out, and she said to the men, "I cannot perceive any design here," and they answered, "No, madam, for you are on the wrong side of the carpet"; but when she went round to the other side, she saw the beauty of the workmanship. Alas! we are at present on the wrong side of God's work; we must get to heaven to see it perfectly, and when we get there, we shall—Sing, with wonder and surprise, His loving-kindness in the skies. and we shall say, It was all right; it could not have been better. Every dark and bending line Meets in the centre of his love. God hath not erred. He has not gone about the longest way to do His work, but He has done in the wisest and most prudent manner all that was for the best and highest interests of His dear covenanted ones.

Thus, I have shown you that sometimes, and it should be always, God's people do see that glorious covenant of grace which is in the temple above.

III. Now I want to have your attention while I say briefly, in the third place, that THE COVENANT CONTAINS MUCH THAT IS WORTH SEEING. Let us think of what was in the ancient ark of the covenant, for all that was in that ark as a type is to be seen in Christ our heavenly covenant ark above.

In that ark, if you and I could have gone into the holy place, and have had our eyes strengthened to look. we should have seen, first, God dwelling among men. What a wonderful thing! Over the top of the lid of that sacred coffer which was called the ark, there shone an amazing light which was the index of the presence of God. He was in the midst of the camp of Israel. He that filleth heaven and earth, the infinite Jehovah, deigned to make that place His special dwelling-place, so that He is addressed as, "Thou that dwellest between the cherubims." Here is a part of the new covenant: "I will dwell in them, and walk in them." It is marvelous that

God does speak with men. He whom you heard thundering, last night, as He drove His chariot through the sky, that God in infinite condescension speaks with us, and has come down to us, and taken us into relationship with Himself in the person of the Lord Jesus Christ, who is at once the fellow of the Almighty, and the brother of the sons of men. O beloved, rejoice in the covenant, that God is no longer divided from men! The chasm made by sin is filled, the gulf is bridged, and God now dwells with me, and manifests Himself to them; and "the secret of the Lord is with them that fear him."

Next, in that ark you would have noticed, if you could have seen into it, God reconciled and communing with men upon the mercy-seat. Over the top of that ark, as I have told you, was a golden lid, which fitted it, and covered it exactly, and that golden lid was called the mercy-seat, the throne of grace. There God spoke with men. He sat there, as it were, enthroned as the Friend of men. Now, it is a part of the covenant that God hears prayer, that God answers our petitions, that He meets us in a way of reconciled love, that He speaks to us in tones which the spirit can hear though the ear cannot. Thank God for a blood-besprinkled mercy-seat. What should we do if we had not that as our meeting-place with the thrice-holy Jehovah?

Then, within the ark, underneath the lid, if we could have looked in, we should have seen the law, the two tables of stone, which represent law fulfilled in Christ, and henceforth laid up in His heart, and laid up in our hearts, too, if we delight in the law of God after the inward man. Now, this is our joy, that the law of God has nothing against the believer. It is fulfilled in Christ, and we see it laid up in Christ, not to be a stone to fall upon us to grind us to powder, but beautiful and fair to look upon as it is in the heart of Christ, and fulfilled in the life of Christ. I rejoice in the covenant which contains in it stipulations all fulfilled, and commands all executed, by our great Representative.

Together with those tables of the law there was laid up a rod, a rod which had originally been a dry stick in the hands of Aaron, but when it was laid up before the Lord it budded, and blossomed, and brought forth almonds. So, in the covenant of grace, we see the kingdom established and flourishing in Christ, and we rejoice in it. Oh how pleased we are to bow before His fruitful sceptre! What wonderful fruit we gather from that blessed rod! Reign, reign, Jesus, reign! The more Thou dost rule us, the more Thou art absolute Sovereign of our hearts, the happier shall we be, and the more shall we delight ourselves in Thee. There is no liberty like complete subjection beneath the sway of Jesus who is our Prophet, Priest, and King.

Then, by the side of that rod there was laid up the golden pot full of manna, the provision made for the wilderness. Let us rejoice that there is in the covenant all the provision that we need. God has laid up for us in Christ all our spiritual meat, all the food that we shall ever need between here and heaven. "Feed me till I want no more," we cry to our blessed covenant Representative, and He will do so.

Then, over the top off the ark, sat the cherubirm with outstretched wings, as, I think, representing how the angels are in league with us, and with the angels all the forces and powers of the universe. This day, the beasts of the field are our friends, and the stones of the field have ceased to be our foes. Child of God, you may travel by land or sea; you may go where you will; for everywhere you are in your Father's house. All that you see about you is a friend to you, since you are a friend to God. I often wonder that the earth bears up ungodly men. It must groan beneath the weight of a swearer; it must want to open and swallow him up. But with the gracious man, the man who fears God, all things are at peace; and we may know it to be so. "Ye shall go out with joy, and be led forth with peace; the mountains and the hills shall break forth before you into singing, and all the trees of the field shall clap their hands." We do not often enough realize, I think, the friendship of all God's creatures to those who are His children. St. Francis, thought he was a Romish monk, yet had a true idea when he used to regard the sparrows and other birds of the air, and even the dogs in the street, as his friends and his brothers, and talked to them as such. And Luther was much of the same mind when he opened His window, and listened to the chirpings of the robins in the early spring, and felt that they had come to teach the theological doctor some lesson which he had not learned. Oh yes, oh yes, we are quite at home anywhere, now that God is our God! True, the earth travaileth, and is in pain, and the creation suffers and will suffer till Christ comes again; but still her travail is our travail, and we are in sympathy with her, and when she doth reflect the glory of her God she is our looking-glass in which we see our Father's face.

Thus, I think, 1 have shown you that there is much to be seen in the ark of the covenant. God give us grace, like the angels, to fix our eyes upon it! "Which things the angels desire to look into." We have more to do with the ark of His covenant than they have; let us be more desirous even than they are to look therein.

IV. I close with this fourth point. THE COVENANT HAS SOLEMN SURROUNDINGS. Listen: "There were lightnings, and voices, and thunderings, and an earthquake, and great hail."

When the people entered into covenant with God on Sinai, the Lord came down upon the top of the mount, and there were thunderings, and lightnings, and voices, and an earthquake. There were all these tokens of His presence, and God will not leave the covenant of his grace without the sanctions of His power; that thunder, that lightning, that storm—all these are engaged to keep His covenant. When they are wanted, the God who smote Egypt with great hailstones, the God who make the Kishon to sweep his enemies away, the God who made the stars in heaven to fight against Sisera, will bring all the overwhelming forces that are at His command to the help of His people, and the fulfilling of the covenant which He has made with them. O you who are His people, fall back in confidence upon the God who has treasures of snow, and hail, and the dread artillery of storms and tempest! Most of you, my hearers, have never seen a great storm yet, no r heard in its majesty the thunder of God's power. You must be in the tropics to know what these can be, and even then you would have to say, "These are but parts of His ways." Oh, how the Lord can shake the earth, and make it tremble even to its deep foundations when He pleases! He can make what we call "the solid earth" to be as weak as water when He doth but lift up His finger. But all the power that God hath—and it is boundless—is all in that right hand which has been lifted high to heaven in the solemn oath that He will save His people.

Wherefore, lean upon God without the shadow of a doubt. He may well put all your fears to rest even by the thunder of His power.

Then reflect that there is another side to this truth. You who are not in covenant with God, you who have not believed that Jesus is the Christ, you who have never fled for refuge to lay hold of the hope set before you, you who refuse the divine mercy which comes to you through the bleeding person of the suffering Christ, do remember that there will be for you the thunderings, and the lightnings, and the voices, and the earthquake, and the great hail, for these set forth the terrors of eternal law, overthrowing God's adversaries. You have no conception of what God will do with the ungodly. False teachers may smooth it down as much as they like, but that Book is full of thunderbolts to you who refuse God's mercy. Listen to this one text: "Consider this, ye that forget God, lest I tear you in pieces, and there be none to deliver." Can you sport with that? Listen to another: "Ah, I will ease me of mine adversaries, and avenge me of mine enemies!" What will you say to that, or to this? "And again they said Alleluia. And her smoke rose up forever and ever." "The same shall drink of the wine of the wrath of God, which is poured out without mixture into the cup of his indignation; and he shall be tormented with fire and brimstone in the presence of the holy angels, and in the presence of the Lamb. And the smoke of their torment ascendeth up forever and ever: and they have no rest day not night, who worship the beast and his image, and whosoever receiveth the mark; of his name." That they talk as if we invented these terrible words, but we do not; we merely quote the Scriptures of truth, and they are terrible indeed to the wicked. That they should make men start in their sleep, and never rest until they find a Savior. A Universalist once said to a Christian man that, whatever he did, God would not punish him, and the other replied, "If I spit on your god, I suppose he will not punish me. If I curse him, if I defy him, it will all come right at last?" "Yes," said the Universalist. "Well," answered the other, "that may be the character of your god; but don't you try that kind of thing with my God, the God of the Scriptures, or else you will find that because He is love He cannot, and He will not, suffer this world to be in anarchy, but he will rule it,;and govern it, and He will punish those that refuse His infinite compassion." So I beseech you, my hearers, fly to Jesus at once; weary, and heavy-laden, look to Him, for He saith especially to you, "Come unto me, and I will give you rest." The Lord add His blessing to the truth I have tried to preach to you, the sweet and the terrible alike, for Jesus' sake! Amen.

Hebrews 9.

Verse 1. Then verily the first covenant had also ordinances of divine service, and a worldly sanctuary.

That is to say, a material sanctuary, a sanctuary made out of such things as this world contains. Under the old covenant, there were certain outward symbols. Under the new covenant, we have not the symbols, but we have the substance itself. The old law dealt with types and shadows, but the gospel deals with the spiritual realities themselves.

2, 3. For there was a tabernacle made; the first, wherein was the candlestick, and the table, and the shewbread' which is called the sanctuary. And after the second veil, the tabernacle which is called the Holiest of all; All this was by divine appointment; the form of the rooms, the style of the furniture, everything was ordained of God; and that not merely for ornament, but for purposes of instruction. As we shall see farther on, the Holy Ghost intended a significance, a teaching, about everything in the old tabernacle, whether it was a candlestick, or a table, or the shewbread.

4, 5. Which had the golden censer, and the ark of the covenant overlaid round about with gold wherein was the golden pot that had manna, and Aaron's rod that budded, and the tables of the covenant; and over it the cherubims of glory shadowing the mercy seat; of which we cannot now speak particularly.

It would not have been to the point which the apostle had in hand, so he waived the explanation of those things for another time.

6–8. Now when these things were thus ordained, the priests went always into the first tabernacle, accomplishing the service of God. But into the second went the high priest alone once every year, not without blood, which he offered for himself, and for the errors of the people: the Holy Ghost this signifying.

It is from this sentence that I am sure that the Holy Ghost had a signification, a meaning; a teaching, for every item of the ancient tabernacle and temple; and we are not spinning fancies out of idle brains when we interpret these types, and learn from them important gospel lessons. "The Holy Ghost this signifying,"—

8. That the way into the holiest of all was not yet made manifest, while as the first tabernacle was yet standing:

It was necessary that you should take away the sacred tent, the tabernacle, ay, and take away the temple, too, before you could learn the spiritual meaning of them. You must break the shell to get at the kernel. So God had ordained. Hence, there is now no tabernacle, no temple, no holy court, no inner shrine, the holy of holies. The material worship is done away with, in order that we may render the spiritual worship of which the material was but the type,

9. Which was a figure for the time then present,

Only a figure, and only meant for "the time then present." It was the childhood of the Lord's people; it was a time when, as yet, the light had not fully broken in upon spiritual eyes, so they must be taught by picture-books. That they must have a kind of Kindergarten for the little children, that they might learn the elements of the faith by the symbols, types, and representations of a material worship. When we come into the true gospel light, all that is done away with; it was only "a figure for the time then present."

9. In which were offered both gifts and sacrifices, that could not make him that did the service perfect, as pertaining to the conscience: All those rites could only give a fleshly purity, but they could not touch the conscience. If men saw what was meant by the outward type, then the conscience was appeased; but by the outward sign itself the conscience was never comforted, if it was a living and lowly conscience.

10. Which stood only in meats and drinks, and divers washings, and carnal ordinances, imposed on them until the time of reformation.

These ordinances were only laid upon the Jews—not upon any other people—and only laid upon them until the better and brighter days of reformation and fuller illumination.

11. But Christ—

Oh, how we seem to rise when we begin to get near to Him, away from the high priests of the Jews! "but Christ"—

11. being come an high priest of good things to come,

Not of the shadows, but of the good things themselves: "an high priest of good things to come,"—

11. by a greater and more perfect tabernacle, not made with hands, that is to say, not of this building;

That tabernacle was His body, which was not made with hands, nor yet formed by carnal generation as our human tabernacle is. This greater and more perfect tabernacle was made according to the power of an endless life.

12. Neither by the blood of goats and calves, but by his own blood he entered in once into the holy place, having obtained eternal redemption for us.

The Jewish high priests went once a year into the Holy of Holies. Each year as it came round demanded that they should go again. Their work was never done; but "He entered in once," and only once, "into the holy place, having obtained eternal redemption for us." I love that expression, "eternal redemption"—a redemption which really does redeem, and redeems forever and ever. If you are redeemed by it, you cannot be lost; if this redemption be yours, it is not for a time, or for a season, but it is "eternal redemption." Oh, how you ought to rejoice in the one entrance within the veil by our great High Priest who has obtained eternal redemption for us!

13–15. For if the blood of bulls and of goats, and the ashes of an heifer sprinkling the unclean. sanctifieth to the purifying of the flesh: how much more shall the blood of Christ, who through the eternal Spirit offered himself without spot to God, purge your conscience from dead works to serve the living God? And for this cause he is the mediator of the new testament, that by means of death, for the redemption of the transgressions that were under the first testament, they which are called might receive the promise of eternal inheritance.

When you come to deal with Christ, you have to do with eternal things. There is nothing temporary about Him, or about His work. It is "eternal redemption" that He has obtained for us, it is an "eternal inheritance" that He has purchased for us.

16, 17. For where a testament is, there must also of necessity be the death of the testator. For a testament is of force after men are dead: otherwise it is of no strength at all while the testator liveth.

Or, "Where a covenant is, there must also be the death of him who covenants, or of that by which the covenant is established." Or read it as we have it in our version, for it seems as if it must be so, although we are loathe to give the meaning of "testament" to the word, since its natural meaning is evidently covenant: "Where a testament is, there must also of necessity be the death of the testator. For a testament is of force after men are dead; otherwise it is of no strength at all while the testator liveth"; or, if you will, while the victim that was to confirm the covenant lived, the covenant was not ratified; it must be slain before it could be thus effective.

18–22. Whereupon neither the first testament was dedicated without blood. For when Moses had spoken every precept to all the people according to the law, he took the blood of calves and of goats, with water, and scarlet wool, and hyssop, and sprinkled both the book, and all the people, saying, This is the blood of the testament which God hath enjoined unto you. Moreover he sprinkled with blood both the tabernacle, and all the vessels of the ministry. And almost all things are by the law purged with blood; and without shedding of blood is no remission.

There is no truth more plain than this in the whole of the Old Testament; and it must have within it a very weighty lesson to our souls. There are some who cannot endure the doctrine of a substitutionary atonement. Let them beware lest they be casting away the very soul and essence of the gospel. It is evident that the sacrifice of Christ was intended to give ease to the conscience, for we read that the blood of bulls and of goats could not do that. I fail to see how any doctrine of atonement except the doctrine of the vicarious sacrifice of Christ can give ease to the guilty conscience. Christ in my stead suffering the penalty of my sin—that pacifies my conscience, but nothing else does: "Without shedding of blood is no remission."

23. It was therefore necessary that the patterns of things in the heavens should be purified with these;

These things down below are only the patterns, the models, the symbols of the heavenly things; they could therefore be ceremonially purified with the blood which is the symbol of the atoning sacrifice of Christ.

23, 24. But the heavenly things themselves with better sacrifices than these. For Christ is not entered into the holy places made with hand, which are the figures of the true; but into heaven itself, now to appear in the presence of God for us:

He never went within the veil in the Jewish temple; that was but the symbol of the true holy of holies. He has gone "into heaven itself, now to appear in the presence of God for us."

25–28. Nor yet that he should offer himself often, as the high priest entereth into the holy place every year with blood of others; for then must he often have suffered since the foundation of the world: but now once in the end of the world hath he appeared to put away sin by the sacrifice of himself. And as it is appointed unto mere once to die, but after this the judgment: so Christ was once offered to bear the sins of many; There is no need that He should die again, His one offering has forever perfected His people. There remains nothing but His final coming for the judgment of the ungodly, and the acquittal of His redeemed.

28. And unto them that look for him shall he appear the second time without sin unto salvation.

Christ's second coming will be "without sin," and without a sin offering, too, wholly apart from sin, unto the salvation of all His chosen. May we all be amongst those who are looking for Him! Amen. HYMNS FROM "OUR OWN HYMN BOOK"—327, 228, 193.

The Bliss of the Glorified

A Sermon (No. 3499) Published on
Thursday, February 17th, 1916.
Delivered by C. H. SPURGEON,
At the Metropolitan Tabernacle, Newington.
ON the Lord's-Day Evening, August 13th, 1871.

"They shall hunger no more, neither thirst any more, neither shall the sun light on them, nor any heat."—Revelation 7:16.

We cannot too often turn our thoughts heavenward, for this is one of the great cures for worldliness. The way to liberate our souls from the bonds that tie us to earth is to strengthen the cords that kind us to heaven. You will think less of this poor little globe when you think more of the world to come. This contemplation will also serve to console us for the loss, as we call it, of those who have gone before. It is their gain, and we will rejoice in it. We cannot have a richer source of consolation than this, that they who have fallen asleep in Christ have not perished; they have not lost life, but they have gained the fullness of it. They are rid at all that molests us here, and they enjoy more than we as yet can imagine. Cheer your hearts, ye mourners, by looking up to the gate of pearl, by looking up—to those who day without night surround the throne of their Redeemer. It will also tend to quicken our diligence if we think much of heaven. Suppose I should miss it after all! What if I should not so run that I may obtain! If heaven be little, I shall be but a little loser by losing it; but if it be indeed such that the half could never be told us, then, may God grant us diligence to make our calling and election sure, that we may be certain of entering into this rest, and may not be like the many who came out of Egypt, but who perished in the wilderness and never entered into the promised land. All things considered, I know of no meditation that is likely to be more profitable than a frequent consideration of the rest which remaineth for the people of God. I ask, then, for a very short time that your thoughts may go upward to the golden streets.

And, first, we shall think a little of the blessedness of the saints as described in the simple words of our text; then we will say a few words as to how they came by that felicity; and thirdly, draw some practical lessons from it. First, then, we have here:—

I. A DESCRIPTION OF THE BLESSEDNESS OF THE GLORIFIED.

We have not the full description of it here; but we have here a description of certain evils from which they are free. You notice they are of two or three kinds—first, such as originate within—"They shall hunger no more, neither thirst any more"—they are free from inward evils; secondly, such as originate without—"Neither shall the sun light on them, nor any heat." They are altogether delivered from the results of outward circumstances.

Take the first: "They shall hunger no more, neither thirst any more." We are never so to strain Scripture for a spiritual sense as to take away its natural sense, and hence we will begin by saying this is no doubt to be understood physically of the body they will have in glory. Whether there will be a necessity for eating and drinking in heaven, we will not say, for we are not told, but anyhow it is met by the text, "The Lamb that is in the midst of the throne shall feed them"—if they need food—"and lead them to living fountains of water" if they need to drink. Whatever may be the necessities of the future, those necessities shall never cause a pang. Here, the man who is hungry may have to ask the question, "What shall I eat?"; the man who is thirsty may have to say, "What shall I drink?"; and we have all to ask, "Wherewithal shall we be clothed?" But such questions shall never arise there. They are abundantly supplied. Children of God have been hungry here: the great Son of God, the head of the household was hungry before them; and they need not wonder if they have fellowship with him in this suffering. Children of God have had to thirst here: their great Lord and Master said, "I thirst"; they need not wonder, therefore, if in his affliction they have to take some share. Should not they who are to be like their head in heaven be conformed unto him on earth? But up yonder there is no poverty, and there shall be no accident that shall place them in circumstances of distress. "They shall hunger no more, neither thirst any more."

While we take this physically, there is no doubt that it is to be understood mentally. Our minds are also constantly the victims of hungerings and thirstings. There are on earth various kinds of this hunger and thirst—in a measure evil, in a measure also innocent. There are many men that in this world are hungering after wealth, and the mouth of avarice can never be filled. It is as insatiable as the horse-leech, and for ever cries, "Give, give!" But such hunger was never known in heaven, and never can be, for they are satisfied there; they have all things and abound. All their enlarged capacities can desire they already possess, in being near the throne of God and beholding his glory; there is no wealth which is denied them. Here, too, some of the sons of men hunger after fame, and oh! what have not men done to satisfy this? It is said that breaks through stone walls; certainly ambition has done it. Death at the cannon's mouth has been a trifle, if a man might win the bubble reputation. But in heaven there is no such hunger as that Those who once had it, and are saved, scorn ambition henceforth. And what room would there be for ambition in the skies? They take their crowns and cast them at their Saviour's feet. They have their palm-branches, for they have won the victory, but they ascribe the conquest to the Lamb, their triumph to his death. Their souls are satisfied with his fame. The renown of Christ has filled their spirit with everlasting contentment. They hunger no more, nor thirst any more, in that respect. And oh! what hunger and thirst there has been on earth by those of tender and large heart for a fit object of love! I mean not now the common thing called "love," but the friendship which is in man's heart, and sends out its tendrils wanting something to which to cling. We must—we are born and created for that very purpose—we must live together, we cannot develop ourselves alone. And oftentimes a lonely spirit has yearned for a brother's ear, into which to pour its sorrows; and doubtless many a man has been brought to destruction and been confined to the lunatic asylum whose reason might have been saved had there been some sympathetic spirit, some kind, gentle heart that would have helped to bear his burden. Oh! the hunger and the thirst of many a soul after a worthy object of confidence. But they hunger and they thirst, up there, no more.

Their love is all centred on their Saviour. Their confidence, which they reposed in him on earth, is still in him. He is their bosom's Lord, their heart's Emperor, and they are satisfied, and, wrapped up in him, they hunger and they thirst no more.

And how many young spirits there are on earth that are hungering after knowledge who would fain get the hammer and break the rock, and find out the history of the globe in the past. They would follow philosophy, if they could, to its source, and find out the root of the matter. Oh! to know, to know, to know! The human mind pants and thirsts for this. But there they know even as they are known. I do not know that in heaven they know all things—that must be for the Omniscient only—but they know all they need or really want to know; they are satisfied there. There will be no longer searching with a spirit that is ill at ease. They may, perhaps, make progress even there, and the scholar may become daily more and more wise; but there shall never be such a hungering and thirsting as to cause their mental faculties the slightest pang. They shall hunger no more, neither thirst any more. Oh! blessed land where the seething ocean of man's mind is hushed, and sleeps in everlasting calm! Oh! blessed country where the hungry spirit, that crieth every hour for bread, and yet for more, and yet for more, and spends its labour for that which satisfieth not, shall be fed with the bread of angels, and be satisfied with favour and full of the goodness of the Lord.

But, dear friends, surely the text also means our spiritual hungering and thirsting. "Blessed is the man that hungers and thirst to-day after righteousness, for he shall be filled." This a kind of hunger that we ought to desire to have; this is a sort of thirst that the more you have of it will be the indication of the possession of more grace. On earth it is good for saints to hunger and to thirst spiritually, but up there they have done even with that blessed hunger and that blessed thirst. Today, beloved, some of us are hungering after holiness. Oh! what would I not give to be holy, to be rid of sin, of every evil thing about me! My eyes—ah! adieu sweet light, if I might also say, "Adieu sin! "My mouth—ah! well would I be content to be dumb if I might preach by a perfect life on earth! There is no faculty I know of that might not be cheerfully surrendered if the surrender of it would deprive us of sin. But they never thirst for holiness in heaven, for this excellent reason, that they are without fault before the throne of God. Does it not make your mouth water?

Why this is the luxury of heaven to be perfect. Is not this—the heaven of heaven, to be clean rid of the root and branch of sin, and not a rag or bone, or piece of a bone of our old depravity left—all gone like our Lord, made perfect without spot or wrinkle, or any such thing. And here, too, brethren and sisters, we very rightly hunger and thirst after full assurance and confidence. Many are hungering after it; they hope they are saved, and they thirst to be assured that they are. But there is no such thirst as that in heaven, for, having crossed the golden threshold of Paradise, no saint ever asks himself, "Am I saved?" They see his face without a cloud between; they bathe in the sea of his love; they cannot question that which they perpetually enjoy. So, too, on earth I hope we know what it is to hunger and thirst for fellowship with Christ. Oh! when he is gone from us—if he do but hide his face from us, how we cry, "My soul desires thee in the night"! We cannot be satisfied unless we have the love of God shed abroad in our hearts by the Holy Ghost. But in heaven they have no such thing. There the shepherd is always with the Sheep, the King is ever near them, and because of his perpetual presence their hungering and their thirsting will be banished for ever. Thus much upon those evils, then, that would arise from within. As they are perfect, whatever comes from within is a source of pleasure to them, and never of pain.

And now, dear friends, the evils that come from without: let us think of them. We no doubt can appreciate in some measure, though not to the degree which we should if we were in Palestine in the middle of summer—we can appreciate the words, "Neither shall the sun light on them, nor any heat." This signifies that nothing external shall injure the blessed. Take it literally. There shall be nothing in the surroundings of heavenly saints that shall cause glorified spirits any inconvenience. I think we may take it mainly in relation to the entire man glorified; and so let us say that on earth the sun lights on us and many heats in the form of affliction. What heats of affliction some here have passed through! Why there are some here who are seldom free from physical pain. There are many of the best of God's children that, if they get an hour without pain, are joyful indeed. There are others that have had a great fight of affliction Through poverty they have fought hard. They have been industrious, but somehow or other God has marked them out for the scant tables and the thread-worn garments. They are the children of poverty, and the furnace heat is very hot about them. With others it has been repeated deaths of those they have loved. Ah! how sad is the widow's case!

How deep the grief of the fatherless! How great the sorrow of bereaved parents! Sometimes the arrows of God fly one after the other; first one falls and then another until we think we shall hardly have one left. These are the heats of the furnace of affliction. And at other times these take the form of ingratitude from children. I think we never ought to repine so much about the death of a child as about the ungodly life of a child. A dead cross is very heavy, but a living cross is heavier far. Many a mother has had a son of whom she might regret that he did not die even the very hour of his birth, for he has lived to be the grief of his parents, and a dishonour to their name. These are sharp trials—these heats—but you shall have done with them soon. "Neither shall the sun light on them, nor any heat." No poverty, no sickness, no bereavement, no ingratitude—nothing of the kind. They for ever rest from affliction. Heat sometimes comes in another form—in the matter of temptation. Oh! how some of God's people have been tried—tried by their flesh! Their constitution, perhaps, has been hot, impulsive, and they have been carried off their feet, or would have been but for the interposing grace of God, many and many a time. They have been tempted, too, in their position, and they of their own household have been their enemies. They have been tempted by their peculiar circumstances; their feet have almost gone many a time.

And they have been tempted by the devil; and hard work it is to stand against Satanic insinuations. It is hot, indeed, when his fiery darts fly. Oh! when we shall have once crossed the river, how some of us who have been much tempted will look back upon that old dog of hell, and laugh him to scorn because he will not be able even to bark at us again! Then we shall be for ever free from him. He worries us now because he would devour us, but there, as he cannot devour, so shall he not even worry us. "Neither shall the sun" of temptation "light on them, nor any heat." Happy are the people that are in such a case. The heats of persecution have often, too, carried about the saints. It is the lot of God's people to be tried in this way. Through much tribulation of this sort they inherit the kingdom; but there are no Smithfields in heaven, and no Bonners to light up the faggots, no Inquisitions in heaven, no slanderers there to spoil the good man's name. They shall never have the heat of persecution to suffer again. And, once more, they shall not have the heat of care. I do not know that we need have it, even here; but there are a great many of God's people who allow care to get very hot about them. Even while sitting in this place to-night while the hymn was going up, "What must it be to be there!" the thoughts of some of you have been going away to your business, or your home. While we are trying to preach and draw your attention upwards, perhaps some housewife is thinking of something she has left out which ought to have been looked up before she came away, or wondering where she left the key.

We make any excuses for care through the cares we continually invent, forgetting the words, "Cast all your care on him, for he careth for you." But they have no cares in heaven. "They hunger no more, neither thirst any more; neither shall the sun light on them, nor any heat." Ah! good man, there shall be no ships at sea by-and-bye-no harvests—to trouble you as to whether the good weather will last! Ah! good woman, you shall have no more children that are sickly to fret over, for there you will have all you desire, and be in a family circle that is unbroken, for all the brothers and sisters of God's family shall by-and-bye be there, and so you shall be eternally blest.

We have thus opened up as well as we could the words of the text on the felicity of the saints. Now, very briefly:—

II. How DO THEY COME TO BE HAPPY?

Well, it is quite clear that they did not come to it because they were very fortunate people on earth, for if you read another passage of the Word of God you will find, "These are they that came out of great tribulation."

Those that have had trial and suffering on earth are amongst those that have the bliss of heaven. Encourage yourselves, you poor and suffering ones. It is quite certain they did not come there from their own merit, for we read, they have "washed their robes"—they wanted washing. They did not keep them always undefiled.

There had been spots upon them. They came there not because they deserved to be there, but because of the rich grace of God. How did they come there then? Well, first, they came there through the lamb that was slain. He bore the sun and the heat, and, therefore, the sun doth not light on them, nor any heat. The hot sun of Jehovah's justice shone full upon the Saviour—scorched, and burned, and consumed him with grief and anguish; and because the Saviour suffered, therefore we suffer it no more. All our hopes of heaven are found at the cross.

But they came there next because the Saviour shed his blood. They washed their robes in it. Faith linked them to the Saviour. The fountain would not have cleansed their robes if they had not washed in it. Oh! there shall be none come to heaven but such as have by faith embraced what God provides. Dear hearer, judge thyself whether thou art right, therefore. Hast thou washed thy robe and made it white in the Lamb's blood? Is Christ all in all to thee? If not, canst thou hope to be there? And they are there in perfect bliss, we are told. No sun lights on them, nor any heat, because the Lamb in the midst of the throne is with them. How could they be unhappy who see Christ? Is not this the secret of their bliss, that Jesus fully reveals himself to them?

And besides, they have the love of God to enjoy, for the last word of the chapter is, "God shall wipe away all tears from their eyes." The blood of Jesus applied, the presence of Jesus enjoyed, and the love of God fully revealed—these are the causes of the bliss of the saved in heaven. But we must close our meditation with the last point, which is:—

III. WHAT THIS TEACHES US.

First, the bliss of the saved in glory teaches us to long for it. It is legitimate to long for heaven—not too long to escape from doing our duty here. It is idleness to be always wanting to have done with this world—it is clear sloth—but to be longing to be where Jesus is, is only natural and gracious. Should not the child long to go home from the school? Should not the captive pine for liberty? Should not the traveller in foreign lands long to see his native country? Should not the bride, the married wife, when she has been long away from her husband, long to see his face? If you did not long for heaven, surely you might question whether heaven belonged to you. If you have ever tasted of the joys of the saints, as believers do on earth, you will sing with full soul:—

"My thirsty spirit faints To reach the land I love The bright inheritance of saints, Jerusalem above."

You may long for this.

And the next lesson is, be patient until you get there. As it will be such a blessed place when you arrive, don't trouble about the difficulties of the way. You know our hymn:—"The way may be rough, but it cannot be long." So "Let us fill it with hope, and cheer it with song." You know how well your horse goes when you turn its head homewards. Perhaps you had to flog him a bit before, but when he begins to know he is going down the long lane which leads home he will soon lift up his ears, and away, away he will go. We ought to have as much sense as horses. Our heads are turned towards heaven We are steering towards that port—homeward bound. It may be rough weather but we shall soon be in the fair haven where not a wave of trouble shall ever disturb us again. Be patient, be patient. The husbandman has waited for the precious fruits of the earth; you can well wait for the precious things of heaven. You sow in tears, but you shall reap in joy. He has promised you a harvest. He who cannot lie has said the seed-time and harvest shall never cease They do not cease below; depend upon it, they won't cease above. There is a harvest for you who have been sowing here below.

Our first lesson, then, is, long for this, and then be patient in waiting. But our next lesson is to be, wait your appointed time. And now the next instruction is, make much of faith. They entered heaven because they had washed their robes in blood. Make much of the blood and much of the faith by which you have washed. Dear hearers, have you all got faith? It is, as it were, the key of blessedness. "But all men have not faith," says the Apostle. Hast thou faith? Dost thou believe in Christ Jesus? In other words, dost thou trust thyself alone with him' Can you sing with our poet:—"Nothing in my hand I bring Simply to thy cross I cling; Naked, come to thee for dress, Helpless, look to thee for grace. Foul, I to the fountain fly, Wash me, Saviour, or I die"? Make much of the faith that will admit you to heaven.

Once more, our text teaches us this lesson—Do any of us want to know what heaven is on earth? Most of us will say, "Aye" to that. Well then, the text tells you how to find heaven on earth. You find it in the same way as they find it in heaven. First, be thou washed in the blood of Christ, and that will be a great help towards happiness on earth. It will give thee peace now, "the peace of God that passeth all understanding." Some people think that heaven on earth is to be found in the theatre, and in the ballroom, and in the giddy haunts of fashion. Well, it may be heaven to some, but if God has any love to you, it won't be heaven to you. Wash your robe, therefore, in the Saviour's blood, and there will be the beginning of heaven on earth.

Then next, it appears, if you read the connection of our text, that those who enjoy heaven serve God day and night in his temple. If you want heaven on earth, serve God continually day and night. Having washed your robe first, then put it on, and go out to serve God. Idle Christians are often unhappy Christians I have met with many a spiritual dyspeptic always full of doubts and fears. Is there a young man here full of doubts and fears who has lost the light he once possessed, and the joy he once had? Dear brother, get to work. In cold weather the best way to be warm is not to get before a fire, but to work. Exercise gives a healthy glow, even amidst the frost. "I am doing something," says one. Yes, with one hand; use the other hand. "Perhaps I should have too many irons in the fire," says one. You cannot have too many. Put them all in, and blow the fire with all the bellows you can get. I do not believe any Christian man works too hard, and, as a rule, if those who kill themselves in Christ's service were buried in a cemetery by themselves, it would be a long while before it would get filled. Work hard for Christ. It makes happy those who are in heaven to serve God day and night, and it will make you happy on earth. Do all you can. Another way is to have fellowship with Christ here. Read again this chapter. "He that sitteth on the throne shall dwell among them—he shall feed them." Oh! if you want to be happy, live near to Jesus. Poor men are not poor when Christ lives in their house. Truly, sick men have their beds made easy when Christ is there. Has he not said, " I will make his bed in all his sickness"? Only get fellowship with Jesus, and outward circumstances won't distress you. The sun will not light on you, nor any heat. You will be like the shepherd on Salisbury Plain, who said it was good weather, though it rained hard.

"It is weather," said he, "that pleases me." "How so?" said a traveller to him. "Well, sir," he said, "it pleases God, and what pleases God pleases me." "Good day!" said one to a Christian man. "I never had a bad day since I was converted," said he. "They are all good now since Christ is my Saviour." Do you not see, then, that if your wishes are subdued, if you do not hunger any more, or thirst any more as you used to do, and if you always live near to Christ, you will begin to enjoy heaven on earth. Begin, then, the heavenly life here below.

The Bible says, "For he hath raised us up, and made us sit together in heavenly places in Christ Jesus." The way to live on earth, according to many, is to live on earth, but to look upward to heaven. That is a good way of living, but I will tell you a better, and that is to live in heaven, and look down on earth. The Apostle had learned that when he said, "Our conversation is in heaven." It is good to be on earth, and look up to heaven; it is better for the mind to be in heaven, and to look down upon earth. May we learn that secret. The Lord lead us into it. Then when faith is strong, and love is ardent, and hope is bright, we shall sing, with Watts:—"The men of grace have found Glory begun below; Celestial fruits on earthly ground From faith and hope may grow."

The Lord grant you a participation in this bliss, beloved, and an abundant entrance into that bliss for ever, for Jesus Christ's sake. Amen.

The Blood-Shedding

A Sermon (No. 118) Delivered on
Sabbath Morning, February 22, 1857,
by the REV. C. H. SPURGEON
At The Music Hall, Royal Surrey Gardens.

"Without shedding of blood is no remission."
—Hebrews 9: 22.

I will show you three fools.

One is yonder soldier, who has been wounded on the field of battle, grievously wounded, well nigh unto death; the surgeon is by his side, and the soldier asks him a question. Listen, and judge of his folly. What question does he ask? Does he raise his eyes with eager anxiety and inquire if the wound be mortal, if the practitioner's skill can suggest the means of healing, or if the remedies are within reach and the medicine at hand? No, nothing of the sort; strange to tell, he asks, "Can you inform me with what sword I was wounded, and by what Russian I have been thus grievously mauled? I want," he adds, "to learn every minute particular respecting the origin of my wound." The man is delirious or his head is affected. Surely such questions at such a time are proof enough that he is bereft of his senses.

There is another fool. The storm is raging, the ship is flying impetuous before the gale, the dark scud moves swiftly over head, the masts are creaking, the sails are rent to rags, and still the gathering tempest grows more fierce. Where is the captain? Is he busily engaged on the deck, is he manfully facing the danger, and skilfully suggesting means to avert it? No sir, he has retired to his cabin, and there with studious thoughts and crazy fancies he is speculating on the place where this storm took its rise. "It is mysterious, this wind; no one ever yet" he says, "has been able to discover it." And, so reckless of the vessel, the lives of the passengers, and his own life, he is careful only to solve his curious questions. The man is mad, sir; take the rudder from his hand; he is clean gone mad! If he should ever run on shore, shut him up as a hopeless lunatic.

The third fool I shall doubtless find among yourselves. You are sick and wounded with sin, you are in the storm and hurricane of Almighty vengeance, and yet the question which you would ask of me, this morning, would be, "Sir, what is the origin of evil?" You are mad, Sir, spiritually mad; that is not the question you would ask if you were in a sane and healthy state of mind; your question would be: "How can I get rid of the evil?" Not, "How did it come into the world?" but "How am I to escape from it?" Not, "How is it that hail descends from heaven upon Sodom?" but "How may I, like Lot, escape out of the city to a Zoar." Not, "How is it that I am sick?" but "Are there medicines that will heal me? Is there a physician to be found that can restore my soul to health?" Ah! you trifle with subtleties while you neglect certainties. More questions have been asked concerning the origin of evil than upon anything else. Men have puzzled their heads, and twisted their brains into knots, in order to understand what men can never know—how evil came into this world, and how its entrance is consistent with divine goodness? The broad fact is this, there is evil; and your question should be, "How can I escape from the wrath to come, which is engendered of this evil?" In answering that question this verse stands right in the middle of the way (like the angel with the sword, who once stopped Balaam on his road to Barak,) "Without shedding of blood is no remission." Your real want is to know how you can be saved; if you are aware that your sin must be pardoned or punished, your question will be, "How can it be pardoned?" and then point blank in the very teeth of your enquiry, there stands out this fact: "Without shedding of blood there is no remission." Mark you, this is not merely a Jewish maxim; it is a world-wide and eternal truth. It pertaineth not to the Hebrews only, but to the Gentiles likewise. Never in any time, never in any place, never in any person, can there be remission apart from shedding of blood. This great fact, I say, is stamped on nature; it is an essential law of God's moral government, it is one of the fundamental principles which can neither be shaken nor denied. Never can there be any exception to it; it stands the same in every place throughout all ages— "Without shedding of blood there is no remission." It was so with the Jews; they had no remission without the shedding of blood. Some things under the Jewish law might be cleansed by water or by fire, but in no case where absolute sin was concerned was there ever purification without blood—teaching this doctrine, that blood, and blood alone, must be applied for the remission of sin. Indeed the very heathen seem to have an inkling of this fact. Do not I see their knives gory with the blood of victims? Have I not heard horrid tales of human immolations, of holocausts, of sacrifices; and what mean these, but that there lies deep in the human breast, deep as the very existence of man, this truth,—"that without shedding of blood there is no remission." And I assert once more, that even in the hearts and consciences of my hearers there is something which will never let them believe in remission apart from a shedding of blood. This is the grand truth of Christianity, and it is a truth which I will endeavour now to fix upon your memory; and may God by his grace bless it to your souls. "Without shedding of blood is no remission."

First, let me show you the blood-shedding, before I begin to dwell upon the text. Is there not a special blood-shedding meant? Yes, there was a shedding of most precious blood, to which I must forthwith refer you. I shall not tell you now of massacres and murders, nor of rivers of blood of goats and rams. There was a blood-shedding once, which did all other shedding of blood by far outvie; it was a man—a God—that shed his blood at that memorable season. Come and see it. Here is a garden dark and gloomy; the ground is crisp with the cold frost of midnight; between those gloomy olive trees I see a man, I hear him groan out his life in prayer; hearken, angels, hearken men, and wonder; it is the Saviour groaning out his soul! Come and see him. Behold his brow! O heavens! drops of blood are streaming down his face, and from his body; every pore is open, and it sweats! but not the sweat of men that toil for bread; it is the sweat of one that toils for heaven—he "sweats great drops of blood!" That is the blood-shedding, without which there is no remission. Follow that man further; they have dragged him with sacrilegious bands from the place of his prayer and his agony, and they have taken him to the hall of Pilate; they seat him in a chair and mock him; a robe of purple is put on his shoulders in mockery; and mark his brow—they have put about it a crown of thorns, and the crimson drops of gore are rushing down his cheeks! Ye angels! the drops of blood are running down his cheeks! But turn aside that purple robe for a moment. His back is bleeding. Tell me, demons who did this. They lift up the thongs, still dripping clots of gore; they scourge and tear his flesh, and make a river of blood to run down his shoulders! That is the shedding of blood without which there is no remission. Not yet have I done: they hurry him through the streets; they fling him on the ground; they nail his hands and feet to the transverse wood, they hoist it in the air, they dash it into its socket, it is fixed, and there he hangs the Christ of God. Blood from his head, blood from his hands, blood from his feet! In agony unknown he bleeds away his life; in terrible throes he exhausts his soul. "Eloi, Eloi, lama sabacthani." And then see! they pierce his side, and forthwith runneth out blood and water. This is the shedding of blood, sinners and saints; this is the awful shedding of blood, the terrible pouring out of blood, without which for you, and for the whole human race, there is no remission.

I have then, I hope, brought my text fairly out: without this shedding of blood there is no remission. Now I shall come to dwell upon it more particularly.

Why is it that this story doth not make men weep? I told it ill, you say. Ay, so I did; I will take all the blame.

But, sirs, if it were told as ill as men could speak, were our hearts what they should be, we should bleed away our lives in sorrow. Oh! it was a horrid murder that! It was not an act of regicide; it was not the deed of a fratricide, or of a parricide; it was—what shall I say?—I must make a word—a deicide; the killing of a God; the slaying of him who became incarnate for our sins. Oh! if our hearts were but soft as iron, we must weep, if they were but tender as the marble of the mountains, we should shed great drops of grief; but they are harder than the nether millstone; we forget the griefs of him that died this ignominious death, we pity not his sorrows, nor do we account the interest we have in him as though he suffered and accomplished all for us.

Nevertheless, here stands the principle—"Without shedding of blood is no remission."

Now, I take it, there are two things here. First, there is a negative expressed: "No remission without shedding of blood." And then there is a positive implied, forsooth, with shedding of blood there is remission.

I. First, I say, here is A NEGATIVE EXPRESSED: there is no remission without blood—without the blood of Jesus Christ. This is of divine authority; when I utter this sentence I have divinity to plead. It is not a thing which you may doubt, or which you may believe; it must be believed and received, otherwise you have denied the Scriptures and turned aside from God. Some truths I utter, perhaps, have little better basis than my own reasoning and inference, which are of little value enough; but this I utter, not with quotations from God's Word to back up my assertion, but from the lips of God himself. Here it stands in great letters, "There is no remission." So divine its authority. Perhaps you will kick at it: but remember, your rebellion is not against me, but against God, If any of you reject this truth, I shall not controvert; God forbid I should turn aside from proclaiming his gospel, to dispute with men. I have God's irrevocable statute to plead now, here it stands: "Without shedding of blood there is no remission." You may believe or disbelieve many things the preacher utters; but this you disbelieve at the peril of your souls. It is God's utterance: will you tell

God to his face you do not believe it? That were impious. The negative is divine in its authority; bow yourselves to it, and accept its solemn warning.

But some men will say that God's way of saving men, by shedding of blood, is a cruel way, an unjust way, an unkind way; and all kinds of things they will say of it. Sirs, I have nothing to do with your opinion of the matter; it is so. If you have any faults to find with your Maker, fight your battles out with him at last. But take heed before you throw the gauntlet down; it will go ill with a worm when he fighteth with his Maker, and it will go ill with you when you contend with him. The doctrine of atonement when rightly understood and faithfully received, is delightful, for it exhibits boundless love, immeasurable goodness, and infinite truth; but to unbelievers it will always be a hated doctrine. So it must be sirs; you hate your own mercies; you despise your own salvation. I tarry not to dispute with you; I affirm it in God's name: "Without shedding of blood there is no remission."

And note how decisive this is in its character: "Without shedding of blood there is no remission." "But, sir, can't I get my sins forgiven by my repentance? if I weep, and plead, and pray, will not God forgive me for the sake of my tears?" "No remission," says the text, "without shedding of blood." "But, sir, if I never sin again, and if I serve God more zealously than other men, will he not forgive me for the sake of my obedience?" "No remission," says the text, "without shedding of blood." "But, sir, may I not trust that God is merciful, and will forgive me without the shedding of blood?" "No," says the text, "without shedding of blood there is no remission;" none whatever. It cuts off every other hope. Bring your hopes here, and if they are not based in blood. and stamped with blood, they are as useless as castles in the air, and dreams of the night. "There is no remission," says the text, in positive and plain words; and yet men will be trying to get remission in fifty other ways, until their special pleading becomes as irksome to us as it is useless for them. Sirs, do what you like, say what you please, but you are as far off remission when you have done your best, as you were when you began, except you put confidence in the shedding of our Saviour's blood, and in the blood-shedding alone, for without it there is no remission.

And note again how universal it is in its character. "What! may not I get remission without blood-shedding?" says the king; and he comes with the crown on his head; "May not I in all my robes, with this rich ransom, get pardon without the blood-shedding?" "None," is the reply; "none." Forthwith comes the wise man, with a number of letters after his name—"Can I not get remission by these grand titles of my learning?" "None; none." Then comes the benevolent man—"I have dispersed my money to the poor, and given my bounty to feed them; shall not I get remission?" "None;" says the text, "Without shedding of blood there is no remission." How this puts everyone on a level! My lord, you are no bigger than your coachman; Sir, squire, you are no better off than John that ploughs the ground; minister, your office does not serve you with any exemption—your poorest hearer stands on the very same footing. "Without shedding of blood there is no remission." No hope for the best, any more than for the worst, without this shedding of blood. Oh! I love the gospel, for this reason among others, because it is such a levelling gospel. Some persons do not like a levelling gospel; nor would I, in some senses of the word. Let men have their rank, and their titles, and their riches, if they will; but I do like, and I am sure all good men like, to see rich and poor meet together and feel that they are on a level; the gospel makes them so. It says "Put up your money-bags, they will not procure you remission; roll up your diploma, that will not get you remission; forget your farm and your park, they will not get you remission; just cover up that escutcheon, that coat of arms will not get you remission. Come, you ragged beggars, filthy off-scourings of the world, penniless; come hither; here is remission as much for you, ill-bred and ill-mannered though ye be, as for the noble, the honorable, the titled, and the wealthy. All stand on a level here; the text is universal: "Without shedding of blood there is no remission."

Mark too, how perpetual my text is. Paul said, "there is no remission;" I must repeat this testimony too. When thousands of years have rolled away, some minister may stand on this spot and say the same. This will never alter at all; it will always be so, in the next world as well as this: no remission without shedding of blood. "Oh! yes there is," says one, "the priest takes the shilling, and he gets the soul out of purgatory." That is a mere pretence; it never was in. But without shedding of blood there is no real remission. There may be tales and fancies, but there is no true remission without the blood of propitiation. Never, though you strained yourselves in prayer; never, though you wept yourselves away in tears; never, though you groaned and cried till your heart-strings break; never in this world, nor in that which is to come, can the forgiveness of sins be procured on any other ground than redemption by the blood of Christ, and never can the conscience be cleansed but by faith in that sacrifice. The fact is, beloved, there is no use for you to satisfy your hearts with anything less than what satisfied God the Father. Without the shedding of blood nothing would appease his justice; and without the application of that same blood nothing can purge your consciences.

II. But as there is no remission without blood-shedding, IT IS IMPLIED THAT THERE IS REMISSION WITHOUT IT. Mark it well, this remission is a present fact. The blood having been already shed, the remission is already obtained. I took you to the garden of Gethsemane and the mount of Calvary to see the bloodshedding. I might now conduct you to another garden and another mount to shew you the grand proof of the remission. Another garden, did I say? Yes, it is a garden, fraught with many pleasing and even triumphant reminiscences. Aside from the haunts of this busy world, in it was a new sepulchre, hewn out of a rock where Joseph of Arimathea thought his own poor body should presently be laid. But there they laid Jesus after his crucifixion.

He had stood surety for his people, and the law had demanded his blood; death had held him with strong grasp; and that tomb was, as it were, the dungeon of his captivity, when, as the good shepherd, he laid down his life for the sheep. Why, then, do I see in that garden, an open, untenanted grave? I will tell you. The debts are paid, the sins are cancelled—, the remission is obtained. How, think you? That great Shepherd of the sheep hath been brought again from the dead by the blood of the everlasting covenant, and in him also we have obtained redemption through his blood. There, beloved, is proof the first.

Do you ask further evidence? I will take you to Mount Olivet. You shall behold Jesus there with his hands raised like the High Priest of old to bless his people, and while he is blessing them, he ascends, the clouds receiving him out of their sight. But why, you ask, oh why hath he thus ascended, and whither is he gone? Behold he entereth, not into the holy place made with hands, but be entereth into heaven itself with his own blood, there to appear in the presence of God for us. Now, therefore, we have boldness to draw near by the blood of Christ. The remission is obtained, here is proof the second. Oh believer, what springs of comfort are there here for thee.

And now let me commend this remission by the shedding of blood to those who have not yet believed. Mr. Innis, a great Scotch minister, once visited an infidel who was dying. When he came to him the first time, he said, "Mr. Innis, I am relying on the mercy of God; God is merciful, and he will never damn a man for ever."

When he got worse and was nearer death, Mr. Innis went to him again, and he said, " Oh! Mr. Innis, my hope is gone; for I have been thinking if God be merciful, God is just too; and what if, instead of being merciful to me, he should be just to me? What would then become of me? I must give up my hope in the mere mercy of God; tell me how to be saved!" Mr. Innis told him that Christ had died in the stead of all believers—that God could be just, and yet the justifier through the death of Christ. " Ah!" said he, " Mr. Innis, there is something solid in that; I can rest on that; I cannot rest on anything else;" and it is a remarkable fact that none of us ever met with a man who thought he had his sins forgiven unless it was through the blood of Christ. Meet a Mussulman; he never had his sins forgiven; he does not say so. Meet an Infidel; he never knows that his sins are forgiven. Meet a Legalist; he says, "I hope they will be forgiven;" but he does not pretend they are. No one ever gets even a fancied hope apart from this, that Christ, and Christ alone, must save by the shedding of his blood.

Let me tell a story to show how Christ saves souls. Mr. Whitfield had a brother who had been like him, an earnest Christian, but he had backslidden; he went far from the ways of godliness; and one afternoon, after he had been recovered from his backsliding, he was sitting in a room in a chapel house. He had heard his brother preaching the day before, and his poor conscience had been cut to the very quick. Said Whitfield's brother, when he was at tea, "I am a lost man," and he groaned and cried, and could neither eat nor drink. Said Lady Huntingdon, who sat opposite, "What did you say, Mr. Whitfield?" "Madam," said he, "I said, I am a lost man." "I'm glad of it," said she; "I'm glad of it." "Your ladyship, how can you say so? It is cruel to say you are glad that I am a lost man." " I repeat it, sir," said she; "I am heartily glad of it." He looked at her, more and more astonished at her barbarity. "I am glad of it," said she, "because it is written, 'The Son of Man came to seek and to save that which was lost.' " With the tears rolling down his cheeks, he said, "What a precious Scripture; and how is it that it comes with such force to me? Oh! madam," said he, "madam, I bless God for that; then he will save me; I trust my soul in his hands; he has forgiven me." He went outside the house, felt ill, fell upon the ground, and expired. I may have a lost man here this morning. As I cannot say much, I will leave you, good people; you do not want anything.

Have I got a lost man here? Lost man! Lost woman! Where are you? Do you feel yourself to be lost? I am so glad of it; for there is remission by the blood-shedding. O sinner, are there tears in your eyes? Look through them. Do you see that man in the garden? That man sweats drops of blood for you. Do you see that man on the cross? That man was nailed there for you. Oh! if I could be nailed on a cross this morning for you all, I know what you would do: you would fall down and kiss my feet, and weep that I should have to die for you.

But sinner, lost sinner, Jesus died for you—for you; and if he died for you., you cannot be lost. Christ died in vain for no one. Are you, then, a sinner? Are you convinced of sin because you believe not in Christ? I have authority to preach to you. Believe in his name and you cannot be lost. Do you say you are no sinner? Then I do not know that Christ died for you. Do you say that you have no sins to repent of? Then I have no Christ to preach to you. He did not come to save the righteous; he came to save the wicked. Are you wicked? Do you feel it? Are you lost? Do you know it? Are you sinful? Will you confess it? Sinner! if Jesus were here this morning, he would put out his bleeding hands, and say, " Sinner, I died for you, will you believe me?" He is not here in person; he has sent his servant to tell you. Won't you believe him? "Oh!" but you say, "I am such a sinner;" "Ah!" says he, "that is just why I died for you, because you are a sinner." "But," you say, "I do not deserve it." "Ah!" says he, "that is just why I did it." Say you, "I have hated him." "But," says he, "I have always loved you." "But, Lord, I have spat on thy minister, and scorned thy word." "It is all forgiven," says he, "all washed away by the blood which did run from my side. Only believe me; that is all I ask. And that I will give you. I will help you to believe." "Ah!" says one, "but I do not want a Saviour." Sir, I have nothing to say to you except this—"The wrath to come! the wrath to come!" But there is one who says, "Sir, you do not mean what you say! Do you mean to preach to the most wicked men or women in the place?" I mean what I say. There she is! She is a harlot, she has led many into sin, and many into hell, There she is; her own friends have turned her out of doors; her father called her a good-for-nothing hussey, and said she should never come to the house again. Woman I dost thou repent? Dost thou feel thyself to be guilty? Christ died to save thee, and thou shalt be saved. There he is. I can see him. He was drunk; he has been drunk very often. Not many nights ago I heard his voice in the street, as he went home at a late hour on Saturday night, disturbing everybody; and he beat his wife, too. He has broken the Sabbath; and as to swearing, if oaths be like soot, his throat must want sweeping bad enough, for he has cursed God often. Do you feel yourself to be guilty, my hearer? Do you hate your sins, and are you willing to forsake them? Then I bless God for you. Christ died for you. Believe! I had a letter a few days ago, from a young man who heard that during this week I was going to a certain town. Said he, "Sir, when you come, do preach a sermon that will fit me; for do you know, sir, I have heard it said that we must all think ourselves to be the wickedest people in the world, or else we cannot be saved. I try to think so, but I cannot, because I have not been the wickedest. I want to think so, but I cannot. I want to be saved, but I do not know how to repent enough." Now, if I have the pleasure of seeing him, I shall tell him, God does not require a man to think himself the wickedest in the world, because that would sometimes be to think a falsehood; there are some men who are not so wicked as others are. What God requires is this, that a man should say, "I know more of myself than I do of other people; I know little about them, and from what I see of myself, not of my actions, but of my heart, I do think there can be few worse than I am. They may be more guilty openly, but then I have had more light, more privileges, more opportunities, more warnings, and therefore I am still guiltier." I do not want you to bring your brother with you, and say, "I am more wicked than he is;" I want you to come yourself, and say, "Father, I have sinned;" you have nothing to do with your brother William, whether he has sinned more or less; your cry should be, "Father, I have sinned;" you have nothing to do with your cousin Jane, whether or not she has rebelled more than you. Your business is to cry, "Lord, have mercy upon me, a sinner!" That is all. Do you feel yourselves lost? Again, I say,—"Come, and welcome, sinner, come!"

To conclude. There is not a sinner in this place who knows himself to be lost and ruined, who may not have all his sins forgiven, and "rejoice in the hope of the glory of God." You may, though black as hell, be white as heaven this very instant. I know 'tis only by a desperate struggle that faith takes hold of the promise, but the very moment a sinner believes, that conflict is past. It is his first victory, and a blessed one. Let this verse be the language of your heart; adopt it, and make it your own: "A guilty weak, and helpless worm. In Christ's kind arms I fall; He is my strength and righteousness, My Jesus and my all."

The Character of Christ's People

A Sermon (No. 78) Delivered on
Thursday Evening, November 22, 1855,
by the REV. C. H. SPURGEON
At New Park Street Chapel, Southwark.

"They are not of the world, even as I am not of the world."—John 17:16.

Christ's prayer was for a special people. He declared that he did not offer an universal intercession. "I pray for them," said he. "I pray not for the world, but for them which thou hast given me, for they are thine." In reading this beautiful prayer through, only one question arises to our minds; Who are the people that are described as "them," or as "they?" Who are these favoured individuals, who share a Saviour's prayers, are recognized by a Saviour's love, have their names written on the stones of his precious breastplate, and have their characters and their circumstances mentioned by the lips of the High Priest before the throne on high? The answer to that question is supplied by the words of our text. The people for whom Christ prays are an unearthly people. They are a people somewhat, above the world, distinguished altogether from it. "They are not of the world, even as I am not of the world."

I shall treat my text, first of all, docrtrinally; secondly, experimentally; and thirdly, practically.

I. First, we shall take our text and look at it DOCTRINALLY.

The doctrine of it is, that God's people are people who are not of the world, even as Christ was not of the world. It is not so much that they are not of the world, as that they are "not of the world, even as Christ was not of the world." This is an important distinction, for there are to be found certain people who are not of the world, and yet they are not Christians. Amongst these I would mention sentimentalists—people who are always crying and groaning in affected sentimental ways. Their spirits are so refined, their characters are so delicate, that they could not attend to ordinary business. They would think it rather degrading to their spiritual nature to attend to anything connected with the world. They live much in the air of romances and novels; love to read things that fetch tears from their eyes; they would like continually to live in a cottage near a wood, or to inhabit some quiet cave, where they could read "Zimmerman on Solitude" for ever; for they feel that they are "not of the world." The fact is, there is something too flimsy about them to stand the wear and tear of this wicked world. They are so pre-eminently good, that they cannot bear to do as we poor human creatures do. I have heard of one young lady, who thought herself so spiritually-minded that she could not work. A very wise minister said to her, "That is quite correct! you are so spiritually-minded that you cannot work; very well, you are so spiritually-minded that you shall not eat unless you do." That brought her back from her great spiritual-mindedness. There is a stupid sentimentalism that certain persons nurse themselves into. They read a parcel of books that intoxicate their brains, and then fancy that they have a lofty destiny. These people are "not of the world," truly; but the world does not want them, and the world would not miss them much, if they were clean gone for ever. There is such a thing as being "not of the world," from a high order of sentimentalism, and yet not being a Christian after all. For it is not so much being "not of the world," as being "not of the world, even as Christ was not of the world." There are others, too, like your monks, and those other made individuals of the Catholic church, who are not of the world. They are so awfully good, that they could not live with us sinful creatures at all. They must be distinguished from us altogether. They must not wear, of course, a boot that would at all approach to a worldly shoe, but they must have a sole of leather strapped on with two or three thongs, like the far-famed Father Ignatius. They could not be expected to wear worldly coats and waistcoats; but they must have peculiar garbs, cut in certain fashions, like the Passionists. They must wear particular dresses, particular garments, particular habits. And we know that some men are "not of the world," by the peculiar mouthing they give to all their words—the sort of sweet, savoury, buttery flavor they give to the English language, because they think themselves so eminently sanctified that they fancy it would be wrong to indulge in anything in which ordinary mortals indulge. Such persons are, however, reminded, that their being "not of the world," has nothing to do with it. It is not being "not of the world," so much as being "not of the world, even as Christ was not of the world."

This is the distinguishing mark—being different from the world in those respects in which Christ was different.

Not making ourselves singular in unimportant points, as those poor creatures do, but being different from the world in those respects in which the Son of God and the Son of man, Jesus Christ, was not of the world in nature; that he was not of the world again, in office; and above all, that he was not of the world in his character.

1. First, Christ was not of the world in nature. What was there about Christ that was worldly? In one point of view his nature was divine; and as divine, it was perfect, pure unsullied, spotless, he could not descend to things of earthliness and sin; in another sense he was human; and his human nature, which was born of the Virgin Mary, was begotten of the Holy Ghost, and therefore was so pure that in it rested nothing that was worldly. He was not like ordinary men. We are all born with worldliness in our hearts. Solomon well says, "Foolishness is bound up in the heart of a child." It is not only there, but it is bound up in it; it is tied up in his heart, and is difficult to remove. And so with each of us; when we were children, earthliness and carnality were bound up in our nature. But Christ was not so. His nature was not a worldly one; it was essentially different from that of every one else, although he sat down and talked with them. Mark the difference! He stood side by side with a Pharisee; but every one could see he was not of the Pharisee's world. He sat by a Samaritan woman, and though he conversed with her very freely, who is it that fails to see that he was not of that Samaritan woman's world—not a sinner like her? He mingled with the Publicans, nay, he sat down at the Publican's feast, and eat with Publicans and sinners; but you could see by the holy actions and the peculiar gestures he there carried with him, that he was not of the Publicans' world, though he mixed with them. There was something so different in his nature, that you could not have found an individual in all the world whom could have set beside him and said, "There! he is of that man's world," Nay, not even John, though he leaned on his bosom and partook very much of his Lord's spirit, was exactly of that world to which Jesus belonged; for even he once in his Boanergean spirit, said words to this effect, "Let us call down fire from heaven on the heads of those who oppose thee,"—a thing that Christ could not endure for a moment, and thereby proved that he was something even beyond John's world.

Well, beloved, in some sense, the Christian man is not of the world even in his nature. I do not mean in his corrupt and fallen nature, but in his new nature. There is something in a Christian that is utterly and entirely distinct from that of anybody else. Many persons think that the difference between a Christian and worldling consists in this: one goes to chapel twice on a Sabbath-day, another does not go but once, or perhaps not at all; one of them takes the sacrament, the other does not; one pays attention to holy things, the other pays very little attention to them. But, ah, beloved, that does not make a Christian. The distinction between a Christian and a worldling is not merely external, but internal. The difference is one of nature, and not of act.

A Christian is as essentially difference from a worldling as a dove is from a raven, or a lamb from a lion. He is not of the world even in his nature. You could not make him a worldling. You might do what you liked; you might cause him to fall into some temporary sin; but you could not make him a worldling. You might cause him to backslide; but you could not make him a sinner, as he used to be. He is not of the world by his nature. He is a twice-born man; in his veins run the blood of the royal family of the universe. He is a nobleman; he is a heaven-born child. His freedom is not merely a bought one, but he hath his liberty his new-born nature; he is essentially and entirely different from the world. There are persons in this chapel now who are more totally distinct from one another than you can even conceive. I have some here who are intelligent, and some who are ignorant; some who are rich, and some who are poor; but I do not allude to those distinctions: they all melt away into nothing in that great distinction—dead or alive, spiritual or carnal, Christian or worldling. And oh! if ye are God's people, then ye are not of the world in your nature; for ye are "not of the world, even as Christ was not of the world."

2. Again: you are not of the world in your office. Christ's office had nothing to do with worldly things. "Art thou a king them?" Yes; I am a king; but my kingdom is not of this world. "Art thou a priest?" Yes; I am a priest; but my priesthood is not the priesthood which I shall soon lay aside, or which shall be discontinued as that of others has been. "Art thou a teacher?" Yes; but my doctrines are not the doctrines of morality, doctrines that concern earthly dealings between man and man simply; my doctrine cometh down from heaven. So Jesus Christ, we say, is "not of the world." He had no office that could be termed a worldly one, and he had no aim which was in the least worldly. He did not seek his own applause, his own fame, his own honour; his very office was not of the world. And, O believer! what is thy office? Hast thou none at all? Why, yes, man! Thou art a priest unto the Lord thy God; thy office is to offer a sacrifice of prayer and praise each day. Ask a Christian what he is. Say to him: "What is your official standing? What are you by office?" Well, if he answers you properly, he will not say, "I am a draper, or druggist," or anything of that sort. No; he will say, "I am a priest unto my God. The office unto which I am called, is to be the salt of the earth. I am a city set on a hill, a light that cannot be hid. That is my

office. My office is not a worldly one." Whether yours be the office of the minister, or the deacon, or the church member, ye are not of this world is your office, even as Christ was not of the world; your occupation is not a worldly one.

3. Again, ye are not of the world in your character; for that is the chief point in which Christ was not of the world. And now, brethren, I shall have to turn somewhat from doctrine to practice before I get rightly to this part of the subject; for I must reprove many of the Lord's people, that they do not sufficiently manifest that they are not of the world in character, even as Christ was not of the world. Oh! how many of you there are, who will assemble around the table at the supper of your Lord, who do not live like your Saviour. How many of you there are, who join our church and walk with us, and yet are not worthy of your high calling and profession. Mark you the churches all around, and let your eyes run with tears, when you remember that of many of their members it cannot be said, "ye are not of this world," for they are of the world. O, my hearers, I fear many of you are worldly, carnal, and covetous; and yet ye join the churches, and stand well with God's people by a hypocritical profession. O ye whitewashed sepulchres! ye would deceive even the very elect! ye make clean the outside of the cup and platter, but your inward part is very wickedness. O that a thundering voice might speak this to your ears!—"Those whom Christ loves are not of the world," but ye are of the world; therefore ye cannot be his, even though ye profess so to be; for those that love him are not such as you. Look at Jesus character; how different from every other man's—pure, perfect, spotless, even such should be the life of the believer. I plead not for the possibility of sinless conduct in Christians, but I must hold that grace makes men to differ, and that God's people will be very different from other kinds of people. A servant of God will be a God's-man everywhere. As a chemist, he could not indulge in any tricks that such men might play with their drugs; as a grocer—if indeed it be not a phantom that such things are done—he could not mix sloe leaves with tea or red lead in the pepper; if he practised any other kind of business, he could not for a moment condescend to the little petty shifts, called "methods of business." To him it is nothing what is called "business;" it is what is called God's law, he feels that he is not of the world, consequently, he goes against its fashions and its maxims. A singular story is told of a certain Quaker. One day he was bathing in the Thames, and a waterman called out to him, "Ha! there goes the Quaker." "How do you know I'm a Quaker?" "Because you swim against the stream; it is the way the Quakers always do." That is the way Christians always ought to do—to swim against the stream. The Lord's people should not go along with the rest in their worldliness. Their characters should be visibly different. You should be such men that your fellows can recognise you without any difficulty, and say, "Such a man is a Christian." Ah! beloved, it would puzzle the angel Gabriel himself, to tell whether some of you are Christians or not, if he were sent down to the world to pick out the righteous from the wicked. None but God could do it, for in these days of worldly religion they are so much alike. It was an ill day for the world, when the sons of God and the daughters of men were mingled together: and it is an ill day now, when Christians and worldlings are so mixed, that you cannot tell the difference between them. God save us from a day of fire that may devour us in consequence! But O beloved! the Christian will be always different from the world. This is a great doctrine, and it will be found as true in ages to come as in the centuries which are past. Looking back into history, we read this lesson: "They are not of the world, even as I am not of the world." We see them driven to the catacombs of Rome; we see them hunted about like partridges; and wherever in history you find God's servants, you can recognise them by their distinct, unvarying character—they are not of the world, but were a people scarred and peeled; a people entirely distinct from the nations. And if in this age, there are no different people, if there are none to be found who differ from other people, there are no Christians; for Christians will be always different from the world. They are not of the world; even as Christ is not of the world. This is the doctrine.

II. But now for treating this text EXPERIMENTALLY.

Do we, dearly beloved, feel this truth? Has it ever been laid to our souls, so that we can feel it is ours? "They are not of the world, even as I am not of the world." Have we ever felt that we are not of the world? Perhaps there is a believer sitting in a pew to-night, who says, "Well, sire, I can't say that I feel as if I was not of the world, for I have just come from my shop, and worldliness is still hanging about me." Another says, "I have been in trouble and my mind is very much harassed—I can't feel that I am different from the world; I am afraid that I am of the world." But, beloved, we must not judge ourselves rashly, because just at this moment we discern not the spot of

God's children. Let me tell you, there are always certain testing moments when you can tell of what kind of stuff a man is made. Two men are walking. Part of the way their road lies side by side.

How do you tell which man is going to the right, and which to the left? Why, when they come to the turning point. Now, to-night is not a turning point, for you are sitting with worldly people here, but at other times we may distinguish.

Let me tell you one or two turning points, when every Christian will feel that he is not of the world. One is, when he gets into very deep trouble. I do believe and protest, that we never feel so unearthly as when we get plunged down into trouble. Ah! when some creature comfort hath been swept away, when some precious blessing hath withered in our sight, like the fair lily, snapped at the stalk; when some mercy has been withered, like Jonah's gourd in the night—then it is that the Christian feels, "I am not of the world." His cloak is torn from him, and the cold wind whistles almost through him; and then he says, "I am a stranger in the world, as all my fathers were. Lord, thou hast been my dwelling-place in all generations." You have had at times deep sorrows. Thank God for them! They are testing moments. When the furnace is hot, it is then that the gold is tried best. Have you felt at such a time that you were not of the world? Or, have you rather sat down, and said, "Oh! I do not deserve this trouble?" Did you break under it? Did you bow down before it and let it crush you while you cursed your Maker? Or did your spirit, even under its load, still lift itself unto him, like a man all dislocated on the battle-field, whose limbs are cut away, but who still lifts himself up as best he can, and looks over the field to see if there be a friend approaching. Did you do so? Or did you lie down in desperation and despair? If you did that, methinks you are no Christian; but if there was a rising up, it was a testing moment, and it proved that you were "not of the world," because you could master affliction; because you could tread it under foot, and say——"When all created streams are dry, His goodness is the same; With this I well am satisfied, And glory in his name." But another testing moment is prosperity. Oh! there have been some of God's people, who have been more tried by prosperity than by adversity. Of the two trials, the trial of adversity is less severe to the spiritual man than that of prosperity. "As the fining pot for silver, so is a man to his praise." It is a terrible thing to be prosperous. You had need to pray to God, not only to help you in your troubles, but to help you in your blessings. Mr. Whitfield once had a petition to put up for a young man who had—stop, you will think it was for a young man who had lost his father or his property. No! "The prayers of the congregation are he has need of much grace to keep him humble in the midst of riches." That is the kind of prayer that ought to be put up; for prosperity is a hard thing to bear. Now, perhaps you have become almost intoxicated with worldly delights, even as a Christian. Everything goes well with you; you have loved, and you are loved.

Your affairs are prosperous; your heart rejoices, your eyes sparkle; you tread the earth with a happy soul and a joyous countenance; you are a happy man, for you have found that even in worldly things, "godliness with contentment is great gain." Did you ever feel,—"These can never satisfy; Give me Christ, or else I die." Did you feel that these comforts were nothing but the leaves of the tree, and not the fruit, and that you could not live upon mere leaves? Did you feel they were after all nothing but husks? Or did you not sit down and say, "Now, soul, take thine ease; thou hast goods laid up for many years; eat, drink, and be merry?" If you did imitate the rich fool, then you were of the world; but if your spirit went up above your prosperity so that you still lived near to God, then you proved that you were a child of God, for you were not of the world. These are testing points; both prosperity and adversity.

Again: you may test yourselves in this way in solitude and in company. In solitude you may tell whether you are not of the world. I sit me down, throw the window up, look out on the stars, and think of them as the eyes of God looking down upon me! And oh! does it not seem glorious at times to consider the heavens when we can say, "Ah! beyond those stars in my house not made with hands; those stars are mile-stones on the road to glory, and I shall soon tread the glittering way, or be carried by seraphs far beyond them, and be there!" Have you felt in solitude that you are not of the world? And so again in company. Ah! beloved, believe me, company is one of the best tests for a Christian. You are invited to an evening party. Sundry amusements are provided which are not considered exactly sinful, but which certainly cannot come under the name of pious amusements. You sit there with the rest; there is a deal of idle chat going on, you would be thought puritanical to protest against it. Have you not come away—and notwithstanding all has been very pleasant, and friends have been very agreeable—have you not been inclined to say, "Ah! that does not do for me; I would rather be in a prayer meeting; I could be with the people of God, than in fine rooms with all the dainties and delicacies that could be provided without the company of Jesus. By God's grace I will seek to shun all these places as much as possible." That is a good test. You will prove in this way that you are not of the world. And you may do so in great many other ways, which I have no time to mention. Have you felt this experimentally, so that you can say, "I know that I am not of the world, I feel it; I experience it." Don't talk of doctrine. Give me doctrine ground into experience. Doctrine is good; but experience is better. Experimental doctrine is the true doctrine which comforts and which edifies.

IV. And now, lastly we must briefly apply this in PRACTICE. "They are not of the world, even as I am not of the world." And, first, allow me, man or woman, to apply this to thee. Thou who art of the world, whose maxims, whose habits, whose behaviour, whose feelings, whose everything is worldly and carnal, list thee to this. Perhaps thou makest some profession of religion. Hear me, then. Thy boasting of religion is empty as a phantom, and shall pass away when the sun rises, as the ghosts sleep in their grave at the crowing of the cock. Thou hast some pleasure in that professioned religion of thine wherewith thou art arrayed, and which thou carriest about thee as a cloak, and usest as a stalking-horse to thy business, and a net to catch the honour of the world, and yet thou art worldly, like other men. Then I tell thee if there be no distinction between thyself and the worldly, the doom of the worldly shall be thy doom. If thou wert marked and watched, thy next door tradesman would act as thou dost, and thou actest as he does; there is no distinction between thee and the world. Hear me, then; it is God's solemn truth. Thou art none of his. If thou art like the rest of the world, thou art of the world. Thou art a goat, and with goats thou shalt be cursed; for the sheep can always be distinguished from the goats by their appearance. O ye worldly men of the world! ye carnal professors, ye who crowd our churches, and fill our places of worship, this is God's truth! let me say it solemnly. If I should say it as I ought, it would be weeping tears of blood. Ye are, with all your profession, "in the gall of bitterness;" with all your boastings, ye are "in bonds of iniquity;" for ye act as others and ye shall come where others come; and it shall be done with you as with more notorious heirs of hell. There is an old story which was once told of a Dissenting minister. The old custom was, that a minister might stop at an inn, and not pay anything for his bed or his board; and when he went to preach, from place to place, he was charged nothing for the conveyance in which he rode. But on one occasion, a certain minister stopped at an inn and went to bed.

The landlord listened and heard no prayer; so when he came down in the morning, he presented his bill. "Oh! I am not going to pay that, for I am a minister." "Ah!" said the landlord, "you went to bed last night like a sinner, and you shall pay this morning like a sinner; I will not let you go." Now, it strikes me, that this will be the case with some of you when you come to God's bar. Though you pretended to be a Christian, you acted like a sinner, and you shall fare like a sinner too. Your actions were unrighteous; they were far from God; and you shall have a portion with those whose character was the same as yours. "Be not deceived;" it is easy to be so. "God is not mocked," though we often are, both minister and people. "God is not mocked; whatsoever a man soweth, that shall he also reap."

And now we want to apply this to many true children of God who are here, by way of caution. I say, my brother Christian, you are not of the world. I am not going to speak hardly to you, because you are my brother, and in speaking to you I speak to myself also, for I am as guilty as thou art. Brother, have we not often been too much like the world? Do we not sometimes in our conversation, talk too much like the world? Come, let me ask myself, are there not too many idle words that I say? Ay, that there are. And do I not sometimes give occasion to the enemy to blaspheme, because I am not so different from the world as I ought to be? Come, brother; let us confess our sins together. Have we not been too worldly? Ah! we have. Oh! let this solemn thought cross our minds: suppose that after all we should not be his! for it is written, "Ye are not of the world." O God! if we are not right, make us so; where we are a little right, make us still more right; and where we are wrong, amend us! Allow me to tell a story to you; I told it when I was preaching last Tuesday morning, but it is worth telling again. There is a great evil in many of us being too light and frothy in our conversation.

A very solemn thing once happened. A minister had been preaching in a country village, very earnestly and fervently. in the midst of his congregation there was a young man who was deeply impressed with a sense of sin under the sermon; he therefore sought the minister as he went out, in hopes of walking home with him. They walked till they came to a friend's house. On the road the minister had talked about anything except the subject on which he had preached, though he had preached very earnestly, and even with tears in his eyes.

The young man thought within himself, "Oh! I wish I could unburden my heart and speak to him; but I cannot. He does not say anything now about what he spoke of in the pulpit." When they were at supper that evening, the conversation was very far from what it should be, and the minister indulged in all kinds of jokes and light sayings. The young man had gone into the house with eyes filled with tears, feeling like a sinner should feel; but as soon as he got outside, after the conversation, he stamped his foot, and said, "It is a lie from beginning to end. That man has preached like an angel; and now he has talked like a devil." Some years after the young man was taken ill, and sent for this same minister. The minister did not know him. "Do you remember preaching at such-and-such a village?" asked the young man. "I do." "your text was very deeply laid to my heart." "Thank God for that," said the minister. "Do not be so quick about thanking God," said the young man. "Do you know what you talked of that evening afterwards, when I went to supper with you. Sir, I shall be damned! And I will charge you before God's throne with being the author of my damnation. On that night I did feel my sin; but you were the means of scattering all my impressions." That is a solemn thought, brother, and teaches us how we should curb our tongues, especially those who are so light hearted, after solemn services and earnest preachings, that we should not betray levity. Oh! let us take heed that we are not of the world, even as Christ was not of the world.

And Christian, lastly, by way of practice, let me comfort thee with this. Thou art not of the world for thy home is in heaven. Be content to be here a little, for thou art not of the world, and thou shalt go up to thine own bright inheritance by-and-bye. A man in travelling goes into an inn; it is rather uncomfortable, "Well," says he, "I shall not have to stay here many nights; I have only to sleep here to-night, I shall be at home in the morning, so that I don't care much about one night's lodging being a little uncomfortable." So, Christian, this world is never a very comfortable one; but recollect, you are not of the world. This world is like an inn; you are only lodging here a little while. Put up with a little inconvenience, because you are not of the world, even as Christ is not of the world; and by-and-bye, up yonder, you shall be gathered into your father's house, and there you will find that there is a new heaven and a new earth provided for those who are "not of the world."

The Christian—A Debtor

A Sermon (No. 96)
Delivered on Sabbath Evening, August 10, 1856,
by the REV. C. H. SPURGEON
At Exeter Hall, Strand.

"Therefore, brethren, we are debtors."
—Romans 8:12.

Observe the title whereby he addressed the Church—"Brethren." It was the gospel which taught Paul how to say brother. If he had not been a Christian, his Jewish dignity would never have condescended to call a Roman—"brother;" for a Jew sneered at the Gentile, and called him "dog." But now in the breast of this "Hebrew of Hebrews," there is the holy recognition of Christian fraternity without reserve or hypocrisy. The gospel softened the breast of Paul, and made him forget all national animosities, otherwise, one of the down-trodden race would not have called his oppressor, "brother." The Roman had his iron foot on the Jew; yet Paul addresses those, who subjugated his race, as "brethren." We repeat, a third time, it was the gospel which implanted in the soul of Paul the feeling of brotherhood, and removed every wall of partition which divided him from any of the Lord's elect. "So then," he said, "we are no more strangers and foreigners, but fellow-citizens with the saints, and of the household of God." He proclaimed the doctrine of the "one blood," and gloried in the fact of "one family" in Christ. He felt within him affinities with all the blood-bought race, and loved them all. He had not seen many of those whom he addressed; yet they were known to him, in the Spirit, as partakers of one glorious and blessed hope, and, therefore, he called them "brethren." My friends, there is a cementing power in the grace of God which can scarcely be over estimated. It resets the dislocated bones of society, rivets the bonds of friendship, and welds the broken metal of manhood into one united mass.

It makes all brethren who feel its power. Grace links mankind in a common brotherhood; grace makes the great man give his hand to the poor, and confess a heavenly relationship; grace constrains the intellectual, the learned, the polite, to stoop from their dignity to take hold of the ignorant and unlettered, and call them friends; grace weaves the threads of our separate individualities into one undivided unity. Let the gospel be really felt in the mind and it will toll the knell of selfishness, it will bring down the proud from their elevated solitude, and it will restore the down-trodden to the rights of our common manhood. We need only the gospel thoroughly preached to bring about "liberty, equality, and fraternity," in the highest and best sense of these words. Not the "liberty, equality and fraternity," which the democrat seeks for, which is frequently another name for his own superiority, but that which is true and real—that which will make us all free in the Spirit, make us all equal in the person of Christ Jesus, and give us all the fraternity of brethren, seeing that we are all one with our Lord, in the common bond of gospel relationship. Let the truths of Christianity work out their perfect work: and pride, bitterness, wrath, envy, and malice, must see their graves. This and this alone can restore the peace of divided families, and unite disputing relatives. Only let the gospel be preached, and there shall be an end of war; let it thoroughly pervade all ranks of society, and saturate the mind of nations, and there shall be no more lifting of the spears, they shall be used for pruning hooks; no bathing of swords in blood, for they shall be turned into the peaceful ploughshares of the soil; we shall then have no hosts encountering hosts; we shall have no millions slain for widows to deplore; but every man shall meet every other man, and call him "brother." And men of every kindred, and of every tribe, shall see in the face of every man, a relative allied to them by ties of blood. I am sure I feel, myself, the force of this word "brother," with regard to many of you. If ye be partakers of that glorious hope, if ye be believers in our glorious Redeemer, if ye have put your trust under the shadow of his wings, my hand and my heart with it, there is that word "brother" for you. And so addressing you, who love the Lord, under that title; I come at one to the text, "Brethren, we are debtors." We are all of us under obligations; let us consider the fact in the following manner:—First, how are we to understand this? and secondly, how ought it to affect us?

I. HOW ARE WE TO UNDERSTAND THIS, "Brethren, we are debtors"? We may understand it in a thousand sense, for indeed we are debtors. Brethren, we who know and love the Lord, are debtors, not to one creditor, but to many.

We are debtors to the past. Methinks I see the fathers at their midnight lamps, the ancient saints in their much-frequented closets, the thrice brave preachers in their pulpits denouncing error, and the faithful pastors reproving wrong. To such who have preceded us we owe the purity of the Church, and to them we are debtors. methinks I see the martyrs and confessors rising from their tombs—I mark their hands still stained with blood, and their bodies scarred with the wound of persecution. They tell me, that they of old maintained the truth, and preached it, in the midst of fire and sword—that they bore death in defence of the cause of God, that they might hand down his holy word inviolate to us! I look on them, and see among their glorious ranks, some whose names are celebrated in every Christian land as the bold "lions of God," the immovable pillars of truth; men of whom the world was not worthy, whose praise is in all the churches, and who are now nearest the eternal throne. And as I look on them, and they on me, I turn to you all and say, "Brethren, we are debtors." We are debtors to the men who crossed the sea, and laughed at the fury of the storm, who risked the journeying, and the weariness, and all the various perils to which they were exposed, by reason of robbers and false brethren; we are debtors to each stake at Smithfield; we are debtors to the sacred ashes of the thousands who have there followed Jesus even unto death; we are debtors to the headless bodies of those who were beheaded for Christ Jesus; we are debtors to those who dared the lions in the amphitheatre and fought with wild beasts at Ephesus; we are debtors to the massacred thousands of the bloody church of Rome, and the murdered myriads of her pagan predecessors; we are debtors to them all. Remember the bloody day of St. Bartholomew, the valleys of Piedmont, and the mountains of Switzerland. Let the sacred mounds of our fathers' sepulchres speak to us. Is not this Bible opened and read by us all, the gift of their self-denying faithfulness? Is not the free air we breathe the purchase of their death? Did not they, by bitter suffering, achieve our liberty for us? And are we not debtors to them? Shall we not, in some degree, repay the immense debt of our obligation by seeking to make the future also debtors to us, that our descendants may look back and acknowledge that they owe us thank for preserving the Scriptures, for maintaining liberty, for glorifying God?

Brethren, we are debtors to the past.

And I am quite sure we are debtors to the present. Wherever we go, we gather fresh proofs of the common observation, that we are living in a most marvellous age. It is an oft-repeated truth, and one which, perhaps, has almost lost its meaning from being so oft repeated, that this is the very crisis. The world has always been in a crisis, but this seems to use to be a peculiar one. We have around us appliances for doing good, such as men never possessed before; we behold around us machinery for doing evil, such as never was at work even in earth's worst days. Good men are labouring, at least with usual zeal, and bad men are strenuously plying their craft of evil. Infidelity, popery, and every other phase of anti-Christ are now straining every nerve. The tug of war is now with us. Look around you and learn your duty. The work is not yet done, the time of folding of hands has not yet arrived; our swords must not yet see their scabbards, for the foe is not yet slain.

We see, in many a land, the proudest dynasties and tyrannies still crushing, with their mountain-weight, every free motion of the consciences and hearts of men. We see, on the other hand, the truest heroism for the right, and the greatest devotion to the truth in hearts that God has touched. We have a work to do, as great as our forefathers, and, perhaps, far greater. The enemies of truth are more numerous and subtle than ever, and the needs of the Church are greater than at any preceding time. If we be not debtors to the present, then men were never debtors to their age and their time. Brethren, we are debtors to the hour in which we live. Oh! that we might stamp it with truth, and that God might help us to impress upon its wings some proof that it has not flown by neglected and unheeded.

And, brethren, we are debtors to the future. If we, the children of God, are not valiant for truth now, if we maintain not the great standard of God's omnipotent truth, we shall be traitors to our liege Lord. Who can tell the fearful consequences to future generations if we now betray our trust. If we suffer orthodoxy to fail, or God's truth to be dishonored, future generations will despise and execrate our name. If we now suffer the good vessel of gospel truth to be drifted by adverse winds upon the rock, if we keep not good watch to her helm, and cry not well to her great Master that she may led to a prosperous end, surely those who are to succeed us will look on us with scorn, and say, "Shame on the men, who had so great and glorious a mission, and neglected it, and handed down to us a beclouded gospel and an impure Church." Stand up ye warriors of the truth, stand up firmly, for ye are debtors to the future, even as ye are debtors to the past. Sow well, for others must reap. You are fountains for coming generations; O, be careful that your streams are pure. May the Spirit of God enable you so to live, that you can bequeath your example as a legacy to the future.

And as we are debtors to all times, so we are all debtors to all classes. But there are some that always get well paid for what they do, and, therefore, I shall not mention them, since I am not aware that their claims need my advocacy. We may be remarkably indebted to members of parliament, but for the little they do they are tolerably well rewarded; at least, we take it that the place is more an honour to some of them than they are to their place. It may be true that we owe a great deal to the higher ranks of society; we may possibly, in some mysterious way, be much under obligation to the sacred personages who are styled lords and bishops, but it is not necessary that I should stand up for their claims, for I have no doubt they will take good care of themselves; at any rate they have usually done so, and have not allowed themselves to be robbed of much of their deservings. (Who would wish that they should? but it is possible to pay too dear, especially when you could get on as well without them as with them.) I shall not refer to any class of society, and say of them, we are debtors, except to one, and that is the poor. My brethren, we are debtors to the poor. "What!" says some one, "I, debtor to the poor?" Yes, my lady, thou art a debtor to the poorest man that ever walked the earth.

The beggar shivering in his rags, may owe thee something, if thou givest him alms; but thou owest him something more. Charity to the poor is a debt. We are not at liberty to give or to refuse. God requires us to remember the poor, and their poverty is a claim upon our generosity. But in the case of the believing poor, their claim upon us is far more binding, and I beseech you do not neglect it. O how much we owe them. When I think how the poor toil day after day and receive barely enough to keep their souls within their bodies: when I think how frequently they serve their Church, unhonored and unrewarded, when I know some of them who perform the hardest deeds of service for our common Christianity, and are yet passed by with neglect and scorn; when I remember how many of them are toiling in the Sabbath-school, having neither emolument nor reward; when I consider how many of the lower classes are as prayerful, as careful, as honest, as upright, as devout, as spiritual as others are, and frequently more so, I cannot but say that we are debtors to all God's poor in a very large degree. We little know how many a blessing the poor man's prayer brings down upon us. I beseech you then, beloved, wherever you see a poor saint, wherever you behold an aged Christian, recollect he cannot be so much in debt to you as you are to him, for you have much, and he has but little, and he cannot be in debt for what he has not. Many of you will not feel the force of Christian reasons, let me remind you, that even you are obliged to the laboring poor. The rich man hoards wealth, the poor man makes it. Great men get the blessing, but poor men bring it down from heaven. Some men are the cisterns that hold God's rain; but other men are those who pray the rain from heaven, like very Elijahs, and many of these are to be found in the lower ranks of society. "Brethren, we are debtors;" what I have is not my own, but God's; and if it be God's, then it belongs to God's poor. What the wealthiest man has is not his own, but God's, and if it be God's then it is Christ's, and if Christ's, then his children's; and Christ's children are often those who are hungry, and thirsty, and destitute, and afflicted, and tormented. Take care then of that class, brethren, for we are debtors to them.

But while I have thus mentioned some of the different classes to whom we are debtors, I have not yet come to the point on which I desire to press your attention. Brethren, we are debtors to our covenant God; that is the point which swallows up all. I owe nothing to the past, I owe nothing to the future, I owe nothing to the rich, and nothing to the poor, compared with what I owe to my God. I am mainly indebted to these because I owe so much to my God. Now, Christian, consider how thou art a debtor to thy God. Remember thou art now a debtor to God in a legal sense, as thou art in Adam, thou art no longer a debtor to God's justice as thou once wast. We are all born God's creatures, and as such we are debtors to him; to obey him with all our body, and soul, and strength. When we have broken his commandments, as we all of us have, we are debtors to his justice, and we owe to him a vast amount of punishment, which we are not able to pay. But of the Christian, it can be said, that he does not owe God's justice a solitary farthing; for Christ has paid the debt his people owed. I am a debtor to God's love, I am a debtor to God's grace, I am a debtor to God's power, I am a debtor to God's forgiving mercy; but I am no debtor to his justice—for he, himself, will never accuse me of a debt once paid.

It was said, "It is finished!" and by that was meant, that what'er his people owed was wiped away for ever from the book of remembrance. Christ, to the uttermost, has satisfied divine justice; the debt is paid, the handwriting is nailed to the cross, the receipt is given, and we are debtors to God's justice no longer. But then because we are not debtors to God in that sense, we become ten times more debtors to God than we should have been otherwise. Because he has remitted all our debt of sin, we are all the more indebted to him in another sense. Oh! Christian, stop and ponder for a moment! What a debtor thou art to Divine Sovereignty!

Thou art not as some, who say, that thou didst choose thyself to be saved; but thou believest that God could have destroyed thee, if he had pleased and that it is entirely of his own good pleasure that thou art made one of his, while others are suffered to perish. Consider, then, how much thou owest to his Sovereignty! If he had willed it, thou wouldst have been among the damned; if he had not willed thy salvation, all thou couldst do would have been utterly powerless to deliver thee from perdition. Remember how much thou owest to his disinterested love, which rent his own Son from his bosom that he might die for thee! let the cross and bloody sweat remind thee of thine obligation. Consider how much you owe to his forgiving grace, that after ten thousand affronts he loves you as infinitely as ever; and after a myriad of sins, his Spirit still resides within you. Consider what you owe to his power; how he has raised you from your death in sin, and how he has preserved your spiritual life, how he has kept you from falling, and how, though a thousand enemies have beset your path, you have been able to hold on your way! Consider what thou owest to his immutability. Though thou hast changed a thousand times, he has not changed once; though thou hast shifted thy intentions, and thy will, yet he has not once swerved from his eternal purpose, but still has held thee fast. Consider thou art as deep in debt as thou canst be to every attribute of God. To God thou owest thyself, and all thou hast.

"Brethren, we are debtors."

We are not only debtors to God in the light of gratitude for all these things; but because of our relationship to him. Are we not his sons, and is there not a debt the son owes to the father which a lifetime of obedience can never remove? I feel that to the knee that dandled me and the breast that gave me sustenance, I owe more than I can ever pay; and to him who taught me, and led me in the paths of truth I owe so much, that I dare not speak of the tremendous weight of obligation due to him. Beloved, if God be a father, where is honor? And if we be his sons, are we not thereby bound to love, serve, and obey him? Sonship towards an earthly parent brings with it a host of duties, and shall the Everlasting Father be unregarded? No. The true son of God will never blush to acknowledge that he is in subjection to the Father of spirits. He will rather glory in his high connection, and with reverence obey the commands of his Heavenly Parent. Remember again, we are Christ's brethren, and there is a debt in brotherhood. Brother owes to brother what he cannot pay until he dies. It is more than some men think to have been rocked in the same cradle and dandled on the same knee. Some esteem it nothing. Alas! it is a well-known truth, that if you want help you must go anywhere for it, save to your brother's house. Go not into thy brother's house in the day of thine adversity. Go to the greatest stranger, and he shall help thee; go to thy brother, and he shall oft upbraid thee. But this should not be so. Brotherhood has its ties of debt, and to my brother I owe what I shall not yet pay him. Beloved, are ye brothers of Christ, and do ye think that ye owe him no love? Are ye brothers and sisters of the saints, and think ye that ye ought not to love and serve them, even to the washing of their feet? Oh, yes, I am sure ye ought. I am afraid none of us feel enough how much we are debtors to God. Yea, I am certain that we do not. It is astonishing how much gratitude a man will feel to you if you have been only the instrument of doing him good; but how little gratitude he feels to God, the first cause of all! There have been many who have been won from drunkenness by hearing the preaching of God's Word even under myself, and those persons have been ready to carry me on their shoulders, from very gratitude, for joy; but I would be bound to say they make a far more feeble display of their thankfulness to my Master. At least, they seem to have lost their first love to him far sooner than they did to his servant. We remember to be grateful to all except our God. Our little debts we can pay. Debts of honor, as we call them—which are no debts in some men's eyes—we can discharge; but the great and solemn debt we owe to God is ofttimes passed by, neglected and forgotten. "Brethren, we are debtors."

II. In the second place, very briefly, WHAT OUGHT WE TO DRAW FROM THIS DOCTRINE, that we are debtors?

First, we think we should learn a lesson of humility. If we be debtors we never ought to be proud. All we can do for God is but a trifling acknowledgment of an infinite obligation; yea, more, our good works are gifts of his grace, and do but put us under greater debt to the author of them. Stay, then, ye who are puffed up by your achievements, consider ye have but poorly performed, not a deed of supererogation, but of ordinary duty. How much have you done after all, young man? I thought I saw you the other day looking amazingly great, because on such an occasion you really had done some little service to Christ's Church; and you looked astonishingly proud about it. Young man, didst thou do more than thou oughtest to have done? "No, I did not," you say; "I was a debtor." Then who should be proud of having paid only a part of his debt, when, after all, he owes a great deal more than he is worth? Is there anything to be proud of in having paid a farthing in the pound? I take it there is not. Let us do what we may, it is but a farthing in the pound that we shall ever be able to pay off the debt of gratitude we owe to God. It is curious to see how some men are proud of being greater debtors than others. One man has ten talents, and oh how proud he is, and how he looks down upon another who has but one, and says: "Ah, you are a mean man; I have ten talents." Well, then, thou owest ten talents, and thy brother owes only one; why should you be proud that you owe more than he does? It would be a foolish pride indeed, if two prisoners in the Queen's Bench were to boast, one saying, "I owe a hundred pounds," and the other replying, "I am a greater gentleman than you are, for I owe a thousand." I have heard that in the Marshalsea of old they did take rank according to the greatness of their debts. It is often so on earth: we take rank at times according to the greatness of our talents. But the greatness of our talents is only the amount of our debt; for, the more we have, the more we owe. If a man walks the streets, sticking his bill upon his breast, and proclaiming with pride that he is a debtor, you would say, "Sure he must be a madman; lock him up." And so if a man walk through the earth and lift up his head because of what God has given him, and say, "I am not to notice the poor, I am not to shake hands with the ignorant, because I am so great and mighty," you may with equal reason say, "Take away that poor creature, his pride is his insanity; put him in safe custody, and let him learn that all he has is his debt, and that he has no cause for pride."

Then again, how zealous we should be for our Master! Though we cannot pay all, we can at least acknowledge the debt. It is something on the part of a debtor if he will but acknowledge the claim of his creditor. Oh! how ought we day by day to seek, by living unto God, to acknowledge the debt we owe to him; and, if we cannot pay him the principal, yet to give him some little interest upon the talent which he has lent to us, and upon those stupendous mercies which he has granted to us. I beseech you, my dear friends, take this thought with you wherever you go: "I am a debtor, I must serve my God. It is not left to my pleasure whether I will do it or no; but I am a debtor, and I must serve him."

If we all believed this, how much easier it would be to get our churches into good order! I go to one brother, and I say, "Brother, there is such-and-such an office in the Sabbath-school; will you take it?" "Well, sir, you know how much I love the cause, and how earnest I am in doing everything that I can to serve my Maker; but (now comes the end of it all) I really work so hard all the week that I cannot afford to go out on the Sabbath to Sunday-schools." There you see, that man does not know that he is a debtor. I take him a bill to-morrow morning, and he says, "Do you coming begging?" I say, "No; I have brought a bill; look at it." "Oh, yes," he says, "I see; there is the cash." Now that is the way to act; to feel and acknowledge that you are a debtor; when there is a thing to be done, to do it, and to say, "Do not thank me for it, I have only done what I ought to have done; I have only paid the debt that I owed."

Then let me give you just one piece of homely advice before I send you away. Be just before you are generous, and especially before you are generous to yourselves. Take care that you pay your debts before you spend money upon your pleasures. I would recommend that to many Christians. Now, there are some of you here incommoding us to-night, and making us very hot. You have been very generous to yourselves by coming here, but not very just to your ministers in neglecting the places of worship where you ought to have gone.

You said to yourselves, "We have no doubt we ought to be there; that is our debt; nevertheless we should like to gratify our curiosity for once, by hearing this singular preacher, who will be sure to say something extravagant that will furnish the occasion for a joke for the next fortnight." Now, why did you come here till you had paid your debt? You should have rallied round your own minister and strengthened his hands in the work of the Lord. Again; how many a man is there who says, "I want such-and-such a luxury; I know the cause of God demands of me more than I give it, but I must have that luxury, that shilling shall go to myself, and not to God." Now if you had a debtor who owed you more than he could pay, and you saw him going off on pleasure in a horse and gig to-morrow, you would say, "It is all very well his having that fine horse and gig, and going down to Greenwich; but I would rather that he should pay me the ten pound note I lent him the other day. If he cannot afford to pay, he ought to keep at home till he can." So in regard to God. We come and spend our time and our money upon our pleasures before we pay our just and fair debts. Now, what is not right towards man is not right towards God. If it is robbing man to spend the money in pleasure wherewith we ought to pay our debts; it is robbing God if we employ our time, our talents, or our money, in anything but his service, until we feel we have done our share in that service. I beseech you, members of churches, deacons, or whatever you may be, lay this to heart. To God's cause you are debtors. Do not expect to get thanked at last for doing much, for after all you have done, you will only have done what is your duty.

Now, farewell to such of you as are debtors in that sense; but just one word to those who are debtors in the other sense; Sinner, thou who owest to God's justice, thou who hast never been pardoned; what wilt thou do when pay-day comes/ My friend over there, you who have run up a score of black sins, what will you do when pay-day comes, and no Christ to pay your debts for you? What will you do if you are out of God and out of Christ at the last pay-day, when the whole roll of your debts to God shall be opened, and you have no Christ to give you a discharge? I beseech thee, "Agree with thy creditor quickly, whilst thou art in the way with him; lest he deliver thee to the judge, and the judge deliver thee to the officer to cast thee into prison: verily I say unto thee, thou shall not come out till thou hast paid the uttermost farthing." But if thou agrest with thy creditor, he will, for Jesus' sake, blot out all thy debts, and set thee at liberty, so that thou shalt never be amenable for thine iniquities.

The Covenant Promise of the Spirit

A Sermon (No. 2200) Delivered on Lord's-Day Morning, April 12th, 1891, by C. H. SPURGEON, At the Metropolitan Tabernacle, Newington.

"And I will put my spirit within you."
—Ezekiel 36:27.

No preface is needed; and the largeness of our subject forbids our wasting time in beating about the bush. I shall try to do two things this morning: first, I would commend the text; and secondly, I would in some measure expound the text.

I. First, as for THE COMMENDATION OF THE TEXT, the tongues of men and of angels might fail. To call it a golden sentence would be much too commonplace: to liken it to a pearl of great price would be too poor a comparison. We cannot feel, much less speak, too much in praise of the great God who has put this clause into the covenant of His grace. In that covenant every sentence is more precious than heaven and earth; and this line is not the least among His choice words of promise: "I will put my spirit within you."

I would begin by saying that it is a gracious word. It was spoken to a graceless people, to a people who had followed "their own way," and refused the way of God; a people who had already provoked something more than ordinary anger in the Judge of all the earth; for He Himself said (verse 18), "I poured my fury upon them." These people, even under chastisement, caused the holy name of God to be profaned among the heathen, whither they went. They had been highly favoured, but they abused their privileges, and behaved worse than those who never knew the Lord. They sinned wantonly, wilfully, wickedly, proudly and presumptuously; and by this they greatly provoked the Lord. Yet to them He made such a promise as this—"I will put my spirit within you." Surely, where sin abounded grace did much more abound.

Clearly this is a word of grace, for the law saith nothing of this kind. Turn to the law of Moses, and see if there be any word spoken therein concerning the putting of the Spirit within men to cause them to walk in God's statutes. The law proclaims the statutes; but the gospel alone promises the spirit by which the statutes will be obeyed. The law commands and makes us know what God requires of us; but the gospel goes further, and inclines us to obey the will of the Lord, and enables us practically to walk in His ways. Under the dominion of grace the Lord worketh in us to will and to do of His own good pleasure.

So great a boon as this could never come to any man by merit. A man might so act as to deserve a reward of a certain kind, in measure suited to His commendable action; but the Holy Spirit can never be the wage of human service: the idea verges upon blasphemy. Can any man deserve that Christ should die for him? Who would dream of such a thing? Can any man deserve that the Holy Ghost should dwell in him, and work holiness in him? The greatness of the blessing lifts it high above the range of merit, and we see that if the Holy Ghost be bestowed, it must be by an act of divine grace—grace infinite in bounty, exceeding all that we could have imagined. "Sovereign grace o'er sin abounding" is here seen in clearest light. "I will put my spirit within you" is a promise which drops with graces as the honeycomb with honey. Listen to the divine music which pours from this word of love. I hear the soft melody of grace, grace, grace, and nothing else but grace.

Glory be to God, who gives to sinners the indwelling of His Spirit.

Note, next, that it is a divine word: "I will put my spirit within you." Who but the Lord could speak after this fashion? Can one man put the Spirit of God within another? Could all the church combined breathe the Spirit of God into a single sinner's heart? To put any good thing into the deceitful heart of man is a great achievement; but to put the Spirit of God into the heart, truly this is the finger of God. Nay, here I may say, the Lord has made bare His arm, and displayed the fulness of His mighty power. To put the Spirit of God into our nature is a work peculiar to the Godhead, and to do this within the nature of a free agent, such as man, is marvellous. Who but Jehovah, the God of Israel, can speak after this royal style, and, beyond all dispute, declare, "I will put my spirit within you?" Men must always surround their resolves with conditions and uncertainties; but since omnipotence is at the back of every promise of God, He speaks like a king; yea, in a style which is only fit for the eternal God. He purposes and promises, and He as surely performs. Sure, then, is this sacred saying, "I will put my spirit within you." Sure, because divine. O sinner, if we poor creatures had the saving of you, we should break down in the attempt; but, behold the Lord Himself comes on the scene, and the work is done! All the difficulties are removed by this one sentence, "I will put my spirit within you."

We have wrought with our spirit, we have wept over you, 'and we have entreated you; but we have failed. Lo, there cometh One into the matter who will not fail, with whom nothing is impossible; and He begins His work by saying, "I will put my spirit within you." The word is of grace and of God; regard it, then, as a pledge from the God of grace.

To me there is much charm in the further thought that this is an individual and personal word. The Lord means, "I will put my spirit within you": that is to say, within you, as individuals. "I will put my spirit within you" one by one. This must be so since the connection requires it. We read in verse 26, "A new heart also will I give you." Now, a new heart can only be given to one person. Each man needs a heart of his own, and each man must have a new heart for himself. "And a new spirit will I put within you." Within each one this must be done. "And I will take away the stony heart out of your flesh, and I will give you an heart of flesh"—these are all personal, individual operations of grace. God deals with men one by one in the solemn matters of eternity, sin, and salvation. We are born one by one, and we die one by one: even so we must be born again one by one, and each one for himself must receive the Spirit of God. Without this a man has nothing. He cannot be caused to walk in God's statutes except by the infusion of grace into him as an individual. I think I see among my hearers a lone man, or woman, who feels himself, or herself, to be all alone in the world, and therefore hopeless. You can believe that God will do great things for a nation, but how shall the solitary be thought of?

You are an odd person, one that could not be written down in any list; peculiar sinner, with constitutional tendencies all your own. Thus saith God, "I will put my spirit within you"; within your heart—even yours. My dear hearers, you who have long been seeking salvation, but have not known the power of the Spirit—this is what you need. You have been striving in the energy of the flesh, but you have not understood where your true strength lieth. God saith to you, "Not by might, nor by power, but by my Spirit, saith the Lord"; and again, "I will put my spirit within you." Oh, that this word might be spoken of the Lord to that young man who is ready to despair; to that sorrowful woman who has been looking into herself for power to pray and believe!

You are without strength or hope in and of yourself; but this meets your case in all points. "I will put my spirit within you"—within you as an individual. Enquire of the Lord for it. Lift up your heart in prayer to God, and ask Him to pour upon you the Spirit of grace and of supplications. Plead with the Lord, saying, "Let thy good Spirit lead me. Even me." Cry, "Pass me not, my gracious Father; but in me fulfil this wondrous word of thine, 'I will put my spirit within you.'"

Note, next, that this is a separating word. I do not know whether you will see this readily; but it must be so: this word separates a man from his fellows. Men by nature are of another spirit from that of God, and they are under subjection to that evil spirit, the Prince of the power of the air. When the Lord comes to gather out His own, fetching them out from among the heathen, He effects the separation by doing according to this word, "I will put my spirit within you." This done, the individual becomes a new man. Those who have the Spirit are not of the world, nor like the world; and they soon have to come out from among the ungodly, and to be separate; for difference of nature creates conflict. God's Spirit will not dwell with the evil spirit: you cannot have fellowship with Christ and with Belial; with the kingdom' of heaven and with this world. I wish that the people of God would again wake up to the truth that to gather out a people from among men is the great purpose of the present dispensation. It is still true, as James said at the Jerusalem Council, "Simeon hath declared how God at the first did visit the Gentiles, to take out of them a people for his name." We are not to remain clinging to the old wreck with the expectation that we shall pump the water out of her and get her safe into port. No; the cry is very different—"Take to the lifeboat! Take to the lifeboat!" You are to quit the wreck, and then you are to carry away from the sinking mass that which God will save. You must be separate from the old wreck, lest it suck you down to sure destruction. Your only hope of doing good to the world is by yourselves being "not of the world," even as Christ was not of the world. For you to go down to the world's level will neither be good for it nor for you. That which happened in the days of Noah will be repeated; for when the sons of God entered into alliance with the daughters of men, and there was a league between the two races, the Lord could not endure the evil mixture, but drew up the sluices of the lower deep and swept the earth with a destroying flood. Surely, in that last day of destruction, when the world is overwhelmed with fire, it will be because the church of God shall have degenerated, and the distinctions between the righteous and the wicked shall have been broken down. The Spirit of God, wherever He comes, doth speedily make and reveal the difference between Israel and Egypt; and in proportion as His active energy is felt, there will be an ever-widening gulf between those who are led of the Spirit and those who are under the dominion of the flesh.

The possession of the Spirit will make you, my hearer, quite another sort of man from what you now are, and then you will be actuated by motives which the world will not appreciate; for the world knoweth us not, because it knew him not. Then you will act, and speak, and think, and feel in such a way, that this evil world will misunderstand and condemn you. Since the carnal mind knoweth not the things that are of God—for those things are spiritually discerned—it will not approve your objects and designs. Do not expect it to be your friend. The spirit which makes you to be the seed of the woman is not the spirit of the world. The seed of the serpent will hiss at you, and bruise your heel. Your Master said, "Because ye are not of this world, but I have chosen you out of the world; therefore the world hateth you." It is a separating word this. Has it separated you? Has the Holy Spirit called you alone and blessed you? Do you differ from your old companions? Have you a life they do not understand? If not, may God in mercy put into you that most heavenly deposit, of which He speaks in our text: "I will put my spirit within you"!

But now notice, that it is a very uniting word. It separates from the world, but it joins to God. Note how it runs: "I will put my Spirit within you." It is not merely a spirit, or the spirit, but my spirit. Now when God's own Spirit comes to reside within our mortal bodies, how near akin we are to the Most High! "Know ye not that your body is the temple of the Holy Ghost?" Does not this make a man sublime? Have you never stood in awe of your own selves, O ye believers? Have you enough regarded even this poor body, as being sanctified and dedicated, and elevated into a sacred condition, by being set apart to be the temple of the Holy Ghost?

Thus are we brought into the closest union with God that we can well conceive of. Thus is the Lord our light and our life; while our spirit is subordinated to the divine Spirit. "I will put my spirit within you"—then God Himself dwelleth in you. The Spirit of Him that raised up Christ from the dead is in you. With Christ in God your life is hid, and the Spirit seals you, anoints you, and abides in you. By the Spirit we have access to the Father; by the Spirit we perceive our adoption, and learn to cry, "Abba, Father"; by the Spirit we are made partakers of the divine nature, and have communion with the thrice holy Lord.

I cannot help adding here that it is a very condescending word—"I will put my spirit within you." Is it really so, that the Spirit of God who displays the power and energetic force of God, by whom God's Word is carried into effect—that the Spirit who of old moved upon the face of the waters, and brought order and life from chaos and death—can it be so that He will deign to sojourn in men? God in our nature is a very wonderful conception! God in the babe at Bethlehem, God in the carpenter of Nazareth, God in the "man of sorrows," God in the Crucified, God in Him who was buried in the tomb—this is all marvellous. The incarnation is an infinite mystery of love; but we believe it. Yet, if it were possible to compare one illimitable wonder with another, I should say that God's dwelling in His people and that repeated ten thousand times over, is more marvellous. That the Holy Ghost should dwell in millions of redeemed men and women, is a miracle not surpassed by that of our Lord's espousal of human nature. For our Lord's body was perfectly pure, and the Godhead, while it dwells with His holy manhood, does at least dwell with a perfect and sinless nature; but the Holy Spirit bows Himself to dwell in sinful men; to dwell in men who, after their conversion, still find the flesh warring against the spirit, and the spirit against the flesh; men who are not perfect, though they strive to be so; men who have to lament their shortcomings, and even to confess with shame a measure of unbelief. "I will put my spirit within you" means the abiding of the Holy Spirit in our imperfect nature. Wonder of wonders! Yet is it as surely a fact as it is a wonder. Believers in the Lord Jesus Christ, you have the Spirit of God, for "if any man have not the Spirit of Christ, he is none of his." You could not bear the suspicion that you are not His; and therefore, as surely as you are Christ's, you have His Spirit abiding in you. The Saviour has gone away on purpose that the Comforter might be given to dwell in you, and He does dwell in you. Is it not so? If it be so, admire this condescending God, and worship and praise His name. Sweetly submit to His rule in all things. Grieve not the Spirit of God. Watch carefully that nothing comes within you that may defile the temple of God. Let the faintest monition of the Holy Spirit be law to you. It was a holy mystery that the presence of the Lord was specially within the veil of the Tabernacle, and that the Lord God spake by Urim and Thummim to His people; it is an equally sacred marvel that now the Holy Ghost dwells in our spirits and abides within our nature and speaks to us whatsoever He hears of the Father. By divine impressions which the opened ear can apprehend, and the tender heart can receive, He speaketh still. God grant us to know His still small voice so as to listen to it with reverent humility and loving joy: then shall we know the meaning of these words, "I will put my spirit within you."

Nor have I yet done with commending my text, for I must not fail to remind you that it is a very spiritual word. "I will put my spirit within you" has nothing to do with our wearing a peculiar garb—that would be a matter of little worth. It has nothing to do with affectations of speech—those might readily become a deceptive peculiarity. Our text has nothing to do with outward rites and ceremonies; but goes much further and deeper.

It is an instructive symbol when the Lord teaches us our death with Christ by burial in baptism: it is to our great profit that He ordains bread and wine to be tokens of our communion in the body and blood of His dear Son; but these are only outward things, and if they are unattended with the Holy Spirit they fail of their design. There is something infinitely greater in this promise—"I will put my spirit within you." I cannot give you the whole force of the Hebrew, as to the words "within you," unless I paraphrase them a little, and read "I will put my spirit in the midst of you." The sacred deposit is put deep down in our life's secret place. God puts His Spirit not upon the surface of the man, but into the centre of his being. The promise means—"I will put my spirit in your bowels, in your hearts, in the very soul of you." This is an intensely spiritual matter, without admixturing of anything material and visible. It is spiritual, you see, because it is the Spirit that is given; and He is given internally within our spirit. It is true the Spirit operates upon the external life, but it is through the secret and internal life, and of that inward operation our text speaks. This is what we so greatly require. Do you know what it is to attend a service and hear God's truth faithfully preached, and yet you are forced to say, "Somehow or other it did not enter into me; I did not feel the unction and taste the savor of it"? "I will put my spirit within you," is what you need. Do you not read your Bibles, and even pray, and do not both devotional exercises become too much external acts? "I will put my spirit within you" meets this evil. The good Spirit fires your heart; he penetrates your mind; he saturates your soul; he touches the secret and vital springs of your existence. Blessed Word! I love my text. It love it better than I can speak of it.

Observe once more that this Word is a very effectual one. "I will put my spirit within you, and cause you to walk in my statutes, and ye shall keep my judgments and do them." The Spirit is operative—first upon the inner life, in causing you to love the law of the Lord; and then it moves you openly to keep His statutes concerning Himself, and His judgments between you and your fellowmen. Obedience, if a man should be flogged to it, would be of little worth; but obedience springing out of a life within, this is a priceless breastplate of jewels. If you have a lantern, you cannot make it shine by polishing the glass outside, you must put a candle within it: and this is what God does, He puts the light of the Spirit within us, and then our light shines. He puts His Spirit so deep down into the heart, that the whole nature feels it: it works upward, like a spring from the bottom of a well. It is, moreover, so deeply implanted that there is no removing it. If it were in the memory, you might forget it; if it were in the intellect, you might err in it; but "within you" it touches the whole man, and has dominion over you without fear of failure. When the very kernel of your nature is quickened into holiness, practical godliness is effectually secured. Blessed is he who knows by experience our Lord's words—"The water that I shall give him shall be in him a well of water springing up into everlasting life."

If I should fail in expounding the text, I hope I have so fully commended it to you, that you will turn it over and meditate upon it yourselves, and so get a home-born exposition of it. The key of the text is within its own self; for if the Lord gives you the Spirit, you will then understand his words—"I will put my spirit within you."

II. But now I must work upon THE EXPOSITION OF THE TEXT. I trust the Holy Spirit will aid me therein.

Let me show you how the good Spirit manifests the fact that He dwells in men. I have to be very brief on a theme that might require a great length of time; and can only mention a part of His ways and workings.

One of the first effects of the Spirit of God being put within us is quickening. We are dead by nature to all heavenly and spiritual things; but when the Spirit of God comes, then we begin to live. The man visited of the Spirit begins to feel; the terrors of God make him tremble, the love of Christ makes him weep. He begins to fear, and he begins to hope: a great deal of the first and a very little of the second, it may be. He learns spiritually to sorrow: he is grieved that he has sinned, and that he cannot cease from sinning. He begins to desire that which once he despised: he specially desires to find the way of pardon, and reconciliation with God.

Ah, dear hearers! I cannot make you feel, I cannot make you sorrow for sin, I cannot make you desire eternal life; but it is all done as soon as this is fulfilled by the Lord, "I will put my spirit within you." The quickening Spirit brings life to the dead in trespasses and sins.

This life of the Spirit shows itself by causing the man to pray. The cry is the distinctive mark of the living child. He begins to cry in broken accents, "God be merciful to me." At the same time that he pleads, he feels the soft relentings of repentance. He has a new mind towards sin, and he grieves that he should have grieved his God. With this comes faith; perhaps feeble and trembling, only a touch of the hem of the Saviour's robe; but still Jesus is his only hope and his sole trust. To Him he looks for pardon and salvation. He dares to believe that Christ can save even him. Then has life come into the soul when trust in Jesus spring up in the heart.

Remember, dear friends, that as the Holy Spirit gives quickening at the first, so He must revive and strengthen it. Whenever you become dull and faint, cry for the Holy Spirit. Whenever you cannot feel in devotion as you wish to feel, and are unable to rise to any heights of communion with God, plead my text in faith, and beg the Lord to do as He hath said, namely, "I will put my spirit within you." Go to God with this covenant clause, even if you have to confess, "Lord, I am like a log, I am a helpless lump of weakness. Unless thou come and quicken me I cannot live to Thee." Plead importunately the promise, "I will put my spirit within you." All the life of the flesh will gender corruption; all the energy that comes of mere excitement will die down into the black ashes of disappointment; the Holy Ghost alone is the life of the regenerated heart. Have you the Spirit? and if you have Him within you, have you only a small measure of His life, and do you wish for more? Then go still where you went at first. There is only one river of the water of life: draw from its floods. You will be lively enough, and bright enough, and strong enough, and happy enough when the Holy Spirit is mighty within your soul.

When the Holy Spirit enters, after quickening He gives enlightening. We cannot make men see the truth, they are so blind; but when the Lord puts His Spirit within them their eyes are opened. At first they may see rather hazily; but still they do see. As the light increases, and the eye is strengthened, they see more and more clearly. What a mercy it is to see Christ, to look unto Him, and so to be lightened! By the Spirit, souls see things in their reality: they see the actual truth of them, and perceive that they are facts. The Spirit of God illuminates every believer, so that he sees still more marvellous things out of God's law; but this never happens unless the Spirit opens his eyes. The apostle speaks of being brought "out of darkness into His marvellous light"; and it is a marvellous light, indeed, to come to the blind and dead. Marvellous because it reveals truth with clearness. It reveals marvellous things in a marvellous way. If hills and mountains, if rocks and stones were suddenly to be full of eyes, it would be a strange thing in the earth, but not more marvellous than for you and me by the illumination of the Holy Spirit to see spiritual things. When you cannot make people see the truth, do not grow angry with them, but cry, "Lord, put thy spirit within them." When you get into a puzzle over the Word of the Lord, do not give up in despair, but believingly cry, "Lord, put thy Spirit within me." Here lies the only true light of the soul. Depend upon it, all that you can see by any light except the Spirit of God you do not spiritually see. If you only see intellectually, or rationally, you do not see to salvation. Unless intellect and reason have received heavenly light, you may see, and yet not see; even as Israel of old. Indeed, your boasted clear sight may aggravate your ruin, like that of the Pharisees, of whom our Lord said, "But now ye say, We see, therefore your sin remaineth." O lord, grant us the Spirit within, for our soul's illumination!

The Spirit also works conviction. Conviction is more forcible than illumination: it is the setting of a truth before the eye of the soul, so as to make it powerful upon the conscience. I speak to many here who know what conviction means; still I will explain it from my own experience. I knew what sin meant by my reading, and yet I never knew sin in its heinousness and horror, till I found myself bitten by it as by a fiery serpent, and felt its poison boiling in my veins. When the Holy Ghost made sin to appear sin, then was I overwhelmed with the sight, and I would fain have fled from myself to escape the intolerable vision. A naked sin stripped of all excuse, and set in the light of truth, is a worse sight than to see the devil himself. When I saw sin as an offence against a just and holy God, committed by such a proud and yet insignificant creature as myself, then was I alarmed. Sirs, did you ever see and feel yourselves to be sinners? "Oh, yes," you say, "we are sinners." O sirs, do you mean it? Do you know what it means? Many of you are no more sinners in your own estimation than you are Hottentots. The beggar who exhibits a sham sore knows not disease; if he did he would have enough of it without pretences. To kneel down and say, "Lord, have mercy upon us miserable sinners," and then to get up and feel yourself a very decent sort of body, worthy of commendation, is to mock Almighty God. It is by no means a common thing to get hold of a real sinner, one who is truly so in his own esteem; and it is as pleasant as it is rare, for you can bring to the real sinner the real Saviour, and He will welcome him. I do not wonder that Hart said: "A sinner is a sacred thing, The Holy Ghost hath made him so." The point of contact between a sinner and Christ is sin. The Lord Jesus gave Himself for our sins, He never gave Himself for our righteousnesses. He comes to heal the sick, and the point He looks to is our sickness. When a physician is called in he has no patience with things apart from his calling. "Tut, tut!" he cries, "I do not care about your furniture, nor the number of your cows, nor what income tax you pay, nor what politics you admire; I have come to see a sick man about his disease, and if you will not let me deal with it I will be gone."

When a sinner's corruptions are loathsome to himself, when his guilt is foul in his own nostrils, when he fears the death that will come of it, then he is really convinced by the Holy Spirit; and no one ever knows sin as his own personal ruin till the Holy Spirit shows it to him. Conviction as to the Lord Jesus comes in the same way.

We do not know Christ as our Saviour till the Holy Spirit is put within us. Our Lord says—"He shall receive of mine, and shall shew it unto you," and you never see the things of the Lord Jesus till the Holy Ghost shows them to you. To know Jesus Christ as your Saviour, as one who died for you in particular, is a knowledge which only the Holy Spirit imparts. To apprehend present salvation, as your own personally, comes by your being convinced of it by the Spirit. Oh, to be convinced of righteousness, and convinced of acceptance in the Beloved! This conviction cometh only of Him that hath called you, even of Him of whom the Lord saith, "I will put my Spirit within you."

Furthermore, the Holy Spirit comes into us for purification. "I will put my spirit within you, and cause you to walk in my statutes, and ye shall keep my judgments, and do them." When the Spirit comes, He infuses a new life, and that new life is a fountain of holiness. The new nature cannot sin, because it is born of God, and "it is a living and incorruptible seed." This life produces good fruit, and good fruit only. The Holy Ghost is the life of holiness. At the same time, the coming of the Holy Ghost into the soul gives a mortal stab to the power of sin. The old man is not absolutely dead, but it is crucified with Christ. It is under sentence, and before the eye of the law it is dead; but as a man nailed to a cross may linger long, but yet he cannot live, so the power of evil dies hard, but die it must. Sin is an executed criminal: those nails which fasten it to the cross will hold it fast till no breath remains in it. God the Holy Ghost gives the power of sin its death wound. The old nature struggles in its dying agonies, but it is doomed, and die it must. But you never will overcome sin by your own power, nor by any energy short of that of the Holy Spirit. Resolves may bind it, as Samson was bound with cords; but sin will snap the cords asunder. The Holy Spirit lays the axe at the root of sin, and fall it must. The Holy Ghost within a man is "the Spirit of judgment, the Spirit of burning." Do you know Him in that character? As the Spirit of judgment, the Holy Spirit pronounces sentence on sin, and it goes out with the brand of Cain upon it. He does more: He delivers sin over to burning. He executes the death penalty on that which He has judged. How many of our sins have we had to burn alive! and it has cost us no small pain to do it. Sin must be got out of us by fire, if no gentler means will serve; and the Spirit of God is a consuming fire. Truly, "our God is a consuming fire." They paraphrase it, "God out of Christ is a consuming fire"; but that is not Scripture: it is, "our God," our covenant God, who is a consuming fire to refine us from sin. Has not the Lord said, "I will purely purge away all thy dross, and take away all thy sin"? This is what the Spirit does, and it is by no means easy work for the flesh, which would spare many a flattering sin if it could.

The Holy Spirit bedews the soul with purity till He saturates it. Oh, to have a heart saturated with holy influences till it shall be as Gideon's fleece, which held so much dew that Gideon could wring out a bowl full from it! Oh, that our whole nature were filled with the Spirit of God; that we were sanctified wholly, body, soul, and spirit! Sanctification is the result of the Holy Spirit being put within us.

Next, the Holy Ghost acts in the heart as the Spirit of preservation. Where He dwells men do not go back unto perdition. He works in them a watchfulness against temptation day by day. He works in them to wrestle against sin. Rather than sin a believer would die ten thousand deaths. He works in believers union to Christ, which is the source and guarantee of acceptable fruitfulness. He creates in the saints those holy things which glorify God, and bless the sons of men. All true fruit is the fruit of the Spirit. Every true prayer must be "praying in the Holy Ghost." He helpeth our infirmities in prayer. Even the hearing of the Word of the Lord is of the Spirit, for John says, "I was in the Spirit on the Lord's day, and heard behind me a great voice."

Everything that comes of the man, or is kept alive in the man, is first infused and then sustained and perfected of the Spirit. "It is the spirit that quickeneth; the flesh profiteth nothing." We never go an inch towards heaven in any other power than that of the Holy Ghost. We do not even stand fast and remain steadfast except as we are upheld by the Holy Spirit. The vineyard which the Lord hath planted He also preserves; as it is written, "I the Lord do keep it; I will water it every moment: lest any hurt it, I will keep it night and day." Did I hear that young man say, "I should like to become a Christian, but I fear I should not hold out? How am I to be preserved?" A very proper inquiry for "He that endureth to the end, the same shall be saved." Temporary Christians are no Christians: only the believer who continues to believe will enter heaven. How, then, can we hold on in such a world as this? Here is the answer. "I will put my spirit within you." When a city has been captured in war, those who formerly possessed it seek to win it back again; but the king who captured it sends a garrison to live within the walls, and he said to the captain, "Take care of this city that I have conquered, and let not the enemy take it again." So the Holy Ghost is the garrison of God within our redeemed humanity, and he will keep us to the end. "May the peace of God, which passeth all understanding, keep your hearts and minds through Christ Jesus." For preservation, then, we look to the Holy Spirit.

Lest I weary you, I will be very brief upon the next point: the Holy Spirit within us is for guidance. The Holy Spirit is given to lead us into all truth. Truth is like a vast grotto, and the Holy Spirit brings torches, and shows us all the splendour of the roof; and since the passage seems intricate, He knows the way, and He lead us into the deep things of God. He opens up to us one truth after another, by His light and by His guidance, and thus we are "taught of the Lord." He is also our practical guide to heaven, helping and directing us on the upward journey. I wish Christian people oftener inquired of the Holy Ghost as to guidance in their daily life. Know ye not that the Spirit of God dwelleth in you? You need not always be running to this friend and to that to get direction: wait upon the Lord in silence, sit still in quiet before the oracle of God. Use the judgment God has given you; but when that suffices not, resort to Him whom Mr. Bunyan calls "the Lord High Secretary," who lives within, who is infinitely wise, and who can guide you by making you to "hear a voice behind you saying, This is the way, walk ye in it." The Holy Ghost will guide you in life; He will guide you in death; and He will guide you to glory. He will guard you from modern error, and from ancient error, too. He will guide you in a way that you know not; and through the darkness He will lead you in a way you have not seen: these things will He do unto you, and not forsake you.

Oh, this precious text! I seem to have before me a great cabinet full of jewels rich and rare. May God the Holy Ghost Himself come and hand these out to you, and may you be adorned with them all the days of your life!

Last of all, "I will put my spirit within you," that is, by way of consolation, for His choice name is "The Comforter." Our God would not have His children unhappy, and therefore, He Himself, in the third Person of the blessed Trinity, has undertaken the office of Comforter. Why does your face such mournful colours wear? God can comfort you. You that are under the burden of sin; it is true no man can help you into peace, but the Holy Ghost can. O God, to every seeker here who has failed to final rest, grant Thy Holy Spirit! Put Thy Spirit within him, and he will rest in Jesus. And you dear people of God, who are worried, remember that worry and the Holy Ghost are very contradictory one to another. "I will put my spirit within you" means that you shall become gentle, peaceful, resigned, and acquiescent in the divine will. Then you will have faith in God that all is well. That text with which I began my prayer this morning was brought home to my heart this week. Our dearly beloved friend Adolph Saphir passed away last Saturday, and his wife died three or four days before him. When my dear brother, Dr. Sinclair Patterson, went to see him, the beloved Saphir said to him, "God is light, and in him is no darkness at all." Nobody would have quoted that passage but Saphir, the Biblical student the lover of the word, the lover of the God of Israel. "God is light, and in him is no darkness at all."

His dear wife is gone, and he himself is ill; but "God is light, and in him is no darkness at all." This is a deep well of overflowing comfort, if you understand it well. God's promise is light as well as his promise, and the Holy Spirit makes us know this. God's word and will and way are all light to his people, and in him is no darkness at all for them. God himself is purely and only light. What if there be darkness in me, there is no darkness in him; and his Spirit causes me to fly to him! What if there be darkness in my family, there is no darkness in my covenant God, and his Spirit makes me rest in him. What if there be darkness in me by reason of my failing strength, there is no failing in him, and there is no darkness in him: his Spirit assures me of this. David says—"God my exceeding joy"; and such He is to us. "Yea, mine own God is he"! Can you say, "My God, my God"? Do you want anything more? Can you conceive of anything beyond your God? Omnipotent to work all for ever! Infinite to give! Faithful to remember! He is all that is good. Light only: "in him is no darkness at all." I have all light, yea, all things, when I have my God. The Holy Spirit makes us apprehend this when He is put within us. Holy Comforter, abide with us, for then we enjoy the light of heaven. Then are we always peaceful and even joyful; for we walk in unclouded light. In Him our happiness sometimes rises into great waves of delight, as if it leaped up to the glory. The Lord make this text your own—"I will put my Spirit within you." Amen.

The Comforter

A Sermon (No. 5) Delivered on
Sabbath Evening, January 21, 1855,
by the REV. C. H. SPURGEON
At New Park Street Chapel, Southwark.

"But the Comforter, which is the Holy Ghost, whom the Father will send in my name, he shall teach you all things and bring all things to your remembrance, whatsoever I have said unto you."
—John 14:26.

Good old Simeon called Jesus the consolation of Israel; and so he was. Before his actual appearance, his name was the day-star; cheering the darkness, and prophetic of the rising sun. To him they looked with the same hope which cheers the nightly watcher, when from the lonely castle-top he sees the fairest of the stars, and hails her as the usher of the morn. When he was on earth, he must have been the consolation of all those who were privileged to be his companions. We can imagine how readily the disciples would run to Christ to tell him of their griefs, and how sweetly, with that matchless intonation of his voice, he would speak to them, and bid their fears be gone. Like children, they would consider him as their Father; and to him every want, every groan, every sorrow, every agony, would at once be carried; and he, like a wise physician, had a balm for every wound; he had mingled a cordial for their every care; and readily did he dispense some mighty remedy to allay all the fever of their troubles. Oh! it must have been sweet to have lived with Christ. Surely, sorrows were then but joys in masks, because they gave an opportunity to go to Jesus to have them removed. Oh! would to God, some of us may say, that we could have lain our weary heads upon the bosom of Jesus, and that our birth had been in that happy era, when we might have heard his kind voice, and seen his kind look, when he said, "Let the weary ones come unto me."

But now he was about to die. Great prophecies were to be fulfilled; and great purposes were to be answered; therefore, Jesus must go. It behoved him to suffer, that he might be made a propitiation for our sins. It behoved him to slumber in the dust awhile, that he might perfume the chamber of the grave to make it—

No more a carnel house to fence
The relics of lost innocence.

It behoved him to have a resurrection, that we, who shall one day be the dead in Christ, might rise first, and in glorious bodies stand upon earth. And if behoved him that he should ascend up on high, that he might lead captivity captive; that he might chain the fiends of hell; that he might lash them to his chariot-wheels, and drag them up high heaven's hill, to make them feel a second overthrow from his right arm, when he should dash them from the pinnacles of heaven down to the deeper depths beneath. "It is right I should go away from you," said Jesus, "for if I go not away, the Comforter will not come." Jesus must go. Weep, ye disciples; Jesus must be gone. Mourn, ye poor ones, who are to be left without a Comforter. But hear how kindly Jesus speaks: "I will not leave you comfortless, I will pray the Father, and he shall send you another Comforter, who shall be with you, and shall dwell in you forever." He would not leave those few poor sheep alone in the wilderness; he would not desert his children, and leave them fatherless. Albeit that he had a mighty mission which did fill his heart and hand; albeit he had so much to perform, that we might have thought that even his gigantic intellect would be overburdened; albeit he had so much to suffer, that we might suppose his whole soul to be concentrated upon the thought of the sufferings to be endured. Yet it was not so; before he left, he gave soothing words of comfort; like the good Samaritan, he poured in oil and wine, and we see what he promised: "I will send you another Comforter—one who shall be just what I have been, yea, even more; who shall console you in your sorrows, remove your doubts, comfort you in your afflictions, and stand as my vicar on earth, to do that which I would have done had I tarried with you."

Before I discourse of the Holy Ghost as the Comforter, I must make one or two remarks on the different translations of the word rendered "Comforter." The Rhenish translation, which you are aware is adopted by Roman Catholics, has left the word untranslated, and gives it "Paraclete." "But the Paraclete, which is the Holy Ghost, whom the Father will send in my name, he shall teach you all things." This is the original Greek word, and it has some other meanings besides "Comforter." Sometimes it means the monitor or instructor: "I will send you another monitor, another teacher." Frequently it means "Advocate;" but the most common meaning of the word is that which we have here: "I will send you another Comforter." However, we cannot pass over those other two interpretations without saying something upon them.

"I will send you another teacher." Jesus Christ had been the official teacher of his saints whilst on earth. They called no man Rabbi except Christ. They sat at no men's feet to learn their doctrines; but they had them direct from the lips of him who "spake as never man spake." "And now," says he, "when I am gone, where shall you find the great infallible teacher? Shall I set you up a pope at Rome, to whom you shall go, and who shall be your infallible oracle? Shall I give you the councils of the church to be held to decide all knotty points?" Christ said no such thing. "I am the infallible paraclete, or teacher, and when I am gone, I will send you another teacher, and he shall be the person who is to explain Scripture; he shall be the authoritative oracle of God, who shall make all dark things light, who shall unravel mysteries, who shall untwist all knots of revelation, and shall make you understand what you could not discover, had it not been for his influence."

And, beloved, no man ever learns anything aright, unless he is taught of the Spirit. You may learn election, and you may know it so that you shall be damned by it, if you are not taught of the Holy Ghost; for I have known some who have learned election to their soul's destruction; they have learned it so that they said they were of the elect, whereas, they had no marks, no evidences, and no works of the Holy Ghost in their souls. There is a way of learning truth in Satan's college, and holding it in licentiousness; but if so, it shall be to your souls as poison to your veins and prove your everlasting ruin. No man can know Jesus Christ unless he is taught of God. There is no doctrine of the Bible which can be safely, thoroughly, and truly learned, except by the agency of the one authoritative teacher. Ah! tell me not of systems of divinity; tell me not of schemes of theology; tell me not of infallible commentators, or most learned and most arrogant doctors; but tell me of the Great Teacher, who shall instruct us, the sons of God, and shall make us wise to understand all things. He is the Teacher; it matters not what this man or that man says; I rest on no man's boasting authority, nor will you.

Ye are not to be carried away with the craftiness of men, nor sleight of words; this is the authoritative oracle—the Holy Ghost resting in the hearts of his children.

The other translation is advocate. Have you ever thought how the Holy Ghost can be said to be an advocate? You know Jesus Christ is called the wonderful, the counsellor, the mighty God; but how can the Holy Ghost be said to be an advocate? I suppose it is thus; he is an advocate on earth to plead against the enemies of the cross. How was it that Paul could so ably plead before Felix and Agrippa? How was it that the Apostles stood unawed before the magistrates, and confessed their Lord? How has it come to pass, that in all times God's ministers have been made fearless as lions, and their brows have been firmer than brass; their hearts sterner than steel, and their words like the language of God? Why, it was simply for this reason; that it was not the man who pleaded, but it was God the Holy Ghost pleading through him. Have you never seen an earnest minister, with hands uplifted and eyes dropping tears, pleading with the sons of men? Have you never admired that portrait from the hand of old John Bunyan?—a grave person with eyes lifted up to heaven, the best of books in his hand, the law of truth written on his lips, the world behind his back, standing as if he pleaded with men, and a crown of gold hanging over his head. Who gave that minister so blessed a manner, and such goodly matter? Whence came his skill? Did he acquire it in the college? Did he learn it in the seminary? Ah, no. He learned it of the God of Jacob; he learned it of the Holy Ghost; for the Holy Ghost is the great counsellor who teaches us how to advocate his cause aright.

But, beside this, the Holy Ghost is the advocate in men's hearts. Ah! I have known men reject a doctrine until the Holy Ghost began to illuminate them. We, who are the advocates of the truth, are often very poor pleaders; we spoil our cause by the words we use; but it is a mercy that the brief is in the hand of a special pleader, who will advocate successfully, and overcome the sinner's opposition. Did you ever know him fail once?

Brethren, I speak to your souls; has not God in old times convinced you of sin? Did not the Holy Ghost come and prove that you were guilty, although no minister could ever get you out of your self-righteousness? Did he not advocate Christ's righteousness? Did he not stand and tell you that your works were filthy rags? And when you had well-nigh still refused to listen to his voice, did he not fetch hell's drum and make it sound about your ears; bidding you look through the vista of future years, and see the throne set, and the books open, and the sword brandished, and hell burning, and fiends howling, and the damned shrieking forever? And did he not convince you of the judgment to come? He is a mighty advocate when he pleads in the soul—of sin, of righteousness, and of the judgment to come. Blessed advocate! Plead in my heart; plead with my conscience. When I sin, make conscience bold to tell me of it; when I err, make conscience speak at once; and when I turn aside to crooked ways, then advocate the cause of righteousness, and bid me sit down in confusion, knowing by guiltiness in the sight of God.

But there is yet another sense in which the Holy Ghost advocates, and that is, he advocates our cause with Jesus Christ, with groanings that cannot be uttered. O my soul! thou art ready to burst within me. O my heart! thou art swelled with grief. The hot tide of my emotion would well-nigh overflood the channels of my veins. I long to speak, but the very desire chains my tongue. I wish to pray, but the fervency of my felling curbs my language. There is a groaning within that cannot be uttered. Do you know who can utter that groaning? who can understand it, and who can put it into heavenly language, and utter it in a celestial tongue, so that Christ can hear it? O yes; it is God the Holy spirit; he advocates our cause with Christ, and then Christ advocates it with his Father. He is the advocate who maketh intercession for us, with groanings that cannot be uttered.

Having thus explained the Spirit's office as a teacher and advocate, we now come to the translation of our version—the Comforter; and here I shall have three divisions: first, the comforter; secondly, the comfort; and thirdly, the comforted.

I. First, then, the COMFORTER. Briefly let me run over in my mind, and in your minds too, the characteristics of this glorious Comforter. Let me tell you some of the attributes of his comfort, so that you may understand how well adapted he is to your case.

And first, we will remark, that God the Holy Ghost is a very loving Comforter. I am in distress, and I want consolation. Some passer-by hears of my sorrow, and he steps within, sits down, and essays to cheer me; he speaks soothing words, but he loves me not; he is a stranger; he knows me not at all; he has only come in to try his skill. And what is the consequence? His words run o'er me like oil upon a slab of marble—they are like the pattering rain upon the rock; they do not break my grief; it stands unmoved as adamant, because he has no love for me. But let some one who loves me dear as his own life, come and plead with me, then truly his words are music; they taste like honey; he knows the password of the doors of my heart, and my ear is attentive to every word; I catch the intonation of each syllable as it falls, for it is like the harmony of the harps of heaven. Oh! there is a voice in love, it speaks a language which is its own; it has an idiom and a brogue which none can mimic; wisdom cannot imitate it; oratory cannot attain unto it; it is love alone which can reach the mourning heart; love is the only handkerchief which can wipe the mourner's tears away. And is not the Holy Ghost a loving comforter? Dost thou know, O saint, how much the Holy Spirit loves thee? Canst thou measure the love of the Spirit? Dost thou know how great is the affection of his soul towards thee? Go measure heaven with thy span; go weigh the mountains in the scales; go take the ocean's water, and tell each drop; go count the sand upon the sea's wide shore; and when thou hast accomplished this, thou canst tell how much he loveth thee. He has loved thee long, he has loved thee well, he loved thee ever, and he still shall love thee; surely he is the person to comfort thee, because he loves. Admit him, then, to your heart, O Christian, that he may comfort you in your distress.

But next, he is a faithful Comforter. Love sometimes proveth unfaithful. "Oh! sharper than a serpent's tooth" is an unfaithful friend! Oh! far more bitter than the gall of bitterness, to have a friend turn from me in my distress! Oh! woe of woes, to have one who loves me in my prosperity, forsake me in the dark day of my trouble. Sad indeed; but such is not God's Spirit. He ever loves, and loves even to the end—a faithful Comforter. Child of God, you are in trouble. A little while ago, you found him a sweet and loving Comforter; you obtained relief from him when others were but broken cisterns; he sheltered you in his bosom, and carried you in his arms. Oh, wherefore dost thou distrust him now? Away with thy fears; for he is a faithful Comforter. "Ah!, but," thou sayest, "I fear I shall be sick, and shall be deprived of his ordinances." Nevertheless he shall visit thee on thy sick bed, and sit by thy side, to give thee consolation. "Ah! but I have distresses greater than you can conceive of; wave upon wave rolleth over me; deep calleth unto deep, at the noise of the Eternal's waterspouts." Nevertheless, he will be faithful to his promise. "Ah! but I have sinned."

So thou hast, but sin cannot sever thee from his love; he loves thee still. Think not, O poor downcast child of God, because the scars of thine old sins have marred thy beauty, that he loves thee less because of that blemish. O no! He loved thee when he foreknew thy sin; he loved thee with the knowledge of what the aggregate of thy wickedness would be; and he does not love thee less now. Come to him in all boldness of faith; tell him thou hast grieved him, and he will forget thy wandering, and will receive thee again; the kisses of his love shall be bestowed upon thee, and the arms of his grace shall embrace thee. He is faithful; trust him, he will never deceive you; trust him, he will never leave you.

Again, he is an unwearied Comforter. I have sometimes tried to comfort persons, and have been tired. You, now and then, meet with a case of a nervous person. You ask, "What is your trouble?" You are told; and you essay, if possible, to remove it; but while you are preparing your artillery to battle the trouble, you find that it has shifted its quarters, and is occupying quite a different position. You change your argument and begin again; but lo, it is again gone, and you are bewildered. You feel like Hurcules, cutting off the evergrowing heads of the Hydra, and you give up your task in despair. You meet with persons whom it is impossible to comfort, reminding one of the man who locked himself up in fetters, and threw the key away, so that nobody could unlock him. I have found some in the fetters of despair. "O, I am the man," say they, "that has seen affliction; pity me, pity me, O, my friends;" and the more you try to comfort such people, the worse they get; and, therefore, out of all heart, we leave them to wander alone among the tombs of their former joys. But the Holy Ghost is never out of heart with those whom he wishes to comfort. He attempts to comfort us, and we run away from the sweet cordial; he gives us some sweet draught to cure us, and we will not drink it; he gives some wondrous potion to charm away all our troubles, and we put it away from us. Still be pursues us; and though we say that we will not be comforted, he says we shall be, and when he has said, he does it; he is not to be wearied by all our sins, nor by all our murmurings.

And oh, how wise a Comforter is the Holy Ghost. Job had comforters, and I think he spoke the truth when he said, "Miserable comforters are ye all." But I dare say they esteemed themselves wise; and when the young man Elihu rose to speak, they thought he had a world of impudence. Were they not "grave and reverend seigniors?" Did not they comprehend his grief and sorrow? If they could not comfort him, who could? But they did not find out the cause. They thought he was not really a child of God, that he was self-righteous, and they gave him the wrong physic. It is a bad case when the doctor mistakes a disease and gives a wrong prescription, and so perhaps kills the patient. Sometimes, when we go and visit people, we mistake their disease; we want to comfort them on this point, whereas they do not require any such comfort at all, and they would be better left alone, than spoiled by such unwise comforters as we are. But oh, how wise the Holy Spirit is! He takes the soul, lays it on the table, and dissects it in a moment; he finds out the root of the matter, he sees where the complaint is, and then he applies the knife where something is required to be taken away, or puts a plaster where the sore is; and he never mistakes. O how wise is the blessed Holy Ghost; from ever comforter I turn, and leave them all, for thou art he who alone givest the wisest consolation.

Then mark, how safe a Comforter the Holy Ghost is. All comfort is not safe, mark that. There is a young man over there very melancholy. You know how he became so. He stepped into the house of God and heard a powerful preacher, and the word was blessed, and convinced him of sin. When he went home, his father and the rest found there was something different about him, "Oh," they said, "John is mad, he is crazy;" and what said his mother? "Send him into the country for a week; let him go to the ball or the theatre." John, did you find any comfort there? "Ah no; they made me worse, for while I was there I thought hell might open and swallow me up." Did you find any relief in the gayeties of the world? "No," say you, "I thought it was idle waste of time." Alas! this is miserable comfort, but it is the comfort of the worldling; and, when a Christian gets into distress, how many will recommend him this remedy and the other. "Go and hear Mr. So-and-so preach;" "have a few friends at you house;" "Read such-and-such a consoling volume;" and very likely it is the most unsafe advice in the world. The devil will sometimes come to men's souls as a false comforter; and he will say to the soul, "What need is there to make all this ado about repentance? you are no worse than other people;" and he will try to make the soul believe, that what is presumption, is the real assurance of the Holy Ghost; thus he deceives many by false comfort. Ah! there have been many, like infants, destroyed by elixirs, given to lull them to sleep; many have been ruined by the cry of "peace, peace," when there is no peace; hearing gentle things, when they ought to be stirred to the quick. Cleopatra's asp was brought in a basket of flowers; and men's ruin often lurks in fair and sweet speeches. But the Holy Ghost's comfort is safe, and you may rest on it. Let him speak the word, and there is a reality about it; let him give the cup of consolation, and you may drink it to the bottom; for in its depths there are no dregs, nothing to intoxicate or ruin, it is all safe.

Moreover, the Holy Ghost is an active Comforter; he does not comfort by words, but by deeds. Some comfort by, "Be ye warmed, and be ye filled, giving nothing." But the Holy Ghost gives, he intercedes with Jesus; he gives us promises, he gives us grace, and so he comforts us. Mark again, he is always a successful Comforter; he never attempts what he cannot accomplish.

Then, to close up, he is an ever-present Comforter, so that you never have to send for him. Your God is always near you; and when you need comfort in your distress, behold the word is nigh thee; it is in thy mouth, and in thy heart. He is an ever-present help in time of trouble. I wish I had time to expand these thoughts, but I cannot.

II. The second thing is the COMFORT. Now there are some persons who make a great mistake about the influence of the Holy Spirit. A foolish man, who had a fancy to preach in a certain pulpit, though in truth he was quite incapable of the duty, called upon the minister, and assured him solemnly, that it had been revealed to him by the Holy Ghost that he was to preach in his pulpit. "Very well," said the minister, "I suppose I must not doubt your assertion, but as it has not been revealed to me that I am to let you preach, you must go your way, until it is." I have heard many fanatical persons say the Holy Spirit revealed this and that to them. Now, that is very generally revealed nonsense. The Holy Ghost does not reveal anything fresh now. He brings old things to our remembrance. "He shall teach you all things, and bring all things to your remembrance, whatsoever I have told you." The canon of revelation is closed, there is no more to be added; God does not give a fresh revelation, but he rivets the old one. When it has been forgotten, and laid in the dusty chamber of our memory, he fetches it out and cleans the picture, but does not paint a new one. There are no new doctrines, but the old ones are often revived. It is not, I say, by any new revelation that the Spirit comforts. He does so by telling us old things over again; he brings a fresh lamp to manifest the treasures hidden in Scripture; he unlocks the strong chests in which the truth has long lain, and he points to secret chamber filled with untold riches; but he coins no more, for enough is done. Believer! there is enough in the Bible for thee to live upon forever. If thou shouldst outnumber the years of Methuselah, there would be no need for a fresh revelation; if thou shouldst live till Christ should come upon the earth, there would be no need for the addition of a single word; if thou shouldst go down as deep as Jonah, or even descend as David said he did into the belly of hell, still there would be enough in the Bible to comfort thee without a supplementary sentence. But Christ says, "He shall take of mine, and show it unto you." Now, let me just tell you briefly what it is the Holy Ghost tells us.

Ah! does he not whisper to the heart, "Saint, be of good cheer; there is one who died for thee; look to Calvary, behold his wounds, see the torrent gushing from his side—there is thy purchaser, and thou art secure. He loves thee with an everlasting love, and this chastisement is meant for thy good; each stroke is working thy healing; by the blueness of the wound thy soul is made better." "Whom he loveth he chasteneth, and scourgeth every son whom he receiveth." Doubt not his grace, because of thy tribulation; but believe that he loveth thee as much in seasons of trouble, as in times of happiness. And then, moreover, he says, "What is all thy suffering compared with that of thy Lord's? or what, when weighed in the scales of Jesus' agonies, is all thy distress?

And especially at times does the Holy Ghost take back the veil of heaven, and lets the soul behold the glory of the upperworld! Then it is that the saint can say, "O thou art a Comforter to me!" "Let cares like a wild deluge come, And storms of sorrow fall; May I but safely reach my home, My God, my heaven, my all." Some of you could follow, were I to tell of manifestations of heaven. You, too, have left sun, moon, and stars at your feet, while, in your flight, outstripping the tardy lightning, you have seemed to enter the gates of pearl, and tread the golden streets, borne aloft on wings of the Spirit. But here we must not trust ourselves; lest, lost in reverie, we forget our theme.

III. And now, thirdly, who are the comforted persons? I like, you know, at the end of my sermon to cry out, "Divide! divide!" There are two parties here—some who are comforted, and others who are the comfortless ones—some who have received the consolations of the Holy Ghost, and some who have not. Now let us try and sift you, and see which is the chaff and which is the wheat; and may God grant that some of the chaff may, this night, be transformed into his wheat!

You may say, "How am I to know whether I am a recipient of the comfort of the Holy Ghost?" You may know it by one rule. If you have received one blessing from God, you will receive all other blessings too. Let me explain myself. If I could come here as an auctioneer, and sell the gospel off in lots, I should dispose of it all.

If I could say, here is justification through the blood of Christ—free; giving away, gratis; many a one would say, "I will have justification; give it to me; I wish to be justified; I wish to be pardoned." Suppose I took sanctification, the giving up of all sin, a thorough change of heart, leaving off drunkenness and swearing; many would say, "I don't want that; I should like to go to heaven, but I do not want that holiness; I should like to be saved at last, but I should like to have my drink still; I should like to enter glory, but then I must have an oath or two on the road." Nay, but, sinner, if thou hast one blessing, thou shalt have all. God will never divide the gospel. He will not give justification to that man, and sanctification to another—pardon to one, and holiness to another. No, it all goes together. Whom he call, them he justifies; whom he justifies, them he sanctifies; and whom he sanctifies, them he also glorifies. Oh; if I could lay down nothing but the comforts of the gospel, ye would fly to them as flies do to honey. When ye come to be ill, ye send for the clergyman. Ah! you all want your minister then to come and give you consoling words. But, if he be an honest man, he will not give some of you a particle of consolation. He will not commence pouring oil, when the knife would be better. I want to make a man feel his sins before I dare tell him anything about Christ. I want to probe into his soul and make him feel that he is lost before I tell him anything about the purchased blessing. It is the ruin of many to tell them, "Now just believe on Christ, and that is all you have to do." If, instead of dying, they get better, they rise up white-washed hypocrites—that is all. I have heard of a city missionary who kept a record of two thousand persons who were supposed to be on their death-bed, but recovered, and whom he should have put down as converted persons had they died; and how many do you think lived a Christian life afterwards out of the two thousand? Not two. Positively he could only find one who was found to live afterwards in the fear of God. Is it not horrible that when men and women come to die, they should cry, "Comfort, comfort?" and that hence their friends conclude that they are children of God, while, after all, they have no right to consolation, but are intruders upon the enclosed grounds of the blessed God. O God, may these people ever be kept from having comfort when they have no right to it! Have you the other blessings?

Have you had the conviction of sin? Have you ever felt your guilt before God? Have your souls been humbled at Jesus' feet? And have you been made to look to Calvary alone for your refuge? If not, you have no right to consolation. Do not take an atom of it. The Spirit is a convincer before he is a Comforter; and you must have the other operations of the Holy Spirit, before you can derive anything from this.

And now I have done. You have heard what this babbler hath said once more. What has it been? Something about the Comforter. But let me ask you, before you go, what do you know about the Comforter? Each one of you, before descending the steps of this chapel, let this solemn question thrill through your souls—What do you know of the Comforter? O! poor souls, if ye know not the Comforter, I will tell you what you shall know—You shall know the Judge! If ye know not the Comforter on earth, ye shall know the Condemner in the next world, who shall cry, "Depart, ye cursed, into everlasting fire in hell." Well might Whitefield call out, "O earth, earth, earth, hear the word of the Lord!" If ye were to live here forever, ye might slight the gospel; if ye had a lease of your lives, ye might despise the Comforter. But, sirs, ye must die. Since last we met together, probably some have gone to their long last home; and ere we meet again in this sanctuary, some here will be amongst the glorified above, or amongst the damned below. Which will it be? Let you soul answer. If to-night you fell down dead in your pews, or where you are standing in the gallery, where would you be? in heaven or in hell? Ah! deceive not yourselves; let conscience have its perfect work; and if in the sight of God, you are obliged to say, "I tremble and fear lest my portion should be with unbelievers," listen one moment, and then I have done with thee. "He that believeth and is baptized shall be saved, and he that believeth not shall be damned." Weary sinner, hellish sinner, thou who art the devil's castaway, reprobate, profligate, harlot, robber, thief, adulterer, fornicator, drunkard, swearer, Sabbath-breaker—list! I speak to thee as well as to the rest. I exempt no man. God hath said there is no exemption here. "Whosoever believeth on the name of Jesus Christ shall be saved." Sin is no barrier; thy guilt is no obstacle. Whosoever—though he were as black as Satan, though he were filthy as a fiend—whosoever this night believes, shall have every sin forgiven, shall have every crime effaced; shall have ever iniquity blotted out; shall be saved in the Lord Jesus Christ, and shall stand in heaven safe and secure. That is the glorious gospel. God apply it to your hearts, and give you faith in Jesus!

> We have listened to the preacher—
> Truth by him has now been shown;
> But we want a GREATER TEACHER,
> From the everlasting throne;
> APPLICATION Is the work of God alone.

The Death of Christ

A Sermon (No. 173) Delivered on Sabbath Morning, January 24, 1858, by the REV. C. H. SPURGEON at the Music Hall, Royal Surrey Gardens.

"Yet it pleased the Lord to bruise him; he hath put him to grief: when thou shalt make his soul an offering for sin, he shall see his seed, he shall prolong his days, and the pleasure of the Lord shall prosper in his hand."—Isaiah 53:10.

That myriads of eyes are casting their glances at the sun! What multitudes of men lift up their eyes, and behold the starry orbs of heaven! They are continually watched by thousands—but there is one great transaction in the world's history, which every day commands far more spectators than that sun which goeth forth like a bridegroom, strong to run his race. There is one great event, which every day attracts more admiration than do the sun, and moon, and stars, when they march in their courses. That event is, the death of our Lord Jesus Christ. To it, the eyes of all the saints who lived before the Christian era were always directed; and backwards, through the thousand years of history, the eyes of all modern saints are looking. Upon Christ, the angels in heaven perpetually gaze. "Which things the angels desire to look into," said the apostle. Upon Christ, the myriad eyes of the redeemed are perpetually fixed; and thousands of pilgrims, through this world of tears, have no higher object for their faith, and no better desire for their vision, than to see Christ as he is in heaven, and in communion to behold his person. Beloved, we shall have many with us, whilst this morning we turn our face to the Mount of Calvary. We shall not be solitary spectators of the fearful tragedy of our Saviour's death: we shall but dart our eyes to that place which is the focus of heaven's joy and delight, the cross of our Lord and Saviour Jesus Christ.

Taking our text, then, as a guide, we propose to visit Calvary, hoping to have the help of the Holy Spirit whilst we look upon him who died upon the cross. I would have you notice this morning, first of all, the cause of Christ's death—"It pleased the Lord to bruise him." "It pleased Jehovah to bruise him," saith the original; "he hath put him to grief." Secondly, the reason of Christ's death—"When thou shalt make his soul an offering for sin." Christ died because he was an offering for sin. And then, thirdly, the effects and consequences of Christ's death. "He shall see his seed, he shall prolong his days, and the pleasure of the Lord shall prosper in his hand." Come, Sacred Spirit, now, whilst we attempt to speak on these matchless themes.

I. First, we have THE ORIGIN OF CHRIST'S DEATH. "It pleased Jehovah to bruise him; he hath put him to griefs." He who reads Christ's life, as a mere history, traces the death of Christ to the enmity of the Jews, and to the fickle character of the Roman governor. In this he acteth justly, for the crime and sin of the Saviour's death must lay at the door of manhood. This race of ours became a deicide and slew the Lord, and nailed its Saviour to a tree. But he who reads the Bible with the eye of faith, desiring to discover its hidden secrets, sees something more in the Saviour's death than Roman cruelty, or Jewish malice: he sees the solemn decree of God fulfilled by men, who were the ignorant, but guilty instruments of its accomplishment. He looks beyond the Roman spear and nail, beyond the Jewish taunt and jeer, up to the Sacred Fount, whence all things flow, and traces the crucifixion of Christ to the breast of Deity. He believes with Peter—"Him, being delivered by the determinate counsel and foreknowledge of God, ye have taken, and by wicked hands have crucified and slain." We dare not impute to God the sin, but at the same time the fact, with all its marvelous effects in the world's redemption, we must ever trace to the Sacred Fountain of divine love. So cloth our prophet. He says, "It pleased Jehovah to bruise him. He overlooks both Pilate and Herod, and traces it to the heavenly Father, the first Person in the Divine Trinity. "It pleased the Lord to bruise him, he hath put him to grief."

Now, beloved, there be many who think that God the Father is at best but an indifferent spectator of salvation. Others do belie him still more. They look upon Him as an unloving, severe Being, who had no love to the human race, and could only be made loving by the death and agonies of our Saviour. Now, this is a foul libel upon the fair and glorious grace of God the Father, to whom for ever be honor: for Jesus Christ did not die to make God loving, but he died because God was loving. "'Twas not to make Jehovah's love Toward his people flame, That Jesus from the throne above,

A suffering man became. "'Twas not the death which he endured, Nor all the pangs he bore, That God's eternal love procured, For God was love before." Christ was sent into the world by his Father, as the consequence of the Father's affection for his people. Yea, he "so loved the world, that he gave his only begotten Son that whosoever believeth in him should not perish, but have everlasting life. The fact is, that the Father as much decreed salvation, as much effected it, and as much delighted in it, as did either God the Son, or God the Holy Spirit. And when we speak of the Saviour of the world, we must always include in that word, if we speak in a large sense, God the Father, God the Son, and God the Holy Ghost, for all these three, as one God, do save us from our sins. The text puts away every hard thought concerning the Father, by telling us that it pleased Jehovah to bruise Jesus Christ. The death of Christ is traceable to God the Father. Let us try if we can see it is so.

1. First it is traceable in decree. God, the one God of heaven and earth, hath the book of destiny entirely in his power. In that book there is nothing written by a stranger's hand. The penmanship of the solemn book of predestination is from beginning to end entirely divine. "Chained to his throne a volume lies, With all the fates of men, With every angel's form and size, Drawn by th' eternal pen." No inferior hand hath sketched even so much as the least minute parts of providence. It was all, from its Alpha to its Omega, from its divine preface to its solemn finis, marked out, designed, sketched, and planned by the mind of the all-wise, all-knowing God. Hence, not even Christ's death was exempt from it. He that wings an angel and guides a sparrow, he that protects the hairs of our head from falling prematurely to the ground, was not likely, when he took notice of such little things, to omit in his solemn decrees the greatest wonder of earth's miracles, the death of Christ. No; the blood-stained page of that book, the page which makes both past and future glorious with golden words,—that blood-stained page, I say,

was as much written of Jehovah, as any other. He determined that Christ should be born of the Virgin Mary, that he should suffer under Pontius Pilate, that he should descend into Hades, that thence he should rise again, leading captivity captive, and then should reign for ever at the right hand of the Majesty on high. Nay, I know not but that I shall have Scripture for my warrant when I say, that this is the very core of predestination, and that the death of Christ is the very center and main-spring by which God did fashion all his other decrees, making this the bottom and foundation-stone upon which the sacred architecture should be builded. Christ was put to death by the absolute foreknowledge and solemn decree of God the Father, and in this sense "it pleased the Lord to bruise him; he hath put him to grief."

2. But a little further, Christ's coming into the world to die was the effect of the Father's will and pleasure. Christ came not into this world unsent. He had laid in Jehovah's bosom from before all worlds, eternally delighting himself in his Father, and being himself his Father's eternal joy. "In the fullness of time" God did rend his Son from his bosom, his only-begotten Son, and freely delivered him up for us all. Herein was matchless, peerless love, that the offended judge should permit his co-equal Son to suffer the pains of death for the redemption of a rebellious people. I want your imaginations for one minute to picture a scene of olden times. There is a bearded patriarch, who rises early in the morning and awakes his son, a young man full of strength, and bids him arise and follow him. They hurry from the house silently and noiselessly, before the mother is awake. They go three days, journey with their men; until they come to the Mount, of which the Lord hath spoken. You know the patriarch. The name of Abraham is always fresh in our memories. On the way, that patriarch speaks not one solitary word to his son. His heart is too full for utterance. He is overwhelmed with grief. God has commanded him to take his son, his only son, and slay him upon the mountain as a sacrifice. They go together; and who shall paint the unutterable anguish of the father's soul, whilst he walks side by side with that beloved son, of whom he is to be the executioner? The third day has arrived; the servants are bidden to stay at the foot of the hill, whilst they go to worship God yonder. Now, can any mind imagine how the father's grief must overflow all the banks of his soul, when, as he walked up that hill-side, his son said to him, "Father, behold the fire and the wood; but where is the lamb for a burnt-offering?" Can you conceive how he stifled his emotions, and, with sobs, exclaimed, "My son, God will provide himself a lamb." See! the father has communicated to his son the fact that God has demanded his life. Isaac, who might have struggled and escaped from his father, declares that he is willing to die, if God hath decreed it. The father takes his son, binds his hands behind his back, piles up the stones, makes an altar, lays the wood, and has his fire ready. And now where is the artist that can depict the anguish of the fathers countenance, when the knife is unsheathed, and he holds it up, ready to slay his son? But here the curtain falls. Now the black scene vanishes at the sound of a voice from heaven. The ram caught in the thicket supplies the substitute, and faith's obedience need go no further. Ah! my brethren, I want to take you from this scene to a far greater one. What faith and obedience made man do, that love constrained God himself to do. He had but one son, that son his own heart's delight: he covenanted to yield him up for our redemption, nor did he violate his promise; for, when the fullness of time was come, he sent his Son to be born of the Virgin Mary, that he might suffer for the sins of man. O! can ye tell the greatness of that love, which made the everlasting God not only put his Son upon the altar, but actually do the deed, and thrust the sacrificial knife into his Son's heart? Can you think how overwhelming must have been the love of God toward the human race, when he completed in act what Abraham only did in intention? Look ye there, and see the place where his only Son hung dead upon the cross, the bleeding victim of awakened justice! Here is love indeed; and here we see how it was, that it pleased the Father to bruise him.

3. This allows me to push my text just one point further. Beloved, it is not only true that God did design and did permit with willingness the death of Christ; it is moreover, true that the unutterable agonies that clothed the death of the Saviour with superhuman terror, were the effect of the Father's bruising of Christ in very act and deed. There is a martyr in prison: the chains are on his wrists, and yet he sings. It has been announced to him that to-morrow is his burning day. He claps his hands right merrily, and smiles while he says, "It will be sharp work to-morrow, I shall breakfast below on fiery tribulations, but afterward I will sup with Christ.

Tomorrow is my wedding-day, the day for which I have long panted, when I shall sign the testimony of my life by a glorious deaths." The time is come; the men with the halberts precede him through the streets. Mark the serenity of the martyrs countenance. He turns to some who look upon him, and exclaims, "I value these iron chains far more than if they had been of gold; it is a sweet thing to die for Christ. There are a few of the boldest of the saints gathered round the stake, and as he unrobes himself, ere he stands upon the fagots to receive his doom, he tells them that it is a joyous thing to be a soldier of Christ, to be allowed to give his body to be burned; and he shakes hands with them, and bids them "Good by" with merry cheer. One would think he were going to a bridal, rather than to be burned. He steps upon the fagots; the chain is put about his middle; and after a brief word of prayer, as soon as the fire begins to ascend, he speaks to the people with manful boldness. But hark! he sings whilst the fagots are crackling and the smoke is blowing upward. He sings, and when his nether parts are burned, he still goes on chanting sweetly some psalm of old. "God is our refuge and strength, a very present help in trouble; therefore will we not fear, though the earth be removed and the mountains be carried into the midst of the sea."

Picture another scene. There is the Saviour going to his cross, all weak and wan with suffering; his soul is sick and sad within him. There is no divine composure there. So sad is his heart, that he faints in the streets. The Son of God faints beneath a cross that many a criminal might have carried. They nail him to the tree. There is no song of praise. He is lifted up in the air, and there he hangs preparatory to his death. You hear no shout of exultation. There is a stern compression of his face, as if unutterable agony were tearing his heart—as if over again Gethsemane were being acted on the cross—as if his soul were still saying, "If it be possible let this cross pass from me; nevertheless, not as I will, but as thou wilt." Hark! he speaks. Will he not sing sweeter songs than ever came from martyr's lips? Ah! no; it is an awful wail of woe that can never be imitated. "My God, my God, why hast thou forsaken me?" The martyrs said not that: God was with them. Confessors of old cried not so, when they came to die. They shouted in their fires, and praised God on their racks. Why this?

Why doth the Saviour suffer so? Why, beloved, it was because the Father bruised him. That sunshine of God's countenance that has cheered many a dying saint, was withdrawn from Christ; the consciousness of acceptance with God, which has made many a holy man espouse the cross with joy, was not afforded to our Redeemer, and therefore he suffered in thick darkness of mental agony. Read the 22nd Psalm, and learn how Jesus suffered. Pause over the solemn words in the 1st, 2nd, 6th, and following verses. Underneath the church are the ever lasting arms; but underneath Christ there were no arms at all, but his Father's hand pressed heavily against him; the upper and the nether mill-stones of divine wrath pressed and bruised him; and not one drop of joy or consolation was afforded to him. "It pleased Jehovah to bruise him; he hath put him to grief." This, my brethren, was the climax of the Saviour's woe, that his Father turned away from him, and put him to grief.

Thus have I expounded the first part of the subject—the origin of our Saviour's worst sufferings, the Father's pleasure.

II. Our second head must explain the first, or otherwise it is an insolvable mystery how God should bruise his Son, who was perfect innocence, while poor fallible confessors and martyrs have had no such bruising from him in the time of their trial. WHAT WAS THE REASON OF THE SAVIOUR'S SUFFERING? We are told here, "Thou shalt make his soul an offering for sin." Christ was thus troubled, because his soul was an offering for sin. Now, I am going to be as plain as I can, while I preach over again the precious doctrine of the atonement of Christ Jesus our Lord. Christ was an offering for sin, in the sense of a substitute. God longed to save; but, if such a word may be allowed, Justice tied his hands. "I must be just," said God; "that is a necessity of my nature. Stern as fate, and fast as immutability, is the truth that I must be just. But then my heart desires to forgive—to pass by man's transgressions and pardon them. How can it be done? Wisdom stepped in, and said, "It shall be done thus;" and Love agreed with Wisdom. "Christ Jesus, the Son of God, shall stand in man's place, and he shall be offered upon Mount Calvary instead of man. Now, mark: when you see Christ going up the Mount of Doom, you see man going there: when you see Christ hurled upon his back, upon the wooden cross, you see the whole company of his elect there; and when you see the nails driven through his blessed hands and feet, it is the whole body of his Church who there, in their substitute, are nailed to the tree.

And now the soldiers lift the cross, and dash it into the socket prepared for it. His bones are every one of them dislocated, and his body is thus torn with agonies which can not be described. 'Tis manhood suffering there; 'tis the Church suffering there, in the substitute. And when Christ dies, you are to look upon the death of Christ, not as his own dying merely, but as the dying of all those for whom he stood as the scape-goat and the substitute. It is true, Christ died really himself; it is equally true that he did not die for himself, but died as the substitute, in the room, place, and stead of all believers. When you die you will die for yourselves; when Christ died, he died for you, if you be a believer in him. When you pass through the gates of the grave, you go there solitary and alone; you are not the representative of a body of men, but you pass through the gates of death as an individual; but, remember, when Christ went through the sufferings of death, he was the representative Head of all his people.

Understand, then, the sense in which Christ was made a sacrifice for sin. But here lies the glory of this matter. It was as a substitute for sin that he did actually and literally suffer punishment for the sin of all his elect. When I say this, I am not to be understood as using any figure whatever, but as saying actually what I mean. Man for his sin was condemned to eternal fire; when God took Christ to be the substitute, it is true, he did not send Christ into eternal fire, but he poured upon him grief so desperate, that it was a valid payment for even an eternity of fire. Man was condemned to live forever in hell. God did not send Christ forever into hell; but he put on Christ, punishment that was equivalent for that. Although he did not give Christ to drink the actual hells of believers, yet he gave him a quid pro quo—something that was equivalent thereunto. He took the cup of Christ's agony, and he put in there, suffering, misery, and anguish such as only God can imagine or dream of, that was the exact equivalent for all the suffering, all the woe, and all the eternal tortures of every one that shall at last stand in heaven, bought with the blood of Christ. And you say, "Did Christ drink it all to its dregs?" Did he suffer it all? Yes, my brethren, he took the cup, and "At one triumphant draught of love, He drank damnation dry." He suffered all the horror of hell: in one pelting shower of iron wrath it fell upon him, with hailstones bigger than a talent; and he stood until the black cloud had emptied itself completely. There was our debt; huge and immense; he paid the utmost farthing of whatever his people owed; and now there is not so much as a doit or a farthing due to the justice of God in the way of punishment from any believer; and though we owe God gratitude, though we owe much to his love, we owe nothing to his justice; for Christ in that hour took all our sins, past, present, and to come, and was punished for them all there and then, that we might never be punished, because he suffered in our stead. Do you see, then, how it was that God the Father bruised him? Unless he had so done the agonies of Christ could not have been an equivalent for our sufferings; for hell consists in the hiding of God's face from sinners, and if God had not hidden his face from Christ, Christ could not—I see not how he could—have endured any suffering that could have been accepted as an equivalent for the woes and agonies of his people.

Methinks I heard some one say, "Do you mean us to understand this atonement that you have now preached as being a literal fact?" I say, most solemnly, I do. There are in the world many theories of atonement; but I can not see any atonement in any one, except in this doctrine of substitution. Many divines say that Christ did something when he died that enabled God to be just, and yet the Justifier of the ungodly. What that something is they do not tell us. They believe in an atonement made for every body; but then, their atonement is just this.

They believe that Judas was atoned for just as much as Peter; they believe that the damned in hell were as much an object of Jesus Christ's satisfaction as the saved in heaven; and though they do not say it in proper words, yet they must mean it, for it is a fair inference, that in the case of multitudes, Christ died in vain, for he died for them all, they say; and yet so ineffectual was his dying for them, that though he died for them they are damned afterward. Now, such an atonement I despise—I reject it. I may be called Antinomian or Calvinist for preaching a limited atonement; but I had rather believe a limited atonement that is efficacious for all men for whom it was intended, than an universal atonement that is not efficacious for anybody, except the will of man be joined with it. Why, my brethren, if we were only so far atoned for by the death of Christ that any one of us might afterward save himself, Christ's atonement were not worth a farthing, for there is no man of us can save himself—no, not under the gospel; for if I am to be saved by faith, if that faith is to be my own act, unassisted by the Holy Spirit, I am as unable to save myself by faith as to save myself by good works. And after all, though men call this a limited atonement, it is as effectual as their own fallacious and rotten redemptions can pretend to be. But do you know the limit of it? Christ hath bought a "multitude that no man can number." The limit of it is just this: He hath died for sinners; whoever in this congregation inwardly and sorrowfully knows himself to be a sinner, Christ died for him; whoever seeks Christ, shall know Christ died for him; for our sense of need of Christ, and our seeking after Christ, are infallible proofs that Christ died for us. And, mark, here is something substantial. The Arminian says Christ died for him; and then, poor man, he has but small consolation therefrom, for he says, "Ah! Christ died for me; that does not prove much. It only proves I may be saved if I mind what I am after. I may perhaps forget myself; I may run into sin and I may perish. Christ has done a good deal for me, but not quite enough, unless I do something." But the man who receives the Bible as it is, he says, "Christ died for me, then my eternal life is sure. I know," says he, "that Christ can not be punished in a man's stead, and the man be punished afterwards. No," says he, "I believe in a just God, and if God be just, he will not punish Christ first, and then punish men afterwards. No; my Saviour died, and now I am free from every demand of God's vengeance, and I can walk through this world secure; no thunderbolt can smite me, and I can die absolutely certain that for me there is no flame of hell, and no pit digged; for Christ, my ransom, suffered in my stead, and, therefore, am I clean delivered. Oh! glorious doctrine! I would wish to die preaching it! What better testimony can we bear to the love and faithfulness of God than the testimony of a substitution eminently satisfactory for all them that believe on Christ? I will here quote the testimony of that pre-eminently profound divine, Dr. John Owen:—"Redemption is the freeing of a man from misery by the intervention of a ransom. Now, when a ransom is paid for the liberty of a prisoner, does not justice demand that he should have and enjoy the liberty so purchased for him by a valuable consideration? If I should pay a thousand pounds for a man's deliverance from bondage to him that retains him, who hath power to set him free, and is contented with the price I give, were it not injurious to me and the poor prisoner that his deliverance be not accomplished? Can it possibly be conceived that there should be a redemption of men, and those men not redeemed? That a price should be paid and the ransom not consummated? Yet all this must be made true, and innumerable other absurdities, if universal redemption be asserted. A price is paid for all, yet few delivered; the redemption of all consummated, yet, few of them redeemed; the judge satisfied, the jailer conquered, and yet the prisoners inthralled! Doubtless 'universal,' and 'redemption,' where the greatest part of men perish, are as irreconcilable as 'Roman, and 'Catholic.' If there be a universal redemption of all, then all men are redeemed. If they are redeemed, then are they delivered from all misery, virtually or actually, whereunto they were inthralled, and that by the intervention of a ransom. Why, then, are not all saved? In a word, the redemption wrought by Christ being the full deliverance of the persons redeemed from all misery, wherein they were inwrapped, by the price of his blood, it can not possibly be conceived to be universal unless all be saved: so that the opinion of the Universalists is unsuitable to redemption."

I pause once more; for I hear some timid soul say—"But, sir, I am afraid I am not elect, and if so, Christ did not die for me." Stop sir! Are you a sinner? Do you feel it? Has God, the Holy Spirit, made you feel that you are a lost sinner? Do you want salvation? If you do not want it, it is no hardship that it is not provided for you; but if you really feel that you want it, you are God's elect. If you have a desire to be saved, a desire given you by the Holy Spirit, that desire is a token for good. If you have begun believingly to pray for salvation, you have therein a sure evidence that you are saved. Christ was punished for you. And if now you can say, "Nothing in my hands I bring, Simply to the cross I cling." you may be as sure you are God's elect as you are sure of your own existence; for this is the infallible proof of election—a sense of need and a thirst after Christ.

III. And now I have just to conclude by noticing the BLESSED EFFECTS of the Saviour's death. On this I shall be very brief.

The first effect of the Saviour's death is, "He shall see his seed." Men shall be saved by Christ. Men have offspring by life; Christ had an offspring by death. Men die and leave their children, and they see not their seed; Christ lives, and every day sees his seed brought into the unity of the faith. One effect of Christ's death is the salvation of multitudes. Mark, not a chance salvation. When Christ died the angel did not say, as some have represented him, "Now by his death many may be saved;" the word of prophecy had quenched all "buts" and "peradventures;" "By his righteousness he shall justify many. There was not so much as an atom of chance work in the Saviour's death. Christ knew what he bought when he died; and what he bought he will have—that, and no more, and no less. There is no effect of Christ's death that is left to peradventure. "Shalls" and "wills" made the covenant fast: Christ's bloody death shall effect its solemn purpose. Every heir of grace shall meet around the throne, "Shall bless the wonders of his grace, And make his glories known." The second effect of Christ's death is, "He shall prolong his days." Yes, bless his name, when he died he did not end his life. He could not long be held a prisoner in the tomb. The third morning came, and the conqueror, rising from his sleep burst the iron bonds of death, and came forth from his prison house, no more to die. He waited his forty days, and then, with shouts of sacred song, he "led captivity captive, and ascended up on high." "In that he died he died unto sin once; but in that he liveth he liveth unto God," no more to die. "Now by his Father's side he Sits, And there triumphant reigns," the conqueror over death and hell.

And, last of all, by Christ's death the Father's good

pleasure was effected and prospered. God's good pleasure is, that that this world shall one day be totally redeemed from sin; God's good pleasure is, that this poor planet, so long swathed in darkness, shall soon shine out in brightness, like a new-born sun. Christ's death hath done it. The stream that flowed from his side on Calvary shall cleanse the world from all its blackness. That hour of mid-day darkness was the rising of a new sun of righteousness, which shall never cease to shine upon the earth. Yes, the hour is coming when swords and spears shall be forgotten things—when the harness of war and the pageantry of pomp shall all be laid aside for the food of the worm or the contemplation of the curious. The hour approacheth when old Rome shall shake upon her seven hills, when Mohammed's crescent shall wane to wax no more, when all the gods of the heathens shall lose their thrones and be cast out to the moles and the bats; and then, when from the equator to the poles Christ shall be honored, the Lord paramount of earth, when from land to land, from the river even to the ends of the earth, one King shall reign, one shout shall be raised, "Hallelujah, hallelujah, the Lord God Omnipotent reigneth." Then, my brethren, shall it be seen what Christ's death has accomplished, for "the pleasure of the Lord shall prosper in his hand."

THE DEATH OF CHRIST FOR HIS PEOPLE

A Sermon (No. 2656) Intended for
Reading on Lord's-Day, January 7th, 1900,
Delivered by C. H. SPURGEON,
At New Park Street Chapel, Southwark.
ON a Lord's-Day Evening in the winter of 1857.

"He laid down his life for us."—1 John 3:16.

Come, believer and contemplate this sublime truth, thus proclaimed to thee in simple monosyllables: "He laid down his life for us." There is not one long word in the sentence; it is all as simple as it can be; and it is simple because it is sublime. Sublimity in thought always needs simplicity in words to express itself. Little thoughts require great words to explain them; little preachers need Latin words to convey their feeble ideas, but great thoughts and great expressers of those thoughts are content with little words.

"He laid down his life for us." Here there is not much upon which any man can display his eloquence; here is little room for metaphysical discussion or for deep thought; the text sets before us a simple yet sublime doctrine. What, then, shall I do with it? If I would speak of it profitably to myself, since I need not employ my wit to dissect it, nor my oratory to proclaim it, let me exercise my adoration to worship it; let me prostrate all my powers before the throne, and, like an angel when his work is done, and he has nowhere else to fly at his Lord's command, let me fold the wings of my contemplation, and stand before the throne of this great truth, and meekly bow myself, and worship him that was, and is, and is to come,—the great and glorious One who "laid down his life for us."

It will be well for me, in commencing my discourse, to remind you that there is no understanding the death of Christ unless we understand the person of Christ. If I were to tell you that God died for us, although I might be telling you a truth, and you might possibly not misunderstand what I meant, yet I should be at the same time uttering an error. God cannot die; it is, of course, impossible, from his very nature, that he could even for a moment cease to exist. God is incapable of suffering. It is true that we sometimes use words to express emotions On the part of God; but, then, we speak after the manner of men. He is impassive; he cannot suffer; it is not possible for him to endure aught; much less, then, is it possible for him to suffer death. Yet we are told, in the verse from which our text is taken, "Hereby perceive we the love of God." You notice that the words "of God" are inserted by the translators. They are in italics because they are not in the original. A better translation would be, "Hereby perceive we love." But when we read "of God," it might lead the ignorant to fancy that God could die; whereas, God could not. We must always understand, and constantly remember, that our Lord Jesus Christ was "very God of very God," and that, as God, he had all the attributes of the Most High, and could not, therefore, be capable either of suffering or death. But then he was also man, "man of the substance of his mother," man, just like ourselves, sin alone excepted. And the Lord Jesus died not as God; it was as man that he gave up the ghost; as man, he was nailed to the cross. As God, he was in heaven, even when his body was in the tomb; as God, he was swaying the sceptre of all worlds even when the mock sceptre of reed was in his hand, and the imperial robe of universal monarchy was on the eternal shoulders of his Godhead when the soldier's old purple cloak was wrapped about his manhood. He did not cease to be God, he did not lose his Omnipotence, and his eternal dominion, when he became man; nor did he, as God, die or suffer; it was as man that he "laid down his life for us."

Come, now, my soul, and worship this man, this God. Come, believer, and behold thy Saviour; come to the innermost circle of all sanctity, the circle that contains the cross of Christ, and here sit down; and, whilst thou dost worship, learn three lessons from the fact that "he laid down his life for us." The first lesson should be,—Did he lay down his life for us? Ah! then, my brethren, how great must have been our sins that they could not have been atoned for at any other price! Secondly, did he lay down his life for us? Ah! then, beloved, how great must have been his love! He would not stop short anywhere, until life itself had been resigned. Thirdly, did he lay down his life for us? Ah! then, my soul, be of good cheer; how safe art thou! If such an atonement hath been offered, if such a sure satisfaction hath been given to Almighty God, how secure thou art! Who is he that can destroy him who hath been bought with the blood of such a Redeemer?

I. Come, then, let me believingly meditate on the first sad fact. Did Christ lay down his life for me? Then, HOW GREAT MUST HAVE BEEN MY SINS!

Ah! my brethren, I will speak a little of my own experience, and in so doing I shall also be describing yours. I have seen my sins in many different ways. I saw them once by the blazing light of Sinai; and, oh! my spirit shrank within me, for my sins seemed exceeding black. When the sound of the trumpet waxed loud and long, and the lighting and fire flashed into my heart, I saw a very hell of iniquity within my soul, and I was ready then to curse the day that I was horn, that I should have had such a heart, so vile and so deceitful. I thought that then I had seen the exceeding blackness of my sin. Alas! I had not seen enough of sin to make me loathe it so as to leave it, for that conviction passed away. Sinai was but a volcano, and it was hushed to silence; and then I began to play with sin again, and loved it as much as ever.

I beheld another sight one day; I saw my sins by the light of heaven. I looked up, and I considered the heavens, the work of God's fingers; I perceived the purity of God's character written on the sunbeams, I saw his holiness engraved upon the wide world, as well as revealed in Scripture; and as I compared myself with him, I thought I saw how black I was. O God! I never knew the heinousness of my own guilt, until I saw the glory of thy character; but now I see the brightness of thy holiness, my whole soul is cast down at the thought of my sinfulness, and my great departure from the living God. I thought that, then, I had seen enough. Ah! I had seen enough to make me worship for a moment; but my gladness was as the early cloud and as the morning dew, and I went my way, and forgot what manner of man I was. When I had lost the sense of the majesty of God, I lost also the consciousness of my own guilt.

Then there came to me another view, and I beheld God's lovingkindness to me; I saw how he had dandled me upon the knee of Providence,—how he had carried me all my life long,—how he had strewn my path with plenty, and given me all things richly to enjoy. I remembered how he had been with me in the hour of trial, how he had preserved me in the day of hurricane, and kept me safe at the moment of storm. I remembered all his goodness to me; and, struck with surprise at his mercy, I looked upon my sin in the light of his grace; and I said, "O sin, how base thou art, what dire ingratitude dost thou manifest against a God so profoundly kind!"

I thought, then, surely I had seen the worst of sin, when I had laid it side by side, first with the character of God, and afterwards with his bounties. I cursed sin from my inmost heart, and thought I had seen enough of it. But, ah! my brethren, I had not. That sense of gratitude passed away, and I found myself still prone to sin, and still loving it.

But, oh, there came a thrice-happy, yet thrice-mournful hour! One day, in my wanderings, I heard a cry, a groan; metought 'twas not a cry such as came from mortal lip, it had in it such unutterable depths of wondrous woe. I turned aside, expecting to see some great sight; and it was indeed a great sight that I saw. Lo, there, upon a tree, all bleeding, hung a man. I marked the misery that made his flesh all quiver on his bones; I beheld the dark clouds come rolling down from heaven, like the chariots of misery; I saw them clothe his brow with blackness; I saw even in the thick darkness, for mine eyes were opened, and I perceived that his heart was as full of the gloom and horror of grief as the sky was full of blackness. Then I seemed to look into his soul, and I saw there torrents of unutterable anguish,—wells of torment of such an awful character that mortal lip dare not sip, lest it should be burned with scalding heat. I said, "Who is this mighty sufferer? Why doth he suffer thus? Hath he been the greatest of all sinners, the basest of all blasphemers?" But a voice came forth from the excellent glory, and it said, "This is my beloved Son; but he took the sinner's sin upon himself, and he must bear its penalty." O God! I thought, I never saw sin till that hour, when I saw it tear Christ's glories from his head,—when it seemed for a moment even to withdraw the lovingkindness of God from him,—when I saw him covered with his own blood, and plunged into the uttermost depths of oceans of grief. Then I said, "Now shall I know what thou art, O sin, as never before I knew it!" Though those other sights might teach me something of the dire character of evil, yet never, till I saw the Saviour on the tree, did I understand how base a traitor man's guilt was to man's God.

O heir of heaven, lift now thine eye, and behold the scenes of suffering through which thy Lord passed for thy sake! Come in the moonlight, and stand between those olives; see him sweat great drops of blood. Go from that garden, and follow him to Pilate's bar. See your Matter subjected to the grossest and filthiest insult; gaze upon the face of spotless beauty defiled with the spittle of soldiers; see his head pierced with thorns; mark his back, all rent, and torn, and scarred, and bruised, and bleeding beneath the terrible lash. And O Christian, see him die! Go and stand where his mother stood, and hear him say to thee, "Man, behold thy Saviour!" Come thou to-night, and stand where John stood; hear him cry, "I thirst," and find thyself unable either to assuage his griefs or to comprehend their bitterness. Then, when thou hast wept there, lift thine hand, and cry, "Revenge!" Bring out the traitors; where are they? And when your sins are brought forth as the murderers of Christ, let no death be too painful for them; though it should involve the cutting off of right arms, or the quenching of right eyes, and putting out their light for ever; do it! For if these murderers murdered Christ, then let them die. Die terribly they may, but die they must. Oh! that God the Holy Ghost would teach you that first lesson, my brethren, the boundless wickedness of sin, for Christ had to lay down his life before your sin could be wiped away.

II. Now we will come to the second head, and here we will lift up our hearts from the depths of sadness to the heights of affection. Did the Saviour lay down his life for me? We will read it now, "He laid down his life for me;" and I pray the Lord to help each of you, by faith, to read it so, because, when we say "us", that is dealing in generalities,—blessed generalities, it is true,—but let us, at this time, deal in specialities, and say, each one of us who can do so truthfully, "He laid down his life for me." Then, HOW GREATLY HE MUST HAVE LOVED ME!

Ah, Lord Jesus! I never knew thy love till I understood the meaning of thy death. Beloved, we shall try again, if we can, to tell the story of our own experience, to let you see how God's love is to be learned. Come, saint, sit down, and meditate on thy creation, note how marvellously thou hast been formed, and all thy bones fitted to one another, and see love there. Mark, next, that predestination which placed thee where thou art; for the lines have fallen unto thee in pleasant places, and, notwithstanding all thy troubles, thou hast, compared with many a poor soul, "a goodly heritage." Mark, then, the love of God displayed in the predestination that has made thee what thou art, and placed thee where thou art. Then look thou back, and see the lovingkindness of thy Lord, as displayed to thee in all thy journey up till now. Thou art getting old, and thy hair is whitening above thy brow; but he hath carried thee all the days of old; not one good thing hath failed of all that the Lord thy God hath promised. Recall thy life-story. Go back now, and look at the tapestry of thy life, which God has been working every day with the golden filament of his love, and see what pictures of grace there are upon it. Canst thou not say that Jesus has loved thee? Turn thine eye back, and read the ancient rolls of the everlasting covenant, and see thy name amongst the firstborn, the elect, the Church of the living God. Say, did he not love thee when he wrote thy name there? Go and remember how the eternal settlements were made, and how God decreed and arranged all things so that thy salvation should come to pass. Say, was there not love there?

Pause at the remembrance of thy convictions; think of thy conversion; recollect thy preservation, and how God's grace hath been working upon thee, in adoption, in justification, and in every item of the new covenant; and when thou hast summed up all these things, let me ask thee this question,—Do all these things produce in thee such a sense of gratitude as the one thing that I shall mention now, the cross of our Lord Jesus Christ?

For, my brother, if thy mind is like mine, although thou wilt think highly enough of all these things that God hath given thee, thou wilt be obliged to confess that the thought of the death of Christ upon the cross swallows them all up. This I know, my brethren, I may look back, I may look forward, but whether I look back to the decrees of eternity, or look forward to the pearl-gated city, and all the splendours that God has prepared for his own beloved children, I can never see my Father's love so beaming forth, in all its effulgence, as when I look at the cross of Christ, and see him die thereon. I can read the love of God in the rocky letters of the eternal covenant, and in the blazing letters of heaven hereafter; but, my brethren, in those crimson lines, those lines written in blood, there is something more striking than there is anywhere else, for they say, "He laid down his life for us" Ah, here it is ye learn love. You know the old story of Damon and Pythias,—how the two friends struggled together as to which should die for the other; there was love there. But, ah! there is no comparison between Damon and Pythias, and a poor sinner and his Saviour. Christ laid down his life, his glorious life, for a poor worm; he stripped himself of all his splendours, then of all his happiness, then of his own righteousness, then of his own robes, till he was naked to his own shame; and then he laid down his life, that was all he had left, for our Saviour had not kept anything back.

Just think of that for a moment. He had a crown in heaven; but he laid that aside, that you and I might wear one for ever. He had a girdle of brightness—brighter than the stars,—about his loins; but he took it off, and laid it by, that you and I might eternally wear a girdle of righteousness. He had listened to the holy songs of the cherubim and seraphim; but he left them all that we might for ever dwell where angels sing; and then he came to earth, and he had many things, even in his poverty, which might have tended to his comfort; he laid down, first one glory, and then another, at love's demand; at last, it came to this, he had nothing left but one poor garment, woven from the top throughout, and that was clinging to his back with blood, and he laid down that also. Then there was nothing left, he had not kept back one single thing. "There," he might have said, "take an inventory of all I have, to the last farthing; I have given it all up for my people's ransom." And there was nought left now but his own life. O love insatiable! couldst thou not stay there? Though he had given up one hand to cancel sin, and the other hand to reconcile us unto God; and had given up one foot that we might have our sinful feet for ever transfixed, and nailed, and fastened, never to wander, and the other foot to be fastened to the tree that we might have our feet at liberty to run the heavenly race; and there was nothing left but his poor heart, and he gave his heart up too, and they set it abroach with the spear, and forthwith there came out thence blood and water.

Ah, my Lord! what have I ever given to thee compared to what thou hast given for me? Some poor things, like some rusty farthings, I have given thee; but how little compared with what thou hast given me! Now and then, my Lord, I have given thee a poor song upon an ill-toned instrument; sometimes, my Lord, I have done some little service for thee; but, alas! my fingers were so black, they spoiled what I intended to have presented to thee white as snow. It is nought I have done for thee, my Lord. No, though I have been a missionary, and surrendered home and friends; no, though I have been a martyr, and given my body to be burned, I will say, in the last hour, "My Master, I have done nothing for thee, after all, in comparison with what thou hast done for me; and yet, what can I do more? How can I show my love to thee, for thy love to me, so peerless, so matchless? What shall I do? I will do nothing but—

Dissolved by thy goodness, I'll fall to the ground,
And weep to the praise of the mercy I've found.

"That is all I can do, and that I must and will do." III. Now, beloved, we will change the theme, and go one note higher. We have run up the gamut a long way, and now we have just reached the height of the octave. But we have something else to get out of the text: "He laid down his life for us." Did my Saviour lay down his life for me? Then, HOW SAFE I AM!

We will have no controversy to-night with those who do not see this truth; the Lord open their blind eyes, and show it to them! That is all we will say. We, who know the gospel, see, in the fact of the death of Christ, a reason that no strength of logic can ever shake, and no power of unbelief can remove, why we should be saved. There may be men, with minds so distorted that they can conceive it possible that Christ should die for a man who afterwards is lost; I say, there may be such. I am sorry to say that there are still to be found some such persons, whose brains have been so addled, in their childhood, that they cannot see that what they hold is both a preposterous falsehood and a blasphemous libel. Christ dies for a man, and then God punishes that man again; Christ suffers in a sinner's stead, and then God condemns that sinner after all! Why, my friends, I feel quite shocked in only mentioning such an awful error; and were it not so current as it is, I should certainly pass it over with the contempt that it deserves. The doctrine of Holy Scripture is this, that God is just, that Christ died in the stead of his people, and that, as God is just, he will never punish one solitary soul of Adam's race for whom the Saviour did thus shed his blood. The Saviour did, indeed, in a certain sense, die for all; all men receive many a mercy through his blood, but that he was the Substitute and Surety for all men, is so inconsistent, both with reason and Scripture, that we are obliged to reject the doctrine with abhorrence. No, my soul, how shalt thou be punished if thy Lord endured thy punishment for thee? Did he die for thee? O my soul, if Jesus was not thy Substitute, and did not die in thy very stead, then he is no Saviour to thee! But if he was thy Substitute, if he suffered as thy Surety, in thy stead, then, my soul, "Who is he that condemneth?" Christ hath died, yea, rather, hath risen again, and sitteth at the right hand of God, and maketh intercession for us. There stands the master-argument: Christ "laid down his life for us," and "if, when we were enemies, we were reconciled to God by the death of his Son, much more, being reconciled, we shall be saved by his life."

If the agonies of the Saviour put our sins away, the everlasting life of the Saviour, with the merits of his death added thereunto, must preserve his people, even unto the end.

This much I know,—ye may hear men stammer when they say it,—but what I preach is the old Lutheran, Calvinistic, Augustinian, Pauline, Christian truth,—there is not one sin in the Book of God against anyone that believeth. Our sins were numbered on the Scapegoat's head, and there is not one sin, that ever a believer did commit, that hath any power to damn him, for Christ hath taken the damning power out of sin, by allowing it, to speak by a bold metaphor, to damn himself, for sin did condemn him; and, inasmuch as sin condemned him, sin cannot condemn us. O believer, this is thy security, that all thy sin and guilt, all thy transgressions and thine iniquities, have been atoned for, and were atoned for before they were committed; so that thou mayest come with boldness, though red with all crimes, and black with every lust, and lay thine hand on that Scapegoat's head, and when thou hast put thine hand there, and seen that Scapegoat driven into the wilderness, thou mayest clap thine hands for joy, and say, "It is finished, sin is pardoned." "Here's pardon for transgressions pest, It matters not how black their cast; And oh, my soul, with wonder view, For sin's to come, here's pardon too!" This is all I want to know; did the Saviour die for me? Then I will not continue in sin that grace may abound; but nothing shall stop me of thus glorying, in all the churches of the Lord Jesus, that my sins are entirely removed from me; and, in God's sight, I may sing, as Hart did sing,—

> With Christ's spotless vesture on,
>   Holy as the Holy One.

O marvellous death of Christ, how securely dost, thou set the feet of God's people on the rocks of eternal love; and how securely dost thou keep them there! Come, dear brethren, let us suck a little honey out of this honeycomb. Was there ever anything so luscious and so sweet to the believer's taste as this all-glorious truth that we are complete in him; that in and through his death and merits we are accepted in the Beloved? Oh, was there ever anything mare sublime than this thought, that he hath already raised us up together, and made us sit together in heavenly places in Christ Jesus, far above all principalities and powers; just where he sits? Surely there is nothing more sublime than that, except it be that a master-thought stamps all these things with more than their own value,—that master-thought that, though the mountains may depart and the hills be removed, the covenant of his love shall never depart from us. "For," saith Jehovah, "I will never forget thee, O Zion;" "I have graven thee upon the palms of my hands; thy walls are continually before me." O Christian, that is a firm foundation, cemented with blood, on which thou mayest build for eternity! Ah, my soul! thou needest no other hope but this. Jesus, thy mercy never dies; I will plead this truth when cast down with anguish,—Thy mercy never dies. I will plead this when Satan hurls temptations at me, and when conscience casts the remembrance of my sin in my teeth; I will plead this ever, and I will plead it now,—"Jesus, thy blood and righteousness

My beauty are, my glorious dress.

> Yea, and after I die, and even when I stand
> before thine eyes, thou dread Supreme,—
>   When from the dust of death I rise,
>   To take my mansion in the skies,
>   E'en then shall this be all my plea,
>   'Jesus hath lived and died for me.'
>   Bold shall I stand in that great day,
>   For who aught to my charge shall lay?
>   While through Christ's blood absolved I am
>   From sin's tremendous curse and shame.

Ah, brethren, if this is your experience you may come to the table of communion now right happily; it will not be coming to a funeral, but to a feast of gladness. "He laid down his life for us."

The Exaltation of Christ

A Sermon (No. 98) Delivered on Sabbath Morning, November 2, 1856, by the REV. C. H. SPURGEON At New Park Street Chapel, Southwark.

"Wherefore God also hath highly exalted him, and given him a name which is above every name: That at the name of Jesus every knee should bow, of things in heaven, and things in earth, and

things under the earth; And that every tongue should confess that Jesus Christ is Lord, to the glory of God the Father."—Philippians 2:9–11.

I almost regret this morning that I have ventured to occupy this pulpit, because I feel utterly unable to preach to you for your profit. I had thought that the quiet and repose of the last fortnight had removed the effects of that terrible catastrophe; but on coming back to the same spot again, and more especially, standing here to address you, I feel somewhat of those same painful emotions which well-nigh prostrated me before.

You will therefore excuse me this morning, if I make no allusion to that solemn event, or scarcely any. I could not preach to you upon a subject that should be in the least allied to it. I should be obliged to be silent if I should bring to my remembrance that terrific scene in the midst of which it was my solemn lot to stand. God shall over-rule it doubtless. It may not have been so much by the malice of men, as some have asserted; it was perhaps simple wickedness—an intention to disturb a congregation; but certainly with no thought of committing so terrible a crime as that of the murder of those unhappy creatures. God forgive those who were the instigators of that horrid act! They have my forgiveness from the depths of my soul. It shall not stop us, however; we are not in the least degree daunted by it. I shall preach there again yet; ay, and God shall give us souls there, and Satan's empire shall tremble more than ever. "God is with us; who is he that shall be against us?" The text I have selected is one that has comforted me, and in a great measure, enabled me to come here to-day—the single reflection upon it had such a power of comfort on my depressed spirit. It is this:—"Wherefore God also hath highly exalted him, and given him a name which is above every name: That at the name of Jesus every knee should bow, of things in heaven, and things on earth, and things under the earth; And that every tongue should confess that Jesus Christ is Lord, to the glory of God the Father."—Philippians 2:9–11.

I shall not attempt to preach upon this text; I shall only make a few remarks that have occurred to my own mind; for I could not preach to-day; I have been utterly unable to study, but I thought that even a few words might be acceptable to you this morning, and I trust to your loving hearts to excuse them. Oh, Spirit of God, magnify thy strength in thy servant's weakness, and enable him to honour his Lord, even when his soul is cast down within him. WHEN the mind is intensely set upon one object, however much it may by divers calamities be tossed to and fro, it invariably returns to the place which it had chosen to be its dwelling place. Ye have noticed in the case of David. When the battle had been won by his warriors, they returned flushed with victory. David's mind had doubtless suffered much perturbation in the mean time; he had dreaded alike the effects of victory and defeat; but have you not noticed how his mind in one moment returned to the darling object of his affections? "Is the young man Absalom safe?" said he, as if it mattered not what else had occurred, it his beloved son were but secure! So, beloved, it is with the Christian. In the midst of calamities, whether they be the wreck of nations, the crash of empires, the heaving of revolutions, or the scourge of war, the great question which he asks himself, and asks of others too, is this—Is Christ's kingdom safe? In his own personal afflictions his chief anxiety is,—Will God be glorified, and will his honour be increased by it? If it be so, says he, although I be but as smoking flax, yet if the sun is not dimmed I will rejoice; and though I be a bruised reed, if the pillars of the temple are unbroken, what matters it that my reed is bruised? He finds it sufficient consolation, in the midst of all the breaking in pieces which he endures, to think that Christ's throne stands fast and firm, and that though the earth hath rocked beneath his feet, yet Christ standeth on a rock which never can be moved. Some of these feelings, I think, have crossed our minds. Amidst much tumult and divers rushings to and fro of troublous thoughts our souls have returned to the darling object of our desires, and we have found it no small consolation after all to say, "It matters not what shall become of us: God hath highly exalted him, and given him a name which is above every name: That at the name of Jesus every knee should bow."

This text has afforded sweet consolation to every heir of heaven. Allow me, very briefly, to give you the consolations of it. To the true Christian there is much comfort in the very fact of Christ's exaltation. In the second place, there is no small degree of consolation in the reason of it. "Wherefore, also, God hath highly exalted him;" that is because of his previous humiliation. And thirdly, there is no small amount of really divine solace in the thought of the person who has exalted Christ. Wherefore God also"—although men despise him and cast him down—"God also hath highly exalted him."

I. First, then, IN THE VERY FACT OF CHRIST'S EXALTATION THERE IS TO EVERY TRUE CHRISTIAN A VERY LARGE DEGREE OF COMFORT. Many of you who have no part nor lot in spiritual things, not having love to Christ, nor any desire for his glory, will but laugh when I say that this is a very bottle of cordial to the lip of the weary Christian, that Christ, after all, is glorified. To you it is no consolation, because you lack that condition of heart which makes this text sweet to the soul. To you there is nothing of joy in it; it does not stir your bosom; it gives no sweetness to your life; for this very reason, that you are not joined to Christ's cause, nor do you devoutly seek to honour him. But the true Christian's heart leapeth for joy, even when cast down by divers sorrows and temptations, at the remembrance that Christ is exalted, for in that he finds enough to cheer his own heart. Note here, beloved, that the Christian has certain features in his character which make the exaltation of Christ a matter of great joy to him. First, he has in his own opinion, and not in his own opinion only, but in reality, a relationship to Christ, and therefore he feels an interest in the success of his kinsman. Ye have watched the father's joy, when step by step his boy has climbed to opulence or fame; ye have marked the mother's eye, as it sparkled with delight when her daughter grew up to womanhood, and burst forth in all the grandeur of beauty. Ye have asked why they should feel such interest; and ye have been told, because the boy was his, or the girl was hers. They delighted in the advancement of their little ones, because of their relationship. Had there been no relationship, they might have been advanced to kings, emperors, or queens, and they would have felt but little delight. But from the fact of kindred, each step was invested with a deep and stirring interest. Now, it is so with this Christian. He feels that Jesus Christ, the glorified "Prince of the kings of the earth." is his brother. While he reverences him as God, he admires him as the man-Christ, bone of his bone, and flesh of his flesh, and he delights, in his calm and placid moments of communion with Jesus, to say to him, "O Lord, thou art my brother." His song is, "My beloved is mine, and I am his." It is his joy to sing—"In the blood with sinners one," Christ Jesus is; for he is a man, even as we are: and he is no less and no more man than we are, save only sin. Surely, when we feel we are related to Christ, his exaltation is the source of the greatest joy to our spirits; we take a delight in it, seeing it is one of our family that is exalted. It is the Elder Brother of the great one family of God in heaven and earth; it is the Brother to whom all of us are related.

There is also in the Christian not only the feeling of relationship merely, but there is a feeling of unity in the cause. He feels that when Christ is exalted, it is himself exalted in some degree, seeing he has sympathy with his desire of promoting the great cause and honour of God in the world. I have no doubt that every common soldier who stood by the side of the Duke of Wellington felt honoured when the commander was applauded for the victory; for, said he, "I helped him, I assisted him; it was but a mean part that I played; I did but maintain my rank; I did but sustain the enemy's fire; but now the victory is gained. I feel an honour in it, for I helped, in some degree, to gain it." So the Christian, when he sees his Lord exalted, says, "It is the Captain that is exalted, and in his exaltation all his soldiers share. Have I not stood by his side? Little was the work I did, and poor the strength which I possessed to serve him; but still I aided in the labour;" and the commonest soldier in the spiritual ranks feels that he himself is in some degree exalted when he reads this—"Wherefore God also hath highly exalted him, and given him a name which is above every name:" a renown above every name—"that at the name of Jesus every knee should bow."

Moreover, the Christian knows not only that there is this unity in design, but that there is a real union between Christ and all his people. It is a doctrine of revelation seldom descanted upon, but never too much thought of—the doctrine that Christ and his members are all one. Know ye not, beloved, that every member of Christ's church is a member of Christ himself? We are "of his flesh and of his bones," parts of his great mystical body; and when we read that our head is crowned, O rejoice, ye members of his, his feet or his hands, though the crown is not on you, yet being on your Head, you share the glory, for you are one with him. See Christ yonder, sitting at his Father's right hand! Believer! he is the pledge of thy glorification; he is the surety of thine acceptance; and, moreover, he is thy representative. The seat which Christ possesses in heaven he has not only by his own right, as a person of the Deity, but he has it also as the representative of the whole church, for he is their forerunner, and he sits in glory as the representative of every one of them. O rejoice, believer, when thou seest thy Master exalted from the tomb, when thou beholdest him exalted up to heaven. Then, when thou seest him climb the steps of light, and sit upon his lofty throne, where angels' ken can scarcely reach him—when thou hearest the acclamations of a thousand seraphs—when thou dost note the loud pealing choral symphony of millions of the redeemed; think, when thou seest him crowned with light—think that thou art exalted too in him, seeing that thou art a part of himself. Happy art thou if thou knowest this, not only in doctrine, but in sweet experience too. Knit to Christ, wedded to him, grown into him, parts and portions of his very self, we throb with the heart of the body; when the head itself is glorified we share in the praise; we felt that his glorification bestows an honour upon us. Ah! beloved, have you ever felt that unity to Christ?

Have you ever felt a unity of desire with him? If so, you will find this rich with comfort; but if not—if you know not Christ—it will be a source of grief rather than a pleasure to you that he is exalted, for you will have to reflect that he is exalted to crush you, exalted to judge you and condemn you, exalted to sweep this earth of its sins, and cut the curse up by the roots, and you with it, unless you repent and turn unto God with full purpose of heart.

There is yet another feeling, which I think is extremely necessary to any very great enjoyment of this truth, that Christ is exalted. It is a feeling of entire surrender of one's whole being to the great work of seeking to honour him. Oh! I have striven for that: would to God I might attain unto it! I have now concentrated all my prayers into one, and that one prayer is this, that I may die to self, and live wholly to him. It seems to me to be the highest stage of man—to have no wish, no thought, no desire but Christ—to feel that to die were bliss, if it were for Christ—that to live in penury and woe, and scorn, and contempt, and misery, were sweet for Christ—to feel that it did not matter what became of one's self, so that one's Master was but exalted—to feel that though, like a sear leaf, you are blown in the blast, you are quite careless whither you are going, so long as you feel that the Master's hand is guiding you according to his will. Or rather to feel that though like the diamond you must be cut, that you care not how sharply you may be cut, so that you may be made fit to be a brilliant in his crown; that you care little what may be done to you, if you may but honour him. If any of you have attained to that sweet feeling of self-annihilation, you will look up to Christ as if he were the sun, and you will say of yourself, "O Lord, I see thy beams; I feel myself to be not a beam from thee—but darkness, swallowed up in thy light. The most I ask is, that thou wouldst live in me, that the life I live in the flesh may not be my life, but thy life in me, that I may say with emphasis, as Paul did, 'For me to live is Christ.'" A man that has attained to this, never need care what is the opinion of this world. He may say, "Do you praise me? Do you flatter me? Take back your flatteries: I ask them not at your hands; I sought to praise my Master; ye have laid the praises at my door; go, lay them at his, and not at mine. Do ye scorn me? Do ye despise me? Thrice happy am I to bear it. If ye will not scorn and despise him!" And if ye will, yet know this, that he is beyond your scorn; and, therefore, smite the soldier for his Captain's sake; ay, strike, strike; but the King ye cannot touch—he is highly exalted—and thou ye think ye have gotten the victory, ye may have routed one soldier of the army, but the main body is triumphant. One soldier seems to be smitten to the dust, but the Captain is coming on with his victorious cohorts, and shall trample you, flushed with your false victory, beneath his conquering feet. As long as there is a particle of selfishness remaining in us, it will mar our sweet rejoicing in Christ; till we get rid of it, we shall never feel constant joy. I do think that the root of sorrow is self. If we once got rid of that, sorrow would be sweet, sickness would be health, sadness would be joy, penury would be wealth, so far as our feelings with regard to them are concerned. They might not be changed, but our feelings under them would be vastly different. If you would seek happiness, seek it at the roots of your selfishness; cut up your selfishness, and you will be happy. I have found that whenever I have yielded to the least joy when I have been prepared to feel acutely the arrows of the enemy; but when I have said of the praises of men, "Yes, what are ye? worthless things!"—then I could also say of their contempt—"Come on! come on! I'll send you all where I sent the praises; you may go together, and fight your battles with one another; but as for me, let your arrows rattle on my mail—they must not, and they shall not, reach my flesh." But if you give way to one you will to another. You must seek and learn to live wholly in Christ—to sorrow when you see Christ maligned and dishonoured, to rejoice when you see him exalted, and then you will have constant cause for joy.

Sit down now, O reviled one, poor, despised, and tempted one; sit down, lift up thine eyes, see him on his throne, and say within thyself, "Little though I be, I know I am united to him; he is my love, my life, my joy; I care not what happens so long as it is written, 'The Lord reigneth.'" II. Now, briefly upon the second point. Here also is the very fountain and well-spring of joy, in THE REASON OF CHRIST'S EXALTATION. "Wherefore God also hath highly exalted him." Why? Because, "he being in the form of God, thought it not robbery to be equal with God: But made himself of no reputation, and took upon him the form of a servant, and was made in the likeness of men: And being found in fashion as a man, he humbled himself, and because obedient unto death, even the death of the cross. Wherefore God also hath highly exalted him." This of course relates to the manhood of our Lord Jesus Christ. As God, Christ needed no exaltation; he was higher than the highest,

"God over all, blessed for ever." But the symbols of his glory having been for a while obscured, having wrapped his Godhead in mortal flesh, his flesh with his Godhead ascended up on high, and the man-God, Christ Jesus, who had stooped to shame, and sorrow, and degradation, was highly exalted, "far above all principalities and powers," that he might reign Prince-regent over all worlds, yea, over heaven itself. Let us consider, for a moment, that depth of degradation to which Christ descended; and then, my beloved, it will give you joy to think, that for that very reason his manhood was highly exalted. Do you see that man—

The humble Man before his foes,
  The weary Man and full of woes?

Do you mark him as he speaks? Note the marvellous eloquence which pours from his lips, and see how the crowds attend him? But do you hear, in the distance, the growling of the thunders of calumny and scorn? Listen to the words of his accusers. They say he is "a gluttonous man and a wine-bibber, a friend of publicans and sinners;" "he has a devil, and is mad." All the whole vocabulary of abuse is exhausted by vituperation upon him. He is slandered, abused, persecuted! Stop! Do you think that he is by this cast down, by this degraded? No, for this very reason: "God hath highly exalted him." Mark the shame and spitting that have come upon the cheek of yonder man of sorrows! See his hair plucked with cruel hands; mark ye how they torture him and how they mock him. Do you think that this is all dishonourable to Christ? It is apparently so; but list to this: "He became obedient," and therefore "God hath highly exalted him." Ah! there is a marvellous connection between that shame, and spitting, and the bending of the knee of seraphs; there is a strange yet mystic link which unites the calumny and the slander with the choral sympathies of adoring angels. The one was, as it were, the seed of the other. Strange that it should be, but the black, the bitter seed brought forth a sweet and glorious flower which blooms for ever. He suffered and he reigned; he stopped to conquer, and he conquered for he stooped, and was exalted for he conquered.

Consider him further still. Do you mark him in your imagination nailed to yonder cross! O eyes! ye are full of pity, with tears standing thick! Oh! how I mark the floods gushing down his cheeks! Do you see his hands bleeding, and his feet too, gushing gore? Behold him! The bulls of Bashan gird him round, and the dogs are hounding him to death! Hear him! "Eloi, Eloi, lama sabachthani?"

The earth startles with affright. A God is groaning on a cross! What! Does not this dishonour Christ? No; it honours him! Each of the thorns becomes a brilliant in his diadem of glory; the nails are forged into his sceptre, and his wounds do clothe him with the purple of empire. The treading of the wine-press hath stained his garments, but not with stains of scorn and dishonour. The stains are embroideries upon his royal robes for ever. The treading of that wine-press hath made his garments purple with the empire of a world; and he is the Master of a universe for ever. O Christian! sit down and consider that thy Master did not mount from earth's mountains into heaven, but from her valleys.

It was not from heights of bliss on earth that he strode to bliss eternal, but from depths of woe he mounted up to glory. Oh! what a stride was that, when, at one mighty step from the grave to the throne of The Highest, the man Christ, the God, did gloriously ascend. And yet reflect! He in some way, mysterious yet true, was exalted because he suffered. "Being found in fashion as a man, he humbled himself, and became obedient unto death, even the death of the cross. Wherefore God also hath highly exalted him, and given him a name which is above every name." Believer, there is comfort for thee here, if thou wilt take it. If Christ was exalted through his degradation, so shalt thou be. Count not thy steps to triumph by thy steps upward, but by those which are seemingly downward. The way to heaven is down-hill. he who would be honoured for ever must sink in his own esteem, and often in that of his fellow-men. Oh! think not of yon fool who is mounting to heaven by his own light opinions of himself and by the flatteries of his fellows, that he shall safely reach Paradise; nay, that shall burst on which he rests, and he shall fall and be broken in pieces. But he who descends into the mines of suffering, shall find unbounded riches there; and he who dives into the depths of grief, shall find the pearl of everlasting life within tis caverns. Recollect, Christian, that thou art exalted when thou art disgraced; read the slanders of thine enemies as the plaudits of the just; count that the scoff and jeer of wicked men are equal to the praise and honour of the godly; their blame is censure, and their censure praise. Reckon too, if thy body should ever be exposed to persecution, that it is no shame to thee, but the reverse; and if thou shouldst be privileged, (and thou mayest) to wear the blood-red crown of martyrdom, count it no disgrace to die. Remember, the most honourable in the church are "the noble army of martyrs." Reckon that the greater the sufferings they endured, so much the greater is their "eternal weight of glory;" and so do thou, if thou standest in the brunt and thick of the fight, remember that thou shalt stand in the midst of glory. If thou hast the hardest to bear, thou shalt have the sweetest to enjoy. On with thee, then—through floods, through fire, through death, through hell, if it should lie in thy path. Fear not. He who glorified Christ because he stooped shall glorify thee; for after he has caused thee to endure awhile, he will give thee "a crown of life which fadeth now away."

III. And now, in the last place, beloved, here is yet another comfort for you. THE PERSON who exalted Christ is to be noticed. "GOD also hath highly exalted him." The emperor of all the Russians crowns himself: he is an autocrat, and puts the crown upon his own head: but Christ hath no such foolish pride. Christ did not crown himself. "GOD also hath highly exalted him." The crown was put upon the head of Christ by God; and there is to me a very sweet reflection in this,—that the hand that put the crown on Christ's head, will one day put the crown on ours;—that the same Mighty One who crowned Christ, "King of kings, and Lord of lords," will crown us, when he shall make us "Kings and priests unto him for ever." "I know," said Paul, "there is laid up for me a crown of glory which fadeth not away, which God, the righteous judge, shall give me in that day."

Now, just pause over this thought—that Christ did not crown himself, but that his Father crowned him; that he did not elevate himself to the throne of majesty, but that his Father lifted him there, and placed him on his throne. Why, reflect thus: Man never highly exalted Christ. Put this then in opposition to it—"God also hath highly exalted him." Man hissed him, mocked him, hooted him. Words were not hard enough—they would use stones. "They took up stones again to stone him." And stones failed; nails must be used, and he must be crucified. And then there comes the taunt, the jeer, the mockery, whilst he hangs languishing on the death-cross. Man did not exalt him. Set the black picture there. Now put this, with this glorious, this bright scene, side by side with it, and one shall be a foil to the other. Man dishonoured him; "God also exalted him." Believer, if all men speak ill of thee, lift up thy head, and say, "Man exalted not my Master; I thank him that he exalts not me. The servant should not be above his master, nor the servant above his lord, nor he that is sent greater than he that sent him." "If on my face for his dear name, Shame and reproach shall be; I'll hail reproach and welcome shame, For he'll remember me." God will remember me, and highly exalt me after all, though man casts me down.

Put it, again, in opposition to the fact, that Christ did not exalt himself. Poor Christian! you feel that you cannot exalt yourself. Sometimes you cannot raise your poor depressed spirits. Some say to you, "Oh! you should not feel like this." They tell you, "Oh! you should not speak such words, nor think such thoughts." Ah! "the heart knoweth its own bitterness, and a stranger intermeddleth not therewith,"—ay, and I will improve upon it, "nor a friend either." It is not easy to tell how another ought to feel and how another ought to act. Our minds are differently made, each in its own mould, which mould is broken afterwards, and there shall never be another like it. We are all different, each one of us; but I am sure there is one thing in which we are all brought to unite in times of deep sorrow, namely, in a sense of helplessness. We feel that we cannot exalt ourselves. Now remember, our Master felt just like it. In the 22nd Psalm, which, if I read it rightly, is a beautiful soliloquy of Christ upon the cross, he says to himself, "I am a worm, and no man." As if he felt himself so broken, so cast down, that instead of being more than a man, as he was, he felt for awhile less than man. And yet, when he could not lift finger to crown himself, when he could scarce heave a thought of victory, when his eye could not flash with even a distant glimpse of triumph,—then his God was crowning him. Art thou so broken in pieces, Christian? Think not that thou art cast away for ever; for "God also hath highly exalted him" who did not exalt himself; and this is a picture and prophecy of what he will do for thee.

And now, beloved, I can say little more upon this text, save that I bid you now for a minutes meditate and think upon it. Oh! let your eyes be lifted up; bid heaven's blue veil divide; ask power of God—I mean spiritual power from on high, to look within the veil. I bid you not look to the streets of gold, nor to the walls of jasper, nor to the pearly-gated city. I do not ask you to turn your eyes to the white-robed hosts, who for ever sing loud hallelujahs; but yonder, my friends, turn your eyes, "There, like a man, the Saviour sits; The God, how bright he shines; And scatters infinite delight

On all the happy minds. "Do you see him?" The head that once was crowned with thorns, Is crowned with glory now; A royal diadem adorns that mighty Victor's brow.

No more the bloody crown, The cross and nails no more: For hell itself shakes at his frown, And all the heavens adore." Look at him! Can your imagination picture him? Behold his transcendent glory! The majesty of kings is swallowed up; the pomp of empires dissolves like the white mist of the morning before the sun; the brightness of assembled armies is eclipsed. He in himself is brighter than the sun, more terrible than armies with banners. See him! See him! O! hide your heads, ye monarchs; put away your gaudy pageantry, ye lords of this poor narrow earth! His kingdom knows no bounds; without a limit his vast empire stretches out itself.

Above him all is his; beneath him many a step are angels, and they are his; and they cast their crowns before his feet. With them stand his elect and ransomed, and their crowns too are his. And here upon this lower earth stand his saints, and they are his, and they adore him; and under the earth, among the infernals, where devils growl their malice, even there is trembling and adoration; and where lost spirits, with wailing and gnashing of teeth for ever lament their being, even there, there is the acknowledgment of his Godhead, even though the confession helps to make the fire of their torments. In heaven, in earth, in hell, all knees bend before him, and every tongue confesses that he is God. If not now, yet in the time that is to come this shall be carried out, that ever creature of God's making shall acknowledge his Son to be "God over all, blessed for ever. Amen." Oh! my soul anticipates that blessed day, when this whole earth shall bend its knee before its God willingly! I do believe there is a happy era coming, when there shall not be one knee unbent before my Lord and Master. I look for that time, that latter-day glory, when kings shall bring presents, when queens shall be the nursing mothers of the church, when the gold of Sheba and the ships of Tarshish, and the dromedaries of Arabia shall alike be his, when nations and tribes of every tongue shall "Dwell on his name with sweetest song, And infant voices shall proclaim Their early blessings on his name." Sometimes I hope to live to see that all-auspicious era—that halcyon age of this world, so much oppressed with grief and sorrow by the tyranny of its own habitants. I hope to see the time, when it shall be said, "Shout, for the great Shepherd reigns, and his unsuffering kingdom now is come"—when earth shall be one great orchestra of praise, and every man shall sing the glorious hallelujah anthem of the King of kings. But even now, while waiting for that era, my soul rejoices in the fact, that every knee does virtually bow, though not willingly, yet really. Does the scoffer, when he mouths high heaven, think that he insults God? He thinks so, but his insult dies long ere it reaches half-way to the stars. Does he conceive, when in his malice he forges a sword against Christ, that his weapon shall prosper? If he does, I can well conceive the derision of God, when he sees the wildest rebel, the most abandoned despiser, still working out his great decrees, still doing that which God hath eternally ordained, and in the midst of his wild rebellion still running in the very track which in some mysterious way before all eternity had been marked as the track in which that being should certainly move. "The wild steeds of earth have broken their bridles, the reins are out of the hands of the charioteer"—so some say; but they are not, or if they are, the steeds run the same round as they would have done had the Almighty grasped the reins still. The world has not gone to confusion; chance is not God; God is still Master, and let men do what they will, and hate the truth we now prize, they shall after all do what God wills, and their direst rebellion shall prove but a species of obedience, though they know it not.

But thou wilt say, "Why dost thou yet find fault; for who hath resisted such a will as that?" "Nay, but O man, who art thou that repliest against God? Shall the thing formed say to him that formed it, why hast thou made me thus? Hath not the potter power over the clay, of the same lump to make one vessel unto honour, and another unto dishonour? What if God, willing to show his wrath, and to make his power known, endured with much longsuffering the vessels of wrath fitted to destruction: and that he might make known the riches of his glory on the vessels of mercy, which he had afore prepared unto glory." Who is he that shall blame him? Woe unto him that striveth with his Maker! He is God—know that, ye inhabitants of the land; and all things, after all, shall serve his will. I like what Luther says in his bold hymn, where, notwithstanding all that those who are haters of predestination choose to affirm, he knew and boldly declared, "He everywhere hath sway, and all things serve his might." Notwithstanding all they do, there is God's sway, after all. Go on, reviler! God knoweth how to make all thy revilings into songs! Go on, thou warrior against God, if thou wilt; know this, thy sword shall help to magnify God, and carve out glory for Christ, when thou thoughtest the slaughter of his church. It shall come to pass that all thou dost shall be frustrated; for God maketh the diviners mad, and saith, "Where is the wisdom of the scribe? Where is the wisdom of the wise?" Surely, "Him hath God exalted, and given him a name which is above every name."

And now, lastly, beloved, if it be true, as it is, that Christ is so exalted that he is to have a name above every name, and every knee is to bow to him, will we not bow our knees this morning before his Majesty? You must, whether you will or no, one day bow your knee. O ironsinewed sinner, bow thy knee now! Thou wilt have to bow it, man, in that day when the lightnings shall be loosed, and the thunders shall roll in wild fury: thou wilt have to bow thy knee then. Oh! bow it now! "Kiss the Son, lest he be angry, and ye perish from the way, when his wrath is kindled but a little." O Lord of hosts! bend the knees of men! Make us all the willing subjects of thy grace, lest afterward, we should be the unwilling slaves of thy terror; dragged with chains of vengeance down to hell. O that now those that are on earth might willingly bend their knees lest in hell it should be fulfilled, "Things under the earth shall bow the knee before him."

God bless you, my friends, I can say no more but that. God bless you, for Jesus' sake! Amen.

Power From On High

By Charles Finney

CHAPTER 1

POWER FROM ON HIGH

Please permit me through your columns to correct a misapprehension of some of the members of the late Council at Oberlin of the brief remarks which I made to them; first on Saturday morning, and afterwards on the Lord's Day. In my first remarks to them I called attention to the mission of the Church to disciple all nations, as recorded by Matthew and Luke, and stated that this commission was given by Christ to the whole Church, and that every member of the Church is under obligation to make it his lifework to convert the world. I then raised two inquiries:

1. What do we need to secure success in this great work?

2. How can we get it?

Answer. 1. We need the enduement of power from on high. Christ had previously informed the disciples that without Him they could do nothing. When He gave them the commission to convert the world, He added, "But tarry ye in Jerusalem till ye be endued with power from on high. Ye shall be baptized with the Holy Ghost not many days hence. Lo, I send upon you the promise of My Father." This baptism of the Holy Ghost, this thing promised by the Father, this enduement of power from on high, Christ has expressly informed us is the indispensable condition of performing the work which he has set before us.

2. How shall we get it? Christ expressly promised it to the whole Church, and to every individual whose duty it is to labour for the conversion of the world. He admonished the first disciples not to undertake the work until they had received this enduement of power from on high. Both the promise and the admonition apply equally to all Christians of every age and nation. No one has, at any time, any right to expect success, unless he first secures this enduement of power from on high. The example of the first disciples teaches us how to secure this enduement. They first consecrated themselves to his work, and continued in prayer and supplication until the Holy Ghost fell upon them on the Day of Pentecost, and they received the promised enduement of power from on high. This, then, is the way to get it.

The Council desired me to say more upon this subject; consequently, on the Lord's Day, I took for my text the assertion of Christ, that the Father is more willing to give the Holy Spirit to them that ask Him than we are to give good gifts to our children.

1. I said, This text informs us that it is infinitely easy to obtain the Holy Spirit, or this enduement of power from the Father.

2. That this is made a constant subject of prayer. Everybody prays for this, at all times, and yet, with all this intercession, how few, comparatively, are really endued with this spirit of power from on high! This want is not met. The want of power is a subject of constant complaint. Christ says, "Everyone that asketh receiveth," but there certainly is a "great gulf" between the asking and receiving, that is a great stumbling-block to many. How, then,

is this discrepancy to be explained? I then proceeded to show why this enduement is not received. I said:

(1) We are not willing, upon the whole, to have what we desire and ask.

(2) God has expressly informed us that if we regard iniquity in our hearts He will not hear us. But the petitioner is often self-indulgent. This is iniquity, and God will not hear him.

(3) He is uncharitable.

(4) Censorious.

(5) Self-dependent.

(6) Resists conviction of sin.

(7) Refuses to confess to all the parties concerned.

(8) Refuses to make restitution to injured parties.

(9) He is prejudiced and uncandid.

(10) He is resentful.

(11) Has a revengeful spirit.

(12) Has a worldly ambition.

(13) He has committed himself on some point, and become dishonest, and neglects and rejects further light.

(14) He is denominationally selfish.

(15) Selfish for his own congregation.

(16) He resists the teachings of the Holy Spirit.

(17) He grieves the Holy Spirit by dissension.

(18) He quenches the Spirit by persistence in justifying wrong.

(19) He grieves Him by a want of watchfulness.

(20) He resists Him by indulging evil tempers.

(21) Also by dishonesties in business.

(22) Also by indolence and impatience in waiting upon the Lord.

(23) By many forms of selfishness.

(24) By negligence in business, in study, in prayer.

(25) By undertaking too much business, too much study, and too little prayer.

(26) By a want of entire consecration.

(27) Last and greatest, by unbelief. He prays for this enduement without expecting to receive it. "He that believeth not God, hath made Him a liar." This, then, is the greatest sin of all. What an insult, what a blasphemy, to accuse God of lying!

I was obliged to conclude that these and other forms of indulged sin explained why so little is received, while so much is asked. I said I had not time to present the other side. Some of the brethren afterward inquired, "What is the other side?" The other side presents the certainty that we shall receive the promised enduement of power from on high, and be successful in winning souls, if we ask, and fulfill the plainly revealed conditions of prevailing prayer. Observe, what I said upon the Lord's Day was upon the same subject, and in addition to what I had previously said. The misapprehension alluded to was this: If we first get rid of all these forms of sin, which prevent our receiving this enduement, have we not already obtained the blessing? What more do we need?

Answer. There is a great difference between the peace and the power of the Holy Spirit in the soul. The disciples were Christians before the Day of Pentecost, and, as such, had a measure of the Holy Spirit. They must have had the peace of sins forgiven, and of a justified state, but yet they had not the enduement of power necessary to the accomplishment of the work assigned them. They had the peace which Christ had given them, but not the power which He had promised. This may be true of all Christians, and right here is, I think, the great mistake of the Church, and of the ministry. They rest in conversion, and do not seek until they obtain this enduement of power from on high. Hence so many professors have no power with either God or man. They prevail with neither. They cling to a hope in Christ, and even enter the ministry, overlooking the admonition to wait until they are endued with power from on high. But let anyone bring all the tithes and offerings into God's treasury, let him lay all upon the altar, and prove God herewith, and he shall find that God "will open the windows of heaven, and pour him out a blessing that there shall not be room enough to receive it."

CHAPTER 2

WHAT IS IT?

The apostles and brethren, on the Day of Pentecost, received it. What did they receive? What power did they exercise after that event?

They received a powerful baptism of the Holy Ghost, a vast increase of divine illumination. This baptism imparted a great diversity of gifts that were used for the accomplishment of their work. It manifestly included the following things: The power of a holy life. The power of a self-sacrificing life. (The manifestation of these must have had great influence with those to whom they proclaimed the gospel.) The power of a cross-bearing life. The power of great meekness, which this baptism enabled them everywhere to exhibit. The power of a loving enthusiasm in proclaiming the gospel. The power of teaching. The power of a loving and living faith. The gift of tongues. An increase of power to work miracles. The gift of inspiration, or the revelation of many truths before unrecognized by them. The power of moral courage to proclaim the gospel and do the bidding of Christ, whatever it cost them.

In their circumstances all these enduements were essential to their success; but neither separately nor all together did they constitute that power from on high which Christ promised, and which they manifestly received. That which they manifestly received as the supreme, crowning, and all-important means of success was the power to prevail with both God and man, the power to fasten saving impressions upon the minds of men. This last was doubtless the thing which they understood Christ to promise. He had commissioned the Church to convert the world to Him. All that I have named above were only means, which could never secure the end unless they were vitalized and made effectual by the power of God. The apostles, doubtless, understood this; and, laying themselves and their all upon the altar, they besieged a Throne of Grace in the spirit of entire consecration to their work.

They did, in fact, receive the gifts before mentioned; but supremely and principally this power to savingly impress men. It was manifested right upon the spot. They began to address the multitude; and, wonderful to tell, three thousand were converted the same hour. But, observe, here was no new power manifested by them upon this occasion, save the gift of tongues.

They wrought no miracle at that time, and used these tongues simply as the means of making themselves understood. Let it be noted that they had not had time to exhibit any other gifts of the Spirit which have been above named. They had not at that time the advantage of exhibiting a holy life, or any of the powerful graces and gifts of the Spirit. What was said on the occasion, as recorded in the gospel, could not have made the impression that it did, had it not been uttered by them with a new power to make a saving impression upon the people. This power was not the power of inspiration, for they only declared certain facts of their own knowledge. It was not the power of human learning and culture, for they had but little. It was not the power of human eloquence, for there appears to have been but little of it. It was God speaking in and through them. It was a power from on high—God in them making a saving impression upon those to whom they spoke. This power to savingly impress abode with and upon them. It was, doubtless, the great and main thing promised by Christ, and received by the apostles and primitive Christians. It has existed, to a greater or less extent, in the Church ever since. It is a mysterious fact often manifested in a most surprising manner. Sometimes a single sentence, a word, a gesture, or even a look, will convey this power in an overcoming manner.

To the honour of God alone I will say a little of my own experience in this matter. I was powerfully converted on the morning of the 10th of October. In the evening of the same day, and on the morning of the following day, I received overwhelming baptisms of the Holy Ghost, that went through me, as it seemed to me, body and soul. I immediately found myself endued with such power from on high that a few words dropped here and there to individuals were the means of their immediate conversion. My words seemed to fasten like barbed arrows in the souls of men. They cut like a sword. They broke the heart like a hammer. Multitudes can attest to this. Oftentimes a word dropped, without my remembering it, would fasten conviction, and often result in almost immediate conversion. Sometimes I would find myself, in a great measure, empty of this power. I would go out and visit, and find that I made no saving impression. I would exhort and pray, with the same result. I would then set apart a day for private fasting and prayer, fearing that this power had departed from me, and would inquire anxiously after the reason of this apparent emptiness. After humbling myself, and crying out for help, the power would return upon me with all its freshness. This has been the experience of my life.

I could fill a volume with the history of my own experience and observation with respect to this power from on high. It is a fact of consciousness and of observation, but a great mystery. I have said that sometimes a look has in it the power of God. I have often witnessed this. Let the following fact illustrate it. I once preached, for the first time, in a manufacturing village. The next morning I went into a manufacturing establishment to view its operations. As I passed into the weaving department I beheld a great company of young women, some of whom, I observed, were looking at me, and then at each other, in a manner that indicated a trifling spirit, and that they knew me. I, however, knew none of them. As I approached nearer to those who had recognized me they seemed to increase in their manifestations of lightness of mind. Their levity made a peculiar impression upon me; I felt it to my very heart. I stopped short and looked at them, I know not how, as my whole mind was absorbed with the sense of their guilt and danger. As I settled my countenance upon them I observed that one of them became very much agitated. A thread broke. She attempted to mend it; but her hands trembled in such a manner that she could not do it. I immediately observed that the sensation was spreading, and had become universal among that class of triflers. I looked steadily at them until one after another gave up and paid no more attention to their looms. They fell on their knees, and the influence spread throughout the whole room. I had not spoken a word; and the noise of the looms would have prevented my being heard if I had. In a few minutes all work was abandoned, and tears and lamentations filled the room. At this moment the owner of the factory, who was himself an unconverted man, came in, accompanied, I believe, by the superintendent, who was a professed Christian. When the owner saw the state of things he said to the superintendent, "Stop the mill." What he saw seemed to pierce him to the heart.

"It is more important," he hurriedly remarked, "that these souls should be saved than that this mill should run." As soon as the noise of the machinery had ceased, the owner inquired: "What shall we do? We must have a place to meet, where we can receive instruction." The superintendent replied: "The muleroom will do." The mules were run up out of the way, and all of the hands were notified and assembled in that room. We had a marvelous meeting. I prayed with them, and gave them such instructions as at the time they could bear. The word was with power. Many expressed hope that day; and within a few days, as I was informed, nearly every hand in that great establishment, together with the owner, had hope in Christ.

This power is a great marvel. I have many times seen people unable to endure the word. The most simple and ordinary statements would cut men off from their seats like a sword, would take away their bodily strength, and render them almost as helpless as dead men. Several times it has been true in my experience that I could not raise my voice, or say anything in prayer or exhortation except in the mildest manner, without wholly overcoming those that were present. This was not because I was preaching terror to the people; but the sweetest sounds of the gospel would overcome them. This power seems sometimes to pervade the atmosphere of one who is highly charged with it. Many times great numbers of persons in a community will be clothed with this power, when the very atmosphere of the whole place seems to be charged with the life of God. Strangers coming into it, and passing through the place, will be instantly smitten with conviction of sin, and in many instances converted to Christ. When Christians humble themselves, and consecrate their all afresh to Christ, and ask for this power, they will often receive such a baptism that they will be instrumental in converting more souls in one day than in all their lifetime before. While Christians remain humble enough to retain this power the work of conversion will go on, till whole communities and regions of country are converted to Christ. The same is true of ministers. But this article is long enough. If you will allow me, I have more to say upon this subject.

CHAPTER 3

THE ENDUEMENT OF THE SPIRIT

Since the publication in the Independent of my article on "The Power from on High" I have been confined with protracted illness. In the meantime I have received numerous letters of inquiry upon that subject. They relate mostly to three particular points of inquiry:

1. They request further illustrations of the exhibition of this power.
2. They inquire, "Who have a right to expect this enduement?"
3. How or upon what conditions can it be obtained?

I am unable to answer these inquiries by letters to individuals. With your leave I propose, if my health continues to improve, to reply to them in several short articles through your columns. In the present number I will relate another exhibition of this power from on high, as witnessed by myself. Soon after I was licensed to preach I went into a region of country where I was an entire stranger. I went there at the request of a Female Missionary Society, located in Oneida County, New York. Early in May, I think, I visited the town of Antwerp, in the northern part of Jefferson County. I stopped at the village hotel, and there learned that there were no religious meetings held in that town at the time. They had a brick meeting-house, but it was locked up. By personal efforts I got a few people to assemble in the parlour of a Christian lady in the place, and preached to them on the evening after my arrival. As I passed round the village I was shocked with the horrible profanity that I heard among the men wherever I went. I obtained leave to preach in the school-house on the next Sabbath; but before the Sabbath arrived I was much discouraged, and almost terrified, in view of the state of society which I witnessed. On Saturday the Lord applied with power to my heart the following words, addressed by the Lord Jesus to Paul (Acts 18:9, 10): "Be not afraid, but speak, and hold not thy peace; for I am with thee, and no man shall set on thee to hurt thee; for I have much people in this city." This completely subdued my fears; but my heart was loaded with agony for the people. On Sunday morning I arose early, and retired to a grove not far from the village to pour out my heart before God for a blessing on the labours of the day. I could not express the agony of my soul in words, but struggled with much groaning, and, I believe, with many tears, for an hour or two, without getting relief. I returned to my room in the hotel; but almost immediately came back to the grove. This I did thrice. The last time I got complete relief, just as it was time to go to meeting. I went to the school-house, and found it filled to its utmost capacity. I took out my little pocket Bible, and read for my text: "God so loved the world that He gave his only begotten Son, that whosoever believeth in Him should not perish, but have everlasting life." I exhibited the love of God as contrasted with the manner in which He was treated by those for whom He gave up His Son. I charged home their profanity upon them; and, as I recognized among my hearers several whose profanity I had particularly noticed, in the fullness of my heart and the gushing of my tears I pointed to them, and said, "I heard these men call upon God to damn their fellows." The Word took powerful effect. Nobody seemed offended, but almost everybody greatly melted. At the close of the service the amiable landlord, Mr. Copeland, rose and said that he would open the meeting-house in the afternoon. He did so. The meeting-house was full, and, as in the morning, the Word took powerful effect. Thus a powerful revival commenced in the village, which soon after spread in every direction. I think it was on the second Sabbath after this, when I came out of the pulpit in the afternoon, an aged man approached, and said to me: "Can you not come and preach in our neighborhood? We have never had any religious meetings there." I inquired the direction and the distance, and appointed to preach there the next afternoon, Monday, at five o'clock, in their school-house. I had preached three times in the village, and attended two prayer-meetings on the Lord's Day; and on Monday I went on foot to fulfill this appointment. The weather was very warm that day, and before I arrived there I felt almost too faint to walk, and greatly discouraged in my mind. I sat down in the shade by the wayside, and felt as if I was too faint to reach there; and if I did, too much discouraged to open my mouth to the people. When I arrived I found the house full, and immediately commenced the service by reading a hymn. They attempted to sing, but the horrible discord agonized me beyond expression. I leaned forward, put my elbows upon my knees and my hands over my ears, and shook my head withal, to shut out the discord, which even then I could barely endure. As soon as they had ceased to sing I cast myself down upon my knees, almost in a state of desperation. The Lord opened the windows of heaven upon me, and gave me great enlargement and power in prayer. Up to this moment I had no idea what text I should use on the occasion. As I rose from my knees the Lord gave me this: "Up, get you out of this place, for the Lord will destroy this city." I told the people, as nearly as I could recollect, where they would find it, and went on to tell them of the destruction of Sodom. I gave them an outline of the history of Abraham and Lot, and their relations to each other; of Abraham's praying for Sodom, and of Lot, as the only pious man that was found in the city. While I was doing this I was struck with the fact that the people looked exceedingly angry about me. Many countenances appeared very threatening, and some of the men near me looked as if they were about to strike me. This I could not understand, as I was only giving them, with great liberty of spirit, some interesting sketches of Bible history. As soon as I had completed the historical sketch I turned upon them, and said that I had understood they had never had any religious meetings in that neighborhood; and, applying that fact, I thrust at them with the sword of the Spirit with all my might. From this moment the solemnity increased with great rapidity. In a few moments there seemed to fall upon the congregation an instantaneous shock. I cannot describe the sensation that I felt, nor that which was apparent in the congregation; but the word seemed literally to cut like a sword. The power from on high came down upon them in such a torrent that they fell from their seats in every direction. In less than a minute nearly the whole congregation were either down on their knees, or on their faces, or in some position prostrate before God. Everyone was crying or groaning for mercy upon his own soul. They paid no further attention to me or to my preaching. I tried to get their attention; but I could not. I observed the aged man who had invited me there as still retaining his seat near the centre of the house. He was staring around him with a look of unutterable astonishment. Pointing to him, I cried at the top of my voice, "Can't you pray?" He knelt down and roared out a short prayer, about as loud as he could holler, but they paid no attention to him. After looking round for a few moments, I knelt down and put my hand on the head of a young man who was kneeling at my feet, and engaged in prayer for mercy on his soul. I got his attention, and preached Jesus in his ear. In a few moments he seized Jesus by faith, and then broke out in prayer for those around him. I then turned to another in the same way, and with the same result; and then another, and another, till I know not how many had laid hold of Christ and were full of prayer for others. After continuing in this way till nearly sunset I was obliged to commit the meeting to the charge of the old gentleman who had invited me, and go to fulfil an appointment in another place for the evening. In the afternoon of the next day I was sent for to go down to this place, as they had not been able to break up the meeting. They had been obliged to leave the school-house, to give place to the school; but had removed to a private house near by, where I found a number of persons still too anxious and too much loaded down with conviction to go to their homes. These were soon subdued by the Word of God, and I believe all obtained a hope before they went home. Observe, I was a total stranger in that place, had never seen or heard of it, until as I have related. But here, at my second visit, I learned that the place was called Sodom, by reason of its wickedness; and the old man who invited me was called Lot, because he was the only professor of religion in the place. After this manner the revival broke out in this neighborhood. I have not been in that neighborhood for many years; but in 1856, I think, while labouring in Syracuse, New York, I was introduced to a minister of Christ from St. Lawrence County by the name of Cross. He said to me, "Mr. Finney, you don't know me; but do you remember preaching in a place called Sodom?" I said, "I shall never forget it." He replied, "I was then a young man, and was converted at that meeting." He is still living, a pastor in one of the churches in that county, and is the father of the principal of our preparatory department. Those who have lived in that region can testify of the permanent results of that blessed revival. I can only give in words a feeble description of that wonderful manifestation of power from on high attending the preaching of the Word.

CHAPTER 4

ENDUEMENT OF POWER FROM ON HIGH

In this article I propose to consider the conditions upon which this enduement of power can be obtained. Let us borrow a little light from the Scriptures. I will not cumber your paper with quotations from the Bible, but simply state a few facts that will readily be recognized by all readers of the Scriptures. If the readers of this article will read in the last Chapter of Matthew and of Luke the commission which Christ gave to His disciples, and in connection read the first and second chapters of the Acts of the Apostles, they will be prepared to appreciate what I have to say in this article.

1. The disciples had already been converted to Christ, and their faith had been confirmed by His resurrection. But here let me say that conversion to Christ is not to be confounded with a consecration to the great work of the world's conversion. In conversion the soul has to do directly and personally with Christ. It yields up its prejudices, its antagonisms, its self-righteousness, its unbelief, its selfishness; accepts Him, trusts Him, and supremely loves Him. All this the disciples had, more or less, distinctly done. But as yet they had received no definite commission, and no particular enduement of power to fulfil a commission.

2. But when Christ had dispelled their great bewilderment resulting from His crucifixion, and confirmed their faith by repeated interviews with them, He gave them their great commission to win all nations to Himself. But He admonished them to tarry at Jerusalem till they were endued with power from on high, which He said they should receive not many days hence. Now observe what they did. They assembled, the men and women, for prayer. They accepted the commission, and, doubtless, came to an understanding of the nature of the commission, and the necessity of the spiritual enduement which Christ had promised. As they continued day after day in prayer and conference they, no doubt, came to appreciate more and more the difficulties that would beset them, and to feel more and more their inadequacy to the task. A consideration of the circumstances and results leads to the conclusion that they, one and all, consecrated themselves, with all they had, to the conversion of the world as their life-work. They must have renounced utterly the idea of living to themselves in any form, and devoted themselves with all their powers to the work set before them. This consecration of themselves to the work, this self-renunciation, this dying to all that the world could offer them, must, in the order of nature, have preceded their intelligent seeking of the promised enduement of power from on high. They then continued, with one accord, in prayer for the promised baptism of the Spirit, which baptism included all that was essential to their success. Observe, they had a work set before them. They had a promise of power to perform it. They were admonished to wait

until the promise was fulfilled. How did they wait? Not in listlessness and inactivity; not in making preparations by study and otherwise to get along without it; not by going about their business, and offering an occasional prayer that the promise might be fulfilled; but they continued in prayer, and persisted in their suit till the answer came. They understood that it was to be a baptism of the Holy Ghost. They understood that it was to be received from Christ. They prayed in faith. They held on, with the firmest expectation, until the enduement came. Now, let these facts instruct us as to the conditions of receiving this enduement of power.

We, as Christians, have the same commission to fulfil. As truly as they did, we need an enduement of power from on high. Of course, the same injunction, to wait upon God till we receive it, is given to us.

We have the same promise that they had. Now, let us take substantially and in spirit the same course that they did. They were Christians, and had a measure of the Spirit to lead them in prayer and in consecration. So have we. Every Christian possesses a measure of the Spirit of Christ, enough of the Holy Spirit to lead us to true consecration and inspire us with the faith that is essential to our prevalence in prayer. Let us, then, not grieve or resist Him: but accept the commission, fully consecrate ourselves, with all we have, to the saving of souls as our great and our only life-work. Let us get on to the altar with all we have and are, and lie there and persist in prayer till we receive the enduement. Now, observe, conversion to Christ is not to be confounded with the acceptance of this commission to convert the world. The first is a personal transaction between the soul and Christ relating to its own salvation. The second is the soul's acceptance of the service in which Christ proposes to employ it. Christ does not require us to make brick without straw. To whom He gives the commission He also gives the admonition and the promise. If the commission is heartily accepted, if the promise is believed, if the admonition to wait upon the Lord till our strength is renewed be complied with, we shall receive the enduement.

It is of the last importance that all Christians should understand that this commission to convert the world is given to them by Christ individually.

Everyone has the great responsibility devolved upon him or her to win as many souls as possible to Christ. This is the great privilege and the great duty of all the disciples of Christ. There are a great many departments in this work. But in every department we may and ought to possess this power, that, whether we preach, or pray, or write, or print, or trade, or travel, take care of children, or administer the government of the state, or whatever we do, our whole life and influence should be permeated with this power. Christ says: "If any man believe in Me, out of his belly shall flow rivers of living water"—that is, a Christian influence, having in it the element of power to impress the truth of Christ upon the hearts of men, shall proceed from Him. The great want of the Church at present is, first, the realizing conviction that this commission to convert the world is given to each of Christ's disciples as his life-work. I fear I must say that the great mass of professing Christians seem never to have been impressed with this truth. The work of saving souls they leave to ministers. The second great want is a realizing conviction of the necessity of this enduement of power upon every individual soul. Many professors of religion suppose it belongs especially and only to such as are called to preach the Gospel as a life-work. They fail to realize that all are called to preach the Gospel, that the whole life of every Christian is to be a proclamation of the glad tidings. A third want is an earnest faith in the promise of this enduement. A vast many professors of religion, and even ministers, seem to doubt whether this promise is to the whole Church and to every Christian. Consequently, they have no faith to lay hold of it. If it does not belong to all, they don't know to whom it does belong. Of course they cannot lay hold of the promise by faith. A fourth want is that persistence in waiting upon God for it that is enjoined in the Scriptures. They faint before they have prevailed, and, hence, the enduement is not received. Multitudes seem to satisfy themselves with a hope of eternal life for themselves. They never get ready to dismiss the question of their own salvation, leaving that, as settled, with Christ. They don't get ready to accept the great commission to work for the salvation of others, because their faith is so weak that they do not steadily leave the question of their own salvation in the hands of Christ; and even some ministers of the Gospel, I find, are in the same condition, and halting in the same way, unable to give themselves wholly to the work of saving others, because in a measure unsettled about their own salvation. It is amazing to witness the extent to which the Church has practically lost sight of the necessity of this enduement of power. Much is said of our dependence upon the Holy Spirit by almost everybody; but how little is this dependence realized. Christians and even ministers go to work without it. I mourn to be obliged to say that the ranks of the ministry seem to be filling up with those who do not possess it. May the Lord have mercy upon us!

Will this last remark be thought uncharitable? If so, let the report of the Home Missionary Society, for example, be heard upon this subject. Surely, something is wrong.

An average of five souls won to Christ by each missionary of that Society in a year's toil certainly indicates a most alarming weakness in the ministry. Have all or even a majority of these ministers been endued with the power which Christ promised? If not, why not? But, if they have, is this all that Christ intended by His promise? In a former article I have said that the reception of this enduement of power is instantaneous. I do not mean to assert that in every instance the recipient was aware of the precise time at which the power commenced to work mightily within him. It may have commenced like the dew and increased to a shower. I have alluded to the report of the Home Missionary Society. Not that I suppose that the brethren employed by that Society are exceptionally weak in faith and power as labourers for God. On the contrary, from my acquaintance with some of them, I regard them as among our most devoted and self-denying labourers in the cause of God. This fact illustrates the alarming weakness that pervades every branch of the Church, both clergy and laity. Are we not weak? Are we not criminally weak? It has been suggested that by writing thus I should offend the ministry and the Church. I cannot believe that the statement of so palpable a fact will be regarded as an offence. The fact is, there is something sadly defective in the education of the ministry and of the Church. The ministry is weak, because the Church is weak. And then, again, the Church is kept weak by the weakness of the ministry. Oh for a conviction of the necessity of this enduement of power and faith in the promise of Christ!

CHAPTER 5

IS IT A HARD SAYING?

In a former article I said that the want of an enduement of power from on high should be deemed a disqualification for a pastor, a deacon or elder, a Sabbath-school superintendent, a professor in a Christian college, and especially for a professor in a theological seminary. Is this a hard saying? Is this an uncharitable saying? Is it unjust? Is it unreasonable? Is it unscriptural? Suppose any one of the Apostles, or those present on the day of Pentecost, had failed, through apathy, selfishness, unbelief, indolence, or ignorance, to obtain this enduement of power, would it have been uncharitable, unjust, unreasonable, or unscriptural, to have accounted him disqualified for the work which Christ had appointed them?

Christ had expressly informed them that without this enduement they could do nothing. He had expressly enjoined it upon them not to attempt it in their own strength, but to tarry at Jerusalem until they received the necessary power from on high. He had also expressly promised that if they tarried, in the sense which He intended, they should receive it "not many days hence." They evidently understood Him to enjoin upon them to tarry in the sense of a constant waiting upon Him in prayer and supplication for the blessing. Now, suppose that any one of them had stayed away and attended to his own business, and waited for the sovereignty of God to confer this power. He of course would have been disqualified for the work; and if his fellow-Christians, who had obtained this power, had deemed him so, would it have been uncharitable, unreasonable, unscriptural?

And is it not true of all to whom the command to disciple the world is given, and to whom the promise of this power is made, if through any shortcoming or fault of theirs they fail to obtain this gift, that they are in fact disqualified for the work, and especially for any official station? Are they not, in fact, disqualified for leadership in the sacramental host? Are they qualified for teachers of those who are to do the work? If it is a fact that they do lack this power, however this defect is to be accounted for, it is also a fact that they are not qualified for teachers of God's people; and if they are seen to be disqualified because they lack this power, it must be reasonable and right and Scriptural so to deem them, and so to speak of them, and so to treat them. Who has a right to complain? Surely, they have not. Shall the Church of God be burdened with teachers and leaders who lack this fundamental qualification, when their failing to possess it must be their own fault? The manifest apathy, indolence, ignorance, and unbelief that exist upon this subject are truly amazing. They are inexcusable. They must be highly criminal. With such a command to convert the world ringing in our ears; with such an injunction to wait in constant, wrestling prayer till we receive the power; with such a promise, made by such a Savior, held out to us of all the help we need from Christ Himself, what excuse can we offer for being powerless in this great work? What an awful responsibility rests upon us, upon the whole Church, upon every Christian! One might ask, How is apathy, how is indolence, how is the common fatal neglect possible, under such circumstances? If any of the primitive Christians to whom this commandment was given had failed to receive this power, should we not think them greatly to blame? If such default had been sin in them, how much more in us with all the light of history and of fact blazing upon us, which they had not received? Some ministers and many Christians treat this matter as if it were to be left to the sovereignty of God, without any persistent effort to obtain this enduement. Did the primitive Christians so understand and treat it? No, indeed. They gave themselves no rest till this baptism of power came upon them. I once heard a minister preaching upon the subject of the baptism of the Holy Ghost. He treated it as a reality; and when he came to the question of how it was to be obtained, he said truly that it was to be obtained as the Apostles obtained it on the day of Pentecost. I was much gratified, and listened eagerly to hear him press the obligation on his hearers to give themselves no rest till they had obtained it. But in this I was disappointed: for before he sat down he seemed to relieve the audience from the feeling of obligation to obtain the baptism, and left the impression that the matter was to be left to the discretion of God, and said what appeared to imply a censure of those that vehemently and persistently urged upon God the fulfilment of the promise. Neither did he hold out to them the certainty of their obtaining the blessing if they fulfilled the conditions. The sermon was in most respects a good one; but I think the audience left without any feeling of encouragement or sense of obligation to seek earnestly the baptism. This is a common fault of the sermons that I hear. There is much that is instructive in them; but they fail to leave either a sense of obligation or a feeling of great encouragement, as to the use of means, upon the congregation. They are greatly defective in their winding up. They neither leave the conscience under a pressure nor the whole mind under the stimulus of hope. The doctrine is often good, but the "what then?" is often left out. Many ministers and professors of religion seem to be theorizing, criticizing, and endeavouring to justify their neglect of this attainment. So did not the Apostles and other Christians. It was not a question which they endeavoured to grasp with their intellects before they embraced it with their hearts. It was with them, as it should be with us, a question of faith in a promise. I find many persons endeavouring to grasp with their intellect and settle as a theory questions of pure experience. They are puzzling themselves with endeavours to apprehend with the intellect that which is to be received as a conscious experience through faith.

There is need of a great reformation in the Church on this particular point. The Churches should wake up to the facts in the case, and take a new position, a firm stand in regard to the qualifications of ministers and Church officers. They should refuse to settle a man as pastor of whose qualifications for the office in this respect they are not well satisfied. Whatever else he may have to recommend him, if his record does not show that he has this enduement of power to win souls to Christ, they should deem him unqualified. It used to be the custom of Churches, and I believe in some places is so still, in presenting a call to the pastorate, to certify that, having witnessed the spiritual fruits of his labours, they deem him qualified and called of God to the work of the ministry. Churches should be well satisfied in some way that they call a fruitful minister, and not a dry stalk—that is, a mere intellect, a mere head with little heart; an elegant writer, but with no unction; a great logician, but of little faith; a fervid imagination, it may be, with no Holy Ghost power.

The Churches should hold the theological seminaries to a strict account in this matter; and until they do, I fear the theological seminaries will never wake up to their responsibility. Some years since, one branch of the Scotch Church was so tried with the want of unction and power in the ministers furnished them by their theological seminary that they passed a resolution that until the seminary reformed in this respect they would not employ ministers that were educated there. This was a necessary, a just, a timely rebuke, which I believe had a very salutary effect. A theological seminary ought by all means to be a school not merely for the teaching of doctrine, but also, and even more especially, for the development of Christian experience. To be sure the intellect should be well furnished in those schools; but it is immeasurably more important that the pupils should be led to a thorough personal knowledge of Christ, and the power of His resurrection, and the fellowship of His sufferings, and to be made conformable to His death. A theological seminary that aims mainly at the culture of the intellect, and sends out learned men who lack this enduement of power from on high, is a snare and a stumbling-block to the Church. The seminaries should recommend no one to the Churches, however great his intellectual attainments, unless he has this most essential of all attainments, the enduement of power from on high. The seminaries should be held as incompetent to educate men for the ministry if it is seen that they send out men as ministers who have not this most essential qualification. The Churches should inform themselves, and look to those seminaries which furnish not merely the best educated, but the most unctuous and spiritually powerful ministers. It is amazing that, while it is generally admitted that the enduement of power from on high is a reality, and essential to ministerial success, practically it should be treated by the Churches and by the schools as of comparatively little importance. In theory it is admitted to be everything; but in practice treated as if it were nothing. From the Apostles to the present day it has been seen that men of very little human culture, but endued with this power, have been highly successful in winning souls to Christ; whilst men of the greatest learning, with all that the schools have done for them, have been powerless so far as the proper work of the ministry is concerned. And yet we go on laying ten times more stress on human culture than we do on the baptism of the Holy Ghost. Practically human culture is treated as infinitely more important than the enduement of power from on high. The seminaries are furnished with learned men, but often not with men of spiritual power; hence, they do not insist upon this enduement of power as indispensable to the work of the ministry. Students are pressed almost beyond endurance with study and the culture of the intellect, while scarcely an hour in a day is given to instruction in Christian experience. Indeed, I do not know that so much as one course of lectures on Christian experience is given in the theological seminaries. But religion is an experience. It is a consciousness. Personal intercourse with God is the secret of the whole of it. There is a world of most essential learning in this direction wholly neglected by the theological seminaries. With them doctrine, philosophy, theology, Church history, sermonizing are everything, and real heart-union with God nothing. Spiritual power to prevail with God and to prevail with man has but little place in their teaching. I have often been surprised at the judgment men form in regard to the prospective usefulness of young men preparing for the ministry. Even professors are very apt, I see, to deceive themselves on this subject. If a young man is a good scholar, a fine writer, makes good progress in exegesis, and stands high in intellectual culture, they have strong hopes of him, even though they must know in many such cases that these young men cannot pray; that they have no unction, no power in prayer, no spirit of wrestling, of agonizing, and prevailing with God. Yet they are expecting them, because of their culture, to make their mark in the ministry, to be highly useful. For my part, I expect no such thing of this class of men. I have infinitely more hope of the usefulness of a man who, at any cost, will keep up daily intercourse with God; who is yearning for and struggling after the highest possible spiritual attainment; who will not live without daily prevalence in prayer and being clothed with power from on high. Churches, presbyteries, associations, and whoever license young men for the ministry, are often very faulty in this respect. They will spend hours in informing themselves of the intellectual culture of the candidates, but scarcely as many minutes in ascertaining their heart culture, and what they know of the power of Christ to save from sin, what they know of the power of prayer, and whether and to what extent they are endued with power from on high to win souls to Christ. The whole proceeding on such occasions cannot but leave the impression that human learning is preferred to spiritual unction. Oh! that it were different, and that we were all agreed, practically, now and for ever, to hold fast to the promise of Christ, and never think ourselves or anybody else to be fit for the great work of the Church till we have received a rich enduement of power from on high. I beg of my brethren, and especially my younger brethren, not to conceive of these articles as written in the spirit of reproach. I beg the Churches, I beg the seminaries, to receive a word of exhortation from an old man, who has had some experience in these things, and one whose heart mourns and is weighed down in view of the shortcomings of the Church, the ministers, and the seminaries on this subject. Brethren, I beseech you to more thoroughly consider this matter, to wake up and lay it to heart, and rest not till this subject of the enduement of power from on high is brought forward into its proper place, and takes that prominent and practical position in view of the whole Church that Christ designed it should.

CHAPTER 6

PREVAILING PRAYER

Prevailing prayer is that which secures an answer. Saying prayers is not offering prevailing prayer. The prevalence of prayer does not depend so much on quantity as on quality. I do not know how better to approach this subject than by relating a fact of my own experience before I was converted. I relate it because I fear such experiences are but too common among unconverted men.

I do not recollect having ever attended a prayer-meeting until after I began the study of law. Then, for the first time, I lived in a neighbourhood where there was a prayer-meeting weekly. I had neither known, heard, nor seen much of religion; hence I had no settled opinions about it. Partly from curiosity and partly from an uneasiness of mind upon the subject, which I could not well define, I began to attend that prayer-meeting. About the same time I bought the first Bible that I ever owned, and began to read it. I listened to the prayers which I heard offered in those prayer-meetings with all the attention that I could give to prayers so cold and formal. In every prayer they prayed for the gift and outpouring of the Holy Spirit. Both in their prayers and in their remarks, which were occasionally interspersed, they acknowledged that they did not prevail with God. This was most evident, and had almost made me a sceptic.

Seeing me so frequently in their prayer-meeting, the leader, on one occasion, asked me if I did not wish them to pray for me. I replied: "No." I said: "I suppose that I need to be prayed for, but your prayers are not answered. You confess it yourselves." I then expressed my astonishment at this fact, in view of what the Bible said about the prevalence of prayer. Indeed, for some time my mind was much perplexed and in doubt in view of Christ's teaching on the subject of prayer and the manifest facts before me, from week to week, in this prayer-meeting. Was Christ a divine teacher? Did He actually teach what the Gospels attributed to Him? Did He mean what He said? Did prayer really avail to secure blessings from God? If so, what was I to make of what I witnessed from week to week and month to month in that prayer-meeting? Were they real Christians? Was that which I heard real prayer, in the Bible sense? Was it such prayer as Christ had promised to answer? Here I found the solution.

I became convinced that they were under a delusion; that they did not prevail because they had no right to prevail. They did not comply with the conditions upon which God had promised to hear prayer. Their prayers were just such as God had promised not to answer. It was evident they were overlooking the fact that they were in danger of praying themselves into scepticism in regard to the value of prayer.

In reading my Bible I noticed such revealed conditions as the following:

(a) Faith in God as the answerer of prayer. This, it is plain, involves the expectation of receiving what we ask.

(b) Another revealed condition is the asking according to the revealed will of God. This plainly implies asking not only for such things as God is willing to grant, but also asking in such a state of mind as God can accept. I fear it is common for professed Christians to overlook the state of mind in which God requires them to be as a condition of answering their prayers.

For example: In offering the Lord's Prayer, "Thy kingdom come," it is plain that sincerity is a condition of prevailing with God. But sincerity in offering this petition implies the whole heart and life devotion of the petitioner to the building up of this kingdom. It implies the sincere and thorough consecration of all that we have and all that we are to this end. To utter this petition in any other state of mind involves hypocrisy, and is an abomination.

So in the next petition, "Thy will be done on earth as it is in heaven," God has not promised to hear this petition unless it be sincerely offered. But sincerity implies a state of mind that accepts the whole revealed will of God, so far as we understand it, as they accept it in heaven. It implies a loving, confiding, universal obedience to the whole known will of God, whether that will is revealed in His Word, by His Spirit, or in His providence. It implies that we hold ourselves and all that we have and are as absolutely and cordially at God's disposal as do the inhabitants of heaven. If we fall short of this, and withhold anything whatever from God, we "regard iniquity in our hearts," and God will not hear us.

Sincerity in offering this petition implies a state of entire and universal consecration to God. Anything short of this is withholding from God that which is His due. It is "turning away our ear from hearing the law." But what saith the Scriptures? "He that turneth away his ear from hearing the law, even his prayer shall be an abomination." Do professed Christians understand this?

What is true of offering these two petitions is true of all prayer. Do Christians lay this to heart? Do they consider that all professed prayer is an abomination if it be not offered in a state of entire consecration of all that we have and are to God? If we do not offer ourselves with and in our prayers, with all that we have; if we are not in a state of mind that cordially accepts and, so far as we know, perfectly conforms to the whole will of God, our prayer is an abomination. How awfully profane is the use very frequently made of the Lord's Prayer, both in public and in private. To hear men and women chatter over the Lord's Prayer, "Thy kingdom come, Thy will be done on earth as it is in heaven," while their lives are anything but conformed to the known will of God is shocking and revolting. To hear men pray, "Thy kingdom come," while it is most evident that they are making little or no sacrifice or effort to promote this kingdom, forces the conviction of bare-faced hypocrisy. Such is not prevailing prayer.

(c) Unselfishness is a condition of prevailing prayer. "Ye ask and receive not, because ye ask amiss, that ye may consume it upon your lusts" (James 4:3).

(d) Another condition of prevailing prayer is a conscience void of offense toward God and man. 1 John 3:20, 22: "If our heart (conscience) condemn us, God is greater than our heart and knoweth all things; if our heart condemn us not, then have we confidence toward God, and whatsoever we ask we receive of Him, because we keep His commandments and do those things that are pleasing in His sight." Here two things are made plain: first, that to prevail with God we must keep a conscience void of offense; and, second, that we must keep His commandments and do those things that are pleasing in His sight.

(e) A pure heart is also a condition of prevailing prayer. Psalm 66:18: "If I regard iniquity in my heart, the Lord will not hear me."

(f) All due confession and restitution to God and man is another condition of prevailing prayer. Proverbs 28:13: "He that covereth his sins shall not prosper. Whoso confesseth and forsaketh them shall find mercy."

(g) Clean hands is another condition. Psalm 26:6: "I will wash mine hands in innocence, so will I compass thine altar, O Lord." I Timothy 2:8: "I will that men pray everywhere, lifting up holy hands, without wrath and doubting."

(h) The settling of disputes and animosities among brethren is a condition. Matthew 5:23,24: "If thou bring thy gift to the altar, and there rememberest that thy brother hath ought against thee, leave there thy gift before the altar and go thy way. First be reconciled to thy brother, then come and offer thy gift."

(i) Humility is another condition of prevailing prayer. James 4:6: "God resisteth the proud, but giveth grace to the humble."

(j) Taking up the stumbling-blocks is another condition. Ezekiel 14:3: "Son of man, these men have set up their idols in their heart, and put the stumbling-block of their iniquity before their face. Should I be inquired of at all by them?"

(k) A forgiving spirit is a condition. Matthew 6:12: "Forgive us our debts as we forgive our debtors"; 15: "But if ye forgive not men their trespasses, neither will your Heavenly Father forgive your trespasses."

(l) The exercise of a truthful spirit is a condition. Psalm 51:6: "Behold, Thou desireth truth in the inward parts." If the heart be not in a truthful state, if it be not entirely sincere and unselfish, we regard iniquity in our hearts; and, therefore, the Lord will not hear us.

(m) Praying in the name of Christ is a condition of prevailing prayer.

(n) The inspiration of the Holy Spirit is another condition. All truly prevailing prayer is inspired by the Holy Ghost. Romans 8:26, 27: "For we know not what we should pray for as we ought, but the Spirit itself maketh intercession for us with groanings which cannot be uttered. And He that searcheth the heart knoweth what is the mind of the Spirit, because He maketh intercession for the saints according to the will of God." This is the true spirit of prayer. This is being led by the Spirit in prayer. It is the only really prevailing prayer. Do professed Christians really understand this? Do they believe that unless they live and walk in the Spirit, unless they are taught how to pray by the intercession of the Spirit in them, they cannot prevail with God?

(o) Fervency is a condition. A prayer, to be prevailing, must be fervent. James 5:16: "Confess your faults one to another, and pray one for another, that ye may be healed. The effectual fervent prayer of a righteous man availeth much."

(p) Perseverance or persistence in prayer is often a condition of prevailing. See the case of Jacob, of Daniel, of Elijah, of the Syrophoenician woman, of the unjust judge, and the teaching of the Bible generally.

(q) Travail of soul is often a condition of prevailing prayer. "As soon as Zion travailed, she brought forth her children." "My little children," said Paul, "for whom I travail in birth again, till Christ be formed in you." This implies that he had travailed in birth for them before they were converted. Indeed, travail of soul in prayer is the only real revival prayer. If anyone does not know what this is, he does not understand the spirit of prayer. He is not in a revival state. He does not understand the passage already quoted—Romans 8:26, 27. Until he understands this agonizing prayer he does not know the real secret of revival power.

(r) Another condition of prevailing prayer is the consistent use of means to secure the object prayed for, if means are within our reach, and are known by us to be necessary to the securing of the end. To pray for a revival of religion, and use no other means, is to tempt God. This, I could plainly see, was the case of those who offered prayer in the prayer-meeting of which I have spoken. They continued to offer prayer for a revival of religion, but out of meeting they were as silent as death on the subject, and opened not their mouths to those around them. They continued this inconsistency until a prominent impenitent man in the community administered to them in my presence a terrible rebuke. He expressed just what I deeply felt. He rose, and with the utmost solemnity and tearfulness said: "Christian people, what can you mean? You continue to pray in these meetings for a revival of religion. You often exhort each other here to wake up and use means to promote a revival. You assure each other, and assure us who are impenitent, that we are in the way to hell; and I believe it. You also insist that if you should wake up, and use the appropriate means, there would be a revival, and we should be converted. You tell us of our great danger, and that our souls are worth more than all worlds; and yet you keep about your comparatively trifling employments and use no such means. We have no revival and our souls are not saved." Here he broke down and fell, sobbing, back into his seat. This rebuke fell heavily upon that prayer-meeting, as I shall ever remember. It did them good; for it was not long before the members of that prayer-meeting broke down, and we had a revival. I was present in the first meeting in which the revival spirit was manifest. Oh! how changed was the tone of their prayers, confessions, and supplications. I remarked, in returning home, to a friend: "What a change has come over these Christians. This must be the beginning of a revival." Yes; a wonderful change comes over all the meetings whenever the Christian people are revived. Then their confessions mean something. They mean reformation and restitution. They mean work. They mean the use of means. They mean the opening of their pockets, their hearts and hands, and the devotion of all their powers to the promotion of the work.

(s) Prevailing prayer is specific. It is offered for a definite object. We cannot prevail for everything at once. In all the cases recorded in the Bible in which prayer was answered, it is noteworthy that the petitioner prayed for a definite object.

(t) Another condition of prevailing prayer is that we mean what we say in prayer; that we make no false pretenses; in short, that we are entirely childlike and sincere, speaking out of the heart, nothing more nor less than we mean, feel, and believe.

(u) Another condition of prevailing prayer is a state of mind that assumes the good faith of God in all His promises.

(v) Another condition is "watching unto prayer" as well as "praying in the Holy Ghost." By this I mean guarding against everything that can quench or grieve the Spirit of God in our hearts. Also watching for the answer, in a state of mind that will diligently use all necessary means, at any expense, and add entreaty to entreaty.

When the fallow ground is thoroughly broken up in the hearts of Christians, when they have confessed and made restitution—if the work be thorough and honest—they will naturally and inevitably fulfill the conditions, and will prevail in prayer. But it cannot be too distinctly understood that none others will. What we commonly hear in prayer and conference meetings is not prevailing prayer. It is often astonishing and lamentable to witness the delusions that prevail upon the subject. Who that has witnessed real revivals of religion has not been struck with the change that comes over the whole spirit and manner of the prayers of really revived Christians? I do not think I ever could have been converted if I had not discovered the solution of the question: "Why is it that so much that is called prayer is not answered?"

CHAPTER 7

HOW TO WIN SOULS

"Take heed unto thyself, and unto the doctrine; continue in them: for in doing this thou shalt both save thyself, and them that hear thee."—1 Timothy 4:16.

I beg leave in this article to suggest to my younger brethren in the ministry some thoughts on the philosophy of so preaching the gospel as to secure the salvation of souls. They are the result of much study, much prayer for divine teaching, and a practical experience of many years.

I understand the admonition at the head of this article to relate to the matter, order, and manner of preaching.

The problem is, How shall we win souls wholly to Christ? Certainly we must win them away from themselves.

1. They are free moral agents, of course—rational, accountable.

2. They are in rebellion against God, wholly alienated, intensely prejudiced, and committed against Him.

3. They are committed to self-gratification as the end of their being.

4. This committed state is moral depravity, the fountain of sin within them, from which flow by a natural law all their sinful ways. This committed voluntary state is their "wicked heart." This it is that needs a radical change.

5. God is infinitely benevolent, and unconverted sinners are supremely selfish, so that they are radically opposed to God. Their committal to the gratification of their appetites and propensities is known in Bible language as the "carnal mind"; or, as in the margin, "the minding of the flesh," which is enmity against God.

6. This enmity is voluntary, and must be overcome, if

at all, by the Word of God, made effectual by the teaching of the Holy Spirit.

7. The gospel is adapted to this end, and when wisely presented we may confidently expect the effectual co-operation of the Holy Spirit. This is implied in our commission, "Go and disciple all nations, and lo! I am with you always, even to the end of the world."

8. If we are unwise, illogical, unphilosophical, and out of all natural order in presenting the gospel, we have no warrant for expecting divine co-operation.

9. In winning souls, as in everything else, God works through and in accordance with natural laws. Hence, if we would win souls we must wisely adapt means to this end. We must present those truths and in that order adapted to the natural laws of mind, of thought and mental action. A false mental philosophy will greatly mislead us, and we shall often be found ignorantly working against the agency of the Holy Spirit.

10. Sinners must be convicted of their enmity. They do not know God, and consequently are often ignorant of the opposition of their hearts to Him. "By the law is the knowledge of sin," because by the law the sinner gets his first true idea of God. By the law he first learns that God is perfectly benevolent, and infinitely opposed to all selfishness. This law, then, should be arrayed in all its majesty against the selfishness and enmity of the sinner.

11. This law carries irresistible conviction of its righteousness, and no moral agent can doubt it.

12. All men know that they have sinned, but all are not convicted of the guilt and ill desert of sin. The many are careless and do not feel the burden of sin, the horrors and terrors of remorse, and have not a sense of condemnation and of being lost.

13. But without this they cannot understand or appreciate the gospel method of salvation. One cannot intelligently and heartily ask or accept a pardon until he sees and feels the fact and justice of his condemnation.

14. It is absurd to suppose that a careless, unconvicted sinner can intelligently and thankfully accept the gospel offer of pardon until he accepts the righteousness of God in his condemnation. Conversion to Christ is an intelligent change. Hence the conviction of ill desert must precede the acceptance of mercy; for without this conviction the soul does not understand its need of mercy. Of course, the offer is rejected. The gospel is no glad tidings to the careless, unconvicted sinner.

15. The spirituality of the law should be unsparingly applied to the conscience until the sinner's self-righteousness is annihilated, and he stands speechless and self-condemned before a holy God.

16. In some men this conviction is already ripe, and the preacher may at once present Christ, with the hope of His being accepted; but at ordinary times such cases are exceptional. The great mass of sinners are careless, unconvicted, and to assume their conviction and preparedness to receive Christ, and, hence, to urge sinners immediately to accept Him, is to begin at the wrong end of our work—to render our teaching unintelligible. And such a course will be found to have been a mistaken one, whatever present appearances and professions may indicate. The sinner may obtain a hope under such teaching; but, unless the Holy Spirit supplies something which the preacher has failed to do, it will be found to be a false one. All the essential links of truth must be supplied.

17. When the law has done its work, annihilated self-righteousness, and shut the sinner up to the acceptance of mercy, he should be made to understand the delicacy and danger of dispensing with the execution of the penalty when the precept of law has been violated.

18. Right here the sinner should be made to understand that from the benevolence of God he cannot justly infer that God can consistently forgive him. For unless public justice can be satisfied, the law of universal benevolence forbids the forgiveness of sin. If public justice is not regarded in the exercise of mercy, the good of the public is sacrificed to that of the individual. God will never do this.

19. This teaching will shut the sinner up to look for some offering to public justice.

20. Now give him the atonement as a revealed fact, and shut him up to Christ as his own sin offering. Press the revealed fact that God has accepted the death of Christ as a substitute for the sinner's death, and that this is to be received upon the testimony of God.

21. Being already crushed into contrition by the convicting power of the law, the revelation of the love of God manifested in the death of Christ will naturally beget great self-loathing, and that godly sorrow that needeth not to be repented of. Under this showing the sinner can never forgive himself. God is holy and glorious; and he a sinner, saved by sovereign grace. This teaching may be more or less formal as the souls you address are more or less thoughtful, intelligent, and careful to understand.

22. It was not by accident that the dispensation of law preceded the dispensation of grace; but it is in the natural order of things, in accordance with established mental laws, and evermore the law must prepare the way for

the gospel. To overlook this in instructing souls is almost certain to result in false hope, the introduction of a false standard of Christian experience, and to fill the Church with spurious converts. Time will make this plain.

23. The truth should be preached to the persons present, and so personally applied as to compel everyone to feel that you mean him or her. As has been often said of a certain preacher: "He does not preach, but explains what other people preach, and seems to be talking directly to me."

24. This course will rivet attention, and cause your hearers to lose sight of the length of your sermon. They will tire if they feel no personal interest in what you say. To secure their individual interest in what you are saying is an indispensable condition of their being converted. And, while their individual interest is thus awakened, and held fast to your subject, they will seldom complain of the length of your sermon. In nearly all cases, if the people complain of the length of our sermons, it is because we fail to interest them personally in what we say.

25. If we fail to interest them personally, it is either because we do not address them personally, or because we lack unction and earnestness, or because we lack clearness and force, or certainly because we lack something that we ought to possess. To make them feel that we and that God means them is indispensable.

26. Do not think that earnest piety alone can make you successful in winning souls. This is only one condition of success. There must be common sense, there must be spiritual wisdom in adapting means to the end. Matter and manner and order and time and place all need to be wisely adjusted to the end we have in view.

27. God may sometimes convert souls by men who are not spiritually minded, when they possess that natural sagacity which enables them to adapt means to that end; but the Bible warrants us in affirming that these are exceptional cases. Without this sagacity and adaptation of means to this end a spiritual mind will fail to win souls to Christ.

28. Souls need instruction in accordance with the measure of their intelligence. A few simple truths, when wisely applied and illuminated by the Holy Ghost, will convert children to Christ. I say wisely applied, for they too are sinners, and need the application of the law, as a schoolmaster, to bring them to Christ, that they may be justified by faith. It will sooner or later appear that supposed conversions to Christ are spurious where the preparatory law work has been omitted, and Christ has not been embraced as a Saviour from sin and condemnation.

29. Sinners of education and culture, who are, after all, unconvicted and sceptical in their hearts, need a vastly more extended and thorough application of truth. Professional men need the gospel net to be thrown quite around them, with no break through which they can escape; and, when thus dealt with, they are all the more sure to be converted in proportion to their real intelligence. I have found that a course of lectures addressed to lawyers, and adapted to their habits of thought and reasoning, is most sure to convert them.

30. To be successful in winning souls, we need to be observing—to study individual character, to press the facts of experience, observation, and revelation upon the consciences of all classes.

31. Be sure to explain the terms you use. Before I was converted, I failed to hear the terms repentance, faith, regeneration, and conversion intelligibly explained. Repentance was described as a feeling. Faith was represented as an intellectual act or state, and not as a voluntary act of trust. Regeneration was represented as some physical change in the nature, produced by the direct power of the Holy Ghost, instead of a voluntary change of the ultimate preference of the soul, produced by the spiritual illumination of the Holy Ghost. Even conversion was represented as being the work of the Holy Ghost in such a sense as to cover up the fact that it is the sinner's own act, under the persuasions of the Holy Ghost.

32. Urge the fact that repentance involves the voluntary and actual renunciation of all sin; that it is a radical change of mind toward God.

33. Also the fact that saving faith is heart trust in Christ; that it works by love, it purifies the heart, and overcomes the world; that no faith is saving that has not these attributes.

34. The sinner is required to put forth certain mental acts. What these are he needs to understand. Error in mental philosophy but embarrasses, and may fatally deceive the inquiring soul. Sinners are often put upon a wrong track. They are put upon a strain to feel instead of putting forth the required acts of will. Before my conversion I never received from man any intelligible idea of the mental acts that God required of me.

35. The deceitfulness of sin renders the inquiring soul exceedingly exposed to delusion; therefore it behoves teachers to beat about every bush, and to search out every nook and corner where a soul can find a false refuge. Be so thorough and discriminating as to render it as nearly impossible as the nature of the case will admit that the inquirer should entertain a false hope.

36. Do not fear to be thorough. Do not through false pity put on a plaster where the probe is needed. Do not fear that you shall discourage the convicted sinner, and turn him back, by searching him out to the bottom. If the Holy Spirit is dealing with him, the more you search and probe the more impossible it will be for the soul to turn back or rest in sin.

37. If you would save the soul, do not spare a right hand, or right eye, or any darling idol; but see to it that every form of sin is given up. Insist upon full confession of wrong to all that have a right to confession. Insist upon full restitution, so far as is possible, to all injured parties. Do not fall short of the express teachings of Christ on this subject. Whoever the sinner may be, let him distinctly understand that unless he forsakes all that he has he cannot be the disciple of Christ. Insist upon entire and universal consecration of all the powers of body and mind, and of all the property, possessions, character, and influence to God. Insist upon the total abandonment to God of all ownership of self, or anything else, as a condition of being accepted.

38. Understand yourself, and, if possible, make the sinner understand, that nothing short of this is involved in true faith or true repentance, and that true consecration involves them all.

39. Keep constantly before the sinner's mind that it is the personal Christ with whom he is dealing, that God in Christ is seeking his reconciliation to Himself, and that the condition of his reconciliation is that he gives up his will and his whole being to God—that he "leave not a hoof behind."

40. Assure him that "God has given to him eternal life, and this life is in His Son"; that "Christ is made unto him wisdom, righteousness, sanctification, and redemption"; and that from first to last he is to find his whole salvation in Christ.

41. When satisfied that the soul intelligently receives all this doctrine, and the Christ herein revealed, then remember that he must persevere unto the end, as the further condition of his salvation. Here you have before you the great work of preventing the soul from backsliding, of securing its permanent sanctification and sealing for eternal glory.

42. Does not the very common backsliding in heart of converts indicate some grave defect in the teachings of the pulpit on this subject?

What does it mean that so many hopeful converts, within a few months of their apparent conversion, lose their first love, lose all their fervency in religion, neglect their duty, and live on in name Christians, but in spirit and life worldlings?

43. A truly successful preacher must not only win souls to Christ, but must keep them won. He must not only secure their conversion, but their permanent sanctification.

44. Nothing in the Bible is more expressly promised in this life than permanent sanctification. 1 Thessalonians 5:23, 24: "The very God of peace sanctify you wholly; and I pray God your whole spirit, soul, and body be preserved blameless unto the coming of our Lord Jesus Christ. Faithful is He that calleth you, who also will do it." This is unquestionably a prayer of the apostle for permanent sanctification in this life, with an express promise that He who has called us will do it.

45. We learn from the Scriptures that "after we believe" we are, or may be, sealed with the Holy Spirit of promise, and that this sealing is the earnest of our salvation. Ephesians 1:13,14: "In whom ye also trusted after that ye heard the word of truth, the gospel of your salvation; in whom also after that ye believed, ye were sealed with the Holy Spirit of promise, which is the earnest of our inheritance until the redemption of the purchased possession, unto the praise of His glory." This sealing, this earnest of our inheritance, is that which renders our salvation sure. Hence, in Ephesians 4:30, the apostle says: "Grieve not the Holy Spirit of God, whereby ye are sealed unto the day of redemption." And in 2 Corinthians 1:21 and 22 the apostle says: "Now He which establisheth us with you in Christ, and hath anointed us, is God, who hath also sealed us and given the earnest of the Spirit in our hearts." Thus we are established in Christ and anointed by the Spirit, and also sealed by the earnest of the Spirit in our hearts. And this, remember, is a blessing that we receive after that we believe, as Paul has informed us in his Epistle to the Ephesians, above quoted. Now, it is of the first importance that converts should be taught not to rest short of this permanent sanctification, this sealing, this being established in Christ by the special anointing of the Holy Ghost.

46. Now, brethren, unless we know what this means by our own experience, and lead converts to this experience, we fail most lamentably and essentially in our teaching. We leave out the very cream and fullness of the Gospel.

47. It should be understood that while this experience is rare amongst ministers it will be discredited by the Churches, and it will be next to impossible for an isolated preacher of this doctrine to overcome the unbelief of his Church. They will feel doubtful about it, because

so few preach it or believe in it; and will account for their pastor's insisting upon it by saying that his experience is owing to his peculiar temperament, and thus they will fail to receive this anointing because of their unbelief. Under such circumstances it is all the more necessary to insist much upon the importance and privilege of permanent sanctification.

48. Sin consists in carnal-mindedness, in "obeying the desires of the flesh and of the mind." Permanent sanctification consists in entire and permanent consecration to God. It implies the refusal to obey the desires of the flesh or of the mind. The baptism or sealing of the Holy Spirit subdues the power of the desires, and strengthens and confirms the will in resisting the impulse of desire, and in abiding permanently in a state of making the whole being an offering to God.

49. If we are silent upon this subject, the natural inference will be that we do not believe in it, and, of course, that we know nothing about it in experience. This will inevitably be a stumbling-block to the Church.

50. Since this is undeniably an important doctrine, and plainly taught in the gospel, and is, indeed, the marrow and fatness of the gospel, to fail in teaching this is to rob the Church of its richest inheritance.

51. The testimony of the Church, and to a great extent of the ministry, on the subject has been lamentably defective. This legacy has been withheld from the Church, and is it any wonder that she so disgracefully backslides? The testimony of the comparatively few, here and there, that insist upon this doctrine is almost nullified by the counter-testimony or culpable silence of the great mass of Christ's witnesses.

52. My dear brethren, my convictions are so ripe and my feelings so deep upon this subject that I must not conceal from you my fears that lack of personal experience, in many cases, is the reason of this great defect in preaching the gospel. I do not say this to reproach you; it is not in my heart to do so. It is not wonderful that many of you, at least, have not this experience. Your religious training has been defective. You have been led to take a different view of this subject. Various causes have operated to prejudice you against this blessed doctrine of the glorious gospel. You have not intellectually believed it; and, of course, have not received Christ in His fullness into your hearts. Perhaps this doctrine to you has been a stumbling-block and a rock of offence; but I pray you let not prejudice prevail, but venture upon Christ by a present acceptance of Him as your wisdom, righteousness, sanctification, and redemption, and see if He will not do for you exceeding abundantly above all that you asked or thought.

53. No man, saint or sinner, should be left by us to rest or be quiet in the indulgence of any sin. No one should be allowed to entertain the hope of heaven, if we can prevent it, who lives in the indulgence of known sin in any form. Our constant demand and persuasion should be, "Be ye holy, for God is holy." "Be ye perfect, even as your Father in heaven is perfect." Let us remember the manner in which Christ concludes His memorable Sermon on the Mount. After spreading out those awfully searching truths before His hearers, and demanding that they should be perfect, as their Father in heaven was perfect, He concludes by assuring them that no one could be saved who did not receive and obey His teachings. Instead of attempting to please our people in their sins, we should continually endeavor to hunt and persuade them out of their sins. Brethren, let us do it, as we would not have our skirts defiled with their blood. If we pursue this course and constantly preach with unction and power, and abide in the fullness of the doctrine of Christ, we may joyfully expect to save ourselves and them that hear us.

CHAPTER 8

PREACHER, SAVE THYSELF

"Take heed unto thyself, and unto the doctrine; continue in them: for in doing this thou shalt both save thyself and them that hear thee."—I Timothy 4:16.

I am not going to preach to preachers, but to suggest certain conditions upon which the salvation promised in this text may be secured by them.

1. See that you are constrained by love to preach the gospel, as Christ was to provide a gospel.

2. See that you have the special enduement of power from on high, by the baptism of the Holy Ghost.

3. See that you have a heart, and not merely a head call to undertake the preaching of the gospel. By this I mean, be heartily and most intensely inclined to seek the salvation of souls as the great work of life, and do not undertake what you have no heart to.

4. Constantly maintain a close walk with God.

5. Make the Bible your book of books. Study it much, upon your knees, waiting for divine light.

6. Beware of leaning on commentaries. Consult them when convenient; but judge for yourself, in the light of the Holy Ghost.

7. Keep yourself pure—in will, in thought, in feeling, in word and action.

8. Contemplate much the guilt and danger of sinners, that your zeal for their salvation may be intensified.

9. Also deeply ponder and dwell much upon the boundless love and compassion of Christ for them.

10. So love them yourself as to be willing to die for them.

11. Give your most intense thought to the study of ways and means by which you may save them. Make this the great and intense study of your life.

12. Refuse to be diverted from this work. Guard against every temptation that would abate your interest in it.

13. Believe the assertion of Christ that He is with you in this work always and everywhere, to give you all the help you need.

14. "He that winneth souls is wise"; and "If any man lack wisdom, let him ask of God, who giveth to all men liberally and upbraideth not, and he shall receive. But let him ask in faith." Remember, therefore, that you are bound to have the wisdom that shall win souls to Christ.

15. Being called of God to the work, make your calling your constant argument with God for all that you need for the accomplishment of the work.

16. Be diligent and laborious, "in season and out of season."

17. Converse much with all classes of your hearers on the question of their salvation, that you may understand their opinions, errors, and wants. Ascertain their prejudices, ignorance, temper, habits, and whatever you need to know to adapt your instruction to their necessities.

18. See that your own habits are in all respects correct; that you are temperate in all things—free from the stain or smell of tobacco, alcohol, drugs, or anything of which you have reason to be ashamed, and which may stumble others.

19. Be not "light-minded," but "set the Lord always before you."

20. Bridle your tongue, and be not given to idle and unprofitable conversation.

21. Always let your people see that you are in solemn earnest with them, both in the pulpit and out of it; and let not your daily intercourse with them nullify your serious teaching on the Sabbath.

22. Resolve to "know nothing" among your people "save Jesus Christ and Him crucified"; and let them understand that, as an ambassador of Christ, your business with them relates wholly to the salvation of their souls.

23. Be sure to teach them as well by example as by precept. Practise yourself what you preach.

24. Be especially guarded in your intercourse with women, to raise no thought or suspicion of the least impurity in yourself.

25. Guard your weak points. If naturally tending to gaiety and trifling, watch against occasions of failure in this direction.

26. If naturally sombre and unsocial, guard against moroseness and unsociability.

27. Avoid all affectation and sham in all things. Be what you profess to be, and you will have no temptation to "make believe."

28. Let simplicity, sincerity, and Christian propriety stamp your whole life.

29. Spend much time every day and night in prayer and direct communion with God. This will make you a power for salvation. No amount of learning and study can compensate for the loss of this communion. If you fail to maintain communion with God, you are "weak as another man."

30. Beware of the error that there are no means of regeneration, and, consequently, no connection of means and ends in the regeneration of souls.

31. Understand that regeneration is a moral, and therefore a voluntary change.

32. Understand that the gospel is adapted to change the hearts of men, and in a wise presentation of it you may expect the efficient co-operation of the Holy Spirit.

33. In the selection and treatment of your texts, always secure the direct teaching of the Holy Spirit.

34. Let all your sermons be heart and not merely head sermons.

35. Preach from experience, and not from hearsay, or mere reading and study.

36. Always present the subject which the Holy Spirit lays upon your heart for the occasion. Seize the points presented by the Holy Spirit to your own mind, and present them with the greatest possible directness to your congregation.

37. Be full of prayer whenever you attempt to preach, and go from your closet to your pulpit with the inward groanings of the Spirit pressing for utterance at your lips.

38. Get your mind fully imbued with your subject, so that it will press for utterance; then open your mouth, and let it forth like a torrent.

39. See that "the fear of man that bringeth a snare" is not upon you. Let your people understand that you fear God too much to be afraid of them.

40. Never let the question of your popularity with your people influence your preaching.

41. Never let the question of salary deter you from "declaring the whole counsel of God, whether men will hear or forbear."

42. Do not temporize, lest you lose the confidence of your people, and thus fail to save them. They cannot thoroughly respect you, as an ambassador of Christ, if they see that you dare not do your duty.

43. Be sure to "commend yourself to every man's conscience in the sight of God."

44. Be "not a lover of filthy lucre."

45. Avoid every appearance of vanity.

46. Compel your people to respect your sincerity and your spiritual wisdom.

47. Let them not for one moment suppose that you can be influenced in your preaching by any considerations of salary, more or less, or none at all.

48. Do not make the impression that you are fond of good dinners, and like to be invited out to dine; for this will be a snare to you, and a stumbling-block to them.

49. Keep your body under, lest after having preached to others, yourself should be a castaway.

50. "Watch for souls as one who must give an account to God."

51. Be a diligent student, and thoroughly instruct your people in all that is essential to their salvation.

52. Never flatter the rich.

53. Be especially attentive to the wants and instruction of the poor.

54. Suffer not yourself to be bribed into a compromise with sin by donation parties.

55. Suffer not yourself to be publicly treated as a mendicant, or you will come to be despised by a large class of your hearers.

56. Repel every attempt to close your mouth against whatever is extravagant, wrong, or injurious amongst your people.

57. Maintain your pastoral integrity and independence, lest you sear your conscience, quench the Holy Spirit, forfeit the confidence of your people, and lose the favour of God.

58. Be an example to the flock, and let your life illustrate your teaching. Remember that your actions and spirit will teach even more impressively than your sermons.

59. If you preach that men should offer to God and their neighbour a love service, see that you do this yourself, and avoid all that tends to the belief that you are working for pay.

60. Give to your people a love service, and encourage them to render to you, not a money equivalent for your labour, but a love reward that will refresh both you and them.

61. Repel every proposal to get money for you or for Church purposes that will naturally disgust and excite the contempt of worldly but thoughtful men.

62. Resist the introduction of tea-parties, amusing lectures, and dissipating sociables, especially at those seasons most favourable for united efforts to convert souls to Christ. Be sure the devil will try to head you off in this direction. When you are praying and planning for a revival of God's work, some of your worldly Church members will invite you to a party. Go not, or you are in for a circle of them, that will defeat your prayers.

63. Do not be deceived. Your spiritual power with your people will never be increased by accepting such invitations at such times. If it is a good time to have parties, because the people have leisure, it is also a good time for religious meetings, and your influence should be used to draw the people to the house of God.

64. See that you personally know and daily live upon Christ.

CHAPTER 9

INNOCENT AMUSEMENTS

We hear much said, and read much, in these days, of indulging in innocent amusements. I heard a minister, some time since, in addressing a large company of young people, say that he had spent much time in devising innocent amusements for the young. Within a few years I have read several sermons and numerous articles pleading for more amusements than have been customary with religious people. With your consent, I wish to suggest a few thoughts upon this subject—first, what are not, and, secondly, what are innocent amusements.

1. This is a question of morals.

2. All intelligent acts of a moral agent must be either right or wrong. Nothing is innocent in a moral agent that is not in accordance with the law and gospel of God.

3. The moral character of any and every act of a moral agent resides in the motive or the ultimate reason for

the act. This I take to be self-evident and universally admitted.

4. Now, what is the rule of judgment in this case? How are we to decide whether any given act of amusement is right or wrong, innocent or sinful?

I answer:

1. By the moral law, "Thou shalt love the Lord thy God with all thy heart," etc., "and thy neighbour as thyself." No intelligent act of a moral agent is innocent or right unless it proceeds from and is an expression of supreme love to God and equal love to man—in other words, unless it is benevolent.

2. The Gospel. This requires the same: "Therefore, whether ye eat or drink, or whatever ye do, do all to the glory of God." "Do all in the name of our Lord Jesus Christ."

3. Right reason affirms the same thing. Now, in the light of this rule, it is plain that it is not innocent to engage in amusements merely to gratify the desire for amusement. We may not innocently eat or drink to gratify the desire for food or drink. To eat or drink merely to gratify appetite is innocent enough in a mere animal, but in a moral agent it is a sin. A moral agent is bound to have a higher ultimate motive—to eat and drink—that he may be strong and healthy for the service of God. God has made eating and drinking pleasant to us; but this pleasure ought not to be our ultimate reason for eating and drinking. So amusements are pleasant, but this does not justify us in seeking amusements to gratify desire. Mere animals may do this innocently, because they are incapable of any higher motive. But moral agents are under a higher law, and are bound to have another and a higher aim than merely to gratify the desire for amusements. Therefore, no amusement is innocent which is engaged in for the pleasure of the amusement, any more than it would be innocent to eat and drink for the pleasure of it. Again, no amusement is innocent that is engaged in because we need amusements. We need food and drink; but this does not justify us in eating and drinking simply because we need it. The law of God does not say, "Seek whatever ye need because ye need it"; but, "Do all from love to God and man." A wicked man might eat and drink selfishly—that is, to make his body strong to execute his selfish plans—but this eating and drinking would be sin, notwithstanding he needed food and drink.

Nothing is innocent unless it proceeds from supreme love to God and equal love to man, unless the supreme and ultimate motive be to please and honour God. In other words, to be innocent, any amusement must be engaged in because it is believed to be at the time most pleasing to God, and is intended to be a service rendered to Him, as that which, upon the whole, will honour Him more than anything else that we can engage in for the time being. I take this to be self-evident. What then? It follows:

1. That none but benevolent amusements can be innocent. Fishing and shooting for amusement are not innocent. We may fish and hunt for the same reason that we are allowed to eat and drink—to supply nature with aliment, that we may be strong in the service of God. We may hunt to destroy noxious animals, for the glory of God and the interests of His kingdom. But fishing and hunting to gratify a passion for these sports is not innocent. Again, no amusement can be innocent that involves the squandering of precious time, that might be better employed to the glory of God and the good of man. Life is short. Time is precious. We have but one life to live. Much is to be done. The world is in darkness. A world of sinners are to be enlightened, and, if possible, saved. We are required to work while the day lasteth. Our commission and work require dispatch. No time is to be lost. If our hearts are right, our work is pleasant. If rightly performed it affords the highest enjoyment and is itself the highest amusement. No turning aside for amusement can be innocent that involves any unnecessary loss of time. No man that realizes the greatness of the work to be done, and loves to do it, can turn aside for any amusement involving an unnecessary waste of time. Again, no amusement can be innocent that involves an unnecessary expenditure of the Lord's money. All our time and all our money are the Lord's. We are the Lord's. We may innocently use both time and money to promote the Lord's interests and the highest interests of man, which are the Lord's interests. But we may not innocently use either for our own pleasure and gratification. Expensive journeys for our own pleasure and amusement, and not indulged in with a single eye to the glory of God, are not innocent amusements, but sinful. Again, in the light of the above rule of judgment, we see that no form of amusement is lawful for an unconverted sinner. Nothing in him is innocent. While he remains impenitent and unbelieving, does not love God and his neighbour according to God's command, there is for him no innocent employment or amusement; all is sin.

And right here I fear that many are acting under a great delusion. The loose manner in which this subject is viewed by many professors of religion, and even ministers, is surprising and alarming. Some time since, in a sermon, I remarked that there were no lawful employments or innocent amusements for sinners. An aged clergyman who was present said, after service, that it was ridiculous to hold that nothing was lawful or innocent in an impenitent sinner. I replied: "I thought you were orthodox. Do you not believe in the universal necessity of regeneration by the Holy Spirit?" He replied: "Yes." I added: "Do you believe that an unregenerate soul does anything acceptable to God? Before his heart is changed, does he ever act from a motive that God can accept, in anything whatever? Is he not totally depraved, in the sense that his heart is all wrong, and therefore his actions must be all wrong?" He appeared embarrassed, saw the point, and subsided.

Whatever is lawful in a moral agent or according to the law of God is right. If anyone, therefore, engages lawfully in any employment or in any amusement, he must do so from supreme love to God and equal love to his neighbour; and is, therefore, not an impenitent sinner, but a Christian. It is simply absurd and a contradiction to say that an impenitent soul does, or says, or omits anything with a right heart. If impenitent, his ultimate motive must necessarily be wrong; and, consequently, nothing in him is innocent, but all must be sinful. What, then, is an innocent amusement? It must be that and that only which not only might be but actually is engaged in with a single eye to God's glory and the interests of His kingdom. If this be not the ultimate and supreme design, it is not an innocent, but a sinful amusement. Now, right here is the delusion of many persons, I fear. When speaking of amusements, they say: "What harm is there in them?" In answering to themselves and others this question, they do not penetrate to the bottom of it. If on the surface they see nothing contrary to morality, they judge that the amusement is innocent. They fail to inquire into the supreme and ultimate motive in which the innocence or sinfulness of the act is found. But apart from the motive no course of action is either innocent or sinful, any more than the motions of a machine or the acts of a mere animal are innocent or sinful. No act or course of action should, therefore, be adjudged as either innocent or sinful without ascertaining the supreme motive of the person who acts.

To teach, either directly or by implication, that any amusement of an impenitent sinner or of a backslider is innocent is to teach a gross and ruinous heresy. Parents should remember this in regard to the amusements of their unconverted children. Sabbath school teachers and superintendents who are planning amusements for their Sabbath schools, preachers who spend their time in planning amusements for the young, who lead their flocks to picnics, in pleasure excursions, and justify various games, should certainly remember that, unless they are in a holy state of heart, and do all this from supreme love to God and a design in the highest degree to glorify God thereby, these ways of spending time are by no means innocent, but highly criminal, and those who teach people to walk in these ways are simply directing the channels in which their depravity shall run. For be it ever remembered that, unless these things are indulged in from supreme love to God and designed to glorify Him, unless they are, in fact, engaged in with a single eye to the glory of God, they are not innocent, but sinful amusements. I must say again, and, if possible, still more emphatically, that it is not enough that they might be engaged in as the best way, for the time being, to honour and please God; but they must be actually engaged in from supreme love to God, with the ultimate design to glorify Him. If such, then, is the true doctrine of innocent amusements, let no impenitent sinner and no backslidden Christian suppose for a moment that it is possible for him to engage in any innocent amusement. If it were true, as the aged minister to whom I have referred and many others seem to believe, that impenitent sinners or backsliders can and do engage in innocent amusements, the very engaging in such amusements, being lawfully right and innocent in them, would involve a change of heart in the unconverted, and a return to God in the backslider. For no amusement is lawful unless it be engaged in as a love-service rendered to God and with design to please and glorify Him. It must not only be a love service, but, in the judgment of the one who renders it, it must be the best service that, for the time being, he can render to God—a service that will be more pleasing to Him and more useful to His kingdom than any other that can be engaged in at the time. Let these facts be borne in mind when the question of engaging in amusements comes up for decision. And remember, the question in all such cases is not, "What harm is there in this proposed amusement?" but, "What good can it do?" "Is it the best way in which I can spend my time?" "Will it be more pleasing to God and more for the interest of His kingdom than anything else at present possible to me?" "If not, it is not an innocent amusement, and I cannot engage in it without sin." The question often arises: "Are we never to seek such amusements?" I answer: It is our privilege and our duty to live above a desire for such things. All that class of desires should be so subdued by living so much in the light of God, and having so deep a communion with Him as to have no relish for such amusements whatever. It certainly is the privilege of every child of God to walk so closely with Him, and maintain so divine a communion with Him, as not to feel the necessity of worldly excitements, sports, pastimes, and entertainments to make his enjoyment satisfactory. If a Christian avails himself of his privilege of communion with God, he will naturally and by an instinct of his new nature repel solicitations to go after worldly amusements. To him such pastimes will appear low, unsatisfactory, and even repulsive. If he is of a heavenly mind, as he ought to be, he will feel as if he could not afford to come down and seek enjoyment in worldly amusements. Surely, a Christian must be fallen from his first love, he must have turned back into the world, before he can feel the necessity or have the desire of seeking enjoyment in worldly sports and pastimes. A spiritual mind cannot seek enjoyment in worldly society. To such a mind that society is necessarily repulsive. Worldly society is insincere, hollow, and to a great extent a sham. What relish can a spiritual mind have for the gossip of a worldly party of pleasure? None whatever. To a mind in communion with God their worldly spirit and ways, conversation and folly is repulsive and painful, as it is so strongly suggestive of the downward tendency of their souls, and of the destiny that awaits them. I have had so marked an experience of both sides of this question that I think I cannot be mistaken. Probably but few persons enjoy worldly pleasure more intensely than I did before I was converted; but my conversion, and the spiritual baptism which immediately followed it, completely extinguished all desire for worldly sports and amusements. I was lifted at once into entirely another plane of life and another kind of enjoyment. From that hour to the present the mode of life, the pastimes, sports, amusements, and worldly ways that so much delighted me before have not only failed to interest me, but I have had a positive aversion to them. I have never felt them necessary to, or even compatible with, a truly rational enjoyment. I do not speak boastingly; but for the honour of Christ and His religion, I must say that my Christian life has been a happy one. I have had as much enjoyment as is probably best for men to have in this life, and never for an hour have I had the desire to turn back and seek enjoyment from anything the world can give. But some may ask: "Suppose we do not find sufficient enjoyment in religion, and really desire to go after worldly amusements. If we have the disposition, is it not as well to gratify it?" "Is there any more sin in seeking amusements than in entertaining a longing for them?" I reply that a longing for them should never be entertained. It is the privilege and therefore the duty of everyone to rise, through grace, above a hungering and thirsting for the fleshpots of Egypt, worldly pastimes and time-wasting amusements. The indulgence of such longings is not innocent. One should not ask whether the longing should be gratified, but whether it should not be displaced by a longing for the glory of God and His kingdom.

Professed Christians are bound to maintain a life consistent with their profession. For the honour of religion, they ought to deny worldly lusts; and not, by seeking to gratify them, give occasion to the world to scoff and say that Christians love the world as well as they do. If professors of religion are backslidden in heart, and entertain a longing for worldly sports and amusements, they are bound by every consideration of duty and decency to abstain from all outward manifestation of such inward lustings. Some have maintained that we should conform to the ways of the world somewhat—at least, enough to show that we can enjoy the world and religion too; and that we make religion appear repulsive to unconverted souls by turning our backs upon what they call their innocent amusements. But we should represent religion as it really is—as living above the world, as consisting in a heavenly mind, as that which affords an enjoyment so spiritual and heavenly as to render the low pursuits and joys of worldly men disagreeable and repulsive. It is a sad stumbling-block to the unconverted to see professed Christians seeking pleasure or happiness from this world. Such seeking is a misrepresentation of the religion of Jesus. It misleads, bewilders, and confounds the observing outsider. If he ever reads his Bible, he cannot but wonder that souls who are born of God and have communion with Him should have any relish for worldly ways and pleasures. The fact is that thoughtful unconverted men have little or no confidence in that class of professing Christians who seek enjoyment from this world. They may profess to have, and may loosely think of such as being liberal and good Christians. They may flatter them, and commend their religion as being the opposite of fanaticism and bigotry, and as being such a religion as they like to see; but there is no real sincerity in such professions on the part of the impenitent.

In my early Christian life I heard a Methodist bishop from the South report a case that made a deep impression on my mind. He said there was in his neighbourhood a slave holder, a gentleman of fortune, who was a gay and agreeable man, and gave himself much to various field sports and amusements. He used to associate much with his pastor, often invite him to dinner, and to accompany him in his sports and pleasure-seeking excursions of various kinds. The minister cheerfully complied with these requests, and a friendship grew up between the pastor and his parishioner that continued till the last sickness of this gay and wealthy man. When the wife of this worldling was apprised that her husband could live but a short time she was much alarmed for his soul, and tenderly inquired if she should not call in their minister to converse and pray with him. He feelingly replied: "No, my dear; he is not the man for me to see now. He was my companion, as you know, in worldly sports and pleasure-seeking; he loved good dinners and a jolly time. I then enjoyed his society and found him a pleasant companion. But I see now that I never had any real confidence in his piety, and have now no confidence in the efficacy of his prayers. I am now a dying man, and need the instruction and prayers of somebody that can prevail with God. We have been much together, but our pastor has never been in serious earnest with me about the salvation of my soul, and he is not the man to help me now." The wife was greatly affected, and said: "What shall I do, then?" He replied: "My coachman, Tom, is a pious man. I have confidence in his prayers. I have often overheard him pray, when about the barn or stables, and his prayers have always struck me as being quite sincere and earnest. I never heard any foolishness from him. He has always been honest and earnest as a Christian man. Call him." Tom was called, and came within the door, dropping his hat and looking tenderly and compassionately at his dying master. The dying man put forth his hand, saying: "Come here, Tom. Take my hand. Tom, can you pray for your dying master?" Tom poured out his soul in earnest prayer. I cannot remember the name of this bishop, it was so long ago; but the story I well remember as an illustration of the mistake into which many professors and some ministers fall, supposing that we recommend religion to the unconverted by mingling with them in their pleasures and their running after amusements. I have seen many illustrations of this mistake. Christians should live so far above the world as not to need or seek its pleasures, and thus recommend religion to the world as a source of the highest and purest happiness. The peaceful look, the joyful countenance, the spiritual serenity and cheerfulness of a living Christian recommend religion to the unconverted. Their satisfaction in God, their holy joy, their living above and shunning the ways and amusements of worldly minds, impress the unconverted with a sense of the necessity and desirableness of a Christian life.

But let no man think to gain a really Christian influence over another by manifesting a sympathy with his worldly aspirations.

Now, is this rule a yoke of bondage? I do not wonder that it has created in some minds not a little disturbance. The pleasure-loving and pleasure-seeking members of the Church regard the rule as impracticable, as a straitjacket, as a bondage. But to whom is it a straitjacket and a bondage? To whom is it impracticable? Surely it is not and cannot be to any who love God with all their heart and their neighbour as themselves. It certainly cannot be so regarded by a real Christian, for all real Christians love God supremely. Their own interests and their own pleasure are regarded as nothing as compared with the interests and good pleasure of God. They, therefore, cannot seek amusements unless they believe themselves called of God to do so. By a law of our nature we seek to please those whom we supremely love. Also, by a law of our nature, we find our highest happiness in pleasing those whom we supremely love; and we supremely please ourselves when we seek not at all to please ourselves, but to please the object of our supreme affection. Therefore, Christians find their highest enjoyment and their truest pleasure in pleasing God and in seeking the good of their fellow-men; and they enjoy this service all the more because enjoyment is not what they seek, but what they inevitably experience by a law of their nature.

This is a fact of Christian consciousness. The highest and purest of all amusements is found in doing the will of God. Mere worldly amusements are cold and insipid and not worthy of naming in comparison with the enjoyment we find in doing the will of God. To one who loves God supremely it is natural to seek amusements, and everything else that we do seek, with supreme reference to the glory of God. Why, then, should this rule be regarded as too strict, as placing the standard too high, and as being a strait-jacket and a bondage? How, then, are we to understand those who plead so much for worldly amusements?

From what I have heard and read upon this subject within the last few years, I have gathered that these pleaders for amusements have thought that there was more enjoyment to be gained from these amusements than from the service of God. They remind me of a sentence that I used to have as a copy when a school-boy: "All work and no play makes Jack a dull boy." They seem to assume that the service of God is work in the sense of being a task and a burden; that to labour and pray and preach to win souls to Christ, to commune with God and perform the duties of religion is so wearisome, not to say irksome, that we need a good many playdays; that the love of Christ is not satisfactory; that we must have frequent resort to worldly amusements to make life tolerable. Christ on one occasion said to His disciples: "Come aside and rest awhile." This is not wonderful when we consider that they were often so thronged as not to have time even to eat their ordinary meals. But it was not amusement that they sought; simply rest from their labours of love, in which labours they must have had the greatest enjoyment.

I often ask myself: "What can it mean that so many of our highly-fed and most popular preachers are pleading so much for amusements?" They seem to be leading the Church off in a direction in which she is the most in danger. It is no wonder that lay-men and women are easily led in that direction, for such teaching exactly accords with the innumerable temptations to worldliness which are presented to the Church on every side. The Bible is replete with instruction upon this subject, which is the direct opposite of these pleas for worldly amusements. These teachers plead for fun, hilarity, jesting, plays, and games, and such things as worldly minds love and enjoy; but the Bible exhorts to sobriety, heavenly-mindedness, unceasing prayer, and a close and perpetual walk with God. The Bible everywhere assumes that all real enjoyment is found in this course of life, that all true peace of mind is found in communion with God and in being given up to seek His glory as the constant and supreme end of life. It exhorts us to watchfulness, and informs us that for every idle word we must give account in the Day of Judgment. It nowhere informs us that fun and hilarity are the source of rational enjoyment; it nowhere encourages us to expect to maintain a close walk with God, to have peace of mind and joy in the Holy Ghost, if we gad about to seek amusements. And is not the teaching of the Bible on this subject in exact accordance with human experience? Do we need to have the pulpit turn advocate of worldly amusements? Is not human depravity strong enough in that direction, without being stimulated by the voice of the preacher? Has the Church worked so hard for God and souls, are Christians so overdone with their exhausting efforts to pull sinners out of the fire, that they are in danger of becoming insane with religious fervour and need that the pulpit and the press should join in urging them to turn aside and seek amusements and have a little fun?

What can it mean? Why, is it not true that nearly all our dangers are on this side? Is not human nature in its present state so strongly tending in these directions that we need to be on our guard, and constantly to exhort the Church not to be led away after amusements and fun, to the destruction of their souls? But to come back to the question: To whom is it a bondage, to be required to have a single eye to the good pleasure and glory of God in all that we do? Who finds it hard to do so? Christ says His yoke is easy and His burden is light. The requirement to do all for the glory of God is surely none other than the yoke of Christ. It is His expressed will. Who finds this a hard yoke and a heavy burden? It is not hard or heavy to a willing, loving mind.

Just the thing here required is natural and inevitable to everyone that truly loves God and is truly devoted to the Saviour. What is devotion to Jesus but a heart set upon rendering Him a loving obedience in all things? What is Christian liberty but the privilege of doing that which Christians most love to do—that is, in all things to fulfil the good pleasure of their blessed Lord? Turn aside from saving souls to seek amusements! As if there could be a higher and diviner pleasure than is found in labouring for the salvation of souls. It cannot be. There can be no higher enjoyment found in this world than is found in pulling souls out of the fire and bringing them to Christ. I am filled with amazement when I read and hear the appeals to the Church to seek more worldly amusements. Do we need, can we have any fuller and higher satisfaction than is found in a close, serious, loving walk with God and co-operation with Him in fitting souls for heaven?

All that I hear said to encourage the people of God in seeking amusements appears to me to proceed from a worldly, instead of a spiritual state of mind. Can it be possible that a soul in communion with God and, of course, yearning with compassion over dying men, struggling from day to day in agonizing prayer for their salvation, should entertain the thought of turning aside to seek amusement? Can a pastor in whose congregation are numbers of unsaved souls, and amongst whose membership are many worldly-minded professors of religion, turn aside and lead or accompany his Church in a backsliding movement to gain worldly pleasure? There are always enough in every Church who are easily led astray in that direction. But who are they that most readily fall in with such a movement? Who are ready to come to the front when a picnic, a pleasure excursion, a worldly party, or other pleasure-seeking movements are proposed? Are they, in fact, the class that always attend prayer-meetings, that are always in a revival state of mind? Do they belong to the class whose faces shine from day to day with the peace of God pervading their souls? Are they the Aarons and Hurs that stay up the hands of their pastor with continual and prevailing prayer? Are they spiritual members, whose conversation is in heaven and who mind not earthly things? Who does not know that it is the worldly members in the Church who are always ready for any movement in the direction of worldly pleasure or amusement, and that the truly spiritual, prayerful, heavenly-minded members are shy of all such movements? They are not led into them without urging, and weep in secret places when they see their pastor giving encouragement to that which is likely to be so great a stumbling-block to both the Church and to the world.

Pres. Finney, in forwarding his revision of the above tract for publication by the Willard Tract Repository, accompanied it with a note to Dr. Cullis, in which he said:

"The previous pages contain a condensation of three short articles that I published in the Independent. I recollect that the editor of the Advance, and one of the editors of the Independent, both of whom had published what I regard as very loose views, approving and recommending the worldly amusements of Christians, criticized those articles with an asperity that seemed to indicate that they were nettled by them. They so far perverted them as to assert that they taught asceticism, and the prohibition of rest, recreation, and all amusements. I regard the doctrine of this tract as strictly Biblical and true. But, to avoid all such unjust inferences and cavils, add the following lines.

"Let no one say that the doctrine of this tract prohibits all rest, recreation, and amusement whatever. It does not. It freely admits all rest, recreation, and amusement that is regarded, by the person who resorts to it, as a condition and means of securing health and vigour of body and mind with which to promote the cause of God. This tract only insists, as the Bible does, that 'whether we eat or drink,' rest, recreate, or amuse ourselves, all must be done as a service rendered to God. God must be our end. To please Him must be our aim in everything, or we sin."

CHAPTER 10

HOW TO OVERCOME SIN

In every period of my ministerial life I have found many professed Christians in a miserable state of bondage, either to the world, the flesh, or the Devil. But surely this is no Christian state, for the apostle has distinctly said: "Sin shall not have dominion over you, because ye are not under the law, but under grace." In all my Christian life I have been pained to find so many Christians living in the legal bondage described in the seventh Chapter of Romans—a life of sinning, and resolving to reform and falling again. And what is particularly saddening, and even agonizing, is that many ministers and leading Christians give perfectly false instruction upon the subject of how to overcome sin. The directions that are generally given on this subject, I am sorry to say, amount to about this: "Take your sins in detail, resolve to abstain from them, and fight against them, if need be with prayer and fasting, until you have overcome them. Set your will firmly against a relapse into sin, pray and struggle, and resolve that you will not fall, and persist in this until you form the habit of obedience and break up all your sinful habits." To be sure it is generally added: "In this conflict you must not depend upon your own strength, but pray for the help of God." In a word, much of the teaching, both of the pulpit and the press, really amounts to this: Sanctification is by works, and not by faith. I notice that Dr. Chalmers, in his lectures on Romans, expressly maintains that justification is by faith, but sanctification is by works. Some twenty-five years ago, I think, a prominent professor of theology in New England maintained in substance the same doctrine. In my early Christian life I was very nearly misled by one of President Edwards's resolutions, which was, in substance, that when he had fallen into any sin he would trace it back to its source, and then fight and pray against it with all his might until he subdued it. This, it will be perceived, is directing the attention to the overt act of sin, its source or occasions. Resolving and fighting against it fastens the attention on the sin and its source, and diverts it entirely from Christ.

Now it is important to say right here that all such efforts are worse than useless, and not infrequently result in delusion. First, it is losing sight of what really constitutes sin; and, secondly, of the only practicable way to avoid it. In this way the outward act or habit may be overcome and avoided, while that which really constitutes the sin is left untouched. Sin is not external, but internal. It is not a muscular act, it is not the volition that causes muscular action, it is not an involuntary feeling or desire; it must be a voluntary act or state of mind. Sin is nothing else than that voluntary, ultimate preference or state of committal to self-pleasing out of which the volitions, the outward actions, purposes, intentions, and all the things that are commonly called sin proceed. Now, what is resolved against in this religion of resolutions and efforts to suppress sinful and form holy habits? "Love is the fulfilling of the law." But do we produce love by resolution? Do we eradicate selfishness by resolution? No, indeed. We may suppress this or that expression or manifestation of selfishness by resolving not to do this or that, and praying and struggling against it. We may resolve upon an outward obedience, and work ourselves up to the letter of an obedience to God's commandments. But to eradicate selfishness from the breast by resolution is an absurdity. So the effort to obey the commandments of God in spirit—in other words, to attempt to love as the law of God requires by force of resolution—is an absurdity. There are many who maintain that sin consists in the desires. Be it so. Do we control our desires by force of resolution? We may abstain from the gratification of a particular desire by the force of resolution. We may go further, and abstain from the gratification of desire generally in the outward life. But this is not to secure the love of God, which constitutes obedience. Should we become anchorites, immure ourselves in a cell, and crucify all our desires and appetites, so far as their indulgence is concerned, we have only avoided certain forms of sin; but the root that really constitutes sin is not touched. Our resolution has not secured love, which is the only real obedience to God. All our battling with sin in the outward life, by the force of resolution, only ends in making us whited sepulchres. All our battling with desire by the force of resolution is of no avail; for in all this, however successful the effort to suppress sin may be, in the outward life or in the inward desire, it will only end in delusion, for by force of resolution we cannot love.

All such efforts to overcome sin are utterly futile, and as unscriptural as they are futile. The Bible expressly teaches us that sin is overcome by faith in Christ. "He is made unto us wisdom, righteousness, sanctification, and redemption." "He is the way, the truth, and the life." Christians are said to "purify their hearts by faith" (Acts 15:9). And in Acts 26:18 it is affirmed that the saints are sanctified by faith in Christ. In Romans 9:31,32 it is affirmed that the Jews attained not to righteousness "because they sought it not by faith, but as it were by the works of the law." The doctrine of the Bible is that Christ saves His people from sin through faith; that Christ's Spirit is received by faith to dwell in the heart. It is faith that works by love. Love is wrought and sustained by faith. By faith Christians "overcome the world, the flesh, and the Devil." It is by faith that they "quench the fiery darts of the wicked." It is by faith that they "put on the Lord Jesus Christ and put off the old man, with his deeds." It is by faith that we fight "the good fight," and not by resolution. It is by faith that we "stand," by resolution we fall.

This is the victory that overcometh the world, even our faith. It is by faith that the flesh is kept under and carnal desires subdued. The fact is that it is simply by faith that we receive the Spirit of Christ to work in us to will and to do, according to His good pleasure. He sheds abroad His own love in our hearts, and thereby enkindles ours. Every victory over sin is by faith in Christ; and whenever the mind is diverted from Christ, by resolving and fighting against sin, whether we are aware of it or not, we are acting in our own strength, rejecting the help of Christ, and are under a specious delusion. Nothing but the life and energy of the Spirit of Christ within us can save us from sin, and trust is the uniform and universal condition of the working of this saving energy within us. How long shall this fact be at least practically overlooked by the teachers of religion? How deeply rooted in the heart of man is self-righteousness and self-dependence? So deeply that one of the hardest lessons for the human heart to learn is to renounce self-dependence and trust wholly in Christ. When we open the door by implicit trust He enters in and takes up His abode with us and in us. By shedding abroad His love He quickens our whole souls into sympathy with Himself, and in this way, and in this way alone, He purifies our hearts through faith. He sustains our will in the attitude of devotion. He quickens and regulates our affections, desires, appetites and passions, and becomes our sanctification. Very much of the teaching that we hear in prayer and conference meetings, from the pulpit and the press, is so misleading as to render the hearing or reading of such instruction almost too painful to be endured. Such instruction is calculated to beget delusion, discouragement, and a practical rejection of Christ as He is presented in the Gospel.

Alas! for the blindness that "leads to bewilder" the soul that is longing after deliverance from the power of sin. I have sometimes listened to legal teaching upon this subject until I felt as if I should scream. It is astonishing sometimes to hear Christian men object to the teaching which I have here inculcated that it leaves us in a passive state, to be saved without our own activity. What darkness is involved in this objection! The Bible teaches that by trusting in Christ we receive an inward influence that stimulates and directs our activity; that by faith we receive His purifying influence into the very centre of our being; that through and by His truth revealed directly to the soul He quickens our whole inward being into the attitude of a loving obedience; and this is the way, and the only practicable way, to overcome sin. But someone may say: "Does not the Apostle exhort as follows: 'Work out your own salvation with fear and trembling; for it is God which worketh in you, both to will and to do of His good pleasure'? And is not this an exhortation to do what in this article you condemn?" By no means. In the 12th verse of the second Chapter of Philippians Paul says: "Wherefore, my beloved, as ye have always obeyed, not as in my presence only, but now much more in my absence, work out your own salvation with fear and trembling, for it is God that worketh in you, both to will and to do of His good pleasure." There is no exhortation to work by force of resolution, but through and by the inworking of God. Paul had taught them, while he was present with them; but now, in his absence, he exhorts them to work out their own salvation, not by resolution but by the inward operation of God. This is precisely the doctrine of this tract. Paul had too often taught the Church that Christ in the heart is our sanctification, and that this influence is to be received by faith, to be guilty in this passage of teaching that our sanctification is to be wrought out by resolution and efforts to suppress sinful and form holy habits. This passage of Scripture happily recognizes both the divine and human agency in the work of sanctification. God works in us to will and to do; and we, accepting by faith His inworking, will and do according to His good pleasure. Faith itself is an active and not a passive state. A passive holiness is impossible and absurd. Let no one say that when we exhort people to trust wholly in Christ we teach that anyone should be or can be passive in receiving and co-operating with the divine influence within. This influence is moral, and not physical. It is persuasion, and not force. It influences the free will, and consequently does this by truth, and not by force. Oh! that it could be understood that the whole of spiritual life that is in any man is received direct from the Spirit of Christ by faith, as the branch receives its life from the vine. Away with this religion of resolutions! It is a snare of death. Away with this effort to make the life holy while the heart has not in it the love of God. Oh! that men would learn to look directly at Christ through the Gospel and so close in with Him by an act of loving trust as to involve a universal sympathy with His state of mind. This, and this alone, is sanctification.

CHAPTER II

THE DECAY OF CONSCIENCE

I believe it is a fact generally admitted that there is much less conscience manifested by men and women in nearly all the walks of life than there was forty years ago. There is justly much complaint of this, and there seems to be but little prospect of reformation. The rings and frauds and villainies in high and low places, among all ranks of men, are most alarming, and one is almost compelled to ask: "Can nobody be safely trusted?" Now, what is the cause of this degeneracy? Doubtless there are many causes that contribute more or less directly to it, but I am persuaded that the fault is more in the ministry and public press than in any and all things else. It has been fashionable now for many years to ridicule and decry Puritanism. Ministers have ceased, in a great measure, to probe the consciences of men with the spiritual law of God. So far as my knowledge extends, there has been a great letting down and ignoring the searching claims of God's law, as revealed in His Word. This law is the only standard of true morality. "By the law is the knowledge of sin." The law is the quickener of the human conscience. Just in proportion as the spirituality of the law of God is kept out of view will there be manifest a decay of conscience. This must be the inevitable result. Let ministers ridicule Puritanism, attempt to preach the Gospel without thoroughly probing the conscience with the divine law, and this must result in, at least, a partial paralysis of the moral sense. The error that lies at the foundation of this decay of individual and public conscience originates, no doubt, in the pulpit. The proper guardians of the public conscience have, I fear, very much neglected to expound and insist upon obedience to the moral law. It is plain that some of our most popular preachers are phrenologists. Phrenology has no organ of free will. Hence, it has no moral agency, no moral law and moral obligation in any proper sense of these terms. A consistent phrenologist can have no proper ideas of moral obligation, of moral guilt, blameworthiness, and retribution. Some years since a brother of one of our most popular preachers heard me preach on the text "Be ye reconciled to God." I went on to show, among other things, that being reconciled to God implied being reconciled to the execution of His law. He called on me the next morning, and among other things said that neither himself nor two of his brothers, whom he named, all preachers, had naturally any conscience. "We have," said he, "no such ideas in our minds of sin, guilt, justice and retribution as you and Father have." "We cannot preach as you do on those subjects." He continued: "I am striving to cultivate a conscience, and I think I begin to understand what it is. But, naturally, neither I nor the two brothers I have named have any conscience." Now, these three ministers have repeatedly appeared in their writings before the public. I have read much that they have written, and not infrequently the sermons of one of them, and have been struck with the manifest want of conscience in his sermons and writings. He is a phrenologist, and, hence, he has in his theological views no free will, no moral agency, and nothing that is really a logical result of free will and moral agency. He can ridicule Puritanism and the great doctrines of the Orthodox faith; and, indeed, his whole teaching, so far as it has fallen under my eye, most lamentably shows the want of moral discrimination. I should judge from his writings that the true ideas of moral depravity, guilt, and ill-desert, in the true acceptation of those terms, have no place in his mind. Indeed, as a consistent phrenologist, such ideas have no right in his mind. They are necessarily excluded by his philosophy. I do not know how extensively phrenology has poisoned the minds of ministers of different denominations, but I have observed with pain that many ministers who write for the public press fail to reach the consciences of men. They fail to go to the bottom of the matter and insist upon obedience to the moral law as alone acceptable to God. They seem to me to "make void the law through faith." They seem to hold up a different standard from that which is inculcated in Christ's Sermon on the Mount, which was Christ's exposition of the moral law. Christ expressly taught in that sermon that there was no salvation without conformity to the rule of life laid down in that sermon. True faith in Christ will always and inevitably beget a holy life. But I fear it has become fashionable to preach what amounts to an antinomian gospel. The rule of life promulgated in the Gospel is precisely that of the moral law. These four things are expressly affirmed of true faith—of the faith of the Gospel:

1. "It establishes the law."
2. "It works by love."
3. "It purifies the heart."
4. "It overcomes the world."

These are but different forms of affirming that true faith does, as a matter of fact, produce a holy life. If it did not, it would "make void the law." The true Gospel is not preached where obedience to the moral law as the only rule of life is not insisted upon. Wherever there is a failure to do this in the instructions of any pulpit, it will inevitably be seen that the hearers of such a mutilated Gospel will have very little conscience. We need more Boanerges or sons of thunder in the pulpit. We need men that will flash forth the law of God like livid lightning and arouse the consciences of men. We need more Puritanism in the pulpit. To be sure, some of the Puritans were extremists. But still under their teaching there was a very different state of the individual and public conscience from what exists in these days. Those old, stern, grand vindicators of the government of God would have thundered and lightened till they had almost demolished their pulpits, if any such immoralities had shown themselves under their instructions as are common in these days. In a great measure the periodical press takes its tone from the pulpit. The universal literature of the present day shows conclusively that the moral sense of the people needs toning up, and some of our most fascinating preachers have become the favourites of infidels, sceptics of every grade, Universalists, and the most abandoned characters. And has the offence of the Cross ceased, or is the Cross kept out of view? Has the holy law of God, with its stringent precept and its awful penalty, become popular with unconverted men and women? Or is it ignored in the pulpit, and the preacher praised for that neglect of duty for which he should be despised? I believe the only possible way to arrest this downward tendency in private and public morals is the holding up from the pulpits in this land, with unsparing faithfulness, the whole Gospel of God, including as the only rule of life the perfect and holy law of God.

The holding up of this law will reveal the moral depravity of the heart, and the holding forth of the cleansing blood of Christ will cleanse the heart from sin. My beloved brethren in the ministry, is there not a great want in the public inculcations of the pulpit upon this subject? We are set for the defence of the blessed Gospel and for the vindication of God's holy law. I pray you let us probe the consciences of our hearers, let us thunder forth the law and Gospel of God until our voices reach the capital of this nation, through our representatives in Congress. It is now very common for the secular papers even to publish extracts of sermons. Let us give the reporters of the press such work to do as will make their ears and the ears of their readers tingle. Let our railroad rings, our stock gamblers, our officials of every grade, hear from its pulpit, if they come within the sound, such wholesome Puritanical preaching as will arouse them to better thoughts and a better life. Away with this milk-and-water preaching of a love of Christ that has no holiness or moral discrimination in it. Away with preaching a love of God that is not angry with sinners every day. Away with preaching a Christ not crucified for sin.

Christ crucified for the sins of the world is the Christ that the people need. Let us rid ourselves of the just imputation of neglecting to preach the law of God until the consciences of men are asleep. Such a collapse of conscience in this land could never have existed if the Puritan element in our preaching had not in great measure fallen out.

Some years ago I was preaching in a congregation whose pastor had died some months before. He seemed to have been almost universally popular with his Church and the community. His Church seemed to have nearly idolized him. Everybody was speaking in his praise and holding him up as an example; and yet both the Church and the community clearly demonstrated that they had had an unfaithful minister, a man who loved and sought the applause of his people. I heard so much of his inculcation and saw so much of the legitimate fruits of his teachings that I felt constrained to tell the people from the pulpit that they had had an unfaithful minister; that such fruits as were apparent on every side, both within and without the Church, could never have resulted from a faithful presentation of the Gospel. This assertion would, doubtless, have greatly shocked them had it been made under other circumstances; but, as the way had been prepared, they did not seem disposed to gainsay it.

Brethren, our preaching will bear its legitimate fruits. If immorality prevails in the land, the fault is ours in a great degree. If there is a decay of conscience, the pulpit is responsible for it. If the public press lacks moral discrimination, the pulpit is responsible for it. If the Church is degenerate and worldly, the pulpit is responsible for it. If the world loses its interest in religion, the pulpit is responsible for it. If Satan rules in our halls of legislation, the pulpit is responsible for it. If our politics become so corrupt that the very foundations of our government are ready to fall away, the pulpit is responsible for it. Let us not ignore this fact, my dear brethren; but let us lay it to heart, and be thoroughly awake to our responsibility in respect to the morals of this nation.

CHAPTER 12

THE PSYCHOLOGY OF FAITH

I have heretofore endeavored to show that sanctification is wrought in the soul by the Spirit of Christ, through faith, with and not without the concurrence of our own activity. I now wish to call attention to the nature or psychology of faith as a mental act or state. My theological teacher held that faith was an intellectual act or state, a conviction or firm persuasion that the doctrines of the Bible are true. So far as I can recollect, this was the view of faith which I heard everywhere advanced.

When it was objected to this that the intellectual convictions and states are involuntary, and could not be produced by any effort of the will, and, consequently, we cannot be under obligations to exercise faith; and, furthermore, that faith, being an intellectual act or state, could not be virtue, it was replied that we control the attention of the mind by an effort of the will, and that our responsibility lay in searching for that degree of evidence that would convince the intellect; that unbelief was a sin, because it was the inevitable result of a failure to search for and accept the evidence of the truths of revelation; that faith was virtue, because it involved the consent and effort of the will to search out the truth.

I have met with this erroneous notion of the nature of Christian faith almost everywhere since I was first licensed to preach. Especially in my early ministry I found that great stress was laid on believing "the articles of faith," and it was held that faith consisted in believing with an unwavering conviction the doctrines about Christ. Hence, an acceptance of the doctrines, the doctrines, the DOCTRINES of the Gospel was very much insisted upon as constituting faith. These doctrines I had been brought to accept intellectually and firmly before I was converted. And, when told to believe, I replied that I did believe, and no argument or assertion could convince me that I did not believe the Gospel. And up to the very moment of my conversion I was not and could not be convinced of my error.

At the moment of my conversion, or when I first exercised faith, I saw my ruinous error. I found that faith consisted not in an intellectual conviction that the things affirmed in the Bible about Christ are true, but in the heart's trust in the person of Christ. I learned that God's testimony concerning Christ was designed to lead me to trust Christ, to confide in His person as my Saviour; that to stop short in merely believing about Christ was a fatal mistake and inevitably left me in my sins. It was as if I were sick almost unto death, and someone should recommend to me a physician who was surely able and willing to save my life, and I should listen to the testimony concerning him until fully convinced that he was both able and willing to save my life, and then should be told to believe in him, and my life was secure. Now, if I understood this to mean nothing more than to credit the testimony with the firmest conviction, I should reply: "I do believe in him with an undoubting faith. I believe every word you have told me regarding him." If I stopped here I should, of course, lose my life. In addition to this firm intellectual conviction of his willingness and ability, it were essential to apply to him, to come to him, to trust his person, to accept his treatment. When I had intellectually accepted the testimony concerning him with an unwavering belief, the next and the indispensable thing would be a voluntary act of trust or confidence in his person, a committal of my life to him, and his sovereign treatment in the cure of my disease.

Now this illustrates the true nature or psychology of faith as it actually exists in consciousness. It does not consist in any degree of intellectual knowledge, or acceptance of the doctrines of the Bible. The firmest possible persuasion that every word said in the Bible respecting God and Christ is true, is not faith. These truths and doctrines reveal God in Christ only so far as they point to God in Christ, and teach the soul how to find Him by an act of trust in His person.

When we firmly trust in His person, and commit our souls to Him by an unwavering act of confidence in Him for all that He is affirmed to be to us in the Bible, this is faith. We trust Him upon the testimony of God. We trust Him for what the doctrines and facts of the Bible declare Him to be to us. This act of trust unites our spirit to Him in a union so close that we directly receive from Him a current of eternal life. Faith, in consciousness, seems to complete the divine galvanic circle, and the life of God is instantly imparted to our souls. God's life, and light, and love, and peace, and joy seem to flow to us as naturally and spontaneously as the galvanic current from the battery. We then for the first time understand what Christ meant by our being united to Him by faith, as the branch is united to the vine. Christ is then and thus revealed to us as God. We are conscious of direct communion with Him, and know Him as we know ourselves, by His direct activity within us. We then know directly, in consciousness, that He is our life, and that we receive from Him, moment by moment, as it were, an impartation of eternal life.

With some the mind is comparatively dark, and the faith, therefore, comparatively weak in its first exercise. They may hold a great breadth of opinion, and yet intellectually believe but little with a realizing conviction. Hence, their trust in Him will be as narrow as their realizing convictions. When faith is weak, the current of the divine life will flow so mildly that we are scarcely conscious of it. But when faith is strong and all-embracing, it lets a current of the divine life of love into our souls so strong that it seems to permeate both soul and body. We then know in consciousness what it is to have Christ's Spirit within us as a power to save us from sin and stay up our feet in the path of loving obedience.

From personal conversation with hundreds—and I may say thousands—of Christian people, I have been struck with the application of Christ's words, as recorded in the fifth Chapter of John, to their experience. Christ said to the Jews: "Ye do search the Scriptures [for so it should be rendered][1]; for in them ye think ye have eternal life, and they are they which testify of Me; and ye will not come unto Me that ye might have life." They stopped short in the Scriptures. They satisfied themselves with ascertaining what the Scriptures said about Christ, but did not avail themselves of the light thus received to come to Him by an act of loving trust in His person. I fear it is true in these days, as it has been in the days that are past, that multitudes stop short in the facts and doctrines of the Gospel, and do not by any act of trust in His person come to Him, concerning whom all this testimony is given. Thus the Bible is misunderstood and abused.

Many, understanding the "Confession of Faith" as summarizing the doctrines of the Bible, very much neglect the Bible and rest in a belief of the articles of faith. Others, more cautious and more in earnest, search the Scriptures to see what they say about Christ, but stop short and rest in the formation of correct theological opinions; while others, and they are the only saved class, love the Scriptures intensely because they testify of Jesus. They search and devour the Scriptures because they tell them who Jesus is and what they may trust Him for. They do not stop short and rest in this testimony; but by an act of loving trust go directly to Him, to His person, thus joining their souls to Him in a union that receives from Him, by a direct divine communication, the things for which they are led to trust Him. This is certainly Christian experience. This is receiving from Christ the eternal life which God has given us in Him. This is saving faith.

There are many degrees in the strength of faith, from that of which we are hardly conscious to that which lets such a flood of eternal life into the soul as to quite overcome the strength of the body. In the strongest exercise of faith the nerves of the body seem to give way for the time being under the overwhelming exercise of the mind. This great strength of mental exercise is perhaps not very common. We can endure but little of God's light and love in our souls and yet remain in the body. I have sometimes felt that a little clearer vision would draw my soul entirely away from the body, and I have met with many Christian people to whom these strong gales of spiritual influence were familiar. But my object in writing thus is to illustrate the nature or psychology and results of saving faith.

The contemplation of the attitude and experience of numbers of professed Christians in regard to Christ is truly lamentable and wonderful, considering that the Bible is in their hands. Many of them appear to have stopped short in theological opinions more or less firmly held. This they understand to be faith. Others are more in earnest, and stop not short of a more or less realizing conviction of the truths of the Bible concerning Christ. Others have strong impressions of the obligations of the law, which move them to set about an earnest life of works which leads them into bondage. They pray from a sense of duty; they are dutiful, but not loving, not confiding. They have no peace and no rest, except in cases where they persuade themselves that they have done their duty. They are in a restless agonizing state.

> Reason they hear, her counsels weigh,
>   And all her words approve,
>   And yet they find it hard to obey,
>   And harder still to love.

They read and perhaps search the Scriptures to learn their duty and to learn about Christ. They intellectually believe all that they understand the Scriptures to say about Him; but when Christ is thus commended to their confidence, they do not by an act of personal loving trust in and committal to Him so join their souls to Him as to receive from Him the influx of His life, and light and love. They do not by a simple act of personal loving trust in His person receive the current of His divine life and power into their own souls. They do not thus take hold of His strength and interlock their being with His. In other words, they do not truly believe. Hence, they are not saved. Oh! what a mistake is this. I fear it is very common. Nay, it seems to be certain that it is appallingly common, else how can the state of the Church be accounted for? Is that which we see in the great mass of professors of religion all that Christ does for and in His people, when they truly believe? No, no! There is a great error here. The psychology of faith is mistaken, and an intellectual conviction of the truth of the Gospel is supposed to be faith. And some whose opinions seem to be right in regard to the nature of faith rest in their philosophy and fall short of exercising faith.

Let no one suppose that I under-estimate the value of the facts and doctrines of the Gospel. I regard a knowledge and belief of them as of fundamental importance. I have no sympathy with those who undervalue them and treat doctrinal discussion and preaching as of minor importance, nor can I assent to the teaching of those who would have us preach Christ and not the doctrines respecting Him. It is the facts and doctrines of the Bible that teach us who Christ is, why He is to be trusted, and for what. How can we preach Christ without preaching about Him? And how can we trust Him without being informed why and for what we are to trust Him?

The error to which I call attention does not consist in laying too much stress in teaching and believing the facts and doctrines of the Gospel; but it consists in stopping short of trusting the personal Christ for what those facts and doctrines teach us to trust Him, and satisfying ourselves with believing the testimony concerning Him, thus resting in the belief of what God has said about Him, instead of committing our souls to Him by an act of loving trust.

The testimony of God respecting Him is designed to secure our confidence in Him. If it fails to secure the uniting of our souls to Him by an act and state of implicit trust in Him—such an act of trust as unites us to Him as the branch is united to the vine—we have heard the Gospel in vain. We are not saved. We have failed to receive from Him that impartation of eternal life which can be conveyed to us through no other channel than that of implicit trust.

CHAPTER 13

THE PSYCHOLOGY OF RIGHTEOUSNESS

During my Christian life I have been asked a great many times, in substance, by thoughtful and anxious souls: "What is the mental act or acts and states that God requires of me?" I have found it profitable, and even indispensable, with the commands of God before me, to question consciousness for a satisfactory answer to this question. I have satisfied myself, and, by the help of God, I trust I have aided many others to their satisfaction. Be it understood, then, that by the psychology of righteousness I mean to designate the mental act and state that constitutes righteousness. I will endeavour to develop this in the following order by showing:

I. What righteousness is not.
II. What it is.
III. How we know what righteousness is.
IV. How a sinner may attain to righteousness.
I. [What Righteousness Is Not.]

1. Righteousness does not consist in the outward life or in any physical or bodily act whatever. All of these acts belong to the category of cause and effect. They are necessitated by an act of the will and have in themselves no moral character whatever.

2. Righteousness does not consist in volition. Volition is an act of will, but necessitated by choice. It is an executive act, and is the product of a purpose or choice. It is designed as a means to an end. It is put forth to control either the attention of the intellect, the states of the sensibility, or the movements of the outward life by force. Volition is both an effect and a cause. It is the effect of a choice, purpose, intention. It is the cause of the outward life and of many of the changes both of the intellect and sensibility. Volition is a doing. Whatever we do we accomplish by the exercise of volition. Volition is not, in the highest sense, a free act, because it is an effect. It is itself caused. Hence, it has no moral character in itself, and moral quality can be predicated of it only as it partakes of the character of its primary cause.

3. Righteousness does not consist in proximate or subordinate choice. I choose an ultimate, supreme end, for its own sake. This choice is not executive. It is not put forth to secure the end, but is simply the choice of an object for its own sake. This is ultimate choice. I purpose, or choose, if possible, to secure this end. This is proximate or subordinate choice. Strictly speaking, this choice belongs also to the category of cause and effect. It results by necessity from the ultimate choice. In the strictest sense, it is not a free act, since it is itself caused. Hence, it has no moral character in itself, but, like volition, derives whatever moral quality it has from its primary cause, or the ultimate choice.

4. Righteousness does not consist in any of the states or activities of the sensibility. By the sensibility I mean that department of the mind that feels, desires, suffers, enjoys. All the states of the sensibility are involuntary, and belong to the category of cause and effect. The will cannot control them directly, nor always indirectly. This we know by consciousness. Since they are caused, and not free, they can have no moral character in themselves, and, like thoughts, volitions, subordinate choices, have no moral quality except that which is derived from their primary cause.

II. What Righteousness Is.

Righteousness is moral rightness, moral rectitude, moral uprightness, conformity to moral law. But what mental act or state is that which the moral law or law of God requires? Law is a rule of action. Moral law requires action—mental action, responsible action, therefore free action. But what particular form of action does moral law require?

Free action is a certain form of action of the will, and this is the only strictly free action. Christ has taught us by His own teaching and through His inspired Prophets and Apostles that the moral law requires love, and that this is the sum of its requirements. But what is this love? It cannot be the involuntary love of the sensibility, either in the form of emotion or affection; for these states of the mind, belonging as they do to the category of cause and effect, cannot be the form of love demanded by the law of God. The moral law is the law of God's activity, the rule in conformity to which He always acts. We are created in God's image. His rule of life is therefore ours. The moral law requires of Him the same kind of love that it does of us. If God had no law or rule of action, He could have no moral character. As our Creator and Lawgiver, He requires of us the same love in kind and the same perfection in degree that He Himself exercises. "God is love." He loves with all the strength of His infinite nature. He requires us to love with all the strength of our finite nature. This is being perfect as God is perfect. But what is this love of God as a mental exercise? It must be benevolence or good will. God is a moral agent. The good of universal being is infinitely valuable in itself. God must infinitely well appreciate this. He must see and feel the moral propriety of choosing this for its own sake. He has chosen it from eternity. By His executive volitions He is endeavouring to realize it. The law which He has promulgated to govern our activity requires us to sympathize with His choice, His benevolence, to choose the same end that He does, for the same reason—that is, for its own sake. God's infinite choice of the good of universal being is righteousness in Him, because it is the choice of the intrinsically and infinitely valuable for its own sake. It is a choice in conformity with His nature and the relations He has constituted. It must be a choice in conformity with His infinitely clear conscience or moral sense. Righteousness in God, then, is conformity to the laws of universal love or good will. It must be an ultimate, supreme, immanent, efficient preference or choice of the highest good of universal being, including His own. It must be ultimate, in that this good of being is chosen for its own sake. It must be supreme, because it is preferred to everything else. It must be immanent, because it is innate and at the very foundation of all His moral activity. It must be efficient, because, from its very nature, it must energize to secure that which is thus preferred or chosen with the whole strength of his infinite nature. This is right choice, right moral action. The moral quality, then, of unselfish benevolence is righteousness or moral rightness. All subordinate choices, volitions and actions, and states of the sensibility which proceed from this immanent, ultimate, supreme preference or choice, have moral character in the sense and only for the reason that they proceed from or are the natural product of unselfish benevolence. This ultimate, immanent, supreme preference is the holy heart of a moral agent. Out of it proceeds, directly or indirectly, the whole moral or spiritual life of the individual.

III. How We Know What Righteousness Is.

I answer: By consciousness.

(a) By consciousness we know that our whole life proceeds from ultimate choice or preference. (b) By consciousness we know that conscience demands perfect, universal love or unselfish benevolence; and, by consequence, it demands all those acts and states of mind and outward courses of life that by a law of our nature proceed from unselfish benevolence. (c) By consciousness we know that conscience is satisfied with this, demands nothing more, and accepts nothing less. (d) By consciousness we know that conscience pronounces this to be right, or righteousness. (e) By consciousness we know that this is obedience to the law of God as revealed in our nature, and that when we render this obedience we are so adjusted in the will of God that we have perfect peace. We are in sympathy with God. We are at peace with God and with ourselves. Short of this we cannot be so. This I understand to be the teaching both of our nature and the Bible. My limits will not allow me to quote Scripture to sustain this view.

IV. Lastly, how a sinner may attain to righteousness.

A sinner is a selfish moral agent. Being selfish, he will, of course, make no other than selfish efforts to become righteous. Selfishness is a state of voluntary committal to the indulgence of the sensibility. While the will is in this state of committal to self-indulgence, the soul will not and cannot put forth any righteous act. The first righteous act possible to an unregenerate sinner is to change his heart, or the supreme ultimate preference of his soul. Without this he may outwardly conform to the letter of God's law; but this is not righteousness. Without this he may have many exercises and states of mind which he may suppose to be Christian experience; but these are not righteousness. Without a change of heart he may live a perfectly outwardly moral and religious life. All this he may do for selfish reasons; but this is not righteousness. I say again his first righteous act must be to change his heart. To say that he will change this for any selfish reason is simply a contradiction, for the change of heart involves the renunciation of selfishness. How, then, can a sinner change his heart or attain to righteousness? I answer: Only by taking such a view of the character and claims of God as to induce him to renounce his self-seeking spirit and come into sympathy with God. To say nothing here of possibility, the Bible reveals the fact and human consciousness attests the truth that a sinner will never attain to such a view of the claims of God as will induce him to renounce selfishness and sympathize with God without the illuminations of the Holy Spirit. A sinner attains, then, to righteousness only through the teachings and inspirations of the Holy Spirit.

But what is involved in this change from sin to righteousness?

(1) It must involve confidence in God, or faith. Without confidence a soul could not be persuaded to change his heart, to renounce self, and sympathize with God.

(2) It must involve repentance. By repentance I mean that change of mind which consists in a renunciation of self-seeking and a coming into sympathy with God.

(3) It involves a radical change of moral attitude in respect to God and our neighbour.

All these are involved in a change of heart. They occur simultaneously, and the presence of one implies the existence and presence of the others. It is by the truths of the Gospel that the Holy Spirit induces this change in sinful man. This revelation of divine love, when powerfully sent home by the Holy Spirit, is an effectual calling. From the above it will be seen that, while a sinner may live a perfectly outwardly moral and religious life, a truly regenerated soul cannot live a sinful life. The new heart does not, cannot sin. This John in his first Epistle expressly affirms. A benevolent, supreme, ultimate choice cannot produce selfish, subordinate choices or volitions. It is possible for a Christian to backslide. If it were not, perseverance would be no virtue. If the change were a physical one, or a change of the very nature of the sinner, backsliding would be impossible and perseverance no virtue. It is objected to this view that backsliding must consist in going back to a selfish, ultimate preference, and, therefore, involve an adverse change of heart. What if it does? Must this not be, indeed, true? Did not Adam and Eve change their hearts from holy to sinful ones? But may a man change his heart back and forth? I answer: Yes; or a sinner could not be required to make to himself a new heart, nor could a Christian sin after regeneration. The idea that the same person can have at the same time both a holy and a sinful heart is absurd in true philosophy, contrary to the Bible, and of most pernicious tendency. When a soul is backslidden, Christ calls upon him to repent and do his first work over again.

Righteousness is sustained in the human soul by the indwelling of Christ through faith and in no other way. It cannot be sustained by purposes or resolutions self-originated and not inwrought by the Spirit of Christ. Through faith Christ first gains ascendancy in the human heart, and through faith He maintains this ascendancy and reigns as king in the soul.

There can be no righteousness in man back of his heart, for nothing back of this can be voluntary; therefore, there can be no righteousness in the nature of man in the sense that implies praiseworthiness or virtue.

All outward conformity to the law and commandments of God that does not proceed from Christ, working in the soul by His Holy Spirit, is self-righteousness. All true righteousness, then, is the righteousness of faith, or a righteousness secured by Christ through faith in Him.

WEIGHED AND WANTING

Addresses on the Ten Commandments
By D. L. Moody 1898

"*Tekel: Thou art weighed in the balances, and art found wanting.*"

THE TEN COMMANDMENTS.

Exodus 20:3–17.

I. Thou shalt have no other gods before me.

II. Thou shalt not make unto thee any graven image, or any likeness of any thing that is in heaven above, or that is in the earth beneath, or that is in the water under the earth: thou shalt not bow down thyself to them, nor serve them: for I the Lord thy God am a jealous God, visiting the iniquity of the fathers upon the children unto the third and fourth generation of them that hate Me; and shewing mercy unto thousands of them that love Me, and keep my commandments.

III. Thou shalt not take the name of the Lord thy God in vain; for the Lord will not hold him guiltless that taketh His name in vain.

IV. Remember the Sabbath day, to keep it holy. Six days shalt thou labour, and do all thy work: but the seventh day is the Sabbath of the Lord thy God: in it thou shalt not do any work, thou, nor thy son, nor thy daughter, thy manservant, nor thy maidservant, nor thy cattle, nor thy stranger that is within thy gates: for in six days the Lord made heaven and earth, the sea, and all that in them is, and rested the seventh day: wherefore the Lord blessed the Sabbath day and hallowed it.

V. Honour thy father and thy mother: that thy days may be long upon the land which the lord thy God giveth thee.

VI. Thou shalt not kill.

VII. Thou shalt not commit adultery.

VIII. Thou shalt not steal.

IX. Thou shalt not bear false witness against thy neighbour.

X. Thou shalt not covet thy neighbour's house, thou shalt not covet thy neighbour's wife, nor his manservant, nor his maidservant, nor his ox, nor his ass, nor any thing that is thy neighbour's.

WEIGHED IN THE BALANCES

In the fifth chapter of Daniel we read the history of King Belshazzar. One chapter tells us all we know about him. One short sight of his career is all we have. He bursts in upon the scene and then disappears.

THE EASTERN FEAST.

We are told that he made a great feast to a thousand of his lords, and drank wine before them. In those days a feast would sometimes last for six months in Eastern countries. How long this feast had been going on we are not told, but in the midst of it, he "commanded to bring the golden and silver vessels which his father Nebuchadnezzar had taken out of the temple which was in Jerusalem; that the king, and his princes, his wives, and his concubines, might drink therein. Then they brought the golden vessels that were taken out of the temple of the house of God which was at Jerusalem; and the king, and his princes, his wives, and his concubines, drank in them.

They drank wine, and praised the gods of gold, and of silver, of brass, of iron, of wood, and of stone."

While this impious act was being committed, "in the same hour came forth fingers of a man's hand, and wrote over against the candlestick upon the plaister of the wall of the king's palace; and the king saw the part of the hand that wrote." We are not told at what hour of the day or the night it happened. Perhaps it was midnight. Perhaps nearly all the guests were more or less under the influence of drink; but they were not so drunk but that they suddenly became sober as they saw something that was supernatural—a handwriting on the wall, right over the golden candlestick.

Every face turned deathly pale. "The king's countenance was changed, and his thoughts troubled him, so that the joints of his loins were loosed, and his knees smote one against another." In haste he sent for his wisest men to come and read that handwriting on the wall. They came in one after another, and tried to make it out; but they could not interpret it. The king promised that whoever could read it should be made the third ruler in the kingdom; that he should have gifts, and that a gold chain should be put round his neck. But the wise men tried in vain. The king was greatly troubled.

At last, in the midst of the consternation, the queen came in, and she told the monarch, if he would only send for one who used to interpret the dreams of Nebuchadnezzar, he could read the writing and tell him the interpretation thereof. So Daniel was sent for. He was very familiar with it. He knew his Father's handwriting.

"This is the writing that was written, *Mene, Mene, Tekel, Upharsin*. This is the interpretation of the thing: *Mene*—God hath numbered thy kingdom and finished it. *Tekel*—Thou art weighed in the balances, and art found wanting. *Peres*—Thy kingdom is divided, and given to the Medes and Persians."

If some one had told the king an hour before that the time had come when he must step into the balances and be weighed, he would have laughed at the thought. But the vital hour had come.

The weighing was soon over. The verdict was announced, and the sentence carried out. "In that night was Belshazzar the king of the Chaldeans slain, and Darius the Median took the kingdom." Darius and his army came marching down those streets. There was a clash of arms. Shouts of war and victory rent the air. That night the king's blood mingled with the wine of the banquet hall. Judgment came upon him unexpectedly, suddenly: and probably ninety-nine out of every hundred judgments come in this way. Death comes upon us unexpectedly; it comes upon us suddenly.

Perhaps you say: "I hope Mr. Moody is not going to compare me with that heathen king."

I tell you that a man who does evil in these Gospel days is far worse than that king. We live in a land of Bibles. You can get the New Testament for a nickel, and if you haven't got a nickel you can get it for nothing. Many societies will be glad to give it to you free. We live in the full blaze of Calvary. We live on this side of the cross, but Belshazzar lived more than five hundred years on the other side. He never heard of Jesus Christ. He never heard about the Son of God. He never heard about God except, perhaps, in connection with his father's remarkable vision. He probably had no portion of the Bible, and if he had, probably he didn't believe it. He had no godly minister to point him to the Lamb of God.

Don't tell me that you are better than that king. I believe that he will rise in judgment and condemn many of us.

All this happened long centuries ago. Let us get down to this century, to this year, to ourselves. We will come to the present time. Let us imagine that now, while I am preaching, down come some balances from the throne of God. They are fastened to the very throne itself. It is a throne of equity, of justice. You and I must be weighed. I venture to say this would be a very solemn audience. There would be no trifling. There would be no indifference. No one would be thoughtless.

Some people have their own balances. A great many are making balances to be weighed in. But after all we must be weighed in God's balances, the balances of the sanctuary. It is a favorite thing with infidels to set their own standard, to measure themselves by other people. But that will not do in the Day of Judgment. Now we will use God's law as a balance weight. When men find fault with the lives of professing Christians, it is a tribute to the law of God.

"Tekel." It is a very short text. It is so short I am sure you will remember it: and that is my object, just to get people to remember God's own Word.

GOD'S HANDWRITING.

Let me call your attention to the fact that God wrote on the tables of stone at Sinai as well as on the wall of Belshazzar's palace.

These are the only messages to men that God has written with His own hand. He wrote the commandments out twice, and spoke them aloud in the hearing of Israel.

If it were known that God Himself was going to speak once again to man, what eagerness and excitement there would be. For nearly nineteen hundred years He has been silent. No inspired message has been added to the Bible for nearly nineteen hundred years. How eagerly all men would listen if God should speak once more. Yet men forget that the Bible is God's own Word, and that it is as truly His message to-day as when it was delivered of old. The law that was given at Sinai has lost none of its solemnity. Time cannot wear out its authority or the fact of its authorship.

I can imagine some one saying—"I won't be weighed by that law. I don't believe in it."

Now men may cavil as much as they like about other parts of the Bible, but I have never met an honest man that found fault with the Ten Commandments. Infidels may mock the Lawgiver and reject Him who has delivered us from the curse of the law, but they can't help admitting that the commandments are right. Renan said that they are for all nations, and will remain the commandments of God during all the centuries.

If God created this world, He must make some laws to govern it. In order to make life safe we must have good laws; there is not a country the sun shines upon that does not possess laws. Now this is God's law. It has come from on high, and infidels and skeptics have to admit that it is pure. Legislatures nearly all over the world adopt it as the foundation of their legal systems.

"The law of the Lord is perfect, converting the soul: the testimony of the Lord is pure, making wise the simple: the statutes of the Lord are right, rejoicing the heart: the commandment of the Lord is pure, enlightening the eyes."

Now the question for you and me is—are we keeping these commandments? Have we fulfilled all the requirements of the law? If God made us, as we know He did, He had a right to make that law; and if we don't use it aright it would have been better for us if we had never had it, for it will condemn us. We shall be found wanting. The law is all right, but are we right?

AN INFIDEL'S TESTIMONY.

It is related of a clever infidel that he sought an acquaintance with the truths of the Bible, and began to read at the books of Moses. He had been in the habit of sneering at the Bible, and in order to be able to refute arguments brought by Christian men, he made up his mind, as he knew nothing about it, to read the Bible and get some idea of its contents. After he had reached the Ten Commandments, he said to a friend:

I will tell you what I *used* to think. I supposed that Moses was the leader of a horde of banditti; that, having a strong mind, he acquired great influence over a superstitious people; and that on Mount Sinai he played off some sort of fireworks to the amazement of his ignorant followers, who imagined in their fear and superstition that the exhibition was supernatural. I have been looking into the *nature* of that law. I have been trying to see whether I could add anything to it, or take anything from it, so as to make it better. Sir, I cannot! It is perfect!

The first commandment directs us to make the Creator the object of our supreme love and reverence. That is right. If He be our Creator, Preserver, and Supreme Benefactor, we ought to treat Him, and *none other*, as such. The second forbids idolatry. That certainly is right. The third forbids profanity. The fourth fixes a time for religious worship. If there be a God, He ought surely to be worshipped. It is suitable that there should be an outward homage significant of our inward regard. If God be worshipped, it is proper that some *time* should be set apart for that purpose, when all may worship Him harmoniously, and without interruption. One day in seven is certainly not too much, and I do not know that it is too little.

The fifth commandment defines the peculiar duties arising from family relations. Injuries to our neighbor are then *classified* by the moral law. They are divided into offences against life, chastity, property, and character; and I notice that the greatest offence in each class is expressly forbidden. Thus the greatest injury to life is murder; to chastity, adultery; to property, theft; to character, perjury. Now the greatest offence must include the least of the same kind. Murder must include every injury to life; adultery every injury to purity; and so of the rest. And the moral code is closed and perfected by a command forbidding every improper *desire* in regard to our neighbors.

I have been thinking, Where did Moses get that law? I have read history. The Egyptians and the adjacent nations were idolaters; so were the Greeks and Romans; and the wisest or best Greeks or Romans never gave a code of morals like this. Where did Moses obtain that law, which surpasses the wisdom and philosophy of the most enlightened ages? He lived at a period comparatively barbarous; but he has given a law in which the learning and sagacity of all subsequent time can detect no flaw. Where did he obtain it? He could not have soared so far above his age as to have devised it himself. I am satisfied where he obtained it. It came down from heaven. It has convinced me of the truth of the religion of the Bible.

The infidel, (now an infidel no longer), remained to his death a firm believer in the truth of Christianity.

We call it the "Mosaic" Law, but it has been well said that the commandments did not originate with Moses, nor were they done away with when the Mosaic Law was fulfilled in Christ, and many of its ceremonies and regulations abolished. We can find no trace of the existence of any lawmaking body in those early times, no parliament or congress that built up a system of laws. It has come down to us complete and finished, and the only satisfactory account is that which tells us that God Himself wrote the commandments on tables of stone.

BINDING TO-DAY.

Some people seem to think we have got beyond the commandments. What did Christ say? "Think not that I am come to destroy the law and the prophets; I am not come to destroy but to fulfil. For verily I say unto you, Till heaven and earth pass away, one jot or one tittle shall in no wise pass from the law, till all be fulfilled." The commandments of God given to Moses in the Mount at Horeb are as binding to-day as ever they have been since the time when they were proclaimed in the hearing of the people. The Jews said the law was not given in Palestine, (which belonged to Israel), but in the wilderness, because the law was for all nations.

Jesus never condemned the law and the prophets, but He did condemn those who did not obey them. Because He gave new commandments it does not follow that He abolished the old. Christ's explanation of them made them all the more searching. In His Sermon on the Mount He carried the principles of the commandments beyond the mere letter. He unfolded them and showed that they embraced more, that they are positive as well as prohibitive. The Old Testament closes with these words: "Remember ye the law of Moses my servant, which I commanded unto him in Horeb for all Israel, with the statutes and judgments. Behold, I will send you Elijah the prophet before the coming of the great and dreadful day of the Lord: and he shall turn the heart of the fathers to the children, and the heart of the children to their fathers, lest I come and smite the earth with a curse."

Does that look as if the law of Moses was becoming obsolete?

The conviction deepens in me with the years that the old truths of the Bible must be stated and restated in the plainest possible language. I do not remember ever to have heard a sermon preached on the commandments. I have an index of two thousand five hundred sermons preached by Spurgeon, and not one of them selects its text from the first seventeen verses of Exodus xx. The people must be made to understand that the Ten Commandments are still binding, and that there is a penalty attached to their violation. We do not want a gospel of mere sentiment. The Sermon on the Mount did not blot out the Ten Commandments.

When Christ came He condensed the statement of the law into this form: "Thou shalt love the Lord thy God with all thy heart and with all thy soul and with all thy strength and with all thy mind; and thy neighbor as thyself." Paul said: "Love is the fulfilling of the law." But does this mean that the detailed precepts of the Decalogue are superseded, and have become back numbers? Does a father cease to give children rules to obey because they love him? Does a nation burn its statute books because the people have become patriotic? Not at all. And yet people speak as if the Commandments do not hold for Christians because they have come to love God. Paul said: "Do we then make void the law through faith? God forbid. Yea, we establish the law." It still holds good. The commandments are necessary. So long as we obey, they do not rest heavy upon us; but as soon as we try to break away, we find they are like fences to keep us within bounds. Horses need bridles even after they have been properly broken in.

"We know that the law is good if a man use it lawfully; knowing this, that the law is not made for a righteous man, but for the lawless and disobedient, for the ungodly and for sinners, for unholy and profane, for murderers of fathers and murderers of mothers, for manslayers, for whoremongers, for them that defile themselves with mankind, for menstealers, for liars, for perjured persons, and if there be any other thing that is contrary to sound doctrine."

Now, my friend, are you ready to be weighed by this law of God? A great many people say that if they keep the commandments, they do not need to be forgiven and saved through Christ. But have you kept them? I will admit that if you perfectly keep the commandments, you do not need to be saved by Christ; but is there a man in the wide world who can truly say that he has done this? Young lady, can you say: "I am ready to be weighed by the law?" Can you, young man? Will you step into the scales and be weighed one by one by the Ten Commandments?

Now face these Ten Commandments honestly and prayerfully. See if your life is right, and if you are treating God fairly. God's statutes are just, are they not? If they are right, let us see if we are right. Let us pray that the Holy Ghost may search each one of us. Let us get alone with God and read His law—read it carefully and prayerfully, and ask Him to show us our sins and what He would have us to do.

FIRST COMMANDMENT

"Thou shalt have no other gods before me."

My friend, are you ready to be weighed against this commandment? Have you fulfilled, or are you willing to fulfil, all the requirements of this law? Put it into one of the scales, and step into the other. Is your heart set upon God alone? Have you no other God? Do you love Him above father or mother, the wife of your bosom, your children, home or land, wealth or pleasure?

If men were true to this commandment, obedience to the remaining nine would follow naturally. It is because they are unsound in this that they break the others.

FEELING AFTER GOD.

Philosophers are agreed that even the most primitive races of mankind reach out beyond the world of matter to a superior Being. It is as natural for man to feel after God as it is for the ivy to feel after a support. Hunger and thirst drive him to seek for food, and there is a hunger of the soul that needs satisfying, too. Man does not need to be commanded to worship, as there is not a race so high or so low in the scale of civilization but has some kind of a god. What he needs is to be directed aright.

This is what the first commandment is for. Before we can worship intelligently, we must know what or whom to worship. God does not leave us in ignorance. When Paul vent to Athens, he found an altar dedicated to "An Unknown God," and he proceeded to tell of Him whom we worship. When God gave the commandments to Moses, He commenced with a declaration of His own character, and demanded exclusive recognition. "I am the Lord thy God, which have brought thee out of the land of Egypt, out of the house of bondage. Thou shalt have no other gods before me."

The Rev. Dr. Dale says these words have great significance. "The Jews knew Jehovah as the God who had held back the waves like a wall while they fled across the sea to escape the vengeance of their enemies; they knew him as the God who had sent thunder, and lightning, and hail, plagues on cattle, and plagues on men, to punish the Egyptians and to compel them to let the children of Israel go; they knew Him as the God whose angel had slain the firstborn of their oppressors, and filled the land from end to end with death, and agony, and terror. He was the same God, so Moses and Aaron told them, who by visions and voices, in promises and precepts, had revealed Himself long before to Abraham, Isaac, and Jacob. We learn what men are from what they say and from what they do. A biography of Luther gives a more vivid and trustworthy knowledge of the man than the most philosophical essay on his character and creed. The story of his imprisonment and of his journey to Worms, his Letters, his Sermons, and his Table-Talk, are worth more than the most elaborate speculations about him. The Jews learned what God is, not from theological dissertations on the Divine attributes, but from the facts of a Divine history. They knew Him for themselves in His own acts and His own words."

Some one asked an Arab: "How do you know that there is a God?" "How do I know whether a man or a camel passed my tent last night?" he replied. God's footprints in nature and in our own experience are the best evidence of His existence and character.

THE ISRAELITES WERE EXPOSED TO DANGER.

Remember to whom this commandment was given, and we shall see further how necessary it was. The forefathers of the Israelites had worshipped idols, not many generations back. They had recently been delivered out of Egypt, a land of many gods. The Egyptians worshipped the sun, the moon, insects, animals, etc. The ten plagues were undoubtedly meant by God to bring confusion upon many of their sacred objects. The children of Israel were going up to take possession of a land that was inhabited by heathen, who also worshipped idols. There was therefore great need of such a commandment as this. There could be no right relationship between God and man in those days any more than to-day, until man understood that he must recognize God alone, and not offer Him a divided heart.

If He created us, He certainly ought to have our homage. Is it not right that He should have the first and only place in our affections?

NO COMPROMISE.

This is one matter in which no toleration can be shown. Religious liberty is a good thing, within certain limits. But it is one thing to show toleration to those who agree on essentials, and another, to those who differ on fundamental beliefs. They were willing to admit any god to the Roman Pantheon. One reason why the early Christians were persecuted was that they would not accept a place for Jesus Christ there. Napoleon is said to have entertained the idea of having separate temples in Paris for every known religion, so that every stranger should have a place of worship when attracted toward that city. Such plans are directly opposed to the Divine one. God sounded no uncertain note in this commandment. It is plain, unmistakable, uncompromising.

We may learn a lesson from the way a farmer deals with the little shoots that spring up around the trunk of an apple tree. They look promising, and one who has not learned better might welcome their growth. But the farmer knows that they will draw the life-sap from the main tree, injuring its prospects so that it will produce inferior fruit. He therefore takes his axe and his hoe, and cuts away these suckers. The tree then gives a more plentiful and a finer crop.

GOD'S PRUNING-KNIFE.

"Thou shalt not" is the pruning-knife that God uses. From beginning to end, the Bible calls for wholehearted allegiance to Him. There is to be no compromise with other gods.

It took long years for God to impress this lesson upon the Israelites. He called them to be a chosen nation. He made them a peculiar people. But you will notice in Bible history that they turned away from Him continually, and were punished with plague, pestilence, war and famine. Their sin was not that they renounced God altogether, but that they wanted to worship other gods beside Him. Take the case of Solomon as an example of the whole nation. He married heathen wives who turned away his heart after other gods, and built high places for their idols, and lent countenance to their worship. That was the history of frequent turnings of the whole nation away from God, until finally He sent them into captivity in Babylon and kept them there for seventy years. Since then the Jews have never turned to other gods.

Hasn't the church to contend with the same difficulty to-day? There are very few who in their hearts do not believe in God, but what they will not do is give Him exclusive right of way. Missionaries tell us that they could easily get converts if they did not require them to be baptized, thus publicly renouncing their idols. Many a person in our land would become a Christian if the gate was not so strait. Christianity is too strict for them. They are not ready to promise full allegiance to God alone. Many a professing Christian is a stumbling-block because his worship is divided. On Sunday he worships God; on week days God has little or no place in his thoughts.

FALSE GODS IN AMERICA TO-DAY.

You don't have to go to heathen lands to-day to find false gods. America is full of them. Whatever you make most of is your god. Whatever you love more than God is your idol. Many a mans heart is like some Kaffirs' huts, so full of idols that there is hardly room to turn around. Rich and poor, learned and unlearned, all classes of men and women are guilty of this sin. "The mean man boweth down, and the great man humbled himself."

A man may make a god of himself, of a child, of a mother, of some precious gift that God has bestowed upon him. He may forget the Giver, and let his heart go out in adoration toward the gift.

Many make a god of pleasure; that is what their hearts are set on. If some old Greek or Roman came to life again and saw men in a drunken debauch, would he believe that the worship of Bacchus had died out? If he saw the streets of our large cities filled with harlots, would he believe that the worship of Venus had ceased?

Others take fashion as their god. They give their time and thought to dress. They fear what others will think of them. Do not let us flatter ourselves that all idolaters are in heathen countries.

With many it is the god of money. We haven't got through worshipping the golden calf yet. If a man will sell his principles for gold, isn't he making it a god? If he trusts in his wealth to keep him from want and to supply his needs, are not riches his god? Many a man says, "Give me money, and I will give you heaven. What care I for all the glories and treasures of heaven? Give me treasures here! I don't care for heaven! I want to be a successful business man." How true are the words of Job: "If I have made gold my hope, or have said to the fine gold, Thou art my confidence; if I rejoiced because my wealth was great, and because mine hand had begotten much; if I beheld the sun when it shined, or the moon walking in brightness; and my heart hath been secretly enticed, or my mouth hath kissed my hand: this also were an iniquity to be punished by the judge: for I should have denied the God that is above."

But all false gods are not as gross as these. There is *the atheist*. He says that he does not believe in God; he denies His existence, but he can't help setting up some other god in His place. Voltaire said, "If there were no God, it would be necessary to invent one." So the atheist speaks of the Great Unknown, the First Cause, the Infinite Mind, etc. Then there is *the deist*. He is a man who believes in one God who caused all things: but he doesn't believe in revelation. He only accepts such truths as can be discovered by reason. He doesn't believe in Jesus Christ, or in the inspiration of the Bible. Then there is *the pantheist*, who says: "I believe that the whole universe is God. He is in the air, the water, the sun, the stars."; the liar and the thief included.

MOSES' FAREWELL MESSAGE.

Let me call your attention to a verse in the thirty-second chapter of Deuteronomy, thirty-first verse: "For their rock is not as our Rock, even our enemies themselves being judges."

These words were uttered by Moses, in his farewell address to Israel. He had been with them forty years. He was their leader and instructor. All the blessings of heaven came to them through him. And now the old man is about to leave them. If you have never read his speech, do so. It is one of the best sermons in print. I know few sermons in the Old or New Testament that compare with it.

I can see Moses as he delivers this address. His natural activity has not abated. He still has the vigor of youth. His long white hair flows over his shoulders, and his venerable beard covers his breast. He throws down the challenge: "Their rock is not as our Rock, even our enemies themselves being judges."

Has the human heart ever been satisfied with these false gods? Can pleasure or riches fill the soul that is empty of God? How about the atheist, the deist, the pantheist? What do they look forward to? Nothing! Man's life is full of trouble; but when the billows of affliction and disappointment are rising and rolling over them, they have no God to call upon. "They shall cry unto the gods unto whom they offer incense; but they shall not save them at all in the time of their trouble." Therefore I contend "their rock is not as our Rock."

My friends, when the hour of affliction comes, they call in a minister to give consolation. When I was settled in Chicago, I used to be called out to attend many funerals. I would inquire what the man was in his belief. If I found out he was an atheist, or a deist, or a pantheist, when I went to the funeral and in the presence of his friends said one word about that man's doctrine, they would feel insulted. Why is it that in a trying hour, when they have been talking all the time against God—why is it that in the darkness of affliction they call in believers in that God to administer consolation? Why doesn't the atheist preach no hereafter, no heaven, no God, in the hour of affliction? This very fact is an admission that "their rock is not as our Rock, even our enemies themselves being judges."

The deist says there is no use in praying, because nothing can change the decrees of deity; God never answers prayer. Is his rock as our Rock?

The Bible is true. There is only one God. How many men have said to me: "Mr. Moody, I would give the world if I had your faith, your consolation, the hope you have with your religion."

Isn't that a proof that their rock is not as our Rock?

Some years ago I went into a man's house, and when I commenced to talk about religion he turned to his daughter and said: "You had better leave the room. I want to say a few words to Mr. Moody." When she had gone, he opened a perfect torrent of infidelity upon me. "Why did you send your daughter out of the room before you said this?" I asked. "Well," he replied, "I did not think it would do her any good to hear what I said."

Is his rock as our Rock? Would he have sent his daughter out if he really believed what he said?

NO CONSOLATION EXCEPT IN GOD.

No. There is no satisfaction for the soul except in the God of the Bible. We come back to Paul's words, and get consolation for time and eternity:—"We know that an idol is nothing in the world, and that there is none other God but one. For though there be that are called gods, whether in heaven or in earth, (as there be gods many, and lords many,) yet to us there is but one God, the Father, of whom are all things, and we in Him; and one Lord Jesus Christ, by whom are all things, and we by Him."

My friend, can you say that sincerely? Is all your hope centred on God in Christ? Are you trusting Him alone? Are you ready to step into the scales and be weighed against this first commandment?

WHOLE-HEARTED ALLEGIANCE.

God will not accept a divided heart. He must be absolute monarch. There is not room in your heart for two thrones. Christ said: "No man can serve two masters; for either he will hate the one and love the other, or else he will hold to the one and despise the other. Ye cannot serve God and Mammon." Mark you, He did not say— "No man *shall* serve....Ye *shall* not serve....", but "No man *can* serve....Ye *can* not serve...." That means more than a command; it means that you cannot mix the worship of the true God with the worship of another god any more than you can mix oil and water. It cannot be done. There is not room for any other throne in the heart if Christ is there. If worldliness should come in, godliness would go out.

The road to heaven and the road to hell lead in different directions. Which master will you choose to follow? Be an out-and-out Christian. "Him only shalt thou serve." Only thus can you be well pleasing to God. The Jews were punished with seventy years of captivity because they worshipped false gods. They have suffered nearly nineteen hundred years because they rejected the Messiah. Will you incur God's displeasure by rejecting Christ too? He died to save you. Trust him with your whole heart, for with the heart man believeth unto righteousness.

I believe that when Christ has the first place in our hearts—when the kingdom of God is first in everything—we shall have power, and we shall not have power until we give Him His rightful place. If we let some false god come in and steal our love away from the God of heaven, we shall have no peace or power.

SECOND COMMANDMENT

"Thou shalt not make unto thee any graven image, or any likeness of any thing that is in heaven above, or that is in the earth beneath, or that is in the water under the earth: thou shalt not bow down thyself to them, nor serve them: for I the Lord thy God am a jealous God, visiting the iniquity of the fathers upon the children unto the third and fourth generation of them that hate Me; and shewing mercy unto thousands of them that love Me, and keep My commandments."

The first commandment, which we have just considered, points out the one true object of worship; this commandment is to tell us the right way in which to worship. The former commands us to worship God alone; this calls for purity and spirituality as we approach Him. The former condemns the worship of false gods; this prohibits false forms. It relates more especially to outward acts of worship; but these are only the expression of what is in the heart.

Perhaps you will say that there is no trouble about this weight. We might go off to other ages or other lands, and find people who make images and bow down to them; but we have none here. Let us see if this is true. Let us step into the scales and see if we can turn them when weighed against this commandment.

I believe this is where the battle is fought. Satan tries to keep us from worshipping God aright, and from making Him first in everything. If I let some image made by man get into my heart and take the place of God the Creator, it is a sin. I believe that Satan is willing to have us worship anything, however sacred,—the Bible, the crucifix, the church,—if only we do not worship God Himself.

You cannot find a place in the Bible where a man has been allowed to bow down and worship any one but the God of heaven and Jesus Christ His Son. In the Book of Revelation, when an angel came down to John, he was about to fall down and worship him, but the angel would not let him. If an angel from heaven is not to be worshipped, when you find people bowing down to pictures, to images, even when they bow down to worship the cross, *it is a sin*. There are a great many who seem to be carried away with these things. "Thou shalt have no other gods before Me." "Thou shalt not bow down thyself to any graven image." God wants us to worship Him only, and if we do not believe that Jesus Christ is God manifest in the flesh we should not worship Him. I have no more doubt about the divinity of Christ than I have that I exist.

Worship involves two things: the internal belief, and the external act. We transgress in our hearts by having a wrong conception of God and of Jesus Christ before ever we give public expression in action. As some one has said, it is wrong to have loose opinions as well as to be guilty of loose practices. That is what Paul meant when he said: "We ought not to *think* that the Godhead is like unto gold or silver or stone, graven by art or man's device." The opinions that some people hold about Christ are not in accordance with the Bible, and are real violations of this second commandment.

A QUESTION.

The question at once arises—is this commandment intended to forbid the use of drawings and pictures of created things altogether? Some contend that it does. They point to the Jews and the Mohammedans as a proof. The Jews have never been much given to art. The Mohammedans to this day do not use designs of animals, etc., in patterns. But I do not agree with them. I think God only meant to forbid images and other representations when these were intended to be used as objects of religious veneration. "Thou shalt not make *unto thee*....Thou shalt not *bow down thyself* to them, nor *serve* them." In Exodus we are told that God ordered the bowls of the golden candlestick for the tabernacle to be made "like unto almonds, with a knop and a flower;" and the robe of the ephod had a hem on which they were to put a bell and a pomegranate alternately. How could God order something that broke this second commandment?

I believe that this commandment is a call for spiritual worship. It is in line with Christ's declaration to that Samaritan woman—"God is a spirit, and they that worship Him must worship Him in *spirit* and in *truth*."

This is precisely what is difficult for men to do. The apostles were hardly in their graves before they began to put up images of them, and to worship relics. People have a desire for something tangible, something that they can see. It is so much easier to live in the sense than in the spirit. That is why there is a demand for ritualism. Some people are born Puritans; they want a simple form of worship. Others think they cannot get along without forms and ceremonies that appeal to the senses. And many a one whose heart is not sincere before God takes refuge in these forms, and eases his conscience by making an outward show of religion.

The second commandment is to restrain this desire and tendency.

God is grieved when we are untrue to Him. God is Love, and He is wounded when our affections are transferred to anything else. The penalty attached to this commandment teaches us that man has to reap what he sows, whether good or bad; and not only that, but his children have to reap with him. Notice that punishment is visited upon the children unto the *third* or the *fourth* generation, while mercy is shown unto thousands, or (as it is more correctly) unto the *thousandth* generation.

THE FOLLY OF IMAGES.

Think for a moment, and you will see how idle it is to try to make any representation of God. Christians have tried to paint the Trinity, but how can you depict the Invisible? Can you draw a picture of your own soul or spirit or will? Moses impressed it upon Israel that when God spake to them out of the midst of the fire they saw no manner of similitude, but only heard His voice.

A picture or image of God must degrade our conception of Him. It fastens us down to one idea, whereas we ought to grow in grace and in knowledge. It makes God finite. It brings him down to our level. It has given rise to the horrible idols of India and China, because they fashion these images according to their own notions. How would the president feel if Americans made such hideous objects to resemble him as they make of their gods in heathen countries? Isaiah bore down with tremendous irony upon the folly of idol makers: upon the smith who fashioned gods with tongs and hammers; and upon the carpenter who took a tree, and used part of it for a fire to warm himself and roast his meat, and made part of it in the figure of a man with his rule and plane and compass, and called it his god and worshipped it. "A deceived heart hath turned him aside."

A man must be greater than anything he is able to make or manufacture. What folly then to think of worshipping such things!

The tendency of the human heart to represent God by something that appeals to the senses is the origin of all idolatry. It leads directly to image-worship. At first there may be no desire to worship the thing itself, but it inevitably ends in that. As Dr. MacLaren says: "Enlisting the senses as allies of the spirit is risky work. They are apt to fight for their own band when they once begin, and the history of all symbolical and ceremonial worship shows that the experiment is much more likely to end in sensualizing religion than in spiritualizing sense."

PICTURES AND IMAGES.

But some one says—"I find pictures are a great help to me, and images. I know that they are not themselves sacred, but they help me in my devotions to fix my thoughts on God."

When Dr. Trumbull was in Northfield, he used an illustration that is a good answer to this. He said, "Suppose a young man were watching from a window for his absent mother's return, with a wish to catch the first glimpse of her approaching face. Would he be wise or foolish in putting up a photograph of her on the window-frame before him, as a help to bear her in as he looks for her coming? As there can be no doubt about the answer to that question, so there can be no doubt that we can best come into communion with God by closing our eyes to everything that can be seen with the natural eye, and opening the eyes of our spirit to the sight of God the Spirit."

I would a great deal sooner have five minutes communion with Christ than spend years before pictures and images of Him. Whatever comes between my soul and my Maker is not a help to me, but a hindrance. God has given different means of grace by which we can approach Him. Let us use these, and not seek for other things that He has distinctly forbidden.

Dr. Dale says that in his college days he had an engraving of our Lord hanging over his mantlepiece. "The calmness, the dignity, the gentleness, and the sadness of the face represented the highest conceptions which I had in those days of the human presence of Christ. I often looked at it, and seldom without being touched by it. I discovered in the course of a few mouths that the superstitious sentiments were gradually clustering about it, which are always created by the visible representations of the Divine. The engraving was becoming to me the shrine of God manifest in the flesh, and I understood the growth of idolatry. The visible symbol is at first a symbol and nothing more; it assists thought; it stirs passion. At last it is identified with the God whom it represents. If, every day, I bow before a crucifix in prayer, if I address it as though it were Christ, though I know it is not, I shall come to feel for it a reverence and love which are of the very essence of idolatry."

Did you ever stop to think that the world has not a single picture of Christ that has been handed down to us from His disciples? Who knows what He was like? The Bible does not tell us how He looked, except in one or two isolated general expressions as when it says—"His visage was so marred more than any man, and His form more than the sons of men." We don't know anything definite about His features, the color of His hair and eyes, and the other details that would help to give a true representation. What artist can tell us? He left no keepsakes to His disciples. His clothes were seized by the Roman soldiers who crucified Him. Not a solitary thing was left to be handed down among His followers. Doesn't it look as if Christ left no relics lest they should be held sacred and worshipped?

History tells us further that the early Christians shrank from making pictures and statues of any kind of Christ. They knew Him as they had seen Him after His resurrection, and had promises of His continued presence that pictures could not make any more real.

I have seen very few pictures of Christ that do not repel me more or less. I sometimes think that it is wrong to have pictures of Him at all.

Speaking of the crucifix Dr. Dale says; "It makes our worship and prayer unreal. We are adoring a Christ who does not exist. He is not on the cross now, but on the throne. His agonies are passed forever. He has risen from the dead. He is at the right hand of God. If we pray to a dying Christ, we are praying not to Christ Himself, but to a mere remembrance of Him. The injury which the crucifix has inflicted on the religious life of Christendom, in encouraging a morbid and unreal devotion, is absolutely incalculable. It has given us a dying Christ instead of a living Christ, a Christ separated from us by many centuries instead of a Christ nigh at hand."

THE INDWELLING CHRIST.

No one can say that we have nowadays any need of such things. "Behold I stand at the door, and knock: if any man hear my voice, and open the door, I will come in to him, and will sup with him, and he with me." If Christ is in our hearts, why need we set Him before our eyes? "Where two or three are gathered together in my name, there am I in the midst of them." If we take hold of that promise by faith, what need is there of outward symbols and reminders? If the King Himself is present, why need we bow down before statues supposed to represent Him? To fill His place with an image (some one has said,) is like blotting the sun out of the heavens and substituting some other light in its place. "You cannot see Him through chinks of ceremonialism; or through the blind eyes of erring man; or by images graven with art and man's device; or in cunningly devised fables of artificial and perverted theology. Nay, seek Him in His own Word, in the revelation of Himself which He gives to all who walk in His ways. So you will be able to keep that admonition of the last word of all the New Testament revelation: 'Little children, keep yourselves from idols.'"

I believe many an earnest Christian would be found wanting if put in the balances against this commandment. "Tekel" is the sentence that would be written against them, because their worship of God and of Christ is not pure. May God open our eyes to the danger that is creeping more and more into public worship throughout Christendom! Let us ever bear in mind Christ's words in the fourth chapter of John's gospel, which show that true spiritual worship is not a matter of special times and special places because it is of all times and all places:

"Believe me, the hour cometh, when ye shall neither in this mountain, nor yet at Jerusalem, worship the Father. But the hour cometh, and now is, when the true worshippers shall worship the Father in spirit and in truth: for the Father seeketh such to worship Him. God is a Spirit: and they that worship Him must worship Him in spirit and in truth."

THIRD COMMANDMENT

"Thou shalt not take the name of the Lord thy God in vain; for the Lord will not hold him guiltless that taketh His name in vain."

I was greatly amazed not long ago in talking to a man who thought he was a Christian, to find that once in a while, when he got angry, he would swear. I said: "My friend, I don't see how you can tear down with one hand what you are trying to build up with the other. I don't see how you can profess to be a child of God and let those words come out of your lips."

He replied: "Mr. Moody, if you knew me you would understand. I have a very quick temper. I inherited it from my father and mother, and it is uncontrollable; but my swearing comes only from the lips."

When God said, "I will not hold him guiltless that takes My name in vain," He meant what He said, and I don't believe any one can be a true child of God who takes the name of God in vain. What is the grace of God for, if it is not to give me control of my temper so that I shall not lose control and bring down the curse of God upon myself? When a man is born of God, God takes the "swear" out of him. Make the fountain good, and the stream will be good. Let the heart be right; then the language will be right; the whole life will be right. But no man can serve God and keep His law until he is born of God. There we see the necessity of the new birth.

To take God's name "in vain" means either (1) lightly, without thinking, flippantly; or (2) profanely, deceitfully.

USING GOD'S NAME IRREVERENTLY.

I think it is shocking to use God's name with so little reverence as is common nowadays, even among professing Christians. We are told that the Jews held it so sacred that the covenant name of God was never mentioned amongst them except once a year by the high priest on the Day of Atonement, when he went into the holy of holies. What a contrast that is to the familiar use Christians make of it in public and private worship! We are apt to rush into God's presence, and rush out again, without any real sense of the reverence and awe that is due Him. We forget that we are on holy ground.

Do you know how often the word "reverend" occurs in the Bible? Only once. And what is it used in connection with? God's name. Psalm cxi. 9: "HOLY AND REVEREND IS HIS NAME." So important did the Jewish rabbis consider this commandment that they said the whole world trembled when it was first proclaimed on Sinai.

USING GOD'S NAME PROFANELY.

But though there is far too much of this frivolous, familiar use of God's name, the commandment is broken a great deal more by profanity. Taking the name of God in vain is blasphemy. Is there a swearing man who reads this? What would you do if you were put into the balances of the sanctuary, if you had to step in opposite to this third commandment? Think a moment. Have you been taking God's name in vain to-day?

I do not believe men would ever have been guilty of swearing unless God had forbidden it. They do not swear by their friends, their fathers or mothers, their wives or children. They want to show how they despise God's law.

A great many men think there is nothing in swearing. Bear in mind that God sees something wrong in it, and He says He will not hold men guiltless, even though society does.

I met a man sometime ago who told me he had never sinned in his life. He was the first perfect man I had ever met. I thought I would question him, and began to measure him by the law. I asked him: "Do you ever get angry?"

"Well," he said, "sometimes I do; but I have a right to do so. It is righteous indignation."

"Do you swear when you get angry?" He admitted he did sometimes. "Then," I asked, "are you ready to meet God?"

"Yes," he replied, "because I never mean anything when I swear."

Suppose I steal a man's watch and he comes after me.

"Yes," I say, "I stole your watch and pawned it, but *I did not mean anything by it*. I pawned it and spent the money, but *I did not mean anything by it*."

You would smile at and deride such a statement.

Ah, friends! You cannot trifle with God in that way. Even if you swear without meaning it, it is forbidden by God. Christ said: "Every idle word that men shall speak, they shall give an account thereof in the day of judgment; for by thy words thou shalt be justified, and by thy words thou shalt be condemned." You will be held accountable whether your words are *idle* or *blasphemous*.

A SENSELESS HABIT.

The habit of swearing is condemned by all sensible persons. It has been called "the most gratuitous of all sins," because no one gains by it; it is "not only sinful, but useless." An old writer said that when the accusing angel, who records men's words, flies up to heaven with an oath, he blushes as he hands it in.

When a man blasphemes, he shows an utter contempt for God. I was in the army during the war, and heard men cursing and swearing. Some godly woman would pass along the ranks looking for her wounded son, and not an oath would be heard. They would not swear before their mothers, or their wives, or their sisters; they had more respect for them than they had for God!

Isn't it a terrible condemnation that swearing held its own until it came to be recognized as a vulgar thing, a sin against society? Men dropped it then, who never thought of its being a sin against God.

There will be no swearing men in the kingdom of God. They will have to drop that sin, and repent of it, before they see the kingdom of God.

HOW TO KEEP FROM SWEARING.

Men often ask: "How can I keep from swearing?" I will tell you. If God puts His love into your heart, you will have no desire to curse Him. If you have much regard for God, you will no more think of cursing Him than you would think of speaking lightly or disparagingly of a mother whom you love. But the natural man is at enmity with God, and has utter contempt for His law. When that law is written on his heart, there will be no trouble in obeying it.

When I was out west about thirty years ago, I was preaching one day in the open air, when a man drove up in a fine turn-out, and after listening a little while to what I was saying, he put the whip to his fine-looking Steed, and away he went. I never expected to see him again, but the next night he came back, and he kept on coming regularly night after night.

I noticed that his forehead itched—you have noticed people who keep putting their hands to their foreheads?—he didn't want any one to see him shedding tears—of course not! It is not a manly thing to shed tears in a religions meeting, of course!

After the meeting I said to a gentleman: "Who is that man who drives up here every night? Is he interested?" "Interested! I should think not! You should have heard the way he talked about you today." "Well," I said, "that is a sign he is interested."

If no man ever has anything to say against you, your Christianity isn't worth much. Men said of the Master, "He has a devil," and Jesus said that if they had called the master of the house Beelzebub, how much more them of his household.

I asked where this man lived, but my friend told me not to go to see him, for he would only curse me. I said: "It takes God to curse a man; man can only bring curses on his own head." I found out where he lived, and went to see him. He was the wealthiest man within a hundred miles of that place, and had a wife and seven beautiful children. Just as I got to his gate I saw him coming out of the front door.

I stepped up to him and said: "This is Mr.—, I believe?"

He said: "Yes, sir; that is my name." Then he straightened up and asked—"What do you want?"

"Well," I said, "I would like to ask you a question, if you won't be angry."

"Well, what is it?"

"I am told that God has blessed you above all men in this part of the country; that He has given you wealth, a beautiful Christian wife, and seven lovely children. I do not know if it is true, but I hear that all He gets in return is cursing and blasphemy."

He said, "Come in; come in." I went in. "Now," he

said, "what you said out there is true. If any man has a fine wife I am the man, and I have a lovely family of children, and God has been good to me. But do you know, we had company here the other night, and I cursed my wife at the table, and did not know it till after the company had gone. I never felt so mean and contemptible in my life as when my wife told me of it. She said she wanted the floor to open and let her down out of her seat. If I have tried once, I have tried a hundred times to stop swearing. You preachers don't know anything about it."

"Yes," I said, "I know all about it; I have been a drummer."

"But," he said, "you don't know anything about a business-man's troubles. When he is harassed and tormented the whole time, he can't help swearing."

"Oh, yes," I said, "he can. I know something about it. I used to swear myself."

"What! You used to swear?" he asked; "how did you stop?"

"I never stopped."

"Why, you don't swear now, do you?"

"No; I have not sworn for years."

"How did you stop?"

"I never stopped. It stopped itself."

He said, "I don't understand this."

"No," I said, "I know you don't. But I came up to talk to you, so that you will never want to swear again as long as you live."

I began to tell him about Christ in the heart; how that would take the temptation to swear out of a man,

"Well," he said, "how am I to get Christ?"

"Get right down here and tell Him what you want."

"But," he said, "I was never on my knees in my life. I have been cursing all the day, and I don't know how to pray or what to pray for."

"Well," I said, "it is mortifying to have to call on God for mercy when you have never used His name except in oaths; but He will not turn you away. Ask God to forgive you if you want to be forgiven."

Then the man got down and prayed—only a few sentences, but thank God, it is the short prayers, after all, which bring the quickest answers. After he prayed he got up and said: "What shall I do now?"

I said, "Go down to the church and tell the people there that you want to be an out-and-out Christian."

"I cannot do that," he said; "I never go to church except to some funeral."

"Then it is high time for you to go for something else," I said.

After a while he promised to go, but did not know what the people would say. At the next church prayer-meeting, the man was there, and I sat right in front of him. He stood up and put his hands on the settee, and he trembled so much that I could feel the settee shake. He said:

"My friends, you know all about me. If God can save a wretch like me, I want to have you pray for my salvation."

That was thirty odd years ago. Sometime ago I was back in that town, and did not see him; but when I was in California, a man asked me to take dinner with him. I told him that I could not do so, for I had another engagement. Then he asked if I remembered him, and told me his name. "Oh," I said, "tell me, have you ever sworn since that night you knelt in your drawing-room, and asked God to forgive you?"

"No," he replied, "I have never had a desire to swear since then. It was all taken away."

He was not only converted, but became an earnest, active Christian, and all these years has been serving God. That is what will take place when a man is born of the divine nature.

Is there a swearing man ready to put this commandment into the scales, and step in to be weighed? Suppose you swear only once in six months or a year—suppose you swear only once in ten years—do you think God will hold you guiltless for that act? It shows that your heart is not clean in God's sight. What are you going to do, blasphemer? Would you not be found wanting? You would be like a feather in the balance.

FOURTH COMMANDMENT

> "Remember the sabbath day, to keep it holy. Six days shalt thou labor, and do all thy work: but the seventh day is the sabbath of the Lord thy God: in it thou shalt not do any work, thou, nor thy son, nor thy daughter, thy manservant, nor thy maidservant, nor thy cattle, nor thy stranger that is within thy gates: for in six days the Lord made heaven and earth, the sea, and all that in them is, and rested the seventh day: wherefore the Lord blessed the sabbath day, and hallowed it."

There has been an awful letting-down in this country regarding the sabbath during the last twenty-five years, and many a man has been shorn of spiritual power, like Samson, because he is not straight on this question. Can *you* say that you observe the sabbath properly? You may be a professed Christian: are you obeying this commandment? Or do you neglect the house of God on the sabbath day, and spend your time drinking and carousing in places of vice and crime, showing contempt for God and His law? Are you ready to step into the scales? Where were you last sabbath? How did you spend it?

I honestly believe that this commandment is just as binding to-day as it ever was. I have talked with men who have said that it has been abrogated, but they have never been able to point to any place in the Bible where God repealed it. When Christ was on earth, He did nothing to set it aside; He freed it from the traces under which the scribes and Pharisees had put it, and gave it its true place. "The sabbath was made for man, not man for the sabbath." It is just as practicable and as necessary for men to-day as it ever was—in fact, more than ever, because we live in such an intense age.

The sabbath was binding in Eden, and it has been in force ever since. This fourth commandment begins with the word "remember," showing that the sabbath already existed when God wrote this law on the tables of stone at Sinai. How can men claim that this one commandment has been done away with when they will admit that the other nine are still binding?

I believe that the sabbath question to-day is a vital one for the whole country. It is the burning question of the present time. If you give up the sabbath the church goes; if you give up the church the home goes; and if the home goes the nation goes. That is the direction in which we are traveling.

The church of God is losing its power on account of so many people giving up the sabbath, and using it to promote selfishness.

HOW TO OBSERVE THE SABBATH.

"Sabbath" means "rest," and the meaning of the word gives a hint as to the true way to observe the day. God rested after creation, and ordained the sabbath as a rest for man. He blessed it and hallowed it. "Remember *the rest-day* to keep it *holy*." It is the day when the body may be refreshed and strengthened after six days of labor, and the soul drawn into closer fellowship with its Maker.

True observance of the sabbath may be considered under two general heads: cessation from ordinary secular work, and religious exercises.

I.—CESSATION FROM SECULAR WORK.

A man ought to turn aside from his ordinary employment one day in seven. There are many whose occupation will not permit them to observe Sunday, but they should observe some other day as a sabbath. Saturday is my day of rest because I generally preach on Sunday, and I look forward to it as a boy does to a holiday. God knows what we need.

Ministers and missionaries often tell me that they take no rest-day; they do not need it because they are in the Lord's work. That is a mistake. When God was giving Moses instructions about the building of the tabernacle, He referred especially to the sabbath, and gave injunctions for its strict observance; and later, when Moses was conveying the words of the Lord to the children of Israel, he interpreted them by saying that not even were sticks to be gathered on the sabbath to kindle fires for smelting or other purposes. In spite of their zeal and haste to erect the tabernacle, the workmen were to have their day of rest. The command applies to ministers and others engaged in Christian work to-day as much as to those Israelite workmen of old.

WORKS OF NECESSITY AND OF EMERGENCY.

In judging whether any work may or may not be lawfully done on the sabbath, find out the reason and object for doing it. Exceptions are to be made for works of necessity and works of emergency. By "*works of necessity*" I mean those acts that Christ justified when He approved of leading one's ox or ass to water. Watchmen, police, stokers on board steamers, and many others have engagements that necessitate their working on the sabbath. By "*works of emergency*" I mean those referred to by Christ when He approved of pulling an ox or an ass out of a pit on the sabbath day. In case of fire or sickness a man is often called on to do things that would not otherwise be justifiable.

A Christian man was once urged by his employer to work on Sunday. "Does not your Bible say that if your ass falls into a pit on the sabbath, you may pull him out?" "Yes," replied the other; "but if the ass had the habit of falling into the same pit every sabbath, I would either fill up the pit or sell the ass."

Every man must settle the question as it effects unnecessary work, with his own conscience.

No man should make another work seven days in the

week. One day is demanded for rest. A man who has to work the seven days has nothing to look forward to, and life becomes humdrum. Many Christians are guilty in this respect.

SABBATH TRAVELING.

Take, for instance, the question of sabbath traveling. I believe we are breaking God's laws by using the cars on Sunday and depriving conductors and others of their sabbath. Remember the fourth commandment expressly refers to "the stranger that is within thy gates." Doesn't that touch sabbath travel?

But you ask, "What are we to do? How are we to get to church?"

I reply, on foot. It will be better for you. Once when I was holding meetings in London, in my ignorance I made arrangements to preach four times in different places one sabbath. After I had made the appointments I found I had to walk sixteen miles; but I walked it, and I slept that night with a clear conscience. I have made it a rule never to use the cars, and if I have a private carriage, I insist that horse and man shall rest on Monday. I want no hackman to rise up in judgment against me.

My friends, if we want to help the sabbath, let business men and Christians never patronize cars on the sabbath. I would hate to own stock in those companies, to be the means of taking the sabbath from these men, and have to answer for it at the day of judgment. Let those who are Christians at any rate endeavor to keep a conscience void of offence on this point.

SABBATH TRADING.

There are many who are inclined to use the sabbath in order to make money faster. This is no new sin. The prophet Amos hurled his invectives against oppressors who said, "When will the new moon be gone, that we may sell corn? and the sabbath, that we may set forth wheat?"

Covetous men have always chafed under the restraint, but not until the present time do we find that they have openly counted on sabbath trade to make money. We are told that many street car companies would not pay if it were not for the sabbath traffic, and the sabbath edition of newspapers is also counted upon as the most profitable.

The railroad men of this country are breaking down with softening of the brain, and die at the age of fifty or sixty. They think their business is so important that they must run their trains seven days in the week. Business men travel on the sabbath so as to be on hand for business Monday morning. But if they do so God will not prosper them.

Work is good for man and is commanded, "Six days shalt thou labor;" but overwork and work on the sabbath takes away the best thing he has.

NECESSARY AND BENEFICIAL.

The good effect on a nation's health and happiness produced by the return of the sabbath, with its cessation from work, cannot be overestimated. It is needed to repair and restore the body after six days of work. It is proved that a man can do more in six days than in seven. Lord Beaconsfield. said: "Of all divine institutions, the most divine is that which secures a day of rest for man. I hold it to be the most valuable blessing conceded to man. It is the cornerstone of all civilization, and its removal might affect even the health of the people." Mr. Gladstone recently told a friend that the secret of his long life is that amid all the pressure of public cares he never forgot the sabbath, with its rest for the body and the soul. The constitution of the United States protects the president in his weekly day of rest. He has ten days, "Sundays excepted," in which to consider a bill that has been sent to him for signature. Every workingman in the republic ought to be as thoroughly protected as the president. If workingmen got up a strike against unnecessary work on the sabbath, they would have the sympathy of a good many.

"Our bodies are seven-day clocks," says Talmage, "and they need to be wound up, and if they are not wound up they run down into the grave. No man can continuously break the sabbath and keep his physical and mental health. Ask aged men, and they will tell you they never knew men who continuously broke the sabbath, who did not fail in mind, body, or moral principles."

All that has been said about rest for man is true for working animals. God didn't forget them in this commandment, and man should not forget them either.

II.—RELIGIOUS ACTIVITY.

But "rest" does not mean idleness. No man enjoys idleness for any length of time. When one goes on a vacation, one does not lie around doing nothing all the time. Hard work at tennis, hunting, and other pursuits fills the hours. A healthy mind must find something to do.

Hence the sabbath rest does not mean inactivity. "Satan finds some mischief still for idle hands to do." The best way to keep off bad thoughts and to avoid temptation is to engage in active religious exercises.

As regards these, we should avoid extremes. On the one hand we find a rigor in sabbath observance that is nowhere commanded in Scripture, and that reminds one of the formalism of the Pharisees more than of the spirit of the gospel. Such strictness does more harm than good. It repels people and makes the sabbath a burden. On the other hand we should jealously guard against a loose way of keeping the sabbath. Already in many cities it is profaned openly.

When I was a boy the sabbath lasted from sundown on Saturday to sundown on Sunday, and I remember how we boys used to shout when it was over. It was the worst day in the week to us. I believe it can be made the brightest day in the week. Every child ought to be reared so that he shall be able to say, with a friend, that he would rather have the other six days weeded out of his memory than the sabbath of his childhood.

PUBLIC WORSHIP.

Make the sabbath a day of religious activity. First of all, of course, is attendance at public worship. "There is a discrepancy," says John McNeill, "between our creed about the sabbath day and our actual conduct. In many families, at ten o'clock on the sabbath, attendance at church is still an open question. There is no open question on Monday morning—'John, will you go to work to-day?'"

A minister rebuked a farmer for not attending church, and said, "You know John you are never absent from market."

"O," was the reply, "we *must* go to market."

Some one has said that without the sabbath the church of Christ could not, as a visible organization, exist on earth. Another has said that "we need to be in the drill of observance as well as in the liberty of faith." Human nature is so treacherous that we are apt to omit things altogether unless there is some special reason for doing them. A man is not likely to worship at all unless he has regularly appointed times and means for worship. Family and private devotions are almost certain to be omitted altogether unless one gets into the habit, and has a special time set apart daily.

A REMINISCENCE.

I remember blaming my mother for sending me to church on the sabbath. On one occasion the preacher had to send some one into the gallery to wake me up. I thought it was hard to have to work in the field all the week, and then to be obliged to go to church and hear a sermon I didn't understand. I thought I wouldn't go to church any more when I got away from home; but I had got so in the habit of going that I couldn't stay away. After one or two sabbaths, back again to the house of God I went. There I first found Christ, and I have often said since,

"Mother, I thank you for making me go to the house of God when I didn't want to go."

Parents, if you want your children to grow up and honor you, have them honor the sabbath day. Don't let them go off fishing, and getting into bad company, or it won't be long before they will come home and curse you. I know few things more beautiful than to see a father and mother coming up the aisle with their daughters and sons, and sitting down together to hear the Word of God. It is a good thing to have the children, not in some remote loft or gallery, but in a good place, well in sight. Though they cannot understand the sermon now, when they get older they won't desire to break away, they will continue attending public worship in the house of God.

But we must not mistake the means for the end. We must not think that the sabbath is just for the sake of being able to attend meetings. There are some people who think they must spend the whole day at meetings or private devotions. The result is that at nightfall they are tired out, and the day has brought them no rest. The number of church services attended ought to be measured by the person's ability to enjoy them and get good from them, without being wearied. Attending meetings is not the only way to observe the sabbath. The Israelites were commanded to keep it in their dwellings as well as in holy convocation. The home, that centre of so great influence over the life and character of the people, ought to be made the scene of true sabbath observance.

HOME OBSERVANCE.

Jeremiah classified godless families with the heathen: "Pour out thy fury upon the heathen that know thee not, and upon the families that call not on thy name: for they have eaten up Jacob, devoured him, and consumed him, and have made his habitation desolate."

Many mothers have written to me at one time or another to know what to do to entertain their children on the sabbath. The boys say, "I do wish 'twas Night," or, "I do hate the sabbath," or, "I do wish the sabbath was over." It ought to be the happiest day in the week to them, one to be looked forward to with pleasure. In order to this end, many suggestions might be followed. Make family prayers especially attractive by having the children learn some verse or story from the Bible. Give more time to your children than you can give on week days, reading to them and perhaps taking them to walk in the afternoon or evening. Show by your conduct that the sabbath is a delight, and they will soon catch your spirit. Set aside some time for religious instruction, without making this a task. You can make it interesting for the children by telling Bible stories and asking them to guess the names of the characters. Have Sunday games for the younger children. Picture books, puzzle maps of Palestine, etc., can be easily obtained. Sunday albums and Sunday clocks are other devices. Set aside attractive books for the sabbath, not letting the children have these during the week. By doing this, the children can be brought to look forward to the day with eagerness and pleasure.

PRIVATE OBSERVANCE.

Apart from public and family observance, the individual ought to devote a portion of the time to his own edification. Prayer, meditation, reading, ought not to be forgotten. Think of men devoting six days a week to their body, which will soon pass away, and begrudging one day to the soul which will live on and on forever: Is it too much for God to ask for one day to be devoted to the growth and training of the spiritual senses, when the other senses are kept busy the other six days?

If your circumstances permit, engage in some definite Christian work—such as teaching in Sunder school, or visiting the sick. Do all the good you can Sin keeps no sabbath, and no more should good deeds. There is plenty of opportunity in this fallen world to perform works of mercy and religion. Make your sabbath down here a foretaste of the eternal sabbath that is in store for believers.

You want power in your Christian life, do you? You want Holy Ghost power? You want the dew of heaven on your brow? You want to see men convicted and converted? I don't believe we shall ever have genuine conversions until we get straight on this law of God.

SABBATH DESECRATION.

Men seem to think they have a right to change the holy day into a *holiday*. The young have more temptations to break the sabbath than we had forty years ago. There are three great temptations: first, the trolley car, that will take you off into the country for a nickel to have a day of recreation; second, the bicycle, which is leading a good many Christian men to give up their sabbath and spend the day on excursions; and the third, the Sunday newspaper.

Twenty years ago Christian people in Chicago would have been horrified if any one had prophesied that all the theatres would be open every sabbath; but that is what has come to pass. If it had been prophesied twenty years ago that Christian men would take a wheel and go off on Sunday morning and be gone all day on an excursion, Christians would have been horrified and would have said it was impossible; but that is what is going on to-day all over the country.

THE SUNDAY NEWSPAPER.

With regard to the Sunday newspaper, I know all the arguments that are brought in its favor—that the work on it is done during the week, that it is the Monday paper that causes Sunday work, and so on. But there are two hundred thousand newsboys selling the paper on Sunday. Would you like to have your boy one of them? Men are kept running trains in order to distribute the papers. Would you like your sabbath taken away from you? If not, then practise the Golden Rule, and don't touch the papers.

Their contents make them unfit for reading any day, not to say Sunday. Some New York dailies advertise Sunday editions of sixty pages. Many dirty pieces of scandal in this and other countries are raked up and put into them. "Eight pages of fun!"—that is splendid reading for Sunday, isn't it? Even when a so-called sermon is printed, it is completely buried by the fiction and news matter. It is time that ministers went into their pulpits and preached against Sunday newspapers if they haven't done it already. Put the man in the scales that buys and reads Sunday papers. After reading them for two or three hours he might go and hear the best sermon in the world, but you couldn't preach anything into him. His mind is filled up with what he has read, and there is no room for thoughts of God. I believe that the archangel Gabriel himself could not make an impression on an audience that has its head full of such trash. If you bored a hole into a man's head, you could not inject any thoughts of God and heaven.

I don't believe that the publishers would allow their own children to read them. Why then should they give them to my children and to yours?

A merchant who advertises in Sunday papers is not keeping the sabbath. It is a master-stroke of the devil to induce Christian men to do this in order to make trade for Monday. But if a man makes money, and yet his sons are ruined and his home broken up, what has he gained?

Ladies buy the Sunday papers and read the advertisements of Monday bargains to see what they can buy cheap. Just so with their religion. They are willing to have it if it doesn't cost anything.

If Christian men and women refused to buy them, if Christian merchants refused to advertise in them, they would soon die out, because that is where they get most of their support.

They tell me the Sunday paper has come to stay, and I may as well let it alone. Never! I believe it is a great evil, and I shall fight it while I live. I never read a Sunday paper, and wouldn't have one in my house. They are often sent me, but I tear them up without reading them. I will have nothing to do with them. They do more harm to religion than any other one agency I know. Their whole influence is against keeping the sabbath holy. They are an unnecessary evil. Can't a man read enough news on week days without desecrating the sabbath? We had no Sunday papers till the war came, and we got along very well without them. They have been increasing in size and in number ever since then, and I think they have been lowering their tone ever since. If you believe that, help to fight them too. Stamp them out, beginning with yourself.

PUNISHMENT OR BLESSING?

No nation has ever prospered that has trampled the sabbath in the dust. Show me a nation that has done this, and I will show you a nation that has got in it the seeds of ruin and decay. I believe that sabbath desecration will carry a nation down quicker than anything else. Adam brought marriage and the sabbath with him out of Eden, and neither can be disregarded without suffering. When the children of Israel went into the Promised Land God told them to let their land rest every seven years, and He would give them as much in six years as in seven. For four hundred and ninety years they disregarded that law. But mark you, Nebuchadnezzar came and took them off into Babylon, and kept them seventy years in captivity, and the land had its seventy sabbaths of rest. Seven times seventy is four hundred and ninety. So they did not gain much by breaking this law. You can give God His day, or He will take it.

On the other hand, honoring the fourth commandment brings blessing. "If thou turn away thy foot from the sabbath, from doing thy pleasure on my holy day; and call the sabbath a delight, the holy of the Lord, honorable; and shalt honor Him, not doing thine own ways, nor finding thine own pleasure, nor speaking thine own words ('thine own' as contrasted with what God enjoins), then shalt thou delight thyself in the Lord; and I will cause thee to ride upon the high places of the earth, and feed thee with the heritage of Jacob thy father, for the mouth of the Lord hath spoken it."

I do not know what will become of this republic if we give up our Christian sabbath. If Satan can break the conscience down on one point, he can break it down on all. When I was in France in 1867, I could not tell one day from the other. On Sunday stores were open and buildings were erected, the same as on other days. See how quickly that country went down. One hundred years ago France and England stood abreast in the march of nations. Where do they stand to-day? France undertook to wipe out the sabbath, and has pretty nearly wiped itself out, while England belts the globe.

A FIRM STAND.

We have a fighting chance to save this nation, and what we want is men and women who have moral courage to stand up and say:

"No, I will not touch the Sunday paper, and all the influence I have I will throw dead against it. I will not go away on Saturday evening if I have to travel on Sunday to get back. I will not do unnecessary work on the sabbath. I will do all I can to keep it holy as God commanded."

But some one says: "Mr. Moody, what are you going to do? I have to work seven days a week or starve."

Then starve! Wouldn't it be a grand thing to have a martyr in the nineteenth century? "The blood of the martyrs is the seed of the church." Some one says the seed is getting very low; it has been a long time since we have had any seed. I would give something to erect a monument to such a martyr to his fidelity to God's law. I would go around the world to attend his funeral.

We want to-day men who will make up their minds to do what is right, and stand by it if the heavens tumble on their heads. What is to become of Christian Associations and Sunday Schools, of churches and Christian Endeavor Societies, if the Christian sabbath is given up to recreation, and made a holiday? Hasn't the time come to call a halt if men want power with God? Let men call you narrow and bigoted, but be man enough to stand by God's law, and you will have power and blessing. That is the kind of Christianity we want just now in this country. Any man can go with the crowd, but we want men who will go against the current.

Sabbath-breaker, are you ready to step into the scales?

FIFTH COMMANDMENT

"Honor thy father and thy mother: that thy days may be long upon the land which the Lord thy God giveth thee."

We are living in dark days on this question too. It really seems as if the days the apostle Paul wrote about are upon us: "In the last days perilous times shall come; for men shall be lovers of their own selves, covetous, boasters, proud, blasphemers, *disobedient to parents, unthankful*, unholy, *without natural affection*, despisers of those that are good,…." If Paul was alive to-day, could he have described the present state of affairs more truly? There are perhaps more men in this country that are breaking the hearts of their fathers and mothers, and trampling on the law of God, than in any other civilized country in the world. How many sons treat their parents with contempt, and make light of their entreaties? A young man will have the kindest care from parents; they will watch over him, and care for all his wants; and some bad companion will come in and sweep him away from them in a few weeks. How many young ladies have married against their parents' wishes, and have gone off and made their own life bitter! I never knew one case that did not turn out badly. They invariably bring ruin upon themselves, unless they repent.

BEGIN IN THE HOME.

The first four commandments deal with our relations to God. They tell us how to worship and when to worship; they forbid irreverence and impiety in word and act. Now God turns to our relations with each other, and isn't it significant that He deals first with family life? "God is going to show us our duty to our neighbor. How does He begin? Not by telling us how kings ought to reign, or how soldiers ought to fight, or how merchants ought to conduct their business, but how boys and girls ought to behave at home."

We can see that if their home life is all right, they are almost sure to fulfil the law both in regard to God and man. Parents stand in the place of God to their children in a great many ways until the children arrive at years of discretion. If the children are true to their parents, it will be easier for them to be true to God. He used the human relationship as a symbol of our relationship to Him both by creation and by grace. God is our Father in heaven. We are His offspring.

On the other hand, if they have not learned to be obedient and respectful at home, they are likely to have little respect for the law of the land. It is all in the heart; and the heart is prepared at home for good or bad conduct outside. The tree grows the way the twig is bent.

"Honor thy father and thy mother." That word "honor" means more than mere obedience—a child may obey through fear. It means love and affection, gratitude, respect. We are told that in the east the words "father" and "mother" include those who are "superiors in age, wisdom and in civil or religious station," so that when the Jews were taught to honor their father and mother it included all who were placed over them in these relations, as well as their parents. Isn't there a crying need for that same feeling to-day? The lawlessness of the present time is a natural consequence of the growing absence of a feeling of respect for those in authority.

HONOR THY MOTHER.

It has been pointed out as worthy of notice that this commandment enjoins honor for *the mother*, and yet in eastern countries to the present day woman is held of little account. When I was in Palestine a few years ago, the prettiest girl in Jericho was sold by her father in exchange for a donkey. In many ancient nations, just as in certain parts of heathendom today, the parents are killed off as soon as they become old and feeble. Can't we see the hand of God here, raising the woman to her rightful position of honor out of the degradation into which she had been dragged by heathenism?

"Honor thy father and thy mother that thy days may be long upon the land which the Lord thy God giveth thee." I believe that we must get back to the old truths. You may make light of it, and laugh at it, young man, but remember that God has given this commandment, and you cannot set it aside. If we get back to this law, we shall have power and blessing.

TEMPORAL BLESSING OR CURSE.

I believe it to be literally true that our temporal condition depends on the way we act upon this commandment.

"Honor thy father and mother, (which is the first commandment with promise), that it may be well with thee, and that thou mayest live long on the earth." "Honor thy father and thy mother, as the Lord thy God hath commanded thee; that thy days may be prolonged, and that it may go well with thee, in the land which the Lord thy God giveth thee." "Cursed is he that setteth light by his father or mother." "Whoso curseth his father or mother, his lamp shall be put out in obscure darkness." It would be easy to multiply texts from the Bible to prove this truth. Experience teaches the same thing. A good, loving son generally turns out better than a refractory son. Obedience and respect at home prepare the way for obedience to the employer, and are joined with other virtues that help toward a prosperous career, crowned with a ripe, honored old age. Disobedience and disrespect for parents are often the first steps in the downward track. Many a criminal has testified that this is the point where he first went astray. I have lived over sixty years, and I have learned one thing if I have learned nothing else—that no man or woman who dishonors father or mother ever prospers.

Young man, young woman, how do you treat your parents? Tell me that, and I will tell you how you are going to get on in life. When I hear a young man speaking contemptuously of his grey-haired father or mother, I say he has sunk very low indeed. When I see a young man as polite as any gentleman can be when he is out in society, but who snaps up his mother and speaks unkindly to his father, I would not give the snap of my finger for his religion. If there is any man or woman on earth that ought to be treated kindly and tenderly, it is that loving mother or that loving father. If they cannot have your regard through life, what reward are they to have for all their care and anxiety? Think how they loved you and provided for you in your early days.

A MOTHER'S LOVE.

Let your mind go back to the time when you were ill. Did your mother neglect you? When a neighbor came in and said, "Now, mother, you go and lie down; you have been up for a week; I will take your place for a night"—did she do it? No; and if the poor worn body forced her to it at last, she lay watching, and if she heard your voice, she was at your side directly, anticipating all your wants, wiping the perspiration away from your brow. If you wanted water, how soon you got it! She would gladly have taken the disease into her own body to save you. Her love for you would drive her to any lengths. No matter to what depths of vice and misery you have sunk, no matter how profligate you have grown, she has not turned you out of her heart. Perhaps she loves you all the more because you are wayward. She would draw you back by the bands of a love that never dies.

FILIAL INGRATITUDE.

When I was in England, I read of a man who professed to be a Christian, who was brought before the magistrate for not supporting his aged father. He had let him go to the workhouse. My friends, I'd rather be content with a crust of bread and a drink of water than let my father or mother go to the workhouse. The idea of a professing Christian doing such a thing! God have mercy on such a godless Christianity as that! It is a withered up thing, and the breath of heaven will drive it away. Don't profess to love God and do a thing like that.

A friend of mine told me of a poor man who had sent his son to school in the city. One day the father was hauling some wood into the city, perhaps to pay his boy's bills. The young man was walking down the street with two of his school friends, all dressed in the very height of fashion. His father saw him, and was so glad that he left his wood, and went to the sidewalk to speak to him. But the boy was ashamed of his father, who had on his old working clothes, and spurned him, and said:

"I don't know you."

Will such a young man ever amount to anything? Never!

I remember a very promising young man whom I had in the Sunday school in Chicago. His father was a confirmed drunkard, and his mother took in washing to educate her four children. This was her eldest son, and I thought that he was going to redeem the whole family. But one day a thing happened that made him go down in my estimation.

The boy was in the high school, and was a very bright scholar. One day he stood with his mother at the cottage door—it was a poor house, but she could not pay for their schooling, and feed and clothe her children, and hire a very good house too, out of her earnings. When they were talking a young man from the high school came up the street, and this boy walked away from his mother. Next day the young man said:

"Who was that I saw you talking to yesterday?"

"Oh, that was my washerwoman."

I said: "Poor fellow! He will never amount to anything."

That was a good many years ago. I have kept my eye on him. He has gone down, down, down, and now he is just a miserable wreck. Of course he would go down. Ashamed of his mother that loved him and toiled for him, and bore so much hardship for him! I cannot tell you the contempt I had for that one act.

Let us look at:

A BRIGHTER PICTURE.

Some years ago I heard of a poor woman who sent her boy to school and college. When he was to graduate, he wrote his mother to come, but she sent back word that she could not because her only skirt had already been turned once. She was so shabby that she was afraid he would be ashamed of her. He wrote back that he didn't care how she was dressed, and urged so strongly that she went. He met her at the station, and took her to a nice place to stay. The day came for his graduation, and he walked down the broad aisle with that poor mother dressed very shabbily, and put her into one of the best seats in the house. To her great surprise he was the valedictorian of the class, and he carried everything before him. He won a prize, and when it was given to him, he stepped down before the whole audience, and kissed his mother, and said:

"Here, mother, here is the prize. It is yours. I would not have had it if it had not been for you."

Thank God for such a man!

The one glimpse the Bible gives us of thirty out of the thirty-three years of Christ's life on earth shows that He did not come to destroy this fifth commandment. The secret of all those silent years is embodied in that verse in Luke's Gospel—"And He went down with them and came to Nazareth, and was subject to them." Did He not set an example of true filial love and care when in the midst of the agonies of the cross He mode provision for His mother? Did He not condemn the miserable evasions of this law by the Pharisees of His own day:

> Well did Isaiah prophesy of you hypocrites, as it is written, This people honoreth me with their lips, but their heart is far from me. But in vain do they worship me, teaching as their doctrines the precepts of men....Full well do ye reject the commandment of God, that ye may keep your tradition. For Moses said, Honor thy father and thy mother; and, He that speaketh evil of father or mother, let him die the death; but ye say, If a man shall say to his father or his mother, That wherewith thou mightest have been profited by me, is Corban, (that is to say, Given to God), ye no longer suffer him to do aught for his father or his mother: making void the word of God by your tradition, which ye have delivered.

I have read of one heathen custom in China, which would do us credit in this so-called Christian country. On every New Year's morning each man and boy, from the emperor to the lowest peasant, is said to pay a visit to his mother, carrying her a present varying in value according to his station in life. He thanks her for all she has done for him, and asks a continuance of her favor another year. Abraham Lincoln used to say: "All I have I owe to my mother."

I would rather die a hundred deaths than have my children grow up to treat me with scorn and contempt. I would rather have them honor me a thousand times over than have the world honor me. I would rather have their esteem and favor than the esteem of the whole world. And any man who seeks the honor and esteem of the world, and doesn't treat his parents right, is sure to be disappointed:

AN EXHORTATION.

Young man, if your parents are still living treat them kindly. Do all you can to make their declining years sweet and happy. Bear in mind that this is the only commandment that you may not always be able to obey. As long as you live, you will be able to serve God, to keep the sabbath, to obey all the other commandments, but the day comes to most men when father and mother die. What bitter feelings you will have when the opportunity has gone by, if you fail to show them the respect and love that is their due! How long is it since you wrote to your mother? Perhaps you have not written home for months, or it may be for years. How often I get letters from mothers urging me to try and influence their sons!

Which would you rather be—a Joseph or an Absalom? Joseph wasn't satisfied until he had brought his old father down into Egypt. He was the greatest man in Egypt, next to Pharaoh; he was arrayed in the finest garments; he had Pharaoh's ring on his hand, and a gold chain about his neck, and they cried before him, "Bow the knee." Yet when he heard Jacob was coming, he hurried out to meet him. He wasn't ashamed of the old man, with his shepherds clothes. What a contrast we see in Absalom. That young man broke his father's heart by his rebellion, and the Jews are said to throw a stone at Absalom's pillar to the present day, whenever they pass it, as a token of their horror of Absalom's unnatural conduct.

Come, now, are you ready to be weighed? If you have been dishonoring your father and mother, step into the scales and see how quickly you will be found wanting. See how quickly you will strike the beam. I don't know any man who is much lighter than one who treats his parents with contempt. Do you disobey them just as much as you dare? Do you try to deceive them? Do you call them old-fashioned, and sneer at their advice? How do you treat that venerable father and praying mother?

You may be a professing Christian, but I wouldn't give much for your religion unless it gets into your life and teaches you how to live. I wouldn't give a snap of my finger for a religion that doesn't begin at home and regulate your conduct toward your parents.

SIXTH COMMANDMENT

"Thou shalt not kill."

I used to say: "What is the use of taking up a law like this in an audience where, probably, there isn't a man who ever thought of, or ever will commit murder?" But as one gets on in years, he sees many a murder that is not outright killing. I need not kill a person to be a murderer. If I get so angry that I wish a man dead, I am a murderer in God's sight. God looks at the heart and says he that hateth his brother is a murderer.

First let us see what this commandment does not mean.

It does not forbid the killing of animals for food and for other reasons. Millions of rams and lambs and turtle-doves must have been killed every year for sacrifices under the Mosaic system. Christ Himself ate of the Passover lamb, and we are told definitely of cases where He ate fish Himself and provided it for His disciples and the people to eat.

It does not forbid the killing of burglars, etc., in self-defence. Directly after the giving of the Ten Commandments, God laid down the ordinance that if a thief be found breaking in and be smitten that he die, it was pardonable. Did not Christ justify this idea of self-defence when He said: "If the goodman of the house had known in what watch the thief would come, he would have watched, and would not have suffered his house to be broken up?"

It does not forbid capital punishment. God Himself set the death penalty upon violations of each of the first seven commandments, as well as for other crimes. God said to Noah after the deluge—"Whoso sheddeth man's blood, by man shall his blood be shed;" and the reason given is just as true to-day as it was then—"for in the image of God made He man."

What it does forbid is the wanton, intentional taking of human life under wrong motives and circumstances. Man is made in God's image. He is built for eternity. He is more than a mere animal. His life ought therefore to be held sacred. Once taken, it can never be restored. In heathen lands human life is no more sacred than the life of animals; even in Christian lands there are heartless and selfish men who hold it cheap; but God has invested it with a high value. An infidel philosopher of the eighteenth century said: "In the sight of God every event is alike important; and the life of a man is of no greater importance to the universe than that of an oyster." "Where is the crime," he asked, "of turning a few ounces of blood out of their channel?" Such language needs no answer.

THE VALUE OF A MAN.

Let me give you a passage from H. L. Hastings: "A friend of mine visited the Fiji Islands in 1844, and what do you suppose an infidel was worth there then? You could buy a man for a musket, or if you paid money, for seven dollars, and after you had bought him you could feed him, starve him, work him, whip him, or eat him—they generally ate them, unless they were so full of tobacco they could not stomach them! But if you go there to-day you could not buy a man for seven million dollars. There are no men for sale there now. What has made the difference in the price of humanity? The twelve hundred Christian chapels scattered over that Island tell the story. The people have learned to read that Book which says: 'Ye were not redeemed with corruptible things as silver and gold, but with the precious blood of Christ'; and since they learned that lesson, no man is for sale there."

Men tell me that the world is getting so much better. We talk of our American civilization. We forget the alarming increase of crime in our midst. It is said that there is no civilized country on the globe where murder is so frequently committed and so seldom punished.

SUICIDE.

There is that other kind of murder that is increasing at an appalling rate among us—suicide. There have been infidels in all ages who have advocated it as a justifiable means of release from trial and difficulty; yet thinking men, as far back as Aristotle, have generally condemned it as cowardly and unjustifiable under any conditions. No man has a right to take his own life from such motives any more than the life of another.

It has been pointed out that the Jewish race, the people of God, always counted length of days as a blessing. The Bible does not mention one single instance of a good man committing suicide. In the four thousand years of Old Testament history it records only four suicides, and only one suicide in the New Testament. Saul, king of Israel, and his armor-bearer, Ahithophel, Zimri and Judas Iscariot are the five cases. Look at the references in the Bible to see what kind of men they were.

OTHER KINDS OF MURDER.

But I want to speak of other classes of murderers that are very numerous in this country, although they are not classified as murderers. The man who is the cause of the death of another through criminal carelessness is guilty. The man who sells diseased meat; the saloon-keeper whose drink has maddened the brain of a criminal; those who adulterate food; the employer who jeopardizes the lives of employees and others by unsafe surroundings and conditions in harmful occupations,—they are all guilty of blood where life is lost as a consequence.

When I was in England in 1892, I met a gentleman who claimed that they were ahead of us in the respect they had for the law. "We hang our murderers," he said, "but there isn't one out of twenty in your country that is hung." I said, "You are greatly mistaken, for they walk about these two countries unhung." "What do you mean?" "I will tell you what I mean," I said; "the man that comes into my house and runs a dagger into my heart for my money, is a prince compared with a son that takes five years to kill me and the wife of my bosom. A young man who comes home night after night drunk, and when his mother remonstrates, curses her grey hairs and kills her by inches, is the blackest kind of a murderer."

That kind of thing is going on constantly all around us. One young man at college, an only son, whose mother wrote to him remonstrating against his gambling and drinking habits, took the letters out of the post-office, and when he found that they were from her, he tore them up without reading them. She said,

"I thought I would die when I found I had lost my hold on that son."

If a boy kills his mother by his conduct, you can't call it anything else than *murder*, and he is as truly guilty of breaking this sixth commandment as if he drove a dagger to her heart. If all young men in this country who are killing their parents and their wives by inches, should be hung this next week, there would be a great many funerals.

How are you treating your parents? Come, are you killing them? This sixth commandment follows very naturally after the fifth,—"Honor thy father and thy mother." Don't put any thorns in their pillows and make their last days miserable. Bear in mind that the commandment refers not only to shooting a man down in cold blood; but he is the worst murderer who goes on, month after month, year after year, until he has crowded the life out of a sainted mother and put a godly father under the sod.

THE WORDS OF CHRIST.

Let us look once again at the Sermon on the Mount, that men think so much of, and see what Christ had to say: "Ye have heard that it has been said by them of old time, Thou shalt not kill; and whosoever shall kill shall be in danger of the judgment: but I say unto you, that whosoever is angry with his brother without a cause shall be in danger of the judgment: and whosoever shall say to his brother, Raca, (an expression of contempt), shall be in danger of the council: but whosoever shall say, Thou fool, (an expression of condemnation), shall be in danger of hell fire." "Three degrees of murderous guilt," as has been said, "all of which can be manifested without a blow being struck; secret anger—the spiteful jeer—the open, unrestrained outburst of violent abusive speech."

Again, what does John say? "Whosoever hateth his brother is a murderer: and ye know that no murderer hath eternal life abiding in him."

Did you ever in your heart wish a man dead? That was murder. Did you ever get so angry that you wished any one harm? Then you are guilty. I may be addressing some one who is cultivating an unforgiving spirit. That is the spirit of the murderer, and needs to be rooted out of your heart.

We can only read man's acts—what they have done. God looks down into the heart. That is the birthplace and home of the evil desires and intentions that lead to the transgression of all God's laws.

Listen once more to the words of Jesus: "From within, out of the heart of men, proceed EVIL THOUGHTS—ADULTERIES—FORNICATIONS—

MURDERS—THEFTS—COVETOUSNESS—WICKEDNESS—DECEIT—LASCIVIOUSNESS—AN EVIL EYE—BLASPHEMY—PRIDE—FOOLISHNESS...."

May God purge our hearts of these evil things, if we are harboring them! Ah, if many of us were weighed now, we should find Belshazzar's doom written against us—"Tekel—wanting!"

SEVENTH COMMANDMENT

"Thou shalt not commit adultery."

An English army-officer in India who had been living an impure life went around one evening to argue religion with the chaplain. During their talk the officer said:

"Religion is all very well, but you must admit that there are difficulties—about the miracles, for instance."

The chaplain knew the man and his besetting sin, and quietly looking him in the face, answered:

"Yes, there are some things in the Bible not very plain, I admit; but the seventh commandment is very plain."

PLAIN SPEAKING.

I would to God I could pass over this commandment, but I feel that the time has come to cry aloud and spare not. Plain speaking about it is not very fashionable nowadays. "Teachers of religion have by common consent banished from their public teaching all advice, warning or allusion in regard to love between the sexes," says Dr. Stalker. These themes are left to poets and novelists to handle. In an autobiography recently published in England, the writer attributed no small share of the follies and vices of his earlier years to his never having heard a plain, outspoken sermon on this seventh commandment.

But though men are inclined to pass it by, God is not silent or indifferent in regard to it. When I hear any one make light of adultery and licentiousness, I take the Bible and see how God has let his curse and wrath come down upon it.

Thou shalt not commit adultery....For this is a heinous crime; yea, it is an iniquity to be punished by the judges. For it is a fire that consumeth to destruction, and would root out all mine increase....By means of a whorish woman a man is brought to a piece of bread: and the adulteress will hunt for the precious life. Can a man take fire in his bosom, and his clothes not be burned? Can one go upon hot coals, and his feet not be burned? So he that goeth in to his neighbor's wife; whosoever toucheth her shall not be innocent.... Whoso committeth adultery with a woman lacketh understanding: he that doeth it destroyeth his own soul. A wound and dishonor shall he get; and his reproach shall not be wiped away....Know ye not that the unrighteous shall not inherit the kingdom of God? Be not deceived: neither fornicators, nor adulterers, nor effeminate, nor abusers of themselves with mankind shall inherit the kingdom of God....But fornication, and all uncleanness, let it not be once named among you, as becometh saints; neither filthiness, nor foolish talking, nor jesting, which are not convenient: but rather giving thanks. For this ye know, that no whoremonger, nor unclean person hath any inheritance in the kingdom of Christ and of God. Let no man deceive you with vain words: for because of these things cometh the wrath of God upon the children of disobedience. Be not ye therefore partakers with them....Whoremongers shall have their part in the lake which burneth with fire and brimstone: which is the second death....For without are whoremongers....

These are a few of the threatenings and warnings contained in the old Book, up to its closing chapter. It speaks plainly, without compromise.

MARRIAGE AND THE HOME.

This commandment is God's bulwark around marriage and the home. Marriage is one of the institutions that existed in Eden; it is older than the fall. It is the most sacred relationship that can exist between human beings, taking precedence even of the relationship of the parent and child. Some one has pointed out that as in the beginning God created one man and one woman, this is the true order for all ages. Where family ties are disregarded and dishonored, the results are always fatal. The home existed before the church, and unless the home is kept pure and undefiled, there can be no family religion and the church is in danger. Adultery and licentiousness have swept nation after nation out of existence. Did it not bring fire and brimstone from heaven upon Sodom and Gomorrah? What carried Rome into ruin? The obscene frescoes and statues at Pompeii and Naples tell the tale. Where there is no sacredness around the home, population dwindles; family virtues disappear; the children are corrupt from their very birth; the seeds of sure decay are already planted. In 1895 there were twenty-five thousand divorces in this country. I was on one of the fashionable streets of a prominent city some time ago, where every family except two in the whole street had either a son or a daughter that had been divorced. Divorce and debauchery go hand in hand. We are not gaining much in turning away from this old law, are we?

THE DEVIL'S COUNTERFEIT.

Lust is the devil's counterfeit of love. There is nothing more beautiful on earth than a pure love, and there is nothing so blighting as lust. I do not know of a quicker, shorter way down to hell than by adultery and the kindred sins condemned by this commandment. The Bible says that with the heart man believeth unto righteousness, but "whoredom and wine and new wine take away the heart." Lust will drive all natural affection out of a man's heart. For the sake of some vile harlot he will trample on the feelings and entreaties of a sainted mother and beautiful wife and godly sister.

Young man, are you leading an impure life? Suppose God's scales should drop down before you, what would you do? Are you fit for the kingdom of heaven? You know very well that you are not. You loathe yourself. When you look upon that pure wife or mother, you say,

"What a vile wretch I am! The harlot is bringing me down to an untimely and dishonored grave."

May God show us what a fearful sin it is! The idea of making light of it! I do not know of any sin that will make a man run down to ruin more quickly. I am appalled when I think of what is going on in the world; of so many young men living impure lives, and talking about the virtue of women as if it didn't amount to anything. This sin is coming in upon us like a flood at the present day. In every city there is an army of prostitutes. Young men by hundreds are being utterly ruined by this accursed sin.

THE PRODIGAL DAUGHTER.

I think that the most infernal thing the sun shines on in America is the way woman is treated after she has been ruined by a man, often under fair promises of marriage. Some one said that when the prodigal son came home he had the best robe and the fatted calf, but what does the prodigal daughter get? Although she may have been more sinned against than sinning, she is cast out and ostracized by society. She is condemned to an almost hopeless life of degradation and shame, sinking step by step into a loathsome grave, unless she hurries her doom by suicide. But the wretch who has ruined her in body and soul, holds his head as high as ever, and society attaches no stain to him. If he had failed to pay his gambling debts or was detected cheating at cards, he would promptly be dropped by society; but he may boast of his impure life, and his companions will think nothing of it. Parents who would not allow their daughters to become acquainted with a man who is rude in manners, sometimes do not hesitate to accept the society of men who are known to be impure.

Talk about stealing—a man who steals the virtue of a woman is the meanest thief that ever was on the face of the earth! One who goes into your house and steals your money is a prince compared with a vile libertine who takes the virtue of your sister, or steals the affection of your wife, and robs you of her; no sneakthief that ever walked the earth is so mean as he. How men pass laws to protect their property, but when that which is far nearer and dearer to them than money is taken, it is made light of! If a man should push a young lady into the river and she should be drowned, the law would lay hold of him, and he would be tried for murder and hung. But if he wins her affection and ruins her, and then casts her off, isn't he worse, than a murderer? There are some sins that are worse than murder, and that is one of them. If some one should treat your wife or sister so, you would want to shoot him as you would a dog. Why do you not respect all women as you do your mother and sister? "What law of justice forgives the obscene bird of prey, while it kicks out of its path the soiled and bleeding dove?"

GOD'S COMING JUDGMENT.

God has appointed a day when this matter will be set right. "Be not deceived: God is not mocked: whatsoever a man soweth, that shall he also reap." He will render to every man according to his deeds. You may walk down the aisle of the church and take your seat, thinking that no one knows of your sin. But God is on the throne, and He will surely bring you to judgment. Do you believe that God will allow this infernal thing to go on,—women bearing all the blame while guilty men go unpunished? God has appointed a day when He will judge this world in righteousness, and the day is fast approaching.

If you are guilty of this sin, do not let the day pass until you repent. If you are living in some secret sin, or are fostering impure thoughts, make up your mind that by the grace of God you will be delivered. I don't believe a man who is guilty of this sin is ever going to see the kingdom of God unless he repents in sackcloth and ashes, and does all he can to make restitution.

AN EVIL HARVEST.

Even in this life adultery and uncleanness bring their awful results, both physical and mental. The pleasure and excitement that lead so many astray at the beginning soon pass away, and only the evil remains. Vice carries a sting in its tail, like the scorpion. The body is sinned against, and the body sooner or later suffers. "Every sin that a man doeth is without the body: but he that committeth fornication sinneth against his own body," said Paul. Nature herself punishes with nameless diseases, and the man goes down to the grave rotten, leaving the effects of his sin to blight his posterity. There are nations whose manhood has been eaten out by this awful scourge.

It drags a man lower than the beasts. It stains the memory. I believe that memory is "the worm that never dies," and the memory is never cleansed of obscene stories and unclean acts. Even if a man repents and reforms he often has to fight the past.

Lust gave Samson into the power of Delilah, who robbed him of his strength. It led David to commit murder and called down upon him the wrath of God, and if he had not repented he would have lost heaven. I believe that if Joseph had responded to the enticement of Potiphar's wife, his light would have gone out in darkness.

It ends in one or other of two ways: either in remorse and shame because of the realization of the loss of purity, with a terrible struggle against a hard taskmaster; or in hardness of heart, brutalizing of the finer senses, which is a more dreadful condition.

We hear a good deal about intemperance nowadays. That sin advertises itself; it shows its marks upon the face and in the conduct. But this hides itself away under the shadow of the night. A man who tampers with this evil goes on step by step until his character is blasted, his reputation ruined, his health gone, and his life made as dark as hell. May God wake up the nation to see how this awful sin is spreading!

Will any one deny that the house of the strange woman is "the way to hell, going down to the chambers of death," as the Bible says? Are there not men whose characters have been utterly ruined for this life through this accursed sin? Are there not wives who would rather sink into their graves than live? Many a man went with a pure woman to the altar a few years ago, and promised to love and cherish her. Now he has given his affections to some vile harlot, and brought ruin on his wife and children!

ARE YOU GUILTY?

Young man, young woman, are you guilty, even in thought? Bear in mind what Christ said: "Ye have heard that it was said by them of old time, Thou shalt not commit adultery: but I say unto you, That whosoever looketh on a woman to lust after her has committed adultery with her already in his heart." How many would repent but that they are tied hand and foot, and some vile harlot, whose feet are fastened in hell, clings to him and says: "If you give me up, I will expose you!" Can you step on the scales and take that harlot with you?

If you are guilty of this awful sin, escape for your life. Hear God's voice while there is yet time. Confess your sin to Him. Ask Him to snap the fetters that bind you. Ask Him to give you victory over your passions. If your right eye offends, pluck it out. If your right hand offends, cut it off. Shake yourself like Samson, and say:

"By the grace of God I will not go down to an adulterer's grave."

There is hope for you, adulterer. There is hope for you, adulteress. God will not turn you away if you truly repent. No matter how low down in vice and misery you may have sunk, you may be washed, you may be sanctified, you may be justified in the name of the Lord Jesus, and by the Spirit of our God. Remember what Christ said to that woman which was a sinner—"Thy sins are forgiven thee; thy faith hath saved thee; go in peace;" and to that woman that was taken in adultery—"Go, and sin no more."

EIGHTH COMMANDMENT

"Thou shalt not steal."

During the time of slavery, a slave was preaching with great power. His master heard of it, and sent for him, and said:

"I understand you are preaching?"

"Yes," said the slave,

"Well, now," said the master, "I will give you all the

time you need, and I want you to prepare a sermon on the Ten Commandments, and to bear down especially on stealing, because there is a great deal of stealing on the plantation."

The slave's countenance fell at once. He said he wouldn't like to do that; there wasn't the warmth in that subject there was in others.

I have noticed that people are satisfied when you preach about the sins of the patriarchs, but they don't like it when you touch upon the sins of to-day. That is coming too near home. But we need to have these old doctrines stated over and over again in our churches. Perhaps it is not necessary to speak here about the grosser violations of this eighth commandment, because the law of the land looks after these; but a man or woman can steal without cracking safes and picking pockets. Many a person who would shrink from taking what belongs to another person, thinks nothing of stealing from the government or from large public corporations, such as street-car companies. If you steal from a rich man it is as much a sin as stealing from a poor man. If you lie about the value of things you buy, are you not trying to defraud the storekeeper? "It is naught, it is naught, saith the buyer: but when he is gone his way, then he boasteth."

On the other hand, many a person who would not steal himself, holds stock in companies that make dishonest profits; but "though hand join in hand, the wicked shall not go unpunished."

A young man in our Bible Institute in Chicago got on the grip-car, and before the conductor came around to take the fare, they reached the Institute and he jumped off without paying his fare. In thinking over that act he said: "That was not just right. I had my ride and I ought to pay the fare."

He remembered the face of the conductor, and he went to the car barns and paid him the five cents.

"Well," the conductor said, "you are a fool not to keep it." "No," the young man said, "I am not. I got the ride, and I ought to have paid for it." "But it was my business to collect it." "No, it was my business to hand it to you." The conductor said, "I think you must belong to that Bible Institute."

I have heard few things said of the Institute that pleased me so much as that one thing. Not long after that the conductor came to the Institute and asked the student to come to see him. A cottage-meeting was started in his house; and not only himself but a number of others around there were converted as a result of that one act.

You can hardly take up a paper now without reading of some cashier of a bank who has become a defaulter, or of some large swindling operation that has ruined scores, or of some breach of trust, or fraudulent failure in business. These things are going on all over the land.

I would to God that we could have all gambling swept away. If Christian men take the right stand, they can check it and break it up in a great many places. It leads to stealing.

WHERE THE STREAM STARTS.

The stream generally starts at home and in the school. Parents are woefully lax in their condemnation and punishment of the sin of stealing. The child begins by taking sugar, it may be. The mother makes light of it at first, and the child's conscience is violated without any sense of wrong. By and by it is not an easy matter to check the habit, because it grows and multiplies with every new commission.

The value of the thing that is stolen has nothing to say to the guilt of the act. Two people were once arguing upon this point, and one said: "Well, you will not contend that a theft of a pin and of a dollar are the same to God?" "When you tell me the difference between the value of a pin and of a dollar to God," said the other, "I will answer your question."

The value or amount is not what is to be considered, but whether the act is *right* or *wrong*. Partial obedience is not enough: obedience must be entire. The little indulgences, the small transgressions are what drive religion out of the soul. They lay the foundation for the grosser sins. If you give way to little temptations, you will not be able to resist when great temptations come to you.

GOD'S WEIGHTS.

Extortioner, are you ready to step into the scales? What will you do with the condemnation of God—"Thou has taken usury and increase, and thou hast greedily gained of thy neighbor's by extortion, and hast forgotten me, saith the Lord God?"

Employer, are you guilty of sweating your employees? Have you defrauded the hireling of his wages? Have you paid starvation wages?

Thou shalt not oppress a hired servant that is poor and needy, whether he be of thy brethren, or of thy strangers that are in thy land within thy gates.…What mean ye that ye beat my people to pieces, and grind the faces of the poor? saith the Lord God of hosts....Behold, the hire of the laborers who have reaped down your fields, which is of you kept back by fraud, crieth: and the cries of them which have reaped are entered into the ears of the Lord of sabaoth.

And you, *employee*, have you been honest with your employer? Have you robbed him of his due by wasting your time when he was not looking? If God should summon you into His presence now, what would you say?

Let the *merchant* step into the scales. See if you will prove light when weighed against the law of God. Are you guilty of adulterating what you sell? Do you substitute inferior grades of goods? Are your advertisements deceptive? Are your cheap prices made possible by defrauding your customers either in quantity or in quality? Do you teach your clerks to put a French or an English tag on domestic manufactures, and then sell them as imported goods? Do you tell them to say that the goods are all wool when you know they are half cotton? Do you give short weight or measure? See what God says in His Word:

Shall I count them pure with the wicked balances, and with the bag of deceitful weights? Thou shalt not have in thy bag divers weights, a great and a small: thou shalt not have in thy house divers measures, a great and a small: but thou shalt have a perfect and just weight, a perfect and just measure shalt thou have: that thy days may be lengthened in the land which the Lord thy God giveth thee.... Ye shall do no unrighteousness in judgment, in meteyard, in weight, or in measure. Just balances, just weights, a just ephah and a just hin, shall ye have." Are you like those who said: "When will the new moon be gone, that we may sell corn? and the sabbath, that we may set forth wheat, making the ephah small, and the shekel great, and falsifying the balances by deceit? that we may buy the poor for silver, and the needy for a pair of shoes; yea, and sell the refuse of the wheat?

"Show me a people whose trade is dishonest," said Fronde, "and I will show you a people whose religion is a sham." Unless your religion can keep you honest in your business, it isn't worth much; it isn't the right kind. God is a God of righteousness, and no true follower of his can swerve one inch to the right or left without disobeying Him.

STOLEN GOODS A BURDEN.

I heard of a boy who stole a cannon-ball from a navy-yard. He watched his opportunity, sneaked into the yard, and secured it. But when he had it, he hardly knew what to do with it. It was heavy, and too large to conceal in his pocket, so he had to put it under his hat. When he got home with it, he dared not show it to his parents, because it would have led at once to his detection. He said in after years it was the last thing he ever stole. The story is told that one of Queen Victoria's diamonds valued at $600,000 was stolen from a jeweler's window, to whom it had been given to set. A few months afterward a miserable man died a miserable death in a poor lodging-house. In his pocket was found the diamond and a letter telling how he had not dared to sell it lest it should lead to his discovery and imprisonment. It never brought him anything but anxiety and pain.

Everything you steal is a curse to you in that way. The sin overreaches itself. A man who takes money that does not belong to him never gets any lasting comfort. He has no real pleasure, for he has a guilty conscience. He cannot look an honest man in the face. He loses peace of mind here, and all hope of heaven hereafter. "As the partridge sitteth on eggs, and hatcheth them not; so he that getteth riches, and not by right, shall leave them in the midst of his days, and at his end shall be a fool....Let no man go beyond and defraud his brother in any matter; because that the Lord is the avenger of all such."

I may be speaking to some clerk who perhaps took five cents to-day out of his employer's drawer to buy a cigar; perhaps he took ten cents to get a shave, and thinks he will put it back to-morrow—no one will ever know it. If you have taken a cent, you are a thief. Do you ever think how those little stealings may bring you to ruin? Let your employer find it out. If he doesn't take you into court, he will discharge you. Your hopes will be blasted, and it will be hard work to get up again. Whatever condition you are in, do not take a cent that does not belong to you. Rather than steal, go up to heaven in poverty—go up to heaven from the poor-house. Be honest rather than go through the world in a gilded chariot of stolen riches.

RESTITUTION.

If you have ever taken money dishonestly, you need not pray God to forgive you and fill you with the Holy Ghost until you make restitution. If you have not got the money now to pay back, will to do it, and God accepts the willing mind.

Many a man is kept in darkness and unrest because he fails to obey God on this point. If the plough has gone deep, if the repentance is true, it will bring forth fruit. What use is there in my coming to God until I am willing to make it good, like Zacchaeus, if I have done any man wrong or have taken anything from him falsely? "If the wicked restore the pledge, give again that he had robbed, walk in the statutes of life, without committing iniquity; he shall surely live, he shall not die. None of his sins that he hath committed shall be mentioned unto him." Confession and restitution are the steps that lead up to forgiveness. Until you tread those steps, you may expect your conscience to be troubled, your sin to haunt you.

I was preaching in British Columbia some years ago, and a young man came to me, and wanted to become a Christian. He had been smuggling opium into the States.

"Well, my friend," I said, "I don't think there is any chance for you to become a Christian until you make restitution."

He said, "If I attempt to do that, I will fall into the clutches of the law, and I will go to the penitentiary."

"Well," I replied, "you had better do that than go to the judgment-seat of God with that sin upon your soul, and have eternal punishment. The Lord will be very merciful if you set your face to do right."

He went away sorrowful, but came back the next day, and said: "I have a young wife and child, and all the furniture in my house I have bought with money I have got in this dishonest way. If I become a Christian, that furniture will have to go, and my wife will know it."

"Better let your wife know it, and better let your home and furniture go."

"Would you come up and see my wife?" he asked; "I don't know what she will say."

I went up to see her, and when I told her, the tears trickled down her cheeks, and she said: "Mr. Moody, I will gladly give everything if my husband can become a true Christian."

She took out her pocketbook, and handed over her last penny. He had a piece of land in the United States, which he deeded over to the government. I do not know in all my backward track of any living man who has had a better testimony for Jesus Christ than that man. He had been dishonest, but when the truth came to him that he must make it right before God would help him, he made it right and then God used him wonderfully.

No amount of weeping over sin, and saying that you feel sorry, is going to help it unless you are willing to confess, and make restitution.

NINTH COMMANDMENT

"Thou shalt not bear false witness against thy neighbor."

Two out of the Ten Commandments deal with sins that find expression by the tongue—the third commandment, which forbids taking God's name in vain, and this ninth commandment, which forbids false witness against our neighbor. This two-fold prohibition ought to impress us as a solemn warning, especially as we find that the pages of Scripture are full of condemnation of sins of the tongue. The Psalms, Proverbs and the epistle of James deal largely with the subject.

TRUTH NECESSARY.

Organized society of a degree higher than that of the herding of animals and flocking of birds depends so much upon the power of speech, that without it we may say society would be impossible. Language is an essential element in the social fabric. To its purpose it must be trustworthy. Words must command confidence. Anything which undermines the truth takes (as it were) the mortar out of the building and if general, must mean ruin. Paul said—"Wherefore putting away lying, speak every man truth to his neighbor: for we are members one of another." Note the reason given—"we are members one of another." All community, all union and fellowship would be shattered if a man did not know whether to believe his neighbor or not.

The transgressions of this commandment are very varied in form, and very frequent. Men and women of all ages have to guard against them. They include some of the most besetting sins. David said in his haste—"All men are liars." Some one has remarked that if he had been living nowadays, he might say it without haste and not be very far wide of the truth.

PERJURY.

The bearing of false witness is forbidden, but this must not be limited merely to testimony given in the law court or under oath. Isn't it a condemnation that men have to be put under oath in order to make sure of their speaking the truth? As a legal offence, *perjury*—the bearing of false witness when under oath—is one of the most serious crimes that can be committed. Nearly every civilized nation visits it with heavy punishment. Unless promptly checked, it would shake the very foundations of justice.

Lying—uttering or acting falsehood—and *slander*—the spreading of false reports tending to destroy the reputation of another—are two of the most common violations of this commandment.

LYING.

We have got nowadays so that we divide lies into white lies and black lies, society lies, business lies, etc. The Word of God knows no such letting-down of the standard. A lie is a lie, no matter what are the circumstances under which it is uttered, or by whom. I have heard that in Siam they sew up the mouth of a confirmed liar. I am afraid if that was the custom in America, a good many would suffer. Parents should begin with their children while they are young and teach them to be strictly truthful at all times. There is a proverb: "A lie has no legs." It requires other lies to support it. Tell one lie and you are forced to tell others to back it up.

SLANDER.

You don't like to have any one bear false witness against you, or help to ruin your character or reputation: then why should you do it to others? How public men are slandered in this country! None escape, whether good or bad. Judgment is passed upon them, their family, their character, by the press and by individuals who know little or nothing about them. If one tenth that is said and written about our public men was true, half of them should be hung. Slander has been called "tongue murder." Slanderers are compared to flies that always settle on sores, but do not touch a man's good parts.

If the archangel Gabriel should come down to earth and mix in human affairs, I believe his character would be assailed inside of forty-eight hours. Slander called Christ a gluttonous man and a winebibber. He claimed to be the Truth, but instead of worshipping Him, men took Him and crucified Him.

When any one spoke evil of another in the presence of Peter the Great, he used promptly to stop him, and say:

"Well, now, has he not got a bright side? Tell me what you know good of him. It is easy to splash mud, but I would rather help a man to keep his coat clean."

I need not stop to run through the whole catalogue of sins that are related to these three. False rumor—exaggeration—misrepresentation—insinuation—gossip—equivocation—holding back of the truth when it is due and right to tell it—disparagement—perversion of meaning: these are common transgressions of this ninth commandment, differing in form and degree of guilt according to the motive or manner of their expression. They bear false witness against a man before the tribunal of public opinion—a court whose judgment none of us escape. As so much of our life is passed in public view, any untruth that leads to a false judgment is a grievous wrong.

A TEST OF TRUE RELIGION.

Government of the tongue is made the test of true religion by James. "If any man among you seem to be religious, and bridleth not his tongue, but deceiveth his own heart, this man's religion is vain.…For in many things we offend all. If any man offend not in word, the same is a perfect man, and able also to bridle the whole body:" Just as a doctor looks at the tongue and can tell the condition of the bodily health, so a man's words are an index of what is within. Truth will spring from a good heart: falsehood and deceit from a corrupt heart. When Ananias kept back part of the price of the land, Peter asked him—"Why hath Satan filled THINE HEART to lie unto the Holy Ghost?" Satan is the father of lies and the promoter of lies:

FOR GOOD OR EVIL.

The tongue can be an instrument of untold good or incalculable evil. Some one has said that a sharp tongue is the only edged tool that grows keener with constant use. "Thy tongue deviseth mischiefs; like a sharp razor, working deceitfully.…They have sharpened their tongues like a serpent; adders' poison is under their lips.…The mouth of a righteous man is a well of life: but violence covereth the mouth of the wicked.…A wholesome tongue is a tree of life: but perverseness therein is a breach in the spirit,…" Bishop Hall said that the tongues of busybodies are like the tails of Samson's foxes—they carry firebrands and are enough to set the whole field of the world in a flame. "Behold, we put bits in the horses' mouths that they may obey us; and we turn about their whole body. Behold also the ships, which though they be so great, and are driven of fierce winds, yet are they turned about with a very small helm, whithersoever the governor listeth. Even so the tongue is a little member, and boasteth great things. Behold how great a matter a little fire kindleth! And the tongue is a fire, a world of iniquity: so is the tongue among our members, that it defileth the whole body, and setteth on fire the course of nature; and it is set on fire of hell. For every kind of beasts, and of birds, and of serpents, and of things in the sea, is tamed and hath been tamed by mankind: but the tongue can no man tame; it is an unruly evil, full of deadly poison. Therewith bless we God, even the Father; and therewith curse we men, which are made after the similitude of God. Out of the same mouth proceedeth blessing and cursing. My brethren, these things ought not so to be. Doth a fountain send forth at the same time sweet water and bitter? Can the fig tree, my brethren, bear olive berries? either a vine figs? so can no fountain both yield salt water and fresh. Who is a wise man and endued with knowledge among you? let him shew out of a good conversation his works with meekness of wisdom. But if ye have bitter envying and strife in your hearts, glory not, and lie not against the truth."

Blighted hopes and blasted reputations are witness to its awful power. In many cases the tongue has murdered its victims. Can we not all recall cases where men and women have died under the wounds of calumny and misrepresentation? History is full of such cases.

WORDS NEVER CALLED BACK.

The most dangerous thing about it is that a word once uttered can never be obliterated. Some one has said that lying is a worse crime than counterfeiting. There is some hope of following up bad coins until they are all recovered; but an evil word can never be overtaken. The mind of the hearer or reader has been poisoned, and human devices cannot reach in and cleanse it. Lies can never be called back.

A woman who was well known as a scandal-monger, went and confessed to the priest. He gave her a ripe thistle-top, and told her to go out and scatter the seeds one by one. She wondered at the penance, but obeyed; then she came and told the priest. He next told her to go and gather again the scattered seeds. Of course she saw that it was impossible. The priest used it as an object-lesson to cure her of the sin of scandalous talk.

THE FATE OF THE LIAR AND SLANDERER.

These sins are devilish, and the Bible is severe in its denunciations of them. It contains many solemn warnings. "Thou shalt destroy them that speak leasing: the Lord will abhor the bloody and deceitful man.... The mouth of them that speak lies shall be stopped. Whoso privily slandereth his neighbor, him will I cut off.... Lying lips are an abomination to the Lord: but they that deal truly are His delight.... By thy words thou shalt be justified, and by thy words thou shalt be condemned.... All liars shall have their part in the lake which burneth with fire and brimstone: which is the second death." Whoso loveth and maketh a lie shall in no wise enter into the new Jerusalem.

HOW TO OVERCOME.

"But, Mr. Moody," you say, "how can I check myself? how can I overcome the habit of lying and gossip?" A lady once said to me that she had got so into the habit of exaggerating that her friends said they could never understand her.

The cure is simple, but not very pleasant. Treat it as a sin, and confess it to God and the man whom you have wronged. As soon as you catch yourself lying, go straight to the person and confess you have lied. Let your confession be as wide as your transgression. If you have slandered or lied about any one in public, let your confession be public. Many a person says some mean, false thing about another in the presence of others, and then tries to patch it up by going to that person alone. That is not making restitution. I need not go to God with confession until I have made it right with that person, if it is in my power to do so; He will not hear me.

Hannah Moore's method was a sure cure for scandal. Whenever she was told anything derogatory of another, her invariable reply was:

"Come, we will go and ask if it be true."

The effect was sometimes ludicrously painful. The talebearer was taken aback, stammered out a qualification, or begged that no notice might be taken of the statement. But the good lady was inexorable. Off she took the scandal-monger to the scandalized to make inquiry and compare accounts.

It is not likely that anybody ventured a second time to repeat a gossipy story to Hannah Moore.

My friend, how is it? If God should weigh you against this commandment, would you be found wanting? "Thou shalt not bear false witness." Are you innocent or guilty?

TENTH COMMANDMENT

"Thou shalt not covet thy neighbor's house, thou shalt not covet thy neighbor's wife, nor his manservant, nor his maidservant, nor his ox, nor his ass, nor anything that is thy neighbor's."

In the twelfth chapter of Luke our Saviour lifted two danger signals. "Beware ye of the leaven of the Pharisees, which is hypocrisy.... Take heed and beware of covetousness."

The greatest dupe the devil has in the world is the hypocrite; but the next greatest is the covetous man, "for a man's life consisteth not in the abundance of the things which he possesseth."

I believe this sin is much stronger now than ever before in the world's history. We are not in the habit of condemning it as a sin. In his epistle to the Thessalonians Paul speaks of "the cloke of covetousness." Covetous men use it as a cloke, and call it prudence, and foresight. Who ever heard it confessed as a sin? I have heard many confessions, in public and private, during the past forty years, but never have I heard a man confess that he was guilty of this sin. The Bible does not tell of one man who ever recovered from it, and in all my experience I do not recall many who have been able to shake it off after it had fastened on them. A covetous man or woman generally remains covetous to the very end.

We may say that covetous desire plunged the human race into sin. We can trace the river back from age to age until we get to its rise in Eden. When Eve saw that the forbidden fruit was good for food and that it was desirable to the eyes, she partook of it, and Adam with her. They were not satisfied with all that God had showered upon them, but coveted the wisdom of gods which Satan deceitfully told them might be obtained by eating the fruit. She saw,—she desired—then she took! Three steps from innocence into sin.

A SEARCHING COMMANDMENT.

It would be absurd for such a law as this to be placed upon any human statute book. It could never be enforced. The officers of the law would be powerless to detect infractions. The outward conduct may be regulated, but the thoughts and intents of a man are beyond the reach of human law.

But God can see behind outward actions. He can read the thoughts of the heart. Our innermost life, invisible to mortal eye, is laid bare before Him. We cannot deceive Him by external conformity. He is able to detect the least transgression and shortcoming, so that no man can shirk detection. God cannot be imposed upon by the cleanness of the outside of the cup and the platter.

Surely we have here another proof that the Ten Commandments are not of human origin, but must be divine.

This commandment, then, did not, even on the surface, confine itself to visible actions as did the preceding commandments. Even before Christ came and showed their spiritual sweep, men had a commandment that went beneath public-conduct and touched the very springs of action. It directly prohibited—not the wrong act, but the wicked desire that prompted the act. It forbade the evil thought, the unlawful wish. It sought to prevent—not only sin, but the desire to sin. In God's sight it is as wicked to set covetous eyes, as it is to lay thieving hands, upon anything that is not ours.

And why? Because if the evil desire can be controlled, there will be no outbreak in conduct. Desires have been called "actions in the egg." The desire in the heart is the first step in the series that ends in action. Kill the evil desire, and you successfully avoid the ill results that would follow upon its hatching and development. Prevention is better than cure.

We must not limit covetousness to the matter of money. The commandment is not thus limited; it reads, "Thou shalt not covet...anything...." That word "anything" is what will condemn us. Though we do not join in the race for wealth, have we not sometimes a hungry longing for our neighbor's goodly lands—fine houses,—beautiful clothes,—brilliant reputation,—personal accomplishments,—easy circumstances,—comfortable surroundings? Have we not had the desire to increase our possessions or to change our lot in accordance with what we see in others? If so, we are guilty of having broken this law.

GODS THOUGHTS ABOUT COVETOUSNESS.

Let us examine a few of the Bible passages that bear down on this sin, and see what are God's thoughts about it.

Know ye not that the unrighteous shall not inherit the kingdom of God? Be not deceived: neither fornicators, nor idolaters, nor adulterers, nor effeminate, nor abusers of themselves with mankind, nor thieves, NOR COVETOUS, nor drunkards, nor revilers, nor extortioners, shall inherit the kingdom of God.

Notice that the covetous are named between thieves and drunkards. We lock up thieves, and have no mercy on them. We loathe drunkards, and consider them great sinners against the law of God as well as the law of the land. Yet there is far more said in the Bible against covetousness than against either stealing or drunkenness.

Covetousness and stealing are almost like Siamese twins—they go together so often. In fact we might add lying, and make them triplets. "The covetous person is a thief *in* the shell. The thief is a covetous person *out of* the shell. Let a covetous person see something that he desires very much; let an opportunity of taking it be offered; how very soon he will break through the shell and come out in his true character as a thief." The Greek word translated "covetousness" means—an inordinate desire of getting. When the Gauls tasted the sweet wines of Italy, they asked where they came from, and never rested until they had overrun Italy.

For this ye know, that no whoremonger, nor unclean person, nor covetous man, who is an idolater, hath any inheritance in the kingdom of Christ and God.

There we have the same truth repeated; but notice that covetousness is called idolatry. The covetous man worships Mammon, not God.

Moreover thou shalt provide out of all the people able men, such as fear God, men of truth, HATING COVETOUSNESS; and place such over them, to be rulers of thousands, and rulers of hundreds, rulers of fifties, and rulers of tens.

Isn't it extraordinary that Jethro, the man of the desert, should have given this advice to Moses? How did he learn to beware of covetousness? We honor men to-day if they are wealthy and covetous. We elect them to office in church and state. We often say that they will make better treasurers just because we know them to be covetous. But in God's sight a covetous man is as vile and black as any thief or drunkard. David said: "The wicked boasteth of his heart's desire, and blesseth the covetous, whom the Lord abhorreth." I am afraid that many who profess to have put away wickedness also speak well of the covetous.

A SORE EVIL.

He that loveth silver shall not be satisfied with silver; nor he that loveth abundance with increase: this is also vanity. When goods increase, they are increased that eat them: and what good is there to the owners thereof, saving the beholding of them with their eyes? The sleep of the laboring man is sweet, whether he eat little or much: but the abundance of the rich will not suffer him to sleep. There is a sore evil which I have seen under the sun, namely, riches kept for the owners thereof to their hurt.

Isn't that true? Is the covetous man ever satisfied with his possessions? Aren't they vanity? Does he have peace of mind? Don't selfish riches always bring hurt?

The folly of covetousness is well shown in the following extract:

If you should see a man that had a large pond of water, yet living in continual thirst, nor suffering himself to drink half a draught for fear of lessening his pond; if you should see him wasting his time and strength in fetching more water to his pond, always thirsty, yet always carrying a bucket of water in his hand, watching early and late to catch the drops of rain, gaping after every cloud, and running greedily into every mire and mud in hopes of water, and always studying how to make every ditch empty itself into the pond; if you should see him grow grey in these anxious labors, and at last end a thirsty life by falling into his own pond, would you not say that such a one was not only the author of his own disquiet, but was foolish enough to be reckoned among madmen? But foolish and absurd as this character is, it does not represent half the follies and absurd disquiets of the covetous man.

I have read of a millionaire in France, who was a miser. In order to make sure of his wealth, he dug a cave in his wine cellar so large and deep that he could go down into it with a ladder. The entrance had a door with a spring lock. After a time, he was missing. Search was made, but they could find no trace of him. At last his house was sold, and the purchaser discovered this door in the cellar. He opened it, went down, and found the miser lying dead on the ground, in the midst of his riches. The door must have shut accidentally after him, and he perished miserably.

A TEMPTATION AND A SNARE.

"They that will be, (that is, desire to be), rich fall into temptation and a snare, and into many foolish and hurtful lusts, which drown men in destruction and perdition."

The Bible speaks of the deceitfulness of two things—"the deceitfulness of sin" and "the deceitfulness of riches." Riches are like a mirage in the desert, which has all the appearance of satisfying, and lures on the traveler with the promise of water and shade; but he only wastes his strength in the effort to reach it. So riches never satisfy: the pursuit of them always turns out a snare.

Lot coveted the rich plains of Sodom, and what did he gain? After twenty years spent in that wicked city, he had to escape for his life, leaving all his wealth behind him.

What did the thirty pieces of silver do for Judas? Weren't they a snare?

Think of Balaam. He is generally regarded as a false prophet, but I do not find that any of his prophecies that are recorded are not true; they have been literally fulfilled. Up to a certain point his character shone magnificently, but the devil finally overcame him by the bait of covetousness. He stepped over a heavenly crown for the riches and honors that Balak promised him. He went to perdition backwards. His face was set toward God, but he backed into hell. He wanted to die the death of the righteous, but he did not live the life of the righteous. It is sad to see so many who know God, miss everything for riches.

Then consider the case of Gehazi. There is another man who was drowned in destruction and perdition by covetousness. He got more out of Naaman than he asked for, but he also got Naaman's leprosy. Think how he forfeited the friendship of his master Elisha, the man of God! So to-day lifelong friends are separated by this accursed desire. Homes are broken up. Men are willing to sell out peace and happiness for the sake of a few dollars.

Didn't David fall into foolish and hurtful lusts? He saw Bathsheba, Uriah's wife, and she was "very beautiful to look upon," and David became a murderer and an adulterer. The guilty longing hurled him into the deepest pit of sin. He had to reap bitterly as he had sowed.

I heard of a wealthy German out west, who owned a lumber mill. He was worth nearly two millions of dollars, but his covetousness was so great that he once worked as a common laborer carrying railroad ties all day. It was the cause of his death.

And Achan answered Joshua, and said, Indeed I have sinned against the Lord God of Israel, and thus and thus have I done: When I saw among the spoils a goodly Babylonish garment, and two hundred shekels of silver, and a wedge of gold of fifty shekels weight, then *I COVETED THEM*, and took them; and, behold, they are hid in the earth in the midst of my tent, and the silver under it.

He saw—he coveted—he took—he hid! The covetous eye was what led Achan up to the wicked deed that brought sorrow and defeat upon the camp of Israel.

We know the terrible punishment that was meted out to Achan. God seems to have set danger signals at the threshold of each new age. It is remarkable how soon the first outbreaks of covetousness occurred. Think of Eve in Eden, Achan just after Israel had entered the Promised Land, Ananias and Sapphira in the early Christian Church.

A ROOT EXTRACTOR.

"For the love of money is the root of all evil, which while some coveted after, they have erred from the faith, and pierced themselves through with many sorrows."

The Revised Version translates it—"a root of all kinds of evil." This tenth commandment has therefore been aptly called a "root-extractor," because it would tear up and destroy this root. Deep down in our corrupt nature it has spread. No one but God can rid us of it.

Matthew tells us that the deceitfulness of riches chokes the Word of God. Like the Mississippi river, which chokes up its mouth by the amount of soil it carries down. Isn't that true of many business-men to day? They are so engrossed with their affairs that they have not time for religion. They lose sight of their soul and its eternal welfare in their desire to amass wealth. They do not even hesitate to sell their souls to the devil. How many a man says, "We must make money, and if God's law stands in the way, brush it aside."

The word "lucre" occurs five times in the New Testament, and each time it is called "filthy lucre."

"A root of all kinds of evil." Yes, because what will not men be guilty of when prompted by the desire to be rich? Greed for gold leads men to commit violence and murder, to cheat and deceive and steal. It turns the heart to stone, devoid of all natural affection, cruel, unkind. How many families are wrecked over the father's will! The scramble for a share of the wealth smashes them to pieces. Covetous of rank and position in society, parents barter sons and daughters in ungodly marriage. Bodily health is no consideration. The uncontrollable fever for gold makes men renounce all their settled prospects, and undertake hazardous journeys—no peril can drive them back. It destroys faith and spirituality, turning men's minds and hearts away from God. It disturbs the peace of the community by prompting to acts of wrong. Covetousness has more than once led nation to war against nation for the sake of gaining territory or other material resources. It is said that when the Spaniards came over to conquer Peru, they sent a message to the king, saying, "Give us gold, for we Spaniards have a disease that can only be cured by gold."

Dr. Boardman has shown how covetousness leads to the transgression of every one of the commandments, and I cannot do better than quote his words:

> Coveting tempts us into the violation of the first commandment, worshipping Mammon in addition to Jehovah. Coveting tempts us into a violation of the second commandment, or idolatry. The apostle Paul expressly identifies the covetous man with an idolater: "Covetousness, which is idolatry." Again: Coveting tempts us into violation of the third commandment, or sacrilegious falsehood: for instance, Gehazi, lying in the matter of his interview with Naaman the Syrian, and Ananias and Sapphira, perjuring themselves in the matter of the community of goods. Again: Coveting tempts us into the violation of the fourth commandment, or Sabbath-breaking. It is covetousness which encroaches on God's appointed day of sacred rest, tempting us to run trains for merely secular purposes, to vend tobacco and liquors, to hawk newspapers. Again: Coveting tempts us into the violation of the fifth commandment, or disrespect for authority; tempting the young man to deride his early parental counsels, the citizen to trample on civic enactments. Again: Covetousness tempts us into violation of the sixth commandment, or murder. Recall how Judas' love of money lured him into the betrayal of his Divine Friend into the hand of His murderers, his lure being the paltry sum of—say—fifteen dollars. Again: Covetousness tempts us into the violation of the seventh commandment, or adultery. Observe how Scripture combines greed and lust. Again: Covetousness tempts us into the violation of the eighth commandment, or theft. Recall how it tempted Achan to steal a goodly Babylonish mantle, and two hundred shekels of silver, and a wedge of gold of fifty shekels weight. Again: Covetousness tempts us into the violation of the ninth commandment, or bearing false witness against our neighbor. Recall how the covetousness of Ahab instigated his wife Jezebel to employ sons of Belial to bear blasphemous and fatal testimony against Naboth, saying, "Thou didst curse God and the king."

HOW TO OVERCOME.

You ask me how you are to cast this unclean spirit out of your heart? I think I can tell you.

In the first place, make up your mind that by the grace of God you will overcome the spirit of selfishness. You must overcome it, or it will overcome you. Paul said: "Mortify therefore your members which are upon the earth; fornication, uncleanness, inordinate affection, evil concupiscence, and covetousness, which is idolatry: for which things' sake the wrath of God cometh on the children of disobedience."

I heard of a rich man who was asked to make a contribution on behalf of some charitable object. The text was quoted to him—"He that hath pity upon the poor lendeth unto the Lord; and that which he hath given will He pay him again." He said that the security might be good enough, but the credit was too long. He was dead within two weeks. The wrath of God rested upon him as he never expected.

If you find yourself getting very miserly, begin to scatter, like a wealthy farmer in New York state I heard of. He was a noted miser, but he was converted. Soon after, a poor man who had been burned out and had no provisions, came to him for help. The farmer thought he would be liberal and give the man a ham from his smoke-house. On his way to get it, the tempter whispered to him:

"Give him the smallest one you have."

He had a struggle whether he would give a large or a

small ham, but finally he took down the largest he could find.

"You are a fool," the devil said.

"If you don't keep still," the farmer replied, "I will give him every ham I have in the smoke house."

Mr. Durant told me he woke up one morning to find that he was a rich man, and he said that the greatest struggle of his life then took place as to whether he would let money be his master, or he be master of money, whether he would be its slave, or make it a slave to him. At last he got the victory, and that was how Wellesley College came to be built.

In the next place, cultivate the spirit of contentment. "Let your conversation be without covetousness; and be content with such things as ye have: for He hath said, I will never leave thee, nor forsake thee. So that we may boldly say, The Lord is my helper, and I will not fear what man shall do unto me."

Contentment is the very opposite of covetousness, which is continually craving for something it does not possess. "Be content with such things as ye have," not worrying about the future, because God has promised never to leave or forsake you. What does the child of God want more than this? I would rather have that promise than all the gold of the earth.

Would to God we might all be able to say with Paul—"I have coveted no man's silver, or gold, or apparel." The Lord had made him partaker of His grace, and he was soon to be a partaker of His glory, and earthly things looked very small. "Godliness with contentment is great gain," he wrote to Timothy; "having food and raiment, therewith let us be content." Observe that he puts godliness first. No worldly gain can satisfy the human heart. Roll the whole world in, and still there would be room.

May God tear the scales off our eyes if we are blinded by this sin. Oh, the folly of it, that we should set our heart's affections upon anything below! "For we brought nothing into this world, and it is certain we can carry nothing out....Be thou not afraid when one is made rich, when the glory of his house is increased; for when he dieth he shall take nothing away: his glory shall not descend after him."

THE HANDWRITING BLOTTED OUT

We have now considered the Ten Commandments, and the question for each one of us is—are we keeping them? If God should weigh us by them, would we be found wanting or not wanting? Do we keep the law, the *whole* law? Are we obeying God with all our heart? Do we render Him a full and willing obedience?

ONE LAW, NOT TEN.

These ten commandments are not ten different laws; they are one law. If I am being held up in the air by a chain with ten links and I break one of them, down I come, just as surely as if I break the whole ten. If I am forbidden to go out of an enclosure, it makes no difference at what point I break through the fence. "Whosoever shall keep the whole law and yet offend in one point, he is guilty of all." "The golden chain of obedience is broken if one link is missing."

We sometimes hear people pray to be preserved from certain sins, as if they were in no danger of committing others. I firmly believe that if a man begins by wilfully breaking one of these commandments it is much easier for him to break the others. I know of a gentleman who had a confidential clerk, and insisted on his going down Sunday morning to work on his books. The young man had a good deal of principle, and at first refused, but he was anxious to keep in the good graces of his employer and finally yielded. He had not done that a great while before he speculated in stocks, and became a defaulter for $120,000. The employer had him arrested and put in the penitentiary for ten years, but I believe he was just as guilty in the sight of God as that young man, for he led him to take the first step on the downward road. You remember the story of a soldier who was smuggled into a fortress in a load of hay, and opened the gates to his comrades. Every sin we commit opens the door for other sins.

ALL HAVE COME SHORT.

For fifteen hundred years man was under the law, and no one was equal to it. Christ came and showed that the commandments went beyond the mere letter; and can any one since say that he has been able to keep them in his own strength? As the plummet is held up, we see how much we are out of the perpendicular. As we measure ourselves by that holy standard, we find how much we are lacking. As a child said, when reproved by her mother and told that she ought to do right: "How can I do right when there is no 'right' in me?" All have sinned and come short of the glory of God. There is none righteous, no, not one.

I do not say that all are equally guilty of gross violations of the commandments. It needs a certain amount of reckless courage openly to break a law, human or divine; but it is easy to *crack* them, as the child said. It has been remarked that the life of many professors of religion is full of fractures that result from little sins, little acts of temper and selfishness. It is possible to crack a costly vase so finely that it cannot be noticed by the observer; but let this be done again and again in different directions, and some day the vase will go to pieces at a touch. When we hear of some one who has had a lifelong reputation for good character and consistent living, suddenly falling into some shameful sin, we are shocked and puzzled. If we knew all, we would find that only the fall has been sudden, that he has been sliding toward it for years. Away back in his life we should find numerous *cracked* commandments. His exposure is only the falling of the vase to pieces.

FALSE WEIGHTS.

Men have all sorts of weights that they think are going to satisfy, but they will find that they are altogether vanity, and lighter than vanity.

The moral man is as guilty as the rest. His morality cannot save him. "Except ye repent, ye shall all likewise perish....Except ye be converted, and become as little children, ye shall not enter into the kingdom of heaven." I have often heard good people say that our meetings were doing good, they were reaching the drunkards, and gamblers, and harlots; but they never realized that they needed the grace of God for themselves.

Nicodemus was probably one of the most moral men of his day. He was a teacher of the law. Yet Christ said to him: "Except a man be born again, he cannot see the kingdom of God." It is much easier to reach thieves and drunkards and vagabonds than self-righteous Pharisees. You do not have to preach to those men for weeks and months to convince them that they are sinners. When a man learns that he has need of God, and that he is a sinner, it is very easy to reach him. But the self-righteous Pharisee needs salvation as much as any drunkard that walks the streets.

I read of a minister traveling in the south who obtained permission to preach in the local jail. A son of his host went with him. On the way back the young man, who was not a Christian, said to the minister: "I hope some of the convicts were impressed. Such a sermon as that ought to do them good."

"Did it do you good?" the minister asked.

"Oh, you were preaching to the convicts!" the young man answered.

The minister shook his head, and said: "I preached Christ, and you need Him as much as they."

If you do not repent of your sins, and ask Him for mercy, there is no hope for you. Let me ask you to take this question home to yourself. If a summons should come at midnight for you to be "weighed in the balances," what would become of your soul?

Many are only making a profession. You belong to the church; but are you ready to be weighed—ready to step into the scales? A great many would be found like those five foolish virgins. When the hour came, they would be found with no oil in their lamps. If you have only an empty lamp, or are living on mere formalism, I beg of you to give it up. Give up that dead, cold, miserable lukewarmness. God will have non of it. Are you trusting to your good works? Do you think your Bible, your crucifix, your prayers, your church-going, will help you?

Or do you set your hope upon your education, your wealth, your earthly distinctions? What will your university education amount to, and all your wealth and honors, if you go down through lust and passion and covetousness, and lose your soul at last? We are not redeemed with corruptible things as silver and gold, but with the precious blood of Christ. If you have not Christ when God weighs you, "Tekel" will be your sentence.

DO NOT DESPAIR.

I can imagine that you are saying to yourself, "If we are to be judged by these laws, how are we going to be saved? Nearly every one of them has been broken by us—in spirit, if not in letter." I almost hear you say: "I wonder if Mr. Moody is ready to be weighed. Would he like to put those tests to himself?"

With all humility I reply that if God commanded me to step into the scales now, I am ready.

"What!" you say, "haven't you broken the law?"

Yes, I have. I was a sinner before God the same as you; but for forty years ago I plead guilty at His bar. I cried for mercy, and He forgave me. If I step into the scales, the Son of God has promised to be with me. I would not dare to step in without Him. If I did, how quickly the scales would fly up!

CHRIST IS ALL.

Christ kept the law. If He had ever broken it, He would have had to die for Himself; but because He was a Lamb without spot or blemish, His atoning death is efficacious for you and me. He had no sin of His own to atone for, and so God accepted His sacrifice. Christ is the end of the law for righteousness to every one that believeth. We are righteous in God's sight because the righteousness of God which is by faith in Jesus Christ is unto all and upon all them that believe.

If we had to live forever with our sins in the handwriting of God on the wall, it would be hell on earth. But thank God for the gospel we preach! If we repent, our sins will all be blotted out. "You, being dead in your sins, hath He quickened together with Him, having forgiven you all your trespasses, blotting out the handwriting of ordinances that was against us, which was contrary to us, and took it out of the way, nailing it to His cross:"

LOVE THE FULFILLING OF THE LAW.

If the love of God is shed abroad in your heart, you will be able to fulfil the law. Paul reduced the commandments to one: "Love is the fulfilling of the law." Some one has written the following:

Love to God will admit no other God.
    Love resents everything that debases its object
        by representing it by an image.
    Love to God will never dishonor His name.
    Love to God will reverence His day.
    Love to parents makes one honor them.
    Hate, not love, is a murderer.
    Lust, not love, commits adultery.
    Love will give, but never steal.
    Love will not slander or lie.
    Love's eye is not covetous.

ARE YOU READY?

It is the height of madness to turn away and run the risk of being called by God to judgment and have no hope in Christ. Now is the day and hour to accept salvation, and then He will be with you. Do you step aside and say: "I'm not ready yet. I want a little more time to prepare, to turn the matter over in my mind?" Well, you have time, but bear in mind it is only the present; you do not know that you will have to-morrow. Wasn't Belshazzar cut off suddenly? Would he have believed that that was going to be his last night, that he would never see the light of another sun? That banquet of sin didn't close as he expected. As long as you delay you are in danger. If you don't enter into the kingdom of heaven by God's way, you cannot enter at all. You must accept Christ as your Savior, or you will never be fit to be weighed.

My friend, have you got Him? Will you remain as you are and be found wanting, or will you accept Christ and be ready for the summons? "This is the record, that God hath given to us eternal life, and this life is in His Son. He that hath the Son hath life: and he that hath not the Son of God hath not life."

May God open your heart to receive His Son now!